WEST'S LAW

Text & Cases

Third Edition

WEST'S
BUSINESS LAW
Text & Cases

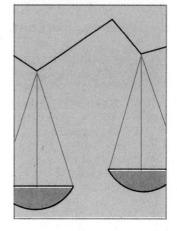

Third Edition

KENNETH W. CLARKSON
Director, Law and Economics Center
and
School of Law
University of Miami

ROGER LeROY MILLER
Center for Policy Studies
and
Department of Economics
Clemson University

GAYLORD A. JENTZ
Herbert D. Kelleher
Professor in Business Law
Chairman, Department of General Business
University of Texas at Austin

WEST PUBLISHING COMPANY
St. Paul   New York   Los Angeles   San Francisco

Library of Congress Cataloging-in-Publication Data

Clarkson, Kenneth W.
    West's business law.

    Includes index.
    1. Commercial law—United States—Cases.
    2. Business law—United States.
    I.   Miller, Roger LeRoy.
    II. Jentz, Gaylord A.
    III. West Publishing Company.   IV.   Title.
    KF888.C55   1986   346.73'07   85-26300
    ISBN 0-314-93162-7   347.3067

A study guide has been developed to assist you in mastering the concepts presented in the text. The study guide includes a "Things to Keep in Mind" section, a list of key terms, an outline of each chapter, a set of fill-in questions (a type of programmed learning device), a set of multiple-choice questions, the answers to the fill-in and multiple choice questions, and a new section entitled Uniform CPA Business Law Examination information. This workbook is available from your local bookstore under the title *Study Guide to Accompany West's Business Law: Text and Cases, Third Edition* prepared by Barbara Behr of Bloomsburg University of Pennsylvania.

PREFACE

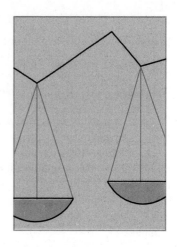

The first course in business law is often an exciting adventure for the student preparing for a career in business, accounting, government, law, and most other careers in today's world. Now, more than ever before, a basic knowledge of business law is an important part of a student's general education, for the law touches on just about every individual at one time or another. All you need to do to confirm this statement is glance through some of the case excerpts contained within the following pages. You will see how the litigation represented by these cases involves many different types of individuals and situations and how the law and the legal process affects people from all walks of life. It is no exaggeration to say that the law provides an all-encompassing framework in our society.

It is with this universal applicability of the law in mind that we have fashioned this text. The result is, we believe, a useful "tool for living" and a text which should satisfy the demands of students preparing for future careers.

In this preface we would like to point out not only the changes that have been made in the Third Edition, but also the numerous pedagogical devices that aid the student-reader in systematically learning the law.

THE THIRD EDITION: THOROUGHLY MODERN

We believe that business law should be taught in a contemporary setting. Consequently, we have included, wherever possible and appropriate, over one hundred court cases and case problems from the 1980s. Approximately half of the case excerpts included within this text are from the past decade; the remainder include some of the tried and true classics pertaining to business law. The basic criterion for inclusion, however, is always the same: the appropriateness of the case to the legal concept being explained.

Also included are the 1984 Bankruptcy Amendments and Federal Judgeship Act, the recent trend in the passage of "lemon laws," new developments in computer-assisted legal research and crimes, the current status of due-on-sale mortgage clauses, and many more recent changes.

New Chapters in the Third Edition

The first and second editions of this text included a number of unique chapters that were necessary to keep pace with contemporary legal trends. These chapters covered special partnerships (including limited partnerships), private franchises, torts related to business, employment and labor relations law, trusts, wills, estates and other topics. These and other chapters from the Second Edition have been retained in this text, appropriately revised or rewritten to reflect current legislation or legal trends.

In addition, at the recommendation of our many faithful users, three new chapters have been added to the Third Edition. They are:

● Constitutional Authority to Regulate Business (Chapter 2)
● The Liability of Accountants (Chapter 56)
● The Effect of International Law in a Global Economy (Chapter 57)

A number of chapters have also been rearranged in the organization of the Third Edition. For example, the chapters on personal property (Chapter 51) and bailments (Chapter 52) are now more logically placed at the beginning of Unit VIII, entitled "The Protection of Property and Other Interests."

In addition, a number of chapters have been substantially rewritten in response to reviewers' suggestions and comments. These chapters include Chapter 14 (Third Party Contract Rights), Chapter 29 (Secured Transactions), and Chapters 32 and 33 (Principal and Agency).

NEW EXHIBITS

A number of new exhibits have been added to the Third Edition to enhance the student's understanding of the text and the forms used in the business world. Included as new exhibits are copies of a purchase order, security agreement, negotiable bill of lading, and nonnegotiable warehouse receipt.

CONCEPT SUMMARIES ADDED

Students often need an explicit review of key concepts. In the Third Edition we have provided what we believe to be an extremely useful pedagogical device in the form of Concept Summaries. These summaries are provided in 21 separate instances. Examples are:

● Valid Business Contracts under the Statute of Frauds (Chapter 13)
● Types and Basic Rules of Contract Discharge (Chapter 15)
● Rules on Passage of Title and Risk of Loss (Chapter 18)
● Termination of Agency by Acts of the Parties and by Operation of Law (Chapter 33)
● Rights and Duties of a Bailee (Chapter 52)

FOCUS ON ETHICS

The teaching of ethics as an integral part of introductory courses in business law is becoming common practice throughout the United States. Additionally, accreditation committees now usually require the inclusion of a minimum of ethical considerations in an introductory business law course. To satisfy this requirement and the increased interest in ethical questions, we have greatly expanded these sections and updated them to include current ethical problems and controversies. These specially prepared sections are found at the end of each of the eight units in the text, and each Focus on Ethics considers ethical problems relating to topics covered in the preceding unit. These sections are not intended as a course in ethics, but are designed to elicit comments and discussion from the student-readers. For this reason, each Focus ends with a set of sample discussion questions.

APPENDICES

Since most students keep their business law text as a future reference source, we have included a full set of appendices. They are as follows:

A How to Brief a Case
B The United States Constitution
C The Uniform Commercial Code, fully updated
D The Uniform Partnership Act
E The Uniform Limited Partnership Act
F The Revised Uniform Limited Partnership Act
G The Model Business Corporation Act
H Selections from the Revised Model Business Corporation Act

Appendix H is new to this edition. Where appropriate, references to these various appendices, including the new one, are given throughout the text.

OTHER SPECIAL FEATURES OF THIS TEXT

In addition to being comprehensive and accurate, our text provides some unique features for the students and the instructor.

1. *Cases fully integrated:* Cases immediately follow the legal point being discussed that they either substantiate or illustrate, rather than appearing at the back of each chapter.
2. *Cases have a unique format:* The case cite is fully presented in the margin. *Background and Facts* are first given and then the actual case excerpts are presented in different type size to differentiate them. Following the excerpts is a *Decision and Remedy* section. Finally, in some cases, a *Comments* section follows.
3. *Vocabulary stressed:* Each time a new important term is introduced, it is presented in boldface. A further explanation of boldfaced terms is given in the glossary at the end of the text. The glossary has been expanded in the Third Edition.
4. *Easy to read and learn from:* The text is written in an easy-to-read manner and is separated into sections by four different levels of subheadings. This greatly eases the learning process and allows for easier outlining by the student-reader.
5. *Case questions and problems:* At the end of each chapter, there are approximately eight to ten questions and case problems. The first four to five questions are usually hypothetical in nature, centering explicitly on specific areas of law treated in the chapter. The remainder of the questions are actual case problems taken from important cases, for which full citations are given. In most chapters one or more new case problems, based on court cases from the 1980s, have been included in the Third Edition. Complete answers to these end-of-chapter hypothetical problems and case questions are presented in a separately bound booklet. The answers to these end-of-chapter problems and questions constitute a complete review of the law.

SUPPLEMENTAL MATERIALS

We realize that most business law teachers face a difficult task in finding the time to teach all of the materials they are required to teach during each term. Therefore, we have developed, with several colleagues, supplementary materials which will ease both the students' and instructors' jobs.

Study Guide to Accompany WEST's BUSINESS LAW, Third Edition

Professor Barbara E. Behr of Bloomsburg University of Pennsylvania has put together what we believe to be the most comprehensive, informative and helpful Study Guide for business law students that exists. It is directly aimed at allowing the student to comprehend not only "black letter" law, but also some of the subtleties behind the legal process. Basically, though, it is designed to allow the student to comprehend each chapter in such a way that exam time will not be a moment of panic. The Study Guide contains:

1. A "things to keep in mind" section.
2. A list of key terms.
3. An outline of the chapter.
4. A set of fill-in questions (a type of programmed learning device).
5. A set of multiple choice questions.
6. The answers to the fill-in and multiple choice questions.
7. A section entitled Uniform CPA Business Law Examination Information.

Instructor's Manual and Test Bank

In this edition, there is a fully revised Instructor's Manual prepared by Professor Frank S. Forbes of the University of Nebraska, Omaha, and Lorne H. Seidman of the University of Nevada, Las Vegas. The Instructor's Manual contains the following materials:

1. Chapter outlines.
2. Major chapter concepts with notes for classroom lectures.
3. Practical teaching suggestions.

4. Questions for the student that are designed to stimulate classroom discussion.

5. Full notes on all cases excerpted within each chapter, including potential classroom discussion questions.

6. A full set of test questions, including approximately 1,000 multiple choice questions with answers and approximately the same number of true/false questions with answers.

7. Additional information to help students who are taking the course in preparation for the CPA examination.

Transparencies

A full set of acetate transparencies are available to qualified adopters.

Legal Business Forms

A separate booklet of approximately forty often-used sample forms is also available.

ACKNOWLEDGMENTS FOR THE FIRST EDITION

Barbara E. Behr, Bloomsburg University of Pennsylvania ; Robert Staaf, Daniel E. Murray, Richard A. Hausler, Irwin Stotzky, Patrick O. Gudridge, all of the University of Miami School of Law; William Auslen, San Francisco City College; Donald Cantwell, University of Texas at Arlington; Frank S. Forbes, University of Nebraska; Bob Garrett, American River College-California; Thomas Gossman, Western Michigan University; Charles Hartman, Wright State University-Ohio; Telford Hollman, University of Northern Iowa; Robert Jesperson, University of Houston; Susan Liebeler, Loyola University; Robert D. McNutt, California State University-Northridge; Roger E. Meiners, Texas A&M University; Gerald S. Meisel, Bergen Community College-New Jersey; James E. Moon, Meyer, Johnson & Moon-Minneapolis; Bob Morgan, Eastern Michigan University; Arthur Southwick, University of Michigan; Raymond Mason Taylor, North Carolina State; Edwin Tucker, University of Connecticut; Gary Victor, Eastern Michigan University; Gary Watson, California State University, Los Angeles.

ACKNOWLEDGMENTS FOR THE SECOND EDITION

Robert Staaf, Kenneth Burns, Judith Kenney, Thomas Crane, all of the University of Miami; Sylvia A. Spade, David A. Escamilla, Peyton J. Paxson, and JoAnn W. Hammer, all of the University of Texas at Austin.

Frank S. Forbes of the University of Nebraska-Omaha, Jeffrey E. Allen, University of Miami; Raymond August, Washington State University; David L. Baumer, North Carolina State; Barbara E. Behr, Bloomsburg University of Pennsylvania; William J. Burke, University of Lowell-Massachusetts; Robert Chatov, State University of New York-Buffalo; Larry R. Curtis, Iowa State University; Gerard Halpern, University of Arkansas; June A. Horrigan, California State University-Sacramento; John P. Huggard, North Carolina State University; John W. McGee, Southwest Texas State University; Robert D. McNutt, California State University-Northridge; Thomas E. Maher, California State University-Fullerton; David Minars, Brooklyn College-New York; Joan Ann Mrava, Los Angeles Southwest College; Thomas L. Palmer, Northern Arizona University; Charles M. Patten, University of Wisconsin-Oshkosh; Arthur D. Wolfe, Michigan State University.

ACKNOWLEDGMENTS FOR THE THIRD EDITION

Numerous individuals throughout the country offered help and criticism on both the Second Edition text and the numerous drafts of the Third Edition prepared over the last few years. In particular, we had help from the following individuals at the University of Texas at Austin: Kristi K. Brown, Kenneth S. Culotta, Michele A. Dunkerley, Karen Kay Matson, Melinda Ann Mora, Dana Blair Smith, Marshall Wilkerson, Elizabeth Anene Wolfe; and from Tamra Kempf from the University of Miami.

We are especially grateful to the following people for the extensive help they gave us: Janine S. Hiller, Virginia Polytechnic Institute and State College; Margaret Jones, Southwest Missouri State College; Carol D. Rasnic, Virginia Commonwealth University; Lorne H. Seidman, Larry Strate and Cotton Meagher of the University of Nevada, Las Vegas. Lorne H. Seidman updated and improved the fine

Instructor's Manual previously authored by Frank S. Forbes of the University of Nebraska, Omaha. A special thanks goes to Professor Seidman for his comments and criticisms throughout the entire process of the third edition. Also a very special thank-you to Lavina Leed Miller for her detailed editing and other manuscript assistance.

We also appreciate the review comments received from the following professors: Thomas M. Apke, California State University, Fullerton; John J. Balek, Morton College, Illinois; Joseph E. Cantrell, DeAnza College, California; Frank S. Forbes, University of Nebraska, Omaha; Chris L. Hamilton, Golden West College, California; Woodrow J. Maxwell, Hudson Valley Community College, New York; David Minars, City University of New York, Brooklyn; Rick F. Orsinger, College of DuPage, Illinois; Ralph L. Quinones, University of Wisconsin, Oshkosh; Jesse C. Trentadue, University of North Dakota; Robert J. Walter, University of Texas, El Paso.

As always, any remaining errors in the text are solely our responsibility. We welcome comments from all users of this text, for it is by incorporating such comments that we can make this text an even better one in future editions.

CONTENTS
IN BRIEF

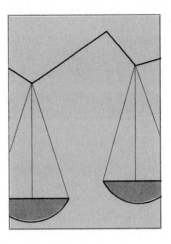

Preface v

Table of Cases xix

UNIT I
The Legal Environment Of
Business

1 Introduction to the Study of Law 3
2 Constitutional Authority to Regulate Business 17
3 Courts and Procedures 33
4 Torts 52
5 Torts Related to Business 75
6 Criminal Law 90
FOCUS ON ETHICS—The Central Problem:
Defining Business Ethics 107

UNIT II
Contracts

7 Contracts/Nature, Form, and Terminology 113
8 Contracts/Agreement 125
9 Contracts/Consideration 149
10 Contracts/Contractual Capacity 168
11 Contracts/Legality 182
12 Contracts/Genuineness of Assent 201
13 Contracts/Writing and Form 217
14 Contracts/Third Party Rights 233

15 Contracts/Performance and Discharge 246
16 Contracts/Breach of Contract and Remedies 263
FOCUS ON ETHICS—Contract Law and the
Application of Ethics 280

UNIT III
Commercial Transactions and the
Uniform Commercial Code

17 Sales/Introduction to Sales Contracts and Their
Formation 287
18 Sales/Title, Risk, and Insurable Interest 312
19 Sales/Performance and Obligation 329
20 Sales/Remedies of Buyer and Seller for Breach of
Sales Contracts 345
21 Sales/Introduction to Sales Warranties 364
22 Sales/Products Liability 383
23 Commercial Paper/Basic Concepts of Commercial
Paper 397
24 Commercial Paper/The Negotiable Instrument 405
25 Commercial Paper/Transferability and
Negotiation 418
26 Commercial Paper/Holder in Due Course 429
27 Commercial Paper/Liability, Defenses, and
Discharge 442
28 Commercial Paper/Checks and the Banking
System 461
29 Secured Transactions 481
FOCUS ON ETHICS—Commercial Transactions and
the Uniform Commercial Code 506

UNIT IV
Creditors' Rights and Bankruptcy

30 Rights of Debtors and Creditors 513
31 Bankruptcy and Reorganization 527
FOCUS ON ETHICS—Creditors' Rights and
Bankruptcy 546

UNIT V
Agency and Employment

32 Agency/Creation, and Duties and Rights of Agents
and Principals 553
33 Agency/Liability of Principals and Agents to Third
Parties and Termination of Agency: Employer-
Employee Relationships 567
FOCUS ON ETHICS—Agency and Employment 592

UNIT VI
Business Organizations

34 Forms of Business Organization 597
35 Partnerships/Creation and Termination 603
36 Partnerships/Operation and Duties 623
37 Partnerships/Limited Partnerships 632
38 Corporations/Nature and Classifications 643
39 Corporations/Formation and Corporate
Financing 656
40 Corporations/Corporate Powers and
Management 677
41 Corporations/Rights and Duties of Directors,
Managers, and Shareholders 689
42 Corporations/Merger, Consolidation, and
Termination 703
43 Corporations/Financial Regulation and Investor
Protection 715
44 Corporations/Private Franchises 730
FOCUS ON ETHICS—Business Organizations 742

UNIT VII
Government Regulation

45 Government Regulation/Regulation and
Administrative Agencies 749

46 Government Regulation/Consumer Protection 760
47 Government Regulation/Environmental
Protection 777
48 Government Regulation/Antitrust: Statutes and
Exemptions 789
49 Government Regulation/Antitrust: Enforcement and
Trends 803
50 Government Regulation/Employment and Labor
Relations Law 819
FOCUS ON ETHICS—Government Regulation 829

UNIT VIII
Protection of Property and Other
Interests

51 Personal Property 835
52 Bailments 848
53 Nature and Ownership of Real Property 865
54 Wills, Trusts, and Estates 893
55 Insurance 913
56 Liability of Accountants 932
57 The Effect of International Law in a Global
Economy 943
FOCUS ON ETHICS—Protection of Property and
Other Interests 954

Appendices

A. How to Brief a Case 959
B. The Constitution of the United States 961
C. The Uniform Commercial Code 971
D. The Uniform Partnership Act 1077
E. Uniform Limited Partnership Act 1087
F. Revised Uniform Limited Partnership Act 1093
G. The Model Business Corporation Act 1105
H. Selected Provisions of Revised Model Business
Corporation Act 1151

Glossary 1161

Index 1187

CONTENTS

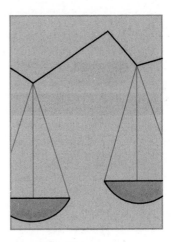

Preface   v

Table of Cases   xix

UNIT I
The Legal Environment of Business

1 Introduction to the Study of Law   3
What Is Law?   3
Schools of Legal, or Jurisprudential, Thought   4
History and Sources of American Law   5
More Recent Sources of Law   6
Sources of Commercial (or Business) Law   7
Classification of Law   8
Remedies at Law versus Remedies in Equity   9
How to Find Case Law   10
How to Analyze Case Law   11
Case Analysis   14

2 Constitutional Authority to Regulate Business   17
Basic Constitutional Concepts   17
The Bill of Rights in a Business Context   25
Other Constitutional Guarantees   31

3 Courts and Procedures   33
Introduction   33
Jurisdiction   33
Venue   34
The Court Systems in the United States   34

The Federal Court System   37
Jurisdiction of Federal Courts   40
Which Cases Reach the Supreme Court?   41
Judicial Procedures: Following a Case through the Courts   42
Arbitration   50

4 Torts   52
Tort Law versus Criminal Law   52
Kinds of Torts   53
Intentional Torts: Wrongs against the Person   53
Intentional Torts: Wrongs against Property   60
Unintentional Torts: Negligence   64
Strict Liability   71

5 Torts Related to Business   75
Wrongful Interference with a Contractual Relationship   75
Wrongful Interference with a Business Relationship   77
Wrongfully Entering into Business   79
Infringement of Trademarks, Trade Names, Patents, and Copyrights   81
Disparagement of Property or Reputation   88
The Future   88

6 Criminal Law   90
The Nature of Crime   90
The Essentials of Criminal Liability   93
Defenses to Criminal Liability   94
Criminal Procedure   98
Crimes Affecting Business   99

White-Collar Crimes 101
FOCUS ON ETHICS—The Central Problem:
  Defining Business Ethics 107

UNIT II
Contracts

7 Contracts/Nature, Form, and
    Terminology 113
  Some Perspectives 113
  The Function of Contracts 114
  Freedom of Contract and Freedom from
    Contract 114
  The Basic Requirements of a Contract 114
  Nature and Types of Contracts 115
  Definition of a Contract 115
  Types of Contracts Explained 115

8 Contracts/Agreement 125
  Mutual Assent 125
  Requirements of the Offer 126
  Termination of the Offer 136
  Acceptance 142

9 Contracts/Consideration 149
  Requirements of Consideration 149
  Moral Obligations 151
  Adequacy of Consideration 151
  Problem Areas in Business Concerning
    Consideration 155

10 Contracts/Contractual Capacity 168
  Minors 168
  Intoxicated Persons 176
  Insane Persons 179
  Aliens 180
  Married Women 180

11 Contracts/Legality 182
  Contracts Contrary to Statute 182
  Contracts Contrary to Public Policy 186
  Effect of Illegality 196

12 Contracts/Genuineness of
     Assent 201
  Mistakes 201
  Misrepresentation—Fraud 205
  Undue Influence 212
  Duress 212
  Adhesion Contracts and Unconscionability 214

13 Contracts/Writing and Form 217
  Contracts That Must Be in Writing 217
  Contracts Involving Interests in Land 218

Contracts Whose Terms Cannot Possibly Be
  Performed Within One Year From the Date of
  Formation or the Making Thereof 219
Collateral Promises 220
Promises Made in Consideration of
  Marriage 224
Contracts for the Sale of Goods 224
Sufficiency of the Writing 225
The Parol Evidence Rule 227

14 Contracts/Third Party Rights 233
  Assignment of Rights and Delegation of
    Duties 233
  Third Party Beneficiary Contracts 241
  Enforceable Rights—When the Rights of a Third
    Party Vest 243

15 Contracts/Performance and
     Discharge 246
  Conditions 246
  Discharge by Performance 249
  Discharge by Agreement 253
  Discharge by Operation of Law 255
  Anticipatory Breach 256
  Discharge by Impossibility of Performance 257

16 Contracts/Breach of Contract and
     Remedies 263
  Damages 263
  Rescission and Restitution 272
  Specific Performance 272
  Reformation 274
  Recovery Based on Quasi-Contract 275
  Election of Remedies 275
  Waiver of Breach 276
  Contract Provisions Limiting Remedies 276
  FOCUS ON ETHICS—Contract Law and the
    Application of Ethics 280

UNIT III
Commercial Transactions and the
Uniform Commercial Code

17 Sales/Introduction to Sales Contracts
     and Their Formation 287
  Historical Perspective 287
  The Scope of Article 2: The Sale of Goods 288
  Formation of a Sales Contract 292

18 Sales/Title, Risk, and Insurable
     Interest 312
  Passage of Title 312
  Identification 312

Risk of Loss   314
Bulk Transfers   322
Sales by Nonowners   323
Insurable Interest   326

19 Sales/Performance and Obligation   329

Duty of Good Faith and Commercial
   Reasonableness   329
Performance of a Sales Contract   331
Concurrent Conditions of Performance   331
Seller's Obligation of Tender of Delivery   331
The Perfect Tender Rule   333
Buyer's Obligations   338

20 Sales/Remedies of Buyer and Seller for Breach of Sales Contracts   345

Remedies of the Seller   345
Remedies of the Buyer   350
Statute of Limitations for Actions Brought under
   the Uniform Commercial Code   356
Contractual Provisions Affecting Remedies   358
Lemon Laws   361

21 Sales/Introduction to Sales Warranties   364

Warranty of Title   364
Express Warranties   366
Implied Warranties   370
Overlapping Warranties   374
Third Party Beneficiaries of Warranties: Express
   or Implied   374
Warranty Disclaimers   375
Unconscionability and Warranty
   Disclaimers   376
Magnuson-Moss Warranty Act   379

22 Sales/Products Liability   383

Warranty Theory   383
Liability Based on Negligence   383
The Doctrine of Strict Liability   387

23 Commercial Paper/Basic Concepts of Commercial Paper   397

Functions and Purposes of Commercial
   Paper   397
Types of Commercial Paper   398
Letters of Credit   400
Other Ways of Classifying Commercial
   Paper   401
Parties to Commercial Paper   401

24 Commercial Paper/The Negotiable Instrument   405

The Requirements for a Negotiable
   Instrument   405

Omissions That Do Not Affect
   Negotiability   415
Other Factors Not Affecting Negotiability   415

25 Commercial Paper/Transferability and Negotiation   418

Assignment and Negotiation   418
Indorsements   419

26 Commercial Paper/Holder in Due Course   429

Contract Law versus the Law of Commercial
   Paper   429
Holder versus Holder in Due Course   430
Requirements for Holder-In-Due-Course
   Status   430
Holders Through a Holder in Due Course   438
Federal Limitations on Holder-In-Due-Course
   Rights   439

27 Commercial Paper/Liability, Defenses, and Discharge   442

Liability Based on Signatures   442
Warranty Liability of Parties   450
Defenses   452
Discharge   458

28 Commercial Paper/Checks and the Banking System   461

Checks   461
The Bank–Customer Relationship   465
Duties of the Bank   465
Honoring Checks   465
Accepting Deposits   474
Technology in Banking Operations—Electronic
   Funds Transfer Systems   477

29 Secured Transactions   481

Article 9 of the UCC   481
Definitions   482
Creating a Security Interest   482
Purchase Money Security Interest   485
Perfecting a Security Interest   485
The Range of Perfection and the Floating Lien
   Concept   490
Priorities   494
Exceptions to Perfection Priority Rules   494
The Rights and Duties of Debtors and Creditors
   under the UCC   497
Default   499
Termination   503
FOCUS ON ETHICS—Commercial
   Transactions and the Uniform Commercial
   Code   506

UNIT IV
Creditors' Rights and Bankruptcy

30 Rights of Debtors and
        Creditors 513
    Laws Assisting Creditors 513
    Protection of the Debtor 522
    Special Protection for the Consumer-
        Debtor 524

31 Bankruptcy and Reorganization 527
    Federal Bankruptcy Law—Historical
        Background 527
    The Bankruptcy Reform Act of 1978 as
        Amended 528
    Chapter 7 Liquidations 528
    Chapter 11 Reorganizations 538
    Chapter 13 Plans 541
    Special Business Function Provisions—1984
        Amendments 543
    Other Amendments 544
    FOCUS ON ETHICS—Creditors' Rights and
        Bankruptcy 546

UNIT V
Agency and Employment

32 Agency/Creation, and Duties and
        Rights of Agents and
        Principals 553
    The Nature of Agency 553
    Kinds of Agency Relationships 553
    Formation of the Agency Relationship 556
    Duties of Agents and Principals 559
    Remedies and Rights of Agents and
        Principals 563

33 Agency/Liability of Principals and
        Agents to Third Parties and
        Termination of Agency
        Relationship: Employer-Employee
        Relationships 567
    Scope of Agent's Authority 567
    Principal's and Agent's Liability for
        Contracts 575
    Principal's and Agent's Liability for Torts of an
        Agent 577
    Termination of an Agency 579
    Employer-Employee Relationships 583
    Employer's Liability for Employee's Intentional
        Torts 589
    FOCUS ON ETHICS—Agency and
        Employment 592

UNIT IV
Business Organizations

34 Forms of Business
        Organization 597
    Sole Proprietorship 597
    Partnership 597
    Business Corporations 598
    Other Forms of Business Organization 598
    The Advantages and Disadvantages of a Sole
        Proprietorship 599
    Comparing a Partnership with a
        Corporation 600

35 Partnerships/Creation and
        Termination 603
    Characteristics of a Partnership 603
    Formation of a Partnership 605
    Partnership Property Rights 613
    Partnership Termination 613

36 Partnerships/Operation and
        Duties 623
    Rights among Partners 623
    Duties and Powers of Partners 627

37 Partnerships/Limited
        Partnerships 632
    Definition of Limited Partnership 632
    History of the Limited Partnership 632
    Formation 633
    Rights and Liabilities of Limited Partners 635
    The Use of a Limited Partnership 640
    Dissolution 640
    Limited Partnership Associations 641

38 Corporations/Nature &
        Classifications 643
    A Brief History of the Corporation 643
    The Corporation as a Creature of Statute 643
    The Nature of a Corporation 644
    Domestic, Foreign, and Alien Corporations 646
    Public and Private Corporations 648
    Nonprofit Corporations 648
    Close Corporations 649
    Subchapter S Corporations 651
    Professional Corporations 652

39 Corporations/Formation and
        Corporate Financing 656
    Promoters' Activities 656
    Incorporation 659
    Disregarding the Corporate Entity 663
    Costs and Benefits of Incorporation 667
    Corporate Financing 669

40   Corporations/Corporate Powers and
     Management   677
     Corporate Powers   677
     Corporate Management—Shareholders   681
     Corporate Management—Directors   685

41   Corporations/Rights and Duties of
     Directors, Managers, and
     Shareholders   689
     The Role of Officers and Directors   689
     Rights of Directors   692
     Rights and Duties of Corporate Officers and
        Other Management Employees   693
     Shareholder Rights   693
     Shareholder Liabilities   700
     Duties and Liabilities of Major
        Shareholders   700

42   Corporations/Merger, Consolidation,
     and Termination   703
     Merger and Consolidation   703
     Termination   711

43   Corporations/Financial Regulation
     and Investor Protection   715
     The Securities and Exchange Commission   715
     The Securities Act of 1933   715
     The Securities Exchange Act of 1934   719
     Regulation of Investment Companies   726
     State Securities Laws   727

44   Corporations/Private Franchises   730
     The Law of Franchising   730
     Types of Franchises   731
     The Franchise Agreement   731
     Regulation of the Franchising Industry   737
     Franchising—Antitrust Implications   739
     FOCUS ON ETHICS—Business
        Organizations   742

UNIT VII
Government Regulation

45   Government Regulation/Regulation
     and Administrative Agencies   749
     Historical Background   749
     Regulated Activities   750
     Types of Regulation   753
     Administrative Agencies   753

46   Government Regulation/Consumer
     Protection   760
     Consumer Protection Sources   760
     Advertising   762
     Sales   766
     Health Protection   767
     Consumer Product Safety Legislation   768
     Real Estate   769
     Credit Protection   770

47   Government Regulation/
     Environmental Protection   777
     Historical Background   777
     Regulation by Administrative Agencies   778
     Private Litigation   778
     Air Pollution   778
     Water Pollution   780
     Noise Pollution   782
     Toxic Substances   783
     Pesticide Control   783
     Waste Disposal   783
     Judicial Limits   785

48   Government Regulation/Antitrust:
     Statutes and Exemptions   789
     Common Law Actions   789
     The Beginnings of U.S. Antitrust Law   790
     The Sherman Antitrust Act   790
     The Clayton Act   795
     The Federal Trade Commission Act   795
     Robinson-Patman Act   796
     Other Antitrust Acts   796
     Summary   796
     Exemptions from Antitrust Laws   797

49   Government Regulation/Antitrust:
     Enforcement and Trends   803
     Enforcement of Prohibitions on Horizontal
        Activities   803
     Enforcement of Prohibitions on Vertical
        Restraints   808
     Mergers   812
     Other Antitrust Enforcement   816

50   Government Regulation/
     Employment and Labor Relations
     Law   819
     Unions and Collective Bargaining   819
     Civil Rights and Equal Opportunity   821
     Injury, Compensation, and Safety   824
     Retirement and Security Income   826
     Other Employment Laws   827
     FOCUS ON ETHICS—Government
        Regulation   829

UNIT VIII
Protection of Property and Other
Interests

51 Personal Property 835
The Nature of Personal Property 835
Property Rights and Ownership Title 836
Acquiring Ownership of Personal Property 837
Mislaid, Lost, and Abandoned Property 841
Special Types of Intangible Personal
Property 845

52 Bailments 848
Elements of a Bailment 848
Ordinary Bailments 851
Rights and Duties of a Bailee 852
Rights and Duties of a Bailor 859
Special Bailments 859

53 Nature and Ownership of Real
Property 865
Nature of Real Property 865
Ownership Interest in Real Property—Estates in
Land 869
Relationship of Landlord and Tenant 873
Concurrent Ownership 875
Transfer of Ownership 876
Future Interests 885
Nonpossessory Interests 886
Land Use Control 887

54 Wills, Trusts, and Estates 893
Origins of Inheritance Laws 893
Purposes of Inheritance Laws 894
Wills 894
Statutes of Descent and Distribution 903
Trusts 907
Estate Administration 908
Estate Taxes 910

55 Insurance 913
The Nature of Insurance 913
The Insurance Contract 916
Types of Insurance 923

56 Liability of Accountants 932
Potential Common Law Liability to Clients 932
Potential Common Law Liability to Third
Persons 935
Potential Statutory Liability 937
Criminal Liability 941

57 The Effect of International Law in a
Global Economy 943
Sources of International Law 943
Transacting Business Abroad 944
Conflicts between International and Municipal
Law 946
The Doctrine of Sovereign Immunity 948
Application of U.S. Antitrust Laws in a
Transnational Setting 950
The Proliferation of Common Markets 950
FOCUS ON ETHICS—Protection of Property
and Other Interests 954

Appendices

A. How to Brief a Case 959
B. The Constitution of the United States 961
C. The Uniform Commercial Code 971
D. The Uniform Partnership Act 1077
E. Uniform Limited Partnership Act 1087
F. Revised Uniform Limited Partnership Act 1093
G. The Model Business Corporation Act 1105
H. Selected Provisions of Revised Model Business
Corporation Act 1151

Glossary 1161

Index 1187

TABLE OF CASES

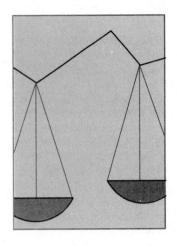

The principal cases are in italic type. Cases cited or discussed are in roman type.

A

ABC Trans, Etc. v. Aeronautics Forwarders, Inc., 560–561

Abell Co. v. Skeen, 590–591

Adams v. Lindsell, 146 n.25

Adams v. Nichols, 336

Adolph Coors Co. v. Federal Trade Commn., 758

Aero Drapery of Kentucky, Inc. v. Engdahl, 701

Affiliated Ute Citizens of Utah v. United States, 940, 941

Agaliotis v. Agaliotis, 427

Alabama Football, Inc. v. Greenwood, 166

Alafoss, H. F., v. Premium Corp. of America, Inc., 354–355

Albrecht v. Herald Co., 808 n.8

Ali v. Playgirl, Inc., 88 n.5

Allen v. Grafton, 372

Allied Bank International v. Banco Credito Agricola de Cartago, 948

All-State Indus. of North Carolina, Inc. v. Federal Trade Comm'n, 765–766

Alport A., & Son, Inc. v. Hotel Evans, Inc., 417

Alyeska Pipeline Serv. Co. v. The Wilderness Soc'y, 762 n.4

Amear v. Hall, 555–556

American Can Co. v. Oregon Liquor Control Comm'n, 784–785

American Home Improvement, Inc. v. MacIver, 308

American Mail Line Limited v. Federal Maritime Comm'n., 817

American Oil Co. v. McMullin, 801–802

American Petroleum v. Occupational Safety and Health Adm'n., 785–786

American Sand & Gravel, Inc. v. Clark & Fray Constr. Co., 311

American Society of Mechanical Engineers, Inc. v. Hydrolevel Corp., 804–805

Arizona Public Serv. Co. v. Federal Power Comm'n., 788 n.10

Amory v. Delamire, 842 n.7

Armour & Co. v. Celic, 154 n.5

Associated Press v. Walker, 27

Atlantic Richfield Co. v. Razumic, 733–735

Auerbach v. Bennet, 688

Austin Road Co. v. Occupational Safety and Health Review Commission, 751

Autry v. Republic Productions, 260

Azar v. Lehigh Corp., 77–78

B

Baden v. Curtiss Breeding Service, 363

Baker v. University of Tennessee at Chattanooga (In re Baker), 536–537
Ballard v. Eldorado Tire Co., 279
Banco National de Cuba v. Sabbatino, 946–948
BankEast Corporation v. Galdi, 714
Bank of Martin v. England, 542 n.23
Barber v. Kimbrell's, Inc., 776
Barnes v. Euster, 247–248
Barton v. Tra-Mo, Inc., 382
Bentall, F. M., v. Koenig Brothers, Inc., 678–679
Berkowitz v. Baron, 942
Bickford v. Mattocks, 838 n.1
Blackett v. Olanoff, 892
Bleecher v. Conte, 116–117
Bloom v. Weiser, 569
Blue Chip Stamps v. Manor Drug Stores, 941 n.12
Bose Corporation v. Consumers Union of United States, Inc., 26–28
Bowles v. City Nat'l Bank and Trust, 505
Boyd v. Aetna Life Ins. Co., 203–204
Brewer v. Dyer, 242
Brind v. International Trust Co., 840 n.2
Broadway Management Corp. v. Briggs, 414–415
Brown v. Board of Education, 6
Brown v. Brown, 642
Brown v. Lober, 878–880
Brown Shoe Co. v. United States, 814 n.19
Buchanan v. Byrd, 864
Budget Rent-A-Car Corp. of America v. Fein, 189–190
Bunny Bear, Inc. v. Peterson, 758
Burbank v. Lockheed Air Terminal, 23–24
Burchett v. Allied Concord Financial Corp., 453 n.5, 454–456
Burnett v. National Enquirer, 57–59
Butler v. Frontier Telephone Co., 865 n.1
Butt, H. E., Grocery Co. v. Hawkins, 74

C

Cal Distributing Co. v. Bay Distributors, Inc., 801
California Liquor Dealers v. Midcal Aluminum, Inc., 799
California State Auto v. Barrett Garages, Inc., 277 n.21
Campbell Soup Co. v. Wentz, 306 n.6, 273–274
Campbell v. Vose, 711 n.4
Cannon v. Texas Gulf Sulphur, 723 n.8
Cappezaro v. Winfrey, 854–855
Carola v. Grogan, 622
Carpenter v. Alberto Culver, 382
Carson v. Here's Johnny Portable Toilets, 88 n.4
Casey v. Kastel, 557 n.4
Catania v. Brown, 373
Central Properties, Inc. v. Robbinson, 148
Chaplinsky v. New Hampshire, 26 n.15
Chemical Bank v. Miller Yacht Sales, 505

Chemical Bank of Rochester v. Ashenburg, 638–639
Chiarella v. United States, 724 n.9, 725
Chicago Roller Skate Manufacturing Company v. Sokol Manufacturing Company, 348–350
Childers v. United States, 618 n.18
Childs v. Philpot, 676
Citizens Against Toxic Sprays, Inc. v. Bergland, 788
Citizens to Preserve Overton Park, Inc. v. Volpe, 757 n.21
City of Delta Junction v. Mack Trucks, Inc., 571–572
City of Lafayette, Louisiana v. Louisiana Power & Light Co., 799 n.20
City of Salinas v. Souza & McCue Constr. Co., 209 n.9
Clark v. Campbell, 911
Clark v. Cloud Brothers, Inc., 311
Clement v. Prestwich, 245
Club Chain of Manhattan, Ltd. v. Christopher & Seventh Gourmet, 231
Cobb, T. M., Co., Inc. v. Superior Court, 138–139
Coca-Cola Co., The, v. The Koke Co. of America et al., 83–84
Colorado Pump and Supply Co. v. Febco, Inc., 817
Columbia Nitrogen Corporation v. Royster Company, 305
Colvin v. Robert E. McKee Inc., 396
Community Communications Co. v. City of Boulder, 799
Conner v. Herd, 889–891
Continental Ore Co. v. Union Carbide and Carbon Corp., 791 n.7
Continental T.V., Inc. v. GTE Sylvania, Inc., 809–810
Corcoran v. Lyle School District No. 406, Klickitat County, Washington, 141–142
Corning Glass Works v. Brennan, 828
Coty v. U.S. Slicing Machine Co., Inc., 741
Courtaulds North America, Inc. v. N. C. Nat. Bank, 953
Crane Ice Cream Co. v. Terminal Freezing Co., 240 n.9
Cranson v. International Business Machines (IBM), Inc., 663 n.4
Crittendon v. State Oil Co., 566
Crocker v. Winthrop Laboratories, Div. of Stirling Drugs, Inc., 387 n.1
Crocker Commercial Services v. Countryside Bank, 945
Cummings General Tire Co. v. Volpe Constr. Corp., 525–526
Curtis Pub. Co. v. Butts, 27

D

Dalsis v. Hills, 788
Danielson v. Roberts, 845 n.8
Danje Fabrics v. Morgan Guaranty Trust Co., 424–425
Davenport Peters Co. v. Royal Globe Ins. Co., 931
Davies v. Arthur Murray, Inc., 259
Davis and Landry, Inc. v. Guaranty Income Life Insurance Company, 917–919

Davis v. Pioneer Bank and Trust Co., 622
Davis v. Western Union Telegraph Co., 427–428
Deesen v. Professional Golfers Ass'n of America, 801
Delaney v. Fidelity Lease Limited, 642
Devlin v. Smith, 384, 385
Diamond Match Company v. Roeber, 200
Dickinson v. Dodds, 148
Dirks v. Securities and Exchange Commission, 724–726
Dr. Miles Medical Co. v. John D. Park & Sons Co., 808 n.7
Dodge v. Ford Motor Co., 686 n.9, 695–696
Dolenz v. National Bank of Texas at Ft. Worth, 62–63
Donnell v. General Motors Corp., 828
Dorf v. Tuscarora Pipeline Co., 876 n.10
Dorman v. International Harvester Co., 382
Dorton v. Collins & Aikman Corp., 298, 301
Douglas v. Citizens Bank of Jonesboro, 480
Dowd More Co. Realtors v. McDonald, 581
Dreyfus Company, Inc. v. Royster Company, 343–344
Durham v. United States, 95 n.4
Dyer's Case, 789

E

Eaton v. Engelcke Mfg., 124
Edward Bankers & Co. v. Spradlin, 872
Embry v. Hargadine McKittrick Dry Goods Co., 147–148
Embs v. Pepsi-Cola Bottling Co. of Lexington, Kentucky, Inc., 393–394
England v. Leithoff, 357
Ernst & Ernst v. Hochfelder, 728–729, 941 n.13
Escott v. BarChris Constr. Corp., 717–718, 938
Estate of: Cancik, 895–897
    Eckert, 912
    Morris, 911
    Murrell, 864
    Piper, 838–839
    Thompson, 901–902
    Thornton *et al.* v. Caldor, Inc., 28, 821 n.6
    Witlin, 627–628
Ethyl Corp. v. Environmental Protection Agency, 779–780
Evergreen Amusement Corp. v. Milstead, 279

F

Fabian v. Wasatch Orchard Co., 231
Faretta v. California, 42 n.10
Farris v. Glen Alden Corp., 709–710
Fedders Corp. v. Federal Trade Comm'n, 817–818
Federal Trade Comm'n: v. Algoma Lumber Co., 764
    v. *Colgate-Palmolive Co., 763–765*
    v. *Procter & Gamble Co., 815–816*
Feinberg v. Pfeiffer Co., 166

Fernandez v. Arizona Water Co., 801
Fink v. Cox, 149 n.2
Firefighters Local Union No. 1784 v. Stotts, 829–830
First Arlington National Bank v. Stathis, 945
First County Nat'l Bank and Trust Co. v. Canna, 504–505
First Federal Sav. & Loan Ass'n v. Branch Banking and Trust Co., 417
First Flight Associates, Inc. v. Professional Golf Co., 591
First Nat. Bank v. Anderson, 441
First National Bank of Boston v. Bellotti, 28, 644 n.2
Flood v. Kuhn, 797
Florida Lime & Avocado Growers v. Paul, 32
Flynn v. Reaves, 631
Flynt Distributing Company., Inc. v. Harvey, 676
Foakes v. Beer, 154 n.4
Forest Products v. White Lumber Sales, Inc., 334 n.3
Fortner Enterprises v. U.S. Steel Corp., 739 n.5
Fradkin v. Ernst, 688
Franklin Life Ins. Co. v. Winney, 147
Frederickson v. Hackney, 369–370
Free For All Missionary Baptist Church, Inc. v. Southeastern Beverage and Ice Equipment Co., Inc., 688
Frostifresh Corp. v. Reynoso, 309
Fuqua Homes, Inc. v. Evanston Building & Loan Co., 328

G

Gabhart v. Gabhart, 714
Galler v. Galler, 650–651
Ganley Bros., Inc. v. Butler Bros. Bldg. Co., 231
Garfield v. Strain, 728
Gartner v. Snyder, 663–664
Gastonia Personnel Corp. v. Rogers, 174–175
Geary v. United States Steel Corporation, 107–108
Ger-Ro-Mar, Inc. v. FTC, 740–741
Gertz v. Robert Welch, Inc., 26
Gibbons v. Ogden, 750 n.1
Giberson v. Ford Motor Co., 393 n.5
Gibson v. Cranage, 252 n.7
Girard Bank v. Haley, 622
Gizzi v. Texaco, Inc., 571
Glover v. Jewish War Veterans of the United States, Post No. 58, 135–136
Goddard v. Ishikawajima-Harima Heavy Industries Co., 344
Goldberg v. Kelly, 759
Goldberg v. Rothman, 431–432
Goldfarb v. Virginia State Bar, 797–798
Goldman v. Allyn & Bacon, Inc., 261
Goldthwaite v. Janney, 626
Golosh v. Cherokee Cab Co., 556
Gonzales v. Schmerler Ford, 776

Goodman v. Darden, Doman and Stafford Assoc., 657–659

Grace v. Grace Institute, 682–683

Grady-Gould Watershed Improvement Dist. v. Transamerica Ins. Co., 279

Graham v. State, 569

Granite Equipment Leasing Corp. v. Hempstead Bank, 467–468

Grant, W. T., Co. v. Walsh, 199

Gray v. Martino, 166

Greenman v. Yuba Power Products, Inc., 388–390

Grey v. European Health Spas, Inc., 775–776

Griffin v. Ellinger, 443–445

Griggs v. Duke Power Co., 822–824

Groban v. S. S. Pegu, 931

Gross v. Waldbaum, Inc., 73

Groulich Caterer, Inc. v. Hans Holterbosch, Inc., 344

Gruenberg v. Goldmine Plantation, Inc., 712–713

Guarino v. Mine Safety Appliance Co., 68–69

Gulf Refining Co. v. Williams, 74

H

Habersham Elec. Membership Corp. v. Dalton, 70–71

Hackbardt v. Cincinnati Bengals, Inc., 593–594

Hadley v. Baxendale, 267–268

Hall v. Hall, 200

Hall v. Marston, 242

Hamer v. Sidway, 150–151

Hammer v. Dagenhart, 750 n.1

Hanigan v. Wheeler, 237–239

Hanson v. Denckla, 648

Harestad v. Weitzel, 631

Harris Corp. v. National Iranian Radio, Etc., 953

Hartung v. Architects Hartung/Odle/Burke, Inc., 701–702

Haven v. Randolph, 566

Hawkins v. McGee, 126 n.7

Haydocy Pontiac, Inc. v. Lee, 172–173

Heart of Atlanta Motel v. United States, 19–20

Heggblade-Marguleas-Tenneco, Inc. v. Sunshine Biscuit, Inc., 304–306

Henningsen v. Bloomfield Motors, Inc., 193 n.9, 376–379

Henshaw v. Kroenecke, 617–618

Herman & MacLean v. Huddleston, 939

Herrin v. Sutherland, 865

Hicks v. Miranda, 41 n.8

Hirsch v. S. C. Johnson & Son, Inc., 88 n.6

Hochester v. De La Tour, 256 n.19

Hodge v. Garrett, 630–631

Hoffman v. Red Owl Stores, Inc., 163–165

Hohenberg Brothers Co. v. Killebrew, 590

Holly v. First National Bank, 154 n.6

Holly Hill Acres, Ltd. v. Charter Bank of Gainesville, 408–409

Home Center Supply v. CertainTeed Corp., 448–449

Hopkins v. United States, 792 n.10

Hotchkiss v. National City Bank of N.Y., 126 n.6

Howard v. Nicholson, 262

Hudson Properties, Inc. v. Citizens & Southern National Bank, 505

Hutchinson v. Proxmire, 74

I

Imperial Ice Co. v. Rossier et al., 89

Imperial Motors, Inc. v. Chrysler Corporation, 732–733

Industrial Lift Truck v. Mitsubishi International Corporation, 120–121

Industrial Union Dept. AFL-CIO v. American Petroleum Institute, 751–752

Ingham Lumber Co. v. Ingersoll & Co., 257 n.24

In the Matter of:
Fontana v. D'ORO Foods Inc., 261–262
the estate of Gray, 591
The Hawaii Corporation, 934–935

In re: Bray, 545
Cady, Roberts & Co., 724, 725
Crisan Estate, 124
Estate of Baldwin, 566
Estate of Unger, 898–899
Goodson Steel Corp., 362
Iacovoni, 542 n.23
Isis Foods, Inc., 328
Johns-Manville Corp., 539–540, 548
Karachi Cab Co., 532–533
Lewis, 545
Tomeo, 545
Tracy Service Co., 545
Wilco Forest Machinery, Inc., 676
Wolfe's Will, 911–912

INS v. Chadha, 758

International Ass'n of Machinists v. Southard, 89

International Business Machines v. United States, 811 n.13

International Shoe Co. v. Washington, 647–648, 953

InterTherm, Inc. v. Olympic Homes Systems, Inc., 666–667

J

Jack Development, Inc. v. Howard Eales, Inc., 515–516

Jackson v. Kusmer, 525

Jacob & Youngs v. Kent, 250 n.6

James v. J. F. K. Carwash, Inc., 680–681

Jefferson Parish Hospital District No. 2 v. Hyde, 817

Jewel v. Boxer, 619–621

Joel v. Morison, 588

Johnson v. K-Mart Enterprises, Inc., 55–56

Johnson v. Nasi, 658

Jones v. Bank of Nevada, 505

Jones & Laughlin Supply v. Dugan Production Corp. 488–489

Jones v. Star Credit Corp., 193 n.10, 307–309

K

Kademenos v. Equitable Life Assur. Soc'y, 566

Kaiser v. Northwest Shopping Center, 480

Kaiser Trading Co. v. Associated Metals & Minerals Corp., 362

Kampman v. Pittsburgh Contracting and Engineering Co., 222 n.15

Kassel v. Consolidated Freightways Corporation of Delaware, 21–22

Kastner v. Husband, 898

Kaufman v. Jaffee, 210 n.11

Keane v. Pan American Bank, 459–460

Kellos, A. J., Constr. Co., Inc. v. Balboa Ins. Co., 526

Kelly v. Kowalsky, 166–167

Kendall Yacht Corp. v. United California Bank, 466–467

Kerr Steamship Co. v. Radio Corp. of America, 279

Kirk Williams Co. Inc. v. Six Industries, Inc., 158–160

Kittredge v. Langley, 638 n.13

Klebanow v. New York Produce Exchange, 640 n.23

Klim v. Jones, 514 n.1

Klinicki v. Lundgren, 701

Kloster-Madsen, Inc. v. Tafi's, Inc., 525

Kruger v. Gerth, 714

Kuchta v. Allied Builders Corp., 739 n.4

Kuss Machine Tool & Die Co. v. El-Tronics, Inc., 294

L

Laemmar v. J. Walter Thompson Co., 216

Lair Distributing Co. v. Crump, 328

Lalli v. Lalli, 906

Lambert v. Home Fed. Sav. and Loan Ass'n, 226–227

Lamson v. Commercial Credit Corporation, 422

Landrine v. Mego Corporation, 392–393

Lane v. Honeycutt, 324–326

Lanfier v. Lanfier, 160–162

Langeveld v. LRZH Corp., 460

Lawrence v. Fox, 242

Lee Oldsmobile, Inc. v. Kaiden, 363

Lefkowitz v. Great Minneapolis Surplus Store, Inc., 129–131

Lehman v. Lehman, 856–858

Libel v. Libel, 213–214

Libra Bank Ltd. v. Banco Nacional de Costa Rica, 946, 952, 953

Lichtyger v. Franchard Corp., 635 n.8

Lieber v. Mohawk Arms, Inc., 847

Lindenfelser v. Lindenfelser, 876 n.10

Little Rock & Ft. Smith Ry. Company v. Eubanks, 191 n.8

L.M.T. Steel Products, Inc. v. Peirson, 566

Loeb & Co. v. Schreiner, 311

LTV Aerospace Corp. v. Bateman, 311

Lucas v. Hamm, 243 n.14

Lucy, W. O., and J. C. Lucy v. A. H. Zehmer and Ida S. Zehmer, 177–179

Lumber Sales, Inc. v. Brown, 317

Lumley v. Gye, 75 n.1

Lund v. Commonwealth of Virginia, 106

Lynch v. Donnelly, 28 n.20

M

McAvoy v. Medina, 847

McCall v. Frampton, 199

McCallum v. Gray, 675–676

McCarty v. E. J. Korvette, Inc., 382

McConnell v. Commonwealth Pictures Corp., 186 n.5

McCutcheon v. United Homes Corp., 191–193

McDonald v. Davis, 581

McGee v. International Life Insurance Co., 648

McGowan v. Maryland, 28 n.18

Mackie v. LaSalle Industries, Inc., 76–77

McLain v. Real Estate Board of New Orleans, 20

McLaughlin Ford, Inc. v. Ford Motor Company, 733

McLouth Steel Corp. v. Jewell Coal & Coke Co., 124

McMeekin v. Gimbel Brothers, Inc., 382

MacPherson v. Buick Motor Co., 384–386

Maras v. Stilinovich, 614–615

Marbury v. Madison, 18 n.3, 36, 787

Marine Midland Bank—New York v. Graybar Electric Co., 427

Marshall v. Barlow's, Inc., 29, 824–826

Martin v. American Exp., Inc., 776

Martin v. Ryder Truck Rental, Inc., 396

Marvin v. Marvin, 186–188, 199

Masheter v. Boehm, 867

Mason v. Blayton, 417

Masterson v. Sine, 229–230

Mattei v. Hopper, 116

Matter of Estate of Weidner, 902

Charles A. Howard, 718

May Dept. Stores Co. v. Pittsburgh Nat. Bank, 424 n.4

Mazer v. Jackson Ins. Agency, 167

Mecham v. United Bank of Arizona, 441

Meinhard v. Salmon, 690 n.2

Mellen v. Johnson, 127–128

Mendelson-Zeller Co., Inc. v. Joseph Wedner & Son Co., 294–295

Merchants and Farmers Bank v. Harris Lumber Co., 688

Merritt v. Railroad Co., 169 n.2

Metro-Goldwyn-Mayer, Inc. v. Showcase Atlantic Coop. Productions, Inc., 89

Michigan-Wisconsin Pipeline Co. v. Kentucky, 655

Miles v. Perpetual Sav. & Loan Co., 566

Miller v. City Bank & Trust Co., N.A., 611–612

Miller v. Plains Ins. Co., 210–211

Mineral Park Land Co. v. Howard, 258 n.29

Minneapolis v. Republic Creosoting Co., 257 n.23

Minton v. Cavaney, 665

Miranda v. Arizona, 98 n.6

Mishara Constr. Co., Inc. v. Transit-Mixed Concrete Corp., 335–337

Missouri Pac. Ry. Co. v. Elmore & Stahl, 860–862

Mitchell v. Reynolds, 789–790

Mitsubishi Motors Corp. v. Solek Chrysler-Plymouth, Inc., 50 n.13

Moe v. Steenberg, 593

Monsanto Co. v. Spray-Rite Service Corp., 817

Moon Over the Mountain, Ltd. v. Marine Midland Bank, 480

Moore v. Kuehn, 118–119

Moore v. Puget Sound Plywood, Inc., 357

Morad v. Coupounas, 691–692

Morris v. Hokosana, 266

Moses v. Newman, 322

Motorists Mutual Insurance Company v. Richmond, 915–916

Mutual Sav. Life Ins. Co. v. Noah, 931

Myzel v. Fields, 729

N

Nagy v. State of New York, 73–74

Nanda v. Ford Motor Co., 396

National Cash Register Co. v. Townsend Grocery Store, 215–216

National Collegiate Athletic Association v. Board of Regents of Oklahoma et al, 802

National Reserve Bank of the City of New York v. The Corn Exchange Bank, 465

National Society of Professional Engineers v. United States, 794, 804

Natural Resources Defense Council, Inc. v. EPA, 779

Nelson v. Shroeder Aerosports, Inc., 849–850

New Liberty Medical and Hospital Corp. v. E. F. Hutton and Co., 676

New York Times v. Sullivan, 26, 27, 57 n.

New York Yellow Pages, Inc. v. Growth Personnel Agency, Inc., 215

Ninth Street East Ltd. v. Harrison, 328

NLRB: v. Bildisco, 11–15, 544, 548–549

    v. Jones & Laughlin Steel Corp., 750 n.2

    v. Retail Store Employees Union, 828

Norfolk Dev. Corp. v. St. Regis Pulp and Paper Corp., 396

Northern Pipeline Co. v. Marathon Pipeline Co., 527

Northwest Airlines, Inc. v. Minnesota, 24

O

Oak Park Currency Exchange, Inc. v. Maropoulos, 451–452

Oberg v. Phillips, 343

O'Callaghan v. Waller & Beckwith Realty Co., 216

Oddo v. Ries, 630

O'Donnell v. MFA Insurance Company, 931

Old American Life Ins. Co. v. Biggers, 162

Olsen v. Hawkins, 179 n.5

Ortelere v. Teachers Retirement Board, 180 n.7

Orzeck v. Englehart, 714

Ossip-Harris Insurance, Inc. v. Barnett Bank of South Florida, N.A., 472–474

Overbeck v. Sears, Roebuck and Company, 199–200

Owens v. Haas, 245

P

Palmer and Ray Dental Supply of Abilene v. First National Bank, 428

Palsgraf v. Long Island R.R. Co., 66–67

Pan American Bank of Tampa v. Sullivan, 460

Pankas v. Bell, 181

Park Cities Corp. v. Byrd, 642

Park City Corp. v. Watchie, 676

Parker v. Arthur Murray, Inc., 258–260

Parker, A. B., v. Bell Ford, Inc., 343

Paset v. Old Orchard Bank & Trust Co., 842–844

Paul v. First Nat'l Bank of Cincinnati, 867–869

Peckham v. Larsen Chevrolet, 340–342

Peddy v. Montgomery, 181

Peerless Glass Co. v. Pacific Crockery Co., 202 n.2

People v. Norwood, 404

Pestana v. Karinol Corp., 315–316

Petersen v. Pilgrim Village, *132–133*

Peterson v. Peterson, 517–518

Petry v. Cosmopolitan Spa International, Inc., 235–236

Philadelphia v. New Jersey, 32

Piehl v. Norwegian Old Peoples' Home Society of Chicago, 194–195

Plante v. Jacobs, 250–251

Plasteel Products Corp. v. Helman, 635 n.12

Plessy v. Ferguson, 6

Prentiss v. Sheffel, 622

Procter & Gamble Distributing Co. v. Lawrence American Field Warehousing Corp., 864

Q

Quaker Hill, Inc. v. Parr, 658

Quality Motors, Inc. v. Hays, 170–171

Quantum Dev. vs. Joy, 423 n.2

R

Raffles v. Wichelhaus and Another, 202–203
Ralston Purina Co. v. McNabb, 311
Ramsey v. Gordon, 563–564
Rapoport v. 55 Perry Co., 622
Raymond Motor Transportation v. Rice, 21, 22
REA and 22 Ford, Inc. v. Ford Motor Co., 736–737
Rea Express, Inc. v. Brennan, 828
Regents of the University of California v. Bakke, 829
Regina v. Faulkner, 105
Rehrig v. Fortunak, 443 n.1
Reliance Cooperage Corp. v. Treat, 257 n.21
Reliance Electric Co. v. Emerson Electric Co., 728
Reserve Mining Co. v. EPA, 783
Reynolds v. Armstead, 265–266
Rhodes v. Wilkins, 225 n.22
Ricchetti v. Meister Brau, Inc., 800–801
Rice v. Santa Fe Elevator Corp., 24
Richelman v. Kewanee Machinery & Conveyer Co., 396
Ricketts v. Scotham, 163 n.11
Ringling Bros.-Barnum and Bailey Combined Shows v. Ringling, 649 n.10
Roberts v. Sears, Roebuck & Co., 584–586
Robertson v. King, 181
Robertson v. Levy, 646 n.
Robinson v. Branch Moving and Storage Co., 382
Rockland Trust Co. v. South Shore Nat'l Bank, 480
Rogers v. Unimac Company, Inc., 390–391
Rohdie v. Washington, 638 n.16
Ronnett v. American Breeding Herds, Inc., 729
Rose v. Lurvey, 152–153
Roseman v. Retail Credit Co., Inc., 775
Rosen v. Deporter-Butterworth Tours, Inc., 576–577
Rosenblum v. Adler, 942
Rossi v. Ventresca Bros. Const. Co., Inc., 61
Roto-Rooter Corp. v. O'Neal, 89
Roy v. Allstate Ins. Co., 920–921
Royal Indem. Company v. Westinghouse Elec. Corp., 279
Royal Store Fixture Co. v. Bucci, 293–294
Rozen v. North Carolina Nat. Bank, 438–439
Runyan v. Pacific Air Indust., Inc., 741
Ryan v. Kanne, 937
Rylands v. Fletcher, 72

S

Safeway Stores v. Suburban Foods, 83 n.2
Saka v. Sahara-Nevada Corp., 441
Sam Goody, Inc. v. Franklin Nat'l Bank of Long Island, 464–465
Save the Bay Committee, Inc. v. Mayor, etc., of the City of Savannah, 777 n.1
Saxe, Bacon and Bolan, P.C. v. Martindale-Hubbell, Inc., 653

Schaefers v. Apel, 892
Schenck v. Nortron Corporation, 89
Schermerhorn v. Vanderheyden, 242
Schnell v. The Vallescura, 862
Schrier v. Home Indemnity Co., 328
Scott v. Fox Brothers Enterprises, Inc., 245
Sears, Roebuck & Co. v. Seven Palms Motor Inn, 892
    v. Stiffel Co., 89
Seattle Times Co. v. Tielsch, 184–185
Seaver v. Ransome, 245
Securities and Exchange Comm. v. Children's Hospital, 728
    v. W. J. Howey Co., 738 n.3, 728
    v. Koenig, 728
    v. Texas Gulf Sulphur Co., 720–723
Seedkem, Inc. v. Safranek, 936–937
Sessa v. Riegle, 366–367
Shakey's Incorporated v. Martin, 741
Shapiro v. Hotel Statler Corp., 372
Sharon v. Time, Inc., 28
Sharp v. Coopers & Lybrand, 939–941
Shelley v. Kraemer, 888
Sherwood v. Walker, 203 n.4
Sherwood & Roberts-Oregon, Inc. v. Alexander, 658
Shuey v. United States, 148
Sierra Club v. Morton, 25 n.13, 32
Simon v. Eastern Kentucky Welfare Rights Organization, 25 n.14
Singleton v. Commissioner of Internal Revenue, 42 n.9
Slaughter v. Jefferson Federal Sav. and Loan Ass'n, 441
Sloane v. Dixie Gardens, Inc., 892
Smith v. Atlantic Properties, Inc., 702
Smith v. Chapman, 771–772
Smith v. Gerrish, 372
Sony Corp. v. Universal City Studios, 86–87, 955
Sonzinsky v. United States, 25 n.10
Southern Baptist Hospital v. Williams, 409 n.1
Southern Pacific Co. v. Arizona, 21 n.7
    v. Loden, 860 n.7
Spaulding v. New England Furniture Co., 181
Sports Factory, Inc. v. Chanoff, 642
S.S.I. Investors Limited v. Korea Tungsten Mining Co., 148
Standard Oil Co. of California v. United States, 811
Standard Oil Co. of New Jersey, The, v. United States, 792–794
State v. Burton, 92
    by Lefkowitz v. ITM, Inc., 308
    v. Mills, 106
    v. Rollins, 216
    of New Jersey v. Canola, 91–92
    of Washington v. Birch, 631
Statler v. Ray Mfg. Co., 384–385
Steele v. Latimer, 873–874
Steigler v. Ins. Co. of North America, 921–922

Stensel v. Stensel, 502–503

Stephen Industries, Inc. v. Haskins and Sells, 942

Sterling Nat'l Bank and Trust Co. v. Fidelity Mortgage Investors, 460

Sternmeyer v. Schroeppel, 281

Stoops v. Smith, 231–232

Strother v. Strother, 625–627

Stuart v. Overland Medical Center, 605–607

Sun Pipe Line Co. v. Altes, 704–706

Sun Printing and Publishing Assn. v. Remington Paper & Power Co., Inc., 506

S. W. Neighborhood Assembly v. Eckard, 788

Sylvestre v. Minnesota, 140 n.16

T

Tampa Elec. Co. v. Nashville Coal Co., 811

Tanbro Fabrics Corp. v. Deering Milliken, Inc., 495–496

Taute v. Econo-Car Int'l, Inc., 741

Taylor v. Caldwell, 280

Tennessee Valley Auth. v. Hill, 786–787

Terminal Grain Corp. v. Freeman, 290–292

Texas Trading v. Federal Republic of Nigeria, 949–950

T.G.I. Friday's, Inc. v. International Restaurant Group, Inc., 89

Theis v. duPont, Glore Forgan Inc., 574–575

Thomas v. Winchester, 384, 385

Thompson v. Occidental Life Ins. Co., 930–931

Thompson Crane & Trucking Co. v. Eyman, 213 n.14

Tigrett v. Pointer, 675

Timmermann v. Timmermann, 622

Transatlantic Financing Corp. v. United States, 258 n.30

Travco Corp. v. Citizens Federal Sav. & Loan Ass'n, 428

Trendtex Trading Corp. v. Central Bank of Nigeria, 949

Troop v. St. Louis Union Trust Co., 847

Turner v. General Motors Corp., 394 n.6

Tuttle v. Buck, 79–81

Two, Inc. v. Gilmore, 208–209

U

Uldrich v. Datasport, Inc., 697–699

Ultramares Corp. v. Touche, 935–936

United States v. Aluminum Co. of America, 808 n.5

   v. Arnold, Schwinn & Co., 739 n.5, 809, 810

   v. Atlantic Richfield Co., 781–782

   v. Barth, 644 n.3, 655

   v. Bower, 96–97

   v. Causby, 866 n.3

   v. Colgate & Co., 811 n.12

   v. General Elec. Co., 808 n.9

   v. General Motors Corp., 806–807

   v. Gonzales, 519–520

   v. Grinnel Corp., 807 n.

   v. Interstate Commerce Commission, 750

   v. Joint Traffic Ass'n, 792 n.11

   v. Kahriger, 25 n.12

   v. Knight, E. C., Co., 792 n.8

   v. Nixon, 36–37

   v. Park, 767 n.10

   v. Philadelphia National Bank, 812

   v. Real Estate Development Corp., 590

   v. Rybicki, 105–106

   v. Sanchez, 25 n.11

   v. Slutsky, 29 n.24

   v. Socony Vacuum Oil Co., 795

   v. Tilton, 102–103

   v. Transmissouri Freight Ass'n., 792 n.9

   v. United States Gypsum Co., 804, 818

   v. Von's Grocery Co., 812–814

United States Steel Corp. v. Fortner Enterprises, Inc., 811

U.S. Trust Company of New York v. McSweeney, 480

United States for the Use of Fram Corp. v. Crawford, 344

Universal C.I.T. Credit Corp. v. Ingel, 417

V

Valley Finance, Inc. v. United States, 655

Valley Forge Christian College v. Americans United, 32

Valley Nat. Bank v. Porter, 434

Van Duyn v. Home Office, 951–952

Varney v. Ditmars, 132–133

Venzke v. Magdanz, 251

Verlinden B. V. v. Central Bank of Nigeria, 953

Vermont Yankee Nuclear Power Corp. v. Natural Resources Defense Council, Inc., 759

Vickrey v. Sanford, 470

VJK Productions, Inc. v. Friedman/Meyer Productions, Inc., 262

Vokes v. Arthur Murray, Inc., 206–208

Vrgora v. Los Angeles United School District, 269–271

Vuitton, et Fils, S.A. v. Crown Handbags, 81–83

W

Wagner v. International Ry. Co., 69

Walls v. Morris Chevrolet, Inc., 410–411

Walraven v. Ramsay, 638 n.14

Warner v. Texas & Pac. Ry. Co., 219 n.10

Wat Henry Pontiac Co. v. Bradley, 368–370

Watertown Federal Sav. and Loan v. Spanks, 426 n.5

W.C.M. Window Co., Inc. v. Bernardi, 644 n.4

Weaver v. Bank of America, 267, 467

Webb v. McGowin, 162

Webster v. Blue Ship Tea Room, 370–372

Weil v. Diversified Properties, 637–638

Welsh v. Independent Bank and Trust Co., 707–708

Welton v. Gallagher, 847

Werner v. So. Calif. etc. Newspapers, 58
Whirlpool Corp. v. Marshall, 587 n.16
White v. Guarente, 942
White v. Randolph, 905–906
Whitehead v. Bishop, 911
Wichita Eagle & B. Pub. Co., Inc. v. Pacific Nat. Bk. of San Fran., 953
Wickard v. Filburn, 19 n.4
Wild v. Brewer, 30
William F. Wilke, Inc. v. Cummins Diesel Engines, Inc., 322
Williams v. Burrus, 616
Williams v. Walker-Thomas Furniture Co., 199, 760 n.
Williams & Associates v. Ramsey Products Corp., 232
Williamson v. Wanless, 417
Willred Co. v. Westmoreland Metal Mfg. Co., 362
Wilson Floors Co. v. Sciota Park, Ltd., 222–224
Wilson Trading Corp. v. David Ferguson, Ltd., 359–361

Winston v. Lee, 29
Wishing Well Club v. Akron, 183 n.3
Womack v. Maner, 199
Wood v. Lucy, Lady Duff-Gordon , 156 n.8
Wudrick v. Clements, 545

Y

Yommer v. McKenzie, 71–72
Younger v. Plunkett, 526

Z

Zabriskie v. Lewis, 728
Zapatha v. Dairy Mart., Inc., 330–331
Zilg v. Prentice-Hall, Inc., 262
Zorach v. Clauson, 28 n.19

WEST'S
BUSINESS LAW
Text & Cases

Third Edition

UNIT I

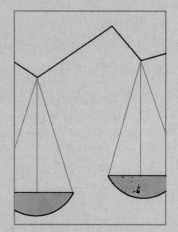

THE LEGAL
ENVIRONMENT
OF BUSINESS

1

Introduction to the Study of Law

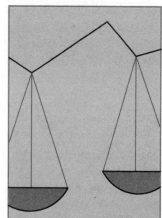

Law has developed because individuals and society need certain standards that govern relationships among individuals and between people and their government. Law works within a social order containing numerous activities, among which are business activities. Thus, the study of law includes the effect of law on business activities. The rules, or laws, to be described exist as an expression of the standards set by society.

WHAT IS LAW?

Aristotle saw law as a rule of conduct. Plato believed law was a form of social control. Cicero contended that law was the agreement of reason and nature, the distinction between the just and the unjust. The British jurist Sir William Blackstone described law as "a rule of civil conduct prescribed by the supreme power in a state, commanding what is right, and prohibiting what is wrong." In America, the eminent jurist Oliver Wendell Holmes contended that law was a set of rules that allowed one to predict how a court would resolve a particular dispute—"the prophecies of what the courts will do in fact, and nothing more pretentious, are what I mean by the law."

There have been and will continue to be different definitions of law. We can begin to understand something about the nature of law by looking at two approaches to the study of it.

The Traditional Approach

The traditional approach sees law as a body of principles and rules that courts apply in deciding disputes, and thus the study of law is the study of these rules and the general principles of right and wrong upon which the rules are based. The traditional approach is based upon the idea that the principles of right and wrong change, if at all, less rapidly than society changes. Hence, this approach fulfills one of the important functions of law—to provide stability, predictability, and continuity so that people can be sure of how to order their affairs.

The Sociological Approach

Many people perceive law as being a social institution and, as such, only one part of the total environment of society. This is a sociological approach to law. In this view, the purpose of law is to create a legal system with the proper incentives to provide and promote justice and stability in a given society. The term **justice,** however, is subject to great controversy. Justice has different meanings to different people, and thus conflicting ideas arise as to how the law should be structured.

Most people, for example, agree that the law should protect individuals from being injured or killed. People also look upon crimes against the government, such as treason and sedition, with disfavor, and consequently, we have laws that prohibit these types of crimes. Laws also protect the public health, safety, and morals. The question frequently arises, however, as to how the public health, safety, and morals can best be protected, and the social environment exercises much influence over what decisions are made. As society changes, its laws must also change. Scientific and technological advances in our culture have often created situations in which there is no existing law to rely upon, and hence new principles of law have had to be developed. Moreover, people's ideas of right and wrong change over time. Thus, law is often perceived as an instrument by which society can go about obtaining *social justice* through the orderly process provided by the legal system.

Most of the material in this book takes the traditional approach. It presents the rules of law that apply to the business world and the principles on which they are based. Remember, however, that *outside forces in the environment do shape the rules*.

SCHOOLS OF LEGAL, OR JURISPRUDENTIAL, THOUGHT

The court opinions in this book show that judges often refer to custom, logic, history, or a philosophy of what is right in making a decision. Sometimes, however, they may seem to ignore custom and history, to stretch their logic to the breaking point, and to depart from previous notions of what is right. Law is often shaped by "legal reasoning"—reasoning that is employed by a judge to achieve justice in an individual case but that is apparently inconsistent with prior decisions. It would be easy to shrug one's shoulders, say "that's legal reasoning," and dismiss the majority of judges as illogical or dishonest. Yet there are reasons for deciding a case one way as opposed to another. Part of the study of law, often referred to as **jurisprudence,** is ascertaining the principles upon which legal rules are actually based.

All legal philosophers agree that custom, history, logic, and ideals have influenced the development of law in some way. These philosophers disagree, however, on the importance that each of these in-

fluences should have in shaping law, and their disagreements have produced different schools, or philosophies, of jurisprudence.

The Natural Law School

The natural law philosopher assumes that there is an ideal state of being, either inherent in the nature of humanity or derived from a divine source. This ideal state, based on **natural law,** presupposes a definite right and wrong. Hence, the purpose of a legal system, according to the natural law philosophers, is to help society approach the ideal of natural law. People do not create this natural law, but rather discover it through the use of reason and the knowledge of good and evil. The natural law school emphasizes ethics as the source of legal authority. Documents such as the Magna Carta, the Declaration of Independence, the U.S. Constitution, and the U.N. Declaration of Human Rights reflect natural law ideals in phrases like: "We hold these truths to be self-evident, that all men are created equal, that they are endowed by their Creator with certain inalienable Rights *   *   *."

The Historical School

The historical school emphasizes the evolutionary process of law by concentrating upon the origin and history of the legal system. Thus, this school looks to the past to discover what the principles of contemporary law should be. The legal principles that have withstood the passage of time—those that have worked in the past—are deemed best suited for shaping present laws. Hence, law derives its legitimacy and authority from adhering to the principles that historical development has shown to be workable. Followers, or adherents, of the historical school are more likely than those of other schools to follow strictly decisions that have been presented in past cases.

The Analytical School

The analytical school uses logic to shape law. A legal analyst examines the structure and subject matter of a legal code and uses logical analysis to extract the principles that underlie it. By analyzing cases and rules, analysts formulate general principles, and these principles become the starting points for legal reasoning. Individual laws are judged on the basis of whether they are in logical agreement with these starting points.

The Legal Realists

Legal realism is based upon the idea that law is shaped by social forces and needs, and hence law may be viewed as an instrument of social control. In addition to stressing the pragmatic and empirical sides of law, legal realists perceive law as a means to a social end, and hence, they desire to predict and influence lawmaking. They believe that, despite moral law, historical development, and logical analysis, the same conclusion will not always follow from the same set of facts. A reviewing court, therefore, may view facts differently than a lower court. For the legal realist, the legitimacy of law and of legal institutions is measured by how well they serve the needs of society.

HISTORY AND SOURCES OF AMERICAN LAW

Because of our colonial heritage, much of American law is based on the English legal system. Without a knowledge of this heritage, one cannot understand the nature of our legal system today.

The Establishment of Courts of Law

In 1066 the Normans conquered England, and William the Conqueror and his successors began the process of unifying the country under their rule. One of the means they used to this end was the establishment of the king's court. Before the Conquest, disputes had been settled locally according to local custom. The king's court sought to establish a common or uniform set of customs for the whole country. The body of rules that evolved under the king's court, called the *Curia Regis*, was the beginning of the *common law*. As the number of courts and cases increased, the more important decisions of each year were gathered together and recorded in year books. Judges, settling disputes similar to ones that had been decided before, used the year books as the basis for their decisions. If a case was unique, judges had to create new laws, but they based their decisions on the general principles suggested by ear-

lier cases. The body of judge-made law that developed under this system is still used today and is known as the **common law.**

Common Law

Common law began as the ancient unwritten law of England, but common law today includes the statutory and case-law background of England and of the American colonies prior to the American Revolution. The **case law** of the United States since the American Revolution is a predominant part of our common law. This case law consists of the rules of law announced in court decisions. It is the aggregate of reported cases. These cases may consist of a court interpretation of a statute, of a regulation, or of a provision in a constitution. Such an interpretation becomes part of the authoritative law on the subject and further serves as a *precedent* in the particular jurisdiction. A prior case that is similar in legal principles or in facts to a case under consideration is referred to as a **precedent.**

Common law must be distinguished from statutory law, such as that enacted by state and federal legislatures. Where common law does not conflict with a statute, it generally has the same force as statutory law, since most states have adopted common law by legislative decree.

Thus, in areas where legislation has not covered the relevant issue, courts still refer to the common law. The history and circumstances of the various states differ, and this has given rise to differences in the common law in each state. Even where legislation has been substituted for common law, courts often rely on common law to interpret the legislation on the theory that the people who drafted the statute intended to codify a previous common-law rule.

Stare Decisis

The practice of deciding new cases with reference to former decisions eventually became a cornerstone of the English and American judicial systems. It forms a doctrine called *stare decisis* ("to stand on decided cases"). The doctrine of *stare decisis* suggests that judges attempt to follow precedents.

The doctrine of *stare decisis* performs many useful functions. First, it helps the courts to be more efficient. It would be very time-consuming if each judge had to reason out the policies for deciding what the law should be for each case brought before the court. If other courts have confronted the same issue and reasoned through the case carefully, their opinions can serve as guides.

Second, *stare decisis* creates a more just and uniform system. The rule of precedent tends to neutralize the prejudices of individual judges. If judges feel pressure to use precedent as the basis for their decisions, they will be less influenced by any personal prejudices. Different states and regions, however, often follow different precedents, and hence variations in rules of law occur.

Third, *stare decisis* makes the law more stable and predictable. If the law on that subject is well settled, someone bringing a case to court can usually rely upon the court to make a decision based on what the law has been.

Finally, *stare decisis* reflects the experience of the past and is based on the wisdom of the past.

Sometimes a court will depart from the rule of precedent because it has decided that the precedent is incorrect. For example, if changes in technology, business practice, or society's attitudes necessitate a change in the law, courts may depart from precedent. Judges are reluctant to overthrow precedent, and whether they do will depend on the subject of the case, the number and prestige of prior decisions, the degree of social change that has occurred, and the identity of the deciding court.

Sometimes there is no precedent on which to base a decision, or there are conflicting precedents. In these situations, a court will: (1) refer to past decisions that may be similar to the current case and decide the case by reasoning through analogy; (2) look at social factors—changes in the status of women, for example—that might influence the issues involved; and (3) consider what the fairest result would be.

Cases that overturn precedent often receive a great deal of publicity. In *Brown v. Board of Education*, for example, the U.S. Supreme Court expressly overturned precedent when it concluded that separate educational facilities for whites and blacks are inherently unequal.[1] Previously, in *Plessy v. Ferguson*, as well as in numerous other cases, the Court had upheld as constitutional the provision of separate but equal accommodations.[2] Thus, the Su-

preme Court's departure from precedent in *Brown* received a tremendous amount of publicity as people began to realize the ramifications of this change in the law. Yet irrespective of the publicity that is typically generated when cases overturn precedent, in reality the majority of cases are decided according to precedent because of the application of the doctrine of *stare decisis*.

MORE RECENT SOURCES OF LAW

Much law has been made since the officials of the king's court made decisions with reference to the year books. Today, courts have sources other than precedent to consider when making their decisions.

Constitutions

The federal government and the states have separate constitutions that set forth the general organization, powers, and limits of their respective governments. The U.S. Constitution[3] is the supreme law of the land. A law in violation of the Constitution, no matter what its source, will be declared unconstitutional and will not be enforced. Similarly, unless they conflict with the U.S. Constitution, state constitutions are supreme within their respective borders.

The U.S. Constitution defines the powers and limitations of the federal government. All powers not granted to the federal government are retained by the states or the people. The Constitution, for example, gives the federal government the power to regulate *interstate* commerce, and thus states retain the power to regulate *intrastate* commerce. The Constitution further delineates how federal powers are divided among the three governmental branches, establishing a system of checks and balances. Hence, the legislative power (power to make laws) is vested in the Congress; the executive power (power to see that laws are carried out) is vested in the president; and the judicial power (power to determine what the law is and whether laws are valid) is vested in the courts.[4]

---

1. 347 U.S. 483, 495 (1954).
2. See *Plessy v. Ferguson*, 163 U.S. 537 (1896).

3. See Appendix B for the complete text of the U.S. Constitution.
4. State governments are generally established and organized in the same way as the federal government.

Codified Law: Statutes and Ordinances

Statutes enacted by the Congress and the various state legislative bodies comprise another source of law which is generally referred to as **statutory law**. The statutory law of the United States further consists of the ordinances passed by cities and counties, none of which can violate the U.S. Constitution or the relevant state constitution. Today legislative bodies and regulatory agencies have assumed an ever-increasing share of lawmaking. Much of the work of modern courts consists of interpreting what the rulemaker meant when the law was passed and applying it to a present set of facts.

Administrative Agency Regulations

An administrative agency is created when the executive or legislative branch of the government delegates some of its authority to an appropriate group of persons. Administrative agencies exercise legislative, executive, and judicial power—in their rulemaking, they are using legislative power; in their regulation and supervision, they are using executive power; and in their adjudication procedures, they are using judicial power. Unlike legislators, presidents, governors, and many judges, administrative agency personnel are rarely chosen by popular elections, and many do not serve fixed terms. As a result, great power is given to people who may not be responsive to the public.

Administrative law is the branch of public law concerned with the executive power and actions of administrative agencies, their officials, and their workers.[5] When an individual has a dispute with such an agency, administrative law comes into play. The scope of administrative law has expanded enormously in recent years, and the scope of administrative agencies has increased so much that their activities have come to be called *administrative process*, in contrast to *judicial process*. Administrative process involves the administration of law by non-judicial agencies, whereas judicial process is the administration of law by judicial bodies (the courts).

---

5. See Chapter 45 for a more extensive discussion of administrative law.

SOURCES OF COMMERCIAL (OR BUSINESS) LAW

The body of law that pertains to commercial dealings is commonly referred to as commercial, or business, law. It includes most of the topics in this text—contracts, partnerships, corporations, and agencies, for example. For business students, the most important codification of commercial law is the Uniform Commercial Code (UCC). Since the UCC forms the basis of many chapters in this book, its origins will be briefly discussed here.

Codification of Commercial Law

In the interests of uniformity and reform, the legal profession, under the leadership of the American Law Institute, has suggested that comprehensive codes of laws be adopted by the states. (These codes of laws are also statutory law).

The National Conference of Commissioners on Uniform State Laws first started to meet in the late 1800s in order to draft uniform statutes. Once these uniform codes were drawn up, the commissioners urged each state legislature to adopt them. Adoption of uniform codes is a state matter, and a state may reject all or part of a code. Hence, the laws throughout the United States are not "uniform."

The first such code, or act, was the Negotiable Instruments Act, which was finally approved in 1896 and was adopted in every state by the early 1920s (though not all states used exactly the same wording). Afterwards, other acts were drawn up in a similar manner; they included the Uniform Sales Act, the Uniform Warehouse Receipts Act, the Uniform Bills of Lading Act, the Uniform Partnership Act, the Model Business Corporation Act (drafted by the American Bar Association), and the Uniform Stock Transfer Act. Recently, a Uniform Probate Code was prepared. The most ambitious uniform act of all, however, was the Uniform Commercial Code.

The Uniform Commercial Code (UCC)

The National Conference of Commissioners on Uniform State Laws and the American Law Institute sponsored and directed the preparation of the Uniform Commercial Code. These two organizations were assisted by literally hundreds of law professors, businesspersons, judges, and lawyers. The complete text of the Code can be found in Appendix C in this book. The District of Columbia, the Virgin Islands, and all fifty states have adopted the Uniform Commercial Code in whole or in part.[6]

The UCC is designed to assist the legal relationship of parties involved in modern commercial transactions by helping to determine the intentions of the parties to a commercial contract and by giving force and effect to their agreement. Moreover, the Code is meant to encourage business transactions by assuring businesspersons that their contracts, if validly entered into, will be enforced.

CLASSIFICATION OF LAW

The body of law is huge. In order to study it, one must break it down by some means of classification. No single system of classification can cover such a large mass of information; consequently, those systems that have been devised tend to overlap. Moreover, they are, of necessity, arbitrary in some respects. A discussion of the best known systems follows.

Substantive versus Procedural Law

Substantive law includes all of those laws that define, describe, regulate, and create legal rights and obligations. A rule stating that promises are enforced only where each party receives something of value from the other party is part of substantive law. So, too, is a rule stating that a person who injures another through negligence must pay damages.

Procedural law (or adjective law) establishes the methods of enforcing the rights that are established by substantive law. Questions about how a lawsuit should begin, what papers need to be filed, to which court the suit should go, which witnesses can be called, and so on are all questions of procedural law. In brief, substantive law tells us our rights; procedural law tells us how to exercise them.

Exhibit 1–1 classifies law in terms of its subject matter, dividing it into law covering substantive issues and law covering procedural issues. Most of this text concerns substantive law.

---

6. Louisiana, for example, has adopted only Articles 1, 3, 4, and 5.

EXHIBIT 1–1 Subject Matter Divided Into Substantive and Procedural[a]	
SUBSTANTIVE	**PROCEDURAL**
Agency	Evidence
Commercial paper	Civil procedure
Contracts	Criminal procedure
Corporation law	Administrative procedure
Property	Appellate procedure
Torts	
Taxation	
Sales	
Real property	
Personal property	
Partnerships	
Trusts and Wills	
Criminal law	
Constitutional law	
Administrative law	

a. The importance of this distinction is more than academic: the *result* of a case may well depend upon the determination that a rule is substantive rather than procedural.

Public versus Private Law

Public law addresses the relationship between persons and their government, whereas **private law** addresses direct dealings between persons.

Criminal law and constitutional law, for example, are generally classified as public law because they deal with persons and their relationships to government. Criminal acts, though they may involve only one victim, are seen as offenses against society as a whole and are prohibited by governments in order to protect the public. Constitutional law is frequently classified as public law since it involves questions of whether the government—federal, state or local—has the power to act in a particular fashion; often the issue is whether a law, duly passed, exceeds the limits set on the government. See Exhibit 1–2 for examples.

Civil versus Criminal Law

Civil law spells out the duties that exist between persons or between citizens and their governments, excluding the duty not to commit crimes. Contract law, for example, is part of civil law. The whole body of tort law, which has to do with the infringement by one person of the legally recognized rights

EXHIBIT 1–2 Examples of Public and Private Law	
PUBLIC LAW	**PRIVATE LAW**
Administrative law	Torts
Constitutional law	Contracts
Criminal law	Partnerships
Civil, criminal, and	Corporation law
appellate procedure	Real property
Evidence	Personal property
Taxation	Agency
	Commercial paper
	Sales
	Trusts and Wills

of another, is an area of civil law. (Tort law is treated in Chapters 4 and 5.)

Criminal law, in contrast to civil law, is concerned with a wrong committed against the public as a whole.[7] Criminal acts are proscribed by local, state, or federal government statutes. Criminal law is always public law, whereas civil law is sometimes public and sometimes private. In a criminal case, the government seeks to impose a penalty upon an allegedly guilty person. In a civil case, one party (sometimes the government) tries to make the other party comply with a duty or pay for the damage caused by failure to so comply.

REMEDIES AT LAW VERSUS REMEDIES IN EQUITY

The distinction between law and equity is primarily of historical interest, but it has special relevance to students of business law. In the early king's courts, the kinds of **remedies** (legal means to recover a right or redress a wrong) that the courts could grant were severely restricted. If one person wronged another in some way, the king's court could award as compensation one or more of the following: (1) land, (2) items of value, or (3) money. The courts that awarded these compensations became known as **courts of law** and the three remedies were called **remedies at law.** Even though such a system introduced uniformity in the settling of disputes, when *plaintiffs* (parties suing) wanted a remedy other than economic

---

7.   Chapter 6 addresses criminal law in greater detail.

compensation, the courts of law could do nothing, so "no remedy, no right."

Equity Courts: Going to the King for Relief

When individuals could not obtain an adequate remedy in a court of law because of strict technicalities, they petitioned the king for relief. Most of these petitions were decided by an adviser of the king, called a **chancellor.** The chancellor was said to be the "keeper of the king's conscience." When the chancellor thought that the claim was a fair one, new and unique remedies were granted. In this way, a new body of chancery rules and reliefs, or remedies, came into being, and eventually formal chancery courts were established. These became known as *courts of equity.*

Equity is that branch of unwritten law, founded in justice and fair dealing, that seeks to supply a more equitable and adequate remedy than any available remedy at law. Thus, two distinct systems were created, each having a different set of judges. There were two bodies of rules and remedies that existed at the same time, *remedies at law* and **remedies in equity.** Plaintiffs had to specify whether they were bringing an "action at law" or an "action in equity," and they chose their courts accordingly. Only one remedy could be granted for a particular wrong, and even in equity the wrong had to be of a type the court would recognize as remediable.

Courts of equity had the responsibility of using discretion in supplementing the common law. Even today, when the same court can award both legal and equitable remedies, such discretion is often guided by so-called **equitable principles and maxims.** Maxims are propositions or general statements of rules of law that courts often invoke. Listed below are a few of the various maxims of equity.

1.   Whoever seeks equity must do equity.
2.   Equity treats as done what ought to be done.
3.   Where there is equal equity, the law must prevail.
4.   One seeking the aid of an equity court must come to the court with clean hands.
5.   Equity will not suffer a right to exist without a remedy.
6.   Equity aids the vigilant, not those who rest on their rights.

The last maxim is worthy of discussion. It means that individuals who fail to look out for their rights until after a reasonable time has passed will not be helped. This maxim has become known as the equitable doctrine of **laches.**

The equitable doctrine of laches can be used as a defense. The doctrine arose to encourage people to bring lawsuits while the evidence is fresh. What constitutes a reasonable time, of course, varies according to the circumstances of the case. Time periods for different types of cases are now usually fixed by **statutes of limitations.** After the time allowed under a statute of limitations has expired, no action can be brought no matter how strong the case was originally.

Equitable Relief

Decrees of Specific Performance   Previously, courts of law and equity were not merged. Hence, a plaintiff might come into a court of equity asking it to order a defendant to perform within the terms of a contract. A *court of law* could not issue such an order because its remedies were limited to payment of money or property as compensation for damages. A *court of equity*, however, could issue a decree of *specific performance*—an order to perform what was promised. Yet this remedy was, and still is, only available when the dispute before the court involves a *contractual* transaction.

Injunctions   If a person wanted a certain activity prevented, he or she would have to go to the chancellor in equity to ask that the person doing the wrongful act be ordered to stop. The order was called an injunction. An **injunction** is an order to a specific person, directing that person to *refrain* from engaging in a particular act. Injunctions are frequently contrasted with decrees of specific performance which require a contracting party *to carry out* his or her duties.

Rescission   Often the legal remedy of the payment of money for damages is unavailable or inadequate when there are disputes over agreements among persons. In such cases, the equitable remedy of rescission is frequently given. **Rescission** is an action to undo an agreement—to return the parties to their *status quo* prior to the agreement. It returns a person to the position he or she occupied before the other

person acted wrongfully. All duties created by the agreement are abolished. If, for example, a sales agreement is made because a seller misrepresents the quality of goods, but the fraud is discovered before any money changes hands, the buyer might want merely to rescind the agreement. If, however, money has been exchanged and the buyer has already resold some of the goods, the buyer might want damages for harm suffered.

The Merging of Law and Equity

Today the courts of law and equity are merged, and thus the distinction between these two types of courts has largely disappeared. A plaintiff (the person bringing the action) may now request both legal and equitable remedies in the same action, and the trial court judge may grant either kind or both forms of relief.

Yet the merging of the courts of law and equity does not diminish the importance of distinguishing legal remedies from equitable remedies. To request the proper remedy, one must know what remedies are available. Therefore, students of business law should be aware of the various equitable as well as legal remedies.

HOW TO FIND CASE LAW

Most trial court decisions are not published. Except for the federal courts and New York and a few other states that publish selected opinions of their trial courts, decisions in trial courts are merely filed in the office of the clerk of the court, where they are available for public inspection.

On the other hand, the written decisions of appellate courts are published and distributed (these reported cases paradoxically are called *unwritten law*, as contrasted with the *written*, or statutory, law). Virtually all of the cases in this book have been taken from decisions of these appellate courts. It is therefore important to understand the case reporting system. The study of law is enhanced by using the so-called *case method* for presentation of subject matter. When students of law study cases, they are engaging in the inductive method of learning.

The reported appellate decisions are published in volumes called *Reports*, which are numbered consecutively. State court decisions are found in the state reports of that particular state. Additionally, state reports appear in regional units of the *National Reporter System*, published by West Publishing Company. Most lawyers and libraries have the West reporters because they report cases more quickly and they are distributed more widely than the state-published reports. In fact, many states have eliminated their own reports in favor of West's *National Reporter System*.

Geographical Areas

West Publishing Company has divided the states into geographical areas: Atlantic (A. or A.2d), Southeastern (S.E. or S.E.2d), Southwestern (S.W. or S.W.2d), Northwestern (N.W. or N.W.2d), Northeastern (N.E. or N.E.2d), Southern (So. or So.2d), and Pacific (P. or P.2d). After appellate decisions are published, they are normally referred to (cited) by giving the name of the case; the volume, name, and page of the state report (if any); the volume and page of the National Reporter; and the volume, name, and page of any other selected case series. For example, consider the following case: Quality Motors, Inc. v. Hays, 216 Ark. 264, 225 S.W.2d 326 (1950). After the names of the parties, we see that the opinion in this case may be found in Volume 216 of the official *Arkansas Reports* on page 264; and in Volume 225 of the *Southwestern Reporter*, Second Series on page 326. (Additionally, when we cite cases in this text, we give the name of the court and the year of filing for the appellate court decision.) See Exhibit 1–3 for West's *National Reporter System*.

Federal court decisions are found in the *Federal Reporter* (F. or F.2d), *Federal Supplement* (F.Supp.), *Federal Rules Decisions* (F.R.D.), *West's Bankruptcy Reporter* (B.R.), *United States Supreme Court Reports* (U.S.), *Supreme Court Reporter* (S.Ct.), and the *Lawyer's Edition* (L.Ed.).

Case Titles

In the title of a case such as *Adams v. Jones*, the v. or vs. stands for versus, which means against. In the trial court, Adams was the plaintiff—the person who filed the suit. Jones was the defendant. When the case is appealed, however, the appellate court will sometimes place the name of the party appealing the decision first, so that the case will be called *Jones v. Adams. Since some appellate courts retain the trial court order of names, it is often impossible to distinguish the plaintiff from the defendant in the title of a reported appellate court decision.* The student must carefully read the facts of each case in order to identify each party. Otherwise, the discussion by the appellate court will be difficult to understand.

HOW TO ANALYZE CASE LAW

The following Supreme Court case is annotated to illustrate how one begins to analyze case law. Case law is critical with respect to the decision making of business people, since businesses must operate within the boundaries established by law. The law consists of case law as well as statutory law, and it is thus essential that business people be able to understand the law as evidenced by adjudicated cases. A substantial number of cases appear throughout this book.

The different sections of the given case are described following the case. Note that the triple asterisks (* * *) indicate that the authors of this book have deleted part of the opinion to make the case more concise and readable. Quadruple asterisks (* * * *) indicate that a paragraph (or more) has been omitted. Where an opinion cites another case, the citations to the referenced case have been omitted to save space and improve readability.

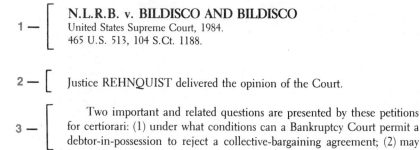

1 — **N.L.R.B. v. BILDISCO AND BILDISCO**
United States Supreme Court, 1984.
465 U.S. 513, 104 S.Ct. 1188.

2 — Justice REHNQUIST delivered the opinion of the Court.

3 — Two important and related questions are presented by these petitions for certiorari: (1) under what conditions can a Bankruptcy Court permit a debtor-in-possession to reject a collective-bargaining agreement; (2) may

EXHIBIT 1-3   National Reporter System   Regional/Federal

Regional Reporters	Coverage Beginning	Coverage
Atlantic Reporter	1885	Connecticut, Delaware, Maine, Maryland, New Hampshire, New Jersey, Pennsylvania, Rhode Island, Vermont, and District of Columbia Municipal Court of Appeals
North Eastern Reporter	1885	Illinois, Indiana, Massachusetts, New York and Ohio
North Western Reporter	1879	Iowa, Michigan, Minnesota, Nebraska, North Dakota, South Dakota and Wisconsin
Pacific Reporter	1883	Alaska, Arizona, California, Colorado, Hawaii, Idaho, Kansas, Montana, Nevada, New Mexico, Oklahoma, Oregon, Utah, Washington and Wyoming
South Eastern Reporter	1887	Georgia, North Carolina, South Carolina, Virgina and West Virginia
South Western Reporter	1886	Arkansas, Kentucky, Missouri, Tennessee, and Texas
Southern Reporter	1887	Alabama, Florida, Louisiana and Mississippi

Federal Reporters		
Federal Reporter	1880	United States Circuit Court from 1880 to 1912; Commerce Court of the United States from 1911 to 1913; District Courts of the United States from 1880 to 1932; U.S. Court of Claims from 1929 to 1932 and since 1960; the U.S. Court of Appeals from its organization in 1891; the U.S. Court of Customs and Patent Appeals from 1929; and the U.S. Emergency Court of Appeals from 1943.
Federal Supplement	1932	United States Court of Claims from 1932 to 1960; United States District Courts since 1932; United States Customs Court since 1956.
Federal Rules Decisions	1939	United States District Courts involving the Federal Rules of Civil Procedure since 1939 and Federal Rules of Criminal Procedure since 1946.
Supreme Court Reporter	1882	U.S. Supreme Court beginning with the October term of 1882.
Bankruptcy Reporter	1980	Bankruptcy decisions of U.S. Bankruptcy Courts, U.S. District Courts, U.S. Courts of Appeals and the U.S Supreme Court.
Military Justice Reporter	1978	United States Court of Military Appeals and Courts of Military Review for the Army, Navy, Air Force and Coast Guard.

NATIONAL REPORTER SYSTEM MAP

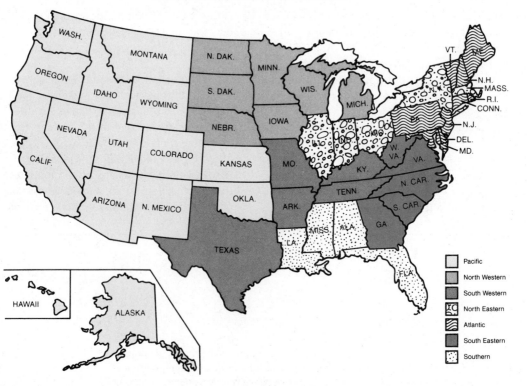

3 — the National Labor Relations Board find a debtor-in-possession guilty of an unfair labor practice for unilaterally terminating or modifying a collective-bargaining agreement before rejection of that agreement has been approved by the Bankruptcy Court. *   *   *

*   *   *   *

4 — On April 14, 1980, respondent Bildisco and Bildisco ("Bildisco"), a New Jersey general partnership in the business of distributing building supplies, filed a voluntary petition in bankruptcy for reorganization under Chapter 11 of the Bankruptcy Code. *   *   * Bildisco was subsequently authorized by the Bankruptcy Court to operate the business as debtor-in-possession under 11 U.S.C. § 1107.

*   *   *   *

5 — In December, 1980, Bildisco requested permission from the Bankruptcy Court, pursuant to 11 U.S.C. § 365(a), to reject the collective-bargaining agreement. *   *   * On January 15, 1981, the Bankruptcy Court granted

6 — Bildisco permission to reject the collective-bargaining agreement and allowed the Union 30 days in which to file a claim for damages against Bildisco stemming from the rejection of the contract. The District Court upheld the order of the Bankruptcy Court, and the Union appealed to the Court of Appeals for the Third Circuit.

7 — During mid-summer 1980, the Union filed unfair labor practice charges with the National Labor Relations Board ("Board"). *   *   * Ultimately the Board found that Bildisco had violated § 8(a)(5) and § 8(a)(1) of the NLRA by unilaterally changing the terms of the collective-bargaining agreement and by refusing to negotiate with the Union. *   *   * The Board petitioned the Court of Appeals for the Third Circuit to enforce its order.

8 — The Court of Appeals consolidated the Union's appeal and the Board's petition for enforcement of its order. *   *   * That court held that a collective-bargaining agreement is an executory contract subject to rejection by a debtor-in-possession under § 365(a) of the Bankruptcy Code.

9 — The Court of Appeals refused to enforce the Board's order, rejecting the Board's conclusion that Bildisco, as debtor-in-possession, was the alter-ego of the pre-petition employer. Under the Bankruptcy Code, a debtor-in-possession was deemed a "new entity" not bound by the debtor's prior collective-bargaining agreement. *   *   *

10 — We granted certiorari to review the decision of the Court of Appeals because of the apparent conflict between that decision and the decision of the Court of Appeals for the Second Circuit in *Brotherhood of Railway Employees v. REA Express, Inc.,* *   *   *.

11 — [1] Section 365(a) of the Bankruptcy Code, 11 U.S.C. § 365, provides in full:

"(a) Except as provided in sections 765 and 766 of this title and in subsections (b), (c), and (d) of this section, the trustee, subject to the court's approval, may assume or reject any executory contract or unexpired lease of the debtor."

*   *   * Obviously, Congress knew how to draft an exclusion for collective bargaining agreements when it wanted to; its failure to do so in this

11 — instance indicates that Congress intended that § 365(a) apply to all collective-bargaining agreements covered by the NLRA.

*   *   *   *

12 — We agree with the Court of Appeals below, and with the Court of Appeals for the Eleventh Circuit in a related case, *In re Brada-Miller Freight System, Inc.*, *   *   * that the Bankruptcy Court should permit rejection of a collective-bargaining agreement under § 365(a) of the Bankruptcy Code if the debtor can show that the collective-bargaining agreement burdens the estate, and that after careful scrutiny, the equities balance in favor of rejecting the labor contract. *   *   *

Before acting on a petition to modify or reject a collective-bargaining agreement, however, the Bankruptcy Court should be persuaded that reasonable efforts to negotiate a voluntary modification have been made and are not likely to produce a prompt and satisfactory solution. *   *   *

13 — [3] Since the policy of Chapter 11 is to permit successful rehabilitation of debtors, rejection should not be permitted without a finding that that policy would be served by such action. The Bankruptcy Court must make a reasoned finding on the record why it has determined that rejection should be permitted. Determining what would constitute a successful rehabilitation involves balancing the interests of the affected parties—the debtor, creditors, and employees. *   *   *

*   *   *   *

14 — [4] The second issue raised by this case is whether the NLRB can find a debtor-in-possession guilty of an unfair labor practice for unilaterally rejecting or modifying a collective-bargaining agreement before formal rejection by the Bankruptcy Court. *   *   *

*   *   *   *

15 — While all parties to this case ultimately concede that the Bankruptcy Court may authorize rejection of a collective-bargaining agreement, the Board and the Union nonetheless insist that a debtor-in-possession violates § 8(a)(5) and § 8(d) of the NLRA if it unilaterally changes the terms of the collective-bargaining agreement between the date of filing the bankruptcy petition and the date on which the Bankruptcy Court authorizes rejection of the agreement. *   *   *

*   *   *   *

16 — *   *   * But while a debtor-in-possession remains obligated to bargain in good faith under NLRA § 8(a)(5) over the terms and conditions of a possible new contract, it is not guilty of an unfair labor practice by unilaterally breaching a collective-bargaining agreement before formal Bankruptcy Court action.

17 — Accordingly, the judgment of the Court of Appeals is affirmed.

CASE ANALYSIS

1. The name of the case is *N.L.R.B. v. Bildisco and Bildisco*. Bildisco is the name of the plaintiff.

When the Bankruptcy Court granted Bildisco permission to reject the collective-bargaining agreement and both the Union and the National Labor Relations Board appealed, Bildisco then became the respondent. A *respondent* is the party who contends against the pending appeal.

The numbers and letters found below the case name, such as 465 U.S. 513, 104 S.Ct. 1188, constitute the **citation**. The citation follows the form prescribed in A *Uniform System of Citation*. The fact that this opinion is a Supreme Court opinion can be determined from the citation. We know that this case can be found in Volume 465 of the United States Supreme Court Reports, on page 513, and in Volume 104 of the *Supreme Court Reporter* on page 1188. The two sets of numbers are frequently referred to as parallel cites since this case appears in two different sets of reporters.

2. Justice Rehnquist is the name of the justice who delivered the opinion of the Court.

3. This sentence indicates what issues are to be decided. An issue is a disputed point of fact or law between the parties. It is directly related to the result, to the facts, and to the holding. In this particular case, the NLRB was alleging that Bildisco had violated the National Labor Relations Act by unilaterally changing the terms of the collective-bargaining agreement and that the language of "executory contract" of the Bankruptcy Code did not include collective-bargaining agreements.

4. This paragraph briefly describes the facts of the case. Bildisco filed a voluntary petition in bankruptcy for reorganization under Chapter 11 of the Bankruptcy Code (Chapter 11 filing is discussed in · Chapter 31 of this text), and was authorized to operate as a debtor-in-possession.

5. This sentence describes the event that subsequently evolves into the issue of this case.

6. The case originated in the Bankruptcy Court, and the District Court upheld the order of the Bankruptcy Court. An appeal was then taken to the Court of Appeals for the Third Circuit.

7. This paragraph summarizes the Union's involvement with the National Labor Relations Board. The NLRB petitioned the Court of Appeals to enforce its order.

8. These sentences describe how the Court of Appeals dealt with the Union's appeal and the Board's petition for enforcement of its order.

9. These sentences further describe the conclusions reached by the Court of Appeals. The Supreme Court of the United States is the highest appellate court in the United States, and it is reviewing the decision of the Court of Appeals. The primary purpose of review by an appellate court is to reexamine judicially a decision made by a lower court. It is a reconsideration of a prior decision made by a lower court.

10. The Supreme Court granted the *writ of certiorari*. A *writ of certiorari* is an order used by an appellate court when the court has the discretion of hearing or not hearing the appeal. When the writ is granted, the lower court is thereby required to produce a certified record of the particular case for the appellate court which has used its discretion to hear the appeal. If, however, the writ is denied, this denial indicates that the appellate court has refused to hear the appeal and thus the judgment of the lower court remains unchanged. The Supreme Court granted certiorari because of the apparent conflict between this decision in the Court of Appeals for the Third Circuit and another decision of the Court of Appeals for the Second Circuit.

11. In these paragraphs, the Supreme Court concluded that a collective-bargaining agreement subject to the National Labor Relations Act is an "executory contract" and, hence, subject to rejection by a debtor-in-possession. This conclusion is the first part of the Supreme Court's holding in this case.

12. In this paragraph, the Supreme Court determined that the Court of Appeals reached the appropriate result. By interpreting § 365(a) of the Bankruptcy Code, the Court concluded that rejection of a collective-bargaining agreement should be permitted if the debtor satisfies certain conditions. The Supreme Court further stated the steps that the Bankruptcy Court should follow before acting on a petition to modify or reject a collective-bargaining agreement.

13. Within its opinion, the Supreme Court emphasized the policy rationale behind Chapter 11 of the Bankruptcy Code. Additional requirements are imposed upon the Bankruptcy Code in the context of rejection of collective-bargaining agreements.

14. The second issue was posed.

15. The Supreme Court discussed the dispute with respect to this issue.

This sentence represents the conclusion reached by the Supreme Court when addressing the second issue.

17. The Supreme Court affirmed the judgment of the Court of Appeals. Thus, the judgment of Court of Appeals was declared to be valid.

QUESTIONS AND CASE PROBLEMS

1. What is the difference between common law and statutory law? Should judges have the same authority to overrule statutory law as they have to overrule common law?

2. What is the difference between common law and *stare decisis?* Should judges have the same power to adopt a rule contrary to common law as they do to depart from *stare decisis?*

3. What is substantive law? What is procedural, or adjective, law? Are there reasons for the two existing side by side?

4. The concept of *equity* was mentioned in this chapter. Courts of equity tend to follow general rules or maxims rather than common law or *stare decisis* as courts of law do. Some of those maxims are: whoever seeks equity must do equity; one seeking the aid of an equity court must come to the court with clean hands; and equity aids the vigilant, not those who rest on their rights. (The last maxim is the equitable doctrine of laches, and it refers to those who do not pursue a remedy within a reasonable time.) Why would equity courts give more credence to such maxims than to a hard and fast body of law?

5. The U.S. Constitution is a document in which the people of the United States give the government the "power to govern." Yet the Constitution was written by a handful of men who represented the aristocracy of the time. Surprisingly, this group of aristocrats wrote a document giving more freedoms to common people than any other constitution in existence. Name some of the basic guarantees found in the Constitution.

2

Constitutional Authority To Regulate Business

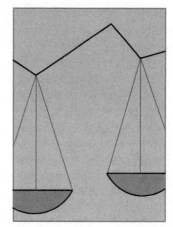

The United States Constitution is the supreme law in this country. Neither Congress nor any state may pass a law that conflicts with the Constitution. In this respect, the U.S. Constitution serves as a limitation upon the power of the government.

Before the Constitution was written, a *federal* form of government existed. A federal form of government is one in which the states form a union and the *sovereign* power is divided between a central governing authority and the member states.[1] The Articles of Confederation, ratified in 1778, established a national government with very limited powers over the states. After the Revolutionary War, however, the states passed laws which hampered national commerce and foreign trade by preventing the free movement of goods and services. Consequently, the Constitutional Convention convened in 1787 to amend the Articles of Confederation to give the national government the power to address the country's commercial problems. Instead of amending the Articles of Confederation, the Con-

vention created the Constitution and a completely new type of federal government which they believed was much better equipped than its predecessor to resolve the problems of the nation.

BASIC CONSTITUTIONAL CONCEPTS

Federalism

Federalism is the basic structure of the government in the United States. Thus, under this form of government state governments and the national government share powers. The Constitution reserves certain powers for the federal government, and the states retain all powers not delegated to the federal government. Neither government is superior to the other except within the particular area of authority granted to it under the Constitution. Hence, the concept of federalism recognizes that society may be best served by distributing functions among local governments and the national government on the basis of which government is better equipped to perform these functions. The Constitution reflects the Federalist belief that a national government can

---

1. Sovereign power refers to that supreme power in which no other person or authority is superior or equal.

handle certain problems better than individual state governments can.

Conflicts frequently arise regarding the question of which government—federal or state—should be exercising power in a particular area. The United States Supreme Court, as the arbiter of the Constitution, resolves such conflicts by deciding which governmental system is empowered to act under the Constitution.

Delegated Powers

Convening in 1787, the Constitutional Convention created a federal government in which the states delegated certain enumerated powers to the federal government and reserved all other powers to themselves. Thus, the federal government has no powers apart from those delegated to it by the states. The federal government is also frequently referred to as one holding only *enumerated powers* since it can only exercise those powers which are expressly or implicitly granted to it.

The Bill of Rights

For various reasons proposals made during the Constitutional Convention of 1787 were rejected. Yet the importance of a written declaration of the rights of individuals eventually caused the first Congress to submit ten amendments to the Constitution for the approval of the states. These amendments, commonly known as the **Bill of Rights,** were adopted in 1791, and embody a series of protections for the individual against various types of interference by the federal government. Among the guarantees provided for by the Bill of Rights are the First Amendment protections of religion, speech, and assembly; the Fourth Amendment provisions regarding arrest, search, and seizure; and the Sixth Amendment rights to counsel, confrontation, and cross-examination in criminal prosecutions. Furthermore, through the Fourteenth Amendment, passed after the Civil War, most of these guarantees have been held to be so fundamental as to be applicable at the state level as well.

Separation of Powers

The federal government is divided into three branches—the executive branch, the legislative branch, and the judicial branch. Article I of the Constitution provides for the legislative branch. The duties of the executive branch and the method of electing the president are set forth in Article II. The federal judicial system was created by Article III.[2]

Deriving its power from the Constitution, each branch performs a separate function, and no branch may exercise the authority of another branch. Each branch, however, has some power to *limit* the actions of the other branches. In each article of the Constitution that grants specific powers to one of the three branches of the government there is also a provision for limiting that power by another branch. Congress, for example, has power over spending and commerce, but the president can veto that legislation. The executive branch is responsible for foreign affairs, but treaties with foreign governments require the advice and consent of the members of the Senate. Under Article III, Congress determines the jurisdiction of the federal courts, but the Supreme court has the power to hold acts of the other branches of the federal government unconstitutional.[3] Thus, with this system of **checks and balances,** no one branch of government can accumulate too much power.

The Commerce Clause

Article I, Section 8, of the United States Constitution grants Congress the power "[t]o regulate Commerce with foreign Nations, and among the several States, and with the Indian Tribes. . . ." This clause has a greater impact on business than any other provision in the Constitution. Theoretically, the power over commerce authorizes the federal government to regulate every commercial enterprise in the United States. This power was delegated to the federal government to insure the uniformity of rules governing the movement of goods through the states.

Traditionally, the commerce power was interpreted as applying only to interstate, not to intrastate, commerce. The Supreme Court, however, now recognizes that Congress has the power to regulate any activity, interstate or intrastate, which "affects" interstate commerce. Wheat production of an individual farmer intended wholly for consumption on

---

2. The Constitution has been included as Appendix B in this text.

3. See Marbury v. Madison, 5 U.S. 137, 2 L.Ed. 60 (1803).

his or her own farm, for example, was held to be subject to federal regulation since such home consumption reduces the demand for wheat and thus may have a substantial economic effect on interstate commerce.[4]

---

4.   See Wickard v. Filburn, 317 U.S. 111, 63 S.Ct. 82 (1942).

The following case, *Heart of Atlanta Motel v. United States*, illustrates the "affectation doctrine." This case specifically demonstrates the Supreme Court's use of the commerce clause to affirm the power of Congress to pass the Civil Rights Act of 1964. The breadth of the commerce clause permits the national government to legislate in areas in which there is no explicit grant of power to Congress.

BACKGROUND AND FACTS   *The owner of a motel, who refused to rent rooms to blacks, despite the Civil Rights Act of 1964, brought an action to have the Civil Rights Act of 1964 declared unconstitutional. The motel owner alleged that Congress, in passing the act, had exceeded its power to regulate commerce.*

HEART OF ATLANTA MOTEL v. UNITED STATES

Supreme Court of the United States, 1964.
379 U.S. 241.

Mr. Justice CLARK delivered the opinion of the Court.
*   *   *   *

This is a declaratory judgment action *   *   * attacking the constitutionality of Title II of the Civil Rights Act of 1964 *   *   *. Appellant owns and operates the Heart of Atlanta Motel which has 216 rooms available to transient guests. *   *   * It is readily accessible to interstate highways 75 and 85 and state highways 23 and 41. Appellant solicits patronage from outside the State of Georgia through various national advertising media, including magazines of national circulation; it maintains over 50 billboards and highway signs within the State, soliciting patronage for the motel; it accepts convention trade from outside Georgia and approximately 75 percent of its registered guests are from out of State. Prior to passage of the Act the motel had followed a practice of refusing to rent rooms to Negroes, and it alleged that it intended to continue to do so. In an effort to perpetuate that policy this suit was filed. [The District Court sustained the Act.] *   *   *

The sole question posed is, therefore, the constitutionality of the Civil Rights Act of 1964 as applied to these facts. The legislative history of the Act indicates that Congress based the Act on § 5 and the Equal Protection Clause of the Fourteenth Amendment as well as its power to regulate interstate commerce under Art. I, § 8, cl. 3 of the Constitution.

The Senate Commerce Committee made it quite clear that the fundamental object of Title II was to vindicate "the deprivation of personal dignity that surely accompanies denials of equal access to public establishments." At the same time, however, it noted that such an objective has been and could be readily achieved "by congressional action based on the commerce power of the Constitution." Our study of the legislative record, made in the light of prior cases, has brought us to the conclusion that Congress possessed ample power in this regard, and we have therefore not considered the other grounds relied upon. *   *   *

While the Act as adopted carried no congressional findings, the record of its passage through each house is replete with evidence of the burdens that discrimination by race or color places upon interstate commerce *   *   *. This testimony included the fact that our people have become increasingly mobile with millions of all races traveling from State to State; that Negroes in particular have been the subject of discrimination in transient accommodations, having to travel great distances to secure the same; that often they have been unable to obtain accommodations and have had to call upon friends to put them up overnight. *   *   * These exclusionary practices were found to be nationwide, the Under Secretary of Commerce testifying that there is "no question that this discrimination in the North still exists to a large degree" and in the West and Midwest as well *   *   *. This testimony indicated a qualitative as well as quantitative effect on interstate travel by Negroes. The former was the obvious impairment of the Negro traveler's pleasure and convenience that resulted when he continually was uncertain of finding lodging. As for the latter, there was evidence that this uncertainty stemming from racial discrimination had the effect of discouraging travel on the part of a substantial portion of the Negro community *   *   *. We shall not burden this opinion with further details since the voluminous testimony presents overwhelming evidence that discrimination by hotels and motels impedes interstate travel *   *   *.

The power of Congress to deal with these obstructions depends on the meaning of the Commerce Clause. [T]he determinative test of the exercise of power by the Congress under the Commerce Clause is simply whether the activity sought to be regulated is "commerce which concerns more States than one" and has a real and substantial relation to the national interest *   *   *.

*   *   *   *

That Congress was legislating against moral wrongs in many of these areas rendered its enactments no less valid. In framing Title II of this Act Congress was also dealing with what it considered a moral problem. But that fact does not detract from the overwhelming evidence of the disruptive effect that racial discrimination has had on commercial intercourse. *   *   *

It is said that the operation of the motel here is of a purely local character. But, assuming this to be true, "if it is interstate commerce that feels the pinch, it does not matter how local the operation that applies the squeeze." Thus the power of Congress to promote interstate commerce also includes the power to regulate the local incidents thereof, including local activities in both the States of origin and destination, which might have a substantial and harmful effect upon that commerce. *   *   *

We, therefore, conclude that the action of the Congress in the adoption of the Act as applied here to a motel which concededly serves interstate travelers is within the power granted it by the Commerce Clause of the Constitution, as interpreted by this Court for 140 years *   *   *.

DECISION AND REMEDY   *The Court upheld the constitutionality of the Civil Rights Act of 1964. The power of Congress to regulate interstate commerce permitted the enactment of legislation that could halt local discriminatory practices.*

Since Heart of Atlanta   Actions are still brought to determine whether a local activity "substantially affects" interstate commerce and is thus subject to regulation by Congress. In *McLain v. Real Estate Board of New Orleans, Inc.*, the Supreme Court held that local real estate brokers, who were licensed to perform their function only in Louisiana, substantially affected financial transactions and title insurance which were clearly interstate in nature.[5] Thus, the brokers' activities sufficiently affected interstate commerce to be regulated by the Sherman Act. The Court acknowledged that the commerce clause has "long been interpreted to extend beyond activities

actually in interstate commerce to reach other activities, while wholly local in nature, which nevertheless substantially affect interstate commerce."[6]

The Power of States to Regulate   Another problem that frequently arises under the commerce clause concerns a state's ability to regulate matters within its own borders. There is no doubt that states have a strong interest in regulating activities within their borders. As part of their inherent sovereignty, states possess **police powers.** In exercising police powers, states may regulate private activities to protect or to promote the public health, safety, morals, or general

---

5.   100 S.Ct. 502 (1980).

6.   100 S.Ct. 502, 508 (1980).

welfare of their citizens. States, for example, have a strong interest in keeping their local roads and highways safe for their residents. However, most state regulations place some burden on interstate commerce, and when state regulations impinge upon interstate commerce, courts must balance the state's interest in the merits and purposes of the regulation against the burden placed on interstate commerce.[7]

Because courts balance the interests involved, it is extremely difficult to predict the outcome in a particular case. State laws enacted pursuant to a state's police powers and affecting the health, safety, and welfare of local citizens do carry a strong presumption of validity. However, in *Raymond Motor Transportation, Inc. v. Rice*, the Supreme Court

invalidated Wisconsin administrative regulations limiting the length of trucks traveling on its highways.[8] The Court weighed the burden on interstate commerce against the benefits of the regulations and concluded that the challenged regulations "place a substantial burden on interstate commerce and they cannot be said to make more than the most speculative contribution to highway safety."[9]

The following case involves virtually the same type of truck-length regulation as in the *Raymond* case, and the Supreme Court went even further to conclude that the state's highway regulation discriminated against interstate commerce and thus had to be invalidated.

---

7. See Southern Pacific Co. v. Arizona, 325 U.S. 761 (1945).

8. 434 U.S. 429 (1978).
9. 434 U.S. 429, 447 (1978).

BACKGROUND AND FACTS   *Unlike all other states in the West and Midwest, Iowa prohibited by statute the use of 65-foot double-trailer trucks within its borders. Use of 55-foot single-trailer trucks and 60-foot double-trailer trucks was allowed. The appellee, Consolidated Freightways, however, owned 65-foot doubles which it was prohibited from using to carry commodities through Iowa on interstate highways. Consequently, Consolidated filed suit, alleging that Iowa's statutory scheme unconstitutionally burdened interstate commerce.*

KASSEL v. CONSOLIDATED FREIGHTWAYS CORPORATION OF DELAWARE
Supreme Court of the United States, 1981.
101 S.Ct. 1309.

Mr. Justice POWELL delivered the opinion of the Court.
*   *   *   *

The question is whether an Iowa statute that prohibits the use of certain large trucks within the State unconstitutionally burdens interstate commerce. *   *   *

Appellee Consolidated Freightways Corporation of Delaware (Consolidated) is one of the largest common carriers in the country. It offers service in forty-eight States under a certificate of public convenience and necessity issued by the Interstate Commerce Commission. Among other routes, Consolidated carries commodities through Iowa on Interstate 80, the principal east-west route linking New York, Chicago, and the West Coast, and on Interstate 35, a major north-south route.

Consolidated mainly uses two kinds of trucks. One consists of a three-axle tractor pulling a 40-foot two-axle trailer. *   *   * Consolidated also uses a two-axle tractor pulling a single-axle trailer which, in turn, pulls a single-axle dolly and a second single-axle trailer. This combination, known as a double, or twin, is 65 feet long overall. Many trucking companies, including Consolidated, increasingly prefer to use doubles to ship certain kinds of commodities. Doubles have larger capacities, and the trailers can be detached and routed separately if necessary. Consolidated would like to use 65-foot doubles on many of its trips through Iowa.

The State of Iowa, however, by statute restricts the length of vehicles that may use its highways. Unlike all other States in the West and Midwest, Iowa generally prohibits the use of 65-foot doubles within its borders. *   *   *
*   *   *   *

Because of Iowa's statutory scheme, Consolidated cannot use its 65-foot doubles to move commodities through the State. Instead, the company must do one of four

things: (1) use 55-foot singles; (ii) use 60-foot doubles; (iii) detach the trailers of a 65-foot double and shuttle each through the State separately; or (iv) divert 65-foot doubles around Iowa. *   *   *
*   *   *   *

In a fourteen-day trial, both sides adduced evidence on safety, and on the burden on interstate commerce imposed by Iowa's law. On the question of safety, the District Court found that the "evidence clearly establishes that the twin is as safe as the semi."
*   *   *   *

*   *   *   *

The Commerce Clause does not, of course, invalidate all state restrictions on commerce. It has long been recognized that, "in the absence of conflicting legislation by Congress, there is a residuum of power in the state to make laws governing matters of local concern which nevertheless in some measure affect interstate commerce or even, to some extent, regulate it."
*   *   *   *

But the incantation of a purpose to promote the public health or safety does not insulate a state law from Commerce Clause attack. Regulations designed for that salutary purpose nevertheless may further the purpose so marginally, and interfere with commerce so substantially, as to be invalid under the Commerce Clause. *   *   *
*   *   *   *

Applying these general principles, we conclude that the Iowa truck-length limitations unconstitutionally burden interstate commerce.
*   *   * This case is *Raymond* revisited. Here, as in *Raymond*, the State failed to present any persuasive evidence that 65-foot doubles are less safe than 55-foot singles. Moreover, Iowa's law is now out of step with the laws of all other Midwestern and Western States. Iowa thus substantially burdens the interstate flow of goods by truck. In the absence of congressional action to set uniform standards, some burdens associated with state safety regulations must be tolerated. But where, as here, the State's safety interest has been found to be illusory, and its regulations impair significantly the federal interest in efficient and safe interstate transportation, the state law cannot be harmonized with the Commerce Clause.
*   *   *   *

The Court normally does accord "special deference" to state highway safety regulations. This traditional deference "derives in part from the assumption that where such regulations do not discriminate on their face against interstate commerce, their burden usually falls on the local economic interests as well as other States' economic interests, thus insuring that a State's own political processes will serve as a check against unduly burdensome regulations." Less deference to the legislative judgment is due, however, where the local regulation bears disproportionately on out-of-state residents and businesses. Such a disproportionate burden is apparent here. Iowa's scheme, although generally banning large doubles from the State, nevertheless has several exemptions that secure to Iowans many of the benefits of large trucks while shunting to neighboring States many of the costs associated with their use.
*   *   *   *

DECISION AND REMEDY   *The Supreme Court held that the Iowa statute that prohibits the use of certain large trucks within the state unconstitutionally burdens interstate commerce.*

COMMENTS   *The Supreme Court further stated that Iowa seemed to have hoped that by deflecting some through traffic, it could limit the use of its highways. Such a purpose is inconsistent with the commerce clause.*

The Supremacy Clause

Article VI of the Constitution provides that the Constitution, laws, and treaties of the United States are "the supreme Law of the Land. . . ." This article, the supremacy clause, is important in the ordering of state and federal relationships. Thus, when there is a direct conflict between a federal law and a state law, the state law is rendered invalid. But because some powers are shared by the federal government and the states—because they are concurrent powers—it is necessary to determine which law should prevail when there is a conflict.

When concurrent federal and state powers are involved, a state law that conflicts with a federal law is prohibited. A federal action pursuant to a power specifically delegated to it by the Constitution always has the capacity to override a state law on the same matter. Therefore, when Congress chooses to act exclusively in a concurrent area, it is said to have *preempted* the area. A federal regulatory scheme will preempt state law whenever there is an outright conflict between the two or when the state regulation interferes with federal objectives. Congress, however, rarely makes clear its intent to preempt an entire subject area against state regulation, and consequently, the courts must determine whether Congress intended to exercise exclusive dominion over a given area. These types of conflicts often arise in the commerce clause context.

When congressional intent as to preemption is unclear, courts use a test in preemption cases that is similar to the analysis used in the interstate commerce cases. Before declaring that federal law preempts a state statute, courts must first determine that Congress intended to supersede state law. The general rule is that such congressional intent will be found if the federal law is so pervasive, comprehensive, or detailed that the states have no room to supplement it.

In the following case, the Supreme Court had to determine whether various federal laws preempted a city ordinance.

BACKGROUND AND FACTS   *The city council of Burbank, California, passed an ordinance making it unlawful for jet aircraft to take off from the Hollywood-Burbank Airport between 11:00 P.M. and 7:00 A.M. Lockheed Air Terminal sought an injunction against enforcement of the ordinance. The District Court found the ordinance to be unconstitutional on both supremacy clause and commerce clause grounds. The Court of Appeals affirmed on the grounds of the supremacy clause.*

BURBANK v.
LOCKHEED AIR
TERMINAL
Supreme Court of the United
States, 1973.
411 U.S. 624.

Mr. Justice DOUGLAS delivered the opinion of the Court.

*   *   *   *

The Federal Aviation Act of 1958, as amended by the Noise Control Act of 1972 and the regulations under it, are central to the question of preemption.

Section 1108(a) of the Federal Aviation Act provides in part, "The United States of America is declared to possess and exercise complete and exclusive national sovereignty in the airspace of the United States *   *   *." By §§ 307(a), (c) of the Act, the Administrator of the Federal Aviation Administration (FAA) has been given broad authority to regulate the use of the navigable airspace, "in order to insure the safety of aircraft and the efficient utilization of such airspace" and "for the protection of persons and property on the ground *   *   *."

*   *   *   *

The original complaint was filed on May 14, 1970; the District Court entered its judgment November 30, 1970; and the Court of Appeals announced its judgment and opinion March 22, 1972—all before the Noise Control Act of 1972 was approved by the President on October 27, 1972. That Act reaffirms and reinforces the conclusion that FAA, now in conjunction with EPA, has full control over aircraft noise, preempting state and local control.

There is, to be sure, no express provision of preemption in the 1972 Act. That, however, is not decisive. As we stated in *Rice v. Santa Fe Elevator Corp.*, 331 U.S. 218, 230:

> "Congress legislated here in a field which the States have traditionally occupied * * *. So we start with the assumption that the historic police powers of the States were not to be superseded by the Federal Act unless that was the clear and manifest purpose of Congress * * *. Such a purpose may be evidenced in several ways. The scheme of federal regulation may be so pervasive as to make reasonable the inference that Congress left no room for the States to supplement it * * *. Or the Act of Congress may touch a field in which the federal interests is so dominant that the federal system will be assumed to preclude enforcement of state laws on the same subject * * *. Likewise, the object sought to be obtained by the federal law and the character of obligations imposed by it may reveal the same purpose * * *. Or the state policy may produce a result inconsistent with the objective of the federal statute."

It is the pervasive nature of the scheme of federal regulation of aircraft noise that leads us to conclude that there is preemption. As Mr. Justice Jackson stated, concurring in *Northwest Airlines, Inc. v. Minnesota*, 322 U.S. 292, 303:

> "Federal control is intensive and exclusive. Planes do not wander about in the sky like vagrant clouds. They move only by federal permission, subject to federal inspection, in the hands of federally certified personnel, and under an intricate system of federal commands. The moment a ship taxis onto a runway it is caught up in an elaborate and detailed system of controls."

* * * *

If we were to uphold the Burbank ordinance and a significant number of municipalities followed suit, it is obvious that fractionalized control of the timing of takeoffs and landings would severely limit the flexibility of FAA in controlling air traffic flow. The difficulties of scheduling flights to avoid congestion and the concomitant decrease in safety would be compounded. In 1960 FAA rejected a proposed restriction on jet operations at the Los Angeles airport between 10:00 P.M. and 7:00 A.M. because such restrictions could "create critically serious problems to all transportation patterns." The complete FAA statement said:

> "The proposed restriction on the use of the airport by jet aircraft between the hours of 10:00 P.M. and 7:00 A.M. under certain surface wind conditions has also been reevaluated and this provision has been omitted from the rule. The practice of prohibiting the use of various airports during certain specific hours could create critically serious problems to all air transportation patterns. The network of airports throughout the United States and the constant availability of these airports are essential to the maintenance of a sound air transportation system. The continuing growth of public acceptance of aviation as a major force in passenger transportation and the increasingly significant role of commercial aviation in the nation's economy are accomplishments which cannot be inhibited if the best interest of the public is to be served. It was concluded therefore that the extent of relief from the noise problem which this provision might have achieved would not have compensated the degree of restriction it would have imposed on domestic and foreign Air Commerce."

This decision, announced in 1960, remains peculiarily within the competence of FAA, supplemented now by the input of EPA. We are not at liberty to diffuse the powers given by Congress to FAA and EPA by letting the States or municipalities in on the planning. If that change is to be made, Congress alone must do it.

DECISION AND REMEDY   *The Supreme Court declared the Burbank ordinance to be unconstitutional. Federal regulation of the airspace preempted the local law.*

The Taxing Power

Article I, Section 8 further provides that Congress has the "Power to lay and collect Taxes, Duties, Imposts, and Excises . . . but all Duties, Imposts and Excises shall be uniform throughout the United States." The requirement of uniformity refers to geographic uniformity among the states, and thus Congress may not tax some states while exempting others. Traditionally, in reviewing cases the courts have examined whether Congress was actually attempting to regulate indirectly by taxation, an area over which it had no authority to regulate directly. If the regulatory effect was one which could have been achieved directly, then the tax would not be stricken as an invalid, disguised regulation. On the other hand, if Congress was attempting to regulate an area over which it had no authority, then such a regulation would be invalidated.

In recent cases, however, the Supreme Court has focused less on the motives of Congress and more on whether the tax can be sustained as a valid exercise of federal regulation. The Court has upheld taxes on dealers in firearms,[10] on the transfer of marijuana,[11] and on persons engaged in the business of accepting wagers.[12] If Congress does not have the power to regulate the activity being taxed, the tax will be upheld only if it is a valid revenue-raising measure. When a tax produces revenues, it is generally held to be within the national taxing power. Moreover, the expansive interpretation of the commerce clause almost always provides a basis for sustaining a federal tax.

The Spending Power

Under Article I, Section 8, Congress has the power "to pay the Debts and provide for the common Defence and general welfare of the United States. . . ." Through the spending power, Congress disposes of the revenues accumulated from the taxing power, and thus this power necessarily involves policy choices. The requirement of **standing to sue** makes it difficult for taxpayers to use the judicial system to object to government spending, and consequently, the spending power is seldom challenged. The doctrine of

standing to sue requires a litigant to demonstrate *a direct and immediate personal injury* due to the challenged action.[13] Thus, a litigant must show that the injury suffered can be fairly traced to the challenged action and will be redressed by the judicial relief sought.[14] Communicating directly with members of Congress has proved to be a more efficient route to curbing or increasing federal allocations.

The spending power exists separately from all other powers delegated to the federal government. Therefore, Congress can spend revenues not only to carry out its enumerated powers but also to promote any objective it deems worthwhile. Grants-in-aid to state and local governments carry with them many federal conditions as to the use of the funds, causing the grants to be known as "strings money." Although there has been a move toward unrestricted block grants—"no-strings money"—federal conditions will exist in most grants to the states.

THE BILL OF RIGHTS IN A BUSINESS CONTEXT

Businesses consist of one or more persons operating under their own names, a common name, or a fictitious name. Some business entities, such as corporations, exist as separate legal entities and enjoy the same rights and privileges as a *natural* person. A corporation is generally identified as an artificial person or legal entity under law. The Bill of Rights guarantees citizens certain protections, and some constitutional protections apply to business entities as well.

Specific actions of the federal government are prohibited by the first ten amendments, and the Fourteenth Amendment further prohibits most of the same actions by state governments. The due process clause of the Fourteenth Amendment makes certain rights guaranteed by the first ten amendments applicable to the states. Under the doctrine of *selective incorporation*, only those guarantees of individual liberty that are fundamental to the American system of law must be protected by the states.

---

10. Sonzinsky v. United States, 300 U.S. 506 (1937).
11. United States v. Sanchez, 340 U.S. 42 (1950).
12. United States v. Kahriger, 345 U.S. 22 (1953).

13. Sierra Club v. Morton, 405 U.S. 727 (1972).
14. Simon v. Eastern Kentucky Welfare Rights Organization, 426 U.S. 26 (1976).

Freedom of Speech

All of the First Amendment freedoms of religion, speech, press, assembly, and petition have been applied to the states through the due process clause of the Fourteenth Amendment. However, none of these freedoms confers an absolute right. It is unclear what types of speech the First Amendment was designed to protect, but constitutional protection has never been afforded to certain classes of speech. In 1942, for example, the U.S. Supreme Court concluded:

> There are certain well-defined and narrowly limited classes of speech, the prevention and punishment of which have never been thought to raise any Constitutional problem. These include the lewd and obscene, the profane, the libelous, and the insulting or "fighting" words—those which by their very utterance inflict injury or tend to incite an immediate breach of the peace. It has been well observed that such utterances are no essential part of any exposition of ideas, and are of such slight social value as a step to truth that any benefit that may be derived from them

is clearly outweighed by the social interest in order and morality.[15]

While the Supreme Court initially took the view that language treated as defamatory under state law was not entitled to First Amendment protection, it subsequently concluded that the First Amendment requires that a defense for honest error be allowed where statements are made about *public officials* relating to their *official conduct*. In the well-known case of *New York Times v. Sullivan*, the Court articulated a formal rule in stating that the First Amendment prohibits public officials from recovering damages for defamatory falsehoods relating to their official conduct unless they prove that the statements were made with "actual malice."[16] Actual malice means that a statement must be made *with knowledge that it was false* or *with reckless disregard of whether it was false or not*. Actual malice is also a requirement for a successful products disparagement suit brought against a competitor.

In the following case, a manufacturer of a loudspeaker system brought a defamation action against a consumer product-testing organization.

---

15.   Chaplinsky v. New Hampshire, 315 U.S. 568 (1942).

16.   376 U.S. 254 (1964).

BOSE CORPORATION v. CONSUMERS UNION OF UNITED STATES, INC.

Supreme Court of the United States, 1984.
104 S.Ct. 1949.

BACKGROUND AND FACTS   *Bose Corporation, the petitioner, is a manufacturer of loudspeaker systems. The respondent, Consumers Union, published an article in its* Consumer Reports *magazine evaluating the quality of various brands of loudspeaker systems, including the one marketed by the petitioner. The petitioner objected to numerous statements in the article concerning the Bose system. Among other things, the article stated that various instruments could be located less easily while using the Bose system than when using a standard speaker and that "individual instruments heard through the Bose system seemed to grow to gigantic proportions and tended to wander about the room."*

Justice STEVENS delivered the opinion of the Court.

*   *   *   *

*   *   * [T]he District Court ruled that the petitioner is a "public figure" as that term is defined in *Gertz v. Robert Welch, Inc.* *   *   * for purposes of this case and therefore the First Amendment, as interpreted in *New York Times v. Sullivan,* *   *   * precludes recovery in this product disparagement action unless the petitioner proved by clear and convincing evidence that respondent made a false disparaging statement with "actual malice."

*   *   *   *

*   *   *[I]n cases raising First Amendment issues we have repeatedly held that an appellate court has an obligation to "make an independent examination of the whole

record" in order to make sure "that the judgment does not constitute a forbidden intrusion on the field of free expression." * * *
* * * *

The First Amendment presupposes that the freedom to speak one's mind is not only an aspect of individual liberty—and thus a good unto itself—but also is essential to the common quest for truth and the vitality of society as a whole. Under our Constitution "there is no such thing as a false idea. However pernicious an opinion may seem, we depend for its correction not on the conscience of judges and juries but on the competiton of other ideas." * * * Nevertheless, there are categories of communication and certain special utterances to which the majestic protection of the First Amendment does not extend because they "are no essential part of any exposition of ideas, and are of such slight social value as a step to truth that any benefit that may be derived from them is clearly outweighed by the social interest in order and morality."
* * *

Libelous speech has been held to constitute one such category. * * * In each of these areas, the limits of the unprotected category, as well as the unprotected character of particular communications, have been determined by the judicial evaluation of special facts that have been deemed to have constitutional significance. * * *
* * * *

The requirement of independent appellate review reiterated in *New York Times v. Sullivan* is a rule of federal constitutional law. * * * It reflects a deeply held conviction that judges—and particularly members of this Court—must exercise such review in order to preserve the precious liberties established and ordained by the Constitution. The question whether the evidence in the record in a defamation case is of the convincing clarity required to strip the utterance of First Amendment protection is not merely a question for the trier of fact. Judges, as expositors of the Constitution, must independently decide whether the evidence in the record is sufficient to cross the constitutional threshold that bars the entry of any judgment that is not supported by clear and convincing proof of "actual malice."

The Court of Appeals was correct in its conclusion (1) that there is a significant difference between proof of actual malice and mere proof of falsity, and (2) that such additional proof is lacking in this case.
* * * *

The statement in this case represents the sort of inaccuracy that is commonplace in the forum of robust debate to which the *New York Times* rule applies. * * * "Realistically, . . . some error is inevitable; and the difficulties of separating fact from fiction convinced the Court in *New York Times, Butts, Gertz,* and similar cases to limit liability to instances where some degree of culpability is present in order to eliminate the risk of undue self-censorship and the suppression of truthful material."
* * *

The Court of Appeals entertained some doubt concerning the ruling that the *New York Times* rule should be applied to a claim of product disparagement based on a critical review of a loudspeaker system. We * * * agree with the Court of Appeals that the difference between hearing violin sounds move around the room and hearing them wander back and forth fits easily within the breathing space that gives life to the First Amendment. * * *
* * * *

DECISION AND REMEDY

The Supreme Court affirmed the judgment of the Court of Appeals. The Court concluded that the record did not contain clear and convincing evidence that respondent's employee prepared the Consumer Reports *article with knowledge that it contained a false statement or with reckless disregard of the truth.*

COMMENTS

In Curtis Pub. Co. v. Butts *and* Associated Press v. Walker, *the* New York Times's *"actual knowledge or reckless disregard of the truth test" was extended to include* public figures. *(Both cases are reported at 388 U.S. 130 [1967].) The petitioner (Bose Corporation) did not contest the conclusion that it was a public figure, and thus the* New York Times's *standard was held to be applicable. In a recent case,* Sharon v. Time, Inc. *[575 F.Supp. 1162 (1983)], the jury found that statements made in a* Time *Magazine article were false, but because there was no actual malice,* Time *won the lawsuit.*

Freedom-of-speech cases generally distinguish between commercial and noncommercial messages. Even though commercial advertising is accorded less constitutional protection than political or private speech, it is not completely outside the First Amendment. As stated in *First National Bank of Boston v. Bellotti,* speech that otherwise would be within the protection of the First Amendment does not lose that protection simply because its source is a corporation.[17] The Supreme Court in *Bellotti,* however, expressly refused to explore the outer boundaries of the Amendment's protection of corporate speech or to address the question of whether corporations have the same measure of rights that individuals enjoy under the First Amendment.

Freedom of Religion

The First Amendment requires that the government neither establish any religion nor prohibit the free exercise of religious practices. Government action, both federal and state, must be neutral toward religion. However, regulation that does not promote, or place a significant burden on, religion is constitutional even if it has some impact on religion. "Sunday closing laws," for example, make some commercial activities illegal if performed on Sunday. These statutes, also known as "blue laws," have been upheld on the ground that it is a legitimate function of government to provide a day of rest. The Supreme Court has held that the closing laws, although originally of a religious character, have taken on the secular purpose of promoting the health and welfare of workers.[18] Even though closing laws admittedly make it easier for Christians to attend religious services, the Court has viewed this effect as an incidental, not a primary, purpose of Sunday closing laws.

Thus, the Constitution does not require a complete separation of church and state but rather affirmatively mandates accommodation, not merely toleration, of all religions and forbids hostility toward any.[19] The Supreme Court recently held that the establishment clause of the First Amendment does not prohibit a municipality from including a Nativity scene in its annual Christmas display.[20] The Court concluded that whatever benefit the Nativity scene provided to religion was indirect, remote, and incidental.

Another freedom of religion involves the accommodation that businesses must make for the religious beliefs of their employees. Title VII of the Civil Rights Act of 1964 prohibits government, and private employers and unions, from discriminating against persons because of their religion.

The U.S. Supreme Court recently addressed this issue in *Estate of Thornton, et al. v. Caldor, Inc.*[21] In this case, the Court held that a Connecticut statute granting employees the absolute right not to work on their Sabbath had the effect of advancing religious practices in violation of the establishment clause of the First Amendment. The Court felt that such a statute discriminated against employees who might want a weekend day off for secular reasons.

Search and Seizure

The Fourth Amendment protects the "right of the people to be secure in their persons, houses, papers, and effects. . . ." Federal, state, and local governments must obtain search warrants unless there is *probable cause* to believe that the items sought will

---

17. 435 U.S. 765, 98 S.Ct. 1407 (1978).
18. McGowan v. Maryland, 366 U.S. 420 (1961).

19. See Zorach v. Clauson, 343 U.S. 306, 72 S.Ct. 679 (1952).
20. See Lynch v. Donnelly, —— U.S. ——, 104 S.Ct. 1355 (1984).
21. 53 U.S.L.W. 4853 (1985).

be removed before a warrant can be obtained. Probable cause requires law enforcement officials to have trustworthy evidence that would convince a reasonable person that it is more likely than not that the proposed search or seizure is justified. Thus, to obtain a warrant, law enforcement officers must convince a judge that they have probable cause to believe a search will reveal a specific illegality.

The Fourth Amendment prohibits general warrants and requires a particular description of that which is to be searched or seized. General searches through a person's belongings are impermissible. Nothing is left to the discretion of the officer executing a search warrant; the search cannot extend beyond what is described in the warrant. The recent case of *Winston v. Lee* deals with a rather unusual type of desired search.[22] In *Winston v. Lee*, a shopkeeper was wounded during an attempted robbery. The shopkeeper, also armed, fired and apparently wounded his assailant in the left side. The assailant fled the scene, and the police shortly thereafter found the defendant eight blocks away from the scene of the shooting and suffering from a gunshot wound to his left chest area. Alleging that a bullet in the defendant's chest would provide evidence of his guilt or innocence, the Commonwealth of Virginia moved for an order directing the defendant to undergo surgery to remove the bullet. The Supreme Court, however, held that the proposed surgery would violate the defendant's right to be secure in his person and also that, under the Fourth Amendment, such a search would be "unreasonable" in this situation. In general, the reasonableness of surgical intrusions is determined by weighing an individual's interests in privacy and security against the interest of society in obtaining evidence to determine fairly guilt or innocence.

Constitutional protection against searches and seizures is extremely important to businesses and professionals. With increased federal and state regulation of commercial activities, frequent and unannounced government inspection to insure compliance with the law would be extremely disruptive. In *Marshall v. Barlow's, Inc.*,[23] the Supreme Court held that government inspectors do not have the right to enter business premises without a warrant.

Lawyers and accountants are frequently in possession of the business records of their clients, and consequently, to inspect these documents while they are out of the hands of their true owner, a warrant is also required.

Self-Incrimination

The Fifth Amendment guarantees that no person "shall be compelled in any criminal case to be a witness against himself." Thus, in any federal proceeding, an accused person cannot be compelled to give evidence of a testimonial or communicative nature which might subject him or her to any criminal prosecution. An accused person cannot be forced to testify against himself or herself in state courts either, because the Fourteenth Amendment due process clause incorporates the Fifth Amendment provision against self-incrimination. However, only the accused has this protection against self-incrimination; there is no protection against the incriminating testimony of witnesses.

The Fifth Amendment's guarantee against self-incrimination extends only to natural persons. Since a corporation is a legal entity and not a natural person, the privilege against self-incrimination is inapplicable to it. Similarly, the business records of a partnership do not receive Fifth Amendment protection.[24] No artificial organization may utilize the personal privilege against compulsory self-incrimination. When records of these organizations are required to be produced, the information must be given even if it incriminates the persons who comprise the business entity.

Sole proprietors and sole practitioners who have not incorporated cannot be compelled to produce their business records. These individuals have the full protection against self-incrimination because they function in only one capacity: There is no separate business entity. In the following case, the sole stockholder in a corporation attempted to assert his Fifth Amendment privilege to prevent the production of his corporation's records.

22. 53 U.S.L.W. 4367 (1985).
23. 430 U.S. 934 (1978).

24. The privilege has been applied to some small family partnerships. See United States v. Slutsky, 352 F.Supp. 1105 (S.D. N.Y. 1972).

WILD v. BREWER
United States Court of Appeals,
Ninth Circuit, 1964.
329 F.2d 924.

BACKGROUND AND FACTS *Brewer, an IRS agent, served Wild with a summons requiring Wild to appear and testify about the tax liability of "Albert J. Wild, President, Air Conditioning Supply Company." The corporation was wholly owned by Wild, and all books and records requested were those of the corporation. Wild appeared but refused to produce the records on the ground that they might tend to incriminate him and hence were protected by the Fifth Amendment. When Wild was cited for contempt, he appealed. The majority of the appellate court affirmed, ordering Wild to produce the corporate books and records. One judge, however, found support for Wild's position.*

MADDEN, Judge [dissenting].
* * * *

The privilege guaranteed by the Fifth Amendment, against the Government of the United States, "in any criminal case" not to be compelled to be a witness against one's self, is available not only to defendants in criminal trials but to witnesses in any kind of official proceeding under the auspices of the United States. It applies not only to the giving of oral testimony, but to the production from one's possession of incriminating documents or objects.
* * * *

There is without question a general doctrine that an officer of a corporation who, as such officer, has custody of its records may not successfully refuse to produce those records in response to a subpoena [court-ordered summons] issued to the corporation and served upon him as custodian, on the ground that the records contain material which would incriminate him. * * *

A corporation does not have the Constitutional privilege against self-incrimination. It therefore cannot, if its records are subpoenaed, assert the Fifth Amendment privilege.
* * *

* * * [But Wild] did not claim the privilege for the corporation, and could not have done so. He claims it for himself, and says that he, and not any artificial legal entity, will be the one to suffer the punishment if he is obliged to furnish to the Government the evidence which will bring about his conviction. * * *

Wild says that since he is the sole owner of his corporation, the corporation does embody the "purely private or personal interests of its [only] constituent(s)," who is Wild himself.

[The dissenting judge was sympathetic to Wild's position. However, the majority decision was binding. A corporation does not enjoy the Fifth Amendment privilege against self-incrimination, even when it is claimed for the benefit of the sole owner.]

DECISION AND REMEDY *The trial court's ruling of contempt was affirmed. Wild was unable to invoke the Fifth Amendment to protect company records. He was required to produce the records in response to the IRS subpoena.*

COMMENTS *A corporation is a legal fiction; that is, it is considered to be a person for most purposes under the law. An unsettled area of corporation law has to do with the criminal acts of a corporation. It is obvious that a corporation cannot be sent to prison even though, under law, it is a person. Most courts hold a corporation that has violated the criminal statutes liable for fines. Where criminal conduct can be attributed to corporate officers or agents, those individuals, as natural persons, are held liable and can be imprisoned for their acts.*

OTHER CONSTITUTIONAL GUARANTEES

Due Process

Both the Fifth and the Fourteenth Amendments provide that no person shall be deprived "of life, liberty, or property, without due process of law." The due process clauses have two aspects: procedural and substantive. Procedural due process requires that any government decision to take life, liberty, or property must be made fairly, and thus there must be fairness in the procedures used to determine that a person will be subjected to punishment or have some burden imposed on him or her.

Substantive due process, on the other hand, focuses on the content or substance of legislation. Unless a law is compatible with the Constitution, it is a violation of substantive due process. For example, if a state legislature enacted a law imposing a fifteen-year term of imprisonment without allowing a trial on all businesspersons who appeared in their own television commercials, the law would be unconstitutional on both substantive and procedural grounds. Substantive review would invalidate the legislation because it abridges freedom of speech. Procedurally, the law is unfair because the penalty is imposed without giving the accused a chance to defend his or her actions. The lack of procedural due process will cause a court to invalidate any statute or prior court decision. Similarly, a denial of substantive due process requires courts to overrule any state or federal law that violates the Constitution.

Equal Protection

Under the Fourteenth Amendment, a state may not "deny to any person within its jurisdiction the equal protection of the laws." The Supreme Court has used the due process clause of the Fifth Amendment to make the equal protection guarantee applicable to the federal government. Equal protection means that the government must treat similarly situated individuals in a similar manner.

Equal protection is concerned with whether there is a rational and legitimate purpose for applying different rules to different people. For example, a law which provides unemployment benefits only to people over six feet tall would violate the guarantee of equal protection. There is no rational basis for determining the distribution of unemployment compensation on the basis of height. Such a distinction could not be in furtherance of any legitimate government objective.[25]

---

25. See Chapter 50 for a more elaborate coverage of these concepts.

QUESTIONS AND CASE PROBLEMS

1. Suppose that in 1973 the Public Service Commission of the State of Illinois ordered that all "promotional advertising" by electric utilities cease. Assume that this order was based upon the Commission's finding that the state in all likelihood did not have sufficient fuel for the upcoming winter. If the Public Service Commission sought to enforce its ban in 1977, when the fuel shortage had eased, would such enforcement be a regulation of commercial speech in violation of the First Amendment? Assume that the Commission's interest in conservation could not have been adequately protected by a less restrictive alternative.

2. Suppose that the Ohio legislature passed a statute prohibiting the issuance of a liquor license to any establishment that is located within 600 feet of a church if the church objects in writing to the issuance of such a license. Would this statute be valid under the establishment clause (of religion) of the First Amendment?

3. A Georgia statute requires the use of contoured rear-fender mudguards on trucks and trailers operating within its state lines. The statute further makes it illegal for trucks and trailers to use straight mudguards. In approximately 35 other states, straight mudguards are legal. Moreover, in Florida, straight mudguards are explicitly required by law. There is some evidence that suggests that contoured mudguards might be a little safer than straight mudguards. Does this Georgia statute violate any constitutional provisions?

4. Florida Lime & Avocado Growers, Inc. is engaged in the business of growing and packing Florida avocados and

marketing them via interstate commerce. Section 792 of the California Agricultural Code requires that avocados contain no less than 8 percent of oil by weight before they may be transported or sold within California. Under the Federal Agricultural Marketing Agreement Act of 1937, Florida avocados may be certified as mature and yet not satisfy the standards prescribed by the California Code. The federal standards attribute no significance to oil content. Should this California statute, as applied, be held unconstitutional under the supremacy clause? Is the California statute displaced by the Federal Agricultural Marketing Agreement Act of 1937? [Florida Lime and Avocado Growers v. Paul, 373 U.S. 132, 83 S.Ct. 1210 (1963)]

5. New Jersey enacted a law prohibiting the importation of most wastes into the state. Some of the landfill operators in New Jersey, however, had agreements with out-of-state residents to dispose of their solid and liquid waste. Philadelphia brought an action claiming that this statute violated the commerce clause by facially discriminating against interstate commerce. New Jersey asserted that its statute was justified since its landfills were inadequate to dispose of its own waste and importation had a significant and adverse potential effect on the environment. Is this state regulation of interstate commerce permissible? [Philadelphia v. New Jersey, 437 U.S. 617, 98 S.Ct. 2531 (1978)]

6. The Mineral King Valley, located in the Sierra Nevada Mountains, is an area of great natural beauty. The United States Forest Service began to give consideration to Mineral King as a potential site for recreational development. In June of 1969 the Sierra Club filed a suit seeking a declaratory judgment that various aspects of the proposed development contravened federal laws and regulations. The Sierra Club sued as a membership corporation *with a special interest* in the conservation of national parks. However, there was no allegation that the members of the Sierra Club would be affected by the proposed action. Has Sierra Club demonstrated a direct and immediate personal injury due to the challenged action, as is required by Article III of the Constitution? [Sierra Club v. Morton, 405 U.S. 727, 92 S.Ct. 1361 (1972)]

7. The plaintiffs, Americans United for Separation of Church and State, Inc., *as taxpayers*, brought an action to challenge a conveyance of land from the Department of Health, Education, and Welfare (HEW) to Valley Forge Christian College, the defendant. The plaintiffs alleged that such a conveyance violated the establishment clause of the First Amendment to the Constitution. The district court dismissed the complaint on the ground that the plaintiffs lacked "standing." What was the result on appeal? [Valley Forge Christian College v. Americans United, 454 U.S. 464, 102 S.Ct. 752 (1982)]

3

Courts and Procedures

INTRODUCTION

In the United States, each state has its own court system. In this chapter both the state and the federal court systems will be examined. Then a typical case will be followed through the court. Remember that an important step in the use of the courts or in the process of adjudication is *determining which rules apply to the facts in the case*. These rules can be *substantive* or *procedural*. They may come from several sources and can cover several areas of the law.

In studying the courts and their procedures, the first question should be which courts have the power to decide a particular case—that is, which courts have jurisdiction.

JURISDICTION

Juris means "law"; *diction* means "to speak." Thus, the power to speak the law is the literal meaning of the term **jurisdiction.** Before any court can hear a case, it must have jurisdiction—that is, the power to hear and decide a case. Without jurisdiction, a court cannot exercise any authority in the case. Thus, in order for a court to exercise valid authority, it must have jurisdiction over both the person against

whom the suit is brought or over the property involved in the suit, and the subject matter of the case.

In personam, In rem, and *Quasi in rem* Jurisdiction

In order to consider a case, a court must have power over the *person or the property* involved in the action. Power over the person is often referred to as **in personam** jurisdiction. *In personam* jurisdiction is required before a court can enter a personal judgment against a party to the action. This type of jurisdiction may be contrasted with **in rem** jurisdiction. An *in rem* proceeding is one which is taken directly against property. In an *in rem* proceeding, for example, a court may use property within a state to help satisfy a general debt.

A third type of jurisdiction, **quasi in rem** jurisdiction, is used when *in personam* jurisdiction is not possible. A *quasi in rem* proceeding is not strictly *in rem* since an action in this situation is brought against the defendant personally. Yet it is the defendant's interest in the property that serves as the basis of the jurisdiction.

Generally, a court's power is limited to the territorial boundaries of the state in which it is located. Thus, a court has jurisdiction over the person of anyone who can be served with a summons within those boundaries. Additionally, if a person is a resident of the state or does business within the state, there will be jurisdiction over that person. Finally, in some cases where an individual has committed a wrong, such as an automobile injury or the sale of defective goods within the state, a court can exercise jurisdiction using the authority of a long arm statute even if the individual is outside the state. A **long arm statute** is a state law permitting courts to obtain jurisdiction over nonresident defendants. A court can further exercise jurisdiction over a corporation in the state where it is incorporated, in the state where it has its main plant or office, and in any state where it does business.

In all cases where a court exercises jurisdiction, the parties must be served either with actual notice that they are involved in a suit (usually by service of a summons) or, where the parties cannot be located, by publication of notice in a newspaper or in some other manner if permitted by statute.

Subject Matter Jurisdiction

Subject matter jurisdiction is a limitation on types of cases a court can hear. For example, probate courts—courts that handle only matters relating to wills and estates—are a common example of limited subject matter jurisdiction. The subject matter jurisdiction of a court is usually defined in the statute or constitution creating the court. A court's subject matter jurisdiction can be limited not only by the subject of the lawsuit, but also by the amount of money in controversy, by whether a case is a felony or misdemeanor, or by whether the proceeding is a trial or an appeal.

General Jurisdiction and Special, or Limited, Jurisdiction
The distinction between courts of general jurisdiction and courts of special, or limited, jurisdiction lies in the subject matter of cases heard. A court of general jurisdiction can decide virtually any type of case. Every state has one level of such courts, which may be called county courts, circuit courts, district courts, or by some other name. On the other hand, at both federal and state levels there are courts that hear only cases of specialized, or limited, subject matter. For example, one court may handle only cases dealing with divorce or child custody. Another may handle disputes over relatively small amounts of money (a small claims court).

Courts of general jurisdiction will not handle cases that are appropriate for these courts of special, or limited, jurisdiction.

Original and Appellate Jurisdiction

The distinction between courts of original jurisdiction and courts of appellate jurisdiction normally lies in whether the case is being heard for the first time. Courts having original jurisdiction are those of the first instance. In other words, they are where the trial of a case begins. In contrast, courts having appellate jurisdiction act as reviewing courts. In general, cases can be brought to them only on appeal from an order or a judgment of a lower court.

VENUE

Jurisdiction is concerned with whether a court has authority over a specific subject matter or individual. **Venue,** on the other hand, is concerned with the particular geographic area within a judicial district where a suit should be brought. It is a question that arises after a determination of jurisdiction. A particular court may have jurisdiction but not venue.

Basically, the concept of venue reflects the policy that a court trying a suit should be in the geographic neighborhood where the incident leading to the suit occurred or where the parties involved in the suit reside. That neighborhood is usually the county where the incident occurred or where the parties live. However, pretrial publicity or other factors may require a change of venue to another community, especially in criminal cases, if the defendant's right to a fair and impartial jury is impaired.

The proper venue for a suit is defined by statute. Improper venue does not deprive the court of power to hear a case, but a party can request a change of venue if venue is not proper.

THE COURT SYSTEMS IN THE UNITED STATES

Today in the United States there are fifty-two separate court systems. Each of the fifty states, in addition to the District of Columbia, has its own fully developed, independent system of courts. Additionally, there is a separate federal court system. It is important to understand that the federal courts—

the system taken as a whole—are not superior to the state courts. They are simply an independent system authorized by Article 3, Section 2, of the United States Constitution. The federal courts were set up to handle matters of particular federal interest. As we shall see, the United States Supreme Court is the final controlling voice over all these fifty-two systems, at least when questions of U.S. constitutional law are involved.

A Typical Court System

Most court systems, including the federal system, are based on a three-tiered model. Any person who is a party to a lawsuit typically has the opportunity to plead the case before a trial court and then, if he or she loses, before two levels of appellate courts. Therefore, in most states a case may proceed first through a trial court, with an automatic right to review by a state appellate court, and then, if accepted, to the state supreme court. Finally, if a federal constitutional issue is involved in the decision of the state supreme court, that decision may be appealed to the United States Supreme Court.

Consider the typical state court system represented in Exhibit 3–1. It has three main tiers: (1) the state trial court of general or limited jurisdiction, (2) the state appellate court, and (3) the state supreme court.

One can view the typical state system as being made up of trial courts and of appellate courts, or courts of appeal and review. Trial courts are exactly what their name implies—courts in which trials are held and testimony is taken. Trial courts may be courts of record, where a written record is taken, or courts not of record. Most are of record today. Most states have trial courts of both limited and general jurisdiction.

Limited-Jurisdiction Trial Courts   Every state has trial courts that have original jurisdiction. Those with limited jurisdiction as to subject matter are often called special inferior trial courts or minor judiciary courts. Some typical courts of limited jurisdiction are domestic relations courts, which handle only divorce actions and child custody cases; local municipal courts, which handle mainly traffic cases; probate courts, which handle the administration of wills and estate settlement problems; and small claims and justice of the peace courts. Typically, the minor judiciary courts do not keep complete written records of trial proceedings.

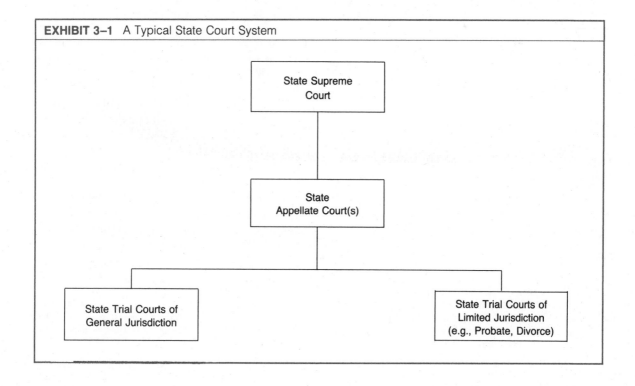

EXHIBIT 3–1 A Typical State Court System

General-Jurisdiction Trial Courts   Trial courts that have general jurisdiction as to subject matter may be called county, district, superior, or circuit courts.[1] The jurisdiction of these courts of general and original jurisdiction is often determined by the size of the county in which the court sits. These courts of general jurisdiction may be supplemented by the courts of limited jurisdiction or the minor judiciary courts discussed above.

One should understand that many important cases involving businesses originate in these general trial courts. Thus, a study of corporate law, contract law, and commercial law must start here.

Appellate Courts, or Courts of Appeal and Review

Although in some states trial courts of general jurisdiction also have limited jurisdiction to hear appeals from the minor judiciary—for example, small claims and traffic cases—when one discusses courts of review, or appellate courts, one usually means courts that are not trial courts.

Every state has at least one court of review, or appellate court. The subject matter jurisdiction of these courts is substantially limited to hearing appeals. Many states have intermediate reviewing courts and one supreme court. The intermediate appellate, or review, court is often called the court of appeals. The highest court of the state is normally called the supreme court.[2] Appellate courts try few cases. They examine the record of the case on appeal and determine whether the trial court committed an error. They look at questions of law and procedure, not questions of fact.[3] The decisions of each state's highest court in all questions of state law are final. It is only when questions of federal law are involved that a state's highest court can be overruled by the Supreme Court of the United States.

---

1.   The name in Ohio is Court of Common Pleas; the name in New York is Supreme Court.
2.   In New York it is called the Court of Appeals.
3.   The only times an appellate court tampers with a trial court's findings of fact are when the finding is clearly erroneous (that is, when it is contrary to the evidence presented at trial) or when there is no evidence to support the finding.

Judicial Review

The problem often arises as to whether or not a law is contrary to the mandates of the Constitution. **Judicial review** is the process for making such a determination. The term judicial review means that the judicial branch of the government has the authority and power to determine if a particular law is in violation of the Constitution.

The power of judicial review was first established in *Marbury v. Madison*. In determining that the Supreme Court had the power to decide that a law passed by Congress violated the Constitution, the Court stated:

> It is emphatically the province and duty of the Judicial Department to say what the law is. Those who apply the rule to a particular case, must of necessity expound and interpret that rule. If two laws conflict with each other, the courts must decide on the operation of each.
>
> So if the law be in opposition to the Constitution, if both the law and the Constitution apply to a particular case, so that the court must either decide that case conformably to the law, disregarding the Constitution; or conformably to the Constitution, disregarding the law; the court must determine which of these conflicting rules governs the case. This is of the very essence of judicial duty.
>
> If, then, the courts were to regard the Constitution and the Constitution is superior to any ordinary Act of the Legislature, the Constitution, and not such ordinary Act, must govern the case to which they both apply.[4]

In another famous case, *United States v. Nixon*, the Supreme Court established its power over actions of the president. In 1974 a grand jury indicted seven individuals for obstruction of justice and conspiracy to defraud (among other things). President Nixon was ordered by the special prosecutor to produce tapes, memoranda, papers, and transcripts. The president attempted to avoid the subpoena on the ground of "executive privilege," but this ground was denied him by the district court.

The president's view of the privilege was broad, and he claimed the courts lacked the power to de-

---

4.   5 U.S. 137, 2 L.Ed. 60 (1803). How to read case citations is explained at the end of Chapter 1. How to brief a case is presented in Appendix A.

mand the records sought. The Supreme Court subsequently heard the case, denied the claim of executive privilege that was at the heart of the controversy, and affirmed the order of the district court. Among other things, the Court balanced the president's claim against the needs of the defendants and the courts to have the records.

THE FEDERAL COURT SYSTEM

The federal court system is similar in many ways to most state court systems. It is also a three-tiered model consisting of: (1) trial courts, (2) intermediate courts of appeals, and (3) the Supreme Court. Exhibit 3–2 shows the organization of the federal court system in some detail.

District Courts

At the federal level, the equivalent of a state trial court of general jurisdiction is the district court. There is at least one federal district court in every state. The number of judicial districts can vary over time, primarily due to population changes and corresponding case loads. Large states, such as California, have more than one. Thus, an entire state can comprise a single district, or a state can be divided into several districts. United States district courts are often referred to as federal trial courts. Most federal cases originate in these courts. When there are two or more district courts within a single state, there is limited geographical jurisdiction in each court. The state of Florida, for example, has district courts for northern, middle, and southern Florida.

In the Federal Judgeship Act of 1984, Congress took the opportunity to increase the total number of judicial circuit court and district court judgeships in the United States. The total number of new judgeships will be increased by 85, and these judges will be appointed by the president, with the advice and consent of the Senate. The law now provides for 168 circuit court judgeships with thirteen circuits and 563 district court judgeships within the ninety-six judicial districts.[5]

U.S. district courts have original jurisdiction in federal matters. In other words, district courts are where federal cases originate. There are other trial courts with original, albeit special (or limited), jurisdiction, such as the U.S. Tax Court, the U.S. Bankruptcy Court, and the U.S. Claims Court. Certain administrative agencies and departments having judicial power also have original jurisdiction. These agencies and departments are listed in Exhibit 3–2.

U.S. Courts of Appeals

Congress has established twelve judicial circuits that hear appeals from the district courts located within their respective circuits. The decisions of the courts of appeals are final in most cases, but appeal to the Supreme Court is possible. Appeals from federal administrative agencies, such as the Federal Trade Commission, are also made to the U.S. circuit courts of appeals. See Exhibit 3–3 for the geographical boundaries of U.S. district courts and U.S. courts of appeals.

The Supreme Court of the United States

The highest level of the three-tiered model of the federal court system is the Supreme Court of the United States. According to the language of Article III of the U.S. Constitution, there is only one Supreme Court. All other courts in the federal system are considered "inferior." Congress is empowered to create such other inferior courts as it deems necessary. Thus, according to this language, the inferior courts that Congress has created include the second tier in our model—the U.S. courts of appeals, as well as the district courts and any other courts of limited, or specialized, jurisdiction.

The Supreme Court of the United States consists of nine justices; these justices are nominated by the president of the United States, and confirmed by the Senate.[6] They receive lifetime appointments (since under Article III they "hold their offices during Good Behavior"). The Supreme Court was created by the U.S. Constitution. Although it has original, or trial, jurisdiction in rare instances, set forth in Article III, Section 2, most of its work is as an appeals court. The Supreme Court can review any case decided by

---

5. See Sections 44(a) and 133 of Title 28, United States Code.

6. Members of the Supreme Court and of some appellate courts are called justices, whereas members of trial courts are called judges. The same distinction often applies in state court systems.

EXHIBIT 3–2 The Organization of The Federal Court System

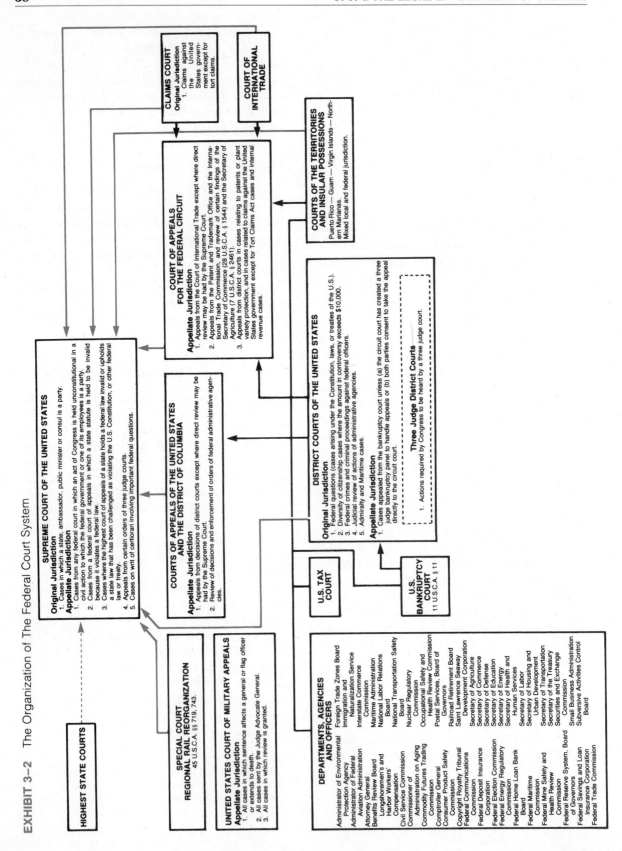

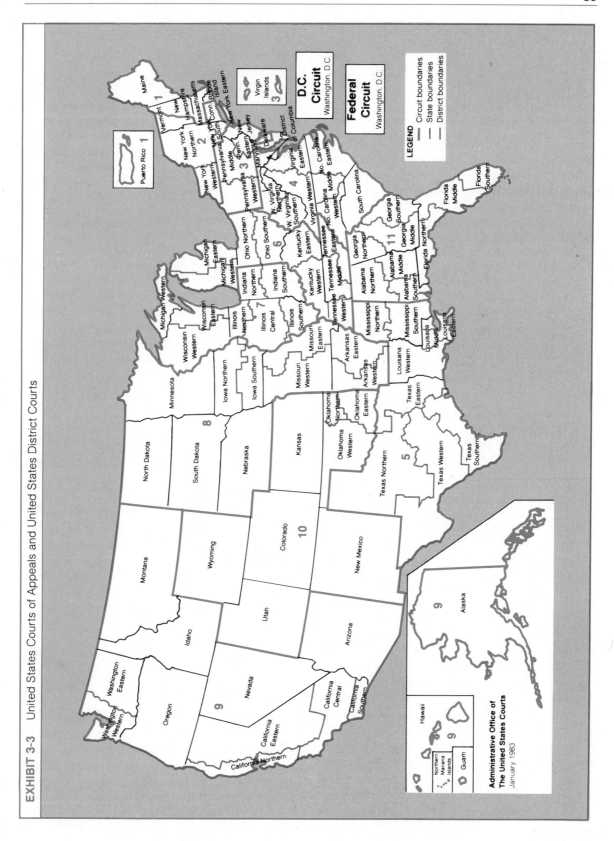

EXHIBIT 3-3 United States Courts of Appeals and United States District Courts

any of the federal courts of appeals, and it also has appellate authority over some cases decided in the state courts.

JURISDICTION OF FEDERAL COURTS

Since the federal government is a government of limited powers, the jurisdiction of the federal courts is limited. Article III of the U.S. Constitution established the boundaries of federal judicial power:

> Section 1.   The judicial power of the United States shall be vested in one supreme Court and in such inferior Courts as the Congress may from time to time ordain and establish. * * *
>
> Section 2.   The judicial power shall extend to all Cases, in Law and Equity, arising under this Constitution, the Laws of the United States, and Treaties made, or which shall be made, under their Authority;—to all Cases affecting Ambassadors, other public Ministers and Consuls;—to all Cases of admiralty and maritime Jurisdiction;—to Controversies to which the United States shall be a Party;—to Controversies between two or more States; between a State and Citizens of another State; 7—between Citizens of different States;—between Citizens of the same State claiming Lands under the Grants of different States, and between a State, or the Citizens thereof, and foreign States, Citizens or Subjects.
>
> In all Cases affecting Ambassadors, other public Ministers and Consuls, and those in which a State shall be a Party, the supreme Court shall have original Jurisdiction. In all the other Cases before mentioned, the supreme Court shall have appellate Jurisdiction, both as to Law and Fact, with such Exceptions, and under such Regulations as the Congress shall make.

In line with the checks and balances system of the federal government, Congress has the power to control the number and kind of inferior courts in the federal system. Except in those cases where the Constitution gives the Supreme Court original jurisdiction, Congress can also regulate the jurisdiction of the Supreme Court. Although the Constitution sets the outer limits of federal judicial power, Congress can set other limits on federal jurisdiction. Furthermore, the courts themselves can promulgate rules that limit the types of cases that they will hear.

---

7.   Amendment XI, passed in 1798, prohibits any exercise of federal judicial power in cases brought against a state by citizens of another state.

Federal Questions

"The Judicial Power shall extend to all cases * * * arising under this Constitution, the laws of the United States and Treaties made * * * under their authority." Thus, federal-question jurisdiction (as well as diversity jurisdiction which will be discussed below) arises from Article III, Section 2 of the Constitution. Whenever a plaintiff's cause of action is based, at least in part, on the United States Constitution, a treaty, or a federal law, then a **federal question** arises, and the case comes under the judicial power of federal courts. People whose claims are based on rights granted by an act of Congress can sue in a federal court. People who claim that their constitutional rights have been violated can begin their suits in federal court.

Any lawsuit involving a federal question can originate in a federal court. In lawsuits involving diversity of citizenship (to be discussed shortly), the amount in controversy must be in excess of $10,000 if the case is to proceed in federal court. In federal-question cases, however, there is no dollar-amount requirement.

Diversity of Citizenship

Another basis for federal district court jurisdiction is *diversity of citizenship*. Diversity of citizenship cases are those arising between (1) citizens of different states, (2) a foreign country and citizens of a state, or different states, and (3) citizens of a state and citizens or subjects of a foreign country. As indicated above, under Title 28, Section 1332, the amount in controversy must be more than $10,000 before a federal court can take jurisdiction. For purposes of diversity of citizenship jurisdiction, a corporation is a citizen of the state where it is incorporated and of the state where it has its principal place of business. Cases involving diversity of citizenship can commence in the appropriate federal court or, if they have started in a state court, can sometimes be transferred.

Diversity jurisdiction originated in 1789. The authors of the Constitution felt that a state might be biased toward its own citizens. Hence, the option of using the federal courts provided by the principle of diversity of citizenship is a means of protecting the out-of-state party. A large percentage of the more than 70,000 cases filed in federal courts each year are based on diversity of citizenship.

Consider some examples. Smith is driving from his home state, New York, to Florida. In Georgia he runs into a car owned by Able, a citizen of Georgia. Able's new Mercedes is demolished, and as a result of the personal injuries she sustained in the accident, Able is unable to work for six months. Thus, the case in question involves more than $10,000 worth of damages. A Georgia court must have *in personam* jurisdiction through a long arm statute, but Smith can have the suit removed to a federal district court on the basis of diversity of citizenship.

Jones, who resides in Texas, is owed $25,000 by Corporation XYZ, which is incorporated and has its principal place of business in Louisiana. XYZ does enough business in Texas to allow Texas courts to exercise *in personam* jurisdiction over it. Since, for purposes of diversity of citizenship jurisdiction, XYZ is a citizen of Louisiana, Jones can begin her suit in a federal district court in Texas or Louisiana or in a state court in Texas or Louisiana.

Concurrent versus Exclusive Jurisdiction

When both federal and state courts have the power to hear a case, such as in cases in which there is diversity of citizenship of the parties, **concurrent jurisdiction** exists. In contrast, when cases can be tried only in federal courts, **exclusive jurisdiction** exists. Federal courts have exclusive jurisdiction in cases involving federal crimes, bankruptcy, patents, and copyrights; in suits against the United States; and in some areas of admiralty law. (States have exclusive jurisdiction in certain subject matters also— for example, in divorce and in adoptions.)

WHICH CASES REACH THE SUPREME COURT?

Many people are surprised to learn that in a typical case there is no absolute right of appeal to the United States Supreme Court. The Supreme Court is given original, or trial court, jurisdiction in a small number of situations. In all other cases, its jurisdiction is appellate "with such Exceptions, and under such Regulations as the Congress shall make." Today the exceptions and rules set by Congress and some rules that the court has set for itself are quite complex. Over 4,500 cases are filed with the Supreme Court each year; yet it hears an average of only 300. There are basically two procedures for bringing a case be-

fore the Supreme Court: by *appeal* or by *writ of certiorari*.

Appeal

Under rules set out by Congress, the Supreme Court must review a decision (that is, an individual has an absolute right to **appeal**) in the following situations:

1. When a federal court of appeals holds that a state statute is invalid because it violates federal law.
2. When the highest state court of appeals holds a federal law invalid or upholds a state law that has been challenged as violating federal law.
3. When a federal court holds an act of Congress unconstitutional and the federal government or one of its employees is a party.
4. When the hearing under appeal is for an injunction in a civil (as opposed to criminal) action that Congress requires a district court of three judges to determine.

Theoretically, the Supreme Court is required to hear any appeal that falls within one of these four categories, but it can decide which of these cases require full consideration, including written briefs from the lawyers and oral arguments before the Court. The Court will give full consideration only if four of the nine justices vote to do so. Otherwise the case will be dismissed. A case can be dismissed because the Court agrees with the lower court's decision, because the federal question presented is not a substantial one, or on some other procedural ground. When a case is dismissed for reasons of substantive law—that is, when the higher court agrees with the lower court or when a substantial federal question is lacking—the Court's decision has value as precedent, and the dismissal can be cited in later cases.[8]

Writ of Certiorari

A **writ of certiorari** is an order issued by the Supreme Court to a lower court requiring the latter to send it the record of the case for review. Parties whose cases do not fall into one of the appeal categories can petition the Supreme Court to issue a *writ of certiorari*, but whether the Court will issue one is

---

8.   Hicks v. Miranda, 422 U.S. 332, 95 S.Ct. 2281 (1975)

entirely within its discretion. In no instance is the Court required to issue a *writ of certiorari*.

Below are some of the situations in which the Supreme Court may issue a *writ of certiorari:*

1. When a state court has decided a substantial federal question that has not been determined by the Supreme Court before, or the state court has decided it in a way that is probably in disagreement with the trend of the Supreme Court's decisions.
2. When two or more federal courts of appeals are in disagreement with each other.
3. When a federal court of appeals has decided an important state question in conflict with state law, has decided an important federal question not yet addressed by the Court but which should be decided by the Court, has decided a federal question in conflict with applicable decisions of the Court, or has departed from the accepted and usual course of judicial proceedings.

Most petitions for *writs of certiorari* are denied. A denial is not a decision on the merits of a case, nor does it indicate agreement with the lower court's opinion. Denial of the writ also has no value as a precedent.[9] The Court will not issue a writ unless at least four justices approve of it. This is called the "rule of four." Typically, only the petitions that raise the possibility of important constitutional questions are granted.

JUDICIAL PROCEDURES: FOLLOWING A CASE THROUGH THE COURTS

American and English courts follow the *adversary system of justice.* The judge's role is viewed as nonbiased and mostly passive. The lawyer functions as the client's advocate, presenting the client's version of the facts in order to convince the judge or the jury (or both) that they are true. Judges do not have to be entirely passive. They are responsible for the appropriate application of the law. They do not have to accept the legal reasoning of the attorneys. They can base a ruling and a decision on a personal study of the law. Judges sometimes ask questions of wit-

nesses and even suggest types of evidence to be presented. For example, if an indigent defendant chooses to act as his or her own counsel, the judge will often play less of a passive role and more of an advocate role, intervening during the trial proceedings to help the defendant.[10]

Procedure

Procedure involves the way in which disputes are handled in the courts. A large body of law, procedural law, establishes the rules and standards for determining disputes in courts. The rules are very complex, and they vary from court to court. There is a set of federal *rules of procedure,* and there are various sets of procedural rules in the state courts. Rules of procedure differ in criminal and civil cases.

We will now follow a civil case through the state court system. The case involves an automobile accident in which John Jones, driving a Cadillac, has struck Jane Adams, driving a Ford. The accident has occurred at an intersection in New York City. Adams has suffered personal injuries, incurring medical and hospital expenses as well as lost wages for four months. Jones and Adams are unable to agree on a settlement, and Adams sues Jones. Adams is the *plaintiff,* and Jones is the *defendant.* Both are represented by lawyers.

The Pleadings

Complaint and Summons   Adams's suit, or action, against Jones will commence when her lawyer files a *complaint* (sometimes called a petition or declaration) with the clerk of the trial court in the appropriate geographic area (the proper venue). In most states it will be a court having general jurisdiction; in others it may be a court having special jurisdiction with regard to subject matter. The complaint will contain: (1) a statement alleging the facts necessary for the court to take jurisdiction, (2) a short statement of the facts necessary to show that the plaintiff is entitled to a remedy, and (3) a statement of the remedy the plaintiff is seeking. A typical complaint is shown in Exhibit 3–4.

The complaint will state that Adams was driving her Ford through a green light at the specified in-

---

9.   Singleton v. Commissioner of Internal Revenue, 439 U.S. 940, 99 S.Ct. 335 (1978).

10.   See Faretta v. California, 422 U.S. 806, 95 S.Ct. 2525 (1975).

EXHIBIT 3–4   Example of A Typical Complaint

IN THE UNITED STATES DISTRICT COURT
FOR THE ___Southern___ DISTRICT OF ___New York___

CIVIL NO. __9–1047__

_____Jane Adams_____ ,
Plaintiff

vs.   COMPLAINT

_____John Jones_____ ,
Defendant.

Comes now the plaintiff and for his cause of action against the defendant alleges and states as follows:

1. This action is between plaintiff, who is a resident of the State of New York, and defendant, who is a resident of the State of New Jersey. There is diversity of citizenship between parties.

2. The amount in controversy, exclusive of interest and costs, exceeds the sum of $10,000.00.

3. On September 10th, 1982 plaintiff, Jane Adams, was exercising good driving habits and reasonable care in driving her car through the intersection of Broadwalk and Pennsylvania Ave. when defendant, John Jones, negligently drove his vehicle through a red light at the intersection and collided with plaintiff's vehicle.

4. As a result of the collision plaintiff suffered severe physical injury, that prevented her from working, and property damage to her car. The cost she incurred included: $85,000 in medical bills, $10,000 in lost wages, $5,000 automobile repair.

WHEREFORE, plaintiff demands judgment against the defendant for the sum of $100,000 plus interest at the maximum legal rate and the costs of this action.

By   _____

Joseph Roe
Attorney for Plaintiff
100 Main Street
New York, New York

1/2/86

tersection, exercising good driving habits and reasonable care, when Jones carelessly drove his Cadillac through a red light and into the intersection from a cross street, striking Adams and causing serious personal injury and property damage. The complaint will go on to state that she is entitled to $85,000 to cover medical bills, $10,000 to cover lost wages, and $5,000 to cover property damage to the car.

After the complaint has been filed, the sheriff or a deputy of the county will serve a *summons* and a copy of the complaint on the defendant Jones. The summons notifies Jones that he is required to prepare an answer to the complaint and to file a copy of his answer with both the court and the plaintiff's attorney within a specified time period (usually twenty to thirty days after the summons has been served). The summons also informs Jones that failure to answer will result in a judgment by default for the plaintiff—the plaintiff would be awarded the damages alleged in her complaint. A typical summons is shown in Exhibit 3–5.

Rules governing the service of a summons vary, but usually *service* is made by handing the summons to the defendant personally or by leaving it at the defendant's residence or place of business. In a few states a summons can be served by mail. When the defendant cannot be reached, special rules sometimes permit serving the summons by leaving it with a designated person, such as the secretary of state.

Choices Available after Receipt of the Summons and Complaint   Once the defendant is served with a copy of the summons and complaint, the defendant must file a responsive pleading (the answer). This filing must be done within the stipulated time period. In the answer, the defendant may file (1) a motion to dismiss, (2) any answer containing an affirmative defense, (3) a counterclaim, or (4) an answer denying the allegations and containing both an affirmative defense and a counterclaim.

Motion to Dismiss   If the defendant challenges the sufficiency of the plaintiff's complaint, the defendant can present to the court a **motion to dismiss,** or **demurrer.** (The rules of civil procedure in many states do not use the term *demurrer;* they use only *motion to dismiss.*) The motion to dismiss is an allegation that even if the facts presented in the complaint are true, their legal consequences are such

that there is no reason to go further with the suit and no need for the defendant to present an answer. It is a contention that the defendant is not legally liable even if the facts are as the plaintiff alleges. If, for example, Adams's complaint alleges facts that exclude the possibility of negligence on Jones's part, Jones can move to dismiss, and he will not be required to answer because his motion will be granted. The motion to dismiss is often used for purposes of delay.

If Adams wishes to discontinue the suit because, for example, an out-of-court settlement has been reached, she can likewise move for dismissal. The court can also dismiss on its own motion. If the court grants the motion to dismiss, the judge is saying that the plaintiff has failed to state a recognized cause of action. The plaintiff generally is given time to file an amended complaint. If the plaintiff does not file this amended complaint, a judgment will be entered against the plaintiff solely on the basis of the pleadings, and the plaintiff will not be allowed to bring suit on the matter again. On the other hand, if the court denies the motion to dismiss, the judge is indicating that the plaintiff has stated a recognized cause of action, and the defendant is given an extension of time to file a further pleading. If the defendant does not do so, a judgment will normally be entered for the plaintiff.

Answer and Counterclaim   If the defendant has not chosen to file a motion to dismiss or has filed a motion to dismiss that has been denied, then an **answer** must be filed with the court. This document either admits the statements or allegations set out in the complaint or denies them and sets out any defenses that the defendant may have. If Jones admits all of Adams's allegations in his answer, a judgment will be entered for Adams. If Jones denies Adams's allegations, the matter will proceed to trial.

Jones can deny Adams's allegations and set forth his own claim that Adams was in fact negligent and therefore owes Jones money for damages to the Cadillac. This is appropriately called a **counterclaim,** or a **cross-complaint.** If Jones files a counterclaim, Adams will have to answer it with a pleading, normally called a *reply,* that has the same characteristics as an answer.

Answer and Affirmative Defenses   Jones can also admit the truth of Adams's complaint but raise new

EXHIBIT 3–5   A Typical Summons

SUMMONS IN A CIVIL ACTION

United States District Court

FOR THE ___Southern___ DISTRICT OF: New York

CIVIL ACTION FILE No. _94047_

Jane Adams

Plaintiff

v.

John Jones

Defendant

SUMMONS

To the above named Defendant:

You are hereby summoned and required to serve upon   Joseph Roe

plaintiff's attorney, whose address is   100 Main Street
                                                 New York, New York

an answer to the complaint which is herewith served upon you, within 20* days after service of this summons upon you, exclusive of the day of service. If you fail to do so, judgment by default will be taken against you for the relief demanded in the complaint.

_____Tom Smith_____
                                    Clerk of Court

_____Mary Doakes_____
                                    Deputy Clerk.

Date: 1/10/86   [Seal of Court]

NOTE:—This summons is issued pursuant to Rule 4 of the Federal rules of Civil Procedure.

facts that will result in dismissal of the action. This is called raising an **affirmative defense.** For example, Jones could admit that he was negligent but plead that the time period for raising the claim has passed and that Adams's complaint must therefore be dismissed because it is barred by the statute of limitations (a statutory limit to the time during which one can raise a claim).

The complaint and answer (and the counterclaim and reply) taken together are called the **pleadings.** The pleadings inform each party of the claims of the other and specify the issues (disputed questions) involved in the case. Pleadings remove the element of surprise from a case. They allow lawyers to gather the most persuasive evidence and to prepare better arguments, thus increasing the probability that a just and true result will be forthcoming from the trial.

Dismissals and Judgments before Trial

Many actions for which pleadings have been filed never come to trial. There are numerous procedural avenues for disposing of a case without a trial. Many of them involve one or the other party's attempts to get the case dismissed through the use of pretrial *motions.* We have already mentioned the motion to dismiss, or the demurrer. Another equally important motion is the motion for a judgment on the pleadings.

Motion for Judgment on the Pleadings   After the pleadings are closed—after the complaint, answer, and any counterclaim and reply have been filed—either of the parties can file a *motion for a judgment on the pleadings.* This motion is basically the same as a motion to dismiss and may be granted or denied on the same grounds.

Motion for Summary Judgment   A lawsuit can be shortened or a trial can be avoided if there are no disagreements about the facts in a case and the only question is which laws apply to those facts. Both sides can agree to the facts and ask the judge to apply the law to them. In this situation, it is appropriate for either party to move for **summary judgment.** Summary judgment will be granted when there are no genuine issues of fact in a case and the only question is one of law. When the court considers a motion for summary judgment, it can take into ac-

count evidence outside the pleadings. This distinguishes the motion for summary judgment from the motion to dismiss. In a pretrial setting, one party can bring in a sworn statement, or affidavit, that refutes the other party's claim. Unless the second party brings in affidavits of conflicting facts, the first party will receive summary judgment.

Jones, for example, can bring in the sworn statement of a witness that Jones was in California at the time of the accident. Unless Adams can bring in other statements raising the possibility that Jones was at the scene of the accident, Jones will be entitled to dismissal on a motion for summary judgment. Motions for summary judgment can be made before or during a trial, but they will be granted only if it is clear that there are no factual disputes.

Discovery

Before a trial begins, the parties can use a number of procedural devices in order to obtain information and gather evidence about the case. Adams, for example, will want to know how fast Jones was driving, whether or not he had been drinking, whether he saw the red light, and so on. The process of obtaining information from the opposing party or from other witnesses is known as **discovery**. Discovery serves several purposes. It preserves evidence from witnesses who might not be available at the time of the trial or whose memories will fade as time passes. It can pave the way for summary judgment if it is found that both parties agree on all facts. It can lead to an out-of-court settlement if one party decides that the opponent's case is too strong to challenge. Even if the case does go to trial, discovery prevents surprises by giving parties access to evidence that might otherwise be hidden, and it serves to narrow the issues so that trial time is spent on the main questions in the case. In addition, discovery procedures may serve to establish a witness's testimony so that the witness's credibility can be attacked at trial if that testimony is changed. The federal rules of civil procedure and similar rules in the states set down the guidelines for discovery activity. Discovery includes gaining access to witnesses, documents, records, and other types of evidence.

Depositions and Interrogatories   Discovery can involve the use of depositions or interrogatories, or both. **Depositions** are sworn testimony by the op-

posing party or any witness, recorded by a court official. The person deposed appears before a court officer and is sworn. That person then answers questions asked by the attorneys from both sides. The questions and answers are taken down, sworn to, and signed. These answers will, of course, help the attorneys prepare their cases. They can also be used in court to impeach a party or witness who changes testimony at the trial. Finally, they can be used as testimony if the witness is not available at trial. Depositions can also be taken with written questions from both sides prepared ahead of time.

Interrogatories are a series of written questions for which written answers are prepared and then signed under oath. The main difference between interrogatories and depositions with written questions is that interrogatories are directed to a party, not to a witness, and the party can prepare answers with the aid of an attorney. The scope of interrogatories is broader because parties are obligated to answer questions even if the answer requires disclosing information from their records and files. Interrogatories are also usually less expensive than depositions.

Request for Admissions   A party can serve a written request to the other party for an admission of the truth of matters relating to the trial. Any matter admitted under such a request is conclusively established for the trial. For example, Adams can ask Jones to admit that he was driving at a speed of forty-five miles an hour. A request for admission saves time at trial because parties will not have to spend time proving facts on which they already agree.

Documents, Objects, and Entry upon Land   A party can gain access to documents and other items not in possession in order to inspect and examine them. Likewise, the party can gain entry upon land to inspect the premises. Jones, for example, can gain permission to inspect and duplicate Adams's medical records and repair bills.

Physical and Mental Examination   Where the physical or mental condition of a party is in question, a party can ask the court to order a physical or mental examination. If the court is willing to make the order, the party can obtain the results of the examination. It is important to note that the court will make such an order only when the need

for the information outweighs the right to privacy of the person to be examined.

The rules governing discovery are designed to make sure that a witness or party is not unduly harassed, that privileged material is safeguarded, and that only matters relevant to the case at hand are discoverable.

Pretrial Hearing

Either party or the court can request a pretrial conference or hearing. Usually the hearing consists of an informal discussion between the judge and the opposing attorneys after discovery has taken place. The purpose of the hearing is to identify the matters that are in dispute and to plan the course of the trial. The pretrial hearing is not intended to compel the parties to settle their case before trial, although judges may encourage them to settle out of court if circumstances suggest that a trial would be a waste of time.

Jury Trials

A trial can be held with or without a jury. If there is no jury, the judge determines the truth of the facts alleged in the case. The Seventh Amendment to the U.S. Constitution guarantees the right to a jury trial for cases at law in federal courts when the amount in controversy exceeds $20. Most states have similar guarantees in their own constitutions, although many states put a higher minimum dollar amount restriction on the guarantee. For example, Iowa requires the dollar amount of damages to be at least $1,000 before there is a right to a jury trial.

The right to a trial by jury does not have to be exercised, and many cases are tried without one. In most states and in federal courts, one of the parties must request a jury or the right is presumed to be waived.

In the case between Adams and Jones, both parties want a jury trial. The jurors are questioned by the judge and by both attorneys to insure that their judgment will be impartial. After the jurors are selected, they are impaneled, sworn in, and the trial is ready to begin.

The Trial

Both attorneys are allowed to make *opening statements* concerning the facts that they expect to prove during the trial. Since Adams is the plaintiff and has the burden of proving that her case is correct, Adams's attorney begins the case by calling the first witness for the plaintiff and examining (questioning) the witness. (For both attorneys, the type of question and the manner of asking are governed by the rules of evidence.) This examination is called *direct examination*. After Adams's attorney is finished, the witness will be questioned by Jones's attorney on *cross-examination*. After that, Adams's attorney has another opportunity to question the witness in *redirect examination*, and Jones's attorney can then follow with *recross-examination*. When both attorneys have finished with the first witness, Adams's attorney will call the succeeding witnesses in the plaintiff's case, each of whom is subject to cross-examination (and redirect and recross, if necessary).

At the conclusion of the plaintiff's case, the defendant's attorney has the opportunity to ask the judge to direct a verdict for the defendant on the ground that the plaintiff has presented no evidence that would justify the granting of the plaintiff's remedy. This is called a *motion for a directed verdict*. In considering the motion, the judge will look at the evidence in the light most favorable to the plaintiff and will grant the motion only if there is insufficient evidence to raise an issue of fact. (Motions for directed verdicts at this stage of trial are seldom granted.)

The defendant's attorney will then present the evidence and witnesses for the defendant's case. Witnesses are called and examined. The plaintiff's attorney has a right to cross-examine them, and there is a redirect and recross-examination if necessary. At the end of the defendant's case, either attorney can again move for a directed verdict, and the test will again be whether the jury can, under any reasonable interpretation of the evidence, find for the party against whom the motion is made.

After the defendant's attorney has finished the presentation of evidence, the plaintiff's attorney can present additional evidence to refute the defendant's case in a **rebuttal**. The defendant's attorney can meet that evidence in a **rejoinder**. After both sides have rested their cases, the attorneys each present a **closing argument**, urging a verdict in favor of their respective clients. The judge instructs the jury (assuming it is a jury trial) in the law that applies to the case. The instructions to the jury are often called *charges*. Then the jury retires to the jury room to deliberate a verdict. In the *Adams v. Jones* case the jury will not only decide for the plaintiff or for the defendant but, if it finds for the plaintiff, it will also decide on the amount of money to be paid to her.

Motion for New Trial At the end of the trial, a motion can be made to set aside an adverse verdict and any judgment, and to hold a new trial. The motion will be granted if the judge is convinced, after looking at all the evidence, that the jury was in error. A new trial can also be granted on the grounds of newly discovered evidence, misconduct by the participants during the trial, or error by the judge.

Judgment N.O.V. (Notwithstanding the Verdict) If Adams wins, and if Jones's attorney had previously moved for a directed verdict, Jones's attorney can now make a motion for a **judgment n.o.v.** (from the Latin *non obstante veredicto*, or notwithstanding the verdict). In other words, Jones can state that even if the evidence is viewed in the light most favorable to Adams, a reasonable jury should not have found a verdict in Adams's favor. If the judge finds this contention to be correct or decides that the law requires the opposite result, the motion will be granted. The standards for granting a judgment n.o.v. are the same as those for granting a motion to dismiss. Assume here that this motion is denied and that Jones appeals the case. (If Adams wins but receives a smaller money award than she sought, she can appeal also.) These events are illustrated in Exhibit 3–6.

The Appeal

A notice of appeal must be filed with the clerk of the trial court within the prescribed time. Jones then becomes the *appellant* or *petitioner*. His attorney files in the reviewing court (usually an intermediate court of appeals) the record on appeal, which contains the following: (1) the pleadings, (2) a transcript of the trial testimony and copies of the exhibits, (3) the judge's rulings on motions made by the parties, (4) the arguments of counsel, (5) the instructions to the jury, (6) the verdict, (7) the posttrial motions, and (8) the judgment order from which the appeal is taken. Jones may also be required to post a bond for the appeal.

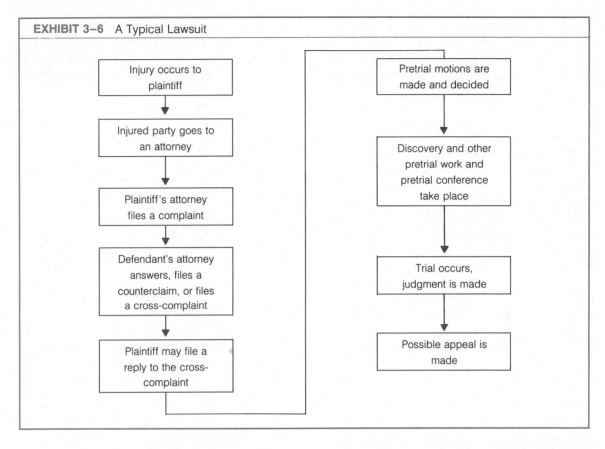

EXHIBIT 3–6   A Typical Lawsuit

Injury occurs to plaintiff

Injured party goes to an attorney

Plaintiff's attorney files a complaint

Defendant's attorney answers, files a counterclaim, or files a cross-complaint

Plaintiff may file a reply to the cross-complaint

Pretrial motions are made and decided

Discovery and other pretrial work and pretrial conference take place

Trial occurs, judgment is made

Possible appeal is made

Jones's attorney is required to prepare a condensation of the record, known as an *abstract*. The abstract, the brief, and the arguments are filed with the reviewing court. The brief contains (1) a short statement of the facts, (2) a statement of the issues, (3) the rulings by the trial court that Jones contends are erroneous and prejudicial, (4) the grounds for reversal of the judgment, (5) a statement of the applicable law, and (6) arguments on Jones's behalf, citing applicable statutes and relevant cases as precedent. The attorney for the *appellee*, or *respondent*, Adams, must now file an answering brief and argument. Jones's attorney can now file a reply (although this is not required). The reviewing court then considers the case.

No Evidence Heard   Appeals courts do not hear any evidence. Their decision concerning a case is based upon the abstracts, the record, and the briefs. The attorneys can present oral arguments, after which the case is taken under advisement. When the court has reached a decision, the decision is written. It contains the opinion (the court's reasons for its decision), the rules of law that apply, and the court's ultimate decision. In general, the appellate courts do not reverse findings of fact unless the findings are unsupported or contradicted by the evidence. Rather, they review the record for errors of law. If the reviewing court believes that a reversible error was committed during the trial or that the jury was improperly instructed, the judgment will be reversed. Sometimes the case will be *remanded* (sent back to the court that originally heard the case) for a new trial. In many cases the decision of the lower court is *affirmed*, resulting in the enforcement of that court's judgment or decree.

Higher Appeals Courts   If the reviewing court is an intermediate appellate court, the losing party (in that court) may seek a reversal of its decision by filing within the prescribed time period a petition for leave to appeal to the state supreme court.[11] Such

11.   In most states, the appeal from the court of original jurisdiction to the state supreme court is a matter of right.

a petition corresponds to a petition for a *writ of certiorari* in the United States Supreme Court. The winning party in the intermediate appellate court can file an answer to the petition for leave to appeal. If the petition is granted, the complete record is certified and forwarded to the higher court. New briefs must be filed before the state supreme court and the attorneys may be allowed or requested to present oral arguments. Whenever the state supreme court concludes that the judgment of the intermediate appellate court is correct, it affirms. If it decides otherwise, it reverses the appellate court's decision and enters an appropriate order of remand. At this point, unless a federal question is at issue, the case has reached its end. If a new trial is ordered, it will start again at the court of origin.

It is important to know that the vast majority of disputes are settled out of court mainly because of the time and expense of trying a case. Furthermore, of those cases that go to trial, about 97 percent are finally resolved at the trial level, as relatively few trial court decisions are changed on appeal.

ARBITRATION

Arbitration is becoming an increasingly popular alternative to the court system and its formalities. In arbitration programs, a dispute is referred to an impartial third person who is chosen by the parties to the dispute. The parties in dispute agree in advance to abide by the arbitrator's decision, which is issued after a hearing in which both parties have an opportunity to be heard. Presently, forty-three of the largest fifty law firms are members of the **American Arbitration Association (AAA)**. The AAA is a major organization that offers arbitration services.

Since trials are often characterized by extensive court delays, going to trial is both costly and time-consuming. Arbitration offers a less formal alternative for the settlement of claims. With the assistance of expert arbitors, disputes can be settled quickly and satisfactorily, without the expense and publicity that would accompany court trials. Because of the advantages of the arbitration process, most states[12] currently have statutes encouraging arbitration in certain types of disputes—the coverage varying from state to state.

The U.S. District Court for the Southern District of New York has adopted a case-referral project. Under this project, participating judges may order the parties to meet within thirty days with the director of the AAA's New York Regional Office. During this meeting, available non-judicial methods for resolving disputes are discussed. Of the cases referred to the AAA, more than half of them have resulted in an agreement to use some method of alternative dispute resolution (ADR).

South Carolina has become the first state to institute a voluntary arbitration program at the *appellate court level*. Appealing a case is very costly and time-consuming, and, hence, arbitration at this level is designed to reduce the time and expense of having an appeal decided. Litigants, under the South Carolina system, must waive the court hearing when requesting arbitration. Moreover, all decisions by the arbitrators are final.

Arbitration is also encouraged on the international level. In a recent landmark case, the U.S. Supreme Court held that even antitrust claims—which in a domestic context are not arbitrable—could be subject to arbitration if they were related to transnational contracts.[13]

---

12. Including Montana, Utah, and Vermont, which enacted such laws in 1985.
13. Mitsubishi Motors Corp. v. Soler Chrysler-Plymouth, Inc., — U.S. —, 53 U.S.L.W. 5069 (U.S., July 2, 1985).

QUESTIONS AND CASE PROBLEMS

1. The American system of government is unique in that it has essentially two sets of governments—state and federal. This is called the dual, or federal, system. One problem that arises in a federal system is that each government tends to duplicate the other's efforts. Can you see any way to avoid such problems of duplication?
2. When a person commits an act that violates both state and federal law, quite often both the federal and the state government have jurisdiction. What problems do you see here?

3. The Constitution says that a person cannot be tried twice for the same crime. Does this problem arise when both the federal and the state government try the same person for the same crime? Explain.

4. (a) Before two parties go to trial, there is an involved process called pleadings and discovery. Until recently, pleadings were very formal, and trials often turned on elements of surprise. For example, a plaintiff would not necessarily know until the trial what the defendant's defense was going to be. Does this seem like a fair way to conduct a trial?

(b) Within the last twenty years, new rules of pleadings and discovery have substantially changed all this. Now each attorney can discover practically all the evidence that the other will be presenting at trial. However, certain information is still not available to the parties—namely, each attorney's work product. *Work product* is not a clear concept. Basically, it includes all the attorney's thoughts on the case. Can you see any reason why such information should not be made available to the opposing attorney?

5. Quite often, trials are concluded before they are begun. If the parties do not disagree on the facts, they simply relate those facts to the judge, and then, through a motion for judgment on the pleadings, they ask the judge to decide what the law is and how it applies to this set of facts. How is it possible that two parties can agree on the facts yet disagree as to which party is liable?

6. If a judge enters judgment on the pleadings, the losing party can usually appeal but cannot present evidence to the appellate court. Does this seem fair? Explain.

7. Once a case is appealed, most appellate courts do not have the power to enter judgment or to award damages to a party who should have received them at trial. Consequently, if the appellate court disagrees with the trial court's decision, it will reverse and remand—in effect, ordering the trial court judge to change the judgment. Why should an appellate court not take a judge's word as final?

8. Sometimes on appeal there are questions of whether the facts presented in a trial support the conclusion reached by the judge or the jury. The appellate court will reverse on the basis of the facts only when so little evidence was presented at trial that no reasonable person could have reached the conclusion that the judge or jury reached. Appellate courts normally defer to a judge's decision with regard to the facts. Can you see any reason for this?

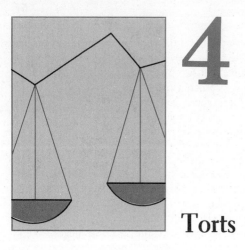

4

Torts

Part of doing business today and, indeed, part of everyday life is the risk of being involved in a lawsuit. A normal and ever-increasing business operating cost is that of liability insurance to protect against lawsuits. The list of circumstances in which business people can be sued is long and varied. An employee injured on the job may attempt to sue the employer because of an unsafe working environment. The consumer who is injured while using a product may attempt to sue the manufacturer because of a defect in the product. The patient who has received negligent treatment may attempt to sue the doctor. The issue in all of these examples is alleged wrongful conduct by one person that causes injury to another. Such wrongful conduct is covered by the law of **torts.** (The word *tort* is French for "wrong.")

Tort law covers a broad variety of injuries. Society recognizes an interest in personal physical safety, and tort law provides a remedy for acts causing physical injury or interfering with physical security and freedom of movement. Society recognizes an interest in protecting personal property, and tort law provides a remedy for acts causing destruction or damage to property. Society recognizes other, more intangible interests in such things as personal privacy, family relations, reputation, and dignity. Tort law provides a remedy for invasion of protected interests in these areas.

Tort law is constantly changing and growing with society. Although many torts have their origin in the old common law, new torts are recognized in order to protect new interests that develop with social change. For example, until recently it was not a legally recognizable tort for a husband to negligently injure his wife or child because of old notions of family structure. But today minors, as well as spouses, receive much more protection. Traditionally, one could not recover for psychological injury unless one had personally risked physical harm. That rule is changing, with more and more courts allowing recovery for emotional damage to those who witness traumatic injury to another.

TORT LAW VERSUS CRIMINAL LAW

Two notions serve as the basis of all torts: wrongs and compensation. Tort law recognizes that some acts are wrong because they cause injury to someone. The one who commits the act is to blame, or bears the fault for these injuries. Of course, this is not the only type of wrong that exists in the law; crimes involve wrongs also. A crime, however, is an act so reprehensible that it is considered to be a wrong against the state or against society as a whole, as well as against the individual victim. Therefore, the *state* prosecutes the criminal. On the other hand, a tort action is a *civil* action in which one person brings a suit of a personal nature against another. The state is not a party to the suit. Thus, for example, an assault could be the basis for a criminal prosecution as well as the basis of an action in tort.[1] In such a case the same act can be a criminal wrong and a civil wrong.

The function of tort law is to provide the injured party with some remedy. The law of torts is used to decide when victims must bear the loss themselves and when the responsibility belongs to someone else. A typical tort action involves a negligent act of one party that causes personal or property damage to another.

KINDS OF TORTS

Determining whether or not some action is a tort involves, in essence, a decision on how losses should be allocated in an increasingly complex society. Thus, the many factors that make up social policy are weighed against one another. Torts are traditionally divided into three categories:

1.   Intentional torts.
2.   Negligence.
3.   Strict liability.

Intentional torts, as the name implies, are injuries caused by intentional acts. Negligence consists of harm caused by careless acts. Strict liability rules require someone to compensate the injured party without regard to fault; generally, strict liability is imposed by law.

INTENTIONAL TORTS: WRONGS AGAINST THE PERSON

An **intentional tort** arises from an act which the defendant consciously desired to perform, either in order to harm another or knowing with substantial certainty that injury to another could result. Note that it is the *intent* to perform the original act that

---

1.   An assault may be described as any word or action intended to cause the person to whom it is directed to be in fear of immediate physical harm.

is important. The nature of the damage ultimately caused is irrelevant in determining whether there was intent. If Johnson intentionally pushes Adams and Adams falls to the ground and breaks her arm, it does not matter that Johnson never wished to break Adams's arm. Johnson did intend to push Adams, and that in itself is a tortious act; Johnson is liable for the consequences, including injury to Adams's arm. If the push were accidental, there would not be an intentional tort, but there might be a negligent injury.

Because intent is a subjective concept, the law generally assumes that one intends the normal consequences of his or her actions. Thus, an angry push is an intentional tort because the object of the push will go flying; however, a playful pat on the shoulder is not an intentional tort even though, in drawing away suddenly, the person touched may be injured. When injury is not a normal consequence of the act, the injured person must prove real harm has occurred in order to recover damages.

Assault

Any intentional, unexcused act that creates in another person a reasonable apprehension or fear of immediate harmful or offensive contact is an **assault**. Apprehension is not the same as fear. If a contact is such that a reasonable person would want to avoid it, and if there is a reasonable basis for believing the contact is coming, then the plaintiff suffers apprehension whether or not he or she is afraid.

The interest protected by tort law concerning assault is the freedom from having to expect harmful or offensive contact. The arousal of apprehension is enough to justify compensation. Of course, the *completion* of the act that caused the apprehension, if it results in harm to the plaintiff, is a battery, discussed next. For example, Jones threatens Smith with a gun, then shoots him. The pointing of the gun at Smith is an assault; the firing of the gun (if the bullet hits Smith) is a battery.

Battery

A **battery** is an unexcused, harmful or offensive physical contact intentionally performed. If Jones intentionally punches Smith in the nose, it is a battery. The interest this tort protects is the right to personal security and safety. The contact can be harmful, or it can be merely offensive (such as an unwelcome kiss). Physical injury does not have to occur. The contact can be to any part of the body or anything attached to it—for example, a hat or other clothing, a purse, a chair, or an automobile in which one is sitting. Whether the contact is offensive or not is determined by the *reasonable person* standard.[2] The contact can be made by the defendant or by some force that the defendant sets in motion—for example, a rock thrown, food poisoned, or a stick swung.

If the plaintiff shows that there was a contact, and the jury agrees that the contact was offensive, that is enough to have a right to some compensation. Furthermore, there is no need to show that the defendant acted out of malice. The person could have been joking or playing or could even have had some benevolent motive. The underlying motive does not matter, only the intent to do the act. In fact, proving a motive is never necessary (but is always relevant). Damages from a battery can be for emotional harm or loss of reputation as well as for physical harm.

Assault and Battery Defenses   A number of legally recognized defenses can be raised by a defendant who is sued for assault or battery, or both. The defenses to be discussed here are (1) **consent**, (2) **self-defense**, (3) **defense of others**, and (4) **defense of property.**

Consent   When a person consents to the act that damages him or her, there is generally no liability for the damage done. A person who voluntarily signs up for a touch football team implicitly consents to the *normal* physical punishment that takes place during such activities. This defense is good only so long as the defendant remains within the boundaries of the consent given—that is, plays football by the normal rules.

Self-defense   An individual who is defending his or her life or physical well-being may use the defense of self-defense. A person is privileged to use whatever force is *reasonably* necessary to prevent harmful con-

tact. This defense extends not only to *real* danger, but also to *apparent* danger. However, reasonable ground must exist for believing the danger is real. Also, force cannot be used once the danger has passed, and revenge is always prohibited.

Defense of Others   An individual can act in a reasonable manner to protect others who are in real or apparent danger.

Defense of Property   Individuals who use reasonable force in attempting to remove intruders from their homes can use defense of property to counter tort lawsuits for assault or battery, or both. The law does value life, though, more than it values property. In principle, force that is likely to cause death or great bodily injury may never be used just to protect property. Setting a trap that fires a gun if an intruder enters an empty house is not considered reasonable by most courts.

False Imprisonment

False imprisonment, sometimes called false arrest, is defined as the intentional confinement or restraint of another person without justification. It involves interference with the freedom to move without restraint. The confinement can be accomplished through the use of physical barriers, physical restraint, or threats of physical force. Moral pressure or future threats are not restraints sufficient to constitute false imprisonment. It is essential that the person being restrained not comply with the restraint willingly. On the other hand, a person is under no duty to risk personal harm in trying to escape.

Business people are often confronted with suits for false imprisonment after they have attempted to confine a suspected shoplifter for questioning. Consider, for example, the case in which a store detective locks an alleged shoplifter in one of the store's offices. If the customer can prove his or her innocence or that the detention was totally unreasonable, the store can be sued for false imprisonment.

The loss to business from shoplifting is estimated to exceed 10 billion dollars a year. Almost all states have adopted so-called merchant protection legislation, which allows a merchant to detain any suspected shoplifter, provided that there is reasonable cause for suspicion and provided that the confinement is carried out in a reasonable way. However,

---

2.   The reasonable person standard is an objective test of how a reasonable (normal) person would have acted under the same circumstances. See Page 65 under "Breach of Duty of Care."

the risk of real injury to an innocent person is great. Educational programs are often offered to all employees; these programs explain the exact procedures to be followed when a customer is suspected of shoplifting. Harm to reputation and mental distress caused by wrongful imprisonment are believed by the law to be so real that damages are presumed and need not be proved to make a case.

A merchant can use the defense of probable cause to justify delaying a suspected shoplifter, but the delay must be *reasonable*. The following case provides a good example.

BACKGROUND AND FACTS *Deborah Johnson, plaintiff, went to defendant's store in Madison at about 7:30 P.M. in September of 1976. She took her small child with her, carrying the child in an infant seat which she had purchased at K-Mart two or three weeks before. After purchasing some diapers and children's clothes, she attempted to leave the store. The store security officer stopped the plaintiff and asked her to come back into the store because a K-Mart employee reported that she had seen plaintiff steal the infant seat. To show ownership, the plaintiff pointed to cat hair, food crumbs, and mild stains on the seat. After a twenty-minute delay, the security officer apologized and let the plaintiff leave. The trial court dismissed the plaintiff's action for false imprisonment. Plaintiff appealed.*

JOHNSON v. K-MART ENTERPRISES, INC.

Court of Appeals of Wisconsin, 1980.

98 Wis.2d 533, 297 N.W.2d 74.

DYKMAN, Judge.

*   *   *   *

Probable Cause

*   *   *   *

Because defendant is a corporation, it must transact business through its officers and employees. Section 943.50(3), Stats., permits a merchant (here K-Mart) to detain a shopper if certain conditions are met, one of which is that the merchant has probable cause for believing that the shopper stole the merchant's goods. Plaintiff's deposition shows that defendant's security officer believed that plaintiff stole the infant seat because another K-Mart employee told him that she saw plaintiff steal it. There is no conflicting evidence on this point. The question is whether the employee who said she saw plaintiff steal the infant seat was fabricating her story. Our inquiry is whether there is an issue of material fact in dispute as to whether the K-Mart employee who detained the plaintiff had probable cause for believing that plaintiff stole the infant seat.

We find no material facts in dispute, nor reasonable alternative inferences to be drawn from the facts. The merchant received word, through one of its employees, that plaintiff removed an infant seat from the shelf, put her child in it, and left the store without paying for the seat. We hold as a matter of law that the merchant, through its security guard, had probable cause based on this report to believe that plaintiff had shoplifted.

Reasonable Manner of Detention

Plaintiff argues that her deposition shows that the place of detention made the detention unreasonable, or at least would permit an inference from which a jury could find that the manner of detention was unreasonable.

Few innocent persons who are detained because they are suspected of shoplifting will feel that their detention was accomplished in a reasonable manner. Plaintiff's complaint is that the place she was detained was public. Yet, plaintiff's deposition shows that defendant's only actions were to stop plaintiff, ask her to return to the store, inform her that she was suspected of shoplifting, produce the witness who allegedly saw plaintiff steal the infant seat, apologize to plaintiff for the detention and release her. There is no suggestion in plaintiff's complaint or deposition that she asked to go to a more private place. Defendant's actions do not permit an inference that the detention was accomplished in an unreasonable manner.

Length of Time Detained

In plaintiff's deposition, she testified that she was detained for 20 minutes. An inference that could be drawn from the entire deposition is that most of this time was spent in obtaining the presence of the K-Mart employee who said she saw plaintiff steal the infant seat. Plaintiff suggests that the employee was not produced more quickly because she was afraid of confronting the person she had falsely accused.

 * * * In determining whether a 20-minute detention is reasonable as a matter of law, we must weigh the customer's important liberty interests against a merchant's need for protection against shoplifters. Such a balancing is evident in the language of the statute which gives merchants the power to detain suspected shoplifters while at the same time safeguarding the customer's rights. We hold that a merchant's interest in detaining suspected shoplifters is such that a 20-minute detention is reasonable. * * * *

DECISION AND REMEDY   *The appellate court upheld the trial court's dismissal of plaintiff's claim. The security officer acted reasonably and with probable cause.*

Infliction of Mental Distress

Recently the courts have begun to recognize an interest in freedom from mental distress as well as an interest in physical security. The tort of infliction of *mental distress* can be defined as an intentional act that amounts to extreme and outrageous conduct resulting in severe emotional distress to another.[3] For example, a prankster telephones an individual and says that the individual's spouse has just been in a horrible accident. As a result, the individual suffers intense mental pain or anxiety. This is deemed to be extreme and outrageous conduct that exceeds the bounds of decency accepted by society and is therefore actionable.

As this is a relatively new tort, it poses some problems. One major problem is that it could flood the courts with lawsuits asserting this basis of recovery. A society in which individuals are rewarded if they are unable to endure the normal mental stresses of day-to-day living is obviously undesirable. Therefore, the law usually focuses on the nature of the acts that come under this tort. Indignity or an-

noyance alone are usually not enough for a lawsuit based on intentional infliction of emotional distress. Many times, however, repeated annoyances, coupled with threats, are enough. Also, an unusually severe emotional reaction, such as the extreme distress of a woman incorrectly informed that her husband and two sons have been killed, may be actionable. Because it is difficult to prove the existence of mental suffering, a few states (such as Texas) require that the mental disturbance be evidenced by some physical illness.

Defamation

The protection of a person's body is involved in the torts of assault, battery, and false imprisonment. **Defamation** of character involves wrongfully hurting a person's good reputation. The law has imposed a general duty on all persons to refrain from making false, defamatory statements about others. Breaching this duty orally involves the tort of **slander;** breaching it in writing involves the tort of **libel.**[4]

---

3.   Restatement, Second, Torts, Section 46, Comment d.

4.   This distinction between oral and written defamation is becoming less meaningful.

The basis of the tort is the *publication* of a statement or statements that hold an individual up to contempt, ridicule, or hatred. *Publication* here means that the defamatory statements are made to or within the hearing of persons other than the defamed party. If Thompson writes Andrews a private letter accusing him of embezzling funds, that does not constitute libel. If Peters calls Gordon dishonest, unattractive, and incompetent when no one else is around, that does not constitute slander. In neither case was the message communicated to a third party. Interestingly, the courts have generally held that dictating a letter to a secretary constitutes publication. Moreover, if a third party overhears defamatory statements by chance, the courts have generally held that this also constitutes publication. Note further that any individual who republishes or repeats defamatory statements is liable even if that person reveals the source of such statements. Most radio stations have instituted seven-second delays for live broadcasts, such as talk shows, to avoid this kind of liability.

The common law has defined four types of false utterances that are considered torts *per se*, or on their face. That means that no proof of damages is required before these false utterances become actionable. They are:

1.   A statement that another has a loathsome communicable disease.
2.   A statement that another has committed improprieties while engaging in a profession or trade.
3.   A statement that another has committed or has been imprisoned for a serious crime.
4.   A statement that an unmarried woman is unchaste.

Defenses against Defamation   Truth is normally an *absolute* defense against a defamation charge. Furthermore, there may be a privilege involved. For example, statements made by attorneys and judges during a trial are *privileged* and therefore cannot be the basis for a defamation charge. Members of Congress making statements on the floor of Congress have an absolute privilege. Legislators have complete immunity from liability for false statements made in debate, even if they make such statements maliciously—that is, knowing them to be untrue. In general, false and defamatory statements that concern public figures and are published in the press are privileged if they are made without malice.[5] Under this rule of privilege, public figures are defined as those who "thrust" themselves into the forefront of public controversy.

Privileged communications are of two types, absolute and qualified. Only in limited cases, such as in judicial proceedings and legislative proceedings mentioned above, is the absolute privilege (immunity) granted. The qualified or conditional privilege is a common law concept based on the philosophy that the right to know or speak is of equal importance to the right not to be defamed. If the communication is conditionally privileged, the plaintiff must show that the privilege was abused in order to recover.

An example of a qualified privilege is found in letters of recommendations and in written evaluations of employees. This privilege allows for some latitude in making mistakes in the communication without defamation liability. Generally, if the communication statements are made in good faith and the publication is limited to those who have a legitimate interest in the communication, the statement falls within the qualified privilege.

In order to prove malice, a plaintiff must show that the defendant acted with either actual knowledge of falsity or a reckless disregard of the truth. The balance between free speech and the torts of slander and libel is delicate. The following case illustrates a libel case involving a public figure and the extent of liability when malice is proved.

---

5.   New York Times Co. v. Sullivan, 376 U.S. 254, 84 S.Ct. 710 (1964).

BACKGROUND AND FACTS   *Plaintiff Carol Burnett, the famous comedienne, believed she was libeled by an article in* The National Enquirer, *the defendant. She decided to sue the* Enquirer *for substantial punitive damages. At trial, she was awarded $300,000 in general damages and $1,300,000 in punitive damages.* The National Enquirer *moved for judgment notwithstanding the verdict and a new trial. The Court replied:*

BURNETT v.
NATIONAL ENQUIRER
California Superior Court, Los Angeles County, 1981.
7 Med.L.Rptr. 1321.

SMITH, J.

It is not the intention of the court to deal at great length with every issue raised by defendant in its motion for judgment notwithstanding the verdict and motion for new trial, but simply to articulate the reasons for denying defendant's motions, save and except the motion for new trial as it relates to the issue of damages.

Initially, defendant contends that its publication of March 2, 1976 about plaintiff was not libelous per se. It is clear to the court that the average reader, viewing the article in its entirety, would conclude that plaintiff was intoxicated and causing a disturbance. The evidence is undisputed that the article was false. There can be little question that the described conduct of plaintiff holds her up to ridicule within the meaning of California Civil Code section 45.

The National Enquirer's protestation that it was not guilty of actual malice borders on absurdity. Not only did plaintiff establish actual malice by clear and convincing evidence, but she proved it beyond a reasonable doubt. At the very minimum Brian Walker, the de facto gossip columnist, had serious doubts as to the truth of the publication. There is a high degree of probability that Walker fabricated part of the publication—certainly that portion relating to plaintiff's row with Henry Kissinger.

* * * *

At this point, it is fair to infer that Walker decided that there was little news value in the fact that Burnett and Kissinger had a good-natured conversation and that Burnett distributed her dessert to other patrons. A little embellishment was needed to "spice up" the item.

An entire afternoon was devoted to the issue of whether the National Enquirer was a newspaper or magazine. The court reaffirms its findings that the defendant does not qualify for the protection of California Civil Code section 48a because, when Exhibits 21, 22, 174 and 175 are viewed as a whole, the predominant function of the publication is the conveying of news which is neither timely nor current. Additionally, the defendant has been registered as a magazine with the Audit Bureau of Circulation since 1963, and carries a designation as a magazine or periodical in eight mass media directories.

In *Werner v. So. Calif. etc. Newspapers*, 35 Cal.2d 121, 128 (1950) our Supreme Court upheld the constitutionality of California Civil Code section 48a against an attack that it unfairly discriminated in favor of newspaper and radio stations. The court articulated its rationale as follows:

"In view of the complex and far flung activities of the news services upon which newspapers and radio stations must largely rely and the necessity of publishing *news while it's news* (emphasis mine), newspapers and radio stations may in good faith publicize items that are untrue but whose falsity they have neither the time nor the opportunity to ascertain."

Since the defendant rarely deals with "news while it's new", it is not entitled to the protection of Civil Code section 48a.

* * * *

While the record is clear that she suffered no actual pecuniary loss as a result of the libelous article, she had every right to suffer anxiety reactions in the immediate aftermath of the March 2, 1976 article and the ineffectual correction. Emotional distress is more difficult to quantify than pain and suffering, but it is no less real. A review of other verdicts for emotional distress is not particularly helpful since the facts of each case vary significantly. The fact that defendant's false publication was communicated to sixteen million readers coupled with an inadequate correction, is of substantial significance in measuring the extent of plaintiff's emotional distress. Finally, the only residual aspect of emotional distress which has lingered with plaintiff since the immediate aftermath of the publication is the fact she occasionally gets a little paranoid about talking too loudly in restaurants.

Defendant points to the fact that Burnett never sought the services of a psychiatrist, psychologist or counselor. Plaintiff acknowledged that she was able to set aside her anxiety to the point where she was able to function in her profession. Miss Burnett should be commended for not seeking the unnecessary services of some "phony build up artist" in order to inflate her damages. She should not be penalized for self-treating.

The court finds that plaintiff was a highly credible witness who did not exaggerate her complaints. Nevertheless, the jury award is clearly excessive and is not supported by substantial evidence. The court finds that the sum of $50,000.00 is a more realistic recompense for plaintiff's emotional distress and special damage.

An award of $1,300,000 will probably not amount to "capital punishment" (bankruptcy), as publicly espoused by defendant's counsel after the jury verdict, because of the defendant's strong cash position. The court finds that it is excessive because it does not bear a reasonable relationship to the compensatory damages that amount to only $50,000. A review of California case law indicates that appellate courts have not sanctioned any particular ratio of general and punitive damages. Each case turns on its own set of facts.

The court found that there was substantial evidence to support an award of punitive damages, but reduced the award to $760,000, a sum the judge felt was sufficient to deter further misconduct. The judge also reduced the amount of general damages to $50,000. Motions for judgement n.o.v. and for a new trial were denied. (The punitive damages were further reduced to $150,000 in 1983 by the California State Court of Appeals.)   **DECISION AND REMEDY**

Slander of Title, Disparagement of Goods, and Defamation by Computer

There are three torts, typically called business torts, that involve defamation. Defamation arising from a false statement made about a person's product, business, or title to property is called *slander of title* or *disparagement of goods*, depending on the case. Erroneous information from a computer about a person's credit standing or business reputation can impair that person's ability to obtain further credit and is called *defamation by computer*. These torts are treated in more detail in the following chapter.

Invasion of the Right to Privacy

A person's right to solitude and freedom from prying public eyes is the interest protected by the tort of invasion of privacy. Four different acts qualify as an invasion of privacy:

1. The use of a person's name or picture for commercial purposes without permission.
2. Intrusion upon an individual's affairs or seclusion.
3. Publication of information that places a person in a false light. This could be a story attributing to

the person ideas that are not held or actions that were not taken. (Publishing such a story could involve the tort of defamation as well.)
4. Public disclosure of private facts about an individual that an ordinary person would find objectionable.

Misrepresentation (Fraud, Deceit)

The tort of misrepresentation involves the use of fraud and deceit for personal gain. It includes several elements:

1. Misrepresentation of facts or conditions with knowledge that they are false or with reckless disregard for the truth.
2. Intent to induce another to rely on the misrepresentation.
3. Justifiable reliance by the deceived party.
4. Damages suffered as a result of reliance.
5. Causal connection between the misrepresentation and the injury suffered.

In general, the reliance must be upon a statement of fact. Reliance on a statement of opinion is not justified unless the person making the statement has a superior knowledge of the subject matter. A lawyer's opinion of the law, for instance, is an example of superior knowledge, and reliance on that opinion will be regarded as reliance upon a statement of fact.

Seller's Talk versus Facts   In order for fraud to occur, more than mere *seller's talk* must be involved. Fraud exists only when a person represents as a material fact something he or she knows is untrue. For example, it is fraud to claim that a building does not leak when one knows it does. Facts are objectively ascertainable, whereas seller's talk is not. "I'm the best lawyer in town," is seller's talk, or "puffing." The speaker is not trying to represent something as fact, because "best" is a subjective, not an objective, term.

The topic of fraud in contracts is important enough to merit an entire chapter. (See Chapter 12.)

INTENTIONAL TORTS: WRONGS AGAINST PROPERTY

Wrongs against property include (1) trespass to land and to personal property, (2) conversion, and (3) nuisance. The wrong is against the individual who has legally recognized rights with regard to land or personal property. The law distinguishes real property from personal property. *Real property* is land and things "permanently" attached thereto. *Personal property* is all other things that are basically movable. Thus, a house and lot are real property, whereas the furniture inside a house is personal property. Money and securities are also personal property.

Trespass to Land

Any time a person enters onto land that is owned by another, or causes anything to enter onto the land, or remains on the land, or permits anything to remain on it, such action constitutes the civil tort called a **trespass to land.** Note that actual harm to the land is not an essential element of this tort, because the tort is designed to protect the right of an owner to exclusive possession. If no harm is done, usually only nominal—in name only, not significant—damages (such as $1) can be recovered by the landowner. Examples of common types of trespass to land include walking or driving on the land,

shooting across it with a gun, throwing rocks or spraying water on a building in the possession of another, building a dam across a river that causes water to back up on someone else's land, and placing part of one's building on the adjoining landowner's property.

In the past, the right to land gave exclusive possession of a space that extended from "the center of the earth to the heavens," but this rule has been relaxed. Today, reasonable intrusions are permitted. Thus, aircraft can normally fly over privately owned land. The temporary invasion of the air space over such land is, in effect, considered privileged as to the aircraft owner. Society's interest in air transportation preempts the individual's interest in the air space.

Trespass Criteria, Rights and Duties   Before a person can be a trespasser, the real property owner (the person who legally controls the realty) must expressly or impliedly establish that person as a trespasser. For example, "posted" trespass signs expressly establish a person as a trespasser when that person ignores these signs and enters upon the property. However, a guest in your home is not a trespasser. Should the guest become unruly, you could *ask* your guest to leave and at that moment establish your guest as a trespasser. Any person who enters upon your property to commit an illegal act (such as a thief entering a lumberyard at night to steal lumber) is impliedly established as a trespasser without verbal establishment or posted signs.

Once a person is established as a trespasser, certain rights and duties are applied to both the owner of the realty and to the trespasser. Some of these are:

1.   A trespasser is liable for any damage caused to the property. The owner does not have to prove negligence.
2.   A trespasser assumes the risks of the premises and cannot hold the owner liable for injuries sustained. This rule does not permit the owner to lay traps with the intent to injure a trespasser. Under the "attractive nuisance" doctrine, infants or young persons do not assume the risks of the premises if they are attracted to the premises. Under some circumstances an owner may even have a duty to warn of dangers on the property, such as guard dogs.

3. As previously discussed, a trespasser can be removed from the premises through the use of reasonable force without the owner being liable for assault and battery. This same basic concept allows an owner to remove, without liability, another's property which constitutes a trespass, if the removal is accomplished by the exercise of reasonable care.

In the following case, a trespasser, even though innocent, is liable for damages.

BACKGROUND AND FACTS *During a severe snowstorm the plaintiff, Ronald Rossi, parked his car in the privately owned parking lot of a shopping center. The car was towed from the lot. Rossi sued the shopping center owners, Ventresca Bros. Const. Co., Inc., and the towing company to recover the $113.40 he paid to retrieve his car.*

ROSSI v. VENTRESCA BROS. CONST. CO., INC.

City Court of the City of White Plains, Westchester County, New York. Small Claims Part, 1978. 94 Misc.2d 756, 405 N.Y.S.2d 375.

BLAUSTEIN, Judge

* * * *

This Court reluctantly finds that the plaintiff was trespassing in parking on private property and the snowstorm does not justify the trespass. Further, the owner of the shopping center has the corollary right to remove any car so parked. The rule is stated in 87 C.J.S. Trespass § 45a:

"He [the owner] may remove chattels which are wrongfully on his land, if he uses due care in the removal. The removal should be effected with as little injury to the chattels removed as is possible, and without the exercise of excessive force."

* * * *

While plaintiff here is not a willful trespasser considering the severity of the storm, still, he was violating the owner's property and is liable for damages. The measure of damages is actual or special damages incurred. Even the most innocent of trespassers is liable for nominal damages as a minimum. (87 C.J.S. Trespass § 117).

Plaintiff was allowed to recover $27 of the towing charge. The court found the $113.40 charge to be excessive damages for the plaintiff's trespass.

DECISION AND REMEDY

Defenses against Trespass to Land Trespass to land involves wrongful interference with another person's real property rights. But if one can show that the trespass was warranted, as when a trespasser enters to assist someone in danger, a complete defense exists. Another defense is to show that the purported owner did not actually have the right to possess the land in question.

In some situations, courts can easily assess damages for trespass to land, especially when the trespasser damages or wrongfully destroys items of value on the land. For example, land purchasers can recover the value of destroyed trees when avoidable errors caused construction crews to knock them down.

Trespass to Personal Property

Whenever any individual unlawfully injures the personal property of another or otherwise interferes with the personal property owner's right to exclusive possession and enjoyment of that property, **trespass to personalty, or personal property,** occurs. Trespass to personal property involves intentional meddling. If a student takes another student's business law book as a practical joke and hides it so that the owner is unable to find it for several days prior to the final examination, the student has engaged in a trespass to personal property.

Defenses against Trespass to Personal Property   If it can be shown that trespass to personal property was warranted, then a complete defense has been made. Many states, for example, allow automobile repair shops to hold a customer's car when he has refused to pay for repairs rendered (under what is called an artisan's, or possessory, lien).

Conversion

Whenever personal property is taken from its rightful owner or possessor and placed in the service of another, the act of **conversion** occurs. Conversion is the civil side of those crimes relating to stealing.[6] A store clerk who steals merchandise from the store commits a crime and the tort of conversion at the same time. Of course, when conversion occurs, the lesser offense of trespass to personal property usually occurs as well. If the initial taking of the property was unlawful, there is trespass. Then, retention of that property is conversion. Even if the initial taking of the property was permitted by the owner or, for some other reason, is not a trespass, failure to return it may be conversion.

---

6.   Theft requires intent, but conversion does not.

Even if a person mistakenly believed that he or she was entitled to the goods, a tort of conversion may take place. In other words, good intentions are not a defense against conversion, and conversion can be an entirely innocent act. To illustrate: ABC Hardware allowed Samuels to take a lawn mower home to try it out. Samuels used the lawn mower once. He then lent it to his neighbor, Nichols. A thief stole the lawn mower from Nichols. When ABC Hardware learned what had happened to the mower, it demanded that Samuels pay for it. Samuels is guilty of conversion because he had no right to lend the mower to Nichols. His misuse of the mower renders him liable. He obviously did not intend for the mower to be stolen, but he intentionally took the mower from ABC and intentionally and knowingly lent it to his neighbor.

Whoever suffers a conversion is generally entitled to recover the reasonable value of the lost goods. If Henries deliberately smashes a vase that Arts, Inc., exhibits for sale in its store, Henries is liable for the value of the vase. Deliberate destruction of the personal property of another is conversion. Henries treated the vase as if he owned it when he asserted a right to destroy it. (When the goods are not destroyed, the owner can either try to get them back through a lawsuit or ask for damages for conversion. The court will not give the owner full value for the goods and return the property as well.)

The following case illustrates the concept of the tort of conversion.

DOLENZ v. NATIONAL BANK OF TEXAS AT FT. WORTH
Court of Civil Appeals of Texas, 1983.
649 S.W.2d 368.

BACKGROUND AND FACTS   *National Bank of Texas, the defendant, held a security interest in four large trailers owned by John Shipplet. When Shipplet became delinquent in paying for the trailers, the bank repossessed three of the trailers. Unknown to the bank, Bernard Dolenz, the plaintiff, had items of personal property, consisting primarily of restaurant equipment, stored inside the trailers. As soon as the bank discovered who owned the equipment, its agent contacted the plaintiff and offered to return the equipment. Plaintiff said he would get back in touch with the bank, but he never did. Instead, he brought suit for conversion of the equipment. The trial court rendered a "take nothing judgment" against plaintiff, and he appealed.*

JORDAN, Justice.
*   *   *   *

Conversion is any distinct act of dominion wrongfully exerted over another person's personal property and denial of, or inconsistent with, that other person's right in the property, either permanently or for indefinite time. * * * Conversion is an offense against possession and not title, and has been defined as the unlawful and wrongful exercise of dominion, ownership, or control by one person over the property of another, to the exclusion of the exercise of the same rights by the owner, either permanently or for an indefinite time, which may be effected by taking actual corporal possession and control over the property of another so as to prevent the owner from the exercise of such rights. * * *

To constitute a conversion of property, there must be some repudiation of the owner's right or an exercise of dominion over the property, wrongfully and in denial of or inconsistent with that right; or, there must be an illegal assumption of ownership. * * *

Before there can be a conversion, there must be an intent on the part of the defendant to assert some right in the property. * * * In this case we have none of the elements of a conversion of appellant's personal property which we have discussed above. Here, appellant's property was taken by appellee without appellee's knowledge, and with no intent to take it, or to exercise dominion and control over it. Appellee bank never, at any time, asserted any claim to or ownership of the property. As soon as it was discovered who was the rightful owner of the property, the bank contacted that owner, appellant here, apprised him of their possession of his property, and asked him to retake it. Appellee did not assert any right inconsistent with the title of or ownership of appellant's property; nor did it do anything except safely preserve and store his property. The property was taken by appellee, not for its use and benefit, but without any knowledge that said property was stored within the trailers repossessed by the bank. * * *

Appellant's position that when the bank unintentionally took his property there was a conversion as a matter of law, and that the bank then owned it, is untenable and erroneous. If, upon being advised by appellee that it had appellant's property, appellant had made demand for the return of it, and that demand had been refused, then, and only then, would there have been a conversion of appellant's property. Appellant made no demand for the return of his property, but, instead, when it was offered to him, he did not claim it. * * * *

The appellate court upheld the trial court's action, and the bank was not liable for the conversion.   **DECISION AND REMEDY**

Stolen Goods Here again, intent to engage in a wrongdoing is not necessary for conversion to exist. Rather, it is the intent to exercise control over property when such control is inconsistent with the plaintiff's rights that constitutes conversion. Therefore, someone who buys stolen goods is guilty of conversion even if he or she did not know the goods were stolen. If the true owner brings a tort action against the buyer, the buyer must pay the owner the full value of the property, despite having already paid some money to the thief.

Defenses against Conversion A successful defense against the charge of conversion is that the purported owner has no title, or right to possess, superior to the holder's rights.

Necessity is another possible defense against conversion. If Abrams takes Stephens's cat, Abrams is guilty of conversion. If Stephens sues Abrams, Abrams must return the cat and pay damages. If, however, the cat has rabies and Abrams took the cat to protect the public, Abrams has a valid defense—necessity (and perhaps even self-defense if he can prove that he was in danger from the cat).

Nuisance

It is possible to commit a tort and be liable because of unreasonable uses of your own property. A **nuis-**

ance is an improper activity that interferes with another's enjoyment or use of his or her property. Nuisances can be either *public* or *private*. A public nuisance disturbs or interferes with the public in general, whereas a private nuisance interferes with the property interest of a limited number of individuals. Reasonable limitations are placed on the use of property in all situations. Such limitations prevent the owner from unreasonably interfering with the health and comfort of neighbors or with their right to enjoy their own private property. One who suffers as a result of a nuisance can have it stopped by seeking an injunction in the courts. An injunction is an equitable remedy. The court, if it grants the injunction, will prohibit the continuation of the undesirable activity.

Nuisances can also involve indecent, improper, or unlawful personal conduct. Obviously, there is an extremely subjective element in any definition of nuisance, particularly when it involves personal conduct. Moreover, a nuisance may be a crime as well as a tort, and the dividing line is difficult to ascertain. Finally, nuisances may result from intentional types of conduct as well as from negligent (careless) conduct. The defendant may even be held liable on the ground of strict liability. The difficulties in applying the nuisance doctrine are apparent.

UNINTENTIONAL TORTS: NEGLIGENCE

Intentional torts normally involve a particular mental state. In negligence, however, the actor neither wishes to bring about the consequences of the act nor believes that they will occur. The actor's conduct merely creates a *risk* of such consequences. Without the creation of a risk, there can be no negligence. Moreover, the risk must be foreseeable; that is, it must be such that a reasonable person would anticipate it and guard against it. In determining what is reasonable conduct, courts consider the nature of the possible harm. A very slight risk of a dangerous explosion might be unreasonable, whereas a distinct possibility of burning one's fingers on a stove might be reasonable.

In examining a question of negligence, one should ask six questions:

1. Does (or did) the defendant owe a duty of care to the plaintiff?
2. What did the person do (act)?
3. Did the act create a foreseeable risk of harm (breach of duty of care)?
4. Was harm done (damages)?
5. Did the act *cause* the harm (causation in fact, or actual cause)?
6. At what point should liability cease (proximate cause)?

Many of the actions discussed in the section on intentional torts would constitute negligence if they were done carelessly, but without intent. For instance, carelessly bumping into someone who falls and breaks an arm constitutes negligence. Likewise, carelessly, as opposed to intentionally, flooding someone's land constitutes negligence. In a sense, negligence is a *way of committing* a tort rather than a distinct *category* of torts.

Negligence involves the allocation of loss between an innocent plaintiff and an innocent, albeit careless, defendant. The extent of duty and liability of both the plaintiff and the defendant is frequently determined by social policy. For example, suppose that XYZ Corporation—selling $600 million of products a year—is sued by Simperman for injuries resulting from negligent manufacturing. Simperman cannot afford to pay his medical expenses, but XYZ Corporation can spread the cost of the damages in its pricing among all its customers. If there is a policy of spreading such costs, a court may find for the plaintiff. In a similar situation, however, the court might not find for the plaintiff if the defendant is an individual rather than a large corporation.

Negligence has been committed when someone has suffered injury caused by the failure of another to live up to a required duty of care. Three elements must be examined here: (1) breach (failure) of duty of care, (2) injury, and (3) causation. Certain defenses must also be examined.

Breach of Duty of Care

The first element in a tort of negligence can also be broken into a two-part question:

1. Is there a duty of care?
2. Did the defendant's action breach (fail to live up to) that duty?

Duty of Care Basically, the concept of duty arises from the notion that if we are to live in society with other people, some actions can be tolerated and some cannot, some actions are right and some are wrong, and some actions are reasonable and some are not. The basic rule of duty is that people are free to act as they please as long as their actions do not infringe on the interests of others.

Tort law measures duty by a standard of reasonableness—the *reasonable person standard*. In determining whether a tort has been committed, the courts ask how a reasonable person would have acted in the same circumstances. The reasonable person standard is said to be (though in an absolute sense it cannot be) objective. It is not necessarily how a particular person would act. It is society's judgment on how people should act. If the so-called reasonable person existed, he or she would be careful, conscientious, even-tempered, and honest. This hypothetical "reasonable person" is frequently used in discussions of law.

Breach of Duty   When someone either intentionally harms another, or fails to comply with the duty of exercising reasonable care, a tortious act may have been committed (but not necessarily a completed tort, since that will depend on whether damage and proximate cause exist). Failure to live up to the standard of care may be an act (setting fire to a building) or an omission (neglecting to put out a fire). It may be an intentional act, a careless act, or a carefully performed but nevertheless dangerous act that results in injury.

Whether or not a person's act or failure to act is unreasonable depends on the interaction of a number of factors. One factor is the nature of the act. Some actions—shooting off a gun in a crowd, for instance—are so outrageous that the actor should pay for what has been done regardless of physical damage. Other acts, like blasting with dynamite, are so dangerous that any damage caused should be paid for. Another factor in determining whether damages should be awarded is the manner in which an act is performed. Intentionally hitting someone on the back probably should be paid for; accidentally doing so probably should not be. A third factor is the nature of the injury—whether it is serious or slight, extraordinary, or simply part of everyday life. Other factors to be considered are whether or not the activity causing the injury was socially useful and how easily the injury could have been guarded against.

Injury

In order for a tort to have been committed, there must be a *legally* recognizable injury to the plaintiff.

The plaintiff must have suffered some loss, harm, wrong, or invasion of a protected interest to recover damages (that is, to receive compensation). The reason for the requirement of injury is obvious. Without an injury of some kind, there can be no compensation. Essentially, the purpose of torts is to compensate for legally recognized injuries resulting from wrongful acts, not to punish these acts. However, for some torts the injured person may be given extra compensation as punitive damages, because society tries to discourage these acts.[7] But few negligent acts are so reprehensible that punitive damages are available.

Causation

The second element necessary to a tort is causation. If a person fails in a duty of care and someone suffers injury, the wrongful activity must have caused the harm for a tort to have been committed. In deciding whether there is causation, the court must actually address two questions:

1.   Is there *causation in fact?*
2.   Was the act the *proximate cause* of the injury?

Causation in Fact   Did the injury occur because of the defendant's act, or would it have occurred anyway? If an injury would not have occurred without the defendant's act, then there is **causation in fact.** If Johnson carelessly leaves a campfire burning, and the fire burns down the forest, there is causation in fact. If Johnson carelessly leaves a campfire burning, but it burns out, and then lightning causes a fire that burns down the forest, there is no causation in fact. In both cases there is a wrongful act and damage. In the second case, however, there is no causal connection and thus no liability. Causation in fact can usually be determined by use of the *but for* test: But for the wrongful act, the injury would not have occurred.

In some cases, causation in fact is difficult to determine. What if Johnson's campfire did spread, but at the same time lightning also started a fire? In this type of situation, the courts apply the *substantial factor* test: If Johnson's conduct was a substantial factor in bringing about the damage, Johnson will be held liable.

---

7.   Even though punitive damages may be awarded in tort actions, they are usually *not* available in breach of contract actions.

Determining causation in fact entails examining the facts portrayed in evidence at a trial. The plaintiff has the burden of proving causation in fact as well as other elements, such as damages. The plaintiff must prove the case by a *preponderance of the evidence* in a civil suit.

Proximate Cause   How far should a defendant's liability extend for a wrongful act that was a substantial factor in causing injury? For example, Johnson's fire not only burns down the forest but also sets off an explosion in a nearby chemical plant that spills chemicals into a river, killing all the fish for a hundred miles downstream and ruining the economy of a tourist resort. Should Johnson be liable to the resort owners? To the tourists whose vacations were ruined? These are questions about the limitation of liability, which is the second element in the general issue of causation. The courts use the term **proximate cause** (or sometimes legal cause) to describe this element. Proximate cause is a question not of fact but of law and policy. The question is whether the connection between an act and an injury is strong enough to justify imposing liability. Probably the most cited case on proximate cause is the *Palsgraf* case.

PALSGRAF v. LONG
ISLAND R.R. CO.
Court of Appeals of New York,
1928.
248 N.Y. 339, 162 N.E. 99.

BACKGROUND AND FACTS   *The plaintiff, Palsgraf, was waiting for a train on a station platform. A man carrying a package was rushing to catch a train that was already moving. As the man attempted to jump aboard the moving train, he seemed unsteady and about to fall. A railroad guard on the car reached forward to grab him, and another guard on the platform pushed him from behind to help him on the train. The man's package, which contained fireworks, fell on the railroad tracks and exploded. There was nothing about the package to indicate its contents. The explosion caused scales located at the other end of the platform to fall upon Palsgraf, causing injuries for which she sued the railroad company. At the trial, the jury found that the railroad guards were negligent in their conduct toward the plaintiff.*

CARDOZO, Chief Justice.
*   *   *   *

The conduct of the defendant's guard, if a wrong in its relation to the holder of the package, was not a wrong in its relation to the plaintiff, standing far away. Relatively to her it was not negligence at all. Nothing in the situation gave notice that the falling package had in it the potency of peril to persons thus removed. *Negligence is not actionable unless it involves the invasion of a legally protected interest, the violation of a right.* "Proof of negligence in the air, so to speak, will not do." [Emphasis added.]
*   *   * If no hazard was apparent to the eye of ordinary vigilance, an act innocent and harmless, at least to outward seeming, with reference to her, did not take to itself the quality of a tort because it happened to be a wrong, though apparently not one involving the risk of bodily insecurity, with reference to someone else. "In every instance, before *negligence* can be predicated of a given act, *back of the act must be sought and found a duty to the individual complaining*, the observance of which would have averted or avoided the injury." [Emphasis added.]
A different conclusion will involve us, and swiftly too, in a maze of contradictions. A guard stumbles over a package which has been left upon a platform. It seems to be a bundle of newspapers. It turns out to be a can of dynamite. To the eye of ordinary vigilance, the bundle is abandoned waste, which may be kicked or trod on with impunity. Is a passenger at the other end of the platform protected by the law against the unsuspected hazard concealed beneath the waste? If not, is the result to be any different, so far as the distant passenger is concerned, when the guard stumbles over a valise which a truckman or a porter has left upon the walk? The passenger far away, if the victim of a wrong at all, has a cause of action, not derivative, but original and primary.

His claim to be protected against invasion of his bodily security is neither greater nor less because the act resulting in the invasion is a wrong to another far removed. In this case, the rights that are said to have been violated, the interests said to have been invaded, are not even of the same order. The man was not injured in his person nor even put in danger. The purpose of the act, as well as its effect, was to make his person safe. If there was a wrong to him at all, which may very well be doubted, it was a wrong to a property interest only the safety of his package. Out of this wrong to property, which threatened injury to nothing else, there has passed, we are told, to the plaintiff by derivation or succession a right of action for the invasion of an interest of another order, the right to bodily security. The diversity of interests emphasizes the futility of the effort to build the plaintiff's right upon the basis of a wrong to someone else. The gain is one of emphasis, for a like result would follow if the interests were the same. Even then, the orbit of the danger as disclosed to the eye of reasonable vigilance would be the orbit of the duty. One who jostles one's neighbor in a crowd does not invade the rights of others standing at the outer fringe when the unintended contact casts a bomb upon the ground. The wrongdoer as to them is the man who carries the bomb, not the one who explodes it without suspicion of the danger. Life will have to be made over, and human nature transformed, before prevision so extravagant can be accepted as the norm of conduct, the customary standard to which behavior must conform.

    *   *   * What the plaintiff must show is "a wrong" to herself; i.e., a violation of her own right, and not merely a wrong to some one else, nor conduct "wrongful" because unsocial, but not "a wrong" to any one. *   *   * The risk reasonably to be perceived defines the duty to be obeyed[.] *   *   * This does not mean, of course, that one who launches a destructive force is always relieved of liability, if the force, though known to be destructive, pursues an unexpected path. "It was not necessary that the defendant should have had notice of the particular method in which an accident would occur, if the possibility of an accident was clear to the ordinarily prudent eye." Some acts, such as shooting are so imminently dangerous to any one who may come within reach of the missile however unexpectedly, as to impose a duty of prevision not far from that of an insurer. Even today, and much oftener in earlier stages of the law, one acts sometimes at one's peril. *   *   * Here, by concession, there was nothing in the situation to suggest to the most cautious mind that the parcel wrapped in newspaper would spread wreckage through the station. If the guard had thrown it down knowingly and willfully, he would not have threatened the plaintiff's safety, so far as appearances could warn him. His conduct would not have involved, even then, an unreasonable probability of invasion of her bodily security. Liability can be no greater where the act is inadvertent.

    *   *   * One who seeks redress at law does not make out a cause of action by showing without more that there has been damage to his person. *If the harm was not willful, he must show that the act as to him had possibilities of danger so many and apparent as to entitle him to be protected against the doing of it though the harm was unintended.* [Emphasis added.] *   *   * The victim does not sue derivatively, or by right of subrogation, to vindicate an interest invaded in the person of another.   *   *   * He sues for breach of a duty owing to himself.

    *   *   * [To rule otherwise] would entail liability for any and all consequences, however novel or extraordinary.

DECISION AND REMEDY

Palsgraf's complaint was dismissed. The railroad was not negligent toward her because injury to her was not foreseeable. Had the owner of the fireworks been harmed, there could well be a different result if he filed suit. Judge Cardozo indicated that while the conduct of the defendant's guards may have been a wrong against the holder of the package, it was not a wrong in relation to the plaintiff who was standing far away.

Foreseeability   Since the decision in the *Palsgraf* case, the courts have used *foreseeability* as the test for proximate cause. The railroad guards were negligent, but the railroad's duty of care did not extend to Palsgraf because she was an unforeseeable plaintiff. If the consequences of the harm done or the victim of the harm are unforeseeable, there is no proximate cause. Of course, it is foreseeable that people will stand on railroad platforms and that objects attached to the platforms will fall as the result of explosions nearby. However, this is not a chain of events against which a reasonable person will normally guard. It is difficult to predict when a court will say that something is foreseeable and when it will say that something is not. This difficulty stems from the fact that proximate cause is tied up with the notion of duty and public policy. (This point is obvious from Chief Justice Cardozo's opinion.) How far a court stretches foreseeability will be determined in part by the extent to which the court is willing to stretch the defendant's duty of care.

Defenses to Negligence

Three basic defenses in negligence cases are: (1) superseding intervening forces, (2) assumption of risk, and (3) contributory and comparative negligence.

Superseding Intervening Forces   A superseding or intervening force may break the connection between a wrongful act and injury to another. If so, it cancels out the wrongful act. For example, keeping a can of gasoline in the trunk of one's car creates a foreseeable risk and is thus a negligent act. If lightning strikes the car, exploding the gas tank *and* can, injuring passing pedestrians, the lightning supersedes the original negligence as a cause of the damage, since it was not foreseeable. This example illustrates that the doctrine of superseding intervening forces is also a question of proximate cause and legal duty.

In other situations, the intervention of a force may not relieve one of liability. If medical maltreatment of an injury aggravates the injury, the person whose negligence originally caused the injury is not relieved of liability. If subsequent disease or a subsequent accident is proximately caused by the original injury, the person who caused the original injury will be liable for the injury caused by the subsequent disease or accident. Where negligence endangers property, and the owner is injured in an attempt to protect the property, the negligent party will be liable for the injury.

In negligence cases, the negligent party will often attempt to show that some act has intervened after his or her action and that this second act was the proximate cause of injury. Typically, in cases where an individual takes a defensive action, such as attempting to escape by swerving or leaping from a vehicle, the original wrongdoer will not be relieved of liability even if the injury actually resulted from the escape attempt. The same is true under the "danger invites rescue" doctrine. Under this doctrine, if Smith commits an act that endangers Jones, and Brown sustains an injury trying to protect Jones, then Smith will be liable for Brown's injury, as well as for any injuries Jones may sustain. Rescuers can injure themselves, or the person rescued, or even a stranger, but the original wrongdoer will still be liable. The following case illustrates this doctrine.

GUARINO v. MINE
SAFETY APPLIANCE
CO.

Court of Appeals of
New York, 1969.
25 N.Y.2d 460, 306 N.Y.S.2d
942, 255 N.E.2d 173.

BACKGROUND AND FACTS   *This case arose out of an accident that killed three men and seriously injured five others. All were sewage treatment workers. After they had corrected a water leakage problem in a New York City sewer, one of the workers, Rooney, was fatally stricken by lethal gas present in the sewer when the oxygen-type protective mask he was wearing failed to operate properly. A companion worker shouted for help. Two other workers responded to the cries for help and were stricken by the gas when they entered the sewer tunnel without masks. The plaintiffs sued the manufacturer of the oxygen masks.*

JASEN J., Judge.
*   *   *   *

This appeal presents for our review the "danger invites rescue" doctrine.
*   *   *   *

Here the defendant committed a culpable act against the decedent Rooney, by manufacturing and distributing a defective oxygen-producing mask * * *. By virtue of this defendant's culpable act, Rooney was placed in peril, thus inviting his rescue by the plaintiffs who were all members of Rooney's sewage treatment crew. There was no time for reflection when it became known that Rooney was in need of immediate assistance in the dark tunnel some 30 to 40 feet below the street level. These plaintiffs responded to the cries for help in a manner which was reasonable and consistent with their concern for each other as members of a crew. To require that a rescuer answering the cry for help make inquiry as to the nature of the culpable act that imperils someone's life would defy all logic.

As Judge Cardozo so eloquently stated in Wagner v. International Ry. Co.: "Danger invites rescue. The cry of distress is the summons to relief. * * * The *wrong* that imperils life is a wrong to the imperilled victim; it is a wrong also to his rescuer." [Emphasis added.]

* * * *

We conclude that a person who by his culpable act, whether it stems from negligence or breach of warranty, places another person in a position of imminent peril, may be held liable for any damages sustained by a rescuer in his attempt to aid the imperilled victim.

The manufacturer of the malfunctioning oxygen mask was held liable for damages sustained by the plaintiffs who sought to rescue the individual overcome by sewer gas when the mask failed.   **DECISION AND REMEDY**

Assumption of Risk   A plaintiff who voluntarily enters into a risky situation, knowing the risk involved, will not be allowed to recover. This is the defense of **assumption of risk.** For example, a driver who enters a race knows that there is a risk of being killed or injured in a crash. The driver has assumed the risk of injury. The two requirements of this defense are: (1) knowledge of the risk and (2) voluntary assumption of the risk.

The risk can be assumed by express agreement, or the assumption of risk can be implied by the plaintiff's knowledge of the risk and subsequent conduct. Of course, the plaintiff does not assume a risk different from or greater than the risk normally carried by the activity. In our example, the race driver assumes the risk of being injured in the race but not the risk that the banking in the curves of the racetrack will give way during the race because of a construction defect.

Risks are not deemed to be assumed in situations involving emergencies. Neither are they assumed where a statute protects a class of people from harm and a member of the class is injured by the harm.

Contributory and Comparative Negligence   All individuals are expected to exercise a reasonable de-

gree of care in looking out for themselves. In some jurisdictions, recovery for injury resulting from negligence is prevented by failure of the injured person to exercise such care over himself or herself. This is the defense of **contributory negligence** where both parties have been negligent, and their combined negligence has contributed to cause the injury. When one party sues the other in tort for damages for negligence, the defendant can claim contributory negligence, which is a complete defense under common law rules. (Contributory negligence is not, however, a defense to intentional torts or to suits based on strict liability, a topic that will be covered later.)

The modern trend is toward narrowing the scope of the defense of contributory negligence. Instead of allowing contributory negligence to negate a cause of action completely, an increasing number of states allow recovery based on the doctrine of **comparative negligence.**[8] This doctrine enables computation of both the plaintiff's and the defendant's negligence. The plaintiff's damages are reduced by a percentage

---

8. Comparative negligence has been adopted in approximately forty-one states.

that represents the degree of his or her contributing fault. In an extreme case, if the plaintiff's negligence is found to be greater than the defendant's, the plaintiff may receive nothing. Indeed, the plaintiff may be subject to counterclaim by the defendant. In jurisdictions that follow the contributory negligence doctrine, negligence on the part of the plaintiff will bar any recovery of damages. In comparative negligence jurisdictions, however, the plaintiff will be able to recover the percentage of damages that was due to the defendant's negligence.

"Last clear chance" is a doctrine that can excuse the effect of a plaintiff's contributory negligence. If applicable, the last clear chance rule allows the plaintiff to recover full damages despite failure to exercise care. This doctrine, or rule, operates when, through his or her own negligence, the plaintiff is endangered (or his or her property is endangered) by a defendant who has an opportunity to avoid causing damage. For example, if Murphy walks across the street against the light, and Lewis, a motorist, sees her in time to avoid hitting her but hits her anyway, Lewis (the defendant) is not permitted to use Murphy's (the plaintiff's) prior negligence as a defense. The defendant negligently missed the opportunity to avoid injuring the plaintiff.

This rule is not easy to apply. Court decisions in which it appears are often in conflict. Its correct application requires knowledge of the nature and time span of the negligence of two or more persons, as well as knowledge of split-second sequences of events and perceptions. The principal variables for last clear chance cases are (1) the nature of the plaintiff's predicament and (2) the degree of the defendant's attentiveness to the plaintiff's peril. The classic last clear chance situation is one with a helpless plaintiff and an observant defendant. In any event, the defendant's ability to have prevented the injury must be proved. It is the existence of this last clear chance that allows a plaintiff to recover damages for injury despite his or her negligence.

The following case briefly summarizes a court's consideration of the elements required for a successful negligence action and the basic defenses of superseding intervening acts, contributory negligence, and assumption of risk.

HABERSHAM ELEC. MEMBERSHIP CORP. v. DALTON

Court of Appeals of Georgia, 1984.
170 Ga.App. 483, 317 S.E.2d 312.

BACKGROUND AND FACTS *Donald Dalton, the defendant of this appeal, suffered electrical burns when a tool he was using to clean a chicken feed bin contacted overhead high-voltage power lines owned by plaintiff Habersham Elec. Membership Corp. Habersham knew the feed bins were constructed under the power lines, and three wires did not meet the clearance requirements of the National Electric Safety Code. Dalton sued Habersham for negligent construction and maintenance of the power lines.*

McMURRAY, Chief Judge.
*   *   *   *

The power company owed a duty to maintain the lines "in such a manner and at such a location as not to injure persons who might be reasonably expected to come in contact with such lines." *   *   * [As an earlier court stated] "(t)he causal connection between an original act of negligence and injury to another is not broken by the 'intervening' act *   *   * if the nature of such intervening act was such that it could reasonably have been anticipated or foreseen by the original wrongdoer." The court further added that "the foreseeability of (an intervening agency) is for the jury where reasonable minds might differ." *   *   *

In light of the evidence presented, we decline to hold that plaintiff's act (of sticking the conduit pipe handle into the overhead high-voltage power lines while cleaning the feed bin in question) was unforeseeable as a matter of law. The evidence was sufficient for the jury to find that the defendant power company should have anticipated that someone in the ordinary and usual course of farming operations, either lawfully or negligently, might strike its alleged negligently maintained wire. Similarly, we cannot conclude as a matter of law that the plaintiff's own negligence was the proximate cause of his injury, nor can we conclude that the plaintiff assumed the risk. "Only in plain and palpable cases will assumption of risk or contributory negligence issues be decided by the court as a matter of law. *   *   * The general grounds are without merit, and the trial court did not err in denying defendant's motion for a directed verdict. *   *   *   *

The appellate court denied Habersham's appeal and upheld the verdict for Dalton reached by the trial court.   **DECISION AND REMEDY**

STRICT LIABILITY

The final category of torts is called **strict liability,** or *liability without fault.* Intentional or negligent torts involve an act that departs from a reasonable standard of care and causes an injury. Under the doctrine of *strict liability*, liability for injury is imposed for reasons other than fault.

Abnormally Dangerous Activities

Strict liability for damages proximately caused by abnormally dangerous activities is one application of this doctrine. Abnormally dangerous activities have three characteristics:

1.   The activity involves potential harm, of a serious nature, to persons or property.

2.   The activity involves a high degree of risk that cannot be completely guarded against by exercising reasonable care.

3.   The activity is not commonly performed in the community or area.

Strict liability is applied because of the extreme risk of the activity. Although an activity such as blasting with dynamite is performed with all reasonable care, there is still a risk of injury. Balancing that risk against the potential for harm, it is fair to ask the person engaged in the activity to pay for injury caused by engaging in the activity. Although there is no fault, there is still responsibility because of the nature of the activity. In other words, it is reasonable to require the person engaged in the activity to carry the necessary insurance or otherwise stand prepared to compensate anyone who suffers.

The following case illustrates a type of abnormally dangerous activity.

BACKGROUND AND FACTS   *The Yommers operated a gasoline station. In December 1967 their neighbors, the McKenzies, noticed a smell in their well water, which proved to be caused by gasoline in the well water. McKenzie complained to the Yommers, who arranged to have one of their underground storage tanks replaced. Nevertheless, the McKenzies were unable to use their water for cooking or bathing until they had a filter and water softener installed. At the time of the trial, in December 1968, they were still bringing drinking water in from an outside source.*

The McKenzies sued the Yommers for nuisance and recovered damages of $3,500. The Yommers appealed the verdict on the grounds that the McKenzies did not prove that there was any negligence and that a gas station is not a nuisance.

YOMMER v. McKENZIE
Court of Appeals of Maryland, 1969.
255 Md. 220, 257 A.2d 138.

SINGLEY, Judge.
*   *   *   *

   We have previously held that the establishment of a gasoline filling station does not constitute a nuisance *per se*, but that it may become a nuisance because of its location or manner in which it is operated.

The argument that the McKenzies must prove negligence in order to recover fails to take into account the doctrine of strict liability imposed by the rule of *Rylands v. Fletcher* which has been adopted by our prior decisions.

*   *   *   *

The black letter of new § 520 sets out the definition:

"520.   *Abnormally Dangerous Activities*

In determining whether an activity is abnormally dangerous, the following factors are to be considered:

(a)   Whether the activity involves a high degree of risk of some harm to the person, land or chattels of others;

(b)   Whether the gravity of the harm which may result from it is likely to be great;

(c)   Whether the risk cannot be eliminated by the exercise of reasonable care;

(d)   Whether the activity is not a matter of common usage;

(e)   Whether the activity is inappropriate to the place where it is carried on; and

(f)   The value of the activity to the community."

We believe that the present case is clearly within the ambit of this definition. Although the operation of a gasoline station does not of itself involve "a high degree of risk of some harm to the person, land or chattels of others," the placing of a large underground gasoline tank in close proximity to the appellees' residence and well does involve such a risk, since it is not a matter of common usage.* The harm caused to the appellees was a serious one, and it may well have been worse if the contamination had not been detected promptly.

Although there is no evidence of negligence on the part of the Yommers (indeed such a showing is not required as will be discussed below), it is proper to surmise that this risk cannot, or at least was not, eliminated by the exercise of reasonable care.

The fifth and perhaps most crucial factor under the Institute's guidelines as applied to this case is the appropriateness of the activity in the particular place where it is being carried on. No one would deny that gasoline stations as a rule do not present any particular danger to the community. However, when the operation of such activity involves the placing of a large tank adjacent to a well from which a family must draw its water for drinking, bathing and laundry, at least that aspect of the activity is inappropriate to the locale, even when equated to the value of the activity.

*   *   *   *

We accept the test of appropriateness as the proper one: that the unusual, the excessive, the extravagant, the bizarre are likely to be non-natural uses which lead to strict liability.

*   *   *   *

It is apparent to us that the storage of large quantities of gasoline immediately adjacent to a private residence comes within this rule and relieved the McKenzies of the necessity of proving negligence. *   *   *

**DECISION
AND REMEDY**

The Yommers lost on appeal; the judgment for the McKenzies was upheld. There was no need to prove negligence in the case because the nature of the activity and the location of the tank caused the Yommers to be held strictly liable for the gasoline seepage.

---

*   "An activity is a matter of common usage if it is customarily carried on by the great mass of mankind, or by many people in the community. *   *   * Gas and electricity in household pipes and wires [are examples of common usage], as contrasted with large gas storage tanks or high tension power lines." Restatement, Torts 2d, *supra*, comment on clause (d) at 65–66.

Other Applications of Strict Liability

There are other applications of the strict liability principle, notably in the workmen's compensation acts and in the area of products liability. Liability here is a matter of social policy, and it is based on two factors: (1) the ability of the employer and man-ufacturer to better bear the cost of injury by spreading it out to society through an increase in the cost of goods and services and (2) the fact that the employer and manufacturer are making a profit from their activities and therefore should bear the cost of injury as an operating expense. Products liability will be considered in depth in Chapter 22.

QUESTIONS AND CASE PROBLEMS

1. Richards is an employee of the Dun Construction Corporation. While delivering materials to a construction site, he carelessly runs Dun's truck into a passenger vehicle driven by Green. This is Richards's second accident in six months. When Dun learns of this latest accident, a heated discussion ensues, and Dun fires Richards. Dun is so angry that he immediately writes a letter to the union of which Richards is a member and to all other construction outfits in the community, stating that Richards is the "worst driver in the city" and that "anyone who hires him is asking for legal liability." Richards files suit against Dun, alleging libel on the basis of the statements made in the letters. Discuss the results.

2. It is a cold, wintry day. Ken needs to do some shopping on his way home from work. He is running late and is in a hurry. He stops at a drugstore to buy a tube of toothpaste on sale. He sticks the toothpaste in his overcoat pocket, laying the correct amount of change for the purchase on the counter. He is proceeding home when he suddenly remembers his wife's request that he pick up some much-needed groceries. He stops at a grocery store and rushes through the store picking up the groceries. He checks out and in a slow trot starts to leave the store when the checkout clerk sees the toothpaste in his overcoat pocket. Believing Ken was attemping to leave the store without declaring the item, the clerk yells, "Stop, thief!" Two bagboys grab Ken and haul him, struggling and protesting, to a small, dark back room, where he is locked in. One hour later, the store manager gets back from dinner, learns of the events, and, after questioning a distraught Ken, lets him go. Ken starts having nightmares, acquires backaches, and becomes extremely nervous when friends and neighbors look at him. Discuss fully whether any torts have been committed against Ken.

3. Frank is a former employee of ABC Auto Repair Company. He enters the property of ABC, claiming the company owes him $150 in back wages. An argument ensues, and the ABC general manager, Steward, orders Frank off the property. Frank refuses to leave, and Steward orders two mechanics to throw him off the property. Frank runs to his truck, but on the way he grabs some tools valued at $150. Frank gets into his truck and, in his haste to drive away, destroys a gatepost. Frank refuses to return the tools.

(a) Discuss whether Frank has committed any torts.

(b) If the mechanics had thrown Frank off the property, would ABC be guilty of assault and battery? Explain.

4. John is a delivery employee for Crystal Glass, Inc. He is making a delivery when, at an intersection, his van and the passenger car of Jane collide. Jane wants to hold both John and Crystal Glass liable for the damages she has sustained. John claims that Jane was also at fault, at least as much at fault as he, and therefore neither he nor Crystal should be liable. Discuss fully these claims.

5. Ruth carelessly parks her car on a tall hill, leaving the car in neutral and failing to engage the parking brake. The car rolls down the hill, knocking down an electric line. The sparks from the broken line ignite a grass fire. The fire speads until it reaches a barn one mile away. The barn has dynamite inside, and the burning barn explodes, causing part of the roof to fall upon and injure a passing motorist, Jim. Can Jim recover from Ruth? Why or why not?

6. A grocery cart in Waldbaum's Store was missing the protective flap in the "jump seat," or "baby seat," that can be raised to cover the opening when the seat is not in use. A shopper using the cart placed a large bottle of soda in the jump seat; the bottle fell through the opening and hit Mrs. Gross's foot, causing her injuries. Is Waldbaum's Store liable for this injury on the ground of negligence? Was the shopper's act of placing heavy or breakable items in the jump seat foreseeable? [Gross v. Waldbaum, Inc., 102 Misc. 2d 175, 423 N.Y.S.2d 123 (Civ.Ct.N.Y.1979)]

7. Yonkers Contracting Co., Inc. (Yonkers) was engaged as the general contractor in the construction of a highway on land owned by defendant State of New York. Plaintiff, an employee of Yonkers, was assisting in preparation for blasting a boulder and was experienced in blasting operations. While so engaged on October 13, 1980, explosives were detonated and plaintiff was hit in the head by a rock propelled through the air as a result of the blast. He and his wife filed a claim against the State. Is blasting

an inherently dangerous activity? Should liability extend to the landowner even though an independent contractor directed the blasting? What if an innocent passerby had been injured? [Nagy v. State of New York, 89 A.D.2d 199, 456 N.Y.S.2d 241 (1982)]

8. Gulf Refining Company sold a drum of gasoline to a farmer for use in his farm tractor. When Williams, an employee of the farmer, attempted to open the drum, he found that the bunghole cap was stuck because the threads were in disrepair. Movement of the worn threads produced a spark that caused an explosion and a fire. When Williams sued Gulf, Gulf admitted that it knew that the threads in the bung cap were in a state of disrepair from repeated hammering on the bung cap over the course of several years. Gulf claimed, however, that it should not be held liable for the injury sustained by Williams because it was so unusual, extraordinary, and improbable that it was not reasonably foreseeable. Is Gulf correct? [Gulf Refining Co. v. Williams, 183 Miss. 723, 185 So. 234 (1938)]

9. Professor Ronald R. Hutchinson received federal funding for animal (monkey) studies on aggression. United States Senator William Proxmire bestowed his Golden Fleece of the Month Award on the federal agency that funded Hutchinson's research. The purpose of the award was to publicize wasteful government spending. Senator Proxmire announced the award in a speech prepared for and given to the Senate. The speech was reprinted in a press release mailed to 275 members of the news media and in a newsletter sent to 100,000 people. Proxmire described the federal grants for Hutchinson's research, among other critical comments, as "monkey business." Hutchinson sued Proxmire for defamation. The district court and U.S. court of appeals confirmed Senator Proxmire's claims that his communication was privileged and that Professor Hutchinson was a public figure who had not proven there was malice. Is either of Senator Proxmire's claims a valid defense? [Hutchinson v. Proxmire, 443 U.S. 111, 99 S.Ct. 2675 (1979)]

10. H. E. Butt Grocery Company (H.E.B.) has numerous retail grocery stores scattered throughout the state of Texas. Hawkins went to grocery shop at one of the H.E.B. stores. A heavy rainstorm and north wind had caused water to be tracked into the store by customers and water to be blown through the door each time it was opened. As Hawkins entered through the automatically opened door, she slipped and fell in approximately one-half inch of rain water which had accumulated on the floor. The manager knew of the weather conditions and had employees mop the floor on numerous occasions. There was no sign posted warning customers of the water hazard. Can Hawkins recover from H.E.B. for injuries sustained from slipping on the water-covered floor? [H. E. Butt Grocery Co. v. Hawkins, 594 S.W.2d 187 (1980)]

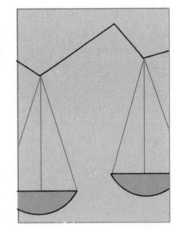

5

Torts Related
To Business

Our economic system of free enterprise is predicated on the ability of individuals, acting either as individuals or as business firms, to compete for customers and for sales. Unfettered competitive behavior has been shown to lead to economic efficiency and economic progress. On the other hand, overly enthusiastic competitive efforts sometimes fall into the realm of intentional torts and crimes. Businesses may, generally speaking, engage in whatever is *reasonably* necessary to obtain a fair share of a market or to recapture a share that has been lost. But they are not allowed to use the motive of completely eliminating competition in order to justify certain business activities. Thus, an entire area of what is called business torts has arisen. **Business torts** are defined as wrongful interference with another's business rights. Included in business torts are such vaguely worded concepts as *unfair competition* and *interfering with the business relations of others*. Because the field is so broad, it is necessary to restrict this discussion to the following causes of action, which are presented in terms of general categories:

1. Wrongful interference with a contractual relationship.
2. Wrongful interference with a business relationship.
3. Wrongfully entering into business.

4. Infringement of trademarks, trade names, patents, and copyrights.
5. Disparagement of property or reputation.

WRONGFUL INTERFERENCE WITH A CONTRACTUAL RELATIONSHIP

Tort law relating to *intentional interference with a contractual relationship* has increased greatly in recent years. A landmark case in this area involved an opera singer, Joanna Wagner, who was under contract to sing for a man named Lumley for a specified period of years.[1] A man named Gye, who knew of this contract, nonetheless "enticed" Wagner to refuse to carry out the agreement, and Wagner began to sing for Gye. Gye's action constituted a tort because it interfered with the contractual relationship between Wagner and Lumley. (Wagner's refusal to carry out the agreement also entitled Lumley to sue for breach of contract.)

In principle, any lawful contract can be the basis for an action of this type. The plaintiff must prove that the defendant actually induced the breach of contractual relationship, not merely that the defendant reaped the benefits of a broken contract. If Jones

---

1. Lumley v. Gye, 118 Eng. Rep. 749 (1853).

has a contract with Smith that calls for Smith to mow Jones's lawn every week for a year at a specified price, Jones cannot sue Miller when Smith breaches the contract merely because Miller now receives gardening services from Smith.

Elements of Wrongful Interference with a Contractual Relationship

Three basic elements are necessary to the existence of wrongful interference with a contractual relationship:

1. A valid, enforceable contract must exist between two parties.
2. A third party must *know* that this contract exists.
3. This third party must *intentionally* cause either of the two parties who have the contract to break

the contract. Whether this third party acts in bad faith or with malice is immaterial to establishing this tort, even though in most cases malice or bad faith is in evidence. However, the interference must be for the purpose of advancing the economic or pecuniary interest of the inducer.

The contract rights interfered with may be those between a firm and its employees or a firm and its customers. Sometimes the competitor of a firm may attempt to draw away a key employee, even to the extent of paying the damages for breach of contract. If the original employer can show that the competitor induced the breach—that is, that the employee would not normally have broken the contract—damages can be recovered.

The following case illustrates the necessity of proving the three basic elements for a wrongful interference with a contractual relationship.

MACKIE v. LASALLE INDUSTRIES, INC.

Supreme Court, Appellate Division, First Department, 1983. 92 A.D.2d 821, 460 N.Y.S.2d 313.

BACKGROUND AND FACTS　*In October 1975, LaSalle Industries, Inc. (LaSalle) orally agreed to employ plaintiff Katherine J. Mackie, for no fixed term, as a sales representative. In April 1976, Mackie acquired for LaSalle the very lucrative Home Box Office (HBO) account.*

On August 30, 1978, individual defendants Arthur Solomon, Jack Gorman, and Daniel Solomon, stockholders and agents of LaSalle, informed plaintiff that the HBO account was being taken away from her because allegedly HBO was dissatisfied with plaintiff's performance. The plaintiff protested because the loss of the HBO account meant reduced commissions to her.

In addition, plaintiff had obtained a printing contract order from Hecht, Higgins, and Petterson Advertising, Inc. (Hecht) for $25,000. Hecht withdrew this order after an argument ensued with Arthur Solomon concerning nonpayment of a previous order by Hecht.

In August 1979 plaintiff commenced the instant action alleging, among other things, interference with a contract as to the HBO account and as to the order with Hecht Advertising. Immediately after Mackie instituted this action, LaSalle terminated her employment.

MURPHY, P. J. (and ROSS, CARRO, ASCH, and ALEXANDER, JJ.)

MEMORANDUM DECISION

*　*　*　*

In the third cause of action the plaintiff seeks $2,500 in damages upon the ground of Arthur Solomon's alleged tortious conduct. It is undisputed that plaintiff obtained a printing order from Hecht, Higgins and Petterson Advertising, Inc. (Hecht) in the amount of $25,000. Hecht withdrew this order, after Arthur Solomon got into an argument with a representative of Hecht over Hecht's non-payment of an earlier printing order in the amount of $50,000. Plaintiff admits (RA 62) in her bill of particulars that her claim is solely based upon the aggressive manner in which Arthur Solomon attempted to collect this old debt, which had nothing to do with the printing order she had obtained. In view of plaintiff's admission, we dismiss this cause of action because we find that Arthur Solomon's behavior was not intended to either tortiously interfere with any contract to which plaintiff was a party * * * or to have been undertaken for the purpose of intentionally harming the plaintiff. * * * "Even under the most liberal construction of this pleading, plaintiff fails to state a valid cause of action" * * *.

The fifth cause of action in substance asserts that the corporate defendant LaSalle and the four individual defendants Messrs. Arthur Solomon, Jack Gorman, Daniel Solomon, and Bernard Jacoby, conspired to interfere with LaSalle's own employment contract with plaintiff by improperly transferring plaintiff's accounts to others. This allegation "that defendant corporation tortiously interfered with its own contract," quite clearly does not state a legally sufficient cause of action and must also be dismissed. * * *.

* * * *

Plaintiff failed to state a cause of action as to any of her complaints, so the appellate court dismissed her case. **DECISION AND REMEDY**

WRONGFUL INTERFERENCE WITH A BUSINESS RELATIONSHIP

Individuals devise countless schemes to attract business, but they are forbidden by the courts to interfere unreasonably with another's business in their attempts to gain a share of the market. There is a difference between *competition* and *predatory behavior*. The distinction usually depends on whether a business is attempting to attract customers in general or to solicit only those customers who have already shown an interest in the similar product or service of a specific competitor. If a shopping center contains two shoe stores, an employee of Store A cannot be positioned at the entrance of Store B for the purpose of diverting customers to Store A. This type of activity constitutes the tort of wrongful interference with a business relationship, or what is commonly considered to be an unfair trade practice. If this type of activity were permitted, Store A would reap the benefits of Store B's advertising.

A salesperson cannot follow another company's salesperson through the city, soliciting the same prospective customers. Even though the people contacted may have purchased nothing from the first salesperson, that salesperson still has a business relationship with them. Courts will issue injunctions against this kind of behavior and will award damages when the business alleging interference can prove it suffered a monetary loss. In the following case a salesman's activities exceeded the bounds of fair competition.

BACKGROUND AND FACTS *Lehigh Corporation, a developer of real estate, obtained a restraining order against one of its former salesmen, Leroy Azar. Lehigh brought prospective customers to its development, Lehigh Acres, and provided accommodations at its company-owned motel. Azar pursued a practice of following Lehigh purchasers and persuading them to rescind their contracts with Lehigh and purchase less expensive property from him.*

The Circuit Court issued the following order:

IT IS HEREBY ORDERED AND ADJUDGED that the Defendant, Leroy Azar, is hereby restrained and enjoined from directly or indirectly contacting or soliciting the Plaintiff's perspective [sic] or actual customers on the premises of the Lehigh Resort

AZAR v. LEHIGH CORP.

District Court of Appeal of Florida, Second District, 1978. 364 So.2d 860.

Motel or at the sales offices of the Plaintiffs if such purchasers are in Lee County as guests of the Plaintiffs. "Guests" of the Plaintiffs shall mean persons who have been invited by the Plaintiffs, either directly or indirectly, to view the Lehigh Acres community and real estate situate therein. "Invited" shall mean those persons who have come to the Lehigh Acres community as a result of any promotional activities of the Plaintiffs wherein some incentive of value has been given or offered to said persons. The "Defendant", Leroy Azar, shall include any person or entity acting in the Defendant's behalf or at the urging of the Defendant, Leroy Azar.

Azar contended that Lehigh's customers had a right under federal law to rescind their contracts within three days and that he was merely providing them with an opportunity to be relieved of their contract and to obtain comparable property for lower prices. Lehigh asserted that Azar was tortiously interfering with the advantageous business relationship between Lehigh and its customers.

GRIMES, Chief Judge.
*   *   *   *

[T]he elements of [the tort of interference with business are] as follows:
(1) the existence of a business relationship under which the plaintiff has legal rights, (2) an intentional and unjustified interference with that relationship by the defendant, and (3) damage to the plaintiff as a result of the breach of the business relationship. *   *   *.
It is not essential, however, that the business relationship be founded upon an enforceable contract. *   *   *

There is a narrow line between what constitutes vigorous competition in a free enterprise society and malicious interference with a favorable business relationship. Under the heading of "Interference with prospective advantage," Prosser states:
Though trade warfare may be waged to the bitter end, there are certain rules of combat which must be observed. . . . W. Prosser, Law of Torts (4th ed. 1971) at 956.

He goes on to say that the courts have generally prohibited such activities as defamation of the competitor, disparagement of his goods and his business methods, and intimidation, harassment and annoyance of his customers. In the final analysis, the issue seems to turn upon whether the subject conduct is considered to be "unfair" according to contemporary business standards.

Keeping in mind the trial judge's broad discretion to enter temporary restraining orders, we believe there is sufficient evidence in this record to support the court's decision. Moreover, we believe the terms of the order are precise enough for the appellant to understand what he cannot do. Considering appellant's knowledge of Lehigh's operation, we are confident that he will have no difficulty in ascertaining which of the motel patrons constitute appellees' guests as defined in the temporary restraining order.

DECISION AND REMEDY
The restraining order against Azar was allowed to stand. Azar remained under court order not to solicit business from those customers brought to Lehigh Acres by Lehigh Corporation.

Defenses to Wrongful Interference with a Contractual or Business Relationship

Justification is the defense used most often against the accusation of the tort of wrongful interference with a contractual or business relationship. For example, bona fide competitive behavior is a privileged interference even if it results in the breaking of a contract. If Jones Meats advertises so effectively that it induces Sam's Restaurant Chain to break its contract with Paul's Meat Company, Paul's Meat Company would be unable to recover against Jones Meats on a wrongful interference theory. After all, the public policy that favors free competition in advertising definitely outweighs any possible instability that such competitive activity might cause in contractual relations.

Permissive Interferences

Permissive interferences are interfering actions that the courts have not held to be tortious interferences. The most common example is a labor union's freedom to encourage a strike. Encouraging a strike interferes with the contractual relationship between employer and employee and may interfere with business relationships; yet it is permitted by the courts.

WRONGFULLY ENTERING INTO BUSINESS

In a freely competitive society it is usually true that any person can enter into any business in order to compete for the customers of extant businesses. Two situations in which this general notion of free competition does not hold, however, are (1) when entering into a business is in violation of law and (2) when competitive behavior is predatory in nature.

Entering a Business in Violation of the Law

Although we live in a free enterprise system, government at all levels—local, state, and federal—restricts who may enter certain businesses. Indeed, there exists a whole area of regulated economic activities in which people cannot engage unless they first obtain permission from a regulatory agency or commission. Although the trend is toward increasing deregulation, the number of businesses under such regulation is still large. For example, a group of people cannot simply agree among themselves to start a business competitive with their local electric company or natural gas company. First they would have to gain approval from the public utility, or service, commission in their particular state, approval which would be highly unlikely. As another example, one cannot simply put up a radio or television transmitter and start transmitting on some frequency believed to be open. A license is necessary. The Federal Communications Commission grants all licenses for both television and radio, and these are only for designated frequencies.

Many occupations require licenses in the United States. Not only are lawyers, physicians, and dentists licensed, but so are palm readers and astrologists. In many states the licensed member of a profession is allowed to bring action on behalf of the entire profession in order to prevent an unlicensed individual from practicing that occupation.

Predatory Competitive Activities

Any business or profession not subject to regulatory agencies or occupational licensing standards is open to an individual; however, no one can open a business for the sole purpose of driving another firm out of business. Such a predatory motive for opening a business is considered to constitute *simulated competition*. What the courts consider normal competitive activity is not always easy to ascertain. One might ask when the normal desire to compete and obtain profits ends and when a tortious action begins. The landmark case that follows illustrates how a Minnesota court grappled with the question of malicious injury to business.

BACKGROUND AND FACTS   *The plaintiff, a barber, filed suit against the defendant for malicious interference with his business. The plaintiff had owned and operated a barbershop for the previous ten years and had been able to maintain himself and his family comfortably from the income of the business.*

The defendant was a banker in the same community. During the past twelve months, the defendant had "maliciously" established a competitive barbershop, employed a barber to carry on the business, and used his personal influence to attract customers from the plaintiff's barbershop. Apparently, the defendant

TUTTLE v. BUCK
Supreme Court of Minnesota,
1909.
107 Minn. 145, 119 N.W. 946.

had circulated false and malicious reports and accusations about the plaintiff and had personally solicited, urged, threatened, and otherwise persuaded many of the plaintiff's patrons to stop using the plaintiff's services and to use the defendant's shop instead. The plaintiff charged that the defendant undertook this entire plan with the sole design of injuring the plaintiff and destroying his business, not for serving any legitimate business interest or as fair competition.

ELLIOTT, Justice.

*   *   *   *

*   *   * It is not at all correct to say that the motive with which an act is done is always immaterial, providing the act itself is not unlawful. *   *   *

*   *   * It must be remembered that the common law is the result of growth, and that its development has been determined by the social needs of the community which it governs. It is the result of conflicting social forces, and those forces which are for the time dominant leave their impress upon the law. It is of judicial origin, and seeks to establish doctrines and rules for the determination, protection, and enforcement of legal rights. Manifestly it must change as society changes and new rights are recognized. To be an efficient instrument, and not a mere abstraction, it must gradually adapt itself to changed conditions. Necessarily its form and substance has been greatly affected by prevalent economic theories. For generations there has been a practical agreement upon the proposition that competition in trade and business is desirable, and this idea has found expression in the decisions of the courts as well as in statutes. But it has led to grievous and manifold wrongs to individuals, and many courts have manifested an earnest desire to protect the individuals from the evils which result from unrestrained business competition. The problem has been to so adjust matters as to preserve the principle of competition and yet guard against its abuse to the unnecessary injury to the individual. So the principle that a man may use his own property according to his own needs and desires, while true in the abstract, is subject to many limitations in the concrete. Men cannot always, in civilized society, be allowed to use their own property as their interests or desires may dictate without reference to the fact that they have neighbors whose rights are as sacred as their own. The existence and well-being of society requires that each and every person shall conduct himself consistently with the fact that he is a social and reasonable person. The purpose for which a man is using his own property may thus sometimes determine his rights. "If there exists, then, a positive duty to avoid harm, much more, then, exists the negative duty of not doing willful harm, subject, as all general duties must be subject, to the necessary exceptions. The three main heads of duty with which the law of torts is concerned, namely, to abstain from willful injury, to respect the property of others, and to use due diligence to avoid causing harm to others, are all alike of a comprehensive nature." Pollock, Torts, (8th Ed.) p. 21.

To divert to one's self the customers of a business rival by the offer of goods at lower prices is in general a legitimate mode of serving one's own interest, and justifiable as fair competition. But when a man starts an opposition place of business, not for the sake of profit to himself, but regardless of loss to himself, and for the sole purpose of driving his competitor out of business, and with the intention of himself retiring upon the accomplishment of his malevolent purpose, he is guilty of a wanton wrong and an actionable tort. In such a case he would not be exercising his legal right, or doing an act which can be judged separately from the motive which actuated him. To call such conduct competition is a perversion of terms. It is simply the application of force without legal justification, which in its moral quality may be no better than highway robbery.

The plaintiff's cause of action was recognized under Minnesota law. The Supreme Court of Minnesota concluded that modern business requires certain protection against abusive business practices. The plaintiff then returned to the trial court to prove his case. From that point forward, Minnesota recognized a cause of action for tortious interference with business relations.

**DECISION
AND REMEDY**

INFRINGEMENT OF TRADEMARKS, TRADE NAMES, PATENTS, AND COPYRIGHTS

Infringement of Trademarks and Service Marks

A **trademark** is a distinctive mark, motto, device, or implement that a manufacturer stamps, prints, or otherwise affixes to the goods it produces, so that they may be identified on the market and their origin vouched for. At common law, the person who used a symbol or mark to identify a business or product was protected in the use of that trademark. Clearly, if one used the trademark of another, one would mislead consumers into believing that one's goods were made by the other. The law seeks to avoid this kind of confusion. Normally, personal names, words, or places that are descriptive of an article or its use cannot be trademarked; they are available to anyone. Words that are used as part of a design or device, however, or words that are uncommon or fanciful may be trademarked.

Consider an example. *English Leather* may not be trademarked to describe leather processed in England. On the other hand, *English Leather* may be, and is, trademarked as a name for aftershave lotion, since this constitutes a *fanciful* use of the words.

Consider also that even the common name of an individual may be trademarked if that name is accompanied by a picture or some fanciful design that allows for easy identification of the product—for example, Smith Brothers' Cough Drops.

A **service mark** is similar to a trademark but is used to distinguish the services of one person from those of another. For example, each airline has a particular mark or symbol associated with its name. Titles or character names used in radio and television are frequently registered as service marks.

When Infringement Occurs Once a trademark has been registered, a firm is entitled to the exclusive use of it for marketing purposes. Whenever that trademark is copied to a substantial degree or used in its entirety by another, intentionally or unintentionally, the trademark has been infringed. The trademark need not be registered with the state or with the federal government in order to obtain protection from the tort of trademark infringement, but registration does furnish proof of the date of inception of its use. Moreover, registration may prolong the life of the trademark. Service marks are registered in the same manner as are trademarks.

The defendant in the following case was liable for trademark infringement even though he did not manufacture the article.

BACKGROUND AND FACTS *Plaintiff, Vuitton, et Fils, S.A., a French corporation that manufactures expensive handbags, sued the defendant, Crown Handbags, for infringement of its registered trademark. The defendant had offered to sell six of the handbags to a private investigator hired by plaintiff.*

**VUITTON ET FILS, S.A.
v. CROWN HANDBAGS**
District Court, Southern District
of New York, 1979.
492 F.Supp. 1071.

BRIEANT, District Judge.

* * * *

The goal of the framers of the Lanham Trade-Mark Act was to secure to the owner of a trademark the goodwill of his business, and at the same time protect the buying public against spurious and falsely marked goods. The Vuitton trademark has been used in connection with the advertising and sale of goods in commerce for over 46 years since its entry upon the Principal Trademark Register of the United States Patent Office in 1932. The trademark, #297,594, specifically refers to "handbags and pocketbooks" as items to which the mark would be affixed. Defendant makes no effort to challenge the validity or ownership of the Vuitton mark.

It remains to be determined whether defendant's actions in offering for sale copies of genuine Vuitton handbags was an infringement of plaintiff's registered mark within the meaning of 15 U.S.C. § 1114 which provides in pertinent part:

"1) Any person who shall, without the consent of the registrant—

(a) use in commerce any reproduction, counterfeit, copy, or colorable imitation of a registered mark in connection with the sale, offering for sale, distribution, or advertising of any goods or services on or in connection with which such use is likely to cause confusion, or to cause mistake, or to deceive . . . shall be liable in a civil action by the registrant for the remedies hereinafter provided."

Where an alleged infringing mark is used in connection with the sale of similar goods, the long standing rule in this Circuit has been that the second comer to the marketplace "has a duty to so name and dress his product as to avoid all likelihood of consumers confusing it with the product of the first comer." The second comer has no right to trade upon the good will of the first comer developed over a period of time and at considerable expense. As our Court of Appeals in this Circuit ruled many years ago:

"It is so easy for the honest business man, who wishes to sell his goods upon their merits, to select from the entire material universe, which is before him, symbols, marks and coverings which by no possibility can cause confusion between his goods and those of his competitors, that the courts look with suspicion upon one who, in dressing his goods for the market, approaches so near to his successful rival that the public may fail to distinguish between them."

The great weight of the evidence in the case leads to the conclusion that the Vuitton trademark is a strong mark, and as such is entitled to broad protection. The strength of the mark stems from its conspicuously distinctive nature. It is unique in its design and color, and during the more than 46 years of its continuous use in this country it has come to represent a source of product of perceived quality and prestige. *   *   *

It would be impossible for one engaged in the same trade as plaintiff is, and defendant is so engaged, to be unaware of the presence of the counterfeits in the trade. Nor could such a person be unaware of the plaintiff's rights to its valued mark. I find that defendant was a willful violator.

*   *   *   *

Both Vuitton and consumers in general would suffer by the purchase of counterfeit bags of inferior quality. Vuitton would soon lose its reputation for quality and exclusivity, and consumers would be deceived into believing they were getting something they were not.

Defendant clearly infringed upon plaintiff's registered trademark in violation of 15 U.S.C. § 1114, by offering for sale a combination of product and trademark which exactly mimics that of plaintiff, resulting in the type of confusion and deception which the Lanham Act was designed to prevent. In doing so, defendant acted willfully and with knowledge of the fact that these handbags which it offered for sale infringed upon the trademark rights of plaintiff. Defendant was in the business of manufacturing leather handbags in New York. As noted earlier, logic dictates that it must be charged with actual as well as constructive knowledge of plaintiff's mark and merchandise. The counterfeit bags were manufactured with the intention to trade upon the plaintiff's established reputation for quality merchandise. Although defendant apparently did not itself manufacture the infringing articles, it took an active part in their distribution and sale, making use of plaintiff's trademark in the process.

Vuitton was granted permanent injunctive relief from Crown Handbag's commercial practices that violated Vuitton's trademark rights. Crown had to pay damages amounting to the sales price of the six handbags offered to Vuitton's investigator. Crown also had to pay Vuitton's attorney's fees.

DECISION AND REMEDY

Certification and Collective Marks   A certification mark is used in connection with the products or services of one or more persons, other than the owner, to certify the region, materials used, mode of manufacture, quality, or accuracy of the goods or services. When used by members of a cooperative, association, or other organization, it is referred to as a collective mark. Examples of certification marks are the "Good Housekeeping Seal of Approval" and "UL Tested." Examples of collective marks are found at the end of the credits of a movie indicating the various associations and organizations who participated in the making of the movie, or the union mark found on the tags of certain products.

Infringement upon Trade Names

The term **trade name** is used to indicate part or all of a business's name, whether that business be a sole proprietorship, a partnership, or a corporation. Generally, a trade name is directly related to a business

and to its goodwill. As with trademarks, words must be unusual or fancifully used in order to be protected as trade names. The word *Safeway* was held by the courts to be sufficiently fanciful to obtain protection as a trade name.[2] The decisions of the courts do not give entirely clear guidelines as to when the name of a corporation can be regarded as a trade name. A particularly thorny problem arises when a trade name acquires generic use. Originally, the following were used only as trade names: Frigidaire, Scotch Tape, Xerox, and Kleenex. Today, a secondary meaning has been acquired by these names. Even so, the courts will not allow another firm to use those names in such a way as to deceive a potential consumer. Consider, for example, the following famous case concerning Coca-Cola, decided by the Supreme Court.

---

2. Safeway Stores v. Suburban Foods, 130 F.Supp. 249 (E.D.Va. 1955).

BACKGROUND AND FACTS   *The plaintiff, Coca-Cola Company, sought to enjoin other beverage companies from using the words "Koke" or "Dope" for their products. The defendants, The Koke Co. of America, et al., contended that the Coca-Cola trademark was a fraudulent representation and that Coca-Cola was therefore not entitled to any help from the courts.*

THE COCA-COLA CO. v. THE KOKE CO. OF AMERICA ET AL.
United States Supreme Court, 1920.
254 U.S. 143, 41 S.Ct. 113.

MR. JUSTICE HOLMES delivered the opinion of the court.

This is a bill in equity brought by the Coca-Cola Company to prevent the infringement of its trade-mark Coca-Cola and unfair competition with it in its business of making and selling the beverage for which the trade-mark is used. The District Court gave the plaintiff a decree [an injunction]. This was reversed by the Circuit Court of Appeals. Subsequently a writ of certiorari was granted by this Court.

*   *   *   *

Of course a man is not to be protected in the use of a device the very purpose and effect of which is to swindle the public. But the defects of a plaintiff do not offer a very broad ground for allowing another to swindle him. The defense relied on here should be scrutinized with a critical eye. The main point is this: Before 1900 the beginning of the good will was more or less helped by the presence of cocaine, a drug that, like alcohol or caffein or opium, may be described as a deadly poison or as a valuable item of the pharmacopœa according to the rhetorical purposes in view. The amount seems to have been very small, but it may have been enough to begin a bad habit and after the Food and Drug Act of June 30, 1906, if not earlier, long before this suit was brought, it was eliminated from the plaintiff's compound. Coca leaves still are used, to be sure, but after they have been subjected to a drastic process that removes from them every characteristic substance except a little tannin and still less chlorophyl. The cola nut, at best, on its side furnishes but a very small portion of the caffein, which now is the only element that has appreciable effect. That comes mainly from other sources. It is argued that the continued use of the name imports a representation that has ceased to be true and that the representation is reinforced by a picture of coca leaves and cola nuts upon the label and by advertisements, which however were many years before this suit was brought, that the drink is an "ideal nerve tonic and stimulant," *   *   * and that thus the very thing sought to be protected is used as a fraud.

The argument does not satisfy us. We are dealing here with a popular drink not with a medicine, and although what has been said might suggest that its attraction lay in producing the expectation of a toxic effect the facts point to a different conclusion. Since 1900 the sales have increased at a very great rate corresponding to a like increase in advertising. The name now characterizes a beverage to be had at almost any soda fountain. It means a single thing coming from a single source, and well known to the community. It hardly would be too much to say that the drink characterizes the name as much as the name the drink. In other words Coca-Cola probably means to most persons the plaintiff's familiar product to be had everywhere rather than a compound of particular substances. The coca leaves and whatever of cola nut is employed may be used to justify the continuance of the name or they may affect the flavor as the plaintiff contends, but before this suit was brought the plaintiff had advertised to the public that it must not expect and would not find cocaine, and had eliminated everything tending to suggest cocaine effects except the name and the picture of the leaves and nuts, which probably conveyed little or nothing to most who saw it. It appears to us that it would be going too far to deny the plaintiff relief against a palpable fraud because possibly here and there an ignorant person might call for the drink with the hope for incipient cocaine intoxication. The plaintiff's position must be judged by the facts as they were when the suit was begun, not by the facts of a different condition and an earlier time.

The decree of the District Court restrains the defendant from using the word Dope. The plaintiff illustrated in a very striking way the fact that the word is one of the most featureless known even to the language of those who are incapable of discriminating speech. In some places it would be used to call for Coca-Cola. It equally would have been used to call for anything else having about it a faint aureole of poison. It does not suggest Coca-Cola by similarity and whatever objections there may be to its use, objections which the plaintiff equally makes to its application to Coca-Cola, we see no ground on which the plaintiff can claim a personal right to exclude the defendant from using it.

The product including the coloring matter is free to all who can make it if no extrinsic deceiving element is present.

DECISION AND REMEDY   *The competing beverage companies were enjoined from calling their products "Koke," but the Court would not prevent them from calling their products "Dope."*

Infringement of Patents

A **patent** is a grant from the government that conveys and secures to an inventor the exclusive right to make, use, and sell an invention for a period of seventeen years. Patents for a lesser period are given for designs, as opposed to inventions. For either a regular patent or a design patent, the applicant must demonstrate to the satisfaction of the patent office that the invention, discovery, or design is genuine, novel, useful, and not obvious in the light of technology of the time. A patent holder gives notice to all that an article or design is patented by placing on it the word "Patent" or "Pat.," plus the patent number.

When Infringement Occurs   If a firm uses a substantial identity of operation and result between its device and a patented device, the tort of patent infringement exists. Patent infringement may exist even though not all features or parts of an invention are copied. (With respect to a patented process, however, all steps or their equivalent must be copied in order for infringement to exist.) Often, litigation for patent infringement is so costly that the patent holder will instead offer to sell to the infringer a license to use the patented design, product, or process. Indeed, in many cases the costs of detection, prosecution, and monitoring are so high that patents are valueless to their owners, since they cannot afford to protect them.

Infringement of Copyright

A **copyright** is an intangible right granted by statute to the author or originator of certain literary or artistic productions. Works created after January 1, 1978, are automatically given statutory copyright protection for the life of the author plus fifty years. Note that it is not possible to copyright an idea. What is copyrightable is the particular way in which an idea is expressed.

Recent legislation permits the copyright of computer programs. The problem arises, however, as to how trade secrets may be protected once a program is registered. This issue is presently being addressed in Congress and will be discussed further in the following chapter.

Under the "fair use" doctrine, the reproduction of copyrighted material is permitted without the payment of royalties. Section 107 of the Copyright Act provides:

Nothwithstanding the provisions of section 106, the fair use of a copyrighted work, including such use by reproduction in copies or phonorecords or by any other means specified by that section, for purposes such as criticism, comment, news reporting, teaching (including multiple copies for classroom use), scholarship, or research, is not an infringement of copyright. In determining whether the use made of a work in any particular case is a fair use the factors to be considered shall include—

(1) the purpose and character of the use, including whether such use is of a commercial nature or is for nonprofit educational purposes;

(2) the nature of the copyrighted work;

(3) the amount and substantiality of the portion used in relation to the copyrighted work as a whole; and

(4) the effect of the use upon the potential market for or value of the copyrighted work.

Unfortunately the act does not *clearly* define this doctrine, and any reproduction can still make the producer thereof subject to a violation.

The act does provide that a copyright owner no longer needs to place a © or ℗ on the work to have the work protected against infringement. Chances are that if somebody created it, somebody owns it.

When an Infringement Occurs   Whenever the form of expression of an idea is copied, an infringement of copyright has occurred. The production does not have to be exactly the same as the original; nor does it have to reproduce the original in its entirety. If a substantial part of the original is reproduced, a copyright infringement exists.

Penalties or remedies can be imposed on those who infringe copyrights. These range from actual damages or statutory damages ($250–$10,000) imposed at the discretion of the court, to criminal proceedings for willful violations which may result in fines and/or imprisonment.

The following case discusses copyright infringement by recording television broadcasts on home videotape recorders.

SONY CORP. v.
UNIVERSAL CITY
STUDIOS
Supreme Court of the United
States, 1984.
104 S.Ct. 774, 78 L.Ed.2d 574.

BACKGROUND AND FACTS   *Universal City Studios, respondents, own the copyrights on some of the television programs that are broadcast on the public airwaves. Sony Corporation, petitioners, manufacture and sell home videotape recorders. Universal alleged that members of the general public used Betamax videotape recorders (VTR) to record some broadcasts of Universal's copyrighted works, thereby infringing Universal's copyrights. Universal then maintained that Sony was liable for these copyright infringements because Sony marketed the Betamax VTRs. Universal sought money damages, an accounting for profits, and an injunction against the manufacture and marketing of Betamax VTRs. The District Court denied Universal any relief, but the Court of Appeals held Sony liable for contributory infringement. The United States Supreme Court took up the case.*

STEVENS, Justice.
*   *   *   *

Copyright protection "subsists . . . in original works of authorship fixed in any tangible medium of expression." 17 U.S.C. § 102(a). This protection has never accorded the copyright owner complete control over all possible uses of his work. Rather, the Copyright Act grants the copyright holder "exclusive" rights to use and to authorize the use of his work in five qualified ways, including reproduction of the copyrighted work in copies. Id., § 106. All reproductions of the work, however, are not within the exclusive domain of the copyright owner; some are in the public domain. Any individual may reproduce a copyrighted work for a "fair use"; the copyright owner does not possess the exclusive right to such a use. Compare Id., § 106 with Id., § 107.

"Anyone who violates any of the exclusive rights of the copyright owner," that is, anyone who trespasses into his exclusive domain by using or authorizing the use of the copyrighted work in one of the five ways set forth in the statute, "is an infringer of the copyright." Id., § 501(a). Conversely, anyone who is authorized by the copyright owner to use the copyrighted work in a way specified in the statute or who makes a fair use of the work is not an infringer of the copyright with respect to such use.
*   *   *   *

The two respondents in this case do not seek relief against the Betamax users who have allegedly infringed their copyrights. Moreover, this is not a class action on behalf of all copyright owners who license their works for television broadcast, and respondents have no right to invoke whatever rights other copyright holders may have to bring infringement actions based on Betamax copying of their works. As was made clear by their own evidence, the copying of the respondent's programs represents a small portion of the total use of VTRs. It is, however, the taping of respondents' own copyrighted programs that provides them with standing to charge Sony with contributory infringement. To prevail, they have the burden of proving that users of the Betamax have infringed their copyrights and that Sony should be held responsible for that infringement.
*   *   *   *

If vicarious liability is to be imposed on petitioners in this case, it must rest on the fact that they have sold equipment with constructive knowledge of the fact that their customers may use that equipment to make unauthorized copies of copyrighted material. There is no precedent in the law of copyright for the imposition of vicarious liability on such a theory. *   *   *
*   *   *   *

*   *   * Accordingly, the sale of copying equipment, like the sale of other articles of commerce, does not constitute contributory infringement if the product is widely used for legitimate, unobjectionable purposes. Indeed, it need merely be capable of substantial noninfringing uses.

* * * *

Even unauthorized uses of a copyrighted work are not necessarily infringing. An unlicensed use of the copyright is not an infringement unless it conflicts with one of the specific exclusive rights conferred by the copyright statute. * * * Moreover, the definition of exclusive rights in § 106 of the present Act is prefaced by the words "subject to sections 107 through 118." Those sections describe a variety of uses of copyrighted material that "are not infringements of copyright notwithstanding the provisions of § 106." The most pertinent in this case is § 107, the legislative endorsement of the doctrine of "fair use."

* * * *

* * * A challenge to a noncommercial use of a copyrighted work required proof either that the particular use is harmful, or that if it should become widespread, it would adversely affect the potential market for the copyrighted work.

* * * *

When these factors are all weighted in the "equitable rule of reason" balance, we must conclude that this record amply supports the District Court's conclusion that home time-shifting is fair use. In light of the findings of the District Court regarding the state of the empirical data, it is clear that the Court of Appeals erred in holding that the statute as presently written bars such conduct.

* * * *

The Supreme Court concluded: First, that a substantial number of television broadcast copyright holders would not object to having their broadcasts recorded; and second, that Universal failed to demonstrate the recordings would cause more than minimal harm to the market for, or value of, their copyrighted works. Therefore, the Betamax VTR is capable of noninfringing uses, so Sony was not liable for contributory infringement.

DECISION AND REMEDY

Theft of Trade Secrets

Some processes or items of information that are not patented, or not patentable, are nevertheless protected by law against appropriation by a competitor. Businesses that have *trade secrets* generally protect themselves by having all employees who use the process or information agree in their contracts never to divulge it. Thus, if a salesperson tries to solicit the company's customers for non-company business, or if an employee copies the employer's unique method of manufacture, he or she has appropriated a trade secret and has also broken a contract, two separate wrongs. Theft of confidential data by industrial espionage, as when a business taps into a competitor's computer, is a theft of trade secrets without any contractual violations and is actionable in itself.

Appropriation

Recently, a number of tort cases have arisen concerning the use of a famous person's name, or a likeness thereof, which results in a benefit to the defendant. This tort is called **appropriation** and seeks to protect an individual's right to have the exclusive use of his or her identity protected from others using the right of publicity to benefit the user.[3]

A typical case concerns the Johnny Carson show which has as its opening "Here's Johnny." A Michigan corporation engaged in the business of renting and selling "Here's Johnny" portable toilets. Johnny Carson brought suit claiming that the Michigan corporation violated his right of privacy and publicity

---

3. Restatement, Second, Torts, Section 652C.

appropriating his celebrity status in commercial exploitation of his identity. The Court held such use to be an appropriation[4] of Carson's identity without using his name.

Similar cases have involved the use of Muhammad Ali's name by describing a nude black man as "The Greatest," [5] and Elroy Hirsch as "Crazylegs" for a shaving gel used by women.[6]

DISPARAGEMENT OF PROPERTY OR REPUTATION

Business firms are encouraged to compete in our society, but they have the right to be reasonably free from disparagement of their products and their reputations.

Disparagement of Product

Disparagement of product or, more generally, disparagement of property, refers to common law torts of *slander of quality* and *slander of title*. Unprivileged publication of false information about another's product, alleging it is not what its seller claims, constitutes a tort of slander of quality. This tort has also been given the name *trade libel*. Actual damages must be proved by the plaintiff to have proximately resulted from the slander of quality. It must be shown that a third person refrained from dealing with the plaintiff because of the improper publication. It is possible for an improper publication to be both a slander of quality and a defamation. For example, a statement that disparages the quality of an article

4. Carson v. Here's Johnny Portable Toilets, 698 F.2d 831 (6th Cir. 1983).
5. Ali v. Playgirl, Inc., 447 F.Supp. 723 (S.D.N.Y. 1978).
6. Hirsch v. S. C. Johnson & Son, Inc., 90 Wis.2d 379, 280 N.W.2d 129 (1979).

may also, by implication, disparage the character of the person who would sell such a product.

When a publication denies or casts doubt upon another's legal ownership of any property, and when this results in financial loss to that property owner, the tort of slander of title may exist. Usually this is an intentional tort in which someone knowingly publishes an untrue statement about property, with the intent of discouraging a third person from dealing with the person slandered. For example, it would be difficult for a car dealer to attract customers after competitors put out a notice that the dealer's stock consisted of stolen autos.

Disparagement of Reputation

In Chapter 4 we discussed defamation, breaking it down into its component parts of libel in written or printed form and slander in oral form. Defamation becomes a business tort when the defamatory matter injures someone else in a profession, business, or trade or when it adversely affects a business entity in its credit rating and other dealings.

THE FUTURE

Torts relating to business, long recognized at common law, are becoming increasingly important in today's competitive world. Courts are ordering redress for more and more of these torts. Suits claiming violation of one or more of the rights of the owners of businesses are proliferating. Computerization, rapid communications, and mass media advertising multiply the means of committing such torts and magnify the effects they can have on the injured party's business. Since the law in this area is primarily case law rather than statutory law, it is free to change to accommodate the new developments that are transforming the business world.

QUESTIONS AND CASE PROBLEMS

1. Stevens owns a bakery. He has been trying to obtain a long-term contract with the owner of Martha's Tea Sa-

lons for some time. Stevens starts a local advertising campaign on radio and television and in the newspaper. This advertising campaign is so persuasive that Martha decides to break the contract she has had with Hank's Bakery so that she can patronize Stevens's bakery. Is Stevens liable to Hank's Bakery for the tort of wrongful interference with contractual relations? Is Martha liable for this tort? For anything?

2. Ann owns the Tasty Pastry Bakery and has been in business at the same location for fifteen years. Half of Ann's business comes from regular local drop-in customers. Also, Ann sells pastries to numerous restaurants, and just recently secured a one-year contract to supply rolls and pastries to a chain of restaurants and coffee shops owned by Eat-Lite. Eat-Lite had previously purchased its rolls and pastries from Green's Pastries, owned by Green. Green is quite upset about losing the Eat-Lite contract to Ann. Green purchases a vacant store in the same block as Ann's bakery and immediately does the following:

(a) Lowers Green's pastry and roll prices substantially below cost at the competing store.

(b) Hires an employee to verbally encourage potential and regular customers outside of Ann's bakery to shop at Green's Pastries.

Taking each act above separately, can Ann hold Green liable? Explain.

3. An Atlanta theater group produced a musical entitled "Scarlett Fever." The production opened with Shady Charlotte O'Mara at her plantation, Tiara, and moved through the major episodes of the film *Gone With The Wind*. This was not a parody or a farce, but another "play." The play also utilized backdrops reminiscent of the settings in the film. Original songs and dances were performed. Did this production infringe copyright interests in the film and the novel *Gone with the Wind*? [Metro-Goldwyn-Mayer, Inc. v. Showcase Atlanta Coop. Productions, Inc., 479 F.Supp. 351 (N.D.Ga.1979)]

4. Franchisees of a "T.G.I. Friday's" restaurant in Jackson, Mississippi, opened a restaurant in Baton Rouge, Louisiana. They named the new restaurant "E.L. Saturday's" or "Ever Lovin' Saturday's." The Baton Rouge restaurant was physically similar to T.G.I. Friday's, in Jackson. Both used a turn-of-the-century motif. "T.G.I. Friday's" is registered as a trademark with the United States patent office. Was the opening of the Baton Rouge restaurant a trademark infringement? [T.G.I. Friday's, Inc. v. International Restaurant Group, Inc., 569 F.2d 895 (5th Cir. 1978)]

5. Southard was stranded in Hawaii as the result of an airline strike. He had purchased a round-trip ticket before leaving his home in Denver. He sued the union for tortious interference with his contract with the airline and sought to recover the additional expense he incurred on another airline. Was the union liable to Mr. Southard?

[International Ass'n of Machinists v. Southard, 170 Colo. 119, 459 P.2d 570 (1969)]

6. California Consumers Company purchased from S. L. Coker an ice distributing business in the city of Santa Monica. In the purchase agreement Coker agreed that he would not engage in the business of selling or distributing ice either directly or indirectly in the city of Santa Monica, so long as the purchasers or anyone later purchasing the business remained in the business. Imperial Ice Company acquired the ice distributing business from California Consumers. Coker subsequently began selling ice in the same territory. The ice was supplied to him by a company owned by Rossier and Matheson on very attractive terms, because they wished to break into that area. Imperial Ice sued to obtain an injunction to restrain Coker from violating his original contract. Did Rossier and Matheson induce Coker to violate his contract, and were they therefore guilty of the tort of wrongful interference with contractual relations? [Imperial Ice Co. v. Rossier et al., 18 Cal.2d 33, 112 P.2d 631 (1941)]

7. Stiffel manufactured a floor lamp that he had patented. Sears, Roebuck and Co. made an identical lamp that it sold at a lower price. Stiffel sought an injunction against Sears, claiming that his patent had been infringed. The patent, however, had expired. Was Sears guilty of infringement of patent and unfair competition? [Sears, Roebuck & Co. v. Stiffel Co., 376 U.S. 225, 84 S.Ct. 784 (1964)]

8. Roto-Rooter was granted a federal registration in 1954 for its service mark "Roto-Rooter" for sewer, pipe, and drain cleaning services. In 1973 O'Neal opened a business with the name "Rotary D-Routing." Roto-Rooter sued for damages for trademark infringement. Could O'Neal continue using the name "Rotary D-Routing?" [Roto-Rooter Corp. v. O'Neal, 513 F.2d 44 (5th Cir. 1975)]

9. In the early 1960s Schenck employees Klaus Federn, Heinrick Geiss, and Alfred Seibert discovered a hard-bearing device for balancing rotors. This invention was registered with the patent office, but it was never used as an automobile wheel balancer. Nortron produced an automobile wheel balancer which used a hard-bearing device with a support plate similar to Schenck's. Is Schenck's patent not infringed because it was not used for automobile wheel balancing? [Schenck v. Nortron Corporation, 570 F.Supp. 810 (M.D.Tenn.1982)].

6

Criminal Law

Previously in this text we referred to a *crime* as being a wrong defined by society and perpetrated against society. A discussion of criminal law is appropriate to a study of business law because the prevention of crime and the effort of capturing and prosecuting those accused of crimes are time-consuming and costly activities. Because of this, these activities must be taken into account by businesses. Consequently, it is important that we understand the nature, extent, and impact of such activities on businesses.

The sanctions used to bring about a peaceful society, in which individuals engaging in business can compete and flourish, include those imposed by the civil law, such as damages for various types of tortious conduct, as discussed in the previous chapters, and damages for breach of contract, to be discussed in detail later. Chapter 1 also pointed out that courts of equity may restrain certain unlawful conduct by issuing injunctions.

These remedies have not been sufficient deterrents in some instances. Consequently, additional sanctions have been developed for particular undesirable activities. As a result, a *criminal law element* exists within the legal environment of business. The prerequisites of *fault* or *guilt* in this area are different from those in the civil law, as are the sanctions and penalties.

A *Concept Summary* showing which types of offenses fall under criminal law and civil law, respectively, can be found on page 104, near the end of this chapter.

THE NATURE OF CRIME

Crimes can be distinguished from other wrongful acts in that they are *offenses against society as a whole*. Crimes are prosecuted by a public official, not by their victims. In addition, those who have committed crimes are punished. Tort remedies—remedies for civil wrongs—are generally intended to compensate the injured (except when damages of a punitive nature are assessed), but criminal law is directly concerned with punishing (and ideally rehabilitating) the wrongdoer. The act of punishment is intended to accomplish four aims:

1. Punishment is supposed to deter not only the wrongdoer in a particular instance, but also all other members of society who might commit a similar wrong. In other words, this theory holds that publicly known acts of punishment indicate to other members of society that costs will be involved if they commit a similar wrong. Thus, punishment for a particular criminal act will, according to this theory, prevent other crimes.

2. Punishment protects society by incapacitating an individual convicted of a crime through imprisonment. If that individual is likely to commit other crimes, imprisonment will remove him or her from potential victims.

3. Punishment serves as a substitute for private vengeance. A society will become chaotic if private

means of "settling the score" are allowed when criminal acts have taken place.

4. Punishment, in theory, will rehabilitate those who have committed crimes. The American penal system has programs for treatment and education of inmates.

A final factor distinguishing criminal sanctions from tortious remedies is that the source of criminal law is primarily statutory. Both the acts that constitute crimes and the resulting punishments are formally and very specifically set out in statutes. A **crime** can thus be defined as a wrong against society proclaimed in a statute and punishable by society if committed.

Classifications of Crimes

Felonies   Crimes are classified as felonies or misdemeanors according to their seriousness. **Felonies** are more serious than misdemeanors and are punishable by death or by imprisonment in a federal or state penitentiary for more than a year. Felonies can also be divided by degrees of seriousness. The Model Penal Code, for example, provides for four degrees of felony: capital offenses where the maximum penalty is death, first degree felonies punishable by a maximum penalty of life imprisonment, second degree felonies punishable by a maximum of ten years' imprisonment, and third degree felonies punishable by up to five years' imprisonment. (It is important to note that these are maximum penalties. The actual sentence served can be less than the maximum.)

Felony Murder   When death occurs during or as the result of a felonious crime, many states have laws whereby the individual accused of the crime is charged with **felony murder** in addition to the crime that was intended. State legislatures determine which crimes can lead to felony murder charges. Most states, however, do not impose the death penalty in felony murder cases, but choose instead to impose a life sentence. The following case illustrates a felony murder statute.

BACKGROUND AND FACTS   *The defendant, Canola, and three other men robbed a jewelry store. During the robbery, the owner of the store, Bahtiarian, and one of the robbers, Lloredo, were killed. Canola did not shoot either man, but he was found guilty of their deaths in accordance with the New Jersey felony murder statute.*

STATE OF NEW
JERSEY v. CANOLA
Superior Court of New Jersey,
Appellate Division, 1975.
135 N.J.Super. 224,
343 A.2d 110.

COLLESTER, Presiding Justice of the Appellate Division.

* * * *

Defendant contends the trial court erred in denying his motion to dismiss the second count of the indictment charging him with the felony murder of Harold Lloredo. He argues here, as he did below, that he cannot be held for felony murder as a matter of law because Lloredo was shot and killed by Bahtiarian, one of the victims of the armed robbery. In denying the motion the trial court held the language of N.J.S.A. 2A:113–1, particularly the clause, "if the death of anyone ensues from the committing or attempting to commit any such crime or act," (hereinafter referred to as the "ensues clause") indicated a legislative policy which holds one (and others in concert with him) who deliberately commits an inherently violent act fully responsible for the probable consequences of the act.

The question of whether a participant in an armed robbery can be held liable for murder when his co-participant is killed by an intended victim in an attempt to abort an armed robbery has not heretofore been considered by our appellate courts. The resolution of the question depends upon the Legislature's intent when N.J.S.A. 2A:113–1 was enacted.

The statute, in pertinent part, reads as follows:

If any person, in committing or attempting to commit arson, burglary, kidnapping, rape, robbery, sodomy or any unlawful act against the peace of this state, of which the probable consequences may be bloodshed, kills another, or if the death of anyone ensues from the committing or attempting to commit any such crime or act; * * * then such person so killing is guilty of murder.

At both common law and today by statute all participants in any of the felonies referred to in the statute are equally guilty as principals.

* * * *

N.J.S.A. 2A:113–1 has no counterpart among the felony murder statutes in other jurisdictions which have considered murder prosecutions predicated upon a killing of an accomplice by one resisting a felony. The distinguishing feature in our statute is the "ensues clause," referred to above. Thus cases of other states are of no aid in deciding the question presented in the instant case.

* * * *

In *State v. Burton,* defendant was indicted for the murder of two of his accomplices who were killed by the police while they and the defendant were committing an armed robbery. In denying a motion to dismiss the indictment the trial judge stated that a reading of the statute indicated the Legislature intended to extend criminal account-ability beyond that imposed upon a felon under the common law. The judge held that the "ensues clause" evidenced a legislative intent to adhere to the proximate cause theory of felony murder and to extend the culpability of a defendant to all deaths which occurred during the commission of any of the offenses designated in the statute.

* * * *

The proximate cause theory simply stated is that when a felon sets in motion a chain of events which were or should have been within his contemplation when the motion was initiated, the felon, and those acting in concert with him, should be held responsible for any death which by direct and almost inevitable consequences results from the initial criminal act.

We agree with the court's interpretation of the statute in *State v. Burton.* In our view the statute indicates an intention on the part of the Legislature to extend criminal responsibility beyond that imposed upon a felon at common law and to hold liable all participants in an armed robbery for deaths which occur during the commission of the crime. We conclude that the trial judge properly denied the motion to dismiss the indictment.

DECISION AND REMEDY   *Canola's conviction, as well as his sentence of two concurrent terms of life imprisonment, was upheld. On further appeal to the Supreme Court of New Jersey, the conviction of Canola for the murder of his co-felon was reversed. Canola was still held guilty for the death of Bahtiarian, the owner of the store, under the felony murder statute.*

Misdemeanors   **Misdemeanors** are crimes punishable by a fine or by confinement for up to a year. Misdemeanors are also sometimes defined as offenses where incarceration takes place in a local jail instead of in a penitentiary. In practice, the jail confinement is usually for no more than a year. Disorderly conduct and trespass are common misdemeanors. Some states have different classes of misdemeanors. For example, in Illinois there are Class A misdemeanors (confinement for up to a year), Class B (not more than six months), and Class C (not more than thirty days). Whether a crime is a felony or a misdemeanor can also determine whether the case is tried in a magistrate court or a general trial court.

Violations   Another kind of wrong is termed a petty offense and often is not classified as a crime. Petty offenses include many traffic violations or violations of building codes. Even for petty offenses, a guilty party can be put in jail for a few days, or fined, or both.

Federal and State Crimes   Criminal law is primarily the province of the states, but the federal government also has a criminal code. Federal crimes relate to federal government functions or involve federal personnel or institutions. Counterfeiting, unlawful immigration, spying, robbing a federally insured bank, or assaulting a federal officer are examples of federal crimes. In other instances, the federal government can use its general regulatory powers to aid state law enforcement agencies in combating crimes that have a national impact. Transportation of stolen vehicles across state lines, kidnapping, and civil rights violations are areas that fall under federal criminal law.

Classification by Nature   Crimes can be classified according to their nature. For example, there are crimes against property (theft, burglary, arson), crimes against the person (murder, assault, rape), and crimes against the government (perjury, bribery). These classifications are used to group crimes within a statutory code.

THE ESSENTIALS OF CRIMINAL LIABILITY

Two elements are necessary for a person to be convicted of a crime: (1) the performance of a prohibited act, and (2) a specified state of mind or intent on the part of the actor. Even when these two elements are satisfied, there are possible defenses which the law deems sufficient to excuse such actions. Defenses will be discussed in the next section.

Performance of Prohibited Acts

Every criminal statute prohibits certain behavior. Most crimes require an act of *commission;* that is, a person must *do* something in order to be accused of a crime.[1] In some cases an act of *omission* can be a crime, but only if what is omitted is a legal duty. Failure to file a tax return is an example of an omission that is a crime.

The *guilty act* requirement is based on one of the premises of criminal law—that a person is punished for *harm done* to society. Thinking about killing someone or about stealing a car may be wrong, but these thoughts in themselves do no harm until they are translated into action. Of course, a person can be punished for attempting murder or robbery, but only if substantial steps toward the criminal objective have been taken.

Even a completed act that harms society is not legally a crime, however, unless the court finds that the required state of mind was present.

State of Mind or Intent

A wrongful mental state[2] is as necessary as a wrongful act to establish criminal liability. What constitutes such a mental state varies according to the wrongful action. Thus, for murder, the *actus reus* (act) is the taking of a life, and the *mens rea* (mental state) is the intent to take life. For theft, the *actus reus* is the taking of another person's property, and the *mens rea* involves both the knowledge that the property belongs to another and the intent to deprive the owner of it. Without the mental state required by law for a particular crime, there can be no crime.

The *mens rea* in which a particular act is committed can vary in the degree of its wrongfulness. The same act—shooting someone—can be committed with varying mental states. It can be done coldly, after premeditation, as in murder in the first degree. It can be done in the heat of passion, as in voluntary manslaughter. Or it can be done as the result of negligence, as in involuntary manslaughter. In each of these situations the law recognizes a different degree of wrongfulness, and the punishment differs accordingly.

The Model Penal Code[3] recognizes four categories of *mens rea:*

1.	Purpose or intent.	formerly covered under the term *specific intent.*
2.	Knowledge.	
3.	Recklessness.	formerly covered by the term *general intent.*
4.	Negligence.	

---

1.   Called the *actus reus,* or guilty act.

2.   Called the *mens rea,* or evil intent.

3.   American Law Institute Model Penal Code, official draft, 1962. This Code contains four parts relating to general provisions, definitions of specific crimes, treatment and correction, and organization of correction.

DEFENSES TO CRIMINAL LIABILITY

The law recognizes certain conditions that will relieve a defendant of criminal liability. These conditions are called defenses, and among the important ones are infancy, intoxication, insanity, mistake, consent, duress, justifiable use of force, entrapment, and statute of limitations. The burden of proving one or more of these defenses lies on the defendant. A criminal defendant can also be given immunity from prosecution.

Infancy

In the common law, children up to seven years of age were considered incapable of committing a crime because they did not have the moral sense to understand that they were doing wrong. Children between the ages of seven and fourteen were presumed to be incapable of committing a crime, but this presumption could be rebutted by showing that the child understood the wrongful nature of the act. (See Exhibit 6–1.)

Today, states vary in their approaches, but all retain the defense of infancy as a bar to criminal liability. Most states retain the common law approach, although age limits vary from state to state. Other states have rejected the rebuttable presumption and simply set a minimum age required for criminal responsibility. All states have juvenile court systems that handle children below the age of criminal responsibility who commit delinquent acts. Their aim is allegedly to reform rather than to punish. In states that retain the rebuttable presumption approach, children who are beyond the minimum age but are still juveniles can be turned over to the criminal courts if the juvenile court determines that they should be treated as adults.

Intoxication

The law recognizes two types of intoxication, whether from drugs or from alcohol: *involuntary* and *voluntary*. Involuntary intoxication occurs when a person is either physically forced to ingest or inject an intoxicating substance or is unaware that a substance contains drugs or alcohol. Involuntary intoxication is a defense to crime if its effect was to make a person either incapable of understanding that the act committed was wrong or incapable of obeying the law.

Voluntary intoxication can also be used as a defense where intoxication precludes having the required *mens rea*. Thus, if Johnson shoots Peters while too drunk to know what she is doing, she cannot be convicted of *murder* because she did not have the required *intent* to kill when she shot Peters.

Voluntary intoxication, however, does not serve as a defense for crimes requiring recklessness or negligence. The law requires that people be aware that intoxication can make it impossible to behave as a reasonable person. Therefore, becoming intoxicated and committing a reckless or negligent act is a crime. In the example above, Johnson could be convicted of the lesser crime of *manslaughter*.

Insanity

Just as a child is judged incapable of the state of mind required to commit a crime, so also is someone suffering from mental illness. Thus, insanity is a defense to a criminal charge. The courts have had difficulty deciding what the test for legal insanity should be, and psychiatrists, as well as lawyers, are critical of the tests used. Almost all federal courts and some states use the standard in the Model Penal Code:

> A person is not responsible for criminal conduct if at the time of such conduct as a result of mental disease or defect he lacks substantial capacity either to appreciate the wrongfulness of his conduct or to conform his conduct to the requirements of the law.

Other states use the *M'Naghten* test, which excuses a criminal act if a mental defect makes a person incapable of appreciating the nature of the act or

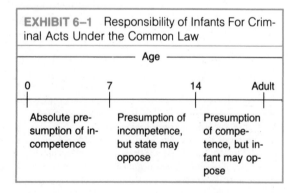

EXHIBIT 6–1 Responsibility of Infants For Criminal Acts Under the Common Law

Age		
0 7 14 Adult		
Absolute presumption of incompetence	Presumption of incompetence, but state may oppose	Presumption of competence, but infant may oppose

incapable of knowing that it was wrong. Some states that follow the *M'Naghten* rule have also adopted the irresistible impulse test. A person operating under an irresistible impulse may know that an act is wrong but may still be unable to keep from doing it. Even if a mental illness is not grave enough to serve as a complete defense, it may render a person legally incapable of certain crimes if the illness precludes the possibility of the required *mens rea*. The *Durham* role is still another alternative to the M'Naghten test. In *Durham* the District of Columbia court held that the proper solution is to discard all tests of insanity.[4] Instead, the *jury* should determine whether the defendant was sane or insane at the time of the alleged crime, and if he was insane, whether the harmful act was the product of his insanity. Even though the *Durham* role has received favorable reactions from commentators, it has received little support from the courts.

Mistake

Everyone has heard the saying "ignorance of the law is no excuse." It may seem harsh to presume that everyone knows or should know the law, but the result of a different rule would be unmanageable. Ordinarily, ignorance of the law or a mistaken idea about what the law requires is not a valid defense. In some states, however, that rule has been modified. A person who claims that he or she honestly did not know that a law was being broken may have a valid defense if: (1) the law was not published or reasonably made known to the public or (2) the person relied on an official statement of the law that was erroneous. An official statement is a statute, judicial opinion, administrative order, or statement by someone responsible for administering, interpreting, or enforcing the law (which does not normally include private attorneys). Statements in newspapers or textbooks are not official statements.

A *mistake of fact*, as opposed to a *mistake of law*, will operate as a defense if it negates the required *mens rea*. If, for example, John Jones mistakenly drives off in Mary Thompson's car because he thinks that it is his, there is no theft. Theft requires knowledge that the property belongs to another. (Of course, this has no bearing on a civil action for the tort of conversion.)

---

4. Durham v. United States, 214 F.2d 862 (1954).

Consent

What if a victim consents to a crime or even encourages the person intending a criminal act to commit it? The law will allow consent as a defense if the consent cancels the harm that the law is designed to prevent. In each case, the question is whether the law forbids an act against the victim's will or forbids the act without regard to the victim's wish. The law forbids murder, prostitution, and drug use whether the victim consents to it or not. Consent operates as a defense most successfully in crimes against property, since one can always give away one's property. Of course, if the act operates to harm a third person who has not consented, there will be no escape from criminal liability. Consent or forgiveness given after a crime has been committed is not really a defense, though it can affect the likelihood of prosecution.

Duress

A person who is asked or instructed to commit a crime is not excused from criminal liability, but committing a crime under *duress* is a valid defense. Duress exists when the *wrongful threat* of one person induces another person to perform an act which he or she would not otherwise perform. In such a situation, duress is said to negate the *mens rea* necessary to commit a crime.

The courts use a number of requirements to measure duress. First, the threat must be of serious bodily harm or death. A person who was threatened with failing a course or losing a job cannot plead duress as a defense. Second, the harm that is threatened must be greater than the harm that will be caused by the crime. A threat to shoot a woman's husband unless she robs a bank would be sufficient; a threat to hit her over the head might not be. The third requirement is that the threat must be immediate and inescapable. Finally, people who plead duress as a defense must have been involved in the situation through no fault of their own. If, for example, a person committing a burglary forces an accomplice to kill someone, the accomplice cannot use duress as an excuse. The act of participating in the burglary carries with it the possibility of being forced to commit a greater crime.

The threat in a duress defense can be to the person under duress or to someone close to him or her, such as a spouse. One crime that cannot be excused by duress is murder. It is difficult to justify taking a life even if one's own life is threatened.

Justifiable Use of Force

Probably the most well known defense to criminal liability is *self-defense*. But there are other situations that justify the use of force: the defense of one's dwelling, the defense of other property, and the prevention of a crime. In all of these situations it is important to distinguish between the use of deadly and nondeadly force. Deadly force is likely to result in death or serious bodily harm. Nondeadly force is force that reasonably appears necessary to prevent the imminent use of criminal force.

Generally speaking, people can use the amount of nondeadly force that seems necessary in order to protect themselves, their dwellings or other property, or to prevent the commission of a crime. Deadly force can be used in self-defense if there is a *reasonable belief* that imminent death or grievous bodily harm will otherwise result, if the attacker is using unlawful force (an example of lawful force would be that exerted by a police officer), and if the person has not initiated or provoked the attack. Deadly force can be used to defend a dwelling only if the unlawful entry is violent and the person believes that deadly force is necessary to prevent imminent death, great bodily harm, or—in some jurisdictions—if the person believes deadly force is necessary to prevent commission of a felony in the dwelling.

In defense of other property, the use of nondeadly force is justified to prevent or to end a criminal attempt to take away or otherwise interfere with the property. Deadly force usually is justifiable only when used in self-defense.

Force reasonably necessary to prevent a serious crime is permissible but, in the majority view, deadly force can be used to prevent only crimes that involve a substantial risk of death or great bodily harm.

Entrapment

Entrapment is a defense designed to prevent the police or other government agents from encouraging criminal acts in order to apprehend persons wanted for criminal acts. In the typical entrapment case, an undercover agent *suggests* that a crime be committed and somehow pressures or induces an individual to commit it. The agent then arrests the individual for the crime. Both the suggestion and the inducement must take place. The defense is not intended to prevent the police from setting a trap for an unwary criminal. It is intended to prevent them from pushing the suspected wrongdoer into it. The crucial issue is whether a person who commited a crime was predisposed to commit the crime or committed the crime because the agent induced it. This is often a question of fact, as illustrated by the following case.

UNITED STATES v.
BOWER

United States Court of Appeals,
Fifth Circuit, 1978.
575 F.2d 499.

BACKGROUND AND FACTS   *This case involves a cocaine transaction that resulted in the defendant's (Bower's) conviction for selling the narcotic to a government Drug Enforcement Administration (DEA) agent, Sylvestri. An informer, Clegg, initiated a relationship with the defendant. The informer encouraged the defendant to supply a quantity of cocaine to an out-of-town buyer. The defendant agreed to meet the buyer and make the exchange. After the defendant delivered the cocaine to the agent, the agent arrested him. The defendant was subsequently found guilty on various charges, including possession and distribution of cocaine. The defendant claimed entrapment on the part of the government agents.*

RONEY, Circuit Judge.
*   *   *   *

Defendant contends the evidence established an entrapment as a matter of law. In support of this claim, defendant relies primarily on his own trial testimony that he had agreed to participate in the criminal enterprise in a moment of extreme depression. Defendant had recently turned 30 and, reflecting upon an uneventful past and contemplating a similar future, had decided to return to college and finish his education. Unfortunately, a year of voluntary unemployment had so depleted his personal finances that he could not return to school without working at least part time. Having hoped to be able to focus his undivided attention on his studies, defendant began to recognize Clegg's proposals as an opportunity to finance his schooling. His depression at this time was heightened by the fact that he and his girlfriend had recently severed their long-standing relationship. Consequently, although he had repeatedly rejected Clegg's earlier entreaties, he could no longer resist the temptation of the promised "exorbitant gains" to be reaped from a single cocaine sale.

Since Clegg did not testify at trial, defendant's account of Clegg's repeated attempts to persuade defendant to procure narcotics is uncontradicted. The record nevertheless contains evidence weighing against the contention that defendant was "an innocent seduced by a government agent." Defendant admitted that he saw the sale as a source of "easy money" and that he expected to make a $1,000 profit on the transaction. He purchased the cocaine from a nongovernment source who trusted defendant enough to defer payment until defendant had resold the drug. Indeed, while negotiating the actual exchange, defendant assured DEA agent Sylvestri that he could handle Sylvestri's future cocaine needs if the amounts were not too large. Both agent Sylvestri and defendant testified that during the transaction, defendant received a telephone call from his source. Defendant interrupted his telephone conversation to ask Sylvestri if he was interested in buying another four ounces of cocaine. When the DEA agent expressed interest, defendant requested his source "not to lock up the other four" and offered to produce the additional cocaine for Sylvestri in 30 minutes.

On this evidence, the trial court did not err in submitting the entrapment issue to the jury. The crucial issue in entrapment cases is whether the defendant was predisposed to commit the crime. The Government's provisions of aid, incentive, and opportunity for commission of the crime amounts to an entrapment only if it appears that the defendant has done that which he would never have done were it not for the inducement of Government operatives. Although the record contains evidence upon which a jury might conclude that defendant was induced by a Government informer to commit a crime that he was not otherwise predisposed to commit, the evidence was not "so overwhelming that it was 'patently clear' or 'obvious' that [defendant] was entrapped as a matter of law."

The appellate court affirmed the defendant's convictions. The evidence supported   **DECISION**
the jury's verdict that the defendant, Bower, was predisposed to commit the   **AND REMEDY**
crime.

Statute of Limitations

An individual can be excused from criminal liability by a statute of limitations. Such statutes provide that the state has only a certain amount of time within which to prosecute a crime. If the state does not do so within the allotted time, it has lost its opportunity, and the suspect is free from prosecution. The idea behind these statutes is that people should not have to live under the threat of criminal prosecution indefinitely. Also, if prosecution is delayed for too

long, it becomes difficult to find out what the truth is because witnesses die or disappear and evidence is destroyed.

Time limits vary from state to state. Felonies usually have a longer statute of limitations than misdemeanors, and there is no time limitation placed on murder. For all other crimes, the time limit runs from the time the crime is committed, unless it is a crime that is difficult to discover. In those cases, the time begins to run when the crime is discovered. A time limitation will be suspended, however, if the suspect leaves the state or cannot be found. Normally, statutes will provide for subtraction of time if the suspect is not available to stand trial.

Immunity

At times, the state may wish to obtain information from a person accused of a crime. Such accused persons, of course, have an absolute privilege against self-incrimination and are understandably reluctant to give information if it will be used to prosecute them. In these cases, the state can grant immunity from prosecution or agree to prosecute for a less serious offense in exchange for the information. Once immunity is given, the person can no longer refuse to testify on Fifth Amendment grounds, since self-incrimination is then impossible. Often a grant of immunity from prosecution for a serious crime is part of the plea-bargaining negotiations between defense and prosecution. The defendant may still be convicted of a lesser offense, but the state uses his or her testimony to prosecute accomplices for serious crimes carrying heavy penalties.

CRIMINAL PROCEDURE

Our criminal justice system operates on the premise that it is far worse for an innocent person to be punished than for a guilty person to go free. A person is innocent until proven guilty, and guilt must be proved beyond a reasonable doubt. The procedure of the criminal legal system is designed to protect the rights of the individual and to preserve the presumption of innocence.

Constitutional Safeguards

Criminal law brings the weighty force of the state, with all its resources, to bear against the individual. Specific safeguards are provided in the Constitution for those accused of crimes. The Supreme Court has ruled that most of these safeguards apply not only in federal but also in state courts by virtue of the due process clause of the Fourteenth Amendment. The safeguards include:

1.   Fourth Amendment protection from unreasonable searches and seizures.
2.   The Fourth Amendment requirement that no warrants for a search or an arrest can be issued without probable cause.

3.   The Fifth Amendment requirement that no one can be deprived of "life, liberty, or property without due process of law."
4.   Fifth Amendment prohibition against double jeopardy (trying someone twice for the same criminal offense).
5.   Sixth Amendment guarantees of a speedy trial, trial by jury, a public trial, the right to confront witnesses, and the right to a lawyer for serious charges.
6.   Eighth Amendment prohibitions against excessive bails and fines, and cruel and unusual punishment.[5]

In recent years the Supreme Court has been active in interpreting these rights. Some of the cases are widely known. The *Miranda* decision, for example, established the rule that individuals who are arrested must be informed of their right to remain silent, of the fact that anything they say can be used against them in court, of their right to have a lawyer present, and of the duty of the state to provide lawyers if individuals cannot pay for them.[6]

Criminal Process

A criminal prosecution differs significantly from a civil case in several respects. These differences reflect the desire to safeguard the rights of the individual against the state.

Arrest   Before a warrant for arrest can be issued, probable cause must exist for believing that the individual in question has committed a crime. **Probable cause** can be defined as a substantial likelihood that the individual has committed or is about to commit a crime. Note that probable cause involves a likelihood, not just a possibility. Arrests may sometimes be made without a warrant when there is no time to get one, but the action of the arresting officer is still judged by the standard of probable cause.

Indictment   Individuals must be formally charged with having committed specific crimes before they can be brought to trial. This charge is called an **indictment** if issued by a grand jury and an **information** if issued by a magistrate. Before a charge can be issued, the grand jury or the magistrate must

5.   See the U.S. Constitution in Appendix B.
6.   Miranda v. Arizona, 384 U.S. 436, 86 S.Ct. 1602 (1966).

determine that there is sufficient evidence to justify bringing the individual to trial. The standard used to make this determination varies from jurisdiction to jurisdiction. Some courts use the probable cause standard. Others use the preponderance of evidence standard, which is a belief based on evidence provided by both sides that it is more likely than not that the individual committed the crime. Still another standard is the *prima facie* case standard, which is a belief based only on the prosecution's evidence that the individual is guilty.

Trial   At the trial the accused person does not have to prove anything. The entire burden of proof is on the prosecution (the state). Guilt is judged on the basis of the **reasonable doubt** test. The prosecution must show that, based on all the evidence, the defendant's guilt is established beyond all reasonable doubt. Note that a verdict of "not guilty" is not the same as a statement that the defendant is innocent. It merely means that not enough evidence was properly presented to the court to prove guilt beyond all reasonable doubt. Courts have complex rules about what types of evidence may be presented and how the evidence may be brought out, especially in jury trials. These rules are designed to insure that evidence in trials is relevant, reliable, and not unfairly prejudicial to the defendant. The defense attorney will cross-examine the witnesses who present evidence against his or her client in an attempt to show that their evidence is not reliable. Of course, the state may also cross-examine any witnesses presented by the defendant.

CRIMES AFFECTING BUSINESS

Forgery

The fraudulent making or alteration of any writing that changes the legal liability of another is **forgery.** If Smith signs Brown's name without authorization to the back of a check made out to Brown, Smith has committed forgery. Forgery also includes changing trademarks, falsifying public records, counterfeiting, and, the alteration of any legal document.

Most states have a special statute, often called a *credit card statute,* to cover the illegal use of credit cards. Thus, the state attorney can prosecute a person who misuses a credit card for violating either the forgery statute or the special credit card statute.

Robbery

At common law, **robbery** was defined as forcefully and unlawfully taking personal property of any value from another. The use of force or fear is usually necessary for an act of theft to be considered a robbery. Thus, pickpocketing is not robbery because the action is unknown to the victim. Typically, states have more severe penalties for *aggravated* robbery—robbery by use of deadly weapon.

Burglary

At common law, **burglary** was defined as breaking and entering the dwelling of another at night with the intent to commit a felony. Originally, the definition was aimed at protecting an individual's home and its occupants. Most state statutes have eliminated some of the requirements found in the common law definition. Thus, the time at which the breaking and entering occurs is usually immaterial. State statutes frequently omit the element of breaking, and some states do not require that the building be a dwelling. Aggravated burglary, which is defined as burglary with the use of a deadly weapon, or burglary of a dwelling, or both, incurs a greater penalty.

Larceny

The wrongful or fraudulent taking and carrying away by any person of the personal property of another is **larceny.** It includes the fraudulent intent to permanently deprive an owner of property. Many business-related larcenies entail fraudulent conduct.

The place from which physical property is taken is generally immaterial. However, statutes usually prescribe a stiffer sentence for property taken from buildings such as banks or warehouses. Larceny is differentiated from robbery by the fact that robbery involves force or fear, and larceny does not. Therefore, pickpocketing is larceny, not robbery.

As society has become more complex, the question often arises as to what is property. In most states, the definition of the property that is subject to larceny statutes has been expanded. Stealing computer programs may constitute larceny even though the programs consist of magnetic impulses. Trade secrets can be subject to larceny statutes. Stealing the use of telephone wires by the device known as a "blue box" is subject to larceny statutes. So, too, is the theft of natural gas.

Distinguishing between Grand and Petit Larceny   The common law distinction between grand and petit larceny depends on the value of the property taken. Many states have abolished this distinction, but in those that have not, grand larceny is a felony and petit larceny a misdemeanor.

Obtaining Goods by False Pretenses

It is a criminal act to obtain goods by means of false pretenses—for example, buying groceries with a check, knowing that one has insufficient funds to cover it. Statutes covering such illegal activities vary widely from state to state.

Receiving Stolen Goods

It is a crime to receive stolen goods. The recipient of such goods need not know the true identity of the owner or of the thief. All that is necessary is that the recipient knows or should have known that the goods are stolen, which implies an intent to deprive the owner of those goods.

Embezzlement

The fraudulent conversion of property or money owned by one person but entrusted to another is **embezzlement.** Typically, it involves an employee who fraudulently appropriates money. Banks face this problem, and so do a number of businesses in which corporate officers or accountants "jimmy" the books to cover up the fraudulent conversion of money for their own benefit. Embezzlement is not larceny because the wrongdoer does not physically take the property from the possession of another, and it is not robbery because there is no taking by use of force or fear.

It does not matter whether the accused takes the money from the victim or from a third person. If, as the comptroller of a large corporation, Saunders pockets a certain number of checks from third parties that were given to her to deposit into the account of another company, she has committed embezzlement.

Misapplication of Trust Funds   Often the owner of property will remit money to a contractor specifically for the contractor to pay various persons who worked on the owner's building. The contractor who does not use the money for this purpose commits a special form of embezzlement called *misapplication of trust funds.* The funds were entrusted to the contractor for a specific purpose and that trust has been violated. The fact that the accused intended eventually to return the embezzled property does not constitute a sufficient defense. In practice, though, an embezzler who returns what has been taken will not ordinarily be prosecuted, because the owner usually will not take the time to make a complaint, give depositions, and appear in court.

Arson

The willful and malicious burning of a building (and in some states personal property) owned by another is the crime of **arson.** At common law, arson applied only to burning down the dwelling house of another. Such law was designed to protect human life. Today, arson statutes apply to other kinds of buildings. Also, if someone is killed as a result of arson, the act is murder because of the application of the murder-felony rule.

Burning to Defraud Insurers   Every state has a special statute that covers burning a building in order to collect insurance. If Allison owns an insured apartment building that is falling apart and burns it himself or pays someone else to set fire to it, Allison is guilty of burning to defraud insurers. Of course, the insurer need not pay the claim when insurance fraud is proven.

Use of the Mails to Defraud

It is a federal crime to use the mails to defraud the public. Illegal use of the mails must involve (1) mailing or causing someone else to mail a writing for the purpose of executing a scheme to defraud and (2) a contemplated or organized scheme to defraud by false pretenses. If, for example, Johnson advertises the sale of a cure for cancer that he knows to be fraudulent because it has no medical validity, he can be prosecuted for fraudulent use of the mails. Federal law also makes it a crime to use a telegram to defraud.

WHITE-COLLAR CRIMES

Although no official definition exists for **white-collar crime**, the term is popularly used to mean an illegal act or series of acts committed by an individual or corporation using some nonviolent means to obtain a personal or business advantage. Usually this kind of crime is committed in the course of a legitimate occupation. The cost to the public of so-called white-collar crimes ranges between $40 billion and $110 billion a year.

Since it is impossible to cover the vast range of what are considered to be white-collar crimes, the efforts in this chapter will center on four areas: (1) computer crimes, (2) bribery, (3) bankruptcy fraud, and (4) corporate crimes.

Computer Crimes

The age of the computer is now upon us. An increasing percentage of business is carried on via computers. Virtually all of the financial transactions of the government and most large businesses are handled by computer. Many of the transfers of money from business to business, from individual to business, from business to individual, and from individual and business to and from government involve not the physical circulation of money but rather the changing of digital information within computer memories.

Clearly, the manipulation of computers for personal or business gain is possible. Detection is often difficult. Certain companies, and even the government, have discovered multimillion dollar thefts made this way only after a significant amount of time has elapsed. Employees of accounting and computer departments have been known to make extra copies of paychecks, transfer monies among accounts, and create fictitious insurance policies to pay out dividends.

Criminal Sanctions   Existing criminal laws are often inadequate to deal with the numerous computer-assisted crimes that take place. Larceny statutes were originally passed to prohibit the theft of *tangible property*. Criminal misuse of a computer, however, frequently relates to computer software. Unlike computer hardware, which consists of the tangible physical parts of the computer, computer software comprises intangibles, such as computer programs.

As mentioned above, some states have expanded their definition of property to allow these new types of crimes to fall within their larceny statutes. In those states that have not expanded their larceny statutes to include intangible types of property, such as computer software, prosecutors have had to rely upon other criminal statutes. However, as a result of the lenient punishments that usually arise in computer crimes, various proposals have been put forward to deal with this new type of crime. The law involving computer crime is clearly still in its formative stage.

The Problem of Secrecy   The full extent of computer crime in our business society is unrevealed. Firms adversely affected by such crime rarely publicize the fact, because they are afraid that their customers will then doubt the accuracy of computer-generated material. Trials of apprehended perpetrators of computer crimes are rare. The affected business usually allows the case to be *plea bargained* instead of going to trial. Sometimes, for fear of publicity, the business will not even report the crime and may be blackmailed into giving the person who committed the crime a reference for another job.

Bribery

Basically, three types of actions called bribery are considered crimes. They involve: (1) bribery of foreign officials, (2) bribery of public officials, and (3) commercial bribery.

Bribery of Foreign Officials   Until the 1970s, bribery of foreign officials to obtain business contracts was rarely, if ever, discussed. Indeed, payments in cash or in-kind benefits to government officials for such purposes are often considered normal practice. This is not to say that the practice is legal. In order to reduce the amount of such bribes given to foreign government officials by representatives of American corporations, Congress passed the Foreign Corrupt Practices Act in 1977 (15 U.S.C. 78).

The act is divided into two major parts. The first part, which applies to all U.S. companies, its directors, officers, shareholders, employers or agents, prohibits bribes (anything of value) to most foreign government officials where the purpose is to obtain or retain business for the U.S. company.

The second part is directed toward accountants because previous bribes were often concealed in corporate financial records. The act requires all companies to keep detailed records which "accurately and fairly" reflect the company's financial activities, and to have an accounting system which provides "reasonable assurance" that all transactions entered into by the company are accounted for and legal. Although this requirement is broad in scope, these requirements should assist in detecting illegal foreign bribes.

The act further prohibits any person in the company from making false statements to accountants, or any person from making any false entry in any record or account. Any violation of the act results in fines of up to $1 million, and the incarceration of officers or directors of convicted companies for up to a maximum of five years. Those officers and directors can also be fined up to $10,000, and the fine cannot be paid by the company.

Bribery of Public Officials The attempt to influence a public official to act in a way that serves a private interest is a crime. As an element of this crime, *intent* must be present and proved. The bribe that is offered can be anything that the recipient of the offer considers to be valuable. *The commission of the crime of bribery occurs when the bribe is tendered.* The recipient does not have to agree to perform whatever action is desired by the person tendering the bribe; nor does the recipient have to accept the bribe.

Commercial Bribery In some states, so-called kickbacks and payoffs from an individual working for one company to another individual or individuals working for another company are crimes. No public official need be involved. Such commercial bribes are typically given with the intent of obtaining proprietary information, covering up an inferior product, or securing new business. Industrial espionage sometimes involves this kind of activity—for example, a payoff of some type to an employee in a competing firm in exchange for trade secrets and pricing schedules.

The following case illustrates an instance of commercial bribery.

UNITED STATES v. TILTON

United States Court of Appeals, Fifth Circuit, 1980.
610 F.2d 302.

BACKGROUND AND FACTS *Defendant Tilton was responsible for locating repair shops to perform work for his employer, Sea-Land Incorporated. Tilton requested and received from the repair shop owners a $20 "commission" on each item sent to the shops. The trial court found Tilton guilty of mail fraud, interstate travel to facilitate an unlawful activity, and conspiracy.*

THORNBERRY, Circuit Judge.
* * * *

Appellant * * * contends that the evidence was not sufficient to support his convictions for conspiracy, mail fraud, and violating the Travel Act. This claim is without merit.

We will first examine appellant's claim with respect to the alleged Travel Act violation. The Travel Act provides in part:

(a) Whoever travels in interstate or foreign commerce or uses any facility in interstate or foreign commerce, including the mail, with intent to—

(1) distribute the proceeds of any unlawful activity; * * * shall be fined not more than $10,000 or imprisoned for not more than five years, or both.

(b) As used in this subsection "unlawful activity" means * * * (2) extortion, *bribery,* or arson in violation of the laws of the State in which committed or of the United States.

The Supreme Court recently held, in an opinion affirming a decision of this court, that "bribery," as mentioned in the Act, includes not only bribery of a public official but also bribery of a private employee in violation of a state criminal statute. The payment of $1,400 by Brenner to Tilton in the lounge of a Charleston, South Carolina

motel constituted the offense of bribery, punishable under South Carolina law. Therefore, the only remaining question is whether Tilton's interstate travel from Florida to
South Carolina was accomplished with the *intent* to facilitate this unlawful activity.
It is enough that the intent is motivated in part by the unlawful activity even if one
motivating factor involves a legitimate purpose. Tilton's acceptance of the bribe soon
after arriving in South Carolina supports the inference that the trip was motivated, at
least in part, by the bribe. The fact that Tilton travelled in part for an improper reason
may be inferred from his actions immediately after the travel. Therefore, the evidence
appears sufficient to support Tilton's conviction for violation of the Travel Act.
*   *   *   *

The evidence is also sufficient to support a finding that Tilton conspired to commit
mail fraud. This court has stated that to sustain a conviction for conspiracy to commit
mail fraud, the evidence must merely show a scheme or artifice to defraud, use of the
mails caused by someone associated with the scheme, and use of the mails in executing
the fraud. The scheme of inflating the invoices that were mailed to Sea-Land in order
to generate the "commissions" to be paid to Tilton defrauded Sea-Land by increasing
the cost of each chassis by at least $20. The UTS conspirators (Gillespie, Cotrone)
executed this fraudulent scheme by mailing the padded invoices to Sea-Land. It is not
necessary to demonstrate which invoices were fraudulent. Since the defrauded funds
were used to pay Tilton his "commissions," the evidence is clearly sufficient to demonstrate that Tilton participated in the *conspiracy* to commit mail fraud through a
scheme to defraud and use of the mails to execute that fraud.

Tilton's conviction and sentence were upheld. The punishment was one year's   **DECISION**
imprisonment for violation of the Travel Act, four years' probation on the mail   **AND REMEDY**
fraud and conspiracy counts, and a $2,000 fine for his part in the conspiracy.

Bankruptcy Fraud

When a business finds itself with an oppressive amount
of debt, its creditors may seek to have the court
adjudge it a bankrupt company. Alternatively, the
individual or business entity may seek voluntary
bankruptcy. Today, individuals or businesses can be
relieved of oppressive debt by federal law under the
Bankruptcy Reform Act of 1978, as amended by the
Bankruptcy Amendments and Federal Judgeship Act
of 1984. We discuss this act in more detail in Chapter 31. In short, the act requires that the debtor
disclose all assets. The assets are then taken into
possession by a trustee, unless they are exempt. The
trustee must follow certain rules in distributing those
assets to creditors. Following are examples of some
of the numerous white-collar crimes that can be
perpetrated throughout the many phases of a bankruptcy proceeding.

False Claims of Creditors   Creditors are required
to file their individual claims against the debtor who
is in bankruptcy proceedings. A creditor who files a
false claim commits a crime.

Transfer of Property   Obviously, a debtor, knowing
that he or she will be in bankruptcy proceedings,
has an incentive to transfer assets to favored parties
before or after the petition for bankruptcy is filed.
For example, a company-owned automobile can be
"sold" at a bargain price to a trusted friend or relative. Closely related to the crime of fraudulent transfer
of property is fraudulent concealment of property.
The number of ways in which debtors have fraudulently concealed assets would require several books
to outline.

Scam Bankruptcies   The term *scam bankruptcy* has
been used to indicate a swindle in which a bankruptcy is planned in advance. The perpetrators purchase a legitimate business that sells highly liquid
goods, such as jewelry or electronic home entertainment equipment. Numerous items are purchased on credit by the new owners. The creditors
are paid off within a relatively short period of time.
This activity continues until the creditors are willing
to offer larger and larger amounts of credit to the

CONCEPT SUMMARY: Classifications of Law	
LAW CLASSIFICATIONS	**TYPES OF OFFENSE**

Criminal law—is concerned with acts against society for which society seeks redress in the form of punishment.	1. Felony
	  a. Homicide
	  b. Manslaughter
	  c. Robbery
	  d. Burglary
	  e. Larceny (grand)
	  f. Bribery
	  g. Arson
	
	2. Misdemeanor
	  a. Public intoxication
	  b. Vagrancy
	  c. Prostitution
	  d. Larceny (petit)
	  e. Assault and battery (simple)
	  f. Trespass
	  g. Disturbing the peace

Civil law—is concerned with acts against a person for which the injured party seeks redress in the form of compensation or other relief.	1. Contract
	  a. Real estate
	  b. Insurance
	  c. Sales
	  d. Business organization formation
	  e. Services
	  f. Commercial paper obligations
	  g. Commercial bailments
	
	2. Tort
	  a. Defamation
	  b. Invasion of privacy
	  c. Assault and battery
	  d. Negligence
	  e. Strict liability
	  f. Trespass
	  g. Fraud

new owners. Finally, the new owners order a very large amount of merchandise on credit, sell it at whatever price is necessary to unload it quickly for cash, and then close down the business. Of course, creditors file an involuntary petition in bankruptcy against the business. The amount that those creditors will recover, however, is typically very small. And the scam operators are nowhere to be found.

Corporate Crimes

Corporations are "artificial" persons created by law. Clearly, they cannot harbor the criminal intent that is required for conviction of a crime, but their officers can. The modern tendency is to hold corporations criminally responsible for their acts or omissions if the assigned penalty is a fine, and if intent either is not an element of the crime or can be implied.

Obviously, a crime such as perjury cannot be committed by a corporation but can be committed by a natural person, such as an officer of the corporation. Furthermore, crimes punishable by imprisonment or corporal punishment cannot be committed by corporations. However, when a statute allows a fine in addition to, or in the place of, these penalties, a corporation can be convicted of that crime. If, for example, a statute requires that adequate safety equipment be installed on machines, and a corporation fails to do so—and if the result is the death of a worker—the corporation can be fined for committing criminal manslaughter. In addition, the corporate officers who were in a position to prevent the wrong can be prosecuted under specific federal and state statutes.

QUESTIONS AND CASE PROBLEMS

1. Civil trials and criminal trials are conducted under essentially the same format. There are, however, several important differences. In criminal trials, the defendant must be proven guilty beyond all reasonable doubt, whereas in civil trials, the defendant need only be proven guilty by a preponderance of the evidence. Can you see any reason for this difference?

2. Crimes are classified as either felonies or misdemeanors. Determine from the facts below what type of crime has been committed and whether the crime is a felony or a misdemeanor.

(a) John is walking through an amusement park when his wallet, with $2,000 in it, is "picked" from his pocket.

(b) Allen and George become involved in a shouting argument. Allen knocks George down, causing a serious head injury to George.

(c) Darrell continually crosses Mary's backyard without permission, despite Mary's notice to Darrell to get off her land.

(d) Harold walks into a camera shop. Without force and without the owner noticing, Harold walks out of the store with a camera.

3. The following fact situations are similar (the theft of Jean's television set); yet three different crimes are described. Identify the three crimes, noting the differences among them.

(a) While passing Jean's house one night, Sam sees a portable television set left unattended on Jean's lawn. Sam takes the television set, carries it home, and tells everyone he owns it.

(b) While passing Jean's house one night, Sam sees Jean outside with a portable television set. Holding Jean at gunpoint, Sam forces her to give up the set. Then Sam runs away with it.

(c) While passing Jean's house one night, Sam sees a portable television set in a window. Sam breaks the front door lock, enters, and leaves with the set.

4. Jack, an undercover police officer, stops Patricia on a busy street. Jack offers to sell Patricia an expensive wristwatch for a fraction of its value. After some questioning, Jack admits that the watch is stolen property, although he says that he was not the thief. Patricia pays for and receives the wristwatch and is immediately arrested by Jack for receiving stolen property. At trial, Patricia contends entrapment. What is the result of the trial?

5. Two basic elements are needed for a person to be convicted of a crime. The first element is called *actus reus*, and the second is called *mens rea*. Explain what these terms mean, and discuss how each is applied to the following:

(a) Murder or manslaughter.

(b) Forgery.

(c) Arson.

6. Faulkner was a seaman on the ship Zemindar. One night while on duty, Faulkner went in search of the rum that he knew the ship was carrying. He found it and opened one of the kegs, but because he was holding a match at the time, he inadvertently ignited the rum and set fire to the ship. Faulkner was criminally prosecuted for setting fire to the ship. At the trial, it was determined that even though he had not intended to set fire to the rum, he had been engaged in the unlawful act of stealing it. Does Faulkner's theft of the rum make him criminally liable for setting fire to the ship? [Regina v. Faulkner, 13 Cox C.C. 550 (Ireland)]

7. In 1965 Rybicki failed to pay the complete amount of income tax he owed the federal government. Attempts by the IRS to collect the tax proved fruitless. Therefore, the IRS, through lawful means, obtained a tax lien on Rybicki's personal property, which included his truck. In February 1967 Rybicki's wife, upon hearing the motor of the truck, awoke her sleeping husband. Wielding a shotgun, Rybicki went to his front door and told the two men who were attempting to take his truck to stop. Rybicki claimed that he did not know that the two men were IRS agents. Subsequently, the federal government indicted Rybicki for obstructing justice. Can Rybicki be held criminally liable if he did not know that the men were IRS agents performing their duty? [United States v. Rybicki, 403 F.2d 599 (6th Cir. 1968)]

8. Pivowar agreed to lend Mills approximately $9,000, and Mills agreed to repay the loan and further agreed that

the loan would be secured by two houses that he owned. Mills showed Pivowar the two houses but falsely represented that Pivowar was to get a first mortgage on the houses. Pivowar later learned that the mortgages he held were not on the two houses but on two vacant lots and, further, that the mortgages were second mortgages and not first mortgages as Mills had promised. Can Mills be prosecuted criminally for false pretenses if he contends that he intended to pay back the loan and that Pivowar never demanded payment on the note? [State v. Mills, 96 Ariz. 377, 396 P.2d 5 (1964)]

9. Lund was working on his doctoral dissertation in statistics at Virginia Polytechnic Institute in Blacksburg, Virginia. He was required to use the computer facilities at the university. His faculty adviser neglected to arrange for the use of the computer. Nonetheless, Lund went ahead and used it without obtaining proper authorization. At trial, Lund was convicted of grand larceny for obtaining approximately $30,000 worth of computer services without authorization. At trial, four faculty members testified that computer time "probably would have been" or "would have been" assigned to Lund if properly requested. Lund appealed his conviction. What was the result? [Lund v. Commonwealth of Virginia, 217 Va. 688, 232 S.E.2d 745 (1977)]

FOCUS ON ETHICS

The Central Problem: Defining Business Ethics

Business people face complicated decisions. A course of action that may mean relatively high short-run profits may also involve conduct that, though legal, is not ethical. How indeed does a manager know that he or she is facing an ethical issue in reaching a particular business decision? To answer this question, we must first look at the concept of ethics and determine what comprises an *ethical issue.*

WHAT IS AN ETHICAL ISSUE?
Essentially, an ethical issue is one that transcends its subject matter to pose a fundamental, structural question such as, What is fair? What is just? or What makes this outcome more socially desirable than another? One of the best definitions of *ethics* from a business point of view appeared in *Ethics in the Corporate Policy Process: An Introduction*: "Ethics is a process by which individuals, social groups, and societies evaluate their actions from the perspective of moral principles and values. This evaluation may be on the basis of traditional convictions, of ideals sought, of goals desired, of moral laws to be obeyed, of an improved quality of relations among humans and with the environment. When we speak of "ethics" and ethical reflection,

we mean the activity of applying these various yardsticks to the actions of persons and groups."*

Thus, a society's ethical values, whether related to business or otherwise, rest on a collection of shared beliefs. Indeed, it is the sharing of beliefs and the desire to spread these beliefs that cause people to organize as groups. The collection of basic values accepted by most members of society constitutes the prevailing morality of that society. We must bear in mind, however, that what constitutes an ethical concern of a society may change as the values of that society change. What was ethical conduct in the United States ten years ago may be considered unethical today, although ten years from now it may once again be considered ethical.

WHY DO ETHICAL ISSUES ARISE?
For business people, ethical issues arise because of competing interests in the business world among buyers, sellers, managers, nonmanagers, and others.

*C. McCoy, et al., Ethics in the Corporate Policy Process: An Introduction, Berkeley, Calif.: Center for Ethics and Social Policy, Graduate Theological Union, 1975, p. 2.

Ethical problems may arise when there is a conflict between the goals of different departments of the same company. It is frequently difficult in a company to determine who has the responsibility to voice concern over the quality or safety of a product being manufactured. It is often the middle management who has the knowledge upon which an ethical dilemma turns. All too often the manager in such a case is in a no-win situation. He or she must be concerned with the reaction of upper-management personnel as well as with the reactions of fellow employees. A middle-manager most likely has also developed a loyalty to the reputation of the company and its long-run interests. Thus, disclosing or not disclosing quality problems places a great deal of pressure upon those middle-managers. How do you decide whether it is "your" ethical responsibility to disclose quality problems? What if the situation is clearly under someone else's control and they obviously are content to ignore what you personally perceive to be unethical conduct?

CONFRONTING ETHICAL DILEMMAS
The case of *Geary* v. *United States Steel Corporation* [319 A.2d 174, 456 Pa. 171 (1974)] illustrates some possible

consequences of an ethical dilemma. George Geary was employed by the United States Steel Corporation to sell tubular products to the oil and gas industry. His employment was at will. Geary alleged that he believed that one of the company's new products, a tubular casing, had not been adequately tested and constituted a serious danger to anyone who used it. Even though Geary at all times performed his duties to the best of his ability, he continued to express his reservations with respect to the company's new product. Geary alleged that because of the above events, he was summarily discharged without notice.

The Supreme Court of Pennsylvania held that Geary had no right of action against his employer for wrongful discharge. The court stated that Geary vigorously expressed his own point of view by bypassing his immediate superiors and by taking his case to a vice-president of the company. It concluded that the most natural inference from the chain of events was that Geary had made a nuisance of himself and, hence, the company had discharged him to preserve administrative order. In addition, the court acknowledged the fact that Geary did not possess any expert qualifications: He was only involved in the sale of company products. The mere fact that Geary may have had "good intentions" was not found to be sufficient to establish a right to litigate a case such as this one.

The court in *Geary* clearly recognized the potential for abuse if a new non-statutory cause of action were to be created. Vexatious suits by

disgruntled employees against a company could severely disrupt its normal operational procedures. Furthermore, there would also be substantial problems of proof in creating a legal forum for this type of plaintiff. How do you actually prove that an employee is discharged for one reason as opposed to another?

Clearly, there are conflicting interests to which our laws must address themselves. On the one hand, our legal system serves to encourage individuals to acknowledge their ethical responsibilities. Yet, on the other hand, our laws must be structured in such a way as to discourage frivolous suits that unnecessarily disrupt business.

WHITE-COLLAR CRIME

White-collar crime is composed of numerous categories of behavior that society considers to be unethical. The term "white-collar crime" generally refers to nonviolent crimes committed by corporations and individuals. Theft, fraud, and embezzlement are examples of white-collar crime.

Increasingly, ethical dilemmas are facing both men and women in their careers. What if the fraud is being committed by your boss? How will you know if the entire company is involved in a fraudulent conspiracy? In this situation, complaining to top management will be of little avail. Furthermore, what if the behavior you regard as unethical is in fact behavior that you have misinterpreted or behavior that is actually quite legal and ethical? Sure, you may have made a mistake, and if the company is engaging in ethical practices, they shouldn't worry. Yet all too often companies may see this inquiry

as a lack of company loyalty. These types of ethical dilemmas are not easy to resolve and indeed can be quite stressful.

WHITE-COLLAR SENTENCING

Ethical issues also arise with respect to the sentencing of those convicted of white-collar crimes. Should they be subject to the traditional penalties— such as imprisonment and fines—or are different modes of punishment more appropriate for these persons? In 1974, in the paper label case, Judge Renfrew of the Northern District of California imposed suspended jail sentences on five corporate executives convicted of conspiring to fix prices in the paper label industry.** The suspension of these jail sentences was conditional upon each of the five defendants making an oral presentation before twelve business, civic, or other groups concerning the circumstances of the case and each defendant's participation therein. The defendants were then further required to submit a written report giving the details of each presentation, the composition of the group, and the response of the group.

Even though Judge Renfrew's sentencing is relatively unique, there is a tendency for judges to impose fines, as opposed to criminal sanctions, upon those who have committed white-collar crimes. Do you think this tendency is justified or desirable? Should white-collar offenders, who otherwise are charitable and law-abiding citizens, be given sentences

---

** Charles B. Renfrew, "The Paper Label Sentences: An Evaluation," 86 *Yale Law Journal* 590 (1977).

other than the traditional forms of punishment? The defense counsel generally argues that "they have suffered enough." Have they? Or is this not the point?

WHISTLE-BLOWING

What happens to those employees who blow the whistle on dangerous or improper business behavior? In the past, employees who exposed illegal activities frequently found themselves disciplined or even fired by their employers. The states, however, are slowly beginning to extend protection to whistle-blowers.

California, Connecticut, Maine, Michigan, and New York have passed special laws with respect to workers and whistle-blowing. Yet many states uphold the "fire at will" doctrine. Furthermore, companies may use subtle techniques, such as transferring a whistle-blower to a less desirable location or otherwise making his or her work hours miserable. Many whistle-blower sympathizers, therefore, are attempting to change business attitudes toward this type of activity. These sympathizers are attempting to impress upon companies that they can benefit in various ways by avoiding improper and dangerous practices. Costly liability actions by injured workers or consumers can often be avoided when dangerous business practices are eliminated.

Regardless of the movement for greater protection of whistle-blowers, the dilemma still remains. How many working men or women with children to feed and to send through school are willing to risk their jobs, or at the least face subtle types of punishment, in order to expose business behavior that they know is unethical and often quite dangerous? Even though whistle-blowing is more often than not in the public interest, all too often the pressure upon individuals to tolerate or ignore unethical behavior deters workers from "blowing the whistle."

WHAT IS CONSIDERED "ETHICAL BEHAVIOR" CHANGES OVER TIME

Law reflects societal values and, hence, when values change, the law also changes. Since law is a response, however, there is a time lag between any changes in society's values and corresponding changes in the law. Before any change in the law occurs, someone must question the fairness of existing laws. Someone must ask whether those laws represent society's values. It would be a mistake to focus on an understanding of what current laws state without questioning why these laws exist or whether they should exist in their current form.

For example, it was only recently that the commercial bribery of foreign government officials was raised as an ethical issue. It took several scandals involving large payoffs to bring this issue to the forefront. Values in the United States had finally changed sufficiently that Congress felt impelled to pass a law making it illegal, under most circumstances, for any corporate official to offer bribes to foreign government officials for the purpose of obtaining business. Corporate leaders have since complained that such legislation has kept U.S. businesses from competing on an equal footing with the corporations of other countries. They argue that other countries have no such law and that corporate officials (or government officials) of other countries feel no compunction about paying bribes in order to consummate business deals. Yet enough groups concluded that this type of behavior was unethical that Congress was induced to pass a law prohibiting these types of bribes.

Throughout this book we will see how the law has been changed when it was revealed to be in conflict with society's prevailing standards of fairness and justice.

DISCUSSION QUESTIONS

1. Should businesses be concerned with ethics? In other words, should companies have social or ethical goals in addition to profit-making goals?
2. If companies should have goals other than making profits, who in the company should set those goals?
3. Should the decision on who sets the goals depend on the type of business conducted by the company or on the current political and environmental climate?
4. Should ethics be a concern of top management alone, or should it be a shared concern of all employees, distributors, suppliers, and so on?

UNIT II

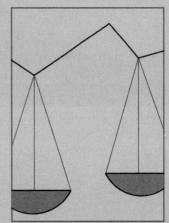

CONTRACTS

7

CONTRACTS
Nature, Form, and Terminology

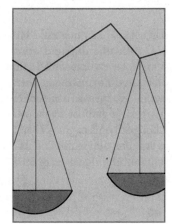

SOME PERSPECTIVES

In the legal environment of business, contracts are one of the most significant bodies of law. Contract law shows to what extent our society allows people to make promises or commitments that are legally binding. It shows what excuses our society will accept for breaking such promises. And it shows what kinds of promises will be considered as being against public policy and therefore legally void.

As a general rule, a promise will be enforced by a court (or damages will be imposed for not keeping the promise) as long as it was made knowingly and voluntarily. Sometimes, however, enforcing a promise will transgress an important public policy. If the promise is against the interests of society as a whole, it will be invalidated. Also, if it was made by a child, or by an insane person, or on the basis of false information, a question will be raised about whether the promise should be enforced. Resolving such questions is the essence of contract law.

Contract law, in effect, governs the relationships between those who make promises to one another. The use of contract principles dates back thousands of years. Very early in history the importance of contracts was recognized and given legal effect. The following chapters will explain how contracts are formed, how they are discharged, and what happens when they are not performed. The rules relating to the formation, discharge, and breach of enforceable promises are called *the law of contracts*.

Society's need of contracts is obvious. The foundation for almost all commercial activity is the contract. The purchase of goods, such as automobiles, is governed by a sales contract; the lease of an apartment or office by a lease agreement; the hiring of people to work for us or to make repairs by service contracts; the sharing of risks on our property by insurance contracts—the list is endless. In short, we could not order our daily activities without contracts.[1] Contract law helps us predict the future because it looks to the future.

Although from state to state the laws concerning certain aspects of contract law may vary, much of the law is based on the common law. In 1932, the American Law Institute compiled the Restatement

---

1. The Soviet Union attempted to eliminate the need for contracts by dispensing with the private ordering of activities. The state required everyone to engage in certain specified activities—work, education, recreation—in the hope of redistributing wealth according to administrative standards and norms. The experiment failed, and Lenin explicitly recognized this when he wrote in 1921, "The private market proved to be stronger than we [thought]. * * * We ended up with ordinary * * * trade." Ultimately, contracts were reintroduced, and contract law was codified along traditional lines. See Loeber, *"Plan and Contract Performance in Soviet Law,"* reprinted in LaFave, *Law in the Soviet Society*, Wayne R. LaFave, ed. Urbana, University of Illinois Press [1965].

of the Law of Contracts. This work is a nonstatutory authoritative exposition of the present law on the subject on contracts. The Restatement is presently in its Second Edition and will be referred to throughout the following contract chapters.

THE FUNCTION OF CONTRACTS

Contract law assures the parties to private agreements that the promises they make will be enforced. Not all promises or obligations are enforceable. Sometimes the promises exchanged create *moral* rather than *legal* obligations. Failure to perform a moral obligation, such as an agreement to take a friend to lunch, does not create a legal liability. Nonperformance of a contract generally does. The promise of a father to pay for the college education of his daughter may be a legal, as well as a moral, question.

Clearly, many promises are kept because of a sense of duty, or because keeping them is in the mutual self-interest of the parties involved, not because the **promisor** (the person making the promise) or the **promisee** (the person to whom the promise is made) are conscious of the rules of contract law. Nevertheless, the rules of contract law are often followed in business agreements in order to avoid potential problems.

By providing procedures for enforcing private agreements, contract law provides an essential condition for the existence of a market economy. Without a legal framework for reasonably assured expectations within which to plan and venture, businesspersons would be able to rely only on the good faith of others. Duty and good faith are usually sufficient, but when price changes or adverse economic factors make it costly to comply with a promise, these elements may not be enough. Contract law is necessary in order to insure compliance with a promise or to entitle the innocent party to some form of relief.

Contract law also provides a foundation upon which more specialized areas of law are built. The sale of goods (Chapters 17–22); the transfer and negotiation of checks, notes, and drafts (Chapters 23–28); the giving of security in goods or land (Chapter 29); the rights of debtors and creditors (Chapter 30); the rights of agents, employees, and their employers (Chapters 32–33); the creation, operation, and ter-

mination of partnerships and corporations (Chapters 35–44); the regulation of trade and monopolies (Chapters 45–50); and the transfer of property (Chapters 51 and 53) all require a basic understanding of contract law.

Since contract law underlies virtually all business relationships, knowledge of it is essential to avoid costly mistakes. Some familiarity with legal thinking can be a valuable asset for anyone dealing with lawyers.

FREEDOM OF CONTRACT AND FREEDOM FROM CONTRACT

As a general rule, the law recognizes everyone's ability to enter freely into contractual arrangements. This recognition is called *freedom of contract*, and this freedom is protected by the U.S. Constitution in Article I, Section 10. But as the character of institutions and society changes, the functions of contract law and its enforcement must also change. Such change can be perceived today in the fact that certain types of agreements are no longer considered valid. For example, illegal bargains, agreements unreasonably in restraint of trade, and contracts made between one party with an inordinate amount of bargaining power and another with little power are generally not enforced. In addition, certain contracts with consumers, as well as certain clauses within those contracts, are not enforceable under the rationale of public policy, fairness, and justice (see Chapter 11 for details). The law of contracts is broadening to include new controls on the manner of contracting and on the allowable terms of agreements. These controls are meant to provide freedom from contract for certain members of society who heretofore may have been forced into making contracts unfavorable to them.

THE BASIC REQUIREMENTS OF A CONTRACT

The many topics that will be discussed in this unit on contracts require an understanding of the basic requirements of a contract and the processes by which one is created. The following list gives a brief description of these requirements. Each will be explained more fully in subsequent chapters.

1. Agreement. An agreement includes an offer and an acceptance. One party must offer to enter into a legal agreement, and another party must accept the terms of the offer.
2. Consideration. Any promises made by parties must be supported by legally sufficient and bargained-for consideration.
3. Contractual capacity. Both parties entering into the contract must have the contractual capacity to do so; they must be recognized by the law to possess characteristics qualifying them as competent parties.
4. Legality. The contract must be made to accomplish some goal that is legal and not against public policy.
5. Reality of assent. Apparent consent of both parties must be genuine.
6. Form. The contract must be in whatever form the law requires, such as in writing.

The first four items given in this list constitute what are formally known as the elements of a contract. The last two are formally known as defenses to the formation or the enforcement of a contract.

NATURE AND TYPES OF CONTRACTS

In order for the detailed elements of a contract to be understood, certain terms and certain types of contracts must be defined. When reading subsequent chapters, refer to the definitions given in this chapter. This effort should enhance and reinforce your understanding of the language of contract law.

DEFINITION OF A CONTRACT

A **contract** is simply any agreement that can be enforced in a court of law or equity. It is formed by two or more parties who agree to perform or refrain from performing some act now or in the future.[2] Generally, contract disputes arise when there is a promise of future performance. A **promise** is an

2. As defined by the American Law Institute, a *contract* is "a promise or a set of promises for the breach of which the law gives a remedy, or the performance of which the law in some way recognizes as a duty." Restatement, Second, Contracts, Section 1.

undertaking that something either will or will not happen in the future. If the contractual promise is not fulfilled, the party who made it is subject to the sanctions of a court of law or equity. That party may be required to pay money damages for failing to perform or, in limited instances, may be required to perform the promised act.

TYPES OF CONTRACTS EXPLAINED

There are numerous types of contracts, and each has a legal significance as to formation, enforceability, or performance (see the *Concept Summary* at the end of this chapter). The various types of contracts are:

1. Bilateral.
2. Unilateral.
3. Express.
4. Implied-in-fact.
5. Quasi-contracts or contracts implied-in-law.
6. Formal.
7. Informal.
8. Executed.
9. Executory.
10. Valid.
11. Voidable.
12. Void.
13. Unenforceable.

In most cases, the best method of explaining each is to compare one type of contract with another. The following section makes these comparisons.

Bilateral versus Unilateral Contracts

Every contract involves at least two parties. The **offeror** is the party making the offer, and the **offeree** is the party to whom the offer is made. The offeror always promises to do or not to do something and thus is also a promisor. Whether the contract is classified as *unilateral* or *bilateral* depends on what the offeree must do to accept the offer and to bind the offeror to a contract. If the offer requires as acceptance only that the offeree promise to perform, the contract formed is called a **bilateral contract.** Hence, a bilateral contract is a "promise for a promise." The exchange of mutual promises (called mutuality of obligation) is the basis of the consideration for the contract and the heart of the formation of a bilateral contract. If the offer is phrased so that the offeree can accept only by complete performance, the contract formed by completion of the act (performance) is called a **unilateral contract.** Hence, a unilateral contract is a "promise for an act."

A problem arises in unilateral contracts when the promisor attempts to revoke the offer after the promisee has begun performance but before performance is completed. Acceptance can occur only upon full performance, and offers are normally revocable until accepted. However, the modern-day view is that the offer becomes irrevocable once performance has begun or has been substantially completed. This does not act as an acceptance but prohibits the offeror from revoking the offer, for a reasonable period of time.

Suppose Ann offers to buy John's sailboat, moored in San Diego, upon delivery to Ann's dock in Newport Beach. John rigs the boat and sets sail. Shortly before his arrival at Newport Beach, John receives a radio message from Ann withdrawing her offer. Ann's offer is for a unilateral contract, and only John's delivery of the sailboat at her dock is an acceptance. Ordinarily her revocation would terminate the offer, but since substantial performance had been completed by John, under the modern-day view her offer is irrevocable. John can deliver the boat and bind Ann to the contract.

The classic illustration of a unilateral contract is that in which Alan says to Barbara, "If you walk across the Brooklyn Bridge, I'll give you $10." Alan promises to pay only if Barbara walks the entire span of the bridge. Only upon Barbara's complete crossing does she accept Alan's offer to pay $10. If she chooses not to walk at all, there are no legal consequences.

The following case illustrates the need for the exchange of mutual promises for the creation of a bilateral contract.

BLEECHER v. CONTE

Supreme Court of California,
1981.
173 Cal.Rptr. 278, 626 P.2d
1051.

BACKGROUND AND FACTS *The plaintiffs entered into an agreement to purchase land from the defendant, Conte. Conte refused to proceed with the transaction, and the buyers brought suit for specific performance. Conte defended her actions by asserting that the agreement lacked mutuality of obligation and imposed no legal obligation on the buyers. The trial court held a bilateral contract was formed and granted the plaintiffs a decree for specific performance.*

BIRD, Chief Justice.
*   *   *   *

The first issue to be decided is whether the agreement lacked mutuality of obligation and, therefore, was unenforceable. A bilateral contract is one in which there are mutual promises given in consideration of each other. The promises of each party must be legally binding in order for them to be deemed consideration for each other.

If a party is not assuming a legal duty in making a promise, the agreement is not binding as a bilateral contract. This court expressed the rule in *Mattei v. Hopper:* "[w]hen the parties attempt *   *   * to make a contract where promises are exchanged as the consideration, the promises must be mutual in obligation. In other words, for the contract to bind either party, both must have assumed some legal obligations. Without this mutuality of obligation, the agreement lacks consideration and no enforceable contract has been created.
*   *   *   *

In the present case, the seller contends that the buyers' promise was illusory since they assumed no real obligations under the agreement. Therefore, she argues, the contract lacked mutuality of obligation and was unenforceable. She claims that the buyers could decline to have a tract map prepared or to obtain city approval for development, renege on the agreement, and still get back their $1,000 escrow deposit.
*   *   *   *

There is one fatal flaw in the seller's argument that this contract lacked mutuality of obligation. She overlooks the buyers' promise to "do everything in their power to expedite the recordation of the final map" and to "proceed with diligence."

The present contract would have no value to the buyers if they did not proceed in good faith and obtain the necessary reports and approvals. The buyers do not have an unfettered right to cancel their contract or ignore their contractual obligations. More importantly, the buyers expressly promised to diligently pursue their obligations and to refrain from withholding their approval unreasonably.
* * * *

In light of the express and implied obligations to proceed in good faith, the buyers here had an enforceable obligation to proceed diligently with the recordation of the tract map and to obtain the city's approval to develop the property. * * *
* * * *

This land sale contract does not lack mutuality of obligation. The buyers are under an express duty to proceed diligently and to refrain from unreasonably denying approval. They have an implied duty to proceed in good faith and to act fairly.
* * * *

The trial court's award of specific performance to the buyers was upheld.   **DECISION AND REMEDY**

Express versus Implied Contracts

An **express contract** is one in which the terms of the agreement are fully and explicitly stated in words, oral or written. A signed lease for an apartment or a house is an express written contract. If a classmate calls you on the phone and agrees to buy your textbooks from last semester for $50, an express oral contract has been made.

A contract that is implied from the conduct of the parties is called an **implied-in-fact contract,** or an implied contract. Implied-in-fact contracts differ from express contracts in that the *conduct* of the parties, rather than their words, creates and defines the terms of the contract. For example, suppose you need a tax consultant or an accountant to fill out your tax return this year. You look through the phone book and find both an accountant and a tax consultant at an office in your neighborhood, so you drop by to see them. You go into the office and explain your problem, and they tell you what their fees are. The next day you return, giving the secretary all of the necessary information such as cancelled checks, W-2 copies, and so on. You say nothing expressly to the secretary; rather, you walk out the door. Nonetheless, you have entered into an implied-in-fact contract to pay the tax consultant and accountant the usual and reasonable fees for their services. The contract is implied by your conduct and by the consultants' conduct. They expect to be paid for preparing your tax return. By bringing

in all of the necessary records that will allow them to do so, you have implied an intent to pay them for their work.

Summary of Steps Necessary for an Implied-in-Fact Contract   The following three steps establish an implied-in-fact contract:

1.   The plaintiff furnished some service or property.
2.   The plaintiff expected to be paid for that service or property and the defendant knew or should have known that payment was expected (by using the objective theory of contracts test).
3.   The defendant had a chance to reject the services or property and did not.

Objective Theory of Contracts   The intent or apparent intent to enter into an express or implied-in-fact contract is of prime importance in the formation of the contract. This intent is determined by what is called the **objective theory of contracts,** not by the personal or subjective intent, or belief, of a party. This is illustrated by the previous tax preparation example. The theory is that a party's intention to enter into a contract is judged by outward, objective facts as interpreted by a **reasonable offeree** (one to whom the offer is being made), rather than by the party's own secret, subjective intentions. Objective facts include: (1) what the party said when entering into the contract, (2) how the party acted or appeared, and (3) the circumstances surrounding the transaction.

Courts need verifiable evidence in order to determine whether a contract has been made, so they usually rely only on objective factors when passing judgment on a contract dispute. Using this approach, they often determine that the parties have entered into contracts that are *implied-in-fact.* In other words, courts examine all the objective facts, conduct, and circumstances surrounding a particular transaction in order to determine if the parties have made a contract.

The following case illustrates a court's use of the objective theory of contracts, reviewing the conduct and circumstances surrounding a transaction in order to determine whether an express or implied-in-fact contract exists.

MOORE v. KUEHN

Missouri Court of Appeals, 1980.
602 S.W.2d 713.

BACKGROUND AND FACTS   *When a fire damaged the building of James and Margaret Kuehn, George Moore was contacted to submit a written estimate for the necessary repair work. When Moore submitted a written proposal of $7,600 to the Kuehns, James Kuehn told him that he, Kuehn, wanted to look over the proposal more closely before signing it. Kuehn, however, told Moore that "the roof ought to be fixed, so get on it." Moore proceeded to complete all the repairs suggested in the proposal and also requested on several occasions that Kuehn sign the written proposal. Kuehn advanced numerous reasons for not signing the proposal, and hence the proposal was never signed. When the insurer settled with the Kuehns for $12,069.48, George Kuehn wrote out checks to the three companies involved in the rebuilding. Kuehn subsequently informed Moore that, as a result of insufficient funds, he could pay Moore only $5,500. Moore filed suit, and the trial court, sitting without a jury, held that a contract existed between Moore and the Kuehns and awarded Moore $2,531. The defendants, James and Margaret Kuehn, claimed no contract was ever entered into and appealed.*

STEPHAN, Presiding Judge.
*   *   *   *

It is a well-settled rule of law that a written offer may be orally accepted.   *   *   *
The result is an oral contract embodying the terms of the writing. In light of this rule, we believe there can be little doubt that Moore and Kuehn entered into an express oral contract for the repair of the roof. Upon receiving the written proposal, Kuehn told Moore, "The roof ought to be fixed, so get on it." The only offer made to Kuehn at that point, and the only offer to which his acceptance could conceivably have had reference, was Moore's proposal. The terms of that writing therefore necessarily controlled the oral contract established at that point.

We find, furthermore, that Kuehn's silent acquiescence in and acceptance of Moore's performance of the other repair work listed in the proposal constituted an implied acceptance of the contract as it related to those items. The manifestation of acceptance of an offer need not be made by the spoken or written word; it may also come through the offeree's conduct or failure to act.   *   *   *

"Frequently, services are rendered under circumstances such that the party benefited thereby knows the terms on which they are being offered. If he receives the benefit of the services in silence, when he had a reasonable opportunity to express his rejection of the offer, he is assenting to the terms proposed and thus accepts the offer.

*   *   *   *

Generally speaking, an offeree need make no reply to offers, and his silence and inaction cannot be construed as an assent to the offer; but the relations between the parties or other circumstances may have been such as to have justified the offeror in expecting a reply, and, therefore, in assuming that silence indicates assent to his proposal. Such cases may be thus classified:

(1) Where the offeree with reasonable opportunity to reject offered goods or services takes the benefit of them under circumstances which would indicate to a reasonable man that they were offered with the expectation of compensation."

*   *   *   *

*   *   * In the instant case, the evidence indicates that the writing was the sole offer made by Moore to Kuehn; that Kuehn was aware of the terms of that offer; that he instructed Moore to complete one of the items proposed; that he subsequently permitted Moore, without objection, to complete all the work proposed in the writing and in fact cooperated with him in one facet of the job; and that appellants accepted the benefit of Moore's performance. There is no evidence that appellants either questioned the necessity of any of the proposed repairs or contested the proposed contract price. In view of this evidence, we do not believe that Kuehn's contemporaneous refusals to sign the proposal *   *   * were such that they indicated that he did not in fact impliedly assent to Moore's full performance in accordance with the proposal. We therefore believe that the trial court was justified in finding a contract to have existed between the litigants for the repairs listed in the proposal. *   *   *

*   *   *   *

The Court of Appeals affirmed the trial court's decision that there was a contract and the judgment against James and Margaret Kuehn in the amount of $2,531, plus interest.

DECISION AND REMEDY

This case illustrates the objective theory of contract formation. The court will look to what was said, the conduct of the parties, and the surrounding circumstances when a party argues that there was no intent to form a contract.

COMMENTS

Quasi-Contracts, or Contracts Implied-in-Law

Quasi-contracts, or **contracts implied-in-law,** should be distinguished from contracts *implied-in-fact.* Quasi-contracts, as their name suggests, are not true contracts. They arise in order to achieve justice rather than from a mutual agreement between the parties. A quasi-contract is imposed on the parties in order to avoid *unjust enrichment.* The doctrine of unjust enrichment holds that people should not be allowed to profit or enrich themselves inequitably at the expense of others. The doctrine is equitable rather than contractual in nature.

The quasi-contract is, in essence, a legal fiction. It is based neither on an expressed promise by the defendant to pay for the benefit received nor on conduct of the defendant implying such a promise. Indeed, the recipient of such a benefit (the defendant) not only has not solicited it but often may be unaware that it has been conferred.

The contract implied-in-fact is a true contract. The parties have expressed their agreement to its terms by their conduct. The only way a contract implied-in-fact differs from an express contract is in its lack of express words or writings. In contrast, a contract implied-in-law (a quasi-contract) exists in the absence of both words and conduct from which a court could imply that a contract had been formed. Rather, a fictional contract is created by the court for reasons of social policy.

Examples of Quasi-Contracts   Suppose Steve enters into an oral agreement with Diane, agreeing to work with Diane for two years to develop a noise reduction turbine for fixed-wing commercial jets. Diane agrees to pay Steve a "fair share of the profit" derived from the sale of the device. After working six months on the project and making considerable headway, Diane tells Steve she will not pay him anything because the terms of the contract are too indefinite. Diane claims that there is no way to "objectively" determine "fair share of the profit." Assuming Diane is correct, Steve cannot sue on the contract itself, since there is no contract. Instead Steve sues on the theory of quasi-contract for the reasonable value of his services. Obviously, it would be unfair to allow Diane to pay nothing for Steve's work, so the court will imply a quasi-contract. Thus, Diane will be required to pay Steve a fair wage for the six months of work.

In another example, a doctor is driving down the highway on vacation and comes upon Smith lying on the side of the road unconscious. The doctor renders medical aid saving Smith's life. Although the injured, unconscious Smith did not solicit the medical aid and was not aware that the aid had been rendered, Smith received a valuable benefit and the requirements for a quasi-contract have been fulfilled.

A Limitation on the Quasi-Contract   The principle underlying quasi-contractual obligations is based on the notion of "unjust enrichment." Nonetheless, there are situations in which the party obtaining the "unjust enrichment" is not liable. Basically, the quasi-contractual principle cannot be invoked by the party who has conferred a benefit on someone else unnecessarily or as a result of misconduct or negligence. Consider the following example. You take your car to the local car wash and ask to have it run through the washer and to have the gas tank filled. While it is being washed, you go to a nearby shopping center for two hours. In the meantime, one of the workers at the car wash has mistakenly believed that your car is the one that he is supposed to hand wax. When you come back, you are presented with a bill for a full tank of gas, a wash job, and a hand wax. Clearly, a benefit has been conferred on you. But this benefit has been conferred because of a mistake by the car wash employee. You have not received an *unjust* benefit under these circumstances. People cannot normally be forced to pay for benefits "thrust" upon them.

Also, the doctrine of quasi-contract cannot normally be used when there is a contract that covers the area in controversy. For example, Gonzales contracts with Mott to deliver a furnace to a building project owned by Mitchell. Mott goes bankrupt without paying Gonzales. Gonzales cannot collect from Mitchell in quasi-contract, because Gonzales had an existing contract with Mott.

The following case illustrates the philosophy behind the creation and enforcement of a quasi-contract and the limitation of its use when there is an express contract covering the subject matter on which the quasi-contractual claim rests.

INDUSTRIAL LIFT TRUCK v. MITSUBISHI INTERNATIONAL COROPRATION

Appellate Court of Illinois, First District, Fourth Division, 1982.
432 N.E.2d 999.

BACKGROUND AND FACTS   *Industrial Lift, the plaintiff, sells and services fork-lift trucks. The defendant, Mitsubishi International Corporation, is the United States distributor of fork-lift trucks. In 1973 Industrial entered into a deal with Mitsubishi whereby the plaintiff would purchase fork-lift trucks from the defendant and use its best efforts to sell the trucks. Under the dealership agreement, the plaintiff was required to service the trucks it sold. In 1976, the original agreement was terminated and replaced by a new agreement, which stated that the plaintiff would use its best efforts to service and sell the defendant's product. A pertinent part of the agreement allowed the defendant to terminate the agreement without just cause by giving ninety days' notice.*

From 1973 to 1977, the plaintiff allegedly became the nation's largest dealer in the product. The plaintiff's success was attributed to its "great expenditures of time, effort, and money," among which were expenditures that went toward design changes in the defendant's product. These changes were made in order to adapt the Japanese product to the American market. The defendant did not request these changes, but it did eventually incorporate the changes into the products it sold to other dealers.

In 1978, the defendant terminated the dealership agreement with the plaintiff. The plaintiff tried to recover for the benefits conferred upon the defendant by the plaintiff's design changes under quasi-contract principles. The plaintiff's action in quasi-contract was dismissed.

LINN, Justice.
*   *   *   *

A contract implied in law, or a quasi-contract, is fictitious and arises by implication of law wholly apart from the usual rules relating to contract. *   *   * Quasi-contractual claims involving services usually arise when there is no contract, either express or implied, between the parties. One party performs a service that benefits another. The benefiting party has not requested the service but accepts the benefit. Circumstances indicate that the services were not intended to be gratuitous. As a result, the law will sometimes impose a duty on the benefiting party to pay for the services rendered despite the lack of a contract. *   *   *

Difficulties arise with quasi-contractual claims when there is an express contract between the parties. The general rule is that no quasi-contractual claim can arise when a contract exists between the parties concerning the same subject matter on which the quasi-contractual claim rests.
*   *   *   *

In the present case, plaintiff obviously made the design changes with a view to being compensated pursuant to the contract terms. By its own admission, the design changes allowed plaintiff to become one of the nation's largest dealers in defendant's product. When the changes were made, plaintiff knew the risk involved. It knew the contract could be terminated as it was terminated, and thus knew when it made the changes that it might not be compensated under the contract to the extent it hoped to be compensated. Now that a situation plaintiff knew could occur has occurred, plaintiff seeks to shift a risk it assumed in light of the contract to defendant. In essence, plaintiff is seeking to use quasi-contract as a means to circumvent the realities of a contract it freely entered into.
*   *   *   *

The contract defined the entire relationship of the parties with respect to its general subject matter—the sale and servicing of defendant's products. Plaintiff's attempt here to bring a quasi-contract action is nothing more than an attempt to unilaterally amend the agreement in a manner prohibited by the agreement. In such circumstances, the benefit received by defendant can hardly be considered unjust. *   *   * Defendant had a right to assume that the contract defined the entire relationship of the parties with respect to all matters related to defendant's product. Defendant had a right to assume, absent a valid amendment to the agreement, that it should not have to compensate plaintiff for any acts done in relation to the subject matter of the contract except pursuant to the contract terms.
*   *   *   *

The specific contract barred the plaintiff's action in quasi-contract and the court held that the plaintiff's actions in quasi-contract were properly dismissed.   **DECISION AND REMEDY**

Formal versus Informal Contracts

Formal contracts are contracts that require a special form or method of creation (formation) to be enforceable. They include: (1) contracts under seal, (2) recognizances, (3) negotiable instruments, and (4) letters of credit.[3] **Contracts under seal** are for-

---

3. Restatement, Second, Contracts, Section 6.

malized writings with a special seal attached.[4] The significance of the seal has eroded, although about ten states require no consideration when a contract is under seal. (See Chapter 9 for details.) A **recognizance** is an acknowledgment in court by a person that he or she will pay a certain sum if a certain event occurs. The most common form of recognizance is the surety bond or criminal recognizance bond. Negotiable instruments and letters of credit are special methods of payment that are designed for use in many commercial settings. **Negotiable instruments** include checks, notes, drafts, and certificates of deposit. **Letters of credit** are agreements to pay contingent on the purchaser's receipt of invoices and bills of lading. Negotiable instruments and letters of credit are discussed at length in subsequent chapters.

Informal contracts include all other contracts. (Such contracts are also called *simple contracts*.) No special form is required (except for certain types of contracts that must be in writing), as the contracts are usually based on their substance rather than their form.

Executed versus Executory Contracts

Contracts are also classified according to their stage of performance. A contract that has been fully performed on both sides is called an **executed contract.** A contract that has not been fully performed on either side is called an **executory contract.** If one party has fully performed but the other has not, the contract is said to be executed on the one side and executory on the other, but the contract would still be classified as executory. For example, assume you agree to buy ten tons of coal from the Wheeling Coal Company. Further assume that Wheeling has delivered the coal to your steel mill, where it is now being burned. At this point, the contract is executed on the part of Wheeling and executory on your part. After you pay Wheeling for the coal, the contract will be executed on both sides.

Valid versus Void, Voidable, and Unenforceable Contracts

A **valid contract** is one with the necessary elements to entitle at least one of the parties to enforce it in court. Those elements consist of an offer and an acceptance, supported by legally sufficient consideration, for a legal purpose, and made by parties who have the legal capacity to enter into the contract. Each element is discussed in detail in the following chapters.

A **void contract** is no contract at all. The terms *void* and *contract* are contradictory. A void contract produces no legal obligations by any of the parties. For example, a contract can be void because one of the parties was adjudged by a court to be legally insane or because the purpose of the contract was illegal.

A **voidable contract** is a *valid* contract in which one or both of the parties has the option of avoiding his or her legal obligations. The party having this option can elect to avoid any duty to perform or can elect to *ratify* the contract. If the contract is avoided, both parties are released from it. If it is ratified, both parties must fully perform their respective legal obligations.

As a general rule, but subject to exceptions, contracts made by minors are voidable at the option of the minor. (See Chapter 10 for details.) Contracts entered into under fraudulent conditions are voidable at the option of the defrauded party. (See Chapter 12 for details.) In addition, some contracts entered into because of mistakes, and all contracts entered into under legally defined duress or undue influence are voidable.

An **unenforceable contract** is one that cannot be enforced because of certain legal defenses against it. It is not unenforceable because of failing to satisfy any of the legal requirements of a contract; rather, it is a valid contract rendered unenforceable by some statute or law. For example, a valid contract barred by a statute of limitations is an unenforceable contract.[5] Likewise, oral contracts under the Statute of Frauds are unenforceable. (See Chapter 13 for details.)

---

4. A seal is usually an impression made on a thin wafer of wax firmly affixed to the writing. In some instances, the word *seal* or the letters *L.S.* appear at the end of the document. *L.S.* stands for *locus sigilli* and means "the place for the seal."

---

5. A statute of limitations prevents a party from suing on a contract after a certain period of time has elapsed.

CONCEPT SUMMARY: Classifications of Contracts	
CLASSIFICATIONS	**TYPES AND DEFINITIONS**
Formation	1. Bilateral—A promise for a promise.
	2. Unilateral—A promise for an act (acceptance is completed by performance of the act).
	3. Express—Formed by words (oral, written, or a combination).
	4. Implied-in-Fact—Formed by conduct of the parties.
	5. Implied-in-Law (Quasi-contract)—Imposed by law to prevent unjust enrichment.
	6. Formal—Requires a special form for creation.
	7. Informal—Requires no special form for creation.
Enforceability	1. Valid—It has the necessary contractual elements of offer and acceptance, consideration, parties with capacity, and it is made for a legal purpose.
	2. Voidable—One party has the option of avoiding or enforcing the contractual obligation.
	3. Void—No contract exists or there is a contract without legal obligations.
	4. Unenforceable—A contract exists, but it cannot be enforced because of a legal defense.
Performance	1. Executed—A fully performed contract.
	2. Executory—A contract not fully performed.

QUESTIONS AND CASE PROBLEMS

1. Suppose Felix, a local businessman, is a good friend of Miller, the owner of a local candy store. Every day at his lunch hour Felix goes into Miller's candy store and usually spends about five minutes looking at the candy. After examining Miller's candy and talking with Miller, Felix usually buys one or two candy bars. One afternoon, Felix goes into Miller's candy shop, looks at the candy, picks up a $1 candy bar and, seeing that Miller is very busy at the time, waves the candy bar at Miller without saying a word and walks out. Is there a contract? If so, classify it within the categories presented in this chapter.

2. Mary is a minor, age sixteen. By letter, Mary offers to buy John's bicycle for $100. John, an adult, accepts by telegram. Mary pays John $100, and John delivers the bicycle to Mary. How would this contract be classified, and what is the legal effect on Mary?

3. James is confined to his bed. He calls a friend who lives across the street and offers to sell her his watch next week for $100. If his friend wishes to accept, she is to put a red piece of paper in her front window. The next morning, she places a red piece of paper in her front window. Is the contract formed bilateral or unilateral? Explain.

4. Air Advertising employed Red, a World War II flying ace, to fly its advertisements above Long Island Sound beaches. Burger Baby restaurants engaged Air Advertising to fly an advertisement above the Connecticut beaches. The advertisement offered $1,000 to any person who could swim from the Connecticut beaches to Long Island across Long Island Sound in less than a day. On Saturday, October 10, at 10:00 a.m., Red flew a sign above the Connecticut beaches that read: "Swim across the Sound and Burger Baby pays $1,000." Upon seeing the sign, Davison dove in. About four hours later, when he was about halfway across the Sound, Red flew another sign over the

Sound that read: "Burger Baby revokes." Is there a contract between Davison and Burger Baby? Can Davison recover anything?

5. Susan contacts Joe and makes the following offer: "When you finish mowing my yard, I'll pay you $25." Joe responds by saying, "I accept your offer." Is there a contract? Is it a bilateral or unilateral contract? What is the legal significance of the distinction?

6. Sosa Crisan, an eighty-seven-year-old widow of Romanian origin, collapsed while shopping at a local grocery store. The Detroit police took her to the Detroit city hospital. She was admitted, and she remained there fourteen days. Then she was transferred to another hospital, where she died some eleven months later. Crisan had never regained consciousness after her collapse at the local grocery store. After she died, the city of Detroit sued her estate to recover the expenses of both the ambulance that took her to the hospital and the expenses of her hospital stay. Is there a contract between Sosa Crisan and the hospital? If so, how much can the Detroit hospital recover? [In Re Crisan Estate, 362 Mich. 569, 107 N.W.2d 907 (1961)]

7. On April 1, 1969, McLouth Steel Corporation entered into a contract with Jewell Coal and Coke Company under which Jewell agreed to supply all McLouth's coal requirements for the next thirty years. The contract mentioned no specific quantities. The price was set at $14.25 a ton for the first six months and was subject to an escalation clause whereby in each subsequent six months the original price would be increased by the cost increases encountered by Jewell. Ten years later Jewell found that even with those cost increases, the price it could charge McLouth was far less than the price it could receive in the open market. Jewell therefore stopped shipping coal. Is the contract executory or nonexecutory on the ground of indefiniteness? [McLouth Steel Corp. v. Jewell Coal and Coke Co., 570 F.2d 594 (6th Cir. 1978)]

8. Engelcke Manufacturing, Inc. planned to design and manufacture "Whizball," an electronic game. Engelcke asked Eaton to design the electronic schematic for the game. Engelcke told Eaton that he would be paid for the reasonable value of his services but no written contract was signed. Eaton had worked on the project for eleven months. Upon completion, Engelcke contends there was an express contract; Eaton contends it was an implied-in-fact contract. Who is correct? [Eaton v. Engelcke Mfg., Inc., 681 P.2d 1312 (Wash.App. 1984)]

8

CONTRACTS
Agreement

Essential to any contract is an **agreement;** that is, an offer must be made by one party and accepted or assented to by the other party. The agreement does not necessarily have to be in writing. Both parties, however, must exhibit what is called a manifestation of assent to the same bargain.[1] If the agreement is supported by legally sufficient consideration,[2] is not illegal,[3] and is entered into freely by parties with contractual capacity,[4] a valid contract is formed, generally creating enforceable rights and duties between the parties.

A contract must include the following terms, either expressed in, or capable of reasonable implication from, the agreement:

1. Identification of the parties.
2. Identification of the object or subject matter of the contract (also quantity, where appropriate), with specific identification of such items as goods, services, and land.
3. The consideration to be paid.
4. The time of performance.

If these terms are expressly stated in the agreement, the contract is definite. Although terms and intent are equally important in both the offer and the acceptance, for simplicity's sake we will discuss the relevant laws only in terms of the offer.

MUTUAL ASSENT

Ordinarily, mutual assent is evidenced by an **offer** and an **acceptance.** One party offers a certain bargain to another party, who then accepts that bargain. The parties are required to manifest to each other their **mutual assent** to the same bargain.[5] Because words often fail to convey the precise meaning intended, the law of contracts generally adheres to the objective theory of contracts, as discussed in Chapter 7. Under this theory, a party's words and conduct are held to mean whatever a reasonable person in the offeree's position would think they mean. The

---

1. Under early English and American law, many contracts were not enforced unless they complied with rigid legal standards requiring a writing and in many cases a seal or impression made on wax, which was firmly affixed to the writing. Today, some contracts must still be in writing (see Chapter 13). The seal has been almost entirely done away with. [UCC 2–203]
2. See Chapter 9.
3. See Chapter 11.
4. See Chapter 10.

---

5. Restatement, Second, Contracts, Section 22.

125

court will give words their usual meaning even if "it were proved by twenty bishops that [the] party * * * intended something else."[6]

REQUIREMENTS OF THE OFFER

The parties to a contract are the **offeror,** the one who makes an offer or proposal to another party, and the **offeree,** the one to whom the offer or proposal is made. An **offer** is a promise or commitment to do or refrain from doing some specified thing in the future. Three elements are necessary for an offer to be effective:

1. There must be a *serious and objective intention* by the offeror to become bound by the offer.
2. The terms of the offer must be reasonably *certain*, or *definite*, so that the parties and the court can ascertain the terms of the contract.
3. The offer must be communicated to the offeree.

Once an effective offer has been made, the offeree has the power to accept the offer. If the offeree accepts, the offer is translated into an agreement (and thus into a contract if other essential elements are present).

Intention

The first element for an effective offer to exist is a serious and objective intent on the part of the offeror. But serious intent is not determined by the *subjective* intentions of the offeror. It is determined instead by whether the offer created a *reasonable* impression in the mind of the offeree. Objective intent is therefore determined from the words and actions of the parties as interpreted by a reasonable person. Offers made in obvious anger, jest, or undue excitement do not meet the serious and objective intent test. Since these offers are not effective, an offeree's acceptance would not create an agreement.

For example, you and three classmates ride to school each day in Jane's new automobile, which has a market value of $8,000. One cold morning the four of you get into the car, but Jane cannot get the car started. She yells in anger, "I'll sell this car to anyone for $500!" You drop $500 in her lap. Given these facts, a reasonable person, taking into consideration Jane's frustration and the obvious difference in value between the car and purchase price, would declare that her offer was not made with serious and objective intent and that you do not have an agreement.

The concept of intention can be further explained by distinguishing between offers and various kinds of non-offers. Consider the following:

1. Expressions of opinion.
2. Statements of intention.
3. Preliminary negotiations.
4. Certain kinds of advertisements, catalogues, and circulars.

In each of these cases, an offer (as legally defined) probably does not exist, because the legal requirement of intention is probably not met.

Expressions of Opinion An expression of opinion is not an offer. It does not evidence an intention to enter into a binding agreement. Hawkins took his son to McGee, a doctor, and asked McGee to operate on the son's hand. McGee said the boy would be in the hospital three or four days and that the hand would *probably* heal within a few days afterward. The son's hand did not heal for a month, but the father did not win a suit for breach of contract. The court held that McGee did not make an offer to heal the son's hand in three or four days. He merely expressed an opinion as to when the hand would heal.[7]

Statements of Intention If Henry says "I *plan* to sell my stock in Ryder Systems for $150 per share," a contract will not be created if Fred "accepts" and tenders the $150 per share for the stock. Henry has merely expressed his intention to enter into a future contract for the sale of the stock. No contract is formed, because a reasonable person would conclude that Henry was only *thinking* about selling his stock, not promising to sell, even if Fred accepts

6. Learned Hand in Hotchkiss v. National City Bank of N.Y., 200 F. 287 (2d Cir. 1911), aff'd 231 U.S. 50, 34 S.Ct. 20 (1913).

7. Hawkins v. McGee, 84 N.H. 114, 146 A. 641 (1929).

and tenders the $150 per share. Henry is stating a future contractual intent, not a present one.

Preliminary Negotiations A request or invitation to negotiate is not an offer. It only expresses a willingness to discuss the possibility of entering into a contract. Included are statements such as "Will you sell Blythe Estate?" or "I wouldn't sell my car for less than $1,000." A reasonable person in the offeree's position would not conclude that these statements evidence an intention to enter into a binding obligation. Likewise, when construction work is done for the government and private firms, contractors are invited to submit bids. The *invitation* to submit bids is not an offer, and a contractor does not bind the government or private firm by submitting a bid. (The bids that the contractors submit *are* offers, however, and the government or private firm can bind the contractor by accepting the bid.)

Consider whether the court was dealing with preliminary negotiations or an actual offer in the following case.

BACKGROUND AND FACTS *Defendant Johnson is the owner of real estate. Johnson's real estate agent wrote a letter to plaintiff Mellen, indicating that certain seashore property that Mellen had expressed an interest in purchasing would be placed on the market. The letter further indicated that several other people who had expressed an interest in purchasing the property were also being informed at the same time before the property went on the open market. Mellen interpreted the letter as an "offer" and promptly "accepted." Mellen, thinking he was entitled to buy the property, sued Johnson to force her to go through with the sale (specific performance). The trial court upheld Mellen's position that the letter was an offer.*

MELLEN v. JOHNSON
Supreme Judicial Court of
Massachusetts, Essex, 1948.
322 Mass. 236, 76 N.E. 2d 658.

WILKINS, Justice.
*   *   *   *

The defendant is the owner of two parcels of land with the buildings thereon at 74 and 75 Willow Road, Nahant. On March 27, 1947, the defendant's son-in-law, Edward Hicks, who was her agent to sell the property, wrote the following letter to the plaintiff's brother-in-law, who was his agent as to this subject matter: "You will perhaps remember that we spent a pleasant visit *   *   * on the break water at Nahant last summer. On that occasion either you or your brother-in-law expressed an interest in my Mother's property which is the Johnson cottage. I told you that I would contact you if and when my Mother expressed a desire to dispose of her property. Well, that time has arrived and her health is such that she will not be able to open the cottage this year. She has, therefore, decided that it will be best to place the property on the market, however, before turning it over to the real estate agents, I am writing the several people, including yourself, who have previously expressed an interest in the property. Our price is $7,500. This property consists of the lot and cottage on the south side of Willow Road, and also a very large plot on which a two car garage is situated running from Willow Road clear through the block to the next street. Just how much property there is in this tract, I cannot tell you at the moment. I can say, however, that it is a large tract which would offer possibilities for further building. The price of $7,500 would include the entire property on both sides of Willow Road. The cottage is in very good condition. There are three rooms downstairs with a large entry hall, and a sun porch, also three good sized bedrooms upstairs, with bath. Hardwood floors throughout, hot water, heat and is suitable for all year round occupancy if desired. The oil burner is in good condition and the house is far better built than most of the new constructions of today. *I will be interested in hearing from you further if you have any interest in this property, for as I said before, I am advising those who have asked for an opportunity to consider it.* [Emphasis added.] I might just add that the property would be available for immediate occupancy. By that I mean within such time as the present furnishings could be removed and title transferred."

On March 28 Hicks received a telegram from the plaintiff's brother-in-law which read: "We are interested in your offer. Will look at house tomorrow. Communicate with you first of week." On the same day shortly after the telegram was received Hicks telegraphed the plaintiff's brother-in-law: "Have heard from three interested buyers tonight which means we must accept highest bid for Nahant property. Suggest you wire or phone us Elmsford N.Y. 7292 Saturday your best offer on cash basis." Before this was received the plaintiff's brother-in-law telegraphed Hicks: "I accept your offer on Nahant cottage. Letter in mail."

It is unnecessary to recount the subsequent communications of the parties other than to state that the defendant entered into a written contract to sell the property to someone other than the plaintiff. This sale has not been completed pending this suit.

*   *   *   *

The letter of March 27 was not an offer. It expressed "a desire to dispose of" the property. It announced that the agent was "writing the several people, including yourself, who have previously expressed an interest in the property." Its conclusion, in part, was "I will be interested in hearing further from you if you have any interest in this property, for as I said before, I am advising those who have asked for an opportunity to consider it." The recipient could not reasonably understand this to be more than an attempt at negotiation. It was a mere request or suggestion that an offer be made to the defendant.

DECISION AND REMEDY   *The trial court was found to be in error; its decision was reversed. The court of appeals decided that the letter was merely a negotiation, and Johnson was not required to sell the property to Mellen.*

COMMENTS   *It is often difficult to distinguish an actual "offer" from preliminary negotiations, or what lawyers call "invitations to offer." The key distinction between preliminary negotiations and offers is that an offer is a definite commitment, whereas a preliminary negotiation is noncommital.*

Advertisements, Catalogues, and Circulars In general, advertisements, mail order catalogues, price lists, and circular letters are treated not as offers to contract but as invitations to negotiate. Suppose Loeser & Co. advertises a used paving machine. The ad is mailed to hundreds of firms and reads, "Used Case Construction Co. paving machine. Builds curbs and finishes cement work all in one process. Price $11,250 firm." If Star Paving calls Loeser and says, "We accept your offer," no contract is formed. Any reasonable person would conclude that Loeser was not promising to sell the paving machine but rather that it was soliciting offers to buy it.

The same result occurs when a new car dealership advertises, "New Lincoln Continentals; loaded with options; now only $13,899." The ad is intended to draw customers who will make offers. If Bill Weinberg goes to the dealership with a check for $13,899, the dealership is not legally bound to sell the Lincoln. (However, federal and state statutes prohibit "false and misleading advertising" that is intended solely to draw customers to the retail outlet.)

Most advertisements are not offers, because the seller never has an unlimited supply of goods. If advertisements were offers, then everyone who "accepted" after the retailer's supply was exhausted could sue for breach of contract. Suppose you put an ad in the classified section of your local newspaper offering to sell a guitar for $75. Suppose further that seven people called and "accepted" your "offer" before you could remove the ad from the newspaper. If the ad were truly an offer, you would be bound on seven contracts to sell your guitar. But since initial advertisements are treated as *invitations* to make offers, rather than as offers, you would have seven offers to choose from, and you could accept the best one without incurring any liability for the six you reject.

Price lists are another form of invitation to negotiate or trade. The price list of the seller is not an offer to sell at that price. It merely invites the buyer to offer to buy at that price. As further evidence of the lack of intent to offer to sell at the listed prices, the words "prices subject to change" are usually printed somewhere on the price list.

Although most advertisements and the like are treated as invitations to negotiate, this does not mean that an advertisement can never be an offer. If the advertisement makes a promise so definite in character that it is apparent that the offeror is binding himself or herself to the conditions stated, the advertisement is treated as an offer. This is particularly true when the advertisement solicits performance—

for example, by offering a reward for the capture of a criminal or for the return of a lost article.

Suppose an advertisement states, "To the first five persons in our store at 8:00 A.M. on May 1, we offer to sell Singer Sewing Machines, Model X, at $50." This statement invites an acceptance of terms stated rather than an offer to buy. If you were one of the first five in the store at the time specified, your acceptance creates a contract. Another example is a reward offered in a newspaper for the return of a lost dog. The finder's return of the dog in response to the advertisement creates a unilateral contract, as the reward obviously invited an acceptance, not an offer, from the offeree.

In the following case, the court had to decide whether a newspaper advertisement announcing a "special sale" in a department store should be construed as an offer, the acceptance of which would complete a contract. (Today the Federal Trade Commission has a set of rules governing such ads.)

BACKGROUND AND FACTS *Plaintiff Lefkowitz read a newspaper advertisement offering certain items of merchandise for sale on a first come-first served basis. Plaintiff went to the store twice and was the first person to demand the merchandise and indicate a readiness to pay the sale price. On both occasions, the defendant department store refused to sell the merchandise to the plaintiff, saying that the offer was intended for women only, even though the advertisement was directed to the general public. The plaintiff sued the store for breach of contract, and the trial court awarded him damages.*

LEFKOWITZ v. GREAT MINNEAPOLIS SURPLUS STORE, INC.
Supreme Court of Minnesota, 1957.
251 Minn. 188, 86 N.W.2d 689.

MURPHY, Justice.
*   *   *   *

This case grows out of the alleged refusal of the defendant to sell to the plaintiff a certain fur piece which it had offered for sale in a newspaper advertisement. It appears from the record that on April 6, 1956, the defendant published the following advertisement in a Minneapolis newspaper:

> "Saturday 9 A.M. Sharp
> 3 Brand New
> Fur
> Coats
> Worth to $100.00
> First Come
> First Served
> $1
> Each"

On April 13, the defendant again published an advertisement in the same newspaper as follows:

"Saturday 9 A.M.
2 Brand New Pastel
Mink 3-Skin Scarfs
Selling for $89.50
Out they go
Saturday. Each . . . $1.00
1 Black Lapin Stole
Beautiful,
worth $139.50 . . . $1.00
First Come
First Served"

The record supports the findings of the court that on each of the Saturdays following the publication of the above-described ads the plaintiff was the first to present himself at the appropriate counter in the defendant's store and on each occasion demanded the coat and the stole so advertised and indicated his readiness to pay the sale price of $1. On both occasions, the defendant refused to sell the merchandise to the plaintiff, stating on the first occasion that by a "house rule" the offer was intended for women only and sales would not be made to men, and on the second visit that plaintiff knew defendant's house rules.

*   *   *   *

The defendant contends that a newspaper advertisement offering items of merchandise for sale at a named price is a "unilateral offer" which may be withdrawn without notice. He relies upon authorities which hold that, where an advertiser publishes in a newspaper that he has a certain quantity or quality of goods which he wants to dispose of at certain prices and on certain terms, such advertisements are not offers which become contracts as soon as any person to whose notice they may come signifies his acceptance by notifying the other that he will take a certain quantity of them. Such advertisements have been construed as an invitation for an offer of sale on the terms stated, which offer, when received, may be accepted or rejected and which therefore does not become a contract of sale until accepted by the seller; and until a contract has been so made, the seller may modify or revoke such prices or terms.

*   *   *   *

[However] *   *   * [t]here are numerous authorities which hold that a particular advertisement in a newspaper or circular letter relating to a sale of articles may be construed by the court as constituting an offer, acceptance of which would complete a contract.

The test of whether a binding obligation may originate in advertisements addressed to the general public is "whether the facts show that some performance was promised in positive terms in return for something requested."

The authorities above cited emphasize that, where the offer is clear, definite, and explicit, and leaves nothing open for negotiation, it constitutes an offer, acceptance of which will complete the contract. *   *   *

Whether in any individual instance a newspaper advertisement is an offer rather than an invitation to make an offer depends on the legal intention of the parties and the surrounding circumstances. We are of the view on the facts before us that the offer by the defendant of the sale of the Lapin fur was clear, definite, and explicit, and left nothing open for negotiation. The plaintiff having successfully managed to be the first one to appear at the seller's place of business to be served, as requested by the advertisement, and having offered the stated purchase price of the article, he was entitled to performance on the part of the defendant. We think the trial court was correct in holding that there was in the conduct of the parties a sufficient mutuality of obligation to constitute a contract of sale.

The defendant contends that the offer was modified by a "house rule" to the effect that only women were qualified to receive the bargains advertised. The advertisement contained no such restriction. This objection may be disposed of briefly by stating that, while an advertiser has the right at any time before acceptance to modify his offer, he does not have the right, after acceptance, to impose new or arbitrary conditions not contained in the published offer.

The Supreme Court affirmed the trial court's judgment, awarding the plaintiff the sum of $138.50 ($139.50 for the Lapin stole less the $1 purchase price) in damages for breach of contract against the defendant department store.   **DECISION AND REMEDY**

Other Non-Offer Situations   Sometimes what appears to be an offer is not sufficient to serve as the basis for formation of a contract.

Auctions   In an auction, a seller "offers" goods for sale through an auctioneer. This is not, however, an offer for purposes of contract. The seller is really only expressing a willingness to sell. Unless the terms of the auction are explicitly stated to be *without reserve*, the seller (through the auctioneer) may withdraw the goods at any time before the auctioneer closes the sale by announcement, or by fall of the hammer. This is called an auction with reserve, and is implied in all auctions unless stated clearly to the contrary.[8] At auctions announced "without reserve," the goods cannot be withdrawn and must be sold to the highest bidder.

In an auction with reserve there is no obligation to sell, and the seller may refuse the highest bid. The bidder is actually the offeror. The auctioneer accepts a bid and completes a contract by knocking the hammer. A bidder can retract an offer while the auctioneer sings "going once, going twice, third and last call." If the bid is not withdrawn and the hammer falls, the contract is formed.

Agreements to Agree   Agreements to agree are not contracts and cannot be enforced. Suppose Zahn Consulting gets together with Leon Construction Company to discuss plans for designing a shopping mall. Zahn and Leon agree further to meet in a month and work out the terms of the contract. The agreement to agree "or make a contract at a future time" is not enforceable. There is nothing to enforce in an agreement to agree because the terms have not yet been agreed upon.

Sham Transactions   A sham transaction is entered into by two parties in order to deceive a third person and is unenforceable. For example, a sham transaction might involve the alleged sale or transfer of a house to make one party's net worth appear larger than otherwise. Suppose that Sneed is trying to get a loan to buy a new BMW. In order to increase his unimpressive net worth on paper, he agrees in a personal letter to a close friend to sell his power boat for $50,000 (it's actually worth only about $25,000), and his friend agrees in a letter to pay that much. In filling out his net worth statement, Sneed claims that his boat is worth $50,000, and, if questioned, he can produce a personal letter from his friend to show that that is the price at which it will be sold. Sneed and his friend entered into the sham transaction knowing that they were not actually going to perform their respective obligations. Sneed cannot attempt now to enforce that transaction by requesting payment of $50,000 for his boat.

Definiteness

The second element for an effective offer is the definiteness of its terms. An offer must have reasonably definite terms so that a court can determine if a breach has occurred and can give an appropriate remedy.[9] An offer may invite an acceptance to be worded in such specific terms that the contract is made definite. For example, assume D'Onfro contacts your corporation and offers to sell "from one to ten sheet metal presses for $1,750 each, state number desired in acceptance." Your corporation agrees to buy two presses. If the quantity had not been specified in the acceptance, the contract would be unenforceable because the terms of the contract

---

8.   See UCC 2–328.

9.   Restatement, Second, Contracts, Section 33.

would have been indefinite. But since the acceptance stated that your corporation wanted two presses, the contract is definite and can be enforced.

Is an employment contract that provides for a salary plus "a share of the profits" too vague and indefinite for a court to enforce? The following case tells the plight of a plaintiff, Victor Petersen, who worked first as construction supervisor and then as manager for the Pilgrim Village Company, the defendant.

PETERSEN v.
PILGRIM VILLAGE
Supreme Court of Wisconsin,
1950.
256 Wis. 621, 42 N.W.2d 273.

BACKGROUND AND FACTS   *Petersen was employed by Pilgrim Village for nearly ten years. His contract of employment provided that he was to be paid a stated salary. Petersen claimed that Pilgrim told him when he began work that he would share in the profits of the corporation and promised him repeatedly throughout the term of his employment that he would share in the profits.*

When Petersen left Pilgrim Village, Pilgrim paid him all but $666.67 of his salary for the time he had worked the previous year.

Petersen sued Pilgrim for the back salary of $666.67 and for $20,000, which he declared was his "reasonable" share of corporate profits. Pilgrim agreed to pay Petersen the salary but objected to paying any amount based on Petersen's claim that he was entitled to "a share of the profits." The trial court instructed the jury to award Petersen whatever part of the $20,000 they thought corresponded to "the reasonable value of services" Petersen had rendered to Pilgrim. The jury decided on $8,000. Pilgrim appealed, arguing that the parties had never come to any definite agreement as to what, if any, the percentage of profits was to be. The Supreme Court of Wisconsin reviewed Pilgrim's arguments.

FRITZ, Chief Justice.
*   *   *   *

As stated in Restatement of the Law on Contracts, sec. 32, pp. 40, 41.

"An offer must be so definite in its terms, or require such definite terms in the acceptance, that the promises and performances to be rendered by each party are reasonably certain.
*   *   *   *

As stated in 12 Am.Jur. sec. 70, p. 561, "The general rule is that price is an essential ingredient of every contract for the transfer of property or rights therein or for the rendering of services. Accordingly, an agreement must be definite as to compensation. In order that an executory agreement may be valid, it is generally necessary that the price must be certain or capable of being ascertained from the agreement itself. By this is not meant that the exact amount in figures must be stated in the agreement; however, where that is not the case, the price must, by the terms of the agreement, be capable of being definitely ascertained. An agreement leaving the price for future determination is not binding. *   *   * (p. 562) Although there is some authority to the contrary, a promise to pay a reasonable sum for goods or services is generally held valid. *   *   * On the other hand, a promise to pay a fair share of profits has been held too indefinite to be valid." Varney v. Ditmars, 217 N.Y. 223, 111 N.E. 822, 823, Ann.Cas. 1916B 758 (1916).

In *Varney v. Ditmars*, supra, the employer promised to pay plaintiff $40 a week and "the first of January next year I will close my books and give you a fair share of my profits." The court said:

"The statement alleged to have been made by the defendant about giving the plaintiff and said designer a fair share of his profits is vague, indefinite, and uncertain, and the amount cannot be computed from anything that was said by the parties or by reference to any document, paper, or other transaction. The minds of the parties never met upon any particular share of the defendant's profits to be given the employes or upon any plan by which such share could be computed or determined. The contract so far as it related to the special promise or inducement was never consummated. It was left subject to the will of the defendant or for further negotiation. It is urged that the defendant by the use of the word 'fair,' in referring to a share of his profits, was as certain and definite as people are in the purchase and sale of a chattel when the price is not expressly agreed upon, and that if the agreement in question is declared to be too indefinite and uncertain to be enforced, a similar conclusion must be reached in every case where a chattel is sold without expressly fixing the price therefor. The question whether the words 'fair' and 'reasonable' have a definite and enforceable meaning when used in business transactions is dependent upon the intention of the parties in the use of such words and upon the subject-matter to which they refer. In cases of merchandising and in the purchase and sale of chattels the parties may use the words 'fair and reasonable value' as synonymous with 'market value.' *   *   *

"The contract in question, so far as it relates to a share of the defendant's profits, is not only uncertain, but it is necessarily affected by so many other facts that are in themselves indefinite and uncertain that the intention of the parties is pure conjecture. *   *   * The courts cannot aid parties in such a case when they are unable or unwilling to agree upon the terms of their own proposed contract."
*   *   *   *

Consequently, *   *   * plaintiff's [claim] *   *   * was merely that he was to be paid "some share of the profits," and as the parties never came to any definite agreement as to what that percentage of the profits was to be, the [trial] court erred.

Petersen left the appellate court without any of the $8,000 in "reasonable profits" the trial court jury had awarded him originally. Even assuming Petersen had been offered some share of the profits, the parties never showed that they had come to any definite agreement as to what that percentage of the profits ought to be. Note, however, that the appellate court allowed Petersen a new trial to establish sufficient evidence that he was entitled to payment of "the reasonable value" of any additional services he had rendered to Pilgrim over and above what he had been paid in his actual salary.	**DECISION AND REMEDY**
Because an offer must be definite, a court can determine and award a monetary remedy if the offer is accepted and thus becomes a contract that is subsequently breached. The terms of the agreement forming the contract between the parties must be specific and firm enough for the court to measure which damages are directly related to the breach of the contract in question.	**COMMENTS**

Relaxation of Definiteness under the Uniform Commercial Code Even before the adoption of the Uniform Commercial Code (UCC), courts were reluctant to declare a contract invalid because of the indefiniteness of its terms when both parties manifested a clear intention to enter into the contract. Therefore, the courts inserted reasonable terms wherever possible to resolve ambiguous or missing terms. In some cases this was impossible.

Clearly, in commercial situations contract law is supposed to aid business, not hinder it. For this reason, the UCC has liberalized the requirement of definiteness as to essential terms, although the common law continues to be much stricter in its interpretation.

Even though one or more of its terms are left open, a contract for the sale of *goods* does not fail for indefiniteness, under the UCC, if the parties have clearly intended to make a contract and if a reasonably certain basis exists for giving an appropriate remedy. [UCC 2-204] Some of the ways in which the UCC fills in missing terms are as follows: If no price is stated, or if the price is left open to be agreed on, "the price is a reasonable price at the time for delivery." [UCC 2-305] If no place of delivery is specified, then delivery is to occur at the seller's place of business. [10] [UCC 2-308(a)] If the time for shipment or delivery is not provided for, then the time shall be a reasonable time after the contract is formed. [UCC 2-309] If the time for payment is not specified, then payment is due at the time and place of delivery. [UCC 2-310(a)]

In addition, under the UCC, omitted terms may be supplied by custom and usage in trade and by prior dealings. If the parties have dealt with each other previously, their past conduct may be used to supply the omitted terms. For example, assume Steven's Poultry has purchased spring chickens from Robinson Farms for the last ten years, and the chickens have always been paid for on credit. Steven's Poultry then enters into a contract to buy 150 chickens, but no mention is made of the terms of payment. Because of prior dealings, Steven's may pay on credit, since the understandings of the past may be implied in the current contract.

Indefiniteness may be cured by *partial performance*, that is, by performance that has already begun. Assume Brown-Crummer, Inc., agrees to buy beans at $4 per bushel from Arkansas Grains. Arkansas Grains, however, has four different grades of beans. This is an indefinite contract since its subject matter is insufficiently described. But if Arkansas Grains ships No. 3 beans and Brown-Crummer accepts them, the indefiniteness is cured. This contract becomes enforceable when Brown-Crummer accepts the beans because Brown-Crummer's acceptance (partial performance) identifies the subject matter of the contract. [UCC 2-606]

Output and Requirements Contracts   The UCC also liberalizes the law for validation of output and requirements contracts. [11] **Output contracts** are agreements to sell all production during a specified period to a buyer. **Requirements contracts** are agreements to buy all production needs, or "requirements," during a specified period from a seller. These contracts do not specifically state the quantity of output or requirements at the time of contract formation, but the quantity may be definitely ascertainable after the time of contract formation, within reasonable limits. The courts have a reasonably certain basis for giving an appropriate remedy if either type of contract is breached.

Communication

A third element for an effective offer is communication, resulting in the offeree's knowledge of the offer. One cannot agree to a bargain without knowing that the bargain exists. Suppose Emerman advertises a reward for the return of her lost dog. Baldwin, not knowing of the reward, finds the dog and returns it to Emerman. Baldwin cannot recover the reward because he did not know it was offered. [12]

Rewards   A reward is a unilateral contract because it can be accepted only by performance. An essential element to the reward contract is that the one who claims the reward must have known that it was offered. Otherwise there can be no contract. This rule follows because it is impossible to have an acceptance under contract law unless the offeree knows that the offer exists. The following case is one of the classic reward cases in the common law dealing with the requirement of communication of the offer.

---

10. But if both parties know the goods are elsewhere when the contract is formed, then the place of delivery is the place where the goods are located.

11. UCC 2-306(1): A term which measures the quantity by the output of the seller or the requirements of the buyer means such actual output or requirements as may occur in good faith, except that no quantity unreasonably disproportionate to any stated estimate or to any normal or otherwise comparable prior output or requirements may be tendered or demanded. See also page 156 in Chapter 9.

12. A few states will allow recovery of the reward but not on contract principles. Since Emerman wanted her dog returned, and Baldwin returned it, these few states would allow Baldwin to recover on the basis that it would be unfair to deny him the reward just because he did not know about it.

BACKGROUND AND FACTS   *The Jewish War Veterans of the United States offered a reward of $500 in a newspaper "to the person or persons furnishing information resulting in the apprehension and conviction of the persons guilty of the murder of Maurice L. Bernstein." A day or so after the notice appeared, one of the men suspected in the crime was arrested and the police received information that the other murderer was the "boyfriend" of a daughter of Mary Glover, the plaintiff and claimant in the present case. That evening, the police visited Mary Glover. She provided names and addresses and possible locations where her daughter and the suspect might be found. The suspect was arrested at one of the places suggested by Glover, and all suspects were subsequently convicted of the crime.*

Glover claimed the $500 reward from the Jewish War Veterans, arguing that the information she gave to the police officers led to the arrest and conviction of the murderers. But there was some question as to whether she was entitled to the reward. At the time she gave the information to the police officers, she did not know that any reward had been offered for information leading to the arrest and conviction of the guilty persons. In fact, she did not learn about the reward until several days afterward. The trial court denied Glover the $500 reward. The appellate court reviewed the law of contracts concerning rewards.

GLOVER v. JEWISH
WAR VETERANS OF
THE UNITED STATES,
POST NO. 58

Municipal Court of Appeals for
the District of Columbia, 1949.
68 A.2d 233.

CLAGETT, Associate Judge.

*   *   *   *

The issue determinative of this appeal is whether a person giving information leading to the arrest of a murderer without any knowledge that a reward has been offered for such information by a nongovernmental organization is entitled to collect the reward. The trial court decided the question in the negative and instructed the jury to return a verdict for defendant.

*   *   *   *

We have concluded that the trial court correctly instructed the jury to return a verdict for defendant. While there is some conflict in the decided cases on the subject of rewards, most of such conflict has to do with rewards offered by governmental officers and agencies. So far as rewards offered by private individuals and organizations are concerned, there is little conflict on the rule that questions regarding such rewards are to be based upon the law of contracts.

Since it is clear that the question is one of contract law, it follows that, at least so far as private rewards are concerned, *there can be no contract unless the claimant when giving the desired information knew of the offer of the reward and acted with the intention of accepting such offer* (emphasis added); otherwise the claimant gives the information not in the expectation of receiving a reward but rather out of a sense of public duty or other motive unconnected with the reward. "In the nature of the case," according to Professor Williston, "it is impossible for an offeree actually to assent to an offer unless he knows of its existence." After stating that courts in some jurisdictions have decided to the contrary, Williston adds, "It is impossible, however, to find in such a case [that is, in a case holding to the contrary] the elements generally held in England and America necessary for the formation of a contract. If it is clear the offeror intended to pay for the services, it is equally certain that the person rendering the service performed it voluntarily and not in return for a promise to pay. If one person expects to buy, and the other to give, there can hardly be found mutual assent. These views are supported by the great weight of authority, and in most jurisdictions a plaintiff in the sort of case under discussion is denied recovery."

The American Law Institute in its Restatement of the Law of Contracts follows the same rule, thus: "It is impossible that there should be an acceptance unless the offeree knows of the existence of the offer." The Restatement gives the following illustration of the rule just stated: "A offers a reward for information leading to the arrest and conviction of a criminal. B, in ignorance of the offer, gives information leading to his arrest and later, with knowledge of the offer and intent to accept it, gives other information necessary for conviction. There is no contract."

We have considered the reasoning in state decisions following the contrary rule. Mostly, as we have said, they involve rewards offered by governmental bodies and in general are based upon the theory that the government is benefited equally whether or not the claimant gives the information with knowledge of the reward and that therefore the government should pay in any event. We believe that the rule adopted by Professor Williston and the Restatement and in the majority of the cases is the better reasoned rule and therefore we adopt it. We believe furthermore that this rule is particularly applicable in the present case since the claimant did not herself contact the authorities and volunteer information but gave information only upon questioning by the police officers and did not claim any knowledge of the guilt or innocence of the criminal but only knew where he probably could be located.

DECISION AND REMEDY   *The trial court judgment was affirmed. The Jewish War Veterans did not have to pay the reward to Glover. No contract existed because Glover's performance was not induced by the offer as she had no knowledge of the offer.*

COMMENTS   *In this case, the court indicated that there is some conflict concerning rewards offered by government officers and agencies. Some courts provide a remedy when a government body offers a reward on the theory that the government is benefited equally whether or not the claimant gave it the information while knowing about the reward. The public good is served regardless. Another rationale is that knowledge of government actions is imputed. Whichever theory the courts use, the result is the same—the government pays the reward.*

TERMINATION OF THE OFFER

The communication of an effective offer to an offeree creates a power in the offeree to transform the offer into a binding, legal obligation (a contract). This power of acceptance, however, does not continue forever. It can be terminated by either *action of the parties* or *operation of law*.

Termination by Action of the Parties

The power of the offeree to transform the offer into a binding, legal obligation can usually be terminated by any of the following actions:

1. Revocation of the offer by the offeror.
2. Rejection of the offer by the offeree.
3. Counteroffer by the offeree.

Revocation of the Offer by the Offeror   **Revocation** is the withdrawal of the offer by the offeror. An offer may be revoked by the offeror, even if the offeror promises to keep the offer open, if a revocation is communicated to the offeree before the offeree accepts. Revocation may be accomplished by expressly repudiating the offer (such as "I withdraw my previous offer of October 17") or by acts inconsistent with the existence of the offer, which are made known to the offeree.

The revocation must be communicated to the offeree before acceptance, or the revocation will be ineffective and a valid contract can be formed. The general rule followed by most states is that a revocation is effective only upon actual receipt of the revocation by the offeree or offeree's agent. Therefore, a letter of revocation that is mailed on April 1 and is delivered at the offeree's residence or place of business on April 3 becomes effective on April 3.

Alternatively, communication to the offeree exists if the offeree indirectly discovers that the offer is revoked. This indirect discovery may occur when a third person tells the offeree that the offer has been revoked prior to the offeree's acceptance, or when the offeree learns that the subject matter of the contract has been sold to a third party.

Offers made to the general public may be revoked by communicating a revocation in the same manner that the offer was originally communicated. For example, suppose Macy's offers a $10,000 reward for anyone giving information leading to the apprehension of the persons who burglarized Macy's downtown store. The offer is published in three local papers and in four papers in neighboring communities. In order to revoke the offer, Macy's must publish the revocation in all seven papers for the same number of days as it published the offer. The revocation will then be accessible to the general public, even if some particular offeree does not know about it.

Irrevocable Offers   Although most offers are revocable, certain offers can be made irrevocable. Three such types of **irrevocable offers** deserve discussion. They are:

1. Option contracts.
2. Firm offers under the UCC.
3. Offeree's detrimental reliance on the offer (promissory estoppel).

Option Contracts   As a general rule, offerors may revoke their offers even if they expressly agreed to hold them open for a specified period of time. When an offeror promises to hold an offer open for a *specified* period of time, however, and the offeree pays for the promise (gives consideration), an **option contract** is created. An option contract is a separate contract which takes away the offeror's power to revoke the offer for the period of time specified in the option. If no time is specified, then a reasonable period of time is implied.

For example, suppose Brennan offers to sell one hundred shares of stock in Texas Instruments to Columbus for $189 per share. Brennan promises to keep the offer open for thirty days. After fourteen days Brennan calls Columbus on the telephone and says that the offer is revoked. If Columbus has not given any consideration (say $25 in cash) for the offer up to this time, Brennan may revoke the offer despite his promise to keep it open for thirty days.

But if Columbus has given some consideration for the offer, Brennan must hold it open for the stated thirty days. This particular option contract (for the purchase of common stock) is becoming increasingly popular, and similar options are traded publicly on numerous exchanges.

Death or incompetency of the offeror does not terminate an offer under an option contract, unless the offeror's personal performance is essential to fulfillment of the contract.[13] For example, assume Vendrick executes an option to Carney entitling Carney to purchase Vendrick's hundred-acre ranch in Costa Rica. Carney pays $750 for the option, but before she can exercise it, Vendrick dies. Carney can still exercise the option against Vendrick's estate, since Vendrick is not required to perform the act of conveying the ranch to Carney personally. In sum, option contract rights and duties are not discharged by the death of either party unless performance is of a personal nature—that is, consists of personal services.

Firm Offers   Under the UCC, certain offers may be irrevocable even if no consideration is given. These are called **firm offers**.[14] If a merchant makes a written, signed offer to buy or sell goods and states that the offer is not revocable, the offer cannot be revoked regardless of the lack of consideration. The offer will remain open for the period of time specified in the offer or, if no time is specified, for a reasonable period; but the period of irrevocability without consideration cannot exceed three months. Note the various elements necessary for a firm offer:

1. The offer must be for the purchase or sale of goods.
2. The offer must be made by a merchant dealing in those goods.
3. The offer must be written and signed by the merchant.
4. The offer must give assurance that it will be held open for some period of time.

Detrimental Reliance on the Offer   Increasingly, courts are refusing to allow an offeror to revoke an offer when the offeree has changed position in justifiable reliance on the offer. In such cases, revocation is considered unjust to the offeree. Consider

---

13. Restatement, Second, Contracts, Section 37.
14. UCC 2-205.

an example. Feinberg has worked for Pfeiffer for thirty-five years. Pfeiffer tells her that whenever she quits, she will be paid $150 a month for the rest of her life. There is no indication by Pfeiffer that she should quit now. In reliance upon Pfeiffer's offer, she works for an additional five years. Just before her announced retirement, Pfeiffer gives Feinberg notice that he is withdrawing his $150 per month offer. Can he effectively revoke his offer?

The argument is that he will not be able to do so because Feinberg has been relying on his promise to pay her $150 a month. Had the promise not been made, she would have rearranged her affairs to obtain other retirement funds. This is a case of a detrimental reliance on a promise, which therefore cannot be revoked. This situation is normally called **promissory estoppel.** To **estop** means to bar or impede, or to preclude. Thus, promissory estoppel means that the promisor (the offeror) is barred or prevented from revoking the offer, in this case because the offeree has already changed her actions in reliance on the offer. We will cover the doctrine of promissory estoppel again in Chapter 9.

Another situation causing detrimental reliance on the part of the offeree is when there is *partial performance* by the offeree in response to a *unilateral* offer prior to revocation. The offer of a unilateral contract invites acceptance only by full performance or forbearance; merely promising to perform does not constitute acceptance. Obviously, injustice can result if an offeree expends time and money in partial performance, and then the offeror revokes the offer before performance is complete. Consequently, many courts will not allow the offeror to revoke after the offeree has performed some substantial part of his or her duties.[15] In effect, partial performance renders the offer irrevocable, giving the original offeree reasonable time to complete performance. Of course, when performance is complete, a unilateral contract exists.

The following case deals with whether homeowners effectively revoked their offer to settle in lieu of continuing their lawsuit for negligent construction of their home.

_____

15.   Restatement, Second, Contracts, Section 25.

T. M. COBB CO., INC.
v. SUPERIOR COURT
Supreme Court of California,
1984.
682 P.2d 338 (Cal. 1984).

BACKGROUND AND FACTS   *Sturm and Conrow brought suit for negligent design and construction of their home against T. M. Cobb. Sturm and Conrow mailed a compromise offer of settlement to Cobb but after discovery of additional damages withdrew the offer. T. M. Cobb received notice of Sturm and Conrow's revocation, but shortly thereafter accepted the offer anyway. T. M. Cobb claims the offer was irrevocable and a binding settlement was entered into. Sturm and Conrow claim their offer was effectively revoked. The Superior Court granted the homeowners' revocation and Cobb now brings the suit to have the Superior Court vacate its order in support of the revocation and to award Cobb a valid acceptance of the offer.*

BIRD, Chief Justice.
*   *   *   *

This court must decide whether an offer of compromise *   *   * may be revoked by the offeror prior to its acceptance by the offeree.
*   *   *   *

It is a well-established principle of contract law that an offer may be revoked by the offeror any time prior to acceptance.
*   *   *   *

Real parties [Sturm and Conrow] *   *   * contend that the policy of encouraging settlements would be frustrated by a holding that *   *   * offers are irrevocable. If offers are irrevocable, real parties argue, fewer offers will be made. Accordingly, there will be fewer offers on which to base any settlement. Thus, to promise settlements, real parties argue, offers *   *   * must be revocable.

Real parties are correct that the policy of encouraging settlements is best promoted by making * * * offers revocable. A party is more likely to make an offer * * * if that party knows that the offer may be revised if circumstances change or new evidence develops. Conversely, a party who knows that he or she is strictly bound to the terms of the first offer made may be reluctant to make such an offer for fear of being locked into a position which becomes unfavorable upon the discovery of additional information. If a party is more likely to make a revocable offer, and less likely to make an irrevocable one, then more offers will be made if revocation is permitted. The more offers that are made, the more likely the chance for settlement. Thus, it is apparent that the general contract law principle that offers are revocable until accepted serves * * * the * * * purpose of encouraging settlements.
* * * *

Petitioner's argument that an irrevocable option contract is created lacks merit. Mutual consent—a prerequisite to the existence of the purported irrevocable option contract—is absent.

"It is universally accepted that an option agreement is a contract distinct from the contract to which the option relates, since it does not bind the optionee to perform or enter into the contract upon the terms specified in the option." * * * However, mutual consent of the parties is essential for a contract to exist * * * and "[c]onsent is not mutual, unless the parties all agree upon the same thing in the same sense * * *." * * * "The existence of mutual consent is determined by objective rather than subjective criteria, the test being what the outward manifestations of consent would lead a reasonable person to believe. * * * Accordingly, the primary focus in determining the existence of mutual consent is upon the acts of the parties involved." * * *

In the present case, the parties never agreed that the offer was irrevocable or that they were consenting to an irrevocable option contract. When real parties made the offer there was no indication that the offer was irrevocable.
* * * *

* * * Since real parties properly revoked their offer prior to any acceptance, petitioner could not thereafter accept the offer.
* * * *

Sturm and Conrow's offer to settle in compromise could be revoked, thereby allowing them to continue their suit for negligent construction of their home. **DECISION AND REMEDY**

Rejection of the Offer by the Offeree The offer may be rejected by the offeree, in which case the offer is terminated. Any subsequent attempt by the offeree to accept will be construed as a new offer, giving the original offeror (now the offeree) the power of acceptance. A rejection is ordinarily accomplished by words or conduct evidencing an intent not to accept the offer.

As in the case of revocation of the offer, rejection is effective only when actually received by the offeror or the offeror's agent.

Suppose you offer to sell Procter & Gamble twenty-five tons of linseed oil at 35 cents per gallon. Procter & Gamble could reject your offer by writing or telephoning you, expressly rejecting the offer (per-

haps by saying, "We are sufficiently stocked in linseed oil and do not need any more"). Alternatively, the company could mail your offer back to you, evidencing an intent to reject the offer. Or it could offer to buy the oil at 20.3 cents per gallon, which would operate as a counteroffer, necessarily rejecting the original offer.

Merely inquiring about the offer does not constitute rejection. For example, a friend offers to buy your bicycle for $75. If you respond, "Is this your best offer?" or "Will you pay me $100 for it?" a reasonable person would conclude that you did not reject the offer but merely made an inquiry for further consideration of the offer. You can still accept and bind your friend to the $75 purchase price.

When the offeree merely inquires as to the firmness of the offer, there is no reason to presume that he or she intends to reject it.

Some responses are borderline in nature. For example, if you respond to your friend's offer with, "The price seems low; I'll bet you can do better than that," it could be argued that you are inquiring about the offer or rejecting it.

Counteroffer by the Offeree   A counteroffer is usually a rejection of the original offer and the simultaneous making of a new offer. Suppose Stewart offers to sell his home to Twardy for $70,000. Twardy responds, "Your price is too high. I'll offer to purchase your house for $65,000." Twardy's response is termed a counteroffer, since it terminates Stewart's offer to sell at $70,000 and creates a new offer by Twardy to purchase at $65,000. At common law, the *mirror image* rule requires the offeree's acceptance to match the offeror's offer exactly—to mirror the offer. Any material change in, or addition to, the terms of the original offer automatically terminates that offer and substitutes the counteroffer, which, of course, need not be accepted. The original offeror can, however, accept the terms of the counteroffer and create a valid contract.

Variance in terms between the offer and the offeree's acceptance, violating the **mirror image rule**, has caused considerable problems in commercial transactions. This is particularly true in contracts for the sale of goods where different standardized purchase forms of the seller and buyer are exchanged in the process of offer and acceptance. Seldom do the terms of both purchase forms match each other exactly. This phenomenon has been called the "battle of the forms" because of the problem of whose form will prevail.

Dealing with contracts for the sale of goods, the UCC in Section 2-207 has addressed this problem by providing that a contract is formed if the offeree makes a definite expression of acceptance, even though the terms of the acceptance modify or add to the terms of the original offer.[16] *Between merchants*, the new terms become part of the contract automatically unless:

1.   The original offer expressly required acceptance of its terms.
2.   The new or changed terms materially alter the contract.
3.   The offeror rejects the new or changed terms within a reasonable period of time.

The Code further provides that if one or both parties are nonmerchants, the contract is formed according to the terms of the offer, not according to the additional terms of the acceptance.

It is possible for an offeree to make a new offer without intending to reject the original offer. In such a case two offers exist, each capable of acceptance. To illustrate, suppose Frank offers to sell his bicycle for $100. Irene's response is, "I do not have $100 but will try to raise that sum. I do have $75 and will offer to purchase your bicycle for that price." Since the offeree did not reject the $100 offer, that offer remains effective. But the offeree did offer to purchase the bicycle for $75. Thus, two offers exist, and the first to be accepted binds the parties to a contract for that amount.

Termination by Operation of Law

The power in the offeree to transform the offer into a binding, legal obligation can be terminated by operation of the law through the following:

1.   Lapse of time.
2.   Destruction of the subject matter of the contract.
3.   Death or incompetency of the offeror or the offeree.
4.   Supervening illegality of the proposed contract.

Lapse of Time   An offer terminates automatically by law when the period of time specified in the offer has passed. For example, suppose Anna offers to sell her boat to Bob if he accepts within twenty days. Bob must accept within the twenty-day period or the offer will lapse (terminate). The period of time specified in an offer begins to run when the offer is actually received by the offeree, not when it is sent or drawn up. When the offer has been delayed, the

---

16.   For example, Sylvestre v. Minnesota, 289 Minn. 142, 214 N.W.2d 658 (1973). See UCC 2-207.

period begins to run from the date the offeree would have received the offer, but only if the offeree knew or should have known the offer was delayed.[17] For example, if Anna had used improper postage when mailing the offer to Bob, but Bob knew Anna had used improper postage, the offer would lapse twenty days after the day Bob would ordinarily have received the offer had Anna used proper postage.

---

17. Restatement, Second, Contracts, Section 49.

If no time for acceptance is specified in the offer, the offer terminates at the end of a *reasonable* period of time. A reasonable period of time is determined by the subject matter of the contract, business and market conditions, and other relevant circumstances. An offer to sell farm produce, for example, will terminate sooner than an offer to sell farm equipment because farm produce is perishable and subject to greater fluctuations in market value. The question of what is a reasonable period of time arises in the next case.

BACKGROUND AND FACTS *Bradley T. Corcoran, plaintiff, appealed his dismissal from the Lyle School District for his failure to accept his employment contract for the 1976–1977 school year in a timely manner. Corcoran is a certified teacher. He received an unsigned copy of his proposed employment contract on June 4, 1976. It provided: "If this contract is not signed by said employee and returned to the Secretary of the school district on or before June 14, 1976, the Board reserves the right to withdraw this offer."*

In addition, the superintendent of schools personally called Corcoran's attention to the time provision contained within the contract. At that time, Corcoran informed the superintendent that he was considering other employment. In any event, Corcoran did not return the contract with his signature on it until June 16. Two days later, he received a letter from the superintendent stating that the school board had decided not to accept any contracts returned after the June 14 deadline. Therefore, Corcoran would not be rehired for the forthcoming school year. The trial court agreed with the school board.

CORCORAN v. LYLE SCHOOL DISTRICT NO. 406, KLICKITAT COUNTY, WASHINGTON
Court of Appeals of Washington, Division 3,
Panel Four, 1978.
20 Wash. App. 621,
581 P.2d 185.

McINTURFF, Judge.
*   *   *   *

Beyond the statutory rights contained in the continuing contract law, the relationship between the school district and its employees is a contractual one governed by general principles of law. *It is well settled that an offeror may require acceptance within a specified reasonable time and that failure of the offeree to so accept constitutes a rejection of the offer.* [Emphasis added.] By his failure to timely return the contract in the face of express written and personal notice that such conduct could result in the school board's rejection of its offer, Mr. Corcoran effectively waived his continuing contract rights.

While certified teachers who have not been given notice of non-retention are entitled to contracts containing terms and conditions substantially identical to those of the previous year, they may not desire such employment. If they fail to accept or reject those contracts within a reasonable time, school districts should be released from their obligations to rehire them under their former contracts. Unless a reasonable contract-return deadline is established and enforced, school districts, as a practical matter, may not know until classes begin how many of their retained teachers will return to the classroom each fall.

Mr. Corcoran does not contend the 10-day contractual limit was unreasonable, nor has he alleged any circumstances which would have prevented him from returning his signed contract within the time established. Therefore, we need not determine the reasonableness of the 10-day return provision.

* * * [B]y his own conduct Mr. Corcoran foreclosed the potential contractual relationship between himself and the school district. * * *

DECISION AND REMEDY *The judgment of the lower court was affirmed. The school district was not required to rehire Corcoran.*

Destruction of the Subject Matter An offer is automatically terminated if the specific subject matter of the offer is destroyed before the offer is accepted. For example, if Watts offers to sell her race horse to Teagle, but the horse dies before Teagle can accept, the offer is automatically terminated.

Death or Incompetency of the Offeror or Offeree An offeree's power of acceptance is terminated when the offeror or offeree dies or is deprived of legal capacity to enter into the proposed contract.[18] An offer is personal to both parties and cannot pass to the decedent's heirs, guardian, or estate. Furthermore, this rule applies whether or not the other party had notice of the death or incompetency of the party. For example, on June 4, Manne offers to sell Clark a rowboat for $300, telling Clark that he, Manne, needs the answer by June 20. On June 10, Manne dies. On June 18, Clark informs the executor of Manne's estate that he has accepted the offer. The executor can refuse to sell the rowboat because the death of the offeror has terminated the offer.

There is an exception to the rule that the death of either the offeror or the offeree before acceptance terminates an offer. The exception applies to *irrevocable offers*—offers that legally cannot be withdrawn by the offeror once made. As previously discussed, an *option* is an example of an irrevocable offer. Although some disagree, many legal scholars believe that the exception also applies to *firm offers* (irrevocable under the UCC).

Supervening Illegality of the Proposed Contract A statute or court decision that makes an offer illegal will automatically terminate the offer. If Barker offers to loan Jackson $20,000 at 15 percent annually, and a usury statute is enacted prohibiting loans at interest rates greater than 14 percent before Jackson

can accept, the offer is automatically terminated. (If, in the above hypothetical case, the usury statute had been passed after Jackson accepted the offer, a valid contract would have been formed, but the contract may be unenforceable.)

ACCEPTANCE

Acceptance is a voluntary act (either words or conduct) by the offeree that shows assent (agreement) to the terms of an offer. The acceptance must be unequivocal and communicated to the offeror.

Who Can Accept?

Generally, a third person cannot interpose himself or herself as a substitute for the offeree and effectively accept the offer. After all, the identity of the offeree is as much a condition of a bargaining offer as any other term contained therein. Thus, except in certain special circumstances to be discussed, only the person to whom the offer is made can accept the offer and create a binding contract. For example, Jones makes an offer to Hanley. Hanley is not interested, but Hanley's friend, Smith, accepts the offer. No contract is formed.

Exceptions The special circumstances in which a third party can accept an offer in place of the offeree are as follows:

1. If the offer is an option contract, the right to exercise the option is generally considered a contract right. As such, it is assignable or transferable to third persons (with exceptions—see Chapter 14).
2. If the offeree is an agent for a principal, the acceptance may be made by the principal and a contract is formed between the principal and the offeror (see Chapter 33).

---

18. Restatement, Second, Contracts, Section 48.

CONCEPT SUMMARY: Methods By Which An Offer Can Be Terminated	
METHODS OF TERMINATION	**BASIC RULES**
By Acts of the Parties:	
1. Revocation	1. An offer can be revoked at any time before acceptance without liability unless the offer is irrevocable. 2. Option contracts, firm offers under UCC 2-205, and the promissory estoppel theory render some offers irrevocable. 3. Except for public offers, revocation is not effective until *known* by the offeree or authorized agent.
2. Rejection	1. Rejection of an offer is accomplished by words or actions that demonstrate a clear intent not to accept or consider the offer further. Inquiries about an offer do not constitute a rejection. 2. A rejection is not effective until *known* by the offeror or an authorized agent of the offeror.
3. Counteroffer	1. A counteroffer is a rejection of the original offer and the making of a new offer. Inquiries are not rejections. 2. Under UCC 2-207, a definite acceptance of an offer is not a counteroffer, even if the acceptance terms modify the terms of the offer.
By Operation of Law:	
1. Lapse of Time	1. If a time period for acceptance is stated in the offer, the offer ends at the stated time. 2. If no time period for acceptance is stated, the offer terminates at the end of a reasonable period.
2. Destruction	Destruction of the subject matter of the offer terminates the offer.
3. Death or Insanity	Death or insanity of either offeror or offeree terminates an offer, unless the offer is irrevocable.
4. Illegality	Supervening illegality terminates an offer.

When the Offer Is Made to Two or More Persons If an offer is made to two or more persons, it must be accepted by all of them. If individual offers are made to two or more persons individually, then contracts are created only with those persons who accept the offer.

Unequivocal Acceptance

In order to exercise the power of acceptance effectively, the offeree must accept unequivocally. This is the *mirror image rule* previously discussed. If the acceptance is subject to new conditions, or if the terms of the acceptance materially change the original offer, the acceptance may be considered a counteroffer that implicitly rejects the original offer. An acceptance may be unequivocal even though the offeree expresses dissatisfaction with the contract. For example, "I accept the goods, but I wish I could have gotten a better price" will operate as an effective acceptance. So, too, will "I accept, but can you shave the price?" On the other hand, the statement

"I accept the goods, but only if I can pay on ninety days' credit" is not an unequivocal acceptance and operates as a counteroffer, rejecting the original offer.

Certain conditions, when added to an acceptance, will not qualify the acceptance sufficiently to reject the offer. Suppose Childs offers to sell her sixty-five-acre cotton farm to Sharif. Sharif replies, "I accept your offer to sell the farm, provided you can supply good title." This condition (providing a good title) does not make the acceptance equivocal. A warranty of good title is normally implied in every offer for the sale of land, so the condition does not add any new or different terms to the offer.

Or suppose that in response to an offer to sell a motorcycle, the offeree replies, "I accept; please send written contract." The offeree has requested a written contract but has not made it a condition for acceptance. Therefore, the acceptance is effective without the written contract. However, if the offeree replies, "I accept if you send a written contract," the acceptance is expressly conditioned on the request for a writing, and the statement is not an acceptance but a counteroffer. (Notice how important *each* word is!) As noted above, under the UCC, an acceptance is still valid even if terms are added. The additional terms are then simply treated as proposals for additions to the contract.[19]

Silence as Acceptance

Ordinarily, silence cannot be acceptance, even if the offeror states, "By your silence and inaction you will be deemed to have accepted this offer." This general rule applies because an offeree should not be put under a burden or liability to act affirmatively in order to reject an offer. No consideration has passed to the offeree to impose such a liability.

On the other hand, silence can operate as an acceptance when an offeree takes the benefit of offered services even though he or she had an opportunity to reject them and knew that they were offered with the expectation of compensation. Suppose Holmes watches while her daughter is given piano lessons. The piano instructor has not been requested to give the daughter lessons but plans to give a series of fifteen. Holmes knows the instructor expects to

be paid but lets the lessons continue nonetheless. Here, her silence constitutes an acceptance, and an implied-in-fact contract is created. She is bound to pay a reasonable value for the lessons. This rule applies only to services and goods from which the offeree has received a benefit.

Silence can also operate as acceptance when the offeree has had prior dealings with the offeror. To illustrate: Brodsky, a salesman, has previously ordered goods from Morales and paid without notifying Morales of his acceptance. Whenever Brodsky receives a shipment from Morales, he sells it and simply sends a check to Morales. Only if the goods are defective does he notify Morales. The last shipment, however, has been neither paid for nor rejected. Nonetheless, Brodsky is bound on a contract and must pay Morales for this last shipment of goods.[20]

In the past, at common law, silence could constitute acceptance in the following situation: Books or magazines are sent to an individual through the mails. The individual did not order the books or magazines and is under no duty to reship them to the seller. However, if he or she uses the books or magazines, acceptance is established, and he or she must pay reasonable value for them. Note that silence does not constitute an acceptance unless the receiver exercises control over the goods. This common law rule of contract law has been changed by statute. The Postal Reorganization Act of 1970 provides that *unsolicited* merchandise sent by U.S. mail may be retained, used, discarded, or disposed of in any manner deemed appropriate, without the individual incurring any obligation to the sender.[21] In addition, the mailing of unordered merchandise (except for free samples) constitutes an unfair trade practice and is not permitted. (Exceptions are mailings by charitable agencies and those made by mistake.)

Another situation where silence creates an acceptance is that in which the offeree solicits the offer. In such a case the offeree has a *duty to speak*, if the offeree wishes to reject. Failure to reject operates as acceptance by silence. For example, Able tells Sallor she is interested in purchasing a complete textbook on business law for approximately $35. Sallor responds that he has just the book Able is looking for, published by West and costing $32. Sallor fur-

---

19. Restatement, Second, Contracts, Section 61 and UCC 2-207.

20. Restatement, Second, Contracts, Section 72.
21. 39 U.S.C.A., Section 3009.

ther informs Able that he has sent the book to Able and unless he hears from Able to the contrary in thirty days, he will bill Able. Since Able solicited Sallor's offer, Able has a duty to reject, and her failure to do so during the thirty-day period will constitute an acceptance.

A similar situation occurs with such organizations as the Book-of-the-Month Club. Once an individual has agreed to this kind of offer, merchandise is shipped periodically (usually every month) unless the customer sends a card indicating that he or she does not want the merchandise. Failure to reject the offered merchandise in this manner operates as acceptance by silence.

Communication of Acceptance

Whether the offeror must be notified of the acceptance depends on the nature of the contract. In a unilateral contract, notification or communication is generally not necessary. Since a unilateral contract calls for the full performance of some act, acceptance is not complete until the act has been fully performed. Therefore, notice of acceptance is usually unnecessary. To illustrate: Beta offers to pay Gamma $150 to paint Beta's garage. Gamma can accept only by painting the garage. Once the garage is completely painted (and hence the acceptance is complete), notification of the acceptance is superfluous. Exceptions do exist. When the offeror requests notice of acceptance or has no adequate means of determining whether the requested act has been performed, or when the law requires such notice of acceptance, then notice is necessary.[22]

In a bilateral contract, *communication* of acceptance is necessary because acceptance is in the form of a promise (not performance), and the contract is formed when the promise is made (rather than when the act is performed). The offeree must use reasonable efforts to communicate the acceptance to the offeror. In a bilateral contract, however, *notification* of acceptance is not necessary if the offer dispenses with the requirement. In addition, if the offer can be accepted by silence, no communication or notification is necessary.

Under the UCC, an order or other offer to buy goods for prompt shipment may be treated as either a bilateral or a unilateral offer and can be accepted by a promise to ship or by actual shipment.[23]

Consider an example. Peters receives a telegram that he is to ship certain goods to Johnson. The UCC provides that Peters can accept by either promptly shipping the goods or sending a telegram to Johnson, saying that he is going to ship the goods. (If the shipment will take a considerable amount of time, Peters would be wise to telegraph Johnson that the goods are in transit.)

Mode and Timeliness of Acceptance in Bilateral Contracts

The general rule is that an acceptance is timely if it is effective within the duration of the offer. Problems arise, however, when the parties involved are not dealing face to face. In such cases, the offeree must use an authorized mode of communication. Acceptance takes effect, thus completing formation of the contract, at the time that communication is sent by the mode expressly or impliedly authorized by the offeror. This is the so-called acceptance-upon-dispatch rule (mailbox rule), which the majority of courts uphold. (Note that this is an exception to the normal rule of bilateral contracts that acceptance requires a completed communication.) What becomes an issue is the *authorized* means of communicating the acceptance. Authorized means can be either expressly stated in the offer or impliedly authorized by facts or by law. In any case, the acceptance becomes effective at the time that it is sent by an authorized means of communication, whether or not the offeror receives that communication.[24]

---

22. UCC 2–206(2).

23. UCC 2–206(1)(b).

24. Restatement, Second, Contracts, Section 30 provides that an offer invites acceptance "by any medium reasonable in the circumstances," unless the offer is specific about the means of acceptance. Under Section 65, a medium is reasonable if it is one used by the offeror or one customary in similar transactions, unless the offeree knows of circumstances that would argue against the reasonableness of a particular medium (e.g., the need for speed because of rapid price changes). Acceptance by mail is ordinarily reasonable where the parties are negotiating at a distance even though the offer was transmitted by telephone or telegraph. However, care must be taken to insure a safe transmission. Under Section 66, "[a]n acceptance by mail or otherwise from a distance is not operative when dispatched, unless it is properly addressed and such other precautions taken as are ordinarily observed to insure safe transmission of similar messages." See also UCC 2-206(1)(a).

When an offeror specifies how acceptance should be sent (for example, by first-class mail or by telegram), *express authorization* is said to exist, and the contract is not formed unless the offeree uses that specified means of acceptance. Moreover, both offeror and offeree are bound in contract the moment such means of acceptance are employed. If telegraph is expressly authorized as the means for acceptance, a contract is established as soon as the offeree gives his or her message to Western Union. Even if Western Union for some reason fails to deliver the message, the contract still exists.

Most offerors do not specify expressly the means by which the offeree is to accept. Thus, the common law and statutes recognize what are called implied authorized means of acceptance. In the absence of expressly authorized means, three implied authorized means have been designated, as follows:

1.   The means chosen by the offeror to make the offer implies that the offeree is authorized to use the *same* or a *faster* means for acceptance.
2.   When two parties are at a distance, unless otherwise inferred, *mailing* (the so-called depository rule) is impliedly authorized.[25]
3.   Under the UCC, acceptance of an offer for sale of goods can be made by any *medium* that is *reasonable* under the circumstances.[26]

Any acceptance sent by means not expressly or impliedly authorized is often not effective until it is received by the offeror.[27]

To illustrate authorized means of acceptance, note the following cases:

1.   On January 1, Jones makes an offer to sell Smith his motorcycle for $450, stipulating that Smith should send acceptance by telegram. On January 2, Jones mails Smith a letter of revocation that is received by Smith at noon on January 4. On January 3, Smith delivers to Western Union his telegram of acceptance. The telegram is incorrectly sent and is not received by Jones until January 5. Are Jones and Smith bound in contract? The answer is yes. Telegram was the expressly stated means of acceptance in the offer; therefore, acceptance is effective the moment Smith delivers his acceptance to Western Union on January 3. A revocation is not effective until it is received by the offeree, in this case on January 4. This is subsequent to the acceptance, and the revocation is ineffective.

2.   On January 1, Jones by telegram offers to sell Smith his motorcycle for $450. The offer contains no expressly stated means for Smith to make his acceptance. The telegram is received by Smith the same day it is sent. On January 2, Smith delivers his acceptance to Western Union. The telegram is lost and is never received by Jones. Jones sells the motorcycle to Green on January 20, believing Smith was not interested in his offer. Can Smith hold Jones liable for breach of contract? The answer is yes. Although the offer did not expressly state a means for Smith's acceptance, telegraph was impliedly authorized. The court here could use either the common law "same or faster means" rule of implied authorization or the UCC "reasonable medium" rule dealing with the sale of goods. Either way, Smith formed a contract with Jones on January 2.

There are three basic exceptions to the rule that a contract is formed when acceptance is sent by authorized means:

1.   If the acceptance is not properly dispatched, in most states it will not be effective until it is received by the offeror.[28] For example, if mail is the authorized means for acceptance, the offeree's letter must be properly addressed and have the correct postage.
2.   The offeror can specifically condition his or her offer on receipt of acceptance by a certain time. For example, an offer may be worded as follows: "Acceptance is not binding unless received by the offeror in her office by 5:00 P.M. on May 1." In this case it is immaterial how the offeree sends acceptance, as the acceptance is effective only when received.

25.   Adams v. Lindsell, 106 Eng.Rep. 250 (K.B. 1818).
26.   UCC 2–206(1)(a) changes the common law rule from "authorized means" to "a reasonable medium."
27.   An exception to this rule is given in Restatement, Second, Contracts, Section 67. Under the Restatement, an acceptance is effective upon dispatch even though the means of transmission is improper or the offeree fails to use care in insuring safe transmission (e.g., wrong address or postage) if (1) the acceptance sent is timely and (2) the offeror receives the communication within the same period of time that a properly transmitted acceptance would have arrived.

28.   But see exception in footnote 27.

3. Sometimes an offeree sends a rejection first, then later changes his or her mind and sends an acceptance. Obviously, this chain of events could cause confusion and even detriment to the offeror, depending on whether the rejection or the acceptance arrived first. Because of this, the law cancels the rule of acceptance upon dispatch, and the first communication to be received by the offeror determines whether a contract is formed. If the rejection is received first, there is no contract.[29]

---

29. Restatement, Second, Contracts, Section 40.

QUESTIONS AND CASE PROBLEMS

1. As a bank officer, you have been given the responsibility of purchasing word processing equipment. On May 6, the ABC Manufacturing Corporation sends you a letter offering to sell your bank some word processing equipment at a price of $10,000, to be shipped via LM Truck Lines. The letter states that the offer is to remain open until May 20. On May 12, you write ABC a letter stating, "Offer appears a little high; I am sure you can do better. I'll need presidential approval for the $10,000 offer. I have authority to purchase word processing equipment for $8,500 and will buy your products at that price." ABC receives this letter on May 16. On May 15, the president of your bank approves the $10,000 purchase. On that same date, ABC sends you a letter revoking its offer. The letter of revocation is received at your bank at 11:00 A.M. on May 19. On May 19 at 11:15 A.M. you send ABC the following telegram: "Accept your offer for $10,000." Because of a delay by the telegraph company, this letter is not delivered until May 21.

(a) Discuss the legal effect of ABC's revocation sent on May 15.

(b) Discuss fully the legal effect of your response sent on May 12.

(c) Discuss whether your bank has a contract in light of the fact that the telegram was not delivered until May 21.

2. Beyer writes Sallor and inquires how much Sallor is asking for a specific forty-acre tract of land Sallor owns. In a letter received by Beyer, Sallor states, "I will not take less than $60,000 for the forty-acre tract as specified." Beyer immediately sends Sallor a telegram stating, "I accept your offer for $60,000." Discuss whether Beyer can hold Sallor to a contract for the land.

3. Smith, operating a sole proprietorship, has a large piece of used equipment for sale. He offers to sell the equipment to Barry for $10,000. Discuss the legal effect of the following events on the offer.

(a) Smith dies prior to Barry's acceptance, and at the time Barry accepts, she is unaware of Smith's death.

(b) The night before Barry accepts, fire destroys the equipment.

(c) Barry pays $100 for a thirty-day option to purchase the equipment. During this period Smith dies and later Barry accepts the offer, knowing of Smith's death.

(d) Barry pays $100 for a thirty-day option to purchase the equipment. During this period Barry dies, and Barry's estate accepts Smith's offer within the stipulated time period.

4. Perez sees an advertisement in the newspaper that the ABC Corporation has for sale a two-volume set of *How to Make Repairs around the House* for $12.95. All Perez has to do is send in a card requesting delivery of the books for a thirty-day trial period of examination. If he does not ship the books back within thirty days of delivery, ABC will bill him for $12.95. Discuss whether or not Perez and ABC have a contract under either of the following circumstances.

(a) Perez sends in the card and receives the books in the U.S. mail. He uses the books to make repairs and fails to return them within thirty days.

(b) Perez does not send in the card, but ABC sends him the books anyway through the U.S. mail. Perez uses the books and fails to return them within thirty days.

5. A plaintiff is attempting to recover death benefits under a life insurance policy. The policy contained a provision that allowed the policy's owner to terminate the policy and receive its cash value. All that the company required was a written request received at the home office. The owner of the policy died after having sent a letter requesting the cash value of the policy (which was much less than the face value). The letter was received *after* the policyowner died. The representative of the deceased owner contended that the estate was entitled to the death benefits of the life insurance policy. What result? [Franklin Life Ins. Co. v. Winney, 469 S.W.2d 21 (Tex.Civ.App. 1971)]

6. McKittrick Co. employed Embry under a written contract at a fixed annual salary. Several times before the contract expired, Embry approached McKittrick's presi-

dent, seeking to have his employment contract extended another year. The president did not make any firm commitments to Embry, and Embry continued working. Eight days after his employment contract had run out, Embry again approached the president, this time threatening to quit if his contract was not extended. The president responded, "Go ahead, you're all right. Get your men out, and don't let that worry you." Two months later Embry was laid off. Can Embry recover his salary under the contract for the entire year? [Embry v. Hargadine, McKittrick Dry Goods Co., 127 Mo.App. 383, 105 S.W. 777 (1907)]

7. Korea Tungsten Mining Co. (KTM) owned a parcel of real estate in midtown Manhattan, and advertised the sale of this property in several prominent newspapers indicating that only "sealed written bids" would be accepted. NOVA bid $750,000 on an all cash basis for the property. However, S.S.I. Investors submitted an alternative bid of $556,000, "and/or one dollar ($1.00) more than the highest bidding price you have received for the above property." While KTM weighed the offers, both NOVA and S.S.I. Investors forwarded a required $10,000 deposit. Approximately ten days later, KTM rejected S.S.I. Investors' bid and returned the deposit. S.S.I. Investors claim that since its bid was the highest, S.S.I. has a binding contract with KTM. Discuss S.S.I.'s contention. [S.S.I. Investors Limited v. Korea Tungsten Mining Co., Ltd., 438 N.Y.S.2d 96, 80 A.D.2d 155 (1981)]

8. John H. Surratt was one of John Wilkes Booth's alleged accomplices in the murder of President Lincoln. On April 20, 1865, the Secretary of War issued and caused to be published in newspapers the following proclamation: "$25,000 reward for the apprehension of John H. Surratt and liberal rewards for any information that leads to the arrest of John H. Surratt." On November 24, 1865, President Johnson revoked the reward and published the revocation in the newspapers. Henry B. St. Marie learned of the reward but left for Rome prior to its revocation. In Rome, St. Marie discovered Surratt's whereabouts; and, in April of 1866, unaware that the reward had been revoked, he reported this information to United States of-

ficials. Pursuant to receiving this information, the officials were able to arrest Surratt. Should St. Marie have received the reward? If so, was he entitled to the full $25,000? [Shuey v. United States, 92 U.S. 73, 23 L.Ed. 697 (1875)]

9. Dodds signed and delivered to Dickinson the following memorandum on Wednesday, June 10:

"I hereby agree to sell to Mr. George Dickinson the whole of the dwelling houses, garden ground, stabling, and outbuildings these to belonging, situated at Croft, belonging to me, for the sum of £800. As witness my hand this tenth day of June, 1874."

"£800 [signed] John Dodds."

"P.S. this offer to be left over until Friday, 9 o'clock A.M. 12th June, 1874."

[Signed] J. Dodds."

The next afternoon (Thursday) Dickinson learned that Dodds was negotiating with a man named Allan. That evening Dickinson went to the house of Dodds's mother-in-law and left her a written acceptance. This document never reached Dodds. The next morning, at 7 A.M., Dickinson's agent gave Dodds a copy of the acceptance. Dodds replied that it was too late as he had already sold the property. Was the memorandum signed by Dodds a binding contract? If it was merely an offer, was Dickinson's acceptance sufficient to form a binding contract? [Dickinson v. Dodds, 2 Ch.D. 463 (1876)]

10. Central Properties entered into a contract with Robbinson and Westside, a real estate development company, whereby Central Properties purchased 60 acres of land. The contract included a "right of first refusal" to purchase the water and sewage system on the remaining property of Westside. Westside wanted to sell the sewage system and over the course of three months exchanged letters with Central asking whether they wished to exercise their "right." Central Properties never affirmatively accepted in any of its responses but requested different terms, price, etc. Central now wishes to hold Westside to a contract for the system. Westside states no contract was formed. Discuss who is right. [Central Properties, Inc. v. Robbinson, 450 So.2d 277 (Fla.App. 1 Dist. 1984)]

9

CONTRACTS
Consideration

A contract cannot be formed without legally sufficient consideration. **Consideration** is defined as the value given in return for a promise. In other words, consideration is something that is exchanged for something else.

Often consideration is broken into two elements: (1) something of *legal* value must be given in exchange for the promise, and (2) there must be a *bargained-for* exchange. The "something of legal value" may consist of a return promise that is bargained for. If it consists of performance, that performance may consist of:

1. An act (other than a promise);
2. A forbearance; or
3. The creation, modification, or destruction of a legal relation.[1]

For example, Earl says to his son, "Upon completion of mowing my yard, I promise to pay you $25." Earl's son mows the yard. The act of mowing the yard is the consideration which creates the contractual obligation of Earl to pay his son $25. However, suppose Earl says to his son, "In consideration of the fact that you are not as wealthy as your broth-

ers, I will pay you $500." This promise is not enforceable because Earl's son has not given any consideration for the $500 promised.[2] Earl has simply stated his *motive* for giving his son a gift. The fact that the word "consideration" is used does not, alone, make it consideration.

REQUIREMENTS OF CONSIDERATION

Legal Sufficiency

In order to create a binding contract, the elements of consideration must not only exist but must be legally sufficient. To be *legally sufficient*, consideration for a promise must be either legally *detrimental to the promisee*—the one receiving the promise—or legally *beneficial to the promisor*—the one making the promise, or both. Legal detriment occurs when one does or promises to do something which there was no prior legal duty to do. It also includes a forbearance, a refraining or promising to refrain from doing something that there was no prior legal duty to refrain from doing. Conversely, legal benefit is obtaining something that there was no prior legal right to obtain. *Legal* detriment or benefit is not

---

1. Restatement, Contracts, Second, Section 71.

2. Fink v. Cox, 18 Johns. 145, 9 Am.Dec. 191 (N.Y. 1820).

synonymous with *actual* (economic) detriment or benefit. In most cases, the promisor's legal benefit is the same as the promisee's legal detriment. However, the existence of *either* a legal detriment to the promisee *or* a legal benefit to the promisor constitutes legally sufficient consideration.

Suppose Myers owns a brickhouse that causes considerable air pollution in and around his property. Myers has been thinking about getting out of the brick-making business since he has not made much profit and his property is constantly enveloped in a thick layer of smoke. Bernard, his neighbor, is sick of the smoke and pollution and offers Myers $1,500 to stop making bricks (and thus stop the smoke). Myers agrees. The consideration flowing from Myers to Bernard is the promise to refrain from doing an act that Myers is legally entitled to do—that is, to earn a living by making bricks. The consideration flowing from Bernard to Myers is the promise to pay a sum of money that is not otherwise legally required to be paid. (Consideration is sufficient even though Myers may have gone out of business without Bernard's offer.)

In the following case, one of the classics of contract law, the court found that refraining from certain behavior at the request of another was sufficient consideration to support a promise to pay a sum of money.

HAMER v. SIDWAY
Court of Appeals of New York,
Second Division, 1891.
124 N.Y. 538, 27 N.E. 256.

BACKGROUND AND FACTS *William E. Story, Sr., was the uncle of William E. Story II. In the presence of family members and guests invited to a family gathering, Story, Sr., promised to pay his nephew $5,000 if he would refrain from drinking, using tobacco, swearing, and playing cards or billiards for money until he became 21. The nephew agreed and fully performed his part of the bargain. When he reached 21, he wrote and told his uncle that he had kept his part of the agreement and was thereby entitled to $5,000. The uncle replied that he was pleased with his nephew's performance, writing, "I have no doubt but you have, for which you shall have five thousand dollars, as I promised you. I had the money in the bank the day you was twenty-one years old that I intend for you, and you shall have the money certain. * * * P.S. You can consider this money on interest."*

The nephew received his uncle's letter and thereafter consented that the money should remain with his uncle according to the terms and conditions of the letter. The uncle died about two years later without having paid his nephew any part of the $5,000 and interest. The executor of the uncle's estate (the defendant in this action) did not want to pay the $5,000 (with interest) to the nephew, claiming that there had been no valid consideration for the promise.

The court disagreed with the executor and reviewed the doctrine of detriment-benefit as valid consideration under the law.

PARKER, Justice.
* * * *

The defendant contends that the contract was without consideration to support it, and therefore invalid. He asserts that the promisee, by refraining from the use of liquor and tobacco, was not harmed, but benefited; that that which he did was best for him to do, independently of his uncle's promise,—and insists that it follows that, unless the promisor was benefited, the contract was without consideration,—a contention which, if well founded, would seem to leave open for controversy in many cases whether that which the promisee did or omitted to do was in fact of such benefit to him as to leave no consideration to support the enforcement of the promisor's agreement. Such a rule could not be tolerated, and is without foundation in the law. The exchequer chamber in 1875 defined "consideration" as follows: "A valuable consideration, in the sense of the law, may consist either in some right, interest, profit, or benefit accruing to the one party, or some forbearance, detriment, loss, or responsibility given, suffered, or undertaken by the other." Courts "will not ask whether the thing which forms the consideration does in fact benefit the promisee or a third party, or is of any substantial value to any one. It is enough that something is promised, done, forborne, or suffered by the party to whom the promise is made as consideration for the promise made to him. In general a waiver of any legal right at the request of another party is a sufficient consideration for a promise. Any damage, or suspension, or forbearance of a right will be sufficient to sustain a promise." *   *   * Now, applying this rule to the facts before us, the promisee used tobacco, occasionally drank liquor, and he had a legal right to do so. That right he abandoned for a period of years upon the strength of the promise of the testator that for such forbearance he would give him $5,000. We need not speculate on the effort which may have been required to give up the use of those stimulants. It is sufficient that he restricted his lawful freedom of action within certain prescribed limits upon the faith of his uncle's agreement, and now, having fully performed the conditions imposed, it is of no moment whether such performance actually proved a benefit to the promisor, and the court will not inquire into it; but, were it a proper subject of inquiry, we see nothing in this record that would permit a determination that the uncle was not benefited in a legal sense.

The court ruled that the nephew had provided legally sufficient consideration by giving up smoking, drinking, swearing, and playing cards or billiards for money until he became twenty-one and was therefore entitled to the money.   **DECISION AND REMEDY**

The Hamer v. Sidway *case is a good illustration of the distinction between benefits to the promisor and detriment to the promisee. Here the court did not inquire as to whether a benefit flowed to the promisor, but required only that there was a legally sufficient detriment to the promisee.*   **COMMENTS**

MORAL OBLIGATIONS

Promises based on moral duty or obligation are not enforceable because a moral obligation is not legally sufficient consideration. Suppose your friend is injured in a distant city and a grocer takes care of him during his injury. Thereafter, feeling a moral obligation to help your friend and aid the grocer, you promise the grocer to pay for your friend's expenses. The promise is unenforceable since it is supported only by your moral obligation, and a moral obligation cannot be legally sufficient consideration.

Sometimes people feel a moral obligation to make a promise to loved ones. A father may promise to pay $10,000 to his daughter "in consideration of the love and affection that I have for you." An employer may promise to give a sum of money to a trusted employee "in consideration of the many acts of kindness and thoughtfulness over the years" that the employee has performed. Frequently, promises to pay for acts already performed (called past consideration, to be discussed later in this chapter) are premised upon moral obligations. This is generally called "good consideration." It is founded on a natural duty and affection or on a strong moral obligation, but such is not legally sufficient consideration, and promises made in exchange for it are unenforceable.

Another example of a promise made out of a moral obligation is a promise to pay the debts of one's parents or a promise to pay for the care rendered to relatives one was under no duty to support. A minority of states enforce such promises supported only by a moral obligation—but only to the extent of the actual obligation or of the services or care rendered. For an example, see California Civil Code, Sec. 1606.

ADEQUACY OF CONSIDERATION

Adequacy of consideration refers to the fairness of the bargain. On the surface, when the values of the items that are exchanged are unequal, fairness would appear to be an issue. If Bryant and Kowalewski make an agreement whereby Bryant is to pay $1 for

Kowalewski's car (with a market value of $1,000), is the agreement supported by consideration? There is no question that $1 is legal value and that Kowalewski is giving up her legal title to the car. Thus, it appears that the requirements of legal value, bargained-for exchange, and legally sufficient consideration have been met. However, the consideration is far from adequate, since Kowalewski does not appear to be getting a fair bargain. Does this unfairness negate the bargain?

In general, a court of law will not question the adequacy of consideration if the consideration is legally sufficient. Under the doctrine of freedom of contract, parties are normally free to bargain as they wish. If people could sue merely because they entered into an unwise contract, the courts would be overloaded with frivolous suits. In extreme cases, a court of law may look to the amount or value (the adequacy) of the consideration because inadequate consideration can indicate fraud, duress, or undue influence. Suppose Lansky has a house worth $25,000, and he sells it for $5,000. A $5,000 sale could indicate that the buyer unduly pressured Lansky into selling or that Lansky was defrauded into selling the house at far below market value.

In an equity suit, courts will more likely question the adequacy of consideration. (Remember from Chapter 1 that actions at law allow for remedies that consist of some form of compensation. Actions in equity allow for remedies that involve specific performance, injunction, or rescission.) The parties in an equity suit must show that the transaction was not unconscionable and that consideration was exchanged. For example, a suit to compel specific performance is equitable and requires the losing party to perform the contract duties rather than pay damages for breach of contract. Assume McMichael agrees to sell land worth $45,000 to Price for only $7,500. After signing the contract, McMichael refuses to deliver possession, and Price sues for specific performance. The court may now look at the relative values of the consideration exchanged in light of the circumstances and may refuse to allow specific performance since the consideration is inadequate.

As a general principle of contract law, the courts will not ordinarily attempt to evaluate the adequacy of the consideration in an agreed-upon exchange. In the following case, however, the court would not allow "peace of mind" and $1.05 to constitute adequate consideration for a $12,000 land sale.

ROSE v. LURVEY
Court of Appeals of Michigan,
1972.
40 Mich.App. 230, 198 N.W.2d
839.

BACKGROUND AND FACTS *When the Rose family ran into marital difficulties, Robert Rose sought the advice and help of his sister, Norma Lurvey. Robert's estranged wife, Barbara, had failed to make several mortgage payments, and was in danger of defaulting on the family home as well as being in arrears on taxes. Norma Lurvey suggested to Robert that her son (his nephew), Wyman Lurvey, might assist financially.*

Robert and Wyman discussed transferring the house, but no price was ever mentioned. Wyman agreed that following such a transfer, he would make the back mortgage payments and pay the taxes that were owing. An attorney drew up the necessary papers. The instruments were executed despite the fact that they failed to specify a sale price. The only money mentioned was $1.05 recited as consideration in the documents. Subsequently, Robert and Barbara Rose reconciled and continued to live in the house, anticipating that Wyman would be paying them some additional money. Wyman instead served them with notice to vacate the premises. The Roses ignored the notice. A month or so later, Robert Rose entered the hospital. During the short time the house was unoccupied, Wyman moved in and began remodeling the interior.

The Rose family (plaintiffs) contended that the quit claim deed and the contract assigning the land to Wyman Lurvey (defendant) should be thrown out because the consideration was so grossly inadequate as to shock the conscience.

LESINSKI, Chief Judge.
*   *   *   *

It is a general principle of contract law that courts will not ordinarily look into the adequacy of the consideration in an agreed exchange. Equity will, however, grant relief where the inadequacy of consideration is particularly glaring. Thus the Michigan Supreme Court stated the rule that:

"Mere inadequacy of consideration, unless it be so gross as to shock the conscience of the court, is not ground for rescission."

In the case at bar [the one under consideration], the trial judge found that plaintiffs received more than just the $1.05 recited consideration from defendants. This additional consideration was said to have been the peace of mind plaintiffs obtained from knowing that they did not have to worry about the ramifications of defaulting on the land contract. This Court believes that this finding of additional consideration was erroneous. What the trial court mistakenly referred to as consideration was in actuality nothing more than the inducements and motives which influenced plaintiffs into making the contract. Inducements and motives are merely the subjective manifestation of plaintiffs' own desires. They are not that bargained for exchange or legal detriment to defendants which is necessary to establish a legally valid contract.

"The motive which prompts one to enter into a contract and the consideration for the contract are distinct and different things. [Emphasis added.] Parties are led into agreements by many inducements, such as the hope of profit, the expectation of acquiring what they could not otherwise obtain, the desire of avoiding a loss, etc. These inducements are not, however, either legal or equitable consideration, and actually compose no part of the contract."

In light of the fact that $1.05 represented the entire consideration for the transfer of an equity in the property worth approximately $12,000, we find ourselves called upon to decide whether such consideration was so grossly inadequate as to "shock the conscience of the court." We believe it was.

[T]he South Carolina Supreme Court *   *   * stated:

" 'Grossly inadequate consideration does not mean simply less than the actual value of the property. It means a consideration so far short of the real value of property as to shock a correct mind.' "

[T]he Virginia Supreme Court of Appeals cited *   *   * grossly inadequate consideration as:

" 'An inequality so strong, gross and manifest that it must be impossible to state it to a man of common sense without producing an exclamation at the inequality of it,'
*   *   *."

This Court reaches the conclusion that the transfer of an equity in property worth $12,000 for $1.05 exhibited an inequality so strong as to amount to a gross inadequacy of consideration.

"Inadequacy of price paid for real property is not sufficient alone to authorize a court of equity to set aside a deed of conveyance, unless it is so gross as to shock a conscientious person; but, if the inadequacy is so great as to shock a conscientious person, it alone may furnish sufficient ground for annulling the conveyance."

DECISION AND REMEDY

The court held that the gross inadequacy of the consideration mandated the cancellation of the quit claim deed and of the contract of assignment. Wyman Lurvey was required to vacate the house. A new trial was ordered to determine whether Wyman owed the Roses rent for the time he occupied the house and whether the Roses owed Wyman the amount of back taxes and mortgage payments he had made on their behalf.

Preexisting Duty Rule

Under most circumstances, a later promise to do what one already has a previous legal duty to do is not legally sufficient consideration because no legal detriment or benefit has been incurred.[3] The preexisting legal duty may arise out of a previous contract or may be imposed by law. A sheriff cannot collect a reward for information leading to the capture of a criminal if the sheriff is under a legal duty to capture the criminal. Similarly, assume Healey agrees to hire Brewster for one year at $175 per week. Brewster begins working. After two months, Healey agrees orally to increase the wages to $195 per week. Healey's promise falls under the preexisting duty rule and is generally held to be unenforceable unless the promise is supported by legally sufficient consideration. Brewster was under a preexisting contractual duty to work for one year, and the performance of that duty cannot serve as consideration for the wage increase.

The harshness of the preexisting duty rule is evident. In the examples above, the sheriff is denied a reward that anyone else could have received, and Brewster, the employee, can be denied his pay raise. Therefore, the courts are alert to finding any legal detriment or benefit that may exist, no matter how small or insignificant it may be, so that the promise will be enforceable. Hence, if Brewster was required to perform any extra duties, the promise modifying his employment contract would be enforceable.[4]

The law recognizes some basic exceptions to the preexisting duty rule, however. They are:

1. Rescission and new contract.
2. Sale of goods—modification of contract without consideration.
3. Unforeseen difficulties.

Rescission and New Contract   The law recognizes that two parties can mutually agree to rescind their contract, at least to the extent that it is executory. For example, suppose Jones contracts with Abel to purchase Abel's watch for $100. Later Jones tells Abel that he would prefer not to purchase the watch. As it happens, Abel no longer desires to sell it, so they call off the deal. This is called **rescission**, defined as the unmaking of a contract in which the parties to it remain in status quo.

Suppose one day later Jones decides he really wants the watch and offers to purchase it once again. Abel is willing to sell, but this time for a price of $125. Jones agrees, and a new contract is formed.

When rescission and the making of the contract take place at the same time, the courts are frequently given a choice of using the preexisting duty rule (not enforcing the new promise) or rescission and new contract. To illustrate, suppose Bauman-Bache, Inc., begins construction on a seven-floor office building and after three months demands an extra $75,000 on its contract or it will stop working. The owner of the land, having no one else to complete construction, agrees to pay the extra $75,000. The agreement is not enforceable because it is not supported by legally sufficient consideration; Bauman-Bache was under a preexisting duty to complete the building. Some courts, however, have held such a modifying agreement to be enforceable by holding that the original contract was rescinded and replaced with the new agreement.[5] Some courts even hold that the original considerations carry over into the new agreement.[6] The conflicting policies are: (1) people should be able to modify their legal relations when circumstances make it equitable to do so; and (2) modification in some cases will resemble duress, as in the Bauman-Bache example.

Sale of Goods—Modification   The UCC deals with the problem of preexisting duty or modification of an existing contract very simply: "[A]n agreement modifying a contract within this Article needs no consideration to be binding." [UCC 2-209(1)]

To illustrate, Smith and Jones have entered into a one-year requirements contract whereby Smith is to supply Jones with all her flour needs for her bakery at $50 per barrel. Subsequently, the price of wheat to Smith increases so sharply that the cost of producing a barrel of flour is now $56. Smith tells Jones he will not ship Jones any more flour unless Jones

3. Foakes v. Beer, 9 App. Cas. 605 (1884).
4. Note, however, that in the example of the sheriff, the person taking the job as sheriff knows ahead of time that he or she will not be allowed to take rewards. But since the modern view of courts seems to skirt the preexisting duty rule, the courts' attitude has broken down much of contract validity.

5. Armour & Co. v. Celic, 294 F.2d 432 (2d Cir. 1961).
6. Holly v. First Nat'l Bank, 218 Wis. 259, 260 N.W. 429 (1935).

agrees to pay $58 per barrel. Jones agrees. This modification of an existing sales contract is enforceable under the UCC even though Smith was under a preexisting duty to supply flour at $50 per barrel. Jones must pay the additional $8 per barrel. The UCC simply eliminates the consideration requirement if both parties in good faith agree to a modification.

Unforeseen Difficulties Sometimes a party to a contract runs into *unforeseen* and substantial difficulties that could not have been anticipated at the time the contract was entered into. If the parties later agree to pay extra compensation for overcoming these unforeseen difficulties, the court may enforce the agreement. It should be noted that these unforeseen difficulties do not include the types of risks ordinarily assumed in business. For example, the increase in the price of wheat in the preceding example would not normally be deemed an unforeseen hardship or difficulty.

Suppose you contract with Carvelli to dig a basement on your vacant lot for $1,000. Carvelli starts to dig the basement and encounters an unforeseen concrete slab reinforced with steel. He will now require special equipment and additional time to finish digging the basement. He asks for an additional $200 to dig the basement, and you agree. Many courts will enforce the modification, under the unforeseen difficulty exception.

PROBLEM AREAS IN BUSINESS CONCERNING CONSIDERATION

Because of the difficulty in clearly defining the requirements for consideration, numerous exceptions have been created in order to enforce contracts without consideration or to emphasize the intent of the parties to contract with one another, rather than to emphasize the existence or nonexistence of consideration.

Businesses face a great deal of uncertainty (risk) in the form of changing market conditions. This uncertainty makes it difficult to define the future rights and duties of parties who contract today. As a result, some output and requirements contracts may not call for any performance in the future under certain market considerations. Yet this does not mean that the contract fails for lack of consideration. Prob-

lems concerning the issue of consideration usually fall into one of the following categories:

1. Promises exchanged where total performance by the parties is uncertain.
2. Settlement of claims.
3. Certain promises enforceable without consideration.

The court's solutions to these types of problems can give you insights into how the law views the complex concept of consideration.

Uncertain Performance— Illusory versus Non-illusory

An exchange of promises where performance may never take place suggests that there is no consideration because there is no detriment incurred by the promisee or benefit received by the promisor. If the terms of the contract express such uncertainty of performance that the promisor has not actually promised to do anything, the promise is said to be *illusory*—without consideration and unenforceable. For example, suppose the president and sole owner of ABC Corporation says to his employees: "All of you have worked hard, and if profits continue to remain high, a 10 percent bonus at the end of the year will be given—if management thinks it is warranted." The employees continue to work hard, and profits remain high, but no bonus is given. This is an illusory promise, or no promise at all, because performance depends solely on the discretion of the president. There is no bargained-for consideration. The statement declares merely that the president may or may not do something in the future. The president is not obligated (incurs no detriment) now or in the future.

The following four types of business contracts have a certain degree of uncertainty as to the amount of performance legally required:

1. Requirements contracts.
2. Output contracts.
3. Exclusive dealing contracts.
4. Option to cancel clauses.

Frequently the determination of whether the promise is illusory or non-illusory is dependent on all the surrounding facts, not just on the terms of the agreement.

Requirements Contracts   A **requirements contract** is a contract in which the buyer agrees to purchase and the seller agrees to sell all or up to a stated amount of what the buyer *needs* or *requires*. If the contract terms permit the buyer to purchase only if the buyer *wishes or desires* to do so, or if the buyer reserves the right to buy the goods from someone other than the seller, the promise is illusory (without consideration), and the agreement is unenforceable.

For example, a manufacturer uses coal to operate and to heat his plant. The manufacturer agrees to purchase from a coal producer all the coal that the manufacturer will require or need to heat and to run his plant for one year at a set price per ton. Since the agreement is based on the *established* needs of the buyer, and since the contract requires the buyer to purchase those needs from this seller, the contract is non-illusory (with consideration) and enforceable, even though the exact amount of coal tonnage to be purchased is unknown. If the agreement stated that the buyer had to buy only the coal he "wanted" or "wished" or "desired," or if the buyer reserved the right to purchase his needs "from any seller whose delivery price is lowest," there is no contract, because the buyer is not obligated to buy any coal from this seller and thus has incurred no legal detriment.

But, one might ask, is there not a possibility that the manufacturer will go out of business and thus have no requirements? Where, then, is the detriment, or consideration? The detriment is that the buyer gives up the opportunity (legal right) to purchase from other sellers, and the seller gives up the opportunity (legal right) to sell to other buyers (who do not have requirements contracts) until he or she has satisfied the obligation under the requirements contract.

Output Contracts   An **output contract** is a contract in which the seller agrees to sell and the buyer agrees to buy all or up to a stated amount of what the seller produces.

For example, if U.S. Steel agrees to sell to Boeing Aircraft all I-beams it produces during the month of March at an agreed-upon price per beam, a binding, non-illusory promise will be made. If the contract terms permit a seller to sell output to others besides the buyer, or if the seller's obligation to produce is based on the seller's want, desire, or wish, the contract is illusory. Therefore, the criteria for a non-illusory output contract are basically the same as for a requirements contract, except that the criteria are applied to the seller's obligation to produce rather than to the buyer's obligation to purchase.

The UCC imposes a *good faith limitation* on output and requirements contracts. The quantity under such contracts is the amount of output or the amount of requirements that occur during a *normal* production year. The actual quantity sold or purchased cannot be unreasonably disproportionate to normal or comparable prior output or requirements.[7]

Exclusive Dealing Contracts—"Best Efforts" Rule   An **exclusive dealing contract** gives a party the sole right to deal in or with the product of the other party. For example, an exclusive dealing contract requires a buyer to carry only products made by the seller. Wood agrees to market only the fabrics, millinery, and dresses upon which Lady Duff-Gordon places her endorsement. Lady Duff-Gordon receives no promise that Wood will market any dresses, but she gives Wood an exclusive right to market whatever number of items Wood deems appropriate. At first glance, Wood's promise appears illusory. He has not agreed to sell anything. However, as in the output and the requirements contracts, Wood is under a duty to use his "best efforts" to market the dresses.[8] This duty, or obligation, is consideration for the promise to either supply or sell.

Consider another example. A real estate broker obtains a thirty-day *exclusive* contract from the seller of a house. The broker has the duty to perform his or her best efforts in selling the house within thirty days and in dealing with potential buyers. The seller's detriment is the loss of the opportunity (legal right) to hire another broker, and a duty to pay the agent if the agent finds a satisfactory buyer for the house. In return for this detriment, the law imposes a legal obligation of "best efforts" on the broker.

Option to Cancel Clauses   A term or time contract may include a clause in which one or both parties may reserve the right to cancel the contract prior to the stated period. For example, consider a three-year lease (a term contract) in which the tenant

---

7. UCC 2-306.
8. Wood v. Lucy, Lady Duff-Gordon, 222 N.Y. 88, 118 N.E. 214 (1917). See UCC 2-306(2).

reserves the right to cancel, with notice, at any time after one year's occupancy. The uncertainty of performance is that the contract may or may not last for the entire three-year period.

The basic rule of law is that, although it is immaterial if one or both parties have the option, the contract with an option to cancel will be enforced if the party having the option has given up an opportunity (legal right). The loss of the opportunity is a detriment and thus constitutes consideration. This point will become clearer as we look at two more examples.

Suppose I contract to hire you for one year at $4,000 per month, reserving the right to cancel the contract at any time. Upon close examination of these words, you can see that I have not actually agreed to hire you, as I could cancel without liability before you start performance. I have not given up the opportunity of hiring someone else. This contract, therefore, is illusory.

Now compare this situation to the previous one. I contract to hire you for one year at $4,000 per month, reserving the right to cancel the contract at any time after you begin performance by giving you thirty days' notice. By saying that I will give you thirty days' notice, I am relinquishing the opportunity (legal right) to hire someone else instead of you for a thirty-day period. Therefore, if you work for one month, at the end of which I give you thirty days' notice, you will be entitled to enforce the contract for $4,000 in salary.

Settlement of Claims

An understanding of the enforceability of agreements to settle claims or discharge debts is important in the business world. The following agreements are the most frequent transactions:

1. Accord and satisfaction.
2. Release, or covenant not to sue.

Accord and Satisfaction The concept of accord and satisfaction deals with a debtor's offer of payment and a creditor's acceptance of a lesser amount than the debt the creditor purports to be owed. The accord is defined as the agreement whereby one of the parties undertakes to give or perform, and the other to accept, in satisfaction of a claim, something other

than that which was originally agreed upon. Satisfaction may take place when the accord is executed (agreement performance completed), after which there has been an accord and satisfaction. Accord and satisfaction deal with an attempt by the obligor to extinguish an obligation. A basic rule is that there can be no satisfaction unless there is first an accord.

This rule does not apply if the debtor presumably has a preexisting legal obligation to perform according to the contract. In other words, the creditor is owed full performance—that is, payment of the debt as per contract terms. When the amount of money owed is not in dispute, we have a situation of a preexisting legal obligation with respect to payment of a liquidated debt, where the legal term *liquidated* means ascertained, agreed-upon, fixed, settled, and determined. For example, if Baker signed an installment loan contract with her banker in which she agreed to pay a specified rate of interest on a specified sum of money borrowed, at timely monthly intervals in the form of a $100-per-month payment for two years, that is a liquidated debt. Reasonable persons will not differ over the amount owed.

The opposite of a liquidated debt is an *unliquidated debt*. Here reasonable persons may differ over the amount owed. It is not settled, fixed, agreed-upon, ascertained, or determined. In these circumstances the accord of the lesser sum is also satisfaction, discharging the purported debt. Suppose that Devereaux goes to the dentist's office. The dentist tells him that he needs three gold inlays. The price is not discussed, and there is no standard fee for this type of work. Devereaux leaves the office. At the end of the month, the dentist sends him a bill for $1,500. Devereaux, believing that this amount is grossly out of proportion with what a reasonable person would believe to be the debt owed, sends a check for $1,000. On the back of the check he writes "payment in full for three gold inlays." The dentist cashes the check. Since we are dealing with an unliquidated debt— the amount has not been agreed upon—partial payment accepted by the dentist will wipe out the debt. One argument to support this rule is that the parties give up a legal right to contest the amount in dispute, and thus consideration passes.

In the majority of states, accord (acceptance of a lesser sum) of a liquidated debt is not satisfaction, and the balance of the debt is still legally owed. The rationale for this rule is that no consideration is given by the debtor to satisfy the obligation of paying the balance to the creditor, since the debtor has a preexisting legal obligation to pay the entire debt.

To illustrate, suppose a debtor, by agreement, borrows $100, payable at the end of one year at 10 percent interest. At the end of the year, the debtor sends the creditor a check for $100 (not $110), marked clearly "payment in full." The creditor, under the

majority rule, could cash the check and still legally sue for the balance of $10.

The importance of being sure that the party receiving the tendered payment knows that the payment is intended as full accord and satisfaction in discharging an unliquidated debt is illustrated by the following case.

KIRK WILLIAMS CO., INC. v. SIX INDUSTRIES, INC.

Court of Appeals of Ohio, 1983.
463 N.E.2d 1266.

BACKGROUND AND FACTS *Six Industries, Inc., the appellee, was the general contractor for the construction of an insurance building in Springfield, Ohio. Appellee entered into a subcontract with Kirk Williams Company, the appellant, for heating and air-conditioning the building. As is standard practice on projects of this size, the contract between the parties was changed by formal written change orders on several occasions. Near completion of the building Six Industries submitted two last change orders. Kirk Williams refused to sign or complete the change order because it was claimed that Six Industries had delayed the project to Kirk Williams' detriment and was soon to file a lawsuit for delay damages. On November 10, 1981, Six Industries issued a check to Kirk Williams for $14,850.04. On the check, the following language appeared: "Endorsement and/or negotiation of the check constitutes a full and complete release of Six Industries, Inc. and acknowledges full payment of all monies due. . . ." Appellant received the check in the normal course of business, and appellant's bookkeeper deposited the check. Soon after, appellant filed suit for delay damages and for declaratory judgment that the check was not an accord and satisfaction. The trial court found the check was an accord and satisfaction. Kirk Williams appealed.*

BROGAN, Presiding Judge.

* * * *

An accord and satisfaction is a method of discharging a contract or settling a cause of action arising either from a contract or tort, by substituting for such contract or cause of action an agreement for the satisfaction thereof an execution of such substituted agreement. * * *

"An accord is a contract under which an obligee promises to accept a stated performance in satisfaction of the obligor's existing duty. Performance of the accord discharges the original duty." Restatement of the Law, Contracts 2d (1981) 381–382, Section 281(1).

An accord and satisfaction is the result of an agreement between the parties, and this agreement, like all others, must be consummated by a meeting of the minds of the parties. * * * An effective assent cannot be given and a meeting of the minds cannot be achieved unless the parties have knowledge of the facts which are material to the agreement. But an agreement intended as an accord and satisfaction of certain claims may be valid as to those claims known to both parties at the time of the execution, notwithstanding that an additional claim was discovered after an accord had been made and executed by satisfaction. * * *

As in the case of the other contracts, when a contract of accord and satisfaction is entered into by an alleged agent on behalf of his principal, in order to bind the principal the agent must have been duly authorized thereto, or his act must have been ratified by the principal. * * *

An accord and satisfaction, being a contract, must be supported by a good or valuable consideration in order to be given effect. 1 American Jurisprudence 2d, supra,

Section 12, at 310. In the case of an unliquidated or disputed demand the consideration rests in part upon the settlement of the dispute. A claim is an "unliquidated demand," as the term is used in connection with an accord and satisfaction, if there is a bona fide dispute as to its existence or amount. *   *   *

A creditor to whom remittance is made as payment in full of an unliquidated or disputed claim has the option either of accepting it upon the condition on which it was sent or of rejecting it, and if it clearly appears that the remittance was sent upon the condition it be accepted in full satisfaction, then failure to reject it will result in an accord and satisfaction. *   *   *

*   *   *   *

The record is clear that Thomas Cooke, appellee's vice-president, had been informed that as late as October 10, 1982, the industrial manager of appellant's firm refused to accept a change order which contained a "notation" that the change order settled all disputed items between the parties on the Credit Life Insurance Building project. Nonetheless, someone in appellee's company mailed a check to appellant for $14,850.04 with the restrictive endorsement containing similar language to the change order.

The evidence revealed that Carl Shaffer, a boookkeeper with Kirk Williams, deposited the Six Industries check containing the restrictive endorsement. Shaffer's training was solely that of a bookkeeper. He also opened the daily mail and distributed it to the various departments within the company. He was given a rubber stamp by his employer stating, "make payable to Kirk Williams Company, Deposit," and it was his duty to prepare deposit slips and to make credit entries on the accounts receivable. The deposit slip was then given to a secretary or the controller for deposit in the bank. He had no authority to settle disputes between his company and other contractors.

*   *   *   *

While the evidence revealed that the responsibilities of various corporate personnel were not clearly delineated, it was clear from the evidence that Shaffer's role was essentially that of a clerk-bookkeeper. There was evidence that several others, either as officers of the corporation, project managers, or estimator engineers, had authority to settle change orders or disputes with contractors.

"Mere authority given an agent to indorse a check for deposit does not effect an accord and satisfaction based upon the receipt of a check for an amount less than that due where the agent does not have knowledge of any controversy as to the amount of the indebtedness or authority to adjust any such controversy." 1 American Jurisprudence 2d, supra, Section 8, at 306–307.

*   *   *   *

The entering into an accord and satisfaction is the making of a new and independent contract in which the minds of the parties to the contract must meet, and the parties who act must be so "authorized," or there must be an acceptance by way of ratification. There was no meeting of minds here. Shaffer's action was ministerial in nature. It was not the result of a conscious decision of the appellant to accept the $14,850.04 in settlement of its delay claim.

*   *   *   *

The appellate court held that the check did not constitute an accord and satisfaction, and ordered the case remanded back to the trial court to determine the issue of delay damages.   **DECISION AND REMEDY**

Usually a clearly worded notation on a check, which calls to the attention of the indorser that the check is intended as a discharge of an obligation (accord and satisfaction), is sufficient to establish accord (an agreement) upon the cashing or depositing of the check. If there is doubt, it is wise to address a letter   **COMMENTS** *to the proper party stating this intent. The letter is usually held to be sufficient notice of intent once the letter is received. Upon cashing of the check the only possible issue then is whether the debt is liquidated or unliquidated.*

Release, or Covenant Not to Sue   A **release** serves to bar any further recovery beyond the terms stated in the release. For example, suppose you are involved in an automobile accident due to the negligence of Jean. Jean offers you $500 if you will release her from any further liability resulting from the accident. You believe that the damages to your car will not exceed $400. You agree to the release. Later you discover that the damage to your car is $600. Can you collect the balance? The answer is no, you are limited to the $500 in the release. Therefore it is important to know the extent of your injuries or damages before signing a release.

Generally, releases are binding if three criteria are proved:

1.   The release is secured and given in good faith—that is, in the absence of fraud and the like.
2.   In many states, the release must be in a signed writing.
3.   Consideration for the release is given.

Consideration in the above case is Jean's promised payment of $500 in return for your promise not to bring an action for a larger amount. Under the UCC, a written, signed waiver or renunciation by an aggrieved party discharges any further liability for a breach even without consideration.[9]

A **covenant not to sue**, in contrast to a release, does not always bar further recovery. The parties simply substitute a contractual obligation for some other type of action. For example, assume that in the accident just described, you say that you are going to sue the negligent party, Jean, in tort (negligence) for your damages. Jean and you agree that

if you will refrain from bringing a tort action, she will pay for all damages to your car. Therefore, a contract is substituted for the tort action. If Jean fails to pay for your damages as agreed, your action is for breach of contract (you do not have to prove negligence). This does not prevent you from bringing a tort-negligence suit; but if you do so, you have breached your contract. The same elements for a binding release are required for a valid covenant not to sue.

Past Consideration

Promises made for events that have already taken place are unenforceable. These promises lack consideration in that the element of bargained-for exchange is missing. In short, you can bargain for something to take place now or in the future, but not for something that has already taken place. Therefore, **past consideration** is no consideration.

Suppose a father tells his son, "In consideration of the fact that you named your son after me when he was born, I promise to pay you $1,000." The promise is for an event that already has taken place, so it is unenforceable. A similar example is a promise to pay for "past love and affection given." Although there are strong moral obligations to fulfill those promises, there is no legal obligation to do so.

Consider instead that the father tells his son, "In consideration of your promise to name your next child after me, I promise to pay you $1,000." The son names his next child after his father. Here is a bargained-for exchange with legally sufficient consideration binding the father to pay.

In the following case, we see an illustration of how "past" and "moral" issues can be involved in consideration.

---

9.   UCC 1-107.

LANFIER v. LANFIER
Supreme Court of Iowa, 1939.
227 Iowa 258, 288 N.W. 104.

BACKGROUND AND FACTS   *This suit concerned title to certain real property. The plaintiff-appellee was a minor bringing suit through his father. The defendants were the heirs of August Schultz and the administratrix of his estate. The case came to court on the basis of an oral contract allegedly made between Schultz and the plaintiff (through the plaintiff's mother).*

The plaintiff was born December 17, 1925 and two days later was named August Dwayne Lanfier after his grandfather August Schultz. Over three months later, Schultz orally agreed to transfer certain real property to the plaintiff, subject to a life estate in plaintiff's parents, if plaintiff's parents would name the plaintiff after him. The plaintiff's parents accepted Schultz's offer. Schultz neglected to perform his oral contract and never arranged for title to the property to pass to plaintiff. However, he did deliver possession of the real estate to plaintiff's parents, who held possession for about twelve years. Among other things, the plaintiff wanted the court to adjudge him the absolute owner of the real estate.

The administratrix of Schultz's estate and the other beneficiaries challenged plaintiff's right to the property. The trial court awarded the property to the plaintiff based on the alleged oral contract between decedent and plaintiff's mother.

MILLER, Justice.

* * * *

"The general principle of the law of contracts, that to be valid and legally enforceable, as between the parties thereto an agreement or undertaking of any kind must be supported by a consideration, is too elementary to call for citation of authorities."

Under the record herein, there is a total absence of any evidence of a legal consideration to support the alleged contract plaintiff seeks to enforce. The evidence is undisputed that plaintiff was born on December 17, 1925, and, two days later, December 19, 1925, he was named August Dwayne Lanfier. He was named August after his grandfather, the decedent herein. * * * There is no evidence of any request on the part of the decedent that plaintiff be named after him until the latter part of March, 1926, over three months after plaintiff had been named. There are several witnesses who testified to conversations between plaintiff's mother and the decedent at that time, the substance of which was that, if plaintiff's mother would name plaintiff after the decedent, decedent would make a will and would thereby devise to plaintiff the real estate in question, subject to a life estate in plaintiff's parents. At the time these conversations were had, plaintiff and his parents were already in possession of the property, as tenants of the decedent. * * *

Counsel for plaintiff assert that the contract was supported by sufficient consideration, in that the prior naming of the plaintiff for the decedent constituted a past or moral consideration, and further that the contract should be supported on the basis of love and affection being good consideration. The contentions of counsel are without merit.

This court has repeatedly held that past or moral consideration is not sufficient to support an executory contract. * * * If the services are gratuitous, no obligation, either moral or legal, is incurred by the recipient. No one is bound to pay for that which is a gratuity. No moral obligation is assumed by a person who receives a gift. Suppose the plaintiff had given the defendant a horse, was he morally bound to pay what the horse was reasonably worth? We think not. In such case there never was any liability to pay, and therefore a subsequent promise would be without any consideration to support it.

* * * *

The contentions of counsel to the effect that love and affection constitute sufficient consideration to support the contract here asserted are likewise without merit. No such consideration is expressed in the contract, and we seriously doubt that the record supports any claim that such might have been consideration for the alleged contract. However, in any event, the proposition of law contended for by counsel has no support in the decisions of this court or in the courts generally.

* * * *

"Although love and affection is a 'good' consideration, it is not a sufficient consideration for a promise. Promises or contracts made on the basis of mere love and affection, unsupported by a pecuniary or material benefit, create at most bare moral obligations, and a breach thereof presents no cause for redress by the court."

DECISION AND REMEDY *Plaintiff was not awarded title to the property. Love and affection are not legally sufficient consideration to support a promise, and thus breach of such a promise presents no legally recognizable cause of action.*

COMMENTS *In rare cases, courts are willing to recognize a moral obligation of the promisor as a substitute for consideration where the promisor receives a material benefit and subsequently expresses a promise to pay for it. For example, in Webb v. McGowin, 27 Ala.App. 82, 168 So. 196 (1935), Webb was maimed for life when he diverted the course of a falling block of wood that otherwise would have killed McGowin. McGowin was so grateful to Webb that he agreed to send him $15 every two weeks for the remainder of Webb's life. But McGowin died before Webb. Ultimately, the court ruled that McGowin's estate was responsible for continuing to pay Webb the $15 every other week. McGowin's promise became a valid and enforceable contract. (See also Old American Life Ins. Co. v. Biggers, 172 F.2d 495 [10th Cir. 1949].)*

Promises Enforceable Without Consideration

There are exceptions to the rule that only promises supported by consideration are enforceable. Other circumstances in which promises will be enforced despite the lack of what one normally considers legal consideration are as follows:

1. Composition of creditors' agreements.
2. Promises to pay debts barred by the statute of limitations.
3. Promises to pay debts barred by discharge in bankruptcy.
4. Detrimental reliance, or promissory estoppel.
5. Charitable subscriptions.

Composition of Creditors' Agreements A composition with creditors is an agreement between an insolvent or financially troubled debtor and his or her creditors that the creditors will accept either a specified amount or a percentage of the full amount owed. A creditors' composition agreement can be fully enforceable without consideration, although courts sometimes find consideration in the mutual promises of the creditors to accept less than the full amount owed.

Promises to Pay Debts Barred by the Statute of Limitations Statutes of limitations in all states require a creditor to sue within a specified period to recover debts. If the creditor fails to sue in time, recovery of the debt is barred by the statute of limitations. A debtor who promises to pay a previous debt barred by the statute of limitations makes an enforceable promise. *The promise needs no consideration.* (Some states, however, require that it be in writing.) In effect, the promise extends the limitations period, and the creditor can sue to recover the entire debt, or at least the amount promised. The promise can be implied if the debtor acknowledges the barred debt by making a partial payment.

Suppose you borrow $5,000 from First National Bank of San Jose. The loan is due in November 1980. You fail to pay, and the bank does not sue you until December 1985. If California's statute of limitations for this debt is five years, recovery of the debt is barred. If you then agree to pay off the loan, First National Bank can sue for the entire amount. This is an example of an express promise, which extends the limitations period. Likewise, you can make a monthly payment and implicitly acknowledge the existence of the debt. Again First National Bank can sue you for the entire debt. This is an example of acknowledgment. Suppose instead that you expressly promise First National Bank to pay it $2,500. This promise is generally enforceable only to the extent of $2,500 (and usually must be in writing).

Promises to Pay Debts Barred by Discharge in Bankruptcy

The Bankruptcy Reform Act of 1978, as amended by the Bankruptcy Amendments and Federal Judgeship Act of 1984, has made substantial changes in the law concerning reaffirmations of debts barred by a discharge in bankruptcy. Prior to the enactment of the law, a former debtor could make a promise in writing to repay a debt totally discharged by a bankruptcy decree, and that promise would be enforced without consideration.

The law severely restricts such reaffirmations, and they are enforceable only under the following conditions:

1. The reaffirmation agreement must be made prior to the debtor's discharge in bankruptcy. Even then, the debtor has a right to rescind the agreement at any time prior to the debtor's discharge decree or within sixty (60) days of the filing of the agreement with the Bankruptcy Court, whichever is later. The right to rescind and the rescission period must be stated clearly and conspicuously in the reaffirmation agreement.

2. The reaffirmation agreement must be filed with the Bankruptcy Court. If the debtor is represented by an attorney, court approval is not required if the attorney files a declaration or affidavit stating that the debtor is fully aware of the consequences of the agreement, the agreement was entered into voluntarily, and the agreement does not impose a hardship on the debtor or on the dependents of the debtor. If the debtor is not represented by an attorney, court approval is required, and the court will only approve if the agreement does not operate as an undue hardship and is in the best interest of the debtor.

Detrimental Reliance, or the Doctrine of Promissory Estoppel

The doctrine of detrimental reliance, or promissory estoppel, involves a promise given by one party that induces another party to rely on that promise to his or her detriment. When the promisor (the person making the promise) can reasonably expect the promisee (the person receiving the promise) to act on the promise, and injustice cannot be avoided any other way, the promise will be enforced.[10] Additionally, the promisee must act with justifiable reliance on the promise—that is, must be justified in relying on it—and the act must be of a substantial nature.

The promise is enforced by refusing to allow the promisor to set up the defense of lack of consideration. The promisor is estopped (prevented) from asserting the lack of consideration. The estoppel arises from the promise, and hence *promissory estoppel* is the term used. (This doctrine is not used in some jurisdictions.)

Imagine that your grandfather tells you, "I'll pay you $75 per week so you won't have to work anymore." Then you quit your job, and your grandfather refuses to pay. You may be able to enforce the promise since you have justifiably relied on it to your detriment.[11]

Traditionally, promissory estoppel has been applied only to gratuitous promises, that is, when the parties are not bargaining in a commercial setting. The trend, however, is to apply it in any situation if justice so requires. A classic case illustrates this point.

---

10. Restatement, Second, Contracts, Section 90 provides: A promise which the promisor should reasonably expect to induce action or forbearance on the part of the promisee or a third person and which does induce such action or forbearance is binding if injustice can be avoided only by enforcement of the promise.
11. Ricketts v. Scothorn, 57 Neb. 51, 77 N.W. 365 (1898).

BACKGROUND AND FACTS *Red Owl Stores, Inc. (defendant), induced the Hoffmans (plaintiffs) to give up their current business and run a Red Owl franchise. The Hoffmans relied on the representations of Red Owl, and when the deal ultimately fell through because of Red Owl's failure to keep its promise concerning the operation of the franchise agency store, the Hoffmans brought this suit to recover their losses, and the trial court found in their favor.*

HOFFMAN v. RED OWL STORES, INC.

Supreme Court of Wisconsin, 1965.
26 Wis.2d 683, 133 N.W.2d 267.

CURRIE, Chief Justice.

*   *   *   *

Recognition of a Cause of Action Grounded on Promissory Estoppel.

Sec. 90 of Restatement, 1 Contracts, provides (at p. 110):

"A promise which the promisor should reasonably expect to induce action or forbearance of a definite and substantial character on the part of the promisee and which does induce such action or forbearance is binding if injustice can be avoided only by enforcement of the promise."

*   *   *   *

Because we deem the doctrine of promissory estoppel, as stated in sec. 90 of Restatement, 1 Contracts, as one which supplies a needed tool which courts may employ in a proper case to prevent injustice, we endorse and adopt it.

Applicability of Doctrine to Facts of this Case.

The record here discloses a number of promises and assurances given to Hoffman by Lukowitz in behalf of Red Owl upon which plaintiffs relied and acted upon to their detriment.

Foremost were the promises that for the sum of $18,000 Red Owl would establish Hoffman in a store. After Hoffman had sold his grocery store and paid the $1,000 on the Chilton lot, the $18,000 figure was changed to $24,100. Then in November, 1961, Hoffman was assured that if the $24,100 figure were increased by $2,000 the deal would go through. Hoffman was induced to sell his grocery store fixtures and inventory in June, 1961, on the promise that he would be in his new store by fall. In November, plaintiffs sold their bakery building on the urging of defendants and on the assurance that this was the last step necessary to have the deal with Red Owl go through.

We determine that there was ample evidence to sustain the answers of the jury to the questions of the verdict with respect to the promissory representations made by Red Owl, Hoffman's reliance thereon in the exercise of ordinary care, and his fulfillment of the conditions required of him by the terms of the negotiations had with Red Owl.

There remains for consideration the question of law raised by defendants that agreement was never reached on essential factors necessary to establish a contract between Hoffman and Red Owl. Among these were the size, cost, design, and layout of the store building; and the terms of the lease with respect to rent, maintenance, renewal, and purchase options. This poses *the question of whether the promise necessary to sustain a cause of action for promissory estoppel must embrace all essential details of a proposed transaction* between promisor and promisee so as to be the equivalent of an offer that would result in a binding contract between the parties if the promisee were to accept the same. [Emphasis added.]

Originally the doctrine of promissory estoppel was invoked as a substitute for consideration rendering a gratuitous promise enforceable as a contract. In other words, the acts of reliance by the promisee to his detriment provided a substitute for consideration. If promissory estoppel were to be limited to only those situations where the promise giving rise to the cause of action must be so definite with respect to all details that a contract would result were the promise supported by consideration, then the defendants' instant promises to Hoffman would not meet this test. However, sec. 90 of Restatement, 1 Contracts, does not impose the requirement that the promise giving rise to the cause of action must be so comprehensive in scope as to meet the requirements of an offer that would ripen into a contract if accepted by the promisee. Rather the conditions imposed are:

(1) Was the promise one which the promisor should reasonably expect to induce action or forbearance of a definite and substantial character on the part of the promisee?

(2) Did the promise induce such action or forbearance?

(3) Can injustice be avoided only by enforcement of the promise?

We deem it would be a mistake to regard an action grounded on promissory estoppel as the equivalent of a breach of contract action. As Dean Boyer points out, it is desirable that fluidity in the application of the concept be maintained. While the first two of the above listed three requirements of promissory estoppel present issues of fact which ordinarily will be resolved by a jury, the third requirement, that the remedy can only be invoked where necessary to avoid injustice, is one that involves a policy decision by the court. Such a policy decision necessarily embraces an element of discretion.

We conclude that injustice would result here if plaintiffs were not granted some relief because of the failure of defendants to keep their promises which induced plaintiffs to act to their detriment.

The trial court's judgment was affirmed. Hoffman was entitled to damages, the exact amount to be determined when the case was returned to the trial court.

DECISION AND REMEDY

Promissory estoppel does not mean that each and every gratuitous promise will be binding merely because the promisee has changed position. Liability is created only when there is "justifiable reliance on the promise." The promisor must have known or had reason to believe that the promisee would likely be induced to change position as a result of the promise.

COMMENTS

Charitable Subscriptions Subscriptions to religious, educational, and charitable institutions are promises to make a gift and are unenforceable on traditional contract grounds because they are not supported by legally sufficient consideration. A gift is the opposite of bargained-for consideration. However, the modern view is to enforce these promises under the doctrine of promissory estoppel, or find consideration simply as a matter of public policy.

The premise for enforcement is that a promise is made, and an institution changes its position because of reliance on that promise. For example, suppose a church solicits and receives donative sub-scriptions to build a new church. On the basis of these pledges, the church purchases land, employs architects, and makes other contracts that change its position. Courts may enforce the pledges under promissory estoppel, or find consideration in the fact that each promise is made in reliance on the other promises of support, or that the trustees, by accepting the subscription, impliedly promise to complete the proposed undertaking. Such cases represent exceptions to the general rule that consideration must exist for the formation of a contract. And these exceptions come about as a result of public policy.

QUESTIONS AND CASE PROBLEMS

1. D'Albergo is the owner of a large bakery. She contracts to purchase from XYZ Flour, Inc., all the flour she might desire for a one-year period at $30 per barrel. Payment terms call for a billing at the end of each month for shipments made, with a 3 percent discount if paid within twenty days of the billing date. During the first month D'Albergo orders and XYZ delivers 1,000 barrels of flour. On the third day of the next month, XYZ sends D'Albergo a bill for $30,000 dated that same day. A dispute develops between the two parties. XYZ refuses to ship any more flour to D'Albergo, and on the thirtieth day of the month, D'Albergo sends XYZ a check for $29,100, marked clearly, "payment in full." Discuss whether XYZ's refusal to ship any more flour places it in breach of contract. Also, if XYZ cashes D'Albergo's check, can XYZ recover in a lawsuit the balance of $900?

2. Tabor is the buyer of widgits manufactured by Martin. Martin's contract with Tabor calls for delivery of 10,000 widgits at $1 per widgit in ten equal installments. After delivery of two installments, Martin informs Tabor that

because of inflation, Martin is losing money and will promise to deliver the remaining 8,000 widgits only if Tabor will pay $1.20 per widgit. Tabor agrees in writing. Discuss whether Martin can legally collect the additional $200 upon delivery to Tabor of the next installment of 1,000 widgits.

3. Star Furniture Company manufactures summer lawn furniture. Its sole product consists of webbed aluminum frame furniture used mainly on outdoor patios and on beaches. As of October 1, Star Furniture was heavily indebted to its three main suppliers—Aluminum Pole, Inc.; Plastic Webbing, Ltd.; and The Little Steel Rivet Company. Star owed each of these suppliers approximately $10,000. Star's president met with the presidents of the three suppliers to work out some arrangement whereby the company could avoid declaring bankruptcy. Since all the parties desired that Star Furniture not go bankrupt, an agreement was made among the four parties that Star would pay each supplier $7,000, which would be accepted as full payment of all outstanding debts as of October 1. Discuss whether this agreement is enforceable.

4. Beyer owns a lot and wants to build a house according to a specific set of plans and specifications. She solicits bids from building contractors and receives three bids: one from Carlton for $60,000, one from Friend for $58,000, and one from Shade for $53,000. She accepts Shade's bid. One month after construction of the house has begun, Shade contacts Beyer and informs her that because of inflation and a recent price hike in materials, he will not finish the house unless Beyer agrees to pay an extra $3,000. Beyer reluctantly agrees to pay the additional sum. After the house is finished, however, Beyer refuses to pay the additional $3,000. Discuss whether Beyer is legally required to pay this additional amount.

5. Daniel, a recent college graduate, is on his way home for the Christmas holidays from his new job. Daniel gets caught in a snowstorm and is taken in by an elderly couple, who provide him with food and shelter. After the snowplows have cleared the road, Daniel proceeds home. Daniel's father, Fred, is most appreciative of the elderly couple's action and in a letter promises to pay them $500. The elderly couple, in need of money, accept Fred's offer. Because of a dispute between Daniel and Fred, Fred refuses to pay the elderly couple the $500. Discuss whether they can hold Fred in contract for the services rendered to Daniel.

6. Greenwood, an established professional football player, signed a contract on May 31, 1974, to play football for three years, beginning in 1975, for the Birmingham Americans. The Birmingham Americans were a team operated by Alabama Football, Inc. (AFI), under a franchise agreement with the World Football League. The contract provided for an initial payment to Greenwood of $25,000 upon signing the contract, a $25,000 payment in September 1974, and a $25,000 payment in April, 1975.

Greenwood received the first two payments of $25,000 each. During the 1974 season, however, AFI experienced extreme financial difficulties, and in January of 1975 it lost its franchise to operate a team in the World Football League. Greenwood subsequently cancelled his agreement with AFI. AFI sued Greenwood to recover the $50,000 already paid, on the theory that Greenwood had not yet earned any compensation under the contract. Greenwood countered that the $50,000 constituted payment for his signing the contract and for the promotional value that AFI derived from the use of his name during 1974. Does the signing of the contract and the use of Greenwood's name during 1974 constitute sufficient consideration to support the early payments made to Greenwood? Was AFI contractually obligated to make those payments, or were they merely unearned advances that must be returned upon cancellation of the contract? [Alabama Football, Inc. v. Greenwood, 452 F.Supp. 1191 (W.D.Pa.1978)]

7. Martino is a police officer in Atlantic City. Gray, who lost a significant amount of her jewelry during a burglary of her home, offered a reward for the recovery of the property. Incident to his job, Martino possessed certain knowledge concerning the theft of Gray's jewelry. When Martino informed Gray of his knowledge of the theft, Gray offered Martino $500 to help her recover her jewelry. As a result of Martino's police work, the jewelry was recovered and returned to Gray. Martino sued Gray for the reward he claimed she promised him. Was there a valid contract between Gray and Martino? [Gray v. Martino, 91 N.J.L. 462, 103 A. 24 (1918)]

8. Feinberg was employed as bookkeeper, office manager, and assistant treasurer of Pfeiffer Company. After she had worked there for forty-seven years, the board of directors, in recognition of her "long and faithful service," passed a resolution whereunder she would be paid $200 a month for the rest of her life at any time she decided to retire. Shortly thereafter, Feinberg retired and for several years received the $200 per month as promised. The president of Pfeiffer eventually died and was succeeded by his son-in-law, who reduced the payments to $100 a month. Feinberg sued Pfeiffer Company. Was she able to recover under contract theory? [Feinberg v. Pfeiffer Co., 322 S.W.2d 163 (Mo.App. 1959)]

9. Kowalsky, a contractor, is required to make periodic payments to a union pension fund administered by Kelly, trustee for the union. Kowalsky and Kelly disagree over the amount of money Kowalsky owes the union. After a number of heated discussions Kowalsky sends Kelly four checks totaling $8,500 and encloses them in a letter saying: "These checks are tendered with the understanding that they are full payment of all claims against Kowalsky." Immediately after receiving the checks, Kelly called Kowalsky and told him the checks were not going to be cashed, but would simply be held and that Kowalsky still owed Kelly money because the $8,500 did not cover late

charges on the deposited payments. Kowalsky did not ask for the return of the checks or stop payment. Kelly retained, but does not cash, the checks and sues Kowalsky for the late charges. Kowalsky claims that retention of the checks constituted full accord and satisfaction of the debt. Who wins and why? [Kelly v. Kowalsky, 186 Conn. 618, 442 A.2d 1355 (1982)]

10. A group of developers in Alabama were planning the development of approximately seventy-five acres as an office park. Part of the proposed development was in the Mountain Brook police jurisdiction, and part was in the Homewood police jurisdiction. In order to facilitate administrative dealings, the developers sought to have Mountain Brook annex the part of the proposed development that was in Homewood and requested the Mountain Brook Planning Commission to pass a resolution containing certain assurances to the homeowners in both Homewood and Mountain Brook who would be affected by the development. In part, the resolution that was passed stated that a buffer zone of about one hundred feet would surround the houses in Homewood. The zone would be maintained at all times, there would be no building or parking permitted in it, and it would be left as natural woodland. Twenty years later, only the hundred-foot buffer zone of natural woodlands separated the homeowners' backyards from the office park that had been developed. The developers announced plans to eliminate the buffer zone and to construct an additional office park. They claimed that the homeowners had no ground for preventing such additional development because there was no detrimental reliance on the alleged promises about maintaining the buffer zone. What was the result? [Mazer v. Jackson Ins. Agency, 340 So.2d 770 (Ala. 1976)]

10

CONTRACTS
Contractual Capacity

Historically, the law has concerned itself with the relative strength of the bargaining power of each contracting party. Thus, special protection is afforded those who bargain with the inexperience of youth or those who lack legally defined mental competence.

Contractual capacity—the competence (legal ability) of the parties—is one element of a valid contract. Full competence exists when both parties have full legal capacity to enter into a contract and to have the contract enforced against them. *No competence* exists when one or both of the parties have been adjudged by a proper court to be insane and therefore have no legal capacity to contract. In this event, an essential element for a valid contract is missing, and the contract is *void. Limited competence* exists when one or both parties are minors in age, intoxicated, or insane (but not yet adjudicated officially as such by a proper court). These parties have full and legal capacity to enter into a contract, but if they so wish, they can avoid liability under the contract. This kind of contract is said to be *voidable*.

MINORS

At common law, a minor was defined as a male who had not attained the age of twenty-one or a female who had not attained the age of eighteen. Today, in most states, the age of majority (when a person is no longer a minor) for contractual purposes has been changed by statute to eighteen years for both sexes.[1] In addition, some states provide for the termination of minority upon marriage. Subject to certain exceptions, the contracts entered into by a minor are voidable at the option of that minor. A **voidable contract** is one in which the minor may avoid legal obligations by exercising the option to *disaffirm* the contract. On the other hand, an adult who enters into a contract with a minor cannot avoid his or her contractual duties on the ground that the minor can do so. Unless the minor exercises the option to avoid the contract, the adult party is bound by it.

Minors' Rights to Disaffirm

The general rule of law is that a minor can enter into any contract that an adult can enter into, provided that the contract is not one prohibited by law for minors (for example, the sale of alcoholic bev-

---

1. Although the age of majority applicable in contracts has been changed to eighteen in many states, it may still be twenty-one for some purposes, including the purchase and consumption of alcohol. The word "infant" is usually used synonymously with the word "minor."

erages). Although minors can enter into contracts, they also have the right to disaffirm their contracts. Exceptions to this rule exist and will be discussed later in this chapter.

Disaffirmance in General   In order for a minor to exercise the option to avoid a contract, he or she need only manifest an intention not to be bound by it. The minor "avoids" the contract by "disaffirming" it. The technical definition of **disaffirmance** is the legal avoidance, or setting aside, of a contractual obligation. Words or conduct may serve to express this intent. Suppose James Caldwell, a seventeen-year-old, enters into a contract to sell his car to Joseph Reed, an adult. Caldwell can avoid the contract and avoid his legal duty to deliver possession of the car to Reed by either telling Reed that he refuses to abide by the contract or by selling the car to a third person. In other words, Caldwell can disaffirm the contract by expressing his intention in words or by acting inconsistently with his duties under the contract.

The contract can ordinarily be disaffirmed at any time during minority or for a reasonable time after the minor comes of age. However, in some states an exception exists in the case of a contract for the sale of land by a minor. There, a minor cannot disaffirm the contract until he or she reaches majority.

If a minor fails to disaffirm a contract within a reasonable time after reaching the age of majority, the court must determine whether the conduct constitutes *ratification*, binding the minor in contract, or *disaffirmance*, allowing the minor's avoidance. Generally, if the contract is fully performed by both parties (executed), the contract is presumed to be ratified. If the contract is still executory (not yet fully performed by both parties), it is considered disaffirmed.

For example, assume that the age of majority in your state is eighteen. Your sister, age seventeen, contracts to purchase a bicycle from an adult for $125. Your sister then turns eighteen. If she has not taken possession of the bicycle or paid the $125 purchase price, an executory contract exists, and most courts would hold her conduct to be an act of disaffirmance. On the other hand, if she has taken possession of the bicycle and paid the purchase price, an executed contract exists, and most courts would hold her failure to actively disaffirm within a rea-

sonable time after her eighteenth birthday to be an act of *ratification*, removing her right of avoidance.

Duty of Restoration   When a contract has been executed, minors cannot disaffirm without returning whatever goods they may have received, or paying for their reasonable value, or at least making an offer to pay. This is called the minor's *duty of restoration*. Although many states recognize this duty, most place certain limitations on it. Under the majority view, the minor need only return the goods (or other consideration), provided such goods are in the minor's possession or control. Suppose Pat Boland, a seventeen-year-old, purchases a used Ford Fairmont from Jane Crow, an adult. Boland is a bad driver and negligently runs the car into a telephone pole. The next day he returns the car to Crow and disaffirms the contract. Under the majority view, this return fulfills Boland's duty even though the auto is now wrecked.

On the other hand, a few states, either by statute or by court decision, have placed an additional duty on the minor—the *duty of restitution*. The theory is that the adult should be returned to his or her position before the contract was made. The duty of restitution requires Boland to pay Crow for the damage done to the car in addition to returning it. Some states do not require full restitution. A minor must pay only a "reasonable" amount to compensate the adult.

A minor must disaffirm the entire contract in order to disaffirm it at all. The minor cannot decide to keep part of the goods and return the remainder. When a minor disaffirms, all property that he or she has transferred to the adult as consideration can be recovered, even if it is then in the hands of a third party. If the property itself cannot be returned, the adult must pay the minor its equivalent value. Under UCC 2-403(1), dealing with the sale of or the contract to sell *goods*, a minor cannot recover the goods transferred to a third party who is a bona fide purchaser[2] ("a good faith purchaser for value"). For example, Mary, a minor, sells her bicycle to Ann, an adult, for $100. Ann immediately sells the bicycle to a fellow employee, Grant, for $110. Later, Mary wishes her bicycle back and notifies Ann of

---

2.   Defined as "a purchaser for a valuable consideration paid or parted with in the belief that the vender had a right to sell, and without any suspicious circumstances to put him on inquiry." [Merritt v. Railroad Co., 12 Barb., N.Y. 605 (1852)].

her intent to disaffirm the contract. Even though Mary has a legal right to disaffirm the contract with Ann, Mary cannot require Grant, a bona fide purchaser, to return the bicycle to her.

In the following case, a minor's father brought an action on behalf of his son to disaffirm the mi-

nor's purchase of an automobile and to recover the purchase price. The court reviewed the contract with the minor and took into account the fact that the seller knew the buyer was a minor when the contract was made.

QUALITY MOTORS, INC. v. HAYS

Supreme Court of Arkansas, 1949.
216 Ark. 264, 225 S.W.2d 326.

BACKGROUND AND FACTS *Johnny Hays, the plaintiff, was a sixteen-year-old minor. He went to Quality Motors, Inc. (the defendant) to inspect and test a car. When the Quality Motors salesman raised the question of Hays's age, he was told that Hays's father in New York had sent him the money to buy the car. The salesman refused to sell the car unless the purchase was made by an adult. Hays left the salesman and returned shortly with a young man of twenty-three, whom he had met that day for the first time.*

The salesman then accepted Hays's cashier's check in payment for the car. The bill of sale was made out to the twenty-three-year-old. The salesman then recommended a notary public to prepare the necessary papers for transfer of the title to Hays, and he drove the two into town for this purpose. The young man did transfer title, and the car was delivered by the salesman to Hays at his college.

When Hays's father, Dr. D. J. Hays, learned of the transaction, he called Quality Motors and asked it to take the car back. The company refused to do so. Dr. Hays was unable at that time to deliver the car back to Quality Motors, since his son had taken it out of town. However, the next day, Dr. Hays retrieved the car from his son and once again called Quality Motors to ask it to take the car back. It again refused. Dr. Hays then went to his attorney's office and, through his attorney, once more attempted to have the company accept the car back. The company refused but said it would try to sell the car for the Hayses if it could. The car was put into storage.

The following week this lawsuit was filed. Plaintiff's attorney indicated in writing to the defendant that the return of the automobile had been refused but that the automobile was now in storage and would be turned over to the defendant any time it would be accepted. Meanwhile, the son found the keys to the car and the bill of sale, took the car out of state, and damaged it in two accidents. At the time of trial, the car was subject to various repair bills and was not in running condition. The defendant continually refused to take the car back.

The special chancellor in the trial court found that, for all intents and purposes, the defendant sold the car to the plaintiff, knowing the plaintiff was a minor. The use of a third person adult was merely a sham.

DUNAWAY, Justice.
*   *   *   *

Johnny M. Hays [plaintiff], by his [father], Dr. D. J. Hays, brought this suit to disaffirm his purchase of a Pontiac automobile and recover the purchase price of $1,750 from defendant Quality Motors, Inc.
*   *   *   *

In the case at bar Johnny Hays testified positively that he desired to disaffirm his purchase and return the car to the seller. *   *   *

The law is well settled in Arkansas that an infant may disaffirm his contracts, except those made for necessaries, without being required to return the consideration received, except such part as may remain in specie in his hands. * * *

We do not find any merit in [Quality Motors's] contention that no proper tender of the car was made when [Johnny Hays through his father] sought to disaffirm his purchase. The undisputed testimony shows that Dr. Hays and his attorney offered to return the car on several occasions, but were informed that [defendant] would not accept it. That it was not actually delivered to Quality Motors when the suit was filed, is [defendant's] own fault. The law does not require that a tender be made under circumstances where it would be vain and useless.

[Quality Motors's] most serious contention is that the plaintiff is liable for damages to the car which occurred while he was driving over the country, after he had slipped the car from its storage place and while the suit to disaffirm was pending. In order to obtain any relief on this score, it must be shown that plaintiff was guilty of conversion in taking the automobile. [See Chapter 4 on torts.] Conversion is the exercise of dominion over property in violation of the rights of the owner or person entitled to possession. In advancing this argument [defendant] is in an inconsistent position. In its answer, [defendant] denied selling the car to [plaintiff] and was stoutly insisting that it did not have to take the car back. If that was true [defendant] was not the owner of nor entitled to possession of the car. Until the court decreed return of the car and recovery of the consideration paid, plaintiff still had title to the car. One cannot be liable for conversion in taking his own property.

* * * *

[I]n the instant case Quality Motors, Inc. was insisting at the time of the alleged conversion by Johnny Hays, that it did not have to accept return of the car. Ebbert, one of the owners of Quality Motors, Inc., testified that during his conversation with his employees in regard to keeping the car in the shop after the first wreck, he told them they could not make Johnny leave it. "Well, it's not our car," was his statement at that time. In these circumstances it certainly cannot be said [plaintiff's] possession was that of a bailee or trustee.

[Defendant] knowingly and through a planned subterfuge sold an automobile to a minor. It then refused to take the car back. Even after the car was wrecked once, it was in [defendant's] place of business, and [defendant] was still resisting disaffirmance of the contract. The loss which [defendant] has suffered is the direct result of its own acts.

DECISION AND REMEDY

The court affirmed the minor's right to avoid the contract. The plaintiff, Johnny Hays, was ordered to return the car to the defendant within seven days. When the wrecked car was returned, plaintiff was allowed to recover the purchase price from the defendant.

COMMENTS

Minors comprise a particular category of persons the law protects from economic exploitation. A minor is not compelled to avoid contracts made before attaining majority. Rather, the minor has the option of keeping the bargain or avoiding it.

The Effect of a Minor's Misrepresentation of Age   Suppose a minor tells a seller that she is twenty-one years old when she is actually only seventeen. Ordinarily, the minor can disaffirm the contract even though she has misrepresented her age. Moreover, the minor is not liable in certain jurisdictions for the tort of deceit for such misrepresentation, the ·

rationale being that such a tort judgment might indirectly force the minor to perform the contract.

Many jurisdictions, however, do find circumstances under which a minor can be bound by a contract when age has been misrepresented. First, several states have enacted statutes for precisely this purpose. In these states misrepresentation of age is enough to prohibit disaffirmance. Other statutes prohibit disaffirmance by a minor who has engaged in business as an adult.[3]

Second, some courts refuse to allow minors to disaffirm executed contracts unless they can return the consideration received. The combination of their misrepresentation and their unjust enrichment has persuaded several courts to estop (prevent) minors from asserting contractual incapacity.

Third, some courts allow a misrepresenting minor to disaffirm the contract but hold the minor

---

3. See, for example, statutes in Iowa, Kansas, Utah, and Washington.

liable for damages in tort. Here, the defrauded party may sue the minor for misrepresentation or fraud. A split in authority exists on this point, since some courts, as previously pointed out, have recognized that allowing a suit in tort is equivalent to the indirect enforcement of the minor's contract.

Basically, a minor's ability to avoid a contractual obligation is allowed by the law as a shield for the minor's defense, not as a sword for his or her unjust enrichment.

In the following case, an Ohio appellate court had to deal with the problem of a contract induced by a false representation of the age of the minor. The age of majority in Ohio at the time this case was decided was twenty-one years of age.

HAYDOCY PONTIAC, INC. v. LEE

Court of Appeals of Ohio, Franklin County, 1969. 19 Ohio App.2d 217, 250 N.E.2d 898.

BACKGROUND AND FACTS *The plaintiff is Haydocy Pontiac, a seller of automobiles. The defendant, Lee, was twenty years of age when she contracted to purchase the automobile, but she represented to the plaintiff, seller, that she was twenty-one years old. The defendant purchased the car by making a trade-in and financing the rest of the purchase price. She executed a note for the unpaid purchase price, including financing charges and insurance charges. The total amount of the note was approximately $2,000.*

Immediately following delivery of the automobile, Lee turned the car over to a third person. She never at any time thereafter had possession of the automobile. She made no further attempt to make payment on the contract, and she attempted to rescind it. She did not return the automobile to the plaintiff-seller; nor did she offer to return it. She merely announced that she was a minor at the time of purchase, that she had not ratified the agreement to purchase the car, and that she was repudiating her contract and would not be bound by it. The trial court applied the general rule of law permitting a minor to avoid a transaction without being required to restore the consideration received.

STRAUSBAUGH, Judge.
*   *   *   *

The cases we have examined in this regard all relate to the question whether the infant can recover from the vendor the purchase price paid and the right of the vendor to counterclaim rather than the facts of this case where the vendor, in the original petition, seeks to recover the property or, in lieu thereof, the balance due on the purchase price. Many of the cases use language to the effect that when the property received by the infant is in his possession, or under his control, to permit him to rescind the contract without requiring him to return or offer to return it would be to permit him to use his privilege as a "sword rather than a shield."
*   *   *   *

To allow infants to avoid a transaction without being required to restore the consideration received where the infant has used or otherwise disposed of it causes hardship on the other party. We hold that where the consideration received by the infant cannot be returned upon disaffirmance of the contract because it has been disposed of the infant must account for the value of it, not in excess of the purchase price, where the other party is free from any fraud or bad faith and where the contract has been induced by a false representation of the age of the infant. *Under this factual situation the infant is estopped [prevented] from pleading infancy as a defense where the contract has been induced by a false representation that the infant was of age.* [Emphasis added.]

The necessity of returning the consideration as a prerequisite to obtaining equitable relief is still clearer where the infant misrepresents age and perpetrated an actual fraud on the other party. The disaffirmance of an infant's contract is to be determined by equitable principles, whether sought in a proceeding in equity or a case at law.

The common law has bestowed upon the infant the privilege of disaffirming his contracts in conservation of his rights and interests. Where the infant, 20 years of age, through falsehood and deceit enters into a contract with another who enters therein in honesty and good faith and, thereafter, the infant seeks to disaffirm the contract without tendering back the consideration, no right or interest of the infant exists which needs protection. The privilege given the infant thereupon becomes a weapon of injustice.

Judgment of the trial court was reversed. The Ohio Appellate Court allowed the seller, Haydocy Pontiac, Inc., to recover the fair market value of the automobile from the defendant, Lee. The only restriction imposed by the court was that the fair market value could not be in excess of the original purchase price of the automobile.

DECISION AND REMEDY

Liability for Necessaries   A minor who enters into a contract for *necessaries* may disaffirm the contract but will still remain liable for the reasonable value of the goods. The legal duty to pay a reasonable value does not arise from the contract itself but is imposed by law under a theory of quasi-contract. One theory is that the minor should not be unjustly enriched and should therefore be liable for those things that fulfill basic needs, such as food, clothing, and shelter.

Another theory is that the minor's right to disaffirm a contract has economic ramifications in that sellers are likely to refuse to deal with minors because of it. If minors can at least be held liable for the reasonable value of the goods, sellers' reluctance to enter into contracts with minors will be offset. This theory explains why the courts narrow the subject matter to necessaries. Without such a rule, minors might be denied the opportunity to purchase necessary goods.

Note, though, that the minor is liable only for the reasonable value (quasi-contract theory) of the goods (because with disaffirmance there is no contract and therefore no contract price to which the court can refer). Suppose Hank Olsen, a minor, purchases a suit that is list priced at $150. After wearing the suit for several weeks, Olsen wants to disaffirm his contract with the clothier. He can do so, but he is liable for the reasonable value of the suit. If the market value is actually $115, then the clothier can recover only that amount, even if this deprives the clothier of all profit on the sale.

For an agreement to be classified as a contract for necessaries, three basic criteria are reviewed by a court. First, the item must be for the minor's very existence. Second, the value of the item must be in accordance with the minor's station in life (that to which the minor is accustomed). Third, the minor must not be under the care of a parent or guardian who has adequately supplied the minor with the items of necessity.

There is no firm, universally accepted definition of necessaries. In recent years, there has been a tendency by the courts to expand the "types" of contracts considered to be necessaries. At a minimum, necessaries include food, clothing, shelter, medicine, and hospital care. However, the term is not construed to be limited to items required for physical support of life, but extends to whatever is needed to maintain a person in his or her established lifestyle. Thus, what are necessaries for one person may not be for another in a different station in life. Moreover, necessaries include education as well as services that are reasonably necessary to enable a minor to earn a living (such as an employment agency fee for obtaining a job).

The following case illustrates what has traditionally been construed by common law to be necessaries and a court's willingness to expand the concept to include a contract with a professional employment agency to assist the minor in finding suitable employment.

GASTONIA
PERSONNEL CORP. v.
ROGERS

Supreme Court of North
Carolina, 1970.
276 N.C. 279, 172 S.E.2d 19.

BACKGROUND AND FACTS   *Bobby L. Rogers, defendant, was nineteen years old, married, and nearing the completion of his associate of arts degree when he went to the office of plaintiff, an employment agency, and signed a contract for assistance in obtaining suitable employment. The contract contained the following provision:*

> *"If I ACCEPT employment offered me by an employer as a result of a lead (verbal or otherwise) from you within twelve (12) months of such lead even though it may not be the position originally discussed with you, I will be obligated to pay you as per the terms of the contract."*

Under the contract, the defendant was otherwise free to continue his own quest for employment. He became obligated to the plaintiff only if he accepted a job to which the plaintiff agency had referred him.

After several telephone calls to prospective employers, the employment agency arranged an interview with an employer who ultimately hired the defendant. The service charge to defendant of $295 was never paid. Plaintiff attempted to collect its fee. Defendant attempted to disaffirm the contract on the theory that services of a professional employment agency are not "necessaries" and hence can be disaffirmed. The trial court agreed with the defendant.

BOBBITT, Chief Justice.

*   *   *   *

Under the common law, persons, whether male or female, are classified and referred to as *infants* until they attain the age of twenty-one years. [Under modern law, the age is lowered to eighteen years.]

*   *   *   *

An early commentary on the common law, after the general statement that contracts made by persons (infants) before attaining the age of twenty-one "may be avoided," sets forth "some exceptions out of this generality," to wit: "*An infant may bind himselfe to pay for his necessary meat, drinke, apparell, necessary physicke, and such other necessaries,* and likewise for his good teaching or instruction, whereby he may profit himselfe afterwards." (Our italics.) Coke on Littleton, 13th ed. (1788), p. 172. If the infant married, "necessaries" included necessary food and clothing for his wife and child.

In accordance with this ancient rule of the common law, this Court has held an infant's contract, unless for "necessaries" or unless authorized by statute, is voidable by the infant, at his election, and may be disaffirmed during infancy or upon attaining the age of twenty-one.

*   *   *   *

The nature of the common law requires that each time a rule of law is applied it be carefully scrutinized to make sure that the conditions and needs of the times have not so changed as to make further application of it the instrument of injustice.

In general, our prior decisions are to the effect that the "necessaries" of an infant, his wife and child, include only such necessities of life as food, clothing, shelter, medical attention, etc. In our view, the concept of "necessaries" should be enlarged to include such articles of property and such services as are reasonably necessary to enable the infant to earn the money required to provide the necessities of life for himself and those who are legally dependent upon him.

*   *   *   *

The evidence before us tends to show that defendant, when he contracted with plaintiff, was nineteen years of age, emancipated, married, a high school graduate, within "a quarter or 22 hours" of obtaining his degree in applied science, and capable of holding a job at a starting annual salary of $4,784.00. To hold, as a matter of law, that such a person cannot obligate himself to pay for services rendered him in obtaining employment suitable to his ability, education and specialized training, enabling him to provide the necessities of life for himself, his wife and his expected child, would place him and others similarly situated under a serious economic handicap.

In the effort to protect "older minors" from improvident or unfair contracts, the law should not deny to them the opportunity and right to obligate themselves for articles of property or services which are reasonably necessary to enable them to provide for the proper support of themselves and their dependents. The minor should be held liable for the reasonable value of articles of property or services received pursuant to such contract.

The services of a professional employment agency were construed to be a "necessary." The case was remanded to the lower court for a new trial. The defendant could be expected to pay the reasonable value of the services rendered to him pursuant to the employment contract.

DECISION AND REMEDY

Although the doctrine of voidability of a minor's contract often seems necessary for the protection of the young person, there are situations in which such a result is unjust. This is consistent with the policy of law that promotes business by allowing contracts to develop between parties whenever possible. Some states allow the parties to submit a proposed contract to a court that removes a minor's right to disaffirm if the court finds the particular contract to be fair or just.

COMMENTS

Insurance and Loans   Traditionally, insurance has not been viewed as a *necessary*, so minors can ordinarily disaffirm their contract and recover all premiums paid. However, some jurisdictions prohibit the right to disaffirm—for example, when minors contract for life or health insurance on their own lives. Other jurisdictions allow a minor to disaffirm but limit recovery to the value of premiums paid, less the insurance company's actual cost of protecting the minor under the policy. Suppose Bob Berzak takes out an automobile insurance policy and pays $125 in premiums. Bob has an accident for which his insurance company, State Farm, pays a claim of $85. In states following the traditional rule, Bob's recovery upon disaffirmance will be $125, the full value of the premiums. In states limiting his recovery, Bob can recover only $40, the excess of the value of the premiums over State Farm's actual cost under the policy.

In and of itself, a loan is seldom viewed as a necessary, even if the minor spends the money on necessaries. However, if the lender makes a loan for the express purpose of enabling the minor to purchase necessaries, and the lender personally makes sure the money is so spent, the minor is normally obligated to repay the loan.

Ratification

Ratification is an act or expression in words by which a minor, upon or after reaching majority, indicates an *intention* to become bound by the contract. Ratification must necessarily occur, if at all, after the individual comes of age, since any attempt to become legally bound prior to majority is no more effective than the original contractual promise. This protects the minor and is consistent with the theory that the contracts of a minor are voidable at his or her option.

Express Ratification   Suppose John Lawrence enters into a contract to sell a house to Carol Ogden. At the time of the contract Carol is a minor. Naturally, Carol can avoid her legal duty to pay for the house by disaffirming the contract. Imagine, instead, that Carol reaches majority and writes a letter to John stating that she still agrees to buy the house. Carol thus ratifies the contract and is now legally bound. John can sue for breach of contract if Carol refuses to perform her part of the bargain. This is an example of *express* ratification.

Implied Ratification   The contract can also be ratified by *conduct*. Suppose, after reaching majority,

Carol lives in the house. This conduct evidences an intent to abide by the contract and is a form of *implied* ratification. Again, Carol is legally bound, and John can sue her for breach of contract if she fails to perform her duty to pay the purchase price. When an individual, after reaching majority, continues to use and make payments on property purchased as a minor, the continued use and payment is inconsistent with disaffirmance and implicitly indicates an intention to be bound by the contract.

In general, any act or conduct showing an intention to affirm the contract will be deemed to be ratification. However, as previously discussed, silence after reaching the age of majority does not in and of itself constitute ratification of an executory contract in most situations. If Carol had said nothing to John and had not entered into possession or made payment, she would not have ratified the contract, since she had expressed no intention to abide by it. On the other hand, the minor may have a duty to speak in some circumstances. Suppose that after coming of age, a former minor seller fails to disaffirm, knowing that the purchaser is making improvements on the property sold. In this case the minor cannot disaffirm the contract.

Non-voidable Contracts and Torts

Minors   Many states have passed statutes restricting the ability of minors to avoid certain contracts. For example, as previously discussed, some states prohibit minors from disaffirming certain insurance contracts. Other states hold that loans for education or medical care received by minors create binding legal duties that they cannot avoid.[4]

In addition, certain statutes specifically require minors to perform legal duties. Suppose James Dornan, a minor, wants to legally seize the property of Davis Snowden for default of a loan. In some states, Dornan is required to file a bond before the legal seizure, or attachment, can occur. After filing the bond, Dornan cannot avoid the obligations of the bonding agreement, since the bond is a legal duty imposed by state statute. In such situations, a minor cannot rely on the common law rule that the bonding contract is voidable. Similar legal duties are imposed on minors with respect to bank accounts and transfers of stocks.

---

4.   New York Education Law, Sec. 281 (McKinney 1969); Cal. Civil Code Sec. 36 (West 1982).

Some contracts cannot be avoided, simply as a matter of law, on the grounds of public policy. For example, marriage contracts and contracts to enlist in the armed services fall into this category.

Torts   In Chapters 4 and 5, we discussed the area of law called torts, defined as private wrongs committed upon a person or property independent of contract. Generally, minors are liable for their torts. Courts do, however, weigh the factors of age, mental capacity, and maturity before determining a minor's liability. As has been pointed out, a breach of contract is normally not treated as a tort for which the minor is liable. However, when the tort is more than a simple misfeasance in the performance of a contract, and when it is separate from and independent of the contract, the court may rule against the minor. The test of action against the minor is whether liability exists without taking notice of the contract. For example, suppose a minor rents a boat. The rental agreement provides that the minor will use due care to prevent damage to the boat. Nonetheless, the minor's careless use of the boat damages it. Will a court uphold an action in tort for negligence? The answer to this question depends on whether imposing tort liability on the minor will directly or indirectly enforce the minor's promise, which, because of a lack of contractual capacity, is voidable.

Parents' Liability

As a general rule, parents are not liable for the contracts made by their minor children. This is why businesses ordinarily require parents to sign any contract made with a minor. The parents then become personally obligated under the contract to perform the conditions of the contract, even if their child avoids liability.

Parents who have neglected the care of their minor child can be held liable for the reasonable value of necessaries supplied to the child, even when they have not signed a contract. In other words, if a child purchases shoes because his or her parents refuse to provide any shoes, the parents can be held liable for the reasonable value of the shoes.

INTOXICATED PERSONS

A contract entered into by an intoxicated person can be either voidable or valid. If the person was drunk enough to lack mental capacity, then the transaction is voidable at the option of the intoxicated person even if the intoxication was purely voluntary. In order for the contract to be voidable, it must be proved that the intoxicated person's reason and judgment were impaired to the extent that he or she did not comprehend the legal consequences of entering into the contract. If, despite intoxication, the person understands these legal consequences, the contract will be enforceable. Simply because the terms of the contract are foolish or obviously favor the other party does not mean that the contract is voidable (unless the other party *fraudulently* induced the person to become intoxicated). Problems often arise in determining whether a party was drunk enough to avoid legal duties. Many courts prefer to look at objective indications to determine whether the contract is voidable because of intoxication rather than inquire into the intoxicated party's mental state.

The following case shows an unusual business transaction in which boasts, brags, and dares "after a few drinks" resulted in a binding sale and purchase transaction. It should be noted that avoidance for intoxication is very rare.

BACKGROUND AND FACTS   *W. O. Lucy and J. C. Lucy filed suit against A. H. Zehmer and Ida Zehmer, the defendants, to compel the Zehmers to perform a contract by which it was alleged that the Zehmers had sold to the Lucys their property, known as the Ferguson Farm, for $50,000. The transaction had come about in a most unusual manner. Lucy had known Zehmer for fifteen or twenty years and for the last eight years or so had been anxious to buy the Ferguson Farm from Zehmer. One night, Lucy stopped in to visit the Zehmers in the restaurant, filling station, and motor court they operated. While there, Lucy tried to buy the Ferguson Farm once again. This time he tried a new approach. According to the trial court transcript, Lucy said to Zehmer, "I bet you wouldn't take $50,000 for that place." Zehmer replied, "Yes, I would too; you wouldn't give fifty."*

Throughout the evening the conversation returned to the sale of the Ferguson Farm for $50,000. At the same time, the parties continued to drink whiskey and engage in light conversation. The conversation repeatedly returned to the subject of the Ferguson Farm. Eventually, Lucy enticed Zehmer to write up an agreement to the effect that Zehmer would agree to sell to Lucy the Ferguson Farm for $50,000 complete. Zehmer first wrote that out on the back of a restaurant check. He tore up the first copy because he had written "I do hereby agree" and thought it had better read "we" because Mrs. Zehmer would have to sign it too. Zehmer rewrote the agreement and asked Mrs. Zehmer to sign it. She agreed.

Lucy sued Zehmer to go through with the sale. Zehmer argued that he was drunk and that the offer was made in jest and hence was unenforceable. The trial court agreed with the Zehmers.

W. O. LUCY AND J. C. LUCY v. A. H. ZEHMER AND IDA S. ZEHMER
Supreme Court of Appeals of Virginia, 1954.
196 Va. 493, 84 S.E.2d 516.

BUCHANAN, Justice.

* * * *

The instrument sought to be enforced was written by A. H. Zehmer on December 20, 1952, in these words: "We hereby agree to sell to W. O. Lucy the Ferguson Farm complete for $50,000.00, title satisfactory to buyer," and signed by the defendants, A. H. Zehmer and Ida S. Zehmer.

A. H. Zehmer admitted that *   *   * W. O. Lucy offered him $50,000 cash for the farm, but that he, Zehmer, considered that the offer was made in jest; that so thinking, and both he and Lucy having had several drinks, he wrote out "the memorandum" quoted above and induced his wife to sign it; that he did not deliver the memorandum to Lucy, but that Lucy picked it up, read it, put it in his pocket, attempted to offer Zehmer $5 to bind the bargain, which Zehmer refused to accept, and realizing for the first time that Lucy was serious, Zehmer assured him that he had no intention of selling the farm and that the whole matter was a joke. Lucy left the premises insisting that he had purchased the farm.

* * * *

The discussion leading to the signing of the agreement, said Lucy, lasted thirty or forty minutes, during which Zehmer seemed to doubt that Lucy could raise $50,000. Lucy suggested the provision for having the title examined and Zehmer made the suggestion that he would sell it "complete, everything there," and stated that all he had on the farm was three heifers.

Lucy took a partly filled bottle of whiskey into the restaurant with him for the purpose of giving Zehmer a drink if he wanted it. Zehmer did, and he and Lucy had one or two drinks together. Lucy said that while he felt the drinks he took he was not intoxicated, and from the way Zehmer handled the transaction he did not think he was either.

* * * *

The defendants insist that * * * the writing sought to be enforced was prepared as a bluff or dare to force Lucy to admit that he did not have $50,000; that the whole matter was a joke; that the writing was not delivered to Lucy and no binding contract was ever made between the parties.

It is an unusual, if not bizarre, defense. * * *

In his testimony, Zehmer claimed that he "was high as a Georgia pine," and that the transaction "was just a bunch of two doggoned drunks bluffing to see who could talk the biggest and say the most." That claim is inconsistent with his attempt to testify in great detail as to what was said and what was done. * * * The record is convincing that Zehmer was not intoxicated to the extent of being unable to comprehend the nature and consequences of the instrument he executed, and hence that instrument is not to be invalidated on that ground. * * *

* * * *

The appearance of the contract, the fact that it was under discussion for forty minutes or more before it was signed; Lucy's objection to the first draft because it was written in the singular, and he wanted Mrs. Zehmer to sign it also; the rewriting to meet that objection and the signing by Mrs. Zehmer; the discussion of what was to be included in the sale, the provision for the examination of the title, the completeness of the instrument that was executed, the taking possession of it by Lucy with no request or suggestion by either of the defendants that he give it back, are facts which furnish persuasive evidence that the execution of the contract was a serious business transaction rather than a casual, jesting matter as defendants now contend.

* * * *

Not only did Lucy actually believe, but the evidence shows he was warranted in believing, that the contract represented a serious business transaction and a good faith sale and purchase of the farm.

In the field of contracts, as generally elsewhere, *"We must look to the outward expression of a person as manifesting his intention rather than to his secret and unexpressed intention. [Emphasis added.]* 'The law imputes to a person an intention corresponding to the reasonable meaning of his words and acts.' "

* * * *

Whether the writing signed by the defendants and now sought to be enforced by the complainants was the result of a serious offer by Lucy and a serious acceptance by the defendants, or was a serious offer by Lucy and an acceptance in secret jest by the defendants, in either event it constituted a binding contract of sale between the parties.

The Supreme Court of Virginia determined that the writing was an enforceable contract and reversed the ruling of the lower court. The Zehmers were required by court order to carry through with the sale of the Ferguson Farm to the Lucys.   **DECISION AND REMEDY**

Avoidance or Ratification

If a contract is held to be voidable because of a person's intoxication, that person has the option of disaffirming (avoiding) it—the same option available to a minor. However, the vast majority of courts require the intoxicated person to make full restitution (fully return consideration received) as a condition of disaffirmance. For example, a person contracts to purchase a set of encyclopedias while intoxicated. If the books are delivered, the purchaser can disaffirm the executed contract (getting back the payment made) only by returning the encyclopedias.

Like a minor, an intoxicated person, after becoming sober, may ratify expressly or implicitly. Implied ratification occurs when a person enters into a contract while drunk and fails to disaffirm the contract within a *reasonable* time after becoming sober. Acts or conduct inconsistent with an intent to disaffirm will also ratify the contract—for example, if a person continues to use property purchased under a voidable contract.

In addition, contracts for necessaries are voidable (as in the case of minors), but the intoxicated person is liable in quasi-contract (implied-in-law contract) for the reasonable value of the consideration received.

The lack of contractual capacity due to intoxication while the contract is being made must be distinguished from capacity (or the lack thereof) of an alcoholic. If a contract is made while an alcoholic is sober, there is no lack of capacity.[5] Exhibit 10-1 illustrates a classification of contracts made by intoxicated persons.

INSANE PERSONS

Contracts made by insane persons can be either void, voidable, or valid. If a person has been adjudged insane by a court of law and a guardian has been appointed, any contract made by the insane person is void—no contract exists. Only the guardian can enter into binding legal duties on behalf of the insane person.

Insane persons not so adjudged by a court may enter into voidable contracts if they do not know they are entering into the contract, or if they lack the mental capacity to comprehend its subject matter, nature, and consequences. In such situations the contracts are voidable at the option of the insane person, although the other party does not have this option.[6]

The contract may be disaffirmed or ratified. Ratification must occur after the person is mentally competent or after a guardian is appointed and ratifies the contract. As in the case of minors and intoxicated persons, insane persons are liable in quasi-contract for the reasonable value of necessaries they receive.

A contract entered into by an insane person may also be valid. A person can understand the nature and effect of entering into a certain contract, yet simultaneously lack capacity to engage in other activities. In such cases the contract will be valid, since the person is not legally insane for contractual pur-

---

5.   Olsen v. Hawkins, 90 Idaho 28, 408 P.2d 462 (1965).

6.   This applies to all voidable contracts.

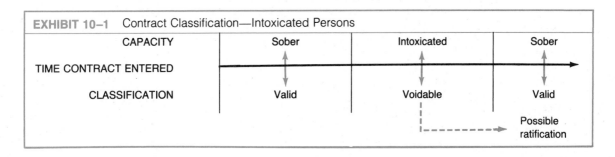

EXHIBIT 10–1   Contract Classification—Intoxicated Persons

CAPACITY	Sober	Intoxicated	Sober
TIME CONTRACT ENTERED			
CLASSIFICATION	Valid	Voidable	Valid
			Possible ratification

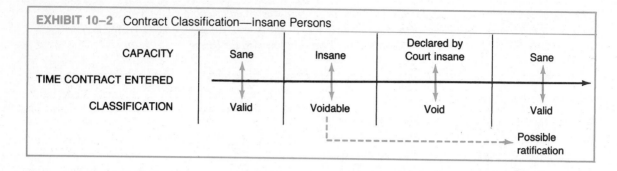

EXHIBIT 10–2 Contract Classification—Insane Persons

CAPACITY	Sane	Insane	Declared by Court insane	Sane
TIME CONTRACT ENTERED				
CLASSIFICATION	Valid	Voidable	Void	Valid

Possible ratification

poses.[7] Exhibit 10-2 illustrates contract classifications of insane persons.

ALIENS

An alien is a citizen of another country who resides in this country. Generally, aliens who are legally in this country have the same contractual rights as U.S. citizens. They may be sued and they may sue in the courts in order to enforce their contractual rights. Some states restrict the right of an alien to own real property. In virtually all cases, an enemy alien (i.e., a citizen of a country with which we are at war) will

not be able to enforce a contract, although the contract can be held in abeyance until the war is over.

MARRIED WOMEN

At common law, a married woman could not make binding contracts even if she lived apart from her husband. In other words, married women's contracts were void rather than voidable. Even after the death of the husband, the married woman was incapable of ratifying a previously drawn contract because that contract was invalid from the beginning. Virtually all states have abolished common law restrictions on the contractual capacity of married women.[8]

---

7.   Modern courts no longer require a person to be *legally* insane to disaffirm contracts. See Ortelere v. Teachers' Retirement Bd., 25 N.Y.2d 196, 303 N.Y.S.2d 362, 250 N.E.2d 460 (1969). The court sets out what the tests for mental incompetency are.

8.   These statutes are normally called Married Women's Property Acts.

QUESTIONS AND CASE PROBLEMS

1.   For most contractual purposes in State X, age eighteen is the age of majority. Martin, age seventeen, contracts to purchase adult Smith's car for $1,200, paying $200 down, with the balance plus interest to be paid at $75 per month. The car is to be used primarily to go back and forth to college and for pleasure. Martin takes possession and starts making payments. He turns eighteen and then makes one additional payment before discovering some defects in the automobile. Martin tenders the car back to Smith, demanding back all payments made, claiming his right to disaffirm the contract. Smith refuses the tender,

claiming Martin is legally liable for the remaining payments. Discuss who is correct and why.

2.   Seling, a minor, sold her bicycle to Adam, an adult, for $100. Adam took possession and paid Seling. Two months later, Adam sold the bicycle to Bonnet, a bona fide purchaser, for value. Seling's parents became upset when they learned of her sale. Seling, before reaching the age of majority, seeks to disaffirm the contract with Adam and recover the bicycle from Bonnet. Discuss whether Seling can recover the bicycle from Bonnet, *and* discuss Adam's liability to Seling.

3.   Treat is a seventeen-year-old minor who has just graduated from high school. She is attending a university 200 miles from home and has contracted to rent an apartment near the university for one year at $250 per month. She is working at a convenience store to earn enough money to be self-supporting. She moves into the apartment and

has paid four months' rent when a dispute arises between her and the landlord. Treat, still a minor, moves out and returns the key to the landlord. The landlord wants to hold Treat for the balance on the lease, $2,000. Discuss fully Treat's liability on the lease.

4. If a college student who is a minor seeks to rent an apartment, he or she may be asked to sign a lease in which there is a clause certifying that the person signing the lease is an adult. What are the possible legal ramifications of such a signed lease?

5. Smith has been the owner of a car dealership for a number of years. One year ago, Smith sold one of his most expensive cars to Beyer. At the time of the sale, Smith thought Beyer acted in a peculiar manner; however, Smith had not thought further about the transaction until today, when Beyer's court-appointed guardian appeared at his office, tendered back the car, and demanded Beyer's money back. The guardian informed Smith that Beyer had been adjudged insane two months ago by a proper court.

(a) Discuss the rights of the parties.

(b) If Beyer had been adjudicated insane at the time of the contract, what would be the legal effect of the contract?

6. Robertson, a minor, entered into a conditional sales agreement whereby he purchased a pickup truck from Julian Pontiac Company for the agreed price of $1,743.85. Robertson traded in a passenger car for which he was given a credit of $723.85 on the purchase price, leaving a balance of $1,020, which he agreed to pay in twenty-three monthly installments. Robertson had already paid one of the installments when the pickup truck began to experience electrical wiring difficulties. Less than a month after the purchase of the truck, Robertson turned eighteen. About two weeks later, as a result of the electrical wiring defects, the truck caught fire and was practically destroyed. Robertson refused to make any further payments under the installment agreement. Julian Pontiac Company sued Robertson to recover the truck. Robertson filed a cross-complaint to rescind the contract and recover the amounts he had paid. Who prevails? [Robertson v. King, 225 Ark. 276, 280 S.W.2d 402 (1955)]

7. Pankas was the owner and operator of a hair styling boutique in downtown Pittsburgh, Pennsylvania. He had maintained his shop in the same location for a number

of years and had built up a substantial clientele. In March 1962, Pankas hired Bell, who was about seventeen years old at the time. Part of Bell's employment included an agreement (called a restrictive covenant) that if he should leave Pankas's employ, he would not work at another beauty parlor within a ten-mile radius of downtown Pittsburgh. Shortly after reaching majority, Bell left Pankas's employ and, along with another Pankas employee, opened a beauty shop only a few blocks away from Pankas's business. In addition, Bell advertised the fact that he and his partner were former employees of Pankas. Pankas sued Bell to enjoin him from further breach of their restrictive covenant. Bell claimed that as a minor he could rescind the agreement. Was he correct? [Pankas v. Bell, 413 Pa. 494, 198 A.2d 312 (1964)]

8. Peddy and Montgomery entered into a contract under which Montgomery agreed to sell a certain parcel of her land to Peddy. At the time of the transaction, Montgomery was a resident of the state of Alabama. Alabama, by statute, prohibited married women from selling real estate without the consent of their husbands. Montgomery's husband refused to consent to the deal, and Montgomery in turn refused to transfer the land to Peddy. Montgomery claimed that because of the statute she was not obligated under the contract since the contract was invalid from the beginning. Peddy responded that the statute violated the equal protection clause of the Constitution since it treated men and women differently with no reasonable basis for the difference in treatment. Was the contract between Montgomery and Peddy void or voidable? What do you think of the constitutional claim? [Peddy v. Montgomery, 345 So.2d 631 (Ala.1977)]

9. Spaulding, a minor, entered into a contract with New England Furniture Co. for the purchase of bedroom furniture and a stove. The purchase included a three-piece bedroom set that was priced significantly higher than most other three-piece bedroom sets and an expensive combination oil-and-gas stove. After making several payments, Spaulding defaulted, disaffirmed his contract, and allowed the company to remove all the furniture and the stove. New England Furniture, however, refused to return the money that Spaulding had already paid. Was Spaulding able to recover these payments? [Spaulding v. New England Furniture Co., 154 Me. 330, 147 A.2d 916 (1959)]

11

CONTRACTS
Legality

In order for a contract to be enforced in court, the contract must call for the performance of a legal act. A contract is illegal if either its formation or its performance is criminal, tortious, or otherwise opposed to public policy. The first part of this chapter will consider what makes a bargain illegal—when the contract is contrary to state or federal statutes and when the contract is contrary to public policy. The second part will consider the *effects* of an illegal bargain. Such contracts are normally void—that is, they really are not contracts.

CONTRACTS CONTRARY TO STATUTE

Usury

Every state has statutes that set the maximum rates of interest that can be charged for different types of transactions, including ordinary loans. A lender who makes a loan at an interest rate above the lawful maximum is guilty of **usury.** The maximum rate of interest varies from state to state.

The maximum rate of interest should not be confused with either the **legal rate of interest** or the **judgment rate of interest.** The legal rate of interest is a rate fixed by statute where the parties to a contract intend an interest rate to be paid but do not fix the

rate in the contract. This rate is frequently the same as the statutory maximum rate of interest permitted. A judgment rate of interest is a rate fixed by statute which is applied to monetary judgments from the moment the judgment is awarded by a court until the judgment is paid.

In order to determine the amount of interest being charged on a loan, and whether the loan is usurious, many states require that fees, service charges, credit insurance, "points,"[1] and the like imposed by the lender be included in the calculation. For example, suppose you are charged $100 per year to borrow $1,000. In addition, the lender charges you $25 in service charges and requires you to take out credit insurance that costs another $25. The true annual rate of interest is then 15 percent (the total of $150 in charges divided by the principal amount of $1,000).

For some loans, the lender imposes a discount from the principal as interest. Suppose that the lender is willing to loan you $1,000, payable at the end of one year at a discount of $150. At the time of receipt

---

1. "Points" are commonly required in the financing of real estate transactions. A point is defined as one percent of the amount of the loan and is classified as a service charge of the lender. See *Real Estate Sales Handbook*, Realtors National Marketing Institute of the National Association of Realtors, Chicago, Illinois, 1979.

of the loan you will receive only $850. At the end of the loan year you must pay the lender $1,000.

Not all charges are included in the calculation for interest. Many statutes provide that charges for additional services primarily of benefit to the borrower should not be included if they are reasonable. Examples of such charges are certain filing fees, attorneys' fees, and inspection or investigation charges.

Exceptions   Because usury statutes place a ceiling on the allowable rates of interest, exceptions have been made in order to facilitate business transactions. For example, many states exempt corporate loans from the usury laws. In addition, almost all states have adopted special statutes allowing much higher interest rates on small loans. In some cases the interest (including other charges) can exceed 100 percent of the loan. Such high rates are allowed because many borrowers simply cannot get loans at interest rates below the lawful maximum and might otherwise be forced to turn to loan sharks.

Installment Loans   Many states have special statutes dealing with allowable charges and interest on installment loans. This is particularly true of retail and motor vehicle installment sales. Each state statute must be checked, as the rates and amounts vary substantially.[2] For example, in some states the maximum amount permitted by law may depend on the age of the motor vehicle subject to the loan agreement.

Add-on interest loans can result in a loan being declared usurious. These types of loans are frequently applied to installment payment loans. For example, a lender loans you $1,000 at an add-on interest rate of 8 percent, payable in twelve equal installments. The lender then adds $80 interest to the $1,000 principal and divides the $1,080 by twelve to compute the monthly payments of $90 per month. The problem is that the borrower is not receiving the full $1,000 during the twelve-month period, as would be the case in a simple interest loan. The

borrower is paying part of the principal back each month. Instead of the borrower getting an 8 percent loan, the calculation to a simple interest loan is almost 15 percent. Lenders use very accurate published actuarial charts to convert the add-on rate to simple interest.

Retail Charge Agreements—Revolving Charge Accounts   Sales agreements often give the purchaser an opportunity to pay all charges from a particular seller or lender by means of a revolving charge account. This means that the purchaser can make numerous credit purchases at a department store (on a credit card, for example) and, upon receiving the bill, can either pay it in full or pay a minimum monthly amount, extending the balance to be paid in the future. For the privilege of paying the balance later, the purchaser is charged a monthly interest on the balance. For example, purchases on a revolving credit account or purchases made with Visa or MasterCard credit cards usually call for interest payments of 1.5 percent per month on the outstanding balance. Some courts have interpreted these transactions as not being "loans of money" and therefore not subject to the usury laws. Some states have passed installment sales statutes that expressly permit such practices.

Effects of Usury   The effects of a usurious loan differ from state to state. A number of states allow the lender to recover the principal of a loan along with interest up to the legal maximum. In effect, the lender is denied recovery of the excess interest. In other states the lender can recover the principal amount of the loan but not the interest. In a few states, a usurious loan is a void transaction, and the lender cannot recover either the principal or the interest (which is very harsh).

Gambling

In general, wagers, lotteries, and games of chance are illegal. All states have statutes that regulate gambling—defined as any scheme for the distribution of property by chance, among persons who have paid a valuable consideration for the opportunity to receive the property.[3] Gambling is the creation of risk for the purpose of assuming it. A few states do permit

---

2.   The complexities of determining the true interest rate for comparative loan shopping led to passage of the federal Truth-in-Lending Law, which primarily requires a seller or lender to disclose not only the charges associated with the loan, or installment sale, but the *annual percentage rate* (APR) by standard procedures. This law does not set maximum rates (state law controls what is usury), but it does provide information on the interest actually being charged.

---

3.   See Wishing Well Club v. Akron, 112 N.E.2d 41 (1951).

gambling, some only as long as the prizes or winnings do not exceed $100 to $500.[4] In addition, a number of states have recognized the substantial revenues that can be obtained from gambling and have legalized state-operated lotteries, horseracing, and lotteries arranged for charitable purposes (such as bingo).

Sometimes it is difficult to distinguish a gambling contract from the risk-sharing inherent in almost all contracts. Suppose Adams takes out a life insurance policy on Ziegler, naming himself as beneficiary under the policy. At first glance, this may seem entirely legal; but further examination shows that Adams is simply gambling on how long Ziegler will live. In order to prevent this type of practice, insurance contracts can be entered into only by someone with an **insurable interest.** An insurable interest, discussed in Chapter 55, is a property or ownership right wherein the insured would derive a pecuniary benefit or advantage for its preservation,

---

4. Iowa and Florida are two such states.

or will suffer pecuniary loss or damage for its destruction. Adams cannot take out an insurance policy on Ziegler's home or auto because Adams does not have an insurable interest in Ziegler's property. But if Adams has a mortgage on Ziegler's house, he can take out an insurance policy because he has a property interest in the house.

Futures contracts, or contracts for the future purchase or sale of commodities such as corn and wheat, are not illegal gambling contracts. It might appear that a person selling or buying a futures contract is essentially gambling on the future price of the commodity. However, since the seller of the futures contract either already has a property interest in the commodity or can purchase the commodity elsewhere and deliver the commodity as required in the futures contract, courts have upheld the legality of such contracts.

The following case illustrates a court's analysis of the difference between a contest of chance and one of skill in forecasting the results of football games to be played.

SEATTLE TIMES CO. v.
TIELSCH

Supreme Court of Washington,
En Banc, 1972.
80 Wash.2d 502, 495 P.2d 1366.

BACKGROUND AND FACTS   *The* Seattle Times *ran a football forecasting contest that it named "Guest-Guesser." The Seattle chief of police claimed that the contest was illegal because it was a lottery. When the* Times *asked for a declaratory judgment action to determine the legality of the contest, the trial court found that the contest was an illegal lottery. The* Times *appealed.*

ROSELLINI, J.
* * * *

The result of a football game may depend upon weather, the physical condition of the players and the psychological attitude of the players. It may also be affected by sociological problems between and among the members of a football team. The element of chance is an integral part of the game of football as well as the skill of the players.

The lure of the "Guest-Guesser" contest is partially the participant's love of football, partially the challenge of competition and partially the hope enticingly held out, which is often false or disappointing, that the participant will get something for nothing or a great deal for a very little outlay * * *.

The elements of a lottery are prize, consideration and chance * * *.

The appellant maintains that chance is not a dominant element in football forecasting contests. * * * The trial court found to the contrary upon that evidence, and we think the finding is justified. The appellant's expert statistician who testified at the trial did not state that chance plays no part in the outcome of such a contest or even that it does not play a dominant role. He merely testified that such a contest is not one of "pure chance." Pure chance he defined as a 50-50 chance. He acknowledged that a contestant who consistently predicted the outcome of 14 out of 20 games correctly would be a "highly skilled" contestant. * * *

Where a contest is multiple or serial, and requires the solution of a number of problems to win the prize, the fact that skill alone will bring contestants to a correct solution of a greater part of the problems does not make the contest any the less a lottery if chance enters into the solution of another lesser part of the problems and thereby proximately influences the final result *   *   *.

Our research has revealed only one case involving a football forecasting game and the game there was a "pool," that is, a gambling game wherein wagers were placed. The Superior Court of Pennsylvania held that it was a lottery. What is most relevant in the case for our consideration here is the court's discussion of the element of chance in forecasting the result of football games. That court said: It is true that for an avid student of the sport of football the chance taken is not so great as for those who have little interest in the game. However, it is common knowledge that the predictions even among these so-called "experts" are far from infallible. Any attempt to forecast the result of a single athletic contest, be it football, baseball, or whatever, is fraught with chance. This hazard is multiplied directly by the number of predictions made. The operators of the scheme involved in this case were all cognizant of this fact for the odds against a correct number of selections were increased from 5 to 1 for three teams picked up to 900 to 1 for fifteen teams.

The trial court in the instant case recognized the same basic realities attendant upon the enterprise of football game-result forecasting. We are convinced that it correctly held that chance, rather than skill, is the dominant factor in the Times' "Guest-Guesser" contest. The very name of the contest conveys quite accurately the promoter's as well as the participants' true concept of the nature of the contest.

We conclude that the contest, however harmless it may be in the opinion of the participants and the promoters, is a lottery. *   *   *

The trial court was upheld. The "Guest-Guesser" game was indeed illegal as a lottery. The contest, even though harmless in the opinion of the participants and the promoters, was illegal.

DECISION AND REMEDY

Sabbath Laws

Statutes called Sabbath, or Sunday, laws prohibit the formation or performance of certain contracts on a Sunday. At common law, in the absence of this statutory prohibition, such contracts are legal. Most states, however, have enacted some type of Sunday statute.

Some states have statutes making all contracts entered into on a Sunday illegal. Statutes in other states prohibit only the sale of merchandise, particularly alcoholic beverages, on a Sunday. (These are often called blue laws.) A number of states have laws that forbid the carrying on of "all secular labor and business on The Lord's Day." In such states, it would appear that all contracts made on a Sunday are illegal and unenforceable *as long as they remain executory*.

Exceptions to Sunday laws permit contracts for necessities, such as food and works of charity. In addition, a contract entered into on a Sunday that has been fully performed (that is, an *executed* con-

tract) cannot be rescinded, or cancelled. Active enforcement of Sunday laws varies from state to state and even among communities within a particular state. Many do not enforce the Sunday laws, and some of these laws have been held to be unconstitutional.

Licensing Statutes

All states require members of certain professions or callings to obtain licenses allowing them to practice. Doctors, lawyers, real estate brokers, construction contractors, electricians, and stockbrokers are but a few of the people who must be licensed. Some licenses are obtained only after extensive schooling and examinations, which indicates to the public that a special skill is involved. Others require only that the particular person be of good moral character.

When a person enters into a contract with an unlicensed individual, the contract may be enforceable despite the lack of a license. The nature of the statute itself often tells if such a contract is enforceable. Some statutes expressly provide that the lack of a license for people engaged in certain occupations will bar enforcement of any work-related contracts they enter into.

If the statute does not expressly state this, one must look to the underlying purpose of the licensing requirements for that occupation. If the underlying purpose is to protect the public from unauthorized practitioners, then the contract will be illegal and unenforceable. For example, if you enter into a contract involving the professional services of an unlicensed chiropractor, the chiropractor cannot enforce the contract. The licensing of chiropractors is designed to protect the public from persons who are not capable (or who have not shown their capability) of practicing their trade. On the other hand, if the underlying purpose of the licensing statute is to raise revenues, contracts entered into with an unlicensed practitioner will be enforceable. The sanction instead will usually be a fine on the unlicensed practitioner.

Contracts to Commit a Crime

Any contract to commit a crime is a contract in violation of a statute.[5] Thus, a contract to sell an

---

5.   See, for example, McConnell v. Commonwealth Pictures Corp., 7 N.Y.2d 465, 199 N.Y.S.2d 483, 166 N.E.2d 494 (1960). In this famous case, the majority view and the dissent clearly showed two different ideas about illegality.

illegal drug (the sale of which is prohibited by statute) is not enforceable. Should the object or performance of the contract be rendered illegal by statute after the contract has been entered into, the contract is said to be discharged by law. (See discussion under "Impossibility of Performance" in Chapter 15).

CONTRACTS CONTRARY TO PUBLIC POLICY

Although contracts are entered into by private parties, some are not enforceable because of the negative impact they would have on society. These contracts are said to be *contrary to public policy*. Numerous examples exist. Any contract to commit an immoral act is in this category. Contracts that prohibit marriage have been held to be illegal on this basis. Suppose Dangerfield promises a young man $500 if he will refrain from marrying Dangerfield's daughter. If the young man accepts, the resulting contract is not formed (is void). Thus, if he married Dangerfield's daughter, Dangerfield could not sue him for breach of contract.

In the following case, a famous movie star was party to an unusual suit brought to enforce an oral contract for property and support growing out of a nonmarital relationship.

MARVIN v. MARVIN
Supreme Court of California,
1976.
18 Cal.3d 660, 134 Cal.Rptr.
815, 557 P.2d 106.

BACKGROUND AND FACTS   *Michelle Marvin lived with Lee Marvin for seven years without marriage and then brought suit to enforce an alleged oral contract existing between them. Michelle Marvin, the plaintiff, claimed that, according to their agreement, she was entitled to half the property that had been acquired in Lee Marvin's name during the seven years of their cohabitation, and she sought support payments.*

The aspect to be dealt with here is the Supreme Court of California ruling that a court can enforce a contract between nonmarital parties unless the contract was explicitly founded on the consideration of meretricious sexual services, which are illegal.

TOBRINER, Justice.
*   *   *   *

During the past 15 years, there has been a substantial increase in the number of couples living together without marrying.[1] Such nonmarital relationships lead to legal

---

1.   "The 1970 census figures indicate that today perhaps eight times as many couples are living together without being married as cohabited ten years ago." [Comment, *In re Cary: A Judicial Recognition of Illicit Cohabitation* (1974) 25 Hastings L.J. 1226.]

controversy when one partner dies or the couple separates. Courts of Appeal, faced with the task of determining property rights in such cases, have arrived at conflicting positions. We [the Supreme Court] take this opportunity to resolve that controversy and to declare the principles which should govern distribution of property acquired in a nonmarital relationship.

* * * *

Although the past decisions hover over the issue in the somewhat wispy form of the figures of a Chagall painting, we can abstract from those decisions a clear and simple rule. *The fact that a man and woman live together without marriage, and engage in a sexual relationship, does not in itself invalidate agreements between them relating to their earnings, property, or expenses.* [Emphasis added.] Neither is such an agreement invalid merely because the parties may have contemplated the creation or continuation of a nonmarital relationship when they entered into it. Agreements between nonmarital partners fail only to the extent that they rest upon a consideration of meretricious sexual services. * * *

In summary, we base our opinion on the principle that adults who voluntarily live together and engage in sexual relations are nonetheless as competent as any other persons to contract respecting their earnings and property rights. Of course, they cannot lawfully contract to pay for the performance of sexual services, for such a contract is, in essence, an agreement for prostitution and unlawful for that reason [because the action is illegal; hence the contract would be illegal and void]. But they may agree to pool their earnings and to hold all property acquired during the relationship in accord with the law governing community property; conversely they may agree that each partner's earnings and the property acquired from these earnings remains the separate property of the earning partner. So long as the agreement does not rest upon illicit meretricious consideration, the parties may order their economic affairs as they choose, and no policy precludes the courts from enforcing such agreements.

In the present instance, plaintiff alleges that the parties agreed to pool their earnings, that they contracted to share equally in all property acquired, and that defendant agreed to support plaintiff. The terms of the contract as alleged do not rest upon any unlawful consideration. We therefore conclude that the complaint furnishes a suitable basis upon which the trial court can render declaratory relief.

* * * *

We conclude that the judicial barriers that may stand in the way of a *policy based upon the fulfillment of the reasonable expectations of the parties to a nonmarital relationship should be removed.* [Emphasis added.] As we have explained, the courts now hold that express agreements will be enforced unless they rest on an unlawful meretricious consideration. We add that in the absence of an express agreement, the courts may look to a variety of other remedies in order to protect the parties' lawful expectations.

The courts may inquire into the conduct of the parties to determine whether that conduct demonstrates an implied contract or implied agreement of partnership or joint venture or some other tacit understanding between the parties. * * * Finally, a nonmarital partner may recover in quantum meruit for the reasonable value of household services rendered less the reasonable value of support received if he can show that he rendered services with the expectation of monetary reward.

DECISION AND REMEDY

The court recognized that a contract can exist between nonmarital parties with regard to their earnings and property rights and that such an agreement can be enforced by the court as long as it is not explicitly founded on the consideration of sexual services. The case was sent back to the trial court to determine if an implied or an express contract existed between the parties and the nature of the terms. Another trial was held, and the court found for Michelle Marvin. The trial court awarded her $104,000 on "equitable" grounds to allow her to gain sufficient education and skills to become economically independent. Lee Marvin appealed this decision, and on appeal the appellate court ruled there was no *basis for the $104,000 award and deleted it from the judgment. In the end, Michelle Marvin did not receive any monetary award. See 122 Cal.App.3d 871, 176 Cal.Rptr. 555 (1981).*

Contracts in Restraint of Trade

An example of contracts that adversely affect the public are contracts in restraint of trade. Public policy favors competition in the economy. In addition, contracts in restraint of trade usually violate one or more statutes.[6] However, prior to the adoption of these federal statutes, case law prohibiting certain contracts had the effect of restraining trade.

Although most contracts in restraint of trade are illegal, an exception is recognized when the restraint is *reasonable* and is an integral part of certain contracts. Many such exceptions are a type of restraint that is called a covenant not to compete, or a restrictive covenant.

Covenants Not to Compete *Covenants not to compete* are often contained in contracts for the sale of an ongoing business. The seller agrees not to open up a new store within a certain geographical area surrounding the old store. When covenants, or agreements, not to compete are accompanied by the sale of an ongoing business, the agreements are usually upheld as legal if they are "reasonable," usually in terms of time and area. The purpose of these covenants is to enable the seller to sell, and the purchaser to buy, the "good will" and "reputation" of an ongoing business. If these covenants were not valid, then the valuable business interest of "good will" and "reputation" could not be transferred. For example, suppose the seller has built up an established clientele because the business is known for its high-quality product and service. If the buyer desires to keep the opportunity to serve the established clientele, he or she will include a covenant that imposes reasonable restrictions on the seller—for example, that the seller shall not establish a similar business within a two-mile radius for a period of five years. The seller, in turn, receives consideration in return for giving up his or her legal right to compete under the conditions prescribed. In this

way, the seller is prevented from opening a similar business right down the block and drawing away the buyer's customers.

If the agreement not to compete is made without an accompanying sales agreement, it is void in that the agreement tends to restrain trade and is contrary to public policy. Even when ancillary to a primary agreement, agreements not to compete can be contrary to public policy if they are unreasonably broad or restrictive as to time or geographic area. Suppose Orian Capital, doing business in San Francisco, sells its loan and finance business to Bankers Life Company. If Orian Capital agrees not to open another business in the whole state of California, the agreement not to compete is unreasonably broad. After all, the threat of losing customers to Orian is not very severe in San Diego. On the other hand, if the agreement covers only the San Francisco Bay area, it will probably be upheld.

Ancillary agreements not to compete can also be held contrary to public policy if they last for an unreasonably long period of time. In the preceding example, if Orian agrees not to compete for a hundred years, the contract will be contrary to public policy. On the other hand, a five-year agreement is reasonable and enforceable (and in some cases, depending on the situation, up to twenty years would be reasonable).

Agreements not to compete can be ancillary to employment contracts. It is common for many middle and upper level management personnel to agree not to work for competitors or not to start a new business for a specified period of time after terminating employment. If such an agreement is not ancillary to an employment contract, it is illegal. If ancillary, it is legal as long as it is not excessive in scope or duration. (The courts are reluctant to enforce these contracts, however.)

On occasion, where the covenant not to compete is unreasonable in its essential terms, the court may *reform* the covenant, converting its terms into reasonable ones. Instead of declaring the covenant illegal and unenforceable, the court applies the rule of reasonableness and changes the contract so that its basic, original intent can be enforced. For ex-

6. Some of these statutes are the Sherman Antitrust Act, the Clayton Act, and the Federal Trade Commission Act. States also have separate antitrust statutes. Antitrust and contracts in restraint of trade are discussed in Chapters 48 and 49.

ample, in the Orian Capital case, if Orian is forbidden to open another business anywhere in California for a period of one hundred years, the court could either declare the entire covenant null and void or could reform the covenant terms to cover only the San Francisco Bay area for a period of five years. (This presents a problem, however, in that the judge becomes a party to the contract. Consequently, contract reformation is usually carried out by a court only when necessary to prevent undue burdens or hardships.)

In the following case, the covenant not to compete was held to be too restrictive and therefore unenforceable.

BACKGROUND AND FACTS   *Budget Rent-A-Car, the plaintiff, franchises and services operators in the discount automobile rental business. Budget brought this lawsuit to enforce a restrictive covenant not to compete against Fein, the defendant.*

Defendant Fein was a prospective purchaser of a Budget franchise. It is standard practice for Budget to require prospective purchasers to sign a standard agreement containing many provisions, one of them requiring the purchaser "not to enter into any daily discount automotive rental business in the western hemisphere for a period of two years" without the written permission of Budget. The agreement also prevents the franchisee from disclosing any information about the operational aspects of the business to any other business or organization.

After Fein signed the standard agreement, Budget divulged to him much of its confidential literature describing its operating technique. Budget believed its knowledge of how to start and operate a local rental agency successfully was akin to a trade secret. Consequently, when the franchise deal between Fein and Budget fell through and Fein acquired another franchise from a competitor, Budget charged that Fein was operating his agency similarly to a Budget agency, apparently using some of the confidential information he had recieved after signing the agreement.

BUDGET RENT-A-CAR
CORP. OF AMERICA
v. FEIN
United States Court of Appeals,
Fifth Circuit, 1965.
342 F.2d 509.

BROWN, Circuit Judge.
*   *   *   *   *

[A]s a matter of public policy, *   *   * this restrictive covenant would be unenforceable—primarily because of the "unreasonable" breadth of the territorial restriction.
*   *   *

Of course the equitable doctrine of restrictive covenants is the law's reflex to the needs of the businessman and the commercial world. Consequently it is the business judgment on the value of the relationship, the nature of acquired trade confidences, the uniqueness of skills and the like which counts for much. In that process it is not for Judges, certainly not initially, to determine independent of the practical appraisal of business what is reasonably necessary to protect these several interests. These practical judgments carry great weight. But in the final analysis a court has to evaluate the competing factors to determine whether the legal sanction sought unduly interferes with personal economic freedom of individuals or the flow of goods and services free of monopolistic restraints. *   *   *

For the covenantee to obtain judicial relief, he must show more than the mere promise of the covenantor. He must bare the soul of the business, or parts of it, even though this breaches for a time or a limited extent the confidences, trade secrets, etc. sought to be protected. *   *   * Before the law will foreclose economic opportunity to an individual for a long period of time because of a covenant exacted as a prelude to the consideration of whether a new relationship is to come into being, it is obvious that what is to be revealed has to be something which is of demonstrable value and deserving of protection.

*   *   *   *

There is another important aspect. *Budget, by extracting this covenant from everyone it talks turkey with, deleteriously affects a far wider range of people than a covenant ancillary to a sale of business where only two parties—the seller and the buyer—are involved.* [Emphasis added. Here the court is saying that true ancillary restrictive agreements are acceptable.] Of course Budget can say that there are only two parties to this particular agreement. The difference is that when a business changes hands, a transaction economically beneficial to the community occurs, but when an individual signs the Budget agreement, looks the deal over, and then does not buy, the only result of economic significance to the community—here the wide, wide world, or at least the half wide world—is that one less individual is free to choose how he will make his living.

*   *   *   *

If Fein had actually bought the franchise and this covenant pertained to the eventuality of his selling out and thereafter competing, * * * a much stronger argument could be made for the enforceability of the covenant. But such is not this case.

* * * Obviously this [covenant] has an anti-competitive effect since anyone talking to Budget is nailed down for two years—anywhere in the western hemisphere. Business necessities justifying such a consequence are not revealed in this record.

Another basis—independent of those already mentioned—why this covenant cannot be enforced is that *the territory encompassed is unreasonably large.* [Emphasis added.] * * * Since Budget does not do business throughout the western hemisphere and the papers utterly fail to demonstrate that there is any reasonably foreseeable likelihood that it will in the near future, it follows that the territorial limitation is unreasonably broad. The covenant is therefore unenforceable.

DECISION AND REMEDY   *Both the trial court and the appellate court agreed that the restrictive covenant was unenforceable. Budget could not prohibit Fein from engaging in the rental car franchise business.*

COMMENTS   *The current view of restraints of trade is that reasonable restraints contained in an employment agreement are enforceable if the purpose of the restraint is to protect a property interest of the promisee (usually the employer) and the conditions of the restraint are reasonable in terms of geographical limitations, duration, and so on. In addition, where confidential or secret information is involved, the courts will occasionally imply a noncompetition agreement where one is not expressly provided.*

Resale Price Maintenance Agreements Another contract in restraint of trade is the resale price maintenance contract between a manufacturer and a dealer or a set of dealers. The dealer or dealers agree not to sell a product at a price below some specified minimum, thereby assuring a certain price level for the product. Between 1937 and 1977, manufacturers could require resale price maintenance on the part of dealers throughout the country (subject to state control). Today such laws (called **fair trade laws**) are against public policy as expressed by federal statute. They are illegal.[7]

---

7. There are exceptions, however. The states can regulate the sale of alcoholic beverages in virtually any way they wish, and many have resale price maintenance for alcoholic beverages.

Unconscionable Contracts (Clauses) and Exculpatory Clauses

Ordinarily, a court will not look at the fairness or equity of a contract. That is, the courts will generally not inquire into the adequacy of consideration, as discussed in Chapter 9. Persons are assumed to be reasonably intelligent, and the courts will not come to their aid just because they have made an unwise or foolish bargain. In certain circumstances, however, bargains are so oppressive that the courts will relieve innocent parties of part or all of their duties. Such bargains are called **unconscionable contracts or clauses.**

Contracts attempting to absolve parties of negligence or other wrongs are often held to be unconscionable. For example, suppose Jones and Laughlin Steel Company hires a laborer and has him sign a contract stating:

Said employee hereby agrees with employer, in consideration of such employment, that he will take upon himself all risks incident to his position and will in no case hold the company liable for any injury or damage he may sustain, in his person or otherwise, by accidents or injuries in the factory, or which may result from defective machinery or carelessness or mis-

conduct of himself or any other employee in service of the employer.

This contract provision attempts to remove Jones and Laughlin's potential liability for injuries occurring to the employee, and it is usually contrary to public policy.[8]

Such clauses, which may also be found in rental or ordinary sales agreements, are called **exculpatory clauses.** They are defined as clauses that release a party from all liability in the event of monetary or physical injury *no matter who is at fault.*

Exculpatory clauses are sometimes found in commercial and noncommercial leases. In the majority of cases in commercial leases, these clauses are held to be contrary to public policy, and almost universally illegal and unenforceable in noncommercial leases. The following case illustrates the illegality of an exculpatory clause in a noncommercial lease.

---

8. For a case with similar facts, see Little Rock & Ft. Smith Ry. Company v. Eubanks, 48 Ark. 460, 3 S.W. 808 (1887). In such a case the clause may also be illegal on the basis of a violation of the state workers' compensation law.

BACKGROUND AND FACTS *Norma McCutcheon was a tenant in a multi-family dwelling complex owned by United Homes Corp. She was injured one evening when she fell down an unlighted flight of stairs leading from her apartment. She claimed that the defendant, United Homes Corp., was negligent because the lights at the top and bottom of the stairwell were not operating. At trial, the defendant claimed that it was not liable since the plaintiff had signed a form called a "month-to-month rental agreement." In the agreement the following exculpatory clause existed:*

Neither the Lessor nor his Agent shall be liable for any injury to Lessee, his family, guests, or employees, or any other person entering the premises or the building of which the demised premises are a part.

The trial court granted a summary judgment of dismissal.

McCUTCHEON v. UNITED HOMES CORP.

Supreme Court of Washington, En Banc, 1971.
79 Wash. 2d 443, 486 P.2d 1093.

STAFFORD, Justice.
* * * *

The question is one of first impression. The issue is whether the lessor of a residential unit within a multi-family dwelling complex may exculpate itself from liability for personal injuries sustained by a tenant, which injuries result from the lessor's own negligence in maintenance of the approaches, common passageways, stairways and other areas under the lessor's dominion and control, but available for the tenants' use. (Hereinafter called the "common areas".)

Basic to the entire discussion is the common law rule that one who leases a portion of his premises but retains control over the approaches, common passageways, stairways and other areas to be used in common by the owner and tenants, has a duty to use reasonable care to keep them in safe condition for use of the tenant in his enjoyment of the demised premises. The landlord is required to do more than passively refrain from negligent acts. He has a duty of affirmative conduct, an affirmative obligation to exercise reasonable care to inspect and repair the previously mentioned portions of the premises for protection of the lessee.

It is readily apparent that the exculpatory clause was inserted in defendant's form "Month to Month Rental Agreement" to bar its tenants from asserting actions for personal injuries sustained through the landlord's own negligence. It was adopted to negative the result of the lessor's failure to comply with its affirmative duty to the tenants.

The defendant asserts that a lessor may contract, in a rental agreement, to exculpate itself from liability to its lessee, for personal injuries caused by lessor's own negligence. It contends such exculpatory clauses are not contrary to public policy because the landlord-tenant relationship *is not a matter of public interest, but relates exclusively to the private affairs of the parties concerned and that the two parties stand upon equal terms. Thus, there should be full freedom to contract.*

*   *   *   *

The importance of "freedom of contract" is clear enough. However, the use of such an argument for avoiding the affirmative duty of a landlord to its residential tenant is no longer compelling in light of today's multi-family dwelling complex wherein a tenant merely rents some space with appurtenant rights to make it more usable or livable. Under modern circumstances the tenant is almost wholly dependent upon the landlord to provide reasonably for his safe use of the "common areas" beyond the four walls demised to him.

*   *   *   *

In other words, such an exculpatory clause may be legal, when considered in the abstract. However, when applied to a specific situation, one may be exempt from liability for his own negligence *only when the consequences thereof do not fall greatly below the standard established by law.*

In the landlord-tenant relationship it is extremely meaningful to require that a landlord's attempt to exculpate itself, from liability for the result of its own negligence, *not fall greatly below the standard of negligence set by law.* As indicated earlier, a residential tenant who lives in a modern multi-family dwelling complex is almost wholly dependent upon the landlord for the reasonably safe condition of the "common areas". However, a clause which exculpates the lessor from liability to its lessee, for personal injuries caused by lessor's own acts of negligence, not only lowers the standard imposed by the common law, it effectively *destroys* the landlord's affirmative obligation or duty to keep or maintain the "common areas" in a reasonably safe condition for the tenant's use.

When a lessor is no longer liable for the failure to observe standards of affirmative conduct, or for *any* conduct amounting to negligence, by virtue of an exculpatory clause in a lease, *the standard ceases to exist.* In short, such a clause *destroys* the concept of negligence in the landlord-tenant relationship. Neither the standard nor negligence can exist in abstraction.

*   *   *   *

*   *   * Furthermore, one must ignore present day realities to say that such an exculpatory clause, which relieves a lessor of liability for personal injuries caused by its own negligence, is purely a "personal and private affair" and "not a matter of public interest".

We no longer live in an era of the occasional rental of rooms in a private home or over the corner grocery. In the relatively short span of 30 years the public's use of rental units in this state has expanded dramatically. In the past 10 years alone, in the state of Washington, there has been an increase of over 77,000 rental units. It takes no imagination to see that a business which once had a minor impact upon the living habits of the citizenry has developed into a major commercial enterprise directly touching the lives of hundreds of thousands of people who depend upon it for shelter.

Thus, we are not faced merely with the theoretical duty of construing a provision in an isolated contract specifically bargained for by *one landlord and one tenant* as a purely private affair. Considered realistically, we are asked to construe an exculpatory clause, the generalized use of which may have an impact upon thousands of potential tenants.

Under these circumstances it cannot be said that such exculpatory clauses are "purely a private affair" or that they are "not a matter of public interest." The real question is whether we should sanction a technique of immunizing lessors of residential units within a multi-family dwelling complex, from liability for personal injuries sustained by a tenant, which injuries result from the lessor's own negligence in maintaining the "common areas"; particularly when the technique employed destroys the concept of negligence and the standard of affirmative duty imposed upon the landlord for protection of the tenant.

An exculpatory clause of the type here involved contravenes long established common law rules of tort liability that exist in the landlord-tenant relationship. As so employed, it offends the public policy of the state and will not be enforced by the courts. It makes little sense for us to insist, on the one hand, that a workman have a safe place in which to work, but, on the other hand, to deny him a reasonably safe place in which to live.

The trial court's ruling was reversed and the case was remanded for a new trial. This particular exculpatory clause was deemed unenforceable. **DECISION AND REMEDY**

Contracts entered into because of one party's vastly superior bargaining power may also be deemed unconscionable. For example, if every auto manufacturer were to insert an exculpatory clause (a clause freeing the manufacturer from liability for personal or monetary damage) in contracts for the sale of autos, consumers presumably would have no chance to bargain for the elimination of the clause in a given contract. (These contracts are also called adhesion contracts.) Essentially, the consumer's choice would be to take it or leave it. In order to combat such clauses, courts have held them to be unconscionable.[9] The consumer has no choice, so the contract is contrary to public policy.

Another example of an unconscionable contract is a contract in which the terms of the agreement "shock the conscience" of the court. Suppose a welfare recipient with a fourth-grade education agrees to purchase a refrigerator for a price of $2,000, signing a two-year, non-usurious installment contract.

The same type of refrigerator usually sells for $400 on the market. Some courts have held this type of contract unconscionable despite the general rule that the courts will not inquire into the adequacy of consideration.[10]

Both the Uniform Commercial Code (UCC) and the Uniform Consumer Credit Code (UCCC) embody the unconscionability concept—the former with regard to the sale of goods[11] and the latter with regard to consumer loans and the waiver of rights.[12]

To illustrate, UCC 2-302, dealing with the sale of goods, basically provides that as a matter of law a court can declare an entire contract or any clause in a contract illegal because it is unconscionable. Whether the court will so hold depends frequently upon the commercial setting and all the circumstances of the transaction, such as the education,

---

9. See Henningsen v. Bloomfield Motors, Inc., 32 N.J. 358, 161 A.2d 69 (1960).

10. Jones v. Star Credit Corp., 59 Misc. 2d 189, 298 N.Y.S. 2d 264 (1969).

11. See, for example, UCC Sections 2-302 and 2-719.

12. See, for example, UCCC Sections 5.108 and 1.107.

income, and position of the buyer relative to the seller (as in the refrigerator example).

Quite often when the plaintiff wishes to set aside a contract as being unconscionable because of the inequity of the terms between the parties, the plaintiff will claim in addition that the contract fails for want of consideration. The following case illustrates an administrator's attempt to set aside a nursing home contract, whereby the nursing home was to provide a woman continuing care in consideraton of the transfer of all her present and future assets to the home.

PIEHL v. NORWEGIAN OLD PEOPLES' HOME SOCIETY OF CHICAGO

Appellate Court of Illinois First District, Third Division, 1984. 469 N.E.2d 705.

BACKGROUND AND FACTS *On October 26, 1981, Mabel Finn signed a document entitled "Continuing Care Contract" with the Norwood Park Home, a nursing facility owned and operated by the Norwegian Old Peoples' Home Society (the Home). The contract provided that the Home would provide continuing care in the form of room, board, and nursing and medical services until Finn left the facility voluntarily, involuntarily, or by reason of death. For these services Finn agreed to transfer all her present and future assets. The Home reserved the right to cancel the contract if Finn failed to qualify for old age assistance benefits once the assets transferred to the Home were exhausted. Five and one-half months later Finn died while a resident of the Home. The Home paid for Finn's funeral expenses but upon demand of Finn's administrator refused to make any accounting for the assets and funds Finn transferred to the Home. Finn's administrator, Piehl, filed suit to set aside the contract based upon lack of mutuality and because the contract terms were oppressive and unconscionable. The trial court granted the Home's petition to dismiss Piehl's action, and Piehl appealed.*

WHITE, Justice.

*   *   *   *

    [Piehl] contends that the "continuing care contract" signed by Mrs. Finn was void for lack of mutuality. Plaintiff argues that the Home's promise to care for Mrs. Finn was illusory since the Home had the option to terminate the contract if Mrs. Finn was ineligible for old age assistance benefits. [Piehl] concludes that the Home was not bound by the contract and therefore neither was Mrs. Finn. A contract does not lack mutuality merely because its obligations appear unequal or because every obligation or right is not met by an equivalent counter obligation or right in the other party. *   *   * The mutuality requirement is satisfied if each party has made a promise to the other and is therefore an obligor and under a duty to the other contracting party. *   *   * In the instant case, the decedent and the Home each assumed obligations which were detrimental to them and could be enforced by the other party. The decedent transferred to the Home her present assets and any and all assets which she might subsequently acquire together with her social security income, her pension benefits, and all other monies or benefits for which she might be eligible. In return the Home agreed to provide room, board, and nursing and medical services until the decedent left the facility voluntarily, involuntarily, or by reason of death. We are aware that section 2.3 of the "continuing care contract" provided that the obligation of the facility to continue care may be terminated at the option of the facility when all of the assets transferred have been used for resident's care if the resident fails to qualify for old age assistance benefits. This provision, however, did not give the Home an absolute right to terminate or cancel the contract at any time. The Home was bound to care for Mrs. Finn until the assets transferred were exhausted or, if Mrs. Finn qualified for old age assistance benefits, until her death. Moreover, it is well settled that want of mutuality is no defense where a contract is executed or where a party who was not bound to perform does perform. * * * In the instant case, the Home provided care for Mrs. Finn until her death. Accordingly, we conclude that the "continuing care contract" had been performed by the Home and that the claim of lack of mutuality was not available.

Plaintiff maintains that the "continuing care contract" was oppressive and unconscionable in that, although it purports to provide care for Mrs. Finn's lifetime, the contract allowed the Home to terminate such care upon exhaustion of the transferred assets or for medical or safety reasons. An unconscionable contract has been defined as a *one-sided contract or one which no man in his senses, not under delusion, would make, on the one hand, and which no fair and honest man would accept on the other.* [Italics added] * * * The term unconscionability encompasses an absence of a meaningful choice on the part of one of the parties together with contract terms which are unreasonably favorable to the other party. * * * Where a contract is found to be unconscionable, courts will refuse to give full effect to it as written. * * * We are of the opinion that the terms of the "continuing care contract" were not unreasonably favorable to the Home. The contract provided that the Home would care for decedent until she left the facility voluntarily, involuntarily, or by reason of death. In the event Mrs. Finn left the facility voluntarily she was entitled to recover the balance then remaining in the account paid or deposited with the facility on her behalf less charges properly allocated to her stay in the facility. Mrs. Finn was also entitled to a refund should the Home request that she leave the facility for medical reasons, safety reasons, or for reasons permitted by law. Lastly, the Home reserved the right to terminate the contract should Mrs. Finn not be eligible for old age assistance benefits. However, the Home incorporated certain safeguards in the contract to insure Mrs. Finn's eligibility for old age assistance benefits. Most importantly, the Home's option could only be exercised once all assets transferred to the Home had been used in the care of Mrs. Finn. Accordingly, we conclude that the "continuing care contract" signed by Mrs. Finn was not unconscionable.
* * * *

DECISION AND REMEDY

The circuit court affirmed the trial court's dismissal of the administrator's petition, and the Home was allowed to keep the assets and funds transferred.

COMMENTS

The mere fact that the terms of a contract favor one party more than the other is insufficient to claim lack of mutuality (because of the adequacy of consideration rule), and until the unfairness hurts the consciousness of society, courts will not set aside the contract. The philosophy is that persons must be bound by their legal agreements, even if the agreement turns out to operate as a hardship on one of the parties.

Discriminatory Contracts

Contracts in which a party promises to discriminate in terms of color, race, religion, national origin, or sex are contrary to statute and contrary to public policy.[13] For example, if a property owner promises in a contract not to sell the property to a member of a particular race, the contract is unenforceable.

Public policy underlying these prohibitions is very strong and the courts are quick to invalidate discriminatory contracts. Thus, the law attempts to insure that people will be treated equally.

Contracts for the Commission of a Tort

Contracts that require a party to commit a civil wrong, or a tort, are illegal. Remember that a *tort* is an act that is wrongful to another individual in a private

---

13. Federal Civil Rights Act of 1964, 42 U.S.C.A., Section 2000e, et seq.

sense, even though it may not necessarily be criminal in nature (an act against society).

Contracts Injuring Public Service

Contracts that interfere with a public officer's duties are contrary to public policy. For example, contracts to pay legislators for favorable votes are obviously harmful to the public. Often, a fine line is drawn between lobbying efforts and agreements to influence voting. When a lobbying group provides certain factual information in order to influence the outcome of legislation, the lobby is not engaging in an illegal activity. But if the lobby enters into a contingency fee agreement, whereby the legislator receives a certain amount of money if a certain bill is passed or a certain contract is awarded, the agreement is illegal because it is deemed contrary to public policy. In the United States, people are not entitled to buy and sell votes. Therefore, agreements to do so are illegal.

Agreements that involve a *conflict of interest* are often illegal. Public officers cannot enter into contracts that cause conflict between their official duties as representatives of the people and their private interests. Statutes require many public officers to liquidate their interests in private businesses before serving as elected representatives. Other statutes merely require them to put their businesses in blind trusts, so that private and public responsibilities remain separate.

Suppose Ladd is a county official in charge of selecting land for the building of a new courthouse. He makes a contract for the state to buy land that he happens to own. This is a conflict of interest. If the state discovers later that Ladd owned the land, it can normally use this information to show a conflict of interest and to void the contract.

Agreements Obstructing Legal Process

Any agreement that intends to delay, prevent, or obstruct the legal process is illegal. For example, an agreement to pay some specified amount if a criminal prosecution is terminated is illegal. Likewise, agreements to suppress evidence in a legal proceeding or to commit fraud upon a court are illegal. Tampering with a jury by offering jurors money in exchange for their votes is illegal.

In a trial, most witnesses (except expert witnesses) are paid a flat fee to compensate them for their expenses. Offering to pay one witness more than another is contrary to public policy, since the extra payment can provide an incentive for the witness to lie.

A promise to refrain from prosecuting a criminal offense in return for a reward is void because it is against public policy. A reward given under the threat of arrest or prosecution is also void.

Forum Selection and Arbitration Clauses Agreements that do not obstruct the legal process include agreements for the preselection of a forum or agreements for the arbitration of a dispute. **Forum selection clauses** are often contained in contracts where the parties are large multinational firms. For example, a contract for the sale of construction machinery made between a French corporation and a Colombian corporation can provide for the resolution of disputes in London, England. Agreements to preselect a forum are usually upheld unless they are designed to discourage litigation (for example, where a consumer in Florida buys an auto from General Motors Corp. and the contract contains a forum selection clause requiring any lawsuit to be brought in Detroit, Michigan).

Arbitration is the negotiation of a dispute before an arbitrator or a panel of arbitrators. Both sides present their stories, and the arbitrator makes the decision. Essentially, arbitration is similar to a trial, although formal rules of pleading, discovery, and evidence are not recognized. After arbitration, the losing party may appeal the arbitrator's decision to a court of law, but with rare success. **Arbitration clauses** (clauses in the contract calling for the settlement of disputes through arbitration) are generally upheld today, although courts previously invalidated such clauses on the basis that they interfered with the jurisdiction of the court. (See Chapter 3.)

EFFECT OF ILLEGALITY

In general, an illegal contract is void. That is, the contract is deemed never to have existed, and the courts will not aid either party. In most illegal contracts both parties are considered to be equally at fault—**in pari delicto.** In such cases the contract is void. If it is executory (not yet fulfilled), neither party can enforce it. If it is executed, there can be neither contractual nor quasi-contractual recovery.

Suppose Sonatrach, Algeria's national oil company, contracts to sell oil to Tenneco without government approval. Algeria has a law that prohibits the export of oil without government approval. Therefore, the contract is illegal and unenforceable. If Tenneco sues to enforce delivery of the oil, the suit will be dismissed since the contract is void. Even if Tenneco has paid for some of the oil, the contract cannot be enforced. Tenneco cannot even get back the money it paid under the illegal contract. In general, the courts take a hands-off attitude toward illegal contracts.

That one wrongdoer in an illegal contract is unjustly enriched at the expense of the other is of no concern to the law—except under certain special circumstances that will be discussed below. The major justification for this hands-off attitude is that it is improper to place the machinery of justice at the disposal of a plaintiff who has broken the law by entering into an illegal bargain. Another justification is the hoped-for deterrent effect of this general rule. A plaintiff who suffers loss because of it should presumably be deterred from entering into similar illegal bargains.

Exceptions to the General Rule

Some persons are excepted from the general rule that neither party to an illegal bargain can sue for breach and neither can recover for performance rendered:

1. Persons justifiably unaware or ignorant of facts that make the agreement illegal.
2. Persons protected by statutory law.
3. Persons who withdraw from an illegal agreement before the transaction is performed (partial performance).
4. Persons induced to enter into an illegal contract through fraud, duress, or undue influence.

Justifiable Ignorance of the Facts   When one of the parties is relatively innocent, that party can often obtain restitution or recovery of benefits conferred in a partially executed contract. In this case, the courts will not enforce the contract but will allow the parties to return to their original position.

It is also possible for an innocent party who has fully performed under the contract to enforce the contract against the guilty party. For example, a truck carrier contracts with Gillespie to carry goods to a specific destination for a normal fee of $500. The truck carrier delivers the goods and later finds out that the contents of the shipped crates were illegal. Although the law specifies that the shipment, use, and sale of the goods were illegal, the carrier, being an innocent party, could still legally collect the $500 from Gillespie.

Members of Protected Classes   An illegal contract can be enforced by a member of a group of persons specifically protected by statute. When a statute is clearly designed to protect certain classes of people, a member of that class can enforce an illegal contract even though the other party cannot. A statute that prohibits employees from working more than a specified number of hours per month is designed to protect those employees. An employee who works more than the maximum can recover for those extra hours of service. Flight attendants are subject to a federal statute that prohibits them from flying more than a certain number of hours every month. Even if an attendant exceeds the maximum, the airline must pay for those extra hours of service.

Another example of statutes designed to protect a particular class of people concerns **Blue Sky Laws,** legislation that regulates and supervises investment companies for the protection of the public. Such laws are intended to stop the sale of stock in fly-by-night concerns such as visionary oil wells and distant gold mines. Investors are protected as a class and can sue to recover the purchase price of stock issued in violation of such laws.

Most states also have statutes regulating the sale of insurance. If the insurance company violates a statute when selling insurance, *the purchaser can nevertheless enforce the policy.* For example, assume Indemnity Insurance Company is not qualified to sell insurance in Montana but does so anyway. A purchaser who buys a policy to insure his auto has an accident and seeks to recover. The insurer cannot resist payment under the policy, even though the contract is illegal. The statutes regulating insurance companies are designed to protect policyholders, so the buyer can recover from the insurer.

Withdrawal from Illegal Agreement   If the illegal agreement has been only partly performed and the illegal part of the bargain has not yet been performed, the party rendering performance can withdraw from the bargain. That party can recover the performance or its value. For example, Sam and Jim decide to wager (illegally) on the outcome of a boxing match. They each deposit money with a stakeholder, who agrees to pay the winner of the bet. At this point, each party has performed part of the agreement, but the illegal part of the agreement will not occur until the money is paid to the winner. Before such payment occurs, either party is entitled to withdraw from the agreement by giving notice of repudiation to the stakeholder.

Illegal Contract through Fraud, Duress, or Undue Influence   Often illegal contracts involve two blameworthy parties, but one party is more at fault than the other. Whenever the plaintiff has been induced to enter into an illegal bargain by fraud, duress, or undue influence of the other party to the agreement, that party will be allowed to recover for performance or its value.

Consider the following example: Mildred Pfeiffer has a number of creditors threatening to file suit for debts she owes. Her friend, Harry, suggests she "sell" to him two very expensive investment diamonds for a nominal price because a judgment creditor could levy execution of judgment on the diamonds as nonexempt property. He promises to "sell" back the diamonds at the same price after she has "gotten her creditors off her back." (This transaction would defraud Mildred's creditors, and if discovered could be set aside by her creditors). Mildred settles with her creditors by making to each an agreed modest payment for release of the debts. Mildred now demands the diamonds from Harry, and Harry re-

fuses to "sell" back the diamonds. Although Mildred's transfer of property was for the purpose of defrauding her creditors and was illegal, the court will allow her to recover her property.

Severable, or Divisible, Contracts

If a contract is severable into legal and illegal portions, and the illegal portion does not go to the essence of the bargain, the legal portion can be enforced. This is consistent with the basic policy of courts to enforce the legal intentions of the parties wherever possible. A *severable* contract consists of distinct parts that can be performed separately, with separate consideration provided for each part.

Suppose Norman Harrington contracts to buy ten pounds of bluegrass seed for $25 and five gallons of herbicide for $30. At the time, Harrington does not know that the Food and Drug Administration has banned sale of the herbicide and that the contract for its sale is therefore illegal. Here, the contract is severable because separate considerations were stated for the bluegrass seed ($25) and the herbicide ($30). Therefore, the portion of the contract for the sale of bluegrass seed is enforceable; the other portion is not.

Another example of a severable contract would be one involving the sale of a business in which a restrictive covenant not to compete is included. The courts may find that the restrictive covenant is too broad, in terms of time or area, and therefore illegal. This covenant could be declared void, but the remainder of the contract for the sale of the business would stand.

QUESTIONS AND CASE PROBLEMS

1. A famous New York City hotel, Hotel Lux, is noted for its food as well as its luxury accommodations. Hotel Lux contracts with a famous chef, Chef Perlee, to become its head chef at $6,000 per month. The contract states

that should Perlee leave the employment of Hotel Lux for any reason, he will not work as a chef for any hotel or restaurant in the states of New York, New Jersey, or Pennsylvania for a period of one year. During the first six months of the contract, Hotel Lux substantially advertises Perlee as its head chef, and business at the hotel is excellent. Then a dispute arises between the hotel management and Perlee, and Perlee terminates his employment. One month later, he is hired by a famous New Jersey restaurant just across the New York state line. Hotel Lux learns of Perlee'e employment through a large advertisement in a New York City newspaper. It seeks to enjoin Perlee from working in that restaurant as a chef for one year. Discuss how successful Hotel Lux will be in its action.

2. State X requires a person to be eighteen years old before being permitted to purchase alcoholic beverages. The state also has passed a law that persons who prepare and serve liquor in the form of drinks in commercial establishments must be licensed. The only requirement for obtaining a yearly license is that the person be at least eighteen years old. Michael, age 35, is hired as a bartender for the Lone Star Restaurant. George, a staunch alumnus of a nearby university, brings twenty of his friends to the restaurant to celebrate a football victory that afternoon. George has ordered four rounds of drinks, and the bar bill exceeds $150. George learns that Michael failed to renew his bartender's license, and George refuses to pay, claiming the contract is unenforceable. Discuss if George is correct.

3. The Constitution provides for the separation of church and state. The government can in no way support or affiliate itself with any particular religion or group of religions. [Note that across-the-board legislation, such as tax exemptions for religious organizations, is not prohibited by this constitutional provision.] Illinois enacted a law requiring all nonfood retailers to remain closed on Sunday. A local retailer challenged the law as a violation of the constitutional provision calling for separation of church and state. Do you think such a "Sunday closing law" is unconstitutional? Discuss fully.

4. Walsh was shopping at W. T. Grant Co. when she was approached by a saleswoman, who asked her if she wanted to open a charge account. The saleswoman's "pitch" was that she needed points for a contest. Walsh agreed to open a charge account and was given a booklet of coupons totaling $200. She was told by the saleswoman that she would be charged only for the coupons she used. In reality, the agreement Walsh signed was an installment sales contract, obligating her to pay a total of $246.01 over a twenty-month period at $10 per month. Walsh failed to make the first payment. W. T. Grant Co. filed suit. Is the agreement illegal? If so, for what reasons? [W. T. Grant Co. v. Walsh, 100 N.J.Super. 60, 241 A.2d 46 (1968)]

5. Womack was a well-known gambler in Saline County. Judge Maner, a friend of Womack, not only knew of Womack's gambling enterprises, but approved of them. From time to time over a period of several years, Womack paid money to the judge to insure that he would not be prosecuted. As a result of this long-standing agreement, Womack paid the judge a total of $1,675. Womack then claimed that the consideration for his paying the judge

was void and unlawful at the time the contract was entered into as well as at the present time. Therefore, Womack sued Judge Maner to rescind the contract and to get back the $1,675 he had paid. Should Womack recover? [Womack v. Maner, 277 Ark. 786, 301 S.W.2d 438 (1957)]

6. McCall and Frampton entered an oral agreement whereby McCall was to leave her husband and her employment and was to live and be intimate with Frampton and to work toward the promotion of his musical career. In return, McCall was to receive, as equal partner, 50 percent of all proceeds from Frampton's work as a musician. McCall did in fact leave her husband, live with Frampton, and devote all her resources, time, and effort to the promotion of Frampton's career. As agreed, they shared all benefits as equal partners from 1973 through July 1978, at which time Frampton unilaterally terminated the agreement. McCall sued to recover 50 percent of Frampton's earnings since 1978 and to obtain an interest in certain real property held by Frampton. McCall relied on *Marvin v. Marvin* to support her argument that the agreement is an enforceable one. Did McCall win? [McCall v. Frampton, 99 Misc. 2d 159, 415 N.Y.S.2d 752 (Sup. Ct. 1979)]

7. Williams, a woman of limited education who was separated from her husband and living on welfare, entered into a series of installment contracts with Walker-Thomas Furniture Company. During the period 1957 to 1962 she purchased various items from Walker-Thomas, including curtains, rugs, chairs, mattresses, a washing machine, and a stereo set. With each purchase, she paid part in cash and signed an installment agreement for the balance. Included in the installment agreement was a paragraph, in extremely fine print, that provided that payments, after the first purchase, were to be prorated on all purchases then outstanding. This had the effect of keeping a balance due on every item until the total bill was paid. Prior to her final purchase, Williams had reduced her outstanding balance to $164. The last purchase, a stereo, increased her balance due to $678. After making several more payments, Williams defaulted. Walker-Thomas attempted to enforce the installment provision allowing it to repossess all the goods previously purchased by Williams. Was this contract enforceable? [Williams v. Walker-Thomas Furniture Company, 198 A.2d 914 (D.C.App.1964)]

8. In 1970 Overbeck received a Sears credit card. In 1974 he charged several purchases on the credit card. If Overbeck had paid for each purchase within thirty days, no service charge would have been added to the outstanding balance. But he chose to let the account "revolve." Therefore, under the credit card agreement between Overbeck and Sears, a service charge of 1.5 percent (18 percent annually) was added each month. Overbeck claimed that the 18 percent annual interest was usurious and con-

trary to the laws of Indiana that set the maximum legal rate at 6 percent. Was Overbeck correct? [Overbeck v. Sears, Roebuck and Company, 169 Ind.App. 501, 349 N.E.2d 286 (1976)]

9. Jo Anne Hall's husband induced her to consent to get divorced. She claimed that her former husband represented that the divorce was needed for business reasons. He promised that after the divorce they would continue living together as man and wife, and he would support her as he had in the past. The divorce was granted and they lived together for three months. He then left her so he could marry another woman. Mrs. Hall filed suit claiming among other allegations breach of contract. Discuss whether a contract to get a divorce and to cohabitate after the divorce is illegal. [Hall v. Hall, 455 So.2d 813 (Ala. 1984)]

10. Roeber and the Swift & Courtney & Beecher Company were both engaged in the business of manufacturing matches. Swift desired to purchase Roeber's business, which was quite lucrative. Pursuant to the sale agreement between Swift and Roeber, Roeber agreed not to engage in the match business in any state in the United States other than Nevada and Montana for ninety-nine years. Was the contract enforceable? [Diamond Match Company v. Roeber, 106 N.Y. 473, 13 N.E. 419 (1801)]

12

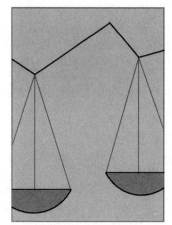

CONTRACTS
Genuineness of Assent

It is possible for a contract to be unenforceable even though two parties, with full legal capacity, have entered into an agreement for a legal purpose and even though it is supported by consideration. This can occur when (1) there is no *genuine assent* to the terms of the contract because of misrepresentation, mistake, duress, or undue influence; and (2) when written evidence is lacking for certain contracts that require it. This chapter will examine the problems of genuine assent, and the next chapter will deal with contracts that require a writing under the Statute of Frauds.

Historically, the law has stressed the necessity of people conducting their affairs in a way that is not injurious to others. This philosophy has already been discussed in the chapters on tort and criminal law. Although parties to a contract must assume certain risks, the law has determined that neither party should be allowed to benefit in contract from deceit, from undue influence, from duress, or from making certain types of mistakes. (The law views different types of mistakes in different ways, as will be discussed in this chapter.) Therefore, certain contracts are voidable either by both parties when there is mutual mistake or by the innocent party in contracts formed by deceit, undue influence, or duress.

MISTAKES

It is important to distinguish between mistakes *as to facts* and mistakes *in judgment as to value or quality.*

Only the former have legal significance. Suppose Jane Simpson plans to buy ten acres of land in Montana. If she believes the land is worth $10,000, and it is worth only $4,000, her mistake is one of value or quality. However, if she believes the land is the ten acres owned by the Boyds, and it is actually the ten acres owned by the Deweys, her mistake is one of fact. Only a mistake as to fact allows a contract to be avoided.

Mistakes occur in two forms—*unilateral* and *mutual,* or *bilateral.* A unilateral mistake is made by only one of the contracting parties; a mutual, or bilateral, mistake is made by both.

Unilateral Mistakes

A unilateral mistake involves some *material fact* that is important to the subject matter of the contract. In general, a unilateral mistake does not afford the mistaken party any right to relief from the contract.[1] For example, John intends to sell his stereo for $550. He learns that Jane is interested in buying a used stereo. John writes a letter to Jane offering to sell his stereo, but he mistakenly types in the figure price of $500. Jane immediately writes back, accepting John's offer. Even though John intended only to sell

---

1. Restatement, Second, Contracts, Section 153, liberalizes this rule to take into account the modern trend of allowing avoidance although only one party has been mistaken.

his stereo for $550, John's unilateral mistake falls on him. He is bound in contract to sell the stereo to Jane for $500.

There are two exceptions to the general rule. First, the rule is not applied when the *other* party to the contract knows or should have known that a mistake was made. Second, some states will not enforce the contract against the mistaken party if the error was due to a mathematical mistake in addition, subtraction, division, or multiplication and if it was done inadvertently and without gross negligence.

For an example of how these exceptions are applied, consider the following case. Odell Construction Co. made a bid to install the plumbing in a proposed apartment building. When Herbert Odell, the president, added up his costs, his secretary forgot to give him the figures for the pipe fittings. Because of the omission, Odell's bid was $6,500 below that of the other bidders. The prime contractor, Sunspan Inc., accepted Odell's bid. If Sunspan was not aware of Odell's mistake and could not reasonably have been aware of it, the contract will be enforceable, and Odell will be required to install the plumbing at the bid price. However, if it can be shown that Odell's secretary mentioned her error to Sunspan,

or if Odell's bid was so far below the others that, as a contractor, Sunspan should reasonably have known the bid was a mistake, the contract can be rescinded. Sunspan would not be allowed to accept the offer knowing it was made by mistake.[2] The law of contracts protects only *reasonable* expectations.

Mutual Mistakes of Material Fact

When both parties are mistaken as to the same material fact, the contract can be rescinded by either party.[3] The mistake must be about a material fact—that is, a fact that is important and central to the contract.

The classic case on mutual mistake of fact involved a ship named "Peerless" that was to sail from Bombay with certain cotton goods on board. However, more than one ship named "Peerless" sailed from Bombay that winter. The mistake was mutual, and it was about a material fact.

---

2. Peerless Glass Co. v. Pacific Crockery Co., 121 Cal. 641, 54 P. 101 (1898).
3. Restatement, Second, Contracts, Section 152.

RAFFLES v. WICHELHAUS AND ANOTHER

2 Hurl & C. 906,
159 Eng. Rep. 375 (1864).
Court of Exchequer (Per Curiam)

BACKGROUND AND FACTS　*The defendant purchased a shipment of Surat cotton from the plaintiff "to arrive ex 'Peerless' from Bombay." The defendant expected the goods to be shipped on the Peerless sailing from Bombay in October. The plaintiff expected to ship the goods on another Peerless, which sailed from Bombay in December. By the time the goods arrived and the plaintiff tried to deliver them, the defendant was no longer willing to accept them.*

*　*　*　*

Declaration. For that it was agreed between the plaintiff and the defendants, to wit, at Liverpool, that the plaintiff should sell to the defendants, and the defendants buy of the plaintiff, certain goods, to wit, 125 bales of Surat cotton, guaranteed middling fair merchant's Dhollorah, to arrive ex "Peerless" from Bombay; and that the cotton should be taken from the quay, and that the defendants would pay the plaintiff for the same at a certain rate, to wit, at the rate of 17¼d. per pound, within a certain time then agreed upon after the arrival of the said goods in England. Averments: that the said goods did arrive by the said ship from Bombay in England, to wit, at Liverpool, and the plaintiff was then and there ready, and willing and offered to deliver the said goods to the defendants, &c. Breach: that the defendants refused to accept the said goods or pay the plaintiff for them.

Plea. That the said ship mentioned in the said agreement was meant and intended by the defendants to be the ship called the "Peerless," which sailed from Bombay, to wit, in October; and that the plaintiff was not ready and willing and did not offer to deliver to the defendants any bales of cotton which arrived by the last mentioned ship, but instead thereof was only ready and willing and offered to deliver to the defendants 125 bales of Surat cotton which arrived by another and different ship, which was also called the "Peerless", and which sailed from Bombay, to wit, in December.

* * * *

There is nothing on the face of the contract to show that any particular ship called the "Peerless" was meant; but the moment it appears that two ships called the "Peerless" were about to sail from Bombay there is a latent ambiguity, and parol evidence may be given for the purpose of shewing that the defendant meant one "Peerless," and the plaintiff another. That being so, there was no consensus ad idem, and therefore no binding contract.

The judgment was for the defendant.

DECISION AND REMEDY

Mutual Mistake in Identity and Mistake in Value

If a mutual mistake concerns the *value* or *quality* of the object of the contract rather than some material fact, the contract can be enforced by either party. This rationale evolves from the theory that certain risks are assumed by both parties who enter into a contract. Without this rule, almost any party who did not receive what he or she considered was a fair bargain could argue bilateral mistake. In essence, this would make *adequacy* of consideration a factor in determining whether a contract existed. As discussed in Chapter 9, the courts normally do not inquire into the adequacy of consideration.

Obviously, the distinction between a mistake *in identity* and a mistake *in value* is central to this issue. Suppose Daniel Murray, after seeing Beverly Beale's violin, buys it for $250. Neither party knows that it is a Stradivarius built in 1717 worth thousands of dollars. Although Beverly may claim a mutual mistake has been made, the mistake is not one which warrants contract rescission or reformation. Both parties knew what the subject matter of the contract was—the violin that Murray had seen. Both Murray and Beale mistook the value of that particular violin. Therefore, the contract cannot be rescinded.

Sometimes courts have difficulty in ascertaining whether the mutual mistake is one of identity (fact) or one of value. For example, an early Michigan case[4] involved two farmers who entered into a contract for the purchase of a cow. Both the owner and purchaser thought the cow was barren (a cow incapable of breeding and producing valuable calves). Based on this belief, the negotiated price was several hundred dollars less than it would have been had the cow been capable of breeding. Just before delivery, the owner discovered the cow had conceived a calf, and he refused to deliver the much more valuable cow to the purchaser, claiming contract rescission due to mutual mistake in identity. In a split decision, the court held that "a barren cow is substantially a different creature than a breeding one." Therefore, the mutual mistake went to the substance (identity) of the contract rather than the value of the cow.

In the following case the court applied the mutual mistake doctrine to a situation where an insurance contract was canceled on the basis of a mutual mistake of fact.

---

4.   Sherwood v. Walker, 66 Mich. 568, 33 N.W. 919 (1887).

BACKGROUND AND FACTS   *The plaintiff, Christine Boyd, was named beneficiary in a policy insuring her husband's life. The policy, issued by Aetna Life (the defendant), contained a provision for payment of benefits in the event of the husband's permanent total disability. The couple separated, but Mrs. Boyd continued to pay the premiums, keeping the policy in force subject to valid claims. Later, since she did not know the whereabouts of her husband or his*

BOYD v. AETNA LIFE INS. CO.
Appellate Court of Illinois, Fourth District, 1941.
310 Ill. App. 547, 35 N.E. 2d 99.

state of health, she contacted the insurance company and it was agreed that she should surrender the policy for the cash surrender value. After she surrendered the policy, Mrs. Boyd learned that her husband had become disabled. His disability had occurred before she surrendered the policy, and had she known about it, she would not have surrendered the policy. She asked the court to rescind her surrender agreement with the Aetna Life Insurance Co. and to pay her the disability (and death) benefits due under the policy on the ground of "mutual mistake of fact." Aetna argued "that notwithstanding her conscious want of ignorance of the condition of health of her husband she had elected to surrender the policy in question and take the cash surrender value thereof, in lieu of paying any further premiums on the policy, and by such action waived any rights she had under the policy of insurance."

STONE, Presiding Justice.
* * * *

The decisive and practically sole question for the consideration of this court is whether the facts alleged in the amended complaint set forth a sufficient mistake of fact, in the legal acceptation of the term, as to justify the intervention of a court of equity, and relieve against the consequences of that alleged mistake of fact, in the entering into the contract of recision.

"Mistake of fact" has been defined to be a mistake, not caused by the neglect of a legal duty on the part of the person making the mistake, and consisting in an unconscious ignorance or forgetfulness of a fact past or present material to the contract, or belief in the present existence of a thing material to the contract which does not exist, or in the past existence of a thing which has not existed. [Emphasis added.]

* * * [A]t the time of cancellation plaintiff had a perfectly valid claim, but she and the company were both at that time * * * ignorant of the fact that there was a claim in existence, due to the total permanent disability of insured. The supposed element of doubt as to the health of Boyd never entered into the contemplation of either party, nor did it form any part of the consideration for the cancellation and surrender of the policy. It would be quite natural that they would assume, as they evidently did, that the insured was in good health. As matter of fact such is the express allegation of the amended complaint.
* * * *

In the instant case, the insured's state of health was not merely incidental, nor was it a matter that would merely enhance the amount of damages. The subject matter of the mistake was intrinsic to the transaction. As set forth in plaintiff's amended complaint, "if she had known the true facts as to said Jimmie Boyd's total permanent disability * * * she would not have surrendered same (the policy) to the defendant." This policy was in full force and effect at the time of total permanent disability. Upon that contingency coming to pass the liability of defendant was fixed. The cancellation was not intended to reach back and absolve defendant from any liability which it had already incurred.

DECISION AND REMEDY

Aetna was held liable to Mrs. Boyd as a beneficiary for payment of benefits under the policy, since she had been paying the policy up to and including the point when her ex-husband became disabled. At the time of his disability, Aetna became indebted to Mrs. Boyd as beneficiary for those payments. Therefore, there was indeed a mutual mistake of fact, since neither she nor Aetna knew of her ex-husband's disability entitling her to payment. The court permitted Mrs. Boyd to rescind her surrender agreement with Aetna and ordered Aetna to pay her the disability benefits.

MISREPRESENTATION—FRAUD

Although fraud is a tort, it also affects the genuineness of the innocent party's consent to the contract. Thus, the transaction is not voluntary in the sense of "mutual assent." When an innocent party consents to a contract with fraudulent terms, the contract normally can be voided because that party has not *voluntarily* consented to its terms.[5] Normally, the innocent party can either rescind the contract and be restored to the original position or can enforce the contract and seek damages for any injuries resulting from the fraud.

When a Misrepresentation Is Fraudulent

The word *fraudulent* is used in various senses in the law. Generally, fraudulent misrepresentation refers only to misrepresentation that is consciously false and is intended to mislead another. That is, the perpetrator of the fraudulent misrepresentation must know or believe that the assertion is not true, or must be lacking the confidence that he or she states or implies in the truth of the assertion, or must know that he or she does not have the basis stated or implied for the assertion.[6]

What is at issue is whether the defendant believes that the plaintiff is substantially certain to be misled as a result of the misrepresentation. For example, Jones makes a statement to ABC Credit Rating Company about his financial condition that he knows is untrue. Jones realizes that ABC will publish this information for its subscribers. Marchetti, a subscriber, receives the published information. Relying on that information, Marchetti is induced to make a contract to lend money to Jones. Jones's statement is a fraudulent misrepresentation. The contract is voidable by Marchetti.

The Four Elements of Fraud

Typically, there are four elements of fraud:

1. A misrepresentation of a material fact has occurred.

2. There is an intent to deceive.
3. The innocent party has justifiably relied on the misrepresentation.
4. The innocent party has been injured.

In the following four sections we will examine each of these elements.

Misrepresentation Has Occurred The first element of proving fraud is to show that misrepresentation of a material fact has occurred. This misrepresentation can be in words or actions. For example, the statement "This sculpture was made by Michelangelo" is an express misrepresentation of fact if the statue was made by another artist. The misrepresentation as to the identity of the artist would certainly be a *material* fact in the formation of a contract.

Misrepresentation can also take place by the conduct of a party. One such form of conduct is concealment. Concealment is basically an act which keeps the other party from learning of a material fact.[7] Suppose Quid contracts to buy a racehorse from Ray. The horse is blind in one eye, but when Ray shows the horse, he skillfully keeps its head turned so that Quid does not see the defect. The concealment constitutes fraud because of Ray's *conduct*. Likewise, if a salesperson shows a sample from the top of a large box, but does not show the inferior samples at the bottom, a misrepresentation *by conduct* has occurred if there is a marked difference in quality between the top and the bottom merchandise.

Representations of future facts (predictions) or statements of opinion are generally not subject to a claim of fraud. Every person is expected to exercise care and judgment when entering into contracts, and the law will not come to the aid of one who simply makes an unwise bargain. For example, statements like, "This land will be worth twice as much next year" or "This car will last for years and years" are statements of opinion, not fact. Hence, contracting parties should recognize them as such and not rely on them. An opinion is usually subject to

5. Restatement, Second, Contracts, Sections 163 and 164.
6. Restatement, Second, Contracts, Section 162.

7. Restatement, Second, Contracts, Section 160.

contrary or conflicting views; a fact is objective and verifiable. Therefore, a seller of goods is allowed to "huff and puff" his wares without liability for fraud.

In certain cases, however, opinions may entitle the innocent party to rescission or reformation. These cases almost always involve some sort of "expert" giving a naive purchaser some opinion, and they are decided on equitable grounds. The courts usually hold it to be unfair to allow an expert to take ad-vantage of a novice, especially if the expert knows the novice is relying on the expert's opinion. Thus, an expert's statement of opinion to a layperson is treated as fact.

The following case illustrates how a dance in-structor with superior knowledge made statements of opinion concerning plaintiff's dance potential, and such were treated as a misrepresentation of a material fact.

VOKES v. ARTHUR MURRAY, INC.

District Court of Appeal of Florida, Second District, 1968.
212 So.2d 906.

BACKGROUND AND FACTS *The defendant, Arthur Murray, Inc., op-erated dancing schools throughout the nation through local, franchised opera-tors, one of whom was the defendant. The plaintiff, Audrey E. Vokes, a widow without family, wished to become "an accomplished dancer" and to find "a new interest in life." In 1961 she was invited to attend a "dance party" at J. P. Davenport's "School of Dancing." Vokes went to the school and received elab-orate praise from her instructor for her grace, poise, and potential as "an excellent dancer." The instructor sold her eight half-hour dance lessons for $14.50 each, to be utilized within one calendar month.*

Subsequently, over a period of less than sixteen months, Vokes bought a total of fourteen dance courses, which amounted to 2,302 hours of dancing lessons for a total cash outlay of $31,090.45, all at Davenport's school.

PIERCE, Judge.
*   *   *   *

These dance lesson contracts and the monetary consideration therefor of over $31,000 were procured from her by means and methods of Davenport and his associates which went beyond the unsavory, yet legally permissible, perimeter of "sales puffing" and intruded well into the forbidden area of undue influence, the suggestion of false-hood, the suppression of truth, and the free exercise of rational judgment, if what plaintiff alleged in her complaint was true. From the time of her first contact with the dancing school in February, 1961, she was influenced unwittingly by a constant and continuous barrage of flattery, false praise, excessive compliments, and panegyric en-comiums, to such extent that it would be not only inequitable, but unconscionable, for a Court exercising inherent chancery power to allow such contracts to stand.

She was incessantly subjected to overreaching blandishment and cajolery. She was assured she had "grace and poise"; that she was "rapidly improving and developing in her dancing skill"; that the additional lessons would "make her a beautiful dancer, capable of dancing with the most accomplished dancers"; that she was "rapidly pro-gressing in the development of her dancing skill and gracefulness", etc., etc. She was given "dance aptitude tests" for the ostensible purpose of "determining" the number of remaining hours instructions needed by her from time to time.

At one point she was sold 545 additional hours of dancing lessons to be entitled to the award of the "Bronze Medal" signifying that she had reached "the Bronze Standard", a supposed designation of dance achievement by students of Arthur Murray, Inc.

Later she was sold an additional 926 hours in order to gain the "Silver Medal", indicating she had reached "the Silver Standard", at a cost of $12,501.35.

At one point, while she still had to her credit about 900 unused hours of instructions, she was induced to purchase an additional 24 hours of lessons to participate in a trip to Miami at her own expense, where she would be "given the opportunity to dance with members of the Miami Studio".

She was induced at another point to purchase an additional 126 hours of lessons in order to be not only eligible for the Miami trip but also to become "a life member of the Arthur Murray Studio", carrying with it certain dubious emoluments, at a further cost of $1,752.30.

At another point, while she still had over 1,000 unused hours of instruction she was induced to buy 151 additional hours at a cost of $2,049.00 to be eligible for a "Student Trip to Trinidad", at her own expense as she later learned.

Also, when she still had 1100 unused hours to her credit, she was prevailed upon to purchase an additional 347 hours at a cost of $4,235.74, to qualify her to receive a "Gold Medal" for achievement, indicating she had advanced to "the Gold Standard".

On another occasion, while she still had over 1200 unused hours, she was induced to buy an additional 175 hours of instruction at a cost of $2,472.75 to be eligible "to take a trip to Mexico".

Finally, sandwiched in between other lesser sales promotions, she was influenced to buy an additional 481 hours of instruction at a cost of $6,523.81 in order to "be classified as a Gold Bar Member, the ultimate achievement of the dancing studio".

All the foregoing sales promotions, illustrative of the entire fourteen separate contracts, were procured by defendant Davenport and Arthur Murray, Inc., by false representations to her that she was improving in her dancing ability, that she had excellent potential, that she was responding to instructions in dancing grace, and that they were developing her into a beautiful dancer, whereas in truth and in fact she did not develop in her dancing ability, she had no "dance aptitude", and in fact had difficulty in "hearing the musical beat". The complaint alleged that such representations to her "were in fact false and known by the defendant to be false and contrary to the plaintiff's true ability, the truth of plaintiff's ability being fully known to the defendants, but withheld from the plaintiff for the sole and specific intent to deceive and defraud the plaintiff and to induce her in the purchasing of additional hours of dance lessons". It was averred that the lessons were sold to her "in total disregard to the true physical, rhythm, and mental ability of the plaintiff". In other words, while she first exulted that she was entering the "spring of her life", she finally was awakened to the fact there was "spring" neither in her life nor in her feet.

*   *   *   *

It is true that "generally a misrepresentation, to be actionable, must be one of fact rather than of opinion". But this rule has significant qualifications, applicable here. It does not apply where there is a fiduciary relationship between the parties, or where there has been some artifice or trick employed by the representor, or where the parties do not in general deal at "arm's length" as we understand the phrase, or where the representee does not have equal opportunity to become apprised of the truth or falsity of the fact represented.

" *   *   * A statement of a party having *   *   * superior knowledge may be regarded as a statement of fact although it would be considered as opinion if the parties were dealing on equal terms."

It could be reasonably supposed here that defendants had "superior knowledge" as to whether plaintiff had "dance potential" and as to whether she was noticeably improving in the art of terpsichore. And it would be a reasonable inference from the undenied averments of the complaint that the flowery eulogiums heaped upon her by defendants as a prelude to her contracting for 1944 additional hours of instruction in order to attain the rank of the Bronze Standard, thence to the bracket of the Silver Standard, thence to the class of the Gold Bar Standard, and finally to the crowning plateau of a Life Member of the Studio, proceeded as much or more from the urge to "ring the cash register" as from any honest or realistic appraisal of her dancing prowess or a factual representation of her progress.

*   *   *   *

" * * * [W]hat is plainly injurious to good faith ought to be considered as a fraud sufficient to impeach a contract", and * * * an improvident agreement may be avoided "because of surprise, or mistake, *want of freedom, undue influence, the suggestion of falsehood, or the suppression of truth*". (Emphasis supplied.)

DECISION AND REMEDY

Vokes's complaint, which had originally been dismissed from the trial court, was reinstated, and the case was returned to the trial court to allow Vokes to prove her case.

COMMENTS

Fraud is an ambiguous concept in law. It includes various degrees of misrepresentation that can be separated into three tort categories: (1) intentional behavior, (2) negligent behavior, and (3) strict liability for certain behavior. In all cases involving the tort of misrepresentation and the contract defense of fraud, the defendant must misrepresent a fact or facts, and the plaintiff must believe the misrepresentation to be true and must rely on it with resulting damages.

Misrepresentation of Law   Misrepresentation of law does not *ordinarily* entitle the party to relief from a contract. For example, Sarah has a parcel of property that she is trying to sell to Brad. Sarah knows that a local ordinance prohibits building anything on the property higher than three stories. Nonetheless, she tells Brad, "You can build a condominium fifty stories high if you want to." Brad buys the land and later discovers that Sarah's statement is false. Normally Brad cannot avoid the contract because at common law people are assumed to know state and local law where they reside. Additionally, a layperson should not rely upon a statement made by a nonlawyer about a point of law.

Exceptions to this rule occur when the misrepresenting party is in a profession that is known to

require greater knowledge of the law than the average citizen possesses. The courts are recognizing an increasing number of such professions. For example, the courts recognize that real estate brokers are expected by their clients to know the law governing real estate sales, land use, and so on. If Sarah, in the preceding example, were a lawyer or a real estate broker, her misrepresentation of the area's zoning status would probably constitute fraud.[8]

The following case demonstrates an attempt by one party to bring an action based on deceit against a hotel owner for his misrepresentation of state law.

---

8.   Restatement, Contracts, Second, Section 170.

TWO, INC. v.
GILMORE
Colorado Court of Appeals, 1984.
679 P.2d 116.

BACKGROUND AND FACTS   *Two, Inc. contacted Gilmore regarding an opportunity to operate a discotheque in Aspen's Jerome Hotel owned by Gilmore. Gilmore represented to Two, Inc. that if they agreed to a "management agreement," by law Two, Inc. could share in Gilmore's liquor license. Gilmore's opinion of the law on this matter had been previously questioned by others. A short time thereafter Gilmore discovered that the agreement was illegal, as it did not conform with state liquor codes. Gilmore contacted Two, Inc. to renegotiate a new agreement but an impasse occurred over the liquor license. Gilmore indicated he would notify the liquor distributors that Two, Inc. did not have a license to buy or sell liquor. Two, Inc. abandoned the premises and Two, Inc. filed a lawsuit seeking damages on grounds of deceit based on fraud. The trial court entered a judgment for Gilmore, and Two, Inc. appealed.*

PIERCE, Judge.

*   *   *   *

The trial court concluded, as a matter of law, that Gilmore's representation to Two that a management agreement was tantamount to a lease and would allow for the sharing of liquor license privileges was a representation of law and, therefore, not actionable. We agree.

A representation of law is only an expression of opinion and is impotent to void a contract or support an action for damages. *   *   * A representation of what the law will or will not permit to be done is one upon which the party to whom it is made has no right to rely. The truth or falsehood of such a representation can be tested by ordinary vigilance and attention. *   *   * Therefore the fact that Gilmore's opinion as to the state of the law had previously been questioned by others is no bar to his defense against this deceit claim. *   *   *

Here, Gilmore's representation to Two constitutes an individual's belief and opinion concerning statutes controlling the dispensation, purchase, and sale of liquor. Therefore, under the facts of this case, Two cannot obtain remedial relief. *   *   *

The court affirmed the ruling of the trial court and denied Two, Inc. any damages.

DECISION AND REMEDY

Silence   Ordinarily, neither party to a contract has a duty to come forward and disclose facts. Therefore, a contract cannot be set aside because certain pertinent information is not volunteered.

For example, suppose you own a car and have an accident that requires extensive body work on one side of the car. After the repair, the car's appearance and operation are the same as they were prior to the accident. One year later you decide to sell your car. Do you have a duty to volunteer the information about the accident to the seller? The answer is no. In this case, silence does not constitute misrepresentation. On the other hand, if the purchaser asks you if the car has had extensive body work and you lie, you have committed a fraudulent misrepresentation.

Some exceptions to this rule exist. If a *serious* defect or *serious* potential problem is known to the seller but cannot reasonably be suspected by the buyer, the seller may have a duty to speak. Expanding the example just given, suppose your car occasionally vibrates dangerously because of the earlier accident. In this case, you would have a duty to speak. In another example, if the foundation of a factory is cracked, creating a potential for serious water damage, the seller must reveal this fact. Likewise, when a city fails to disclose to bidders subsoil conditions that will cause great expense in constructing a sewer, the city is guilty of fraud.[9]

Failure to disclose important facts also constitutes fraud if the parties have a relationship of trust and confidence called a *fiduciary relationship*. In such a relationship, if one party knows any facts that materially affect the other's interests, they must be disclosed. An attorney, for example, has a duty to disclose material facts to a client. Other such relationships include partners in a partnership, directors of corporations and the shareholders, and guardians and wards.[10]

Knowledge of the Fact's Falsity—Intent to Deceive   The *second* element of fraud is knowledge on the part of the misrepresenting party that facts have been falsely represented. This element, normally called **scienter**, or "guilty knowledge," signifies that there was an *intent to deceive*. Proof of intent

---

9.   City of Salinas v. Souza & McCue Constr. Co., 66 Cal. 2d 217, 57 Cal. Rptr. 337, 424 P. 2d 921 (1967). Normally the seller must disclose only "latent" defects—that is, ones that would not readily be discovered even by an expert. Thus, termites in a house would not be a latent defect, since an expert could readily discover their presence.

10.   Restatement, Contracts, Second, Sections 161 and 173.

is not necessary if the circumstances surrounding a transaction are such that one can *infer* the intent. The act of misrepresentation combined with the knowledge of its falsity normally constitutes an intent to deceive.

Suppose that Roper has owned a 1980 Oldsmobile for two years and suddenly, for no apparent reason, quits driving it. Roper then advertises the automobile for sale. Chipper asks Roper how the engine runs, and Roper says, "This Olds runs like a Swiss watch; there is nothing wrong with it." So Chipper buys the Olds, only to discover the next day that there is a crack in the engine block requiring replacement of the entire engine. Here a court can *infer* that Roper knew that the engine block was cracked (at least in the absence of another explanation from Roper), since he suddenly quit driving the two-year-old car and put it up for sale.

Reliance on the Misrepresentation The *third* element of fraud is reasonably *justifiable reliance* on the misrepresentation of fact. The deceived party must have justifiable reason for relying on the misrepresentation, and the misrepresentation must be an important factor in inducing the party to enter into the contract. It need not be the sole factor in order to satisfy the requirement of reliance.

Reliance is not justified if the innocent party knows the true facts or relies on obviously extravagant statements. Suppose a used-car dealer tells you, "This old Cadillac will get fifty miles to the gallon." You would not normally be justified in relying on the statement. Or suppose Phelps, a bank director, induces Scott, a co-director, into signing a guarantee that the bank's assets will satisfy its liabilities, stating, "We have plenty of assets to satisfy our creditors." If Scott knows the true facts, he will not be justified in relying on Phelps's statement. However, if Scott does not know the true facts *and has no way of finding them out*, he will be justified in relying on the statement. The same rule applies to defects in property sold. If the defects are obvious, the buyer cannot justifiably rely on the seller's representations. If the defects are hidden or latent (that is, not ap-

pearing on the surface), the buyer is justified in relying on the seller's statements.

Injury to the Innocent Party The final element of fraud is injury to the innocent party. The courts are divided on this issue. Some do not require a showing of injury when the action is to *rescind or cancel* the contract. Since rescission returns the parties to the position they were in prior to the contract, showing injury to the innocent party has been held to be unnecessary.[11]

In an action to recover *damages* caused by the fraud, proof of an injury is universally required. The measure of damages is ordinarily equal to what the value of the property would have been if it had been delivered as represented, less the actual price paid for the property. In effect, this gives the innocent (non-breaching) party the benefit of the bargain, rather than reestablishing the party's position prior to the contract. In actions based on fraud, courts will often award **exemplary**, or **punitive**, **damages**, which are defined as those damages awarded to a plaintiff over and above the proved, actual compensation for the loss. Punitive damages are based on the public policy consideration of *punishing* the defendant or setting an example for similar wrongdoers.

In the following case, Hazel Gales applied for auto insurance, stating falsely that she had not been in an auto accident in the past five years and had not received a ticket for a moving violation in the past three years. The defendant, Plains Insurance Co., claimed that such false representations made her policy void from the beginning (void *ab initio*). The company contended that it would not have sold the policy at the specified rate and perhaps would not have sold it at all if Gales had provided true information about her driving record. Thus, the insurance company contended that it had not engaged in a genuine assent (that is, there was no reality of consent).

---

11. For example, Kaufman v. Jaffee, 244 App.Div. 344, 279 N.Y.S. 392 (1935).

MILLER v. PLAINS INS. CO.

Springfield Court of Appeals, Missouri 1966. 409 S.W.2d 770.

BACKGROUND AND FACTS *The plaintiff in this action, D. C. Miller, is suing the insurance company of the owner and driver of the automobile in which his wife was killed. The owner and operator of the automobile, Hazel Gales, also perished in the crash. She was insured by Plains Insurance Company, the defendant. The policy provided, among other things, $500 medical expense* *coverage and up to $10,000 uninsured motorists coverage. This coverage provides for payment to the insured in case the insured is involved in an accident where someone else is at fault and does not have any insurance.*

At the trial, Miller was awarded both $500 in medical expenses and $10,000 under the uninsured motorists provision. On appeal, the defendant argued that had it known certain representations were untrue, it would not have undertaken the risk in insuring Gales, who had a record for moving traffic violations and, in particular, for which she had been cited in another state, for hazardous driving and did not disclose it when applying for the policy.

TITUS, Judge.

*   *   *   *

What is a material misrepresentation? A misrepresentation that would likely affect the conduct of a reasonable man in respect to his transaction with another is material. [Emphasis added.] Materiality, however, is not determined by the actual influence the representation exerts, but rather by the possibility of its so doing. A representation made to an insurer that is material to its determination as to what premium to fix or to whether it will accept the risk, relates to a fact actually material to the risk which the insurer is asked to assume. The word "risk" does not relate to an actual increase in danger but to a danger determined by the insurer's classification of the various circumstances affecting rates and insurability. That the fact misrepresented has no actual subsequent relation to the manner in which the event insured against occurred, does not make it any the less material to the risk. Thus, whether a misrepresentation is material in an application for an automobile insurance policy, is determined by whether the fact, if stated truthfully, might reasonably have influenced the insurance company to accept or reject the risk or to have charged a different premium, and not whether the insurer was actually influenced.

*   *   *   *

It is a well-known fact insurance companies rely on expense, loss, and other statistical data to measure differences among risks and thus ascertain rates to be charged for individual risks in accordance with standards for measuring variations in hazards. This is recognized and, to some extent, controlled by our statutes. Questions as to traffic violations of prospective insureds and as to previous accidents in which they have been involved are legitimate fields of research for insurance companies, for these are not only rate-determining facts but may also determine if the risk will even be insured. In consideration of the authorities previously cited, *   *   * we are of the opinion the misrepresentations involved in this case might reasonably be expected to have influenced the insurance company to have accepted or rejected Mrs. Gales as an insured or to have charged her a different premium for issuing her a policy. As the only evidence in this case is that if defendant had known the truth it would have declined the risk, we are drawn to the conclusion the misrepresentations were material and should permit defendant to avoid its liability under the policy.

The trial court's ruling was reversed. The defendant, Plains Life Insurance Company, did not have to pay the $10,000 uninsured motorists claim or the $500 medical expense coverage because of the material misrepresentation of fact made by Hazel Gales when she filled out the application on which her insurance policy was issued. In essence, the court decided there was no true assent by the insurance company to insure Gales under that premium for that policy. No insurance contract ever came into existence.

**DECISION
AND REMEDY**

Innocent Misrepresentation If a person makes a statement that he or she believes to be true, but that actually misrepresents material facts, the person is guilty only of an **innocent misrepresentation,** not of fraud. If an innocent misrepresentation occurs, the aggrieved party can rescind the contract but usually cannot seek damages. Basically, an innocent misrepresentation, in the contract sense, is viewed as a mistake rather than as a fraud.

Negligent Misrepresentation Suppose a salesperson tells a customer, "This air conditioner will cool your whole house," without knowing the size of the house. This person is acting in a negligent manner with reckless disregard for the truth. Consider another example: A real estate broker assures Sneed that a particular house is insulated, even though the broker does not know whether the house is insulated. In virtually all states, such *negligent misrepresentation* is equal to *scienter*, or to knowingly making a misrepresentation. In other words, culpable ignorance of the truth supplies the intention to mislead, even if the defendant can claim, "I didn't know."

UNDUE INFLUENCE

Undue influence arises from special kinds of relationships in which one party can greatly influence another party, thus overcoming that party's free will. Minors and elderly people are often under the influence of guardians. If the guardian induces a young or elderly ward to enter into a contract that benefits the guardian, undue influence is likely being exerted. Undue influence can arise from a number of fiduciary or confidential relationships: attorney-client, doctor-patient, guardian-ward, parent-child, husband-wife, or trustee-beneficiary. The essential feature of undue influence is that the party being taken advantage of does not, in reality, exercise free will in entering into a contract. A contract entered into under excessive or undue influence lacks genuine assent and is therefore voidable.[12]

In the final analysis, the court must ask the following question in order to determine undue influence: To what extent was the transaction induced by dominating the mind or emotions of the person in question? It follows, then, that the mental state of the person in question will often show to what extent the persuasion from the outside influence was "unfair."

Whenever a contract is challenged on the basis of the particular relationship between the parties, the court will often *presume* that the contract was made under undue influence. For example, if a ward challenges a contract made with his or her guardian, the presumption will normally be that the guardian has taken advantage of the ward. To rebut this presumption successfully, the guardian has to show that full disclosure was made to the ward, that consideration was adequate, and that the ward received independent and competent advice before completing the transaction.

In cases where the relationship is one of trust and competence, such as between an attorney and a client, the dominant party (the attorney) is held to extreme or utmost good faith in dealing with the subservient party. Suppose a long-time attorney for an elderly man induces him to sign a contract for the sale of some of his assets to a friend of the attorney at below-market prices. The contract is probably voidable. The attorney has not upheld good faith in dealing with the man (unless this presumption can be rebutted).

DURESS

Assent to the terms of a contract is not genuine if one of the parties is *forced* into agreement. Recognizing this, the courts allow that party to rescind the contract. Forcing a party to enter into a contract under the fear of threats is legally defined as **duress.**[13] For example, if Piranha Loan Co. threatens to harm you or your family unless you sign a promissory note for the money that you owe, Piranha is guilty of using duress. In addition, threatening blackmail or extortion to induce consent to an informal contract constitutes duress. Duress is both a defense to the enforcement of a contract and a ground for rescission or cancellation. Therefore, the party upon whom the duress is exerted can choose to carry out the contract or to avoid the entire transaction. (This is true in most cases in which assent is not real.)

Generally, the threatened act must be wrongful or illegal. Threatening civil litigation (if the claim

---

12. Restatement, Second, Contracts, Section 177.

13. Restatement, Second, Contracts, Sections 174 and 175.

is bona fide) does not constitute duress, but threatening a criminal suit does.

Suppose that Donovan injures Jaworski in an auto accident. The police are not called. Donovan has no automobile insurance, but she has substantial assets. Jaworski is willing to settle the potential claim out of court for $3,000. Donovan refuses. After much arguing, Jaworski loses her patience and says, "If you don't pay me $3,000 right now, I'm going to sue you for $35,000." Donovan is frightened and gives Jaworski a check for $3,000. Later in the day she stops payment on the check. Jaworski comes back to sue her for the $3,000. Donovan argues that she was the victim of duress. However, the threat of a civil suit is normally not duress. Had Jaworski threatened to have Donovan arrested unless Donovan paid her $3,000, Donovan's check would have been secured under duress.

Economic need is generally not sufficient to constitute duress, even when one party exacts a very high price for an item the other party needs. However, if the party exacting the price also creates the need, economic duress may be found. For example,

the Internal Revenue Service assessed a large tax and penalty against Sam Thompson. Thompson retained Earl Eyman to resist the assessment. The last day before the deadline for filing a reply with the Internal Revenue Service, Eyman declined to represent Thompson unless he signed a very high contingency fee agreement for his services. The agreement was unenforceable.[14] Although Eyman had threatened only to withdraw his services, something that he was legally entitled to do, he was responsible for delaying the withdrawal until the last day. Since it would have been impossible at that late date to obtain adequate representation elsewhere, Thompson was forced into either signing the contract or losing his right to challenge the IRS assessment.

In the following case, the court examines some of the factors that are necessary in order for a court to be able to conclude that the consent obtained in an agreement was the result of duress.

---

14. Thompson Crane & Trucking Co. v. Eyman, 123 Cal. App. 2d 904, 267 P. 2d 1043 (1954).

BACKGROUND AND FACTS *John and Janet Libel entered into a post-divorce agreement that provided nine months' extension of alimony to Janet Libel beyond that fixed in the parties' separation agreement. The separation agreement had been approved and incorporated into the divorce decree. The appellant, John Libel, however, subsequently asserted that his consent to the post-divorce agreement was invalid because it was obtained under duress. The trial court upheld the post-divorce agreement against assertions of duress, and hence John Libel appealed.*

LIBEL v. LIBEL
Court of Appeals of Kansas, 1980.
616 P. 2d 306.

HARMAN, Chief Judge Retired.
*   *   *   *

Appellant admits he signed the agreement, indeed he penciled the body of it himself, but he urges his consent was invalid because it was obtained under duress because of appellee's threats to curtail his visitation privileges with his two sons.

> To constitute duress by threats the actor's manifestation must be made for the purpose of coercing the other; must have for its object the securing of undue advantage with respect to the other; must be of such a character that it is adapted to overpower the will of the other and is reasonably adequate for the purpose; must in fact deprive the other of free exercise of will; and must cause the other to act to his detriment. *   *   *

Thus, the important question in cases of this character is whether the party threatened was, by such threats, deprived of the exercise of his free will.

Generally, absent a confidential or fiduciary relationship between the parties, one who asserts duress to avoid an agreement has the burden of proof to establish that claim, *   *   * and such evidence must be of a substantial nature. *   *   *

Appellant did testify that appellee was very emotional and upset and told him she needed one thousand dollars per month for herself and her children to continue her education, and that she said that his conduct in that respect would govern the extent of his child visitation. * * * Both parties seemed genuinely concerned for the boys' best interest. More could be said, but the matter need not be further labored. We cannot say that the trial court erred in determining this factual issue.

* * * *

The judgment is affirmed.

* * * *

DECISION AND REMEDY

The Court of Appeals affirmed the trial court's holding that John Libel's consent to the post-divorce agreement was not invalid as obtained under duress.

COMMENTS

The court emphasized the fact that an attorney who had served as John Libel's business counsel was consulted at the time of the signing. John Libel was also aware that visitation rights could be the subject of judicial action.

ADHESION CONTRACTS AND UNCONSCIONABILITY

Modern courts are beginning to strike down terms that are dictated by one of the parties with overwhelming bargaining power. **Adhesion contracts** arise when one party forces the other party to adhere to dictated terms or go without the commodity or service in question. An adhesion contract is written *exclusively* by one party (the dominant party) and presented to the other party (the adhering party) with no opportunity to negotiate. Adhesion contracts usually contain copious amounts of fine print disclaiming the maker's liability for everything imaginable. Standard lease forms are often called adhesion contracts. Many automobile retailers have used contracts containing several pages of fine print when selling a car. In the past, nearly every company excluded liability for personal injuries suffered as a result of using the product. The average consumer buying a car for $8,000 or $9,000 was in no position to bargain for personal injury coverage. The consumer could either go without an automobile or buy the auto, risking personal injury for which he could not hold the auto manufacturer liable.

Standard form contracts are used by a variety of businesses and include life insurance policies, residential leases, loan agreements, and employment agency contracts. In order to avoid enforcement of the contract or of a particular clause, the aggrieved party must show substantially unequal bargaining positions and show that enforcement would be "manifestly unfair" or "oppressive." If the required showing is made, the contract or particular term is deemed *unconscionable* and not enforced. Technically, unconscionability under the UCC applies only to contracts for the sale of goods.[15] Many courts, however, have broadened the concept and applied it in other situations.

Although unconscionability was discussed in the preceding chapter under the subject of legality, it is important to note here that the great degree of discretion permitted a court to invalidate or strike down a contract or clause as being unconscionable has met with resistance. As a result, some states have not adopted Section 2-302 of the UCC. In those states the legislature and the courts prefer to rely on traditional notions of fraud, undue influence, and duress. In one respect, this gives certainty to contractual relationships, since parties know they will be held to the exact terms of their contracts. But on the other hand, public policy does dictate that there be some limit on the power of individuals and businesses to dictate the terms of a contract.

---

15. See UCC 2-302.

QUESTIONS AND CASE PROBLEMS

1. In front of witnesses, Juanita informs Sue that she is going to offer to sell her car to Nick for $950. That evening, Juanita types a letter offering to sell her car to Nick, but in her haste she types the figure $900 instead of $950. Nick receives the letter and by return letter accepts. At the time for transfer of title, Nick tenders $900, but Juanita refuses to transfer title to the car unless he pays $950. She claims she has witnesses to her intent. Discuss whether, despite the witnesses, Nick can hold Juanita to a contract for $900. Would your answer be any different if Juanita in her haste had typed $95 instead of $950? Explain.

2. Pam owns two 1981 Buicks, one valued at $8,000 and the other valued at $9,000. She needs money and decides to sell one of her cars. Mary knows of this and offers to purchase Pam's Buick for $8,500. Pam signs a contract for the purchase price. At the time for transfer and payment, Pam attempts to deliver the Buick valued at $8,000. Mary believes she is buying the Buick valued at $9,000. Pam wants to hold Mary in contract for the 1981 Buick valued at $8,000, and Mary wants to hold Pam in contract for the 1981 Buick valued at $9,000. Discuss who can hold the other in contract.

3. Martin owns a forty-room motel on Highway 100. Tanner is interested in purchasing the motel. During the course of negotiations, Martin tells Tanner that the motel netted $30,000 last year and that it will net at least $45,000 next year. The motel books, which Martin turns over to Tanner before the purchase, clearly show that Martin's motel netted only $15,000 last year. Also, Martin fails to tell Tanner that a bypass to Highway 100 is being planned that will redirect most traffic away from the front of the motel. Tanner purchases the motel. During the first year under Tanner's operation, the motel nets only $18,000. It is at this time that Tanner learns of the previous low profitability of the motel and the planned bypass. Tanner wants his money back from Martin. Discuss fully Tanner's probable success in getting his money back.

4. Discuss which of the following contracts are fully enforceable:

(a) Simmons finds a stone in his pasture that he believes to be quartz. Jenson, who also believes that the stone is quartz, contracts to purchase it for $10. Just before delivery, the stone is discovered to be a diamond worth $1,000.

(b) Jacoby's barn is burned to the ground. He accuses Goldman's son of arson and threatens to bring criminal action unless Goldman agrees to pay him $5,000. Goldman agrees to pay.

(c) Student Velikovski threatens to tell teacher O'Brien's wife that O'Brien is having a sexual relationship with a student—unless O'Brien agrees to pay Velikovski $200. O'Brien agrees to pay.

(d) Sallor is a *new* salesperson and innocently tells Beyer that a lawn mower he is selling has a five-year manufacturer's warranty. Beyer contracts to purchase the lawn mower in reliance thereon. Beyer and Sallor are transacting business for the first time. At the time of delivery, it is discovered that the manufacturer only warrants the lawn mower for one year.

5. Joshua and Adam are brothers and have been close for many years. Adam is the oldest and has been acting as a father figure for fifteen years, since the death of their father. Joshua married Mary, and Adam and Mary do not get along together. During the past year, Adam has told Joshua that Mary is unfaithful and is out to get all his worldly possessions. Furthermore, he advises Joshua to sell his lake property (held in Joshua's name) before Mary moves in. Adam suggests that Joshua sell the property to a friend of Adam's immediately, and that although the value of the property is $20,000, a sale of $14,000 is better than nothing. Joshua contracts with his brother's friend at that price, but before the closing to transfer title, Joshua dies. Mary is executrix of his estate and wants to set aside the contract to sell the lake property. Discuss how successful she will be.

6. Plaintiff publishes a directory entitled *New York Yellow Pages*, which is strikingly similar in format, print style, and paper color to the *New York Telephone Company Yellow Pages*, but which in fact is part of an independent business enterprise. In addition, the *New York Yellow Pages* has on its cover the legend "Let your fingers do the walking!" along with the familiar logo of walking fingers that appears on the *Telephone Company Yellow Pages*. Plaintiff's representative, stating that this publication would replace the bulkier *New York Telephone Company Yellow Pages*, sold advertising space to Grossman for $1,492.80. Grossman made a down payment of $118.40 and one installment payment of $65.20 and thereafter refused to make payments. Plaintiff sued. Grossman claims that plaintiff fraudulently induced him to enter into the contract by leading him to believe plaintiff's book was a new, improved version of the *New York Telephone Company Yellow Pages*. Can Grossman rescind the contract on grounds of fraudulent inducement? [New York Yellow Pages, Inc. v. Growth Personnel Agency Inc., 98 Misc. 2d 541, 414 N.Y.S. 2d 260 (Civ. Ct. 1979)]

7. Stronach was a salesman for National Cash Register Company. Over the years he had sold cash registers to a number of retail establishments. Stronach approached Townsend, a retail merchant, to sell him a cash register. Stronach told Townsend that he would save the cost of a

bookkeeper and perhaps half the cost of a sales clerk if he bought a cash register. Relying on this, Townsend bought the cash register. After several months, he realized that the cash register was not bringing about the savings that Stronach had promised. Can Townsend rescind the agreement? [See National Cash Register Co. v. Townsend Grocery Store, 137 N.C. 652, 50 S.E. 306 (1905)]

8. Laemmar was an employee of J. Walter Thompson Co. During the years of his employment, he purchased shares of common stock from the company. Laemmar's stock was to be subject to repurchase by the company if Laemmar's employment were terminated for any reason. The officers and directors of the company decided to increase their control and demanded that Laemmar and several other employees sell their stock back or lose their jobs. Although Laemmar did not wish to sell his stock, he did so to keep his job. The officers and directors never made any physical threats or suggestions of physical harm to Laemmar. Several years later Laemmar instituted a lawsuit to rescind his sale of the stock. Can Laemmar rescind? [Laemmar v. J. Walter Thompson Co., 435 F.2d 680 (7th Cir. 1970)]

9. W & B Realty Company owned and operated an apartment building in Chicago and rented one of the apartments to O'Callaghan. O'Callaghan signed a lease with a clause relieving W & B from all liability for any injuries that O'Callaghan might sustain anywhere on the premises of the apartment area, regardless of any negligence by W & B Realty. One evening, while crossing the courtyard, O'Callaghan fell because the pavement in the courtyard had been improperly maintained. O'Callaghan sued W & B for her injuries. W & B claimed that it was not liable because of the exculpatory clause contained in the lease. Is W & B correct? [O'Callaghan v. Waller & Beckwith Realty Co., 15 Ill.2d 436, 155 N.E.2d 545 (1958)]

10. Rollins was a prisoner in Rhode Island State Prison. While he was incarcerated, a prisoners' uprising occurred in which prison personnel were held as hostages. Rollins and other prisoners were promised immunity from prosecution by the director of the Department of Corrections if they would stop their violent actions and release the hostages. They did so. Nonetheless, they were later indicted and prosecuted for the crimes they committed during the prison revolt. Can Rollins and the others raise the defense that the promise of immunity had been made to them? [State v. Rollins, 116 R.I. 528, 359 A.2d 315 (1976)]

13

CONTRACTS
Writing and Form

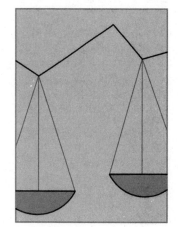

Suppose I meet you on the street and orally offer to sell you my used personal computer (PC) for $800. You accept my offer. Later, upon your tender of the $800, I refuse to transfer my personal computer to you because I have a better offer from another person. You threaten to sue me. After all, we did have an *oral* contract. The question is whether an oral contract is enforceable. In most cases, it is, but the party seeking to enforce it must establish the existence of the contract as well as its actual terms. Naturally, when the parties have no writing or memorandum about the contract, only oral testimony can be used in court to establish the existence of the terms of the contract. The problem with oral testimony is that parties are sometimes willing to perjure themselves in order to win lawsuits.

Therefore, at early common law, parties to a contract were not allowed to testify. This led to the practice of hiring third party witnesses. As early as the seventeenth century, the English recognized the many problems presented by this practice and enacted a statute to help deal with it. The statute was known as "An Act for the Prevention of Frauds and Perjuries."[1] The act required that certain types of contracts, in order to be enforceable, had to be evidenced by a writing and signed by the party against

whom enforcement was sought. For example, our oral contract for the sale of my PC would fall under the act and could not be enforced by you in a court action. In the United States, the descendant of the British Act is called the Statute of Frauds.

CONTRACTS THAT MUST BE IN WRITING

Today almost every state has a Statute of Frauds, modeled after the English act. The actual name of the Statute of Frauds is misleading since it neither applies to fraud nor invalidates any type of contract. Rather, it denies enforceability to certain contracts that do not comply with its requirements. The primary purpose of the act is evidentiary, to provide reliable evidence of the existence and terms of certain classes of contracts deemed historically to be important or complex. Although the statutes vary slightly from state to state, they all require the following types of contracts to be in writing or evidenced by written memorandum.[2]

1. Contracts involving interests in land.
2. Contracts that cannot *by their terms* be performed within one year from date of formation.

---

1. The English Parliament passed the act in 1677.

2. Restatement, Second, Contracts, Section 110.

3. Collateral contracts such as promises to answer for the debt or duty of another and promises by the administrator or executor of an estate to pay a debt of the estate personally, that is, out of his or her own pocket.
4. Promises made in consideration of marriage.
5. Contracts for the sale of goods for more than $500.

CONTRACTS INVOLVING INTERESTS IN LAND

Sale of Land

A contract calling for the sale of, or transfer of an interest in, land is not enforceable unless it is in writing or evidenced by a written memorandum. Land is real property and includes all physical objects that are permanently attached to the soil, such as buildings, plants, trees, and the soil itself. The Statute of Frauds operates as a *defense* to the enforcement of an oral contract for the sale of land. Therefore, even if both parties acknowledge the existence of an oral contract for the sale of land, under most circumstances the contract will still not be . enforced.[3] If Sam contracts orally to sell Blackacre to Betty but later decides not to sell, Betty cannot enforce the contract. Likewise, if Betty refuses to close the deal, Sam cannot force Betty to pay for the land by bringing a lawsuit. The Statute of Frauds is a defense to the enforcement of this type of oral contract.

Frequently it is necessary to distinguish between real property, which is property affixed to the land, and personal property. A contract for the sale of land ordinarily involves the entire interest in the real property, including buildings, growing crops, vegetation, minerals, timber, and anything else affixed to the land. Therefore, a fixture (personal property so affixed or so used as to become a part of the realty) is treated as real property. But anything else, say a couch, is treated as personal property.

The Statute of Frauds requires written contracts for the transfer of other interests in land. Interests in land include life estates, real estate mortgages, easements, and leases.

Life Estates   A **life estate** is an ownership interest in land that lasts for a person's lifetime. For example, if Sally Manne sells Edenfarm to Mary Johnson "for life, then after Johnson's death, to Nancy Smole," Johnson has a life estate in the farm. This means that Johnson can live on and farm the land during her lifetime, but when Johnson dies Smole will have a full estate in the farm—that is, she will own it entirely.[4]

Mortgages   A real estate **mortgage** is a conveyance of an interest in land as a security for repayment of a loan. If Nancy Smole, now full owner of Edenfarm, wants to borrow money from First National Bank, First National will require *collateral* for the loan. By giving conditional title of Edenfarm to the bank, Smole can get the loan.[5] When Smole pays off the debt, Edenfarm will be hers once again in total ownership.

Easements   An **easement** is a legal right to use land without owning it. Easements are created expressly or impliedly. An express easement arises when the owner of land expressly agrees to allow another person to use the land. To be enforceable the agreement must be in writing. Implied easements can arise from the past conduct of the parties. For example, when a farmer has used a certain path to reach the back forty acres of his farm for twenty years, and the path goes across a neighbor's property, the farmer has an *implied* easement to cross the neighbor's property. Implied easements need not be in writing and rarely are, because of the way they are created. Another example of an implied easement involves the ownership of adjacent properties by one person. The owner establishes an apparent and permanent use of, say, a road through one property onto the other. He or she then sells that property without specifying the road as an easement to the other property. It is implied nonetheless if the other property is otherwise landlocked without ingress or egress.

---

3. However, the contract will be enforced if the parties admit to the existence of the oral contract in court or admit to its existence pursuant to discovery before trial.

4. Full ownership like Nancy Smole's is called a fee simple absolute. See Chapter 53.
5. Technically, only in "title" states will Nancy Smole be required to convey title to First National Bank. In "lien" states, she can enter into a mortgage contract giving the bank a lien against the farm. Today, many of the distinctions between title states and lien states have essentially been eliminated.

Leases A lease is a transfer without title of real property for a certain period of time.[6] Most states have statutes dealing specifically with leases apart from the Statute of Frauds and exempt leases of one year or less from the writing requirements. Thus, any lease lasting more than one year must be in writing. Some states extend this period. For example, Indiana allows leases to be oral for up to three years.

Partial Performance—Exception

Since the Statute of Frauds is a defense against the enforcement of an oral contract for the sale of land or an interest in land, problems arise when an oral contract has been partially performed. For example, the buyer may have paid part of the purchase price and then taken possession of the premises or made permanent improvements to the property.[7] If the parties cannot be returned to their status quo, the courts may grant *specific performance* of the oral contract.

Whether the courts will enforce an oral contract for an interest in land, where partial performance has taken place, is usually determined by the degree of injury which would be suffered if the court chose not to enforce the oral contract.[8] The following three examples will illustrate:

1. The purchase price of the land has been paid, but the buyer has not taken possession. In this case, since the parties can be returned to their original positions without injury, the courts will usually not grant specific performance.
2. The buyer has paid part of the purchase price and entered into possession. Some states allow enforcement of the contract since the parties cannot be returned to their status quo.
3. When part of the purchase price has been paid, possession has been taken by the buyer, and permanent improvements have been made on the land, most states allow enforcement of the contract. Once

these three things have been done, the courts can be fairly sure that there was actually a contract in existence, even if it was an oral contract. The parties could not be returned to their status quo without substantial injury.

CONTRACTS WHOSE TERMS CANNOT POSSIBLY BE PERFORMED WITHIN ONE YEAR FROM THE DATE OF FORMATION

Contracts that cannot, *by their own terms*, be performed within one year from the date the contract is formed must be in writing to be enforceable.[9] Since disputes over such contracts are unlikely to occur until some time after the contracts are made, resolution of these disputes is difficult unless the contract terms have been put in writing.

In order for a particular contract to fall into this category, contract performance must be objectively impossible to perform within a year from the date of contract formation. If the contract, by its terms, makes performance within the year *possible* (not probable), the contract is not within the Statute of Frauds and need not be in writing.

Suppose Bankers Life orally contracts to loan $40,000 to Janet Lawrence "as long as Lawrence and Associates operates its financial consulting firm in Omaha, Nebraska." The contract is not within the Statute of Frauds—no writing is required—because Lawrence and Associates could possibly go out of business in one year or less. In this event, the contract would be fully performed within one year. Although this occurrence is unlikely, it is nevertheless possible, and that possibility removes the contract from the province of the Statute of Frauds.[10]

Suppose, on the other hand, that Bankers Life agrees to loan the money to Lawrence "for a period of two years with the provision that there will be no acceleration or prepayment for the period." Lawrence and Associates could go out of business in one year or less. Since the debtor is not allowed to accelerate payments on the loan or prepay the remainder at any time, he or she cannot perform the contract within one year without breaching the con-

---

6. Although a lease is technically a conveyance of an interest in land, it is usually accompanied by a contract, rather than a deed.
7. Executed contracts—that is, contracts that have been fully performed—are not subject to the Statute of Frauds.
8. In some states, mere *reliance* on an oral contract is enough to remove it from the Statute of Frauds.

---

9. Restatement, Second, Contracts, Section 130.
10. See Warner v. Texas & Pac. Ry. Co., 164 U.S. 418, 17 S.Ct. 147 (1896).

tract's terms. Therefore, this contract is subject to the Statute of Frauds and must be evidenced by a writing. Compare the specified two years in this contract to the statement in the preceding example, where the words "as long as" were used.

Next assume that the contract states that the loan will last for two years "terminable at the end of six months, subject to review of Lawrence and Associates' financial condition." Here the contract is not subject to the Statute of Frauds because, by the terms of the contract, it can be fully performed within one year.

The one-year period begins to run *the day after the contract is made.*[11] Suppose you graduate from college on June 1. An employer orally contracts to hire you immediately (June 1) for one year at $2,000 per month. This contract is not subject to the Statute of Frauds (need not be in writing in order to be enforceable) because the one-year period to measure performance begins on June 2. Since your performance of one year can begin immediately, it would take you exactly one year from the date of entering the contract to perform.

Suppose that on March 1 the dean of your college, in your presence, orally contracts to hire your professor for the next academic year (a nine-month period) at a salary of $35,000. The academic year begins on September 1. Does this contract have to be in writing to be enforceable? The answer is yes. The one-year period used to measure whether performance by contract terms is possible begins on March 2. Since the nine-month contract could not begin until September 1 and would end on May 31 of the next year, the contract performance period

exceeds the one-year measurement period by three months. Thus, this contract is within the Statute of Frauds. But if this oral contract had been entered into at any time between June 1 and September 1, the contract, by its terms, would be performed within one year of the date of contract formation (acceptance of the offer), and the oral contract would be enforceable.

In summary, the test to determine whether an oral contract is enforceable under the one-year rule of the Statute of Frauds is not whether an agreement is *likely* to be performed within a year from the date of making the contract. Rather, the question revolves around whether performance within a year is *possible.* Conversely, when performance of an oral contract is impossible during a one-year period, this provision of the Statute of Frauds will bar recovery on an oral contract.

Exhibit 13–1 illustrates the basic determination of when contracts whose performance cannot be performed within one year must be in writing to be enforceable.

COLLATERAL PROMISES

A collateral, or secondary, promise is one ancillary to an integrated contractual relationship. This term is used to refer to any promise that is ancillary to a principal transaction. Two collateral promises are covered by the Statute of Frauds. They are:

1.   Promises by the administrator or executor of an estate to pay personally the debts of the estate.
2.   Promises to answer for the debt or duty of another.[12]

---

11.   2 Corbin on Contracts, Sec. 444.

12.   Restatement, Second, Contracts, Section 112.

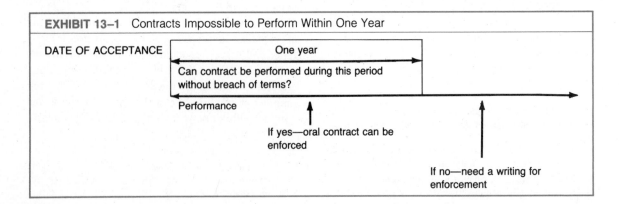

EXHIBIT 13–1   Contracts Impossible to Perform Within One Year

DATE OF ACCEPTANCE

One year

Can contract be performed during this period without breach of terms?

Performance

If yes—oral contract can be enforced

If no—need a writing for enforcement

Promises by the Administrator or Executor of an Estate to Pay Personally the Debts of the Estate

The administrator (or executor) of an estate has the duty of paying the debts of the deceased and distributing any remainder to the deceased's heirs. The administrator can contract orally on behalf of the estate. A writing is required only when the administrator promises to pay the debts of the estate personally. Suppose Edward Post (administrator) contracts with Martha Lynch for legal services. If Post contracts on behalf of the estate, an oral contract is valid, and the estate is bound to pay Lynch for her legal services. But if Post agrees to pay Lynch's legal fees personally out of his own pocket, the contract must be in writing. Otherwise it is not enforceable, and Lynch cannot recover.

Promises to Answer for the Debt or Duty of Another

Promises made by one person to pay the debts or discharge the duties of another if the latter fails to perform are subject to the Statute of Frauds and must be in writing. Three elements must be present in this collateral promise situation in order to require that the agreement be in writing. They are:

1. Three parties are involved.
2. Two promises are involved.
3. The secondary, or collateral, promise is to pay a debt or fulfill a duty only if the first promisor fails to do so.

This set of requirements is illustrated in Exhibit 13–2.

The Statute of Frauds applies only to contracts that are promises of guaranty or suretyship. Only the promise between the guarantor and the creditor falls under the Statute of Frauds. Any other promise, such as the promise to incur the primary debt between the debtor and the creditor, or a promise of reimbursement between the guarantor and debtor, does not fall within the Statute of Frauds as applied to guaranty or suretyship contracts.

The key point here is that the debt of the guarantor is secondary. The debtor's obligation is primary. The Statute of Frauds applies if, and only if, the guarantor's obligation is contingent upon the

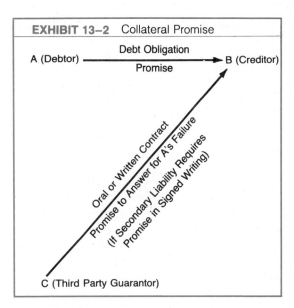

EXHIBIT 13–2   Collateral Promise

debtor's refusal or inability to pay the creditor. Consider some examples.

Suppose that Occidental Petroleum has signed an agreement with Husky Oil to ship 40,000 barrels of crude oil to Husky for a specified price. In other words, Husky has incurred an initial, or primary, obligation to Occidental Petroleum. To insure delivery to Husky, a president of European Caveham, Ltd., a major distributor of Husky, makes a *collateral* promise with Occidental Petroleum that, if Husky does not pay for the oil, European will pay for it. If the collateral promise to pay the debt of Husky is not in writing, it is not enforceable. The nature of European's liability is secondary (European is liable only if Husky Oil does not pay). When the promise creates secondary liability, it falls under this section of the Statute of Frauds.

As another example, suppose John orally contracts with Green Florist to send his mother a dozen roses for Mother's Day. John's oral contract with Green Florist provides that he will pay for the roses if his mother does not do so. Is the contract enforceable against John? The answer is yes. John's mother is not a debtor; nor is she obligated to pay Green Florist. John's obligation is primary, not secondary, because John's mother has no obligation as a promisor under the contract. The third element that makes writing necessary is missing. John's oral contract is supported by legally sufficient consideration and is enforceable.[13]

---

13.   Restatement, Second, Contracts, Section 112.

Now suppose John's mother owes $1,000 to the Third Bank of Austin on a promissory note payable on June 1. John knows that his mother cannot pay on the due date. John orally contracts with the Third Bank for the bank to extend the note payment for six months. Should the note not be paid at the end of that period by John's mother, John agrees to pay the note. Does this oral contract fall within the Statute of Frauds?

The answer is yes. The contract was express, made between the guarantor, John, and the creditor, Third Bank, and John's obligation is secondary— he is obligated to pay only if his mother does not pay. Therefore, this contract is not enforceable unless it is supported by a writing. Had John co-signed the note (and become a co-maker), allowing the bank to collect from either John or his mother, John's obligation would be *primary* and the contract would fall outside the Statute of Frauds and would not need to be in writing. Had John secured his mother's release from the debt from the bank for his promise to pay, the release being a discharge of her primary obligation to pay, John's promise to pay would become the *primary* liability and would fall outside the Statute of Frauds and would not need to be in writing in order to be enforceable.

The "Main Purpose" Rule—Consideration of Benefit to Promisor   The oral promise to answer for the debt of another is covered by the Statute of Frauds unless the guarantor is effectively a debtor because his or her main purpose in accepting secondary liability is to secure a pecuniary benefit. This type of contract need not be in writing.[14] The as-

sumption is that a court can infer from the circumstances of any given case whether the "leading objective" of the promisor was to secure a pecuniary advantage and thus, in effect, to answer for his or her own debt.

Consider an example. The General Contracting Corporation agrees to build a home for Oswald. General Contracting subcontracts part of its work to Ace Construction Company. After several weeks, Ace refuses to supply further labor or materials because General is in shaky financial condition and Ace is worried about being paid. Oswald is anxious to inhabit the house so that his children may start school on time in their new neighborhood. Therefore, Oswald orally agrees to pay Ace's debts if General fails to pay. Oswald's oral promise is enforceable (even though collateral) because the primary, or main, purpose in making the guarantee was to get the house built.[15]

Another typical application of the so-called main purpose doctrine is when one creditor guarantees the debtor's debt to another creditor for the purpose of forestalling litigation so as to allow the debtor to remain in business long enough to generate enough profits to pay *both* creditors.

The following case illustrates the main purpose doctrine application where a creditor of a development complex guaranteed the general contractor's payments to a subcontractor to insure that the development would be completed on time. Failure of the development project to be completed as contracted would markedly decrease tenant revenue, placing the principal debtor in default on its loan to the bank.

---

14.   Restatement, Second, Contracts, Section 116.

15.   Kampman v. Pittsburgh Contracting and Engineering Co., 316 Pa. 502, 175 A.396 (1934).

WILSON FLOORS CO.
V. SCIOTA PARK, LTD.
Supreme Court of Ohio, 1978.
54 Ohio St.2d 451,
377 N.E.2d 514.

BACKGROUND AND FACTS   *Wilson Floors contracted to provide flooring materials for a residential and commercial development known as "The Cliffs," which was owned by the defendant Sciota Park, Ltd. When the general contractor for Sciota fell behind in payments to Wilson, Wilson stopped work on the project. The bank financing the development assured Wilson that he would be paid if he returned to work. After Wilson's final bill was not paid Wilson proceeded with this action against the bank.*

SWEENEY, Justice.

The central issue in this cause is whether the bank's oral promise to Wilson that payments would be forthcoming upon a resumption of work at The Cliffs project constituted an enforceable oral contract.

R.C. 1335.05 provides:

"No action shall be brought whereby to charge the defendant, upon a special promise, to answer for the debt, default, or miscarriage of another person * * * unless the agreement upon which such action is brought, or some memorandum or note thereof, is in writing and signed by the party to be charged therewith or some other person thereunto by him or her lawfully authorized."

"When the leading object of the promisor is not to answer for another, but to subserve some pecuniary or business purpose of his own, involving a benefit to himself, or damage to the other contracting party, his promise is not within the statute of frauds, although it may be in form a promise to pay the debt of another, and its performance may incidentally have the effect of extinguishing that liability."

In applying the leading object rule to the facts in this cause, the Court of Common Pleas, finding that the bank assumed a "direct undertaking" when it guaranteed Wilson payment for future services rendered, held that the bank's promise was enforceable by Wilson. No significance was given to the fact that [the general contractor] remained primarily liable for the debt owed Wilson; *i.e.*, that Wilson continued to send its progress billings to [the general contractor] for reimbursement.

The Court of Appeals, on the other hand, finding that the bank became only secondarily liable to Wilson when it guaranteed payment to the subcontractor, held that the bank's promise came within the provisions of the statute of frauds and therefore was unenforceable. The fact that the promise by the bank to guarantee payments was made to further the bank's own business interest was found not to be determinative of the cause.

* * * *

"In many cases the test whether a promise is or is not within the statute of frauds is to be found in the fact that the original debtor does or does not remain liable on his undertaking; if he is discharged by a new arrangement made on sufficient consideration, with a third party, this third party may be held on his promise though not in writing; but if the original debtor remains liable and the promise of the third party is only collateral to his, it will in strictness be nothing more than a promise to answer for the other's debt. But where the third party is himself to receive the benefit for which his promise is exchanged, it is not usually material whether the original debtor remains liable or not."

The above explanation of the leading object rule indicates that, in a determination of whether an oral promise is enforceable to pay the debt of another, the court may employ one of two tests. The court may inquire as to whether the promisor becomes primarily liable on the debt owed by another to a third party. If it is found that the promisor does not become primarily liable for payment of the debt, the court may inquire as to whether the promisor's leading object was to subserve his own business or pecuniary interest.

Because it is unquestioned that the bank in the instant cause did not become primarily liable when it guaranteed the subcontractors that they would be paid the court must apply the second test * * * to determine the enforceability of the verbal agreement.

Under the second test, it is of no consequence that when such promise is made, the original obligor remains primarily liable or that the third party continues to look to the original obligor for payment. So long as the promisor undertakes to pay the subcontractor whatever his services are worth irrespective of what he may owe the general contractor, and so long as the main purpose of the promisor is to further his own business or pecuniary interest, the promise is enforceable. Thus, under this test it is not required to show as a condition precedent for enforceability of the oral contract that the original debt is extinguished.

The facts in the instant cause reflect that the bank made its guarantee to Wilson to subserve its own business interest of reducing costs to complete the project. Clearly, the bank induced Wilson to remain on the job and rely on its credit for future payments. To apply the statute of frauds and hold that the bank had no contractual duty to Wilson despite its oral guarantees would not prevent the wrong which the statute's enactment was to prevent, but would in reality effectuate a wrong.

DECISION AND REMEDY   *Judgment was entered in favor of Wilson. The bank's main purpose (leading object) was to derive a benefit for itself. Therefore, the promise to pay the general contractor's debts was not within the Statute of Frauds.*

PROMISES MADE IN CONSIDERATION OF MARRIAGE

A unilateral promise to pay a sum of money or to give property in consideration of a promise to marry must be in writing. If Bill MacAdams promises $10,000 to Bruce Coby if Coby promises to marry his daughter, Sally MacAdams, MacAdams's promise must be in writing. The same rule applies to *prenuptial agreements* (agreements made before marriage), which define the ownership rights of each partner in the other partner's property. For example, a prospective husband may wish to limit the amount his prospective wife could obtain if the marriage should end in divorce. Another common situation involving prenuptial agreements occurs when a man and woman who wish to get married both have separate assets and children from prior marriages. A prenuptial arrangement may be highly desirable in this case, particularly in a community property state. Prenuptial arrangements must be in writing to be enforceable, and there must be consideration. (Some states do not require consideration—Florida, for example.)

CONTRACTS FOR THE SALE OF GOODS

The UCC contains several Statute of Frauds provisions that require written evidence of a contract. Section 2-201 contains the major provision, which generally requires a writing or memorandum for the sale of goods priced at $500 or more.[16] A writing

that will satisfy the Code requirement need only state the quantity term, and that need not be stated "accurately," as long as it adequately reflects both parties' intentions. The contract will not be enforceable, however, for any quantity greater than that set forth in the writing. In addition, the writing must be signed by the person to be charged—that is, the person who refuses to perform or the one being sued. Beyond these two requirements, the writing need not designate the buyer or seller, the terms of payment, or the price.

Exceptions to the writing requirements, contained in UCC 2–201, are discussed in detail in Chapter 17. A few of the more important exceptions are also discussed in this chapter.

Partial Performance

The Statute of Frauds provides that an oral contract will be enforceable to the extent a seller accepts payment or to the extent a buyer accepts delivery of the goods contracted for.[17] For example, Windblown Sailboats makes an oral contract with Sunset Sails to have Sunset make 750 sails for Windblown's new nineteen-foot Day Sailer. Windblown repudiates the agreement after the sails have been made and after two dozen have been delivered. The contract will be enforceable to the extent of the two dozen sails accepted by Windblown.

Goods Made Specially to Order

Contracts for goods made specially for the buyer— that is, goods that cannot be resold by the seller in the ordinary course of the seller's business—are enforceable even when not in writing, provided that

---

16.   UCC 2–201, reads in part:

   [A] contract for the sale of goods for the price of $500 or more is not enforceable by way of action or defense unless there is some writing sufficient to indicate that a contract for sale has been made between the parties and been signed by the party against whom enforcement is sought. *   *   * A writing is not

insufficient because it omits or incorrectly states a term agreed upon but the contract is not enforceable under this paragraph beyond the quantity of goods shown in the writing. *   *   *

17.   UCC 2-201(3)(c).

the seller has made a substantial beginning of manufacture or commitment for their procurement.[18] Suppose that Wilt Chamberlain orally contracts with a furniture factory for $250,000 of furniture specially designed on a larger than normal scale to accommodate his larger than normal physique. Once the factory has committed itself to the manufacture of, or has made a substantial beginning in manufacturing, the furniture, the oral contract is enforceable.

Consider another example. Smith orally contracts with Green for 10,000 calendars at a price of $10,000 imprinted with Smith's business name and address. Once Green has made a substantial beginning in the printing of the calendars, the oral contract is enforceable.

Confirmation of an Oral Contract between Merchants

If one merchant sends another written confirmation of an oral contract, the merchant receiving the confirmation (with knowledge of its terms) must object in writing within ten days of its receipt, or the oral contract will be enforceable by either party.[19]

Suppose Rodriguez in Los Angeles calls Cohen in New York City on June 1, and an oral contract is formed for Cohen's purchase of a new $10,000 machine. The next day Rodriguez sends Cohen a telegram that states, "This is to confirm our telephone contract of June 1 for * * * machine at $10,000. Thank you for your order." Cohen receives the telegram the same day. On June 15 Cohen discovers that a similar machine can be purchased for $9,000. Cohen claims the Statute of Frauds as a defense for his refusal of Rodriguez's tender of the machine. Cohen will lose against Rodriguez's suit for breach because he failed to object within ten days of receiving Rodriguez's confirmation.

Admissions

If a party to an oral contract "admits" in "pleading, testimony or otherwise in court that a contract for sale was made," the contract will be enforceable, but only to the extent of the quantity admitted.[20] Thus,

if the president of Windblown Sailboats admits under testimony that an oral agreement was made for fifty sails, the agreement will be enforceable to that extent.

SUFFICIENCY OF THE WRITING

To be safe, all contracts should be fully set forth in a writing signed by all the parties. This assures that if any problems arise concerning performance of the contract, a written agreement can be introduced into court. The Statute of Frauds and the UCC require either a written contract or a *written memorandum* signed by the party against whom enforcement is sought or a legally recognized exception, such as partial performance. For a memorandum, any confirmation, invoice, sales slip, check, or telegram can constitute a writing sufficient to satisfy the Statute of Frauds.[21] The signature need not be placed at the end of the document but can be anywhere in the writing. It can even be an initial rather than the full name.

A memorandum evidencing the oral contract need only contain the essential terms of the contract. Under the UCC, for the sale of goods, the writing need only name the quantity term and be signed by the party to be charged. Under most provisions of the Statute of Frauds, the writing must ordinarily name the parties, subject matter, consideration, and quantity. Contracts for the sale of land are exceptions. In some states the memorandum must, in addition, state the *essential* terms of the contract, such as location and price, with sufficient clarity to allow the terms to be determined from the memo itself, without reference to any outside sources.[22]

Only the party to be held liable on the oral contract need sign the writing. Therefore, a contract may be enforceable by one of its parties but not by the other. Suppose Ota and Warrington orally contract for the sale of Ota's lake house and lot for $25,000. Ota writes Warrington a letter confirming the sale by identifying the parties and the essential terms—price, method of payment, and legal address—and signs the letter. Ota has made a written

---

18.   UCC 2-201(3)(a).
19.   UCC 2-201(2).
20.   UCC 2-201(3)(b).

---

21.   Even if the Statute of Frauds is satisfied, the existence and terms of the contract must be proven in court.
22.   Rhodes v. Wilkins, 83 N.M. 782, 498 P.2d 311 (1972).

memorandum of the oral land contract. Since she signed the letter, she can be held to the oral contract by Warrington. However, since Warrington has not signed or entered into a written contract or memorandum, he can plead the Statute of Frauds as a defense, and Ota cannot enforce the contract against him.

The following case illustrates the importance of meeting the writing criteria required in a given state before a memorandum satisfies the Statute of Frauds.

LAMBERT v. HOME FED. SAV. AND LOAN ASS'N

Supreme Court of Tennessee, 1972.
481 S.W.2d. 770.

BACKGROUND AND FACTS *Home Federal Savings and Loan Association, through its agent Marx and Bensdorf, loaned the Lamberts $672,000 for apartment construction. The loan was evidenced by a one-year note combined with a deed in trust. At about the same time, Home Federal agreed to loan the Lamberts $2,910,000 (as a long-term loan), but this agreement was not reduced to writing. When the Lamberts tried to obtain the long-term loan, Home Federal refused to make the loan. Lambert claimed that, since Home Federal could use the trust deed as security for further loans, it was a sufficient memorandum to meet Statute of Frauds requirements. The Lamberts produced thirteen documents at trial, but none referred to nor made commitments for a long-term loan. The lower court held for Home Federal.*

HUMPRHEYS, Justice.
*   *   *   *

To meet the requirements of the Statute of Frauds, the Lamberts produced memoranda which they contended would, when considered in connection with this [original construction] mortgage to Marx & Bensdorf, furnish written memoranda of the transaction which would satisfy the Statute of Frauds.

The memoranda relied on by the Lamberts consists of thirteen documents which, considered separately, and collectively, made no commitments whatsoever by Home Federal or Marx & Bensdorf to lend [an additional $2,910,000 of] money to the Lamberts and take a trust deed as security. Nor is any commitment made by the Lamberts to Home Federal and Marx & Bensdorf to accept such a loan and to give a trust deed to secure the same on any described real property. [In other words, there was no written document specifically showing a bilateral agreement, or a "promise for a promise."]

Marx & Bensdorf is not involved in the memoranda other than by the note and deed of trust for the construction loan of $672,000.00. [Moreover], this deed of trust by its terms became null and void upon payment and release, which was done October 1, 1968; and contains no terms which considered alone or with the thirteen instruments satisfies the statute.

The deed of trust does not, and could not, under its terms, secure any greater amount than the $672,000.00 for which it was intended to furnish security. No other amounts are mentioned in the instrument and there is no language therein indicating any intention that it shall apply to any other loan than the single one mentioned.

A mortgage, or a deed of trust, in its legal aspect is a conveyance of an estate or an interest in land and as such within the meaning of the Statute of Frauds. A mortgage or deed of trust of land cannot be made by parol [orally].

*   *   * It is also the rule that a mortgage cannot be modified or extended by an oral agreement to secure further indebtedness.

On the basis of this authority the Lamberts' contention that the trust deed to Marx & Bensdorf to secure the single $672,000.00 loan can be looked to as memorandum satisfying the Statute of Frauds must be rejected.

The rule by which the thirteen instruments exhibited to the bill as memoranda satisfying the Statute of Frauds must be tested is well stated thusly: "The general rule is that the memorandum, in order to satisfy the statute, must contain the essential terms of the contract, expressed with such certainty that they may be understood from the memorandum itself or some other writing to which it refers or with which it is connected, without resorting to parol evidence. A memorandum disclosing merely that a contract had been made without showing what the contract is, is not sufficient to satisfy the requirement of the Statute of Frauds that there be a memorandum in writing of the contract."

Considered in the light of this statement of what is required of memoranda to satisfy the statute, the conclusion is unavoidable that the memoranda does not satisfy the statute.

The appeal was dismissed. The Lamberts could not enforce the loan contract for $2,910,000. The court required that in order to satisfy the Statute of Frauds, the writing had to include the essential terms of the contract.

DECISION AND REMEDY

The writing should specify the parties, subject matter, and any special conditions or terms with certainty. Documenting consideration is a matter of state law. Some states require it; some do not. If the writing consists of several pages, each page should be signed separately and clearly identified as part of the same transaction.

COMMENTS

THE PAROL EVIDENCE RULE

The **parol evidence rule** prohibits the introduction at trial of words (parol) that contradict or vary the terms of written contracts.[23] The written contract is ordinarily assumed to be the complete embodiment of the parties' agreement. Courts are reluctant to recognize oral or other written evidence of prior or contemporaneous agreements that conflict with the terms of the written agreement. Therefore, courts assume that all prior negotiations and oral agreements are embodied in the written contract.

Because of the rigidity of the parol evidence rule, courts make several exceptions.

First, evidence of *subsequent modification* of a written contract can be introduced into court. Since courts assume all prior negotiations and oral agreements are merged in the written contract, there is no reason to forbid changes in the written contract as long as they occur after the writing. Keep in mind that the oral modifications may not be enforceable if they come under the Statute of Frauds—for example, if they increase the price of the goods for sale to over $500 or increase the term for performance to more than one year. Also, oral modifi-

cations will not be enforceable if the original contract provides that any modification must be in writing.[24]

Second, oral evidence can be introduced in all cases to show that the contract was voidable or void (for example, induced by mistake, fraud, or misrepresentation). In this case, if one of the parties was deceived into agreeing to the terms of a written contract, oral evidence attesting to fraud should not be excluded. Courts frown upon bad faith and are quick to allow such evidence when it establishes fraud.

Third, when the terms of a written contract are ambiguous, oral evidence is admissible to show the meaning of the terms.

Fourth, oral evidence is admissible when the written contract is incomplete in that it lacks one or more of the essential terms. The courts allow oral evidence to fill in the gaps in this case.

Fifth, under the UCC, oral evidence can be introduced to explain or supplement a written contract by showing a prior course of dealing or usage of trade.[25] When buyers and sellers deal with each other over extended periods of time, certain customary practices develop. They are often overlooked when writing the contract, so courts allow the in-

---

23. Restatement, Contracts, Second, Section 213.

24. UCC 2-209(2)(3).
25. UCC 1-205, 2-202.

CONCEPT SUMMARY: Valid Business Contracts under the Statute of Frauds	
TYPES OF CONTRACTS	**APPLICATIONS AND EXCEPTIONS**
Contract to guaranty the debt of another	Application—Applies only to express contracts made between the guarantor and creditor, whose terms make the guarantor secondarily liable. Exception—Main purpose or leading object doctrine.
Contract involving an interest in realty	Application—Applies to any contract for an interest in realty, such as sale, lease, mortgage, easement grant, life tenancy interest, and real estate broker contracts. Exceptions—1. Statute: most statutes permit short-term leases (usually of a year or less) to be orally enforceable. 2. Partial performance: principle in equity where parties cannot be restored to status quo.
Contract whose terms are impossible to perform within one year of contract formation	Application—Applies only to contracts objectively impossible to perform fully within one year from the date of the contract's formation. Exception—None. (Some courts ignore option to cancel clauses in term contracts for Statute of Fraud purposes.)
Sale of goods priced at $500 or more	Application—Applies only to the sale of goods, and where the purchase price (excluding taxes) is $500 or more. UCC 2-201(1) Exceptions—1. Between merchants, where one sends a written confirmation and the receiver does not object in writing within ten (10) days. UCC 2-201(2) 2. Specially ordered goods where the seller has made a substantial beginning of manufacture or commitment for procurement. UCC 2-201(3)(a) 3. Admission under oath of an oral contract. UCC 2-201(3)(b) 4. Partial performance by buyer's payment or possession, at least to the extent paid or quantity possessed. UCC 2-201(3)(c)
EXCEPTION TO ALL STATUTE OF FRAUDS CONTRACTS	
Memorandum—Written evidence of an oral contract signed by the party against whom enforcement is sought. Generally, the writing must name the parties, identify the subject matter of the contract, and, in the sale of goods, the quantity; in the sale of land, it must name essential terms, such as land description and price.	

troduction of oral evidence to show how the parties have acted in the past.

Sixth, the parol evidence rule does not apply if the existence of the entire written contract is subject to an orally agreed upon condition. Proof of the condition does not *alter* or *modify* the written terms but involves the very *enforceability* of the written contract. Suppose Carvelli agrees in writing to buy Jackson's real property for $100,000. The terms are written on a note pad, and the pad is signed by both parties. Prior to the signing, the parties orally agree that the contract is binding *only on condition* that the terms as written are approved by Carvelli's attorney. Evidence of the oral condition can be proved and is not a violation of the parol evidence rule. What is at issue here is the intention of the parties to have an enforceable agreement.

Seventh, when an *obvious* or *gross* clerical (or typographic) error exists which would clearly not represent the agreement of the parties, parol evidence is admissible to correct the error. For example, Karen agrees to lease 1,000 square feet of office space at the current monthly rate of $1.50 per square foot from Smith Enterprises. The signed written lease provides for a monthly lease payment of $15.00 rather than the $1,500 agreed to by the parties. Since the error is obvious, Smith Enterprises would be allowed to admit evidence to correct the mistake.

The major key in determining if the general rule excluding parol evidence is applied is basically whether the written contract is intended to be a complete and final embodiment of the terms of the agreement. If so intended, it is referred to as an integrated contract, and parole evidence is excluded. If only partially integrated, evidence of consistent additional terms are admissible to supplement the written agreement.[26]

The following often-cited case deals with the problem of determining if the parties have entered into an integrated or partially integrated contract.

---

26.   Restatement, Contracts, Second, Section 216.

BACKGROUND AND FACTS   *Masterson sold his ranch to Sine, his brother-in-law. Their contract of purchase included a clause giving Masterson a ten-year option to repurchase the ranch for the same price plus a percentage of the cost of any improvements Sine might have made over the course of the years. Masterson went bankrupt sometime after the sale. His trustee in bankruptcy attempted to exercise this option clause to repurchase the ranch to obtain funds to satisfy Masterson's debts. The trial court refused to allow Sine to introduce extrinsic evidence showing the meaning the parties attached to the option clause, specifically that it was personal to Masterson. Thus, the trial court permitted the trustee to enforce the option to repurchase on Masterson's behalf. Defendant Sine appealed.*

MASTERSON v. SINE
Supreme Court of California,
1968.
68 Cal.2d 222, 65 Cal.Rptr. 545,
436 P.2d 561.

TRAYNOR, Chief Justice.

*   *   *   *

When the parties to a written contract have agreed to it as an "integration"—a complete and final embodiment of the terms of an agreement—parol evidence cannot be used to add to or vary its terms. *   *   * When only part of the agreement is integrated, the same rule applies to that part, but *parol evidence may be used to prove elements of the agreement not reduced to writing.*[Emphasis added.]

*   *   *   *

The crucial issue in determining whether there has been an integration is whether the parties intended their writing to serve as the exclusive embodiment of their agreement. The instrument itself may help to resolve that issue. It may state, for example, that "there are no previous understandings or agreements not contained in the writing," and thus express the parties' "intention to nullify antecedent understandings or agreements." Any such collateral agreement itself must be examined, however, to determine whether the parties intended the subjects of negotiation it deals with to be included in, excluded from, or otherwise affected by the writing. Circumstances at the time of the writing may also aid in the determination of such integration.

*   *   *   *

In formulating the rule governing parol evidence, several policies must be accommodated. One policy is based on the assumption that written evidence is more accurate than human memory. This policy, however, can be adequately served by excluding parol evidence of agreements that directly contradict the writing. Another policy is based on the fear that fraud or unintentional invention by witnesses interested in the outcome of the litigation will mislead the finder of facts.

Legal authorities have suggested that the party urging the spoken as against the written word is most often the economic underdog, threatened by severe hardship if the writing is enforced. [This] view [of] the parol evidence rule arose to allow the court to control the tendency of the jury to find through sympathy and without a dispassionate assessment of the probability of fraud or faulty memory that the parties made an oral agreement collateral to the written contract, or that preliminary tentative agreements were not abandoned when omitted from the writing. [It] recognizes, however, that if this theory were adopted in disregard of all other considerations, it would lead to the exclusion of testimony concerning oral agreements whenever there is a writing and thereby often defeat the true intent of the parties.

Evidence of oral collateral agreements should be excluded only when the fact finder [the judge or the jury] is likely to be misled. The rule must therefore be based on the credibility of the evidence. One such standard, adopted by section 240(1)(b) of the Restatement of Contracts, permits proof of a collateral agreement if it "is such an agreement as might *naturally* be made as a separate agreement by parties situated as were the parties to the written contract." The draftsmen of the Uniform Commercial Code would exclude the evidence in still fewer instances: "If the additional terms are such that, if agreed upon, they would *certainly* have been included in the document in the view of the court, then evidence of their alleged making must be kept from the trier of fact." [UCC Sec. 2-202] (Italics added.)

The option clause in the deed in the present case does not explicitly provide that it contains the complete agreement, and the deed is silent on the question of assignability. Moreover, the difficulty of accommodating the formalized structure of a deed to the insertion of collateral agreements makes it less likely that all the terms of such an agreement were included. The statement of the reservation of the option might well have been placed in the recorded deed solely to preserve the grantors' rights against any possible future purchasers and this function could well be served without any mention of the parties' agreement that the option was personal. There is nothing in the record to indicate that the parties to this family transaction, through experience in land transactions or otherwise, had any warning of the disadvantages of failing to put the whole agreement in the deed. This case is one, therefore, in which it can be said that a collateral agreement such as that alleged "might naturally be made as a separate agreement." A *fortiori*, the case is not one in which the parties "would certainly" have included the collateral agreement in the deed.

DECISION AND REMEDY *Since the writing did not constitute an integrated contract, extrinsic (parol) evidence could be used to show that the option was personal to the grantors and, therefore, not assignable. As a result, the trial court judgment was reversed because that court had excluded parol evidence improperly.*

QUESTIONS AND CASE PROBLEMS

1. On May 1, by telephone, Yu offers to hire Benson to perform personal services. On May 5, Benson returns Yu's call and accepts the offer. Discuss fully whether this contract falls under the Statute of Frauds under the following circumstances:

(a) The contract calls for Benson to be employed for one year, with the right to begin performance immediately.

(b) The contract calls for Benson to be employed for nine months, with performance of services to begin on September 1.

(c) The contract calls for Benson to submit a written research report, with a deadline of two years for submission.

2. In December 1984, Kaplin ordered 11,000 yards of madras at 75 cents a yard from Reich. The order was

made over the telephone. On January 9, 1985, Reich sent Kaplin a bill that included a statement of the quantity that Reich had sent Kaplin. On February 18, 1985, Kaplin wrote to Reich, stating:

> Replying to your letter of the 18th, please be advised that we examined a few pieces of merchandise that were billed to us against your invoice No. 10203, and found that it was not up to our standard. We are, therefore, unable to accept this shipment. * * * Very truly yours, (signed) Isador Kaplin.

Reich sued Kaplin for payment owed under the contract. Kaplin defended on the ground that the contract was entered into over the telephone and therefore failed to meet Statute of Frauds requirements. Is Kaplin's argument convincing?

3. William Rowe was admitted to General Hospital, suffering from the effects of a severe gastric hemorrhage. On the day Rowe was admitted, Rowe's son informed an agent for the hospital that his father had no financial means but that he would pay for his father's medical services. Subsequently, the son stated, "Well, we want you to do everything you can to save his life, and we don't want you to spare any expense. Whatever he needs, Doctor, you go ahead and get it, and I will pay you." After Rowe was discharged from the hospital, his son refused to pay the medical bills. Can the hospital enforce the son's oral promise?

4. Roger is interested in starting a restaurant on Lake Faithful. He locates an old, vacant mansion on the lake, which, with alterations, would be ideal for the restaurant. The mansion is owned by Striker. Roger calls Striker on the telephone and contracts to lease the mansion, to be used as a restaurant with agreed alterations, for ten years at a lease price of $12,000 per year, with Roger to pay six months' rent in advance. Roger is to have immediate right to possession. He sends Striker a check for $6,000, noting on the check, "six months advance payment on ten-year lease—Striker mansion." Striker cashes the check upon receipt. Roger does not take immediate possession, but he does contract with Smith & Associates to make alterations to the mansion. Work on the alterations had not yet begun when, one month later, Striker has an opportunity to sell the mansion to a buyer at a substantial price. Striker tenders back to Roger $6,000, claiming the ten-year lease is unenforceable under the Statute of Frauds. Is Striker correct? Discuss fully.

5. The following oral contracts deal with the sale of goods. Discuss fully which of them are enforceable and which are unenforceable under the Statute of Frauds:

(a) Carrigan contracts to purchase for $2,000 napkins and tablecloths with the name of his restaurant, "Harvest House," embroidered on each.

(b) Harper, a merchant, sends Proctor, another merchant, a confirmation of their oral contract. Proctor receives this confirmation on May 1 and does not respond until May 20, at which time he refutes the contract.

6. "Man's Country," a health club and bathhouse in Manhattan, leased a billboard from Christopher at a monthly rental of $400. The lease allowed termination by either party on ninety days' notice. In August 1978, Christopher threatened to terminate the lease if the club did not agree to a higher rental. The club alleges that it agreed to the higher rental in exchange for a new lease agreement that was to last seven and one-half years and that did not include a termination provision. It sent a written version of this oral lease agreement to Christopher for execution, and it immediately began paying the higher rental of $600 per month. In addition, the club undertook to make changes in the artwork on the billboards. In June 1979, Christopher again demanded a rent increase and threatened to terminate the lease if the club refused. The club sued for enforcement of the new lease agreement, which precluded such increases and gave Christopher no right of termination. Christopher countered that the Statute of Frauds barred the club's suit. Christopher, not wanting to relinquish its right of termination, had never executed the written lease that the club had drawn up. Can the new lease agreement be enforced? [Club Chain of Manhattan, Ltd. v. Christopher & Seventh Gourmet, Ltd., 74 A.D.2d 277, 427 N.Y.S.2d 627 (Sup.Ct. 1980)]

7. Wasatch Orchard Company entered into an oral agreement with Fabian to have him sell its canned asparagus for a three-year period. Wasatch agreed to pay Fabian a 2.5 percent commission on all sales he made. Within six months, Fabian had secured orders totaling $30,000. Thereafter, Wasatch refused to honor its oral commitment. Can Fabian sue under the oral agreement? What, if anything, can Fabian recover? [Fabian v. Wasatch Orchard Co., 41 Utah 404, 125 P. 860 (1912)]

8. Butler Brothers was the main contractor for a highway construction project near Minneapolis. Butler hired another contractor, Ganley Brothers, to perform some of the highway construction work. At the time the contract was formed, Butler made several false representations to Ganley. If Ganley had known Butler's statements were fraudulent, Ganley would never have entered into the contract. The written contract between Butler and Ganley included the following clause: "The contractor [Ganley] has examined the said contracts * * * and is not relying upon any statement made by the company in respect thereto." In light of this clause, can Ganley introduce evidence of Butler's fraudulent misstatements at trial? [Ganley Bros. Inc. v. Butler Bros. Bldg. Co., 170 Minn. 373, 212 N.W. 602 (1927)]

9. Rimshot, director of a local basketball camp, wished to increase his business by advertising his camp. He dis-

cussed with Lyal, a local printer, the possibility of Lyal printing up flyers about the camp. Rimshot told Lyal that not only did he want Lyal to print the flyers, he wanted him to distribute them to local merchants. Lyal said that he usually distributed about 20 flyers to each one and charged a small publication fee. Subsequently, Lyal and Rimshot entered into a written agreement under which Lyal agreed to print 1,000 flyers for Rimshot and to "publish the same locally." Lyal printed the flyers but distributed them to only four merchants, giving 250 to each. After the poorest turnout in his basketball camp's history, Rimshot sued Lyal for breach of contract. Can he introduce parol evidence concerning Lyal's statements about how he normally distributed flyers? [See similar fact pattern in Stoops v. Smith, 100 Mass. 63, 97 Am.Dec. 76 (1868)]

10. Ramsey Products Corporation entered into negotiations with Williams & Associates, architects, to design a new factory for Ramsey. After several days of negotiations, Ramsey and Williams signed a contract under which Williams promised to design the factory. The contract was brief, containing a short description of the type of plant as well as the number of offices that Ramsey wanted. Over the next several months, Williams drew up plans for a new factory that would cost between $400,000 and $500,000. Since this was much more than what Ramsey expected to pay, Ramsey officials changed their minds and refused to compensate Williams for his plans. Williams sued Ramsey to recover for his services. Ramsey wished to defend against Williams's claim on the ground that Williams had not performed the contract as discussed by the parties. Specifically, Ramsey wanted to introduce evidence about oral negotiations made before the written contract, which said that Williams would design a building costing about $250,000. Can Ramsey introduce this evidence? [Williams & Associates v. Ramsey Products Corp., 19 N.C.App. 1, 198 S.E.2d 67 (1973)]

14

CONTRACTS
Third Party Rights

Once it has been determined that a valid and legally enforceable contract exists, attention can be turned to the rights and duties of the parties to the contract. Since a contract is a private agreement between the parties who have entered into it, it is fitting that these parties alone should have rights and liabilities under the contract. This idea is referred to as **privity of contract,** and it establishes the basic concept that third parties have no rights in a contract to which they are not a party.

To illustrate, suppose I offer to sell you my watch for $100, and you accept. Later, I refuse to deliver the watch to you even though you tender the $100. You decide to overlook my breach, but your close friend, Ann, is unhappy with my action and files suit. Can she receive a judgment? The answer is obviously no, as she was not a party to the contract. You, as a party, have rights under the contract and could file a successful suit, but Ann has *no standing in court* (right to sue).

There are two exceptions to this rule. The first involves an **assignment of rights** or **delegation of duties**. Here, one of the original parties transfers contractual rights or obligations to a third party, giving the third party the rights or obligations of the transferor. The second involves a **third party beneficiary contract.** Here, the rights of a third party against the promisor arise from the original contract,

and the parties to the original contract normally make it with the intent to benefit the third party.

ASSIGNMENT OF RIGHTS AND DELEGATION OF DUTIES

When third parties acquire rights or assume duties arising from a contract to which they were not parties, the rights are transferred to them by *assignment* and the duties are transferred by *delegation*. Assignment, or delegation, occurs *after* the original contract is made, when one of the parties transfers an interest or duty in the contract to another party.

A distinction must also be made between assignment (or delegation), and *novation* (see Chapter 15). A novation is a written agreement entered into by *all* the parties whereby one party is substituted for another party; that is, one party is completely dismissed from the contract, and another is substituted. The dismissed party is no longer liable under the original contract. In an assignment, or delegation, the original party remains liable on the contract.

Assignments

In every bilateral contract the two parties have corresponding rights and duties. One party has a *right*

233

to require the other to perform some task, and the other has a *duty* to perform it. The transfer of *rights* to a third person is known as an *assignment*. When rights under a contract are assigned unconditionally, the rights of the assignor (the party making the assignment) are extinguished.[1] The third party (the assignee, or party receiving the assignment) has a right to demand performance from the other original party to the contract (the obligor). This is illustrated in Exhibit 14–1.

Once Able has assigned her rights under the original contract with Baker to Carlson, Carlson can enforce the contract against Baker if Baker fails to perform. The assignee takes only those rights that the assignor originally had. For example, suppose Baker owes Able $50, and Able assigns to Carlson the right to receive the $50. Here, a valid assignment of a debt exists, and Baker must pay the $50 to Carlson, or Carlson will be entitled to enforce payment in a court of law.

Furthermore, the assignee's rights are subject to the defenses that the obligor has against the assignor. To illustrate, suppose Baker contracts to sell her boat to Able for $40,000. The contract calls for delivery of the boat to Able or his assignee upon presentation of a receipt of payment signed by Baker. Able fraudulently gives Baker a worthless check, and Baker signs the receipt, noting thereon "payment by check." Able is in debt to Carlson and in satisfaction of the debt assigns to Carlson the contract rights for the delivery of the boat. Baker, upon discovery of the worthless check, has a legal right to avoid the contractual obligation to deliver the boat to Able. Since the assignee Carlson's rights are subject to this same defense, Carlson also cannot require Baker to transfer the boat, even though she is an innocent party to these events.

Statute of Frauds   In general, an assignment can take any form, oral or written. Naturally, it is more difficult to prove the occurrence of an oral assignment, so it is practical to put all assignments in writing.

Assignments covered by the Statute of Frauds must be in writing to be enforceable. As noted in Chapter 13, assignments of an interest in land, contracts not to be performed within one year, promises

EXHIBIT 14–1   Assignment Relationships

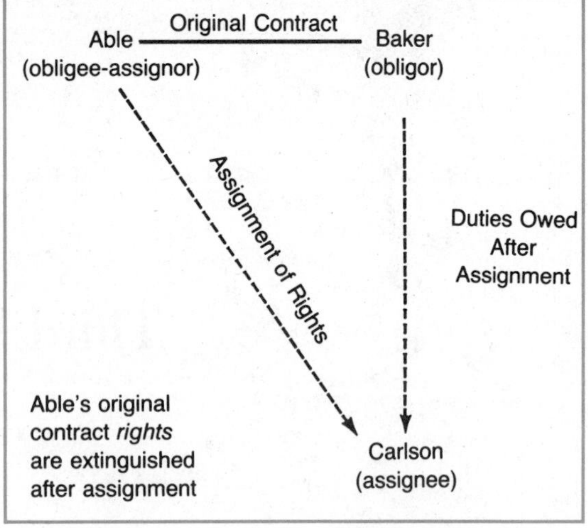

to answer for the debts of another, promises in consideration of marriage, and promises of an administrator or an executor to personally pay the debts of an estate must also be in writing. In addition, most states require contracts for the assignment of wages to be in writing.[2]

Consideration   An assignment need *not* be supported by *legally sufficient consideration* to be effective. A gratuitous assignment is just as effective as an assignment made for money. However, the absence of consideration becomes significant when the assignor wants to revoke the assignment. If the assignment was made for consideration, the assignor cannot revoke it. If no consideration is involved, the assignor can revoke, thereby cancelling the right of the third party to demand performance or to sue for failure to render that performance.[3] Gratuitous assignments can be revoked by:

1.   The subsequent assignment of the same right to another third party.
2.   The death of the assignor.
3.   The bankruptcy of the assignor.
4.   A notice of revocation given to the assignee.

---

1.   Restatement, Second, Contracts, Section 317.

2.   See, for example, California Labor Code, Sec. 300.
3.   Restatement, Second, Contracts, Section 332.

Rights That Can Be Assigned

As a general rule, all rights can be assigned, except in special circumstances. The following is a list of these special circumstances with examples:

1. If a statute expressly prohibits assignment, the particular right in question cannot be assigned. Suppose John is a new employee of Craft, Inc. Craft is an employer under Workers' Compensation statutes in this state, and thus John is a covered employee. John has a relatively high risk job. In need of a loan, John borrows the money from Shady, assigning to Shady all Workers' Compensation benefits due him should he be injured on the job. This type of assignment of *future* Workers' Compensation benefits is prohibited by state statute and thus cannot be assigned.

2. If a contract stipulates that the rights cannot be assigned, then, *ordinarily*, they cannot be assigned.[4] Suppose Baker agrees to build a house for Able. The contract between Able and Baker states: "The contract cannot be assigned by Able. Any assignment renders this contract void, and all rights hereunder will thereupon terminate." Able then attempts to assign her rights to Carlson. Carlson cannot enforce the contract against Baker by trying to get Baker to

build the house because the contract expressly prohibits the assignment of rights. (But once the house is built, the rights to the monetary payment are assignable.)

3. When a contract is *personal* in nature, the rights under the contract cannot be assigned unless all that remains is a money payment. Suppose Baker signs a contract to be a tutor for Able's children. Able then attempts to assign her right in Baker's services to Carlson. Carlson cannot enforce the contract against Baker because the contract called for the rendering of a personal service.[5]

4. Finally, a right cannot be assigned if assignment will materially increase or alter the duties of the obligor.[6] Assume Able takes out an insurance policy on her hotel with Preventive Casualty, an insurance company. The policy insures against fire, theft, floods, and vandalism. Able then attempts to assign the insurance policy to Carlson, who also owns a hotel. The assignment is ineffective because it substantially alters Preventive Casualty's *duty of performance*. Insurance companies evaluate the particular risk of a certain party and tailor their policies to fit the exact risk of that party. If the policy is assigned to a third party, the insurance risk will be materially altered. Therefore, the assignment will not operate to give Carlson any rights against Preventive Casualty.

In the following case, the central issue was whether a seller of a spa could assign membership contracts which included an exculpatory clause which limited liability for personal injuries. The claim of nonassignability due to the personal nature of the contract is discussed.

---

4. Several exceptions to this rule exist. First, a contract cannot prevent assignment of the right to receive money. This exception exists to encourage the free flow of money and credit in modern business settings. Second, the assignment of rights in real estate normally cannot be prohibited because this would be contrary to public policy. Such prohibitions are called *restraints against alienation*. Third, the assignment of negotiable instruments cannot be prohibited. Fourth, in a sale of goods contract, the right to receive damages for breach of contract, or for payment of an account owed, may be assigned even though the sales contract prohibits assignment [UCC 2-210(2)].

---

5. Restatement, Second, Contracts, Sections 317 and 318.
6. See UCC 2-210(2).

BACKGROUND AND FACTS *On August 8, 1978, the plaintiff, Shirley Petry, entered into a contract with the defendant, Cosmopolitan Spa International, Inc. (Cosmopolitan). The contract was for a spa membership that was to include "processing, program counseling, and facilities usage . . . ." The written contract contained an exculpatory clause. The pertinent part of the clause stated, "Member fully understands and agrees that in participating in one or more of the courses, or using the facilities maintained by Cosmopolitan, there is the possibility or [sic] accidental or other physical injury. Member further agrees to assume the risk of such injury and further agrees to indemnify Cosmopolitan from any and all liability to Cosmopolitan by either the Member or*

PETRY v.
COSMOPOLITAN SPA
INTERNATIONAL, INC.
Court of Appeals of Tennessee,
Eastern Section, 1982.
641 S.W.2d 202.

third party as the result of the use by the Member of the facilities and instructions as offered by Cosmopolitan."

On or around January 1, 1980, Cosmopolitan sold the spa to Holiday Spa of Tennessee, Inc. (Holiday). On February 25, 1980, the plaintiff, Shirley Petry, injured her back when she sat on an exercise machine and it collapsed under her. She brought this suit against both Cosmopolitan and Holiday for damages for personal injuries resulting from the defendants' negligence in properly maintaining the exercise machine. The defendants claimed that the exculpatory clause negated their liability. The trial court granted a summary judgment to the defendants.

PARROTT, Presiding Judge.
*   *   *   *

The Supreme Court of Tennessee [has] held *   *   * that an exculpatory clause of almost the exact type and wording as the one in this case was valid and enforceable. That case is both factually and legally on point with this one. The trial judge below correctly recognized this in his summary judgment opinion. Like the court below, we are compelled by the doctrine of stare decisis to follow this holding. [The Supreme Court case referred to above] is a clear and unambiguous decision by the highest court of this state and has never been altered or overruled.
*   *   *   *

Appellant also contends that even if the exculpatory clause is valid, it does not protect appellee, Holiday, from liability because it could not be assigned. Again, we must disagree. The exculpatory clause in this contract was a right of appellee Cosmopolitan. Generally, contractual rights can be assigned:

(2) A contractual right can be assigned unless

(a) the substitution of a right of the assignee for the right of the assignor would materially change the duty of the obligor, or materially increase the burden or risk imposed on him by his contract, or materially impair his chance of obtaining return performance, or materially reduce its value to him, or

(b) the assignment is forbidden by statute or is otherwise inoperative on grounds of public policy, or

(c) assignment is validly precluded by contract. *Restatement (Second) of Contracts* § 317(2)(1981).

None of the above exceptions to assignability can be successfully raised as to this exculpatory clause. Appellant contends that the assignment was invalid because the contract was of a personal nature and that she never consented to the assignment. We find this unpersuasive. This contract was primarily for the use of spa facilities and not of a personal nature.

DECISION AND REMEDY

The exculpatory clause in this case was clearly enforceable, and the contract containing it was assignable to Holiday. Appellant's suit was barred as a matter of law and was properly dismissed by summary judgment.

Anti-Assignment Clauses

Anti-assignment clauses in contracts are increasing in both number and importance. If the promisor, in clear language, evidences the intention to create a right in the promisee that is *not* to be assignable, generally no subsequent assignment can affect the promisor or third parties.

Anti-assignment clauses have appeared in leases for many years. Now they are being used more frequently in other types of contracts as well. Recently, they have appeared in mortgage contracts in an attempt to restrict the assumption of mortgages by new owners of real property. The typical lease or mortgage today cannot be assigned without the landlord's or mortgagee's consent.

Typical clauses in mortgages are due-on-sale (DOS) provisions. This means that an owner of realty with a lower than market interest rate cannot sell the property to a buyer with an assumption of this low interest rate mortgage. The due-on-sale provision accelerates the entire loan, making the mortgage fully payable. Therefore the loan would have to be fully paid (by the buyer) or the buyer would have to secure a new mortgage (at the current interest rate). The Supreme Court has upheld such clauses for federally insured financial institutions.

In 1982, Congress enacted the Garn-St. Germain Act. Provisions of that act dealt with state laws (legislative or court decisions) which prohibit or limit DOS clauses.[7] The act provides that any state which presently declares invalid or limits DOS provisions can continue to do so provided that the legislature of that state passes a statute extending the prohibition on or before October 15, 1985. Should the legislature fail to do so, DOS clauses will become valid and legally enforceable. Presently, most states, either by statute or judicial decision, permit and enforce DOS clauses in mortgage contracts.

Certain contracts provide that if the promisee assigns his or her rights under the contract to a third party, the contract itself will become void. These contract provisions are frequently found in insurance policies. They stipulate the forfeiture of the policy rights if the policyholder assigns the policy. If the assignment is attempted before a loss is incurred, the company can declare that the policy is void. (On the other hand, if the assignment is made after the loss, the claim is reduced to a monetary right and the assignee can recover.)

Typically, when an anti-assignment clause restrains the alienation of property, the clause becomes subject to judicial review. In the following case the court examined an anti-assignment clause in a franchise agreement in terms of its reasonableness and its effect on public policy.

---

7.   At the time of passage of the Garn–St. Germain Act, states that had limited DOS clause enforceability included Arizona, California, Colorado, Florida, Georgia, Illinois, Iowa, Mississippi, New Mexico, Ohio, South Carolina, and Washington.

BACKGROUND AND FACTS *This case centered around an anti-assignment clause in an agreement for a franchise business that required the consent of the area franchise holder before the business could be transferred. The proceeding was brought for a declaratory judgment. (In a declaratory judgment, a court merely declares the rights and duties of parties without awarding damages. Such judgments are given to prevent disputes from arising.)*

The appellant, George Hanigan, entered into a "Dairy Queen Store Agreement" with the appellee, Eileen A. LeMoines. The contract contained a provision that read as follows: "Second Party shall not assign or transfer this Agreement without the written approval of First Party." Subsequently, LeMoines entered into a deposit and receipt agreement with Wheeler for the sale of the Dairy Queen franchise as well as the real property located at and built specifically for the franchise.

A few days later, Hanigan was told about the sale, and an attempt was made to gain his approval. Hanigan refused to approve the sale. He stated that the price of $90,000 was too high and that, in his experience, an inflated sale price was detrimental to the Dairy Queen business. Hanigan also stated that the Wheelers were inexperienced in business and that they were too young to run the franchise properly. (Mr. Wheeler was a dentist, and Mrs. Wheeler was a housewife.) The trial court declared that the clause disallowing assignment without Hanigan's consent was unenforceable as against public policy. The franchise holder, Hanigan, appealed.

HANIGAN v. WHEELER
Court of Appeals of Arizona,
Division 2, 1972.
19 Ariz.App. 49, 504 P.2d 972.

HOWARD, Judge.

*   *   *   *

The primary question dispositive of this appeal is whether the trial court erred in determining that the contract provision precluding the franchise transfer without the area franchise holder's approval is unenforceable as against public policy. A review of the record and the relevant law leads us to answer this question in the affirmative. Given the instant fact situation, the law in this area does not warrant the trial court's order requiring Hanigan to consent to the subject transaction:

"As a general rule, a contract is not assignable where the nature or terms of the contract make it nonassignable, [footnote omitted] unless such provision is waived. *   *   * The parties may in terms, by a provision in the contract, prohibit an assignment thereof, *   *   *." 6 C.J.S. Assignments § 24.b (1937).

"Provisions in bilateral contracts which forbid or restrict assignment of the contract without the consent of the obligor have generally been upheld as valid and enforceable when called into question, [footnote omitted] although the meaning of such terms becomes a matter of interpretation. *   *   *" 6 Am.Jur.2d Assignments § 22 (1963).

These general statements are in accord with the Restatement of the Law of Contracts § 151, which reads as follows:

"A right may be the subject of effective assignment unless, *   *   * (c) the assignment is prohibited by the contract creating the right."

*   *   *   *

A leading case stated the law as follows:

*   *   * we think it is reasonably clear that, while the courts have striven to uphold freedom of assignability, they have not failed to recognize the concept of freedom to contract. In large measure they agree that, where appropriate language is used, assignments of money due under contracts may be prohibited. When 'clear language' is used, and the 'plainest words *   *   * have been chosen' parties may 'limit the freedom of alienation of rights and prohibit the assignment.'

*   *   *   *

In opposition to the above principles, appellees contend that more than a contract right is involved in the case at bench in that the subject clause restricting assignment without Hanigan's approval serves as an unreasonable and unlawful restraint on the right of alienation of property, since the Store Agreement provides no guidelines by which the area franchise holder is to base his approval or disapproval of potential buyers, and that hypothetically, through the whim or arbitrariness of the holder, the LeMoines could be prevented from ever selling their franchise and the property associated with the franchise.

We accept the fundamental principle that one of the primary incidents inherent in the ownership of property is the right of alienation or disposition. However, this right is not limitless. The right to make an assignment of property can be defeated where there is a clear stipulation to that effect. The current state of the law in this area appears to be that a restraint on the alienation of property may be sustained when the restraint is reasonably designed to attain or encourage accepted social or economic ends.

*   *   *   *

We also perceive that despite the restriction on assignment of the store agreement, the LeMoines are not entirely powerless. Where a contract contains a *promise* to refrain from assigning, an assignment which violates it would not be ineffective. "The promise creates a *duty* in the promisor not to assign. It does not deprive the assignor of the *power* to assign and its breach, therefore, would simply subject the promisor to an action for damages while the assignment would be effective. *   *   *"

In summary, we hold that the law as set forth above demonstrates that the contract limitation against assignment of the Store Agreement without the approval of the area franchise holder is proper and valid. The trial court erred in concluding that the provision limiting assignability was unenforceable as against public policy. The court also erred in ruling that defendants had a duty to consent to the franchise sale, for this is contrary to the manifested intention of the parties to the contract. The general proposition is that " 'a covenantor [promisor] is not to be held beyond his undertaking and he may make that as narrow as he likes.' "

The trial court was incorrect. The appellate court declared that it was the right of the area franchise holder to consent or refuse to consent to the sale (assignment) of a franchise.

DECISION AND REMEDY

The trial court had ordered Hanigan to consent to the transaction. Hanigan wanted the appeals court to declare affirmatively that, as a matter of law, he was not required to approve the transfer. The court had to use a declaratory judgment because no sale had occurred yet. In this particular case, judicial scrutiny was fact oriented rather than public policy oriented.

COMMENTS

Notice of the Assignment   Once a valid assignment of rights has been made to a third party, the third party should notify the obligor (Baker in Exhibit 14–1) of the assignment. This is not legally necessary because an assignment is effective immediately, whether or not notice is given. Two major problems arise, however, when notice of the assignment is not given the obligor:

1.   If the assignor assigns the same right to two different assignees, the question arises as to which assignee has priority (right) to the performance by the obligor. Although the majority rule in the United States is that the first assignment in time is the first in right, some states follow the English rule, which basically gives priority to the first assignee who gives notice.[8]

For example, suppose Baker owes Able $1,000 on a contractual obligation. On May 1, Able assigns this monetary claim to Carlson. No notice of assignment is given Baker. On June 1, for services Dullus has rendered to Able, Able assigns the same

monetary claim from Baker to Dullus. Dullus immediately notifies Baker of the assignment. Although in the majority of states Carlson has priority to receive payment, because Carlson's assignment was first in time, in some states Dullus would have priority because Dullus gave first notice.

2.   Until the obligor has notice of assignment, the obligor can discharge his or her obligation by performance to the assignor, and performance by the obligor to the assignor constitutes a discharge to the assignee. Once the obligor receives proper notice, only performance to the assignee can discharge the obligor's obligations.

To illustrate, suppose Baker owes Able $1,000 on a contract obligation. Able assigns this monetary claim to Carlson. No notice of assignment is given to Baker. Baker pays Able the $1,000. Although the assignment was valid, Baker's payment to Able was a discharge of the debt, and Carlson's failure to give notice to Baker of the assignment caused Carlson to lose the right to collect the money from Baker. If Carlson had given Baker notice of the assignment, Baker's payment to Able would not discharge the debt, and Carlson would have a legal right to require payment from Baker.

Delegation of Duties

Just as a party can transfer rights under a contract through an assignment, a party can also transfer duties. Duties are not assigned, however. They are delegated. Normally, a delegation of duties does not

---

8.   At common law, there were three different rules. The first rule was called the English rule. Assignees, second in time to the first assignee, prevailed in every case in which they had paid value, had taken the assignment without notice of the prior assignment, and had given the *obligor* notice of the assignment before the first assignee gave such notice. Another rule, called the New York rule, essentially stated that the first assignment in time is first in right. Finally, the third rule was the Massachusetts rule. The first assignee prevailed provided the first assignment was not revocable at the time the second assignment was made.

relieve the party making the delegation—the delagator—of the obligation to perform in the event that the party who has been delegated the duty—the delagatee—fails to perform.

Form of the Delegation No special form is required to create a valid delegation of duties. As long as the delegator (the party delegating the duty) expresses a present intention to make the delegation, it will be effective. The delegator need not even use the word "delegate."

Duties That Can Be Delegated As a general rule, any duty can be delegated. Exhibit 14–2 illustrates the relationships involved in a delegation. There are, however, some exceptions to this rule. Delegation is prohibited:

1. When performance depends on the *personal* skill or talents of the obligor.
2. When special trust has been placed in the obligor.
3. When performance by a third party will vary materially from that expected by the obligee under the contract.

Suppose Baker contracts with Able to tutor Able in the various aspects of financial underwriting and investment banking. Baker is an experienced businessman who is well known for his expertise in finance. Further, assume that Baker wants to delegate his duties to teach Able to a third party, Carlson. This delegation would be ineffective since Baker has contracted to render a service to Able that is founded upon Baker's *expertise*. It is a change from Able's expectancy under the contract. Therefore, Carlson cannot perform Baker's duties.

Suppose Baker, an attorney, contracts with Able, a bank, to advise Able on a proposed merger with a savings and loan association. Baker wishes to delegate her duty to advise the bank to Carlson, a law firm across town. Services of an attorney are *personal in nature*. Baker's delegation will be ineffective.

Finally, assume that Baker contracts with Able to pick up and deliver heavy construction machinery to Able's property. Baker then delegates this duty to Carlson, who is in the business of delivering heavy machinery. The delegation is effective. The performance required is of a *routine* and *nonpersonal nature* and does not change Able's expectancy under the contract.

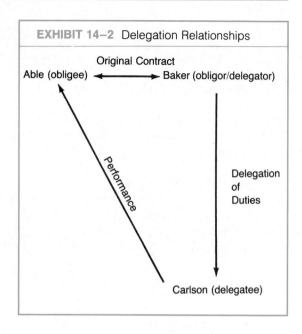

EXHIBIT 14–2 Delegation Relationships

Original Contract

Able (obligee) ←——→ Baker (obligor/delegator)

Performance

Delegation of Duties

Carlson (delegatee)

Effect of a Delegation of Duties If a delegation of duties is enforceable, the obligee (Able in the exhibit) must accept performance from the delegatee. The obligee can legally refuse performance from the delegatee only if the duty is one that may not be delegated. A valid delegation of duties does *not relieve* the delegator (Baker in the exhibit) of obligations under the contract.[9] If the delegatee (Carlson in the exhibit) fails to perform, the delegator is still liable to the obligee.

Liability of the Delegatee to the Obligee. If the delegatee fails to perform, whether the obligee can hold the delegatee liable comes into issue. If the delegatee has made a promise of performance which will benefit directly the obligee, there is an "assumption of duty." Breach of this duty makes the delegatee liable to the obligee.

Suppose Baker contracts to build Able a house according to Able's blueprint plans. Baker becomes seriously ill and contracts to have Carlson build the house for Able. Carlson fails to build the house. Since the delegatee Carlson contracted with Baker to build the house for the benefit of Able, Able can sue Baker, or Carlson, or both.

If the delegatee has made no promise to benefit the obligee, a "mere declaration" takes place, and

9. Crane Ice Cream Co. v. Terminal Freezing Co., 147 Md. 588, 128 A. 280 (1925).

the delegatee cannot be held liable by the obligee. To illustrate, Baker contracts to build Able a house complete with a swimming pool. Baker falls behind schedule and contracts to have Carlson build the swimming pool. Carlson fails to do so. Since Carlson's obligation was for the *primary* benefit of Baker, Carlson has no liability to Able, only to Baker.

When a contract provides for "assignment of all rights," this wording may also be treated as an "assumption of duties." The traditional view was that under this type of assignment, Carlson did not assume any duties. This view was based on the theory that the acceptance of the benefits of the contract was not sufficient to imply a promise to assume the duties of the contract.

Modern authorities, however, take the view that the probable intention in using such general words is to create both an assignment of rights and an assumption of duties.[10] Therefore, when general words are used (for example, "I assign the contract" or "all my rights under the contract"), the contract is construed as implying both an assignment of rights and an assumption of duties.

THIRD PARTY BENEFICIARY CONTRACTS

Unless you are a party to a contract formation, you have no contractual rights in that contract. There is an exception to this rule when the original parties to the contract intend at the time of contracting that the contract performance directly benefit a third person. The third person becomes a beneficiary of the contract, and as a beneficiary has legal rights in the contract to insure that the benefits intended are performed.

In general, the law recognizes the rights of two types of beneficiaries—creditor and donee—but not the rights of an incidental beneficiary.[11] For ex-

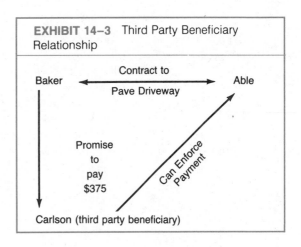

EXHIBIT 14–3 Third Party Beneficiary Relationship

ample, Able contracts with Baker to pave Baker's driveway upon Baker's promise to pay Carlson $375. Carlson is the third party beneficiary (since he is benefiting from Baker's promise). The courts will usually uphold Baker's promise if Carlson is a creditor or donee beneficiary but not if Carlson is an incidental beneficiary. In order to determine whether the third party beneficiary has enforceable rights, the **intent** of Able in Exhibit 14–3 must be examined.

Creditor Beneficiaries

If a promisee's main purpose in making a contract is to discharge a duty or debt he or she already owes to a third party, then the third party is a **creditor beneficiary**.[12] There must be a debtor-creditor relationship established or existing. The debtor then makes a contract with another person, which is intended to discharge the debt of the debtor and at the same time confer a benefit on the debtor's creditor. The creditor, although not a party to the contract between the debtor and the other person, was intended to benefit. The creditor becomes a creditor beneficiary and therefore can enforce the promise against the other person (the promisor).

The following classic case is an illustration of the third-party-beneficiary theory. This case is often cited in modern-day court decisions.

---

10. UCC 2-210(1) (where there is a general assignment of a contract for the sale of goods). Restatement, Second, Contracts, Section 328.

11. Restatement, Second, Contracts, Section 302. This is the traditional terminology used to describe the various types of third party beneficiaries. Under the Restatement of Contracts, the term "intended beneficiary" replaces "creditor beneficiary" and "donee beneficiary." However, a majority of state courts still distinguish between donee and creditor beneficiaries, so the traditional terms will be used here.

---

12. Restatement, Second, Contracts, Section 302(1)(a).

LAWRENCE v. FOX
Court of Appeals of New York,
1859.
20 N.Y. 268.

BACKGROUND AND FACTS *Holly owed the plaintiff $300. The defendant suggested that Holly give him the money and promised to pay it to the plaintiff to discharge Holly's debt. (Sufficient consideration was present in this transaction to create a contract between Holly and the defendant.) The defendant never paid the plaintiff, so the plaintiff sued the defendant, considering himself a third party beneficiary of the contract between Holly and the defendant. The court decided that the plaintiff had a legal right to sue the defendant for failing to pay the $300 as promised, even though the plaintiff was never "in privity"; that is, he was never a direct participant or party to the contract.*

H. GRAY, Justice.
*   *   *   *

In this case the promise was made to Holly and not expressly to the plaintiff; *   *   * As early as 1806 it was announced by the Supreme Court of this State, upon what was then regarded as the settled law of England, "That where one person makes a promise to another for the benefit of a third person, that third person may maintain an action upon it." *Schermerhorn v. Vanderheyden* (1 John. R., 140), has often been re-asserted by our courts and never departed from.
*   *   *   *

In *Hall v. Marston* the court [said]: "It seems to have been well settled that if A promises B for a valuable consideration to pay C, the latter may maintain assumpsit [the agreement] for the money;" and in *Brewer v. Dyer*, the recovery was upheld, as the court said, "upon the principle of law *long recognized and clearly established*, that when one person, for a valuable consideration, engages with another, by a simple contract, to do some act for the benefit of a third, the latter, who would enjoy the benefit of the act, may maintain an action for the breach of such engagement; that it does not rest upon the ground of any actual or supposed relationship between the parties as some of the earlier cases would seem to indicate, but upon the broader and more satisfactory basis, that the law operating on the act of the parties creates the duty, establishes a privity, and implies the promise and obligation on which the action is founded."
*   *   *   *

In this case the defendant, upon ample consideration received from Holly, promised Holly to pay his debt to the plaintiff; the consideration received and the promise to Holly made it as plainly his duty to pay the plaintiff as if the money had been remitted to him for that purpose, and as well implied a promise to do so as if he had been made a trustee of property to be converted into cash with which to pay.
*   *   *   *

No one can doubt that he [Holly] owes the sum of money demanded of him, or that in accordance with his promise it was his duty to have paid it to the plaintiff; nor can it be doubted that whatever may be the diversity of opinion elsewhere, the adjudications in this State, from a very early period, approved by experience, have established the defendant's liability *   *   *."

The judgment should be affirmed.

DECISION AND REMEDY *Judgment was for the plaintiff. The defendant was required to pay the plaintiff $300 to fulfill his original contract with Holly.*

Assumption of a Mortgage The assumption of a real estate mortgage is a type of third party creditor beneficiary contract. Suppose some years ago your parents purchased their home. Unable to pay cash, they contracted to borrow the money from Thrift Home and Loan at a rate of 8.5 percent interest, with Thrift taking a mortgage on the home purchased. Today your parents decide to sell their home to Braico. Braico is interested in the 8.5 percent loan rate of interest and agrees to pay your parents for their equity (value of the home less the mortgage amount) and to assume the mortgage held by Thrift. Even though Thrift is not a party to the present contract for the sale of the home to Braico, does Thrift have any rights in this contract?

The answer is yes, if the assumption is not prohibited in the mortgage contract. When your parents purchased the home through a mortgage, they became debtors and Thrift a creditor. When your parents sold the home to Braico, Braico's assumption of their mortgage created a benefit for Thrift in that Thrift could then hold Braico personally liable on the loan—in addition to holding your parents liable or gaining the property should there be a default. Thus, Thrift is a creditor beneficiary of certain terms of the contract between your parents and Braico and can enforce the monthly mortgage payments against Braico.

Donee Beneficiaries

If a promisee's main purpose in making a contract is to confer a benefit upon a third party, then the third party is a *donee beneficiary*.[13] A donee beneficiary can enforce the promise of a promisor just as a creditor beneficiary can. To illustrate, suppose Able goes to her attorney, Baker, and enters into a contract in which Baker promises to draft a will naming Able's son, Carl, as an heir. Carl is a donee beneficiary, and if Baker does not prepare the will properly, Carl can sue Baker.[14] Or suppose Able offers to paint Baker's house if Baker pays $750 to Carl, Able's son. Able wants to give the money to Carl as a gift. Carl is a donee beneficiary and can enforce Baker's promise to pay $750.

The most common third party beneficiary contract involving a donee beneficiary is a life insurance contract. In a typical contract, Able, the promisee, pays premiums to Old Life, a life insurance company, and Old Life promises to pay a certain amount of money upon Able's death to anyone Able designates as beneficiary. The designated beneficiary, Carl, is a donee beneficiary under the life insurance

13. Restatement, Second, Contracts, Section 302(1)(b).
14. Lucas v. Hamm, 56 Cal.2d 583, 15 Cal.Rptr. 821, 364 P.2d 685 (1961).

policy and can enforce payment against the insurance company upon Able's death.

Incidental Beneficiaries

The benefit that an *incidental beneficiary* receives from a contract between two parties is unintentional. Therefore, an incidental beneficiary cannot enforce a contract to which he or she is not a party. Several factors must be examined to determine whether a party is an incidental beneficiary. The presence of one or more of the factors listed below strongly indicates an *intended* (rather than an incidental) benefit to the third party.

1. Performance rendered directly to the third party.
2. The rights of the third party to control the details of performance.
3. Express designation in the contract.

The following are examples of incidental beneficiaries. The third party has no rights in the contract and cannot enforce it against the promisor.

1. B contracts with A to build a factory on A's land. B's plans specify that Ad Pipe Company pipe fittings must be used in all plumbing. Ad Pipe Company is an incidental beneficiary and cannot enforce the contract against B by attempting to require B to purchase its pipe.
2. B contracts with A to build a recreational facility on A's land. Once the facility is constructed, it will greatly enhance the property values in the neighborhood. If B subsequently refuses to build the facility, C, a neighboring property owner, cannot enforce the contract against B by attempting to require B to build the facility.
3. B is an employee of A. B has been promised a promotion if his employer obtains a contract with C. A is unable to obtain the contract with C. B is an incidental beneficiary to that contract. B has no right to sue C for being the cause of his nonpromotion to a better-paying position. Indeed, B cannot sue C even if B loses his job as the result of the failure of A and C to reach an agreement.

ENFORCEABLE RIGHTS— WHEN THE RIGHTS OF A THIRD PARTY VEST

Until the rights of a third party *vest*, the third party cannot enforce a contract against the original parties.

When a right is vested, it is fixed or it takes effect. The rights of a third party vest when the original parties *cannot rescind or change the contract without the consent of the third party.*

The rights of a third party beneficiary (donee or creditor) vest (and the power of the original contracting parties to change, alter, or rescind the contract terminates) whenever one of the following three things happen:

1.   The third party beneficiary learns of and consents to the contract.[15]
2.   The third party beneficiary brings suit upon the contract.
3.   The third party materially alters his or her position in detrimental reliance on the contract.

---

15.   Restatement, Second, Contracts, Section 311(3), says that the promisor and the promisee have to request assent.

Suppose, for example, that Carlson learns of Baker's intention to give $375 to Carlson after the driveway is paved. Before Carlson agrees to accept the payment, however, Baker decides to make payment elsewhere. Carlson's rights to the payment will not have been vested since Carlson did not assent prior to the contract revision.

If the contract expressly reserves the right to cancel, rescind, or modify the contract, the rights of the third party beneficiary are subject to any change that results. In such a case, the vesting of the third party's rights will not terminate the power of the original contracting parties to alter their legal relationships.[16] This is particularly true in most life insurance contracts, where the right to change the beneficiary is reserved.

---

16.   Defenses raised against third party beneficiaries are given in Restatement, Second, Contracts, Section 309.

QUESTIONS AND CASE PROBLEMS

1. John has been accepted as a freshman to attend a college 200 miles from his home for the fall semester. John's roommate is his close friend, Daniel. John's father, Michael, makes a contract with auto dealer Jackson to purchase a new car for $10,000 to be delivered to John, with the title in John's name. Daniel is delighted to hear of Michael's purchase for John, since Daniel will not have a car of his own at college and will benefit if John has a car. Michael pays the full purchase price and takes off for a six-month vacation in Europe. Jackson never delivers the car, and John files an action against Jackson. Discuss fully whether John can recover for Jackson's breach of contract. Would your answer be any different if Daniel sued Jackson for breach of contract?

2. Five years ago Jane purchased a house. At that time, being unable to pay the full purchase price, she borrowed money from Thrift Savings and Loan, which in turn took an 8 percent mortgage on the house. The mortgage contract did not prohibit the assignment of the mortgage. Now Jane has secured a new job in another city and sells the house to Sylvia. The purchase price includes payment to Jane of the value of her equity and the assumption of the mortgage held by Thrift. At the time of this contract,

Thrift did not know of or consent to the sale. On the basis of these facts, if Sylvia defaults in making the house payments to Thrift, what are Thrift's rights?

3. Thomas is a student attending college. He signs a one-year lease agreement that runs from September 1 to August 31. The lease agreement specifies that the lease cannot be assigned without the landlord's consent. Thomas decides not to go to summer school and assigns the balance of the lease (three months) to a close friend, Fred. The landlord objects to the assignment and denies Fred access to the apartment. Thomas claims Fred is financially sound and should be allowed the full rights and privileges of an assignee. Discuss fully whether the landlord or Thomas is correct.

4. Ben Cartwright sells the mineral rights to 1,000 acres on the Ponderosa to Ajax Mining Company for royalty payments of $1,000 per month for the term of the agreement. One month later, Ben assigns the royalties to his son, Little Joe, as a gift. Later, Little Joe's actions around the Ponderosa cause him to fall out of favor with his father. Ben, in need of working capital, contracts with banker John for a loan of $50,000, with Ben assigning the royalty payments to John for the repayment of this loan. The next royalty payment arrives. Discuss who is entitled to the royalty payment, Little Joe or banker John?

5. Diane has a specific set of plans to build a sailboat. The plans are detailed in nature, and any boat builder can build the boat. Diane secures bids, and the low bid is by the Whale of a Boat Corporation. Diane contracts

with Whale to build the boat for $4,000. Whale then receives unexpected business from elsewhere. In order to meet the delivery date in the contract with Diane, Whale assigns (delegates) the contract, without Diane's consent, to Quick Brothers, a reputable boat builder. When the boat is ready for delivery, Diane learns of the assignment and refuses to accept delivery, even though the boat is built to specifications. Discuss fully whether Diane is obligated to accept and pay for the boat. Would your answer be any different if Diane did not have a specific set of plans but instead contracted with Whale to design and build a sailboat for $4,000? Explain.

6. Christopher wrote a letter to Donald claiming that Donald owed him $3,000 for the shipment of string bikinis sent Donald three months ago. Donald wrote back, saying that the bikinis were defective and that therefore he refused to pay. Christopher wrote back that his lawyer had advised him that it was questionable whether Donald had informed him of the defect in time and that Christopher might have a valid claim for the purchase price of $3,000 despite any defects. About a month later, Donald wrote back to Christopher informing him that Jerry, who owed Donald $3,000 from a previous contract, had agreed with Donald to make the payment to Christopher. Thereafter, Jerry failed to make the payment to Christopher. Can Christopher sue Jerry?

7. Owens, a federal prisoner, was transferred from federal prison to the Nassau County Jail pursuant to a contract between the U.S. Bureau of Prisons and the county. The contract included a policy statement that required the receiving prison to provide for the safekeeping and protection of transferred federal prisoners. While in the Nassau County Jail, Owens was beaten severely by prison officials, suffering lacerations, bruises and a lasting impairment that caused blackouts. Can Owens, as a third party beneficiary, sue the county for breach of its agreement with the U.S. Bureau of Prisons? [Owens v. Haas, 601 F.2d 1242 (2d Cir. 1979)]

8. Beman wrote his wife's will as she was about to die. When he read the will to her, she said that it was not the way she wanted it and that she wanted to leave her house to her niece, Seaver. Beman offered to write her another will, but she said she was afraid she would not hold out long enough to sign it. Beman told her that if she would sign the will, he would leave Seaver enough in his will to make up the difference. When Beman died, no provision was made for Seaver to receive the monetary value of the house. Seaver brought an action against Beman's estate, claiming a contract right for the value of the house. What was the result? [Seaver v. Ransom, 224 N.Y. 233, 120 N.E. 639 (1918)]

9. Clement was seriously injured in a car accident with King. Clement sued King. King retained Prestwich as her attorney. Due to the alleged negligence of Prestwich, Clements was able to obtain a $21,000 judgment on her claim against King. Clement received from King a purported written assignment of King's malpractice claim against Prestwich, as settlement for the judgment against her. Can King assign her cause of action against Prestwich to Clement? [Clement v. Prestwich, 448 N.E.2d 1039 (Ill.App. 2 Dist. 1983)]

10. Fox Brothers agreed to convey to Canfield Lot 23 together with a one year option to purchase Lot 24 in a subdivision known as Fox Estates. The agreement did not contain any prohibitions, restrictions, or limitations against assignments. Canfield paid the price of $20,000 and took title to Lot 23. Thereafter, Canfield assigned his option rights in Lot 24 to the Scotts. When the Scotts tried to exercise their right to the option, Fox Brothers refused to convey the property to them. The Scotts then brought suit for specific performance. What was the result? [Scott v. Fox Brothers Enterprises, Inc., 667 P.2d 773 (Colo.App. 1983)]

15

CONTRACTS
Performance and Discharge

Just as rules are necessary to determine when a legally enforceable contract exists, so rules are also necessary to determine when one of the parties can justifiably say, "I have fully performed, so I am now discharged from my obligations on this contract." The legal environment of business requires some point at which one or both parties can reasonably know their duties are at an end. This chapter deals with this issue.

The **discharge** (termination) of a contract is ordinarily accomplished when both of the parties perform those acts promised in the contract. For example, a buyer and seller have a contract for the sale of a bicycle for $50. This contract will be discharged upon buyer's payment of $50 to the seller, and the seller's transfer of possession of the bicycle to the buyer.

However, discharge can occur in other ways. Some of the more important of these,[1] which will be discussed later in this chapter, are:

1. The occurrence or failure of a *condition*.
2. *Performance*.
3. *Agreement*.
4. *Operation of law*.

5. *Breach of contract*.
6. *Impossibility of performance*.

CONDITIONS

In most contracts, promises of performance are not *expressly* conditioned or qualified. They are called *absolute promises*. They must be performed, or the party promising the act will be in breach of contract. For example, I contract to sell you my watch for $100. Our promises are unconditional: my transfer of the watch to you and your payment of $100 to me. The $100 does not have to be given if the watch is not.

However, in some cases performance may be beneficial only if a certain event either does or does not occur. Therefore, *a condition* is inserted into the contract, either expressly by the parties or impliedly by courts. If this condition is not satisfied, the obligations of the parties are discharged.

Suppose I offer to purchase a tract of your land on the condition that your neighbor to the south agrees to sell me her land. You accept my offer. Our obligations (promises) are conditioned upon your neighbor's willingness to sell her land. Should this condition not be satisfied (for example, if your

---

1. Looking at *all* of them would take an entire book.

neighbor refuses to sell), our obligations to each other are discharged and cannot be enforced.

Thus, a **condition** is a possible future event, the occurrence or nonoccurrence of which will trigger the performance of a legal obligation or terminate an existing obligation under a contract.[2]

Although there is a fundamental distinction between the breach of an absolute promise and the failure or nonoccurrence of an express condition, both can occur in a single contract.

For example, suppose you promise to buy a corn futures contract from Merrill Lynch *if the price of number 2 yellow corn reaches $2.25 per bushel.* The condition to your promise to buy is that the price of number 2 yellow corn will reach $2.25 per bushel. If there is a failure of that condition—if number 2 yellow corn never reaches $2.25 per bushel and, therefore, you do not buy—the contract is not breached. However, once the price of corn does reach $2.25, your promise to buy becomes absolute, and if you do not buy, the contract is breached.

Types of Conditions

Three types of conditions can be present in any given contract—conditions *precedent,* conditions *subsequent,* and conditions *concurrent.*

Conditions Precedent

A condition that must be fulfilled before a party's promise becomes absolute is called a **condition precedent.**[3] The condition precedes the absolute duty to perform. For example, Fisher promises to contribute $1,000 to the Salvation Army if Calvin completes college. Fisher's promise is subject to the (express) condition precedent to Calvin's completing college. Until the condition is fulfilled or satisfied, Fisher's promise to donate to charity does not become absolute.

The following Maryland case illustrates in a contract for the sale of land a condition precedent that certain zoning variances would be obtained.

---

2. Restatement, Second, Contracts, Section 224, "An event, not certain to occur, which must occur, unless its non-occurrence is excused, before performance under a contract becomes due."

3. Restatement, Second, Contracts, Section 224, eliminates the terms *condition precedent* and *condition subsequent.*

BACKGROUND AND FACTS *A contract for the sale of a tract of land by the appellee (seller) to the appellant (buyer) was subject to a condition precedent that certain zoning variances be obtained. Generally, applications for zoning can be filed only during each of two specified months of the year, six months apart. The parties had included in their contract a provision that "this sale [is] subject to the obtaining of necessary zoning for the erection of general offices for use of doctors within the next zoning application term." The parties had further agreed that the provision meant the six-month period following the first day of the month in which zoning applications could be filed after the signing of the contract.*

The zoning application was timely filed (that is, within the legal, necessary, or reasonable period) but not obtained "within the next zoning application term." The sellers then notified the buyer in writing that the contract was terminated and that the buyer's 10 percent deposit was being returned. The land was sold to another purchaser. The buyer (appellant) attempted to obtain damages from the seller (appellee) for having sold the land to another purchaser. The buyer took the position that the contract was still in force.

BARNES v. EUSTER
Court of Appeals of Maryland, 1965.
240 Md. 603, 214 A.2d 807.

HAMMOND, Judge.

* * * *

The contract provision was that it was "subject" to the specified rezoning being obtained within the current zoning application term, and "where a contractual duty is subject to a condition precedent, whether express or implied, there is no duty of performance and there can be no breach by nonperformance until the condition precedent is either performed or excused." Here it was not performed, and, if the further assumption be made that the condition * * * was for the protection only of the buyer, it could have been excused or waived by him as being a provision for his benefit, but the excusing or waiving would have had to be done before the expiration of the current zoning application term or within a reasonable time thereafter.

    * * * *

In mid-1960 the buyer knew the condition had not been met, but it was not until three years later, * * * that he first indicated by word or act that he was willing to excuse or waive the condition and take the land as it was. Some sixteen months after the last day of the critical zoning application term, when the sellers wrote that the contract had terminated, he took the position it was still in force, subject to the condition.

    * * * *

His delay in excusing or waiving the condition was unreasonable as a matter of law in light of the notification of termination by the sellers and the rapidly rising prices of real estate. * * *

DECISION AND REMEDY *The appellate court affirmed the trial court's order. The prospective buyer had no right to damages from the seller for the sale of the land to another purchaser since the condition precedent had never been fulfilled or excused within a reasonable time.*

Conditions Subsequent When a condition operates to terminate a party's absolute promise to perform, it is called a **condition subsequent.**[4] The condition follows, or is subsequent to, the absolute duty to perform. If the condition occurs, the party need not perform any further. For example, if Hartman promises to work for the San Pedro Company for one year unless he is admitted to Stanford's Graduate School of Business, the absolute duty to work is conditioned upon not being admitted. Hartman's promise to work for San Pedro continues to be absolute until he is admitted to Stanford. Once Hartman is officially admitted, the absolute duty to work for San Pedro ends, and Hartman is released from the contract.

Concurrent Conditions Where each party's absolute duty to perform is conditioned on the other party's absolute duty to perform, there are **concurrent conditions.** Concurrent conditions occur only when the parties expressly or impliedly are to perform their respective duties *simultaneously*. For example, if a buyer promises to pay for goods when they are delivered by the seller, each party's absolute duty to perform is conditioned upon the other party's absolute duty to perform. The buyer's duty to pay for the goods does not become absolute until the seller either delivers or tenders the goods. Accordingly, the seller's duty to deliver the goods does not become absolute until the buyer tenders or actually makes payment. Therefore, neither can recover from the other for breach unless he or she first tenders his or her own performance.

Express and Implied Conditions Conditions can also be classified as:

1. Express.
2. Implied-in-fact.
3. Implied-in-law.

Express conditions are provided for by the parties' agreement. An express condition is usually prefaced by "if," "provided," "after," or "when." Conditions *implied-in-fact* are similar to express conditions because they are understood to be part of the agreement, but they are not expressly found in the language of the agreement. The court infers them from the promises.

---

4. Restatement, Second, Contracts, Section 224. It is possible that a condition may be subsequent in form but precedent in fact. Further, if there is any difference at all between the two, it is as to burdens of proof and pleading. For this reason, the draft of the Restatement, Second, Contracts drops the distinction between the two.

Suppose Silverman and Lyon enter into two agreements. The first states, "Silverman promises to pay Lyon $1,500 *if* Lyon delivers 100 cases of oranges to Silverman's business office. Lyon promises to deliver 100 cases of oranges to Silverman's business office *if* Silverman pays $1,500 for the oranges." The second agreement states, "Silverman promises to pay $1,500 for 100 cases of Lyon's oranges to be delivered at Silverman's business office."

In the first agreement, Silverman's promise to pay is expressly conditioned on Lyon's promise to deliver. Also, Lyon's promise to deliver is expressly conditioned on Silverman's promise to pay. As noted above, these are *concurrent conditions*.

In the second agreement, Silverman's promise to pay is conditioned on Lyon's promise to deliver, and Lyon's promise to deliver is conditioned on Silverman's promise to pay. The conditions are implied-in-fact because they are necessarily implied by the promise contained in the contract. In other words, it is obvious from custom and context that the duties here are conditional.

Finally, *implied-in-law*, or *constructive*, conditions are imposed by the law in order to achieve justice and fairness. They are not contained in the language of the contract or even necessarily implied.[5] For example, a contract in which a builder is supposed to build a house for a buyer can omit the date on which the buyer is supposed to pay the builder. Nonetheless, the court will imply a condition that the buyer is not obliged to pay the builder until the house is fully or substantially completed. This is done because the buyer should not be compelled to perform unless the builder has performed.

The distinction between conditions is important because if these conditions are expressed, the plaintiff has a duty to allege that all conditions antecedent to his or her responsibility have occurred. Thus, when they are expressed, the burden of proof is on the plaintiff.

DISCHARGE BY PERFORMANCE

The great majority of contracts are discharged by performance. The contract comes to an end when both parties fulfill their respective duties by performing the acts they have promised. Performance can

---
5. Restatement, Second, Contracts, Section 226.

also be accomplished by tender. **Tender** is an unconditional offer to perform by one who is ready, willing, and able to do so. Therefore, a seller who places goods at the disposal of a buyer has tendered delivery and can demand payment. A buyer who offers to pay for goods has tendered payment and can demand delivery of the goods. Once performance has been tendered, the party making the tender has done everything possible to carry out the terms of the contract. If the other party then refuses to perform, the party making the tender can consider the duty discharged and sue for breach of contract.

The Degree of Performance Required

It is important to distinguish among three types of performance:

1. Complete.
2. Substantial.
3. Definitely inferior and constituting a material breach of the contract.

One typically uses *a reasonable expectations test* for determining which of these categories a performance fits. *Complete performance* occurs when performance is within the bounds of reasonable expectations. *Substantial performance* occurs when performance is slightly below reasonable expectations. A *material breach* occurs when performance is far below reasonable expectations.

Although in most contracts the parties fully discharge their obligations by complete performance, sometimes a party fulfills most, but not all, the duties or completes the duties in a manner contrary to the terms of the contract. The issue then arises as to whether this failure of complete performance acts as a discharge of performance for the other party.

For example, a home building contract specifies installation of Fuller brand plasterboard for the walls. The builder cannot secure the Fuller brand and installs Honeyrock. All other aspects of construction conform to the contract. Does this deviation discharge the buyer from paying for the house upon completion?

The answer usually depends on one or two basic questions:

1. Does the term in dispute constitute an express condition?

2. Can only "complete performance" discharge the promise?

If both answers are affirmative, only *complete* performance acts as a discharge of performance. If the terms of the contract do not fit both these categories, *substantial*, not complete, performance is required. In this event, it must be determined whether the performance is substantial. If it is not, the party is then in *material breach* (a topic to be discussed later).

Conditions and Complete Performance Normally, conditions expressly stated in the contract must fully occur in all aspects. Any deviation operates as a discharge. In the illustration given above, if the terms in the specifications had stated that *only Fuller brand* plasterboard was to be used, a court could construe this term as a condition. The builder's use of the Honeyrock brand, even though it is of equal quality to Fuller, would not fulfill this express condition precedent to payment, and therefore the builder would not be entitled to payment.

A typical illustration of a condition precedent to payment is a life insurance policy in which one of the conditions for enforcing the policy is the payment of the life insurance premium. The premium must be paid prior to the death of the insured, or the insurance company will not be obligated to pay benefits.

Substantial Performance Most terms or promises are not made or construed as conditions. Human nature dictates that performance will not always fully satisfy the parties. Therefore, for the sake of justice and fairness, the courts hold that a party's obligation is not discharged as long as the other party has fulfilled the terms of the contract with *substantial performance*. In order to qualify as substantial, the performance must not vary greatly from the performance promised in the contract. If performance is substantial, the other party's duty to perform remains absolute, less damages, if any, for the minor deviations.

In the "Fuller" illustration, if the specification for Fuller plasterboard is not construed as a condition, then the only issue is whether the substitution of Honeyrock plasterboard is substantial performance. Obviously, if Honeyrock is of similar quality, substantial performance by the builder has taken place, and either the buyer is obligated to pay,[6] or the contractor is required to tear out all the Honeyrock brand plasterboard and replace it with the Fuller brand. However, this kind of deviation from the terms of a contract must not be willful or grossly negligent but must result only from an oversight.

Substantial performance does not operate to eliminate any breach of contract arising from less than full performance. Although substantial performance does not prevent discharge (as the breach is not material), a breach of contract—however slight—has occurred. If the plasterboard substituted for Fuller brand had been of a somewhat lesser quality than Fuller, reducing the value of the house by $300, the builder would still be allowed to recover the contracted building price but less the $300. Remedies will be discussed in detail in the next chapter.

The following case, also involving a contract for the construction of a house, will help to clarify when there has been substantial performance by the contractor.

---

6.   For an excellent analysis of substantial performance, see Judge Cardozo's opinion in Jacob & Youngs v. Kent, 230 N.Y. 239, 129 N.E. 889 (1921).

PLANTE v. JACOBS
Supreme Court of Wisconsin,
1960.
10 Wis.2d 567, 103 N.W.2d 296.

BACKGROUND AND FACTS *The Jacobses entered into a written contract with the plaintiff, Plante, to furnish the materials and construct a house on their lot, in accordance with plans and specifications, for a sum of $26,765. During the course of construction, the plaintiff was paid $20,000. Disputes arose between the parties concerning the work being done. The Jacobses refused to continue paying. The plaintiff did not complete the house. The trial court found that the contract was substantially performed. The Jacobses were told to pay $4,152.90 plus interest and court costs.*

HALLOWS, JUSTICE.

*   *   *   *

The defendants argue the plaintiff cannot recover any amount because he has failed to substantially perform the contract. The plaintiff conceded he failed to furnish the kitchen cabinets, gutters and downspouts, sidewalk, closet clothes poles, and entrance seat amounting to $1,601.95. This amount was allowed to the defendants. The defendants claim some 20 other items of incomplete or faulty performance by the plaintiff and no substantial performance because the cost of completing the house in strict compliance with the plans and specifications would amount to 25 or 30 per cent of the contract price. The defendants especially stress the misplacing of the wall between the living room and the kitchen, which narrowed the living room in excess of one foot. The cost of tearing down this wall and rebuilding it would be approximately $4,000. The record is not clear why and when this wall was misplaced, but the wall is completely built and the house decorated and the defendants are living therein. Real estate experts testified that the smaller width of the living room would not affect the market price of the house.

*   *   *   *

Substantial performance as applied to construction of a house does not mean that every detail must be in strict compliance with the specifications and the plans. Something less than perfection is the test of specific performance unless all details are made the essence of the contract. This was not done here. There may be situations in which features or details of construction of special or of great personal importance, if not performed, would prevent a finding of substantial performance of the contract. In this case the plan was a stock floor plan. No detailed construction of the house was shown on the plan. There were no blueprints. The specifications were standard printed forms with some modifications and additions written in by the parties. Many of the problems that arose during the construction had to be solved on the basis of practical experience. No mathematical rule relating to the percentage of the price, of cost of completion or of completeness can be laid down to determine substantial performance of a building contract. Although the defendants received a house with which they are dissatisfied in many respects, the trial court was not in error in finding the contract was substantially performed.

The next question is what is the amount of recovery when the plaintiff has substantially, but incompletely, performed. For substantial performance the plaintiff should recover the contract price less the damages caused the defendant by the incomplete performance. Both parties agree. Venzke v. Magdanz, 1943, 243 Wis. 155, 9 N.W.2d 604, states the correct rule for damages due to faulty construction amounting to such incomplete performance, which is the difference between the value of the house as it stands with faulty and incomplete construction and the value of the house if it had been constructed in strict accordance with the plans and specifications. This is the diminished-value rule. The cost of replacement or repair is not the measure of such damage, but is an element to take into consideration in arriving at value under some circumstances. The cost of replacement or the cost to make whole the omissions may equal or be less than the difference in value in some cases and, likewise, the cost to rectify a defect may greatly exceed the added value to the structure as corrected. The defendants argue that under the Venzke rule their damages are $10,000. The plaintiff on review argues the defendants' damages are only $650. Both parties agree the trial court applied the wrong rule to the facts.

The reviewing court upheld the trial court's judgment. Substantial performance was evident.   **DECISION AND REMEDY**

Performance to the Satisfaction of Another
Contracts will often state that completed work must personally satisfy one of the parties or a third person. The question then arises as to whether this satisfaction becomes a condition precedent, requiring actual personal satisfaction or approval for discharge, or whether the test of satisfaction is an absolute promise requiring such performance as would satisfy a "reasonable person" (substantial performance).

When the subject matter of the contract is personal, a contract to be performed to the satisfaction of one of the parties is conditioned, and performance must actually satisfy that party. For example, contracts for portraits, works of art, medical or dental work, and tailoring are considered personal. Therefore, only the personal satisfaction of the party will be sufficient to fulfill the condition. Suppose Williams agrees to paint a portrait of Hirshon's daughter for $500. The contract provides that Hirshon must be satisfied with the portrait. If Hirshon is not, she will not be required to pay for it. The only requirement imposed on Hirshon is that she act honestly and in good faith. If she expresses dissatisfaction only to avoid paying for the portrait, the condition of satisfaction is excused, and her duty to pay becomes absolute. (Of course, the jury, or judge acting as a jury, will have to decide whether she is acting honestly.)[7]

Contracts that involve mechanical fitness, utility, or marketability need only be performed to the satisfaction of a reasonable person unless they *expressly state otherwise*. For example, construction contracts or manufacturing contracts are usually *not* considered to be personal, so the party's personal satisfaction is normally irrelevant. As long as the performance will satisfy a reasonable person, the contract is fulfilled. For example, assume Duplex Safety Boiler Company agrees to rebuild Garden's boiler "to Garden's satisfaction." After rebuilding the boiler, it operates properly, but Garden is dissatisfied and refuses to pay for the repair work. Most courts would not construe these terms as a condition and if a reasonable person would be satisfied with the boiler's operation, Duplex is entitled to be paid for the repair work.[8]

At times, contracts also require performance to the satisfaction of a third party (not a party to the contract). For example, assume you contract to pave several city streets. The contract provides that the work will be done "to the satisfaction of Phil Hopper, the supervising engineer." In this situation, the courts are divided. A minority of courts require the personal satisfaction of the third party, here Phil Hopper. If Hopper is not satisfied, you will not be paid, even if a reasonable person would be satisfied. Again, the personal judgment must be made honestly or the condition will be excused. A majority of courts require the work to be satisfactory to a reasonable person. So even if Hopper were dissatisfied with the cement work, you would be paid, as long as a qualified supervising engineer would have been satisfied.

All of the above examples demonstrate the necessity for *clear, specific wording in contracts*. That is, in all states the parties could provide that the performance must meet the *personal and subjective* satisfaction of the party who is paying for the work being done. One must never underestimate the importance of reading the small print in contracts.

Material Breach of Contract

A **breach of contract** is the nonperformance of a contractual duty. When the breach is *material*,[9] or performance is not substantial, the nonbreaching party is excused from the performance of contractual duties and has a cause of action to sue for damages caused by the breach. If the breach is *minor* (not material), the nonbreaching party's duty to perform can sometimes be suspended until the breach is remedied but is not entirely excused. Once the minor breach is cured, the nonbreaching party must then resume performance of the contractual obligations undertaken. Any breach entitles the nonbreaching party to sue for damages, but only a material breach discharges the nonbreaching party from the contract. The policy underlying these rules allows contracts to go forward when only minor problems occur but terminates them if major problems occur.[10]

Suppose Raytheon Corp. contracts with the United States government to build an all-weather

---

7. For a classic case, see Gibson v. Cranage, 39 Mich. 49 (1878).
8. If, however, the contract specifically states that it is to be fulfilled to the "personal" satisfaction of one or more of the parties,

and the parties so intended, the outcome will probably be different.
9. Restatement, Second, Contracts, Section 241.
10. See UCC 2-612 dealing with installment contracts for the sale of goods.

tactical strike force system and to test equipment for the Hawk missile system. Raytheon is to complete the project in two years and has certain schedules to meet for each stage of the production. Every six months Raytheon is to receive $3.8 million of the total $15.2 million contract price. If Raytheon is four months late in completing the first stage of production, the government will be entitled to treat the contract as discharged. Taking ten months to complete a stage that was scheduled for six months is a material breach of contract. In addition, the government can sue Raytheon for breach of contract and recover damages caused by the four-month delay. If, on the other hand, Raytheon is two days late in completing the first stage, the government will not be entitled to treat the contract as discharged. Two days is only a minor breach. However, the government can sue Raytheon for damages caused by the minor delay.

A nonbreaching party need not treat a material breach as a discharge of the contract, but can treat the contract as being in effect and simply sue for damages. In the above example, if Raytheon delays four months on the first stage, the government can treat the contract as still being in effect and sue for damages caused by the delay.

Time for Performance

If no time for performance is stated in the contract, a reasonable time is implied.[11] If a specific time is stated, the parties must usually perform by that time. However, unless time is expressly stated to be vital, a delay in performance will not destroy the performing party's right to payment. When time is expressly stated to be vital, or when "time is of the essence," the time for performance must usually be strictly complied with. The time element becomes a condition.

For example, a contract for the sale of soybeans must be performed within a reasonable time, even if it does not mention time. A contract for the sale of soybeans "on or before April 1" may be performed by April 2 or 3. (But the party rendering late performance will have to pay for any damages caused by the delay.) A contract for the sale of soybeans "on or before April 1—necessary for immediate shipment abroad on April 2" must be performed by

April 1. Time is of the essence because the buyer plans on immediate resale. Delivery after April 1 will prevent the buyer from exporting the soybeans.

DISCHARGE BY AGREEMENT

Any contract can be discharged by agreement of the parties. The agreement can be contained in the original contract, or the parties can form a new contract for the express purpose of discharging the original contract.

Discharge by Rescission

Rescission is the process whereby the parties cancel the contract and are returned to the positions they occupied prior to forming it. In order for **mutual rescission** to take place, the parties must make another agreement, which must also satisfy the legal requirements for a contract. There must be an *offer*, an *acceptance*, and *consideration*. Ordinarily, if the parties agree to rescind the original contract, their promises not to perform those acts promised in the original contract will be legal consideration for the second contract. This occurs when the performance of each is executory, in whole or in part.

The rescission agreement is generally enforceable even if made orally. This applies even if the original agreement was in writing. There are two basic exceptions. One applies to transfers of realty. The other applies to the sale of goods under the UCC, where the sales contract requires written rescission.[12]

When one party has fully performed, however, an agreement to call off the original contract will not normally be enforceable. Because the performing party has received no consideration for the promise to call off the original bargain, additional consideration will be necessary.

To illustrate: Suppose Alberto's Food Company contracts to buy forty truckloads of oranges from Citrus Products, Inc. Later, representatives of Alberto's and Citrus get together and decide to call off the deal or rescind the original contract. This agreement is enforceable since neither party has yet performed. The consideration that Citrus receives for calling off the deal is freedom from performing what

---

11. See UCC 1-204.

12. UCC 2-209(2)(4).

it was legally bound to perform under the contract—that is, not having to deliver the forty truckloads of oranges. The consideration Alberto's receives for calling off the deal is not having to pay for the oranges, an obligation it otherwise had to honor.

On the other hand, if Citrus had already delivered the oranges, an agreement to call off the deal would not normally be enforceable. In this case, Citrus would receive no consideration for its promise to call off the deal.

In sum, contracts that are *executory* on *both* sides (contracts where neither party has performed) can be rescinded solely by agreement.[13] But contracts that are *executed on one side* (contracts where one party has performed) can be rescinded only if the party who has performed receives consideration for the promise to call off the deal.

Discharge by Novation or Substituted Agreement

The process of **novation** substitutes a new party for one of the original parties. Essentially, the parties to the original contract and one or more new parties all get together and agree to substitute the new party for one of the original parties. The requirements of a novation are:

1. A previous valid obligation.
2. An agreement of all the parties to a new contract.
3. The extinguishment of the old obligation (discharge of the prior party).
4. A new contract that is valid.

Suppose Union Carbide Corporation contracts to sell its petrochemical business in Europe, Bakelite Xylonite, Ltd., to British Petroleum Company for 200 million dollars. Before the transfer is completed, British Petroleum learns from its financial experts that this acquisition is not in its best interests at this time. British Petroleum has known for sometime that BP Chemicals has a strong interest in acquiring

Bakelite to expand its European market. British Petroleum wants to substitute BP Chemicals as purchaser of Bakelite. In order to accomplish this, the parties agree to a novation. Union Carbide, British Petroleum, and BP Chemicals all get together and agree that BP Chemicals will buy the Bakelite Xylonite stock from Union Carbide. As long as the new contract is supported by consideration, the novation will discharge the original contract (between Union Carbide and British Petroleum) and replace it with the new contract (between Union Carbide and BP Chemicals).

A *substituted* agreement is a new contract between the same parties that expressly or impliedly revokes and discharges a prior contract.[14] The parties involved may simply want a new agreement with somewhat different terms. So they expressly state in a new contract that the old contract is now discharged. They can also make the new contract without expressly stating that the old contract is discharged. If the parties do not expressly discharge the old contract, it will be *impliedly* discharged due to the change or different terms of the new contract.

For example, suppose Triangle Pacific Corp. contracts to sell its lumber manufacturing facilities in Slocan, British Columbia, to a Canadian investor group for $7.9 million in cash and $800,000 in five-year subordinated debentures. Before the sale is closed, however, Triangle Pacific Corp. decides that it wants $6.9 million in cash and $1.8 million in five-year subordinated debentures. The Canadian investor group agrees, and the parties draw up a new contract with these terms of sale. If the second agreement states, "Our previous contract to accept payment of $7.9 million in cash, balance in five-year subordinated debentures is hereby revoked," the original contract will be expressly discharged by substitution. If the second agreement does not state this, the original contract will nevertheless be discharged by implication. Triangle Pacific Corp. cannot sell the same lumber manufacturing facilities under two different terms of payment. Since the terms are inconsistent, a court will enforce the terms that were decided upon most recently. In this case, the sale would be for

---

13. Certain sales made to consumers at their homes can be rescinded by the consumer within three days for no reason at all. This three-day "cooling-off" period is designed to aid consumers who are susceptible to high-pressure door-to-door sales tactics. See Chapter 46 and 15 USC, Section 1635(a).

14. It is this immediate discharge of the prior contract that distinguishes a substituted contract from accord and satisfaction, discussed in the next section.

$6.9 million in cash and $1.8 million in five-year subordinated debentures.

A *compromise*, or settlement agreement, that arises out of a bona fide dispute over the obligations under an existing contract will be recognized at law. Such an agreement will be substituted as a new contract, and it will either expressly or impliedly revoke and discharge the obligations under any prior contract.

Discharge by Accord and Satisfaction

For a contract to be discharged by *accord* and *satisfaction*, the parties must agree to accept performance different from the performance originally promised. An *accord* is defined as an executory contract (that is, one that has not yet been performed) to perform some act to satisfy an existing contractual duty.[15] The duty is not yet discharged. A *satisfaction* is the performance of the accord agreement. An **accord** *and* its **satisfaction** (performance) discharge the original contractual obligation.

Once the accord has been made, the original obligation is merely suspended unless the accord agreement is breached. Thus the obligor can discharge the obligation by performance of the obligation agreed to in the accord. Likewise, if the obligor refuses to perform the accord, the obligee can bring action on the original obligation or seek a decree for specific performance on the accord.

To illustrate, Matthews obtains a judgment against Brown for $3,000. Later both parties agree that the judgment can be satisfied by Brown's transfer of her automobile to Matthews. This agreement to accept the automobile in lieu of $3,000 in cash is the accord. If Brown transfers her automobile to Matthews, the accord agreement has been fully performed and the $3,000 debt is discharged. If Brown refuses to transfer her car, the accord has been breached. Since the original obligation is merely suspended, Matthews can bring action to enforce the judgement for $3,000 in cash or, in most states, obtain a decree for specific performance for the transfer of the automobile and the discharge of the debt.

As pointed out in Chapter 9 on consideration, acceptance by a creditor of a debtor's payment on a disputed or unliquidated debt operates as both accord and satisfaction of the debt claim of the creditor, resulting in a discharge.

---

15. Restatement, Second, Contracts, Section 281.

DISCHARGE BY OPERATION OF LAW

Alteration of the Contract

In order to discourage parties from altering written contracts, the law operates to allow an innocent party to be discharged when the other party has materially altered a written contract without consent. For example, contract terms such as quantity or price might be changed without the knowledge or consent of all parties. If so, the party who was unaware of the change can treat the contract as discharged or terminated.[16]

Statutes of Limitations

Statutes of limitations limit the period of time during which a party can sue on a particular cause of action. A cause of action is the basis or reason for suing or bringing an action. After the applicable limitations period has passed, suit can no longer be brought in a court of law or equity.

For example, the limitations period for oral contracts is usually two to three years; for written contracts, four to five years; for recovery of judgments, ten to twenty years, depending on state law.

Section 2-725 of the UCC deals with the statute of limitations applicable to contracts for the sale of goods. The UCC does not distinguish between oral and written contracts. Section 2-725 provides that an action for the breach of any contract for sale must be commenced within four years after the cause of that action has occurred. The cause of action starts to accrue when the breach occurs, regardless of the aggrieved party's lack of knowledge of the breach. By original agreement, the parties can reduce this four-year period to a one-year period. They cannot, however, extend the statute beyond the four-year limitation period.

Technically, the running of a statute of limitations bars access only to *judicial* remedies; it does not extinguish the debt or the underlying obligation. The statute precludes access to the courts for col-

---

16. The contract is voidable and the innocent party can also treat the contract as in effect, either on the original terms or on the terms as altered. A buyer who discovers that a seller altered the quantity of goods in a sales contract from 100 to 1,000 by secretly inserting a zero can purchase either 100 or 1,000 of the items.

lection. But if the party who owes the debt or obligation agrees to perform (that is, makes a new promise to perform), the cause of action barred by the statute of limitations will be revived. For the old agreement to be revived by a new promise in this manner, many states require that the promise be in writing or that there be evidence of partial performance.

For example, suppose Burlington Northern Railroad contracts for sixty-three new miles of track to be laid between Dalhart and Amarillo, Texas. Martin Marietta Corp. supplies four tons of cast iron railway for the project and is paid $22,000 of the $30,000 purchase price. Texas's statute of limitations for collection of this debt is five years, but Martin Marietta Corp. fails to collect the debt or sue for collection during that five-year period after delivery of the iron. Therefore, Martin Marietta Corp. can no longer sue. It is barred by the statute of limitations. But if Burlington Northern Railroad agrees, in writing, to pay the remaining $8,000, or if it actually pays part of the $8,000, Marietta Corp. can again sue to collect the full debt. The statute of limitations is no longer a bar, and the cause of action for recovery of the full debt is revived.

Bankruptcy

A discharge in bankruptcy will ordinarily bar enforcement of a debtor's contract by the creditor. (Bankruptcy is fully discussed in Chapter 31.) Bankruptcy can be entered into voluntarily or involuntarily.[17] A proceeding in bankruptcy attempts to allocate the assets the debtor owns at bankruptcy to the creditors in a fair and equitable fashion. Once the assets are allocated, the debtor receives a **discharge in bankruptcy**. Partial payment of a debt barred *after* discharge in bankruptcy will not revive the debt.

ANTICIPATORY BREACH

Duties of the nonbreaching party can be discharged by *anticipatory repudiation* of the contract by the other party. This type of repudiation constitutes a material breach.

Before either party to a contract has a duty to perform, one of the parties may refuse to perform his or her contractual obligations. This is called **anticipatory breach,** or **repudiation.**[18] For example, De La Tour made a contract with Hochester in March to employ Hochester as a courier for three months—June, July, and August. On April 1, De La Tour told Hochester, "I am going abroad this summer and will not need a courier." This is an anticipatory breach of the employment contract. Since De La Tour repudiated the contract, Hochester *could* treat the act as a present, material breach. Furthermore, he could sue to recover damages *immediately*, without having to wait until June 1 to sue.[19]

There are two reasons for treating an anticipatory breach as a present, material breach:

1. The nonbreaching party should not be required to remain ready and willing to perform when the other party has already repudiated the contract.
2. The nonbreaching party should have the opportunity to seek a similar contract elsewhere.

Thus, Hochester should not be required to remain ready to serve as De La Tour's courier until June 1 since that would be a waste of time. In the meantime, Hochester could be working elsewhere.

It is important to note that until the nonbreaching party treats this early repudiation as a breach, the breaching party can retract his or her anticipatory repudiation by proper notice and restore the parties to their original obligations.[20]

Quite often an anticipatory breach occurs when a sharp fluctuation in market prices causes the contract, if performed, to be extremely unfavorable to one of the parties. For example, Martin Corporation contracts to manufacture and sell 100,000 personal computers to Com-age, a retailer of computer equipment who has 500 outlet stores. Delivery is to be made six months from the date of the contract. The contract price is based upon the seller's present costs

---

17. A Chapter 13 case can be initiated only by a debtor's filing of a voluntary petition.

18. Restatement, Second, Contracts, Section 253, and UCC 2-610.

19. The doctrine of anticipatory breach first arose in the landmark case of Hochester v. De La Tour, 2 Ellis and Blackburn Reports 678 (1853) when the English court recognized the delay and expense inherent in a rule requiring a nonbreaching party to wait until the time for performance to sue on an anticipatory breach.

20. See UCC 2-611.

of acquiring inventory parts purchased from others. One month later three inventory suppliers raise their prices to Martin. Based on these prices, if Martin manufactures and sells the personal computers to Com-age at the contract price, Martin stands to lose $500,000. Martin immediately writes Com-age that Martin cannot deliver the 100,000 at the contract price. Even though you feel sorry for Martin, Martin's letter is an anticipatory repudiation of the contract, allowing Com-age the option to treat the repudiation as a material breach and to proceed immediately to pursue remedies, even though the actual contract delivery date is still five months away.[21]

DISCHARGE BY IMPOSSIBILITY OF PERFORMANCE

After a contract has been made, performance may become impossible in an objective sense. This is known as **impossibility of performance** and may discharge a contract.[22] This *objective impossibility* ("It can't be done") must be distinguished from *subjective impossibility* ("I can't do it"). Examples of subjective impossibility include contracts in which goods cannot be delivered on time because of freight car shortages[23] and contracts in which money cannot be paid on time because the bank is closed.[24] In effect, the party in these cases is saying "It is impossible for *me* to perform," not "It is impossible for anyone to perform." Accordingly, such excuses will not discharge a contract, and the nonperforming party will normally be held in breach of contract.

Objective Impossibility

Four basic types of situations generally qualify under the objective impossibility of performance rules that discharge contractual obligations:

1. Where one of the parties to a personal contract *dies or becomes incapacitated prior* to performance.[25]

2. Where the *specific* subject matter of the contract is destroyed.[26]
3. Where a change in *law* renders performance illegal.[27]
4. Where performance becomes *commercially impracticable*.[28]

To illustrate the first type of impossibility, suppose Jane, a famous actress, contracts to play the leading role in a movie. Before the picture starts, she becomes ill and dies. Her personal performance was essential to the completion of the contract. Thus her death discharges the contract and her estate's liability for her nonperformance.

The second type of impossibility can occur when, for example, Pappagoras contracts to sell 10,000 bushels of apples to be harvested "from his Green Valley apple orchard in the state of Washington." Volcanic ash from Mount St. Helens destroys his apples. Because the contracted apples were to come specifically from his Green Valley orchard, his performance has been rendered impossible by the eruption of Mount St. Helens. Thus this contract is discharged.

Another example of the second type of impossibility is a contract to lease a building where the building is destroyed by fire, or a contract to sell oil from a particular well where the well goes dry.

Examples of the third type include a contract to loan money at 20 percent where the usury rate is changed to make loans in excess of 12 percent illegal, or a contract to build an apartment building where the zoning laws are changed to prohibit the construction of residential rental property. Both changes render the contracts impossible to perform.

The fourth type of impossibility is the result of a growing trend to allow parties to discharge contracts in which the performance that was originally contemplated turns out to be more difficult or more expensive than anticipated. This is known as the doctrine of commercial impracticability. In order for someone to successfully invoke this doctrine, the anticipated performance must become extremely difficult or costly.

---

21. See Reliance Cooperage Corp. v. Treat, 195 F.2d 977 (8th Cir. 1952) as a further illustration.
22. Restatement. Second, Contracts, Section 261.
23. Minneapolis v. Republic Creosoting Co., 161 Minn. 178, 201 N.W. 414 (1924).
24. Ingham Lumber Co. v. Ingersoll & Co., 93 Ark. 447, 125 S.W. 139 (1910).
25. Restatement, Second, Contracts, Section 262.

---

26. Restatement, Second, Contracts, Section 263.
27. Restatement, Second, Contracts, Section 264.
28. Restatement, Second, Contracts, Sections 265 and 266, and UCC 2–615.

To illustrate, the California Supreme Court held that a contract was discharged because it would cost ten times more than the original estimate to excavate a certain amount of gravel.[29] In another case, commercial impracticability was not found where a carrier of goods was to deliver wheat from the West Coast of the United States to a safe port in Iran.[30] The Suez Canal, the usual route, was nationalized by Egypt and closed, forcing the carrier to travel around Africa and the Cape of Good Hope, through the Mediterranean and on to Iran. The added expense was approximately $42,000 above and beyond the contract price of $306,000, and the original journey of 10,000 miles was extended by an additional 3,000 miles. Nevertheless, the court held that the contract was not commercially impracticable to perform because the closing of the Suez Canal was foreseeable. Therefore, caution should be used in invoking commercial impracticability. The added burden of performing must be *extreme* and, more importantly, must *not* be within the cognizance of the parties when the contract was made.

The following case illustrates objective impossibility where the plaintiff could not continue to take dance lessons under a contract due to a serious automobile accident injury.

---

29. Mineral Park Land Co. v. Howard, 172 Cal. 289, 156 P. 458 (1916).
30. Transatlantic Financing Corp. v. United States, 363 F.2d 312 (D.C. Cir. 1966).

PARKER v. ARTHUR MURRAY, INC.

Appellate Court of Illinois, Second Division, First District, 1973.

10 Ill.App.3d 1000, 295 N.E.2d 487.

BACKGROUND AND FACTS *In November 1959, the plaintiff, Parker, went to the Arthur Murray Dance Studio to redeem a certificate entitling him to three free dance lessons. At the time, Parker was a thirty-seven-year-old college-educated bachelor who lived alone in a one-room attic apartment. During the free lessons, the instructor told Parker that he had exceptional potential to become an accomplished dancer and generally encouraged him to take more lessons. Parker signed a contract for seventy-five hours of lessons at a cost of $1,000. At the bottom of the contract, "NON-CANCELLABLE NEGOTIABLE CONTRACT" was printed in boldface type.*

Parker attended lessons regularly. He was praised and encouraged by the instructors despite his lack of progress. Contract extensions and new contracts for additional instructional hours were executed. Each contract and each extension contained the same boldface words: "NON-CANCELLABLE CONTRACT." Some of the agreements contained the statement, "I UNDERSTAND THAT NO REFUNDS WILL BE MADE UNDER THE TERMS OF THIS CONTRACT," also in boldface.

On September 24, 1961, Parker was seriously injured in an automobile collision. The accident rendered him incapable of continuing his dance lessons. By that time, he had contracted for a total of 2,734 hours of lessons for which he had paid $24,812.80. Despite repeated written demand, the defendants, the Arthur Murray Dance Studio, refused to return any of Parker's money. This lawsuit ensued.

STAMOS, Presiding Justice.

The sole issue raised by defendants is whether the terms of the contracts barred plaintiff from asserting the doctrine of impossibility of performance as the basis for seeking rescission.

* * * *

Plaintiff was granted rescission [by the trial court] on the ground of impossibility of performance. The applicable legal doctrine is expressed in the Restatement of Contracts, § 459, as follows:

A duty that requires for its performance action that can be rendered only by the promisor or some other particular person is discharged by his death or by such illness as makes the necessary action by him impossible or seriously injurious to his health, unless the contract indicates a contrary intention or there is contributing fault on the part of the person subject to the duty.

Similarly, § 460 of the Restatement states:

(1) Where the existence of a specific thing or person is, either by the terms of a bargain or in the contemplation of both parties, necessary for the performance of a promise in the bargain, a duty to perform the promise . . . (b) is discharged if the thing or person subsequently is not in existence in time for seasonable performance, unless a contrary intention is manifested, or the contributing fault of the promisor causes the nonexistence.

In Illinois impossibility of performance was recognized as a ground for rescission in Davies v. Arthur Murray, Inc., 124 Ill.App.2d 141, 260 N.E.2d 240, wherein the court nonetheless found for the defendant because of the plaintiff's failure adequately to prove the existence of an incapacitating disability.

Defendants do not deny that the doctrine of impossibility of performance is generally applicable to the case at bar. Rather they assert that certain contract provisions bring this case within the Restatement's limitation that the doctrine is inapplicable if "the contract indicates a contrary intention." It is contended that such bold type phrases as "NON-CANCELLABLE CONTRACT," "NON-CANCELLABLE NEGOTIABLE CONTRACT" and "I UNDERSTAND THAT NO REFUNDS WILL BE MADE UNDER THE TERMS OF THIS CONTRACT" manifested the parties mutual intent to waive their respective rights to invoke the doctrine of impossibility. This is a construction which we find unacceptable. Courts engage in the construction and interpretation of contracts with the sole aim of determining the intention of the parties. We need rely on no construction aids to conclude that plaintiff never contemplated that by signing a contract with such terms as "NON-CANCELLABLE" and "NO REFUNDS" he was waiving a remedy expressly recognized by Illinois courts. Were we also to refer to established tenets of contractual construction, this conclusion would be equally compelled. An ambiguous contract will be construed most strongly against the party who drafted it. Exceptions or reservations in a contract will, in case of doubt or ambiguity, be construed least favorably to the party claiming the benefit of the exceptions or reservations. Although neither party to a contract should be relieved from performance on the ground that good business judgment was lacking, a court will not place upon language a ridiculous construction. We conclude that plaintiff did not waive his right to assert the doctrine of impossibility.

Defendants have also contended, albeit indirectly, that plaintiff failed to establish the existence of an incapacitating disability. In contrast to Davies v. Arthur Murray, Inc., *supra*, wherein the plaintiff relied solely upon his own uncorroborated testimony, plaintiff in the case at bar produced both lay witnesses and expert medical testimony corroborating the severity and permanency of his injuries. That testimony need not be recited; suffice it to say that overwhelming evidence supported plaintiff's contention that he was incapable of continuing his lessons.

The trial court's ruling that impossibility of performance was grounds for rescission was upheld. Parker was entitled to recover the prepaid sums of money representing unused lessons.

DECISION AND REMEDY

A closely allied theory is the doctrine of frustration of purpose. In principle, a contract will be discharged if supervening circumstances make it impossible to attain the purpose both parties had in mind when making the contract. The origins of the doctrine lie in the old English "coronation cases." A coronation procession was planned for Edward VII when he became king of England following the death of his mother, Queen Victoria. Hotel rooms along the coronation route were rented at exorbitant prices for that day. When the king became ill and the procession was cancelled, the purpose of the room contracts

COMMENTS

was "frustrated." A flurry of lawsuits resulted. Hotel and building owners sought to enforce the room rent bills against would-be parade observers, and would-be parade observers sought to be reimbursed for rental monies paid in advance on the rooms. It was from this situation that the court developed its theory of recovery known as frustration of purpose.

Temporary Impossibility

An occurrence or event that makes it temporarily impossible to perform the act for which a party has contracted will operate to *suspend* performance until the impossibility ceases. Then, ordinarily, the parties must perform the contract as originally planned. However, if the lapse of time and the change in circumstances surrounding the contract make it substantially more burdensome to perform the promised acts, the parties will be discharged.

The leading case on this subject, *Autry v. Republic Productions*,[31] involved an actor who was drafted into the army in 1942. Being drafted rendered his contract temporarily impossible to perform, and it was suspended until the end of the war. When the actor got out of the army, the value of the dollar had so changed that performance of the contract would have been substantially burdensome for him. Therefore, the contract was discharged.

31. 30 Cal.2d 144, 180 P.2d 888 (1947).

CONCEPT SUMMARY: Discharge of Contracts	
METHOD	**TYPES AND BASIC RULES**
Discharge by action of the parties	1. Performance—Complete or substantial (if terms are construed as promises). 2. Breach—Material nonperformance discharges the nonbreaching party's performance. 3. Mutual Rescission—An enforceable agreement to restore parties to their precontract positions. 4. Novation—By valid contract; a new party is substituted for an original party thereby terminating the old contract. 5. Accord and Satisfaction—An agreement whereby the original contract can be discharged by a different performance.

Discharge by operation of the law	1. Alteration—An innocent party is discharged by material alteration without consent.
	 2. Bankruptcy—The decree discharges most of the debtor's contractual obligations.
	 3. Statute of Limitations—The plaintiff's delay in filing suit bars availability of judicial remedies, thus discharging the defendant's legal liability.
	 4. Rendition of Judgment—A contractual duty is merged by court into a judgment discharging the contract.
	 5. Objective Impossibility of Performance—
	   a. Death or incapacity of a person whose performance is essential to completion of the contract.
	   b. The specific subject matter of the contract is destroyed prior to transfer.
	   c. Performance is declared illegal.
	   d. Performance becomes commercially impracticable.

QUESTIONS AND CASE PROBLEMS

1. The Rosenbergs own a real estate lot, and they contract with Faithful Construction, Inc., to build a house thereon for $60,000. The specifications list "all plumbing bowls and fixtures . . . to be Crane brand." The Rosenbergs leave on vacation, and during their absence Faithful is unable to buy and install Crane plumbing fixtures. Instead, Faithful installs Kohler brand fixtures, an equivalent in the industry. Upon completion of the building contract, the Rosenbergs, on inspection, discover the substitute and refuse to accept the house, claiming Faithful had breached the conditions set forth in the specifications. Discuss fully the Rosenbergs' claim.

2. Junior owes creditor Carlton $1,000, which is due and payable on June 1. Junior has been in a car accident, missed a great deal of work, and consequently will not have the money on June 1. Junior's father, Fred, offers to pay Carlton $1,100 in four equal installments if Carlton will discharge Junior from any further liability on the debt. Carlton accepts. Discuss the following:

    (a) Is the transaction a novation, or is it accord and satisfaction? Explain.

    (b) Does the contract between Fred and Carlton have to be in writing to be enforceable? (Review the Statute of Frauds.) Explain.

3. ABC Clothiers, Inc., has a contract with retailer Taylor & Sons to deliver 1,000 summer suits to Taylor's place of business on or before *May 1*. On *April 1*, Taylor senior receives a letter from ABC informing him that ABC will not be able to make the delivery as scheduled. Taylor is very upset, as he had planned a big ad sale campaign. He wants to file suit against ABC immediately (April 2). Taylor's son, Tom, tells his father that a suit is not proper until ABC actually fails to deliver the suits on May 1. Discuss fully who is correct, Taylor or his son Tom?

4. The following events take place after the formation of the contracts. Discuss which of these contracts are now discharged by virtue of the events rendering the contracts impossible of performance.

    (a) Jimenez, a famous singer, contracts to perform in your nightclub. He dies prior to performance.

    (b) Raglione contracts to sell you her land. Just before title is to be transferred, she dies.

    (c) Oppenheim contracts to sell you 1,000 bushels of apples from her orchard in the state of Washington. Because of a severe frost, she is unable to deliver the apples.

    (d) Maxwell contracts to lease a service station for ten years. His principal income is from the sale of gasoline. Due to an oil embargo by foreign oil nations, gasoline is rationed, cutting sharply into Maxwell's gasoline sales. He cannot make his lease payments.

5. Murphy contracts to purchase from Lone Star Liquors six cases of French champagne for $1,200. The contract states that delivery is to be made at the Murphy residence "on or before June 1, to be used for daughter's wedding reception on June 2." The champagne is carried regularly in Lone Star's stock. On June 1, Lone Star's delivery van is involved in an accident, and the champagne is not delivered that day. On the morning of June 2, Murphy discovers the nondelivery. Unable to reach Lone Star because its line is busy, Murphy purchases the champagne from another dealer. That afternoon, just before the wedding reception, Lone Star tenders delivery of the champagne at Murphy's residence. Murphy refuses tender, and Lone Star sues for breach of contract. Discuss fully the result.

6. In 1972 Allyn & Bacon, publishers, contracted with two authors, Goldman and Traschen, to produce a second edition of their drama anthology. After the authors had selected the plays, obtained copyright consents, and completed the editorial comment, they received two letters from Allyn & Bacon discouraging them from going forward with the revision. The first letter stated that the company was phasing out its English department and urged the authors to consider submitting their work to another publisher. The second letter advised them that there would be little funding for promotion or advertising of the book. It stated that "from a business and financial standpoint, we are simply not in a position to launch your revision."

Goldman and Traschen, alleging anticipatory repudiation, sued for breach of contract. Will their claim succeed? Alternatively, could they recover for their own substantial performance of the contract? [Goldman v. Allyn & Bacon, Inc., 482 F. Supp. 963 (D.C. Mass. 1979)]

7. John Agosta and his brother Salvatore had formed a corporation, but disagreements between the two brothers caused John to petition for voluntary dissolution of the corporation. The dissolution agreement was based upon the total assets of the corporation, which included a warehouse and inventory, being split between the brothers by Salvatore selling his stock to John for $500,000. This agreement was approved but shortly before the payment was made, a fire totally destroyed the warehouse and inventory which was the major asset of the corporation. John refused to pay Salvatore the $500,000 and Salvatore brought suit for breach of contract. Discuss whether the subsequent fire destroying the major assets of the corporation affect John's required performance. [In the Matter of Fontana v. D'ORO Foods Inc., 472 N.Y.S.2d 528 (Sup. 1983)]

8. Zilg is author of *DuPont: Behind the Nylon Curtain*, a historical account of the DuPont family in America's social, political, and economic affairs. Prentice-Hall signed

Zilg to a contract to exclusively publish the book. There was no provision to have Prentice-Hall use its best efforts to promote the book, but rather it was left up to the publisher to use its discretion as to the number of volumes printed and the level of promotion. Prentice-Hall printed 13,000 volumes, authorized an advertising budget of $5,500, distributed over 600 copies to reviewers, and purchased ads in major newspapers. Zilg claims that Prentice-Hall cut its first printing by 5,000 copies and its advertising budget by $9,500, and these cuts were evidence that Prentice-Hall had not made a "best effort" to fully promote the book. Prentice-Hall claimed that its reduction came after careful review and was based on sound and valid business decisions. Based on these facts only, discuss whether Prentice-Hall has fulfilled its contractual duty to Zilg. [Zilg v. Prentice-Hall, Inc., 717 F.2d 671 (2d Cir. 1983)]

9. Nicholson hired Howard Construction Company to build a building for use as a bridal salon. At the time, Nicholson had arranged that Honey's International would be the tenant. Once built, the building would be suitable only for a bridal salon. After Nicholson and Howard had entered into their contract but before construction had begun, Honey's International went bankrupt. Nicholson thereafter refused to pay Howard to go through with the contract since Nicholson's intended tenant was no longer in existence. Howard sues Nicholson for breach of contract. Can Howard recover? [Howard v. Nicholson, 556 S.W.2d 477 (Mo.App. 1977)]

10. In March of 1980, Friedman/Meyer, motion picture producers, entered into an agreement with I.F.I. in which I.F.I. agreed to provide partial financing for a proposed motion picture called "Brenda Star." Because Friedman and Meyer were being investigated by a federal grand jury, a separate letter agreement provided that should either Friedman or Meyer be indicted, I.F.I. would assume all of Friedman/Meyer's rights and functions to the film. In September of 1980 Friedman/Meyer entered into an employment contract with Victor Kemper to serve as Director of Photography on the film. Kemper was to be paid whether the film went forward or not. In November of 1980, the grand jury returned an indictment against both Friedman and Meyer. I.F.I. took over the film, and Kemper was never paid. Kemper sued Friedman/Meyer for the salary he never received. Friedman/Meyer claimed that I.F.I.'s taking control of the film was a novation and that the contract with Kemper was frustrated and rendered their performance impossible. Discuss fully their contentions. [VJK Productions, Inc. v. Friedman/Meyer Productions, Inc., 565 F.Supp. 916 (S.D.N.Y. 1983)]

16

CONTRACTS
Breach of Contract and Remedies

Whenever a party fails to perform part or all of the duties under a contract, that party is in *breach of contract*. Breach of contract is the failure to perform what a party is under an absolute duty to perform.[1] Once a party fails to perform or performs inadequately, the other party—the nonbreaching party—can choose one or more of several remedies. A *remedy* is the relief provided for an innocent party when the other party has breached the contract. It is the means employed to enforce a right or to redress an injury. Strictly speaking, the "remedy" is not a part of a lawsuit, but the result thereof, the object for which the lawsuit is presented and the end to which all litigation is directed. The most common remedies available to a nonbreaching party include:

1. Damages.
2. Rescission and restitution.
3. Specific performance.
4. Reformation.

DAMAGES

A breach of any contract entitles the nonbreaching party to sue for money damages. *Damages* are de-

signed to compensate the nonbreaching party for the loss of the bargain. When a party loses the benefit of the bargain or contract, the breaching party must make up this loss to the nonbreaching party. Often, courts say that innocent parties are to be placed in the position they would have occupied had the contract been fully performed.[2]

Types of Damages

There are four broad categories of damages that will be discussed in this chapter. They are:

1. Compensatory.
2. Consequential.
3. Punitive.
4. Nominal.

Compensatory Damages Damages compensating the nonbreaching party for the *loss* of the bargain are known as **compensatory damages.** These damages compensate the injured party only for injuries actually sustained and proved to have arisen directly from the loss of the bargain due to the breach of contract. They simply replace the loss caused by the

---

1. Restatement, Second, Contracts, Section 235(2).

2. Restatement, Second, Contracts, Section 347, and UCC 1-106(1).

wrong or injury. In a breach of contract, compensatory damages are usually the only damages recoverable. To illustrate: Wilcox contracts to perform certain services exclusively for Hernandez during the month of March for $2,000. Hernandez cancels the contract and is in breach. Wilcox is able to find another job during the month of March, but can only earn $500. He can sue Hernandez for breach and recover $1,500 as compensatory damages.

The measurement of compensatory damages varies by type of contract. Certain types of contracts deserve special mention. They are contracts for the sale of goods, land contracts, and construction contracts.

Sale of Goods   In a contract for the sale of goods, the usual measure of compensatory damages is an amount equal to the difference between the contract price and the market price.[3] Suppose Chrysler Corporation contracts to buy ten model UTS 400 computer terminals from Sperry Rand Corporation for $8,000 apiece. If Sperry Rand fails to deliver the ten terminals, and the current market price of the terminals is $8,150, Chrysler's measure of damages in this case is $1,500 (ten times $150).

Sale of Land   The measure of damages in a contract for the sale of land is ordinarily the same as the measure in contracts for the sale of goods—that is, the difference between the contract price and the market price of the land. The majority of states follow this rule regardless of whether it is the buyer or the seller who breaches the contract. A minority of states, however, follow a different rule when the seller breaches the contract and the breach is not deliberate.[4] In such a case, these states allow the prospective purchaser to recover any down payment plus any expenses incurred (such as fees for title searches, attorneys, and escrows). This minority rule effectively places purchasers in the position they occupied prior to the sale.

Construction Contracts   The measure of damages in a building or construction contract varies depending upon which party breaches and at what stage the breach occurs. The owner can breach at three different stages of the construction:

1.   Before performance begins.
2.   During performance.
3.   After performance is complete.

If the owner breaches *before performance begins*, the contractor can recover only the profits that would have been made on the contract (that is, the total contract price less the cost of materials and labor). To illustrate: Goodyear Tire & Rubber Co. wants to build an international research center at its industrial and film products plant in Craigavon, Northern Ireland. Goodyear makes a contract for the 54,000-square-foot center with your corporation. The contract price is $5 million, and your company plans to spend $4.3 million in materials and labor. However, before construction begins, Goodyear's president calls you and unequivocally repudiates the contract. Your measure of damages is $700,000.

If the owner breaches *after performance begins*, the contractor can recover the profits plus the costs incurred in partially constructing the building. Assume you begin work on the research center, but after you spend $1.2 million, Goodyear throws your crews off the land and refuses to allow any more construction to go on. Your measure of damages is $1.9 million ($700,000 of lost profit plus $1.2 million in costs).

If the owner breaches *after the construction is complete*, the contractor can recover the entire contract price.[5] Assume you are able to complete the research center, but Goodyear breaches the contract by refusing to pay. Your measure of damages is $5 million (the full contract price).

When the *construction contractor breaches the contract* by stopping halfway through the project, the measure of damages is the cost of completion. If the contractor substantially performs, the courts may use the cost of completion formula, but only

---

3.   At the time and place where the goods were to be delivered or tendered. See UCC 2-708 and UCC 2-713.

4.   A deliberate breach includes the vendor's failure to convey the land because the market price has gone up. A nondeliberate breach includes the vendor's failure to convey the land because an unknown easement rendered title unmarketable. See Chapter 53.

---

5.   Actually, this is true for most contracts; the nonbreaching party is normally owed the contract profit plus the cost of performance.

if there is no substantial economic waste in requiring completion.[6] If the contractor finishes late, the measure of damages will be the *loss of use*. As examples, assume three situations:

1. The builder of a house quits working after the foundation is built.
2. The builder of a house completes the construction, but the paneling is one-quarter-inch thick instead of five-sixteenths-inch thick.
3. The builder completes the house one week late.

In situation 1, the measure of damages equals the cost of getting another builder to complete the house. In situation 2, the cost to complete the house in-

---

6.   Economic waste occurs when the cost of additional resources to finish the project exceeds any conceivable value placed on the additional work done. For example, if a contractor discovers that it will cost $10,000 to move a large coral rock eleven inches as specified in the contract, and the change in the rock's position will alter the appearance of the project only a trifle, full completion will involve an economic waste.

cludes the cost of tearing out the walls and installing the thicker paneling. This additional cost is economic waste and a needless expense (which the owner probably would not incur anyway), so the courts will usually give the owner the difference between the value of the house as it is and the value of the house if it had been completed as promised. If the house is worth $2,000 less because of the thinner paneling, that will be the amount of damages recoverable. In situation 3, the measure of damages is the cost incurred by the owner to live elsewhere for a week and any other costs incident to the delay.

Often, the party suing for compensatory damages has failed to perform completely his or her part of the bargain. Faced with this situation in the following case, two courts arrived at the same figure for damages but used different theories. The trial court used the theory of *substantial performance*; the appellate court insisted that the proper action was *quantum meruit* (recovery of fair value). In either event, a contractor who did not live up to the requirements of his contract was not entitled to full payment of the contract price.

BACKGROUND AND FACTS   *Armstead Masonry Company brought this action against Roper (and Reynolds), the defendants, to collect $535.25 in damages for nonpayment of an oral contract whereby Roper agreed to pay Armstead to do some brick veneer work on Roper's house. The record showed that the parties entered into this oral contract, and Armstead expressly promised to use new brick matching as closely as possible the color and appearance of the existing brick on Roper's house. Armstead failed to use brick that conformed reasonably to Roper's existing brick work, although Armstead's veneer work was sound in all other respects.*

Since the work was completed, Armstead was entitled to a certain amount of payment on the contract. However, the trial court assessed Roper's damages at $267.63 and awarded Armstead $267.62—the contract price of $535.25 less damages of $267.63.

REYNOLDS v.
ARMSTEAD

Supreme Court of Colorado,
1968.
166 Colo. 372, 443 P.2d 990.

MOORE, Chief Justice.
*   *   *   *

This court has repeatedly held that a contractor may recover the agreed price for substantial performance of his contract, subject to a deduction for damages for the contractor's failure to adhere to the contract in minor details.

The question presented here, however, is whether as a matter of law Armstead substantially performed his contract with Roper, and therefore became entitled to a recovery on the contract. Our authorities judiciously decline to state a formula determining with mathematical certainty what constitutes substantial performance, but instead rely upon the application of general principles. Thus, in *Morris v. Hokosona,* supra, we stated:

"* * * [S]ubstantial performance permitting a recovery on the contract means an attempt in good faith to strictly and fully perform and is not satisfied unless there has been only slight or inadvertent omissions or departures which have not affected the value of the structure and which are capable of remedy and for which the employer may be compensated by a reduction of the contract price."

* * * "Substantial compliance with reference to contracts, means that although the conditions of the contract have been deviated from in trifling particulars not materially detracting from the benefit the other party would derive from a literal performance, he has received substantially the benefit he expected, and is, therefore, bound to pay."

* * * *

In the instant case the trial court, in legal effect, found that there had not been a substantial compliance with the terms of the contract, and that to the extent of fifty per cent of the contract price there was a failure to perform. Armstead's failure to install brick which reasonably matched the existing veneer damaged the appearance of Roper's house to the extent of half the value of the contract. The parties entered into their agreement with the acknowledged intent that Armstead's brickwork should be aesthetically, as well as functionally, acceptable. Consequently, we hold that as a matter of law Armstead's breach was material and cannot be deemed a "slight and trivial defect" "not materially detracting from the benefit the other party would derive from a literal performance."

Armstead's failure to substantially perform his contract deprived him of the right to recover under the "theory" of express contract.

* * * *

Upon a "theory" of quantum meruit the plaintiff, under the evidence, was entitled to the judgment entered by the trial court.

DECISION AND REMEDY *The trial court's judgment was affirmed. Armstead was entitled to collect for the work he did, but his failure to perform in compliance with the terms of his agreement with Roper resulted in a substantial reduction in the amount of money he could collect from Roper.*

Consequential (Special) Damages Foreseeable damages which result from a party's breach of contract are called *consequential damages.* They differ from compensatory damages in that they are caused by special circumstances beyond the contract itself. They flow only from the consequences or results of a breach.

For example, if a seller fails to deliver goods with knowledge that a buyer is planning to resell these goods *immediately,* consequential damages will be awarded for the loss of profit from the planned resale. The buyer will also recover compensatory damages for the difference between the contract price and the market price of the goods.

In order to recover consequential damages, the breaching party must know (or have reason to know) that special circumstances will cause the nonbreach-

ing party to suffer an additional loss. The rationale here is to give the nonbreaching party the whole benefit of the bargain, provided the breaching party knew of the special circumstances when the contract was made.

For example, Leed contracts to have a specific part shipped to her—one that she desperately needs to repair her printing press. In contracting with the shipper who is to return the part, Leed tells the shipper that she must receive it by Monday or she will not be able to print her paper and will lose $750. If the shipper is late, Leed can recover the consequential damages caused by the delay (that is, the $750 in lost profits).

Likewise, when a bank wrongfully dishonors a check, the drawer of the check (customer of the bank) may recover consequential damages (such as those resulting from slander of credit or reputation) if he or she is arrested or prosecuted.[7] Another example of consequential damages is when an ice company fails to deliver ice to keep a butcher's meat cold. The ice company can be held liable for meat spoilage if it does not deliver the ice on time.

A leading case on the necessity of giving notice of "consequential" circumstances is *Hadley v. Bax-*

---

7. Weaver v. Bank of America, 59 Cal.2d 428, 30 Cal.Rptr. 4, 380 P.2d 644 (1963). A checking account is a contractual arrangement. See UCC 4-402.

endale, decided in 1854. The case involved a broken crankshaft used in a mill operation. In the mid-1800s, it was very common for large mills, such as the one the plaintiffs operated, to have more than one crankshaft in case the main one broke and had to be repaired, as it did in this case. Also, in those days it was common knowledge that flour mills had spares. It is against this background that the parties argued whether or not the damages resulting from lost profits while the crankshaft was out for repair were "too remote" to be recoverable.

BACKGROUND AND FACTS *The plaintiffs ran a flour mill in Gloucester. The crankshaft attached to the steam engine broke, causing the mill to shut down. The shaft had to be sent to a foundry located in Greenwich so that the new shaft could be made to fit the other parts of the engine. The defendants were common carriers, who transported the shaft from Gloucester to Greenwich. The plaintiffs claimed that they had informed the defendants that the mill was stopped and that the shaft must be sent immediately. The freight charges were collected in advance, and the defendants promised to deliver the shaft the following day. They did not do so, however. As a consequence, the mill was closed for several days. The plaintiffs sued to recover their lost profits during that time. The defendants contended that the loss of profits was "too remote." The court held for the plaintiffs, and the jury was allowed to take into consideration the lost profits.*

HADLEY v. BAXENDALE
9 Exch. 341, 156 Eng.Rep. 145, 1854.

ALDERSON, B.
*   *   *   *

Now we think the proper rule in such a case as the present is this:—Where two parties have made a contract which one of them has broken, the damages which the other party ought to receive in respect of such breach of contract should be such as may fairly and reasonably be considered either arising naturally, i.e., according to the usual course of things, from such breach of contract itself, or such as may reasonably be supposed to have been in the contemplation of both parties, at the time they made the contract, as the probable result of the breach of it. Now, if the special circumstances under which the contract was actually made were communicated by the plaintiffs to the defendants, and thus known to both parties, the damages resulting from the breach of such a contract, which they would reasonably contemplate, would be the amount of injury which would ordinarily follow from a breach of contract under these special circumstances so known and communicated. But, on the other hand, if these special circumstances were wholly unknown to the party breaking the contract, he, at the most, could only be supposed to have had in his contemplation the amount of injury which would arise generally, and in the great multitude of cases not affected by any special circumstances, from such a breach of contract. For, had the special circumstances been known, the parties might have specially provided for the breach of contract by special terms as to the damages in that case; and of this advantage it would be very unjust to deprive them. Now the above principles are those by which we think the jury ought to be guided in estimating the damages arising out of any breach of contract.
*   *   *   *

Now, in the present case, if we are to apply the principles above laid down, we find that the only circumstances here communicated by the plaintiffs to the defendants at the time the contract was made, were, that the article to be carried was the broken shaft of a mill, and that the plaintiffs were the millers of that mill. But how do these circumstances show reasonably that the profits of the mill must be stopped by an unreasonable delay in the delivery of the broken shaft by the carrier to the third person? Suppose the plaintiffs had another shaft in their possession put up or putting up at the time, and that they only wished to send back the broken shaft to the engineer who made it; it is clear that this would be quite consistent with the above circumstances, and yet the unreasonable delay in the delivery would have no effect upon the intermediate profits of the mill. Or, again, suppose that, at the time of the delivery to the carrier, the machinery of the mill had been in other respects defective, then, also, the same results would follow. Here it is true that the shaft was actually sent back to serve as a model for a new one, and that the want of a new one was the only cause of the stoppage of the mill, and that the loss of profits really arose from not sending down the new shaft in proper time, and that this arose from the delay in delivering the broken one to serve as a model. But it is obvious that, in the great multitude of cases of millers sending off broken shafts to third persons by a carrier under ordinary circumstances, such consequences would not, in all probability, have occurred; and these special circumstances were here never communicated by the plaintiffs to the defendants. It follows, therefore, that the loss of profits here cannot reasonably be considered such a consequence of the breach of contract as could have been fairly and reasonably contemplated by both the parties when they made this contract.

DECISION AND REMEDY   *The Court of Exchequer ordered a new trial. According to the court, the special circumstances that caused the loss of profits had never been sufficiently communicated by the plaintiffs to the defendants. The plaintiffs would have to have given express notice of these circumstances in order to collect consequential damages.*

COMMENTS   *In awarding damages, compensation is given only for those injuries that the defendant could reasonably have foreseen as a probable result of the usual course of events following a breach. If the injury complained of is outside the usual and foreseeable cause of events, it must be shown specifically that the defendant had reason to know the facts and foresee the injury.*

Punitive Damages   Punitive, or exemplary, damages are generally not recoverable in a breach of contract action. Punitive damages are designed to punish a guilty party and to make an example of the party in order to deter similar conduct in the future. Such damages have no legitimate place in contract law since they are, in essence, penalties, and a breach of contract is not unlawful in a criminal or societal sense. A contract is simply a civil relationship between the parties. The law may compensate one party for the loss of bargain, no more and no less.

In a few situations, a person's actions can cause both a breach of contract and a tort. For example, the parties can establish by contract a certain reasonable standard or duty of care. Failure to live up to that standard is a breach of contract, and the act itself may constitute negligence.

A careful review of Chapter 4, dealing with torts, will indicate that some intentional torts could also be tied to a breach of the terms of the contract. In these cases it is possible for the nonbreaching party to recover punitive damages for the commission of the tort in addition to compensatory and consequential damages for breach of contract.

Nominal Damages   Nominal damages have been defined as those that are awarded when only a technical injury is involved and no actual damages have been suffered. In other words, when no financial loss is involved because of a breach of contract, the court may award nominal damages to the innocent party. Nominal damage awards are often trifling, such as a dollar, but they do establish that the defendant acted wrongfully. For example, suppose that Jackson contracts to buy potatoes from Stanley at 50 cents a pound. Stanley breaches the contract and does not deliver the potatoes. In the meantime, the price of potatoes has fallen. Jackson is able to buy them in the open market at half the price he contracted for with Stanley. He is clearly better off because of Stanley's breach. Thus, in a breach of contract suit, Jackson may be awarded only nominal damages for the technical injury he sustained, because no monetary loss was involved. Most law suits for nominal damages are brought as a matter of principle under the theory that a breach has occurred and some damages must be imposed regardless of actual loss.

Mitigation of Damages

In most situations, when a breach of contract occurs, the innocent injured party is held to a duty to mitigate, or reduce, the damages that he or she suffers. Under this **mitigation of damages** doctrine, whatever duty is owed depends on the nature of the contract. For example, some states require the lessor to use reasonable means to find a new tenant if the lessee abandons the premises and fails to pay rent. If an acceptable tenant becomes available, the landlord is required to lease the premises to this tenant to mitigate the damages recoverable from the former lessee. The former lessee is still liable for the difference between the amount of the rent under the original lease and the rent received from the new lessee. If the lessor had not taken the reasonable means necessary to find a new tenant, presumably a court could reduce the award made by the amount of rent he or she could have received had such reasonable means been taken.

In the majority of states, wrongfully terminated employees owe the duty to mitigate damages suffered by their employers' breach. The damages they receive are their salaries less the incomes they would have received in similar jobs that they could have obtained by reasonable means. It is the employer's burden to prove the existence of such a job and to prove that the employee could have been hired. (The employee is, of course, under no duty to take a job that is not of the same type and rank.)

Liquidated Damages versus Penalties

A **liquidated damages** provision in a contract specifies a certain amount to be paid in the event of a future default or breach of contract. For example, a provision requiring a construction contractor to pay $100 for every day he or she is late in completing the construction is a liquidated damages provision. Liquidated damages differ from penalties. **Penalties** specify a certain amount to be paid in the event of a default or breach of contract *and are designed to penalize* the breaching party. Liquidated damage provisions are enforceable; penalty provisions are not.

In order to determine if a particular provision is for liquidated damages or for a penalty, two questions must be answered. First, were the damages difficult to estimate when the contract was entered into? Second, was the amount set as damages a reasonable estimate and not excessive? [8] If both answers are yes, the provision will be enforced. If either answer is no, the provision will not be enforced.

In a construction contract, it is difficult to estimate the amount of damages caused by a delay in completing construction, so liquidated damage clauses are often used. On the other hand, the damage caused by failure to pay rent is easily estimated, so in leases, liquidated damage clauses are normally not enforced. [9]

The following case demonstrates the application of liquidated damages to a contractor who was responsible for delays in the completion of a project.

---

8.   Restatement, Second, Contracts, Section 356(1).
9.   But compare with K. W. Clarkson, R. L. Miller, and T. J. Muris, "Liquidated Damages vs. Penalty: Sense or Nonsense?" *Wisconsin Law Review*, Spring 1978.

BACKGROUND AND FACTS   *Vrgora, a general contractor, entered into a contract with the Los Angeles Unified School District (LAUSD) to construct an "automotive service shed" and to construct a specifically enclosed room outfitted with an electronic vehicle performance tester. The contract contained a price of $167,195.09, a completion time of 250 days from commencement, and a liquidated damages clause of $100 per day for late completion.*

VRGORA v. LOS ANGELES UNITED SCHOOL DISTRICT

Court of Appeal, Second District, 1984.

152 Cal. App. 3d 1178.

Vrgora began construction on January 31, 1977, with an expected com-
pletion date of July 29, 1977. Delays in the project arose when the manufacturer
of the tester did not receive approval for the tester until September 23, 1977 (a
delay of over six months). The tester arrived on November 15, 1977, but due
to a conflict over its payment, the manufacturer removed the tester. Upon
payment, the manufacturer re-delivered the tester on December 23, 1977, and
Vrgora completed the project on May 2, 1978. LAUSD assessed $20,700 as
liquidated damages against Vrgora. In a suit that followed, the trial court
determined that Vrgora was liable for the damages and Vrgora appealed.

STEPHENS, Associate Justice.

* * * *

"A judgment . . . of the lower court is presumed correct." * * * "The presumption being in favor of the judgment . . ., the court must consider the evidence in a light most favorable to the *prevailing party*, giving him the benefit of *every reasonable inference*, and *resolving conflicts* in support of the judgment." * * *

* * * *

In essence, Vrgora first argues that no justification for the liquidated damages assessment exists because the delay resulting in same is attributable to LAUSD's failure to forewarn him of anticipated difficulties in obtaining approval of the vehicle performance testing machine. More specifically, Vrgora suggests that prior to submitting his bid on the underlying contract, he was never placed on notice nor under a duty to discover whether or not he could anticipate problems in obtaining the appropriate test lab approval for the testing machine. Further, he asserts that the architect responsible for the project plans (including specific reference to the subject machine), not only knew that the machine was unapproved, but also knew that another machine of the same type suffered serious and lengthy approval problems.

* * * *

The evidence in the form of testimony and exhibits, as introduced at trial, establishes that there has never been any mystery surrounding the fact that the purpose of the contract was to construct both an edifice housing a vehicle performance tester as well as a structure to park cars to be tested or otherwise worked on. In that same vein, a portion of the contract appropriately entitled "DIVISION 11 [¶] SECTION 11D [¶] VEHICLE PERFORMANCE TESTER" clearly provides under the subheading of "EQUIPMENT" that: ". . . The vehicle performance tester shall be the Sun Road-A-Matic Model RAM 937-1, 460 Volt, 30, as manufactured by the Sun Electric Corporation. All electrical equipment shall have UL Label or City of Los Angeles Test Laboratory Label."

If anything, it appears that the foregoing proviso was such that it should have aroused, at the very minimum, the suspicions of any prospective contract bidder, that by so bidding or otherwise agreeing to the contract, that party was affirmatively undertaking to ensure the subject machine's compliance with the qualifications specified by LAUSD. Thus, appellant knew or had reason to inquire as to the exact nature of his obligations at the very inception of the contract.

* * * *

In light of the evidence outlined above, it is manifest that neither artifice nor sleight of hand nor ambiguity played any part in inducing appellant Vrgora to bid and accept the instant contract. In fact, the record makes it quite clear that Vrgora entered into the contract wholly on his own volition and that he had ample notice so as to reasonably foresee the material portions of his anticipated performance *at the formative stages of the contract*. If at all, the mistake of material or collateral fact, at which appellant

hints, must be attributed to his own neglect. Furthermore, the evidence blatantly suggests that LAUSD did not possess any "special knowledge" by which it was affirmatively obligated to cure appellant's so-called carelessness or dereliction of duty. Thus, as a matter of law, it was appellant's duty to discover the foreseeable problems affecting his performance, and any "hinted" claim of impracticability or frustration of performance which might discharge said duty is meritless.
* * * *

[Vrgora's] final argument rests with the fact that LAUSD actually used and occupied a portion of the facility prior to its completion. With this premise, appellant insists that LAUSD should not be allowed to claim full liquidated damages. Particularly, appellant maintains that "[i]f the specified daily rate is a reasonable approximation of the amount necessary to compensate [LAUSD] because [it] cannot occupy the entire building, then, presumably, it would not be a reasonable approximation as to only a portion of the building when another portion is actually occupied." Although at first blush the argument appears plausible, appellant's logic is flawed.

Under California law, liquidated damages are viable if it is established that at the formative stages of the contract that: (1) it was mutually recognized that damages from a breach would be impracticable or extremely difficult to determine with certainty; and (2) that the amount or formula stipulated by the parties represented a reasonable endeavor to ascertain what such damages might be. * * * In the context of a public construction contract, it has often been determined as a matter of law that contractor-induced damages, described as "inconvenience and loss of use by the public," are incalculable. * * * Further, this type of liquidated damages provision is legislatively presumed valid ". . . unless manifestly unreasonable under the circumstances existing at the time the contract was made." * * *

In the case at bench, it is most evident that at the formative stages of the contract damages in the event of a breach could not have been ascertained with any reasonable degree of certainty. Moreover, the per diem assessment does *not* appear manifestly unreasonable. Yet, with the use of double negatives, appellant ostensibly argues that the above authority mandates a finding that the liquidated damages formula in the contract is a reasonable approximation of the actual damages incurred by LAUSD. To hold as such, however, would thwart one of the major purposes of the allowance of liquidated damages—to provide a remedy—where damages are not easily ascertainable.
* * * *

For our purposes, we find it significant that the appellate court's award was made *notwithstanding the fact that the school district occupied and used some of the school rooms.* * * *
* * * *

Because the judgment is supported by substantial evidence in the record, an implicit finding that appellant was sufficiently on notice that the vehicle performance ·tester's laboratory approval was his contractual responsibility negates his contentions to the contrary. Likewise, substantial evidence requires that we affirm an implicit finding that appellant was the sole source of any delays and thus was obligated under the terms of the contract for the agreed liquidated damages. Finally, the fact that actual injury is uncertain militates against any "setoff" due to possible unjust enrichment of LAUSD.
* * * *

The court upheld the lower court's finding sustaining the liquidated damages to Vrgora of $20,700.

DECISION AND REMEDY

RESCISSION AND RESTITUTION

Rescission is essentially an action to undo, or cancel, a contract—to return the contracting parties to the positions they occupied prior to the transaction.[10] Where fraud, a mistake, duress, or failure of consideration are present, rescission is available.[11] The failure of one party to perform entitles the other party to rescind the contract. The rescinding party must give prompt notice to the breaching party. In order to rescind a contract, both parties must make **restitution** to each other by returning goods, property, or money previously conveyed.[12] If the goods or property received can be restored *in specie*—that is, if the actual goods or property can be returned—they must be. If the goods or property have been consumed, restitution must be made in an equivalent amount of money.

Essentially, restitution refers to the recapture of a benefit conferred on the defendant through which the defendant has been unjustly enriched. For example, Ann conveys $10,000 to Bob in return for Bob's promise to design a house for Ann. The next day Bob calls Ann and tells her that he has taken a position with a large architectural firm in another state and cannot design the house. Ann decides to hire another architect that afternoon. Ann can get restitution of the $10,000 because now an unjust benefit of $10,000 was conferred on Bob.

SPECIFIC PERFORMANCE

The equitable remedy of *specific performance* calls for the performance of the act promised in the contract. This remedy is quite attractive to the nonbreaching party since it provides the exact bargain promised in the contract. It also avoids some of the problems inherent in a suit for money damages.

(Specific performance is a rare remedy, only available in unique situations.)

There are three basic reasons for the attractiveness of the remedy of specific performance. First, the nonbreaching party need not worry about collecting the judgment.[13] Second, the nonbreaching party need not look around for another contract. Third, the actual performance is more valuable than the money damages.

Although the equitable remedy of specific performance is often preferable to other remedies, specific performance will not be granted unless the party's legal remedy (money damages) is inadequate.[14] For example, contracts for the sale of goods rarely qualify for specific performance. The legal remedy, money damages, will ordinarily be adequate in such situations because substantially identical goods can be bought or sold in the market. If the goods are unique, however, a court of equity will decree specific performance. For example, paintings, sculptures, or rare books or coins are so unique that money damages will not enable a buyer to obtain substantially identical substitutes in the market.

Sale of Land

Specific performance is granted to a buyer in a contract for the sale of land. The legal remedy for breach of a land sales contract is inadequate because every piece of land is considered to be unique. Money damages will not compensate a buyer adequately because the same land in the same location obviously cannot be obtained elsewhere.

Contracts for Personal Services

Personal service contracts require one party to work personally for another party. Courts of equity uniformly refuse to grant specific performance of personal service contracts. If the contract is not deemed personal, the remedy at law may be adequate if substantially identical service is available from other persons (for example, if you hire someone to mow your lawn). In most personal service contracts, courts

---

10. The rescission discussed here refers to *unilateral* rescission, where only one party wants to undo the contract. In mutual rescission, both parties agree to undo the contract. Mutual rescission discharges the contract; unilateral rescission is generally available as a remedy for breach of contract.
11. States often have statutes allowing consumers to rescind unilaterally contracts made at home with door-to-door salespersons. Rescission is allowed within three days for any reason or for no reason at all. See, for example, California Civil Code, Section 1689.5.
12. Restatement, Second, Contracts, Section 370.

13. Courts enter judgments as final dispositions of cases. The judgment, of course, must be collected. Collection, however, poses problems. For example, the judgment debtor may be broke or have only a very small net worth.
14. Restatement, Second, Contracts, Section 359.

are very hesitant to order specific performance by a party because public policy strongly discourages involuntary servitude.[15] Moreover, the courts do not want to have to monitor a continuing service contract.

Therefore, specific performance will be denied if it is impossible or impractical to enforce performance. Courts do not want to become entangled in personal service transactions and will not decree specific performance if supervision will be prolonged

_____

15. The Thirteenth Amendment to the United States Constitution prohibits involuntary servitude, but *negative* injunctions (that is, prohibiting rather than ordering certain conduct) are possible. Thus, whereas you may not be able to compel a person to perform under a personal service contract, you may be able to restrain that person from engaging in similar contracts for a period of time.

or difficult. For this reason, courts refuse to order specific performance that requires the exercise of personal judgment or talent. For example, if you contract with a brain surgeon to perform brain surgery on you, and the surgeon refuses to perform, the court would not compel (and you certainly would not want) the surgeon to perform under these circumstances. There is no way the court can assure meaningful performance in such a situation.[16]

In the following case, a question arose as to whether a particular variety of carrots, which became scarce, was so unique that specific performance would be an appropriate remedy.

_____

16. Similarly, courts often refuse to order specific performance of construction contracts because courts are not set up to operate as construction supervisors or engineers.

BACKGROUND AND FACTS *Campbell Soup Company made a written contract with farmer defendant, Wentz. Wentz was to deliver all the Chantenay red carrots he grew on his fifteen-acre farm that year for $30 per ton. The contract provided that only those carrots that conformed to company specifications would be accepted, but Campbell retained the right to prohibit the sale of those carrots elsewhere without consent.*

During the year, the market price of these carrots rose sharply to about $90 per ton, and Chantenay red carrots became virtually unobtainable. The defendant told a Campbell representative that he would not deliver his carrots at the contract price. Then, he sold the rest of his carrots to a neighboring farmer. Campbell bought about half the shipment from the neighboring farmer and then realized that it was purchasing its own "contract carrots." Campbell refused to purchase any more and sought an injunction against both the defendant and the neighboring farmer to prohibit them from selling any more of the contract carrots to others. In addition, Campbell sought to compel specific performance of the contract by Wentz. The trial court denied the equitable relief requested by Campbell.

CAMPBELL SOUP CO. v. WENTZ
United States Court of Appeals, Third Circuit, 1948.
172 F.2d 80.

GOODRICH, Circuit Judge.
* * * *

The trial court denied equitable relief. We agree with the result reached, but on a different ground from that relied upon by the District Court.
* * * *

We think that on the question of adequacy of the legal remedy the case is one appropriate for specific performance. It was expressly found that at the time of the trial it was "virtually impossible to obtain Chantenay carrots in the open market." This Chantenay carrot is one which the plaintiff uses in large quantities, furnishing the seed to the growers with whom it makes contracts. It was not claimed that in nutritive value it is any better than other types of carrots. Its blunt shape makes it easier to handle in processing. And its color and texture differ from other varieties. The color is brighter than other carrots. The trial court found that the plaintiff failed to establish what proportion of its carrots is used for the production of soup stock and what proportion is used as identifiable physical ingredients in its soups. We do not think lack of proof on that point is material. It did appear that the plaintiff uses carrots in fifteen of its twenty-one soups. It also appeared that it uses these Chantenay carrots diced in some of them and that the appearance is uniform. The preservation of uniformity in appearance in a food article marketed throughout the country and sold under the manufacturer's name is a matter of considerable commercial significance and one which is properly considered in determining whether a substitute ingredient is just as good as the original.

* * * *

Judged by the general standards applicable to determining the adequacy of the legal remedy we think that on this point the case is a proper one for equitable relief. There is considerable authority, old and new, showing liberality in the granting of an equitable remedy. We see no reason why a court should be reluctant to grant specific relief when it can be given without supervision of the court or other time-consuming processes against one who has deliberately broken his agreement. Here the goods of the special type contracted for were unavailable on the open market, the plaintiff had contracted for them long ahead in anticipation of its needs, and had built up a general reputation for its products as part of which reputation uniform appearance was important. We think if this were all that was involved in the case specific performance should have been granted.

* * * *

We are not suggesting that the contract is illegal. Nor are we suggesting any excuse for the grower in this case who has deliberately broken an agreement entered into with Campbell. We do think, however, that a party who has offered and succeeded in getting an agreement as tough as this one is, should not come to a chancellor and ask court help in the enforcement of its terms. That equity does not enforce unconscionable bargains is too well established to require elaborate citation.

DECISION AND REMEDY

Campbell's petition for an injunction and for specific performance was denied by the appellate court. The court ruled that the contract was unconscionable, as the terms placed undue restrictions on the small farmer to achieve a supply of a specific type of carrots for Campbell, a large corporation. The court recognized, however, that if the contract had not been unconscionable (see Chapter 11), specific performance would have been available to Campbell. The fact that these carrots were different in shape, color, and texture and that they were not available on the open market met the tests of uniqueness and the remedy for specific performance.

REFORMATION

Reformation is an equitable remedy used when the parties have *imperfectly* expressed their agreement in writing. Reformation allows the contract to be rewritten to reflect the parties' true intentions. It applies most often where fraud or mutual mistake (for example, a clerical error) are present. If Gilge contracts to buy a certain piece of land from Cav-

endish, but both parties are mistaken about what piece of land is to be sold, a mutual mistake has occurred. Accordingly, a court of equity could reform the contract so that Gilge and Cavendish can agree on which piece of land is being sold.

Two other examples deserve mention. The first involves two parties who have made a binding oral contract. They further agree to reduce the oral contract to writing, but in doing so, they make an error in stating the terms. Universally, the courts will allow into evidence the correct terms of the oral contract, thereby reforming the written contract.

The second example deals with written agreements (covenants) not to compete (see Chapter 11 on Legality). If the covenant is for a valid and legitimate purpose (such as the sale of a business) but the area or time restraints of the covenant are unreasonable, some courts will reform the restraints by making them reasonable and will enforce the entire contract as reformed. Other courts, however, will throw the entire restrictive covenant out as illegal.

RECOVERY BASED ON QUASI-CONTRACT

As stated in Chapter 7, a quasi-contract is not a true contract but an equitable theory *imposed* on the parties to obtain justice and to prevent unjust enrichment. Hence, a quasi-contract becomes an equitable basis for equitable relief. The legal obligation, or duty, arises because the law *implies* a promise to pay for benefits received by a party. Generally, when one party has conferred a benefit on another party, justice requires the party receiving the benefit to pay the reasonable value for it. The party receiving the benefit should not be unjustly enriched at the other party's expense.

Quasi-contractual recovery is useful where one party has *partially* performed under a contract that is unenforceable. It can be used as an alternative to a suit for damages and will allow the party to recover the reasonable value of the partial performance.

In order to recover on a quasi-contract, the party seeking recovery must show that:

1. A benefit has been conferred on the other party.
2. The benefit was conferred with the expectation of being paid.
3. The party seeking recovery did not act as a volunteer in conferring the benefit.
4. Retention of the benefit without being paid would result in unjust enrichment of the party receiving the benefit.

For example, suppose Abrams contracts to build two oil derricks for the Texas Gulf Sulfur Co. The derricks are to be built over a period of three years, but the parties do not make a written contract. En-

forcement of the contract will therefore be barred by the Statute of Frauds.[17] If Abrams completes one derrick before Texas Gulf Sulfur tells him that the contract is unenforceable, Abrams can sue in quasi-contract because: First, a benefit has been conferred on Texas Gulf Sulfur, since one oil derrick has been built. Second, Abrams built the derrick (conferred the benefit) expecting to be paid. Third, Abrams did not volunteer to build the derrick; he built it under an unenforceable oral contract. Fourth, allowing Texas Gulf Sulfur to retain the derrick would enrich the company unjustly. Therefore, Abrams should be able to recover the reasonable value of the oil derrick (under the theory of *quantum meruit*—"as much as he deserved"). This is ordinarily equal to the fair market value of the derrick.

ELECTION OF REMEDIES

In many cases, a nonbreaching party will have several remedies available, but they may be inconsistent with each other. Therefore, the party must choose which remedy to pursue. For example, a person who buys a fraudulently represented car can sue either to cancel (rescind) the sales contract or to recover damages. Obviously, these remedies are inconsistent. An action to rescind undoes the contract; an action for damages affirms it.

The purpose of the *election of remedies* doctrine is to prevent double recovery. Suppose McCarthy agrees to sell his land to Tally. Then McCarthy changes his mind and repudiates the contract. Tally can sue for compensatory damages or for specific performance. If she receives damages caused by the breach, she should not be able to get specific performance of the sales contract, since failure to deliver possession of the land was the cause of the injury for which she received damages. If Tally could seek compensatory damages in addition to specific performance, she would recover twice for the same breach of contract. The doctrine of election of remedies requires Tally to choose the remedy she wants, and it eliminates any possibility of double recovery.

Unfortunately, the doctrine has been applied in a rigid and technical manner, leading to some harsh

---

17. Contracts which by their terms cannot be performed within one year must be in writing to be enforceable. See Chapter 13.

results.[18] Therefore, the doctrine of election of remedies has been eliminated in contracts for the sale of goods. The UCC expressly rejects the doctrine. (See UCC 2-703 and UCC 2-711.) Remedies under the UCC are essentially cumulative in nature and include all the available remedies for breach of contract.

WAIVER OF BREACH

Under certain circumstances, a nonbreaching party may be willing to accept a defective performance of the contract. This knowing relinquishment of a legal right (that is, the right to require satisfactory and full performance) is called a **waiver**.[19] When a waiver of a breach of contract occurs, the party waiving the breach cannot take any later action on the theory that the contract was broken. In effect, the waiver erases the past breach; the contract continues as if the breach had never existed. Of course, the waiver of breach of contract extends only to the matter waived and not to the whole contract. Businesspersons often waive breaches of contract by the other party in order to get whatever benefit possible out of the contract.

For example, a seller contracts with a buyer to deliver to the buyer 10,000 tons of coal on or before November 1. The contract calls for the buyer's payment to be made by November 10 for coal delivered. Because of a coal miners' strike, coal is scarce. The seller breaches the contract by not tendering delivery until November 5. The buyer may well be advised to waive the seller's breach, accept delivery of the coal, and pay as contracted.

Ordinarily, the waiver by a contracting party will not operate to waive subsequent, additional, or future breaches of contract. This is always true when the subsequent breaches are unrelated to the first

breach. For example, an owner who waives the right to sue for late completion of a stage of construction does not waive the right to sue for failure to comply with engineering specifications.

A waiver will be extended to subsequent defective performance if a reasonable person would conclude that similar defective performance in the future would be acceptable. Therefore, a *pattern of conduct* that waives a number of successive breaches will operate as a continued waiver. In order to change this result, the nonbreaching party should give notice to the breaching party that full performance will be required in the future.

To illustrate: Suppose the construction contract above was to be completed in six stages, each two months apart, spanning a period of one year. The question is whether the waiver of the right to object to lateness of performance of stage 1 will operate as a waiver of the time requirements of performance for stages 2 through 6. If only stage 1's time requirements have been waived, the waiver will not extend to the other five stages. However, if the first five stages were all late (and the right to object to the lateness was always waived), the waivers will extend to stage 6 unless the owner has given proper notice that future performance is to be on time.

The party who has rendered defective or less than full performance remains liable for the damages caused by the breach of contract. In effect, the waiver operates to keep the contract going. The waiver prevents the nonbreaching party from calling the contract to an end or rescinding the contract. The contract continues, but the nonbreaching party can recover damages caused by defective or less than full performance.

CONTRACT PROVISIONS LIMITING REMEDIES

A contract can include provisions stating that no damages can be recovered for certain *types* of breaches or that damages must be limited to a *maximum amount*. In addition, the contract can provide that the only remedy for breach is replacement, repair, or refund of the purchase price. Provisions stating that no damages can be recovered are called *exculpatory clauses*. (See Chapter 11). Provisions that affect the availability of certain remedies are called *limitation of liability clauses*.

18. For example, in a Wisconsin case, Carpenter was fraudulently induced to buy a piece of land for $100. He spent $140 moving onto the land and then discovered the fraud. Instead of suing for damages, Carpenter sued to rescind the contract. The court denied recovery of the $140 because the seller, Mason, did not receive the $140 and was therefore not required to reimburse Carpenter for his moving expenses. So Carpenter suffered a net loss of $140 on the transaction. If Carpenter had sued for damages, he could have recovered the $100 and the $140. See Carpenter v. Mason, 181 Wis. 114, 193 N.W. 973 (1923).

19. Restatement, Second, Contracts, Sections 84, 246, and 247. The Restatement uses the term *promise* rather than *waiver*.

Because of the importance of these clauses and their uses, some discussion and illustrative situations will follow. It is important to keep in mind that the following is an overview and not an exhaustive explanation or a complete coverage of this topic.

Mutual Assent of Limitation Required

Initially, a court must determine if the provision has been made a part of the contract by offer and acceptance. In order for a term or provision to become part of a contract, both parties must consent to it. Therefore, courts will analyze whether the provision was noticed by the parties—whether, for example, the provision was in fine print or on the back of a lengthy contract. If either party did not know about the provision, it will not be a part of the contract and will not be enforced.[20]

For example, motorists often park their cars in lots and receive a small ticket stub that excludes liability for damages to cars parked in the lot. Since there is an implied duty to read a contract, if a reasonable person would have noticed such an exculpatory clause, it will be enforced. If the clause is not conspicuous and a reasonable person would not have noticed it, the clause will not be enforced, and the motorist can sue for damage caused to his or her car.[21]

Type of Breach Covered

Once it has been determined that the provision or clause is part of the contract, the analysis must focus on the type of breach that is exculpated. For example, a provision excluding liability for fraudulent or intentional injury will not be enforced. Likewise, a clause excluding liability for illegal acts or violations of law will not be enforced. On the other hand, a clause excluding liability for negligence may be enforced in appropriate cases. When an exculpatory clause for negligence is contained in a contract made between parties with roughly equal bargaining positions, the clause usually will be enforced.

For example, assume Delta Airlines buys six DC-9s from Douglas Aircraft. In the contract for sale,

a clause excludes liability for errors in design and construction of the aircraft. The clause will be upheld because both parties are large corporations with roughly equal bargaining positions. The equality of bargaining power assures that the exculpatory clause was not dictated by one of the parties and forced upon the other.

Limited Remedies—UCC

Under the UCC, in a contract for the *sale of goods*, remedies can be limited, but rules different from those just discussed apply. If only a certain remedy is desired, the contract must state that the remedy is exclusive. Suppose you buy an automobile, and the sales contract limits your remedy to repair or replacement of defective parts. Under the UCC, the sales contract must state that the *sole* and *exclusive* remedy available to the buyer is repair and/or replacement of the defective parts.[22] If the contract states that the remedy is exclusive, then the specified remedy will be the only one ordinarily available to the buyer (provided the contract is not unconscionable).

When circumstances cause an exclusive remedy to fail in its essential purpose, then it will not be exclusive. [See UCC 2-719(2).] In the preceding example, if your car breaks down several times, and the dealer is unable to fix or replace the defective parts, the exclusive remedy fails in its essential purpose. Then all the other remedies under the UCC become available.

Under the UCC, a sales contract may also limit or exclude consequential damages, provided the limitation is not *unconscionable*.[23] Where the buyer is purchasing consumer goods, the limitation of liability for personal injury is *prima facie* unconscionable and will not normally be enforced. Where the buyer is purchasing goods for commercial use, the limitation of liability for personal injury is not necessarily unconscionable.

Suppose that you have purchased a small printing press for your teenage son. It is a present to him for his birthday. He will be using it to print leaflets and pamphlets for his social club. The contract for

---

20. See, for example, the Magnuson-Moss Warranty Act discussion in Chapter 21.
21. See California State Auto v. Barrett Garages, Inc., 257 Cal.App.2d 84, 64 Cal.Rptr. 699 (1967).

22. UCC 2-719(1).
23. See Chapter 11 for a discussion of unconscionability and UCC 2-719(3).

purchase states that consequential damages, arising from personal injury as a result of a defect in the small printing press, are excluded. This exclusion or limitation of liability is *prima facie* unconscion-able (illegal). It will not be enforced. On the other hand, if you buy a printing press for your business, the limitation will not necessarily be unconscionable and may be enforceable.

QUESTIONS AND CASE PROBLEMS

1. Discuss fully under which of the following breach of contract situations specific performance would be an appropriate remedy:

(a) Thompson contracts to sell her house and lot to Cousteau. Then, upon finding another buyer willing to pay a higher purchase price, she refuses to deed the property to Cousteau.

(b) Amy contracts to sing and dance in Fred's nightclub for one month, beginning May 1. She then refuses to perform.

(c) Hoffman contracts to purchase a rare coin owned by Erikson, as Erikson is breaking up his coin collection. At the last minute, Erikson decides to keep his coin collection intact and refuses to deliver the coin to Hoffman.

(d) There are three shareholders of the ABC Corporation: Panozzo, who owns 48 percent of the stock; Chang, who owns another 48 percent; and Ryan, who owns 4 percent. Ryan contracts to sell her 4 percent to Chang. Later, Ryan refuses to transfer the shares to Chang.

2. Cohen contracts to sell his house and lot to Windsor for $100,000. The terms of the contract call for Windsor to put up 10 percent of the purchase price as "earnest money," a down payment. The terms further stipulate that should the buyer breach the contract, the earnest money would be treated as liquidated damages. Windsor puts up the earnest money, but because her expected financing of the $90,000 balance falls through, she breaches the contract. Two weeks later Cohen sells the house and lot to Ballard for $105,000. Windsor demands her $10,000 back, but Cohen refuses, claiming that Windsor's breach and contract terms entitle him to keep the "earnest money" payment. Discuss who is correct.

3. Ken owns and operates a famous candy store. He makes most of the candy sold in the store, and business is particularly heavy during the Christmas season. Ken contracts with Sweet, Inc. to purchase 10,000 pounds of sugar to be delivered on or before November 15. Ken has informed Sweet that this particular order is to be used for the Christmas season business. Because of production problems the sugar is not tendered to Ken until December 10, at which time Ken refuses it as being too late. Ken has been unable to purchase the quantity of sugar needed to meet the Christmas orders and has had to turn down numerous regular customers, some of whom have indicated that they will purchase candy elsewhere in the future. What sugar Ken has been able to purchase has cost him 10 cents per pound above the price contracted for with Sweet. Ken sues Sweet for breach of contract, claiming as damages the higher price paid for sugar from others, lost profits from this year's lost Christmas sales, future lost profits from customers who have indicated that they will discontinue doing business with him, and punitive damages for failure to meet the contracted delivery date. Sweet claims Ken is limited to compensatory damages only. Discuss who is correct.

4. Wallechinsky purchases an automobile from Anderson Motors, paying $1,000 down and agreeing to pay off the balance in thirty-six monthly payments of $200 each. The terms of the agreement call for Wallechinsky to make each payment on or before the first of each month. During the first six months, Anderson receives the $200 payments before the first of each month. During the next six months, Wallechinsky's payments are never made until the fifth of each month. Anderson has accepted and cashed the payment check each time. When Wallechinsky tenders the thirteenth payment on the fifth of the next month, Anderson refuses to accept the check, claiming that Wallechinsky is in breach of contract and demands the entire balance owed. Wallechinsky claims that Anderson cannot hold her in breach. Discuss the result fully.

5. Putnam contracts to buy a new Oldsmobile from Old Century Motors, paying $2,000 down and agreeing to make twenty-four monthly payments of $350 each. He takes the car home and, after making one payment, learns that his Oldsmobile has a Chevrolet engine in it rather than the famous Olds Super V-8 engine. Old Century never informed Putnam of this fact. Putnam immediately notifies Old Century of his dissatisfaction and tenders back the car to Old Century. Old Century accepts the car and returns to Putnam the $2,000 down payment plus the one $350 payment. Two weeks later Putnam, without a car and angry, files a suit against Old Century, seeking damages for breach of warranty and fraud. Discuss the effect of Putnam's actions.

6. The Grady-Gould Watershed Improvement District contracted with Kellett Company to have twenty miles of ditches sprayed to remove vegetation. Kellett guaranteed a 95 percent kill rate. The contract required that the level of kill be determined by inspection of the ditches after notice to Kellett. Kellett completed spraying and was paid the full contract price. Grady-Gould subsequently had representatives of the Soil Conservation Service appraise the kill level. No notice of this inspection was given to Kellett. However, Kellett conducted its own inspection, determined that a 95 percent kill had not been achieved, and promised Grady-Gould that the area would be resprayed. Kellett never resprayed, and Grady-Gould subsequently sued. Kellett asserts by way of defense Grady-Gould's failure to give notice of inspection, as required by the contract, in order that Kellett's representative could be present at such inspection. Is this defense valid? [Grady-Gould Watershed Improvement Dist. v. Transamerica Ins. Co., 570 F.2d 720 (8th Cir. 1978)]

7. Ballard was working for Eldorado Tire Company. He was discharged and sued for breach of the employment contract. The trial court awarded damages to Ballard, and Eldorado Tire appealed. In the appeal, Eldorado claimed that the trial court failed to reduce Ballard's damages by the amount that he might have earned in other employment during the remainder of the breached contract. Eldorado Tire introduced as evidence the fact that there was an extremely low rate of unemployment for professional technicians and managers in the area. The implication was that Ballard had not taken advantage of the opportunity for mitigating damages. Was Eldorado correct? [Ballard v. Eldorado Tire Co., 512 F.2d 901 (5th Cir. 1975)]

8. Westinghouse entered into a contract with New Jersey Electric to manufacture and install a turbine generator for producing electricity. The contract price was over $10 million. The parties engaged in three years of negotiations and bargaining before they agreed on a suitable contract. The ultimate contract provided, among other things, that Westinghouse would not be liable for any injuries to the property belonging to the utility or to its customers or employees. Westinghouse warranted only that it would repair any defects in workmanship and materials appearing within one year of installation. After installation, part of New Jersey Electric's plant and several of its employees were injured because of a defect in the turbine. New Jersey Electric sued Westinghouse, claiming that Westinghouse was liable for the damages because the exculpatory provisions in the contract were unconscionable. What was the result? [Royal Indem. Company v. Westinghouse Elec. Corp., 385 F.Supp. 520 (D.C.N.Y. 1974)]

9. Evergreen Amusement Corporation purchased a parcel of land for use as a drive-in movie theater. Evergreen contracted with Milstead to have the lot cleared and graded according to specifications that would make it adequate for a drive-in theater. Milstead was supposed to complete the work by June 1, and Evergreen planned to open the theater at about that time. However, Milstead did not finish clearing and grading the lot until the third week in August. Evergreen sued Milstead, claiming as damages the profits that it could have made on the drive-in theater had it been in operation. Are lost profits the proper measure of damages here? [Evergreen Amusement Corp. v. Milstead, 206 Md. 610, 112 A.2d 901 (1955)]

10. Kerr Steamship Company delivered to RCA a twenty-nine-word coded message to be sent to Kerr's agent in Manila. The message included instructions on loading cargo onto one of Kerr's vessels. Kerr's profits on the carriage of the cargo were to be about $6,600. RCA mislaid the coded message, and it was never sent. Kerr sued RCA for the $6,600 in profits that it lost because RCA never sent the message. Can Kerr recover? [Kerr Steamship Co. v. Radio Corp. of America, 245 N.Y. 284, 157 N.E. 140 (1927)]

FOCUS ON ETHICS

Contract Law and the Application of Ethics

Numerous areas of contract law lend themselves to ethical analysis. Business people certainly face ethical questions when they deal with the application of black-letter law to contracts. Courts, for example, generally will not inquire into the adequacy of the consideration given in a contract. In other words, a court will not reevaluate a contract to determine whether what each party gave is equivalent to what each party received. As long as each party gives some sort of consideration, the courts will conclude that the parties intended to make a binding agreement. The requirement that contracts be supported by consideration also makes parties aware that they can be bound by the contract. Thus, a businessperson could knowingly arrange an exchange in which consideration is greatly less than value received and successfully argue in court that the consideration was adequate enough to make the contract legally enforceable. Nonetheless, that person may still be violating the ethics of society.

CONTRACT LAW AND CHANGE

Much of contract law has changed to coincide with the changing ideas of fairness.

Consider several examples that are, of course, not exhaustive of ethical concerns in contract law.

Impossibility

The doctrine of impossibility is based to some extent on the ethical question of whether one party should suffer economic loss when it is impossible to perform a contract. The rule that one is "bound by his or her contracts" is not followed when performance is made impossible. The doctrine of impossibility is applied to relieve a contracting party of liability for failure to perform. However, this doctrine is applied only when the parties themselves did not allocate the risk of the events that would have rendered performance impossible. Furthermore, this doctrine rests upon the assumption that the party claiming the defense of impossibility has acted ethically. In other words, a party cannot arrange events in order to intentionally make performance impossible.

A contract is discharged, for example, if the performance of the contract calls for the delivery of a particular good, such as a car, and through no fault of either party this car is stolen and completely demolished in an accident. Yet the doctrine of impossibility is not available if the party agreeing to sell his or

her car either crashed the car to avoid performance of the contract or the car's destruction was caused by his or her negligence. The well-known English case of *Taylor* v. *Caldwell* is also illustrative of the doctrine of impossibility [122 Eng.Rep. 309 (K.B. 1863)]. In *Taylor,* the plaintiff entered into a contract with the defendant to rent the defendant's music hall for a series of concerts. Before the first concert, but after the contract was entered into, the music hall was destroyed by fire. The court held that the defendant was discharged from performing. Furthermore, because performance was impossible, his failure to perform was not a breach of contract.

Prior to the late nineteenth century, courts were reluctant to discharge a contract even when it appeared that performance was literally impossible. However, just as society's ethics change with the passage of time, law also makes a transition to reflect society's new perceptions of ethical behavior. Today courts are much more willing to discharge a contract when its performance has become literally impossible. Holding a party in breach of contract, when performance has become literally impossible through no fault of the party claiming the defense of impossibility, no longer coincides with society's notions of fairness.

Frustration of Purpose

The doctrine of frustration of purpose is based upon the idea that when one party's purpose is completely or almost completely frustrated by supervening events, that party should not be required to perform the contract. Thus, even though performance of the contract itself is not rendered impossible, events occur that subvert one party's purpose in entering into the contract. When such a "frustration of purpose" occurs, most courts will discharge a party from performing.

In determining whether to discharge a party from performing a contract, courts will frequently consider whether the alleged frustrating event was foreseeable. The more foreseeable the event, the less likely it is that a court will allow this defense. Hence, the doctrine of frustration of purpose embodies society's ethical notion that it is unfair to require a party to perform a contract in a situation in which the party's object in making the contract is frustrated.

Mistake

The notion that mistake in contracts should release the contracting parties from their obligations has gained strength as the ethics of society have changed. If one were to study the cases of several hundred years ago, one would find much less acceptance of mistake as an excuse to avoid a contractual obligation than exists today.

Mistakes can arise in numerous contexts surrounding the making of a contract. A mistake may be unilateral in the sense that the mistake is made by only one party. In *Sternmeyer* v. *Schroeppel* [226

Ill. 9 (1907)], for example, a bidder on a construction project incorrectly calculated his costs and therefore submitted an offer that was substantially lower than it would have been if he had correctly calculated his costs. The Illinois court held that the bidder was not entitled to rescind the contract. The court further stated that rescission based upon a unilateral mistake may not be obtained when the mistake results from a failure to exercise reasonable care and diligence. More recent court cases, however, appear to be less harsh. Some courts have concluded that rescission on account of computation errors is permissible when the only injury to the other party is the disappointment of losing an expectation interest. Thus, ideas of fairness to each of the contracting parties change over time.

Unconscionability

Ethical consideration clearly inspired the concept of unconscionability embodied in the Uniform Commercial Code 2–302. This section provides that if a court as a matter of law finds a contract or any clause of a contract to have been unconscionable at the time it was made, the court may refuse to enforce the contract, or it may enforce the contract without the unconscionable clause, or it may limit the application of any unconscionable clause so as to avoid an unconscionable result. The question arises, however, as to what unconscionability is.

Irrespective of the fact that the UCC has a particular provision regarding the doctrine of unconscionability, nowhere in the Code is there a definition of the term "unconscionability." The Comment 1 to UCC 2–302 suggests that the basic test for

unconscionability is whether, under the circumstances existing at the time of the making of the contract, the clauses in question are so one-sided as to be unconscionable. This test is to be applied against the general commercial background. The comments to UCC 2–302, like the provision itself, refrain from defining the term "unconscionable," and hence the basic test set forth in the guidelines provides only general guidance.

The recognition that "unconscionability" is incapable of precise definition corresponds to much of what we have discussed in the context of ethics in general. If there were an attempt to define precisely this term, it is likely that such a definition would be over-inclusive or under-inclusive. Determining what is unconscionable is very similar to determining what is ethical. Both determinations must be made on the basis of particular facts and specific circumstances. These two terms preclude precise definition.

The "court as a matter of law," not the jury, must find that a contract or a clause of a contract was unconscionable at the time it was made. Furthermore, the party who desires to assert the defense of unconscionabililty must plead and prove it.

Contractual Capacity

Chapter 10 pointed out that in order for a contract to be valid, the individuals entering into it must have contractual capacity. Consequently, except under certain circumstances, minors can avoid contractual obligations. The question of whether or not a minor should be held responsible for his or her acts is clearly an ethical one. Our set of shared beliefs currently dictates that minors should not be held responsible for contracts except under special circumstances.

For example, in most states minors are allowed to avoid contracts for the sale of nonnecessaries. Merely by making a good faith attempt to return the purchased goods, a minor can receive a full refund of any monies paid. An ethical issue arises, however, when the minor has diminished the value of the goods prior to returning them or is unable to return them. Because it does not seem "fair" to most people that the merchant should suffer because of the minor's actions, some states require that the merchant be compensated for any reduction in value of the goods.

The Equitable Remedy of Quasi-Contract

Quasi-contracts, often referred to as contracts implied in law, arise to establish justice and fairness. However, the term quasi-contract is misleading in the sense that a quasi-contract is not a contract at all. The parties have not made any agreement. Rather, a court imposes a quasi-contract upon the parties when justice requires; these contracts are used to prevent unjust enrichment. The doctrine of unjust enrichment is based upon the theory that individuals should not be allowed to profit or enrich themselves inequitably at the expense of others. This belief is fundamental in our society. Thus, imposing contract liability on an unconsenting party in order to prevent a result perceived by society as unfair (unjust enrichment) is clearly an action inspired by ethical considerations.

A typical situation in which a court, as a matter of judicial

policy, may impose a quasi-contract upon the parties arises when one person renders emergency services to another person without first entering into a contract. In these circumstances, courts generally allow the person who renders the emergency services to recover in quasi-contract the reasonable fee for his or her emergency services. This recovery is allowed irrespective of the fact that the parties never entered into a contract. Thus, ethical considerations suggest that it is sometimes necessary for courts to imply a contract in order to avoid unfairness or unjust enrichment.

ETHICS VERSUS EFFICIENCY

Contracts can be analyzed in terms of economic efficiency. Economic efficiency exists when, *ex ante*, no change in the current use of resources will result in the increasing material welfare of society. It can be argued that the law of contracts leads to economic efficiency because it establishes a set of rules that businesspersons can rely on when they engage in commercial transactions. When such persons know what the outcome of court cases will be, they have an incentive to avoid behavior that is not in conformance with the law of contracts. In other words, businesspersons attempt to minimize the amount of their resources spent on litigation, since litigation expenses increase costs and lower profits.

Much contractual litigation results in reduction in the wealth of one party and an increase in the wealth of the other. Consider the following example: An individual enters into a contract with a merchant. For a specified sum of money, the

merchant is to provide a certain tool. The tool is to be used for a specified activity. The purchaser of the tool uses it for another activity and in so doing permanently injures himself. He sues the merchant, which is an extremely large company. If the trier of fact rules in favor of the merchant, the wealth of the injured plaintiff will be decreased and the company is better off than if it would have been had it been forced to compensate the plaintiff for the injuries resulting from the use of its tool. If, on the other hand, the trier of fact rules in favor of the plaintiff, the plaintiff's wealth will be increased, and the company's wealth will be correspondingly decreased. From an ethical point of view, is it fair to require the company to compensate the plaintiff when the plaintiff's injuries resulted from a disregard for the company's explicit instructions? Some people argue that, since the company can better "afford" to lose wealth (via payment to the injured plaintiff for injuries), the trier of fact should rule in favor of the plaintiff. Others, however, question the fairness of determining the outcome of a particular case on the basis of who can best absorb the cost.

From an economic-efficiency point of view, placing liability on the merchant will lead to less efficiency. After all, the contract between the two parties was for a tool to be used in a specified activity. The plaintiff did not use the tool in that activity. If, because of injury from improper use of the tool, the plaintiff is awarded damages, a signal will be generated to other individuals in society that they too will be awarded compensation for any injuries sustained by careless or negligent use of such tools. Arguably, this rule will lead to greater carelessness by consumers since they will no longer need to be concerned with suffering the consequences of their carelessness. The company, on the other hand, will now be the subject of many more suits by consumers who are suing to recover damages for injuries sustained by their careless use of the merchant's tool. Paying out compensation to those injured, careless plaintiffs will increase the company's costs. If other companies that produce substantially the same tool are also sued and the courts similarly award damages to the careless plaintiffs, the price of this tool will eventually go up to reflect the costs of compensating careless plaintiffs. Consumers in general will have to pay more for this tool because of the carelessness of a relatively few individuals. Economic efficiency clearly will suffer.

The results of recent court cases involving personal injuries indicate a greater concern in our society for proper compensation of injuries as opposed to economic efficiency. The ethical concern that victims who are injured using products of a manufacturer deserve to be compensated appears to predominate in court cases, irrespective of how careless the plaintiff may have been. Thus, particularly in the area of products liability, the increasing number of actions brought by plaintiffs has frequently resulted in defendant companies settling questionable claims in order to save the expense of litigation.

CONTRACT LAW, THE INDIVIDUAL, AND BIG BUSINESS

According to one school of legal and economic thought, contract law as interpreted in this unit does not mesh with reality. This school asserts that the individual as a consumer no longer contracts in the traditional sense with multi-billion-dollar companies such as Exxon and General Motors. Consequently, it is suggested that the traditional contract notions of offer, acceptance, consideration, and so on may not be the most appropriate way to analyze consumer purchases.

Some critics argue that an individual consumer has no bargaining position and, hence, must buy on the merchant's terms or not at all. If this theory is correct, ethical considerations no longer play as important a part in understanding common law contract doctrine as they did a hundred years ago. In other words, the relationship between the (seller) corporation and the eventual (buyer) consumer has become so attenuated that the traditional personal interaction between buyers and sellers is no longer present to inspire ethical considerations. A company produces a product, sells it to a wholesaler, who then sells it to a distributor-dealer, who in turn may sell the product to the ultimate consumer. This school of thought de-emphasizes the effect of ethical considerations on the part of companies and thus concludes that big business in general has had a detrimental effect on society.

Another school of thought asserts that no matter how large a firm is, it must please the consumer in order to maximize profits. That is, the ultimate "director" of the firm is the consumer, who still has the choice of buying a smaller quantity or none at all of whatever products are offered in the marketplace. This school of thought perceives consumers to be relevant actors. Furthermore, in those markets where more than one firm exists, competition forces the firms to offer the consumer products at a price and quality that will maximize profits. Because most producers make the highest profits by inducing repeat sales, they have a profit incentive to treat their clients ethically—in a way that pleases them. Thus, to some extent, the ethical issues here are hidden by the effect of the producers' notion of profit maximization.

Since both schools of thought are convinced that they are right, the debate may continue indefinitely.

DISCUSSION QUESTIONS

1. Is the nature of a company's business an ethical concern? That is, is it ethical for a company to produce and market goods of varying quality and to place the burden of purchasing goods of the desired quality on the consumer?

2. U.S. automobile manufacturers have recently been attempting to produce higher-quality cars. Did this result from an ethical concern of the companies? If so, why did this concern not exist before? Or is the attempt to produce higher-quality cars merely a result of Japanese competition, and will such an attempt cease when and if the Japanese competition disappears?

3. To what extent should a company offer advantageous prices and pursue a high standard of honesty by refraining from advertising only its loss leader articles?

UNIT III

COMMERCIAL TRANSACTIONS AND THE UNIFORM COMMERCIAL CODE

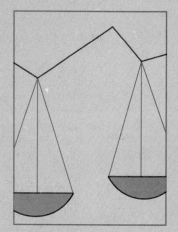

17

SALES
Introduction to Sales Contracts and Their Formation

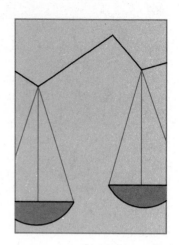

Almost every day of our lives we make purchases—the daily newspaper, groceries, clothes, textbooks, a stereo, a car, and so on. Most of our purchases are of "goods" rather than real property. For this reason studying the law relating to the sale of goods is relevant to our daily lives.

The people from whom we buy our goods are, to us, "sellers." But our "sellers" are in turn "buyers" from their suppliers, who are in turn, "buyers" from manufacturers. The law of sales is the study of the rights and responsibilities of those in the purchase-and-sale of goods chain, from the original maker of the item to the ultimate user. A **sale** is a contract that, by its terms, transfers title to goods from a seller to a buyer for a price.

HISTORICAL PERSPECTIVE

Today's law of sales originated centuries ago in the customs and traditions of merchants and traders. The *Lex Mercantoria* (Law Merchant) was a system of rules, customs, and usages self-imposed by early commercial traders and merchants to settle disputes and to enforce obligations among themselves. These rules were established at "fairs," where merchants met to exchange goods and settle differences through "fair courts" established and operated by the merchants themselves.

By the end of the seventeenth century, the principles of the Law Merchant were widely accepted and quite naturally became part of the common law. From that time on, judges, not merchants, refined the principles of mercantile law into the modern commercial law of sales.

Numerous attempts were made in the United States to produce a uniform body of laws relating to commercial transactions. Two major enactments, the Uniform Negotiable Instruments Law (1896) and the Uniform Sales Act (1906) were widely adopted by the states. Several other proposed "uniform acts" followed, although most were not widely adopted.

In the 1940s the need to integrate the half-dozen or so uniform acts covering commercial transactions into a single, comprehensive body of statutory law was recognized. Accordingly, the Uniform Commercial Code (UCC, or simply "the Code") was developed to serve that purpose.

Shift from Common Law to Statutory Law

It is important to note that when we focus on sales contracts, the subject of this chapter, we move away from common law principles and into a body of statutory law. The UCC is the statutory framework we will use, since it has been adopted as law by all states (with the exception of Louisiana, which has adopted only part of it). Relevant sections of the UCC are noted in the following discussion of sales contracts. The reader should refer to the appendix in the back of the book while examining these notations. Many similarities to the contract law previously studied in Chapters 7 through 16 will be apparent. Indeed, such similarities should be expected, since the UCC represents the codification of much of the existing common law of contracts.

The Uniform Commercial Code

The UCC is the single most comprehensive codification of the broad spectrum of laws involved in a total commercial transaction. The Code views the entire "commercial transaction for the sale of and payment for goods" as a single legal occurrence having numerous facets.

To illustrate: Review the titles of the ten articles of the UCC in Appendix C. Now consider a consumer who buys a refrigerator from an appliance store and agrees to pay for it on an installment plan. Several articles of the UCC could be applied to this single commercial transaction. Since there is a contract for sale of goods, Article 2 would apply. If a check is given as the down payment on the purchase price, it will be negotiated and ultimately passed through one or more banks for collection. This process is the subject matter of Article 3, Commercial Paper, and Article 4, Bank Deposits and Collections. If the appliance store extends credit to the consumer through the installment plan, and if it retains a right in the refrigerator (collateral), then Article 9, Secured Transactions, will be applicable.

Suppose, in addition, the appliance company must first obtain the refrigerator from its manufacturer's warehouse, after which it is to be delivered by common carrier to the consumer. The storage and shipment of goods is the subject matter of Article 7, Documents of Title. If the appliance company arranges to pay the manufacturer, located in another state, for the refrigerator supplied, a letter of credit, which is the subject matter of Article 5, may be used.

Thus, the Code attempts to provide a consistent and integrated framework of rules to deal with all the phases *ordinarily arising* in a commercial sales transaction.[1]

THE SCOPE OF ARTICLE 2: THE SALE OF GOODS

No body of law operates in a vacuum removed from other principles of jurisprudence. A sales contract is governed by the same common law principles applicable to all contracts—offer, acceptance, consideration, capacity, and legality—and these principles should be reexamined when studying sales. The law of sales, found in Article 2 of the UCC, is a part of the law of contracts.

Two things should be kept in mind. First, Article 2 deals with the sale of *goods*, not real property (real estate), services, or intangible property such as stocks and bonds. Second, in some cases, the rules may vary quite a bit, depending upon whether the buyer or seller is a *merchant*.

It is always a good idea to note the subject matter of a dispute and the kind of people involved. If the subject is goods, then the UCC will govern. If it is real estate or services, then the common law will apply. Although the vast majority of the rules under Article 2 apply to all sellers and buyers of goods, some specific rules apply only if the seller or buyer, or both, are merchants.

What Is a Sale?

Section 2-102 of the Code states that Article 2 "applies to transactions in goods." This implies a broad scope for this article, covering leases, gifts, bailments, and purchases of goods. However, for the purposes of this chapter (and most authorities and courts would agree), we will treat Article 2 as ap-

---

1. Two articles of the UCC seemingly do not fit into the "ordinary" commercial sales transaction. Article 6, Bulk Transfers, involves merchants who sell off the major part of their inventory (sometimes pocketing the money and disappearing, leaving creditors unpaid). Since such "bulk sales" do not "ordinarily arise" in a commercial transaction for the sale of goods, they are treated separately. Article 8, Investment Securities, deals with negotiable securities (stocks and bonds), transactions that do not fall within the concept of sale of or payment for *goods*. However, the subject matter of Articles 6 and 8 was considered by the Code's drafters to be related *sufficiently* to commercial transactions to warrant inclusion in the UCC.

plicable only to an actual sale. A sale is officially defined ". . . as the passing of title from the seller to the buyer for a price." [UCC 2-106(1)] The price may be payable in money or in other goods, services, or realty (real estate).

What Are Goods?

To be characterized as a *good*, an item must be *tangible*, and it must be *movable*.

A tangible item has physical existence—it can be touched or seen, as a horse, a car, or a chair. Thus, intangible property such as corporate stocks and bonds, promissory notes, bank accounts, patents and copyrights, or ordinary contract rights have only conceptual existence and do not come under Article 2.

A *movable* item can be carried from place to place. Hence, real estate is excluded from Article 2.

Two basic areas of dispute arise in determining whether the object of the contract is goods, and thus whether Article 2 is applicable. One dispute concerns *goods associated with realty*, such as crops or timber, and the other concerns contracts involving a combination of *goods and services*.

Goods versus Realty   *Goods associated with real estate* fall under Article 2. Section 2-107 provides the following rules:

1.   A contract for the sale of minerals or the like (including oil and gas) or a structure (such as a building) is a contract for the sale of goods *if severance is to be made by the seller*. If the buyer is to sever them from the land, the contract is considered a sale of real estate governed by the principles of real property law, not the UCC.

To illustrate: Sue agrees to sell Ben a quantity of oil that is located under Sue's property. If Ben is to drill the wells to remove the oil, the contract is a sale of real estate. If the agreement provides that Sue is to drill the wells to obtain the oil, the transaction is a sale of goods. Similarly, if Sue agrees to sell Ben an old barn located on Sue's farm with Ben to remove the barn, it is a contract for the sale of real estate. If Sue is to remove the barn, the contract is characterized as a sale of goods under UCC Article 2.

2.   A sale of growing crops or timber to be cut is a contract for the sale of goods *regardless of who severs them*.

3.   Other "things attached" to realty but capable of severance without material harm to the land are considered goods regardless of who severs them.[2]

Examples of such things are a furnace or window air-conditioner in a house, or counters and stools in a luncheonette. The test is whether removal will cause *material harm* to the realty to which the item is attached. Removal of a window air-conditioner would be a sale of goods, but removal of a central air-conditioning system would probably do a great deal of damage to the realty and would be treated as a sale of real estate. When the parties do not envision any items being removed (severed) from the realty, such as in the sale of "ten acres with corn standing," then the transaction is characterized as the sale of real estate.

Goods versus Services   Where goods and services are combined, courts have disagreed over whether a particular transaction involves the sale of goods or the rendering of a service. For example, is the blood furnished to a patient during an operation a "sale of goods" or the "performance of a medical service"? Some courts say "a good"; some say "a service." In discussing their decisions, the courts try to determine which factor is predominant—the good or the service.

The same kind of "mixed transaction" problem is encountered when a beautician applies hair dye to a customer in a beauty shop. The Code does not provide the answer, and court decisions are in conflict.

The Code does stipulate, however, that serving food or drink to be consumed either on or off restaurant premises is the "sale of goods," at least for the purpose of an implied warranty of merchantability. [UCC 2-314(1)] Whether the transaction in question involves the sale of goods or services is important because the majority of courts treat services as being excluded by the UCC.

Also, a contract for specially manufactured goods is one for goods, not services. [UCC 2-105(1)] Sev-

---

2.   The Code avoids using the word "fixtures" here because of the numerous definitions of this term. (See Chapter 53.)

eral other special cases are explicitly characterized as goods by the Code, including the unborn young of animals, rare coins, and other forms of money as a commodity.

Who Is a Merchant?

Article 2 governs the sale of goods in general. It applies to sales transactions between all buyers and sellers. In a limited number of instances, however, the Code presumes that in certain phases of sales transactions involving *professional merchants*, special business standards ought to be imposed because of the merchants' degree of commercial expertise.[3] Such standards do not apply to the casual or inexperienced seller or buyer. Section 2-104 defines three ways that *merchant* status occurs:

1. A merchant is a person who *deals in goods of the kind* involved in the sales contract. Thus, a retailer, a wholesaler, or a manufacturer is a merchant of those goods sold in the business. A merchant for

---

3. The provisions that apply only to merchants deal principally with the Statute of Frauds, firm offers, confirmatory memoranda, warranties, and contract modification. These special rules reflect expedient business practice commonly known to merchants in the commercial setting. They will be discussed later in this chapter.

one type of goods is not necessarily a merchant for any other type. For example, a sporting equipment retailer is a merchant when buying tennis equipment but not when buying stereo equipment.

2. A merchant is a person who, by occupation, *holds himself or herself out as having knowledge and skill peculiar to the practices or goods involved in the transaction*. This is a broad definition that can include banks or universities as merchants.

3. A person who employs a merchant as a broker, agent, or other intermediary has the status of merchant in that transaction. Hence, if a "gentleman farmer" who ordinarily does not run the farm hires a broker to purchase livestock, the farmer is considered a merchant in the livestock transaction.

In summary, a person is a merchant when that person, acting in a mercantile capacity, possesses or uses an expertise specifically related to the goods being sold. This basic distinction, however, is not always clear-cut. For example, disagreement has arisen over whether a farmer is a merchant. The answer depends upon the particular goods involved, the transaction, and whether, in the particular situation, the farmer has special knowledge concerning the goods involved in the transaction. The following case illustrates how the courts decide whether or not a person is a merchant and therefore subject to the UCC version of the Statute of Frauds.

TERMINAL GRAIN CORP. v. FREEMAN

Supreme Court of South Dakota, 1978.
270 N.W.2d 806.

BACKGROUND AND FACTS *The plaintiff, a grain company, brought this action against a farmer for the farmer's failure to deliver grain pursuant to an alleged oral contract. The grain company had issued, and the farmer had received, a written confirmation for the sale. This was the only writing, and it was for more than $500. The trial court entered a judgment for the farmer, and the grain company appealed.*

HANSON, Retired Justice.

*   *   *   *

Terminal Grain *   *   * alleges error on the refusal of the trial court to instruct the jury on the Uniform Commercial Code provisions contained in [UCC 2-201(1) and (2)]. [UCC 2-201(1)] is a general statute of frauds providing as follows:

Except as otherwise provided in [this section] a contract for the sale of goods for the price of five hundred dollars or more is not enforceable by way of action or defense unless there is some writing sufficient to indicate that a contract for sale has been made between the parties and signed by the party against whom enforcement is sought or by his authorized agent or broker. A writing is not insufficient because it omits or incorrectly states a term agreed upon but the contract is not enforceable under this section beyond the quantity of goods shown in such writing.

The above statute of frauds has been held applicable in similar actions for damages involving oral contracts in excess of $500.00 between an elevator/buyer and a farmer/seller for nondelivery of grain at a future date. However, the court had no occasion to consider the application of [UCC 2-201(2)] in either case. This exception to the Uniform Commercial Code general statute of frauds provides:

Between merchants if within a reasonable time a writing in confirmation of the contract and sufficient against the sender is received and the party receiving it has reason to know its contents, it satisfies the requirements of [subsection (1)] against such party unless written notice of objection to its contents is given within ten days after it is received.

As a farmer, Freeman contends he is not a "merchant" within the contemplation of the above statute and it, therefore has no application to him. The term "merchant" is defined in [UCC 2-104(1)] as meaning

a person who deals in goods of the kind or otherwise by his occupation holds himself out as having knowledge or skill peculiar to the practices or goods involved in the transaction or to whom such knowledge or skill may be attributed by his employment of an agent or broker or other intermediary who by his occupation holds himself out as having such knowledge or skill.

Also, the term "between merchants" is defined to mean "in any transaction with respect to which both parties are chargeable with the knowledge or skill of merchants."

The official comment to § 2-104 of the Uniform Commercial Code definition of "Merchant" and "Between Merchants" states in part:

1. This Article assumes that transactions between professionals in a given field require special and clear rules which may not apply to a casual or inexperienced seller or buyer. *   *   *

2. The term 'merchant' as defined here roots in the 'law merchant' concept of a professional in business. The professional status under the definition may be based upon specialized knowledge as to the goods, specialized knowledge as to business practices, or specialized knowledge as to both and which kind of specialized knowledge may be sufficient to establish the merchant status is indicated by the nature of the provisions.

In similar factual cases the courts which have considered whether or not a "farmer" is or may be considered a "merchant" under the above Uniform Commercial Code provisions are almost equally divided in their opinions. The courts in Illinois, Texas, Missouri, Ohio, and North Carolina have held farmers to be merchants under various facts and circumstances *   *   *.

On the other hand the courts in Iowa, New Mexico, Utah, Kansas, Arkansas, and Alabama have held that a farmer is not a merchant *   *   *.

In arriving at its conclusion that the defendant farmer/seller was not a "merchant" within the meaning of the Uniform Commercial Code, the Kansas Court said:

[T]he appellee neither 'deals' in wheat, as that term is used in 2-104 nor does he by his occupation hold himself out as having knowledge or skill peculiar to the practices or goods involved in the transaction. The concept of professionalism is heavy in determining who is a merchant under the statute. The writers of the official UCC comment virtually equate professionals with merchants—the casual or inexperienced buyer or seller is not to be held to the standard set for the professional in business. The defined term 'between merchants', used in the exception proviso to the statute of frauds, contemplates the knowledge and skill of professionals on each side of the transaction. The transaction in question here was the sale of wheat. Appellee as a farmer undoubtedly had special knowledge or skill in raising wheat but we do not think this factor, coupled with annual sales of a wheat crop and purchases of seed wheat, qualified him as a merchant in that field. The parties' stipulation states appellee has sold only the products he raised. There is no indication any of these sales were other than cash sales to local grain elevators, where conceivably an expertise reaching professional status could be said to be involved.

We agree with the reasoning of the Kansas Court and with the other courts which hold the average farmer, like Freeman, with no particular knowledge or experience in selling, buying, or dealing in future commodity transactions, and who sells only the crops he raises to local elevators for cash or who places his grain in storage under one of the federal loan programs, is not a "merchant" within the purview of the exception provision to the Uniform Commercial Code statute of frauds. Through training and years of experience a farmer may well possess or acquire special knowledge, skills, and expertise in the production of grain crops but this does not make him a "professional," equal in the marketplace with a grain buying and selling company, whose officers, agents, and employees are constantly conversant with the daily fluctuations in the commodity market, the many factors affecting the market, and with its intricate practices and procedures. Accordingly, the trial court did not err in refusing to instruct the jury on this issue.

DECISION AND REMEDY   *The decision was affirmed for the farmer, and the grain company could not recover damages for the farmer's failure to deliver the wheat. The Statute of Frauds was applicable to the transaction. Since the farmer was not a "merchant," the confirmation sent by the grain company was insufficient to bind the farmer to the alleged oral contract.*

COMMENT   *Whether a farmer is a merchant will be decided on the facts of each case. If the farmer deals extensively in contracts for future delivery, the courts are more likely to determine that he or she is a merchant than if the farmer deals only in cash sales to grain elevators.*

FORMATION OF A SALES CONTRACT

The policy of the UCC is to recognize that the law of sales is part of the general law of contracts. The Code often restates general principles or is silent on certain subjects. In those situations, the common law of contracts and applicable state statutes govern. The following sections summarize the ways that UCC provisions *change* the effect of the general law of contracts.

Offer

In general contract law, the moment a definite offer is met by an unqualified acceptance, a binding contract is formed. In commercial sales transactions, the verbal exchanges, the correspondence, and the actions of the parties may not reveal exactly when a binding contractual obligation arises. The Code states that an agreement sufficient to constitute a contract can exist even if the moment of its making is undetermined. [UCC 2-204(2)]

Open Terms   According to contract law, an offer must be definite enough for the parties (and the courts) to ascertain its essential terms when it is accepted. The UCC states that a sales contract will not fail for indefiniteness even if one or more terms are left open as long as: (1) the parties intended to make a contract and (2) there is a reasonably certain basis for the court to grant an appropriate remedy. [UCC 2-204(3)]

The Code provides numerous *open term* provisions that can be used to fill in the gaps in a contract. Two factors should be kept in mind. First, the more terms left open, the less likely the courts will find that the parties intended to form a contract. Second, as a general rule, if the *quantity* term is left open, the courts will have no basis for determining a remedy, and the sales contract will fail unless the contract is either an output or a requirements contract. [UCC 2-306]

Open Price Term   If the parties have not agreed on a price, the court will determine "a reasonable price *at the time for delivery."* [UCC 2-305(1)] If either the buyer or the seller is to determine the price, it means a price fixed in good faith. [UCC 2-305(2)]

Sometimes the price fails to be fixed through the fault of one of the parties. In that case, the other party can treat the contract as cancelled or fix a reasonable price. For example, Axel and Beatty enter into a contract for the sale of goods and agree that Axel will fix the price. The agreement becomes economically burdensome to Axel, and Axel refuses to fix the price. Beatty can either treat the contract as cancelled or can set a reasonable price. [UCC 2-305(3)]

Open Payment Term When parties do not specify payment terms, payment is due at the time and place at which the buyer is to receive the goods. [UCC

2-310(a)] Generally, cash, not credit, is used. The buyer can tender payment using any commercially normal or acceptable means, such as a check or a credit card. If the seller demands payment in cash, however, the buyer must be given a reasonable time to obtain it. [UCC 2-511(2)] This would be especially important when a definite and final time for performance is stated in the contract.

Although the UCC has radically lessened the requirements for definiteness of essentials in contracts of sale, it has not removed the common law requirement that the contract be at least definite enough for the court to identify the agreement, so that it can either enforce it or award appropriate damages if it is breached. In the following case, the absence of the price term and the absence of the specific goods to be purchased caused the court to find that there was no contract.

BACKGROUND AND FACTS *Bucci, the defendant, purchased some land, intending to build a combination restaurant and delicatessen on it, and contacted several contractors and suppliers for estimates. Bucci ultimately made a written agreement with the Royal Store Fixture Co., the plaintiff, "to purchase the store fixtures and refrigeration equipment required" for the new store. Subsequently, the plaintiff submitted various proposals for an equipment layout to the defendant. The defendant also received bids from other companies and ultimately purchased the required equipment from one of the plaintiff's competitors. The plaintiff insisted that the defendant was bound by the writing— that is, by a valid agreement to buy all store fixtures and equipment requirements through the plaintiff at competitive prices. The defendant argued, on the other hand, that the document signed by the parties was too vague and indefinite to be a binding contract.*

ROYAL STORE
FIXTURE CO. v. BUCCI
Pennsylvania County Court, 1969.
7 UCC Rep. Serv. 1193.

MEADE, Judge.
* * * *

The Uniform Commercial Code (UCC) § 2-204 * * * provides that "(3) Even though one or more terms are left open a contract for sale does not fail for indefiniteness if the parties have intended to make a contract and there is a *reasonably certain basis for giving an appropriate remedy*." (Italics supplied.) The commentary to the code * * * points out that, as to contract rules "The prime test is simply that the parties intended to make a contract and that 'there is a reasonably certain basis for giving an appropriate remedy'. It is specifically provided that the price, particulars of performance, the time for performance and the duration of the contract must not necessarily be fixed by the agreement of the parties." The authors of the code itself point out in the comment to § 2-204 that "The more terms the parties leave open, the less likely it is that they have intended to conclude a binding agreement, but their actions may be frequently conclusive on the matter despite the omissions."

The subject matter in the case sub judice [the case at bar or the case under study] is described only as "store fixtures and refrigeration equipment." This description is wholly inadequate to give the requisite clarity to the agreement so as to make it an enforceable contract.

* * * *

Nor do we believe that the price of the unspecified store fixtures and refrigeration equipment could ever be reduced to reasonable certainty. While § 2-305 of the UCC dealing with "open price term", has been construed to call for a reasonable price [*Kuss Machine Tool & Die Co. v. El-Tronics, Inc.*, 393 Pa 353 (1958)], this may not necessarily be the same as the "competitive prices" called for in the writing. The testimony is clear that the parties left open the term of price, because it was to be agreed upon at a later date. Whether the court could arrive at a "reasonable" price is doubted in view of plaintiff's testimony on that question.

* * * *

For the foregoing reasons, we hold that the instrument signed by the parties was not an enforceable agreement. * * *

Judgment must be entered in favor of defendant and against plaintiff.

DECISION AND REMEDY   *Judgment was for the defendant. Bucci was allowed to purchase store fixtures and refrigeration equipment from another supplier. The sales contract, or agreement, was too vague because it did not state the price of the unspecified goods that were to be sold, and, more importantly, it was not possible for the court to determine exactly what goods Bucci was to purchase under the agreement.*

Open Delivery Term   When no delivery terms are specified, the buyer normally takes delivery at the seller's place of business. [UCC 2-308(a)] If the seller has no place of business, then the seller's residence is used. When goods are located in some other place and both parties know it, then delivery is made there. When the time for shipment or delivery has not been clearly specified in the sales contract, the court will infer a "reasonable" time under the circumstances for performance. [UCC 2-309(1)]

The following case illustrates a court's determination of what constitutes a reasonable time for the delivery of produce to be sold at market.

MENDELSON-ZELLER CO., INC. v. JOSEPH WEDNER & SON CO.

U.S. Department of Agriculture, 1970.
7 UCC Rep. Serv. 1045.

BACKGROUND AND FACTS   *The dispute here concerned 400 cartons of lettuce. The contract provided that the lettuce would be shipped from El Centro, California, on January 18 and that the lemons would be loaded at Yuma, Arizona. The parties estimated that delivery to Pittsburgh, Pennsylvania, would be in time for the market on Monday morning, January 22, 1968.*

Mendelson-Zeller, the plaintiff, shipped the lettuce on January 18, 1968, at 9:40 P.M. from El Centro, California, and the lemons on January 19, 1968, at 4:30 A.M. from Yuma, Arizona, in a truck. The truckload of produce arrived at Wedner & Son's (the defendant's) place of business at 12:30 P.M., January 22, 1968. Wedner's docking superintendent refused to unload the truck and instructed the driver to return the next morning at 2:00 A.M. to have the truck unloaded for Tuesday's market. The driver locked the truck and did not return until 6:30 A.M. on Tuesday. Thus, the produce was delivered on the scheduled delivery date, but, according to Wedner, it arrived nine and one-half hours late. Wedner claimed that the agreement indicated that the goods would arrive between 2:00 and 3:00 A.M. so they would be available when the produce market opened. Mendelson-Zeller claimed that neither the time of loading nor the time of arrival was guaranteed.

Wedner eventually sold the lettuce and remitted the net proceeds of $1,028.93 to Mendelson-Zeller, along with the net proceeds from the consignment sale of the lettuce. Mendelson-Zeller sued for the difference between the contract price and the amount remitted.

FLAVIN, Judicial Officer. [Functions as a judge or magistrate.]
* * * *

There is evidence that the trucker was under some pressure to get the lettuce to respondent [Wedner & Son] for Monday morning's market.
* * * *

It is evident * * * that [seller] * * * distinguishes between an estimated delivery time and a delivery time which is specified as a part of the contract terms. Neither party submitted a broker's memorandum covering the sale which would presumably show whether there was a specified contract delivery time. In addition the bill of lading does not disclose a specified arrival time though a blank space is provided in which such information can be entered. All of the statements relevant to arrival time other than [buyer] Wedner's statement can be interpreted to mean estimated or anticipated arrival time rather than a time specified as a contract condition.

Respondent [Wedner] as the party alleging that a specified arrival time was a part of the contract of sale had the burden of proving by a preponderance of the evidence that its allegation was true. In view of the foregoing discussion we conclude that respondent has not met its burden of proof.

Section 2-309(1) of the Uniform Commercial Code provides that the time for delivery in the absence of an agreed time shall be a reasonable time. Section 2-503(1) provides that tender of delivery must be at a reasonable hour. The evidence shows that the truck left Yuma at 4:30 a.m. January 19 and arrived at respondent's warehouse at 12:30 p.m. January 22. Although the trucker offered to pay overtime for unloading, respondent's docking superintendent refused to unload. Wedner testified that he thought the truck arrived well after business hours. However, he also testified that respondent's office hours are 9 a.m. to 5 p.m. and the hours at its warehouse and terminal on Mondays are 4 a.m. to anywhere from 11:30 to 12:30 p.m. There is no evidence as to the exact time the warehouse closed on January 22. It is unnecessary to resolve whether the tender on January 22 was within a reasonable hour or whether, as complainant contends, respondent accepted delivery by ordering the truckers to return the next morning. The load was tendered and accepted at 6:30 a.m. January 23, about 97 hours after the truck left Yuma. Although there was some testimony indicating that the normal transit time is 72 hours, the trucking company states that this is an impossibility in the winter time. The truck was actually in transit about 80 hours between Yuma and Pittsburgh. Under the circumstances, we are unable to say that delivery on January 23, was not within a reasonable time.

The seller, Mendelson-Zeller Co., prevailed. The delivery was made in reasonable time; hence Wedner's failure to pay the full contract price of the lettuce was a breach of contract. The court awarded Mendelson-Zeller damages plus interest on the amount owing.

DECISION AND REMEDY

Duration of an Ongoing Contract A single contract might specify successive performances, but may not indicate how long the parties are required to deal with one another. Although either party may terminate the ongoing contractual relationship, principles of good faith and sound commercial practice call for reasonable notification before termination so as to give the other party reasonable time to seek a substitute arrangement. [UCC 2-309(2)(3)]

Options and Cooperation Regarding Performance   When specific shipping arrangements have not been made but the contract contemplates shipment of the goods, the *seller* has the right to make these arrangements in good faith, using commercial reasonableness in the situation. [UCC 2-311]

When terms relating to the assortment of goods are omitted from a sales contract, the *buyer* can specify the assortment. For example, Able and Baker contract for the sale of 1,000 pens. The pens come in a variety of colors, but the contract is silent on which color is ordered. Baker, the buyer, has the right to take 600 blue pens and 400 green pens if he wishes. However, Baker must make the selection in good faith and must use commercial reasonableness. [UCC 2-311]

Merchant's Firm Offer   The firm offer is in the special category of rules applicable only to *merchants*. Under regular contract principles, an offer can be revoked any time before acceptance. The major common law exception is an option contract in which the offeree pays consideration for the offeror's irrevocable promise to keep the offer open for a stated period.

The UCC creates a second exception that applies only to *firm offers* for the sale of goods made *by a merchant* (regardless of whether or not the offeree is a merchant). If the merchant gives *assurances* in a *signed writing* that the offer will remain open for the stated period or, if no definite period is specified, a reasonable period (neither to exceed three months), the *merchant's firm offer* is irrevocable without the necessity of consideration.[4] [UCC 2-205]

To illustrate: Daniels, a used-car dealer, writes a letter to Peters on January 1 stating, "I have a 1974 Dodge Dart on the lot that I'll sell you for $2,200 any time between now and the end of the month." By January 18, Daniels has heard nothing from Peters so he sells the Dodge Dart to another person. On January 23, Peters tenders $2,200 to Daniels and asks for the car. When Daniels tells him the car has already been sold, Peters claims that Daniels

has breached a good contract. Peters is right. Since Daniels is a merchant of used cars, he is obligated to keep his offer open until the end of January. Since he has not done so, he is liable for breach.

It is necessary, however, that the offer be both *written and signed* by the offeror.[5] Where a firm offer is contained in a form contract prepared by the offeree, a *separate* firm offer assurance must be signed in addition. The purpose of the merchant's firm offer rule is to give effect to a merchant's deliberate intent to be bound to a firm offer. If the firm offer is buried in one of the pages of the offeree's form contract amid copious language, the offeror might inadvertently sign the contract without realizing it, thus defeating the purpose of the rule.

Acceptance

Methods of Acceptance   The general common law rule is that an offeror can specify, or authorize, a particular means of acceptance, making that means the only one effective for the contract. The common law rule has been altered recently, however, so that even unauthorized means of communication are effective as long as the acceptance is received by the specified deadline. For example, suppose the offer states, "Answer by telegraph within five days." If the offeree sends a letter, and it is received by the offeror within five days, a valid contract is formed.

When the offeror does not specify a means of acceptance, the Code provides that acceptance can be made by any means of communication reasonable under the circumstances, even if the acceptance is not received within the designated time. [UCC 2-206(1)] For example, Alpha Corporation writes Beta Corporation a letter offering to sell Beta $1,000 worth of goods. The offer states that Alpha will keep the offer open for only ten days from the date of the letter. Before the ten days have lapsed, Beta sends Alpha a telegram of acceptance. The telegram is misdirected by the telegraph company and does not reach Alpha until after the ten-day deadline. Is a valid contract formed? The answer is probably yes, since telegraph appears to be a commercially rea-

---

4.   If the offeree pays consideration, then an *option contract* and not a *merchant's firm offer* is formed.

5.   "Signed" includes any symbol executed or adopted by a party with present intention to authenticate a writing. [UCC 1-201(39)] A complete signature is not required. Therefore, initials, a thumbprint, a tradename, or any mark used in lieu of a written signature will suffice, regardless of its location on the document.

sonable medium of acceptance under the circumstances. Acceptance would be effective upon Alpha's delivery of the message to the telegraph office, which occurred before the offer lapsed.

The UCC permits acceptance of an offer to buy goods for current or prompt shipment by either a *promise* to ship or *prompt shipment* of the goods to the buyer. [UCC 2-206(1)(b)] This provision of the Code retains the common law acceptance of an offer (performance by delivery of conforming goods to the carrier) and adds as acceptance the commercial practice of sellers who send promises to ship conforming goods. These promises are effective when sent, if they meet the test of being sent by a medium that is commercially reasonable under the circumstances.

The Code goes one step further and provides that if the seller does not promise to ship conforming goods but instead ships (in response to the order) *nonconforming goods*, this shipment constitutes both an *acceptance* (contract) and a *breach*. This specific rule (dealing with nonconforming goods shipped) does not apply if the seller seasonably notifies the buyer that the nonconforming shipment is offered only as an accommodation. The notice of accommodation must clearly indicate to the buyer that the shipment does not constitute an acceptance and that, therefore, no contract has been formed at this time.

For example, Beyer orders 1,000 *blue* widgets from Sallor. Sallor ships 1,000 *black* widgets to Beyer, notifying Beyer that since Sallor has only black widgets in stock, these are sent as an accommodation. The shipment of black widgets is not an acceptance, but an offer (usually a counter offer), and a contract will be formed only if Beyer accepts the black widgets.

If, however, Sallor ships 1,000 black widgets instead of blue without notifying Beyer that the goods are being shipped *as an accommodation*, Sallor's shipment acts as both an acceptance of Beyer's offer and a *breach* of the resulting contract. Beyer may sue Sallor for any appropriate damages.

At common law, since a unilateral offer invites acceptance by a performance, the offeree need not notify the offeror of performance unless the offeror would not otherwise know about it. The UCC is more stringent than common law, stating that "Where the beginning of requested performance is a reasonable mode of acceptance an offeror who is not notified of acceptance within a reasonable time may treat the offer as having lapsed before acceptance." [UCC 2-206(2)]

To illustrate: Johnson writes the Scroll Bookstore on Monday, "Please send me a copy of *West's Book of Business Law* for $35, C.O.D.," signed "Johnson." Scroll receives the request on Tuesday. Scroll immediately prepares the book for shipment but does not ship it for four weeks. Upon its arrival, Johnson rejects the shipment, claiming that the book has arrived too late to be of value.

In this case, since Johnson heard nothing from Scroll for a month, he was justified in assuming that the store did not intend to deliver *West's Book of Business Law*. Johnson could consider that the offer lapsed because of the length of time.

Additional Terms   Under traditional common law, if Able makes an offer to Baker, and Baker in turn accepts but adds some slight qualification, there is no contract. The so-called "mirror-image rule" of offer-to-acceptance makes Baker's action a rejection of, and a counter offer to, Able's offer.

The UCC generally takes the position that if the offeree's response indicates a *definite* acceptance of the offer, a contract is formed, even if the acceptance includes terms in addition to or different from the original offer. [UCC 2-207(1)] However, the Code provides that the offeree's expression cannot be construed as an acceptance if the modifications are subject to (conditional upon) the offeror's "assent."

For example, Sallor offers to sell Beyer 500 pounds of chicken breasts at a specified price and on specified delivery terms. Beyer responds, "I accept your offer for 500 pounds of chicken breasts, *as evidenced by a city scale weight certificate*, at the price and delivery terms stated in your offer."

Beyer's response constitutes a contract even though the acceptance adds the words "as evidenced by a city scale weight certificate." However, if Beyer says, "I accept your offer for 500 pounds of chicken breasts on the condition that the weight be evidenced by a city scale weight certificate," there will be no contract unless Sallor so agrees.

If it is determined that a contract exists, the issue then becomes one of determining under whose terms we measure performance: the offeror's or the offeree's (with modifications). The Code also addresses this issue in an attempt to solve the so-called battle of the forms between commercial buyers and sellers.

Exhibit 17–1 is an example of a purchase order. The front of the form is the actual order for particular goods. The back contains standard contract clauses and terms governing the sale. These clauses are sometimes modified to meet a particular purchase requirement. These clauses will have even more meaning as you read the following materials and chapters on sales.

Rules Where Seller or Buyer Is a Non-merchant

When either the seller or the buyer is a non-merchant, or when both are non-merchants, the additional terms are construed as mere proposals (suggestions), and the modified terms do not become a part of the contract. Thus, the contract is formed on the offeror's terms. [UCC 2-207(2)]

For example, Smith offers to sell his *personal* car to Green for $1,000. Green replies, "I accept your offer to purchase your car for $1,000. I would like a new spare tire to be included as part of the purchase price." Green has given Smith a definite expression of acceptance, creating a contract, even though Green's acceptance also suggests an added term for the offer. Since Green is not a merchant, the additional term is merely a proposal (suggestion), and Green is not legally obligated to comply. On the other hand, if Smith made the spare tire a *condition* of acceptance, then Smith would be making a counteroffer and rejecting the original offer.

Rules between Merchants

The Code rule for *additional* terms in the acceptance is a little different when the transaction occurs between merchants (that is, when both buyer and seller are merchants). Between merchants the additional proposed terms *automatically* become part of the contract unless:

1. They *materially alter* the original contract.
2. The *offer expressly states* that no terms other than those in the offer will be accepted.
3. The offeror timely objects to the modified terms. [UCC 2-207(2)]

Suppose Sallor and Beyer are merchants. Sallor offers to sell Beyer 1,000 ballpoint pen and pencil sets at a price of $10 per set *plus* freight. Beyer responds, "I accept your offer. Price is $10.01 per set, *including* freight." There is a contract between Sallor and Beyer because Beyer made a definite expression of acceptance. Unless Sallor objects to the freight modification within a reasonable time after receiving notice of the change, Sallor is bound to the $10.01 price per set including freight.

Such is not the case, however, if the modification is one that materially alters the contract. What constitutes a material alteration is frequently a question of fact that only a court can decide. Generally, if the modification involves no unreasonable element of surprise or hardship for the offeror, the court will hold that it did not materially alter the contract. If, in the example just presented, the actual freight charge and the 1¢ per set are within a reasonable range of each other, the modification would *probably* not be considered material.

Now suppose that Sallor's offer states, "1,000 ballpoint pen and pencil sets at a price of $10 per set plus freight. Your acceptance on these terms and these terms only." Beyer's definite expression of acceptance with the modified freight terms still constitutes a contract, but because Sallor's offer specifically restricts his obligations to the terms of his offer, the contract is formed on Sallor's terms of "$10 per set plus freight."

In this next case, the court considers the question of whether a carpet manufacturer's written confirmation of a carpet dealer's oral orders for carpet was an "acceptance expressly conditioned on the buyer's consent to additional terms" (specifically, an arbitration provision), which would bring their situation within UCC 2-207(1), and whether the written confirmation between merchants automatically became part of the contract unless they "materially altered it," which would bring the action within the provisions of UCC 2-207(2).

DORTON v. COLLINS & AIKMAN CORP.

United States Court of Appeals, Sixth Circuit, 1972. 453 F.2d 1161.

BACKGROUND AND FACTS *The Carpet Mart, a carpet dealer, and Collins & Aikman Corp., a carpet manufacturer, typically did business orally, followed with acknowledgment forms that were generally recognized as confirmations of prior oral agreements. In this particular instance, Collins & Aikman attempted to introduce in their confirmation form an additional term concerning an arbitration provision. The court was not able to resolve who should prevail*

EXHIBIT 17–1   An Example of a Purchase Order (Front)

IBM   **Purchase Order**

NUMBER   DATE

IBM DATA

| SUPPLIER | MACH | U/M | O/C | SUC | P P E | R E X | E C P | COMMODITY | M M | DEPT. ORDER | A L T | JOB NO. | DEPT. CHG. | APPROP. | C C | PR ORIG. | CHG. RN |

REC. NO.   B.J. S.O. OR REF. NO.   ACCOUNT NO.   COMMITMENT

REMIT TO→

NOTIFY BUYER IMMEDIATELY IF REMIT TO ADDRESS IS DIFFERENT ON INVOICE.

S H I P T O   **IBM**   11400 BURNET ROAD AUSTIN, TEXAS 78758   BLDG.

OTHER THAN ABOVE

| CODE | TAXES |
DO NOT CHARGE TEXAS SALES USE TAX SINCE WE PAY DIRECT OUR DIRECT PAY AUTHORIZATION NUMBER IS:
3-000001-7281-4

SPECIFICATION CODE
1. Print Attached.
2. Specifications Attached.
3. Sample Attached.
4. Print in Your Possession.
5. Specification in Your Possession.
6. Sample in Your Possession.

SEE CODE BELOW   SHIP VIA   IBM DATA   F.O.B. SHIP POINT   DESTINATION   IBM DATA   YOUR TERMS OF PAYMENT

TRANSPORTATION ROUTING GUIDELINES *(DO NOT INSURE OR DECLARE VALUE)*

{ 0-99 (45kg.) United Parcel Service, if available. If not,
0-40 (18kg.) Parcel Post *(Zones 1-8)* up to $1000 value.
All other   Ship as indicated in "ship via" block.

IMPORTANT
1. SHOW OUR COMPLETE ORDER NUMBER, ITEM NUMBER AND IBM PART NUMBER (IF ANY) ON ALL INVOICES, SHIPPING CONTAINERS, PACKING LISTS AND CORRESPONDENCE
2. SECURELY ATTACH PACKING SLIP TO OUTSIDE OF CARTON.
3. PACKAGES WEIGHING OVER 75 LBS MUST BE PACKAGED FOR HANDLING WITH A MECHANICAL DEVICE.

ITEM	PART NUMBER	E/C LEVEL	SHIP TO ARRIVE	QUANTITY	U/M	UNIT PRICE	U/M

*TOTAL QUANTITY OF ITEM ORDERED

"SUBJECT TO THE TERMS AND CONDITIONS ON THE BACK HEREOF WHICH ARE INCORPORATED AND MADE A PART HEREOF"

ADDRESS ALL INVOICES TO:
INTERNATIONAL BUSINESS MACHINES CORP.
Attn: Accounts Payable
P. O. Box 9928
Austin, Texas 78766

AUTHORIZED SIGNATURE   512-838-3300   EXT.

942-0262-4

Source: Reprinted with the permission of the IBM Corporation. © 1985. Copyright: IBM.   *(continued on next page)*

EXHIBIT 17–1 An Example of a Purchase Order (Backside)

STANDARD TERMS AND CONDITIONS

IBM EXPRESSLY LIMITS ACCEPTANCE TO THE TERMS SET FORTH ON THE FACE AND REVERSE SIDE OF THIS PURCHASE ORDER AND ANY ATTACHMENTS HERETO:

PURCHASE ORDER CONSTITUTES COMPLETE AGREEMENT

This Purchase order, including the terms and conditions on the face and reverse side hereof and any attachments hereto, contains the complete and final agreement between International Business Machines Corporation (IBM) and Seller. Reference to Seller's bids or proposals, if noted on this order, shall not affect terms and conditions hereof, unless specifically provided to the contrary herein, and no other agreement or quotation in any way modifying any of said terms and conditions will be binding upon IBM unless made in writing and signed by IBM's authorized representative.

ADVERTISING

Seller shall not, without first obtaining the written consent of IBM, in any manner advertise, publish or otherwise disclose the fact that Seller has furnished, or contracted to furnish to IBM, the material and/or services ordered hereunder.

APPLICABLE LAW

The agreement arising pursuant to this order shall be governed by the laws of the State of New York. No rights, remedies and warranties available to IBM under this contract or by operation of law are waived or modified unless expressly waived or modified by IBM in writing.

CASH DISCOUNT OR NET PAYMENT PERIOD

Calculations will be from the date an acceptable invoice is received by IBM. Any other arrangements agreed upon must appear on this order and on the invoice.

CONFIDENTIAL INFORMATION

Seller shall not disclose to any person outside of its employ, or use for any purpose other than to fulfill its obligations under this order, any information received from IBM pursuant to this order, which has been disclosed to Seller by IBM in confidence, except such information which is otherwise publicly available or is publicly disclosed by IBM subsequent to Seller's receipt of such information or is rightfully received by Seller from a third party. Upon termination of this order, Seller shall return to IBM upon request all drawings, blueprints, descriptions or other material received from IBM and all materials containing said confidential information. Also, Seller shall not disclose to IBM any information which Seller deems to be confidential, and it is understood that any information received by IBM, including all manuals, drawings and documents will not be of a confidential nature or restrict, in any manner, the use of such information by IBM. Seller agrees that any legend or other notice on any information supplied by Seller, which is inconsistent with the provisions of this article, does not create any obligation on the part of IBM.

GIFTS

Seller shall not make or offer gifts or gratuities of any type to IBM employees or members of their families. Such gifts or offerings may be construed as Seller's attempt to improperly influence our relationship.

IBM PARTS

All parts and components bailed by IBM to Seller for incorporation in work being performed for IBM shall be used solely for such purposes.

OFF-SPECIFICATION

Seller shall obtain from IBM written approval of all off-specification work.

PACKAGES

Packages must bear IBM's order number and show gross, tare and net weights and/or quantity.

PATENTS

Seller will settle or defend, at Seller's expense (and pay any damages, costs or fines resulting from), all proceedings or claims against IBM, its subsidiaries and affiliates and their respective customers, for infringement, or alleged infringement, by the goods furnished under this order, or any part or use thereof of patents (including utility models and registered designs) now or hereafter granted in the United States or in any country where Seller, its subsidiaries or affiliates, heretofore has furnished similar goods. Seller will, at IBM's request, identify the countries in which Seller, its subsidiaries or affiliates, heretofore has furnished similar goods.

PRICE

If price is not stated on this order, Seller shall invoice at lowest prevailing market price.

QUALITY

Material is subject to IBM's inspection and approval within a reasonable time after delivery. If specifications are not met, material may be returned at Seller's expense and risk for all damages incidental to the rejection. Payment shall not constitute an acceptance of the material nor impair IBM's right to inspect or any of its remedies.

SHIPMENT

Shipment must be made within the time stated on this order, failing which IBM reserves the right to purchase elsewhere and charges Seller with any loss incurred, unless delay in making shipment is due to unforeseeable causes beyond the control and without the fault or negligence of Seller.

SUBCONTRACTS

Seller shall not subcontract or delegate its obligations under this order without the written consent of IBM. Purchases of parts and materials normally purchased by Seller or required by this order shall not be construed as subcontracts or delegations.

(NON-U.S. LOCATIONS ONLY)

Seller further agrees that during the process of bidding or production of goods and services hereunder, it will not re-export or divert to others any IBM specification, drawing or other data, or any product of such data.

TAXES

Unless otherwise directed, Seller shall pay all sales and use taxes imposed by law upon or on account of this order. Where appropriate, IBM will reimburse Seller for this expense.

TOOLS

IBM owned tools held by Seller are to be used only for making parts for IBM. Tools of any kind held by Seller for making IBM's parts must be repaired and renewed by Seller at Seller's expense.

TRANSPORTATION

Routing—As indicated in transportation routing guidelines on face of this order.
F.O.B.—Unless otherwise specified, ship collect, F.O.B. origin.
Prepaid Transportation (when specified)—Charges must be supported by a paid freight bill or equivalent.

Cartage	) No charge allowed
Premium Transportation	) unless authorized
Insurance	) by IBM.

Consolidation—Unless otherwise instructed, consolidate all daily shipments to one destination on one bill of lading.

COMPLIANCE WITH LAWS AND REGULATIONS

Seller shall at all times comply with all applicable Federal, State and local laws, rules and regulations.

EQUAL EMPLOYMENT OPPORTUNITY

There are incorporated in this order the provisions of Executive Order 11246 (as amended) of the President of the United States on Equal Employment Opportunity and the rules and regulations issued pursuant thereto with which the Seller represents that he will comply, unless exempt.

EMPLOYMENT AND PROCUREMENT PROGRAMS

There are incorporated in this order the following provisions as they apply to performing work under Government procurement contracts: Utilization of Small Business Concerns (if in excess of $10,000) (Federal Procurement Regulation (FPR) 1-1.710-3(a)); Small Business Subcontracting Program (if in excess of $500,000) (FPR 1-1.710-3 (b)); Utilization of Labor Surplus Area Concerns (if in excess of $10,000) (FPR 1-1.805-3(a)); Labor Surplus Area Subcontracting Program (if in excess of $500,000) (FPR 1-1.805-3 (b)); Utilization of Minority Enterprises (if in excess of $10,000) (FPR 1-1.1310-2 (a)); Minority Business Enterprises Subcontracting Program (if in excess of $50,000) (FPR 1-1.1310-2(b)); Affirmative Action for Handicapped Workers (if $2,500 or more) (41 CFR 60-741.4); Affirmative Action for Disabled Veterans and Veterans of the Vietnam Era (if $10,000 or more) (41 CFR 60-250.4); Utilization of Small Business Concerns and Small Business Concerns Owned and Controlled by Socially and Economically Disadvantaged Individuals (if in excess of $10,000) (44 Fed. Reg. 23610 (April 20, 1979)); Small Business and Small Disadvantaged Business Subcontracting Plan (if in excess of $500,000) (44 Fed. Reg. 23610 (April 20, 1979)).

WAGES AND HOURS

Seller warrants that in the performance of this order Seller has complied with all of the provisions of the Fair Labor Standards Act of 1938 of the United States as amended.

WORKERS' COMPENSATION, EMPLOYERS' LIABILITY INSURANCE

If Seller does not have Workers' Compensation or Employer's Liability Insurance, Seller shall indemnify IBM against all damages sustained by IBM resulting from Seller's failure to have such insurance.

because a final decision required additional findings of fact from the trial court. So, the court merely provided a framework within which the trial court could proceed after the additional information had been gathered. The case should be read for an understanding of the law.

CELEBREZZE, Circuit Judge.

*   *   *   *

*   *   * *Under the common law, an acceptance or a confirmation which contained terms additional to or different from those of the offer or oral agreement constituted a rejection of the offer or agreement and thus became a counter-offer.* [Emphasis added.] The terms of the counter-offer were said to have been accepted by the original offeror when he proceeded to perform under the contract without objecting to the counter-offer. Thus, a buyer was deemed to have accepted the seller's counter-offer if he took receipt of the goods and paid for them without objection.

Under Section 2-207 the result is different. This section of the Code recognizes that in current commercial transactions, the terms of the offer and those of the acceptance will seldom be identical. Rather, under the current "battle of the forms", each party typically has a printed form drafted by his attorney and containing as many terms as could be envisioned to favor that party in his sales transactions. Whereas under common law the disparity between the fine-print terms in the parties' forms would have prevented the consummation of a contract when these forms are exchanged, Section 2-207 recognizes that in many, but not all, cases the parties do not impart such significance to the terms on the printed forms. *   *   *

*   *   *   *

Assuming, for purposes of analysis, that the arbitration provision was an addition to the terms of The Carpet Mart's oral offers, we must next determine whether or not Collins & Aikman's acceptances were "expressly made conditional on assent to the additional *   *   * terms" therein, within the proviso of Subsection 2-207(1).

Because Collins & Aikman's acceptances were not expressly conditional on the buyer's assent to the additional terms within the proviso of Subsection 2-207(1) a contract is recognized under Subsection (1), and the additional terms are treated as "proposals" for addition to the contract under Subsection 2-207(2). Since both Collins & Aikman and The Carpet Mart are clearly "merchants" as that term is defined in Subsection 2-104(1), the arbitration provision will be deemed to have been accepted by The Carpet Mart under Subsection 2-207(2) unless it materially altered the terms of The Carpet Mart's oral offers.

DECISION AND REMEDY

If Collins & Aikman's acknowledgments are in fact acceptances and the arbitration provision is additional to the terms of Carpet Mart's oral orders, the contracts will be recognized under the provisions of UCC 2-207(1). The arbitration clause will then be viewed as a "proposal" under UCC 2-207(2), and it will be deemed to have been accepted by Carpet Mart, as both parties are merchants, unless it materially altered the oral agreement.

Consideration

The UCC radically changes the common law rule that contract modification must be supported by new consideration. Section 2-209(1) states that "an agreement modifying a contract needs no consideration to be binding." Of course, contract modification must be sought in good faith. [UCC 1-203] Modifications *extorted* from the other party are in bad faith and, therefore, unenforceable.

For example, Hal agrees to manufacture and sell certain goods to Betty for a stated price. Subsequently, a sudden shift in the market makes it difficult for Hal to sell the items to Betty at the given price without suffering a loss. Hal tells Betty of the situation, and Betty agrees to pay an additional sum for the goods. Later Betty reconsiders and refuses to pay more than the original price. Under Section 2-209(1) of the UCC, Betty's promise to modify the contract needs no consideration to be binding. Hence, Betty is bound by the modified contract.

In the example above, a shift in the market provides an example of a *good faith* reason for contract modification. In fact, Section 1-203 states that "Every contract or duty within this act imposes an obligation of good faith in its performance or enforcement." Good faith in the case of a merchant is defined to mean honesty in fact and the observance of reasonable commercial standards of fair dealing in the trade. [UCC 2-103(1)(b)] But what if there really were no shift in the market, and Hal knew that Betty needed the goods immediately but refused to deliver unless Betty agreed to pay an additional sum of money? This sort of extortion of a modification without a legitimate commercial reason would be ineffective because it would violate the duty of good faith. Hal would not be permitted to enforce the higher price.

When Modification Without Consideration Requires a Writing

There are situations in which modification without consideration must be written in order to be enforceable. For example, the contract itself may prohibit any modification or rescission of the contract unless such is in a signed writing. Therefore, only those changes agreed to in the signed writing are enforceable. [UCC 2-209(2)] If a consumer (nonmerchant buyer) is dealing with a merchant, *and* the merchant supplies the form that contains a prohibition against oral modification, the consumer must sign a separate acknowledgment of such a clause.

Also, any modification that brings the contract under the Statute of Frauds will usually require the modification to be in writing to be enforceable. Thus, if an oral contract for the sale of goods priced at $400 is modified so that the contracted goods are now priced at $600, the modification will have to be in writing to be enforceable. [UCC 2-209(3)] If, however, the buyer accepts delivery of the goods after the modification, he or she is bound to the $600 price. [UCC 2-201(3)(c)]

Statute of Frauds

Section 2-201(1) of the UCC contains a Statute of Frauds provision that applies to contracts for the sale of goods. The provision requires a writing for the contract to be enforceable if the price is $500 or more. The parties can have an initial oral agreement, however, and satisfy the Statute of Frauds by having a subsequent written memorandum of their oral agreement. In each case the writing must be signed by the party against whom enforcement is sought.

Between Merchants—Written Confirmation

Once again the UCC provides a special rule for a contract for the sale of goods between merchants. Merchants can satisfy the requirements of a writing for the Statute of Frauds if, after the parties have agreed orally, one of the merchants sends a signed written confirmation to the other merchant. The communication must indicate the terms of the agreement, and the merchant receiving the confirmation must have reason to know of its contents. Unless the merchant who receives the confirmation gives written notice of objection to its contents within ten days after receipt, the writing will be sufficient against the receiving merchant even though he or she has not signed anything.

For example, Beyer is a Miami merchant buyer. He contracts over the telephone to purchase $5,000 worth of goods from Sallor, a New York City merchant seller. Two days later Sallor sends written confirmation detailing the terms of the oral contract, and later Beyer receives it. If Beyer wishes to use the Statute of Frauds as a defense against enforcement of the contract against him, Beyer must give Sallor written notice of objection to the contents of the written confirmation within ten days of receipt.

Relaxed Requirements

The UCC has greatly relaxed the requirements for the sufficiency of a writing to satisfy the Statute of Frauds. A written contract or a memorandum will be sufficient as long as a sales contract (agreement) is indicated and as long as it is signed by the party (or agent) against whom enforcement is sought. The single term that must be included in the writing is the quantity (except in the case of output and requirements contracts). All other terms can be proved in court by oral testimony.

Often, terms that are not agreed upon can be supplied by the open term provisions of Article 2 itself.

Exceptions Section 2-201 defines three exceptions to the Statute of Frauds requirement. [UCC 2-201(3)] A contract, if proved to exist, will be enforceable despite the absence of a writing even if it involves a sale of goods for $500 or more if:

1. *The oral contract is for (a) specially manufactured goods for a particular buyer, (b) these goods are not suitable for resale to others in the ordinary course of the seller's business, and (c) the seller has substantially started to manufacture the goods or made commitments for the manufacture of the goods.* In this situation, once the seller has taken action, the buyer cannot repudiate the agreement claiming the Statute of Frauds as a defense.

To illustrate: Archer ordered a uniquely styled cabinet from Collins, a cabinetmaker. The price of the cabinet is $1,000, and the contract is oral. Collins finishes the cabinet and tenders delivery to Archer. Archer refuses to pay for it even though the job is completed on time. Archer claims that he is not liable because the contract is oral. Clearly, if the unique style of the cabinet makes it improbable that Collins can find another buyer, then Archer is liable to Collins. Also, Collins must have made a substantial beginning in manufacturing the specialized item prior to Archer's repudiation. Of course, the court must still be convinced that there was an oral contract.

2. *A party to a contract can admit in pleadings (written answers), testimony, or other court proceedings that a contract for sale was made.* In this case the contract will be enforceable even though it was oral, but enforceability is limited to the quantity of goods admitted.

To illustrate: Archer and Collins negotiate an agreement over the telephone. During the negotiations, Archer requests a delivery price for 500 gallons of gasoline and a separate price for 700 gallons of gasoline. Collins replies that the price would be the same, $1.10 per gallon. Archer verbally orders 500 gallons. Collins honestly believes that Archer has ordered 700 gallons and tenders that amount. Archer refuses the shipment of 700 gallons, and Collins sues for breach. Archer's answer and testimony admit an oral contract was made, but only

for 500 gallons. Since Archer admits the existence of the oral contract, Archer cannot plead the Statute of Frauds as a defense. However, the contract is enforceable only to the extent of the quantity admitted, 500 gallons.

3. *An oral agreement will be enforceable to the extent that payment has been made and accepted or to the extent that goods have been received and accepted.* This is the "partial performance" exception. The oral contract will be enforced at least to the amount of performance that *actually* took place.

For example, Archer orally contracts to sell Collins ten chairs at $100 each. Before delivery, Collins sends Archer a check for $500, which Archer cashes. Later, when Archer attempts to deliver the chairs, Collins refuses delivery, claiming the Statute of Frauds as a defense, and demands the return of his $500. Under the UCC's partial performance rule, Archer can enforce the oral contract by tender of delivery of five chairs for the $500 accepted. Similarly, if Collins had made no payment but had accepted the delivery of five chairs from Archer, the oral contract would have been enforceable against Collins for $500, the price of the five chairs delivered.

Parol Evidence

If the parties to a contract set forth its terms in a confirmatory memorandum (a writing expressing offer and acceptance of the deal) or in a writing intended as their final expression, the terms of the contract cannot be contradicted by evidence of any prior or contemporaneous oral or written agreements. However, the terms of the contract can be explained or supplemented by consistent additional terms, or by *course of dealing, usage of trade, or course of performance.* [UCC 2-202]

Consistent Additional Terms If the court finds an ambiguity in a writing that is supposed to be a complete and exclusive statement of the agreement between the parties, it may accept evidence of consistent additional terms to clarify or remove the ambiguity. The court will not, however, accept evidence of contradictory terms. This is the rule under both the Code and the common law of contracts.

Course of Dealing and Usage of Trade In construing a commercial agreement, the court will assume that the course of prior dealing between the parties and the usage of trade were taken into account when the agreement was phrased. [UCC 2-202 and 1-201(3)] The Code states, "A course of dealing between the parties and any usage of trade in the vocation or trade in which they are engaged or of which they are or should be aware give particular meaning to [the terms of an agreement] and supplement or qualify the terms of [the] agreement." [UCC 1-205(3)]

The Code has determined that the meaning of any agreement, evidenced by the language of the parties and by their action, must be interpreted in light of commercial practices and other surrounding circumstances.

A *course of dealing* is a sequence of previous conduct between the parties to a particular transaction that establishes a common basis for their understanding. [UCC 1-205(1)] Course of dealing is restricted, literally, to the sequence of conduct be-

tween the parties that has occurred prior to the agreement in question.

Usage of trade is defined as any practice or method of dealing having such regularity of observance in a place, vocation, or trade as to justify an expectation that it will be observed with respect to the transaction in question. [UCC 1-205(2)] Further, the expressed terms of an agreement and an applicable course of dealing or usage of trade will be construed to be consistent with each other whenever reasonable. However, when such construction is *unreasonable*, the expressed terms in the agreement will prevail. [UCC 1-205(4)]

In the following case, the court permitted the introduction of evidence of usage and custom in the trade to explain the meaning of quantity figures that the parties took for granted when the contract was formed.

HEGGBLADE-MARGULEAS-TENNECO, INC. v. SUNSHINE BISCUIT, INC.

Court of Appeals of California, 5th District, 1976.
59 Cal. App. 3d 948,
131 Cal. Rptr. 183.

BACKGROUND AND FACTS   *Heggblade-Marguleas-Tenneco (HMT) contracted with Sunshine Biscuit (Bell Brand) to supply potatoes to be used in the production of potato-snack foods. HMT had never marketed processing potatoes before. The quantity mentioned in their contract negotiations was 100,000 sacks of potatoes. It was agreed that the amount of potatoes to be supplied would vary somewhat with Sunshine Biscuit's needs. Subsequently, a decline in demand for Sunshine Biscuit's products severely reduced its need for potatoes, and it prorated the reduced demand among its suppliers, including HMT, as fairly as possible. Sunshine Biscuit was able to take only 60,105 sacks out of the 100,000 previously estimated. In HMT's suit for breach of contract, Sunshine Biscuit attempted to introduce evidence that it is customary in the potato-processing industry for the number of potatoes specified in sales contracts to be reasonable estimates rather than exact numbers that a buyer intends to purchase. The trial court held for Sunshine Biscuit.*

FRANSON, Acting Presiding Justice.
*   *   *   *

California Uniform Commercial Code section 2202 states the parol evidence rule applicable to the sale of personal property:

"Terms with respect to which the confirmatory memoranda of the parties agree or which are otherwise set forth in a writing intended by the parties as a final expression of their agreement with respect to such terms as are included therein may not be contradicted by evidence of any prior agreement or of a contemporaneous oral agreement but may be explained or supplemented "(a) By course of dealing or usage of trade (Section 1205) *   *   *.""

California Uniform Commercial Code section 2202, subdivision (a), permits a trade usage to be put in evidence "as an instrument of interpretation." The Uniform Commercial Code comment to subdivision (a) of section 2202 states that evidence of trade usage is admissible "*   *   * in order that the true understanding of the parties as to the agreement may be reached. Such writings are to be read on the assumption that * * * the usages of trade were taken for granted when the document was phrased. Unless *carefully negated* they have become an element of the meaning of the words used. Similarly, the course of actual performance by the parties is considered the best indication of what they intended the writing to mean."

A case factually similar to the instant case is *Columbia Nitrogen Corporation v. Royster Company* (4th Cir. 1971), 451 F.2d 3. There the seller sued the buyer for breach of contract for the purchase of a specified quantity of phosphate. The buyer's defense was a trade usage which imposed no duty to accept at the quoted prices the minimum quantity stated in the contract. The trial court had excluded this evidence because "* * * 'custom and usage * * * are not admissible to contradict the express, plain, unambiguous language of a valid written contract, which by virtue of its detail negates the proposition that the contract is open to variances in its terms. * * *' " The Court of Appeal interpreted Virginia Uniform Commercial Code section 2-202, which is identical to California Uniform Commercial Code section 2202(a), as meaning that where the contract does not expressly state that trade usage cannot be used to explain or supplement the written terms, the evidence of trade usage should be admitted to interpret the contract. "The contract is silent about adjusting prices and quantities to reflect a declining market. It neither permits nor prohibits adjustment, and this neutrality provides a fitting occasion for recourse to usage of trade and prior dealing to supplement the contract and explain its terms."

We find *Columbia Nitrogen Corporation* persuasive. Under subdivision (a) of section 2202, established trade usage and custom are a part of the contract unless the parties agree otherwise. Since the contracts in question are silent about the applicability of the usage and custom, evidence of such usage and custom was admissible to explain the meaning of the quantity figures.

* * * *

Appellant's [HMT's] argument that the evidence of custom should not have been considered by the jury in interpreting the contracts because the officers of HMT were inexperienced in the marketing of processing potatoes and lacked knowledge of the custom is similarly without merit. Mr. Hoffman was knowledgeable in the processing potato business and was aware of the trade custom. Since appellant pleaded that the contracts had been entered into on October 15, 1970, and Hoffman had been employed by HMT on October 1, 1970, his knowledge was imputed to HMT.

Moreover, persons carrying on a particular trade are deemed to be aware of prominent trade customs applicable to their industry. The knowledge may be actual or constructive, and it is constructive if the custom is of such general and universal application that the party must be presumed to know of it.

* * * Because potatoes are a perishable commodity and their demand is dependent upon a fluctuating market, and because the marketing contracts are signed eight or nine months in advance of the harvest season, common sense dictates that the quantity would be estimated by both the grower and processor. Thus, it cannot be said as a matter of law that HMT was ignorant of the trade custom.

We conclude that the trial court properly admitted the evidence of usage and custom to explain the meaning of the quantity figures in the contracts.

The trial court's judgment was affirmed. Bell Brand did not have to pay HMT for the difference between the 100,000 estimated hundredweight sacks of potatoes and the 60,105 actual sacks of potatoes that were purchased.

DECISION AND REMEDY

Parol evidence of usage and custom that is not inconsistent with the terms of the written agreement can be introduced in situations where both parties knew or should have known of the existence of the particular custom or usage in that industry in that locality. Such evidence is supplemental and shows the meaning

COMMENTS

that the parties attach to the particular language. It does not alter or change the contract terms. Just as a previous course of dealing between parties can be regarded as establishing a common basis for interpreting their expressions and conduct [UCC 1-205(1)], so, too, a usage of trade is a regularly observed practice or method of dealing that is normally accepted and followed in a place, vocation, or trade and that establishes a common basis for interpreting expressions or conduct. [UCC 1-205(2)]

Course of Performance   Course of performance is the conduct that occurs under the terms of a particular agreement. The course of performance actually undertaken is the best indication of what the parties to an agreement intended it to mean. Presumably, the parties themselves know best what they meant by their words, and their action under that agreement is the best indication of what they meant. [UCC 2-208]

To illustrate: Able Lumber Company contracts with Baker to sell Baker a specified number of "2-by-4s." The lumber in fact does not measure 2 inches by 4 inches but rather 1⅞ inches by 3¾ inches. If Baker objects to the lumber delivered, Able can prove that "2-by-4s" are never exactly 2 inches by 4 inches by applying usage of trade or course of prior dealings, or both. Able can show in previous transactions that Baker took 1⅞ inch by 3¾ inch lumber without objection. In addition, Able can show that in the trade, 2-by-4s are commonly 1⅞ inches by 3¾ inches. Both usage of trade and course of prior dealings are relevant in determining and explaining what the parties meant by 2-by-4s.

Using the same example, suppose that Able agrees to deliver the lumber in five separate deliveries. The fact that Baker has accepted lumber without objection in three previous deliveries under the agreement (course of performance) is relevant in determining that the words 2-by-4 actually mean 1⅞ by 3¾.

The Code provides *rules of construction*. Express terms, course of performance, course of dealing, and usage of trade are to be construed together when they do not contradict one another. When such construction is unreasonable, however, the following order of priority controls: (1) express terms, (2) course of performance, (3) course of dealing, and (4) usage of trade. [UCC 1-205(4) and 2-208(2)]

Unconscionability

An unconscionable contract is one that is so unfair and one-sided that it would be unreasonable to enforce it. Section 2-302 allows the court to evaluate a contract or any clause in a contract, and if the court deems it to be unconscionable *at the time it was made*, the court can (1) refuse to enforce the contract, or (2) enforce the remainder of the contract without the unconscionable clause, or (3) limit the application of any unconscionable clauses to avoid an unconscionable result.

The court, in determining whether a contract or clause is unconscionable, must decide whether, in light of general commercial practice and the commercial needs of the particular trade involved, the clauses are so one-sided as to be unconscionable under the circumstances at the time the contract was made. In this day of consumer law, more and more consumer sales contracts are being attacked as unconscionable. Typical cases involve high pressure salespersons and uneducated consumers who contract away their basic rights. In general, the courts have concluded that unequal bargaining power, coupled with unscrupulous dealings by one party, will result in an unenforceable, unconscionable contract.

It is noteworthy that the doctrine of unconscionability expressed explicitly in Section 2-302 is a codification of a pre-UCC notion that was of uncertain application. The right of the courts to refuse to enforce all of the terms agreed to by the parties to a contract has been recognized for centuries. Equity courts have refused to grant performance of a contract deemed unfair (unconscionable). One of the leading cases involved Campbell Soup Company.[6]

---

6. Campbell Soup Co. v. Wentz, 172 F.2d 80 (3d Cir. 1948). See Chapter 16 for case excerpts.

The form contract prepared by Campbell Soup contained a clause that excused Campbell Soup from accepting goods under certain circumstances. Additionally, the clause prohibited the seller of the goods from selling them elsewhere without Campbell's written consent. The court refused to grant specific performance in this classic case on the basis that this clause was unconscionable.

The inclusion of Section 2-302 in the UCC reflects an increased sensitivity to certain realities of modern commercial activities. Classical contract theory holds that a contract is a bargain in which the terms have been worked out *freely* between parties that are equals. In many modern commercial transactions, this premise is invalid. Standard form contracts are often signed by consumer-buyers who understand few of the terms used and who often do not even read them. Virtually all of the terms are advantageous to the parties supplying the standard form contract. With Section 2-302, the courts have a powerful weapon for policing such transactions, as the next case illustrates.

BACKGROUND AND FACTS *The purchasers of a freezer brought this action to reform the contract of sale. The purchasers alleged the contract was unconscionable.*

JONES v. STAR CREDIT CORP.

Supreme Court of New York, Nassau County, 1969.
59 Misc. 2d 189, 298 N.Y.S.2d 264.

WACHTLER, Justice.

*   *   *   *

On August 31, 1965 the plaintiffs, who are welfare recipients, agreed to purchase a home freezer unit for $900 as the result of a visit from a salesman representing Your Shop At Home Service, Inc. With the addition of the time credit charges, credit life insurance, credit property insurance, and sales tax, the purchase price totalled $1,234.80. Thus far the plaintiffs have paid $619.88 toward their purchase. The defendant claims that with various added credit charges paid for an extension of time there is a balance of $819.81 still due from the plaintiffs. The uncontroverted proof at the trial established that the freezer unit, when purchased, had a maximum retail value of approximately $300. The question is whether this transaction and the resulting contract could be considered unconscionable within the meaning of Section 2-302 of the Uniform Commercial Code which provides in part:

(1) If the court as a matter of law finds the contract or any clause of the contract to have been unconscionable at the time it was made the court may refuse to enforce the contract, or it may enforce the remainder of the contract without the unconscionable clause, or it may so limit the application of any unconscionable clause as to avoid any unconscionable result.

(2) When it is claimed or appears to the court that the contract or any clause thereof may be unconscionable the parties shall be afforded a reasonable opportunity to present evidence as to its commercial setting, purpose and effect to aid the court in making the determination.

There was a time when the shield of "caveat emptor" would protect the most unscrupulous in the marketplace—a time when the law, in granting parties unbridled latitude to make their own contracts, allowed exploitive and callous practices which shocked the conscience of both legislative bodies and the courts.

The effort to eliminate these practices has continued to pose a difficult problem. On the one hand it is necessary to recognize the importance of preserving the integrity of agreements and the fundamental right of parties to deal, trade, bargain, and contract. On the other hand there is the concern for the uneducated and often illiterate individual who is the victim of gross inequality of bargaining power, usually the poorest members of the community.

*   *   *   *

The law is beginning to fight back against those who once took advantage of the poor and illiterate without risk of either exposure or interference. From the common law doctrine of intrinsic fraud we have over the years, developed common and statutory law which tells not only the buyer but also the seller to beware. This body of laws recognizes the importance of a free enterprise system but at the same time will provide the legal armor to protect and safeguard the prospective victim from the harshness of an unconscionable contract.

Section 2-302 of the Uniform Commercial Code enacts the moral sense of the community into the law of commercial transactions. It authorizes the court to find, as a matter of law, that a contract or a clause of a contract was "unconscionable at the time it was made," and upon so finding the court may refuse to enforce the contract, excise the objectionable clause or limit the application of the clause to avoid an unconscionable result. "The principle", states the Official Comment to this section, "is one of the prevention of oppression and unfair surprise". It permits a court to accomplish directly what heretofore was often accomplished by construction of language, manipulations of fluid rules of contract law and determinations based upon a presumed public policy.

There is no reason to doubt, moreover, that this section is intended to encompass the price term of an agreement. In addition to the fact that it has already been so applied, the statutory language itself makes it clear that not only a clause of the contract, but the contract in toto, may be found unconscionable as a matter of law. Indeed, no other provision of an agreement more intimately touches upon the question of unconscionability than does the term regarding price.

Fraud, in the instant case, is not present; nor is it necessary under the statute. The question which presents itself is whether or not, under the circumstances of this case, the sale of a freezer unit having a retail value of $300 for $900 ($1,439.69 including credit charges and $18 sales tax) is unconscionable as a matter of law. The court believes it is.

Concededly, deciding the issue is substantially easier than explaining it. No doubt, the mathematical disparity between $300, which presumably includes a reasonable profit margin, and $900, which is exhorbitant on its face, carries the greatest weight. Credit charges alone exceed by more than $100 the retail value of the freezer. These alone, may be sufficient to sustain the decision. Yet, a caveat is warranted lest we reduce the import of Section 2-302 solely to a mathematical ratio formula. It may, at times, be that; yet it may also be much more. The very limited financial resources of the purchaser, known to the sellers at the time of the sale, is entitled to weight in the balance. Indeed, the value disparity itself leads inevitably to the felt conclusion that knowing advantage was taken of the plaintiffs. In addition, the meaningfulness of choice essential to the making of a contract, can be negated by a gross inequality of bargaining power.

There is no question about the necessity and even the desirability of instalment sales and the extension of credit. Indeed, there are many, including welfare recipients, who would be deprived of even the most basic conveniences without the use of these devices. Similarly, the retail merchant selling on instalment or extending credit is expected to establish a pricing factor which will afford a degree of protection commensurate with the risk of selling to those who might be default prone. However, neither of these accepted premises can clothe the sale of this freezer with respectability.

Support for the court's conclusion will be found in a number of other cases already decided. In *American Home Improvement, Inc. v. MacIver*, the Supreme Court of New Hampshire held that a contract to install windows, a door and paint, for the price of $2,568.60, of which $809.60 constituted interest and carrying charges and $800 was a salesman's commission was unconscionable as a matter of law. In *State by Lefkowitz v. ITM, Inc.*, a deceptive and fraudulent scheme was involved, but standing alone, the court held that the sale of a vacuum cleaner, among other things, costing the defendant $140 and sold by it for $749 cash or $920.52 on time purchase was unconscionable as a matter of law. Finally, in *Frostifresh Corp.* v. *Reynoso*, the sale of a refrigerator costing the seller $348 for $900 plus credit charges of $245.88 was unconscionable as a matter of law. * * *

Having already paid more than $600 toward the purchase of this $300 freezer unit, it is apparent that the defendant has already been amply compensated. In accordance with the statute, the application of the payment provision should be limited to amounts already paid by the plaintiffs and the contract be reformed and amended by changing the payments called for therein to equal the amount of payment actually so paid by the plaintiffs.

Judgment was entered for the plaintiffs. The contract was reformed so that no further payments were required to be made. **DECISION AND REMEDY**

A court may be reluctant to find a contract unconscionable if the retail price and the time purchase price vary only slightly, or if credit charges are reasonable in light of current interest rates. **COMMENTS**

SUMMARY OF SPECIAL RULES

An outline of special rules for contracts for the sale of goods and the Code sections of Article 2 that apply are presented in summary form below in Ex-

hibit 17–2. All of these rules have either been treated in this chapter or will be treated in Chapters 18 through 22.

EXHIBIT 17–2 UCC Rules for Contracts for the Sale of Goods		
	RULE	**UCC SECTION**
OFFER AND ACCEPTANCE	1. The acceptance of unilateral offers can be made by a promise to ship or by shipment itself.	2-206(1)(b)
	2. Not all terms have to be included for a contract to result.	2-204
	3. Particulars of performance can be left open.	2-311(1)
	4. Firm written offers by *merchants* for three months or less cannot be revoked.	2-205
	5. Acceptance by performance requires notice within a reasonable time; otherwise the offer can be treated as lapsed.	2-206(2)
	6. The price does not have to be included to have a contract.	2-305
	7. Variations in terms between the offer and the acceptance may not be a rejection but may be an acceptance.	2-207
	8. Acceptance can be made by any reasonable means of communication; it is effective when deposited.	2-206(1)(a)
CONSIDERATION	1. A modification of a contract for the sale of goods does not require consideration.	2-209(1)
	2. Adding a seal has no effect on the validity of the contract.	2-203
ILLEGALITY	1. Unconscionable bargains will not be enforced.	2-302
VOIDABLE CONTRACTS	1. Rescission for fraud does not prevent a lawsuit for monetary damages.	2-721
	2. A person with voidable title has power to transfer a good title to a good faith purchaser for value.	2-403

(continued on next page)

EXHIBIT 17–2 (Continued)

	RULE	UCC SECTION
FORM OF THE AGREEMENT	1. The Statute of Frauds covers: (a) All sales of goods for a price of $500 or more. (b) Written confirmations between merchants. (c) Specially manufactured goods. (d) Memoranda that do not include all the agreement terms. (e) Goods for which payment has been made and accepted; goods which have been received and accepted. (f) Admission in pleadings or court proceedings that a contract for sale was made.	2-201
RIGHTS OF THIRD PARTIES	1. Delegation of duties is included when a contract, or the rights under a contract, are assigned.	2-210
PERFORMANCE OF CONTRACTS	1. Tender of payment is a condition precedent to a tender of delivery, unless a credit sale was agreed upon. 2. Anticipatory breach cannot be withdrawn if the other party gives notice that it is final. 3. Claims and rights can be waived without consideration.	2-511 2-611 1-107
DISCHARGE	1. The statute of limitations is four years. Mutual agreement can reduce it to not less than one year.	2-725

QUESTIONS AND CASE PROBLEMS

1. A. B. Smith, Inc. is the manufacturer of washing machines. Over the *telephone*, Smith offers to sell Radar Appliances 100 Model-Z washers at a price of $150 per unit. Smith agrees to keep this offer open for ninety days. Radar tells Smith that the offer appears to be a good one and that Radar will let Smith know of its acceptance within the next two to three weeks. One week later, Smith sends and Radar receives notice that Smith has withdrawn its offer. Radar immediately thereafter telephones Smith and accepts the $150-per-unit offer. Smith claims, first, that there never was a sales contract formed between it and Radar and, second, that if there was a contract, the contract is unenforceable. Discuss Smith's contentions.

2. Beyer, a retailer of television sets, orders 100 Model Color-X sets from manufacturer Martin. The order specifies the price and that the television sets are to be *shipped* by Humming Bird Express on or before October 30. The order is received by Martin on October 5. On October 8 Martin writes Beyer a letter indicating the order was received and that the sets will be shipped as directed, at the specified price. This letter is received by Beyer on October 10. On October 28 Martin, in preparing the shipment, discovers it has only 90 Color-X sets in stock. Martin ships the 90 Color-X sets and 10 television sets of a different model, stating clearly on the invoice that the 10 are being shipped only as an accommodation. Beyer claims Martin is in breach of contract. Martin claims the shipment was not an acceptance, and therefore no contract was formed. Explain who is correct and why.

3. Beyer has a requirements contract with Sallor that obligates Sallor to supply Beyer with all the gasoline Beyer needs for his delivery trucks for one year at $1 per gallon. A clause inserted in small print in the contract by Beyer, and not noticed by Sallor, states, "The buyer reserves the right to reject any shipment for any reason without liability." For six months Beyer has ordered and Sallor has delivered under the contract without any controversy. Because of price actions by OPEC, the price of gasoline to Sallor has increased substantially. Sallor contacts Beyer and tells Beyer he cannot possibly fulfill the requirements contract unless Beyer agrees to pay $1.10 per gallon. Beyer, in need of the gasoline, agrees in writing to modify the contract. Later that month, Beyer learns he can buy gasoline at $1.05 per gallon from Collins. Beyer refuses delivery of his most recent order to Sallor, claiming, first, that the contract allows Beyer to do so without liability and second, that he is required to pay only $1 per gallon if he accepts the delivery. Discuss fully Beyer's contentions.

4. Sallor owns 360 acres of land in Bear County. Sallor makes three separate contracts, in writing, with Beyer concerning the land. First, Sallor contracts to sell to Beyer

500 tons of gravel from a quarry located on the land for a stated price. The contract calls for Beyer to remove the gravel. The second contract sells to Beyer all the wheat presently growing on a forty-acre tract. Sallor is obligated under the contract to harvest and deliver the wheat to Beyer. The third contract is for the sale of the northeast ninety acres with all corn standing. Discuss fully which of these contracts, if any, fall under the UCC.

5. Sallor offers to sell Beyer 1,000 shirts for a stated price. The offer states that shipment will be by the ABC Truck Line. Beyer replies, "I accept your offer for 1,000 shirts at the price quoted. Delivery to be by Yellow Express Truck Line." Both Sallor and Beyer are merchants. Three weeks later, Sallor ships the shirts by the ABC Truck Line, and Beyer refuses shipment. Sallor sues for breach of contract. Beyer claims, first, that there never was a contract because the modification of carriers did not constitute an acceptance and, second, even if there was a contract, Sallor is in breach by shipping the shirts by ABC contrary to the contract terms. Discuss fully Beyer's claims.

6. The Singleton family hired Duewaine Clark d/b/a Clark Construction to repair a damaged portion of their home. During the reconstruction, Clark sent the Singletons to Cloud Brothers, Inc., a furniture, appliance, and carpet wholesaler, to select some necessary items. They ordered merchandise amounting to $7,311. The merchandise was picked up by Clark and delivered to the Singletons. In addition, the invoices were sent directly to Clark, who added his mark-up and then billed the Singletons. Soon after that, the Singletons filed bankruptcy and were unable to pay part of the bill. Cloud Brothers file suit against Clark for the balance owed on the merchandise selected by the Singletons. Clark claims he was not the purchaser and never agreed to pay Cloud for the goods sold to the Singletons. Cloud claims that the facts and conduct of Clark clearly formed a contract. Discuss whether Clark and Cloud have a contract for the sale of goods. [Clark v. Cloud Brothers, Inc., 406 N.E.2d 260, (Ind.App. 1980)]

7. In 1961 Clark and American Sand & Gravel discussed the possibility of a purchase by Clark of 25,000 tons of sand at 45 cents per ton. Although both parties found the terms of the possible sale agreeable, no sale was ever made. About eighteen months later, Clark requested his truck driver to obtain about 1,500 tons of sand from American Sand & Gravel. American Sand & Gravel supplied the sand, but no purchase price was ever mentioned. Subsequently, American charged Clark 55 cents per ton for the sand. Is there a contract between American and Clark? If so, what price can American charge for the sand? [American Sand & Gravel, Inc. v. Clark and Fray Constr. Co., 2 Conn.Cir. 284, 198 A.2d 68 (1964)]

8. Loeb & Company entered into an oral agreement with Schreiner, a farmer, whereby Schreiner was to sell Loeb 150 bales of cotton, each weighing 480 pounds. Shortly thereafter, Loeb sent Schreiner a letter confirming the terms of the oral contract. Schreiner neither acknowledged receipt of the letter nor objected to its terms. When delivery came due, Schreiner ignored the oral agreement and sold his cotton on the open market because the price of cotton had more than doubled (from 37 cents to 80 cents per pound) since the oral agreement was made. In a lawsuit by Loeb & Company against Schreiner, can Loeb & Company recover? [Loeb & Co. v. Schreiner, 294 Ala. 722, 321 So.2d, 199 (1975)]

9. McNabb agreed to sell soybeans to Ralston Purina Company. Severe weather damaged a significant portion of all soybean crops that year. When McNabb was unable to meet the November 30th delivery deadline, Ralston Purina modified the contracts monthly without additional consideration to allow delivery as late as February 28th of the following year. Between November and February, the price of soybeans rose substantially. If Ralston Purina's extensions of the delivery date were intended to *maximize* damages in the event of McNabb's breach, would the modifications to the contract be enforceable? [Ralston Purina Co. v. McNabb, 381 F.Supp. 181 (D.Tenn. 1974)]

10. The LTV Aerospace Corporation publicly solicited bids from local suppliers to manufacture shipping containers to specifications and in quantities to 8,000. The containers were to be delivered on a periodic basis to be specified by LTV to fit its production schedule. Bateman, having obtained a copy of the invitation to bid from a third party, submitted a detailed written bid to LTV. After some oral changes on both specifications and price, an agreement was reached, and the bid was accepted by LTV. Bateman made substantial beginnings in the production of the packing cases. LTV refused to take delivery of the cases after it stopped production of the specific product for which the cases were needed. When Bateman sued for breach of contract, LTV claimed that there was no writing to satisfy the Statute of Frauds. The trial court ruled against LTV, and LTV appealed. What was the result? [LTV Aerospace Corp. v. Bateman, 492 S.W.2d 703 (Tex.Civ.App. 1973)]

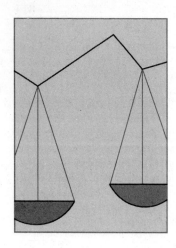

18

SALES
Title, Risk, and Insurable Interest

The sale of goods transfers ownership (title) from seller to buyer. Often a sales contract will be signed before the actual goods are available. For example, a sales contract for oranges is signed in May, but the oranges are not ready for picking and shipment until October. Any number of things can happen between the time that a sales contract is signed and the time that the goods are actually transferred to the buyer's possession. Fire, flood, or frost can destroy the orange groves. The oranges may be lost or damaged in transit. The parties may want to obtain casualty insurance on the goods. The government may levy a tax on the oranges.

Before the creation of the UCC, *title*—right of ownership—was the central concept in sales law, controlling all issues of rights and remedies of the parties to a sales contract. However, it was difficult to determine when title actually passed from seller to buyer. Therefore, the UCC divorced the question of title as completely as possible from the question of the rights and obligations of buyers, sellers, or third persons (such as subsequent purchasers, creditors, or the tax collector).

In some situations title is still relevant under the Code, and the UCC has special rules for locating title. These rules will be discussed in the materials that follow. In most situations, however, the Code replaces the concept of title with three other concepts: (1) identification, (2) risk of loss, and (3) insurable interest.

PASSAGE OF TITLE

Before any interest in specific goods can pass from the seller to the buyer, two conditions must prevail: (1) The goods must be in existence, and (2) they must be identified to the contract. If either condition is lacking, only a contract *to sell* (not a sale) exists. [UCC 2-105(2)] Goods that are not both existing and identified to the contract are called "future goods." For example, a contract to purchase next year's crop of hay would be a contract for future goods, a crop yet to be grown.

IDENTIFICATION

For passage of title, the goods must be identified in a way that will distinguish the particular goods to be delivered under the sales contract from all other similar goods.[1] **Identification** is a designation of goods as the subject matter of the sales contract.

---

1. According to UCC 2-401, each provision of Article 2 "with respect to the rights, obligations, and remedies of the seller, the buyer, purchasers or other third parties applies irrespective of title to the goods except where the provisions refer to such title." These provisions referring to title include: UCC 2-312, warranty of title by seller; UCC 2-326(3), consignment sales; UCC 2-327(1)(a), sale on approval and "risk of loss"; UCC 2-403(1), entrustment; UCC 2-501(2), insurable interest in goods; and UCC 2-722, who can sue third parties for injury to goods.

In many cases identification is simply a matter of specific designation. For example, you contract to purchase a fleet of five cars by the serial numbers listed for the cars, or you agree to purchase all the wheat in a specific bin at a stated price per bushel. Problems usually occur only when a quantity of goods is purchased from a larger mass, such as 1,000 cases of peas from a 10,000-case lot.

There is a general rule that when a purchaser buys a quantity of goods to be taken from a larger mass, identification can be made only by separating the contracted goods from the mass. Therefore, until the seller separates the 1,000 cases of peas from the 10,000-case lot, title and risk of loss remain with the seller.

There are a few exceptions to this general rule. For example, a seller owns approximately 5,000 chickens (hens and roosters). A buyer agrees to purchase all the hen chickens at a stated price. Most courts would hold that "all the hen chickens" is a sufficient identification, and title and risk can pass to the buyer without the goods identified in the contract being physically separated from the other goods (the hens from the roosters). The reasoning is that the contract identification serves as sufficient separation.

The most common exception deals with fungible goods. [UCC 1-201(17)] Fungible goods are goods that are alike naturally, by agreement or trade usage. Typical examples are wheat, oil, and wine. If these goods are held or intended to be held as tenants in common (owners have an undivided share of the entire mass), a seller-tenant can pass title and risk of loss to the buyer without an actual separation. The buyer replaces the seller as a tenant in common. [UCC 2-105(4)]

For example, Able, Baker, and Clark are farmers. They deposit, respectively, 5,000 bushels, 3,000 bushels, and 2,000 bushels of the same grade of grain in a bin. The three become tenants in common, with Able owning 50 percent of the 10,000 bushels, Baker 30 percent, and Clark 20 percent. Able could contract to sell 5,000 bushels of grain to Thomas and, since the goods are fungible, pass title and risk of loss to Thomas without physically separating 5,000 bushels. Thomas now becomes a tenant in common with Baker and Clark.

Identification is significant because it gives the buyer the right to obtain insurance (insurable interest) on the goods and the right to recover from third parties who damage the goods. In certain circumstances, identification allows the buyer to take the goods from the seller. In other words, the concept of identification is easier to understand if one looks at its consequences.

Parties can agree on when identification will take place in their contract; but if they do not so specify, in addition to the preceding rules, the following rules apply: [UCC 2-501(1)]

1. Identification takes place at the time the contract is made *if the contract calls for the sale of specific and ascertained goods already existing.*
2. If the sale involves unborn young animals that will be born within twelve months from the time of the contract, or if it involves crops to be harvested within twelve months (or the next harvest season occurring after contracting, whichever is longer), identification will take place, in the first case, when the young are conceived and, in the second case, when the crops are planted or begin to grow.
3. In other cases, identification takes place when the goods are marked, shipped, or somehow designated by the seller as the particular goods to pass under the contract. The seller can delegate the right to identify goods to the buyer.

When Title Passes

Once goods exist and are identified, the provisions of UCC 2-401 apply to the passage of title.

By Agreement Parties can expressly agree to the conditions under which title will pass to the buyer and to the time. In virtually all subsections of UCC 2-401, the words "unless otherwise explicitly agreed" appear, meaning that any explicit understanding between the buyer and the seller will determine when title passes.

In Absence of Agreement Unless an agreement is explicitly made, title passes to the buyer at the time and the place the seller performs the *physical* delivery of the goods. [UCC 2-401(2)] The delivery arrangements determine when this occurs.

Shipment Contracts Under shipment contracts (the seller is required or authorized to ship goods by carrier), the seller is required only to deliver the goods into the hands of a carrier (such as a trucking company), and title passes to the buyer at the time and place of shipment. [UCC 2-401(2)(a)]

Destination Contracts   With destination contracts, the seller is required to deliver the goods to a particular destination, usually directly to the buyer but sometimes to the buyer's designate. Title passes to the buyer when the goods are tendered at that destination. [UCC 2-401(2)(b)]

Contracts for Delivery without Seller Moving the Goods   Where the contract of sale does not call for the seller's shipment or delivery (buyer to pick up), the passage of title depends on whether the seller must deliver a document of title, such as a bill of lading or a warehouse receipt, to the buyer. When a document of title is required, title passes to the buyer *when and where the document is delivered.* Thus, if the goods are stored in a warehouse, title passes to the buyer when the appropriate documents are delivered. The goods never move. In fact, the buyer can choose to leave the goods at the same warehouse for a period of time, and the buyer's title to those goods will be unaffected.

When no documents of title are required, and delivery is made without moving the goods, title passes at the time and place the sales contract was made, if the goods have already been identified. If the goods have not been identified, then title does not pass until identification occurs. Consider an example: Fein sells lumber to Ozo. It is agreed that Ozo will pick up the lumber at the yard. If the lumber has been identified (segregated, marked, or in any other way distinguished from all other lumber), title will pass to Ozo when the contract is signed. If the lumber is still in storage bins at the mill, however, title will not pass to Ozo until the particular pieces of lumber to be sold under this contract are identified. [UCC 2-401(3)]

RISK OF LOSS

Under the UCC, several concepts replace the concept of title in determining the rights and remedies of parties to a sales contract. For example, risk of loss does not necessarily pass with title. The question of who suffers a financial risk if goods are damaged, destroyed, or lost is resolved primarily under Sections 2-509 and 2-319. Risk of loss depends on whether or not a sales contract has been breached at the time of loss. [UCC 2-510]

Passage of Risk of Loss Absent a Breach of Contract

By Agreement   Risk of loss can be assigned through an agreement by the parties, preferably in writing. Therefore, the parties can generally control the exact moment risk of loss passes from the seller to the buyer. Of course, at the time so agreed, the goods must be in existence and identified to the contract for this contract provision to be enforceable.

Carrier Cases—Sales Requiring Delivery by Movement of Goods   Assuming that there is no specification in the agreement, the following rules will apply to so-called carrier cases.

Shipment Contracts   In a shipment contract, if the seller is required or authorized to ship goods by carrier (not required to deliver them to a particular destination), risk of loss passes to the buyer when the goods are duly delivered to the carrier. [UCC 2-509(1)(b)]

For example, a seller in New York sells 10,000 tons of sheet metal to a buyer in California, F.O.B. New York (free on board in New York—that is, buyer pays the transportation charges from New York). The contract authorizes a shipment by carrier; it does not require the seller to tender the metal in California. Risk passes to the buyer when the conforming goods are properly placed in the possession of the carrier. If the goods are damaged in transit, the loss falls on the buyer. (Actually, buyers have recourse against carriers, subject to tariff rule limitations, and they usually insure the goods from the time they leave the seller.) Generally, all contracts are assumed to be shipping contracts if nothing is stated in the contract.

Destination Contracts   In a destination contract, the seller is required to deliver the goods at a particular destination. The risk of loss passes to the buyer when the goods are tendered to the buyer at that destination. In the preceding example, if the contract had been F.O.B. California, risk of loss during transit to California would have fallen on the seller.

Contract Terms Specific *terms* in the contract, even though used in connection with a stated price, assist one in determining when risk of loss passes to the buyer. Four such terms should be noted:

1. **F.O.B.** (free on board) can be either at place of shipment (for example, seller's city or place of business) or at place of destination (for example, buyer's city or place of business). In absence of agreement, the risk of loss rules pertaining to shipment and destination as stated above basically apply. [UCC 2-319(1)]

2. **F.A.S.** (free alongside) vessel requires the seller at his own expense and "risk" to deliver the goods alongside the vessel before risk passes to the buyer. [UCC 2-319(2)]

3. **CIF or C&F** (cost, insurance, and freight, or just cost and freight) requires, among other things, the seller to "put the goods in possession of a carrier" before risk passes to the buyer. [UCC 2-320(2)] (These are basically pricing terms and remain shipment contracts, not destination contracts.)

4. **Delivery ex-ship** (from the carrying vessel) means that risk of loss does not pass to the buyer until the goods leave the ship or are otherwise properly unloaded. [UCC 2-322]

In the following case the court reviewed UCC 2-509(1) as it relates to passage of the risk of loss. Under the Code, an F.O.B. term indicates whether the contract is a "shipment" contract or a "destination" contract, with the risk of loss passing at different times in each of these contracts. The F.O.B. terminology controls. In this case a "shipment" contract shifted the risk of loss to the buyer when the goods were delivered to a carrier. The fact that there was a "ship to" address had no significance in changing the UCC presumption that the contract was a "shipment" contract.

BACKGROUND AND FACTS *Defendant Karinol Corp. contracted "to ship" watches to the plaintiff in Chetumal, Mexico. The contract contained no delivery terms, such as F.O.B., nor specific terms for allocation of loss while goods were in transit. The plaintiff-buyer had made a deposit, the watches were shipped, but they were lost in transit. The plaintiff sought a refund for the deposit, claiming risk of loss was on the seller. Defendant-seller Karinol claimed that the plaintiff suffered the risk of loss and owed the balance of the purchase price. The trial court held for the defendant.*

PESTANA v. KARINOL CORP.

District Court of Appeal of Florida, Third District (1979). 367 So. 2d 1096.

HUBBART, Judge.
* * * *

The central issue presented for review is whether a contract for the sale of goods, which stipulates the place where the goods sold are to be sent by carrier but contains (a) no explicit provisions allocating the risk of loss while the goods are in the possession of the carrier and (b) no delivery terms such as F.O.B. place of destination, is a shipment contract or a destination contract under the Uniform Commercial Code. We hold that such a contract, without more, constitutes a shipment contract wherein the risk of loss passes to the buyer when the seller duly delivers the goods to the carrier under a reasonable contract of carriage for shipment to the buyer. Accordingly, we affirm.
* * * *

Where the risk of loss falls on the seller at the time the goods sold are lost or destroyed, the seller is liable in damages to the buyer for non-delivery unless the seller tenders a performance in replacement for the lost or destroyed goods. On the other hand, where the risk of loss falls on the buyer at the time the goods sold are lost or destroyed, the buyer is liable to the seller for the purchase price of the goods sold.

In the instant case, we deal with the normal shipment contract involving the sale of goods. The defendant Karinol pursuant to this contract agreed to send the goods sold, a shipment of watches, to the plaintiff's decedent in Chetumal, Mexico. There was no specific provision in the contract between the parties which allocated the risk of loss on the goods sold while in transit. In addition, there were no delivery terms such as F.O.B. Chetumal contained in the contract.

All agree that there is sufficient evidence that the defendant Karinol performed its obligations as a seller under the Uniform Commercial Code if this contract is considered a shipment contract. Karinol put the goods sold in the possession of a carrier and made a contract for the goods safe transportation to the plaintiff's decedent; Karinol also promptly notified the plaintiff's decedent of the shipment and tendered to said party the necessary documents to obtain possession of the goods sold.

The plaintiff Pestana contends, however, that the contract herein is a destination contract in which the risk of loss on the goods sold did not pass until delivery on such goods had been tendered to him at Chetumal, Mexico—an event which never occurred. He relies for this position on the notation at the bottom of the contract between the parties which provides that the goods were to be sent to Chetumal, Mexico. We cannot agree. A "send to" or "ship to" term is a part of every contract involving the sale of goods where carriage is contemplated and has no significance in determining whether the contract is a shipment or destination contract for risk of loss purposes. As such, the "send to" term contained in this contract cannot, without more, convert this into a destination contract.

DECISION AND REMEDY   *The buyer was liable to the seller for the full contract price of the watches.*

Delivery without Movement of Goods   The Code also addresses situations in which the seller is required neither to ship nor to deliver the goods. Frequently the buyer is to pick up the goods from the seller, or the goods remain in a warehouse, or they are held by a bailee (the person to whom they are entrusted). [UCC 2-509(2)(3)]

When the goods are held by a bailee, they are usually represented by a negotiable or nonnegotiable document of title (a bill of lading or warehouse receipt). If the goods are held by the seller, a document of title is usually not used. This distinction is important in applying the rules governing passage of risk of loss to the buyer. [UCC 2-509(2)(3)]

Merchant Seller   If the seller is a merchant, risk of loss to goods held by the seller passes to the buyer when the buyer actually takes physical possession of the goods. [UCC 2-509(3)] For example, a merchant sells goods to a buyer who is supposed to pick them up. Risk of loss does not pass to the buyer until the goods are actually picked up. (Tender is not enough.)

Nonmerchant Seller   If the seller is not a merchant, the risk of loss to goods held by the seller passes to the buyer upon *tender of delivery*. [UCC 2-509(3)] A tender of delivery is the seller's placing or holding of conforming goods at the buyer's disposition (with any necessary notice), enabling the buyer to take delivery. [UCC 2-503(1)]

To illustrate: Jones has cut down a tree in her backyard. The tree has been cut into a pile of firewood. On May 1, Jones contracts to sell the wood to Farber. At the time of their contract, Jones tells Farber that he can take the wood with him on that day if he wishes. Farber tells Jones to keep the wood until May 15, so that he, Farber, can arrange for a place to keep it after taking possession. The firewood burns up three days later through no fault of Jones. Jones claims that Farber is obligated to pay for the wood, even though it has been destroyed. Jones is right. Jones, a nonmerchant, tendered delivery when she offered to let Farber take the wood with him on May 1.

The question of tender of delivery arises in the following case.

BACKGROUND AND FACTS   *Brown contracted to purchase carloads of lumber from Lumber Sales, Inc. The contract terms did not include an F.O.B. term but did require Lumber Sales to deliver the boxcar of lumber to the Nashville Railroad Company depot in Nashville. The boxcar of lumber arrived at the depot at approximately 8:00* A.M. *on November 27, the day before Thanksgiving. Inspection by a carrier employee showed the boxcar to be fully loaded, and at 11:07* A.M. *Brown's office was notified of the boxcar arrival, location, and availability for unloading. Brown did not attempt to unload the lumber. On the day following Thanksgiving, an employee of the carrier inspected the car and found it empty. Brown claimed the lumber was not duly tendered and, since risk of loss was still with Lumber Sales, Brown was not liable for payment. Lumber Sales sued for the purchase price and the trial court held Brown liable.*

LUMBER SALES, INC.
v. BROWN

Court of Appeals of Tennessee, 1971.
63 Tenn.App. 189, 469 S.W.2d 888.

PURYEAR, Judge.
*   *   *   *

The particular Code Section applicable here is Sub-section (1) of [the Tennessee Code] as follows:

"47-2-509. *Risk of loss in the absence of breach.*—(1) Where the contract requires or authorizes the seller to ship the goods by carrier (a) (this portion not applicable) (b) if it does require him to deliver them at a particular destination and the goods are there duly tendered while in the possession of the carrier, the risk of loss passes to the buyer when the goods are there duly so tendered as to enable the buyer to take delivery."

*   *   *   *

Counsel for defendant argues that the lumber in question was not duly so *tendered as to enable the buyer to take delivery"* as required by [UCC Sec. 2-509(1)(b)].

However, this argument seems to be based upon the premise that it was not convenient for the defendant to unload the lumber on November 27th, the day on which it was delivered at track location 609-A and defendant was duly notified of such delivery.

This was an ordinary business day and the time of 11:07 A.M. was a reasonable business hour. If it was not convenient with the defendant to unload the lumber within a few hours after being duly notified of delivery, then he should have protected himself against risk of loss by directing someone to guard the cargo against loss by theft and other hazards.

To hold that the seller or the carrier should, under the circumstances existing in a case of this kind, continue to protect the goods until such time as the buyer may find it convenient to unload them would impose an undue burden upon the seller or the carrier and unnecessarily obstruct the channels of commerce.

The language of subsection (1)(b) of [the Tennessee Code] does not impose such a burden upon the seller, in the absence of some material breach of the contract for delivery, and we think a reasonable construction of such language only requires the seller to place the goods at the buyer's disposal so that he has access to them and may remove them from the carrier's conveyance without lawful obstruction, with the proviso, however, that due notice of such delivery be given to the buyer.

The trial court's judgment was affirmed. Risk of loss had passed to the buyer, and the buyer was liable to the seller for the contract price of the carload of lumber. Basically, the UCC and the court indicated that the buyer should have provided insurance in kind by having someone physically protect the lumber, or he should have purchased a regular insurance policy against theft.

**DECISION
AND REMEDY**

Cases Involving Bailees When a bailee is holding goods for a person who has contracted to sell them, and the goods are to be delivered without being moved, the risk of loss passes to the buyer when: (1) the buyer receives a negotiable document of title for the goods, or (2) the bailee acknowledges the buyer's right to possess the goods, or (3) the buyer receives a nonnegotiable document of title *and* has had a *reasonable time* to present the document to the bailee and demand the goods. Obviously, if the bailee refuses to honor the document, the risk of loss remains with the seller. [UCC 2-509(2) and 2-503(4)(b)]

See Exhibit 18–1 for a sample negotiable bill of lading and Exhibit 18–2 for a sample nonnegotiable warehouse receipt.

To illustrate: McKee stores goods in Hardy's warehouse and takes a negotiable warehouse receipt for them. On the following day, McKee indorses and sells the receipt to Byne for cash. The day after that, Hardy's warehouse burns down, and the goods are completely destroyed. At the time of the fire, Hardy had not been informed of the sale of the warehouse receipt. The risk of loss is on Byne because it accompanies the negotiable warehouse receipt that gave him title to the goods.

The *Concept Summary* below gives the basic rules discussed previously on passage of title and risk of loss.

Sale on Approval and Sale or Return Contracts

A **sale on approval** is not a sale until the buyer accepts (approves) the offer. A **sale or return** is a sale that can be rescinded by the buyer without liability. In each case, passage of title and risk of loss depend

---

CONCEPT SUMMARY: Passage of Title and Risk of Loss for Goods in Existence and Identified in Absence of Express Agreement

SITUATION	BASIC RULES
Contract terms call for goods to be *shipped* (i.e., F.O.B. seller's business or city)	1. In absence of agreement, title and risk pass upon seller's delivery of conforming goods to the carrier. UCC 2-401(2)(a), UCC 2-509(1)(a)
Contract terms call for goods to be delivered at *destination* (i.e., F.O.B. buyer's warehouse)	1. In absence of agreement, title and risk pass upon seller's *tender* of delivery of conforming goods to the buyer at the point of destination. UCC 2-401(2)(b), UCC 2-509(1)(b)
Contract terms call for goods to be delivered *without physical movement* (i.e., the buyer must pick up the goods)	1. In absence of agreement, if the goods are not represented by a document of title— a. Title passes upon the formation of the contract. UCC 2-401(3)(b) b. Risk passes to the buyer, if seller is a merchant, upon buyer's *receipt* of the goods; if the seller is a nonmerchant, upon seller's *tender* of delivery of the goods. UCC 2-509(3) 2. In absence of agreement, if the goods are represented by a document of title— a. If negotiable, title and risk pass upon the buyer's *receipt* of the document. UCC 2-401(3)(a), UCC 2-509(2)(a) b. If nonnegotiable, title passes upon the buyer's receipt of the document, but risk does *not* pass until the buyer, after receipt of the document, has had reasonable time to present the document to demand the goods. UCC 2-401(3)(a), UCC 2-509(2)(c), UCC 2-503(4)(b)

EXHIBIT 18–1 A Sample Negotiable Bill of Lading

UNIFORM MOTOR CARRIER ORDER BILL OF LADING   **1st Sheet**

Shipper's No._____

Original—Domestic

Agent's No._____

CENTRAL FREIGHT LINES INC.

RECEIVED, subject to the classifications and tariffs in effect on the date of the issue of this Bill of Lading,

From _____ , Date _____ 19 ____

At _____ Street, _____ City, _____ County, _____ State

the property described below, in apparent good order, except as noted (contents and condition of contents of packages unknown) marked, consigned and destined as shown below, which said company (the word company being understood throughout this contract as meaning any person or corporation in possession of the property under the contract) agrees to carry to its usual place of delivery at said destination, if within the scope of its lawful operations, otherwise to deliver to another carrier on the route to said destination. It is mutually agreed, as to each carrier of all or any of said property over all or any portion of said route to destination, and as to each party at any time interested in all or any of said property, that every service to be performed hereunder shall be subject to all the conditions not prohibited by law, whether printed or written, herein contained, including the conditions on back hereof, which are hereby agreed to by the shipper and accepted for himself and his assigns.

The surrender of this Original ORDER Bill of Lading properly indorsed shall be required before the delivery of the property. Inspection of property covered by this bill of lading will not be permitted unless provided by law or unless permission is indorsed on this original Bill of lading or given in writing by the shipper.

Consigned to Order of _____

Destination	Street,	City,	County,	State

Notify _____

At	Street,	City,	County,	State

I. C. C. No. _____   Vehicle No. _____

Routing _____

No. Pack- ages	Description of Articles, Special Marks, and Exceptions	*Weight (Subject to Correction)	Class or Rate	Check Column	Subject to Section 7 of Conditions, if this shipment is to be delivered to the consignee without recourse on the consignor, the consignor shall sign the following statement:
					The carrier shall not make delivery of this shipment without payment of freight and all other lawful charges.
					(Signature of consignor.)
					If charges are to be prepaid write or stamp here, "To be Prepaid."
					Received $_____ to apply in prepayment of the charges on the property described hereon.
					Agent or Cashier.
					Per_____ (The signature here acknowledges only the amount prepaid.)

*If the shipment moves between two ports by a carrier by water, the law requires that the bill of lading shall state whether it is "carrier's or shipper's weight."

Note—Where the rate is dependent on value, shippers are required to state specifically in writing the agreed or declared value of the property.

The agreed or declared value of the property is hereby specifically stated by the shipper to be not exceeding

_____ per _____

Charges advanced:

$_____

Shipper _____		Agent.
Per _____	Per _____	
Permanent address of Shipper _____	Street, _____ City,	State

MOORE BUSINESS FORMS, INC., WACO, TEX. M

Source: Reprinted with permission of Central Freight Lines Inc. © 1985 Central Freight Lines, Inc.
Note: This form is printed in yellow to warn holders that it is an order bill of lading. The back of the form permits negotiation by indorsement.

EXHIBIT 18–2   A Sample Nonnegotiable Warehouse Receipt

Warehouse Receipt – Not Negotiable

Agreement No. _____   Vault No. _____

Service Order _____   _____

Receipt and
Lot Number_____   Date of Issue_____ 19____

Received for the account of and deliverable to • _____

whose latest known address is _____

SAMPLE

_____ the goods enumerated on the inside or attached schedule to be

stored in Company warehouse, located at _____
which goods are accepted only upon the following conditions set forth below:

READ CAREFULLY► That the value of all goods stored, including the contents of any container, and all goods hereafter
stored for Depositor's account to be not over $_____ per pound † per article unless a higher value is noted
in the schedule, for which an additional monthly storage charge of _____ ¢ on each $_____
valuation in excess of $_____ per pound † per article or fraction thereof will be made.

If there are any items enumerated in this receipt valued in excess of the above limitations per pound
per article and not so noted in the schedule, return this receipt within 10 days with proper values so indicated
in writing in order that the receipt may be re-issued and proper higher storage rates assessed.

OWNERSHIP. The Customer, Shipper, Depositor, or Agent represents and warrants that he is lawfully possessed of goods to be stored and/or has the authority to store or ship said goods. (If the goods are mortgaged, notify the Company the name and address of the mortgagee.)

PAYMENT OF CHARGES. Storage bills are payable monthly in advance for each month's storage or fraction thereof. Labor charges, cartage and other services rendered are payable upon completion of work. All charges shall be paid at the warehouse location shown hereon, and if delinquent, shall incur interest monthly at the rate of _____ per cent ( ) per year.

The Depositor will pay reasonable attorney's fee incurred by The Company in collecting delinquent accounts.

LIABILITY OF COMPANY. The company shall be liable for any loss or injury to the goods caused by its failure to exercise such care as a reasonably careful man would exercise under like circumstances. The company will not be liable for loss or damage to fragile articles not packed, or articles packed or unpacked by other than employees of this company. Depositor specifically agrees that the warehouse will not be liable for contamination of or for insect damage to articles placed in drawers of furniture by the depositor. Periodic spraying of the warehouse premises shall constitute ordinary and proper care, unless the Depositor requests in writing and pays for anti-infestation treatment of articles in drawers and compartments of stored furniture.

CHANGE OF ADDRESS. Notice of change of address must be given the Company in writing, and acknowledged in writing by the Company.

TRANSFER OR WITHDRAWAL OF GOODS. The warehouse receipt is not negotiable and shall be produced and all charges must be paid before delivery to the Depositor, or transfer of goods to another person; however, a written direction to the Company to transfer the goods to another person or deliver the goods may be accepted by the Company at its option without requiring tender of the warehouse receipt.

ACCESS TO STORAGE, PARTIAL WITHDRAWAL. A signed order from the person in whose name the receipt is issued is required to enable others to remove or have access to goods. A charge is made for stacking and unstacking, and for access to stored goods.

BUILDING—FIRE—WATCHMAN. The Company does not represent or warrant that its building cannot be destroyed by fire or that the contents of said buildings including the said property cannot be destroyed by fire. The Company shall not be required to maintain a watchman or sprinkler system and its failure to do so shall not constitute negligence.

CLAIMS OR ERRORS. All claims for non-delivery of any article or articles and for damage, breakage, etc., must be made in writing within ninety (90) days from delivery of goods stored or they are waived. Failure to return the warehouse receipt for correction within ( ) days after receipt thereof by the depositor will be conclusive that it is correct and delivery will be made only in accordance therewith.

FUTURE SERVICE. This Contract shall extend and apply to future services rendered to the Depositor by the Company and to any additional goods deposited with the Company by the Depositor.

WAREHOUSEMAN'S LIEN. The Company reserves the right to sell the goods stored, in accordance with the provisions of the Uniform Commercial Code (Business and Commerce Code if stored in Texas), for all lawful charges in arrears.

TERMINATION OF STORAGE. The Company reserves the right to terminate the storage of the goods at any time by giving to the Depositor thirty (30) days' written notice of its intention so to do, and, unless the Depositor removes such goods within that period, the Company is hereby empowered to have the same removed at the cost and expense of the Depositor, or the Company may sell them at auction in accordance with state law.

DEPOSITOR WILL PAY REASONABLE LEGAL FEES INCURRED BY WAREHOUSE IN COLLECTING DELINQUENT CHARGES.

THIS DOCUMENT CONTAINS THE WHOLE CONTRACT BETWEEN THE PARTIES AND THERE ARE NO OTHER TERMS, WARRANTIES, REPRESENTATIONS, OR AGREEMENTS OF EITHER DEPOSITOR OR COMPANY NOT HEREIN CONTAINED.

Storage per month
or fraction thereof . . . . $_____
Warehouse labor . . . . . $_____
Cartage . . . . $_____
Packing at residence . . . $_____
Wrapping and preparing
for storage . . . . . . $_____
Charges advanced . . . . $_____
_____ $_____

*By*_____

*Insert "Mr. and/or Mrs." or, if military personnel, appropriate rank or grade.
†Delete the words "per pound" if the declared value is per article.
For goods stored for military personnel under PL 245, the contractor's liability for care of goods is as provided in Basic Agreement with U.S. Government.

THIS PROPERTY HAS NOT BEEN INSURED BY THIS COMPANY FOR FIRE OR ANY OTHER CASUALTY
SCHEDULE OF GOODS ON FOLLOWING PAGE OR ATTACHED

W-1 (1981) Approved by S W W T 4 ©   Re-order from Hart Graphics, Austin, Texas

Source: Reprinted with permission of Hart Graphics, Inc. of Austin, Texas. © 1985 Hart Graphics, Inc.

upon the happening or nonhappening of the conditional event, since these transactions are conditional by their very nature.

Sale on Approval   When a seller offers to sell goods to a buyer and permits the buyer to take the goods on a trial basis, a sale on approval is made. The term *sale* here is a misnomer, since only an *offer* to sell has been made, along with a bailment created by the buyer's possession.

Therefore, title and risk of loss (from causes beyond the buyer's control) remain with the seller until the buyer accepts (approves) the offer. Acceptance can be made expressly, by any act inconsistent with the *trial* purpose or seller's ownership, or by the buyer's election not to return the goods within the trial period. If the buyer does not wish to accept, the buyer may notify the seller of such fact within the trial period, and the return is at the seller's expense and risk. [UCC 2-327(1)] Goods held on approval are not subject to the claims of the buyer's creditors until acceptance.

Sale or Return   The sale or return (sometimes called *sale and return*) is a species of contract by which the seller delivers a quantity of goods to the buyer, on the understanding that if the buyer wishes to retain any portion of those goods (for use or resale), the buyer will consider the portion retained as having been sold to him or her and will pay accordingly. The balance will be returned to the seller or will be held by the buyer as a bailee subject to the seller's order. When the buyer receives possession at the time of sale, the title and risk of loss pass to the buyer. Both remain with the buyer until the buyer returns the goods to the seller within the time period specified. If the buyer fails to return the goods within this time period, the sale is finalized. The return of the goods is at the buyer's risk and expense. The goods held on a sale or return contract are subject to the claims of the buyer's creditors while they are in the buyer's possession.

Under a contract of sale or return, the title vests immediately in the buyer, who has the privilege of rescinding the sale. [UCC 2-326] It is often difficult to determine from a particular transaction which exists—a sale on approval or a contract for sale or return. The Code states that (unless otherwise agreed) if the goods are for the buyer to use, the transaction

is a sale on approval; if the goods are for the buyer to resell, the transaction is a sale or return. [UCC 2-326(1)]

Risk of Loss in a Breached Sales Contract

There are many ways to breach a sales contract, and the transfer of risk operates differently depending on whether the seller or the buyer breaches. Generally, the party in breach bears the risk of loss.

Seller's Breach   If the goods are so nonconforming that the buyer has the right to reject them, the risk of loss will not pass to the buyer until the defects are cured or until the buyer accepts the goods in spite of their defects (thus waiving the right to reject). For example, a buyer orders blue widgets from a seller, F.O.B. seller's plant. The seller ships black widgets, giving the buyer the right to reject. The widgets are damaged in transit. The risk of loss falls on the seller (although the risk would have been on the buyer if blue widgets had been shipped under a shipment contract). [UCC 2-510]

If a buyer accepts a shipment of goods and later discovers a latent defect, acceptance can be revoked. Revocation allows the buyer to pass the risk of loss back to the seller, at least to the extent that the buyer's insurance does not cover the loss. [UCC 2-510(2)]

Buyer's Breach   The general rule is that when a buyer breaches a contract, the risk of loss *immediately* shifts to the buyer. There are three important limitations to this rule:

1.   The seller must have already identified the goods under the contract. (Regardless of the delivery arrangements, the risk will shift.)
2.   The buyer will bear the risk for only a *commercially reasonable time* after the seller learns of the breach.
3.   The buyer will be liable only to the extent of any *deficiency* in the seller's insurance coverage. [UCC 2–510(3)]

The following case is a good example of the effect of a seller's failure to conform to the contract resulting in the risk of loss remaining with the seller.

MOSES v. NEWMAN

Court of Appeals of Tennessee,
1983.
658 S.W.2d 119.

BACKGROUND AND FACTS *Newman, the plaintiff, in response to an advertisement offering a "trailer, complete set-up," purchased a mobile home from Moses, the defendant, on February 7, 1981. On February 9, 1981, the defendant delivered the mobile home to the plaintiff's lot, blocked up and leveled the home, removed the tires and axles, and connected sewer and water pipes. The defendant failed to anchor the mobile home. The plaintiff notified the defendant that the home had a broken window and water pipe and that there were no door keys. An installation crew was to return the following day; however, on February 10, 1981, a windstorm totally destroyed the mobile home. Newman claimed the loss of the mobile home fell on the seller. On appeal the appellate court first held that the plaintiff had not accepted tender of the mobile home, then addressed the issue of which party had the risk of loss.*

FRANKS, Judge.

*   *   *   *

The risk of loss provisions of the Uniform Commercial Code are contained in T.C.A., §§ 47-2-509, 47-2-510. In the instant case defendant argues T.C.A., § 47-2-509(3) applies and passes the risk of loss to the buyer on receipt of the goods where the seller is a merchant. Plaintiff argues T.C.A., § 47-2-510(1) applies, which provides: "Where a tender or delivery of goods so fails to conform to the contract as to give a right of rejection the risk of their loss remains on the seller until cure or acceptance."

Under the chancellor's factual determination the delivery of the trailer failed to conform to the contract giving rise to a right of rejection. The right of rejection under T.C.A., § 47-2-601 arises if the goods "fail in any respect to conform to the contract." *   *   * Whether the mobile home conformed to the contract is tested by the definition in T.C.A., § 47-2-106(2): "Goods or conduct including any part of a performance are 'conforming' or conform to the contract when they are in accordance with the obligations under the contract." In this case, plaintiff contracted for a habitable mobile home plus the installation. Accordingly, since the loss occurred before the installation was complete, the defendant had not delivered conforming goods which would shift the risk of loss to plaintiff.

For the risk to shift to the purchaser, the purchaser must receive the goods and the seller must fulfill his contractual obligations. "Under subsection (1) the seller by his individual action cannot shift the risk of loss to the buyer unless his action conforms with all the conditions resting on him under the contract." Comment 1 to T.C.A., § 47-2-510. See *William F. Wilke, Inc. v. Cummins Diesel Engines, Inc.*, 252 Md. 611, 250 A.2d 886 (1969), where the court held, notwithstanding the fact that the goods were delivered to the buyer, the risk of loss remained with the seller where the seller had not conducted testing or the inspection specified by the contract of sale.

*   *   *   *

**DECISION
AND REMEDY**

The appellate court upheld the chancellor's determination that the risk of loss had not shifted from defendant seller to the plaintiff. The seller had to bear the cost of the loss due to his failure to conform completely to the contract.

BULK TRANSFERS

Special problems arise when a major portion of a business's assets are transferred. This is the subject matter of UCC Article 6, Bulk Transfers, which are defined as any transfer of a major part of the material, supplies, merchandise, or other inventory *not made in the ordinary course of the transferor's busi-*

ness. [UCC 6-102(1)] Problems arise, for example, when a business owing numerous creditors sells a substantial part of its equipment and inventories to a buyer. If the merchant uses the proceeds to pay off debts, no problems arise. But what if the merchant spends the money on a trip around the world, leaving the creditors without payment? Can the creditors lay any claim to the goods that were transferred in bulk to the buyer? To prevent this problem from arising, Article 6 lays out certain requirements for bulk transfer.

Requirements of Article 6

A bulk transfer of assets is ineffective against any creditor of the transferor unless the following requirements are met:

1. The seller (transferor) must furnish to the transferee a sworn list of the person's existing creditors. This list must include those whose claims are disputed, stating names, business addresses, and amounts due. [UCC 6-104(1)(a)]
2. The buyer and the seller must prepare a schedule of the property transferred. [UCC 6-104(1)(b)]
3. The buyer must preserve the list of creditors and the schedule of property for six months. He or she must permit inspection thereof by any creditor of the seller or file the list and the schedule of property in a designated public office. [UCC 6-104(1)(c)]
4. Notice of the proposed bulk transfer must be given by the buyer to each creditor of the seller at least ten days before the buyer takes possession of the goods or makes payments for them, whichever happens first. [UCC 6-105]

If all four steps are undertaken, then the bulk transfer complies with the statutory requirements. The buyer acquires title to the goods free of all claims of creditors of the seller.

Notice to Creditors

The specific requirements for the contents of the notice to creditors are:

1. A statement that a bulk transfer is about to be made.
2. Names and business addresses of the seller in bulk and buyer in bulk.

3. Information about whether all debts of the seller in bulk are to be paid in full as a result of the bulk transfer and if so, the addresses to which creditors should send their bills. [UCC 6-107(1)]

Whenever the debts of the transferor in bulk are not to be paid in full as they fall due, the notice to creditors must also state such things as the location and general description of the property to be transferred, the address where the schedule of property and list of creditors may be inspected, and whether the transfer is for new consideration. [UCC 6-107(2)]

When Failure to Comply Occurs

When the requirements of Article 6 are not complied with, goods in possession of the transferee continue to be subject to the claims of the unpaid creditors of the seller for a period of six months. [UCC 6-111] Nonetheless, a bona fide purchaser of these goods from the transferee who pays value in good faith, not knowing that the goods are still subject to the claims of the transferor's creditors, acquires the goods free of any claim of those creditors.

If the creditor did not receive notice and such is due to the fault of the seller (such as not being on the seller's list), the seller is liable to the buyer for any loss incurred by the buyer. If the failure to receive notice is the buyer's fault and the seller's creditor satisfies his or her claim from the property transferred, the buyer can only recover from the seller the amount of the debt the seller owed to that creditor (quasi-contractual theory).

SALES BY NONOWNERS

Special problems arise when persons who acquire goods with imperfect titles attempt to resell them. UCC 2-402 and 2-403 deal with the rights of two parties who lay claim to the same goods, sold with imperfect titles.

Imperfect Title

Void Title   A buyer acquires at least whatever title the seller has to the goods sold. A buyer may unknowingly purchase goods from a seller who is not the owner of the goods. If the seller is a thief, the seller's title is *void*—legally, no title exists. Thus, the buyer acquires no title, and the real owner can reclaim the goods from the buyer.

For example, if Thomas steals goods owned by Able, Thomas has *void title* (no legally recognized title) to those goods. If Thomas sells the goods to Beyer, Able can reclaim them from Beyer even though Beyer acted in good faith and honestly had no knowledge that the goods were stolen.

Voidable Title   A seller will have a *voidable title* if the goods that he or she is selling were obtained by fraud; paid for with a check that is later dishonored; purchased on credit, when the seller was insolvent; or if the goods were purchased from a minor. Purchasers of goods acquire all title that their transferors either had or had the power to transfer. However, a purchaser of a limited interest acquires rights only to the extent of the interest purchased. A seller with *voidable title* has power, nonetheless, to transfer a good title to a **good faith purchaser** for value.

A good faith purchaser is one who buys without knowledge of the circumstances that would make a person of ordinary prudence inquire about the title of the seller of the goods. In other words, such circumstances exist, but the purchaser is unaware of them. The real owner cannot recover goods from a good faith purchaser for value. [UCC 2-403(1)] If the buyer of the goods is not a good faith purchaser for value, then the actual owner of the goods can reclaim them from the buyer (or from the seller if the goods are still in the seller's possession).

To illustrate: Martin, a minor, sells his bicycle to Able, an adult. Since Martin is a minor, with the right to avoid this contract, Able has a voidable title. If Able sells the bicycle to Beyer, a good faith purchaser, Martin cannot use his minority, when he later disaffirms his contract with Able, to recover the bicycle from Beyer.

The defendant in the following case had some warning that there was something suspicious about the transaction in which he was participating.

LANE v. HONEYCUTT

Court of Appeals of North
Carolina, 1972.
14 N.C.App. 436, 188 S.E.2d
604.

BACKGROUND AND FACTS   *The plaintiff was engaged in the business of selling boats, motors, and trailers. He sold a new boat, motor, and trailer to a person who called himself John W. Willis. Willis took possession of the goods and paid for them with a check for $6,285. The check was later dishonored.*

About six months later, the defendant, Jimmy Honeycutt, bought the boat, motor, and trailer from a man identified as "Garrett," who was renting a summer beach house to the defendant that year. The defendant had known Garrett for several years.

The plaintiff sought to recover the boat, motor, and trailer from the defendant. The defendant's sole defense was that he was a good faith purchaser, and therefore the plaintiff should not be able to recover from him.

VAUGHN, Judge.
*   *   *   *

Contrary to the contentions of plaintiff, we hold that the goods were delivered under a transaction of purchase and that the consequences of this purchase are governed by G.S. [General Statutes] § 25-2-403, which, in part, is as follows:

"Power to transfer; good faith purchase of goods; 'entrusting.'—(1) A purchaser of goods acquires all title which his transferor had or had power to transfer except that a purchaser of a limited interest acquires rights only to the extent of the interest purchased. A person with voidable title has power to transfer a good title to a good faith purchaser for value. When goods have been delivered under a transaction of purchase the purchaser has such power even though
(a) the transferor was deceived as to the identity of the purchaser, or
(b) the delivery was in exchange for a check which is later dishonored, or
(c) it was agreed that the transaction was to be a 'cash sale,' or

(d) the delivery was procured through fraud punishable as larcenous under the criminal law."

* * * *

The question * * * which we consider to be determinative of this appeal is whether there is any evidence to support the following findings of fact by the court. "(2) The Defendant, Jimmy Honeycutt, did not purchase the boat, motor and trailer in good faith."

* * * *

[Next, the court carefully reviewed the defendant's testimony concerning "Mr. Garrett," who had sold the defendant a boat, motor, and trailer worth over $6,000 for a mere $2,500.]

"Mr. Garrett first approached me about buying his house on the beach that I was staying in, and told me he wanted $50,000.00 for it, and I told him I couldn't afford anything like that. He said, 'Well, let me sell you a boat out there.' And I said, 'Well, I couldn't afford that either.' * * *"

* * * *

"* * * As to whether or not, in other words, this boat looked like it was fairly expensive, well, I thought it would be a little more than it was. He told me the price and I was very pleasantly surprised * * *. [H]e sells fishing tackle and stuff of that nature, and beer. He also sells gasoline for boats. Yes, sir, that is about all he sells down there. He rents small fishing boats and motors too. No, he doesn't sell them, he doesn't sell boats as far as I know * * *."

Garrett told defendant he would let defendant have the boat for $2500. Defendant then paid Garrett a deposit of $100. Garrett had nothing to indicate that he was the owner of the boat, motor or trailer. Garrett told defendant he was selling the boat for someone else. "This guy comes down, you know, and does some fishing."

Two weeks later defendant returned to Garden City, South Carolina, with $2400, the balance due (on a boat, motor and trailer which had been sold new less than six months earlier for $6,285.00). On this occasion,

"Mr. Garrett had told me—well, he always called him, 'this guy' see, so I really didn't know of any name or anything, but he told me, 'this guy does a lot of fishing around here but I can't seem to get ahold of him.' He said, 'I've called him, but I can't get ahold of him, so since you have the money and you're here after the boat' * * * [s]ince you have the money and I can't seem to find him,' he said, 'I don't believe he would object, so I'll just go ahead and sign this title for you so you can go on and get everything made out to you.' He then signed the purported owner's name on the documents and he signed the title over to me then."

The so-called "document" and "title," introduced as defendant's exhibit No. 8, was nothing more than the "certificate of number" required by G.S. § 75A-5 and issued by the North Carolina Wildlife Resources Commission. This "certificate of number" is not a "certificate of title" to be compared with that required by G.S. § 20-50 for vehicles intended to be operated on the highways of this State. Upon the change of ownership of a motor boat, G.S. § 75A-5(c) authorizes the issuance of a new "certificate of number" to the transferee upon proper application. The application for transfer of the number, among other things, requires the seller's *signature*. A signature is "the name of a person written with his own hand." Webster's Third New International Dictionary (1968). Defendant observed Garrett counterfeit the signature of the purported owner, John P. Patterson, on the exhibit. Following the falsified signature on defendant's exhibit No. 8, the "date sold" is set out as "June 12, 1970" and the buyer's "signature" is set out as "George (illegible) Williams." There was no testimony as to who affixed the "signature" of the purported buyer, George Williams, and there is no further reference to him in the record.

* * * *

We hold that the evidence was sufficient to support the court's finding that defendant was not a good faith purchaser. * * *

DECISION AND REMEDY   *The trial court's ruling was affirmed. The defendant was not a good faith purchaser. The plaintiff was determined to be the owner and was entitled to immediate possession of the boat, motor, and trailer. The plaintiff was also awarded damages against the defendant for wrongful detention of the property.*

Entrustment   According to Section 2-403(2), entrusting goods to a merchant *who deals in goods of that kind* gives the merchant the power to transfer all rights to a *buyer in the ordinary course of business. Entrusting* includes both delivering the goods to the merchant and leaving the purchased goods with the merchant for later delivery or pickup. [UCC 2-403(3)] A "buyer in the ordinary course" is a person who buys in good faith from a person who deals in goods of that kind. The buyer cannot have knowledge that the sale violates the ownership rights of a third person.

For example, Sue leaves her watch with a jeweler to be repaired. The jeweler sells both new and used watches. The jeweler sells Sue's watch to Ann, a customer, who does not know that the jeweler has no right to sell it. Ann gets *good title* against Sue's claim of ownership.[2]

The good faith buyer, however, obtains only those rights held by the person entrusting the goods. For example, Sue's watch is stolen by Thomas. Thomas leaves the watch with a jeweler for repairs. The jeweler sells the watch to Betty, who does not know that the jeweler has no right to sell it. Betty gets good title against Thomas, the entrustor, but not against Sue, who neither entrusted the watch to Thomas nor authorized Thomas to entrust it.

Seller's Retention of Sold Goods   Ordinarily, sellers do not retain goods in their possession or their use after the goods are sold. A seller who retained goods after they were sold could mislead creditors into believing that the seller's assets were more substantial than they really were.

Retention of the goods, and particularly their use by the seller, is basic evidence of an intent to defraud creditors. If a creditor can prove that the retention is *in fact* fraud, or if the state has a *statute* providing that such retention creates a *presumption*

of fraud (and if such is unrebutted), the creditor can set aside the sale to the buyer.

However, UCC 2-402(2) recognizes that it is not necessarily a fraud upon creditors if a *merchant* seller retains possession in good faith for a "commercially reasonable time" in order to accomplish some legitimate purpose (for example, repairs or adjustments). In such situations, the seller's unsecured creditors cannot void the sale.

A seller can defraud creditors by selling items at something substantially less than "fair consideration," thereby depleting the seller's assets. This is fraud on the seller's creditors if the seller is insolvent at the time of the sale, is made insolvent by the sale, or actually intended to defraud or delay actions by the creditors. Assets sold at less than "fair consideration" often are sold to a friend or relative of the seller. Such sales are considered sham transactions used to conceal assets.

For example, suppose that FL Boat Company is on the verge of bankruptcy. Many of the loans that FL's owner had taken out were personally secured by him, so his creditors can go after his personal assets to recover what he owes them. Knowing this, FL's owner sells several expensive cars to his father for only $3,000 apiece, and he sells his personal yacht to his brother-in-law for $10,000 (when it is worth $110,000). He has an implicit understanding with his father and his brother-in-law that he will retain control over these assets but that they will have title. If the creditors find out about the sham transactions, they can void the sales.

INSURABLE INTEREST

Buyers and sellers often obtain insurance coverage to protect against damage, loss, or destruction of goods. But any party purchasing insurance must have a "sufficient interest" in the insured item to obtain a valid policy. Insurance laws—not the Code—determine "sufficiency." (See Chapter 55.) However, the Code is helpful because it contains certain rules

---

2. In the case of entrustment, no transaction of purchase is required between the entrustor (true owner) and the entrustee in order for the good faith purchaser to prevail.

regarding a buyer's and a seller's insurable interest in goods on a sales contract.

Buyer's Insurable Interest

Buyers have an insurable interest in *identified* goods. The moment the goods are identified to the contract by the seller, the buyer has this "special" property interest that allows the buyer to obtain necessary insurance coverage for those goods even before the risk of loss has passed. [UCC 2-501(1)]

Consider an example: In March a farmer sells a cotton crop he hopes to harvest in October to a buyer. After the crop is planted, the buyer insures it against hail damage. In September a hailstorm ruins the crop. When the buyer files a claim under her insurance policy, the insurer refuses to pay the claim, asserting that the buyer has no insurable interest in the crop. The insurer is not correct. The buyer acquired an insurable interest in the crop when it was planted, since she had a contract to buy it.

The rule in UCC 2-501(1)(c) states that a buyer obtains an insurable interest in the goods by identification, which occurs "when the crops are planted or otherwise become growing crops * * * if the contract is * * * for the sale of crops to be harvested within twelve months or the next normal harvest season after contracting, whichever is longer."

Seller's Insurable Interest

Sellers have an insurable interest in goods as long as they retain title to the goods. However, even after title passes to a buyer, a seller who has a "security interest" in the goods (a right to secure payment) still has an insurable interest and can insure the goods. [UCC 2-501(2)]

Hence, both a buyer and a seller can have an insurable interest in identical goods at the same time. In all cases, one must sustain an actual loss in order to have the right to recover from an insurance company.

QUESTIONS AND CASE PROBLEMS

1. On May 1 Beyer goes into Smith's retail clothing store to purchase a suit. Beyer finds the suit he is interested in for $190 and buys it. The suit needs alteration. Beyer is to pick up the altered suit at Smith's store on May 10. Assume separately:
   (a) One of Smith's major creditors has a judgment against Smith and levies execution on that judgment against all clothing in Smith's possession.
   (b) On May 9, through no fault of Smith, his store burns down, and all contents are a total loss.
Discuss *Beyer's* rights to the suit on which the major creditor has levied. Between Smith and Beyer, who suffers the loss of the suit destroyed by fire? Explain.

2. Beyer orders from Sallor 1,000 cases of Greenie brand peas from Lot A at list price to be shipped F.O.B. Sallor's city via Fast Freight Lines. Sallor receives the order and immediately sends Beyer an acceptance of the order with a promise to ship promptly. Sallor later separates the 1,000 cases of Greenie peas and prints Beyer's name and address on each case. The peas are placed on Sallor's dock, and Fast Freight is notified to pick up the shipment. The night before the pickup by Fast Freight, through no fault of Sallor, a fire destroys the 1,000 cases of peas. Sallor claims

title passed at the time the contract was made, and risk of loss passed to Beyer upon the marking of the goods with Beyer's name and address. Discuss Sallor's contentions.

3. Sallor sells lawn mowers. Beyer is a regular customer who comes in to see Sallor. Sallor has a special promotional campaign. He tells Beyer about it. It involves a down payment of $50. Upon receipt of the down payment, Sallor will sell Beyer a new Universal lawn mower for $200, even though it normally sells for $350. Sallor further states to Beyer that if Beyer does not like the performance of the lawn mower, Beyer can return the mower within thirty days and Sallor will refund the $50 down payment. Beyer pays the $50 and takes the mower. On the tenth day the lawn mower is stolen through no fault of Beyer. Beyer calls Sallor and demands the return of his $50. Sallor claims Beyer should suffer the risk of loss and that he still owes Sallor the remainder of the purchase price, $150. Discuss whether Beyer or Sallor is correct.

4. In the following situations, two parties lay claim to the same goods sold. Discuss which of the parties would prevail in this claim to the television set in each situation.
   (a) Thomas steals Able's television set and sells the set to Beyer, an innocent purchaser, for value. Able learns Beyer has the set and demands its return.
   (b) Able takes her television set for repair to Martin, a merchant who sells new and used television sets. By accident, one of Martin's employees sells the

set to Beyer, an innocent purchaser-customer, who takes possession. Able wants her set back from Beyer.

5. Beyer contracts to purchase from Sallor 100 cases of Knee High Corn to be shipped F.O.B. Sallor's warehouse by ABC Truck Lines. Sallor, by mistake, delivers 100 cases of Green Valley Corn to the ABC Truck Lines. While in transit, the Green Valley Corn is stolen. As between Beyer and Sallor, who suffers the loss?

6. Crump, a television fanatic, purchased a television antenna and antenna tower from Lair Company. Crump purchased the antenna and tower under a ten-year conditional sales contract that obligated him to make monthly payments. The sales contract provided that Lair Company would retain title until Crump had completed all payments under the contract. The purchase contract stated, among other things, that Crump was not to move or tamper with the antenna during the ten-year payment period. About a year later, lightning struck and destroyed Crump's new antenna. At Crump's request, Lair Company performed extensive repairs on the antenna. Crump refused to pay, claiming that risk of loss or damage resulting from the lightning should be borne by Lair Company. Will Lair be successful in a suit for the cost of its repairs? [Lair Distributing Co. v. Crump, 48 Ala.App. 72, 261 So. 2d 904 (1972)]

7. Isis Foods, Inc., located in St. Louis, desired to purchase a shipment of food from Pocasset Food Sales, Inc. The sale of food was initiated by a purchase order from Isis stating that the shipment was to be made "F.O.B. St. Louis." Pocasset made the shipment by delivery of the goods to the carrier. Pocasset's invoices contain a provision stating: "Our liability ceases upon delivery of merchandise to carrier." The shipment of food was destroyed in transit before reaching St. Louis. Discuss which party has the risk of loss and why? [In re Isis Foods, Inc., 38 B.R. 48 (B.C.W.D. Mo. 1983)]

8. A new car owned by a New Jersey car rental agency was stolen in 1967. The agency collected the full price of the car from its insurance company, Home Indemnity Company, and assigned all its interest in the automobile to the insurer. Subsequently, a thief sold the car to an automobile wholesaler, who in turn sold it to a retail car dealer. Schrier purchased the automobile from the car dealer without knowledge of the theft. Home Indemnity Insurance Company sued Schrier to recover the car. Can Home Indemnity recover? [Schrier v. Home Indemnity Co., 273 A.2d 248 (D.C.App. 1971)]

9. The Ryans borrowed money from Evanston Building & Loan Company to buy a modular home manufactured by Fuqua Homes. They purchased the home from a partnership acting as an intermediary-dealer for Fuqua. After receiving the proceeds of the sale, the partners in the intermediary-dealership disappeared without making any payment to Fuqua Homes. Fuqua claimed that since it had not been paid, it was still the holder of the certificate of origin of the modular home, and it still had title to the home. Is Fuqua correct? [Fuqua Homes, Inc. v. Evanston Building & Loan Co., 52 Ohio App.2d 399, 370 N.E.2d 780 (1977)]

10. A men's clothing manufacturer in Los Angeles sold $2,216 of men's clothing to a store in Westport, Connecticut. The contract stated that the shipment was to be "F.O.B. Los Angeles." The Los Angeles manufacturer arranged for shipping via common carrier to Connecticut. Upon arrival of the clothes, the purchaser's agent refused to unload them, as did the carrier's agent, indicating that it was the purchaser's obligation to unload. The carrier left with the shipment, which subsequently disappeared. The Los Angeles manufacturer sued the purchaser for the contract price. Had the risk of loss passed to the Connecticut purchaser at the time of delivery of the clothes to the common carrier? [Ninth Street East Ltd. v. Harrison, 5 Conn.Cir. 597, 259 A.2d 772 (1968)]

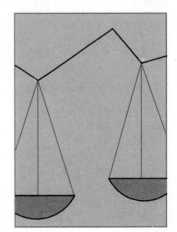

19

SALES
Performance
and Obligation

DUTY OF GOOD FAITH AND COMMERCIAL REASONABLENESS

To understand the performance that is required of a seller and of a buyer under a sales contract, it is necessary to know the duties and obligations each party has assumed under the terms of the contract. Keep in mind that "duties and obligations" under the terms of the contract here include those specified in the agreement, the custom, and the Code.

Sometimes the sales contract leaves open some particulars of performance and permits one of the parties to specify them. The obligations of "good faith" and "commercial reasonableness," however, underlie every sales contract within the UCC. They are objective obligations, and they can form the basis for a breach of contract suit later on. These standards are read into every contract, and they provide a framework in which the parties can specify particulars of performance. "Any such specification must be made in good faith and within limits set by commercial reasonableness." [UCC 2-311(1)]

The duty of cooperation between the parties required by Section 2-311 must be read along with the Code's "good faith" provision, which can never be disclaimed. "Every contract or duty within this

Act imposes an obligation of good faith in its performance or enforcement." [UCC 1-203] "Good faith" in the case of a merchant means honesty in fact *and* the observance of reasonable commercial standards of fair dealing in the trade. [UCC 2-103(1)(b)]

Thus, when one party delays specifying particulars of performance for an unreasonable period of time or fails to cooperate with the other party, the innocent party is excused from any resulting delay in performance. In addition, the innocent party can proceed to perform in any reasonable manner. If the innocent party has performed as far as is reasonably possible under the circumstances, then the other party's failure to specify particulars or failure to cooperate can be treated as a breach of contract.

Good faith can mean that one party must not take advantage of another party by manipulating contract terms. Good faith applies to both parties, even the nonbreaching party. The principle of good faith applies through both the performance and the enforcement of all agreements or duties within a contract. Good faith is a question of fact for the jury. As previously mentioned, it means honesty in fact.

The following case deals with the issue of good faith in the termination of a franchise contract.

ZAPATHA v. DAIRY
MART, INC.
Massachusetts Supreme Judicial
Court, 1980.
408 N.E.2d 1370, 29 UCC
Rep. Serv. 1121.

BACKGROUND AND FACTS *In 1973 the Zapathas entered into a franchise agreement with the defendant. The agreement permitted either party to terminate the relationship without cause on ninety days' written notice. A second franchise agreement was executed in 1974, when the Zapathas moved their store to a new location. In 1977 the Zapathas refused to sign a new agreement submitted by the defendant. Dairy Mart then gave written notice to the Zapathas that their contract would be terminated in ninety days. The Zapathas brought this action seeking to enjoin the termination of the agreement, alleging that the contract provision allowing termination without cause was unconscionable and that Dairy Mart had not acted in good faith. The trial court held for the Zapathas and Dairy Mart appealed.*

WILKINS, Judge.
* * * *

We start with the recognition that the Uniform Commercial Code itself implies that a contract provision allowing termination without cause is not per se unconscionable. Section 2-309(3) provides that "[t]ermination of a contract by one party except on the happening of an agreed event requires that reasonable notification be received by the other party and an agreement dispensing with notification is invalid if its operation would be unconscionable." This language implies that termination of a sales contract without agreed "cause" is authorized by the Code, provided reasonable notice is given. There is no suggestion that the ninety days' notice provided in the Dairy Mart franchise agreement was unreasonable.

We find no potential for unfair surprise to the Zapathas in the provision allowing termination without cause. We view the question of unfair surprise as focused on the circumstances under which the agreement was entered into. The termination provision was neither obscurely worded, nor buried in fine print in the contract. The provision was specifically pointed out to Mr. Zapatha before it was signed; Mr. Zapatha testified that he thought the provision was "straightforward," and he declined the opportunity to take the agreement to a lawyer for advice. The Zapathas had ample opportunity to consider the agreement before they signed it. * * *
* * * *

We further conclude that there was no oppression in the inclusion of a termination clause in the franchise agreement. We view the question of oppression as directed to the substantive fairness to the parties of permitting the termination provisions to operate as written. The Zapathas took over a going business on premises provided by Dairy Mart, using equipment furnished by Dairy Mart. As an investment, the Zapathas had only to purchase the inventory of goods to be sold but, as Dairy Mart concedes, on termination by it without cause Dairy Mart was obliged to repurchase all the Zapathas' saleable merchandise inventory, including items not purchased from Dairy Mart, at 80% of its retail value. There was no potential for forfeiture or loss of investment. There is no question here of a need for a reasonable time to recoup the franchisees' initial investment. The Zapathas were entitled to their net profits through the entire term of the agreement. They failed to sustain their burden of showing that the agreement allocated the risks and benefits connected with termination in an unreasonably disproportionate way and that the termination provision was not reasonably related to legitimate commercial needs of Dairy Mart. To find the termination clause oppressive merely because it did not require cause for termination would be to establish an unwarranted barrier to the use of termination at will clauses in contracts in this Commonwealth, where each party received the anticipated and bargained for consideration during the full term of the agreement.

We see no basis on the record for concluding that Dairy Mart did not act in good faith, as that term is defined in the sales article ("honesty in fact and the observance of reasonable commercial standards of fair dealing in the trade"). There was no evidence that Dairy Mart failed to observe reasonable commercial standards of fair dealing in the trade in terminating the agreement. If there were such standards, there was no evidence of what they were.

The question then is whether there was evidence warranting a finding that Dairy Mart was not honest "in fact." The judge concluded that the absence of any commercial purpose for the termination other than the Zapathas' refusal to sign a new franchise agreement violated Dairy Mart's obligation of good faith. Dairy Mart's right to terminate was clear, and it exercised that right for a reason it openly disclosed. The sole test of "honesty in fact" is whether the person was honest. We think that, whether or not termination according to the terms of the franchise agreement may have been arbitrary, it was not dishonest.

*　*　*　*

The lower court's judgment for the plaintiffs was reversed. Dairy Mart was allowed to terminate the agreement.

DECISION AND REMEDY

PERFORMANCE OF A SALES CONTRACT

A seller has the basic obligation to *transfer and deliver conforming goods.* The buyer has the basic obligation to *accept and pay for conforming goods* in accordance with the contract. [UCC 2-301] Overall performance of a sales contract is controlled by the agreement between the buyer and the seller. When the contract is unclear, or when terms are indefinite in certain respects and disputes arise, the Code provides built-in standards and rules for interpreting their agreement.

CONCURRENT CONDITIONS OF PERFORMANCE

The delivery of goods by the seller and the payment of the purchase price by the buyer are said to be *concurrent conditions*—those that are mutually dependent and are to be performed at the same time. The theoretical assumption is that delivery and payment can occur simultaneously. In reality this rarely happens.

Section 2-301 of the Code provides that "the obligation of the seller is to transfer and deliver and that of the buyer is to accept and pay *in accordance with the contract*" (emphasis added). If the contract expressly provides that the seller must first deliver the goods before receiving payment or that the buyer must pay before receiving the goods, then the terms of the contract control. However, where the agree-

ment does not specifically provide, the Code charges both parties with the duty to proceed. In other words, in order for either party to maintain an action against the other for breach, the party bringing suit must put the other party in default by performing. This is accomplished in one of three ways—through: (1) performance according to the contract, (2) tender of performance according to the contract, or (3) excuse from tender of performance.[1]

For example, Laval agrees to deliver goods to Boyd on September 1, and Boyd agrees to pay on September 15. If Laval fails to deliver the goods, Boyd can sue Lavel on or after September 2. Since Laval is in default, Boyd can proceed without first tendering the purchase price.

SELLER'S OBLIGATION OF TENDER OF DELIVERY

Tender of Delivery

Tender of delivery requires that the seller have and hold *conforming* goods at the buyer's disposal and give the buyer whatever notification is reasonably necessary to enable the buyer to take delivery. [UCC 2-503(1)]

Tender must occur at a *reasonable hour* and in a *reasonable manner.* In other words, a seller cannot call the buyer at 2:00 A.M. and say, "The goods are

---

1.　To tender is to offer or make available money or property in pursuance of a contract in such a way that nothing further remains to be done to fulfill the obligation of the party tendering.

ready. I'll give you twenty minutes to get them." Unless the parties have agreed otherwise, the goods must be tendered for delivery at a reasonable time and must be kept available for a reasonable period of time in order to enable the buyer to take possession of them. [UCC 2-503(1)(a)]

All goods called for by a contract must be tendered in a single delivery unless the parties agree otherwise [UCC 2-612] or the circumstances are such that either party can rightfully request delivery in lots. [UCC 2-307] Hence, an order for 1,000 shirts cannot be delivered two at a time. If seller and buyer contemplated, though, that the shirts would be delivered in four orders of 250 each as they are produced, for summer, winter, fall, and spring stock, and the price can be apportioned accordingly, it may be commercially reasonable to do so.

Place of Delivery

Non-Carrier Cases If the contract does not designate where the goods will be delivered, and the buyer is expected to pick them up, the place of delivery is the *seller's place of business* or, if the seller has none, the *seller's residence*. [UCC 2-308] If the contract involves the sale of *identified goods* (see Chapter 18 for a discussion of such goods), and the parties know when they enter into the contract that these goods are located somewhere other than at the seller's place of business (such as at a warehouse or in the possession of a bailee), then the *location of the goods* is the place for their delivery. [UCC 2-308]

For example, Laval and Boyd live in San Francisco. In San Francisco, Laval contracts to sell to Boyd five used railroad dining cars, which both parties know are located in Atlanta. If nothing more is specified in the contract, the place of delivery for the railroad cars is Atlanta.

Assume further that the railroad cars are stored in a warehouse and that Boyd will need some type of document to show the warehouse (bailee) in Atlanta that Boyd is entitled to take possession of the five dining cars. The seller "tenders delivery" without moving the goods. The seller may "deliver" either by giving the buyer a *negotiable document of title* or by obtaining the *bailee's* (warehouse's) *acknowledgment* that the buyer is entitled to possession.[2]

Carrier Cases There are many instances, resulting either from attendant circumstances or from delivery terms contained in the contract, when it is apparent that the parties intend that a carrier be used to move the goods. There are two ways a seller can complete performance of the obligation to deliver the goods—through a shipment contract or a destination contract.

Shipment Contracts A shipment contract requires or authorizes the seller to ship goods by a carrier. The contract does not require the seller to deliver the goods at a particular destination. [UCC 2-509 and 2-319] Unless otherwise agreed, the seller must [UCC 2-504]:

1. Put the goods into the hands of the carrier.
2. Make a contract for their transportation that is reasonable according to the nature of the goods and their value. (For example, certain types of goods need refrigeration in transit.)
3. Obtain and promptly deliver for tender to the buyer any documents necessary to enable the buyer to obtain possession of the goods from the carrier.
4. Promptly notify the buyer that shipment has been made.

If the seller fails to notify the buyer that shipment has been made or fails to make a proper contract for transportation, and a *material loss* of the goods or a *delay* results, the buyer can reject the shipment. Of course, the parties can agree that a lesser amount of loss or a delay will be grounds for rejection.

Destination Contracts Under destination contracts, the seller agrees to see that the goods will be duly tendered to the buyer at a particular destination. Once the goods arrive, the seller must tender the goods at a reasonable hour and hold conforming goods at the buyer's disposal for a reasonable length of time, giving appropriate notice. The seller must also provide the buyer with any documents of title necessary to enable the buyer to obtain delivery from the carrier. This is often done by tendering the documents through ordinary banking channels. Although not a part of the seller's tender, unless other-

---

2. If the seller delivers a nonnegotiable document of title or merely writes instructions to the bailee to release the goods to the

buyer without the bailee's *acknowledgment* of the buyer's rights, this will also be a sufficient tender, unless the buyer objects. [UCC 2-503(4)] But risk of loss would not pass until the buyer had a reasonable time to present the document or the instructions.

wise agreed, the buyer must furnish facilities reasonably suited for the receipt of the goods. [UCC 2-503]

Contract Terms As previously discussed in Chapter 18, specific terms in the sales contract, such as F.O.B., F.A.S., Delivery Ex-ship, and C.I.F. (C&F), are also delivery terms. As a brief review:

F.O.B. Contracts In contracts specifying that the goods, price, or delivery are F.O.B. (free on board) to a particular point, the F.O.B. point is the delivery point. [UCC 2-319(1)]

F.A.S. Contracts F.A.S. contracts involve transportation by ship or other seagoing vessel. In contracts specifying that the goods, price, or delivery are F.A.S. (free alongside ship), the seller must deliver the goods alongside the vessel, usually on a dock designated by the buyer. The seller must obtain and tender a receipt, which is delivered to the buyer, ordinarily through banking channels. Once delivered, the F.A.S. contract is complete. [UCC 2-319(2)]

Ex-ship Contracts If the contract specifies for delivery of goods "ex-ship" (from the carrying vessel), the shipper must ship conforming goods, and unload the goods at the port of destination.

C.I.F. Contracts In C.I.F. ("cost, insurance, and freight") or C&F (cost and freight) contracts, unless otherwise agreed, the seller is required to deliver and load the goods on board the carrier, obtain a bill of lading showing freight has been paid, obtain proper insurance coverage, prepare an invoice and other necessary documents, and forward all documents to the buyer. [UCC 2-320 and 2-321]

THE PERFECT TENDER RULE

As previously noted, the seller has an obligation to ship or tender *conforming goods*, and this entitles the seller to acceptance by and payment from the buyer according to the terms of the contract. At common law the seller was obligated to deliver goods in conformity with the terms of the contract in every detail. This was called the *perfect tender* doctrine. The UCC, in Section 2-601, preserves the perfect tender doctrine by providing "if goods or tender of

delivery fail *in any respect* to conform to the contract" (emphasis added), the buyer has the right to accept the goods, reject the entire shipment, or accept part and reject part.

For example, the buyer contracts to purchase 100 cases of brand X peas to be delivered at the buyer's place of business on or before October 1. On September 28 the seller discovers that there are only 99 cases of brand X in inventory, but there will be another 500 cases within the next two weeks. So the seller tenders delivery of the 99 cases of brand X on October 1, with the promise that the other case will be delivered within three weeks. Since the seller failed to make a perfect tender of 100 cases of brand X, the buyer has the right to reject the entire shipment and hold the seller in breach. (Such a rigid rule, however, seems uncharacteristic of the Code's philosophy of finding and preserving a contract whenever possible and inconsistent with the idea that good faith permeates the Code.)

Exceptions to the Perfect Tender Rule

Agreement of the Parties If the parties have agreed, for example, that defective goods or parts will not be rejected if the seller is able to repair or replace them within a reasonable time, then the perfect tender rule does not apply.

Cure The term **cure** is not specifically defined in the Code, but it refers to the seller's right to repair, adjust, or replace defective or nonconforming goods. [UCC 2-508]

When any tender or delivery is rejected because of *nonconforming goods* and the time for performance has not yet expired, the seller can notify the buyer promptly of the intention to cure and can then do so *within the contract time for performance.* [UCC 2-508(1)]

For example, Horn sells Gill a white refrigerator, to be delivered on or before September 15. Horn delivers a yellow refrigerator on September 10, and Gill rejects it. Horn can cure by notifying Gill that he intends to cure and by delivering a white refrigerator on or before September 15.

Once the time for performance under the contract has *expired*, the seller can still exercise the right to cure if the seller had *reasonable grounds to believe that the nonconforming tender would be acceptable to the buyer.*

Although frequently the seller tenders nonconforming goods with some type of price allowance, he or she may still have a reasonable belief that the goods will be accepted by the buyer for other reasons. For example, Demsetz has been supplying auto body paint to Hall Body, an auto body paint shop, for several years. Demsetz and Hall have a contract for R-Z type paint. In the past, when Demsetz could not obtain R-Z type paint, he substituted R-Y type paint, and Hall accepted without any objection. Hall signs a new contract for R-Z type paint to be delivered on April 30. Demsetz realizes that, with the paint supply on hand, only half the order can be filled with R-Z type paint, so he completes the other half of the order with R-Y type paint. The order is delivered on April 30. Hall rejects. Demsetz, knowing from their prior course of dealing that R-Y had always been an acceptable substitute, has "reasonable grounds to believe" that R-Y would be acceptable. Therefore, Demsetz can cure within a reasonable time, even though conforming delivery will occur after the actual time for performance under the contract.

As just pointed out, the seller may offer a price allowance with the tender of nonconforming goods. This frequently creates a presumption that a buyer will accept the fortuitous offer. Suppose a buyer contracts to purchase 100 Model Z hand calculators at a price of $20 each from a seller, to be delivered on or before October 1. The seller cannot deliver 100 Model Z calculators but tenders 100 new, more sophisticated, more expensive Model A–1 calculators at the same price as the 100 Model Z calculators contracted for on October 1. The buyer rejects the delivery. If the seller *notifies* the buyer of intent to cure, the seller has a *reasonable time* (after October 1) to substitute a conforming tender of Model Z calculators.

The seller's right to cure substantially restricts the buyer's right to reject. If the buyer refuses a tender of goods as nonconforming but does not disclose the nature of the defect to the seller, the buyer cannot later assert the defect as a defense if the defect is one that the seller could have cured. The buyer must act in good faith and state specific reasons for refusing to accept the goods. [UCC 2-605]

Substitution of Carriers   Where an agreed manner of delivery (berthing, loading, or unloading facilities) becomes impracticable or unavailable through no fault of either party, but a commercially reasonable substitute is available, this substitute performance is sufficient tender to the buyer. [UCC 2-614(1)]

For example, a sales contract calls for the delivery of a large piece of machinery to be shipped by ABC Truck Lines on or before June 1. The contract terms clearly state the importance of the delivery date. The employees of ABC Truck Lines go on strike. The seller will be entitled to make a reasonable substitute tender, perhaps by rail. Note that the seller here is responsible for any additional shipping costs, unless contrary arrangements have been made in the sales contract.

Installment Contracts   An **installment contract** is a single contract that requires or authorizes delivery in two or more separate lots to be accepted and paid for separately. In an installment contract, a buyer can reject an installment *only if the nonconformity substantially impairs the value* of the installment and cannot be cured. [UCC 2-612(2) and 2-307] Notice, then, how this is a substantial limitation on the perfect tender rule.

The entire installment contract is breached only when one or more nonconforming installments *substantially* impair the value of the *whole contract*. If the buyer subsequently accepts a nonconforming installment and fails to notify the seller of cancellation, then the contract is reinstated, however. Also, if the buyer brings an action with respect only to past installments or demands performance as to future installments, the aggrieved party has reinstated the contract. [UCC 2-612(3)]

A major issue to be determined is what constitutes *substantial* impairment of the "value of the whole." For example, consider an installment contract for the sale of twenty carloads of plywood. The first carload does not conform to the contract because 9 percent of the plywood in the car deviates from the thickness specifications. The buyer cancels the contract, and immediately thereafter the second and third carloads of plywood arrive at the buyer's place of business. The court would have to grapple with the question of whether the 9 percent of nonconforming plywood substantially impaired the value of the whole.[3]

---

3.   Forest Products v. White Lumber Sales, Inc., 256 Or. 466, 474 P.2d 1, 8 UCC 178 (1970). The court held that the deviation did not substantially impair the value of the whole contract. Additionally, the court stated that the nonconformity could be cured by an adjustment in the price.

A more clear-cut example is an installment contract that involves parts of a machine. Suppose that the first part is delivered and is irreparably defective but is necessary for the operation of the machine. The failure of this first installment will be a breach of the whole contract. Even when the defect in the first shipment is such that it gives the buyer only a "reasonable apprehension" about the ability or willingness of the seller to properly complete the other installments, the breach on the first installment may be regarded as a breach of the whole.

The point to remember in this discussion is that the UCC substantially alters the right of a buyer to reject the entire contract in installment sales contracts. Such contracts are broadly defined in the UCC, which strictly limits rejection to cases of substantial nonconformity.

Commercial Impracticability Whenever occurrences unforeseen by either party when the contract was made make performance commercially impracticable, the rule of perfect tender no longer holds. According to UCC 2-615(a), delay in delivery or nondelivery in whole or in part is not a breach when performance has been made impracticable "by the occurrence of a contingency the nonoccurrence of which was a basic assumption on which the contract was made * * *." However, the seller must notify the buyer as soon as it is practicable to do so that there will be a delay or nondelivery.

The notion of commercial impracticability is derived from contract law theories of impossibility and frustration of purpose.[4] Increased costs resulting from inflation do not in and of themselves excuse performance. This is the kind of risk ordinarily assumed by a seller conducting business. The unforeseen

contingency must be one that would have been impossible to contemplate in a given business situation.

For example, a major oil company that receives its supplies from the Middle East has a contract to supply a buyer with 100,000 gallons of oil. Because of an oil embargo by OPEC, the seller is prevented from securing oil supplies to meet the terms of this contract. Because of the same embargo, the seller cannot secure oil from any other source. This situation comes fully under the commercial impracticability exception to the perfect tender doctrine.

Sometimes the unforeseen event only *partially* affects the seller's capacity to perform. As a result, the seller is able to fulfill the contract *partially* but cannot tender total performance. In this event, the seller is required to allocate in a fair and reasonable manner any remaining production and deliveries among the contracted customers. The buyer must receive notice of the allocation, with the obvious right to accept or reject the allocation.

For example, a grower of cranberries in the state of Washington, Cran Plan, has contracted to sell this season's production to a number of customers, including the G & G grocery chain. G & G has contracted to purchase 2,000 crates of cranberries. Cran Plan has sprayed *some* of its bogs of cranberries with a chemical called Green. The Department of Agriculture discovers that there is a potential danger that persons who eat products sprayed with Green may develop cancer. An order prohibiting the sale of these products is effected. Cran Plan has harvested all the bogs not sprayed with Green, but the production will not allow it to fully meet all contract deliveries. In this case, Cran Plan is required to allocate its production, notifying G & G of the amount it is able to deliver.

Does a picket line at a job site cause a party's performance to become so "impracticable" that the excuse of "impossibility" becomes a valid defense to performance? That is the question to be answered in the following case.

---

4. See Chapter 15 under "Discharge by Impossibility of Performance."

BACKGROUND AND FACTS *The plaintiff, Mishara Construction Company, Inc., was a general contractor. Mishara was under contract with the Pittsfield Housing Authority for the construction of Rose Manor, a housing project for the elderly. In September 1966, Mishara negotiated with the defendant, Transit-Mixed Concrete Corp., for the supply of ready-mixed concrete to be used on the project. An agreement was reached that Transit would supply all the concrete needed on the project at a price of $13.25 per cubic yard, with*

MISHARA CONSTR. CO., INC. v. TRANSIT-MIXED CONCRETE CORP.
Supreme Judicial Court of Massachusetts, 1974.
310 N.E.2d 363.

deliveries to be made at the times and in the amounts ordered by Mishara. The two parties signed a purchase order on September 21, 1966. The purchase order identified the Rose Manor project and indicated that delivery was to be made as required by the Mishara Construction Company. Performance under this contract was satisfactory to both parties until April 1967.

In that month a labor dispute disrupted work on the job site. Although work resumed on June 15, 1967, a picket line was maintained on the site until the project was completed in 1969. Throughout this period, with very few exceptions, Transit delivered no concrete because of the picket line, despite frequent requests by Mishara. After notifying Transit of its intention, Mishara purchased the balance of its concrete requirements elsewhere. Mishara then sought damages for the additional cost of the replacement concrete and for the expenses it incurred in locating an alternate source of ready-mixed concrete.

REARDON, Justice.

* * * *

The principal issue in the case was the defendant's claimed excuse of impossibility of performance. The determination of that issue depended on facts and circumstances which were for the jury to decide. * * *

* * * *

The excuse of impossibility in contracts for the sale of goods is controlled by the appropriate section of the Uniform Commercial Code, * * * § 2-615. That section sets up two requirements before performance may be excused. First, the performance must have become "impracticable." Second, the impracticability must have been caused "by the occurrence of a contingency the non-occurrence of which was a basic assumption on which the contract was made." This section of the Uniform Commercial Code has not yet been interpreted by this court. Therefore it is appropriate to discuss briefly the significance of these two criteria.

With respect to the requirement that performance must have been impracticable, the official Code comment to the section stresses that the reference is to "*commercial impracticability*" as opposed to strict impossibility. [Emphasis added.] This is not a radical departure from the common law of contracts as interpreted by this court. Although a strict rule was originally followed denying any excuse for accident or "inevitable necessity," e.g., *Adams v. Nichols*, 19 Pick. 275 (1837), it has long been assumed that circumstances drastically increasing the difficulty and expense of the contemplated performance may be within the compass of "impossibility." By adopting the term "impracticability" rather than "impossibility" the drafters of the Code appear to be in accord with Professor Williston who [prior to enactment of the UCC] stated that "the essence of the modern defense of impossibility is that the promised performance was at the making of the contract, or thereafter became, impracticable owing to some extreme or unreasonable difficulty, expense, injury, or loss involved, rather than that it is scientifically or actually impossible."

The second criterion of the excuse, that the intervening circumstance be one which the parties assumed would not occur, is also familiar to the law of Massachusetts. The rule is essentially aimed at the distribution of certain kinds of risks in the contractual relationship. By directing the inquiry to the time when the contract was first made, we really seek to determine whether the risk of the intervening circumstance was one which the parties may be taken to have assigned between themselves. It is, of course, *the very essence of contract that it is directed at the elimination of some risks for each party in exchange for others. Each receives the certainty of price, quantity, and time, and assumes the risk of changing market prices, superior opportunity, or added costs.* [Emphasis added.] It is implicit in the doctrine of impossibility (and the companion rule of "frustration of purpose") that certain risks are so unusual and have such severe consequences that they must have been beyond the scope of the assignment of risks inherent in the contract, that is, beyond the agreement made by the parties. To require performance in that case would be to grant the promisee an advantage for which he could not be said to have bargained in making the contract. "The important question is whether an unanticipated circumstance has made performance of the promise vitally different from what should reasonably have been within the contemplation of both parties when they entered into the contract. If so, the risk should not fairly be thrown upon the promisor." Williston, Contracts (Rev. ed.) § 1931 (1938). The emphasis in contracts governed by the Uniform Commercial Code is on the commercial context in which the agreement was made. The question is, given the commercial circumstances in which the parties dealt: *Was the contingency which developed one which the parties could reasonably be thought to have foreseen as a real possibility which could affect performance?* [Emphasis added.] Was it one of that variety of risks which the parties were tacitly assigning to the promisor by their failure to provide for it explicitly? If it were, performance will be required. If it could not be so considered, performance is excused. The contract cannot be reasonably thought to govern in these circumstances, and the parties are both thrown upon the resources of the open market without the benefit of their contract.

With this backdrop, we consider Mishara's contention that a labor dispute which makes performance more difficult never constitutes an excuse for nonperformance. We think it is evident that in some situations a labor dispute would not meet the requirements for impossibility discussed above. A picket line might constitute a mere inconvenience and hardly make performance "impracticable." Likewise, in certain industries with a long record of labor difficulties, the nonoccurrence of strikes and picket lines could not fairly be said to be a basic assumption of the agreement. Certainly, in general, labor disputes cannot be considered extraordinary in the course of modern commerce. See Restatement: Contracts, § 461, illustration 7 (1932). Admitting this however, we are still far from the proposition implicit in the plaintiff's requests. Much must depend on the facts known to the parties at the time of contracting with respect to the history of and prospects for labor difficulties during the period of performance of the contract, as well as the likely severity of the effect of such disputes on the ability to perform. From these facts it is possible to draw an inference as to whether or not the parties intended performance to be carried out even in the face of the labor difficulty. *Where the probability of a labor dispute appears to be practically nil, and where the occurrence of such a dispute provides unusual difficulty, the excuse of impracticability might well be applicable.* [Emphasis added.] * * * "Rather than mechanically apply any fixed rule of law, where the parties themselves have not allocated responsibility, justice is better served by appraising all of the circumstances, the part the various parties played, and thereon determining liability."

DECISION AND REMEDY

The plaintiff was unsuccessful in obtaining damages from the defendant. The jury determined that this labor dispute would be considered a commercial impracticability under the UCC. Therefore, the defendant was excused from performing under the terms of the contract.

COMMENTS

Many commentators on this case do not agree with the judgment. Strikes in and of themselves do not normally excuse performance, so the outcome of this case cannot be considered the general rule.

Destruction of Identified Goods The Code provides that when a casualty occurs that totally destroys *identified goods* under a sales contract through no fault of either party and *before risk passes to the buyer*, the seller and buyer are excused from performance. [UCC 2-613(a)] However, if the goods are only partially destroyed, the buyer can inspect them and either treat the contract as void or accept the damaged goods with an allowance off the contract price.

Consider an example. Acme Appliances has on display six ABC dishwashers of a discontinued model. Five are white, and one is harvest gold. No others of that model are available. Jones, who is not a merchant, clearly specifies that she needs the harvest gold dishwasher because it fits into her kitchen's color scheme. Jones buys the harvest gold dishwasher. Unfortunately, before Acme can deliver it, it is destroyed by a fire. In such a case, under Section 2-613, Acme Appliance will not be liable to Jones for failure to deliver the harvest gold dishwasher. The goods here suffered a casualty without fault of either party before the risk of loss passed to the buyer, and the loss was total, so the contract is avoided. Clearly, Acme has no obligation to tender that dishwasher. Of course, Jones has no obligation to pay for it either.

Change the example somewhat. Jones purchases a discontinued dishwasher model but does not specify the color. If the harvest gold dishwasher is destroyed by fire, Acme is still obliged to tender one of the other discontinued models, and Jones is obligated to accept and to make payment. Only if Acme's entire stock of the discontinued model were destroyed by the fire would Acme be excused from performance in this instance.

Assurance and Cooperation   Two other exceptions to the perfect tender doctrine apply equally to the seller and buyer.

The right of assurance stems from the concept that the essential purpose of a contract is performance by both parties, and thus when one party has reason to believe the other party will not perform, it is an undue hardship to force the first party to perform.

The Code provides that should a seller (or buyer) have "reasonable grounds" to believe the buyer (or seller) will not perform as contracted, he or she may "in writing demand adequate assurance of due performance" from the other party; and until such assurance is received, he or she may "suspend" further performance without liability. The grounds for such belief and action must be reasonable. Between merchants, the grounds are determined by commercial

standards. [UCC 2-609] The assurances requested also must be reasonable. If such assurances are not forthcoming within a reasonable time (not to exceed thirty days), the failure to respond may be treated as a *repudiation* of the contract.

For example, Sallor has contracted to ship Beyer 100 dozen shirts on or before October 1, with Beyer's payment due within thirty days of delivery. Sallor has made two previous shipments, neither of which has been paid for by Beyer. On September 20, Sallor demands in writing certain assurances of payment (such as payment of the last two orders to bring the account up to date) before Sallor will ship the 100 dozen shirts. If this assurance is reasonable, Sallor can suspend shipment of the shirts without liability pending Beyer's compliance. If Beyer does not provide the payments within a reasonable time (no longer than thirty days), Sallor can hold Beyer in breach of contract without having made the contracted shipment.

Sometimes performance of one party depends on the cooperation of the other. The Code provides that when such cooperation is not forthcoming, the other party can suspend his or her own performance without liability and hold the uncooperative party in breach. [UCC 2-311(3)]

For example, Sallor is required by contract to deliver 1,200 Model Z washing machines to locations within the state of California to be specified later by Beyer. Deliveries are to be made on or before October 1. Sallor has repeatedly requested the delivery locations, and Beyer has not responded. The 1,200 Model Z machines are ready for shipment on October 1, but Beyer still refuses to give Sallor the delivery locations. Sallor does not ship on October 1. Can Sallor be held liable? The answer is no. Sallor is excused for any resulting delay of performance because of Beyer's failure to cooperate.

BUYER'S OBLIGATIONS

Once the seller has adequately tendered delivery, the buyer is obligated to accept the goods and pay for them according to the terms of the contract. In the absence of any specific agreements, the buyer must:

1.   Furnish facilities reasonably suited for receipt of the goods. [UCC 2-503(1)(b)]

2. Make payment at the time and place the buyer *receives* the goods, even if the place of shipment is the place of delivery. [UCC 2-310(a)]

Payment

When a sale is made on credit, the buyer is obliged to pay according to credit terms (for example, 60, 90, or 120 days), *not* when the goods are received. The credit period usually begins on the *date of shipment*. [UCC 2-310(d)]

Payment can be made by any means agreed upon between the parties. Cash can be used, but the buyer can also use any other method generally acceptable in the commercial world. If the seller demands cash when the buyer offers a check, credit card, or the like, then the seller must permit the buyer reasonable time to obtain legal tender. [UCC 2-511]

Right of Inspection

Unless otherwise agreed, or for C.O.D. (collect on delivery) goods, the buyer's right to inspect the goods is absolute. This right allows the buyer to verify, before making payment, that the goods tendered or delivered are what were contracted for or ordered. If the goods are not what the buyer ordered, there is no duty to pay. *An opportunity for inspection is therefore a condition precedent to the seller's right to enforce payment.* [UCC 2-513(1)]

Unless otherwise agreed, inspection can take place at any reasonable place and time and in any reasonable manner. Generally, what is reasonable is determined by custom of the trade, past practices of the parties, and the like. The Code also provides for inspection after arrival when goods are to be shipped.

Costs of inspecting conforming goods are borne by the buyer unless agreed otherwise. [UCC 2-513(2)]

C.O.D. Shipments If a seller ships goods to a buyer C.O.D. (or under similar terms), the buyer can rightfully *reject* them (unless the contract expressly provides for a C.O.D. shipment). This is because C.O.D. does not permit inspection before payment, and the effect is a denial of the buyer's right of inspection. But when the buyer has agreed to a C.O.D. shipment in the contract or has agreed to pay for the goods upon the presentation of a bill of lading, no right of inspection exists because it was negated by the agreement. [UCC 2-513(3)]

Payment Due—Documents of Title Under certain contracts, payment is due on the receipt of the required documents of title even though the goods themselves may not have arrived at their destination. With C.I.F. and C&F contracts, payment is required upon receipt of the documents unless the parties have agreed to the contrary. Thus, payment is required prior to inspection, and it must be made unless the buyer knows that the goods are nonconforming. [UCC 2-310(b) and 2-513(3)]

Acceptance

The buyer can manifest assent to the delivered goods in different ways, each of which will constitute acceptance:

1. The buyer can expressly accept the shipment by words or conduct. For example, there is an acceptance if the buyer, after having reasonable opportunity to inspect, signifies agreement to the seller that either the goods are conforming or they are acceptable despite their nonconformity. [UCC 2-606(1)(a)]
2. Acceptance will be presumed if the buyer has had a reasonable opportunity to inspect the goods and has failed to reject them within a reasonable period of time. [UCC 2-606(1)(b) and 2-602(1)]
3. The buyer accepts the goods by performing any act inconsistent with the seller's ownership. For example, any use or resale of the goods will generally constitute an acceptance. Limited use for the sole purpose of testing or inspecting the goods is not an acceptance, however. [UCC 2-606(1)(c)]

Revocation of Acceptance

Acceptance of the goods by the buyer precludes the buyer from exercising the right of rejection. Acceptance does not in and of itself impair the right of the buyer to pursue remedies. (Remedies are discussed in Chapter 20.) But if the buyer accepts the nonconforming goods and fails to notify the seller of the breach when it is discovered (or when it should have been discovered), then the buyer is barred from pursuing any remedy against the seller. What is at issue here is the necessity of the buyer informing the seller of the breach within a reasonable time. The burden is on the buyer to establish the existence of a breach of contract once the goods are accepted. [UCC 2-607(3)]

After a buyer accepts a lot or a commercial unit, acceptance can still be revoked if the nonconformity *substantially* impairs the value of the unit or lot and if one of the following factors also is present:

1. If acceptance was predicated on the reasonable assumption that the conformity would be cured, and it has not been cured within a reasonable time. [UCC 2-608(1)(a)]

2. If the buyer does not discover the nonconformity, either because it is difficult to discover before acceptance or because the seller's assurance that the goods are conforming kept the buyer from inspecting the goods. [UCC 2-608(1)(a)]

In the following case, the court made it clear that "substantial impairment of the value to the buyer" is the test of whether revocation of purchased goods can occur once the buyer has accepted the goods.

PECKHAM v. LARSEN CHEVROLET

Supreme Court of Idaho, 1978.
99 Idaho 675, 587 P.2d 816.

BACKGROUND AND FACTS   *Peckham purchased a new car from Larsen Chevrolet. During the first month and a half after the purchase of the car, he discovered that there was a dent in the hood, the gas tank contained no baffles, the emergency brake was inoperable, the clock and speedometer did not work, and there was no jack or spare tire. Peckham made repeated attempts to have those defects repaired. The repairs were finally completed three months after purchase. Then, a couple of days after that, a fire occurred in the dashboard of the car, damaging the dashboard and the carpeting and rendering the vehicle inoperable. Peckham took the car back to Larsen Chevrolet, demanding that the vehicle be repaired at Larsen's expense, or that the contract be rescinded, or that a new car be provided. A discussion between Peckham and Larsen Chevrolet did not satisfy Peckham, so he orally informed Larsen that he was electing to rescind the contract and demand the return of the purchase price. At a hearing for a summary judgment, Larsen Chevrolet argued that the alleged defects were known by Peckham at the time of purchase. Larsen further denied having received the alleged oral notice of rescission.*

A summary judgment was entered in favor of Larsen Chevrolet. The Idaho Supreme Court stated that "although the action was brought for 'rescission,' we treat it as one for revocation of acceptance under the Uniform Commercial Code."

SHEPARD, Chief Justice.

*   *   *   *

Sale of the automobile here is a sale of goods governed by Article 2 of the Uniform Commercial Code. I.C. § 28-2-711 sets forth in general a buyer's remedies. It is provided therein that a buyer may cancel the contract if the seller's delivery is such that it gives the buyer a right to reject or a right to revoke acceptance of the goods.

As noted, this action was originally brought as one for "rescission" and Larsen Chevrolet and General Motors argue that because there is no provision in the Uniform Commercial Code for this remedy, it is unavailable to the buyer. The Code has, in most instances, abandoned the use of the term "rescission" in favor of terms such as "cancellation or termination." However, it has been held, and the commentators agree, that rescission and revocation of acceptance amount to the same thing under the Uniform Commercial Code, particularly since cancellation is a remedy available to a buyer who has established justifiable grounds for revocation of acceptance. I.C. § 28-2-711(1); We, therefore, view and treat Peckham's action for "rescission" as one for "revocation of acceptance" under I.C. § 28-2-608. The principal issue in this case is whether Peckham has sufficiently established the elements necessary for a revocation of acceptance under I.C. § 28-2-608, so as to avoid a summary judgment in favor of the defendants.

Before a buyer may revoke acceptance under § 28-2-608, he must first show that the goods are nonconforming and that the nonconformity substantially impairs the value of the goods to the buyer. *   *   *

Thereafter, if the buyer knew of the nonconformity when he accepted the goods, it is necessary that he show he acted with a reasonable assumption that the nonconformity would be cured, but that it was not seasonably cured. I.C. § 28-2-608(1)(a). If the buyer did not know of the nonconformity when he accepted, he must show that his acceptance was reasonably induced, either by the difficulty of discovering the nonconformity before acceptance or by the seller's assurances. I.C. § 28-2-608(1)(b); [citation.] Finally, the revocation of acceptance by the buyer must occur within a reasonable time after the buyer discovers the defect or should have discovered it, and before any substantial change in condition of the goods which is not caused by their own defects. Such revocation of acceptance is not effective until the buyer notifies the seller. I.C. § 28-2-608(2).

*   *   *   *

Considering the requisite elements for a revocation of acceptance and the facts construed most favorably toward Peckham, a factual dispute exists as to whether Peckham orally notified Larsen Chevrolet of his desire to cancel or rescind the contract (revocation of acceptance) immediately following the fire. Such is denied by Larsen Chevrolet. Depending upon the resolution of that disputed fact, also unresolved is whether Peckham's alleged oral or written notice of cancellation of the contract took place within a reasonable time.

As explained by comment 4 to § 28-2-608(2) of the Uniform Commercial Code, revocation of acceptance is required within . . . a reasonable time after discovery of the grounds for such revocation. Since this remedy will be generally resorted to only after attempts at adjustment have failed, the reasonable time period should extend in most cases beyond the time in which notification of breach must be given, beyond the time for discovery of non-conformity after acceptance and beyond the time for rejection after tender. The parties may by their agreement limit the time for notification under this section, but the same sanctions and considerations apply to such agreements as are discussed in the comment on manner and effect of rightful rejection.

It would appear that no particular form or content of notice of revocation of acceptance is required if the notice is sufficient to inform the seller that the buyer has revoked and identify the particular goods as to which he has revoked.

A further factual issue appears to remain regarding the conformity of the goods. Here there appears to be a dispute as to whether the goods were accepted by Peckham in a defective nonconforming condition or whether he accepted the goods upon assurance by the seller that the defects would be remedied. As stated by I.C. § 28-2-608, comment 2:

> [r]evocation of acceptance is possible only where the nonconformity substantially impairs the value of the goods to the buyer. For this purpose, the test is not what the seller had reason to know at the time of contracting; the question is whether the nonconformity is such as will in fact cause a substantial impairment of value to the buyer though the seller had no advance knowledge as to the buyer's particular circumstances.

An exhaustive discussion of what constitutes substantial impairment to a buyer is unnecessary since it is held each case must be examined on its own merits to determine what is a substantial impairment of value to the particular buyer.

DECISION   *The court reversed the summary judgment in favor of the defendant. The case*
AND REMEDY   *was remanded for further proceedings consistent with the opinion.*

Notice of Revocation Required Revocation of acceptance will not be effective until notice is given to the seller, and that must occur within a reasonable time after the buyer either discovers *or should have discovered* the grounds for revocation. Also, revocation must occur before the goods have undergone any substantial change that was not caused by their own defects (such as spoilage). [UCC 2-608(2)]

Partial Acceptance If some of the goods delivered do not conform to the contract, and the seller has failed to cure, the buyer can make a *partial* acceptance. [UCC 2-601(c)] The same is true if the nonconformity was not reasonably discoverable before acceptance. A buyer cannot accept less than a single *commercial unit*, however. According to Section 2-105, "commercial unit" means a unit of goods that, by commercial usage, is viewed as a "single whole" for purposes of sale, division of which would materially impair the character of the unit, its market value, or its use. A commercial unit can be a single article (such as a machine), or a set of articles (such as a suite of furniture or an assortment of sizes), or a quantity (such as a bale, gross, or carload), or any other unit treated in the trade as a single whole.

Anticipatory Repudiation

The buyer and the seller have *concurrent* conditions of performance. But what if, before the time for either performance, one party clearly communicates to the other the intention not to perform? Such an action is a breach of the contract by *anticipatory repudiation*. When this occurs, the aggrieved party can, according to UCC 2-610:

1. For a commercially reasonable time await performance by the repudiating parties.
2. Resort to any remedy for breach even if the aggrieved party has notified the repudiating party that he or she awaits the latter's performance and has urged retraction.
3. In either case, *suspend performance* or proceed in accordance with the provisions of this article on the seller's right to identify goods notwithstanding

breach or to salvage unfinished goods. [Emphasis added.]

The key to anticipatory breach is that the repudiation takes place *prior* to the time that the party is required under contract to tender performance. The nonbreaching party has a choice of two responses. He or she can treat the repudiation as a final breach by pursuing a remedy; or he or she can wait, hoping that the repudiating party will decide to honor the obligations required by the contract despite the avowed intention to renege.

Should the latter course be pursued, the Code permits the breaching party (subject to some limitations) to "retract" his or her repudiation. The retraction can be by any method that clearly indicates an intent to perform. Once retraction is made, the rights of the repudiating party under the contract are reinstated. [UCC 2-611]

To illustrate: Sallor has contracted to deliver to Beyer 100,000 tons of coal on or before October 1. On September 15, Sallor tells Beyer that he will not make delivery until December 1. This statement of intent not to deliver until two months after the required delivery date is an anticipatory breach, and Beyer could pursue any of the remedies discussed in the next chapter.

But suppose Beyer responds that he expects Sallor to perform as obligated. Then, on September 28, Sallor informs Beyer that the 100,000 tons will be delivered as contracted, and a tender is made on October 1. Beyer has learned in the meantime that the same amount of coal can be purchased elsewhere (later in October) at a lower price. Therefore, Beyer refuses the tender, claiming Sallor breached the contract on September 15.

In this case Beyer, not Sallor, is in breach of contract. Sallor's notice was a retraction of the earlier repudiation. Since Beyer had not resorted to a remedy, or materially changed his position, or indicated the repudiation was final, the retraction reinstated Sallor's rights under the contract. Therefore, Sallor's proper tender obligated Beyer to accept and pay for the coal tendered, and Beyer's refusal constitutes a breach.

QUESTIONS AND CASE PROBLEMS

1. Sallor contracts to ship to Beyer 100 Model Z television sets. The terms of delivery are F.O.B. Sallor's city, by Green Truck Lines, with delivery on or before April 30. On April 15, Sallor discovers that because of an error in inventory control, all Model Z sets have been sold and the stock has not been replenished. Sallor has Model X, a similar but slightly more expensive unit, in stock. On April 16, Sallor ships 100 Model X sets, with notice that Beyer will be charged the Model Z price. Beyer (in a proper manner) rejects the Model X sets tendered on April 18. Sallor does not wish to be held in breach of contract, even though he has tendered nonconforming goods. Discuss Sallor's options.

2. Sallor contracts to deliver to Beyer 1,000 bushels of corn at market price. Delivery and payment are to be made on October 1. On September 10, Beyer informs Sallor that because of financial reverses she cannot pay on October 1. Sallor immediately notifies Beyer that he is holding Beyer in breach of contract. On September 15, Sallor files suit for breach of contract. On October 3, Beyer files an answer to Sallor's lawsuit. Beyer claims that had Sallor tendered delivery on October 1, she would have paid for the corn. Since no delivery was tendered, Beyer claims she cannot be held liable. Discuss whether Sallor can hold Beyer liable in breach.

3. Sallor has contracted to deliver to Beyer 1,000 cases of brand Greenie peas on or before October 1. Beyer is to specify the means of transportation twenty days prior to date of shipment. Payment for the peas is to be made by Beyer upon tender of delivery. On September 10, Sallor prepares the 1,000 cases for shipment. Sallor asks Beyer how he would like the goods to be shipped, but Beyer does not respond. On September 21, Sallor demands in writing assurance that Beyer will be able to pay upon tender of the peas. Sallor's demand is that the money be placed in escrow prior to October 1 in a bank in Beyer's city named by Sallor. Beyer does not respond to any of the requests made by Sallor, but on October 5 he wants to file suit against Sallor for breach of contract for failure to deliver the peas as contracted. Discuss Sallor's liability for failure to tender delivery on October 1.

4. Sallor contracts to deliver 100 Model X color television sets to a new retail customer, Beyer, on May 1, with payment to be made upon delivery. Sallor tenders delivery in her own truck. Beyer notices that one or two cartons have scrape marks on them. Beyer inquires of Sallor whether the sets might have been damaged upon loading. Sallor assures Beyer that the sets are in perfect condition. Beyer tenders Sallor a check, but Sallor refuses the check, claiming that the first delivery to new customers is always for cash. Beyer promises to have the cash within two days. Sallor leaves the sets with Beyer, who stores them in a warehouse pending an "opening sale" date. Two days later, Beyer opens some of the cartons and discovers that a number of the televisions are damaged beyond ordinary repair. Sallor claims Beyer has accepted the sets and is in breach by not paying on delivery. Discuss fully Sallor's claims.

5. Oberg purchased a car from Phillips. Soon after the purchase, Oberg discovered several defects with the automobile, including problems with the engine, the body paint, and the steering. Oberg returned the car to Phillips for repairs on numerous occasions. Phillips had the car at the shop for almost half of a three-month period. Oberg felt these repairs were unsatisfactory and gave Phillips a deadline in which to complete repairs. Phillips did not meet this deadline, and Oberg gave written notification of revocation of his acceptance. Oberg brings a suit against Phillips for breach of contract. Phillips insists that the defects were only minor, that the car was under a one-year express warranty, and that these factors do not give Oberg a basis for his revocation. Does Oberg have a valid claim for revoking his acceptance of the car under this contract and suing for breach of contract? [Oberg v. Phillips, 615 P.2d 1022 (Okla.App. 1980)]

6. In August of 1979, A. B. Parker purchased a Ford-manufactured F-100 pickup truck from Bell Ford, Inc. for $6,155.40. Parker made several complaints to Bell Ford of excessive tire wear, and Bell Ford gave Parker a purchase order to have the vehicle aligned at an independent alignment shop. Though the problem was not cured, Parker never returned the vehicle to Bell Ford nor did he make further complaint. A later inspection of the vehicle disclosed a defective wheel housing causing the tires to wear excessively. Parker sued Bell Ford and Ford Motor Company for breach of warranty. Bell Ford and Ford Motor Company claim Parker's continued acceptance of the vehicle under the circumstances precludes Parker's action. Discuss Bell Ford and Ford Motor Company's contention. [A. B. Parker v. Bell Ford, Inc., 425 So.2d 1101 (Ala. 1983)]

7. On February 6, 1978, Dreyfus Company, Inc. entered into a contract for the sale to Royster Company of 5,000 bushels of Arkansas Certified Bragg soybean seed at $13.50 per bushel. The contract of sale was conditioned on certification of the beans. Dreyfus informed Royster that the beans being sold would have to be purchased by Dreyfus from a company in Parkin, Arkansas. The parties

did not communicate until May when Dreyfus informed Royster that the beans had failed certification. Hours later, Dreyfus phoned and informed Royster that replacement certified beans had been located. Royster refuses delivery, claiming the original beans suffered a casualty loss by failing certification under Section 2-613 of the UCC. Dreyfus sues for breach of contract. Discuss Royster's contention that UCC 2-613 relieves him from liability. [Dreyfus Company, Inc. v. Royster Company, 501 F.Supp. 1169 (E.D.Arkansas 1980)]

8. Goddard and Ishikawajima-Harima Heavy Industries entered into a contract under which Ishikawajima agreed to furnish Goddard with as many boats as Goddard would require. On January 28, 1965, Goddard sent a written order to Ishikawajima for a number of boats. On February 17, 1965, just after Ishikawajima had begun manufacturing the boats, its plant was completely destroyed by fire. Is Ishikawajima liable to Goddard for its failure to deliver the boats? [Goddard v. Ishikawajima-Harima Heavy Industries Co., 29 A.D.2d 754, 287 N.Y.S.2d 901 (1968)]

9. Fram Corp. furnished eighteen fuel filter/separator units called for by a contract with Crawford, who was constructing a building for the United States Navy. Crawford received and installed all eighteen units. The contract price for the units was $55,564.20. Crawford did not pay $6,298.50 of the total, claiming that he had not accepted the equipment because it was defective. Was Crawford right? [United States for the Use of Fram Corp. v. Crawford (C.A.5 Ga.) 443 F.2d 611 (1971)]

10. Holterbosch contracted with Groulich to provide quality food for a pavilion at the 1964 New York World's Fair. The food was to be equal in quality to that presented to agents of Holterbosch at a meeting (prior to the contract signing) where different platters of food were displayed and sampled. The contract was for 1 million units of food to be delivered in installments over a one-year period. On April 23, 1964, the first delivery of food—955 units—was found to be inferior to the contract samples presented at the prior meeting and was therefore rejected as unacceptable. Holterbosch agreed to allow Groulich to tender another batch of food. Groulich delivered 2,520 units. Many of them were found to be unacceptable by both employees of Holterbosch and patrons at the New York World's Fair exhibit. Holterbosch cancelled the entire contract. Groulich sued for out-of-pocket expenses and lost profits. Who wins? [Groulich Caterer, Inc. v. Hans Holterbosch, Inc., 243 A.2d 253 (N.Y. 1968)]

20

SALES
Remedies of Buyer and Seller for Breach of Sales Contracts

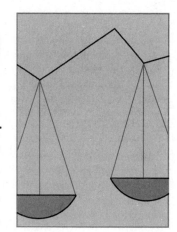

When a sales contract is breached, the aggrieved party may have a number of remedies from which to choose. [UCC 2-703 and 2-711] These remedies range from retaining the goods to requiring the breaching party's performance under the contract. The general purpose of these remedies is to put the aggrieved party "in as good a position as if the other party had fully performed." It is important not only that the nonbreaching party know what remedies are available but that he or she know which remedy is most appropriate for a given situation. [UCC 1-106(1)]

REMEDIES OF THE SELLER

The remedies available to a seller when the buyer is in breach under the UCC include:

1. The right to withhold delivery of the goods.
2. The right to stop a carrier or bailee from delivering goods to an insolvent or defaulting buyer.
3. A limited right to reclaim goods in the possession of an insolvent buyer.
4. The right to identify and/or resell goods to the contract.

The right to recover the purchase price plus incidental damages in certain cases.

6. The right to recover damages for the buyer's wrongful repudiation or nonacceptance of the contract.
7. The right to cancel the sales contract.

The Right to Withhold Delivery of the Goods

In general, sellers can withhold or discontinue performance of their obligations under a sales contract when buyers are in breach. If the breach is due to the buyer's insolvency, the seller can refuse to deliver the goods unless the buyer pays in cash. [UCC 2-702(1)]

Consider an example. On September 1, Simpson receives an order from Bentley for ten cases of ballpoint pens to be shipped on September 13. Bentley wants the goods put on his thirty-day open account. On September 6, Bentley files involuntary bankruptcy. On September 9, Simpson learns of Bentley's bankruptcy and therefore refuses to ship the goods on September 13. The court-appointed trustee of Bentley's assets now claims that Simpson has breached his contract with Bentley by not shipping the goods on September 13 as agreed. The trustee will not prevail because Simpson was under no obligation to ship goods on credit to an insolvent

345

buyer. The trustee, of course, could still obtain the goods for the benefit of Bentley's bankrupt estate by paying cash for them.

If a buyer has wrongfully rejected, revoked acceptance, failed to make proper and timely payment, or repudiated a part of the contract, the seller can withhold delivery of the particular goods in question. Furthermore, the seller can withhold the entire undelivered balance of the goods if the buyer's breach is material. [UCC 2-703]

The Right to Stop a Carrier or Bailee from Delivering Goods in Transit

If the seller has delivered the goods to a carrier or bailee, but the buyer has not as yet received them, the goods are said to be *in transit*. If the seller learns of the buyer's insolvency while the goods are in transit, the seller can stop the carrier or bailee from delivering the goods to the buyer on the basis of the buyer's insolvency, regardless of the quantity shipped. A person is insolvent under the UCC when that person ceases to pay "his debts in the ordinary course of business or cannot pay his debts as they become due or is insolvent within the meaning of the federal bankruptcy law." [UCC 1-201(23)]

If the buyer is not insolvent but repudiates the contract or gives the seller some other right to withhold or reclaim the goods, the seller can stop the goods in transit only if the quantity shipped is at least a carload, a truckload, a planeload, or a larger shipment. [UCC 2-705(1)]

Consider an example. On January 1, Beel orders a carload of onions from Sneed. Sneed is to ship them on January 8, and Beel is to pay for them on January 10. Sneed ships on time, but Beel does not pay on January 10. As soon as Sneed learns of this, she orders the carrier to stop the carload in transit. Since the carload is still on its way to Beel's city, the carrier is able to stop shipment. Beel cannot claim that Sneed and the carrier have performed a wrongful act by stopping the shipment, for a seller can always stop a carload of goods in transit when a buyer commits some breach of contract that gives the seller the right to withhold or reclaim the goods. Had the contract called for a shipment of ten bags of onions, rather than a carload, Sneed could not have stopped the goods in transit unless Beel was unable to pay for the goods (insolvent).

In order to stop delivery, the seller must *timely notify* the carrier or other bailee that the goods are to be returned or held for the seller. If the carrier has sufficient time to stop delivery, then the goods must be held and delivered according to the instructions of the seller, who is liable to the carrier for any additional costs incurred. If the carrier fails to act properly, it will be liable to the seller for any loss. [UCC 2-705(3)]

The right of the seller to stop delivery is lost when:

1. The buyer obtains possession of the goods.
2. The carrier acknowledges the buyer's rights by reshipping or storing the goods for the buyer.
3. A bailee of the goods other than a carrier acknowledges that he or she is holding the goods for the buyer.
4. A negotiable document of title covering the goods has been negotiated to the buyer. [UCC 2-705(2)]

The Right to Reclaim Goods in the Possession of an Insolvent Buyer

Whenever a seller discovers that the buyer has *received* goods on credit while insolvent (as previously defined), the seller can demand return of the goods, if such demand is made within ten days of the buyer's receipt of the goods. The seller can demand and reclaim the goods at any time if the buyer misrepresented his or her solvency in writing within three months prior to the delivery of the goods. [UCC 2-702(2)]

The seller's right to reclaim, however, is subject to the rights of a good faith purchaser or other buyer in the ordinary course of business who purchases the goods from the buyer before the seller reclaims.[1]

It is obvious that successful reclamation of goods under the UCC constitutes preferential treatment as against the buyer's other creditors. Because of this, the Code provides that reclamation *bars* the seller from pursuing any other remedy as to these goods. [UCC 2-702(3)]

This section of the UCC is extremely important should the buyer go through federal bankruptcy. The 1978 Bankruptcy Reform Act, as amended, has a provision [Section 546(c)] which provides that the rights and powers of the bankruptcy trustee are "sub-

---

1. A *buyer in the ordinary course of business* is a person who, in good faith and without knowledge that the sale violates the ownership rights or security interest of a third party, buys in ordinary course from a person (other than a pawnbroker) in the business of selling goods of that kind. [UCC 1-201(9)]

ject to any statutory right or common law right of a seller . . . if the debtor has received such goods while insolvent. . . ." The seller need only make a demand for the return of the goods within ten days after receipt of the goods by the buyer.

The Right to Identify and/or Resell Goods to the Contract after the Buyer Has Breached

Sometimes a buyer breaches or repudiates a sales contract while the seller is still in possession of finished or partially manufactured goods. In this event, the seller can identify to the contract the conforming goods that are still in his or her possession or control, even if they were not identified at the time of the breach. Then the seller can resell the goods, holding the buyer liable for any loss. [UCC 2-704]

When the goods contracted for are unfinished at the time of breach, the seller can treat the unfinished goods in two ways. First, the seller can cease manufacturing the goods and resell them for scrap or salvage value. Second, the seller can complete the manufacture, identify the goods to the contract, and resell them, holding the buyer liable for any deficiency. In choosing between these two alternatives, the seller must exercise reasonable commercial judgment in order to mitigate the loss and obtain maximum realization of value from the unfinished goods. [UCC 2-704(2)]

When a seller possesses or controls the goods at the time of the buyer's breach (because of the buyer's wrongful rejection or revocation of acceptance, failure to pay, or repudiation of the contract), or when the seller rightfully reacquires the goods by stopping them in transit, then the seller has the right to resell the goods. The resale must be made in good faith and in a commercially reasonable manner. The seller can recover any deficiency between the sales price and the contract price, along with **incidental damages,** defined as those costs to the seller resulting from the breach. [UCC 2-706(1) and 2-710] Obviously, it would be unfair for a buyer to profit from his or her own breach. Therefore, the Code encourages the seller's use of the remedy of resale by providing that the seller is *not liable* to the buyer for any profits made on the resale. [UCC 2-706(6)]

Consider some examples. Sallor contracts on Monday to sell his car to Beyer for $5,000, with delivery of the car and payment for it due on the following Monday. When Sallor tenders delivery on

Monday, Beyer refuses to accept or pay for the car. Sallor informs Beyer that he will resell the car at a private sale. Sallor sells the car to Devins for $2,000 on Tuesday. The following day, Sallor sues Beyer for $3,200—$3,000 being the difference between the resale price and the contract price and $200 being the value of incidental damages—the expense of arranging the sale. In this example, the seller would be unlikely to recover the $3,000 difference between the resale price and the contract price, because the resale was obviously not made in good faith or in a commercially reasonable manner. But if Sallor can prove incidental damages of $200, he will be likely to recover them.

Suppose that Sallor contracts to sell Beyer a prize bull for $10,000, with delivery and payment due on Monday. On Monday, Sallor tenders delivery of the prize bull, but Beyer refuses to accept or pay for it. Sallor tells Beyer that he is going to sell the bull at an area livestock auction the next day. At the auction, there are few bidders for the prize bull. Beyer decides to bid on the bull himself and obtains it for $9,000. Sallor then demands $1,100 in damages from Beyer—$1,000 for the contract price less the resale price plus $100 for incidental expenses in getting the prize bull to the auction. In this example, the total sum could probably be recovered by Sallor, assuming he can substantiate his incidental expenses. The livestock auction was a reasonable place for resale, and the resale was done in a commercially reasonable manner.

As a third example, Sallor contracts on Monday to sell 4,000 heads of romaine lettuce to Beyer for 30 cents per head, with delivery and payment due on Friday. On Wednesday, Sallor has 14,000 heads of romaine lettuce in his inventory, but he has not yet identified the 4,000 he intends to sell to Beyer. On that day, Beyer telephones Sallor to inform him that he will not accept or pay for the lettuce. Beyer claims that, since the 4,000 heads of romaine lettuce for his contract have not yet been identified, Sallor cannot resell and recover damages from Beyer. Beyer is incorrect here. Sallor has the right to identify the 4,000 heads of lettuce for Beyer's contract and the right to resell the lettuce. Sallor can recover the difference between the resale price received and the contract price of 30 cents per head, plus any incidental damages. [UCC 2-704(1), 2-706(1), and 2-710]

The resale can be private or public, and the goods can be sold as a unit or in parcels. The seller must give the original buyer reasonable notice of the resale, unless the goods are perishable or will rapidly decline in value. [UCC 2-706(2) and 2-706(3)] In the latter case, the seller has a duty to resell the goods as rapidly as possible in order to mitigate damages. A bona fide purchaser in a resale takes the goods free of any of the rights of the original buyer, even if the seller fails to comply with these requirements of the Code. [UCC 2-706(5)]

The Right to Recover the Purchase Price Plus Incidental Damages

Before the UCC was adopted, a seller could not sue for the purchase price of the goods unless title had passed to the buyer. Under the Code, an unpaid seller can bring an action to recover the purchase price and incidental damages, but only under one of the following unusual circumstances:

1. When the buyer has accepted the goods and has not revoked acceptance, in which case title would have passed to the buyer.
2. When conforming goods have been lost or damaged after the risk of loss has passed to the buyer.
3. When the buyer has breached after the goods have been identified to the contract and the seller is unable to resell the goods. [UCC 2-709(1)]

An action to recover the purchase price and incidental damages, available to the seller only under the circumstances just described, is distinct from an action to recover damages for breach of the sales contract.

If a seller sues for the contract price of goods that he or she has been unable to resell, the goods must be held for the buyer. The seller can resell at any time prior to the collection of the judgment from the buyer, but the net proceeds from the sale must be credited to the buyer. This is an example of the duty to mitigate damages.

To illustrate: Suppose Sallor has contracted to sell Beyer 200 tablecloths with the name of Beyer's restaurant inscribed on them. Sallor delivers the 200 tablecloths to Beyer, but Beyer refuses to pay. Or suppose Sallor tenders the 200 tablecloths to Beyer, but Beyer refuses to accept them. In either case, Sallor has, as a proper remedy, an action for the purchase price.

In the first situation, Beyer accepted conforming goods, but he is in breach by failure to pay. In the second situation, the goods have been identified to the contract, but it is obvious that Sallor could not sell the tablecloths inscribed with Beyer's restaurant's name to anyone else. Thus, both situations fall under UCC 2-709.

The Right to Recover Damages for Buyer's Wrongful Repudiation or Non-acceptance

If a buyer repudiates a contract or wrongfully refuses to accept the goods, a seller can maintain an action to recover the damages that were sustained. Ordinarily, the amount of damages will equal the difference between the contract price and the market price (at the time and place of tender of the goods) plus incidental damages. [UCC 2-708(1)] The time and place of tender are frequently given by such terms as F.O.B., F.A.S., C.I.F., and the like, which determine whether there is a shipment or destination contract.

If the difference between the contract price and the market price is too small to place the seller in the position that he or she would have been in if the buyer had fully performed, the proper measure of damages is the seller's lost profits, including a reasonable allowance for overhead and other incidental expenses. [UCC 2-708(2)]

The question of wrongful repudiation of a sales contract concerning specially manufactured roller wheels for skateboards is the subject of the next case.

CHICAGO ROLLER SKATE MANUFACTURING COMPANY v. SOKOL MANUFACTURING COMPANY

Supreme Court of Nebraska, 1970.
185 Neb. 515, 177 N.W.2d 25.

BACKGROUND AND FACTS   *Chicago Roller Skate Manufacturing Company entered into a sales contract with Sokol Manufacturing Company to provide the latter with truck and wheel assemblies with plates and hangers for use in the manufacture of skateboards. Chicago sent the requested goods to Sokol. At that time there was a balance due of $12,860. But since the skateboard fad had ended, Sokol decided to return, without Chicago's consent, a quantity of the goods purchased. These goods were not suitable for any other use; nor could they be resold. Chicago held them for seven months. Chicago offered Sokol a credit of 70 cents per unit, which Sokol neither accepted nor rejected. Finally,*

Chicago disassembled, cleaned, and rebuilt the units to make them suitable for use on normal roller skates. The rebuilt units had a reasonable value of between 67 cents and 69 cents. Thus, the salvage operation cost Chicago Roller Skate $3,540.76. Profits lost amounted to an additional $2,572. Chicago, disregarding its expense, credited Sokol with 70 cents per unit and brought suit for the balance due of $4,285. It recovered this sum in a judgment in the trial court. Sokol appealed.

NEWTON, Justice.

*   *   *   *

Section 1-103, U.C.C., provides: "Unless displaced by the particular provisions of this act, the principles of law and equity, including the law merchant and the law relative to capacity to contract, *   *   * or other validating or invalidating cause shall supplement its provisions."

Section 1-106, U.C.C., provides in part: "(1) The remedies provided by this act shall be liberally administered to the end that the aggrieved party may be put in as good a position as if the other party had fully performed but neither consequential or special nor penal damages may be had except as specifically provided in this act or by other rule of law."

Section 1-203, U.C.C. states: "Every contract or duty within this act imposes an obligation of good faith in its performance or enforcement."

Section 2-718(4), U.C.C., provides: "Where a seller has received payment in goods their reasonable value or the proceeds of their resale shall be treated as payments *   *   *."

In accordance with section 2-709, U.C.C., plaintiff was entitled to hold the merchandise for defendant and recover the full contract price of $12,860. Plaintiff did not elect to enforce this right, but recognizing that there was no market for the goods or resale value and that they were consequently worthless for the purpose for which they were designed, it attempted to mitigate defendant's damages by converting the goods to other uses and credited defendant with the reasonable value of the goods as converted or rebuilt for use in roller skates. In so doing, plaintiff was evidencing good faith and conforming to the general rule requiring one damaged by another's breach of contract to reduce or mitigate damages. *   *   *

The Uniform Commercial Code contemplates that it shall be supplemented by existing principles of law and equity. It further contemplates that the remedies provided shall be liberally administered to the end that an aggrieved party shall be put in as good a position as it would have been in if the contract had been performed. Here the buyer was demanding of the seller credit for the full contract price for goods that had become worthless. The seller was the aggrieved party and a return of worthless goods did not place it in as good a position as it would have been in had the contract been performed by the buyer paying the contract price. On the other hand, the crediting to defendant of the reasonable value of the rebuilt materials and recovery of the balance of the contract price did reasonably reimburse plaintiff. This procedure appears to be contemplated by section 2-718(4), U.C.C., which requires that a seller paid in goods credit the buyer with the reasonable value of the goods.

It is the defendant's theory that since the goods were not resold or held for the buyer, the seller cannot maintain an action for the price. We agree with this proposition. We also agree with defendant in its contention that the controlling measure of damages is that set out in section 2-708(2), U.C.C. This section provides that the measure of damages is the profit which the seller would have made from full performance by the buyer, together with any incidental damages resulting from the breach and costs reasonably incurred. Defendant overlooks the provision for allowance of incidental damages and costs incurred. The loss of profits, together with the additional costs or damage sustained by plaintiff amount to $6,112.76, a sum considerably in excess of that sought and recovered by plaintiff. Although the case was tried by plaintiff and determined on an erroneous theory of damages, the error is without prejudice to defendant. There being no cross-appeal, the judgment of the district court is affirmed.

DECISION AND REMEDY

Sokol had to pay the $4,285 to Chicago Roller Skate Manufacturing Company.

The Right to Cancel the Sales Contract

A seller can cancel a contract if the buyer wrongfully rejects or revokes acceptance of conforming goods, fails to make proper payment, or repudiates the contract in part or in whole. The contract can be canceled with respect to the goods directly involved, or the entire contract can be canceled if the breach is material. A material breach is one that substantially impairs the value of the entire contract. [UCC 2-703]

The seller must *notify* the buyer of the cancellation, and at that point all remaining obligations of the seller are discharged. The buyer is not discharged from all remaining obligations but is in breach and can be sued under any of the subsections mentioned in UCC 2-703 and in UCC 2-106(4).

If the seller's cancellation is not justified, then the seller is in breach of the contract, and the buyer can sue for appropriate damages.

Seller's Lien

Under certain circumstances, a seller's rights go beyond the remedies provided for under the UCC. One such right is a seller's common law lien in the goods being sold. Technically, a lien is a right that is incident to the sale rather than a remedy for breach of contract.

A seller's lien enables the seller to retain possession of the goods until the buyer pays for them.

The seller's lien can be waived or lost by: (1) express agreement, (2) acts inconsistent with the lien's existence, (3) payment or tender of payment by the buyer, or (4) voluntary and unconditional delivery of the goods to a carrier or other bailee or to the buyer or an authorized agent of the buyer.

If the sales agreement provides for an extension of credit to the buyer, the seller normally has no lien on the goods, since the act of extending credit is inconsistent with the existence of the lien. The seller will have a lien on the goods, however, if the buyer becomes insolvent or if the credit period expires while the goods are still in the seller's possession.

The tender of payment or the actual payment of the debt that the lien secures will ordinarily discharge the lien. This occurs when the buyer pays the full price for the goods and the seller gives up possession. When the buyer gives a promissory note, the lien ordinarily will *not* be discharged until the note is paid even if the seller relinquishes possession of the goods.

Finally, sellers lose their liens when they voluntarily deliver possession of the goods to the buyer or to an authorized agent of the buyer. The lien is not lost, though, where delivery is qualified or where the buyer obtains possession fraudulently.

Consider the following illustration. Williams, the plaintiff, sold his Chevrolet sedan to the Greers, the defendants. The defendants paid $235 by check and $90 in cash. After the Greers received possession of the Chevrolet, they stopped payment on the check. Williams went to court to regain possession of the auto by enforcing his seller's lien. The court upheld his complaint, allowing him to regain possession of the auto and to keep it until the Greers paid the $235. Essentially, the Greers had obtained possession fraudulently; therefore, they had a voidable title. Williams could validly enforce his lien because he had the right to void the title.

REMEDIES OF THE BUYER

Under the UCC, the remedies available to the buyer include:

1. The right to reject nonconforming or improperly delivered goods.
2. The right to recover identified goods upon the seller's insolvency.
3. The right to obtain specific performance.

CONCEPT SUMMARY: Seller's Remedies For Buyer's Breach	
SITUATIONS	**SELLER'S REMEDIES**
	(The remedies available to a seller are basically determined by who has possession of the goods at the time of the buyer's breach.)
Goods are in the seller's possession	1. Withhold delivery. UCC 2-703(a) 2. Identify goods to the contract. UCC 2-704 3. Resale. UCC 2-706 4. Sue for breach of contract. UCC 2-708 5. Cancel (and rescind). UCC 2-703
Goods are in transit	1. Stoppage in transit. UCC 2-705
Goods are in the buyer's possession	1. Sue for purchase price. UCC 2-709 2. Reclaim goods received by insolvent buyer (excludes all other remedies on reclamation). UCC 2-702

4. The right to replevy the goods.
5. The right to retain the goods and enforce a security interest in them.
6. The right to cancel the contract.
7. The right of cover.
8. The right to recover damages for nondelivery or repudiation by the seller.
9. The right to recover damages for breach in regard to accepted goods.

The Right to Reject Nonconforming or Improperly Delivered Goods

If either the goods or the seller's tender of the goods fails to conform to the contract *in any respect*, the buyer can reject the goods. If some of the goods conform to the contract, the buyer can keep the conforming goods and reject the rest. [UCC 2-601]

Timeliness and Reason for Rejection Required Goods must be rejected within a reasonable time and the seller must be seasonably notified. [UCC 2-602] Furthermore, the buyer must designate particular defects that are ascertainable by reasonable inspection. Failure to do so precludes the buyer from using such defects to justify rejection or to establish breach when the seller could have cured the defects if they had been stated seasonably. [UCC 2-605] After rejecting the goods, the buyer cannot exercise

any right of ownership over them. If the buyer acts inconsistently with the seller's ownership rights, the buyer will be deemed to have accepted the goods. [UCC 2-606]

Merchant Buyer's Duties When Goods Are Rejected If a *merchant buyer* rightfully rejects goods, and the seller has no agent or business at the place of rejection, the buyer is required to follow any reasonable instructions received from the seller with respect to the goods controlled by the buyer. The buyer is entitled to reimbursement for the care and cost entailed in following the instructions. [UCC 2-603] The same requirement holds if the buyer rightfully revokes acceptance. [UCC 2-608(3)]

If no instructions are forthcoming and the goods are perishable or threaten to decline in value quickly, the buyer can resell the goods in good faith, taking the appropriate reimbursement from the proceeds. [UCC 2-603(1)] If the goods are not perishable, the buyer may store them for the seller's account or reship them to the seller. [UCC 2-604]

The Right to Recover Identified Goods from an Insolvent Seller

If a buyer has made a partial or a full payment for goods that remain in the possession of the seller, the buyer can recover the goods if the seller becomes insolvent within ten days after receiving the first payment and if the goods are identified to the contract. To exercise this right, the buyer must tender to the seller any unpaid balance of the purchase price. [UCC 2-502]

The Right to Obtain Specific Performance

A buyer can obtain specific performance when the goods are unique or when the buyer's remedy at law is inadequate. [UCC 2-716(1)] Ordinarily, a suit for money damages will be sufficient to place a buyer in the position he or she would have occupied if the seller had fully performed. However, when the contract is for the purchase of a particular work of art, patent, copyright, or similarly unique item, money damages may not be sufficient. Under these circumstances, equity will require the seller to perform exactly (a remedy of specific performance) by delivering the particular goods identified to the contract.

To illustrate: Casey contracts to sell an antique car to Smith for $30,000, with delivery and payment due on June 14. Smith tenders payment on June 14, but Casey refuses to deliver. Can Smith force delivery of the car? Probably, because the antique car is unique. Therefore, Smith can obtain specific performance of the contract from Casey.

The Right to Replevy the Goods

Replevin is an action to recover specific goods in the hands of a breaching party who is unlawfully withholding them from the other party. The buyer can replevy goods *identified* to the contract if the seller has repudiated or breached the contract. *Additionally*, buyers must usually show that they were *unable to cover* for the goods after a reasonable effort. [UCC 2-716(3)]

Consider the following example. On July 1, Sallor contracts to sell her tomato crop to Beyer, with delivery and payment due on August 10. By August 1, it is clear that the local tomato crop will be bad and that the price of tomatoes is going to rise. Sallor contracts to sell her tomato crop to Green for a higher price and then informs Beyer that she will not deliver on August 10 as agreed. Beyer indicates that cover is unavailable and that he is therefore going to bring a replevin action against Sallor to force her to deliver her tomatoes to Beyer on August 10.

This replevin action will succeed. Although a tomato crop is not unique, a buyer of scarce goods for which no cover is available has a right to a replevin. In a normal tomato year, cover would probably have been available and Beyer would be limited to an action for damages.

The Right to Retain and Enforce a Security Interest in the Goods

Buyers who rightfully reject goods or who justifiably revoke acceptance of goods that remain in their possession or control have a security interest in the goods (basically a lien to recover expenses, costs, and the like). The security interest encompasses any payments the buyer has made for the goods as well as any expenses incurred with regard to inspection, receipt, transportation, care, and custody of the goods. [UCC 2-711(3)] A buyer with a security interest in the goods is a "person in the position of a seller." This gives the buyer the same rights as an unpaid seller. Thus, the buyer can resell, withhold delivery, or stop delivery of the goods. A buyer who chooses to resell must account to the seller for any amounts received in excess of the security interest. [UCC 2-711(3) and 2-706(6)]

The Right to Cancel the Contract

When a seller fails to make proper delivery or repudiates the contract, the buyer can cancel or rescind the contract. In addition, a buyer who has rightfully rejected or revoked acceptance of the goods can cancel or rescind. Under these circumstances, the buyer can cancel or rescind that portion of the contract directly involved in the breach. If the seller's breach is material and substantially impairs the value of the whole contract, the buyer can cancel or rescind the whole contract. Upon notice of cancellation, the buyer is relieved of any further obligations under the contract but still retains all remedy rights that can be assessed against the seller.

The Right of Cover

In certain situations, buyers can protect themselves by obtaining *cover*, that is, by substituting goods for those that were due under the sales contract. This option is available to a buyer who has rightfully rejected goods or revoked acceptance. It is also available where the seller repudiates the contract or fails to deliver the goods. In obtaining cover, the buyer must act in good faith without unreasonable delay. [UCC 2-712]

After purchasing substitute goods, the buyer can recover from the seller the difference between the cost of cover and the contract price, plus incidental and consequential damages less the expenses (such as delivery costs) that were saved as a result of the seller's breach. [UCC 2-712 and 2-715]

Consequential damages are any loss suffered by the buyer that the seller could have foreseen (had reason to know) at the time of contract and any injury to the buyer's person or property proximately resulting from a breach of warranty. [UCC 2-715(2)]

Suppose Sallor contracts to sell Beyer 10,000 pounds of sugar at 20 cents per pound. Delivery is to be on or before November 15. Sallor knows that Beyer is going to use the sugar to make candy for Christmas sales. Beyer usually makes a $15,000 profit from these sales. Sallor fails to deliver on November 15. Beyer attempts to purchase the sugar on the open market, but she must pay 30 cents a pound and take delivery on December 8. Because of this late delivery date, Beyer can prepare and sell only half as much Christmas candy as usual.

Beyer can recover from Sallor the difference between the cover price and the contract price of sugar ($3,000 − $2,000 = $1,000) plus any incidental damages (costs incurred in effecting the cover). In addition, since Sallor knew the reason for Beyer's purchase (sale of Christmas candy), Beyer is entitled to consequential damages. In this case, Beyer could probably include as part of her damages against Sallor the lost profits from the Christmas candy sales ($7,500—half of the $15,000 profit usually made).

Buyers are not required to cover, and failure to do so will not bar them from using any other remedies that are available under the UCC. [UCC 2-712(3)] But a buyer who fails to cover may *not* be able to collect the consequential damages that could have been avoided by purchasing substitute goods. [UCC 2-715(2)(a)] Thus the UCC encourages buyers to cover in order to mitigate damages.[2] For example, if a wholesaler is supposed to supply a grocer wth eggs for resale, and the wholesaler is unable to deliver them, the grocer has the option of covering. If the grocer covers, he or she can recover any lost

profits resulting from the wholesaler's breach of the contract. If the grocer does not cover, and has no eggs to sell, he or she cannot recover lost profits.

The Right to Recover Damages for Nondelivery or Repudiation

If a seller repudiates the sales contract or fails to deliver the goods, the buyer can sue for damages. The measure of recovery is the difference between the contract price and the market price of the goods at the time that the buyer *learned* of the breach. The market price is determined at the place where the seller was supposed to deliver the goods. In appropriate cases, the buyer can also recover incidental and consequential damages less the expenses that were saved as a result of the seller's breach. [UCC 2-713] Note that the damages here are based upon the time and place a buyer would normally obtain cover.

Consider an example. Billings orders 10,000 bushels of wheat from Sneed for $5 a bushel, with delivery due on June 14 and payment due on June 20. Sneed does not deliver on June 14. On June 14, the market price of wheat is $5.50 per bushel. Billings chooses to do without the wheat. He sues Sneed for damages for nondelivery. Billings can recover $5,000 plus any expenses the breach may have caused him to incur. Here the measure of damages is the market price less the contract price at the date that Billings was to have received delivery. (Any expenses Billings saved by the breach would have to be deducted from the damages.)

The Right to Recover Damages for Breach in Regard to Accepted Goods

A buyer who has accepted nonconforming goods must notify the seller of the breach within a reasonable time after the defect was or should have been discovered. Otherwise, the buyer cannot complain about defects in the goods. [UCC 2-607(3)] In addition, the parties to a sales contract can insert a provision requiring the buyer to give notice of any defects in the goods within a certain prescribed period. Such a requirement is ordinarily binding on the parties.

Measure of Damages If a Warranty is Breached
When the seller breaches a warranty, the measure of damages equals the difference between the value

---

2. UCC 2-712(3) and UCC 2-715(2)(a) are inconsistent.

of the goods as accepted and their value if they had been delivered as warranted. As illustrated by the following case, the buyer can recover only the actual damages resulting from the breach of warranty as well as incidental and consequential damages. [UCC 2-714]

ALAFOSS, H. F. v.
PREMIUM CORP. OF
AMERICA, INC.
United States Court of Appeals,
Eighth Circuit, 1979.
599 F.2d 232.

BACKGROUND AND FACTS *Alafoss agreed to sell Premium Corp. of America (PCA) a large quantity of women's coats made of Icelandic sheep wool. PCA approved samples and ordered 8,200 coats. One of the special features of the samples was a detachable solid white fur collar. Several months after delivery of the coats, PCA discovered that, among other defects, the majority of the coats had discolored fur collars. After an unsuccessful attempt at treating the collars (paid for by Alafoss), PCA was able to obtain an offer of only $25 per coat, apparently because of the defects and discoloration. Alafoss was unable to produce a higher offer, so PCA sold 3,376 nonconforming coats to a third party for approximately $20 per coat. Alafoss then sued for the unpaid contract price. PCA counterclaimed for damages for breach of warranty. At trial, the court held that Alafoss had indeed breached warranties of quality, and it entered a net judgment for PCA in the amount of $133,275 (plus costs). The U.S. Court of Appeals now examines the question of whether PCA adequately proved its damages.*

BRIGHT, Circuit Judge.
* * * *

The legal standard for determining PCA's damages in this case is set forth in Minn. Stat. Ann. § 336.2-714(2), which provides:

"(2) The measure of damages for breach of warranty is the difference at the time and place of acceptance between the value of the goods accepted and the value they would have had if they had been as warranted, unless special circumstances show proximate damages of a different amount."

In applying that standard, the district court took the unit cost of the wrap coats to PCA, $88.11, as the value of each coat as warranted, at the time and place of acceptance. The court determined the actual value of each nonconforming coat at the time and place of acceptance to be $25. The court then calculated PCA's damages from the breach by multiplying both unit values by 3,736, the number of nonconforming coats left over after the sales program ended, and subtracting the total value of the coats as accepted from the value they would have possessed if they had been as warranted. The resulting difference amounted to $238,758.96.

In calculating the damage PCA sustained because of the nonconforming coats in the above manner, the district court appears to have overlooked certain "special circumstances show[ing] proximate damages of a different amount." [UCC 2-714(2)] First, evidence introduced at trial indicates that PCA anticipated that, even if all of the wrap coats conformed to sample, it would be unable to sell somewhere between twenty-five and fifty percent of the coats during the mail-marketing program. Such "normal leftover" coats would have been sold in bulk at a price less than cost, precisely as PCA did here with the leftover nonconforming coats. To the extent that such normal leftover coats would have existed in the absence of any breach by Alafoss, the proper measure of damages proximately caused by Alafoss' breach is the difference between the value of leftover conforming coats if sold in bulk and the value of the nonconforming coats sold in bulk.

Second, because the nonconformities for which Alafoss is responsible may have caused more coats to be left over than would have been the case absent the breach, the district court should have distinguished between the number of coats that would normally have been left over and the number of additional coats left over due to the nonconformities. As to those additional leftover coats (but not as to the coats that would have been left over even if no breach existed), the proper measure of damages is that applied by the district court to all coats—that is, at the time and place of acceptance, the difference between the value of the coats if they had been as warranted and the coats' value as actually delivered.

Thus, the proper computation of PCA's damages proximately resulting from Alafoss' breach requires, in addition to the findings already made by the district court, a determination of (1) the number of coats that would have been left over absent any breach, and (2) the value of those normal leftover coats. The record as it stands does not reveal those quantities. We note, however, that the PCA customers' letters referred to above, indicating that coats were returned by customers for reasons other than the nonconformities attributable to Alafoss, constitute strong evidence that such returned coats would have been left over even if Alafoss had complied fully with the terms of the sales agreement. Therefore, the damage award should be substantially reduced to reflect the actual loss PCA sustained for coats that would have been left over regardless of the breach.

The Court of Appeals affirmed the district court's determination of the liability of Alafoss for breach of warranties. However, it reversed the damage award and remanded the case for further consideration of damages consistent with this opinion. In particular, the trial court was directed to receive additional evidence concerning the number of coats that normally would have been left over (unsold) absent any breach.

DECISION AND REMEDY

Suit by a Buyer's Customer Resulting from the Seller's Breach of Warranty   When a buyer resells defective goods that were originally sold by a breaching seller, the buyer's customer can sue the buyer. Under these circumstances the buyer has two alternatives:

1.   The buyer can notify the seller of the pending litigation. The notice should state that the seller can come in and defend, and it should also state that the seller will be bound by the buyer's action if the seller does not defend within a reasonable time after receipt of the notice. [UCC 2-607(5)(a)]

2.   The buyer can also defend against the customer's suit and later bring an action against the original seller. This situation arises most frequently where there is a manufacturer-dealer arrangement—for example, where a car dealer sells a defective automobile and the customer sues the dealer but not the manufacturer.

Other Measures of Damages   The Code also allows for two additional methods or remedies for damages

for accepted goods. Both can also be applied where there has been a breach of warranty.

The first applies where the buyer has accepted *nonconforming* goods. The buyer is entitled to recover for any loss "resulting in the ordinary course of events * * * as determined in any manner which is reasonable." Thus, this remedy is available for both a breach of warranty situation and any other failure of the seller to perform according to the contracted obligations. [UCC 2-714(1)]

The second remedy is extremely important to a buyer, as the buyer not only has possession of the goods but also determines the amount of damages. The UCC permits the buyer, with proper notice to the seller, to deduct all or any part of the damages from the price still due and payable to the seller. [UCC 2-717]

Suppose Sallor is under contract to deliver 100 pairs of dress shoes at $50 each to Beyer. The shoes are tendered, and upon inspection Beyer discovers that 10 pairs are high-quality work shoes, not dress shoes. Beyer accepts all 100 pairs and notifies Sallor of the breach. At the time for contracted payment by Beyer, Beyer notifies Sallor that she will not be able to sell the work shoes as quickly or for the same price or profit as the dress shoes, and she is therefore tendering a check for $4,750 instead of the full $5,000 to reflect this loss. If Sallor accepts and cashes Beyer's check, Beyer's measurement of damages is final.

When the buyer still has the goods, the courts often must grapple with the interpretation of the basic damages formula in UCC 2-714(2) versus circumstances where damages of different amounts are proved.

STATUTE OF LIMITATIONS FOR ACTIONS BROUGHT UNDER THE UNIFORM COMMERCIAL CODE

An action brought by a buyer or seller for breach of contract must be commenced under the Code *within four years after the cause of action accrues*. In addition to filing suit within the four-year period, an aggrieved party must ordinarily notify the breaching party of a defect within a reasonable time. [UCC 2-607(3)(a)] By agreement in the contract, the parties can reduce this period to not less than one year, but they cannot extend the period beyond the stated four years. [UCC 2-725(1)]

A cause of action accrues for breach of warranty when the seller makes *tender* of delivery. This is the rule even if the aggrieved party is unaware that the cause of action has accrued. [UCC 2-725(2)] Remember, tender of delivery takes place in a shipment contract upon delivery of the goods to the carrier, and in a destination contract upon tender of the goods at the specified destination delivery location. The one-year limitation in these cases may have a tremendous impact if the goods purchased are going to be stored primarily for future use. To avoid this impact, a purchaser may want to include a clause in the sales contract which delays the time at which the cause of action accrues until a future date, such as at the time of first performance of the goods.

Future performance warranties (those that expressly or impliedly take effect in the future) are not breached until the time for performance begins. The statute of limitations also begins to run at that time.

For example, Beyer purchases a central air-conditioning unit for Beyer's restaurant. The unit is warranted to keep the temperature below a certain level. The unit is installed in the winter, but when summer comes, the restaurant does not stay cool. Therefore, this warranty was breached in the summer and not when the unit was delivered in the winter. The statute of limitations did not begin to run until the summer.

CONCEPT SUMMARY: Buyer's Remedies For Seller's Breach	
SITUATIONS	**BUYER'S REMEDIES**
	(The remedies available to a buyer are basically determined by the facts of the situation.)
The seller refuses to deliver or seller tenders nonconforming goods and buyer rejects them	1. Cancel and, with notice, rescind. UCC 2-711 2. Cover. UCC 2-712 3. Sue for breach of contract. UCC 2-713
Seller tenders nonconforming goods and buyer accepts them	1. Sue for ordinary damages. UCC 2-714(1) 2. Sue for breach of warranty. UCC 2-714(2) 3. Deduct damages from the price of the goods. UCC 2-717
Seller refuses delivery and buyer wants the goods	1. Sue for specific performance. UCC 2-716(1) 2. Replevin. UCC 2-716(3) 3. Recover goods from the seller on seller's insolvency where the buyer has paid part or all of the purchase price. UCC 2-502

The following case illustrates how the expectation of the parties extends the time of warranty performance to a future date for statute of limitation purposes. The case deals with express warranties made at the time of the purchase of "siding" for a home, and whether these representations were intended to last for the lifetime of the house.

BACKGROUND AND FACTS   *Puget Sound Plywood, Inc. manufactured certain lauan siding that Dennis and Lois Moore purchased during the construction of their house in 1970–71. By October 1977, the Moores noticed some "problems" with the appearance of the siding. The problem, delamination, resulted because the particular species of lauan tree used in making the siding was not susceptible to being glued together with the resin that Puget Sound used. The Moores began investigating a remedy for the situation in 1979, but they had difficulty determining who manufactured the siding. This action was filed in April of 1981. The Moores alleged damages of $4,550, but the two lower courts both dismissed their case, holding that the period of limitations had lapsed. The Moores appealed.*

MOORE v. PUGET SOUND PLYWOOD, INC.

Supreme Court of Nebraska, 1983.

214 Neb. 14, 332 N.W.2d 212.

CAPORALE, Justice.

*   *   *   *

This analysis is required by reason of the operation of Neb. U.C.C. § 2-313(1)(b) (Reissue 1980) as delineated in England v. Leithoff, 212 Neb. 462, 323 N.W.2d 98 (1982), decided after the municipal court trials herein. That opinion foreshadows the outcome of this case. We held therein that an oral representation concerning the origin of goods, made in the course of a sale, constitutes an express warranty under § 2-313(1)(b), which provides, among other things, that any description of goods which becomes a part of the basis of the bargain creates an express warranty that the goods shall conform to the description. According to the parties, the description of the goods as "siding" carried with it the representation that it would last the lifetime of the house. Therefore, the requisite elements of § 2-313(1)(b) are present; that is, the description of the goods became a part of the bargain and created in the minds of the parties the expectation that the siding would last the lifetime of the house. Section 2-725(2) provides in part: "A breach of warranty occurs when tender of delivery is made, except that where a warranty explicitly extends to future performance of the goods and discovery of the breach must await the time of such performance the cause of action accrues when the breach is or should have been discovered." The instant breach did not occur upon tender of delivery since, in light of the expectations of the parties, the warranty herein necessarily extended explicitly to future performance.

The case *   *   * relied upon by Puget Sound is not factually apposite here. Therein, discovery could, and in fact did, occur shortly after completion of the construction project; that is, the plaintiff knew about the defect prior to the tolling of the period of limitations but failed to act until after it had tolled. In this case, discovery could occur at any time between installation and the "life" of the house. The Moores acted within a reasonable period of time after they discovered the latent defect.

*   *   *   *

The Supreme Court agreed with the Moores that the two lower courts were in error. The Court remanded the case with instructions that a judgment be entered in favor of the Moores in the sum of $4,550.

DECISION AND REMEDY

Actions Not Falling within the Uniform Commercial Code

When a buyer or seller brings suit on a legal theory unrelated to the Code, the limitations periods specified above do not apply, even though the claim relates to goods.

For example, Beyer buys tires for his automobile. The tires prove to have an inherently dangerous defect. Four years and one month after purchasing the tires, Beyer loses control of the car and injures several passengers as well as himself. Beyer can bring a suit against the tire manufacturer based on strict liability in tort. The suit will not be governed by the Code's statute of limitations, but rather by the state's tort statute of limitations.

CONTRACTUAL PROVISIONS AFFECTING REMEDIES

The parties to a sales contract can vary their respective rights and obligations by contractual agreement. Certain restrictions are placed on the ability of parties to contract to limit their rights and remedies under the Code, but the common provisions that the parties frequently include are:

1. The liquidation or limitation of damages.
2. The limitation of remedies.
3. The waiver of defenses.

Liquidated Damages and Limitation of Damages

The parties can provide that a specified amount of damages will be paid in the event that either party breaches. These damages, called liquidated damages, must be reasonable in amount and approximately equal to the anticipated or actual loss caused by the breach. If the provision is valid, the aggrieved party is limited to recovering only the amount of damages as agreed. If the amount of liquidated damages is unreasonably large, the provision is void as a penalty, and the court will determine the appropriate damage. [UCC 2-718]

Consider as an example the sale of an uncommon antique. Sallor contracts with Beyer to sell it for $3,000. The contract contains a liquidated damages clause that holds the breaching party liable for $1,000 in case of a breach by either party. Payment

and delivery of the antique are due on January 1. Beyer tenders payment on that date, but Sallor refuses to deliver for no valid reason. Can Beyer demand $1,000 in damages? Because we are dealing with an uncommon antique, Beyer will probably be able to recover. Sallor's breach might cause Beyer a loss of $1,000 in that the object in question is probably not easily acquired on the open market for the price of $3,000. If, instead, the object in question were easily obtainable for the agreed price, then Beyer probably would not be able to recover the $1,000. The normal measure of damages would then be the market price of the object less the contract price. The $1,000 damage clause in the contract would, in essence, be imposing a penalty upon Sallor and therefore would be void under UCC 2-718(1). The court could determine that a smaller damage was appropriate, however.

A buyer often makes a down payment when a contract is executed. If the buyer defaults and the contract contains a liquidated damages provision, the seller retains the down payment as damages, and the buyer can recover only the part of the down payment that exceeded the amount specified as liquidated damages. The buyer is entitled to this sum as restitution. If the contract contains no provision for liquidated damages, the seller's damages are deemed to be 20 percent of the purchase price or $500, whichever is less. [UCC 2-718(2)(b)] The amount by which the buyer's down payment exceeded this sum must be returned to the buyer. If the seller can prove that his or her actual damages are higher, the buyer can recover only the excess over the seller's actual damages.

For example, Beyer pays $1,250 down on a $10,000 lathe. Beyer then breaches, and Sallor offers no proof of the actual damages. In the absence of a liquidated damages clause, Beyer is entitled to restitution of $750 ($1,250 less $500). If Beyer had put $350 down on a $500 lathe, Beyer would be entitled to $250 ($350 less $100, which is 20 percent of the purchase price).

Limitation of Remedies

A seller and a buyer can expressly provide for remedies in addition to those provided in the Code. They can also provide remedies in lieu of those provided in the Code, or they can change the measure of damages. The seller can provide that the buyer's only remedy upon breach of warranty will be repair or replacement of the item, or the seller can limit the buyer's remedy to return of the goods and refund of the purchase price. A remedy that is so provided is in addition to remedies provided in the Code unless the parties expressly agree that the remedy is exclusive of all others. [UCC 2-719(1)]

If the parties state that a remedy is exclusive of all other remedies, then it is the sole remedy. But when circumstances cause an exclusive remedy to fail of its essential purpose, the remedy will no longer be exclusive. [UCC 2-719(2)]

For example, a sales contract that limits the buyer's remedy to repair or replacement fails of its essential purpose if the item cannot be repaired and no replacements are available.

For example, Bing buys a motorcycle from merchant Simple. The sales contract is accompanied by an express warranty stating that there is an exclusive remedy of repair or replacement of defective parts. The contract explicitly provides that Simple will not be responsible for consequential loss. Bing discovers numerous defects in her motorcycle after only a few days' use. After discovering each defect, she returns the motorcycle for repairs. Some of the parts are out of stock and will take months to arrive at Simple's repair station. Bing sues Simple. A trier of fact in this situation may return a verdict for Bing in an amount far exceeding the cost of repairs. The reason is that the exclusive remedy of repair or replacement of defective parts would have failed in its essential purpose, since the motorcycle could not operate as it should, free of defects.

In the following case, the court examines a limitation clause in a sales contract concerning *when* a claim can be brought for inferior quality wool.

BACKGROUND AND FACTS *Wilson Trading Corp. entered into a contract with David Ferguson, Ltd. for the sale of yarn. A clause in the contract stated that "no claims relating to excessive moisture content, short weight, count variations, twist, quality or shade shall be allowed if made after weaving, knitting, or processing, or more than 10 days after receipt of shipment." In an apparent contradiction to this clause, defendant David Ferguson, Ltd., failed to make payment because, according to the defendant, after the yarn was cut and knitted into sweaters and then washed, the color changed in a way that made the sweaters unmarketable. At trial, plaintiff Wilson Trading Corp. won summary judgment for the contract price of the yarn, on the ground that the notice of the alleged breach of warranty for defect in the coloration of the yarn was not given within the time expressly limited by the contract. The appellate division affirmed the trial court's decision without an opinion and the buyer appealed.*

WILSON TRADING
CORP. v. DAVID
FERGUSON, LTD.
Court of Appeals of New York, 1968.
23 N.Y.2d 398, 297 N.Y.S.2d 108, 244 N.E.2d 685.

JASEN, Judge.
*   *   *   *

The defendant on this appeal urges that the time limitation provision on claims in the contract was unreasonable since the defect in the color of the yarn was latent and could not be discovered until after the yarn was processed and the finished product washed.

Defendant's affidavits allege that its sweaters were rendered unsaleable because of latent defects in the yarn which caused "variation in color from piece to piece and within the pieces." *   *   * Indeed, the plaintiff does not seriously dispute the fact that its yarn was unmerchantable, but instead *   *   * relies upon the failure of defendant to give notice of the breach of warranty within the time limits prescribed by paragraph 2 of the contract.

Subdivision (3) (par. [a]) of section 2-607 of the Uniform Commercial Code expressly provides that a buyer who accepts goods has a reasonable time after he discovers or should have discovered a breach to notify the seller of such breach. Defendant's affidavits allege that a claim was made immediately upon discovery of the breach of warranty after the yarn was knitted and washed, and that this was the earliest possible moment at which the defects could reasonably be discovered in the normal manufacturing process. * * *

However, the Uniform Commercial Code allows the parties, within limits established by the code, to modify or exclude warranties and to limit remedies for breach of warranty. * * *

We are, therefore, confronted with the effect to be given the time limitation provision in paragraph 2 of the contract.

* * * *

Parties to a contract are given broad latitude within which to fashion their own remedies for breach of contract (Uniform Commercial Code, § 2-316, subd. [4]; §§ 2-718–2-719). Nevertheless, it is clear from the official comments to section 2-719 of the Uniform Commercial Code that it is the very essence of a sales contract that at least minimum adequate remedies be available for its breach. "If the parties intend to conclude a contract for sale within this Article they must accept the legal consequence that there be at least a fair quantum of remedy for breach of the obligations or duties outlined in the contract. Thus any clause purporting to modify or limit the remedial provisions of this Article in an *unconscionable manner* is subject to deletion and in that event the remedies made available by this Article are applicable as if the stricken clause had never existed." (Uniform Commercial Code, § 2-719, official comment 1; emphasis supplied.)

It follows that contractual limitations upon remedies are generally to be enforced unless unconscionable. * * *

However, it is unnecessary to decide the issue of whether the time limitation is unconscionable on this appeal for section 2-719 (subd. [2]) of the Uniform Commercial Code provides that the general remedy provisions of the code apply when "circumstances cause an exclusive or limited remedy to fail of its essential purpose". As explained by the official comments to this section: "where an apparently fair and reasonable clause because of circumstances fails in its purpose or operates to deprive either party of the substantial value of the bargain, it must give way to the general remedy provisions of this article." (Uniform Commercial Code, § 2-719, official comment 1.) Here, paragraph 2 of the contract bars all claims for shade and other specified defects made after knitting and processing. Its effect is to eliminate any remedy for shade defects not reasonably discoverable within the time limitation period. It is true that parties may set by agreement any time not manifestly unreasonable whenever the code "requires any action to be taken within a reasonable time" (Uniform Commercial Code, § 1-204, subd. [1]), but here the time provision eliminates all remedy for defects not discoverable before knitting and processing and section 2-719 (subd. [2]) of the Uniform Commercial Code therefore applies.

Defendant's affidavits allege that sweaters manufactured from the yarn were rendered unmarketable because of latent shading defects not reasonably discoverable before knitting and processing of the yarn into sweaters. If these factual allegations are established at trial, the limited remedy established by paragraph 2 has failed its "essential purpose" and the buyer is, in effect, without remedy. The time limitation clause of the contract, therefore, insofar as it applies to defects not reasonably discoverable within the time limits established by the contract, must give way to the general code rule that a buyer has a reasonable time to notify the seller of breach of contract after he discovers or should have discovered the defect. (Uniform Commercial Code, § 2-607, subd. [3], par. [a].) * * *

In sum, there are factual issues for trial concerning whether the shading defects alleged were discoverable before knitting and processing, and, if not, whether notice of the defects was given within a reasonable time after the defects were or should have been discovered. If the shading defects were not reasonably discoverable before knitting and processing and notice was given within a reasonable time after the defects were or should have been discovered, a further factual issue of whether the sweaters were rendered unsaleable because of the defect is presented for trial.

The judgment in favor of the seller was reversed. The case was remanded for a new trial.

DECISION AND REMEDY

Limiting Consequential Damages A contract can limit or exclude consequential damages provided the limitation is not unconscionable. When the buyer is a consumer, the limitation of consequential damages for personal injuries resulting from a breach of warranty is *prima facie* unconscionable. The limitation of consequential damages is not necessarily unconscionable where the loss is commercial in nature—for example, lost profits and property damage. [UCC 2-719(3)]

Waiver of Defenses

A buyer can be precluded from objecting to a breach of warranty by a seller in certain situations. For example, when a buyer purchases on credit, the seller usually assigns the note or account to a financial institution in order to obtain ready cash. In order to facilitate the assignment of these notes or accounts, the seller will include a waiver of defense clause in the sales contract. By entering into the contract, the buyer agrees not to assert against the assignee defenses that may apply to the seller. In essence, the buyer must complain directly to the seller, and the buyer cannot withhold payment for breach of warranty. If the owner of the assignment clause is a holder in due course of the buyer's note, no defenses can be asserted against the owner-assignee, even if the contract contains no waiver of defense clause. [UCC 9-206]

In such a case buyers are in the same position they would be in if they had signed a waiver. Because of this, many states, including those that have adopted the Uniform Consumer Credit Code, have invalidated such clauses when the sale is for consumer goods. In addition, Federal Trade Commission rules provide that in consumer purchases on credit, any personal defense of the debtor-buyer against the seller

is equally applicable against *any* holder, including a holder in due course. Therefore, these clauses are invalid in consumer transactions.

LEMON LAWS

Some purchasers of automobiles found that the remedies provided by the UCC, after limitations imposed by the seller, were inadequate when they purchased what was called a "lemon." Their frustrations grew to the point that legislatures during the early 1980s enacted what are called *lemon laws*. The majority of the states have enacted such laws.[3]

Basically these laws provide that if a warranty defect substantially affects the vehicle's value or use, *and* the defect has not been remedied by the seller within a specified number of opportunities (usually four), the buyer is entitled to a new car, replacement of defective parts, or return of all consideration paid.

Because disputes would arise concerning the above criteria, most state statutes require the aggrieved purchaser to state his or her case before an appeal jury, whose decisions are binding on the car manufacturers (cannot be appealed), but not usually on the purchaser.

To date, the car manufacturers have set up a network of appeal juries to hear these purchaser complaints. For example, General Motors has contracted with numerous Better Business Bureaus throughout the United States to act as appeal juries.

---

3. As of January 1, 1985, approximately thirty-three states have enacted Lemon Laws. Some of these states are Arizona, Colorado, Connecticut, Delaware, Illinois, Iowa, Kentucky, Missouri, New York, North Carolina, Oregon, Pennsylvania, Tennessee, Texas, Vermont, Washington, Wisconsin, and Wyoming.

QUESTIONS AND CASE PROBLEMS

1. Sallor contracts to ship to Beyer via ABC Truck Line 100 cases of Knee High brand corn, F.O.B. Sallor's city, at $6.50 per case. Beyer is to make a 10 percent down payment on the date of shipment. The payment is to be received at Sallor's place of business before shipment occurs. Sallor ships the corn as contracted, although he has not yet received the down payment, and the goods arrive in Beyer's city. There they remain in the delivery van. Since Beyer failed to make the down payment, Sallor orders ABC not to make the delivery to Beyer's warehouse. Beyer claims that the transit had ended and that Sallor had no right to stop the delivery of the corn. Discuss the validity of Beyer's claim and Sallor's action.

2. Sallor has contracted to sell Beyer 500 washing machines of a certain model at list price. Sallor is to ship the goods on or before December 1. Sallor produces 1,000 of this model washing machine but has not as yet prepared Beyer's shipment. On November 1, Beyer repudiates the contract. Discuss the remedies available to Sallor.

3. Beyer has contracted with Sallor for the purchase and delivery of 100 Model Z dryers. At the time for that contracted tender, Sallor tenders 80 Model Z dryers and 20 Model X dryers. Sallor does not have 100 Model Z dryers in stock and does not expect to acquire any for at least three months. Beyer wants 100 Model Z dryers or none at all. Discuss the remedies available to Beyer under these circumstances.

4. Beyer has contracted to purchase 500 pairs of shoes from Sallor. Sallor manufactures the shoes and tenders delivery to Beyer. Beyer accepts the shipment. Later, upon inspection, Beyer discovers that 10 pairs of the shoes are poorly made and will have to be sold to customers as seconds. If Beyer decides to keep all 500 pairs of shoes, what remedies are available to her?

5. Beyer is an antique car collector. He contracts to purchase spare parts for a 1938 engine from Sallor. These parts are not made any more and are scarce. To get the contract with Sallor, Beyer has had to pay 50 percent of the purchase price in advance. On May 1, Beyer sends the payment, which is received on May 2. On May 3, Sallor, having found another buyer willing to pay substantially more for the parts, informs Beyer that he will not deliver as contracted. That same day Beyer learns that Sallor is insolvent. Sallor has the parts, and Beyer wants them. Discuss fully any possible remedies available to Beyer to get these parts.

6. As a result of inquiries by Sumitomo, a steel manufacturer, Goodson supplied Sumitomo with a written statement of its solvency on February 7, 1968. On February 25, 1968, Goodson and Sumitomo entered into a contract for the sale of steel to be shipped from Japan. Goodson received the steel on June 24, 1968, about two months after Sumitomo had shipped it. On July 30, 1968, Sumitomo learned that Goodson was insolvent and had been insolvent for the entire month of February 1968. The same day, Sumitomo attempted to reclaim the steel from Goodson's trustee in bankruptcy. Will Sumitomo succeed? In Re Goodson Steel Corp., 488 F.2d 776 (5th Cir. 1974).

7. Westmoreland Metal Manufacturing Company made school furniture. In 1955 Willred Company entered into a contract with Westmoreland to be its exclusive distributor of school furniture in the metropolitan New York area. Under this contract, Westmoreland made a number of shipments of furniture to Willred, which Willred resold to the New York Board of Education. The distributorship contract between Willred and Westmoreland was to end in December 1957, but Westmoreland, without legal justification, terminated the contract in February 1956. Just before Westmoreland breached the contract, it made a large shipment of furniture to Willred that amounted to about half the furniture that Willred had just ordered from Westmoreland. Much of the furniture was shipped in damaged condition, requiring Willred to repair it extensively before it could be resold. In addition, Willred was forced to purchase a large quantity of school furniture on the open market to satisfy a current contract with the New York Board of Education. Finally, Willred had to rent a small amount of furniture in order to satisfy its contractual obligations to the New York Board of Education. Which of these expenditures, if any, can Willred recoup from Westmoreland? [Willred Co. v. Westmoreland Metal Mfg. Co., 200 F.Supp. 59 (E.D.Pa. 1961)]

8. In a contract between Associated Metals & Minerals Corp. and Kaiser Trading Company, Associated promised to deliver to Kaiser 4,000 tons of cryolite over the next sixteen months. After Associated had delivered about one-eighth of the cryolite to Kaiser, it repudiated the contract. Kaiser sought to enforce the contract and requested the court to grant it specific performance against Associated. Kaiser presented convincing proof at trial that only a few hundred tons of cryolite were available on the open market and that Kaiser needed the 4,000 tons that Associated had promised to deliver in order for Kaiser to fulfill its contractual obligations to a number of other industrial companies. Should the court grant specific performance in this case? [Kaiser Trading Co. v. Associated Metals and Minerals Corp., 321 F.Supp. 923 (N.D.Cal. 1970)]

9. Kaiden placed a $5,000 deposit on a Rolls-Royce in August. The order form did not specify a delivery date, but correspondence between the parties indicated delivery was expected in November. On November 21, Kaiden

notified the automobile dealer that she had purchased another Rolls-Royce elsewhere and requested a refund of her deposit. Under the liquidated damages clause of the written contract, the dealer was to retain the entire cash deposit in the event of a breach by the purchaser. The car was sold before Kaiden brought suit to recover her deposit. The dealer's actual damages amounted to $2,075. Should the court allow the dealer to retain the $5,000? [Lee Oldsmobile, Inc. v. Kaiden, 32 Md.App. 556, 363 A.2d 270 (1976)]

10. Rancher Baden purchased bull semen from Curtiss Breeding to use for artificial insemination. The semen was defective, so no calves were born. When Baden sued Curtiss, he contended that his consequential damages should include not only the value of the calf crop not born that year, but also the calf crop that would have been born the following year from the first calf crop. Should Baden be awarded these additional consequential damages? [Baden v. Curtiss Breeding Service, 380 F. Supp. 243 (D.Mont. 1974)]

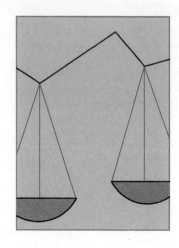

21

SALES
Introduction to
Sales Warranties

Until recently, *caveat emptor*—let the buyer beware—was the prevailing philosophy in sales contract law. In twentieth-century America, however, this outlook has given way to a more enlightened consumer approach (although many sellers argue that today's standards of liability are unrealistic and excessive). This chapter will review the concept of product warranty as it occurs in a sales contract under the UCC.

The concept of *warranty* is based upon the seller's assurance to the buyer that the goods will meet certain standards. The UCC designates five types of warranties that can arise in a sales contract:

1. Warranty of title. [UCC 2-312]
2. Express warranty. [UCC 2-313]
3. Implied warranty of merchantability. [UCC 2-314]
4. Implied warranty of fitness for a particular purpose. [UCC 2-315]
5. Implied warranty arising from the course of dealing or trade usage. [UCC 2-314(3)]

In the law of sales, since a warranty imposes a duty upon the seller, a breach of warranty is a breach of the seller's promise, and a buyer can sue to recover

damages against the seller. Also, a breach can allow the buyer to rescind the agreement.[1]

WARRANTY OF TITLE

Title warranty arises automatically in most sales contracts. UCC 2-312 imposes three types of warranties of title.

Good Title

In most cases, sellers warrant that they have good and valid title to the goods sold and that transfer of the title is rightful. [UCC 2-312(1)(a)] For example, Alice steals goods from Ophelia and sells them to Betty, who does not know that they are stolen. If Ophelia discovers that Betty has the goods, then Ophelia has the right to reclaim them from Betty. Under this Code provision, however, Betty can then sue Alice for breach of warranty, because a thief has no title to stolen goods and thus cannot give good

---

1. Rescission can occur in two ways: It can occur by rejection of goods before acceptance or by revocation by the buyer after acceptance, returning the parties to their original positions.

title in a subsequent sale. When Alice sold Betty the goods, Alice *automatically* warranted to Betty that the title conveyed was valid and that its transfer was rightful. Since this was not in fact the case, Alice has breached the warranty of title imposed by UCC 2-312(1)(a), and Alice becomes liable to the buyer for appropriate damages.

No Liens

A second warranty of title provided by the Code protects buyers who are *unaware* of any encumbrances (claims or liens) against goods at the time of the contract. [UCC 2-312(1)(b)] This warranty protects buyers who, for example, unknowingly purchase goods that are subject to a creditor's security interest. (See Chapter 29.) If a creditor legally repossesses the goods from a buyer who *had no actual knowledge of the security interest*, then the buyer can recover from the seller for a breach of warranty. (The buyer who has *actual knowledge* of a security interest has no recourse against a seller.)

To illustrate: Henderson buys a used color television set from Sneed for cash. A month later, Reynolds repossesses the set from Henderson, proving that she, Reynolds, has a valid security interest in the set. She proves that Sneed is in default, having missed five payments. Henderson demands his money back from Sneed. Under Section 2-312(2)(b), Henderson will be able to recover because the seller of goods warrants that the goods shall be delivered free from any security interest or other lien of which the buyer has no knowledge.

No Infringements

A third "category" of title warranty is the warranty against infringement. A merchant is deemed to warrant that the goods delivered are free from any patent, trademark, or copyright claims of a third person.[2] [UCC 2-312(3)] If this warranty is breached and the buyer is sued by the claim holder, the buyer

---

2. Recall from Chapter 17 that a *merchant* is defined in UCC 2-104(1) as a person who deals in goods of the kind involved in the sales contract or who, by occupation, presents himself or herself as having knowledge or skill peculiar to the goods involved in the transaction.

must notify the seller of litigation within a reasonable time to enable the seller to decide whether to defend the lawsuit. If the seller states in writing that he or she has decided to defend and agrees to bear all expenses, including that of an adverse judgment, then the buyer must let the seller undertake litigation; otherwise the buyer loses all rights against the seller if any infringement liability is established. [UCC 2-607(3)(b) and (5)(b)]

To illustrate: Green buys a machine from Brown, a manufacturer of such machines, for use in his factory. Three years later, Patton sues Green for damages for patent infringement. Patton claims that he has a patent on the machine and that it cannot be used without his permission. At once, Green informs Brown of this suit and demands that Brown take over the defense. Brown refuses to do so, claiming that Patton has no case. Green goes to court and loses. Patton obtains a judgment against Green, which Green pays off. Green now demands that Brown reimburse him for this amount. Brown must reimburse Green because merchant sellers of goods warrant to buyers that the goods they regularly sell are free of infringement claims by third parties.

This infringement warranty does not apply to buyers who furnish specifications for the goods to be made in a particular way. In fact, it is the buyer who must hold the seller harmless (i.e., not liable) against any third person's claims of infringement arising out of the goods manufactured to the buyer's specifications. [UCC 2-312(3)] The same requirements of notice apply to a seller who is sued for breach of an infringement warranty for which the buyer is answerable by virtue of the "hold harmless" agreement. [UCC 2-607(6)]

To illustrate: Green orders a custom-made machine from Brown, who is a manufacturer of such machines. It is built strictly to Green's specifications. While the machine is being built, Patton files a suit against Brown for patent infringement. Brown immediately informs Green in writing of this suit and demands that Green take over the expense of the litigation. Green refuses to do so. Brown settles with Patton out of court by paying Patton modest damages. Brown now wishes to be reimbursed by Green. Brown will be able to collect because a buyer who orders custom-built goods from a seller, and who furnishes the seller with the specifications, warrants to the seller that the specifications do not infringe any patent.

Disclaimer of Title Warranty

In an ordinary sales transaction, the title warranty can be disclaimed or modified only by *specific language* in a contract. For example, sellers assert that they are transferring only such rights, title, and interest as they have in the goods.

In certain cases, the circumstances of the sale are sufficient to indicate clearly to a buyer that no assurances as to title are being made. The classic example is a sheriff's sale, where buyers know that the goods have been seized to satisfy debts and it is apparent that the goods are not the property of the person who is selling them. [UCC 2-312(2)]

EXPRESS WARRANTIES

A seller can create an **express warranty** by making representations concerning the quality, condition, description, or performance potential of the goods. Under UCC 2-313, express warranties arise when a seller indicates that:

1.   The goods will conform to any *affirmation or promise* of fact that the seller makes to the buyer about the goods. Such affirmations or promises are usually made during the bargaining process. Statements such as "These drill bits will *easily* penetrate stainless steel—and without dulling" constitute express warranties.

2.   The goods will conform to any *description* of them. For example, "Crate contains one 150-horse-power diesel engine," or the contract calls for delivery of a "camel's hair coat."

3.   The goods will conform to any *sample* or *model*.

Basis of the Bargain

The Code requires that for any express warranty to be created, the affirmation, promise, description, or sample must become part of the "basis of the bargain." Just what constitutes the basis of the bargain is hard to say. The Code does not define the concept, and each case presents a question of fact to determine whether a representation came at such a time and in such a way that it induced the buyer to enter the contract.

Are certain vague telephone statements part of the basis of the bargain? That is the question addressed in the following case.

SESSA v. RIEGLE

United States District Court, Eastern District of Pennsylvania, 1977.
427 F.Supp. 760, affirmed without opinion 568 F.2d 770 (3d Cir. 1978).

BACKGROUND AND FACTS   *Riegle sold a standard-bred race horse to Sessa for $25,000. Prior to the sale, Sessa sent a friend, Maloney, to examine the horse. Maloney reported that he "liked him." Additionally, during a telephone conversation, Riegle stated to Sessa that Sessa would like the horse and that he was a "good one" and "sound." After the sale was consummated and after delivery, the horse almost immediately went lame in the hind legs. Experts were unable to identify the cause. They could not establish if the condition was present before Riegle shipped the horse. Even though the horse—Tarport Conaway—was later able to race, Sessa sued for damages.*

HANNUM, District Judge.

*   *   *   *

Sessa contends that certain statements made by Riegle during that conversation constitute express warranties on which Riegle is liable in this action. The most important of these is Riegle's alleged statement that, "The horse is sound," or words to that effect.

In deciding whether statements by a seller constitute express warranties, the court must look to UCC § 2-313 which presents three fundamental issues. First, the court must determine whether the seller's statement constitutes an "affirmation of fact or promise" or "description of the goods" under § 2-313(1)(a) or (b) or whether it is rather "merely the seller's opinion or commendation of the goods" under § 2-313(2). Second, assuming the court finds the language used susceptible to creation of a warranty, it must then be determined whether the statement was "part of the basis of the bargain." If it was, an express warranty exists and, as the third issue, the court must determine whether the warranty was breached.

With respect to the first issue, the court finds that in the circumstances of this case, words to the effect that "The horse is sound" spoken during the telephone conversation between Sessa and Riegle constitute an opinion or commendation rather than express warranty. This determination is a question for the trier of fact. There is nothing talismanic or thaumaturgic about the use of the word "sound." Whether use of that language constitutes warranty, or mere opinion or commendation depends on the circumstances of the sale and the type of goods sold. While § 2-313 makes it clear that no specific words need be used and no specific intent need be present, not every statement by a seller is an express warranty.

*   *   *   *

Also mitigating against a finding of express warranty is the nature of the conversation between Sessa and Riegle. It seemed largely collateral to the sale rather than an essential part of it. Although Sessa testified that Riegle's "personal guarantee" given during the conversation was the quintessence of the sale, the credible evidence suggests otherwise. While on the telephone, Riegle made statements to the effect that "the horse is a good one" and "you will like him." These bland statements are obviously opinion or commendation, and the statement, "The horse is sound," falling within their penumbra takes on their character as such.

Under all the facts and circumstances of this case, it is clear to the court that Riegle's statements were not of such a character as to give rise to express warranties under § 2-313(1) but were opinion or commendation under § 2-313(2).

Even assuming that Riegle's statements could be express warranties, it is not at all clear that they were "part of the basis of the bargain," the second requisite of § 2-313. This is essentially a reliance requirement and is inextricably intertwined with the initial determination as to whether given language may constitute an express warranty since affirmations, promises, and descriptions tend to become part of the basis of the bargain. It was the intention of the drafters of the U.C.C. not to require a strong showing of reliance. In fact, they envisioned that all statements of the seller became part of the basis of the bargain unless clear affirmative proof is shown to the contrary. See Official Comments 3 and 8 to U.C.C. § 2-313, 12A P.S. § 2-313.

It is Sessa's contention that his conversation with Riegle was the principal factor inducing him to enter the bargain. He would have the court believe that Maloney was merely a messenger to deliver the check. The evidence shows, however, that Sessa was relying primarily on Maloney to advise him in connection with the sale. Maloney testified that he had talked to Sessa about the horse on several occasions and expressed the opinion that he was convinced "beyond the shadow of a doubt" that he was a good buy. With respect to his authority to buy the horse he testified

"Well, Mr. Sessa said he had enough confidence and faith in me and my integrity and honesty that I, what I did say about the horse, I was representing the horse as he is or as he was, and that if the horse, in my estimation, was that type of a horse and at that given price, the fixed price of $25,000, he would buy the horse."

When, at the airport, Maloney protested that he did not want to accept full responsibility to go to Ohio alone, Sessa told him "*   *   * I take your word. I—I trust your judgment and I trust your—your honesty, that if this horse is right, everything will be all right." In Ohio, Maloney examined the horse, jogged him, and reported to Sessa over the telephone that he "liked him."

The court believes that Maloney's opinion was the principal, if not the only, factor which motivated Sessa to purchase the horse. The conversation with Riegle played a negligible role in his decision.

The court decided that no express warranty had been made. The court further concluded that even if the defendant's statements gave rise to an express warranty, those statements were not relied on as part of the bargain.

DECISION AND REMEDY

Statements of Opinion and Value—Use of Formal Words Not Required

According to Section 2-313(2), "It is not necessary to the creation of an express warranty that the seller use formal words such as 'warrant' or 'guarantee' or that he has a specific intention to make a warranty * * *." It is necessary only that a reasonable buyer would regard the representation as part of the basis of the bargain.

On the other hand, if the seller merely makes a statement that relates to the value or worth of the goods, or makes a statement of opinion or recommendation about the goods, the seller is not creating an express warranty. [UCC 2-313(2)] For example, a seller claims, "This is the best used car to come along in years; it has four new tires and a 350-horsepower engine just rebuilt this year." The seller has made several *affirmations of fact* that can create a warranty: The automobile has an engine; it is a 350-horsepower engine; it was rebuilt this year; there are four tires on the automobile; the tires are new. But the seller's *opinion* that it is "the best used car to come along in years" is known as "puffing" and creates no warranty. (Puffing is the expression of an opinion by a seller that is not made as a representation of fact.) A statement relating to the value of the goods, such as "it's worth a fortune" or "anywhere else you'd pay $10,000 for it," will not normally create a warranty.

The ordinary seller can give an *opinion* that is not a warranty. However, if the seller is an expert and gives an opinion as an expert, then a warranty can be created. For example, Saul is an art dealer and an expert in seventeenth-century paintings. If Saul states to Beyer, a purchaser, that in his opinion a particular painting is a Rembrandt, and Beyer buys the painting, Saul has warranted the accuracy of his opinion.

What constitutes an express warranty and what constitutes puffing is not easy to resolve. Merely recognizing that some statements are not warranties does not tell us where one should draw the line between puffs and warranties. The reasonableness of the buyer's reliance appears to be the controlling criterion in many cases. For example, a salesperson's statements that a ladder "will never break" and will "last a lifetime" are so clearly improbable that no reasonable buyer should rely on them. Also, the context within which a statement is made might be relevant in determining the reasonableness of the buyer's reliance. For example, any statement made in a written advertisement is more likely to be relied upon by a reasonable person than a statement made orally by a salesperson.

The following case involves the question of puffing. It is a classic pre-UCC case that is not inconsistent with the Code.

WAT HENRY PONTIAC CO. v. BRADLEY
Supreme Court of Oklahoma, 1949.
202 Okl. 82, 210 P.2d 348.

BACKGROUND AND FACTS *The plaintiff, Bradley, alleged that on October 22, 1944, she purchased a used Buick automobile from the defendant, Wat Henry Pontiac Co., paying $890 in cash. At that time, the defendant assured her orally that the vehicle was in first-class condition, usable and serviceable in every respect. The plaintiff relied on that representation and purchased the vehicle. But as it turned out, the car was not in first-class, usable condition. In fact, it was necessary to have the vehicle repaired and have parts replaced. Ultimately, the plaintiff spent $249.56 in repair and replacement and suffered damages, expenses, and inconvenience in the amount of $75.*

The defendant argued, in the first place, that the expression was mere opinion and did not constitute a warranty and, in the second place, that no implied warranty of quality or fitness is ever present in the sale of a second-hand automobile. The trial court held for the plaintiff.

JOHNSON, Justice.
* * * *

We now consider defendant's proposition one: "Generally, no implied warranty of quality or fitness is present in sale of a secondhand automobile, but the doctrine of caveat emptor applies."

This is the general rule as to implied warranties. However, the plaintiff in this case does not rely on an implied warranty, but upon an express verbal warranty, and the rule of caveat emptor does not apply where there is an express warranty of condition, and does not apply to hidden defects which are not open to discovery by the buyer.

[The court thus found that the rule of *caveat emptor* did not apply in this case. The court looked next at the defendant's other contention—that he had not asserted a warranty but merely stated an opinion.]

The salesman who sold the car testified in substance that he had been an auto mechanic for about twelve years before becoming a salesman; that he was engaged in demonstrating and selling cars; that he did not warrant the car, but explained to the buyer that the sale was without a warranty, but did state that after the deal was closed that he told plaintiff, "I would not be afraid to start, and I wouldn't have been afraid to start any place in the car, because it run as nice as you would expect a car that age to run. There wasn't anything to indicate to me that there was anything wrong with the car, if there was anything wrong with it."

The evidence adduced as to the issues involved was in conflict, each side having witnesses to substantiate their theory. Now, did these facts as stated by plaintiff, if true, constitute an oral warranty?

The rule is that to constitute an express warranty no particular form of words is necessary, and any affirmation of the quality or condition of the vehicle, not uttered as a matter of opinion or belief, made by a seller at the time of sale for the purpose of assuring the buyer of the truth of the fact and inducing the buyer to make the purchase, if so received and relied on by the buyer, is an express warranty.

This court * * * [has stated the rule of law as follows:]

" 'Warranty' is a matter of intention. A decisive test is whether the vendor assumes to assert a fact of which the buyer is ignorant, or merely states an opinion, or his judgment, upon a matter of which the vendor has no special knowledge, and on which the buyer may also be expected to have an opinion and to exercise his judgment. In the former case there is a warranty; in the latter case there is not. * * *

"The buyer knew nothing about the capacity of the automobile purchased. The seller was an expert in the handling of automobiles, and was engaged in the business of demonstrating and selling the same. Held, a statement made by the seller that the automobile could be driven over the roads in a certain vicinity satisfactorily constituted a warranty and was not the expression of a mere opinion."

The facts in this case bring it squarely within the above well-settled principles of law, and the jury was justified in finding that there was an oral warranty.

DECISION AND REMEDY

The court held that the defendant's statements about the mechanical condition of the car constituted a warranty. The defendant was liable to the plaintiff, who was awarded $324.56 in damages for breach of the express oral warranty of the used car.

COMMENTS

A similar case, Frederickson v. Hackney [159 Minn. 234, 198 N.W. 806 (1924)], was decided differently. In that case, the seller of a bull calf stated to the buyer that the purchase would put "the buyer on the map" and that the father of the bull calf was "the greatest living dairy bull." The bull proved sterile, so the buyer sued. The Minnesota court considered the statements made by the seller to represent only trade talk, not a warranty of productive capacity. Apparently, the most persuasive difference between the two cases was that in the Wat Henry *case it was a woman who bought the car to make a trip with her seven-month-old child in 1944 to visit her husband in the Army, and the car broke down en route. Presumably, it was the natural compassion that the trier of fact felt for a World War II service wife who was stranded with a seven-*

month-old child that distinguishes this case from the Frederickson *case. This analysis is supported by the fact that oral statements by used car salespeople are notoriously unreliable and, indeed, archetypal puffs.*

IMPLIED WARRANTIES

An **implied warranty** is one that *the law derives* by implication or inference from the nature of the transaction or the relative situation or circumstances of the parties.

For example: Kaplan buys an axe at Enrique's Hardware Store. There are no express warranties made. The first time she chops wood with it, the axe handle breaks, and Kaplan is injured. She immediately notifies Enrique. Examination shows that the wood in the handle was rotten but that the rottenness could not have been noticed by either Enrique or Kaplan. Nonetheless, Kaplan notifies Enrique that she will hold him responsible for the medical bills. Enrique is responsible because a merchant seller of goods warrants that the goods he sells are fit for normal use. This axe was obviously not fit for normal use.

Implied Warranty of Merchantability

An **implied warranty of merchantability** automatically arises in every sale of goods made *by a merchant* who deals in goods of the kind sold. [UCC 2-314] Thus, a retailer of ski equipment makes an implied warranty of merchantability every time the retailer sells a pair of skis, but a neighbor selling skis at a garage sale does not.

Goods that are *merchantable* are "reasonably fit for the ordinary purposes for which such goods are used." They must be of at least average, fair, or medium-grade quality. The quality must be comparable to quality that will pass without objection in the trade or market for goods of the same description. In addition, the goods, to be merchantable, must be adequately packaged and labeled as provided by the agreement, and they must conform to the promises or affirmations of fact made on the container or label, if any.

Some examples of nonmerchantable goods include: light bulbs that explode when switched on, pajamas that burst into flames upon slight contact with a stove burner, high heels that break off shoes under normal use, or shotgun shells that explode prematurely.

A sale is also accompanied by an implied warranty of merchantability that imposes on the merchant liability for the safe performance of the product. It makes no difference whether the merchant knew of or could have discovered a defect that makes the product unsafe. (Of course, merchants are not absolute insurers against *all* accidents arising in connection with the goods. For example, a bar of soap will not be unmerchantable merely because a user can slip and fall by stepping on it.) In an action based on breach of warranty, it is necessary to show:

1. The existence of the implied warranty,
2. That the warranty was broken, and
3. That the breach of warranty was the proximate cause of the damage sustained.

The serving of food or drink to be consumed on or off the premises is recognized as a sale of goods subject to the warranty of merchantability. [UCC 2-314(1)] "Merchantable" food means food that is fit to eat. Therefore, any object within the food that a buyer would ordinarily expect to accompany the food would not render the food nonmerchantable. Thus, a pearl swallowed by a buyer eating oysters would not subject the merchant seller to liability, but a nail would.

The following is a classic case of a court's interpretation of whether a fish bone in fish chowder is a foreign substance rendering the chowder unwholesome or not fit to be eaten.

WEBSTER v. BLUE
SHIP TEA ROOM

Supreme Judicial Court of
Massachusetts, 1964.
347 Mass. 421, 198 N.E.2d 309.

BACKGROUND AND FACTS   *Webster brought the following action against the Blue Ship Tea Room for personal injuries she sustained when consuming a bowl of their fish chowder. Her theory was breach of implied warranty of merchantability. A jury rendered a verdict for the plaintiff.*

REARDON, Justice.

This is a case which by its nature evokes earnest study not only of the law but also of the culinary traditions of the Commonwealth [Massachusetts] which bear so heavily upon its outcome. It is an action to recover damages for personal injuries sustained by reason of a breach of implied warranty of food served by the defendant in its restaurant. * * *

* * * On Saturday, April 25, 1959, about 1 P.M., the plaintiff, accompanied by her sister and her aunt, entered the Blue Ship Tea Room operated by the defendant. The group was seated at a table and supplied with menus.

This restaurant, which the plaintiff characterized as "quaint," was located in Boston "on the third floor of an old building on T Wharf which overlooks the ocean."

The plaintiff, who had been born and brought up in New England (a fact of some consequence), ordered clam chowder and crabmeat salad. Within a few minutes she received tidings to the effect that "there was no more clam chowder," whereupon she ordered a cup of fish chowder. Presently, there was set before her "a small bowl of fish chowder." She had previously enjoyed a breakfast about 9 A.M. which had given her no difficulty. "The fish chowder contained haddock, potatoes, milk, water and seasoning. The chowder was milky in color and not clear. The haddock and potatoes were in chunks" (also a fact of consequence). "She agitated it a little with the spoon and observed that it was a fairly full bowl * * *. It was hot when she got it, but she did not tip it with her spoon because it was hot * * * but stirred it in an up and under motion. She denied that she did this because she was looking for something, but it was rather because she wanted an even distribution of fish and potatoes." "She started to eat it, alternating between the chowder and crackers which were on the table with * * * [some] rolls. She ate about 3 or 4 spoonfuls then stopped. She looked at the spoonfuls as she was eating. She saw equal parts of liquid, potato and fish as she spooned it into her mouth. She did not see anything unusual about it. After 3 or 4 spoonfuls she was aware that something had lodged in her throat because she couldn't swallow and couldn't clear her throat by gulping and she could feel it." This misadventure led to two esophagoscopies at the Massachusetts General Hospital, in the second of which, on April 27, 1959, a fish bone was found and removed. The sequence of events produced injury to the plaintiff which was not insubstantial.

We must decide whether a fish bone lurking in a fish chowder, about the ingredients of which there is no other complaint, constitutes a breach of implied warranty under applicable provisions of the Uniform Commercial Code,[1] the annotations to which are not helpful on this point. As the judge put it in his charge, "Was the fish chowder fit to be eaten and wholesome? * * * [N]obody is claiming that the fish itself wasn't wholesome. * * * But the bone of contention here—I don't mean that for a pun—but was this fish bone a foreign substance that made the fish chowder unwholesome or not fit to be eaten?"

The defendant asserts that here was a native New Englander eating fish chowder in a "quaint" Boston dining place where she had been before; that "[f]ish chowder, as it is served and enjoyed by New Englanders, is a hearty dish, originally designed to satisfy the appetites of our seamen and fishermen"; that "[t]his court knows well that we are not talking of some insipid broth as is customarily served to convalescents." We are asked to rule in such fashion that no chef is forced "to reduce the pieces of fish in the chowder to miniscule size in an effort to ascertain if they contained any pieces of bone." "In so ruling," we are told (in the defendant's brief), "the court will not only

---

1. "(1) Unless excluded or modified by section 2-316, a warranty that the goods shall be merchantable is implied in a contract for their sale if the seller is a merchant with respect to goods of that kind. Under this section the serving for value of food or drink to be consumed either on the premises or elsewhere is a sale. (2) Goods to be merchantable must at least be such as * * * (c) are fit for the ordinary purposes for which such goods are used * * *." G.L. c. 106, § 2-314.

uphold its reputation for legal knowledge and acumen, but will, as loyal sons of Massachusetts, save our world-renowned fish chowder from degenerating into an insipid broth containing the mere essence of its former stature as a culinary masterpiece." Notwithstanding these passionate entreaties we are bound to examine with detachment the nature of fish chowder and what might happen to it under varying interpretations of the Uniform Commercial Code.

＊　＊　＊ It is not too much to say that a person sitting down in New England to consume a good New England fish chowder embarks on a gustatory adventure which may entail the removal of some fish bones from his bowl as he proceeds. We are not inclined to tamper with age old recipes by any amendment reflecting the plaintiff's view of the effect of the Uniform Commercial Code upon them. We are aware of the heavy body of case law involving foreign substances in food, but we sense a strong distinction between them and those relative to unwholesomeness of the food itself, e.g., tainted mackerel (*Smith v. Gerrish*, 256 Mass. 183, 152 N.E. 318), and a fish bone in a fish chowder. Certain Massachusetts cooks might cavil at the ingredients contained in the chowder in this case in that it lacked the heartening lift of salt pork. In any event, we consider that the joys of life in New England include the ready availability of fresh fish chowder. We should be prepared to cope with the hazards of fish bones, the occasional presence of which in chowders is, it seems to us, to be anticipated, and which, in the light of a hallowed tradition, do not impair their fitness or merchantability. While we are bouyed up in this conclusion by *Shapiro v. Hotel Statler Corp.*, 132 F.Supp. 891 (S.D.Cal.), in which the bone which afflicted the plaintiff appeared in "Hot Barquette of Seafood Mornay," we know that the United States District Court of Southern California, situated as are we upon a coast, might be expected to share our views. We are most impressed, however, by *Allen v. Grafton*, 170 Ohio St. 249, 164 N.E.2d 167, where in Ohio, the Midwest, in a case where the plaintiff was injured by a piece of oyster shell in an order of fried oysters, Mr. Justice Taft (now Chief Justice) in a majority opinion held that "the possible presence of a piece of oyster shell in or attached to an oyster is so well known to anyone who eats oysters that we can say as a matter of law that one who eats oysters can reasonably anticipate and guard against eating such a piece of shell ＊　＊　＊."

DECISION AND REMEDY   *The court "sympathized with a plaintiff who has suffered a peculiarly New England injury," but entered a judgment for the defendant, Blue Ship Tea Room.*

Implied Warranty of Fitness for a Particular Purpose

The implied warranty of fitness for a particular purpose arises when *any seller* (merchant or nonmerchant) knows the particular purpose for which a buyer will use the goods *and* knows that the buyer is relying upon the seller's skill and judgment to select suitable goods. [UCC 2-315]

A "particular purpose of the buyer" differs from the "ordinary purpose for which goods are used" (merchantability). Goods can be merchantable but still not fit for the buyer's particular purpose. For example, house paints suitable for ordinary walls are not suitable for painting over stucco walls.

A contract can include both a warranty of merchantability *and* a warranty of fitness for a particular purpose, which relates to a specific use or to a special situation in which a buyer intends to use the goods. For example, a seller recommends a particular pair of shoes, *knowing* that a customer is looking for mountain climbing shoes. The buyer purchases the shoes *relying* on the seller's judgment. If the shoes are found to be not only improperly made but suitable only for walking, not for mountain climbing, the seller has breached both the warranty of fitness for a particular purpose, and the warranty of merchantability.

A seller does not need "actual knowledge" of the buyer's particular purpose. It is sufficient if a seller "has reason to know" the purpose. However, the buyer must have *relied* upon the seller's skill or judgment in selecting or furnishing suitable goods in order for an implied warranty to be created.

For example, Josephs buys a shortwave radio from Radio Shack, telling the salesperson that she wants a set strong enough to pick up Radio Luxemburg, which is 8,000 miles away. Radio Shack sells Josephs a Model XYZ set. The set works, but it will not pick up Radio Luxemburg. Josephs wants her money back. Here, since Radio Shack is guilty of a breach of implied warranty of fitness for the buyer's particular purpose, Josephs will be able to recover. The salesperson knew specifically that she wanted a set that would pick up Radio Luxemburg. Furthermore, Josephs relied upon the salesperson to furnish a radio that would fulfill this purpose. Radio Shack did not do so. Therefore, the warranty was breached.

In the next case, a seller helped a buyer solve a painting problem and became the defendant in a lawsuit for breach of an implied warranty of fitness.

BACKGROUND AND FACTS   *The defendant, Brown, was engaged in the retail paint business. Catania, the plaintiff, asked Brown to recommend a paint to cover the exterior stucco walls of his house. Brown recommended and sold to Catania a certain brand of paint called "Pierce's Shingle and Shake" paint. Brown also advised Catania how to prepare the walls before applying the paint and how to mix the paint in proper proportion to the thinner. Catania followed Brown's instructions, but the paint blistered and peeled soon after it was applied.*

CATANIA v. BROWN
Circuit Court of Connecticut,
Appellate Division, 1967.
4 Conn.Cir. 344, 231 A.2d 668.

JACOBS, Judge.
*   *   *   *

Under the statute governing implied warranty of fitness for a particular purpose (§ 42a-2-315), two requirements must be met: (a) the buyer relies on the seller's skill or judgment to select or furnish suitable goods; and (b) the seller at the time of contracting has reason to know the buyer's purpose and that the buyer is relying on the seller's skill or judgment. "It is a question of fact in the ordinary case whether these conditions have been met and the warranty arises."

*   *   * "The raising of an implied warranty of fitness depends upon whether the buyer informed the seller of the circumstances and conditions which necessitated his purchase of a certain character of article or material and left it to the seller to select the particular kind and quality of article suitable for the buyer's use. *   *   * So when the buyer orders goods to be supplied and trusts to the judgment or skill of the seller to select goods or material for which they are ordered, there is an implied warranty that they shall be reasonably fit for that purpose." "Reliance can, of course, be more readily found where the *retailer* selects the product or recommends it."

*   *   * [T]he buyer, being ignorant of the fitness of the article offered by the seller, justifiably relied on the superior information, skill and judgment of the seller and not on his own knowledge or judgment, and under such circumstances an implied warranty of fitness could properly be claimed by the purchaser.

The plaintiff prevailed on the theory of implied warranty of fitness for a particular purpose. The defendant had created and breached a warranty of fitness by recommending the particular paint as suitable for stucco walls.

**DECISION
AND REMEDY**

Implied Warranty Arising from the Course of Dealing or Trade Usage

The Code recognizes in Section 2-314(3) that implied warranties can arise (or be excluded or modified) from course of dealing, course of performance, or usage of trade. [UCC 2-316(3)(c)] In the absence of evidence to the contrary, when both parties to a sales contract have knowledge of a well-recognized trade custom, the courts will infer that they both intended that custom to apply to their contract. For example, in the sale of a new car, where the industry-wide custom includes lubricating the car before delivery, a seller who fails to do so can be held liable to a buyer for resulting damages for breach of implied warranty. This, of course, would also be negligence on the part of the dealer.

OVERLAPPING WARRANTIES

Sometimes two or more warranties are made in a single transaction. An implied warranty of merchantability or of fitness for a particular purpose, or both, can exist in addition to an express warranty. For example, where a sales contract for a new car states that "this car engine is warranted to be free from defects for 12,000 miles or 12 months, whichever occurs first," there is an express warranty against all defects and an implied warranty that the car will be fit for normal use.

The rule of UCC 2-317 is that express and implied warranties are construed as *cumulative* if they are consistent with one another. If the warranties are *inconsistent*, the courts will usually hold that:

1. *Express* warranties will displace inconsistent *implied* warranties except implied warranties of fitness for a particular purpose.
2. Samples will take precedence over inconsistent general descriptions.
3. Technical specifications will displace inconsistent samples or general descriptions.

Suppose that when Josephs buys a shortwave radio at Radio Shack, the contract expressly warrants radio receivership to a maximum range of 4,000 miles. She tries to pick up Radio Luxembourg—the stated purpose of her purchase—which is 8,000 miles away. The set cannot perform that well. Josephs claims that Radio Shack is guilty of breach of war-

ranty of fitness. The express warranty, however, takes precedence over any implied warranty of merchantability that a shortwave set should pick up any station anywhere in the world. Josephs does have a good claim for the breach of implied warranty of fitness for a specific purpose because she had made it clear that she was buying the set to pick up Radio Luxembourg. In cases of inconsistency between an express warranty and a warranty of fitness for a buyer's particular purpose, the warranty of fitness for the buyer's particular purpose normally prevails. [UCC 2-317(c)]

THIRD PARTY BENEFICIARIES OF WARRANTIES: EXPRESS OR IMPLIED

One of the general principles of contract law is that unless you are one of the parties to a contract, you have no rights under the contract. (Notable exceptions are assignments and third party beneficiary contracts. See Chapter 14.) In short, common law established that **privity** must exist between a plaintiff and a defendant with respect to the matter under dispute in order to maintain any action based upon a contract.

For example, I purchase a ham from retailer Ralph. I invite you to my house that evening. I prepare the ham properly. You are served first, since you are my guest, and you become severely ill because the ham is spoiled. Can you sue retailer Ralph for breach of the implied warranty of merchantability? Since warranty is based on a contract for the sale of goods, under the common law you would normally have warranty rights only if you were a party to the purchase of the ham. Therefore, the warranty would extend only to me, the purchaser.

In the past this hardship was sometimes resolved by court decisions removing privity as a requirement to hold manufacturers and sellers liable for certain defective products (notably food, drugs, and cosmetics) that were sold. The UCC, reflecting some of these decisions, has addressed the problem of privity, at least to the extent of giving the state the option to determine with whom privity is no longer required.

There is sharp disagreement over how far warranty liability should extend. In order to satisfy opposing views of the various states, the drafters of the

UCC proposed three alternatives for liability under UCC 2-318. Accordingly, some states have adopted alternative A; others, alternative B; and still others, alternative C. All three alternatives are intended to eliminate the privity requirement with respect to certain enumerated types of injuries (personal versus property) for certain beneficiaries (for example, household members or bystanders).

Alternative A   All sellers' warranties (express or implied) extend to any *natural person* in the buyer's family or household or to anyone who is a guest in the home, when it is reasonable to expect that such persons will use, consume, or be affected by the goods or be personally injured because of a breach of the warranty. Consider this example: Anderson buys an electric washing machine from E-Z Appliances. One month after the purchase, Anderson's mother-in-law, who has been living with his family for a year, receives a severe electric shock from a defective wire while using the machine. Anderson's mother-in-law claims damages from E-Z Appliances for breach of warranty of merchantability. She can recover because the defective wire made the washing machine unfit for normal use. Since she was living with Anderson's family, she naturally would use the washing machine if she helped with housekeeping chores. Anderson's mother-in-law therefore qualifies as a third party beneficiary of the warranty.

Alternative B   Alternative B extends the seller's warranty (express or implied) to any *natural person* who can reasonably be expected to use, consume, or be affected by the goods and who suffers personal injury because of the breach of warranty. This is a broader basis for liability than alternative A since protection is not limited to family or household members.

Note the restrictions here. As with alternative A, the seller's warranty extends only to persons, not corporations. It also limits the right of recovery to personal injury damages and therefore eliminates the possibility of suing for property damages. A seller may not exclude or limit the warranties given under alternatives A or B.

Alternative C   Alternative C offers the broadest coverage of all. It extends to any person who is injured. (It also extends the rule to damages beyond injuries to the person.) It does not allow the seller to exclude or limit the operation of liability for personal injury of an individual to whom the warranty extends.

WARRANTY DISCLAIMERS

Since each warranty is created in a special way, the manner in which each one can be disclaimed or qualified by the seller varies.

Express Warranties

Any affirmation of fact or promise, description of the goods, or use of samples or models by a seller will create an express warranty. Obviously, then, express warranties can be excluded if the seller has carefully refrained from making any promise or affirmation of fact relating to the goods, or describing the goods, or selling by means of a sample model. [UCC 2-313]

The Code does permit express warranties to be negated or limited by specific and unambiguous language, provided this is done in a manner that protects the buyer from surprise. Therefore, a written disclaimer in language that is clear and conspicuous, called to a buyer's attention, could negate all oral express warranties not included in the written sales contract. This permits the seller to avoid false allegations that oral warranties were made, and it insures that only representations by properly authorized individuals are included as part of the bargain. [UCC 2-316(1)]

Implied Warranties

Generally speaking, and unless circumstances indicate otherwise, implied warranties (merchantability and fitness) are disclaimed by the expressions "as is," "with all faults," or other similar expressions that in common understanding for *both* parties call the buyer's attention to the fact that there are no implied warranties. [UCC 2-316(3)(a)]

The Code also permits a seller to specifically disclaim the implied warranty either of fitness *or* of merchantability. [UCC 2-316(2)] To disclaim the implied warranty of fitness, the disclaimer *must* be in writing and conspicuous. The word "fitness" does not have to be mentioned in the writing; it is sufficient if, for example, the disclaimer states, "There are no warranties that extend beyond the description on the face hereof."

A *merchantability disclaimer* must be more specific; it must mention *merchantability*. It need not be written; but if it is, the writing must be conspicuous. According to UCC 1-201(10):

> A term or clause is conspicuous when it is so written that a reasonable person against whom it is to operate ought to have noticed it. A printed heading in capitals is conspicuous. Language in the body of a form is conspicuous if it is in large or other contrasting type or color.

To illustrate: Merchant Smith sells Beyer a particular lawn mower selected by Smith with the characteristics clearly requested by Beyer. At the time of the sale, Smith orally tells Beyer that he does not warrant the merchantability of the mower, as it is last year's model. The mower proves to be defective and will not work. Beyer wishes to hold Smith for breach of implied warranty of merchantability and of fitness for a particular purpose.

Beyer can hold Smith for breach of the warranty of fitness but not of the warranty of merchantability. Smith's oral disclaimer mentioning the word *merchantability* is a proper disclaimer. For Smith to have disclaimed the implied warranty of fitness, a conspicuous writing would have been required. Since no written disclaimer was made, Smith can still be held liable.

Buyer's Refusal to Inspect

If a buyer actually examines the goods (or a sample or model) as fully as desired before entering a contract, or if the buyer refuses to examine the goods, *there is no implied warranty with respect to defects that a reasonable examination will reveal.*

Suppose, in the illustration concerning Kaplan's purchase of the axe from Enrique's Hardware Store, the defect in Kaplan's axe could easily have been spotted by normal inspection. Kaplan, even after Enrique asks, refuses to inspect the axe before buying it. After being hurt by the defective axe, she will not be able to hold Enrique for breach of warranty of merchantability because she could have spotted the defect during an inspection. [UCC 2-316(3)(b)]

Failing to examine the goods is not a refusal to examine them; it is not enough that the goods were available for inspection and the buyer failed to examine them. A "refusal" occurs only when the seller *demands* that the buyer examine the goods. Of course, the seller always remains liable for all latent (hidden) defects that ordinary inspection would not reveal. What the examination ought to reveal depends on a particular buyer's skill and method of examination. Therefore, an auto mechanic purchasing a car should be responsible for the discovery of some defects that a nonexpert would not be expected to find. The circumstances of each case determine what defects a so-called reasonable inspection should reveal.

UNCONSCIONABILITY AND WARRANTY DISCLAIMERS

The Code sections dealing with warranty disclaimers do not refer specifically to unconscionability as a factor. Eventually, however, the courts will test warranty disclaimers with reference to the unconscionability standards of Section 2-302. Such things as lack of bargaining position, "take it or leave it" choices, and failure of a buyer to understand or know of a warranty disclaimer provision will become relevant to the issue of unconscionability. Note in the following pre-UCC landmark decision the court's recognition of the consumer's "bargaining" position with respect to large auto manufacturers.

HENNINGSEN v.
BLOOMFIELD
MOTORS, INC.
Supreme Court of New Jersey,
1960.
32 N.J. 358, 161 A.2d 69.

BACKGROUND AND FACTS   *This case involves the recovery of damages from an automobile manufacturer for injuries sustained by the owner and driver of a new car manufactured by Chrysler. The standard form purchase order used in the transaction contained an express warranty by which the manufacturer warranted the vehicle to be free from defects in material or workmanship. If any defects were found, the manufacturer promised to correct them without cost to the purchaser for a ninety-day period or four thousand miles, whichever occurred first. In addition, the purchase order contained a disclaimer in fine* print, *of any and all other express or implied warranties. The disclaimer purported to absolve Chrysler and the dealer from all liability for the implied warranty of merchantability against injuries suffered. The standard form purchase order became part of the Chrysler contract when a consumer purchased an automobile. Hence, the express warranty that was offered instead of all other warranties, express or implied, was intended to provide the limits of Chrysler's liability.*

FRANCIS, Justice.
*   *   *   *

Plaintiff Claus H. Henningsen purchased a Plymouth automobile, manufactured by defendant Chrysler Corporation, from defendant Bloomfield Motors, Inc. His wife, plaintiff Helen Henningsen, was injured while driving it and instituted suit against both defendants to recover damages on account of her injuries. *   *   * The complaint was predicated upon breach of express and implied warranties and upon negligence.
*   *   *

The facts are not complicated, but a general outline of them is necessary to an understanding of the case.
*   *   *   *

The new Plymouth was turned over to the Henningsens on May 9, 1955. *   *   * It had no servicing and no mishaps of any kind before the event of May 19. That day, Mrs. Henningsen drove to Asbury Park. On the way down and in returning the car performed in normal fashion until the accident occurred. She was proceeding north on Route 36 in Highlands, New Jersey, at 20–22 miles per hour. The highway was paved and smooth, and contained two lanes for north-bound travel. She was riding in the right-hand lane. Suddenly she heard a loud noise "from the bottom, by the hood." It "felt as if something cracked." The steering wheel spun in her hands; the car veered sharply to the right and crashed into a highway sign and a brick wall. No other vehicle was in any way involved. A bus operator driving in the left-hand lane testified that he observed plaintiff's car approaching in normal fashion in the opposite direction; "all of a sudden [it] veered at 90 degrees *   *   * and right into this wall." As a result of the impact, the front of the car was so badly damaged that it was impossible to determine if any of the parts of the steering wheel mechanism or workmanship or assembly were defective or improper prior to the accident. The condition was such that the collision insurance carrier, after inspection, declared the vehicle a total loss. It had 468 miles on the speedometer at the time.

I.
The Claim of Implied Warranty against the Manufacturer.

In the ordinary case of sale of goods by description an implied warranty of merchantability is an integral part of the transaction. If the buyer, expressly or by implication, makes known to the seller the particular purpose for which the article is required and it appears that he has relied on the seller's skill or judgment, an implied warranty arises of reasonable fitness for that purpose. The former type of warranty simply means that the thing sold is reasonably fit for the general purpose for which it is manufactured and sold. *   *   *
*   *   *   *

Of course such sales, whether oral or written, may be accompanied by an express warranty. *   *   * [A]ny affirmation of fact relating to the goods is an express warranty if the natural tendency of the statement is to induce the buyer to make the purchase.
*   *   *   *

*   *   * [A] question of first importance to be decided is whether an implied warranty of merchantability by Chrysler Corporation accompanied the sale of the automobile to Claus Henningsen.
*   *   *   *

Chrysler points out that an implied warranty of merchantability is an incident of a contract of sale. It concedes, of course, the making of the original sale to Bloomfield Motors, Inc., but maintains that this transaction marked the terminal point of its contractual connection with the car. Then Chrysler urges that since it was not a party to the sale by the dealer to Henningsen, there is no privity of contract between it and the plaintiffs, and the absence of this privity eliminates any such implied warranty.

* * * *

Under modern conditions the ordinary layman, on responding to the importuning of colorful advertising, has neither the opportunity nor the capacity to inspect or to determine the fitness of an automobile for use; he must rely on the manufacturer who has control of its construction, and to some degree on the dealer who, to the limited extent called for by the manufacturer's instructions, inspects and services it before delivery. In such a marketing milieu his remedies and those of persons who properly claim through him should not depend "upon the intricacies of the law of sales. The obligation of the manufacturer should not be based alone on privity of contract."

* * *

Accordingly, we hold that under modern marketing conditions, when a manufacturer puts a new automobile in the stream of trade and promotes its purchase by the public, an implied warranty that it is reasonably suitable for use as such accompanies it into the hands of the ultimate purchaser. [Emphasis added.] Absence of agency between the manufacturer and the dealer who makes the ultimate sale is immaterial.

II.

The Effect of the Disclaimer and Limitation of Liability Clauses on the Implied Warranty of Merchantability.

* * * In a society such as ours, where the automobile is a common and necessary adjunct of daily life, and where its use is so fraught with danger to the driver, passengers and the public, the manufacturer is under a special obligation in connection with the construction, promotion and sale of his cars. Consequently, the courts must examine purchase agreements closely to see if consumer and public interests are treated fairly.

What influence should these circumstances have on the restrictive effect of Chrysler's express warranty in the framework of the purchase contract? As we have said, *warranties originated in the law to safeguard the buyer and not to limit the liability of the seller or manufacturer.* [Emphasis added.] * * * But does the doctrine that a person is bound by his signed agreement, in the absence of fraud, stand in the way of any relief?

* * * *

The traditional contract is the result of free bargaining of parties who are brought together by the play of the market, and who meet each other on a footing of approximate economic equality. * * * But in present-day commercial life the standardized mass contract has appeared. It is used primarily by enterprises with strong bargaining power and position. * * *

* * * *

The warranty before us is a standardized form designed for mass use. It is imposed upon the automobile consumer. He takes it or leaves it, and he must take it to buy an automobile. No bargaining is engaged in with respect to it. In fact, the dealer through whom it comes to the buyer is without authority to alter it; his function is ministerial— simply to deliver it. The form warranty is not only standard with Chrysler but, as mentioned above, it is the uniform warranty of the Automobile Manufacturers Association. * * *

The gross inequality of bargaining position occupied by the consumer in the automobile industry is thus apparent. * * *

* * * *

* * * Courts keep in mind the principle that the best interests of society demand that persons should not be unnecessarily restricted in their freedom to contract. But they do not hesitate to declare void as against public policy contractual provisions which clearly tend to the injury of the public in some way.

* * * *[W]e are of the opinion that Chrysler's attempted disclaimer of an implied warranty of merchantability and of the obligations arising therefrom is so inimical to the public good as to compel an adjudication of its invalidity.* [Emphasis added.]
* * * *

III.
The Dealer's Implied Warranty.

The principles that have been expounded as to the obligation of the manufacturer apply with equal force to the separate express warranty of the dealer. This is so, irrespective of the absence of the relationship of principal and agent between these defendants, because the manufacturer and the Association establish the warranty policy for the industry. The bargaining position of the dealer is inextricably bound by practice to that of the maker and the purchaser must take or leave the automobile, accompanied and encumbered as it is by the uniform warranty.
* * * *

For the reasons set forth in Part I hereof, *we conclude that the disclaimer of an implied warranty of merchantability by the dealer, as well as the attempted elimination of all obligations other than replacement of defective parts, are violative of public policy and void.* [Emphasis added.]

The court upheld the right of the plaintiffs, the Henningsens, to recover damages for injuries notwithstanding the attempted warranty disclaimer on the part of the defendants, Chrysler Corporation and Bloomfield Motors, Inc.

DECISION AND REMEDY

MAGNUSON-MOSS WARRANTY ACT

The Magnuson-Moss Warranty Act was designed to prevent deception in warranties by making them easier to understand.[3] The Magnuson-Moss Warranty Act is mainly enforced by the Federal Trade Commission (FTC). Additionally, the attorney general or a consumer who has been injured can enforce the act if informal procedures for settling disputes prove to be ineffective. The Magnuson-Moss Warranty Act modifies UCC warranty rules to some extent where *consumer* sales transactions are involved. However, the UCC remains the primary codification of warranty rules for industrial and commercial transactions.

No seller is *required* to give a written warranty for consumer goods sold under the Warranty Act. But if a seller chooses to make an express written warranty, and the cost of the consumer goods is more than $10, the warranty must be labeled as "full" or "limited." In addition, if the cost of the goods is

more than $15 (FTC regulation), the warrantor is required to make certain disclosures fully and conspicuously in a single document in "readily understood language." This disclosure states the names and addresses of the warrantor(s), what specifically is warranted, procedures for enforcement of the warranty, any limitations on warranty relief, and that the buyer has legal rights.

Although a *full warranty* may not cover every aspect of the consumer product sold, what it covers insures some type of buyer satisfaction in case the product is defective. Full warranty requires free repair or replacement of any defective part; if it cannot be repaired within a reasonable time, the consumer has the choice of either a refund or a replacement without charge. The full warranty frequently does not have a time limit on it. Any limitation on consequential damages must be *conspicuously* stated. Also, the warrantor need not perform warranty services if the problem with the product was caused by damage to the product or unreasonable use by the consumer.

A *limited warranty* arises when the written warranty fails to meet one of the minimum requirements for a full warranty. The fact that a seller is

---

3. 15 U.S.C.A., Sections 2301-12.

CONCEPT SUMMARY: Warranties Under the UCC

TYPE OF WARRANTY	HOW CREATED	POSSIBLE DEFENSES

Warranty of Title
UCC 2-312
	1. Upon transfer of title, the seller warrants—
	  a. the right to pass good and rightful title,
	  b. that the goods are free from unstated liens or encumbrances,
	  c. (merchant) the goods are free from infringement claims.
		1. Exclusion or modified only by specific language or circumstances. UCC 2-312(2)

Express Warranty UCC 2-313	As part of a sale or bargain— 1. An affirmation of fact or promise. 2. A sale by description. 3. A sample shown as conforming to bulk.	1. Opinion. 2. Exclusion or limitation. UCC 2-316(1) 3. No statement by seller.
Warranty of Merchantability UCC 2-314	1. Where the seller is a merchant, and 2. Goods are properly packaged and labeled, of proper quality, and fit for ordinary use or resale.	1. Specific disclaimer—can be oral or in writing, but must mention "merchantability" and if in writing must be conspicuous. UCC 2-316(2) 2. Sales stated "as is" or "with all faults." UCC 2-316(3)(a) 3. If there is an examination by the buyer, the buyer is bound by all defects found, or which should have been found, or if the buyer refuses or fails to examine, the buyer is bound by patent defects. UCC 2-316(3)(b) 4. Course of dealing, performance, or usage of trade. UCC 2-316(3)(c)
Warranty of Fitness for a Particular Purpose UCC 2-315	1. The buyer's purpose or use must expressly or impliedly be known by the seller, and 2. The buyer must purchase in reliance of the seller's selection.	1. Specific disclaimer—must be in writing and be conspicuous. "There are no warranties which extend beyond the description on the face hereof." UCC 2-316(2) 2. Same as merchantability (2–4) above.
Implied Warranty Arising from Course of Dealing or Trade Usage UCC 2-314(3)	1. By prior dealings and/or custom of trade.	1. Exclusion by specific language or as provided under UCC 2-316.

giving only a limited warranty must be conspicuously designated. If it is only a time limitation that distinguishes a limited warranty from a full warranty, then the Warranty Act allows the seller to indicate it as a full warranty by such language as "full 12-month warranty."

Creating an express warranty under the Warranty Act differs from creating one under the UCC.[4]

1. An express warranty is *any written promise* or *affirmation of fact* made by the seller to a consumer indicating the quality or performance of the product and affirming or promising that the product is either free of defects or will meet a specific level of performance over a period of time. For example, "this watch will not lose more than one second a year."

2. An express warranty is a written agreement to refund, repair, or replace the product if it fails to meet written specifications. This is typically a service contract.

Implied warranties do not arise under the Magnuson-Moss Warranty Act. They continue to be created according to the UCC provisions. Where an express warranty is made in a sales contract or a combined sales and service contract (where the service contract is undertaken within ninety days of the sale), the Magnuson-Moss Warranty Act prevents sellers from disclaiming or modifying the implied warranties of merchantability and fitness for a particular purpose. However, sellers can impose a time limit on the duration of an implied warranty, but such time limit has to correspond to the duration of the express warranty.[5]

---

4. For example, express warranties created by description or sample or model will continue to be governed under UCC provisions because only written promises or affirmations of fact are covered by the Magnuson-Moss Warranty Act.

5. The time limit on an implied warranty occurring by virtue of the seller's express warranty must, of course, be reasonable, conscionable, and set forth in clear and conspicuous language on the face of the warranty.

QUESTIONS AND CASE PROBLEMS

1. Beyer contracts to purchase a used car from Johnson's Quality Used Cars. During the oral negotiations for the sale, Johnson told Beyer that this used car was in "A-1 condition" and would get sixteen miles to the gallon. Beyer asked if the car used oil. Johnson replied that he had personally checked the car, and in his opinion the car did not use oil. After delivery, Beyer has used the car for one month (400 miles of driving) and is unhappy with it. The car needs numerous repairs, does not get sixteen miles to the gallon, and has used two quarts of oil. Beyer claims Johnson is in breach of express warranties as to the condition of the car, gas mileage, and oil use. Johnson claims no express warranties were made. Discuss who is correct.

2. Beyer is a farmer who needs to place a 2,000 pound piece of equipment in his barn. This will require lifting the equipment 30 feet up into a hayloft. Beyer goes to Davidson Hardware and tells Davidson that he needs some heavy-duty rope to be used on his farm. Davidson recommends a one-inch thick nylon rope, and Beyer purchases 200 feet of the rope. Beyer ties the rope around the piece of equipment and puts it through a pulley, and, with a tractor, lifts the equipment off the ground. Suddenly the rope breaks. In the crash to the ground the

equipment is severely damaged. Beyer files suit against Davidson for breach of implied warranty of fitness. Discuss how successful Beyer will be with his suit.

3. Beyer purchases a new car from Smith Motors. The retail installment contract states immediately above the buyer's signature in large, bold type, "There are no warranties that extend beyond the description on the face hereof" and "There are no express warranties that accompany this sale unless expressly written in this contract." In purchasing the car, Beyer specifically informed Smith's salesperson that he wanted a car that could be driven in a dusty area without needing mechanical repairs. Smith's salesperson said to Beyer, "Nothing will go wrong with this car, but if it does, return it to us, and we will repair it without cost to you." Neither this statement nor any similar to it appears in the retail sales contract. Beyer drives the car into a dust storm. The air filter gets plugged up and the car engine overheats, causing motor damage. Smith refuses to repair the engine under any warranty. Beyer claims Smith is liable for breach of the implied warranty of fitness, that such cannot be disclaimed because of the Magnuson-Moss Warranty Act, and that there is a breach of the salesperson's express warranty. Discuss Beyer's claims.

4. Sallor has a used television set that she wishes to sell. Beyer contracts to purchase the set. At the time of the making of the contract, Sallor demands that Beyer inspect the set to be sure it is exactly what he wants. Beyer tells Sallor that he does not have the time to do so. The set is delivered and paid for. Beyer, upon using the set, discovers

that the picture has a tendency to "jump" and that the vertical control does not always correct that tendency. The cost to repair the set is $50. Beyer claims that the set is neither merchantable nor fit for its purpose. Sallor claims no liability. Discuss who is correct.

5. John buys a one-karat diamond ring from Shady Sallor for $500. John is assured by Shady that the ring belonged to his deceased mother and that the only reason the price is so low is that he is behind in making payments on his car. John has no reason to believe differently. Beyer, a neighbor, admires the ring and offers to purchase it for $1,000. John agrees to sell the ring to Beyer, stating that he is transferring only such right and title as he has. Two months later, the police confiscate the ring as property stolen in a burglary of Owen's home. Beyer seeks to hold John liable. Discuss Beyer's action under warranty laws.

6. Myrtle Carpenter purchased hair dye from a drugstore. The use of the dye caused an adverse skin reaction. She sued the local drugstore and the manufacturer of the dye, Alberto Culver Company. She claimed that a sales clerk indicated that several of Myrtle's friends had used the product and that their hair came out "very nice." The clerk purportedly also told Myrtle that she would get very fine results. On the package, there were cautionary instructions telling the user to make a preliminary skin test to determine if the user was susceptible in any unusual way to the product. Myrtle stated that she did not make the preliminary skin test. Did the seller make an express warranty about the hair dye? [Carpenter v. Alberto Culver Co., 28 Mich. App. 399, 184 N.W. 2d 547 (1970)]

7. McCarty purchased four tires from a Korvette store. The sales invoice clearly stated that the tires were guaranteed for 36,000 miles against all road hazards, including blowouts, when the tires were used in normal, noncommercial passenger car service. One of the rear tires on McCarty's car blew out. The car swerved and turned over. McCarty and his wife were injured, and the car was severely damaged. McCarty claimed that the clause in the sales invoice was an express warranty against blowouts. Was it? [McCarty v. E. J. Korvette, Inc., 28 Md. App. 421, 347 A. 2d 253 (1975)]

8. In July 1959, McMeekin purchased a lawn mower from Gimbel Brothers. In June of 1960, while McMeekin was mowing his lawn, his son was struck in the eye by an unknown object and subsequently lost sight in the eye. In a suit filed by McMeekin on behalf of his son against Gimbels, McMeekin sought recovery on the theory that Gimbels had breached its warranty of merchantability. McMeekin claimed that "somehow, part of the lawn mower broke off and flew into my son's eye." Can McMeekin recover? [McMeekin v. Gimbel Brothers, Inc., 223 F. Supp. 896 (W.D. Pa. 1963)]

9. Barton sells plastic auxiliary fuel tanks for diesel-powered passenger cars. Barton approaches Tra-Mo, Inc., a plastic manufacturer, about the possibility of Tra-Mo producing tanks from a less expensive material than Barton has used in the past. Tra-Mo suggests using high-density polyethylene and demonstrates the strength by using water tanks made of the material. Tra-Mo also produced five to eight tanks from Barton's molds and subjected them to strength tests. Barton, impressed by Tra-Mo's demonstration, entered into an agreement to purchase over 2000 tanks. After delivery, approximately 600 of these tanks bulged, split or shattered under normal use. Is Tra-Mo liable for breach of express warranty by sample or model? Explain. [Barton v. Tra-Mo, Inc., 69 Or. App. 295, 686 P. 2d 423 (1984)]

10. A disclaimer of the implied warranty of fitness must be in writing and must be conspicuous. If the implied warranty of merchantability is to be excluded by means of a writing, it must also be conspicuous. The following paragraph appeared in a sales contract. The page contained other type of larger and smaller sizes and boldface print, but no other words on the page were printed in italics.

> The equipment covered hereby is sold subject only to the applicable manufacturer's standard printed warranty, if any, in effect at the date hereof, receipt of a copy of which is hereby acknowledged, and no other warranties, express or implied, including without limitation, the implied warranties of *merchantability and fitness for a particular purpose shall apply.*

Is this an effective disclaimer of the implied warranties according to UCC 2-316? [Dorman v. International Harvester Co., 46 Cal. App. 3d 11, 120 Cal. Rptr. 516 (1975)]

11. Robinson purchased a truck from Branch Moving and Storage Company "as it was" without inspecting the truck. Branch diligently and repeatedly advised Robinson of the risk he was taking by purchasing the unit without inspection. When the truck required a number of repairs because of defects in it, Robinson sued Branch for breach of warranty. At trial, Robinson won. Branch appealed. What was the result? [Robinson v. Branch Moving and Storage Co., 28 N.C. App. 244, 221 S.E. 2d 81 (1976)]

22

SALES
Products Liability

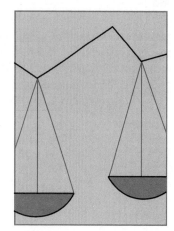

Often retailers serve simply as go-betweens, selling manufacturers' goods to consumers in prepackaged, sealed containers. Even so, retailers may be liable to purchasers on express or implied warranties despite the fact that they cannot always examine the goods prior to resale. In the past, courts frequently addressed the question of whether the injured party should recover from the manufacturer, the processor, or the retailer for damages caused by a defective product. Today, liability has been extended to manufacturers and processors through the application of new and old principles of the law.

Manufacturers and sellers of goods can be held liable to consumers, users, and bystanders for physical harm or property damage that is caused by the goods. This is called *products liability*, and it encompasses the contract theory of *warranty* and tort theories such as *negligence* and *strict liability*.

WARRANTY THEORY

Today, warranty law is an important part of the entire spectrum of laws relating to products liability. Consumers, purchasers, and even users of goods can recover *from any seller* for losses resulting from breach of implied and express warranties. A manufacturer is a *seller*. Therefore, a person who purchases goods from a retailer can recover from the retailer or manufacturer if the goods are not merchantable, because in most states *privity of contract* is no longer a prerequisite for breach-of-warranty recovery.

Since warranty laws were discussed in Chapter 21, the balance of this chapter will deal with the tort theories of recovery for damages and injuries caused by defective products.

LIABILITY BASED ON NEGLIGENCE

Chapter 4 defined *negligence* as failure to use that degree of care that a reasonable, prudent person would have used under the circumstances. The failure to exercise reasonable care under the circumstances that cause an injury is the basis of liability for negligence. Thus, the manufacturer of a product must exercise "due care" to make that product safe to be used as it was intended. Due care must be exercised in designing the product, in selecting the materials, in using the appropriate production process, in assembling and testing the product, and in

383

placing adequate warnings on the label informing the user of dangers of which an ordinary person might not be aware. The duty of care extends to the inspection and testing of purchased products used in the final product sold by the manufacturer. The failure to exercise due care is negligence.

In the following landmark case, the New York court dealt with the liability of a manufacturer who failed to exercise reasonable care in manufacturing a finished product.

MacPHERSON v. BUICK MOTOR CO.

Court of Appeals of New York, 1916.

111 N.E. 1050, 217 N.Y. 382.

BACKGROUND AND FACTS   *The MacPherson case is the classic negligence case in which privity of contract was not required between the plaintiff and the defendant to establish liability. This is a forerunner to products liability, although it does not use products liability theory. Its subject matter, defectively manufactured wooden wheels for automobiles, is dated, but the principles involved are not.*

The defendant, Buick Motor Company, was sued by Donald C. MacPherson, the plaintiff, who suffered injuries while riding in a Buick automobile that suddenly collapsed because one of the wheels was made of defective wood. The spokes crumbled into fragments, throwing MacPherson out of the vehicle and injuring him.

The wheel itself had not been made by Buick Motor Company; it had been bought from another manufacturer. There was evidence, however, that the defects could have been discovered by reasonable inspection and that such an inspection had not taken place. Although there was no charge that Buick knew of the defect and willfully concealed it, MacPherson charged Buick with negligence for putting a human life in imminent danger.

Keep in mind that MacPherson sued the manufacturer directly, despite the fact that the automobile was purchased from a retail Buick dealer.

CARDOZO, Justice.
 *   *   *   *

The question to be determined is whether the defendant owed a duty of care and vigilance to any one but the immediate purchaser.

The foundations of this branch of the law, at least in this state, were laid in *Thomas v. Winchester*, 6 N.Y. 397, 57 Am.Dec. 455. A poison was falsely labeled. The sale was made to a druggist, who in turn sold to a customer. The customer recovered damages from the seller who affixed the label. "The defendant's negligence," it was said, "put human life in imminent danger." A poison, falsely labeled, is likely to injure any one who gets it. *Because the danger is to be foreseen, there is a duty to avoid the injury.* [Emphasis added.] *   *   * *Thomas v. Winchester* became quickly a landmark of the law. In the application of its principle there may, at times, have been uncertainty or even error. There has never in this state been doubt or disavowal of the principle itself. *   *   *

These early cases suggest a narrow construction of the rule. Later cases, however, evince a more liberal spirit. First in importance is *Devlin v. Smith*, 89 N.Y. 470, 42 Am.Rep. 311. The defendant, a contractor, built a scaffold for a painter. The painter's servants were injured. The contractor was held liable. He knew that the scaffold, if improperly constructed, was a most dangerous trap. He knew that it was to be used by the workmen. He was building it for that very purpose. Building it for their use, he owed them a duty, irrespective of his contract with their master, to build it with care.

From *Devlin v. Smith* we *   *   * turn to the latest case in this court in which Thomas v. Winchester was followed. That case is *Statler v. Ray Mfg. Co.*, 195 N.Y. 478, 480, 88 N.E. 1063. The defendant manufactured a large coffee urn. It was installed in a restaurant. When heated, the urn exploded and injured the plaintiff. We held that the manufacturer was liable. We said that the urn "was of such a character inherently that, when applied to the purposes for which it was designed, it was liable to become a source of great danger to many people if not carefully and properly constructed."

It may be that *Devlin v. Smith* and *Statler v. Ray Mfg. Co.* have extended the rule of *Thomas v. Winchester*. If so, this court is committed to the extension. The defendant argues that things imminently dangerous to life are poisons, explosives, deadly weapons—things whose normal function it is to injure or destroy. But whatever the rule in *Thomas v. Winchester* may once have been, it has no longer that restricted meaning. A scaffold (*Devlin v. Smith*, supra) is not inherently a destructive instrument. It becomes destructive only if imperfectly constructed. A large coffee urn (*Statler v. Ray Mfg. Co.*, supra) may have within itself, if negligently made, the potency of danger, yet no one thinks of it as an implement whose normal function is destruction. * * * * * * *

We hold, then, that the principle of *Thomas v. Winchester* is not limited to poisons, explosives, and things of like nature, to things which in their normal operation are implements of destruction. If the nature of a thing is such that it is reasonably certain to place life and limb in peril when negligently made, it is then a thing of danger. Its nature gives warning of the consequences to be expected. If to the element of danger there is added knowledge that the thing will be used by persons other than the purchaser, and used without new tests, then, irrespective of contract, the manufacturer of this thing of danger is under a duty to make it carefully. * * * It is possible to use almost anything in a way that will make it dangerous if defective. That is not enough to charge the manufacturer with a duty independent of his contract. * * * There must also be knowledge that in the usual course of events the danger will be shared by others than the buyer. Such knowledge may often be inferred from the nature of the transaction. But it is possible that even knowledge of the danger and of the use will not always be enough. The proximity or remoteness of the relation is a factor to be considered. We are dealing now with the liability of the manufacturer of the finished product, who puts it on the market to be used without inspection by his customers. If he is negligent, where danger is to be foreseen, a liability will follow.

We are not required, at this time, to say that it is legitimate to go back of the manufacturer of the finished product and hold the manufacturers of the component parts. To make their negligence a cause of imminent danger, an independent cause must often intervene; the manufacturer of the finished product must also fail in his duty of inspection. It may be that in those circumstances the negligence of the earlier members of the series is too remote to constitute, as to the ultimate user, an actionable wrong. * * * There is here no break in the chain of cause and effect. In such circumstances, the presence of a known danger, attendant upon a known use, makes vigilance a duty. * * *

From this survey of the decisions, there thus emerges a definition of the duty of a manufacturer which enables us to measure this defendant's liability. Beyond all question, the nature of an automobile gives warning of probable danger if its construction is defective. This automobile was designed to go 50 miles an hour. Unless its wheels were sound and strong, injury was almost certain. It was as much a thing of danger as a defective engine for a railroad. The defendant knew the danger. It knew also that the car would be used by persons other than the buyer. This was apparent from its size; there were seats for three persons. It was apparent also from the fact that the buyer was a dealer in cars, who bought to resell. The maker of this car supplied it for the use of purchasers from the dealer just as plainly as the contractor in *Devlin v. Smith* supplied the scaffold for use by the servants of the owner. * * * * * * *

It is true that * * * "an automobile is not an inherently dangerous vehicle." * * * The meaning is that danger is not to be expected when the vehicle is well constructed. The court left it to the jury to say whether the defendant ought to have foreseen that the car, if negligently constructed, would become "imminently dangerous." Subtle distinctions are drawn by the defendants between things inherently dangerous and things imminently dangerous, but the case does not turn upon these verbal niceties. If danger was to be expected as reasonably certain, there was a duty of vigilance, and this whether you call the danger inherent or imminent. *   *   *

We think the defendant was not absolved from a duty of inspection because it bought the wheels from a reputable manufacturer. It was not merely a dealer in automobiles. It was a manufacturer of automobiles. It was responsible for the finished product. It was not at liberty to put the finished product on the market without subjecting the component parts to ordinary and simple tests. *   *   * The obligation to inspect must vary with the nature of the thing to be inspected. The more probable the danger the greater the need of caution.

DECISION AND REMEDY *The New York Court of Appeals, the highest court in the New York state system, affirmed the judgment of the original trial court and the intermediate review court that the defendant, Buick Motor Company, was liable to Donald C. MacPherson for the injuries he sustained when he was thrown from the vehicle.*

COMMENTS *This case has been interpreted to cover all articles that imperil life whenever negligently made. Prior to* MacPherson, *manufacturers escaped liability to consumers whenever their contractual dealings were with middlemen or retailers. Since* MacPherson, *that is no longer the case.*

Privity of Contract Not Required

An action based upon negligence does not require privity of contract between the injured plaintiff and the negligent defendant-manufacturer. Section 395 of the Restatement, Second, Torts states:

A manufacturer who fails to exercise reasonable care in the manufacture of a chattel [movable good] which, unless carefully made, he should recognize as involving an unreasonable risk of causing substantial bodily harm to those who lawfully used it for a purpose for which it was manufactured and to those whom the supplier should expect to be in the vicinity of its probable use, is subject to liability for bodily harm caused to them by its lawful use in a manner and for a purpose for which it is manufactured.

Simply stated, a manufacturer is liable for its failure to exercise due care to any person who sustained an injury proximately caused by a negligently made (defective) product regardless of whether there was a sale or contract to sell.

Defenses to Negligence

Any manufacturer, seller, or processor who can prove due care was used in the manufacture of its product has an appropriate defense against a negligence suit, since failure to exercise due care is one of the major elements of negligence.

But there are other defenses, and their use and application vary from state to state. One area of variation is the tying of the breach (failure to exercise reasonable care) to the injury, referred to as causation (see Chapter 4). Numerous events, involving different people, take place between the time a product is manufactured and the time of its use. Thus, if any of these events can be shown to have caused or contributed to the injury, the manufacturer will claim no liability on the basis of this intervening cause.

Two other defenses are contributory negligence and, where recognized, assumption of risk (both also discussed in Chapter 4). For example, assume a person used a lotion on her or his body, knowing that the ingredients of that lotion would cause the skin to blister. The plaintiff files suit claiming that the manufacturer was negligent in failing to warn of the possibility of blisters on the label. The manufacturer-defendant would claim that the plaintiff's own knowledge of the risk and voluntary use of the product with such knowledge was an unreasonable assumption of risk and was the proximate cause of the injury.

Likewise, any time a plaintiff misuses a product or fails to make a reasonable effort at preserving his or her own welfare, the manufacturer or seller will claim that the plaintiff contributed to causing the injuries. The claim is that the plaintiff's negligence offsets the negligence of the manufacturer or seller. In some states, the contributory negligence of the plaintiff is an absolute defense for the defendant-manufacturer or seller. In many others, the negligence of each is compared (comparative negligence), and damages are based on the proportion of negligence attributed to the defendant.

Basis of Liability— Violation of Statutory Duty

Numerous federal and state laws impose duties upon manufacturers of cosmetics, drugs, foods, toxic substances, and flammable materials. These duties involve appropriate description of contents, labeling, branding, advertising, and selling. For example, federal statutes include the Federal Flammable Fabrics Act; the Federal Food, Drug, and Cosmetics Act; and the Federal Hazardous Substances Labeling Act. In a civil action for damages (tort), a violation of statutory duty is often held to constitute *negligence per se.*

Consider an example: Jason Manufacturing Company produces pipe fittings *specifically* for use in the construction of homes in Monroe County only. The fittings do not comply with county building codes. One of the pipe fittings bursts in a home, allowing hot water to spray on the homeowner. The homeowner can bring a negligence action for personal damages on the ground that failure to comply with the building codes is in and of itself an automatic breach of the manufacturer's duty of reasonable care. Of course, the homeowner has to show proximate cause—that is, he or she must relate the injury to the careless act.

Fraudulent and Nonfraudulent Misrepresentation

When a fraudulent misrepresentation has been made to a user or consumer, and that misrepresentation ultimately results in an injury, the basis of liability may be the tort of **fraud.** Examples are the intentional mislabeling of packaged cosmetics or the intentional concealment of a product's defects. A more interesting basis of liability is nonfraudulent mis-

representation, when a merchant *innocently* misrepresents the character or quality of goods.

A famous example involved a drug manufacturer and a victim of addiction to a prescription medicine called Talwin. The manufacturer, Winthrop Laboratories, a division of Stirling Drug, Inc., innocently indicated to the medical profession that the drug was not physically addictive. Using this information, a physician prescribed the drug for his patient, who developed an addiction that turned out to be fatal. Even though the addiction was a highly unusual reaction resulting from the victim's highly unusual susceptibility to this product, the drug company was still held liable.[1]

THE DOCTRINE OF STRICT LIABILITY

A fairly recent development of tort law is the revival of the old doctrine of strict liability. Under this doctrine, people are liable for the results of their acts regardless of their intentions or their exercise of reasonable care. For example, a company that uses dynamite to blast for a road is strictly liable for any damages that it causes, even if it takes reasonable and prudent precautions to prevent such damages. In essence, the blasting company becomes liable for any personal injuries it causes and thus is an absolute insurer.

The English courts accepted the doctrine of strict liability for many years. Often persons whose conduct resulted in the injury of another were held liable for damages, even if they had not intended to injure anyone and had exercised reasonable care. This approach was abandoned around 1800 in favor of the *fault* approach in which an action was considered tortious only if it was wrongful or blameworthy in some respect.

Strict liability was reapplied to manufactured goods in several landmark cases in the 1960s and has since become a common method of holding manufacturers liable. Basically, if the purchaser of a product is injured through use of the product, that person can show a cause of action against the manufacturer by proving (1) that the product was defective, (2) that the defect made the product unreasonably dan-

---

1. Crocker v. Winthrop Laboratories, Div. of Stirling Drugs, Inc., 514 S.W.2d 429 (Tex. 1974).

gerous, and (3) that the defect was the proximate cause of the injury.

The Restatement of Torts

The Restatement, Second, Torts designates how the doctrine of strict products liability should be applied. It is a precise and widely accepted statement of the liabilities of sellers of goods (including manufacturers) and deserves close attention. Section 402A of Restatement, Second, Torts states:

(1) One who sells any product in a defective condition unreasonably dangerous to the user or consumer or to his property is subject to liability for physical harm thereby caused to the ultimate user or consumer or to his property, if
    (a) the seller is engaged in the business of selling such a product, and
    (b) it is expected to and does reach the user or consumer without substantial change in the condition in which it is sold.
(2) The rule stated in Subsection (1) applies although
    (a) the seller has exercised all possible care in the preparation and sale of his product, and

(b) the user or consumer has not bought the product from or entered into any contractual relation with the seller.

Thus, liability is imposed by law as a matter of public policy. It does not depend on privity of contract or on proof of negligence. The manufacturer's liability to an injured party is virtually unlimited.[2] The injured party does not have to be the buyer or a third party beneficiary, as required under contract warranty theory. [UCC 2-318] Indeed, this type of liability in law is not governed by the provisions of the UCC.

An important case that started the trend toward strict liability involved the use of a power tool.

---

2. Some states have enacted what are called statutes of repose. Basically, these statutes provide that after a specific statutory period of time from date of manufacture or sale, a plaintiff is precluded from pursuing a cause of action for injuries or damages sustained from a product, even though the product is defective. States such as Illinois, Indiana, Alabama, Tennessee, Florida, and Nebraska are illustrative.

GREENMAN v. YUBA POWER PRODUCTS, INC.

Supreme Court of California, 1962.
27 Cal.Rptr. 697, 377 P.2d 897.

BACKGROUND AND FACTS *California was the first state to impose strict liability in tort on manufacturers. In this landmark decision, the California Supreme Court sets out the reasons for applying tort law rather than contract law to cases in which a consumer is injured by a defective product.*

TRAYNOR, Justice.
* * * *

Plaintiff brought this action for damages against the retailer and the manufacturer of a Shopsmith, a combination power tool that could be used as a saw, drill, and wood lathe. He saw a Shopsmith demonstrated by the retailer and studied a brochure prepared by the manufacturer. He decided he wanted a Shopsmith for his home workshop, and his wife bought and gave him one for Christmas in 1955. In 1957 he bought the necessary attachments to use the Shopsmith as a lathe for turning a large piece of wood he wished to make into a chalice. After he had worked on the piece of wood several times without difficulty, it suddenly flew out of the machine and struck him on the forehead, inflicting serious injuries. About ten and a half months later, he gave the retailer and the manufacturer written notice of claimed breaches of warranties and filed a complaint against them alleging such breaches and negligence.
* * * *

Plaintiff introduced substantial evidence that his injuries were caused by defective design and construction of the Shopsmith. His expert witnesses testified that inadequate set screws were used to hold parts of the machine together so that normal vibration caused the tailstock of the lathe to move away from the piece of wood being turned permitting it to fly out of the lathe. They also testified that there were other more positive ways of fastening the parts of the machine together, the use of which would have prevented the accident. The jury could therefore reasonably have concluded that the manufacturer negligently constructed the Shopsmith. The jury could also reasonably have concluded that statements in the manufacturer's brochure were untrue, that they constituted express warranties, and that plaintiff's injuries were caused by their breach.

The manufacturer contends, however, that plaintiff did not give it notice of breach of warranty within a reasonable time and that therefore his cause of action for breach of warranty is barred *   *   *.

*   *   *   *

[The California Sales Act] does not provide that notice must be given of the breach of a warranty that arises independently of a contract of sale between the parties. Such warranties are not imposed by the sales act, but are the product of common-law decisions that have recognized them in a variety of situations. It is true that in many of these situations the court has invoked the sales act definitions of warranties in defining the defendant's liability, but it has done so, not because the statutes so required, but because they provided appropriate standards for the court to adopt under the circumstances presented.

The notice requirement is not an appropriate one for the court to adopt in actions by injured consumers against manufacturers with whom they have not dealt. *   *   * We conclude, therefore, that even if plaintiff did not give timely notice of breach of warranty to the manufacturer, his cause of action based on the representations contained in the brochure was not barred.

Moreover, to impose strict liability on the manufacturer under the circumstances of this case, it was not necessary for plaintiff to establish an express warranty *   *   *. A manufacturer is strictly liable in tort when an article he places on the market, knowing that it is to be used without inspection for defects, proves to have a defect that causes injury to a human being. Recognized first in the case of unwholesome food products, such liability has now been extended to a variety of other products that create as great or greater hazards if defective.

*   *   *   [The] theory of an express or implied warranty running from the manufacturer to the plaintiff, the abandonment of the requirement of a contract between them, the recognition that the liability is not assumed by agreement but imposed by law, and the refusal to permit the manufacturer to define the scope of its own responsibility for defective products make clear that the liability is not one governed by the law of contract warranties but by the law of strict liability in tort. Accordingly, rules defining and governing warranties that were developed to meet the needs of commercial transactions cannot properly be invoked to govern the manufacturer's liability to those injured by their defective products unless those rules also serve the purposes for which such liability is imposed.

*   *   * The purpose of such liability is to insure that the costs of injuries resulting from defective products are borne by the manufacturers that put such products on the market rather than by the injured persons who are powerless to protect themselves. Sales warranties serve this purpose fitfully at best. In the present case, for example, plaintiff was able to plead and prove an express warranty only because he read and relied on the representations of the Shopsmith's ruggedness contained in the manufacturer's brochure. Implicit in the machine's presence on the market, however, was a representation that it would safely do the jobs for which it was built. Under these circumstances, it should not be controlling whether plaintiff selected the machine because of the statements in the brochure, or because of the machine's own appearance of excellence that belied the defect lurking beneath the surface, or because he merely assumed that it would safely do the jobs it was built to do. It should not be controlling whether the details of the sales from manufacturer to retailer and from retailer to plaintiff's wife were such that one or more of the implied warranties of the sales act arose. "The remedies of injured consumers ought not to be made to depend upon the intricacies of the law of sales." To establish the manufacturer's liability it was sufficient

that plaintiff proved that he was injured while using the Shopsmith in a way it was intended to be used as a result of a defect in design and manufacture of which plaintiff was not aware that made the Shopsmith unsafe for its intended use.

DECISION   *The jury verdict for the plaintiff was upheld.*
AMD REMEDY

Requirements of Strict Products Liability

The six basic requirements of strict products liability are:

1. The defendant must sell the product in a defective condition.
2. The defendant must normally be engaged in the business of selling that product.
3. The product must be unreasonably dangerous to the user or consumer because of its defective condition.[3]
4. The plaintiff must incur physical harm to self or property by use or consumption of the product.

---

3. This element is no longer required in some states, for example, California.

5. The defective condition must be the proximate cause of the injury or damage.
6. The goods must not have been substantially changed from the time the product was sold to the time the injury was sustained.

Thus, in any action against a manufacturer or seller, the plaintiff does not have to show why or in what manner the product became defective. The plaintiff does, however, have to show that at the time the injury was sustained, the condition of the product was essentially the same as it was when it left the hands of the defendant manufacturer or seller.

In the following case, the question of strict liability comes into play. The court attempts to answer the question of whether the product was manufactured in such a way that it would become unreasonably dangerous.

ROGERS v. UNIMAC COMPANY, INC.

Supreme Court of Arizona, 1977.
115 Ariz. 304, 565 P.2d 181.

BACKGROUND AND FACTS   *Plaintiff Rogers, a car wash employee, brought this action against the manufacturer of a commercial washer-extractor machine (an appliance used for drying towels). When the lid of the machine was raised, a mechanical brake stopped the spinning basket. The extractor also had a timer that stopped the basket at a pre-set time. During peak hours, the employees used the lid-activated brake. The brake frequently failed to operate, and the employees pressed down on the rim of the spinning basket to stop its motion. In November 1972, while Rogers was attempting to stop the washer-extractor in this manner, his arm became entangled in the machine. An examination of the brake unit after the accident revealed that it had not been properly maintained. Rogers contended that the machine was defectively designed and that the manufacturer should have placed a warning on the extractor to indicate this type of hazard.*

CAMERON, Chief Justice.
*   *   *   *

The Unimac 202, when shipped to the Country Club Car Wash in 1967, was equipped with two safety features. First, a micro switch cut off the electrical current to the motor when the lid was raised. This prevented the motor from running while the lid was open. Second, raising the lid applied a mechanical brake which stopped the cylinder within ten seconds. That the Unimac Company could have adopted a different type of safety device, i.e., a lid lock, is not in itself sufficient evidence to establish defective design. Under strict liability principles, a manufacturer is required to adopt those safety devices which would prevent the product from becoming unreasonably dangerous.

We do not believe the evidence showed a defect in design which made the Unimac 202 unreasonably dangerous. The most the evidence presented by the plaintiff showed was improper maintenance and repair of the machine and not defective design. The safety features of the Unimac 202 were a reasonable preventative of injury so long as the machine was properly maintained. The manufacturer is not liable for lack of normal maintenance.

* * * *

The plaintiff * * * contends that the Unimac Company should have placed a warning on the extractor of the hazard involved in reaching into the spinning cylinder. He argues that a warning was necessary because the machine was so designed that the operator had to lift the lid to apply the brake, and was thus exposed to the spinning cylinder for at least ten seconds or longer, depending upon the condition of the brake.

The brake design of the Unimac 202 was, at the time of manufacture and is today, a common and accepted safety design. But we need not decide whether this ten-second interval was an unreasonably dangerous defect because the lack of a warning was not the proximate cause of the injury. * * *

* * * *

Furthermore, we are unwilling to impose liability upon the manufacturer of an appliance for failure to warn of those dangers which may arise because of lack of normal repair.

* * * *

A warning on the Unimac 202 extractor would not have prevented this injury. The owners and managers of the County Club Car Wash required their young employees to work with an extractor made hazardous because of lack of repair. The Unimac 202 presented no unreasonable danger of injury so long as it was properly maintained.

The judgment for the defendant-manufacturer was affirmed. Rogers was unable to prove that a defect in the product was the proximate cause of his injury.

DECISION AND REMEDY

Limitations on Recovery

Some courts have limited the application of the strict liability doctrine to cases in which personal injuries have occurred. Thus, when a defective product causes only *property damage*, the seller may not be liable under a theory of strict liability, depending on the law of the particular jurisdiction. In addition, until recently, recovery for *economic* loss was not available in an action based on strict liability (and even today this is rarely available). Note, however, that recovery for *breach of warranty* may be available, depending upon the type of injury and which alternative section of UCC 2-318 is in effect.

Lastly, statutes enacted by a number of states limit the seller's (manufacturer's) liability to injuries occurring within a specified period (for example, five to twelve years) from the date of *sale* or *manufacture* of the defective product. Therefore, it is immaterial that the product is defective or causes the injury if the injury occurs after the statutory period has lapsed. In addition, some of these legislative enactments have limited the application of the doctrine of strict liability to new goods. Some states, such as Massachusetts, have refused to recognize products liability. In these states, recovery is gained mainly via breach of warranty or negligence.

Defenses

Assumption of Risk Assumption of risk can be used as a defense in an action based on strict liability in tort. Whenever consumers or users use goods improperly under unreasonable circumstances, they assume the risk of injury. In order for such a defense to be established, the defendant must show the following basic elements (previously discussed):

1.   That the plaintiff voluntarily engaged in the risk while realizing the potential danger.
2.   That the plaintiff knew and appreciated the risk created by the defect.
3.   That the plaintiff's decision to undertake the known risk was unreasonable.

Misuse of the Product   Similar to the defense of voluntary assumption of risk is that of misuse of the

product. Here the injured party does not know that the product is dangerous for a particular use, but that use is not the one for which the product was designed. (Contrast this with assumption of risk.) This defense has been severely limited by the courts, however. Even if the injured party does not know about the inherent danger of using the product in a wrong way, if the misuse is foreseeable nonetheless, the seller must take measures to guard against it.

In the following case, the court examines the question of whether the injured party's misuse of the product was foreseeable by the manufacturer.

LANDRINE v. MEGO CORPORATION

Supreme Court, Appellate Division, 1983.
464 N.Y.S.2d 516.

BACKGROUND AND FACTS   *The plaintiff, Beverly Landrine, sued on behalf of her deceased infant daughter. The infant died after she swallowed a balloon while playing with a doll known as "Bubble Yum Baby." The doll could simulate the blowing of a bubble gum bubble by inserting a balloon, which was inflated by pumping the doll's arm, into the doll's mouth. The balloon was manufactured by the defendant, Perfect Products Co. and distributed by Mego Corporation. The plaintiff claimed that the balloon was defectively made or inherently unsafe when used by children and that the defendant failed to warn of dangers associated with the balloon's usage. The defendant moved for summary judgment, which the trial court denied, and then the defendant appealed.*

MEMORANDUM DECISION
*   *   *   *

A cause of action in strict products liability arises when a manufacturer places on the market a product which has a defect that causes injury. *   *   * "[A] defectively designed product is one which, at the time it leaves the seller's hands, is in a condition not reasonably contemplated by the ultimate consumer and is unreasonably dangerous for its intended use; that is one whose utility does not outweigh the danger inherent in its introduction into the stream of commerce." *   *   * On this record neither plaintiff nor the crossclaimants have established that the balloons were unreasonably dangerous or defectively made. Absent a finding that all balloons are inherently dangerous, and that consequently a warning of the possible dangers must be given, Perfect cannot be held liable. Balloons in and of themselves are not dangerous. Their characteristics, features, and propensities are well-known, to children and adults alike. No duty to warn exists where the intended or foreseeable use of the product is not hazardous. Furthermore, "there is no necessity to warn a customer already aware—through common knowledge or learning—of a specific hazard." *   *   * Digestion of a balloon is not an intended use, and to the extent it is a foreseeable one, it is a misuse of the product for which the guardian of children must be wary. Were it otherwise, anything capable of being swallowed would have to be kept from a child. Even if a warning were required in this case it would have had to be directed to the guardian since the "legal responsibility, if any, for injury caused by [a product] which has possible dangers incident to its use should be shouldered by the one in the best position to have eliminated those dangers." *   *   * We see no need for such a warning. The ingestion of a balloon—which is not its intended use—is an act fraught with peril. Like a caution to drive carefully when operating heavy equipment * * * a self-evident warning is unnecessary.

* * * *

The appellate court reversed the trial court and granted summary judgment to Perfect, thereby freeing it of any liability for the infant's death.

DECISION AND REMEDY

This case illustrates that a manufacturer is not an absolute insurer of the product it produces. The basic elements of strict liability must still be met; i.e., the product must be defective and unreasonably dangerous (which is the foreseeable cause of an injury or damage) when sold by a merchant.

COMMENTS

Contributory Negligence   As pointed out in Chapter 4, at common law, in any action based on negligence, contributory negligence of the injured party either completely barred recovery or reduced the amount of recovery under the rule of comparative negligence. In principle, negligence and contributory negligence are immaterial in any action based on the theory of strict liability in tort.

Recent developments in the area of comparative negligence are affecting the doctrine of strict liability. Whereas previously the plaintiff's conduct was not a defense to strict liability, today a growing number of jurisdictions consider the negligent or intentional actions of the plaintiff in the apportionment of liability and damages. This "comparing" of the plaintiff's conduct to the defendant's strict liability results in an application of the doctrine of comparative negligence. Some states which have adopted this doctrine are Texas, California, Oregon, Florida, and Hawaii.[4] Although comparative negligence in

strict liability is presently the minority view, its recent growth may indeed have a pervasive effect on this area of tort law.

Strict Liability to Bystanders

All courts extend the strict liability of manufacturers and other sellers to injured bystanders, although the drafters of Restatement, Second, Torts, Section 402A did not take a position on bystanders. For example, the manufacturer of an automobile was held liable for injuries caused by the explosion of the car's motor while in traffic. A cloud of steam that resulted from the explosion caused multiple collisions because other drivers could not see well.[5]

In the following case, the court looks at the fact that bystanders as a class are purchasers of most of the same products to which they are exposed as bystanders. Thus, someone injured by an exploding bottle in a supermarket seems to be covered by Section 402A, Restatement, Second, Torts.

---

4. Keeton, *et al.*, *Prosser and Keeton on Torts*, 5th Ed. (St. Paul: West Publishing Co., 1984), pp. 478–499, 565.

5. Giberson v. Ford Motor Co., 504 S.W.2d 8 (Mo. 1974).

BACKGROUND AND FACTS   *The plaintiff, Embs, was buying some groceries at Stamper's Cash Market. Unnoticed by her, a carton of 7-Up was sitting on the floor at the edge of the produce counter about one foot from where she was standing. Several of the 7-Up bottles exploded. Embs's leg was injured severely enough that Embs had to be taken to the hospital by a managing agent of the store. The trial court dismissed the claim. The appellate court now takes up her case.*

EMBS v. PEPSI-COLA BOTTLING CO. OF LEXINGTON, KENTUCKY, INC.

Court of Appeals of Kentucky, 1975.
528 S.W.2d 703.

LUKOWSKY, Judge.

* * * *

Our expressed public policy will be furthered if we minimize the risk of personal injury and property damage by charging the costs of injuries against the manufacturer who can procure liability insurance and distribute its expense among the public as a cost of doing business; and since the risk of harm from defective products exists for mere bystanders and passersby as well as for the purchaser or user, there is no substantial reason for protecting one class of persons and not the other. The same policy requires us to maximize protection for the injured third party and promote the public interest in discouraging the marketing of products having defects that are a menace to the public by imposing strict liability upon retailers and wholesalers in the distributive chain responsible for marketing the defective product which injures the bystander. The imposition of strict liability places no unreasonable burden upon sellers because they can adjust the cost of insurance protection among themselves in the course of their continuing business relationship.

We must not shirk from extending the rule to the manufacturer for fear that the retailer or middleman will be impaled on the sword of liability without regard to fault. Their liability was already established under Section 402A of the Restatement of Torts 2d. As a matter of public policy the retailer or middleman as well as the manufacturer should be liable since the loss for injuries resulting from defective products should be placed on those members of the marketing chain best able to pay the loss, who can then distribute such risk among themselves by means of insurance and indemnity agreements.

* * * *

The result which we reach does not give the bystander a "free ride." When products and consumers are considered in the aggregate, bystanders, as a class, purchase most of the same products to which they are exposed as bystanders. Thus, as a class, they indirectly subsidize the liability of the manufacturer, middleman and retailer and in this sense do pay for the insurance policy tied to the product.

Public policy is adequately served if parameters are placed upon the extension of the rule so that it is limited to bystanders whose injury from the defect is reasonably foreseeable.

For the sake of clarity we restate the extension of the rule. The protections of Section 402A of the Restatement, Second, Torts extend to bystanders whose injury from the defective product is reasonably foreseeable.

* * * *

It matters not that the evidence be circumstantial for as Thoreau put it "Some circumstantial evidence is very strong, as when you find a trout in the milk." There are some accidents, as where a beverage bottle explodes in the course of normal handling, as to which there is common experience that they do not ordinarily occur without a defect; and this permits the inference of a defect. This is particularly true when there is evidence in the case of the antecedent explosion of other bottles of the same product.

In cases involving multiple defendants the better reasoned view places the onus of tracing the defect on the shoulders of the dealers and the manufacturer as a policy matter, seeking to compensate the plaintiff and to require the defendants to fight out the question of responsibility among themselves.

DECISION AND REMEDY *The appellate court reversed the trial court's directed verdict that dismissed Embs's claim. The case was remanded to the lower court for a new trial.*

Crash-worthiness Doctrine

Certain courts have adopted the doctrine of crashworthiness, which imposes liability for defects in the design or construction of motor vehicles that increase the extent of injuries to passengers if an ac-

cident occurs. The doctrine holds even when the defects do not actually cause the accident.[6] By ac-

---

6. Turner v. General Motors Corp., 514 S.W.2d 497 (Texas Civ. App. 1974).

cepting the crash-worthiness doctrine, the courts reject the argument of automobile manufacturers that involving a car in a collision does not constitute "ordinary use" of a car. There are, however, strong differences of opinion among the courts on this issue.

Strict Liability of Suppliers of Component Parts and Lessors of Movable Goods

Under the rule of strict liability in tort, the basis of liability has been expanded to include suppliers of component parts and lessors of movable goods. Thus, if General Motors buys brake pads from a subcontractor and puts them in Chevrolets without changing their composition, and those pads are defective, both the supplier of the brake pads and General Motors will be held strictly liable for the damages caused by the defects.

Liability for personal injuries caused by defective goods extends to those who lease such goods. Section 408 of the Restatement, Second, Torts states that:

> One who leases a chattel as safe for immediate use is subject to liability to those whom he should expect to use the chattel, or to be endangered by its probable use, for physical harm caused by its use in a manner for which and by a person for whose use it is leased, if the lessor fails to exercise reasonable care to make it safe for such use or to disclose its actual condition to those who may be expected to use it.

Some courts have held that a leasing agreement gives rise to a contractual *implied warranty* that the leased goods will be fit for the duration of the lease. Under this view, if Hertz Rent-a-Car leases a Chevrolet that has been improperly maintained, and a passenger is injured in an accident, the passenger can sue Hertz. (Liability is based on the contract theory of warranty, not tort.)

QUESTIONS AND CASE PROBLEMS

1. Susan buys a television set manufactured by Quality TV Appliance, Inc. She is going on vacation, so she takes the set to her mother's house for her mother to use. Because the set is defective, it explodes, causing considerable damage to her mother's house. Susan's mother sues Quality for the damages to her house. Discuss under what theories Susan's mother can recover from Quality.

2. Acme Drug Company manufactures, and has placed on the market, a drug for airsickness. Beyer purchases the drug from Green's Drug Store. Beyer is going on a trip and takes two of the tablets as directed. Beyer loses consciousness because of the side effects of the drug, and he falls down a flight of stairs at the airport, breaking an arm and a leg. Acme knew of the possible side effects but did not place any warning on the label. Also, it is learned that Acme failed to meet minimum federal drug standards in the manufacture of the drug—standards that would have reduced the side effects. Beyer wants to file an action based on Acme's negligence.
   (a) Discuss Beyer's burden of proof.
   (b) Discuss how the situation would change if a warning had been placed on the package and minimum standards had been met.

3. Colt manufactures a new pistol. Firing of the pistol is dependent on an enclosed high-pressure device. The pistol has been thoroughly tested in two laboratories in the Midwest, and it has been designed and manufactured according to all known technology. Beyer purchases one of the new pistols from Smith's Gun and Rifle Emporium. When he uses the pistol in the high altitude of the Rockies, the difference in pressure causes the pistol to misfire, resulting in serious injury to Beyer. Colt can prove that all due care was used in the manufacturing process, and it refuses to pay for Beyer's injuries. Discuss Colt's liability in tort.

4. Baxter manufactures electric hair dryers. Beyer purchases a Baxter dryer from her local Ace Drug Store. Green, a friend and guest in Beyer's home, has taken a shower and wants to dry her hair. Beyer tells Green to use the new Baxter hair dryer, which Beyer has just purchased. As Green plugs in the dryer, sparks fly out from the motor and continue to do so as she operates it. Despite this, Green begins drying her hair. Suddenly, the entire dryer ignites into flames, severely burning Green's scalp. Green sues Baxter on the basis of the torts of negligence and strict liability. Baxter admits the dryer was defective but denies liability, particularly since Green did not purchase the dryer. Discuss the validity of any defense claimed by Baxter.

5. Green is standing on a street corner waiting for a ride to work. Beyer has just purchased a new car manufactured by Able Motors. Beyer is driving down the street when suddenly the steering mechanism breaks, causing Beyer to run over Green. Green suffers permanent injuries. Beyer's total income per year has never exceeded $15,000. Green files suit against Able under the theory of strict

liability in tort. Able pleads no liability because (1) due care was used in the manufacture of the car, (2) Able is not the manufacturer of the steering mechanism (Smith is), and (3) the Restatement governing strict liability applies only to users or consumers, and Green is neither. Discuss the validity of the defenses claimed by Able.

6. Ryder Truck Rental leased one of their trucks to Gagliardi Brothers, Inc. While the truck was operated by one of Gagliardi's employees in the scope of his employment, the brakes failed. The truck struck one car, which then collided with a car driven by Martin. Martin's car was damaged and she received injuries. If Martin wishes to sue Ryder, can she bring her suit under the theory of strict liability? [Martin v. Ryder Truck Rental, Inc., 353 A.2d 581 (Del. 1976)]

7. Ford Motor Company manufactured and distributed the Ford Cortina, which had only a cardboard shield separating the fuel tank from the passenger compartment. Nanda suffered severe disabling burns when the gas tank in his car exploded upon being struck in the rear by another car. In a strict liability action by Nanda against Ford Motor Company, Nanda argued that the absence of a fire wall or metal shield between the fuel tank and passenger compartment constituted an unreasonably dangerous defect in the product, and that his injuries were caused by this defect. What was the result? [Nanda v. Ford Motor Co., 509 F.2d 213 (7th Cir. 1974)]

8. Larry Colvin, an iron worker, was setting a steel truss on a concrete column while in a squatting position. He reached above his head to pull himself up and grabbed an I-beam, known as a purlin, which was eight or ten feet long and was not yet welded into place. The purlin failed to support Colvin's weight, and he fell. The plans for the building called for the purlins to be over forty feet long, but only seven were that length. The remaining purlins were substantially shorter and were welded together to serve their purpose as spacers between the trusses and the roof. The purlins were supplied by Red Steel Company. Explain whether Red Steel is strictly liable for Colvin's injury due to the short length of the purlins. [Colvin v. Robert E. McKee, Inc., 671 S.W.2d 556 (Tex.App.–Dallas 1984, writ granted)]

9. In 1961, Gillette Dairy, Inc. purchased a compressor from St. Regis Corp. for use in its dairy processing plant. In 1965 the compressor exploded, resulting in a fire that caused extensive damage to Gillette's plant. The explosion was caused by a defect in the manufacture of the pistons. Gillette sought to recover from St. Regis for damage done to the plant and for the profits it lost while the plant was closed for repairs. What was the result? [Norfolk Dev. Corp. v. St. Regis Pulp and Paper Corp., 338 F.Supp. 1213 (D.C.Neb. 1972)]

10. A two-year-old child lost his leg when he became entangled in a grain auger on his grandfather's farm. The auger had a safety guard that prevented any item larger than 4⅝ inches from coming into contact with the machine's moving parts. The child's foot was smaller than the openings in the safety guard. Was such an injury reasonably foreseeable? [Richelman v. Kewanee Machinery & Conveyor Co., 375 N.E.2d 885 (1978)]

23

COMMERCIAL PAPER
Basic Concepts of Commercial Paper

To some extent, commercial law is a reflection of customs and usages of trade in the business world. The development of the law concerning commercial paper grew from commercial necessity. As early as the thirteenth century, merchants dealing in foreign trade were using commercial paper in order to finance and conduct their affairs. Problems in transportation and in the safekeeping of gold or coins had prompted this practice. Since the king's common law courts of those times did not recognize the validity of commercial paper, the merchants had to develop their own rules governing its use, and these rules were enforced by "fair" or "borough" courts. For this reason, the early law governing commercial paper was part of the "Law Merchant." (See Chapter 17.)

Later, the Law Merchant was codified in England in the Bills of Exchange Act of 1882. In 1896, the National Conference of Commissioners on Uniform Laws drafted the Uniform Negotiable Instruments Law. This law was reviewed by the states, and by 1920 all the states had adopted it. The Uniform Negotiable Instruments Law was the forerunner of Article 3 of the Uniform Commercial Code.

Commercial paper can be defined as any written promise or order to pay a sum of money. Drafts, checks, and promissory notes are typical examples. Commercial paper is transferred more readily than ordinary contract rights, and persons who acquire it are normally subject to less risk than the ordinary assignee of a contract right.

FUNCTIONS AND PURPOSES OF COMMERCIAL PAPER

Commercial paper has two functions. It serves as a substitute for money and/or as a credit device.

A Substitute for Money

Debtors sometimes use currency, but for convenience and safety they often use commercial paper instead. For example, commercial paper is being used when a debt is paid by check. The substitute-for-money function of commercial paper developed in the Middle Ages. As mentioned previously, merchants deposited their precious metals with bankers in order to avoid the dangers of loss or theft. When they needed funds to pay for the goods that they were buying, they gave the seller a written order addressed to the bank. This authorized the bank to deliver part of the precious metals to the seller. These orders, called *bills of exchange*, were sometimes used as a substitute for money. Today people use checks the same way. They also use drafts, promissory notes, and certificates of deposit that are payable either on demand or on some specified date in the future. Commercial paper as a substitute for money is further indicated by the Federal Reserve's official definition of what is called the "narrow" money supply—(M1–B) currency (dollar bills and coins) in the hands of the public and checking-like account balances held in all financial institutions.

A Credit Device

Commercial paper may represent an extension of credit. When a buyer gives a seller a promissory note, the terms of which provide that it is payable within sixty days, the seller has essentially extended sixty days of credit to the buyer. The credit aspect of commercial paper was developed in the Middle Ages soon after bills of exchange began to be used as substitutes for money. Merchants were able to give to sellers bills of exchange that were not payable until a future date. Since the seller would wait until a maturity date to collect, this was a form of extending credit to the buyer.

Discounting The holder of a promissory note payable in sixty or ninety days who wishes to sell this instrument to a third party may do so for immediate cash. Typically, banks buy these instruments and wait until their maturity date to receive payment. In order to induce a bank to buy a promissory note, the holder of the instrument accepts a discount of,

say, 5, 10, or 15 percent of the face amount. In effect, the bank pays less than the amount it will eventually collect as a way of charging interest.

Collectibility For commercial paper to operate *practically* either as a substitute for money or as a credit device or as both, it is essential that the paper be easily transferable without danger of being uncollectible. This is the function that characterizes negotiable commercial paper. Each rule studied in this chapter can be examined in light of this function.

TYPES OF COMMERCIAL PAPER

UCC 3-104 specifies four types of instruments— drafts, checks, notes, and certificates of deposit.

Drafts

A **draft** (bill of exchange) is an unconditional written order. The party creating it (the drawer) orders another party (the drawee) to pay money, usually to a third party (the payee). Exhibit 23–1 shows a typical draft. The drawee must be obligated to the drawer either by agreement or through a debtor-creditor relationship before the drawee is obligated to the drawer to honor the order.

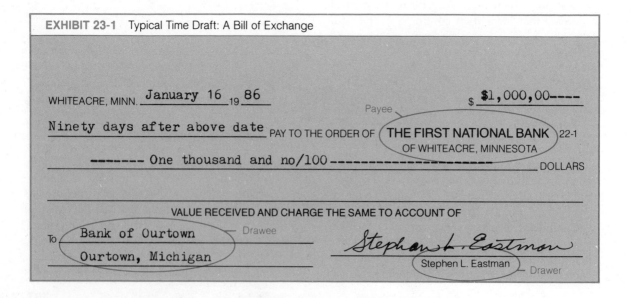

EXHIBIT 23-1 Typical Time Draft: A Bill of Exchange

WHITEACRE, MINN. January 16, 19 86 $ $1,000,00----

Ninety days after above date PAY TO THE ORDER OF THE FIRST NATIONAL BANK 22-1 OF WHITEACRE, MINNESOTA

-------- One thousand and no/100 -------------------- DOLLARS

VALUE RECEIVED AND CHARGE THE SAME TO ACCOUNT OF

To Bank of Ourtown — Drawee
Ourtown, Michigan

Stephen L. Eastman
Stephen L. Eastman — Drawer

Time and Sight Drafts A time draft is a draft that is payable at a definite future time. A sight (or demand) draft is payable on sight, that is, when the holder presents it for payment.[1] A draft can be both a time and sight draft; such a draft is one payable at a stated time after sight.

Trade Acceptances The **trade acceptance** is a draft that is frequently used with the sale of goods. The seller is both the drawer and the payee on this draft. Essentially, the draft orders the buyer to pay a specified sum of money to the seller usually at a stated time in the future.

To illustrate: Good Yard Company sells $50,000 of fabric to Lane Dresses, Incorporated each fall on terms requiring payment to be made in ninety days. One year Good Yard needs cash, so it draws a *trade acceptance* that orders Lane to pay $50,000 to the order of Good Yard Company ninety days hence. Good Yard presents the paper to Lane. Lane *accepts* by signing the face of the paper and returns it to Good Yard. Lane's acceptance creates an enforceable promise to pay the instrument when it comes due in ninety days. Good Yard can sell the trade acceptance in the commercial money market more easily than it can assign the $50,000 account receivable (for the reasons covered in Chapter 14, on assignments, and in subsequent chapters in this area). Thus, trade acceptances are the standard credit instruments in sales transactions. Exhibit 23–2 shows a trade acceptance.

Checks

A **check** is a distinct type of draft, *drawn* on a *bank* and payable on *demand*. Checks are discussed more fully in Chapter 28. Note here, however, that with certain types of checks, the bank is both the drawer and the drawee. For example, cashier's checks drawn by the bank on itself are payable on demand when issued. In addition, a check can be drawn by a bank on another bank. This instrument is known as a bank draft.

When traveler's checks are drawn on a bank, they are checks, but they require the payee's authorized signature before becoming payable. (Technically, most traveler's checks are not checks but drafts, because the drawee—for example, American Express—is ordinarily not a bank.)

Promissory Notes

The **promissory note** is a written promise between two parties. One party is the maker of the promise to pay, and the other is the payee, or the one to whom the promise is made. A promissory note,

---

1. Or a sight draft is payable on acceptance. Acceptance is the drawee's written promise (engagement) to pay the draft when it comes due. The usual manner of accepting is by writing the word *accepted* across the face of the instrument, followed by the date of acceptance and the signature of the drawee.

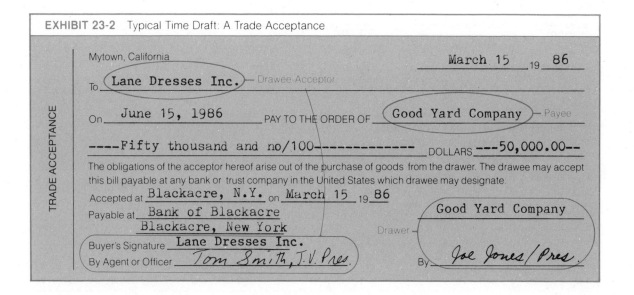

EXHIBIT 23-2 Typical Time Draft: A Trade Acceptance

TRADE ACCEPTANCE

Mytown, California

March 15 19 86

To (Lane Dresses Inc.) — Drawee-Acceptor

On June 15, 1986 PAY TO THE ORDER OF (Good Yard Company) — Payee

----Fifty thousand and no/100------------ DOLLARS ---50,000.00--

The obligations of the acceptor hereof arise out of the purchase of goods from the drawer. The drawee may accept this bill payable at any bank or trust company in the United States which drawee may designate.

Accepted at Blackacre, N.Y. on March 15 19 86

Payable at Bank of Blackacre
Blackacre, New York

Buyer's Signature Lane Dresses Inc.
By Agent or Officer Tom Smith, J.V. Pres.

Drawer —

Good Yard Company

By Joe Jones/Pres.

commonly referred to as a **note,** can be made payable at a definite time or on demand. It can name a specific payee or merely be payable to bearer. A sample promissory note is shown in Exhibit 23–3.

Notes are used in a variety of credit transactions and often carry the name of the transaction involved. For example, in real estate transactions, promissory notes for the unpaid balance on a house, secured by a mortgage on the property, are called *mortgage notes.* A note that is secured by personal property is called a *collateral note.* And a note payable in installments, such as for payment of a color television set over a twelve-month period, is called an *installment note.*

Certificates of Deposit

A **certificate of deposit** (CD) is an acknowledgment by a bank of the receipt of money with an engagement to repay it. [UCC 3-104(2)(c)] Certificates of deposit in small denominations are often sold by savings and loan associations, savings banks, and commercial banks. They are called small CDs and are for amounts up to $100,000. Certificates of deposit for amounts over $100,000 are called large CDs.[2] Exhibit 23–4 shows a typical small CD.

---

2.   Large CDs are included in certain definitions of the money supply because they are fully negotiable and because the interest they pay is not regulated by the Federal Reserve. Large CDs may, however, be subject to regulation by the state banking authority of the state in which they are issued.

Large and small certificates of deposit pay interest and most large CDs are negotiable. Their negotiability allows them to be sold, to be used to pay debts, or to serve as security (collateral) for a loan.

LETTERS OF CREDIT

A **letter of credit** is neither a draft nor a note. It is an agreement that the issuer will pay drafts drawn by the creditor. Letters of credit are made by a bank or other person at the request of a customer and can be revocable or irrevocable commitments. Letters of credit are frequently used by buyers in the purchase of goods in commerce.

For example, a corporate buyer in California wishes to purchase manufacturing equipment from a West German seller. The buyer goes to its bank and through a loan agreement gets the bank to issue and to send a letter of credit to the seller in West Germany. The letter of credit provides that upon the seller's presentation of certain documents (bill of lading, invoice, customs receipts, and the like) to the bank, the bank will pay any drafts drawn by the seller on the buyer up to a stated amount. As the drafts are presented to the bank for payment, the bank remits the funds to the seller. The bank then collects the amount from the buyer under the terms of the loan agreement.

Today, letters of credit are used for a variety of lending arrangements (such as the development of real estate) for both domestic and foreign commer-

---

EXHIBIT 23-3   Typical Promissory Note

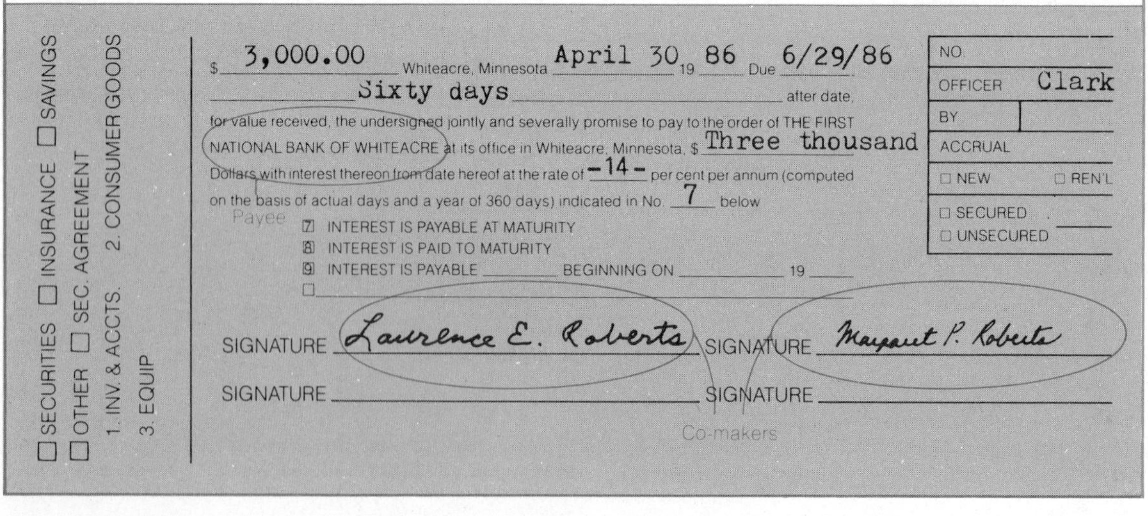

cial purposes. Much of the law governing letters of credit is found in Article 5 (Letters of Credit) in the UCC.

OTHER WAYS OF CLASSIFYING COMMERCIAL PAPER

The preceding classifications of commercial paper follow the language of the UCC. There are numerous other ways to classify commercial paper, some of which are treated here.

Demand Instruments and Time Instruments

Commercial paper can be classified as demand instruments or as time instruments. A demand instrument is payable on demand, that is, whenever the holder—a possessor *to whom the instrument runs*—chooses to present it to the maker in the case of a note or to the drawee in the case of a draft. (Instruments payable on demand include those payable on sight or on presentation, and in which no time for payment is stated.) [UCC 3-108] All checks are demand instruments because, by definition, they must be payable on demand; therefore, checking accounts are called **demand deposits.** Time instruments are payable at a future date.

Orders to Pay and Promises to Pay

Commercial paper involving the payment of money must contain either a *promise* to pay or an *order* to

pay. Thus, commercial paper can be classified as either promises to pay or orders to pay. Accordingly, a check or a draft is an order to pay. On the other hand, a certificate of deposit and a promissory note are promises to pay.

Negotiable and Nonnegotiable Instruments

All commercial paper is either *negotiable* or *nonnegotiable*. This serves as another means of classification. Both its form and its content determine whether commercial paper is negotiable. All the elements listed in UCC 3-104 must be present for negotiability. This topic is of sufficient importance that all of Chapter 24 is devoted to it. Note that when an instrument is negotiable, its transfer from one person to another is governed by Article 3 of the UCC. Indeed, UCC 3-102(e) defines *instrument* as a "negotiable instrument." For that reason, wherever the term *instrument* is used in this book, it refers to a negotiable instrument. Transfers of nonnegotiable instruments are governed by rules of assignment of contract rights. (See Chapter 14).

PARTIES TO COMMERCIAL PAPER

To review, a note (or a certificate of deposit) has two original parties—the maker and the payee. A draft, or check, has three original parties—the drawer, the drawee, and the payee. Sometimes two of the parties to a draft can be the same person (drawer-drawee or

---

EXHIBIT 23-4   Typical Small CD

THE FIRST NATIONAL BANK OF WHITEACRE   22-1 / 960   NUMBER 332
NEGOTIABLE CERTIFICATE OF DEPOSIT
                                         WHITEACRE, MINN. __February 15_____ 19 _86____

THIS CERTIFIES to the deposit in this Bank the sum of $ __5,000.00__

-------- Five thousand and no/100 -------------------------------- DOLLARS

Payee (Bearer)
which is payable to bearer on the ____15th____ day of _____July_____, 19 _86__, against presentation and surrender of
this certificate, and bears interest at the rate of 9 3/4 % per annum, to be computed (on the basis of 360 days and actual days
elapsed) to, and payable at, maturity. No payment may be made prior to, and no interest runs after, that date. Payable at maturity in federal
funds, and if desired, at Manufacturers Hanover Trust Company, New York.

                                                         THE FIRST NATIONAL BANK OF WHITEACRE

                                              By ____John Doe_____
                                                                                          Signature
                                                                                   Maker

drawer-payee). Once an instrument is issued, additional parties can become involved. **Issue** is defined as the "first delivery of an instrument to a holder."[3] [UCC 3-102(1)(a)] The liability of these parties is discussed in Chapter 27.

Makers

A **maker** is the person who issues a promissory note or a CD promising to pay a certain sum of money to a payee or bearer. The maker's signature must appear on the face of the promissory note or CD for the maker to be liable on the note.

Drawers, Drawees, and Payees

When a check or other draft is issued, the person who issues it, known as the **drawer**, orders the **drawee** (who is a bank in the case of a check) to pay a certain sum of money to a **payee** (or to the bearer of the instrument).

To illustrate: Smith has a checking account with West Wind Bank. At the end of the month, Smith receives his utility bill of $52 from the Tower Power and Light Corporation. Smith writes a check payable to the order of the utility, signing it in the lower right-hand corner. Smith is the *drawer* of the check. The West Wind Bank, which has been ordered to pay the check, is the *drawee*. Tower Power and Light, to which Smith has issued the check, is the *payee*.

Indorsers

The payee of a note or draft may transfer it by signing (indorsing) it and delivering it to another person. By doing this, the payee becomes an **indorser**. For example, Carol receives a graduation check for $25. She can transfer the check to her mother (or anyone) by signing it on the back. Carol is an indorser.

Indorsees

The person who receives the indorsed instrument is the **indorsee**. In the example above, Carol's mother is the indorsee. She is entitled to the $25 payment by virtue of Carol's indorsement. Carol's mother can indorse the check to someone else and thus become an indorser as well.

The Bearer

A **bearer** is any person who has physical possession of an instrument that either is payable to anyone without specific designation or is indorsed in blank. If a note is expressly made "payable to bearer," the person who possesses that note is the bearer. A person possessing a note or check payable to "cash" is also a bearer. A check payable to the order of a named person and indorsed by that named person in blank on the back makes its possessor a bearer also.

Holders

The term **holder** includes any person in possession of an instrument drawn, issued, or indorsed to him or her or to his or her order or to bearer or in blank.[4] To illustrate: A check made payable to the order of John Doe, in his possession, makes John Doe a holder. A promissory note written by Sarah Smith promises to pay a sum of money to the order of Tom Jones. While the note is in Jones's possession, Jones is a holder. If Jones signs (indorses) the back of the note and transfers (negotiates) it to Adam White, the note becomes bearer paper, and White becomes the holder.

The holder and the owner of negotiable paper can often be the same person, but not necessarily. For example, a thief who steals a bearer instrument is a *holder* under commercial law principles (but obviously the thief is not the owner). Nonetheless, the thief can legally transfer (negotiate) the bearer instrument to another person, who then becomes a *holder*.

Holder in Due Course   Under UCC 3-302, a holder in due course (HDC) is a person who acquires an instrument for value in a good faith transaction without notice that it is defective or overdue. It is easier for an HDC to collect payment on an instrument

---

3. One can also refer to primary and secondary parties. Primary parties are makers of notes and acceptors of drafts. These parties promise to pay the instrument according to its terms. A signature of a person other than as the maker or the acceptor makes that person a secondary party.

---

4. UCC 1-201(20) defines *holder* as "a person who is in possession of a document of title or an instrument or an investment security drawn, issued, or indorsed to him or to his order or to bearer or in blank."

than it is for an assignee of a contract to collect payment. The assignee is subject to all outstanding defenses of prior parties; the HDC is protected from all but a few defenses.[5]

Holder through a Holder in Due Course An ordinary holder whose manner of acquisition fails to meet the requirements of a holder in due course can still be afforded HDC protection by proving that any prior holder qualified as a holder in due course. [UCC 3-201(1)]

Acceptors

An **acceptor** is a drawee of a draft or check who has, by signing the instrument, manifestly agreed to pay the draft when due. For example, when the buyer "agrees" to pay the trade acceptance of the seller, drawn on the buyer (drawee), the buyer becomes an acceptor of the draft. (See Exhibit 23–2). The same

---

5. The HDC is subject to real defenses. These generally involve the validity of the instrument—for example, legal capacity or certain sorts of forgery or alteration. [UCC 3-305] An HDC is free from all personal defenses between prior parties—for example, breach of contract.

result takes place when a drawee bank certifies a check drawn on that bank.

Accommodation Parties

An **accommodation party** is one who signs an instrument in any capacity to lend "his name to another party to it." [UCC 3-415(1)] The accommodation party actually lends his or her credit to the party to whom the accommodation is made and is classified accordingly.

For example, Barrow seeks a loan from the West Wind Bank. The bank will make the loan only if Barrow will get a third party with a good credit rating to co-sign the note. Able qualifies and agrees to accommodate Barrow by signing the note below Barrow's signature. Barrow is the *maker*, and Able is the *accommodation maker*. If, prior to the instrument's due date, Smith takes it for value, Able is still liable in the capacity in which she signed, even though Smith knows of the accommodation. [UCC 3-415(2)]

In any case, Able, as the accommodation party, is not liable to Barrow. Able is liable to Smith who took for value. She is normally liable only to the West Wind Bank. But if Able pays the instrument, she has the right of recourse on the instrument against Barrow. [UCC 3-415(5)]

QUESTIONS AND CASE PROBLEMS

1. Adam Smith, a college student, wished to purchase a new component stereo system from John Locke Stereo, Inc. Since Smith did not have the cash to pay for the entire stereo system, he offered to sign a note promising to pay $150 per month for the next six months. Locke Stereo, anxious to sell the system to Smith, agreed to accept the promissory note as long as Smith had one of his professors sign it. Smith did this and tendered a note to John Locke Stereo that stated, "I, Adam Smith, promise to pay John Locke Stereo or its order the sum of $150 per month for the next six months." The note was signed by Adam Smith and his business law professor. About a week later, John Locke Stereo, which was badly in need of cash, signed the back of the note and sold it to Fidelity

Bank. Give the specific designation of the four parties on this note.

2. A partnership called Larson and Adkins is a law firm. Larson had just won a case for her client, Brown, against Bill Bucks. When Larson went to collect the judgment from Bucks, Bucks wrote out a check that read: "Pay to the order of Larson and Adkins $60,000 [Signed] Bill Bucks." On the top of the check were the words "Hanover Trust." When Larson went to deposit the check in the trust account that she had set up for her client, she signed the back of the check "L. Larson." How are each of these parties designated in commercial paper law?

3. Negotiable instruments play an important part in commercial transactions. Different needs can be fulfilled by using different types of instruments in certain ways. For instance, many insurance companies use a form of draft instead of a check to remit insurance benefits. The insurance company is both the drawer and the drawee; the beneficiary (the person receiving the money) is the payee; and the draft is made payable through a named bank in

which the insurance company maintains a large account. What are the advantages of using such a draft?

4. Often when two parties to a sale are strangers to each other, and the sale is for a substantial amount of money, the selling party will insist that the purchaser make payment with a cashier's check. A cashier's check is a check for which the bank is both the drawer and the drawee. To purchase a cashier's check, a person goes to a bank teller, tenders the amount of money for which the check is to be payable, and supplies the teller with the name of the person who is to be the payee of the check. Once the payee's name is inscribed on the check, only the payee (or a person to whom the payee negotiates the check) will be able to receive money for the check. What problem might arise if a seller asks a prospective buyer of goods to make payment with a cashier's check, and the buyer purchases the check, naming the seller as the payee? How can this problem be avoided?

5. Identify the following types of commercial paper *or* parties involved in commercial paper.

   (a) A draft drawn on a bank payable to a payee on demand.
   (b) A written acknowledgment by a bank of a receipt of money with an obligation to repay it.
   (c) A written promise to pay another (or holder) a certain sum of money.
   (d) An instrument drawn by a bank on itself payable on demand.
   (e) Any person who acquires the instrument as a payee, by indorsement, or by delivery.
   (f) A person who issues a promissory note payable to a named payee.
   (g) A payee who transfers an order instrument by signing the instrument.
   (h) A person who indorses a check on behalf of the payee upon the payee's transfer to an indorsee.

6. A California statute makes possession of a check with intent to defraud a crime. Norwood had in his possession an instrument that had the following title in the upper right-hand corner: "AUDITOR CONTROLLER'S GENERAL WARRANT COUNTY OF LOS ANGELES." Below this the instrument stated, "The treasurer of the County of Los Angeles will pay to the order of John Norwood $5,000." At trial the district attorney proved that Norwood had intended to defraud the County of Los Angeles of $5,000 while in possession of the above instrument. You are Norwood's attorney, and you are now appealing the case. What argument would appear to be the strongest to overturn Norwood's conviction? [People v. Norwood, 26 Cal.3d 148, 103 Cal.Rptr. 7 (1972)]

24

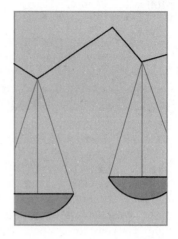

COMMERCIAL PAPER
The Negotiable Instrument

For businesses and commerce to operate smoothly, commercial paper must be generally accepted as money. For it to be readily accepted, it must be freely transferable. The law creating and governing the negotiable instrument is primarily designed, therefore, to urge its use as a substitute for money.

In this chapter, we will examine the elements of a negotiable instrument. Whenever a dispute arises over the enforceability of an instrument, it is vital to know whether the instrument is negotiable. If it is, all disputes are resolved under Article 3 of the UCC. If it is not, disputes must be resolved under ordinary contract law. For example, the holder-in-due-course doctrine is recognized only under Article 3. Thus, anyone attempting to utilize this doctrine in enforcing an instrument must show that the instrument is negotiable. If it is not, transfer of such instrument is by assignment and is governed by the rules of contract law.

This chapter deals with the requirements of what must appear *on the face* of negotiable instruments. All matters relating to the requirements for a proper indorsement usually appear *on the back* of the instrument and are covered in Chapter 25.

THE REQUIREMENTS FOR A NEGOTIABLE INSTRUMENT

UCC 3-104(1) specifies that in order for an instrument to be negotiable, it must:

1. Be in writing.
2. Be signed by the maker or drawer.
3. Be an unconditional promise or order to pay.
4. State a specific sum of money.
5. Be payable on demand or at a definite time.
6. Be payable to order or to bearer.

A Writing

Negotiable instruments must be in *written form*. Clearly, an oral promise can create the danger of fraud or make it difficult to determine liability. Negotiable instruments must possess the quality of certainty that only formal written expression can give.

Practical Limitations on the Writing   There are certain practical limitations concerning the writing and the substance on which it is placed.

1. The writing must be on material that lends itself to *permanence*. Instruments have been carved in blocks of ice and recorded on other impermanent surfaces. They are in writing, but only for a relatively short period of time. For example, if Mary writes in the sand, "I promise to pay $100 to the order of Tom," this is not a writing because it lacks permanence.

2. The writing must have *portability*. This is not a legal requirement, but if an instrument is not movable, it cannot meet the requirement that it be freely transferable. A promise to pay written on the side of a cow, for example, is technically correct, but a cow cannot easily be transferred in the ordinary course of business.

Signed by the Maker or the Drawer

For an instrument to be negotiable, it must be signed by the maker if it is a note or certificate of deposit, or by the drawer if it is a draft or check. [UCC 3-104(1)(a)]

Extreme latitude is granted in determining what constitutes a **signature**. UCC 1-201(39) defines the word *signed* as "[including] any symbol executed or adopted by a party with present intention to authenticate a writing." UCC 3-401(2) expands upon this: "A signature is made by use of any name, including any trade or assumed name, upon an instrument, or by any word or mark used in lieu of a written signature." Thus, initials, an X, or a thumbprint will suffice. A trade name or an assumed name is sufficient even if it is false. A "rubber stamp" bearing a person's signature is permitted and frequently used in the business world. If necessary, parol evidence (Chapter 13) is admissible in identifying the signer. When the signer is identified, the signature becomes effective.

Placement of the Signature   The location of the signature on the document is unimportant. The usual place is the lower right-hand corner, but this is not required. A *handwritten* statement on the body of the instrument, such as "I, Mary Jones, promise to pay John Doe," is sufficient to act as Mary's signature.

There are virtually no limitations on the manner in which a signature can be made, but it is necessary to be careful when receiving an instrument that has been signed in an unusual way. The burden of proving the genuineness of a signature rests on the recipient. Furthermore, an unusual signature clearly decreases the marketability of an instrument because it creates uncertainty.

Signature by Authorized Representative   If a person signs an instrument as the agent for the maker or drawer, the maker or drawer has effectively signed the instrument if the agent had *authority* to do so. No particular form of appointment as an agent is necessary to show such authority; all that is needed is proof that the agent has such authority. [UCC 3-403]

If the agent has authority, the maker or drawer is liable on the instrument, just as if he or she had actually signed it. If the agent has authority and clearly has signed the instrument in a representative capacity, he or she will not be personally liable. If the agent has no such authority, or if the agent did not clearly sign in a representative capacity, the agent is personally liable. The importance of the liability of the parties in these situations will be discussed in detail in Chapter 33.

Unconditional Promise or Order To Pay

The terms of a promise or order must be included in the writing on the face of a negotiable instrument. These terms must not be conditioned upon the occurrence or nonoccurrence of some other event or agreement. Nor can the promise state that it is to be paid only out of a particular fund or source. [UCC 3-105(2)]

Promise or Order   In order for an instrument to be negotiable, it must contain an express order or promise to pay. A mere acknowledgment of the debt, which might logically *imply* a promise, is not sufficient under the UCC because the promise must be an *affirmative* undertaking. [UCC 3-102(1)(c)]

For example, the traditional I.O.U. is only an acknowledgment of indebtedness. Therefore, it is not a negotiable instrument. But if such words as *to be paid on demand* or *due on demand* are added, the need for an affirmative promise is satisfied. For example, if a buyer executes a promissory note using the words, "I promise to pay $1,000 to the order of the seller for the purchase of goods X, Y, Z," then the requirement for a negotiable instrument is satisfied.

A certificate of deposit is different. Here, the requisite promise is satisifed because the bank's acknowledgment of the deposit and the other terms of the instrument clearly indicate a promise.

An order is associated with three-party instruments, such as trade acceptances, checks, and drafts. An order directs a third party to pay the instrument as drawn. In the typical check, the word *pay* (to the order of a payee) is a command to the drawee bank to pay the check when presented, and thus it is an order. The order is mandatory even if it is written in a courteous form with words like *please pay* or *kindly pay*. However, precise language must be used. An order stating, "I wish you would pay," does not fulfill the requirement of precision.

In addition to being precise, an effective order must specifically identify the drawee (the person who must pay). [UCC 3-102(1)(b)] A bank's name printed on the face of a check, for example, sufficiently designates the bank as drawee.

Unconditional   A negotiable instrument's utility as a substitute for money or as a credit device would be dramatically reduced if it had *conditional* promises attached to it. It would be expensive and time-consuming to investigate such conditional promises, and, therefore, the free transferability of negotiable instruments would be greatly reduced. There would be substantial administrative costs associated with processing conditional promises. Furthermore, the payee would risk the possibility of the condition not occurring.

If Martin promises to pay Paula $10,000 only if a certain ship reaches port safely, anyone interested in purchasing the promissory note would have to investigate whether the ship arrived. Additionally, the facts that the investigation disclosed might be incorrect. To avoid such problems, the UCC provides that only unconditional promises or orders can be negotiable. [UCC 3-104(1)(b)]

However, the Code expands the definition of *unconditional* in order to make sure that certain conditions commonly used in business transactions do *not* render an otherwise negotiable instrument nonnegotiable. These are resolved by UCC 3-105:

A promise or order otherwise unconditional is not made conditional by the fact that the instrument

(a) is subject to implied or constructive conditions; or

(b) states its consideration * * * or the transaction which gave rise to the instrument * * *; or

(c) refers to or states that it arises out of a separate agreement * * *; or

(d) states that it is drawn under a letter of credit; or

(e) states that it is secured, whether by mortgage, reservation of title or otherwise; or

(f) indicates a particular account to be debited or any other fund or source from which reimbursement is expected; or

(g) is limited to payment out of a particular fund or the proceeds of a particular source, if the instrument is issued by a government or governmental agency unit; or

(h) is limited to payment out of the entire assets of a partnership, unincorporated association, trust or estate * * *.

Some of these conditions are very common and will be briefly discussed.

Implied or Constructive Conditions   Without the rule allowing implied or constructive conditions, no instrument could be negotiable. Implied conditions, such as good faith and commercial reasonableness, appear in virtually every example of a negotiable instrument.

Statements of Consideration   Many instruments state the terms of the underlying agreement as a matter of standard business practice. Somewhere on its face, the instrument refers to the transaction or agreement for which it is being used in payment. The policy of the UCC is to integrate standard trade usages into its provisions.

For example, the words *as per contract* or *this debt arises from the sale of goods X and Y* do not render an instrument nonnegotiable.

If James Quinta writes, "On July 14, 1982, I promise to pay to the order of Louis Sneed $100 in full payment for the television set that Louis Sneed delivered to me on July 2, 1982, [signed] James Quinta," this promissory note is a negotiable instrument. The statement concerning the television set is not a condition. It describes the consideration for which the note is given. On the other hand, if the following words were added, the instrument would become nonnegotiable: "If this television set does not suit my tastes and preferences in any way whatsoever on July 13, then the maker's obligation hereunder shall be null and void."

Reference to Other Agreements   The UCC provides that mere reference to another agreement does not affect negotiability. If, on the other hand, the instrument is made subject to the other agreement, it will be nonnegotiable. [UCC 3-105(2)(a)] A reference to another agreement is normally inserted for the purpose of keeping a record or giving information to anyone who may be interested. Notes frequently refer to separate agreements that give special rights to a creditor for an acceleration of payment or to a debtor for prepayment. References to these rights do not destroy the negotiability of the instrument.

For example, an instrument states, "On January 23, 1985, I promise to pay to the order of Patricia Senior $1,000, this note being secured under a security agreement and lien upon my 1974 Dodge Dart, noted upon the title certificate thereof [signed] Henry Winn." This instrument is negotiable. A statement that an instrument's payment is secured by collateral will not render an otherwise negotiable instrument nonnegotiable. [UCC 3-112(1)(b)] In fact, this statement adds to the salability and marketability of the instrument.

In the following case, a promissory note that incorporated another agreement was rendered nonnegotiable.

HOLLY HILL ACRES, LTD. v. CHARTER BANK OF GAINESVILLE

District Court of Florida, 1975.
314 So.2d 209.

BACKGROUND AND FACTS   *A promissory note and purchase money mortgage were executed by the appellant, Holly Hill Acres, and given to a third party, Rogers and Blythe. Subsequently, Rogers and Blythe assigned the promissory note and mortgage in question to the appellee, Charter Bank of Gainesville, to secure its own note. Ultimately, the Holly Hill note went into default. The bank sued both Holly Hill and Rogers and Blythe to recover payment on the note. The trial court allowed the bank to recover. Holly Hill appealed that ruling, claiming that the note contained a stipulation that rendered it nonnegotiable. Hence, Holly Hill's defense against paying Rogers and Blythe was equally effective as a defense against paying the bank.*

The bank argued that it was a special type of assignee called a holder in due course because the promissory note was a negotiable instrument. On this basis, the bank claimed the unhampered right to recover on the note despite any underlying disputes between Holly Hill and Rogers and Blythe. (A holder in due course takes a negotiable instrument free of most claims of other parties when negotiable commercial paper is involved. See Chapter 27.) Hence, the key to the bank's claim for recovery was that the promissory note was negotiable.

The trial court ruled that the note was negotiable and that the bank could recover. Holly Hill appealed this ruling, claiming that, because the note was made subject to the mortgage agreement, it was nonnegotiable.

SCHEB, Judge.
*   *   *   *

The note, executed April 28, 1972, contains the following stipulation:
This note with interest is secured by a mortgage on real estate, of even date herewith, made by the maker hereof in favor of the said payee, and shall be construed and enforced according to the laws of the State of Florida. *The terms of said mortgage are by this reference made a part hereof.* [Emphasis supplied.]
*   *   *   *

The note having incorporated the terms of the purchase money mortgage was not negotiable. The appellee Bank was not a holder in due course. *   *   *
The note, incorporating by reference the terms of the mortgage, did not contain the unconditional promise to pay required by [UCC Sec. 3-104(1)(b)]. Rather, the note

falls within the scope of [UCC Sec. 3-105(2)(a)]. Although negotiability is now governed by the Uniform Commercial Code, this was the Florida view even before the U.C.C. was adopted.

* * * Mere reference to a note being secured by mortgage is a common commercial practice and such reference in itself does not impede the negotiability of the note. There is, however, a significant difference in a note stating that it is "secured by a mortgage" from one which provides, "the terms of said mortgage are by this reference made a part hereof." In the former instance the note merely refers to a separate agreement which does not impede its negotiability, while in the latter instance the note is rendered non-negotiable.

The appellate court ruled that the note was nonnegotiable and that the bank was not a holder in due course. A new trial was ordered—one in which Holly Hill could assert its defenses against the bank. **DECISION AND REMEDY**

Secured by a Mortgage A simple statement in an otherwise negotiable note, indicating that the note is secured by a mortgage, does not destroy its negotiability. Actually, such a statement might make the note even more acceptable in commerce. Note that the statement that a note is secured by a mortgage must not stipulate that the maker's promise to pay is *subject* to the terms and conditions of the mortgage.

Indication of Particular Funds or Accounts In many instruments, it is indicated expressly or impliedly that payment should come from a particular fund or that a particular account is to be debited. For example, a check is drawn impliedly on funds in a particular checking account.

Generally, mere reference to the account to be debited, or to the fund from which payment is preferred, will not affect the negotiability of the instrument. However, if payment is expressly limited to payment *only* from a particular fund, the instrument is rendered nonnegotiable. [UCC 3-105(2)(b)] The condition obviously restricts the acceptability of the instrument as a substitute for money, as a holder's payment now depends on whether such a fund exists and whether it is sufficient to pay the instrument.

For example, a note dated March 3, 1986, reads, "Gilbert Corporation promises to pay to the order of the Miami Herald $150 on demand, charged to advertising expense, signed Harold Henry, Treasurer, Gilbert Corporation." This note is negotiable. The phrase "charged to advertising expense" is merely a posting instruction to the corporation's accounting department. If a note states that "Jones plans to

liquidate real estate to pay this obligation," the note is still considered negotiable.[1] On the other hand, if a note reads "payment to be made within the next thirty days from jobs now under construction," the note will be held nonnegotiable because it does not contain an unconditional promise.

Consider another example. A note states that "payment of said obligation is restricted to payment from accounts receivable." In this case, payment is conditioned from only one particular source—accounts receivable—and therefore renders the instrument nonnegotiable. This does not make the note uncollectible, however. The contract may still be assigned under contract rules of assignment.

The two exceptions to this rule are instruments issued by government agencies that are payable out of particular revenue funds and instruments limited to partnership, unincorporated association, estate, or trust assets. [UCC 3-105(1)(g) and (h)]

Sum Certain in Money

Negotiable instruments must state the amount to be paid in a *sum certain in money*. This requirement promotes clarity and certainty in determining the value of the instrument. [UCC 3-104(1)(b)] Any promise to pay in the future is risky because the value of money (purchasing power) fluctuates. Nonetheless, the present value of such an instrument can still be estimated with a reasonable degree

---

1. Southern Baptist Hospital v. Williams, 89 So.2d 769 (La.App. 1956).

of accuracy by financial experts. If the instrument's value were stated in terms of goods or services, it would be too difficult to ascertain the market value of those goods and services at the time the instrument was to be discounted.

The UCC mandates that negotiable commercial paper be paid wholly in money. For example, a promissory note that provides for payment in diamonds, or in 1,000 hours of services, would not be payable in money. Thus, the note would be nonnegotiable.

Sum Certain The term *sum certain* means an amount that is ascertainable from the instrument itself without reference to an outside source. A demand note payable with 12 percent interest meets the requirement of sum certain because its amount can be determined at the time it is payable. UCC 3-106(1) states that the sum is not rendered uncertain by the fact that it is to be paid:

(a) with stated interest or by stated installments; or
(b) with stated different rates of interest before and after default or a specified date; or
(c) with a stated discount or addition if paid before or after the date fixed for payment; * * *

The basic test is whether any holder who receives the instrument can determine by calculation the amount required to be paid when the instrument is due. Thus, instruments that provide simply for payment of interest at prevailing bank rates are generally nonnegotiable, because bank rates fluctuate. A mortgage note tied to a variable rate of interest that fluctuates as a result of market conditions would not be negotiable. However, when an instrument is payable at the legal rate, or at a judgment rate, or as fixed by state law, the instrument can be negotiable.

In international trade, notes that are to be paid in another currency satisfy the sum certain requirement. If X promises to pay 1,000 French francs, this note meets the certainty requirement even though the parties must refer to exchange rates that are not embodied in the instrument. The Code, therefore, makes an exception to its own general rule because of the realities of international trade. [UCC 3-107(2)]

Often, instruments have provisions authorizing collection costs and attorneys' fees upon default. UCC 3-106(1)(e) indicates that an instrument with such provisions still meets the sum certain requirement and therefore is still negotiable. Providing for collection costs and attorneys' fees lessens some of the costs and risks that a bank (or other institution) dealing in commercial paper would otherwise incur. Note, though, that a few states have invalidated such provisions either by statute or by judicial decision. In states where such provisions are legal, the fees must be reasonable, or the clause will be voided as against public policy.

The elements that determine negotiability must be present on the face of the instrument. In the following case, the amount of a finance charge was not apparent from the face of the note.

WALLS v. MORRIS CHEVROLET, INC.

Court of Appeals of Oklahoma, 1973.
515 P.2d 1405.

BACKGROUND AND FACTS *This transaction involved a consumer credit sale in which a note and a security agreement, written on the same sheet of paper, were executed. The note provided that any unearned finance charges would be refunded if the consumer prepaid the full credit amount. The court had to determine whether the note and the security agreement, when read together, constituted a negotiable instrument. The defendant, Morris Chevrolet, Inc., was a merchant and needed to know because a statute prohibits any seller of consumer goods from taking a negotiable instrument other than a check in conjunction with a consumer credit sale. If a merchant transgresses this statute, the purchaser can recover three times the amount of the credit charge from the merchant. Morris Chevrolet therefore used the defense that the paper signed by the plaintiff, Walls, did not include a negotiable instrument. The reasoning was that the note lacked a sum certain. Walls took the position that a sum certain could be ascertained by looking at the note and the security agreement, which were contained on the same piece of paper. The trial court agreed with the defendant, Morris Chevrolet, that the note was not negotiable. The trial court therefore dismissed the plaintiff's petition. Walls appealed.*

BAILEY, Presiding Judge.

*   *   *   *

First, both parties assume that the note, considered by itself, is not negotiable. So do we. The sum payable from the face of the note does not appear to be a sum certain because of the privilege stated in the note of refund of any unearned finance charge upon prepayment of the balance. The amount of the finance charge is not apparent from the face of the note and therefore the sum to be paid is uncertain in the event of prepayment. Under [UCC Sec. 3-106]: "(1) The sum payable is a sum certain even though it is to be paid *   *   * (c) with a stated discount *   *   * if paid before *   *   * the date fixed for payment *   *   *." In this instance the amount of the discount is not stated in the note and cannot be computed from its face. As is stated in the Uniform Commercial Code Comment to this section: "A stated discount or addition for early or late payment does not affect the certainty of the sum so long as the computation can be made *   *   * from the instrument itself *   *   *."

To overcome the absence of a sum certain on the face of the note, the plaintiff argues that the amount of the finance charge appears in the accompanying security agreement, that the security agreement and the note should be considered one instrument because on the same sheet of paper, that so construed the missing term is supplied and both note and security agreement are negotiable.

*   *   *   *

*   *   * We have been cited to no case, nor have we found one, in which a note on its face non-negotiable has been found to be negotiable by reference to an attached security agreement.

It is our opinion that a note cannot depend upon another agreement for elements of negotiability whether that agreement is attached to the note or separate from it except in those rare instances where such an incorporation is sanctioned by the Uniform Commercial Code expressly or by necessary implication. Negotiable notes are designed to be couriers without excess luggage under both the prior law and under the Code and so negotiability must be determined from the face of the note without regard to outside sources (with rare exceptions) so that the taker may know that he takes a negotiable instrument with the insurance of collectability provided by the Code and not an ordinary contract subject to the possibility of all defenses by the maker.

The note was not negotiable on its face. A separate agreement cannot supply **DECISION**
the elements of negotiability to a note that, from its very nature, must be **AND REMEDY**
negotiable on its face. Therefore, the defendant prevailed.

Money and No Other Promise   UCC 3-104(1)(b) provides that a sum certain is to be payable in "money and no other promise." The Code defines money as "a medium of exchange authorized or adopted by a domestic or foreign government as a part of its currency." [UCC 1-201(24)]

Suppose that the maker of a note promises "to pay on demand $1,000 in U.S. gold." Since gold is not a medium of exchange adopted by the U.S. government, the note is not payable in money. The same result would occur if the maker promised "to pay $1,000 *and* fifty liters of 1964 Chateau Lafite-Rothschild wine," as the instrument is not payable *entirely* in money.

An instrument "payable in $1,000 U.S. currency or an equivalent value in gold" would render the instrument nonnegotiable, if the maker reserved the option of paying in money or gold. If the option were left to the payee, some legal scholars argue that the instrument would be negotiable.

The UCC has a special provision for such instruments. [UCC 3-107(2)] Any instrument payable in the U.S. with a face amount stated in a foreign currency can be paid in the equivalent in U.S. dollars at the due date, unless the paper expressly requires payment in the foreign currency.

To summarize, only instruments payable in money are negotiable. An instrument payable in

U.S. government bonds or in shares of IBM stock is not negotiable, because neither bonds nor stocks are a medium of exchange recognized by the U.S. government.

Payable on Demand or at a Definite Time

UCC 3-104(1)(c) requires that a negotiable instrument "be payable on demand or at a definite time." Clearly, in order to ascertain the value of a negotiable instrument, it is necessary to know when the maker, drawee, or acceptor is required to pay. It is also necessary to know when the obligations of secondary parties—drawers, indorsers and accommodation parties—will arise. Furthermore, it is necessary to know when an instrument is due in order to calculate when the statute of limitations may apply. And finally, with an interest-bearing instrument, it is necessary to know the exact interval during which the interest will accrue in order to determine the present value of the instrument.

Payable on Demand Instruments that are payable on demand include those that contain the words *payable at sight* or *payable upon presentment* and those that say nothing about when payment is due. The very nature of the instrument may indicate that it is payable on demand. For example, a check, by definition, is payable on demand. [UCC 3-104(2)(b)] If no time for payment is specified and the person responsible for payment must pay upon the instrument's presentment, the instrument is payable on demand. [UCC 3-108]

Payable at a Definite Time To be negotiable, time instruments must be payable at a definite time that is specified on the face of the instrument. The maker or drawee is under no obligation to pay until the specified time has elapsed.

Often instruments contain additional terms that seem to conflict with the definite time requirement. UCC 3-109 attempts to clear up some of these potential problems:

(1) An instrument is payable at a definite time if by its terms it is payable:
  (a) on or before a stated date or at a fixed period after a stated date; or
  (b) at a fixed period after sight; or
  (c) at a definite time subject to any acceleration; or

  (d) at a definite time subject to extension at the option of the holder, or to extension to a further definite time at the option of the maker or acceptor or automatically upon or after a specified act or event.
(2) An instrument which by its terms is otherwise payable only upon an act or event uncertain as to time of occurrence is not payable at a definite time even though the act or event has occurred.

To illustrate: An instrument dated June 1, 1981, states, "One year after the death of my grandfather, James Taylor, I promise to pay to the order of Henry Winkler $500. [Signed] Mary Taylor." This instrument is nonnegotiable. Because the date of the grandfather's death is uncertain, the maturity date is uncertain, even though the event is bound to occur.

When an instrument is payable on or before a stated date, it is clearly payable at a definite time, although the maker has the option of paying before the stated maturity date. This uncertainty does not violate the definite time requirement. If Lee gives Zenon an instrument dated May 1, 1981, which indicates on its face that it is payable on or before May 1, 1982, it satisfies the requirement. On the other hand, an instrument that is undated and made payable "one month after date" is clearly nonnegotiable. There is no way to determine the maturity date from the face of the instrument.

Drafts stating that they are payable at a fixed period after sight are considered payable at a definite time. [UCC 3-109(1)(b)] The term *sight* means the moment that the draft is presented for payment or for acceptance by the drawee. The Code further requires that such instruments be presented for acceptance to the drawee in order to determine the maturity date. [UCC 3-501(1)(a)] Presenting an instrument for acceptance to the drawee establishes the sight and the time period, which runs from the date the instrument is presented.

Acceleration Clauses An **acceleration clause** is one that allows a payee or other holder of a time instrument to demand payment of the entire amount due, with interest, if a certain event occurs, such as a default in payment of an installment when due. There must be, of course, a good faith belief that payment will not be made before an acceleration clause is invoked.

For example, Carl lends $1,000 to Debra. Debra makes a negotiable note promising to pay $100 per month for eleven months. The note may contain a provision that permits Carl or any holder to accelerate all the payments plus interest if Debra fails to pay an installment in any given month. If, for example, Debra fails to make the third payment, the note will be due and payable in full. If Carl accelerates the unpaid balance, Debra will owe Carl the remaining principal plus interest.

Under UCC 3-109(1)(c), instruments that include acceleration clauses are negotiable because the exact value of the instrument can be ascertained, and the instrument will be payable on a fixed date if the event allowing acceleration does not occur. Thus, the fixed date is the outside limit used to determine the value of the instrument.

Furthermore, the payee or holder cannot accelerate the instrument even if it contains an acceleration clause unless it is done in good faith. Section 1-208 indicates that the acceleration clause "* * * shall be construed to mean that * * * [the holder of the instrument] shall have the power * * * [to accelerate] only if he in good faith believes that the prospect of payment or performance is impaired." But the burden of proving a lack of good faith is on the borrower—the maker of the note.

Extension Clauses   The reverse of an acceleration clause is an extension clause, which allows the date of maturity to be extended into the future. To keep the instrument negotiable, the interval of the extension must be specified if the right to extend is given to the maker of the instrument. If, on the other hand, the holder of the instrument can extend it, the maturity date does not have to be specified.

Suppose a note reads, "The maker [obligor] has the right to postpone the time of payment of this note beyond its definite maturity date of January 1, 1983. However, this extension shall be for no more than a reasonable time." Any note with this language is not negotiable because it does not satisfy the definite time requirement. The right to extend is the maker's, and the maker has not indicated when the note will become due after the extension.

If a note reads, "The holder of this note at the date of maturity, January 1, 1985 can extend the time of payment until the following June 1 or later, if the holder so wishes," this is a negotiable instrument. The length of the extension does not have to be specified because the option to extend is solely that of the holder. After January 1, 1985, the note is, in effect, a demand instrument.

Payable to Order or to Bearer

Since one of the functions of a negotiable instrument is to substitute for money, freedom to transfer is an essential requirement. To be sure that a proper transfer can be made, one of the requirements of a negotiable instrument is that it be "payable to order or to bearer." [UCC 3-104(1)(d)] These required words indicate that at the time of issuance it is expected that future unknown persons—not just the immediate party—will eventually be the owners. If these words are not present, the instrument is nonnegotiable and therefore only assignable and governed by contract law.

Order Instruments   UCC 3-110(1) defines an instrument as an order to pay "when by its terms it is payable to the order * * * of any person therein specified with reasonable certainty * * *." This section goes on to state that an order instrument can be payable to the order of:

(a) the maker or drawer; or
(b) the drawee; or
(c) a payee who is not maker, drawer, or drawee; or
(d) two or more payees together or in the alternative; or
(e) the representative of an estate, trust, or fund or his successor; or
(f) an office or officer by title [such as a tax assessor]; or
(g) a partnership or unincorporated association.

The purpose of order paper is to allow the maker or drawer to transfer the instrument to a specific person. This in turn allows that person to transfer the instrument to whomever he or she wishes. Thus the maker or drawer agrees to pay the person so specified or to pay whomever that person designates. In this way, the instrument retains its transferability.

Suppose an instrument states, "payable to the order of Sam Smith," or, "pay to Sam Smith or order." Clearly the maker or drawer has indicated that a payment will be made to Smith or to whomever Smith designates. The instrument is negotiable.

However, if the instrument states, "payable to Sam Smith," or, "pay to Sam Smith only," the instrument loses its negotiability. (The maker or drawer indicates only that Smith will be paid.)

In addition, except for bearer paper, the person specified must be named with *certainty* because the transfer of an order instrument requires an indorsement. (See Chapter 25.) If an instrument is "payable to the order of my kissing cousin," the instrument is nonnegotiable, as a holder could not be sure which cousin was intended to indorse and properly transfer the instrument.

Bearer Instrument UCC 3-111 defines a bearer instrument as one that does not designate a specific payee. The term *bearer* means the person in possession of an instrument that is payable to bearer or indorsed in blank. [UCC 1-201(5)] This means that the maker or drawer agrees to pay anyone who presents the instrument for payment, and complete transferability is implied.

Any instrument containing the following terms is a bearer instrument: "Payable to the order of bearer," "Payable to Sam Sneed or bearer," "Payable to bearer,"

"Pay cash," or "Pay to the order of cash." In addition, an instrument that contains "any other indication which does not purport to designate a specific payee" is bearer paper. [UCC 3-111(c)] The use of such designations can cause problems and should be avoided. Therefore, a check made payable to the order of "Uncle Sam" would probably be to a designated payee, the United States government, and be an order instrument. An instrument "payable to the order of a bucket of milk" would not be a designation of a specific payee, and the instrument would be a bearer instrument.

Where an instrument is made payable to order *and* to bearer, if the bearer words are handwritten or typewritten, the instrument is a bearer instrument. But if the bearer words are in a printed form, it is an order instrument. [UCC 3-110(3)] The next case distinguishes bearer paper from order paper.

BROADWAY MANAGEMENT CORP. v. BRIGGS

Appellate Court of Illinois, Fourth District, 1975. 30 Ill. App. 3d 403, 332 N.E. 2d 131.

BACKGROUND AND FACTS *Defendant Briggs signed a note that read in part* "Ninety days *after date, I, we, or either of us, promise to pay to the order of* Three Thousand Four Hundred Ninety Eight and ⁴⁵⁄₁₀₀ . . . . . . .dollars." *The words and symbols in roman print were typed out. The remainder of the words in the quote were printed. No blanks had been left on the face of the instrument; any unused space had been filled in with hyphens. The note contained several clauses that permitted acceleration in the event the holder deemed itself insecure. When the note was not paid at maturity, Broadway Management Corp. brought suit on the note for full payment. Broadway prevailed at trial; Briggs appealed. The appeal centered on the question of whether the note was order or bearer paper.*

CRAVEN, Justice.
* * * *

The trial court determined this instrument to be non-negotiable paper, yet applied certain elements of the law of negotiable instruments in arriving at its conclusion. We believe the instrument to be negotiable. Uniform Commercial Code, section 3-109 establishes that an acceleration clause does not affect negotiability; * * *

Thus, the critical question of whether this is order or bearer paper is to be determined by section 3 of the Uniform Commercial Code, which governs negotiable instruments. If this is bearer paper, the plaintiff's possession was sufficient to make it a holder (Uniform Commercial Code, section 1-201(20))
* * * *

On the other hand, if the instrument is order paper, it becomes apparent that the payee cannot be determined upon the face of the instrument.
* * * *

Under the Code, an instrument is payable to bearer only when by its terms it is payable to:

(a) bearer or the order of bearer; or (b) a specified person or bearer; or (c) 'cash' or the order of 'cash', or any other indication which does not purport to designate a specific payee. (U.C.C., § 3-111.)

The official comments to the section note that an instrument made payable "to the order of _____" is not bearer paper, but an incomplete order instrument unenforceable until completed in accordance with authority. U.C.C., § 3-115.

The instrument here is not bearer paper. We cannot say that it "does not purport to designate a specific payee." Rather, we believe the wording of the instrument is clear in its implication that the payee's name is to be inserted between the promise and the amount, so that the literal absence of blanks is legally insignificant.

Because the payee's name was not inserted in the blank reserved for the payee's name, the instrument was an incomplete order instrument, so the holder could not be determined from the face of the instrument. The trial court's decision was reversed, and the case was remanded.

DECISION AND REMEDY

OMISSIONS THAT DO NOT AFFECT NEGOTIABILITY

UCC 3-112 lists the following terms and omissions that do not affect negotiability:

1. The omission of a statement of any consideration.
2. The omission of the place where the instrument is drawn or payable.
3. The promise or power to maintain or protect collateral or to give additional collateral.
4. The term in a draft indicating that the payee, by indorsing or cashing the draft, acknowledges full satisfaction of the obligation of the drawer.

OTHER FACTORS NOT AFFECTING NEGOTIABILITY

There are other factors that do not affect the negotiability of an instrument, and the UCC provides rules for clearing up ambiguous terms. Some of these rules are:

1. Unless the date of an instrument is necessary to determine a definite time for payment, the fact that an instrument is undated does not affect its negotiability. A typical example is an undated check. [UCC 3-114(1)]
2. Postdating or antedating an instrument does not affect negotiability. [UCC 3-114(1)]
3. Handwritten terms outweigh typewritten and printed terms. [UCC 3-118(b)] For example, if your check is printed "Pay to the order of," and in handwriting you insert in the blank "John Smith or bearer," the check is a bearer instrument.
4. Words outweigh figures unless the words are ambiguous. [UCC 3-118(c)] This is important where the numerical amount and written amount on a check differ.
5. Where an interest rate is specified but not stated, "with interest," the interest rate is the judgment rate, not the legal rate. [UCC 3-118(d)]

CONCEPT SUMMARY: Eight Requirements For Negotiable Instruments	
REQUIREMENTS	**BASIC RULES**
Must Be in Writing UCC 3-104(1)	1. A writing can be on anything readily transferable which has a degree of permanence.
Must Be Signed by the Maker or Drawer UCC 3-104(1)(a) UCC 3-401(2) UCC 1-201(39)	1. The signature can be any place on the instrument. 2. It can be in any form (such as a word, mark, or rubber stamp) which purports to be a signature, and authenticates the writing. 3. It can be signed in a representative capacity.

(continued on next page)

CONCEPT SUMMARY, continued

REQUIREMENTS	BASIC RULES
Must Be a Definite Promise or Order UCC 3-104(1)(b)	1. A promise must be more than a mere acknowledgement of a debt. 2. The words "I/We promise" or "Pay" meet this criterion.
Must Be Unconditional UCC 3-104(1)(b) UCC 3-105	1. Payment cannot be expressly conditional upon the occurrence of an event. 2. Payment cannot be made subject to or governed by another agreement. 3. Payment cannot be paid only out of a particular fund (except for a government-issued instrument).
Must Be an Order or Promise to Pay a Sum Certain UCC 3-104(1)(b) UCC 3-106	1. An instrument is a sum certain even if paid in installments, with interest, at a stated discount, or at an exchange rate. 2. Inclusion of costs of collection and attorneys' fees does not disqualify as a sum certain.
Must Be Payable in Money UCC 3-104(1)(b) UCC 3-107	1. Any medium of exchange recognized as the currency of a government is money. 2. The maker or drawer cannot retain the option to pay the instrument in money or something else.
Must Be Payable on Demand or at a Definite Time UCC 3-104(1)(c) UCC 3-108 UCC 3-109	1. Any instrument payable on sight, presentation, or issue is a demand instrument. 2. An instrument is still payable at a definite time even though payable on or before a stated date, within a fixed period after sight, or the drawer or maker has an option to extend time for a definite period. 3. Acceleration clauses, even if unenforceable, do not affect the negotiability of the instrument.
Must Be Payable to Order or Bearer UCC 3-104(1)(d) UCC 3-110 UCC 3-111	1. An order instrument must name the payee with reasonable certainty. 2. An instrument whose terms intend payment to no particular person is payable to bearer.

QUESTIONS AND CASE PROBLEMS

1. The following note is written by Mary Ellen on the back of an envelope: "I, Mary Ellen, promise to pay to Kathy Martin or bearer $100 on demand." Discuss fully if this constitutes a negotiable instrument.

2. A promissory note is signed by Peter Paul. The note is dated May 1, 1985. Assuming that all other terms in the note meet the requirements for negotiability, discuss fully whether the following clause would render the note nonnegotiable: "This note is payable 100 years from date, but payment of principal plus interest is due and payable immediately upon the death of the maker."

3. The following instrument was written on a sheet of paper by Moss Martin: "I, the undersigned, do hereby acknowledge that I owe Sam Smith one thousand dollars, with interest, payable out of the proceeds of the sale of my horse, Thundercloud, next month. Payment is to be made on or before six months from date." Discuss specifically why this instrument is nonnegotiable.

4. You have signed a year's lease for an apartment near campus. The October rent is due and payable. You write a check for the rent due. On the check you write the following, "Payment for October rent as per lease agreement."

    (a) Does this statement render the instrument nonnegotiable? Explain.

    (b) Would your answer be any different if the written clause read, "Payment subject to the terms of a signed lease dated September 1, 1985"?

5. Martin Moss is in need of a loan. He borrows $500 from his friend, Paula Peters, signing a promissory note. Two clauses in the note are as follows:

    (a) "On or before July 1, 1986, I promise to pay to Paula Peters or bearer $550 in cash or title to my 1978 car, at the holder's option."

    (b) "The maker hereof reserves the right to extend the time of payment of said note for six months; however, the holder reserves the right to extend the time of payment indefinitely."

Explain whether either or both clauses render Martin's note nonnegotiable.

6. Ingel entered into a contract with Allied Aluminum Associates, Inc., to have aluminum siding put on his home. Ingel executed a promissory note naming Allied as payee, and, at the same time, both Ingel and the Allied representative signed a completion certificate that bound Allied to complete the job satisfactorily. The completion certificate was not mentioned in or attached to the promissory note. Allied Aluminum Associates later negotiated the promissory note to Universal C.I.T. Credit Corp. Allied never finished the aluminum siding work and was never heard from again. In a suit by Universal to collect on the note, Ingel's defense turned on whether the promissory note was negotiable. Ingel contended that it was not negotiable since it was accompanied by a completion certificate that contained promises other than the promise merely to pay a sum certain in money. Will Ingel's argument succeed? [Universal C.I.T. Credit Corp. v. Ingel, 347 Mass. 119, 196 N.E.2d 847 (1964)]

7. Joe Jones Trucking Co. owed Mason, a lessor, $3,000 for the rental of certain trucking equipment. Mason in-

formed the president of Joe Jones Trucking, Blayton, that unless he issued his personal check for $3,000 immediately, Mason would sue the company. Mason promised to hold onto the check for two days to allow Joe Jones Trucking time to pay the arrearages. When the company failed to do so, Mason attempted to deposit the check, but Blayton had stopped payment on it. Blayton claimed that the check was subject to a condition—that it would be void if the company failed to pay the arrearages within two days—and that therefore the check was not negotiable. If Mason's agreement not to cash the check was first made orally over the phone and later put in writing, will this affect the negotiability of the check issued by Blayton? [Mason v. Blayton, 119 Ga.App. 203, 166 S.E.2d 601 (1969)]

8. Hotel Evans, Inc., issued two promissory notes, as maker, to A. Alport & Son, Inc., payee. One note contained a promise by Hotel Evans to pay Alport $1,600 "with interest at bank rates." The other note, for $900, had "bank rates" typed in after the printed word "interest." Are either of these promissory notes negotiable? [A. Alport & Son, Inc. v. Hotel Evans, Inc., 65 Misc.2d 374, 317 N.Y.S.2d 937 (1970)]

9. In October 1970, Hall issued a draft that included the following: "Pay to L. Westmoreland and B. Bridges or order $1,000 on demand." Before he handed it to Bridges, Hall scratched out the words *or order* with his pen. Does the fact that the draft is payable to two payees destroy its negotiability? Does the scratching out of the words *or order* destroy the draft's negotiability? [First Federal Sav. and Loan Ass'n v. Branch Banking and Trust Co., 282 N.C. 44, 191 S.E.2d 683 (N.C. 1972)]

10. The Williamsons held a note secured by a second mortgage on a farm they had sold to the Wanlesses. The Wanlesses sometimes made payments later than the first of the month, but they never missed a payment. The Williamsons brought suit to enforce the acceleration clause in the note. Could the Williamsons prove that they believed in good faith that payment or performance might be impaired? [Williamson v. Wanless, 545 P.2d 1145 (1976)]

25

COMMERCIAL PAPER
Transferability and Negotiation

Commercial paper must be freely transferable. Once a negotiable instrument circulates beyond the original parties, the commercial law principles of negotiation come into play. The method of transfer that is used to pass a negotiable instrument from person to person determines the rights and duties that are passed with it.

Strictly speaking, negotiation occurs at the first delivery of a negotiable instrument to a holder, when the maker or drawer *issues* the instrument. [UCC 3-102(1)(a)] Typically, however, in commercial practice, the term *negotiation* is used to identify transfers occurring in a particular way after the instrument has been issued.

As already pointed out, the method of transfer determines the rights and duties that are passed with the negotiable instrument. Furthermore, whether the instrument is an order or bearer instrument (as discussed in Chapter 24) will determine how one *initially* negotiates it.

ASSIGNMENT AND NEGOTIATION

Once issued, a negotiable instrument can be transferred by *assignment* or by *negotiation*.

Assignment

Recall from Chapter 14 that under general contract principles, a transfer by assignment to an assignee gives the assignee only those rights that the assignor possessed. Assignment is a transfer of rights under a contract. Any defenses that can be raised against an assignor can be raised against the assignee (unless there is an enforceable waiver of defense clause). Article 3 applies only to negotiable instruments; there can be no *negotiation* of a nonnegotiable instrument. Furthermore, when a transfer fails to qualify as a negotiation, it becomes an assignment. The transferee is then an *assignee*, rather than a *holder*.

Negotiation

Negotiation is the transfer of an instrument in such form that the transferee becomes a holder. [UCC 3-202(1)] Under UCC principles, a transfer by negotiation creates a holder who, at the very least, receives the rights of the previous possessor. [UCC 3-201(1)] Unlike an assignment, a transfer by negotiation can make it possible for a holder to receive more rights in the instrument than the prior possessor. [UCC 3-305] (A holder who receives greater rights is known as a *holder in due course*. See Chapter 26). There are two methods of negotiating an instrument so that the receiver becomes a holder.

Negotiating Order Paper   **Order paper** contains the name of a payee capable of indorsing, as in "pay to the order of Jane Smith." Order paper is also paper that has as its last or only indorsement a *special* indorsement, as in "pay to Smith. [Signed] Jones."

If the instrument is order paper, it is negotiated by delivery with any necessary indorsements. For example, the Transco Company issues a payroll check "to the order of Jane Smith." Smith takes the check to the supermarket, signs her name on the back (an indorsement), gives it to the cashier (a delivery), and receives cash. Smith has negotiated the check to the supermarket. [UCC 3-202(1)]

Negotiating Bearer Paper   If an instrument is payable to bearer, it is negotiated by delivery—that is, by transfer into another person's possession. Indorsement is not necessary. [UCC 3-202(1)] The use of *bearer paper* involves more risk through loss or theft than the use of order paper.

Assume Bob Brown writes a check "payable to cash" and hands it to Debbie Myers (a delivery). Brown has negotiated the check (a bearer instrument) to Myers. Myers places the check in her wallet, which is subsequently stolen. The thief has possession of the check. At this point, negotiation has not occurred, because delivery must be voluntary on the part of the transferor. However, if the thief "delivers" the check to an innocent third person, negotiation will be complete. All rights to the check will be passed *absolutely* to that third person, and Myers will lose all right to recover the proceeds of the check from that third person. [UCC 3-305] Of course, she can recover her money from the thief if the thief can be found.

Converting Order to Bearer Paper and Vice Versa   The method used for negotiation depends upon the character of the instrument at the time the negotiation takes place. For example, a check originally payable to "Cash," but subsequently indorsed "Pay to Jones," must be negotiated as order paper (by indorsement and delivery) even though it was previously bearer paper. [UCC 3-204(1)]

An instrument payable to the order of a named payee and indorsed in blank (see Exhibit 25–1) becomes a bearer instrument. [UCC 3-204(2)] To illustrate: A check is made payable to the order of John Smith. The check is issued to Smith, and Smith indorses his name on the back of it. The instrument can now be negotiated by delivery only. Smith can negotiate the check to whomever he wishes by delivery, and that person in turn can negotiate by delivery without indorsement. If Smith, after such indorsement, loses the check, then a finder can negotiate it further.

INDORSEMENTS

Indorsements are required whenever the instrument being negotiated is classified as an order instrument. (Many transferees of bearer paper require indorsement for identification purposes even though the UCC does not require it.) An **indorsement** is a signature with or without additional words or statements. It is most often written on the back of the instrument itself. If there is no room on the instrument, indorsements can be written on a separate piece of paper called an **allonge**. The allonge must be "so firmly affixed" to the instrument "as to become a part thereof." [UCC 3-202(2)] Pins or paper clips will not suffice. Some courts hold that staples are sufficient.

One purpose of an indorsement is to effect the negotiation of order paper. Sometimes the transferee of bearer paper will request the holder-transferor to indorse. This is done to impose liability on the indorser. The liability of indorsers will be discussed later, in Chapter 27.

Once an instrument qualifies as a negotiable instrument, the form of indorsement will have no effect on the character of the underlying instrument. Indorsement relates to the right of the holder to negotiate the paper and the manner in which it must be done.

Types of Indorsements

We will examine four categories of indorsements:

1. Blank.
2. Special.
3. Qualified.
4. Restrictive.

Blank Indorsements   A **blank indorsement** specifies no particular indorsee and can consist of a mere signature. [UCC 3-204(2)] Hence, a check payable "to the order of Rosemary White" can be indorsed in blank simply by having her signature written on the back of the check. Exhibit 25–1 shows a blank endorsement.

An instrument payable to order and indorsed in blank becomes payable to bearer and can be negotiated by delivery alone. [UCC 3-204(2)] In other words, a blank indorsement converts an order instrument to a bearer instrument, which anybody can

---

EXHIBIT 25–1   Blank Indorsement

Rosemary White

EXHIBIT 25–2   Special Indorsement

Pay to Sam Wilson
Arthur Engles

---

cash. If De Wert indorses a check payable to her order in blank and then loses it on the street, Jones can find it and sell it to Smith for value without indorsing it. This constitutes a negotiation because Jones makes delivery of a bearer instrument (which was an order instrument until it was indorsed).

Special Indorsements   A **special indorsement** indicates the specific person to whom the indorser intends to make the instrument payable; that is, it names the indorsee. [UCC 3-204(1)] No special words of negotiation are needed. Words such as "pay to the order of Wilson" or "pay to Wilson" followed by the signature of the indorser are sufficient. When an instrument is indorsed in this way, it is order paper. Had the words "pay to Wilson" been used on the face of the instrument to indicate the payee, the instrument would not have been negotiable.

To avoid the risk of loss from theft, one may convert a blank indorsement to a special indorsement. This returns the bearer paper to order paper. UCC 3-204(3) allows a holder to "convert a blank indorsement into a special indorsement by writing over the signature of the indorser in blank any contract consistent with the character of the indorsement."

For example, a check is made payable to Arthur Engles. He indorses his name by blank indorsement on the back of the check and negotiates the check to Sam Wilson. Sam, not wishing to cash the check immediately, wants to avoid any risk should he lose the check. He therefore writes "pay to Sam Wilson" above Arthur's blank indorsement. In this manner Sam has converted Arthur's blank indorsement into a special indorsement. Further negotiation now requires Sam Wilson's indorsement plus delivery. (See Exhibit 25–2.)

Qualified Indorsements   Generally, an indorser, *merely by indorsing*, impliedly promises to pay the holder, or any subsequent indorser, the amount of the instrument in the event that the drawer or

maker defaults on the payment. [UCC 3-414(1)] A **qualified indorsement** is used by an indorser to disclaim or limit this liability on the instrument. In this form of indorsement, the notation *without recourse* is commonly used. A sample is shown in Exhibit 25–3.

EXHIBIT 25–3   Qualified Indorsement

Without recourse
Arthur Engles

A qualified indorsement is often used by persons acting in a representative capacity. For instance, insurance agents sometimes receive checks payable to them that are really intended as payment to the insurance company. The agent is merely indorsing the payment through to the principal and should not be required to make good on the check if it is later dishonored. The "without recourse" indorsement absolves the agent. If the instrument is dishonored, the holder cannot obtain recovery from the agent who indorsed "without recourse" unless the indorser has breached one of the warranties listed in UCC 3-417(2).

Usually blank and special indorsements are *unqualified* indorsements. That is, the blank or special indorser is guaranteeing payment of the instrument *in addition to* transferring title to it. The qualified indorser is not guaranteeing such payment. Nonetheless, the qualified indorsement ("without recourse") still transfers title to the indorsee; an instrument bearing a qualified indorsement can be further negotiated.

Qualified indorsements are accompanied by either a special or a blank indorsement that determines further negotiation. Therefore, a special qualified indorsement makes the instrument an order instrument, and it requires an indorsement plus delivery for negotiation. A blank qualified indorsement makes the instrument a bearer instrument, and only delivery is required for negotiation.

To illustrate: A check is made payable to the order of Mary Smith. Mary wants to negotiate the check specifically to Harold Hollis with a qualified indorsement. Mary would indorse the check, "Pay to Harold Hollis, without recourse. [Signed] Mary Smith." For Harold to further negotiate the check to George Green, Harold would have to indorse and deliver the check to George.

Restrictive Indorsements   Prior to the existence of the UCC, a restrictive indorsement was thought to prohibit the further negotiation of an instrument. Although some who indorse in this manner still believe the restrictive indorsement prevents any further transfer, the Code holds to the contrary. UCC 3-206(1) states that "no restrictive indorsement prevents further transfer or negotiation of the instrument." The **restrictive indorsement** requires indorsees to comply with certain instructions regarding the funds involved. Restrictive indorsements come in many forms. UCC 3-205 categorizes four separate types.

Conditional Indorsements   When payment is dependent on the occurrence of some specified event, the instrument has a conditional indorsement. [UCC 3-205(a)] For example, Ted Smith indorses a note to read as follows (Exhibit 25-4):

EXHIBIT 25-4   Conditional Indorsement

Pay to Bob Block, provided he complete renovations on building number 23 by September 1, 1985

Jed Smith

Except against intermediary banks (defined in Chapter 28), the indorsement is enforceable, and neither Bob Block nor any subsequent holder has the right

to enforce payment against Block on the note before the condition is met. [UCC 3-206(3)]

It is important to note that a conditional indorsement does not prevent further negotiation of the instrument. However, if the conditional language had appeared on the face of the instrument, it would not have been negotiable because it would not have met the requirement that the note contain an unconditional promise to pay.

Indorsements Prohibiting Further Indorsement   An indorsement such as "pay to Bill Jones only. [Signed] X," does not destroy negotiability. Jones can negotiate the paper to a holder just as if it had read "pay to Bill Jones. [Signed] X." [UCC 3-206(1)] This type of restrictive indorsement has the same legal effect as a special indorsement. It is rarely used. [UCC 3-205(b)]

Indorsement for Deposit or Collection   A common type of restrictive indorsement is one that makes the indorsee (almost always a bank) a collecting *agent* of the indorser. (See Exhibit 25-5 for an illustration where the check is payable and issued to Mary Smith.)

EXHIBIT 25-5   For Deposit—For Collection Indorsement

For Deposit
Mary Smith
or
For Collection Only

In particular, a "Pay any bank or banker" or "For deposit only" indorsement has the effect of locking the instrument into the bank collection process. Only a bank can acquire rights of a holder following this indorsement until the item has been specially indorsed by a bank to a person who is not a bank. [UCC 4-201(2)] A bank's liability for payment of an instrument with a restrictive indorsement is discussed in Chapter 28. The court deals with a bank's special indorsement by an *allonge* after its *restrictive indorsement* in the next case.

LAMSON v.
COMMERCIAL CREDIT
CORPORATION

Supreme Court of Colorado,
1975.
531 P.2d 966.

BACKGROUND AND FACTS *Defendant Commercial Credit Corporation issued two checks payable to the order of Rauch Motor Co. Rauch Motor indorsed the checks in blank and deposited them in its account with University National Bank. University National stamped the checks "pay any bank" and sent them through the collection process. The checks were subsequently returned to University National marked "payment stopped." Several months later, University National indorsed the checks to Lamson, who sued Commercial Credit Corporation for the face amount of the checks. The trial court entered judgment for Lamson. The Court of Appeals reversed, and the Supreme Court of Colorado agreed to hear the case.*

DAY, Justice.

*   *   *   *

In reversing the trial court the Court of Appeals held as a matter of law that the plaintiff Lamson was not a holder of the checks. It arrived at the decision by ruling that the Bank's indorsement to Lamson was not in conformance with the Uniform Commercial Code because it was stapled to the checks. It was this interpretation of [UCC] 3-202(2) which prompted us to grant certiorari. It is that holding of the Court of Appeals which we expressly reverse.

When Rauch deposited the checks, it indorsed them in blank, transforming them into bearer paper. [UCC] 1-201(5) and 3-204(2). The Bank in turn indorsed the checks "pay any bank." That is a restrictive indorsement. [UCC]3-205(c). After a check has been restrictively indorsed, "only a bank may acquire the rights of a holder *   *   * [u]ntil the item has been specially indorsed by a bank to a person who is not a bank." [UCC] 4-201(2)(b).

There is no question that the checks were indorsed to Lamson by name, thus qualifying as a special indorsement. [UCC] 3-204(1). The problem is whether the special indorsement was correctly and properly affixed to the checks under [UCC] 3-202(2). It provides *inter alia* that "[a]n indorsement must be written *   *   * on behalf of the holder and on the instrument or on a paper so firmly affixed thereto as to become a part thereof."

*   *   *   *

We agree with the Court of Appeals' statement that a separate paper pinned or paper-clipped to an instrument is not sufficient for negotiation. [UCC] 3-202(2), comment 3. However, we hold, *contra* to its decision, that the section does permit stapling as an adequate method of firmly affixing the indorsement. *   *   * Therefore we hold that under the circumstances described, stapling an indorsement to a negotiable instrument is a permanent attachment to the checks so that it becomes "a part thereof."

[UCC] 1-201(20) defines a holder as "a person who is in possession of *   *   * an instrument *   *   * indorsed to him *   *   *." The Bank's special indorsement, stapled to the two checks, effectively made Lamson a holder, although not a holder in due course.

**DECISION
AND REMEDY**

The trial court's judgment for Lamson was reinstated.

Trust or Agency Indorsements Indorsements that are for the benefit of the indorser or a third person are trust, or agency, indorsements. Samples are shown in Exhibit 25–6.

The indorsement results in legal title vesting in the original indorsee. To the extent that the original indorsee pays or applies the proceeds consistently with the indorsement (for example, "in trust for Johnny

---

EXHIBIT 25-6 Trust Indorsements

Pay to Ann North
in trust for
Johnny North

R. P. North

or

Pay to Ann North
as agent for R. P. North

R. P. North

North * * *"), the indorsee is a holder and can become a holder in due course. (See Chapter 26.) [UCC 3-205(d) and 3-206(4)]

The fiduciary restrictions on the instrument do not reach beyond the original indorsee.[1] Any subsequent purchaser can qualify as a holder in due course unless he or she has actual notice that the instrument was negotiated in breach of the fiduciary duty.[2]

Unauthorized Signatures

People are not normally liable to pay on negotiable instruments unless their signatures appear on the instruments. Hence, an unauthorized signature is wholly inoperative and will not bind the person whose name is forged.[3] There are exceptions to this rule, found in UCC 3-404(1). If the person whose unauthorized signature was used ratifies that signature or is in some way precluded from denying it, then the unauthorized signature is operative. Addition-

ally, an unauthorized signature will operate as "the signature of the unauthorized signer in favor of any person who in good faith pays the instrument or takes it for value." [UCC 3-404(1)]

Generally when there is a forged or unauthorized *indorsement*, the burden of loss falls on the first party to take the forged indorsement. However, there are two situations in which the resulting loss falls on the drawer or maker. These situations are:

1. When an imposter induces the maker or drawer of an instrument to issue it to the imposter.
2. When a person signs as or on behalf of a maker or drawer, intending that the payee will have no interest in the instrument, and an agent or employee of the maker or drawer has supplied him or her with the name of the payee, also *intending* the payee to have no such interest. [UCC 3-405(1)] These situations often involve an employee who wishes to swindle an employer by padding bills or payrolls. This is frequently referred to as the *fictitious payee* rule.

Imposters: Signature and Name of Payee

An **imposter** is one who, by use of the mails, telephone, or personal appearance, induces a maker or drawer to issue an instrument in the name of an impersonated payee. The maker or drawer honestly believes that the imposter is actually the named payee and issues the instrument to the imposter. Since the maker or drawer did issue and intend the imposter to receive the instrument, the indorsement by the imposter is not treated as unauthorized when transferred to an innocent party.

In these situations, the unauthorized indorsement of a payee's name can be as effective as if the real payee had signed. The *imposter rule* of UCC 3-405 provides that an imposter's indorsement will be effective—that is, not a "forgery"—insofar as the drawer goes.

For example, a man walks into John Green's clothing store and purports to be Jerry Lewis soliciting contributions for his annual fund raising for muscular dystrophy. John Green has heard of the Lewis Telethon but has never met or seen Jerry Lewis. Wishing to support a worthy cause, Green writes out a check for $500 payable to Jerry Lewis and hands it to the imposter. The imposter forges the signature of Jerry Lewis and negotiates the check

---

1. Compare this to the rule governing conditional indorsements. A conditional indorsement binds all subsequent indorsers (except certain banks) and primary parties to see that the money is applied consistently with the condition. Agency or trust indorsements limit this responsibility only to the original indorsee. Subsequent parties are not encumbered with this restriction.
2. See Quantum Dev. v. Joy, 397 F.Supp. 329 (D.C.Virgin Is. 1975).
3. On the other hand, a drawee is charged with knowledge of the *drawer's* signature. The drawee cannot recover money it pays out to a holder in due course on a negotiable instrument bearing a forged drawer's signature. (See UCC 3-418)

to a Stop and Shop convenience store. Green discovers the fraud and stops payment on the check, claiming the payee's signature is forged. Since the imposter rule is in effect, Green cannot claim a forgery against Stop and Shop, and he must seek redress from the imposter. If Green had sent the check to the real Jerry Lewis, but the check had been stolen and negotiated to the store by a forged indorsement, the imposter rule would not apply, and Stop and Shop would have to seek redress against the forger.

Fictitious Payee

The so-called **fictitious payee** rule deals with the intent of the maker or drawer to issue an instrument to a payee who has *no interest* in the instrument. This most often takes place when (1) a dishonest employee deceives the employer-maker or drawer into signing an instrument payable to a party with no right to receive the instrument, or (2) the dishonest employee or agent has the authority to so issue the instrument on behalf of the maker or drawer. In these situations, the payee's indorsement is not treated as a forgery, and the maker or drawer is held liable on the instrument by an innocent holder.

Assume that the Revco Company gives its bookkeeper, Sam Snyde, general authority to issue checks in the company name drawn on Second Federal Bank so that Snyde can pay employees and pay other corporate bills. Snyde decides to cheat Revco out of $10,000 by issuing a check payable to Fanny Freid, an old acquaintance of his. Snyde does not intend Freid to receive any of the money, and Freid is not an employee or creditor of the company.

Snyde indorses the check in Freid's name, naming himself as indorsee. Snyde cashes the check with a local bank, which collects payment from the drawee bank, Second Federal. Second Federal then charges Revco's account $10,000.

Revco discovers the fraud and demands that its account be recredited. Who bears the loss? Neither the local bank that first accepted the check nor Second Federal are liable. The rule of UCC 3-405 provides the answer. Since Snyde's indorsement in the name of a payee with no interest in the instrument is "effective," there is no "forgery." Hence, the collecting bank is protected in paying on the check, and the drawee bank is protected in charging Revco's account. It is the employer-drawer, Revco, that bears the loss.[4]

Whether a dishonest employee actually signs the check or merely supplies his or her employer with names of fictitious creditors (or with true names of creditors having fictitious debts), the Code makes no distinction in result. For example, Ned Norris draws up the payroll list from which employee checks are written. Norris fraudulently adds the name Sue Swift (a fictitious person) to the payroll, thus causing checks to be issued to her. Again, it is the employer-drawer who bears the loss because the employer is in the best position to prevent such fraud.

In the following case, the court must determine whether an employer should bear the loss for checks wrongfully indorsed by an employee.

---

4.   May Dept. Stores Co. v. Pittsburgh Nat. Bank, 374 F.2d 109 (3rd Cir. 1967).

DANJE FABRICS v.
MORGAN GUARANTY
TRUST CO.

New York Supreme Court, 1978.
24 UCC Rep. Serv. 188.

BACKGROUND AND FACTS   *Danje Fabrics, a company that converted yarn into fabric, hired Caulder as its bookkeeper. Specialty Dyers dyed fabrics for Danje. Caulder prepared checks in payment of Specialty Dyers's invoices and submitted them to Danje's president for signature. After Caulder's employment was terminated, it was discovered that he had taken twenty-seven checks payable to Specialty Dyers and diverted them into an account he opened at Citibank in the name of Specialty Dyers. Danje sought recovery from Morgan, the drawee bank, for wrongfully deducting the amount of these checks from Danje's account.*

GROSSMAN, Judge.
*   *   *   *

Citibank contends that Morgan has a complete defense to the claim set forth by Danje in its complaint by reasons of the provisions of § 3-405 of the Uniform Commercial Code.

This section provides in pertinent part:

"Section 3-405. Imposters; Signatures in Name of Payee. (1) An indorsement by any person in the name of a named payee is effective if * * * (c) an agent or employee of the maker or drawer has supplied him with the name of the payee intending the latter to have no such interest."

Since it was Caulder who was responsible for the preparation of checks based upon invoices given to him by plaintiff Danje's production department and who presented such checks to the individual who was authorized to sign them, Citibank argues, and Morgan agrees, that, based upon the facts as herein set forth, Caulder "supplied" the plaintiff with the name of the payee intending the latter to have no such interest and therefore the endorsements in question are effective. Danje's position is that, since the twenty-seven checks in question were prepared as a result of bona fide business transactions between Dyers, the named payee, and Danje, Caulder did not "supply" plaintiff with the name of the payee but simply converted the checks to his own use, and that therefore § 3-405(1)(c) of the Uniform Commercial Code has no application to the instant case.

Therefore, the issue to be decided in this case is what scope the word "supplied", as used in § 3-405(1)(c) of the Uniform Commercial Code was intended to have. Was it the legislature's intent for it to cover all instances where an employee presents an instrument to the maker for signature or must a line be drawn to distinguish between those instances where the instrument is based upon a fraudulent transaction and those where the instrument is based upon a bona fide transaction occurring in the regular course of business?

* * * *

Although the Official Comment [to UCC 3-405] makes mention only of "padded payroll" cases, it is clear that the provisions of the Code extend beyond these to other "padded" cases where the operative facts are present, i.e., where the drawer's agent or employee prepares the checks, presumably drawn for payroll or other valid purposes, for signature or otherwise furnishes the signing officer with the name of the payee.

* * * *

In our present case, the checks stolen by Caulder were legitimate and bona fide payments due and owing to Dyers. The checks themselves involved in our case were not fraudulent in any respect and the facts herein indicate that proper and careful business procedures were followed in the drawing and making of said checks. The undisputed facts herein further show that it was only the criminal conduct of Caulder in appropriating, stealing and falsely endorsing said checks, which constituted legitimate payments to the named payee, that resulted in the loss herein incurred by Danje.

* * * *

In our instant case, the checks involved were based upon bona fide transactions and obligations of the plaintiff which arose out of the normal business relationship with the payee named on said checks. In such instance, it cannot be claimed that the employee, Caulder, supplied his employer, Danje, with the name of the payee, Dyers, as said checks were legitimately based upon open invoices due and owing to the payee, Dyers.

The indorsements forged by Caulder were ineffective. Danje was entitled to have its account credited by Morgan. Morgan could then recover from Citibank under the warranties made by Citibank as the collecting bank. **DECISION AND REMEDY**

Miscellaneous Indorsement Problems

No Standard Category Sometimes an indorsement does not seem to fit into any of the standard categories. For example, the indorsement can read: "I hereby assign all my right and title and interest in this note. [Signed] Bob Smith." The signature is an effective indorsement despite the additional language of transfer. Use of the word *assign* does not change the negotiation into a mere assignment. Clearly Bob Smith did not intend to limit the rights of the person to whom he was transferring the instrument. [UCC 3-202(4)]

Correction of Name An indorsement should be identical to the name that appears on the instrument. The payee or indorsee whose name is misspelled can indorse with the misspelled name, or the correct name, or both. [UCC 3-203]

For example, Susan Lock receives a check payable to the order of "Susan Locke." She can indorse the check either "Susan Locke" or "Susan Lock." The usual practice is to indorse the name as it appears on the instrument and follow it by the correct name.[5]

Bank Indorsements When a customer deposits a check with a bank and fails to indorse it, the bank has the right to supply any necessary indorsement for its customer unless the instrument *specifically prohibits it*. [UCC 4-205(1)]

For example, Bob Adams deposits his government check with First National Bank and forgets to indorse it. Since government checks typically state, "Payee's indorsement required," the bank will not supply the indorsement. The check will be returned to Adams for his signature.

Ordinarily, checks do not specifically require the payee's indorsement. The bank merely stamps or marks the check, indicating that it was deposited by the customer or credited to the customer's account. [UCC 4-205]

Commercial paper must move rapidly through banking channels. In the process of clearing through

collection, a check can be transferred between banks using any agreed-upon method of indorsement that identifies the transferor bank. [UCC 4-206] For example, a bank can indorse using its Federal Reserve number instead of its name.

Multiple Payees An instrument payable to two or more persons *in the alternative* (for example, "Pay to Able or Baker") requires the indorsement of one of the payees. [UCC 3-116(a)] However, if an instrument is payable to two or more persons *jointly* (for example, "Pay Carl and Doris" or "Pay Glenda, Harold"), then all the payees' indorsements are necessary for negotiation. [UCC 3-116(b)]

Unindorsed Order Paper If order paper is transferred without indorsement, it is a transfer by assignment, not by negotiation. The receiver is merely a transferee, not a holder, and does not qualify as a holder in due course. If, however, the transfer is made for value given, the unqualified indorsement of the transferor can be compelled by law by the transferee unless the parties have agreed otherwise. The effect is the negotiation of the instrument. The transferee becomes a holder and can negotiate the instrument further. [UCC 3-201(3)] Compare this rule with that of the bank's right, upon deposit of an unindorsed check, as previously discussed.

Agents or Officers A negotiable instrument can be drawn payable to a legal entity such as an estate, a partnership, or an organization. For example, if a check reads "Pay to the Red Cross," an authorized representative of the Red Cross can negotiate it.

Similarly, negotiable paper can be payable to a public officer. For example, checks reading "Pay to the order of the County Tax Collector," or "Pay to Larry White, Receiver of Taxes," can be negotiated by whoever holds the office. [UCC 3-110(1)(b)]

---

5. Watertown Federal Sav. and Loan v. Spanks, 346 Mass. 398, 193 N.E.2d 333 (1963).

QUESTIONS AND CASE PROBLEMS

1. A check drawn by Daniel for $200 is made payable to the order of Paula. The check is issued to Paula. Paula owes her landlord $200 in rent and transfers the check to her landlord with the following indorsement: "For rent

paid. [Signed] Paula." Paula's landlord has contracted to have Peter Plumber repair a number of apartment leaks. The plumber insists on immediate payment. The landlord transfers the check to Peter without indorsement. Later, in order to pay for plumbing supplies at Facet's Store, Peter transfers the check with the following indorsement: "Pay to Facet's Store, without recourse. [Signed] Peter Plumber." Facet sends the check to its bank indorsed "For deposit only. [Signed] Facet's Store."

(a) Classify each of these indorsements.

(b) Was the transfer from Paula's landlord to Peter Plumber, without indorsement, an assignment or a negotiation? Explain.

2. Dan David drafts a check for $500 payable to the order of Jane Petrie. Petrie wants to purchase Fred Flint's 1972 Chevy for $500 and contracts to do so, with payment to be immediate and delivery of the car to be seven days thereafter. Petrie indorses David's check to Flint as "Pay to Flint, upon condition of delivery of his 1972 Chevy. [Signed] Jane Petrie." Flint takes the check and indorses it, "For deposit. [Signed] Fred Flint."

On his way to the bank to deposit the check, Flint is sidetracked by a flea market sale. Flint purchases an old clock and gives the indorsed check to Gary Gambler, the seller of the clock. Gambler deposits the check with his bank.

Assume Dan David has a legal right to stop payment on the check, and assume that Flint has not delivered the car.

    (a) How would each of the above indorsements be classified?

    (b) What is the legal effect of Petrie's indorsement under the circumstances?

    (c) Could Flint legally negotiate the check to Gambler with an indorsement "for deposit"? Explain.

3. Able Ledger has been Ann Green's employee accountant for five years. During that time, Green has relied more and more on Ledger to prepare payment checks for suppliers, payroll checks, and the like. Unknown to Green, Ledger is a compulsive gambler and is deeply in debt. Ledger, believing that his life is at stake, prepares two checks payable to nonexistent suppliers. Green signs both checks without knowledge of these events. Ledger indorses both suppliers' names and adds "pay to Able Ledger" above both names. Ledger takes the checks and deposits them at his bank without indorsement. Later, he withdraws the funds from his bank. His bank sends the checks through the collection process. The checks are paid by Green's bank, the drawee. Green discovers Ledger's action after Ledger has left town. Green claims that Ledger's indorsement of the suppliers' names constituted a forgery, that Ledger's bank did not have Ledger's indorsement, and that therefore the bank must recredit her account. Discuss Green's contentions.

4. John and Mary Smith ordered a clock from a catalog seller. John sent the seller a check for $50 with the order. The seller cashed the check. When the seller found she could not deliver the clock, she drew and sent a refund check to the Smiths. When the Smiths received the check, they noticed that it was made payable to Jonathan and Mary Smith. Mary Smith is now away visiting her mother, and John needs to negotiate the check to pay an overdue bill.

    (a) Can John properly negotiate the check without Mary's indorsement? Explain.

    (b) John is concerned that the check is made payable to Jonathan, not John. Would this prohibit John from negotiating the check under any circumstances? Explain.

5. Jay Jones is an Elevated Party candidate for the city council in a large city. It is common knowledge that Jones is personally soliciting funds throughout the neighborhood. Frank Francis has been a member of the Elevated Party for years. He receives a phone call from Sam Shady, who pretends to be Jay Jones and asks for financial help. Over the phone Francis agrees to write a check for $200 payable to Jay Jones. Shady gives Jones a post office box address. Francis writes the check and sends it to the box as directed. Shady has nothing to do with the campaign of Jones, and the box is his own. Shady immediately takes the check and indorses the name of Jones and then his own name. Shady now negotiates the check to a friend, Judy Green, who has no knowledge of Shady's activities. Shady leaves the country. Later, Francis learns of the fraud. Francis claims that since the signature of Jones was forged by Shady, Francis is not liable to Green on the check. Discuss the contention of Francis.

6. Dynamics Corp. and Marine Midland Bank had a long-standing agreement under which Marine Midland received checks payable to Dynamics and indorsed and deposited them in Dynamics' account. Dynamics never saw the checks. They were made out to the order of Dynamics and delivered directly to Marine Midland. Marine Midland stamped the backs of the checks with Dynamics' name and insignia and transferred them. Within the meaning of the UCC, is the act of sending checks to Marine Midland Bank a negotiation? If Marine Midland transfers the checks to other parties, is this a negotiation? [Marine Midland Bank–New York v. Graybar Electric Co., 41 N.Y.2d 703, 363 N.E.2d. 1139 (1977)]

7. A life insurance policy was taken out on the life of Robert Agaliotis by Louis Agaliotis, his father. A provision in the policy allowed Louis to request $1,852 be paid to him as the owner of the policy. Through a clerical error, the insurance company made the check payable to Robert, but was correctly delivered to Louis. If Louis indorses Robert's name and cashes the check, will he be liable for wrongfully indorsing the check? [Agaliotis v. Agaliotis, 247 S.E.2d 28 (N.C. 1978)]

8. Davis, a Marine, often ran out of money and telegraphed his father to wire him extra cash. On August 1, 1945, the father received a telegram, purportedly from his son, requesting $250. The father wired a money order to the Western Union office nearest his son's base. Though the Western Union money order application contained an option whereby the father could require positive identification of the recipient at the other end, the father failed to sign for this special provision. Later, when the father learned that an imposter, not his son, had received the $250, he demanded his money back from Western Union.

Western Union declined. Should the father recover? [Davis v. Western Union Telegraph Co., 4 D. & C.2d. 264 (Pa. 1956)]

9. F. Mitchell, assistant treasurer of Travco Corporation, caused two checks payable to a fictitious company, L. and B. Distributors, to be drawn on the corporation's account. Mitchell took both checks to his personal bank, indorsed them "F. Mitchell," and gave them to the teller. The teller cashed them. When Travco learned of the embezzlement, it demanded reimbursement from the bank. The bank contended that under the rule concerning fictitious payees and imposters, Mitchell's indorsement was valid and that therefore the bank should be allowed to collect. Is the bank's contention true? [Travco Corp. v. Citizens Federal Sav. & Loan Ass'n, 42 Mich.App. 291, 201 N.W.2d. 675 (1972)]

10. Wilson was the bookkeeper for Palmer and Ray Dental Supply. Wilson was to deposit several checks into Palmer and Ray's account. However, Wilson, using a rubber stamp with the company's name and address, indorsed the checks and then cashed them.
   (a) Did Wilson effectively change the checks from order paper to bearer paper?
   (b) If the checks were effectively changed to bearer paper, could Palmer and Ray recover the money from the bank that cashed the checks?
[Palmer and Ray Dental Supply of Abilene v. First National Bank, 447 S.W.2d 954 (Tex.Civ.App., 1972)]

26

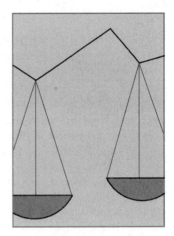

COMMERCIAL PAPER
Holder in Due Course

Commercial paper is not money; rather, it is an instrument that is payable in money. Litigation concerning commercial paper occurs when there is a dispute about who should be paid. Issues of litigation usually turn on which party can obtain payment on an instrument when it is due or on whether or not some defense can be asserted to discharge or to cancel liability on an instrument. For these reasons, it becomes important for a person seeking payment to have the rights of a holder in due course.

A holder in due course takes a negotiable instrument free of all claims and most defenses of other parties. That means that the holder in due course has the right to collect payment on that instrument, and this right will take priority over the claims of other parties.[1]

CONTRACT LAW VERSUS THE LAW OF COMMERCIAL PAPER

The basic principles of contract law govern when simple contract rights are assigned to a third party,

when a nonnegotiable instrument is transferred to a third party, or when a negotiable instrument is improperly negotiated to a third party (transferee). The contract rights of assignees or transferees are burdened with every legal defense that existed between prior parties regardless of the extent of their knowledge of them. Persons who transfer or assign contractual or nonnegotiable rights pass on only the rights that they had.

For example, Martin contracts in writing to purchase a used word processor from Francis for $600. Martin needs the word processor in his business. Martin pays $200 down and agrees to pay the balance, plus 10 percent interest, in six equal installments. Francis, as part of the sale, made express warranties as to the amount of prior use and the condition of the word processor. Shortly after the sale and transfer, Francis sells and assigns the contract and the balance due to Arlene. Martin learns that Francis has lied about the prior use, and the processor is not in the condition warranted. Martin refuses to make any further payments on the contract, claiming breach of warranty. Arlene insists that she has no knowledge of the deceit, is an innocent party, and wants to enforce the contractually obligated payments against Martin. Because Arlene as assignee is subject to any defense Martin has against the assignor, Francis, Arlene is subject to the claims and defenses of Martin.

---

1. UCC 3-305(2) specifically sets forth the very limited number of real *defenses* that defeat payment to a holder in due course. A holder in due course takes commercial paper free from personal (as opposed to real) defenses. These are discussed more thoroughly in Chapter 27.

The body of rules contained in Article 3 of the UCC govern a party's right to payment of a check, draft, note, or certificate of deposit.[2] The third party is characterized as either an ordinary *holder* or a *holder in due course*.[3] (The party can also be a transferee according to UCC 3-201.) Our discussion of holders in due course will be concerned primarily with *negotiable* instruments that have been negotiated.

HOLDER VERSUS HOLDER IN DUE COURSE

As pointed out in Chapter 23, a holder is a person who possesses a negotiable instrument "drawn, issued, or indorsed to him or his order or to bearer or in blank." [UCC 1-201(20)] In other words, the holder is the person who, by the terms of the instrument, is legally entitled to payment. The holder of an instrument need not be its owner in order to transfer it, negotiate it, discharge it, or enforce payment of it in his or her own name. [UCC 3-301]

A holder has the status of an assignee of a contract right. A transferee of a negotiable instrument who is characterized merely as a holder (as opposed to a holder in due course) obtains only those rights that the predecessor-transferor had in the instrument. In the event that there is a conflicting, superior claim or defense to the instrument, an ordinary holder will not be able to collect payment.

A **holder in due course** (HDC) is a special-status transferee of a negotiable instrument who, by meeting certain acquisition requirements, takes the instrument *free* of most defenses or adverse claims to it. Stated another way, an HDC can normally acquire a higher level of immunity to defenses against payment on the instrument or claims of ownership to the instrument by other parties.

REQUIREMENTS FOR HOLDER-IN-DUE-COURSE STATUS

The basic requirements for attaining HDC status are set forth in UCC 3-302. An HDC must first be a holder of a negotiable instrument. The holder must take the instrument (1) for value, (2) in good faith, and (3) without notice that it is overdue, or that it has been dishonored, or that any person has a defense against it or a claim to it.

The underlying requirement of "due course" status is that a person must first be a holder on that instrument. Regardless of other circumstances surrounding acquisition, only a holder has a chance to become an HDC.

Taking for Value

An HDC must have given *value* for the instrument. [UCC 3-303] A person who receives an instrument as a gift or who inherits it has not met the requirement of value. In these situations, the person becomes an ordinary holder and does not possess the rights of an HDC.[4]

The concept of value in the law of negotiable instruments is not the same as the concept of consideration in the law of contracts. An executory promise (a promise to give value in the future) is a clearly valid consideration to support a contract. [UCC 1-201(44)] It does not, however, normally constitute value sufficient to make one an HDC. UCC 3-303 provides that a holder takes the instrument for value only to the extent that the agreed-upon consideration has been performed. Therefore, if the holder plans to pay for the instrument later or plans to perform the required services at some future date, the holder has not yet given value. In that case, the holder is not yet a holder in due course.

Suppose Ted Green draws a $500 note payable to Roger Evans in payment for goods. Evans negotiates the note to Irene Franks, who promises to pay him for it in thirty days. During the next month, Franks learns that Evans breached the contract by

---

2. The rights and liabilities on checks, drafts, notes, and certificates of deposit are determined under Article 3 of the UCC. Other kinds of commercial paper, such as stock certificates or bills of lading and other documents of title, meet the requirements of negotiable instruments, but the rights and liabilities of the parties on these documents are covered by Articles 7 and 8 of the Code.

3. A holder, as the term is used in Article 3 of the UCC, applies here only in the context of negotiable instruments.

4. There is one way an ordinary holder who fails to meet the value requirement can qualify as a holder in due course. The "shelter provision" of the Code allows an ordinary holder to succeed to HDC status if any prior holder was an HDC. This exception is discussed later in the chapter. [UCC 3-201(1)]

delivering defective goods and that Green will not honor the $500 note. Evans has left town. Whether Franks can hold Green liable on the note will depend on Franks's status as a holder in due course. Since Franks has given no value at the time of having learned of Green's defense, Franks is a mere holder, not a holder in due course. Thus, Green's defense is valid not only against Evans but also against Franks. If Franks had paid Evans for the note on the transfer (which would mean the agreed-upon consideration had been performed), she would be a holder in due course and could hold Green liable on the note even though Green had a valid breach of contract or warranty defense against Evans.

The Code provides for a holder to take the instrument for value in one of three ways. Basically, a holder gives value:

1. To the extent that the agreed-upon consideration has been paid or a security interest or lien acquired.
2. By payment of or as security for an antecedent debt.
3. By giving a negotiable instrument or irrevocable commitment as payment.

In the following case, the court takes up the question of value.

BACKGROUND AND FACTS *The plaintiff, Ethel Goldberg, sought to recover the sum of $7,500 on four promissory notes in which she was designated the payee. The notes were executed by six individual defendants. At the time the notes were made, the plaintiff's husband, Donald Goldberg, and the defendants were all stockholders in a corporation known as 86th Street Bay 40th Corporation. The notes were given in consideration for the sale of Donald Goldberg's interest in the corporation to the defendants. At Donald Goldberg's request, the notes were made payable to his wife, the plaintiff, who otherwise had no interest in or connection with the corporation.*

The defendants alleged that they had a valid cause of action that they should be able to assert against Donald Goldberg and against Ethel Goldberg as payee on the promissory notes because, at the time the notes were executed, Donald Goldberg specifically said that certain monies would be paid for goods that had been sold pursuant to a business deal in which the corporation was involved.

The defendants claimed that a balance of $7,643.33 was due as a result of this other business deal and that they should be able to bring an action against Donald Goldberg as a counterclaim, or, at least, as a setoff against the plaintiff's cause of action. [Background and Facts substantially as stated by the court.]

GOLDBERG v. ROTHMAN
Civil Court of the City of New York, 1971.
66 Misc.2d 981, 322 N.Y.S.2d 931.

BOYERS, Justice.
* * * *

There is no explanation or reason as to why plaintiff was designated payee of the subject notes other than it was done in compliance with Donald Goldberg's request. Nor does it appear that plaintiff took the instruments for "value" as that term is defined by § 3-303 of the Uniform Commercial Code. For ought that appears Donald Goldberg gave these notes as a gift to the plaintiff, but such a determination is not relevant to the issues herein. It is clear that a payee may be a holder in due course (see § 3-302, Uniform Commercial Code), but since the plaintiff herein did not take the instruments for value she is an ordinary holder. Nonetheless she has the rights of a holder and may enforce payment in her own name (§ 3-301, Uniform Commercial Code). * * *
[T]he court feels the merits or lack of merits of defendants' contention of an assignment and the promise of Donald Goldberg that the debt owing [to defendants] could be set

off against the notes is not relevant to plaintiff's cause of action for reasons hereafter set forth.

Under § 3-306, Uniform Commercial Code, plaintiff not having the rights of a holder in due course takes the instrument here, the notes in question, "subject to (b) all defenses of any party which would be available in an action on simple contract."

＊　＊　＊　＊

Plaintiff sues herein in her own right. Defendants have not shown that any defenses exist against her in relation to the validity of the notes nor have they established that they have any right of setoff because of an alleged claim against plaintiff's husband.

DECISION AND REMEDY   *The court held that Ethel Goldberg was entitled to recover $7,500 from the defendants. However, her award did not prejudice any cause of action the defendants had against Donald Goldberg. The court made it clear that the plaintiff's right to recover was independent of her husband's possible liability in another lawsuit.*

Agreed-upon Consideration Performed A holder takes an instrument for value to the extent that agreed-upon consideration has been performed. In the typical situation, the holder is a purchaser for money.

Performance of agreed-upon consideration can also include an act such as the delivery of goods. Harper holds a note from Barton and agrees to negotiate the note to Thompson in payment for a purchase of goods. Delivery of the goods is Thompson's agreed-upon performance, that is, the value given for the note.

UCC 3-303(a) provides that a holder takes an instrument for value only to the extent that the agreed-upon consideration has been performed. For example, Arnolds negotiates a $1,000 note to Raymonds for a total price of $950, with $700 payable now and $250 due in thirty days. Raymonds is immediately an HDC to the extent of $700, and when she completes payment of $250, she will become an HDC for the full $1,000 face amount of the note.

Do not be confused when the value of the agreed-upon consideration differs from the face amount of the instrument. When a time instrument is sold, it is usually discounted to allow for transfer costs, collection costs, and interest charges. Thus, a $1,000 note due in ninety days may be sold for $950 cash to a financial institution. The requirement of agreed-upon consideration is satisfied by the $950 payment. And when the instrument comes due, the holder will collect the full $1,000. If the discrepancy between the purchase amount and face value is great, however, this discrepancy can be considered along

with other factors to indicate either that the purchaser lacks good faith or that only a partial payment is being made, reducing the HDC status to this amount. The good faith element will be discussed later in this chapter.

A holder takes an instrument for value to the extent that the holder acquires a security interest in or lien on the instrument.[5] It is not unusual for an instrument to be given as security for a loan or other obligation.

If, for example, Norris issues a $1,000 note payable to Lomond, Lomond can use the note to secure a $700 loan from Hilton. (Lomond gets $700 cash; Hilton holds the note as security.) Hilton's $700 loan qualifies her as a holder for value. If Lomond does not repay the $700, Hilton can collect the note. But what if Norris has a personal defense against Lomond? Hilton, as an HDC, is free and clear of the defense, but *only to the extent of $700.* Hence, the rule is, "a purchaser of a limited interest can be a holder in due course only to the extent of the interest purchased." [UCC 3-302(4)]

A holder can also take for value by acquiring a lien on the instrument through an agreement rather than through operation of law. For example, a payee of a note pledges it to a bank as security for a loan. The terms of the pledge agreement give the bank a lien on the instrument. The bank is a holder for value to the extent of its lien.

---

5. A holder does not become an HDC of an instrument by purchasing it at a judicial sale or by taking it under legal process. [UCC 3-302(3)(a)]

Antecedent Claim When an instrument is given in payment of an **antecedent claim** (or as security for an antecedent, or prior, debt), the value requirement is met. [UCC 3-303(b)] Here again, commercial law and contract law produce different results. An antecedent debt is not valid consideration under general contract law, but it does constitute value sufficient to satisfy the requirement for HDC status in commercial law.

Assume Cary owes Dwyer $2,000 on a past due account. If Cary negotiates a $2,000 note to Dwyer and Dwyer accepts it to discharge the overdue account balance, Dwyer has given value for the instrument.

Negotiable Instrument as Value Merely promising to pay money or to perform an act in the future does not constitute giving value. However, if a purchaser's promise to pay money is made in the form of a negotiable instrument or irrevocable commitment (for example, a check or an irrevocable letter of credit), the requirement of value is met. UCC 3-303(c) provides that a holder takes the instrument for value "when he gives a negotiable instrument for it, or makes an irrevocable commitment to a third person."

To illustrate: Martin has issued a $500 negotiable promissory note to Paula. The note is due six months from the date issued. Paula's financial circumstances are such that she does not want to wait for the maturity date to collect. Therefore, Paula negotiates the note to her friend Susan, who pays Paula $200 in cash and writes Paula a negotiable check for the balance of $300. Susan has given full value for the note by paying $200 in cash and issuing Paula the check for $300.

A negotiable instrument has value when issued, not when the underlying obligation is finally paid. In the preceding example, assume that before Paula cashes Susan's check, Susan learns that the maker of the note has a personal defense against Paula. In this event, Susan has the protection of HDC status. Commercial practicality requires this rule because a negotiable instrument, by its nature, carries the possibility that it might be negotiated to a holder in due course. If it is, the party that issued it generally cannot refuse to pay. [UCC 3-303]

Check Deposits and Withdrawals Occasionally, a commercial bank can become an HDC when hon-

oring other banks' checks for its own customers. In this situation the bank becomes an "involuntary" holder in due course, in that at the time of giving value the bank has no intention of becoming an HDC.

Assume that on Monday morning at the end of the month Pat Stevens has $400 in her checking account at the First National Bank. That morning Stevens deposits her payroll check for $300 drawn by her employer on the Second National Bank. During her lunch hour she issues a check to her landlord for $425. The landlord cashes the check at the First National Bank. Later, the Second National Bank returns the payroll check marked "insufficient funds." In most cases, First National would charge this check against Stevens's account. If such cannot be done, however, is the First National Bank an HDC of the employer's check? The answer is yes. According to what is referred to as the first-money-in, first-money-out rule, First National Bank has paid to the landlord $25 of its own funds. [UCC 4-208(2)] Therefore, First National is an HDC to the extent it has given value—$25.

Special Cases In a few exceptional circumstances, a holder can take an instrument even for value but still not be accorded HDC status. UCC 3-302(3) specifies the following situations:

1. Purchase at a judicial sale (for example, a bankruptcy sale) or taking under legal process.
2. Acquisition when taking over an estate (as administrator).
3. Purchase as part of a bulk transfer (for example, a corporation buying the assets of another corporation).

This provision limits the rights of the holder to that of an ordinary holder.

Taking in Good Faith

The second requirement for HDC status is that the holder take the instrument in good faith. [UCC 3-302(1)(b)] This means that the purchaser-holder must have acted honestly in the process of acquiring the instrument. **Good faith** is defined in UCC 1-201(19) as "honesty in fact in the conduct or transaction concerned."

The good faith requirement *applies only to the holder.* It is immaterial whether the transferor acted in good faith. Thus, a person who in good faith takes a negotiable instrument from a thief can be an HDC. The reason is simple. An inherent characteristic of negotiable paper is that any person in possession of an instrument that runs to him or her by its terms is a holder. Also, anyone can deal with the possessor as a holder.

Because of the good faith requirement, one must ask whether the purchaser, when acquiring the instrument, honestly believed the instrument was not defective. If a person purchases a $10,000 note for $100 from a stranger on a street corner, the issue of good faith can be raised on the grounds of the suspicious circumstances *and* the grossly inadequate consideration. The Code does not provide clear guidelines to determine good faith. Thus, each situation will be examined separately.

In the following case the court focused on the issue of whether the IRS acquired a check in good faith.

VALLEY NAT. BANK v. PORTER

United States Court of Appeals, Eighth Circuit, 1983. 705 F.2d 1027.

BACKGROUND AND FACTS   *During 1975 and 1976 the plaintiff, Valley National Bank, made over $100,000 in loans to Van Dyck Heating and Air Conditioning, Inc., and the plaintiff took a security interest in all accounts and third-party checks payable to Van Dyck. When the defendant, an IRS agent, questioned Van Dyck about its slowness in making federal employment tax payments, Van Dyck began indorsing checks received from customers directly to the IRS. Over a five-month period, the defendant accepted twenty-five third-party checks from Van Dyck, amounting to $32,237.19. The plaintiff sued the defendant for wrongful conversion of the checks. At trial, the district judge ruled that the IRS was a holder in due course of the checks.*

PER CURIAM

*   *   *   *

On appeal the bank primarily contends that the district court erred in finding that the appellee was a holder in due course in that the evidence showed that IRS officers acted in bad faith and that under the totality of the circumstances they must be viewed as having notice of appellant's security interest.

Under the holder in due course doctrine, "good faith" is defined as "honesty in fact in the conduct or transition concerned." Iowa Code Ann. § 554.1201(19) (West 1967). This has been construed as requiring only honesty of intent measured under a subjective standard. *   *   * Mere negligence or knowledge of suspicious circumstances is not sufficient to show bad faith. *   *   * The definition of notice pertinent to the instant case is that a person has notice of a claim if "from all the facts and circumstances known to him at the time in question he has reason to know that it exists." Iowa Code Ann. § 554.1201(25) (West 1967). This is essentially an objective test of what a reasonable person in the holder's position would know, *   *   * and the issue has been phrased as whether a holder had "actual knowledge of facts from which it could reasonably infer the probable existence of the *   *   * claim?" *   *   *

The district court applied the foregoing principles to the evidence in the present case and concluded that: (1) the defendant had proved that the IRS agents acted in subjective good faith in accepting the third-party checks, *   *   * and (2) "[w]hen considered in the aggregate, the 'suspicious' circumstances cited by plaintiff could not have reasonably afforded [the defendant] constructive notice that the third-party checks *   *   * represented secured proceeds."

DECISION AND REMEDY   *The Court of Appeals upheld the district court's ruling. Valley Bank was unable to recover the $32,237.19 because the IRS was an HDC.*

Taking without Notice

The third requirement for HDC status involves notice. [UCC 3-304] A person will not be afforded HDC protection if he or she acquires an instrument knowing, or having reason to know, that it is defective in any one of the following ways: [UCC 3-302(1)(c)]

1. It is overdue.
2. It has been dishonored.
3. There is a defense against it.
4. There is another claim to it.

The main provisions of UCC 3-304 spell out the common circumstances that, as a matter of law, constitute notice of a claim or defense and notice of an overdue instrument. However, UCC 3-304(4) specifies certain facts that a purchaser might know about an instrument but that do not constitute notice of a defense or claim. These facts do not disqualify the purchaser from HDC status.

Notice of a fact involves [UCC 1-201(25)]: (1) Actual knowledge of it, (2) receipt of a notice about it, and (3) reason to know that a fact exists, given all the facts and circumstances known at the time in question.

Overdue Instruments   All negotiable paper is either payable at a definite time (time instrument) or payable on demand (demand instrument). What will constitute notice that an instrument is overdue or has been dishonored will vary depending upon whether a person takes demand or time paper.

Time Instruments   A holder of a time instrument who takes the paper the day after its expressed due date is "on notice" that it is overdue. Nonpayment by the due date should indicate to any purchaser who is obligated to pay that the primary party has a defense to payment. Thus, a promissory note due on May 15 must be acquired before midnight on May 15. If it is purchased on May 16, the purchaser will be an ordinary holder, not an HDC.

Sometimes instruments read, "Payable in thirty days." A note dated December 1 that is payable in thirty days is due by midnight on December 31. But, what if a note is dated December 2 and is payable in thirty days? When is it due? If the payment date falls on a Sunday or holiday, the instrument is payable on the next business day, so the note is due on January 2.

A large debt is often broken down into successive payments. The debt can be evidenced by a single, large-denomination note payable in installments, or there can be a series of notes in smaller denominations issued, each identified as part of the same indebtedness. In the case of an installment note, notice that the maker has defaulted on any installment of principal (but not interest payments) will prevent a purchaser from becoming an HDC. [UCC 3-304(3)(a)] Most installment notes provide specifically that any payment made on the note shall be applied first to interest, with the balance to principal. Thus, any installment payment submitted that is less than the amount owed on that installment would put a holder on notice that the note is overdue.

The same result occurs when a series of notes, each with successive maturity dates, is issued at the same time for a single indebtedness. An uncured default in payment of any one note of the series will constitute overdue notice for the entire series. Prospective purchasers then know that they cannot qualify as HDCs.

Suppose a note reads, "Payable May 15, but may be accelerated if the holder feels insecure." A purchaser, unaware that a prior holder has elected to accelerate the due date on the instrument, buys the instrument prior to May 15. UCC 3-304(3)(b) provides that such a purchaser can be a holder in due course unless he or she has reason to know that the acceleration has occurred.

Demand Instruments   A purchaser has notice that a demand instrument is overdue if he or she takes the instrument knowing that demand has been made or takes it an unreasonable length of time after its issue. "A reasonable time for a check drawn and payable within the states and territories of the United States and the District of Columbia is *presumed* to be 30 days." [UCC 3-304(3)(c)] [Emphasis added]

Obviously, what constitutes a reasonable time period depends on the circumstances. Except for a domestic check, in which a reasonable time is presumed to be thirty days, there are no exact measurements for determining a reasonable time. Past cases indicate, however, that a reasonable time for payment of an interest-bearing demand instrument is longer than for one payable without interest.

Dishonored Instruments   Actual knowledge that an instrument was previously dishonored, or knowledge of facts that would lead a holder to suspect that such had happened, puts a holder on notice. Thus, a check clearly stamped "insufficient funds," taken by a person, would put that person on notice. No notice exists without this knowledge. For example, Burton holds a demand note dated March 1 on Kayto, Inc., a local business firm. On March 19, she demands payment, and Kayto refuses (that is, dishonors the instrument). On March 20, Burton negotiates the note to Reynolds, a purchaser who lives in another state. Reynolds does not know and has no reason to know that the note has been dishonored, so Reynolds is not put on notice and therefore can become an HDC.

Claims against or Defenses to an Instrument   Knowledge of claims or defenses can be imputed to the purchaser in certain situations because (1) they are apparent from an examination of the face of the instrument or (2) they are extraneous to the instrument but apparent from the facts surrounding the transaction.

The Code provides that a purchaser of a negotiable instrument has "notice of a claim or defense if * * * the instrument is so incomplete, bears such visible evidence of forgery or alteration, or is otherwise so irregular as to call into question its validity, terms of ownership * * * or * * * that the obligation of any party is voidable in whole or in part, or that all parties have been discharged." [UCC 3-304(1)(a)(b)]

Incomplete Instruments   A purchaser cannot expect to become an HDC when an instrument is so incomplete on its face that an element of negotiability is lacking (for example, the name of the payee on order paper is missing, or the amount is not filled in). Minor omissions are permissible because these do not call into question the validity of the instrument.

For example, omission of connective words, such as the "on" in "pay to Smith on order," does not affect negotiability and neither does omission of the date from a check that has the month and year. [UCC 3-304(1)(a) and 3-114(1)]

When a person accepts an instrument without knowing that it is incomplete, then that person can take as an HDC and enforce the instrument as completed. To illustrate: Stuart Morgan asks Joan Nelson to buy a textbook for him when she goes to the campus bookstore. Morgan writes a check payable to the campus store, leaves the amount blank, and tells her to fill in the price of the textbook. Assume the textbook costs $15.50 in each of the following situations.

1.   If Nelson gives the store the check with the amount entirely blank, the check is so incomplete that not only is it nonnegotiable (it has no certain amount), but also the bookstore cannot qualify as an HDC.

2.   If the cashier sees that the check is blank, watches Nelson complete the amount as $65.50, and then gives her $50 in change, the store will probably still be an HDC if the cashier is without notice that the filling in of the amount is improper. [UCC 3-304(4)(d)]

3.   If Nelson fills in the check for $65.50 before she gets to the bookstore, the store sees only a properly completed instrument. Therefore it will take the check as an HDC and can enforce it for the full $65.50. The unauthorized completion is not a sufficient defense against the store in this situation. [UCC 3-407 and 3-115]

Irregular Instruments   Any noticeable irregularity on the face of an instrument that should indicate to a purchaser that something is wrong with the paper will bar HDC status. For example, a note bearing a payee's signature that has been lined through with bold strokes, with the second name penciled above it, is highly irregular and will disqualify a taker from HDC status. [UCC 3-304(1)(a)]

On the other hand, a note that is otherwise negotiable, containing the notation "payable at Newark," will not be the subject of inquiry because such notation does not raise questions essential to the terms, ownership, or validity of the note, nor does it create an ambiguity as to who is the party required to pay. [UCC 3-304(1)(a)]

Different handwriting used in the body of a check and in the signature will not in and of itself make an instrument irregular. Postdating or antedating a check, or stating the amount in digits but failing to write out the numbers, will not make a check irregular. [UCC 3-114(2)]

Visible evidence of forgery or alterations to material elements of negotiable paper will disqualify a purchaser from HDC status. Conversely, a careful forgery or alteration can go undetected by reasonable examination, and, therefore, the purchaser can qualify as an HDC. [UCC 3-304(1)(a)] However, losses that result from careful forgeries usually fall on the party to whom the forger transferred the instrument (assuming, of course, that the forger cannot be found).

Voidable Obligations It stands to reason that a purchaser who knows that a party to an instrument has a defense that entitles that party to avoid the obligation in any way cannot be a holder in due course. At the very least, good faith requires *honesty in fact* of the purchaser in a transaction. For example, a potential purchaser who knows that the maker of a note has breached the underlying contract with the payee cannot thereafter purchase the note as an HDC. [UCC 3-304(1)(b)]

Knowledge of one defense precludes a holder from becoming an HDC to all other defenses. Jones, knowing that the note he has taken was previously forged, presents it to the maker for payment. The maker refuses to pay on the grounds of breach of the underlying contract by the payee, Smith. The maker can assert this defense against Jones even though Jones had no knowledge of the breach because his knowledge of the forgery alone prevents him from being an HDC in *all* circumstances.

Knowledge that a fiduciary has wrongfully negotiated an instrument is sufficient notice of a claim against the instrument to disqualify HDC status. Suppose Jordan, a trustee of a university, improperly writes a check on the university trust account to pay a personal debt. Farley knows that the check has been improperly drawn on university funds, but she accepts it anyway. Farley cannot claim to be an HDC. When a purchaser knows that a fiduciary is acting in breach of trust, HDC status is denied. [UCC 3-304(2)]

There is a strong policy against *imputing* notice to an otherwise good faith purchaser on a negotiable instrument. Not all knowledge charges the purchaser with notice of a claim or defense. UCC 3-304(4) contains a list of specific facts that do not in themselves constitute notice of a defense or claim. The list can be reviewed in the full text of the Code contained in Appendix C. In short, the Code's position is that certain kinds of information about the instrument or about parties to it can raise some suspicion regarding the ultimate enforceability of the paper, but the information falls short of indicating a defense or claim.

Finally, knowledge from a public notice, for example, through newspapers or official records, is not automatically imputed to a purchaser; it must be shown that the information was read. [UCC 3-304(5)]

Recall that the basic test of good faith is honesty in fact. The key concern is whether this particular purchaser honestly knew or had reason to know something was wrong with a particular instrument at the time it was acquired.

Payee as HDC Under certain circumstances, a payee may qualify as an HDC. [UCC 3-302(2)] In order to be an HDC, a payee must exercise good faith, give value, and take the instrument without notice of a defense against it or claim to it.

To illustrate, Marshall Reed is an attorney for Dana Smith. Marshall recently had minor office surgery performed by Dr. Peters, and owes Dr. Peters $300. Marshall has agreed to draft a land sales contract for Dana next week, on condition that Dana issue a check payable to Dr. Peters for $300. Dana sends the check to Dr. Peters with a note, "in payment of medical services rendered to Marshall Reed." Marshall leaves town and never performs the services for Dana. Dana stops payment on the check. Can Dr. Peters enforce payment as an HDC? The answer is yes. Although Dr. Peters is the payee, she has given value (medical services), took the check in good faith, and took without notice of dishonor, defense, claim, or that the check was overdue.

Logic dictates that in the majority of instances, if there are defenses to the instrument, the payee will know or have reason to know about them. To illustrate: Baker Painters contracts with Amex Company to paint the exterior of its new office building for $2,000. Amex issues a negotiable promissory note to Baker Painters for $2,000, due thirty days later. When the note comes due, Baker tries to collect the $2,000 from Amex. Amex refuses to pay the note, claiming that the paint was defective; it washed off during a rainstorm. Since Baker Painters obviously knows about the defective paint, Baker Painters is not an HDC. Amex can disavow liability on the note based on the breach of the underlying contract.

HOLDERS THROUGH A HOLDER IN DUE COURSE

A person who does not qualify as a holder in due course but who derives his or her title *through a holder in due course* can acquire the rights and privileges of a holder in due course. According to UCC 3-201(1):

> Transfer of an instrument vests in the transferee such rights as the transferor has therein, except that a transferee who has himself been a party to any fraud or illegality affecting the instrument or who as a prior holder had notice of a defense or claim against it cannot improve his position by taking from a later holder in due course.

This is sometimes called the **shelter principle.** This rule seems to detract from the basic holder-in-due-course philosophy. It is, however, in line with the concept of marketability and free transferability of commercial paper, as well as with contract law, which provides that assignees acquire the rights of assignors. The transfer rule extends the holder-in-due-course benefits, and it is designed to aid the HDC to dispose of the instrument readily. Since any instrument in the hands of an HDC is free from personal defenses (by definition), an HDC should reasonably have the privilege of transferring all rights in the instrument.

Anyone, no matter how far removed from an HDC, who can trace his or her title ultimately back to an HDC, comes within the shelter principle.

Normally, a person who acquires an instrument from an HDC or from someone with HDC rights gets HDC rights on the principle that the transferee of an instrument gets at least the rights that the transferor had.

Limitations on the Shelter Principle

However, UCC 3-201(1) explicitly indicates that certain persons who formerly held instruments cannot improve their positions by later reacquiring them from HDCs. Thus, if a holder was a party to fraud or illegality affecting the instrument, or if, as a prior holder, he or she had notice of a claim or defense against an instrument, that holder is not allowed to improve his or her status by repurchasing from a later HDC. In other words, a person is not allowed to "launder" the paper by passing it into the hands of an HDC and then buying it back.

To illustrate: Bailey and Zopa collaborate to defraud Manor. Manor is induced to give Zopa a negotiable note payable to Zopa's order. Zopa then specially indorses the note for value to Adams, an HDC. Bailey and Zopa split the proceeds. Adams negotiates the note to Stanley, another HDC. Stanley then negotiates the note for value to Bailey. Bailey, even though he got the note through an HDC, is not a holder through an HDC, for he participated in the original fraud and can never acquire HDC rights in this note.

The following case demonstrates the importance of establishing a prior transferor as an HDC to gain the rights of an HDC under the shelter principle.

ROZEN v. NORTH CAROLINA NAT. BANK
United States Court of Appeals, Fourth Circuit, 1978.
588 F.2d 83.

BACKGROUND AND FACTS   *The defendant, North Carolina National Bank (NCNB), had made a long-term loan to Sharpe Hosiery Mill. In October of 1974 NCNB issued a $20,000 certificate of deposit (CD) to Sharpe. A few days later Allen Stein bought Sharpe. As a result of the sale, NCNB was able to call for payment of the long-term loan and set off the CD against the unpaid balance. Stein refused to return the CD, and instead used it as partial collateral for a personal loan from Manufacturers Hanover Bank and Trust, which did not know of the NCNB claim. When the CD matured, Manufacturers sent the CD to NCNB for collection. NCNB dishonored and retained the CD. Thereafter Stein had plaintiff, Rozen, his brother-in-law, purchase all rights in the CD from Manufacturers. Rozen claimed the rights of an HDC as to the CD. However, when plaintiff sued NCNB for the value of the CD, the trial court held plaintiff was not protected by the "shelter principle."*

HAYNSWORTH, Chief Judge.

* * * *

Rozen argues that Manufacturers enjoyed holder-in-due-course status and that, under § 3-201, Manufacturers transferred this protection to him along with its assignment of rights in the paper. Therefore, Rozen argues, the trial judge should have directed a verdict in his favor, since a holder in due course takes an instrument free from "all claims to it on the part of any person . . . and . . . all defenses of any party to the instrument with whom the holder has not dealt." U.C.C. § 3-305.

The difficulty with this contention, however, is that the jury was thoroughly justified in finding that Rozen's assignor was Allen Stein, not Manufacturers.

* * * *

Even if we should consider Manufacturers as being Rozen's assignor, however, it does not assist Rozen. The pledgee of a negotiable instrument may qualify as a holder in due course, U.C.C. § 3-302, Comment 4, but the pledgee's rights are limited by his secured creditor's status. * * * A secured creditor's interest in collateral ceases when the debt is paid in full, see U.C.C. § 1-201(37), so whatever rights Manufacturers had as a holder in due course of the NCNB certificate were terminated when Allen Stein paid Manufacturers the money he owed. Thus at the time that Manufacturers executed the purported assignment to Rozen, the only rights it had in the NCNB certificate of deposit were those of a secured creditor which had been paid in full, and those rights are nothing.

Because Stein was not a holder in due course, Rozen could not have become a holder in due course derivatively. See U.C.C. § 3-201. Not surprisingly, Rozen makes no claim of having independently acquired the status of a holder in due course. See U.C.C. § 3-302. Since he never had possession of the certificate of deposit, he never became a holder of any kind. See U.C.C. § 1-201(20).

The shelter principle seeks to ensure that a holder in due course always enjoys a ready market for the paper he owns. This principle applies with greatest vigor to holders of time instruments yet to come due, for in such cases the holder cannot collect from the maker. If the holder needs immediate funds, he must turn to the market. If, however, notice of claims and defenses are widespread, free transfer will be inhibited. Thus, § 3-201 protects the transferee so as to create a market for the transferor.

In this case, however, Manufacturers never sought the benefits of § 3-201 for itself.

* * * *

Moreover, the policy underlying the exception to the shelter principle counsels affirmance. The exclusion from the shelter principle of one who, having had notice of prior claims, takes back an instrument from a holder in due course rests upon sound principle and simple logic. Operation of the shelter principle in favor of such a person would defeat the purpose of subjecting him to defenses of the maker. Without the exception to the shelter principle, one not a holder in due course, by a transfer and an agreement to repurchase, could readily avoid the limitations under which he held the instrument in the first place.

Because Manufacturers held the CD as collateral on Stein's loan, Stein was the true assignor of the CD. Stein was not an HDC, so Rozen could not become an HDC under the "shelter principle."   **DECISION AND REMEDY**

FEDERAL LIMITATIONS ON HOLDER-IN-DUE-COURSE RIGHTS

A relatively recent Federal Trade Commission (FTC) rule has severely limited the preferential position enjoyed by a holder in due course in certain circumstances. This so-called FTC rule limits the rights of an HDC over an instrument that evidences a debt arising out of a *consumer credit* transaction. (Payment by check is not a credit transaction.) The rule, entitled "Preservation of Consumers' Claims and Defenses," is an attempt to prevent a situation in which a consumer is required to make payment for a defective product to a third party who is a holder in due course of a promissory note that formed part of the contract with the dealer who sold the defective good.

The FTC rule[6] makes the following provision for any seller or lessor of goods or services who takes or receives a consumer credit contract or who accepts as full or partial payment for such sale or lease the proceeds of any purchase money loan made in connection with any consumer credit contract:

---

6.   Section 433 of Title 15, U.S.C., Sections 41 et seq., effective May 14, 1976.

NOTICE

ANY HOLDER OF THIS CONSUMER CREDIT CONTRACT IS SUBJECT TO ALL CLAIMS AND DEFENSES WHICH THE DEBTOR COULD ASSERT AGAINST THE SELLER OF GOODS OR SERVICES OBTAINED PURSUANT HERETO OR WITH THE PROCEEDS HEREOF. RECOVERY HEREUNDER BY THE DEBTOR SHALL NOT EXCEED AMOUNTS PAID BY THE DEBTOR HEREUNDER.

Obviously, the purpose of this notice is to inform any holder that, upon acquisition of a negotiable commercial paper, he or she is subject to all claims and demands that the debtor could assert against the promisee or payee named in the paper. In essence, the FTC rule places a holder in due course of the paper or of the negotiable instrument in the position of a contract assignee. The FTC rule clearly reduces the degree of transferability of commercial paper resulting from consumer credit contracts.

QUESTIONS AND CASE PROBLEMS

1. Janice Smith issues a ninety-day negotiable promissory note payable to the order of Dennis Jones. The amount of the note is left blank, pending a determination of the amount of money Jones will need to purchase a bull for Smith. Smith authorizes any amount not to exceed $2,000. Jones, without authority, fills in the note in the amount of $5,000 and thirty days later sells the note to the First National Bank of Texas for $4,500. Jones not only does not buy the bull but has left the state. The First National Bank had no knowledge that the instrument was incomplete when issued or that Jones had no authority to complete the instrument in the amount of $5,000.
  (a) Does the bank qualify as a holder in due course, and, if so, for what amount? Explain.
  (b) If Jones had sold the note to a stranger in a bar for $500, would the stranger qualify as a holder in due course? Explain.
2. Dana draws and issues a $100 check to Peter. The check is dated and issued on May 1. On May 25, Peter indorses the check in blank to Sam as a gift. On June 5, Sam delivers the check for value without indorsement to Helen. Dana has stopped payment on the check, claiming that Peter is in breach of contract. Helen claims that she has the rights of a holder in due course. Discuss Helen's contention.

3. Daniel is a well-known industrialist in the community. He has agreed to purchase a rare coin from Helen's Coin Shop. The purchase price is to be determined by independent appraisal. Payment is to be by Daniel's check. Daniel is going out of town and informs Helen that his agent will bring her a check during his absence. Daniel draws up a check payable to Helen, leaves the amount blank, and gives the check to his agent, Able. Able, without authority, fills in the amount for $10,000, and presents it to Helen, who now has the appraisal. The appraisal price is $7,000. Able tells Helen that Daniel wanted to be sure the check would cover the appraisal and that he (Able) is authorized to receive the coin plus the balance in cash. Helen gives Able the coin plus $3,000. When Daniel discovers Able's fraud, Daniel stops payment on the check and offers Helen $7,000 for the coin. Helen claims she is a holder in due course and is entitled to the face value of the check, $10,000. Discuss whether Helen is an HDC and can therefore successfully pursue her claim.
4. Martha has just opened a small copy reproduction store. She has numerous clients, and she bills them at the end of the month. Her operation was begun with limited financial resources. Her bank balance with the First National Bank is $200. She receives in the morning mail two checks. One is from the Buckhorn Corporation for $500, and the other is from Shady Acres Magazine Sales for $300. Martha deposits both checks at the First National Bank. Later, a paper supply saleswoman presents Martha with an overdue bill of $800. Martha writes a check in that amount, and the check is paid by the First

National Bank. Later, one of the checks deposited by Martha is returned to the First National Bank. It is from Shady Acres and is marked "insufficient funds." Can the First National Bank be a holder in due course to the check written by Shady Acres? Explain.

5. Daniel is going on a fishing trip with two friends. Upon packing, he discovers that his fishing rod and reel are broken. He immediately goes to George's Rod & Reel Store and purchases a rod and reel from Charles, a clerk, in the store. The cost of the rod and reel is $70. Daniel has always paid cash at this store in the past, but he has only $63 cash in his pocket. He pays the $63 in cash and gives the clerk a check intended to cover the balance. He signs the check but in his haste, leaves the payee's name and amount blank, telling the clerk to properly fill them in. Charles rings up a $63 sale on the cash register. He then inserts his name as payee on the check. George, the owner, owes Charles $7 in overtime pay. George fills in the amount on the check for $7. Charles negotiates the check to Altari in payment of a loan. Altari *cleverly* raises the amount of the check from $7 to $70 by adding a zero behind the 7 and a "ty" on the word seven. The changes are made in the same color ink. Altari transfers the check to Harold for value. Daniel's purchased rod and reel are defective, and he has stopped payment on the check. All the above events are now known. Harold claims that he has the status of an HDC. Discuss whether Harold is correct.

6. The Sahara-Nevada Hotel billed Affinity Pictures for hotel charges in the amount of $3,046. Affinity's president, Saka, refused to pay the full amount, claiming that only $800 was owed. Saka signed a blank check and gave it to his agent. He instructed the agent to make the check out for $800, cash it, and give the cash to the Sahara-Nevada Hotel. Instead, the agent made the check payable for $3,046, the amount claimed by the hotel, and delivered it to the hotel's manager without mentioning the instructions. Is the Sahara-Nevada Hotel, the payee, a holder in due course? [Saka v. Sahara-Nevada Corp., 92 Nev. 703, 558 P.2d 535 (1976)]

7. By making several fraudulent misrepresentations, a builder induced several homeowners in Washington, D.C.,

to sign contracts authorizing home improvements. The homeowners obtained financing to pay the builder's fees from Jefferson Federal Savings and Loan Association, a local lending institution. In exchange for the financing, the homeowners each issued promissory notes to Jefferson. The builder's fees were exorbitant, and the promissory notes were issued by the homeowners in the exact amounts of the fees charged. In addition, it was the builder's agent who introduced the homeowners to the loan manager of Jefferson Savings and Loan. The loan manager was aware of the fact that this person was the builder's agent. About a month later, after the homeowners realized that the prices for the home improvements were exorbitant, they refused payment on the notes held by Jefferson. If Jefferson qualifies as a holder in due course, it will have every right to payment. Does Jefferson qualify? [Slaughter v. Jefferson Federal Sav. and Loan Ass'n, 538 F.2d 397 (D.C.Cir. 1976)]

8. Anderson entered into a contract with Atlantic Storm Window Company for the installation of storm windows in his home. He signed a promissory note and a contract. They were stapled together, and neither had any dollar amounts filled in. Atlantic Storm Window had orally agreed with Anderson that the price would be $744, but it later filled in both the contract and the promissory note for $895. Shortly thereafter, Atlantic sold the promissory note with the contract still attached to First National Bank. Atlantic installed the windows improperly, and Anderson refused to pay on the note. If First National Bank qualifies as a holder in due course, Anderson will be obligated on the promissory note. What was the result? [First Nat. Bank v. Anderson, 7 D. & C. 2d 661 (Pa. 1956)]

9. Mecham signed a note payable to Munson for a brokerage fee on a mortgage Munson's firm was obtaining for him. Munson gave the note to his bank as security for a debt. Mecham maintained that Munson did not obtain the type of mortgage on which they had agreed, and he refused to make payment on the note. Can the bank recover from Mecham as an HDC? [Mecham v. United Bank of Arizona, 107 Ariz. 437, 489 P.2d 247 (1971)]

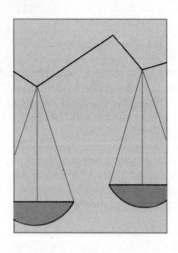

27

COMMERCIAL PAPER
Liability, Defenses, and Discharge

Two kinds of liability are associated with negotiable instruments: liability based on contract and warranty liability. *Liability based on contract* is likely to arise not from a specific contract but from UCC rules relating to the signature on the instrument. Those who sign commercial paper are potentially liable for payment of the amount stated on the instrument. *Warranty liability*, on the other hand, extends to both signers and nonsigners. A breach of warranty can occur when the instrument is transferred or presented for payment.

This chapter covers the liability of the parties who sign the instrument—for example, drawers of drafts and checks, makers of notes and certificates of deposit, and indorsers. It also covers the liability of accommodation parties and the warranty liability of those who *transfer* with or without a signature.

Since liability is not always absolute on a negotiable instrument, even for a holder in due course, in this chapter we will consider the defenses available to prevent liability and then will review the various ways a person can be discharged from an obligation on a negotiable instrument. Note that the focus here is on liability *on the instrument itself or on warranties connected with transfer or presentment of the instrument* as opposed to liability for the underlying contract.

LIABILITY BASED ON SIGNATURES

The key to liability on a negotiable instrument is a **signature,** which is defined in UCC 3-401(2) as "any

name, including any trade or assumed name, upon an instrument, or * * * any word or mark used in lieu of a written signature." A signature can be handwritten, typed, or printed; or it can be made by mark, by thumbprint, or in virtually any manner. According to UCC 1-201(39), "signed" means any symbol executed or adopted by a party with the "present intention to authenticate a writing."

The requirement of a signature has its origin in the Law Merchant and is based simply on the need to know whose obligation the instrument represents. The critical element with any signature is a "present intention to authenticate a writing." Parol evidence can be used to identify the signer, and, once identified, the signature is effective against the signer no matter how it is made. UCC 3-401(1) states the general rule: "No person is liable on an instrument unless his [or her] signature appears thereon."

The few exceptions to the general rule are contained in UCC 3-404, covering unauthorized signatures:

1. Any unauthorized signature is wholly inoperative unless the person whose name is signed ratifies it or is precluded from denying it. [UCC 3-404(1)] For example, a signature made by an agent exceeding the scope of actual, implied or apparent authority can be ratified by the principal. A Pennsylvania court held that a wife's acceptance and retention of benefits from a promissory note constituted ratification of an otherwise unauthorized signature made

442

by her husband.[1] Moreover, a person who writes and signs a check, leaving blank the amount and the name of the payee, and who then leaves the check in a place available to the public can be estopped (prevented), on the basis of negligence, from denying liability for its payment. [UCC 3-115, 3-406, and 4-401(2)(b)]

2. An unauthorized signature operates as the signature of the unauthorized signer in favor of an HDC. For example, a person who forges a check can be held personally liable by an HDC. [UCC 3-404 and 3-401(2)]

Agent's Signatures

The general law of agency covered in Chapters 32 and 33 applies to negotiable instruments. Agents can sign negotiable instruments and thereby bind their principals. [UCC 3-403(1)] Without such a rule, all corporate commercial business would stop. As Chapter 41 will show, every corporation can and must act through its agents. However, because of the critical function the signature plays in determining liability on a negotiable instrument, this chapter will go into some detail concerning the potential problems of agents' signatures.

Generally, an authorized agent will not normally bind a principal on the instrument unless the agent indicates that he or she is signing on behalf of a *clearly named* principal. The agent must write out the principal's name (by signature, mark, or some symbol) and his or her own name, or the agent can supply only the principal's signature.[2]

To illustrate: The following signatures by Able as agent for Peter would bind Peter on the instrument:

1. Peter, by Able, agent.
2. Peter.
3. Peter, Able. (By parol evidence.)

If an authorized agent signs just his or her own name, the principal will not be bound on the instrument. The agent will be personally liable. In these situations, form prevails over intent.

Under UCC 3-403(2)(a), when an agent carelessly signs just his or her own name, the agent is *personally* liable on the instrument even though the parties know of the agency relationship. In addition, the parol evidence rule precludes the introduction of evidence to establish that the signature was made for a principal (see Chapter 13).

Under UCC 3-403(2)(b), two other situations in which an agent is held personally liable on a negotiable instrument can arise. If the instrument is signed in both the agent's name and the principal's name—"John Jones, Bob Smith"—but nothing on the instrument indicates the agency relationship, the agent cannot be distinguished from the principal. In such a case, the form of the signature binds the agent (and it can also bind the principal). Since inclusion of both the agent's and the principal's names without indicating their relationship is ambiguous, parol evidence is admissible *as between the original parties* to prove the agency relationship.

Another situation envisioned under UCC 3-403(2)(b) occurs when an agent signs a negotiable instrument and indicates agency status but fails to name the principal—for example, "Barry Scott, agent." Against any subsequent holder the agent is *personally* liable, but the unnamed principal cannot be held on the instrument. But, since the indication of agency status without naming the principal is ambiguous, parol evidence is admissible *as between the original parties* to prove the agency relationship and to establish the liability of the unnamed principal. [UCC 3-403(2)(b)]

The following case illustates the personal liability of an agent who signed a check without disclosing that he was signing in a representative capacity.

---

1. Rehrig v. Fortunak, 39 D. & C.2d 20, (Pa. 1966).
2. If the agent signs the principal's name, the Code presumes that the signature is authorized and genuine. [UCC 3-307(1)(b)]

BACKGROUND AND FACTS *Plaintiff, O. B. Ellinger, doing business as Ellinger Paint and Dry Wall, sued Percy Griffin, the defendant, on three checks drawn on the account of Greenway Building Company and signed by Griffin, the company president. The checks, totaling $3,950, were issued to Ellinger in*

GRIFFIN v. ELLINGER
Supreme Court of Texas, 1976.
538 S.W.2d 97.

payment for labor and materials furnished to Greenway for a construction project. Greenway was the prime contractor for the project, and Griffin was authorized to sign checks as president of the company. The bank refused to honor the checks because of insufficient funds in the Greenway account.

The major question before the court was whether Griffin's signature on a corporate check, without any indication of his representative capacity, obligated him personally and individually for the amount of the check.

DOUGHTY, Justice.

The question presented by this case is whether a corporate officer who signs a check on a corporate account without designating the capacity in which he signs is personally liable as the drawer of the check. * * *

* * * *

* * * [Defendant] contends that the drafts show conclusively on their face that he was signing in a representative capacity only. Second, petitioner contends that extrinsic evidence establishes as a matter of law that the parties understood his signature to be in a representative capacity.

* * * To determine whether an authorized representative is personally liable on an instrument which he signs on behalf of his principal, we must look to Section 3-403 of the Code[.] * * *

Each of the three drafts signed by Griffin were in essentially the same form. A copy of one of the drafts is reproduced below.

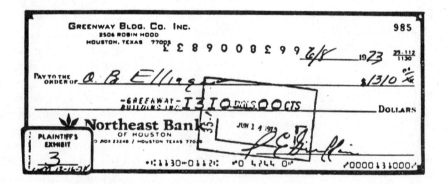

The first question is whether the draft shows on its face that Griffin signed in a representative capacity only. Although the draft clearly names the person represented, it does not show that Griffin signed only in his capacity as president of Greenway. Griffin contends, however, that considering the instrument as a whole, and taking into account the normal business usage of personalized checks, it should be apparent from the instrument itself that Griffin signed only as an authorized agent of Greenway. We disagree. We recognize that it is unusual to demand the individual obligation of a corporate officer on checks drawn on the corporate account, and that the more usual way of obtaining the personal obligation of an officer on such a check would be by endorsement. Business practice and usage are proper factors to be considered in construing the particular instrument under consideration. We also recognize that an instrument may disclose on its face that a signature was executed only in a representative capacity even though the particular office or position of the signer is not disclosed thereon.

* * * [W]e can find nothing on the face of the checks in the present case to show that Griffin intended to sign only in a representative capacity. [Defendant] points out that each check is stamped by a "check protector," which imprinted not only the

amount of the draft but also the company's name. Although the stamp clearly reveals the name of the principal, it does not aid [defendant] because it gives no information as to the capacity in which *he* signed the instrument.

The fact that the name of the corporation appears on the check indicates that the account drawn upon is that of the corporation and that the funds in the account are the corporation's. While the drawer of a check is ordinarily the owner of the funds in the account drawn upon, the Code does not require that this be so. Under Section 3.413, *any person* who signs a draft engages that, upon dishonor, he will pay the amount thereof to the holder. Indeed, under Section 3.404, the signer of a draft who has no authority to draw upon the account is nevertheless liable upon his contract as drawer to any person who takes the instrument in good faith for value. [Defendant] points out that, since a corporation can only act through its agents, a personal signature is always required to authorize withdrawal of funds from a corporate account. Under Section 3.403, however, one signing an instrument is personally liable thereon even though he is authorized to and does in fact bind his principal, if he does not disclose that he is signing only in a representative capacity. In short, the burden is on the signer to relieve himself of personal liability by disclosing his agency. The fact that the instrument is an authorized draft drawn on a corporate account is not enough to disclose the representative character of the signature thereon. Section 3.403(c) expressly provides that the signer of an instrument may avoid personal liability by disclosing both the name of the organization of which he is an agent and the office he holds with the organization. Absent such a disclosure or its equivalent, the signer is personally liable on the instrument according to its terms, unless "otherwise established between the immediate parties" under subsection (b)(2). We hold that the checks in question do not show on their face that Griffin signed only in a representative capacity. * * *

The plaintiff, Ellinger, was able to collect the $3,950 from Griffin personally because Griffin failed to disclose the representative character of his signature.

**DECISION
AND REMEDY**

Although this case represents the majority rule, there are differences among states on the issue of personal liability. When the question of personal liability arises, the signer can offer evidence to prove that he or she acted in a representative capacity and may thus overcome the presumption that he or she is personally obligated.

COMMENTS

When a negotiable instrument is signed in the name of an organization, and the organization's name is preceded or followed by the name and office of an authorized individual, the organization will be bound; the individual who has signed the instrument in the representative capacity will not be bound. [UCC 3-403(3)]

If the agent had no authority, either apparent or implied, to sign the principal's name, the "unauthorized signature is wholly inoperative as that of the person whose name is signed * * *." [UCC 3-404(1)] Assume that Mary Night is the principal and Arthur King is her agent. King, without authority, signs a promissory note as follows: "Mary Night, by Arthur King, agent." Since Mary Night's

"signature" is unauthorized, she cannot be held liable on the note, but King will be liable. This would be true even if King had merely signed the note "Mary Night," without indicating any agency. In either case, the unauthorized signer, King, is liable on the instrument.

Signature Liability

Primary and Secondary Liability   Every party, except a *qualified indorser*,[3] who signs a negotiable

---

3. A "qualified" indorser—one who indorses "without recourse"—undertakes no obligation to pay. A qualified indorser merely assumes warranty liability, which is discussed later in this chapter.

instrument is either primarily or secondarily liable for payment of that instrument when it comes due.

If a person is primarily liable on a negotiable instrument, then that person is absolutely required to pay the instrument, subject to certain real defenses. [UCC 3-305] Only *makers* and *acceptors* are primarily liable. [UCC 3-413(1)]

The liability of a party who is secondarily liable on a negotiable instrument is similar to that of a guarantor (surety) in a simple contract. Drawers and indorsers have secondary liability. Secondary liability is "contingent liability." In the case of notes, an indorser's secondary liability does not arise until the maker, who is primarily liable, has defaulted on the instrument. [UCC 3-413(1) and 3-414]

With regard to drafts and checks, a drawer's secondary liability does not arise until the drawee fails to pay or to accept the instrument, whichever is required. Note, however, that a drawee is not primarily liable. Makers of notes promise to pay, but drawees are ordered to pay. Therefore, drawees are not primarily liable unless they promise to pay—for example, by certifying a check. Nor are drawees even secondarily liable on an instrument. As stated in UCC 3-409, "a check or draft does not of itself operate as an assignment of any funds in the hands of the drawee available for its payment * * *." Thus, unless a drawee *accepts*, the drawee's only obligation is to honor the drawer's orders.

The parties to a negotiable instrument are bound by all of the terms implied by their signatures by operation of law. Once it is established that a party signed the instrument (or that it was signed by that party's authorized agent), the Code defines the party's liability. The liability is contractual in the sense that each party voluntarily incurs it and thus can modify it.

Primary Liability of the Maker or Acceptor The maker of a note promises to pay the note. The words "I promise to pay" embody the maker's obligation to pay the instrument according to the terms as written at the time of the signing. If the instrument is incomplete when the maker signs it, then the maker's obligation is to pay it as completed, assuming that the instrument is properly completed. [UCC 3-413(1) and 3-115]

A maker guarantees that certain facts are true by signing a promissory note. In particular, Section 3-413(3) specifies that a maker admits to all subsequent parties that the payee in fact exists and that the payee has current capacity to indorse the note (for example, that the payee is not a minor at the time the note is signed). Primary liability is unconditional. The primary party's liability is immediate when the note becomes due. No action by the holder of the instrument is required.

The drawee/acceptor is in virtually the same position as the maker of a note. [UCC 3-413(1) (3)] A drawee who does not accept owes a contractual duty to the drawer to pay in accordance with the drawer's orders, but a drawee owes no duty to either the payee or any holder.

For example, Beyer buys from Sallor goods costing $2,000. The goods will be shipped to arrive on September 1. Instead of giving Sallor cash, Beyer draws a draft on Finance Company for $2,000 payable to Sallor on September 1. At this point, Finance is not liable on the draft, and it will not become liable on the draft unless and until it accepts the draft.

Three situations under which a holder must present the instrument to a drawee for acceptance are:

1. Where the instrument requires such presentation (see trade acceptances, discussed in Chapter 23).
2. Where the draft is to be payable at an address different from that of the drawee.
3. Where the draft's payment date is dependent on such presentment [UCC 3-501(1)(a)]—for example, if the draft is payable thirty days after acceptance or sight.

Presentment in these situations is required to charge the drawer and indorsers with secondary liability.

If the drawee accepts the instrument as presented, the drawee becomes an acceptor and is primarily liable to all subsequent holders. A drawee who refuses to accept such a draft has dishonored the instrument. In refusing to accept, the drawee retains his original status and owes no duty to the payee or any holder.

A check is a special type of draft that is drawn on a bank and is payable on demand. Acceptance of a check is called certification. Certification is not necessary on checks, and a bank is under no obligation to certify. (See Chapter 28 for details.) However, upon certification, the drawee bank occupies the position of an acceptor and is primarily liable on the check to holders. [UCC 3-411]

Secondary Liability Dishonoring an instrument triggers the liability of secondarily liable parties on the instrument—that is, the drawer, "unqualified indorsers," and accommodation indorsers. Parties who are secondarily liable on a negotiable instrument promise to pay on that instrument only if:

1. The instrument is properly and timely presented.
2. The instrument is dishonored.
3. Notice of dishonor is timely given to the secondarily liable party.[4]

These requirements are necessary for a secondarily liable party to have signature liability on a negotiable instrument, but they are not necessary to hold a secondarily liable party to warranty liability (to be discussed later). [UCC 3-414, 3-501, and 3-502]

UCC 3-413(2) provides that "upon dishonor of the draft and any necessary notice of dishonor * * * [the drawer] will pay the amount of the draft to the holder or to any indorser who takes it up." For example, Nancy Jones writes a check on her account at Third National Bank payable to the order of Joel Andrews. If Third National does not pay the check when Andrews presents it for payment, then Jones is liable to Andrews on the basis of her secondary liability. Drawers are secondarily liable on drafts unless they disclaim their liability by drawing the instruments "without recourse." [UCC 3-413(2)]

Since drawers are secondarily liable, their liability does not arise until presentment and notice of dishonor have been made *properly* and in a *timely* way. If a draft (or check) is payable at a bank, improper presentment or notice relieves the drawer from secondary liability only when the drawee bank is insolvent.

An *unqualified indorser* promises that in the event of presentment, dishonor, and notice of dishonor, the indorser will pay the instrument. Thus, the liability of an indorser is much like that of a drawer, with one major exception: Indorsers are *relieved* of

their contractual liability to the holder of the instrument by (1) improper (late) presentment or (2) late notice or failure to notify the indorser of dishonor. [UCC 3-414, 3-501, and 3-502]

When an indorser has actively caused an instrument to be dishonored, the requirements of presentment and notice of dishonor are excused. [UCC 3-511(2)(b)]

Proper Presentment The Code spells out what constitutes a proper presentment. Basically, presentment by a holder must be to the proper person, must be in a proper manner, and must be timely. [UCC 3-503 and 3-504]

A note or CD must be presented to the maker for payment. A draft is presented by the holder to the drawee for acceptance or payment, or both, whichever is required. A check is presented to the drawee for payment. [UCC 3-504]

The proper manner for presentment can be in any one of the following three ways, depending on the type of instrument: [UCC 3-504(2)]

1. By mail. But presentment is not effective until receipt of the mail.
2. Through a clearinghouse procedure, such as deposited checks.
3. At the place specified in the instrument for acceptance or payment—or, if the instrument is silent as to place, at the place of business or the residence of the person required to accept or pay.

One of the most crucial criteria for proper presentment is timeliness. [UCC 3-503] Failure to present on time is the most prevalent reason for improper presentment and consequent discharge of unqualified indorsers from secondary liability. See Exhibit 27–1, bearing in mind that its contents are somewhat oversimplified.

Proper Notice Once the instrument has been dishonored, proper notice must be given to hold secondary parties liable. The rules of proper notice are basically as follows: [UCC 3-508]

1. Notice must be given to the party to be held secondarily liable, but such notice can come from any person who could be liable on the instrument. Once proper notice is received, that notice is effective for all subsequent holders. [UCC 3-508(8)]

---

4. An instrument can be drafted to provide a waiver of the presentment, dishonor, and notice of dishonor requirements. Presume for simplicity's sake that such waivers have not been incorporated into the instruments described in this chapter.

EXHIBIT 27–1   Time For Proper Presentment [UCC 3-503]

Type of Instrument	For Acceptance	For Payment
Time	On or before due date	On due date
Demand	Within a reasonable time (after date or issue, or after secondary party becomes liable thereon)	
Check (domestic)	Not applicable	Presumed to be: Within thirty days (of date or issue) to hold drawer secondarily liable Within seven days (of indorsement) to hold indorser secondarily liable

2.   Except for dishonor of foreign drafts, notice may be given in any reasonable manner. This includes oral or written notice and notice written or stamped on the instrument itself. [UCC 3-508(3)] To give notice of dishonor of a foreign draft (a draft drawn in one country and payable in another country), a formal notice called a *protest* is required. [UCC 3-509]

3.   Any necessary notice must be given by a bank before its midnight deadline (midnight of the next banking day after receipt) [UCC 4-104(1)(h)] and by all others before midnight of the third *business* day after either dishonor or receipt of notice of dishonor [UCC 3-508(2)]. Written notice is effective when sent, not when received.

4.   Notice to a partner is notice to a partnership. Similarly, when a party is deceased, incompetent, or bankrupt, notice may be given to his or her representative.

Accommodation Party   An **accommodation party** is one who signs an instrument for the purpose of lending his or her name to another party in credit to the instrument. [UCC 3-415(1)] Accommodation parties are one form of security against nonpayment on a negotiable instrument.

For example, a bank about to lend money, a seller taking a large order for goods, or a creditor about to extend credit to a prospective debtor all want some reasonable assurance that the debts will be paid. A party's uncertain financial condition or the fact that the parties to a transaction are complete strangers can make a creditor reluctant to rely solely on the prospective debtor's ability to pay. To reduce the risk of nonpayment, the creditor can require the joining of a third person as an accommodation party on the instrument.

If the accommodation party signs on behalf of a maker, he or she will be an *accommodation maker* and will be primarily liable on the instrument. If the accommodation party signs on behalf of a payee or other holder (usually to make the instrument more marketable), he or she will be an *accommodation indorser* and will be secondarily liable. Any indorsement not in the ordinary chain of title is notice of its accommodation character. [UCC 3-415(2)(4)]

The following case discusses some of the differences between an accommodation maker and an accommodation indorser.

HOME CENTER
SUPPLY v.
CERTAINTEED CORP.

Court of Special Appeals of
Maryland, 1984.
59 Md. App. 495, 476 A.2d 724.

BACKGROUND AND FACTS   As of March 1982, Home Center Supply of Maryland, Inc., owed the plaintiff, CertainTeed Corporation, over $170,000 for building materials, of which about $100,000 was delinquent. In order to alleviate the situation, in May 1982 CertainTeed agreed to reduce a portion of the indebtedness by having Home Center Supply sign a promissory note so that the existing past due debt could be removed from CertainTeed's books. Joseph DelPo, president of Home Center, personally indorsed the note. After Home Center made five payments, no further payments were forthcoming.

CertainTeed accelerated the balance due on the note, $24,481, and when no payment was made, initiated suit to recover the balance. At trial the only issue contested was DelPo's liability on the note made by Home Center. DelPo appealed the $24,481 judgment against him entered by the trial court.

BELL, Judge.
* * * *

At the outset * * * we note the status of DelPo as an indorser and his obligations resulting therefrom. In this case, DelPo, by his personal indorsement, undertook to "back up" the performance of Home Center and thereby give CertainTeed the added assurance of having another party to the obligation. It is a common practice for a surety such as DelPo to appear on a note as either a co-maker or as an indorser. In either case, he becomes an accommodation party and owes the holder of the note the obligation of either the maker or the indorser. It makes little difference in this case whether appellant is a maker or an indorser, though, since the contract and warranty liabilities of each class of signatories to a note are not so dissimilar as to predicate liability upon the distinction between a maker and an indorser. * * *

As between the surety, DelPo, and the debtor, Home Center, Home Center has the primary obligation to pay the debt. Since the creditor, CertainTeed, is entitled to only one performance and the debtor receives the benefit of the transaction, the surety's obligation is undertaken with the expectation that the debtor will meet his commitment to the creditors; thus, if the surety is made to pay the principal's debt, he has the right to recover from the principal. White and Summers, Uniform Commercial Code, § 13-12 (1980).

Section 3-415 of the Commercial Code defines accommodation party as "one who signs the instrument in any capacity for the purpose of lending his name to another party to it." Md. Code (1974, Repl. Vol. 1975) *Commercial Law Article*, § 3-415 (1). It is readily apparent that DelPo lent his name to Home Center to facilitate the continuation of the business relationship with CertainTeed. The actual language of § 3-415 (1) indicates that an accommodation party also signs in a particular capacity, as a maker, acceptor, or indorser of an instrument. The Official Comment 1 to § 3-415 explains that:

> Subsection (1) recognizes that an accommodation party is always a surety (which includes a guarantor), and it is his only distinguishing feature. He differs from other sureties only in that his liability is on the instrument and he is a surety for another party to it. His obligation is therefore determined by the capacity in which he signs. An accommodation maker or acceptor is bound on the instrument without any resort to his principal, while an accommodation indorser may be liable only after presentment, notice of dishonor, and protest.

Moreover, § 3-415 (2) refers specifically to liability of an accommodation party "in the capacity in which he has signed." It follows therefore that DelPo is an accommodation party with liability as an indorser of the note. As an indorser, DelPo promised that "upon dishonor and any necessary notice of dishonor and protest he will pay the instrument according to its tenor at the time of his indorsement to the holder. . . ."
* * * *

The appellate court held that the note was negotiable, and that CertainTeed was a holder in due course. Home Center's antecedent obligation to CertainTeed was consideration for the note, so DelPo had no defense against liability. The court upheld the $24,481 judgment against DelPo.

DECISION AND REMEDY

WARRANTY LIABILITY OF PARTIES

In addition to the signature liability discussed in the preceding sections, transferors make certain implied warranties regarding the instruments that they are negotiating. Liability under these warranties is not subject to the conditions of proper presentment, dishonor, and notice of dishonor. These warranties arise even when a transferor does not indorse the instrument (as in delivery of bearer paper). [UCC 3-417] Sometimes it is more expedient to compel a transferor to take back an instrument on the basis of breach of warranty than it is to prove a case of signature liability as a holder in due course against the maker or drawer. Warranties fall into two categories, those that arise upon the *transfer* of a negotiable instrument and those that arise upon *presentment*.

Transfer Warranties

The five *transfer warranties* are described in UCC 3-417(2). They provide that any person who *indorses* an instrument and *receives consideration* warrants to all subsequent transferees and holders who take the instrument in good faith that:

1.   The transferor has good title to the instrument or is otherwise authorized to obtain payment or acceptance on behalf of one who does have good title.
2.   All signatures are genuine or authorized.
3.   The instrument has not been materially altered.
4.   No defense of any party is good against the transferor.
5.   The transferor has no knowledge of any insolvency proceedings against the maker, the acceptor, or the drawer of an unaccepted instrument.

A qualified indorser who indorses an instrument "without recourse" limits the fourth warranty to a warranty that he or she has "no knowledge" of such a defense rather than that there is no defense. [UCC 3-417(3)]

The Extent of Transfer Warranties

of transfer and the negotiation that is used determine how far and to whom a transfer warranty will run. Transfer by indorsement and delivery of order paper extends warranty liability to any subsequent holder who takes the instrument in good faith. However, the warranties of a person who transfers without indorsement (by delivery of bearer paper) will extend only to the immediate transferee. [UCC 3-417(2)]

For example, Able forges Martin's name as maker of a promissory note. The note is made payable to Able. Able indorses the note in blank and negotiates it to Paula. Able has left the country. Paula, without indorsement, delivers the note to Bill. Bill, in turn without indorsement, delivers the note to Helen. Upon Helen's presentment of the note to Martin, the forgery is discovered. Helen can hold Bill (the immediate transferor) liable for breach of warranty that all signatures are genuine. Helen cannot hold Paula liable, because Paula is not Helen's immediate transferor but is a prior non-indorsing transferor. This example shows the importance of the distinction between transfer by indorsement and delivery of order paper and transfer by delivery of bearer paper without indorsement.

See page 452 for a summary of the law on transfer warranty liability.

Presentment Warranties

When a person presents an instrument for payment or acceptance to a maker or a drawer, a **presentment warranty** will protect the person to whom the instrument is presented. As a general rule, when payment or acceptance of an instrument is made, it is final in favor of a holder in due course, or any person, who in good faith has changed his or her position in reliance on that payment. [UCC 3-418] Three exceptions to this general rule, under UCC 3-417(1), are often referred to as the presentment warranties. They provide the following:

1.   The party presenting has good title to the instrument or is authorized to obtain payment or acceptance on behalf of a person who has good title.
2.   The party presenting has no knowledge that the signature of a maker or the drawer is unauthorized.
3.   The instrument has not been materially altered.

The second and third warranties do not apply in certain cases (to certain persons) where the presenter is a holder in due course. It is assumed, for example, that a drawer or maker will recognize his or her own signature or that a maker or acceptor will recognize whether an instrument has been materially altered.

Both transfer and presentment warranties attempt to shift liability back to a wrongdoer or to the person who dealt face to face with a wrongdoer and thus was in the best position to prevent the wrongdoing.

The following case illustrates an accommodation indorser's possible signature and warranty liability.

BACKGROUND AND FACTS *Bugay came into the possession of a check drawn to the order of Henry Sherman, Inc. He fraudulently indorsed "Henry Sherman" on the back side of the check. Then Bugay asked the defendant, Maropoulos, to help him cash it. Maropoulos took Bugay to the Oak Park Currency Exchange, Inc., the plaintiff, because Maropoulos was known by the personnel of that company. While on the company premises, Maropoulos identified himself and induced the company to cash the check. Oak Park Currency Exchange agreed to cash the check only if Maropoulos would indorse it. He did so, received the money, and immediately gave it to Bugay. When Oak Park subsequently indorsed the check and deposited it in the Belmont National Bank, the "Henry Sherman" indorsement was found to be a forgery. The bank recovered full payment from plaintiff Oak Park. Plaintiff in turn attempted to receive reimbursement from defendant Maropoulos on his indorsement and for breach of warranty. At trial, the court directed a verdict in favor of defendant Maropoulos. Oak Park appealed.*

OAK PARK CURRENCY EXCHANGE, INC. v. MAROPOULOS

Appellate Court of Illinois, 1977. 48 Ill.App.3d 437, 6 Ill.Dec. 525, 363 N.E.2d 54.

GOLDBERG, Presiding Justice.
* * * *

In this court, plaintiff urges that defendant breached his warranty of good title when he obtained payment of a check on which the payee's indorsement was forged and that there was sufficient evidence to support a directed verdict in favor of plaintiff. Plaintiff's contentions are based exclusively on Section 3-417(1) of the Code. Defendant contends that an accommodation indorser does not make warranties under Section 3-417(1) and that the trial court properly directed a verdict for the defendant.

A party who signs an instrument "for the purpose of lending his name to another party to * * *" that instrument is an accommodation party. Section 3-415(1). Such a party "is liable in the capacity in which he has signed * * *." Section 3-415(2). Therefore defendant is an accommodation indorser and would be liable to plaintiff under his indorser's contract, provided that he had received timely notice that the check had been presented to the drawee bank and dishonored. Section 3-414. Because these conditions precedent to the contractual liability of an indorser have not been met, defendant is not liable on his contract as an accommodation indorser.

Furthermore, the drawee bank, American National, did not dishonor the check but paid it. This operated to discharge the liability of defendant as an accommodation indorser.

The portion of the Code upon which plaintiff seeks to hold defendant liable is Section 3-417 entitled "Warranties on Presentment and Transfer." * * * Section 3-417(1) sets out warranties which run only to a party who "pays or accepts" an instrument upon presentment. We note that presentment is defined as "a demand for acceptance or payment made upon the maker, acceptor, drawee, or other payor * * *." Section 3-504(1). As applied to the instant case, the warranties contained in Section 3-417(1) * * * run only to the payor bank and not to any other transferee who acquired the check. In the case before us, plaintiff is not a payor or acceptor of the draft. * * * The case before us involves a transferee, not a party who paid or accepted the instrument.
* * * *

An additional theory requires affirmance of the judgment appealed from. Subsection 3-417(2) of the Code provides that one "who transfers an instrument and receives consideration warrants to his transferee * * * " that he has good title. * * * The evidence presented in the case at bar establishes that defendant received no consideration for his indorsement. Though [plaintiff's employee] testified that she saw Bugay hand defendant some money as the two left the currency exchange, she also testified that defendant stated that he was doing a favor for his friend; that she was not paying close attention to the two men and that she did not watch them as they walked away from her. Thus her testimony was considerably weakened by her own qualifying statements and it was strongly and directly contradicted by the positive and unshaken testimony of defendant that he received nothing in return for his assistance. The simple fact standing alone that this witness saw Bugay hand some money to defendant, even if proved, would have no legal significance without additional proof of some type showing that the payment was consideration for defendant's indorsement.

DECISION AND REMEDY *The appellate court affirmed the trial court's directed verdict in favor of Maropoulos. He was not required to repay Oak Park Currency Exchange, Inc.*

DEFENSES

Depending upon whether it is a holder or an HDC (or a holder through an HDC) who makes the demand for payment, certain defenses will be effective to bar collection from persons who would otherwise be primarily or secondarily liable on an instrument.

Defenses fall into two general categories—real (or universal) defenses and personal defenses. Real defenses are used to avoid payment to all holders of a negotiable instrument including an HDC or a holder through an HDC (Shelter Principle). [UCC 3-305(2)] Personal defenses are used to avoid payment to an *ordinary holder* of a negotiable instrument. [UCC 3-306]

Real Defenses

Real (universal) defenses are valid against *all* holders, including HDCs or holders who take through an HDC.

CONCEPT SUMMARY: Transfer Warranty Liability For Types of Indorsers Who Receive Consideration	
TYPES	**TO WHOM WARRANTIES EXTEND**
General Indorsers	The five transfer warranties listed below extend to *all* subsequent holders: 1. Transferor has good title or is otherwise authorized to obtain payment or acceptance on behalf of one who does have good title. 2. All signatures are genuine or authorized. 3. Instrument has not been materially altered. 4. No defense of any party is good against transferor. 5. Transferor has no knowledge of insolvency proceedings against the maker, acceptor or drawer of an accepted instrument.
Non-Indorsers	Same as for the general indorser, but warranties extend *only* to the *immediate transferee.*
Qualified Indorsers	The same five transfer warranties as the general indorser except a qualified indorsement (without recourse) limits the fourth warranty to a warranty of "no knowledge" of such a defense rather than that there is no defense. These warranties extend to *all* subsequent holders.

Forgery   Forgery of a maker's or a drawer's signature cannot bind the person whose name is used (unless that person ratifies the signature or is precluded from denying it). [UCC 3-401 and 3-404(1)] Thus, when a person forges an instrument, the person whose name is used has no liability to pay any holder or any HDC the value of the forged instrument. In addition, a principal can assert the defense of unauthorized signature against any holder or HDC when an agent exceeds his or her authority to sign negotiable paper on behalf of the principal. [UCC 3-403] (Forgery is discussed briefly in Chapter 25, and unauthorized signatures have been discussed earlier in this chapter in the section on liability.)

Fraud in the Execution (in factum) or Inception   If a person is deceived into signing a negotiable instrument, believing that he or she is signing something other than a negotiable instrument (such as a receipt), fraud in execution is committed against the signer. For example, a consumer unfamiliar with the English language signs a paper presented by a salesperson as a request for an estimate when in fact it is a promissory note. Even if the note is negotiated to an HDC, the consumer has a valid defense against payment. This defense cannot be raised, however, when a reasonable inquiry would have revealed the nature and terms of the instrument.[5] Thus the signer's age, experience, and intelligence are relevant, since they frequently determine whether the signer should have known the nature of the transaction before he or she signed.

Material Alteration   An alteration is material if it changes the contract terms between any two parties in any way. Examples of material alterations are [UCC 3-407(1)]:

1. A change in the number or relations of the parties.
2. The completion of an instrument in an unauthorized manner.
3. Adding to the writing as signed or removing any part of it.

Thus, cutting off part of the paper of a negotiable instrument, adding clauses, or any change in the

amount, the date, or the rate of interest—even if the change is only one penny, one day, or 1 percent—is material. But it is not a material alteration to correct the maker's address, to have a red line drawn across the instrument to indicate that an auditor has checked it, or to correct the total final payment due when a mathematical error is discovered in the original computation. If the alteration is not material, any holder is entitled to enforce the instrument according to its original terms.

Material alteration is a *complete* defense against an ordinary holder but is at best only a *partial* defense against an HDC. An ordinary holder can recover nothing on an instrument if it has been materially altered. [UCC 3-407(2)]

If the original terms have been altered, such as the monetary amount payable, the HDC can enforce the instrument against the maker or drawer according to the original terms (tenor). If the instrument was incomplete and later completed in an unauthorized manner, alteration no longer can be claimed as a defense against a HDC, as the HDC can enforce the instrument as completed. [UCC 3-407(2)(3)] If the alteration is readily apparent, then obviously the holder has notice of some defect or defense, and such a holder cannot be an HDC. [UCC 3-302(1)(c) and 3-304(1)(a)]

Discharge in Bankruptcy   Discharge in bankruptcy is an absolute defense on any instrument regardless of the status of the holder because the purpose of bankruptcy is to settle finally all of the insolvent party's debts. [UCC 3-305(2)(d)]

Minority   Minority, or infancy, is a real defense only to the extent that state law recognizes it as such. [UCC 3-305(2)(a)] (See Chapter 10.) Thus, this defense renders the instrument voidable rather than void, as discussed in the next three sections ("Illegality," "Mental Incapacity," and "Extreme Duress"). Since state laws on minority vary, so do determinations on whether minority is a real defense as against an HDC.

For example, in some states, when a minor misrepresents his or her age, the minor is prohibited from exercising the right of disaffirmance. In those states, minority is not allowed as a real defense if a minor who signs a negotiable instrument misrepresents his or her age. (In those states a minor can disaffirm if no misrepresentation of age took place.)

---

5. Burchett v. Allied Concord Financial Corp., 74 N.M. 575, 396 P.2d 186 (1964), *infra.*

In other states, a minor is allowed to disaffirm (liable only for a tort of deceit) despite the misrepresentation of age, and therefore minority is a real defense.

Illegality   When the law declares that an instrument is *void* because it has been executed in connection with illegal conduct, then the defense is absolute against both an ordinary holder and an HDC. If the law merely makes it *voidable*, as in the personal defense of illegality to be discussed below, then it is still a defense against a holder, but not against an HDC. The courts are sometimes prone to treat the word *void* in a statute as meaning "voidable" in order to protect a holder in due course.[6] [UCC 3-305(2)(a)]

Mental Incapacity   If a person is adjudicated mentally incompetent by state proceedings, then any instrument issued by that person thereafter is null and void. The instrument is *void ab initio* (from the beginning) and unenforceable by any holder or any HDC. [UCC 3-305(2)(a)]

Extreme Duress   When a person signs and issues a negotiable instrument under such extreme duress as an immediate threat of force or violence (for example, at gunpoint), the instrument is *void* and unenforceable by any holder or HDC. (Ordinary duress, to be discussed, is only a personal defense.) [UCC 3-305(2)(a)]

Personal Defenses

As mentioned above, personal defenses are used to avoid payment to an ordinary holder of a negotiable instrument.

Breach of Contract   When there is a breach of the underlying contract for which the negotiable instrument was issued, the maker of a note can refuse to

---

6.   Hawkland, *Commercial Paper and Bank Deposits and Collections* (Brooklyn: Foundation Press, 1979), p. 249.

pay it or the drawer of a check can stop payment. Breach of the contract can be claimed as a defense to liability on the instrument. For example, Peter purchases several cases of imported wine from Walter. The wine is to be delivered in four weeks. Peter gives Walter a promissory note for $1,000, which is the price of the wine. The wine arrives, but many of the bottles are broken, and several bottles that are tested have turned to vinegar. Peter refuses to pay the note on the basis of breach of contract and breach of warranty. (Under sales law, a seller impliedly promises that the goods are at least merchantable; see Chapter 21.) If the note is no longer in the hands of the payee seller but is presented for payment by an HDC, the maker buyer will not be able to plead breach of contract as a defense against liability on the note.

Fraud in the Inducement   A person who issues a negotiable instrument based on false statements by the other party will be able to avoid payment on that instrument. To illustrate: Peter agrees to purchase Sam's used tractor for $2,800. Sam, knowing his statements to be false, tells Peter that the tractor is in good working order and that it has been used for only one harvest. In addition, he tells Peter that he owns the tractor free and clear of all claims. Peter pays Sam $500 in cash and issues a negotiable promissory note for the balance. As it turns out, Sam still owes the original seller $500 on the purchase of the tractor, and the tractor is subject to a filed security interest. In addition, the tractor is three years old and has been used in three harvests. Peter can refuse to pay the note if it is held by an ordinary holder; but if Sam has negotiated the note to an HDC, Peter must pay the HDC. Of course, Peter can then sue Sam.

   The following case illustrates not only the importance of reading a contract before signing, but also that fraud in this case is only a personal defense and cannot be used against a holder in due course.

BURCHETT v. ALLIED
CONCORD FINANCIAL
CORP.

Supreme Court of New Mexico,
1964.
74 N.M. 575, 396 P.2d 186.

BACKGROUND AND FACTS   *Mr. and Mrs. Burchett and Mr. and Mrs. Beevers, the plaintiff appellees, signed contracts with Kelly, a representative of Consolidated Products, to install aluminum siding on their homes. The original offer (made orally and accompanied by a written statement) indicated that each house would serve as a show house for advertising purposes and that the owners would receive $100 credit on each contract sold in a specific area of their town. Neither the Burchetts nor the Beeverses read their contract. In a few days, the first installment of the contract that they had actually signed—a mortgage* *contract that had been recorded against their property—came due. The mortgage note had been purchased from Consolidated Products by the appellant in this case, Allied Concord Financial Corporation. When Allied Concord notified the appellees that payment was due, the appellees realized the nature of the contracts they had signed and brought this action against the finance company to have the notes and mortgages canceled and declared void. The trial court determined that since the notes and mortgages were obtained fraudulently, Allied Concord Financial Corporation could not recover.*

CARMODY, Justice.

*   *   *   *

Following the explanation by Kelly, both families agreed to the offer and were given a form of a printed contract to read. While they were reading the contract, Kelly was filling out blanks in other forms. After the appellees had read the form of the contract submitted to them, they signed, *without reading,* the form or forms filled out by Kelly, assuming them to be the same as that which they had read and further assuming that what they signed provided for the credits which Kelly assured them they would receive. Needless to say, what appellees signed were notes and mortgages on the properties to cover the cost of the aluminum siding, and contracts containing no mention of credits for advertising or other sales.

*   *   *   *

Within a matter of days after the contracts were signed, the aluminum siding was installed, although in neither case was the job completed to the satisfaction of appellees. Sometime later, the appellees received letters from appellant, informing them that appellant had purchased the notes and mortgages which had been issued in favor of Consolidated Products and that appellees were delinquent in their first payment. Upon the receipt of these notices, appellees discovered that mortgages had been recorded against their property and they immediately instituted these proceedings.

*   *   *   *

[The] trial court found that the notes and mortgages, although signed by the appellees, were fraudulently procured. The court also found that the appellant paid a valuable consideration for the notes and mortgages, although at a discount, and concluded as a matter of law that the appellant was a holder in due course. *   *   *

*   *   *   *

*   *   * The only real question in the case is whether, under these facts, appellees, by substantial evidence, satisfied the provisions of the statute relating to their claimed defense as against a holder in due course.

In 1961, by enactment of ch. 96 of the session laws, our legislature adopted, with some variations, the Uniform Commercial Code. The provision of the code applicable to this case is as follows:

"To the extent that a holder is a holder in due course he takes the instrument free from

"*   *   *

"(2) all defenses of any party to the instrument with whom the holder has not dealt except

"*   *   *

"(c) such misrepresentation as has induced the party to sign the instrument with neither knowledge nor reasonable opportunity to obtain knowledge of its character or its essential terms; *   *   *

We believe that the official comments following § 3-305(2)(c), Comment No. 7, provide an excellent guideline for the disposition of the case before us.

*   *   *   *

The test of the defense here stated is that of excusable ignorance of the contents of the writing signed. The party must not only have been in ignorance, but also have had no reasonable opportunity to obtain knowledge. In determining what is a reasonable opportunity all relevant factors are to be taken into account, including the age and sex of the party, his intelligence, education and business experience; his ability to read or to understand English, the representations made to him and his reason to rely on them or to have confidence in the person making them; the presence or absence of any third person who might read or explain the instrument to him, or any other possibility of obtaining independent information; and the apparent necessity, or lack of it, for acting without delay.

"Unless the misrepresentation meets this test, the defense is cut off by a holder in due course."

* * * *

Applying the elements of the test to the case before us, Mrs. Burchett was 47 years old and had a ninth grade education, and Mr. Burchett was approximately the same age, but his education does not appear. Mr. Burchett was foreman of the sanitation department of the city of Clovis and testified that he was familiar with some legal documents. Both the Burchetts understood English and there was no showing that they lacked ability to read. Both were able to understand the original form of contract which was submitted to them. * * * (T)he Burchetts had never had any prior association with Kelly and the papers were signed upon the very day that they first met him. There was no showing of any reason why they should rely upon Kelly or have confidence in him. The occurrences took place in the homes of appellees, but other than what appears to be Kelly's "chicanery," no reason was given which would warrant a reasonable person in acting as hurriedly as was done in this case. None of the appellees attempted to obtain any independent information either with respect to Kelly or Consolidated Products, nor did they seek out any other person to read or explain the instruments to them. As a matter of fact, they apparently didn't believe this was necessary because, like most people, they wanted to take advantage of "getting something for nothing." There is no dispute but that the appellees did not have actual knowledge of the nature of the instruments which they signed, at the time they signed them. Appellant urges that appellees had a reasonable opportunity to obtain such knowledge but failed to do so, were therefore negligent, and that their defense was precluded.

We recognize that the reasonable opportunity to obtain knowledge may be excused if the maker places reasonable reliance on the representations. The difficulty in the instant case is that the reliance upon the representations of a complete stranger (Kelly) was not reasonable, and all of the parties were of sufficient age, intelligence, education, and business experience to know better. In this connection, it is noted that the contracts clearly stated, on the same page which bore the signatures of the various appellees, the following:

"No one is authorized on behalf of this company to represent this job to be 'A SAMPLE HOME OR A FREE JOB.' " * * *

Although we have sympathy with the appellees, we cannot allow it to influence our decision. They were certainly victimized, but because of their failure to exercise ordinary care for their own protection, an innocent party cannot be made to suffer.

DECISION AND REMEDY

The finance company, Allied Concord Financial Corporation, as holder in due course, took the instrument free from the defenses claimed. Thus, the Burchetts and the Beeverses were liable for the amount of the notes.

COMMENTS

Consumer protection legislation might alter the outcome of similar cases in some states. Also, had this action been brought after the FTC holder in due course rule was put into effect in 1976 (see Chapter 26), then the outcome might have been different. Remember that the FTC rule requires that the subsequent holder of a promissory note resulting from a consumer credit contract be informed that he or she takes the note simply as a contract assignee and that the consumer credit contract is subject to all claims and demands that the debtor could assert against the promisee or payee named therein.

Illegality Certain types of illegality constitute personal defenses. Other types constitute real defenses. Some transactions are prohibited under state statutes or ordinances, and some of these applicable statutes fail to provide that the prohibited transactions are void. If a statute provides that an illegal transaction is voidable, the defense is personal. If a statute makes an illegal transaction void, the defense is a real defense and can successfully be asserted against an HDC. For example, a state may make gambling contracts illegal and void, but be silent on payments of gambling debts. Thus, the payment of a gambling debt becomes voidable.

Ordinary Duress or Undue Influence Duress involves threats of harm or force. Ordinary duress— for example, the threat of a boycott—is a personal defense. When the threat of force or harm becomes so violent and overwhelming that a person is deprived of his or her free will (aggravated duress), it becomes a real defense, good against all holders, including HDCs. [UCC 3-305]

Mental Incapacity There are various types and degrees of incapacity. Incapacity is ordinarily only a personal defense. If a maker or drawer is so extremely incapacitated that the transaction becomes a nullity, then the instrument is void. In that case, the defense becomes real, and it is good against an HDC as well. [UCC 3-305(2)(b)]

If the maker drafts a negotiable instrument while insane, but before a formal court hearing declares (adjudicates) him or her insane, many courts declare the obligation thereon as voidable. If, however, the maker has been declared by a court as being insane, a guardian has been appointed, and then the note is written, many courts would hold the obligation null and void.

Discharge by Payment or Cancellation If commercial paper is paid before its maturity date, the maker will ordinarily demand the return of the instrument itself or will note on the face of the instrument that payment has been made. Otherwise, it is possible for the instrument to continue circulating. If it comes into the hands of an HDC who demands payment at maturity, the defense of discharge by payment, which is merely a personal defense, will not allow the maker to avoid paying a second time on the same note. [UCC 3-601(1)(a) and 3-602]

Unauthorized Completion of an Incomplete Instrument It is unwise for a maker or drawer to

CONCEPT SUMMARY: Valid Defenses Against Holders of a Negotiable Instrument	
DEFENSES	**TYPES**
Real Defenses UCC 3-305 Valid against all holders, including holders in due course or holders with the rights of a holder in due course (shelter rule)	1. Minority—If the contract is voidable. 2. Other incapacity, duress, or illegality—If the contract is void. 3. Fraud in the execution. 4. Discharge in bankruptcy. 5. Forgery. 6. Material alteration—Generally only to the alteration.
Personal Defenses UCC 3-306 Valid against mere holders; not valid against holders in due course or holders with the rights of a holder in due course	1. Breach of contract. 2. Incapacity (other than minority), duress, or illegality—If the contract is voidable. 3. Breach of warranty. 4. Failure or lack of consideration. 5. Nondelivery of the instrument. 6. Previous payment of the instrument. 7. Fraud in the inducement.

sign any negotiable instrument that is not complete. For example, Daniel signs a check, leaves the amount blank, and gives it to Able, an employee, instructing Able to make certain purchases and to complete the check "for not more than $500." Able fills in the amount as $5,000 *contrary to instructions*. If Daniel can stop payment in time, Daniel *may* be able to assert the defense of unauthorized completion and avoid liability to an ordinary holder. However, if the check is negotiated to an HDC, the instrument is payable as completed. [UCC 3-115, 3-407, 3-304(4)(d), and 4-401(2)(b)]

Nondelivery   If a bearer instrument is lost or stolen, the maker or drawer of the instrument has the defense of nondelivery against an ordinary holder. Recall that delivery means "voluntary transfer of possession." [UCC 1-201(14)] This defense, however, is not good against an HDC. [UCC 3-305 and UCC 3-306(c)]

DISCHARGE

Discharge from liability on an instrument can come from payment, cancellation, or material alteration, as previously discussed. Discharge can also occur if a party reacquires an instrument, if a holder impairs another party's right of recourse, or if a holder surrenders collateral without consent. [UCC 3-601]

Discharge by Payment

According to UCC 3-601(1)(a) and 3-603, all parties to a negotiable instrument will be discharged when the party primarily liable on it pays to a holder the amount due in full.[7] The same is true if the drawee of an unaccepted draft or check makes payment in good faith to the holder. In these situations, all parties on the instruments are usually discharged. By contrast, such payment made by any other party (for example, an indorser) will discharge only the indorser and subsequent parties on the instrument. The party making such a payment still has the right to recover on the instrument from any prior parties.

---

7.   This is true even if the payment is made "with knowledge of a claim of another person to the instrument unless prior to such payment or satisfaction the person making the claim either supplies indemnity deemed adequate by the party seeking the discharge or enjoins payment or satisfaction by order of a court of competent jurisdiction in an action in which the adverse claimant and the holder are parties." [UCC 3-603(1)]

Instruments Acquired by Theft or Restrictively Indorsed   A party will not be discharged when paying in bad faith to a holder who acquired the instrument by theft or who obtained the instrument from someone else who acquired it by theft (unless, of course, the person has the rights of a holder in due course). [UCC 3-603(1)(a)] Finally, a party who pays on a restrictively indorsed instrument cannot claim discharge if the payment is made in a manner inconsistent with the terms of the restrictive indorsement. [UCC 3-603(1)(b)]

Once payment or other satisfaction is made to the holder in return for the surrender of the instrument, the liability of the maker or drawer is discharged and the transaction comes to an end. There are numerous acts by which makers or drawers can fulfill payment or satisfaction.

Discharge by Cancellation

The holder of a negotiable instrument can discharge any party to the instrument by cancellation. UCC 3-605(1)(a) explains how cancellation can occur: "The holder of an instrument may even without consideration discharge any party in a manner apparent on the face of the instrument or the indorsement, as by intentionally cancelling the instrument or the party's signature by destruction or mutilation, or by striking out the party's signature." For example, to write the word "Paid" across the face of an instrument constitutes cancellation. Tearing up a negotiable instrument cancels the instrument. Crossing out a party's indorsement cancels that party's liability and the liability of subsequent indorsers who have already indorsed the instrument, but not the liability of any prior parties.

Destruction or mutilation of a negotiable instrument is considered cancellation only if it is done with the intention of eliminating obligation on the instrument. [UCC 3-605(1)(a)] Thus, if destruction or mutilation occurs by accident, the instrument is not discharged, and the original terms can be established by parol evidence. [UCC 3-804]

Discharge by Reacquisition

A person reacquiring an instrument that he or she held previously discharges all intervening indorsers against subsequent holders who do not qualify as holders in due course. [UCC 3-208 and 3-601(3)(a)]

Discharge by Impairment of Recourse or of Collateral

Sometimes a party to an instrument will post or give collateral to secure that his or her performance will occur. When a holder surrenders that collateral without consent of the parties who would benefit from the collateral in the event of nonpayment, those parties to the instrument are discharged. [UCC 3-606(1)(b)]

QUESTIONS AND CASE PROBLEMS

1. On December 1, Daniel draws a check payable to Peter for $100 for services to be rendered on or before January 1. Peter indorses the check in blank to Smith on December 15 as payment of a debt he owed. Smith has been unable to cash the check during the Christmas holidays. Finally, on January 5 he negotiates the check to Harold, without indorsement, as payment for a cord of wood delivered. Peter never performs the services, and Daniel has stopped payment on the check by the time Harold attempts to cash it. Harold contends that he can hold Daniel liable on the check. Daniel claims that his defense is good against Harold. Discuss the contentions of Daniel and Harold.

2. Jim Hartman is vice-president of Harvey Waller's Construction Corporation. As vice-president, Hartman has authority to draft checks on behalf of the corporation. He draws two corporate checks, one for $20,000 to ABC Auto Inc. for a new Mercedes, signed "Harvey Waller's Construction Corporation," and the other to Suppliers, Inc., for $2,000 for purchase of materials, signed "Jim Hartman." Harvey Waller, president of Harvey Waller's Construction Corporation, learns of the purchases and stops payment on both checks, claiming no liability for the corporation, based on the fact that Hartman had no authority to purchase the car and that the corporation does not need the materials Hartman purchased. Discuss whether the corporation is liable on these checks.

3. Martin makes out a negotiable promissory note payable to the order of Peter. Peter indorses the note "without recourse, Peter" and transfers the note for value to Susan. Susan, in need of cash, negotiates the note to Helen by indorsing it "Pay to Helen, Susan." On the due date, Helen presents the note to Martin for payment, only to learn that Martin has filed for bankruptcy and will have all debts (including the note) discharged in bankruptcy. With these facts, discuss fully whether Helen can hold Martin, Peter, and Susan liable on the note.

4. Daniel draws a check on his bank, the First National West Bank, for $500, payable to Susan. She indorses the check in blank and negotiates it to Helen for value. Helen is about to purchase a piece of real estate in Daniel's city and goes to the First National West Bank to have the check certified. The bank refuses to certify the check and, after an argument, refuses even to cash the check, despite the fact that Daniel has sufficient funds in his checking account and has not issued a stop-payment order.

   (a) Is the bank's refusal to certify the check a dishonor? Explain.

   (b) Can the bank be held liable by Helen for its refusal to pay the check? Explain.

   (c) If the bank does certify the check, what is the status of the bank as to the real estate agent to whom Helen would negotiate the check? Explain.

5. Martin makes out a $500 negotiable promissory note payable to the order of Peter. By special indorsement, Peter transfers the note for value to Susan. By blank indorsement, Susan transfers the note for value to Martha. By special indorsement, Martha transfers the note for value to Harold. In need of cash, Harold transfers the instrument for value by blank indorsement *back* to Susan. When told that Peter has left the country, Susan strikes out Peter's indorsement. Later she learns that Peter is a wealthy restaurant owner in Miami and that Martin is financially unable to pay the note. Susan contends she can hold either Peter, Martha, or Harold liable on the note as an HDC. Discuss fully Susan's contentions.

6. George Sackett is president of G & J Wood Products Company. On October 14, 1968, Sackett personally co-signed, along with a sawmill operator named Bennington, a promissory note to Deerfield State Bank. When Bennington went out of business because of financial difficulties, G & J Wood Products paid the balance due on the note. What status did G & J Wood Products have before and after it paid the note?

7. In January 1971 the law firm of Harkavy, Moxley, and Keane was dissolved. Keane left the firm, which continued under the names of the other two partners. Prior to its dissolution, the law firm maintained a business account at Pan American Bank in which the signature of any one of the partners was sufficient for the deposit or withdrawal of funds. After dissolution of the firm, the account was kept open to take care of the former firm's receivables. In May 1971 a check payable to Keane and Moxley in the amount of $16,500 was received by Harkavy

for business carried on by the former firm. The check was deposited in the former firm's account after the bookkeeper for the firm had rubber-stamped the check "For Deposit Only, Harkavy, Moxley and Keane 035-602." The $16,500 was thereafter withdrawn by Harkavy and Moxley and deposited into the account of the new firm. If the stamping of the check is deemed to be an improper indorsement, then Keane cannot recover from Pan American Bank. Can Keane recover? [Keane v. Pan American Bank, 309 So.2d 579 (Fla.App. 1975)]

8. Fidelity Mortgage Investors established a line of credit with Sterling National Bank and Trust Company in the amount of $2,000,000. In exchange for the credit, Fidelity issued a promissory note to Sterling for this same amount. Interest on the note was 9¼ percent. A notation "9¼" was penciled on the face of the note by Sterling. This accorded with standard bank practices in that locality. Fidelity later claimed that this notation constituted a fraudulent and material alteration of the instrument in that it represented an attempt by Sterling to set the post-maturity interest at the same rate as the pre-maturity interest. In the absence of agreement, the post-maturity rate would be 6 percent (by statute). What effect did the notation "9¼" have on each of the parties to the promissory note? [Sterling Nat'l Bank and Trust Co. v. Fidelity Mortgage Investors, 510 F.2d 870 (2d Cir. 1975)]

9. The LRZH Corporation borrowed from Langeveld and gave in exchange its promissory note, which was guaranteed by Joseph Higgins. The note was secured by a third mortgage on property owned by LRZH. Langeveld failed to record this mortgage until nearly one year after the loan was made. LRZH defaulted on the note. Foreclosure proceedings yielded only enough money to pay the holders of the first and second mortgages. Receiving nothing from the sale of the property, Langeveld sued Higgins on the basis of his guaranty. Higgins argued that Langeveld's failure to record the mortgage impaired the collateral held by Langeveld and hence discharged Higgins from liability on the note. What was the result? [Langeveld v. LRZH Corp., 130 N.J.Super. 486, 327 A.2d 683 (1974)]

10. A bank sued an accommodation indorser for payment of a note. The indorser asserted as a defense that the bank could not collect because the purpose of the loan was to purchase the bank's own stock—a transaction prohibited under the Federal Banking Law. The federal statute does not make this type of loan void. Was the indorser's defense of illegality successful? [Pan American Bank of Tampa v. Sullivan, 375 So.2d 338 (Fla.App. 4th Dist. 1979)].

28

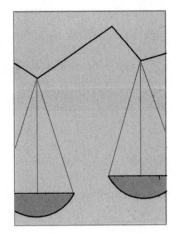

COMMERCIAL PAPER
Checks and the
Banking System

Checks are the most common kind of commercial paper regulated by the Uniform Commercial Code. Checks, credit cards, and charge accounts are rapidly replacing currency as a means of payment in almost all transactions for goods and services. It is estimated that approximately 57 billion personal and commercial checks are written each year in the United States. Checks are more than a daily convenience; checkbook money is an integral part of the economic system.

This chapter will identify the legal characteristics of checks and the legal duties and liabilities that arise when a check is issued. Then it will consider the check deposit and collection process—that is, the actual procedure by which checkbook money moves through banking channels, causing the underlying cash dollars to be shifted from bank account to bank account.

CHECKS

A **check** is a special type of draft that is drawn on a *bank*, ordering it to pay a sum of money on *demand*. [UCC 3-104(2)(b)] The person who writes the check is called the drawer and is usually a depositor in the bank on which the check is drawn. The person to whom the check is payable is the payee. The bank or financial institution on which the check is drawn

is the drawee. If Anne Gordon writes a check from her checking account to pay her school tuition, she is the *drawer*, her bank is the *drawee*, and her school is the *payee*.

The payee can indorse the check to another person, thereby making that receiver a holder. Recall from Chapter 26 that a holder is a person who is in rightful possession of an instrument that is drawn to that person's order (or drawn to bearer) or that is indorsed to that person (or in blank). [UCC 1-201(20)] The *payee as a holder* of a check has the right to transfer or negotiate it or to demand its payment in his or her own name, *as does any subsequent holder*.

A check does not, in and of itself, operate as an assignment of funds [UCC 3-409(1)], because it does not show an intention to make present transfer of the right to the specified sum. Thus, the drawee bank is not liable to a payee or holder who presents the check for payment, even though the drawer has sufficient funds to pay the check. The payee's, or holder's, only recourse is against the drawer. (The drawer, however, may subsequently hold the bank liable for its wrongful refusal to pay.)

Cashier's Checks

Checks are usually three-party instruments, but on certain types of checks, the bank can serve as both the drawer and the drawee. For example, when a bank draws a check upon itself, the check is called a **cashier's check** and is a negotiable instrument upon issue. (See Exhibit 28–1.) In effect, with a cashier's check, the bank lends its credit to the purchaser of the check, thus making it available for immediate use in banking circles. (The drawee is treated similar to an acceptor.) A cashier's check is therefore an acknowledgment of a debt drawn by the bank upon itself.

Traveler's Checks

A traveler's check is generally not a check, but a straight draft. It is an instrument on which a financial institution is both the drawer and the drawee. (It is most often a regular draft since a bank is seldom the drawee.) On traveler's checks, however, there is an additional requirement that the payee must provide his or her authorized signature in order for it to become a negotiable instrument. A traveler's check has the characteristics of a cashier's check from the issuing bank. It is drawn by the issuer upon itself. (See Exhibit 28–2.)

Certified Checks

When a person writes a check, it is assumed that he or she has money on deposit to cover that check when it is presented for payment. To insure against dishonor for insufficient funds, a check may be certified by the drawee bank. A **certified check** is rec-

ognized and accepted by a bank officer as a valid appropriation of the specified amount that is drawn against the funds held by the bank. (See Exhibit 28–3.) The usual method of certification is for the cashier or teller to write across the face of the check, over the signature, a statement that it is good when properly indorsed.

The certification should contain the date, the amount being certified, and the name and title of the person certifying. Certification prevents the bank from denying liability. It is a promise that sufficient funds are on deposit and *have been set aside* to cover the check. Certified checks are used in many business dealings, especially when the buyer and seller are strangers. Sometimes, certified checks are the required form of payment under state law—for example, in purchases at a sheriff's sale.

A drawee bank is not obligated to certify a check, and failure to do so is not a dishonor of the check. [UCC 3-411(2)] When a bank agrees to certification, it immediately charges the drawer's account with the amount of the check and transfers those funds to its own certified check account. In effect, the bank is agreeing in advance to accept that check when it is presented for payment and to make payment from those funds reserved in the certified check account. [UCC 3-411(1)]

Drawer's Request for Certification   The legal liability of the drawer differs on the basis of whether

---

EXHIBIT 28-1   Cashier's Check

| F 537 M | THE FIRST NATIONAL BANK OF WHITACRE
332 MAIN STREET   WHITEACRE, MINNESOTA — Drawee-Bank | NUMBER
644848 |

EXHIBIT 28-2 Traveler's Check

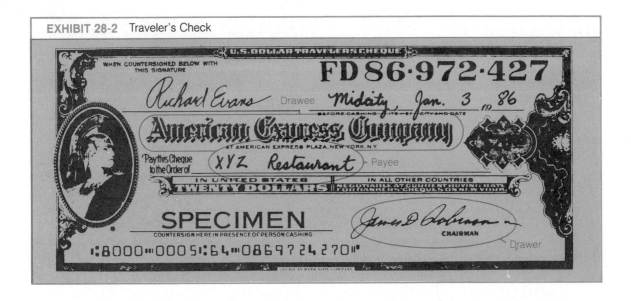

EXHIBIT 28-3 Certified Check

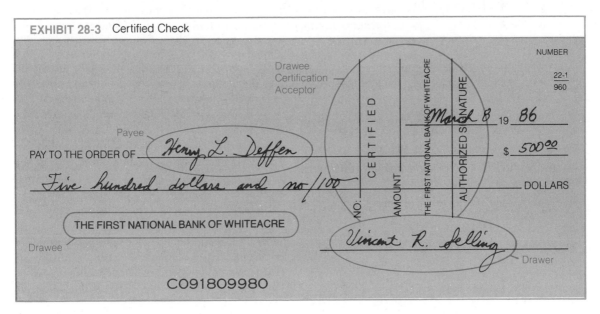

the certification is requested by the drawer or the holder. The drawer who obtains certification remains *secondarily liable* on the instrument if for some reason the certifying bank cannot or does not honor the check when it is presented for payment.

For example, Epstein buys Stiple's car for $500. Epstein writes out a check for that amount and takes it to the bank where it is certified. In the unlikely event that the bank fails to honor the check when it is presented for payment, Stiple can hold Epstein liable for payment of the $500.

Holder's Request for Certification If the check is certified at the request of the holder, then the drawer and any indorsers prior to certification are completely discharged. A holder's request for certification is viewed as an affirmative choice for the bank's promise to pay over the drawer's and any indorser's promises. In this situation, the holder can look only to the bank for payment. In the example above, Epstein writes a $500 check to Stiple, but Stiple takes the check to the drawee bank for certification. Upon certification, Epstein is released from all liability, and Stiple can look only to the bank for his $500. [UCC 3-411(1)]

Revocation of Certification   The bank's ability to revoke certification is extremely limited. If a good faith holder has changed position in reliance on that certification, the bank cannot revoke. Furthermore, since certification constitutes *acceptance* of an instrument under the Uniform Commercial Code, a bank can never revoke certification against an HDC regardless of whether the HDC has changed position in reliance on the certification. [UCC 3-418]

Alteration of a Certified Check   A bank will be liable for payment of an altered check only if the check was altered prior to certification. Upon certification, the drawee bank becomes an acceptor and becomes liable for the instrument according to its tenor at the time of certification. Alterations after certification are not binding on the bank.

The following case involves a certified check that was altered. Because of the alteration, it was dishonored when presented to the bank. The court held the bank liable for only the original amount of the check.

SAM GOODY, INC. v. FRANKLIN NAT'L BANK OF LONG ISLAND

Supreme Court of New York, 1968.

57 Misc.2d 193, 291 N.Y.S.2d 429.

BACKGROUND AND FACTS   *The Franklin National Bank (defendant) certified a check payable to Sam Goody, Inc., in the amount of $16. The certification stamp of the defendant bank did not show the amount for which the check was certified. The check had been presented to the defendant bank for certification by either the depositor or an accomplice. After the certification was procured, the amount of the check was altered from $16 to $1,600. The check was later presented to the plaintiff, Sam Goody, Inc., in payment for merchandise. The customer who presented the check represented that it was a bonus check. The customer had ordered the merchandise on the previous day and had stated that he would secure from his employer a certified check drawn directly to the plaintiff, Sam Goody, to pay the balance owing. Subsequently, the bank refused to honor the check because of the alteration. The plaintiff sued the bank for the full $1,600. The bank asserted that it was responsible only for the amount it had certified originally—that is, $16.*

FARLEY, Justice.
*   *   *   *

The fraudulent scheme perpetrated in this case was obviously made possible by the knowledge that the certification stamp of the defendant Bank would not disclose the amount for which the check was certified. The plaintiff claims the negligence of the Bank in this respect caused the loss and that the Bank is estopped from asserting the defense of alteration under section 3-406 of the Uniform Commercial Code.
*   *   *   *

A bank, when certifying a check, does no more than to affirm the genuineness of the signature of the maker, that he has funds on deposit to meet the item, and that the funds will not be withdrawn to the prejudice of the holder. The certification constitutes an acceptance of the check to this extent (U.C.C., § 3-411), but the bank by its certification does not guaranty the body thereof *   *   * and engages only to pay the item according to its tenor at the time certification is procured (U.C.C., § 3-413). Furthermore, a holder of a check, by having it certified, is deemed to have warranted to the bank that the instrument has not been materially altered. The Code makes one exception to this rule by providing that the same warranty is not given by a holder in due course whether the alteration is made before or after certification (U.C.C., §§ 3-417 subd. (1) [c. iii, iv]; 3-413). Consequently, under the Code, where a check is certified *after the amount has been altered*, the bank runs the risk of sustaining the loss if the instrument passes into the hands of a holder in due course. [Emphasis added.] The Code in this respect changes the law which previously obtained in New

York (*National Reserve Bank of the City of New York v. The Corn Exchange Bank, supra*).

The rule, however, is otherwise where the certification of the check is procured by the maker. In such case, the bank does not incur the risk of an alteration prior to its acceptance, and only agrees to pay the instrument according to its tenor at the time of certification even as to a holder in due course (U.C.C., § 3-413[1]).

The evidence in this case does not disclose whether the maker or his accomplice procured certification of the check, but the controlling fact that alteration occurred after certification of the instrument is not disputed. The bank, in checking its records, discovered the alteration and refused payment. Under these circumstances, the negligence of the bank, if any, is not a substantial or proximate cause of the loss, and in accordance with the rules mentioned above, it is not liable to the plaintiff except for the amount for which the check was originally drawn.

The defendant, Franklin National Bank, was liable for only $16, the original amount of the certified check.

DECISION AND REMEDY

Notice that the court did not discuss UCC 3-406 at length. Rather, the court made it clear that it did not believe that the bank was negligent.

COMMENT

THE BANK–CUSTOMER RELATIONSHIP

The bank-customer relationship begins when the customer opens a checking account and deposits money that will be used to pay for checks written. The rights and duties of the bank and the customer are contractual and depend upon the nature of the transaction.

Article 4 of the UCC is a statement of the principles and rules of modern bank deposit and collection procedures. It governs the relationship of banks with one another as they process checks for payment, and it establishes a framework for deposit and checking agreements between a bank and its customers.

Article 3 of the UCC, dealing with the use of commercial paper, sets forth the requirements for negotiable instruments. The extent to which any party is either charged or discharged from liability on a check is established according to the provisions of Article 3. Note that a check can fall within the scope of Article 3 as a negotiable instrument and yet be subject to the provisions of Article 4 while it is in the course of collection. In the case of a conflict between Articles 3 and 4, Article 4 controls. [UCC 4-102(1)]

A creditor-debtor relationship is created between a customer and a bank when, for example, the customer makes cash deposits into a checking account or when final payment is received for checks drawn on other banks.

A principal-agent relationship underlies the check collection process. A check does not operate as an immediate legal assignment of funds between the drawer and the payee. [UCC 3-409] The money in the bank represented by that check does not move from the drawer's account to the payee's account; nor is any underlying debt discharged until the drawee bank honors the check and makes final payment. To transfer checkbook dollars among different banks, each bank acts as the agent of collection for its customer. [UCC 4-201(1)]

DUTIES OF THE BANK

A commercial bank serves its customers primarily in two ways:

1. By honoring checks for the withdrawal of funds on deposit in its customers' accounts.
2. By accepting deposits in U.S. currency and collecting checks written to or indorsed to its customers that are drawn on other banks.

HONORING CHECKS

When a commercial bank provides checking services, it agrees to honor the checks written by its customers with the usual stipulation that there be sufficient funds available in the account to pay each check. When a drawee bank *wrongfully* fails to honor a check, it is liable to its customer for damages resulting from its refusal to pay. The Code does not attempt to specify the theory under which the customer may recover for wrongful dishonor; it merely states that the drawee is liable. Thus, the drawer customer no longer has to prove that the drawee bank breached its contractual commitment, or slandered the customer's credit, or was negligent. [UCC 4-402] When the bank properly dishonors a check for insufficient funds, it has no liability to the customer.

On the other hand, a bank may charge against a customer's account a check that is payable from that account even though the account contains insufficient funds to cover the check. [UCC 4-401(1)]

Once a bank makes special arrangements with its customer to accept overdrafts on an account, the payor bank can become liable to its customer for damages proximately caused by its wrongful dishonor of overdrafts. The charging of overdrafts will be discussed later in this chapter.

The customer's agreement with the bank includes a general obligation to keep sufficient money on deposit to cover all checks written. The customer is liable to the payee or to the holder of a check in a civil suit if a check is not honored. If intent to defraud can be proved, the customer can also be subject to criminal prosecution for writing a bad check.

The following case illustrates that when a bank agrees with a customer to pay overdrafts, the bank's refusal to honor checks on an overdrawn account is a wrongful dishonor.

KENDALL YACHT CORP. v. UNITED CALIFORNIA BANK

Court of Appeals of California, 1975.
50 Cal.3d 949, 123 Cal.Rptr. 848.

BACKGROUND AND FACTS *Lawrence and Linda Kendall were officers and the principal shareholders of Kendall Yacht Corporation, a corporation formed to build yachts upon special order from customers. The corporation had never issued stock and was undercapitalized.*

The corporation had a payroll checking account and a general business checking account with United California Bank. When the corporation ran into some financial problems, Mr. Kendall spoke with Ron Lamperts, a loan officer at the bank, in an effort to obtain financing for the corporation.

The bank agreed to honor overdrafts on the corporate account until such time as the corporation was financially more stable. The Kendalls continued to write checks for supplies, payroll, and other operating expenses of the corporation from about mid-October through December. The corporate bank account was badly overdrawn, and a number of the checks had been dishonored by the bank.

The Kendalls brought this lawsuit against United California Bank, charging that its wrongful dishonor of checks that it had initially agreed to accept as overdrafts caused damage to the Kendalls' personal and credit reputation.

McDANIEL, Associate Justice.
* * * *

During October, November, and December, the Bank honored overdrafts of the Corporation totaling in excess of $15,000. There were also a number of overdrafts written during these months which were not honored by the Bank. Some of these were to suppliers and others were payroll checks to employees. In addition, the Bank failed to honor a check written to Insurance Company of North America to cover a premium for workmen's compensation insurance. The Kendalls were not aware that this check had been "bounced" until after one of their employees had been injured and they had been notified by Insurance Company of North America that their insurance had been terminated for nonpayment of premium.

After the collapse of the business, the Kendalls understandably had a number of enemies in the community. They were accused of having breached the trust of their former suppliers and employees and of having milked the Corporation of its funds and placed them in a Swiss bank account. They were repeatedly threatened with legal action and physical harm; they suffered acts of vandalism such as eggs and oil being thrown at their cars. Mr. Kendall's subsequent employer was contacted and threatened by creditors of the Corporation. Criminal charges were brought against Mrs. Kendall for writing checks against insufficient funds; the charges were dismissed shortly before she was brought to trial on them. The Kendalls were required to appear and answer charges in administrative proceedings involving dishonored payroll checks and the Corporation's failure to carry workmen's compensation insurance. Each testified to experiencing severe emotional distress and humiliation as a result of these matters. They also testified to marital problems which were allegedly caused by the stress brought on by the failure of the business.

* * * *

The Bank contends first that under Commercial Code section 4402 the wrongful dishonor of a check of a *corporation* does not give a cause of action for damages to individual officers and shareholders of the corporation. Commercial Code section 4402, which represents section 4-402 of the Uniform Commercial Code, reads as follows: "A payor bank is liable to its customer for damages proximately caused by the wrongful dishonor of an item. When the dishonor occurs through mistake liability is limited to actual damages proved." [Footnote omitted.]

[It] was entirely foreseeable that the dishonoring of the Corporation's checks would reflect directly on the personal credit and reputation of the Kendalls and that they would suffer the adverse personal consequences which resulted when the Bank reneged on its commitments.

* * * *

[It] has been held in this state that a cause of action for wrongful dishonor of a check sounds in tort as well as in contract (*Weaver v. Bank of America*, 59 Cal.2d 428, 431, 30 Cal.Rptr. 4, 380 P.2d 644), and "if the conduct is tortious, damages for emotional distress may be recovered despite the fact that the conduct also involves a breach of contract."

The court awarded the Kendalls $26,000 each as compensatory damages for the bank's wrongful dishonor of the checks.

DECISION AND REMEDY

Stale Checks

The bank's responsibility to honor its customers' checks is not absolute. A bank is not obliged to pay an uncertified check presented more than six months from its date. [UCC 4-404] Commercial banking practice regards a check outstanding for longer than six months as *stale*. UCC 4-404 gives a bank the option of paying or not paying on a **stale check**. The usual banking practice is to consult the customer, but if a bank pays in good faith without consulting the customer, it has the right to charge the customer's account for the amount of the check.

In the following case, a bank's payment of a stale check is at issue. The court's discussion of this issue is illustrative.

BACKGROUND AND FACTS *Granite Equipment Leasing Corporation issued a check to Overseas Equipment Company. After five days, Overseas indicated that the check had not been received. Granite ordered payment on the check stopped and wired the funds to Overseas. Approximately one year later, the check cleared and Granite's account was charged. Granite sued the bank for return of the funds to its account, maintaining that the bank had a duty to inquire into the circumstances of the stale check. The bank based its*

GRANITE EQUIPMENT LEASING CORP. v. **HEMPSTEAD BANK**
Supreme Court of New York, 1971.
68 Misc.2d 350, 326 N.Y.S.2d 881.

defense on the premise that the stop-payment order had expired and that it had acted in good faith.

HARNETT, Justice.

* * * *

Under the Uniform Commercial Code, does a bank have a duty of inquiry before paying a stale check? Does it matter that the stale check had been previously stopped under a stop payment order which expired for lack of renewal? So this case goes.

* * * *

There is no doubt the check is stale. There is no doubt the stop payment order was properly given at the outset, and that it was never renewed. Granite essentially maintains the Bank had a duty to inquire into the circumstances of that stale check, and should not have paid in face of a known lapsed stop order without consulting its depositor.

The Uniform Commercial Code, which became effective in New York on September 27, 1964, provides that:

"(1) A customer may by order to his bank stop payment of any item payable for his account *   *   * (2) *   *   * A written [stop] order is effective for only six months unless renewed in writing". UCC § 4-403.

* * * *

Granite cannot be permitted to predicate liability on the part of the Bank on its failure to inquire about and find a stop payment order which had become terminated in default of renewal.

* * * *

Neither may Granite predicate a claim of liability upon the Bank's payment of a stale check. The legal principles applicable to this circumstance are codified in UCC § 4-404, which provides that:

"[a] bank is under no obligation . . . to pay a check, other than a certified check, which is presented more than six months after its date, but *it may charge its customer's account for a payment made thereafter in good faith*". (Emphasis added.) *   *   *

There is no obligation under the statute of the Bank to search its records to discover old lapsed stop payment orders. The Bank does not have to pay a stale check, but it may pay one in "good faith". Significantly, UCC § 1-201(19) defines "good faith" as "honesty in fact in the conduct or transaction concerned". In the absence of any facts which could justify a finding of dishonesty, bad faith, recklessness, or lack of ordinary care, in the face of circumstances actually known, or which should have been known, the Bank is not liable to Granite for its payment of the check drawn to Overseas.

Granite's complete remedy lies in its pending Florida action against Overseas to recover the extra payment.

DECISION AND REMEDY   *The court dismissed the complaint and entered judgment in favor of the bank, which was not required to pay Granite Equipment the amount of the check. The court ruled that Hempstead Bank had acted in good faith.*

Missing Indorsements

Depositary institutions are allowed to supply any necessary indorsements of a customer. This rule does not apply if the item expressly requires the payee's indorsement. The depositary bank places a statement on the item to the effect that it was deposited by a customer or credited to that customer's account. [UCC 4-205(1)]

Death or Incompetence of a Customer

UCC 4-405 provides that if, at the time a check is issued or its collection has been undertaken, a bank does *not know* of an adjudication of incompetence, an item can be paid and the bank will not incur liability. Neither death nor incompetency revokes the bank's authority to pay an item until the bank knows of the situation and has had reasonable time to act. Even when a bank *knows* of the *death* of its customer, for ten days after the date of death, it can pay or certify checks drawn on or prior to the date of death—unless a person claiming an interest in that account, such as an heir or an executor of the estate, orders the bank to stop all payment. Without this provision, banks would constantly be required to verify the continued life and competency of their drawers.

Stop-Payment Orders

Only a customer can order his or her bank to pay a check, and only a customer can order payment to be stopped. This right does not extend to holders—that is, payees or indorsees—because the drawee bank's contract is only with its drawers. A customer has no right to stop payment on a check that has been certified or where there has been acceptance by a bank. A stop-payment order must be received within a reasonable time and in a reasonable manner to permit the bank to act on it. [UCC 4-403(1)]

A stop-payment order can be given orally, usually by phone, and it is binding on the bank for only fourteen calendar days unless confirmed in writing.[1] (See Exhibit 28–4.) A written stop-payment order

---

1. Some states do not recognize oral stop-payment orders; they must be in writing.

or oral order confirmed in writing is effective for six months only, unless renewed in writing. [UCC 4-403(2)]

Should the drawee bank pay the check over the customer's properly instituted stop-payment order, the bank will be obligated to recredit the account of the drawer customer. However, the bank is liable for no more than the actual loss suffered by the drawer because of such wrongful payment.

For example, Pat Davis orders one hundred used typewriters at $50 each from Jane Smith. Davis pays in advance for the goods with her check for $5,000. Later that day, Smith tells Davis that she is not going to deliver any typewriters. Davis immediately calls her bank and stops payment on the check. Two days later, in spite of this stop-payment order, the bank inadvertently honors Davis's $5,000 check to Smith for the undelivered typewriters. The bank will be liable to Davis for the full $5,000.

The result would be different if Smith had delivered ninety-nine typewriters. Since Davis would have owed Smith $4,950 for the goods delivered, she would have been able to establish actual losses of only $50 resulting from the bank's payment over her stop-payment order. The bank would be liable to Davis for only $50.

A stop-payment order has its risks for a customer. The drawer must have a *valid legal ground* for issuing such an order; otherwise the holder can sue the drawer for payment. Moreover, defenses sufficient to refuse payment against a payee may not be

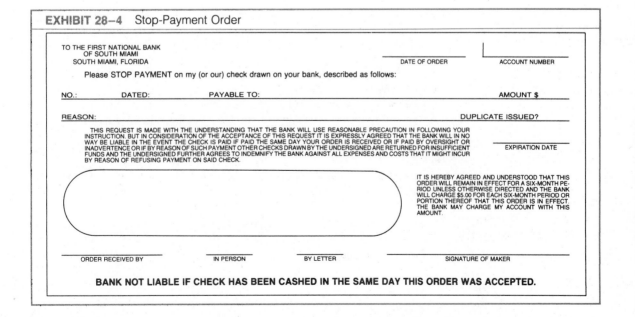

EXHIBIT 28–4 Stop-Payment Order

TO THE FIRST NATIONAL BANK OF SOUTH MIAMI
SOUTH MIAMI, FLORIDA

DATE OF ORDER _____   ACCOUNT NUMBER _____

Please STOP PAYMENT on my (or our) check drawn on your bank, described as follows:

NO.: _____   DATED: _____   PAYABLE TO: _____   AMOUNT $ _____

REASON: _____   DUPLICATE ISSUED? _____

THIS REQUEST IS MADE WITH THE UNDERSTANDING THAT THE BANK WILL USE REASONABLE PRECAUTION IN FOLLOWING YOUR INSTRUCTION. BUT IN CONSIDERATION OF THE ACCEPTANCE OF THIS REQUEST IT IS EXPRESSLY AGREED THAT THE BANK WILL IN NO WAY BE LIABLE IN THE EVENT THE CHECK IS PAID IF PAID THE SAME DAY YOUR ORDER IS RECEIVED OR IF PAID BY OVERSIGHT OR INADVERTENCE OR IF BY REASON OF SUCH PAYMENT OTHER CHECKS DRAWN BY THE UNDERSIGNED ARE RETURNED FOR INSUFFICIENT FUNDS AND THE UNDERSIGNED FURTHER AGREES TO INDEMNIFY THE BANK AGAINST ALL EXPENSES AND COSTS THAT IT MIGHT INCUR BY REASON OF REFUSING PAYMENT ON SAID CHECK.

EXPIRATION DATE _____

IT IS HEREBY AGREED AND UNDERSTOOD THAT THIS ORDER WILL REMAIN IN EFFECT FOR A SIX-MONTH PERIOD UNLESS OTHERWISE DIRECTED AND THE BANK WILL CHARGE $5.00 FOR EACH SIX-MONTH PERIOD OR PORTION THEREOF THAT THIS ORDER IS IN EFFECT. THE BANK MAY CHARGE MY ACCOUNT WITH THIS AMOUNT.

ORDER RECEIVED BY _____   IN PERSON _____   BY LETTER _____   SIGNATURE OF MAKER _____

BANK NOT LIABLE IF CHECK HAS BEEN CASHED IN THE SAME DAY THIS ORDER WAS ACCEPTED.

valid grounds to prevent payment against a subsequent holder in due course. [UCC 3-305]

A person who wrongfully stops payment on a check will not only be liable to the payee for the amount of the check, but might also be liable for *special* damages resulting from the wrongful order. Special damages, however, must be separately pleaded and proved at trial. The following case illustrates the problem of proving special damages for wrongful stop payment of a check.

VICKREY v. SANFORD
Court of Appeals of Texas,
1974.
506 S.W.2d 270.

BACKGROUND AND FACTS   *Sanford was fired from a restaurant by his supervisor, Vickrey. Vickrey gave him a number of checks for wages due along with a check for $720 to reimburse him for shares of stock that he had purchased in one of Vickrey's other companies. After depositing the checks, Sanford returned to the restaurant and verbally insulted and threatened Vickrey. Following the incident, Vickrey stopped payment on the check for $720. Sanford sued Vickrey for $720 plus interest.*

BREWSTER, Justice.
*   *   *   *

On the occasion when Vickrey had given the $720.00 check to Sanford, Sanford had advised Vickrey that he needed the money to pay up bills and to get to Las Vegas, Nevada, at which place he could get a job.

After Sanford had done the cursing at the "Sirloin Stockade", he, on the same day, left for Las Vegas, Nevada, and was there hired at the Golden Nugget as a dealer and to work at the roulette wheel.

A few days later Sanford called home and was told by his wife that payment had been stopped on the $720.00 check and that Mr. Allen, a vice-president of Denton County National Bank, where he had cashed it, wanted to get in touch with him. He called Allen and Allen wanted him to sign a note for the $720.00.
*   *   *   *

Sanford sought in this case to recover the amount of the check ($720.00) plus interest thereon, plus the expenses that he incurred in making the two trips back to Denton, plus exemplary (punishment) damages.
*   *   *   *

[The court had no trouble deciding that Vickrey was responsible for paying the $720 plus interest. It was Sanford's most unusual request for the cost of traveling between Nevada and Texas to straighten out the mess that gave the court cause for concern.]

If plaintiff, Sanford, is legally entitled to recover for expenses incurred in making the two trips from Nevada back to Texas plus the loss of salary due to losing his job, it would only be on the theory that they were special damages that were within the contemplation of the parties at the time the contract was executed. This is a necessary element if the expenses sought to be recovered are in the category of special damages.
*   *   *   *

There was no evidence tending to show that the entire transaction with reference to Sanford signing the note to the Bank could not have been handled by mail, thus rendering both of Sanford's trips to Texas unnecessary. There was no evidence offered to the effect that it was necessary that this note be signed in Denton.

DECISION AND REMEDY   *The court permitted Sanford to recover only the amount of the $720 check in damages. The court held that there was insufficient evidence to uphold Sanford's claim for special damages.*

Overdrafts

When the bank receives an item properly payable from its customer's checking account, but there are insufficient funds in the account to cover the amount of the check, the bank can either dishonor the item or it can pay the item and charge the customer's account, creating an overdraft. [UCC 4-401(1)] The bank can subtract the difference from the customer's next deposit because the check carries with it an enforceable implied promise to reimburse the bank.

When a check "bounces," a holder can resubmit the check, hoping that at a later date sufficient funds will be available to pay it. The holder must notify any indorsers on the check of the first dishonor; otherwise they will be discharged from their signature liability.

Payment on a Forged Signature of the Drawer

A forged signature on a check has no legal effect as the signature of a drawer. [UCC 3-404(1)] Banks require signature cards from each customer who opens a checking account. The bank is responsible for determining whether the signature on a customer's check is genuine. The general rule is that the bank must recredit the customer's account when it pays on a forged signature.

Customer Negligence   When the customer's negligence substantially contributes to the forgery, the bank will not normally be obliged to recredit the customer's account for the amount of the check. Suppose Axelrod Corporation uses a mechanical check-writing machine to write its payroll and business checks. Axelrod discovers that one of its employees used the machine to write himself a check for $10,000 and that the bank subsequently honored it. Axelrod requests the bank to recredit $10,000 to its account for incorrectly paying on a forged check. If the bank can show that Axelrod failed to take reasonable care in controlling access to the check-writing equipment, Axelrod cannot require the bank to recredit its account for the amount of the forged check. [UCC 3-406]

Timely Examination Required   A customer has an *affirmative duty* to examine monthly statements and canceled checks promptly and with reasonable care and to report any forged signatures promptly. [UCC 4-406(1)] This includes forged signatures of indorsers, to be discussed later. [UCC 4-406]

Failure to so examine and report, or any carelessness by the customer that results in a loss to the bank, makes the customer liable for the loss. [UCC 4-406(2)(a)] Even if the customer can prove that reasonable care was taken against forgeries, the Code provides that discovery of such forgeries and notice to the bank must take place within specific time frames, or the customer cannot require the bank to recredit his or her account.

When a series of forgeries by the same wrongdoer takes place, the Code provides that the customer, in order to recover for all the forged items, must discover and report the forgery to the bank within fourteen calendar days of the receipt of the bank statement and canceled checks that contain the forged item. [UCC 4-406(2)(b)] Failure to notify within this period of time discharges the bank's liability for all similar forged checks prior to notification.

For example, Middletown Bank sends out monthly statements and canceled checks on the last day of each month. Bradley, owner of a small store, unknowingly has had a number of his blank checks stolen by employee Harry. On April 20 Harry forges Bradley's signature and cashes check number 1. On April 22, Harry forges and cashes check number 2. The checks canceled in April (including the forged ones) and the April statement from the Middletown Bank are received on May 1. Bradley sets aside the statement and does not reconcile his checking account. On May 20 Bradley forges check number 3. The checks canceled in May and the May statement are received by Bradley on June 1. Upon immediate examination of both statements, Bradley discovers the forgeries.

Can Bradley demand that the bank recredit his account for all forged checks? The answer is no, assuming the bank was not negligent in paying the forged checks. [UCC 4-406(3)] A series of forgeries by the same wrongdoer has been committed. The two forged checks in April were made available to Bradley for inspection on May 1. Liability for any forged check in the series written after May 15 (fourteen days after receipt of the April statement) falls on Bradley. In addition, if Bradley's negligence in failing to examine his April statement promptly results in a loss to the Middletown Bank, the bank's liability to recredit Bradley's account for any forged item would be reduced by the amount of any loss the bank suffered by reason of Bradley's failure to promptly notify the bank.

Had Bradley examined his April statement immediately upon receipt and reported the two April forgeries, the bank would have been obligated to fully recredit Bradley's account. However, if the bank can prove that Bradley's carelessness in permitting the blank checks to be stolen substantially contributed to the forgery, Bradley—not the bank—will be liable. [UCC 3-406 and 4-406]

Regardless of the degree of care exercised by the customer or the bank, the Code has placed an absolute time limit on the liability of a bank for forged customer signatures. UCC 4-406(4) provides that a customer who fails to report his or her forged signature one year from the date that the statement and canceled checks were made available for inspection loses the legal right to have the bank recredit his or her account.

Payment on a Forged Indorsement

A bank that pays a customer's check bearing a forged indorsement must recredit the customer's account or be liable to the customer-drawer for breach of contract.

For example, Baker issues a $50 check "to the order of Thelma." Larry steals the check, forges Thelma's indorsement and cashes the check. When the check reaches Baker's bank, the bank pays it and debits Baker's account. Under UCC 4-401, the bank must recredit Baker's account $50 because it failed to carry out Baker's order to pay "to the order of Thelma." (Baker's bank will in turn recover—under breach of warranty principles—from the bank that cashed the check. [UCC 4-207(1)(a)]

By comparison, the bank has no right to recover from a holder who, without knowledge, cashes a check bearing a *forged drawer's signature.* The holder merely guarantees that he or she has no knowledge that the signature of the drawer is unauthorized. Unless the bank can prove such knowledge, its only recourse is against the forger. [UCC 3-418 and 4-207(1)(b)]

The customer, however, has a duty to examine the returned checks and statements received by the bank and to report forged indorsements upon discovery or notice. Failure to report forged indorsements within a three-year period after such forged items are made available to the customer relieves the bank of liability. [UCC 4-406(4)]

In the following case, the customer's duty to discover and report an unauthorized signature was at issue.

OSSIP-HARRIS INSURANCE, INC. v. BARNETT BANK OF SOUTH FLORIDA, N.A.
District Court of Appeal of Florida, 1983.
428 So.2d 363.

BACKGROUND AND FACTS *Ossip-Harris Insurance Company, Inc., the plaintiff, maintained a checking account with Barnett Bank of South Florida, N.A., the defendant, during 1980 and 1981. From May 1980 through June 1981, Ossip's bookkeeper, Edgerly, used a facsimile signature stamp to forge the name of Ossip's president, Harris, to ninety-nine checks totaling $19,711.90. When the cancelled checks came back to Ossip, Edgerly would replace the payee name with one of a legitimate Ossip business expense. Throughout this period, Harris periodically reviewed the monthly statements and cancelled checks, but did not detect the forgeries until June of 1981. At that time, Harris notified Barnett, and no further forged instruments were paid by Barnett. Ossip alleged that Barnett wrongfully paid the ninety-nine checks drawn on Ossip's account, but the trial court entered a summary judgment in favor of Barnett. Ossip appealed the summary judgment.*

HENDRY, Judge.
* * * *

Resolution of this dispute turns on the provisions of subsections (1) through (3) of Section 674.406, Florida Statutes (1981), which state:
(1) When a bank sends to its customer a statement of account accompanied by items paid in good faith in support of the debit entries or holds the statement and

items pursuant to a request or instructions of its customer or otherwise in a reasonable manner makes the statement and items available to the customer, the customer must exercise reasonable care and promptness to examine the statement and items to discover his unauthorized signature or any alteration on an item and must notify the bank promptly after discovery thereof.

(2) If the bank establishes that the customer failed with respect to an item to comply with the duties imposed on the customer by subsection (1) the customer is precluded from asserting against the bank:

(a) His unauthorized signature or any alteration on the item if the bank also establishes that it suffered a loss by reason of such failure; and

(b) An unauthorized signature or alteration by the same wrongdoer on any other item paid in good faith by the bank after the first item and statement was available to the customer for a reasonable period not exceeding 14 calendar days and before the bank receives notification from the customer of any such unauthorized signature or alteration.

(3) The preclusion under subsection (2) does not apply if the customer establishes lack of ordinary care on the part of the bank in paying the item(s).

Subsection (1) of the statute clearly requires a bank customer such as Ossip to "exercise reasonable care and promptness" in examining bank statements and items to discover any unauthorized signatures or alterations. If this duty is not complied with, paragraph (b) of subsection (2) of the statute precludes recovery from the bank on any checks containing an unauthorized signature which were paid by the bank at least fourteen days after the first item and statement were made available to the customer. * * * Subsection (3) of the statute provides, however, that subsection (2) is inapplicable where the "customer establishes lack of ordinary care on the part of the bank in paying the item(s)."

We find that Barnett met its burden, as movant for summary judgment, of conclusively showing that Ossip failed to meet its initial burden under subsection (1) of the statute in that it did not "exercise reasonable care and promptness to examine the statement and items to discover" the unauthorized signatures. The undisputed evidence demonstrates that Ossip received bank statements from Barnett each month from May 1980 to June 1981 and that the statements contained the cancelled checks alleged to be forgeries. In response to a question posed by Ossip's own attorney, Edward Harris admitted that he did not actually review the signature on all of the company's cancelled checks and even admitted that he didn't pay attention to the signatures on the checks but was more concerned with the amounts and whether it was "the kind of check [Ossip-Harris] would normally pay." The checks were thus not scrutinized for unauthorized signatures as required by statute, nor was reasonable notice given to Barnett of any wrongdoing after the first statement and checks were made available to Ossip within the meaning of Section 674.406 (2)(b). Consequently, the evidence supports the conclusion, as a matter of law, that Ossip failed to exercise the degree of care required by statute * * * [and] is therefore precluded from recovering against Barnett unless it can establish lack of ordinary care by Barnett in paying the forgeries.

Under Section 674.406(3), the burden of proving Barnett's lack of ordinary care falls squarely on Ossip-Harris. * * * Deposition testimony by Estella Brown, an employee of Barnett that handled the Ossip-Harris account, established that she had received six months of on-the-job training and that she examined each check against the signature card on file with the bank to determine the validity of the signature. When any problems arose with regard to signatures, she would bring the checks to the attention of her supervisor. Ossip presented no evidence of either the accepted standard of ordinary care in the banking world, or that Barnett's method of detecting forgeries did not meet this standard. Ossip's only argument in this regard, that the bank was negligent in not detecting the forgery, is particularly unavailing in light of the fact that Edward Harris failed to detect the forgery of his own signature. To require Barnett's employees to be handwriting experts as Ossip seems to imply, would establish a higher standard than that required by the statute, which is simply ordinary care.

*   *   *   *

DECISION AND REMEDY   *The appellate court sustained the summary judgment entered by the trial court. Plaintiff Ossip could not recover the $19,711.90 paid out of its account by the defendant, Barnett Bank.*

COMMENTS   *This case illustrates the importance of reconciling your bank statement promptly upon receipt and notifying your bank of any alteration or unauthorized signature.*

Payment on an Altered Check

The customer's instruction to the bank is to pay the exact amount on the face of the check to the holder. The bank must examine each check before making final payment. If it fails to detect an alteration, it is liable to its customer for the loss because it did not pay as the drawer customer ordered. The loss is the difference between the original amount of the check and the amount actually paid. Suppose a check written for $11 is raised to $111. The customer's account will be charged $11 (the amount the customer ordered it to pay). The bank will be responsible for the $100. [UCC 4-401(2)(a)]

The bank is entitled to recover the amount of loss from the transferor who, by presenting the check for payment, warrants that the check has not been materially altered. No customer or collecting bank or other holder in due course who acts in good faith gives this warranty to:

1. The maker of a note,
2. The drawer of a draft,
3. The acceptor of an item with respect to an alteration made prior to the acceptance if the holder in due course took the item after the acceptance, or
4. The acceptor of an item with respect to an alteration made after the acceptance. [UCC 4-207(1)(c) and 3-417(1)(c)]

A customer's negligence can shift the risk of loss. A common example occurs when a person carelessly writes a check, leaving large gaps around the numbers and words so that additional numbers and words can be inserted. (See, for example, Exhibit 28–5.)

Similarly, a person who signs a check and leaves the dollar amount for someone else to fill in is barred from protesting when the bank unknowingly and in good faith pays whatever amount is shown. [UCC 4-401(2)(b)] Finally, if the bank can trace its loss on successive altered checks to the customer's failure to discover the initial alteration, then the bank can alleviate its liability for reimbursing the customer's account.[2] [UCC 4-406] The law governing the customer's *duty* to examine monthly statements and canceled checks, and to discover and report alterations to the drawee bank, is the same as that applied to forged customer signatures.

In every situation involving a forged drawer's signature or alteration, a bank must observe reasonable commercial standards of care in paying on a customer's checks. [UCC 4-406(3)] The customer's contributory negligence can be asserted only if the bank has exercised ordinary care.

ACCEPTING DEPOSITS

A second fundamental service a commercial bank provides for its checking account customers is that of accepting deposits of cash and checks. Cash deposits made in U.S. currency are received into the customer's account without being subject to further collection procedures. This section will focus on the check after it has been deposited. In the vast majority of cases, deposited checks are from parties who do business at different banks, but sometimes checks

---

2. The bank's defense is the same whether successive payments were made on either a forged drawer's signature or an altered check. The bank must prove that prompt notice would have prevented its loss. For example, notification might have alerted the bank to stop paying further items or enabled it to catch the forger.

EXHIBIT 28–5   A Poorly Filled Out Check

XYZ CORPORATION
10 INDUSTRIAL PARK
ST. PAUL, MINN.

NUMBER

June 8 19 86

22 - 1
960

PAY
TO THE
ORDER OF   *John Doe* $ *100.00*

One hundred and no/100 ————————— DOLLARS

THE FIRST NATIONAL BANK OF MYTOWN
332 MINNESOTA STREET
MYTOWN, MINNESOTA 55555

Stephanie Roe

⑨4⋯775771⋯ 0885

---

are written between customers of the same bank. Either situation brings into play the bank collection process as it operates within the statutory framework of Article 4 of the UCC.

Definitions

The first bank to receive a check for payment is the **depositary bank.**[3] When a person deposits his or her IRS tax refund check into a personal checking account at the local bank, the bank acts as a *depositary* bank. The bank on which a check is drawn (the drawee bank) is called the **payor bank.** Any bank except the payor bank that handles a check during some phase of the collection process is a **collecting bank.** Any bank except the payor bank or depositary bank to which an item is transferred in the course of this collection process is called an **intermediary bank.**

The Collection Process

During the collection process, any bank can take on one or more of the above roles. For example, a buyer in New York writes a check on her New York bank and sends it to a seller in San Francisco. The seller deposits the check in her San Francisco bank account. The seller's bank is both a *depositary bank* and *a collecting bank.* The buyer's bank in New York is the *payor bank.* As the check travels from San Francisco to New York, any collecting bank

---

3.   All definitions in this section are found in UCC 4-105.

(other than the depositary bank and the payor bank) handling the item in the collection process is also called an *intermediary bank.*

Bank's Liability for Restrictive Indorsements Banks handling commercial paper in the normal course of collection are called *intermediary* banks [UCC 4-105(c)], and banks paying on commercial paper are called *payor* banks. [UCC 4-105(b)] Neither type of bank is bound by any restrictive indorsements of any person except the immediate holder who transfers or presents the instrument for payment. [UCC 3-206(2)] This means that only the first bank to which the item is presented for collection must pay in a manner consistent with any restrictive indorsement. [UCC 3-206(3)] This bank is called the depositary bank. [UCC 4-105(a)] This is true even if the depositary bank is also the payor bank (that is, where only one bank is involved).

To illustrate: Elliott writes a check on his New York bank account and sends it to Barton. Barton indorses the check with a restrictive indorsement that reads, "For deposit into Account #4921 only." A Miami bank is the first bank to which this check is presented for payment (the depositary bank), and it must act consistently with the terms of the restrictive indorsement. Therefore, it must credit account #4921 with the money or be liable to Barton for conversion. Elliot's check leaves the Miami bank indorsed "for collection." As the check moves through the collection network of intermediary banks to Elliot's New York bank for payment, each intermediary bank is only bound by the preceding bank's indorsement to collect.

CONCEPT SUMMARY: Bank-Customer Relationships

SITUATION	BASIC RULES
Bank's Charge Against Customer's Account UCC 4-401	The bank has the right to charge a customer's account for any item properly payable even if the charge results in an overdraft.
Wrongful Dishonor UCC 4-402	The bank is liable to its customer for wrongful dishonor due to mistake for actual damages proven. Damages can include those proximately caused for arrest or prosecution, or other consequential damages.
Stop-Payment Orders UCC 4-403	The customer must make a stop-payment order in time for the bank to have a reasonable opportunity to act. Oral orders are binding for only 14 days unless they are confirmed in writing. Written orders are effective for only six months, unless renewed in writing. The bank is liable for wrongful payment over a timely stop-payment order.
Stale Check UCC 4-404	The bank is not obligated to pay an uncertified check presented more than six months after its date, but may do so in good faith without liability.
Death or Incompetence of Customer UCC 4-405	As long as the bank does not know of the death or incompetence of a customer, the bank can pay an item without liability to the customer's estate. Even with knowledge of a customer's death, a bank can honor or certify checks (in the absence of a stop-payment order) for ten days after the date of the customer's death.
Unauthorized Signature or Alteration UCC 4-406	The customer has a duty to examine account statements with reasonable care upon receipt and to notify the bank promptly of any unauthorized signatures or alterations. On a series of unauthorized signatures or alterations by the same wrongdoer, examination and report must be given within fourteen calendar days of receipt of the statement. Failure to comply releases the bank from any liability unless the bank failed to exercise reasonable care. Regardless of care or lack of care, the customer is estopped from holding the bank liable after one year for unauthorized customer signatures or alterations, and after three years for unauthorized indorsements.

The division of responsibility between types of banks is necessary. Collecting banks process huge numbers of commercial instruments, and there is no practical way for them to examine and comply with the effect of each restrictive indorsement. Therefore, the only reasonable alternative is to charge the depositary bank with the responsibility of examining and complying with any restrictive indorsements.

Check Collection between Customers of the Same Bank An item that is payable by the depositary bank that receives it is called an "on-us item." If the bank does not dishonor the check by the opening of the second banking day following its receipt, it is considered paid. [UCC 4-213(4)(b)] For example, Harriman and Goldsmith each have a checking account at First National Bank. On Monday morning, Goldsmith deposits into his own checking account a $300 check from Harriman. That same day, First National issues Goldsmith a "provisional credit" for $300. When the bank opens on Wednesday, Harriman's check is considered honored and Goldsmith's provisional credit becomes a final payment.

Check Collection between Customers of Different Banks Millions of checks circulate throughout the United States each day, and every check must be physically transported to its payor bank before final payment is made. Once a depositary bank receives a check, it must arrange to present it either directly or through intermediary banks to the appropriate payor bank. Each bank in the collection chain must pass the check on before midnight of the next banking day following its receipt. [UCC 4-202(2)]

The bank has a duty to use ordinary care in performing its collection functions. [UCC 4-202(1)] This duty requires banks to conform to general banking usage as established in the Uniform Commercial Code, Federal Reserve regulations, clearinghouse rules, and so on.[4] [UCC 4-103(1)] Banks also have a duty to act seasonally. This means that a bank is generally required to take appropriate action before the midnight deadline following the receipt of a check, a notice, or a payment. [UCC 4-104(1)(h)] So, for example, a collecting bank that receives a check on Monday must forward it to the next collection bank prior to midnight on Tuesday.

Upon receipt of a check by a *payor* bank through the collection process, the midnight deadline for action becomes extremely important. Unless the payor bank dishonors the check or returns it by midnight on the next banking day following receipt, the payor bank is accountable for the face amount of the check. [UCC 4-302]

Because of this and of the need for an even work flow of the many items handled by banks daily, the Code permits what is called deferred posting, or delayed return. *Deferred posting* permits checks received after a certain time (say 2:00 P.M.) to be deferred until the next day. Thus, a check received by a payor bank at 3:00 P.M. on Monday would be deferred for posting until Tuesday. In this case, the payor bank's deadline would be midnight Wednesday. [UCC 4-301(1)]

The Federal Reserve System Clears Checks The Federal Reserve System has greatly simplified the clearing of checks—that is, the method by which checks deposited in one bank are transferred to the banks on which they were written. Suppose Smith of Chicago writes a check to John Jones in San Francisco. When John receives the check in the mail, he deposits it in his bank. His bank then deposits the check in the Federal Reserve Bank of Chicago. That Federal Reserve Bank then sends the check to Smith's bank, where the amount of the check is deducted from Smith's account. Exhibit 28–6 illustrates this process.

TECHNOLOGY IN BANKING OPERATIONS—ELECTRONIC FUNDS TRANSFER SYSTEMS

The present basis of the payment-collection process is the check, but banks are finding it increasingly difficult to cope with trillions of pieces of paper that evidence funds. New systems of automatic payments and direct deposits, known as electronic funds transfer systems (EFTS), promise to rid banks of the burden of transferring money by moving mountains of paper. There are basically three parts to an EFTS system: (1) teller machines, (2) point-of-sale systems, and (3) automated clearinghouses.

Teller Machines

A recent EFTS development has involved teller machines, which are also called customer bank communication terminals or remote service units. They are located either on the bank's premises or at convenient locations such as stores, supermarkets, drugstores, and shopping centers.

Automated teller machines receive deposits, dispense funds from checking or savings accounts, make credit card advances, and receive payment. The devices are connected on-line to the bank's computers.

Point-of-Sale Systems

Point-of-sale systems allow the consumer to transfer funds to merchants in order to make purchases. On-line terminals are located at check-out counters in the merchant's store. When making a purchase, the customer's card is inserted into the terminal, which reads the data encoded on it. The computer at the customer's bank verifies that the card and identification code are valid and that there is enough money in the customer's account. After the purchase is made, the customer's account is debited for the amount of the purchase.

---

4. The Code is explicit that "the obligations of good faith, diligence, reasonableness and care * * * may not be disclaimed. * * * " [UCC 1-102(3)]

EXHIBIT 28–6   How A Check Is Cleared

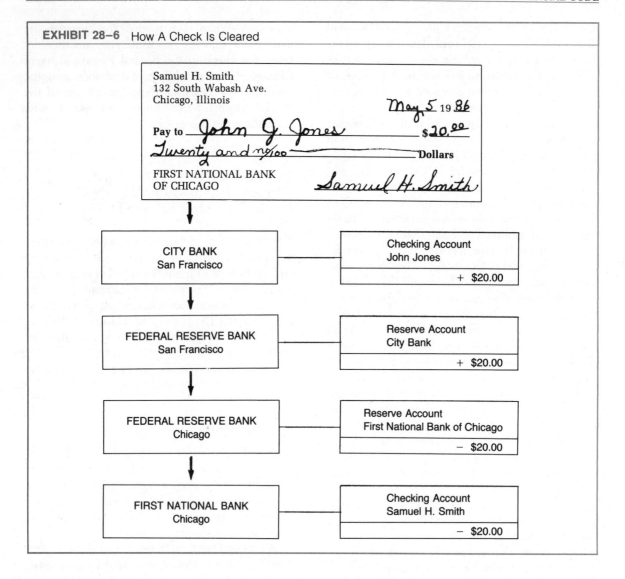

Automated Clearinghouses

Automated clearinghouses are similar to ordinary clearinghouses in which checks are cleared between banks. The main difference is that entries are made in the form of electronic signals; no checks are used. These systems do not further automate the handling of paper checks; they replace checks. Such systems are especially useful to businesspersons for recurrent payments, such as payroll, social security, or pension fund payments.

This new technology, however, has aroused some serious consumer concerns. For example:

1. It is difficult to issue stop-payment orders.
2. Fewer records are available.

3. The possibilities for tampering (with a resultant decrease in privacy) are increased.
4. The time between the writing of a check and its deduction from an account ("float" time) is lost.

The Bank's Liability in EFTS

In response to customer concern over EFTS, Congress has passed legislation which affects the liability of both customers and banks. These new rules relate to electronic funds transfer accounts that are operated by telephone, automatically, or by presenting a customer debit card to merchants when making purchases. Some of the major rules that apply are:

1. If a customer's debit card is lost or stolen and used without his or her permission, the customer

has to pay only $50. However, the customer must notify the bank of the loss or theft within *two* days of learning about it. Otherwise, the liability increases to $500. The customer is liable for more than $500 if the unauthorized use is not reported within sixty days after it appears on the customer's statement. (Even the $50 limit does not apply if the customer gives his or her card to someone who uses it improperly or if fraud is committed.)

2. Any error on the monthly statement must be picked up by the customer within *sixty* days, and the bank must be notified. The bank then has *ten* days to investigate. If the bank takes longer than ten days, it must return the disputed amount of money to the customer's account until the error is found. If there is no error, the customer has to give the money back to the bank.

3. The bank must furnish receipts for transactions made through computer terminals, but it is not obliged to do so for telephone transfers.

4. A monthly statement must be made for every month in which there is an electronic transfer of funds. Otherwise, statements must be made every quarter. The statement must show the amount and date of the transfer, the names of the retailers involved, the location or identification of the terminal, and the fees. Additionally, the statement must give an address and phone number for inquiries and error notices.

5. Any authorized prepayment for utility bills and insurance premiums can be stopped three days before the scheduled transfer.

6. There are certain limitations to the federal government's access to these financial records, but a bank is not prohibited from giving the customer's records to a retailer who might want information on the customer's spending habits.

All of the above information must be given to the customer who opens an EFTS account.[5]

---

5. The $50 limit on consumer liability went into effect February 10, 1978. The other provisions of this new law took effect in May 1980.

QUESTIONS AND CASE PROBLEMS

1. Daniel drafts a check for $1,000 payable to Paula and drawn on the West Bank. After issue of the check, Paula, by blank indorsement, negotiates the check to Fred. Fred finds an ideal real estate lot for sale, but to close the deal he needs to make a $1,000 down payment by certified check. Fred takes the check to West Bank and requests West Bank to certify Daniel's check.

    (a) If West Bank refuses to certify Daniel's check, can either Daniel or Fred hold the bank liable? Explain.

    (b) If West Bank certifies the check, explain fully the liability of Daniel as drawer to Fred and to Paula as indorser.

2. On January 5 Daniel drafts a check for $3,000 drawn on the East Bank and payable to his secretary, Sylvia. Daniel puts last year's date on the check by mistake. Before Sylvia can get to the East Bank to cash the check, on January 7, Daniel is killed in an automobile accident. The East Bank is aware of Daniel's death. On January 10 Sylvia presents the check to the East Bank, and the bank honors the check by payment to Sylvia. Daniel's widow, Martha, claims that the East Bank wrongfully paid Sylvia since it knew of Daniel's death and also paid a check that was by date over one year old. Martha, as executrix of Daniel's estate and sole heir by his will, demands that East Bank recredit Daniel's estate for the check paid Sylvia. Discuss fully East Bank's liability in light of Martha's demand.

3. Daniel goes grocery shopping and carelessly leaves his checkbook in his shopping cart. His checkbook, with two blank checks remaining, is stolen by Thomas. On May 5 Thomas forges Daniel's name on a check for $100 and cashes the check at Daniel's bank, the First of Jonestown Bank. Daniel has not reported the theft to his bank. On June 1 Daniel receives his monthly bank statement and cancelled checks from Jonestown Bank, including the forged check by Thomas. Daniel does not reconcile his checking account. On June 20 Thomas forges Daniel's last check. This check is for $1,000 and is cashed at the West Bank, a bank with which Thomas has previously done business. The West Bank sends the check through the collection process, and the Jonestown Bank honors it. On July 1, upon receipt of Jonestown Bank's statement and cancelled checks, Daniel discovers both forgeries and immediately notifies Jonestown Bank. Thomas cannot be found. Daniel claims that Jonestown must recredit his account for both checks, as his signature was forged. Discuss fully Daniel's claim.

4. Diana takes her television set to Honest John's TV Service Store for repairs. The set is supposedly repaired, at a cost of $125. On Saturday Diana writes out a check payable to Honest John drawn on the First Greenville Bank. Diana takes the set home and discovers that virtually no repairs have been made. On Monday Diana calls Honest John to complain about his lack of performance. Honest John insists the repairs were made and refuses to even look at the television set. Diana immediately calls the First Greenville Bank and issues a stop-payment order over the phone. Three weeks later, Honest John cashes Diana's check at a drive-in window of the First Greenville Bank. Diana is furious upon discovery of the bank's payment to Honest John and wants the bank to recredit her account. Discuss fully the First Greenville Bank's liability in this matter.

5. Daniel has $5,000 in his checking account with the Second Bank of Fielder. Daniel writes a check for $500 payable to Peter. This check is in settlement of a long-standing dispute between the two. Peter deposits the check in his bank. Peter's bank sends the check through the collection process. The Second Bank, by mistake, returns the check to Peter's bank marked "insufficient funds." Peter's bank returns the check to Peter, charging his account for $500, plus the bank's service charge of $10 for returned checks. Peter is furious and files criminal charges against Daniel. Discuss fully the Second Bank of Fielder's liability for wrongful dishonor of Daniel's check.

6. In September 1976, Edward and Christine McSweeney opened a joint checking account with the United States Trust Company of New York. Between April of 1978 and July of 1978, 195 checks totaling $99,063 were written. In July 1978 activity in the account ceased. Ninety-five of the 195 checks were written by Christine totaling $16,811, and the balance were written by Edward. After crediting deposits during the period, the checks amounted to a cumulative overdraft of $75,983. Can a bank knowingly honor a check when payment creates an overdraft or must the bank dishonor the check? If the bank pays a check creating an overdraft, can the bank collect the amount of overdraft from it's customer? [U.S. Trust Company of New York v. McSweeny, 457 N.Y.S.2d 276, 91 A.D.2d 7 (1982)]

7. Rees Plumbing Company, Inc., and Weldon Douglas both maintained checking accounts at the Citizens Bank of Jonesboro. On August 19, 1966, Rees drew a check payable to Douglas in the amount of $1,000 and delivered it to Douglas. On that same day Douglas presented the check to Citizens Bank for deposit in his own checking account. Deposit slips were prepared, and a teller of the bank stamped the back of the check with the August 19 date, and a statement, "pay to any bank—prior indorsement guaranteed, Citizens Bank of Jonesboro, Jonesboro, Arkansas." On August 20, 1966, the bank dishonored the check because of insufficient funds and debited the amount of the check from Douglas's account. Did the bank, by stamping the indorsement upon the check deposited by Douglas and by delivering a deposit slip to Douglas, "accept" the check? Assume that instead of giving Douglas a provisional credit to his account, the Citizens Bank had cashed the check. Could it then have debited Douglas's account upon dishonor of the check? [Douglas v. Citizens Bank of Jonesboro, 244 Ark. 168, 424 S.W.2d 532 (1968)]

8. Reinhard purchased a cashier's check made payable to The Patchworks Co. from Marine Midland Bank. The check was delivered to The Patchworks in exchange for goods purchased by Reinhard. Because he was dissatisfied with the goods, Reinhard told the bank that he had lost the check and asked that payment be stopped. Can Reinhard stop payment? [Moon Over the Mountain, Ltd. v. Marine Midland Bank, 87 Misc.2d 918, 386 N.Y.S.2d 974 (1976)]

9. Northwest Shopping Center owned and operated a shopping center in Texas. Kaiser was one of its tenants. Pursuant to the rental agreement, Kaiser paid a monthly rent of $500 with a check that it mailed to Northwest. Northwest retained one of these rent checks for over nine months before presenting it to the bank for payment. If Northwest now presents to Kaiser's bank for payment, must the bank pay? If the bank refuses to pay, is Kaiser still liable? [Kaiser v. Northwest Shopping Center, 544 S.W.2d 785 (Tex. Civ. App. 1976)]

10. Ralston pledged stock certificates as collateral for a loan. The proceeds of the loan, $38,000, were used to open a new checking account at the lending bank. Ralston immediately had the bank certify a $21,000 check payable to a second bank. Later that day the lending bank learned that the stock certificates were stolen and notified the payee bank that certification of the check was rescinded. The payee bank had accepted the check for deposit to Ralston's account but had given no value for it (no checks had been honored against the deposit). As a holder of the certified check, could the payee bank prevent the lending bank's revocation of certification? [Rockland Trust Co. v. South Shore Nat'l Bank, 366 Mass. 74, 314 N.E.2d 438 (1974)].

29

Secured Transactions

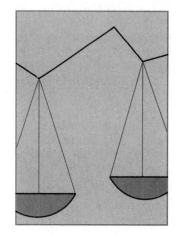

The concept of a secured transaction is as basic to modern business practice as the concept of credit. Few purchasers (manufacturers, wholesalers, retailers, consumers) have the resources to pay cash for goods being purchased. Lenders are reluctant to lend money to a debtor solely upon the debtor's promise to repay the debt. The simple fact is that sellers and lenders want to minimize the risk of loss due to nonpayment and will not sell goods or lend money unless the promise of payment is somehow guaranteed.

To minimize the risk of loss, the creditor often requires the debtor to provide some type of security beyond the mere promise that the debt will be paid. When this security takes the form of personal property owned by the debtor, or in which the debtor has a legal interest, the transaction becomes known as a **secured transaction.**

The importance of being a secured creditor should not be overemphasized. Business, as we know it, could not exist without the presence of secured transaction law. Secured creditors are generally not hampered by state exemption laws favorable to debtors, and secured creditors have a favored position should the debtor become bankrupt.

The underlying philosophy of secured transaction law deals with two major concerns of the creditor should the debtor default on the obligation:

1. Can the debt be satisfied from some *specific property offered as security* (collateral) by the debtor?
2. Will satisfaction of that particular debt from that collateral be given *priority* over the claims of other creditors?

The answers form the basis for the law of secured transactions.

ARTICLE 9 OF THE UCC

Prior to adoption of the UCC, there were a great number of security devices used by creditors, such as chattel mortgages, conditional sales contracts, assignment of accounts, and trust receipts. Each had separate rules, and each had different terminology. Article 9 of the UCC has eliminated the distinctions among the various forms of financing, simplified the terminology, and provided a framework for the law of secured transactions.

Article 9 applies to any transaction that is intended to create a security interest in personal property, the sale of accounts, chattel paper, and fixtures. Transactions excluded from Article 9 include real estate mortgages, landlords' liens, mechanics' liens, claims arising from judicial proceedings, and so on. [UCC 9-104] In general, these transactions do not deal with personal property and are excluded because they are extensively treated in other areas of the law.

As will become evident, the law of secured transactions tends to favor the rights of creditors; but, to a lesser extent, it offers debtors some protection, too.

DEFINITIONS

The terminology used under the Code is now uniformly adopted in all documents drawn in a secured transaction situation:

1. **Security interest.** Every interest "in *personal property or fixtures* [emphasis added] which secures payment or performance of an obligation" is a security interest. [UCC 1-201(37)]
2. **Secured party.** A lender, seller, or any person in whose favor there is a security interest, including a person to whom accounts or chattel paper have been sold, is a secured party. [UCC 9-105(1)(m)]
3. **Debtor.** The party who owes payment or performance of the secured obligation, whether or not that party actually owns or has rights in the collateral, is a debtor. The term *debtor* includes sellers of accounts or chattel paper. When the debtor and owner of the collateral are not the same person, the term *debtor* refers to the actual owner of the collateral or describes the obligor on an obligation, or both, depending upon the context in which the term is used. [UCC 9-105(1)(d)]
4. **Security agreement.** The agreement that creates or provides for a security interest between the debtor and a secured party is called a security agreement. [UCC 9-105(1)(*l*)]
5. **Collateral.** The property subject to a security interest, including accounts and chattel paper that have been sold, is collateral. [UCC 9-105(1)(c)] See Exhibit 29–4 on page 491 for definitions.

These basic definitions form the concept under which a debtor-creditor relationship becomes a secured transaction relationship. See Exhibit 29–1.

CREATING A SECURITY INTEREST

Before a creditor can become a secured party, the creditor must have a security interest in the collateral of the debtor. Three requirements must be met in

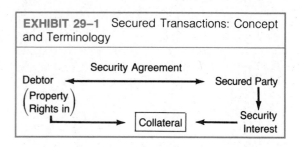

EXHIBIT 29–1 Secured Transactions: Concept and Terminology

order for a creditor to have an enforceable security interest.

1. Unless the creditor has possession of the collateral, there must be an agreement in writing.
2. The creditor must give value to the debtor.
3. The debtor must have rights in the collateral.

Once these requirements are met, the creditor's rights are said to "attach" to the collateral. This means that the creditor has an *enforceable* security interest against the debtor. Attachment insures that the security interest between the debtor and the secured party is effective. [UCC 9-203]

Written Agreement

Unless the collateral is in the possession of the secured party (the creditor), there must be a *written security agreement* describing the collateral and signed by the debtor. See Exhibit 29–2 for a detailed sample agreement. The security agreement creates or provides for a security interest. For example, it might read "Debtor hereby grants to secured party a security interest in the following goods." There are three requirements for the agreement to be valid:

1. The agreement must be signed by the debtor.
2. The agreement must contain a description of the collateral.
3. The description must reasonably identify the collateral. [UCC 9-203(1) and 9-110]

Value Given to Debtor

The secured party must give *value*. According to UCC 1-201(44), value is any consideration that supports a simple contract. In addition, value can be security given for a preexisting (antecedent) obligation or any binding commitment to extend credit.

EXHIBIT 29–2 A Sample Security Agreement

SECURITY AGREEMENT

DEBTOR _____

DEBTOR'S RESIDENCE _____
      OR
PLACE OF BUSINESS _____

SECURED PARTY _____

SECURED PARTY'S ADDRESS _____

_____

SECURITY INTEREST In order to secure the payment of the Debt described below and the obligations of this Security Agreement, Debtor gives Secured Party a security interest in the following Collateral under Article 9 of the Uniform Commercial Code (UCC):

COLLATERAL_____

_____

_____

_____

AFTER-ACQUIRED PROPERTY AND PROCEEDS The Collateral includes: all proceeds, increases, substitutions, replacements, additions, improvements and accessions to the Collateral, all proceeds from insurance on the Collateral, and all refunds of unearned premiums for insurance; but does not include any consumer goods (other than accessions) acquired by Debtor more than 10 days after the loan proceeds are advanced. This provision shall not be construed to mean that Debtor is authorized to sell, lease, or dispose of the Collateral without the consent of Secured Party.

DEBT $_____ Note dated _____, 19____ payable to Secured Party.

FUTURE ADVANCES AND OTHER DEBTS The debt includes: any renewals or extensions of the Note; any amounts advanced by Secured Party to protect its security interest in the Collateral; any future amounts advanced by Secured Party at its option to Debtor; any and all other liabilities of Debtor to Secured Party, now existing or later incurred, matured or unmatured, direct or contingent; any costs or expenses that may be lawfully assessed against Debtor for the collection of the Debt, including attorney's fees.

LOCATION OF COLLATERAL Debtor agrees to keep the Collateral
[ ] at the Debtor's address stated above;
[ ] at the following location: _____

_____

REAL ESTATE If marked here [ ], the Collateral is either [ ] a fixture that is, or will be, attached to the following described real estate; or [ ] crops growing or to be grown upon the following described real estate: _____

_____

whose record owner is: _____ .

FARM PRODUCTS If marked here [ ], the Collateral is farm products and includes the offspring and increase of any livestock or crops given as such Collateral and all feed, seed, fertilizer and other supplies now owned or later acquired in connection with such farming operations, all of which is located upon the above described real estate.

LOCATION OF RECORDS If marked here [ ], the Collateral consists of accounts, instruments, chattel paper, documents or other general intangibles and the records concerning such Collateral are kept at _____

_____

POSSESSION BY SECURED PARTY If marked here [ ], the Collateral will be retained in the possession of Secured Party, and the following provisions in this section shall be applicable. Secured Party's duty with reference to the Collateral shall be solely to use reasonable care in the custody and preservation of the Collateral in its possession and to receive collections, earnings, dividends, remittances and payments on such Collateral as and when made. Secured Party shall have the option of applying the amounts so received, after deduction for any collection costs that may be lawfully charged, as payment of any debt secured by this Security Agreement, or holding such amounts for the benefit of Debtor. Secured Party shall not be responsible in any way for any depreciation in value of the Collateral, nor shall Secured Party have any duty or responsibility to take any steps to preserve rights against other parties or to enforce collection of the Collateral.

USE OF COLLATERAL The Collateral will be used primarily for the purposes checked below:
[ ] Personal, family, or household purposes
[ ] Business operations (other than farming)
[ ] Farming operations

OWNERSHIP OF COLLATERAL Debtor is the owner of the Collateral, or if marked here [ ], Debtor is purchasing the Collateral with the proceeds of the Note described above. Except for the security interest created by this Security Agreement, the Collateral is free from any lien, security interest, encumbrance, or claim. With respect to any instruments, chattel paper, documents or other general intangibles given as Collateral, Debtor warrants and represents that: they are genuine, free from adverse claims, default, prepayment or defenses; all persons appearing to be obligated thereon have authority and capacity to contract and are bound thereon; and they comply with applicable laws concerning form, content, and manner of preparation and execution. Debtor will, at Debtor's cost and expense, defend any action which may affect Secured Party's security interest in, or Debtor's title to, the Collateral.

FINANCING STATEMENT No Financing Statement covering the Collateral or any part thereof or any proceeds thereof is on file in any public office and, at Secured Party's request, Debtor will join in executing all necessary Financing Statements in forms satisfactory to Secured Party and will pay the cost of filing and will further execute all other necessary instruments deemed necessary by Secured Party and pay the cost of filing.

SALE OR ENCUMBRANCE OF COLLATERAL Debtor will not, without the written consent of Secured Party, sell, contract to sell, lease, encumber, or dispose of the Collateral or any interest therein until this Security Agreement and all debts secured thereby have been fully satisfied.

(continued on next page)

EXHIBIT 29–2   Continued

INSURANCE   If the Collateral is tangible property and is insurable, Debtor will insure the Collateral with companies acceptable to Secured Party against such casualties and in such amounts as Secured Party shall reasonably require with a loss payable clause in favor of Debtor and Secured Party as their interest may appear, and Secured Party is hereby authorized to collect sums which may become due under any of said policies and apply the same to the obligations hereby secured.

PROTECTION OF COLLATERAL   If the Collateral is tangible property, Debtor will keep the Collateral in good order and repair and will not waste or destroy the Collateral or any part thereof. Debtor will not use the Collateral in violation of any statute or ordinance and Secured Party will have the right to examine and inspect the Collateral at any reasonable time.

TAXES   Debtor will pay promptly when due all taxes and assessments on the Collateral or for its use and operation.

DECREASE IN VALUE OF COLLATERAL   If in Secured Party's judgment the Collateral has materially decreased in value or if Secured Party shall at any time deem that Secured Party is insecure, Debtor shall either provide enough additional Collateral to satisfy Secured Party, or shall reduce the total indebtedness by an amount sufficient to satisfy Secured Party.

REIMBURSEMENT OF EXPENSES   At the option of Secured Party, Secured Party may discharge taxes, liens, interest, or perform or cause to be performed for and on behalf of Debtor any actions and conditions, obligations, or covenants which Debtor has failed or refused to perform, and may pay for the repair, maintenance, and preservation of the Collateral, including, to the extent but only to the extent such amounts may be lawfully collected, attorney's fees, court costs, agent's fees, or commissions, or any other costs or expenses. All sums so expended shall bear interest from the date of payment at the rate of interest stated in the Note described above, if such rate of interest can be lawfully collected and if not then at the maximum legal rate, and shall be payable on demand at the place designated in the Note and shall be secured by this Security Agreement.

CHANGE OF RESIDENCE OR PLACE OF BUSINESS   Debtor will promptly notify Secured Party of any change of the Debtor's residence, place of business, or place where records are kept.

TIME OF PERFORMANCE AND WAIVER   In performing any act under this Security Agreement and the Note secured thereby, time shall be of the essence. Secured Party's acceptance of partial or delinquent payments, or the failure of Secured Party to exercise any right or remedy shall not be a waiver of any obligation of Debtor or right of Secured Party or constitute a waiver of any other similar default subsequently occurring.

DEFAULT   Debtor shall be in default under this Security Agreement on the happening of any of the following events or conditions:

(1) Default in the payment or performance of any obligation, covenant, or liability contained or referred to in the Note or in this Security Agreement;

(2) Any warranty, representation, or statement made or furnished to Secured Party by or on behalf of Debtor proves to have been false in any material respect when made or furnished;

(3) Loss, theft, substantial damage, destruction, sale, or encumbrance to or of any of the Collateral, or the making of any levy, seizure, or attachment thereof or thereon;

(4) Any time Secured Party believes that the prospect of payment of any indebtedness secured hereby or the performance of this Security Agreement is impaired;

(5) Death, dissolution, termination of existence, insolvency, business failure, appointment of a receiver for any part of the Collateral, assignment for the benefit of creditors or the commencement of any proceeding under any bankruptcy or insolvency law by or against Debtor or any guarantor or surety for Debtor.

REMEDIES   Upon the occurrence of any such event of default, and at any time thereafter, Secured Party may declare all obligations secured immediately due and payable and may proceed to enforce payment of the same and exercise any and all of the rights and remedies provided by the Uniform Commercial Code as well as other rights and remedies either at law or in equity possessed by Secured Party.

Secured Party shall have the right to remove the Collateral from the premises of Debtor and, for purposes of removal and possession, Secured Party or its representatives may enter any premises of the Debtor without legal process and the Debtor hereby waives and releases Secured Party of and from any and all claims in connection therewith or arising therefrom.

Secured Party may require Debtor to assemble the Collateral and make it available to Secured Party at any place to be designated by the Secured Party which is reasonably convenient to both parties. Unless the Collateral is perishable or threatens to decline speedily in value or is of a type customarily sold on a recognized market, Secured Party will give the Debtor reasonable notice of the time and place of any public sale thereof or of the time after which any private sale or any other intended disposition thereof is to be made. The requirements of reasonable notice shall be met if such notice is mailed, postage prepaid, to the address of Debtor shown at the beginning of this Security Agreement at least five days before the time of the sale or disposition. Expenses of retaking, holding, preparing for sale, selling, or the like shall include Secured Party's reasonable attorney's fees and legal expenses, to the extent but only to the extent such amounts may be lawfully collected.

TEXAS LAW TO APPLY   This Agreement shall be construed under and in accordance with the Uniform Commercial Code and other applicable laws of the State of Texas and all obligations of the parties created hereunder are performable in the County of the Secured Party's address stated above.

PARTIES BOUND   This Agreement shall be binding on and inure to the benefit of the parties hereto and their respective heirs, executors, administrators, legal representatives, successors, and assigns. If there is more than one Debtor, their obligations shall be joint and several.

LEGAL CONSTRUCTION   In case any one or more of the provisions contained in this Agreement shall for any reason be held to be invalid, illegal, or unenforceable in any respect, such invalidity, illegality, or unenforceability shall not affect any other provision thereof and this Agreement shall be construed as if such invalid, illegal, or unenforceable provision had never been contained herein. Notwithstanding anything else herein to the contrary, if the Debt secured by this Security Agreement is a loan made under any chapter of the Texas Credit Code that limits charges and expenses that may be collected by Secured Party, the provisions of such Code shall govern in the event of any conflict between the provisions of this Security Agreement and the provisions of such Code.

Executed   ....,19........ .

Secured Party: Debtor:

_____   _____

_____   _____

Source: Reprinted with permission of Hart Graphics Inc. of Austin, Texas. © 1985 Hart Graphics Inc.

Normally, the value given by a secured party is in the form of a direct loan, or it involves a commitment to sell goods on credit.

Debtor Has Rights in Collateral

The debtor must have *rights* in the collateral; that is, the debtor must have some ownership interest or right to obtain possession of that collateral. The debtor's rights can represent either a current or a future legal interest in the collateral. For example, a retail seller-debtor can give a secured party a security interest not only in existing inventory owned by the retailer, but also in future inventory to be acquired by the debtor.

PURCHASE MONEY SECURITY INTEREST

Often, sellers of consumer durable goods, such as stereos and television sets, agree to extend credit for part of the purchase price of those goods.[1] Also, lenders not necessarily in the business of selling such goods often agree to lend much of the purchase price for such goods. There is a special name for the security interest that the seller or the lender obtains when such a transaction occurs. It is called a **purchase money security interest.** Formally, such an interest obtains when:

1.   A security interest is retained in, or taken by the seller of, the collateral in order to secure part or all of its price; or
2.   A security interest is taken by a person who, by making advances or incurring an obligation, gives something of value that enables the debtor to acquire rights in the collateral or to use it. [UCC 9-107]

In either case, a lender or seller has essentially provided a buyer with the "purchase money" to buy goods. To illustrate, suppose Barbara wants to purchase a combination color television-stereo set from Sallor. The purchase price is $900. Not being able

to pay cash, Barbara signs a security agreement to pay $100 down and $50 per month until the balance plus interest is fully paid. Sallor is to retain a security interest in the purchased set until full payment has been made. Since the security interest was created as part of the purchase agreement, it is a purchase money security interest.

The same result would occur if Barbara went to the West Bank and borrowed the $900 to buy the combination set from Sallor. After Barbara signs a security agreement with West Bank, with the to-be-purchased set as collateral, West Bank has a purchase money security interest the moment the set is purchased from Sallor. Obviously if Barbara used the money for other purposes, West Bank would not have a security interest. For this reason, West Bank might arrange to pay the $900 directly to Sallor.

The importance of a purchase money security interest is basically two-fold:

1.   It allows for an automatic perfection of a purchase money security in consumer goods without the secured party's possession or filing (to be discussed shortly).
2.   It ordinarily gives a secured party priority over a non-purchase money security interest in the same collateral (to be discussed later).

PERFECTING A SECURITY INTEREST

A creditor has two main concerns if the debtor defaults—satisfaction of the debt out of certain predesignated property and priority over other creditors. The concept of *attachment*, which establishes the criteria for creating an enforceable security interest, deals with the former concern; the concept of *perfection* deals with the latter.

Even though a security interest has attached, the secured party *must* take steps in order to protect its claim to the collateral over claims that third parties may have, such as other secured creditors, general creditors, trustees in bankruptcy, and purchasers of the collateral that is the subject matter of the security agreement. Perfection represents the legal process by which a secured party protects itself against the claims of third parties who may wish to have their debts satisfied out of the same collateral.

---

1.   Under the FTC's "unfair credit practices" rules, it is a violation of Section 5 of the FTC Act for a lender or retail seller to take or receive a *nonpossessory, nonpurchase* money security interest in household goods.

Methods of Perfection

There are basically three methods of perfection:

1. *By transfer of collateral.* The debtor can transfer possession of the collateral itself to the secured party. This occurs, for example, when the debtor gives the secured party stocks or bonds, or even a piece of jewelry, provided that it is collateral securing the debt. For most collateral, possession by the secured party is impractical as it denies the debtor the right to use, sell, or derive income from the property to pay off the debt. With respect to instruments (negotiable as per UCC 3-104) or a certificated security (as defined in UCC 8-102), except for a few cases of temporary perfections, the *only* way for proper perfection is by possession by the secured party. This type of transfer is called a **pledge.** [UCC 9-302(1)(a), 9-304(1), 9-305]

Consider an example. Ulster borrows $2,000 from Levine, giving Levine possession of three antique guns as collateral for the loan. Several months later, before Ulster has repaid the loan, a creditor obtains a judgment against Ulster. The creditor seeks to have the sheriff take the valuable antique guns away from Levine. Even though no financing statement has been filed, the creditor cannot touch the antique guns because Levine perfected his security interest in them when he took possession of them.

2. *By attachment of a purchase money security interest in consumer goods.* In certain circumstances, the security interest can be perfected automatically at the time of a credit sale—that is, at the time that the security interest is created under a written security agreement. Note that this *automatic perfection rule* with regard to purchase money security interests applies only when the goods are *consumer goods* (defined as goods bought or used by the debtor primarily for personal, family, or household purposes). The seller in this situation need do nothing more to protect his or her interest. There are exceptions to this rule, however, that cover security interests in fixtures and in motor vehicles. [UCC 9-302(1)(d)] For those states that have not adopted the 1972 UCC amendments,[2] a purchase money security interest in farm equipment under a certain

statutory value is also automatically perfected by attachment.

Another instance of automatic perfection occurs when a person assigns a small portion of his or her accounts receivable—usually to a collecting agent known as a *factor.* Perfection is automatic as long as the assignment does not by itself or in conjunction with other assignments to the same assignee constitute a transfer of a significant part of the outstanding accounts of the debtor. Other situations where perfection is automatic (but which are somewhat less important) are listed in UCC 9-302(1).

3. *By filing.* The third and most common method of perfection is by filing a *financing statement.* The UCC requires a financing statement to have: (a) the signature of the debtor, (b) the addresses of both the debtor and the creditor, and (c) a description of the collateral by type or item.[3] [UCC 9-402(1)] Filing is generally the means of perfection to use—unless, of course, the collateral is the kind that a secured party can take possession of, or is required to take possession of, in order to perfect (such as a money pledge), or unless the creditor has a purchase money security interest in consumer goods. See Exhibit 29–3 for a sample financing statement.

Both the security agreement and the financing statement must contain a description of the collateral in which the secured party has a security interest. The UCC requires that the security agreement include a description of the collateral because no security interest in goods could exist unless the parties agree on which goods are subject to the security interest and then describe these goods in writing. On the other hand, the purpose of including a description of collateral in a financing statement is to put persons who might later wish to lend to the debtor on notice that certain goods in the debtor's possession are already subject to a security interest. Sometimes the descriptions vary, with the description in the security agreement being more precise and the description in the financing statement more general. For example, a commercial security agreement loan to a manufacturer may list all the manufacturer's equipment (subject to the loan) by serial number, whereby the financing statement may sim-

---

2. The following states have *not* adopted the 1972 amendments in whole or in part: Indiana, Kentucky, Louisiana, Missouri, South Carolina, Tennessee, Vermont, and Wyoming.

3. Certain types of collateral—crops, timber to be cut, minerals, accounts, or goods that are to become fixtures—require more than mere description, i.e., a description of the real estate concerned. [UCC 9-402(1)(5), 9-103(5), and 9-313]

EXHIBIT 29–3 Sample Financing Statement

This FINANCING STATEMENT is presented for filing pursuant to the California Uniform Commercial Code.

1. DEBTOR (LAST NAME FIRST—IF AN INDIVIDUAL)	1A. SOCIAL SECURITY OR FEDERAL TAX NO.	
1B. MAILING ADDRESS	1C. CITY, STATE	1D. ZIP CODE
2. ADDITIONAL DEBTOR (IF ANY) (LAST NAME FIRST—IF AN INDIVIDUAL)	2A. SOCIAL SECURITY OR FEDERAL TAX NO.	
2B. MAILING ADDRESS	2C. CITY, STATE	2D. ZIP CODE
3. DEBTOR'S TRADE NAMES OR STYLES (IF ANY)	3A. FEDERAL TAX NUMBER	

4. SECURED PARTY

    NAME

    MAILING ADDRESS

    CITY   STATE   ZIP CODE

4A. SOCIAL SECURITY NO., FEDERAL TAX NO. OR BANK TRANSIT AND A.B.A. NO.

5. ASSIGNEE OF SECURED PARTY (IF ANY)

    NAME

    MAILING ADDRESS

    CITY   STATE   ZIP CODE

5A. SOCIAL SECURITY NO., FEDERAL TAX NO. OR BANK TRANSIT AND A.B.A. NO.

6. This FINANCING STATEMENT covers the following types or items of property **(include description of real property on which located and owner of record when required by instruction 4).**

As security for and in consideration of all present and any future advances or other obligations debtor hereby grants United California Bank a security interest in all of the following types or items of property ("Collateral" herein) in which the debtor now has or hereafter acquires any right, title, or interest, or rights present and future, wheresoever located and whether in the possession of the debtor, a warehouseman, bailee, trustee or any other person, and all increases, therein and replacements, products, and proceeds thereof. Proceeds include but are not limited to inventory, returned merchandise, accounts, chattel paper, general intangibles, insurance proceeds, documents, money, goods, equipment, instruments, and any other tangible or intangible property arising under the sale, lease or other disposition of collateral:

7. CHECK IF APPLICABLE ☒	7A. ☐ PRODUCTS OF COLLATERAL ARE ALSO COVERED	7B. DEBTOR(S) SIGNATURE NOT REQUIRED IN ACCORDANCE WITH INSTRUCTION 5(c) ITEM: ☐ (1) ☐ (2) ☐ (3) ☐ (4)

8. CHECK IF APPLICABLE ☒ ☐ DEBTOR IS A "TRANSMITTING UTILITY" IN ACCORDANCE WITH UCC § 9105 (1) (n)

9. ▶ SIGNATURE(S) of DEBTOR(S) DATE:	C O D E	10. THIS SPACE FOR USE OF FILING OFFICER (DATE, TIME, FILE NUMBER AND FILING OFFICER)
TYPE OR PRINT NAME(S) OF DEBTOR(S)	1	
▶ SIGNATURE(S) OF SECURED PARTY(IES)	2 / 3	
TYPE OR PRINT NAME(S) OF SECURED PARTY(IES)	4	
11. *Return copy to:*	5	
NAME	6	
ADDRESS	7	
CITY	8	
STATE	9	
ZIP CODE	0	

(1) FILING OFFICER COPY   FORM UCC-1—FILING FEE $3.00
Approved by the Secretary of State

MS-336 10-78

ply state "all equipment owned or hereafter acquired. . . ."

To avoid problems of different descriptions, a secured party may repeat exactly the security agreement's description in the financing statement, file the security agreement as a financing statement assuming such meets the previously discussed criteria,

or, where permitted, file a combination security agreement-financing statement form.

The following case illustrates the importance of an accurate and adequate description of the collateral and the different reasons for including a description of the collateral in the security agreement and the financing statement.

JONES & LAUGHLIN SUPPLY v. DUGAN PRODUCTION CORP.

Court of Appeals of New Mexico, 1973.
85 N.M. 51, 508 P.2d 1348.

BACKGROUND AND FACTS *Dugan Production Corporation, the defendant, purchased oil drilling equipment previously owned by Lucky Drilling Company at a sheriff's sale. Plaintiff Jones & Laughlin Supply claimed that it held a security interest in the property. However, although the security agreement between Lucky Drilling Company and Jones & Laughlin described numerous pieces of equipment, it did not include the equipment purchased by Dugan. Jones & Laughlin argued that it could prove that the security agreement was intended to include the equipment at issue by introducing into evidence a loan and mortgage agreement between Jones and Lucky Drilling Company, plus an unsigned filed financial statement.*

LOPEZ, Judge.

*   *   *   *

The case arose out of a sheriff's sale in which certain pieces of equipment belonging to Lucky Drilling Company were sold to the defendants [Dugan and McDonald]. At the sheriff's sale, Dugan *   *   * purchased the Whealand rotary table in question. The defendant, George McDonald, purchased the Waukesha gasoline engine. Prior to the sheriff's sale, Lucky Drilling Company mortgaged certain equipment to plaintiff and plaintiff took a security agreement and mortgage. *   *   * A review of the record reveals that this security agreement, together with an unsigned financing statement with exhibits, was filed *   *   * in the office of the County Clerk of San Juan County, New Mexico, and *   *   * in the office of the New Mexico Secretary of State.

*   *   * [T]he two items in question were not specifically described in the security agreement or in the financing statement. *   *   * The financing statement was not signed by the debtor or the secured party as required by [UCC] 9-402.

The financing statement contains the wording: " *   *   * all hand tools, drill collars, drill pipe, equipment, accessories, parts, exchanges, substitutions, additions, accretions, betterments, supplies and items that Debtor may now have or hereafter acquire and use with or as part of such collateral or in connection therewith. *   *   * "

The security agreement which is signed by all the parties contains the wording: " *   *   * together with all hand tools, drill collars, drill pipe and together with all equipment, accessories, parts, exchanges, additions, betterments, and appliances that Debtor may hereafter acquire and use with or as a part of the above described goods. *   *   *" *The security agreement does not contain the language "equipment, parts, supplies and items which the Debtor may now have" as does the financing statement.* [Emphasis added.]

Plaintiff would have the two disputed items included within the security agreement on the basis of the "used with" language of the security agreement and on the basis of similar language included in certain of the exhibits referred to in the security agreement. This argument is without merit[.] *   *   * [T]he "used with" phrase in the security agreement applies only to after-acquired property and the disputed items are not in that category. The disputed items cannot be included in the security agreement on the basis of "used with" language in the security agreement[.] *   *   *

The financing statement was not signed pursuant to the provisions of [UCC Sec.] 9-402. There is a conflict in the language of the security agreement and the financing statement. We follow the reasoning in the Anderson Uniform Commercial Code, Vol. 4 at 124 (2d Ed. 1971) referring to Uniform Commercial Code which states:

"* * * § 9-110:17.—Conflicting descriptions in security agreement and financing statement:

"When there is a conflict between the financing statement on file and the security agreement as to the property involved, the latter prevails for the reason that no security interest can exist in the absence of a security agreement, and therefore a financing statement which goes beyond the scope of the agreement has no effect to that extent." Thus, the "may now have" language of the unsigned financing statement does not provide plaintiff with a security interest in the disputed items.

Plaintiff contends the disputed items were included within the security agreement because they were reasonably described therein. [UCC Sec.] 9-110. Plaintiff contends this reasonable description is provided by "external evidence." This "external evidence" consists of the unsigned financing statement and evidence at trial to the effect that Lucky Drilling Company mortgaged and plaintiff took, pursuant to the mortgage, security on *all* of the equipment of Lucky Drilling Company.

* * * Plaintiff's security agreement neither refers to "now owned equipment" or to "all" equipment of Lucky Drilling Company.

A security agreement is effective according to *its* terms. [UCC Sec.] 9-201. A security interest is not effective against third parties unless the debtor has signed a security agreement which contains a description of the collateral. [UCC Sec.] 9-203(1)(a). The disputed items cannot be included within the security agreement by the "outside evidence" relied on by plaintiff because the disputed items are not described in the security agreement. * * *

* * * We hold that the security agreement did not cover the two disputed items.

The plaintiff, Jones & Laughlin, did not have a security interest in the Whealand rotary table purchased by Dugan or in the Waukesha gasoline engine purchased by McDonald. The defendants had the right to these items bought at the sheriff's sale, and the plaintiff had no claim against them.

DECISION AND REMEDY

Where to File Depending upon the classification of collateral, filing is with either the secretary of state or the county clerk or other official, or both, according to state law. According to UCC 9-401, a state may choose one of these three alternatives.[4] In general, financing statements for consumer goods or for any collateral used or arising from a farmer's business should be filed with the county clerk. Other kinds of collateral require filing with the secretary of state. [UCC 9-401]

When the secured party obtains a security interest in *unissued* shares of stock, UCC 9-302(1) prevails, because unissued securities are categorized as general intangibles under UCC 9-106. "General

intangibles means any personal property (including things in action) other than goods, accounts, chattel paper, documents, instruments, and money." Under UCC 9-301(1), a security interest in unissued stock is perfected by filing a financing statement with the secretary of state.

Classification of Collateral Determines Where to File The classification of collateral is important in many situations. To determine the place of filing, goods must be classified as consumer goods, equipment, farm products, or inventory. Collateral also may be classified by legal scholars as indispensable paper, consisting of chattel paper, documents of title, and instruments; or intangible collateral, such as accounts and general intangibles. The classes of goods are mutually exclusive; *the same property can-*

---

4. Approximately half the states have adopted the second alternative. Filing fees range from as low as $2.00 to as high as $15.00.

not at the same time and to the same person be both equipment and inventory. Is a physician's car equipment or a consumer good? Is a farmer's jeep equipment or a consumer good? The principal *use* to which the property is put by the debtor determines its classification. If the physician uses the car primarily for personal use, then it is a consumer good; if it is used primarily for medical practice, then it is equipment. If a farmer's jeep is necessary for farming operations and is used primarily for that, then the jeep is classified as farm equipment. But the car and jeep can never be categorized as both equipment and inventory. [UCC 9-109]

Goods can fall into different classes at different times. For example, a CB radio is *inventory* when it is in the hands of a dealer. [UCC 9-109(4)] But when it is purchased by a consumer for use in a private car, it becomes a *consumer good.* [UCC 9-109(1)] When it is bought and then put in a patrol car, it is *equipment.* [UCC 9-109(2)] Under the Code, the majority rule is that the classification and filing are based on the *primary use* being made of the collateral at the time of filing.

It is important to note that if a secured party fails to perfect properly, the perfection is void and a later properly perfected security interest has priority. For example, suppose a state had adopted the second alternative of UCC 9-401. This alternative provides for central filing (usually with the secretary of state) if the collateral is inventory. West Bank loans retail seller Beyer $5,000 with Beyer putting up all existing inventory and any after-acquired inventory as collateral. Beyer signs a security agreement and a financing statement. By error, West files the financing statement locally. Later Beyer, in need of working capital, secures a loan from Friendly Savings and Loan. Beyer puts up some newly acquired inventory paid for previously by Beyer with cash. Beyer signs a security agreement and a financing statement. Friendly perfects its security interest by filing centrally. If Beyer goes into default on both loans, Friendly's proper perfection gives it priority to the after-acquired inventory because West Bank's perfection, although prior in time, was improperly filed and therefore void.

According to UCC 9-401, once the security agreement is properly filed, any change in the use of that collateral will not endanger the security interest of the secured party. State laws other than the UCC control where filing is done for each category of collateral. Exhibit 29–4 summarizes the various classifications of collateral and the methods of perfecting a security interest.

THE RANGE OF PERFECTION AND THE FLOATING LIEN CONCEPT

A security agreement can cover various types of property in addition to collateral already in the debtor's possession—the proceeds of sale, after-acquired property, and future advances.

Proceeds

Proceeds include whatever is received when collateral is sold, exchanged, collected, or disposed of. A secured party has an interest in the proceeds of the sale of collateral. To illustrate, suppose a bank has a perfected security interest in the inventory of a retail seller of TV sets. The retailer sells a TV set out of this inventory to you, a buyer in the ordinary course of business. You cannot pay cash and have agreed to a twenty-four-month-payment retail security agreement. If the retailer should go into default on the loan from the bank, the bank is entitled to the remaining payments you owe to the retailer as proceeds.

Perfection of the proceeds is available automatically upon perfection of the secured party's security interest and remains perfected for ten days after receipt of the proceeds by the debtor. One way to extend the ten-day automatic period is to provide for such extended coverage in the original security agreement. This is typically done when the collateral is the type that is likely to be sold.

The UCC provides three methods by which the security interest in proceeds remains perfected for longer than ten days after the receipt of the proceeds by the debtor. They are:

1. When a filed financing statement covers the original collateral, and the proceeds are collateral in which a security interest may be perfected by filing in the office or offices where the financing statement has been filed. Furthermore, if the proceeds are acquired with cash proceeds, the description of collateral in the financing statement must indicate the

EXHIBIT 29–4	Types Of Collateral and Methods Of Perfection		
Type of Collateral	**Definitions**	**Perfection Method**	**UCC Sections**
Tangible Goods	All things which are *moveable* at the time the security interest attaches or which are *fixtures* (emphasis added) [UCC 9-105(1)(h)]. This includes timber to be cut, growing crops, and unborn young animals.		
1. Consumer Goods	Goods used or bought primarily for personal, family, or household purposes—for example, household furniture [UCC 9-109(1)].	For purchase money security interest, attachment is sufficient; for boats, motor vehicles, and trailers, there is a requirement of filing or compliance with a certificate of title statute; for other consumer goods, general rules of filing or possession apply.	9-302(1)(d); 9-302(3); 9-302(4); 9-305
2. Equipment	Goods bought for or used primarily in business—for example, a delivery truck [UCC 9-109(2)].	Filing or possession by secured party.	9-302(1); 9-305
3. Farm Products	Crops, livestock, and supplies used or produced in a farming operation in the possession of a farmer debtor. This includes products of crops or livestock—for example, milk, eggs, maple syrup, and ginned cotton [UCC 9-102(3)].	Filing or possession by secured party.	9-302(1); 9-305
4. Inventory	Goods held for sale or lease, and materials used or consumed in the course of business—for example, raw materials or floor stock of a retailer [UCC 9-109(4)].	Filing or possession by secured party.	9-302(1); 9-305
5. Fixtures	Goods which become so affixed to realty that an interest in them arises under real estate law—for example, a central air conditioning unit [UCC 9-313(1)(a)].	Filing only.	9-313(1)
Indispensable Paper			
1. Chattel Paper	Any writing(s) that evidences both a *monetary obligation and a security interest*—for example, a thirty-six-month-payment retail security agreement and note signed by a buyer to purchase a car [UCC 9-105(1)(b)].	Filing or possession by secured party.	9-304(1); 9-305
2. Documents of Title	Paper which entitles the person in possession to hold, receive, or dispose of the paper or goods the document covers—for example, bills of lading, warehouse receipts, and dock warrants [UCC 9-105(1)(f), 1-201(15), 7-201].	Filing or possession by secured party.	9-304(1)(3); 9-305
3. Instruments	Any writing(s) which evidences a right to payment of money which is not a security agreement or lease, and any negotiable instrument or certificated security, which in the ordinary course of business is transferred by delivery with any necessary indorsement or assignment—for example, stock certificates, promissory notes, and certificates of deposit [UCC 9-105(1)(i), 3-104, 8-102(1)(a)].	Unless temporary perfected status, possession only.	9-304(1)(4) (5); 9-305

(continued on next page)

EXHIBIT 29–4 Continued

Type of Collateral	Definitions	Perfection Method	UCC Sections
Intangible Collateral			
1. Accounts	Any right(s) to payment of goods sold or leased or services *rendered* that are not evidenced by an instrument or chattel paper—for example, accounts receivable, contract right payments [UCC 9-106].	Filing required (with exceptions).	9-302(1)(e) (g)
2. General Intangibles	Any personal property other than that defined above—for example, a patent, copyright, goodwill, or trademark [UCC 9-106].	Filing only.	9-302(1)

types of property constituting the proceeds. [UCC 9-306(3)(a)]

2. Whenever there is a filed financing statement that covers the original collateral and the proceeds are identifiable cash proceeds. [UCC 9-306(3)(b)]

3. Whenever the security interest in the proceeds is perfected before the expiration of the ten-day period. [UCC 9-306(3)(c)]

After-acquired Property

After-acquired property of the debtor is property acquired after the execution of the security agreement. The security agreement itself may provide for coverage of after-acquired property. [UCC 9-204(1)] This is particularly useful for inventory financing arrangements, because a secured party whose security interest is in existing inventory knows that the debtor will sell that inventory, thereby reducing the collateral subject to the security interest. Generally, the debtor will purchase new inventory to replace the inventory sold. The secured party wants this newly acquired inventory to be subject to the *original* security interest. Thus, the after-acquired property clause continues the secured party's claim onto any inventory acquired thereafter. This is not to say that such original security interest will be superior to the rights of all other creditors with regard to this after-acquired inventory, as will be discussed later.

An after-acquired property clause normally does not allow for attachment of a security interest in consumer goods "unless the debtor acquires rights in them within 10 days after the secured party gives value." [UCC 9-204(2)] Presumably, this protects consumers from encumbering all their present and future property.

Consider a typical example. Anderson buys factory equipment from Blonsky on credit, giving as security an interest in all of her equipment—both what she is buying and what she already owns. The security interest with Blonsky contains an after-acquired property clause. Six months later, Anderson pays cash to another seller for more equipment. Six months after that, Anderson goes out of business before she has paid off her debt to Blonsky. Blonsky has a security interest in *all* of Anderson's equipment, even the equipment bought from the other seller.

Future Advances

Often a debtor will have a continuing *line of credit* under which the debtor can borrow intermittently. This is often done with a *letter of credit*—an agreement in which the issuer of the letter agrees to pay drafts drawn on it by the creditor (as explained earlier). It is an advance arrangement of financing with the maximum amount of advance that the debtor can obtain. A letter of credit, typically issued by a bank, has three parties: the issuer, the customer, and a beneficiary who will draw the drafts under it. Letters of credit typically specify not only a maximum amount but a specified time duration. Letters of credit (sometimes called lines of credit) can be subject to a security interest in certain properly perfected collateral.

The security agreement may provide that any future advances made against that line of credit are also subject to the security interest in the same collateral. For example, Smith is the owner of a small manufacturing plant with equipment valued at $1,000,000. Smith is in immediate need of $50,000 working capital. Smith secures a loan from West Bank, signing a security agreement putting up his entire equipment as security. In the security agreement Smith can borrow up to $500,000 in the future, using the same equipment as collateral (future advances.) In such cases, it is not necessary to execute a new security agreement and perfect a security interest in the collateral each time an advance is made to the debtor. [UCC 9-204(3)]

The Floating Lien Concept

When a security agreement provides for the creation of a security interest in proceeds of the sale of the collateral that was the subject matter of the secured transaction, after-acquired property or future advances, or both, it is referred to as a **floating lien.** Floating liens commonly arise in the financing of inventories, for example. A creditor is not interested in specific pieces of inventory, because they are constantly changing.

Suppose that Ptarmigan Mountaineering, a cross-country ski dealer, has a line of credit with Seattle First National Bank to finance an inventory of cross-country skis. Ptarmigan and Seattle First enter into a security agreement that provides for coverage of proceeds, after-acquired property, inventory, and future advances.

This security interest in inventory is perfected by filing centrally (with the secretary of state). One day, Ptarmigan sells a new pair of the latest cross-country skis, for which it receives a used pair in trade. That same day, it purchases two new pairs of skis from a local manufacturer with an additional amount of money obtained from Seattle First. Seattle First gets a perfected security interest in the used pair of cross-country skis under the proceeds clause, has a perfected security interest in the two new pairs of skis purchased from the local manufacturer under the after-acquired property clause, and has the new amount of money advanced to Ptarmigan secured by the future-advance clause. All of this is done under the original perfected security agreement. The various items in the inventory have changed, but Seattle First still has a perfected security interest in Ptarmigan's inventory, and hence it has a floating lien on the inventory.

The concept of a floating lien can also apply to a shifting stock of goods. Under Section 9-205, the lien can start with raw materials and follow them as they become finished goods and inventories and as they are sold, turning into accounts receivable, chattel paper, or cash.

Collateral Moved to Another Jurisdiction

Obviously, collateral may be moved by the debtor from one jurisdiction (state) to another. When this occurs, a problem arises in that a secured party's perfection by filing serves as notice only to the third parties who check the records in the county (local filing) or state (central filing) where the perfection properly took place. Frequently, the secured party is not even aware of the collateral being moved out of the jurisdiction.

The Code addresses this problem and at the same time furthers the concept of the floating lien. In general, a properly perfected security interest in collateral moved into a new jurisdiction continues to be perfected in the new jurisdiction for a period of up to four months from the date it was moved, or for the period of time remaining under the perfection in the original jurisdiction, whichever expires first. [UCC-9-103(1)(d) and 9-103(3)(e)] However, collateral moved from county to county *within* a state (where local filing is required) may not have a four-month limitation, and the original filing would have continuous priority. [See UCC 9-403(3)]

To illustrate: Suppose that on January 1 Calvin secures a loan from a Kansas bank by putting up all his wheat threshing equipment as security. The Kansas bank files the security interest centrally with the secretary of state. In June, Calvin has an opportunity to harvest wheat crops in South Dakota and moves his equipment into that state on June 15. Applying the above law, the Kansas bank's perfection remains effective in South Dakota for a period of four months from June 15. If the Kansas bank wishes to retain its perfection priority, the bank must perfect properly in South Dakota during this four-month period. Should the bank fail to do so, its perfection is lost after four months, and subsequent perfected security interests in the same collateral in South Dakota would prevail.

In mobile goods, automobiles pose one of the biggest problems. If either the new or the original jurisdiction requires a certificate of title as part of its perfection process in regard to an automobile, perfection does not automatically end after four months. Instead, perfection ends as soon as the automobile is registered again (after the end of the four-month period) and a "clean" certificate of title is obtained. [UCC 9-103(2)]

The Effective Time of Perfection

The Code furthers the floating lien concept with provisions affecting the time period during which a properly perfected security interest has priority. A filing statement is effective for five years from the date of filing. [UCC 9-403(2)] If a continuation statement is filed *within six months* prior to the expiration date, the effectiveness of the original statement is continued for another five years, starting with the expiration date of the first five-year period. [UCC 9-403(3)] The effectiveness of the statement can be continued in the same manner indefinitely.

PRIORITIES

The consequences of perfection and nonperfection are important in determining priorities among parties having conflicting interests in the *same* collateral.

Perfection is important because the Code makes it clear that an *unperfected* security interest is of little value when challenged by a third party. According to UCC 9-301, certain categories of persons prevail over the unperfected security interest:

1. Persons who have a perfected security interest in the same collateral.
2. Lien creditors—that is, creditors who acquire a lien on property by attachment or **levy** (judicial process), including trustees in bankruptcy. [9-301(3)]
3. A person who is a transferee in bulk (see UCC Article 6) or other buyer not in the ordinary course of business (or who is a buyer of farm products in the ordinary course of business) to the extent that that person gives value and receives delivery of the collateral without knowledge of the security interest and before it is perfected.
4. A person who is a transferee of accounts or general intangibles to the extent that the transferee gives value without knowledge of the security interest and before it is perfected.

Assuming a party has an enforceable security interest, his or her priority will depend upon the time when the security interest attached (became enforceable) or the time when it became perfected, or both, according to the following rules:

1. *Conflicting perfected security interests.* When two or more secured parties have perfected security interests in the same collateral, generally the *first to perfect* (file or take possession of collateral) wins. [UCC 9-312(5)(a)]
2. *Conflicting unperfected security interests.* When two conflicting security interests are unperfected, the *first in time* to attach has priority. [UCC 9-312(5)(b)]
3. *Conflicting perfected security interests in commingled or processed goods.* When goods, with two or more perfected security interests, are so manufactured or commingled that they lose their identity into a product or mass, the perfected parties' security interests attach to the new product or mass "according to the ratio that the cost of goods to which each interest originally attached bears to the cost of the total product or mass." [UCC 9-315(2)]

EXCEPTIONS TO PERFECTION PRIORITY RULES

Under certain circumstances, the perfection of a security interest will not protect a secured party against certain other third parties having claims to the collateral. The following discussion covers these exceptions to perfection priority rules.

Non-purchase versus Purchase Money Perfected Security Interests

The general rule, as previously stated, is that the first in time to perfect is first in priority rights to the collateral. This rule is always applicable when the first in time to perfect is a purchase money security interest. However, the Code provides that under certain conditions a purchase money security interest, properly perfected, will prevail over a non-purchase money security interest in after-acquired collateral, even though the non-purchase money security interest was perfected first in time.

If the collateral is *inventory*, a perfected purchase money security interest will prevail over a previously perfected non-purchase security interest, provided (generally) that the purchase money secured party perfects *and* gives the non-purchase secured party written notice of his or her interest *before* the debtor takes possession of the newly acquired inventory. [UCC 9-312(3)]

If the collateral is other than inventory, a purchase money security interest will have priority over a previously perfected non-purchase security interest provided that the purchase money security interest is perfected either before or within ten days *after* the debtor takes possession. No notice is required. [UCC 9-312(4)]

To illustrate: Retailer Mary needs a loan of money to be used as working capital. On May 1, she secures a one-year installment loan from West Bank, signing a security agreement and putting up her present inventory plus any after-acquired inventory as collateral. That same date West Bank perfects by filing a financing statement centrally. On August 1 Mary learns that she can purchase directly from Martin, a manufacturer, $10,000 worth of new inventory, which is a bargain. Since she cannot pay this amount in cash, she signs a security agreement with Martin, giving Martin a security interest in the newly purchased inventory. Delivery of the new inventory is to be on September 1. The new inventory is delivered on September 1 as ordered. On September 7 a fire destroys most of Mary's store and warehouse. There remains only a part of the new inventory, and its value is insufficient to cover both debts. Who has priority on the remaining inventory, West Bank or Martin?

If Martin perfected by filing and gave West Bank notice of its security interest prior to September 1, the date Mary received possession, Martin prevails. If Martin did not meet these conditions, West Bank prevails.

Suppose the collateral is equipment, rather than inventory, and Martin perfected on September 8, after the fire. Since Martin properly perfected his purchase money security interest within ten days after Mary received delivery, Martin prevails over West Bank for the remaining after-acquired equipment.

Buyers in the Ordinary Course of Business

Since buyers should not be required to find out if there is an outstanding security interest on a merchant's inventory, the Code provides that a person who buys "in the ordinary course of business" will take the goods free from any security interest in the merchant's inventory, even if the security interest is perfected and even if the buyer knows of its existence. [UCC 9-307(1)] A *buyer in the ordinary course of business* is defined as any person who in good faith, and without knowledge that the sale is in violation of the ownership rights or security interest of a third party in the goods, buys in ordinary course from a person in the business of selling goods of that kind. [UCC 1-201(9)]

Suppose retail seller Carla secures a loan from West Bank putting up her existing appliance inventory and any appliance inventory thereafter acquired. Carla signs a security agreement and a financing statement, which West Bank properly perfects. Later Carla sells an appliance from her inventory under the security agreement to Lee, with Lee paying cash. If Carla goes into default on the loan, West Bank's prior perfected security has no effect upon Lee. Lee took the appliance completely free of West Bank's security interest, even though perfected, and West Bank loses this piece of collateral for satisfaction of the default.

In the following case, the court must determine whether a sale was in the ordinary course of the seller's business.

BACKGROUND AND FACTS *Tanbro finishes textile fabrics (griege goods) into dyed and patterned fabrics. Tanbro, known in the trade as a "converter," sought damages for the tortious conversion of unfinished textile fabrics from Deering Milliken, a textile manufacturer. The goods in question had been manufactured by Deering and sold to Mill Fabrics. Mill Fabrics resold the goods to Tanbro, while the goods were still in Deering's warehouse. Deering refused to deliver the goods to Tanbro because, although these goods had been paid for, Mill Fabrics owed Deering on other accounts. Deering claimed a perfected security interest in the goods.*

TANBRO FABRICS CORP. v. DEERING MILLIKEN, INC.

Court of Appeals of New York, 1976.
39 N.Y.2d 632, 385 N.Y.S.2d 260, 350 N.E.2d 590.

BREITEL, Chief Judge.

*   *   *   *

*   *   * [U]nder the terms of the Deering sales agreements with Mill Fabrics, Deering retained a security interest in Mill Fabrics' "property" on a bill and hold basis, whether paid for or not. This security interest was perfected by Deering's continued possession of the goods (Uniform Commercial Code, § 1-201, subd. [37]; § 9-305). Tanbro argued that if it had title by purchase its goods were excluded from the security arrangement which was literally restricted to the "property of the buyer", that is, Mill Fabrics. In any event, unless prevented by other provisions of the code, or the sale was not unauthorized, Tanbro took title subject to Deering's security interest.

Under the code (§ 9-307, subd. [1]) a buyer in the ordinary course of the seller's business takes goods free of even a known security interest so long as the buyer does not know that the purchase violates the terms of the security agreement. As defined in the code (§ 1-201, subd. [9]) "a buyer in ordinary course" is "a person who in good faith and without knowledge that the sale to him is in violation of the ownership rights or security interest of a third party in the goods buys in ordinary course from a person in the business of selling goods of that kind but does not include a pawnbroker. 'Buying' may be for cash or by exchange of other property or on secured or unsecured credit and includes receiving goods or documents of title under a preexisting contract for sale but does not include a transfer in bulk or as security for or in total or partial satisfaction of a money debt." Critical to Tanbro's claim is that it purchased the goods in the ordinary course of Mill Fabrics' business and that it did not purchase the goods in knowing violation of Deering's security interest.

Under the code whether a purchase was made from a person in the business of selling goods of that kind turns primarily on whether that person holds the goods for sale. Such goods are a person's selling inventory. (Uniform Commercial Code, § 1-201, subd. [9]; § 9-307, subd. [1]; Official Comment, at par. 2.) Note, however, that not all purchases of goods held as inventory qualify as purchases from a person in the business of selling goods of that kind. The purpose of section 9-307 is more limited. As indicated in the Practice Commentary to that section, the purpose is to permit buyers "to buy goods from a dealer in such goods without having to protect himself against a possible security interest on the inventory". Hence, a qualifying purchase is one made from a seller who is a dealer in such goods.

A former Mill Fabrics' employee testified that there were times when Mill Fabrics, like all converters, found itself with excess goods. When it was to their business advantage, they sold the excess fabrics to other converters. Although these sales were relatively infrequent they were nevertheless part of and in the ordinary course of Mill Fabrics' business, even if only incidental to the predominant business purpose. Examples of a nonqualifying sale might be a bulk sale, a sale in distress at an obvious loss price, a sale in liquidation, a sale of a commodity never dealt with before by the seller and wholly unlike its usual inventory, or the like.

All subdivision (1) of section 9-307 requires is that the sale be of the variety reasonably to be expected in the regular course of an on-going business. *   *   *

DECISION AND REMEDY

Tanbro recovered damages from Deering to compensate for the wrongful conversion of the goods.

Secondhand Goods: Goods Sold by a Consumer to a Consumer

Carla is a consumer who purchases a refrigerator on credit because she cannot pay the full purchase price.

A written security agreement exists in which the seller takes a purchase money security interest in the consumer goods under this type of credit plan. Further, the seller need not file a financing statement because, when a purchase money security interest is taken in consumer goods, *perfection occurs automatically*. [UCC 9-302(1)(d)] Later, Carla sells the refrigerator to her next door neighbor, Nan, who purchases it for home use without any knowledge of the credit arrangements between Carla and the original seller. Subsequently, Carla defaults on the credit payments to the seller. What are the seller's rights? The seller had a perfected purchase money security interest in the refrigerator when it was held by Carla. However, under UCC 9-307(2), the perfection is not good against the next door neighbor.

UCC 9-307(2) requires that the "next door neighbor" must purchase (give value for) the goods for personal, family, or household use, without knowledge of the original seller's security interest, and the purchase must take place *before* the secured party files a financing statement. In this case, recall that the seller took a purchase money security interest, which is perfected automatically. No filing was required. Hence, the next door neighbor purchased the refrigerator free and clear before the seller had filed a financing statement. The seller could have avoided this possibility simply by *filing* a financing statement, even though a purchase money security interest had been perfected.

Buyers of Chattel Paper and Instruments

Another purchaser not subject to a secured party's interest despite perfection is the purchaser of chattel paper and instruments. This protection is provided by Section 9-308(a). As defined before, *chattel paper* is a writing or writings that evidence both a monetary obligation and a security interest in specific goods. *Instrument* means a negotiable instrument as defined in UCC 3-104, or a certificated security as defined in UCC 8-102, or basically any other writing that evidences a right to the payment of money and is not itself a security agreement or lease transferred in the ordinary course of business. [UCC 9-105(1)(i)]

Chattel paper is a very important class of collateral used in financing arrangements, especially in automobile financing. When it is sold by a creditor, the creditor can deliver it over to the assignee, who is then responsible for collecting the debt directly from the debtor. This arrangement is known as *notification* or *direct collection*. As an alternative, a creditor can sell chattel paper to an assignee with the understanding that the creditor will retain the chattel paper, make collections from the debtor, and then remit the money to the assignee. This kind of

transaction is *nonnotification* or *indirect collection*. The chattel paper is usually not delivered to the assignee. The widespread use of both methods of dealing with chattel paper is recognized by the Code, and hence the Code permits perfection of a chattel paper security interest either by filing or by taking possession.

Problems arise when perfection is made by filing only. If the chattel paper is thereafter sold to another purchaser who gives *new value* and takes *possession* of the paper in the *ordinary course of business without knowledge* that it is subject to a security interest, the new purchaser usually will have priority over the secured creditor. (Of course, the creditor has rights in the proceeds.)

The *Concept Summary* on the next page deals with priority of claims to a debtor's collateral.

THE RIGHTS AND DUTIES OF DEBTORS AND CREDITORS UNDER THE UCC

The security agreement itself determines most of the rights and duties of the debtor and the creditor. The UCC, however, imposes some rights and duties that are applicable in the absence of a security agreement to the contrary.

Information Request by Creditors

Under UCC 9-407(1), a creditor has the option, when making the filing, of asking the filing officer to make a note of the file number, the date, and the hour of the original filing on a copy of the financing statement. The filing officer must send this copy to the person making the request. Under UCC 9-407(2), a filing officer must also give information to a person who is contemplating obtaining a security interest from a prospective debtor. The filing officer must give a certificate that provides information on possible perfected financing statements with respect to the named debtor. The filing officer will charge a fee for the certification or information copies provided.

Assignment, Amendment, and Release

Whenever desired, a secured party of record can release part or all of the collateral described in a filed financing statement. This ends his or her se-

CONCEPT SUMMARY: The Priority of Claims to a Debtor's Collateral	
PARTIES	**PRIORITY**
Unperfected Secured Party	Prevails over unsecured creditors and unlevied judgment creditors. UCC 9-301
Purchasers of Debtor's Collateral	1. Goods purchased in the ordinary course of business prevail over a secured party's security interest, even if perfected and even if the purchaser knows of the security interest. UCC 9-307(1)
	2. Consumer goods purchased out of the ordinary course of business prevail over a secured party's interest, even if perfected, providing purchaser purchased— a. For value. b. Without actual knowledge of the security interest. c. For use as a consumer good. d. Prior to secured party's perfection by *filing*. UCC 9-307(2)
	3. The chattel paper purchaser prevails over a perfected secured party providing the purchaser— a. Gave new value. b. Took possession. c. Took in the ordinary course of business. d. Took without *actual* knowledge of secured party's perfection. UCC 9-308
	4. Negotiable instruments, documents, and securities purchased prevail over a perfected secured party, particularly if the purchaser is a holder in due course, a holder to whom the document has been duly negotiated, or a bona fide purchaser of a security. UCC 9-308, UCC 9-309

Perfected Secured Parties to Same Collateral	As between two perfected secured parties in the same collateral, the general rule is that first in time of perfection is first in right to the collateral. UCC 9-312(5). Exceptions are—
	 a. Crops—New value to produce crops given within three months of planting has priority over prior six-month perfected interest. UCC 9-312(2)
	 b. Purchase money security interest—Even if second in time of perfection (first in time of perfection is a nonpurchase money security interest), it has priority providing—
	   i. Inventory—Purchase money security interest is perfected and proper notice is given to nonpurchase money perfected security interest holder *on* or *before* debtor takes possession. UCC 9-312(3)
	   ii. Other collateral—Purchase money security interest has priority providing such is perfected within ten (10) days after debtor receives possession. UCC 9-312(4)

curity interest in the collateral. [UCC 9-406] A secured party can assign part or all of the security interest to another, called the assignee. That assignee becomes the secured party of record if, for example, he or she either makes a notation of the assignment somewhere on the financing statement or files a written statement of assignment. [UCC 9-405(2)]

It is also possible to amend a financing statement that has already been filed. The amendment must be signed by *both* parties. The debtor has to sign the security agreement, the original financing statement, and the amendments. [UCC 9-402] All other secured transaction documents, such as releases, assignments, continuations of perfection, perfections of collateral moved into another jurisdiction, or termination statements, need only be signed by the secured party.

Reasonable Care of Collateral

If a secured party is in possession of the collateral, he or she must use reasonable care in preserving it. Otherwise, the secured party is liable to the debtor. [UCC 9-207 (1) and (3)] If the collateral increases in value, the secured party can hold this increased value or profit as additional security unless it is in the form of money, which must be remitted to the debtor or applied toward reducing the secured debt. [UCC 9-207(2)(c)] Additionally, the collateral must be kept in identifiable condition unless it is fungible. [UCC 9-207(2)(d) Finally, the debtor must pay for all reasonable charges incurred by the secured party in preserving, operating, and taking care of the collateral in possession. [UCC 9-207(2)(a)]

The Status of the Debt

During the time that the secured debt is outstanding, the debtor may wish to know the status of the debt. If so, the debtor need only sign a statement that indicates the aggregate amount of the unpaid debt at a specific date (and perhaps a list of the collateral covered by the security agreement). The secured party must then approve or correct this statement in writing. The creditor must comply with the request within two weeks of receipt; otherwise, the creditor is liable for any loss caused to the debtor by the failure to do so. [UCC 9-208(2)] One such request is allowed without charge every six months. For each additional request, the secured party can require a fee not exceeding $10 per request. [UCC 9-208(3)]

DEFAULT

Article 9 defines the rights, duties, and remedies of a secured party and of the debtor upon a debtor's default. Should the secured party fail to comply with its duties, the debtor is afforded particular rights and remedies.

The topic of default is one of great concern to secured lenders and to the lawyers who draft security agreements. What constitutes default is not always clear. In fact, Article 9 does not define the term. Thus, parties are encouraged in practice and by the Code to include in their security agreements certain standards to be applied in the event that default actually comes about. Consequently, parties can stipulate the conditions that will constitute a default. [UCC 9-501(1)]

Typically, because of the unusual disparity in the bargaining position between a debtor and a creditor, these critical terms are shaped with exceeding breadth by the creditor in order to arrive at some sense of security. The ultimate terms, however, are not allowed to go beyond the limitations imposed by the good faith requirement of UCC 1-208 and the unconscionability doctrine.

Although any breach of the terms of the security agreement can constitute default, default occurs most commonly when the debtor fails to meet the scheduled payments that the parties have agreed upon or when the debtor becomes bankrupt. However, if the security agreement covers equipment, the debtor may have warranted that he or she is the owner of the equipment or that no liens or other security interests are pending on that equipment. Breach of any of these representations can result in default.

Basic Remedies

According to UCC 9-501, upon default, a secured creditor can reduce a claim to judgment, foreclose, or enforce a security interest by any available judicial process. Where the collateral consists of documents of title, a secured party can proceed against either the documents or the underlying goods.

A secured party's remedies can be divided into two basic categories:

1. A secured party can relinquish a security interest and proceed to judgment on the underlying debt, followed by execution and levy. This is rarely done unless the value of the secured collateral has been greatly reduced below the amount of the debt, and the debtor has other nonexempt assets available to satisfy the debt. [UCC 9-501(1)]

2. A secured party can take possession of the collateral covered by the security agreement. [UCC 9-503] Upon taking possession, the secured party can retain the collateral covered by the security agreement for satisfaction of the debt [UCC 9-505(2)] or can resell the goods and apply the proceeds toward the debt. [UCC 9-504]

The rights and remedies under UCC 9-501(1) are *cumulative*; therefore, if a creditor is unsuccessful in enforcing rights by one method, another method can be pursued. The UCC does not require election of remedies between an action on the obligation or repossession of the collateral.[5]

When a security agreement covers both real and personal property, the secured party can proceed against the personal property in accordance with the remedies of Article 9. On the other hand, the secured party can proceed against the entire collateral under procedures set down by local real estate law, in which case the Code does not apply. [UCC 9-501(4)]

For example, this situation occurs when the security interest on a corporate loan applies to the manufacturing plant (real property) and also to the inventory (personal property). Determining whether particular collateral is personal or real property can prove to be difficult, especially when dealing with fixtures—things affixed to real property. Under certain circumstances, the Code allows the removal of fixtures upon default; however, such removal is subject to the provisions of Article 9. [UCC 9-313]

The Secured Party's Right to Take Possession

The secured party has the right to take possession of the collateral upon default unless the security agreement states otherwise. As long as there is no breach of the peace, the secured party can simply repossess the collateral. Otherwise the secured party must resort to the judicial process. [UCC 9-503]

What constitutes a breach of the peace is of prime importance to both parties, for such an act can open the secured party to tort liability. The Code

does not define *breach of the peace*. Therefore, parties must resort to state law to determine it.

Generally, the creditor or the creditor's agent cannot enter a debtor's home, garage, or place of business without permission. Consider a situation where an automobile is collateral. If the repossessing party walks onto the debtor's premises, proceeds up the driveway, enters the vehicle without entering the garage, and drives off, it probably will not amount to a breach of the peace. However, in some states, an action for wrongful trespass could meet the threshold test and start a cause of action for breach of the peace. (Most car repossessions occur when the car is parked on a street or in a parking lot.)

Reasonable Care of the Collateral Required   Once the secured party comes into possession of the collateral by repossession after breach, the rights, remedies, and duties provided by Section 9-207, as previously discussed, come into play. The main requirement of that section calls for the secured party to exercise "reasonable care" in the custody and preservation of any collateral in its possession.

This duty cannot be disclaimed, and any exculpatory clause will be unenforceable. [UCC 1-102(3)] Reasonable limitations as to what will be required, however, can be agreed upon by the parties. Where the collateral consists of instruments or chattel paper, reasonable care extends to taking necessary steps to preserve rights against prior parties unless otherwise agreed. Should the secured party fail to meet its obligations as prescribed in UCC 9-207, he or she will be liable for any damages occasioned by such failure. The secured party does not, however, lose the security interest for failure to exercise reasonable care.

Assembling the Collateral   UCC 9-503 provides authorization for security agreements to require that, upon default, the debtor assemble the collateral and make it available to the secured party at a location designated by that party. The location must be reasonably convenient to both parties. This provision is important to a creditor when the collateral is located in several locations or when the debtor is in a better position to assemble it.

The Code also recognizes the inherent practical problems involved in removal and disposition of collateral when it is heavy equipment. Removal and

---

5. See White and Summers, *Uniform Commercial Code*, 2nd Ed. (St. Paul: West Publishing Co., 1980), pp. 1093–1094.

storage costs could quickly reach an impractical level. The Code therefore authorizes the secured party to render such equipment "unusable" and to dispose of the collateral on the debtor's premises. [UCC 9-503] This authorization does not permit unreasonable action by the secured party, because every aspect of the repossession and disposition must comply with the standards of commercial reasonableness of Section 9-504.

Disposition of Collateral

Once default has occurred, the secured party is faced with several alternatives to secure payment of the debt. The party can sell, lease, or otherwise dispose of the collateral in any commercially reasonable manner. [UCC 9-504(1)] Any sale is always subject to procedures established by state law.

Retention of Collateral by Secured Party after Default   The Code recognizes that parties are sometimes better off if they do not sell the collateral. Therefore, a secured party can retain collateral, but this general right is subject to several conditions. The secured party must send written notice of the proposal to the debtor if the debtor has not signed a statement renouncing or modifying his or her rights after default. With consumer goods, no *other* notice has to be given. In all other cases, notice must be sent to any other secured party from whom the secured party has received written notice of a claim of interest in the collateral in question. If within twenty-one days after the notice is sent the secured party receives an objection in writing from a person entitled to receive notification, then the secured party must dispose of the collateral under UCC 9-504. If no such written objection is forthcoming, the secured party can retain the collateral in full satisfaction of the debtor's obligation. [UCC 9-505(2)]

Consumer Goods   When the collateral is *consumer goods* with a *purchase money security interest*, and the debtor has paid *more* than 60 *percent* of the *cash price*, or *loan*, then the secured party must dispose of the collateral under UCC 9-504 within ninety days. Failure to comply opens the secured party to an action for conversion or other liability under UCC 9-507(1) unless the consumer-debtor signed a written statement *after default* renouncing or modifying

the right to demand the sale of the goods. [UCC 9-505(1)]

Disposition Procedures   A secured party who does not choose to retain the collateral must resort to the disposition procedures prescribed under UCC 9-504. The Code allows a great deal of flexibility with regard to disposition. The only real limitation is that it must be accomplished in a commercially reasonable manner. UCC 9-507(2) supplies some examples of what does or does not meet the standard of commercial reasonableness:

> The fact that a better price could have been obtained by a sale at a different time or in a different method from that selected by the secured party is not of itself sufficient to establish that the sale was not made in a commercially reasonable manner. If the secured party either sells the collateral in the usual manner in any recognized market therefor or if he sells at the price currently in such a market at the time of sale or if he has otherwise sold in conformity with reasonable commercial practices among dealers in the type of property sold, he has sold in a commercially reasonable manner.

A secured party is not compelled to resort to public sale to dispose of the collateral. The party is given the latitude under the Code to seek out the best terms possible in a private sale. Generally, no specific time requirements must be met; however, the time must ultimately meet the standard of commercial reasonableness.

Notice must be sent by the secured party to the debtor if the debtor has not signed a statement renouncing or modifying the right to notification of sale after default. For consumer goods, no other notification need be sent. In all other cases, notification must be sent to any other secured party from whom the secured party has received written notice of claim of an interest in the collateral. [UCC 9-504(3)] Such notice is not necessary, however, when the collateral is perishable or threatens to decline speedily in value, or when it is of a type customarily sold on a recognized market.

To be classified as a sale conducted in a commercially reasonable manner, generally notice of the place, time, and manner of sale is required. The following case illustrates the importance of compliance with such requirement.

STENSEL v. STENSEL

Appellate Court of Illinois,
Fourth District, 1978.
63 Ill.App.3d 639, 20 Ill.Dec.
548, 380 N.E.2d 526.

BACKGROUND AND FACTS *Glenn Stensel borrowed $35,000 from a bank, pledging sixteen mobile homes that he owned as collateral. Glenn's father, Vernell Stensel, co-signed the notes. Glenn defaulted in payments on the notes, and his father sold the mobile homes at a public auction. Using the proceeds of the sale and his own funds, Vernell satisfied his son's debt. After Vernell's death, his widow sought a deficiency judgment against Glenn. The trial court entered judgment for the widow. Glenn contended he was not liable for the money his father added to the auction proceeds because he was not notified of the sale.*

WEBBER, Justice.

*   *   *   *

Plaintiff contends that no notice was required because the collateral was in danger of destruction and threatened to decline speedily in value, and in any event, Glenn renounced his right to notice by sending certain written instructions to the bank and to Vernell.

The pertinent provision of the Code relating to the secured party's right to dispose of collateral is section 9-504(3) which reads as follows:

"Disposition of the collateral may be by public or private proceedings and may be made by way of one or more contracts. Sale or other disposition may be as a unit or in parcels and at any time and place and on any terms but every aspect of the disposition including the method, manner, time, place and terms must be commercially reasonable. *Unless collateral is perishable or threatens to decline speedily in value or is of a type customarily sold on a recognized market, reasonable notification of the time and place of any public sale or reasonable notification of the time after which any private sale or other intended disposition is to be made shall be sent by the secured party to the debtor, if he has not signed after default a statement renouncing or modifying his right to notification of sale.* In the case of consumer goods no other notification need be sent. In other cases notification shall be sent to any other secured party from whom the secured party has received (before sending his notification to the debtor or before the debtor's renunciation of his rights) written notice of a claim of an interest in the collateral. The secured party may buy at any public sale and if the collateral is of a type customarily sold in a recognized market or is of a type which is the subject of widely distributed standard price quotations he may buy at private sale."

We are not persuaded that a mobile home is collateral which "threatens to decline speedily in value." *   *   * In our opinion, that application of this provision to chattel property would be a rarity. Its obvious intent was to apply to securities in a rapidly falling market, or any other item, such as gold bullion, which is subject to price fluctuations on a daily basis.

*   *   * Plaintiff makes much of some letters in the record from Glenn to the bank and to Vernell. *   *   *

While the letters *prima facie* authorize a sale, nothing in either of them can be construed as a waiver of notice of the time and place of the sale. This is especially true in view of section 9-501(3) of the Code which reads, in part, as follows:

"To the extent that they give rights to the debtor and impose duties on the secured party, the rules stated in the subsections referred to below *may not be waived or varied* except as provided with respect to compulsory disposition of collateral (subsection (3) of Section 9-504 and Section 9-505 and with respect to redemption of collateral (Section 9-506)) but the parties may by agreement determine the standards by which the fulfillment of these rights and duties is to be measured if such standards are not manifestly unreasonable."

We have already held that the disposition here was not one under compulsion and there is nothing in the record to indicate that the parties made any other agreement regarding these rights. Under the authority just set forth, Glenn could not legally waive his rights to notice and since he received none, the purported sale was void as to him.

* * * *

Since the sale was void as to Glenn, the remaining problem is whether a deficiency judgment could be obtained against him.

The commentary to section 9-504 of the Code indicates that there is a divergence of authority in the United States on this subject. One line holds that any damages recoverable by the debtor must be offset by any deficiency on the sale, but the burden shifts to the secured party to prove that he obtained a commercially reasonable sale, especially in the absence of notice to the debtor.

Another line of cases holds that a failure of the secured party to give notice of sale to the debtor absolutely bars any deficiency judgment.

We are persuaded that the latter line of authority is the better reasoned. The deprivation of the ability to be present at the sale and guard one's interests is serious and allows the secured party too free a hand in making disposition.

The judgment of the trial court was reversed. Vernell's widow could not recover because Glenn was not given proper notice of the sale. **DECISION AND REMEDY**

Proceeds from Disposition   Proceeds from the disposition must be applied in the following order:

1. Reasonable expenses stemming from the retaking, holding, or preparing for sale are covered first. When authorized by law and if provided for in the agreement, these can include reasonable attorneys' fees and legal expenses.
2. Satisfaction of the balance of the debt owed to the secured party must then be made.
3. Subordinate security interests whose written demands have been received prior to the completion of distribution of the proceeds are covered third. [UCC 9-504(1)]
4. Any surplus generally goes to the debtor.

Deficiency Judgment   Often, after proper disposition of the collateral, the secured party does not collect all that is still owed by the debtor. Unless otherwise agreed, the debtor is liable for any deficiency. On the other hand, if the underlying transaction was a sale of accounts or of chattel paper, the secured party can collect a deficiency judgment only if the security agreement so provides. [UCC 9-504(2)]

Redemption Rights   Any time before the secured party disposes of the collateral or enters into a contract for its disposition, or before the debtor's obligation has been discharged through the secured party's retention of the collateral, the debtor or any other secured party can exercise the right of *redemption* of the collateral. The debtor can do this by tendering performance of *all* obligations secured by the collateral, by paying the expenses reasonably incurred by the secured party, and by retaking the collateral and maintaining its care and custody. [UCC 9-506]

TERMINATION

When a debt is paid, the secured party generally must send to the debtor or file with the filing officer to whom the original financing statement was given a termination statement. If the financing statement covers consumer goods, the termination statement must be filed by the secured party within one month after the debt is paid, or if the debtor requests the termination statement in writing, it must be filed within ten days after the debt is paid, whichever is earlier. [UCC 9-404(1)] In all other cases, the termination statement must be filed or furnished to the debtor within ten days after a written request is made by the debtor. If the affected secured party fails to file such a termination statement, as required by UCC 9-404(1), or fails to send the termination statement within ten days after proper demand, the secured party shall be liable to the debtor for $100. Additionally, the secured party will be liable for any loss caused to the debtor.

QUESTIONS AND CASE PROBLEMS

1. Discuss how each secured party would properly perfect his or her security interest in the following cases.
   (a) Martin is the manufacturer of refrigerators. Ray, a retailer, buys a number of these refrigerators. Ray signs a security agreement giving Martin a security interest in the refrigerators.
   (b) Mary sells a refrigerator to Carla, to be used in Carla's home. Carla signs a security agreement giving Mary a security interest in the refrigerator.
   (c) Ray sells a refrigerator to Dr. Dodd, to be used in his office to store medicines. Dr. Dodd signs a security agreement giving Ray a security interest in the refrigerator.
   (d) Mary sells a refrigerator to farmer Jones, who needs it to store excess eggs not sold at market. Jones signs a security agreement giving Mary a security interest in the refrigerator.

2. Smith has a prize horse named Thunderbolt. Smith is in need of working capital. To secure it, she borrows $5,000 from Rodriguez, with Rodriguez taking possession of Thunderbolt as security for the loan. No written agreement is signed. Discuss whether, in absence of written agreement, Rodriguez has a security interest in Thunderbolt *and* whether Rodriguez is a perfected secured party without filing a financing statement.

3. Ray is a seller of electric generators. He purchases a large quantity of generators from manufacturer Martin Corp. by making a down payment and signing a security agreement to make the balance of payments over a period of time. The security agreement gives Martin Corp. a security interest in the generators sold and the proceeds. Martin Corp. files a financing statement on its security interest centrally. Ray receives the generators and immediately sells one of them to Green on an installment contract, with payment to be made in twelve equal installments. At the time of sale, Green knows of Martin's security interest. Two months later Ray goes into default on his payments to Martin. Discuss Martin's rights against purchaser Green in this situation.

4. Martin Corporation is a manufacturer of washing machines. On September 1, in need of working capital,

Martin contacts Smith, a loan officer for the First Bank. Martin asks to borrow $200,000, putting up all its equipment as security. Smith agrees to make the loan. In the security agreement signed by Martin's president is a clause stating that this loan is secured not only by the existing equipment presently located at Martin's plant but by any equipment acquired in the future by Martin. The First Bank files a financing statement centrally on *September 5*. On *November 1* Martin has an opportunity to purchase from Daniel Equipment Corporation some newly manufactured Daniel equipment at a bargain price of $50,000. On that same date Martin contracts by a security agreement to purchase the equipment from Daniel, paying $20,000 down and the balance in monthly payments over a three-year period, with Daniel having a security interest in the purchased equipment. The new equipment is delivered on *December 1*. On *December 7* Daniel perfects its security interest in the newly delivered equipment by filing a financing statement centrally. Later Martin goes into default to both parties. Discuss who has priority over the new equipment, the First Bank or Daniel.

5. Ray is a retail seller of television sets. Ray sells a color television set to Clara for her apartment for $600. Clara cannot pay cash and signs a security agreement, paying $100 down and agreeing to pay the balance in twelve equal installments of $50 each. The security agreement gives Ray a security interest in the television set sold. Clara makes six payments on time; then she goes into default because of unexpected financial problems. Ray repossesses the set and wants to keep it in full satisfaction of the debt. Discuss Ray's rights and duties in this matter.

6. Denise owns and operates a successful restaurant. One year ago she borrowed money from West Bank to make two purchases, an expensive television set for her home and a piece of restaurant equipment. Denise signed security agreements for both purchases with West Bank, giving West Bank a security interest in all of the collateral. West Bank filed a financing statement locally for perfection of its security interest in the television set and centrally for the restaurant equipment. Denise has now made the last payments on both. Discuss West Bank's duties and liabilities to Denise for its failure to file termination statements on the security interests.

7. Canna loaned Diodato a sum of money for the purchase of an automobile. Diodato signed a promissory note and procured a title certificate for the automobile. The title certificate included a typed notation designating Canna

as a secured party. First County National Bank sued Diodato for money that Diodato owed the bank. The bank obtained a judgment against Diodato and attempted to levy execution upon the automobile in Diodato's possession. When it did, it became aware of Canna's claim of a prior lien. The bank then attempted to have Canna's lien set aside. Did Diodato and Canna create a valid security interest in the automobile in Canna's favor? [First County Nat'l. Bank and Trust Co. v. Canna, 124 N.J. Super. 154, 305 A.2d 442 (1973)]

8. Federal Bank made a loan to Pre-Fab in the amount of $325,000. In return for the loan, Pre-Fab signed a promissory note and entered into a security agreement whereby Federal Bank took a security interest in Pre-Fab's assets, accounts receivable, and monies due. Federal Bank immediately filed a financing statement that described in detail all of the above items. Pre-Fab subsequently acquired two promissory notes for the sale of some stock it owned. It used these notes as security for a second loan from a different bank. Federal Bank claims priority in the notes by virtue of its prior filing. Does Federal Bank have a perfected security interest in the notes and other described items? [Bowles v. City Nat'l Bank and Trust Co., 537 P.2d 1219 (Okl.App.1975)]

9. In 1969 Jones and Percell executed a promissory note and a security agreement covering a converted military aircraft built in the 1950s. Upon default, the Bank of Nevada repossessed the aircraft. After providing the required notice to Jones and Percell, the bank placed advertisements in several trade journals as well as in major newspapers in several large cities. In addition, the bank sent 2,000 brochures to 240 sales organizations. A sales representative was hired to market the aircraft. The plane was later sold for $71,000 to an aircraft broker, who in turn resold it for $123,000 after spending $33,000 on modifications. Since the price obtained on the sale of the plane was about $75,000 less than the amount Jones and Percell owed the bank, the bank initiated a lawsuit to obtain the amount of the deficiency. Can Jones and Percell object to the bank's manner of resale? [Jones v. Bank of Nevada, 91 Nev. 368, 535 P.2d 1279 (1975)]

10. Mueller bought a 32-foot motor boat for a cash sale price of $29,000. Part of the sale was financed by Chemical Bank. The retail installment contract security agreement was assigned to Chemical on June 15, 1976. Ten days after the assignment, Chemical Bank filed a financing statement. Approximately a year later, Mueller, now representing himself as Lawrence J. Miller, traded the 32-foot boat in on a 36-foot boat at Miller Yacht Sales. Mueller made a down payment of $2,000. He was given a trade-in allowance of $22,500. The balance due was financed with another bank. When Miller Yacht Sales took possession of the 32-foot boat as Mueller's trade-in, it resold it to someone else. Then Mueller defaulted on his payments on the original retail installment contract to Chemical Bank and disappeared. Chemical Bank notified Miller Yacht Sales that it had a security interest. Since Miller Yacht Sales had already resold the boat, Chemical brought suit against Miller Yacht Sales. What was the result? [Chemical Bank v. Miller Yacht Sales, 173 N.J.Super. 90, 413 A.2d 619 (1980)]

11. In July of 1978, Dr. Jose B. Namer executed to Citizens and Southern National Bank a note in the amount of $35,000 with an accompanying security agreement in the following property: "All equipment of the debtor of every description used or useful in the conduct of the debtor's business, now or hereafter existing or acquired . . . . The listed assets held for collateral are presently located at 4385 Hugh Howell Rd., Tucker, Ga." In July of 1980 Dr. Namer moved some of his equipment to a new office owned by Hudson Properties, Inc. in Fairburn, Georgia. In order to finance this move, Dr. Namer procured a loan from a Fairburn bank, and Hudson co-signed the note. The Fairburn bank prepared a security agreement covering the same equipment as the 1978 security agreement. In September of 1980 Dr. Namer defaulted on the first note and absconded with the equipment in the Fairburn office. Hudson received an insurance payment as cash proceeds for the missing equipment. Citizens and Southern National Bank claim priority rights to the missing equipment or proceeds even though the equipment was moved to Fairburn. Can Citizens and Southern National Bank recover this insurance money from Hudson? [Hudson Properties, Inc. v. Citizens & Southern National Bank, 168 Ga.App. 331, 308 S.E.2d 708 (1983)]

FOCUS ON ETHICS

Commercial Transactions and the Uniform Commercial Code

Transactions involving the sale of goods constitute a major portion of business activity in the commercial and manufacturing sectors of this economy. Since the 1960s, the sale of goods has been governed by the Uniform Commercial Code in virtually every state. Many of the Code provisions express our ethical standards. Much of the conduct of businesspersons in the business world has an ethical basis.

INDEFINITENESS IN THE SALES CONTRACT

It would seem that the requirements for the formation of the sales contract would be detailed and explicit. In fact, there is no contract if the terms are unduly indefinite. However, the UCC [2–204(3)] states that a sales contract will not fail for indefiniteness even if one or more terms are left open, so long as the parties intend to make the contract and there is a reasonably certain basis for the court to grant an appropriate remedy. For example, there can be open price and quantity terms, open delivery terms, and open payment terms, and a valid contract will still exist.

Yet the tolerance for indefiniteness in contracts was not always so great. Older common law cases required a much higher degree of specificity with respect to the terms of a contract. In the often-cited case of *Sun Printing and Publishing Assn.* v. *Remington Paper & Power Co., Inc.* [235 N.Y. 338 (1923)], Judge Cardozo, writing for the New York Court of Appeals, held that the contract that stated that the price of the newsprint was to be agreed upon by the parties, but in no event was the price to be higher than the contract price charged by the Canadian Export Paper Company, failed for indefiniteness. Cardozo concluded that since the contract did not specify how the fluctuations in the Canadian price were to affect the contract price, it must fail. But over time, society's perceptions of the contracting environment, as well as its ideas on fairness, have changed. Thus, a lesser degree of specificity is presently tolerated with respect to the terms of a contract.

As long as the court determines that the parties have intended to make a contract and that there is any reasonably certain basis for granting a remedy, it may attempt to supply the missing term. The Code attempts to maximize the probability that two willing parties will engage in a mutually beneficial economic transaction. Underlying this effort is the notion that commercial transactions form the basis of our country's economic well-being. Rather than make such transactions difficult, the UCC attempts to facilitate commercial transactions.

Businesspersons at times try to take advantage of the flexibility of the UCC's requirements for a valid sales contract. Occasionally, one reads of a business scandal in which an unscrupulous seller, for example, requires buyers of a product to sign a written sales contract with a number of blanks. The contract's blanks are filled in later in a manner not agreed upon by the two parties prior to signature. Our shared beliefs reject the notion that businesspersons should be able to take advantage of customers in such a way. And, in fact, both the competitive nature of the marketplace and the UCC's imposition of an obligation of good faith and commercial reasonableness in the performance of every contract minimize the success of unscrupulous businesspersons who desire to operate in an unethical fashion.

THE EFFECT OF A COMPETITIVE MARKETPLACE

The competitive marketplace limits unethical behavior by

businesspersons. Virtually all successful businesses, particularly those dealing in goods, must have "repeat" customers to be successful. Unethical dealings with customers invariably become publicly known, and hence repeat customers dwindle as well as act as deterrents to other potential customers. In this type of situation, the unethical businessperson will often eventually go out of business. Unfortunately for the consumer, this process may take a long time. And during this time, some consumers will be harmed.

GOOD FAITH AND COMMERCIAL REASONABLENESS

"Good faith" and "commercial reasonableness" are two key concepts that permeate the Uniform Commercial Code and help to prevent the success of unethical behavior by businesspersons. These standards are objective, even though the terms are subjective.

The concepts of good faith and commercial reasonableness are read into every contract and impose certain duties on all parties. Section 2–311(1) indicates that when parties leave the particulars of performance to be specified by one of the parties, "[a]ny such specification must be made in good faith and within limits set by commercial reasonableness." The requirement of commercial reasonableness means that the term subsequently supplied should not come as a surprise to one party. Thus, commercial reasonableness indicates that there is a permissible variation that is determined according to commercial standards. Courts frequently look to course of dealing, usage of trade, and the surrounding circumstances in determining commercial reasonableness.

Even though all commercial actions, including performance and enforcement of contract terms, must exhibit commercial reasonableness, the UCC makes it clear that innocent parties can be excused from certain types of nonperformance. Nonperformance of a contract may be excused when the nonperformance is the result of a commercially reasonable intervening phenomenon. Indeed, the doctrine of commercial impracticability relies on a theory of reasonablility. The fact that the word "reasonable" appears about ninety times in Article II of the UCC demonstrates the UCC's opposition to imposing undue hardship upon merchants and upon those with whom they deal. A merchant is expected to act in a reasonable manner according to reasonable commercial customs. Also, throughout the UCC merchants are held to a higher standard than are nonmerchants. Under UCC 2–314(1), for example, a warranty that goods shall be merchantable is only implied in a contract for their sale if the seller is "a merchant with respect to goods of that kind." This higher standard clearly represents an ideal that the drafters of the UCC were seeking.

With respect to good faith, under previous law, the only time this concept was discussed in any detail was normally in an equitable proceeding where the "ethics" of a situation has always been emphasized more strongly (for example, "He who seeks equity must do equity"). By making good faith a clear obligation in every contract for the sale of goods, and then defining good faith as *honesty in fact,* the drafters of the UCC are stating a very broad policy principle—one that maintains a high standard. Present UCC law does not require that actions be "fair," only that they be honest in fact.

The concept of good faith, which is read into every contract, implies that one party will not take advantage of another party by manipulating contract terms. Furthermore, it is implicitly understood that good faith applies to both *actions* and *intent.* The obligation of good faith is particularly important in "requirements" and "output" contracts. Requirements contracts provide that the buyer purchase all of his or her needs for a specific good from the seller. An output contract provides that the buyer will purchase the seller's entire output. Without the obligation of good faith, it is clear that the potential for abuse would be tremendous. If, for example, the cost of producing the good that is the subject of a requirements contract suddenly increases and the market price of the good unexpectedly quadruples, the buyer could claim that his or her needs are now equivalent to the entire output of the seller. Then, after buying all the seller's output at a price that is substantially below the market price, the buyer could turn around and resell the goods the buyer does not need for his or her own use at the new, higher market price.

Under the UCC, however, this type of unethical behavior is prohibited. Even though contracts that call for the buyer to purchase all of his or her needs from the seller are explicitly authorized under the Code, such contracts are construed to involve actual requirements that may occur in good faith. Under UCC 2–306(1), no quantity "unreasonably disproportionate to any stated estimate or in the absence of a stated estimate to any normal or otherwise comparable prior output or requirements may be tendered or demanded." Thus, the requirements of "good faith" and of not demanding a quantity "unreasonably disproportionate" make it clear that *no speculation* is allowed under requirements contracts. The UCC reflects ethical considerations in prohibiting such abuses of contracts.

WARRANTIES

The higher standard to which merchants must conform carries over to warranties. The term "warranty" is used in the UCC to reflect a promise or a guarantee made by a seller of goods that these goods will have certain characteristics. In expressing ideas of fairness in particular situations, the UCC makes it difficult for merchants to disclaim warranties and requires that any such disclaimers be conspicuous. In other words, disclaimers must not be hidden.

Both express and implied warranties are recognized by the Code. Under UCC 2–314(2) goods sold by a merchant must be fit for the ordinary purposes for which such goods are used, be of proper quality, and be properly labeled and packaged. A description of goods is an express warranty, and, hence, a seller of goods may be found in breach of contract if the goods fail to conform to the previously made description. Recognizing

descriptions as express warranties is an effort by the Code to inject greater fairness into contractual situations. The UCC acknowledges the fact that a buyer may often reasonably believe that a seller is warranting his or her product, even though the seller may not use formal words such as "warrant" or "guarantee." Thus, the law imposes an ethical obligation upon merchants in statutory form.

It is generally believed that the implied warranties of merchantability and fitness for a particular purpose are necessary to help the consumer in a world of complex problems (although some scholars have argued that, in fact, the UCC sections addressing disclaimer, waiver, and modification, when properly used, have *reduced* the effectiveness of such warranty protection for the consumer). The creation of the Consumer Product Safety Commission (CPSC) occurred after numerous congressional studies showed a need for greater consumer protection. The CPSC presumably was created because the marketplace somehow failed to provide products that were sufficiently safe. Apparently, it was concluded that the warranty provisions of the UCC had failed to provide adequate protection for consumers.

The businessperson has not only a legal obligation to provide safe products, but also an ethical one. When faced with the possibility of providing additional safety at no extra cost, every ethical businessperson will indeed opt for a safer product. At issue, however, is the policy relating to what a producer should do when a safer product requires

higher costs and therefore higher consumer prices. The marketplace presumably will determine the optimal level of safety; however, that level has been deemed too low by many, and for this reason the Consumer Product Safety Commission was created. Arguably, unsafe products lead to social costs because injured individuals must sometimes receive medical care, and often at public expense. Furthermore, dependents of injured individuals may find themselves in financial difficulties and require "welfare" payments from the state.

PRODUCTS LIABILITY

The broader issue of products liability is certainly susceptible to the same analysis. Section 402A of the Restatement, Second, Torts, embodies a doctrine of strict tort liability. The doctrine of strict liability implies that even if the consumer is careless, the manufacturer is liable for any resulting damages from a defective product. This result leads not only to an ethical question but to an economic-efficiency question as well. As increasing liability is imposed upon manufacturers, consumers have less incentive to be careful when they use products. In the insurance industry, this phenomenon is called *moral hazard.* An important question therefore arises: To what extent should consumers be responsible for their own actions? No one has ethical qualms about requiring that the manufacturer of an exploding soft drink bottle pay for damages, but what about a situation where a user of a rotary lawn mower leaves it running and sticks his or her hand underneath to remove a rock and is subsequently injured? Should the manufacturer of the lawn mower be held 100 percent liable for such damages? Or should the user of the machinery be completely responsible for his or her negligent action? Or is there a middle ground?

The fact is that whatever rule of liability is decided upon, future activities will be affected. For example, the Consumer Product Safety Commission may require that all lawn mowers be made in such a way that it is impossible for anyone, no matter how negligent, to touch a moving blade. This requirement may sound like a "good" rule, but such a rule will require an additional use of resources. After all, the construction of safer lawn mowers costs more. These costs will be passed on to the consumer. We then must ask an economic question: What are the costs and what are the benefits? If the anticipated aggregate costs of protection far exceed the anticipated long-run benefits, should the Consumer Product Safety Commission be allowed to pass such a rule? Or do we have an ethical obligation, no matter what the economic cost, to provide maximum safety for every product that is generated in our economic system?

CHECKS AND THE BANKING SYSTEM

Numerous moral and ethical questions face members of the banking community. Banks and other financial institutions offer a variety of services to their customers. Some financial institutions would certainly like to prevent customers from using stop-payment orders. Stop payment occurs when a financial institution permits its customers to stop payment on a check for whatever reason. The marketplace, as well as custom and law, nonetheless provides for the customer's use of such stop payments. How much should a bank or other financial institution be allowed to charge a customer for the use of a stop payment? If the bank or other financial institution charges too much for this service, is it in fact effectively removing that service by over-pricing it? The same issue applies to returned checks (usually for insufficient funds). What is the appropriate bank charge?

DISCUSSION QUESTIONS

1. To what extent does competition in the marketplace obviate the need for ethical business standards?
2. Should the question of product safety be decided according to economic analysis only? Or is product safety simply an ethical consideration? How far removed is economic analysis from ethical considerations here?
3. Can a human life be subjected to a cost-benefit analysis? For example, consider the following situation: A rule is proposed that will require all commercial airlines to use jets that have two additional emergency exit doors. Given the average number of airline crashes per year and the average number of individuals injured or killed in such crashes, it is estimated that the new safety standard will save an additional ten lives per year. Should the standard therefore be instituted? What if it costs $10 million? $50 million? $3 billion? To what extent, if any, is cost relevant where human life is concerned?

UNIT IV

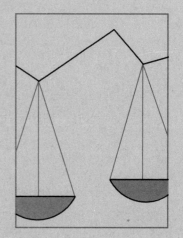

CREDITORS' RIGHTS AND BANKRUPTCY

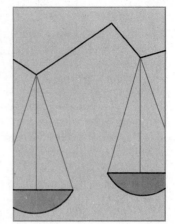

30

Rights of Debtors and Creditors

The law of debtor-creditor relations has undergone various changes over the years. Historically, debtors and their families have been subjected to terrible punishment for their inability to pay debts, including involuntary servitude, imprisonment, and dismemberment. The modern legal system has moved away from a punishment philosophy in dealing with debtors. In fact, many people say that it has moved too far in the other direction, to the detriment of creditors. Today, consumer protection is emphasized, and the legal system is designed to aid and protect the debtor and the debtor's family.

This chapter deals with various rights and remedies available through statutory laws, common law, and contract law to assist the debtor and creditor in resolving their disputes without the debtor having to resort to bankruptcy. The next chapter discusses bankruptcy as a so-called last resort to resolve debtor-creditor problems.

LAWS ASSISTING CREDITORS

Mechanic's Lien on Real Property

When a person contracts for labor, services, or material to be furnished for the purpose of making improvements on real property but does not immediately pay for the improvements, a creditor can place a **mechanic's lien** on the property. This creates a special type of debtor-creditor relationship wherein the real estate itself becomes security for the lien (debt).

For example, a roofer repairs a leaky roof at the request of a homeowner. The homeowner owes the roofer the agreed-upon price for the materials, labor, and services performed. If the homeowner cannot pay or pays only a portion of the charges, a mechanic's lien against the property can be created. The roofer is the lienholder, and the real property is encumbered with a mechanic's lien for the amount owed. If the homeowner does not pay the lien, the property can be sold to satisfy the debt.

The procedures by which a mechanic's lien is created are controlled by state statutory law. Generally, the lienholder must file a written notice of lien against the particular property involved. The notice of lien must be filed within a specific time period, measured from the last date that materials or labor were provided (usually within 60 to 120 days). Failure to pay the debt entitles the lienholder to foreclose on the real estate where the improvements were made and to sell it in order to satisfy the amount of the debt. Of course, the lienholder is required by statute to give notice to the owner of the property prior to foreclosure and sale. The sale proceeds are used to pay the debt and the costs of the legal proceedings, and the surplus, if any, is paid to the former owner.

Artisan's and Hotelkeeper's Liens on Personal Property

An **artisan's lien** and a **hotelkeeper's lien** are security devices, created at common law, similar to a mechanic's lien but used to charge personal property with the payment of a debt for labor done, for value added, or for caring for the personal property (bailee or warehousing costs).

For example, Ann leaves her watch at the jeweler's to be repaired and to have her initials engraved on the back. In absence of agreement, the jeweler can keep the watch until Ann pays for the repairs and services that the jeweler provides. Should Ann fail to pay, the jeweler has a lien on Ann's watch for the amount of the bill and can sell the watch in satisfaction of the lien.

An artisan's lien is a *possessory lien*. The lienholder ordinarily must have retained possession of the property and have expressly or impliedly agreed to provide the services on a *cash, not a credit, basis*. Usually the lienholder retains possession of the property. When this occurs, the lien remains in existence as long as the lienholder maintains possession and is terminated once possession is voluntarily surrendered—unless the surrender is only temporary. If it is a temporary surrender, there must be an agreement that the property will be returned to the lienholder. Even with such an agreement, if a third party obtains rights in that property while it is out of the possession of the lienholder, the lien is lost. The only way a lienholder can protect a lien and surrender possession at the same time is to record notice of the lien in accordance with state lien and recording statutes.

Modern statutes permit the holder of an artisan's lien to foreclose and sell the property subject to the lien in order to satisfy payment of the debt. As with the mechanic's lien, the lienholder is required to give notice to the owner of the property prior to foreclosure and selling. The sale proceeds are used to pay the debt and the costs of the legal proceedings, and the surplus, if any, is paid to the former owner.

A hotelkeeper's lien is given on the baggage of guests for the agreed-upon charges that remain unpaid. If no express agreement was made on those charges, then the lien will be the reasonable value of the accommodations furnished. The hotelkeeper's lien is terminated either by the guest's payment of the hotel's charges or by surrender of the baggage to the guests, unless such surrender is temporary. Also, the lien is terminated by conversion of the guest's baggage by the hotelkeeper. Although state statutes permit such conversion by means of a public sale, there is a trend toward requiring that the guest first be given an impartial judicial hearing.[1]

Writ of Execution

A debt must be past due in order for a creditor to commence legal action against a debtor. If the creditor is successful, the court awards the creditor a judgment against the debtor (usually for the amount of the debt plus any interest and legal costs incurred in obtaining the judgment). Attorneys' fees are not included in this amount unless provided for by statute or contract.

Frequently it is easy to secure a judgment, but this is only half the battle. If the debtor does not or cannot pay the judgment, the creditor is entitled to go back to the court and obtain a **writ of execution.** This writ is an order, usually issued by the clerk of the court, directing the sheriff to seize (levy) and sell any of the debtor's nonexempt real or personal property that is within the court's geographic jurisdiction (usually the county in which the courthouse is located). The proceeds of the sale are used to pay off the judgment and the costs of the sale. Any excess is paid to the debtor. The debtor can pay the judgment and redeem the nonexempt property any time before the sale takes place. Because of exemption and bankruptcy laws, many judgments are virtually uncollectible.

Attachment

Attachment is a court-ordered seizure and taking into custody of property that is in controversy over a debt. Attachment rights are created by state statutes. Attachment is normally a *prejudgment* remedy. It occurs either at the time of or immediately after the commencement of a lawsuit but before the entry of a final judgment. By statute, the restrictions and requirements for a creditor to attach before judgment are very specific and limited. The due process clause of the Fourteenth Amendment to the Constitution limits courts' power to authorize seizure of debtors' property without notice to the debtor or a hearing on the facts. In recent years, a number of

---

1. Klim v. Jones, 315 F.Supp. 109 (D.C.N.D.Cal. 1970).

state attachment laws have been held to be unconstitutional.

In order to use attachment as a remedy, the creditor must have an enforceable right to payment of the debt under law and the creditor must follow certain procedures. Otherwise, the creditor can be liable for damages for wrongful attachment. He or she must file with the court an affidavit stating that the debtor is in default and stating the statutory grounds under which attachment is sought. A bond must be posted by the creditor to cover court costs, the value of the loss of use of the good suffered by the debtor, and the value of the property attached. When the

court is satisfied that all the requirements have been met, it issues a **writ of attachment.** This writ is similar to a writ of execution in that it directs the sheriff or other officer to seize nonexempt property. If the creditor prevails at trial, the seized property can be sold to satisfy the judgment.

The following case illustrates that strict compliance with every specific procedure established by the state's attachment statute is required before the property is subject to an enforceable writ of attachment because a writ of attachment operates against a debtor's property simply on the strength of the creditor's sworn statement that a debt is owed.

BACKGROUND AND FACTS *Corcoran was the owner of a large building in Washington, D.C. In April 1976 Eales, a creditor of Corcoran, obtained a prejudgment writ of attachment from a Washington, D.C., court against the building. In June 1976 notice of the writ was posted on the building. In October 1976 Corcoran conveyed the building to Jack Development, Inc. Up to this time, Eales had been unable to serve notice on Corcoran as required by a Washington, D.C., statute. In the alternative, the statute allowed the notice requirement to be fulfilled by a three-week publication of the writ in a local newspaper. Eales first published notice of the writ in February 1977. Jack Development argues that it is the owner since title was transferred to it before the writ "attached"—that is, before the statutory notice requirements had been fulfilled. Eales argues that the writ attached when notice was posted on the building, and therefore Corcoran was unable to transfer clear title.*

JACK DEVELOPMENT, INC. v. HOWARD EALES, INC.
District of Columbia Court of Appeals, 1978.
388 A.2d 466.

PER CURIAM [By the Court—an opinion of the whole court].
*   *   *   *

The sequence of relevant events therefore was:
April 15, 1976—Writ of attachment before judgment issued by trial court against defendant's realty [real estate].
June 21, 1976—Marshal posts realty with writ.
October 19, 1976—Defendant conveys realty to Jack Development, Inc., by quitclaim deed [a deed passing title, but not professing that the title is valid or not containing any warranty for title].
December 10, 1976—Quitclaim deed to realty recorded by Jack Development, Inc.
February 2, 1977—Marshal signs and files the indorsement on the writ of attachment before judgment which he had posted on the realty the previous June.
February 28, 1977—First date of service of process on defendant by publication.
*   *   *   *

Appellant Jack Development argues that it acquired title to the property at 1718 Corcoran Street, N.W., free of the writ of attachment before judgment which had been issued against the transferor, since the defendant transferred his interest *prior to service upon the transferor of the writ of attachment and the indorsement and notice,* as required by D.C.Code 1973, §§ 16-502, -508. *   *   *
*   *   *   *

Initially, we note that because a writ of attachment before judgment is a harsh and drastic remedy, strict compliance with the procedures established by the statute is required. In this case, the delivery of the writ of attachment before judgment to the marshal did create an inchoate [contingent] lien on the defendant's property. The mere posting of the property did *not* comply, however, with the notice procedures mandated by D.C.Code 1973 §§ 16-502, -508.

[The code in Washington, D.C., provides that if a debtor cannot be found within the district, the creditor must obtain a court order granting permission to inform the debtor by publication (for three consecutive weeks) that said debtor must appear and show cause why the property conditionally attached should not be subject to final attachment and sale.]

The statutory requirements were not completed in this case until three weeks after the first date of publication on February 28, 1977. At that time, the attachment normally would relate back to the date of the delivery of the writ to the marshal, *i.e.*, April 15, 1976. Here, however, the defendant during the intervening period had transferred the property by quitclaim deed to Jack Development and appellant had recorded its deed on December 10, 1976—all such dates being prior to appellee's full compliance with the attachment statute.   *   *   *

*   *   *   *

*   *   * Here, a valid transfer occurred before the defendant himself had been given notice of a sufficiently levied writ of attachment in compliance with the statute. D.C.Code 1973, § 16-508. Jack Development therefore took the property free of the writ of attachment which had been sought against the transferor.

DECISION AND REMEDY   *The appellate court quashed the writ of attachment. Jack Development kept title to the property free of the writ of attachment. The judgment of the trial court was reversed.*

COMMENTS   *Attachment does not always prevent a subsequent transfer of the attached property. If the attachment has been perfected under statutory requirements, the transferee takes the property subject to the terms and conditions of the attachment and its underlying lien. The buyer, however, would ordinarily be aware of this, since the public records would indicate it.*

Garnishment

Garnishment is similar to attachment except that it is a collection remedy that is directed not at the debtor but at the debtor's property or rights held by a third person. The third person, the garnishee, owes a debt to the debtor or has property that belongs to the debtor, such as wages or a bank account. The typical garnishee is an employer. The wages an employer owes to the debtor-employee are subject to garnishment. Both state and federal laws, however, permit only a limited portion of the debtor's wages to be garnished.[2]

Federal laws and state laws limit the amount of money that can be garnished from a debtor's weekly take-home pay. Typically, a garnishment judgment will be served on a person's employer so that part of the person's usual paycheck will be paid to the creditor. Federal law provides a minimal framework to protect debtors from losing all their income in order to pay judgment debts.[3] State laws also provide dollar exemptions, and these amounts are often larger than those provided by federal law. State and federal statutes can be applied together to help create a pool of funds sufficient to enable a debtor to continue to provide for family needs while also reducing the amount of the judgment debt in a reasonable way.

---

2.   Some states (for example, Texas) do not permit garnishment of wages by private parties.

3.   For example, the federal Consumer Credit Protection Act, 15 U.S.C.A., Section 1601 et seq., provides that a debtor can retain either 75 percent of the disposable earnings per week or the sum equivalent to thirty hours of work paid at federal minimum wage rates, whichever is greater.

Garnishment of an employee's wages cannot be grounds for dismissal of an employee because federal law prohibits any employer from discharging an employee who has been involved in only one garnishment proceeding.

The legal proceeding for a garnishment action is governed by state law. As a result of a garnishment proceeding, the debtor's employer is ordered by the court to turn over a portion of the debtor's wages to pay the debt. However, garnishment operates differently from state to state. According to the laws in some states, the judgment creditor needs to obtain only one order of garnishment that will then continuously apply to the judgment debtor's weekly wages until the entire debt is paid. In other states, the judgment creditor must go back to court for a separate order of garnishment for each pay period.

The court must always be sure that it is the debtor's property that is actually being taken in a garnishment or attachment proceeding. The following case illustrates that, in a situation where garnishment is sought against property not owned by the debtor, the garnishment will be refused by the courts.

BACKGROUND AND FACTS   *The plaintiff and the defendant were divorced. The defendant was delinquent in making child support payments, and the plaintiff obtained a judgment against him. The plaintiff then sought a writ of garnishment against funds deposited in a checking account held in the defendant's name. The defendant was successful in having the garnishment writ set aside by establishing in the lower court that the funds in the garnished account were not his but belonged to his second wife.*

PETERSON v.
PETERSON
Supreme Court of Utah, 1977.
571 P.2d 1360.

WILKINGS, Justice.
*   *   *   *

At the hearing on defendant's motion to set aside the garnishment execution, the evidence demonstrated that the garnished account was held in defendant's name; that only his name was on the bank's signature card and, therefore, only he was authorized to write checks against the account. However, defendant had not worked for over a year, and the funds in the account were almost exclusively derived from the paychecks of defendant's present wife; and these checks were routinely endorsed to the defendant by her and deposited by him. During the course of the year, defendant did deposit some of his funds in the account, but they amounted to less than $1,000. The money in the account was used for defendant's child support payments to plaintiff, totaling $1,200, as well as for the general living expenses of defendant and his wife. The defendant and his wife each considered the money in the account to be the wife's money though the defendant withdrew for his personal obligations more than he contributed to the account. On the basis of these facts, the District Court found that none of the money belonged to the defendant and all of the funds remaining in the account belonged to defendant's wife, and were not subject to garnishment for the defendant's debts.
*   *   *   *

[The plaintiff insisted that her former husband had the burden of proof to show by clear and convincing evidence that he had no ownership rights to the money in the checking account.]

Among the classes of cases to which this special standard of persuasion (clear and convincing proof) has been applied are the following: (1) charges of fraud, and undue influence, (2) suits on oral contracts to make a will, and suits to establish the terms of a lost will, (3) suits for the specific performance of an oral contract, (4) proceedings to set aside, reform or modify written transactions or official acts on grounds of fraud, mistake or incompleteness, and (5) miscellaneous types of claims and defenses, varying from state to state, where there is thought to be special danger of deception, or where the court considers that the particular type of claim should be disfavored on policy grounds.

We agree with plaintiff that persuasion by defendant of a clear and convincing nature is required in this matter, believing that there is a "special danger of deception" in cases such as this one but hold that the defendant sustained that burden and the evidence below was sufficient to support the Court's finding, especially in view of the fact that both defendant and his present wife testified that defendant had not been working and earning money for a year because of his medical problems and plaintiff presented no evidence to rebut that testimony.

DECISION AND REMEDY   *The judgment was affirmed. The wrongful garnishment was correctly set aside by the lower court.*

Composition of Creditors' Agreements

As discussed in Chapter 9, creditors may contract with a debtor for discharge of the debtor's liquidated debts upon payment of a sum less than that owed. These agreements are called compositions or creditors' composition agreements and are usually held to be enforceable.

Secured Transactions—Article 9

Chapter 29 discussed in detail a secured party's rights upon a debtor's default. One such right is the repossession of the collateral upon breach of the security agreement. Upon repossession, the secured party has the right to keep the collateral in full satisfaction of the debt (unless there is a purchase money security interest in consumer goods with 60 percent or more of the price paid or unless proper objection is received). Alternatively, the secured party may sell the collateral and use the proceeds to discharge the debt. If the proceeds are insufficient to cover the balance owed, the secured party is entitled to a deficiency judgment and can proceed with a writ of execution, as previously discussed. Therefore, either way, a debt resolution can be accomplished.

Assignment for Benefit of Creditors

Both common law and statutes may provide for a debtor's assignment of assets to a trustee or assignee for the benefit of the debtor's creditors. In these situations the debtor voluntarily transfers title to assets owned to a trustee or assignee, who in turn sells

or liquidates these assets, tendering payment to the debtor's creditors on a pro rata basis.

The creditors have a choice of accepting or rejecting the tender. Those who accept it effectively discharge the debt owed to them. Those who do not accept it can proceed against any remaining non-exempt assets, or they may elect to petition the debtor into involuntary bankruptcy. This differs from a composition of creditors' arrangement in that there is no agreement made between the debtor and creditors as to the amount acceptable to discharge the debt.

Suretyship and Guaranty

When a third person promises to pay a debt owed by another in the event the debtor does not pay, a suretyship or guaranty relationship is created. Exhibit 30–1 illustrates these relationships. The third person's credit becomes the security for the debt owed.

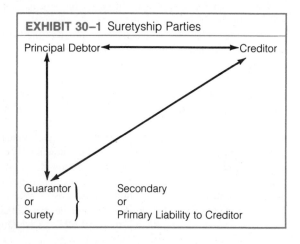

EXHIBIT 30–1 Suretyship Parties

Principal Debtor ⟷ Creditor

Guarantor or Surety } Secondary or Primary Liability to Creditor

Surety   A contract of strict suretyship is a promise made by a third person to be responsible for the debtor's obligation. Suretyship is an express contract between the surety and the creditor. The surety in the strictest sense is *primarily* liable for the debt of the principal. The creditor can demand payment from the surety from the moment that the debt is due. A suretyship is not a form of indemnity; that is, it is not merely a promise to make good any loss that a creditor may incur as a result of the debtor's failure to pay. The creditor need not exhaust all legal remedies against the principal debtor before holding the surety responsible for payment. A surety agreement does not have to be in writing to be enforceable, but it usually is.

For example, David Brown wants to borrow money from the bank to buy a used car. Because David is still in college, the bank will not lend him the money unless his father, John Brown, who has dealt with the bank before, will co-sign the note. When Mr. Brown co-signs the note he becomes primarily liable to the bank. On the note's due date the bank has the option to seek payment from either David or Mr. Brown or both, jointly.

Guaranty   A guaranty contract is similar to a suretyship in that it includes a promise to answer for the debt or default of another. With suretyship, however, the surety is primarily liable for the debtor's obligation of the principal. With a guaranty arrangement, the guarantor—the third person making the guaranty—is *secondarily* liable. The guarantor can be required to pay the obligation only after the debtor defaults, and then usually only after the creditor has made an attempt to collect from the principal debtor.

For example, a closely held corporation, A. B. Corporation, needs to borrow money to meet its payroll. The bank is skeptical about the credit worthiness of A. B., and requires Smith, A. B.'s president and a wealthy business man who owns seventy percent of A. B., to sign an agreement making Smith personally liable for payment if A. B. does not pay off the loan. Smith is a guarantor of the loan, and the bank cannot hold Smith liable until A. B. Corporation is in default.

A guaranty contract between the guarantor and creditor must be in writing to be enforceable unless the "main purpose" exception applies. Briefly, this exception provides that if the main purpose of the guaranty agreement is to benefit the guarantor, then the contract need not be in writing to be enforceable. (See Chapter 13 for a more detailed discussion.)

The guaranty contract terms determine the extent and time of the guarantor's liability. For example, a guaranty can be *continuing*, designed to cover a series of transactions by the debtor. Also, the guaranty can be *unlimited* or *limited* as to time and amount. In addition, the guaranty can be *absolute*, wherein the guarantor becomes liable immediately upon the debtor's default, or *conditional*, wherein the guarantor becomes liable only upon the happening of a certain event.

The following case discusses the characteristics of a guaranty relationship between the borrower and the guarantor.

BACKGROUND AND FACTS   *On November 3, 1972, Gilbert Gonzales, the defendant, executed a promissory note for the sum of $1,500. This note was subsequently assigned to Commerce Bank of Kansas City, Missouri, which demanded repayment from the defendant when the note was due under its terms. Defendant never made repayment of the note and went into default in August of 1974. However, repayment of the note was guaranteed by the United States under a federal program of student loan insurance, and the United States repaid the note in February of 1976. The United States seeks recovery from Gonzales. On guarantees of student loans, there is a six-year statute of limitations from the date the action accrues. Gonzales claims that the United States is a mere assignee of the Commerce Bank, and that the statute bars the United States' action against him. The United States claims that it is a guarantor and that the statute begins on the date of its repayment of the student loan to the Commerce Bank.*

UNITED STATES v.
GONZALES
United States District Court,
Kansas, 1982.
541 F.Supp. 783.

SAFFELS, District Judge.

*   *   *   *

A surety or guarantor is one who promises to answer for the debt, default, or miscarriage of another. *   *   * The distinguishing feature of a guaranty is that the obligation is collateral to another's contractual duty to perform. Thus, if the obligation sought to be enforced is a primary or unconditional promise, so that the promisor is primarily liable, independent of the failure of some other party to perform his contractual duty, then the obligation is not a contract of guaranty. It is clear from the language of the Act that the government was liable to the lender only upon default by the student borrower. 20 U.S.C. § 1080(a). Thus, the obligation of the United States is collateral to the student's contractual duty to repay his loan. The Court therefore concludes that the law of guaranty applies to this case.

A guarantor or surety who discharges the obligation of its principal is entitled to be reimbursed by the principal. The language of the Act does not limit the government to the rights of an assignee, and does not destroy this common-law right of a surety or guarantor to seek reimbursement from the principal obligator. The statute of limitations does not begin to run on the surety's cause of action against the principal until the surety has made a payment on the debt to the creditor. In its status as a surety or guarantor, the statute of limitations began to run against the United States only when the United States paid the Commerce Bank on February 26, 1976.

The Court therefore concludes that the statute of limitations does not bar this lawsuit. Plaintiff is entitled to judgment as a matter of law.

*   *   *   *

DECISION AND REMEDY   *The Court held the United States to be a guarantor and that the statute of limitations began on the date of repayment of the student loan. The Court ordered that the plaintiff's motion for summary judgment be granted.*

COMMENTS   *If the United States had been an assignee of the note rather than a guarantor, the statute of limitations would have begun to run against the United States upon defendant's default, and the United States would not have been able to recover.*

The rights and defenses of the surety and guarantor are basically the same. Therefore, the following discussion applies to both.

Defenses of the Surety   A creditor must try to prevent certain actions that will release the surety from the obligation. Any material change made in the terms of the original contract between the principal debtor and the creditor, including the awarding of a binding extension of time for making payment without first obtaining the consent of the surety, will discharge the surety either completely or to the extent that the surety suffers a loss.

When a creditor discharges the principal debtor (or debtors), discharge of any one of them releases the surety from any obligation unless the surety agrees to the discharge. Naturally, if the principal obliga-tion is paid by the debtor or by another person on behalf of the debtor, the surety is discharged from obligation. Similarly, if valid tender of payment is made, and the creditor for some reason rejects it with knowledge of the surety's existence, then the surety is released from any obligation on the debt.

Generally, any defenses available to a principal debtor can be used by the surety to avoid liability on the obligation to the creditor; the defenses that cannot be used are incapacity, bankruptcy, and the statute of limitations. The ability of the surety to assert any defenses the debtor may have against the creditor is the most important concept in suretyship, since most defenses available to the surety are those of the debtor.

Obviously, a surety may have his or her own defenses—for example, incapacity or bankruptcy.

Another defense is when the creditor fraudulently induced the surety to guaranty the debt of the debtor. In most states, prior to formation of the suretyship contract, the creditor has a legal duty to inform the surety of material facts known by the creditor that would materially increase the surety's risk. Failure to so inform is fraud and makes the suretyship obligation voidable.

In addition, if a creditor surrenders or impairs the debtor's collateral while knowing of the surety and without the surety's consent, the surety is released to the extent that the surety would suffer a loss from the creditor's actions. The primary reason for this is to protect the surety who agreed to become obligated only because the debtor's collateral was in the possession of the creditor.

Rights of the Surety   When the surety pays the debt owed to the creditor, the surety is entitled to certain rights. First, the surety has a legal **right of subrogation**. Simply stated, this means that any right the creditor had against the debtor now becomes the right of the surety. Included are creditor rights in bankruptcy, rights to collateral possessed by the creditor, and rights to judgments secured by the creditor. In short, the surety now stands in the shoes of the creditor.

Second, the surety has a **right of reimbursement** from the debtor. This right either stems from the suretyship contract or from equity. Basically, the surety is entitled to receive from the debtor all outlays the surety has made on behalf of the suretyship arrangement. This can include expenses incurred as well as the actual amount of the debt paid the creditor.

Third, if there are co-sureties (two or more sureties on the same obligation owed by the debtor), a surety who pays more than his or her proportionate share upon a debtor's default is entitled to recover from the co-sureties the amount paid above the surety's obligation. This is referred to as the surety's **right of contribution**. Generally, a co-surety's liability either is determined by agreement or, in absence of agreement, is set at the maximum liability under the suretyship contract.

For example, two co-sureties are obligated under a suretyship contract to guarantee the debt of a debtor. One surety's maximum liability is $15,000, and the other's is $10,000. The debtor owes $10,000 and is in default. The surety with the $15,000 maximum

liability pays the creditor the entire $10,000. In the absence of other agreement, this surety can recover $4,000 from the other surety ($10,000/$25,000 × $10,000 = $4,000, this co-surety's obligation).

Mortgage
Foreclosure on Real Property

A real estate mortgage agreement provides that when the **mortgagor** (debtor/borrower) *defaults* in making payment in accordance with the terms of the agreement, the **mortgagee** (creditor/lender) can declare that the entire mortgage debt is due immediately. The mortgagee/creditor can enforce payment in full by a legal action called **foreclosure.**

There are four statutory methods of foreclosure permitted in the United States:

1.   Strict foreclosure—permitted in only a few states. Upon default and after a specified period, the mortgagee acquires absolute title to the property.
2.   Entry or writ of entry—permitted in only a few states. Upon default, the mortgagee gets a writ entitling him or her to possession; after a specified statutory period, the mortgagee receives absolute title.
3.   Power of sale—permitted in most states. Instead of following a statutory judicial sale of the property, the sale provisions are stated in the mortgage agreement.
4.   Foreclosure sale—usual method (to be discussed). Statutory procedures must be followed to protect the rights of the mortgagor.

A **deed of trust** is used in some states as being basically equivalent to a mortgage. The major difference between a mortgage and a deed of trust is that the legal title to the real property is placed with a trustee to secure payment of the loan for the realty. In most states, upon the debtor's default, the terms of the deed of trust and the statutory treatment thereof results in a foreclosure similar to a mortgage.

Foreclosure Sales   In this action, the real estate that is covered by the mortgage is sold at a judicial sale.[4]

---

4.   This is true even if the property is the debtor's homestead. A mortgage is one debt that is *not* subject to the homestead statutory exemption that exempts the homestead from execution of any general debts of a householder or head of a family.

If the proceeds of the sale are sufficient to cover both the costs of the foreclosure and the mortgaged debt, any surplus is received by the debtor. If, on the other hand, the sale proceeds are insufficient to cover the foreclosure costs and the mortgaged debt, the mortgagee can seek to recover the difference from the mortgagor by obtaining a *deficiency judgment*. This type of judgment represents the "deficiency amount"—that is, the difference between the mortgaged debt and the amount actually received from the proceeds of the foreclosure sale. A deficiency judgment is obtained in a separate legal action that is pursued subsequent to the foreclosure action. It entitles the creditor to recover from other nonexempt property owned by the debtor. A number of states do not allow for a deficiency judgment for certain types of real estate interests.

From the time of default until the time of the foreclosure sale, a mortgagor can redeem the property by paying the full amount of the debt, plus any interest and other costs that have accrued. This mortgagor's right is known as the **equity of redemption.** In some states, the mortgagor may even redeem within a statutory period after the judicial sale. This is called a **statutory period of redemption**, and the deed to the property is usually not delivered to the purchaser until the expiration of this period.

Bulk Sales—Article 6 of the UCC

As discussed in Chapter 18, a creditor may have certain rights when a seller-debtor sells a substantial portion of the assets of the business to a purchaser. This is referred to as a bulk sale or transfer—that is, one not normally made in the seller's ordinary course of business. Because a creditor's recovery against the debtor could be substantially diminished with the sale of bulk assets being transferred to an innocent purchaser, the Code treats such transfer as a potential fraud on creditors.

To avoid any possibility of fraud and protect the rights of the creditors and of the purchaser of the bulk goods, the UCC sets forth certain procedures for bulk transfers. Basically, the bulk seller is required to give the purchaser a sworn list of creditors, and the purchaser is obligated to give the seller's creditors notice of the pending sale at least ten days prior to payment or to the purchaser taking possession. Creditors who receive notice must act within that ten-day period or their claims are cut off by the sale to the purchaser. However, any creditor not receiving notice of the sale can take action against the debtor-seller and levy against the goods so transferred to the purchaser for a period of up to six months. In this way, creditors' interests are protected in the bulk transfer of a debtor's business assets.

Fraudulent Conveyances

As also discussed in Chapter 18, any conveyance by a debtor through sale (or gift) to a third person that is expressly or impliedly *fraudulent* allows the creditor to set aside the transfer and proceed against the property (even if the property is in the possession of a third person).

There are two types of fraud: fraud in fact and fraud implied in law. Fraud in fact is the transfer of the property with the *intent* to defraud the creditor. Fraud implied in law occurs when the transfer is made in such a manner that a non-merchant transferor retains *possession* (and usually the use) of the property. In the latter case fraud is presumed, but it can be rebutted.

PROTECTION OF THE DEBTOR

Exemptions

In most states, certain types of real and personal property are exempt from levy of execution or attachment. Probably the most familiar of these exemptions is the **homestead exemption.** Each state permits the debtor to retain the family home, either in its entirety or up to a specified dollar amount, free from the claims of unsecured creditors or trustees in bankruptcy. The purpose is to insure that the debtor will retain some form of shelter.

For example, Daniels owes Carey $40,000. The debt is the subject of a lawsuit, and the court awards Carey a judgment of $40,000 against Daniels. The homestead of Daniels is valued at $50,000. There are no outstanding mortgages or other liens on his homestead. To satisfy the judgment debt, Daniels's family home is sold at public auction for $45,000. Assume the homestead exemption is $25,000. The

CONCEPT SUMMARY	Remedies Available To Creditors
REMEDIES	**DEFINITIONS**
Mechanic's Lien	A nonpossessory, filed lien on an owner's real estate for labor, services, or materials furnished to or made on the realty.
Artisan's and Hotelkeeper's Liens	A possessory lien on an owner's personal property for labor performed, value added, or care of said personal property which was not paid for.
Writ of Execution	In cases of unsatisfied judgments, a court order directing the sheriff to seize and sell sufficient nonexempt property of the judgment debtor to satisfy the judgment.
Attachment	A court-ordered seizure of property (generally prior to full resolution of the creditor's rights resulting in judgment). Attachment is only available upon posting of bond and in strict compliance with the applicable state statutes.
Garnishment	A collection remedy that allows the creditor to attach a debtor's money (such as wages owed or bank accounts) and property that is held by a third person.
Suretyship or Guaranty	Under contract, a third person agrees to be primarily or secondarily liable for the debt owed by the principal debtor. A creditor can turn to this third person for satisfaction of the debt.
Secured Transaction UCC Article 9	Upon the debtor's default, a secured party has the right to repossess collateral subject to the secured party's security interest and either keep or sell the collateral to satisfy the debt.
Mortgage Foreclosure	Upon the debtor's default, the entire mortgage debt is due and payable, allowing the creditor to foreclose on the realty by selling it or taking title to it to satisfy the debt.
Composition of Creditors' Agreements	A contract between the debtor and creditors whereby the debtor's debts are discharged by payment of a sum less than that owed in the original debt.
Assignment for Benefit of Creditors	The debtor assigns certain assets to a trustee or assignee, who sells or liquidates these assets and tenders payments to creditors on a pro rata basis. Acceptance of this payment by a creditor is discharge of the debt.
Fraudulent Conveyance (Express or Implied)	If a conveyance is fraudulent, the creditor may set aside the transfer to a third party and proceed against the property conveyed.

proceeds of the sale are distributed as follows:

1. Daniels is paid $25,000 as his homestead exemption.

2. Carey is paid $20,000 toward the judgment debt, leaving a $20,000 deficiency judgment (that is, "left-over debt") that can be satisfied (paid) from any other nonexempt property (personal or real) that Daniels may have, if allowed by state law.

In some states, statutes permit the homestead exemption only if the judgment debtor has a family. The policy behind this type of statute is to protect the family. If a judgment debtor does not have a family, a creditor may be entitled to collect the full amount realized from the sale of the debtor's home.

State exemption statutes usually include both real and personal property. Personal property that is most often exempt from satisfaction of judgment debts includes:

1. Household furniture up to a specified dollar amount.
2. Clothing and certain personal possessions, such as family pictures or a bible.
3. A vehicle (or vehicles) for transportation (at least up to a specified dollar amount).
4. Certain classified animals, usually livestock but including pets.

SPECIAL PROTECTION FOR THE CONSUMER-DEBTOR

There are numerous *consumer* protection statutes and rules that apply to the debtor-creditor relationship. Although most of these are discussed in detail in Chapter 46, a brief listing and discussion here will illustrate the breadth and importance of these consumer-oriented protection laws.

Consumer Credit Protection Act (CCPA)

This federal statute is commonly known as the Truth-in-Lending Act. It is basically a *disclosure law*, administered by the Federal Reserve Board, that requires sellers and lenders to disclose credit terms and loans so that a consumer-debtor can shop around for the best financing arrangements. Generally, the creditor must clearly indicate to the consumer-debtor what charges are being made for the privilege of paying the debt over a period of time, including what the total annual percentage rate is.

Uniform Consumer Credit Code (UCCC)

In an attempt to make consumer credit laws at the state level uniform, the National Conference of Commissioners on Uniform Laws proposed legislation called the Uniform Consumer Credit Code (UCCC).

The essential points of the UCCC are as follows:

1. To place statutory ceilings on interest rates and other charges.
2. To require disclosure similar to that required by the truth-in-lending law.

3. To limit garnishment actions against take-home wages to a certain amount and to prohibit discharge of an employee solely because of garnishment proceedings.
4. To allow cancellation of a contract solicited by a seller in the consumer-debtor's home within three business days of the solicitation.
5. To limit the holder-in-due-course concept to the acceptance of a check, rather than any other type of negotiable instrument, from the consumer-debtor.
6. To prohibit referral sales, which are sales in which a seller offers a rebate or discount to a buyer for furnishing the names of other prospective purchasers.
7. To provide criminal as well as civil penalties for violations.

Only a handful of states have adopted the UCCC even though it has undergone numerous drafts. Some other states have passed laws similar to some of the provisions of the UCCC, such as laws concerning the home-solicitation sales.

Federal Trade Commission Rule—Holder in Due Course (HDC)

As part of the consumer protection movement, the FTC promulgated a rule that limited the rights of an HDC where the debtor-buyer executes a negotiable promissory note as a part of a consumer transaction. As stated in Chapter 26, the rule provides basically that any personal defenses the buyer could assert against the seller can also be asserted against an HDC. The seller must disclose this rule clearly on the sales agreement.

This rule basically eliminates the use of a buyer's waiver of defense clause in a consumer transaction. These clauses in security agreements, otherwise permitted under UCC 9-206, waive any claim or defense the debtor might have against a good faith assignee for value of a security interest.

For example, a buyer purchases a refrigerator for home use from a seller by means of a retail installment security agreement and negotiable promissory note. In the agreement and note is a clause that prohibits the buyer from asserting against a good faith assignee for value any defense available against the seller. The seller sells the security interest installment agreement to a financial institution. One month later, the refrigerator stops working because of a defect. The buyer wants to return the refrigerator, rescind the contract, and receive a refund. The seller refuses. The buyer stops making payments. Under UCC 9-206, the financial institution could enforce the payment agreement, as the buyer by waiver could not assert the breach of warranty defense against the assignee. Under the FTC rule, however, which supersedes state law, the financial institution is subject to the same defense the buyer has against the seller.

QUESTIONS AND CASE PROBLEMS

1. Sylvia takes her car to Crank's Auto Repair Shop. A sign in the window states that all repairs must be paid for in cash unless credit is approved in advance. Sylvia and Crank agree that Crank will repair Sylvia's car engine and put in a new transmission. No mention is made of credit. Because Crank is not sure how much engine repair will be necessary, he refuses to give Sylvia an estimate. He repairs the engine and puts in a new transmission. When Sylvia comes to pick up her car, she learns that the bill is $795. Sylvia is furious, refuses to pay Crank that amount, and demands possession of her car. Crank demands payment. Discuss the rights of the parties in this matter.

2. James is employed by the Cross-Bar Packing Corporation and earns take-home pay of $400 per week. He is $2,000 in debt to the Holiday Department Store for goods purchased on credit over the past eight months. Most of this property is nonexempt and is presently located in James's apartment. James is in default on his payments to Holiday. Holiday learns that James has a girlfriend in another state and that he plans on giving her most of this property for Christmas. Discuss what actions are available and should be taken by Holiday to resolve the debt owed by James.

3. Ann is a student at Slippery Stone University. In need of funds to pay tuition and books, she attempts to secure a short-term loan from West Bank. The bank agrees to make a loan if Ann will have someone financially responsible guarantee the loan payments. Sheila, a well-known businesswoman and a friend of Ann's family, calls the bank and agrees to pay the loan if Ann cannot. Because of Sheila's reputation, the loan is made. Ann is making the payments, but because of illness she is not able to work for one month. She requests that West Bank extend the loan for three months. West Bank agrees, raising the interest rate for the extended period. Sheila has not been notified of the extension (and therefore has not consented to it). One month later Ann drops out of school. All attempts to collect from Ann have failed. West Bank wants to hold Sheila liable. Discuss West Bank's claim against Sheila.

4. Smith is the owner of a relatively old home valued at $45,000. He notices that the bathtubs and fixtures in both bathrooms are leaking and will need to be replaced. He contracts with Plumber to replace the bathtubs and fixtures. Plumber replaces them, and on June 1 she submits her bill of $4,000 to Smith. Because of financial difficulties, Smith does not pay the bill. Smith's only asset is his home, which, under state law, is exempt up to $40,000 as a homestead. Discuss fully Plumber's remedies in this situation.

5. Kloster-Madsen, Inc., a general contractor, entered into a contract with the owner of a building to do certain remodeling work. About a month later, pursuant to the contract, an electrical subcontractor proceeded to remove several light fixtures from one of the ceilings, cutting four holes in the ceiling and placing the removed light fixtures in the holes. Immediately after this work was begun, a new owner, Tafi's, Inc., purchased the building. Several thousand dollars' worth of material and labor was expended before Tafi's informed the general contractor that it did not wish to have the building remodeled. Can Kloster-Madsen impose a mechanic's lien on the building even though the building contract was entered into with a different owner? [Kloster-Madsen, Inc. v. Tafi's, Inc., 303 Minn. 59, 226 N.W.2d 603 (1975)]

6. Jackson, the owner of a trailer with a refrigeration unit, brought the trailer to North Broadway Service Station for repairs. When the service station owner finished the repairs, Jackson was unable to pay. He pleaded with the owner to permit him to use the trailer to enable him to earn the money necessary to pay the repair bill. The owner kindheartedly returned the trailer to Jackson. Shortly thereafter, the trailer was repossessed by the Trailer Refrigeration Company, which held a mortgage on the trailer on which Jackson had defaulted. The service station owner then attempted to enforce an artisan's lien against the trailer, claiming priority over Trailer Refrigeration Company's mortgage. Will he succeed? What if the owner of the service station had obtained a written memorandum from Jackson at the time he released the trailer to him, stating that he retained an artisan's lien on the trailer and was releasing it only to enable Jackson to earn the money to pay the repair bill? Would the results be different? [Jackson v. Kusmer, 411 S.W.2d 257 (Mo. App. 1967)]

7. One of the ways in which a plaintiff can collect a money judgment from a defendant is by garnishing a debt

that is due from a garnishee to the defendant. Garnishment is allowed only where the debt due from the garnishee is unconditional. With this in mind, discuss the following situation. Cummings Company sued C & E Excavating Company. C & E had a contract with Volpe Construction Company to do certain excavating work for Volpe. Can Cummings garnish the money owed under this contract? What must be known about the contract in order to answer this question? [Cummings General Tire Co. v. Volpe Constr. Co., 230 A.2d 712 (D.C.App. 1967)]

8. A. J. Kellos Construction Co. was the general contractor for the construction of a building in Georgia. Kellos entered into a subcontract with Roofing Specialists, Inc., for the construction of the roof of this project. A performance bond was executed by Balboa Insurance Co. in favor of Kellos that Roofing Specialists would faithfully perform its contract. When the roofing was condemned by the state architect, Kellos sued Balboa on the bond for damages resulting from Roofing Specialists default on the contract. Is the bond executed by Balboa in favor of Kellos a contract of liability insurance or a suretyship? [A. J. Kellos Const. Co., Inc. v. Balboa Ins. Co., 495 F.Supp. 408 (S.D. Georgia, 1980)]

9. John Shumate parked his car in a vacant lot where he had left it several times previously. When he returned, he was informed that the car had been towed at the property owner's request. Thomas Younger had a collision with another car. His car was towed from the scene of the accident at the request of the police while Younger was discussing his accident with the police. The towing companies informed both car owners that they must pay towing and storage charges before their autos would be returned. The car owners sued to challenge this claim of a possessory lien asserted by the towing companies. Could the owners be prevented from removing their cars until payment was made? [Younger v. Plunkett, 395 F.Supp. 702 (E.D.Pa. 1975)]

31

Bankruptcy and Reorganization

The U.S. Constitution, Article I, Section 8, provides that "The Congress shall have the power * * * to establish * * * uniform laws on the subject of bankruptcies throughout the United States." Bankruptcy proceedings are therefore rooted in federal laws; bankruptcy courts are special federal courts; and bankruptcy judges are federally appointed.

FEDERAL BANKRUPTCY LAW— HISTORICAL BACKGROUND

Bankruptcy law is designed to accomplish two main goals. The first is to provide relief and protection to debtors who have "gotten in over their heads." The second major goal of bankruptcy is to provide a fair means of distributing a debtor's assets among all creditors.

The original Bankruptcy Act was enacted in 1898 and was amended by the 1938 Chandler Act. A major overhaul of the federal bankruptcy law occurred in 1978 with the passage of the Bankruptcy Reform Act of 1978. The Bankruptcy Reform Act became effective on October 1, 1979.

This act soon became the center of controversy. Critics claimed that the act favored debtors, that bankruptcy judges appointed for fourteen-year periods had excessively broad jurisdiction, and that the

act permitted abuses and misuses detrimental to the debtor-creditor relationship.

The entire matter came to a head with the Supreme Court's decision in *Northern Pipeline Co. v. Marathon Pipeline Co.*,[1] holding that the broad judicial jurisdiction given by Congress to the bankruptcy judges was a violation of Article III of the U.S. Constitution.[2] This decision virtually brought the proceedings in bankruptcy to a standstill. To allow Congress to act, the Supreme Court stayed its decision until December 24, 1983.

The *Northern Pipeline* decision prompted Congress to review the 1978 Reform Act, and in doing so Congress passed the Bankruptcy Amendments and Federal Judgeship Act of 1984.[3] The amendments created two hundred thirty-two bankruptcy judgeships in various judicial districts throughout the United States.[4] The bankruptcy judges will still have fourteen-year appointments, but will be under the authority of the U.S. district courts. The bankruptcy

---

1. 458 U.S. 50 (1982).
2. See Appendix B.
3. See Chapter 3 for details on additional district and circuit court judgeships.
4. For example, twelve judgeships were assigned to the Central District of California, while states such as Alaska, Delaware, Hawaii, Idaho, Montana, Nebraska, New Hampshire, North Dakota, Rhode Island, South Carolina, South Dakota, Vermont, and Wyoming were assigned one.

courts' primary function is to hold *core proceedings*[5] dealing with the procedures required to administer the estate of the debtor in bankruptcy. Fundamentally, bankruptcy courts fulfill the role of an administrative court for the district court concerning matters in bankruptcy. Decisions on personal injury, wrongful death, and other civil proceedings affecting the debtor will now be resolved in federal or state courts. The jurisdiction of bankruptcy courts became effective on July 10, 1984.

The balance of the 1984 amendments was enacted primarily to remedy apparent abuses, misuses, resulting delays, and ambiguous provisions discovered after the passage of the 1978 act. These amendments covered both basic and special business provisions. The majority of these provisions became effective October 7, 1984. Most of the amendments are incorporated in the text material that follows.

Although the Bankruptcy Act is a federal law, state laws on secured transactions, liens, judgments, and exemptions also play a role in a federal bankruptcy proceeding.

THE BANKRUPTCY REFORM ACT OF 1978 AS AMENDED

The Bankruptcy Reform Act of 1978, as amended by the Bankruptcy Amendments and Federal Judgeship Act of 1984 (hereinafter the Code), is contained in Title 11 of the United States Code and has eight odd-numbered chapters. Chapters 1, 3, and 5 include general definitional provisions and provisions governing case administration, creditors, the debtor,[6] and the estate. These three chapters apply generally to all kinds of bankruptcies. The next four chapters set forth the different types of bankruptcy relief that debtors or creditors may seek. Chapter 7 provides for liquidations. Chapter 9 governs the adjustment of debts of a municipality. Chapter 11 governs reorganizations, and Chapter 13 provides for the adjustment of debts of individuals with regular income.

The last chapter, Chapter 15, sets up a pilot United States trustee system.

The following sections deal with Chapter 7 liquidations, Chapter 11 reorganizations, and Chapter 13 plans. The latter two chapters have been referred to as "rehabilitation" chapters.

The 1984 Bankruptcy Amendments require the clerk of the court to give all *consumer debtors*[7] written notice of each chapter under which the debtor may proceed prior to the commencement of a filing. The purpose of this amendment is to fully inform a debtor of the various chapters available to this type of debtor, i.e, Chapters 7, 11, and 13.

CHAPTER 7 LIQUIDATIONS

This is the most familiar type of bankruptcy proceeding and is often referred to as an ordinary or "straight" bankruptcy. Put simply, a debtor in a straight bankruptcy states his or her debts and turns his or her assets over to a trustee. The trustee sells the assets and distributes the proceeds to creditors. With certain exceptions, the balance of the debts is then discharged (extinguished) and the debtor is relieved of his or her obligation to pay the debts. Any "person"—defined as including individuals, partnerships and corporations[8]—may be a debtor under Chapter 7. Railroads, insurance companies, banks, savings and loan associations, and credit unions cannot be Chapter 7 debtors. Other chapters of the Code, or federal or state statutes, apply to them.

Filing the Petition

A straight bankruptcy may be commenced by the filing of either a voluntary or an involuntary petition.

Voluntary Bankruptcy   A voluntary petition is brought by the debtor, who files official forms designated for that purpose in the bankruptcy court. The 1984 amendments require a consumer-debtor who has selected Chapter 7 to state in the petition, at the time of filing, that he or she understands the relief available under Chapters 11 and 13, and has

---

5.   Core proceedings are procedural functions, such as allowance of claims, decisions on preferences, automatic stay proceedings, confirmation of bankruptcy plans, discharge of debts, etc.

6.   It is noteworthy that the term *bankrupt* no longer exists under the Code. Those who were formerly *bankrupts* under the old Bankruptcy Act are now merely *debtors* under the Code.

7.   Defined here as an individual whose debts are primarily consumer debts.

8.   The definition of a *corporation* includes unincorporated companies and associations. It also covers labor unions.

chosen to proceed under Chapter 7. If the consumer-debtor is represented by an attorney, the attorney must file an affidavit stating that the attorney has informed the debtor of the relief available under each chapter. Anyone who is liable on a claim held by a creditor can do this. The debtor does not even have to be insolvent to file a petition.

The voluntary petition contains the following schedules:

1. A list of both secured and unsecured creditors, their addresses, and the amount of debt owed to each.
2. A statement of the financial affairs of the debtor.
3. A list of all property owned by the debtor, including property claimed by the debtor to be exempt.
4. A listing of current income and expenses. (This schedule was added by the 1984 amendments to provide creditors and the court with relevant information on the debtor's ability to pay creditors a reasonable amount from future income. This information *could* permit a court, on its own motion, to dismiss a consumer-debtor's Chapter 7 petition after a hearing,[9] encouraging a Chapter 13 petition where such would result in a substantial improvement of a creditor's receipt of payment.)

The official forms must be completed accurately, sworn to under oath, and signed by the debtor. To conceal assets or knowingly supply false information on these schedules is a crime under the bankruptcy laws. If the voluntary petition for bankruptcy is found to be proper, the filing of the petition will itself constitute an *order for relief.* Once a consumer-debtor's voluntary petition has been filed, the clerk of the court (or person directed) must give the trustee and creditors mailed notice of the order of relief not more than twenty days after entry of said order.

A new feature allows a husband and wife to file jointly for bankruptcy under a single petition. As mentioned previously, debtors do not have to be insolvent (when debts exceed fair market value of assets exclusive of exempt property) to file for voluntary bankruptcy.

Involuntary Bankruptcy   An involuntary bankruptcy occurs when the debtor's creditors force the debtor into bankruptcy proceedings. An involuntary case cannot be commenced against a farmer[10] or a charitable institution. For an involuntary case to be filed against other debtors, the following requirements must be met. If the debtor has twelve or more creditors, three or more of these creditors having unsecured claims aggregating at least $5,000 must join in the petition. If a debtor has fewer than twelve creditors, one or more creditors having a claim of $5,000 may file.

If the debtor challenges the involuntary petition, a trial will be held and the bankruptcy court will enter an *order for relief* if it finds that:

1. The debtor is generally not paying debts as they become due.[11]
2. A custodian was appointed or took possession of a portion of the debtor's property within 120 days before the filing of the petition for the purpose of enforcing a lien against such property.

If the court grants an order for relief, the debtor will be required to supply the information in the bankruptcy schedules discussed above.

An involuntary petition should not be used as an everyday debt-collection device, and the Code provides penalties for the filing of frivolous petitions against debtors. Judgment may be granted against the petitioning creditors for the costs and attorneys' fees incurred by the debtor in defending against an involuntary petition that is dismissed by the court. If the petition is filed in bad faith, damages can be awarded for injury to the debtor's reputation. Punitive damages may also be awarded.

Automatic Stay

The filing of a petition, either voluntary or involuntary, operates as an automatic stay or suspension of virtually all litigation and other action by creditors

---

9. The law does give the debtor a presumption in favor of granting an order of relief for whatever chapter is requested by the debtor.

10. The definition of *farmer* includes persons who receive more than 80 percent of their gross income from farming operations, such as tilling the soil, dairy farming, ranching, or the production or raising of crops, poultry, or livestock. Corporations and partnerships can be *farmers.*

11. The inability to pay debts as they become due is known as *equitable* insolvency. A *balance sheet* insolvency, which exists when a debtor's liabilities exceed assets, is not the test. Thus, it is possible for debtors to be thrown into involuntary bankruptcy even though their assets far exceed their liabilities. This may occur when a debtor's cash flow problems become severe.

against the debtor or the debtor's property. In other words, once a petition is filed, creditors cannot commence or continue most legal actions against the debtor to recover claims they have against him or her. Nor can creditors take any action to repossess property in the hands of the debtor. However, a secured creditor may petition the bankruptcy court for relief from the automatic stay in certain circumstances.

Underlying the Code's automatic stay provision for a secured creditor is a concept known as *adequate protection*. The adequate protection doctrine, among other things, protects secured creditors from losing their security as a result of the automatic stay. The bankruptcy court can provide adequate protection by requiring the debtor or trustee to make periodic cash payments, or a one-time cash payment (or provide additional collateral or replacement liens) to the extent that the stay causes the value of the property involved to decrease. Or the court may grant other relief that is the "indubitable equivalent" of the secured party's interest in the property, such as a guaranty by a solvent third party to cover losses suffered by the secured party as a result of the stay.

For example, suppose Speedy Express, a delivery service, owns three delivery trucks in which First Bank has a security interest. Speedy Express has failed to make its monthly payments for two months. Speedy Express files a petition in bankruptcy, and the automatic stay prevents First Bank from repossessing the trucks. Meanwhile, the trucks (whose collective value is already less than the balance due) are depreciating at a rate of several hundred dollars a month. First Bank's inability to repossess and immediately resell the delivery trucks is harming First Bank to the extent of several hundred dollars per month. The bankruptcy court may prevent First Bank from being harmed by requiring Speedy Express to make a one-time cash payment or periodic cash payments (or provide additional collateral or replacement liens) to the extent that the delivery trucks are depreciating in value. If the debtor is unable to provide adequate protection, the court may vacate the stay and allow First Bank to repossess the trucks.

A creditor's failure to abide by an automatic stay imposed by the filing of a petition could be costly. The 1984 amendments provide that if a creditor *knowingly* violates the automatic stay (a willful violation), any party injured is entitled to recover actual damages, costs, and attorney fees, and may be entitled to recover punitive damages.

The Trustee

Promptly after the order for relief has been entered, an interim or provisional trustee is appointed to preside over the debtor's property until the first meeting of creditors.[12] At this first meeting, either a permanent trustee is elected or the interim trustee becomes the permanent trustee. The trustee's principal duty is to collect and reduce to money the "property of the estate" for which he serves, and to close up the estate as expeditiously as is compatible with the best interests of the parties. Trustees are entitled to compensation for services rendered, plus reimbursement for expenses.

Creditors' Meeting

Within a reasonable time after the order of relief is granted (not less than ten days or more than thirty days) the bankruptcy court must call a meeting of creditors listed in the schedules filed by the debtor. The bankruptcy judge does not attend or preside at this meeting.

At this meeting a permanent trustee is elected (by 20 percent or more of the unsecured creditors with fixed claims), and the interim trustee's duties are discharged or, more typically, in the absence of election the interim trustee becomes the permanent trustee. The debtor is required to attend this meeting (unless excused by the court) and to submit to examination under oath by the creditors and the trustee. Failure to appear when required or false statements made under oath may result in the debtor being denied a discharge of bankruptcy.

Proof of claims by creditors must normally be filed within six months of this meeting. (The Code merely calls for "timely filing," without specifying the length of time.)

Property of the Estate

Upon commencement of a Chapter 7 proceeding, an *estate in property* is created. The estate consists of all the debtor's legal and equitable interests in property presently held, wherever located, together

---

12. The 1978 Reform Act provides for a pilot program whereby the attorney general appoints U.S. trustees (to act in ten districts). A U.S. trustee in that district becomes the trustee for the debtor's estate, rather than having a trustee elected or appointed by the court.

with community property, property transferred in a transaction voidable by the trustee, proceeds and profits from the property of the estate, and certain after-acquired property. Interests in certain property, such as gifts, inheritances, property settlements (divorce), or life insurance death proceeds, to which the debtor becomes entitled *within 180 days after filing* may also become part of the estate. Thus, the filing of a bankruptcy petition generally fixes a dividing line: Property acquired prior to the petition becomes property of the estate, and property acquired after the filing of the petition, except as just noted, remains the debtor's.

Exemptions

An individual debtor is entitled to exempt certain property from the property of the estate. Prior to the enactment of the Code, state law exclusively governed the extent of the exemptions. (See Chapter 30.) However, the Code establishes a federal exemption scheme. An individual debtor (or husband and wife who file jointly) now has the option of choosing between the exemptions provided under the applicable state law or the federal exemptions.[13] The Code exempts the following property:

1. Up to $7,500 in equity in the debtor's residence and burial plot.
2. Interest in a motor vehicle up to $1,200.
3. Interest, up to $200 for *any* particular item, in household goods and furnishings, wearing apparel, appliances, books, animals, crops, or musical instruments (the 1984 amendments limit, however, an aggregate total of all items to $4,000).
4. Interest in jewelry up to $500.
5. Any other property worth up to $400, plus any unused part of the $7,500 homestead exemption up to an amount of $3,750.[14]

6. Up to $750 interest in any tools of the debtor's trade.
7. Any unmatured life insurance contract owned by the debtor.
8. Certain interests in accrued dividends or interest under life insurance contracts owned by the debtor.
9. Professionally prescribed health aids.
10. The right to receive Social Security and certain welfare benefits, alimony and support, and certain pension benefits.
11. The right to receive certain personal injury and other awards.

Trustee's Powers

The basic duty of the trustee is to collect the debtor's available estate and reduce it to money for distribution, preserving the interests of both the debtor and unsecured creditors. This requires that the trustee be accountable for administering the debtor's estate. To enable the trustee to accomplish this duty, the Code gives the trustee certain powers, stated in both general and specific terms.

General powers are vouchsafed by the statement that the trustee occupies a position *equivalent* in rights to that of other parties. For example, the trustee has the same rights as a *lien creditor* on a simple contract who could have obtained a judicial lien on the debtor's property or who could have levied execution on the debtor's property. This means that a trustee has priority over an unperfected secured party to the debtor's property. A trustee also has power equivalent to that of a *bona fide purchaser* of real property from the debtor. Thus, the trustee would prevail in priority over a secured party's *unperfected* fixture security interest.

In addition, the trustee has specific powers of avoidance. These powers include any voidable rights available to the debtor, preferences, certain statutory liens, and fraudulent transfers by the debtor. Each will be discussed in more detail in this chapter.

With these powers, persons holding the debtor's property at the time the petition is filed are required to deliver the property to the trustee.

The following case illustrates the trustee's rights and powers in a dispute with a secured party over the collateral of the debtor, upon the secured party's making of an improper perfection of her security interest.

---

13. Individual states are given the power to pass legislation precluding the use of the federal exemptions by debtors in their states. As of July 1984, the following states have such legislation: Alabama, Alaska, Arizona, Arkansas, California, Delaware, Florida, Georgia, Idaho, Illinois, Indiana, Iowa, Kentucky, Louisiana, Maine, Maryland, Missouri, New York, North Carolina, North Dakota, Oregon, South Carolina, South Dakota, Tennessee, and Utah. In these states, only state exemptions are available.

14. The 1984 amendments placed a cap of $3,750 on the unused part of the homestead exemption to prevent some debtors from receiving a windfall.

IN RE KARACHI CAB CO.

United States Bankruptcy Court for the Southern District of New York, 1982.
21 B.R. 822.

BACKGROUND AND FACTS   *The Karachi Cab Co. negotiated a loan from Ruth Wapnick. Ms. Wapnick wanted her loan to be secured so she asked the Karachi Cab Co. to put up two of their medallions (i.e., licenses to operate a cab in the city of New York) as collateral. Karachi Cab signed the proper security agreement, and Ms. Wapnick attempted to perfect her interest by filing the financing statement (UCC-1) in the office of the County Clerk of New York. Later Karachi Cab filed for bankruptcy. The trustee attempted to avoid the security interest of Ms. Wapnick, arguing that it was not properly perfected because the filing was improper.*

RYAN, Bankruptcy Judge.

*   *   *   *

The taxi medallions listed as collateral in the security agreement were used or bought for use primarily in the debtor's business and as such are classified as equipment within the meaning of UCC § 9-109(2). *   *   * The perfection of a security interest in equipment requires filing of a financing statement pursuant to UCC § 9-401(1)(c) which provides in pertinent part:

(1) The proper place to file [a financing statement] in order to perfect a security interest [in equipment] is as follows:

(c) . . ., in the department of state and in addition, if the debtor has a place of business in this state and in only one county of this state, also in the office of the filing officer of such county.

Section 9-401 is explicit in mandating that a financing statement filing with the New York Secretary of State is necessary for the proper perfection of a security interest in equipment. Defendant has produced no evidence establishing that a financing statement had been filed with the Secretary of State. In fact, she has admitted that she did not file a UCC-1 financing statement with the Secretary of State and filed only with the County Clerk of New York. Consequently, the security interest asserted cannot be held to have been perfected within the meaning of UCC § 9-401(1)(c). *   *   *

The trustee in bankruptcy has the status of a lien creditor without notice under section 544(a) of the Bankruptcy Code and UCC § 9-301(3). Section 544(a) of the Bankruptcy Code states in pertinent part:

(a) The trustee shall have, as of the commencement of the case, and without regard to any knowledge of the trustee or of any creditor, the rights and powers of, or may avoid any transfer of property of the debtor or any obligation incurred by the debtor that is avoidable by—

(1) A creditor that extends credit to the debtor at the time of the commencement of the case, and that obtains, at such time and with respect to such credit, a judicial lien, . . . whether or not such creditor exists.

Section 544(a) giving the trustee lien creditor status derives from § 70(c) of the former Bankruptcy Act and is a "strong arm" clause available to the trustee. This provision gives the trustee the rights of a creditor on a simple contract with a judicial lien on the property of the debtor as of the date of the petition which commenced the bankruptcy action. The practical effect of section 544(a) is to give the trustee all the rights which a hypothetical creditor would have on the property regardless of whether the creditor actually exists.

UCC § 9-301 provides in pertinent part:

(1) . . ., an unperfected security interest is subordinate to the rights of

(b) a person who becomes a lien creditor before the security interest is perfected.

(3) A "lien creditor" means . . . a trustee in bankruptcy from the date of the filing of the [bankruptcy] petition.

UCC § 9-301(1)(b) makes the unperfected security interest subordinate to one who "becomes a lien creditor before the security interest is perfected." Section 544(a) of the Bankruptcy Code, coupled with UCC § 9-301(1)(b), requires that the trustee in this case prevail over the unperfected security interest of Wapnick.

In summary:

Wapnick was required, pursuant to § 9-401 of the Uniform Commercial Code of the State of New York, to file a UCC-1 financing statement in the Department of State of New York in order to properly perfect the security interest granted to Wapnick by the debtor in the security agreement between the parties dated August 1, 1979.

In only filing a financing statement with the County Clerk of New York County, Wapnick's security interest was not properly perfected on the date of bankruptcy.

The trustee in bankruptcy as a hypothetical lien creditor under § 544(a) of the Bankruptcy Code has priority over the unsecured defendant with respect to the collateral.

Wapnick's secured claim must be and it is disallowed and reclassified as wholly unsecured.

*   *   *   *

The court adjudged the security interest of Ms. Wapnick unperfected, and allowed the trustee properly to avoid it as inferior to the rights of the trustee as a lien creditor.

DECISION AND REMEDY

Voidable Rights   A trustee steps into the shoes of the debtor. Thus, any reason that a debtor can use to obtain return of his or her property can be used by the trustee as well. These grounds include fraud, duress, incapacity, and mutual mistake.

For example, Ben sells his boat to Frank. Frank gives Ben a check, knowing that there are insufficient funds in the bank account to cover the check. Frank has committed fraud. Ben has the right to avoid that transfer and recover the boat from Frank. Once an order for relief has been entered for Ben, the trustee can exercise the same right to recover the boat from Frank.

Preferences   A debtor should not be permitted to transfer property or to make a payment that favors one creditor over others. Thus, the trustee is allowed to recover payments made both voluntarily and involuntarily to one creditor in preference to another.

To constitute a preference that can be recovered, an *insolvent* debtor *generally* must have transferred property, for a *preexisting* debt, within *ninety days* of the filing of the petition in bankruptcy. The transfer must give the creditor more than would have been received if the case were a Chapter 7 liquidation proceeding. The trustee does not have to prove insolvency, as the Code provides that the debtor is presumed to be insolvent during this ninety-day period. Sometimes the creditor receiving the pref-

erence is an "insider." An insider is an individual, partner, partnership, officer, or director of a corporation (or relative of these) who has a close relationship with the debtor. If such is the case, the avoidance power of the trustee is extended to transfer preferences made within *one year* before the petition is filed; however, the *presumption* of insolvency is confined to the ninety-day period. Therefore, the trustee must prove that the debtor was insolvent at the time of earlier transfer.

Not all transfers and conveyances are preferences. To be a preference, the transfer must be made for something other than current consideration. Therefore, it is generally assumed by most courts that payment for services rendered within ten to fifteen days prior to the payment of the current consideration is not a preference. If a creditor receives payment in the ordinary course of business, such as payment of last month's telephone bill, the payment cannot be recovered by the trustee in bankruptcy. To be recoverable, a preference must be a transfer for an antecedent debt, such as a year-old telephone bill. In addition, the 1984 amendments permit a consumer-debtor to transfer any property to a creditor up to a total value of $600, without the transfer constituting a preference.

If a preferred creditor has sold the property to an innocent third party, the property cannot be recovered from the innocent party, but in such circumstances the creditor generally can be held accountable for the value of the property.

Liens on Debtor's Property　The trustee is permitted to avoid the fixing of certain statutory liens, such as a landlord's lien, on property of the debtor. Liens that first become effective on the bankruptcy or insolvency of the debtor are voidable by the trustee. Liens that are not perfected or enforceable on the date of the petition against a bona fide purchaser are voidable.

Fraudulent Transfers　The trustee may avoid fraudulent transfers or obligations if made within one year of the filing of the petition and/or if made with actual intent to hinder, delay, or defraud a creditor. Transfers made for less than a reasonably equivalent consideration are also vulnerable if the debtor thereby became insolvent, was engaged in business with an unreasonably small capital, or intended to incur debts that would be beyond his or her ability to pay.

The debtor shares most of the trustee's avoiding powers. Thus, if the trustee does not take action to enforce one of his or her rights (for example, to recover a preference), the debtor in a Chapter 7 bankruptcy would nevertheless be able to enforce that right.[15]

Claims of Creditors

Generally, any legal obligation of the debtor is a claim. In the case of disputed or unliquidated claims, the bankruptcy court will estimate the value of the claim. Any creditor holding a debtor's obligation can file a claim against the debtor's estate.

These claims are automatically allowed unless contested by the trustee, debtor, or another creditor. However, the Code does not allow claims for breach of employment contracts or real estate leases for terms longer than one year. Such claims are limited to one year's rent or wages, despite the remaining length of either contract in breach. Therefore, an employee who has a three-year employment contract that is breached during the first year by the employer's bankruptcy would be limited to damages

accruing during one year from the filing of the petition, or the date the employment contract was repudiated, whichever is earlier.

Distribution of Property

Creditors are either *secured or unsecured.* (The rights of secured creditors were discussed in Chapter 29.) A *secured* creditor has a security interest in collateral that secures the debt. Before the 1984 amendments, secured parties were frequently put on a hold for months concerning the disposition of the secured collateral held by the debtor because of the automatic stay provisions. Today, the law provides that a consumer-debtor within thirty (30) days of the filing of a Chapter 7 petition, or before the date of the first meeting of the creditors (whichever is first), must file with the clerk a statement of intention with respect to the secured collateral. That intent must state whether the debtor will retain or surrender the collateral to the secured party.[16] The trustee is obligated to enforce the debtor's intent within forty-five (45) days after the intent is filed.

If the secured collateral is surrendered to the secured party, the secured creditor can enforce the security interest either by accepting the property in full satisfaction of the debt or by foreclosing on the collateral and using the proceeds to pay off the debt. In this way, the secured party has priority over unsecured parties to the proceeds from the disposition of the secured collateral. Indeed, the Code provides that if the value of the secured collateral exceeds the secured party's claim, the secured party also has priority to the proceeds in an amount that will cover reasonable fees and costs incurred because of the debtor's default. Any excess over this amount is used by the trustee to satisfy the claims of unsecured creditors. Should the secured collateral be insufficient to cover the secured debt owed, the "secured" creditor becomes an unsecured creditor for the difference.

Bankruptcy law establishes an order or priority for classes of debts owed to *unsecured* creditors, and they are paid in the order of their priority. Each class of debt must be fully paid before the next class is entitled to any of the proceeds—if there are suf-

---

15.　In a rehabilitation proceeding—Chapter 11 or Chapter 13, to be discussed later—where no trustee generally exists, the debtor has the same avoiding powers as a trustee under Chapter 7.

16.　Also, if applicable, the debtor must specify if the collateral will be claimed as exempt property, and that the debtor intends to redeem the property or reaffirm the debt secured by the collateral.

ficient funds to pay the entire class. If not, the proceeds are distributed *proportionately* to each creditor in a class, and all classes lower in priority on the list receive nothing. The order of priority among classes of unsecured creditors is as follows:

1. All costs and expenses for preserving and administering the estate, including such items as court costs and trustee and attorney fees and costs incurred by the trustee during the administration of the estate, such as rental fees and appraisal fees.

2. Unsecured claims in an involuntary proceeding arising in the ordinary course of the debtor's business after commencement of the case but before the appointment of a trustee or issuance of an order for relief.

3. Claims for wages, salaries, and commissions up to an amount of $2,000 per claimant, provided that they were earned within ninety days of the filing of the petition in bankruptcy. Any claims in excess of $2,000 are treated as the "claims of general creditors" (listed as number 8 below).

4. Unsecured claims for contributions to employee benefit plans arising under services rendered within 180 days before filing the petition and limited to the number of employees covered by the plan multiplied by $2,000.

5. Farm producers and fishermen, up to $2,000 against debtors who own or operate grain storage facilities or a fish produce storage or processing facility (1984 amendments).

6. Unsecured claims for money deposited (up to $900) with the debtor before the filing of the petition in connection with the purchase, lease, or rental of property or services that were not delivered or provided. Any claim in excess of $900 is treated as a "claim of a general creditor" (listed as number 8 below).

7. Certain taxes and penalties legally due and owing various governmental units (rules vary depending on type of tax owed).

8. Claims of general creditors. These debts have the lowest priority and are paid on a pro rata basis if, and only if, funds remain after all the debts having priority are paid in full.

9. Any remaining balance is returned to the debtor.

Discharge

From the debtor's point of view, the primary purpose of a Chapter 7 liquidation is to obtain a fresh start

through the discharge of debts.[17] However, there are circumstances in which a claim will not be discharged.

Exceptions to Discharge   A debt may not be discharged because of the nature of the claim or the conduct of the debtor. Claims that are not dischargeable include (the 1984 amendments added 9–11):

1. Claims for back taxes accruing within three years prior to bankruptcy.

2. Claims against property or money obtained by the debtor under false pretenses or by false representations.

3. Unscheduled claims.

4. Claims based on fraud or misuse of funds while the debtor was acting in a fiduciary capacity, or claims involving the debtor's embezzlement or larceny.

5. Alimony and child support.

6. Claims based on willful or malicious injury by the debtor to another or to the property of another.

7. Certain fines and penalties payable to governmental units.

8. Certain student loans, unless such imposes an undue hardship on the debtor and the debtor's dependents.

9. Consumer debts of more than $500 for luxury goods or services owed to a single creditor incurred within forty (40) days of the order of relief. This denial of discharge is a rebuttable presumption, and any debts reasonably acquired to support or maintain the debtor or dependents are not classified as luxury goods or services.

10. Cash advances aggregating more than $1,000 as extensions of open-end consumer credit obtained by the debtor within twenty (20) days of the order of relief. This is also a rebuttable presumption.

11. Judgments or consent decrees awarded against a debtor for liability incurred as a result of the debtor's operation of a motor vehicle while legally intoxicated.

In the following case, the question of the discharge of a student loan is at issue.

---

17. Discharges are granted only to "individuals" who are debtors under Chapter 7, not to corporations or partnerships. The latter may use Chapter 11, or they may liquidate under state law.

BAKER v. UNIVERSITY
OF TENNESSEE AT
CHATTANOOGA
(IN RE BAKER)
United States Bankruptcy Court,
E.D. Tennessee, 1981.
10 B.R. 870.

BACKGROUND AND FACTS   *The facts of this case are stated by the court.*

KELLEY, Bankruptcy Judge.

This cause came on to be heard on May 5, 1981, on debtor's complaint to determine dischargeability of certain educational loans. The complaint alleges that debtor is entitled to relief under 11 U.S.C. 523(a)(8) which reads as follows:

Exceptions to discharge.

(a) A discharge under section 727, 1141, or 1328(b) of this title does not discharge an individual debtor from any debt—

*   *   *   *

(8) to a governmental unit, or a nonprofit institution of higher education, for an educational loan, unless—

(B) excepting such debt from discharge under this paragraph will impose an undue hardship on the debtor and the debtor's dependents;

*   *   *   *

In her trial memorandum the debtor states:

Plaintiff will show that it would be an undue hardship on her to repay the loans. She will show that the student loans would require payments which she will not be able to make. She will show that without consideration of the student loans, her expenses are several hundred dollars in excess of her monthly income. She will show that she has had to get financial aid from her church and from relatives to meet her monthly expenses.

She would further show that her husband has left town and she is not receiving regular financial aid from him. She would further show that she has been unable to locate his whereabouts, even though governmental institutions have also attempted to help find him.

*   *   *   *

From the record in this cause it appears that debtor has three educational loans in the amounts indicated:

University of Tennessee at Chattanooga	$ 600.00
Cleveland State Community College	2,335.00
Baroness Erlanger School of Nursing	3,700.00
Total	$6,635.00

From the proof the court finds that debtor is employed and has take home pay of less than $650.00 a month. She has monthly expenses of $925.00 for herself and three children. She receives no child support. She receives no public support. She has no other income.

The debtor prepared a list of her monthly expenses *   *   *.

After carefully listening to direct and cross examination the court finds no irregularities regarding the monthly expenses. Debtor could possibly reduce expenses some, but the court finds that debtor's reasonable expenses each month far exceed her income.

In January 1981 debtor's church paid $306.00 to the Chattanooga Gas Company so that debtor and her children could have heat in their home. Debtor has not been well. She has not been able to pay all of her medical bills. Debtor used 200 hours sick leave last year. One child has a reading difficulty. Another requires special shoes which are expensive.

In 1976 the Congress passed the Educational Amendments which restricted a discharge in bankruptcy. The restriction was designed to remedy an abuse by students who, immediately upon graduation, would file bankruptcy to secure a discharge of educational loans. These students often had no other indebtedness and could easily pay their debts from future wages. See: *Discharging Student Loans in Bankruptcy*, 52 Am.Bkcy.L.J. 201.

In the present case the debtor did not file bankruptcy to secure a discharge only from her educational loans. Her petition shows that she had been sued and her wages were subject to garnishment. This situation often triggers bankruptcy. The debtor's present income is not sufficient to maintain her and her three children.

As noted in 3 *Collier on Bankruptcy*, 15th edition, at paragraph 523.18:

> Paragraph (B) of subdivision (a)(8) is the "hardship" provision that permits the court to discharge a student loan otherwise nondischargeable, if excepting the debt from discharge will impose an undue hardship on the debtor or the debtor's dependents. This exemption from the exception to discharge is discretionary with the bankruptcy judge who will have to determine whether payment of the debt will cause undue hardship on the debtor and his dependents thus defeating the "fresh start" concept of the bankruptcy laws. There may well be circumstances that justify failure to repay a student loan such as illness, incapacity or other extenuating circumstances. Where the court finds that such circumstances exist, it may order the debt discharged.

The court concludes that under the circumstances of this case, requiring the debtor to repay the debts owed to the *three* defendants in the amount of $6,635.00 plus interest would impose upon her and her dependents an undue hardship. In passing the Educational Amendments of 1976 and including these amendments in the Bankruptcy Reform Act of 1978, Congress intended to correct an abuse. It did not intend to deprive those who have truly fallen on hard times of the "fresh start" policy of the new Bankruptcy Code.

The debtor's student loans were discharged.

DECISION AND REMEDY

The Code makes it appear that student loans are not dischargeable. But the preceding case tells us that in hardship situations equity can step in to alter this rule.

COMMENTS

Objections to Discharge   In addition to the exceptions to discharge previously listed, there are other circumstances that will cause a discharge to be denied. When a discharge is denied, the assets of the debtor are still distributed to the creditors, but the debtor remains liable for the unpaid portions of all claims. Some grounds for the denial of discharge include:

1.   Debtor's concealment or destruction of property with the intent to hinder or delay or defraud a creditor.

2.   Debtor's fraudulent concealment or destruction of records of his or her financial condition.

3.   Debtor's refusal to obey a lawful order of a bankruptcy court.

4.   Debtor's failure to satisfactorily explain the loss of assets.

5.   Grant of a discharge to debtor within six years of the filing of the petition.[18]

6.   Debtor's written waiver of discharge approved by the court.

Prior to the 1984 amendments, creditors were reluctant to challenge and object to the granting of a discharge to a debtor. If the challenge was denied, the creditor was liable in judgment to the debtor for

---

18.   A discharge under Chapter 13 of the Code within six years of the filing of the petition does not bar a subsequent Chapter 7 discharge where a good faith Chapter 13 plan paid at least 70 percent of all allowed unsecured claims.

all costs and reasonable attorney fees. To encourage legitimate objections, the amendments provide that even if the creditor loses on the challenge, the creditor is liable for costs and attorney's fees only if the challenge was not *substantially justified*.

Effect of Discharge The primary effect of a discharge is to void any judgment on a discharged debt and enjoin any action to collect a discharged debt. A discharge does not affect the liability of a codebtor.

Revocation of Discharge The Code provides that a debtor may lose his or her bankruptcy discharge by revocation. The bankruptcy court may within one year revoke the discharge decree if it is discovered that the debtor was fraudulent or dishonest during the bankruptcy proceedings. The revocation renders the discharge null and void, allowing creditors not satisfied by the distribution of the debtor's estate to proceed with their claims against the debtor.

Reaffirmation of Debt A debtor may voluntarily wish to pay off a discharged debt. This is called a reaffirmation of the debt. The 1984 amendments completely revised the procedure and rules concerning reaffirmation agreements. To be enforceable, reaffirmation agreements must be made before a debtor is granted a discharge. The agreement must be filed with the court. If the debtor is represented by an attorney, court approval is not required if the attorney files a declaration or affidavit stating that the debtor has been fully informed of the consequences of the agreement, the agreement is voluntarily made, and the agreement does not impose a hardship on the debtor or dependents. If the debtor is not represented by an attorney, court approval will be required and the agreement will be approved only if the court finds no undue hardship and if the agreement is in the best interest of the debtor.

In addition, the debtor will now have the ability to rescind the agreement at any time prior to discharge or within sixty (60) days[19] of the filing of the agreement, whichever is later. This rescission period must be stated *clearly* and *conspicuously* in the reaffirmation agreement.

---

19. Formerly, the time limit was thirty (30) days.

CHAPTER 11
REORGANIZATIONS

The type of bankruptcy proceeding used most commonly by a corporate debtor is a Chapter 11 reorganization. In a reorganization the creditors and the debtor formulate a plan under which the debtor pays a portion of his or her debts and is discharged of the remainder. The debtor is allowed to continue in business. Although this type of bankruptcy is commonly a corporate reorganization, any debtor who is eligible for Chapter 7 relief is eligible for Chapter 11 relief. In addition, railroads are also eligible for Chapter 11 relief.

The same principles that govern the filing of a Chapter 7 petition apply to Chapter 11 proceedings. The case may be brought either voluntarily or involuntarily. The same principles govern the entry of the order for relief. The automatic stay and adequate protection provisions previously discussed are applicable in reorganizations. The automatic stay provisions and use of a plan to discharge unsecured debts and obligations have been used to prevent injured parties from securing judgments in lawsuits and debtors from breaking of collective bargaining agreements. This has resulted in much controversy. The courts and the 1984 amendments have attempted to clarify some of these issues, particularly collective bargaining agreements, which will be discussed later in this chapter.

In some instances, creditors may prefer private, negotiated adjustments of creditor-company relations, also known as **workouts,** to bankruptcy proceedings. Quite frequently, these out-of-court workouts are much more flexible and thus more conducive to a speedy settlement. Speed is critical since delay is one of the most costly elements in any bankruptcy proceeding.

Another advantage of workouts is that they avoid the various administrative costs of bankruptcy proceedings. Thus, under Section 305(a) of the Bankruptcy Code, a court, after notice and a hearing, may dismiss or suspend all proceedings in a case at any time if such a dismissal or suspension would better serve the interests of the creditors of the debtor. Section 1112 also allows a court, at the request of a party in interest, and after notice and a hearing, to dismiss a case under Chapter 11 for cause. Cause includes an absence of a reasonable likelihood of rehabilitation, the inability to effectuate a plan, and an unreasonable delay by the debtor that is prejudicial to creditors.[20]

---

20. See 11 U.S.C., Section 1112(b).

In the following case, creditors of Johns-Manville Corporation seek to dismiss, under Section 1112, a voluntary petition filed by Manville.

BACKGROUND AND FACTS *On August 26, 1982, Johns-Manville Corporation, a highly successful industrial enterprise, filed for protection under Chapter 11 of the Bankruptcy Code. This filing was quite a surprise to some of Manville's creditors as well as to some of the other corporations that were also being sued, along with Manville, for injuries caused by asbestos exposure. Manville was asserting that the approximately 16,000 lawsuits pending as of the filing date and the potential lawsuits of people who had been exposed but who would not manifest the asbestos-related diseases until sometime in the future necessitated its filing. The creditors of Manville were contending that Johns-Manville did not file in good faith, and thus the voluntary Chapter 11 petition should be dismissed under Section 1112 of the Bankruptcy Code.*

IN RE JOHNS–
MANVILLE CORP.
United States Bankruptcy Court
for the Southern District of
New York, 1984.
36 B.R. 727.

BURTON R. LIFLAND, Bankruptcy Judge.
*   *   *   *

It is the propriety of the filing by Manville which is the subject of the instant decision. Four separate motions to dismiss the petition pursuant to Section 1112(b) of the Code have been lodged before this Court. *   *   *

Manville has opposed all four dismissal motions and has been joined in opposition to them by the Unofficial Committee of School Creditors and the Equity Holders Committee. *   *   *
*   *   *   *

*   *   * Preliminarily, it must be stated that there is no question that Manville is eligible to be a debtor under the Code's statutory requirements. *   *   *
*   *   *   *

Moreover, it should also be noted that neither Section 109 nor any other provision relating to voluntary petitions by companies contains any insolvency requirement. *   *   * "[I]t is no longer necessary for a petitioner for reorganization to allege or show insolvency or inability to pay debts as they mature." *   *   *
*   *   *   *

Accordingly, it is abundantly clear that Manville has met all of the threshold eligibility requirements for filing a voluntary petition under the Code. This Court will now turn to the issue of whether any of the movants have demonstrated sufficient "cause" pursuant to Code Section 1112(b) to warrant the dismissal of Manville's petition.
*   *   *   *

In determining whether to dismiss under Code Section 1112(b), a court is not necessarily required to consider whether the debtor has filed in "good faith" because that is not a specified predicate under the Code for filing. Rather, according to Code Section 1129(a)(3), good faith emerges as a requirement for the confirmation of a plan. *   *   * It is thus logical that the good faith of the debtor be deemed a predicate primarily for emergence out of a Chapter 11 case. It is after confirmation of a concrete and immutable reorganization plan that creditors are foreclosed from advancing their distinct and parochial interests in the debtor's estate.

A "principal goal" of the Bankruptcy Code is to provide "open access" to the "bankruptcy process." *   *   *

Accordingly, the drafters of the Code envisioned that a financially beleaguered debtor with real debt and real creditors should not be required to wait until the economic situation is beyond repair in order to file a reorganization petition. The "Congressional purpose" in enacting the Code was to encourage resort to the bankruptcy process. This philosophy not only comports with the elimination of an insolvency requirement, but also is a corollary of the key aim of Chapter 11 of the Code, that of avoidance of liquidation. * * *

In the instant case, not only would liquidation be wasteful and inefficient in destroying the utility of valuable assets of the companies as well as jobs, but, more importantly, liquidation would preclude just compensation of some present asbestos victims and all future asbestos claimants. This unassailable reality represents all the more reason for this Court to adhere to this basic potential liquidation avoidance aim of Chapter 11 and deny the motions to dismiss. Manville must not be required to wait until its economic picture has deteriorated beyond salvation to file for reorganization. * * * *

In sum, Manville is a financially beseiged enterprise in desperate need of reorganization of its crushing real debt, both present and future. The reorganization provisions of the Code were drafted with the aim of liquidation avoidance by great access to Chapter 11. Accordingly, Manville's filing does not abuse the jurisdictional integrity of this Court. . . . * * *
* * * *

DECISION AND REMEDY   *The motions to dismiss the Manville petition were denied. The court concluded that a bankruptcy proceeding was appropriate in this situation.*

Debtor-in-Possession

Upon entry of the order for relief, the debtor generally continues to operate his or her business as a *debtor-in-possession*. However, the court may appoint a trustee to operate the debtor's business if gross mismanagement of the business is shown or if it is in the best interests of the estate. As soon as practicable after entry of the order for relief, a creditors' committee of unsecured creditors is appointed. The committee may consult with the trustee or the debtor-in-possession concerning the administration of the case or the formulation of the plan.

Creditors' Committees

Additional creditors' committees may be appointed to represent special interest creditors. The creditors' committee is, in a sense, a party in interest in the proceedings. Orders affecting the estate generally will not be entered without either the consent of the committee or after a hearing in which the judge hears the position of the creditors' committee.

The Plan

Filing the Plan   Only the debtor may file a plan within the first 120 days after the date of the order for relief. However, if the debtor does not meet the 120-day deadline, or if the debtor fails to obtain the required creditor consent within 180 days, any party may propose a plan.

Contents of the Plan   A Chapter 11 plan must be "fair and equitable" and must:

1.   Designate classes of claims and interests under the plan.
2.   Specify the treatment to be afforded the classes. The plan must provide the same treatment for each claim in a particular class.
3.   Provide an adequate means for the plan's execution.

Acceptance of the Plan   Once the plan has been developed, it is submitted to each class of creditors for acceptance. Acceptance of a plan is required by each class unless the class is not impaired. [11 U.S.C.A., Section 1129(8)] A class of claims has accepted the plan when a majority of the number of creditors, representing two-thirds of the amount of the total claim, vote to approve the plan.

Confirmation of the Plan   The plan must be "in the best interests of the creditors." Each plan submitted is almost a case history in itself, and each plan varies. Even when all classes of claims accept the plan, the court may refuse to confirm it if it fails to meet this requirement. Also, even if only one class of claims has accepted the plan, the court may still confirm it under the Code's so-called "cram down" provision. The plan is binding upon confirmation. Upon confirmation, the debtor is given a Chapter 11 discharge from all claims not protected under the plan. However, this discharge does not apply to any claims denied discharge under Chapter 7 (as previously discussed).

CHAPTER 13 PLANS

The former Bankruptcy Act provided for the formulation of "wage earner" plans as a means of allowing wage earners to pay off their debts free from the harassment of creditors. Under these plans, the wage earner avoided the stigma of being adjudicated a "bankrupt." Chapter 13 of the Bankruptcy Code provides for "Adjustment of Debts of an Individual with Regular Income."

Individuals (not partnerships or corporations) with *regular income* who owe noncontingent, liquidated, unsecured debts of less than $100,000 or similar secured debts of $350,000 may take advantage of Chapter 13. This includes individual proprietors and individuals on welfare, Social Security, fixed pensions, or investment income.[21] Many small business debtors will have a choice of filing a plan either under Chapter 11 or Chapter 13. There are several advantages in filing a Chapter 13 plan when eligible. One of these advantages is that it is less expensive and less complicated than a Chapter 11 proceeding, or even a Chapter 7 liquidation.

Filing the Petition

A Chapter 13 case can be initiated only by the filing of a voluntary petition by the debtor. Certain Chapter 7 and Chapter 11 cases may be converted to Chapter 13 cases with the consent of the debtor. A trustee must be appointed.

Automatic Stay

Upon the filing of a Chapter 13 petition, the automatic stay previously discussed takes effect. It en-

joins creditors from taking action against co-obligors of the debtor. Although it applies to all or part of a consumer debt, it does not apply to any business debt incurred by the debtor. A creditor has the right to seek relief from the automatic stay. A 1984 amendment was enacted to save the creditor time and money in seeking court approval to vacate the stay and recover from the codebtor. The new law provides that upon the creditor's request to vacate the stay against the codebtor, unless written objection is filed, twenty (20) days later the stay against the codebtor is automatically terminated without a hearing.

The Plan

Filing the Plan Only the debtor may file a plan under Chapter 13. This plan may provide either for the payment of all obligations in full or for payment of an amount less than 100 percent.

Contents of the Plan A Chapter 13 plan must:

1. Provide for the turnover of such future earnings or income of the debtor to the trustee as is necessary for execution of the plan.
2. Provide for full payment in deferred cash payments of all claims entitled to priority.
3. Provide for the same treatment of each claim within a particular class. (The 1984 amendments permit the debtor to list codebtors, such as guarantors or sureties, as a separate class.)

The time for payment under the plan may not exceed three years unless the court approves an extension. The term, with extension, may not exceed five years.

The 1984 amendments require the debtor to make "timely payments," and the trustee is required to "insure" these payments. The law now provides that the debtor shall commence making payments under the proposed plan within thirty (30) days after the plan has been *filed*. If the plan has not been confirmed, the trustee is instructed to retain the payments until the plan is confirmed and then distribute accordingly. If the plan is denied, the trustee will return the payments to the debtor less any costs. Failure of the debtor to make timely payments or to commence payments within the thirty (30) day period will allow the court to convert the case to a Chapter 7 bankruptcy or to dismiss the petition.

---

21. Prior to the new Bankruptcy Act, self-employed persons could not file under Chapter 13.

Confirmation of the Plan   After the plan is filed, the court holds a confirmation hearing at which interested parties may object to the plan. The court will confirm a plan with respect to each claim of a secured creditor:

1.   If the secured creditors have accepted the plan.
2.   If the plan provides that creditors retain their liens and if the value of the property to be distributed to them under the plan is not less than the secured portion of their claims.
3.   If the debtor surrenders the property securing the claim to the creditors.

Prior to the 1984 amendments, unsecured creditors had little protection under a debtor's plan filed under Chapter 13. The court was required to confirm the plan providing:

1.   The plan conformed to the requirements (including payments of fees) of Chapter 13.
2.   The plan was proposed in "good faith."
3.   The value of the property to be distributed would not be less than that paid if the estate were to be liquidated under Chapter 7.
4.   The debtor would be able to make all payments under the plan. [22]

Some courts interpreted these criteria as permitting the confirmation of zero plans (unsecured creditors receive nothing). These courts found no statutory requirement suggesting that a Chapter 13 debtor pay more than what a creditor would get in a straight liquidation proceeding. If the creditor would receive nothing under Chapter 7, there was no requirement to pay the unsecured creditor anything to obtain a Chapter 13 discharge.

Other courts interpreted the criteria much differently. These courts held that the very title of Chapter 13 requires that the petitioner have "regular income" and infers that the debtor will use future income to make payments to creditors. In addition, a prerequisite to confirmation is that the debtor be able to make "all payments" under the plan. This very section anticipates that a debtor must live within a proposed budget to make some payments to an unsecured creditor. Lastly, these courts held that the "good faith" test requires the court to insure that

all parties are treated fairly. Therefore, if "no meaningful repayment can be proposed, the debtor is not entitled to Chapter 13 relief." [23]

Objection to the Plan   Unsecured creditors do not have a vote to confirm a Chapter 13 plan. However, the 1984 amendments attempted to address zero plans and to give the trustee and unsecured creditors a meaningful right of objection to a plan submitted by a debtor. The amendments provide that the court *cannot* approve a plan over the objection of the trustee or any unsecured creditor unless:

1.   The value of the property to be distributed under the plan is at least equal to the amount of the claim; *or*
2.   All the debtor's projected disposable income to be received during the three-year plan period will be applied to making payments. Disposable income is all income received *less* amounts needed to support the debtor and dependents, and/or amounts needed to meet ordinary expenses to continue the operation of a business.

Modification of the Plan   Prior to completion of payments, the plan may be modified upon request of either the debtor, the trustee, or an unsecured creditor. If there is an objection by any interested party to the modification, the court must hold a hearing to determine approval or disapproval of the modified plan.

Discharge

After completion of all payments under a Chapter 13 plan, the court grants a discharge of all debts provided for by the plan. The exemptions to discharge are for certain long-term debts. Except for claims constituting a priority debt and except for alimony and child support, all other debts are dischargeable. Priority debts must be paid because the priority claims are a minimum requirement of what must be included in a plan. That means that the

---

22.   11 U.S.C., Section 1325(a).

23.   In re Iacovoni, 2 B.R. 256 (D. Utah C.D. 1980). The court in its opinion cited Justice Douglas in Bank of Martin v. England, 385 U.S. 99, 103, 87 S.Ct. 274, 277 (1966): "Yet we do not read these statutory words with the ease of a computer. There is an overriding consideration that equitable principles govern the exercise of bankruptcy jurisdiction."

present status of the law allows a Chapter 13 discharge to include fraudulently incurred debt and claims resulting from malicious or willful injury. Therefore, a Chapter 13 discharge is much more beneficial to the debtor than a Chapter 7 discharge.

Even if the debtor does not complete the plan, a "hardship" discharge may be granted if the failure to complete the plan was due to circumstances beyond the debtor's control and if the property distributed with the plan was of greater value than would have been paid in a Chapter 7 liquidation. A discharge can be revoked within one year if it was obtained by fraud.

SPECIAL BUSINESS FUNCTION PROVISIONS—1984 AMENDMENTS

There are five special business function areas affected by the amendments. These are grain storage facilities, leasehold management agreements, repurchase agreements, timeshare consumer agreements, and collective bargaining agreements. Each will be discussed briefly.

Grain Storage Facilities

The amendments dealing with grain storage facilities arose as an attempt to remedy several bankruptcy problems that farm producer and fisherman groups were experiencing. These problems ranged from conflicts of jurisdiction over the control of these facilities to delays in adjudication of the rights and payments to farm producers. The latter even led to a farmer's seizure of his grain held in bailment by a grain storage facility, resulting in the farmer being held in contempt of court.

As previously stated, the amendments now give farm producers and fishermen a *priority* claim of up to $2,000 against debtors who own or operate grain storage facilities or a fish produce storage or processing facility.

In addition, the farmer or fishermen has reclamation rights for ten (10) days after the facility has received the grain or fish, if written notice is given. Most other provisions expedite procedures (most procedures cannot exceed 120 days) for determination of interests of the parties and resolving jurisdictional conflicts.

Leasehold Management Amendments

Long-term lease shopping center vacancies are another area addressed by the act. Prior to the amendments only a Chapter 7 debtor was required to decide whether to assume or reject an unexpired lease within sixty days after the bankruptcy petition was filed. In a Chapter 11 case, there was no deadline. The new law requires the trustee to decide whether to approve or reject within sixty days after the order for relief, regardless of what chapter is used in the case. If no decision is made as to acceptance or rejection within the sixty-day period, the lease is deemed rejected and the trustee must surrender the property to the lessor.

This change will definitely improve landlord creditor positions in shopping centers. Previously, bankrupt Chapter 11 debtors virtually held up decisions on use and payment of rent for leased premises pending submission of plans. In addition, pending such a decision, the trustee had to continue to pay rent and perform other lease obligations.

The balance of the amendments deals mainly with assignments of these leases and rights of a landlord upon termination of the lease.

Repurchase Agreements

Repurchase agreements, commonly referred to as REPOs, were treated with some uncertainty under prior law, particularly as applied to holders of a variety of securities (including CDs, bankers' acceptances, guaranteed government obligations, etc.) subject to a repurchase agreement. The amendments are limited to only a few types of agreements, and are intended to prevent insolvencies of a securities or commodities firm from spreading to the REPO markets.

Timesharing Amendments

The act provides protection to individuals who purchase timeshares in homes or condominiums. The timeshare gave the purchaser a "right-to-use" the premises owned by a debtor-in-possession developer. The problem arose when courts held the "right-to-use" timeshare purchase agreement to be an executory contract. This allowed the debtor to reject the contract, terminate the timeshare interest, and sell the property free and clear of this interest.

Under the 1984 amendments, holders of time-share interests are afforded the same protections extended to lessees of unexpired leases in real property of the debtor. The timeshare consumer, upon rejection by the debtor, has the option of remaining in possession for the balance of the plan or for any renewal or extension enforceable by the timeshare interest purchaser, making whatever rent payments are due with the right to offset damages incurred, or the timeshare consumer can treat the timeshare plan as terminated.

Collective Bargaining Amendments

Under the 1978 Reform Act, questions arose as to whether a Chapter 11 debtor could reject a recently negotiated collective-bargained labor contract. In the recent case of *National Labor Relations Board* v. *Bildisco and Bildisco*, the Supreme Court held that a collective-bargaining agreement subject to the National Labor Relations Act is an "executory contract" and thus subject to *rejection* by a debtor in possession.[24] The Court emphasizes that such a rejection should not be permitted unless there is a finding that the policy of Chapter 11 would be served by such action. (The policy of Chapter 11 is to permit successful rehabilitation of debtors.) Hence, when the bankruptcy court determines that a rejection of a collective-bargaining agreement should be permitted, it must make a reasoned finding *on the record*

---

24. 465 U.S. 513, 104 S.Ct. 1188 (1984). See Chapter 1 for excerpts from this case.

as to *why* it has determined that such a rejection should be permitted.

The 1984 amendments are an attempt to reconcile federal policies favoring collective bargaining while still allowing a debtor company to reject executory labor contracts while trying to reorganize under Chapter 11 of the Code. A new section has been added to the Bankruptcy Code that sets forth standards and procedures under which collective bargaining contracts can be assumed or rejected under a Chapter 11 filing.

In general, a collective bargaining contract can be rejected if the debtor has first proposed "necessary" contractual modifications to the union, and the union has failed to adopt them without "good cause." The company is required to provide the union with the relevant information needed to evaluate this proposal and to confer in good faith in attempting to reach a mutually satisfactory agreement on the modifications.

OTHER AMENDMENTS

There are numerous other amendments, most of which are technical in nature or are clarifications or expansions of existing law. For example, bankruptcy of a debtor cannot be a basis of employment discrimination in the private sector. Before this amendment, such prohibition was applied only to governmental units. Other examples are new provisions to limit the use of consecutive filings where prior petitions have been dismissed, new and clarified definitions, and increased compensation for trustees.

QUESTIONS AND CASE PROBLEMS

1. Carlton has been a rancher all his life, raising cattle and crops. His ranch is valued at $500,000, almost all of which is exempt under state law. Carlton has eight creditors and a total indebtedness of $70,000. Two of his largest creditors are Samson ($30,000 owed) and Greed ($25,000 owed). The other six creditors have claims of less than $5,000 each. A drought has ruined all of Carlton's crops and forced him to sell many of his cattle at a loss. He cannot pay off his creditors.

(a) Under the Code, can Carlton, with a $500,000 ranch, voluntarily petition himself into bankruptcy? Explain.
(b) Could either Samson or Greed force Carlton into involuntary bankruptcy? Explain.

2. Sam is a retail seller of television sets. He sells Martha a $900 set on a retail installment security agreement in which she pays $100 down and agrees to pay the balance in equal installments. Sam retains a security interest in the set sold, and he perfects that security interest by filing a financing statement locally. Two months later Martha is in default on her payments to Sam and is involuntarily petitioned into bankruptcy by her creditors. Sam wants to repossess the television set as provided for in the security agreement, and he wants to have priority over the trustee

in bankruptcy to any proceeds from the disposal of the set. Discuss fully Sam's right to repossess and whether he has priority over the trustee in bankruptcy to any proceeds from disposal of the set.

3. Green is not known for his business sense. He started a greenhouse and nursery business two years ago and because of his lack of experience, he soon was in debt to a number of creditors. On February 1 Green borrowed $5,000 from his father to pay some of these creditors. On May 1 Green paid back the $5,000, depleting his entire working capital. One creditor, the ABC Nursery Supply Corporation, had extended credit to Green on numerous purchases. ABC has pressured Green for payment, and on July 1 Green pays ABC half the money owed. On September 1 Green voluntarily petitions himself into bankruptcy. The trustee in bankruptcy claims that both Green's father and ABC must turn over to the debtor's estate the amounts Green paid to them. Discuss fully the trustee's claims.

4. Smith petitions himself into voluntary bankruptcy. Smith has three major claims against his estate. One is by Carlton, a friend who holds Smith's negotiable promissory note for $2,500; one is by Elmer, an employee who is owed three months' back wages of $4,500; and one is by the United Bank of the Rockies on an unsecured loan of $5,000. In addition, Able, an accountant retained by the trustee, is owed $500, and property taxes of $1,000 are owed to Rock County. If Smith's nonexempt property has been liquidated, with proceeds of $5,000, discuss fully what amount will be received by the United Bank of the Rockies.

5. The East Bank is a secured party on a loan of $5,000 it has made to Sally. Sally later got into financial difficulty, and creditors other than the East Bank petitioned her into involuntary bankruptcy. The value of the secured collateral has substantially decreased in value and, upon sale, the debt to East Bank was reduced to only $2,500. Sally's estate consisted of $100,000 in exempt assets and $2,000 in nonexempt assets. After the bankruptcy costs and back wages to Sally's employees were paid, nothing was left for unsecured creditors. Sally received a discharge in bankruptcy. Later she decided to go back into business. By selling a few exempt assets and getting a small loan, she would be able to buy a small but profitable restaurant. She went to East Bank for the loan. East Bank claimed that the balance of its secured debt was not discharged in bankruptcy. Sally agreed and signed an agreement to pay East Bank the $2,500, as the bank was not a party to the petitioning of Sally into bankruptcy. Because of this, East Bank made the new unsecured loan to Sally.

  (a) Discuss East Bank's claim that the balance of its secured debt was not discharged in bankruptcy.

  (b) Discuss the legal effect of Sally's agreement to pay East Bank $2,500 after the discharge in bankruptcy.

  (c) If one year later Sally went into voluntary bankruptcy, what effect would the bankruptcy proceedings have on the new unsecured loan.

6. Tracey Service Co., Inc., filed a petition for a Chapter 11 reorganization. Acar Supply Co., one of Tracey's creditors, filed a motion to convert the case to a Chapter 7 liquidation. The court found that the debtor corporation had no place of business, no inventory, no equipment, no employees, and no business phone. Should Tracey Service be permitted to reorganize under Chapter 11? [In Re Tracey Service Co., Inc., 17 B.R. 405 (1982)]

7. Donald Lewis filed a voluntary petition for bankruptcy. One of the debts on which he sought discharge was a $1,500 judgment that had been entered against him for assault on Betty Dunson. Lewis testified in the bankruptcy court that he "put both hands around [Dunson's] neck and told her to leave his wife alone or he would break her neck." Will the court grant a discharge of the judgment claim? [In Re Lewis, 17 B.R. 341 (1982)]

8. Mr. and Mrs. Tomeo obtained a loan from HCC Consumer Discount Company and gave HCC a security interest in their household goods, which Mr. Tomeo had valued at $5,000. Four months later the Tomeos filed a voluntary petition in bankruptcy and listed the value of the same household items at $600. HCC objected to the discharge of the debt on the ground that Mr. Tomeo had made materially false representations for the purpose of deceiving HCC. Mr. Tomeo stated that he had valued the items at what he had paid for them ten years previously. Was the debt nondischargeable? [In Re Tomeo, 1 B.R. 673 (1979)]

9. Would a Chapter 13 plan that absorbed the debtor's entire income after expenses, and proposed a 100 percent repayment to secured creditors to the extent of their security, and a 1 percent repayment over a three-and-one-half-year period of general unsecured creditors be approved by the court? [In Re Barnes, 5 B.R. 376 (1980)]

10. Prior to filing for bankruptcy, Bray was making loan payments to his company's credit union through payroll deductions. Bray's employer continued to deduct the loan payments from Bray's paychecks after being notified of the bankruptcy petition. Is this a violation of the Bankruptcy Code? [In Re Bray, 17 B.R. 152 (1982)]

11. Does conversion of nonexempt property to exempt property on the eve of a bankruptcy constitute a fraudulent conveyance? (E.g., purchasing a home could convert $7,500 in cash to $7,500 in exempt property.) [Wudrick v. Clements, 451 F.2d 988 (9th Cir. 1971)].

FOCUS ON ETHICS

Creditors' Rights and Bankruptcy

We are certainly many years away from that period in our history when debtors' prisons existed. Some say, however, that we have proceeded too far in the opposite direction, making it too easy for debtors to avoid what they legally owe.

THE GENERAL QUESTION OF CREDITORS' RIGHTS

When a debtor fails to meet his or her financial obligations, the creditor has numerous remedies, such as a mechanic's lien on real property, an artisan's lien on personal property, foreclosure, attachment, and garnishment. When such rights and remedies are invoked, the creditor is often considered by the general public to employ "unfair" tactics. There is clearly a distinction in the public's mind between the nonrepayment of a loan and the theft of personal property. But from a purely economic point of view, the result is the same—the wealth of the creditor-seller is reduced.

An ethical question arises as to whether the creditor or the debtor should be favored when the debtor has not performed. For many, this ethical question revolves around the way in which the debtor has reduced the net worth of the creditor. Also, the public at large often judges the debtor's action on

the basis of the purpose for which the debt was incurred. If the debt was incurred for a "needed" item, such as a refrigerator, then common opinion seems to be that such a debtor should be dealt with in a lenient manner. On the other hand, if the debt was incurred for a trip to the Bahamas, the ethical issue appears to be significantly different.

THE EFFECT OF NONPAYMENT OF LOANS

Whatever the ethical issue may be when a debtor fails to perform, the economic consequence is clear: The cost of nonperformance is imposed on all of those debtors who do perform. This cost is in the form of higher average interest rates to obtain credit. That is to say, the greater the percentage of loan agreements not consummated as per the agreement, the larger the "risk factor" added to normal interest rates. Creditors deal in a highly competitive market. They expect to earn a normal rate of return for investment in such an industry. If costs increase because of nonperformance by debtors, those costs will have to be recouped somewhere. In general, the only way to recoup them is to charge all debtors a higher interest rate.

Now let us reconsider the ethical question regarding creditors' rights. The more creditors are able to enforce their rights and thereby obtain greater performance on loan agreements, the lower will be the interest rate paid by debtors as a group. Who, then, has a greater right in this situation—the debtor who has not performed or the group of debtors that has, does, and will perform?

ETHICS VERSUS ECONOMICS: AN EXAMPLE

Consider an example of a court decision and the ethical versus the economic issues involved. To purchase furniture and consumer durable goods, residents in low-income areas must sign an agreement that includes a statement that failure to make timely payment can result in the repossession not only of the goods purchased under the instant contract, but also of any prior goods purchased under similar contracts from the same vendor. This provision is often referred to as an add-on clause.

Suppose that Mrs. Brown, a poor, single mother of three children, makes three separate purchases at a furniture store. First she buys a television, then a stereo, and then a couch. Each one of these items is purchased on credit. Each time she purchases an item, she makes a down payment and signs a contract containing the clause stated above. She duly makes payments on the first two items but fails to make payments on time for the last item. The vendor, invoking its rights under the so-called add-on clause, repossesses not only the couch but also the stereo and television. Mrs. Brown sues.

What should the court decide? For many, the add-on clause offends their sense of justice. After all, why should Mrs. Brown relinquish those items for which she has properly paid according to the sales agreement? Indeed, when similar cases have reached the courts, judgments have tended to favor the plaintiffs on the grounds of public policy.

But now consider the long-run implications of such a court decision. Add-on clauses allowing for the repossession (replevin) of previously purchased items, in addition to the one under contract, give vendors in low-income areas additional security to reduce the costs of nonperformance. The reason, presumably, that one does not find such add-on clauses in similar sales agreements in middle-income areas is because vendors do not find it necessary to seek the additional security. Without this additional security in a low-income area, vendors will reduce the amount of credit offered. How? They will screen applicants more carefully, eliminating those who previously might have been able to obtain credit. The long-term result of Mrs. Brown's successful litigation will be a reduction in the amount of credit given in low-income areas. Those buyers

with the lowest credit ratings are the ones who will be hurt. How appealing is this result?

Now try to determine whether the vendor's business conduct in repossessing the stereo and the television, in addition to the couch, was ethically appropriate.

GARNISHMENT OF WAGES

Ethical considerations are invariably involved in the whole issue of garnishment of wages. There will always be a conflict between creditors' rights and the needs of the debtor, plus those of the employer. Certainly many an employer would like to terminate an individual's employment because of garnishment proceedings. Certainly a creditor would like garnishment to allow for repayment of a debt at the earliest possible date. But the employee must continue working. Also, there must be enough income left over after garnishment for the employee to survive and indeed to have an incentive to continue working.

Most states have statutes that allow for garnishment of wages to enforce compliance with child-support orders. By 1983, forty-eight states had enacted this type of statute as a remedy for the noncompliance of child-support obligation. Is this an acceptable form of government intrusion? Texas, one of the two remaining states that did not (until recently) allow garnishment of wages for any purpose, has a long history of protecting the rights of individuals against excessive governmental intrusion. It is difficult to balance the rights of an individual against the legal duty of parents to support their minor children. Yet a balance must be made, and, since the garnishment of wages has

proved to be the most effective method for enforcing child-support payments, society has generally concluded that the garnishment of wages in situations in which child support is not being paid is the most equitable solution. After all, noncompliance with child-support orders transfers the burden of child support onto the public—a situation that many regard as unfair. Therefore, in 1984 Texas changed its law and now permits garnishment of wages to enforce child-support orders.

BANKRUPTCY

The first goal of bankruptcy law is to provide relief and protection to debtors who have "gotten in over their heads." The U.S. Constitution provides that Congress shall have the power to establish uniform laws on the subject of bankruptcies throughout the United States. Our first bankruptcy law was enacted in 1898 and was amended in 1938. In 1978 the Bankruptcy Reform Act was passed and became effective on October 1, 1979. It was further amended in 1984. In addition to the general issue of creditors' versus debtors' rights, there is the specific issue of the rights of those in bankruptcy relative to the rights of the bankrupt party's creditors.

Consider the concept of bankruptcy from the point of view of the creditor. The creditor has extended a transfer of purchasing power from himself or herself to the debtor. That transfer of purchasing power represents a transfer of an asset for an asset. The debtor obtains the asset of money, goods, or services; and the creditor obtains the asset called a *secured* or *unsecured* legal obligation to pay. Once the debtor is in bankruptcy, voluntarily or involuntarily, the asset that the creditor owns most often has a diminished value. Indeed, in many circumstances that asset will have a zero value. Bankruptcy law attempts to provide a "fair" means of distributing to creditors the assets remaining in the debtor's possession.

Society has generally concluded that everyone should be given the chance to start over again. Thus, bankruptcy law is a balancing act between providing such a chance and insuring that creditors are given "a fair shake." But the question of "moral hazard" arises with bankruptcy law just as it does with products liability law. The easier it becomes for debtors to hide behind bankruptcy laws, the greater will be the incentive for debtors to use such laws to avoid payment of legally owed sums of money. That also means that the more easily a debtor can hide behind bankruptcy laws, the more a creditor will charge for a higher degree of risk-taking. The fact is that the total number of bankruptcies has more than doubled since the enactment of the Bankruptcy Reform Act of 1978. What this phenomenon means is that creditors will incur higher risks in making loans. In order to compensate for these higher risks, creditors will do one or more of the following: increase the interest rates charged to everyone, require more security (collateral), or be more selective in the granting of credit. Thus, a trade-off situation exists: The more lenient bankruptcy laws are, the better off will be those debtors who find themselves in bankruptcy; but those debtors who will never be in bankruptcy will be worse

off. Ethical concerns here must be matched with the economic concerns of other groups of individuals affected by the law.

CHAPTER 11 FILING

Particularly controversial is the question concerning at what point and in which circumstances companies should be entitled to file a Chapter 11 petition for reorganization under the Bankruptcy Reform Act of 1978. Filing a Chapter 11 petition automatically stays the commencement, continuation, or enforcement of proceedings against the debtor. As previously stated, the bankruptcy law attempts to provide a refuge to the honest debtor who is unable to pay his or her debts. The "rehabilitation" of the debtor, rather than the liquidation of the debtor's estate (Chapter 7) is the primary purpose of Chapter 11.

Manville Corporation's Chapter 11 filing raises many ethical issues. Many critics argue that the Manville filing was an abuse of the federal bankruptcy law since the company was still earning profits. The Manville Corporation filed for Chapter 11 reorganization on August 26, 1982, and at that time the corporation's reported assets were valued at $2.2 billion. The fact that Manville Corporation was solvent when it filed for Chapter 11 reorganization led many people to question the "fairness" behind Chapter 11. Should a bankruptcy court be used by a solvent company facing potential tort liability? Do companies such as Manville deserve the "fresh start" available under Chapter 11— which allows debtors to escape the pressures that drove them into bankruptcy?

Manville officials contended that the petition for corporation reorganization was the only way to save the corporation from the pending 16,500 lawsuits for asbestos-related diseases. A research firm commissioned by Manville in 1982 estimated liability as high as $4.8 billion by the year 2009. Furthermore, the Bankruptcy Code is drafted so as to allow the filing for Chapter 11 reorganization by a "solvent" debtor. The theory behind allowing solvent debtors to file is that creditors will be better protected if debtors file for reorganization while their assets are still available to pay creditors' claims. As long as a debtor is "honest," bankruptcy courts have been willing to discharge the debtor from pre-petition debts and some post-petition debts.

Yet even though the filing by Manville may stick to the letter of the Bankruptcy Code, the question still arises as to whether Manville filed in good faith and was deserving of a "fresh start." There is no doubt that Manville knew that exposure to asbestos resulted in asbestos-related diseases such as asbestosis, lung cancer, and cancer of the stomach, colon, and rectum. Court cases also resulted in findings that Manville withheld this knowledge from its employees. Given this evidence of social irresponsibility, is Manville truly deserving of a fresh start?

The recent case of *N.L.R.B. v. Bildisco and Bildisco,* [465 U.S. 513, 104 S.Ct. 1188 (1984)], also raises ethical considerations. In *Bildisco,* the debtor, a building-supplies distributor, filed a voluntary petition in bankruptcy for reorganization under Chapter 11 and was thereafter authorized by the bankruptcy court to operate the business as a debtor-in-possession. The debtor's employees were represented by the union with whom the debtor had negotiated a collective-bargaining agreement. When the debtor became unable to meet some of its obligations under the agreement, it requested and received permission from the bankruptcy court to reject the agreement.

The Supreme Court, upon granting the petition for certiorari, held that collective-bargaining agreements subject to the National Labor Relations Act are executory contracts, and hence they are subject to rejection by debtors-in-possession. Is such a result ethical? Should the "fresh start" policy of the Bankruptcy Code extend to the rejection of collective-bargaining agreements? Doesn't this opinion give businesses a real bargaining chip in dealing with unions? If the unions refuse to take pay cuts or other concessions, can't businesses just turn to Chapter 11?

The 1984 Bankruptcy Amendments attempted to answer some of these questions. In general, a collective-bargaining contract can be rejected in a Chapter 11 bankruptcy if the debtor has first proposed "necessary" contractual modifications to the union, and if the union has failed to accept them without "good cause." Good faith negotiations to reach an agreement are required from both sides.

COMPETITION AND CHAPTER 11

Competition often induces manufacturers to take risks that may subsequently harm society, thus precipitating the manufacturer's own economic downfall. Some critics also argue, however, that the imposition of punitive damages in products liability cases may in effect be "overkill." In other words, punitive damages administered to punish the offender and to deter this type of conduct in the future may make the difference between a company's filing or not filing a petition for Chapter 11 reorganization. Thus, the economic consequences of our punishment and deterrence objectives appear much more complex than upon first glance. How can we punish and deter unethical conduct by a company that has done much good in the past and has the potential to do much good in the future without inviting it to file for Chapter 11? Remember, the filing of a petition in bankruptcy automatically stays the commencement of proceedings against the debtor. What happens to potential plaintiffs then?

Another aspect of Chapter 11 also raises ethical considerations (and is controversial as well). In recent years competition in many industries has increased dramatically. After the deregulation of the airline industry, for example, some airlines overexpanded and eventually became insolvent. Furthermore, as the industry grew from 36 to 156 airlines, fare wars began to characterize the industry. Thus, some companies—such as Braniff, Continental, and Air Florida—were unsuccessful under deregulation and ultimately declared bankruptcy. Others—such as Eastern and Pan Am—have high debts and little cash. In this type of situation, it may be tempting for a company not to deal in good faith because it knows that resort to Chapter 11 is always available. Chapter 11 may become a bargaining chip for management to use against labor during wage negotiations. The potential threat of Chapter 11 can leave employees in a very vulnerable position when trying to predict whether a company is actually considering Chapter 11 as a viable alternative or is merely bluffing.

DISCUSSION QUESTIONS

1. What inadequacies existed in the private legal system (mostly contract law) and the private market system to prompt so much federal and state legislation concerning debtors' and creditors' rights?
2. Does this legislation accomplish what was intended?
3. What should be the balance between creditors' and debtors' rights?
4. Who gains and who loses from usury laws? What are the ethical issues concerned here?
5. How moral-ethical is it for a business to refuse to deal with a customer simply because that person once went into bankruptcy, even though that person is now a good credit risk in every other way?

UNIT V

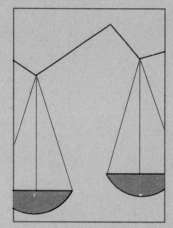

AGENCY AND EMPLOYMENT

32

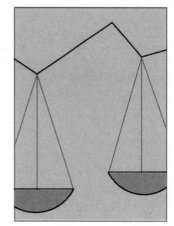

AGENCY
Creation, and Duties and Rights of Agents and Principals

One of the most common, important, and pervasive legal relationships is that of agency. In an **agency** relationship between two parties, one of the parties, called the **agent**, agrees to represent or act for the other, called the **principal**. The principal has the right to control the agent's conduct in matters entrusted to the agent. More formally, the Restatement, Second, Agency,[1] defines *agency* as "the fiduciary relation[2] which results from the manifestation of consent by one person to another that the other shall act in his behalf and subject to his control, and consent by the other so to act." In general, the law of agency is based on the maxim that "one acting by another is acting for himself."

THE NATURE OF AGENCY

An agent acts for his or her principal. By using agents a principal can conduct multiple business operations simultaneously in various locations. Thus, for example, contracts which bind the principal can be

made at different places with different persons at the same time. A familiar example of an agent is a corporate officer who serves in a representative capacity for the owners of the corporation. In this capacity, the officer has the authority to bind the principals to a contract. Indeed, agency law is essential to the existence and operation of a corporate entity, because only through its agents can a corporation function and enter into contracts.

KINDS OF AGENCY RELATIONSHIPS

The first step in analyzing an agency relationship is to determine whether such a relationship exists. Traditional analysis in the law of agency distinguishes three categories of relationships:

1. Principal and agent.
2. Master and servant.
3. Principal or employer and independent contractor.

It is important to note that the principal-and-agency relationship can also be found within a master-servant or a principal-or-employer/independent-contractor relationship.

---

1. Restatement, Second, Agency, Section 1(1). This is an authoritative summary of the law of agency, which is often referred to by jurists in decisions and opinions.
2. A duty to act for someone else's benefit, coupled with a relationship of trust.

553

Principal-Agent

In a principal-agent relationship, the parties have agreed that the agent will act *on behalf of and instead of* the principal in negotiating and transacting business with third persons. This relationship will affect the principal's rights and duties. Thus, an agent is empowered to perform legal acts that are binding on the principal. For example, an agent can bind a principal in a contract with a third person.

An agent has *derivative authority* in carrying out the principal's business. For example, Earl is hired as a booking agent for a rock group—Harry and the Rockets. As the group's agent, Earl can negotiate and sign contracts for the rock group to appear at concerts. The contracts will be binding and thus legally enforceable against the group.

Master-Servant

Today's law defines *servant* as an employee—one employed by a master to perform services; the servant's physical conduct is *controlled* or is subject to control by the master. A servant can be a species of agent. The term *master-servant relationship* is anachronistic. Employees are not referred to as servants. For that matter, employers are not called masters. The current terminology for the old master-servant relationship is *employer-employee*.

The term *employee* had no significance for common law rules of agency. However, with the industrial revolution and recent social legislation, the term has come into prominence. An **employee** can also be an agent (other than an independent contractor) if the employee has an appointment or contract for hire with authority to represent the employer.

For example, Dana owns a dress shop. She employs Sandy, Sheila, and Sue as salespeople, and Sara, as a janitor. Dana is the employer (master); the other women are the employees (servants). The key feature of the employer-employee relationship is that the employer controls, or at least has the right to control, the employee in the performance of the tasks involved in the employment. The employees do not have *independent* business discretion. The dress shop salespeople not only can be told to sell the dresses but also can be told how to sell them. However, in selling the dresses, they are agents as well as employees. They have been given the authority by Dana to contract for and represent Dana

in creating sales with customers. On the other hand, Sara is merely an employee and not an agent. Dana completely controls her work place and work habits, and Sara has no authority to represent Dana in dealings with others.

All employment laws (state and federal) apply only to the employer-employee relationship. Statutes governing Social Security, withholding taxes, workers' compensation, unemployment compensation, work-place safety laws, and the like, are applicable only if there is an employer-employee status. These laws do not apply to the independent contractor.

Principal or Employer– Independent Contractor

Independent contractors are not employees (servants), because their employers have no control over the details of their physical performance. Restatement, Second, Agency, Section 2, defines an independent contractor as:

> * * * a person who contracts with another to do something for him but who is not controlled by the other nor subject to the other's right to control with respect to his physical conduct in the performance of the undertaking. He may or may not be an agent.

The following factors are relevant in determining the status of independent contractors:

1. What is the extent of control that the employer can exercise over the details of the work?
2. Is the employed person engaged in an occupation or business distinct from that of the employer?
3. Is the work usually done under the employer's direction, or is it done by a specialist without supervision?
4. Does the employer supply the tools at the place of work?
5. For how long is the person employed?
6. What is the method of payment—by time period or at the completion of the job?
7. What is the degree of skill required by the person employed?

Building contractors and subcontractors are independent contractors, and a property owner does not control the acts of either of these professionals.

CONCEPT SUMMARY: Agency: Legal Relationships

TYPES OF LEGAL RELATIONSHIPS	DEFINITIONS
Principal-Agent	An agent acts on behalf of and instead of the principal, using a certain degree of his or her own discretion.
Master-Servant (Employer-Employee)	The "servant" is an employee whose physical conduct is controlled or subject to control by an employer. A servant can also be an agent.
Principal or Employer-Independent Contractor	The contractor is not an employee, and the employer or principal has no control over the details of physical performance. Except for real estate and collection agencies, the contractor is not usually an agent.

Truck drivers who own their equipment and hire out on an *ad hoc* basis are independent contractors; however, truck drivers who drive company trucks on a regular basis are usually employees (servants). A collection agency is another example of an independent contractor.

Commingling of the Relationships

It is important to note that the employer-employee (master-servant) relationship may or may not necessarily involve an agency relationship. The same holds true for the relationship between a principal or employer and an independent contractor. To illustrate: An employer who hires a traveling salesperson as an employee has created not only an

employer-employee relationship but one of agency as well. A seller-owner of real estate who hires a real estate broker to negotiate a sale of his or her property has not only contracted with an independent contractor (the real estate broker) but has also established an agency relationship for the specific purpose of assisting in the sale of the property. On the other hand, an employer who hires someone exclusively as a delivery person has created only an employer-employee relationship, and the delivery person is not an agent.

The following case demonstrates the criteria by which courts decide whether a master-servant (employer-employee) or principal or employer-independent contractor relationship exists.

BACKGROUND AND FACTS *Dr. George Hall, the defendant, normally worked from 8:00 A.M. to 6:00 P.M. on weekdays, and frequently on weekends. He had neither the time nor the capacity for household maintenance, so he hired Ivan Davey, who was the partner of plaintiff, Tom Amear, to do landscaping and other work around the house. Dr. Hall would tell Davey what needed to be done, then Davey, Amear, or other employees would accomplish the work. Davey and Amear controlled their own hours and method of accomplishing the work. In February of 1977 Hall asked Davey to install fiberglass over four spaces formed by exposed beams connecting the carport and the house. The beams were purely decorative with no structural purpose, and Dr. Hall did not instruct Davey how to install the fiberglass. It was Amear's idea to climb out on the beams to install it. Once on the beams, the nails in each end of the beam supporting Amear pulled through the beam, and Amear fell and severely injured himself. Amear claims he is an employee and that Dr. Hall failed to provide and maintain safe working conditions. Dr. Hall claims Amear*

AMEAR v. HALL
Court of Appeals of Georgia, 1982.
296 S.E.2d 611, 164 Ga.App. 163.

is an independent contractor. The trial court entered judgment in favor of Dr. Hall, and the plaintiff, Amear, appealed.

QUILLIAN, Chief Justice.
*   *   *   *

"The test to be applied in determining whether the relationship of the parties under a contract for the performance of labor is that of employer and servant, or employer and independent contractor, lies in whether the contract gives, or the employer assumes, the right to control the time, manner and method of executing the work, as distinguished from the right merely to require certain definite results in conformity to the contract. . . . 'Where one is employed generally to perform certain services for another, and there is no specific contract to do a certain piece of work according to specifications for a stipulated sum, it is inferable that the employer has retained the right to control the manner, method and means of the performance of the contract, and that the employee is not an independent contractor.' The test is not whether the employer did in fact control and direct the employee in the work but it is whether the employer had that right under the employment contract." *Golosh v. Cherokee Cab Co.*, 226 Ga. 636, 637–639, 176 S.E.2d 925.

The test historically applied by this Court [in determining] *   *   * whether a person employed is a servant or an independent contractor is whether the employer, under the contract, whether oral or written, has the right to direct the time, the manner, the methods, and the means of the execution of the work, as contradistinguished from the right to insist upon the contractor producing results according to the contract, or whether the contractor in the performance of the work contracted for is free from any control by the employer of the time, manner, and method in the performance of the work. *   *   * Under either test, the evidence demanded a finding that plaintiff was an independent contractor.
*   *   *   *

An individual contractor is expected to determine for himself whether his place of employment is safe or unsafe, and ordinarily may not recover against the owner for injuries sustained in the performance of the contract. *   *   * Unless the owner and an injured employee have a relationship of master-servant, the employer is generally not responsible for injuries occasioned by the method by which work is done by the employee. *   *   * "It is also the general rule that the employer is under no duty to take affirmative steps to guard or protect the [individual] contractor's employees against the consequences of the contractor's negligence or to provide for their safety." *   *   *
*   *   *   *

DECISION AND REMEDY   *The Court of Appeals found Davey and Amear to be independent contractors. Therefore, Dr. Hall was not liable for the injury to Amear, and the judgment of the trial court was affirmed.*

FORMATION OF THE AGENCY RELATIONSHIP

The following discussions will emphasize the usual form that an agency relationship takes. An agency relationship is a *consensual* relationship; that is, it comes about by voluntary consent and agreement between the parties. Generally, the agreement need not be in writing, and consideration is not required.[3]

---

3.   There are two main exceptions to oral agency agreements:
    a. In many states, the Statute of Frauds makes the following requirement. Whenever agency authority empowers the agent to enter into a contract that the Statute of Frauds requires to be in

A principal must have legal capacity to enter contracts. The logic is simple. A person who cannot legally enter contracts directly should not be allowed to do it indirectly through an agent. An agent derives the authority to enter contracts from the principal, and a contract made by an agent is legally viewed as a contract of the principal. It is immaterial whether the agent personally has the legal capacity to make that contract. Thus, a minor can be an agent but cannot be a principal appointing an agent (in some states).[4] Where permitted, however, any resulting contracts will be voidable by the minor principal, but not by the adult third party.

Thus, any person can be an agent, regardless of whether he or she has the capacity to contract. Even a person who is legally incompetent can be appointed an agent if that person is capable of performing the required functions.

An agency relationship can be created for any *legal* purpose. One created for an illegal purpose or contrary to public policy is unenforceable. If Jones (as principal) contracts with Smith (as agent) to sell illegal narcotics, the agency relationship is unenforceable because it is a felony and therefore against public policy to sell narcotics illegally. It is also illegal for medical doctors and other licensed professionals to employ unlicensed agents to perform professional actions.

Generally, no formalities are required to create an agency. The agency relationship can arise by acts of the parties in one of four ways:

1. By agreement.
2. By ratification.
3. By apparent authority, or estoppel.
4. By operation of law.

---

writing, then the agent's authority from the principal must likewise be in writing. This is known as the "equal dignity rule." It occurs most frequently in contracts for the sale of an interest in land or contracts that cannot be performed within one year. The Statute of Frauds is discussed in Chapter 13.

b. A power of attorney is written authority conferred to an agent. It is conferred in a formal writing, usually acknowledged by a notary public, whose seal is attached to the formal document. A power of attorney can be general, giving the agent broad powers, or it can grant the agent only restricted authority.

4. Exceptions have been granted by some courts to allow a minor to appoint an agent for the limited purpose of contracting for the minor's necessities of life. [Casey v. Kastel, 237 N.Y. 305, 142 N.E. 671 (1924)]

Agency by Agreement

Agency is a consensual relationship, because it must be based on some *affirmative* indication that the agent agrees to act for the principal and the principal agrees to have the agent so act.

An agency agreement can take the form of an express written contract. For example, Paula enters into a sales agreement with Adam, a realtor, to sell Paula's house. An agency relationship exists between Paula and Adam for the sale of the house. Most express agreements can be oral. For example, Paula asks Bob, a gardener, to contract with others for the care of her lawn on a regular basis. Bob agrees. An agency relationship exists between Paula and Bob for the lawn care.

An agency agreement can be implied from conduct. For example, a hotel expressly allows Jack Andrews to park cars, but Andrews has no employment contract there. The hotel's conduct amounts to a manifestation of its willingness that Jack park its customers' cars, and Jack can infer from the hotel's conduct that he has authority to act as a valet. It can be implied that he is an agent for the hotel. His purpose is to provide valet parking services for hotel guests.

Agency by Ratification

On occasion, a person who is in fact not an agent, or who is an agent acting outside the scope of his or her authority, may make a contract on behalf of another (a principal). If the principal approves or affirms that contract by word or by action, an agency relationship is created by **ratification.** Ratification is a question of intent, and intent can be expressed by either words or conduct. The basic requirements for ratification are summarized in Chapter 33.

For example, Alfred James is a clerk (employee) of Anne Paul's Chic Fashion Store. Alfred contracts to purchase a tract of land in Paul's name without her authority to do so. Paul learns of James's actions and decides that the land is of great value and that she will go through with the sale. When a principal accepts the benefits or in some way affirms the conduct of one purporting to act on his or her behalf, an agency relationship is created. In this case, Paul has *ratified* James's acts, thereby creating an agency relationship between them. (The creation of the agency "relates back" to the time of James's unauthorized act.) The third party may revoke the offer or rescind the contract if he or she does so before ratification by the principal.

Agency by Estoppel

When a *principal causes* a third person to believe that another person is his or her agent, and the third person deals with the supposed agent, the principal is "estopped to deny" the agency relationship. In these situations, the principal's actions create the *appearance* of an agency that does not in fact exist. For example: Martin accompanies Paul to call on a customer, Sam, the proprietor of the General Store. Martin has done sales work but is not employed by Paul at this time. Paul boasts to Sam that he wishes he had three more assistants "just like Martin." Sam has reason to believe from Paul's statements that Martin is an agent for Paul. Sam then places seed orders with Martin. If Paul does not correct the impression that Martin is an agent, Paul will be bound to fill the orders just as if Martin were really Paul's agent. Paul's representation to Sam created the impression that Martin was Paul's agent and had authority to solicit orders.

Agency by estoppel does not extend to all acts under all circumstances. For example, the acts or declarations of the purported agent in and of themselves do not create an agency by estoppel. It is the deeds or statements of the *principal* that create an agency. Suppose Jane walks into Ann's Dress Boutique and claims to be a sales agent for an exclusive Paris dress designer, Pierre Damon. Ann has never had business relations with Pierre Damon. Based on Jane's claim, Ann gives Jane an order and prepays fifteen percent of the sales order. Jane is not an agent and the dresses are never delivered. Ann cannot hold Pierre Damon liable. Jane's acts and declarations, in and of themselves, do not create an agency by estoppel.

In addition, the third person must prove that he or she *reasonably* believed that an agency relationship existed and that the agent had authority. Facts and circumstances must show that an ordinary, prudent person who is familiar with business practice and custom would be justified in concluding that the agent had authority.

Agency by Operation of Law

In some cases, the courts have found it desirable to find an agency relationship in the absence of a formal agreement. This may occur in family relationships. For example, suppose one spouse purchases certain basic necessaries and charges them to the other spouse's charge account. The courts will often rule that the latter is liable for payment of such necessaries either because of a social policy of promoting the general welfare of the other spouse or because of a legal duty to supply necessaries to family members. Sometimes agency by operation of law is created, giving an agent emergency power to act under unusual circumstances that are not covered by the agreement when failure to act would cause a principal substantial loss. If the agent is unable to contact the principal, the courts will often grant this emergency power.

CONCEPT SUMMARY: Formation of Principal-Agent Relationship	
METHOD OF FORMATION	**DEFINITIONS**
By Agreement	Through express consent (oral or written), or implied from conduct.
By Ratification	Principal either by act or agreement ratifies conduct by a person who is not in fact an agent or who acted outside the scope of authority.
By Estoppel	When the principal causes a third person to believe that another person is his or her agent.
By Operation of Law	Based on a social duty (such as the need to support family members), or in emergency situations where the agent is unable to contact the principal.

DUTIES OF AGENTS AND PRINCIPALS

Once the principal-agent relationship has been created, both parties have duties that govern their conduct. The principal-agent relationship is *fiduciary*—one of trust. In it, each party owes the other the duty to act with the utmost good faith. Neither party may keep from the other information that has any bearing on their agency relationship.

It is logical to discuss separately the agent's duty to the principal and the principal's duty to the agent.

The Agent's Duty to the Principal

The duties that an agent owes to a principal are set forth in the agency agreement or arise by operation of law. They are implied from the agency relationship *whether or not the identity of the principal is disclosed to a third party*. Generally, the agent owes the principal the following five duties:

1. Performance.
2. Notification.
3. Loyalty.
4. Obedience.
5. Accounting.

Duty of Performance   An implied condition in every agency contract is the agent's agreement to use reasonable diligence and skill in performing the work. When an agent fails to perform his or her duties entirely, liability for breach of contract generally will occur.

The degree of skill or care required of an agent is usually that expected of a reasonable person under similar circumstances. Although in most cases this is interpreted to mean ordinary care, an agent may have presented himself or herself as possessing special skills (such as those that an accountant or attorney possesses). In these situations, the agent is expected to exercise the skill or skills claimed. Failure to do so constitutes a breach of the agent's duty.

For example, an insurance agent who fails to obtain the insurance coverage requested by a principal is guilty of breach of contract. When an agent performs carelessly or negligently, the agent can be liable in tort as well.

In many situations, an agent who does not act for money (a gratuitous, or free, agent) can be subject to the same standards of care and duty to perform as other agents. A gratuitous agent cannot, however, be liable for breach of contract, because there is no contract. A gratuitous agent is subject only to tort liability. However, once the agent has begun to act in an agency capacity, he or she has the duty to continue to perform in this capacity in an acceptable manner.

For example, Alex Paul's friend, Amy Foster, is a real estate broker. She (the agent) gratuitously offers to sell Paul's (the principal's) farm, Black Acre. If she never attempts to sell Black Acre, Paul has no legal cause of action to force her to do so. But assume that Foster finds a buyer. She keeps promising the buyer a sales contract but fails to provide one within a reasonable period of time. The buyer becomes disgruntled and seeks another property, and the sale ultimately falls through. Paul has a cause of action in tort for negligence—because Foster failed to use the degree of care reasonably expected of real estate brokers.

Duty of Notification   There is a maxim in agency law that all the agent knows, the principal knows. Thus, it is only logical that the agent is required to notify the principal of all matters that come to his or her attention concerning the subject matter of the agency. This is the duty of notification. What the agent actually tells the principal is not relevant; what the agent *should have told* the principal is crucial.

For example, Able is Paula's agent for the purchase of a certain property from Tom. In the course of dealing, Able discovers that many years ago, Green obtained subsurface mineral rights. Thinking that this is unimportant, Able neglects to tell Paula. The purchase of the land takes place subject to Green's right to mine and remove the minerals. Paula does not have recourse against Tom; that is, Paula cannot rescind the sale or use the existence of Green's right to remove minerals as a defense to avoid going through with the sale. Able had the duty to notify Paula. The fact that he failed to do so and breached his fiduciary duty cannot be allowed to prejudice the rights of the innocent third party, Tom. Paula, however, does have recourse against Able.

Duty of Loyalty   Loyalty is one of the most fundamental duties in a fiduciary relationship. Basically stated, the agent has the duty to act solely for the benefit of his or her principal and not in the interest of the agent or a third party.

Numerous principles result from this duty. For example, an agent cannot represent two principals in the same transaction unless both know of the dual capacity and consent to it. Thus, a real estate agent cannot represent both the seller and the buyer in collecting commissions, unless the seller and the buyer so agree. A salesperson representing Avon cannot sell products of a competing line at the same time unless Avon consents. In addition, an agent who owns property cannot sell the property to the principal without indicating that ownership prior to the sale. Furthermore, an agent employed by a principal to buy cannot buy from himself or herself, and an agent employed to sell cannot become the purchaser without the principal's consent. In short, the

agent's loyalty must be undivided. The agent's actions must be strictly for the benefit of the principal and must not result in any secret profit for the agent.

The duty of loyalty means that any information or knowledge acquired through the agency relationship is considered confidential. It would be a breach of loyalty to disclose such information both during the agency relationship and after its termination. Typical examples of confidential information are trade secrets and customer lists compiled by the principal. Note, however, that an agent has the right to use skills and basic knowledge acquired during the course of agency employment in his or her own behalf (such as using sales techniques learned during the agency relationship), as long as such actions do not violate confidentiality.

The following case involves an employee-agent's use of customer lists that were clearly confidential.

ABC TRANS, ETC. v.
AERONAUTICS
FORWARDERS, INC.

Appellate Court of Illinois, 1978.
62 Ill. App. 3d 671, 20 Ill. Dec.
160, 379 N.E. 2d 1228.

BACKGROUND AND FACTS   *ABC Trans, Etc. (the plaintiff) was involved in freight forwarding, which is a highly competitive business. Salespersons in this kind of business often expend considerable time soliciting prospective clients to ascertain their specialized needs. The corporation hired Robert Agnes as its president, and after a few years the corporation began to operate at a profit. Agnes made increasing salary demands and finally tendered his resignation, but not before copying customer lists and actively recruiting a vice-president, Brownstein, to leave and set up a competing air forwarding company, Aeronautics Forwarders, Inc. (the defendant). The plaintiff sought an injunction to restrain Agnes's new corporation from soliciting or servicing plaintiff's former customers. The trial court denied the injunction.*

SULLIVAN, Presiding Justice.
*   *   *   *

While acting as an agent or employee of another, one owes the duty of fidelity and loyalty; accordingly, a fiduciary cannot act inconsistently with his agency or trust; *i.e.*, solicit his employer's customers for himself, entice coworkers away from his employer, or appropriate his employer's personal property. However, "[i]t is not necessarily a breach of duty for an agent to form a rival concern and purchase machinery for it while working for his principal, though it would be for an agent to continue to work for his principal after a rival corporation which he also served as agent begins business." Thus, as a means of fostering free enterprise, the employee who gains general skills and knowledge and forms relationships with customers and coworkers during the course of his employment may use such skills, knowledge and relationships to compete with his former employer once the employment is terminated but may not compete while still employed as his employer who, lulled by trust in the employee's fidelity and loyalty, is deprived of the opportunity to compete with that employee.

Turning to the question of relief where a betrayal of confidence and trust has been demonstrated, we note that equity will prevent the continuance of such conduct in a proper case and will compel the former employee to turn over the gains to one equitably entitled thereto. * * *

* * * *

During January, 1978, plaintiff's facilities, funds and personal property had been used by its employees under the direction of [defendant] Brownstein to pre-stamp Aeronautics's air bills, to furnish office supplies and airline containers to Aeronautics, and to prepare Aeronautics's daily station report forms. Furthermore, Brownstein continued to meet with plaintiff's customers in order to obtain commitments for Aeronautics on the basis that plaintiff was in financial trouble and would suffer a massive employee walkout. He also had meetings with plaintiff's employees to inform them of the nationwide plan to leave work on a certain Friday, and to devastate plaintiff's ability to compete by simply reporting to Aeronautics on the following Monday morning.

Brownstein admitted securing equipment and supplies for Aeronautics while still employed by plaintiff but denied that plaintiff's funds were used for this purpose. He also admitted that he told plaintiff's staff he would be following Agnes; that he expressed the hope that circumstances would then allow him to ask them to join him; and that he had informed plaintiff's clients of its unhealthy financial prognosis and its management by untrustworthy executives while asking them for the opportunity to solicit their business once he had changed jobs.

The appellate court reversed the trial court's denial of injunctive relief. The case was remanded to the lower court for a hearing on whether the injunction should be issued.

DECISION AND REMEDY

Duty of Obedience   When an agent is acting on behalf of the principal, a duty is imposed on the agent to follow all lawful and clearly stated instructions of the principal. The agent violates this duty whenever the agent deviates from such instructions. However, during emergency situations, when the principal cannot be consulted, the agent may deviate from such instructions without violating this duty if the circumstances so warrant. Whenever instructions are not clearly stated, the agent can fulfill the duty of obedience by acting in good faith and in a reasonable manner under the circumstances.

Duty of Accounting   Unless an agent and a principal agree otherwise, the agent has the duty to keep and make available to the principal an account of all property and money received and paid out on behalf of the principal. This includes gifts from third persons in connection with the agency. For example, a gift from a customer to a salesperson for prompt deliveries made by the principal belongs to the principal. The agent has a duty to maintain separate accounts for the principal's funds and for personal funds, and no intermingling of these accounts is allowed. Whenever a licensed professional violates this duty to account, he or she may be subject to disciplinary proceedings by the appropriate regulatory institution. Such proceedings would be in addition to the agent's liability to the principal for failure to account.

Duties Owed by Subagents   A subagent is any person employed or appointed by an agent to assist the agent in transacting the affairs of the principal. If the agent has authority to appoint a subagent, the subagent has authority to bind the principal. Consequently, there exists a fiduciary relationship between the subagent and the principal as well as between the subagent and the agent. Generally, the principal's authorization is needed for the hiring of subagents except in emergencies. On the other hand, if the agent is normally expected in his or her line of work to hire subagents, they may be hired without the *explicit* authorization of the principal. For example, agents typically may hire subagents to do mechanical or ministerial duties without the explicit authorization of the principal. Subagents owe the same duties to agents and to principals as agents owe to principals.

Unauthorized Subagents If an agent hires a subagent without the principal's authority, then the subagent has no legal relationship to the principal—expressed, implied, or apparent. Since the subagent and the principal have no agency relationship to one another, no duties arise between them. A principal will not be liable to third parties for that subagent's acts. However, the agent who hires the subagent without authority will be liable to the principal if the subagent acts wrongfully, and the agent will bear the loss.

Principal's Duties to the Agent

The principal also has certain duties to the agent. Generally these duties include:

1. Compensation.
2. Reimbursement and indemnification.
3. Cooperation.
4. Safe working conditions.

The principal's duties to an agent may be expressed or they may be implied by law.

Duty of Compensation Except in a gratuitous agency relationship, the principal must pay the agreed-upon value (or reasonable value) for an agent's services. Whenever the amount of compensation is agreed upon by the parties, the principal owes the duty to pay it upon completion of the agent's specified activities. If no amount is expressly agreed upon, then the principal owes the agent the customary compensation for such services. If no amount is established either by custom or by law, the principal owes the agent the reasonable value of his or her services.

In general, when a principal requests certain services from an agent, the agent reasonably expects payment. A duty is therefore implied for the principal to pay the agent for services rendered. For example, when an accountant or an attorney is asked to act as an agent, compensation is implied. The principal has the duty to pay that compensation in a timely manner.

Duty of Reimbursement and Indemnification Whenever an agent disburses sums of money at the request of the principal, and whenever the agent disburses sums of money to pay for necessary expenses in the course of a reasonable performance of his or her agency duties, the principal has the duty to reimburse. Agents cannot recover for expenses incurred by their own misconduct or negligence, however.

Subject to the terms of the agency agreement, the principal has the duty to reimburse an agent for authorized payments or indemnify (compensate) an agent for liabilities incurred because of authorized and lawful acts and transactions and also for losses suffered because of the principal's failure to perform any duties. Additionally, the principal must indemnify the agent for the value of benefits that the agent confers upon the principal unofficially.

The amount of indemnification is usually specified in the agency contract. If it is not, the courts will look to the nature of the business and the type of loss in order to determine the amount.

Authorized subagents can recover from either the principal or the agent who hires them, since the subagent is in a fiduciary relationship to both. If the authorized subagent obtains indemnification from the agent who does the hiring, the agent can then seek indemnification from the principal.

Duty of Cooperation A principal has a duty both to cooperate with and to assist an agent in performing his or her duties. The principal must do nothing to prevent such performance. For example, when a principal grants an agent an exclusive territory, the principal cannot compete with the agent or appoint or allow another agent to so compete in violation of the *exclusive agency*. Such competition would expose the principal to liability for the agent's lost sales or profits.

Duty to Provide Safe Working Conditions The common law requires the principal to provide safe premises, equipment, and conditions for all agents and employees. The principal has a duty to inspect working conditions and to warn agents and employees about any unsafe areas. If the agency is one of employment, the employer's liability is frequently covered by worker's compensation insurance, which is the primary remedy for an employee's injury on the job.

REMEDIES AND RIGHTS OF AGENTS AND PRINCIPALS

It is said that every wrong has its remedy. In business situations, disputes between agents and principals may arise out of either contract or tort laws and carry corresponding remedies. These remedies include monetary damages, termination of the agency relationship, injunction, and required accountings.

Agent's Rights and Remedies Against Principal

For every duty of the principal, the agent has a corresponding right. Therefore, the agent has the right to be compensated, reimbursed, idemnified, and to work in a safe environment. An agent also has the right to perform agency duties without interference by the principal.

Remedies of the agent for breach of duty by the principal follow normal contract and tort remedies. In addition, an agent can:

1. Withhold further performance.
2. Counterclaim if the principal sues.
3. Demand that the principal give an accounting.

These contract remedies are all for damages. Since the principal-agent relationship is deemed to be consensual in nature, an agent has no right to specific performance in an ordinary agency contract. An agent can recover for past services and future damages but cannot force the principal to allow him or her to continue acting as an agent.

Principal's Rights and Remedies Against Agent

In general, a principal has contract remedies for an agent's breach of fiduciary duties. The principal also has tort remedies for fraud, misrepresentation, negligence, deceit, libel, slander, and trespass committed by the agent. In addition, any breach of a fiduciary duty by an agent may justify the principal's termination of the agency.

The main actions of the principal are:

1. Constructive trust.
2. Avoidance.
3. Indemnification.

Constructive Trust Anything an agent obtains by virtue of the employment or agency relationship belongs to the principal. It is a breach of an agent's fiduciary duty to secretly retain benefits or profits that, by right, belong to the principal. Courts in this case will imply a **constructive trust.** The agent actually holds the money on behalf of the principal, and the principal can recover it in a lawsuit. For example, Andrews, a purchasing agent, gets cash rebates from a customer. If Andrews keeps the rebates, he violates his fiduciary duty to his principal, Metcalf. Upon finding out about the cash rebates, Metcalf can sue Andrews and recover them.

The rules against self-purchase prohibit an agent from taking advantage of the agency relationship to obtain goods or property that the principal wants to purchase. For example, Peterson (the principal) wants to purchase property in the suburbs. Cox, Peterson's agent, learns that a valuable tract of land has just become available. Cox cannot buy the land for herself. Peterson gets the right of first refusal. If Cox purchases the land for her benefit, the courts will impose a constructive trust on the land; that is, the land will be held for and on behalf of the principal despite the fact that the agent attempted to buy it in her own name.

Avoidance When an agent breaches the agency agreement or agency duties under contract, the principal has a right to avoid any contract entered into with the agent. This right of avoidance is at the election of the principal.

In the following case, a real estate agent was supposedly acting on behalf of a landowner for the sale of a piece of property. The trial court decided that the agent had no cause of action.

BACKGROUND AND FACTS *Ramsey, the plaintiff, was a licensed real estate broker and was also in the business of buying and holding land for resale. Gordon, the defendant, was the owner of approximately 181 acres of land. Gordon agreed to sell Ramsey the tract of land for $800 per acre. A contract*

RAMSEY v. GORDON
Court of Civil Appeals of Texas, Waco, 1978.
567 S.W.2d 868.

of sale to convey the property was drawn up; but before the contract was executed, Gordon conveyed the property to a third party for the same price ($800 per acre).

Meanwhile, Ramsey, acting for himself, began negotiating for the resale of that property to another customer for a price of $1,250 per acre. Naturally, when Ramsey learned that Gordon had conveyed the property to another buyer, he blamed Gordon for his lost profits. Ramsey claimed that he lost over $90,000 in profits on the resale of the property.

HALL, Justice.

*   *   *   *

Ramsey [the plaintiff] testified that he operated two businesses, "Ramsey Realty" and "Ramsey Properties," that both are sole proprietorships owned by him, that under Ramsey Realty he acts as a real estate agent selling others' property for a commission, and that under Ramsey Properties he purchases property for himself. Although Ramsey now claims he was only a purchaser in the transaction with Gordon [the defendant], he testified on the trial that he was both agent and purchaser—that he was "a purchasing agent." Specifically, Ramsey testified again and again that under the contract he was Gordon's agent for the sale of the property. The trial court expressly found that he was Gordon's agent. The court also found that Ramsey knew the property was appreciating in value when the contract was made, and "up until and through January, 1974," that Ramsey failed to disclose that fact to Gordon; that he became personally interested in the property transaction by attempting to purchase the property himself, that the appreciation in value of the property from $800.00 per acre to $1,000.00 per acre was a material fact relating to the sale of the property; and that Ramsey failed to find a purchaser for Gordon for the best price available. Upon these findings the court concluded that Ramsey had breached his agency agreement and duties under the contract, and that the contract was therefore voidable at Gordon's election.

Ramsey does not challenge the finding that the property was increasing in value when the contract was being negotiated and made with Gordon, nor the findings that he knew the value was increasing and failed to disclose that fact to Gordon. Indeed, he may not do so because they are amply supported by the evidence and its inferences. His response to the conclusion that he breached his duties as Gordon's agent is to argue that he was only a purchaser and to cite Gordon's testimony that Gordon believed $800.00 per acre was a fair price when he made the contract. The over-all import of the record is that when it served Ramsey's purposes he would claim that under the contract he was Gordon's agent, but that in fact he used the contract to speculate with the property to his personal advantage without disclosure to Gordon. As we have said, the [trial] court found that Ramsey was Gordon's agent. Ramsey's testimony supports that finding.

Whenever an agent breaches his duty to his principal by becoming personally interested in an agency agreement, the contract is voidable at the election of the principal without full knowledge of all the facts surrounding the agent's interest. [Emphasis added.] *   *   * [It is a] "settled rule" that "an agent in dealing with a principal on his own account owes it to the principal not only to make no misstatements concerning the subject matter of the transaction, but also to disclose to him fully and completely all material facts known to the agent which might affect the principal; and that unless this duty on the part of the agent has been met, the principal cannot be held to have ratified the transaction."

DECISION AND REMEDY   *The judgment of the trial court was affirmed. Ramsey was denied recovery because an agency relationship existed between Ramsey and Gordon, and Ramsey had breached his duties under this relationship.*

Indemnification   A principal can be sued by a third party for an agent's negligent conduct, and in certain situations the principal can sue the agent for an equal amount of damages. This is called **indemnification.** The same holds true if the agent violates the principal's instructions. For example, Lewis (the principal) tells his agent, Moore, who is a used car salesman, to make no warranties for the used cars. Moore is eager to make a sale to Walters, the third party, and makes a warranty for the car's engine. Lewis is not absolved from liability to Walters for engine failure, but if Walters sues Lewis, Lewis can then sue Moore for indemnification for violating his instructions.

Sometimes it is difficult to distinguish between instructions of the principal that limit an agent's authority and those that are merely advice. For example, Willis (the principal) owns an office supply company; Jones (the agent) is the manager. Willis tells Jones, "Don't order any more supplies this month." Willis goes on vacation. A large order comes in from a local business, and the present inventory is insufficient to meet it. What is Jones to do? In this situation, Jones probably has the inherent power to order more supplies despite Willis's statement. It is unlikely that Jones would be required to indemnify Willis in the event that the local business subsequently canceled the order.

QUESTIONS AND CASE PROBLEMS

1. Paul Gett is a well-known, wealthy financier living in the city of Torris. Adam Wade, a friend of Gett, tells Timothy Brown that he is Gett's agent for the purchase of rare coins. Wade even shows Brown a local newspaper clipping mentioning Gett's interest in coin collecting. Brown, knowing of Wade's friendship with Gett, contracts with Wade to sell a rare coin valued at $25,000 to Gett. Wade takes the coin and disappears with it. On the date of contract payment Brown seeks to collect from Gett, claiming Wade's agency made Gett liable. Gett does not deny that Wade was a friend, but he claims that Wade was never his agent. Discuss fully whether an agency was in existence at the time the contract for the rare coin was made.

2. Adam is hired by Peter as an agent to sell a piece of property owned by Peter. The price to be obtained is to be not less than $30,000. Adam discovers that because a shopping mall is planned for the area of Peter's property, the fair market value of the property will be at least $45,000 and could be higher. Adam forms a real estate partnership with his cousin Carl, and Adam prepares for Peter's signature a contract for $32,000 for sale of the property to Carl. Peter signs the contract. Just before closing and passage of title, Peter learns about the shopping mall and the increased fair market value of his property. Peter refuses to deed the property to Carl. Carl claims that Adam, as agent, solicited a price above that agreed upon in the creation of the agency and that the contract is therefore binding and enforceable. Discuss fully whether Peter is bound to this contract.

3. John Paul Corporation made the following contracts:
   (a) A contract with Able Construction to build an addition to the corporate office building.
   (b) A contract with a CPA, a recent college graduate, to head the cost accounting section.
   (c) A contract with a saleswoman to travel a designated area to solicit orders (contracts) for the corporation.

Able contracts with Apex for materials for the addition; the CPA hires an experienced accountant to advise her on certain accounting procedures; and the saleswoman contracts to sell a large order to Green, agreeing to deliver the goods in person within twenty days. Able refuses to pick up the materials, the CPA is in default in paying the hired consultant, and the saleswoman does not deliver on time. Apex, the accountant, and Green claim John Paul Corporation is liable under agency law. Discuss fully whether an agency relationship was created by John Paul with Able, the CPA, or the saleswoman.

4. Able is hired by Peters as a traveling salesman. Able not only solicits orders but delivers the goods and collects payments from his customers. Able places all payments in his private checking account and at the end of each month draws sufficient cash from his bank to cover the payments made. Peters is totally unaware of this procedure. Because of a slowdown in the economy, Peters tells all his salespeople to offer 20 percent discounts on orders. Able solicits orders, but he offers only 15 percent discounts, pocketing the extra 5 percent paid by customers. Able has not lost any orders by this practice, and he is rated one of Peters's top salespersons. Peters now learns of Able's actions. Discuss fully Peters's rights in this matter.

5. When the Mileses applied for a mortgage loan, the bank president told them a termite inspection was always required and arranged for by the bank. The bank president

was advised that termites were found on the property and that extermination would be necessary, but he did not advise the Mileses. Do the Mileses have a cause of action against the bank? [Miles v. Perpetual Sav. & Loan Co., 58 Ohio St.2d 93, 388 N.E.2d 1364 (1979)]

6. L.M.T. Steel Products contracted with a school to install numerous room partitions. To accomplish this work, L.M.T. hired a man by the name of Webster. Webster was not a regular employee of L.M.T., and was to be paid by the number of feet of partitions installed. Webster did not have a contractor's license. Webster hired other workers to do the installing, and these workers were paid by L.M.T. Webster was given blueprints by L.M.T., but he was not otherwise at any time actively supervised by L.M.T. on the job. Webster, in need to call L.M.T., drove his own personal vehicle to a public telephone. On the way, he negligently collided with another car, and an occupant of that car, Ms. Peirson, was injured. Peirson sues L.M.T. claiming that Webster was an employee. L.M.T. claims Webster to be an independent contractor. Who is correct? [L.M.T. Steel Products, Inc. v. Peirson, 425 A.2d 242, 47 Md.App. 633 (1981)]

7. Roy Haven brought a medical malpractice action against his surgeon, Judson Randolph, M.D., and the hospital where the surgery had been performed. Haven claimed that the doctor's negligence caused him to suffer paralysis as a result of minor surgery. Haven also wished to hold the hospital responsible as Randolph's principal. Randolph was not employed by the hospital, and any services that the hospital provided were at Randolph's direction. Would Randolph be deemed an agent of the hospital? [Haven v. Randolph, 342 F.Supp. 538 (D.C. D.C.1972)]

8. Crittendon took his Chevrolet to a service station operated by Mendenhall and discussed the problem of its faulty wheel bearings. During the conversation, Mendenhall stated that he had previously worked at a Chevrolet garage and was familiar with the repair of Chevrolets. The service station at which Mendenhall worked was owned by State Oil Company and displayed two signs, each containing only the word *State*. Mendenhall leased the service station from State but received neither a salary nor repair tools from State. Crittendon left his car for Mendenhall to repair. After Mendenhall repaired it, he took it out for a test drive, went off the road, and damaged it extensively. Crittendon wished to establish an agency relationship between State and Mendenhall so he could recover from State. Does Crittendon have any grounds to argue for the existence of a principal-agent relationship? [Crittendon v. State Oil Co., 78 Ill.App.2d 112, 222 N.E.2d 561 (1966)]

9. Sam Kademenos was about to sell a $1 million life insurance policy to a prospective customer when he resigned from the company, Equitable Life. Before resigning, however, he had expended substantial company money and had utilized Equitable's medical examiners in order to procure the $1 million sale. After resigning, Kademenos joined a competitor, Jefferson Life Insurance Company, and made the sale through it. Has he breached any duty to Equitable? [Kademenos v. Equitable Life Assur. Soc'y, 513 F.2d 1073 (3d Cir. 1975)]

10. During the course of the administration of the estate of Baldwin M. Baldwin, it became necessary to sell a vast apartment complex owned by the estate, known as "Baldwin Hills Village." Lemby, a real estate broker, doing business as Skyline Realty, was commissioned to make the sale. A number of prospective purchasers were contacted, and they were present at the private sale of Baldwin Hills Village. On a number of prior occasions, Lemby had indicated to the executors of Baldwin's estate that he was interested in purchasing the property. At the private sale, Lemby outbid all others and bought Baldwin Hills Village. Lemby then sought his commission on the sale from the Baldwin estate. Will anything in agency law prevent Lemby from recovering? [In re Estate of Baldwin, 34 Cal.App.3d 596, 110 Cal.Rptr. 189 (1973)]

33

AGENCY
Liability of Principals and Agents to Third Parties and Termination of Agency Relationship: Employer-Employee Relationships

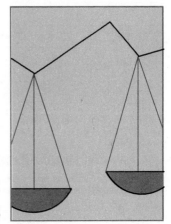

Once the principal-agent relationship is created, attention often focuses on the rights of third persons who deal with the agent. The first part of this chapter is concerned with the rights of these third parties when they *contract* with agents. Such contracts will make an agent's principal liable to the third party only if the agent had authority to make the contract or if the principal ratified, or was estopped from denying, the agent's acts.

The second part of this chapter will deal with an agent's liability to third parties in contract and tort, and the principal's liability to third parties due to an agent's torts. The third part deals with termination of the agency and agent's authority. The chapter concludes with a basic discussion of employer-employee relationships.

SCOPE OF AGENT'S AUTHORITY

A principal's liability in a contract with a third party arises from the authority given the agent to enter legally binding contracts on the principal's behalf. An agent's authority to act stems from three types of sources:

1. Express (or specific).⎫
2. Implied.   ⎬ Actual Authority
3. Apparent (or by estoppel).

If an agent contracts outside the scope of his or her authority, the principal may still be liable by ratifying the contract.

Express Authority

Express authority is embodied in that which the principal has engaged the agent to do. It can be given orally or in writing. For example, giving an agent a power of attorney confers express authority.[1] The power of attorney is a written document and is usually notarized. Like all agency relationships, a power of attorney can be special—permitting the agent to do specified acts only—or it can be general—permitting the agent to transact all business dealings for the principal. See Exhibit 33–1.

The **equal dignity** rule in most states requires that if the contract being executed is or must be in writing, then the agent's authority must also be in writing.[2] Failure to comply with the equal dignity rule can make a contract voidable *at the option of the principal.* The law regards the contract at that

---

1. An agent who holds the power of attorney is called an attorney-in-fact for the principal. The holder does not have to be an attorney-at-law.
2. An exception to the equal dignity rule exists in modern business practice. An executive officer of a corporation, when acting for the corporation in an ordinary business situation, is not required to obtain written authority from the corporation.

567

EXHIBIT 33–1 Sample Power of Attorney

POWER OF ATTORNEY
GENERAL

Know All Men by These Presents: That I, _____

_____

the undersigned (jointly and severally, if more than one) hereby make, constitute and appoint _____

_____

any true and lawful Attorney for me and in my name, place and stead and for my use and benefit:

(a) To ask, demand, sue for, recover, collect and receive each and every sum of money, debt, account, legacy, bequest, interest, dividend, annuity and demand (which now is or hereafter shall become due, owing or payable) belonging to or claimed by me, and to use and take any lawful means for the recovery thereof by legal process or otherwise, and to execute and deliver a satisfaction or release therefor, together with the right and power to compromise or compound any claim or demand;

(b) To exercise any or all of the following powers as to real property, any interest therein and/or any building thereon: To contract for, purchase, receive and take possession thereof and of evidence of title thereto; to lease the same for any term or purpose, including leases for business, residence, and oil and/or mineral development; to sell, exchange, grant or convey the same with or without warranty; and to mortgage, transfer in trust, or otherwise encumber or hypothecate the same to secure payment of a negotiable or non-negotiable note or performance of any obligation or agreement;

(c) To exercise any or all of the following powers as to all kinds of personal property and goods, wares and merchandise, choses in action and other property in possession or in action: To contract for, buy, sell, exchange, transfer and in any legal manner deal in and with the same; and to mortgage, transfer in trust, or otherwise encumber or hypothecate the same to secure payment of a negotiable or non-negotiable note or performance of any obligation or agreement;

(d) To borrow money and to execute and deliver negotiable or non-negotiable notes therefor with or without security; and to loan money and receive negotiable or non-negotiable notes therefor with such security as he shall deem proper;

(e) To create, amend, supplement and terminate any trust and to instruct and advise the trustee of any trust wherein I am or may be trustor or beneficiary; to represent and vote stock, exercise stock rights, accept and deal with any dividend, distribution or bonus, join in any corporate financing, reorganization, merger, liquidation, consolidation or other action and the extension, compromise, conversion, adjustment, enforcement or foreclosure, singly or in conjunction with others of any corporate stock, bond, note, debenture or other security; to compound, compromise, adjust, settle and satisfy any obligation, secured or unsecured, owing by or to me and to give or accept any property and/or money whether or not equal to or less in value than the amount owing in payment, settlement or satisfaction thereof;

(f) To transact business of any kind or class and as my act and deed to sign, execute, acknowledge and deliver any deed, lease, assignment of lease, covenant, indenture, indemnity, agreement, mortgage, deed of trust, assignment of mortgage or of the beneficial interest under deed of trust, extension or renewal of any obligation, subordination or waiver of priority, hypothecation, bottomry, charter-party, bill of lading, bill of sale, bill, bond, note, whether negotiable or non-negotiable, receipt, evidence of debt, full or partial release or satisfaction of mortgage, judgment and other debt, request for partial or full reconveyance of deed of trust and such other instruments in writing of any kind or class as may be necessary or proper in the premises.

Giving and Granting unto my said Attorney full power and authority to do and perform all and every act and thing whatsoever requisite, necessary or appropriate to be done in and about the premises as fully to all intents and purposes as I might or could do if personally present, hereby ratifying all that my said Attorney shall lawfully do or cause to be done by virtue of these presents. The powers and authority hereby conferred upon my said Attorney shall be applicable to all real and personal property or interests therein now owned or hereafter acquired by me and wherever situate.

My said Attorney is empowered hereby to determine in his sole discretion the time when, purpose for and manner in which any power herein conferred upon him shall be exercised, and the conditions, provisions and covenants of any instrument or document which may be executed by him pursuant hereto; and in the acquisition or disposition of real or personal property, my said Attorney shall have exclusive power to fix the terms thereof for cash, credit and/or property, and if on credit with or without security.

The undersigned, if a married woman, hereby further authorizes and empowers my said Attorney, as my duly authorized agent, to join in my behalf, in the execution of any instrument by which any community real property or any interest therein, now owned or hereafter acquired by my spouse and myself, or either of us, is sold, leased, encumbered, or conveyed.

When the contest so requires, the masculine gender includes the feminine and/or neuter, and the singular number includes the plural.

WITNESS my hand this _____ day of _____ , 19____

_____   _____

_____   _____

State of California,
      County of _____ } SS.

On _____ , before me, the undersigned, a Notary Public in and for said
State, personally appeared _____

known to me to be the person _____ whose name _____ subscribed
to the within instrument and acknowledged that _____ executed the same.
                                                (Seal) _____
Witness my hand and official seal.   Notary Public in and for said State.

point as a mere offer. If the principal decides to accept the offer, acceptance must be ratified in writing. For example, Palmer (the principal) orally asks Larkins (the agent) to sell a ranch that Palmer owns. Larkins finds a buyer and signs a sales contract (a contract for an interest in realty must be in writing) on behalf of Palmer to sell the ranch. The buyer cannot enforce the contract unless Palmer subsequently ratifies Larkins's agency status *in writing*. Once the contract is ratified, either party can enforce rights under the contract.

The equal dignity rule does not apply when an agent acts in the presence of a principal or when the agent's act of signing is merely perfunctory. For example, Lucas (the principal) negotiates a contract, but the day it is to be signed, Lucas is called out of town. Lucas authorizes Hilton to sign the contract. In that case, oral authorization is sufficient.

The following case illustrates the formalities required for a power of attorney to give the holder the right to convey real estate.

BACKGROUND AND FACTS   *Joseph Weinberg purchased a condominium unit with Rachela Weiser as joint tenants with right of survivorship. Thereafter Weinberg executed a general power of attorney making his son, Arthur Winters, his agent. Winters conveyed Weinberg's one-half interest in the condominium to Weinberg's daughter, Miriam Bloom. After Weinberg's death, Bloom wanted to sell the condominium, but Weiser claimed complete ownership by right of survivorship on the ground that the agent had no authority to transfer the real estate to Bloom.*

BLOOM v. WEISER
District Court of Appeal of Florida, Third District, 1977.
348 So.2d 651.

HAVERFIELD, Judge.
*   *   *   *

The established rule is that a power of attorney must be strictly construed and the instrument will be held to grant only those powers which are specified. We are of the view that for a power of attorney to authorize a conveyance of real estate, the authority of the agent to do so must be plainly stated. Reviewing the power of attorney granted Winters, we find the instrument contains no specific grant of power authorizing him to convey real estate. Therefore, the July 18 deed executed by Winters and purporting to convey Weinberg's one-half interest in the subject condominium unit to Miriam Bloom is void.

It is interesting to note that the instant power of attorney, prepared and executed in New York, contains almost the identical wording of the power of attorney found to be insufficient to authorize the agent to convey or dispose of real estate in *Graham v. State*, Ct.Cl., 51 N.Y.S.2d 437 (1944) where the court at page 441 explained:

"A power of attorney to convey real estate is an instrument of title. Either expressly or by necessary implication it should state the authority of the agent without leaving it to be established by parol, inferred from coincidences or based on speculation. *   *   * It is not merely a matter between principal and attorney. The deed and the agent's authority are instruments of equal dignity. The language of the so-called power of attorney herein confers no authority on Robert H. Dunnets [the agent]. It lacks an operative clause. It is not a general power of attorney; he is authorized to act only 'in and about the premises.' It is not a special power of attorney; no premises or things to be done appear on the face of the instrument. The document states nothing to which the grant of powers can be related. Drawn, as it would seem, on the usual blank form of special power of attorney, it omits after the words, 'for me and in my name, place and stead,' the usual statement of specific acts authorized."

The deed executed by Winters was void. Title to the condominium belonged to Weiser.

**DECISION
AND REMEDY**

Implied Authority

Implied authority is conferred by custom, can be inferred from the position the agent occupies, or is implied by virtue of being reasonably necessary to carry out express authority.

For example, Adams is employed by Packard Grocery to manage one of its stores. Packard has not specified (expressly stated) Adams's authority to contract with third persons. In this situation, authority to manage a business implies authority to do what is reasonably required (as is customary or can be inferred from a manager's position) to operate the business. This includes contracts for employee help, for buying merchandise and equipment, and even for advertising the products sold in the store.

Because implied authority is conferred on the basis of custom, it is important for the third person to be familiar with the custom of the trade. For example, a traveling salesperson normally may have implied authority to solicit orders for the principal but may not have implied authority to collect for goods unless the salesperson is in possession of the goods.

The list of basic principles of implied authority based on custom or on the agent's position is extensive. It suffices to state that implied authority is always authority customarily associated with the position occupied by the agent, or authority that can be inferred from the express authority given to the agent to fully perform his or her duties. The test is whether it was reasonable for the agent to believe that he or she had the authority to enter the contract in question.

Apparent Authority—Estoppel

Apparent authority, or authority by estoppel, exists when the principal, by either word or action, causes a third party reasonably to believe that an agent has authority to act, even though the agent has no express or implied authority.

For example, a traveling salesperson has no express authority to collect for orders solicited from customers. Since the agent neither possesses the goods ordered nor delivers them, the agent also has no implied authority to collect. Assume that a customer, Carla, pays an agent, Adam, for a solicited order. Adam then takes the payment to the principal's accounting department. An accountant accepts payment and sends Carla a receipt. This procedure is thereafter followed for other orders solicited and paid for by Carla. Later Adam solicits an order, and Carla pays Adam as before. This time, however, Adam absconds with the money. Can Carla claim that the payment to Adam was authorized and thus, in effect, a payment to the principal? The answer is yes, because the principal's *repeated* acts of accepting Carla's payment led Carla reasonably to believe that Adam had authority to receive payments for goods solicited. Although Adam did not have express or implied authority, the principal's conduct gave Adam apparent authority to collect. The principal could not claim the agent had no authority to collect in this particular case.

Sometimes a principal will go beyond mere statements or actions that convince a third party that a certain person is the principal's agent. If, for example, the principal has "clothed the agent" with both possession and apparent ownership of the principal's property, the agent will have very broad powers and can deal with the property as if he or she were the true owner.

For example, to deceive certain creditors, Baker (the principal) and Hunter (the agent) agree verbally that Hunter will hold certain stock certificates for Baker. Hunter's possession and apparent ownership of the stock certificates are such strong indications of ownership that a reasonable person would conclude that Hunter was the actual owner. If Hunter negotiates the stock certificates to a third person, Baker will be estopped from denying Hunter's authority to transfer the stock.

Where land is involved, courts have held that possession alone is not a sufficient indication of ownership. Therefore, if an agent has mere possession of realty, a reasonable person should realize that possession alone is not an adequate assurance of ownership. (See Chapter 53 for details.) If, on the other hand, the agent also possesses the deed to the property and sells the property against the principal's wishes to an unsuspecting buyer, the principal cannot cancel the sale or assert a claim to title.

The next case illustrates the issue of whether there is apparent authority to bind a principal when the principal allows the agent to use the principal's corporate name as part of the agent's corporate name and in the agent's advertising.

BACKGROUND AND FACTS   *In 1975, the city of Delta Junction, the plaintiff, received a grant from the State of Alaska for firefighting equipment. The city decided to purchase a fire tanker from Alaska Mack, Inc., located in Fairbanks. Alaska Mack, a Mack Trucks, Inc. dealer, modified a Mack chassis to carry a 5,000-gallon tank, but the truck exceeded manufacturer's specified weight limits and was dangerously unbalanced and difficult to drive. When subsequent modifications failed to remedy these problems, the city brought suit for breach of warranty against the defendants, Alaska Mack as seller of the truck and against Mack Trucks, Inc. as a principal, under the theory of apparent agency (authority). The trial court granted a directed verdict for Mack, Inc., and the city appealed.*

CITY OF DELTA
JUNCTION v. MACK
TRUCKS, INC.
Supreme Court of Alaska, 1983.
670 P.2d 1128.

BURKE, Chief Justice.
*   *   *   *

"Apparent authority may . . . arise because the agent has been placed in such a position that a person of ordinary prudence, who was conversant with the nature of the particular business and its usages, would be justified in believing that the agent was authorized." W. Sell, Agency § 35, at 26 (1975). See W. Seavey, Handbook of the Law of Agency § 8, at 13 (1964). Apparent authority is easily distinguished from an agent's power to bind the principal with the principal's consent. Both, however, result in the principal's liability for the acts of the agent or apparent agent, including liability for breach of warranty. *   *   *

The general rule for creation of apparent authority is contained in Restatement (Second) of Agency § 27:

[A]pparent authority to do an act is created as to third persons by written or spoken words or any other conduct of the principal which, reasonably interpreted, causes the third person to believe that the principal consents to have the act done on his behalf by the person purporting to act for him.

It is important to note that it is the *principal's* conduct that gives rise to his liability. Thus, "the one dealing with the agent must prove that the principal was responsible for the appearance of authority by doing something or permitting the agent to do something that led others, including the plaintiff, to believe that the agent had the authority he purported to have."

The question of apparent authority often arises in the context of franchise businesses or dealerships where consumers or suppliers attempt to hold the franchisor liable for the acts of the franchisee. Whether or not the franchisor's acquiescence in a franchisee's use of a corporate logo or a name incorporating a trade name creates apparent authority in the franchisee is a question of fact for determination by the jury. *   *   *

In *Gizzi v. Texaco, Inc.*, 437 F.2d 308, a service station patron brought a personal injury action against Texaco, Inc. under an apparent authority theory of liability. An independent service station displaying the Texaco insignia and the nationally advertised slogan, "Trust your car to the man who wears the star," had repaired the brakes of a used van and sold it to the plaintiff. The brakes failed soon after the plaintiff took possession. The trial court granted Texaco's motion for a directed verdict. The United States Court of Appeals, Third Circuit, vacated the judgment and remanded, holding that it was the province of the jury to determine the apparent authority question.
*   *   *   *

The evidence in this case, viewed in the light most favorable to the City, is as follows: Mack, Inc. allowed Alaska Mack to use the term "Mack" as part of its corporate name. Alaska Mack was listed in trade journals and the Fairbanks telephone directory under the heading "MACK TRUCKS." The telephone directory listing displayed the familiar Mack bulldog trademark *   *   *.
*   *   *   *

Delta's Mayor and fire chief at the time of acquisition testified that they believed they were dealing with Mack, Inc. when they contacted Alaska Mack. The fire chief stated that the city council was persuaded to accept Alaska Mack's proposal, the most expensive of the proposals received, on the basis of the manufacturer's reputation. Similarly, the chief of maintenance of the City's volunteer fire department was not aware that Alaska Mack and Mack, Inc. were separate entities. The fire chief who assumed control of Delta's fire department during the unsuccessful attempts to repair the vehicle testsified, by deposition, that when he talked to Alaska Mack about the truck's deficiencies he believed he was communicating with Mack, Inc.

It is fair to say, as did one of Alaska Mack's advertisements, that "Mack" has become part of the language. The corporate name and trademark, the latter being surely the most famous bulldog ever to stand atop a radiator, have been part of the American scene for decades, as familiar to most as apple pie and baseball. The average citizen, who couldn't name five vice-presidents to save himself from eternal damnation, will recognize a Mack advertisement as far as the eye can see. It makes little difference to him whether the particular advertiser is Alaska Mack or Mack, Inc. The important thing, we have been taught to believe, is that the product is a "Mack," and built accordingly.

Mack Inc., therefore, has a vital interest in the use of the name "Mack," and advertisements such as those used by Alaska Mack; its nationwide business and reputation are at stake. It is unlikely that an unauthorized use of these symbols would have gone unnoticed by Mack, Inc., and that has not been suggested. Thus, it can reasonably be inferred that Alaska Mack's use of these items was with Mack, Inc.'s knowledge and approval. Whether its acquiescence in their use was sufficient to bind Mack, Inc. under Delta's theory of apparent authority, was a jury question.

We express no opinion on whether these indices of authority are, in fact, sufficient. We hold, only, that reasonable jurors could disagree on the impression that may have been conveyed to the public.   *   *   *

*   *   *   *

DECISION AND REMEDY   *The Alaska Supreme Court remanded the case back to the trial court, so a jury could decide whether the facts in this case created an apparent agency.*

Emergency Powers

When an unforeseen emergency demands action by the agent to protect or preserve the property and rights of the principal, but the agent is unable to communicate with the principal, the agent has emergency power.

For example, Fisher (the agent) is a brakeman on Pacific Railroad (the principal). While Fisher is acting within the scope of his employment, he falls under the train many miles from home and is severely injured. Davis, the conductor (also an agent), directs Thompson, a doctor, to give medical aid to Fisher and to charge Pacific for the doctor's medical services. Davis has no express authority to bind Pacific Railroad for the services of Thompson. Yet, because of the emergency situation, the law recog-

nizes him as having authority to act appropriately under the circumstances.

Ratification

Ratification is the affirmation of a previously unauthorized contract or act. Ratification can be either express or implied. Generally, only a principal can ratify. The principal must be aware of all material facts; otherwise, the ratification is not effective. Ratification binds the principal to the agent's acts and treats the acts or contracts as if they had been authorized by the principal *from the outset*. If the principal does not ratify, there is no contract binding the principal, and the third-party agreement with the agent is viewed merely as an unaccepted offer. Because the third party's agreement is treated merely as an unaccepted offer, the third party can revoke the offer (rescind the agreement) at any time before the principal ratifies, without liability. The agent, however, may well be liable to the third party for misrepresenting his or her authority.

The principal's acceptance (that is, the ratification) is binding only if the principal *knows* all the terms of the contract. If not, the principal can thereafter rescind ratification unless, of course, the third party has proceeded to change position in reliance on the contract.

Suppose an agent, without authority, contracts with a third person on behalf of a principal for repair work to the principal's office building. The principal learns of the contract from the agent and agrees to "some repair work," thinking that it will involve only patching and painting the exterior of the building. In fact, the contract includes resurfacing the parking lot, which the principal does not want done. Upon learning of the additional provision, the principal rescinds the contract. If the third party has made no preparations to do the work (such as purchasing materials, hiring additional workers, or renting equipment), then the principal can still rescind. But if the third party has, to his or her detriment, relied on the principal's ratification by making preparations, the principal must reimburse the third party for the cost of the preparations.

Two important points must be stressed. First, it is immaterial whether the principal's lack of knowledge results from the agent's fraud or is simply a mistake on the principal's part. If the third party has not changed position in reliance on the principal, the principal can repudiate the ratification. The unauthorized contract remains an offer, and the principal's acceptance is not valid, because contract law provides that one cannot accept terms one does not know about. Second, the whole transaction must be ratified; a principal cannot affirm the desirable parts of a contract and reject the undesirable parts.

Death or incapacity of the third party *before* ratification will void an unauthorized contract. Most courts will also recognize intervening and extraordinary change of circumstances as a basis for setting aside a principal's ratification to permit a third party to revoke.

Assume that Able, without authority, enters into a contract with a third party who wants to purchase Paula's shopping center. The following night the shopping center is destroyed by fire. Paula's subsequent ratification will not be effective to bind the third party. The courts will reason that it is unjust to hold a third party liable in such a case and will permit the transaction to be avoided despite ratification.

Express Ratification   If a principal's statements or conduct express an intent to be bound, the prior unauthorized act will be ratified, and the principal will become a party to the contract.

For example, Smith (the agent) negotiates the sale of a shipment of oranges to World Markets without the authorization of Samuelson (the principal). Samuelson sees the completed paperwork and tells Smith to go ahead with it. Samuelson thus expressly ratifies the sale and is now bound to the terms of the sales contract.

Implied Ratification   Implied ratification occurs most commonly when a principal decides to accept the benefits of a previously unauthorized transaction. In the preceding example, if Samuelson had known of the unauthorized acts and failed to repudiate or object to them within a reasonable time, the contract would be ratified. In addition, if World Markets had paid for the oranges, and if Samuelson, upon learning that World Markets had paid, did not object or repudiate, Samuelson would have impliedly ratified the contract.

Requirements for Ratification Summarized   The previous discussion can be put in the form of a list of requirements for ratification, as follows:

1.   The presumptive agent must have acted on behalf of a principal who subsequently ratifies, although some states permit ratification by an undisclosed principal.
2.   The principal must know of all material facts involved in the transaction.
3.   The agent's act must be affirmed in its entirety by the principal.
4.   The principal must have the legal capacity to authorize the transaction at the time the agent engages in the act and at the time the principal ratifies.
5.   The principal's affirmance must occur prior to the withdrawal of the third party from the transaction or prior to a changing of the circumstances in such a way that it would be unjust to hold the third party to the transaction.

6. The principal must observe the same formalities when he or she approves the act purportedly done by the agent on his or her behalf as would have been required to authorize it initially.

The following case illustrates the need of the principal promptly to repudiate unauthorized acts of an agent, once known by the principal, to avoid ratification.

THEIS v. duPONT, GLORE FORGAN INC.
Supreme Court of Kansas, 1973.
212 Kan. 301, 510 P.2d 1212.

BACKGROUND AND FACTS *Charles Theis, the plaintiff, maintained an investment account with the brokerage firm of duPont, Glore Forgan Inc., the defendant. Theis discovered that Benjamin, a duPont account executive, was making unauthorized transactions in his account and reprimanded him. Theis finally closed the account when Benjamin directly contravened Theis's order not to buy on May 24, 1968. Theis filed suit against duPont for all the unauthorized trading by Benjamin from the inception of the Theis account. The trial court allowed recovery on only the May 24 transaction.*

FROMME, Justice.
*   *   *   *

Ratification is the adoption or confirmation by a principal of an act performed on his behalf by an agent which act was performed without authority. The ratification by the principal of an unauthorized act of his agent is equivalent to an original grant of authority. On acquiring knowledge of the unauthorized act of an agent, the principal should promptly repudiate the act, otherwise it will be presumed he has ratified and affirmed the act.

The principles governing ratification, including the requirement of prompt repudiation of an unauthorized act of an agent, are applicable in brokerage transactions.
*   *   *   *

The record is clear the trial court correctly applied these principles to this entire period. During this period of time there were 36 transactions in the Theis account. The court determined that by Theis's failure to promptly repudiate unauthorized transactions he had either authorized or ratified the first 35 transactions. However, the court found that Theis promptly repudiated the final transaction of May 24 when he learned it had been made contrary to his express orders. This was evidenced not only by registering a protest with Benjamin but also by closing his commodities account with the broker.

It is pointed out the requirement of prompt repudiation is to prevent an investor from withholding his disapproval until the market has taken a turn for the worse, and then deciding to assert the alleged wrongdoing. In such case if prompt repudiation were not required he might sit back and quietly accept profits resulting from an unauthorized trade when it turned out to be to his advantage.

In the present case Theis had previously absorbed the losses, as well as the gains, resulting from Benjamin's unauthorized transactions. However, on May 24 Theis did not hesitate in closing his account as soon as he learned that Benjamin had bought in his short position contrary to express instructions. The record shows he did so without waiting to see whether the market price would ultimately rise or fall. His actions indicate he was unconcerned with the wisdom of the May 24 purchase. He was irate over the unauthorized purchase by Benjamin. The action of Theis in closing his account with duPont was found by the trial court to be an express repudiation of the May 24 transaction and this finding is supported by substantial evidence. Whether there has been a repudiation within a reasonable time is a question of fact and the ratification of a former unauthorized act is not the ratification of another entirely distinct act.

Although the court found Theis had ratified Benjamin's earlier actions, duPont, Glore Forgan Inc. was liable for the unauthorized act of its employee on May 24.   **DECISION AND REMEDY**

PRINCIPAL'S AND AGENT'S LIABILITY FOR CONTRACTS

Principals are classified as **disclosed, partially disclosed,** or **undisclosed.**[3] A *disclosed principal* is a principal whose identity is known by the third party at the time the contract is made by the agent. A *partially disclosed principal* is a principal whose identity is not known by the third party, but the third party knows that the agent is or may be acting for a principal at the time the contract is made. An *undisclosed principal* is a principal whose identity is totally unknown by the third party, and the third party has no knowledge that the agent is acting in an agency capacity at the time the contract is made.

Disclosed and Partially Disclosed Principals

If an agent acts within the scope of his or her authority, a disclosed or partially disclosed principal is liable to a third party for a contract made by the agent. In these situations, an agent has no contractual liability for the nonperformance of the principal or of the third party.

If the agent is not authorized to contract, or exceeds the scope of authority, unless the principal ratifies the contract, the principal cannot be held liable in contract by a third party. The agent is also not liable in contract, unless the agent has personally guaranteed the performance of the principal. The agent's liability is not on the contract because the agent was never personally intended as a party to the contract.

In most states, if the principal is partially disclosed, the principal and agent are both treated as parties to the contract and the third party can hold either liable for contractual nonperformance.[4]

Undisclosed Principals

When neither the fact of agency nor the identity of the principal is disclosed, a third party is deemed to be dealing with the agent personally, and the agent is liable as a party on the contract.

For example, in a contract for the sale of a horse, a third party knows only that Scammon (the agent) wants to purchase the horse. The third party does not know that Scammon is actually negotiating for Johnson (the principal). Scammon signs a written contract in her own name, not indicating any agency relationship. She delivers the horse to Johnson, who is in fact the principal, but Johnson refuses to pay her. Scammon tries to return the horse to the third party, who refuses to take it. The third party is entitled to hold Scammon liable for payment. The agent's subjective intent is not relevant. The third party contracted with the agent on the basis of the *agent's* credit and reputation, not the undisclosed principal's. Therefore, the agent is liable.

If the agent has acted within the scope of authority, the undisclosed principal is fully bound to perform just as if the principal had been fully disclosed at the time the contract is made. Conversely, the undisclosed principal can hold the third party to the contract unless:

1. The undisclosed principal was expressly excluded as a party in the contract. For example, an agent contracts for a lease of a building with a landlord. The landlord does not know of the agency and the lease specially lists the agent as tenant, with no right of assignment without the landlord's consent. The undisclosed principal cannot enforce the lease.

2. The contract is a negotiable instrument, whereby the UCC provides that only the agent is liable if the instrument neither names the principal nor shows that the agent signed in a representative capacity.[5]

3. The performance of the agent is personal to the contract, allowing the third party to refuse the prin-

---

3. Restatement, Second, Agency, Section 4.
4. Restatement, Second, Agency, Section 321.

5. UCC 3-401(1) and 3-403(2)(a). Extrinsic evidence to show an agency relationship is not normally admissible.

cipal's performance. Typical examples involve extensions of credit or highly personal service contracts.

If the agent is forced to pay the third party, and if the agent has contracted within the scope of authority granted,[6] the agent is entitled to indemnification by the principal. It was the principal's duty to perform even though his or her identity was un-

disclosed,[7] and failure to do so will make the principal ultimately liable. Once the undisclosed principal's identity is revealed, the third party has the right to elect to hold either the principal or the agent liable on contract. (In some states no election is necessary.)

In the following case, the undisclosed principal creates a liability problem for the travel agent.

---

6.   The agent can never establish apparent authority because the principal has not previously been revealed and cannot, therefore, have informed the third party of an agency relationship.

7.   If A is a gratuitous agent, and P accepts the benefits of A's contract with a third party, then P will be liable to A on the theory of quasi-contract.

ROSEN v. DEPORTER-BUTTERWORTH TOURS, INC.

Appellate Court of Illinois, 1978.
62 Ill.App.3d 762, 19 Ill.Dec.
743, 379 N.E.2d 407.

BACKGROUND AND FACTS   *The plaintiff, Rosen, purchased a package tour for an African safari from the defendant, Deporter-Butterworth Tours, Inc. The travel bureau failed to disclose that it was in fact a special agent for the tour's sponsor, World Trek. Prior to the purchase of the package, the plaintiff had direct contact with the travel bureau but never with the tour sponsor. Hence, the tour sponsor, World Trek, was an undisclosed principal.*

The plaintiff planned to travel through Europe and then to join the tour in Egypt. Before leaving the United States, the plaintiff informed the travel bureau of where he could be reached in Europe and in Egypt prior to the start of the tour. The tour itinerary had to be changed. The travel bureau failed to contact the plaintiff overseas, leaving the plaintiff stranded in Egypt for a week. The plaintiff sued the travel bureau for damages sustained. The travel bureau claimed that it was not liable because it was merely an agent for World Trek and that World Trek was the proper party to the lawsuit.

BARRY, Presiding Justice.
*   *   *   *

The final issue presented for review is whether the trial court erred in finding defendant [the travel bureau] liable to the plaintiff for the price of the tour. Inherent in a decision of this issue is a determination of the relationship between plaintiff and defendant and defendant and the tour sponsor, World Trek. *   *   * [I]n the normal situation between a travel bureau and its traveler client a special agency relationship arises for the limited object of the one business transaction between the two parties. It is clear in the present case that the plaintiff employed the defendant travel bureau as his special agent for the limited purpose of arranging the African Safari Tour sponsored by World Trek.

Although the sponsor of the tour, World Trek, as advertised in the brochure, was not a party to this lawsuit, their relationship to the defendant is an important factor in deciding liability. The record contains a letter from defendant to World Trek as plaintiff's exhibit No. 4, which admits to defendant's selling of World Trek's tour to the plaintiff and hints of a principal-agency relationship between World Trek and the defendant. The evidence also disclosed that the defendant received a 10% commission from World Trek for selling its tour. *The legal principle that an agent is liable as a principal [to] a third party in the case of an undisclosed agency relationship* is well established and needs no citation for authority. [Emphasis added.] In the instant case the plaintiff was aware that World Trek was sponsoring the tour but was without knowledge as to whether the defendant was truly representing him as his special agent for arranging the tour or whether defendant was acting as an agent for World Trek in selling its tour to plaintiff.

The traditional relationship between a travel bureau, such as defendant, and the tour sponsors of the various tours sold has been categorized as one of agent and principal particularly in the field of tort liability of the travel bureau for injuries that occur to the traveler. No sound reason exists for not finding the same principal-agent relationship between a tour sponsor and a travel bureau in the case of alleged liability for breach of an agreement involving the ultimate sale of the tour to an ordinary member of the traveling public, such as the plaintiff.

* * * *[I]f an agent does not disclose the existence of an agency relationship and the identity of his principal, he binds himself to the third party with whom he acts as if he, himself, were the principal.* [Emphasis added.] * * * The fact that the plaintiff knew that World Trek and not defendant was the tour sponsor does not satisfy the necessary disclosure to prevent defendant from becoming liable as principal. * * *

The court held that the travel bureau was liable to the plaintiff because the travel bureau did not reveal that it was acting as an agent for World Trek as an undisclosed principal.

DECISION AND REMEDY

Warranties of Agent

Whenever the agent lacks authority or exceeds the scope of authority, the agent's liability to a third party is based on the theory of breach of implied warranty of authority, not on breach of the contract itself.[8]

The agent's implied warranty of authority can be breached intentionally or by a good faith mistake.[9] The agent's liability remains, as long as the third party has relied on agency status. Conversely, where the third party knows at the time of the contract that the agent is mistaken, or the agent indicates to the third party *uncertainty* about the extent of authority, the agent is not personally liable for breach of warranty.

PRINCIPAL'S AND AGENT'S LIABILITY FOR TORTS OF AN AGENT

Obviously, an agent is liable to third persons for his or her own torts and crimes. A principal becomes liable for an agent's torts if the torts are committed

within the scope of the agency or the scope of employment.

The Restatement, Second, Agency, Section 229, indicates the general factors that courts will consider in determining whether or not a particular act occurred within the course and scope of employment. They are:

1. Whether the act was authorized by the employer.
2. The time, place, and purpose of the act.
3. Whether the act was one commonly performed by employees on behalf of their employers.
4. The extent to which the employer's interest was advanced by the act.
5. The extent to which the private interests of the employee were involved.
6. Whether the employer furnished the means or instrumentality (for example, a truck or a machine) by which the injury was inflicted.
7. Whether the employer had reason to know that the employee would do the act in question and whether the employee had ever done it before.
8. Whether the act involved the commission of a serious crime.

A principal or employer is not, however, liable for an agent's or employee's crimes, unless he or she participates by conspiracy or other action.

---

8. The agent's liability is not on the contract because the agent was never personally intended as a party to the contract.
9. If the agent intentionally misrepresents his or her authority, then the agent can also be liable in tort for misrepresentation.

A principal is liable if:

1. He or she directs the agent to do the act.
2. There is a negligent entrustment.
3. The principal fails properly to supervise the agent-employee.

Misrepresentation

A principal is exposed to tort liability whenever a third person sustains loss due to the agent's misrepresentation. The key to a principal's liability is whether or not the agent was actually or apparently authorized to make representations, and whether such representations were made within the scope of the agency.

Assume Lewis is a demonstrator for Moore's products. Moore sends Lewis to a home show to demonstrate products and to answer questions from consumers. Moore has given Lewis authority to make statements about the products. If Lewis makes only true representations, all is fine; but if he makes false claims, Moore will be liable for any injuries or damages sustained by third parties in reliance on Lewis's false representations.

An interesting series of cases has arisen on the theory that when a principal has placed an agent in a position to defraud a third party, the principal is liable for the agent's fraudulent acts.

For example, Pratt is a loan officer at First Security Bank. In the ordinary course of the job, Pratt approves and services loans and has access to the credit records of all customers. Pratt falsely represents to a borrower, McMillan, that the bank feels insecure about McMillan's loan and intends to call it in unless McMillan provides additional collateral such as stocks and bonds. McMillan gives Pratt numerous stock certificates that Pratt keeps in her own possession, later using them to make personal investments. The bank is liable to McMillan for losses sustained on the stocks even though the bank had no direct role or knowledge of the fraudulent scheme.

The legal theory used here is that the agent's position conveys to third persons the impression that the agent has the authority to make statements and perform acts that are consistent with the ordinary duties that are within the scope of the position. When an agent appears to be acting within the scope of the authority that the position of agency confers but is actually taking advantage of a third party, the principal who placed the agent in that position is

liable. In the example above, if a bank teller or security guard had told McMillan that the bank required additional security for a loan, McMillan would not be justified in relying on either person's authority to make that representation. However, McMillan could reasonably expect that the loan officer was telling the truth.

Innocent Misrepresentation Tort liability based on fraud requires proof that a material misstatement was made knowingly and with the intent to deceive. An agent's innocent mistakes occurring in a contract transaction or involving a warranty contained in the contract can provide grounds for the third party's rescission of the contract and the award of damages. Moreover, justice dictates that where a principal knows that an agent is not accurately advised of facts but does not correct either the agent's or the third party's impressions, the principal is directly responsible to the third party for resulting damages. The point is that the principal is always directly responsible for an agent's misrepresentation made within the scope of authority.

Negligence: Personal Injury

The principal (employer) is liable for the physical harm caused by an agent (employee) that occurs in the scope of the principal's authority (scope of employment) and furtherance of the principal's business. The theory of liability used here involves the doctrine of *respondeat superior*.

The Doctrine of *Respondeat Superior* The theory of liability based on **respondeat superior**[10] imposes vicarious (strict) liability on the principal or employer (that is, liability without regard to the personal fault of the principal or employer for torts committed by an agent or employee in the course of employment).[11]

---

10. The theory of *respondeat superior* is similar to the theory of strict liability covered in Chapter 22. This doctrine may not apply if the principal or employer has sovereign or charitable organization immunity. The practice of granting such immunity is diminishing in most states.

11. The doctrine of *respondeat superior* applies not only to master-servant relationships but also to principal-agent relationships as long as there is the right of control by the principal over the agent.

Principals are liable only for the negligence of their agents that causes physical harm to third persons, *if* the act takes place within the scope of the agent's employment. Therefore, the liability of a principal for an agent's negligence is dependent upon whether the agent is also an employee (and the employer has control of the conduct of the agent).

The general rule concerning liability for the acts of an independent contractor is that the principal-employer is not liable for physical harm caused to a third person by the negligent act of an independent contractor in the performance of the contract. A principal-employer who has no legal power to control the details of the physical performance of a contract cannot be held liable. Here again the test is the *right to control*. Since a principal-employer bargains with an independent contractor only for results and retains no control over the manner in which those results are achieved, the principal-employer is generally not expected to bear the responsibility for torts committed by an independent contractor. A collection agency is a typical example of an independent-contractor relationship. The creditor is generally not liable for the acts of the collection agency because collection is a distinct business occupation.

Generally, an exception to this doctrine prevails when exceptionally hazardous activities are involved. Typical examples of such activities include blasting operations, the transportation of highly volatile chemicals, or the use of poisonous gases. In these cases an employer cannot be shielded from liability merely by using an independent contractor. Strict liability is imposed upon the employer as a matter of law. Also, in some states, strict liability is imposed by statute.

Subagents As stated before, there are three instances in which an agent can hire a subagent (subservant):

1. To perform ministerial or mechanical duties.
2. Whenever it is the business custom.
3. For unforeseen emergencies.

If an agent is authorized to hire subagents for the principal-employer under any one of these three circumstances, then the principal-employer is liable for the acts of the subagents. There is a slight difference in result if the agent hires for an *undisclosed principal* (employer). In that case, the agent is responsible for the subagent in contract law for such things as wages. However, the undisclosed principal (employer) is generally held to be liable for tort injuries. The doctrine of *respondeat superior* imposes liability on the true "master." An agent's unauthorized hiring of a subagent generally will not create any legal relationship between the principal and the subagent.

TERMINATION OF AN AGENCY

Agency law is similar to contract law in that both an agency and a contract terminate by an act of the parties or by operation of law. Once the relationship between the principal and agent has ended, the agent no longer has the right to bind the principal. However, third persons may also need to be notified when the agency has been terminated in order to terminate an agent's apparent authority.

Termination by Act of the Parties

Lapse of Time An agency agreement may specify the time period during which the agency relationship will exist. If so, the agency ends when that time expires. For example, Able signs an agreement of agency with Paula "beginning January 1, 1983, and ending December 31, 1988." The agency is automatically terminated on December 31, 1988. Of course, the parties can agree to continue the relationship, in which case the same terms will apply.

If no definite time is stated, then the agency continues for a reasonable time and can be terminated at will by either party. A "reasonable time" depends upon the circumstances and the nature of the agency relationship. For example, Paula asks Able to sell Paula's car. After two years, if Able has not sold Paula's car and there has been no communication between Paula and Able, it is safe to assume that the agency relationship has terminated. Able no longer has the authority to sell Paula's car.

Purpose Achieved An agent can be employed to accomplish a particular objective, such as the purchase of stock for a cattle rancher. In that case, the agency automatically ends after the cattle have been purchased.

If more than one agent is employed to accomplish the same purpose, such as the sale of real estate, the first agent to complete the sale automatically terminates the agency relationship for all the others.

Occurrence of a Specific Event

An agency can be created to terminate upon the happening of a certain event. For example, Paula appoints Able to handle her business affairs while she is away. When Paula returns, the agency automatically terminates.

Sometimes one aspect of the agent's authority terminates on the occurrence of a particular event, but the agency relationship itself does not terminate. For example, Paula, a banker, permits Able, the credit manager, to grant a credit line of $1,000 to certain depositors who maintain $1,000 in a savings account. If any customer's savings account falls below $1,000, Able can no longer continue making the credit line available to that customer. But Able's right to extend credit to the other customers maintaining the minimum balance will continue.

Mutual Agreement

Recall from basic contract law that parties can cancel (rescind) a contract by mutually agreeing to terminate the contractual relationship. The same holds true in agency law regardless of whether the agency contract is in writing or whether it is for a specific duration. For example, Paula no longer wishes Able to be her agent, and Able does not want to work for Paula any more. Either party can communicate to the other the intent to terminate the relationship. Agreement to terminate effectively relieves each of the rights, duties, and powers inherent in the relationship.

Termination by One Party

As a *general* rule, either party can terminate the agency relationship. The agent's act is said to be a renunciation of authority. The principal's act is a revocation of authority. Although both parties may have the *power* to terminate, they may not each possess the *right*. Wrongful termination can subject the canceling party to a suit for damages.

For example, Able has a one-year employment contract with Paula to act as her agent for $18,000. Paula can discharge Able before the contract period expires (Paula has the *power* to breach the contract); however, Paula will be liable to Able for money

damages because Paula has no *right* to breach the contract.

Even in an agency at will, the principal who wishes to terminate must give the agent a reasonable notice, that is, at least sufficient notice to allow the agent to recoup his or her expenses and, in some cases, to make a normal profit.

Agency Coupled with an Interest

An agency *coupled with an interest* is a relationship created for the benefit of the agent. The agent actually acquires a beneficial interest in the subject matter of the agency. Under these circumstances it is not equitable to permit a principal to terminate at will. Hence, this type of agency is "irrevocable."

For example, Sarah Roberts (principal) owns Blackacre. She needs some immediate cash, so she enters into an agreement with John Hartwell that Hartwell will lend her $10,000, and she agrees to grant Hartwell a one-half interest in Blackacre and "the exclusive right to sell" it for $25,000 if she fails to repay the $10,000. The loan is to be repaid out of the sale's proceeds. Hartwell's power to sell Blackacre is coupled with a beneficial interest of one-half ownership in Blackacre created at the time of the loan for the purpose of supporting it and securing its repayment. Hartwell's agency power is irrevocable.

An agency coupled with an interest should not be confused with situations in which the agent merely derives proceeds or profits from the sale of the subject matter. For example, an agent who merely receives a commission from the sale of real property does not have a beneficial interest in the property itself. Likewise, an attorney whose fee is a percentage of the recovery (a contingency fee) merely has an interest in the proceeds. These agency relationships are revocable by the principal, subject to any express contractual arrangements that the principal has with the agent.

Since, in an agency coupled with an interest, the interest is not created for the benefit of the principal, it is not really an agency in the usual sense. Therefore, any attempt by the principal to revoke an agency coupled with an interest normally has no legal force or effect and is not terminated by the death of either the principal or the agent.

The next case involves the premature termination of an agency relationship.

BACKGROUND AND FACTS *The appellant, a real estate broker, had an exclusive listing contract for the sale of the appellees' home. During the time the contract was in force, the McDonalds sold their home to a third party and refused to pay the realtor's commission. The broker brought suit for its commission. The trial court held for the McDonalds on the theory that the sale to the third party revoked the agency agreement.*

DOWD MORE CO. REALTORS v. McDONALD

Court of Civil Appeals of Texas, Houston (1st Dist.), 1973.
494 S.W.2d 282.

EVANS, Justice.

*   *   *   *

In this case the appellants Dowd More established the essential facts which entitle them to a recovery for breach of contract. While the appellants were admittedly not the procuring cause of the sale, it is undisputed that appellants had initiated performance under the contract and had advertised the property for sale, had placed their "For Sale" sign in the yard, had listed the property with Multiple Listing Service and had shown the property to prospective customers. The contract was no longer nudum pactum [a voluntary promise for good will only] but on the contrary was a bilateral agreement which appellees could not unilaterally revoke by a sale to a third party.

This principle is, we believe, clearly set forth in McDonald v. Davis, 389 S.W.2d 494, wherein this court speaking through Chief Justice Bell at page 496, said:

*   *   *   *

"The principal may of course revoke an agent's authority where not coupled with an interest, but there is a distinction between his power to revoke and his right to revoke. He at any time before full performance can revoke the authority of an agent so the agent will lose his authority to bring the principal into legal relations with a third party. However, if he has no right to revoke it, he will be liable for damages suffered by the agent by reason of the wrongful revocation. Where, as here, there is a bilateral contract, the principal has no right to revoke to the prejudice of the agent.

Where a principal breaches the contract, he becomes liable in damages. Where, as here, suit is for breach of a contract granting the agent the exclusive right for a definite period of time to sell property, the damages are for breach of contract and not for the commission promised if the agent sold. He is entitled to recover the reasonable profit he would have made. Prima facie that profit is the amount represented by the stipulated commission."

As stated above, appellants' compensation under the exclusive real estate listing contract was stipulated to be 6% of the listed price of $18,500.00, or $1100.00. In the absence of satisfactory evidence that appellants' reasonable profits were in a lesser sum than the stipulated commission the sum specified in the contract is prima facie evidence of their damages. Accordingly, the judgment of the trial court is reversed and judgment is rendered for the appellants in the amount of $1100.00 with interest at 6% per annum from and after September 3, 1971.

The trial court's judgment for the McDonalds was reversed. The McDonalds were liable for the full amount of the real estate commission.

DECISION AND REMEDY

Termination by Operation of Law

Death or Insanity The general rule is that death or insanity of either the principal or the agent automatically and immediately terminates the ordinary agency relationship. Knowledge of the death is not required.[12] For example, Paula sends Able to the Far East to purchase a rare book. Before Able makes

---

12. An exception to virtually all notice and termination rules occurs in an agency coupled with an interest, which is not automatically terminated by death or incapacity.

the purchase, Paula dies. Able's agent status is terminated at the moment of death, even though Able does not know that Paula has died. Some states, however, have changed this common law by statute.

Agents' transactions that occur after the death of the principal are not binding on the principal's estate. Assume Able is hired by Paula to collect a debt from Tom (a third party). Paula dies, but Able still collects the money from Tom, not knowing of Paula's death. Tom's payment to Able is no longer legally sufficient to discharge Tom's debt to Paula because Able no longer has Paula's authority to collect the money. If Able absconds with the money, Tom must again pay the debt to Paula's estate.

Impossibility   When the specific subject matter of an agency is destroyed or lost, the agency terminates. For example, Paula employs Able to sell Paula's house. Prior to any sale, the premises are destroyed by fire. Able's agency and authority to sell Paula's house terminate. When it is impossible for the agent to perform the agency lawfully, because of war or because of a change in the law, the agency terminates.

Cha ged Circumstances   When an event occurs that has such an unusual effect on the subject matter of the agency that the agent can reasonably infer that the principal will not want the agency to continue, the agency terminates. Paula hires Able to sell a tract of land for $10,000. Subsequently, Able learns that there is oil under the land and that the land is therefore worth $1 million. The agency and Able's authority to sell the land for $10,000 are terminated.

Bankruptcy   Bankruptcy of the principal or the agent *usually* terminates the agency relationship.[13] Some situations, such as a serious financial loss, might indicate that future contracts should not be made.

War   When the principal's country and agent's country are at war with each other, the agency is terminated or at least suspended.

Notice Required for Termination

When an agency terminates by operation of law because of death, insanity, or some other unforeseen circumstance, there is no duty to notify third persons, unless the agent's authority is coupled with an interest.[14] However, if the parties themselves have terminated the agency (although notice may be given by others), it is the principal's duty to inform any third parties who know of the existence of the agency that it has been terminated.

An agent's *authority* continues until the agent receives some notice of termination. Notice to third parties, however, follows the general rule that an agent's *apparent authority* continues until the third person is notified (from any source of information) that such authority has been terminated.

The principal is expected to notify *directly* any third person who the principal knows has dealt with the agent. For third persons who have heard about the agency but have not dealt with the agent, *constructive* notice is sufficient.[15]

No particular form of notice is required to be effective. The principal can actually notify the agent, or the agent can learn of the termination through some other means. For example, Marshall bids on a shipment of steel, and Smith is hired as an agent to arrange transportation of the shipment. When Smith learns that Marshall has lost the bid, Smith's authority to make the transportation arrangement terminates.

If the agent's authority is written, it must be revoked in writing, and the writing must be shown to all people who saw the original writing that established the agency relationship. Sometimes a written authorization (like that granting power of attor-

---

13.   Insolvency, as distinguished from bankruptcy, will not necessarily terminate the relationship. Most states do not consider the appointment of a receiver grounds for terminating the agency.

---

14.   There is an exception to this rule in banking. UCC 4-405 provides that the bank as the agent can continue to exercise specific types of authority even after the customer's death or insanity unless it has knowledge of the death or insanity. When it has knowledge of the customer's death, it has authority for ten days after the death to pay checks (but not notes or drafts) drawn by the customer unless the bank receives a stop-payment order from someone who has an interest in the account, such as an heir. (This rule does not apply to insanity.)

15.   Constructive notice is information or knowledge of a fact imputed by law to a person if he or she could have discovered the fact by proper diligence. Constructive notice is often accomplished pursuant to a statute by newspaper publication.

CONCEPT SUMMARY: Termination of an Agency		
TYPES OF TERMINATION OF THE AGENCY	**RULES**	**TERMINATION OF THE AGENT'S AUTHORITY**
ACT OF THE PARTIES		NOTICE TO THIRD PERSONS REQUIRED
1. Lapse of Time	Automatic at end of stated time	1. Direct to those who previously have dealt with agency
2. Purpose Achieved	Automatic upon completion of purpose	
3. Mutual Rescission	Need mutual consent or acceptance of consideration	2. Constructive to all others
4. Termination by One Party		
a. Option Contract Clause	Only upon notice of exercise of option	
b. Revocation by Principal	At will agencies—generally no breach	
c. Renunciation by Agent	Specified time agencies—breach unless legal cause. Cannot revoke an agency coupled with an interest	
OPERATION OF LAW		
1. Death or insanity	Automatic upon death or insanity of either principal or agent—except an agency coupled with an interest	
2. Impossibility— Destruction of the Specific Subject Matter	Applies any time objectively agency cannot be performed due to event beyond parties' control	NO NOTICE REQUIRED— AUTOMATIC UPON THE HAPPENING OF THE EVENT
3. Changed Circumstances	Events so unusual, unequitable to allow agency to continue to exist	
4. Bankruptcy	Bankruptcy decree terminates—not mere insolvency	
5. War between Principal's and Agent's Countries	Automatically suspends or terminates— no way to enforce legal rights	

ney) contains an expiration date. The passage of the expiration date is sufficient notice of termination for third parties.

EMPLOYER-EMPLOYEE RELATIONSHIPS

Employer-employee relationships are generally created by an express or implied contract. The contract gives the employer the right basically to control the employee's conduct, workplace and habits, and the benefits enjoyed within the scope of the employee's employment.

If the employee is also an agent of the employer, the employee has the authority to act on behalf of the employer. The rights, duties, and liabilities afforded this relationship have been discussed previously.

Statutory regulations that deal with employment discrimination, the health of the employee, the safety of the workplace, minimum wage, unemployment compensation, labor-management agreements, and the like apply only to the employer-employee relationship. These laws are briefly discussed in Chapter 50.

Employment Contracts

An employment contract is generally a mutual agreement formed by an employer and an employee. Basic contract rules apply. The parties can include any contract terms they desire, as long as these terms are not in violation of statute or against public policy. For example, a contract for wages so low as to be in violation of the Fair Labor Standards Act would be illegal. Frequently, employment contracts are governed by collective bargaining agreements made on behalf of the employees by a union with the employer.

Covenants Not to Compete In some employment contracts, an employee agrees that should the employee ever leave his or her employment, for whatever reason, the employee will not accept another employment position with an employer who is presently a competitor. These are called covenant not to compete clauses. When these clauses are ancillary to the total employment contract, and the scope of the prohibition is reasonable in geographic area and duration, the convenant is generally enforceable by injunction.

Compensation The duties of the employee are set forth generally in the contract and for fulfillment of these duties the employee is entitled to compensation. Where permitted, a creditor, through a legal procedure, can garnish the wages of an employee in satisfaction of a debt.

Shop Right An interesting question occurs when an employee invents a product and the employer (or principal as an employer) claims a right to the invention or to the patent. The **shop right doctrine**, or rule, is involved here. This doctrine says that if the employee's duties do not include conducting research and making inventions, the employer is not entitled to the invention but merely has a shop right interest in it. This interest allows the employer a nonexclusive right to use the invention without paying any royalties to the employee. The employee retains ownership and, subject to the shop right interest, full rights to the invention. The employer's right is irrevocable even after the employment relationship ends.

The following well-known case involves an invention created by a sales clerk at Sears, Roebuck & Co. during his off-duty hours. As you will see, the court considered whether the employer had a right to the invention even after the employment relationship had ended.

ROBERTS v. SEARS, ROEBUCK & CO.

Court of Appeals of the United States, Seventh Circuit, 1978. 197 U.S.P.Q. (BNA) 516, 573 F.2d 976, U.S. Cert. Den. in 199 U.S.P.Q. (BNA) 640.

BACKGROUND AND FACTS *Peter Roberts, the plaintiff, sued Sears, Roebuck & Co., the defendant, for damages for fraud, breach of a confidential relationship, and negligent misrepresentation. The case arose from Roberts's assignment to Sears of a patent for a new type of socket wrench that Roberts had invented (during his off-duty hours) while in the employment of Sears. After Roberts learned that Sears had misrepresented to him the potential market value of the wrench, Roberts brought suit. The trial court entered a judgment in favor of Roberts, and Sears appealed.*

SPRECHER, Circuit Judge.

* * * *

This case involves the efforts of one of this nation's largest retail companies, Sears, Roebuck & Co. (Sears), to acquire through deceit the monetary benefits of an invention of a new type of socket wrench created by one of its sales clerks during his off-duty hours. That sales clerk, Peter M. Roberts (Plaintiff), initiated the unfortunate events that led to this appeal in 1963, when at the age of 18 he began work on a ratchet or socket wrench that would permit the easy removal of the sockets from the wrench. He, in fact, designed and constructed a prototype tool with a quick-release feature in it that succeeded in permitting its user to change sockets with one hand. Based on that prototype, plaintiff filed an application for a United States patent. In addition, since he was in the employ of Sears, a company that sold over a million wrenches per year, and since he had only a high school education and no business experience, he decided to show his invention to the manager of the Sears store in Gardner, Massachusetts, where he worked. Plaintiff was persuaded to submit formally his invention as a suggestion to Sears. In May 1964, the prototype, along with a completed suggestion form, was sent to Sears' main office in Chicago, Illinois. Plaintiff, thereafter, left Sears' employ when his parents moved to Tennessee.

It was from this point on that Sears' conduct became the basis for the jury's determination that Sears appropriated the value of the plaintiff's invention by fraudulent means. Plaintiff's evidence proved that Sears took steps to ascertain the utility of the invention and that based on the information it acquired, Sears became convinced that the invention was in fact valuable. *   *   *

Sears also took pains to ascertain the patentability of the quick-release feature. In April 1965, it received outside patent counsel's advice that there was "some basis for limited patentability" *   *   *. It had previously learned in February 1965 from plaintiff's lawyer, Charles Fay, that he believed the invention was patentable based on a limited search. In addition, Sears was informed in early May 1965, by plaintiff's lawyer that a patent had been issued to plaintiff.[1]

With all of this information either available or soon to be available, Sears contacted plaintiff in January 1965, and began negotiations regarding the purchase of rights to use plaintiff's invention. During these negotiations, conducted with plaintiff's attorney, Sears' lawyer, Leonard Schram, made various representations to plaintiff that serve as the essential basis for plaintiff's complaint. In April 1965, in a letter seeking merely a license, Schram first told plaintiff that the invention was not new and that the claims in any patent that would be permitted would be "quite limited."

Based on this letter, plaintiff entered into the agreement on July 29, 1965, which provided for a two cent royalty per unit up to a maximum of $10,000 to be paid in return for a complete *assignment* of all of plaintiff's rights. In fact, for no extra charge, plaintiff's attorney gave Sears all of plaintiff's foreign patent rights. A provision was included in the contract regarding what would happen if Sears failed to sell 50,000 wrenches in a given year, thus reinforcing the impression that the wrenches might not sell very well. Also, a provision was inserted dealing with the contingency that a patent might not be issued, notwithstanding that Sears already knew, and plaintiff did not, that the patent had been granted.

By July, Sears knew that it planned to sell several hundred thousand wrenches with a cost per item increase of only 20 cents, that a patent had been issued and that this product in all likelihood would have tremendous appeal with mechanics. Nonetheless, it entered into this agreement both having failed to disclose vital information about the product's appeal and structural utility and having made representations to plaintiff that were either false at the time they were made or became false without disclosure prior to the time of the signing of the contract.

*   *   * Within *nine months*, Sears had sold over 500,000 wrenches and paid plaintiff his maximum royalty thereby acquiring all of plaintiff's rights. Between 1965 and 1975, Sears sold in excess of 19 million wrenches, many at a premium of one to two dollars profit because no competition was able to market a comparable product for several years. To say the least, plaintiff's invention has been a commercial success.

Plaintiff, a Tennessee resident, filed suit against Sears, an Illinois Corporation, in federal district court in December 1969, based on diversity jurisdiction, seeking alternatively return of the patent and restitution or damages for fraud, breach of a confidential

---

1. We might note here that Mr. Fay contacted Sears before informing plaintiff that a patent had been issued. In addition, it was shown that Sears had contacted Mr. Fay during the period of these negotiations about doing some work for it and that he, in fact, did perform a couple of routine matters for Sears, thus raising some doubt about the independence of his advice to plaintiff.

relationship and negligent misrepresentation. A jury trial was held from December 20, 1976, until January 18, 1977. During the trial, plaintiff basically proved the facts as presented above. Sears argued that it did not misrepresent any facts to plaintiff, that he had a lawyer and thus there was no confidential relationship and that the success of the wrenches was a function of advertising and the unforeseeable boom in do-it-yourself repairs, and thus Sears did not misrepresent the salability of plaintiff's wrenches. * * * The jury apparently believed the plaintiff's evidence because it found Sears guilty * * * and entered judgment for one million dollars.
*   *   *   *

Sears' final argument in its cross-appeal is that plaintiff failed to prove the existence of a confidential relationship between himself and Sears. In assessing that argument, we recognize at the outset that there are no hard and fast rules for determining whether a confidential relationship exists. The trier of fact must examine all of the circumstances surrounding the relationship between the parties and determine whether "one person reposes trust and confidence in another who thereby gains a resulting influence and superiority over the first."

Various factors have been recognized judicially as being of particular relevance to that inquiry. Among them are disparity of age, education and business experience between the parties. Additional factors are the existence of an employment relationship and the exchange of confidential information from one party to the other. All five of those factors are present in this case. In addition, one of Sears' witnesses admitted that the company expected plaintiff to "believe" and to "rely" on various representations that Sears made to him.

DECISION AND REMEDY   *The verdict of $1 million was affirmed.*

COMMENTS   *In April 1982, a jury awarded Roberts an additional $5 million after concluding that Sears was guilty of patent infringement with respect to 15 million wrenches sold after the original trial.*

Termination   Contracts of employment are either at will (involving no specific time period) or for a specific term. Contracts at will can generally be terminated by proper notice at any time without liability, unless the termination violates discrimination laws.

Contracts for a specified duration can usually only be terminated, without employer liability, for good and sufficient cause, or by the employee's acceptance of some form of severance consideration. A termination without cause is a breach of contract and can make the employer liable for the balance of the term contract compensation due and/or damages. On occasion, the employer may be required to reinstate the employee.

What is good and sufficient cause for termination is sometimes the heart of an employee's lawsuit. Generally, an employee's serious nonperformance of duties, insubordination, disloyalty, incompetency or disability that seriously affects work performance,

and wrongful conduct are grounds for a good cause termination.

An employee can be held liable by an employer for wrongful termination under a contract for a specific duration. The employer cannot force (through specific performance) the employee to continue to work for the employer, as that would constitute a form of involuntary servitude, which is a constitutional violation. However, the employer can seek damages, making termination by the employee less attractive.

Employment Torts

Considerable legal attention is given to an employer's tort liability for injuries suffered by the employee and to suits by third persons who are harmed by the torts of the employee. This section briefly discusses the employer's liability in these situations.

Employer's Negligence   Under common law, the employer is required to provide the employee with a safe place to work. In the event the employee is injured within the scope of employment, the employee will usually be entitled to worker's compensation or, if the employer's negligence caused the injury, to actual damages. An employee can refuse to work in an unsafe environment and such refusal cannot be a basis for termination of employment.[16]

Frequently an employee is injured by a fellow worker. Under common law, the employer has no liability for injuries caused by a fellow-servant, unless the employer hired an irresponsible worker who caused the injury (negligence on the part of the employer), or a superior or supervisor injured the employee. If the employee falls under worker's compensation law, the employee is entitled to a fixed compensation set forth by statute. This compensation must be paid by the employer or by the employer's insurance.

Employer Liability for Employee's Negligence Third persons injured through the negligence of an employee can sue either the employee who was negligent, or the employer if the employee's negligent conduct occurred while the employee was acting within the scope of employment. Liability of the employer, when the employer is not personally at fault, is based on the doctrine of *respondeat superior*.

At early common law, a servant (employee) was viewed as the master's (employer's) property. The master was deemed to have absolute control over the servant's acts and was held strictly liable for them no matter how carefully the master supervised the servant. The rationale for the doctrine of *respondeat superior* is based on the principle of social duty. Every person shall manage his or her own affairs, whether alone or through agents or servants, so as not to injure another. Liability is imposed on employers because they are deemed to be in better financial positions to bear the loss. The superior financial position carries with it the duty to be responsible for damages.

Today the doctrine continues, but employers carry liability insurance and spread the cost of risk over the entire business enterprise. Public policy requires that an injured person be afforded effective relief, and recovery from a business enterprise provides far more effective relief than recovery from an individual employee. Liability rights exist under law due to public policy protections of third parties. Thus, a master (employer) cannot contract with a servant (employee) to disclaim responsibilities for injuries resulting from the servant's acts, because such disclaimers are against public policy.

The act causing injury must have occurred as part of the employee's regular duties in employment. For example, Sutton (the employee) is a delivery driver for Schwartz (the employer). Schwartz provides Sutton with a vehicle and instructs him to use it for making company deliveries. Nevertheless, one day Sutton drives his own car instead of the company vehicle and negligently injures Walker. Even though Sutton's act (driving the car) was unauthorized, the negligence occurred as part of Sutton's regular duties of employment (making deliveries). Hence, Schwartz is still liable to Walker for the injuries caused by Sutton, even though Sutton used his own car contrary to Schwartz's instructions. Only if Sutton's acts exceed the scope of employment duties in a way that the employer would not reasonably expect to happen will Schwartz be relieved of liability.

An employee going to and from work or to and from meals is usually considered outside the scope of employment. All travel time of a traveling salesperson, however, is normally considered within the scope of employment for the duration of the business trip, including the return trip home.

When an employee goes on a frolic of his or her own—that is, departs from the employer's business to take care of personal affairs—is the employer liable? It depends. If the employee's activity is a substantial departure akin to an utter abandonment of the employer's business, then the employer is not liable.

For example, a traveling salesperson is driving the employer's vehicle to call on a customer for a possible sales order. On the way to the customer's place of business, the employee deviates one block to mail a letter at the post office. As the employee approaches the post office, the employee negligently runs into a parked vehicle owned by Ann. The departure of the employee from the employer's business to take care of a personal affair is not substantial. The employee is still within the scope of employment and the employer is liable to Ann. If the em-

---

16. For example, under the Occupational Safety and Health Act of 1970, employees are protected from discharge or discrimination for refusal to work because of a reasonable apprehension of death or serious injury. See Whirlpool Corp. v. Marshall, 445 U.S. 1, 100 S.Ct. 883 (1980).

ployee decided to pick up a few friends for cocktails in another city, and in the process negligently ran the vehicle into Ann, Ann could not hold the employer liable, only the employee.

The following case is a classic in master-servant law. Although it is over 150 years old, the legal principle for which it stands is still viable in employment law today.

JOEL v. MORISON
Court of Exchequer, England,
1834.
6 Carrington & Payne Reports
501.

BACKGROUND AND FACTS   *The plaintiff was walking across Bishops-gatestreet when he was knocked down by a cart driven negligently by a servant of the defendant. The plaintiff suffered a fractured leg and multiple injuries. The plaintiff took the position that the defendant was liable for his injuries because the defendant's servant was driving the cart that caused the injuries. The defendant argued that his cart was never driven in the neighborhood in which the plaintiff was injured. Moreover, it was suggested that the defendant's servant had gone out of his way for his own purposes and might have taken the cart at a time when it was not wanted for business purposes to pay a visit to some friends.*

PARKE, Judge.
*   *   *   *

His Lordship afterwards, in summing up, said—This is an action to recover damages for an injury sustained by the plaintiff, in consequence of the negligence of the defendant's servant. There is no doubt that the plaintiff has suffered the injury, and there is no doubt that the driver of the cart was guilty of negligence, and there is no doubt also that the master, if that person was driving the cart on his master's business, is responsible. If the servants, being on their master's business, took a detour to call upon a friend, the master will be responsible. If you think the servants lent the cart to a person who was driving without the defendant's knowledge, he will not be responsible. Or, if you think that the young man who was driving took the cart surreptitiously, and was not at the time employed on his master's business, the defendant will not be liable. The master is only liable where the servant is acting in the course of his employment. If he was going out of his way, against his master's implied commands, when driving on his master's business, he will make his master liable; but if he was going on a frolic of his own, without being at all on his master's business, the master will not be liable. As to the damages, the master *   *   * [although not himself] guilty of any offence, *   *   * is only responsible in law, therefore the amount should be reasonable.

**DECISION
AND REMEDY**   *The verdict was for the plaintiff, and he was awarded damages of £30. In this case, the master was held liable for the acts of his servant.*

Borrowed Servants   Employers can lend the services of their employees to other employers. Suppose that an employer leases ground-moving equipment to another employer and sends along an employee to operate the machinery. Who is liable for injuries caused by the employee's negligent actions on the job site? Liability turns on *which employer had the right to control* the employee at the time the injuries occurred. Generally, the employer who rents out

the equipment is presumed to retain control over his or her employee. If the rental is for a relatively long period of time, however, control may be deemed to pass to the employer who is renting the equipment and presumably controlling and directing the employee.

Notice of Dangerous Conditions   The employer is charged with knowledge of any dangerous conditions discovered by an employee and pertinent to the employment situation. To illustrate, a maintenance employee in Martin's apartment notices a lead pipe protruding from the ground. The employee neglects either to fix it or to inform the employer of the danger. Sam falls on the pipe and is injured. The employer is charged with knowledge of the dangerous condition regardless of whether or not the employee actually informed the employer. That knowledge is imputed to the employer by virtue of the employment relationship.

EMPLOYER'S LIABILITY FOR EMPLOYEE'S INTENTIONAL TORTS

Under *respondeat superior*, the employer is liable for intentional torts of the employee committed within the scope of employment, just as the employer is liable for negligence. For example, an employer is liable for an employee's assault and battery or an employee's false imprisonment while acting within the scope of employment. Also, an employer is liable for permitting an employee to engage in reckless acts that can injure others. For example, an employer observes an employee smoking while filling containerized trucks with highly flammable liquids. Failure to stop the employee will cause the employer to be liable for any injuries that result.

An employee acting at the employer's direction can be liable as a tortfeasor (one who commits a wrong, or tort), along with the employer, for committing the tortious act even if the employee was unaware of the wrongfulness of the act. For example, an employer directs an employee to burn out a field of crops. The employee does so, assuming that the field belongs to the employer, which it does not. Both can be found liable to the owner of the field for damages.

An employer who knows or should know that an employee has a propensity for committing tortious acts is liable for the employee's acts even if they would not ordinarily be considered within the scope of employment. For example, the Blue Moon employs Joe Green as a bouncer, knowing that he has a history of arrests for assault and battery. While he is working one night within the scope of his employment, he viciously attacks a patron who "looks at him funny." The Blue Moon will bear the responsibility for Green's acts because it knew that he had a propensity for committing tortious acts.

QUESTIONS AND CASE PROBLEMS

1. Adam is a traveling salesman for Peter Petri Plumbing Supply Corporation. Adam has express authority to solicit orders from customers and to offer a 5 percent discount if payment is made within thirty days of delivery. Petri has said nothing to Adam about extending credit. Adam calls on a new prospective customer, John's Plumbing Firm. John tells Adam that he will place a large order for Petri products if Adam will give him a 10 percent discount with payment in installments on a thirty-sixty-ninety-day basis. Adam says he has authority to make such a contract. John calls Petri and asks if Adam is authorized to make contracts giving a discount. No mention is made of payment terms. Petri replies that Adam has authority to make discounts on purchase orders. On the basis of this information, John orders $10,000 worth of plumbing supplies and fixtures. The goods are delivered and are being sold. One week later John receives a bill for $9,500, if paid in thirty days. John insists he owes only $9,000 and can pay it in three equal installments, at thirty, sixty, and ninety days from delivery. Discuss the liability of Petri and John only.

2. Alice Adams is a purchasing agent-employee for the A & B Coal Supply partnership. Adams has authority to purchase the coal needed by A & B to satisfy the needs of its customers. While Adams is leaving a coal mine from which she just purchased a large quantity of coal, her car breaks down. She walks into a small roadside grocery store for help. While there, she runs into Will Wilson. Wilson owns 360 acres back in the mountains with all mineral rights. Wilson, in need of money, offers to sell Adams the property at $1,500 per acre. Upon inspection, Adams believes the subsurface contains valuable coal deposits. Adams contracts to purchase the property for A & B Coal Company, signing the contract, "A & B Coal Supply, Alice Adams, agent." The closing date is August 1. Adams takes the contract to the partnership. The managing partner is furious, as A & B is not in the property business. Later, just before closing, both Wilson and the partnership learn that the value of the land is at least $15,000 per acre. Discuss the rights of A & B and Wilson concerning the land contract.

3. Paula Development Enterprises hires Able to act as its agent to purchase a 1,000-acre tract of land from Thompson for $1,000 per acre. Paula Enterprises does

not wish Thompson to know that it is the principal or that Able is its agent. Paula wants the land for a new country housing development, and Thompson may not sell the land for that purpose or may demand a premium price. Able makes the contract for the purchase, signing only Able's name as purchaser and not disclosing to Thompson the agency relationship. The closing and transfer of deed is to be September 1.

(a) If Thompson learns of Paula's identity on August 1, can Thompson legally refuse to deed the property on September 1? Explain.

(b) Paula gives Able the money for the closing, but Able absconds with the money, causing a breach of Able's contract at the date of closing. Assume Thompson now learns of Paula's identity and wants to enforce the contract. Discuss fully Thompson's rights under these circumstances.

4. Able is hired as a traveling salesperson for the ABC Tire Corporation. Able has a designated geographic area and time schedule within which to solicit orders and service customers. Able is given a company car to be used in covering the territory. One day Able decides to take his personal car to cover part of his territory. It is 11:00 A.M., and Able has just finished calling on all customers in the city of Tarrytown. Able's next appointment is in the city of Austex, twenty miles down the road, at 2:00 P.M. Able starts out for Austex, but halfway there he decides to visit a former college roommate who runs a farm ten miles off the main highway. Able is enjoying his visit with his former roommate when he realizes that it is 1:45 P.M. and that he will be late for the appointment in Austex. Driving at a high speed down the country road to reach the main highway, Able crashes his car into Thomas's tractor, severely injuring Thomas, a farmer. Thomas claims he can hold the ABC Tire Corporation liable for his injuries. Discuss fully ABC's liability in this situation.

5. Adam is an agent for Fish Galore, Inc. Adam has express authority to solicit orders and receive payments in advance of shipment. He is well known as an agent in the region. One of his customers, Seafood Quality, has been a regular customer for five years, has usually made large orders, and has always paid Adam in advance to get the discount offered by Fish Galore. Fish Galore learns that Adam has incurred large gambling debts and has recently used some of the customers' payments to pay off these debts. When Adam cannot reimburse Fish Galore, he is fired. Fish Galore hires a new agent and publishes in the regional newspapers that the new agent will be covering the territory. Desperately in need of cash, Adam solicits a large order from Seafood Quality and receives payment. Then he calls on a new customer, Catfish Heaven, who also gives Adam an order and payment. Adam absconds with the money. Fish Galore refuses to honor either order. Seafood Quality and Catfish Heaven claim

Fish Galore is in breach of contract. Discuss fully their claims.

6. Paula owes Adam $1,000, and the debt is due and payable. Paula does not have the cash to pay the debt, but she has some stereo equipment valued at $1,800. Paula gives Adam authority to sell the stereo equipment to satisfy the debt, with any surplus being paid back to Paula. Later Paula and Adam have a severe disagreement over another matter, and Paula sends a letter to Adam terminating his authority and agency to sell the stereo equipment. Despite receiving the letter, Adam contracts to sell the equipment to Francis for $1,200. Francis pays Adam, but Paula refuses to turn over the stereo equipment to Francis or accept the $200 from Adam. Paula claims that at the time the contract with Francis was made no agency existed. Discuss fully Paula's contention.

7. Under the Fair Housing Act, racial discrimination in housing practices (including the renting of apartments) is prohibited. Leach owned two apartment complexes in Columbus, Mississippi, and employed Jenkins as office manager of the apartments. For the entire time that she managed the apartments, Jenkins did not rent to any blacks, even though blacks make up about 37 percent of the local population. The United States Attorney General brought suit against Leach for violations of the Fair Housing Act. Leach contended that Jenkins did all the renting and made all the decisions as to whom she rented the apartments. Will the government win its case against Leach? [United States v. Real Estate Development Corp., 347 F.Supp. 776 (N.D.Miss. 1972)]

8. Hohenberg Brothers was a Memphis-based cotton merchandiser, and Killebrew was a Mississippi cotton farmer. Both parties were represented by D. T. Syle, Jr., a cotton agent. In February 1973, Killebrew signed and delivered to Syle a one-page purchase and sales agreement form covering the sale of Killebrew's 1973 cotton crop. All of the blanks in this document were completed, except for the name and signature of the purchaser, who was still unknown. On March 2, Syle secured an oral commitment that Hohenberg would purchase Killebrew's crop at the prices set forth in the one-page contract. Hohenberg immediately sent Syle its standard three-page purchase and sales agreement, the terms of which were identical to Syle's one-page document. Syle signed Killebrew's name and returned it to Hohenberg. Has Syle acted beyond the scope of his agency in signing Killebrew's name? [Hohenberg Brothers Co. v. Killebrew, 505 F.2d 643 (5th Cir. 1974)]

9. For many years Abell Company, publisher of the *Sun* newspaper in Baltimore City, ran advertisements for Warner and Company, a long-established and well-known haberdashery located in Baltimore City. Each February two contracts were entered into; they provided that morning, evening, and Sunday editions would advertise the

clothing store's merchandise. Skeen, Warner's advertising manager, was responsible for procuring the advertisements, and he always signed the contracts with his name followed by the words "Warner & Co." When Warner and Company went bankrupt, Abell argued that Skeen was personally responsible for the advertising debt owed by the company. Abell contended that the use of the name "Warner & Co." was not sufficient to indicate the corporate status of Warner, and thus Skeen should be held personally liable. Will Skeen be liable? [Abell Co. v. Skeen, 265 Md. 53, 288 A.2d 596 (1972)]

10. Pro Golf manufactured and marketed golfing equipment both in the United States and abroad. In 1961 Robert Wynn became Pro Golf's sales representative in the Far East. Wynn and Pro Golf did not have a formal contract, but letters exchanged between them indicated the type of relationship they had. In a 1970 letter from Pro Golf to Wynn, Pro Golf stated, "You will continue to have the exclusive right to import and promote the sale of golfing equipment in the Far East market. However, this is not an irrevocable right but would remain in effect only so long as you did a satisfactory business in this market." Several years later Pro Golf terminated Wynn's exclusive right, but first it gave Wynn five months' notice of its desire to terminate. Was Pro Golf's termination proper? What if Pro Golf had given Wynn no notice? [First Flight Associates, Inc. v. Professional Golf Co., 527 F.2d 931 (6th Cir. 1975)]

11. On October 11, 1973, John Gray, owner of a 50 percent interest in a government oil and gas lease, assigned 20 percent of the operating rights and working interest to John Tylle in consideration of Tylle's payment of $10,000. The assignment was in writing and stated: "Until further notice assignee hereby appoints and designates assignor as agent and operator of the said lease for the purpose of development and management." A few weeks later, John Gray died unexpectedly. Tylle filed a claim against Gray's estate, seeking to recover the $10,000 he paid Gray. In order for Tylle to be successful, he must show that the agency relationship between him and Gray had been terminated. Will Tylle be successful? [In the matter of the estate of Gray, 37 Colo.App. 47, 541 P.2d 336 (1975)]

FOCUS ON ETHICS

Agency and Employment

Agency law is concerned with the duties, rights, and liabilities of principals and agents. Foremost within the area of agency is the nature of duty.

THE DUTY OF THE AGENT TO THE PRINCIPAL

What is the nature of the duty that an agent owes to a principal in an employment situation? Does the agent have the duty to disclose all favorable information that could be used by the principal to increase the principal's profits? Or does the agent have the right to use some of the information gleaned during the course of normal employment for his or her own benefit? In order to understand the answers to these questions, we must understand the kind of relationship that exists between a principal and an agent.

The very nature of the principal-agent relationship is one of trust, which we call a fiduciary relationship. Because of this, it is expected that an agent owes certain duties to the principal. These duties include loyalty and obedience, informing the principal of important facts concerning the agency, accounting to the principal for property or money received, and performing with reasonable diligence and skill.

Thus, ethical conduct would prevent an agent from representing two principals in the same transaction, or making a secret profit from the agency, or failing to disclose the interest of the agent in property the principal was purchasing. The expected ethical conduct of the agent has evolved into rules that, if breached, cause the agent to be held liable.

What about looking beyond the duty of the principal in considering one's duty to society? Those employees of Firestone who knew of the company's defective tires in the early 1980s presumably could have divulged that information to the public (at the risk of losing their jobs, of course). Furthermore, employees aware of deliberate and fraudulent cost overruns on government contracts could make this information public, once again at the risk of losing their jobs. Some scholars have argued that many of the greatest "evils" in the past twenty-five years have been accomplished in the name of "duty" to the principal. Duty in this context means placing the well-being of the principal above that of the public.

AGENCY BY ESTOPPEL

Sometimes a third person may be led to believe, either by the agent or the principal, that an individual is acting in the capacity of an agent for a principal. The notion of agency by estoppel certainly involves ethical issues. To the extent that a third person is in fact led to believe that an agency relationship exists, to what extent should that third person be able to rely on the apparent agency relationship? For the most part, agency law seems to follow ethical considerations in such situations; the notion of agency by estoppel is one in which the potential harm caused by the apparent agency relationship to the innocent third party is either prevented altogether or minimized.

THE DUTY OF PRINCIPALS

A principal has the duty to the agent of providing adequate compensation and reimbursement, cooperation, and safe working conditions. Think about the ethical implications of the last point. To what extent does a businessperson have an ethical mandate to provide a safe working environment for employees? To what extent, for example, should a company use its own resources to eliminate reproductive risks to both men and women from some type of airborne by-product of production? Should individual employees, who are willing to work notwithstanding the

592

possibility of exposure to dangerous chemicals, bear such a responsibility, or should businesses be constrained by government to eliminate such risks?

To insure that employers provide safe working conditions for their employees, government regulation of the workplace has increased dramatically in the last decade. Such government regulation, mostly carried out by the Occupational Safety & Health Administration (OSHA), was a result of presumed inadequate action on the part of employers. Nonetheless, not all scholars agree with OSHA's operating methods. One can argue that there is such a thing as "too much" safety in the workplace. We are then faced with the trade-off between economic and ethical concerns. For many employers, the safer the workplace or the less monotonous the work, the higher the cost related to the labor input in the production process. That higher cost is paid by consumers in the form of higher prices, by stockholders in the form of lower profits, or by employees in the form of lower wages. Some studies have shown that in the long run, the higher costs for safer working conditions are paid almost entirely by employees in the form of lower wages.

To understand the last point, consider an example that has to do with smog. Smog affects the health and well-being of all residents and employees in a geographical area. Wage rates for the same type of work, holding all other things constant, are in general higher in smoggy environments than they are in cleaner environments. In the long run, workers who care more about higher wages and less about clean air will gravitate

toward work environments with more smog. If a law is passed requiring all factories in a smoggy environment to reduce smog output, wage rates in that area will fall. They will fall because workers concerned about air quality will now be able to move into the area to offer their labor services, and this increase in the supply of labor will drive down wages to levels comparable to those in other areas where the air is already clean. Those previously working at higher wage rates, but breathing bad air, will now find their wages reduced. This process of long-run economic equilibrium demonstrates that some workers will lose wages because of the imposition of a higher-quality work environment.

The ethical issue is, who should be protected? Clearly, there is a trade-off involved here. A businessperson, considering the rate of return to investment, may feel totally unconstrained to provide a safe working environment for employees. To the extent that society, in the form of government regulation of the workplace, desires safer working conditions, it must bear the cost. The ethical question, ultimately, is how much safety are we willing to pay for?

RESPONDEAT SUPERIOR

Over the past few years, violence in professional sports has increased dramatically. Traditionally, the doctrine of assumption of risk has prevented plaintiffs from recovering damages for sports injuries on the assumption that the players have "consented" to participation in the sports. Thus, in *Moe v. Steenberg* [275 Minn. 448, 147 N.W.2d 587 (1966)], a

plaintiff ice skater was denied recovery for injuries sustained when another skater, the defendant, was skating backwards and collided with the plaintiff. The general notion prevailed that the participant in a sport assumes the risks that are inherent in it. The question arises, however, as to what type of recovery should be allowed with respect to intentional actions committed by members of a professional sports team. More specifically, should potential plaintiffs be allowed to bring an action against professional sports-team owners under the doctrine of *respondeat superior,* and to recover damages for intentional torts committed by the teams' players? Does our collection of shared beliefs require that this doctrine be extended in such a way? Several cases have indicated a new trend for recovery by a professional athlete against an opposing team.

In 1973, in a game between the Denver Broncos and the Cincinnati Bengals, Dale Hackbardt was playing safety for the Broncos and Charles Clark was playing fullback for the Bengals. When Hackbardt attempted to block Clark to make room for his teammate to run with the intercepted pass, Clark hit the plaintiff (Hackbardt) in the back of the head with his right forearm. This blow resulted in a severe neck injury, which forced the plaintiff to end his career. The trial court dismissed Hackbardt's actions on the grounds that he had assumed the risk of such an injury and that the judiciary was not "well suited" to determine which civil restraints should be applied to professional football. The Tenth Circuit, in *Hackbardt v. Cincinnati Bengals, Inc.* [601

F.2d 516 (10th Cir. 1979)], however, reversed and held that the owner of the team, as well as Clark, was liable under the doctrine of *respondeat superior*.

Do you agree with the Tenth Circuit's recognition of a cause of action based on *respondeat superior* and its conclusion that an owner of a professional sports team may be held liable for intentional torts committed by team members? Even though it doesn't seem "fair" to treat professional sports differently than other master-servant relationships, it is still interesting to explore the policy rationales behind the doctrine of *respondeat superior* as applied in this context.

The prevailing rationale for retaining *respondeat superior* in our laws is based upon the employer's assumed ability to pay. Our collection of shared beliefs suggests that an injured party should be afforded the most effective relief possible. Thus, even though an employer may be absolutely innocent, the employer has a "deeper pocket" and will be more likely to have the funds necessary to make the injured party whole. Yet this rationale begins to weaken in the area of professional sports. Professional athletes are presently among the highest-paid employees in our society. In this context, does it seem ethical to apply the doctrine of *respondeat superior* and impose liability upon owners without fault? Unlike many other employment relationships, professional athletes frequently have the ability to pay a substantial damage claim.

Another rationale for the doctrine of *respondeat superior* is based upon the theory of deterrence. This rationale proposes that employers will take greater precautions to deter wrongful acts by their employees if they know that they may be liable for their employees' wrongful conduct. Yet wouldn't holding a player liable for his or her own wrongful conduct be more effective in deterring this type of undesirable behavior? Isn't it reasonable to assume that deterrence might be better served if a player knew that he or she, not the team owner, would be solely held liable for such conduct?

DISCUSSION QUESTIONS

1. How much obedience and loyalty does an employee owe an employer?

2. If an agent injures a third party during the course of employment, to what extent should the employer be held liable for the agent's actions? Does the amount of negligence on the part of the agent have any bearing on your answer? Is there any situation in which the agent should be held personally liable for his or her actions that harm third parties?

3. The above question relates to the doctrine of *respondeat superior*. What ethical considerations generated this doctrine?

4. Agency by estoppel occurs when the principal's actions create the appearance of apparent authority by a presumed agent. Do you think that agency by estoppel should be allowed under all circumstances? Or, rather, do you believe that the third person must prove that he or she reasonably believed that the agent had authority?

5. The termination of an agency agreement can occur by operation of law. In particular, when unforeseen circumstances (such as impossibility or bankruptcy) occur, termination by operation of law may take place. What ethical considerations are involved here?

UNIT VI

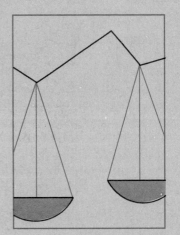

BUSINESS ORGANIZATIONS

34

Forms of Business Organization

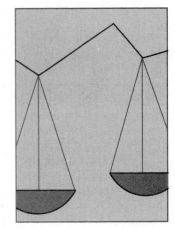

There are basically three types of business organizations—sole proprietorships, partnerships, and corporations. Additionally, there are two types of partnerships—limited partnerships and general, or unlimited, partnerships—and various classifications of corporations, such as closely held corporations and S corporations.

Other types of business organizations also exist—among them joint ventures, syndicates or investment groups, joint stock companies, business trusts, and cooperatives—but these are essentially hybrid forms of partnerships or of corporations.

This chapter will first describe the form of these business organizations. Then it will compare a partnership with a corporation in more detail. Persons starting out in business will most often choose between these two forms when deciding how a business should be organized.

SOLE PROPRIETORSHIP

The simplest form of business is a sole proprietorship. The owner is the business. This form is used by anyone who does business without creating an organization. One usually associates a sole proprietorship with small enterprises, although this is not necessarily the case. The owner's personal estate is liable for his or her business debts. The advantages

and disadvantages of a sole proprietorship are discussed later in this chapter.

PARTNERSHIP

A partnership arises from an agreement, express or implied, between two or more persons to carry on a business for profit. Partners are co-owners of a business and have joint control over its operation and the right to share in its profits. Both partnerships and sole proprietorships are creatures of common law rather than of statutes. No particular form of partnership agreement is necessary for the creation of a partnership, although it is desirable that the agreement be in writing. The Uniform Partnership Act (UPA), adopted in forty-eight states,[1] governs the operation of partnerships *in the absence* of express agreements. Basically, the partners may agree to almost any terms when establishing the partnership so long as they are not illegal or contrary to public policy. The UPA comes into play only if the partners have neglected to include a necessary term. In a sense, then, the UPA is a gap-filler. It is not a

---

1. Only the states of Louisiana and Georgia have not adopted the UPA. Guam, the District of Columbia, and the Virgin Islands have also adopted the UPA. See Appendix D for the text of the UPA.

code that must be followed in order to create the legal entity called a partnership.

A partnership is a legal entity for limited purposes, such as the partnership name and title of ownership and property. Otherwise, it is not a legal entity. Rather, the personal net worth of the partners is subject to partnership obligations. The partnership itself is not subject to levy for federal income taxes; only an information return must be filed. However, a partner's profit from the partnership (whether or not distributed) is taxed as individual income to the individual partner.

Chapter 35 will detail the creation and termination of general partnerships. Chapter 36 will deal with the duties, rights, and liabilities of partners to each other and to third persons.

Limited Partnerships

The most popular special form of a partnership is the limited partnership, which consists of at least one general partner and one or more limited partners. The limited partnership is created by an agreement; but unlike a general partnership, the limited partnership does not come into existence until a certificate of partnership is filed appropriately in a state.

Furthermore, unlike a general partnership, a limited partnership is completely a creature of statute. If the statute is not followed almost to the letter, the courts will hold that a general partnership exists instead. Then those who thought their liability was limited by their investment in a limited partnership will be held generally liable to the full extent of their personal net worth.

Once a limited partnership is created, the law treats the general partner(s) exactly the same as any partner in ordinary partnership. The limited partner(s) is treated basically as an investor; that is, the limited partner contributes capital but does not participate in the management or control of the partnership. As long as the limited partner's activities are confined to the investor role only, the limited partner will have limited liability. This means that the liability of the limited partner, if he or she refrains from management activities, is limited to his or her capital contribution, and personal assets are not subject to partnership obligations. Limited partnerships are discussed in more detail in Chapter 37. All states permit limited partnerships. Twenty-seven states have adopted the Uniform Limited Partnership Act (ULPA) and twenty-two its revision (see Appendices E and F), which govern the organization and operation of limited partnerships.

BUSINESS CORPORATIONS

The most important form of business organization is the corporation. A corporation comes into existence by an act of the state, and therefore it is a legal entity. It typically has perpetual existence. One of the key features of a corporation is that the liability of its owners is limited to their investments. Their personal estates are usually not liable for the obligations of the corporation.

Corporations consist of shareholders, who are the owners of the business. A board of directors, elected by the shareholders, manages the business. The board of directors normally employs officers to oversee day-to-day operations.

The law on the formation, management and operation, liability, and termination of corporations will be discussed in detail in Chapters 38 to 42.

OTHER FORMS OF BUSINESS ORGANIZATION

There are a number of other, less common forms of business organization. They include joint ventures, syndicates or investment groups, joint stock companies, business trusts, and cooperatives.

Joint Ventures

When two or more persons or entities combine their interests in a particular business enterprise and agree to share in losses or profits jointly or in proportion to their contributions, they are engaged in a joint venture. The joint venture is treated much like a partnership, but it differs in that its creation is in contemplation of a limited activity or a single transaction.

For example, Able and Cain pool their resources to buy an old boat, remodel it, and sell it, dividing the profits. This creates not a partnership but a joint venture. The same is true if Able, owning a piece of land, and Cain, owning an adjoining piece of land, agree to sell both parcels together as one unit to the highest bidder and then divide the proceeds proportionately to the value of each parcel of land held.

Members of a joint venture usually have limited powers to bind their co-venturers. A joint venture is normally not a legal entity and therefore cannot be sued as such, but its members can be sued individually. Usually joint ventures are taxed like partnerships. They range in size from very small activities to huge, multimillion-dollar joint actions engaged in by some of the world's largest corporations.

Syndicates, or Investment Groups

A group of individuals getting together to finance a particular project, such as the building of a shopping center or the purchase of a professional basketball franchise, is called a syndicate or an investment group. The form of such groups varies considerably. They may exist as corporations or as general or limited partnerships. In some cases, the members merely own property jointly and have no legally recognized business arrangement.

Joint Stock Companies

A joint stock company or association is a true hybrid of a partnership and a corporation. It has many characteristics of a corporation but is usually treated like a partnership. For example, the joint stock company resembles a corporation in that its ownership is represented by transferable shares of stock, it is usually managed by directors and officers of the company or association, and it can have a perpetual existence.

However, most other features are more characteristic of a partnership. For example, the joint stock company is formed by agreement (not statute); property is usually held in the names of the members; shareholders have personal liability; and generally the company is not treated as a legal entity for purposes of a lawsuit. However, shareholders are not treated as agents of each other, as would be the case if the company were a true partnership.

The joint stock company is not widely used, but a modern example is the American Express Company, which was a joint stock association until 1965.

Business Trusts

A business trust is created by a written trust agreement that sets forth the interests of the beneficiaries and the obligations and powers of the trustees. With a business trust, legal ownership and management of the property of the business stays with one or more of the trustees, and the profits are distributed to the beneficiaries.

The business trust was started in Massachusetts in an attempt to obtain the limited liability advantage of corporate status while avoiding certain restrictions on a corporation's ownership and development of real property.

The business trust resembles a corporation in many aspects. Death or bankruptcy of a beneficiary does not terminate the trust, and beneficiaries are not personally responsible for the debts or obligations of the business trust. In fact, in a number of states business trusts must pay corporate taxes. The business trust was more popular at the turn of the century than it is today. Its decline is a result of antitrust laws (discussed in detail in Chapters 48 and 49).

In a few states only, the beneficiaries are treated as partners and they are personally liable to business creditors; thus the limited liability advantage is eliminated.

Cooperatives

A cooperative is an association, either incorporated or not, that is organized to provide an economic service without profit to its members (or shareholders). An incorporated cooperative is subject to state laws governing nonprofit corporations. It will make distributions of dividends, or profits, to its owners on the basis of their transactions with the cooperative rather than on the basis of the amount of capital they contributed. Cooperatives that are unincorporated are often treated like partnerships. The members have joint liability for the cooperatives' acts. Cooperatives are generally formed by groups of individuals who wish to pool their resources in order to gain some advantage in the marketplace. Consumer purchasing co-ops are formed to obtain lower prices through quantity discounts. Seller marketing co-ops are formed to control the market and thereby obtain higher sales prices from consumers. Often cooperatives are exempt from certain federal laws—for example, antitrust statutes—because of their special status.

THE ADVANTAGES AND DISADVANTAGES OF A SOLE PROPRIETORSHIP

A major advantage of a sole proprietorship is that the proprietor receives all the profits because he or she takes all the risk. In addition, it is often easier and less costly to start a sole proprietorship than to start any other kind of business. Few legal forms must be completed, and since the proprietor makes all the decisions, the problem of reaching agreement among all the people involved is avoided. The sole proprietor is also free from corporate income taxes, paying only personal income taxes on profits. However, these taxes are not necessarily lower than those for a corporation.

A major disadvantage of the sole proprietorship is that, as sole owner, the proprietor alone bears the risk of losses. In addition, the proprietor's opportunity to raise capital is limited to personal funds and the funds of those who are willing to make loans. Additionally, and perhaps more importantly for many potential entrepreneurs, the sole proprietor has unlimited liability, or legal responsibility, for all obligations incurred in doing business.

COMPARING A PARTNERSHIP WITH A CORPORATION

Exhibit 34–1 is an abbreviated comparison between a partnership and a corporation, giving the essential

EXHIBIT 34–1 Comparing A Partnership With A Corporation		
CHARACTERISTIC	**PARTNERSHIP**	**CORPORATION**
1. Method of Creation	Created by agreement of the parties.	Charter issued by state—created by statutory authorization.
2. Legal Position	Not a separate legal entity in many states.	Always a legal entity separate and distinct from its owners—a legal fiction for the purposes of owning property and being party to litigation.
3. Liability	Unlimited liability (except for limited partners in a limited partnership).	Limited liability of shareholders—shareholders are not liable for the debts of the corporation.
4. Duration	Terminated by agreement of the partners, by the death of one or more of the partners, by withdrawal of a partner, by bankruptcy, etc.	Can have perpetual existence.
5. Transferability of Interest	Although partnership interest can be assigned, assignee does not have full rights of a partner.	Shares of stock can be transferred.
6. Management	Each general partner has a direct and equal voice in management unless expressly agreed otherwise in the partnership agreement. (Limited partner has no rights in management in a limited partnership.)	Shareholders elect directors who set policy and appoint officers.
7. Taxation	Each partner pays pro rata share of income taxes on net profits, whether or not they are distributed.	Double taxation—corporation pays income tax on net profits, with no deduction for dividends, and shareholders pay income tax on disbursed dividends they receive.
8. Organizational Fees, Annual License Fees, and Annual Reports	None.	All required.
9. Transaction of Business in Other States	Generally no limitation.[a]	Normally must qualify to do business and obtain certificate of authority.
[a]A few states have enacted statutes requiring that foreign partnerships qualify to do business there—for example, 3 N.H.Rev.Stat.Ann. Chapter 305-A in New Hampshire.		

advantages and disadvantages of each. Other points of comparison concern the liability of owners, tax considerations, and the need for capital."

Liability of Owners

The form of the organization does not always in and of itself determine the liability of the owners. Generally, sole proprietorships and general partners have personal liability and limited partners and shareholders of corporations have liability limited to their investment. Because of this, creditors frequently look to personal liability in extending credit. It simply determines who is liable. For example, a bank may be unwilling to lend money to a corporation that is relatively small and has only a few shareholders. The corporate form for the business does not guar-antee that it is a better risk for the bank. Typically, in such situations the relatively few shareholders must personally sign for any loans made to the corporation. That is, the shareholders agree to become personally liable for the loan. In essence, they must be guarantors for the corporation's debt. Hence, the corporate form of business does not prevent them from having personal liability in such a case, because they have assumed the liability voluntarily.

Tax Considerations

Various tax considerations must be taken into account when one compares a partnership with a corporation. These considerations are listed in Exhibit 34–2.

EXHIBIT 34–2 Partnership Versus Corporation—Tax Considerations

TAX ASPECT	PARTNERSHIP	CORPORATION
1. Federal Income Tax	Partner is taxed on proportionate share of partnership income, even if not distributed; the partnership files information returns only.	Income of the corporation is taxed; stockholders are also taxed on distributed dividends. Must file corporate income tax forms.
2. Accumulation	Partners taxed on accumulated as well as distributed earnings.	Corporate stockholders not taxed on accumulated earnings. There is, however, a penalty tax, in some instances, that the corporation must pay for accumulations of income.
3. Capital Gains and Losses	All partners taxed on their proportionate share of capital gains and losses.	Corporation taxed on capital gains and losses. There is no special deduction to reduce taxes for any excess of long-term gains over short-term losses, but there is a special rate.
4. Exempt Interest	Partners are not taxed on exempt interest received from the firm.	Any exempt interest distributed by a corporation is fully taxable income to the stockholders. Exempt interest can come, for example, from municipal bonds.
5. Pension Plan	Partners are not eligible for an exempt pension trust. The firm cannot deduct payments for partners except under what is called a Keogh Plan.	Employees and officers who are also stockholders can be beneficiaries of a pension trust. The corporation can deduct its payments to the trust.
6. Social Security	Partners do not pay social security tax, but often must pay a self-employment tax.	All compensation to officers and employee stockholders subject to social security taxation up to the maximum.
7. Death Benefits (excluding those provided by insurance)	There is no exemption for payments to partners' beneficiaries.	Benefits up to $5,000 can be received tax-free by stockholders' and employees' beneficiaries.
8. State Taxes	In many states, the partnership is not subject to state income taxes.	The corporation is subject to state income taxes (although these taxes can be deducted on federal returns).

Need for Capital

One of the most common reasons for changing from a sole proprietorship to a partnership or a corporation is the need for additional capital to finance expansion. A sole proprietor can seek partners who will bring capital with them. The partnership might be able to secure more funds from potential lenders than could the sole proprietor. But when a firm wants to expand greatly, simply increasing the number of partners can lead to too many partners and make it difficult for the firm to operate effectively. Therefore, incorporation might be the best choice for an expanding business organization. There are many possibilities for obtaining more capital by issuing shares of stock. The original owners will find that although their proportion of the company is reduced, they are able to expand much more rapidly by selling shares in the company.

QUESTIONS AND CASE PROBLEMS

1. Suppose Ann, Betty, and Carla are college graduates, and Ann has come up with an idea for a new product that she believes could make the three of them very rich. Her idea is to manufacture beer dispensers for home use, and her goal is to market them to consumers throughout the Midwest. Ann's personal experience qualifies her to be both first line supervisor and general manager of the new firm. Betty is a born salesperson. Carla has little interest in sales or management but would like to invest a large sum of money that she has inherited from her aunt. What should Ann, Betty, and Carla consider in deciding which form of business organization to adopt?

2. In the situation described in Question 1, assume that Carla is willing to put her inherited money in the business, but she does not want any further liability should the beer dispenser manufacturing business fail. The bank is willing to lend some capital at a 20 percent interest rate, but it will do so only if certain restrictions are placed on management decisions. This is not satisfactory to Ann or Betty, and the two decide to bring Carla into the business. Under these circumstances, discuss which types of business organizations are best suited to meet the needs of Carla.

3. The limited-liability aspect of the corporation is one of the most important reasons that firms choose to organize as corporations rather than as partnerships or sole proprietorships. Limited liability means that if a corporation is not able to meet its obligations with corporate assets, creditors will not be allowed to look to the owners (stockholders) of the corporation to satisfy their claims. Assume that Ann and Betty (from Problem 1) do not have a wealthy friend like Carla who wishes to go into business with them and that therefore they must borrow money to start their business. Ann and Betty decide to incorporate. What do you think a lender will ask them when they seek a loan? What effect does this have on the "advantage" of limited liability under incorporation?

4. Assume that XYZ Corporation is considering entering into two contracts, one with a joint stock company that distributes home products east of the Mississippi River, and the other with a business trust formed by a number of sole proprietors who were sellers of home products on the West Coast. Both contracts involve large capital outlays for the XYZ Corporation in supplying each business with beer dispensers. In both business organizations, at least two shareholders or beneficiaries are personally wealthy, but each business organization has limited financial resources. The owner-managers of XYZ Corporation are not familiar with either form of business organization. Since each form resembles a corporation, they are concerned with the possibility of liability in the event that either business organization breaches the contract by failing to make the deferred payments. Discuss fully XYZ's concern.

5. Assume Adams and Beatty formed a general partnership. After six months the partnership had assets of $100,000 and debts totaling $150,000. Adams and Beatty decide to dissolve their partnership. How will the debts that the partnership could not pay be handled?

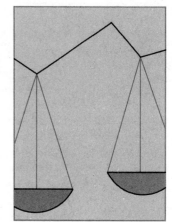

35

PARTNERSHIPS
Creation and Termination

To a great extent, partnership law derives from agency law. Each partner is considered an agent of every other partner. Thus, the agency concepts of imputing knowledge and responsibility for acts done within the scope of the partnership relationship will apply.

In one important way, however, partnership law is distinct from agency law. A partnership is based on a voluntary contract between two or more competent persons, who agree to place some or all of their money, effects, labor, and skill in a business with the understanding that profits and losses will be proportionately shared. On the other hand, in an agency relationship, one person (the agent) can be compensated from business profits but does not agree to share the ordinary business losses and has no ownership interest in the business.

Partnership law in the United States is codified in the *Uniform Partnership Act (UPA.)* The UPA, which has been adopted in forty-eight states, replaces the body of common law principles dealing with partnerships.[1] As pointed out in the last chapter, a partnership agreement can include virtually any terms that the partners wish, unless they are illegal or contrary to public policy. Only when certain essential terms are left out does the UPA come into play.

In the past, attempts to formulate a concrete definition of the term *partnership* caused endless controversy among judges, lawyers, and members of the business community. A **partnership** is defined by the UPA as "an association of two or more persons to carry on as co-owners a business for profit."[2] Therefore, three essential elements of a partnership are (1) a common ownership interest in a business, (2) the sharing of the profits and losses of the business, and (3) the right to manage the operations of the partnership.

CHARACTERISTICS OF A PARTNERSHIP

A partnership is sometimes called a *firm*, or a company, terms that connote an entity separate and apart from its aggregate members. Sometimes the law of partnership recognizes the independent entity, but for certain other purposes, the law treats it as an aggregate of individual partners. At common law, a partnership was never treated as a separate legal entity. Thus, a common law suit could never be brought by or against the firm in its own name; each individual partner had to sue or be sued.

---

1. The UPA was first passed in 1914 by Pennsylvania.

2. UPA Section 6(1).

Partnership as an Entity

Many states today provide specifically that the partnership can be treated as an entity for certain purposes. This usually includes the capacity to sue or be sued, to collect judgments, and to have all accounting procedures in the name of the partnership. In addition, the UPA recognizes that partnership property may be held in the name of the partnership rather than in the names of the individual partners. Finally, federal procedural laws frequently permit the partnership to be treated as an entity in such matters as suits in federal courts, bankruptcy proceedings, and filing of informational federal tax returns. These will be discussed here in some detail.

Legal Capacity   States vary on how a partnership is viewed as a party in a legal suit. Some permit a partnership to sue and be sued in the firm name; others allow a partnership to be sued as an entity but not to sue others in its firm name (that is, the partnership must use the names of the individual partners). Federal courts recognize the partnership as an entity that can sue or be sued when a federal constitutional question is involved. Otherwise, federal courts follow the practice adopted by the state in which the federal court is located.

Judgments   Partnership liability is first paid out of partnership assets when a judgment is rendered *against the firm name*. In a general partnership, the personal assets of the individual members are subject to liability if the partnership's assets are inadequate. Even in limited partnerships, at least one of the partners—called a general partner—subjects his or her personal assets to liability for the partnership's obligations. Good legal practice dictates that where state law permits a firm to be sued, the partners should be joined as parties to the suit. This insures that a wide range of assets will be available for paying the judgment.

The general rule is that a judgment creditor of a partnership can execute the judgment against the partners either jointly or severally. In some states, the judgment creditor must, however, exhaust the remedies against partnership property before proceeding to execute against the individual property of the partners. This is referred to as the doctrine of **marshalling assets**. Marshalling assets is a common law equitable doctrine; it is not statutory.

Marshalling Assets   The arrangement or ranking of assets in a certain order toward the payment of debts

outstanding is involved in marshalling assets. In particular, when there are two classes of assets, and some creditors can enforce their claims against both whereas others can enforce their claims against only one, then the creditors of the former class are compelled to exhaust the assets against which they alone have a claim before they can have recourse to the other assets. This provides for the settlement of as many claims as possible.

As applied to a partnership, the doctrine of marshalling assets requires that the partnership's creditors have first priority to the partnership's assets; and personal creditors of the individual partners have first priority to the individual assets of that partner. When the partnership's assets are insufficient to satisfy a partnership creditor, that partnership creditor does not have access to the assets of any individual partner until the personal creditors of that partner have been satisfied from such assets. This doctrine does not apply to partnerships which are in Chapter 7 proceedings in bankruptcy.

Consider an example. X, Y, and Z are equal partners. On dissolution of the partnership, the partnership has assets of $100,000 and liabilities of $70,000. The partners therefore have a net equity of $10,000 each. X, Y, and Z have no personal assets but owe $10,000 each in personal debts. Under the rule of marshalling of assets, the personal creditors of X, Y, and Z cannot reach the partnership assets until the $70,000 of partnership liabilities have been paid off. After that each partner's personal creditors may resort to each partner's $10,000 equity to satisfy their personal claims.

Now assume that in the preceding example the partnership liabilities are $130,000 rather than $70,000. Assume also that partners X and Y are insolvent. Z, on the other hand, has personal assets of $25,000 and personal liabilities of $25,000. The partnership's creditors cannot resort to Z's personal assets because Z's personal creditors come first and will, in this hypothetical example, exhaust them.

Bankruptcy   In federal court, an adjudication of bankruptcy *in the firm name* applies only to the partnership entity. It does not constitute personal bankruptcy for the partners. Similarly, the personal bankruptcy of an individual partner does not bring the partnership entity or its assets into bankruptcy.

The doctrine of marshalling assets is modified when a partnership is granted an order of relief in bankruptcy. In such situations, if there is a deficiency of partnership assets to cover debts owed to partnership creditors, each general partner becomes personally liable to the bankruptcy trustee for the amount of the deficiency.

Conveyance of Property   The title to real or personal property can be held in the firm name. This means that the partnership as an entity can own property apart from that owned by its individual members.[3] As such, the property can be conveyed (transferred) without having each individual partner join in the transaction.

At common law, title to real estate could not be held in a partnership's firm name. Each partner was regarded as a co-owner (known in legal terminology as a *tenant in partnership*).[4] Each partner had to join in all conveyances. Although the modern rule of partnership property ownership disregards the need for aggregate action to convey property, there are some practical difficulties to consider.

Most states do not require public records to keep lists of members of a partnership, although other states have statutes that require the filing of a certificate of co-partnership. Hence, in determining the validity of a conveyance in a partnership name, it may be impossible to tell whether the person executing the deed is actually a partner and has authority to convey. Some states have passed laws requiring firms to file a statement of partnership. This list names members of the firm authorized to execute conveyances on behalf of the firm.

Aggregate Theory of Partnership

When the partnership is not regarded as a separate legal entity, it is treated as an *aggregate* of the individual partners. For example, for federal income tax purposes, a partnership is not a tax-paying entity. The income or losses incurred by it are "passed through" the partnership framework and attributed to the partners on their individual tax returns. The

---

3.   UPA Section 8(3).
4.   UPA Section 25(1).

partnership as an entity has no tax identity or liability. It is an entity only for the filing of an informational return with the IRS, indicating the profit and loss that each partner will report on his or her individual tax return.

FORMATION OF A PARTNERSHIP

A partnership is ordinarily formed by an explicit agreement among the parties. The law does recognize another form of partnership—*partnership by estoppel*. This form arises when persons who are not partners represent or hold themselves out as partners when dealing with third parties. The liability of partners by estoppel is covered later in this chapter.

This section will describe the requirements for the creation of a true partnership, including references to the liability of "alleged partners." The next section will deal with the process by which partnerships are terminated.

A partnership is a voluntary association of individuals. As such, a *true partnership* is generally based on an agreement among the parties that reflects their intention to create a partnership, contribute capital, share profits and losses, and participate in management. The partnership relationship involves a high degree of trust and reliance. Each partner is an agent for the other partners.

Parties cannot avoid partnership liability, even by *expressly* designating themselves as some other business form, if the evidence establishes the essential elements of a partnership. In the following case, a physician purchased an interest in a medical center along with numerous other doctors. The amount of money each doctor received for practicing at the center was based upon the billing for the services that each performed. The bills were collected in the name of the center. From the total billing, a percentage was deducted to cover expenses and profit sharing. The center's method of allocating expenses to the doctors bore no direct relationship to their actual expenses.

BACKGROUND AND FACTS   *The plaintiff, Stuart, was a physician who sued to settle a dispute arising out of his withdrawal from a claimed professional partnership. The trial court concluded that the plaintiff practiced medicine in a partnership with the defendants at the Overland Medical Center. The court further determined that the partnership between the plaintiff and the defendants*

STUART v. OVERLAND
MEDICAL CENTER
Missouri Court of Appeals, 1978.
510 S.W.2d 494.

was dissolved by the plaintiff's lawsuit. The court evaluated the dollar amount of the plaintiff's interest in the partnership, and after deducting certain amounts due the defendants for expenses, the court entered a judgment for the plaintiff.

The defendants not only challenged the formula used by the lower court in determining the value of the plaintiff's interest in the medical center, but they also challenged the court's conclusion that the relationship between the plaintiff and the defendants was a partnership. In support of their contention, the defendants tried to show that the relationship was one of expense-sharing rather than partnership.

WEIER, Judge.

*   *   *   *

Under the Uniform Partnership Law which was adopted in this state in 1949, a partnership is defined as "an association of two or more persons to carry on as co-owners a business for profit." A partnership is defined judicially as "a contract of two or more competent persons to place their money, effects, labor and skill, or some or all of them, in lawful commerce or business and to divide the profits and bear the loss in certain proportions." The contract creating the partnership need not be written, but may be expressed orally or implied from the acts and conduct of the parties. The primary consideration in determining the existence of a partnership is whether the parties intended to carry on as co-owners a business for profit. With this general background in mind, we proceed to the facts in this case.

*   *   *   *

The amount of money each doctor received for practicing his profession at the Center was based upon billing for services performed by each doctor and collected by and in the name of the Center less a percent of the expenses. By way of illustration, if one doctor collected $1,000.00 and the amount collected by all the doctors was $10,000.00, the doctor who collected $1,000.00 would receive $1,000.00 less 10% of the expenses since the $1,000.00 was ten percent of the total amount collected by all the doctors. The amount of expenses to which each doctor's income was subject was determined by the same method used to allocate collections. Again by way of illustration, if the expenses of all the doctors totaled $2,000.00 for the year in which they collected $10,000.00, the doctor who collected $1,000.00 would be liable for ten percent of the expenses or $200.00. Thus, at the end of this hypothetical year, the doctor who collected $1,000.00 would receive $800.00 as income. Defendants argue that since this method of allocating income is not a profit sharing arrangement but rather an expense sharing arrangement, the relationship between the doctors at the Center cannot be denominated a partnership. We find this argument unconvincing. Each doctor received compensation for the services he performed at the Center. The amount each doctor received as compensation may properly be called income or profit as the two terms are often used interchangeably and, for the most part, have the same meaning. Each doctor shared to some extent in the income or profit of the other doctors although the sharing was not the result of proportionally dividing the total amount of money collected by all the doctors without considering the amount of money each doctor collected individually. Rather, the profit sharing was accomplished by the Center's method of allocating the expenses to be deducted from each doctor's collections. For example, if the doctor referred to in our illustration above had actual expenses of $100.00, $100.00 of the $200.00 he had to pay as expenses was used to pay or help pay another doctor's expenses. It was in this manner that the doctors in the Center actually shared profits. Because the expenses each doctor had to pay bore no relationship to the actual expenses of each doctor, some doctors were receiving profits that otherwise might have been distributed to the doctor or doctors whose actual expenses were slight when compared to the actual expenses of other doctors.

Thus the evidence proved that plaintiff was practicing his profession with the other doctors in the Center as a co-owner of the Center's facilities for a profit. While co-ownership and the sharing of profits by those engaged in business are not factors which conclusively establish the parties' relationship as that of partnership, they are prima facie evidence of partnership. As such, the presumption of partnership prevails unless evidence sufficient to rebut the presumption is brought forward. In this case, defendants presented no evidence which would lead to the conclusion that the relationship between plaintiff and them was anything other than a partnership.

DECISION AND REMEDY

The appellate court affirmed the trial court's judgment that the professional arrangement between the plaintiff and the defendants was a partnership. The plaintiff's interest in the partnership was evaluated by the trial court, and that determination of value was upheld by the appellate court.

COMMENTS

The rights and liabilities of the partners among themselves, although fixed by law, are subject to agreements between the parties insofar as such agreements— and intentions—can be ascertained. Even an oral agreement can be sufficient to establish a framework for a partnership. If there are sufficient circumstances to indicate the intent to carry on a business for profit as co-owners, and if the court can ascertain a method for determining the value of any partner's interest, then a partnership will be presumed unless sufficient contrary evidence is introduced.

Formalities

As a general rule, agreements to form a partnership can be *oral, written,* or *implied by contract.* Some partnership agreements, however, must be in writing to be legally enforceable within the Statute of Frauds. (See Chapter 13 for details.) For example, a partnership agreement that, by its terms, is to continue for more than one year or one that authorizes the partners to deal in real property transfers must be evidenced by a sufficient writing. A sample partnership agreement is shown in Exhibit 35–1.

Practically speaking, it is better if the provisions of any partnership agreement are in writing. The terms of an oral agreement are difficult to prove, because a court must evaluate oral testimony given by persons with an interest in the eventual decision. In addition, in the course of drafting a written agreement, the partners may see potential problems that they would not see if they were making an oral agreement.

For instance, Tomkins and Fredericks plan to enter into a partnership agreement to sell tires. Among the provisions to be included is that Tomkins is to provide two-thirds of the capital to start up the business and is to receive two-thirds of the profits in

return. The agreement is made orally. Tomkins now sues because Fredericks claims that one-half of the profits should be his. Without a writing, Tomkins may have a hard time overcoming the presumption that he is entitled to only one-half of the profits of a two-person partnership.[5] A partnership agreement, called *articles of partnership*, usually specifies each partner's share of the profits and is binding regardless of how uneven the distribution appears to be.

Duration of Partnership

The partnership agreement can specify the duration of the partnership in terms of a date or the completion of a particular project. This is called a *partnership for a term*. A dissolution without the consent of all the partners prior to the expiration of the partnership term constitutes a breach of the agreement, and the responsible partner can be liable for any losses resulting from it.

If no fixed duration is specified, the partnership is a *partnership at will*. This type of partnership can

---

5. The law assumes that members of a partnership share profits and losses equally unless a partnership agreement provides otherwise [UPA Section 18(a)].

EXHIBIT 35–1 Sample Partnership Agreement

PARTNERSHIP AGREEMENT

This agreement, made and entered into as of the _____, by and among _____ _____ (hereinafter collectively sometimes referred to as "Partners").

WITNESSETH:

Whereas, the Parties hereto desire to form a General Partnership (hereinafter referred to as the "Partnership"), for the term and upon the conditions hereinafter set forth;

Now, therefore, in consideration of the mutual covenants hereinafter contained, it is agreed by and among the Parties hereto as follows:

Article I
BASIC STRUCTURE

Form. The Parties hereby form a General Partnership pursuant to the Laws of _____ _____.

Name. The business of the Partnership shall be conducted under the name of _____ _____.

Place of Business. The principal office and place of business of the Partnership shall be located at _____, or such other place as the Partners may from time to time designate.

Term. The Partnership shall commence on _____, and shall continue for _____years, unless earlier terminated in the following manner: (a) By the completion of the purpose intended, or (b) Pursuant to this Agreement, or (c) By applicable _____law, or (d) By death, insanity, bankruptcy, retirement, withdrawal, resignation, expulsion, or disability of all of the then Partners.

Purpose—General. The purpose for which the Partnership is organized is _____

Article II
FINANCIAL ARRANGEMENTS

Each Partner has contributed to the initial capital of the Partnership property in the amount and form indicated on Schedule A attached hereto and made a part hereof. Capital contributions to the Partnership shall not earn interest. An individual capital account shall be maintained for each Partner. If at any time during the existence of the Partnership it shall become necessary to increase the capital with which the said Partnership is doing business, then (upon the vote of the Managing Partner(s)): each party to this Agreement shall contribute to the capital of this Partnership within _ days notice of such need in an amount according to his then Percentage Share of Capital as called for by the Managing Partner(s).

The Percentage Share of Profits and Capital of each Partner shall be (unless otherwise modified by the terms of this Agreement) as follows:

Names	Initial Percentage Share of Profits and Capital

No interest shall be paid on any contribution to the capital of the Partnership. No Partner shall have the right to demand the return of his capital contributions except as herein provided. Except as herein provided, the individual Partners shall have no right to any priority over each other as to the return of capital contributions except as herein provided.

Distributions to the Partners of net operating profits of the Partnership, as hereinafter defined, shall be made at _____. Such distributions shall be made to the Partners simultaneously.

For the purpose of this Agreement, net operating profit for any accounting period shall mean the gross receipts of the Partnership for such period, less the sum of all cash expenses of operation of the Partnership, and such sums as may be necessary to establish a reserve for operating expenses. In determining net operating profit, deductions for depreciation, amortization, or other similar charges not requiring actual current expenditures of cash shall *not* be taken into account in accordance with generally accepted accounting principles.

EXHIBIT 35–1 Continued

No Partner shall be entitled to receive any compensation from the Partnership, nor shall any Partner receive any drawing account from the Partnership.

Article III
MANAGEMENT

The Managing Partner(s) shall be _____.

The Managing Partner(s) shall have the right to vote as to the management and conduct of the business of the Partnership as follows:

Names   **Vote**

Article IV
DISSOLUTION

In the event that the Partnership shall hereafter be dissolved for any reason whatsoever, a full and general account of its assets, liabilities and transactions shall at once be taken. Such assets may be sold and turned into cash as soon as possible and all debts and other amounts due the Partnership collected. The proceeds thereof shall thereupon be applied as follows:

(a) To discharge the debts and liabilities of the Partnership and the expenses of liquidation.

(b) To pay each Partner or his legal representative any unpaid salary, drawing account, interest or profits to which he shall then be entitled and in addition, to repay to any Partner his capital contributions in excess of his original capital contribution.

(c) To divide the surplus, if any, among the Partners or their representatives as follows: (1) First (to the extent of each Partner's then capital account) in proportion to their then capital accounts. (2) Then according to each Partner's then Percentage Share of [*Capital/Income*].

No Partner shall have the right to demand and receive property in kind for his distribution.

Article V
MISCELLANEOUS

The Partnership's fiscal year shall commence on January 1st of each year and shall end on December 31st of each year. Full and accurate books of account shall be kept at such place as the Managing Partner(s) may from time to time designate, showing the condition of the business and finances of the Partnership; and each Partner shall have access to such books of account and shall be entitled to examine them at any time during ordinary business hours. At the end of each year, the Managing Partner(s) shall cause the Partnership's accountant to prepare a balance sheet setting forth the financial position of the Partnership as of the end of that year and a statement of operations (income and expenses) for that year. A copy of the balance sheet and statement of operations shall be delivered to each Partner as soon as it is available.

Each Partner shall be deemed to have waived all objections to any transaction or other facts about the operation of the Partnership disclosed in such balance sheet and/or statement of operations unless he shall have notified the Managing Partner(s) in writing of his objectives within thirty (30) days of the date on which such statement is mailed.

The Partnership shall maintain a bank account or bank accounts in the Partnership's name in a national or state bank in the State of _____. Checks and drafts shall be drawn on the Partnership's bank account for Partnership purposes only and shall be signed by the Managing Partner(s) or their designated agent.

Any controversy or claim arising out of or relating to this Agreement shall only be settled by arbitration in accordance with the rules of the American Arbitration Association, one Arbitrator, and shall be enforceable in any court having competent jurisdiction.

Witnesses   **Partners**

_____   _____

_____   _____

Dated: _____

be dissolved any time by any partner without violating the agreement and without incurring liability for resulting losses to other partners because of the termination.

Capacity

Any person having the capacity to enter a contract can become a partner. A partnership contract entered into with a minor as a partner is voidable and can be disaffirmed by the minor. (See Chapter 10 for details.)

Lack of legal capacity due to insanity at the time of the agreement likewise allows the purported partner either to avoid the agreement or to enforce it. If a partner becomes insane and is adjudicated mentally incompetent during the course of the partnership, the partnership is not automatically dissolved, but dissolution can be decreed by a court upon petition.

The Corporation as Partner

Disagreement exists on whether a corporation can become a partner. After all, general partners are personally liable for the debts incurred by the partnership. But if one of the general partners is a corporation, then what does personal liability mean?

One view is that a corporation cannot be a partner unless the corporation's articles of incorporation specifically empower it to enter into a partnership as a partner. The opposite view, which prevails today, is contained in the Model Business Corporation Act which allows corporations to generally make contracts and incur liabilities. Basically, then, the capacity of corporations to contract is a question of corporation law. The UPA, on the other hand, specifically permits a corporation to be a partner. By definition, "a partnership is an association of two or more persons," and the UPA defines a person as including corporations.[6]

Many states have restrictions on corporations becoming partners, though such restrictions have become less common over the years. Many decisions in jurisdictions that do not permit corporate partners nevertheless validate the arrangements by characterizing them as joint ventures rather than as partnerships.

Mutual Consent

A partnership is a voluntary association of co-owners. It cannot be forced upon anyone. The *intent* to associate is a key element of a partnership, and one cannot join a partnership unless all other partners consent.[7]

Indications of Partnership

Parties commonly find themselves in conflict over whether their business enterprise is a legal partnership, especially in the absence of a formal written contract. To answer this question, the UPA and the courts have developed broad guidelines for interpreting partnership status.

In determining whether a partnership is created, the court usually looks for three factors:

1. A sharing of profits or losses.
2. A joint ownership of the business.
3. An equal right of management of the business.

A problem arises when evidence is insufficient to establish all three factors. The UPA provides a set of guidelines in this event. For example, the sharing of profits and losses from a business is considered *prima facie* evidence that a partnership is created. However, no such inference is made, for example, if the profits were received as payment of:

1. A debt by installments or interest on a loan.
2. Wages of an employee.
3. Rent to a landlord.
4. An annuity to a widow or representative of a deceased partner.
5. A sale of goodwill of a business or property.[8]

To illustrate: A debtor businessperson owes a creditor $5,000 on an unsecured debt. To repay the debt, the debtor agrees to pay (and the creditor to accept) 10 percent of the debtor's monthly profits until the loan with interest is paid. Although the creditor is sharing profits from the business, the debtor and creditor are not presumed to be partners.

Take, for example, a young college graduate who wants to start a retail dress shop. The graduate leases a building from the landlord. Both the landlord and

---

6. UPA Section 2.

7. UPA Section 18(g).
8. UPA Section 7(4).

graduate know that it will take time to establish a clientele, and standard equal rental payments could severely restrict the graduate's ability to purchase inventory. Thus, the lease calls for a minimum low rental payment plus a percentage of the monthly profits for the term of the lease. This sort of arrangement does not make the landlord and tenant partners, even though there is a sharing of profits.

Joint ownership of property, obviously, does not in and of itself create a partnership. Therefore, the fact that Able and Baker own real property as joint tenants or as tenants-in-common (a form of joint ownership) does not establish a partnership. In fact, the sharing of gross returns and even profits from

such ownership will usually not be enough to create a partnership.[9] Thus, if Able and Baker jointly own a piece of rural property and lease the land to a farmer, the sharing of the profits from the farming operation by the farmer in lieu of set rental payments would ordinarily not make Able, Baker, and the farmer partners.

In the following case, a widow attempted to persuade the court that she and her late husband were business partners.

---

9. UPA Section 7(2)(3).

BACKGROUND AND FACTS *The plaintiff, Miller, was a widow who, for tax reasons, attempted to establish that a partnership had existed between herself and her late husband. At the trial, she testified that her deceased husband asked her to marry him and move with him to another city to help run his nursery business. They married, and the plaintiff gave up her well-paying job to move south with her new husband. Although the plaintiff did not make any capital contributions to the partnership, she held a management position in the nursery business, and she did physical labor. In addition, she kept all the books and hired and fired employees. She received periodic payments of $50 or $100. Whenever the plaintiff received a check, her husband also received one for the same amount. Money for household expenses was taken out of the business account.*

Along with the nursery business, her husband had been engaged in making land sales. However, no land had ever been conveyed to the partnership.

The year after the plaintiff married her husband, a business registration certificate was filed for the nursery, indicating that the business was a partnership. Checking accounts, vehicles, and other equipment were bought and held under the business name. On the other hand, annual tax forms and schedules listed the business as a sole proprietorship and the plaintiff's occupation as housewife. A Michigan business activities form also indicated a sole proprietorship. Finally, in applying for a self-employment and pension and profit-sharing plan, the husband stated in his application that his business was a sole proprietorship.

There was never any formal, written partnership agreement. The plaintiff, however, stated that her husband had described the relationship when he asked her to marry him and at all times since as one of partnership. She was under the impression that they were business partners. Furthermore, the plaintiff testified that her husband told her that she was "the best partner he ever had."

MILLER v. CITY BANK & TRUST CO., N.A.
Court of Appeals of Michigan, 1978.
82 Mich.App. 120, 266 N.W.2d 687.

DANHOF, Chief Judge.
* * * *

The burden of proof to show a partnership is on the one alleging the partnership, and the burden is stricter when relatives are the alleged partners. Also the fact that the alleged partner is deceased further raises the burden of proof.

* * * The elements of a partnership are generally considered to include a voluntary association of two or more people with legal capacity in order to carry on, via co-ownership, a business for profit. Co-ownership of the business requires more than merely joint ownership of the property and is usually evidenced by joint control and the sharing of profits and losses. With the intentions of the party to form a partnership as our polestar we will review the trial court's finding.

It is not disputed that the parties were involved in a business venture for profit and had the legal capacity to form a partnership. However, the evidence relating to co-ownership does not indicate that a legal partnership was contemplated. Prior to the marriage, Mr. Miller [the plaintiff's husband] operated the business and owned all the property. Mrs. Miller [the plaintiff] made no capital contributions except her services. Even though plaintiff worked long and hard hours, this does not establish that the parties had an agreement to form a partnership. This evidence could also be viewed as consistent with an employee-employer relationship or that of a helpful wife who assisted her husband without them intending a legal partnership.

Co-ownership is also indicated by profit sharing. In fact, profit sharing is prima facie evidence of a partnership. However, the [trial] court did not find an agreement to share profits and we cannot say that this was clearly erroneous. [When an appellate court reviews a trial court's findings of fact, it will not disturb the resulting judgment unless there is absolutely no factual evidence to support the trial court's conclusion. In this case, the appellate court showed that there were many possible interpretations to be made from the fact that Mr. and Mrs. Miller each received monthly payments from the business.] That Mr. and Mrs. Miller each received monthly payments from the nursery checking account does not necessarily establish profit sharing. The payments could also be reasonably viewed as salary or wages. Another possible interpretation would be that Mr. Miller was withdrawing money from his sole proprietorship and was dividing it equally because he felt an obligation to share equally with his wife, as a wife rather than a business partner.

Another indicia of co-ownership is mutual agency and control. That Mrs. Miller kept the books, wrote checks, and hired and fired does not necessarily establish any control other than that which might be given to a trusted employee. However, it is not necessary that this control be exercised as long as it exists. In view of the absence of the exercise of control or mutual agency, evidence of an agreement in respect to the division of control is about the only way to prove mutual agency and control. However, no evidence of an agreement with respect to mutual control was presented. * * * * *

The evidence introduced against these claims indicated that the deceased did not intend to form a legal partnership with his wife. First, there is no written agreement and there is only plaintiff's testimony in support of an oral one. The income tax returns and schedules listed the business as a sole proprietorship, listed Mr. Miller's income as wages and Mrs. Miller's occupation as a housewife. In 1964, Mr. Miller applied for a self-employee retirement deduction plan as a sole proprietorship. Mr. Miller's social security forms listed the business as a sole proprietorship. All the capital contributions came from Mr. Miller and the property remained in his name (or his and his wife's name), and none was transferred to the partnership. Shortly before his death, Mr. Miller deeded his homestead to his wife and himself as tenants by the entirety and this would seem needless if they already owned it as partners. Although none of these facts are conclusive, they are all factors to be weighed in the decision.

DECISION AND REMEDY

After reviewing the entire trial court record, the appellate court agreed that the presumption of partnership established by the filing of business registration papers was rebutted by other competent evidence, which tended to show that Mr. Miller intended the business to be run as a sole proprietorship. The trial court's judgment that no partnership existed was affirmed.

Partnership by Estoppel

Parties who are not partners can hold themselves out as partners and make representations that third persons rely on in dealing with these alleged partners. The law of partnership imposes liability on the alleged partner or partners, but it does not confer any partnership rights on these persons.

There are two aspects of liability. The person representing himself or herself to be a partner in an actual or alleged partnership is liable to any third person who extends credit in good faith reliance on such representations. Similarly, a person who expressly or impliedly *consents* to such misrepresentation of an alleged partnership relationship is also liable to third persons who extend credit in good faith reliance.[10]

For example, Moore owns a small shop. Knowing that the Midland Bank will not make a loan on his credit alone, Moore represents that Lewis, a financially secure businesswoman, is a partner in Moore's business. Lewis knows of Moore's misrepresentation but fails to correct the bank's information. Midland Bank, relying on the strength of Lewis's reputation and credit, extends a loan to Moore. Moore will be liable to the bank for the loan repayment. In many states, Lewis would also be held liable to the bank in such a loan transaction. Lewis has impliedly consented to such misrepresentation and will normally be estopped from denying that she is a partner of Moore. She will be regarded as if she were in fact a partner in Moore's business to the extent that this loan is concerned.

When a real partnership exists, and a partner represents that a non-partner is a member of the firm, the non-partner is regarded as an agent whose acts are binding on the partner.

For example, Middle Earth Movers has three partners—Johnson, Mathews, and Huntington. Mathews represents to the business community that Thompson is a partner. If Thompson negotiates a contract in Middle Earth Movers' name, the contract will be binding on Mathews, but normally not on Johnson and Huntington (unless, of course, Johnson and Huntington knew and consented to Mathews's representation).

In summary, partnership by estoppel requires that a third person reasonably and detrimentally rely

on the representation that a person was part of the partnership.

PARTNERSHIP PROPERTY RIGHTS

For financial and credit reasons it is frequently necessary to distinguish between property belonging to the firm and property belonging to each individual partner, particularly in bankruptcy proceedings. A partnership can own any real or personal property, unless the partnership agreement contains some prohibition or limitation on what it can acquire. Holding property in the firm name can be merely a convenience, so *title alone is not conclusive* in establishing that a particular asset belongs to the partnership.

Factors Indicating Partnership Property

UPA Section 8(1) provides that "all property originally brought into the partnership's stock or subsequently acquired, by purchase or otherwise, *on account of the partnership*, is partnership property." (Emphasis added.) For example, in the formation of a partnership, a partner may bring into the partnership property he or she owns as a part of his or her capital contribution. This property becomes partnership property even though title is still in the name of the contributing partner.

Indications that the assets were acquired with the intention that it be a partnership asset is the heart of the phrase *on account of the partnership*. Thus, the more closely an asset is associated with the business operations of the partnership, the more likely it is to be a partnership asset. Moreover, when such an asset is purchased with partnership funds, it will belong to the partnership unless a contrary intention is shown. If, for example, a piece of property is purchased with the use of partnership funds, it is presumed to be partnership property even if title is taken in the name of one of the partners.

PARTNERSHIP TERMINATION

Any change in the relations of the partners that demonstrates unwillingness or inability to carry on partnership business dissolves the partnership, re-

---

10. UPA Section 16.

sulting in termination.[11] If any of the partners wish to continue the business, they are free to reorganize into a *new* partnership.

The termination of a partnership has two stages— dissolution and winding up. Both must take place before termination is complete.

Dissolution occurs when any partner (or partners) indicates an intention to disassociate from the partnership. *Winding up* is the actual process of collecting and distributing the partnership's assets.

Dissolution is the principal remedy of a partner against co-partners. Events causing the dissolution can be grouped into three basic categories:

1. Acts of partners.[12]
2. Operation of law.[13]
3. Judicial decree.[14]

Dissolution terminates the right of a partnership to exist as a going concern, but the partnership continues to exist long enough to wind up its affairs. When winding up is complete, the partnership's *legal* existence is terminated. The concepts of dissolution and winding up are discussed by the Supreme Court of Minnesota in the next case.

---

11. UPA Section 29.

12. UPA Section 31(1)(2).
13. UPA Section 33(4)(5).
14. UPA Section 32.

MARAS v. STILINOVICH

Supreme Court of Minnesota, 1978.

268 N.W.2d 541.

BACKGROUND AND FACTS *The plaintiff, Mary Stilinovich, brought this appeal to contest the finding of a referee appointed to liquidate the assets of a partnership between herself and the defendant, Nick Maras. The referee ordered the dissolution of the partnership due to irreconcilable differences between the partners. The plaintiff and the defendant were a sister and brother who had formed a partnership by oral agreement with assets left to them by their deceased father. There were accusations of misappropriation on both sides, and a referee was appointed. Maras tendered a written offer to buy out his sister for $65,000. No such offer was submitted by the plaintiff. A hearing was held, and the referee ordered an accounting. After the accounting, he ordered the business to be sold to Maras for the $65,000. The plaintiff contended that the referee erred in his order.*

YETKA, Justice.

*   *   *   *

[This] was essentially a partnership dissolution in which the undivided two-thirds interest in the land and building was treated as a partnership asset. *   *   * [W]hether a sale could be ordered to one partner over the objection of the other [is contested.] The parties stipulated that the assets were partnership assets and not subject to mere partition. We find the stipulation is broad enough to allow sale to one partner where the other fails to tender a timely bid.

*   *   *   *

After dissolution, a partnership continues until liquidated or wound up. Although dissolution of a partnership is usually followed by liquidation, a withdrawing partner may be paid his partnership contribution and share of accumulated profits and no liquidation need occur. Minn. [law] provides, in effect, that the partnership affairs must be wound up after dissolution unless otherwise agreed. Crane and Bromberg, Law of Partnership, § 86, suggests that the most logical buyers of a dissolved partnership are the remaining partners, and in the stipulation the parties agreed to one of the partners carrying on the business. Agreements for continuation of partnership business after dissolution are generally valid and enforceable. Oral agreements are generally sufficient to establish a partnership relationship, and we hold that the oral agreement in this case was sufficient to establish the framework for dissolution of a partnership.

The referee was clearly acting within the scope of his powers by ordering the sale to Nick Maras.

* * * *

The method of conducting and confirming a judicial sale is within the discretion of the court, and the policy of the law should be to sustain judicial sales where no injustice occurs. Thus, if the parties were treated fairly and the rights of [plaintiff] were not prejudiced by the terms of the sale, then the trial court [judgment] should be affirmed.

The court examined the proceedings and concluded that the dissolution was fair. The trial court's judgment was therefore affirmed.

DECISION AND REMEDY

Dissolution by Acts of the Partners

Dissolution of a partnership may come about through the following acts of the partners: by agreement, by the withdrawal of a partner, by the addition of a partner, or by the transfer of a partner's interest.

By Agreement A partnership can be dissolved if certain events stipulated in the partnership agreement occur. For example, when a partnership agreement expresses a fixed term or a particular business objective to be accomplished, the passing of the date or the accomplishment of the project dissolves the partnership. However, partners do not have to abide by the stipulations in the agreement. They can mutually agree to dissolve the partnership early or to extend it. If they agree to continue in the partnership, they become *partners at will*, with all the rights and duties remaining as originally agreed.

Partner's Power to Withdraw A partnership is a personal legal relationship among co-owners. No person can be compelled either to be a partner or to remain one. Implicit in a partnership is each partner's *power* to disassociate from the partnership at any time. For example, Able and Carla form a partnership with no definite term or particular undertaking specified—that is, a partnership at will. Both Able and Carla have the power and the right to withdraw from the partnership. The partnership continues for three years, until one day Carla announces that she no longer wishes to continue in the partnership. Assuming that Carla's sudden withdrawal will not do irreparable damage to the firm, her act is sufficient to begin the process of dissolution.

Admission of New Partners Any change in the composition of the partnership, whether by withdrawal of a partner or by *admission of a new partner*, results in dissolution. In practice, this result is usually modified by providing that the remaining or new partners continue in the firm's business. Nonetheless, a new partnership arises. The new partnership carries over the debts of the dissolved partnership. Creditors of the prior partnership become creditors of the one that is continuing the business. [15]

Transfer of a Partner's Interest The UPA provides that voluntary transfer [16] or involuntary sale of a partner's interest for the benefit of creditors does not by itself dissolve the partnership. [17] However, either occurrence can ultimately lead to judicial dissolution of the partnership, as will be discussed.

Dissolution by Operation of Law

A partnership is dissolved by operation of law in the event of death, bankruptcy, or illegality.

Death A partnership is dissolved upon the death of any partner, even if the partnership agreement provides for carrying on the business with the executor of the decedent's estate. Any change in the composition among partners results in a new partnership. (But there is always the possibility of a ref-

---

15. UPA Section 41.
16. A single partner cannot make another person a partner in a firm merely by transferring his or her interest to that person [UPA Section 27].
17. UPA Section 28.

ormation of the partnership upon the death of a partner.)

Bankruptcy   Because a partner's credit reputation is an intrinsic part of his or her contribution to a partnership, the bankruptcy of a partner will dissolve a partnership. Insolvency alone will not result in dissolution. Naturally, bankruptcy of the firm itself will result in dissolution.

Illegality   Any event that makes it unlawful for the partnership to continue its business or for any partner to carry on in the partnership will result in dissolution. However, even if the illegality of the partnership business is a cause for dissolution, the partners can decide to change the nature of their business and continue in the partnership.

For example, Able and Baker enter a partnership agreement to run a tuna fishing business. Subsequently, a maritime law prohibiting tuna fishing by private concerns is passed. Able and Baker must dissolve their partnership if their sole business is to fish for tuna. However, they can choose to remain partners and fish for something that is not prohibited.

When the illegality applies to an individual partner, then dissolution *must* occur. For example, suppose the state legislature passes a law making it illegal for magistrate judges to engage in the practice of law. If an attorney in a law firm is appointed a magistrate, the partnership must be dissolved. The next case deals with dissolution of a partnership due to illegality.

WILLIAMS v. BURRUS
Court of Appeals of Washington,
Division 1, 1978.
20 Wash.App. 494, 581 P.2d
164.

BACKGROUND AND FACTS   *Plaintiff Williams sued the defendant, Burrus, for an accounting and dissolution of their partnership. Burrus bought the partnership asset, a restaurant, in his name alone because Williams could not secure a liquor license. If disclosure of Williams's interest had been known, the license would have been denied. The only issue to be considered on appeal was whether the trial court erred in refusing to give Williams any relief in the form of his share of partnership assets.*

ANDERSEN, Judge.
*   *   *   *

Courts will not assist in the dissolution of an illegal partnership or entertain an action for an accounting or distribution of its assets. The trial court's decision was not erroneous.
*   *   *   *

No state retail liquor license of any kind can be issued to a partnership unless all of the members thereof are qualified to obtain a license, and no licenseholder can allow any other person to use such a license.

Furthermore, a partnership is dissolved by any event which makes it unlawful for the business of the partnership to be carried on or for the members to carry it on in partnership.

The issue of illegality may be raised at any time.

Under the general rule that the courts will not aid either party to an illegal agreement where a partnership is formed to carry out an illegal business or to conduct a lawful business in an illegal manner, the courts will refuse to aid any of the parties thereto in an action against the other. *   *   *

**DECISION
AND REMEDY**   *The appellate court affirmed the trial court's dismissal of Williams's case. Since the partnership was illegal, neither party had any rights that a court would enforce. (They were* in pari delicto.*)*

Dissolution by Judicial Decree

Dissolution of a partnership can result from judicial decree. For dissolution to occur, an application or petition must be made in an appropriate court. The court then either denies the petition or grants a decree of dissolution. UPA Section 32 cites the following situations in which a court can dissolve a partnership: insanity, incapacity, business impracticality, and improper conduct.

Insanity   A partnership can obtain a judicial declaration of dissolution when a partner is adjudicated insane or is shown to be of unsound mind. This action often involves a series of complex tests and standards.

Incapacity   When it appears that a partner has become incapable of performing his or her duties under the partnership agreement, a decree of dissolution may be required. It must appear that the incapacity is permanent and will substantially affect the partner's ability to discharge his or her duties to the firm.

Business Impracticality   When it becomes obvious that the firm's business can be operated only at a loss, judicial dissolution may be ordered.

Improper Conduct   A partner's impropriety involving partnership business (for example, fraud perpetrated upon the other partners) or improper behavior reflecting unfavorably upon the firm (for example, habitual drunkenness) will provide grounds for a judicial decree of dissolution.

Dissolution may also be granted when personal dissension between partners becomes so persistent and harmful as to undermine the confidence and cooperation necessary to carry on the firm's business. (In general, courts are reluctant to allow partners to sue each other except for dissolution.)

Notice of Dissolution

Dissolution ends the partnership as a business enterprise. Thereafter, it remains viable only for the purpose of winding up its affairs. In some circumstances, however, a partnership or a withdrawing partner can become bound to a contract made after dissolution has begun but before winding up is complete.

Notice to Partners   The intent to dissolve or to withdraw from a firm must be communicated *clearly* to each partner. This notice of intent can come from the actions or the words of a partner. All partners will share liability for the acts of any partner who continues conducting business for the firm without knowing that the partnership has been dissolved. For example, Ann, Baker, and Carl have a partnership. Ann tells Baker of her intent to withdraw. Before Carl learns of Ann's intentions, Carl enters a contract with a third party. The contract is equally binding on Ann, Baker, and Carl. Unless the other partners have notice, the withdrawing partner will continue to be bound as a partner to all contracts created for the firm.

The following case illustrates that notice of an intention to terminate a partnership relationship can come from both the acts and the words of a partner.

BACKGROUND AND FACTS   *Gene Henshaw and Lou Kroenecke executed a partnership agreement in 1972, which provided that if Kroenecke voluntarily terminated the partnership and breached the covenant not to compete, he would pay to Henshaw as liquidated damages "12 times the average monthly partnership billing to each client or prior client with whom Kroenecke does business." In 1974, Henshaw and Kroenecke individually formed their respective partnership interests into corporations and executed a partnership agreement between their corporations that did not alter or amend the 1972 agreement. The new agreement required the execution of a covenant not to compete to which Kroenecke refused to agree. Henshaw, contending that Kroenecke had voluntarily terminated the partnership agreement, set the termination date at July 31, 1976. Kroenecke responded that it was never his intention to terminate the*

HENSHAW v.
KROENECKE
Court of Appeals of Texas,
Houston (1st Dist.), 1984.
671 S.W.2d 117.

partnership, but he would agree to the terminating date. Following dissolution, Henshaw sued for the liquidated damages as provided in the 1972 partnership agreement. A take-nothing judgment of the trial court was affirmed by the Court of Civil Appeals, but was reversed and remanded by the Supreme Court. The Court of Appeals heard the case on remand to determine if the evidence permitted a finding of voluntary termination of the partnership by Kroenecke.

BASS, Justice.

* * * *

* * * The record reflects that Kroenecke left Henshaw two notes demanding that the covenant not to compete be removed, and reiterated this demand in a meeting. He sent Henshaw a letter demanding the elimination of the covenant, conditioning his continued participation in the partnership upon this demand. He was uncooperative, and would neither disclose to Henshaw necessary billing information nor allow assistance in servicing clients. * * *

* * * *

* * * Kroenecke contends that the events leading up to the alleged termination grew out of negotiations on amending the existing partnership agreements. In support of his [position] he cites Henshaw's admission that all matters were negotiable except for the execution of the non-competition agreement; that Henshaw originally agreed to sign an agreement but later refused, which resulted in Kroenecke's insistence that Henshaw execute one; and that Kroenecke alternatively suggested a lump sum buyout agreement applicable to both parties that Henshaw refused to consider. Kroenecke argues that his insistence that Henshaw do only what he had promised to do can not be construed as a violation of the partnership agreement, and Henshaw's refusal was the only reason he accepted the termination.

The record further reflects, however, that Kroenecke was demanding renegotiation of compensation or partnership equity interest, and moving the office space, in addition to his demand that Henshaw also execute a covenant and replace the liquidated damage provision with a lump sum provision. Henshaw testified that "Mr. Kroenecke stated orally you will make those changes or the partnership will be terminated."

The jury observed the demeanor and determined the credibility of the witnesses and under the evidence presented found that Kroenecke voluntarily terminated the partnership by his words and/or conduct. We hold the evidence to be sufficient to support the jury's finding.

DECISION AND REMEDY   *The court reversed the judgment of the trial court, determining that Kroenecke voluntarily terminated the partnership, and awarded Henshaw $67,689.60 in liquidated damages.*

Notice to Third Parties   Dissolution of a partnership by the act of a partner requires notice to all affected third persons. The manner of giving notice depends upon the third person's relationship to the firm. Any third person who has dealt with the firm must receive *actual notice*. For all others, a newspaper announcement or similar public notice is sufficient. Dissolution resulting from operation of law generally requires *no notice* to third parties.[18]

Winding Up

Once dissolution occurs and partners have been notified, they cannot create new obligations on behalf of the partnership. Their only authority is to complete transactions begun but not finished at the time of dissolution and to wind up the business of the partnership. Winding up includes collecting and preserving partnership assets, discharging liabilities (paying debts), and accounting to each partner for the value of his or her interest in the partnership.

Where dissolution is caused by a partner's act that violates the partnership agreement, the inno-

---

18.   Childers v. United States, 442 F.2d 1299 (5th Cir. 1971).

cent partners may have rights to damages resulting from the dissolution. Also, the innocent partners have the right to buy out the offending partner and to continue the business instead of winding up the partnership.

Dissolution resulting from the death of a partner vests all partnership assets in the surviving partners. The surviving partners act as a fiduciary in settling partnership affairs in a quick, practicable manner and in accounting to the estate of the deceased part-

ner for the value of the decedent's interest in the partnership. The surviving partners are entitled to payment for their services in winding up the partnership as well as to reimbursement for any costs incurred in the process.[19]

The following case deals with the allocation of income generated through the winding up of unfinished business of a dissolved law partnership.

---

19.   UPA Section 18(f).

BACKGROUND AND FACTS   *On December 2, 1977, the law firm of Jewel, Boxer, and Elkind was dissolved by the mutual consent of its four partners, Jewel, Boxer, Elkind, and Leary. Two new partnerships were formed, one between Jewel and Leary, and the other between Boxer and Elkind. The original partnership had no written partnership agreement nor an agreement concerning allocation of fees from actual cases on dissolution of the partnership. On the date of dissolution the original partnership had numerous active cases. Jewel and Leary filed a complaint for an accounting of the attorneys' fees received from the cases, contending they were assets of the dissolved partnership. The trial court allocated post-dissolution income to the old and new firms on a* quantum meruit *basis, and Jewel and Leary appealed.*

JEWEL v. BOXER

California Court of Appeal, First Division, 1984.
156 Cal.App.3d 171, 203 Cal.Rptr. 13.

KING, Associate Justice.

*   *   *   *

In this case we hold that in the absence of a partnership agreement, the Uniform Partnership Act requires that attorneys' fees received on cases in progress upon dissolution of a law partnership are to be shared by the former partners according to their right to fees in the former partnership, regardless of which former partner provides legal services in the case after the dissolution. The fact that the client substitutes one of the former partners as attorney of record in place of the former partnership does not affect this result.

*   *   *   *

In a nonjury trial the court first determined that the partnership interests in income of the old firm were 30% for Jewel, 27% each for Boxer and Elkind, and 16% for Leary. The court then allocated the disputed fees among the old and new firms by considering three factors: the time spent by each firm in the handling of each case, the source of each case (always the old firm), and, in the personal injury contingency fee cases, the result achieved by the new firm. *   *   * Under this formula, Jewel and Leary was determined to owe $115,041.16 to the old firm, and Boxer and Elkind was determined to owe $291,718.60 to the old firm.

*   *   *   *

Under the Uniform Partnership Act (Corp.Code, § 15000 et seq.), a dissolved partnership continues until the winding up of unfinished partnership business. (Corp.Code, § 15030.) No partner (except a surviving partner) is entitled to extra compensation for services rendered in completing unfinished business. (Corp.Code, § 15018, subd. (f).) Thus, absent a contrary agreement, any income generated through the winding up of unfinished business is allocated to the former partners according to their respective interests in the partnership.

*   *   *   *

*   *   * The Uniform Partnership Act unequivocally prohibits extra compensation for post-dissolution services, with a single exception for surviving partners. (Corp.Code, § 15018, subd. (f).) The definition of "business" in the Uniform Partnership Act as including "every trade, occupation, or profession" (Corp.Code, § 15002) precludes an exception for law partnerships. *   *   *

Accordingly, several courts in other states have held that after dissolution of a law partnership, income received by the former partners from cases unfinished at the time of dissolution is to be allocated on the basis of the partners' respective interests in the dissolved partnership, not on a *quantum meruit* basis.
*   *   *   *

There are sound policy reasons for applying the rule against extra compensation to law partnerships. The rule prevents partners from competing for the most remunerative cases during the life of the partnership in anticipation that they might retain those cases should the partnership dissolve. It also discourages former partners from scrambling to take physical possession of files and seeking personal gain by soliciting a firm's existing clients upon dissolution. Boxer and Elkind argue that application of the rule in the present context will discourage continued representation of clients by the attorney of their choice, as former partners will not want to perform all of the post-dissolution work on a particular case while receiving only a portion of the income generated by such work. Of course, this is all the former partners would have received had the partnership not dissolved. Additionally, the former partners will receive, in addition to their partnership portion of such income, their partnership share of income generated by the work of the other former partners, without performing any post-dissolution work in those cases. On balance, the allocation of fees according to each partner's interest in the former partnership should not work an undue hardship as to any partner where each partner completes work on the partnership's cases which are active upon its dissolution.
*   *   *   *

At first glance, strict application of the rule against extra compensation might appear to have unjust results. *   *   * But undue hardship should be prevented by two basic fiduciary duties owed between the former partners. First, each former partner has a duty to wind up and complete the unfinished business of the dissolved partnership. This would prevent a partner from refusing to furnish any work and imposing this obligation totally on the other partners, thus unfairly benefiting from their efforts while putting forth none of his or her own. Second, no former partner may take any action with respect to unfinished business which leads to purely personal gain. *   *   * Thus the former partners are obligated to ensure that a disproportionate burden of completing unfinished business does not fall on one former partner or one group of former partners, unless the former partners agree otherwise. It is unlikely that the partners, in discharging their mutual fiduciary duties, will be able to achieve a distribution of the burdens of completing unfinished business that corresponds precisely to their respective interests in the partnership. But partners are free to include in a written partnership agreement provisions for completion of unfinished business that ensure a degree of exactness and certainty unattainable by rules of general application. If there is any disproportionate burden of completing unfinished business here, it results from the parties' failure to have entered into a partnership agreement which could have assured such a result would not occur. The former partners must bear the consequences of their failure to provide for dissolution in a partnership agreement.

In short, the trial court's allocation of post-dissolution income to the old and new firms on a *quantum meruit* basis constituted error. The appropriate remedy is to remand the cause for post-trial proceedings to allocate such income to the former partners of the old firm in accordance with their respective percentage interests in the former partnership. *   *   *

Under the provisions of the Uniform Partnership Act, the former partners will be entitled to reimbursement for reasonable overhead expenses (excluding partners' salaries) attributable to the production of post-dissolution partnership income; in other words, it is *net* post-dissolution income, not gross income, that is to be allocated to the former partners. * * *

The court reversed the judgment of the trial court and remanded the case for allocation based upon the respective partners' interests in the former partnership.   **DECISION AND REMEDY**

Distribution of Assets

Both creditors of the partnership and creditors of the individual partners can make claims on the partnership's assets. In general, creditors of the partnership have priority over creditors of individual partners in the distribution of partnership assets; the converse priority is usually followed in the distribution of individual partner assets, except under the new Bankruptcy Act.

The distribution of a partnership's assets is made *after* third-party debts are paid. The priorities, after third-party debts, are as follows:[20]

1.   Refund of advances (loans) made to or for the firm by a partner.
2.   Return of capital contribution to a partner.
3.   Distribution of the balance, if any, to partners in accordance with their respective share in the profits.

---

20.   UPA Section 40(b).

QUESTIONS AND CASE PROBLEMS

1. Daniel is the owner of a chain of shoe stores. He hires Martin as a manager of a new store, which is to open in Grand Rapids, Michigan. Daniel, by written contract, agrees to pay Martin a monthly salary. In addition, Daniel and Martin have agreed to an 80-20 percent split in profits. Without Daniel's knowledge, Martin represents himself to Carlton as Daniel's partner, showing Carlton the agreement to share profits. Carlton extends credit to Martin. Martin defaults. Discuss whether Carlton can hold Daniel liable as a partner.

2. Adam wishes to purchase some real property owned by Tropical Gardens. He learns that Tropical Gardens is a partnership owned by Smith, Jones, and Green. He also learns that the partnership needs capital and that the partnership's need for capital is one of the major reasons the partners are selling their real property. Since Tropical Gardens is a partnership, Adam has the following concerns:
   (a) Can the partnership convey the land in the name of Tropical Gardens?
   (b) If there is a breach of contract, against whom must Adam file a lawsuit?
   (c) If he obtains a judgment against Tropical Gardens, against whom can he execute it?

Discuss Adam's concerns.

3. Two individuals, Able and Baker, orally agree to form a partnership to run a television sales and repair business. No specific term of partnership duration is stated. Able is an adult, and Baker is a minor. The oral partnership agreement provides for each partner to contribute capital of $5,000, with Baker's contribution due at the end of the first year's operation. Two months prior to the end of the first year's operation, Able and Baker orally agree to take in Super TV Supply Corporation as a third partner. Two weeks later, both Super TV Supply Corporation and Baker assert that neither of them had the capacity to be a partner and that, in any event, there was no written agreement to form a partnership. Discuss whether Baker and Super TV Supply Corporation can disclaim partnership responsibility to Able.

4. Able, Baker, and Carlton have formed a twenty-year partnership to purchase land, develop it, manage it, and then sell the property. The partnership agreement calls for the partners to devote their full time to the business. Assume one of the following events takes place:
   (a) After two years, Baker and Carlton agree that the working hours of the partnership will be from 8:00 A.M. to 6:00 P.M. rather than the previously established schedule of 9:00 A.M. to 5:00 P.M. Able refuses to come to work before 9:00 A.M. and quits promptly at 5:00 P.M.
   (b) After two years, Able quits the partnership and walks out.
   (c) After two years, Able becomes insolvent.

(d) After two years, Able dies.
Discuss fully which of the above acts constitutes a dissolution and whether there is any ensuing liability of Able.

5. Able and Baker have formed a partnership. At the time of formation Able's capital contribution was $10,000, and Baker's was $15,000. Later Able made a $10,000 loan to the partnership when it needed working capital. The partnership agreement provides that profits are to be shared, with 40 percent for Able and 60 percent for Baker. The partnership is dissolved by Baker's death. At the end of the dissolution and the winding up of the partnership, the partnership's assets are $50,000, and the partnership's debts are $8,000. Discuss fully how the assets will be distributed.

6. Able, Baker, and Charlie were partners in a partnership at will. Able and Baker excluded Charlie from partnership management affairs and then sought a dissolution of the partnership. A trial court dissolved the partnership and ordered a sale of the partnership asset, a shopping center. Able and Baker were the highest bidders at the court-ordered sale and were therefore able to retain the shopping center. Will the courts protect Charlie from this type of freeze-out? [Prentiss v. Sheffel, 20 Ariz.App. 415, 513 P.2d 953 (1973)]

7. In April 1970 Harber, Pittman, and Calvert entered into an oral agreement to build and sell 235 houses. Following their agreement, Harber withdrew $6,000 in partnership funds and purchased three lots on which houses were to be built. The lots were purchased in his name, and after the homes were constructed, title was also in his name. When Harber sells the houses (at a profit) can he retain the proceeds for himself? [Davis v. Pioneer Bank and Trust Co., 272 So.2d 430 (La.App. 1973)]

8. In 1969 Simon, Genia, and Ury Rapoport entered into an agreement with Morton, Gerome, and Burton Parnes to form the partnership known as Perry Company. Each of the families owned 50 percent of the partnership interests. In December 1974 Simon and Genia Rapoport assigned a 10 percent interest of their share in the partnership to their adult children, Daniel and Kalia. An amended partnership certificate was filed in the county clerk's office, as required by law, indicating the addition of Daniel and Kalia as partners. However, when the Rapoports requested the Parneses to execute an amended partnership agreement reflecting this change in the partnership, the Parneses refused. In a court action by the Rapoports to force the Parneses to execute the amended partnership agreement, what will be the result? What interest in the partnership, if any, can Daniel and Kalia Rapoport take without the Parneses' consent? [Rapoport v. 55 Perry Co., 50 A.D.2d 54, 376 N.Y.S.2d 147 (1975)]

9. Lynne, Ernest, and Stanley Timmermann established a partnership in 1965 for the purpose of engaging in farming activities. In January 1969 Lynne stated to the other two partners that he no longer wished to be involved in the partnership. It was not until August 31, 1970, however, that Lynne ceased to participate in the farming activities of the partnership. In January 1972 Lynne attempted to bring about a forced liquidation of the partnership through a lawsuit. In January 1969 the value of the partnership was approximately $50,000. On August 31, 1970 the value of the partnership was slightly less than $10,000; and in January 1972 the value of the partnership was in excess of $300,000. Assuming Lynne had a one-third interest in the partnership, approximately how much should he receive when he withdraws? Explain your answer. [Timmermann v. Timmermann, 272 Or. 613, 538 P.2d 1254 (1975)]

10. On September 28, 1958, Reid and three others entered into a written partnership agreement for the purpose of leasing for profit certain real property located in Montgomery County, Pennsylvania. Reid was to manage the property, and the others were to perform the physical labor necessary to maintain the premises in good condition. One year later, Reid notified the others that she was dissolving the partnership and requested that the partnership assets be liquidated as soon as possible. Has dissolution occurred? Assuming dissolution has occurred, can the other partners recover damages for breach of partnership agreement on the ground that the partnership was a partnership for a particular undertaking and hence not terminable at will? [Girard Bank v. Haley, 460 Pa. 237, 332 A.2d 443 (1975)]

11. Carola and Grogan were partners in a law firm. The partnership began business in 1974 and was created by an oral agreement. On September 6, 1976, Carola withdrew from the partnership some of its files, furniture, books, and various other items of office equipment. The next day, Carola informed Grogan he had withdrawn from the partnership. Were Carola's actions on September 6, 1976 effective notice of dissolution to Grogan? [Carola v. Grogan, 102 A.D.2d 934, 477 N.Y.S.2d 525 (A.D. 3 Dept. 1984)]

36

PARTNERSHIPS
Operation and Duties

The rights and duties of partners are governed largely by the specific terms of their partnership agreement. In the absence of provisions to the contrary in the partnership agreement, the law imposes the rights and duties discussed in this chapter. The character and nature of the partnership business generally influence the application of these rights and duties.

RIGHTS AMONG PARTNERS

The rights held by partners in a partnership relate to the following areas: management, interest in the partnership, compensation, inspection of books, accounting, and property rights. We discuss each of these areas below.

Management

"All partners have equal rights in the management and conduct of partnership business."[1] Management rights belong to all partners in an ordinary partnership.[2] Each partner has one vote in management

matters *regardless of the proportional size of his or her interest in the firm*. Often, in a large partnership, partners will agree to delegate daily management responsibilities to a management committee made up of one or more of the partners.

The majority rule controls decisions in ordinary matters connected with partnership business, unless otherwise specified in the agreement. However, unanimous consent of the partners is required to bind the firm in any of the following actions:

1.   To alter the essential nature of the firm's business as expressed in the partnership agreement or to alter the capital structure of the partnership.[3]
2.   To admit new partners or to enter a wholly new business.
3.   To assign partnership property into a trust for the benefit of creditors.
4.   To dispose of the partnership's goodwill.
5.   To confess judgment against the partnership or submit partnership claims to arbitration.
6.   To undertake any act that would make further conduct of partnership business impossible.[4]

Each of these matters significantly affects the nature of the partnership.

---

1.   UPA Section 18(e).
2.   Compare the management rights of general and limited partners in limited partnerships. The absence of management responsibility and the concomitant liability limitations are distinguishing characteristics of such partnerships. See the discussion on limited partnership in Chapter 37.

---

3.   UPA Section 18(h).
4.   UPA Section 9(3), various subsections.

Interest in the Partnership

Each partner is entitled to the proportion of business profits and losses that is designated in the partnership agreement. If the agreement does not apportion profits or losses, the UPA provides that profits shall be shared equally and losses shall be shared in the same ratio as profits.[5]

For example, Able and Baker form a partnership. The partnership agreement provides for capital contributions of $6,000 from Able and $4,000 from Baker, but it is silent as to how Able and Baker will share profits or losses. In this case, Able and Baker would share both profits and losses equally. Had the partnership agreement provided for profits to be shared in the same ratio as capital contributions, the profits would be shared 60 percent for Able and 40 percent for Baker; and had it been silent as to losses, losses would be shared in the same ratio as the profits (60/40 percent).

Compensation

A partner's time, skill, and energy on behalf of partnership business is a duty and generally not a compensable service. Partners can, of course, agree otherwise. For example, the managing partner of a law firm often receives a salary in addition to his or her share of profits for performing special administrative duties in office and personnel management. UPA Section 18(f) provides that a surviving partner is entitled to compensation for services in winding up partnership affairs (and reimbursement for expenses incurred in the process) above and apart from his or her share in the partnership profits.

Each partner impliedly promises to devote full time and render exclusive service to the partnership. Assume that Hunter, Brooks, and Palmer enter into a partnership. Palmer undertakes independent consulting for an outside firm without the consent of Hunter and Brooks. Palmer's compensation from the outside firm is considered partnership income.[6] A partner cannot engage in any independent competitive or even noncompetitive activities that involve the partnership's time.

If Palmer engages in an activity that competes with the partnership, then Palmer has breached the fiduciary duty that he owes it. Even with a noncompetitive activity, Palmer can breach his fiduciary duty if the partnership suffers a loss from his efforts. Of course, the partnership agreement or the unanimous consent of the partners can permit a partner to engage in any activity.

Inspection of Books

Partnership books and records must be kept accessible to all partners. Each partner has the right to receive (and each partner has the corresponding duty to produce) full and complete information concerning the conduct of all aspects of partnership business.[7] Each firm retains books in which to record and secure such information. Partners contribute the information, and a bookkeeper typically has the duty to preserve it. The books must be kept at the firm's principal business office and cannot be removed without the consent of all the partners.[8] Every partner, whether active or inactive, is entitled to inspect all books and records upon demand and can make copies of the materials. The personal representative of a deceased partner's estate has the same right of access to partnership books and records that the decedent would have had.

Accounting

An accounting of partnership assets or profits is done to determine the value of each partner's proportionate share in the partnership. An accounting can be performed voluntarily, or it can be compelled by the order of a court in equity.[9] Formal accounting occurs by right in connection with dissolution proceedings, but, under UPA Section 22, a partner also has the right to a formal accounting in the following situations:

1. When the partnership agreement provides for a formal accounting.

---

5. UPA Section 18(a).
6. UPA Section 21.
7. UPA Section 20.
8. UPA Section 19.
9. The principal remedy of a partner against co-partners is an equity suit for dissolution, an accounting, or both. With minor exceptions, a partner cannot maintain an action against other firm members for damages until partnership affairs are settled and an accounting is done. This rule is necessary because legal disputes between partners invariably involve conflicting claims to shares in the partnership. Logically, the value of each partner's share must first be determined by an accounting.

2.   When a partner is wrongfully excluded from the business, from access to the books, or both.

3.   When any partner is withholding profits or benefits belonging to the partnership in breach of the fiduciary duty.

4.   When circumstances "render it just and reasonable."

Property Rights

A partner has three basic property rights. They are:

1.   An interest in the partnership.
2.   A right in specific partnership property.
3.   A right to participate in the management of the partnership, as previously discussed. [10]

There is an important legal distinction between a partner's rights in specific property belonging to the firm to be used for business purposes, and a partner's right to share in the firm's earned profits to the extent of his or her interest in the firm. No individual partner has an absolute right to specific property of the firm. A partner is co-owner with his or her partners of specific partnership property, holding as a tenant in partnership. Chapter 35 discussed the factors that the courts use in determining property rights of partners and the rights of creditors in regard to partnerships. A judgment creditor of an individual partner has no right to execute or attach specific partnership property, but he or she can obtain the partner's share of profits. A creditor of the firm can levy directly upon partnership property (as will be discussed).

Partner's Interest in the Firm

A partner's interest in the firm is a personal asset consisting of a proportionate share of the profits earned [11] and a return of capital after dissolution and winding up.

A partner's interest is susceptible to assignment or to a judgment creditor's lien. Judgment creditors

10.   UPA Section 24.
11.   UPA Section 26.

can attach a partner's interest by petitioning the court that entered the judgment to grant the creditors a *charging order*. This order entitles the creditors to profits of the partner and to any assets available to the partner upon dissolution. [12] Neither an assignment nor a court's charging order entitling a creditor to receive a share of the partner's money will cause dissolution of the firm. [13]

Partnership Property

Partners are *tenants in partnership* of all firm property. [14] Tenancy in partnership has several important effects. If a partner dies, the surviving partners, not the heirs of the deceased partner, have the right of survivorship to the specific property. Although surviving partners are entitled to possession, they have a duty to account to the decedent's estate for the *value* of the deceased partner's interest in said property. [15]

A partner has no right to sell, assign, or in any way deal with a particular item of partnership property as an exclusive owner. [16] Nor is a partner's personal credit related to partnership property; creditors cannot use partnership property to satisfy the personal debts of a partner. Partnership property is available only to satisfy partnership debts, to enhance the firm's credit, or to achieve other business purposes.

Every partner is a co-owner with all other partners of specific partnership property, such as office equipment, paper supplies, and vehicles. Each partner has equal rights to possess partnership property for business purposes or in satisfaction of firm debts, but not for any other purpose without the consent of all the other partners.

The following case deals with an attempt by the surviving brothers of a partnership to breach their duty to account to their deceased brother's estate for the value of his interest in partnership property.

12.   UPA Section 28.
13.   UPA Section 27.
14.   UPA Section 25(1).
15.   UPA Section 25(2)(d)(e).
16.   UPA Section 25(2)(a)(b).

BACKGROUND AND FACTS   *Three brothers, James, John, and Claude, purchased several parcels of land, taking title to the lands either in their names or in their partnership name, Strother Brothers. In 1966, James Strother died, and his estate languished in probate. Approximately ten years later, John and Claude, along with their mother Minnie, brought suit to have Minnie declared*

STROTHER v. STROTHER

Supreme Court of Alabama, 1983.

436 So.2d 847.

*owner of a one-fourth interest in the lands. Prior to trial Minnie died, leaving
all her property to John and Claude. The trial court entered judgment against
such a declaration and the case was appealed to the Supreme Court.*

ALMON, Justice.

*   *   *   *

The Strother Brothers partnership operated a cattle business, but the Strothers never
executed a written partnership agreement. The issue at trial and before this Court is
whether Minnie Strother was a partner with her sons and, if so, whether the lands
were taken as partnership property of which Minnie Strother owned a one-fourth
interest. Stated otherwise, the issue is whether she contributed part of the purchase
price for the lands in question so as to be entitled to a resulting trust. If so, the heirs
of James Strother take only a one-fourth interest in the lands, whereas if Minnie Strother
is not entitled to a one-fourth interest, as the trial court held, the heirs of James Strother
take a one-third share.

In Goldthwaite v. Janney, 102 Ala. 431, 15 So. 560 (1894), this Court cited
authorities for the proposition that real estate may be partnership property even though
taken in individual partners' names if it is bought with partnership funds or credit for
partnership purposes. The Court stated:

"Whether the land belongs to a firm or to one of the individuals composing it,—
when the title is in his name, and not in that of the firm,—must be solved by
what appears to have been the intention of the parties. Prima facie, ownership is
where the muniment of title places it, but if by all the circumstances attending the
transaction, *   *   * it is made to appear, that in the intention of the parties, it
was purchased for and was treated as partnership property, that presumption of
ownership arising from the face of the deed will be overcome, and the property
will be treated as belonging to the partnership." *   *   *

*   *   *   *

In the case at bar no detailed factual presentation was made to support the contention
that Minnie Strother was an equal partner with her sons and that the land was partnership property bought with partnership funds or on partnership credit. No written
partnership agreement was ever executed. The evidence that Minnie was a partner
consisted chiefly of testimony by the accountant for Strother Brothers that one-fourth
of the partnership profits were paid to Minnie and Claude Strother's bare assertion that
his mother's funds were part of the purchase money used to buy the lands. We find
no error in the trial court's finding, as follows:

". . . There was absolutely no evidence to establish that Minnie C. Strother ever
intended, during her lifetime, to have any interest in the lands until this suit was
instituted, which was after Minnie C. Strother had become a very old person and
her two (2) sons were the principals of the institution of the suit. The muniment
of title standing in the names of the three (3) sons in each of the Deeds spoke the
truth. Some of the Deeds are the only written evidence that establishes the members
of the Partnership of Strother Brothers and these members were James B. Strother,
Claude C. Strother, and John C. Strother, Jr. All of the evidence disclosed that
before the death of James B. Strother the Partnership was engaged in the cattle
business and it appears from the evidence that this Partnership that was created
before the death of James B. Strother was nothing more than an operating Partnership."

*   *   *   *

"The contents of the James B. Strother Will referring to the Partnership strongly
establishes that the Partnership, prior to his death, consisted only of he [sic] and
his two brothers. *   *   * Due to the large acreage, the Court is of the opinion
said lands may be equitably divided among the owners without a sale of said lands."

The decision of the trial court is in accordance with the evidence of record and the applicable law. The Judgment is affirmed.

* * * *

The Supreme Court's decision gave each brother a one-third interest in the partnership property, thus defeating John and Claude's attempt to enlarge their partnership share.

DECISION AND REMEDY

DUTIES AND POWERS OF PARTNERS

The duties and powers of partners consist of a fiduciary duty of each partner to the other and general agency powers, to be discussed below.

Fiduciary Duty

Partners stand in a fiduciary relationship to one another the way that principals and agents do. (See Chapter 32.) It is a relationship of extraordinary trust and loyalty. The fiduciary duty imposes a responsibility upon each partner to act in good faith for the benefit of the partnership. It requires that each partner subordinate his or her personal interests in the event of conflict to the mutual welfare of the partners.

This fiduciary duty underlies the entire body of law pertaining to partnership and to agency. From it, certain other duties are commonly implied. Thus, a partner must account to the partnership for any personal profits or benefits derived without the consent of all of the partners in any partnership transaction.[17] These include transactions among partners or with third parties connected with the formation, conduct, or liquidation of the partnership, or with any use of partnership property.[18]

Upon the death of a partner, the surviving partner is under a fiduciary duty to liquidate partnership assets without delay and to credit the estate of the deceased partner for the value of the decedent's interest in the partnership. The fiduciary duty of good faith owed the deceased partner extends by implication to the personal representative of the deceased partner's estate as well. The principles of fiduciary duty and property rights are illustrated in the next case.

---

17. In this sense, "to account" to the partnership means not only to divulge the information but also to determine the value of any benefits or profits derived and to hold that money or property in trust on behalf of the partnership.
18. UPA Section 21.

BACKGROUND AND FACTS *About forty-five doctors, including Dr. Witlin, owned and operated a health center as partners. When Dr. Witlin died, the other doctors, in accordance with their partnership agreement, purchased his share of the center, paying his widow $65,228. The partnership agreement provided that on Witlin's death a management committee of the partnership was required to make a good faith determination of the fair market value of Witlin's share. The partnership had the option to offer this amount to Witlin's widow. The $65,228 offer, however, was based only on the book value of the partnership's assets. In addition, although the partnership was in the process of bargaining to sell the health center at a price which would have doubled Dr. Witlin's widow's proportionate share, the partnership did not inform her of that fact. Mrs. Witlin now seeks a greater amount for her husband's share, even though she accepted the partnership's offer. The trial court held for Dr. Witlin's widow, and the doctors appealed.*

ESTATE OF WITLIN

California Court of Appeal, 1978.
83 Cal.App.3d 167, 147
Cal.Rptr. 723.

COBEY, Associate Justice.
* * * *

Appellants [the forty-five doctors] owed [a fiduciary] * * * duty to plaintiff as the widow and executrix of their deceased partner in purchasing from her their deceased partner's interest in the partnership. Throughout the transaction they were bound to act toward her "in the highest good faith" and they were forbidden to obtain any advantage over her in the matter by, among other things, the slightest concealment. Yet the management committee never revealed to plaintiff or her representative, King, that the basic value in their formula for determining the fair market value of the partnership was book value alone. Likewise, as already noted, the management committee did not mention to King the possibility that the hospital might be shortly sold.

This possibility of sale was quite real. It appears from plaintiff's improperly rejected offers of proof that the management committee reached in 1969 a tentative agreement with General Health Services to sell the partnership's assets to it for approximately $60,000 a percentage point, that between April and September 28, 1971, the management committee and the American Cyanamid Corporation were discussing a sale of the partnership to it for at least $93,000 a percentage point, and, as already noted from the evidence itself, that the partnership's assets were finally sold in June 1972 to Hospital Corporation of America for about $84,000 a percentage point.

The management committee knew all of this, but they apparently never breathed a word of it to either plaintiff or her attorney. It seems that in discussing the fair market value of the partnership they talked out of both sides of their mouths. They talked to plaintiff and her attorney in terms of $16,000 and $24,600 per percentage point while they were more or less simultaneously talking to conglomerates interested in purchasing the hospital and the other assets of the partnership in terms of selling prices ranging from $60,000 to $93,500 per percentage point. Given this situation, how could their offer of $24,600 per percentage point to plaintiff have been a good faith determination on their part of the fair market value of the partnership? Obviously the jury's verdict was correct and solidly supported in this respect.

DECISION AND REMEDY   *The trial court's judgment was affirmed on appeal. The partners were held to have breached their fiduciary duty to their deceased partner by failing to make a full and fair disclosure.*

General Agency Powers

Each partner is an *agent* of every other partner and acts as both a principal and an agent in any business transaction within the scope of the partnership agreement. Each partner is a general agent of the partnership in carrying out the usual business of the firm. Thus, every act of a partner in every contract and in every contract signed in the partnership name, concerning partnership business, binds the firm.[19]

The UPA affirms general principles of agency law that pertain to the authority of a partner to bind a partnership in contract or tort. When a partner is apparently carrying on partnership business with third persons in the usual way, both the partner and the firm share liability. It is only when third persons *know* that the partner has no such authority that the partnership is not liable.

For example, Peter, a partner in Firm X, applies for a loan on behalf of the partnership without authorization from the other partners. The bank manager knows Peter has no authority. If the bank manager grants the loan, Peter will be personally bound, but the firm will not be liable.

Joint Liability   Partners have only joint liability on all partnership debts and contracts. Partners are jointly and severally liable for tort actions and breaches of trust to third persons.[20]

---

19. UPA Section 9(1).

20. UPA Section 15.

Joint liability means that the group of partners wins or loses as a group. One partner cannot be singled out to be sued. Unless the partnership is treated as an entity, every partner's name must be listed in the suit, and the individual assets of each partner are equally exposed to potential liability (although the actual contribution in the event of a judgment is calculated on each partner's proportionate share of the firm). If the court awards the claimant a judgment, the claimant is barred from further suits against the partners and against the firm, once satisfaction (that is, payment) of the judgment is made.

In states that allow a firm to be sued in its own name, a contract claimant or a creditor claimant can sue the firm as an *entity* without joining each partner. A judgment against the partnership binds only partnership assets. In such states, the better practice is to sue both the firm as an *entity* and all partners *jointly*. Then, judgment is enforceable against the assets of the partnership and the assets of the individual partners. The judgment rendered in such a case must be internally consistent. For example, if Carl sues Firm X and all its partners jointly for breach of contract and the court finds the firm liable, then it must hold the partners liable (and vice versa).

Joint and several liability means that a claimant can sue one partner without joining the others. Moreover, regardless of the outcome of the suit against the first partner, **res judicata** (a matter or thing settled by judgment in the courts) does not protect the other partners in subsequent suits filed against them.

Liability of Incoming Partner   A newly admitted partner to an existing partnership has limited liability for whatever debts and obligations the partnership incurred prior to the new partner's admission. UPA Section 17 provides that the new partner's liability can be satisfied only from partnership assets. This means that the new partner has no personal liability for these debts and obligations, but any capital contribution made by him or her is subject to these debts.

Trading versus Non-Trading Partnerships—A Digression   At common law, prior to the UPA, a distinction was drawn between trading and non-trading partnerships. Essentially, any partnership business that had goods in inventory and made profits in buying and selling those goods was considered a trading partnership. All other partnerships were non-trading. The distinction between these two types of partnerships is important in discussing the apparent authority of the partnership and of its individual members. The UPA does not expressly adopt the distinction between these two types of partnerships, but many cases decided under the UPA nonetheless followed the distinction.

Authority of Partners   Agency concepts relating to apparent authority, actual authority, and ratification are also applicable to partnerships. The extent of *implied authority* is generally broader for partners than for ordinary agents. The character and scope of the partnership business and the customary nature of the particular business operation determine the scope of implied powers. For example, the usual course of business in a trading partnership involves buying and selling commodities. Consequently, each partner in a trading partnership has a wide range of implied powers to borrow money in the firm name and to extend the firm's credit in issuing or indorsing negotiable instruments.

In an ordinary partnership, firm members can exercise all implied powers reasonably necessary and customary to carry on that particular business. Some customarily implied powers include the authority to make warranties on goods in the sales business, the power to convey real property in the firm name where such conveyances are part of the ordinary course of partnership business, the power to enter contracts consistent with the firm's regular course of business, and the power to make admissions and representations concerning partnership affairs.[21]

If a partner acts within the scope of authority, the partnership is bound to third parties. For example, a partner's authority to sell partnership products carries with it the implied authority to transfer title and to make usual warranties. Hence, in a partnership that operates a retail tire store, any partner negotiating a contract with a customer for the sale of a set of tires can warrant that "each tire will be warranted for normal wear for 40,000 miles."

However, this same partner would not have the authority to sell office equipment, fixtures, or the partnership office building without the consent of all of the other partners. In addition, since partnerships are formed for profit, a partner does not gen-

---

21.   UPA Section 11.

erally have the authority to make charitable contributions without the consent of the other parties. Any such actions are not binding on the partnership unless they are ratified by all of the other partners.

As in the law of agency, the law of partnership imputes one partner's knowledge to all other partners because members of a partnership stand in a fiduciary relationship to one another. Such a fiduciary relationship implies that each partner willfully discloses to every other partner all relevant information pertaining to the business of the partnership. The same rule applies to members of a joint venture.

QUESTIONS AND CASE PROBLEMS

1. Able, Baker, and Clark form a partnership to operate a window washing service. Able contributes $10,000 to the partnership, and Baker and Clark contribute $1,000 each. The partnership agreement is silent on how profits and losses will be shared. One month after the partnership is in operation, Baker and Clark vote, over Able's objection, to purchase another truck for the firm's operation. Able believes that since he contributed $10,000, a major commitment to purchase by the partnership cannot be made over his objection. In addition, Able claims that, in absence of agreement, profits must be divided in the same ratio as each partner's capital contribution. Discuss Able's contentions.

2. Able, Betty, and Carla form a partnership to operate a hairstyling salon. After one year's operation, the salon has become very busy and profitable. Most customers prefer one of the partners to perform the various services offered. Able becomes ill, and Betty and Carla start working sixty-hour weeks. It appears that Able will not return to work for at least two months. Betty and Carla want to bring in Dana as a new partner. Able objects to Dana and refuses to consent to Dana's admission into the partnership. Betty and Carla insist that they be paid extra compensation for having to work additional hours because of Able's illness. Discuss whether Betty and Carla are entitled to the compensation claimed and whether Dana can be admitted as a new partner by majority vote.

3. Able and Baker are partners in a law firm. Able has substantial personal assets. Able, driving his own car, is on his way to take a deposition from a witness when he negligently runs into Thomas. The damages and injuries to Thomas amount to $5,000. Unknown to Able, Baker at the same time has contracted to purchase $9,000 worth of word processing equipment from Copycat, Inc. Both partners have express partnership authority to purchase office equipment. Able is angry about the purchase and wrongfully cancels the contract with Copycat. Both Copycat and Thomas want to sue. Discuss the nature of the partners' liability in both cases.

4. Able and Baker operate as partners a car dealership. The partnership has existing debts of $300,000 with General Motors. Able and Baker take in a new partner, Carlson. Carlson contributes to the partnership land valued at $100,000 to be used by the partnership as a used car lot. Carlson is new to the car dealership business and, in making his first sale, warrants to a customer that the partnership will repair the car at no cost for a period of two years regardless of mileage. General Motors sues the partners jointly on the debt and obtains a judgment. Able and Baker insist that Carlson's warranty to the customer is not binding on the partnership.

  (a) Discuss Carlson's liability to General Motors.

  (b) Discuss Able's and Baker's claim that Carlson's warranty is not binding on the partnership.

5. Able, Baker, and Carlson form a television repair partnership. Profits are to be shared equally. Each partner draws a monthly salary of $1,000. Without Able and Baker's knowledge, Carlson, who has principal authority to purchase supplies and equipment, is receiving a rebate from large orders made with a supplier. Also, Carlson keeps the books and records at his home and continually denies Able and Baker access to the books. Able and Baker want an accounting. Discuss fully whether they are entitled to it.

6. Oddo and Ries entered into a partnership agreement in March 1978 to create and publish a book describing how to restore F-100 pickup trucks. Oddo was to write the book and Ries was to provide the capital. Oddo supplied Ries with the manuscript, but Ries was dissatisfied and hired someone else to revise the manuscript. Ries published the book containing substantial amounts of Oddo's work. Can Oddo require Ries to formally account for the profits on the book? [Oddo v. Ries, 743 F.2d 630 (9th Cir. 1984)]

7. Plaintiff Hodge brought an action against a partnership that owned a movie theater. Volar, the managing partner of the partnership, signed a contract for the sale to Hodge of real estate adjacent to the theater and belonging to the partnership. The agreement reserved an easement for use as a driveway into the premises. At trial, Volar claimed that prior to signing he had told Hodge that Hodge would have to present him with a plan of the property and that Volar's other partners would have to approve before the sale of the property. At trial, Hodge

denied this. The partners argued that, in any event, Volar did not have authority to sell the property. Did he? [Hodge v. Garrett, 101 Idaho 397, 614 P.2d 420 (1980)]

8. A patient sued a physician for medical malpractice and successfully obtained a money judgment. The patient did not sue the partnership to which the physician belonged and made no allegation against the partnership. Injury to the patient occurred in the course of partnership business. Can the physician now recover from his co-partners for damages that he paid out of his personal funds? [Flynn v. Reaves, 135 Ga. App. 651, 218 S.E.2d 661 (1975)]

9. Harestad and Weitzel entered into an oral agreement in August 1970 to be "partners in a real estate and building business," and each contributed equal amounts to the partnership. In October 1970, Weitzel purchased an apartment project in his own name with his own funds. Over the next two years, he oversaw the development and consummated the sale of the apartment project for a hand-some profit. Upon voluntary dissolution of the partnership by both parties, Harestad sought half the profit that Weitzel had made from his apartment project deal. Can she recover? (Harestad v. Weitzel, 272 Or. 199, 536 P.2d 522 (1975)]

10. Birch and DeLong formed Birch-DeLong Construction Company in 1972 as a partnership. They agreed that all proceeds from the sale of houses would be deposited in a bank, and that disbursement of the funds would only be by mutual agreement or authorization. Initially, both men signed all the checks, but in 1974 DeLong agreed that Birch would take over the accounting and disburse funds for the business. In 1980 the business was suffering and DeLong realized Birch had been paying some personal expenses out of partnership funds. Would DeLong have a valid claim to an accounting of the funds Birch made to cover his personal expenses? [State of Washington v. Birch, 36 Wn.App. 405, 675 P.2d 246 (1984)]

37

PARTNERSHIPS
Limited Partnerships

This chapter will look in detail at the management, formation, and termination of limited partnerships. It will also look at a highly specialized form of partnership, the limited partnership association.

DEFINITION OF LIMITED PARTNERSHIP

Limited partnerships are formed by compliance with statutory requirements. They consist of at least one general partner and one or more limited partners.[1] The general partner (or partners) assumes management responsibility of the partnership and, as such, has full personal liability for all debts of the partnership. The limited partner (or partners) contributes cash (or other property) and owns an interest in the firm but does not undertake any management responsibilities and is not personally liable for partnership debts beyond the amount of his or her investment. A limited partner can forfeit limited liability by taking part in managing the business. In many respects, limited partnerships are like general partnerships, discussed in Chapters 35 and 36. They are sometimes referred to as special partnerships, in contrast to general partnerships.

HISTORY OF THE LIMITED PARTNERSHIP

All businesses require capital. A need therefore exists for a form of organization that permits capital investment without responsibility for management and without liability for losses beyond the initial investment. Such an organization should also allow the right to share in the profits with limited liability for losses.

During the Middle Ages, this kind of organization was called a *commenda*.[2] In a commenda, the *commendator* supplied money to the *tractator* and received a major portion of the profits but was not liable for losses. If the tractator lost the capital investment, the commendator was liable only if proven negligent. This particular institution was sanctioned by the French Commercial Code in 1707, Sections 23–28. Over a century later, the first limited partnership acts were adopted in New York (in 1822) and in Connecticut and Pennsylvania (in 1836).

Limited Partnership Statutes—Early Versions

All states have enacted limited partnership statutes. The earlier interpretations of such acts displayed an

---

1. ULPA Section 1.

2. W. Holdsworth, *History of English Law* (London: Methuen and Co. Ltd., 1956), p. 195.

obvious hostility toward limited liability that derived from the common law. Courts imposed full liability on limited partners when there were only trivial failures to comply with the law.

The Uniform Limited Partnership Act

The Uniform Limited Partnership Act (ULPA) was promulgated in 1916. At one time forty-eight states (not Delaware or Louisiana), the District of Columbia, and the Virgin Islands had adopted the 1916 version of the ULPA. Today this number now stands at twenty-seven,[3] as twenty-two states (including Delaware)[4] have adopted the revised ULPA discussed below. Its thirty-one sections are set forth in Appendix E of this book. The great virtue of the ULPA is that it expressly provides protection against technical defects if there has been a substantial compliance in good faith.[5] Under the ULPA, a limited partnership can conduct any business that can be carried on by a general partnership unless there is an exception in the state statutes.[6] The most predominant exceptions are banking and insurance.

The Revised Uniform Limited Partnership Act

On August 5, 1976, the National Conference of Commissioners on Uniform State Laws approved a Revised Uniform Limited Partnership Act (RULPA). It contains eleven articles and sixty-four sections (set forth in Appendix F), and it was made available to state legislatures in 1977.

For a comparison of the basic characteristics of general partnerships, limited partnerships, and those limited partnerships formed under the Revised Uniform Limited Partnership Act, see Exhibit 37–1.

FORMATION

The creation of a limited partnership is a public and formal proceeding that must follow statutory requirements. Contrast this with the informal, private, and voluntary agreement that usually suffices for a general partnership as described in Chapter 35. For a limited partnership, there must be two or more partners, and they must sign a certificate that sets forth, at a minimum, the following information:[7]

1. Firm name.
2. Character of the business.
3. Location of the principal place of business.
4. Name and place of residence of each member and whether each is a general or a limited partner.
5. Duration of the partnership.
6. Amount of cash and a description and agreed-upon valuation of any other property contributed by each limited partner.
7. Additional contributions (if any) to be made by each limited partner and the times at which they are to be made.
8. Rights for changes in partnership personnel (if any) and subsequent continuance of the business.
9. Share of profits or other compensation that each limited partner is entitled to receive.

In essence, the content of the certificate and the method of filing resemble that for the corporate charter. Often, there are private, informal agreements covering matters that do not have to be stated in the certificate, such as the profit shares of the general partners. See Exhibit 37–2 for a sample certificate of limited partnership.

Where to File Certificates

The certificate must be filed with the designated state official. It is usually open to public inspection. The official is normally in the county where the principal business of the firm will be carried on. Some states require multiple filings if the business is carried on in numerous counties. Others require only one filing, usually at the state capital. The revised ULPA requires the filing of the certificate in the office of the Secretary of State. Constructive notice (by reason

---

3. Alaska, Florida, Georgia, Hawaii, Illinois, Indiana, Kentucky, Maine, Mississippi, Missouri, Nevada, New Hampshire, New Mexico, New York, North Carolina, North Dakota, Ohio, Oregon, Pennsylvania, Rhode Island, South Carolina, South Dakota, Tennessee, Texas, Utah, Vermont, and Virginia (as of 5/1/84).
4. Alabama, Arizona, Arkansas, California, Colorado, Connecticut, Delaware, Idaho, Iowa, Kansas, Maryland, Massachusetts, Michigan, Minnesota, Montana, Nebraska, New Jersey, Oklahoma, Washington, West Virginia, Wisconsin, Wyoming (as of 5/1/84).
5. ULPA Section 2(2).
6. ULPA Section 3.

---

7. ULPA Section 2(1), RULPA Section 201.

EXHIBIT 37–1   Basic Comparison Of Partnerships

CHARACTERISTIC	GENERAL PARTNERSHIP	LIMITED PARTNERSHIP	REVISED LIMITED PARTNERSHIP
Creation	By agreement of two or more persons to carry on a business as co-owners for profit.	By agreement of two or more persons, under the laws of the state, having one or more general partners and one or more limited partners to carry on a business as co-owners for profit. Filing of certificate in appropriate state office is required.	Same as limited partnership, except filing of certificate with Secretary of State is required.
Sharing of profits and losses	By agreement, or in absence thereof, profits are shared equally by partners and losses are shared in same ratio as profits.	Profits are shared as required in certificate agreement, and losses shared likewise, except limited partners share losses only up to their capital contribution.	Same as limited partnership, except in absence of provision in certificate agreement, profits and losses are shared on basis of percentages of capital contributions.
Liability	Unlimited personal liability of all partners.	Unlimited personal liability of all general partners; limited partners only to extent of capital contributions.	Same as limited partnership.
Capital contribution	No minimal or mandatory amount; set by agreement.	Set by agreement; may be cash, property, or any obligation except services.	Same as limited partnership; contribution of services is allowed.
Management	By agreement, or in absence thereof, all partners have an equal voice.	General partners by agreement, or else each has an equal voice. Limited partners have no voice, or else subject to liability as a general partner.	Same as limited partnership, except limited partner involved in partnership management is liable as a general partner *only* if third party has knowledge of such involvement. Limited partner may act as agent or employer of partnership, and vote on amending certificate or sale or dissolution of partnership.
Duration	By agreement, or can be dissolved by action of partner (withdrawal), operation of law (death or bankruptcy), or court decree.	By agreement in certification, or by withdrawal, death, or insanity of general partner in absence of right of other general partners to continue the partnership. Death of a limited partner, unless he or she is only remaining limited partner, does not terminate partnership.	Same as limited partnership, except it enlarges class of activities by general partner that result in termination. (Section 402)
Assignment	Interest can be assigned, although assignee does not have rights of substituted partner, without consent of other partners.	Same as general partnership. If partners consent to assignee becoming a partner, certificate must be amended.	Same as limited partnership. Upon assignment of all interest, partner ceases to be a partner.

EXHIBIT 37–1 Continued			
CHARACTERISTIC	GENERAL PARTNERSHIP	LIMITED PARTNERSHIP	REVISED LIMITED PARTNERSHIP
Priorities (order) upon liquidation	1. Outside creditors. 2. Partner creditors. 3. Capital contribution of partners. 4. Profits of partners.	1. Outside creditors. Limited partner creditors. 2. Profits to limited partners. 3. Limited partner capital contributions. 4. General partner creditors. 5. Profits to general partners. 6. Capital contributions of general partners.	1. Outside creditors. Partner creditors. 2. Amounts before withdrawal to which partners are entitled. 3. Capital contributions—limited and general partners. 4. Profits—limited and general partners.

of law) does not usually exist for a certificate filed in another state. Thus, if a limited partnership chooses to do business where a certificate is not filed, a court can rule that its failure to file locally makes it a general partnership. This is similar to the qualification rules for foreign corporations. Some states require newspaper publication of certificates, or at least a summary of them, in addition to a filing.

Number of Limited Partners

Originally, limited partnerships were conceived to accommodate only a few limited partners. There seems, however, to be no statutory limit to their numbers and, in some cases, very large groups have been assembled. In a 1966 case, the limited partners of a real estate syndicate brought a class action suit against the general partners and some outsiders.[8] The limited partners numbered several hundred.

RIGHTS AND LIABILITIES OF LIMITED PARTNERS

General partners, unlike limited partners, are personally liable to the partnership's creditors; thus at least one general partner is necessary in a limited partnership, so that someone has personal liability. This policy can be circumvented in states that allow a corporation to be the general partner in a partnership. Since the corporation has limited liability

by virtue of corporate laws, no one in the limited partnership actually has personal liability.

Limited Partners Cannot Participate in Management

The exemptions from personal liability of the limited partners rest on their not participating in management.[9] First, the contribution of a limited partner cannot be in his or her services as manager—it has to be in cash or other property.[10] Second, the surname of a limited partner cannot be included in the partnership name.[11] A violation of either of these provisions renders the limited partner just as liable as a general partner to any creditor who does not know that he or she is a limited partner.

Note that no law expressly bars the participation of limited partners in the management of the partnership. Rather, the threat of personal liability deters their participation.

The revised ULPA does restrict a limited partner's liability. Only if the third party had knowledge of the limited partner's management activities is the limited partner liable as a general partner. How much actual review and advisement a limited partner can engage in before being exposed to liability is an unsettled question.[12]

The issue of the degree of control of the limited partner comes up in the following case.

---

8. Lichtyger v. Franchard Corp., 18 N.Y.2d 528, 223 N.E.2d 869 (1966).

9. ULPA Section 7.
10. ULPA Section 4.
11. ULPA Section 5.
12. See Plasteel Products Corp. v. Helman, 271 F.2d 354 (1st Cir. 1959) (interpreting Massachusetts law).

EXHIBIT 37–2 Sample Certificate Of Limited Partnership

CERTIFICATE OF LIMITED PARTNERSHIP

The undersigned, desiring to form a Limited Partnership under the Uniform Limited Partnership Act of the State of _____ , make this certificate for that purpose.

§ 1. **Name.** The name of the Partnership shall be "_____ _____ ".

§ 2. **Purpose.** The purpose of the Partnership shall be to [*describe*].

§ 3. **Location.** The location of the Partnership's principal place of business is _____County, _____ .

§ 4. **Members and Designation.** The names and places of residence of the members, and their designation as General or Limited Partners are:

_____	[*Address*]	General Partner
_____	[*Address*]	General Partner
_____	[*Address*]	Limited Partner
_____	[*Address*]	Limited Partner

§ 5. **Term.** The term for which the Partnership is to exist is indefinite.

§ 6. **Initial Contributions of Limited Partners.** The amount of cash and a description of the agreed value of the other property contributed by each Limited Partner are:

[*Name*]	[*Describe*]
[*Name*]	[*Describe*]

§ 7. **Subsequent Contributions of Limited Partners.** Each Limited Partner may (but shall not be obliged to) make such additional contributions to the capital of the Partnership as may from time to time be agreed upon by the General Partners.

§ 8. **Profit Shares of Limited Partners.** The share of the profits which each Limited Partner shall receive by reason of his contribution is:

[*Name*]	_____ %
[*Name*]	_____ %

Signed _____ , 19____

_____
_____
_____
_____

Signed and sworn before me, the undersigned authority, this _____ _____ , 19____ .

Notary Public

_____County, _____

BACKGROUND AND FACTS *Weil, the general partner, sought to have the court declare the limited partners as general partners because of their participation in management activities. The limited partnership was having financial difficulties, and creditors were seeking payment from Weil, who was the sole general partner. He wished to spread the liability to all the limited partners.*

WEIL v. DIVERSIFIED
PROPERTIES
U.S. District Court, District of Columbia, 1970.
319 F.Supp. 778.

GESELL, District Judge.

* * * *

Cases relating to whether or not limited partners have taken part in control of the business and are thus to be treated as general partners involve claims by creditors against the partners. No case has been found where a general partner has invoked Section 7 of the Act against his own limited partners. The purpose of Section 7 is to protect creditors:

> The Act proceeds on the assumption that no public policy requires a person who contributes to the capital of a business, acquires an interest in its profits, and some degree of control over the conduct of the business to become bound for the obligations of the business, provided creditors have no reason to believe that when their credits were extended that such persons were so bound.

* * * *

Even if a general partner might hold his limited partners to account as general partners under certain circumstances, Weil cannot do so on the facts of this case. Weil considers himself still a general partner and recognizes that the written partnership agreement by its terms is a bona fide limited partnership under the Code. As between themselves, partners may make any agreement they wish which is not barred by prohibitory provisions of statutes, by common law, or by considerations of public policy. Whatever may be the obligations of the limited partners as against creditors or third parties, Weil may not prevail against them if they have not breached the terms of the agreement. Having entered into the partnership agreement with advice of counsel, an agreement made largely for his own benefit in a field where he was especially experienced, he is bound by its terms. Accordingly, the initial inquiry must be to determine whether the limited partners have in any way violated the terms of the written agreement.

* * * *

Thus it is apparent that the partners contemplated the general partner would receive a substantial salary and have the day-to-day management of the properties. * * * After May 1, 1969, the partnership operation became a matter of salvaging what could be salvaged in the enterprise as it then existed. This naturally involved refinancing and sale of properties and other matters not in the normal course of day-to-day business. As to these non-routine matters, the limited partners by the very terms of their agreement had a majority vote, and were certainly authorized to comment upon them. Weil believes he should have had exclusive say as to how and what bills were to be paid with any money available beyond immediate operating needs, but under the prevailing conditions this clearly was not a normal day-to-day business question; it involved the very ability of the enterprise to survive. Moreover, the funds coming in were far from sufficient to meet current obligations, and no partnership account was being accumulated.

* * * *

* * * Weil was employed in another business, creditors were harassing him, his affairs were in disarray and he could not always be reached. * * *

Weil has not by a preponderance of the evidence established any violation by the limited partners of terms of the agreement with him, which at the very most is all that Weil can complain of in his effort to have the limited partners declared general partners.

Since the partnership agreement was not violated by the limited partners, Weil has no cause of action and his request for the appointment of a receiver and an accounting will be denied. The provisions of the Limited Partnership Act were primarily designed to protect creditors. So long as the provisions of the agreement were followed, no partner can complain.

DECISION AND REMEDY   *Weil's case was dismissed.*

COMMENTS   *A creditor can seek to have a limited partner declared a general partner because of participation in management, but a general partner can complain of violation of the partnership agreement only if a limited partner interferes with management of the partnership.*

Liability to Creditors   A limited partner is liable to creditors to the extent of any contribution that had been promised to the firm or any part of a contribution that was withdrawn from the firm.[13] If the firm is defectively organized, and the limited partner fails to renunciate (withdraw from the partnership) on discovery of the defect, the partner can be held personally liable to the firm's creditors. Note, though, that the ULPA and the revised ULPA allow people to remain limited partners regardless of whether they comply with statutory technicalities. Decisions on liability for false statements in a partnership certificate run in favor of persons relying on the false statements and against members who sign the certificate knowing of the falsity.[14] A limited partnership is formed by good faith compliance with the requirements for signing and filing the certificate even

if it is incomplete or defective. When a limited partner discovers a defect in the formation of the limited partnership, he or she can obtain shelter from future liability by renouncing an interest in the profits of the partnership, thereby avoiding any future reliance by third parties.[15]

Liability of Limited Partners   The liability of a limited partner is limited to the capital that he or she contributes or agrees to contribute to the partnership. By contrast, the liability of a general partner for partnership indebtedness is virtually unlimited. In a recent case, the general partner of a limited partnership remained personally liable for partnership debts after the limited partnership went through a Chapter 7 bankruptcy.[16]

The following case deals with an attempt by a bank creditor to hold the limited partners personally liable for actions of the general partner.

---

13.   See Kittredge v. Langley, 252 N.Y. 405, 169 N.E. 626 (1930).
14.   See Walraven v. Ramsay, 335 Mich. 331, 55 N.W.2d 853 (1953) and ULPA Section 6.

15.   ULPA Section 11.
16.   Rohdie v. Washington, 641 S.W.2d 317 (Tex.Ct.App. 1982).

CHEMICAL BANK OF ROCHESTER v. ASHENBURG
Supreme Court of Monroe County, 1978.
94 Misc.2d 64, 405 N.Y.S.2d 175.

BACKGROUND AND FACTS   *Chemical Bank of Rochester filed suit against the limited partners of a partnership to recover funds advanced on a note. Stanndco Developers was the sole general partner in Meadowbrook Farm Apartments. In exchange for Stanndco's promise to transfer apartment units to the Meadowbrook limited partnership, eighteen limited partners executed promissory notes payable to Meadowbrook for their "shares" in the limited partnership. The notes totaled $101,000. Stanndco later sought a $101,000 bank loan for purposes unrelated to Meadowbrook and used the notes given by the Meadowbrook limited partners as collateral. Stanndco indorsed the notes to itself without the consent or ratification of the limited partners. The bank sought to collect on the notes from the limited partners.*

SCHNEPP, Justice.

* * * *

Plaintiff [bank] had knowledge that Stanndco was negotiating the instruments in a transaction for its own benefit, without authority, and in breach of its duty as a fiduciary. Plaintiff knew from the outset of the transaction, when Stanndco first approached it for a corporate loan, that the notes were not being used by Stanndco for a partnership purpose. * * * In the face of these facts, plaintiff acted in bad faith. Chemical Bank had actual knowledge or knowledge of facts sufficient to impute notice on the infirmities, defects and defenses to the instrument. In short, plaintiff, having taken the notes with notice and in bad faith, is not entitled to the rights of a holder in due course.

* * * *

It is held that plaintiff takes subject to the defendants' claim that the notes were negotiated for the individual purpose of a general partner in breach of its fiduciary duty. Plaintiff, a non-holder in due course, may not recover on the notes against the defendant makers * * *.

* * * The defendants, as both makers of the notes and limited partners, had a legitimate expectation that the provisions of the Partnership Law would be followed. They had no cause to anticipate that a general partner would exceed his authority by assigning their rights in specific partnership property without their written consent or ratification and thus effectively terminate their right to have their contribution returned. It was the written consent or ratification of each defendant limited partner that was required for the proper negotiation of the notes—and this is what Stanndco failed to secure. Clearly, each defendant maker is offended and damaged by Stanndco's breach of duty, because each is a limited partner.

* * * Plaintiff's conduct permitted the diversion of the partnership assets and it should not profit from its own wrongdoing. Under these circumstances it would be unconscionable not to permit the defendants to assert their claim as a defense against plaintiff. * * *

The court dismissed Chemical Bank's lawsuit against the limited partners. Since Chemical Bank knew that Stanndco was transferring the notes for other than legitimate partnership purposes, it was not permitted to recover any money from the limited partners.

DECISION AND REMEDY

Restrictions on What the Limited Partner Can Do   As already mentioned, the limited partner cannot take control of the firm, cannot contribute services, and cannot allow his or her name to appear in the firm name. Additionally, the limited partner has no authority to bind the firm, even though, in some sense, he or she is a "member" of it.

Rights of the Limited Partner

Subject to the above limitations, limited partners have essentially the same rights as general partners: the right of access to partnership books, the right to an accounting of partnership business, and the right to participate in the dissolution if the winding up and distribution of partnership assets is by court decree. They are entitled to a return of their contri-

butions in accordance with the partnership certificate.[17] They can also assign their interests subject to specific clauses in the certificate.[18]

Limited Partner's Right to Sue   In jurisdictions that have considered the matter, courts seem to recognize fully the limited partner's right to sue, either individually or on behalf of the firm, for economic injury to the firm by the general partners or by outsiders. In addition, investor protection legislation, such as security laws (discussed in Chapter 43), may give some protection to limited partners.

---

17.   ULPA Section 10.
18.   ULPA Section 19.

THE USE OF A LIMITED PARTNERSHIP

The limited partnership is a less effective liability shield than the corporation. In many respects, the corporation is more flexible, and its charter does not require the frequent amendments that a limited partnership certificate does.[19] One might conclude that limited partnerships have little utility, except for special reasons.

Before World War II, limited partnerships were used sparingly, but during and after the war their number increased, largely because of high federal income tax rates, particularly on corporations. A limited partnership allows the limited partners to deduct expenses or losses against other income directly and to be protected from personal liability.

There are three primary uses for limited partnerships today:

1. To buy, build, and lease commercial property, hold it for a period of five or more years, and then resell it.
2. To purchase and lease heavy equipment.
3. To loan money and take back first mortgages.

Limited partnerships are also popular with people who start new Individual Retirement Accounts (IRAs) and are used extensively for oil and gas ventures.

DISSOLUTION

A limited partnership is dissolved in much the same way as an ordinary partnership. The retirement, death, or insanity of a general partner can dissolve the partnership, but not if the business can be continued by one or more of the other general partners in accordance with their certificate or by consent of all members.[20] The death or assignment of interest of a limited partner does not dissolve the limited partnership.[21] With respect to dissolution, limited partnerships resemble corporations more closely than they do general partnerships. Public filings, passive investors, and limited liability are all features of both corporations and limited partnerships.

Causes of Dissolution

A limited partnership is dissolved by the expiration of its term or the completion of its undertaking. When there is no definite term or undertaking, the express will of any general partner will usually dissolve the partnership. Limited partners do not have the power to dissolve unless they have rightfully, but unsuccessfully, demanded the return of their contribution.[22] If, however, the general partners dissolve the partnership without the consent of the limited partners before the end of the term fixed by the certificate, this dissolution is considered a breach.

Illegality, expulsion, and bankruptcy of the general partners dissolve a limited partnership. However, bankruptcy of a limited partner does not dissolve the partnership unless it causes the bankruptcy of the firm.

The retirement of a general partner causes a dissolution unless the members consent to a continuation by the remaining general partners or unless this contingency is provided for in the certificate.

Consequences of Dissolution

The consequences of the dissolution of general partnerships apply to limited partnerships (see Chapter 35). Therefore, the firm continues in operation while winding up. The general partners of a limited partnership have the authority to wind up, as in an ordinary partnership. The representatives of general partners, not the limited partners, succeed the general partners. Limited partners have the right to obtain dissolution and winding up by a court decree.[23]

Assuming that the general partners continue the business, the limited partners generally have the right to be paid the value of their interests at dissolution, plus profits or interest on that value from dissolution until payment.

Priorities in Distribution of Assets

Upon dissolution, creditors' rights to assets precede partners' rights, and limited partners' rights precede general partners' rights. Limited partners take both

---

19. ULPA Section 24(2).
20. ULPA Section 20.
21. ULPA Section 21.

22. ULPA Section 16.
23. Klebanow v. New York Produce Exchange, 344 F.2d 294 (2d Cir. 1965).

their share of profits and of contributed capital before general partners receive anything.[24]

LIMITED PARTNERSHIP ASSOCIATIONS

Certain states allow the formation of limited partnership associations. They are legal hybrids that actually resemble corporations, although they are called partnership associations in some states. They originated in Pennsylvania in 1874, and the capital subscribed to the association was solely responsible for its debts. In 1966, the Pennsylvania Act was repealed except for professions not permitted to incorporate. Three other states have similar laws: Michigan, New Jersey, and Ohio. (Virginia had one from 1874 to 1918.) This type of organization is seldom seen outside of Pennsylvania and Michigan.

---

24. ULPA Section 23, and see Exhibit 37–1. Note differences under RULPA.

The organizational document is publicly filed and can be changed by amendment. It fixes the capital of the association, and there is no maximum or minimum amount. Each member contributes a designated part of the capital.

The association's life is restricted—usually to twenty years. There must be at least three members, and Ohio has established a maximum of twenty-five. The word *limited* must be the last word in the association's name, and it must be conspicuously used on advertisements, signs, and stationery. Dissolution of the limited partnership association occurs when the prescribed term expires or by a majority vote of the members.

An important difference between this type of association and corporations involves the transfer of shares. The shares are freely transferable in a limited partnership association, but the new transferee does not become a member of the association unless duly elected by the other members. When membership is refused, however, the transferee can recover the value of his or her shares from the association.

QUESTIONS AND CASE PROBLEMS

1. Able and Baker form a limited partnership with Able as the general partner and Baker as the limited partner. Baker puts up $15,000, and Able contributes some office equipment that he owns. A certificate of limited partnership is properly filed, and business is begun. One month later Able becomes ill. Instead of hiring someone to manage the business, Baker takes over complete management himself. While Baker is in control, he makes a contract with Thomas involving a large sum of money. Able returns to work. Because of other commitments, the Thomas contract is breached. Thomas contends that he can hold Able and Baker personally liable if his judgment cannot be satisfied out of the assets of the limited partnership. Discuss this contention.

2. Able, Baker, and Clark want to form a limited partnership. Able and Baker are recent college graduates with no business experience. They are to be the general partners. Clark, an experienced businesswoman, is to be the limited partner. Clark is to put up $10,000 and to manage the business for the first six months, until Able and Baker get experience. For this, the partnership will list her capital contribution as $15,000. Profits are to be divided

equally. The limited partnership name has not been determined. For the present the partners plan on simply using their surnames. Discuss what advice an attorney might give Able, Baker, and Clark on forming a limited partnership.

3. Ann, Betty, and Carla form a limited partnership. Ann is a general partner, and Betty and Carla are limited partners. Assume each of the separate events below were to take place. Discuss fully which acts constitute a dissolution of the limited partnership.

(a) Betty assigns her partnership interest to Diana.
(b) Carla is petitioned into involuntary bankruptcy.
(c) Ann dies.

4. Able and Baker form a limited partnership to operate a retail jewelry business. Able is the general partner and Baker the limited partner. The certificate of partnership does not specify a definite term for the partnership existence. Able and Baker disagree over the management of the business by Able. Baker demands, in writing, the return of his contribution. Discuss fully the following:

(a) Can a limited partner dissolve the partnership?
(b) If the limited partnership is dissolved, who has authority to wind up the affairs of the partnership?

5. Able and Baker form a limited partnership, with Able as the general partner. During the existence of the partnership, Able's contribution of capital is $2,000, and Baker's is $50,000. The limited partnership is dissolved, and the sale of partnership assets in winding up the partnership

affairs results in proceeds of $100,000. Partnership creditors have claims totaling $45,000, and the profit accounts of Able and Baker are $5,000 each. Discuss the priorities to the $100,000.

6. In a limited partnership having one general partner, the general partner loaned over $1 million to the partnership and executed notes payable to herself. The limited partner knew that these notes were carried as outstanding debts on the partnership books for seven years. When the general partner died, the limited partner maintained that the partnership agreement did not authorize the general partner to borrow money and that the $1 million-plus constituted a contribution to capital rather than loans. How did the court treat the money? [Park Cities Corp. v. Byrd, 522 S.W.2d 572 (Tex.Civ.App. 1975)]

7. The Ponderosa Land Company was a properly established limited partnership whose members were Harold Brown, Walter Brown, and W. D. Blaster. The Browns were general partners, and Blaster was the sole limited partner. His only contribution to the firm was start-up capital of $50,000. After a number of years of successful operation, Blaster decided to withdraw from the firm since he was badly in need of cash. He requested that the partnership return his capital contribution. Is the partnership dissolved? [Brown v. Brown, 15 Ariz.App. 333, 488 P.2d 689 (1971)]

8. Fidelity Lease Limited, a limited partnership, had over twenty limited partners and one general partner. The general partner was a corporation, Interlease Corporation, and was managed by Sanders, Kahn, and Crombie, all three of whom happened to be limited partners of Fidelity Lease Limited. Assuming that in Texas, where this partnership was established, corporations are allowed to be partners in a limited partnership, what will the liability of Sanders, Kahn, and Crombie be in a suit against Fidelity Lease Limited? Will their liability be limited? [Delaney v. Fidelity Lease Limited, 526 S.W.2d 543 (1975)]

9. The Sports Factory, Inc. executed a lease with Ridley Park Associates, a limited partnership, to operate a health and racquetball club. William Chanoff was the general partner of Ridley Park Associates. Over several months Ridley Park failed to meet the original agreement with Sports Factory, Inc., including the altering of architectural plans for the racquetball courts and the failure to acquire the zoning changes needed for operation of a health spa. If Sports Factory would bring a cause of action for breach of their agreement with Ridley Park, who would be liable? [Sports Factory, Inc. v. Chanoff, 586 F.Supp. 342 (E.D.Pa. 1984)]

38

CORPORATIONS
Nature &
Classifications

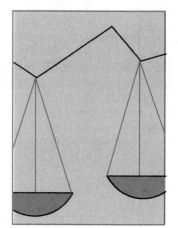

A BRIEF HISTORY
OF THE CORPORATION

The corporation can be owned by a single person, or it can have hundreds, thousands, or even millions of shareholders. The shareholder form of business organization developed in Europe at the end of the seventeenth century. The firms were called joint stock companies, and they frequently collapsed because their organizers absconded with the funds or proved to be incompetent.

The most famous collapse involved the South Sea Company, which assumed England's national debt in 1711 and obtained in return a monopoly over British trade with the South Sea Islands in South America plus an annual interest payment. The shares of the company were driven up by speculation, fraud was exposed, and a collapse followed. The event came to be known as the South Sea Bubble, and it led to the Bubble Act of 1720, a law that curtailed the use of joint stock companies in England for over a hundred years. Because of this history of fraud and collapse, organizations resembling corporations were regarded with suspicion in the United States during its early years.

In the eighteenth century, a typical U.S. corporation was a municipality. Although several business corporations were formed after the Revolution-

ary War, it was not until the nineteenth century that the corporation came into common use for private business. In 1811, New York passed a general incorporation law allowing businesses to incorporate. Incorporation was permissible by five or more persons for the manufacture of textiles, glass, metals, and paint. The corporation could have capital of only $100,000 and a life of twenty years.

The significance of the New York law was that it allowed voluntary incorporation using standard bureaucratic procedures rather than special acts of the legislature, which were usually available only to businesspersons with political influence. By the mid-nineteenth century, railroads predominated among corporations. After the Civil War, manufacturing corporations became numerous.

THE CORPORATION AS
A CREATURE OF STATUTE

The corporation is a creature of statute. Its existence depends generally upon state law, although some corporations, especially public organizations, can be created under federal law. Each state has its own body of corporate law, and these laws are not entirely uniform. The Model Business Corporation Act (often called the Model Act) is a codification of modern

643

corporation law. It enunciates principles of corporate law that have been adopted to some degree or another by every state. (See Appendix G for the complete text of the Model Business Corporation Act.)

The Model Business Corporation Act and the Revised Model Business Corporation Act

The Model Business Corporation Act (MBCA) was originally patterned after the Illinois Business Corporation Act of 1933. It was first published in its complete form in 1933 by the Committee on Corporate Laws of the American Bar Association. Since 1933, the act has undergone several changes and was subsequently revised and renumbered in 1969.

As could be expected, modern business has changed dramatically over the last fifteen years. The 1969 act has undergone revisions over the years and the Committee on Corporate Laws decided that all provisions of the act should be revised so that its language would be internally consistent and uniform.

The Revised Model Business Corporation Act (RMBCA), as approved in June, 1984, was drafted as a convenient guide for revision of state business corporation acts. It was designed for use by both publicly held and closely held corporations and includes provisions for the rights and duties of shareholders, management, and directors. (Selected sections of the RMBCA have been included as Appendix H illustration. Already a number of states have amended their corporation laws, to a limited degree, based on the RMBCA.)

Neither the 1969 act nor the 1984 act has been totally adopted by any state in its current form. However, the 1969 act has been influential in codification of corporation statutes in more than thirty-seven states[1] and the District of Columbia. It should be kept in mind, however, that there is considerable variation among the statutes of the states that have

---

used the Model Act for a basis for their statutes. Because of this, individual state corporation laws should be relied upon rather than the MBCA.

THE NATURE OF A CORPORATION

A **corporation** is a legal entity created and recognized by state law. It can consist of one or more *natural* persons identified under a common name.

The Corporation as a Legal "Person"

A corporation is recognized under state and federal law as a "person," and it enjoys many, but not all, of the same rights and privileges that U.S. citizens enjoy.

The Bill of Rights guarantees a "person," as a citizen, certain protections, and corporations are considered citizens in most instances. For example, a corporation has the same right as a natural person to equal protection of the laws under the Fourteenth Amendment. It has the right of access to the courts as an entity that can sue or be sued. It also has the right of due process before denial of life, liberty, or property, as well as freedom from unreasonable search and seizures and from double jeopardy.

Under the First Amendment, corporations are entitled to freedom of speech;[2] however, only the corporation's individual officers and employees possess the Fifth Amendment right against self-incrimination.[3] In addition, the privilege and immunities clause of the federal Constitution (Article 4, Section 2) does not protect corporations nor does it protect an unincorporated association.[4]

An unsettled area of corporation law has to do with the criminal acts of a corporation. It is obvious that a corporation cannot be sent to prison even though, under law, it is a person. Most courts hold a corporation that has violated the criminal statutes liable for fines. Where criminal conduct can be attributed to corporate officers or agents, those individuals, as natural persons, are held liable and can be imprisoned for their acts.

---

1. Alaska, Alabama, Arizona, Arkansas, Colorado, Connecticut, Florida, Georgia, Idaho, Iowa, Kentucky, Louisiana, Maine, Maryland, Massachusetts, Michigan, Mississippi, Montana, Nebraska, New Jersey, New Mexico, New York, North Carolina, North Dakota, Oregon, Rhode Island, South Carolina, South Dakota, Tennessee, Texas, Utah, Vermont, Virginia, Washington, West Virginia, Wisconsin, Wyoming.

2. First National Bank of Boston v. Bellotti, 435 U.S. 765, 98 S.Ct. 1407 (1978).
3. United States v. Barth, 745 F.2d 184 (2nd Cir. 1984).
4. W.C.M. Window Co., Inc., v. Bernardi, 730 F.2d 486 (7th Cir. 1984).

Characteristics of the Corporate Entity

A corporation is an artificial person, with its own corporate name, owned by individual shareholders. It is a legal entity with rights and responsibilities. The corporation substitutes itself for its shareholders in conducting corporate business and in incurring liability. Its authority to act and the liability for its actions are separate and apart from the individuals who own it, although in certain limited situations the "corporate veil" can be pierced (that is, liability for the corporation's obligations can be extended to shareholders). In some instances, shareholders can voluntarily make themselves personally liable for some or all of the debts of the corporation. This is particularly true with smaller corporations that attempt to obtain financing.

Responsibility for overall management of the corporation is entrusted to a board of directors, which is elected by shareholders.[5] Corporate officers and other employees are hired by the board of directors to run the daily business operations of the corporation.

The following sections briefly discuss the relationships and responsibilities of the shareholders, the board of directors, the officers, and the employees in the management of the corporation. More detail will be found in Chapter 41.

Shareholders   The acquisition of a share of stock makes a person an owner or shareholder in a corporation. Unlike the members in a partnership, the body of shareholders can change constantly without affecting the continued existence of the corporation. Thus, a corporation is not affected by the death of a shareholder, whereas the death of a partner would dissolve a partnership.

As a general rule, a shareholder is not personally liable for the corporation's business debts; nor is the corporation responsible for a shareholder's personal debts. Each shareholder's liability is limited to the amount of the investment (that is, the money actually paid when the stock was acquired).[6]

Thus, if Paul Ginsberg purchases one hundred shares of Ace Manufacturing stock at $1 per share, and Ace Manufacturing goes bankrupt owing creditors millions of dollars, Ginsberg's loss is limited to the $100 purchase price that he originally paid for the shares. The converse is also true. If Ginsberg declares bankruptcy and owes creditors thousands of dollars, Ace Manufacturing Company is not liable, and the creditors can claim only the one hundred shares of stock.

Shareholders have no legal title to corporate property vested in the corporation, such as buildings and equipment. They have only an *equitable* interest in the corporation.

A shareholder can sue the corporation, and the corporation can sue a shareholder. The shareholder's derivative suit and the special responsibility of majority shareholders of the corporation will be discussed in the next two chapters. Briefly, a **derivative suit** is an action by a shareholder to enforce a corporate cause of action. It occurs when the action is based upon a primary right of a corporation but is asserted on its behalf by the stockholder because of the corporation's failure, deliberate or otherwise, to act upon the primary right.

Shareholders are owners without direct control over the management of the corporation's business. Only through the election of the board of directors can they exercise influence over corporate policy. They are neither managers nor agents of the corporation. In a partnership, on the other hand, general partners have control and responsibility for the management of the business, and each partner is an agent who can bind all other partners in the course of business.

Board of Directors   A general rule in corporate law says, "Directors must direct the corporate business affairs." The board of directors is elected by shareholders and is periodically accountable to them for reelection.

The board is responsible for making decisions about overall policy. Directors declare dividends, authorize major corporate contracts, appoint or remove officers and set their salaries, issue authorized shares of stock, and recommend changes in the corporate charter. They delegate the day-to-day operation of corporate affairs to the officers and other employees of the corporation. The board can organize itself into executive committees and delegate to these committees particular responsibilities to act on behalf of the entire board or to report back to it. Then, it acts as a unit.

---

5.   MBCA, Section 35, and RMBCA, Section 8.01.
6.   MBCA, Section 25, and RMBCA, Section 6.22.

Officers and Other Employees   Officers are agents of the corporation. They answer to the board of directors rather than to the shareholders directly, and they can be removed at any time by the board.

Tax Considerations   Since a corporation is a separate legal entity, corporate profits are taxed by the state and federal governments. Corporations can do one of two things with corporate profits—retain them or pass them on to shareholders in the form of dividends. The corporation receives no tax deduction for dividends distributed to shareholders.

When dividends are money payments, they are again taxable (except when they represent distributions of capital) as ordinary income to the shareholder receiving them. This double taxation feature of the corporate organization is one of its major disadvantages. On the other hand, retained earnings, if invested properly, will yield higher corporate profits in the future and thus cause the price of the company's stock to rise. Individual shareholders can then reap the benefits of these retained earnings in the gains they receive when they sell their shares. These gains are treated for tax purposes as capital gains.

DOMESTIC, FOREIGN, AND ALIEN CORPORATIONS

Except for alien corporations, corporations are incorporated in a particular state. The corporation is referred to as a **domestic corporation** by its home state (the state in which it incorporates). A corporation formed in one state but doing business in another is referred to in that other state as a **foreign corporation.** A corporation formed in another country, say Mexico, doing business within the United States is referred to in the United States as an **alien corporation.**

A foreign corporation does not have an automatic right to do business in a state other than its state of incorporation. It must obtain a *certificate of authority* in the states where it plans to do business. Usually, the process of obtaining a certificate is a mere formality, but often the foreign corporation must comply with standards of financial responsibility before the certificate will be issued.

Should a foreign corporation actually do business without obtaining a certificate, the state can fine it, deny it the privilege of using state courts, and even hold its officers, directors, or agents personally liable for corporate obligations incurred in that state.[7]

Once the certificate has been issued, the powers conferred upon a corporation by its home state generally can be exercised in the other state. Numerous states have specific laws designed to regulate foreign corporations. One such law is the requirement that foreign corporations maintain a registered office or agent (address) in the state. One of the purposes of such a statute is to provide a place to serve process in the event of a suit against the corporation. Frequently, state laws governing corporations apply equally to domestic and foreign corporations. However, when these statutes relate to internal corporate affairs, they normally do not apply to foreign corporations.

Some jurisdictions require a foreign corporation to post a bond before the corporation is permitted to do business. This bond is intended to insure the performance of the foreign corporation's contracts within the state.

Frequently, the biggest issue in dealing with foreign corporations is whether such corporations are actually doing business within the state. A single transaction or the mere presence of the corporation's product in the state or contacts with the state may not be enough to constitute doing business there.

Before a state court can hear a dispute in which a foreign corporation is the defendant, the state court must have *jurisdiction* over the defendant. A state court only has jurisdiction over foreign corporations which have sufficient *contacts* with the state. A foreign corporation which has its home office within the state or has manufacturing plants in the state meets this "contacts" requirement. A foreign corporation whose only contact with the state is the fact that one of its directors resides there does not have sufficient contact with the state for the state court to exercise jurisdiction over it.

The following landmark case established the modern view of jurisdiction over foreign corporations.

---

7.   Robertson v. Levy, 197 A.2d 443 (D.C. Ct. of App. 1964).

BACKGROUND AND FACTS *The State of Washington sought to collect unemployment contributions from International Shoe based on commissions paid by the corporation to its Washington-based salespeople. International Shoe was asserting that its activities within the State of Washington were not sufficient to manifest its "presence" there and thus the state courts could not constitutionally exercise jurisdiction over it.*

INTERNATIONAL SHOE CO v. WASHINGTON
United States Supreme Court, 1945.
326 U.S. 310, 66 S.Ct. 154.

Mr. Chief Justice STONE delivered the opinion of the Court.
* * * *

The facts as found by the appeal tribunal and accepted by the state Superior Court and Supreme Court, are not in dispute. Appellant is a Delaware corporation, having its principal place of business in St. Louis, Missouri, and is engaged in the manufacture and sale of shoes and other footwear. It maintains places of business in several states, other than Washington, at which its manufacturing is carried on. * * *

Appellant has no office in Washington and makes no contracts either for sale or purchase of merchandise there. It maintains no stock of merchandise in that state and makes there no deliveries of goods in intrastate commerce. During the years from 1937 to 1940, now in question, appellant employed eleven to thirteen salesmen under direct supervision and control of sales managers located in St. Louis. These salesmen resided in Washington; their principal activities were confined to that state; and they were compensated by commissions based upon the amount of their sales. The commissions for each year totaled more than $31,000. Appellant supplies its salesmen with a line of samples, each consisting of one shoe of a pair which they display to prospective purchasers. On occasion they rent permanent sample rooms, for exhibiting samples, in business buildings, or rent rooms in hotels or business buildings temporary for that purpose. The cost of such rentals is reimbursed by appellant.

The authority of the salesmen is limited to exhibiting their samples and soliciting orders from prospective buyers at prices and on terms fixed by appellant. * * * No salesman has authority to enter into contracts or to make collections.
* * * *

Appellant also insists that its activities within the state were not sufficient to manifest its "presence" there and that in its absence the state courts were without jurisdiction, that consequently it was a denial of due process for the state to subject appellant to suit. * * * And appellant further argues that since it was not present within the state, it is a denial of due process to subject it to taxation or other money exaction. It thus denies the power of the state to lay the tax or to subject appellant to a suit for its collection.

Historically the jurisdiction of courts to render judgment in personam is grounded on their *de facto* power over the defendant's person. Hence his presence within the territorial jurisdiction of a court was prerequisite to its rendition of a judgment personally binding him. * * * But now that the *capias ad respondendum* has given way to personal service of summons or other form of notice, due process requires only that in order to subject a defendant to a judgment in personam, if he be not present within the territory of the forum, he have certain minimum contacts with it such that the maintenance of the suit does not offend "traditional notions of fair play and substantial justice." * * *
* * * *

It is evident that the criteria by which we mark the boundary line between those activities which justify the subjection of a corporation to suit, and those which do not, cannot be simply mechanical or quantitative. * * * Whether due process is satisfied must depend rather upon the quality and nature of the activity in relation to the fair and orderly administration of the laws which it was the purpose of the due process clause to insure. * * *

But to the extent that a corporation exercises the privilege of conducting activities within a state, it enjoys the benefits and protection of the laws of that state. The exercise of that privilege may give rise to obligations; and, so far as those obligations arise out of or are connected with the activities within the state, a procedure which requires the corporation to respond to a suit brought to enforce them can, in most instances, hardly be said to be undue. * * *

Applying these standards, the activities carried on in behalf of appellant in the State of Washington were neither irregular nor casual. They were systematic and continuous throughout the years in question. They resulted in a large volume of interstate business, in the course of which appellant received the benefits and protection of the laws of the state, including the right to resort to the courts for the enforcement of its rights. The obligation which is here sued upon arose out of those very activities. It is evident that these operations establish sufficient contacts or ties with the state of the forum to make it reasonable and just according to our traditional conception of fair play and substantial justice to permit the state to enforce the obligations which appellant has incurred there. * * *

* * * *

DECISION AND REMEDY   *In finding that International Shoe had minimum contacts with the State of Washington, the Supreme Court affirmed the Supreme Court of Washington.*

COMMENTS   *The Supreme Court, in* International Shoe, *established a new test for jurisdiction over foreign corporations. In order for a state to exercise jurisdiction constitutionally over a foreign corporation, the corporation must have minimum contacts with the forum state. Several subsequent Supreme Court cases have dealt with the limits of "minimum contacts." (See* McGee v. International Life Insurance Co., *355 U.S. 220 [1957]; and* Hanson v. Denckla, *357 U.S. 235 [1958].)*

PUBLIC AND PRIVATE CORPORATIONS

A public corporation is one formed by the government to meet some political or governmental purpose. Cities and towns that incorporate are common examples. In addition, many federal government organizations, such as the U.S. Postal Service, the Tennessee Valley Authority, and Amtrak, are public corporations.

Private corporations are created either wholly or in part for private benefit. Most corporations are private. Private corporations can serve a public purpose, such as a public utility does, but they are nonetheless owned by private persons rather than the government.

NONPROFIT CORPORATIONS

Some corporations are formed without a profit-making purpose. These are called nonprofit, not-for-profit, or eleemosynary (charitable) corporations. They are usually (although not necessarily) private corporations. They can be used in conjunction with an ordinary corporation to facilitate making contracts with the government. Private hospitals, educational institutions, charities, religious organizations, and the like are frequently organized as nonprofit (not-for-profit) corporations.

Although shares of stock can be issued, dividends are not paid to the members. Formation of nonprofit corporations often follows state statutes that are based on the Model Nonprofit Corporation Act. At least eleven states plus the District of Columbia have adopted this act (or a modified form of it). In any event, the corporation statutes provide for the organization of nonprofit corporations in much the same way that other types of corporations are formed. The nonprofit corporation is a convenient form of organization that allows various groups to own property and to form contracts without the individual members being personally exposed to liability.

CLOSE CORPORATIONS

This section deals with close corporations—more often referred to as closed corporations, closely held corporations, family corporations, or privately held corporations. A close corporation is one whose shares are closely held by members of a family or by relatively few persons. Usually, the members of the small group that is involved in a close corporation are personally known to each other. Because there is such a small number of shareholders, there is no trading market for the shares. In practice, a close corporation is often operated like a partnership. A few states recognize this in the special statutory provisions that cover close corporations.

Close Corporation Statutes

In order to be eligible for close corporation status, a corporation has to have a limited number of shareholders, the transfer of corporation stock must be subject to certain restrictions, and the corporation must not make any public offering of its securities.[8] Close corporation statutes provide greater flexibility by expressly permitting electing corporations to vary significantly from traditional corporation law.[9]

Management

The close corporation has a single shareholder or a closely knit group of shareholders who usually hold the positions of directors and officers. The manage-

ment of a close corporation resembles that of a sole proprietorship or a partnership. In the eyes of the law, however, it is still a corporation and must meet the same legal requirements as other corporations subject to the special statutes mentioned previously. In states where special statutes have not been enacted, close corporations have sometimes had to circumvent the law.

Consider an example where a state law requires that a corporation have two directors, and a close corporation has only one shareholder. In the articles of incorporation, the number of directors can be set at two, but the corporation can operate with a permanent vacancy on the board of directors. Alternatively, a disinterested person, usually a friend, can be convinced to put his or her name down as director.

Transfer of Shares

Since, by definition, a close corporation has a small number of shareholders, the transfer of shares of one shareholder to someone else can cause serious management problems. In other words, the other shareholders can find themselves required to share control with someone they may not know or like. To avoid this problem, it is usually advisable for the close corporation with several shareholders to specify restrictions on the transferability of stock in its articles of incorporation.

Consider an example. Tom, Dick, and Harry Smith are the only shareholders of Smith Boat Company. Tom and Dick Smith do not want Harry to sell his shares to an unknown third person. The articles of incorporation might therefore restrict the transferability of shares to outside persons. For example, the articles might stipulate that shareholders offer their shares to the corporation or other shareholders before going to an outside purchaser.

Another way that control of a close corporation can be stabilized is through the use of a shareholder agreement. Agreements among shareholders to vote their stock in a particular way are generally upheld.[10] Shareholder agreements can also provide that when one of the original shareholders dies, his or her shares of stock in the corporation will be divided in

---

8. See, for example, 8 Del. Code Annotated, Section 342. This section provides that electing corporations must have a maximum limitation on the number of shareholders, not exceeding thirty.
9. For example, in some states (such as Maryland), the close corporation need not have a board of directors.

---

10. Ringling Bros.-Barnum and Bailey Combined Shows v. Ringling, 53 A.2d 441, 29 Del.Ch. 610 (1947).

such a way that the proportionate holdings of the survivors, and thus their proportionate control, will be maintained.

The following case deals with the enforcement of a provision of a shareholder agreement.

GALLER v. GALLER

Supreme Court of Illinois, 1965.
32 Ill.2d 16, 203 N.E.2d 577.

BACKGROUND AND FACTS   *Benjamin and Isadore Galler were brothers and 50 percent shareholders in a wholesale drug business that was incorporated under Illinois law as the Galler Drug Company.*

The corporation prospered, and in July 1955 Benjamin and Isadore and their wives entered into a carefully drafted agreement among themselves and the corporation. The written agreement purported to provide that, in the event of the death of either brother, the corporation would provide income for the support and maintenance of his immediate family. In addition, the family of the deceased brother would have equal control over the corporation.

Benjamin died in 1957. Shortly thereafter, his widow, Emma, requested that Isadore, the surviving brother, comply with the terms of the 1955 agreement. Isadore refused to cooperate. Emma sued, seeking specific performance of the 1955 agreement. The trial court agreed with Emma, holding that the shareholder agreement was valid. The intermediate appellate court subsequently held that the 1955 agreement was void on the ground of public policy. The Illinois Supreme Court reviewed the case.

UNDERWOOD, Justice.

*   *   *   *

The power to invalidate the agreements on the grounds of public policy is so far reaching and so easily abused that it should be called into action to set aside or annul the solemn engagement of parties dealing on equal terms only in cases where the corrupt or dangerous tendency clearly and unequivocally appears upon the face of the agreement itself or is the necessary inference from the matters which are expressed, and the only apparent exception to this general rule is to be found in those cases where the agreement, though fair and unobjectionable on its face, is a part of a corrupt scheme and is made to disguise the real nature of the transaction.

*   *   *   *

At this juncture it should be emphasized that we deal here with a so-called close corporation. Various attempts at definition of the close corporation have been made. For our purposes, a close corporation is one in which the stock is held in a few hands, or in a few families, and wherein it is not at all, or only rarely, dealt in by buying or selling. Moreover, it should be recognized that shareholder agreements similar to that in question here are often, as a practical consideration, quite necessary for the protection of those financially interested in the close corporation. While the shareholder of a public-issue corporation may readily sell his shares on the open market should management fail to use, in his opinion, sound business judgment, his counterpart of the close corporation often has a large total of his entire capital invested in the business and has no ready market for his shares should he desire to sell. He feels, understandably, that he is more than a mere investor and that his voice should be heard concerning all corporate activity. Without a shareholder agreement, specifically enforceable by the courts, insuring him a modicum of control, a large minority shareholder might find himself at the mercy of an oppressive or unknowledgeable majority. Moreover, as in the case at bar, the shareholders of a close corporation are often also the directors and officers thereof. With substantial shareholding interests abiding in each member of the board of directors, it is often quite impossible to secure, as in the large public-issue corporation, independent board judgment free from personal motivations concerning corporate policy. For these and other reasons too voluminous to enumerate here, often the only sound basis for protection is afforded by a lengthy, detailed shareholder agreement securing the rights and obligations of all concerned.

* * * *

The Appellate Court correctly found many of the contractual provisions free from serious objection, and we need not prolong this opinion with a discussion of them here. That court did, however, find difficulties in the stated purpose of the agreement as it relates to its duration, the election of certain persons to specific offices for a number of years, the requirement for the mandatory declaration of stated dividends (which the Appellate Court held invalid), and the salary continuation agreement.

* * * While limiting voting trusts in 1947 to a maximum duration of 10 years, the [Illinois State] legislature has indicated no similar policy regarding straight voting agreements although these have been common since prior to 1870. In view of the history of decisions of this court generally upholding, in the absence of fraud or prejudice to minority interests or public policy, the right of stockholders to agree among themselves as to the manner in which their stock will be voted, we do not regard the period of time within which this agreement may remain effective as rendering the agreement unenforceable.

The clause that provides for the election of certain persons to specified offices for a period of years likewise does not require invalidation.

We turn next to a consideration of the effect of the stated purpose of the agreement upon its validity. The pertinent provision is: "The said Benjamin A. Galler and Isadore A. Galler desire to provide income for the support and maintenance of their immediate families." Obviously, there is no evil inherent in a contract entered into for the reason that the persons originating the terms desired to so arrange their property as to provide post-death support for those dependent upon them. Nor does the fact that the subject property is corporate stock alter the situation so long as there exists no detriment to minority stock interests, creditors or other public injury.

The Illinois Supreme Court held that the provisions of the shareholder agreement were enforceable.

DECISION AND REMEDY

SUBCHAPTER S CORPORATIONS

Certain corporations can choose to qualify under Subchapter S of the Internal Revenue Code to avoid the imposition of income taxes at the corporate level while retaining all the advantages of a corporation, particularly limited legal liability. In 1982, Congress enacted the Subchapter S Revision Act, the purpose of which was "to minimize the effect of Federal income taxes on choices of the form of business organizations and to permit the incorporation and operation of certain small businesses without the incidence of income taxation at both the corporated and shareholder level." [11]

Additionally, Congress decreed that all corporations are divided into two groups: S Corporations (formerly Subchapter S Corporations) which have elected Subchapter S treatment, and C Corporations, which are all other corporations.

While the S Corporation has the advantages of the corporate form without the double taxation of income (corporate income is not taxed separately),

---

11.   Senate Committee Report No. 97-640.

it does have some disadvantages. One of the most important disadvantages relates to the amount of income that can be placed in pension plans that permit corporate shareholders to shelter income from personal federal income taxes.

Requirements for S Corporation Qualification

There are numerous requirements for S Corporation qualification. The following are some of the more important:

1.   The corporation must be a domestic corporation.
2.   The corporation must not be a member of an affiliated group of corporations.
3.   The shareholders of the corporation must be either individuals, estates, or certain trusts that are treated as owned by an individual who is a citizen or resident of the United States. Corporations and partnerships cannot be shareholders.
4.   The corporation must have thirty-five or fewer shareholders.
5.   The corporation can have only two classes of stock. Not all shareholders need have the same voting rights.
6.   The corporation must not derive more than 20 percent of its gross receipts from passive investment income.
7.   No shareholder of the corporation can be a nonresident alien.

Benefits of S Corporation Election

At times it is beneficial for a regular corporation to elect S Corporation status. The following is a checklist of situations where S Corporation election can be beneficial.

1.   When the corporation has losses, the S election allows the shareholders to use such losses to offset other income.
2.   Whenever the stockholders are in a lower tax bracket than the corporation, the S election causes their entire income to be taxed in the shareholders' bracket, whether or not it is distributed. This is par-

ticularly attractive when the corporation wants to accumulate earnings for some future business purpose.
3.   Taxable income of an S corporation is taxable only to those who are shareholders at the end of the corporate year when that income is distributed.
4.   The S corporation can choose a fiscal year that will permit it to defer some of its shareholders' taxes. This is important because undistributed earnings of the shareholder are not taxed until after the corporation's (not the shareholder's) year.
5.   The shareholder in an S corporation can give some of his or her stock to other members of the family who are in a lower tax bracket.
6.   An S corporation can still offer some tax-free corporate benefits. These fringe benefits can mean federal tax savings to the shareholders.

PROFESSIONAL CORPORATIONS

Professional corporations are relatively new in corporate law. In the past, professional persons such as physicians, lawyers, dentists, and accountants could not incorporate. Today they can, and their corporations are typically called professional service associations or professional corporations. They can be identified by the letters S.C. (service corporation), P.C. (professional corporation), Inc. (incorporated), or P.A. (professional association). In general, a professional corporation is formed like an ordinary business corporation.

The professional corporation equalized the tax burden on professionals who, due to their ethical principles, could not incorporate their businesses. However, by 1981, this form of enterprise had come to be widely viewed as permitting unacceptable tax avoidance through many areas including the use of "defined benefit" pension plans. Since 1981, however, stringent limitations exacted by Congress have helped stop the growth of professional corporations and eliminate the tax loopholes available to those who formed this type of corporation.

State statutes regarding the operations of corporations have been applied to professional corporations. The following case illustrates the application of New York Corporate Law to a professional corporation.

BACKGROUND AND FACTS   *Plaintiffs Saxe, Bacon and Bolan brought suit against Martindale-Hubbell, Inc. for violation of New York's Donnelly Act, which prohibits contracts, agreements, arrangements, or combinations that establish a monopoly or restrain the free exercise of competition in any business, trade, or commerce. Saxe, Bacon and Bolan is a New York professional legal service corporation. Martindale-Hubbell, Inc., the defendant, is a Delaware corporation with its principal place of business in New Jersey. Martindale publishes a Law Directory that rates various law firms from a high of "a" to a low of "c". Only firms with "a" or "b" ratings are included in a Biographical Section that publishes the "professional cards" of the law offices. Saxe, Bacon and Bolan were not listed in the Biographical Section and filed suit in a state court. Martindale sought to move the action to a federal district court, claiming Saxe was a corporation for diversity of citizenship purposes. The federal district court held it had jurisdiction and gave Martindale a summary judgment dismissing Saxe's action. Saxe appealed.*

SAXE, BACON AND BOLAN, P.C. v. MARTINDALE-HUBBELL, INC.

United States Court of Appeals
Second Circuit, 1983.
710 F.2d 87.

VAN GRAAFEILAND, Circuit Judge.

* * * *

Saxe, Bacon says that the district court's decision not to remand this suit was in error, since, in Saxe, Bacon's view, professional corporations must be treated as partnerships for diversity purposes. We disagree. For purposes of removal under section 1441(a), a corporation is deemed a citizen of any State by which it has been incorporated and of the State where it has its principal place of business. 28 U.S.C. § 1332(c). Whether Saxe, Bacon, a New York firm, is a corporation for diversity purposes must be determined by New York law. * * *

* * * *

Saxe, Bacon was organized under Article 15 of the New York Business Corporation Law. * * * Article 15 was enacted to permit professionals "to utilize the corporate form of business to permit them to organize their activities more efficiently and to make available to them and to their employees Federal tax benefits now accorded to executives and employees in all other business endeavors." * * * Although the ethical and professional obligations which individual shareholders of professional corporations owe their clients preclude the grant to them of all the benefits of incorporation, * * * except as so limited, the provisions of New York's Business Corporation Law applicable to ordinary business corporations are also applicable to professional corporations. * * * Saxe, Bacon is a corporation under New York Law and is therefore a citizen of New York for purposes of 28 U.S.C. § 1332(c).

* * * *

The court determined that Saxe, Bacon and Bolan was a corporation under New York law for purposes of diversity jurisdiction, and affirmed the district court's judgment denying damages to Saxe, Bacon and Bolan.

DECISION AND REMEDY

Liability of Members

Subject to certain exceptions, the shareholders of a professional corporation have limited liability. There are three basic areas of liability that deserve brief attention:

1. Malpractice of a member.
2. Ordinary tort committed by other members.
3. Shareholder liability for his or her own torts.

Malpractice of a Member   The liability of a shareholder in a professional association for the malpractice of another member is not clear. In a partnership, dentists Able, Baker, and Carl are each unlimitedly liable for whatever malpractice liability is incurred by the others within the scope of the partnership. If the three formed a professional corporation, the orthodox corporate law rule would apply, and none of the dentists would be liable for the malpractice of the others. As far as statutory reference to malpractice liability is concerned, a conservative court might interpret the statutory preservation of malpractice liability, thus causing the individual shareholder in a professional association to be liable for the acts of his or her associates as if the professional corporation were a partnership.

Torts Unrelated to Professional Activities   Torts that are not related to malpractice are often treated differently from malpractice. A shareholder in a professional corporation is protected from the liability imposed because of torts committed by other members. If a secretary has been sent from the office to pick up tax forms from the IRS and, in the process,

runs into another car, both the corporation and the secretary will be held liable. Ordinarily, the shareholder in a professional corporation will not be personally liable.

Shareholder Liability   Any shareholder of a professional corporation who engages in a negligent action and who is guilty of malpractice is *personally* liable for the damage caused. Basically, this is the same rule of law that applies to ordinary business corporations. On the other hand, many professional corporation statutes retain personal liability of professional persons for their acts and the professional acts performed under their supervision.

Tax Benefits

The tax benefits of the professional corporation are basically those that apply to all corporations. One of the major benefits is that pension and profit-sharing plans can be set up. These plans are discussed in the next chapter in the section on benefits of incorporating.

QUESTIONS AND CASE PROBLEMS

1. Able, Baker, and Carter are active members of a partnership called Swim City. The partnership manufactures, sells, and installs outdoor swimming pools in the states of Texas and Arkansas. The partners want to continue to be active in management and to expand the business into other states as well. They are concerned about rather large recent judgments being entered against swimming pool companies throughout the United States. Based on these facts only, discuss whether the partnership should incorporate.

2. The Swim City partnership decides to incorporate in the state of Texas under the name of Swim City, Inc. The partners also decide that they want to continue to do business in the state of Arkansas. Later, a man from Oklahoma comes into the corporate office in Texas and purchases an outdoor swimming pool. The swimming pool is shipped to Oklahoma and installed personally by the new owner. Later the owner is injured while swimming in the pool and claims his injury is due entirely to the

defective manufacture of the pool. Discuss fully how the corporation can continue to do business in Arkansas. Also discuss the liability the corporation has in a suit filed by the injured man in an Oklahoma state court.

3. When the partnership of Able, Baker, and Carter decided to form the Texas corporation, Swim City, Inc., it was their desire that the only shareholders be the former partners. Discuss what the partners can and should do to limit the management, ownership, and control to the three of them and still incorporate.

4. Able, Baker, and Carter, as partners of Swim City, decide that they need to incorporate in order to have limited personal liability. However, they wish to avoid double taxation—that is, the corporation paying corporate income taxes on profits and then the shareholders paying personal income taxes on dividends they receive. Discuss whether, upon incorporation, there is any way the partners can avoid paying corporate income taxes without criminal liability.

5. Able, Baker, and Clark are doctors who have formed a partnership. Recently they have become concerned about their individual personal liability in the event of a malpractice suit against one of the doctors or even in the event of ordinary negligence on the part of a doctor in the course of driving his or her personal car to make a

house call. Discuss how the doctors can avoid personal liability from any of these kinds of torts committed by another doctor in the partnership.

6. Leslie R. Barth was president of five corporations. During the course of an IRS investigation for failure to file corporate and personal income tax returns, the IRS served an administrative summons for Barth to turn over prescribed corporate records. Barth only partially complied, and the IRS took Barth to district court. The court ordered the corporations to furnish the requested information and to designate an agent to testify for the corporations "without revoking their personal privileges against self-incrimination." Barth appealed the order, claiming that such an order violated the "agent's" (his) constitutional right against self-incrimination, and that this Fifth Amendment protection extended to the corporations. Discuss whether the corporations possess Fifth Amendment privileges against self-incrimination, and whether Barth's individual officer self-discrimination privilege was denied by the district court's order. [United States v. Barth, 745 F.2d 184 (2nd Cir. 1984)]

7. Pacific Development, Inc., was incorporated in the District of Columbia for the purpose of international brokerage consulting. Pacific's founder, president, and sole shareholder was Tongsun Park, a South Korean who was on close terms with South Korea's president, Park Chung Hee. The government alleged that Park's main purpose was to influence Congress to give economic and military aid to South Korea. The IRS assessed $4.5 million in back taxes against Park in 1977. It then seized the assets of Pacific Development, Inc., claiming that the company was a mere alter ego of Park. Valley Finance, Inc., was another of Park's wholly owned corporations. It had loaned money to Pacific Valley Finance, and it held a second deed of trust on the real property that the IRS had seized. Both Pacific Development and Valley Finance attempted to obtain the return of Pacific Development's assets that the IRS had seized. The plaintiffs claimed that the IRS had improperly pierced the corporate veil of Pacific. Do you agree? [Valley Finance, Inc. v. United States, 629 F.2d 162 (D.C. Cir. 1980)]

8. Michigan-Wisconsin Pipeline Company was a Delaware corporation. It operated a natural gas pipeline that extended through more than a dozen states, including Kentucky. In that state, it had a warehouse as well as a compressor station. Twenty-one individuals were employed by Michigan-Wisconsin to carry on its business in Kentucky. No gas was either acquired or marketed in Kentucky. It simply flowed through a pipeline. The pipeline company claimed that it was exempt from Kentucky regulations because it was not doing business there. Do you agree? [Michigan-Wisconsin Pipeline Co. v. Kentucky, 474 S.W.2d 873 (Ky. 1971)]

39

CORPORATIONS
Formation and
Corporate Financing

Incorporation refers to the procedural mechanics of forming a corporation. The corporation is entirely a creature of statute. Therefore, it must meet the requirements of the state's statutes. Although state statutes differ, their basic requirements for incorporation are similar. This chapter will not only deal with these basic requirements but will discuss pre-incorporation arrangements and activities.

In addition, since corporations need financing to be formed and to continue to exist, this chapter will briefly discuss the various methods, called securities, used to finance corporations.

PROMOTERS' ACTIVITIES

Before a corporation becomes a reality, people invest in the proposed corporation as subscribers, and contracts are frequently made by **promoters** on behalf of the future corporation. Promoters are those who, for themselves or others, take the preliminary steps in organizing a corporation. They issue the prospectus[1] for the proposed organization and secure a charter.

It is not unusual for a promoter to purchase or lease property with a view to selling it to the corporation to be organized. In addition, the promoter enters into contracts with attorneys, accountants, architects, or other professionals whose services will be needed in planning for the proposed corporation. Finally, a promoter induces people to purchase stock in the corporation.

Some interesting legal questions arise in regard to the promoter's activities. The most important problem centers on whether the promoter is personally liable for contracts made on behalf of a corporation that does not yet have any legal existence. In addition, once the corporation is formed, does it assume liability on these contracts, or is the promoter still personally liable?

As a general rule, a promoter is held personally liable on pre-incorporation contracts. Courts simply hold that promoters are not agents where a corporation has yet to come into existence. However, if the promoter secures the contracting party's agreement to hold only the corporation (not the promoter) liable on the contract, the promoter will not be liable in the event of any breach of contract.

Basically, the same rule of personal liability of the promoter continues even after incorporation unless the third party *releases* the promoter. In most states this rule is applied whether or not the promoter

---

1. A prospectus is a document, required by federal or state securities laws and regulations, which contains material facts concerning the financial operations of the corporation, allowing an investor to make an informed decision.

made the agreement in the name of, or with reference to, the proposed corporation.

Once the corporation is formed (the charter issued), the promoter remains personally liable until the corporation assumes the pre-incorporation contract by *novation*. (See Chapter 15). Novation releases the promoter and makes the corporation personally liable for performing the contractual obligations. In some cases the corporation *adopts* the promoter's contract by undertaking to perform it. Most courts hold that adoption in and of itself does not discharge the promoter from contractual liability. Obviously, a corporation cannot normally

ratify a pre-incorporation contract, as there was no principal in existence at the time the contract was made.

Incorporation does not make the corporation automatically liable for pre-incorporation contracts. Until the newly formed corporation consents, the third party cannot enforce the promoter's contract against the corporation.

In the following case, a promoter attempted to limit his liability by showing that the parties contracting with him were in agreement to look solely to the corporation for performance of the contract.

BACKGROUND AND FACTS   *John Goodman, as president of a corporation "in formation," signed a renovation contract with Darden, Doman and Stafford Assoc. (hereafter DDS). During the course of negotiations, Goodman informed Doman, the managing partner of DDS, that he would be forming a corporation in order to limit his liability. A contract was executed in August 1979 between DDS and "BUILDING DESIGN AND DEVELOPMENT INC. (In Formation), John A. Goodman, President." DDS knew the corporation was not yet in existence, and they testified at trial that they never agreed to look solely to the corporation for performance of the contract. The work was to be completed by October 15 and contained an arbitration clause. The work was not completed by October 15 and was allegedly of poor quality. On November 1, Goodman filed articles of incorporation. The corporation license (charter) was issued November 2 under the name of "Building Renovation and Design Consultants, Inc." Between August and December of 1979 DDS made five payments, with the first made out to "Building Design Inc.—John Goodman." Goodman struck out his name and indorsed it in the old corporate name. He instructed all further payments to go to the corporation only. In May 1980 DDS served Goodman with a demand for arbitration. Goodman petitioned the court for a stay from arbitration and an order dismissing him from these proceedings. The trial court dismissed Goodman, as an individual, from the proceedings. DDS appealed and the Court of Appeals reversed the trial court's decision.*

GOODMAN v.
DARDEN, DOMAN
AND STAFFORD
ASSOC.

Supreme Court of Washington,
1983.
670 P.2d 648.

DIMMICK, Justice.

* * * *

The issue in this appeal is whether Goodman, as a promoter, is a party to the preincorporation contract and as such whether he is required to take part in the arbitration. As a general rule

> where a corporation is contemplated but has not yet been organized at the time when a promoter makes a contract for the benefit of the contemplated corporation, the promoter is personally liable on it, even though the contract will also benefit the future corporation.

* * * There is a "strong inference that a person intends to make a present contract with an existing person." * * * *

An exception to the general rule is that if the contracting party knew that the corporation was not in existence at the time of contracting but nevertheless agreed to look solely to the corporation for performance, the promoter is not a party to the contract. * * *

As the proponent of the alleged agreement to look solely to the corporation, Goodman has the burden of proving the agreement. *Johnson* v. *Nasi*, 50 Wash. 2d 87, 309 P. 2d 380 (1957). As with any agreement, release of the promoter depends on the intent of the parties. The parties did not manifest their intentions in the contract. Goodman argues that the language indicating that the corporation was "in formation" was an expression by the parties of their intent to make the corporation alone a party to the contract. * * * The mere signing of a contract with a corporation "in formation" does not suffice to show an agreement to look solely to the corporation. It simply begs the question to say that such language in a contract with a promoter in and of itself constitutes an agreement to release the promoter from the contract. Rather, the language raises the question of the parties' intent. Given the "strong inference" that DDS intended to contract with an existing party, the "in formation" language drafted by Goodman is at best ambiguous as to the parties' intentions.
* * * *

We do not believe the agreement to release a promoter from liability must say in so many words, "I agree to release." Where the promoter cannot show an express agreement, existence of the agreement to release him from liability may be shown by circumstances. Of course, where circumstantial evidence is relied on, the circumstances must be such as to make it reasonably certain that the parties intended to and did enter into the agreement. * * *

Goodman cites *Quaker Hill, Inc.* v. *Parr*, 148 Colo. 45, 364 P. 2d 1056 (1961) and *Sherwood & Roberts-Oregon, Inc.* v. *Alexander, supra*, as cases similiar to this one. The courts in those cases found that the promoter had been released from liability. Among the circumstances considered by those courts was the fact that the parties seeking personal liability on the part of the promoter actually urged that the contract be made in the name of the proposed corporation. DDS did not so urge Goodman or even suggest incorporation to him.

The trial court did not make a written finding that the parties intended to look solely to the corporation for performance. Thus we may look to the oral decision to clarify the theory on which the trial court decided the case. * * * From its oral opinion it is clear that the trial court relied on three considerations in holding that the parties agreed to release Goodman from the contract: (1) DDS knew of the corporation's nonexistence; (2) Goodman told Doman that he was forming a corporation to limit his personal liability; and (3) the progress payments were made to the corporation.

The fact that DDS knew of the corporation's nonexistence is not dispositive in any way of its intent. The rule is that the contracting party may know of the nonexistence of the corporation but nevertheless may agree to look solely to the corporation. The fact that a contracting party knows that the corporation is nonexistent does not indicate any agreement to release the promoter. To the contrary, such knowledge alone would seem to indicate that the members of DDS intended to make Goodman a party to the contract. They could not hold the corporation, a nonexistent entity, responsible and of course they would expect to have recourse against someone (Goodman) if default occurred. This consideration also related to another factor the trial court apparently had in mind—that the members of DDS were all educated people. Goodman argues that as such they should have expressly requested that he be personally liable. This was unnecessary because under the law as set out above, Goodman was liable until the partners of DDS agreed otherwise. Thus, they were not required to specify personal liability.

The fact that Goodman expressed a desire to form the corporation to limit his liability also is not dispositive of the intentions of the members of DDS. * * * Apparently Goodman believed that incorporation would automatically limit his liability thus misunderstanding the rules regarding promoter liability. * * *

The only other evidence of the parties' intent to make the corporation the sole party to the contract is that the progress payments were made payable to the corporation.

However, they were so written only at the instruction of Goodman and in fact the first check written by DDS after the signing of the contract was written to the corporation and Goodman as an individual. This evidence does not show by reasonable certainty that DDS intended to contract only with the corporation. *   *   *

*   *   * From the oral decision it is clear that the court made a finding tht DDS intended to look solely to the corporation as a party to the contract on the items of evidence discussed above. We can uphold this finding of intent only if the evidence supporting it is substantial; we find that it is not.

*   *   *   *

The court determined that the trial court erred in dismissing Goodman from the arbitration proceedings and remanded this case for trial.

DECISION AND REMEDY

Subscribers and Subscriptions

Prior to the actual formation of the corporation, the promoter can contact potential individual investors and they can agree to purchase capital stock in the future corporation. This agreement is often called a subscription agreement, and the potential investor is called a subscriber. Depending on state law, subscribers become shareholders as soon as the corporation is formed or as soon as the corporation accepts the agreement. Thus, if the XYZ Corporation becomes insolvent, the trustee in bankruptcy can collect the consideration for any unpaid stock from a pre-incorporation subscriber.

Most courts view the pre-incorporation subscriptions as continuing offers to purchase corporate stock. On or after its formation, the corporation can choose to accept the offer to purchase. Most courts also treat a subscription as a contract between the subscribers. It is therefore irrevocable except with the consent of *all* of the subscribers. Under Section 17 of the Model Business Corporation Act, a subscription is irrevocable for a period of six months unless otherwise provided in the subscription agreement or unless all the subscribers agree to the revocation of the subscription.[2]

A minority of courts do not follow the Model Act, and in those jurisdictions the pre-incorporation subscriber can revoke the offer to purchase before acceptance without liability.

There are various ways that a promoter can avoid the problem of revocation. One way is to set up a trust with the promoter as trustee and the corporation as beneficiary (under the law of trusts, a beneficiary need not exist at the creation of the trust). Then the promoter-trustee enters a contract with the subscriber. By the terms of the contract, the subscriber promises to buy the stock. If the subscriber fails to subscribe or fails to pay, he or she is liable to the promoter-trustee for breach of contract. Additionally, many statutes permit a forfeiture of partial payments on subscriptions, if later installments are not paid.

A typical problem in pre-incorporation subscription agreement cases arises when the corporation actually formed differs from the corporation in which the subscriber originally agreed to invest. The rule of thumb is that if the departure is minimal (for example, merely a change in name), the agreement is likely to be upheld. But if the change is material (such as entering a different business entirely), the agreement will not be enforced against an unwilling investor. More important problems arise, however, when the corporation is not formed or when it fails after formation.

INCORPORATION

Exact procedures for incorporation differ among states, but the basic requirements are relatively similar.

Incorporation Procedures and Requirements

State Chartering   Since state incorporation laws differ, individuals have found some advantage in looking for the states that offer the most advantageous tax or incorporation provisions. Delaware has historically had the least restrictive laws. Consequently, a significant number of corporations, in-

---

2.   See RMBCA, Section 6.20, for the same irrevocable period.

cluding a number of the largest, have incorporated there. Delaware's statutes permit firms to incorporate in Delaware and carry out business and locate operating headquarters elsewhere. (Most other states now permit this.)

On the other hand, closely held corporations, particularly those of a professional nature, generally incorporate in the state where their principal stockholders live and work. In recent years, a number of policymakers have suggested that the differences among state corporation statutes have led to some undesirable consequences. This has prompted various proposals, including a proposal for federal chartering with a more standardized and restrictive incorporation process.[3]

Articles of Incorporation   The primary document needed to begin the incorporation process is called the charter, the articles, or the certificate of incorporation (see Exhibit 39–1). The articles include basic information about the corporation and serve as a primary source of authority for its future organizational and business functions. The person or persons who execute the articles are called "incorporators." Incorporators will be discussed later in this chapter.

Generally, the following should be included in the articles of incorporation:

1. Corporate name.
2. Nature and purpose.
3. Duration.
4. Capital structure.
5. Internal organization.
6. Registered office and agent.
7. Incorporators.

Corporate Name   Choice of a corporate name is subject to state approval to insure against duplication or deception. Fictitious-name statutes usually require that the secretary of state run a check on the proposed name in the state of incorporation. Once cleared, a name can be reserved for a short time, for a fee, pending the completion of the articles of incorporation. All corporate statutes require the cor-

poration name to include the word *Corporation*, *Incorporated*, *Limited*, or abbreviations of these terms.

Some states require that the name of the corporation be expressed in English letters or characters. States usually require that a corporate name not be the same as, or deceptively similar to, the name of an existing corporation doing business within the state.

For example, if an existing corporation is named General Dynamics, Inc., the state will not allow another corporation to be called General Dynamic, Inc. Not only would that name be deceptive to third parties, but it impliedly transfers a part of the goodwill established by the first corporate user to the second corporation.

Nature and Purpose   The intended business activities of the corporation must be specified in the articles, and naturally, they must be lawful. A general statement of corporate purpose is usually sufficient to give rise to all of the powers necessary or convenient to the purpose of the organization. The corporate charter can state, for example, that the corporation is organized "to engage in the production and sale of agricultural products." There is a trend toward allowing corporate charters to state that the corporation is organized for any legal business with no mention of specifics.

Some states have prohibitions against the incorporation of certain professionals, such as doctors or lawyers, except pursuant to a professional incorporation statute. In some states, certain industries, such as banks, insurance companies, or public utilities, cannot be operated in the general corporate form and are governed by special incorporation statutes.

Duration   A corporation can have perpetual existence under most state corporate statutes. However, a few states prescribe a maximum duration after which the corporation must formally renew its existence.

Capital Structure   The capital structure of the corporation is generally set forth in the articles. A few state statutes require a minimum capital investment (for example, $1,000) for ordinary business corporations, while those engaged in insurance or banking can be required to have a greater capital investment. The number of shares of stock authorized for issuance, their par value, the various types or classes of

---

3.   See, for example, Symposium, Federal Chartering of Corporations, 61 GEO.L.J. 71 (1972); Carey, Federalism and Corporate Law: Reflections upon Delaware, 83 YALE L.J. 663 (1974).

EXHIBIT 39–1 Articles Of Incorporation (Minimum Requirements) For the Hypothetical State Of New Pacum

ARTICLE ONE

The name of the corporation is _____.

ARTICLE TWO

The period of its duration is perpetual (may be a number of years or until a certain date).

ARTICLE THREE

The purpose or purposes for which the corporation is organized are _____
_____ .

ARTICLE FOUR

The aggregate number of shares that the corporation shall have authority to issue is _____ of the par value of _____ dollars each (or without par value).

ARTICLE FIVE

The corporation will not commence business until it has received for the issuance of its shares consideration of the value of $1,000 (can be any sum not less than $1,000).

ARTICLE SIX

The address of the corporation's registered office is _____ , New Pacum and the name of its registered agent at such address is _____ . (Use the street or building or rural route address of the registered office, not a post office box number.)

ARTICLE SEVEN

The number of initial directors is _____ , and the names and addresses of the directors are _____ .

ARTICLE EIGHT

The name and address of the incorporator is _____
_____ .

(signed) _____
                    Incorporator

Sworn to on _____ by the above-named incorporator.
            (date)

_____
Notary Public _____County, New Pacum

(Notary Seal)

---

stock authorized for issuance, and other relevant information concerning equity, capital, and credit must be outlined in those provisions of the articles. The range of possibilities is discussed later in this chapter.

Internal Organization Whatever the internal management structure of the corporation, it should be described in the articles, although it can be included in bylaws adopted after the corporation is formed. The articles of incorporation commence the corporation; the bylaws are formed after commencement by the board of directors.

Bylaws are subject to and cannot conflict with the incorporation statute or the corporation's charter. Section 27 of the Model Act, for example, provides that "the power to alter, amend, or repeal the bylaws or adopt new bylaws shall be vested in the board of directors unless reserved to the shareholders by the articles of incorporation." That section further indicates that the bylaws must be consistent with the articles of incorporation. Typical bylaw provisions describe the quorum and voting requirements for shareholders, the election of the board of directors, the methods of replacing directors, and the manner and time of fixing shareholder and board meetings.

Registered Office and Agent   The corporation must indicate the location and address of its registered office within the state. Usually the registered office is also the principal office of the corporation. The corporation must give the name and address of a specific person who has been designated as an *agent* and who can receive legal documents on behalf of the corporation. These legal documents include service of process.

Incorporators   Each incorporator must be listed by name and must indicate an address. An incorporator is a person (or persons) who applies to the state on behalf of the corporation to obtain its corporate charter. The incorporator need not be a subscriber and need not have any interest at all in the corporation. Many states do not impose residency or age requirements for incorporators. States vary on the required number of incorporators; it can be as few as one or as many as three. Incorporators *must* sign the articles of incorporation when they are submitted to the state; often this is their only duty. In some states, they participate at the first organizational meeting of the corporation.

Certificate of Incorporation   Once the articles of incorporation have been prepared, signed, and authenticated by the incorporators, they are sent to the appropriate state official, usually the secretary of state, along with the appropriate filing fee. In many states, the secretary of state then issues a *certificate of incorporation* representing the state's authorization for the corporation to conduct business. The certificate and a copy of the articles are returned to the incorporators, who then hold the initial organizational meeting that completes the details of incorporation.

First Organizational Meeting   The first organizational meeting is provided for in the articles of incorporation but is held after the charter is actually granted. At this meeting, the incorporators elect the first board of directors and complete the routine business of incorporation (pass bylaws, issue stock,

and so forth). Sometimes, the meeting is held after the election of the board of directors, and the business to be transacted depends upon the requirements of the state's incorporation statute, the nature of the business, the provisions made in the articles, and the desires of the promoters.

Adoption of bylaws is probably the most important function of the first organizational meeting. The bylaws are the internal rules of management for the corporation. The shareholders, directors, and officers must abide by them in conducting corporate business. Unless they have knowledge of the bylaws, corporation employees and third persons dealing with the corporation are not bound by them.

Corporate Status

The procedures for incorporation are very specific. If they are not followed precisely, errors can be made that allow others to challenge the existence of the corporation.

Improper Incorporation   Proper incorporation procedures can become important when, for example, a third person attempts to enforce a contract or bring suit for a tort injury and fortuitously learns of the defect in the incorporation procedure. The plaintiff could then seek to make the would-be shareholders personally liable.

Also, when the corporation seeks to enforce a contract against a defaulting party, if the defaulting party learns of the defective incorporation, he or she may seek to avoid liability on that ground. Courts have developed three theories to prevent the windfall that would occur in giving a contracting party the benefit of the stockholders' personal liability. The theories are *de jure* corporation, *de facto* corporation, and corporation by estoppel.

De Jure Corporation   If there is at least substantial compliance with all conditions precedent to incorporation, the corporation is said to have *de jure* existence in law. In most states the certificate of incorporation is viewed as evidence that all mandatory statutory provisions have been met. This means that the corporation is properly formed, and neither the state nor a third party can attack its existence.

To illustrate, Brown Motor Company, Inc., a domestic corporation, is being sued by a customer, Fred Muris, for an injury sustained at Brown's headquarters. Muris wants to challenge Brown's corporate status because he knows that the personal assets of the owners, Gary and Edward Brown, far exceed the company's assets. Muris discovers that the address of one of the incorporators is incorrectly listed in the articles and argues that this error means that the corporation was improperly formed. Hence it is not a duly authorized corporation and Gary and Edward Brown are personally liable. The law regards such inconsequential procedural defects as substantial compliance, and courts will uphold the *de jure* status of Brown Motor Company. Fred Muris can sue only Brown Motor Company as a corporate entity.

De Facto Corporations   In some situations, there is a defect in compliance with statutory mandates— for example, the expiration of the corporation charter. Under these circumstances, the corporation may have a *de facto* status, and its existence cannot be challenged by third persons (except for the state). The following elements are required for *de facto* status:

1.   There must be a state statute under which the corporation can be incorporated validly.
2.   The parties must have made a *good faith* attempt to comply with the statute.
3.   The enterprise must have already undertaken to do business as a corporation.

Practically speaking, the concept of *de facto* status has limited utility in modern corporate law. The Model Business Corporation Act (Section 56) and most state statutes agree that the issuance of a certificate of incorporation (charter) by the secretary of state is *prima facie* evidence of corporate status (that is, *de jure* corporation). However, the right of the state to command a corporation to correct irregularities in corporate formation can be enforced under the *de facto* doctrine.

Corporation by Estoppel   Sometimes a corporation has neither *de jure* nor *de facto* status. When justice requires, the courts treat an alleged corporation as if it were an actual corporation for the purpose of determining the rights and liabilities involved in a particular situation. Corporation by estoppel is thus determined by the situation. It does not extend recognition of corporate status beyond the resolution of the problem at hand.

For example, suppose a buyer in good faith believes erroneously that the articles of his or her corporation have been filed. Based on this belief, the buyer enters into a contract with a seller to purchase typewriters. The seller is relying solely on the credit of the corporation. The corporation is not formed and the buyer breaches the contract. The seller wants to hold the buyer personally liable. Based on these facts, the seller is "estopped" to deny existence of the corporation, and can look only to the corporation for liability.[4]

If an association which is neither an actual corporation nor a *de facto* or *de jure* corporation holds itself out as being a corporation, it will be estopped from denying corporate status in a lawsuit by a third party. This usually occurs when a third party contracts with an association that claims to be a corporation but does not hold a certificate of incorporation. When the third party brings suit naming the "corporation" as the defendant, the association may not escape from liability on the ground that no corporation exists.

DISREGARDING THE CORPORATE ENTITY

In some unusual situations, a corporate entity is used by its owners to perpetrate a fraud, circumvent the law, or in some other way accomplish an illegitimate objective. In these cases, the court will ignore the corporate structure by "piercing the corporate veil," exposing the shareholders to personal liability.

In the next case, the court must determine whether the corporate owner should be held personally liable for the judgment against his corporation.

---

4.   Cranson v. International Business Machines (IBM), Inc., 200 A.2d 33 (Md. 1964).

BACKGROUND AND FACTS   *Plaintiff Gartner contracted to purchase a home from defendant Snyder-Westerlind Enterprises (referred to as Enterprises by the court). Gartner obtained a judgment against Enterprises for breach of the contract to deliver the home by a certain date. Enterprises was one of three*

GARTNER v. SNYDER
United States Court of Appeals, Second Circuit, 1979.
607 F.2d 582.

corporations owned by Snyder. Enterprises had no major assets with which to satisfy the judgment, and the trial judge ruled that Snyder was personally liable to Gartner.

LUMBARD, Circuit Judge.
* * * *

* * * Because New York courts disregard corporate form reluctantly, they do so only when the form has been used to achieve fraud, or when the corporation has been so dominated by an individual or another corporation (usually a parent corporation), and its separate identity so disregarded, that it primarily transacted the dominator's business rather than its own and can be called the other's alter ego. The court will also generally consider whether the corporation was adequately capitalized in determining whether to disregard the corporate form.

The district court held that Snyder had inadequately capitalized Enterprises, had disregarded its separate identity, had used it to a fraudulent end, and should therefore be personally liable for its breach. As badly as Snyder conducted the Hunter Highlands project, we cannot say that Gartner has shown by a preponderance of evidence either that Snyder engaged in a fraud to get more than the contract price for Unit C-21, or that he transacted purely personal business through Enterprises to the extent that the corporation became his alter ego.
* * * *

The district court found as a further reason for disregarding Enterprises' corporate form the fact that Snyder himself failed to observe Enterprises' separate identity. To be sure, Snyder does not deny that Enterprises had no books, files, or office distinct from those of the other corporations he controlled, nor that the Hunter Highlands files did not distinguish among the different corporations involved in the project. But we do not think that the district court properly applied New York law to those facts. Snyder's disregard suggests that Enterprises was simply one arm of a larger corporate combine; it does not prove that Snyder used Enterprises, or the larger combine, to conduct his purely personal business. * * *

Similarly, the fact that Enterprises conveyed its two parcels of land to another Snyder-controlled corporation, while it suggests that Gartner may have claims against the larger Snyder-controlled corporate combine, does not show that Snyder used Enterprises to conduct purely personal business. * * * Snyder ignored the separate identities of the corporations he controlled, but did not use them to pursue personal business.

Thus, while it may be appropriate to disregard Enterprises' form and hold Snyder's larger corporate combine liable for Enterprises' breach—although we of course make no judgment on that question because the other Snyder-controlled corporations were not parties to this action—we do not find evidence in the record to justify holding Snyder personally liable for Enterprises' breach. Although Enterprises was thinly capitalized, that alone is not a sufficient ground for disregarding the corporate form. We know of no New York authority that disregards corporate form solely because of inadequate capitalization.

DECISION AND REMEDY

The judgment against Snyder was reversed. Snyder's actions were not sufficient to expose him to personal liability.

COMMENTS

It is important to note that courts tend to be reluctant to impose personal liability on the directors of a corporation.

Inadequate Capitalization

In other typical cases, a corporation may have insufficient capital at the time it is formed to meet its prospective debts or potential liabilities. Such "thin capitalization" is exacerbated when a corporation fails to obtain the amount of insurance that any reasonable business can be expected to have in the interest of public responsibility. In such situations, victims who are injured may be able to reach the personal assets of stockholders to satisfy their claims. This is illustrated by the following case.

BACKGROUND AND FACTS   *The plaintiff's (Minton's) daughter drowned in a public swimming pool operated by Seminole Hot Springs Corporation (Seminole). The defendant, Cavaney, was a director and the secretary-treasurer of Seminole. Cavaney stated that Seminole had never had any assets and had never functioned as a corporation. No stock was ever issued. The trial court entered a judgment for the plaintiff, Minton.*

MINTON v. CAVANEY
Supreme Court of California, 1961.
56 Cal.2d 576, 15 Cal.Rptr. 641, 364 P.2d 473.

TRAYNOR, Justice.

*   *   *   *

The figurative terminology "alter ego" and "disregard of the corporate entity" is generally used to refer to the various situations that are an abuse of the corporate privilege. The equitable owners of a corporation, for example, are personally liable when they treat the assets of the corporation as their own and add or withdraw capital from the corporation at will, when they hold themselves out as being personally liable for the debts of the corporation or when they provide inadequate capitalization and actively participate in the conduct of corporate affairs.

In the instant case the evidence is undisputed that there was no attempt to provide adequate capitalization. Seminole never had any substantial assets. It leased the pool that it operated, and the lease was forfeited for failure to pay the rent. Its capital was " 'trifling compared with the business to be done and the risks of loss' *   *   *."

The Supreme Court of California concluded that defendant Cavaney could be liable as an individual for the debts of the corporation. It held that a new trial would be required to determine whether plaintiff could pierce the corporate veil to recover from Cavaney, since undercapitalization is only one factor to be considered in such a decision.

**DECISION
AND REMEDY**

Additional Factors That May Cause Courts to "Pierce the Corporate Veil"

There are other factors which frequently cause the court to pierce the corporate veil. Some of these are:

1.   A party is tricked or misled into dealing with the corporation rather than the individual.
2.   The corporation is set up to never make a profit or will always be insolvent.
3.   The shareholder or director unconditionally guarantees to be personally liable for corporate obligations and/or debts.

4.   Failure to follow statutory corporate formalities, such as calling required corporation meetings.

Commingling of Personal and Corporate Interest

Often corporations are formed according to law by a single person or by a few family members. The corporate entity and the sole stockholder (or family member stockholders) must carefully preserve the separate status of the corporation and its owners. Certain practices invite trouble for the one-person or family-owned corporation—the commingling of corporate and personal funds, the failure to hold and record minutes of board of directors' meetings, or the shareholders' continuous, personal use of corporate property (for example, vehicles). When the corporate privilege is abused for personal benefit and the corporate business is treated in such a careless manner that the corporation and the shareholder in control are no longer separate entities, the court will require an owner to assume personal liability to creditors for the corporation's debts.

In short, where the facts show that great injustice would result from use of a corporation to avoid individual responsibility, a court of equity will look behind the corporate structure to the individual stockholder.

General corporation law has no specific prohibition against a stockholder lawfully lending money to his or her corporation. However, when an officer or director lends money and takes back security in the form of corporate assets, the courts will scrutinize the transaction closely. Any such transaction must be made in good faith and for fair value.

In the following case, two shareholders made a lawful loan of money to a corporation (which later became insolvent) and in return took a security interest in certain pieces of corporate property. When the corporation became insolvent, some creditors charged that the shareholders' loan transaction was not made in good faith and that therefore their security interest should be set aside.

INTERTHERM, INC. v.
OLYMPIC HOMES
SYSTEMS, INC.

Court of Appeals of Tennessee,
1978.
569 S.W.2d 467.

BACKGROUND AND FACTS   *The plaintiffs (InterTherm, Inc.) were creditors of the Olympic Homes Systems Corporation (Olympic). Two of Olympic's shareholders, Langley and Clayton, the defendants, had made a sizable loan to the corporation. In return, they took a security interest in certain corporate property.*

When the corporation became insolvent, the general creditors attempted to set aside the priority of the defendants' security interest. The defendants argued that the general creditors failed to show either that there was any fraud involved in making the loan or that the loan was not an "arm's length" transaction. Moreover, the general creditors did not establish that the defendants were in a fiduciary capacity with the corporation or that they showed a lack of good faith in the loan transaction. The trial court entered judgment for the general creditors, and the shareholders appealed.

DROWOTA, Judge.
*   *   *   *

This is a suit by general creditors against an insolvent corporation and three of its shareholders. The issue is whether a security interest taken by two of the shareholders in personal property of the corporation is valid, and whether it entitles the two shareholders to priority over the general creditors as to the property covered by it.
*   *   *   *

It is true, in Tennessee as elsewhere, that there is no general prohibition against a good faith transaction between a shareholder and his corporation. Accordingly, a shareholder may lawfully loan money to his corporation and receive security therefor.

It is also generally held that officers and directors may, in good faith, lawfully loan money to the corporation they serve and take security therefor. This rule is clearly followed in Tennessee. The rule further provides, however, that "such transactions will invite the closest investigation by the courts, and must be characterized by the utmost good faith." The burden of proving good faith is on the officer or director.
*   *   * As a fiduciary, the officer or director has a strong influence on how the corporation conducts its affairs, and a correspondingly strong duty not to conduct those affairs to the unfair detriment of others, such as minority shareholders or creditors, who also have legitimate interests in the corporation but lack the power of the fiduciary.

It is also generally held that courts will closely scrutinize the transactions of a majority, dominant, or controlling shareholder with his corporation, and will place the burden of proof upon the shareholder when the good faith and fairness of such a transaction is challenged. * * * It is obvious, however, that the reason for applying the rule to a shareholder is the same as the reason for applying it to an officer or director, that is, that he occupies a fiduciary position with regard to the corporation and those interested in it. Unless it is shown that a shareholder owns a majority of the stock or that he otherwise controls or dominates a corporation, however, a shareholder cannot be said to be a fiduciary and the reason for closely scrutinizing his transactions with the corporation disappears. Further, in reviewing the cases in which the courts have closely scrutinized transactions between a corporation and a shareholder and have put the burden of justifying them on the latter, we find that they almost invariably involve a majority, dominant, or controlling shareholder. Accordingly, it is clear that courts should apply the rule of close scrutiny and place the burden on the shareholder to justify a transaction with his corporation only when the shareholder owns a majority of stock, or is shown to dominate or control the corporation to a significant degree in some other way.

In the instant case, defendants contend that their secured loan to Olympic should be upheld under the general rule that shareholders may lawfully contract with their corporation. Plaintiffs, on the other hand, argue that this Court should scrutinize this transaction closely and put the burden of justifying it on defendants who, plaintiffs further argue, have failed to carry that burden. We hold that the instant transaction should not be subjected to close scrutiny, and that the burden of proof should not be on defendant shareholders, because plaintiffs have offered no evidence from which we could conclude that defendants owned a majority of Olympic's stock or otherwise dominated it in such a way as to justify imposing fiduciary responsibilities on them.

There is no evidence in this record that either defendant Langley or defendant Clayton was ever an officer or director of Olympic. The evidence is that each owned 15% of the capital stock of Olympic. It is clear that both were involved in setting up the corporation, but there is nothing to show that they participated in the business afterward. There is evidence that they did not intend to participate in the corporation's everyday affairs. * * * In short, there is no evidence of any degree of power or control by defendants over the corporation at any time. As far as we can tell from this record, defendants were simply two 15% shareholders who, although they participated in setting up the corporation, were not even its promoters. It is our conclusion that plaintiffs are required to present at least some evidence that defendant shareholders were also officers or directors, or that they in some significant way dominated the corporation, in order to invoke close scrutiny of the transaction and place the burden of justifying it on defendants. Plaintiffs have failed to do so here.

Plaintiffs, then, by failing to show that defendants Langley and Clayton had any fiduciary capacity with Olympic, have failed to shift from themselves the burden of proving fraud or absence of good faith in the loan transaction. * * *

The Supreme Court of Tennessee reversed the lower court and held that the defendants, Langley and Clayton, held a valid security interest in the property of Olympic and were entitled to priority over the general creditors. **DECISION AND REMEDY**

COSTS AND BENEFITS OF INCORPORATION

Just about anyone in any state can start a corporation. There are, however, numerous costs, as well as benefits, associated with starting and running such a venture.

The Costs of Incorporating

Some of the costs of starting a corporation include the following:

1. *Lawyers' fees.* Most can range from a minimum of $250 to as much as $5,000.

2. *Accountants' fees.* It can cost several hundred dollars to establish a bookkeeping system for a corporation.

3. *Fees to the state.* The state can require an annual corporate fee ranging from a few dollars to several hundred dollars.

4. *Unemployment insurance taxes.* Even if the corporation has only one employee, and it is clearly set up for tax reasons only, it must still pay unemployment insurance taxes, either to the state in which it is registered or to the federal government.

5. *Employer's contribution to social security.* Even if a person is a salaried employee of some other company, or, as an employee of his or her own corporation, he or she must pay employer's "contribution" to social security. This "contribution" is nonrefundable and seems to be on the rise.

6. *Annual legal and accounting fees.* Forms must be filed for corporations. In addition, corporate records and minute books must be maintained. Typically, an accountant or a lawyer does this. Annual fees for such services can run into many hundreds or thousands of dollars. Numerous forms must be filled out every year for retirement funds in particular.

The Benefits of Incorporating

Some of the major benefits of incorporating include the tax benefit of starting a pension or profit-sharing plan and the tax-related benefits associated with fringe benefits.

Pension and Profit-Sharing Plans Employee-shareholders of corporations are allowed to participate in pension and profit-sharing plans. For example, the IRS might allow a pension plan that consists of a contribution by the corporation for every qualified employee of 10 percent of that employee's gross salary. A separate profit-sharing plan might be allowed in which 15 percent of each qualified employee's gross salary is contributed by the corporation. These contributions are tax-deductible to the corporation and are not immediately taxed to the individual employee. The major benefit here is that the payment of the employee's income taxes is deferred until some later date. Moreover, the tax-exempt pension and profit-sharing plans do not pay taxes on the interest income earned until the proceeds of the plans are distributed to the individual

employee upon retirement. To be sure, one does not have to incorporate to participate in tax-exempt retirement plans. Keogh plans and Individual Retirement Accounts (IRAs) are available. However, for the high-income individual, these two plans do not allow for as much sheltering of income as do corporate pension and profit-sharing plans.

Fringe Benefits An individual who starts a corporation can take advantage of a number of fringe benefits that provide items that might otherwise have to be bought with after-tax dollars.

Term Life Insurance An individual, through his or her own corporation, can purchase up to $50,000 of term life insurance every year with dollars out of the corporation. Because these dollars are a cost to the corporation, they are not taxable. If the person is in the 50 percent tax bracket, for example, that means that he or she is buying $50,000 of term insurance for "fifty-cent dollars." In this example, the cost of that insurance is essentially one-half what it would have been if it had been purchased outside the corporate structure.

Disability Insurance An individual can purchase, with before-tax dollars, long-term disability insurance through the corporation. In other words, a person can buy a salary-continuation policy with before-tax dollars that might otherwise have to be bought with after-tax dollars. Such policies pay a certain amount of money every month if the person becomes disabled and is unable to work.

A Medical Plan An individual can set up a completely comprehensive medical plan to cover virtually all kinds of medical expenses. Thus, the corporation can reimburse the individual with before-tax dollars for any payments made for medical insurance. The corporation can pay for all medicines, dental work, and anything that relates to physical well-being. For someone with a large family, this comprehensive medical plan can mean substantial savings every year.

The benefit of a medical plan is reduced by the availability of medical deductions that the individual could have taken off his or her income before figuring federal income taxes. Part of the person's medical insurance, plus any medical expenses exceeding 5 percent of the adjusted gross income, can be itemized as specific deductions on his or her personal federal income tax return. Essentially, then, a medical plan within the corporation for the individual and his or her dependents provides a method for the corporation to deduct medical expenses that generally are not deductible for the individual.

The Revenue Act of 1978 requires that a medical plan not discriminate among employees. In other words, if it is made available to the president of the corporation, it must also be made available to all employees in the corporation.

CORPORATE FINANCING

In order to obtain financing, corporations issue **securities**—evidence of the obligation to pay money or of the right to participate in earnings and the distribution of corporate trusts and other property. The principal method of long-term and initial corporate financing is the issuance of stocks—**equity**—and bonds—**debt**—both of which are sold to investors. Stocks, or **equity securities,** represent the purchase of ownership in the business firm. Bonds (debentures), or **debt securities,** represent the borrowing of money by firms (and governments).[5] Of course, not all debt is in the form of debt securities. Some is in the form of accounts payable, some in the form of notes payable, and still more in the form of leaseholds. Accounts and notes payable are typically short-term debts. Bonds are simply a way for the corporation to split up its long-term debt so that it can market it more easily.

Bonds

Bonds are issued by business firms and by governments at all levels as evidence of the funds they are borrowing from investors. Bonds almost always have a designated maturity date—the date when the principal or face amount of the bond (or loan) is returned to the investor. Bonds are sometimes referred to as *fixed income securities* because their owners receive a fixed dollar interest payment during the period of time prior to maturity.

In the bond trade, the word *bond* refers specifically to a debenture with a face value of $1,000.

Bonds can be sold below their face value at a *discount* or above their face value at a *premium*. Bonds sold at premiums have yields that are less than their coupon, or stated, rates; those sold at a discount have yields that are greater than the face rate.

Corporate Bonds   The characteristics of corporate bonds vary widely, in part because corporations differ in their ability to generate the earnings and cash flow necessary to make interest payments and to repay the principal amount of the bonds at maturity. Furthermore, corporate bonds are only a part of the total debt and the overall financial structure of corporate business.

Because debt financing represents a legal obligation on the part of the corporation, various features and terms of a particular bond issue are specified in a lending agreement called a **bond indenture.** A corporate trustee, often a commercial bank trust department, represents the collective well-being of all bondholders in insuring that the terms of the bond issue are met by the corporation.

The bond indenture specifies the maturity date of the bond and the pattern of interest payments until maturity. Most corporate bonds pay semiannually a coupon rate of interest on the $1,000 face amount of the bond.

For example, the owner of a 6 percent corporate bond would receive $30 interest every six months. The indenture indicates whether any portion of the bond is to be retired each year in a series of *sinking fund payments*, and it specifies any collateral for the bond issue, such as buildings or equipment. Additionally, the indenture indicates how the bondholder (and other creditors of the business firm) will fare if the firm gets into serious financial difficulty and is unable to meet all its legal obligations.

There are a number of different types of corporate bonds, designated below.

Debentures   No specific assets of the corporation are pledged as backing for debentures. Rather, they are backed by the general credit rating of the corporation, plus any assets that can be seized if the corporation allows the debentures to go into default.

Mortgage Bonds   Mortgage bonds pledge specific property. If the corporation defaults on the bonds, the bondholders can take the mortgage property.

---

5. The term *bonds* is often used to describe both secured and unsecured obligations. Technically, however, bonds are secured by a lien or other security interest; debentures are unsecured.

Equipment Trust Bonds   The collateral for the equipment trust bond or chattel mortgage bond (loan) is a specific piece of equipment. Title to the equipment is vested in a trustee, who holds it for the benefit of the bond owners.

Collateral Trust Bonds   Collateral trust bonds are secured by intangibles. They can be shares of stock in another corporation or accounts receivable.

Convertible Bonds   Convertible bonds can be exchanged for a specified number of shares of common stock when and if the bondholder so desires. The rate of conversion is determined when the convertible bond is issued.

Callable Bonds   Callable bonds, which may be debentures or any other kind of bonds, may be called in and the principal repaid at specified times or under specified conditions. The callable provision is included in the bond when it is issued.

Stocks

Issuing stocks is another way corporations obtain financing. Stocks represent ownership in a business firm; bonds represent borrowing by the firm.

The most important characteristics of stock are:

1.   They need not be paid back.
2.   The stockholder receives dividends only when so voted by the directors.
3.   Stockholders are the last investors to be paid off upon dissolution.
4.   Stockholders vote for management and on major issues.

The two major types of stock are preferred stock and common stock.

Common Stock   **Common stock** represents the true ownership of a corporation. Ownership of this stock represents a threefold proportionate interest in the corporation with regard to:

1.   Control.
2.   Earning capacity.
3.   Net assets.

A shareholder's interest is generally in proportion to the number of shares owned out of the total number of shares issued.

Voting rights in a corporation apply to election of the firm's board of directors and to any proposed changes in the ownership structure of the firm.[6] For example, a holder of common stock generally has the right to vote in a decision on a proposed merger, since mergers can change the proportion of ownership. Many small investors in giant corporations probably feel that their small number of votes has little impact on the business firm—particularly when incumbent management owns or obtains the right to vote shares by proxy and thus has a significant and often controlling proportion of the total votes. Still, voting rights are an important characteristic of common stock and one that some investors take seriously.

There is no obligation to return a principal amount per share to each holder of common stock. No firm can insure that the market price per share of its common stock will not go down over time. Neither does the issuing firm guarantee a dividend; indeed, some business firms never pay dividends. Considering these negative aspects, why would an individual even consider investing in common stock? The answer, of course, is that all owners are entitled to their proportional share of the corporation's after-tax earnings. If Janet Gray owns 100 shares (0.01 percent of 1 million shares outstanding) of a firm that earns $3 million after taxes, she will receive a proportional share of those earnings, or $300. Earnings are the key to the benefits that an investor receives from common stock.

Either the earnings of a corporation are paid out in the form of cash dividends to shareholders, or they are retained in the business for the express purpose of enhancing future earnings. If the board of directors of Janet Gray's firm (and it is *her* firm because she owns common stock) declares a dividend of $1.20 per share, then $120 of her $300 earnings is received now as a tangible benefit, and the other $180 is retained by the corporation. Her other tangible benefit is the market price per share that she will receive if and when she ultimately sells part or all of her 100 common shares. Market price

---

6.   State corporation law specifies the types of issues on which shareholder approval must be obtained.

depends, among other things, on the recent earnings (and dividends) of the firm and, more importantly, on the expectations for future earnings and dividends, as well as on the overall economic well-being of the country.

Holders of common stock, then, are a group of investors who assume a *residual* position in the overall financial structure of a business. In terms of receiving payment for their investment, they are last in line. The earnings to which they are entitled also depend on all the other groups—suppliers, employees, managers, bankers, governments, bondholders, and holders of preferred stock—being paid what is due them first. Once those groups are paid, however, the owners of common stock may be entitled to *all* the remaining earnings. (But the board of directors is not normally under any duty to declare the remaining earnings as dividends.) This is the central feature of ownership in any business, be it a corner newsstand, a retail store, an architectural firm, or a giant international oil corporation. In each instance, the owners of common stock occupy the riskiest position, but they can expect a correspondingly greater return on their investment. Again, it can be seen why the return and risk pattern holds. As one moves from savings accounts and U.S. government bonds to corporate bonds with different ratings to preferred stock and, finally, to common stock, expected returns increase to compensate for the higher risks that are undertaken. Exhibit 39–2 is a comparison of stocks and bonds.

Authorized, Issued, and Outstanding Shares A share of stock is the basic unit of ownership of the corporation. **Authorized shares** are those that the corporation is allowed to issue by its articles of incorporation. Under modern law, there generally is no limit on the number of authorized shares. **Issued shares** are those that are actually issued to shareholders. There is no specific percentage of authorized shares that must be issued. The number of issued shares does not always equal the number of outstanding shares because corporations sometimes repurchase some of their shares. **Outstanding shares** are those that are still held by the shareholders. Repurchased shares are known as **treasury shares;** these shares are authorized and issued, but not outstanding.

Par Value and No Par Shares The specific monetary value assigned to shares in the articles of incorporation is called *par value*. It is the *stated* value of a share. Although of historical interest, par value is no longer of primary importance. Its one lingering effect is that the price per common share initially sold must be greater than or equal to par value. This creates no problem when nominal amounts are used for par value.

The issuance of *no par shares* is permitted in most jurisdictions. As their name implies, these shares are assigned no dollar value. Some statutes provide that the board of directors has the right to fix the price for no par shares issued, but the articles of

Exhibit 39–2 How Do Stocks and Bonds Differ?	
STOCKS	**BONDS**
1. Stocks represent ownership.	1. Bonds represent owed debt.
2. Stocks (common) do not have a fixed dividend rate.	2. Interest on bonds must always be paid, whether or not any profit is earned.
3. Stockholders can elect a board of directors, which controls the corporation.	3. Bondholders usually have no voice in or control over management of the corporation.
4. Stocks do not have a maturity date; the corporation does not usually repay the stockholder.	4. Bonds have a maturity date when the bondholder is to be repaid the face value of the bond.
5. All corporations issue or offer to sell stocks. This is the usual definition of a corporation.	5. Corporations do not necessarily issue bonds.
6. Stockholders have a claim against the property and income of a corporation after all creditors' claims have been met.	6. Bondholders have a claim against the property and income of a corporation that must be met before the claims of stockholders.

incorporation may expressly reserve this right for the shareholders. One of the most attractive features of no par stock is that in most states the entire consideration received constitutes the stated capital. These states even permit the board of directors to allow this consideration to be split between stated capital and capital surplus.

Stated capital represents the basic capital of the corporation. Generally, it consists of the sum of the par values for all issued shares, plus the consideration received for the no par shares. In many jurisdictions, the stated capital amount cannot be used as dividends or otherwise unless the corporation is liquidated.

Preferred Stock   **Preferred stock** is stock with *preferences*. Usually this means that holders of preferred stock have priority over holders of common stock to dividends and to payment upon dissolution of the corporation. Preferred stock shareholders may or may not have the right to vote.

From an investment standpoint, preferred stock is more similar to bonds than to common stock. It is not included among the liabilities of a business because it is equity. Like all equity securities, preferred shares have no fixed maturity date when they must be retired by the firm. Occasionally, firms do retire preferred stock, but they are not legally obligated to do so.

Preferred shareholders receive periodic dividend payments, usually established as a fixed percentage of the face amount of each preferred share. A 7 percent preferred stock with a face amount of $100 per share would pay its owner a $7 dividend each year. This is not a legal obligation on the part of the firm, but the interest payments due to bondholders are legal obligations.

There are a number of different types of preferred stock, which are designated as follows:

Cumulative Preferred Stock   Any dividend payment on cumulative preferred stock not made in a given year must be paid in a subsequent year before any dividends can be paid to owners of common stock. In other words, the corporation is liable to the preferred shareholders for past dividends not yet paid (called dividend arrearages). If, for example, a corporation fails to pay dividends for three years on a stock with a $100 par value and a $5 annual dividend preference, then the company must pay the cumulative preferred stock owners $15 per share at the end of the three years before any dividends can be paid to owners of common stock. Sometimes there are limits as to how far back dividends have to be paid—for example, there may be three- or five-year cumulative limits.

Participating Preferred Stock   With participating preferred stock, the owner can share to some extent in additional dividends that are paid by the firm. Usually, the preferred stockholders are paid their agreed-upon rate of, say, $8 per share (the dividend preference), and then common stockholders are paid an equal percentage rate, after which any additional dividends declared by the board of directors are distributed equally among preferred and common stockholders.

Convertible Preferred Stock   The owner of shares of convertible preferred stock has an option of converting each share into a specified number of common shares. Sometimes convertible preferred stock can be exchanged for common stock in another company. In any event, the exchange ratio is determined when the convertible preferred shares of stock are issued. Hence, if there is an increase in the market value of the corporation's common stock, the market value of the convertible preferred stock also rises. See Exhibit 39–3 for a cumulative convertible preferred stock certificate.

Redeemable, or Callable, Preferred Stock   Redeemable, or callable, preferred stock is issued by a corporation under the express condition that the corporation has the right to buy back the shares of stock from the preferred stockholders at some future time. The terms of such a buy-back arrangement are specified when the preferred stock is issued. Corporations issue callable preferred stock so that they can call in the higher-cost preferred stock and reissue lower-cost shares if interest rates fall in the future.

The Cautious Position of the Preferred Stockholder   Holders of preferred stock are investors who have assumed a rather cautious position in their relationship to the corporation. They have a stronger position than common shareholders with respect to dividends and claims on assets, but as a result, they will not share in the full prosperity of the firm if it grows successfully over time.

EXHIBIT 39–3   A Sample Cumulative Convertible Preferred Stock Certificate

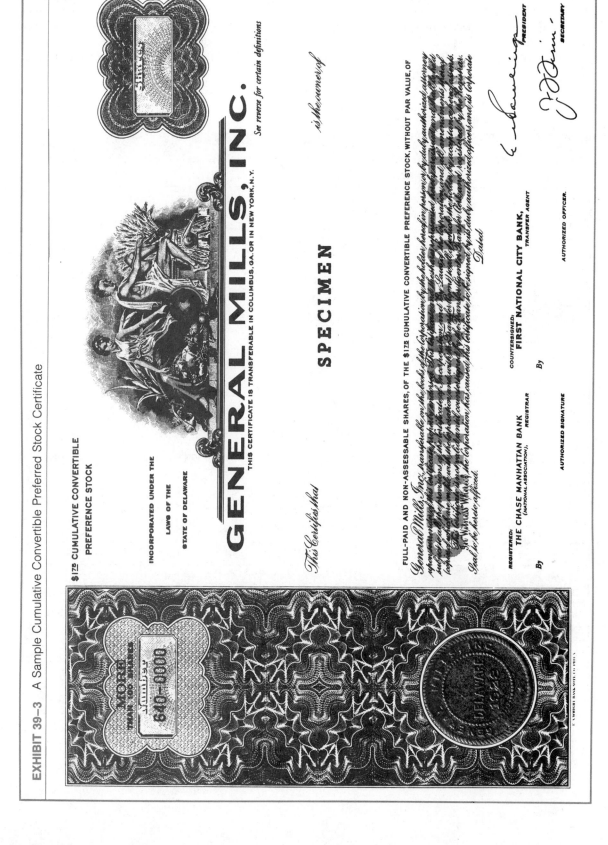

A preferred stockholder receives fixed dividends periodically, and there may be changes in the market price of the shares. The return and the risk for a share of preferred stock lie somewhere between those of bonds and common stock. As a result, preferred stock is often categorized with corporate bonds as a fixed income security, even though the legal status is not the same. As mentioned above, preferred stock is more similar to a bond than common stock, even though preferred stock appears in the ownership section of the firm's balance sheet (financial statements).

CONCEPT SUMMARY: Stocks	
TYPES	**DEFINITIONS**
Common Stock	Voting shares that represent ownership interests in a corporation with lowest priorities with respect to payment of dividends and distribution of assets upon the corporation's dissolution.
Preferred Stock	Shares of stock that have priority over common stock shares as to payment of dividends and distribution of assets upon corporate dissolution. Dividend payments are usually a fixed percentage of the face value of the share.
Cumulative Preferred Stock	Required dividends not paid in a given year must be paid in a subsequent year before any common stock dividends are paid.
Participating Preferred Stock	The owner is entitled to receive dividends from funds available after preferred shareholders receive required agreed dividends, and common shareholders receive prescribed dividends.
Convertible Preferred Stock	Preferred shareholders with the option to convert their shares into a specified number of common shares either in the issuing corporation or, sometimes, in another corporation.
Redeemable or Callable Preferred Stock	Preferred shares issued with the express condition that the issuing corporation has the right to repurchase the shares as specified.
Authorized Shares	Shares allowed to be issued by the articles of incorporation.
Issued Shares	Shares that are actually transferred to shareholders.
Outstanding Shares	Authorized and issued shares still held by shareholders.
Treasury Shares	Shares that are authorized and issued, but are not outstanding (reacquired by the corporation).
No Par Value	Shares issued with no stated value. The price is usually fixed by the board of directors or shareholders.
Par Value	Shares issued and priced at a stated value per share.
Watered Shares (See Chapter 41)	Shares issued (as fully paid) for transfer of property or services rendered, where in fact the value of such property or services is less than the par value or stated board or shareholder price for no par shares.

QUESTIONS AND CASE PROBLEMS

1. Able, Baker, and Carter are recent college graduates who want to form a corporation to manufacture and sell personal computers. Peterson tells them he will set in motion the formation of their corporation. First, Peterson makes a contract for the purchase of a piece of land for $20,000 with Owens. Owens does not know of the prospective corporate formation at the time of the signing of the contract. Second, Peterson makes a contract with Beyer to build a small plant on the property being purchased. Beyer's contract is conditional on the corporation's formation. Peterson secures all necessary subscription agreements and capitalization, and he files the articles of incorporation. A charter is issued.

(a) Discuss whether the newly formed corporation or Peterson or both are liable on the contracts with Owens and Beyer.

(b) Discuss whether the corporation is automatically liable to Beyer upon being formed.

2. As a promoter forming a new corporation, Peterson enters into three pre-incorporation subscription agreements with Mary, Anne, and Harry. The three subscribers each agree to purchase a thousand shares of stock of the future corporation for $2,000. Two months later, just prior to the issuance of the corporate charter, Mary tells Peter she is withdrawing from the agreement. The charter is issued the next week. Just before the first organizational meeting of the corporation, Harry also withdraws from the agreement. Discuss fully whether Mary or Harry or both can withdraw from their subscription agreements without liability.

3. Able, Baker, and Carter form a corporation. The state laws governing incorporation require that the articles of incorporation be signed by three incorporators. A charter is issued, and the corporation begins to do business. Thomas extends credit to the corporation. Because of a national recession, the corporation becomes insolvent. At this time Thomas learns that Able failed to sign the articles of incorporation. Thomas claims that the corporation's formation was improper and that Able, Baker, and Carter are personally liable. Discuss Thomas's claim.

4. Able, Baker, and Carter are brothers who form a corporation to build swimming pools. They are the sole shareholders, members of the board of directors, and officers of the corporation. No meetings are held, and corporate trucks are used on weekends for personal use. In addition, the brothers lend the corporation money, taking a security interest in the corporate property when they

cannot get unsecured credit from others because of previous unsecured indebtedness. The corporation becomes insolvent, and the brothers claim they have priority over unsecured creditors on the basis of their security interest. The unsecured creditors claim not only that the security interest can be set aside but that the brothers are personally liable. Discuss these claims.

5. A new corporation is formed. By its articles of incorporation it has 100,000 shares of authorized common stock at a par value of $2 per share. The corporation has limited property assets, since its major function is that of a service corporation. The corporation issues 50,000 shares. Soon the corporation needs additional financing. Assume that profits for the first year are relatively low but that the future of the corporation is bright. The corporation needs $90,000 of additional financing, but it wants to plow back next year's profits into the corporation.

(a) Would you recommend funding by issuance of corporate bonds? Discuss.

(b) Would you recommend the issuance of preferred or common stock? Discuss.

6. Pointer formed a corporation with $1,000 capital and later loaned over $400,000 to the corporation. Six days after he was notified that Tigrett had filed suit against his corporation, Pointer transferred corporate assets amounting to $400,000 to himself as repayment of the loans. Pointer then transferred these assets to another corporation, of which he was the sole shareholder. The second corporation took over all the business and duties of the original corporation. At the time that Pointer undertook these transfers, Tigrett had not obtained a judgment against the corporation and so was not one of its creditors. By the time Tigrett was awarded a judgment against the original corporation, it had no assets. Is there any way for Tigrett to collect the amount of her judgment? [Tigrett v. Pointer, 580 S.W.2d 375 (Tex.Civ.App. 1978)]

7. Donald McCallum, John Gray, and Lee Evans entered into a pre-incorporation agreement that provided: (1) the three named persons would cause a corporation to be organized under the laws of Oregon with an authorized capital of a thousand shares, (2) each would receive one-third of the shares, and (3) no shareholder would sell, transfer, or in any way dispose of his shares unless and until he offered to sell the shares to the other shareholders. Subsequently, Lee Evans wished to withdraw from the corporation and offered his shares to both McCallum and Gray. Gray declined, but McCallum agreed to purchase all the shares. Thereafter, at a stockholders' meeting with McCallum and Gray both present, McCallum voted, over Gray's objections, to amend the bylaws, allowing an additional thousand shares to be issued. Since Gray had no money to invest at the time, the shares would be purchased by outsiders. Gray objected to the dilution of his interest

in the company. Does Gray have any legal grounds to object to McCallum's action? [McCallum v. Gray, 273 Or. 617, 542 P.2d 1025 (1975)]

8. Watchie, an entrepreneur, acquired the rights to buy certain property that was later to be developed into a large shopping center. Watchie interested a group of Seattle investors, known as the Seattle Syndicate, in the purchase of the land. Over the next two years, Watchie was the promoter of a corporation whose investors contributed approximately $1.5 million for the purchase of the land sold to the Seattle Syndicate. Watchie then convinced the Seattle Syndicate to sell the land to the newly formed corporation for $1,458,000 and convinced the investors that this was a good price. The Seattle Syndicate made a handsome profit on the sale, but Watchie shared in none of it. He was, however, paid a commission of $162,000 on the sale by the Seattle Syndicate. He failed to report this amount to the investors of the newly formed corporation. Can he retain it? [Park City Corp. v. Watchie, 249 Or. 493, 439 P.2d 587 (1968)]

9. New Liberty Medical and Hospital Corporation entered into an agreement with New Liberty Hospital District under which the hospital district agreed to purchase the hospital's debentures under the sole condition that the debentures be legally issued. The district then attempted to avoid its obligation under the agreement with the hospital, claiming that, even though the hospital held a proper certificate of incorporation issued by the secretary of state of Missouri, it did not properly comply with all of the statutory requirements of nonprofit corporations. In a suit by the hospital against the district to enforce the agreement, can the district raise this defense? Explain. [New Liberty Medical and Hospital Corp. v. E. F. Hutton and Co., 474 S.W.2d 1 (Mo. 1971)]

10. Wesley Philpot and his wife engaged the services of Bob Childs Realty Company, Inc., to sell a tract of real estate. Childs Realty sold the property and demanded a commission from the Philpots. The Philpots refused to pay on the ground that Childs Realty had not complied with the Arkansas brokers' law, which required brokers to be incorporated before they could be licensed. Childs Realty argued that it should be deemed a corporation since its president had signed articles of incorporation, and it held itself out as a corporation by use of the designation "Inc." Has Bob Childs Realty Company complied with the Arkansas statute requiring licensed real estate brokers to be incorporated? [Childs v. Philpot, 253 Ark. 589, 487 S.W.2d 637 (1972)]

11. Harvey's is a group of New York corporations. Five of these entered into an agreement with Flynt Distributing Company for Flynt to distribute their magazines. Following this agreement, Harvey failed to pay Flynt or to ship their magazines to Flynt, causing Flynt injury. Two of Harvey's shareholders converted the assets of the five corporations to their own use, which left the corporations undercapitalized. Discuss if this conduct amounts to an abuse of corporate business, allowing Flynt to pierce the corporate veil? [Flynt Distributing Company, Inc. v. Harvey, 734 F.2d 1389 (9th Cir. 1984)]

12. During the early months of 1971, a number of persons began to organize a company later known as Timberjack of Alabama, Inc. On June 8, 1971, a day before the company was formally incorporated, it was assigned certain rights in collateral that was held by Eaton Yale, Ltd. On June 8 Timberjack repossessed the collateral, and on June 9 Timberjack was formally incorporated. Eaton then demanded that Timberjack return the collateral since the right to repossess it was in Timberjack, Inc., and Timberjack, Inc., did not exist on the day repossession took place. Can Eaton reclaim the goods? [In re Wilco Forest Machinery, Inc., 491 F.2d 1041 (5th Cir. 1974)]

40

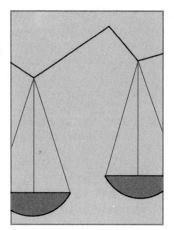

CORPORATIONS
Corporate Powers and Management

CORPORATE POWERS

Corporations have both express and implied powers. These are distinguished and defined below.

Express Powers

The express powers of a corporation are found in its articles of incorporation, in the law of the state of incorporation, and in the state and federal constitutions. The order of priority used when conflicts arise among documents involving corporations is:

1. The U.S. Constitution.
2. State constitutions.
3. State statutes.
4. The certificate of incorporation (charter).
5. Bylaws.
6. Resolutions of the board of directors.

It is important to keep in mind that the corporation is a "legal person." Under modern law, except as limited by charters, statutes, or constitutions, *a corporation can engage in all acts and enter into any contract available to a natural person in order to accomplish the purposes for which it was created.*

Implied Powers

Certain inherent powers attach when a corporation is created. Barring express constitutional, statutory, or charter prohibitions, the corporation has the implied power to do all acts reasonably appropriate and necessary to accomplish its corporate purposes. For this reason, a corporation has the implied power to borrow money within certain limits, to lend money or to extend credit to those with whom it has a legal or contractual relationship, and to make charitable contributions.[1]

To borrow money, the corporation acts through its board of directors to authorize the execution of negotiable paper. Most often, the president or chief executive officer of the corporation will execute the necessary papers on behalf of the corporation. In so doing, corporate officers have the implied power to bind the corporation in matters directly connected with the *ordinary* business affairs of the enterprise. This is the issue in the next case.

---

1. The right of a corporation to make political contributions in federal elections is prohibited by the Federal Elections Campaign Act. [18 USC Section 321] Early law held that a corporation had no implied authority to make charitable contributions, as such was contrary to the primary purpose of the corporation to make a profit. Modern law, by statutes and court decisions, now holds that a corporation has such implied power.

**F.M. BENTALL v.
KOENIG BROTHERS,
INC.**

Supreme Court of Montana,
1962.
140 Mont. 339, 372 P.2d 91.

BACKGROUND AND FACTS   *The plaintiff, F. M. Bentall, loaned $5,000 to the defendant corporation, Koenig Brothers, Inc. The corporation, through its president, executed a promissory note for $5,000 plus interest. The promissory note became overdue. The plaintiff demanded payment from the defendant many times, but the defendant corporation refused to pay any part of the note.*

The corporation acknowledged that there was a note executed and delivered to the plaintiff by its president, Arne Poulsen, but it alleged that Poulsen had neither the power nor the authority to make or deliver the note on behalf of the corporation or to bind the corporation to the payment of such an obligation. Further, the corporation contended that Poulsen's act was not properly approved by the board of directors.

HARRISON, Justice.

*   *   *   *

It is the defendant corporation's contention that the note in question was executed and delivered by the president, Arne Poulsen, without having been so directed or authorized by any order or resolution of the corporation's board of directors, and hence the authority for the execution and delivery thereof to the plaintiff must rest upon the evidence of the defendant corporation's alleged ratification of those acts by the board of directors or upon such general authority as must be ascribed to the president of the corporation who signed the note.

In the instant case, the defendant corporation's articles of incorporation provided for three members to act as directors of the corporation. At the time of the execution of the note in question, R. W. Brenneke, Alvin F. Koenig, and Arne Poulsen were its directors. It is undisputed that Alvin Koenig and Arne Poulsen authorized the execution of the note in question. They constituted a quorum and their action, which was not contrary to law nor contrary to the articles of incorporation or by-laws of the defendant corporation, was binding on the defendant corporation.

The defendant corporation, however, argues that "Arne Poulsen had a conflicting or adverse interest with respect to this loan, and therefore, could not be counted either as part of a quorum of the board of directors, or in any vote by said board, insofar as this loan was concerned."

It is true that a director of a corporation may not cast a vote upon an issue in which he has an adverse interest. However, here, Arne Poulsen, as a director of the defendant corporation, had no interest adverse to that of the defendant corporation.

First of all, *   *   * the $5,000, which is covered by the note in question, was a loan to the defendant corporation and was not *   *   * [a personal loan to Poulsen].

Secondly, the record discloses that the defendant corporation, at the time the note to the plaintiff was executed, was in debt and in immediate need of money to cover current operating expenses. *   *   * When he [Poulsen] obtained the $5,000 loan from the plaintiff for the defendant corporation, he was acting as an agent of the defendant corporation. *   *   *

*   *   *   *

In the case at bar, *   *   * two of the three directors of the defendant corporation, in the absence of the third director, authorized the execution of a promissory note *to a third party*, the plaintiff. These directors did not execute the note to themselves nor did they stand to profit from its execution.

Arne Poulsen, as president of the defendant corporation, not only had express authority to execute the note in question, but he also had *implied* authority.

In the absence of special authority, the president of a corporation has no power, merely by virtue of his office alone, to execute negotiable paper in the name of the corporation. "Where, however, such power is specially conferred upon him [president]

* * * by the corporate charter or by a resolution or by-law of the board of directors, or, *where such power exists, by implication* from the nature of the agency or *by reason of his* * * * being held out by custom or course of dealing as having such authority, or being *intrusted with the conduct and management of the corporate affairs, which requires the use of such instruments in the ordinary course of the business, the president* * * * *may bind the corporation by the execution* * * * *of negotiable paper."*

The plaintiff's case does not here rest upon the proposition that Poulsen's authority to bind the corporation by promissory notes executed for it or in its name may be implied from the mere fact of his official position. To the proof of the fact that he was president, or chief executive officer of the defendant corporation, is added other evidence that he was also one of its three directors and the *manager* of its business. The entire corporation was made up of Poulsen, Alvin Koenig, and one R. W. Brenneke, who is not shown to have any active hand in the business. The record shows that Poulsen had and exercised "full management and control of the affairs of said corporation." The evidence as to the whole course of conduct of the directors and stockholders of the defendant corporation in allowing Poulsen such "full management and control" was sufficient to justify a finding that he was thereby vested with power to borrow money on the note of the corporation.

The defendant corporation was in debt and Poulsen, as a faithful servant intent on saving his corporation, did what the ordinary prudent business man would do in carrying on the affairs of the corporation (i.e., borrow money in the name of the corporation and bind it by a note evidencing the same) and, in so doing, violated no statute of this state, nor the articles of incorporation or any by-law of the defendant corporation. Poulsen was dealing with a matter directly connected with the ordinary business affairs of the defendant corporation and the promissory note to the plaintiff was such as was usual, proper, and necessary, under the circumstances, in the ordinary prosecution of the corporation's business.

The Supreme Court of Montana affirmed the lower court's decision that the corporation was liable on the $5,000 note.

DECISION AND REMEDY

Ultra Vires Doctrine

The term *ultra vires* means "beyond the powers." In corporate law, acts of a corporation that are beyond the authority given to it under its charter or under the statutes by which it was incorporated are **ultra vires** acts.

Ultra vires acts can be understood only within the context of the particular stated purpose for which the corporation was organized. Acts in furtherance of the corporation's expressed purposes are within the corporate power; acts beyond the scope of corporate business as described in the charter are *ultra vires*.

The stated purposes in the articles of the corporation set the limits of the activities the corporation can legally pursue. Any time the corporation takes on activities outside the stated purpose(s), the corporation can be charged with committing an *ultra vires* act. Because of this, corporations are increasingly aware of the benefit of adopting a very broad statement of purpose in their articles of incorporation to include virtually all conceivable activities. Corporate statutes in many states permit the expression "any lawful purpose" to be a legally sufficient stated purpose in the articles of incorporation.

A majority of cases dealing with *ultra vires* acts have involved contracts made for unauthorized purposes. For example, it is difficult to see how a contract made by a plumbing company for the purchase of six thousand cases of vodka is reasonably related to the conduct and furtherance of the corporation's stated purpose of providing plumbing installation and services. Hence, such a contract would probably be held *ultra vires*.

Corporate acts can be *ultra vires* simply in the sense of being beyond corporate powers. Such acts are not necessarily illegal; however, all illegal acts are inherently *ultra vires*. Modern areas of *ultra vires* concern include whether a corporation has the power to make charitable or political contributions, to grant employee fringe benefits, to make loans to directors or officers, or to acquire shares of other corporations. The prudent corporate executive will always check applicable statutes and the articles of incorporation before taking these actions.

In certain cases, the law recognizes the right of a shareholder to sue the board of directors for its alleged wrongful action of pursuing *ultra vires* acts. A stockholder can bring what is called a *derivative suit* against the corporation by first demanding that the directors correct the wrong. Failing that, the stockholder can ask the court to enforce the corporate right.

Certain acts of the board of directors can be unauthorized at the time they first occur but ratified later by a majority vote of the stockholders. Such ratification of the board of directors' actions by a majority of shareholders will ordinarily cure an otherwise voidable wrong. However, certain acts, such as the waste of corporate assets, will usually require unanimous shareholder action for ratifying or condoning the wrong.

Judicial Treatment of *Ultra Vires* Contracts

The courts have treated *ultra vires* contracts in a variety of ways. One treatment is based upon the common law principle of agency, whereby an unauthorized contract made by an agent is void—no rights or duties arise for either party. Early decisions often held that *ultra vires* contracts were void.

The more modern approach is to uphold the validity of contracts that have been performed by all sides. In some states, when a contract is entirely executory, neither party having performed, a defense of *ultra vires* can be used by either party to prevent enforcement of the contract.

Sometimes an *ultra vires* contract is only partially executed at the time of challenge. Courts may still enforce the contract where the circumstances are such that it would be inequitable to allow a party to assert the defense of *ultra vires*.

The current trend in dealing with *ultra vires* contracts is embodied in statutory enactments similar to Section 7 of the Model Act, which upholds the validity and enforceability of an *ultra vires* contract as between the parties involved. However, the right of shareholders on behalf of the corporation, the right of the corporation itself to recover damages from the officers and directors who caused the transaction, and the right of the attorney general of the state to institute an injunction against the transaction or to institute dissolution proceedings against the corporation for *ultra vires* acts have been upheld.

The following case illustrates a court's willingness to embrace the Model Business Corporation Act's policy of denying to a corporation the right to avoid an *ultra vires* contract.

JAMES v. J.F.K. CARWASH, INC.
Supreme Court of Arkansas,
1982.
628 S.W.2d 299.

BACKGROUND AND FACTS *Mansell, Grubbs, and James each owned a one-third interest in J.F.K. Carwash, Inc., an Arkansas corporation. James wanted out of the operation and all three agreed that the corporation would repurchase his shares. A corporate promissory note for the amount of the repurchase was issued by Carwash and secured by the personal guarantees of Mansell and Grubbs. At the time the note was issued, Carwash had deficit of $16,184.36 and had no unrestricted earned surplus. Arkansas law requires that a corporation repurchase its stock out of unrestricted earned surplus. Carwash was unable to make its payments on the promissory note, and James filed suit to recover the unpaid principal. Mansell and Grubbs maintained that the note was void because it was* ultra vires.

DUDLEY, Justice.
*   *   *   *

The issues on appeal are whether a corporate promissory note which was given for an ultra vires repurchase of corporate stock is void and whether there is liability because of an accompanying personal guaranty of the corporate promissory note. *   *   *
*   *   *   *

The ability of a corporation to acquire and dispose of its own shares is one of the segments of a symmetrical statutory structure dealing with corporations. Section 64–104 [Arkansas Statutes Annotated] grants general powers to a corporation. Section 64–105 delineates the restrictions on a corporation purchasing its own stock and § 64–106 provides that when a corporation acts in excess of its powers such action will not be invalid solely because the corporation was without either the capacity or the power to do such act. This latter section provides:

> Defense of ultra vires.—No act of a corporation and no conveyance or transfer of real or personal property to or by a corporation shall be invalid by reason of the fact that the corporation was without capacity or power to do such act or to make or receive such conveyance or transfer, but such lack of capacity or power may be asserted: . . .

None of the conditions for asserting lack of capacity or power are applicable to this case. They are:

A. A shareholder may sue the corporation to enjoin the performance of an ultra vires contract.

B. A stockholder may bring a derivative suit for damages in favor of the corporation against officials who have diverted business by ultra vires acts.

C. The Attorney General is authorized to enjoin unauthorized or ultra vires acts.

The juxtaposition of the statutes is not mere coincidence; it is because the General Assembly wanted to confer limited powers on corporations and to limit causes of action and defenses based on an act in excess of those powers. None of the statutory conditions are present for an assenting stockholder to assert the defense of ultra vires. The promissory note is not invalid as an ultra vires instrument and, accordingly, the underlying personal guarantee is not invalid. *   *   *

*   *   *   *

DECISION AND REMEDY

Although the promissory note was executed in violation of the Arkansas statute governing corporate repurchase of stock, and was therefore ultra vires, *the court would not allow the doctrine to be used by the corporation to an inequitable end.*

COMMENTS

The ultra vires *doctrine is generally not available to release a corporation from its commitments when there is an execution of those commitments. Often, if an* ultra vires *transaction is partially executed, elements of fairness, unjust enrichment, or estoppel will prevent courts from releasing the corporation from its obligations.*

Torts and Criminal Acts

A corporation is liable for the torts committed by its agents or officers within the course and scope of their employment. A corporation can act only through its agents and servants. This principle applies to a corporation exactly as it applies to the ordinary agency relationships discussed in Chapter 33. It follows the doctrine of *respondeat superior*.

At common law, a corporation could not be held liable for a crime, particularly one that required intent. However, under modern criminal law, a corporation can sometimes be held liable for the crim-inal acts of its agents and employees, provided the punishment can be applied to the corporation.[2]

CORPORATE MANAGEMENT—SHAREHOLDERS

Shareholder Powers

Shareholders must approve fundamental changes affecting the corporation before the changes can be

---

2. Obviously, a corporation cannot be imprisoned; however, it can be fined and possibly dissolved.

effected. Hence, shareholders are empowered to amend the articles of incorporation (charter) and bylaws, approve merger or dissolution of the corporation, and approve the sale of all or substantially all of the corporation's assets. Some of these powers are subject to prior board approval.

Election and removal of the board of directors are accomplished by a vote of the shareholders. The first board of directors is either named in the articles of incorporation or chosen by the incorporators to serve until the first shareholders' meeting. From that time on, selection and retention of directors are exclusively a shareholder function.

Directors usually serve their full term. If they are unsatisfactory, they are simply not reelected. Shareholders have the inherent power to remove a director from office *for cause* (breach of duty or misconduct) by a majority vote.[3] Some state statutes

permit removal of directors without cause by the vote of a majority of the holders of outstanding shares entitled to vote.[4] Some corporate charters expressly provide that shareholders, by majority vote or larger than majority vote, can remove a director at any time *without cause*.

The following case illustrates an unusual directorship, that of a life member of an institute, and what consists of removal *for cause*.

---

4. Most states allow cumulative voting for directors. In states in which voting for directors is by cumulative ballot, a director cannot be removed without cause over the negative vote that would be sufficient to elect that director in the first place. See, for example, California Corporate Code, Section 303A. Also see Section 39 of the Model Act. (Cumulative voting is discussed later in this chapter.)

---

3. A director can often demand court review of removal for cause.

GRACE v. GRACE
INSTITUTE

Court of Appeals of New York,
1967.
19 N.Y.2d 307, 279 N.Y.S.2d
721, 226 N.E.2d 531.

BACKGROUND AND FACTS   *The Grace Institute was incorporated by an act of the legislature of the state of New York to provide women with instruction in trades and occupations and in branches of the domestic arts and sciences. The corporation was formed under the general corporation law of New York. Three members of the Grace family and their successors were named original life members of the board of trustees. All the powers and privileges of the corporation were to be exercised by these three life members together with such other persons as they might select to be trustees.*

The plaintiff in this action, Michael P. Grace II, was a successor to one of the original life members and, by virtue of that position, became a member of the board of trustees of the Institute. During his tenure in office, he brought several lawsuits against the Institute, all of which he lost. As a result of these unsuccessful lawsuits, certain charges were drawn up against him, and a hearing was held. Thereafter, the board of trustees removed him as a trustee and a life member of the Grace Institute, despite the fact that no provision in the incorporating statute or the bylaws of the corporation related to the removal of a life member.

KEATING, Judge.

*   *   *   *

The law is settled that a corporation possesses the inherent power to remove a member, officer or director for cause, regardless of the presence of a provision in the charter or by-laws providing for such removal.

The question with which we are presented in this case is whether there exists any triable issues relating to the manner in which this petitioner was removed from his position as a life member and trustee.

It has been the consistent policy of the courts of this State to avoid interference with the internal management and operation of corporations. Although we are dealing here with a charitable corporation over which the Supreme Court is vested with supervisory powers, the Legislature in creating it set up a governing board of trustees and vested in them the power and authority necessary for the management and operation of the Institute. That body, after hearings and deliberation, has decided that the petitioner's conduct was so inimical to the corporate interests as to require his removal. In reaching that conclusion, the trustees had before them evidence of a series of lawsuits commenced by the petitioner against the corporation in each of which he was unsuccessful and in none of which did any of the 13 jurists who took part find even so much as a single triable issue.

After reviewing each of these actions and after studying the entire record in this case, we have reached the conclusion that the evidence clearly supported the finding of the trustees that Michael had embarked on a course of conduct designed to involve the Institute in endless and costly litigation and that the suits were undertaken for the purpose of harassing the Institute and its members. Under these circumstances, courts should not substitute their judgment for the judgment of those charged by the Legislature with the responsibility of running the corporation and seeing to it that it fulfills the purposes for which it was created.

In addition, we have examined the procedure by which the petitioner was removed and we have concluded there is no question but that he was given a reasonable opportunity to be heard and to answer the charges leveled against him. At the hearing during which the charges were aired, he was represented by three attorneys and a law assistant. His attorneys were permitted to cross-examine one of the parties who had been instrumental in preparing the charges against Michael and they could have exercised their right to examine others. Yet despite this opportunity to be heard and to present evidence, Michael never took the stand and never even attempted to answer the charges. The objections of Michael to the hearing we find to be without merit. The things to which he objects in no way detracted from his opportunity to be heard or the validity of his removal.

Michael argues, however, that the position of life member was created by the Legislature and "only the Legislature has the power to change the rights and privileges specifically granted by the act of incorporation." Michael obviously misapprehends the nature of the rights and privileges accorded to him. The Legislature surely could not have intended that a life member retain his position regardless of the manner in which he acted and regardless of the manner in which he abused his trust. The petitioner may not be removed so long as he adheres to what must be regarded as an implied condition of his position—that is, so long as he faithfully serves the Institute. Once he breaches that condition and engages in activities that obstruct and interfere with the operation of the corporation and the purposes for which the Legislature created it, he may be removed.

The New York Court of Appeals reached the conclusion that Michael P. Grace II had been rightfully removed from his position as a life member and trustee of the Grace Institute.   **DECISION AND REMEDY**

The Relationship between the Shareholder and the Corporation

As a general rule, shareholders have no responsibility for the daily management of the corporation, although they are ultimately responsible for choosing the board of directors, which does have such control. Ordinarily, corporate officers and other employees owe no direct duty to individual stockholders. Their duty is to the corporation as a whole. However, a director is in a fiduciary relationship to the corporation and therefore serves the interests of the shareholders as a whole.

Generally, there is no legal relationship between shareholders and creditors of the corporation. Shareholders can, in fact, be creditors of the corporation and have the same rights of recovery against the corporation as any other creditor. The rights and liabilities of shareholders are discussed in Chapter 41.

Shareholders' Forum

Shareholders' meetings must occur at least annually, but special meetings can be called to take care of urgent matters. Since it is usually not practical for owners of only a few shares of stock of publicly traded corporations to attend the shareholders' meetings, they normally give third persons a written authorization to vote their shares at the meeting. This authorization, called a *proxy*, is often solicited by management, as will be discussed later.

Notice of Meetings   The notice and time of meetings, including the day and the hour, is announced in writing to each shareholder at a reasonable length of time prior to the date of the shareholders' meeting.[5] Special meeting notices must include a statement of the purpose of the meeting; business transacted at a special meeting is limited to that purpose.

Shareholder Voting   In order for shareholders to act, a minimum number of them (in terms of number of shares held) must be present at a meeting. This minimum number, called a *quorum*, is generally more than 50 percent. Corporate business matters are presented in the form of *resolutions*, which shareholders vote to approve or disapprove. Some state statutes have set forth voting limits, and corporations' articles or bylaws must remain within the statutory limitations. Some states provide that the unanimous written consent of shareholders is a permissible alternative to holding a shareholders' meeting.

Once a quorum is present, a majority vote of the shares represented at the meeting is usually required to pass resolutions. Assume that Midwestern Supply, Inc., has 10,000 outstanding shares of voting stock. Its articles set the quorum at 50 percent of outstanding shares and provide that a majority

vote of shares present is necessary to pass on ordinary matters. At the shareholders' meeting, a *quorum* of stockholders representing 5,000 outstanding shares must be present to conduct business, and a *vote* of at least 2,501 of those shares represented at the meeting is needed to pass ordinary resolutions. If more than 5,000 are present, a larger vote will be needed.

At times, a larger-than-majority vote will be required either by statute or by corporation charter. Extraordinary corporate matters, such as merger, consolidation, or dissolution of the corporation (to be discussed in Chapter 42), will require a higher percentage of the representatives of *all* corporate shares entitled to vote, not just a majority of those present at that particular meeting.

Voting Lists   Voting lists are prepared by the corporation prior to each shareholders' meeting. Persons whose names appear on the corporation's stockholder records as the record owners of the shares are the persons ordinarily entitled to vote.[6] The voting list contains the name and address of each shareholder as shown on the corporate records on a given cutoff date (record date). It also includes the number of voting shares held by each owner. The list is usually kept at the corporate headquarters and is available for shareholder inspection.

Voting Techniques   Most states permit or require shareholders to elect directors by *cumulative voting*, a method of voting designed to allow minority shareholders representation on the board of directors.[7] Cumulative voting operates as follows: The number of members of the board to be elected is multiplied by the total number of voting shares held. The result equals the number of votes a shareholder has, and this total can be cast for one or more nominees for director. All nominees stand for election at the same time. Where cumulative voting is not required either by statute or under the articles, the entire board can be elected by a majority of shares at a shareholders' meeting.

To illustrate: A corporation has 10,000 shares issued and outstanding. The minority shareholders

---

5.   The shareholder can waive the requirement of written notice by signing a waiver form. A shareholder who did not receive written notice, but who learned of the meeting and attended without protesting the lack of notice, is said to have waived notice by such conduct. State statutes and corporate bylaws typically set forth a minimum allowance notice requirement.

6.   Where the legal owner is deceased, bankrupt, incompetent, or in some other way under a legal disability, his or her vote can be cast by a person designated by law to control and manage the owner's property.

7.   See, for example, the California Corporate Code, Section 708.

hold only 3,000 shares, and the majority share-holders hold the other 7,000 shares. Three members of the board are to be elected. The majority share-holders' nominees are Able, Baker, and Carter. The minority shareholders' nominee is Diamond. Can Diamond be elected by the minority shareholders?

If cumulative voting is allowed, the answer is yes. The minority shareholders have 9,000 votes among them (the number of directors to be elected times the number of shares equals $3 \times 3,000$, which equals 9,000 votes). All of these votes can be cast to elect Diamond. The majority shareholders have 21,000 votes (3 times 7,000 equals 21,000 votes), but these votes have to be distributed among their three nominees. The principal of cumulative voting is that no matter how the majority shareholders cast their 21,000 votes, they will not be able to elect all three directors if the minority shareholders cast all of their 9,000 votes for Diamond, as illustrated in the chart below.

Shareholder Agreements   A group of shareholders can agree in writing prior to the meeting to vote their shares together in a specified manner. Voting agreements are usually held to be valid and enforceable.

Proxy Voting   A shareholder can appoint a voting agent. A proxy is a written authorization to cast the shareholder's vote, and a person can solicit proxies from a number of shareholders in an attempt to concentrate voting power.

Voting Trust   Shareholders can enter into an agreement (a trust contract) whereby legal title (record ownership on the corporate books) is transferred to a trustee who is responsible for voting the shares. The agreement can specify how the trustee is to vote, or it can allow the trustee to use his or her discretion. The trustee takes physical possession of the actual stock certificate and in return gives the shareholder

a *voting trust certificate*. The shareholder retains all of the rights of ownership (for example, the right to receive dividend payments) except for the power to vote.

A voting trust is not the same thing as a proxy, for the latter can be revoked more easily. The holder of a proxy has neither legal title to the stock nor possession of the certificates, whereas voting trustees have both. [8]

CORPORATE MANAGEMENT—DIRECTORS

Every corporation is governed by directors. Subject to statutory limitations, the number of directors is set forth in the corporation's articles or bylaws. Historically, the minimum number of directors has been three, but today many states permit fewer.

Directors' Election and Term of Office

The first board of directors is normally appointed by the incorporators upon the creation of the corporation, or directors are named by the corporation itself in the articles. The first board serves until the first annual shareholders' meeting. Subsequent directors are elected by majority vote of the shareholders.

The term of office for a director is usually one year—from annual meeting to annual meeting. Longer and staggered terms are permissible under most state statutes. A common practice is to elect one-third of the board members each year for a three-year term. In this way, there is greater management continuity.

A director can be removed *for cause*, either as specified in the articles or bylaws or by shareholder

---

8.   Under Section 34 of the Model Act, the term of a voting trust cannot exceed ten years.

Ballots	Majority Shareholders Votes			Minority Shareholder Votes	Directors Elected
	Able	*Baker*	*Carter*	*Diamond*	
1	10,000	10,000	1,000	9,000	Able, Baker, Diamond
2	9,001	9,000	2,999	9,000	Able, Baker, Diamond
3	6,000	7,000	8,000	9,000	Baker, Carter, Diamond

action. Even the board of directors itself may be given power to remove a director for cause, subject to shareholder review. Unless the shareholders have reserved the right at the time of election, a director cannot be removed without cause.

When vacancies occur on the board of directors due to death or resignation, or when a new position is created through amendment of the articles or by-laws, either the shareholders or the board itself can fill the position, depending on state law or the provisions of the bylaws.

Directors' Qualifications and Compensation

Few qualifications are legally required of directors. Only a handful of states retain minimum age and residency requirements. A director is sometimes a shareholder, but this is not a necessary qualification unless, of course, statutory provisions, corporate articles, or bylaws require ownership.

Compensation for directors is ordinarily specified in the corporate articles or bylaws. Because directors have a *fiduciary* relationship to the shareholders and to the corporation, an express agreement or provision for compensation is necessary for them to receive money from the funds they control or for which they have responsibilities.

Management Responsibilities

Directors have responsibility for all policymaking decisions necessary to the management of all corporate affairs. Just as shareholders cannot act individually to bind the corporation, the directors must act as a body in carrying out routine corporate business. One director has one vote, and generally the majority rules.

The general areas of responsibility of the board of directors include:

1. Declaration and payment of corporate dividends to shareholders.[9]
2. Authorization for major corporate policy decisions—for example, the initiation of proceedings for the sale or lease of corporate assets outside of the regular course of business, the determination of new

product lines, and the overseeing of major contract negotiations and major management-labor negotiations.
3. Appointment, supervision and removal of corporate officers and other managerial employees and the determination of their compensation.
4. Financial decisions involving such things as the issuance of authorized shares or bonds.

Directors' Liability

Honest mistakes of judgment and poor business actions on the part of the directors do not make them liable to the corporation for damages sustained. After all, directors are not insurers of the business success of the corporation. Usually, the business judgment rule applies to the actions of directors. In general, this rule sustains corporate transactions and immunizes management (the directors) from liability where the transaction is within the powers of the corporation and within the authority of management, as long as that transaction involves the exercise of due care and compliance with the duties of management.

Of course, directors must be loyal, honest, and reasonably careful at all times. If directors (and their officers) hire employees carefully, they are not personally liable for the willful wrongs and negligent acts of such employees; rather, the corporation is liable.

However, when a director neither attends board meetings nor examines records and books, he or she can be held liable for losses resulting from unsupervised acts of officers and employees. Also, when directors (and officers) allow the assets of the corporation to be diverted to objectives outside of the charter or statutory powers, they may be held liable for damages to the corporation, to a trustee appointed for the corporation, or to the shareholders in a derivative suit.

The Board of Directors' Forum

The board of directors conducts business by holding formal meetings with recorded minutes.[10] The date

---

9. See Dodge v. Ford Motor Co. in Chapter 41.

10. Some states, such as Michigan and Texas (and the Model Act, Section 43), now have a corporate statute authorizing conference telephone calls for board of directors' meetings.

upon which regular meetings are held is usually established in the articles and bylaws or by board resolution, and no further notice is customarily required. Special meetings can be called with notice sent to all directors.

Quorum requirements can vary among jurisdictions. Many states leave the decision to the corporate articles or bylaws. In the absence thereof, most states provide that a quorum is a majority of the number of directors authorized in the articles or bylaws. Voting is done *in person* (unlike voting at shareholders' meetings, which can be done by proxy).[11] The rule is one vote per director. Ordinary matters generally require a majority vote; certain extraordinary issues can require a larger-than-majority vote.

Delegation of Board of Directors' Powers

The board of directors can delegate some of its functions to an executive committee or to corporate officers. In doing so, the board does not avoid its responsibility for directing the affairs of the corporation. Rather, the daily responsibilities of corporate management are given over to corporate officers and managerial personnel, who are empowered to make

---

11. Except in Louisiana, where a director can vote by proxy under certain circumstances.

decisions relating to ordinary corporate affairs within well-defined guidelines.

Executive Committee   Most states permit the board of directors to elect an executive committee from among the directors to handle the interim management decisions between board of directors' meetings, as provided in the bylaws. The *executive committee* is limited to making management decisions about ordinary business matters.

Corporate Officers   The officers and other executive employees are hired by the board of directors or, in rare instances, by the shareholders. In addition to the duties that are articulated in the bylaws, corporate and managerial officers are agents of the corporation, and the ordinary rules of agency apply or have been applied to their employment (unlike the board of directors, whose powers are conferred by the state).

Qualifications are determined at the discretion of the corporation and are included in the articles or bylaws. In most states, a person can hold more than one office and can be both an officer and a director of the corporation. Corporate officers can be removed by the board of directors at any time with or without cause and regardless of the terms of the employment contract, although the corporation can still be liable for breach-of-contract damages.

QUESTIONS AND CASE PROBLEMS

1. The Board of Directors of Able, Inc., has to decide whether or not to make the following three transactions, none of which is expressly covered in the articles or bylaws of the corporation: a charitable gift of $100,000 to a private university noted for the education of minority students, a secured loan of corporate surplus funds at a high interest rate, and an extension of credit to another corporation that Able owns shares in. Discuss whether Able, Inc., through action by its board, has the authority and the power to make the above transactions.
2. Baker, Inc., was formed for the purpose of drilling and servicing water wells. This purpose is specifically stated in its articles of incorporation. One year after the formation of the corporation, the board of directors entered

into a contract with an independent oil driller, Thomas, to purchase and market all the oil Thomas produced from his wells during a five-year period. The contract has been performed for two years, and Baker has expended corporate funds to set up storage and marketing facilities. Thomas now refuses to sell any more oil to Baker, claiming the corporation contracted outside its powers. Discuss this claim.
3. Ann owns ten shares of Monmouth Corporation. Monmouth Corporation has 100,000 outstanding issued common shares. Ann believes that many decisions of the board of directors do not consider the preservation of the environment. Two pending proposals approved by the board deal with the purchase of timberland for conversion into condominiums. Both proposals require an amendment to the corporate charter and thus need a two-thirds shareholder vote. Ann knows other shareholders who she believes would oppose these proposals. Unfortunately, most shareholders live a considerable distance from the site of the shareholders' meeting and will be unable to attend.

Discuss any techniques Ann can use to oppose these proposals.

4. Carter Corporation has issued and has outstanding 100,000 shares of common stock. Four stockholders own 60,000 of these shares, and for the past six years they have nominated a slate of people for membership on the board, all of whom get elected. John and twenty other shareholders, owning 20,000 shares, are dissatisfied with corporate management and want a representative on the board who shares their views. Explain under what circumstances John and the minority shareholders can elect their representative to the board.

5. Kathy is elected to the board of directors of a corporation. The board consists of nine members. The articles and bylaws are silent as to what constitutes a quorum. The bylaws do permit the board itself, by majority vote, to elect board members to fill vacancies created by death or resignation. The bylaws also require majority votes for ordinary corporate decisions made at regular corporate board meetings. Just prior to a regular meeting, a board member dies. At the scheduled regular meeting a proposal is made that Kathy opposes. She cannot attend the meeting and sends her proxy. The meeting takes place with five members in attendance. By a vote of three to two, John is elected to fill the board vacancy, and the proposal is passed. Kathy's proxy is declared invalid by the chairman of the board. Kathy challenges both votes. Discuss whether her challenges will be successful.

6. A stockholder learned that the corporation had paid over $11 million in kickbacks and bribes. The board of directors investigated the allegations and determined that they were true but decided not to file suit. The directors decided that the corporation's actions were excused by the business-judgment doctrine (or rule). The stockholder then brought a derivative suit. The directors maintained that the business-judgment doctrine was a complete defense to their payment of bribes and sought immediate dismissal of the suit. Is the business-judgment doctrine a complete defense to this type of corporate activity? [Auerbach v. Bennett, 64 A.D.2d 98, 408 N.Y.S.2d 83 (1978)]

7. Free For All Missionary Baptist Church, Inc., by and through its pastors (who were also its president and secretary), leased from Southeastern Beverage and Ice Equipment Company, Inc., certain liquor dispensary equipment for use in an establishment known as Soul On Top of Peachtree. The church made an initial payment of $1,575 and then defaulted on the monthly rental payments. Southeastern brought suit against the church corporation, seeking damages for the balance of the lease. The shareholders of the church corporation defended on the ground that the action by its president and secretary and by the church were all *ultra vires*. Is this a valid defense? [Free For All Missionary Baptist Church, Inc. v. Southeastern Beverage and Ice Equipment Co., Inc., 135 Ga.App. 498, 218 S.E.2d 169 (1975)]

8. Mohawk Rubber Company was a corporation organized under the law of the state of Ohio. Fawcett and Ernst are the principle executives of Mohawk. The Board of Directors of Mohawk include Fawcett and Ernst, and five outside directors. The board directed Ernst to consider a new stock option plan as Mohawk was profiting nicely and would likely be the target of a takeover bid. On January 4, 1983, sixteen days before the regularly scheduled board of directors meeting at which Ernst was to present his stock option plan, Ernst telephoned each of the directors individually to obtain their approval for the plan. No prior written notice was given to the directors, and the plan was not before them in written form prior to the telephone calls. Each director orally approved the plan as it was described to him. "Minutes of the Board of Directors Meeting" were prepared that outlined the events of January 4, 1983, as if it had been a formal meeting. Later a proxy statement was issued urging the shareholders to give prompt attention to the plan and indicating that the board of directors had unanimously recommended a vote for the plan. Fradkin, a Mohawk shareholder, filed a derivative suit to stop the plan. To cure the omission of the formal meeting, Ernst and Fawcett presented a document entitled "Approval of Directors of the Mohawk Rubber Company to Action Without a Meeting" at a subsequent board meeting. All of the directors signed the document. Discuss whether Fradkin will be successful in his derivative suit? [Fradkin v. Ernst, 571 F.Supp. 829 (N.D.Ohio, 1983)]

9. Harris Lumber Company was a corporation organized under the law of the state of Arkansas. Harris was the president of the corporation; Nelson was its secretary and treasurer; and Jones was its remaining director and shareholder. Several years after its incorporation, Harris Lumber owed Merchants and Farmers Bank $4,500. A promissory note was executed for the amount of the debt, and a mortgage was executed on certain personal property owned by Harris Lumber to secure payment. Nelson, who at the time was general manager of Harris Lumber, signed both the note and the mortgage. Payments amounting to $2,150 were made over the next two-and-one-half years on the promissory note. At that point payment ceased, and Merchants Bank brought this suit to recover the balance of the sum owed. Harris Lumber Company never objected to the execution of the mortgage or the note or to any of the payments under the note until Merchants Bank filed this suit. However, at that point, Harris Lumber claimed that Nelson did not have the authority to sign promissory notes or to execute mortgages on behalf of Harris Lumber. In fact, neither the corporate charter nor any of the board of directors' resolutions vested the general manager with any authority to bind the corporation. Will Merchants Bank be successful in its suit against Harris Lumber Company? [Merchants and Farmers Bank v. Harris Lumber Co., 103 Ark. 283, 146 S.W. 508 (1912)]

41

CORPORATIONS
Rights and Duties of Directors, Managers, and Shareholders

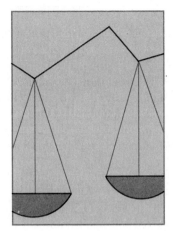

A corporation joins the efforts and resources of a large number of individuals for the purpose of producing greater returns than those individuals could have obtained individually. Sometimes actions that benefit the corporation as a whole do not coincide with the separate interests of these individuals. This chapter focuses on the rights and duties of directors, managers, and shareholders and the ways in which conflicts among them are resolved.

THE ROLE OF OFFICERS AND DIRECTORS

A director occupies a position of responsibility unlike that of other corporate personnel. Directors are sometimes inappropriately characterized as *agents* because they act for and on behalf of the corporation. However, no *individual* director can act as an agent to bind the corporation, and, as a group, directors collectively control the corporation in a way that no agent can control a principal. Directors are often incorrectly characterized as *trustees* because they occupy positions of trust and control over the corporation. However, unlike trustees, they do not own or hold title to property for the use and benefit of others.

Directors manage the corporation through the officers who are selected by the board; these officers

are agents of the corporation. Directors and officers are deemed *fiduciaries* of the corporation. Their relationship with the corporation and its shareholders is one of trust and confidence. The fiduciary duties of the directors and officers include the duty of care and the duty of loyalty.

The Duty of Care

Directors are obligated to be honest and to use prudent business judgment in the conduct of corporate affairs. The so-called business-judgment rule does not require directors to insure the success of every venture that the corporation undertakes. The test most often used is objective—the directors must exercise the same degree of care that reasonably prudent people use in the conduct of their own personal business affairs. Thus, corporate losses resulting merely from poor business judgment or an honest mistake in judgment will not normally result in the imposition of legal liability on directors.

Breach of the Duty of Care   Directors can be held answerable to the corporation and to the shareholders for breach of their duty of care. When directors delegate work to corporate officers and employees, they are expected to use a reasonable amount of supervision. Otherwise, they will be held liable for *negligence* or *mismanagement* of corporate personnel.

For example, a corporate bank director failed to attend any board of directors' meetings in five and a half years and never inspected any of the corporate books or records. Meanwhile, the bank president made various improper loans and permitted large overdrafts. The corporate director was held liable to the corporation for losses of nearly $20,000 resulting from the unsupervised actions of the bank president and the loan committee.

The standard of due care has been variously described and codified in many corporation codes and by judicial decisions.[1] The impact of the standard is to require that directors carry out their responsibilities in an informed, businesslike manner.

Depending on the nature of the business, directors and officers are often expected to act in accordance with their own knowledge and training. However, most states (and Section 35 of the Model Act) allow a director to make decisions in reliance on information furnished by competent officers or employees, professionals such as attorneys and accountants, or even an executive committee of the board, without being accused of acting in bad faith or failing to exercise due care if such information turns out to be faulty.

Directors are expected to attend board of directors' meetings, and their votes should be entered into the minutes of corporate meetings. Unless a dissent is entered, the director is presumed to have assented. Directors who dissent rarely are held individually liable for mismanagement of the corporation. It is for this reason that a director who is absent from a given meeting sometimes registers with the secretary of the board a dissent to actions taken at the missed meeting with which he or she disagrees.

Directors are expected to be informed on corporate matters and to understand legal and other professional advice rendered to the board. A director

who is unable to carry out such responsibilities must resign. Even when the required duty of care has not been exercised, directors and officers are liable only for the damages caused to the corporation by their negligence.

The Duty of Loyalty

Perhaps the best way to describe the concept of loyalty is by a definition given by Justice Cardozo:

> Many forms of conduct permissible in a workaday world for those acting at arm's length, are forbidden to those bound by fiduciary ties. Not honesty alone, but the punctilio of an honor the most sensitive, is then the standard of behavior. As to this there has developed a tradition that is unbending and inveterate.[2]

The essence of the fiduciary duty requires subordination of self-interest to the interest of the entity to which the duty is owed. It presumes constant loyalty to the corporation on the part of the directors and officers. In general, the duty of loyalty prohibits directors from using corporate funds or confidential corporate information for their personal advantage. It requires officers and directors to disclose fully any corporate opportunity or any possible conflict of interest that might occur in a transaction involving the directors and the corporation.

Cases dealing with fiduciary duty typically involve one or more of the following:

1. Competing with the corporation.
2. Usurping a corporate opportunity.
3. Having an interest that conflicts with the interest of the corporation.
4. Engaging in insider trading.
5. Authorizing some corporate transaction that is detrimental to minority shareholders.
6. Selling control over the corporation.

In the following case, the Alabama court reviewed a situation in which officers, directors, and shareholders attempted to secure advantages for themselves at the expense of the corporation.

---

1. See, for example, Section 35 of the Model Business Corporation Act, which provides that "a director shall perform his duties as a director, including his duties as a member of any committee of the board upon which he may serve, in good faith, in any manner he reasonably believes to be in the best interest of the corporation, and with such care as an ordinarily prudent person in a like position would use under similar circumstances."

---

2. Meinhard v. Salmon, 249 N.Y. 458, 464, 164 N.E. 545, 546 (1928).

BACKGROUND AND FACTS *The defendants, Morad and Thomson, were officers, directors, and shareholders of Bio-Lab, Inc. Bio-Lab had one additional shareholder, the plaintiff, Coupounas. While serving as officers and directors of Bio-Lab, the defendants incorporated and operated a competing business, Med-Lab, Inc. The plaintiff brought a derivative suit on behalf of Bio-Lab against the defendants and Med-Lab, alleging that, in opening the competing business, they had usurped a corporate opportunity of Bio-Lab.*

MORAD v.
COUPOUNAS
Supreme Court of Alabama,
1978.
361 So.2d 6.

FAULKNER, Justice.

*   *   *   *

"It is well settled that directors and other governing members of a corporation are so far agents of the corporation that in their dealings respecting corporate interests, they are subject to the rules which apply generally to persons standing in fiduciary relations and which forbid such persons to secure an advantage for themselves which fidelity to the trust reposed in them would carry to others whose interests they ought to represent."

*   *   *   *

"[I]n general the legal restrictions which rest upon such officers in their acquisitions are generally limited to property wherein the corporation has an interest already existing, or in which it has an expectancy growing out of an existing right, or to cases where the officers' interference will in some degree balk the corporation in effecting the purposes of its creation." *   *   *

"[I]f there is presented to a corporate officer or director a business opportunity which the corporation is financially able to undertake, is, from its nature, in the line of the corporation's business and is of practical advantage to it, is one in which the corporation has an interest or a reasonable expectancy, and, by embracing the opportunity, the self-interest of the officer or director will be brought into conflict with that of his corporation, the law will not permit him to seize the opportunity for himself." *   *   *

"[N]umerous factors are to be weighed, including the manner in which the offer was communicated to the officer; the good faith of the officer; the use of corporate assets to acquire the opportunity; the financial ability of the corporation to acquire the opportunity; the degree of disclosure made to the corporation; the action taken by the corporation with reference thereto; and the need or interest of the corporation in the opportunity. These, as well as numerous other factors, are weighed in a given case. The presence or absence of any single factor is not determinative of the issue of corporate opportunity." *   *   *

Here the trial court specifically found that one of the corporate purposes of Bio-Lab was to expand into specific new areas, including Tuscaloosa. Ample evidence in the record supports this conclusion. Bio-Lab's certificate of incorporation declared that one of the purposes of the business was "to have one or more offices." *   *   *

*   *   *   *

*   *   * [T]estimony revealed that $44,000 had been required to establish Med-Lab. At the end of 1974 Bio-Lab had only $24,300 available for this purpose. But, Raburn [a certified public accountant, familiar with the books of both Med-Lab and Bio-Lab] also testified that in 1974 Bio-Lab had paid a "rather high" dividend of $20,000. His testimony indicated that the payment of dividends is often restricted when a corporation wishes to expand. Thus, if the dividend had not been paid, Bio-Lab clearly should have had the financial ability to expand to Tuscaloosa, with or without a loan. In light of this testimony the trial court's finding that defendants improperly formed Med-Lab to the detriment of Bio-Lab is clearly supportable and will not be disturbed by this Court on appeal.

<table>
<tr><td>

DECISION AND REMEDY

</td><td>

The Alabama Supreme Court determined that the appropriate remedy for the defendants' breach of duty of loyalty was for the court to impose a "constructive trust," which would require all profits of Med-Lab to be paid to Bio-Lab.

</td></tr>
<tr><td>

COMMENTS

</td><td>

Directors and officers of a corporation are expected to act with undivided loyalty. This rule restricts them from competing with the corporation, and, at the very least, it requires fiduciaries to offer business opportunities to the corporation.

</td></tr>
</table>

Conflicts of Interest

Corporate directors often have many business affiliations, and they can even sit on the board of more than one corporation. Of course, they are precluded from entering into or supporting any business that operates in direct competition with the corporation. The fiduciary duty requires them to make a full disclosure of any potential *conflicts of interest* that might arise in any corporate transaction.

Contracts Between Director and Corporation

Sometimes the corporation will enter into a contract or engage in a transaction in which an officer or director has a material interest. The director or officer must make a *full disclosure* of that interest and should abstain from voting on the proposed transaction.

For example, Pacific Business Corporation needs office space. Louis Allen, one of its five directors, owns the building adjoining the corporation. He negotiates a lease with Pacific Business for the space, making a full disclosure to Pacific Business and the other four board directors. The lease arrangement is fair and reasonable, and it is unanimously approved by the corporation's board of directors. In such a case, the contract is valid. The rule is one of reason; otherwise, directors would be prevented from ever giving financial assistance to the corporations they serve.

The various state statutes contain different standards, but a contract will generally not be voidable if:

1. It was fair and reasonable to the corporation at the time the contract was made.
2. There is a full disclosure of the interest of the officers or directors in the transaction.

3. The contract is approved by a majority of the disinterested directors or shareholders.

(See Section 41 of the Model Business Corporation Act.)

Contracts Between Corporations Having Common Directors

Often contracts are negotiated between corporations having one or more directors who are members of both boards. Such transactions require great care, as they are closely scrutinized by courts.

RIGHTS OF DIRECTORS

A director of a corporation has a number of rights. These include the right of participation, the right of inspection, the right of indemnification, and the right of compensation. These rights are discussed below.

Right of Participation

A corporate director must have certain rights in order to function properly in that position. The main right is to be notified of board of directors' meetings, so as to participate in them. As pointed out in Chapter 40, regular board meetings are usually established by the bylaws or board resolution, and no notice of these meetings is required. If special meetings are called, however, notice is required unless waived by the director.

Right of Inspection

A director must have access to all corporate books and records in order to make decisions and to exercise the necessary supervision. This right is virtually absolute and cannot be restricted.

Right of Indemnification

It is not unusual for corporate directors to become involved in lawsuits by virtue of their position and their actions as directors. Most states (and the Model Act, Section 5) permit a corporation to indemnify a director for legal costs, fees, and judgments involved in defending corporation-related suits.

At common law, a director had no right to be indemnified; however, there was little objection to indemnification if the director was absolved of liability. Today statutes and court decisions allow indemnification even if the director is not absolved of liability, as long as his or her actions were made in good faith, based on a reasonable belief that such actions were in the best interests of the corporation.

Criminal convictions usually require bad faith, but bad faith is not presumed merely because the director settles the litigation, pleads *nolo contendere* (no contest), or even is found liable civilly. Many states specifically permit a corporation to purchase liability insurance for the directors and officers to cover indemnification. Where the statutes are silent on this matter, the power to purchase such insurance is usually considered to be part of the corporation's implied power.

Right of Compensation

Historically, directors have had no inherent right to compensation for their services as directors. Officers receive compensation, and nominal sums are often paid as honoraria to directors. In many cases, directors are also chief corporate officers and receive compensation in their managerial positions. Most directors, however, gain through indirect benefits, such as business contacts, prestige, and other rewards.

There is a growing trend toward providing more than nominal compensation for directors, especially in large corporations where directorships can be enormous burdens in terms of time, work, effort, and risk. Many states permit the corporate articles or bylaws to authorize compensation for directors, and in some cases the board can set its own compensation unless the articles or bylaws provide otherwise.

RIGHTS AND DUTIES OF CORPORATE OFFICERS AND OTHER MANAGEMENT EMPLOYEES

Corporate officers and other high-level managers are employees of the company, and their rights are defined by employment contracts.

The duties of corporate officers are the same as the duties of directors because their respective corporate positions involve both of them in decision making and place them in similar positions of control. Hence, they are viewed as having the same fiduciary duty of care and loyalty in their conduct of corporate affairs. Officers are subject to the same obligations concerning corporate opportunities and conflicts of interest as are directors.

SHAREHOLDER RIGHTS

Shareholders own the corporation. Their rights are established in the articles of incorporation and under the state's general incorporation law.

The Right to a Stock Certificate

A stock certificate evidences ownership, and shareholders have the right to demand that the corporation issue a certificate and record their names and addresses in the corporate stock record books. Stock is *intangible* personal property—the ownership right exists independently of the certificate itself. A stock certificate may be lost or destroyed, but ownership is not destroyed with it. Corporate records reflect ownership but do not determine it.

A new certificate can be issued to replace one that has been lost or destroyed.[3] Notice of shareholder meetings, dividends, and operational and financial reports are all distributed according to the recorded ownership listed in the corporation's books, not on the basis of possession of the certificate.

Assume that Betty Anderson's certificate showing ownership of corporate stock in Chrysler Cor-

---

3. To have a lost or destroyed certificate reissued, a shareholder is normally required to furnish an indemnity bond to protect the corporation against potential loss should the original certificate reappear at some future time in the hands of a bona fide purchaser. [UCC 8-302 and 8-405(2)]

poration is destroyed in a fire on September 1. The corporation declares a dividend on September 5. According to corporate records, Betty Anderson is the "record owner" and receives the dividend even though she no longer has the certificate.

Of course, to sell or otherwise transfer the shares, indorsement and delivery of the actual certificate to the transferee are required.

Preemptive Rights

A **preemptive right** is a common law concept in which a preference is given to a shareholder over all other purchasers to subscribe to or purchase a pro-rated share of a new issue of stock. This allows the shareholder to maintain his or her portion of control, voting power, or financial interest in the corporation. Most statutes either grant preemptive rights (but allow them to be negated in the corporation's articles) or deny preemptive rights (except to the extent that they are granted in the articles). The result is that the articles of incorporation determine the existence and scope of preemptive rights. Generally, preemptive rights apply only to additional stock sold for cash. They do not apply to treasury shares reissued or to authorized but unissued shares. Generally, such rights must be exercised within a specified time period (usually thirty days).

For example, Paula Smith purchases one hundred shares of National Clothing stock. National Clothing had authorized and issued one thousand shares, of which Paula now owns 10 percent. Subsequently, National Clothing, by vote of its shareholders, authorizes the issuance of another one thousand shares (amending the articles of incorporation). This increases its capital stock to a total of two thousand shares.

If preemptive rights have been provided, Smith can purchase one additional share of the new stock being issued for each share currently owned—or one hundred additional shares. Thus she can own two hundred of the two thousand shares outstanding, and her relative position as a shareholder will be maintained. If preemptive rights are not reserved, her proportionate control and voting power will be diluted from that of a 10 percent shareholder to that of a 5 percent shareholder because of the issuance of the additional one thousand shares.

Preemptive rights are far more significant in a close corporation because of the relatively few number of shares and the substantial interest each shareholder controls.

Stock Warrant Rights

When preemptive rights exist and a corporation is issuing additional shares, each shareholder is usually given *stock warrants*. A **stock warrant** is a transferable option to acquire a given number of shares from the corporation at a stated price (usually below the current market price). Warrants are often publicly traded on securities exchanges. When the warrant option is for a short period of time, the stock warrants are usually referred to as *rights*.

Dividend Rights

A dividend is a distribution of corporate profits or income *ordered by the directors* and paid to the shareholders in proportion to their respective shares in the corporation. Dividends can be paid in cash, property, stock of the corporation that is paying the dividends, or stock of other corporations.[4]

State laws vary, but every state determines the general circumstances and legal requirements under which dividends are paid. State laws also control the sources of revenue to be used; only certain funds are legally available for paying dividends. Once declared, a cash dividend becomes a corporate debt enforceable at law like any other debt.[5]

Dividends payable from limited funds are prescribed by various state statutes as follows:

1. Current net earnings.
2. Net profits.
3. Surplus.

Dividends can be paid only from the following sources of funds:

1. *Retained earnings.* All states allow dividends to be paid from the undistributed net profits earned by the corporation, including capital gains from the sale of fixed assets. The undistributed net profits are called earned surplus or retained earnings.

---

4. Technically, dividends paid in stock are not dividends. They maintain each shareholder's proportional interest in the corporation. On one occasion a distillery declared and paid a "dividend" in bonded whiskey.
5. An insolvent corporation cannot declare a dividend.

2. *Net profits.* A few state statutes allow dividends to be issued from current net profits without regard to deficits in prior years.

3. *Surplus.* A number of state statutes allow dividends to be paid out of any kind of surplus.

When directors fail to declare a dividend, shareholders can ask a court of equity for an injunction to compel the directors to meet and to declare a dividend. It must be shown that the directors have acted so unreasonably in withholding the dividend that their conduct is an abuse of discretion.

Often large money reserves are accumulated for a bona fide purpose such as expansion, research, or other legitimate corporate goals. The mere fact that sufficient corporate earnings or surplus are available to pay a dividend is not enough to compel directors to distribute funds that, in the board's opinion, should not be paid. The courts are circumspect about interfering with corporate operations and will not compel directors to declare dividends unless abuse of discretion is clearly shown. Thus, directors are not ordinarily *required* to declare dividends to shareholders. A striking exception to this rule is made in the following classic case.

BACKGROUND AND FACTS   *Ford Motor Company was formed in 1903. Henry Ford, the president and majority shareholder, attempted to run the corporation as if it were a one-man operation. The business expanded rapidly and, in addition to regular quarterly dividends, often paid special dividends. Sales and profits were:*

DODGE v. FORD MOTOR CO.
Supreme Court of Michigan, 1919.
204 Mich. 459, 170 N.W. 668.

1910   18,664 cars $4,521,509 profit
1911   34,466 cars $6,275,031 profit
1912   68,544 cars $13,057,312 profit, $14,475,095 surplus
1913   168,304 cars $25,046,767 profit, $28,124,173 surplus
1914   248,307 cars $30,338,454 profit, $48,827,032 surplus
1915   264,351 cars $24,641,423 profit, $59,135,770 surplus

By 1916, surplus above capital was $111,960,907.

Originally, the Ford car sold for more than $900. From time to time, the price was reduced, and in 1916 it sold for $440. For the year beginning August 1, 1916, the price was reduced again, to $360. In the interests of setting aside money for future investment and expansion, Ford Motor Company paid no special dividend after October 1915. The plaintiffs were minority stockholders, who owned one-tenth of the shares of the corporation. They petitioned the court to compel the directors to declare a dividend.

OSTRANDER, Chief Justice.

*   *   *   *

[I]t is charged that notwithstanding the earnings for the fiscal year ending July 31, 1916, the Ford Motor Company has not since that date declared any special dividends:

"And the said Henry Ford, president of the company, has declared it to be the settled policy of the company not to pay in the future any special dividends, but to put back into the business for the future all of the earnings of the company, other than the regular dividend of five per cent (5%) monthly upon the authorized capital stock of the company—two million dollars ($2,000,000)."

This declaration of the future policy, it is charged in the bill, was published in the public press in the city of Detroit and throughout the United States in substantially the following language:

" 'My ambition,' declared Mr. Ford, 'is to employ still more men; to spread the benefits of this industrial system to the greatest possible number, to help them build up their lives and their homes. To do this, we are putting the greatest share of our profits back into the business.' "

It is charged further that the said Henry Ford stated to plaintiffs personally, in substance, that as all the stockholders had received back in dividends more than they had invested they were not entitled to receive anything additional to the regular dividend of 5 per cent a month, and that it was not his policy to have larger dividends declared in the future, and that the profits and earnings of the company would be put back into the business for the purpose of extending its operations and increasing the number of its employes, and that, inasmuch as the profits were to be represented by investment in plants and capital investment, the stockholders would have no right to complain.

* * *

* * * *

"It is a well-recognized principle of law that the directors of a corporation, and they alone, have the power to declare a dividend of the earnings of the corporation, and to determine its amount. Courts of equity will not interfere in the management of the directors unless it is clearly made to appear that they are guilty of fraud or misappropriation of the corporate funds, or refuse to declare a dividend when the corporation has a surplus of net profits which it can, without detriment to its business, divide among its stockholders, and when a refusal to do so would amount to such an abuse of discretion as would constitute a fraud, or breach of that good faith which they are bound to exercise towards the stockholders."

* * * *

There is committed to the discretion of directors, a discretion to be exercised in good faith, the infinite details of business, including the wages which shall be paid to employes, the number of hours they shall work, the conditions under which labor shall be carried on, and the price for which products shall be offered to the public.

* * * [I]t is not within the lawful powers of a board of directors to shape and conduct the affairs of a corporation for the merely incidental benefit of shareholders and for the primary purpose of benefiting others, and no one will contend that, if the avowed purpose of the defendant directors was to sacrifice the interests of shareholders, it would not be the duty of the courts to interfere.

* * * *

Defendants say, and it is true, that a considerable cash balance must be at all times carried by such a concern. But, as has been stated, there was a large daily, weekly, monthly, receipt of cash. The output was practically continuous and was continuously, and within a few days, turned into cash. Moreover, the contemplated expenditures were not to be immediately made. The large sum appropriated for the smelter plant was payable over a considerable period of time. *So that, without going further, it would appear that, accepting and approving the plan of the directors, it was their duty to distribute on or near the 1st of August, 1916, a very large sum of money to stockholders.* [Emphasis added.]

In reaching this conclusion, we do not ignore, but recognize, the validity of the proposition that plaintiffs have from the beginning profited by, if they have not lately, officially, participated in, the general policy of expansion pursued by this corporation. We do not lose sight of the fact that it had been, upon an occasion, agreeable to the plaintiffs to increase the capital stock to $100,000,000 by a stock dividend of $98,000,000. These things go only to answer other contentions now made by plaintiffs, and do not and cannot operate to estop them to demand proper dividends upon the stock they own. It is obvious that an annual dividend of 60 per cent upon $2,000,000, or $1,200,000, is the equivalent of a very small dividend upon $100,000,000, or more.

DECISION AND REMEDY   *The defendant, Ford, was ordered by the court to declare a dividend.*

Illegal Dividends   Whenever a dividend is paid while the corporation is *insolvent*, it is automatically an illegal dividend, and shareholders can be liable for returning the payment to the corporation or its creditors.

Dividends are generally required by statute to be distributed only from certain authorized corporate accounts representing profits. Sometimes dividends are improperly paid from an unauthorized account, or their payment causes the corporation to become insolvent. Generally, in this case, shareholders must return illegal dividends only if they knew that the dividends were illegal when they received them.

In all cases of illegal and improper dividends, the board of directors can be held personally liable for the amount of the payment. However, when directors can show that a shareholder *knew* a dividend was illegal when it was received, the directors are entitled to contribution from the shareholder.

The Right to Vote

Shareholders exercise ownership control through the power of their votes. In the early development of corporate law, each shareholder was entitled to one vote per share. This rule still holds today, but the voting techniques discussed in Chapter 40 (shareholder agreements, voting trusts, cumulative voting methods, and so on) all enhance the power of the shareholder's vote.

The articles can exclude or limit voting rights, particularly to certain classes of shares. For example, owners of preferred shares are usually denied the right to vote. Treasury shares, held by the corporation, cannot be voted until they have been reissued by the corporation.

Inspection Rights

Shareholders in a corporation enjoy both common law and statutory inspection rights. Shareholders at common law enjoyed qualified rights to inspect and copy corporate books and records, such as the bylaws and minutes of the board of directors' meetings and the shareholders' meetings, as well as documents such as contracts, correspondence, and tax returns. They even had the right to inspect the corporate headquarters. The shareholder's right of inspection is limited, however, to inspection and copying of corporate books and records for a *proper purpose*, provided they make the request in advance. Either the shareholder can inspect in person, or an attorney, agent, accountant, or other assistant can do so.

The power of inspection is fraught with potential abuses, and the corporation is allowed to protect itself from them. For example, a shareholder can properly be denied access to corporate records to prevent harassment or to protect trade secrets or other confidential corporate information. Section 52 of the Model Act imposes various standard requirements on the shareholder's inspection right:

> Any person who shall have been a holder of record shares * * * at least six months immediately preceding his [or her] demand or [who is] * * * the holder of * * * at least 5 percent of all the outstanding shares of the corporation, upon written demand stating the purpose thereof, shall have the right to examine, in person, or by agent or attorney, at any reasonable time or times, for any proper purpose its relevant books and records of accounts, minutes, and record of shareholders and to make extracts therefrom.

However, a corporation's improper refusal to allow access to its records can result in severe and costly liability to the corporation. Under Section 52 of the Model Act, the penalty is 10 percent of the value of the shares owned by the shareholder who has been denied access to the books.

The following case illustrates a court's dilemma in holding that a stockholder-competitor could inspect the corporate books for limited purposes.

BACKGROUND AND FACTS   *The plaintiff, Uldrich, was a shareholder and former director, officer, and employee of Datasport, Inc., the defendant, a Minnesota corporation. Datasport terminated Uldrich's employment, directorship, and office. Aside from Uldrich maintaining his status as a stockholder, he was also a competitor of Datasport. While Uldrich was still a director and an officer of Datasport, he was prohibited from marketing his competing product for one year, by a court order upon Datasport's request. Since his dismissal,*

ULDRICH v.
DATASPORT, INC.
Court of Appeals of Minnesota,
1984.
349 N.W.2d 286.

Uldrich has been denied access to Datasport's books and records. He seeks a writ of mandamus from the court commanding Datasport to permit inspection.

PARKER, Judge.

*   *   *   *

*   *   * The matter was tried before the district court, which ordered a writ of mandamus directing Datasport to allow examination of:

   a. the general ledger;

   b. the cash and disbursements general journal;

   c. a computer printout of customers, customers' contract terms and contract prices and associated historical data;

   d. the receipts and disbursements journal;

   e. purchase and sales journal;

   f. state and federal income tax returns;

   g. cancelled checks;

   h. bank statements;

   i. deposit tickets;

   j. vendors' sales invoices;

   k. expense vouchers;

   l. entertainment receipts;

   m. vendors' supply vouchers.

In its order, the trial court enjoined Uldrich from making competitive use of such information. Datasport appeals from the order for writ of mandamus.

The right to inspect corporate books and records is guaranteed to shareholders by Minn.Stats. §§ 301.34, subd. 5, and 300.32 (1982), which provide in pertinent parts:

> 301.34, Subd. 5, *Examinations by Shareholders.* Every shareholder *   *   * shall have a right to examine, in person or by agent or attorney, at any reasonable time or times, *for any proper purpose,* and at the place or places where usually kept or at such other place as the court may order, *the share register, books of account and records of the proceedings of the shareholders and directors, and to make extracts therefrom.*

> 300.32. In all stock corporations the directors shall cause accurate and complete records to be kept of all corporate proceedings and of all stock subscribed, transferred, canceled, or retired and proper books, accounts, files, and records of all other business transacted. All such books and records shall, at all reasonable times and for all proper purposes, be open to the inspection of any stockholder. *   *   * (Emphasis added.)

To enforce this right, the remedy of mandamus is available to force a corporate defendant to comply. However, mandamus will not be issued to enforce the mere naked right of inspection or to gratify idle curiosity; rather, it is necessary for the petitioner to set out the interest at stake rendering an inspection necessary. *   *   *

The trial court found that Uldrich has good faith reasons for seeking access to the corporate books and records of Datasport, i.e., to place a monetary value on his stock interests and to evaluate the conduct and affairs of the other shareholders, officers and directors. [In a previous case] the Supreme Court held such reasons sufficient to compel inspection of corporate books and records by mandamus.

Respondent is concerned that the corporate records reflect that virtually all of Datasport's sales revenues are "eaten up" by operating expenses. He is concerned about the other shareholders (who are officers and directors) using Datasport assets to benefit their other business interests. The other shareholders of Datasport own a partnership called Studio Time; Studio Time leases office space to Datasport. These shareholders also own a corporation called Multi-Data, which promotes a product relating health and weather; Multi-Data offices are also located in the same space as Datasport offices.

The officers of Multi-Data are also the officers of Datasport. Datasport sold computer time to Multi-Data and Multi-Data's services were used by Datasport at one time. All of the remaining shareholders, officers and directors of Datasport own a company called Reel Time, a television production company which was operated out of the Datasport offices. In three and one-half years, with over $1.5 million in sales, [Uldrich] has received less than $1,000 in return on his investment.

Datasport contends that the documents requested are "confidential business information" and that the order directs Datasport to make available "significant portions of its corporate records which cannot be included within any reasonable definition of books of account under Minn.Stat § 301.34, subd. 4 and subd. 5."

Neither the statute nor case law defines "books of account." [Datasport] argues that the trial court's order includes information in these various records that are the supporting documentation for the books of account, "but do not themselves form a part of the books of account."

Under the circumstances here, when the shareholders, officers and directors of Datasport have multiple business interests operated on the same premises as, and doing business with, Datasport, and when [Uldrich's] return on his investment appears trivial in view of a substantial sales record, the trial court properly recognized that equity required a broad scope be given to the concept of shareholder access.

The trial court recognized that misuse might be made of some of the information sought and enjoined use of it for any competitive purpose.

*   *   *   *

The court of appeals affirmed Uldrich's writ of mandamus compelling Datasport to allow Uldrich to exercise his shareholder's right of inspection.

DECISION AND REMEDY

The court's order in this case balanced the interests of the shareholder's access to corporate records and the sensitivities of a corporation to its competitors. Apparently because of this, the court did not impose a 10 percent penalty.

COMMENTS

The Right to Transfer Shares

Corporate stock represents an ownership right in intangible personal property. The law generally recognizes the right of an owner to transfer property to another person unless there are valid restrictions on its transferability. Although stock certificates are negotiable and freely transferable by indorsement and delivery, transfer of stock in closely held corporations is generally restricted by contract, the bylaws, or a restriction stamped on the stock certificate. The existence of any restrictions on transferability should always be noted on the face of the stock certificate, and these restrictions must be reasonable.

The Right of First Refusal   Sometimes corporations or their shareholders restrict transferability by reserving the option to purchase any shares offered for resale by a shareholder. The option remains with the corporation or the shareholders for only a spec-

ified or reasonable time. Variations on the purchase option are possible. For example, a shareholder might be required to offer the shares to other shareholders or to the corporation first.

Corporate Records   When shares are transferred, a new entry is made in the corporate stock book to indicate the new owner. Until the corporation is notified and the entry is complete, voting rights, notice of shareholders' meetings, dividend distribution, and so forth are all held by the current record owner.

Rights upon Dissolution

When a corporation is dissolved and its outstanding debts and the claims of its creditors have been satisfied, the remaining assets are distributed on a pro rata basis among the shareholders. Certain classes of preferred stock can be given priority to the extent of their contractual preference. If no preferences to distribution of assets upon liquidation are given to any class of stock, then the stockholders share the remaining assets.

Compelling Receivership Suppose a minority shareholder knows that the board of directors is mishandling corporate assets or is permitting a deadlock to threaten or irreparably injure the corporation's finances. The minority shareholder is not powerless to intervene. He or she can petition a court to appoint a receiver and to liquidate the business assets of the corporation.

The Model Act, Section 97, permits any shareholder to institute such an action when it appears that:

1. The directors are deadlocked in the management of corporate affairs, shareholders are unable to break that deadlock, and irreparable injury to the corporation is being suffered or threatened.
2. The acts of the directors or those in control of the corporation are illegal, oppressive, or fraudulent.
3. Corporate assets are being misapplied or wasted.

SHAREHOLDER LIABILITIES

One of the hallmarks of the corporate organization is that shareholders are not personally liable for the debts of the corporation. If the corporation fails, shareholders can lose their investment, but that is generally the limit of their liability. In certain instances of fraud, undercapitalization, or careless observance of corporate formalities, a court will pierce the corporate veil (disregard the corporate entity) and hold the shareholders individually liable. But these situations are the exception, not the rule.

Although rare, there are three additional situations in which a shareholder can be personally liable. These situations relate to:

1. Stock subscriptions.
2. Watered stock issued.
3. Illegal dividends (previously discussed).

Stock Subscriptions

A preincorporation stock subscription agreement is treated as a continuing offer, and it is usually irrevocable (for up to six months under the Model Act).

Once the corporation has been formed, it can sell shares to shareholder investors. In either case, once the subscription agreement or stock offer is accepted, a binding contract is formed. Any refusal to pay constitutes a breach resulting in the personal liability of the shareholder.

Watered Shares

Shares of stock can be paid for by property or by services rendered, instead of cash. Shares cannot be purchased with promissory notes. The general rule is that for par value shares sold, the corporation must receive a value at least equal to the par value amount. For any no par shares sold, the corporation must receive the value of the shares as determined by the board or shareholders. When shares are issued by the corporation for less than these stated values, the shares are referred to as **watered stock.** In most cases, the shareholder who receives watered stock must pay the difference to the corporation (the shareholder is personally liable). In some states, the shareholder who receives watered stock may be liable to creditors of the corporation for unpaid corporate debts.

To illustrate the concept of watered stock, suppose that during the formation of a corporation, Garcia, as one of the incorporators, transferred his property, Greenacre, to the corporation for 10,000 shares of stock at a par value of $100 per share for a total price of $1 million. The property is transferred and the shares are issued. Greenacre is carried on the corporate books at a value of $1 million. Upon appraisal, it is discovered that the market value of the property at the time of transfer was only $500,000. The shares issued to Garcia are therefore watered stock and he is liable to the corporation for the difference.

DUTIES AND LIABILITIES OF MAJOR SHAREHOLDERS

In some cases, a majority shareholder is regarded as having a fiduciary duty to the corporation and to the minority shareholders. This occurs when a single shareholder (or a few acting in concert) owns a sufficient number of shares to exercise *de facto* control over the corporation. In these situations, majority shareholders owe a fiduciary duty to the minority shareholders and creditors when they sell their shares, because it is in fact a transfer of control of the corporation.

QUESTIONS AND CASE PROBLEMS

1. Acme Corporation negotiates with the Jones Construction Company for the renovation of the Acme corporate headquarters. Jones, owner of the Jones Construction Company, is also one of the five members of the board of directors of Acme. The contract terms are standard for this type of contract. Jones had previously informed two of the other directors of his interest in the construction company. The contract was approved by Acme's board on a three-to-two vote, with Jones voting with the majority. Discuss whether this contract is binding on the corporation.

2. Acme, Inc., has a board of directors consisting of three members (Able, Baker, and Carter) and approximately five hundred shareholders. At a regular meeting of the board, the board selects Green as president of the corporation by a two-to-one vote, with Able dissenting. The minutes of the meeting do not register Able's dissenting vote. Later, upon an audit, it is discovered that Green is a former convict and has openly embezzled $500,000 from Acme, Inc. This loss is not covered by insurance. The corporation wants to hold directors Able, Baker, and Carter liable. Able claims no liability. Discuss the personal liability of the directors to the corporation.

3. Ann owns 10,000 shares (10 percent) of Superal Corporation. Superal authorized 100,000 shares and issued all of them during its first six months in operation. Later Superal reacquired 10,000 of these shares. With shareholder approval, Superal amended its articles so as to authorize and issue another 100,000 shares, and, also, by a resolution of the board of directors, to reissue the 10,000 shares of treasury stock. There is no provision in the corporate articles dealing with shareholder preemptive rights. Because of her previous ownership of 10 percent of Superal, Ann claims that she has the preemptive right to purchase 10,000 shares of the new issue and 1,000 shares of the stock being reissued. Discuss her claims.

4. Jane has acquired one share of common stock of a multimillion-dollar corporation with over 500,000 shareholders. Jane's ownership is so small that she is questioning what her rights are as a shareholder. For example, she wants to know whether this one share entitles her to:

(a) Attend and vote at shareholder meetings.
(b) Inspect the corporate books.
(c) Receive yearly dividends.

Discuss Jane's rights in these three matters.

5. Smith has made a preincorporation subscription agreement to purchase 500 shares of a newly formed corporation. The shares have a par value of $100 per share.

The corporation is formed, and Smith's subscription is accepted by the corporation. Smith transfers a piece of land he owns to the corporation, and the corporation issues 250 shares for it. One year later, with the corporation in serious financial difficulty, the board declares and pays a $5 per share dividend. It is now learned that the land transferred by Smith had a market value of $18,000. Discuss any liability shareholder Smith has to the corporation or to creditors of the corporation.

6. Klinicki and Lundgren formed Berlinair, a closely held Oregon corporation, to provide air transportation out of West Germany. Klinicki, who owned 33 percent of the company stock, was the vice-president and a director. Lundgren, who also owned 33 percent of the stock, was the president and a director. Lelco, Inc., a corporation owned by Lundgren and his family, owned 33 percent of Berlinair, and Berlinair's attorney owned the last 1 percent of stock. One of the goals of Berlinair was to obtain the contract with BFR, a West German consortium of travel agents, to provide BFR with air charter service.

Later, Lundgren learned that the BFR contract might become available. Lundgren then incorporated Air Berlin Charter Company, of which he was the sole owner, and bid for the BFR contract. Lundgren won the BFR contract for Air Berlin while using Berlinair working time, staff, money, and facilities without the knowledge of Klinicki. When Klinicki learned of the BFR contract he filed a derivative suit, as a minority stockholder, against Air Berlin for usurping a corporate opportunity. Should Klinicki recover against Air Berlin? If so, what should Klinicki be awarded as damages? [Klinicki v. Lundgren, 67 Or.App. 160, 678 P.2d 1250 (1984)]

7. Engdahl was a 10 percent stockholder, a director, and the treasurer of Aero Drapery, Inc. In May of 1967 several Aero employees expressed to Engdahl their dissatisfaction with their employment with Aero. Later that month, at Engdahl's suggestion, Engdahl met with the employees and suggested that they join together and form a new enterprise. In early June, they decided to go into the custom-drapery business in direct competition with Aero. Later that month the new business associates decided upon a location for the new business, contacted suppliers, and secured an advertisement in the Yellow Pages. In July 1967, Engdahl tendered his resignation as director and treasurer of Aero Drapery, Inc. Has Engdahl breached any duty to Aero Drapery, Inc.? Would your answer be different if Engdahl had resigned early in May of 1967? (What additional fact do you need to know to answer the latter question?) [Aero Drapery of Kentucky, Inc. v. Engdahl, 507 S.W.2d 166 (Ky.App. 1974)]

8. Hartung, Odle, and Burke were architects. In 1971 they organized as a corporation. Their association, however, was riddled with dissent from the start. As it became apparent that the corporate turmoil would eventually re-

sult in reorganization of the corporation, Hartung began conferring with several clients of the firm, informing them that he was willing to continue as their architect after his withdrawal from the corporation. The corporation was later dissolved, and several of its clients continued to do business with Hartung. Do Odle and Burke have any recourse against Hartung for his activities? [Hartung v. Architects Hartung/Odle/Burke, Inc., 157 Ind.App. 546, 301 N.E.2d 240 (1973)]

9. Atlantic Properties, Inc., had only four shareholders, each of whom owned 25 percent of the capital stock. The bylaws required an 80 percent affirmative vote of the shareholders on all actions taken by the corporation. This provision had the effect of giving any of the four original shareholders a veto in corporate decisions. One shareholder refused for seven years to vote for any dividends, although he was warned that his actions might expose the corporation to Internal Revenue Service penalties for unreasonable accumulation of corporate earnings and profits. The Internal Revenue Service did impose such penalties on the corporation. Can the dissenting shareholder be held personally liable for these penalties? [Smith v. Atlantic Properties, Inc., Mass. App. 1981, 422 N.E.2d 798]

42

CORPORATIONS
Merger, Consolidation, and Termination

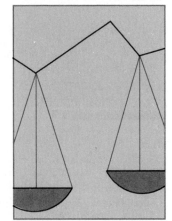

Corporations increase their holdings for a number of reasons. They may wish to enlarge their physical plants, increase their property or investment holdings, or acquire the assets, know-how, or goodwill of another corporation. Sometimes acquisition is motivated by a desire to eliminate a competitor, to accomplish diversification, or to insure adequate resources and markets for the acquiring corporation's product. Whatever the reason, the corporation typically extends its operations by combining with another corporation through:

1. Merger.
2. Consolidation.
3. Purchase of assets.
4. Purchase of a controlling interest of the other corporation.

This chapter will examine the various ways that merger or consolidation alters the fundamental structure of the corporation. Dissolution and liquidation are the combined processes by which a corporation terminates its existence. The last part of this chapter will discuss the typical reasons for and methods used in terminating a corporation.

MERGER AND CONSOLIDATION

The terms *merger* and *consolidation* are often used interchangeably, but they refer to two legally distinct proceedings. Whether a combination is in fact a merger or a consolidation, the rights and liabilities of shareholders, the corporation, and its creditors are the same.

Mergers

A **merger** involves the legal combination of two or more corporations. After a merger, only one of the corporations continues to exist. For example, Corporation A and Corporation B decide to merge. It is agreed that A will absorb B, so upon merger, B ceases to exist as a separate entity and A continues as the *surviving corporation*.

A merger can be represented symbolically as A + B = A. After the merger, A is recognized as a single corporation, possessing all the rights, privileges, and powers of itself and B. A automatically acquires all of B's property and assets without the necessity of formal transfer or deed. A becomes liable for all B's debts and obligations. Finally, A's articles of incorporation are deemed *amended* to include any changes that are stated in the *articles of merger*.

Consolidations

In the case of a **consolidation,** two or more corporations combine so that each corporation ceases to exist and a new one emerges. Corporation A and Corporation B consolidate to form an entirely new organization, Corporation C. In the process, A and B both terminate. C comes into existence as an entirely new entity.

A symbolic representation of a consolidation, then, is A + B = C. The results of a consolidation are essentially the same as the results of merger. C is recognized as a new corporation and a single entity; A and B cease to exist. C accedes to all the rights, privileges, and powers previously held by A and B. Title to any property and assets owned by A and B passes to C without formal transfer. C assumes liability for all debts and obligations owed by A and B. The articles of consolidation *take the place of* A's

and B's original corporate articles and are thereafter regarded as C's corporate articles.

When a merger or a consolidation takes place, the surviving corporation or newly formed corporation will issue shares or pay some fair consideration to the shareholders of the corporation that ceases to exist.

In a merger, the surviving corporation is vested with the disappearing corporation's preexisting legal rights and obligations. For example, if the disappearing corporation had a right of action against a third party, the surviving corporation could bring suit after the merger to recover the disappearing corporation's damages.

The corporation statutes of many states, as illustrated in the following case, provide that a successor (surviving) corporation inherits a *chose in action* (a right to sue for a debt or sum of money) from a merging corporation as a matter of law. So, too, the common law rule recognizes that a chose in action to enforce a property right upon merger will vest with the successor (surviving) corporation, and no right of action will remain with the disappearing corporation.

SUN PIPE LINE CO. v. ALTES

United States Court of Appeals, Eighth Circuit, 1975. 511 F.2d 280.

BACKGROUND AND FACTS   *Sun Pipe Line Company (Sun) merged with OMR, Inc., in August 1972. Sun, the plaintiff in this case, was the surviving corporation. As part of the merger agreement, Sun succeeded to all of OMR's rights and liabilities. State law provided that surviving corporations were entitled to maintain legal actions for damages based on the disappearing corporation's rights and liabilities.*

The disappearing corporation, OMR, had acquired a right-of-way to lay pipeline across certain property. The property was subsequently sold to the defendant, Altes. At the time he purchased the land in early 1972, Altes knew that there was an easement for the pipeline across it and that the pipeline did in fact exist.

Altes owned and operated a rock quarrying and landfill business which was conducted on the parcel of property in question. The operations consisted of removing rock from below the surface, crushing it, selling it, and then filling the excavation with trash and covering it with soil. Defendant Altes warned his workers not to conduct the quarrying operation in the area where the pipeline was buried. Nonetheless, on March 16, 1972, one of his employees did operate a front-end loader in the vicinity of the pipeline and, while digging into the soil, he punctured it. A considerable amount of gasoline being pumped at high pressure escaped through the hole, and the pipeline had to be shut down for repairs. There was no question that Altes's employee had been negligent and that this negligence was attributable to Altes.

At the time of the break in the pipeline, it was owned by OMR, but this litigation was initiated by Sun Pipe Line Company (the plaintiff) after its merger with OMR in August 1972.

The trial court refused to instruct the jury that Sun Pipe Line Company had the right, under state law, to bring this lawsuit. The jury was never instructed as to the law of merger. Instead, the trial judge merely told the members of the jury that it was up to them to determine the effect of the merger.

ROSS, Circuit Judge.

Sun Pipe Line Company (Sun), a Pennsylvania corporation with its principal place of business in Oklahoma, brought this diversity action against Robert Altes, a resident of Arkansas, seeking to recover in excess of $35,000 for damages incurred when one of Altes' employees, while operating an earth moving machine, punctured a pipeline [now] owned by Sun. After a trial in the district court the jury returned a verdict for defendant Altes, and judgment was entered accordingly. Sun appeals, alleging that the court erred in * * * refusing to instruct the jury that Sun had the right to bring this action. * * *

* * * *

[The] issue which developed at trial was whether Sun had a right to prosecute the action. It was revealed that at the time of the break the pipeline was owned by OMR, Inc., a successor firm to Oklahoma Mississippi River Products, Inc., but that the litigation was initiated by Sun after its merger with OMR in August, 1972, in which Sun was the surviving corporation. Evidence was received on this issue, including the articles of merger.

Since the issue of Sun's right to bring the action had been injected into the trial, Sun requested that the district judge instruct the jury that, in accordance with the merger agreement between Sun and OMR, Sun succeeded to all of OMR's rights and liabilities and was entitled to maintain an action for damages against Altes. The court refused to give this instruction.

During his closing argument Altes' attorney argued to the effect that, since OMR owned the pipeline at the time of the accident, Sun had failed to prove that it had sustained any damages. When Sun objected to this line of argument on the ground that it had the right to bring suit for damages to OMR as a matter of law, the trial judge merely told the jury that it is "for you to determine the effect of the merger." Altes' counsel continued to argue that Sun had sustained no damages.

The instruction requested by Sun was not given and neither was the jury informed as to the law of merger. On the other hand, the jury was told that, before it could award damages to Sun, it must find that Sun had sustained damages. Thus, the jury was left in the position of determining whether Sun could recover for damages to OMR. This was error.

Fed.R.Civ.P. 17(b) states that "[t]he capacity of a corporation to sue or be sued shall be determined by the law under which it was organized." Sun is a Pennsylvania corporation, so the law of that state determines whether it can sue to recover premerger damages to OMR.

Pa.Stat.Ann. tit. 15, § 1907 (1974 Supp.) deals with the effect of a merger or consolidation of corporations and provides:

All the property, real, personal, and mixed and franchises of each of the corporations parties to the plan of merger or consolidation, *and all debts due on whatever account to any of them, including subscriptions to shares and other choses in action belonging to any of them*, shall be taken and deemed to be transferred to and vested in the surviving or new corporation, as the case may be, without further act or deed. (Court's emphasis.)

This statute makes it explicitly clear that Sun, the surviving corporation, was vested with OMR's chose in action against Altes and could bring this lawsuit to recover for OMR's damages. In addition, we note that the merger agreement itself conformed to the Pennsylvania statute by providing that Sun would be vested with "all property, real, personal and mixed, and all debts due to each" of the corporations.

Finally, this Court has stated that statutes, such as Pennsylvania's, which provide that a successor corporation inherits a chose in action from a merging corporation as a matter of law merely serve to codify the common law rule "which recognizes that a chose in action to enforce a property right upon merger vests in the successor corporation and no right of action remains in the merging corporation."

In light of this well settled statutory and common law rule, the trial court should have given Sun's requested instruction. The effect of the court's instructions combined with the argument of Altes' attorney was to leave this question of law to the unfettered and unguided discretion of the jury, and this constituted prejudicial error.

DECISION AND REMEDY   *The circuit court reversed the district court ruling and held that the lower court erred in refusing to instruct the jury that, as a matter of law, Sun had the right to bring the suit. The case was returned to the trial court for further proceedings consistent with the principle of law that the surviving corporation inherits any claims for damages belonging to the disappearing corporation.*

The Procedure

All states have statutes authorizing mergers and consolidations for *domestic* corporations, and most states allow the combination of domestic (in-state) and foreign (out-of-state) corporations. Although the procedures vary somewhat among jurisdictions, in each case the basic requirements are as outlined below:

1. The board of directors of *each* corporation involved must approve a merger or consolidation plan.
2. The shareholders of *each* corporation must vote approval of the plan at a shareholders' meeting. Most state statutes require the approval of two-thirds of the outstanding shares of voting stock, although some states require only a simple majority and others require a four-fifths vote. Frequently, statutes require that each class of stock approve the merger; thus, the holders of non-voting stock must also approve. A corporation's bylaws can dictate a stricter requirement.
3. Once approved by *all* the directors and the shareholders, the plan (articles of merger or consolidation) is filed, usually with the secretary of state.
4. When state formalities are satisfied, the state issues a certificate of merger to the surviving corporation or a certificate of consolidation to the newly consolidated corporation.

Short-Form Merger Statutes (or Parent-Subsidy Mergers)

The Model Act in most states provides a simplified procedure for the merger of a substantially owned subsidiary corporation into its parent corporation. Under these provisions, a **short-form merger** can be accomplished *without approval of the shareholders* of either corporation.

The short-form merger can be utilized only when the parent corporation owns 90 to 95 percent of the outstanding shares of each class of stock of the subsidiary corporation. The simplified procedure requires that a plan for the merger be approved by the board of directors of the parent corporation before it is filed with the state. A copy of the merger plan must be sent to each shareholder of record of the subsidiary corporation.

Appraisal Rights

What if a shareholder disapproves of the merger or consolidation, but is outvoted by the other shareholders? The law recognizes that a dissenting shareholder should not be forced to become an unwilling shareholder in a corporation that is new or different from the one in which the shareholder originally invested. The shareholder has the right to dissent and may be entitled to be paid *fair value* for the number of shares held on the date of the merger or consolidation.

This right is referred to as the shareholder's **appraisal right**. An appraisal right is given by state statute. It is available only when the statute specifically provides for it. It may be lost if the elaborate statutory procedures are not precisely followed. Whenever the right is lost, the dissenting shareholder must go along with the objectionable transaction.

The appraisal right is normally extended to regular mergers, consolidations, short-form mergers, sales of substantially all the corporate assets not in the ordinary course of business, and, in certain states, adverse amendments to the articles of incorporation.

One of the basic procedures usually requires that a written notice of dissent be filed by the dissenting shareholder prior to the vote of the shareholders on the proposed transaction. This notice of dissent is also basically a notice to all shareholders of costs which may be imposed by dissenting shareholders should the merger or consolidation be approved. In addition, after approval the dissenting shareholders must make a written demand for payment and for fair value.

Valuation of shares is often a point of contention between the dissenting shareholder and the corporation. The Model Act, Section 81, provides that the "fair value of shares" is the value on the day prior to the date on which the vote was taken.[1] The corporation must make a *written* offer to purchase a dissenting shareholder's stock, accompanying the offer with a current balance sheet and income statement for the applicable (appropriate) corporation. If the shareholder and the corporation do not agree on the fair value, a court will determine it.

Once a dissenting shareholder elects appraisal rights under statute, *most* courts[2] hold that the shareholder may not withdraw from the appraisal process without securing the approval of the board of directors.

The following case illustrates the frequently encountered problem in determining the fair value of shares under appraisal rights.

---

1. Section 81 of the Model Act provides for excluding any appreciation or depreciation of the stock in anticipation of the approval.
2. For example, Rhode Island provides that a stockholder may withdraw his or her demand at any time prior to the appraiser's report.

BACKGROUND AND FACTS   *Two Connecticut banks, the Willimantic Trust Company and the Norwich State Bank and Trust Company, proposed a merger to their stockholders. Willimantic was to be the surviving bank. After the merger, the stockholders voted to change Willimantic's name to the Independent Bank and Trust Company, the named defendant in this case. The bank determined that the fair market value of the stock was $76 on the day prior to the date the notice of the proposed merger was mailed out. The dissenting shareholders rejected the $76 valuation and sought judicial determination of the fair value of their shares. The trial judge set the value of the stock at $105 per share and the bank appealed.*

WELSH v.
INDEPENDENT BANK
AND TRUST CO.
Appellate Court of Connecticut, 1983.
467 A.2d 941.

TESTO, Judge,
*   *   *   *

The history and growth of the Willimantic Bank is undisputed. The testimony of one of its directors at the trial stated that it has been a very successful bank and one of the most successful in Connecticut. This statement was corroborated by the appraisal report of Keefe, Brayette and Woods, Inc. The bank was characterized as being an above-average performer, having abundant capital, good asset quality, but under reserved.

The shares of Willimantic were not listed on any stock exchange. The shares were bought and sold by brokers as principals or agents and by individuals negotiating between themselves. The shares of stocks that were sold between January 12, 1976, and April 21, 1981, are recorded on the bank's stock transfer book and are listed in exhibit A. Between the dates of October 7, 1980 (the date immediately prior to the first newspaper announcement about the proposed merger), and December 30, 1980, exhibit A lists transfers at prices between $100 and $105.50 per share. *   *   *

The [Bank] contends that the trial judge, in setting the value of the stock at $105 per share, exclusively relied on the "market value" approach in finding what the "fair value" of the shares of stock was under General Statutes § 33–374(g). Its claim that other measures of value are used in other jurisdictions and should have been used in this case, namely, earnings value, book value and dividend yield is the basis of this appeal.

The basic concept of value under the appraisal statute, § 33–374(g) of the General Statutes, is that the stockholder is entitled to be paid for that which has been taken from him, viz, his proportionate interest in a going concern. This is the true or intrinsic value of his stock which has been taken by the merger.

General Statutes § 33–374(g) does not state what measuring stick to use to determine the "fair value" of stocks. It gives to the trier of fact the authority to "determine the fair value of the share of the shareholders entitled to payment therefor. . . ."

In determining fair value a court may rely on a legally recognized measure of value which is supported by the subordinate facts. No single method of valuation will control in all cases. *   *   * It is within the discretion of the trier of fact to "select the most appropriate method of valuation under the facts properly found by him." *   *   * Valuation is a matter of fact to be determined by the trier's independent judgment of what is just compensation. Thus, valuation rests largely within the discretion of the lower court *   *   *

Where General Statutes § 33–374(g) gives the trier of fact the right to determine the fair value of stocks and where the trier bases his judgment on supportive and reliable evidence, he may select a legally recognized measure of value (market value) in order to determine the fair value of share of stock in accordance with the statute as provided
*   *   *

*   *   *   *

DECISION AND REMEDY   *The appeals court found that the trial judge was correct in using the "market value" approach in finding the "fair value" of the shares of stock.*

COMMENTS   *Although there are many methods of determining the "fair value" of shares of stock, a judge has the discretion to choose which method of valuation is used. It will be difficult to find an abuse of discretion on the part of the trial judge if he uses one of the standard approaches (i.e., market value, earnings value, book value, or dividend yield) in determining the fair value of the stock.*

Shareholder Approval

Shareholders invest in a corporate enterprise with the expectation that the board of directors will manage the enterprise and will approve ordinary business matters. Actions taken on extraordinary matters must be authorized by the board of directors and the shareholders. Often modern statutes will require that certain types of extraordinary matters be approved by a prescribed voter consent of the shareholders. Typi-

cally, matters requiring shareholder approval include sale, lease, or exchange of all or substantially all corporate assets outside of the corporation's regular course of business. Other examples include amendments to the articles of incorporation, transactions concerning merger or consolidation, and dissolution.

Hence, when any extraordinary matter arises, the corporation must proceed as authorized by law to obtain shareholder and board of director approval.

Sometimes a transaction can be characterized in such a way as not to require shareholder approval, but a court will use its equity powers to require such approval. In order to determine the nature of the transaction, the courts will look not only to the details of the transaction but also to its consequences. In the following case, a "reorganization agreement" seemed to be a guise for a merger.

BACKGROUND AND FACTS *Plaintiff Farris, a shareholder, filed suit to enjoin the Glen Alden Corporation and the List Corporation from carrying out a proposed reorganization agreement that would, in effect, transform Glen Alden (a coal mining company) into a diversified holding company (ranging from the motion picture industry to textiles). Under the agreement, Glen Alden (the smaller company) purchased the assets of List Corporation (the larger company) in exchange for a large amount of Glen Alden stock. At a shareholders' meeting, the reorganization agreement was approved. Farris claimed that this action was invalid as the true intent of the agreement was a merger, and, as a merger, shareholders of both corporations would have been entitled to appraisal rights requiring management to buy out a dissenting shareholder's stock.*

FARRIS v. GLEN ALDEN CORP.

Supreme Court of Pennsylvania, 1958.

393 Pa. 427, 143 A.2d 25.

COHEN, Justice.

We are required to determine on this appeal whether, as a result of a "Reorganization Agreement" executed by the officers of Glen Alden Corporation and List Industries Corporation, and approved by the shareholders of the former company, the rights and remedies of a dissenting shareholder accrue to the plaintiff.

* * * In October 1957, List, a Delaware holding company owning interests in motion picture theaters, textile companies and real estate, and to a lesser extent, in oil and gas operations, warehouses and aluminum piston manufacturing, purchased through a wholly owned subsidiary 38.5% of Glen Alden's outstanding stock. This acquisition enabled List to place three of its directors on the Glen Alden board.

* * * *

Two days after the agreement was executed notice of the annual meeting of Glen Alden to be held on April 11, 1958, was mailed to the shareholders together with a proxy statement analyzing the reorganization agreement and recommending its approval as well as approval of certain amendments to Glen Alden's articles of incorporation and bylaws necessary to implement the agreement. At this meeting the holders of a majority of the outstanding shares (not including those owned by List) voted in favor of a resolution approving the reorganization agreement.

On the day of the shareholders' meeting, plaintiff, a shareholder of Glen Alden, filed a complaint in equity against the corporation and its officers seeking to enjoin them temporarily until final hearing, and perpetually thereafter, from executing and carrying out the agreement.

The gravamen of the complaint was that the notice of the annual shareholders' meeting did not conform to the requirements of the Business Corporation Law, 15 P.S. § 2852-1 et seq., in three respects: (1) It did not give notice to the shareholders that the true intent and purpose of the meeting was to effect a merger or consolidation of Glen Alden and List; (2) It failed to give notice to the shareholders of their right to dissent to the plan of merger or consolidation and claim fair value for their shares, and (3) It did not contain copies of the text of certain sections of the Business Corporation Law as required.

By reason of these omissions, plaintiff contended that the approval of the reorganization agreement by the shareholders at the annual meeting was invalid and unless the carrying out of the plan were enjoined, he would suffer irreparable loss by being deprived of substantial property rights.

* * * *

When use of the corporate form of business organization first became widespread, it was relatively easy for courts to define a "merger" or a "sale of assets" and to label a particular transaction as one or the other. But prompted by the desire to avoid the impact of adverse, and to obtain the benefits of favorable, government regulations, particularly federal tax laws, new accounting and legal techniques were developed by lawyers and accountants which interwove the elements characteristic of each, thereby creating hybrid forms of corporate amalgamation. Thus, it is no longer helpful to consider an individual transaction in the abstract and solely by reference to the various elements therein determine whether it is a "merger" or a "sale". Instead, to determine properly the nature of a corporate transaction, we must refer not only to all the provisions of the agreement, but also the consequences of the transaction and to the purposes of the provisions of the corporation law said to be applicable. We shall apply this principle to the instant case.

*   *   *   *

We hold that the combination contemplated by the reorganization agreement, although consummated by contract rather than in accordance with the statutory procedure, is a merger within the protective purview of the corporation law. The shareholders of Glen Alden should have been notified accordingly and advised of their statutory rights of dissent and appraisal. The failure of the corporate officers to take these steps renders the stockholder approval of the agreement at the 1958 shareholders' meeting invalid. The lower court did not err in enjoining the officers and directors of Glen Alden from carrying out this agreement.

DECISION AND REMEDY   *The appellate court held that the shareholders were entitled to appraisal rights.*

Purchase of Assets

When a corporation acquires all or substantially all of the assets of another corporation by direct purchase, the purchasing or *acquiring* corporation simply extends its ownership and control over more physical assets. Since no change in the legal entity occurs, the *acquiring corporation* is not required to obtain shareholder approval for the purchase.[3]

Although the acquiring corporation may not be required to obtain shareholder approval for such an acquisition, the Department of Justice has issued guidelines that significantly constrain and often prohibit mergers that could result from a purchase of assets, including takeover bids. These guidelines are part of the federal antitrust laws to enforce Sec-

tion 7 of the Clayton Act (discussed in Chapters 48 and 49).

Note that the corporation that is *selling* all its assets is substantially changing its business position and perhaps its ability to carry out its corporate purposes. For that reason, the corporation whose assets are *acquired* must obtain both board of director and shareholder approval. In some states, a dissenting shareholder of the selling corporation can demand appraisal rights.

To illustrate, the Southwestern Cotton Oil Company created a wholly owned subsidiary called Machine Works and transferred substantially all its assets to the subsidiary. A minority shareholder of Southwestern objected to the transaction and demanded appraisal rights, as provided in the Oklahoma statutes. The Oklahoma statute provided for appraisal rights for a dissenting shareholder when a corporation undertook the "sale, lease, exchange or other disposition of all or substantially all" of a corporation's assets. Southwestern refused the minority shareholder's demand. In a subsequent action the court denied Southwestern's claim that the transfer of its assets to a wholly owned subsidiary did not

---

3.   If the acquiring corporation plans to pay for the assets with its own corporate stock and not enough authorized unissued shares are available, the shareholders must vote to approve issuance of additional shares by amendment of the corporate articles. Also, acquiring corporations whose stock is traded in a national stock exchange can be required to obtain their own shareholders' approval if they plan to issue a significant number of shares, such as 20 percent or more of the outstanding shares.

come within the statute. Therefore, shareholder approval was required and the transfer created appraisal rights for dissenting shareholders.[4]

Purchase of Stock

An alternative to the purchase of another corporation's assets is the purchase of a substantial number of the voting shares of its stock. This enables the acquiring corporation to control the acquired, or *target*, corporation. The acquiring corporation deals directly with the shareholders in seeking to purchase the shares they hold.

A so-called "take-over bid" is subject to state and federal securities regulations. When the acquiring corporation makes a public offer to all shareholders of the target corporation, it is called a *tender offer* (an offer that is publicly advertised and addressed to all shareholders of the target company). The price of the stock in the tender offer is generally higher than the market price of the target stock prior to the announcement of the tender offer. The higher price induces shareholders to tender their shares to the acquiring firm.

The tender offer can be conditional upon the receipt of a specified number of outstanding shares by a specified date. The offering corporation can make an *exchange* tender offer in which it offers target stockholders its own securities in exchange for their target stock. In a cash tender offer, the offering corporation offers the target stockholders cash in exchange for their target stock.

Federal securities laws strictly control the terms, duration, and circumstances under which most tender offers are made. In addition, over thirty states have passed take-over statutes that impose additional regulations on tender offers.

The use of the tender offer as a method of gaining corporate control began in the mid-1960s. Highly contested legal battles and enormous expenses involved in complying with federal and state regulations have worked in some cases to discourage the use of tender offers as a vehicle for obtaining control of a corporation through stock purchase.

Recently many tender offers have received national attention, such as T. Boone Picken's (Mesa Petroleum) attempts to take over Gulf Oil Corporation and Phillips Petroleum, Inc., Ted Turner's tender offer to acquire CBS, and Carl Icahn's hostile tender offer to take over Uniroyal, Inc. In some cases, tenders have resulted in millions of dollars being made by the purchaser under a buy-out agreement with the target corporation.

TERMINATION

Termination of a corporate life, like termination of a partnership, has two phases—liquidation and dissolution. **Liquidation** is the process by which corporate assets are converted into cash and distributed among creditors and shareholders according to specific rules of preference.[5] **Dissolution** is the legal death of the artificial "person" of the corporation.

Dissolution can be brought about in any of the following ways:

1. An act of a legislature in the state of incorporation.
2. The expiration of the time provided in the certificate of incorporation.
3. The voluntary approval of the shareholders and the board of directors.
4. Unanimous action by all shareholders.
5. Court decree brought about by the attorney general of the state of incorporation for any of the following reasons: (a) failure to comply with administrative requirements (for example, failure to pay annual franchise taxes or to submit an annual report or to have a designated registered agent), (b) the procurement of a corporate charter through fraud or misrepresentation upon the state, (c) the abuse of corporate powers (*ultra vires* acts), (d) the violation of the state criminal code after the demand to discontinue has been made by the secretary of state, (e) the failure to commence business operations, or (f) the abandonment of operations before starting up.

The following case illustrates a minority shareholder's attempt to have a close corporation dissolved by court decree.

---

4. Campbell v. Vose, 515 F.2d 256 (10th Cir. 1975).

5. Upon dissolution, the liquidated assets are first used to pay creditors. Any remaining assets are distributed to shareholders according to their respective stock rights; preferred stock has priority over common stock, generally by charter.

GRUENBERG v.
GOLDMINE
PLANTATION, INC.

Court of Appeal of Louisiana,
Fourth Circuit, 1978.
360 So.2d 884.

BACKGROUND AND FACTS   *The plaintiff, Howard Gruenberg, a minority shareholder of a close corporation, instituted this action for involuntary dissolution. The defendant corporation was Goldmine Plantation, Inc. Goldmine's principal asset was a nine-hundred-acre tract of land fronting on the east bank of the Mississippi River. In 1941 the land was acquired for $65,000. In 1975 the property was appraised at $3,000 per acre, giving it a value of $2,700,000.*

The land had been used to grow sugar cane, and the mineral rights had been leased. Between 1966 and the date of the lawsuit, various industrial enterprises had expressed the desire to buy the land. The last price offered was about $3,600 per acre net to vendor.

Although none of the attempts to purchase the land had taken the form of a written or binding offer, evidence presented at the trial court suggested that prospective offers were substantial, and a contract to sell could have materialized had the Goldmine board of directors expressed any interest. However, the board decided not to sell the real estate.

Minority shareholders, frustrated by the board's disinterest in selling the property and by low dividends from the sugar cane operations, petitioned the court for involuntary dissolution under the provisions of the state's corporate statute.

STOULIG, Judge.
*   *   *   *

In the light of this situation, we consider whether plaintiffs and intervenors have sustained the proof to support their demands for involuntary dissolution under [any grounds permitted by state law]:

"A.   The court may entertain a proceeding for involuntary dissolution under its supervision when it is made to appear that:
*   *   *   *

(2) The objects of the corporation have wholly failed, or are entirely abandoned, or their accomplishment is impracticable; or

(3) It is beneficial to the interests of the shareholders that the corporation should be liquidated and dissolved; or
*   *   *   *

(7) The corporation has been guilty of gross and persistent ultra vires acts *   *   *."

First we hold the evidence does not support our concluding the objects of incorporation have "wholly failed" or "been abandoned" or that "their accomplishment is impracticable." [Thus the proof required by (A)(2) is lacking].
*   *   *   *

*   *   * [Second], [i]t can be urged validly in this case that the low returns of the past have been more than offset by the appreciation of the corporate assets. With the completion of the river bridge at Luling within the next few years, the land value, according to Kuebel, should increase tremendously. Thus the proof required by (A)(3) is lacking.

Finally, we consider the contention that the majority shareholders and the board have been guilty of gross and persistent ultra vires acts. While we question the wisdom of the board's approach in reaching a decision not to sell the real estate, we conclude the action taken is within the scope of the board's authority and therefore legal.

"Unless it clearly appears that the act is an abuse of discretion, intra vires, legal and good faith acts of the board of directors, other corporate officers, or the majority stockholders, i.e., acts pertaining to the internal management, of the corporation, where they are not fraudulent or unfair to minority stockholders, will not be interfered with or remedied at the instance of minority stockholders, regardless of whether such acts are wise or expedient. In other words, to warrant the interposition of a court in favor of the minority shareholders in a corporation, as against the contemplated action of the majority, where such action is within the corporate powers, a case must be made out which plainly shows that such action is so far opposed to the true interests of the corporation itself as to lead to the clear inference that no one thus acting could have been influenced by any honest desire to secure such interests, but that he must have acted with an intent to subserve some outside purpose, regardless of the consequences to the company and in a manner inconsistent with its interests." *   *   *

We appreciate the frustrations of the minority who are locked into a financial situation in which they have a substantial interest but no control. Appellants suggest the shareholders be equated to partners and be permitted to disengage from the corporation as they could were Goldmine operated as a partnership. Our substantive law provides for involuntary dissolution but offers no remedy for the minority shareholder with substantial holdings who is out of control and trapped in a closed corporation. We will not abrogate the legislative function to provide relief.

The judgment of the trial court was affirmed. The appellate court concluded that it would not permit the minority shareholder to force involuntary dissolution under the provisions of the statute and that the officers of the corporation had acted within the scope of their delegated authority. The objects of incorporation had not wholly failed, and dissolution was not essential to protect the minority shareholder's interests.

**DECISION
AND REMEDY**

Process of Liquidation

When dissolution takes place by voluntary action, the members of the board of directors act as trustees of the corporate assets. As trustees, they are responsible for winding up the affairs of the corporation for the benefit of corporate creditors and shareholders. This makes the board members personally liable for any breach of their fiduciary trustee duties.

Liquidation can be accomplished without court supervision unless the members of the board do not wish to act in this capacity, or unless shareholders or creditors can show cause to the court why the board should not be permitted to assume the trustee function. In either case, the court will appoint a receiver to wind up the corporate affairs and liquidate corporate assets. A receiver is always appointed by the court if the dissolution is involuntary.

Involuntary Dissolution

Sometimes an involuntary dissolution of a corporation is necessary. For example, boards of directors may be deadlocked. Courts hesitate to order involuntary dissolution in such circumstances unless there is specific statutory authorization to do so, but if the deadlock cannot be resolved by the shareholders and if it will irreparably injure the corporation, the court will proceed with an involuntary dissolution. Courts can also dissolve a corporation for mismanagement.

QUESTIONS AND CASE PROBLEMS

1. Smith is chairman of the board of directors of Acme, Inc., and Williams is chairman of the board of directors of Firebrand, Inc. Acme is a manufacturing corporation, and Firebrand is a transportation corporation. Smith and Williams meet to consider the possibility of combining their corporations and activities into a single corporate entity. They consider two alternative courses of action: Acme acquiring all the stock and assets of Firebrand, or both corporations combining to form a new corporation, called Acbrand, Inc. Both chairmen are concerned about the necessity of formal transfer of property, liability for existing debts, and the problem of amending articles of incorporation. Discuss what the two proposed combinations are called and the legal effect each has on the transfer of property, the liabilities of the combined corporations, and the need to amend the articles of incorporation.

2. Ann owns 10,000 shares of Ajax Corporation. Her shares represent a 10 percent ownership in Ajax. Zeta Corporation is interested in acquiring Ajax in a merger, and the board of directors of each corporation has approved the merger. The shareholders of Zeta have already approved the acquisition, and Ajax has called for a shareholder meeting to approve the merger. Ann disapproves of the merger and does not want to accept Zeta shares for the Ajax shares she holds. The market price of Ajax shares is $20 per share the day before the shareholder vote and drops to $16 on the day the shareholders of Ajax approve the merger. Discuss Ann's rights in this matter, beginning with the notice of the proposed merger.

3. Green Corporation wants to acquire all the assets of Red Dot Corporation. Green plans to pay for the assets by issuing its own corporate stock. Green's board of directors has already approved the merger. Discuss whether shareholder approval is required for this merger.

4. Acme Corporation is a small midwestern business that owns a valuable patent. Acme has approximately 1,000 shareholders with 100,000 authorized and outstanding shares. Block Corporation would like to have use of the patent, but Acme refuses to give Block a license. Block has tried to acquire Acme by purchasing Acme's assets, but Acme's board of directors has refused to approve the acquisition. Acme's shares are presently selling for $5 per share. Discuss how Block Corporation might proceed in order to gain the control and use of Acme's patent.

5. Smith Corporation has been losing money for several years but still has valuable fixed assets. The shareholders see little hope of the corporation ever making a profit. Another corporation, Acme Corporation, has failed to pay state taxes for several years or to file annual reports required by statute. In addition, Acme is accused of being guilty of gross and persistent *ultra vires* acts. Discuss whether these corporations will be terminated and how the assets of each would be handled upon dissolution.

6. Galdi was a shareholder of BankEast Corporation. BankEast proposed a merger with another bank, and Galdi voted against the merger and perfected her right to statutory appraisal. BankEast and Galdi could not agree on the value of the stock, so they each appointed an appraiser, who appointed a third appraiser. All three appraisers agreed on the value of the stock. Galdi, still not pleased with the

price, withdrew from the appraisal process. BankEast went to court to compel Galdi to accept the appraisal and transfer the stock. What was the result? [BankEast Corporation v. Galdi, 480 A.2d 136 (1984)]

7. For many years, Bellanca Corporation had been in the business of manufacturing airplanes. In recent years, however, it had engaged in no business operations, had been delisted by the American Stock Exchange, and had in fact become an "empty shell." In 1961, through a series of agreements, the majority shareholder of Bellanca agreed to purchase all the stock of seven California corporations engaged in the egg business and in turn agreed to sell his majority share in Bellanca to Dean and Glen Olson. Orzeck, a minority shareholder of Bellanca, objected to the entire transaction, but it was carried through in spite of her objections. Orzeck felt that she should have been given appraisal rights, which are available when a minority shareholder objects to a company's merger. Should Orzeck have been granted dissenter's appraisal rights? [Orzeck v. Englehart, 41 Del.Ch. 361, 195 A.2d 375 (1963)]

8. Arthur Gerth owned 53 percent of the XYZ Corporation's common stock and half of its preferred stock. His brother, Harry, owned 1 percent of its common stock, and Kruger owned the remainder of its common and preferred stock. The XYZ Corporation was in the retail lumber business. Of the three shareholders, Gerth was the only employee of the corporation. As its president, he paid himself a combined salary and bonus of approximately $15,000 annually. This left less than $2,000 in profits to be distributed as dividends. Kruger brought suit to have XYZ Corporation dissolved on the ground that Gerth was drawing an excessive salary and bonus and was thus wasting corporate assets and leaving an insufficient amount available for dividends. Under Gerth's leadership, the XYZ Corporation had become quite successful, and Gerth claimed that he deserved the salary and bonus because of his efforts. Should XYZ be dissolved? [Kruger v. Gerth, 22 A.D.2d 916, 255 N.Y.S.2d 498 (1964)]

9. Gabhart was one of five shareholders in a corporation in which all the shareholders were also directors. Gabhart resigned as a director but refused to sell his shares. The other four shareholders formed a new corporation and merged the old one into it. Gabhart was not a stockholder in the new corporation, which was the surviving company. The only reason for the merger was to obtain Gabhart's shares. Could this action by the corporation be viewed as a dissolution? If so, how would this affect Gabhart's rights? [Gabhart v. Gabhart, 267 Ind. 370, 370 N.E.2d 345 (1977)]

43

CORPORATIONS
Financial Regulation
and Investor Protection

After the great stock market crash of 1929, various studies showed a need for regulation of securities markets. Basically, securities regulation legislation was enacted to provide investors with more information in order to help them to make buying and selling decisions. Furthermore, this regulation was designed to prohibit deceptive, unfair, and manipulative practices. Today, the sale and transfer of securities are heavily regulated by federal and state statutes and by government agencies. This is a complex area of the law. This chapter will outline the nature of federal securities regulations and their effect on the business world.

The most important federal securities regulations are the Securities Act of 1933 and the Securities Exchange Act of 1934. These acts and others are administered by the Securities and Exchange Commission.

THE SECURITIES AND EXCHANGE COMMISSION

Congress has delegated to the Securities and Exchange Commission (SEC) the responsibility of administering all federal securities law. The SEC is an independent regulatory agency established by the Securities and Exchange Act of 1934. Its major responsibilities are:

1. Requiring disclosure of facts concerning offerings of securities listed on national securities exchanges and of certain securities traded over the counter.
2. Regulating the trade in securities on the thirteen national and regional securities exchanges and in the over-the-counter markets.
3. Investigating securities frauds.
4. Regulating the activities of securities brokers, dealers, and investment advisers and requiring their registration.
5. Supervising the activities of mutual funds.
6. Recommending administrative sanctions, injunctive remedies, and criminal prosecution against those who violate securities laws.

Securities take many forms, the most common form being stock issued by corporations. Investment contracts in condominiums, franchises, limited partnerships, oil or gas or other mineral rights, and farm animals accompanied by care agreements are considered securities.

THE SECURITIES ACT OF 1933

The Securities Act of 1933 [1] was designed to prohibit various forms of fraud and to stabilize the securities

---

1. 48 Stat. 74, 15 U.S.C. 77a.

industry by requiring that all essential information concerning the issuance of stocks be made available to the investing public. The 1933 act basically requires disclosure.

Requirements of the Registration Statement

Section 5 of the act broadly provides that if a security does not qualify for an exemption, that security must be *registered* before it is offered to the public through the use of either the mails or any facility of interstate commerce, including securities exchanges. Issuing corporations must file a *registration statement* with the SEC. Investors must be provided with a *prospectus* that describes the security being sold, the issuing corporation, and the investment or risk attaching to the security. In principle, the registration statement and the prospectus supply sufficient information to enable unsophisticated investors to evaluate the financial risk involved.

Contents of the Registration Statement   The registration statement must include the following:

1.   A description of the significant provisions of the security offered for sale, including the relationship between that security and the other capital securities of the registrant. Also, the corporation must disclose how it intends to use the proceeds of the sale.
2.   A description of the registrant's properties and business.
3.   A description of the management of the registrant, its security holdings, remuneration, and other benefits, including pensions and stock options. Any interests of directors or officers in any material transactions with the corporation must be disclosed.
4.   A financial statement certified by an independent public accounting firm.
5.   A description of threatened or pending lawsuits.

What the Registering Corporation Can Do before, during, and after Registration   Before filing the registration statement and the prospectus with the SEC, the corporation is allowed to obtain an underwriter who will monitor the distribution of the new issue. There is a twenty-day waiting period after registration before the sale can take place. During this period, oral offers between interested investors and the issuing corporation concerning the purchase and sale of the proposed securities may take place; very limited written advertising is allowed. At this time the so-called *red herring* prospectus may be distributed. It gets its name from the red legend printed across it stating that the registration has been filed but has not become effective.

After the waiting period, the registered securities can be legally bought and sold. Written advertising is allowed in the form of a so-called *tombstone ad*, so named because the format resembles a tombstone. Such ads simply tell the investor where and how to obtain a prospectus. Normally, any other type of advertising is prohibited.

Exemptions

A corporation can avoid the high cost and complicated procedures associated with registration by taking advantage of certain exemptions. The SEC reworked the small business offerings exemptions in 1982 by providing that:

1.   Offers up to $500,000 in any one year are exempt if no general solicitation or advertising is used;[2] and
2.   Offers up to $5,000,000 in any one year with less than 35 unaccredited investors are exempt if no general solicitation or advertising is used;[3] and
3.   Offers in unlimited amounts that are not generally solicited nor advertised are exempt if the issuer believes that each unaccredited investor "has such knowledge and experience in financial and business matters that he is capable of evaluating the merits and the risks of the prospective investment."[4]

Transactions are also exempt if they do not involve a public offering. Some exempt transactions are private offerings to a limited number of persons, offerings to an institution that has access to the required information,[5] and offerings restricted to residents of the state in which the issuing company is organized and doing business (but these are still subject to state law).[6] The SEC also has the power to exempt small issues under $1,500,000 from the registration requirement.[7]

---

2.   Securities Act, Regulation D, 17 C.F.R. § 230.504.
3.   Securities Act, Regulation D, 17 C.F.R. § 230.505.
4.   Securities Act, Regulation D, 17 C.F.R. § 230.506.
5.   Securities Act, Section 4(2), 15 U.S.C.A. Section 77d(2).
6.   Securities Act, Section 3(a)(11), 15 U.S.C.A. Section 77c(a)(11).
7.   Securities Act, Section 3(b), 15 U.S.C.A. Section 77(b). For issues of less than $1,500,000, the commission has adopted a simplified registration process under Regulation A.

Additional Exempt Securities

Other exempt securities are:

1. All bank securities sold prior to July 27, 1933.
2. Commercial paper if the maturity date does not exceed nine months.
3. Securities of charitable organizations.
4. Exchange securities where there has been a corporate reorganization.
5. Stock dividends and stock splits.
6. Securities issued by a common carrier or a contract carrier.

7. Any insurance, endowment, or annuity contract issued by an insurance company.

Registration violations of the 1933 act are not treated lightly. In the following case, the BarChris Construction Corporation was sued by the purchasers of the corporation's debentures under Section 11 of the Securities Act of 1933. Section 11 imposes liability when a registration statement or a prospectus contains material false statements or material omissions.

BACKGROUND AND FACTS *This lawsuit was brought by purchasers of BarChris debentures (bonds) under Section 11 of the Securities Act of 1933. The plaintiffs alleged that the registration statement filed with the Securities and Exchange Commission, which became effective on May 16, 1961, contained material false statements and material omissions.*

The defendants fell into three categories: (1) the persons who signed the registration statement, (2) the underwriters (consisting of eight investment banking firms), and (3) BarChris's auditors—Peat, Marwick, Mitchell & Co. Included in the group of defendants who signed the registration statement were: (1) BarChris's nine directors, (2) BarChris's controller, (3) one of BarChris's attorneys, (4) two investment bankers who were later named as directors of the BarChris Corporation, and (5) numerous other persons participating in the preparation of the registration statement.

BarChris grew out of a business that was started in 1946 as a bowling alley building company. The introduction of automatic pin-setting machines in 1952 sparked rapid growth in the bowling industry. BarChris benefited from this increased interest in bowling, and its construction operations expanded rapidly. It was estimated that in 1960 BarChris installed approximately 3 percent of all bowling lanes built in the United States. BarChris's sales increased dramatically between 1956 and 1960, and the company was recognized as a significant factor in the bowling construction industry.

BarChris was in constant need of cash to finance its operations, a need which grew more and more pressing as the operations expanded. In 1959, BarChris sold over a half-million shares of its common stock to the public. By early 1961 it needed additional working capital, and this time it decided to sell debentures.

BarChris filed a registration statement of the debentures with the SEC and received the proceeds of the financing. Nevertheless, it experienced increasing financial difficulties, which in time became insurmountable. By early 1962, it was painfully apparent that BarChris was beginning to fail. In October of that year BarChris filed a petition for an arrangement under the Bankruptcy Act, and it defaulted on the interest due in November on the debentures.

ESCOTT v. BARCHRIS CONSTR. CORP.
United States District Court, S.D. New York, 1968.
283 F.Supp. 643.

The plaintiffs challenged the accuracy of the registration statement and charged that the text of the prospectus—including many of the figures—was false and that material information had been omitted.

The federal district court reviewed all of the figures and statements included in the prospectus.

McLEAN, District Judge.

*   *   *   *

The action is brought under Section 11 of the Securities Act of 1933. Plaintiffs allege that the registration statement [and the prospectus included in it] with respect to these debentures filed with the Securities and Exchange Commission, which became effective on May 16, 1961, contained material false statements and material omissions.

*   *   *   *

On the main issue of liability, the questions to be decided are (1) did the registration statement contain false statements of fact, or did it omit to state facts which should have been stated in order to prevent it from being misleading; (2) if so, were the facts which were falsely stated or omitted "material" within the meaning of the Act.

*   *   *   *

It is a prerequisite to liability under Section 11 of the Act that the fact which is falsely stated in a registration statement, or the fact that it is omitted when it should have been stated to avoid misleading, be "material." The regulations of the Securities and Exchange Commission pertaining to the registration of securities define the word as follows:

"The term 'material', when used to qualify a requirement for the furnishing of information as to any subject, limits the information required to those matters as to which an average prudent investor ought reasonably to be informed before purchasing the security registered."

What are "matters as to which an average prudent investor ought reasonably to be informed"? It seems obvious that they are matters which such an investor needs to know before he can make an intelligent, informed decision whether or not to buy the security.

Early in the history of the Act, a definition of materiality was given in *Matter of Charles A. Howard*, which is still valid today. A material fact was there defined as:

" *   *   * a fact which if it had been correctly stated or disclosed would have deterred or tended to deter the average prudent investor from purchasing the securities in question."

The average prudent investor is not concerned with minor inaccuracies or with errors as to matters which are of no interest to him. The facts which tend to deter him from purchasing a security are facts which have an important bearing upon the nature or condition of the issuing corporation or its business.

Judged by this test, there is no doubt that many of the misstatements and omissions in this prospectus were material. This is true of all of them which relate to the state of affairs in 1961, i.e., the overstatement of sales and gross profit for the first quarter, the understatement of contingent liabilities as of April 30, the overstatement of orders on hand and the failure to disclose the true facts with respect to officers' loans, customers' delinquencies, application of proceeds and the prospective operation of several alleys.

DECISION AND REMEDY   *BarChris Corporation itself and all the signers of the registration statement for the debentures, the underwriters, and the corporation's auditors were held liable.*

THE SECURITIES EXCHANGE ACT OF 1934

The Securities Exchange Act provides for the regulation and registration of security exchanges, brokers, dealers, and national securities associations (such as NASD). It regulates the markets in which securities are traded by maintaining a continuous disclosure system for all corporations with securities on the securities exchanges and for those companies that have assets in excess of $1 million and five hundred or more shareholders. These corporations are referred to as Section 12 companies, since they are required to register their securities under Section 12 of the 1934 act. The act regulates proxy solicitation for voting, and it allows the SEC to engage in market surveillance to regulate undesirable market practices such as fraud, market manipulation, misrepresentation, and stabilization. (*Stabilization* is a market manipulating technique whereby securities underwriters bid for securities to stabilize their price during their issuance.)

Insider Trading

One of the most important parts of the 1934 act relates to so-called *insider trading*. Because of their positions, corporate directors and officers often obtain advance inside information that can affect the future market value of the corporate stock. Obviously, their positions can give them a trading advantage over the general public and shareholders. The 1934 Securities Exchange Act defines and extends liability to officers and directors in their personal transactions for taking advantage of such information when they know it is unavailable to the person with whom they are dealing. In addition, in order to deter the use of inside information, the 1934 act requires officers, directors, and certain large shareholders (those holding 10 percent or more of the issued stock) to turn over to the corporation all short-term profits (within six months) realized on the purchase and sale of corporate stock.

SEC Rule 10b-5

Section 10(b) of the 1934 act and SEC Rule 10b-5 cover not only corporate officers, directors, and majority shareholders but also any persons having access to or receiving information of a nonpublic nature on which trading is based. Those persons to whom the material information is transmitted are known as *tippees*.

Disclosure under Rule 10b-5

Any material omission or misrepresentation of material facts in connection with the purchase or sale of a security may violate Section 10(b) and Rule 10b-5. The key to liability (which can be civil or criminal) under this rule is whether the insider's information is "material."

Following are some examples of material facts calling for a disclosure under the rule:

1. A new ore discovery.
2. Fraudulent trading in the company stock by a broker-dealer.
3. A dividend change (whether up or down).
4. A contract for the sale of corporate assets.
5. A new discovery (process or product).
6. A significant change in the firm's financial condition.

When Must Disclosure under Rule 10b-5 Be Made?   Courts have struggled with the problem of when information becomes public knowledge. Clearly, when inside information becomes public knowledge, all insiders should be allowed to trade without disclosure. The courts have suggested that insiders should refrain from trading for a "reasonable waiting period" when the news is not readily translatable into investment action. Presumably, this gives the news time to filter down and to be evaluated by the investing public. What constitutes a reasonable waiting period is not at all clear.

The following is one of the landmark cases interpreting Rule 10b-5. The SEC sued Texas Gulf Sulphur for issuing a misleading press release. The release underestimated the magnitude and the value of a mineral discovery. The SEC also sued several of Texas Gulf Sulphur's directors, officers, and employees under Rule 10b-5 after these persons had purchased large amounts of the corporate stock prior to the announcement of the corporation's rich ore discovery.

SECURITIES AND EXCHANGE COMM. v. TEXAS GULF SULPHUR CO.

United States Court of Appeals,
Second Circuit, 1968.
401 F.2d 833.

BACKGROUND AND FACTS *Texas Gulf Sulphur Co. (TGS) drilled a hole on November 12, 1963, near Timmins, Ontario. It appeared to yield a core with exceedingly high mineral content. Since TGS did not own the mineral rights in the surrounding regions, it maintained secrecy about the results of the core sample. Evasive tactics were undertaken to camouflage the drill site, and a second hole was drilled. TGS completed an extensive land acquisition program and then began drilling this lucrative site. Rumors began to spread, and by early April 1964, a "tremendous staking rush [was] going on."*

On April 11, 1964, an unauthorized report of the extraordinary mineral find hit the papers. On April 12, TGS announced to the press a strike of at least 25 million tons of ore. Charles Fogarty, executive vice-president of TGS, had already purchased 1,700 shares of stock during the month of November 1963 and an additional 300 shares in December. In March 1964 he bought 400 shares, and in April he bought 300 shares. Other TGS officials also purchased stock. They accepted stock options on February 20, 1964.

The Securities and Exchange Commission filed suit against TGS and several of its officers, directors, and employees to enjoin (prevent) TGS's continued violation of the Securities Exchange Act of 1934 and to compel the individual defendants to rescind the securities transactions they had made. The complaint alleged that, on the basis of material inside information concerning the results of TGS's drilling, the defendants either personally or through agents purchased TGS stock, while the information concerning the drill site remained undisclosed to the investing public. The SEC further charged that certain of the defendants (tippers) had divulged information to certain others (tippees) for their use in purchasing TGS stock before the information was disclosed to the public or to other sellers. In addition, certain defendants had accepted options to purchase TGS stock without disclosing material information about the progress of the drilling to either the stock option committee or the TGS board of directors. Finally, the complaint charged that TGS issued a deceptive press release on April 12, 1964.

The deceptive press release should be the focus while reading the following case. The trial court judge held that the issuance of the press release was lawful because it was not issued for the purpose of benefiting the corporation, and there was no evidence that any insider had used the information in the press release to personal advantage. Thus it was not "misleading or deceptive on the basis of the facts then known." The trial court went on to find that most of the defendants had not violated Rule 10b-5.

WATERMAN, Circuit Judge.

* * * *

This action was commenced in the United States District Court for the Southern District of New York by the Securities and Exchange Commission (the SEC) pursuant to * * * the Securities Exchange Act of 1934 (the Act) against Texas Gulf Sulphur Company (TGS) and several of its officers, directors and employees, to enjoin certain conduct by TGS and the individual defendants said to violate Section 10(b) of the Act, * * * and Rule 10b-5 * * * (the Rule), promulgated thereunder.

* * * *

I.   THE INDIVIDUAL DEFENDANTS

A. *Introductory*

Rule 10b-5, 17 CFR 240.10b-5, on which this action is predicated, provides:

It shall be unlawful for any person, directly or indirectly, by the use of any means or instrumentality of interstate commerce, or of the mails, or of any facility of any national securities exchange,

(1)   to employ any device, scheme, or artifice to defraud,

(2)   to make any untrue statement of a material fact or to omit to state a material fact necessary in order to make the statements made, in the light of the circumstances under which they were made, not misleading, or

(3)   to engage in any act, practice, or course of business which operates or would operate as a fraud or deceit upon any person, in connection with the purchase or sale of any security.

Rule 10b-5 was promulgated pursuant to the grant of authority given the SEC by Congress in Section 10(b) of the Securities Exchange Act of 1934 (15 U.S.C. § 78j(b)). By that Act Congress purposed to prevent inequitable and unfair practices and to insure fairness in securities transactions generally, whether conducted face-to-face, over the counter, or on exchanges. The Act and the Rule apply to the transactions here, all of which were consummated on exchanges. [T]he Rule is based in policy on the justifiable expectation of the securities marketplace that all investors trading on impersonal exchanges have relatively equal access to material information. The essence of the Rule is that anyone who, trading for his own account in the securities of a corporation has "access, directly or indirectly, to information intended to be available only for a corporate purpose and not for the personal benefit of anyone" may not take "advantage of such information knowing it is unavailable to those with whom he is dealing," i.e., the investing public. Insiders, as directors or management officers are, of course, by this Rule, precluded from so unfairly dealing, but the Rule is also applicable to one possessing the information who may not be strictly termed an "insider" within the meaning of Sec. 16(b) of the Act. Thus, anyone in possession of material inside information must either disclose it to the investing public, or if he is disabled from disclosing it in order to protect a corporate confidence, or he chooses not to do so, must abstain from trading in or recommending the securities concerned while such inside information remains undisclosed. So, it is here no justification for insider activity that disclosure was forbidden by the legitimate corporate objective of acquiring options to purchase the land surrounding the exploration site; if the information was, as the SEC contends, material, its possessors should have kept out of the market until disclosure was accomplished.

B. *Material Inside Information*

An insider is not, of course, always foreclosed from investing in his own company merely because he may be more familiar with company operations than are outside investors. An insider's duty to disclose information or his duty to abstain from dealing in his company's securities arises only in "those situations which are essentially extraordinary in nature and which are reasonably certain to have a substantial effect on the market price of the security if [the extraordinary situation is] disclosed." Fleischer, Securities Trading and Corporate Information Practices: The Implications of the Texas Gulf Sulphur Proceeding, 51 Va.L.Rev. 1271, 1289.

Nor is an insider obligated to confer upon outside investors the benefit of his superior financial or other expert analysis by disclosing his educated guesses or predictions. The only regulatory objective is that access to material information be enjoyed equally, but this objective requires nothing more than the disclosure of basic facts so that outsiders may draw upon their own evaluative expertise in reaching their own investment decisions with knowledge equal to that of the insiders.

*   *   *   *

In each case, then, whether facts are material within Rule 10b-5 when the facts relate to a particular event and are undisclosed by those persons who are knowledgeable thereof will depend at any given time upon a balancing of both the indicated probability that the event will occur and the anticipated magnitude of the event in light of the totality of the company activity. Here, notwithstanding the trial court's conclusion that the results of the first drill core, * * * were "too 'remote' * * * to have had any significant impact on the market, i.e., to be deemed material," knowledge of the possibility, which surely was more than marginal, of the existence of a mine of the vast magnitude indicated by the remarkably rich drill core located rather close to the surface (suggesting mineability by the less expensive openpit method) within the confines of a large anomaly (suggesting an extensive region of mineralization) might well have affected the price of TGS stock and would certainly have been an important fact to a reasonable, if speculative, investor in deciding whether he should buy, sell, or hold. After all, this first drill core was "unusually good and * * * excited the interest and speculation of those who knew about it."

* * * *

Finally, a major factor in determining whether the * * * discovery was a material fact is the importance attached to the drilling results by those who knew about it. In view of other unrelated recent developments favorably affecting TGS, participation by an informed person in a regular stock-purchase program, or even sporadic trading by an informed person, might lend only nominal support to the inference of the materiality of the * * * discovery; nevertheless, the timing by those who knew of it of their stock purchases and their purchases of *short-term* calls—purchases in some cases by individuals who had never before purchased calls or even TGS stock—virtually compels the inference that the insiders were influenced by the drilling results.

* * * *

We hold, therefore, that all transactions in TGS stock or calls by individuals apprised of the drilling results * * * were made in violation of Rule 10b-5. Inasmuch as the visual evaluation of that drill core (a generally reliable estimate though less accurate then a chemical assay) constituted material information, those advised of the results of the visual evaluation as well as those informed of the chemical assay traded in violation of law.

II.   THE CORPORATE DEFENDANT

Introductory

At 3:00 P.M. on April 12, 1964, evidently believing it desirable to comment upon the rumors concerning the Timmins project, TGS issued the press release. * * * It read in pertinent part as follows:

* * * *

> "Recent drilling on one property near Timmins has led to preliminary indications that more drilling would be required for proper evaluation of this prospect. The drilling done to date has not been conclusive, but the statements made by many outside quarters are unreliable and include information and figures that are not available to TGS.
>
> "The work done to date has not been sufficient to reach definite conclusions and any statement as to size and grade of ore would be premature and possibly misleading. When we have progressed to the point where reasonable and logical conclusions can be made, TGS will issue a definite statement to its stockholders and to the public in order to clarify the Timmins project."

* * * *

It does not appear to be unfair to impose upon corporate management a duty to ascertain the truth of any statements the corporation releases to its shareholders or to the investing public at large. Accordingly, we hold that Rule 10b-5 is violated whenever assertions are made, as here, in a manner reasonably calculated to influence the investing public, e.g., by means of the financial media, Fleischer, supra, 51 Va.L.Rev. at 1294-95, if such assertions are false or misleading or are so incomplete as to mislead irrespective of whether the issuance of the release was motivated by corporate officials for ulterior purposes. It seems clear, however, that if corporate management demonstrates that it was diligent in ascertaining that the information it published was the whole truth and that such diligently obtained information was disseminated in good faith, Rule 10b-5 would not have been violated.

* * * *

We conclude, then, that, having established that the release was issued in a manner reasonably calculated to affect the market price of TGS stock and to influence the investing public, we must remand to the district court to decide whether the release was misleading to the reasonable investor and if found to be misleading, whether the court in its discretion should issue the injunction the SEC seeks.

DECISION AND REMEDY

The appellate court's judgment was favorable to the SEC. The information contained in the press release was material, and the transaction in stock by the insiders who knew of it had violated Rule 10b-5. Thus, the options of the individual defendants were rescinded. However, the questions of whether the press release was misleading and what remedies should be imposed were remanded to the trial court for decision. A trial court is bound to apply the law as enunciated by the court of appeals in making this type of decision.

COMMENTS

Texas Gulf Sulphur Company was not only sued by the SEC, but numerous civil actions for damages were brought against it by plaintiff-investors who had sold their TGS stock as a result of the deceptively gloomy press release regarding the corporation's mineral exploration. All these suits were settled in 1972.[8] In a federal lawsuit filed against TGS some two years after the initial case, a court of appeals held that investors who had sold stock due to their reliance upon the representations in the press release could recover damages from the corporation and the officers who drafted the release. The court went on to state that the proper measure of damages was the difference between the selling price and the price at which the investors could have reinvested within a reasonable period of time after they became aware of a curative press release made by TGS.

After TGS issued its curative press release, the court held that a diligent and reasonable investor would have become informed of it within four days, and investors who sold their stock more than four days after the second press release was issued could not recover under the Securities Exchange Act on the basis of reliance on the earlier, deceptive release.

---

8.   Cannon v. Texas Gulf Sulphur, 55 F.R.D. 308 (S.D.N.Y. 1972).

When Does Rule 10b-5 Apply?   Rule 10b-5 applies in virtually all cases concerning the trading of securities, whether on organized exchanges, in over-the-counter markets, or in private transactions. The rule covers notes, bonds, certificates of interest and participation in any profit-sharing agreement, agreements to form a corporation, and joint venture agreements; in short, it covers just about any form of security. It is immaterial whether a firm has securities registered under the 1933 act for the 1934 act to apply.

Rule 10b-5 is applicable only when the requisites of federal jurisdiction, such as the use of the mails, of stock exchange facilities, or of any instrumentality of interstate commerce, are present. However, virtually no commercial transaction can be completed without such contact. In addition, the states have corporate securities laws, many of which include provisions similar to Rule 10b-5.

In *Chiarella* v. *United States* the Supreme Court considered the role of Rule 10b-5 when there is no use of interstate commerce, the mails, or any of the facilities of any national securities exchange.[9] Chiarella was a printer who worked at a New York composing room and handled announcements of corporate takeover bids. Even though the documents that were delivered to the printer concealed the identity of the target corporations by blank spaces and false names, Chiarella was able to deduce the names of the target companies. Without disclosing his knowledge, he purchased stock in the target companies and sold the shares immediately after the takeover attempts were made public. He realized a gain of slightly more than $30,000 in the course of fourteen months.

---

9.   445 U.S. 222, 100 S.Ct. 1108 (1980).

In 1978 Chiarella was indicted on seventeen counts of violating Section 10b of the Securities Exchange Act of 1934 and SEC Rule 10b-5. The trial court convicted him on all counts and the court of appeals affirmed that conviction. The Supreme Court, however, reversed. The Court held that Chiarella could not be convicted for his failure to disclose his knowledge to stockholders or to target companies since he was under no duty to disclose his knowledge. Chiarella was under no duty to disclose because he had no prior dealings with the stockholders and was not their agent, nor was he a person in whom sellers had placed their trust and confidence. Thus, an "outsider" such as Chiarella who comes into possession of nonpublic market information does not violate Rule 10b-5 if he or she fails to disclose this information. A duty to disclose does not arise from mere possession of nonpublic market information.

In the following case, the Supreme Court examines the liability of a person who had received material nonpublic information from "insiders" of a corporation with which he had no connection.

DIRKS v. SECURITIES AND EXCHANGE COMMISSION

Supreme Court of the United States, 1983.
463 U.S. 646, 103 S.Ct. 3255 (1983).

BACKGROUND AND FACTS *Dirks was an officer of a New York broker-dealer firm who specialized in providing investment analysis of insurance company securities to institutional investors. On March 6, 1973, Dirks received information from Ronald Secrist, a former officer of Equity Funding of America. Secrist alleged that the assets of Equity Funding were vastly overstated as a result of fraudulent corporate practices, and he urged Dirks to verify the fraud and disclose it publicly. Dirks decided to investigate the allegations, and through his investigation he openly discussed the information he had obtained with a number of clients and investors. The Securities and Exchange Commission (SEC) subsequently filed a complaint against Equity Funding and also found that Dirks had aided and abetted violations of Section 17(a) of the Securities Act of 1933, Section 10(b) of the Securities Exchange Act of 1934, and SEC Rule 10b-5 by repeating the allegations of fraud to members of the investment community who later sold their Equity Funding stock. Dirks sought review in the court of appeals, which entered a judgment against him. The Supreme Court granted certiorari.*

POWELL, Justice.
*   *   *   *

In the seminal case of *In re Cady, Roberts & Co.* *   *   * the SEC recognized that the common law in some jurisdictions imposes on "corporate 'insiders,' particularly officers, directors, or controlling stockholders" an "affirmative duty to disclosure . . . when dealing in securities." *   *   * The SEC found that not only did breach of this common-law duty also establish the elements of a Rule 10b-5 violation, but that

individuals other than corporate insiders could be obligated either to disclose material nonpublic information before trading or to abstain from trading altogether. *   *   *
*   *   *   *

We were explicit in *Chiarella* in saying that there can be no duty to disclose where the person who has traded on inside information "was not [the corporation's] agent, . . . was not a fiduciary, [or] was not a person in whom the sellers [of the securities] had placed their trust and confidence." *   *   *

The SEC's position, as stated in its opinion in this case, is that a tippee "inherits" the *Cady, Roberts* obligation to shareholders whenever he receives inside information from an insider. *   *   *
*   *   *   *

In effect, the SEC's theory of tippee liability in both cases appears rooted in the idea that the antifraud provisions require equal information among all traders. This conflicts with the principle set forth in *Chiarella* that only some persons, under some circumstances, will be barred from trading while in possession of material nonpublic information. *   *   *

Imposing a duty to disclose or abstain solely because a person knowingly receives material nonpublic information from an insider and trades on it could have an inhibiting influence on the role of market analysts, which the SEC itself recognizes is necessary to the preservation of a healthy market. *   *   * It is in the nature of this type of information, and indeed of the markets themselves, that such information cannot be made simultaneously available to all of the corporation's stockholders or the public generally.

The conclusion that recipients of inside information do not invariably acquire a duty to disclose or abstain does not mean that such tippees always are free to trade on the information. The need for a ban on some tippee trading is clear. Not only are insiders forbidden by their fiduciary relationship from personally using undisclosed corporate information to their advantage, but they may not give such information to an outsider for the same improper purpose of exploiting the information for their personal gain. *   *   *
*   *   *   *

In determining whether a tippee is under an obligation to disclose or abstain, it thus is necessary to determine whether the insider's "tip" constituted a breach of the insider's fiduciary duty. All disclosures of confidential corporate information are not inconsistent with the duty insiders owe to shareholders. *   *   * Thus, the test is whether the insider personally will benefit, directly or indirectly, from his disclosure. Absent some personal gain, there has been no breach of duty to stockholders. And absent a breach by the insider, there is no derivative breach. *   *   *
*   *   *   *

Under the inside-trading and tipping rules set forth above, we find that there was no actionable violation by Dirks. It is undisputed that Dirks himself was a stranger to Equity Funding, with no pre-existing fiduciary duty to its shareholders. He took no action, directly or indirectly, that induced the shareholders or officers of Equity Funding to repose trust or confidence in him. There was no expectation by Dirks' sources that he would keep their information in confidence. Nor did Dirks misappropriate or illegally obtain the information about Equity Funding. Unless the insiders breached their *Cady, Roberts* duty to shareholders in disclosing the nonpublic information to Dirks, he breached no duty when he passed it on to investors as well as to the *Wall Street Journal*.
*   *   *   *

The judgment of the court of appeals was reversed. Dirks, under the circum- **DECISION**
stances of this case, had no duty to refrain from the use of the inside information **AND REMEDY**
that he had acquired.

COMMENTS   *There was no breach of duty to the stockholders of Equity Funding, since neither Secrist nor the other employees of Equity Funding benefited directly or indirectly by their disclosure, under the test established by the Supreme Court in this case. Thus, in the absence of a breach of duty to the shareholders by the insiders, there could be no derivative breach by Dirks.*

Insider Reporting and Trading— Section 16(b)

Officers, directors, and certain large stockholders[10] of Section 12 corporations are required to file reports with the SEC concerning their ownership and trading of the corporation's securities.[11] In order to discourage such insiders from using nonpublic information about their company to their personal benefit in the stock market, Section 16(b) of the 1934 act provides for the recapture by the corporation of all profits realized by the insider on any purchase and sale or sale and purchase of the corporation's stock within any six-month period.[12] It is irrelevant whether the insider actually used inside information; all such "short-swing" profits must be returned to the corporation.

Section 16(b) applies not only to stock but to warrants, options, and securities convertible into stock. In addition, the courts have fashioned complex rules for determining profits. Corporate insiders are wise to seek competent counsel prior to trading in the corporation's stock. Exhibit 43–1 compares the effects of Rule 10b-5 and Section 16b.

Proxy Statements

Section 14(a) of the Securities and Exchange Act of 1934 regulates the solicitation of proxies from shareholders of Section 12 companies. The SEC regulates the content of proxy statements sent to shareholders by corporate managers who are requesting authority to vote on behalf of the shareholders in a particular election on specified issues. Whoever solicits a proxy must fully and accurately disclose all facts that are pertinent to the matter to be voted on. SEC Rule 14a-9 is similar to the antifraud provisions of Rule

10b-5. Remedies for violation are extensive, ranging from injunctions to preventing a vote from being taken, to monetary damages.

REGULATION OF INVESTMENT COMPANIES

Investment companies, and mutual funds in particular, grew rapidly after World War II. Such companies were at that time regulated by the Investment Company Act of 1940.[13] This act provides for SEC regulation of investment company activities. It was expanded by the Investment Company Act Amendments of 1970. Further minor changes were made in the Securities Act Amendments of 1975.

The 1940 Act Coverage

The 1940 act requires that every investment company register with the SEC and imposes restrictions on the activities of such companies and persons connected with them. For the purposes of the act, an investment company is defined as any entity that (a) "is * * * engaged primarily * * * in the business of investing, reinvesting, or trading in securities" or (b) is engaged in such business and more than 40 percent of the company's assets consist of investment securities. Excluded from coverage of the act are banks, insurance companies, savings and loan associations, finance companies, oil and gas drilling firms, charitable foundations, tax-exempt pension funds, and other special types of institutions, such as closely held corporations.

Regulation of Mutual Fund Activities

All investment companies must register with the SEC by filing a notification of registration. Each

---

10.   Those stockholders owning 10 percent of the class of equity securities registered under Section 12 of the 1934 act.

11.   1934 act, Section 16(a), 15 U.S.C.A. Section 78.

12.   In a declining stock market, one can realize profits by selling at a high price and repurchasing at a later time at a lower price.

---

13.   15 U.S.C. 80a.

EXHIBIT 43–1 Comparison of Coverage, Application, and Liabilities Under Rule 10b-5 and Section 16(b)

	RULE 10b-5	SECTION 16(b)
1. Subject matter of transaction.	Any security (does not have to be registered).	Any security (does not have to be registered).
2. Transactions covered.	Purchase or sale.	Short-swing purchase and sale or short-swing sale and purchase.
3. Who is subject to liability?	Virtually anyone with inside information—including officers, directors, controlling stockholders, and tippees.	Officers, directors, and certain 10 percent stockholders.
4. Is omission, scheme, or misrepresentation necessary for liability?	Yes.	No.
5. Any exempt transactions?	No.	Yes, there are a variety of exemptions.
6. Is direct dealing with the party necessary?	No.	No.
7. Who can bring an action?	A person transacting with an insider or the SEC or a purchaser or a seller damaged by a wrongful act.	Corporation and shareholder by derivative action.

year registered companies must file reports with the SEC.

In order to safeguard company assets, all securities must be held in the custody of a bank or stock exchange member, and that bank or stock exchange member must follow strict procedures laid down by the SEC.

No dividends may be paid from any source other than accumulated, undistributed net income. Furthermore, there are restrictions on investment activities. For example, investment companies are not allowed to purchase securities on the margin, sell short, or participate in joint trading accounts.

STATE SECURITIES LAWS

Today, all states have their own corporate securities laws that regulate the offer and sale of securities within individual state borders.[14] Often referred to as *blue sky* laws, they are designed to prevent "spec-

ulative schemes which have no more basis than so many feet of blue sky."

Since the adoption of the 1933 and 1934 federal securities acts, the state and federal governments have regulated securities concurrently. Indeed, both acts specifically preserve state securities laws. Certain features are common to all state blue sky laws. They have antifraud provisions, many of which are patterned after Rule 10b-5. Also, most state corporate securities laws regulate securities brokers and dealers.

Typically, these laws also provide for the registration or qualification of securities offered or issued for sale within the state. Unless an applicable exemption from registration is found, issuers must register or qualify their stock with the appropriate state official, often called a corporations commissioner. There is a difference in philosophy among state statutes. Many are like the Securities Act of 1933 and mandate certain disclosures before registration is effective and a permit to sell the securities is issued. Others have fairness standards that a corporation must meet in order to offer or sell stock in the state. The Uniform Securities Act, which has been adopted in part by several states, was drafted to be acceptable to states with differing regulatory philosophies.

---

14. These laws are catalogued and annotated in CCH, *Blue Sky Law Reporter*, a loose-leaf service.

QUESTIONS AND
CASE PROBLEMS

1. Maresh, an experienced geologist, owned certain oil and gas leases covering land in Nebraska. To raise money for the drilling of a test well, he undertook to sell fractional interests in the leases. He approached Garfield, a man with whom he had done business in the past. Garfield had mentioned that he would be interested in investing in some of Maresh's future oil ventures. Garfield had wide business experience in the stock market and in oil stocks. He felt that the investment in Maresh's gas leases could be lucrative. Based on Garfield's promise to wire the money promptly, Maresh began drilling. Soon after, when Maresh realized that the land was dry, Garfield refused to pay his share of the investment. Garfield claimed that he could rescind the agreement to invest since the investment offered by Maresh was a security within the meaning of the Securities Act of 1933, and it had not been registered. Did Maresh offer a security within the meaning of the 1933 act? [Garfield v. Strain, 320 F.2d 116 (10th Cir. 1963)]

2. The Howey Company owned large tracts of citrus acreage in Lake County, Florida. For several years it planted about five hundred acres annually, keeping half of the groves itself and offering the other half to the public to help finance additional development. Howey-in-the-Hills Service, Inc., was a service company engaged in cultivating and developing these groves, including the harvesting and marketing of the crops. Each prospective customer was offered both a land sales contract and a service contract, after being told that it was not feasible to invest in a grove unless service arrangements were made. Of the acreage sold by Howey, 85 percent was sold with a service contract with Howey-in-the-Hills Service, Inc. Must Howey register the sales of these parcels of citrus groves with the Securities and Exchange Commission? [Securities and Exchange Comm. v. W. J. Howey Co., 328 U.S. 293, 66 S.Ct. 1100 (1946)]

3. Zabriskie purchased certain notes from Lewis in connection with a real estate venture that Lewis was trying to establish. The notes bore a maturity date of eight months after the date of purchase. The Securities Act of 1933 excludes from its definition of securities any note that has a maturity date not exceeding nine months at the time of issue. Knowing that the Securities Act is an attempt to control the sales of *investment* securities, can a better test be devised than this strict nine-month rule? [Zabriskie v. Lewis, 507 F.2d 546 (10th Cir. 1974)]

4. Children's Hospital offered and sold a number of 8 percent mortgage bonds in order to raise enough money to begin operation. Its promoters solicited purchasers mainly through the mails and through local newspaper advertisements. Children's Hospital was to be a nonprofit medical organization established mainly to serve the needs of children in the local community. The promoters, however, expected to earn large profits from organizing the hospital. Must the promoters of Children's Hospital register the sale of the mortgage bonds with the Securities and Exchange Commission? [Securities and Exchange Comm. v. Children's Hospital, 214 F.Supp. 883 (D.Ariz. 1963)]

5. On September 1, 1971, the Ecological Science Corporation issued a press release stating, in part, that it had renegotiated the terms of approximately $14 million in loans from its prime lender and that, under the renegotiated agreement, $4 million was due upon demand and the remainder on a specified date. The press release, however, failed to mention that, on the same date as the renegotiated loan agreement, an insurance and annuity association had refused to provide the corporation with the $4 million loan that it had planned to use to repay the demand loan. Moreover, while discussing its European prospects in the press release, Ecological Science Corporation failed to mention the proposed transfer of voting control among its European subsidiaries. Has Ecological Science Corporation violated any of the provisions of the Securities Exchange Act of 1934? [Securities and Exchange Comm. v. Koenig, 469 F.2d 198 (2d Cir. 1972)]

6. Emerson Electric Company owned 13.2 percent of Dodge Manufacturing Company's stock. Within six months of the purchase of this stock, Emerson sold enough shares to a broker to reduce its holding to 9.96 percent of its former Dodge holdings. One week later (but still less than six months after Emerson's initial purchase), Emerson sold its remaining shares of Dodge stock. The sole purpose of Emerson's initial sale of just over 3 percent of its Dodge stock was to avoid liability under Section 16 of the Securities Exchange Act of 1934, which prohibits short-swing trading. Assuming Emerson made no profit on the initial sale of stock but made substantial profits when it sold the remaining 9.96 percent of Dodge stock, must it disgorge the profits it made on the sale? [Reliance Electric Co. v. Emerson Electric Co., 404 U.S. 418, 92 S.Ct. 596 (1972)]

7. Leston Nay owned 90 percent of the stock of First Securities Company. Between the years 1942 and 1966, Hochfelder sent large sums of money to Nay to be invested in escrow accounts of First Securities. The whole investment scheme was a fraud, and Nay converted the money sent by Hochfelder to his own use. Hochfelder then sued Ernst & Ernst, First Securities' auditor, for failing to use proper auditing procedures and thus negligently failing to discover the fraudulent scheme. Will Ernst & Ernst be found guilty of violating Section 10(b) and Rule 10b-5 of

the 1934 Securities Exchange Act? [Ernst & Ernst v. Hochfelder, 425 U.S. 185, 96 S.Ct. 1375 (1976)]

8. Lakeside Plastics and Engraving Company was a close corporation incorporated in Minnesota. The company suffered losses from the time it was incorporated in 1946. Of its four shareholders, only one was involved in management of the firm. Notwithstanding its earlier difficulties, by 1954 the firm was apparently about to become profitable. Without informing the other shareholders of this fact, the shareholder-manager bought out the remaining shareholders. He accomplished this by making numerous misrepresentations to them. Assuming the shareholder-manager used none of the instrumentalities of interstate commerce, including the mails or the telephone, in making these misrepresentations, can the remaining shareholders bring an action under Section 10(b) of the Securities Exchange Act of 1934? If not, do the remaining shareholders have any legal recourse? [Myzel v. Fields, 386 F.2d 718 (8th Cir. 1967)]

9. American Breeding Herds (ABH) offered a cattle breeding plan for which Ronnett contracted to buy 36 Charolais cows at $3,000 per head and a one-quarter interest in a Charolais bull at $5,000, totalling $113,000. The ABH agreement described itself as a "tax shelter program * * * unlike the purchase of securities such as stocks and bonds." Ronnett entered into the agreement after receiving investment advice from Shannon, an investment counselor. The cows were tagged and sent to an ABH approved breeding ranch. Ronnett signed a maintenance agreement and paid a monthly maintenance fee. Was the ABH plan a security and should it have been registered under the Securities Law? [Ronnett v. American Breeding Herds, Inc., 464 N.E.2d 1201 (1984)]

44

CORPORATIONS
Private Franchises

The Federal Trade Commission has defined a **franchise** as "an arrangement in which the owner of a trademark, a trade name, or a copyright licenses others, under specified conditions or limitations, to use the trademark, trade name, or copyright in purveying goods or services." The franchise system has also been described as an organization composed of distributive units established and administered by a supplier as a medium for expanding and controlling the market of its products. Each franchise dealer is a legally independent but economically dependent unit of the integrated business system. The individual *franchisee* (the holder of the franchise) can operate as an independent business; yet it can obtain the advantages of a regional or national organizational affiliation to supply products, advertising, and other services.

The franchise system also provides the consumer public with an opportunity to obtain uniform products at numerous distribution points from small independent contractors. The system therefore seems good for the businessperson, good for the consumer, and good for the economy.

The use of franchises has expanded rapidly in recent years. It began in the early part of the century. Between 1910 and 1940, franchising was used in the automobile industry, sports, and the soft drink bottling industry. Now franchises account for about

25 percent of all retail sales and more than 13 percent of the gross national product in the United States. The franchise pattern of business development is a particularly appealing form of capitalistic enterprise. It has the advantage of enabling groups of individuals with small amounts of capital to become entrepreneurs.

THE LAW OF FRANCHISING

The growth in franchise operations has outdistanced the law of franchising. There has yet to be developed a solid body of appellate decisions under federal or state laws relating to franchise law. Because of the absence of law precisely addressed to franchising, the courts tend to apply general common law principles and the federal or state statutory definitions where they are appropriate. The franchise relationship has characteristics associated with agency law, employment law, and independent contracting; yet it does not truly fit into any of these traditional classifications. Some statutory requirements relating to franchising, however, have been enacted under the Automobile Dealers' Day in Court Act (15 U.S.C.A. Section 1221).

About twenty states currently have statutes dealing with franchise law. Although these statutes are not uniform, the following definition was adopted by two states as a basic definition of franchising:

> "Franchise" means a written agreement for a definite or indefinite period, in which a person grants to another person a license to use a trade name, trademark, service mark, or related characteristics, and in which there is a community of interest in the marketing of goods or services at wholesale, retail, by lease, agreement, or otherwise.[1]

TYPES OF FRANCHISES

There are three types of franchises: distributorships, chain-style businesses, and manufacturing or processing plants.

1. A *distributorship* relationship occurs where a manufacturing concern (franchisor) licenses a dealer (franchisee) to sell its product. Often, a distributorship covers an exclusive territory. An example of this type of franchise is an automobile dealership.

2. A *chain-style business* operation occurs when a franchisee operates under a franchisor's trade name and is identified as a member of a select group of dealers that engages in the franchisor's business. The franchisee is generally required to follow standardized or prescribed methods of operations. Often, the franchisor requires that minimum prices and standards of operation be maintained. In addition, sometimes the franchisee is obligated to deal exclusively with the franchisor to obtain materials and supplies. An example of this type of franchise is McDonald's, or most other fast food chains.

3. A *manufacturing or processing plant* arrangement is one in which the franchisor transmits to the franchisee the essential ingredients or formula to make a particular product. The franchisee then markets it either at wholesale or at retail in accordance with the franchisor's standards. An example of this type of franchise is Coca-Cola and other soft drink corporations.

THE FRANCHISE AGREEMENT

The franchise relationship is defined by a contract between the franchisor and the franchisee. Each

1. N.J. Rev. Stat. Section 56:10-3 (Supp. 1972) Wash. Rev. Code Ann. Section 19.100.010 (Supp. 1972).

franchise relationship and each industry has its own characteristics, so it is difficult to describe the broad range of details a franchising contract will include. The following sections, however, will define the essential characteristics of the franchise relationship.

Entering the Franchise Relationship

Prospective franchisees must initially decide on the type of business they wish to undertake. Then they must obtain information about the business from the franchisor. Usually, franchisors will have numerous statistics and market studies available for prospective franchisees to examine. Of course, people who acquire franchised businesses vary greatly in their degree of business acumen. Some are experienced business people with a firm grasp of the economic realities of how to operate a franchise. Others have no business experience. The inexperienced franchisee must rely heavily on the franchisor in evaluating and setting up the initial business organization.

Payment for Franchise

The franchisee ordinarily pays an initial fee or lump sum price for the franchise license (the privilege of being granted a franchise). This fee is separate from the various products that the franchisee purchases from or through the franchisor. In some industries, the franchisor relies heavily on the initial sale of the franchise for realizing a profit. In other industries, the continued dealing between the parties brings profit to both.

In most situations, the franchisor will receive a stated percentage of the annual sales or annual volume of business done by the franchisee. The franchise agreement may also require the franchisee to pay a percentage of advertising costs and certain administrative expenses incurred throughout the franchise arrangement.

Location and Business Organization

Typically, the franchisor will determine the territory to be served. The franchise agreement can specify whether the premises for the business must be leased or purchased outright. In some cases, construction of a building is necessary to meet the terms of the franchise agreement.

In addition, the agreement will specify whether the franchisor supplies equipment and furnishings for the premises or whether this is the responsibility of the franchisee. When the franchise is a service operation such as a motel, the contract often provides that the franchisor will establish certain standards for the facility and will make inspections to insure that the standards are being maintained in order to protect the franchise name and reputation.

The business organization of the franchisee is of great concern to the franchisor. Depending on the terms of the franchise agreement, the franchisor may specify particular requirements for the form and capital structure of the business. The franchise agreement can provide that standards of operation, such as sales quotas, quality standards, or record keeping, be conducted by the franchisor. Furthermore, a franchisor may wish to retain stringent control over the training of personnel involved in the operation and over administrative aspects of the business. Although the day-to-day operation of the franchise business is normally left up to the franchisee, the franchise agreement can provide for whatever amount of supervision and control the parties agree upon.

One area of franchises that causes a great deal of conflict is the territorial exclusivity of the franchise. Many franchise agreements, while they do define the territory alloted to a particular franchise, specifically state that the franchise is non-exclusive. The ramifications of non-exclusivity can be severe because it allows the franchisor to establish additional franchises in the same territory as the existing franchisee. This problem is illustrated by the following case.

IMPERIAL MOTORS, INC. v. CHRYSLER CORPORATION
United States District Court, D. Massachusetts, 1983. 559 F.Supp. 1312.

BACKGROUND AND FACTS *In 1976, plaintiff Imperial Motors, Inc. entered into direct dealer agreements for Chrysler and Plymouth dealerships with the defendant, Chrysler Corporation. The direct dealer agreements explicitly provided that Imperial would not have the exclusive right to purchase for resale defendant's cars in a four-town area of South Carolina. However, the Chrysler district manager told Imperial that Imperial's Chrysler-Plymouth dealership would be the only one in these four towns.*

In August of 1976, Chrysler allowed another Chrysler-Plymouth dealer, Carroll Motors, to move to a new showroom seven miles from Imperial's location. Imperial claimed that Chrysler had violated the Automobile Dealers' Day in Court Act by approving the relocation of Carroll Motors. Chrysler moved for summary judgment.

ZOBEL, District Judge.
* * * *

Defendant's motion for summary judgment is proper as to that part of plaintiff's claim which alleges that defendant's approval of Carroll's relocation was a violation of the Act. The Act covers only those actions of a franchisor which amount to a "failure . . . to act in good faith in performing or complying with any of the terms or provisions of the franchise, or in terminating, cancelling, or not renewing the franchise with a dealer." 15 U.S.C. § 1222. Good faith is narrowly defined as "the duty of each party . . . to act in a fair and equitable manner toward each other so as to guaranty the one party freedom from coercion, intimidation or threats of coercion or intimidation by the other party. 15 U.S.C. § 1221. The failure to abide by the terms of a franchise agreement cannot by itself constitute a violation of the act. * * * Moreover, the Act explicitly defines a franchise as a "written agreement"; accordingly, oral promises are not part of a franchise agreement and cannot form the basis of a claim of bad faith.
* * *

* * * *

DECISION AND REMEDY *Chrysler's motion for summary judgment was granted, and it was held that allowing a franchise to Carroll in the same area was not a violation of the franchise agreement or of the Automobile Dealers' Day in Court Act.*

The franchisee in this case was left unprotected by his franchise agreement as far as territorial exclusivity was concerned. The same denial of relief has been the result under the Unfair Trade Practices Act, when a Ford automobile dealer (with a non-exclusive franchise agreement) filed suit after Ford Motor Company granted another Ford dealership in close proximity to his own. [See McLaughlin Ford, Inc. v. Ford Motor Company, 473 A.2d 1185, (1984)].

COMMENTS

Price and Quality Controls

Franchises provide the franchisor with an outlet for the firm's goods and services. Depending upon the nature of the business, the franchisor may require the franchisee to purchase products from the franchisor at an established price. Of course, a franchisor cannot set the prices at which the franchisee will resell the goods, as this is a violation of state or federal antitrust laws, or both. A franchisor can suggest retail prices but cannot insist on them.

Although a franchisor can require franchisees to purchase supplies from it, requiring a franchisee to purchase *exclusively* from the franchisor may violate federal antitrust laws. The implications of antitrust violations on territorial restrictions, restrictions on products sold, resale price fixing, and price discrimination will be discussed briefly later.

As a general rule, there is no question of the validity of a provision permitting the franchisor to enforce certain quality standards. Since the franchisor has a legitimate interest in maintaining the quality of the product or service in order to protect its name and reputation, it can exercise greater control in this area than would otherwise be tolerated.

Termination of the Franchise Arrangement

The duration of the franchise is a matter to be determined between the parties. Generally, a franchise will start out for a short period, such as a year, so that the franchisee and the franchisor can determine

whether they want to stay in business with one another. Usually the franchise agreement will specify that termination must be "for cause," such as death or disability of the franchisee, insolvency of the franchisee, breach of the franchise agreement, or failure to meet specified sales quotas. Most franchise contracts provide that notice of termination must be given. If no set time for termination is given, then a reasonable time with notice will be implied. A franchisee must be given reasonable time to wind up the business—that is, to do the accounting and return the copyright or trademark or any other property of the franchisor.

Much franchise litigation has arisen over termination provisions. Since the franchise agreement is normally a form contract drawn and prepared by the franchisor, and since the bargaining power of the franchisee is rarely equal to that of the franchisor, the termination provisions of contracts are generally more favorable to the franchisor. It is in this area that the lack of statutory law and case law is felt most keenly by the franchisee. In some states, franchisees in automobile dealerships and gasoline stations have some statutory protection, however.

The franchisee normally invests a substantial amount of time and money in the franchise operation to make it successful. Despite this fact, the franchisee may receive little or nothing for the business upon termination. The franchisor owns the trademark and hence the business. The courts have often struggled to offer a terminated franchisee some kind of relief, as is illustrated in the next case.

BACKGROUND AND FACTS *The plaintiff, Atlantic Richfield Company (Arco), entered into a "dealer lease" with the defendant, Razumic, in 1953. The defendant expended $5,000 for inventory, equipment, and capital. Arco financed the initial supply of gasoline to get the service station on its feet, and the defendant opened for business. Over the years, the parties signed numerous agreements resembling the first dealer lease, as well as various forms concerning*

ATLANTIC RICHFIELD CO. v. RAZUMIC
Supreme Court of
Pennsylvania, 1978.
480 Pa., 366, 390 A.2d 736.

the use of Arco's promotional campaign materials, the purchase of fuel, and credit card sale arrangements.

In 1970, Razumic moved into a new service station built by Arco and signed a three-year dealer lease. On June 29, 1973, Arco notified Razumic that the lease would not be renewed and directed Razumic to vacate the premises in thirty days. Razumic refused to leave, and Arco filed suit to force termination of the lease agreement. The trial court found for Arco, holding that the dealership agreement could be terminated at will for any reason.

ROBERTS, Justice.

* * * *

In his pleadings, at trial, and on appeal to this Court, Razumic has urged that he and Arco were parties to a franchise agreement Arco could not terminate at will. Arco, on the other hand, has contended throughout that the dealership agreement could be terminated for any reason. We agree with Razumic.

* * * *

We believe that the 1970 writing and its riders embody a franchise agreement.

"In its simplest terms, a franchise is a license from the owner of a trademark or trade name permitting another to sell a product or service under the name or mark. More broadly stated, the franchise has evolved into an elaborate agreement by which the franchisee undertakes to conduct a business or sell a product or service in accordance with methods and procedures prescribed by the franchisor, and the franchisor undertakes to assist the franchisee through advertising, promotion and other advisory services.

"[T]he cornerstone of a franchise system must be the trademark or trade name of a product. It is this uniformity of product and control of its quality and distribution which causes the public to turn to franchise stores for the product."

Given the comprehensive terms of the writing obligating Razumic to operate the Arco service station in a manner Arco determined would reflect favorably upon the public image of the Arco trademark, report and share gross receipts with Arco pursuant to a "FRANCHISE RENT SCHEDULE," and allow Arco to inspect the station to assure Razumic's continued compliance with the many provisions of the form writing, it is clear that Razumic was not pursuing solely his own business interests. Rather, Razumic conducted his business and sold his products in accordance with methods prescribed by Arco.

* * * *

The writing provides Arco the right to terminate the "lease" should Razumic abandon the premises or close them "for a period of seventy-two hours." Razumic's negligence or willful misconduct causing damages to a substantial portion of the premises gives Arco "the right to terminate this lease without liability." Razumic's failure to make timely payment of rent, his death or insolvency, or governmental taking also permit Arco to terminate the "lease." Further, Razumic's "fail[ure] to comply with any of his other obligations" set forth in the writing permits Arco to terminate the agreement if Razumic fails to remedy the situation after fifteen days' notice of non-compliance.

The writing does not, however, contain any provision granting Arco the right to terminate the franchise agreement at will. In view of the provisions authorizing Arco to terminate the parties' franchise agreement for limited, business reasons and an additional provision authorizing Razumic, upon giving "at least sixty days advance written notice," to terminate the agreement without reason upon the anniversary of a term where the stated term exceeds one year, the absence of a similar term authorizing Arco to terminate the agreement without reason is striking.

* * * *

An Arco dealer has his own expectations. He knows that his good service will in many instances produce regular customers. He also realizes, however, that much of his trade will be attracted because his station offers the products, services, and promotions of the well-established and well-displayed name "Arco." Unlike a tenant pursuing his own interests while occupying a landlord's property, a franchisee such as Razumic builds the goodwill of both his own business and Arco.

In exchange, an Arco dealer such as Razumic can justifiably expect that his time, effort, and other investments promoting the goodwill of Arco will not be destroyed as a result of Arco's arbitrary decision to terminate their franchise relationship. Consistent with these reasonable expectations, and Arco's obligation to deal with its franchisees in good faith and in a commercially reasonable manner, Arco cannot arbitrarily sever its franchise relationship with Razumic. A contrary conclusion would allow Arco to reap the benefits of its franchisees' efforts in promoting the goodwill of its name without regard for the franchisees' interests.

* * * *

For the above reasons, the writing's leasehold terminology stating a three year term of occupancy does not govern the duration of the comprehensive contractual business relationship between Razumic and Arco. Rather, the language establishes a right of occupancy which the franchisee Razumic can reasonably expect will not be abruptly halted. Consistent with Razumic's reasonable expectations, principles of good faith and commercial reasonableness, Arco may not arbitrarily recover possession of the service station and thereby summarily terminate the franchise relationship.

The Supreme Court of Pennsylvania reversed the trial court's decision. Arco was prohibited from terminating the franchise agreement without good cause. **DECISION AND REMEDY**

The UCC requirements of good faith in contract dealings are often applied to ongoing franchise relationships when the franchise involves the sale of goods. However, the UCC provisions have ordinarily not been applied to franchise agreements that extend to the leasing of premises. **COMMENTS**

Determination of Relief The courts and legal commentators have tried to apply many theories to protect a franchisee's rights upon termination. Some courts have held that every contract contains an implied covenant of good faith and fair dealing. Others have held that if a franchise investment is substantial and the relationship has been established for an indefinite duration, it cannot be terminated until after a reasonable period of time has elapsed. What a reasonable time is will depend upon the circumstances in each case. Some of the circumstances that the courts consider are:

1. The amount of preliminary and promotional expenditures made.
2. The length of time the franchise has been in operation before notice of termination was given.
3. The prospects for forfeiture of profits.
4. Whether or not the franchise has proved to be profitable during its actual operation.

If contract provisions allow for termination, even though the provisions may be unfair to the franchisee, it is possible that no cause of action will be found. The Uniform Commercial Code, Section 2-302, has been used by some courts to find that termination provisions dispensing with notification are invalid if their effect is unconscionable. The courts have generally refused to find that franchises terminable by notice at any time or at the end of a specific time are unconscionable *per se.*

Measure of Damages The courts, as illustrated in the *Rea* case following, have also struggled to determine how best to measure damages to prevent injustice or unfairness when misconduct occurs in a franchise relationship. Since franchising is a rather peculiar form of capitalist enterprise, serious franchising problems warrant legislative attention. As mentioned previously, Congress enacted statutory requirements under the Automobile Dealers' Day in Court Act (15 U.S.C.A., Section 1221) and thus, in some cases, a franchisee need not rely on common law principles to obtain protection in the courts from franchisor abuses.

REA AND 22 FORD, INC. v. FORD MOTOR CO.

United States Court of Appeals, Third Circuit, 1977. 560 F.2d 554.

BACKGROUND AND FACTS   *This case involved both an individual and a corporate plaintiff. Both plaintiffs filed the action to recover from the automobile manufacturer (franchisor) for damages based on alleged violations of the Automobile Dealers' Day in Court Act. The suit was under litigation for more than ten years. The basic controversy arose when the manufacturer required the plaintiff to resign his holdings in a competing manufacturer's dealership as a condition for obtaining a Ford franchise.*

In February 1964 the plaintiff, Rea, was given a franchise for a Ford dealership in Pennsylvania. At that time he was already a principal stockholder of an Oldsmobile dealership in Pennsylvania. Rea told Ford that he would acquire the assets needed to operate the Ford dealership by liquidating the Oldsmobile business, and Ford had him sign a letter committing him to taking that step.

Subsequently, Rea suggested to a Ford representative that the Oldsmobile operation might not be closed. The Ford representative then warned Rea that unless he got out of the Oldsmobile business, Ford might not ship him the cars needed to operate the Ford franchise. Shortly thereafter, Rea gave up his interest in the Oldsmobile franchise, kept part of its assets to be used in operating the Ford franchise, and sold the rest.

At the trial, it was established that the manufacturer's requirement was a violation of the Automobile Dealers' Day in Court Act. On appeal, Ford's liability was upheld; the only issue remaining was the measure of damages.

HUNTER, Circuit Judge.

* * * *

At the outset, Ford argues that the trial court erred in refusing to allow Ford to introduce evidence tending to establish that: (1) Ford's acts were not the proximate cause of the sale of Rea's Oldsmobile business; (2) Ford's acts were not the proximate cause of any loss in profits by Rea's corporate entities; and (3) Rea failed to "mitigate" damages and, therefore, Ford had not caused any real harm. These elements of causation, says Ford, go to damages alone and were not foreclosed by this court's affirmance of the finding of liability under the Automobile Dealers' Day in Court Act.

We do not agree. Causation is an element of liability. Our remand left open only the amount of damages, not the fact of damage.

[The court refused to allow Ford to challenge the question of liability. It then went on to discuss the elements of damage and the appropriate calculation.]

Ford also claims that the court below erred in including Rea's projected salary and bonuses at the last Oldsmobile franchise in the damage calculation.

[Ford continued to argue that Rea's compensation should be limited to what he would have received as a principal stockholder.]

Again, we do not agree. The corporate entity that suffered harm was the Oldsmobile franchise, which ceased to exist; the "dealer" for purposes of the action under the Auto Dealers' Act was Edward Rea in his capacity as a *Ford* dealer. In that capacity, he personally suffered damage not only through loss of income as a shareholder of the Oldsmobile business Ford forced him to close, but also through loss of the salary and bonuses he could have earned in that business. Since Rea was injured in both respects by Ford's action, he can be made whole only by recovering both types of compensation.

Ford's last point of appeal is that the trial court erred in awarding Rea damages covering the period between Ford's successful first appeal and the retrial as to damages. Ford claims to have been "penalized" for taking an appeal.

We do not agree. The court merely exercised its ordinary powers. Lost profits are recoverable in an action for the destruction or interruption of an established business, whenever they are not merely speculative or conjectural. And, in general, a court has the power to award damages occurring up to the date of the ultimate judgment in the case. Ford does not claim that the damages were too speculative; indeed the fact that the injured party—Rea—had survived the intervening period meant precisely that any objection that he might not have lived to suffer "future damages"—those occurring after the first trial—was obviated. As for the supposed "penalty," Ford might likewise claim that it was "penalized" by defending the action at all, since that also prolonged the period for which lost profits might have been recovered.

[The court went on to evaluate certain other calculations. It found that certain deductions were properly made but certain others were improper, so it reversed the latter. After the court assessed the value of all of the assets involved, it arrived at its decision to adjust the award given by the district court.]

The court of appeals upheld both the liability and damages award of the district court. However, the court recalculated the value of the assets and hence the damages suffered by the plaintiff and vacated the district court's judgment, remanding the case with instructions to the district court to add approximately $160,934 to the judgment awarded the plaintiff. In addition, the court of appeals determined that the Oldsmobile dealership as a corporate entity had no right of action. Only the individual plaintiff, Rea, could collect damages.

DECISION AND REMEDY

Consumer and Franchisee Protection The consumer protection movement and pressures from certain industries (primarily car dealers) have prompted the passage of numerous statutes to protect franchisees from bad faith termination of their franchise contracts. For example, the Automobile Dealers' Day in Court Act allows an auto dealer who contends that the franchisor did not act in good faith in terminating the franchise to take the matter to court for a judicial termination. Moreover, various states have passed laws in recent years that spell out certain conditions and circumstances under which a franchise can be terminated. However, these laws are subject to serious constitutional challenges under the impairment of contracts clause, the due process clause, and the interstate commerce clause of the U.S. Constitution.

The realities of the franchise industry demonstrate a need for uniform regulation. Common law theories and existing statutory remedies have little application to franchising problems. The franchise system is a complex and unique business enterprise. It is growing so fast that it seems almost impossible to design a regulatory scheme that is both comprehensive and flexible enough to meet the needs of this system of business enterprise.

REGULATION OF THE FRANCHISING INDUSTRY

Any industry that expands rapidly without a uniform regulatory scheme is likely to engage in certain abusive and destructive practices. The franchising industry is no exception. The Federal Trade Commission has recently begun investigations to determine whether illegal methods have been used to compel restaurant franchises to purchase goods and services at artificially inflated prices. Other abusive practices have been discovered in the form of hidden markups on the capital assets and equipment that must be purchased by a franchisee either from the franchisor or from approved vendors. Cases of misrepresentation occur in the initial sale of many franchises. More than a few unsuspecting franchisees have learned, after entering into the franchise contract, that in order to operate the business and to meet the established sales quotas, they must work an inordinate number of hours a week.

The franchise relationship grows out of a contract. But because of the nature of the franchise system, the common law remedies that have been applied to contract and sales contract situations do not provide adequate relief. Furthermore, only about twenty states have enacted statutory laws to govern franchise relationships. Thus, what is permissible in one state may not be permissible in another. Such lack of uniformity places a great hardship on franchise arrangements, especially when they are operated on a national scale.

Within the last ten years, regulation of the franchise industry has finally begun at the federal level. Most federal remedies deal with violations of antitrust laws. Attempts at control using the federal securities laws have been less effective. The courts, the state legislatures, and the Congress are all attempting to develop uniform regulations for the franchising industry.

The Franchise Contract: Disclosure Protection

A franchise purchaser can suffer substantial losses if the franchisor has not provided full and complete information regarding the franchisor-franchisee relationship, as well as the details of the contract under which the business will be operated. When misrepresentation permeates the initial sale of a franchise operation, the common law remedy of fraud in the inducement provides inadequate relief. In most cases, the franchisee has already paid the franchise purchase price and may also have incurred substantial losses in the initial operating phases of the business. The elements of fraud are exceedingly difficult to prove. Even the tort of intentional misstatement or misrepresentation of a material fact upon which the franchisee relied places a great burden on the franchisee to show that the franchisor's original offer was misleading or fraudulent.

Only a few of the states that have enacted legislation concerning franchising have included disclosure provisions. California was the first state to enact a franchise disclosure law, and it has served as a model for other disclosure statutes. The California Franchise Investment Law sets out twenty-two items that must be disclosed in a registration

filed with the state. Some of the items of disclosure include:

1.   The name and business address of the franchisor.
2.   The business experience of any persons affiliated with the franchisor.
3.   Whether any person associated with the franchisor has been convicted of a felony.
4.   A recent financial statement.
5.   A typical franchise agreement.
6.   A statement of all fees that the franchisee is required to pay.
7.   Other information that the commissioner of corporations may reasonably require.[2]

Some courts have attempted to apply the Securities Act of 1933 and various state blue sky laws to franchise agreements. The franchise agreement could possibly be considered an "investment contract" within the meaning of blue sky laws and the 1933 Securities Act. Thus, it would be subject to the registration and disclosure requirements of the securities laws. It has been argued that a franchise arrangement is an investment contract that is a security under the Securities Act.

This theory, however, has not met with much success on the federal level. The United States Supreme Court has defined an investment contract as "a contract, transaction or scheme whereby a person invests his (or her) money in a common enterprise and is led to expect profits solely from the efforts of the promoter or third party."[3] The typical franchise agreement fails this test for determining "investment contracts" because a franchisee must make an effort to make money. Thus, franchise agreements are usually not considered securities under the Securities Act.

---

2.   Cal. Corp. Code Section 31001 (West Supp. 1975). The California Franchise Investment Law provides: "California franchisees have suffered substantial losses where the franchisor or his (or her) representative has not provided full and complete information regarding the franchisor-franchisee relationship, the details of the contract between the franchisor and the franchisee, and the prior business experience of the franchisor." It is the intent of this law to provide each prospective franchisee with the information necessary to make an intelligent decision regarding the franchise being offered. As cited in 59 Minn.Law Rev. 1027 (1975). Casenote: Franchise Regulation.
3.   SEC v. W.J. Howey Co., 328 U.S. 293, 66 S.Ct. 1100 (1946).

Federal law prohibits mail fraud. According to 18 U.S.C.A., Section 1341, the U.S. mails cannot be used to further a scheme to defraud. Like Section 5 of the FTC Act, the mail fraud provision penalizes misrepresentations made by use of the mails. This is not a very effective means for preventing fraud or misrepresentation in a franchisor's negotiations with a potential franchisee because it affords only an after-the-fact remedy.

Similarly, the Federal Trade Commission, under Section 5 of the FTC Act, has the power to stop unfair or deceptive practices in commerce and to prohibit deceptive advertising. Both the FTC provisions and the mail fraud provisions lack the affirmative protection that disclosure laws would afford a potential purchaser of a franchise.

The FTC Franchise Rule

The FTC franchise rule was promulgated in response to widespread evidence of deception and unfair practices in connection with the resale of franchises and business opportunity ventures. This rule requires that, within a specified time, franchisors and franchise brokers furnish the information that prospective franchisees need in order to make an informed decision about entering into a franchise relationship. The rule sets forth the circumstances under which a franchisor or broker can make claims about the projected sales income or profits of existing or potential outlets. The rule also imposes requirements that concern the establishment and termination of the franchise relationship.

Franchisee's Relationship to Franchisor: Agent or Independent Contractor?

The mere licensing of a trade name does not create an agency relationship. However, the courts have determined that certain factors in the franchisor-franchisee relationship indicate the existence of an agency relationship:

1. The terms of the agreement create an agency relationship.
2. The franchisor exercises a high degree of control over the franchisee's activities.
3. A third person looking at the relationship between the franchisor and the franchisee would reasonably believe that there is an agency relationship.

4. The franchisor derives an especially great benefit from the franchisee's activities. The greater the benefit, the more likely an agency relationship will be found.[4]

If these factors show a very close relationship between the franchisor and the franchisee, then their relationship will be deemed to be that of an employer-employee or principal-agent. If the factors show a high degree of independence between the franchisee and franchisor, then the franchisee will be deemed an independent contractor.

The characterization of the relationship has tax implications and implications for the regulatory treatment of the business organization. In addition, if an agency relationship is found, the franchisor is liable for the franchisee's improper actions or injuries to third parties both in tort and in contract.

FRANCHISING— ANTITRUST IMPLICATIONS

Two categories of antitrust problems relating to franchises have recently developed. The first involves the distribution of the product. Generally, the franchisor uses the franchise to distribute its goods. Antitrust problems arise when the franchisor attempts to restrict its distributors to selling in only certain areas. Additionally, this action is often accompanied by an attempt by the manufacturers to control or regulate the prices of the goods. Either can be held as a violation of the Sherman Antitrust Act of 1890.

The second major antitrust problem involves trademark licensing arrangements. One of the most notable advantages to a franchisee is the ability to do business under a well-known and respected name. However, the franchise arrangement often produces problems concerning exclusive dealing. In general, the owner of the franchise is required to use only certain products and must buy them from the manufacturer.

These two categories of antitrust problems are vast and complex. They can be avoided by proper drafting of the franchise agreement.[5]

---

4. See Kuchta v. Allied Builders Corp., 21 Cal. App. 3d 541, 98 Cal. Rptr. 588 (1971).
5. For two landmark cases in these areas, see United States v. Arnold, Schwinn & Co., 388 U.S. 365, 87 S.Ct. 1856 (1967); and Fortner Enterprises v. U.S. Steel Corp., 394 U.S. 495, 89 S.Ct. 1252 (1969).

QUESTIONS AND CASE PROBLEMS

1. John Jefferson has a franchise beer distributorship. He has built this distributorship up over ten years into a very profitable business. Last year Jefferson decided to sell a soft drink and distribute it to the outlet retailers and businesses who purchased the beer. The beer company franchisor was unhappy with the arrangement. There was nothing in the franchise agreement to prohibit Jefferson from distributing a noncompeting product, but there was a provision that required Jefferson to give his full attention to the franchise. The beer company demanded that Jefferson cease distributing the soft drink, and Jefferson refused. The franchisor beer company immediately terminated the franchise agreement. Discuss the franchisee's rights in this matter.

2. Ann has been interested in securing a particular high-quality ice cream franchise. The franchisor is willing to give Ann a franchise. A franchise agreement is made that calls for Ann to sell the ice cream only at a specific location, to buy all the ice cream from the franchisor, to order and sell all the flavors produced by the franchisor, and to refrain from selling any ice cream stored for more than two weeks after delivery by the franchisor, as this ice cream decreases in quality after that period. After two months of operation, Ann believes that she can increase her profits by moving the store to another part of the city. She also refuses to order even a limited quantity of the "fruit delight" flavor because of its higher cost, and she has sold ice cream that has been stored longer than two weeks without customer complaint. Ann claims that the franchisor has no right to restrict her in these practices. Discuss her claims.

3. Smith is approached by Apex Company, a franchisor, to sell Apex products under a franchise arrangement. The franchise contract calls for Smith to pay Apex $20,000 and for Apex to supply Smith with all Apex products on low-interest credit terms. The contract also provides that Apex will advertise its products in the area and furnish Smith, who has had no previous business experience, with bookkeeping and other management services. Smith borrows the money and pays Apex $20,000. Apex is a sole proprietorship on shaky financial ground. Not only does Apex fail to provide the promised management services to Smith, but it also fails to advertise its products in Smith's area. In addition, Apex is often late in filling Smith's orders. Smith wants to hold Apex liable for substantial losses. Discuss under what theories Smith will claim relief.

4. Blake is interested in becoming a service station dealer. He contacts Esco Oil Corporation and obtains a franchise contract in which Esco agrees to furnish Blake all gasoline, oil, and related products necessary to run the service station. In addition, Esco provides Blake with Esco signs and promotional materials. A sign reading "Blake's Esco Service" is provided for the front of the station. In return for supplying all the products Blake requires, promotional materials and signs, and other services, Esco is to receive a percentage on all products sold. Esco advertises that it stands behind its dealers. The relationship between Blake and Esco is challenged. Discuss whether the relationship is strictly franchisor-franchisee or whether it is a principal-agent (employer-employee) relationship.

5. Four franchisees of a bicycle manufacturer are located in Clover City. The franchisor-franchisee agreements of each carry the following terms:
   (a) Each franchisee is given a specific territory, and in no case does one territory overlap another. Each franchisee is prohibited from selling a bicycle to any customer who lives in another territory.
   (b) Franchisees must resell bicycles at a price equal to or higher than the suggested retail price furnished by the franchisor.
   (c) Although the franchisee can use any business name, the franchisee must represent himself or herself as an authorized dealer of the franchisor and cannot sell or service other brands of bicycles.

Discuss whether this franchise agreement violates antitrust laws.

6. Ger-Ro-Mar, Inc., was a manufacturer and distributor of lingerie and swimwear. Through its multi-level marketing program, Ger-Ro-Mar enlisted the services of men and women throughout the country to sell its products at wholesale and retail. Under the selling arrangement, franchisees were required to buy an inventory before they could participate in the program. A prospective franchisee could enter at any of three levels—key distributor, senior key, or supervisor. Entry at a particular level was based on the amount of inventory initially purchased by the franchisee. To induce individuals to become franchisees, Ger-Ro-Mar distributed various promotional materials that described the marketing system and illustrated how an individual could earn large sums of money by building a large personal group of salespeople through recruitment. The illustration in Ger-Ro-Mar's brochures promised that district managers could earn up to $56,000 and regional managers up to $90,000 yearly. Concerning the regional manager position, Ger-Ro-Mar's promotional brochure promised, "ANYONE CAN ACHIEVE THIS LEVEL." An investigation by the FTC revealed that the

success promised in the brochure was dependent upon the franchisee's recruitment of salespersons, who in turn would recruit salespersons under them. Is there anything wrong with Ger-Ro-Mar's franchising scheme? Why might the FTC wish to order Ger-Ro-Mar to cease and desist distribution of its promotional brochure? [Ger-Ro-Mar, Inc. v. FTC, 518 F.2d 33 (2d Cir. 1975)]

7. A franchise agreement entered into between Shakey's Incorporated, as franchisor, and Charles Martin, as franchisee, included the following provision: "Upon termination of this agreement, for a period of one year thereafter, the franchisee shall not engage in the production or sale of pizza products in a location within a radius of thirty miles from the franchised premises." After operating a Shakey's pizza franchise for several years, Martin ceased doing business as Shakey's, removed all indications of Shakey's trade name from the premises, and proceeded to do business as "Martin's Pizza Parlor." Has Martin violated his agreement not to compete? What protectable business interest does Shakey's have, if any? Is the agreement not to compete a reasonable one? [Shakey's Incorporated v. Martin, 91 Idaho 758, 430 P.2d 504 (1967)]

8. E. T. Runyan and Pacific Air Industries, Inc., entered into a written franchise agreement whereby, in consideration of Runyan's payment of $25,000, he was awarded an exclusive photogrammetric franchise for four southern California counties. Under the agreement, Pacific was obligated to train Runyan in the rudiments of photogrammetry, including twenty-five hours of sales and technical assistance for an initial period. In the meantime, Runyan resigned his position with Tidewater Oil Company. Since Runyan was entering a technical field in which he had no experience, he relied on Pacific's promise. Pacific's training program proved to be entirely inadequate. Runyan nevertheless attempted to operate his franchise, but when he realized that he was unable to do so, he attempted to rescind. Can Runyan rescind the franchise agreement? [Runyan v. Pacific Air Indust., Inc., 2 Cal.3d 304, 85 Cal.Rptr. 138, 466 P.2d 682 (1970)]

9. In June 1963, Econo-Car granted Carl Taute a franchise to operate a rent-a-car business in Billings, Montana. Burko, an Econo-Car agent, told Taute at the time that as a result of a study for Burko, Econo-Car knew the three best locations for a rent-a-car business in Billings, that Burko would send three men to Billings to help Taute during his first few weeks, and that the entire franchise fee paid by Taute would be spent for three pages of newspaper advertisements during the grand opening. In August 1963, while the contract was still in its early stages of performance and very little time or money had been spent by either party, Taute learned that Burko's statements were false. Nevertheless, Taute continued with his preparations to go into business and, in fact, conducted business for about sixteen months. Thereafter, Taute sued Econo-Car to rescind the franchise agreement, claiming that Econo-Car's agent fraudulently induced him into becoming a franchisee. Will Taute be successful in rescinding the franchise agreement? [Taute v. Econo-Car Int'l, Inc., 414 F.2d 828 (9th Cir. 1969)]

10. A fifteen-year-old employee was injured while using a slicing machine at a fast food franchise, the Yankee Doodle Dandy restaurant. Federal law prohibits the operation of meat-slicing machines by persons under eighteen years of age. Under the franchise agreement, the franchisor had the power to terminate the agreement if the franchisee failed to comply with local, state, and federal laws. The franchisor knew that the franchisee was not conforming to the law. Can the franchisor be held liable for the negligent supervision of the franchisee? [Coty v. U.S. Slicing Machine Co., Inc., 58 Ill.App.3d, 15 Ill.Dec. 687, 373 N.E.2d 1371 (1978)]

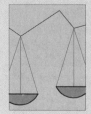

FOCUS ON ETHICS

Business Organizations

Whenever a discussion of business organizations occurs, the central issue is usually the large American business corporation. To be sure, numerous ethical issues are involved in partnership law and in the nature of other specialized forms of business organizations. For example, what should be the treatment of joint ventures—should the individuals involved be treated simply as partners? What about the use of hybrid forms of business organization that are devised to gain either a limitation of liability (e.g., limited partnerships) or tax advantages (e.g., S corporations)? Even though the ethical questions about these other forms of business organizations are important, the issue of big business dominates ethical concerns in both economics and in law in this country. One of the most important ethical considerations is the nature of the control of the large corporation.

WHO CONTROLS THE CORPORATION?
Consider a corporation with literally millions of shareholders. Does any one shareholder affect the way in which the modern corporation governs itself? The answer has to be no. Indeed, the question of the separation of ownership and

management is basic. Management of a corporation apparently can do whatever it wants within the scope of the charter of the corporation. The directors and officers have a duty to perform, but perform for whom? If a director's action cannot be controlled by the owners of the corporation, then by what means is such an action controlled?

There is an ethical question at the heart of all actions of directors and officers. What is the nature of their duty to the entity called the corporation? What is the nature of their duty to society? What is the nature of their duty to the corporation's employees? All of these ethical responsibilities can be considered elements of the question of corporate social responsibility.

CORPORATE SOCIAL RESPONSIBILITY
For a number of years now, numerous speakers have debated the social responsibility of the corporation as an institution. What should be the primary corporate goal? Should the growth of the firm or long-term profit maximization be the primary corporate goal, or should social responsibility be given considerable weight in assessing corporate goals? The way in which corporate goals and social responsibility are

perceived ultimately involves ethical considerations.

At one end of the spectrum is the notion that the corporation's sole responsibility is to maximize profits within the limits set by the law. Commentators at this end of the spectrum assert that the social duty of a business enterprise is actually long-term profit maximization. From this perspective, professional managers are regarded as trustees and the corporation is simply viewed as an extension of its shareholders. Thus, nonprofit-making activities will diminish the shareholders' wealth and therefore are not considered appropriate corporate conduct. Residual profits belong to the stockholders and are not to be devoted to the public interest.

At the other end of the spectrum is the notion that the directors and officers of a corporation have a duty higher than that of mere profit-maximization or growth of the firm. According to this view, corporate management should engage only in those activities that benefit society as a whole. Therefore, if the corporation produces a type of baby food that babies like and that mothers buy but one that is not "good" for babies because of a high MSG or sugar content, the corporation should not market the baby food.

Defining Corporate
Responsibility

One of the major problems in
discussing corporate social
responsibility is our inability to
objectively define it. We might
have some notion of the nature
of socially responsible actions
when publicly appointed or
elected officials are under study,
but we have much less clear-cut
notions about socially
responsible actions when the
directors or officers of a private
corporation are concerned. In
addition, critics of the entire
concept of corporate social
responsibility argue that they do
not want private citizens, in their
roles as directors and officers of
private corporations, engaging in
activities that those individuals
have judged to be socially
responsible. Besides, are
business executives equipped to
fashion appropriate corporate
responses to social demands?
What exactly is in society's best
interest? This query has been a
subject of dispute for decades,
and hence many critics contend
that the political process is the
appropriate forum for decisions
concerning social responsibility,
and not the corporate
boardroom.

The December 1984 Union
Carbide tragedy in Bhopal,
India, has raised numerous
ethical considerations. Was this
company exhibiting corporate
responsibility in its Bhopal
operations? When the U.S.-
owned Union Carbide company
leaked twenty-five tons of the
agricultural pesticide methyl
isocyanate from its Bhopal plant,
2,000 deaths and 100,000
injuries resulted in the city of
Bhopal. Union Carbide insisted
that the Bhopal factory was built
according to the same safety
standards as its U.S. factories.
There was, however, no
computerized safety system

installed in the Bhopal plant,
even though one was installed
in a sister plant in West Virginia.

Many experts contend that
U.S. companies frequently
locate factories in developing
countries in order to escape the
many U.S. environmental and
safety regulations. Is it ethical
for a company to take
advantage of lax regulations in
Third World countries? Such
companies are not *violating* any
laws.

It is further alleged that
companies such as Union
Carbide are lacking in social
responsibility when they locate
factories with lethal materials in
areas of high population density.
Many of the survivors of the
Bhopal tragedy alleged that they
were completely unaware of the
fact that lethal materials were
manufactured so near to them.
Do companies have a
responsibility to inform residents
near their factories as to the
nature of their products? If so,
how far should this responsibility
extend?

CORPORATE SOCIAL RESPONSIVENESS

At early common law, a
corporation was absolutely
prohibited from giving to charity.
However, the law has changed
to allow private corporations to
give to charity. Corporate
nonprofit activity is justified by
public-policy reasons. The
argument is that the wealth of
the nation is no longer primarily
in the hands of private
individuals. Much of the nation's
wealth is in corporate hands.
Additionally, since the size of
government has increased
dramatically since the 1930s,
taxation has increased
accordingly. Thus, the
philanthropic abilities of private

individuals have been
diminished.

Despite criticisms of a lack of
corporate social responsiveness,
most major corporations do
engage in philanthropic
activities. Corporations routinely
donate to hospitals, the arts,
universities, and the like. Most
major corporations employ one
or more individuals to screen
charitable requests and to
determine which organizations
should be the recipients of
charitable contributions.
B. Dalton Bookseller, for
example, put up three million
dollars to launch a massive
drive against functional illiteracy.
Over the next four years, this
contribution will help support
50,000 volunteer literacy tutors.
The Bank of America has
created a ten-million-dollar
revolving-loan program in which
funds are loaned to community
development groups at a three-
percent interest rate.

A considerable number of
corporations have also
acknowledged moral and
political considerations in their
social responsiveness. In 1983
the Bank of America announced
that future loans would be
barred to the South African
government or to governmental
entities until concrete steps
have been taken to dismantle
the apartheid laws. Coca-Cola
has established the National
Hispanic Business Agenda—a
major program to expand ties
with the Hispanic community.
This corporation has agreed to
patronize more Hispanic firms,
employ more Hispanic
employees, and support
Hispanic educational and job-
training programs. Launching a
nationwide boycott of Allstate
Insurance in 1983, the National
Organization for Women (NOW)
alleged that this company
discriminates by paying female

744

UNIT VI: BUSINESS ORGANIZATIONS

employees less than it pays their male counterparts.

SOCIAL INVESTING

Social investing, the buying and selling of securities on the basis of moral or social criteria, has become a popular subject of debate. The question frequently arises: How do you determine whether a company is socially responsible? Socially conscious investors have begun using social-responsibility criteria— such as pollution control, charitable donations, safety conditions, and equal employment opportunities—in identifying socially responsible companies. Some investment advisors rely upon the nature of the products or services that a company provides in order to determine whether a company is socially responsible. Others, however, look to the internal operations of a company in evaluating social responsibility.

Yet irrespective of the wide-spread attention recently given to the subject of social investing, the goal of most people is still simply to make a profit. Even though people claim to be, and probably are, concerned with social responsibility, they still don't really want to commit their funds on any basis other than expected profits. Moral and social scrutiny is appealing, but it does have its problems. How exactly do you determine which company is socially responsible and which is not? How far do you have to look to determine whether a company is socially responsible? Furthermore, does social investing make good financial sense at all? Many individuals allege that when social investing is done properly, the corporation and the public do see a benefit.

THE CORPORATION'S DUTY TO THE CONSUMER

What is the nature of the corporation's duty to the consumer? This issue often dominates discussions of product quality, pricing, and advertising. The layperson's notion is that he or she has absolutely no effect on the pricing, quality, and nature of the products and services offered by the modern-day giant corporation. Therefore, some consumers believe that corporations should be severely regulated by the government and the courts in order to maintain the consumer's rights.

But what, really, is at issue here? Can the corporation willfully ignore the well-being of the consumer? As previously discussed, the critics of modern-day corporations assert that profit maximization is basically the only duty of a corporation. The supporters of modern-day corporations, however, claim that it is impossible for the well-being of the consumer to be ignored. In fact, they take one further step and assert that the ultimate control of the corporation actually lies in the hands of the consumer. After all, they argue, the consumer freely chooses to buy or not to buy a corporation's product. Even in the absence of effective competition, the consumer can purchase a smaller quantity of the product being offered. Thus, it is in the corporation's best interest to attempt to satisfy the consumer.

Irrespective of the alleged power of the consumer to control the corporation, an ethical question remains. The process of competition takes time. Information is costly to obtain and never perfect. If corporate leaders know or suspect that certain of their products may have deleterious long-run effects on the consumer, shouldn't such corporate leaders have an ethical responsibility to inform the consumer? Eli Lilly, for example, failed to recognize an ethical responsibility that resulted in the death of an 81-year-old woman who had taken Lilly's arthritis drug, Oraflex, and a $6 million punitive verdict was rendered against Lilly. Lilly had had Oraflex approved for sale in the United States without informing the Food and Drug Administration of thirty-two overseas deaths associated with the use of this drug.

Furthermore, what about an ethical responsibility to citizens in other countries? If the Food and Drug Administration has prohibited the sale of a particular substance in the United States because it might have long-run carcinogenic effects, should the producer attempt to sell it in those countries where it is still legal?

THE CORPORATION'S DUTY TO ITS EMPLOYEES

What are the corporation's duties to its employees? The answer to this ethical question is not an easy one because of the necessary trade-offs involved. To the extent that the corporation provides higher than competitive wages, better than "reasonable" working conditions, and the like, its costs per unit of production will be higher. That means that the price of the product will be higher. Who has a greater "right," the employee or the consumer? Also, as previously mentioned, there is a conflict between the shareholder and the employee. The more employees obtain, presumably the less shareholders will obtain. No easy solution to such conflict is available.

THE CORPORATION'S DUTY TO ITS SHAREHOLDERS

Particular ethical problems arise with respect to the relationship between the shareholders and the corporate management. The shareholders' derivative suit is the principal means available to minority shareholders to correct abuses committed by corporate management. However, through the application of the business judgment rule, courts have begun to limit the availability of this action. The business judgment rule allows the board

of directors to dismiss the derivative suit if it believes that the suit is not in the corporation's best interests. The directors, however, must be disinterested in the sense that they must not have participated in the challenged transactions or have a personal interest in the outcome of the suit. Therefore, ethically, interested directors cannot dismiss a suit brought against them. Yet how exactly do you go about determining a personal interest? How strong or how weak can this personal interest be? How do you know whether the directors have exercised good faith in their business decisions?

DISCUSSION QUESTIONS

1. If shareholders as individuals own too small a

percentage of a corporation to have an effect on its actions, how do shareholders exhibit control over the corporation? Some argue that their control is via the sale of shares in companies with whose actions they are dissatisfied. How would such a sale of shares have any effect on the company's future activities?

2. Should a company act ethically toward its competitors? Toward its suppliers? If so, in what way?

3. Is energy conservation an ethical concern of business?

4. Should conservation of natural resources and other environmental considerations become ethical concerns to which businesses should address themselves?

UNIT VII

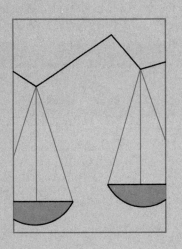

GOVERNMENT REGULATION

45

GOVERNMENT
REGULATION
Regulation and
Administrative Agencies

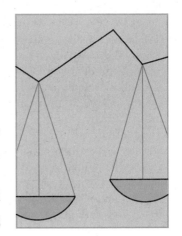

In some of the preceding chapters, we have concentrated on court decisions that constrain or encourage business decisions on the basis of common law. Today's business decisions, however, are often constrained by statutes and rules enforced by administrative agencies. These constraints are called "government regulation."

HISTORICAL BACKGROUND

Regulation of private business activities has been with us, to some extent, since the early years of our nation's history. It was during the Great Depression, however, that such government regulation was dramatically increased. Regulation has always increased during major conflicts, such as World Wars I and II. Yet, in the last decade or so, the regulation of business activities has shifted from rules that primarily evolved from the common law and judicial interpretation of statutory regulations to rules and regulations established by agencies.

Until recently, the functions and authority of many government agencies were primarily ministerial. Agencies' actions were generally limited to carrying out specific activities mandated by legislatures. Thus, Social Security offices gave information and advice to individuals filing for benefits but possessed relatively few discretionary powers. In contrast, current constraints placed on business transactions by regulatory agencies probably have more impact on the economy than those that stem from the common law and the courts.

Beginning in the late 1960s, an increasing number of new rules and regulations were established, along with new federal regulatory agencies. Seven new regulatory agencies—including the Occupational Safety and Health Administration (OSHA), the Consumer Product Safety Commission (CPSC), and the Environmental Protection Agency (EPA)—were created in the early 1970s. The first four years of the 1970s saw a doubling of the number of pages in the Federal Register, the primary document for notification of federal rules and regulations.

Much of this growth can be attributed to a greater emphasis on administrative agencies for the development of policy. Federal regulatory agencies have several features that allow them to deal with certain problems more effectively than the legislatures or the courts. To begin with, an agency is responsible only for a limited area of regulation. Consequently, an agency can develop an expertise from its continuous exposure to a particular area. An agency may be able to specify detailed rules of conduct in the development of sound and coherent policies that the legislature, with its limited resources and competing demands, is simply unable to particularize. Furthermore, a major reason to use a regulatory agency

749

is that such agencies generally consist of very specialized staffs. The jurisdiction of administrative trial judges—in comparison with the jurisdiction of state and federal court judges—is restricted, and frequently the judges are experts, or at least familiar with the subject matter.

Regulatory agencies do not exist without their criticisms, however. Many people contend that agencies have too much "unchecked" power and that the existing constraints on agencies' powers are really quite ineffective. It is further argued that the regulation of activities by agencies is merely another instance of unnecessary intervention by the federal government into the private sector. Frequently referred to is the deregulation of the airline industry, which resulted in substantially lower air fares for many consumers. But because not all activities are as suitable for deregulation and because government regulation is very much present in our society, it is necessary to understand how government regulation affects business activities.

REGULATED ACTIVITIES

Virtually every economic activity is subject to some regulation at one stage or another in the process of manufacturing, wholesaling, retailing, or other activity. A few of those activities are discussed here.

Transportation

Most forms of transportation—surface, air, and water—are subject to a multitude of government regulations. The commerce clause of the Constitution (Article I, Section 8) grants Congress the power to "regulate Commerce with foreign Nations, and among the several States, and with the Indian Tribes." In attempting to define the scope of federal power, earlier Supreme Court decisions endeavored to define "interstate commerce." [1] The Supreme Court now recognizes, however, that Congress has the power to regulate any activity, interstate or intrastate, which has any appreciable effect upon interstate commerce. An activity may take place in one state or in many states and still be subject to regulation by Congress under the commerce clause. This doc-

trine, often referred to as the "affectation doctrine," first appeared in *NLRB* v. *Jones & Laughlin Steel Corp.* [2]

In *Jones & Laughlin Steel Corp.*, the Supreme Court upheld the National Labor Relations Act, which set forth the rights of employees to bargain collectively, and further empowered the National Labor Relations Board (created by the act) to prevent unfair labor practices in all industries "affecting" interstate commerce. The Court stated that intrastate activities, by reason of their close and intimate relationship with interstate commerce, may bring the subject within the reach of federal power, even though the industry—when separately viewed—is local. Thus, Congress has the power to regulate an activity carried on in one or more states that "affects" interstate commerce. Freight service transportation, for example, is regulated by the Interstate Commerce Commission (ICC). The ICC, created by the Act to Regulate Commerce in 1887, regulates lease rates on railroad freight cars and other rolling stock.

In some cases, the ICC's regulatory powers exceed those of other government agencies. For example, in *United States* v. *Interstate Commerce Commisson* the Justice Department unnecessarily attempted to block the commission's approval of the merger of the Great Northern Railway Company and the Northern Pacific Railway Company. [3] The ICC admitted in its First Report that such a merger would result in a "drastic lessening of competition." The Justice Department was asserting that the potential anticompetitive effects of the proposed merger should preclude its approval. The Supreme Court, however, emphasized that the 1920 Transportation Act did not confine mergers to combinations that result in the joining of a "sick" with a strong carrier. Rather, the act embodied a concern for economy and efficiency in rail operations. Since the act vested in the ICC the responsibility of balancing the values of competition against the need for consolidation of rail transportation units, the Supreme Court was unable to conclude that the district court erred in upholding the orders of the ICC, which conditionally approved the application of railroads to merge. Thus, the Justice Department was unsuccessful in setting aside these orders of the ICC.

1. See Gibbons v. Ogden, 22 U.S. 1 (1824); and Hammer v. Dagenhart, 247 U.S. 251 (1918).

2. NLRB v. Jones & Laughlin Steel Corp., 301 U.S. 1 (1937).
3. 396 U.S. 491, 90 S.Ct. 708 (1970).

Utilities

Because of the specific monopoly status of utilities, local and state governments have regulated the provision of electrical power and water, gas, and phone service. Public utility commissions determine recoverable revenue on the basis of cost. The cost estimates are crucial in the negotiations between the regulated electrical utility and the Public Service Commission. Regulatory commissions also institute requirements to serve new customers or to prohibit individuals from purchasing services. In Santa Barbara, California, for example, the local government placed a moratorium on new construction by prohibiting water and sewer hookups for new homes.

Communications

The most prominent form of regulation of communications is concerned with the right to transmit or broadcast signals in the electromagnetic spectrum. Various regulatory agencies, including the Department of Defense and the Federal Communications Commission, have the right to allocate the airwaves. Licenses are generally granted for specific periods of time, and they regulate the mixture of programming that the station can offer its audience. Licenses also specify the station's maximum and minimum wattage power for transmission without interference.

In the past, the Federal Communications Commission (FCC) has severely regulated alternative forms of electromagnetic-signal transmission, such as pay television, cable television, and satellite television. After many years of strict regulation, however, the FCC has now deregulated much of the cable and pay television industry.

Consumer Products

Ultimately, consumers are subject to a multitude of regulations, since virtually every regulation has its final impact on the price of the commodity. Some regulations, however, are more direct. The Consumer Product Safety Commission (CPSC), for example, has been given the authority to establish mandatory safety standards, to require warnings by manufacturers, to require producers to give rebates to consumers, and to ban or recall products without a court hearing. The CPSC can impose criminal penalties, making it possible for executives in firms with violations to face jail sentences.[4] This commission has jurisdiction over more than ten thousand products.

Health and Safety

In 1970, Congress passed the Williams-Steiger Occupational Safety and Health Act (OSHA) to regulate occupational safety and health. OSHA delegated broad authority to the Secretary of Labor to "set mandatory occupational safety and health standards applicable to businesses affecting interstate commerce."[5] Section 651(a) of OSHA states that Congress has found that the personal injuries and illnesses arising out of work situations impose a substantial burden upon interstate commerce in terms of lost production, wage loss, medical expenses, and disability compensation payments.

In enacting OSHA, Congress exercised its authority granted by the commerce clause of the Constitution. As previously stated, Congress has the power to regulate activities that affect commerce, even though the activity may be purely intrastate in nature.[6] An employee thus falls within the act by merely affecting commerce: It is not necessary that the employee be directly engaged in interstate commerce. However, in *Austin Road Co.* v. *Occupational Safety and Health Review Commission*, the court found that the secretary of labor failed to establish that the Texas contractor's activities affected interstate commerce. The secretary, therefore, was unable to demonstrate the applicability of OSHA to the contractor's activities, and hence there could be no violation of the act.[7] Under OSHA, the secretary has the burden of demonstrating that the employer's activities affect interstate commerce.

Section 651 of OSHA does not give the secretary of labor the discretion to adopt standards that are designed to create absolutely risk-free workplaces irrespective of cost. As stated in *Industrial Union Dept. AFL-CIO* v. *American Petroleum Institute*, the "statute was not designed to require employers to provide absolutely risk-free workplaces whenever it

---

4. Consumer Product Safety Act, Public Law 92–573. 42 U.S.C.A. Section 3124–T, 29 U.S.C.A. Section 661.
5. 29 U.S.C., Section 651(b)(3).
6. See Wickard v. Filburn, 317 U.S. 111, 63 S.Ct. 82 (1942).
7. 683 F.2d 905 (5th Cir. 1982).

is technologically feasible to do so."[8] Rather, the court stated that the secretary must make a threshold finding of "significant risk" before he or she can promulgate any permanent health or safety standard. The secretary of labor has adopted standards that apply to fire extinguishers, electrical groundings, exits from buildings, guards for machines, and other resources or activities that affect production in industry.

The regulations implementing OSHA essentially cover all employers and require them to meet certain health and safety standards. Section 652 of the regulations defines an employer as "a person engaged in a business affecting commerce who has employees, but does not include the U.S. or any State or political subdivision of a State."[9] Thus, OSHA does not provide employees with a case of action against federal employers. When an attorney or physician employs one or more employees, he or she comes within the definition of an employer as defined in the act. OSHA also applies to any person engaged in an agricultural activity or business that employs one or more employees. In this situation, members of the immediate family of the farmer-employer are not regarded as employees. Charitable, nonprofit organizations, churches, and religious organizations are also considered to be employers and are subject to the health and safety standards established by the secretary. The regulations implementing OSHA, however, specifically exempt individuals who, in their own residences, privately employ domestic help.[10]

Innovation and Investments

Many federal regulations directly and indirectly affect innovation and investment. In some industries government regulations dramatically influence innovation when applied to the research and development process. For example, the 1962 Kefauver-Harris amendments to the Food, Drug, and Cosmetic Act of 1938 eliminated the time constraint for the Food and Drug Administration's approval of a new drug application. After 1962, the FDA could withhold a drug from the market indefinitely until

the agency was satisfied that the drug was both safe and effective for its intended use. This elimination of a time constraint for approval of a new drug application clearly affected both innovation and investment.

Patent and Copyright

The Constitution delegates to Congress the power "to promote the progress of science and useful arts, by securing limited times to authors and inventors concerning the exclusive right to their respective writings and discoveries *   *   *." As early as 1790, a number of statutes implementing this power were passed.

The patent laws exclude others, for a period of seventeen years, from making, using, or selling inventions that are claimed and determined to be patentable. Patent laws are unique in that they permit a number of practices that are considered to be anti-competitive. For example, the owner of a patent can fix prices to at least one licensee—a *per se* violation of antitrust laws in the absence of a patent. Thus, the patent law deviates from the general policy of preventing monopolies by offering economic protection for a limited time in order to encourage the development and production of goods and services.

In a similar manner, authors or their estates hold exclusive rights to the authors' published or unpublished works for life plus fifty years. For works that are anonymous or pseudonymous, protection is given for a minimum of seventy-five years from publication or one hundred years from creation.

Trademarks

At common law, merchants acquire legal rights to the words or symbols they use to distinguish their goods from others by adoption and use. Trademarks include "any word, name, symbol, or device, or any combination thereof adopted and used by the manufacturer [or] merchant to identify its goods and distinguish them from those manufactured or sold by others." Congress, acting under the commerce clause of the Constitution, enacted legislation long ago to facilitate the acquisition and enforcement of trademark rights. In 1946, the Lanham Act permitted registration of any distinctive mark indicative of its source or origin. Existing law, however, has

---

8.   100 S.Ct. 2844, 2863 (1980).
9.   29 U.S.C., Section 652(5).
10.   29 C.F.R., Sections 1975.4 and 1975.6 (1979).

determined that if the trademark becomes accepted as a generic term for the commodity and loses its association with a particular producer, then it is no longer valid. The trademarks *linoleum* and *aspirin*, for example, were lost when they became generally accepted as the generic name of the goods.

TYPES OF REGULATION

Within each regulated sector there are numerous types of regulation. In Exhibit 45–1 we examine some of the more important forms of regulation.

ADMINISTRATIVE AGENCIES

Administrative agencies are the primary interpreters and enforcers of many legislative statutes that focus on business regulation. Sometimes these agencies are part of a traditional executive branch of the government. For example, the Justice Department enforces the Sherman Act, the Clayton Act, and other antitrust laws. The National Highway Traffic Safety Administration and the Department of Transportation enforce regulations regarding safety, emissions, controls, and fuel economy of automobiles.

EXHIBIT 45–1 Types of Regulation

PROFIT REGULATION:	Profit regulation most often arises where the government has granted exclusive rights to produce a commodity. Most electric and water public utilities fall into this category.
PRICE REGULATION:	Price regulation can take the form of maximum, minimum, or uniform prices. New York City, for example, establishes the maximum price that certain apartment owners can charge their tenants. Minimum prices are often established as floors for certain agricultural products, such as wheat.
ADVERTISING:	Restrictions on professional advertising—for lawyers, doctors, and dentists—have survived many constitutional challenges in the past, but they appear to be weakening today. Restrictions on cigarette advertising continue.
QUOTAS AND DUTIES:	Explicit import duties or taxes are often applied to various products. In addition, some products, like petroleum, have been subject to absolute limits or quotas for importation.
LICENSING AND ALLOCATING RIGHTS:	Through their exercise of licensing power, agencies control entry into and operation of given economic activities. No rail, motor, or water carrier, for example, can extend its routes without a license from the Interstate Commerce Commission.
STANDARD SETTING:	Government agencies establish many standards for consumers. The U.S. Department of Agriculture, for example, grades beef and issues standards for other meat and poultry products.
DISCLOSURE REQUIREMENTS:	Sellers may be required to disclose certain information prior to the completion of a sale. For example, television ads for automobiles that give specific payment periods must also give the down payment, the amount of monthly payment, and the annual percentage rate of interest.
CONTRACT REVISIONS:	Regulatory agencies may limit the ability of parties to write contracts. For example, in recent years there have been movements to limit the remedies, such as wage attachments, available to creditors for defaults on consumer loans.
MATERIALS AND PROCESS REGULATION:	Regulatory agencies can also specify the type of material or process that can be used in the manufacture of certain goods. The Food and Drug Administration (FDA), for example, has prohibited the use of red dye number 2 in food and cosmetics.
TAXES AND SUBSIDIES:	Taxes and subsidies may be used as a means of changing economic behavior. For example, if taxes are imposed on inputs—factors of production such as raw materials and labor—then firms that use those inputs will be likely to substitute lower-cost alternatives.

Congress, on the other hand, has established some administrative agencies that are *independent of the executive branch*. The Interstate Commerce Commission, for example, regulates most service transportation within the United States as well as the service transportation of foreign countries that takes place within the boundaries of the United States. The Federal Aviation Administration, the Federal Trade Commission, the Federal Communications Commission, and the National Labor Relations Board are a few of the most important agencies with rulemaking powers. Exhibit 45–2 lists the most important agencies with rulemaking powers.

Combined Powers

Administrative agencies have judicial, executive, and legislative powers. Because Congress has delegated certain powers to agencies, they are able to combine the legislative, judicial, and executive powers that are traditionally separated under the Constitution. Thus, a single agency often formulates rules having the effect of law (a legislative function), adjudicates individual cases (a judicial function), and prosecutes actions in court (an executive function). It is frequently stated that administrative agencies act as judge, jury, and prosecutor.

Legislative Powers

Administrators' legislative powers have grown considerably over time. Initially, administrators' actions were more ministerial than legislative, and were often explicitly specified by statute. Over the years, as society has become more complex, Congress has authorized administrators to formulate rules and guidelines under the general authority granted to administrative agencies. The safety and health administrator, for example, is authorized to make rules that protect the safety and health of individuals in their places of employment. An authorization to protect the safety and health of individuals grants an agency discretion and effectively transmits legislative power to them. Administrative agencies have been delegated the power to prohibit unfair methods of competition, to grant licenses as public interest, convenience, or necessity requires, and to prevent or promote other generally specified goals.

Rulemaking Powers   Agencies develop and implement policy through both rulemaking and adjudi-

cation. Rulemaking is a legislative power, whereas adjudication is a judicial power. The question then arises as to whether, in a given situation, rulemaking or adjudication is appropriate. It has been suggested that rulemaking procedures are appropriate for decisions of general, "legislative" questions of law and policy, whereas adjudicative procedures are suitable for decisions of specific, "adjudicative" facts about particular parties.[11]

General rulemaking powers have been established by statute for a number of administrative agencies. In recent years there has been an increase in the extent and importance of agency rulemaking. During the 1970s many statutes were enacted that required agencies to promulgate rules. Rules were also perceived by agencies as an effective way to deal with the many new programs that were also created.

Purpose of Rulemaking   Under the Administrative Procedure Act (APA), a rule is defined as "the whole or a part of an agency statement of general or particular applicability and future effect designed to implement, interpret, or prescribe law or policy * * * or practice requirements of an agency."[12] Rules are used when an agency is prepared to announce a broadly applicable, prospective policy. It is future standards of conduct, rather than a past or current act, that a rule addresses. In many situations a rule is more appropriate and efficient than a case-by-case approach. Rules are often more specific and easier to follow than adjudicative precedents.

Procedural Requirements for Rulemaking   APA procedural requirements for rulemaking vary, depending upon whether an agency engages in "formal" or "informal" rulemaking. Some rulemaking is even exempted from the APA's procedural requirements. The APA further distinguishes between "substantive" and "interpretive" rules. Substantive rules are based upon a specific statutory authority to issue rules. Interpretive rules, on the other hand, are issued by an agency to interpret an existing statute.

---

11.   See K. Davis, *Administrative Law Text*, Section 7.03 (3e. 1972).

12.   5 U.S.C.A., Section 551(4).

EXHIBIT 45–2 Agencies With Rule-Making Powers

MAJOR REGULATORY AGENCIES

Consumer Product Safety Commission
Environmental Protection Agency
Equal Employment Opportunity Commission
Federal Communications Commission
Federal Deposit Insurance Corporation
Federal Energy Regulatory Commission
Federal Reserve System
Federal Trade Commission
Food and Drug Administration
Interstate Commerce Commission
National Labor Relations Board
Occupational Safety and Health Administration
Securities and Exchange Commission

OTHER REGULATORY AGENCIES

Civil Aeronautics Board
Commodity Futures Trading Commission
Economic Regulatory Administration
Farm Credit Administration
Federal Election Commission
Federal Home Loan Bank Board
Federal Maritime Commission
National Credit Union Administration
National Mediation Board
National Transportation Safety Board
Nuclear Regulatory Commission
Pension Benefit Guaranty Corporation
Postal Rate Commission
Small Business Administration
U.S. International Trade Commission
U.S. Postal Service
Veterans Administration

AGRICULTURE DEPARTMENT

Agricultural Marketing Service
Agricultural Stabilization and Conservation Service
Animal and Plant Health Inspection Service
Commodity Credit Corporation

Farmers Home Administration
Federal Grain Inspection Service
Food and Nutrition Service
Food Safety and Quality Service
Foreign Agricultural Service
U.S. Forest Service

COMMERCE DEPARTMENT

Economic Development Administration
Industry and Trade Administration
Maritime Administration
National Bureau of Standards
National Oceanic and Atmospheric Administration
Patent and Trademark Office

HEALTH AND HUMAN SERVICES DEPARTMENT

Office for Civil Rights
Social Security Administration
Public Health Service
Health Care Financing Administration
Office of Human Development Services
Child Support Enforcement Administration

HOUSING AND URBAN DEVELOPMENT DEPARTMENT

Office of Fair Housing and Equal Opportunity
Office for Neighborhoods, Voluntary Associations and Consumer Protection
Office of Community Planning and Development
Government National Mortgage Association
New Community Development Corporation

INTERIOR DEPARTMENT

Bureau of Indian Affairs
Bureau of Land Management
U.S. Fish and Wildlife Service
Geological Survey
Office of Surface Mining Reclamation and Enforcement

JUSTICE DEPARTMENT

Antitrust Division
Civil Rights Division
Drug Enforcement Administration
Immigration and Naturalization Service
Office of Justice and Research Statistics

LABOR DEPARTMENT

Employment Standards Administration
Employment and Training Administration
Labor-Management Services Administration
Mine Safety and Health Administration

TRANSPORTATION DEPARTMENT

Federal Aviation Administration
Federal Highway Administration
Federal Railroad Administration
Materials Transportation Bureau
National Highway Traffic Safety Administration
St. Lawrence Seaway Development Corporation
U.S. Coast Guard
Urban Mass Transportation Administration

TREASURY DEPARTMENT

Bureau of Alcohol, Tobacco and Firearms
Comptroller of the Currency
Internal Revenue Service
U.S. Customs Service
Secret Service

REGULATORY OVERSIGHT AND COORDINATION

Administrative Conference of the United States
Consumer Affairs Council
General Accounting Office
Interagency Regulatory Liaison Group
Office of Management and Budget
Task Force on Regulatory Relief

Informal rulemaking is generally used when an agency adopts substantive rules. When an agency engages in informal rulemaking, it must publish notice of the proposed rule, give interested persons an opportunity to participate in the rulemaking, and incorporate in the rules adopted a concise general statement of their basis and purpose.[13] Informal rulemaking is frequently referred to as "notice-and-

---

13. See 5 U.S.C.A., Section 553.

comment rulemaking." In contrast, formal rule-making compels an agency to conduct a trial-type hearing in which a party is entitled to present his or her case or defense by oral or documentary evidence, to submit rebuttal evidence, and to conduct cross-examination.[14] In many respects, formal rulemaking is similar to adjudication.

Judicial Powers

Administrative agencies also develop policy through adjudication—a judicial power. Adjudication is often appropriate when a decision relates to specific facts and to particular parties, or when an agency is not ready to announce a rule and desires to take a more cautious, case-by-case approach. The number of adjudications each year is substantial.

Procedures for Administrative Adjudication Administrative agencies adjudicate individual claims or cases in hearings conducted by administrative law judges assigned to the agency. Administrative law judges are employees of the agency; they are not members of the state or federal judiciary. Furthermore, there is no jury. An administrative law judge conducts the hearing and rules on all motions. He or she decides both the facts and the law to be applied in a case.[15]

An administrative proceeding is initiated with a complaint from the agency to one or more businesses that the agency believes have violated a particular rule or standard. Unlike state and federal courts, which have adopted highly restrictive exclusionary rules of evidence, administrative hearings permit the introduction of evidence that may be less reliable. Liberal administrative evidentiary rules create a strong presumption in favor of admitting challenged evidence.

An agency is represented by counsel, who presents evidence in support of the complaint. The respondent is then entitled to present his or her case. As in other courtroom trials, witnesses may be cross-examined and objections may be raised. Both parties generally submit legal briefs and proposed findings to the law judge. The administrative law judge may

then render an "initial" or a "recommended" order. An order is defined by the APA as "the whole or a part of a final disposition, whether affirmative, negative, injunctive, or declaratory in form, of an agency in a matter other than rulemaking."[16]

An initial order becomes the order of the agency unless it is appealed. In contrast, a recommended order is one in which the presiding employee or an employee qualified to preside at hearings recommends the order to the agency.[17] The recommended order is generally adopted if neither the agency counsel nor the respondent objects.

Although an administrative law judge's initial decision is likely to carry considerable weight with the agency, APA Section 557(b) specifically states that "on appeal from review of the initial decision, the agency has all the powers which it would have in making the initial decision, except as it may limit the issues on notice or by rule." Unlike other courtroom trials, the agency is not required to defer to the administrative law judge's factual conclusions.

Scope of Review Administrative law seeks to achieve bureaucratic justice, but unfortunately this goal is not always attained. Most final actions and orders emanating from administrative agencies can be appealed to the courts. Courts consider whether an agency action is:

1. Pursuant to a statute that is constitutional.
2. Authorized by a statute.
3. The result of fair and proper procedures.
4. Substantively rational.

Judicial review is generally authorized by the enabling statute or by common law precedents. The APA also provides for review when a person suffers a legal wrong because of an agency action or is adversely affected or aggrieved by an agency action.[18] The reviewing court is normally limited to and bound by the findings of fact reached during the original administrative hearing. Federal courts are not supposed to displace the discretion delegated to administrative agencies by substituting their judgment for

14. See 5 U.S.C.A., Section 556.
15. Federal Administrative Law Judge Hearings, *Statistical Report for 1976–1978,* p. 33.

16. See 5 U.S.C.A., Section 551(6).
17. See 5 U.S.C.A., Section 557(b).
18. See 5 U.S.C.A., Section 702.

that of the agency. The legislature delegates discretion to administrative agencies—not to the reviewing courts. Yet, to achieve bureaucratic justice, administrative agencies must be held accountable, and judicial review is one potential check.

Standards of Review   Section 706 of the APA prescribes various levels of judicial deference to agencies' determinations of questions of facts. Depending upon the circumstances, there are three different standards of fact review: (1) the "arbitrary and capricious" test; (2) the "substantial evidence" test; and (3) the "unwarranted by the facts" test.

A judge's ruling may be overturned if it fails to meet the appropriate standard of review. The arbitrary and capricious standard is the most lenient of the tests and is usually applied unless a court determines that one of the other tests is applicable. This test is generally used when reviewing informal actions. However, even when using an arbitrary and capricious standard, courts vary in the amount of deference that they are willing to give to agency fact-findings.

A less lenient standard, the substantial evidence test, is applied when an agency is subject to APA Section 556 and is required to make a record, or when the agency action is reviewed on the record of an agency hearing provided by statute.[19] Basically, this standard is applicable to formal proceedings that are subject to a requirement that there be a formal record.

Rarely used is the third standard of review—"unwarranted by the facts." This standard is relevant only if the facts are subject to trial "de novo" by the reviewing court.[20] De novo review is one in which a reviewing court tries the case as if it had not been heard before. Judicial review is generally of a limited nature, and thus de novo review is infrequent. The Supreme Court has held that de novo review of whether a decision is "unwarranted by the facts" is authorized in two circumstances:

1.   When the action is adjudicatory in nature and the agency fact-finding procedures are inadequate;

2.   When issues that were not before the agency are raised in a proceeding to enforce nonadjudicatory agency action.[21]

Executive Powers

Administrative agencies perform executive functions, such as investigation and prosecution. In order for agencies to regulate businesses, they must be able to obtain information. When, by statute, an agency has been delegated the power to issue rules prescribing standards of conduct, it is essential that the agency have access to complete and accurate information before engaging in rulemaking. Businesses, on the other hand, often consider it to be in their best interests to resist disclosure in an effort to avoid or impede regulation. Consequently, Congress has delegated to agencies various degrees of investigatory powers. Subpoenas for documents or testimony, inspection of records, and information requests are some of the investigatory powers delegated to agencies.

Investigatory powers of agencies, however, are constrained by major constitutional limitations. Both procedural and substantive due process protect businesses against arbitrary, capricious, and unreasonable agency action. Substantive due process arises with issues involving property or other rights affected by government. Procedural due process focuses on proper notice and hearing procedures.

Enforcement powers are also delegated to agencies. All final orders carry the weight of statutory law and have prescribed penalties for violations. These penalties are enforceable unless a reviewing court reverses the agency decision. Failure to comply with the prescribed penalties is treated like any other violation of the law. In most cases, violations are considered to be civil matters, and thus a business is held liable for money damages or is required to take some specific action, such as the installation of pollution-control equipment. However, in recent years there has been a trend toward issuing criminal penalties as well, and violaters, including corporate officers, can be subject to jail sentences. Both the Securities Act of 1933 and the Securities Exchange Act of 1934 prescribe criminal penalties for violations of various sections of their respective acts.

---

19.   See 5 U.S.C.A., Section 706(2)(E).
20.   See 5 U.S.C.A., Section 706(2)(F).

21.   See Citizens to Preserve Overton Park, Inc. v. Volpe, 401 U.S. 402 (1971).

QUESTIONS AND CASE PROBLEMS

1. Assume Congress, under the power of the Constitution to provide for the general welfare of the United States, passes federal legislation creating an administrative agency to deal with the soaring divorce rate. The new agency is called the Federal Anti-Divorce Service (FADS). Congress gives the agency both *rulemaking* and *adjudicatory* powers. Discuss *fully* whether you could justify the creation of such an agency.

2. Assume that once the FADS in Question 1 is created, FADS issues a policy requiring that any married couple seeking a divorce must attend, at a minimum, four counseling sessions with a staff counselor in their state before a petition for a divorce can be filed by either party. Discuss what power FADS is exercising, and what procedures are necessary before implementing this policy as an order.

3. Suppose a married couple seeking a divorce has complied with the FADS "four counseling sessions" rule under Question 2 above and would now like their case to be heard pursuant to the statute creating FADS and granting it adjudication powers. The FADS administrative judge hears the case and awards most of the couple's joint assets and custody of their two children to the husband. The wife is outraged and seeks review. What can the court review and what standard of review will be used?

4. Article III of the Constitution provides that the judicial power shall reside in the Supreme Court of the United States and in such inferior courts as the Congress shall from time to time create. Judicial power is the power to resolve disputes and includes the power to determine whether an individual has committed certain acts and whether the commission of such acts constitutes the breach of a duty owed to another or to society as a whole. Administrative agencies have the power to determine whether a person is guilty or innocent of violating agency rules and regulations. Does this contradict the mandate of Article III?

5. All actions taken by an administrative agency, whether legislative or judicial, are subject to review by the courts. The relevant test for review is whether the agency acted in an "arbitrary or capricious" manner in promulgating the rule. This question was posed in the following case: The secretary of commerce issued a flammability standard that required all mattresses, including crib mattresses, to pass a test that involved contact with a burning cigarette. The manufacturers of crib mattresses petitioned the court to excuse crib mattresses from the flammability standard. These manufacturers said that applying such a rule to crib mattresses would not only be unreasonable but arbitrary

and capricious since infants do not smoke. How should the court rule? [Bunny Bear, Inc. v. Peterson, 473 F.2d 1002 (5th Cir. 1973)]

6. In the past Congress employed a legislative veto in hundreds of statutes. The purpose of such a veto was to allow Congress to retain a check on agency action. When a statute delegated broad legislative rulemaking power to a particular agency, for example, Congress would often retain the power to veto the rules after they were adopted. In 1983, however, the Supreme Court held that Congress cannot retain a "legislative veto" for administrative adjudication or rulemaking. Why was such a veto invalidated? Furthermore, in the future, how might this decision affect Congress when it passes a new statute? [INS v. Chadha, 462 U.S. 919, 103 S.Ct. 2764 (1983)]

7. If an administrative agency acts arbitrarily or capriciously, the reviewing court will strike down its rule. Agencies, however, are given wide latitude or discretion in formulating agency rules. Only when an agency abuses this discretion will a reviewing court reverse it. In Question 5, the administrative agency promulgated a single flammability standard for more than one type of mattress. If the crib mattress manufacturer had clearly demonstrated by proof that a flammability test used on infant mattresses in Europe was as satisfactory as the "cigarette test" and had been used with good results for years in Europe, would the secretary of commerce have abused his discretion in adopting the cigarette test? What if the crib mattress manufacturer proved that the flammability test used in Europe was better than the cigarette test? Would the secretary of commerce have abused his discretion?

8. Reviewing courts readily support rules promulgated by administrative agencies, but they require that the adjudicative findings of an agency be supported by "substantial evidence on the record." When an administrative agency conducts an adjudicative hearing, a record is made of all the evidence and testimony presented at the hearing. If the finding of the hearing is supported by the evidence contained in the record, a reviewing court will uphold the agency's finding. The Adolph Coors Company was accused by the Federal Trade Commission of engaging in certain price-fixing agreements in violation of the Sherman Antitrust Act. After a complete adjudicative hearing, the commission concluded that Coors had in fact engaged in illegal price fixing. Substantial evidence was presented at the hearing in support of the commission's findings. But Coors also presented substantial evidence that it had never entered into any price-fixing arrangements. Should a reviewing court uphold the FTC's findings? [Adolph Coors Co. v. Federal Trade Comm., 497 F.2d 1178 (10th Cir. 1974)]

9. Section 553 of the Administrative Procedure Act prescribes the procedures that agencies must follow in their rulemaking proceedings. In the case of *Vermont Yankee*,

the lower court examined the rulemaking proceedings of the Atomic Energy Commission and concluded that the proceedings were inadequate and thus overturned the rule. This decision was reached despite the fact that the agency employed all the procedures required by Section 553 and more. What was the result reached by the Supreme Court as to whether or not courts are free to require agencies to follow additional rulemaking procedures? [Vermont Yankee Nuclear Power Corp. v. Natural Resources Defense Council, Inc., 435 U.S. 519, 98 S.Ct. 1197 (1978)]

10. Notice and a hearing must be provided whenever an agency action would deprive a party of interests protected by due process. New York State and New York City officials administered various federally assisted welfare programs. A complaint alleged that the state and the city terminated, or were about to terminate, such aid without prior notice and a hearing, thereby denying the plaintiffs due process of law. The state and the city, however, had adopted procedures for notice and hearing *after* suits were brought. Does the failure to provide a welfare recipient with a pre-termination evidentiary hearing violate procedural due process? [Goldberg v. Kelly, 397 U.S. 254, 90 S.Ct. 1011 (1970)]

46

GOVERNMENT REGULATION
Consumer Protection

Consumer grievances about the quality of retail goods and services, the price and terms of credit, repossession practices, warranties and other aspects of the sale, financing, and service of consumer goods represent some of the more important concerns facing individuals in society today. These grievances have prompted ever-growing judicial, legislative, and administrative actions designed to protect the consumer in selecting, purchasing, financing and obtaining service for consumer goods in a seemingly impersonal, urbanized marketplace.

Consumer protection arises from three distinct sources—from the common law through judicial rulings; from the simplification and codification of common law, through federal, state, and local statutes, including the Uniform Commercial Code; and from administrative law, through rulemaking and enforcement activities.

Since parties who make contracts are generally given the right to specify the terms, consumer protection under the common law is sometimes limited. As Chapter 11 illustrated, the interests of consumers are an important consideration in judicial decisions. For example, the unconscionability doctrine (which deals with contracts that would be grossly unfair to enforce) protects consumers from certain pricing techniques for goods that are sold on credit. Consider the example of Williams, who made a series

of purchases from Walker-Thomas Furniture Company from 1957 to 1962. Each of the time-payment contracts that she signed contained the clause that all payments would be credited pro rata on all outstanding accounts. In 1962 she purchased furniture for $164, bringing her total purchases since 1957 to $1,800. The pro rata claim, however, meant that she still owed money on all items, despite the fact that she had paid a total of $1,400 through 1962. A court found this clause to be unconscionable and unenforceable.[1]

CONSUMER PROTECTION SOURCES

Consumers are given protection by federal and state laws, by administrative agencies, by the courts, and by private organizations.

Federal Laws

A number of federal laws—such as the Consumer Credit Protection Act and the Magnuson-Moss Warranty Act—have been passed to provide more explicit direction on the duties of sellers and the rights

---

1. Williams v. Walker-Thomas Furniture Co., 198 A.2d 914 (D.C.App. 1964).

of consumers. In recent years, the pressure on Congress to enact further laws to protect consumers has increased. Exhibit 46-1 lists the major consumer protection statutes by popular name.

State Statutes

In addition to the Uniform Commercial Code's consumer protection provisions,[2] a number of statutes in California, Florida, New York, and other states provide explicit protection to consumers. For example, the California Civil Code permits consumers to keep unsolicited goods. If they are billed for the

goods, they can seek an injunction to stop billing, and they can collect reasonable attorneys' fees.[3]

Administrative Agencies

Administrative agencies provide an important form of consumer protection. For example, the Federal Trade Commission has been given extensive enforcement responsibilities in a number of statutes, some of which are discussed here. The most important authority, however, is Section 5 of the original Federal Trade Commission Act of 1914, as amended in 1938. It permits the commission to stop

---

2. The UCC is discussed more fully in Unit III of this text.

3. Section 1584.5.

EXHIBIT 46–1　Consumer Protection Statutes

Popular Name	Purpose	Statute Reference
ADVERTISING		
Federal Trade Commission Act	Prohibits deceptive and unfair trade practices	15 U.S.C. 45, 341 *et seq.*
CERTIFICATION AND LABELING		
Child Protection	Requires child-proof devices and special labeling	15 U.S.C. 1261 *et seq.*
Smoking Act of 1969	Warns of possible health hazard by surgeon general	15 U.S.C. 1331 *et seq.*
Fair Packaging and Labeling Act	Requires accurate names, quantities, weights	15 U.S.C. 1451 *et seq.*
Fur Products Labeling Act	Prohibits misbranding of fur products	15 U.S.C. 69
Wool Products Labeling Act of 1939	Requires accurate labeling of wool products	15 U.S.C. 68
SALES AND WARRANTIES		
Magnuson-Moss Warranty	Provides rules that govern content of warranties	15 U.S.C. 2301 *et seq.*
Real Estate Settlement Procedures Act of 1974	Requires disclosure of home buying costs	12 U.S.C. 2601 *et seq.*
Uniform Commercial Code (UCC)	Covers unconscionable sales contracts	UCC 2-302 (adopted by all states except Louisiana)
CREDIT		
Consumer Credit Protection Act	Offers comprehensive protection covering all phases of credit transactions	15 U.S.C. 1601 *et seq.*
Equal Credit Opportunity Act	Prohibits discrimination in the extending of credit	15 U.S.C. 1691 *et seq.*
Fair Credit Collection Practices Act	Prohibits debt collectors' abuses	15 U.S.C. 1692
Fair Credit Reporting Act	Protects consumers' credit reputations	15 U.S.C. 1681 *et seq.*
Truth-in-Lending Act	Requires full disclosure of credit terms	15 U.S.C. 1601 *et seq.*
Uniform Consumer Credit Code	Requires full disclosure of credit terms	Adopted by Colorado, Idaho, Indiana, Kansas, Maine, Oklahoma, Utah, Wyoming

"unfair or deceptive acts or practices" that influence, inhibit, or restrict consumers unfairly in their purchasing decisions. Many of these practices are prohibited by industry guidelines or by trade regulation rules. Violations are punishable by law and can occur in two circumstances. A company can engage in a practice prohibited by a trade regulation, or it can violate a known cease and desist order issued against *another* party.

Other agencies of the federal government, such as the Department of Housing and Urban Development, are also engaged in consumer protection activities. HUD, for example, enforces provisions of the National Mobile Home Construction and Safety Standards Act of 1974, requiring periodic inspections and investigations to enforce federal standards. It also enforces the Interstate Land Sale Full Disclosure Act, which requires that sellers of subdivided lots provide certain statements of record that must include a legal description of the land, who has title to the land, and the present condition of the land.

The Courts

Finally, consumers themselves can use the courts to obtain remedies for their grievances. Since the time, embarrassment, and cost to consumers of private lawsuits can be prohibitive, various mechanisms have been developed not only to remove these barriers but to also encourage consumer actions. They include free legal services, small claims courts, and the recovery of attorneys' fees in class actions. Attorneys' fees, however, are generally recoverable only when there is an express statutory authorization.[4] Class actions have become a relatively more common form of addressing consumer grievances, but these actions are subject to certain rules and limitations that make them difficult to pursue.

Private Organizations

Consumers also have access to the Better Business Bureau (BBB) system, a national organization of independent, nonprofit organizations financed by businesses to regulate themselves. The main orga-

nization, the Council of Better Business Bureaus, Inc., has established the following priority projects:

1.   Expanding and improving the services of BBB and seeking standardization and coordination among the parts of the network.
2.   Establishing consumer arbitration as a means of achieving consumer justice.
3.   Establishing a consumer education program to include the traditional information booklets, audiovisual material, school curriculum material, and programs tailored to meet the needs of minority, low-income, and elderly groups.
4.   Establishing a top-level procedure for voluntary self-regulation of advertising.[5]

ADVERTISING

The increased protection received by consumers during the past two decades against deceptive advertising derives more from statutory and administrative sources than from common law. Common law protection is based on fraud and requires proof of intent to misrepresent facts and other criteria. Statutory law and administrative regulations, on the other hand, focus on whether the advertising is likely to be misleading, regardless of intent. This approach arises from the idea that false advertising should be prohibited in order to protect the consumer rather than to punish the seller or advertiser.

The Federal Trade Commission Act empowers the FTC to determine what constitutes a deceptive practice within the meaning of Section 5 of the act. The FTC's judgment can be appealed to a court, but it is accorded great weight by the reviewing court. When the commission renders an opinion or issues an order, appeal can be taken through judicial channels. The commission is responsible for enforcing the legislative policy of the act it administers, and the courts will recognize that the administrative agency that deals continually with cases in the area is often in a better position than the courts are to determine when a practice is deceptive within the meaning of the act.

---

4.   See Alyeska Pipeline Serv. Co. v. The Wilderness Soc'y, 421 U.S. 240, 95 S.Ct. 1612 (1975).

5.   H. Bruce Palmer, *Association Management Magazine*, November 1970. These projects continue to have priority today.

Defining Deceptive Advertising

As defined by the FTC, deception generally means that the advertisement may be interpreted in more than one way and that one of those interpretations is false or misleading. Deception may involve a false statement or claim about the product's quality, effects, price, origin, or availability. Deception also may occur when an advertisement omits important facts or information about the product. Advertisements may contain "half-truths" if the presented material is true but additional information would be required to prevent consumers from being misled.

Finally an advertisement will often be considered deceptive if its statements are not supported by adequate scientific evidence. When, however, the claim is incapable of measurement, as in "When you're out of Schlitz, you're out of beer," no problem of deception is perceived by the FTC.[6]

The following case illustrates an FTC decision that a TV mock-up advertisement was deceptive.

---

6. For a brief article dealing with deceptive advertising, see Gaylord A. Jentz, "Federal Regulation of Advertising: False Representation," *Am.Bus.Law.J.* (Spring 1968), pp. 409–427.

BACKGROUND AND FACTS *The Federal Trade Commission issued a complaint against Colgate-Palmolive Company and Ted Bates & Company, Inc., an advertising agency, for using commercials that misrepresented the characteristics of Colgate's Rapid Shave. Bates had prepared television commercials that showed how Rapid Shave could soften something as tough as sandpaper. In the commercial, Rapid Shave was applied to something that looked like sandpaper, and shortly thereafter a razor shaved it clean. Unknown to the viewers, the "sandpaper" was actually a piece of Plexiglas with sand on it.*

Initially, a hearing examiner concluded that Rapid Shave could shave sandpaper, although not as quickly as the advertisement suggested, so the examiner dismissed the complaint, saying that the misrepresentation was not a material one that would mislead the public.

The commission, however, reversed the hearing examiner's finding and held that, since Rapid Shave could not shave the sandpaper within the time depicted in the commercials, the product's moisturizing power had been misrepresented. In addition, the use of a Plexiglas substitute for sandpaper was a material misrepresentation because it misled viewers into believing that they had seen something which, in fact, they had not. As a result of these findings, the commission entered a cease and desist order against Colgate-Palmolive.

The court of appeals then set aside the order because it was so broadly written that it forbade all use of undisclosed simulations in television commercials. Five months later, the commission issued a revised order prohibiting Colgate-Palmolive from presenting advertisements depicting a test, an experiment, or a demonstration represented as actual proof of a product claim but not in fact constituting proof because of the use of an undisclosed mock-up.

Once again, the court of appeals set aside the commission's order, so the commission petitioned the Supreme Court to set forth a legal standard of the words, deceptive practice, *within the meaning of Section 5 of the Federal Trade Commission Act.*

FEDERAL TRADE COMM'N v. COLGATE-PALMOLIVE CO.
Supreme Court of the United States, 1965.
380 U.S. 374, 85 S.Ct. 1035.

WARREN, Chief Justice.
* * * *

The basic question before us is whether it is a deceptive trade practice, prohibited by § 5 of the Federal Trade Commission Act, to represent falsely that a televised test, experiment, or demonstration provides a viewer with visual proof of a product claim regardless of whether the product claim is itself true.

*   *   *   *

In reviewing the substantive issues in the case, it is well to remember the respective roles of the Commission and the courts in the administration of the Federal Trade Commission Act. When the Commission was created by Congress in 1914, it was directed by § 5 to prevent "[u]nfair methods of competition in commerce." Congress amended the Act in 1938 to extend the Commission's jurisdiction to include "unfair or deceptive acts or practices in commerce"—a significant amendment showing Congress' concern for consumers as well as for competitors. *   *   *

This statutory scheme necessarily gives the Commission an influential role in interpreting § 5 and in applying it to the facts of particular cases arising out of unprecedented situations. *   *   *

The Commission's interpretation of what is a deceptive practice seems more in line with the decided cases than that of respondents. This Court said in *Federal Trade Comm'n v. Algoma Lumber Co.*, "[T]he public is entitled to get what it chooses, though the choice may be dictated by caprice or by fashion or perhaps by ignorance." It has long been considered a deceptive practice to state falsely that a product ordinarily sells for an inflated price but that it is being offered at a special reduced price, even if the offered price represents the actual value of the product and the purchaser is receiving his money's worth. Applying respondents' arguments to these cases, it would appear that so long as buyers paid no more than the product was actually worth and the product contained the qualities advertised, the misstatement of an inflated original price was immaterial.

*   *   *[T]he present case is not concerned with a mode of communication, but with a misrepresentation that viewers have objective proof of a seller's product claim over and above the seller's word. Secondly, *   *   * the present case, deal[s] with methods designed to get a consumer to purchase a product, not with whether the product, when purchased, will perform up to expectations. *   *   *

It is generally accepted that it is a deceptive practice to state falsely that a product has received a testimonial from a respected source. *   *   *

*   *   * We find it an immaterial difference that in one case the viewer is told to rely on the word of a celebrity or authority he respects, in another on the word of a testing agency, and in the present case on his own perception of an undisclosed simulation.

*   *   *   *

We agree with the Commission, therefore, that the undisclosed use of plexiglass in the present commercials was a material deceptive practice, independent and separate from the other misrepresentation found. Respondents claim that it will be impractical to inform the viewing public that it is not seeing an actual test, experiment or demonstration, but we think it inconceivable that the ingenious advertising world will be unable, if it so desires, to conform to the Commission's insistence that the public be not misinformed. If, however, it becomes impossible or impractical to show simulated demonstrations on television in a truthful manner, this indicates that television is not a medium that lends itself to this type of commercial, not that the commercial must survive at all costs. *   *   * If the inherent limitations of a method do not permit its use in the way a seller desires, the seller cannot by material misrepresentation compensate for those limitations.

*   *   * [W]hen the commercial not only makes a claim, but also invites the viewer to rely on his own perception for demonstrative proof of the claim, the respondents will be aware that the use of undisclosed props in strategic places might be a material deception. *   *   *

The judgment of the court of appeals was reversed, and the case was remanded for entry of a judgment enforcing the commission's revised cease and desist order prohibiting Colgate-Palmolive from using the commercials.

DECISION AND REMEDY

Bait and Switch

In some cases, the Federal Trade Commission has promulgated specific rules to govern advertising. One of its more important rules is called "Guides on Bait Advertising,"[7] and it is designed to prohibit advertisements that specify a very low price for a particular item. The low price is the bait to lure the consumer into the store. Then the salesperson tries to switch

the consumer to some other, more expensive item. According to the FTC guidelines, bait advertising occurs if the seller refuses to show the advertised item, fails to have adequate quantities of it available, fails to promise or deliver the advertised item within a reasonable time, or discourages employees from selling the item.

Numerous techniques fall into the bait-and-switch category. In the following case, sales personnel not only were directed to engage in certain baiting practices but were rewarded for doing so.

---

7. 16 C.F.R. 238 (1968).

BACKGROUND AND FACTS   *All-State Industries, a producer of residential aluminum siding, storm windows, and other products, used a bait-and-switch sales technique in selling its products. The "ADV" lower-cost grade of aluminum was featured in the company's ads, but salespersons, following the training manual, attempted instead to sell the "PRO" grade after contacting the customers. The Federal Trade Commission found this practice to be an "unfair and deceptive" practice under Section 5(b) of the FTC Act and issued a cease and desist order. All-State Industries appealed.*

ALL-STATE INDUS. OF NORTH CAROLINA, INC. v. FEDERAL TRADE COMM'N
United States Court of Appeals, Fourth Cir., 1970.
423 F.2d 423.

BRYAN, Circuit Judge.
*   *   *   *

From the Hearing Examiner's findings of fact, the following account unfolds of how they vend their products. These are of two grades. The "ADV" is the cheaper. It is extensively advertised, primarily through mailouts to people whose names and addresses are culled from telephone directories. "PRO," the other grade, is of a higher quality and not so widely publicized.

Respondents' sales technique, or "pitch," is devised to create, first, a demand for the "ADV" product. Through inflated promotion it is presented as a "special offer" with "limited time" prices. But the Examiner found the "ADV" is actually priced uniformly and without time limit. He held as untrue All-State's claim that they deal directly from their factory with the output "100% guaranteed."

Inquiries or "leads" are answered by a supposed "sales manager." He attempts to pressure the prospect into signing a contract, a note and a deed, committing him to the purchase of "ADV" articles but leaving blank the monetary obligation. As soon as the contract is executed, the salesperson brings out a sample of the "ADV" and points out deficiencies in it, "whether real or imaginary." The "PRO" is then shown in contrast, to the detriment of the "ADV." Whenever possible the "PRO" is then sold "at the highest price obtainable from the individual customer." The salesmen have incentives to substitute the "PRO"—they receive no commission on "ADV" but only on "PRO" sales.

This "bait and switch" artifice, the Examiner discovered, was fully set forth in the sales force's training manual and was employed generally. He also reported that All-State's agents utilized "gimmicks whereby the original prices quoted for respondents' products can be reduced." For example, the representative would promise a potential buyer a special discount, even below the quoted sale price, if the latter would allow the use of his home for demonstration or display purposes. Rarely, however, would a patron's home be so utilized. It was found as a bare inducement to overcome "sales resistance at a higher price" and provide "some apparently reasonable basis for the reduction in price."

*   *   *   *

DECISION AND REMEDY *The cease and desist order was enforced against All-State Industries as well as against each of All-State's sales agents. Such a bait-and-switch scheme is clearly in violation of the Federal Trade Commission's "Guides on Bait Advertising."*

Labeling and Packaging

A number of federal and state laws that govern labeling and packaging have been passed to provide the consumer with accurate information or warnings about the use or possible misuse of the product. The Fur Products Labeling Act, the Wool Products Labeling Act, the Cigarette Labeling and Advertising Act, the Food, Drug and Cosmetic Act, the Flammable Fabrics Act, and the Fair Packaging and Labeling Act are a few of the acts that have been enacted in part to reduce the amount of incorrect labeling and packaging in consumer products.

In general, labels must be accurate, which means that they must use words as they are ordinarily understood by consumers. For example, a regular size box of cereal cannot be labeled "giant" if that word would exaggerate the amount of cereal. Labels often must specify the raw materials used in the product, such as the percentage of cotton, nylon, or other fibers used in a shirt. The Fair Packaging Act requires that consumer goods have labels that identify the product, the manufacturer, the packer or distributor and its place of business, the net quantity of the contents, and the quantity of each serving if the number of servings is stated.[8] Additional authority is also included in this statute to add requirements governing words that are used to describe packages, terms that are associated with savings claims, information disclosure for ingredients in nonfood products, and standards for the partial filling of packages. The provisions are enforced by the Federal

---

8.   15 U.S.C.A., Section 1451 et seq.

Trade Commission and the Department of Health and Human Services.

SALES

A number of statutes that protect the consumer in sales transactions concern the disclosure of certain terms in sales, rules governing home or door-to-door sales, mail-order transactions, referral sales, and unsolicited merchandise. The Federal Reserve Board of Governors, for example, has issued Regulation Z, which governs credit provisions associated with sales contracts, and numerous states have passed laws governing the remedies available to consumers in home sales. Furthermore, states have adopted a number of consumer protection provisions by incorporating the UCC and the Uniform Consumer Credit Code into their statutory codes.

In 1968, Congress passed the first of a series of statutes regarding the content of information contained in written and oral messages. If, for instance, certain credit terms are used in an advertisement, other credit information is also required. Thus, if Prolific Pontiac Sales states in a newspaper advertisement that individuals have thirty-six months to pay, the firm must also include the cash price of the automobiles, the down payment, the amount of each periodic payment, and the annual percentage rate of interest.

The Postal Reorganization Act of 1970 provides that unsolicited merchandise sent by U.S. mail may be retained, used, discarded, or disposed of in any manner deemed appropriate, without the individual incurring any obligation to the sender.[9] In addition, the mailing of unordered merchandise (except for free samples) constitutes an unfair trade practice and is not permitted. (Exceptions are mailings by charitable agencies and those made by mistake.)

Door-to-Door Sales

Door-to-door sales are singled out for special treatment in the laws of most states. This special treatment stems in part from the nature of the sales transaction if the salesperson is able to gain entrance. A door-to-door seller usually has a captive audience because many individuals are actually immobilized at home. Since repeat purchases are not as likely as they are in stores, the seller has little incentive to cultivate the good will of the purchaser. Furthermore, the seller is unlikely to present alternative products and their prices. Thus, a number of states have passed statutes that permit the buyers of goods sold door-to-door to cancel their contracts within a specified period of time, usually two to three days after the sale.

A Federal Trade Commission regulation also makes it a Section 5 violation for door-to-door sellers to fail to give consumers three days to cancel any sale. This rule applies as well to state statutes so that consumers are given the most favorable benefits of the FTC rule and their own state statute. In addition, the FTC rule requires that the notification be given in Spanish if the oral negotiations for the sale were in that language.

Mail-Order Transactions

Consumers buying from mail-order houses have typically been given less protection than when they purchase in stores. Many mail-order houses are outside the state, and it is more costly to seek redress for grievances in that situation. In addition to the federal statute that prevents the use of mails to defraud individuals, several states have passed statutes governing certain practices by sellers, including insurance companies, that solicit through the mails. The state statutes parallel the federal statutes governing mail fraud.

HEALTH PROTECTION

Health protection laws govern the processing and distribution of such diverse products as meat and poultry, poisonous substances, and drugs and cosmetics. For some products, such as cigarettes, explicit warnings about health hazards are required.

Food

In 1906, Congress passed its first act regulating drugs. Early laws protected consumers against adulteration and misbranding of food and drug products. In subsequent amendments, standards for foods, specification of safe levels of potentially dangerous food additives, and control of classifications of foods and food advertising were established. The most restrictive amendment was passed in 1958, giving the Food and Drug Administration the right to define food additives and to set safe levels. In addition, this amendment forbids the use of any food additive that can be shown to be carcinogenic (cancer-causing) to humans or animals. In general, the law makes manufacturers responsible for insuring that the food they offer for sale contains no substances that could cause injury to health.[10]

Food Inspection

A number of laws have been passed to establish standards for meat and poultry shipped interstate. All such meat and poultry used for human consumption is subject to inspection for its wholesomeness and accuracy in labeling. Although federal law does not require grade standards, official grading is offered by the Department of Agriculture to packers, processors, and distributors who are willing to pay a fee. Among the statutes enforced by the Food Safety and Quality Service of the Department of Agriculture are the Agricultural Marketing Act of 1946,[11] the Egg Products Inspection Act of 1970,[12] the Poultry Products Inspection Act of 1957,[13] and the Wholesome Meat Act of 1967.[14]

---

9.   39 U.S.C.A. 3009.

10.   United States v. Park, 421 U.S. 658, 95 S.Ct. 1903 (1975).
11.   60 Stat. 1087, 7 U.S.C. 1621.
12.   84 Stat. 1620, 21 U.S.C. 1031.
13.   71 Stat. 441, 21 U.S.C. 451.
14.   81 Stat. 584, 21 U.S.C. 601.

Drugs and Cosmetics

Some regulations regarding drugs and cosmetics are set forth in the original Food, Drug and Cosmetic Act of 1938.[15] In addition, a number of amendments, particularly those of 1962, require that all drugs be proven effective as well as safe before they can be marketed.

Food and Drug Administration (FDA)

Most of the statutes involving food and drugs are monitored and enforced by the Food and Drug Administration. FDA responsibilities include (but are not limited to):

1. The inspection of manufacturing facilities for compliance with FDA standards.
2. The establishment of written and physical standards for biological products.
3. The development of policy regarding the safety, effectiveness, and labeling of all drugs for human use.
4. The evaluation of new drug applications and requests to approve drugs for experimental use.
5. The development of standards for the safety and effectiveness of over-the-counter drugs.
6. The distribution of information on the toxicity of household products and medicines.
7. The conducting of research and the development of standards on the composition, quality, nutrition, and safety of food, food additives, colors, and cosmetics.
8. The development of regulations for food standards to permit the safe use of color and food additives.

Labeling

Congress has also enacted a number of statutes to protect individuals by providing them with information about products.

Fair Packaging and Labeling Act   In 1976, Congress enacted a law that requires manufacturers to provide consumers with accurate information about the quantity of the contents of products. Moreover, the net quantities must be conspicuously displayed in a uniform location on the package. This law facilitates comparisons among similar products by consumers.

Public Health Cigarette Smoking Act   For years, the statement: "Warning: the Surgeon General Has Determined That Cigarette Smoking Is Dangerous to Your Health" was required to appear on both cigarette and little cigar packages. Effective October 12, 1985, major brand cigarette producers must rotate four new warning labels on a quarterly basis. Smaller companies may use all four warnings at the same time on a random basis.

Each warning begins, "SURGEON GENERAL'S WARNING" and then either states:

1. Smoking Causes Lung Cancer, Heart Disease, Emphysema, And May Complicate Pregnancy; or
2. Quitting Smoking Now Greatly Reduces Serious Risks to Your Health; or
3. Smoking By Pregnant Women May Result in Fetal Injury, Premature Birth, And Low Birth Weight; or
4. Cigarette Smoke Contains Carbon Monoxide.

Poison Prevention Packaging Act   A 1970 amendment to the Fair Packaging and Labeling Act requires that manufacturers provide so-called child-proof devices on all household products that could harm young children if mishandled or ingested by them.

CONSUMER PRODUCT SAFETY LEGISLATION

Consumer product safety legislation began in 1953 with the enactment of the Flammable Fabrics Act, which prohibits the sale of highly flammable clothing or materials.[16] Between 1953 and 1972, Congress enacted legislation regulating specific classes of products or product design or composition, rather than the overall safety of consumer products. Finally, as a result of 1970 recommendations of the National Commission on Product Safety, the Consumer Product Safety Act was passed in 1972, creating the Consumer Product Safety Commission (CPSC) to regulate all potentially hazardous consumer products.[17]

---

15.   52 Stat. 1040, 21 U.S.C. 301.

16.   67 Stat. 111, 15 U.S.C. 1191.
17.   86 Stat. 1207, 15 U.S.C. 2051.

Until the 1960s, manufacturers that developed, designed, produced, or marketed a product in a reasonable manner would generally avoid liability for injury or damage from consumer products. In addition to the changing liability discussed in Chapter 22, manufacturers are now subject to a number of statutes regulating product safety. The Consumer Product Safety Act of 1972, for example, protects consumers from unreasonable risk of injury from hazardous products.

Products Subject to the 1972 Act

The 1972 act states that " *   *   * any article, or component part thereof produced or distributed for sale to a consumer for use in or around a permanent or temporary household or residence, a school, in recreation or otherwise, or for the personal use, consumption or enjoyment of a consumer" shall be subject to regulation by the CPSC. As further evidence of how comprehensive the act is, the authority to administer other acts is transferred to the CPSC. These acts include the Federal Hazardous Substance Act, the Child Protection and Toy Safety Act, the Poison Prevention Packaging Act, the Flammable Fabrics Act, and the Refrigerator Safety Act.

Purposes of the 1972 Act

As stated in the act, the Consumer Product Safety Commission was created:

1. To protect the public against unreasonable risk of injury associated with consumer products.
2. To assist consumers in evaluating the comparative safety of consumer products.
3. To develop uniform safety standards for consumer products and to minimize conflicting state and local regulations.
4. To promote research and investigation into the causes and prevention of product-related deaths, illnesses, and injuries.

Form and Functions of the CPSC

The CPSC was set up to conduct research on product safety and maintain a clearinghouse to "collect, investigate, analyze, and disseminate injury data, and information, relating to the causes and prevention of death, injury, and illness associated with consumer products *   *   *."

To this end, the CPSC immediately started gathering data on the two hundred most hazardous consumer products in the nation. The commission required hospital emergency wards to indicate the particular cause of any injury, illness, or death related to a consumer product.

Powers of the CPSC

Not only can the CPSC set safety standards for consumer products, it can also ban the manufacture and sale of any product deemed hazardous to consumers. The commission has the authority to remove products from the market that are deemed imminently hazardous. It also has the power to require manufacturers to report information about any products already sold or intended for sale that have proved to be hazardous.

Impact of the CPSC

Congress sought to create an agency with broad powers to regulate the sale and manufacture of all consumer products. The CPSC could have increasingly profound effects upon the consumer products industry. At the very least, it will give consumers more information about the safety of the products that they buy.

To date, most critics point out that the CPSC's performance has been less than spectacular. There have not been notable reductions in consumer product--related injuries, and where regulations have resulted in safer products, the products are more expensive. It is not unusual for proposed regulations concerning consumer goods to be challenged on the ground that they raise the price of such goods too much. Thus, the thorny problem of weighing the costs of safety against the benefits arises.

REAL ESTATE

Various statutes and regulations have been passed at both the state and federal levels to prevent fraud in real estate transactions and/or to provide a buyer with information concerning such a transaction. The Truth-in-Lending Act, discussed in the next section, applies its disclosure requirements to a substantial number of real estate transactions. However, it should be noted that some differences exist between the disclosure requirements for real estate and for non-real estate transactions. In certain real estate transactions, for example, consumers are given a right of rescission which must be disclosed by providing the consumer with two copies of a notice of the right to rescind. Furthermore, under certain circumstances the Truth-in-Lending Act provides the consumer with a right to rescind even though the creditor has made all of the required disclosures.[18]

Two other federal acts, the Interstate Land Sales Full Disclosure Act[19] and the Real Estate Settlement Procedures Act,[20] provide consumer protection in real estate transactions.

Interstate Land Sales Full Disclosure Act

The Interstate Land Sales Full Disclosure Act (1968) is administered by the Department of Housing and Urban Development (HUD), and its focus is to furnish facts and information to potential buyers so they can make intelligent decisions about whether or not to purchase land. The act is similar to the Securities Act of 1933 in that it requires any seller or lessor of 100 or more lots of unimproved land which is a part of a common promotional plan in interstate commerce to file initially a "statement of record" with the Office of Interstate Land Sales Registration, a division of HUD. The statement must then be approved by HUD before the developer may proceed to offer the land for sale or lease. Under Section 1410 of the act, purchasers are provided with a private right of action for fraud, misrepresentation, or noncompliance. Criminal penalties are also provided for willful violations in Section 1418, and HUD is given certain rights with respect to investigations, injunctions, and the prosecution of offenses. The most important provisions of the act, however, are considered to be the three that provide purchasers with rights of rescission. Yet these provisions in no way preclude or preempt the purchaser's right of rescission under Section 125 of the Truth-in-Lending Act.

Land sale abuses have been occurring for years. Everyone has heard about purchasers who invest their life savings in one hundred acres of land for a $10 down payment and $10 a month only to find that the land is under ten feet of water. Federal law does not prohibit land under water from being sold; it merely requires that the seller inform the buyer that it is under water.

Real Estate Settlement Procedures Act

A recent federal law requires that all closing costs be specifically outlined before a person buys a home. The 1976 revisions of the Real Estate Settlement Procedures Act make the following stipulations about buying a house and borrowing money to pay for it:

1. Within three business days after a person applies for a mortgage loan, the lender must send a booklet, prepared by the U.S. Department of Housing and Urban Development, that outlines the applicant's rights and explains settlement procedures and costs.
2. The lender must give an estimate of most of the settlement costs within that three-day period.
3. The lender must clearly identify individuals or firms that the applicant is required to use for legal or other services, including title insurance and search.
4. If the loan is approved, the lender must provide a truth-in-lending statement that shows the annual percentage rate on the mortgage loan.
5. Lenders, title insurers, and others involved in the real estate transaction cannot pay kickbacks for business referred to them.

CREDIT PROTECTION

One of the more important areas of consumer protection concerns the rights of consumers in credit transactions. Credit has become the American way of life; nearly all major purchases are financed by some form of credit.

Consumer Credit Protection Act (CCPA)

The Consumer Credit Protection Act (CCPA) is commonly called the Truth-in-Lending Act. It is basically a "disclosure law," administered by the Federal Reserve Board, that requires sellers and lenders to disclose credit terms or loan terms so that a debtor can shop around for the best financing arrangements.

Disclosure Requirements under the Truth-in-Lending Act The disclosure requirements of the Truth-in-Lending Act apply to any installment sales

---

18. See CCPA, Section 25.
19. 15 U.S.C.A. 1701 (Supp. 1979).
20. 12 U.C.S.A. 2601 (Supp. 1979).

contract in which payment is to be made in more than four installments. Some of the disclosure requirements that might apply to such a transaction include the specific cash price, the finance charge, premiums or points, the number, amounts, and due dates of payments, and any penalties imposed upon delinquent payments or prepayments.

Who Is Subject to Truth-in-Lending? Only certain creditors or lenders and only certain types of transactions are subject to the Truth-in-Lending Act. It applies to persons who, in the ordinary course of their business, lend money or sell on credit or arrange for the extension of credit. For this reason, sales or loans made between two consumers do not come under the act. Only debtors who are *natural* persons are protected by this law; corporations or other legal entities are not. Transactions involving purchases of property (real or personal) for personal, family, household, or agricultural use come within

the terms and provisions of the act if the amount being financed is less than $25,000. Transactions covered by the act typically include retail and installment sales and installment loans, car loans, home improvement loans, and certain real estate loans.

Violations of the Truth-in-Lending Act A creditor who fails to comply with the disclosure requirements may be liable to the consumer for twice the amount of the finance charge, plus attorneys' fees. In no event will that penalty be less than $100 or more than $1,000 for a violation against an individual consumer. The consumer has one year from the date of the violation to bring suit against a creditor who has failed to provide the disclosure statement or who has failed to discover and correct an error in the disclosure statement provided.

The following case illustrates the need for creditors to comply with all of the requirements of the Truth-in-Lending Act.

BACKGROUND AND FACTS *Mary Smith, the plaintiff, purchased a car from Don Chapman Motor Sales, the defendant. Smith brought an action alleging that the sales contract violated the Truth-in-Lending Act and the Texas Consumer Credit Code. Chapman argued that, although he had not specifically complied with the terms of the two consumer protection statutes, he was in substantial compliance, and further, that since Smith understood all the terms of the contract, Chapman had achieved the purposes of the statutes and should not be penalized.*

SMITH v. CHAPMAN
United States Court of Appeals,
Fifth Circuit, 1980.
614 F.2d 968.

BROWN, Circuit Judge.
*　*　*　*

First, the purpose of TILA is to promote the "informed use of credit *　*　* [and] an awareness of the cost thereof by consumers" by assuring "a meaningful disclosure of credit terms so that the consumer will be able to compare more readily the various credit terms available to him. *　*　* "

It is now well-settled that an objective standard is used in determining violations of TILA. It is not necessary that the plaintiff-consumer actually have been deceived in order for there to be a violation. TILA is primarily enforced through lawsuits filed by consumers acting as "private attorneys general." In fact, consumers who are aware of the true terms of a contract are more able to see that these terms are not clearly and conspicuously disclosed on the installment sales contract form. Thus, the purpose of the Act is more readily served by allowing lawsuits by these consumers who are less easily deceived.

Second, the applicable standard is strict compliance with the technical requirements of the Act. Only adherence to a strict compliance standard will promote the standardization of terms which will permit consumers readily to make meaningful comparisons of available credit alternatives.
*　*　*　*

The "Motor Vehicle Contract" that Smith entered into with Chapman Motors was a one-page document with terms printed on both sides of the page. The front of this document did not mention the security interest that the seller retained in the car; this was set forth as Condition No. 1 on the back of the page. Delinquency charges were stated on the front and as Condition No. 6 on the back of the document as follows:

> The Seller, at its option, shall collect a delinquency charge on each installment in default for a period of more than ten days in an amount not to exceed 5% of each installment or $5.00 whichever is less, or, in lieu thereof, interest after maturity on each such installment, not to exceed the highest lawful contract rate.

The specific interest rate after maturity, imposed by Condition No. 10 on the back of the contract, was ten percent (10%) per annum. At the bottom of both sides of the page was printed: "NOTICE, SEE REVERSE SIDE FOR IMPORTANT INFOR-MATION, ALL TERMS OF WHICH ARE INCORPORATED BY REFERENCE."

Smith alleged in her complaint that the failure to state these provisions on the front side of the page was a violation of Regulation Z, 12 CFR § 226.8(a)(1) *   *   *.

The general rule for disclosures is that they "be made clearly, conspicuously, in meaningful sequence, in accordance with the further requirements of [§ 226], and at the time and in the terminology prescribed in applicable sections."

Chapman first contends that he has complied with the requirements of § 226.8(a)(1) by including the notice of incorporation by reference of terms on both sides of the page. Under a strict compliance standard, incorporating by reference terms on the backside of a page when it is explicitly required that these terms appear on the front side, would be a violation of TILA.

*   *   *   *

Chapman next takes issue with the District Court's holding that the listing of the sales tax on the automobile contract form as an "official fee," and not in the blank labelled "Cash Price (Including Sales Tax)," violated Regulation Z and the TCCC.

*   *   *   *

The District Court inferred from § 226.4(b)(3) that taxes must be included either in the cash price or be listed as a finance charge. We are mindful of the confusion potentially created when taxes, which are imposed regardless of whether or not credit is extended, are listed as finance charges and how, as Chapman urges, this goes against the policy of TILA to make installment sales contracts more easily understood by consumers. Yet, this is what the regulation implies, and this is how we have interpreted it in the past. Any changes in the regulation are not for us, but for the Federal Reserve Board to make. We agree with the District Court's interpretation of § 226.4(b)(3).

*   *   *   *

We reiterate that the purpose of TILA is to "assure a meaningful disclosure of credit terms," and that Regulation Z, § 226.6(a), requires that disclosures be made clearly, conspicuously and in meaningful sequence. To place the tax figure in the wrong space when another space is specifically provided is not a clear disclosure in a meaningful sequence. And when the form states the sales tax is included in the figure stated, but in fact it is not, it is, furthermore, misleading. A misleading disclosure is as much a violation of TILA as a failure to disclose at all.

Because this disclosure is misleading, and because it contradicts the definition of "official fees," which under Texas law do not include sales taxes, it is also in violation of TCCC.

DECISION AND REMEDY   *The judgment of the district court was affirmed. Statutory penalties of twice the amount of the finance charges in connection with the transaction, plus attorneys' fees, were imposed for violation of the federal law and for violation of the state regulations. The entire penalty totaled four times the finance charge.*

Equal Credit Opportunity Act (CCPA)   In 1974, Congress enacted the Equal Credit Opportunity Act as part of the Truth-in-Lending Act to prohibit discrimination based on race, religion, national origin, color, sex, marital status, age, or whether an individual is receiving certain types of income, such as public assistance benefits. Creditors are permitted to request any information from a credit applicant except that which could be used for the type of discrimination covered in the act and its amendments.

Fair Credit Billing Act (CCPA)   In 1974, Congress passed an amendment to the Truth-in-Lending Act called the Fair Credit Billing Act.[21] Basically, under the rules set up pursuant to this act, a purchaser can withhold payment until a dispute over a faulty product that was purchased and paid for by credit card is resolved. It is up to the credit card issuer to intervene and attempt a settlement between the credit card user and the seller. A purchaser, however, does not have an *unlimited* right to stop payment. A good faith effort to get satisfaction from the seller must first be exercised. If such an effort fails, the purchaser is not legally required to notify the credit card company that payment for the item is being stopped. The purchaser can wait for the issuer to respond to the stopped payment. To minimize settlement difficulties, it is probably a good idea to advise the company.

Other provisions of this act relate to disputes over billing. If the debtor thinks that there is an error in a bill, the credit card company must investigate, and the debtor can suspend payments until it does so. The cardholder simply writes to the company within sixty days of receipt of the bill and briefly explains the circumstances and why he or she thinks there is an error. Under the law, the company must acknowledge the letter within thirty days and solve the dispute within ninety days. During that period, the debtor does not have to pay the amount in dispute or make any minimum payment of the amount in dispute. The creditor cannot impose finance charges during that period for unpaid balances in dispute, nor can it close the account. However, if it turns out that there was no error, the creditor can then attempt to collect finance charges for the entire period for which payments were not made.

---

21.   15 U.S.C.A. 1681.

Credit Card Rules (CCPA)   The Truth-in-Lending Act contains two important provisions regarding credit cardholders. One provision limits the liability of a cardholder to $50 per card for unauthorized charges made prior to the time the creditor is notified. The second provision prohibits a credit card company from billing a consumer for *any* unauthorized charges if the credit card is improperly issued by the company.

Suppose, for example, that Jones loses his MasterCard in the street. Bilas finds it and buys $200 worth of goods with the card. The next day Jones informs MasterCard of his loss. MasterCard later bills Jones for the $200 worth of goods that Bilas bought. Clearly, MasterCard can collect only $50 (or nothing if Jones notified it of the loss before the card was used by Bilas) because that is the maximum liability imposed on the loser of a credit card.

Now consider that MasterCard mails a credit card to Farmer, who has not applied for a card or held one in the past. The envelope is stolen out of Farmer's mailbox, and the thief signs the card and buys $200 worth of goods. MasterCard bills Farmer for the $200. Farmer does not have to pay anything at all, not even $50, because MasterCard performed a prohibited act by sending an unsolicited card.

Credit Reports (CCPA)   Over the years there has been a concern that the government might be monitoring the actions of its citizens too closely, and investigative reports on the credit status of consumers have heightened this concern. One serious objection to this practice is that consumers have no access to the contents of the reports and can in no way control their use. Inaccuracies, once reported, have been almost impossible to uncover, much less to correct.

In 1970, Congress enacted the Fair Credit Reporting Act (Title VI) as a part of the Truth-in-Lending Act. This act provides that consumers are entitled, upon request, to be informed of the nature and scope of a credit investigation, the kind of information that is being compiled, and the names of persons who will be receiving the report. They must make the request within specific time limits, however. Consumers have the right to require that any inaccurate or misleading material be reinvestigated and, if not verified, be removed from the file. If there is a dispute about the accuracy of certain parts of the report, consumers have the right to include their own one-hundred-word statement in the file to set forth their position with regard to disputed matters. Such statements become part of the permanent record.

Although the law provides that consumers have the right to be informed of the contents of their files, the Truth-in-Lending Act limits that access for others. A person who wishes to obtain information contained in a consumer's credit file must have either a court order or a legitimate business need for the information or must have the permission of the consumer. Consumer reporting agencies must inform the consumer when an investigative report is being compiled and of the right to disclosure. A consumer credit reporting agency that fails to comply with the terms of the act can be held liable not only for actual damages but for punitive damages and attorneys' fees resulting from a lawsuit brought by the consumer.

Fair Debt Collection Practices Act (1977)

In 1977, Congress enacted the Fair Debt Collection Practices Act (FDCPA).[22] The FDCPA does not apply to all consumer credit collection efforts. Rather, it governs the conduct of debt collectors—persons who regularly collect debts owed to someone else. Those who attempt to collect debts owed to themselves are not covered by this act, except when, in the process of collecting their own debts, such creditors use a name other than their own, leading a debtor to believe that a third person is attempting to collect the debts.

The FDCPA prohibits the following actions on the part of debt collectors:

1. Contacting the consumer at his or her place of employment if the employer objects.
2. Contacting the consumer at inconvenient or unusual times, such as 3 o'clock in the morning, or contacting the consumer at any time if he or she is represented by an attorney.
3. Contacting third parties other than parents, spouses, or financial advisers about the payment of a debt unless the court so authorizes.

4. Using harassment and intimidation, such as abusive language, or using false or misleading information, such as posing as a police officer.
5. Communicating with the consumer after receipt of notice that the consumer is refusing to pay the debt, except to advise the consumer of further action to be taken by the collection agency.

States that have enacted collection practice legislation prohibit these kinds of practices but do not prohibit *all* phone calls. Many states provide penalty provisions that include levying a flat penalty fee against the collector and that permit damages for emotional distress. Although debtors have always been able to use traditional tort law to protect themselves from abuse, clearly the trend of the law, at the state and federal levels, is toward limiting abusive action in the debt collection process.

The Uniform Consumer Credit Code

In 1968, the National Conference of Commissioners on the Uniform State Laws promulgated the Uniform Consumer Credit Code (UCCC). The UCCC has been controversial, but it has been adopted in approximately 20 percent of the states.[23] The UCCC is an attempt to promulgate a comprehensive body of rules governing the most important aspects of consumer credit. Sections of the UCCC, for example, focus on truth in lending, maximum credit ceilings, door-to-door sales, and referral sales. The UCCC is also concerned with materials contained in fine-print clauses and various provisions of creditor remedies, including deficiency judgments (personal judgments for the amount of a debt that is not secured by property) and garnishments (proceedings where property, money, or wages controlled by a third person are transferred to the court to satisfy a judgment). (See Chapter 30 for details.) The UCCC applies to most types of sales, including real estate. It also replaces existing state consumer credit laws as well as installment loan, usury, and retail installment sale acts.

22. See 15 U.S.C.A. 1692. The Federal Trade Commission prosecutes overly zealous debt collectors under federal regulations for unfair and deceptive trade practices.

23. By 1974 the UCCC had undergone six redrafts. Furthermore, in those jurisdictions where the law has been adopted, it is not uniform among them. The states that have adopted some form of the UCCC are Colorado, Idaho, Indiana, Iowa, Kansas, Maine, South Carolina, Utah, Wisconsin, and Wyoming.

QUESTIONS AND CASE PROBLEMS

1. Andrew, a California resident, received a flyer in the U.S. mail announcing a new line of regional cookbooks distributed by the Every-Kind Cookbook Company. Andrew was not interested in regional cookbooks and threw the flyer away. Two days later, Andrew received in the mail an introductory cookbook entitled "Lower Mongolian Regional Cookbook," as announced in the flyer, on a "trial basis" from Every-Kind. Although Andrew was not interested in the Lower Mongolian Regional Cookbook, he did not go to the trouble of mailing it back to Every-Kind. Every-Kind demanded payment of $20.95 for the Lower Mongolian Regional Cookbook. Discuss *fully* whether Andrew is required to pay for this cookbook under present consumer protection laws.

2. Harry's Home-Sweet-Home Rocking Chair Company advertised in the newspaper a special sale price of $159 on machine-caned rocking chairs. In. the advertisement was a drawing of a natural wood rocking chair with a caned back and seat. The average person would not be able to tell from the drawing whether the rocking chair was machine-caned or hand-caned. The hand-caned rocking chairs sold for $259. John and Joanne Wolf went to Harry's because they had seen the ad for the machine-caned rocking chair and were very interested in purchasing one. The Wolfs arrived on the morning the sale opened. Harry said the only machine-caned rocking chairs he had were painted lime green and were priced at $159. He immediately turned the Wolfs' attention to the rocking chairs he had hand-caned, praising their workmanship, and pointing out that for the extra $100, the hand-caned chairs were surely a good value. The Wolfs, preferring the natural wood, machine-caned rocking chair for $159 as pictured in the advertisement, said they would like to order the one in the ad. Harry said he could not order a natural wood, machine-caned rocking chair. Discuss *fully* whether Harry has violated any consumer protection laws.

3. Suppose that Joyce, a homemade toy manufacturer, began a new line of homemade dolls. These stuffed dolls were especially appealing because they had real glass marbles for eyes. Young Samantha received one of these marble-eyed dolls for her birthday. Like everyone else who received the dolls, Samantha was captivated by the shiny marble eyes. Unfortunately, after a month of use, the glue holding the marbles on the face of the doll disintegrated to the point that Samantha was able to pull the marbles off and put one in her mouth. She began to choke on the marble and was rushed to the hospital where her stomach was pumped. Can the manufacture of these marble-eyed dolls be regulated by a federal agency? If so, which agency would regulate it and under what act? What will the agency be able to do to regulate the marble-eyed dolls?

4. Green receives two new credit cards on May 1. One was *solicited* from the King Department Store and the other was *unsolicited* from the Flyways Airline. During the month of May Green makes numerous credit card purchases from King, but she does not use the Flyways Airline card. On May 31 a burglar breaks into Green's home and, along with other items, steals both credit cards. Green notifies the King Department Store of the theft on June 2, but she fails to notify Flyways Airline. Using the King credit card, the burglar makes a $500 purchase on June 1 and a $200 purchase on June 3. The burglar then charges a vacation flight on the Flyways Airline card for $1,000 on June 5. Green receives the bills for these charges and refuses to pay them. Discuss Green's liability in these situations.

5. Roseman was employed as a debit agent for the John Hancock Insurance Company. He resigned, following accusations that he had been dishonest with his company expense account. Before his resignation he reimbursed the account. Part of the information concerning Roseman's resignation was contained in a credit report held by the Retail Credit Co., Inc. Subsequently, Roseman was denied a position with another insurance company after it consulted the Retail Credit Company's report. Assuming that the information held by Retail Credit was accurate, was its circulation of such information illegal?

Roseman felt that he was unfairly treated by Retail Credit because there were two sides to the story of his resignation, and his side was not included in the company's files. He complained that Retail Credit should have informed him that it had such information, and he claimed further that he had the right to include a statement in the files setting forth his version of the circumstances surrounding his resignation. Is Roseman correct? [Roseman v. Retail Credit Co., Inc., 428 F.Supp. 643 (E.D.Pa. 1977)]

6. Harold Grey signed an installment contract as payment for membership in European Health Spas Club, Inc. The disclosure documents that accompanied the installment loan contract were printed in regular type, with the exception of the words, which were printed in capital letters: "FINANCE CHARGE," "ANNUAL PERCENTAGE RATE," and "MEMBER ACKNOWLEDGES THAT HE HAS READ AND RECEIVED A FILLED-IN SIGNED COPY OF THIS AGREEMENT." In addition, at the top of the disclosure statement, the words "NOTICE TO BUYER" were printed. Under federal truth-in-lending regulations, the words *finance charge* and *annual per-*

centage rate must be printed conspicuously in the truth-in-lending disclosure statements. Otherwise, the creditor is deemed in violation of the act. Has the requirement of conspicuousness been met? [Grey v. European Health Spas Inc., 428 F.Supp. 841 (D.C.Conn. 1977)]

7. Roger Gonzalez purchased a Ford from Schmerler Ford on credit. The installment credit agreement that Gonzalez signed named Ford Motor Credit Corporation as the payee of the loan. Nowhere on the loan form or the disclosure documents did the name Schmerler Ford appear. Schmerler Ford, however, helped Gonzalez fill out the loan forms and then forwarded them to Ford Motor Credit Corporation. Schmerler lacked the authority to negotiate the interest rate charged on the loan and lacked the ability to approve Gonzalez's loan. Gonzalez's loan was made solely by Ford Motor Credit Corporation. Later it was discovered that the loan forms failed to disclose all of the relevant information that was required under the Truth-in-Lending Act. Who can be held liable as having violated the act—Schmerler Ford, Ford Motor Credit Corporation, or both? [Gonzalez v. Schmerler Ford, 397 F.Supp. 323 (N.D.Ill. 1975)]

8. In the summer of 1972, Robert Martin applied for and was issued an American Express credit card. Approximately three years later, in April 1975, Martin gave his card to E. L. McBride, a business associate, and orally authorized McBride to charge up to $500 on the credit card. He also wrote to American Express requesting that charges on his account be limited to $1,000. However, in June 1975 Martin received a statement from American Express indicating that the amount owed on his credit card account was approximately $5,300. Under the Truth-in-Lending Act, for how much will Martin be liable to American Express? [Martin v. American Exp., Inc., 361 So.2d 597 (Ala.Civ.App. 1978)]

9. On July 16, Polly Ann Barber entered into a retail installment contract with Kimbrell's, Inc., for the purchase of various items of household furniture totaling $592. Barber later sued Kimbrell's for violating the Truth-in-Lending Act because Kimbrell's used the term *total time balance* in its disclosure document rather than *total of payments* as the act required. At the same time, Barber sued Furniture Distributors, Inc., claiming that it too was liable as a creditor under the act. Furniture Distributors, Inc., participated in the development and preparation of the standard contract form and distributed it for use in all the retail stores in the Kimbrell's chain. It was also the parent company of Kimbrell's and had extensive knowledge of the credit terms for all the consumer credit sales that Kimbrell's made. Each time one of the Kimbrell's stores made a consumer credit sale, the installment contract was sent to Furniture Distributors for review. If Kimbrell's is in violation of the Truth-in-Lending Act, can Barber also hold Furniture Distributors liable? [Barber v. Kimbrell's, Inc., 577 F.2d 216 (4th Cir. 1978)]

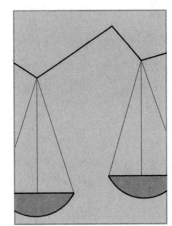

47

GOVERNMENT REGULATION
Environmental Protection

The traditional belief that air, water, and land will absorb all waste products without being harmed has been refuted by a considerable body of evidence. Furthermore, as society has become more urbanized, concern about future degradation of the environment has been heightened. These forces, plus general economic growth, greater wealth, and the proliferation of synthetic products that resist decomposition, have caused policymakers and some individuals to seek methods to reduce or to prevent pollution.

HISTORICAL BACKGROUND

In one sense, concerns about the environment are not new. The English Parliament, for example, passed a number of acts that regulated the burning of soft coal in medieval England. Moreover, through common law nuisance statutes, property owners were given relief from pollution in situations where the individual could identify a distinct harm separate from that affecting the general public. Thus, if a factory polluted the air and killed a farmer's crops, the farmer could seek an injunction and damages against the factory.

Needless to say, nuisance suits that granted specific relief for individuals were inadequate when the harm from pollution could not be identified with groups separate from the public at large. Under the common law, citizens were denied *standing* (access to the courts) unless specific harm could be shown. Therefore, a group of citizens who wished to stop a new development that would cause significant water pollution would be denied access to the courts on the ground that the harm to them did not differ from the harm borne by the general public.[1] A public authority, however, could sue for public nuisance.

The common law further limited relief from pollution in situations where the harm was caused by two or more independent sources. For example, if a number of firms were polluting the air, a harmed individual could sue any individual firm; however, until early in the twentieth century, the plaintiff was not able to sue all of the factories simultaneously. Consequently, specific proof of damages in individual actions was often impossible. These difficulties in seeking relief in pollution cases, along with the forces creating additional pollution, have been largely responsible for the development of statutory regulations of environmental quality.

---

1. Save the Bay Committee, Inc. v. Mayor, etc., of the City of Savannah, 227 Ga. 436, 181 S.E.2d 351 (1971).

REGULATION BY ADMINISTRATIVE AGENCIES

Beginning in 1970, Congress passed a number of federal statutes directing administrative agencies to study the effects of pollution on the environment. On January 1, 1970, the National Environmental Policy Act (NEPA) created the Council of Environmental Quality and mandated that an environmental statement be prepared for every recommendation or report on legislation or major federal action that significantly affects the quality of the environment.[2] Since that time, the government has passed a number of acts that govern air quality, such as the Clean Air Act. In addition, a number of regulations have been promulgated for water quality. They include the Federal Water Pollution Control Act of 1965,[3] the Marine Protection and Research and Sanctuaries Act of 1972,[4] and the Safe Drinking Water Act of 1974.[5] Additional regulations governing the use of pesticides,[6] radiation,[7] solid toxic substances,[8] and noise[9] have also been promulgated.

Environmental Protection Agency

The Environmental Protection Agency (EPA) was created in 1970 to assemble the various agencies responsible for environmental protection. It is primarily an administrative organization. It employs approximately ten thousand individuals who carry out the directives of the numerous and complex regulations of federal statutes affecting the environment.

One of the important responsibilities of the EPA is to insure that all proposed federal legislation affecting the environment be analyzed and an environmental impact statement be issued. This state-

ment has become an instrument for private citizens, consumer interests, businesses, and federal agencies to help shape the final outcome of regulatory actions. Even if an agency's analysis concludes that the impact statement is unnecessary, a statement supporting this conclusion must be filed.[10]

PRIVATE LITIGATION

Private parties continue to recover damages or obtain injunctions for environmental harms under a combination of statutory and common law provisions. The Clean Air Act Amendments of 1972, the Water Pollution and Prevention Control Act of 1972, and the Noise Control Act of 1972, for example, authorize private lawsuits for violations of air, water, and noise pollution standards. Furthermore, some courts have held that organizations can have standing in representing members' interests even if there is no direct organizational interest in the dispute.

On the other hand, some federal statutes give the government exclusive rights to lawsuits for violations of environmental protection regulations. For example, the Environmental Protection Agency is given the exclusive right to bring suits involving the violation of the Federal Water Pollution Control Act.

AIR POLLUTION

Federal involvement with air pollution goes back to the 1950s, when Congress authorized funds for air pollution research. In 1963 the federal government passed the Clean Air Act, which focused on multistate air pollution and provided assistance to states. Various amendments, particularly in 1970 and 1977,[11] strengthened the government's authority to regulate the quality of air.

Automobile Pollution

Regulations governing air pollution from automobiles and other mobile sources specify pollution standards and time schedules. For example, the 1970

2. National Environmental Policy Act of 1969, 42 U.S.C.A. 4321 et seq.
3. Federal Water Pollution Control Act, 33 U.S.C.A. 1151 (1965).
4. Marine Protection and Research and Sanctuaries Act of 1972, 16 U.S.C.A. 1431 et seq.; 33 U.S.C.A. 1407 et seq.
5. Safe Drinking Water Act, 21 U.S.C.A. 349, 42 U.S.C.A. 201, 300F et seq. (1974).
6. Federal Insecticide, Fungicide and Rodenticide Act of 1972, 7 U.S.C.A. 135 et seq. (1947), as amended May 12, 1964.
7. Resource Conservation Recovery Act of 1976, 42 U.S.C.A. 6901 et seq. (1976).
8. Toxic Substances Control Act of 1976, 15 U.S.C.A. 2602 (1976).
9. Noise Control Act of 1972, 42 U.S.C.A. 1604 (1972).

10. Arizona Public Serv. Co. v. Federal Power Comm'n, 483 F.2d 1275 (D.C.Cir. 1973).
11. Clean Air Act Amendments of 1970, 42 U.S.C. 7521, and the Clean Air Act Amendments of 1977, 42 U.S.C. 7521-25, 7541-51.

Clean Air Act required a reduction of 90 percent in the amount of carbon monoxide and hydrocarbons emitted from automobiles by 1975.[12] Similar regulations for aircraft are administered by the Federal Aviation Administration.

---

12. Carbon monoxide, a colorless, odorless gas, can reduce mental performance and result in death if inhaled in sufficient quantities. Hydrocarbons are unburned fuel, one of the principal ingredients that generate smog.

The 1977 amendments to the Clean Air Act establish multilevel standards. For example, they attempt to prevent the deterioration of air quality even in areas where the existing quality exceeds that required by federal law. Present regulations intend to eliminate completely lead in gasoline sold within the next few years.

In the following case the court reviewed an EPA order regulating the lead content of gasoline, the validity of which had been challenged by Ethyl Corporation.

BACKGROUND AND FACTS *Ethyl Corporation, a leading producer of antiknock compounds for increasing gasoline octane rating, filed for judicial review of the Environmental Protection Agency order that required annual reductions in the lead content of gasoline. The Clean Air Act authorized the agency to regulate gasoline additives that are a danger to public health and welfare. Review of agency actions under the Clean Air Act is available only in the U.S. Court of Appeals for the District of Columbia Circuit.*

ETHYL CORP. v. ENVIRONMENTAL PROTECTION AGENCY

United States Court of Appeals, District of Columbia Circuit, 1976.
541 F.2d 1.

WRIGHT, Circuit Judge.

*   *   *   *

Man's ability to alter his environment has developed far more rapidly than his ability to foresee with certainty the effects of his alterations. It is only recently that we have begun to appreciate the danger posed by unregulated modification of the world around us, and have created watchdog agencies whose task it is to warn us, and protect us, when technological "advances" present dangers unappreciated—or unrevealed— by their supporters. Such agencies, unequipped with crystal balls and unable to read the future, are nonetheless charged with evaluating the effects of unprecedented environmental modifications, often made on a massive scale. Necessarily, they must deal with predictions and uncertainty, with developing evidence, with conflicting evidence, and, sometimes, with little or no evidence at all. Today we address the scope of the power delegated one such watchdog, the Environmental Protection Agency (EPA). We must determine the certainty required by the Clean Air Act before EPA may act to protect the health of our populace from the lead particulate emissions of automobiles.

*   *   *   *

On October 28, 1973, as a result of a motion filed in *Natural Resources Defense Council, Inc. v. EPA*, this court ordered EPA to reach within 30 days a final decision on whether lead additives should be regulated for health reasons. *   *   * [The EPA Document] candidly discusses the various scientific studies, both pro and con, underlying this information, and ultimately concludes that lead from automobile emissions will endanger the public health. *   *   * Under the final regulations, lead in all gasoline would be reduced over a five-year period to an average of 0.5 grams per gallon.

*   *   * Our scope *   *   * requires us to strike "agency action, findings, and conclusions" [only if] we find [them] to be "arbitrary, capricious, an abuse of discretion, or otherwise not in accordance with law." This standard of review is a highly deferential one. It presumes agency action to be valid. Moreover, it forbids the court's substituting its judgment for that of the agency *   *   *.

This is not to say, however, that we must rubber-stamp the agency decision as correct. To do so would render the appellate process a superfluous (although time-consuming) ritual. Rather, the reviewing court must assure itself that the agency decision was "based on a consideration of the relevant factors *   *   *."

Petitioners [Ethyl Corp.] vigorously attack both the sufficiency and the validity of the many scientific studies relied upon by the Administrator, while advancing for consideration various studies allegedly supportive of their position. The record in this case is massive—over 10,000 pages. Not surprisingly, evidence may be isolated that supports virtually any inference one might care to draw. *   *   *

Because of the importance of the issues raised, we have accorded this case the most careful and exhaustive consideration. We find that in this rule-making proceeding the EPA has complied with all the statutory procedural requirements and that its reasons as stated in its opinion provide a rational basis for its action. Since we reject all of petitioners' claims of error the Agency may enforce its low-lead regulations.

DECISION   *The Environmental Protection Agency regulations were affirmed by the U.S.*
AND REMEDY   *Court of Appeals. The Court accorded substantial deference to the EPA's con-*
                  clusion, and thus the EPA was permitted to enforce its low-lead regulations.

Acid Pollution

In 1978, Congress enacted the National Energy Act, which consists of five statutes. These statutes were intended to reduce dependence on imported oil and domestic natural gas by encouraging conservation measures, the use of renewable energy resources, and the use of more abundant domestic fuels. One of these statutes, the Powerplant and Industrial Fuel Use Act (PIFUA), requires certain electrical power plants and major fuel-burning installations to switch from gas and oil to coal and other alternate fuels. The conversion to coal, however, has resulted in the environmental hazard of *acid rain.*

Acid rain is caused by sulfuric oxide omissions. Sulfuric oxide emissions in the atmosphere can be converted by oxidation into sulfuric acid, which may subsequently return to the earth in rain or snow. Acid precipitation into lakes in North America and Scandinavia has made many of these lakes so acidic that they can no longer support fish life. However, there is a great deal of scientific debate as to the exact causes and repercussions of acid rain.

The Clean Air Act directs the EPA to establish ambient limits which correspond to pollutant concentrations demonstrated to cause adverse health effects. The EPA has considered promulgating a new ambient standard which focuses specifically on sulfate particles. Unfortunately, documentation with respect to the health effects of exposure to low levels of these pollutants has been sparse. Because of the

insufficient documentation of health effects associated with acid precipitation, the EPA has been unable to conclude that adequate scientific data exist to support a regulatory program. The fact that acid pollution is affected by wind and weather patterns and that acid precipitation crosses the jurisdictional limits of governmental institutions charged with pollution control make these studies difficult to conduct. Yet as more scientific data are accumulated and environmental pressure from the United States and other countries affected by our sulfuric oxide emissions mounts, the EPA may conclude that adequate data exist to support regulation of the causes of acid rain.

WATER POLLUTION

Federal regulations governing the pollution of water can be traced back nearly a century to the River and Harbor Act of 1886, as amended in 1899.[13] These regulations required a permit for discharging or depositing refuse in navigable waterways. The courts have even determined that hot water can be considered refuse.[14] In 1965 Congress passed the Federal Water Pollution Control Act, which strengthened the Environmental Protection Agency's enforcement powers.

---

13.   33 U.S.C. 407.
14.   33 U.S.C. 1254(t).

Clean Water Regulation

Perhaps the most important regulations that govern the quality of water were instituted in 1972 by Congress. These regulations establish goals to (1) make waters safe for swimming, (2) protect fish and wildlife, and (3) eliminate the discharge of pollutants into the water. They set forth specific time schedules, which were extended by amendment in 1977. The 1972 Clean Water Act also specifies a number of regulations with time schedules for controlling industrial water pollution. Regulations for the most part specify that the best available technology be installed.

Consequences of Violating Regulations

In most cases, explicit penalties are imposed on parties that pollute the water. The polluting party can also be required to clean up the pollution or pay for the cost of doing so, as is illustrated by the following case.

BACKGROUND AND FACTS   *In this action, a number of oil companies, including Atlantic Richfield Company and Gulf Oil Company, were assessed monetary penalties that included paying for the cost of cleaning up oil discharges. The defendants (Atlantic Richfield and Gulf Oil) argued that the imposition of such penalties in an accidental oil spill when the reporting and cleaning requirements had been satisfied constituted a criminal action. Therefore, the defendants believed that they had the right to a jury trial. The court had to determine whether these penalties denied due process.*

Two cases were consolidated and heard by the district court simultaneously. In one case, Atlantic Richfield Company (Arco) was the defendant; in the other, Gulf Oil Company was the defendant.

UNITED STATES OF AMERICA v. ATLANTIC RICHFIELD CO.

Eastern District of Pennsylvania, 1977.

429 F.Supp. 830.

BECKER, District Judge.
* * * *

These cases raise issues concerning the proper construction and the constitutionality of the "civil penalty" provision of the oil and hazardous substance sections of the Federal Water Pollution Control Act Amendments of 1972. * * * The constructional issues boil down to whether Congress intended to impose the civil penalty on persons who spill oil accidentally, report such spill to the appropriate authorities, and clean it up at their own expense (hereinafter "accidental, reporting self-cleaners").
* * *

Turning now to the operative facts, we note that the stipulations as to the relevant events in each of the cases before us track essentially the same pattern. In each case either Arco or Gulf owned or operated a vessel or facility from which oil was discharged in harmful quantity into the navigable waters of the United States. The discharges were "accidental" or "unintentional," but, perforce, they violated the prohibition on discharge of (b)(3); hence, without more, they subjected the owners (defendants) to liability for the civil penalty under (b)(6). However, the appropriate defendant (or its agent) promptly reported each spill and cleaned it up within the limits of technological feasibility and to the satisfaction of the Coast Guard. Despite defendants' compliance with their reporting and clean up duties, the Coast Guard, following the prescribed administrative procedure, assessed a civil penalty in each case. Upon defendants' refusal to pay, the government sued.
* * * *

The first prong of defendants' argument goes as follows: The stipulated facts would not survive a motion to dismiss for failure to state a claim under the common law of negligence; *i.e.*, although the facts reveal "accidental" spills, they do not reveal a basis for inferring that defendants caused the spills through a lack of due care; but "negligence" is the lowest level of "fault" recognized by our law; *i.e.*, non-negligent conduct is reasonable conduct; therefore, if the spills were not negligent, we can infer that there was no reasonable means for defendants to prevent the spills.

We find that defendants' argument makes most sense when translated into simple economic terms. A rational owner of an oil facility, recognizing his potential liabilities for clean ups * * * (and for damages under common law damage remedies which § 1321 [of the act] leaves untouched), will attempt to minimize the costs of spills. To accomplish this he will calculate the marginal costs of preventing spills and of potential liabilities. He will thereupon engage in prevention to the point where the marginal cost of prevention equals his marginal liability for spills. Because that point defines *reasonable* spill prevention, a reasonable person will spend money for just that much prevention and no more. To spend less would be negligent. * * * To spend more would be wasteful or inefficient. * * *

* * * While it is true that the stipulated facts about the spills themselves would not be sufficient to support an action in negligence, this is not such an action, but rather an action to enforce a penalty.

The elements of this statutory action are only that defendant violated (b)(3) and that the Coast Guard following the appropriate procedure assessed the (b)(6) penalty. The statute does not make "fault" an element of the cause of action, but rather a factor in the administrative penalty setting procedure. This is proper because there is no principle of law which requires that civil regulability through imposition of penalty be predicated upon a finding of fault. Moreover, a number of factors support civil regulability here in the absence of fault. First, as we explain more fully in our discussion of the Constitutional issues, *infra*, the principal goal of (b)(6) is to *deter* spills. Second, the Congressional purpose here was to impose a standard of conduct higher than that related just to economic efficiency. Additionally, the Congress obviously believed: (a) that no clean up effort could be complete because, after discharge, it is impossible to guarantee against residual harm from quantities of oil too small or too well dispersed to be detectable; and (b) that even the transitory pollution of waters was deleterious to the environment.

* * * *

In view of the foregoing analysis we must reject defendant's contention that, as applied to accidental, reporting, self-cleaners, (b)(6) is really criminal rather than civil because, (1) the statutory language is not ambiguous; and (2) even where defendants are not at fault, the penalty does not act only as a punishment but serves the ends of civil regulation.

DECISION AND REMEDY — *The district court held that the penalties provided under the Federal Water Pollution Control Act Amendments of 1972 were civil, not criminal, penalties. Therefore, the government could continue to assess and collect them against Atlantic Richfield, Gulf, and other oil companies for accidental oil spills.*

NOISE POLLUTION

The Noise Control Acts of 1970 and 1972 established the goal of creating an environment free from noise that is injurious to the health and welfare of the public. In 1972, Congress prescribed standards and regulations for the control of aircraft noise, including sonic booms, and for the control of noise emissions of railroad and motor vehicles involved in interstate commerce.

Regulations promulgated by the noise control acts are administered by the Federal Aviation Administration, the Environmental Protection Agency, and the Department of Transportation. The EPA, for example, is authorized to establish noise emission levels for equipment, motors, and engines.

It also reviews production processes, verifies reports for compliance with the law, conducts audit tests, and makes inspections of manufacturer records.

TOXIC SUBSTANCES

The Toxic Substances Control Act was passed in 1976 to regulate chemicals and chemical compounds that are known to be toxic and to institute investigation of any possible harmful effects from new chemical compounds. The regulations authorize the Environmental Protection Agency to require that manufacturers, processors, and other organizations planning to use chemicals first determine their effect on human health and the environment.

Lack of Scientific Certainty   Regulation of toxic substances frequently takes place at or beyond the edge of scientific knowledge. The Eighth Circuit, in *Reserve Mining Co. v. EPA*, dealt with scientific uncertainty in the area of asbestos—a toxic substance.[15] In *Reserve Mining Co.* an action was brought against a taconite processing company to prevent it from discharging great quantities of mining by-products into the air and water of Lake Superior. These mining by-products contained asbestos. The district court found that the company's discharges gave rise to a potential threat to the public health, and thus the court issued an injunction. On appeal, the Eighth Circuit considered the conflicting evidence with respect to asbestos as well as the appropriate remedy.

A scientific study produced negative results concerning carcinogenic effects of asbestos fibers. However, strong evidence also existed which indicated that workers exposed to asbestos dust suffered from a moderately increased rate of gastrointestinal cancer. After considering the totality of the evidence, the circuit judge held that the company's discharges gave rise to a potential threat which was of sufficient gravity to be legally cognizable. Thus, while the danger to health was not imminent, the court found that it did call for preventive and cautionary steps.

In determining the appropriate form of relief, the Eighth Circuit concluded that no reason existed which required the company to terminate its operations immediately. Rather, the company was entitled to reasonable opportunity and reasonable time to change its operations. This remedy varied tremendously from that of the district court—which had ordered an immediate halt to discharges.

PESTICIDE CONTROL

The use of chemical pesticides to kill insects and weeds has significantly increased agricultural productivity. Unfortunately, there is a growing body of evidence that residuals from these chemicals have not been absorbed by the environment. In some cases, buildups of residuals have killed animals, and some potential long-term effects detrimental to the public have also been identified.

The Environmental Protection Agency has been given the authority to control the introduction of pesticides. Pesticides must be (1) registered before they can be sold, (2) certified and used only for approved applications, and (3) used in amounts that meet established limits when they are applied to crops that provide food for animals or people. The EPA also has the right to inspect manufacturing establishments. In some situations, the supply of pesticides is controlled to keep hazardous chemicals off the market.

WASTE DISPOSAL

Waste disposal can occur on land, in the water, or in the air; thus regulations protecting these resources from pollution also apply to waste disposal. In 1970 Congress passed the Materials Policy Act, an act designed to reduce solid waste disposal by encouraging the recycling of waste and the reuse of materials by society. The act also provides for pilot waste disposal projects utilizing modern technology. For example, the development and use of technology that converts garbage into useful products have been greatly encouraged by the solid waste programs of the Environmental Protection Agency.

Federal statutes also attempt to generate state and local community initiative for solving solid waste disposal problems by providing monies and expert guidance for state and local studies. A number of states have sought to reduce the problem of solid waste disposal by requiring recycling or reuse of various products. One such state is Oregon, whose statute was challenged in the following case.

---

15.   514 F.2d 492 (8th Cir. 1975).

AMERICAN CAN CO. v.
OREGON LIQUOR
CONTROL COMM'N

Court of Appeals of Oregon,
1974.
15 Or. App. 618, 517 P.2d 691.

BACKGROUND AND FACTS *The State of Oregon adopted a law prohibiting the use of nonreturnable containers for beer and carbonated beverages. It also prohibited the sale of metal beverage containers that used detachable pull-top opening devices. The American Can Company instituted an action against the Oregon Liquor Control Commission, as well as other administrative bodies of the State of Oregon, and appealed the initial decision that upheld the law.*

TANZER, Judge.

* * * *

The bottle bill, enacted by the Oregon legislature in 1971, became effective on October 1, 1972. The statute's principal provisions are as follows:

1. Every retailer of the covered beverages (beer or carbonated beverages) in Oregon is required to "accept from a consumer any empty beverage containers of the kind, common size and brand sold by the dealer" and to pay the consumer the statutory "refund value" of the container. * * *

* * * *

Metal beverage containers, a part of which is wholly detachable in opening without a can opener ("pull top" cans), may not be sold at retail in Oregon.

* * * *

The primary legislative purpose of the bottle bill is to cause bottlers of carbonated soft drinks and brewers to package their products for distribution in Oregon in returnable, multiple-use deposit bottles toward the goals of reducing litter and solid waste in Oregon and reducing the injuries to people and animals due to discarded "pull tops."

As bases for attacking the validity of the statute, plaintiffs [the American Can Company] invoke the Equal Protection and Due Process Clauses of the Fourteenth Amendment to the United States Constitution, and the Commerce Clause, art. 1, § 8, clause 3, of the United States Constitution. In addition, plaintiffs cite various provisions of the Oregon Constitution.

One of the plaintiffs' main objectives at trial was to show that the bottle bill would have an effect not only upon manufacturers of bottles and cans, but also upon an entire distribution chain including brewers, soft drink bottlers and canners, beer wholesalers, retailers and, ultimately, consumers. The evidence in this regard demonstrated that the consumption of malt beverages and soft drinks had increased greatly in the United States in recent years, and that a large part of this increase could be attributed to the use of convenient "one-way" packages, including both cans and non-returnable bottles. Plaintiffs assert that non-returnable containers are essential to the existence of national and regional beer markets, and that non-returnable containers are also essential to the continued existence of soft drink enterprises. The non-returnable containers were shown to have provided economies in the packaging and distribution of soft drinks and beer by eliminating the cost of shipping the containers both ways, thus causing an increase in feasible shipping distances and enlarging the market each manufacturer could cover.

* * *

* * * *

The Oregon legislature was persuaded that the economic benefit to the beverage industry brought with it deleterious consequences to the environment and additional cost to the public. The aggravation of the problems of litter in public places and solid waste disposal and the attendant economic and esthetic burden to the public outweighed the narrower economic benefit to the industry. Thus the legislature enacted the bottle bill over the articulate opposition of the industries represented by plaintiffs.

As with every change of circumstance in the market place, there are gainers and there are losers. Just as there were gainers and losers, with plaintiffs apparently among the gainers, when the industry adapted to the development of non-returnable containers, there will be new gainers and losers as they adapt to the ban. The economic losses complained of by plaintiffs in this case are essentially the consequences of readjustment of the beverage manufacturing and distribution systems to the older technology in order to compete in the Oregon market.

*   *   *   *

Economic loss restricted to certain elements of the beverage industry must be viewed in relation to the broader loss to the general public of the state of Oregon which the legislature sought, by enactment of the bottle bill, to avoid. The availability of land and revenues for solid waste disposal, the cost of litter collection on our highways and in our public parks, the depletion of mineral and energy resources, the injuries to humans and animals caused by discarded pull tops, and the esthetic blight on our landscape, are all economic, safety and esthetic burdens of great consequence which must be borne by every member of the public. The legislature attached higher significance to the cost to the public than they did to the cost to the beverage industry and we have no cause to disturb that legislative determination.

*   *   *   *

Plaintiffs' and intervenors' constitutional challenges having failed, we hold the bottle bill to be a valid exercise of Oregon's police power. In doing so, we acknowledge having had the benefit of an able analysis by the trial court.

The appellate court affirmed the trial court's ruling that Oregon had legitimately exercised its state police power in passing laws concerning solid waste disposal. The additional cost to the beverage industry was recognized, but the court would not accept it as a justification for overturning a legislative enactment. Hence, the bottle bill was upheld.

DECISION AND REMEDY

Hazardous Waste

In 1976 Congress passed the Resource Conservation and Recovery Act (RCRA) in response to an ever-increasing concern with the effects of hazardous waste materials on the environment. By this act the Environmental Protection Agency was required to establish regulations to monitor and control hazardous waste disposal and to determine which forms of solid waste should be considered hazardous and thus subject to regulation. Under the authority granted by this act, the EPA has promulgated various technical requirements for limited types of hazardous waste storage and treatment facilities. It also requires all producers of hazardous waste materials to label and package properly any hazardous waste to be transported.

The RCRA was amended in 1984 to extend the program to 1988 and to add several new regulatory requirements to those already monitored and enforced by the EPA. The basic aims of the amendments are to decrease the use of land containment in disposing of hazardous waste and to reduce the "safe harbor" provisions that had been created by

the EPA in administering the 1976 act. Safe harbor provisions had allowed some generators of hazardous waste—such as those generating less than 1,000 kilograms a month—to be excluded from regulation under the RCRA.

JUDICIAL LIMITS

In the first half of the 1970s, federal and state legislators enacted many statutes that regulate environmental quality. Judicial interpretations of these statutes have generally given broad discretionary powers to the administrative agencies that carry out their directives. Beginning in the mid-1970s, however, the courts began to place stricter limits on administrative discretion. Recent court decisions that impose a cost-benefit standard on administrative decisions are likely to limit discretion in the environmental area as well.

In *American Petroleum v. Occupational Safety and Health Adm'n*, an OSHA regulation limiting benzine exposure in the workplace was invalidated by the Fifth Circuit Court of Appeals.[16] In 1977, OSHA promulgated regulations reducing permissible exposure by 90 percent from the 1971 standard. This action was based primarily on the results of three studies that showed an increased risk of leu-

kemia in workers who had been exposed to benzine at levels in excess of one hundred times the 1977 permissible levels.

The following classic case deals with judicial interpretation of an environmental statute, the Endangered Species Act.

---

16.   581 F.2d 493 (5th Cir. 1978).

TENNESSEE VALLEY AUTH. v. HILL

Supreme Court of the United States, 1978.
437 U.S. 153, 98 S.Ct. 2279.

BACKGROUND AND FACTS   *The Endangered Species Act of 1973 authorizes the secretary of the interior to declare a species of life "endangered." The secretary listed a small fish popularly known as the snail darter as an endangered species under this act. The snail darter lived in a portion of the Little Tennessee River in which the Tellico Dam was under construction. The secretary ordered all federal agencies to take action to insure that the critical habitat of the snail darter was not modified or destroyed. An association of scientists, a conservation group, and citizens of the Little Tennessee Valley brought this suit to enjoin completion of the dam, claiming that impoundment of the waters would violate the act by causing the snail darter's extinction.*

MR. Chief Justice BURGER delivered the opinion of the court.
*   *   *   *

We begin with the premise that operation of the Tellico Dam will either eradicate the known population of snail darters or destroy their critical habitat. Petitioner does not now seriously dispute this fact. *   *   * As we have seen, the Secretary promulgated regulations which declared the snail darter an endangered species whose critical habitat would be destroyed by creation of the Tellico Reservoir. Doubtless petitioner would prefer not to have these regulations on the books, but there is no suggestion that the Secretary exceeded his authority or abused his discretion in issuing the regulations. Indeed, no judicial review of the Secretary's determinations has ever been sought and hence the validity of his actions are not open to review in this Court.

Starting from the above premise, two questions are presented: (a) would TVA be in violation of the Act if it completed and operated the Tellico Dam as planned? (b) if TVA's actions would offend the Act, is an injunction the appropriate remedy for the violation? For the reasons stated hereinafter, we hold that both questions must be answered in the affirmative.

It may seem curious to some that the survival of a relatively small number of three-inch fish among all the countless millions of species extant would require the permanent halting of a virtually completed dam for which Congress has expended more than $100 million. The paradox is not minimized by the fact that Congress continued to appropriate large sums of public money for the project, even after congressional Appropriations Committees were apprised of its apparent impact upon the survival of the snail darter. We conclude, however, that the explicit provisions of the Endangered Species Act require precisely that result.

One would be hard pressed to find a statutory provision whose terms were any plainer than those in § 7 of the Endangered Species Act. Its very words affirmatively command all federal agencies "to *insure* that actions *authorized, funded,* or *carried out* by them do not *jeopardize* the continued existence" of an endangered species or *"result in the destruction or modification of habitat of such species.* *   *   * " 16 U.S.C. § 1536 (1976 ed.). (Emphasis added.) This language admits of no exception. Nonetheless, petitioner urges, as do the dissenters, that the Act cannot reasonably be interpreted as applying to a federal project which was well under way when Congress passed the Endangered Species Act of 1973. To sustain that position, however, we would be forced to ignore the ordinary meaning of plain language. * * *

Concededly, this view of the Act will produce results requiring the sacrifice of the anticipated benefits of the project and of many millions of dollars in public funds. But examination of the language, history, and structure of the legislation under review here indicates beyond doubt that Congress intended endangered species to be afforded the highest of priorities.

* * * *

Having determined that there is an irreconcilable conflict between operation of the Tellico Dam and the explicit provisions of § 7 of the Endangered Species Act, we must now consider what remedy, if any, is appropriate. It is correct, of course, that a federal judge sitting as a chancellor is not mechanically obligated to grant an injunction for every violation of law. As a general matter it may be said that "[s]ince all or most all equitable remedies are discretionary, the balancing of equities and hardships is appropriate in almost any case as a guide to the chancellor's discretion." D. Dobbs, Remedies 52 (1973). * * *

But these principles take a court only so far. Our system of government is, after all, a tripartite one, with each branch having certain defined functions delegated to it by the Constitution. While "[i]t is emphatically the province and duty of the judicial department to say what the law is," *Marbury* v. *Madison,* 1 Cranch 137, 177 (1803), it is equally—and emphatically—the exclusive province of the Congress not only to formulate legislative policies and mandate programs and projects, but also to establish their relative priority for the Nation. Once Congress, exercising its delegated powers, has decided the order of priorities in a given area, it is for the Executive to administer the laws and for the courts to enforce them when enforcement is sought.

Here we are urged to view the Endangered Species Act "reasonably," and hence shape a remedy "that accords with some modicum of common sense and the public weal." But is that our function? We have no expert knowledge on the subject of endangered species, much less do we have a mandate from the people to strike a balance of equities on the side of the Tellico Dam. Congress has spoken in the plainest of words, making it abundantly clear that the balance has been struck in favor of affording endangered species the highest of priorities, thereby adopting a policy which it described as "institutionalized caution."

Our individual appraisal of the wisdom or unwisdom of a particular course consciously selected by the Congress is to be put aside in the process of interpreting a statute. Once the meaning of an enactment is discerned and its constitutionality determined, the judicial process comes to an end. We do not sit as a committee of review, nor are we vested with the power of veto. * * *

* * * *

We agree with the Court of Appeals that in our constitutional system the commitment to the separation of powers is too fundamental for us to pre-empt congressional action by judicially decreeing what accords with "common sense and the public weal." Our Constitution vests such responsibilities in the political branches.

The Supreme Court enforced the Endangered Species Act by enjoining completion of the Tellico Dam.   **DECISION AND REMEDY**

It was later determined that snail darters could live in another area of the Little Tennessee River that would be unaffected by the dam. The snail darters were moved at government expense, making it possible to complete the Tellico Dam.   **COMMENTS**

QUESTIONS AND CASE PROBLEMS

1. Moonbay is a development home building corporation that primarily develops retirement communities. Farmtex owns a number of feedlots in Sunny Valley. Moonbay purchased 20,000 acres of farmland in the same area and began building and selling homes on this acreage. In the meantime Farmtex continued to expand its feedlot business, and eventually only 500 feet separated the two operations. Because of the odor and flies from the feedlots, Moonbay found it difficult to sell the homes in its development. Moonbay wants to enjoin Farmtex from operating its feedlots in the vicinity of its retirement home development. Discuss under what theory Moonbay would file this action. Discuss whether Farmtex has violated any federal environmental laws.

2. Hardbottle, Inc. is a processor of a soft drink called "Fizz-Bizz." Hardbottle uses returnable bottles and uses a special acid to clean its bottles for further beverage processing. The acid is diluted by water and then allowed to pass into a navigable stream. Hardbottle crushes its broken bottles and throws the crushed glass into the stream. Discuss *fully* any federal environmental laws which Hardbottle has violated.

3. Spark Electric, Inc. is a privately owned electric utility company. Based on the Powerplant and Industrial Fuel Use Act to reduce dependence on imported oil and domestic gas, Spark converted its generation plants to coal. In doing so, due to technological difficulties and a breach of contract by a low sulfur coal supplier, Spark has had excessive sulfur dioxide emissions from its plants. Spark claims that if it is forced to install additional expensive sulfur dioxide equipment, it would have to shut down its operations. This would seriously affect the economy in the area and the lives of its customers. Spark seeks from the EPA a variance. EPA denies Spark's variance request. In addition, two hundred miles north and east, lake fish suddenly are dying. No smoke from Spark's plants travels that far, but the Sierra Club claims Spark is violating environmental laws. Discuss *fully* the issues involved.

4. Lightair, Inc. is a manufacturer of a new 300-seat passenger airplane which is fuel-efficient and travels at a cruising speed of 900 miles per hour. The plane would only be cost effective for flights of 1,000 miles or more.

Traveling at 900 miles per hour creates a sonic boom lasting for no more than five seconds. The sound measured during the five-second period exceeds aircraft noise levels established by the EPA. Discuss *fully* whether Lightair aircraft can be banned from flying over the United States.

5. Citizens Against Toxic Sprays, Inc., was an organization established to challenge the use of toxic sprays in places where they could be harmful to humans, animals, or vegetation. The group sought to enjoin the United States Forest Service from using the herbicide TCDD because of its hazardous effect on people who breathed it. TCDD was used only in national forests, not in any residential areas. Citizens Against Toxic Sprays alleged that some of its members were affected by the use of TCDD in two of the national forests because they lived near them, worked in them, or used them for recreational activities. Does Citizens Against Toxic Sprays have *standing* to sue the United States Forest Service? [Citizens Against Toxic Sprays, Inc. v. Bergland, 428 F.Supp. 908 (D.C.Or. 1977)]

6. Virginia Dalsis, the proprietor of a small store in the city of Olean, New York, brought a suit to enjoin the construction of a mall because of its projected size. Dalsis alleged that the large size of the shopping center would have an adverse environmental effect on the downtown area, causing economic blight and deterioration to the section in which her business was located. Dalsis, however, did not bring the suit until three months after construction of the shopping mall had begun, even though she was aware of the mall's potential size almost a year before construction started. Should Dalsis be allowed to enjoin the construction of the shopping mall under the National Environmental Policy Act? [Dalsis v. Hills, 424 F.Supp. 784 (W.D.N.Y. 1976)]

7. The Government Services Administration (GSA) entered into an agreement with a private individual under which the individual was to construct a building to GSA's specifications and lease it to the GSA. Under the contemplated lease provision, GSA would have use of the entire building for a five-year (renewable) period. As many as 2,300 government employees would be assigned to the building, and most would commute by automobile. The cost of the lease was approximately $11 million. GSA proceeded with its plans for the building without preparing any environmental impact statement. Was a statement necessary? [S. W. Neighborhood Assembly v. Eckard, 445 F.Supp. 1195 (D.C.D.C. 1978)]

48

GOVERNMENT REGULATION
Antitrust: Statutes and Exemptions

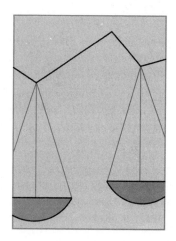

Competition is the socially desired type of market organization in the United States today. Because of this, antitrust laws have been enacted by Congress and enforced to improve business behavior and to keep markets competitive. Antitrust laws reflect a distrust of largeness and any concentration of power. This chapter will discuss the major antitrust statutes that are enforced by the Department of Justice and the Federal Trade Commission. Particular emphasis will be placed on arrangements that create monopolies, since monopolies have the effect of eliminating competition. The next chapter will look at the important developments in the field of antitrust law and how they affect business today.

COMMON LAW ACTIONS

Today's antitrust laws are the direct descendants of common law actions intended to limit restraints of trade. That is not to say, however, that a neat classification of trade restraints can be found in the common law.

Common Law in England

One of the earliest recorded cases about trade restraints in the common law involved a man named John Dyer and has become known as Dyer's Case.[1] Dyer had agreed not to "use his art of a dyer's craft within the town * * * for half a year." The court denied the plaintiff the ability to collect on a bond for Dyer's breach of his agreement. The effect of the agreement was to restrain trade, according to the common law. At that time, restraint of trade was defined as the failure to promote "fair" commercial activity.

A celebrated case occurred in 1711 when a man named Mitchell leased a baking shop for five years, subject to the condition that the lessor, Reynolds, who was also a baker, would not practice the baking art in the immediate area for the term of the lease. Reynolds also agreed to pay Mitchell the sum of £50 if he (Reynolds) engaged in the baking trade within the term of five years. When Reynolds subsequently continued his trade as a baker during the five-year period, Mitchell brought an action against Reynolds on the bond.

Reynolds, when sued, alleged that he was a baker by trade, that he had served his apprenticeship, and that the bond was void in law. When confronted with the issue of whether or not this bond, made in

---

1. Y. B. Pasch. 2 Hen. 5 f. 5, PL. 26 (1414).

restraint of trade, was valid, the court ruled in favor of Reynolds.[2]

This case is significant because the court's opinion systematically classified trade restraints into those that were good and those that were bad. Lord Parker, who rendered the opinion, distinguished between general and particular restraints, the former being invalid and the latter valid. *General restraints* were defined as those used for the purpose of limiting competition. On the other hand, certain *particular restraints* that were supported by "good consideration" were acceptable. These *partial*, or *ancillary*, *restraints*, as they became known, were generally upheld if limited in time and place.

Thus, *Mitchell v. Reynolds* provided the basis for the modern formulation of the so-called rule of reason, in which the court determines whether the restraint in question is reasonable. Since the case of *Mitchell v. Reynolds*, the rule of reason has played an important role in antitrust litigation. In order to determine whether a partial restraint is reasonable (that is, legal), the courts inquire into its purpose and its probable effect.

THE BEGINNINGS OF U.S. ANTITRUST LAW

With the growth of national markets after the Civil War, a number of small companies were combined to form large companies, and they started to engage in practices that were seen as monopolistic. Reported abusive practices by corporate giants in the second half of the nineteenth century finally led to legislation restricting the power of these so-called trusts. The first piece of legislation was the Interstate Commerce Act of 1887, and in 1890 the Sherman Act was passed. These acts were designed to prevent trusts from acting against the public interest.

The Formation of Trusts

Interestingly, *trusts* were a legal innovation that was made famous by John D. Rockefeller's Standard Oil Company. Standard's attorneys established an arrangement whereby owners of stock in several companies could transfer their stock to a set of trustees. In return, the owners received consideration in the

form of certificates entitling them to a specified share in the pooled earnings of the jointly managed companies.

In the late 1800s, the term *trust* was randomly, and sometimes questionably, applied to business combinations of many different types. There were trusts in oil, sugar, cotton, linseed oil, whiskey, and other industries, and the trusts seemed to absorb new enterprises at an expanding rate. Furthermore, some observers felt that the process of consolidation was achieved by *predatory* tactics, that is, tactics that advanced the competitive position of one business by threatening to drive another business out of the market. In fact, the activities of the Standard Oil Company are sometimes presented as the prime example of such tactics. Because of its size, Standard Oil was able to sell kerosene at a price below its cost. Standard's lower prices forced many competitors to sell or close down. As total industry output declined, Standard Oil raised the price and presumably obtained monopoly power.[3]

The 1890 Sherman Act was the response, and its purpose was to promote competition within the U.S. economy.[4] The author of the legislation, Senator Sherman, told Congress that the Sherman Act "does not announce a new principle of law, but applies old and well-recognized principles of the common law." [5] However, the common law regarding trade regulation was not always consistent. Certainly it was not very familiar to the legislators of the Fifty-first Congress of the United States. Most likely, the Sherman Act was an attempt by Congress to prompt the federal courts to create a common body of federal antitrust law.

THE SHERMAN ANTITRUST ACT

Sections 1 and 2 contain the main provisions of the Sherman Act. They are:

§ 1: Every contract, combination in the form of trust or otherwise, or conspiracy, in restraint of trade or commerce among the several States, or with foreign

---

2. 1 P. Wms. 181, 24 Eng. Rep 347 (1711).

3. Not everyone agrees with this rendition of the facts. See, for example, John S. McGee, "Predatory Price Cutting: The Standard Oil (New Jersey) Case," *Journal of Law and Economics* 1 (1958). McGee finds that the facts are consistent with a competitive market with increased supply.

4. 26 Stat 209 (1890) as amended 15 U.S.C. 1–7.

5. 21 Congressional Record 2456 (1890).

nations, is hereby declared to be illegal [and is a felony punishable by fine and/or imprisonment]. * * *

§ 2: Every person who shall monopolize, or attempt to monopolize, or combine or conspire with any other person or persons, to monopolize any part of the trade or commerce among the several States, or with foreign nations, shall be deemed guilty of a felony [and is similarly punishable]. * * *

Sections 1 and 2 Compared

The two main sections of the Sherman Act are quite different. Section 1 requires two or more persons, since a person cannot combine or conspire alone. Thus, the essence of the illegal activity is *the act of joining together*. Section 2 applies to both an individual person and several people because it states, "[e]very person who * * *." Thus, unilateral conduct can result in a violation of Section 2. The cases brought to court under Section 1 of the Sherman Act differ from those brought under Section 2. Section 1 cases are often concerned with finding an agreement (written or oral) that leads to a restraint of trade. Section 2 cases deal with the structure of a monopoly that exists in the marketplace. Thus, Section 1 focuses on agreements that are restrictive—that is, agreements that have a wrongful purpose. Section 2 looks at the so-called misuse of monopoly power in the marketplace. However, both sections seek to curtail market industrial practices that result in undesired monopoly pricing and output behavior. Any case brought under Section 2, however, must be one in which the "threshold" or "necessary" amount of monopoly power already exists.

The Proscriptive Nature of the Sherman Act

The Sherman Act does not tell businesses how they should act. It tells them how they should *not* act. In this sense, the act is *proscriptive* rather than *prescriptive*. It is the basis for *policing* rather than *regulating* business conduct.

Other Aspects of the Sherman Act

Jurisdiction The Sherman Act applies only to restraints that have a significant impact on commerce. Because Congress can only regulate interstate commerce, in principle only interstate commerce is af-

fected by this Act.[6] State regulation of anticompetitive practices addresses purely local restraints on competition. Courts, however, have construed the meaning of *interstate* commerce more and more broadly, thus bringing even local activities within the purview of the Sherman Act if such activities have a significant anticompetitive effect on interstate commerce.

The Sherman Act extends to U.S. nationals abroad who are engaged in activities that will affect U.S. foreign commerce. It was applied, for example, in *Continental Ore Co. v. Union Carbide and Carbon Corp.*[7] In that case, the defendant, Union Carbide, tried to monopolize the market in Canada by excluding competitors. The U.S. plaintiff, Continental Ore Company, was effectively prohibited from entering Canadian markets.

Standing The Department of Justice is not the only entity that can file suit under the Sherman Act. Some private parties can also sue for damages or other remedies. The courts have determined that the test of ability to sue depends on the directness of the injury suffered by the purported plaintiff. Thus, a person wishing to sue under the Sherman Act must prove that (1) the antitrust violation either directly caused or was at least a substantial factor in causing the injury that was suffered, and (2) the unlawful actions of the purported defendant affected business activities of the plaintiff that were protected by the antitrust laws.

One of the unique features of the Sherman Antitrust Act is that it allows any person injured as a result of violations of the act to bring a suit for treble damages against the defendants in addition to reasonable attorneys' fees. In the 1960s General Electric Company, along with other major electrical equipment manufacturers, paid over $200 million in treble damage claims. Certain of the corporate officers were fined, and some of them even went to jail.

Remedies and Sanctions Any person found guilty of violating either Section 1 or Section 2 of the Sherman Act is subject to criminal prosecution for a felony. Currently, upon conviction, a person can

---

6. See the discussion under "The Commerce Clause" in Chapter 2.

7. 370 U.S. 690, 82 S.Ct. 1404 (1962).

be fined up to $100,000 or imprisoned for three years, or both. A corporation can be fined $1 million. The Department of Justice can simultaneously institute civil proceedings to restrain the conduct that is in violation of the act.

The various remedies that the Justice Department has asked the court to impose include divestiture, dissolution, and divorcement, or making a company give up one of its operating functions. A group of meat packers, for example, can be forced to divorce itself from controlling or owning butcher shops.

The Courts' Initial Reaction to the Sherman Act

Initially, the Sherman Act was stripped of any effectiveness because the courts interpreted it so narrowly. For example, five years after passage of the act, the Supreme Court refused to apply the Sherman Act to a sugar trust.[8] The Court held that the law did not extend to restraints affecting *just* the manufacture of commodities. According to the Court, "commerce secedes to manufacturer, and is not a part of it." In other words, the manufacturer of a commodity does not control commerce and therefore cannot violate the Sherman Act.

---

8.   United States v. E. C. Knight Co., 156 U.S. 1, 15 S.Ct. 249 (1895).

Then the Court swung the other way and declared illegal certain price-fixing agreements and territorial divisions because Section 1 of the Sherman Act condemned *every* restraint of trade.[9] This absolute position clearly could not hold for long. The Court then retreated once again. It first condemned direct restraints.[10] It then came to the conclusion that restraints that were lawful at common law might not be prohibited by the Sherman Act.[11]

The Rule of Reason

This change in the Court's view was expressed in its 1911 case against Standard Oil Company of New Jersey, which follows. In this landmark Section 1 decision, the Supreme Court ordered the dissolution of the oil trust into approximately thirty companies. The Court also ruled that only those restraints whose character was *unreasonably* anticompetitive were outlawed by the Sherman Act. Beginning with this decision, a "standard of reason" was applied to determine the purpose of the arrangement, the powers of the parties, and the effect of their actions in restraining of trade.

---

9.   See U.S. v. TransMissouri Freight Ass'n, 166 U.S. 290, 17 S.Ct. 540 (1897).
10.   Hopkins v. United States, 171 U.S. 578, 19 S.Ct. 40 (1898).
11.   United States v. Joint Traffic Ass'n, 171 U.S. 505, 19 S.Ct. 25 (1898).

THE STANDARD OIL CO. OF NEW JERSEY v. UNITED STATES
221 U.S. 1, 31 S.Ct. 502 (1911).

BACKGROUND AND FACTS *Standard Oil Company of New Jersey and thirty-three other corporations, John D. Rockefeller, William Rockefeller, and five other individual defendants were the appellants in this case. They attempted to reverse a decree holding that they were conspiring "to restrain the trade and commerce in petroleum, commonly called 'crude oil,' in refined oil, and in the other products of petroleum, among several States and Territories of the United States and District of Columbia and with foreign nations, and to monopolize the said commerce."*

The government charged that John D. Rockefeller, William Rockefeller, and several other named individuals organized the Standard Oil Corporation of Ohio and soon afterwards became participants in an illegal plan to acquire substantially all of the oil refineries located in Cleveland, Ohio.

In addition, the government charged that there was a trust agreement in which the stock of over forty corporations, including Standard Oil of Ohio, was held for the benefit of the members of the combination. The trust agreement was adjudged void because it was in restraint of trade, and the trust was ordered dissolved.

In the third phase of its case, the government charged that the individual defendants operated a holding company through Standard Oil Company of New Jersey. This company acquired the majority of stock in various other corporations engaging in the purchasing, transporting, refining, shipping, and selling of oil in the United States, the District of Columbia, and foreign nations.

WHITE, Chief Justice.
* * * *

It is sufficient to say that, whilst admitting many of the alleged acquisitions of property, the formation of the so-called trust of 1882, its dissolution in 1892, and the acquisition by the Standard Oil Company of New Jersey of the stocks of the various corporations in 1899, * * * [the appellants] deny all the allegations respecting combinations or conspiracies to restrain or monopolize the oil trade; and particularly that the so-called trust of 1882, or the acquisition of the shares of the defendant companies by the Standard Oil Company of New Jersey in 1899, was a combination of *independent or competing* concerns or corporations. * * *

The [lower] court decided in favor of the United States. In the opinion delivered, all the multitude of acts of wrong-doing charged in the bill were put aside, in so far as they were alleged to have been committed prior to the passage of the Anti-trust Act, "except as evidence of their (the defendants') purpose, of their continuing conduct and of its effect."
* * * *

Giving to the facts just stated, the weight which it was deemed they were entitled to, in the light afforded by the proof of other cognate facts and circumstances, the court below held that the acts and dealings established by the proof operated to destroy the "potentiality of competition" which otherwise would have existed to such an extent as to cause the transfers of stock which were made to the New Jersey corporation and the control which resulted over the many and various subsidiary corporations to be a combination or conspiracy in restraint of trade in violation of the first section of the act, but also to be an attempt to monopolize and a monopolization bringing about a perennial violation of the second section.

We see no cause to doubt the correctness of these conclusions, considering the subject from every aspect, that is, both in view of the facts established by the record and the necessary operation and effect of the law as we have construed it upon the inferences deducible from the facts, for the following reasons:

a. Because the unification of power and control over petroleum and its products which was the inevitable result of the combining in the New Jersey corporation by the increase of its stock and the transfer to it of the stocks of so many other corporations, aggregating so vast a capital, gives rise, in and of itself, * * * to the *prima facie* presumption of intent and purpose to maintain the dominancy over the oil industry, not as a result of normal methods of industrial development, but by new means of combination which were resorted to in order that greater power might be added than would otherwise have arisen had normal methods been followed, the whole with the purpose of excluding others from the trade and thus centralizing in the combination a perpetual control of the movements of petroleum and its products in the channels of interstate commerce.

b. Because the *prima facie* presumption of intent to restrain trade, to monopolize and to bring about monopolization resulting from the act of expanding the stock of the New Jersey corporation and vesting it with such vast control of the oil industry, is made conclusive by * * * what was done under those agreements and the acts which immediately preceded the vesting of power in the New Jersey corporation as well as by * * * the modes in which the power vested in that corporation has been exerted and the results which have arisen from it.

* * * [W]e think no disinterested mind can survey the * * * question without being irresistibly driven to the conclusion that the very genius for commercial development and organization which it would seem was manifested from the beginning soon begot an intent and purpose to exclude others which was frequently manifested by acts and dealings wholly inconsistent with the theory that they were made with the single conception of advancing the development of business power by usual methods, but which on the contrary necessarily involved the intent to drive others from the field and to exclude them from their right to trade and thus accomplish the mastery which was the end in view. * * * The exercise of the power which resulted from that organization fortifies the foregoing conclusions, since the development which came, the acquisition here and there which ensued of every efficient means by which competition could have been asserted, the slow but resistless methods which followed by which means of transportation were absorbed and brought under control, the system of marketing which was adopted by which the country was divided into districts and the trade in each district in oil was turned over to a designated corporation within the combination and all others were excluded, all lead the mind up to a conviction of a purpose and intent which we think is so certain as practically to cause the subject not to be within the domain of reasonable contention.

The inference that no attempt to monopolize could have been intended, and that no monopolization resulted from the acts complained of, since it is established that a very small percentage of the crude oil produced was controlled by the combination, is unwarranted. As substantial power over the crude product was the inevitable result of the absolute control which existed over the refined product, the monopolization of the one carried with it the power to control the other, and if the inferences which this situation suggests were developed, which we deem it unnecessary to do, they might well serve to add additional cogency to the presumption of intent to monopolize which we have found arises from the unquestioned proof on other subjects. * * *

DECISION AND REMEDY

The Supreme Court concluded that the decree issued by the lower court was right and should be affirmed. It forbade Standard Oil from engaging in any future combinations in violation of the Sherman Antitrust Act. In addition, it attempted to neutralize the effect of the monopoly that Standard Oil had created by commanding the dissolution of the combination (the trust) and causing the New Jersey corporation to divest itself of the numerous shares of stock that it controlled.

COMMENTS

The rule of reason was interpreted and modified many times. For example, it was recently broadened to cover a new situation. In National Society of Professional Engineers v. United States *[435 U.S. 679, 98 S.Ct. 1355 (1978)], the court argued that the rule of reason would be applied to anticompetitive situations that were ancillary to a legitimate transaction, such as an employment contract or the sale of an ongoing business. The Court in that case concluded that the rule may sometimes require courts to weigh all the facts of a case, including facts peculiar to the business, the history of the restraint, and the reason why it was imposed, before deciding whether the effect upon trade was unreasonable.*

The Development of Per Se Violations

According to the rule of reason, only unreasonable restraints were illegal at common law. However, with respect to certain restraints on competition, Section 1 will be read literally. Certain kinds of restrictive contracts will be deemed inherently anticompetitive—that is, in restraint of trade as a *matter of law*. In such *per se violations* of Section 1 there is no need to examine any other facts.

In *United States v. Socony Vacuum Oil Co.*[12] the Supreme Court set forth a per se standard, condemning all price-fixing arrangements. Footnote 59 of that opinion has become the most famous footnote in antitrust law. In that footnote Justice Douglas wrote:

> [I]t is well established that a person "may be guilty of conspiring, although incapable of committing the objective offense." * * * And it is likewise well settled that conspiracies under the Sherman Act are not dependent on any overt act other than the act of conspiring. * * * It is the "contract, combination * * * or conspiracy, in restraint of trade or commerce" which § 1 of the Act strikes down, whether the concerted activity be wholly nascent or abortive on the one hand, or successful on the other. * * * And the amount of interstate or foreign trade involved is not material, since § 1 of the Act brands as illegal the character of the restraint not the amount of commerce affected. * * * In view of these considerations a conspiracy to fix prices violates § 1 of the Act though no overt act is shown, though it is not established that the conspirators had the means available for accomplishment of their objective, and though the conspiracy embraced but a part of the interstate or foreign commerce in the commodity. Whatever may have been the status of price-fixing agreements at common law the Sherman Act has a *broader* [emphasis added] application to them than the common law prohibitions or sanctions. * * * Price-fixing agreements may or may not be aimed at complete elimination of price competition. The group making those agreements may or may not have power to control the market. But the fact that the group cannot control the market prices does not necessarily mean that the agreement as to prices has no utility to the members of the combination. The effectiveness of price-fixing agreements is dependent on many factors, such as competitive tactics, position in the industry, the formula underlying price policies. Whatever economic justification particular price-fixing agreements may be thought to have, the law does not permit an inquiry into their reasonableness. They are all banned because of their actual or potential threat to the central nervous system of the economy. * * *

THE CLAYTON ACT

In 1914 Congress attempted to strengthen federal antitrust laws by adopting the Clayton Act, which was aimed at specific monopolistic practices. The important sections of the Clayton Act are Sections 2, 3, 7, and 8. Briefly, these sections state:

> Section 2: [It is illegal to] discriminate in price between different purchasers [except in cases where the differences are due to differences in selling or transportation costs].
>
> Section 3: [Producers or lessors cannot sell or lease] on the condition, agreement or understanding that the * * * purchaser or lessee thereof shall not use or deal in the goods * * * of a competitor or competitors of the seller.
>
> Section 7: [A person or business organization cannot hold stock and/or assets in another business] where the effect * * * may be to substantially lessen competition.
>
> Section 8: * * * [N]o person at the same time shall be a director in any two or more competing corporations, any one of which has capital, surplus, and undivided profits aggregating more than $1 million, engaged in whole or in part in commerce, other than banks, banking associations, trust companies, and common carriers.

Thus, the Clayton Act outlaws price discrimination, exclusive dealing and tying contracts, the purchase of enough stock in a competing business to reduce competition, and interlocking directorates. Most of these actions are discussed in the context of current antitrust enforcement in the next chapter.

THE FEDERAL TRADE COMMISSION ACT

In 1914 Congress passed the Federal Trade Commission Act, which created a bipartisan, independent administrative agency headed by five commissioners, no more than three of whom could be of the same political party.[13] Section 5 of the act gives the FTC broad powers to prevent "unfair methods of competition in commerce and unfair or deceptive acts or practices in commerce." Amendments, particularly in 1975, have broadened the commission's powers.[14] The FTC also has the authority to conduct investigations relating to alleged violations of antitrust statutes and to make reports and recommendations to Congress regarding legislation. More im-

---

12. 310 U.S. 150, 60 S.Ct. 811 (1940).

13. 15 U.S.C.A. 41–51 (1914).
14. Magnuson-Moss FTC Improvements Act of 1975.

portantly, the FTC can promulgate interpretive rules and general statements of policy with respect to unfair or deceptive acts or practices. It can also promulgate trade regulation rules, which *define* particular unfair or deceptive acts or practices, including requirements for the purpose of preventing such acts or practices. The commission has issued guidelines defining unfair practices, but these guidelines are very broad, and many seemingly unfair practices are allowed.[15]

The FTC initiates most of its investigations because of oral or written communications from the general public and private business firms. The primary enforcement mechanism of the FTC is **cease and desist orders** (orders to stop certain activities or practices) against violators of the Federal Trade Commission Act. Furthermore, businesses that disregard these orders are subject to fines of up to $10,000 per day for each day of continued violation. Cease and desist orders can be appealed to the courts. Unlike the Sherman Act, the FTC Act does not allow for treble damage actions.

Additional Authority

Section 5 of the Federal Trade Commission Act overlaps a number of other antitrust statutes, including the Sherman Act, the Clayton Act, and other laws designed to reduce unfair methods of competition. The FTC initiates investigations and issues cease and desist orders, particularly for violations of Sections 2, 3, 7, and 8 of the Clayton Act, as amended by the Celler-Kefauver Act, the Robinson-Patman Act, and other acts.

ROBINSON-PATMAN ACT

One of the more important activities of the Federal Trade Commission has been the detection and prohibition of **price discrimination** (that is, charging different prices to different purchasers for identical goods), when such discrimination lessens competition or tends to create a monopoly.

Subsequent judicial interpretation and responses by businesses effectively circumvented the original intent of Section 2 of the Clayton Act, so in 1936 Congress responded by enacting the Robinson-Patman Act. This act tightened the prohibition against price discrimination. If goods of *similar grade and quality* were sold at different prices, and these differences could not be justified by differences in production and distribution costs, the practice would violate the Robinson-Patman Act even if the Clayton Act could be circumvented. In addition, the act prohibited sellers from cutting prices to levels substantially below those charged by their competitors.[16]

OTHER ANTITRUST ACTS

Both the Justice Department and the Federal Trade Commission enforce other statutes concerning antitrust. Some of these statutes merely amend the basic Sherman or Clayton Acts,[17] whereas others, such as the Emergency Petroleum Allocation Act, focus on a particular industry.

A number of statutes deal directly with *potential* competition in the economy. For example, the FTC is responsible for registering the articles of association or incorporation for associations that are organized under the Export Trade Act. It is also responsible for receiving and monitoring regulations governing mandatory allocations of crude oil, residual fuel oil, and refined petroleum products under the Emergency Petroleum Act of 1973. And it is responsible for working with the Justice Department in developing voluntary agreements under the International Energy Program. The Energy Policy and Conservation Act also creates responsibilities relating to automobile fuel economy, appliance efficiencies, and recycled oil.

SUMMARY

Overall, the major statutes concerning antitrust activities can be summarized as follows:

1.   Those that limit combinations through agreement, merger, or interlocking directorates.

---

15.   The commission, for example, has indicated that a practice is "unfair" if it offends public policy or is immoral, unethical, oppressive, unscrupulous, or causes substantial injury to consumers.

16.   Robinson-Patman Act, Subsection B.
17.   See, for example, the Hart-Scott-Rodino Antitrust Improvement Act, 15 U.S.C.A. 18 (1976).

2. Those that limit contractual and business actions, including price-fixing, boycotts, market division, price discrimination, and other such acts.
3. Those that limit price controls.

Exhibit 48-1 summarizes the major statutes and their principal amendments in these three categories.

EXEMPTIONS FROM ANTITRUST LAWS

In a sense, Congress's attention to the antitrust laws since the Clayton Act has focused primarily on writing *exceptions* to the coverage of the Sherman Act.

Labor and Agriculture

Labor and agricultural organizations are exempted from the Sherman Antitrust Act by Section 6 of the Clayton Act. Agriculture's exemption from antitrust legislation is further extended by the Capper-Volstead Act (1922), the Cooperative Marketing Act (1926), and certain provisions of the Robinson-Patman Act. Labor's exemption was strengthened by the Norris-La Guardia Act of 1932.

The National Labor Relations Act of 1935 protected unions from antitrust legislation. Today, therefore, unions can lawfully engage in actions that are normally prohibited as long as they act in their self-interest and do not conspire or combine with nonlabor groups to accomplish their goals.

Sports

Most commercial sporting activities are subject to the antitrust laws, but there are exceptions. For example, baseball remains untouched by the antitrust laws; it was not thought to be commerce in the

---

EXHIBIT 48-1 Major Antitrust Laws

Statutes Limiting Combinations	Statutes Limiting Contractual and Business Actions	Statutes Controlling Prices
Sherman Act (1890) Section 2* prohibits monopolies and attempts or conspiracies to monopolize.	**Sherman Act** (1890) Section 1* prohibits combinations and conspiracies in restraint of trade, including vertical and horizontal price-fixing, group boycotts, division of markets, and other practices.	**Emergency Price Control Act of 1942** set up the Office of Price Administration to control prices and rents during World War II.
Clayton Act (1914) Section 7 prohibits mergers, when the effect may be to substantially lessen competition or to create a monopoly. Amended (1950)—Celler-Kefauver Act clarified application of Section 7 to acquisition of assets.	**Clayton Act** (1914) Section 2 prohibits price discriminations, substantially lessening sellers' competition (primary violations). Amended (1936)—Robinson-Patman Act prohibits price discriminations, substantially lessening buyers' competition (secondary violation).	**Defense Production Act of 1950** was passed to control prices during the Korean War. **Economic Stabilization Act of 1970** gave the president the power to control prices during a period of high inflation.
Clayton Act (1914) Section 8 prohibits interlocking directorates.	**Clayton Act** (1914) Section 3 prohibits exclusive dealing and tying arrangements where the effect may be to substantially lessen competition.	
	Federal Trade Commission Act (1914) Section 5† prohibits unfair methods of competition; it established and defined powers of FTC. Amended (1938)—Wheeler-Lea Act prohibits unfair trade practices and false advertising. Amended (1976)—Hart-Scott-Rodino Act increases merger-reporting requirements.	

*Amended in 1974 and 1976 to increase penalties and broaden enforcement.
†Amended in 1973 and 1975 to increase penalties and grant industry-wide, rule-making power.

Sherman Act's original contemplation and is thus not commerce today. In *Flood v. Kuhn*, the Supreme Court concluded that if an earlier decision placing baseball outside the scope of the antitrust laws was wrong, Congress could change the rule.[18] The Court emphasized the fact that the baseball industry had been built on the assumption that it was free from the antitrust laws. Yet the exemption for baseball seems to be anomalous, especially since no other professional sport receives such treatment.

---

18.   407 U.S. 258, 92 S.Ct. 2099 (1972).

Professionals

A current controversial topic in antitrust law is the regulation of professionals, such as lawyers and doctors, who have traditionally been exempt from antitrust law. The traditional incantations about the maintenance of high quality no longer shield professionals from the antitrust laws, and professional organizations are no longer exempt from antitrust enforcement. As illustrated in the following case, professional organizations cannot establish minimum-fee schedules or prohibit competitive bidding in any way.

GOLDFARB v.
VIRGINIA STATE BAR

Supreme Court of the United
States, 1975.
421 U.S. 773, 95 S.Ct. 2004.

BACKGROUND AND FACTS *When Mr. and Mrs. Goldfarb contracted to purchase a home in Fairfax County, Virginia, they were unable to find a lawyer who would examine the title for less than the fee prescribed in a minimum-fee schedule published by the Fairfax County Bar Association and enforced by the Virginia State Bar. The Goldfarbs brought this action seeking injunctive relief and damages. They alleged that the minimum-fee schedule and its enforcement mechanism, as applied to fees for legal services relating to residential real estate transactions, constituted price-fixing in violation of Section 1 of the Sherman Act.*

BURGER, Chief Justice.
*   *   *   *

Our inquiry can be divided into *   *   * steps: did respondents engage in price fixing? If so, are their activities in interstate commerce or do they affect interstate commerce? If so, are the activities exempt from the Sherman Act because they involve a "learned profession?" *   *   *

The County Bar argues that because the fee schedule is merely advisory, the schedule and its enforcement mechanism do not constitute price fixing. Its purpose, the argument continues, is only to provide legitimate information to aid member lawyers in complying with Virginia professional regulations. Moreover, the County Bar contends that in practice the schedule has not had the effect of producing fixed fees. The facts found by the trier belie these contentions, and nothing in the record suggests these findings lack support.

A purely advisory fee schedule issued to provide guidelines, or an exchange of price information without a showing of an actual restraint on trade, would present us with a different question. The record here, however, reveals a situation quite different from what would occur under a purely advisory fee schedule. Here a fixed, rigid price floor arose from respondents' activities: every lawyer who responded to petitioners' inquiries adhered to the fee schedule, and no lawyer asked for additional information in order to set an individualized fee. The price information disseminated did not concern past standards, but rather minimum fees to be charged in future transactions, and those minimum rates were increased over time. *   *   * The County Bar makes much of the fact that it is a voluntary organization; however, the ethical opinions issued by the State Bar provide that any lawyer, whether or not a member of his county bar association, may be disciplined for "*habitually* charg[ing] less than the suggested minimum fee schedule adopted by his local bar Association. *   *   *" These factors coalesced to create a pricing system that consumers could not realistically escape. On this record respondents' activities constitute a classic illustration of price fixing.

*   *   *   *

The County Bar argues that Congress never intended to include the learned professions within the terms "trade or commerce" in § 1 of the Sherman Act, and therefore the sale of professional services is exempt from the Act. No explicit exemption or legislative history is provided to support this contention; rather, the existence of state regulation seems to be its primary basis. *   *   *

In arguing that learned professions are not "trade or commerce" the County Bar seeks a total exclusion from antitrust regulation. Whether state regulation is active or dormant, real or theoretical, lawyers would be able to adopt anticompetitive practices with impunity. We cannot find support for the proposition that Congress intended any such sweeping exclusion. The nature of an occupation, standing alone, does not provide sanctuary from the Sherman Act, nor is the public-service aspect of professional practice controlling in determining whether § 1 includes professions. Congress intended to strike as broadly as it could in § 1 of the Sherman Act, and to read into it so wide an exemption as that urged on us would be at odds with that purpose.

The language of § 1 of the Sherman Act, of course, contains no exception. "Language more comprehensive is difficult to conceive." And our cases have repeatedly established that there is a heavy presumption against implicit exemptions. Indeed, our cases have specifically included the sale of services within § 1. Whatever else it may be, the examination of a land title is a service; the exchange of such a service for money is "commerce" in the most common usage of that word. It is no disparagement of the practice of law as a profession to acknowledge that it has this business aspect, and § 1 of the Sherman Act

"[o]n its face *   *   * shows a carefully studied attempt to bring within the Act every person engaged in business whose activities might restrain or monopolize commercial intercourse among the states."

In the modern world it cannot be denied that the activities of lawyers play an important part in commercial intercourse, and that anticompetitive activities by lawyers may exert a restraint on commerce.

The minimum-fee schedule violated the Sherman Act. The case was remanded to the district court for issuance of an injunction against the legal associations and for determination of the damages suffered by the Goldfarbs.	**DECISION AND REMEDY**

Insurance

The 1945 McCarran-Ferguson Act exempts from the antitrust laws "any law enacted by any State for the purpose of regulating the business of insurance."[19] Thus, insurance is exempt from the antitrust laws by the McCarron-Ferguson Act since it is generally extensively regulated by state law.

State Action Exemption

Previously, actions taken by state, local, and other public jurisdictions were exempt from antitrust laws.

In 1978 it was held, however, that the doctrine of *state action* does not exempt all government entities from federal antitrust law merely because of their status.[20] In *California Liquor Dealers v. Midcal Aluminum, Inc.*, the Supreme Court formally recognized two requirements for obtaining antitrust immunity under the state action doctrine. First, the challenged restraint must be "one clearly articulated and affirmatively expressed as state policy," and, second, the policy must be "actively supervised" by the state itself.[21]

The Supreme Court decision in *Community Communications Co. v. City of Boulder* also has

---

19.   59 Stat. 33 (1945), as amended by 15 U.S.C.A., Sections 1011–15.

20.   City of Lafayette, Louisiana v. Louisiana Power and Light Co., 435 U.S. 389, 98 S.Ct. 1123 (1978).
21.   445 U.S. 97, 105 (1980).

implications which challenge the exercise of many municipal activities that were previously thought to be protected from antitrust scrutiny.[22] In *City of Boulder*, Boulder claimed that its ordinance placing a moratorium on the expansion of cable television was an act of government performed by the city acting as the state in local matters which enjoyed the *state action* exemption from Sherman Act lia-

---

22.   455 U.S. 40 (1982).

bility. The Supreme Court held that the requirement of "clear articulation and affirmative expression" was not fulfilled by the Colorado Home Rule Amendment, which granted autonomy to municipalities with respect to local matters. The implications in *City of Boulder* with respect to municipal corporations are so critical because they challenge many municipal activities which were previously thought to be shielded from the Sherman Act. Anticompetitive activities will now be subjected to a much closer antitrust scrutiny.

QUESTIONS AND CASE PROBLEMS

1. Assume the following events take place. Discuss which antitrust law has been *primarily* violated.
   (a) Acme, Inc. and Jiminez, Ltd. are interstate competitors selling similar appliances principally in the states of Wisconsin, Illinois, Minnesota, and Iowa. Acme and Jiminez agree that Acme will no longer sell in Wisconsin and Minnesota, and Jiminez will no longer sell in Iowa and Illinois.
   (b) The partnership of Montoya and Marsh is engaged in the oil well-head service industry in the states of New Mexico and Colorado. They presently have about 40 percent of the market for this service. The firm of West, Williams, and Wilson, Inc. are engaged in competition with the Montoya-Marsh partnership in the same state area. The West corporation has approximately 35 percent of the market. Montoya and Marsh acquire the stock and assets of the West corporation.

2. The Fuller Corporation, the leading manufacturer of electric transformers, and five other major manufacturers of electric transformers, agree to a five-year price maintenance maximum increase of 10 percent per year over their current prices. Green Interstate, an electric cooperative, who purchases large quantities of transformers on competitive bidding, purchased over $500,000 worth of transformers from Fuller over a three-year period. Green learns of the price maintenance agreement. The Department of Justice has filed no action against Fuller and the five other manufacturers. Discuss *fully* whether Green can bring a private action against Fuller.

3. Suntex, Inc. is an interstate manufacturer and seller of hair dryers. These hair dryers are sold directly to whole-

sale distributors at a price of $8.00 per unit. Suntex sells to two competing interstate wholesalers, Appliance Limited and Plug-In Appliances, Inc. Plug-In is the largest purchaser of hair dryers in the United States but usually only orders in quantities of 1,000. Appliance Limited is a smaller purchaser in total sales, but also orders in quantities of 1000 dryers. Plug-In threatens to purchase its dryers from Moontex, Inc., a competitor of Suntex Inc., unless Plug-In gets a 10 percent discount on its 1,000 dryer unit purchases. Suntex agrees to the 10 percent discount for Plug-In only. Discuss *fully* whether this is an antitrust violation.

4. Aztec, Inc. presently controls 55 percent of the market in the manufacture and sale of computers. The balance of the market is controlled by five other manufacturers, with Orange, Inc. having 25 percent of the market. Orange has an innovative research staff, but every time Orange introduces a faster, more powerful and efficient computer in the market, Aztec immediately informs its customers of the upcoming development of a competing computer which they will sell at 30 percent below the Orange price. Orange claims these activities of Aztec are an antitrust violation. Discuss *fully* whether this unilateral action by Aztec is an antitrust violation.

5. Meister Brau, Inc., was engaged in the business of brewing beers, malts, and ales. It acquired the Berger Meister Beer Company through a purchase of the latter's common stock. Berger Meister sold the beer it brewed through distributors who operated as individual businesses separate from Berger Meister. Soon after Meister Brau acquired Berger Meister, it terminated some of Berger Meister's distributors. The distributors handled the products of a number of other breweries, but they complained that the reduced sales volume that would result from their being terminated by Meister Brau would drive them out of business. The distributors thus brought suit against Meister Brau, alleging that its agreement with its new subsidiary, Berger Meister, to terminate the distributors

constituted a conspiracy in restraint of trade in violation of Section 1 of the Sherman Act. The distributors alleged that the terminations would reduce competition in a market that was already tending toward concentration. Has Meister Brau violated Section 1 of the Sherman Act? [Ricchetti v. Meister Brau, Inc., 431 F.2d 1211 (9th Cir. 1970)]

6. Since 1946 Bay Distributors, Inc., a Florida corporation located in the Tampa Bay area, had been engaged in the wholesale distribution and sale of various brands of wines and distilled spirits in approximately a thirteen-county area of the west coast of Florida. The wines that Bay sold included a line produced by United Vintners, Inc., most of which was marketed under the trade name "Italian Swiss Colony." Bay was the exclusive distributor in the Florida west coast area of United Vintners' wines. Between March 1965 and May 1970, Cal Distributing Company acted as Bay's subdistributor in the Sarasota area, which included two of the thirteen counties mentioned above. Cal sold no wine outside the Sarasota area. Although customers in the Sarasota area could have purchased United Vintners' products from either Cal or Bay, neither actually solicited customers from the other. On May 5, 1970, Bay notified Cal that it would no longer sell Cal United Vintners' wines. It would, however, continue to sell Cal all other wines for which Bay was the exclusive distributor. After Bay refused to sell United Vintners' products to Cal as a subdistributor, Bay started selling them directly to the retail businesses to which Cal had been selling them. Considering these facts, along with the other facts given below, answer the following questions. [Cal Distributing Co. v. Bay Distributors, Inc., 337 F.Supp. 1154 (M.D.Fla. 1971)]

(a) Which, if any, of the antitrust statutes discussed in this chapter might Bay have violated when it terminated Cal as its subdistributor? Be specific.

(b) Gallo Wines provides the primary competition to United Vintners. However, both Gallo and United Vintners face direct competition from all other wines. This competition prevents Bay from raising its prices without losing business. The competition provided by Gallo was described by Calvin LaHurd, the president of Cal Distributing Company, as "very, very vigorous." In fact, sales of Gallo Wines at wholesale have exceeded Bay's sales of United Vintners continuously for each month since December 1968. In addition, since December 1968, the monthly sales of United Vintners have never exceeded 22 percent of the total volume of wine sold to retailers in the relevant geographic area. In contrast, the monthly sales of Gallo wines by Tampa Wholesale Liquor Company, one of the area distributors, have averaged more than 22 percent of monthly wholesale wine sales in the relevant geographic area during the same period. In order to be deemed in violation of the antitrust laws, Bay Distributors must be shown to possess the power to control prices or

exclude competition in the relevant market. In order to establish this, Cal must show that there exists a dangerous probability of monopoly power over prices and competition within the relevant market, coupled with a specific intent to monopolize. On the basis of all the facts given, can Cal establish that Bay possessed the necessary *monopoly power* just described?

7. On August 5, 1969, at a hearing held before the Arizona Corporation Commission, the Arizona Water Company, a private corporation, sought and was granted the right to deliver water in a specified geographic area. Subsequently, the State of Arizona issued the company a "certificate of convenience and necessity," which confirmed the company's exclusive right to sell water in the specified area. In light of antitrust laws that prohibit the exercise of monopoly powers, should Arizona Water Company be granted this exclusive right? Under what conditions should the State of Arizona be allowed to withdraw the "certificate of convenience and necessity" that it awarded Arizona Water Company? [Fernandez v. Arizona Water Co., 21 Ariz.App. 107, 516 P.2d 49 (1974)]

8. The Professional Golfers Association of America (PGA) was founded in 1916 as a voluntary, unincorporated, nonprofit association. It has some 4,300 members, and it sponsors or cosponsors substantially all of the professional golf tournaments held in the United States. In order to compete in these tournaments, a player must be either a member of the PGA, an approved tournament player, or one of the limited number of participants designated or invited by the local sponsor of the tournament. Because of the increasing popularity of professional tournament golf, some means had to be found to limit the number of golfers who could enter these tournaments. PGA rules limiting entry to the categories of persons named above and defining the qualifications necessary for nonmember entrance were intended to accomplish this purpose. PGA gives official recognition to many tournaments that it neither sponsors nor cosponsors. These "approved tournaments" are free from any PGA control; yet PGA plans its schedule around them and counts them in determining its official standings. Herbert C. Deesen was a professional golfer who competed for several years in PGA-sponsored tournaments. Deesen sued the PGA, alleging that its sheer size and vast control over professional golf tournaments in the United States amounted to monopoly control in violation of Section 2 of the Sherman Antitrust Act. Do the PGA's activities violate the Sherman Act? [Deesen v. Professional Golfers Ass'n of America, 358 F.2d 165 (9th Cir. 1966)]

9. American Oil Company was a producer and distributor of oil, gas, and related products. Olson was engaged in bulk distribution and retail sales of oil products. Early in 1967, American decided to acquire control of Olson's bulk distribution operations, and it purchased substantially all of Olson's assets. Thereafter, American hired

Lawrence McMullin to assume control of the Olson operation for American. Under the agreement, McMullin was to take charge of the Olson plant and was to be paid on a commission basis in lieu of salary for the bulk petroleum sales that he procured. In addition, the contract between American and McMullin imposed certain territorial limitations and price restrictions on sales by the operations that McMullin was to control. Could the agreement between McMullin and American Oil imposing price restrictions and territorial controls on the operations of which McMullin took charge constitute a violation of Section 1 of the Sherman Antitrust Act? Explain. [American Oil Co. v. McMullin, 508 F.2d 1345 (10th Cir. 1975)]

10. The National Collegiate Athletic Association (NCAA) plays an important role in regulating amateur collegiate sports. As a result of various surveys and reports, the NCAA concluded that television adversely affects college football game attendance and, further, that the telecasting of such games seriously threatens the athletic system in the United States. The NCAA subsequently imposed regulations that restrained the ability of member colleges to negotiate and contract for the telecasting of college football games. Some member colleges began to assert that colleges with major football programs deserved to have a greater imput in the formulation of football television policy than they presently had in the NCAA. In addition, when some member colleges proceeded to enter into a television agreement with NBC on its own, NCAA announced that it would take disciplinary action against any member that complied with this contract. Has there been a Sherman Act violation here? If so, does the *rule of reason* or *per se* analysis apply to the NCAA's television plan? [National Collegiate Athletic Association v. University of Oklahoma *et al.*, 468 U.S. ——, 104 S.Ct. 2948, 82 L.Ed.2d 70 (1984)]

49

GOVERNMENT REGULATION
Antitrust: Enforcement and Trends

In the last half-century, numerous court decisions and several amendments to the antitrust statutes have modified and narrowed the range of acceptable business behavior. Such behavior often involves potential violations of more than one statute. At the federal level, public enforcement activities have been divided between the Antitrust Division of the Justice Department and the Bureau of Competition of the Federal Trade Commission. There are also various subunits at the state level.

Antitrust and trade regulation enforcement is generally categorized in one of two ways: either as dealing with *horizontal activities* or as dealing with *vertical activities*. Horizontal activities are those that involve two or more firms at the same level in an industry, whereas vertical activities are those that comprise *various* levels of production, distribution, and marketing within an industry. A third category, *mergers*, involves conglomerates in which unrelated and diversified businesses are acquired by a conglomerate firm.

ENFORCEMENT OF PROHIBITIONS ON HORIZONTAL ACTIVITIES

The probability of a costly prison sentence or the payment of damages deters most, if not all, business people from openly entering into agreements or con-

spiracies to fix prices, boycott competitors, or perform other unlawful activities. However, often the courts must determine whether the parties acted in concert on the basis of an implicit agreement to perform such unlawful activities. Such implicit agreements are difficult to detect. The courts must also investigate business behavior suspected of violating the antitrust statutes or associated administrative rules.

Enforcement of prohibitions against certain activities has caused well-defined areas of antitrust action to emerge. These areas include concerted action, certain information exchanges, horizontal market divisions, group boycotts, monopolization, and other horizontal actions.

Defining Concerted Action

Businesspersons are not likely to enter into open agreements to restrain trade. Consequently, the courts must infer the purpose of agreements, combinations, and contracts to determine whether they violate the antitrust laws. In other words, what intent is evidenced by the conduct of the business?

Until recently courts looked at the *effect* of the business practice to determine the intent of the participants. If the effect was to reduce competition in the market, a criminal conspiracy existed as a matter of law. In 1978, however, the Supreme Court reversed that trend in *United States v. United States Gypsum Co.*[1] The Supreme Court held that a defendant's *state of mind or intent* is an element that must be considered in determining guilt. The Court stated that "an effect on prices, without more, will not support a criminal conviction under the Sherman Act."[2]

Trade Associations

Exchanges of information between related businesses pose special antitrust problems. Competitors often organize trade associations in order to pursue common interests. These associations disseminate information, represent the members' business interests before governmental bodies, initiate joint ad-

vertising campaigns, and attempt to police their own industry. Trade association activities are by their very nature joint actions and are subject to the antitrust laws.

In some cases the court looks beyond the agreement to a particular effect on prices. In *National Soc'y of Professional Engineers v. United States*,[3] the government found that the Society's Code of Ethics, which prohibited discussion of prices with a potential customer until after the customer had chosen an engineer, was a Section 1 violation. The court found that this ban on competitive bidding was "nothing less than a frontal assault on the basic policy of the Sherman Act."

In the following case, a standard-setting organization is held liable, on an apparent authority theory, for the antitrust violations of its agents.

---

1.   438 U.S. 422, 98 S.Ct. 2864 (1978).
2.   438 U.S. 422, 435 (1978).

---

3.   435 U.S. 679, 98 S.Ct. 1355 (1978).

AMERICAN SOCIETY OF MECHANICAL ENGINEERS, INC. v. HYDROLEVEL CORP.

Supreme Court of the United States, 1982.
456 U.S. 556, 102 S.Ct. 1935, pet. for rehearing denied 102 S.Ct. 3502.

BACKGROUND AND FACTS   *The petitioner, The American Society of Mechanical Engineers, Inc. (ASME), is a nonprofit corporation with over 90,000 members. It promulgates engineering codes mainly through the work of volunteers from all fields of mechanical engineering, and many of these codes are incorporated into federal, state, and local laws. Two of ASME's volunteer workers, James and Hardin, issued an advisory opinion on ASME's letterhead stating that a product manufactured by the respondent, Hydrolevel Corporation, was unsafe. James, who worked for a company that competes with Hydrolevel, used this fraudulent letter to discourage customers from dealing with the respondent.*

Having learned of the letter, Hydrolevel urged ASME to issue a correction explaining that the Hydrolevel product conformed to ASME's safety codes. ASME, unaware of James's motives in issuing the letter, declined to refute the dishonest statements. Hydrolevel sued ASME for violations of Sections 1 and 2 of the Sherman Act. Both the district court and the court of appeals ruled in favor of Hydrolevel. The jury awarded Hydrolevel $7.5 million in damages. ASME petitioned the Supreme Court for certiorari.

Justice BLACKMUN delivered the opinion of the Court.
*   *   *   *

As the Court of Appeals observed, under general rules of agency law, principals are liable when their agents act with apparent authority and commit torts analogous to the antitrust violation presented by this case. *   *   *
*   *   *   *

ASME's system of codes and interpretative advice would not be effective if the statement of its agents did not carry with them the assurance that persons in the affected industries could reasonably rely upon their apparent trustworthiness. Behind the principal's liability under an apparent authority theory, then, is "business expediency—the

desire that third persons should be given reasonable protection in dealing with agents."
Restatement § 262, Comment a, p. 572. *   *   *
*   *   *   *

In addition, ASME contends it should not bear the risk of loss for antitrust violations committed by its agents acting with apparent authority because it is a nonprofit organization, not a business seeking profit. But it is beyond debate that nonprofit organizations can be held liable under the antitrust laws. *   *   * Although ASME may not operate for profit, it does derive benefits from its codes, including the fees the Society receives for its code-related publications and services, the prestige the codes bring to the Society, the influence they permit ASME to wield, and the aid the standards provide the profession of mechanical engineering. Since the antitrust violation in this case could not have occurred without ASME's codes and ASME's methods of administering them, it is not unfitting that ASME be liable for the damages arising from that violation. *   *   * Furthermore, as shown above, ASME is in the best position to take precautions that will prevent future antitrust violations. Thus, the fact that ASME is a nonprofit organization does not weaken the force of the antitrust and agency principles that indicate that ASME should be liable for Hydrolevel's antitrust injuries.

We need not delineate today the outer boundaries of the antitrust liability of standard-setting organizations for the actions of their agents committed with apparent authority. There is no doubt here that Hardin acted within his apparent authority when he answered an inquiry about ASME's Boiler and Pressure Vessel Code as the chairman of the relevant ASME subcommittee. And in this case, we do not face a challenge to a good-faith interpretation of an ASME code reasonably supported by health or safety considerations. *   *   *

When ASME's agents act in its name, they are able to affect the lives of large numbers of people and the competitive fortunes of businesses throughout the country. By holding ASME liable under the antitrust laws for the antitrust violations of its agents committed with apparent authority, we recognize the important role of ASME and its agents in the economy, and we help to ensure that standard-setting organizations will act with care when they permit their agents to speak for them. *   *   *
*   *   *   *

The judgment of the court of appeals was affirmed. Thus ASME, a nonprofit, standard-setting organization, was held liable on an apparent authority theory for the antitrust violations of its agents.   **DECISION AND REMEDY**

Horizontal Market Divisions

Dividing a territory for the sale of a specific product into two or more divisions allocated by agreement specifically to individual, competing companies is also a per se violation of the Sherman Act. For example, if two cement companies normally sell cement throughout the entire state of California, they cannot enter into an agreement in which one of them sells only in southern California and the other sells only in northern California. As a matter of law, this is illegal, even if it might seem "reasonable."

Joint Refusals to Deal, or Group Boycotts

Sellers of goods and services generally have the right to select customers, provided that such a selection is not based on a customer's religious beliefs, color, sex, or place of natural origin. However, when two or more sellers act in concert to refuse to sell to a particular buyer or class of buyers, the courts have generally found such acts unlawful under either the Sherman Act or the Clayton Act, or both. In the following classic case, a group of automobile dealers encouraged General Motors to stop further sales to a discount automobile sales outlet.

**UNITED STATES v.
GENERAL MOTORS
CORP.**

Supreme Court of the United
States, 1966.
384 U.S. 127, 86 S.Ct. 1321.

BACKGROUND AND FACTS   *Beginning in the late 1950s, "discount houses" and "referral services" began offering to sell new cars to the public at allegedly bargain prices. By 1960 about eighty-five Chevrolet dealers, without authorization from General Motors, furnished cars to the discount houses. As the volume of these sales grew, the nonparticipating Chevrolet dealers located near one or more of these discount outlets began to feel the financial pinch.*

The nonparticipating dealers became increasingly disgruntled. They began to flood the Chevrolet division of General Motors with letters and telegrams asking for help. Within a month, General Motors had elicited from each dealer a promise not to do business with any discounters. But such agreements would require policing—a fact that had been anticipated. General Motors elicited the help of three of its associations and a number of individual dealers.

The associations made spot checks to assure that no Chevrolet dealer continued to supply a discounter with cars. They did this by hiring professional investigators to purchase cars from dealers suspected of cooperating with discounters. Each association contributed $5,000 to provide a fund with which the "professional" shopper would pay for the automobile.

Armed with information about violations obtained from the dealers or their associations, General Motors's staff asked the offending dealer to come in and talk with them. The dealer was then confronted with the car purchased by the "professional shopper," the documents of the sale, and, in most cases, a tape recording of the transaction. In every instance, the embarrassed dealer repurchased the car, sometimes at a substantial loss, and promised to stop such sales in the future.

The government charged that these practices were unlawful and that they constituted a conspiracy to restrain trade in violation of the Sherman Act.

FORTAS, Justice.

*   *   *   *

Both the Government and the appellees urge the importance, for purposes of decision, of the "location clause" in the Dealer Selling Agreement which prohibits a franchised dealer from moving to or establishing "a new or different location, branch sales office, branch service station, or place of business *   *   * without the prior written approval of Chevrolet." The appellees contend that this contractual provision is lawful, and that it justifies their actions. They argue that General Motors acted lawfully to prevent its dealers from violating the "location clause," that the described arrangements with discounters constitute the establishment of additional sales outlets in violation of the clause, and that the individual dealers—and their associations— have an interest in uniform compliance with the franchise agreement, which interest they lawfully sought to vindicate.

The Government invites us to join in the assumption, only for purposes of this case, that the "location clause" encompasses sales by dealers through the medium of discounters. But it urges us to hold that, so construed, the provision is unlawful as an unreasonable restraint of trade in violation of the Sherman Act.

*   *   * We have here a classic conspiracy in restraint of trade: joint, collaborative action by dealers, the appellee associations, and General Motors to eliminate a class of competitors by terminating business dealings between them and a minority of Chevrolet dealers and to deprive franchised dealers of their freedom to deal through discounters if they so choose. Against this fact of unlawful combination, the "location clause" is of no avail. * * * And, because the action taken constitutes a combination or conspiracy, it is not necessary to consider what might be the legitimate interest of a dealer in securing compliance by others with the "location clause," or the lawfulness of action a dealer might individually take to vindicate this interest.

* * * Neither individual dealers nor the associations acted independently or separately. The dealers collaborated, through the associations and otherwise, among themselves and with General Motors, both to enlist the aid of General Motors and to enforce dealers' promises to forsake the discounters. The associations explicitly entered into a joint venture to assist General Motors in policing the dealers' promises, and their joint proffer of aid was accepted and utilized by General Motors.

* * * General Motors sought to elicit from all the dealers agreements, substantially interrelated and interdependent, that none of them would do business with the discounters. These agreements were hammered out in meetings between nonconforming dealers and officials of General Motors' Chevrolet Division, and in telephone conversations with other dealers. It was acknowledged from the beginning that substantial unanimity would be essential if the agreements were to be forthcoming. And once the agreements were secured, General Motors both solicited and employed the assistance of its alleged co-conspirators in helping to police them. What resulted was a fabric interwoven by many strands of joint action to eliminate the discounters from participation in the market, to inhibit the free choice of franchised dealers to select their own methods of trade and to provide multilateral surveillance and enforcement. This process for achieving and enforcing the desired objective can by no stretch of the imagination be described as "unilateral" or merely "parallel."

The protection of price competition from conspiratorial restraint is an object of special solicitude under the antitrust laws. We cannot respect that solicitude by closing our eyes to the effect upon price competition of the removal from the market, by combination or conspiracy, of a class of traders. Nor do we propose to construe the Sherman Act to prohibit conspiracies to fix prices at which competitors may sell, but to allow conspiracies or combinations to put competitors out of business entirely.

The Supreme Court found that, beyond question, these activities were a conspiracy to restrain trade in violation of Section 1 of the Sherman Act.

DECISION AND REMEDY

Monopolization

Section 2 of the Sherman Act makes practices to "monopolize or attempt to monopolize" unlawful behavior. In practice, "to monopolize" has often been interpreted to mean actions that aggressively exclude a competitor.

A number of factors are considered. In 1966, the Supreme Court defined two essential elements of monopolization.[4] These elements are:

1. The possession of monopoly power in the relevant market.
2. The willful acquisition or maintenance of that power as distinguished from growth or development

as a consequence of a superior product, business acumen, or historic accident.

Monopoly power is usually measured in terms of the size of the market share held by the defendant company. Significant monopoly is associated with a total market share of 75 percent or more, whereas a market share of 25 percent or less is generally considered to be insufficient market power to support most antitrust actions.

Defining the Relevant Market One of the most important questions facing the courts is: What is the relevant market for measuring monopoly power? Over time the courts have narrowed the definition of the relevant market by considering more information about the characteristics of the product, its substitutes, and the geographic area where the product is

---

4. United States v. Grinnel Corp., 384 U.S. 563, 86 S.Ct. 1698 (1966).

sold. Because determination of the market share is extremely sensitive to the definition of the relevant market, considerable care is taken by both sides in assembling and presenting evidence to determine the market.

The importance of market-sharing was well illustrated in the 1945 Alcoa decision.[5] If the relevant market consisted only of those who bought a virgin ingot, then Alcoa was the sole producer at that time. Another definition of the relevant market included those who bought secondary aluminum, which is an almost perfect substitute for virgin ingot, and thus significantly broadened the relevant market and lowered the measure of Alcoa's share. And when the market was further broadened to include imported fabricated and secondary aluminum, the measure of Alcoa's share fell to roughly 33 percent of the aluminum production market.

Once the relevant market is determined, the court then looks at the extent to which the defendant has exerted pressures on competitors, has prevented potential firms from entering the market, or has engaged in other actions not associated with "natural" growth.

Other Horizontal Restraints

Over the years, the traditional methods for fixing prices, such as allocating territories or boycotting competitors, have been rapidly disappearing. Consequently, the Federal Trade Commission has revised its enforcement approach to focus more on the hidden forms of restricting competition. In the early 1970s, the commission began the first of a number of cases attacking shopping center leases that give major tenants a veto over other tenants. For example, in the case of *Tysons Corner*,[6] the three major department stores had been given lease arrangements that permitted them to disapprove prospective tenants who wished to rent space in the shopping center. These clauses were ruled to be *prima facie* evidence of an unreasonable restraint of trade. The commission ruled that agreements creating approval rights as broad as those involved in the *Tysons Corner* case are per se illegal and amount to an agreement to fix prices.

ENFORCEMENT OF PROHIBITIONS ON VERTICAL RESTRAINTS

Vertical restraints involve the distribution of goods, the power of suppliers to engage in exclusionary practices, and price discrimination. They include those situations where manufacturers attempt to restrict the prices, locations, customers, or retailing methods of goods being sold.

Distribution Restrictions

Restriction on the distribution of goods may come in the form of resale price maintenance, consignment through agents, or territorial or customer restrictions.

Resale Price Maintenance   Resale price maintenance, or "fair trade," agreements arise when the manufacturers specify what the retail price to consumers must be. Usually, either a minimum or a maximum retail price will be specified in these cases. In the well-known *Dr. Miles* decision, the Supreme Court held that a manufacturer who sold medicine to wholesalers was not entitled to restrict resale of the medicine by specifying minimum prices for retailers.[7] Later, this rigid rule against vertical price-fixing was extended to prohibit the specifying of maximum as well as minimum prices.[8]

Consignment through Agents   The antitrust laws are more lenient in permitting manufacturers who continue to retain title and to bear most of the associated risk of ownership to specify the terms of sale, including limits on resale prices. Until 1974, General Electric sold its light bulbs on consignment with retail outlets. In turn, retailers sold the light bulbs at prices specified by General Electric and received commissions on sales. The court concluded that this was an agency relationship and upheld General Electric's right to specify the retail price of the light bulbs.[9]

5.   United States v. Aluminum Co. of America, 148 F.2d 416 (2d Cir. 1945).
6.   Tysons Corner Regional Shopping Center, 85 FTC 970 (1975).

7.   Dr. Miles Medical Co. v. John D. Park & Sons Co., 220 U.S. 373, 31 S.Ct. 376 (1911).
8.   Albrecht v. Herald Co., 390 U.S. 145, 88 S.Ct. 869 (1968).
9.   United States v. General Elec. Co., 272 U.S. 476, 47 S.Ct. 192 (1926).

Territorial and Customer Restrictions In arranging for the distribution of a firm's products, manufacturers often wish to insulate dealers from direct competition from other dealers selling the firm's product. In this case, they may institute territorial restrictions or they may attempt to prohibit wholesalers or retailers from reselling the products to certain classes of buyers, such as competing retailers.

In *United States v. Arnold, Schwinn & Co.*,[10] such restrictions (of either the territorial or consumer type) in manufacturer contracts with wholesalers or retailers were held to be a Section 1 Sherman Act violation. As illustrated in the following case, territorial and customer restrictions are lawful unless their use unreasonably restricts trade.

10. 388 U.S. 365, 87 S.Ct. 1856 (1967).

BACKGROUND AND FACTS *Prior to 1962, like most other television manufacturers, Sylvania sold its televisions to independent or company-owned distributors, who in turn resold to a large and diverse group of retailers. In 1962, Sylvania phased out its wholesale distributors and began to sell its televisions directly to a smaller and more select group of franchised retailers. Sylvania limited the number of franchises granted for any given area and required each franchisee to sell the Sylvania products from only the locations of the franchise. A franchise did not constitute an exclusive territory, and Sylvania retained sole discretion to increase the number of retailers in an area, depending on the success or failure of existing retailers in developing their market. Continental T.V., a Sylvania franchisee, withheld all payments due for Sylvania products after a dispute over additional locations sought by Continental. John P. Maguire & Co., the finance company that handled the credit arrangements between Sylvania and its franchisees, sued Continental for payment and for return of secured merchandise. Continental claimed that Sylvania had violated Section 1 of the Sherman Act by entering into and enforcing franchise agreements that permitted the sale of Sylvania products only in specified locations.*

CONTINENTAL T.V., INC. v. GTE SYLVANIA, INC.
Supreme Court of the United States, 1977.
433 U.S. 36, 97 S.Ct. 2549.

POWELL, Justice.

*   *   *   *

In the present case it is undisputed that title to the televisions passed from Sylvania to Continental. Thus, the *Schwinn per se* rule applies unless Sylvania's restriction on locations falls outside Schwinn's prohibition against a manufacturer's attempting to restrict a "retailer's freedom as to where and to whom it will resell the products." As the Court of Appeals conceded, the language of *Schwinn* is clearly broad enough to apply to the present case. Unlike the Court of Appeals, however, we are unable to find a principled basis for distinguishing *Schwinn* from the case now before us.

Both Schwinn and Sylvania sought to reduce but not to eliminate competition among their respective retailers through the adoption of a franchise system. Although it was not one of the issues addressed by the District Court or presented on appeal by the Government, the Schwinn franchise plan included a location restriction similar to the one challenged here. These restrictions allowed Schwinn and Sylvania to regulate the amount of competition among their retailers by preventing a franchisee from selling franchised products from outlets other than the one covered by the franchise agreement. To exactly the same end, the Schwinn franchise plan included a companion restriction, apparently not found in the Sylvania plan, that prohibited franchised retailers from selling Schwinn products to nonfranchised retailers. In *Schwinn* the Court expressly held that this restriction was impermissible under the broad principle stated there. In intent and competitive impact, the retail-customer restriction in *Schwinn* is indistinguishable from the location restriction in the present case. In both cases the restrictions limited the freedom of the retailer to dispose of the purchased products as he desired. The fact that one restriction was addressed to territory and the other to customers is irrelevant to functional antitrust analysis and, indeed, to the language and broad thrust of the opinion in *Schwinn*. As Mr. Chief Justice Hughes stated: "Realities must dominate the judgement. * * * The Anti-Trust Act aims at substance."

* * * *

Vertical restrictions reduce intrabrand competition by limiting the number of sellers of a particular product competing for the business of a given group of buyers. Location restrictions have this effect because of practical constraints on the effective marketing area of retail outlets. Although intrabrand competition may be reduced, the ability of retailers to exploit the resulting market may be limited both by the ability of consumers to travel to other franchised locations and, perhaps more importantly, to purchase the competing products of other manufacturers. None of these key variables, however, is affected by the form of the transaction by which a manufacturer conveys his products to the retailers.

Vertical restrictions promote interbrand competition by allowing the manufacturer to achieve certain efficiencies in the distribution of his products. These "redeeming virtues" are implicit in every decision sustaining vertical restrictions under the rule of reason. Economists have identified a number of ways in which manufacturers can use such restrictions to compete more effectively against other manufacturers. For example, new manufacturers and manufacturers entering new markets can use the restrictions in order to induce competent and aggressive retailers to make the kind of investment of capital and labor that is often required in the distribution of products unknown to the consumer. Established manufacturers can use them to induce retailers to engage in promotional activities or to provide service and repair facilities necessary to the efficient marketing of their products. Service and repair are vital for many products, such as automobiles and major household appliances. The availability and quality of such services affect a manufacturer's goodwill and the competitiveness of his product. Because of market imperfections such as the so-called "free rider" effect, these services might not be provided by retailers in a purely competitive situation, despite the fact that each retailer's benefit would be greater if all provided the services than if none did.

DECISION AND REMEDY *The Supreme Court reversed the trial court's holding that Sylvania had violated Section 1 of the Sherman Act.*

COMMENTS *In this case, the Supreme Court focused directly on the applications of a strict per se rule. Its rejection of a rigid rule in favor of a "rule of reason" approach has been extended to other important areas of antitrust law. Thus the courts and antitrust enforcers will look at the challenged restraint's impact on competition. In the case of* Coors,[11] *the Federal Trade Commission found that territorial restrictions on Coors distributors with simultaneous wholesale and retail minimum prices reduced competition in the beer industry.*

---

11.   83 F.T.C. 32 (1973).

Exclusionary Practices

Exclusionary practices involve refusals to deal and so-called tying arrangements in which firms refuse to sell or lease a good unless the buyer agrees to purchase other goods or articles produced or distributed by the seller. Exclusionary practices also include arrangements wherein the seller requires the purchaser, usually a retailer, not to sell products of competing firms.

Refusals to Deal   Refusals to deal were discussed under the topic of prohibitions on horizontal activities. In vertical arrangements, the Supreme Court has generally given firms the freedom to refuse to sell to individual buyers. In *United States v. Colgate & Co.*,[12] the Court held that a manufacturer's advance announcement that it would not sell to price cutters was not a violation of the Sherman Act.

Tying Arrangements   A tying arrangement is one in which the seller of a product conditions the sale of that product upon the buyer's agreement to purchase another product produced or distributed by the seller. For example, the seller of a copier machine may tie the sale of a *tying product* (the copier) to the purchase of a *tied product* (paper). The legality of such arrangements depends on many factors, particularly the business purpose or effect of the arrangement.

In 1936, the Supreme Court held that International Business Machines' practice of requiring the purchase of cards (the tied product) as a condition of leasing its tabulation machines (the tying product) was unlawful.[13] The Court, however, has not applied a strict rule against tying arrangements. In *United States Steel Corp. v. Fortner Enterprises, Inc.*,[14] the Court ruled in favor of U.S. Steel despite the existence of a tie-in between the purchase of prefabricated homes (the tied product) and credit (the tying product). There was no evidence that U.S. Steel had significant economic power in the tying product or credit market, and its arrangement was therefore found to be lawful.

Exclusive Dealings   Section 3 of the Clayton Act as amended prohibits exclusive dealing contracts when the effect of these contracts would be "to substantially lessen competition or tend to create a monopoly."

Exclusive dealing contracts arise when a seller or manufacturer requires that the buyer not purchase the products of competitive sellers. Despite its similarity with a tying contract, an exclusive dealing arrangement is subject to a different judicial standard. In general, the courts apply a modified rule of reason in determining whether the arrangement will substantially lessen competition.

The leading exclusive dealing decision is that of *Standard Oil Co. of California v. United States*.[15] In this case, the largest gasoline seller in the nation made exclusive dealing contracts with independent stations in seven western states. The contracts involved 16 percent of all retail outlets, whose sales were approximately 7 percent of all retail sales in that market. The Supreme Court found that these contracts were a Section 3 violation of the Clayton Act.

Requirements Contracts   Another type of exclusive dealing arrangement requires that the buyer of a particular commodity purchase all that the buyer will use of that commodity for a specified period of time. This is called a requirements contract. Its legality is judged by whether or not it results in a substantial lessening of competition. In *Tampa Elec. Co. v. Nashville Coal Co.*,[16] the Supreme Court upheld a contract for the Nashville Coal Company to supply all the coal required by Tampa Electric Company for its electricity generation. The Court defined the relevant geographic market as one involving at least seven states, yielding a contract market share of less than 1 percent, an amount judged to be insubstantial.

Price Discrimination

Although price discrimination that potentially lessens competition or creates a monopoly is unlawful, two difficulties arise in enforcing Section 2 of the Clayton Act (Robinson-Patman Act). First, the various exemptions—such as changing market conditions, meeting price competition from other competitors, and passing on actual cost savings to customers—make proof of a violation difficult. Second, the Federal Trade Commission only sporadically enforces the act.

---

12.   250 U.S. 300, 39 S.Ct. 465 (1919).
13.   International Business Machines v. United States, 298 U.S. 131, 56 S.Ct. 701 (1936).
14.   429 U.S. 610, 97 S.Ct. 861 (1977).

15.   337 U.S. 293, 69 S.Ct. 1051 (1949).
16.   365 U.S. 320, 81 S.Ct. 623 (1961).

Other Vertical Restraints

Antitrust enforcers also investigate other vertical restraints, such as *reciprocal buying*, that promote unfair practices or impede competition. Reciprocal arrangements exist when the seller of one good is required to purchase one or more goods provided by the buyer of the initial good. Thus, if an automobile manufacturer sells autos to a leasing company, and in exchange the leasing company requires employees of the automobile manufacturer to rent cars from the leasing company, a reciprocal buying arrangement exists; and this is illegal.

MERGERS

The statutory authority for enforcing anticompetitive mergers is Section 7 of the Clayton Act. This section was introduced because it was feared that concentration would potentially facilitate collusion among sellers in the market, and that such collusion would be difficult to detect.

Horizontal Mergers

In general, the FTC and Antitrust Division of the Justice Department determine the legality of **horizontal mergers** by looking at the degree of concentration or market shares of merging firms, although the Court has indicated that it will look at the likely effects of the merger as well. Thus, if a merger facilitates horizontal collusion without increasing production or marketing efficiencies, it will be declared unlawful.

Mergers will be permitted when they enhance consumer welfare by increasing efficiency if they do not increase the probability of horizontal collusion. In the case of *U.S. v. Philadelphia National Bank*,[17] the commission held that even in situations with low entry barriers, there may be a loss of actual competition. Thus, mergers can be declared illegal even where entry is relatively easy, as illustrated by the following case.

---

17.   374 U.S. 321 (1963).

UNITED STATES v.
VON'S GROCERY CO.
Supreme Court of the United
States, 1966.
384 U.S. 270, 86 S.Ct. 1478.

BACKGROUND AND FACTS   *In 1958, Von's Grocery Company ranked third in retail sales in the Los Angeles area. Its largest direct competitor, Shopping Bag Food Stores, ranked sixth in retail sales for the same period. The merger of these two highly successful, expanding, and aggressive competitors created the second largest grocery chain in Los Angeles, with sales of almost $173 million annually. The number of small business owners operating single grocery stores in the Los Angeles retail grocery market had been dropping in the years prior to the merger, and after it, the number dropped still further. The grocery business in the Los Angeles area was being concentrated in the hands of fewer and fewer owners, as small grocery companies were continually being absorbed by the larger firms through mergers.*

*On March 25, 1960, the United States brought this action, charging that Von's Grocery Company's acquisitions of its direct competitor, Shopping Bag Food Stores, violated Section 7 of the Clayton Act, which, as amended in 1950 by the Celler-Kefauver Anti-Merger Act, provides in relevant part: "That no corporation engaged in commerce * * * shall acquire the whole or any part of the assets of another corporation engaged also in commerce, where in any line of commerce in any section of the country, the effect of such acquisition may be substantially to lessen competition, or to tend to create a monopoly."*

On March 28, 1960, three days later, the district court refused to grant the government's motion for a temporary restraining order. After a hearing, the district court concluded that there was not a reasonable probability that the merger would tend "substantially to lessen competition" or "create a monopoly" in violation of Section 7. Immediately, Von's took over all of Shopping Bag's capital stock and assets, including its thirty-six grocery stores in Los Angeles. The government appealed directly to the Supreme Court of the United States.[18]

BLACK, Justice.

*　*　*　*

　*　*　* The sole question here is whether the District Court properly concluded on the facts before it that the Government had failed to prove a violation of § 7.

*　*　*　*

From this country's beginning there has been an abiding and widespread fear of the evils which flow from monopoly—that is the concentration of economic power in the hands of a few. On the basis of this fear, Congress in 1890, when many of the Nation's industries were already concentrated into what it deemed too few hands, passed the Sherman Act in an attempt to prevent further concentration and to preserve competition among a large number of sellers. Several years later, in 1897, this Court emphasized this policy of the Sherman Act by calling attention to the tendency of powerful business combinations to restrain competition "by driving out of business the small dealers and worthy men whose lives have been spent therein, and who might be unable to readjust themselves to their altered surroundings." The Sherman Act failed to protect the smaller businessmen from elimination through the monopolistic pressures of large combinations which used mergers to grow ever more powerful. As a result in 1914 Congress, viewing mergers as a continuous, pervasive threat to small business, passed § 7 of the Clayton Act which prohibited corporations under most circumstances from merging by purchasing the stock of their competitors. Ingenious businessmen, however, soon found a way to avoid § 7 and corporations began to merge simply by purchasing their rivals' assets. This Court in 1926, over the dissent of Justice Brandeis, joined by Chief Justice Taft and Justices Holmes and Stone approved this device for avoiding § 7 and mergers continued to concentrate economic power into fewer and fewer hands until 1950 when Congress passed the Celler-Kefauver Anti-Merger Act now before us.

Like the Sherman Act in 1890 and the Clayton Act in 1914, the basic purpose of the 1950 Celler-Kefauver Act was to prevent economic concentration in the American economy by keeping a large number of small competitors. *　*　* "The dominant theme pervading congressional consideration of the 1950 amendments was a fear of what was considered to be a rising tide of economic concentration in the American economy." To arrest this "rising tide" toward concentration into too few hands and to halt the gradual demise of the small businessman, Congress decided to clamp down with vigor on mergers. It both revitalized § 7 of the Clayton Act by "plugging its loophole" and broadened its scope so as not only to prohibit mergers between competitors, the effect of which "may be substantially to lessen competition, or to tend to create a monopoly" but to prohibit all mergers having that effect. By using these terms in § 7 which look not merely to the actual present effect of a merger but instead to its effect upon future competition, Congress sought to preserve competition among many small businesses by arresting a trend toward concentration in its incipiency before that trend developed to the point that a market was left in the grip of a few big companies.

*　*　*

The facts of this case present exactly the threatening trend toward concentration which Congress wanted to halt. The number of small grocery companies in the Los Angeles retail grocery market had been declining rapidly before the merger and continued to decline rapidly afterwards. This rapid decline in the number of grocery store owners moved hand in hand with a large number of significant absorptions of the small

---

18.　Direct appeal is authorized by Section 2 of the expediting act, 15 U.S.C. 29.

companies by the larger ones. In the midst of this steadfast trend toward concentration, Von's and Shopping Bag, two of the most successful and largest companies in the area, jointly owning 66 grocery stores merged to become the second largest chain in Los Angeles. This merger cannot be defended on the ground that one of the companies was about to fail or that the two had to merge to save themselves from destruction by some larger and more powerful competitor. What we have on the contrary is simply the case of two already powerful companies merging in a way which makes them even more powerful than they were before. If ever such a merger would not violate § 7, certainly it does when it takes place in a market characterized by a long and continuous trend toward fewer and fewer owner-competitors which is exactly the sort of trend which Congress, with power to do so, declared must be arrested.

DECISION AND REMEDY *The judgment of the district court was reversed and the case was remanded to the district court to order that Von's Grocery Company divest itself of Shopping Bag's capital stock and assets, including the thirty-six grocery stores in the Los Angeles area.*

COMMENTS *This 1966 Supreme Court decision has recently come under attack. In its opinion, the Supreme Court suggests that the rapid decline in the number of small grocery companies increases the very concentration that Congress wanted to halt. However, a decline of the number of firms in the market does not necessarily increase concentration. Concentration pertains to the market shares held by the largest four or eight firms; it does not refer to the total number of firms in the market. Yet United States v. Von's Grocery Co. is illustrative of the legislative histories behind the Sherman and Clayton Acts. The Court emphasizes that Section 7 of the Clayton Act deals with probabilities, not certainties, since by its terms Section 7 looks to both the present and future effects of a proposed merger.*

Vertical Mergers

Vertical mergers occur when a company at one stage of production acquires a company at a higher or lower stage of production. Thus, the acquisition of a tire plant by an automobile manufacturer would constitute a backward vertical integration, while acquisition of a car-renting agency would constitute a forward vertical integration. The FTC's approach to vertical mergers depends on a number of factors, including the definition of the relevant product in geographic markets as well as the characteristics identified as impeding competition. For example, the commission will attack any vertical merger that prevents competitors of either party from competing in a segment of the market that otherwise would be open to them.[19]

Conglomerate Mergers

Conglomerate mergers often extend product lines at the retail level, particularly among products that are complementary, although mergers can also occur among firms using similar suppliers. A large number of conglomerate mergers, however, occur when the merging firms have no direct functional business link. In such mergers there are no changes in market structure, market shares, or concentration ratios. In many cases, conglomerate mergers serve to reduce overhead costs by spreading them over a larger range of output and reducing advertising and other promotional costs. The following case is illustrative of a *product extension* conglomerate merger.

---

19.   Brown Shoe Co. v. United States, 370 U.S. 294, 82 S.Ct. 1502 (1962).

BACKGROUND AND FACTS   *The Federal Trade Commission argued that Procter & Gamble's acquisition of Clorox Chemical Company violated the Clayton Act and lessened competition in the household liquid bleach market. At the time of the merger, Clorox was the leading manufacturer of household bleach (49 percent of national sales) in a highly concentrated market. The commission found that extensive advertising expenditures could increase Clorox's market share. Purex, the major competitor, did not sell its product in some markets, primarily in the Northeast and Mid-Atlantic states. Procter & Gamble was a large, diversified producer of high-turnover household products primarily sold in grocery stores and drugstores. Through its large advertising budget, Procter & Gamble was able to obtain substantial price reductions. The commission argued that its acquisition of Clorox would discourage entry and competition in this market.*

FEDERAL TRADE
COMM'N v. PROCTER
& GAMBLE CO.
Supreme Court of the United
States, 1967.
386 U.S. 568, 87 S.Ct. 1224.

DOUGLAS, Justice.
*   *   *   *

At the time of the acquisition, Clorox was the leading manufacturer of household liquid bleach, with 48.8% of the national sales—annual sales of slightly less than $40,000,000. Its market share had been steadily increasing for the five years prior to the merger. *   *   * The industry is highly concentrated; in 1957, Clorox and Purex accounted for almost 65% of the Nation's household liquid bleach sales, and, together with four other firms, for almost 80%. *   *   *

Since all liquid bleach is chemically identical, advertising and sales promotion are vital. In 1957 Clorox spent almost $3,700,000 on advertising, imprinting the value of its bleach in the mind of the consumer. *   *   * The Commission found that these heavy expenditures went far to explain why Clorox maintained so high a market share despite the fact that its brand, though chemically indistinguishable from rival brands, retailed for a price equal to or, in many instances, higher than its competitors.

Procter is a large, diversified manufacturer of low-price, high-turnover household products sold through grocery, drug, and department stores. Prior to its acquisition of Clorox, it did not produce household liquid bleach. *   *   * Its primary activity is in the general area of soaps, detergents, and cleansers; in 1957, of total domestic sales, more than one-half *   *   * were in this field. Procter was the dominant factor in this area.
*   *   *   *

In the marketing of soaps, detergents, and cleansers, as in the marketing of household liquid bleach, advertising and sales promotion are vital. *   *   * Due to its tremendous volume, Procter receives substantial discounts from the media. As a multi-product producer Procter enjoys substantial advantages in advertising and sales promotion. Thus, it can and does feature several products in its promotions, reducing the printing, mailing, and other costs for each product. It also purchases network programs on behalf of several products, enabling it to give each product network exposure at a fraction of the cost per product that a firm with only one product to advertise would incur.
*   *   *   *

The decision to acquire Clorox was the result of a study conducted by Procter's promotion department designed to determine the advisability of entering the liquid bleach industry. *   *   *

The final report confirmed the conclusions of the initial report and emphasized that Procter would make more effective use of Clorox's advertising budget and that the merger would facilitate advertising economies. A few months later, Procter acquired the assets of Clorox in the name of a wholly owned subsidiary, the Clorox Company, in exchange for Procter stock.

The Commission * * * found that the substitution of Procter with its huge assets and advertising advantages for the already dominant Clorox would dissuade new entrants and discourage active competition from the firms already in the industry due to fear of retaliation by Procter. * * *

The anticompetitive effects with which this product-extension merger is fraught can easily be seen: (1) the substitution of the powerful acquiring firm for the smaller, but already dominant, firm may substantially reduce the competitive structure of the industry by raising entry barriers and by dissuading the smaller firms from aggressively competing; (2) the acquisition eliminates the potential competition of the acquiring firm.

The liquid bleach industry was already oligopolistic before the acquisition, and price competition was certainly not as vigorous as it would have been if the industry were competitive. * * *

DECISION AND REMEDY   *The FTC order that Procter & Gamble divest itself of the Clorox Company was upheld by the Supreme Court of the United States.*

OTHER ANTITRUST ENFORCEMENT

The Federal Trade Commission investigates and enforces regulations in the context of industry-wide matters. Industry-wide problems may be indicated by high prices, profits, lack of product innovation, or the absence of entry by new firms. In such cases, the exact cause of reduced performance may not be readily identifiable. Determining the problem and selecting the appropriate remedy require a more extensive analysis than is necessary in other FTC investigations. Industry-wide matters include investigations of the petroleum and automobile industries, as well as the breakfast cereal industry as part of the food program investigation.

QUESTIONS AND CASE PROBLEMS

1. Discuss *fully* whether each of the following situations is in violation of the Sherman Act.

   (a) Trujillo Foods, Inc. is the leading seller of frozen Mexican foods in three southwestern states. The various retail outlets which sell Trujillo products are in close competition, and customers are very price conscious. Trujillo has conditioned its sales to retailers with the agreement that the retailer will not sell below a minimum price nor above a maximum price. Except for these limits, the retailer is allowed to set any price the retailer feels appropriate.

   (b) Franklin, Inc., Green, Inc., and Fill-It, Inc. are competitors in the manufacture and sale of microwave ovens sold primarily east of the Mississippi River. As a patriotic gesture, and to assist the unemployed, the three competitors agree to lower their prices on all microwave models by 20% for a three-month period which includes July 4th and Labor Day.

   (c) Foam Beer, Inc. sells its beer to distributors all over the United States. Foam sends to each of its distributors a recommended price list, explaining that past records indicate that beer sold at those prices should insure the distributor a reasonable rate of return. The price list clearly states that the sale of the beer by Foam to the distributor is not conditioned upon the distributor reselling the beer at the recommended price, and the distributor is free to set the price.

2. Mickey's Appliance Store is new retail seller of appliances in Sunwest City. Mickey's innovative sales techniques and financing have caused a substantial loss of sales from the appliance department of Luckluster De-

partment Store. Luckluster is a large department store, and part of a large chain with substantial buying power. Luckluster told a number of appliance manufacturers that if they continued to sell to Mickey's, Luckluster would discontinue its large volume of purchases from these manufacturers. The manufacturers immediately stopped selling appliances to Mickey's. Mickey's files suit against Luckluster and the manufacturers, claiming their actions constituted an antitrust violation. Luckluster and the manufacturers can prove that Mickey's is a small retailer with a small portion of the market, and, since the relevant market was not substantially affected, they claim they are not guilty of restraint of trade. Discuss *fully* whether there is an antitrust violation.

3. Quick Photo, Inc. is a manufacturer of photography film. At the present time Quick Photo has approximately 50 percent of the market. Quick Photo launches a campaign whereby when a customer purchases Quick Photo film, the purchase price includes photo processing by Quick Photo, Inc. Quick Photo claims that its film processing is specially designed to improve the quality of the finished photos when using Quick Photo's film. Discuss *fully* whether Quick Photo's combination of purchase and film processing is an antitrust violation.

4. Bock Brewery, Inc. is a regional five-state producer and seller of Suds Beer. In the five-state area Bock has 15 percent of the beer market. Barrel Tap, Inc. is a corporation which has exclusive beer sales concession taverns in all major airports in a twenty-state area. Barrel Tap purchases beer from Bock, Miller, and Anheuser-Busch, Inc. Bock acquires the stock and assets of Barrel Tap, Inc. What type of merger is this? Discuss *fully* whether this merger is in violation of the Clayton Act, Section 7.

5. The plaintiff, Spray-Rite, was an authorized distributor of Monsanto herbicides from 1957 to 1968, and the defendant, Monsanto Company, manufactures chemical products, including agricultural herbicides. In October 1968 Monsanto declined to renew Spray-Rite's distributorship. Spray-Rite subsequently brought an action under Section 1 of the Sherman Act.

In its complaint, Spray-Rite alleged that Monsanto and some of its distributors conspired to fix the resale price of Monsanto herbicides. Monsanto contended, however, that Spray-Rite's distributorship had been terminated because of its failure to hire trained sales personnel and to promote sales to dealers adequately.

The court of appeals concluded that proof of Spray-Rite's termination subsequent to competitor complaints is sufficient to support an inference of concerted action. Can price-fixing be inferred from the fact that a manufacturer terminated a price-cutting distributor in response to complaints from other distributors? What is the standard of proof necessary to establish a vertical price-fixing conspiracy in violation of Section 1 of the Sherman Act? [Monsanto Co. v. Spray-Rite Service Corp., —— U.S.

——, 104 S.Ct. 1464, rehearing denied —— U.S. —— 80, 104 S.Ct. 2378 (1984)]

6. The plaintiff, Edwin G. Hyde, being a certified anesthesiologist, applied for a position on the medical staff of the defendant, East Jefferson Parish Hospital. Because the hospital had entered into a contract in which all anesthesiological services required by the hospital's patients were to be performed by a professional medical corporation, it denied the plaintiff's application. The plaintiff subsequently brought an action, alleging that the contract violates Section 1 of the Sherman Act. Does this contract *per se* violate Section 1 of the Sherman Act since every patient undergoing surgery at Jefferson Hospital must use the services of one firm of anesthesiologists? Tying arrangements are subject to the *per se* rule. [Jefferson Parish Hospital District No. 2 v. Hyde, —— U.S. ——, 104 S.Ct. 1551 (1984), remanded to Hyde v. Jefferson Parish Hosp. Dist. No. 2, 764 F.2d 1139 (5th Cir. 1985)]

7. Febco, Inc. manufactured lawn and turf equipment. The Colorado Pump and Supply Company was a wholesale distributor of such equipment in the Colorado area. An important item that Colorado Pump distributed was a control device for sprinkling systems. Although Febco manufactured one of the better sprinkler controls, a number of other manufacturers competed in the field with competitive and satisfactory substitutes for the Febco controllers. In an agreement between Febco and Colorado Pump under which Colorado Pump was given the right to distribute Febco products, Colorado Pump was required to stock a complete line of Febco products. Industry data proved that, in this line of goods, it was important for distributors to protect the "good will" of manufacturers by carrying a complete line of a manufacturer's goods or none at all. Does the requirement by Febco that Colorado Pump stock an entire line of Febco products constitute an illegal tying arrangement? [Colorado Pump and Supply Co. v. Febco, Inc., 472 F.2d 637 (10th Cir. 1973)]

8. In 1972, the Federal Maritime Commission approved an agreement under which the world's two largest containership operators—Sea Land Service, Inc., and United States Lines, Inc.—would become subsidiaries of the same corporate parent—R. J. Reynolds Tobacco Company. The commission approved the acquisition agreement on the condition that the subsidiaries would remain independent companies in competition with each other. The Federal Maritime Commission, however, does not have the power to immunize companies from the antitrust laws. Knowing this, does the agreement violate any of the antitrust statutes discussed in this chapter? [American Mail Line Limited v. Federal Maritime Comm'n, 503 F.2d 157 (D.C.Cir. 1974)]

9. Fedders Corporation was a manufacturer of air conditioners and air-conditioning systems. Fedders claimed in its advertising that its air conditioners were unique because they had "reserved cooling power," a phrase that

Fedders admitted was intended to imply "an unusual ability to produce cold air under extreme conditions of heat and humidity." In fact, however, Fedders air-conditioners had no technical advantage over the equipment manufactured by its competitors. Accordingly, the Federal Trade Commission concluded that Fedders was engaging in misrepresentations in its advertising in violation of Section 5 of the Federal Trade Commission Act. Was the Federal Trade Commission's conclusion correct? [Fedders Corp. v. Federal Trade Comm'n, 529 F.2d 1398 (2nd Cir. 1976)]

10. Typically, a market will operate much more efficiently if sellers are well informed about how much buyers are willing to pay for a particular product, how much the industry is producing, what the capacity of various firms is, etc. The dissemination of information, however, is also likely to stablize prices by reducing the *disperson* of prices. The question then arises as to whether or not an exchange of price information for purposes of compliance with the Robinson-Patman Act is beyond the reach of the

Sherman Act. [See 15 U.S.C.A., Section 13(a). The Robinson-Patman Act forbids price discrimination—the discrimination in price between different purchasers of commodities of like grade and quality.] Consider, for example, the situation in which manufacturers of gypsum board were charged with a combination and conspiracy for allegedly contacting competitors about current and future prices before making price concessions to buyers. The defendants asserted that they had only contacted their competitors on prices and sales terms in order to meet the prices of competitors. Under the Robinson-Patman Act, a seller may justify its price discrimination by demonstrating that the lower price in one locality was charged "in good faith to meet an equally low price of a competitor." Thus, is there a conflict between the two antitrust statutes—the behavior proscribed by the Sherman Act and the meeting-competition defense of the Robinson-Patman Act? [United States v. United States Gypsum Co., 438 U.S. 422, 98 S.Ct. 2864 (1978)]

50

GOVERNMENT REGULATION
Employment and Labor Relations Law

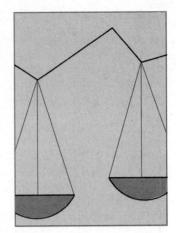

Government regulation of employment and labor relations is very much present in our society. Businesses must operate within the confines established by statutes regulating employment and labor relations. Over the years, legislation has greatly affected the rights and liabilities of employees, as well as employers.

Until the early 1930s, laws at the federal and state levels generally favored management. Collective activities such as unions were discouraged, sometimes forcibly, by employers. Early legislation protecting the rights of employees, such as the National War Labor Board that operated during World War I, was often temporary. Additionally, this type of legislation was frequently restricted to a particular industry, such as the Railway Labor Act of 1926, which required railroads and their employees to attempt to make employment agreements through representatives chosen by each side. Beginning in 1932, however, a number of statutes were enacted that greatly increased employees' rights to join unions, to engage in collective bargaining, to receive retirement and income security benefits, to be protected against various discrimination practices, and to have a safe place to work.

UNIONS AND COLLECTIVE BARGAINING

Most of the early legislation to protect employees focused on the rights of workers to join unions and to engage in collective bargaining.

Norris-LaGuardia Act

Congress protected peaceful strikes, picketing, and boycotts in 1932 in the Norris-LaGuardia Act.[1] The statute restricted federal courts in their power to issue injunctions against unions engaged in peaceful strikes. In effect, the act declared a national policy permitting employees to organize.

National Labor Relations Act

The National Labor Relations Act of 1935 (the Wagner Act)[2] established the rights of employees to engage in collective bargaining and to strike. It also created the National Labor Relations Board to oversee elections and to prevent employers from engag-

---

1. 29 U.S.C. 101–10, 113–15 (1973).
2. 49 Stat. 449, 20 U.S.C. 151.

ing in unfair and illegal union-labor activities and unfair labor practices. The act defined a number of practices as unfair to labor:

1. Interference with the efforts of employees to form, join, or assist labor organizations or to engage in concerted activities for their mutual aid or protection. [Section 8(a)(1)]
2. An employer's domination of a labor organization or contribution of financial or other support to it. [Section 8(a)(2)]
3. Discrimination in the hiring or awarding of tenure to employees for reason of union affiliation. [Section 8(a)(3)]
4. Discrimination against employees for filing charges under the act or giving testimony under the act. [Section 8(a)(4)]
5. Refusal to bargain collectively with the duly designated representative of the employees. [Section 8(a)(5)]

Labor-Management Relations Act

The Labor-Management Relations Act (Taft-Hartley Act)[3] was signed by President Truman on June 23, 1947, after being passed over his veto. Intended to amend the Wagner Act, it contained provisions *protecting employers* as well as employees. The act was bitterly opposed by organized labor groups. It provided a detailed list of unfair labor activities that unions as well as management were now forbidden to practice. Moreover, a "free speech" amendment allowed employers to propagandize against unions prior to any National Labor Relations Board election.

The Closed Shop Made Illegal   A **closed shop** is a firm that requires union membership by its workers as a condition of employment. It was made illegal under the Taft-Hartley Act, which left the union shop legal. A **union shop** does not require membership as a prerequisite for employment but can, and usually does, require that workers join the union after a specified amount of time on the job. Furthermore, the Taft-Hartley Act allowed individual states to pass their own right-to-work laws. A **right-**

to-work law makes it illegal for union membership to be required for *continued* employment in any establishment. Thus, union shops are technically illegal in states with right-to-work laws.

The Eighty-Day Cooling-Off Period   One of the most controversial aspects of the Taft-Hartley Act was the eighty-day cooling-off period. This is a provision in the act that allows federal courts to issue injunctions against strikes that would create a national emergency. The President of the United States can obtain a court injunction that will last for eighty days. Presidents have occasionally used this provision. For example, President Eisenhower applied the eighty-day injunction order to striking steel workers in 1959, President Nixon applied it to striking longshoremen in 1971, and President Carter applied it to striking coal miners in 1978.

Labor-Management Reporting and Disclosure Act of 1959

The Labor-Management Reporting and Disclosure Act of 1959 (Landrum-Griffin Act)[4] established an employee bill of rights and reporting requirements for union activities. This act strictly regulated internal union business procedures.

Union elections, for example, are regulated by this act. The act requires that regularly scheduled elections of officers occur and that secret ballots be used. Ex-convicts and communists are prohibited from holding union office. Moreover, union officials are made accountable for union property and funds. Members have the right to attend and to participate in union meetings, to nominate officers, and to vote in most union proceedings.

Hot Cargo Contracts   In principle, the Taft-Hartley Act made all secondary boycotts illegal. Loopholes, however, appeared. For example, *hot cargo contracts*—wherein employers voluntarily agreed with unions not to handle, use, or deal in the nonunion-produced goods of other employers—became common. This particular type of secondary boycott was not made illegal by the Taft-Hartley Act because the act prevented only unions from inducing employees of an employer to strike or otherwise act to force the employer not to handle such goods. The Landrum-

---

3.   61 Stat. 136, 29 U.S.C. 141.

4.   73 Stat. 519, 29 U.S.C. 401.

Griffin Act plugged this loophole and outlawed hot cargo contracts by Section 8(e):

> It shall be unfair and unfair labor practice for any labor organization and any employer to enter into any contract or agreement * * * whereby such employer * * * agrees to refrain from handling, using, selling, transporting or otherwise dealing in any of the products of any other employer, or to cease doing business with any other person * * *

CIVIL RIGHTS AND EQUAL OPPORTUNITY

At common law, employment was terminable "at will." Any employer could establish the terms and conditions of employment and the rules that the employer wanted the employees to follow. Labor unions were deemed private associations. Therefore, they could determine all membership requirements without oversight of the courts. In the past several decades, however, as a result of judicial decisions, of administrative agency actions, and of legislation, employers and unions have been restricted in their ability to discriminate on the basis of race, religion, creed, age, or sex. The most important statute relating to fair employment practices is Title VII of the Civil Rights Act of 1964.[5]

General Provisions of the Civil Rights Act

Basically, the act and its amendments eliminate job discrimination against employees, applicants, and union members on the basis of race, color, national origin, religion, and sex.

Title VII of the act applies to employers with fifteen or more employees, to labor unions with fifteen or more members, to all labor unions that operate hiring halls, and to all employment agencies. The 1972 amendments extend coverage to all state and local governments, government agencies, political subdivisions, and departments. A special section forbids discrimination in most federal government employment.

Race, Color, and National Origin Discrimination   If a company's standards or policies for selecting or promoting employees have the effect of discriminating against minorities and do not have a substantial, demonstrable relationship to qualifications for the job in question, they are illegal. Discrimination in employment conditions and benefits is also illegal. Thus, an employer cannot maintain all-white or all-black crews for no demonstrable reason. Nor can an employer grant higher average Christmas bonuses to whites than to blacks.

Religious Discrimination   Employers, except for religious corporations, associations, or societies, are not allowed to discriminate in their employment practices on the basis of religion. Moreover, employers must make reasonable accommodation to the religious needs of their employees.

A few states have passed legislation which specifically allows employees to declare a specific day of the week as a "religious day." In those states employers cannot require an employee to work on such a day. A Connecticut statute, for example, provides that, "No person who states that a particular day of the week is observed as his Sabbath may be required by his employer to work on such a day. An employee's refusal to work on his Sabbath shall not constitute grounds for his dismissal." This statute was challenged in a recent Supreme Court decision as going beyond the civil rights rule of employers' reasonable accommodation.[6]

The Supreme Court, in an opinion delivered by Chief Justice Burger, held that the Connecticut statute, by providing Sabbath observers with an absolute and unqualified right not to work on their chosen Sabbath, violates the establishment clause of the First Amendment to the U.S. Constitution. The Court stated that the state statute commanded that Sabbath religious concerns automatically controlled all secular interests and the statute took no account of the convenience or interests of the employer or those other employees who do not observe a Sabbath. Thus the statute had a primary effect of impermissibly advancing a particular religious practice.

Sex Discrimination   Even though states have enacted laws to protect women, they also prohibit by statute the employment of women in certain occupations. Many state statutes have barred women from working during the night or from working more

---

5.   78 Stat. 241, 42 U.S.C. 2000e *et seq.*

6.   Estate of Thornton *et al* v. Caldor, Inc., 472 U.S. ——, 105 S.Ct. 2948, 86 L.Ed.2d 557 (1985)]. See also Chapter 2 under "Freedom of Religion."

than a given number of hours per day or per week. Under the Equal Employment Opportunity Act of 1972, federal courts have struck down many of these laws. EEOC guidelines forbid employers from clasifying jobs as male or female and from advertising in help-wanted columns that are designated male or female unless sex is a bona fide job qualification. Furthermore, employers cannot have separate male and female seniority lists.

Testing and Educational Requirements Employers often find it necessary to use interviews and test-

ing procedures in order to choose among a large number of applicants for job openings. Consequently, personnel tests are common devices for screening applicants. Minimum educational requirements are also common. In the following case, the Supreme Court of the United States had to grapple with the thorny problem of whether minimum educational requirements and the use of standardized general intelligence tests as a condition for employment violated Title VII of the Civil Rights Act.

GRIGGS v. DUKE
POWER CO.
Supreme Court of the United
States, 1971.
401 U.S. 424, 91 S.Ct. 849.

BACKGROUND AND FACTS *The defendant, Duke Power Company, was sued by a number of its black employees for practicing racial discrimination in hiring and assigning employees at its Dan River plant. The plant was organized into five operating departments: (1) labor, (2) coal handling, (3) operation, (4) maintenance, and (5) laboratory testing. Blacks were employed only in the labor department, where the highest-paying jobs paid less than the lowest-paying jobs in the other four departments (which employed only whites). Promotions were normally made within each department on the basis of seniority. Transferees into a department usually began at the lowest position.*

In 1955, the company began to require a high school education for an initial assignment into any department except the labor department. In addition, it required a high school education for any transfer from the coal handling department to any inside department (operations, maintenance, or laboratory). For ten years, this company-wide policy was enforced.

In 1965, when the company abandoned its policy of restricting blacks to the labor department, a high school diploma was nevertheless made a prerequisite to transfer from the labor department into any other department.

From the time the high school requirement was instituted in 1955 to the time the lawsuit was filed, white employees hired before the high school education requirement became effective continued to perform satisfactorily and to achieve promotions in the operating departments.

Then in 1965, the company added further requirements for any new employees. To qualify for placement in any but the labor department it became necessary to score satisfactorily on two professionally prepared aptitude tests as well as to have a high school education. Completion of high school alone, however, continued to make employees eligible for transfer into the four desirable departments. Of course, blacks who had been employed prior to the time of this new requirement had been ineligible for transfer.

In September 1965, the company began to permit employees who lacked a high school education to qualify for transfer from the labor or coal handling department to an inside job by passing two tests—the Wonderlic Personnel Test, which purported to measure general intelligence, and the Bennett Mechanical Comprehension Test. Neither of these tests measured the ability to learn to perform a particular job or category of job. The requisite scores used both for initial hiring and for transfer approximated the national median for high school graduates. Enforcing the median standard screened out approximately half of all high school graduates across the country, not to mention those within the company attempting to pass with a sufficient score. Hence, these two requirements, the diploma and the tests, rendered a markedly disproportionate number of blacks ineligible for employment advancement in the company.

The district court hearing the case concluded that, even though the company had followed a policy of overt racial discrimination prior to the passage of the Civil Rights Act, such conduct had since ceased. Consequently, it held that the impact of the prior inequities was beyond the reach of the act. The court of appeals further concluded that Duke Power Company had no discriminatory intent in adopting the diploma and test requirements and that the standards had been applied fairly to both whites and blacks. On this basis, it affirmed the district court's holding that there was no violation of the Civil Rights Act. The case was then appealed to the Supreme Court.

BURGER, Chief Justice.
*   *   *   *

We granted the writ in this case to resolve the question whether an employer is prohibited by the Civil Rights Act of 1964, Title VII, from requiring a high school education or passing of a standardized general intelligence test as a condition of employment in or transfer to jobs when (a) neither standard is shown to be significantly related to successful job performance, (b) both requirements operate to disqualify Negroes at a substantially higher rate than white applicants, and (c) the jobs in question formerly had been filled only by white employees as part of a longstanding practice of giving preference to whites.
*   *   *   *

The objective of Congress in the enactment of Title VII is plain from the language of the statute. It was to achieve equality of employment opportunities and remove barriers that have operated in the past to favor an identifiable group of white employees over other employees. Under the Act, practices, procedures, or tests neutral on their face, and even neutral in terms of intent, cannot be maintained if they operate to "freeze" the status quo of prior discriminatory employment practices.
*   *   *   *

Congress did not intend by Title VII, however, to guarantee a job to every person regardless of qualifications. In short, the Act does not command that any person be hired simply because he was formerly the subject of discrimination, or because he is a member of a minority group. Discriminatory preference for any group, minority or majority, is precisely and only what Congress has proscribed. What is required by Congress is the removal of artificial, arbitrary, and unnecessary barriers to employment when the barriers operate invidiously to discriminate on the basis of racial or other impermissible classification.
*   *   *   *

The Act proscribes not only overt discrimination but also practices that are fair in form, but discriminatory in operation. The touchstone is business necessity. If an employment practice which operates to exclude Negroes cannot be shown to be related to job performance, the practice is prohibited.

On the record before us, neither the high school completion requirement nor the general intelligence test is shown to bear a demonstrable relationship to successful performance of the jobs for which it was used. Both were adopted, as the Court of Appeals noted, without meaningful study of their relationship to job-performance ability. *   *   *

The evidence, however, shows that employees who have not completed high school or taken the tests have continued to perform satisfactorily and make progress in departments for which the high school and test criteria are now used. The promotion record of present employees who would not be able to meet the new criteria thus suggests the possibility that the requirements may not be needed even for the limited

purpose of preserving the avowed policy of advancement within the Company.   *   *   *
    *   *   *   *

DECISION AND REMEDY   *In concluding that the two tests and the high school diploma requirement did not bear a demonstrable relationship to successful job performance, the U.S. Supreme Court held that the Duke Power Company had in fact violated Title VII of the Civil Rights Act. Accordingly, the company was prohibited from requiring a high school education or the passing of a standardized general intelligence test as a condition of employment or as a prerequisite to transferring from one job to another.*

INJURY, COMPENSATION, AND SAFETY

Numerous state statutes are designed to protect employees and their families from the risk of accidental injury, death, or disease resulting from their employment. This section discusses state workers' compensation acts and the Occupational Safety and Health Act of 1970, which are specifically designed to protect employees and their families.

State Workers' Compensation Acts

Workers' compensation laws are usually administered by some administrative agency or board that has quasi-judicial powers. All rulings of such boards are subject to review by the courts.

In general, the right to recover under workers' compensation laws is given to the injured employee without regard to the existence of negligence or of fault in the traditional sense. Thus, the right of recovery is predicated on the employment relationship and the fact that the injury *arose out of and/or was in the course of normal employment*. Some states require that just one of these conditions be satisfied, whereas other states require that both be satisfied. A simple, two-pronged test for determining whether an employee can receive workers' compensation is:

1. Was the injury accidental?
2. Did the injury arise out of and/or in the course of employment?

Intentionally inflicted self-injury, for example, would not be considered accidental and, hence, it would not be covered under the workers' compensation laws. In the past, heart attacks or other medical problems arising out of preexisting disease or physical conditions were not covered, but recently some states have allowed recovery.

Basically, employers are under a system of strict liability (see Chapter 4). Few, if any, defenses exist for them. Therefore, the costs of treating workers' injuries are considered a cost of production and are passed on to consumers.

Health and Safety Protection

At the federal level the primary legislation for employee health and safety protection is the Occupational Safety and Health Act of 1970 (OSHA).[7] This act was passed to insure safe and healthful working conditions for practically every employee in the country.[8]

In the past, OSHA inspectors conducted warrantless inspections. However, as illustrated in the following case, such inspections violate the warrant clause of the Fourth Amendment.

---

7. 84 Stat. 1590, 29 U.S.C. 553, 651–678.
8. See also the OSHA discussion in the context of administrative agencies in Chapter 45.

MARSHALL v. BARLOW'S, INC.

Supreme Court of the United States, 1978.
436 U.S. 307, 98 S.Ct. 1816.

BACKGROUND AND FACTS   *Prior to 1978, inspectors of the Occupational Safety and Health Administration were not required to obtain permission to enter the work areas of firms subject to OSHA's jurisdiction. In 1975, an OSHA inspector entered the customer service area of Barlow's Inc., an electrical and plumbing installation business. After showing his credentials, the inspector* *informed the president and general manager, Barlow, that he wished to conduct a search of the working areas of the business.*

Upon inquiry, Barlow learned that no complaint had been received about his company. The inspection was simply the result of a random selection process. On further questioning of the inspector, Barlow learned that he did not have a search warrant. Thereupon, Barlow refused to permit the inspector to enter the working area of his business. He said that he was relying on his rights guaranteed by the Fourth Amendment of the United States Constitution.

OSHA filed suit in the United States District Court and was ultimately successful in having that court issue an order compelling Barlow to admit the inspector for purposes of conducting an occupational safety and health inspection.

Once again, this time with court order in hand, the OSHA inspector presented himself at Barlow's, Inc., and Barlow again refused admission. This time Barlow went to court seeking an injunction to prohibit the inspector from making a warrantless search on the ground that it violated the Fourth Amendment of the Constitution.

A court composed of three judges was convened, and it ruled in Barlow's favor, holding that the Fourth Amendment required a warrant for the type of search involved and that the statutory authorization for warrantless inspections under the OSHA statute was unconstitutional. Therefore, a permanent injunction against such searches or inspections was entered. This appeal challenged the validity of that injunction.

WHITE, Justice.

*   *   *   *

The Warrant Clause of the Fourth Amendment protects commercial buildings as well as private homes. To hold otherwise would belie the origin of that Amendment, and the American colonial experience. An important forerunner of the first 10 Amendments to the United States Constitution, the Virginia Bill of Rights, specifically opposed "general warrants, whereby an officer or messenger may be commanded to search suspected places without evidence of a fact committed." The general warrant was a recurring point of contention in the colonies immediately preceding the Revolution.

*   *   *

*   *   *   *

The Secretary urges that an exception from the search warrant requirement has been recognized for "pervasively regulated business[es]."

*   *   *   *

Invoking the Walsh-Healey Act of 1936, the Secretary attempts to support a conclusion that all businesses involved in interstate commerce have long been subjected to close supervision of employee safety and health conditions. But the degree of federal involvement in employee working circumstances has never been of the order of specificity and pervasiveness that OSHA mandates. It is quite unconvincing to argue that the imposition of minimum wages and maximum hours on employers who contracted with the government under the Walsh-Healey Act prepared the entirety of American interstate commerce for regulation of working conditions to the minutest detail. Nor can any but the most fictional sense of voluntary consent to later searches be found in the single fact that one conducts a business affecting interstate commerce; under current practice and law, few businesses can be conducted without having some effect on interstate commerce.

*   *   *   *

We conclude that the concerns expressed by the Secretary do not suffice to justify warrantless inspections under OSHA or vitiate the general constitutional requirement that for a search to be reasonable a warrant must be obtained.

DECISION   *The permanent injunction was upheld. OSHA inspections conducted without*
AND REMEDY *warrants were held to be unconstitutional.*

COMMENTS   *The Fourth Amendment provides that, except upon* probable cause *supported
            by oath or affirmation, people have a right to be secure in their persons, houses,
            papers, and effects against unreasonable searches and seizures. Thus, OSHA
            inspectors are now required to obtain warrants before conducting an inspection.
            However, a warrant for an OSHA inspection is much easier to obtain than one
            involving a criminal investigation. All that is required is proof that there was
            a reasonable and "uniformly applied" basis for selecting a particular workplace
            for inspection.*

RETIREMENT AND SECURITY INCOME

Social Security

Federal and state governments participate in programs of insurance designed to protect employees and their families by covering the financial impact of retirement, disability, death, hospitalization, and unemployment. The key federal law on this subject is the Social Security Act of 1935.[9]

Old Age, Survivors, and Disability Insurance (OASDI) Both employers and employees must "contribute" under the Federal Insurance Contributions Act (FICA)[10] to help pay for the loss of income benefits on retirement. The basis for the employee's contribution is the employee's annual wage base—the maximum amount of an employee's wages that are subject to the tax. Benefits are fixed by statute but increase automatically with increases in the cost of living of 3 percent or more between specified periods.

Medicare A health insurance program, Medicare is administered by the Social Security Administration for people sixty-five years of age and older and for some under sixty-five who are disabled. It has two parts, one pertaining to hospital costs and the other to nonhospital medical costs, such as doctors' office visits. People who have Medicare hospital insurance can also obtain additional federal medical insurance if they pay small monthly premiums that increase as the cost of medical care increases.

Private Retirement Plans

There has been significant legislation to regulate retirement plans set up by employers. These plans are used to supplement Social Security benefits. The major piece of this type of legislation is the Employee Retirement Income Security Act of 1974 (ERISA).[11] This act empowers the Labor Management Services Administration of the Department of Labor to enforce its provisions to regulate individuals who operate private pension funds.

Unemployment Compensation

The United States has a system of unemployment insurance in which employers pay into a fund, the proceeds of which are paid out to qualified unemployed workers. The major piece of federal legislation involved is the Federal Unemployment Tax Act (FUTA).[12] This act created a state system that provides unemployment compensation to eligible individuals, and employers who are within the provisions of the act are taxed quarterly. Taxes are typically collected by the employers and submitted to the states, which then deposit them with the federal government. The federal government maintains an Unemployment Insurance Fund, in which each state has an account.

---

9. 49 Stat. 620, 42 U.S.C. 301.
10. 26 U.S.C. 3101.

11. 88 Stat. 829, 29 U.S.C. 1001.
12. 68A Stat. 439, 26 U.S.C. Chapter 23.

OTHER EMPLOYMENT LAWS

Among the numerous other employment laws affecting U.S. workers and their employers are the Fair Labor Standards Act, the Davis-Bacon Act, and the Walsh-Healy Public Contracts Act.

Fair Labor Standards Act

The Fair Labor Standards Act (also known as the Wage-Hour Law) was signed by the president on June 25, 1938.[13] It covers child labor, maximum hours, and minimum wages.

Child Labor   The act prohibits oppressive child labor. Children under sixteen years of age cannot be employed full time except by a parent under certain circumstances; nor can children between the ages of sixteen and eighteen be employed in hazardous jobs or in jobs detrimental to their health and well-being. Most states require children under sixteen years of age to obtain work permits.

Maximum Hours   Under this act, any employee who agrees to work more than forty hours per week must be paid no less than one-and-a-half times his or her regular pay for all hours over forty. Exceptions are made for employees working under the terms of collective bargaining agreements and in some other circumstances.

Minimum Wage   The Fair Labor Standards Act provides that a minimum hourly wage of a specified amount (currently $3.35 per hour) must be paid to employees in covered industries. Congress periodically revises such minimum wages. The term *wages* is meant to include the reasonable cost of the employer in furnishing employees with board, lodging, and other facilities if they are customarily furnished by that employer.

Other Government-Enforced Minimum-Wage Laws

In 1931, during the Great Depression, the president signed the Davis-Bacon Act.[14] This act requires the payment of "prevailing wages" to employees of contractors or subcontractors working on government construction projects. In 1936, an act that extended the Davis-Bacon Act was put into effect—the Walsh-Healy Public Contract Act.[15] This act requires a minimum wage as well as overtime pay of time-and-a-half to employees of manufacturers or suppliers entering into contracts with agencies of the federal government.

---

13.   52 Stat. 1060, 29 U.S.C. 201.

14.   46 Stat. 1494, 40 U.S.C. 276a.
15.   49 Stat. 2036, 41 U.S.C. 35.

QUESTIONS AND CASE PROBLEMS

1. Discuss *fully* which of the following constitutes a violation of the 1964 Civil Rights Act, Title VII, as amended.
   (a) Causeway, Inc. is a consulting firm and has ten employees. These employees travel on consulting jobs in seven states. Causeway has an employment record of hiring only white males.
   (b) Filmtex, Inc. is making a film about Africa. Filmtex needs to employ approximately one hundred extras for this picture. Filmtex advertises in all major newspapers in Southern California for the hiring of these extras. The ad states only black persons need apply.
   (c) Green Belt is a major processor of cheese sold throughout the United States. Green employs one hundred employees at its principal processing plant. The plant is located in Windward City, whose population is 50 percent white, 25 percent black, and the balance Hispanic, Oriental, etc. Green requires a high school diploma as a condition of employment on its clean-up crew. Three-fourths of the white population complete high school, as compared to only one-fourth of the minority children. Green has an all white cleaning crew.
2. Joseph's is an interstate business engaged in manufacturing and selling boats. Joseph has five hundred nonunion employees. Representatives of these employees approach Joseph seeking a four-day, ten-hours-per-day, work week. Joseph is concerned this proposal will require him to pay his employees time and a half after eight hours per day. Discuss fully which federal act Joseph is concerned

about and whether the proposal will require Joseph to pay for time and a half.

3. Johnson is an employee of Burns, Inc. Burns is a cannery of peas, and has a three-storied plant. On top of the third story is a flagpole. The company has a set lunch break during which time the plant is shut down. The employees are not allowed to leave the plant property, and most eat their lunch outside on a grassy area. However, some employees eat their lunch on top of the third-story roof. Johnson was known as a cut-up and one afternoon in order to show off, Johnson climbed the flagpole, waving wildly at his fellow employees. In the process Johnson lost his grip and fell, suffering numerous injuries. Discuss *fully* whether Johnson is entitled to workers' compensation.

4. Discuss *fully* which of the following boycotts are illegal.

    (a) Hanover, a manufacturer, produces and sells toasters. Hanover employees go out on strike and form picket lines in front of the Hanover plant; they also peacefully picket customers of stores that carry and sell Hanover toasters.

    (b) Suppose Hanover's employees picket not only the Hanover plant, but picket Tough Steel, Inc., which sells to Hanover the steel used to make the toasters.

    (c) Suppose Tough Steel, Inc. is a nonunion shop. Hanover's union employees threaten Hanover with a strike unless Hanover agrees to refuse to buy its steel from Tough Steel. The union wants to organize the Tough Steel workers. To avoid a strike, Hanover agrees to the union demands.

5. Local 1001 of the Retail Store Employees Union became the certified bargaining representative of some of the employees of Safeco Title Insurance Company in the state of Washington. Contract negotiations between Safeco and the union ended in a deadlock. At this point, the union began picketing the five local independent title companies, as well as the main Safeco office. The picketers carried signs indicating that Safeco was a nonunion employer. Safeco declared that Local 1001 was engaging in a secondary boycott in violation of the National Labor Relations Act. It argued that the union was directing its appeal against Safeco insurance policies. The title companies that were being picketed were not owned by Safeco, and none of the daily operations of the title companies was controlled by Safeco. Rather, the title companies simply derived most of their income from the sale of Safeco title insurance policies. Was the Retail Store Employees

Union indeed engaging in a secondary boycott? [NLRB v. Retail Store Employees Union, 439 U.S. 819, 99 S.Ct. 81 (1980)]

6. Donnell was a black General Motors employee in St. Louis who applied for admission into a GM skilled trade apprenticeship program that was established jointly by the company and the United Auto Workers. He was rejected for failure to meet the requirement that all applicants have completed high school. He brought action under Title VII of the Civil Rights Act against both GM and the UAW, claiming that the requirement was discriminatory against blacks as well as unjustified as a business necessity. What was the result? [Donnell v. General Motors Corp., 576 F.2d 1292 (8th Cir. 1978)]

7. Beginning in June 1966, Corning Glass Works started to open up jobs on the night shift to women. The previously separate male and female seniority lists were consolidated, and the women became eligible to exercise their seniority on the same basis as men and to bid for higher-paid night inspection jobs as vacancies occurred. But on January 20, 1969, a new collective bargaining agreement went into effect; it established a new job evaluation system for setting wage rates. This agreement abolished (for the future) separate base wages for night and day shift inspectors and imposed a uniform base wage for inspectors that exceeded the wage rate previously in effect for the night shift. The agreement, however, did allow for a higher "red circle" rate for employees hired prior to January 20, 1969, when working as inspectors on the night shift. This "red circle" wage served essentially to perpetuate the differential in base wages between day and night inspectors. Was Corning in violation of the Civil Rights Act of 1964? [Corning Glass Works v. Brennan, 417 U.S. 188, 94 S.Ct. 839 (1974)]

8. At an REA shipping terminal, a conveyor belt was inoperative because an electrical circuit had shorted out. The manager called a licensed electrical contractor. When the contractor arrived, REA's maintenance supervisor was in the circuit breaker room. The floor was wet, and the maintenance supervisor was using sawdust to try to soak up the water. While the licensed electrical contractor was attempting to fix the short circuit, standing on the wet floor, he was electrocuted. Simultaneously, REA's maintenance supervisor, who was standing on a wooden platform, was burned and knocked unconscious. OSHA wanted to fine REA Express $1,000 for failure to furnish a place of employment free from recognized hazards. What was the result? [REA Express, Inc. v. Brennan, 495 F.2d 822 (2d Cir. 1974)]

FOCUS ON ETHICS

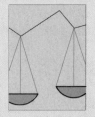

Government Regulation

Government regulation is all-pervasive in our economic and legal system. It includes consumer protection, environmental protection, antitrust law, employment, and labor relations law. In all areas of government regulation, one can ask the question, "Why does government regulation exist?" Pure capitalist ideology has as its basis a minimum of government intervention in the economic system. Yet today virtually every area of economic activity is regulated by government. Is this increased government regulation due to a change in the capitalist ideology, or is it because the ethical concerns of society have changed?

EMPLOYMENT DISCRIMINATION

Society has definitely changed its thinking with respect to employment. In the past, traditional concerns in the area of employment discrimination centered on the failure to hire, retain, and promote with equality. Equal opportunity regulations were therefore designed to reduce or eliminate discriminatory practices. Attempts at "making up" for past patterns of discrimination have resulted in affirmative action programs. Many of these affirmative action programs have resulted in what has been

termed "reverse discrimination" against majority groups. Such reverse discrimination raises the ethical issue of how far society should go in trying to remedy the effects of past discrimination against minorities.

In the well-known case of *Regents of the University of California v. Bakke,* [438 U.S 265, 98 S.C. 2733 (1978)], for example, Alan Bakke, a Vietnam veteran and engineer who had been turned down for medical school at the Davis campus of the University of California, discovered that his academic record was better than those of some of the minority applicants who had been admitted to the program. He sued the University of California regents, alleging reverse discrimination. The Supreme Court held that a public university may give favorable weight to minority applicants, as part of a plan to increase minority enrollment. The Court, however, stated that a quota system, in which a certain number of seats is explicitly reserved for minority applicants, is unconstitutional. In other words, public universities may consider race or ethnic background as a factor in attempting to obtain the benefits that flow from an ethnically diverse student body but they may not utilize a quota system for the benefit of minorities.

Burlington Northern settled a ten-year-old discrimination case by agreeing not only to pay $10 million in back wages to current and former black employees, but also to give priority consideration to black applicants who had been previously rejected for jobs. Unlike the *Bakke* case, however, Burlington Northern is not using a quota system in which a certain number of jobs are reserved for black applicants. Rather, Burlington Northern is merely obliged to give priority preference to the black applicants previously rejected.

Reverse discrimination was also addressed in the recent case of *Firefighters Local Union No. 1784 v. Stotts,* [104 S.Ct. 2576 (1984)]. In this case, Stotts, a black member of the Memphis, Tennessee, Fire Department filed a class action alleging that the department and certain city officials were violating Title VII of the Civil Rights Act of 1964 by engaging in a pattern or practice of making hiring and promotion decisions on the basis of race. A consent decree was subsequently entered into for the purpose of remedying the department's hiring and promotion practices with respect to blacks.

After the consent decree was entered into, the City of

829

Memphis announced that projected budget deficits necessitated a reduction of city employees. The district court proceeded to enjoin the department from adhering to its seniority system in determining who would be laid off. The court concluded that the proposed layoffs would have a racially discriminatory effect and that the seniority system was not a bona fide one. The court of appeals affirmed and the Supreme Court granted the petitions for certiorari.

The Supreme Court held that the consent decree did not include the displacement of white employees with seniority over blacks, and hence the district court's injunction did not merely enforce the agreement of the parties as embodied in the consent decree. The court concluded that, while Title VII protects bona fide seniority systems, it is inappropriate to deny an innocent employee the benefits of his or her seniority in order to provide a remedy in a pattern-or-practice suit. Thus, the Supreme Court's decision prevented the use of reverse discrimination in the area of seniority in hiring in order to remedy past discrimination.

How much should the current generation of white employees and other members of majority groups have to pay for past discriminatory practices of employers? To what extent, and in what ways, should the government regulate employment conditions to insure equal opportunity? These are the questions facing society— and the courts—today.

ENVIRONMENTAL CONCERNS

To what extent is business required to concern itself with the conservation of natural resources? Does a company have to wait until it is besieged by protesters before it acts, such as in the case of Weyerhauser in the Northwest? This forest products company found itself under attack by protesters who accused it of raping the forest. It ultimately set up an extensive program of replanting trees and became more selective in its cutting, thereafter cutting in a manner to conserve natural resources.

For business enterprises generally, the emphasis has been on maximizing short-term profits and, thus, taking the minimal environmental protections required by law. Yet the effect large corporations' activities have on the environment has now become a subject of public concern. Throughout this nation's history Americans have tended to view large corporations with a somewhat critical eye. Whereas in the past corporations have been criticized for failing to create enough jobs or for failing to produce a sufficient quantity or quality of goods and services, these same corporations are now being criticized for failing to consider as their ethical responsibility the protection of the environment. Yet the fact is that companies typically cannot protect the environment without incurring higher production costs, costs that are ultimately passed on to the consumer. This result is generally not happily received by stockholders—even those having environmentalist leanings. Pollution control clearly involves costs that must be absorbed somewhere—by paying out smaller dividends, raising prices, or lowering employee wages.

In a competitive economic system, companies cannot be socially responsible alone. If an individual firm tries to accept this responsibility, and other firms don't, it may lead to lower profits for the socially responsible firm and eventually to its demise. Consequently, we can argue that it is because of our competitive system that we require government regulation and that this need is particularly great in the environmental protection area.

But does this mean that it is only through government regulation of all competitors that we will achieve a reduction in the amount of environmental destruction due to production processes? Is it possible to combine profit-making activities *and* environmental protection programs? Dow Chemical thought so. That firm devised and implemented a massive program of pollution control directed toward waste reduction and the conservation of raw materials. Manufacturing processes were closely scrutinized to increase operating efficiency, to recycle raw materials formerly vented into the air or lost to the sewer, and to use waste products. While in its press releases Dow emphasized its good citizenship, it nonetheless profited by these programs. Pollution control meant savings that could be transferred directly into higher company profits.

ANTITRUST QUESTIONS

In the last quarter-century, antitrust sanctions have been applied to individual corporate officers and directors who have knowingly violated antitrust laws. Jail sentences were given to officers and directors of a corporation due to antitrust violations for the first time in the 1960s. One must ask whether a director or officer of a corporation knowingly should allow the corporation to engage in activities that are clearly in violation of antitrust laws? Again we are faced with the problem of where the duty of loyalty lies for a director or officer of a corporation. If the only duty is to the shareholders, then we would not have a difficult time arguing that directors and officers of a corporation should ignore antitrust laws "as long as they can get away with it." On the other hand, if the ethical responsibility of directors and officers of a corporation is to the public at large, then deliberate acts in violation of antitrust laws should never be performed.

But what about antitrust laws that, in fact, seem unreasonable? In particular, the Robinson-Patman Act has been lambasted by lawyers, businesspersons, and economists alike for many years. In principle, this statute was passed to protect the small businessperson from the buying power of chain stores by limiting price concessions granted to powerful buyers. Thus, the statute prohibited price discrimination unless such discrimination was supported by cost savings or was otherwise necessary to meet a competitor's price. In practice,

however, it has been used on numerous occasions by small stores to effectively extort tribute from large firms. In other words, every time a large operation was able to undercut the price of a smaller operation in the same line of business, the smaller concern entered into antitrust litigation citing violation of Robinson-Patman Act. This use of the Robinson-Patman Act has been severely criticized as being anticompetitive and contrary to the guiding principles of the antitrust laws.

Numerous economic studies have shown that the Robinson-Patman Act has probably resulted in economic inefficiency. But does that mean it should be repealed? Not necessarily, because we may have an ethical responsibility to maintain a large number of small businesses in the United States. After all, the larger the business, presumably the greater the amount of political power. Thus, an objective of antitrust policy may be to limit the social and political power of big business and to increase that of small business. This objective is quite logical, considering the fact that the antitrust laws were enacted during a period of distrust of largeness and concentrations of power. Therefore, we should not

be surprised when the free play of market forces is interrupted in favor of ethical responsibilities such as preserving and encouraging small business. If we wish to maintain a diffuse amount of political power within our society, perhaps we should foster legislation such as the Robinson-Patman Act, which prevents small firms from being forced out of business by larger businesses—even if the latter are more efficient.

DISCUSSION QUESTIONS

1. Does government regulation work? Why or why not?

2. "The only necessary antitrust legislation we need is that which already exists in the competitive marketplace, and it is called competition." Discuss and analyze this extreme view of antitrust legislation.

3. It is often said that the regulated industries capture the regulators. What does this mean? Is there any way to avoid this "capture" phenomenon?

4. What is a company's ethical responsibility to its workers? How can a company balance its ethical responsibilities to its workers and its legal responsibilities to its shareholders?

UNIT VIII

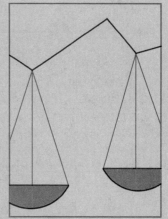

PROTECTION OF PROPERTY AND OTHER INTERESTS

51

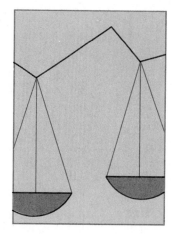

Personal Property

Property consists of the legally protected rights and interests a person has in anything with an ascertainable value that is subject to ownership. Property would have little value (and the word would have little meaning) if the law did not define the right to use it, to sell or dispose of it, and to prevent trespassing upon it. In the United States, the ownership of property receives unique protection under the law. The Bill of Rights states that "no person shall . . . be deprived of life, liberty, or property, without due process of law; nor shall private property be taken for public use, without just compensation." The Fourteenth Amendment provides that "no State shall . . . deprive any person of life, liberty, or property, without due process of law."

THE NATURE OF PERSONAL PROPERTY

Property may be divided into real property and personal property. **Real property** (sometimes called "realty" or "real estate") means the land and everything permanently attached to the land. Where structures are permanently attached to the land, then everything attached permanently to the structures is also realty. (Real property is discussed in detail in Chapter 53.) Everything else is **personal property** ("personalty").

Since personal property and real property differ significantly, the law has developed different sets of rules to deal with their acquisition and disposition. For example, a lease of real property conveys a *property interest* from the landlord (lessor) to the tenant (lessee). A lease of personal property merely transfers a *possessory interest*, creating a bailment (to be discussed in the next chapter).

There are occasions when it is difficult to determine whether the items transferred are realty or personalty. This can be particularly important when dealing with the sale of the item. For example, two such issues deal with *fixtures* and contracts for the sale of *minerals* (including oil, gas, and the like), *structures*, *crops*, and *timber* to be removed from the realty. Because of classification ambiguities, special rules have evolved recently to clarify and even change past rules (for example, the UCC with respect to timber—UCC 2–107[2]).

A **fixture** is personal property attached to the realty or used in such a manner that it becomes a part of the realty. Fixtures pass as part of the realty, unless the seller expressly excludes them from the sale. Until personal property becomes a fixture, it remains personal property and does not pass as part of the realty.

For example, whether a dishwasher is part of the realty as a fixture or is a piece of personal property owned by a seller can be important in the sale of a house. If the dishwasher is built into a kitchen counter, it probably will be considered a fixture and pass with the title of the house from the seller to the buyer. If it is not so attached (that is, if it is portable), it remains personalty and will not pass with the title of the house.

Personal property can be tangible or intangible. *Tangible personal property*, like a TV set, heavy construction equipment, or a car, has physical substance. *Intangible personal property* represents some set of rights and duties, but it has no real physical existence. Stocks and bonds are intangible personal property.

Attorneys sometimes refer to all personal property as **chattel,** a more comprehensive term than *goods* because it includes living as well as inanimate property. Often, instead of saying personal property, the law will refer to goods as chattel.

The Expanding Nature of Personal Property

In a dynamic society, the concept of personal property must expand to take account of new types of ownership rights. For example, gas, water, and telephone services are now considered personal property for the purpose of criminal prosecution when they are stolen or used without payment. Federal and state statutes protect against the copying of musical compositions. It is a crime now to engage in the "bootlegging"—illegal copying for resale—of records and tapes. The theft of computer programs is usually considered a theft of personal property.

PROPERTY RIGHTS AND OWNERSHIP TITLE

Property can be viewed as a bundle of rights. These rights include:

1. Possession.
2. Disposition—sale, gift, rental, lease, and so on.

There are two principal ways for more than one person to hold this bundle at one time. These types of concurrent ownerships are:

1. Tenancy in common.
2. Joint tenancy with right of survivorship, commonly called joint tenancy.

Fee Simple

When a person or persons holds the entire bundle of rights, they are said to be the owner or owners in **fee simple.** The owner or owners in fee simple are entitled to use, possess, or dispose of the property as they choose during their lifetime, and upon death, their interests in the property descend to their heirs.

Tenancy in Common

Tenancy in common is co-ownership in which two or more persons own an undivided fractional interest in the property, but upon one tenant's death, that interest passes to his or her heirs. For example, Reband and Charnock own a rare stamp collection as tenants in common. Should Reband die before Charnock, one-half of the stamp collection would become the property of Reband's heirs. If Reband sold her interest to French before she died, French and Charnock would be co-owners as tenants in common. If French died, his interest in the personal property would pass to his heirs, and they in turn would own the property with Charnock as tenants in common.

Joint Tenancy with Right of Survivorship

In a **joint tenancy with right of survivorship,** two or more persons own an undivided interest in the whole (personal property). Joint tenancy with right of survivorship can be terminated any time before the joint tenant's death by gift or by sale. If no termination occurs, then upon the death of a joint tenant, his or her interest transfers to the remaining joint tenants, not to the heirs of the deceased joint tenant. In the preceding example, if Reband dies before Charnock, the entire collection becomes the property of Charnock. Reband's heirs receive absolutely no interest in the collection. If, prior to Reband's death, she sells her interest to French, French and Charnock become co-owners. Reband's sale, however, terminates the joint tenancy with the right of survivorship, and French and Charnock become owners as tenants in common.

Less Common Ways of Holding Property

There are two less common types of concurrent ownership. One is tenancy by the entirety, and the other is community property.

Tenancy by the Entirety This type of co-ownership is less common today than it used to be. Typically, it is created by a conveyance (transfer) to a husband and wife. It is distinguished from joint tenancy with right of survivorship by the inability of either spouse to transfer separately his or her interest during his or her life. In some states where statutes give the wife the right to convey her property, this form of concurrent ownership has been effectively abolished. A divorce will terminate a tenancy by the entirety. A partitioning of the property will create separate interests in it.

Community Property This type of ownership applies only in Arizona, California, Idaho, Louisiana, Nevada, New Mexico, Texas, Washington, and Wisconsin. Each spouse technically owns an *undivided* one-half interest in the property. This type of ownership applies to most personal property acquired by the husband and/or wife during the course of marriage. It generally does not apply to property acquired prior to the marriage.

ACQUIRING OWNERSHIP OF PERSONAL PROPERTY

The ownership of personal property can be acquired in the following ways:

1. By possession.
2. By purchase.
3. By production.
4. By gift.
5. By will or inheritance.
6. By accession.

Each of these is discussed in turn below.

Possession

A particularly interesting example of acquiring ownership by possession is the capture of wild animals. Wild animals belong to no one in their natural state, and the first person to take possession of a wild animal normally owns it. The killing of a wild animal amounts to assuming ownership of it. Merely being in hot pursuit does not give title, however. There are two exceptions to this basic rule. First, any wild animals captured by a trespasser are the property of the landowner, not the trespasser. Second, if wild animals are captured or killed in violation of wild

game statutes, the capturer does not obtain title to the animals; rather, the state does. Other illustrations of acquiring ownership by possession are presented later in this chapter.

Purchase

Purchase is one of the most common means of acquiring and transferring ownership of personal property. The purchase or sale of personal property (called goods) is covered in depth in Chapters 17 to 20.

Production

Production—the fruits of labor—is another means of acquiring ownership of personal property. Nearly everyone in the United States today is involved in some sort of production. For example, writers, inventors, and manufacturers all produce personal property and thereby acquire title to it. (In some situations—for example, where researchers are hired for that purpose—the producer does not own what is produced.)

Gifts

A **gift** is another fairly common means of both acquiring and transferring ownership of real and personal property. A gift is essentially a *voluntary* transfer of property ownership. It is not supported by legally sufficient consideration since the very essence of a gift is giving without consideration. A gift must be transferred or delivered in the present rather than in the future. For example, suppose that your aunt tells you that she is going to give you a new Mercedes-Benz for your next birthday. This is simply a *promise* to make a gift. It is not considered a gift until the Mercedes-Benz is delivered to the donee.

The Requirements of an Effective Gift There are three requirements for an effective gift:

1. Delivery.
2. Donative intent.
3. Acceptance by the donee.

Delivery Delivery is obvious in most cases, but some objects cannot be relinquished physically. Then the question of delivery depends upon the surrounding circumstances. When the physical object cannot be delivered, a symbolic or **constructive delivery** will be sufficient. Constructive delivery does not confer actual possession of the object in question. It is a general term for all those acts that the law holds to be equivalent to acts of real delivery. Suppose that you want to make a gift of various old rare coins that you have stored in a safety deposit box. You certainly cannot deliver the box itself to the donee, and you do not want to take the coins out of the bank. Instead, you can simply deliver the key to the box to your donee. This constitutes symbolic, or constructive, delivery of the contents of the box.

Delivery of intangible personal property must be accomplished by symbolic or constructive delivery. For example, ownership interests in firms are often represented by stock certificates, and delivery of the certificate entitles the holder to dividends. Other examples of intangible personal property that must be constructively delivered include insurance policies, contracts, promissory notes, and chattel mortgages.

An effective delivery also requires giving up *complete dominion and control* (ownership rights) over the subject matter of the gift. The outcome of disputes often turns on the retaining or relinquishing of control over the subject matter of the gift. The Internal Revenue Service scrutinizes transactions between relatives when one relative has given away income-producing property. A relative who does not relinquish complete control over a piece of property will have to pay taxes on the income from that property. Under the tax laws, it may be illegal to assign or to give away income while retaining control over

the property that produces the income (unless a special trust is set up).

Delivery can be accomplished by means of a third person. The third person may be the agent of the donor or the donee. If the person is the agent of the donor, the gift is effective when the agent delivers to the donee. If, on the other hand, the third person is the agent of the donee, the gift is effective when the donor delivers the property to the donee's agent.[1] Where there is doubt as to whose agent the third party is, he or she is generally presumed to be the agent of the donor. Naturally, no delivery is necessary if the gift is already in the hands of the donee. All that is necessary to complete the gift in such a case is the required intent and acceptance by the donee.

Donative Intent   Donative intent is determined from the language of the donor and the surrounding circumstances. For example, when a gift is challenged in court, the court may look at the relationship between the parties and the size of the gift in relation to the donor's other assets. A gift to an archenemy will be viewed with suspicion. Likewise, when people give away a large portion of their assets, the courts will scrutinize the transaction to determine the mental capacity of the donor and whether there is any fraud or duress.

In the following case, the court looks at the intent of the donor and the question of delivery.

---

1.   Bickford v. Mattocks, 95 Me. 547, 50 A. 894 (1901).

ESTATE OF PIPER
Missouri Court of Appeals, 1984.
676 S.W.2d 897.

BACKGROUND AND FACTS   *Gladys Piper died intestate in 1982. At the time of her death, she owned personal property consisting of household goods, two old automobiles, farm machinery, and "miscellaneous" items totalling $5,150. This did not include jewelry or cash. When Gladys died, she had $206.57 in cash and her two diamond rings, known as the "Andy Piper" rings, in her purse. The contents of Gladys's purse were taken by her niece Wanda Brown upon Gladys' death allegedly to preserve them for the estate. Clara Kauffmann, a friend of Gladys Piper, filed a claim against the estate for $4,800 because from October 1974 until Gladys's death in 1982, Clara took Gladys to the doctor, beauty shop, and grocery store, wrote her checks to pay her bills and helped her care for her home. Clara maintained that Gladys had promised to pay Clara for these services and that the diamond rings were a gift. The trial court denied Clara's request for payment of $4,800 on the basis that the services had been voluntary. Clara then filed a petition for delivery of personal property, the rings, which was granted by the trial court. The defendants appealed.*

GREENE, Judge

* * * *

* * * Named defendants were the administrator of the estate as well as the nieces and nephews, including Wanda Brown, of Gladys Piper. The petition, authorized by § 473.240, RSMo 1978, as amended, alleged that the "Andy Piper" rings, of the appraised value of $2,500, were in the possession of Wanda Brown, having never been surrendered to the estate's administrator, and that the rings were the property of Clara, "having been a consummated gift long prior to the death of Gladys Piper." Clara requested an order from the trial court directing Wanda Brown to deliver the rings to Clara and, if Wanda did not comply, that Clara have judgment "against the defendants in the sum of $2,500."

In his answer, the administrator requested the court to determine the rights of the estate and the parties to the property in question. In her answer, Wanda Brown admitted possession of the rings and cash, and that her custody of them had been necessary to preserve the assets until an administrator was appointed. Her answer included "[f]or Estate inventory purposes," an appraisal of the rings by one Dan H. Maxey of Reno, Nevada, which showed their wholesale value as $875.

After hearing evidence, the trial court judgment directed Wanda Brown to deliver the rings and the cash to the administrator of the estate. The judgment further found that the value of the rings was $2,500, that they were the property of Clara Kauffman, and that Clara was entitled to possession of them. The judgment concluded by saying that if the rings were not delivered to Clara that she was entitled to a judgment of $2,500 against the estate. All defendants appealed from the judgment.

* * * *

We direct our attention to that portion of the judgment declaring that the rings were the property of Clara Kauffman. Clara's petition claimed the rings belonged to her by reason of "a consummated gift long prior to the death of Gladys Piper." The only evidence on the gift issue came from two witnesses. James Naylor, who had known Gladys for over 20 years, testified that when he saw Gladys "[b]etween the time of her last admission to the hospital and the date of her death," Gladys told him, after Naylor had complimented her on her rings, that "these are Clara's, but I am wearing them until I am finished with them, or until I am dead or whatever she may have said * * *." Beverly Marcus testified that Gladys told her "'when she was through with those rings, they were to be Clara's.'"

There was no evidence of any actual delivery to Clara, at any time, of the rings. A person claiming an inter vivos gift of personal property has the burden of proving it by clear and convincing evidence. * * * The essentials of such a gift are 1) a present intention to make a gift on the part of the donor, 2) a delivery of the property by donor to donee, and 3) an acceptance by donee, whose ownership takes effect immediately and absolutely. * * *

While no particular form is necessary to effect a delivery, and while the delivery may be actual, constructive, or symbolical, there must be some evidence to support a delivery theory. What we have here, at best, through the testimony of James Naylor and Beverly Marcus, was an intention on the part of Gladys, at some future time, to make a gift of the rings to Clara. Such an intention, no matter how clearly expressed, which has not been carried into effect, confers no ownership rights in the property in the intended donee. * * * Language written or spoken, expressing an intention to give, does not constitute a gift, unless the intention is executed by a complete and unconditional delivery of the subject matter, or delivery of a proper written instrument evidencing the gift. * * * There is no evidence in this case to prove delivery, and, for such reason, the trial court's judgment is erroneous.

* * * *

The judgment of the trial court was reversed because Gladys never delivered the rings to Clara.

DECISION AND REMEDY

Acceptance The final requirement of a valid gift is acceptance by the donee. This rarely presents any problems since most donees readily accept their gifts. The courts generally assume acceptance unless shown otherwise.

Gifts *Inter Vivos* and Gifts *Causa Mortis* Gifts **inter vivos** are made during one's lifetime. Gifts **causa mortis** are made in contemplation of imminent death. Gifts *causa mortis* do not become absolute until the donor dies from the contemplated illness or disease. The donee must survive to take the gift, and the donor must not have revoked the gift prior to death. A gift *causa mortis* is revocable at any time up to the death of the donor and is automatically revoked if the donor recovers.

Suppose Stevens is to be operated on for a cancerous tumor. Before the operation, he delivers an envelope to a close business associate. The envelope contains a letter saying, "I realize my days are numbered and I want to give you this check for $1,000,000 in the event of my death from this operation." The business associate cashes the check. The surgeon begins the operation and decides not to remove the tumor. Stevens recovers fully from the operation. Several months later Stevens dies from a heart attack that is totally unrelated to the operation. If Stevens's personal representative tries to recover the $1,000,000, she will succeed. The gift *causa mortis* is automatically revoked if the donor recovers. The *specific event* that was contemplated in making the gift was death from a particular operation. Since Stevens's death was not the result of a cancerous tumor, the gift is revoked and the $1,000,000 passes to Stevens's personal representative when Stevens dies.[2]

Will or Inheritance

Ownership of property may be transferred by will or by inheritance under state statutes. These transfers, called bequests, devices, or inheritances, are dealt with in Chapter 54.

Accession

Accession means "adding on" to something. It occurs when someone adds value to a piece of personal property by either labor or materials. Generally, there is no dispute about who owns the property after accession has occurred, especially when the accession is accomplished with the owner's consent.

For example, a Corvette customizing specialist comes to Smith's house. Smith has all the materials necessary. The customizing specialist uses them to add a unique bumper to Smith's Corvette. Smith simply pays the customizer for the value of the labor in improving the property, obviously retaining title to the property.

Two situations in which ownership can be in issue after the occurrence of an accession are:

1. Where a party has wrongfully caused the accession.
2. Where the materials added or labor expended greatly increase the value of the property or change the identity of the property.

Some general rules can be applied when either or both situations occur.

If the accession was caused wrongfully (without the owner's consent) and in bad faith, the courts will generally favor the owner over the improver, even if the value of the property was increased substantially. In addition, many courts would deny the improver (wrongdoer) any compensation for the value added; for example, a car thief who put new tires on the stolen car would obviously not be compensated for the value of the new tires.

If the accession is performed in good faith, however, even without the owner's consent, ownership of the improved item most often depends on the actual increase in the value of the property by the accession or change of identity of the property. The greater the increase, the more likely it is that ownership will pass to the improver. Obviously, when this occurs, the improver must compensate the original owner for the value of the property prior to the accession. If the increase in value is not sufficient to pass ownership to the improver, most courts require the owner to compensate the improver for the value added.

To illustrate: Suppose Angelo is walking in a large country field and discovers a huge stone lying near a fence that is shaped approximately like the Lone Ranger's horse, Silver. Angelo comes back for twenty-seven weeks and transforms the stone into an exact replica of Silver. Angelo's artist friends are very

---

2. Brind v. International Trust Co., 66 Colo. 60, 179 P. 148 (1919).

impressed and convince him to move the stone horse to a gallery, where it is valued at $50,000. The owner of the field where Angelo found the stone now wants to claim title to it. Normally, the courts will give Angelo title to the stone because the changes he made caused it to greatly increase in value and the accession was performed in good faith. But Angelo will have to pay the owner of the field for the reasonable value of the stone before it was altered.

Confusion

When the personal property of two persons becomes intermingled, this is called **confusion.** Confusion is defined as the commingling of goods such that one person's personal property cannot be distinguished from another's. It frequently occurs when the goods are fungible.[3] *Fungible goods* are goods of which each particle is identical with every other particle, such as grain and oil. For example, if two farmers put their number 2 grade winter wheat into the same silo, confusion will occur. If the confusion of goods is caused by a person who wrongfully and willfully mixes goods with those of another in order to render them indistinguishable, the innocent party acquires title to the total.

This rule does not apply when confusion occurs by:

1. Agreement.
2. Honest mistake.
3. The act of some third party.

When any of these three events occurs, the owners all share ownership equally as tenants in common. Suppose that you enter into a cooperative arrangement with five other farmers in your local community of Midway, Iowa. Each fall everyone harvests the same amount of number 2 yellow corn. The corn is stored in silos that are held by the cooperative. Each of you owns one-sixth of the total corn in the silos. If anything happens to the corn, each of you will bear the loss in equal proportions of one-sixth.

Often, though, each owner will not have an interest equal to the other owners. In such a case, the owners must keep careful records of their respective proportions. If a dispute over ownership or loss arises, the courts will presume that everyone has an equal interest or proportion of the goods. So you must be prepared to prove that you own more or less than an equal part.

Suppose you own two-thirds of the corn in the Midway Co-op silos above. Further assume that the silos are partially damaged by a tornado and thunderstorm. How much have you lost of your total if one-half of the corn is blown away by the storm? You have lost one-half of your two-thirds, or one-third. When corn is stored by several owners, each owning a different proportion of the total, any loss is shared proportionally.

Confusion that results from intentional wrongdoing or negligent conduct creates a different problem. When there is a loss by fire, theft, or destruction, the person responsible for the commingling must bear the entire loss. However, if the wrongdoer can show that no injury occurred, and can prove what portion he or she contributed to the whole, then the wrongdoer can recover that portion.

Suppose you are the vice-president in charge of purchasing for a salad oil company. You buy 10,000 gallons of high-grade salad oil and have it delivered to a field warehouse company. The warehouse company stores many grades of oil, and your oil is negligently mixed with a much lower grade of oil. The oil was worth $.64 per gallon before it was confused, but now it is worth only $.32 per gallon. Here you should be entitled to claim your 10,000 gallons of oil and sue the warehouse for $3,200 in damages caused by the negligent confusion. On the other hand, suppose the grades of oil were exactly the same but you contracted to have your oil stored in a separate bin? There may have been a technical breach of contract, but you will not recover any damages because there has been no injury.[4]

MISLAID, LOST, AND ABANDONED PROPERTY

Mislaid Property

Property that has been placed somewhere by the owner voluntarily and then inadvertently forgotten

---

3. See UCC 1-201(17).

4. As a matter of commercial reality, very few, if any, warehouses contract for storage in separate facilities. If they did, many people would want separate facilities for fear of confusion. But, this would negate the savings in warehouse storage. Here we are really dealing with *fungible* goods.

is **mislaid property**. Suppose you go to the theater and leave your gloves on the concession stand. The gloves are mislaid property, and the theater owner is entrusted with the duty of reasonable care for the goods. Whenever mislaid property is found, the finder does not obtain title to or possession of the goods.[5] Instead, the owner of the place where the property was mislaid becomes the caretaker of the property because it is highly likely that the true owner will return.[6]

Lost Property

Property that is *not* voluntarily left and forgotten is **lost property**. A finder of lost property can claim title to the property against the whole world, *except the true owner*. If the true owner demands that the lost property be returned, the finder must do so. If a third party attempts to take possession of lost property from a finder, the third party cannot assert a better title than the finder.

Whenever a finder knows who the true owners of property are and fails to return it to them, that finder is guilty of a tort known as *conversion* (see Chapter 4). Finally, many states require the finder to make a reasonably diligent search to locate the true owner of lost property.

Suppose Arnolds works in a large library at night. In the courtyard on her way home, she finds a piece of gold jewelry that looks like it has several precious stones in it. Arnolds decides to take it to a jeweler

to have it appraised. While pretending to weigh the jewelry, an employee of the jeweler removes several of the stones. If Arnolds brings an action to recover the stones from the jeweler, she will win because she found lost property and holds valid title against everyone *except the true owner*. Since the property was *lost* and not *mislaid*, the owner of the library is not the caretaker of the jewelry. Instead, Arnolds acquires title good against the whole world (except the true owner.)[7]

Many states have **estray statutes** to encourage and facilitate the return of property to its true owner and then to reward a finder for honesty if the property remains unclaimed. Such statutes provide an incentive for finders to report their discoveries by making it possible for them, after passage of a specified period of time, to acquire legal title to the property they have found. The statute usually requires the county clerk to advertise the property in an attempt to enhance the opportunity of the owner to recover what has been lost.

There are always some preliminary questions to be resolved before the estray statute can be employed. The item must be *lost property*, not merely mislaid or abandoned property. When the situation indicates that the property was probably lost and not mislaid or abandoned, as a matter of public policy, loss is presumed and the estray statute applies. Such a situation occurred in the following case.

---

5.   The finder is an involuntary bailee. See Chapter 52.
6.   He or she is a bailee with right of possession against all except the true owner.

7.   See Armory v. Delamire, 1 Strange 505 (K.B. 1722). However, if Arnolds had found the jewelry during the course of her employment, her employer would be the involuntary bailee. Further, many courts now say that lost property recovered in a private place allows the owner of the place, *not* the finder, to become the bailee (even if the finder is not a trespasser).

PASET v. OLD
ORCHARD BANK &
TRUST CO.

Appellate Court of Illinois, First
District, Third Division, 1978.
62 Ill. App. 3d 534, 19 Ill. Dec.
389, 378 N.E. 2d 1264.

BACKGROUND AND FACTS   *Paset, a safety deposit box subscriber, brought this action against the Old Orchard Bank and Trust Co, the defendant, seeking a declaratory judgment that the state estray statute applied to her finding $6,325 on a chair in the examination booth in the bank's safety deposit vault area. The money was not claimed within the statutory time period of one year. Hence, the plaintiff petitioned the court to grant her ownership of the money. The trial court entered an order refusing to determine ultimate ownership of the money.*

SIMON, Justice.

On May 8, 1974, the plaintiff, Bernice Paset, a safety deposit box subscriber at the defendant Old Orchard Bank (the bank), found $6,325 in currency on the seat of a chair in an examination booth in the safety deposit vault. The chair was partially under a table. The plaintiff notified officers of the bank and turned the money over to them. She then was told by bank officials that the bank would try to locate the owner, and that she could have the money, if the owner was not located within 1 year.

The bank wrote to everyone who had been in the safety deposit vault area either on the day of, or on the day preceding, the discovery, stating that some property had been found and inviting the customers to describe any property they might have lost. No one reported the loss of currency, and the money remained unclaimed a year after it had been found. However, when the plaintiff requested the money, the bank refused to deliver it to her, explaining that it was obligated to hold the currency for the owner.

*   *   *   *

The bank's position is that the estray statute is not applicable because the money was not lost in the sense the word "lost" is used in that statute. The bank contends that, under the common law, the money was mislaid by its owner rather than lost, and that the estray statute does not apply to mislaid property. In the alternative, the bank argues that the money was discovered not in a public place, but in a private area with access restricted to safety deposit box subscribers. The bank claims, therefore, that the money always was in its constructive possession or custody, either as owner of the premises or as bailee for an unknown and unidentified safety deposit box subscriber, and that property in someone's constructive possession or custody cannot be lost. As against the plaintiff, the bank claims to have the superior right to hold the money indefinitely, and in fact is required to do so until the true owner puts in his appearance.

*   *   *   *

The estray statute provides in [relevant part]:

"If any person or persons find any lost goods, money, bank notes, or other choses in action, of any description whatever, such person or persons shall inform the owner thereof, if known. *   *   * If the owner is unknown and if such property found is of value of $15 or upwards, the finder or finders shall, within 5 days after such finding as aforesaid, appear before some circuit judge residing in the county, and make affidavit of the description thereof, the time and place when and where the same was found, that no alteration has been made in the appearance thereof since the finding of the same, that the owner thereof is unknown to him and that he has not secreted, withheld or disposed of any part thereof. The judge shall enter an order stating the value of the property found as near as he can ascertain. A certified copy of such order and the affidavit of the finder shall, within 10 days after the order has been entered, be transmitted to the county clerk to be recorded in his estray book, and filed in his office.

" *   *   * If the value thereof exceeds the sum of $15, the county clerk, within 20 days after receiving the certified copy of the judge's order shall cause an advertisement to be set up on the court house door, and in 3 other of the most public places in the county, and also a notice thereof to be published for 3 weeks successively in some public newspaper printed in this state and if the owner of such goods, money, bank notes, or other choses in action does not appear and claim the same *   *   * within one year after the advertisement thereof as aforesaid, the ownership of such property shall vest in the finder."

*   *   *   *

Traditionally, the common law has treated lost and mislaid property differently for the purposes of determining ownership of property someone has found. Mislaid property is that which is intentionally put in a certain place and later forgotten; at common law a finder acquires no rights to mislaid property. The element of intentional deposit present in the case of mislaid property is absent in the case of lost property, for property is deemed lost when it is unintentionally separated from the dominion of its owner. The general rule is that the finder is entitled to possession of lost property against everyone except the true owner. We are not concerned in this case with abandoned property where the owner, intending to relinquish all rights to his property, leaves it free to be appropriated by any other person. Although at common law the finder is entitled to keep abandoned property, the plaintiff has not taken the position that the money here was abandoned.

*   *   *   *

[W]e do not accept the bank's initial argument that the money was mislaid rather than lost. It is complete speculation to infer, as the bank urges, that the money was deliberately placed by its owner on the chair located partially under a table in the examining booth, and then forgotten. If the money was intentionally placed on the chair by someone who forgot where he left it, the bank's notice to safety deposit box subscribers should have alerted the owner. The failure of an owner to appear to claim the money in the interval since its discovery is affirmative evidence that the property was not mislaid.

Because the evidence, though ambiguous, tends to indicate that the money probably was not mislaid, and because neither party contends that the money was abandoned, we conclude that the ambiguity should, as a matter of public policy, be resolved in favor of the presumption that the money was lost. *   *   * Accordingly, we reject the bank's first contention that the money was mislaid and the estray statute irrelevant, and conclude that the money was "lost," and so encompassed by the Illinois estray statute.

We also reject the bank's alternative argument that the money, having been found in a place from which the general public was excluded, was always in the bank's constructive custody or possession, and therefore could not have been "lost," as that word is used in the estray statute.

*   *   *   *

*   *   * The bank's record of its safety deposit box subscribers who visited the vault on the day of or the day preceding the plaintiff's discovery gave the bank the opportunity to search for the owner among this limited group. The bank also had sufficient time to contact any subscriber who had not been in his box since the date the plaintiff discovered the money. Consequently, in view of the opportunities the bank had to search out the owner of the money among this limited group, of the notice the bank gave to that group and of the plaintiff's undisputed compliance with the estray statute, vesting the ownership of the money in the finder is a more pragmatic and sensible solution than having the bank continue to hold the money indefinitely.

DECISION   *The appellate court decided that the estray statute should be applied and that*
AND REMEDY   *the ownership of the money should be vested in the finder.*

Abandoned Property

Property that has been *discarded* by the true owner with *no intention* of claiming title to it is **abandoned property**. Someone who finds abandoned property acquires title to it, and such title is good against the whole world, *including the original owner*. The owner of lost property who eventually gives up any further attempt to find the lost property is frequently held to have abandoned the property.

To illustrate the concept of lost property becoming abandoned property, we will assume that Starr is driving with the windows down in her car. Somewhere along her traveled route, a valuable scarf blows out the window. Despite retracing her route, she cannot find the scarf. She finally decides that any

further search is useless and proceeds to her destination 500 miles away. Starr makes no further attempt to find the scarf. Six months later, Frye, a hitchhiker, finds the scarf. Frye has acquired title, which is good even against Starr. (Of course, the same result would occur if Starr had deliberately discarded the scarf along the highway.)

If, however, a finder is trespassing and finds abandoned property, title does not become vested in the finder but vests with the owner of the land. This is also true of lost property. Suppose Callahan employs Allen and Billheimer to clean out a henhouse. Callahan has recently purchased a home that previously had changed hands a number of times. Allen and Billheimer find a tin can full of gold buried in a corner of the henhouse. The can is extremely old and rusty, suggesting that it has been buried there for quite some time. Callahan, the owner of the land, takes the coins from Allen and Billheimer and claims that they belong to her. Allen and Billheimer bring suit to recover the coins. Allen and Billheimer may be able to recover the coins because they were lost articles found concealed in the earth. Such articles, commonly known as *treasure trove*, are usually coin, gold, or silver found hidden in the earth or other private place. In England, treasure trove belongs to the crown, but in the United States, it is treated like lost property and becomes the property of the finder, subject to the rights of the true owner. Note in this example that Allen and Billheimer are not trespassers. If they were trespassers, they would not be entitled to retain the title to the treasure trove.[8]

SPECIAL TYPES OF INTANGIBLE PERSONAL PROPERTY

There are numerous types of intangible personal property. Three such types, briefly discussed in Chapter 5 (Torts Related to Business), are:

1. Patents.
2. Trademarks.
3. Copyrights.

Patents

A patent is a grant from the government that conveys and secures to an inventor the exclusive right to make, use, and sell an invention for seventeen years. Patents are typically given for new articles, but *design patents* are given for manufactured articles that have been changed in a way that will enhance their sale. *Plant patents* are given to individuals who invent, discover, or reproduce a new variety of plant. Patent law has been evolving with respect to computer programs. Initially, computer programs could not be patented, but the commercial necessity of protecting them has led to a revised view.

Trademarks

A trademark is a distinctive mark, model, device, or emblem that manufacturers stamp, print, or

otherwise affix to the goods they produce so that the goods can be identified in the market and their origin verified. Federal statute allows a trademark to be registered by its owner or user. Exclusive use of the trademark can be perpetual. Protection depends on adoption and use; if the owner continues to use the trademark, no one can infringe upon it. International protection can also be afforded by various registrations. Registration is made before using the trademark in most other countries.

A trademark must be distinctive in order to be registered. It is not enough merely to describe an article or to name a city. For example, it would be hard to register the trademark "New York Clothes." Exceptions to this rule, of course, exist. When particular words have been used for such a long time that the public identifies them with a particular product and its origin, then those words can be registered as a trademark. The same holds for geographic terms that have acquired a meaning other than their location.

Trademarks can become so common that they become generic names. For example, "Thermos" was originally a brand name for a thermal food-storage container. Now the term has become synonymous with such containers and therefore can no longer be used solely as one company's trademark.

Copyrights

A copyright is an intangible right granted by statute to the author or originator of certain literary or artistic productions. With a copyright, the owner is vested for a limited time period with the sole and exclusive privilege of reproducing copies of the work for publication and sale.

At common law, any author or compiler of data who prevented others from using the work without permission by keeping it secret had a common law copyright. Such a copyright ended when the work was published. (Publication meant any communication to others, not necessarily in written or printed form.) Federal statutes now govern virtually all copyright law in this country.

On January 1, 1978, a new copyright law became effective, completely replacing Title 17 of the United States Code, which had been used since 1909. The new law is divided into eight chapters, beginning with a discussion of the subject matter and scope of copyright. It includes chapters relating to copyright duration, notice, deposit and registra-

---

8. Danielson v. Roberts, 44 Or. 108, 74 P. 913 (1904).

tion requirements, infringement, manufacturing requirements, administration, and the like. The new copyright law has four essential purposes:

1. To maximize the availability of creative works to the public.
2. To give creators of copyrighted works a fair return and to provide users of copyrighted works with a fair income.
3. To balance the interest of copyright users and owners.
4. To minimize any negative impact on industries regulated by change in the copyright law.

Works created after January 1, 1978, are given statutory copyright protection for the life of the author plus fifty years. Pseudonymous and anonymous publications, as well as those done "for hire" (ghosted), have a copyright term of seventy-five years from publication or one hundred years from creation, whichever is shorter. For those works already under copyright protection, their present term of twenty-eight years from date of first publication will remain. If a renewal is asked for, the second term will be increased to forty-seven years.

Exclusive Use of Copyright   The copyright holder is entitled to the exclusive use of all those materials that are copyrighted, subject to a number of exceptions, such as fair use and library reproduction.

Fair Use   Under the doctrine of fair use, some copying is allowed without payment of fees or permission of the copyright holder. "Fair use" allows reproduction of copyrighted material without permission if the use of the material is "reasonable" and not harmful to the rights of the copyright owner. Section 107 of the new copyright law mentions permissible purposes such as criticism, comment, news reporting, teaching (including multiple copies for classroom use), scholarship, or research. Four criteria are used in considering whether a particular use is reasonable:

1. The purpose and character of the use, including whether it is of a nonprofit, educational nature or of a commercial nature.
2. The amount and importance of the material used in relation to the work as a whole.
3. The nature of the copyrighted work.
4. The effect of the use on the potential market or value of the copyrighted work.

Library Reproduction   Libraries and archives can reproduce single copies of certain copyrighted items for noncommercial purposes without violating the copyright law. Notice of copyright on the library or archive reproduction is necessary, however. Wholesale copying of periodicals is not permitted.

QUESTIONS AND CASE PROBLEMS

1. John has a severe heart attack and is taken to the hospital. He is not expected to live, and he knows it. As a bachelor without close relatives nearby, John gives his car keys to his close friend, Fred, telling Fred that he is expected to die and that the car is Fred's. John survives the heart attack, but two months later he dies from pneumonia. Uncle Sam is executor of John's estate and wants Fred to return the car. Fred refuses, claiming the car was given to him by John as a gift. Discuss whether Fred will be required to return the car to John's estate.

2. Sally goes into Meyer's Department Store to do some Christmas shopping. She becomes engrossed in looking over a number of silk blouses when she suddenly realizes she has a dinner engagement. She hastily departs from the store, inadvertently leaving her purse on a sales counter. Julie, a sales clerk at the store, notices the purse on the counter but leaves it there, expecting Sally to return for it. Later, when Sally returns, the purse is gone. Sally files an action against Meyer's Department Store for the loss of her purse. Discuss the probable success of her suit.

3. Bill Heise is a janitor for the First Mercantile Department Store. While walking to work, Bill discovers an expensive watch lying on the curb. Later that day, while Bill is cleaning the aisles of the store, he discovers a wallet containing $500 but no identification. Bill turns over the wallet to his superior, Joe Frances. Bill gives the watch to his son, Gordon. Two weeks later, Martin Avery, the owner of the watch, discovers that Bill found the watch and demands it back from Gordon. Bill decides now to claim the wallet with its $500, but Joe refuses to turn it

over, saying that Bill is not the true owner and that the money is really the property of the store. Discuss who is entitled to the watch and who is entitled to the wallet containing $500.

4. Fred McDuff has a son named Don. Fred wants to give his son a new car that he has recently purchased. Fred and his son have not gotten along during the past few years, and Fred feels part of this is his fault. He goes to his son's house, wanting to make amends by giving the car to Don. When Fred arrives at Don's house, his daughter-in-law (Don's wife) tells Fred that Don is out of town and will return the next day. Fred gives the keys to the new car to his daughter-in-law, tells her to hold the keys for his son, and says that he will return the next day. Two hours later, Fred has second thoughts about giving Don a car. He retrieves the keys from his daughter-in-law before she can turn them over to Don. Don returns from his trip, learns of the events, and demands possession of the car, claiming a gift was made. Is Don entitled to the car?

5. James DeCante owns a 1967 Chevy. The car has been having continual mechanical problems, and James's repair expenses have been considerable. One day, in disgust, James parks the car on a city-owned vacant lot two blocks from his house. The car sits there for four months. During this period Sam Green observes the car, which has been unattended by James. Sam takes the car and makes improvements and repairs valued at $500. Later, James learns that Sam has the car, has it running smoothly, and is treating the car as if it were his. James demands the car, claiming title. Sam refuses to surrender the car, claiming that he has title. Discuss who is correct and what rights, if any, each person has against the other.

6. Welton is an experienced businessperson. Welton transferred to Gallagher "bearer bonds" stating that the bonds were hers with "no strings attached" and that she should place the bonds in her safe deposit box for safe keeping. Later, Welton wanted Gallagher to return the bonds to him, claiming that he was still the owner. Gallagher refused claiming that Welton's transfer was a gift of the bonds to her. Discuss *fully* whether Welton's transfer of the bearer bonds was a gift. [Welton v. Gallagher, 2 Hawaii App. 242, 630 P.2d 1077 (1981)]

7. McAvoy owned a barbershop. Medina, a regular customer, spotted a pocketbook lying on one of the tables where McAvoy kept magazines for his customers. Medina pointed out the pocketbook to McAvoy. McAvoy put the purse aside and told Medina that he would hold it until its owner returned. Several weeks passed, and no one claimed the pocketbook. Medina returned to the barbershop and claimed that, since the pocketbook was lost property and he was the finder, and since the owner had not reclaimed it, it was his. Who should get possession of the

pocketbook—McAvoy or Medina? [McAvoy v. Medina, 93 Mass. (11 Allen) 548 (1866)]

8. Troop and Rust were partners in an oil and gas operation. Troop owned a three-fourths interest in the operation, and Rust owned a one-fourth interest. After eight years of operation, a dispute arose as to whether Rust had contributed his share of the expenses. As a result of the dispute, the partnership was dissolved. In attempting to divide up the oil, Rust learned that Troop had commingled the partnership's oil with oil from another lease that Troop owned. At trial, Troop was unable to show how much of the commingled oil had come from his other operation. How much of the oil should each of the parties receive? [Troop v. St. Louis Union Trust Co., 25 Ill. App. 2d 143, 116 N.E. 2d 116 (1960)]

9. Richard Coddington, a single man, opened a joint savings account with his mother. They signed a signature card that stated that the account was owned by them as joint tenants with the right of survivorship. New York banking law provides that joint tenancy has been created when a bank account is opened in the names of two persons and is "payable to either or the survivor." However, there was no statement made on the passbook as to survivorship. Later, Richard married Margaret. Richard died. Margaret claimed a share of the savings account on the ground that it was not a joint tenancy because the passbook did not contain words of survivorship. She also claimed that the statutory presumption of a joint tenancy was negated by Richard's past behavior—his withdrawal of substantial sums from the account throughout his life. At trial, the court awarded the entire account to Richard's mother. Margaret appealed. What was the result? [56 App. Div. 2d 697, 391 N.Y.S. 2d 760 (1977)]

10. In 1945 Lieber, then in the U.S. Army, was one of the first soldiers to occupy Munich, Germany. He and some of his friends entered Adolf Hitler's apartment and removed various items of his personal belongings. Lieber brought home his share, including Hitler's uniform jacket and cap and some of his decorations and personal jewelry. Lieber's possession of these articles was publicly known because Louisiana newspapers published pictures and stories about the collection. Lieber was the subject of a feature story in the Louisiana State University Alumni News of October 1945. In 1968, Lieber's collection was stolen by his chauffeur. The chauffeur sold it to a New York dealer. The dealer then sold it to Mohawk Arms, who purchased it in good faith. When Lieber discovered the whereabouts of his stolen property, he made a demand for it that was refused. The trial court granted summary judgment to Lieber. Mohawk Arms then appealed. What was the result? [Lieber v. Mohawk Arms, Inc., 64 Misc. 2d 206, 314 N.Y.S. 2d 510 (1970)]

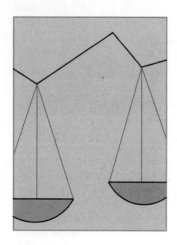

52

Bailments

Virtually every individual and business is affected by the law of bailments at one time or another (and sometimes even on a daily basis). When individuals deal with bailments, whether they realize it or not, they are subject to the obligations and duties that arise from the bailment relationship. A **bailment** is formed by the delivery of personal property, without transfer of title, by one person, called a **bailor,** to another, called a **bailee,** usually under an agreement for a particular purpose (for example, loan, storage, repair, or transportation). Upon completion of the purpose, the bailee is obligated to return the bailed property to the bailor or to a third person or to dispose of it as directed. Most bailments are created by agreement, but not necessarily by contract, because in many bailments not all of the elements of a contract (such as mutual assent or consideration) are present. For example, if you loan your business law text to a friend so that your friend can read tomorrow's assignment, a bailment is created, but not by contract, because there is no consideration. On the other hand, many commercial bailments, such as the delivery of your suit or dress to the cleaners for dry cleaning, are based on contract.

A bailment is distinguished from a sale or a gift in that possession is transferred without passage of title or intent to transfer title. In a sale or a gift, title is transferred from the seller or donor to the buyer or donee.

The number, scope, and importance of bailments created daily in the business community and in everyday life make it desirable for any person to understand the elements necessary for the creation of a bailment and to know what rights, duties, and liabilities flow from bailments.

ELEMENTS OF A BAILMENT

Not all transactions involving the delivery of property from one person to another create a bailment. The basic elements of bailment creation are:

1. Personal property.
2. Delivery of possession (without title).
3. Agreement.

Personal Property Requirement

Bailment involves only personal property. A bailment of persons is not possible. Although a bailment of your luggage is created when it is transported by an airline, as a passenger you are not the subject of a bailment. Also, you cannot bail realty; thus, leasing your house to a tenant is not bailment.

Bailments involving *tangible* items, such as jewelry, cattle, or automobiles, are more frequent than

848

bailments of *intangible* personal property, such as promissory notes and shares of corporate stock.

Delivery of Possession

Delivery of possession means transfer of possession of property to the bailee in such a way that:

1. The bailee is given exclusive possession and control over the property.
2. The bailee *knowingly* accepts the personal property.[1]

Suppose that Stevenson is in a hurry to catch his plane. He has a package he wants to check at the airport. He arrives at the airport check-in station, but the person in charge has gone on a coffee break. Stevenson decides to leave the package on the counter. Even though there has clearly been physical transfer

of the package, the person in charge of the check-in station did not knowingly accept the personal property and therefore there was no effective delivery. The same result would occur in the following example: Delacroix checks her coat at a restaurant. In the coat pocket is a $20,000 diamond necklace. By accepting the coat, the bailee does not *knowingly* accept the necklace.

If either delivery of possession or knowing acceptance is lacking, there is no bailment relationship. To illustrate: As a general rule valet parking constitutes a bailment, but self-parking does not. The difference is found in the control of the car keys. When a car owner is required to leave the car keys with the parking attendant, the owner transfers a sufficient amount of control over the car to the parking company to constitute a bailment. When the car is parked and locked and the keys retained by the owner, the parking garage is merely a *lessor* of space and the car owner a lessee.

The following case distinguishes between a lease of space and a bailment.

---

1. We are dealing here with *voluntary* bailments.

BACKGROUND AND FACTS *Plaintiff Nelson parked his airplane at a facility owned and operated by the defendant, Schroeder Aerosports, Inc. The parking spaces contained tie-down facilities to secure the aircraft. Nelson tied his plane down when he left it at the facility. The defendant later moved Nelson's plane to another space and tied it down. A later attempt was made by the defendant to move the aircraft, but the tie-down knots were so secure that the aircraft was not disturbed. At all times Nelson retained the keys to the plane. After the weather bureau issued a storm warning, the defendant checked all aircraft in tie-down spaces and found that the tie-downs for Nelson's plane were securely tied. During the storm, Nelson's plane was turned over by high winds, and Nelson sought recovery from the defendant for the damage. The trial court held for the defendant.*

NELSON v. SHROEDER AEROSPORTS, INC.
Supreme Court of South Dakota, 1979.
280 N.W.2d 107.

DUNN, Justice.

Plaintiff argues that a bailor-bailee relationship arose between the parties in that a prima facie case was presented for the existence of a bailment. Plaintiff correctly states the elements for a showing of such a prima facie case, to wit: (1) the delivery of the property to defendant, (2) its value, (3) defendant's failure to return the property in good condition upon demand, and (4) the damages resulting from the failure to deliver.

Plaintiff fails, however, to recognize that the delivery contemplated above for the existence of a bailment turns on whether possession and control of the property is retained by the owner or is delivered to defendant. To constitute sufficient delivery, the generally recognized test is whether there is a full transfer of the property so as to amount to relinquishment of exclusive possession, control and dominion over the property for the duration of the relationship so that the person to whom delivery is made can exclude the possession of the owner and all other persons within the limits of the agreement between the parties.

*   *   *   *

The evidence shows that plaintiff kept the keys to the aircraft and gave a third party permission to fly the aircraft. This exhibits plaintiff's retained control over the aircraft.

*   *   *

We must conclude that plaintiff did not relinquish exclusive possession, control and dominion over the aircraft. We hold that under the circumstances present in this case, where plaintiff's aircraft was placed in the airport parking or tie-down space and defendant was not given and did not assert exclusive control over the aircraft, there was no delivery giving rise to a bailor-bailee relationship and only a lease relating to the space occupied by the aircraft was created as opposed to a bailment of the aircraft into the hands of defendant.

DECISION AND REMEDY   *The trial court's judgment for the defendant was upheld. There are, however, cases dealing with* paid-for *public parking privileges in which the court has held that a bailment is created even though the car owner locks up the car and retains the keys.*

There are two types of delivery that will result in the bailee's exclusive possession of and control over the property. One is a *physical delivery*, and the other is a *constructive delivery*.

Physical Delivery   A distinction is made between a restaurant patron who checks a coat with an attendant and a patron who hangs the coat on a coat-rack. The coat given to the attendant constitutes a physical delivery and therefore a bailment. The attendant (hence the restaurant) has exclusive possession and control over the retention and removal of the coat. By contrast, the self-hung coat can be removed at any time by the patron or anyone else so inclined. The restaurant does not have substantial control over the property and is not considered a bailee.

Constructive Delivery—Bailment without Physical Delivery   Constructive delivery is a substitute delivery or symbolic delivery. What is physically delivered to the bailee is not the actual property bailed, but something so related to the property that the requirement of delivery is satisfied. For example, Lyssenko owns a boat that she loans to Brady for the weekend. It is moored at a municipal marina. Lyssenko gives Brady the boat registration papers so that the harbor master will allow Brady to board the boat. Lyssenko has made constructive delivery of the boat to Brady.

There are certain unique situations in which a bailment is found despite the apparent lack of the requisite elements of control or knowledge. In particular, safe deposit box rental is usually held to constitute a bailor-bailee relationship between the bank and its customer, despite the bank's lack of knowledge of the contents and its inability to have exclusive control of the property.[2]

Another example of such a situation is where the bailee acquires the property accidentally or by mistake—such as in finding someone else's lost or mislaid property. A bailment is created even though the bailor did not voluntarily deliver the property to the bailee. These are called *constructive* or *involuntary* bailments.

The Bailment Agreement

A bailment agreement can be *express* or *implied*. Although a written agreement is not required for bailments of less than one year (that is, the Statute of Frauds does not apply), it is a good idea to have one, especially when valuable property is involved.

The bailment agreement expressly or impliedly provides for the return of the bailed property to the bailor or to a third person, or provides for disposal by the bailee. The agreement presupposes that the

---

2.   By statute or by express contract, however, a safe deposit box may be a lease of space or license, depending on the jurisdiction or the facts or both.

bailee will return the identical goods originally given by the bailor. However, in bailment of *fungible goods* [3]—uniform identical goods—or bailments with the *option to purchase*, only equivalent property must be returned.

For example, Sanchez, Basen, and Kerlly each store 1,000 pounds of grain in Hansen's Warehouse every year, and each receives receipts. When Sanchez returns to reclaim "his grain," Hansen's Warehouse is obligated to give him 1,000 pounds of wheat grain—but not necessarily the particular kernels he originally deposited. Sanchez cannot claim that Hansen's Warehouse is guilty of conversion (see Chapter 4) in not returning to him the exact wheat that he put into storage. As long as the warehouse returns goods of the same *type, grade,* and *quantity,* Hansen's Warehouse—the bailee—has performed its obligation.

A bailment with an option or offer to purchase allows the prospective buyer the right to hold or use the property while deciding whether to purchase. At the end of an agreed-upon period, the bailee must either return the property to the bailor-seller or agree to purchase the property (such as by paying cash to the seller). In the latter case, the bailee-buyer returns to the bailor-seller "equivalent" property (promise or payment of money), terminating the bailment and creating a sale.

A typical example is a *sale on approval.* Suppose Rand is interested in buying a lawn mower. The seller gives him possession of a new model, telling him to take it home and try it out. The sales price is $280. If Rand does not like the lawn mower, he can bring it back within two weeks. If he does not bring it back within this period, or if he approves the offer, the seller will bill him. Thus, a bailment is created, and Rand has the duty to either return the lawn mower or approve the offer and return the equivalent in the form of the purchase price.

ORDINARY BAILMENTS

Bailments are either "ordinary" or "special" ("extraordinary"). There are three types of ordinary bailments. The distinguishing feature among them is

---

3. Fungible goods are defined in UCC 1-201(17) and discussed in Chapter 18 (Sales—Title, Risk, and Insurable Interest). UCC 7-207(1) states clearly, "Fungible goods may be commingled."

---

which party receives a benefit from the bailment. Ultimately, the courts will use this factor to determine the standard of care required by the bailee while in possession of the personal property, and this factor will dictate the rights and liabilities of the parties. Modern courts tend to use *reasonable standards of care* regardless of the type of bailment arrangement in effect, but, obviously, who derives the benefit of the bailment does effect the amount of care required.

Bailments for the Sole Benefit of the Bailor

When one person takes delivery of personal property for safekeeping as a favor to another, a bailment for the sole benefit of the bailor is in effect. It is a *gratuitous bailment* for the convenience and benefit of the bailor. In such a situation, the bailee is expected to use *slight care* to preserve the bailed property.

Consider an example. Michael is leaving for a two-week trip to Jamaica. He asks Susan if he can store his Celebrity automobile in her garage. He gives her the keys. She promises not to use the car for personal use. She is not paid any rent. One day, her children happen to be playing in her garage. When the children leave the garage, they fail to close and lock the door. Michael's car is stolen.

When Michael returns, he complains that Susan should pay for the loss of the car. She probably will not have to unless he can prove that she was guilty of negligence. The fact that the children failed to lock the garage door would not normally be considered negligence.

Bailments for the Sole Benefit of the Bailee

The loan of an article to a person (the bailee) solely for that person's convenience and benefit is the essence of a *bailment for the sole benefit of the bailee.* Under such circumstances, the bailee must use *great care* to preserve the bailed item from damage. If your best friend loans you a car so you can go out on a date, you must exercise great care in driving that car. If the car is dented because you parked it in a crowded parking lot, you will have trouble proving that you used great care, and, normally, you will be liable.

Bailments for the Mutual Benefit of the Bailee and the Bailor (Contractual Bailments)

Mutual benefit bailments are by far the most common kind, and they involve some form of compensation between the bailee and the bailor for the service provided—for example, repair work, transporting foods, storing items, renting goods, or holding property.

A mutual benefit bailment need not involve the payment of a fee. All that is required is that both bailor and bailee receive a benefit. For example, many corporations provide locker and cloakroom facilities for their employees' personal belongings because employees are not permitted to bring these items into the work area. The employee (bailor) benefits by receiving storage facilities. The employer (bailee) benefits by keeping the work area uncluttered, thus decreasing the chances of minor accidents.

The duty of care required in a mutual benefit bailment is that of *reasonable care*. Obviously, the exact measurement of that standard depends on the facts of each situation. A general rule, however, is that the standard of care required will be more than what would be expected in a bailment for the sole benefit of the bailor but less than what would be expected in a bailment for the sole benefit of the bailee.

RIGHTS AND DUTIES OF A BAILEE

Rights of the Bailee

The bailee takes possession of personal property for a specified purpose after which that property is returned (in the same or *pre*specified altered form). Thus, implicit in the bailment agreement is the right of the bailee to take possession, to utilize the property in accomplishing the purpose of the bailment, and to receive some form of compensation (unless the bailment is intended to be gratuitous). Depending upon the nature of the bailment and the terms of the bailment agreement, these bailee rights are present (with some limitations) in varying degrees in all bailment transactions.

Right of Possession Temporary control and possession of property that ultimately is to be returned to the owner is the hallmark of a bailment. The meaning of "temporary" depends upon the terms of the bailment agreement. If a specified period is expressed in the bailment agreement, then the bailment is continuous for that time period. Earlier termination by the bailor is a breach of contract (if it is for consideration), and the bailee can recover damages from the bailor. If no duration is specified, the bailment ends when either the bailor or the bailee so demands.

A bailee's right of possession, even though temporary, permits the bailee to recover damages from any third persons for damage or loss to the property. For example, No Spot Dry Cleaners sends all suede leather garments to Cleanall Company for special processing. If Cleanall loses or damages any leather goods, No Spot has the right to recover against Cleanall.

If the personal property is stolen from the bailee during the bailment, the bailee has a legal right to regain possession (recapture) of the goods or to obtain damages from any third person who has wrongfully interfered with the bailee's possessory rights.

Right to Use Bailed Property Naturally, the extent to which bailees can use the personal property entrusted to them depends upon the terms of the bailment contract. Where no provision is made, the extent of use depends upon how necessary it is to have the goods at the bailee's disposal in order to carry out the ordinary purpose of the bailment. For example, when leasing drilling machinery, the bailee is expected to use the equipment to drill. On the other hand, in long-term storage of a car, the bailee is not expected to use the car because the ordinary purpose of a storage bailment does not include use of the property.

Right of Compensation A bailee has a right to be compensated as provided for in the bailment agreement or reimbursed for costs and services rendered in the keeping of the bailed property, or both. In commercial mutual benefit bailments, the amount of compensation is often expressed in the bailment contract. For example, in a rental (bailment) of a car, the contract provides charges on a basis of time, mileage, or a combination of the two, plus other possible charges. In nonrental bailments, such as leaving your car for an oil change, the bailee makes a service charge.

Even in gratuitous bailments, a bailee has a right to be reimbursed or compensated for costs incurred in the keeping of the bailed property. For example, Ann loses her pet dog, which is found by Jesse. Jesse takes Ann's dog to his home and feeds it. Even though he takes good care of the dog, it becomes ill, and a veterinarian is called. The bill for the veterinarian's services and the medicine is paid for by Jesse. Jesse is normally entitled to be reimbursed by Ann for all reasonable costs incurred in the keeping of her dog.

To enforce a bailee's right of compensation, the bailee has a right to place a *possessory* lien (claim) on the specific bailed property until he or she has been fully compensated. This lien on specific bailed property is sometimes referred to as an **artisan's lien**. The lien is effective only as long as the bailee retains possession over the bailed property.

If the bailor refuses to pay or cannot pay the charges (compensation), the bailee is entitled in most states to foreclose on the lien. This means that the bailee can sell the property and be paid out of the proceeds for the amount owed from the bailment, returning any excess to the bailor.

For example, Peter takes his car (that he has just paid cash for) to the garage and enters into an agreement for repairs. The repairs are to be paid in cash. Upon completion of the repairs, the garage tenders Peter his car, but because of unexpected bills he cannot pay the garage. The garage has a right to retain possession of Peter's car, exercising a *bailee's lien*. Unless Peter can make arrangements for payment, the garage will be entitled to sell the car in order to be compensated for the repairs.

Right to Limit Liability "Ordinary" bailees have the right to limit their bailment liability by type of risk or by monetary amount, or both, as long as:

1. The limitations are called to the attention of the bailor.
2. The limitations are not against public policy.

Any enforceable limitation imposed by the ordinary bailee must be brought to the bailor's attention. Although the bailee is not required to read orally or interpret the limitation for the bailor, it is essential that the bailor in some way know of the limitation. Thus, a sign in Joe's garage stating that Joe will not be responsible "for loss due to theft, fire, or vandalism" may or may not be held to be notice to the bailor. Whether the notice will be effective will depend on the size of the sign, its location, and any other circumstances affecting the likelihood of its being noticed by Joe's patrons. The same holds true with limitations placed on the back of identification receipts (stubs) for parked cars, checked coats, or stored bailed goods. Most courts would require additional notice, since the bailor rarely reads the receipt and usually treats it merely as an identification number to be used when reclaiming the bailed goods.

Even if the bailor has notice, certain types of disclaimers of liability are considered to be against public policy and therefore illegal. Clauses, called *exculpatory clauses*, which limit a person's liability for his or her own wrongful acts are carefully scrutinized by the courts, and in bailments they are quite often held to be illegal. The classic illustration of an exculpatory clause is found on parking receipts: "We assume no risk for damage to or loss of automobile or its contents regardless of cause. It is agreed that the vehicle owner assumes all such risks." Even though the language may vary, if the bailee attempts to exclude liability for the bailee's own negligence, the result is the same—the clause is unenforceable as being against public policy. This is especially true in the case of bailees providing quasi-public services.

Duties of the Bailee

The bailee has two basic responsibilities: (1) to take proper care of the property and (2) to surrender or dispose of the property at the end of the bailment. The bailee's duties are based on a mixture of tort law and contract law. The duty of care involves the standards and principles of tort law discussed in Chapter 4. A bailee's failure to exercise appropriate care in handling the bailor's property results in tort liability. The duty to relinquish the property in a mutual benefit bailment at the end of the bailment is grounded in contract law principles. Failure to return the property is a breach of contract, and, with one exception, the bailee is liable for damages. The exception exists when the obligation is excused because the goods or chattel have been destroyed, lost, or stolen through no fault of the bailee (or claimed by a third party with a superior claim).

Duty of Care As previously discussed, bailees must exercise proper care over the property in their possession to prevent its loss or damage. The three types of bailments demand different degrees of care (although the trend is toward reasonable standards of care). When a bailment exists for the sole benefit of the bailee, great care, or the highest level of care, is required. When the bailment exists for the mutual benefit of the bailor and the bailee, reasonable care is the standard. When the bailment exists for the sole benefit of the bailor, slight care, or something less than ordinary or reasonable care, is expected.

Duty to Return Bailed Property   At the end of the bailment, the bailee normally must relinquish the identical undamaged property (unless it is fungible) to either the bailor or someone the bailor designates or otherwise dispose of it as directed. This is usually a *contractual* duty arising from the bailment agreement (contract). Failure to give up possession at the time the bailment ends is breach of a contract term and could result in a tort of conversion.

As noted previously, there are recognized exceptions from tort law that will excuse contract liability. If the bailee does not or cannot return the property at the end of the bailment because it has been lost, stolen, or damaged *through no negligence* (fault) on the part of the bailee, then the contractual obligation to return the property is excused. (There are a number of exceptions to this rule that concern common carriers, public warehouse companies, and innkeepers. They usually cannot limit liability except as provided by statute because they have a higher duty of care. Exceptions also exist when the bailee deviates from the bailment agreement.) Also, if a third party with a superior claim takes the property, the bailee normally is not liable.

Delivery of Goods to the Wrong Person   A bailee may be liable if the goods being held or delivered are given to the wrong person. Hence, a bailee must be satisfied that the person to whom the goods are being delivered is the actual owner or has authority from the owner to take possession of the goods. Should the bailee deliver in error, particularly when the bailee knows that the goods are stolen or that there is another claim of ownership against the goods, then the bailee may be liable for conversion or mis-delivery.

The following case presents an example of this principle.

CAPEZZARO v.
WINFREY

Superior Court of New Jersey,
1977.
153 N.J.Super. 267, 379 A.2d
493.

BACKGROUND AND FACTS   *The plaintiff was a robbery victim who sued the city and its police officers after the police arrested a suspect who the plaintiff claimed had stolen money. During their apprehension of the suspect, the police had removed the money from the suspect's clothing, and the police department kept it.*

When the suspect was released from custody, she went to the police station and demanded return of the money. The police officers gave it to her. The robbery victim claimed to be the rightful owner of the money and sued the city for negligence because police officers in the city's employ had released the money.

The jury found for the robbery victim, and the police officers and the city appealed this judgment.

LORA, SEIDMAN and MILMED, Judges.
PER CURIAM
*   *   *   *

It has been said that a constructive bailment or a bailment by operation of law may be created when a person comes into possession of personal property of another, receives nothing from the owner of the property, and has no right to recover from the owner for what he does in caring for the property. Such person is ordinarily considered to be a gratuitous bailee, liable only to the bailor for bad faith or gross negligence.

Where possession has been acquired accidentally, fortuitously, through mistake or by an agreement for some other purposes since terminated, the possessor, "upon principles of justice," should keep it safely and restore or deliver it to its owner. Under such circumstances, the courts have considered the possessions *quasi-contracts* [implied contracts created by law] of bailment or constructive and involuntary bailments.

Here the police seized and obtained custody of the money which was found in Winfrey's [the robbery suspect's] girdle during a search in her cell after her arrest on the robbery charge and after plaintiff claimed Winfrey had stolen it from him. It is undisputed that the money was being kept by the police as evidence for use in Winfrey's prosecution. It follows, then, that the City of Newark, through its police department, was holding the money for its own benefit as well as for the benefit of its rightful owner.

Ordinarily, a person who has possession of property may be presumed by another to be the rightful owner thereof in the absence of any knowledge to the contrary. However, here the police were fully aware of plaintiff's adverse claim, but notwithstanding such knowledge and without notice to plaintiff turned the money over to Winfrey.

In view of the mutual benefit attendant upon custody of the money in the case before us, we find no error in the trial judge's refusal to charge that the police department was a gratuitous bailee. * * *

Defendants further contend that when the indictment was dismissed any claim by plaintiff lost its validity and they were obligated to return the monies in question to Winfrey as bailor. We disagree. A bailee with knowledge of an adverse claim makes delivery to the bailor at his peril, and only if he is ignorant of such a claim will he be protected against a subsequent claim by the rightful owner. The position of a bailee in such situation and his possible courses of action are set forth in 9 *Williston on Contracts* (3 ed. 1967), § 1036 at 897–898:

* * * If a bailee knows goods are stolen, or that the bailor is acting adversely to a clearly valid right, even though the true owner has as yet made no demand for them, the bailee will be liable to him for conversion if delivery is made to the bailor. In case, therefore, that the bailee knows or has been notified of an adverse claim, he will deliver to the bailor at his peril. The bailee must, for his own protection, choose one of two courses:

First, he may satisfy himself of the validity of one of the two claims and obtain authority from the owner of the claim to refuse delivery to all other claimants. In such a case he may plead at law to an action by any but the rightful owner the title of the latter, or the right of one having a superior right to immediate possession. If this title or right can be proved, a perfect defense is established. Second, if no actual adverse claim has been made, but the bailee knows of the existence of adverse right, or if the bailee cannot determine which of two claimants has the better title, and neither claimant will give a bond indemnifying the bailee from all damage caused by delivery to him, the only course open to the bailee is to file a bill of interpleader against the several possible owners, praying a temporary injunction against actions against himself until the true ownership of the goods is determined. And it should be added that a bailee who redelivers the goods to the bailor, or upon his order, in ignorance of his lack of title, is fully protected against subsequent claims of the rightful owner.

The police returned the money to Winfrey after being informed by the warden of the county jail that the indictments had been dismissed. They did not contact plaintiff before doing so, even though they were on notice of his adverse claim. The dismissal of the indictment for the reasons here present did not vitiate plaintiff's adverse claim to the money. Inherent in the jury's verdict is a finding that defendants were negligent in releasing the money without a determination of the validity of the adverse claim. Such finding and the verdict are amply supported by the evidence.

The judgment of the trial court was affirmed. The police officers and the city were liable to the robbery victim.

DECISION AND REMEDY

Presumption of Negligence Sometimes the duty to return and duty of care are combined to determine bailee liability. At the end of the bailment, a bailee has the duty to return the bailor's property in the condition it was received (allowing for ordinary wear and aging). In some cases, the bailor can sue the bailee in tort (as well as contract) for damages or lost goods on the theory of *negligence* or *conversion*. But often it is not possible for the bailor to discover and prove the specific acts of negligence or conversion committed by the bailee that caused damage or loss to the property.[4] Thus, the law of bailments recognizes a rule whereby a bailor's proof that damage or loss to the property has occurred will, in and of itself, raise a *presumption* that the bailee is guilty of negligence or conversion. Once this is shown, the bailee must prove that he or she was not at fault. A bailee who is able to *rebut* (contradict) the pre-

---

4. The basic formula for finding negligence requires proof that (1) a duty exists, (2) a breach of that duty occurred, and (3) the breach is the proximate cause of damage or loss.

sumption is not liable to the bailor. When damage to goods is normally of the type that results only from someone's negligence, and when the bailee had full control of the goods, it is more likely than not that the damage was caused by the bailee's negligence. Therefore, the bailee's negligence is presumed.

Determining whether a bailee exercised an appropriate degree of care is usually a question of fact. This means that the trier-of-fact (a judge or a jury) weighs the facts of a particular situation and concludes that the bailee did or did not exercise the requisite degree of care at the time the loss or damage occurred. The failure to exercise appropriate care is negligence, and the bailee is liable for the loss or damage in tort.

The following case illustrates that once a bailment is created, failure of the bailee to return the bailed property to the bailor upon demand results in a presumption of conversion (or negligence). Because this presumption was not rebutted, the bailee was held liable.

LEHMAN v. LEHMAN
United States District Court, S.D.
New York, 1984.
591 F.Supp. 1523.

BACKGROUND AND FACTS *Robert Owen Lehman, the plaintiff, sued his former wife, Aki Eveline Lehman, the defendant, to recover possession, or in the alternative, the value of forty-three objects of art that he claims to own. Plaintiff alleged that the defendant breached a bailment "agreement" because she refused to return the artwork to her former husband and she could not adequately explain the whereabouts of some of the missing pieces.*

SPRIZZO, District Judge
* * * *

Mr. and Mrs. Lehman were married in April 1964. They physically separated in late 1971. At that time, the Lehmans were living in their London home (the "White House") with their two young children. At the time of the Lehmans' separation, the items of art at issue in this proceeding were all in the White House.

When the parties separated, Mrs. Lehman retained the forty-three items of art in the White House. Shortly thereafter, in February 1972, she and the children moved to a house in Paris, France (the "Paris House") and took the art work with them.

In October 1974, the Lehmans entered into a separation agreement which, *inter alia*, provided for alimony and support for Mrs. Lehman and set forth who was entitled to which items of art. That agreement, however, specifically stated that, in the event the Lehmans were not divorced by June 30, 1976, its terms would not take effect and the rights of the parties would revert to the status quo existing prior to the execution of the agreement.

Although Mr. Lehman commenced a divorce action in a New York state court, a judgment of divorce was not obtained prior to June 30, 1976. As a result, Mrs. Lehman became entitled to an independent determination of her alimony and support, and ownership of the artwork reverted to the status existing prior to the execution of the separation agreement.

From July 1976 until January 1980, the parties intermittently negotiated and lit-
igated over the issues of alimony and support. On several occasions during this period,
Mr. Lehman, either personally or through his attorneys, demand that the artwork be
returned to him. On each occasion, counsel mutually decided to wait to resolve issues
concerning the artwork until after they settled the alimony and support issues.

Ownership of the Artwork

Each of the parties claims to own all forty-three items of art. Mr. Lehman contends
that, with one exception, he acquired ownership of the items by either purchasing
them himself or receiving them as gifts from his father. Mrs. Lehman claims that she
and/or her children acquired ownership of the items in a variety of ways—by purchasing
them herself with her own or joint funds, by her husband's purchase of them with
joint funds, and by gift from her husband or her father-in-law.

Mrs. Lehman's claim of ownership over all of the artwork is inconsistent with the
position she took earlier in this litigation in responding to one of plaintiff's interrogatories—when she asserted ownership over only eight items. It is also inconsistent with
her conduct prior to the commencement of this litigation. First, between July 1976
and December 1979, Mr. Lehman or his attorneys made several requests that Mrs.
Lehman return the artwork to her husband. At no time did she respond to those requests
by contesting her husband's claim to the property and asserting instead that she was
the proper owner. Second, when questioned in the state matrimonial proceeding regarding the artwork, she also did not claim to own all forty-three items.

Since Mrs. Lehman's interrogatory response only asserted ownership of eight items,
and in light of her previous failure to claim onwership over all of the artwork, the
Court finds that plaintiff, Robert Lehman, is the exclusive owner of thirty-five of the
forty-three items. In so finding, the Court primarily relies upon Mrs. Lehman's response
to plaintiff's interrogatory; however, it also relies upon her overall lack of credibility
in explaining how she came to own those thirty-five items.

[The Court further held that five of the remaining pieces of artwork belonged to
Mr. Lehman.]

*   *   * In so finding, the Court specifically rejects the testimony of Mrs. Lehman
as to how she came to own the artwork and accepts the testimony of plaintiff and his
witness, Dr. George Szabo, curator of the Robert Lehman Art Collection at the Metropolitan Museum of Art.

*   *   *   *

Possession of the Property

Mr. Lehman left the items in London, in his wife's possession, at the time of their
separation. He did so for safekeeping and with the understanding that he owned the
items and could repossess them on demand.

Mrs. Lehman took the items with her when she and the children moved to Paris
in 1972.

At no time was any of the artwork returned to plaintiff.

Items **2, 3, 5, 6, 7, 12, 22, 23, 24, 37, 40, 41, and three of the twenty-two
drawings comprised by item #37 were in Mrs. Lehman's possession when this action
commenced.

The Court is unable to find by a preponderance of the evidence that the remaining
items were in defendant's possession in July 1980, when this action was commenced.
The Court does, however, find that Mrs. Lehman has failed to explain adequately
what happened to those items. Her testimony that they were somehow destroyed, lost,
stolen, or are missing was incredible and supported by no corroborating evidence.

Plaintiff, Robert Lehman, is the exclusive owner of all of the items of art except
##3, 37, and 40, which he owns jointly with the defendant.

When Mr. Lehman left the artwork in his wife's possession at the time of their
separation, his wife became a bailee of the property. That bailment continued after
the terms of the separation agreement became a nullity in 1976.

Plaintiff established his *prima facie* case for conversion by showing that he owned the artwork, that he placed the property in his wife's possession, and that she refused to return it upon demand. * * *

Since Mrs. Lehman refused to return the property to the plaintiff, and since she failed to explain adequately what became of the missing items, she is liable as a converter with respect to all items not in her possession at the time this action was commenced.

With respect to the jointly owned property (items ##3, 37, and 40), plaintiff is entitled to one half the value of those items at the time of trial.

* * * *

DECISION AND REMEDY   *The court found that when Robert Lehman left artworks which he owned in his wife's possession at the time of their separation, his wife became a bailee of the property. The court also found that under New York law, Robert Lehman could recover on his* prima facie *case when the bailee failed to come forward with a satisfactory explanation of what had happened to the property, and in such a situation the bailor need not prove the bailee's negligence.*

CONCEPT SUMMARY: Rights and Duties of a Bailee

BAILEE	BASIC RULES
Rights	1. A bailee has the right to be compensated or reimbursed for keeping bailed property. This right is based in contract or quasi-contract.
	2. Unpaid compensation or reimbursement entitles the bailee to a lien (usually possessory) on the bailed property and the right of foreclosure.
	3. A bailee has the right to limit his or her liability. An ordinary bailee can limit risk or monetary amount or both, provided proper notice is given and the limitation is not against public policy. In special bailments, limitations on types of risk are usually not allowed, but limitations on the monetary amount at risk are permitted by regulation.
	4. The right of possession allows actions against third persons who damage or convert the bailed property, and allows actions against the bailor for wrongful breach of the bailment.
	5. The right to an insurable interest in the bailed property allows the bailee to insure and recover under the insurance policy for loss or damage to the property.
Duties	1. A bailee must exercise reasonable care over property entrusted to him or her. A common carrier (special bailee) is held to a standard of care based on *strict liability* unless the bailed property is lost or destroyed due to: (a) an act of God, (b) an act of a public enemy, (c) an act of a governmental authority, (d) an act of a shipper, or (e) the inherent nature of the goods.
	2. Bailed goods in a bailee's possession must be returned to the bailor, or disposed of according to bailor's directions.
	3. A bailee cannot use or profit from bailed goods except by agreement or in situations where the use is implied to further the bailment purpose.

RIGHTS AND DUTIES OF A BAILOR

Rights of a Bailor

The bailor's rights are essentially a complement to each of the bailee's duties. A bailor has the right to expect the following:

1. The property will be protected with reasonable care while in the possession of the bailee.
2. The bailee will utilize the property as agreed in the bailment agreement (or not at all).
3. The property will be relinquished at the conclusion of the bailment according to directions given by the bailor.
4. The bailee will not convert (alter) the goods except as agreed.
5. The bailor shall not be bound by any bailee limitations of liability unless such are known and are enforceable by law.
6. Repairs or service on the property will be completed without defective workmanship.

Duties of a Bailor

A bailor has a single, all-encompassing duty to provide the bailee with goods or chattel that are free from hidden defects that could cause injury to the bailee. This duty translates into two rules:

1. In a *mutual benefit bailment*, the bailor must notify the bailee of all known defects and any hidden defects that the bailor could have discovered with reasonable diligence and proper inspection.
2. In *bailments for the sole benefit of the bailee*, the bailor must notify the bailee of any known defects.

The bailor's duty to reveal defects is based on a negligence theory of tort law. A bailor who fails to give the appropriate notice is liable to the bailee and to any other person who might reasonably be expected to come into contact with the defective article.

To illustrate: Rentco (bailor) leases four tractors to Hopkinson. Unknown to Rentco (but discoverable by reasonable inspection), the brake mechanism on one of the tractors is defective at the time the bailment is made. Hopkinson uses the defective tractor without knowledge of the brake problem and injures herself and two other field workers when the tractor rolls out of control. Rentco is liable on a negligence theory for injuries sustained by Hopkinson and the two employees.

This is the analysis: Rentco has a mutual benefit bailment and a *duty* to notify Hopkinson of the discoverable brake defect. Rentco's failure to notify is the *proximate cause* of injuries to farm workers who might be expected to use or have contact with the tractor. Therefore, Rentco is *liable* for the resulting injuries.

A bailor can also incur *warranty liability* based on contract law for injuries resulting from bailment of defective articles. Property leased by a bailor must be *fit for the intended purpose of the bailment*. The bailor's knowledge or ability to discover any defects is immaterial. Warranties of fitness arise by law in sales contracts and by judicial interpretation in the case of bailments "for hire."

Termination of Bailment

Bailments for a specific term end when the stated period lapses. When no duration is specified, the bailment can be terminated at any time by the following events:

1. The mutual agreement of both parties.
2. A demand by either party.
3. The completion of the purpose of the bailment.
4. An act by the bailee that is inconsistent with the terms of the bailment.
5. The operation of law.

SPECIAL BAILMENTS

Most of this chapter has concerned itself with ordinary bailments. Special, or extraordinary, bailments include (1) common carriers, (2) warehouse companies, and (3) innkeepers or hotel owners.

Common Carriers

Common carriers are publicly licensed to provide transportation services to the general public. They are distinguished from private carriers that operate transportation facilities for a select clientele. A private carrier is not bound to provide service to every person or company making a request. The common carrier, however, must arrange carriage for all who apply, within certain limitations.[5] The delivery of goods to a common carrier creates a bailment relationship between the shipper (bailor) and the common carrier (bailee).

The common carrier contract of transportation creates a *mutual benefit bailment*. But, unlike ordinary mutual benefit bailments, the common carrier is held to a standard of care based on *strict liability*, rather than reasonable care, in protecting the bailed personal property. This means that the common carrier is absolutely liable, regardless of negligence, for all loss or damage to goods except damage caused by one of the five common law exceptions:

1. An act of God.
2. An act of a public enemy.
3. An order of a public authority.
4. An act of the shipper.
5. The inherent nature of the goods.

Common carriers are treated as if they were absolute insurers for the safe delivery of goods to the destination, but actually they are not. They cannot contract away this liability for damaged goods; but, subject to government regulations, they are permitted to limit their dollar liability to an amount stated on the shipment contract.[6]

Except for the five exceptions given, any damage to goods in shipment, even that caused by the willful acts of third persons or by sheer accident, does not relieve the common carrier from liability. Thus, a common carrier trucking company moving cargo is liable for acts of vandalism, mechanical defects in refrigeration units, or a dam bursting, if any of these acts results in damage to the cargo. But damage caused by acts of God—an earthquake or lightning, for example—are the shipper's loss.

There are many interesting cases concerning what constitutes an "act of God." The following extract is from a case in which a common carrier learned that a flood was *not* necessarily enough of an "act of God" to excuse liability:

> The only acts of God that excuse common carriers from liability for loss or injury to goods in transit are those operations of the forces of nature that could not have been anticipated and provided against and that by their super human force unexpectedly injure or destroy goods in the custody or control of the carrier. Extreme weather conditions which operate to foil human obligations of duty are regarded as acts of God. However, every strong wind, snowstorm, or rainstorm cannot be termed an act of God merely because it is of unusual or more than average intensity. Ordinary, expectable, and gradual weather conditions are not regarded as acts of God even though they may have produced a disaster, because man had the opportunity to control their effects.[7]

Shipper's Loss The shipper bears any loss occurring through its own faulty or improper crating or packaging procedures. For example, if a bird dies because its crate was poorly ventilated, the shipper bears the loss, not the carrier.

In the following case, the U.S. Supreme Court deals with the question of whether a common carrier that has exercised reasonable care and has complied with the instructions of the shipper is nonetheless liable to the shipper for spoilage in transit of an interstate shipment of perishable commodities.

---

5. A common carrier is not required to take any and all property anywhere in all instances. Public regulatory agencies, such as the Interstate Commerce Commission, govern commercial carriers, and carriers can be restricted to geographical areas. They can also be limited to carrying certain kinds of goods or to providing only special types of transportation equipment.

6. For example, federal laws and Interstate Commerce Commission regulations require common carriers to offer shippers the opportunity to obtain higher dollar limits for loss by paying a higher fee for the transport.

7. Southern Pac. Co. v. Loden, 508 P.2d 347 (Ariz. App. 1972).

MISSOURI PAC. RY. CO. v. ELMORE & STAHL

United States Supreme Court, 1964.
377 U.S. 134, 84 S.Ct. 1142.

BACKGROUND AND FACTS *Elmore & Stahl, a fruit shipper, contracted with Missouri Pac. Ry. Co. to ship melons from Rio Grande City, Texas, to Chicago. At trial, the jury was convinced that Missouri Pac. Ry. Co. and its connecting carriers performed all the required transportation services without negligence. The jury also found that a preponderance of evidence showed that the condition of the melons on arrival in Chicago was defective and that the* *defective condition was not due solely to an inherent defect in the melons. The trial judge ruled against the carrier, and the Texas Court of Appeals affirmed, as did the Texas Supreme Court. The ground for affirmation was that, basically, Missouri Pac. Ry. Co. did not show that the spoilage or decay was due entirely to the inherent nature of the goods or, in other words, that the damage was caused solely by natural deterioration. The U.S. Supreme Court reviewed the case.*

Mr. Justice STEWART delivered the opinion of the Court.

*   *   *   *

The Carmack Amendment of 1906, § 20(11) of the Interstate Commerce Act, makes carriers liable "for the full actual loss, damage, or injury *   *   * caused by" them to property they transport, and declares unlawful and void any contract, regulation, tariff, or other attempted means of limiting this liability. It is settled that this statute has two undisputed effects crucial to the issue in this case: First, the statute codifies the common-law rule that a carrier, though not an absolute insurer, is liable for damage to goods transported by it unless it can show that the damage was caused by "(a) the act of God; (b) the public enemy; (c) the act of the shipper himself; (d) public authority; (e) or the inherent vice or nature of the goods." *   *   * Second, the statute declares unlawful and void any "rule, regulation, or other limitation of any character whatsoever" purporting to limit this liability. *   *   * Accordingly, under federal law, in an action to recover from a carrier for damage to a shipment, the shipper establishes his prima facie case when he shows delivery in good condition, arrival in damaged condition, and the amount of damages. Thereupon, the burden of proof is upon the carrier to show both that it was free from negligence and that the damage to the cargo was due to one of the excepted causes relieving the carrier of liability *   *   *.

The disposition of this case in the Texas courts was in accordance with these established principles. It is apparent that the jury were unable to determine the cause of the damage to the melons. "[T]he decay of the perishable cargo is not a cause; it is an effect. It may be the result of a number of causes, for some of which, such as the inherent defects of the cargo *   *   * the carrier is not liable." But the jury refused to find that the carrier had borne its burden of establishing that the damaged condition of the melons was due solely to "inherent vice," as defined in the instruction of the trial judge—including "the inherent nature of the commodity which will cause it to deteriorate with a lapse of time." The petitioner [Missouri Pac. Ry. Co.] does not challenge the accuracy of the trial judge's instruction or the jury's finding. Its position is simply that if goods are perishable, and the nature of the damage is spoilage, and the jury affirmatively find that the carrier was free from negligence and performed the transportation services as required by the shipper, then the law presumes that the cause of the spoilage was the natural tendency of perishables to deteriorate even though the damage might, in fact, have resulted from other causes, such as the acts of third parties, for which no exception from carrier liability is provided. Consequently, it is argued, the question of "inherent vice" should not have been submitted to the jury, since the carrier in such a case does not bear the affirmative burden of establishing that the damage was caused by the inherent vice exception of the common law.

*   *   *   *

Finally, all else failing, it is argued that as a matter of public policy, the burden ought not to be placed upon the carrier to explain the cause of spoilage, because where perishables are involved, the shipper is peculiarly knowledgeable about the commodity's condition at and prior to the time of shipment, and is therefore in the best position to explain the cause of the damage. Since this argument amounts to a suggestion that we now carve out an exception to an unquestioned rule of long standing upon which both shippers and carriers rely, and which is reflected in the freight rates set by the carrier, the petitioner must sustain a heavy burden of persuasion. The general rule of carrier liability is based upon the sound premise that the carrier has peculiarly within its knowledge "[a]ll the facts and circumstances upon which [it] may rely to relieve [it] of [its] duty. * * * In consequence, the law casts upon [it] the burden of the loss which [it] cannot explain or, explaining, bring within the exceptional case in which [it] is relieved from liability." Schnell v. The Vallescura, 293 U.S. 296, 304, 55 S.Ct. 194, 196, 79 L.Ed. 373. We are not persuaded that the carrier lacks adequate means to inform itself of the condition of goods at the time it receives them from the shipper, and it cannot be doubted that while the carrier has possession, it is the only one in a position to acquire the knowledge of what actually damaged a shipment entrusted to its care.

**DECISION
AND REMEDY**   *The U.S. Supreme Court upheld the judgment of the Texas Supreme Court. Even if a common carrier exercises reasonable care, it is liable for spoilage in transit unless it can prove that the cause of the spoilage was the natural tendency of the commodities to deteriorate.*

Connecting Carriers   Where connecting carriers are involved in transporting goods, the shipper can recover from the original carrier or any connecting carrier. Normally, the *last* carrier is presumed to have received the goods in good condition.

Warehouse Companies

Warehousing is the business of providing storage of property for compensation.[8] A warehouse company is a professional bailee whose responsibility differs from an ordinary bailee in two important aspects. First, a warehouse company is empowered to issue documents of title, in particular, warehouse receipts.[9] Second, warehouse companies are subject to an extraordinary network of state and federal statutes and Article 7 of the UCC (as are carriers).

Like ordinary bailees, a warehouse company is liable for loss or damage to property and possession resulting from *negligence* (and therefore does not have the same liability as a common carrier). The duty is one of reasonable care to protect and preserve the goods. A warehouse company can limit the dollar amount of liability, but the bailor must be given the option of paying an increased storage rate for an increase in the liability limit.

A warehouse company accepts goods for storage and issues a warehouse receipt describing the property and the terms of the bailment contract. The warehouse receipt can be negotiable or nonnegotiable depending on how it is written. The warehouse receipt is negotiable if its terms provide that the warehouse company will deliver the goods "to the bearer" of the receipt, or "to the order of" a person named on the receipt.[10]

The warehouse receipt serves multiple functions. It is a receipt for the goods stored; it is a contract of bailment; it also represents the goods (that is, it indicates title) and hence has value and utility in financing commercial transactions. For example, Oakner, a processor and canner of corn, delivers 6,000 cases of corn to Shaw, the owner of a warehouse. Shaw issues a negotiable warehouse receipt payable "to bearer" and gives it to Oakner. Oakner sells the warehouse receipt to a large supermarket chain, "I. M. Plenty." Oakner delivers the warehouse receipt to I. M. Plenty. I. M. Plenty is now the owner of the corn and has the right to obtain the cases from Shaw. It will present the warehouse receipt to Shaw, who in return will release the cases of corn to the chain.

Innkeepers

At common law, innkeepers, hotel owners, or similar operators were held to the same strict liability

---

8. UCC 7–102(h) defines the person engaged in the storing of goods for hire as a "warehouseman."

9. Document of title is defined in UCC 1-201(15) as any "document which in the regular course of business or financing is treated as adequately evidencing that the person in possession of it is entitled to receive, hold, and dispose of the document and the goods it covers. To be a document of title, a document must purport to be issued by or addressed to a bailee and purport to cover goods in the bailee's possession * * *."

10. UCC 7–104.

as common carriers with respect to property brought into the rooms by guests. Today, only those who provide lodging to the public for compensation as a *regular* business are covered under this rule of strict liability. Moreover, the rule applies only to those lodgers who are *guests*, as opposed to *lodgers*. A lodger is a permanent resident of the hotel or inn, whereas a guest is a traveler.

Statutory Changes In many states, innkeepers can avoid strict liability for loss of guests' valuables and money by providing a safe in which to keep them. Each guest must be clearly notified of the availability of such a safe. When articles are not kept in the safe, or when they are of such a nature that they are not normally kept in a safe, statutes will often limit innkeepers' liability.

Consider an example covering personal property that cannot be put in a safe. Jackson stays for a night at Hideaway Hotel. When he returns from eating breakfast in the hotel restaurant, he discovers that the people in the room next door have forced the lock on the door between the two rooms and stolen his suitcase. Jackson claims that the hotel is liable for his loss. The hotel denies liability due to the lack of negligence on its part. At common law, innkeepers are actually insurers of the property of their guests and the hotel will be liable.

Today, however, state statutes limit the strict liability of the common law. These statutes vary from state to state. In many states, the monetary damages for which the innkeeper is liable are limited in amount. Indeed, these statutes may even provide that the innkeeper has no liability in the absence of negligence. Many statutes require these limitations to be posted or the guest to be notified, and the posting (notice) is frequently found on the door of each room in the motel or hotel.

Normally, the innkeeper assumes no responsibility for the safety of a guest's automobile because the guest usually retains possession and control. If, on the other hand, the innkeeper provides parking facilities, and the guest's car is entrusted to the innkeeper or to an employee, the innkeeper will be liable under the rules that pertain to parking lot bailees (ordinary bailments).

QUESTIONS AND CASE PROBLEMS

1. Curtis is an executive on a business trip to the West Coast. He has driven his car on this trip and checks into the Hotel Ritz. The hotel has a guarded underground parking lot. Curtis gives his car keys to the parking lot attendant but fails to notify the attendant that his wife's $10,000 fur coat is in a box in the trunk. The next day, upon checking out, he discovers that his car has been stolen. Curtis wants to hold the hotel liable for both the car and the coat. Discuss the probable success of his claim.

2. Discuss the standard of care required from the bailee for the bailed property in the following situations, and determine whether the bailee breached that duty:

   (a) Adam borrows Tom's lawn mower because his own lawn mower needs repair. Adam mows his front yard. In order to mow the back yard, he needs to move some hoses and lawn furniture. He leaves the mower in front of his house while doing so. When he returns to the front, he discovers the mower has been stolen.

   (b) Mary owns a valuable speedboat. She is going on vacation and asks her neighbor, Regina, to store the boat in one stall of Regina's double garage. Regina consents, and the boat is moved into the garage. Regina, in need of some grocery items for dinner, drives to the store. In doing so, she leaves the garage door open, as is her custom. While she is at the store, the speedboat is stolen.

3. Lee owns and operates a service station. Walter's car needs some minor repairs. Walter takes his car to Lee's station. Lee tells Walter that he will be unable to do the work until the next day and that Walter can either bring the car back at that time or leave it overnight. Walter leaves the car with Lee. The next afternoon Walter comes to pick up his car. Lee presents Walter with a bill for $220 and refuses to return the car until he is paid. Upon inspecting the car, Walter discovers that the mileage indicator shows 150 more miles on the car than when he brought it in. Lee claims he was legally allowed to let one of his employees road-test the car by taking it to his home and driving it last evening. Discuss Walter's and Lee's legal rights under these circumstances.

4. Paul borrows from his neighbor, Max, a gasoline-driven lawn edger. Max has not used the lawn edger for two years. Paul is not familiar with using a lawn edger since

he has never owned one. Max previously used this edger numerous times, and if he had made a reasonable inspection, he would have discovered that the blade was loose. Paul is injured when the blade becomes detached while he is edging his yard.

(a) Can Paul hold Max liable for his injuries?

(b) Would your answer be any different if Paul had rented the edger from Max and paid a fee? Explain.

5. Franklin Washer, Inc. delivered to the Western Central Railroad one hundred crated washing machines to be shipped to Rocky High Appliance Store in Denver, Colorado. Western Central received the goods on Thursday and stored them in its warehouse pending loading into boxcars the next day. On the shipping invoice, Western Central had a clause printed in big bold type that excluded the carrier from liability resulting from loss of goods under control of the carrier because of acts of vandalism, fire, or theft. The clause also limited liability to $500 per shipment unless a higher evaluation was declared and a fee paid. That evening a riot broke out, and in the process some of the one hundred crated washing machines were stolen, some were damaged by the rioters, and some were destroyed by fire. Franklin wants to hold the carrier liable for the entire value of the one hundred machines. Western claims, first, that it has no liability by virtue of the contractual limitation against liability for loss by fire, theft, or vandalism; and second, that if there was liability, its damage cost responsibility would be only $500. Discuss the validity of Western's claims.

6. Procter & Gamble was a distributor of soybean oils. Its buyer, Allied Crude Vegetable Oil Refining Corp., persuaded Procter & Gamble to engage in a practice known as field warehousing. Under this arrangement, Procter & Gamble shipped oil to Field Warehousing Corp., which stored the oil in its tanks. In exchange for the oil, Field Warehousing gave Procter & Gamble "warehousing receipts." This allowed Procter & Gamble to sell the oil to Allied by merely selling the receipts (which were evidence of title to the oil). Thus, Procter & Gamble did not have to ship any of the oil in order to make a sale. About six months after it began storing oil at Field Warehousing, Procter & Gamble sold a large number of its warehouse receipts to Allied, it was discovered that the oil was missing. Who was liable for the missing oil? [Procter & Gamble Distributing Co. v. Lawrence American Field Warehousing Corp., 16 N.Y.2d 344, 266 N.Y.S.2d 785, 213 N.E.2d 873 (1965)]

7. Buchanan entered into an agreement with Byrd and Barksdale in which Buchanan would pay $40 a month for Byrd and Barksdale to feed and keep Buchanan's horse on their five-acre tract in Irving, Texas. One night, the horses were in one of the pastures rather than in their stalls. All of them escaped around midnight, apparently through an open gate. Two were killed by a train a mile away. One of them was Buchanan's. He sued for damages. What was the result? [Buchanan v. Byrd, Supreme Court of Texas, 519 S.W.2d 841 (1975)]

8. Rena, in her will, bequeathed her jewelry to her daughter Linda. Upon Rena's death, Edward, Rena's husband and Linda's stepfather, gave Linda one ring, a gift to Rena from a prior husband, but put the other jewelry in his home in a dresser drawer. While Edward was in the hospital with a heart ailment, the jewelry was stolen from the dresser drawer. Edward never told Linda, nor filed an insurance claim, nor a police report. When Linda found out, she sued her stepfather for negligence for failure to exercise reasonable care over her bailed property. What result? [Estate of Murrell, Supreme Court of Mississippi, 454 So.2d 437 (1984)].

53

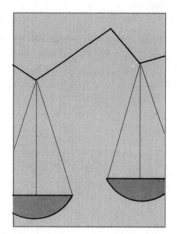

Nature and Ownership of Real Property

From earliest times, property has provided a means for survival. Primitive peoples lived off the fruits of the land, eating the vegetation and wildlife. Later, as the wildlife was domesticated and the vegetation cultivated, property provided pasturage and farmland. In the twelfth and thirteenth centuries the power of feudal lords was exemplified by the amount of land that they held; the more land they held, the more powerful they were. After the age of feudalism passed, property continued to be an indicator of family wealth and social position.

NATURE OF REAL PROPERTY

Real property consists of land and the buildings, plants, and trees that it contains. Whereas personal property is movable, real property—also called real estate or realty—is immovable. Real property usually means land, but it also includes subsurface and air rights, plant life and vegetation, and fixtures.

Land

Land includes the soil on the surface of the earth and the natural or artificial structures that are attached to it. It further includes all the waters contained on or under the surface and much, but not necessarily all, of the air space above it. The exterior boundaries of land extend straight down to the center of the earth and straight up to the farthest reaches of the atmosphere (subject to certain qualifications).

Subsurface and Air Rights

The owner of real property has relatively exclusive rights to the air space above the land as well as the soil and minerals underneath it. Until fifty years ago, the right to use air space was not too significant, but today, commercial airlines and high-rise office buildings and apartments use the air space regularly. Early cases involving air rights dealt with matters such as the right to run a telephone wire across a person's property when the wire did not touch any of the property[1] and whether a bullet shot over the person's land constituted trespass.[2]

Today, cases involving air rights present questions such as the right of commercial and private planes to fly over property, and the right of individuals and governments to seed clouds and produce

---

1. Butler v. Frontier Telephone Co., 186 N.Y. 486, 79 N.E. 716 (1906). Stringing a wire across someone's property violates the air rights of that person. Leaning walls, buildings, projecting eave spouts and roofs also violate the air rights of the property owner.
2. Herrin v. Sutherland, 74 Mont. 587, 241 P. 328 (1925). Shooting over a person's land constitutes trespass.

artificial rain. Flights over private land do not normally violate the property owners' rights unless the flights are low and frequent, causing a direct interference with the enjoyment and use of the land.[3]

Significant limitations on either air rights or subsurface rights normally have to be indicated on the deed transferring title at the time of purchase. Where no such encumbrances are noted, a purchaser can expect unfettered right to possession of the property. If any preexisting covenant unknown to the purchaser interferes with these rights, the purchaser can sue the seller for breach of warranty of title. However, most state statutes limit the time period in which the purchaser can sue. An alternative lawsuit is for breach of the covenant of quiet enjoyment. There is also a limit on the time for bringing such a suit, but it does not begin to run until after the discovery of the breach.

Separation of Surface and Subsurface Rights In many states, the owner of the surface of a piece of land is not the owner of the subsurface, and hence the land ownership may be separated. Subsurface rights can be extremely valuable, as these rights include the ownership of minerals and, in most states, oil and natural gas. Water rights are also extremely valuable, especially in the West.

When the ownership is separated into surface and subsurface rights, each owner can pass title to what he or she owns without the consent of the other. Each owner has the right to use the land owned, and in some cases a conflict will arise between a surface owner's use and the subsurface owner's need to extract minerals, oil, and natural gas.

Plant Life and Vegetation

Plant life, both natural and cultivated, is also considered to be real property. In many instances, the natural vegetation, such as trees, adds greatly to the value of the realty. When a parcel of land is sold and the land has growing crops on it, the sale includes the crops, unless otherwise specified in the sales contract. However, when crops are sold by themselves, they are considered to be personal property or goods. Consequently, the sale of crops is a sale of goods, and it is governed by the Uniform Commercial Code rather than by real property law [UCC 2-107(2)].

Fixtures

Certain personal property can become so closely associated with the real property to which it is attached that the law views it as real property. Such property is known as a **fixture**—a thing affixed to realty. A thing is *affixed* to realty when it is attached to it by roots, embedded in it, or permanently attached by means of cement, plaster, bolts, nails, or screws. The fixture can be physically attached to real property, be attached to another fixture, or even be without any actual physical attachment to the land, as long as the owner *intends* the property to be a fixture.

Fixtures are included in the sale of land if the sales contract does not provide otherwise. The sale of a house includes the land and the house and garage on it, as well as the cabinets, plumbing, and windows. Since these are permanently affixed to the property, they are considered to be a part of it. However, unless otherwise agreed, the curtains and throw rugs are not included. Items such as drapes and window-unit air conditioners are difficult to classify. Thus, a contract for the sale of a house or commercial realty should indicate which items of this sort are included in the sale.

In order to determine whether or not a certain item is a fixture, the *intention* of the party who placed the property must be examined. If the facts indicate that the person intended the item to be a fixture, then it will be a fixture.

When the intent of the party who placed the fixture on the realty is in dispute, the courts usually determine the intent based on either or both of the following factors:

1. If the property attached cannot be removed without causing substantial damage to the remaining realty, it is usually deemed a fixture.
2. If the property attached is so adapted to the rest of the realty as to become a part thereof, it is usually deemed a fixture.

Sometimes the intent of the owner is not readily implied by the circumstances. To illustrate: The owner of a house buys a workbench for the garage. The workbench is not bolted to the wall, but it

---

3. United States v. Causby, 328 U.S. 256, 66 S.Ct. 1062 (1946).

cannot be easily removed. If the owner intended the workbench to become a fixture—part of the garage—then it is a fixture. If the owner plans to remove it after a couple of months, then it is not a fixture. The objective intention of the owner will control.

Certain items can only be attached to property permanently; such items are fixtures. It is assumed that the owner intended them to be fixtures, since they had to be permanently attached to the property.

A tile floor, cabinets, and carpeting are examples. Also, when a piece of property is custom-made for installation on real property, such as storm windows, the property is usually classified as a fixture. Again, it is assumed that the owner intended the piece of property to become part of the real property.

The following case illustrates the court's interpretation of whether certain items are considered fixtures.

BACKGROUND AND FACTS *The plaintiff, Paul, purchased an elegant residence known as Long Acres from the defendant bank, First National Bank of Cincinnati, the executor of the estate of Augustine Long. When possession was delivered to plaintiff, he found items missing from the property. Long's will left to his children "all household furnishings, appliances, decoration, and equipment." Plaintiff claimed the children had wrongfully removed and converted certain fixtures that should have remained with the property.*

PAUL v. FIRST NAT'L BANK OF CINCINNATI
Common Pleas Court of Ohio, Hamilton County, 1976.
52 Ohio Misc. 77, 369 N.E.2d 488.

BLACK, Judge.
*   *   *   *

The converted items must be considered in two groups, as follows:
(1) 4 Handmade lighting fixtures around swimming pool
    Lighting fixture in living quarters of apartment over stable
    2 Lighting fixtures removed from chapel
    3 Metal cranes
    4 Garden statues.
(2) Ornamental housing over well
    Mercury statue
    Walnut organ bench.

In the court's judgment, group (1) are legally classified as "fixtures," and group (2) are "appurtenances" [articles adapted for use to the property to which they are connected], under the intent and meaning of the purchase contract. This conclusion is based on three considerations: the law of fixtures, the intent and meaning of the purchase contract, and the intent and meaning of the testamentary gift to the children.
*   *   *   *

In Masheter v. Boehm (1974), 37 Ohio St.2d 68, 307 N.E.2d 533, the Supreme Court designated, in paragraph two of the syllabus, six "facts" to be considered in determining whether an item is a fixture:

(1) The nature of the property;
(2) The manner in which the property is annexed to the realty;
(3) The purpose for which the annexation is made;
(4) The intention of the annexing party to make the property a part of the realty;
(5) The degree of difficulty and extent of any loss involved in removing the property from the realty; and
(6) The damage to the severed property which such removal would cause.
*   *   *   *

Using the Supreme Court's considerations, the light "fixtures" (there is no other available word) from the swimming pool, the stable apartment and the chapel are clearly fixtures in contemplation of law. They are of a type universally recognized as fixtures. This is true even though the pool "fixtures" were hung on brackets and could be unplugged and simply lifted off the brackets. But they were designed and produced solely and only for the swimming pool, from the same design as was used for the light fixture in the porte cochere (which was not removed). Further, the poles from which they were taken are barren and incomplete without them.

The three metal cranes and the four garden statues also meet five of the six criteria, in the judgment of the court. The "nature" of these items is that they were a part of the total elegance of Long Acres. They are not the type of fixture which would be commonly found on other lawns or in other gardens in Hamilton County, but they are an integral part of this sumptuous country estate. The cranes were "annexed" by being bolted or screwed into concrete foundations in a manner similar to the annexation of the marble table in the Great Hall, an item clearly admitted by all defendants to be a fixture passing with the real estate. The 4 garden statues (busts?) were not simply placed on top of their columns, but were held in place by 6-inch pipe protruding from the columns into the bases of the statues. The purpose of fixing these into position was to ensure their presence and preservation as part and parcel of the landscape and approach to Long Acres. These cranes and statues were not items moved about at the whim of the owner or according to the seasons: they were permanent implacements, intended to be part of the continuing visual effect of the estate. *   *   *

Group (2), being the ornamental well housing, the Mercury statue and the organ bench, were not attached in a permanent way. However, interpreting the contract from its four corners, in the light of all the facts and circumstances in evidence, the Court concludes that these items were "appurtenances" to the real estate, both in contemplation of law and in interpretation of this word as used in the purchase contract.

The word "appurtenance" means more than rights of way or other incorporeal rights: it includes an article adapted to the use of the property to which it is connected and which is intended to be a permanent accession to the freehold.

All three items in group (2) form a part of the character of Long Acres and enhance the style of its elegance. They are appurtenant to Long Acres in the sense that they are necessarily connected with the use and enjoyment of this country estate. They are incidental to the total value of this estate. The source of that value is not only the grand design but also all of the details whereby that design is executed: the location of the house on the property, the sweep of the driveway as it approaches the porte cochere, the spread-out location of the barns and other outbuildings, the majesty of the formal gardens, the spaciousness of the lawns on every side, and all the details of the exterior and interior of the mansion itself.
*   *   *   *

The Mercury statue is pictured in two photographs included in the appraisal of Long Acres which was considered by plaintiff before purchase. It may have been moved from the pedestal from time to time by the Long family, and it was not a "sun dial," despite this label in the appraisal. But interpreting the contract in the light of all facts and circumstances in evidence, the Court concludes that these items were appurtenances passing with the real estate.

The stove was not "built-in." It was surrounded by cabinets and an overhead fan and shield. But it could be pulled out from that location, it is a replaceable item, it is an "appliance" under the terms of the will, and it was listed as a chattel in the probate inventory and so disposed of in settling the probate estate.

The term "stair carpeting" is a misnomer. This was a small oriental rug of a size commonly called a "throw rug." It was tacked down to the short set of stairs from the Great Hall to the music room, but that was to keep it from slipping and causing injury. It was a floor rug adapted to this location on what the court considers a temporary basis. It was a "furnishing" which was given to the children by the will; and it was listed as a chattel in the probate inventory and was so disposed of in settling the probate estate.
*   *   *   *

However, the Long children plainly had no right to cut down and remove light fixtures, or to remove and refuse to return the other items comprising group (1). The status of these items is not and was not in doubt, in the judgment of this Court, and the taking was accomplished with knowledge (both actual and constructive) of the legal status of the items, with purpose to deprive the purchaser of them permanently, without a reasonable or lawful excuse, and to the purchaser's injury.

*   *   *   *

The conclusion of the court is that with respect to the conversion of property (Count 1), damages shall be the fair market value of replacement articles (determined as of the day of taking); the principle is to restore plaintiff fairly and reasonably to his position before the wrongful taking of these articles.

The trial court's judgment for the plaintiff was affirmed. The plaintiff recovered the fair market value of the fixtures and appurtenances improperly taken from the estate.

DECISION AND REMEDY

OWNERSHIP INTEREST IN REAL PROPERTY—ESTATES IN LAND

Ownership of property is an abstract concept that cannot exist independently of the legal system. No one can actually possess or *hold* a piece of land, the air above, the earth below, and all the water contained on it. The legal system therefore recognizes certain rights and duties that constitute the ownership interest in real property.

Freehold Estates

Rights of ownership in real property, called **estates,** are classified according to their nature, interest, and extent. Two major categories of estates are freehold estates, which are held indefinitely, and less than freehold estates, which are held for a predetermined time. There are two kinds of freehold estates—estates in fee and life estates.

Estates in Fee   There are two kinds of estates in fee: fee simple absolute and fee simple defeasible.

The Fee Simple Absolute   In a **fee simple absolute,** or fee simple, the owner has the greatest aggregation of rights, privileges, and power possible. The fee simple is limited absolutely to a person and his or her heirs and is assigned forever without limitation or condition. The rights that accompany a fee simple include the right to use the land for whatever purpose the owner sees fit, subject to laws that prevent the owner from unreasonably interfering with another person's land, and subject to applicable zoning laws.

A fee simple is potentially infinite in duration and can be disposed of by deed or by will (by selling or giving it away). When the owner of a fee simple dies without a will, the fee simple passes to the owner's legal heirs. The owner of a fee simple absolute also has the rights of *exclusive* possession and waste. *Waste* means that the owner can use the land without replenishing what is used. If Albert Samuelson has fee simple absolute ownership of fifteen acres in the mountains, he can mine any ore on that land without replacing it. The term *waste* refers to injury done to the land by one rightfully in possession of the land.

At early common law, a fee simple absolute could be conveyed only by stating that the conveyance was "to A and his heirs." The words "and his heirs" denoted the fee simple as infinite in duration and distinguished it from other estates such as the *fee simple defeasible* (which is defined below). In the United States today, these so-called words of limitation have been eliminated and a conveyance "to A" as well as "to A and his heirs" will convey a fee simple.

The Fee Simple Defeasible   A **fee simple defeasible** [4] encompasses a number of estates that

---

4.   The word *defeasible* refers to an owner's ability to lose ownership of property, whether the loss is voluntary or involuntary.

almost constitute absolute ownership.[5] Essentially, a fee simple defeasible is a fee simple that can end if a specified condition or event occurs.

A conveyance, for example, "to A and his heirs as long as the land is used for charitable purposes" creates a fee simple defeasible. In this type of conveyance, the original owner retains a *partial* ownership interest. As long as the specified condition occurs, A has full ownership rights, but if the specified condition does not occur and the land ceases to be used for charitable purposes, then the land reverts, or returns, to the original owner.[6] The interest that the original owner retains is called a *future interest* since, if it arises, it will arise in the future.[7] (But a so-called future interest is still a form of present property ownership that has a current market value.)

Consider another example. Simon deeds some land to XYZ Church "for as long as this land is used for church purposes and no longer." For two years, the land is used by the church for a playground for the children going to Sunday School. The church then sells the land to Smith, who intends to build an apartment building on it. As soon as Simon learns of the sale to Smith, he begins a court action to have himself declared the owner of the land.[8] Since Simon deeded a fee simple determinable to XYZ Church, he will succeed in his court action.

The church has absolute ownership of the land as long as it is used for church purposes. XYZ Church can even sell the land or otherwise dispose of it to those who will also use it for church purposes. However, as soon as the land stops being used for the specified purpose, the fee simple determinable terminates and ownership reverts to Simon.

The Life Estate   A **life estate** is an estate that lasts for the life of some specified individual. A conveyance "to A for his life" creates a life estate.[9] Estates for life can be created by an act of law or by an act of the parties.

In a life estate, the life tenant has fewer rights of ownership than the holder of a fee simple defeasible. The life tenant has the right to use the land provided no waste (injury to the land) is committed. In other words, the life tenant cannot injure the land in a manner that would adversely affect the owner of the future interest in it. The life tenant can use the land to harvest crops or, if mines and oil wells are already on the land, can extract minerals and oil from it. But the life tenant cannot exploit the land by creating new wells or mines.

Consider some examples. Michaelson deeds land to Hitchcock for life. Oil is found under that land. Agents of Mobil Oil Company negotiate an oil and gas lease with Hitchcock, but Mobil never contacts Michaelson. Mobil merely starts drilling an oil well. When Michaelson learns of this, he demands that Mobil stop drilling or negotiate a lease with him. Michaelson can enforce his demand because a life tenant alone cannot make a binding oil and gas lease upon the property if no drilling was taking place at the time the life estate was created. By the same token, Hitchcock cannot sell any of the timber that is on the land without Michaelson's approval, because the removal of standing timber will reduce the value of the land.

Yet, Hitchcock has the right to possess the land and, if it is farmland, to cultivate it and grow cash crops, retaining the proceeds, or to raise animals for market. Neither activity will reduce the value of the land, and such use is what was intended when the life estate was created.

The life tenant has the right to mortgage the life estate and create liens, easements, and leases; but none can extend beyond the life of the tenant. In addition, the owner of a life estate has exclusive right of possession during his or her life. Exclusive possession, however, is subject to the rights of the future interest holder to come onto the land and protect the future interest.

---

5. The term *fee simple defeasible* encompasses the fee simple determinable, the fee simple subject to special limitation, the fee simple subject to condition subsequent, and the fee simple subject to an executory interest.

6. If the original owner is not living at the time, the land passes to his or her heirs. In other words, once the condition occurs, A is divested of rights regardless of whether the original owner to (or through) whom the land reverts is alive.

7. In the specific example given in the text, the future interest that the owner holds is known as a *possibility of reverter*. In the conveyance "to A, but if the premises are ever used for the sale of alcoholic beverages then to B," the original owner has conveyed the entire interest. The owner has conveyed a fee simple defeasible to A and a future interest to B.

8. Note that the instant the condition is broken, legal ownership automatically vests in Simon.

---

9. A less common type of life estate is created by the conveyance "to A for the life of B." This is known as an estate *pur autre vie*, or an estate for the life of another.

Along with these rights, the life tenant also has some *duties*—to keep the property in repair and to pay property taxes. In short, the owner of the life estate has the same rights as a fee simple owner except that the value of the property must be kept intact for the future interest holder, less the decrease in value resulting from normal use of the property allowed by the life tenancy.

Nonfreehold Estates

The **less than freehold estates** are possessory real estate interests treated for some purposes as personal rather than real property. They are covered in this chapter for the sake of convenience because they relate to ownership of an interest in land. These estates include:

1. The tenancy for years.
2. The tenancy from period to period.
3. The tenancy at will.
4. The tenancy by sufferance.

All involve the transfer of the right to possession for *a specified period of time*.

The owner or lessor (landlord) conveys the property to the lessee (tenant) for a certain period of time. In every nonfreehold estate, the tenant has a *qualified* right to exclusive possession (qualified by the right of the landlord to enter upon the premises to assure that no waste is being committed). This is called a **leasehold estate.** The tenant can use the land, for example, by harvesting crops, but cannot injure the land by such activities as cutting down timber for sale or extracting oil.

Tenancy for Years   A **tenancy for years** is created by express contract (which can sometimes be oral) by leasing the property for a specified period of time. For example, signing a one-year lease to rent an apartment creates a tenancy for years. At the end of the period specified in the lease, the lease ends (without notice) and possession of the apartment returns to the lessor. If the tenant dies during the period of the lease, the lease passes to the tenant's heirs as personal property. Often, leases include renewal or extension provisions.

Tenancy from Period to Period   A **tenancy from period to period** is created by a lease that does not specify how long it is to last but does specify that rent is to be paid at certain intervals. This type of tenancy is automatically renewed for another rental period unless properly terminated. For example, a tenancy from period to period is created by a lease that states, "Rent is due on the tenth day of every month." This provision creates a tenancy from month to month. This type of tenancy can also be from week to week or from year to year. A tenancy from period to period sometimes arises when a landlord allows a tenant under a tenancy for years to hold over and continue paying monthly or weekly rent.

At common law, in order to terminate a tenancy from period to period, the landlord or tenant must give one period's notice to the other party. If the tenancy is month to month, one month's notice must be given. If the tenancy is week to week, one week's notice must be given. State statutes often define the required notice of termination in a tenancy from period to period. Therefore, the particular statute in question should be referred to in order to determine the proper time for notice of termination.

Tenancy at Will   Suppose a landlord rents an apartment to a tenant "for as long as both agree." In such a case, the tenant receives a leasehold estate known as a **tenancy at will.** At common law, either party can terminate the tenancy without notice. This type of estate usually arises when a tenant who has been under a tenancy for years retains possession after the termination date of that tenancy with the landlord's consent. Before the tenancy has been converted into a tenancy from period to period (by the periodic payment of rent), it is a tenancy at will, terminable by either party without notice. Once the tenancy is treated as a tenancy from period to period, a termination notice must conform to the one already discussed. The death of either party or the voluntary commission of waste by the tenant will terminate a tenancy at will.

Tenancy by Sufferance   A **tenancy by sufferance** is not a true tenancy. It is the mere possession of land without right. A tenancy by sufferance is not an estate, since it is created by a tenant *wrongfully* retaining possession of property. Whenever a life estate, tenancy for years, tenancy from period to period, or tenancy at will ends, and the tenant continues to retain possession of the premises without the owner's permission, a tenancy by sufferance is created.

Termination   As long as a tenancy exists, a landlord can collect rent in full, regardless of whether the premises are actually occupied by the tenant. Thus, when a tenant wrongfully abandons the premises and refuses to pay rent, the landlord can permit the premises to remain vacant, refuse to recognize the attempted surrender by the tenant, and bring a lawsuit to collect the rent as it comes due. A tenant who wrongfully abandons the premises and refuses to pay rent cannot require that the landlord find another tenant to pay the rent. In many circumstances, however, the landlord has a duty created by statute or judicial decisions to mitigate his or her damages. As a result, if other tenants are available, the landlord may be unable to collect damages for the tenant's breach of the lease. The issue of termination of tenancy is examined in the following case.

EDWARD BANKERS & CO. v. SPRADLIN

Court of Civil Appeals of Texas, Houston (1st Dist.), 1978. 575 S.W.2d 585.

BACKGROUND AND FACTS   *The defendant, Spradlin, leased space, known as Suite 325, in an office building managed and owned by the plaintiff, Edward Bankers & Co. The lease was for a five-year term. Two years after the lease was signed, Spradlin moved to Suite 1000, a larger and more expensive space in the same building. Both Suite 325 and Suite 1000 were owned and managed by the same company. The move to the larger suite was made after an oral agreement between Spradlin and the plaintiff. After Spradlin moved his offices to Suite 1000, he made no further payments on Suite 325. The plaintiff brought this action against him for recovery of the rental payments on Suite 325.*

EVANS, Justice.
*   *   *   *

The surrender of leased premises by a tenant and the acceptance of possession by the landlord ordinarily releases the tenant from further obligation to pay rentals. An agreement of surrender and release may be express, or it may be implied from the circumstances and acts of the parties. The question of whether there has been an acceptance by the landlord releasing the tenant from further obligations under the lease involves a determination of the intent of the parties, and this may present an issue of fact.

The jury could have concluded from the testimony that Spradlin agreed to vacate his office space in suite 325 and to move his offices to suite 1000, with a substantial increase in his monthly rent, upon the assurance of the plaintiff's building manager that he would not have any further obligation to make rental payments on suite 325. The jury might also have inferred from the testimony that the plaintiff accepted Spradlin's surrender of the office space in suite 325 and that when Spradlin vacated those premises, the plaintiff resumed possession and made use of the space for its own purposes. Thus, from the circumstances presented by the evidence the jury could have concluded that there was a mutual understanding and agreement beween the parties to terminate Spradlin's lease on suite 325 and to enter into a new lease arrangement covering suite 1000. Where the circumstances and acts of the parties are equivalent to an agreement on the part of the tenant to vacate the leased premises and on the part of the landlord to resume possession, a surrender results by operation of law.

The evidence is legally and factually sufficient to support the jury's finding that the plaintiff released Spradlin from liability under the lease covering suite 325.

DECISION AND REMEDY   *The jury verdict for the tenant was affirmed. The landlord by his actions had released the tenant from the rental obligation.*

RELATIONSHIP OF LANDLORD AND TENANT

Much real property is used by those who do not own it. A **lease** is a contract by which the owner—the landlord—grants the tenant an exclusive right to use and possess the land, usually for an ascertainable period of time. The basic characteristic of this particular estate is that it continues for the ascertainable term and carries with it the obligation by the tenant to pay rent to the landlord. Thus an individual who *leases* property must pay rent unless some other form of payment is agreed upon. Usually, the creation of the leasehold estate by contract for terms longer than a year (or three years in some jurisdictions) must be in writing.

Warranties of the Landlord

When a landlord leases premises to a tenant, a **warranty of possession** and a **covenant of quiet enjoyment** are implied by law. Under the *warranty of possession*, the landlord warrants that the premises have been leased only to one tenant, and that the premises will be available for occupancy at the agreed time. This is particularly important in leasing apartments, offices, and the like in buildings under construction.

Under the *covenant of quiet enjoyment*, the landlord promises that the tenant or grantee shall enjoy the possession of the premises in peace and without disturbance. Generally, questions regarding a breach of the covenant of quiet enjoyment arise when the landlord's action (or inaction) affects the tenant's use and enjoyment of the premises in such a way that the tenant is constructively evicted. *Constructive eviction* occurs when the landlord fails to perform any of the undertakings required by the lease, if such failure causes a substantial and lasting injury to the tenant's beneficial enjoyment of the premises. This failure is regarded as an eviction of the tenant.

For example, suppose Smith, a quiet minister, rents half of a duplex from Lawson. Lawson rents the other half of the duplex to three members of a rock band. The band rehearses in the duplex every night from about 11:00 in the evening to 5:00 in the morning. Smith complains to Lawson that strange people are constantly entering and leaving the premises and that the noise is unbearable. If Lawson fails to take any action, he has breached his covenant of quiet enjoyment to Smith and has *constructively evicted* him from the premises. Smith can probably rescind the rental agreement.

At common law, the landlord was under no duty to repair the premises rented by a tenant or to warrant that the premises were habitable or suitable for the particular purpose for which they were rented. Under most state statutes today, however, and under judicial decisions, a landlord of residential premises impliedly warrants that the premises are *habitable* and cannot disclaim this warranty unless the landlord and the tenant have equal bargaining power. Additionally, unless otherwise stated in the lease, a landlord is under an affirmative duty to repair and maintain the structure and all its *common areas* and fixtures. The landlord will be held liable for injuries resulting from negligent failure to maintain the rented premises.

The following case illustrates the development of the doctrine of an implied warranty of habitability in *residential leases*.

BACKGROUND AND FACTS *Plaintiff, Shirley Steele, and her six young children rented a house from Marvin Latimer, the defendant. When Latimer failed to make repairs to the premises, Steele brought this action to compel the repairs and sought damages from the landlord. The trial court ruled that there was no implied warranty of habitability existing in Kansas but concluded that "if there was such an implied warranty of habitability that in this case plaintiff would be entitled to recover because the conditions of the house are such that it does violate the principle or theory of implied warranty of habitability." The Kansas Supreme Court reviewed the case.*

STEELE v. LATIMER
Supreme Court of Kansas, 1974.
214 Kan. 329, 521 P.2d 304.

FONTRON, Justice.

* * * *

It has been said that the development of the common law has been determined largely by the social needs of the society it was designed to serve, and that the capacity for growth and change is one of its most significant features. The most casual student of ages past would agree that the principle of change runs deeply through human history and like a golden thread weaves new "people requirements" into the fabrics of altered social patterns.

* * * *

In recent years there has been a noticeable trend among courts in this country to recognize an implied warranty on the part of the lessor of urban residential property that the premises leased by him are suitable for human habitation and will be maintained in suitable condition throughout the duration of the tenancy.

* * * *

The feudal concept that a lease is simply the sale or conveyance of an interest in land has given way to the more realistic view that a lease is essentially a contract.

The relationship of landlord and tenant being contractual in character, it follows that mutually dependent rights and obligations arise therefrom, binding alike on lessor and lessee.

* * * *

In discussing the housing problems with which today's urban populations are confronted, the Wisconsin Supreme Court phrased the situation this way:

" * * * To follow the old rule of no implied warranty of habitability in leases would, in our opinion, be inconsistent with the current legislative policy concerning housing standards. The need and social desirability of adequate housing for people in this era of rapid population increases is too important to be rebuffed by that obnoxious legal cliché, *caveat emptor.* Permitting landlords to rent 'tumble-down' houses is at least a contributing cause of such problems as urban blight, juvenile delinquency, and high property taxes for conscientious landowners."

Building codes are common today in many urban centers throughout the United States and the modern weight of authority in this country appears to be that the minimum standards embraced within a housing ordinance, building code or other municipal regulation are to be read into and will be implied by operation of law in housing contracts.

[T]he Wichita Housing Code was in full force and effect at all times material to this action. The Code is broad and comprehensive in its outreach; it sets basic standards to be met by city housing and requires lessors and lessees to meet the same as provided therein; it provides for inspections, notices of violations and procedures for conducting hearings and appeals; and it provides criminal penalties for violating the act. The trial court found that the house at 3138 Ethel did not meet the standards set by the Wichita Housing Code in that (1) the windows and front door were not reasonably tight; (2) that there was excess air leakage; and (3) the cabinet top and bathroom floors were unsanitary and dangerous to health.

Under familiar legal principles the provisions of the city's housing code relating to minimum housing standards were by implication read into and became a part of the rental agreement between Shirley Steele and Marvin E. Latimer.

Where a breach of an implied warranty of habitability has occurred traditional remedies for breach of contract are available to the tenant, including the recovery of damages.

DECISION AND REMEDY   *The court held that in Kansas a warranty of habitability is implied in all residential leases. The case was remanded for a new trial on the issue of damages resulting from the breach of the implied warranty.*

Duties Owed by the Tenant

Tenant's Obligation to Pay   The tenant has an implied obligation to pay reasonable rent to the landlord. Most lease contracts contain an express promise, known as a covenant, that indicates that the tenant is to pay a specific amount at specified times. Generally, if the express promise is not in the lease agreement, then the tenant is obliged to pay only rent that is reasonable and only at the end of the term.

Assignment   An assignment of a tenant's lease to another is an agreement to transfer all rights, title, and interest in the lease to the assignee. It is a complete transfer. Many leases require that the assignment have the landlord's written consent, and an assignment that lacks consent can be avoided by the landlord. A landlord who knowingly accepts rent from the assignee, however, will be held to have waived the requirement. Once waived, it cannot later be revised unless new grounds appear.

A tenant does not end his or her liabilities on a lease upon assignment. The tenant may assign rights but not duties. Thus, even though the assignee of the lease is required to pay rent, the original tenant is not released from the contractual obligation to pay rent. Whenever the assignee fails to pay, the landlord can look to the original tenant for compensation.

Subleasing   Subleasing involves a partial transfer of the original tenant's rights to the lease. Frequently, the tenant is prohibited from subleasing the premises without the landlord's consent. By subleasing, the original tenant is not relieved of any obligations to the landlord under the lease.

To illustrate: A student named Ann leases an apartment for a two-year period. Although Ann had planned on attending summer school, she is offered a vacation job in Europe for the summer months and accepts. Ann does not wish to be stuck with three months' rent for an unoccupied apartment. Unless prohibited by a lease requiring landlord permission, she can sublease the apartment to another student (sublessee). The sublessee is bound by the same terms of the lease as the tenant, and should the sublessee violate the lease, Ann can be held liable by the landlord.

Destruction of the Premises and the Obligation to Pay Rent   At common law, destruction by fire or flood of a whole building leased by a tenant did not relieve the tenant of the obligation to pay rent or permit the termination of the lease. Today, however, state statutes have altered the common law rule. Thus, if the building burns down, apartment dwellers in most states are not continuously liable to the landlord for the payment of rent.

CONCURRENT OWNERSHIP

Property owned by one person is said to be held severally, that is, apart from others. When two or more persons own property, it is said to be held concurrently. There are several types of **concurrent estates,** including tenancy in common, joint tenancy, tenancy by the entirety, and community property.

Tenancy in Common

One type of concurrent estate is a **tenancy in common.** Suppose Henry conveys land "to Able and Baker and Carter." This conveyance creates a tenancy in common among Able, Baker, and Carter, whereby each takes a one-third interest. In a tenancy in common, each tenant has the right to convey his or her interest in the property. When one of the tenants dies, that tenant's interest passes to his or her heirs (or, by will, to someone else). Essentially, tenants in a tenancy in common each own an undivided fractional share of the property, an interest that can be conveyed to another.

Joint Tenancy

In a **joint tenancy,** each tenant owns an undivided interest in the property. However, unlike a tenancy in common, each joint tenant has a *right of survivorship.* For example, if there are two joint tenants and one dies, the other becomes the sole owner of this interest. No property passes to the heirs of the deceased—even by will.

At common law, unless a clear intention to create a tenancy in common was shown, there was a presumption that any co-tenancy was a joint tenancy. Modern statutes, however, reverse this presumption. Most statutes now presume that a co-tenancy is a tenancy in common unless there is a clear intention to establish a joint tenancy. Thus, the language "to Able and Baker as joint tenants with right of survivorship, and not as tenants in common" would create a joint tenancy.

A joint tenancy is transformed into a tenancy in common when one of the joint tenants transfers his or her interest to another party. A joint tenancy can also be transferred by *partition*; that is, the tenants can physically divide the property into equal parts. Since a joint tenant's interest is capable of being conveyed without the consent of the other joint tenants, it can be levied against by the tenant's creditors. This characteristic is also true of the tenancy in common.

Tenancy by the Entirety

Another type of concurrent estate is the **tenancy by the entirety**—a joint tenancy between a husband and wife. At common law, a tenancy by the entirety could be created in a husband and wife only where the conveyance was to, say, "Daniel and Harriet Campbell, husband and wife, and their heirs and assigns." A tenancy by the entirety differs from a joint tenancy and tenancy in common in that neither spouse can convey his or her interest without the express consent of the other. Since neither can voluntarily convey his or her interest, the creditors of one spouse cannot levy on the property.

Divorce terminates a tenancy by the entirety and, in most states, creates a tenancy in common. The tenancy by the entirety is not recognized in many states.[10]

Community Property

Nine states provide for concurrent ownership of property by what is called community property.[11] Generally, any property acquired by a husband and wife during the period of their marriage becomes community property, with each owning an undivided half interest. Property acquired by gift or in-

heritance, however, is not included within the category of community property.

The community property systems are based upon the theory that both spouses contribute to acquisitions during marriage. Hence, it is recognized that the activity of each spouse is directed toward making the marriage a "going concern." It is immaterial, therefore, who actually earned or acquired the property. There is an irrefutable presumption of equal contribution.

TRANSFER OF OWNERSHIP

There are a number of ways ownership of real property can pass from one person to another. They include inheritance or will, eminent domain, adverse possession, and deed. Conveyance by deed includes transfer by sale and by gift.

Transfer by Inheritance or Will

Property that is transferred on an owner's death is passed either by *will* or by *inheritance*. If the owner of land dies with a will, the land that the owner had prior to death passes according to the terms of the will. If the owner dies without a will, state statutes prescribe how and to whom the property will pass.

Eminent Domain

Even where ownership in real property is fee simple absolute, there is still a superior ownership that limits the fee simple absolute. It is called **eminent domain,** and it is sometimes referred to as the condemnation power of the government to take land for public use. It gives a right to the government to acquire possession of real property in the manner directed by the Constitution and the laws of the state whenever the public interest requires it.

For example, when a new public highway is to be built, the government must decide where to build it and how much land to condemn. The power of eminent domain is generally invoked through condemnation proceedings. After the government determines that a particular parcel of land is necessary for public use, it brings a judicial proceeding to obtain title to the land. Then, in another proceeding, the court further determines the *fair value* of the land, which is usually approximately equal to its market value. Under the Fifth Amendment, pri-

10.   See Dorf v. Tuscarora Pipeline Co., 48 N.J.Super. 26, 136 A.2d 778(1957) and Lindenfelser v. Lindenfelser 396 Pa. 530, 153 A.2d 901 (1959). Some of the states that recognize tenancy by the entirety require express language to create it.
11.   Arizona, California, Idaho, Louisiana, Nevada, New Mexico, Texas, Washington. As a result of the Wisconsin Marital Property Act, Wisconsin became a community property state as of January 1, 1986.

CONCEPT SUMMARY: The Basic Forms of Ownership of Real Property	
FORMS OF OWNERSHIP	**TYPES AND DEFINITIONS**

Freehold Estate (Held indefinitely)	1. Estates in Fee—
	   a. Fee Simple Absolute—Most complete form of ownership.
	   b. Fee Simple Defeasible—Fee Simple that can end if specified condition or event occurs.
	2. Life Estates—Lasts for life of a specified individual; rights subject to the rights of the future interest holder.

Nonfreehold Estates (Possessory interests held for a specified period of time)	1. Tenancy for Years—Lasts for periods of time stated by express contract. 2. Tenancy from Period to Period—Period determined by frequency of rent payments; automatically renewed unless proper notice is given. 3. Tenancy at Will—For as long as both parties agree; no notice of termination required. 4. Tenancy by Sufferance—Possession of land without legal right.
Concurrent Ownership (Jointly held ownership)	1. Tenancy in Common—Each tenant owns an undivided fractional share of the property. Such interests can be conveyed without consent, and, upon death, pass to tenant's heirs. 2. Joint Tenancy (with right of survivorship)—Each tenant owns an undivided share of the property. Such interest can be conveyed without consent, converting the interest to tenancy in common. Upon death, interest passes to surviving joint tenant, not heirs. 3. Tenancy by the Entirety—A joint tenancy with right of survivorship between husband and wife. 4. Community Property—Most property acquired during marriage by either or both spouses is owned equally by each spouse.

vate property may not be taken for public use without "just compensation."

Adverse Possession

Adverse possession is a means of obtaining title to land without a deed being delivered. Essentially, when one person possesses the property of another for a certain statutory period of time (three to thirty years, with ten years being most common), that person, called the adverse possessor, acquires title to the land and cannot be removed from the land by the original owner. The adverse possessor is vested with a perfect title just as if there had been a conveyance by deed.

In order to hold property adversely, four elements must be satisfied:

1. Possession must be actual and exclusive; that is, the possessor must take sole physical occupancy of the property.

2. The possession must be open, visible, and notorious, not secret or clandestine. The possessor must occupy the land for all the world to see.

3. Possession must be continuous and peaceable for the required period of time. This requirement means that the possessor must not be interrupted in the occupancy by the true owner or by the courts.

4. Possession must be hostile and adverse. In other words, the possessor must claim the property as against the whole world. He or she cannot live on the property with the permission of the owner.

Conveyance by Deed

Possession and title to land are also passed from person to person by means of a **deed**—the instrument of conveyance of real property. A deed is a writing signed by an owner of property by which title to it is transferred to another. Deeds must meet certain requirements.

Requirements of a Valid Deed   Unlike a contract, a deed does not have to be supported by legally sufficient consideration. Gifts of real property are common, and they require deeds even though there is no consideration for the gift. The necessary requirements for a valid deed are:

1.   The names of the buyer (grantee) and seller (grantor).
2.   Words evidencing an intent to convey (for example, "I hereby bargain, sell, grant, or give").
3.   A legally sufficient description of the land.
4.   The grantor's (and usually the spouse's) signature.
5.   Delivery of the deed.

Types of Deeds

General Warranty Deed   General warranty deeds warrant the greatest number of things and thus provide the most extensive protection against defects of title. In most states, special language is required to make a general warranty deed. Thus, if a contract calls for "a general warranty deed" without specifying the covenants to be included in the deed, or if a deed states that the seller is providing the "usual covenants," most courts will infer from this language all of the following covenants (warranties) of title:

1.   A *covenant of seisin and a covenant of the right to convey* warrant that the seller has title and the power to convey the estate that the deed describes.

For example, if Able, the owner of a life estate in Whiteacre, attempts to convey a fee simple to Baker, Able has breached the covenant of seisin. If Baker is damaged by Able's breach, then Baker is entitled to recover from Able.

2.   A *covenant against encumbrances* guarantees that the property being sold or conveyed is not subject to any outstanding rights or interests that will diminish the value of the land, except as stated. Examples of common encumbrances include mortgages, liens, profits, easements, and private deed restrictions on the use of land. Unless the deed expressly states that the conveyance is subject to a particular encumbrance, a covenant against encumbrances will be breached if the buyer discovers an undisclosed encumbrance. Again, as in the case of a covenant of seisin, the buyer is entitled to recover for any damage caused by the breach of this covenant.

3.   A *covenant for quiet enjoyment* guarantees that the grantee or buyer will not be disturbed in his or her possession of the land by the grantor or any third persons. For example, suppose Janet Parker sells her two-acre lot and office building by general warranty deed. Subsequently, a third person shows better title than Janet had and proceeds to evict the buyer. Here the covenant for quiet enjoyment has been breached, and the buyer can recover the purchase price of the land plus any other damages incurred in being evicted.

The following case illustrates these covenants.

BROWN v. LOBER
Supreme Court of Illinois 1979.
75 Ill.2d 549, 27 Ill.Dec. 780,
389 N.E.2d 1188.

BACKGROUND AND FACTS   *The plaintiff, Brown, purchased real property in 1957 and received a warranty deed. The deed contained no list of encumbrances. In 1974, the plaintiff granted a call option to Consolidated Coal Company, permitting the company rights to subsurface coal. Consolidated agreed to pay the plaintiff $6,000 for these rights. In 1976, it was discovered that the plaintiff did not own the subsurface mineral rights free and clear as indicated by the warranty deed of 1957. Instead, the plaintiff owned only one-third of the rights. The rights to the remaining two-thirds had been deeded away in 1947 by a prior grantor.*

The plaintiff had already been paid $2,000 by the coal company for its one-third interest. The coal company would not pay the remaining $4,000. The plaintiff then filed this lawsuit, seeking the $4,000 in damages against the prior grantor, Lober, the defendant.

Lober asserted that the ten-year statute of limitations for covenant of seisin barred the lawsuit. Brown asserted that a right of action was permitted for breach of the covenant of quiet enjoyment.

The trial court found for Lober, deciding that the ten-year statute of limitations had run from the time the deed was issued in 1957. Brown appealed.

UNDERWOOD, Justice.

* * * *

The deed which plaintiffs received * * * was a general statutory form warranty deed meeting the requirements of section 9 of "An Act concerning conveyances."

* * *

The effect of this provision is that certain covenants of title are implied in every statutory form warranty deed. Subsection 1 contains the covenant of seisin and the covenant of good right to convey. These covenants, which are considered synonymous, assure the grantee that the grantor is, at the time of the conveyance, lawfully seized and has the power to convey an estate of the quality and quantity which he professes to convey.

* * * *

Subsection 3 sets forth the covenant of quiet enjoyment, which is synonymous with the covenant of warranty in Illinois. By this covenant, "the grantor warrants to the grantee, his heirs and assigns, the possession of the premises and that he will defend the title granted by the terms of the deed against persons who may lawfully claim the same, and that such covenant shall be obligatory upon the grantor, his heirs, personal representatives, and assigns."

* * * *

Since the deed was delivered to the plaintiffs on December 21, 1957, any cause of action for breach of the covenant of seisin would have accrued on that date. The trial court held that this cause of action was barred by the statute of limitations. No question is raised as to the applicability of the 10-year statute of limitations. We conclude, therefore, that the cause of action for breach of the covenant of seisin was properly determined by the trial court to be barred by the statute of limitations since plaintiffs did not file their complaint until May 25, 1976, nearly 20 years after their alleged cause of action accrued.

* * * *

This court has stated on numerous occasions that, in contrast to the covenant of seisin, the covenant of warranty or quiet enjoyment is prospective in nature and is breached only when there is an actual or constructive eviction of the covenantee by the paramount titleholder.

The cases are also replete with statements to the effect that the mere existence of paramount title in one other than the covenantee is not sufficient to constitute a breach of the covenant of warranty or quiet enjoyment: "[T]here must be a union of acts of disturbance and lawful title, to constitute a breach of the covenant for quiet enjoyment, or warranty * * *. '[T]here is a general concurrence that something more than the mere existence of a paramount title is necessary to constitute a breach of the covenant of warranty.' A mere want of title is no breach of this covenant. There must not only be a want of title, but there must be an ouster under a paramount title."

* * * *

Since no one has, as yet, undertaken to remove the coal or otherwise manifested a clear intent to exclusively "possess" the mineral estate, it must be concluded that the subsurface estate is "vacant." As in *Scott*, plaintiffs "could at any time have taken peaceable possession of it. [They have] in no way been prevented or hindered from the enjoyment of the possession by any one having a better right." Accordingly, until such time as one holding paramount title interferes with plaintiffs' right of possession (*e.g.*, by beginning to mine the coal), there can be no constructive eviction and, therefore, no breach of the covenant of quiet enjoyment.

DECISION
AND REMEDY   *The judgment of the trial court was affirmed. The statute of limitations barred an action for breach of the covenant of seisin. The Browns also could not recover for breach of the covenant of quiet enjoyment because no one had interfered with their right of possession.*

Special Warranty Deed   In contrast to the general warranty deed, the special warranty deed (also known as deed with covenant against grantor's acts) warrants only that the grantor or seller has not previously done anything to lessen the value of the real estate. If the special warranty deed discloses all liens or other encumbrances, the seller will not be liable to the buyer if a third person subsequently interferes with the buyer's ownership. However, if the third person's claim arises out of, or is related to, some act of the seller, the seller will be liable to the buyer for damages.

Both the special warranty deed and the general warranty deed warrant that the seller has "marketable" title. Common defects that may render a title unmarketable include variations in the names of grantors and grantees, breaks in the chain of title, outstanding liens, and defectively executed deeds in the chain of title.

Quitclaim Deed   A **quitclaim deed** warrants less than any other deed. Essentially, it simply conveys to the grantee whatever interest the grantor had. In other words, if the grantor had nothing, then the grantee receives nothing. Naturally, if the grantor had a defective title, or no title at all, a conveyance by general warranty deed or special warranty deed will not cure the defects. A quitclaim deed gives no cause of action unless the seller had one. Such deeds, however, will give the buyer a cause of action to sue the seller. See Exhibit 53–1 for a typical quitclaim deed.

Grant Deed (Bargain and Sale Deed)   With a grant deed, the grantor simply states, "I grant the property to you." Or the grantor may state, "I convey, or bargain and sell, the property to you." By state statute, grant deeds carry with them an implied warranty that the grantor either owns the property being transferred or has not previously encumbered it or conveyed it to someone else.

Recording Statutes

Recording statutes are in force in every jurisdiction. The purpose of these statutes is to provide prospec-

tive buyers with a way to check whether there has been an earlier transaction. Hence, recording a deed gives notice to the world that a certain person is now the owner of a particular parcel of real estate. Placing everyone on notice as to the true owner is intended to prevent the previous owners from fraudulently conveying the land to a subsequent purchaser.

Deeds are generally recorded in the presence of a notary public in the county where the property is recorded. Many state statutes require that the grantor sign the deed in the presence of two attesting witnesses before it can be recorded. There are three basic types of recording statutes:

1.   A *race statute* provides that a subsequent purchaser must record before an earlier purchaser, but he or she is protected whether or not he or she has actual notice of this earlier conveyance. [12]
2.   A *pure notice statute* states that an unrecorded instrument is invalid as against any subsequent purchaser without notice, whether or not the subsequent purchaser records prior to the first purchaser.
3.   A *notice-race statute* protects the subsequent purchaser only if he or she records before the earlier purchaser and he or she takes without actual notice of this earlier conveynace.

Irrespective of the particular type of recording statute adopted by a state, there is a fee involved when a deed is recorded. The grantee typically pays this fee since he or she is the one who will be protected by recording the deed.

Warranty of Habitability

The common law rule of *caveat emptor* ("let the buyer beware") held that the seller of a home made no warranties with respect to the soundness or fitness of the home unless such a warranty was specifically included in the deed or contract of sale. While *caveat emptor* is still the rule of law in many states,

---

12.   Only two states use a race type of recording statute. The rest of the states are split about evenly with respect to the use of a pure notice statute and a notice-race statute.

EXHIBIT 53–1 A Typical Quitclaim Deed

RECORDING REQUESTED BY

AND WHEN RECORDED MAIL THIS DEED AND, UNLESS
OTHERWISE SHOWN BELOW, MAIL TAX STATEMENTS TO:

NAME

ADDRESS

CITY &
STATE
ZIP

Title Order No. _____   Escrow No. _____

———— SPACE ABOVE THIS LINE FOR RECORDER'S USE ————

Quitclaim Deed

The undersigned declares that the documentary transfer tax is $ _____and is
☐ computed on the full value of the interest or property conveyed, or is
☐ computed on the full value less the value of liens or encumbrances remaining thereon at the time of sale. The land, tenements or realty is
located in
☐ unincorporated area   ☐ city of _____ and

FOR A VALUABLE CONSIDERATION, receipt of which is hereby acknowledged

do   hereby remise, release and forever quitclaim to

the following described real property in the   county of
state of California:

Dated _____

STATE OF CALIFORNIA   } ss.
COUNTY OF _____
On _____before me, the under-
signed, a Notary Public in and for said County and State, personally
appeared_____

_____, known to me
to be the person _____ whose name _____ subscribed to the within instrument and acknowledged that _____ executed the same.

_____
          Signature of Notary

FOR NOTARY SEAL OR STAMP

Assessor's Parcel No. _____

MAIL TAX STATEMENTS TO PARTY SHOWN ON FOLLOWING LINE IF NO PARTY SO SHOWN, MAIL AS DIRECTED ABOVE

Name	Street Address	City & State

L-11-A (G.S.) (Rev. 8-75) (8 pt.)

there is currently a strong trend against it and in favor of an *implied* warranty of habitability. Under this new approach, the courts hold that the seller of a new house warrants that it will be fit for human habitation regardless of whether any such warranty is included in the deed or contract of sale. In recent years, some states, such as Virginia, have passed legislation creating such warranties for newly constructed residences.

Essentially, under an implied warranty of habitability, the seller warrants that the house is in reasonable working order and is of reasonably sound construction. The purchaser is only required to prove that the home he or she has purchased was somehow defective and to prove the damages caused by the defect in order to recover. Thus, under the warranty of habitability theory, the seller of a new home is in effect a guarantor of the home's fitness.

Sale of Real Estate

Transfers of ownership interest in real property are frequently accomplished by means of a sale. The sale of real estate is similar to the sale of goods since it involves a transfer of ownership, often with certain warranties. However, in the sale of real estate, certain formalities are observed that are not required in the sale of goods. To meet the requirements of law, a deed must be signed and delivered.[13] In order to illustrate how a transfer of ownership in real property is accomplished, a typical real estate transaction is outlined here.

A Typical Procedure in the Sale of Real Estate

Suppose Janet Parker owns a parcel of real estate—a two-acre lot with an office building. Since her business is expanding to a new location, she has decided to sell the property. The first thing she will do is attempt to locate a buyer. She can put the property up for sale herself, or she can employ a real estate broker or agent to help her locate a buyer.

---

13.   The phrase *signed, sealed, and delivered* used to refer to the requirements for transferring title to real property by deed. The seal has fallen from use, but signature and delivery are still required.

Locating a Buyer   A broker can put Parker's property on an *open listing*. An open listing contract allows Parker (the landowner) to find a buyer herself and/or to hire brokers with nonexclusive rights to sell the property. In the latter case, the broker who is the first to produce such a buyer is entitled to the commission.

Alternatively, Parker can have an *exclusive agency* with the broker. In this type of arrangement, the broker has the exclusive right as an agent to sell the property. Parker can employ another broker, but if she does, the first broker is still entitled to a commission. However, if Parker sells the property without the assistance of the broker, she need not pay the commission.

Finally, Parker can give the broker an *exclusive right to sell*. In this situation, the broker is normally entitled to a commission no matter who sells the real estate—Parker, this broker, or another broker. An exclusive right to sell usually lasts for a specified period of time; after that time, Parker is free to make arrangements with another broker if the property has not yet been sold.

Contract of Sale   Once a buyer is located, a contract for the sale of the land must be negotiated. Here Parker must determine the cost of title examination and insurance, how to allocate property taxes, and what the actual purchase price will be. The Statute of Frauds also requires that the contract for the sale of real estate must be evidenced by writing to be enforceable. Even though the writing need not specify all the details of the transaction, it should contain the essential terms of the bargain. The essential elements of a contract of sale are:

1.   An identification of the parties.
2.   The description of the land to be conveyed.
3.   The purchase price.
4.   The signatures.

Often, the sales contract requires a buyer to purchase *title insurance*—an insurance that protects the buyer in the event that someone is shown to have a better title. Generally, title insurance—as well as title examination, which is discussed below—is merely an option that is available to buyers to protect themselves. See Exhibit 53–2 for a contract for the sale of real estate.

EXHIBIT 53–2 A Hypothetical Example of a Typical Contract

Contract for Sale of Real Estate

I, --
seller, have sold and agree to convey to --
-- (in joint tenancy)
purchaser, upon the terms hereinafter set forth, the following described real estate, situate in Ramsey County, Minnesota,
namely: ---

----

according to the plat thereof, subject, however, to any change in the size of said property caused by the vacating, opening,
widening, narrowing or grading of any street or alley, said property being also known as number ---------------------------
-- Saint Paul, Minnesota.

I, --
have viewed, examined and purchased said real estate and agree to pay therefor the total purchase price of
--Dollars ($--------------------------)
of which --Dollars ($--------------------------)
have been paid at the date hereof, the receipt of which is hereby acknowledged, and the further sum of ---------------------
---Dollars ($--------------------------)
is to be paid by said purchaser to said seller as follows: ---
--Dollars ($--------------------------)
in cash on execution and delivery of a --- Warranty Deed.
---Dollars ($--------------------------)
by assuming and agreeing to pay one certain—proposed mortgage, now—to become a lien against said property, same
bearing—to bear interest at ---------------------% per annum, interest and principal being payable as follows $--------------------
monthly—quarterly—semi-annually with the privilege of multiple payments of $----------------- on any ----------------------
payment date, and $-------------------- in monthly—quarterly—semi-annual—annual installments of $-------------------, or more each;
from the monthly—quarterly—semi-annual—annual payments shall first be deducted the accumulated interest on deferred
payments at ---------------------% per annum; and the balance then remaining, shall be applied in reduction of the principal
indebtedness; and in addition thereto, the purchaser shall add to said -------------------- payments, beginning -------------------
---------------- 19------, an amount sufficient to provide payment before penalties accrue of taxes and assessments; fire, windstorm
and other hazard insurance, as estimated by seller ---

It is understood and agreed that this sale is made subject to the approval within -------------------- days by the owner of said
premises in writing, and that the undersigned agent is in no manner liable or responsible on account of this agreement, except
to return or account for any of the purchase money paid to him under this contract.

Said purchaser agrees to pay the purchase price in the manner and at the times aforesaid, and further to pay all taxes
and assessments on said premises, commencing with those assessed thereon for the present year, but not payable until the
first Monday in January next, together with assessments and deferred instalments thereof, if any, heretofore levied against said
land, the payment of which is not yet enforcible.

Said seller shall, within fifteen days inclusive from the date hereof, deliver to said purchaser a properly certified to date
abstract of title or Abstractor's Registered Property Certificate to said land. Said purchaser shall be allowed ten days after
delivery of said Abstract or Certificate for examination of title and report in writing to seller and within which to perform this
contract, provided that, if the title to said real estate, or any part thereof shall be found to be unmarketable, and can be made
marketable in said seller within ninety days after the delivery of said abstract or certificate, said purchaser shall be allowed
ten days after he shall have been notified in writing of the correcting of such title, to perform this contract on his part, and
payments falling due before the time allowed for the correction of such title shall be postponed until such title is corrected, if
corrected within the time specified.

If such title is found to be unmarketable in said seller and cannot be made marketable within ninety days, or said purchaser
does not waive the same, then this contract shall be void, and neither party shall be liable for damages hereunder, and earnest
money shall be refunded forthwith.

Upon the performance of this contract by said purchaser, said seller shall deliver to said purchaser an Abstract of Title
or the owner's duplicate Torrens Certificate of Title, and a duly acknowledged Contract for --
Warranty Deed entitled to record of said land and all thereof, free from dower or statutory rights, taxes, assessments, mortgages
and all other adverse claims or liens, except as stated above ---
----

The purchaser agrees that Abstract of Title or Torrens Certificate of Title and fire, windstorm and other hazard insurance
policies shall remain in possession of mortgagee and or contract seller until all said indebtedness is paid in full.

(OVER)

(continued on next page)

EXHIBIT 53–2 Continued

If said purchaser agrees in this contract to assume or join in a mortgage, said purchaser and seller and their respective spouses, if any, shall join in executing the necessary papers for renewing said mortgage or placing a new mortgage for any sum not to exceed $............... so as to keep a mortgage of not to exceed $............... in effect until the property herein described is conveyed in accordance with terms of this contract and said purchaser agrees to pay all usual and reasonable expenses for the renewing of the present mortgage or the making of a new one.

All storm sheds, sash and doors; screens, awnings, shades and venetian blinds; all porch windows and doors; gas or electric fixtures, oil burners, stokers, air conditioners and motors pertaining to the same; drapes and carpets in public halls; radiators and all other like appliances and betterments, plants and shrubbery (if any) which are now provided for or used in or on said premises; and, except in single residences, stoves, ranges and refrigerator units, plant or system; and, except such as are the property of the tenants, are included in this sale.

All papers shall bear even date herewith, and liability as between the parties hereto to pay taxes and assessments on said property shall be determined as of the date hereof. The policies of insurance shall on final closing of this sale be so written or endorsed as to protect the interests of seller, purchaser and mortgagee, and shall be taken by said purchaser at their pro rata value from the date hereof. Rentals and interest shall be adjusted as follows: ....
....
....
....

Possession of the property herein described shall be given .... , 19........... subject however to the rights of the tenants in possession.

All tenders and delivery of papers hereunder shall be made at the office of .... in Saint Paul, Minn.

Time is of the essence hereof, and if such purchaser shall fail to perform this contract within the time herein limited, said seller or his agent shall retain the earnest money hereof as a part of his just compensation for such failure, and may declare this contract terminated and proceed for damages, or specific performance against such purchaser. Action to enforce this contract shall be commenced within ninety (90) days from the date of forfeiture of this contract.

Dated at Saint Paul, Minnesota, ... , 19...........

Signed, Sealed and Delivered in Presence of

....Agent (SEAL)

....Seller (SEAL)

....(SEAL)

....Purchaser (SEAL)

....(SEAL)

Adopted by St. Paul Real Estate Board 1943

Contract for Sale of Real Estate

TO

Brady-Margulis Co., St. Paul, Minn.

Title Examination After the sales contract has been negotiated, the buyer or buyer's attorney (or the broker, escrow agent, or title insurance company) will begin the *title examination*. Essentially, a title examination is an examination of the history of all past transfers and sales of the piece of property in question. Every county has a filing system where deeds, plats, and other instruments are recorded.

The title examiner will generally obtain an *abstract* from a private abstract company. This document lists all of the records relating to a particular parcel of land. These records, known as the chain of title, go back to the original grant or deed from the United States or to the particular state where the land is located.[14] After reading the abstract, the examiner will give an opinion as to the validity of the title.

Obtaining a Mortgage Ordinarily, since most buyers do not have enough cash to buy real estate outright, they arrange for a loan. To obtain a loan, the purchaser may put the property up as *collateral*. *Mortgages* are essentially liens against the property that enable the lender to foreclose and sell the real estate if the borrower fails to make timely payments (see Chapter 30). In most cases, a bank or savings and loan association is contacted for financing. In some cases, the seller may agree to loan the buyer the purchase price in exchange for the buyer's promissory note and mortgage. Either type of mortgage is known as a *(first) purchase money mortgage* because the seller or lender supplies the buyer with the money to purchase the house.

Closing The final stage of the sale is called the *closing*. In principle, the transaction is closed by the buyer paying the purchase price and the seller delivering the deed to the buyer. Often, however, the buyer's agent delivers the check and the mortgage papers. The seller's agent (broker) turns over the keys and necessary papers to the buyer. Sometimes, when the property is being mortgaged, the lender (for example, a bank) will close the mortgage deal, paying the seller for the property and receiving a lien (mort-

gage) on the property at the same time. Alternatively, all these matters may be handled by the escrow agent.

FUTURE INTERESTS

The common law recognizes a number of estates that are nonpossessory. **Future estates** consist of estates that *may* or *will* become possessory in the future. These estates are in direct contrast to estates that are *possessory*.

A person can convey an estate that is limited by a specified period of time; by the life of the grantor, grantee, or other person; or by an occurrence. The person to whom such an estate is conveyed has a *present possessory interest*. Life estates, terms for years, and fee simple determinable estates are examples of estates that carry present possessory interests. These estates, however, unlike other possessory estates, are accompanied by a residuary interest that may or may not have been disposed of by the grantor. This residuary interest is a *future interest*, and it can take several forms. If it remains in the grantor, it is called a *reversion*, a *possibility of reverter*, or a *power of termination*. If the future interest is not retained by the grantor, then it is called either a *remainder* or an *executory interest*. Remainders can be either *vested* or *contingent*, depending upon the terms of the conveyance.

Reversionary Interests and Powers of Termination

When a grantor owns a fee simple estate in land and conveys an estate to another with a duration that is less than the duration of the estate that the grantor owns, there is an undisposed residue remaining in the grantor. That undisposed residue is called a **reversion.**

Suppose, for example, that Owen owns a fee simple estate and conveys a life estate in Blackacre to Ann. Owen has not disposed of the interest in the land remaining after Ann's life. Thus, Owen has automatically retained a reversion that will become possessory, upon Ann's death, in Owen or his heirs. Ann's life estate is an estate in possession, whereas Owen has a *vested* future interest—that is, an absolute right to possession of Blackacre at some point in the future. Furthermore, even though Owen holds a future interest, this interest exists in the

---

14. Today the title search need not go back all the way to the grant from the government. Nearly every state has a marketable record title act that provides that the roots of title older than thirty or forty years are conclusively presumed to be valid. In other words, if the chain of title can be traced back thirty or forty years with no defects, no further search need be made.

present in the sense that Owen can convey his future interest.

Suppose, however, that Owen conveys Blackacre "to Ann and her heirs." It is clear that there is no future interest in Blackacre since Owen has conveyed his entire estate to Ann as a fee simple absolute. If, on the other hand, Owen conveys a fee simple determinable (which is one of the estates that is less than a fee simple, such as "to Ann and her heirs as long as the property is used for educational purposes"), Owen has retained a **possibility of reverter.** A possibility of reverter is a future interest in favor of the grantor that is contingent on the happening of the event named in the conveyance. The conveyance of a fee simple determinable that gives rise to a possibility of reverter usually includes the words "so long as," "until," "while," or "during."

Remainders and Executory Interests

When an owner of real property conveys an estate that is less than a fee simple absolute and does not retain the residuary interest, then that interest will take the form of either a **remainder** or an **executory interest.** A remainder differs from an executory interest in that a remainder occurs upon the *natural termination* of a preceding estate—such as a life estate. As mentioned previously, a remainder can be either *vested* or *contingent.* Both are future interests, but the holder of a vested remainder has an absolute right to possession at the end of the prior estate, whereas the owner of a contingent remainder has only a *conditional* right to possession when the prior estate ends. Yet, both are estates in land in favor of persons other than the grantor, and both can be transferred to other persons.

Executory interests, like remainders, are future possessory interests in real property that are conveyed to persons other than the grantor at the time of a conveyance. Executory interests, however, take effect either *before* or *after* the natural termination of a preceding estate. To illustrate: Owen conveys Blackacre "to Ann for twenty years, but *if* Ann should divorce, *then* Blackacre is to pass immediately to Carla." Carla has a future interest in Blackacre that will become a present possessory interest if Ann becomes divorced. Carla's future interest is known as a *shifting executory interest*, since the possessory interest would shift from Ann to Carla if Ann should divorce.

NONPOSSESSORY INTERESTS

Some interests in land do not include any rights of possession. These interests, known as nonpossessory interests, include easements, profits, and licenses. Because easements and profits are similar, and the same rules apply to both, they will be discussed together.

Easements and Profits

An **easement** is the right of a person to make limited use of another person's property without taking anything from the property. An easement, for example, can be the right to walk across another's property. In contrast, a **profit** is the right to go onto land in possession of another and take away some part of the land itself or some product of the land. For example, Owen, the owner of Sandy View, gives Ann the right to go there and remove all the sand and gravel that Ann needs for her cement business. Ann has a profit. The difference between an easement and a profit is that an easement merely allows a person to use land without taking anything from it, whereas a profit allows a person to take something from the land.

Classification of Easements and Profits Easements and profits can be classified as either *appurtenant* or *in gross.*

Easement (or Profit) Appurtenant An easement or profit appurtenant arises when the owner of one piece of land has a right to go onto (or remove things from) an adjacent piece of land owned by another. Suppose Owen, the owner of Whiteacre, has a right to drive his car across Green's land, Greenacre, which is adjacent to Whiteacre. This right of way over Greenacre is an easement appurtenant to Whiteacre and can be used only by the owner of Whiteacre. Owen can convey the easement when he conveys Whiteacre. The outstanding feature of an easement appurtenant is that it involves two neighboring pieces of land owned by two different persons.

Easement (or Profit) in Gross An easement or profit in gross exists when the right to use or take things from another's land is not dependent upon *the owner of the easement or profit also owning an adjacent tract of land.* Suppose Owen owns a parcel of land with a marble quarry. Owen conveys to the XYZ Corporation, which owns no land, the right to come onto Owen's land and remove up to five hundred pounds of marble per day. XYZ Corporation owns a profit in gross. An easement or profit in gross requires the existence of only one piece of land that must be owned by someone other than the owner of the easement or profit in gross. Another illustration is that of a utility company which is granted an easement to run its power lines across another's property.

Effect of Sale of Property   Whenever a parcel of land that is *benefited* by an easement or profit appurtenant is sold, the property carries the easement or profit along with it. Thus, if Owens sells Whiteacre to Thomas and includes the appurtenant right-of-way across Greenacre in the deed to Thomas, Thomas will own both the property and the easement that benefits it.

When a piece of land that has the *burden* of an easement or profit appurtenant is sold, the new owner must recognize its existence only if he or she knew or should have known of it or if it was recorded in the appropriate office of the county. Thus, if Owen records his easement across Greenacre in the appropriate county office before Green conveys the land, the new owner of Greenacre will have to allow Owen, or any subsequent owner of Whiteacre, to continue to use the path across Greenacre.

Creation of an Easement (or Profit)   Profits and easements can be created by *deed* or *will* or by *implication, necessity*, or *prescription*. Creation by *deed* or *will* simply involves the delivery of a deed or a disposition in a will by the owner of an easement stating that the grantee (the person receiving the profit or easement) is granted the rights in the easement or profit that the grantor had. An easement or profit, however, may be created by *implication* when the circumstances surrounding the division of a piece of property imply its creation. If Barrow divides a parcel of land that has only one well for drinking water and conveys the half without a well to Dan, a profit by implication arises, since Dan needs drinking water. An easement may also be created by necessity. An easement by *necessity* does not require division of property for its existence. A person who rents an apartment, for example, has an easement by necessity in the private road leading up to it.

Easements and profits by *prescription* arise when one person uses another person's land for a period of time equal to the statute of limitations for recovery of property. If the owner of the land does not object to the use of the land for the required period of time, the person using the land has an easement or profit by prescription.

Termination of an Easement (or Profit)   An easement or profit can be terminated or extinguished in several ways. The simplest way is to deed it back to the owner of the land that is burdened by it. Second, the owner of an easement or profit can abandon it and create evidence of his or her intent to relinquish the right to use it. Mere nonuse will not extinguish an easement or profit *unless it is accompanied by an intent to abandon.* Third, when the owner of an easement or profit becomes the owner of the property burdened by it, then it is merged into the property.

Licenses

A license is the revocable right of a person to come onto another person's land. It is a personal privilege that arises from the consent of the owner of the land and that can be revoked by the owner. A ticket to attend a movie at a theater is an example of a license. If a theater owner issues a ticket entitling the holder to enter the property of the owner, and Ann subsequently acquires the ticket and is refused entry into the theater, she has no right to force her way into the theater. The ticket is only a revocable license, not a conveyance of an interest in property.

LAND USE CONTROL

Land use control deals with the *limitations* placed upon property owners that either arise by agreement (covenants running with the land, equitable servitudes) or are imposed by the government (zoning).

Covenants Running with the Land

A **covenant running with the land** is an agreement under which a landowner either acquires certain rights or is under certain obligations merely because he or she owns the land that is bound by the covenant.

Consider an example. Owen is the owner of Grasslands, a twenty-acre estate whose northern half contains a small reservoir. Owen wishes to convey the northern half to Arid City, but before he does, he digs an irrigation ditch connecting the reservoir with the lower ten acres that he uses as farmland. When Owen conveys the northern ten acres to Arid City, he enters into an agreement with the city. The agreement, which is contained in the deed, states, "Arid City, its heirs and assigns, promises not to remove more than five thousand gallons of water per day from the Grasslands reservoir." Owen has created a *covenant running with the land* under which Arid City and all future owners of the northern ten acres of Grasslands are limited as to the amount of water they can draw from its reservoir.

Four requirements must be met for a covenant running with the land to be enforceable. If they are not met, a simple contract is created between the two original parties only.

1. The covenant running with the land must be created in a written agreement (covenant). It is usually contained in the document that conveys the land.
2. The parties must intend that the covenant *run with the land*. In other words, the instrument that contains the covenant must state not only that the promisor is bound by the terms of the covenant but that all the promisor's "successors, heirs, or assigns" will be bound.
3. The covenant must *touch and concern* the land. The limitations on the activities of the owner of the burdened land must have some connection with the land. For example, a purchaser of land cannot be bound by a covenant requiring him or her to drive only Ford pickups, since such a restriction has no relation to the land purchased.
4. The original parties to the covenant must be in *privity of estate* at the time the covenant is created. This requirement means that the relationship between them must be landlord-tenant, vendor-purchaser, testator-devisee, and so forth.

Equitable Servitudes

Because of the confusion over the meaning and application of the *privity of estate requirement*, covenants running with the land have not been a very effective device for guiding the development of residential and commercial land. Therefore, courts of equity have created an alternative means of private land use control known as **equitable servitudes.**

Covenants running with the land and equitable servitudes are similar in their application and effect, but the requirements for enforcing an equitable servitude are less stringent. An equitable servitude is created by an instrument that complies with the Statute of Frauds, an intention that the use of land be restricted, and *notice* of the restriction to the person acquiring the burdened land.

Equitable servitudes are usually upheld; however, equitable servitudes and covenants running with the land have sometimes been used to perpetuate neighborhood segregation, and in these cases they have been invalidated by the courts. In the Supreme Court case of *Shelley* v. *Kraemer*, restrictive covenants proscribing resale to minority groups were declared unconstitutional and could no longer be enforced in a court of law.[15] In addition, the Civil Rights Act of 1968 (also known as the Fair Housing Act) prohibits all discrimination based on race, color, religion, or national origin in the sale and leasing of housing.

Zoning

The government is by far the most potent force in guiding the development and use of land. State and local governments have far greater resources and enforcement powers than do private individuals to control land use. Moreover, since ideally the government represents majority interests, it is in the best position to determine what land uses reflect the needs of society as a whole.

The state's power to control the use of land is derived from two sources: eminent domain and police power. Through eminent domain, the government can take land for public use, but it must pay just compensation. Consequently, eminent domain is an expensive method of land use control. Under its police power, however, the state can pass laws aimed at protecting public health, safety, morals, and general welfare. These laws can affect owners' rights and uses of land, without the state having to compensate the landowner. If a state law restricts a landowner's property rights too much, the state's regulation will be deemed a *confiscation* and subject to the eminent domain requirements that just compensation be paid.

---

15.   334 U.S. 1, 68 S.Ct. 836 (1948).

Suppose Perez owns a large tract of land that she purchased with the intent to subdivide and develop into residential properties. At the time of the purchase, there were no zoning regulations restricting use of the land. If the government attempts to zone Perez's entire tract of land as "parkland only" and prohibits her from developing any part of it, the action will be deemed confiscatory, since the government will be denying her the ability to use her property for any purpose for which it is reasonably suited. The government will have to compensate Perez, since it has effectively confiscated her land. However, if the government zones Perez's parcel of land as "three-fourths residential, one-fourth park area" after her purchase, this zoning regulation is not confiscatory since she will be able to use most of the property for building residences.

The state's power to regulate the use of land is limited in two other ways, both of which arise from the Fourteenth Amendment. First, the state cannot regulate the use of land arbitrarily or unreasonably, since this would be a denial of property without due process. There must be a *rational basis* for the classifications that the state imposes on property. Any act that is reasonably related to the health or general welfare of the public is deemed to have a rational basis.

Second, a state's regulation of land use control cannot be discriminatory. The state is prohibited from discriminating against any race, religion, or nationality. The state is generally prohibited from discriminating against any other group as well. Discrimination on the basis of race, religion, or national origin is never justifiable. However, discrimination based on other factors (for example, low-income versus high-income groups) may be upheld if there is a rational basis for the discrimination.

Floating Zones Generally, the state agency charged with the responsibility of land use planning can take one of two approaches. The first is to designate, all at once, use restrictions on each parcel of land located within the entire area to be zoned (usually a city or town). Alternatively, the state agency can use "floating zones," deciding initially how much land should be designated for each of a variety of particular uses (commercial, residential, park, farming) and later assigning such designations at the request of landowners. Under the "floating zone" concept, the amount of land to be used for any one purpose is determined at the outset, but it is not assigned in what otherwise might be an arbitrary manner. This allows for flexibility in zoning.

Variance A landowner whose land has been limited by a zoning ordinance to a particular use cannot make an alternative use of the land unless he or she first obtains a zoning variance. A landowner must meet three criteria to be entitled to a variance:

1. The landowner must find it impossible to realize a reasonable return on the land as zoned.
2. The adverse effect of the zoning ordinance must be particular to the person seeking the variance and not one that has a similar effect on the other landowners within the same zone.
3. A granting of the variance must not alter the essential character of the zoned area substantially.

By far the most important criterion used in granting a variance is whether it will alter the character of the neighborhood substantially. Courts tend to be rather lenient about the first two requirements. As the following case illustrates, courts also tend to defer to the discretion of zoning boards unless the board has abused its authority.

BACKGROUND AND FACTS *The city of Moline planned to build a new firehouse on land that was appropriately zoned for construction of a firehouse. However, the proposed firehouse was slightly larger than the zoning ordinances permitted. Thus, in April 1963 Moline filed with the Board of Zoning Adjustment of St. Louis County for variances from the set-back and building line provisions in the ordinance. Essentially, the city's plans called for construction of a building that would be set back about four feet farther than the zoning allowed. Alfred and Marie Conner, who owned adjacent property facing the site of the new construction, objected to the variance. The variance was granted, and the Conners appealed the board's ruling to the courts.*

CONNER v. HERD
Court of Appeals of Missouri, 1970.
452 S.W.2d 272.

SMITH, Commissioner.

*   *   *   *

The genesis of the litigation was the filing by Moline in April, 1963, of an application to the Board for variances from the set-back and building line provisions.

*   *   *   *

*   *   * [A]ppellants contend the findings of the Board were arbitrary and capricious and not based upon competent and substantial evidence. We take these in order.

*   *   *   *

"JURISDICTION AND POWERS.—The Board of Zoning Adjustment is hereby authorized to: (5) Permit a variation in the yard requirements of any Zoning District or the building and set back lines for Major Highways as provided by law where there are practical difficulties or unnecessary hardships in the carrying out of these provisions due to an irregular shape of the lot, topographical or other conditions, provided such variation will not seriously affect any adjoining property or the general welfare."

This provision, under which the Board acted here, empowers the Board to give variances under specified circumstances where strict enforcement of the regulations would be unjust. It imposes standards for the Board's action and is not a grant of legislative power.

This brings us to the heart of this appeal, appellants' contention that the action of the Board was not based on competent and substantial evidence and was arbitrary and capricious. Neither this court nor the trial court can substitute its judgment on the evidence for that of the Board. We may only determine whether the Board could reach the conclusion it did upon the evidence before it. We hold it could.

*   *   *   *

Having in mind the limited scope of our review of the findings of the Board we turn to the evidence which supports the Board's order. The property in question is on the northwest corner of Chambers Road and Clairmont Drive in an unincorporated portion of St. Louis County. Chambers Road is a major thoroughfare which was widened shortly before the application for variance. The land in question is owned by Moline and has been the site for its fire station since at least 1946. The old fire house complied with the Chambers Road set-back line but not with the Clairmont Drive building line upon which it encroached approximately 4¼ feet as a pre-existing use.

*   *   *   *

The most efficient and satisfactory type of fire station for Moline's purposes is one where returning trucks can enter the back of the station from Clairmont Drive, remove the hoses and other equipment for cleaning, put clean equipment on the truck and move the truck into position for exit through the front onto Chambers Road for the next call. The lot in question is 165 feet in depth (after the widening of Chambers to 80 feet) and 80 feet in width. If the set-back line on Chambers Road, 80 feet, is adhered to there would not be enough room at the rear of the station (39 feet) for the large fire trucks to negotiate the turn from Clairmont Drive into the rear of the station. The entrance from Clairmont would also obviate the need for the trucks to back into the station from Chambers Road. There was also testimony that having the station located nearer the road than the old station would allow greater traffic safety in leaving the station in that both the dispatcher and the driver would have greater visibility along Chambers. *   *   *

The width of the lot is such that a 2 foot variance on the building line of Clairmont Drive would be necessary to get the proposed fire station on the property if the regulation of a 6 foot side yard on the west (next to appellants) is met. The granted variance is less than the previously existing encroachment.

*   *   *   *

The Board could find here that in the absence of a variance Moline would be confronted with substantial additional expense, interruption of fire protection service during the period of construction, and unnecessary inconvenience if not outright danger to the residents of the district. The Board is not required to ignore the source of the funds available to the district (taxpayers) in determining that additional expense constitutes an unnecessary hardship. Under *Rosedale-Skinker*, there exist sufficient "practical difficulties" and "unnecessary hardships" to the district to permit a variance and these arise from the inadequate size of the lot to contain a fire station. This was the essence of the Board's finding "that because of the requirements, the proposed new building and facilities cannot be erected as the eighty foot set back line on Chambers Road and the thirty foot building line on Clairmont Drive are intended."

*   *   *   *

The effect on general welfare finding is supported by the evidence of the need for the new building to render adequate fire protection to the district and by the testimony on the beneficial effect of the proposed construction upon traffic safety on Chambers Road, including the installation of a traffic light on Chambers Road to be controlled by the dispatcher when trucks leave the station.

The court held that the zoning board had enough evidence to grant the variance in accordance with the requirements of the zoning ordinance. The judgment of the circuit court, which had affirmed the action taken by the zoning board, was affirmed by the appellate court.

DECISION AND REMEDY

QUESTIONS AND CASE PROBLEMS

1. Goodman contracts to lease an apartment near the campus from landlord Lopez for one year, with the monthly rent due and payable on the first of each month. At the end of the year, Goodman does not vacate the apartment, and Lopez does not object. Goodman continues to pay the rent on the first day of the month, and it is accepted by Lopez. Six months later, Lopez informs Goodman that the apartment has been leased to Green and that Goodman must vacate the premises by the end of the week. Goodman refuses to leave, and Lopez threatens eviction proceedings. Discuss the rights of the parties under these circumstances.

2. Robert and Maria are neighbors. Robert's lot is extremely large, and his present and future use of it will not involve the entire area owned. Maria wants to build a single-car garage and driveway along the present lot boundary. Because of ordinances requiring buildings to be set back fifteen feet from an adjoining property line, and because of the placement of her existing structures, she cannot build the garage. Marie contracts to purchase ten feet of Robert's property along their boundary line for $3,000. Robert is willing to sell but will give Maria only a quitclaim deed, whereas Maria wants a general warranty deed. Discuss the differences between these deeds as they

affect the rights of the parties in case the title to this ten feet of land later proves to be defective.

3. Harold was a wanderer twenty-two years ago. It was at that time that he decided to settle down on a vacant three-acre piece of land, which he did not own. People in the area indicated to him that they had no idea who owned it. Harold built a house on the land, got married, and raised three children while living there. He fenced in the land, placed a gate with a sign, "Harold's Homestead," above it, and had trespassers removed. Harold is now confronted by Joe Moonfeld, who has a deed in his name as owner of the property. Moonfeld orders Harold and family off the property, claiming his title ownership. Discuss who has best "title" to the property.

4. Anthony is the owner of a lakeside house and lot. He deeds the house and lot to "my wife, Sylvia, for life, with remainder to my son, David, providing he graduates from college with a B or better average during Sylvia's lifetime." Answer the following questions:
   (a) Does Anthony have any interest in the deeded lakeside house? Explain.
   (b) What is Sylvia's interest called? Explain.
   (c) What is David's interest called? Explain.

5. Turner owns an apartment building. She contracts with Alvarez for one year to place coin-operated washing machines and dryers in laundry rooms in the building complex. The contract requires Alvarez to service the washers and dryers within twenty-four hours after notice is given that service is necessary. Some of the apartment lease-holders complain to Turner that Alvarez's service is

poor and that Alvarez does not promptly refund money lost in the machines. After an argument, Turner orders Alvarez to remove all the machines within one week and not to come on the property again. Alvarez claims that he has a lease of the laundry rooms for one year. Discuss fully the property rights of the parties in this matter.

6. Murray owns 640 acres of rural land. A new highway is being built nearby by Ajax Corporation, Inc. Ajax purchases from Murray the rights to build and use a road across Murray's land for construction vehicles to pass over and to remove sand and gravel required to build the highway. A deed is prepared and filed in the county by Ajax. Later, a dispute arises between Murray and Ajax, and Murray refuses Ajax the right to use the road or to remove sand and gravel. Ajax claims its property rights cannot be revoked by Murray. Discuss fully what property rights Ajax has in this matter.

7. The owners of the Seven Palms Motor Inn decided that their motel was in need of renovation. Accordingly, they ordered a large quantity of bedspreads, curtain rods, and drapes from Sears, Roebuck and Company. Thereafter, Seven Palms Motor Inn failed to pay its bill, which amounted to approximately $8,000, including installation. Under Missouri law, a supplier of fixtures can establish a lien on the land and the building to which the fixtures become attached. Sears sought to establish such a lien to make it easier to recover the debt that Seven Palms owed it. Which, if any, of the above-named items will Sears be able to argue are fixtures? [Sears, Roebuck & Co. v. Seven Palms Motor Inn, 530 S.W.2d 695 (Mo. 1975)]

8. A landlord of residential premises leased a building he owned nearby for use as a cocktail lounge. The residential tenants complained to the landlord about the late evening and early morning music and disturbances coming from the lounge. Although the lease for the lounge provided that entertainment had to be conducted so that it could not be heard outside the building and would not disturb residents of the apartments, the landlord was un-

successful in remedying the problem. The tenants vacated their apartments. Will the landlord be successful in a suit to collect rent from the tenants who vacated? [Blackett v. Olanoff, 371 Mass. 714, 358 N.E.2d 817 (1977)]

9. Dixie Gardens, Inc., was a developer in Pasco County, Florida. Henry Sloane purchased a lot and residence in a Dixie Gardens development. The deed read in part as follows: "If the developer or the Crestridge Utilities Corporation causes garbage collection service bi-weekly to be made available, the owner of each lot shall pay the developer or its assigns, the sum of $1.75 per month therefor." Sloane wished to employ another contractor for garbage collection, but Dixie Gardens argued that Sloane was bound by the provision quoted above, which amounted to a covenant running with the land. Is Dixie Gardens correct? [Sloane v. Dixie Gardens, Inc., 278 So.2d 309 (Fla.App. 1973)]

10. In 1961, Mary Schaefers divided her real property and conveyed it to her children, William, Elfreda, Julienne, and Rosemary. The deed from Mary Schaefers to her daughter Rosemary contained the following language: "It is further mutually agreed by and between the grantor and the grantee that as part of the consideration set out above, the grantee agrees to provide a permanent home for my daughter, Elfreda, should she desire or request one, and for my son, William Schaefers, should he desire or request one. Failure to perform the above will be considered a material breach of the consideration set out herein." In 1974, Rosemary conveyed her portion of her mother's property to Edward and Arthur Apel. Subsequently, William Schaefers attempted to prevent the sale to the Apels from taking place by telling them that the house was encumbered by a covenant running with the land and that if they purchased the house, they would be bound to provide a home for William and Elfreda Schaefers. Is Rosemary's promise to provide a home for William and Elfreda (should they demand one) a covenant running with the land? [Schaefers v. Apel, 295 Ala. 277, 328 So.2d 274 (1976)]

54

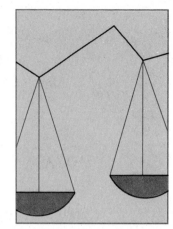

Wills, Trusts, and Estates

The laws of succession of property are a necessary corollary to the concept of private ownership of property. The law requires that, upon death, title to the decedent's property must vest (to deliver full possession) somewhere. The decedent can direct the passage of property after death by *will*, subject to certain limitations imposed by the state. If no valid will has been executed, the decedent is said to have died *intestate*, and state law prescribes the distribution of the property among heirs or next of kin. If no heirs or kin can be found, the property escheats (title is transferred) to the state.

In addition, a person can transfer property through a *trust*.[1] The owner (settlor) of the property transfers legal title to a *trustee*, who has a duty imposed by law to hold the property for the use or benefit of another (the beneficiary).

Following a brief discussion of the origins and purposes of inheritance laws, this chapter will describe how testamentary dispositions are made by *will*, by *statutes of descent and distribution*, or by *trusts*. The chapter concludes with sections on estate administration and taxes.

ORIGINS OF INHERITANCE LAWS

At common law, persons had no power to control the distribution of their property after death. The power of transfer or distribution is derived solely from statutes originating in feudal England, where the transfer of property at death was strictly controlled. The heir (the one who inherited) was required to pay the feudal lord a sum of money[2] for the privilege of succeeding to his or her ancestor's lands. When a tenant died without heirs, the land escheated (title passed) to the feudal lord of the manor.[3]

Sweeping land reforms in England during the 1920s replaced inheritance payments and escheat to the feudal lord with the right of the crown to receive inheritance taxes and to take property of an intestate without heirs. Modern legislation has changed the terminology but not the result. In all states, title to land of persons who die intestate and without heirs vests in the state; the right to make a will and the ways to make one are determined by state law. To be valid, wills normally must follow statutory requirements. Furthermore, taxes are imposed upon

---

1. A trust can be set up by the property owner *during his or her life* (by a deed accompanied by a trust document) or *at his or her death* (by a will containing or accompanied by a trust document). This chapter discusses both.

2. The sum, called a relief, was usually equivalent to one year's rent.

3. C. J. Moynihan, *Introduction to the Law of Real Property* (St. Paul, Minn: West Publishing, 1962), p. 22.

the transfer of property at death by state and federal governments.

PURPOSES OF INHERITANCE LAWS

State regulation of inheritance has developed in response to certain desirable social and political goals. Four principles underlie U.S. inheritance and succession laws.[4]

1. *The concept of private property.* Any system of laws to regulate the passage of a decedent's estate must do so in the context of a firmly rooted tradition of private ownership of property.

2. *Effectuating the individual's testamentary intent.* The right to direct the distribution of one's own property to whomever one chooses (subject to the rights of the surviving spouse and children) is often taken as a basic tenet of U.S. jurisprudence. Many formalities surround the court's duty to insure that when a will is offered for authentication, it is in fact the genuine and final expression of the decedent's wishes. The seriousness of this function is reflected in the highly publicized controversy over the numerous proffers of "authentic" wills belonging to billionaire Howard Hughes. The freedom of an individual to have his or her intentions satisfied after death is subject to limitations imposed by law.

3. *The policy favoring family.* Protection of the family has been a cornerstone of inheritance laws throughout history. As noted earlier, intestate succession is inheritance by heirs of the deceased. In contemporary law, this goal is reinforced by state statutes guaranteeing that an absolute portion of the decedent's estate will be allotted to the surviving spouse and children.

4. *Reflection of societal interests.* State succession laws perpetuate certain social and political goals by: (a) protecting a decedent's family from absolute poverty against creditors' claims (and preventing the family's dependency on the state), (b) obtaining money through escheat (transfer of abandoned property to the state), (c) encouraging educational and scientific research and other civic programs through estate tax exemptions or deductions, and (d) maintaining social stability and confidence in the legal system by adhering to traditional principles of law.

WILLS

A **will** is the final declaration of the disposition that a person desires to have made of his or her property after death, as opposed to an *inter-vivos* trust, which is created and becomes effective during one's lifetime. A will is referred to as a *testamentary disposition* of property. It is a formal instrument that must follow exactly the requirements of the Statute of Wills in order to be effective. The reasoning behind such a strict requirement is obvious. A will becomes effective only after death. No attempts to modify it after the death of the maker are allowed because the court cannot ask the maker to confirm the attempted modifications. (But sometimes the wording must be "interpreted" by the courts.)

A will can serve other purposes besides the distribution of property. It can appoint a guardian for minor children or incapacitated adults. It can appoint a personal representative to settle the affairs of the deceased.

Vocabulary of Wills

Every area of law has its own special vocabulary, and the area of wills is no exception. A man who makes out a will is known as a **testator**, and a woman who makes out a will is called a **testatrix**. The court responsible for administering any legal problems surrounding a will is called a **probate court**. When a person dies, a *personal representative* settles the affairs of the deceased. An **executor** or **executrix** is the personal representative named in the will; an **administrator** or **administratrix** is the personal representative appointed by the court for a decedent who dies without a will, who fails to name an executor in the will, who names an executor lacking the capacity to serve, or who writes a will that the court refuses to admit to probate. A gift of real estate by will is generally called a **devise**, and a gift of personal property under a will is called a **bequest** or **legacy**.

---

4. For a discussion of the goals of succession laws and the need for increasing flexibility in applying these laws, see John T. Gaubatz, "Notes toward a Truly Modern Wills Act," 31 *University of Miami Law Review* 497 (Spring 1977).

Types of Gifts

Gifts by will can be *specific, general,* or *residuary.* A *specific* devise or bequest (legacy) describes particular property that can be distinguished from all the rest of the testator's property. For example, Johnson's will provides, "I give my nephew, Tom, my gold pocket watch with the initials MTJ on it." Should the gold watch not be in existence or part of Johnson's property at the time of Johnson's death (if, for example, it has been sold, destroyed, or given away), an extinguishment, or cancellation, of the legacy (*ademption*) exists.

A *general* devise or bequest (legacy) does not single out any particular item of property to be transferred by will. For example, "I give to my daughter, Dana, $10,000" is a general bequest. Usually, general legacies specify a sum of money.

On occasion, assets are insufficient to pay in full all general bequests provided for in a will. When this happens, an *abatement*, by which the legatees receive reduced benefits, takes place. For example, Johnson's will leaves "$15,000 each to my children, Mary and Sam." Upon Johnson's death only $10,000 is available to honor these bequests. By abatement, each child will receive $5,000.

A testator or testatrix may wish that a legatee receive a gift whether or not a particular source of assets is available at the time of death. This is accomplished by means of a *demonstrative* bequest. In the will, the testator or testatrix designates a particular source from which the gift is to be made, additionally instructing that if that source is insufficient or no longer existing, the bequest be paid out of the general assets.

If the legatee dies prior to the death of the testator or testatrix or before the legacy is payable, a *lapsed legacy* occurs. At common law, the legacy failed. Today, the legacy may not lapse if the legatee is in a certain blood relationship to the testator or testatrix, such as a child, grandchild, brother or sister, if the legatee also left a child or other surviving descendant.

Sometimes a will provides that any assets remaining after specific gifts are made and debts are paid are to be distributed through a *residuary* clause. A residuary provision is used because the exact amount to be distributed cannot be determined until all other gifts and payouts are made. A residuary estate can pose problems, however, when the will does not specifically name the beneficiaries to receive the residue. In such a case, if the court cannot determine the testator's intent, the remainder of the residuary passes according to state laws of intestacy.

In the following case, the court had to decide how to distribute the residual assets of an estate.

BACKGROUND AND FACTS *Edward Cancik, the testator, died having a net estate valued at more than $200,000. Edward had intentionally omitted all his relatives from his will except his cousin Charles Cancik. Edward specifically willed to Charles all his personal and household goods, and placed the residue in a testamentary trust for the maintenance of the Cancik family mausoleum. After Edward's death, Charles filed a complaint alleging that the value of the trust corpus vastly exceeded the amount necessary to accomplish its purpose (i.e., to maintain the mausoleum), and asked that the "residuum" be distributed to him as the testator's only heir at law. Thomas, another relative of Edward's, acting as guardian* ad litem *for any unknown heirs, filed a petition to have the residuum distributed to all the testator's heirs by intestacy, twelve of whom were later found to be living in Czechoslovakia. The trial court held that the residue passed to all the heirs by the laws of intestacy.*

ESTATE OF CANCIK

Appellate Court of Illinois, First District, Fifth Division, 1984.
495 N.E.2d 296.

SULLIVAN, Justice.

*   *   *   *

During his lifetime, Edward Cancik (testator) entered into a contract with the Woodlawn Cemetery Association (Woodlawn) whereby he paid $4,150 to the Woodlawn Trust Fund for an endowment policy for the care and maintenance of the Cancik Family Mausoleum (mausoleum). Thereafter, in September 1978, he executed a will in which he bequeathed, in clause IV, all of his personal and household effects to Charles; and then, in clause V, placed the residue of his estate into a testamentary trust, the income of which was to be used for the perpetual maintenance of the mausoleum. The First National Bank of Cicero was named executor of the will and trustee of the residuary funds. In the final clause of the will (clause VII), testator stated:

"I have intentionally omitted the names of any of my relatives from this my Last Will and Testament for reasons I deem good and sufficient with the exception of my aforesaid cousin, CHARLES E. CANCIK."

*   *   *   *

*   *   * Woodlawn agreed to provide the perpetual care described in the terms of the testamentary trust upon receipt of an additional payment of $10,850.

Both parties submitted memoranda of law, and after consideration thereof, the trial court found that the residuary bequest was against public policy and invalid because of the inexhaustible residuum that would result from the investment of the trust funds; that it was, in effect, a lapsed legacy which passed as intestate property; and that clause VII of the will did not effectively disinherit testator's other heirs or constitute an alternate residual bequest to Charles. The court then denied Charles's claim to the residuum and ordered that it be distributed to testator's heirs at law as provided in the [Illinois] statute of descent and distribution.

OPINION

Charles contends that the trial court erred in finding that the undisposed residuary estate is intestate property which must pass to testator's heirs. He reasons that (a) since the purpose of the trust has been accomplished without depleting its assets, the surplus should be held upon a resulting trust for the estate of the testator; (b) the property must then pass under the will in accordance with the intention expressed therein; and (c) an alternate gift, by implication, of the residuary estate was made to him by the language of clause VII, wherein testator expressed his intention to disinherit all other heirs.

*   *   *   *

The object of testamentary construction is to ascertain the intention of the testator and, in so doing, the intention which must be given effect is that expressed in the language of the will, not one which the testator may have had in his mind but failed to express. *   *   * Although there is a presumption against intestacy, it is only a presumption and may not be used to overcome the language of the will or to supply language which has been omitted. Thus, where the testator has overlooked a contingency for which he probably would have provided had it occurred to him, the court may not speculate as to what that provision might have been *   *   * rather, any property not specifically devised or bequeathed will pass under the residuary clause, but where there is no residuary provision or that clause itself has failed for some reason, the undisposed portion of the estate becomes intestate property and vests in the heirs of the testator according to their proportionate statutory shares. *   *   *

Here, Charles concedes that the will contained no specific dispository provision for the unused trust funds; nevertheless, he maintains that clause VII effectively disinherits all other heirs and thus creates, by implication, an alternate residuary bequest to him as the only heir who was not excluded from participating in the distribution of the estate. We find this argument unpersuasive. First, it is well-settled that heirs cannot be disinherited merely by a declaration that they are excluded from the will or that they take only a certain amount *   *   * The only means by which a testator can disinherit an heir is to give the property to someone else *   *   * thus, no matter how strong the intention to disinherit may be expressed in a will, the testator is presumed to know the law that where a testamentary gift fails, for whatever reason, and no alternate dispositional intention is expressed, the property passes by intestacy to the heirs at law.

* * * Furthermore, while gifts by implication have long been recognized in Illinois, our supreme court has repeatedly held:

> "[T]hey can only be given effect in cases of such clear necessity that from the will itself no reasonable doubt of the intention can exist. Probabilities as to the testator's intention cannot be weighed, but the implication must be so strong that an intention contrary to that imputed to the testator cannot be supposed to have existed in his mind. [Citation omitted.] It must be such as to leave no hesitation in the mind of the court and permit no other reasonable inference. * * * "

In our view, a reading of the will in its entirety, and of the language of clause VII in particular, does not give rise to an implication so strong as to leave no reasonable doubt that the testator intended Charles to inherit the entire excess residuum of his estate. It appears that his major concern was for the care and maintenance of the family mausoleum, and it was to this purpose that he directed, through clause V, the overwhelming bulk of his assets; and although he referred to Charles with a certain degree of affection, as his "beloved cousin," the bequest to Charles in clause IV of the will consisted of only personal property of minimal value when compared to the total estate. In the light of this vastly disproportionate division of property between the trust and Charles, we cannot conclude, as Charles suggests, that he (Charles) was so favored by the overall scheme of the will as to raise an inference that clause VII evidenced testator's intention to disinherit all other heirs; or, more importantly, that it created an alternate residuary bequest to him upon the termination or failure of the trust. As noted earlier, where a will is silent or where its provisions lend themselves to more than one interpretation, the courts may not supply gifts not found therein, and the property left undisposed then passes by intestacy to the heirs of the testator notwithstanding any attempts in the will to disinherit them.

* * * *

The court held that the residuum of Edward's estate must go to his heirs rather than to Charles, who was merely the beneficiary of Edward's personal belongings.

DECISION AND REMEDY

The Uniform Probate Code

Probate laws vary from state to state. In 1969, the American Bar Association and the National Conference of Commissioners on Uniform State Laws approved the Uniform Probate Code (UPC). The UPC codifies general principles and procedures for the resolution of conflicts in settling estates and relaxes some of the requirements for a valid will contained in earlier state laws. Fourteen states have adopted some form of the UPC. References to UPC provisions will be included in the remainder of this chapter where general practice in most states is consistent. However, since succession and inheritance laws vary widely among different states, one should always check the particular laws of the state involved.[5]

---

5. For example, California law differs *substantially* from the UPC.

Testamentary Capacity

Not everyone who owns property necessarily qualifies to make a valid disposition of that property by will. *Testamentary capacity* requires the testator to be of legal age and sound mind *at the time the will is made*. The legal age for executing a will varies, but in most states and under the UPC the minimum age is eighteen years. [UPC 2-501] Thus, a will of a twenty-one-year-old decedent written when the person was sixteen is invalid.

The concept of "being of sound mind" refers to the testator's ability to formulate and to comprehend a personal plan for the disposition of property. Further, a testator must intend the document to be his or her will.

Courts have grappled with the requirement of *sound mind* for a long time, and their decisions have been inconsistent. Mental incapacity is a highly subjective matter and thus is not easily measured. The general test for testamentary capacity has the following provisions:

1. The testator must comprehend and remember the "natural objects of his or her bounty" (usually family members, but including persons for whom the testator has affection).
2. The testator must comprehend the kind and character of the property being distributed.
3. The testator must understand and formulate a plan for disposing of the property.

Less mental ability is required to make a will than to manage one's own business affairs or to enter into a contract. Thus, a testator may be feeble, aged, eccentric, or offensive in behavior and still possess testamentary capacity. Moreover, a person can be judged insane or have insane delusions about certain subjects yet, during lucid moments, still be of *sound mind* and make a valid will.

The problem of determining testamentary mental capacity is illustrated by the following case dealing with a testatrix in a nursing home.

IN RE ESTATE OF
UNGER
Court of Appeals of Oregon,
1980.
47 Or.App. 951, 615 P.2d 1115.

BACKGROUND AND FACTS   *The appellate court examines the testamentary capacity of the testatrix in the following case. She was confined to a nursing home when the will was executed, and the staff testified that she was in a state of mental confusion at the time.*

ROBERTS, Judge.

The issue on appeal in this will contest case is whether testatrix, Lena L. Unger, had sufficient testamentary capacity to execute a last will and testament on February 25, 1976. The probate court found that testatrix had sufficient testamentary capacity. We disagree.

The requirements of testamentary capacity were summarized in *Kastner v. Husband*, as follows:

" *   *   * (1) the person must be able to understand the nature of the act in which he is engaged; (2) know the nature and extent of his property; (3) know, without prompting, the claims, if any, of those who are, should or might be, the natural objects of his bounty; and (4) be cognizant of the scope and reach of the provisions of the document. If the foregoing conditions are found to prevail at the time of executing the instrument, the testator is deemed to have sufficient capacity to make a will. *   *   * "

*   *   *   *

The attorney was one of the subscribing witnesses. He testified that he felt testatrix was competent to make the will as he had no data to indicate otherwise. The other subscribing witness, the attorney's secretary, also testified that, in her opinion, testatrix was competent, as she, too, had no reason to believe otherwise. The secretary was present when respondent read aloud the provisions of the will to testatrix in the reception area, but was unable to hear anything said by testatrix although testatrix appeared to the secretary to be asking questions. After respondent's explanation to testatrix and prior to testatrix's execution of the will, testatrix approached the secretary, asking something to the effect of "What is this, what am I doing, what do you want me to do?" The secretary did not recall that an explanation was given to testatrix by anyone. The secretary testified that the attorney then appeared and asked some cursory questions about testatrix's satisfaction with the document. The secretary did not hear testatrix say anything, but she did appear to nod her head. Testatrix then signed the document at the place indicated to her.

The testimony of the subscribing witnesses, aided by the presumption of competency which accompanies a will that has been duly executed, carries great weight in the determination of decedent's testamentary capacity. The reason for this is that the determination of testamentary capacity must focus on the moment the will is executed and subscribing witnesses are in a position to observe the decedent at the time of the execution. Nevertheless, this heavy reliance on the subscribing witnesses' testimony is not always appropriate.

* * * *

Other witnesses who testified were nursing home personnel who had observed testatrix for a period of eight days prior to the signing of the will, and the physician who examined testatrix three days prior to the date the will was executed. These witnesses were disinterested and unanimous in their opinion that at the time the will was executed, testatrix was without testamentary capacity. Those on the nursing staff who were familiar with testatrix until her death, two and one-half years later, also indicated that at no time was she competent.

* * * *

Those individuals who testified that they observed testatrix frequently both prior to and subsequent to the execution of the will were a registered nurse, a licensed practical nurse, the nursing home's activities director, and the home's administrator. They all indicated that testatrix lacked testamentary capacity. Testatrix was described as being very confused; as wandering aimlessly about the nursing home; as being unable to distinguish her room or her possessions from [those of] other patients; as being unable to recognize the staff; as being unable to carry on a conversation; and as being able to communicate only on the most basic level and only if a short answer was required. Testimony indicated that her mental confusion left her unable to dress herself appropriately and caused her to have difficulty feeding herself and maintaining personal hygiene.

* * * *

We conclude the evidence of testatrix's mental acuity is not as persuasive as the testimony from the examining physician and the nursing home personnel, who were disinterested and who were dealing with testatrix on a more constant basis than the other witnesses during the period of time surrounding the date of the will's execution.

The trial court's judgment was reversed. The testatrix was determined to have lacked testamentary capacity, and, therefore, the will executed on February 25, 1976, was invalid. **DECISION AND REMEDY**

Unger died intestate. The property passed as though there had never been any will. It is important to stress that incapacity is difficult to prove. **COMMENTS**

Formal Requirements of a Will

A will must comply with statutory formalities designed to insure that the testator or testatrix understood his or her actions at the time the will was made. These formalities are intended to help prevent fraud. Unless they are followed, the will is declared void and the decedent's property is distributed according to the laws of intestacy of that state. The requirements are not uniform among the jurisdictions. However, most states uphold the following basic requirements for executing a will.

1. *A will must be in writing.* A written document is generally required, although in some cases oral wills, called nuncupative wills (to be discussed later), are found valid. [UPC 2-502] The writing itself can be informal as long as it substantially complies with the statutory requirements. In some states a will can be handwritten in crayon or ink. It can be written on a sheet or scrap of paper, on a paper bag, or on a piece of cloth. A will that is completely in the handwriting of the testator is called a **holographic** (or olographic) **will**.

A will also can refer to a written memorandum that itself is not a will but that contains information necessary to carry out the will. For example, Thelma's will provides that a certain sum of money be divided among a group of charities named in a written memorandum that Thelma gave to the trustee *the same day the will was signed.* The written list of charities will be "incorporated by reference" into the will only if it was in existence when the will was executed (signed) and if it is sufficiently described so that it can be identified.

2. *A formal (nonholographic) will must be signed by the testator.* It is a fundamental requirement in almost all jurisdictions that the testator's or testatrix's signature appear, generally at the end of the will. Each jurisdiction dictates by statute and court decision what constitutes a signature. Initials, an "X" or other mark, and words like "Mom" have all been upheld as valid when it was shown that the testator intended them to be a signature.

3. *A formal (nonholographic) will must be witnessed.* A will must be attested by two and sometimes three witnesses. The number of witnesses, their qualifications, and the manner in which the witnessing must be done are generally set out in a statute.

A witness can be required to be disinterested— that is, not a beneficiary under the will. By contrast, the UPC provides that a will is valid even if it is attested by an interested witness. [UPC 2-505] There are no age requirements for witnesses, but they must be mentally competent.

Witnesses function to verify that the testator actually executed (signed) the will and had the requisite intent and capacity at the time. A witness does not have to read the contents of the will. Usually, the testator and witnesses must all sign in the sight or the presence of one another, but the UPC deems it sufficient if the testator acknowledges his or her signature to the witnesses. [UPC 2-502] The UPC does not require all parties to sign in the presence of one another.

4. *A will may be required to be "published."* Publication is an oral declaration by the maker to the witnesses that the document they are about to sign is his or her "last will and testament." Publication is becoming an unnecessary formality in most states, and it is not required under the UPC.

In general, strict compliance with the preceding formalities (except for the one relating to witnesses and the one relating to publication) is required before a formal document is accepted as the decedent's will. Holographic wills constitute another exception in some jurisdictions. However, holographic wills must be signed by the decedent, and its material provisions must be in the testator's handwriting in order for them to be probated (validated). [UPC 2-503]

Nuncupative Wills   A nuncupative will is an oral will made before witnesses. It is not permitted in most states. Where authorized by statute, such wills are generally valid only if made during the last illness of the testator or testatrix. They are sometimes referred to as death-bed wills. Only personal property (not real property) can be transferred by a nuncupative will. Statutes frequently permit soldiers and sailors to make nuncupative wills when on active duty.

Undue Influence

A valid will is one that represents the maker's intention to transfer and distribute his or her property. When it can be shown that the decedent's plan of distribution was the result of improper pressure brought by another person, the will is declared invalid.

Undue influence may be inferred by the court if the testator or testatrix ignores blood relatives and names as beneficiary a nonrelative who is in constant close contact and in a position to influence the making of the will. For example, if a nurse or friend caring for the deceased at the time of death is named as beneficiary to the exclusion of all family members, the validity of the will might well be challenged on the basis of undue influence.

Revocation of Wills

An executed will is revocable by the maker at any time during the maker's lifetime. Wills can also be revoked by operation of law. Revocation can be partial or complete, and it must follow certain strict formalities.

Act of the Maker   Revocation of an executed will by the maker can be effected in either of two ways— by physical act or in writing.

Revocation by Physical Act   The testator or testatrix may revoke a will by intentionally burning, tearing, canceling, obliterating, or destroying it, or by having someone else do so in the presence of the maker and at the maker's direction.[6] In some states, partial revocation by physical act of the maker is recognized. Thus, those portions of a will lined out or torn away are dropped, and the remaining parts of the will are valid. In no case, however, can a provision be crossed out and an additional or substitute provision written in. Such altered portions require reexecution (resigning) and reattestation (rewitnessing).

To revoke a will by physical act, it is necessary to follow the mandates of a state statute exactly. Where a state statute prescribes the exact methods for revoking a will by physical act, those are the only methods that will revoke the will.

Revocation in Another Writing   A **codicil** is a written instrument separate from the will that amends

---

6. The destruction cannot be inadvertent. The maker's intent to revoke must be shown. Where a will has been burned or torn accidentally, it is normally recommended that the maker have a new document created so that it will not falsely appear that the maker intended to revoke the will.

or revokes provisions in the will. It eliminates the necessity of redrafting an entire will merely to add to it or amend it. A codicil can also be used to revoke an entire will. The codicil must be executed with the same formalities required for a will. It must refer expressly to the will. In effect, it updates a will because the will is "incorporated by reference" into the codicil.

A *second will* can be executed that may or may not revoke the first or a prior will, depending upon the language used. The second will must use specific language like, "This will hereby revokes all prior wills." If the second will is otherwise valid and properly executed, it will revoke all prior wills. If the express *declaration of revocation* is missing, then both wills are read together. If any of the dispositions made in the second will are inconsistent with the prior will, the second will controls.

Where a state statute details the requirements for revoking a will with another writing, those requirements must be strictly complied with, as illustrated by the following case.

BACKGROUND AND FACTS   *Frances Maude Thompson, the decedent, executed a will on September 2, 1964, in Nebraska. Upon her death, Victor E. Thompson, her husband, filed a petition for the probate of her will. John E. Finley, son of the decedent through a prior marriage, filed a petition seeking a formal adjudication of his deceased mother's estate by intestacy. Finley's petition claimed that his mother executed a subsequent will that revoked the 1964 document offered for probate by the husband. However, Finley could not find the subsequent will.*

ESTATE OF
THOMPSON
Supreme Court of Nebraska,
1983.
336 N.W.2d 590.

CAPORALE, Justice.
*   *   *
*   *   * The only evidence concerning the issue is the testimony of the contestant son and his wife. It is to the effect that in July of 1965 they examined and read a one- or two-page typewritten document which the decedent, a Nebraska resident, showed them while she was visiting at their home in Colorado, and which she said was her will. The document began with the words, "Last Will and Testament of Frances Maude Thompson." It contained two signatures in addition to that of his mother, but they could not recall whose they were. According to the son, there was also "some kind of a mark on it for a notary." It bore a 1965 date, but he could not recall the month. The son believed, but could not "swear," that the document contained a clause revoking former wills. His wife recalled such a clause. The son testified further that "The Will specified that if [sic] the property was first to go to Vic Thompson and then to me without restriction, in other words, he wouldn't be deprived of this property during his lifetime. . . . It had nothing in there that said, specific words, for life." His wife generally corroborated the son in this regard. They could recall no other specific portions of the document.

It is the son's contention that although the above-cited testimony is insufficient to establish the distributive provisions of the 1965 will so as to entitle it to probate, the evidence is sufficient to establish that a will was duly made and executed after the 1964 will such as to destroy the earlier will. The effect of that circumstance would be that his mother would have died intestate and her property would therefore be subject to distribution under the laws of descent rather than under the 1964 document. * * *

[Neb. Rev. Stat.] Section 30–2332 provides: "A will or any part thereof is revoked (1) by a subsequent will which, as is evident either from its terms or from competent evidence of its terms, revokes the prior will or part expressly or by inconsistency; or (2) by being burned, torn, canceled, obliterated, or destroyed, with the intent and for the purpose of revoking it by the testator or by another person in the presence of and by the direction of the testator." * * *

In the posture of this case the threshold question becomes whether the contestant's evidence meets the "clear, unequivocal, and convincing" standard required to establish that a subsequent will was duly executed. We find that it does not.

One need look no further than the first two sentences of the Comment to § 30–2332 to reach that conclusion. Those sentences read: "Revocation of a will may be by either a subsequent will or an act done to the document. If revocation is by a subsequent will, it must be *properly executed*." (Emphasis supplied.) The evidence does not tell us where the will was executed, what formalities, if any, the witnesses observed in affixing their signatures to the document, or what role a notary, if any, played in the execution process.

* * * *

In 1965, Neb. Rev. Stat. § 30–204 (Reissue 1964) provided that, except for nuncupative wills, and wills properly executed in other jurisdictions, wills must be signed by the testator, or some person in his presence, and by his express direction, and attested and subscribed in the presence of the testator by two or more competent witnesses. No showing exists that these formalities were followed. Faced with the same language as to method of execution presently contained in Neb. Rev. Stat. § 30–2327 (Reissue 1979) that, except for holographic wills, certain written statements, and wills properly executed in other jurisdictions, every will is required "to be signed by at least two individuals each of whom witnessed either the signing or the testator's acknowledgement of the signature or of the will," the court in *Matter of Estate of Weidner*, Mont., 628 P.2d 285 (1981), held that where it could not be established that there was a second individual who had witnessed either the signing or the testator's acknowledgment of her signature, there was insufficient evidence to support a finding that the will was fully executed and thus it could not revoke a prior will. * * *

There was no evidence before the trial court herein as to the manner in which the 1965 document was executed. We conclude, therefore, that as a matter of law the evidence does not clearly, unequivocally, and convincingly establish that the 1965 document was properly executed as the last will and testament of the contestant's mother.

* * * *

DECISION AND REMEDY   *The testatrix did not revoke her validly executed will by writing a second will because she did not strictly adhere to the state formalities of a properly executed will.*

Revocation by Operation of Law Revocation by operation of law occurs when marriage, divorce or annulment, or the birth of children takes place after a will has been executed.

Marriage In the vast majority of states, when a testator marries *after* executing a will, which does not include the new spouse, the spouse can still receive the amount the spouse would have taken had the testator died intestate. In effect, this revokes the will to the point of providing the spouse with an intestate share. The rest of the estate is passed under the will. [UPC 2–301, 2–508] If, however, the omission of a future spouse is intentional in the existing will, or the spouse is otherwise provided for in the will (or by transfer of property outside of the will), the omitted spouse will not be given an intestate amount.

Divorce or Annulment   At common law and under the UPC, divorce does not necessarily revoke the entire will. A divorce or an annulment occurring after a will has been executed will revoke those dispositions of property made under the will to the former spouse. [UPC 2–508]

Children Born after a Will is Executed   If a child is born after a will has been executed and if it appears that the testator would have made a provision for the child, then the child is entitled to receive whatever portion of the estate he or she is allowed under state intestate laws. Most state laws allow a child to receive some portion of the estate if no provision is made in a will, unless it appears from the terms of the will that the testator intended to disinherit the child. Under the UPC, the rule is the same. The effect is to partially revoke the parent's will. [UPC 2-302]

Rights Under a Will

The law imposes certain limitations on the way a person can dispose of property in a will. For example, a married person who makes a will cannot avoid leaving a certain portion of the estate to the surviving spouse. In most states this is called a "forced share," "widow's share," or "elective share," and it is often one-third.

Beneficiaries under a will have rights as well. A beneficiary can renounce his or her share of the property given under a will.[7] Further, a surviving spouse can renounce the amount given under a will and elect to take the "forced share" if the forced share is larger than the amount of the gift. State statutes provide the methods by which a surviving

spouse accomplishes renunciation. The purpose of these statutes is to allow the spouse to obtain whichever distribution would be most advantageous. The UPC gives the surviving spouse an elective right to take one-third of the total estate. [UPC 2-201]

STATUTES OF DESCENT AND DISTRIBUTION

The rules of descent are statutory. That means each state can regulate how property shall be distributed when a person dies without a will. State laws attempt to carry out the likely intent and wishes of the decedent. These statutes are called **intestacy laws.**

The rules of descent vary widely from state to state. However, there is usually a special statutory provision for the rights of the surviving spouse and children. In addition, the law provides that first the debts of the decedent must be satisfied out of his or her estate, and then the remaining assets can pass to the surviving spouse and to the children.

A surviving spouse usually receives a share of the estate—one-half if there is also a surviving child and one-third if there are two or more children. Only where no children or grandchildren survive the decedent will a surviving spouse succeed to the *entire estate.* The UPC is more generous to the surviving spouse than most state statutes. [UPC 2–102]

Assume that Able dies intestate and is survived by his wife, Barbara, and his children, Carl and Diane. Able's property passes according to intestacy laws. After Able's outstanding debts are paid, Barbara will receive the homestead (either in fee simple or as a life estate) and ordinarily a one-third to one-half interest in all other property. The remaining real and personal property will pass to Carl and Diane in equal portions.

Distribution

State statutes of descent and distribution specify the order in which heirs of an intestate share in the estate. When there is no surviving spouse or child, then grandchildren, brothers and sisters, and, in some states, parents of the decedent are the next in line to share. These relatives are usually called *lineal descendants.* If there are no lineal descendants, then

---

7.   This is usually done for tax reasons or because the recipient would fare better by taking his or her elective share.

CONCEPT SUMMARY: Wills

TYPES OF WILLS	DEFINITIONS
Holographic	A will completely in the handwriting of the testator; valid where permitted by state statute.
Attested	A written will, signed by the testator, properly witnessed, and, where required, published; one which meets formal statutory requirements for a valid will.
Nuncupative	An oral will made before witnesses during the deathbed illness of the testator; it is only valid to transfer personal property, not real property.
METHODS OF REVOCATION OR MODIFICATION OF WILLS	**DEFINITIONS**
By acts of the maker:	
Physical act	Tearing up, canceling, obliterating, or deliberately destroying part or all of a will.
Codicil	A formal separate document to amend or revoke an existing will.
New will	A new, properly executed will, expressly revoking the existing will.
By operation of the law:	
Marriage	Generally revokes a will written before the marriage.
Divorce or annulment	Revokes dispositions made under a will to a former spouse.
Subsequently born children	It is *implied* that the child is entitled to receive the portion of the estate granted under intestate distribution laws.
TYPES OF GIFTS	**DEFINITIONS**
Specific	A devise or bequest of a particular piece of property in the testator's estate.
General	A devise or bequest that does not single out a particular item in the testator's estate, usually a sum of money.
Residuary	A devise or bequest of any properties left in the estate after all specific and general gifts have been made.

collateral heirs are the next group to share. Collateral heirs include nieces, nephews, aunts, and uncles of the decedent.

If there are still no survivors in any of those groups of people related to the decedent, most statutes provide that the property shall be distributed among the next of kin of any of the collateral heirs. Stepchildren are not considered kin. However, legally adopted children are recognized as lawful heirs of their adoptive parents.

Whether or not an illegitimate child inherits depends on state statute. In all states, intestate succession between the mother and the child exists. In some states, intestate succession between the father and the child can occur only where the child is "legitimized" by ceremony or the child has been "acknowledged" by the father. The constitutionality of these illegitimacy statutes has recently been upheld by the Supreme Court, and affirmed by the Ohio Supreme Court—as illustrated by the following case.

BACKGROUND AND FACTS *An illegitimate child contested the constitutionality of an Ohio statute that prevented her from inheriting from her natural father's estate.*

WHITE v. RANDOLPH
Supreme Court of Ohio, 1979.
59 Ohio St.2d 6, 391 N.E.2d
333.

PER CURIAM [by the Whole Court].

The issue certified for resolution is as follows: "Whether the provisions of R.C. Chapter 2105 denying to one who is illegitimate any right to inherit from the natural father, unless the father has taken certain steps such as *marrying* the mother, *acknowledging* the child, designating the child as an heir-at-law, adoption, or making a provision in a will, are violative of equal protection as guaranteed by the Fourteenth Amendment of the United States Constitution and Article I, Section 2 of the Ohio Constitution."

The unanimous opinion of the Court of Appeals in the cause at bar was written by Judge Robert E. Holmes, now a Justice of this court. In our view, the position taken by Justice Holmes represents the correct one under the instant facts and, therefore, is incorporated at length:

Holmes, P. J.

*   *   *   *

"The facts relevant to this appeal are in brief that Clarence Jackson died testate on January 17, 1975. His will was duly admitted to probate. The will devised all of decedent's property to his wife, but failed to provide for its disposition in the event that she did not survive him. She did not.

"The administrator then brought this action in the Common Pleas Court of Franklin County, Probate Division, for a determination of decedent's heirs-at-law, joining appellant Alice Marie Jackson, who claimed to be decedent's illegitimate daughter, as one of the defendants. Following a hearing on the matter, Judge Metcalf held, as a matter of law, that appellant was not entitled to inherit from the estate of Clarence Jackson because she introduced no evidence tending to show:

" ' *   *   * that the decedent, alleged father, legitimized his illegitimate daughter, or formally acknowledged his daughter in Probate Court, or adopted such daughter, or provided for her in his will, or designated her as his heir at law *   *   *.'

"In Ohio, a child born out of wedlock is capable of inheriting from and through his mother, but may inherit from his father only under certain circumstances. The father may legitimatize an illegitimate child by afterwards marrying the mother of the illegitimate child and acknowledging the child as his. Further, the natural father of an illegitimate child may confer upon such child a right of inheritance from such father by several means: (1) by formal acknowledgement in Probate Court that the child is his with consent of the mother; (2) by designating the illegitimate child as his heir-at-law; (3) by adopting the illegitimate child; and (4) by making a provision for the child in his will.

"Appellant concededly cannot meet any of the above criteria. However, appellant contends that the equal protection clause requires that she be permitted to inherit from decedent if she can establish with sufficient competent evidence that decedent is, in fact, her father. In the cases considering this general issue before us, it has been rather uniformly pointed out that the rationality of the classification must be examined in light of the legitimate state purposes to which it is related.

"It has long been recognized in Ohio that proof of paternity, especially after the death of the alleged father, is difficult, and peculiarly subject to abuse. One of the resultants of such abuse would be the instability of land titles of real estate left by intestate fathers of illegitimate children.

*   *   *   *

"[W]e believe that the Ohio statutory provisions present a reasonable middle ground for the recognition of certain categories of illegitimate children of intestate men. Through these laws inheritance rights may be reasonably recognized without jeopardizing the orderly settlement of estates or the dependability of titles to property passing under intestate laws.

"Clearly, the Ohio classification scheme is rationally related to the legitimate state purpose of assuring efficient disposition of property at death while avoiding spurious claims. Moreover, the Ohio provisions do not discriminate between legitimate and illegitimate children *per se*. All children may inherit from their mothers. Some illegitimate children and all legitimate children may inherit from their fathers. The group 'discriminated against' is that class of illegitimate children whose fathers did not formally acknowledge them or designate them as heirs-at-law."

*   *   *   *

Subsequent to the decision of the Court of Appeals in the instant cause, the United States Supreme Court, in the case of *Lalli v. Lalli* (1978), upheld the constitutionality of a New York statute which allowed illegitimate children to inherit from their father only if a court of competent jurisdiction, during the father's lifetime, entered an order declaring the child's paternity.

Recognizing the difficulty of proving paternity and the possibility of fraudulent assertions of paternity upon the estate of the decedent, the court found that the statutory differences afforded legitimate and illegitimate heirs under intestate succession were justified in furtherance of New York's substantial interest in the just and orderly disposition of property at death. In that regard, we conclude that the Ohio statutes in question in the cause at bar are substantially related to the important state interests discussed by the court in *Lalli, supra*.

DECISION AND REMEDY   *The judgments of the probate court and the appellate court were affirmed. The Ohio statute was not unconstitutional. Ohio has a sufficient state interest in the disposition of property at death to justify different laws regarding intestate succession for legitimate and illegitimate children.*

COMMENTS   *Most states have amended their intestacy statutes dealing with illegitimate children to provide a more liberal test for establishing inheritance rights. These states allow paternity to be established by evidence that the parents married after the child's birth, or by an adjudication before the death of the father, or by clear and convincing proof after the father's death. [UPC 2–109]*

Because state statutes differ so widely, few generalizations can be made about the laws of descent and distribution. It is extremely important to refer to the exact terms of the applicable state statutes when addressing any problem of intestacy distribution.

The UPC provides that a surviving spouse, in addition to taking an elective share of one-third of the decedent's estate, is entitled to the following:

1. A homestead allowance of $5,000.
2. A household and personal effects exemption to a value not to exceed $3,500.

3. A family allowance for a period of up to one year after the death occurs to provide for daily expenses before the estate is settled, up to the amount of $6,000. [UPC 2-401, 402, 403, and 404]

The Pattern of Intestacy Distribution for Grandchildren   When an intestate is survived by descendants of deceased children, a question arises as to what share the descendants (that is, grandchildren of the intestate) will receive. **Per stirpes** is a method of dividing an intestate share where a class or group of distributees (for example, grandchildren) take the share that their deceased parent *would have been* entitled to inherit had that child lived.

Assume that John, a widower, has three children, Able, Barbara, and Clara. Able has two children (Mark and Sally), Barbara has one child (Greg), and Clara has one child (Peter). At the time of John's death, Able and Barbara have predeceased their father. If John's estate is distributed *per stirpes*, the following distribution would take place:

1. Mark and Sally: one-sixth each, taking Able's one-third.
2. Greg: one-third, taking Barbara's share.
3. Clara: one-third, as the surviving child (Peter does not inherit).

Another type of distribution of an estate is on a **per capita** basis. This means that each person takes an equal share of the estate. Assume that John, a widower, has two children, Able and Barbara. Able has two children (Mark and Sally), and Barbara has one child (Greg). At the time of John's death, Able and Barbara have predeceased their father. If John's estate is distributed *per capita*, Mark, Sally, and Greg will each receive a one-third share.

In most states and under the Uniform Probate Code, in-laws do not share in an estate. If a child dies before his or her parents, the child's spouse will not receive an inheritance. Assume that John, a widower, has two married children, Able and Barbara, and no grandchildren. If Able predeceases his father, John's entire estate will go to Barbara. Able's surviving wife will not inherit.

TRUSTS

A trust involves any arrangement whereby property is transferred from one person to be administered by a trustee for a third party's benefit. It can also be defined as a right or property, real or personal, held by one party for the benefit of another. A trust can be created for any purpose that is not illegal or against public policy. The essential elements of a trust are:

1. A designated beneficiary.
2. A designated trustee.
3. A fund sufficiently identified to enable title to pass to the trustee.

4. Actual delivery to the trustee with the intention of passing title.

If Sanford conveys his farm to South Miami First National Bank to be held for the benefit of his daughters, Sanford has created a trust. Sanford is the settlor, South Miami First National Bank is the trustee, and Sanford's daughters are the beneficiaries.

Express Trusts

An express trust is one created or declared in expressed terms, usually in writing. It differs from one that is inferred by the law from the conduct or dealings of the parties (an implied trust, to be discussed later). The two types of express trusts that will be discussed here are *inter vivos* trusts and *testamentary* trusts.

Inter Vivos Trusts   An **inter vivos trust** is a trust executed by a grantor during his or her lifetime. The grantor executes a "trust deed," and legal title to the trust property passes to the named trustee. The trustee has a duty to administer the property as directed by the grantor for the benefit and in the interest of the beneficiaries. The trustee must preserve the trust property, make it productive, and, if required by the terms of the trust agreement, pay income to the beneficiaries, all in accordance with the terms of the trust. Once the *inter vivos* trust is created, the grantor has, in effect, given over the property for the benefit of beneficiaries. Often, tax-related benefits exist in setting up an *inter vivos* trust.

Testamentary Trusts   A **testamentary trust** is a trust created by will to come into existence upon the settlor's death. Although a testamentary trust has a trustee who maintains legal title to the trust property, actions of the trustee are subject to judicial approval. The trustee of a testamentary trust can be named in the will or be appointed by the court. Unlike the *inter vivos* trust, a testamentary trust will not fail because a trustee has not been named in the will. The legal responsibilities of the trustees are the same in both kinds of trusts. If the will setting up a testamentary trust is invalid, then the trust will also be invalid. The property that was supposed to be in the trust will then pass according to intestacy laws, not according to the terms of the trust.

Implied Trusts

Sometimes a trust will be imposed by law, even in the absence of an express trust. Customarily, these implied trusts are divided into **constructive** and **resulting trusts.**

Constructive Trust

A constructive trust differs from an express trust in that it arises by operation of law. Whenever a transaction takes place in which the person who takes the legal estate in property cannot also enjoy the beneficial interest without violating some established principle of equity, the court will create a constructive trust. In effect, the legal owner becomes a trustee for the parties who, in equity, are actually entitled to the beneficial enjoyment that flows from the trust. One element of a constructive trust is a wrongful action, whether it be active or constructive.

To illustrate: Able and Baker are partners in buying, developing, and selling real estate. Able learns through the staff of the partnership that a piece of land will soon come on the market that the staff will recommend that the partnership purchase. Able purchases the property secretly in his own name, violating his fiduciary relationship. When these facts are discovered, a court will determine that Able must hold the property in trust for the partnership.

Resulting Trust

A resulting trust arises from the conduct of the parties. Here the trust results, or is created from, the *apparent intentions* of the parties. Since the trust is created by law, the conduct of the parties evidencing the intent to create a trust relationship is carefully scrutinized.

To illustrate: Smith purchases one acre of land from Green. Because Smith is going out of the country for a period of two years and will be unable to attend the closing, she asks Green, at the closing, to deed the property to Smith's good friend, Crenshaw. Green does indeed convey the property to Crenshaw. Since the intent of the transaction is not to make a gift of the land to Crenshaw, the property will be held in trust (a resulting trust) with Crenshaw as the trustee for the benefit of Smith.

Other Kinds of Trusts

Certain trusts are created for special purposes. Three such trusts that warrant discussion are charitable, spendthrift, and totten trusts.

Charitable Trust

A trust designed for the benefit of a segment of the public or of the public in general is a **charitable trust.** It differs from a private trust in that the identities of the beneficiaries are uncertain. Usually, to be deemed a charitable trust, a trust must be created for charitable, educational, religious, or scientific purposes.

Spendthrift Trust

A trust created to provide for the maintenance of a beneficiary by preventing his or her improvidence with the bestowed funds is a **spendthrift trust.** Essentially, the beneficiary is permitted to draw only a certain portion of the total amount to which he or she is entitled at any one time. The majority of states allow spendthrift trust provisions that prohibit creditors from attaching such trusts.

Totten Trust

A special type of trust created when one person deposits money in his or her own name as a trustee for another is a **totten trust.** This trust is tentative in that it is revocable at will until the depositor dies or completes the gift in his or her lifetime by some unequivocal act or declaration (for example, delivery of the funds to the intended beneficiary). If the depositor should die before the beneficiary dies and if the depositor has not revoked the trust expressly or impliedly, a presumption arises that an absolute trust has been created for the benefit of the beneficiary. At the death of the depositor, the beneficiary obtains property rights to the balance on hand.

ESTATE ADMINISTRATION

The orderly procedure used to collect assets, settle debts, and distribute the remaining assets when a person dies is the subject matter of estate administration. This section will look at the duties of the personal representative of the deceased.

Principal Duties of the Personal Representative

The rules and procedures for managing the estate of a deceased are controlled by statute. Thus, they vary from state to state. In every state, there is a special court, often called a probate court, which oversees the management of estates of decedents.

The first step after a person dies is usually to determine whether or not the decedent left a will. In most cases the decedent's attorney will have that information. If it is not known for some time whether a valid will exists, the personal papers of the deceased must be reviewed. If a will exists, it probably names a personal representative (executor) to administer the estate. If there is no will, or if the will fails to name a personal representative, then the court must appoint an administrator. Under the UPC, the term *personal representative* includes the executor (person named in the will) and administrator (person appointed by the court). [UPC 1-201(30)]

The first duty of the personal representative is to inventory and collect the assets of the decedent. If necessary, the assets must be appraised to determine their value. Both the rights of creditors and the rights of beneficiaries must be protected during the estate administration proceedings. In addition, the personal representative is responsible for managing the assets of the estate during the administration period

and for not allowing them to be wasted or unnecessarily depleted.

The personal representative receives and pays valid claims of creditors and arranges for the estate to pay federal and state income taxes and estate taxes (or inheritance taxes, depending on the state). A personal representative is required to post a bond to insure honest and faithful performance. Usually the bond exceeds the estimated value of the personal estate of the decedent. In some cases, the will can specify that the personal representative need not post a bond.

When the ultimate distribution of assets to the beneficiaries is determined, the personal representative is responsible for distributing the estate pursuant to the court order. Once the assets have been distributed, an accounting is rendered to the court, the estate is closed, and the personal representative is relieved of any further responsibility or liability for the estate. Exhibit 54–1 lists the duties of the personal representative.

EXHIBIT 54–1 The Duties Of The Personal Representative

It would be impossible to indicate all the duties the executor must perform, but here are some.

1. Managing the estate until it is settled, including
   a. Collecting debts due the estate.
   b. Managing real estate; arranging for maintenance and repairs.
   c. Registering securities in the name of the estate.
   d. Collecting insurance proceeds.
   e. Running family business, if necessary.
   f. Arranging for the family's support during probate.
   g. Properly insuring assets.

2. Collecting all assets and necessary records, including
   a. Locating the will, insurance policies, real estate papers, car registrations, and birth certificates.
   b. Filing claims for pension, social security, profit sharing and veteran's benefits.
   c. Taking possession of bank accounts, real estate, personal effects, and safe deposit boxes.
   d. Obtaining names, addresses, and social security numbers of all heirs.
   e. Making an inventory of all assets.
   f. Setting up records and books.

3. Determining the estate's obligations, including
   a. Determining which claims are legally due.
   b. Obtaining receipts for all claims paid.
   c. Checking on mortgages and other loans.

4. Computing and then paying all death taxes due, which requires
   a. Selecting the most beneficial tax alternatives.
   b. Deciding which assets to sell to provide necessary funds.
   c. Paying taxes on time to avoid penalties.
   d. Opposing any unfair evaluations of estate property established by governmental taxing authorities.

5. Computing beneficiaries' shares and then distributing the estate, which includes
   a. Determining who gets particular items and settling family disputes.
   b. Transferring title to real estate and other property.
   c. Selling off assets to pay cash legacies.
   d. Paying final estate costs.
   e. Preparing accountings for the court's approval.

Probate versus Nonprobate

To probate a will means to establish its validity and to carry the administration of the estate through a court process. The process of probate is time-consuming and costly, and the court is involved in every step of the proceedings. Attorneys and personal representatives often become involved in probate.

Many states have statutes that allow for the distribution of assets without probate proceedings. Faster and less expensive methods are then used. For example, property can be transferred by affidavit, and problems or questions can be handled during an administrative hearing. In addition, some state statutes provide that title to cars, savings and checking accounts, and certain other property can be passed merely by filling out forms. This is particularly true when most of the property is held in joint tenancy with right of survivorship or when there is only one heir.

Family Settlement Agreements   A majority of states provide for *family settlement agreements*, which are private agreements among the beneficiaries. Once a will is admitted to probate, the family members can agree to settle among themselves the distribution of the decedent's assets. Although a family settlement agreement speeds the settlement process, a court order is still needed to protect the estate from future creditors and to clear title to the assets involved.

Summary Procedures   The use of summary procedures in estate administration can save time and money. The expense of a personal representative's commission, attorneys' fees, appraisers' fees, and so forth can be eliminated or at least minimized if the parties utilize summary administration procedures. But in some situations—for example, where a guardian for minor children or for an incompetent person must be appointed and a trust has been created to protect the minor or the incompetent person—probate procedures cannot be avoided. In the ordinary situation, a person can employ various will substitutes to avoid the cost of probate—for example, *inter vivos* trusts, life insurance policies with named beneficiaries, or joint tenancy arrangements. Not all methods are suitable for every estate, but there are alternatives to a complete probate administration.

ESTATE TAXES

The death of an individual may result in tax liabilities at both the federal and state levels.

Federal Estate Tax

At the federal level, there is a tax levied upon the total value of the estate after debts and expenses for administration have been deducted and after various exemptions are allowed. The tax is on the estate itself rather than on the beneficiaries. Therefore, it does not depend on the character of any bequests or on the relationship of the beneficiary to the decedent, unless a gift to charity that is recognized by the IRS as deductible from the total estate for tax purposes is involved. However, bequests to a surviving spouse do affect federal estate taxation.

State Inheritance Taxes

The majority of states assess a death tax in the form of an inheritance tax imposed on the recipient of a bequest rather than on the estate. Some states also have a state estate tax similar to the federal estate tax. In general, inheritance tax rates are graduated according to the type of relationship between the beneficiary and decedent. The lowest rates and largest exemptions are applied to a surviving spouse and the children of the decedent.

QUESTIONS AND CASE PROBLEMS

1. John is a widower who has two married children, Frank and Amy. Amy has two children, Phil and Paula.

Frank has no children. John dies, leaving a typewritten will that gives all his property equally to his children, Frank and Amy, and provides that should a child predecease him, leaving grandchildren, the grandchildren are to take *per stirpes*. The will was witnessed by Amy and John's lawyer and was signed by John in their presence. Amy has predeceased John. Frank claims the will is invalid.

(a) Discuss whether the will is valid.

(b) Discuss the distribution of John's estate if the will is invalid.

(c) Discuss the distribution of John's estate if the will is valid.

2. James was a bachelor. While single, he made out a will naming his mother, Carol, as the sole beneficiary. Later James married Lisa. Discuss the results of each of the following possible events:

(a) If James died while married to Lisa without changing his will, would the estate go to his mother, Carol? Explain.

(b) Assume James made out a new will upon his marriage to Lisa, leaving his entire estate to Lisa. Later he divorces Lisa and marries Sue, but he does not change his will. Discuss the rights of Lisa and Sue to his estate when he dies.

(c) Assume James divorces Lisa, marries Sue, and changes his will leaving his estate to Sue. Later a daughter, Lori, is born. James dies without having included Lori in his will. Discuss fully whether Lori has any rights in the estate.

3. Ann has drafted and properly executed a will. Assume the following clauses in her will and the following events:

(a) Her will provides, "I leave my two-carat diamond ring to my sister, Sylvia." At the time of Ann's death, Sylvia had predeceased Ann, leaving one child, Lindsay.

(b) Her will provides, "I leave $5,000 to each of my nieces, Fern and Dorothy." At the time of Ann's death, only $4,000 remains in her estate.

(c) Her will provides, "I leave to my nephew, Donald, my $10,000 Cadillac or equivalent value." Just prior to Ann's death she sold the Cadillac.

Discuss fully each situation, giving its name and describing its effect on the legatees.

4. Sam, an eighty-three-year-old invalid, employs a nurse, Sarah, to care for him. Prior to Sarah's employment, Sam had executed a will leaving his entire estate to his only living relative—his great-grandson Fred. Sarah convinces Sam that Fred is dead and gets Sam to change his will, naming Sarah as his sole beneficiary. After Sam's death, Fred appears and contests the will. Discuss the probable success of Fred's action.

5. The following transfers and events take place:

(a) John lives in Europe. He transfers $20,000 to his good friend, Kate, and orally instructs her to invest and distribute the $20,000 and whatever it accrues so as to finance the MBA education of his daughter, JoAnn.

(b) Fred is on the board of directors of the ABC Corporation and is the chairman of its research policy committee. Through his chairmanship he learns that ABC has come up with a cure for cancer. Fred purchases on the open market 20,000 shares

of ABC stock at $10 per share. When the announcement of the cure is made, the market value of ABC's stock increases to $200 per share.

(c) Sue is a successful businesswoman. She is engaged to marry John, a man of modest means who has ambitions to be an inventor. Sue creates a $20,000 joint savings account in the name of "Sue, in trust for John." Sue tells John that the purpose of the account is to encourage him to move forward in his business ventures.

Discuss fully whether a valid trust has been created in each situation, what each trust is called, and, where applicable, what its effect is.

6. Jesse Butterfield Morris died on February 11, 1967. On April 6, 1967, the Security First National Bank offered a document for probate as Morris's holographic will. The document was entirely in Morris's handwriting, but it contained no signatures of witnesses. The document was dated (November 1, 1965), was addressed to the Security First National Bank, and contained the initials J. B. M. at the end. Should Morris's will be probated? [In re Estate of Morris, 268 Cal. App. 2d 638, 74 Cal. Rptr. 32 (1969)]

7. Harris executed a written instrument in which he named Bishop as trustee of $17,000 in bonds, notes, mortgages, and money. The instrument declared that Harris was hereby transferring these assets to Bishop in trust for the benefit of the public library in Alexandria, Ohio, but Harris never delivered the instrument. Thereafter, Harris received interest on some of the notes and still had access to the money and instruments that were the subject of the trust. Has Harris created a valid trust? Consider the requirements of making a valid gift. [Whitehead v. Bishop, 23 Ohio App. 315, 155 N.E. 565 (1925)]

8. In 1925 Campbell died, leaving a will in which the ninth clause read as follows: "My good friends Clark and Smith I appoint as my trustees. Each of my trustees is competent by reason of familiarity with the property, my wishes and friendships, to wisely distribute some portion at least of said property. I therefore give and bequeath to my trustees all my property in trust to make disposal by the way of a memento from myself, of such articles to such of my friends as they, my trustees, shall select. All of said property, not so disposed of by them, my trustees are directed to sell and the proceeds of such sale or sales to become and be disposed of as a part of the residue of my estate." Is this a valid trust? [Clark v. Campbell, 82 N.H. 281, 133 A. 166 (1926)]

9. H. W. Wolfe died at the age of sixty-seven, leaving personal property worth about $4,000 and more than five hundred acres of land. Just before he died, on July 31, 1911, he properly executed a will that contained the following provision: "I, H. W. Wolfe, will and bequeath to Miss Mary Lilly Luffman, a tract of land near Roaring Gap Post Office, on State Road and South Fork, adjoining the lands of J. M. Royal and others, the land bought by

me from H. D. Woodruff. Witness my hand and seal, this thirty-first day of July, 1911." On August 14, 1911, Wolfe wrote another will that provided in part: "I, H. W. Wolfe, do make and declare this to be my last will and testament. I will and bequeath all my effects to my brothers and sisters, to be divided equally among them. Witness my hand and seal, this the fourteenth day of August, 1911." Both wills were properly signed and attested. Who is entitled to what under these wills? [In re Wolfe's Will, 185 N.C. 563, 117 S.E. 804 (1923)]

10. An elderly, childless widow had nine nieces and nephews. She devised her entire estate to be divided equally among two nieces and the husband of one of the nieces, who was also the attorney-draftsman of the will and the executor named in the will. The testatrix was definitely of sound mind when the will was executed. If you were one of the seven nieces or nephews omitted from the will, could you think of any way to have the will invalidated? [Estate of Eckert, 93 Misc.2d 677, 403 N.Y.S.2d 633 (1978)]

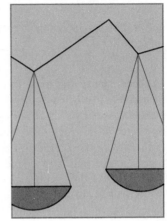

55

Insurance

THE NATURE OF INSURANCE

Insurance is a contract by which the insurance company (insurer) promises to pay a sum of money or give something of value to another (to either the insured or the beneficiary) in the event that the insured is injured or sustains damage as the result of particular stated contingencies. Basically, insurance is an arrangement for *transferring and allocating risk*. In many cases, **risk** can be described as a prediction concerning potential loss, based on known and unknown factors. However, insurance involves much more than a game of chance, and insurers have an interest in seeing that risk is minimized. Many familiar safety devices are now commonplace because of insurer concerns or insurance laws—automobile seat belts, fire escapes, train whistles, railroad-crossing lights, reflecting road signs, and break-away highway lightposts, among others.

The Concept of Risk Pooling

All types of insurance use the principle of pooling of risk; that is, they spread the risk among a large number of people—the pool—to make the premiums small compared to the coverage offered. Consider life insurance. For any particular age group, only a small number of individuals will die in any one year. If a large percentage of this age group pays premiums to a life insurance company in exchange for a benefit payment in case of premature death, there will be a sufficient amount of money to pay the beneficiaries of the policyholders who do die. Given a long enough time for correlation of data about the group and the particular disaster—in this case premature death—insurance companies can predict the total number of premature deaths in any one year with great accuracy. Thus, they can estimate the total amount they will have to pay if they insure the group, and they can predict the rates they will have to charge each member of the group in order to make the necessary payments and make a profit for the company.

Classification of Insurance

Insurance is classified according to the nature of the risk involved. For example, fire insurance, casualty insurance, life insurance, and title insurance each apply to a different type of risk. The persons and interests protected under each of these types of insurance policies differ. This is reasonable because, depending upon the nature of the activity, certain types of losses are expected, certain types are foreseeable, and certain others are unforeseeable.

Terminology

An insurance contract is called a **policy**; the consideration paid to the insurer is called a **premium**;

and the insurance company is sometimes called an **underwriter**.

Parties   The *parties* to an insurance policy are the *insurer* (the insurance company) and the *insured* (the person covered by its provisions). Insurance contracts are usually obtained through an *agent*, who ordinarily works for the insurance company, or a *broker*, who is ordinarily an independent contractor. When a broker deals with an applicant for insurance, the broker is, in effect, the applicant's agent. By contrast, an insurance agent is an agent of the insurance company. Thus, an insurance agent's relationship with the applicant for insurance is controlled by ordinary rules of agency law (see Chapter 33).

As a general rule, the insurance company is bound by the acts of its agents when they act within the agency relationship. On the other hand, a broker has no relationship with the insurance company and is an agent of the applicant for insurance. The status of agent or broker can be extremely important in determining liability. In most situations, state law determines the status of all parties writing or obtaining insurance.

Insurable Interest   A person can insure anything in which he or she has an *insurable interest*. Without this insurable interest, there is no enforceable contract, and a transaction to insure would have to be treated as a wager.

In the case of real and personal property, an insurable interest exists when the insured derives a pecuniary benefit from the preservation and continued existence of the property. That is, one has an insurable interest in property when one would sustain a pecuniary loss from its destruction. In the case of life insurance, one needs to have a reasonable expectation of benefit from the continued life of another in order to have an insurable interest in that person's life. The benefit may be pecuniary or it may be founded upon the relationship between the parties (by blood or affinity).

For example, a person has an insurable interest in his or her own health or life and in the health or life of his or her spouse. But a person cannot obtain fire insurance on the White House or auto insurance on A. J. Foyt's race cars. A mortgagor and

a mortgagee would both have an insurable interest in the mortgaged property. So would a landlord and a tenant in leased property, a secured party in the property in which he or she has an interest, a partner in partnership property, and a stockholder in corporate property.

Close family relationships give a person an insurable interest in the life of another. Generally, blood or marital relationships fit this category. A husband can take out an insurance policy on his wife and vice versa, parents can take out life insurance policies on their children, brothers and sisters on each other, and grandparents on grandchildren, as all these are close family relationships.

To further illustrate the concept of insurable interest, assume that James Jones insures his life for $100,000 with Continental Insurance Company, naming Henry Mason as beneficiary of the policy. When Jones dies, Continental Insurance cannot refuse to pay Mason merely because he had no insurable interest in the life of Jones. The *beneficiary* of a life insurance policy need not have an insurable interest in the insured. Jones was actually insuring his own life for the benefit of Mason and is the owner of the policy. Obviously, Jones has an insurable interest in his own life. On the other hand, if Jones bought a policy with Continental Insurance to insure the life of his next door neighbor, Robert Samuel, Continental Insurance could refuse to pay the face value of the policy upon Samuel's death because Jones had no insurable interest in Samuel's life.

The insurable interest in life insurance must exist *at the time the policy is obtained*. This is exactly the opposite of property insurance, where the insurable interest must exist at the time the loss occurs and not necessarily when the policy is purchased. Because of this rule involving life insurance, in most states a divorce will not affect a policy. If the divorced spouse is named as beneficiary, the divorce action will not automatically divest that spouse's right to the proceeds or to an insurable interest.

The existence of an insurable interest is a primary concern when determining liability under an insurance policy. In the following case, the insurance company claimed that the insured possessed no insurable interest in her former husband's house since she had deeded her interest to him one year before his death.

BACKGROUND AND FACTS *Linda Richmond and Eddie Durham were married, the parents of two children, and homeowners in Kentucky. When Richmond and Durham divorced, Richmond, the plaintiff, deeded her legal interest in the title to their home to Durham and moved out with their children. Shortly thereafter Durham died, leaving the two children as his only legal heirs. Richmond returned to the home with the children. She had been living there, making the mortgage payments, for more than one year when the home was totally destroyed by fire. Ten months prior to the fire, Richmond had secured fire insurance with the defendant, Motorists Mutual Insurance Company. She sought payment from Motorists for the destruction of the house, but Motorists refused to pay, claiming that she had no insurable interest in the house. The trial court awarded Linda Richmond, her children, and the mortgage company $29,000. Motorists appealed.*

MOTORISTS MUTUAL INSURANCE COMPANY v. RICHMOND

Court of Appeals of Kentucky, 1984.
676 S.W.2d 478.

CLAYTON, Judge.

*   *   *   *

*   *   * The sole question on appeal is whether the appellees had an insurable interest in the insured property at the time of issuance of the policy and the time of the loss. *   *   *

*   *   *   *

Seeking to avoid payment under the contract, Motorists would now cast Richmond as nothing more than a trespassing squatter who "surreptitiously" returned to the residence and thereafter fraudulently represented her true lack of ownership interest. Motorists would further tacitly imply that the fire was of mysterious origin by its statement that "[a]t the time of the fire she and her new husband had moved out." We cannot accept these base characterizations. They are not supported by the record or the law.

Linda Richmond, both before and after the death of her late former husband, made substantial monetary contribution to the maintenance and improvement of the destroyed residence. As natural guardian for her minor children, and later as administratrix of the Durham estate, she was obligated to provide for the care and custody of their offspring, including the duty to protect their home, of which the children became sole owners in fee simple by statute of descent upon the death of their father. KRS 391.010 Thus, when Richmond returned to the property following Durham's death she was not a surreptitious trespasser. Her offspring and she as their guardian were fully entitled to use and dominion over the premises. While not possessed of title, Richmond certainly possessed an insurable interest in the residence: first, by her status as natural guardian for the protection of her minor children's interest; and second, by her extensive pecuniary investment in the residence. *   *   *

Nor does the present record contain any suggestion of fraud or unwitting assumption of risk by Motorists. Richmond made no claim of ownership to the residence. Her only direct action with regard to the so-called "receipt" was to place her signature upon it. Motorists' own agent, Mosely, was responsible for completing the remainder of the document including the portion indicating Richmond's ownership. Had he so chosen, he could have easily verified his assumptions concerning Richmond's ownership simply by calling Farmers State Bank. It is a well settled principle of law in this state that an insurer as

> principal is bound by the acts of his agent within the scope of his apparent authority, though his authority may in fact be limited, if the person dealing with him is ignorant of the limitation upon his authority. Few persons understood insurance who have not made it a special study. The agent who comes to get the insurance

is the only person they deal with or know in the transaction. The rule that he represents the company and not the insured in taking the application is just and is generally recognized.

*   *   * Thus, the burden of any error in the nature of Richmond's insurable interest, rather than its existence, falls upon Motorists via the actions of its agent.

Motorists is further obligated to make payment by the definition provisions of its policy. Under that policy "insured" is defined as

You and the following representatives of your household:

a. your relatives

b. *any other person under the age of 21 who is in the care of any person named above.* (emphasis added by court)

At the time of issuance of the policy, Linda's children, Melody and James, were each, by statute of descent, fee simple owners of an indivisible one-half interest in the residence. As minors under the age of 15, neither child was legally capable of contracting for insurance in his or her own behalf. KRS 391.010. Therefore, absent Linda's efforts in securing insurance, neither Melody nor James could have directly protected his or her ownership interest in the home. By defining the terms of its policy so as to include the ownership interest of the children, Motorists undertook exactly the risk it bargained for and should not now be able to successfully deny payment. In this respect no liberal construction of the policy of insurance is necessary to protect the insured.*   *   *

*   *   *   *

DECISION AND REMEDY   *The court held that Linda Richmond had an insurable interest in the home for which Motorists was required to pay.*

COMMENTS   *Although the plaintiff held no legal title to the home, she held an insurable interest in the home. This case also demonstrates the agency principle upon which insurance companies and their agents operate. The agents could have checked the title to the home, but did not, and thus bound Motorists to the insurance contract.*

Key Person Insurance   Key person insurance involves an organization insuring the life of a person who is important to that organization. Because the organization expects to receive some pecuniary gain from the fact that the key person's life continues or expects to suffer a financial loss if the key person dies, the organization has an insurable interest.

Typically, a partnership will insure the life of each partner because the death of any one partner will legally dissolve the firm and cause some degree of loss to the partnership. So, too, a corporation has an insurable interest in the life expectancy of a key executive whose death would result in financial loss to the company.

Indemnity   In fire insurance policies, insurance coverage is usually an *indemnity*; that is, the insurance pays only for what is actually lost. This is usu-

ally the replacement value of the property minus any depreciation. In addition, once payment is made, the insurance company is entitled to "stand in the shoes" of the insured in pursuing any lawsuits arising from the incident. This is called the right of subrogation.

THE INSURANCE CONTRACT

An insurance contract is governed by the general principles of contract law. The application for insurance is usually attached to the policy and made a part of the insurance contract. An insurance applicant is bound by any false statements that appear in the application (subject to certain exceptions). Because the insurance company evaluates the risk factors based on the information included in the insurance application, misstatements or misrepresentations can void a policy, especially if the insurance company can show that it would not have extended insurance if it had known the facts.

Timing

The effective date of an insurance contract is important. In some instances, the insurance applicant is not protected until a formal written policy is issued. In other situations, the applicant is protected between the time the application is received and the time the insurance company either accepts or rejects it. Four facts should be kept in mind:

1. A broker is merely the agent of an applicant. Therefore, if the broker fails to procure a policy, the customer is not insured. According to general principles of agency law, if the broker fails to obtain policy coverage and the applicant is damaged as a result, then the broker is liable to the damaged applicant/principal for the loss.

2. A person who seeks insurance from an insurance company's agent will usually be protected from the moment the application is made, provided some form of premium has been paid. Between the time the application is received and either rejected or accepted, the applicant is covered (possibly subject to certain conditions, such as successfully passing a medical examination). Usually the agent will write a memorandum or **binder** indicating that a policy is pending and stating its essential terms.

3. If the parties agree that the policy will be issued and delivered at a later time, the contract is not effective until the policy is issued and delivered or sent to the applicant, depending upon the agreement. Thus, any loss sustained between the time of application and the delivery of the policy is not covered.

4. Parties can agree that a life insurance policy will be binding at the time the insured pays the first premium. The policy, however, can be *expressly contingent* upon the applicant's passing a physical examination. If the applicant pays the premium and passes the examination, then the policy coverage is continuously in effect. If the applicant pays the premium but dies before having the physical examination, then the applicant's estate must show that the applicant would have passed the examination had he or she not died.

Coverage on an insurance policy can begin when a binder is written, when the policy is issued, or, depending upon the terms of the contract, after a certain period of time has elapsed.

The following case illustrates some of these factors in determining when an insurance contract comes into effect.

BACKGROUND AND FACTS *On October 22, 1981, the partnership of Davis and Landry, Inc., the plaintiff, mailed two applications to Guaranty Income Life Insurance Co., the defendant, for $500,000 life insurance policies and a check for two years' advance premiums to insure the lives of the two principals, Davis and Landry. Pending delivery of the policy, Davis and Landry believed they received a $100,000 coverage under specific terms stated in a premium receipt. On October 27, 1981, the remainder of Davis's application package, a form entitled "Answers Made to the Medical Examiner," executed by a doctor, was received by Guaranty Income. Based on the answers given in this form, Guaranty Income decided it needed to obtain an "attending physician's statement" from the doctor. The request for this further statement was mailed to the doctor on November 2, 1981, and had not been returned by November 10, 1981, when Davis died. The partnership sued Guaranty Income to recover benefits under the insurance policy for Davis's death. The trial court granted a summary judgment for the insurance company, from which the plaintiff appealed.*

DAVIS AND LANDRY, INC. v. GUARANTY INCOME LIFE INSURANCE COMPANY
Court of Appeal of Louisiana, First Circuit, 1983.
442 So.2d 621.

SHORTESS, Judge.

*   *   *   *

An insurance company is under a duty to act upon an application for insurance within a reasonable time, and a violation of that duty with resultant damages will subject the company to liability for negligence. What is a reasonable period must depend upon the facts in each case, and the burden is on plaintiff to show that a policy would have issued but for the delay caused by the neglect of the insurer. *   *   *

*   *   * [In one previous case,] the applicant became ill and was admitted to a hospital five days after applying for a health and accident policy. The court found that the five-day delay in issuing the policy could not be construed as negligence on the part of the defendant insurer. *   *   * [Another case] involved an application for a disability coverage policy. The applicant became disabled three days after applying for the policy and paying the initial premium. The application warned that the insurance company could take as much as 60 days to approve or reject the policy. The company actually took 22 days beyond the sixty-day period in deciding to reject plaintiff's application and refund his premium. Plaintiff was notified of his nonacceptance even later, after a period of four and one-half months had elapsed from the date of the application. Because defendant's delay in rejecting the application was partially caused by plaintiff's failure to make full disclosures of his prior medical history and attending physicians, the court found that the delay was not unreasonable.

Based on the foregoing, we find that the insurer did not breach any duty when it did not inform plaintiff that the physician had not returned Davis' APS. The APS had only been in the physician's possession on the date of the applicant's death for, at most, seven working days. This is simply not an unreasonable amount of time for the insurer to allow the physician to complete and return the APS. Moreover, even if it can be said that defendant breached a duty to this plaintiff, it is clear from the deposition of Fowler, the underwriter, that the policy would not necessarily have issued even upon prompt return of the APS. The APS, as returned on November 17, showed that Davis had suffered tingling and numbness in his hands and "a vague, interior chest wall discomfort" and that Dr. Walker had referred him to a neurosurgeon, Dr. John Clifford, regarding this symptom. Fowler testified that, based upon this information, additional statements would have been required from Dr. Clifford. This testimony, though self-serving, is completely logical and would be the only reasonable action to be taken by defendant faced with that information. Using the "but for" test enunciated in *Brunt*, it would be impossible for plaintiff here to prove that the policy would have issued "but for" the negligence of defendant, because the testimony of Fowler that defendant would *not* have issued the policy is supported by a medical report justifying a genuine uncertainty as to the applicant's acceptability. Even assuming that the APS had been returned to defendant immediately upon receipt by the physician, there is no way for plaintiff to establish that the report which *would* have been requested by defendant from Dr. Clifford would have reached defendant before Davis' death. In other words, given that a report from Dr. Clifford would have been required by defendant, the amount of time it would have taken Dr. Clifford to return his report is a totally unknown and unknowable element which plaintiff would have to prove in order to show that "but for" defendant's negligence the application would have been approved.

*   *   *   *

There is no genuine issue as to the fact that the policy of insurance had not been issued on the life of Robert Davis before or on the date of his death. Plaintiff presented no policy or evidence of one issued other than the assignment of a "policy number" to Davis' application. The assignment of this number was explained in defendant's witnesses' depositions and affidavits as a mere form of registration, such number being composed of the month, day, year, and chronological sequence of the receipt of that application on that day. Such number would be used on a policy in the future should a policy be issued.

Plaintiff claims that it is entitled to a $100,000.00 coverage under the terms of the premium receipt. The receipt provides for a limited amount of coverage after the fulfillment of certain conditions, but before the delivery of the policy. The conditions are:

PARAGRAPH A

(1) Any check for which this receipt has been issued must be honored on first presentation.

(2) The amount paid equals or exceeds the monthly premium for the policy applied for and is paid at the time of application.

(3) Each person to be insured must be acceptable to the company (after investigation and medical examination, if required) under its underwriting rules, limits and standards for the plan and amount applied for, without modification, at the Company's standard rates.

PARAGRAPH B

If the above conditions have been fulfilled and the Company actually approves this application, until the policy applied for is actually delivered, the amount of insurance, including accidental death benefits, which may become effective under this receipt, shall not exceed the amount of insurance applied for or $100,000 whichever is smaller.

Paragraph A, conditions (1) and (2), were fulfilled by plaintiff. Condition (3) was not fulfilled at any point before Davis' death. Plaintiff contends that the information eventually received from Dr. Clifford established that Davis had merely a minor nerve problem which caused his tingling and numbness and chest discomfort. According to plaintiff, this establishes that Davis was at the time of his death "acceptable" to the company. However, plaintiff neglects to read the entire text of the condition. It requires that the person be acceptable after an investigation and medical examination, if required under its underwriting rules.

Defendant was involved in investigating Davis' medical record, pursuant to the decision of its underwriter (Fowler) and the requirements of its underwriting rules, up until and including the date of Davis' death. Therefore, he could not have been acceptable *after* investigation because an investigation was taking place when he died. Furthermore, Section B adds a fourth requirement that the company "actually approves" the application in order for the receipt coverage to become effective. The fact that the company was still conducting an investigation of Davis' health negates any possibility that it had actually approved his application. Its approval of the application of the other principal of plaintiff, Landry, and issuance of a policy on his life on the date of Davis' death, have no bearing on its actions regarding Davis' application. We therefore find that no policy had been issued and that the receipt coverage was not in effect due to nonfulfillment of all the conditions contained in the receipt.

Based on the foregoing, we find that there is no genuine issue of material fact and that defendant is entitled to a judgment as a matter of law. *   *   *

The appellate court affirmed the lower court's grant of summary judgment for the defendant insurance company.

DECISION AND REMEDY

This case illustrates the predicament of the "hopefully insured" waiting for the insurance application to be approved. The courts have granted insurance companies a "reasonable time" to act upon an application. What is a "reasonable time" depends upon the facts of each case. The premium receipt proved to be inadequate in protecting the plaintiff, so the plaintiff was left waiting without any coverage at all.

COMMENTS

Interpreting Provisions of an Insurance Contract

The courts are increasingly cognizant of the fact that most people do not have the special training that is necessary to understand the intricate terminology used in insurance policies. The words used in an insurance contract have their ordinary meaning and are interpreted in light of the nature of the coverage involved. Where there is an ambiguity in the policy, the provision is interpreted against the insurance company. When it is unclear whether an insurance contract actually exists because the written policy has not been delivered, the uncertainty will be determined against the insurance company. The court will presume that the policy is in effect unless the company can show otherwise.

The following case illustrates the problem of interpretation.

ROY v. ALLSTATE INS. CO.

Superior Court of Connecticut, Appellate Session, 1978. 34 Conn.Sup. 650, 383 A.2d 637.

BACKGROUND AND FACTS *Roy (the plaintiff) was covered by an accidental death and dismemberment policy with Allstate Insurance Co., the defendant, that provided full coverage in the event of "total and irrecoverable loss of entire sight of an eye." The plaintiff was in an accident and had a traumatic cataract surgically removed from his eye. After surgery, the plaintiff was fitted with a contact lens in his right eye. He had some amount of vision with the contact lens but could not tolerate wearing it. In effect, his eye was of little functional value, and there was no medical assurance that his eyesight could ever be regained. The insurance company denied coverage under the policy.*

ARMENTANO, Judge.

*   *   *   *

"[A]n insurance policy is a contract to be interpreted and enforced in accordance with the real intent of the parties. The language used in the policy must be given its ordinary meaning unless some special or technical meaning is intended." In considering the meaning of the phrase "irrecoverable loss of sight," we must ascertain the meaning of the contract which the insured would reasonably expect and consider the intent of the insured in procuring the insurance.

It has been held generally that policies which insure against the total and irrecoverable loss of entire sight protect the insured against the irrecoverable loss of the practical use of sight. *   *   * Recently, the word "irrecoverable," as used in an insurance contract similar to the one in this case, was defined to mean "not able to regain [put back to a former state, or recapture]." Therefore, we hold that an insured should recover under this kind of insurance contract if, within the [one year] period of time limited by the policy, he has, owing to an accident, lost the practical use of an eye which he will never be able to regain or recapture.

*   *   * [The Court then applied its definition of irrecoverable to this case.] Two doctors who examined the plaintiff concluded that he had sustained a permanent disability and that his right eye was of little functional value without the use of the contact lens. Without the contact lens which the plaintiff first started to wear in April or May, 1974, he had no vision in his right eye. The longest period of time during which the plaintiff could wear the contact lens in any given day in April or May, 1974, was four hours. Sometime after May 22, 1974, he stopped wearing the contact lens because he was unable to get used to it.

*   *   * In any event a continuous loss of functional use of the eye came about when the plaintiff concluded some time later, for reasons which are not challenged, that he could no longer wear the contact lens and stopped using it *   *   *. [T]he plaintiff could not continue to use the lens and *   *   * his loss of sight, which he previously may have thought could be regained by use of the lens, was never actually recoverable because of his inability to wear the lens. *   *   *

It is clear that the average man purchasing a policy similar to the one in this case would reasonably expect to be insured for an injury to his eye of the type involved in this case where, within the [one year] period of coverage, vision could be restored only to the limited extent that it was restored here. * * *

The trial court was judged correct in permitting the plaintiff to recover insurance benefits under the policy.

DECISION AND REMEDY

Cancellation of Insurance Policies

Under most state laws, once the initial premium on a policy has been paid, the policy does not automatically lapse if the next premium is not paid on the due date. Most policies allow a **grace period** of thirty or thirty-one days.

Moreover, a default in the payment of a life insurance premium may require the insurer to issue a paid-up policy in a smaller amount than originally contracted for, to provide extended insurance for a period of time, or to pay the cash surrender value of the policy. These are alternatives to cancellation. When the insurance contract expressly declares that the insurance company cannot cancel the policy, these alternatives are important.

When the insurance company can cancel the policy, contract provisions or state statutes usually require that the insurer give advance written notice of cancellation.

Cancellation can occur for varying reasons depending on the type of insurance. For example, in California, auto insurance can be cancelled for nonpayment of premiums or a suspension of the insured's driver's license. Property insurance, on the other hand, can be cancelled for many reasons, including non-payment of premiums, conviction of the insured of a crime that increases the hazard insured against, fraud or misrepresentation, gross negligence committed by the insured that increases the hazard insured against, or physical changes in property that result in it being uninsurable.

An insurer cannot normally cancel a policy (or refuse to write a renewal policy) because of the national origin or the race of an applicant. Moreover, an insurance company cannot cancel a policy in order to penalize an insured who has just appeared as a witness in a case against the company.

Defenses Against Payment to the Insured

An insurance company can raise any of the defenses that would be valid in any ordinary action on a contract and some defenses that do not apply in ordinary contract actions. If the insurance company can show that the policy was procured by fraud, misrepresentation, or violation of warranties, it may have a valid defense for not paying on a claim. (The insurance company may also have the right to disaffirm or rescind an insurance contract.) Improper actions, such as those that are against public policy or that are otherwise illegal, can give the insurance company a defense against the payment of a claim or allow it to rescind the contract.

The following case involved the issue of liability for fire damage resulting from the actions of one of the insured persons under a contract of insurance. Because the insured individuals were married, the company claimed that the wrongful act of one spouse was attributable to the other, thereby preventing either from recovering fire insurance proceeds.

BACKGROUND AND FACTS *The plaintiffs sued on an insurance policy issued by the defendant, the Insurance Company of North America (INA), for fire damage to their home. The lower court denied the plaintiffs' recovery. The plaintiffs were a husband and wife who owned the property as tenants in the entirety and who were insured under an INA policy. It was undisputed that*

STEIGLER v. INS. CO. OF NORTH AMERICA
Supreme Court of Delaware, 1977.
384 A.2d 398.

the husband deliberately set fire to the house, that his actions constituted fraud under the terms of the policy, and that the policy was void and he could not recover under it. It was equally undisputed that the wife was not involved in any way in the act. The wife claimed that she was not barred from recovering under the policy since she was an innocent co-tenant and that she was entitled to her pro rata share of the fire insurance proceeds.

DUFFY, Justice.
*   *   *   *

As we have noted, the policy contained a standard fraud provision rendering the policy void "in case of any fraud *   *   * by the *insured* relating thereto" (emphasis added); and the policy insured two persons: "Herbert F. Steigler and Arlene R. Steigler."

The [first] critical question, of course, relates to the meaning of the word "insured" in the fraud provision. Does it mean one or both of the Steiglers? The answer is by no means clear because the word "insured" is singular while two persons are named as the "insured," i.e., Herbert F. Steigler and Arlene R. Steigler. Thus, construction of the term is required.

In resolving the ambiguity in the Steigler-INA contract we refer to two rules of construction. First, where ambiguous, the language of an insurance contract is always construed most strongly against the insurance company which has drafted it.

Second, "an insurance contract should be read to accord with the reasonable expectations of the purchaser so far as the language will permit."

Applying these principles, we hold that an "ordinary person owning an undivided interest in property, not versed in the nice distinctions of insurance law, would naturally suppose that his individual interest in the property was covered by a policy which named him without qualification as one of the persons insured."

In our judgment *   *   * Mrs. Steigler had an interest in the property, the policy named her without qualification as one of the persons insured and she should not be barred from recovering under the policy by the fraud of the other co-tenant.

INA contends that because the Steiglers are married the arson of the husband bars recovery by his wife. The theory is that the contract terms govern any claim, the contract is voided by fraud, and that husband and wife are one person, i.e., together and inseparably they hold the entire estate.

We are not persuaded that the "oneness" theory which is, to say the least, somewhat "quaint" in this day and age, should override the other principles at stake here. When two persons own property as tenants in common, it is generally recognized, as INA concedes, that the interests may be separable and, therefore, an innocent tenant in common can recover a *pro rata* [proportionate] share of fire insurance proceeds. Thus, for example, had the Steiglers owned the property and the policy as "co-habitants" rather than as spouses, the general rule would have permitted rather than have barred her recovery. Without pausing to explore the equal protection problems which such a result might raise, we conclude that barring a wife from recovering because she is a wife would be contrary to the public policy clearly mandated by the Married Women's Act.

DECISION AND REMEDY   *The lower court's ruling was reversed. The wife was entitled to half the insurance policy proceeds for the fire damage. The case was remanded to the trial court's jurisdiction under instruction to enter a ruling in the wife's favor and award her half the insurance proceeds.*

Rebuttal of the Defenses of the Insurance Company

There are certain ways in which the insurance company can be prevented from asserting some defenses that are normally available. State statutes and case law provide for such estoppel.

For example, if a company tells an insured that information requested on a form is optional, and the insured provides it anyway, the company cannot use the information to avoid its contractual obligation under the insurance contract. In the life insurance field, certain clauses become incontestable after a stated period of time. For example, statements as to the age of the insured, even though incorrect, normally do not allow the insurance company to escape payment upon the death of the insured. Typically, the time period after which estoppel for such defenses occurs is two years. Incontestable clauses will be discussed later in this chapter.

TYPES OF INSURANCE

Three general types of insurance coverage held by an individual will be covered here:

1. Life insurance.
2. Fire and homeowner's insurance.
3. Automobile insurance.

These will be discussed in detail with special emphasis on life and fire insurance policies in regard to the law.

Life Insurance

There are four basic types of life insurance:

1. **Whole life**, sometimes referred to as straight life, ordinary life, or cash value insurance. This type of insurance provides protection with a cumulated cash surrender value that can be used as collateral for a loan. Premiums are paid by the insured during the insured's entire lifetime, with a fixed payment to the beneficiary upon death.
2. **Limited payment life**, such as a twenty-payment life policy. Premiums are paid for a stated number of years, after which the policy is paid up and fully effective during the insured's life. Naturally, pre-

miums are higher than for whole life. This insurance does have a cash surrender value.

3. **Term** insurance, providing for a fixed premium for a specified term. Payment on the policy is due only if death occurs within the term period. Premiums are less expensive than for whole life or limited payment life, and there is usually no cash surrender value. Frequently, this type of insurance can be converted to another type of life insurance.
4. **Endowment** insurance, providing for fixed premium payments for a definite term. At the end of the term a fixed amount is to be paid to the insured or, upon the death of the insured during the specified period, to a beneficiary. This type of insurance represents both a term insurance and a form of annuity or savings. It has a rapidly increasing cash surrender value, but premiums are high, as payment is required at the end of the term even if the insured is still living.

Because term and whole life insurance are the most common forms of life insurance, each will be discussed further here.

Term Insurance   There are three basic types of term insurance:

1. Level.
2. Decreasing.
3. Mortgage.

The premiums vary in cost according to the protection afforded. A person whose current income is low but who expects a higher income in the future can afford a greater amount of term insurance than of whole life insurance by choosing level term insurance, since in level term insurance, premium increases come in later years. Alternatively, the insured can keep the premiums at the same level but receive decreasing protection over the years (decreasing term insurance).

Level Term   Premiums for level term insurance commonly increase at the end of each term, such as every five years, if the insured wishes to keep the same face value on the insurance policy. The increased premium reflects the rising probability of death as age increases.

Decreasing Term   Decreasing term insurance has a level premium but a decreasing face value. It is desirable when a person needs maximum protection early in life, with a relatively low premium, but anticipates that the need for this protection will decrease with changes in family and financial accumulations.

For example, a young person with minor children may want a substantial amount of term insurance to protect these children should he or she die while they are still young. After the children have grown into adulthood and are on their own, however, the need for protection will be substantially decreased. Decreasing term insurance is desirable for a person in this situation.

Mortgage Term   Mortgage term insurance, or home protection insurance, declines in face value by an amount equal to the mortgage left to be paid. The idea is that if the insured dies, the home can be paid off with the proceeds. A mortgage term insurance policy decreases in uneven dollar amounts. (This type of insurance can insure other types of consumer debt also.)

Whole Life Insurance   Whole life insurance premiums generally remain at the same level throughout the life of a policy, unless it is a mutual life insurance policy in which dividends are received from the insurer which are then applied to reduce the actual premium level. As a result, the policyholder pays more than is necessary to cover the insurance company's risk in the early years and less than is necessary to cover the company's risk in later years. Compared with term insurance, whole life is relatively more costly because it is a form of financial investment as well as insurance protection. The investment feature of the policy is known as its cash value.

Living Benefits   Living benefits of a whole life policy include converting it into some sort of lump sum payment or stream of retirement income. When the insured reaches retirement age, premium payments on whole life can be discontinued and one of the following living benefit programs can be started:

1.   Protection for the rest of the insured's life but at a lower face value.

2.   Full protection but for a definite number of years in the future (extended term insurance).
3.   A cash settlement that returns whatever savings and dividends have not been used to pay off the insurance company for excessive costs incurred for the particular age group of the insured (the cash surrender fund).
4.   Conversion of a whole life policy into an annuity whereby the insured receives a specified amount of income each year for a certain number of years or for the rest of the insured's life.

Death Benefits   In most life insurance policies, the insured specifies a beneficiary, who receives the death benefits of that policy. If Ken Kerr buys a $10,000 ordinary life policy and does not borrow any money on it, his beneficiary will receive $10,000 plus any paid up accumulations when he dies. However, there are certain options for settling a life insurance policy. The first plan involves a lump sum payment. In the second plan, the face value of the insurance policy is retained by the insurance company, but a small interest payment is made to the beneficiary for a certain number of years or for life. At the end of the specified period, the principal (face value) is then paid according to the terms in the contract. In the third plan, the face value is paid to the beneficiary in the form of annual, semiannual, quarterly, or monthly installments. The company makes regular payments of equal amounts until the fund is depleted. The insurance company guarantees a specific number of payments or payments that will total the face value of the policy. If, however, the beneficiary dies before the guaranteed payments have been made, the remainder goes to the estate of the beneficiary or as otherwise directed in the contract. This is sometimes called an annuity plan.

Special Features and Provisions of Life Insurance   The rights and liabilities of the parties in life insurance are basically dependent upon the insurance contract. There are a few features that deserve additional attention, and they will be discussed below.

Liability   The insurance contract determines not only the extent of the insurer's liability but generally when the insurer is liable upon the death of the insured. Most life insurance contracts exclude liability of the insurer if the death of the insured is caused by one or more of the following: suicide, military action during war, execution by a state or federal government, or even while a passenger in a commercial vehicle. In the absence of exclusion, most courts today construe any cause of death to be one of the insurer's risks.

Incontestable Clause   Generally, life insurance contracts contain an incontestable clause which provides that after the expiration of a specified period, the policy cannot be avoided by the insurer due to errors (misstatements) and the like made by the insured. The specified period is usually two years and covers most defenses which would allow the insurer to cancel the policy. The incontestable clause, however, does not include nonpayment of premiums, failure to file proof of death within a required period, lack of insurable interest, and risks expressly excluded by the policy itself.

Adjustment Due to Misstatement of Age   The insurance policy constitutes the agreement between the parties. The application for insurance is part of the policy and is usually attached to the policy. When the insured misstates his or her age in the application, an error takes place particularly as to the amount of premiums paid. Misstatement of age is not a sufficient material error to allow the insurer to void the policy. Instead, upon discovery of the error the insurer will adjust the premium payments and/or benefits accordingly.

Assignment   Most life insurance policies permit the insured to change beneficiaries. Where this is the case, in the absence of any prohibition or notice requirement, the insured has a right to assign the life insurance contract without consent of the insurer or the beneficiary. If the beneficiary right is vested (insured cannot change), the contract cannot be assigned without the consent of the beneficiary. The vast majority of life insurance contracts permit assignment and only require notice to the insurer to be effective on the insurer.

Creditors' Rights   Unless exempt under state law, judgment creditors can resort to the life insured's interest as an asset. These creditors generally can reach insurance proceeds payable to the insured's estate, proceeds payable to anyone if the payment of premiums constituted a fraud on creditors, and any proceeds payable to a named beneficiary if the insured has reserved the right to change beneficiaries. However, creditors cannot compel the insured to make available the cash surrender value of the policy or to change the named beneficiary to that of the creditor. Almost all states exempt at least a part of the proceeds of life insurance from creditors' claims.

Termination   Although the insured can cancel and terminate the policy, the insurer cannot do so. Therefore, termination usually takes place only upon the occurrence of the following:

1.   Default in premium payments causing the policy to lapse (no cash surrender value to purchase paid-up insurance remains).
2.   Death and payment of benefits.
3.   Expiration of term of policy.
4.   Cancellation by the insured.

Fire and Homeowner's Insurance

There are basically two types of insurance policies for a home—standard fire insurance policies and homeowner's policies.

Standard Fire Insurance Policies   The standard fire insurance policy protects the homeowner against fire and lightning as well as damage from smoke and water caused by the fire or the fire department. Paying slightly more will extend the coverage to damage caused by hail, windstorms, explosions, and so on. Personal theft and a comprehensive liability policy can also be added.

Most fire insurance policies are classified according to what type of property is covered and to what extent (amount) the issuer is liable. The following are typical:

1.   **Blanket policy.**   This policy covers a class of property rather than specific property, since the property is anticipated to shift or vary in nature. A policy covering the inventory of a business is an example.
2.   **Specific policy.**   This policy covers a specific item of property at a specific location. An example

would be a particular painting located in a residence or a piece of machinery located in a factory or business.

3. **Floater policy.** This policy usually supplements a specific policy. It is intended to cover property that may change in either location or quantity. To illustrate, if the painting mentioned in the preceding example were to be exhibited during the year at numerous locations throughout the state, a floater policy would be desirable.

4. **Valued policy.** This policy is one in which, by agreement, a specific value is placed on the subject to be insured to cover the eventuality of its total loss.

5. **Open policy.** This policy is one in which the value of the property insured is not agreed upon. The policy usually provides for a maximum liability of the insurer, but payment for loss is restricted to fair market value of the property at time of loss or to the maximum limit, whichever is less.

Special Features and Provisions of Fire Insurance As with life insurance, certain features and provisions of fire insurance deserve special mention. In reading the following, it is important to note some basic differences in the treatment of life and fire policies.

Liability As with all forms of insurance, the insurer's liability is determined from the terms of the policy. However, most policies limit recovery only to *hostile* fires and loss resulting therefrom due to smoke, water, and the like. A hostile fire is basically one that breaks out or begins in a place where the fire was not intended to burn. A *friendly* fire is not covered. A friendly fire is one burning in a place where such was intended to burn. Therefore, smoke from a fireplace would not be covered, but smoke due to a fire caused by a defective electrical outlet would. Sometimes an owner will add "extended coverage" to the fire policy to cover losses from friendly fires.

If the policy is a valued policy and the subject matter is completely destroyed, the insurer is liable for the amount specified in the policy. If it is an open policy, then the extent of actual loss must be determined, and the insurer is liable only for the amount of the loss or for the maximum amount specified in the policy, whichever is less. For partial losses, actual loss must always be determined, and

the insurer's liability is limited to that amount. Most insurance policies permit the insurer either to restore or replace the property so destroyed, or to monetarily pay for the loss.

Coinsurance Owners of property often insure their property for less than its full value. Part of the reason for this is that most fires do not result in a total loss. To encourage owners to insure their property to as close to full value as possible, coinsurance clauses are frequently placed in fire insurance policies. Coinsurance clauses provide that if the owner insures his or her property up to a given percentage (usually 80 percent) of the property's actual value, the owner can recover up to the full amount provided for in the policy. If the owner insures for less than this percentage, the owner must bear proportionately the loss. The formula for recovery is thus:

$$\frac{\text{Amount of insurance (Policy)}}{80\% \text{ of actual value of property at time of loss}}$$
$$\times \text{ Actual loss } = \text{ Recovery by owner}$$

To illustrate, Perez has a fire which causes $2,500 worth of damage to the roof of the house. The replacement value or actual value of the house at the time of the loss is $50,000, and Perez has fire insurance coverage of $30,000. The recovery for Perez from the insurance coverage is determined as follows:

$$\frac{\$30,000 \text{ (policy)}}{\$40,000 - 80\% \text{ value of house}}$$
$$\times \$2,500 \text{ (actual loss) } = \$1,875 \text{ recovery}$$

Had Perez increased the insurance to $40,000, Perez would receive the full $2,500 loss.

Coinsurance clauses are only applicable to partial losses (not total losses). Coinsurance clauses are found in most homeowners' policies and are implied in marine insurance policies.

Pro Rata Clause On occasion, an owner of property insures the property with more than one insurance carrier. Frequently, a fire insurance policy will include a pro rata clause which requires any loss to be proportionately shared by all carriers. Proportionate means that, by percentage, each carrier insures the property to its total amount of coverage.

To illustrate, Jane has two insurance policies covering her home. One policy with Ajax is for $50,000 and another policy with Beta is for $25,000. Jane suffers a $6,000 loss that is fully covered. If the policies have pro rata clauses, Ajax would be required to pay Jane $4,000 ($50,000/$75,000 × $6,000) and Beta $2,000 ($25,000/$75,000 × $6,000).

Proof of Loss   Fire insurance policies require the insured to file with the insurer a proof of loss as a condition for recovery within a specified period or immediately (reasonable time). Failure to comply *could* allow the insurance carrier to avoid liability. Courts vary somewhat on the enforcement of such clauses. To avoid this becoming a legal issue, the insured should always report a loss immediately to the insurer and file the proper statements covering the loss.

Occupancy Clause   Most standard policies require occupancy of the premises at the time of loss. Therefore, a clause is inserted that if the premises become vacant or unoccupied for a given period, unless consent by insurer is given, the coverage is suspended until the premises are reoccupied. Persons going on extended vacations should check their policies on this matter.

Assignment   Fire insurance policies are not assignable without the consent of the insurer. The theory is that the fire insurance policy is a personal contract between the insured and the insurer. After a loss has occurred, any recovery entitlement is freely assignable without the consent of the insured. The nonassignability of the policy is extremely important in the purchase of a house. The purchaser must procure his or her own insurance. If the purchaser is assuming the remaining insurance coverage period of the seller, consent of the insurer is essential.

To illustrate, Ann is selling her home and lot to Sam. Ann has a one-year fire policy with Ajax Insurance Company, with six months remaining at date of closing the sale. Ann agrees to assign the balance of her policy, but Ajax has not given its consent. One day after passage of the deed, a fire totally destroys the house. Can Sam recover from Ajax?

The answer is no, as the policy is actually voided upon the closing of the transaction and deeding the property. The reason the policy is voided is that Ann no longer has an insurable interest at the time of loss, and Sam has no rights in a nonassignable policy.

Cancellation   Generally, either the insured or the insurer can cancel a fire insurance policy by giving the other notice. Notice usually must be given five days (or more) before cancellation is effective.

Homeowners' Policies   A homeowners' policy provides protection against a number of risks under a single policy, allowing the policyholder to save over the cost of buying each protection separately. In addition to a standard fire policy, liability coverage is also available.

There are basically two types of homeowner's policy coverage:

1.   *Property coverage* includes garage, house, and other private buildings on the policyholder's lot. It also includes the personal possessions and property of the policyholder at home, in traveling, or at work. It pays additional living expenses for living away from home because of a fire or some other covered peril.
2.   *Liability coverage* is for personal liability in case someone is injured on the insured's property, the insured damages someone else's property, or the insured injures someone else who is not in an automobile. It generally does not cover liability for professional malpractice.

Similar to liability coverage is coverage for medical payments for injury to others who are on the policyholder's property and for the property of others that is damaged by a member of the policyholder's family.

Forms of Homeowners' Policies   There are basically five forms of homeowners' and condominium owners' policies. Exhibit 55–1 describes each type. The basic form covers eleven perils, or risks; the broad form covers eighteen, and the comprehensive form covers those eighteen and all others.

Homeowners are not the only ones who take out insurance policies to cover losses. There is also renter's insurance, called "residence contents broad form" (HO-4). It covers personal possessions against the eighteen perils described in Exhibit 55–1. It also

EXHIBIT 55–1   Guide To Package Policies For Homeowners

These are the principal features of standard types of homeowners' insurance policies.

The amount of insurance provided for specific categories, such as personal property and comprehensive personal liability, can usually be increased by paying an additional premium.

The special limits of liability refer to the maximum amounts the policy will pay for the types of property listed in the notes. Usually, jewelry, furs, boats and other items subject to special limits have to be insured separately to obtain greater coverage. Adapted from New Jersey Insurance Department, *A Shopper's Guide to Homeowners Insurance, 1977.*

	Basic Form Homeowners HO-1	Broad Form Homeowners HO-2	Special Form Homeowners HO-3	Comprehensive Form Homeowners HO-5	(For Condominium Owners) HO-6
Perils Covered (see key)	Perils 1–11	Perils 1–18	Perils 1–18 on personal property except glass breakage; all risks, except those specifically excluded, on buildings	All risks except those specifically excluded	Perils 1–18 except glass breakage
Standard Amount of Insurance on: House, attached structures	Based on property value; minimum $8,000	Based on property value; minimum $8,000	Based on property value; minimum $8,000	Based on property value; minimum $15,000	$1,000 on owner's additions and alterations to unit
Detached structures	10% of amount of insurance on house	10% of amount of insurance on house	10% of amount of insurance on house	10% of amount of insurance on house	no coverage
Trees, shrubs, and plants	5% of amount of insurance on house; $250 maximum per item	5% of amount of insurance on house; $250 maximum per item	5% of amount of insurance on house; $250 maximum per item	5% of amount of insurance on house; $250 maximum per item	10% of personal property insurance; $250 maximum per item
Personal property on premises	50% of insurance on house	50% of insurance on house	50% of insurance on house	50% of insurance on house	Based on value of property; minimum $4,000
Personal property away from premises	10% of personal property insurance (minimum $1,000)	10% of personal property insurance (minimum $1,000)	10% of personal property insurance (minimum $1,000)	50% of insurance on house	10% of personal property insurance (minimum $1,000)
Additional living expense	10% of insurance on house	20% of insurance on house	20% of insurance on house	20% of insurance on house	40% of personal property insurance

---

EXHIBIT 55–1 Continued

Special Limits of Liability*	Standard	Standard	Standard	Standard	Standard

KEY TO PERILS COVERED:

1. fire, lightning
2. damage to property removed from premises endangered by fire
3. windstorm, hail
4. explosion
5. riots
6. damage by aircraft
7. damage by vehicles not owned or operated by people covered by policy
8. damage from smoke
9. vandalism, malicious mischief
10. glass breakage
11. theft

12. falling objects
13. weight of ice, snow, sleet
14. collapse of building or any part of building
15. bursting, cracking, burning, or bulging of a steam or hot water heating system, or of appliances for heating water
16. leakage or overflow of water or steam from a plumbing, heating or air-conditioning system
17. freezing of plumbing, heating and air-conditioning systems and domestic appliances
18. injury to electrical appliances, devices, fixtures and wiring (excluding tubes, transistors and similar electronic components) from short circuits or other accidentally generated currents

*Special limits of liability: Money, bullion, numismatic property, bank notes-$100; securities, bills, deeds, tickets, etc.-$500; manuscripts-$1,000; jewelry, furs-$500 for theft; boats, including trailers and equipment-$500; trailers-$500.

---

includes additional living expenses and liability coverage.

Adding a Personal Articles or Effects Floater Policy An insured may wish to pay a slightly higher premium to insure specific personal articles—for example, cameras, musical instruments, works of art, jewelry, and other valuables. This is accomplished by adding a personal articles floater to a homeowner's policy. The insured submits a list of the things to be covered and some affidavits giving their current market value. Insuring under a floater provides all-risk insurance, and the covered property can therefore be omitted from fire and theft policies.

A personal effects floater policy covers personal items when traveling. In most cases, it is not necessary because a regular homeowner's policy provides sufficient coverage. This floater covers the articles only when they are taken off the insured's property. It does not cover theft from an unattended automobile unless there is evidence of forced entry, and even then, the company's liability is generally limited to 10 percent of the amount of insurance and to not more than $250 for all property in any one loss. This restriction in the policy can be removed by paying an additional premium.

Automobile Insurance

There are basically two kinds of automobile insurance: liability insurance and collision and comprehensive insurance.

Liability Insurance One kind of automobile insurance covers bodily injury and property damage liability. Liability limits are usually described by a series of three numbers, such as 25/50/5. This means that the policy will pay a maximum of $25,000 for bodily injury to one person, $50,000 to more than one person, and a maximum of $5,000 for property damage in one accident. Most insurance companies offer liability up to $300,000 and sometimes $500,000.

Individuals who are dissatisfied with the maximum liability limits offered by regular automobile insurance coverage can purchase a separate amount of coverage under an *umbrella* policy. Umbrella limits sometimes go as high as $5 million. They also cover personal liability in excess of homeowner's liability limits.

Collision and Comprehensive Insurance Another kind of automobile insurance covers damage to the insured's car in any type of collision. Usually, it is not advisable to purchase full collision coverage (otherwise known as zero deductible). The price per year is quite high because it is likely that small but costly repair jobs will be required each year. Most people prefer to take out $50 or $100 deductible coverage, which costs about one-fourth the price of zero deductible coverage.

Comprehensive insurance covers loss, damage, and destruction by fire, hurricane, hail, vandalism, and theft. It can be obtained separately from collision insurance.

Other Automobile Insurance   Other types of automobile insurance coverage include the following:

1.   *Uninsured motorist coverage.* Uninsured mo-

torist coverage insures the driver and passengers against injury caused by any driver without insurance or by a hit-and-run driver. Certain states require that it be included in all insurance policies sold to drivers.

2.   *Accidental death benefits.* Sometimes called double indemnity, accidental death benefits provide a lump sum to named beneficiaries if the policyholder dies in an automobile accident. It generally costs very little, but it may not be necessary if the insured has a sufficient amount of life insurance.

3.   *Medical payment coverage.* Medical payments provided for in an auto insurance policy cover hospital and other medical bills and sometimes funeral expenses. This type of insurance protects all the passengers in the insured's car when the insured is driving.

QUESTIONS AND CASE PROBLEMS

1. Ann owns a house and has an elderly third cousin living with her. Ann decides she needs fire insurance on the house and a life insurance policy on her third cousin to cover any funeral and other expenses should her cousin die. Ann takes out a fire insurance policy from Ajax Insurance Company and a $10,000 life insurance policy from Beta Insurance Company on her third cousin. Six months later, Ann sells the house to John and transfers title to him. Ann and her cousin move into an apartment. With two months remaining on the Ajax policy, a fire totally destroys the house; at the same time, Ann's third cousin dies. Both insurance companies tender back premiums but claim they have no liability under the insurance contracts, as Ann did not have an insurable interest. Discuss their claims.

2. John contracts with an Ajax Insurance Company agent for a $50,000 ordinary life insurance policy. The application form is filled in to show that John's age is thirty-two. In addition, the application form asks whether John has ever had any heart ailments or problems. John answers no, forgetting that as a young child he had been diagnosed as having a slight heart murmur. A policy is issued. Three years later John becomes seriously ill. A review of the policy discloses that John was actually thirty-three at the time of application and issuance of the policy and that he erred in answering the question about a history of heart ailments. Discuss whether Ajax can void the policy and escape liability upon John's death.

3. Ann has an ordinary life insurance policy on her life and a fire insurance policy on her house. Both policies have been in force for a number of years. Ann's life insurance names her son, Rory, as beneficiary. Ann has specifically removed her right to change beneficiaries, and the life policy is silent on right of assignment. Ann is going on a one-year European vacation and borrows money from Leonard to finance the trip. Leonard takes an assignment of the life insurance policy as security for the loan, as the policy has accumulated a substantial cash surrender value. Ann also rents out her house to Leonard and assigns to him her fire insurance policy. Discuss fully whether Ann's assignment of these policies is valid.

4. Frank has an open fire insurance policy on his home for a maximum liability of $60,000. The policy has a number of standard clauses, including the right of the insurer to restore or rebuild the property in lieu of a monetary payment, and it has a standard coinsurance clause. A fire in Frank's house virtually destroys a utility room and part of the kitchen. The fire was caused by an electric water heater overheating. The total damage to the property is $10,000. The property at the time of loss is valued at $100,000. Frank files a proof of loss claim for $10,000. Discuss the insurer's liability in this situation.

5. Lori has a large house. She secures two fire insurance open value policies on the house. Her policy with the Ajax Insurance Company is for a maximum of $100,000, and her policy with Beta Insurance Company is for a maximum of $50,000. Each insurance policy contains a pro rata clause. Lori's house burns to the ground. The value of the house at the time of the loss is $120,000. Discuss the liability of Ajax and Beta to Lori.

6. Thompson contracted with Occidental Life Insurance Company of California for an insurance policy on

his life. The beneficiary of the policy was his wife. Before Occidental issued the policy to Thompson, Thompson filled out an application in which he was asked several questions regarding his health. One of the questions was whether Thompson had ever had pressure in his chest. Another was whether he had any disorder with his blood or blood vessels. Thompson entered negative answers to each of these questions since, earlier that morning, one of Occidental's physicians had asked him about these conditions. At that time, he had explained to the physician that two months earlier he had been treated for phlebitis (vein inflammation) and, at about the same time, had experienced minor chest pains. Thompson died in an accident shortly thereafter, and Occidental refused to pay on this life insurance policy, claiming that Thompson misrepresented facts on the application. Under these circumstances, is Thompson's wife entitled to Thompson's life insurance benefits? [Thompson v. Occidental Life Ins. Co., 109 Cal.Rptr. 473, 513 P.2d 353 (1973)]

7. Donald R. Noah was the beneficiary of three life insurance policies that insured the life of William L. Noah, Donald's brother. The insurer was Mutual Savings Life Insurance Company. While the policies were in force, William Noah drowned in Galveston, Texas. Mutual Savings Life refused to pay Donald Noah on the ground that he did not have an insurable interest in his brother's life. Donald Noah sued the company. Is Donald Noah entitled to collect under the policies? Would the answer be the same if William Noah had been Donald's cousin? What if he had been Donald's nephew? [Mutual Sav. Life Ins. Co. v. Noah, 291 Ala. 444, 282 So.2d 271 (1973)]

8. In June 1961, Groban contracted to purchase an inventory of Caterpillar tractor parts from SLDC. Before that purchase was concluded, Groban contracted to resell the inventory to Union. At Union's request, Groban agreed to obtain marine war risk insurance on the shipment at Union's expense. Groban subsequently purchased two contracts of insurance, one naming itself as beneficiary and the second naming Union as beneficiary. The goods were destroyed during shipment. If Groban attempts to recover under the insurance policy, will it have an insurable interest? If Union attempts to recover, will it have an insurable interest? [Groban v. S. S. Pegu, 331 F.Supp. 883 (S.D.N.Y. 1971)]

9. Claude and Mildred owned their home in Lexington and had a fire insurance policy on the home. Claude and Mildred contracted with Benjamin to build a new home for them in exchange for cash and transfer of their present home. After conveying the home to Benjamin, Claude and Mildred continued living there and paid both rent and the insurance premium. The fire insurance policy was never assigned to Benjamin. While Claude and Mildred were still living in their old home a fire occurred. The insurance company would not pay because they claimed Claude and Mildred had no insurable interest in the property at the time of the loss. Discuss *fully* how a court will rule? [O'Donnell v. MFA Insurance Company, 671 S.W.2d 302, (Mo.Ct.App., W.D. 1984)]

10. The insured brought an action to recover losses in excess of $100,000 sustained because of employee theft. The thefts occurred during the terms of two different policies but were not discovered until the second policy had replaced the first. Each policy limited recovery to $50,000 for employee dishonesty and provided that for a loss "which occurs partly during the Effective Period of this endorsement and partly during the period of other policies, the total liability of the Company shall not exceed in the aggregate the amount of this endorsement." The insured maintained that he was entitled to recover $50,000 on each policy. What did the court decide? [Davenport Peters Co. v. Royal Globe Ins. Co., 490 F.Supp. 286 (Mass. 1980)]

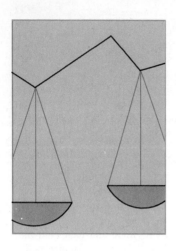

56

Liability of Accountants

Accountants play a major role in a business's financial system. Accountants are subject to standards of conduct established by codes of professional ethics, by state statutes, and by judicial decisions. They are also governed by the contracts they enter into with their clients. When accountants enter into a contract, they must perform all the services for which they were hired, in addition to following the standard accounting procedures. Accountants must comply with generally accepted accounting principles (GAAP) and generally accepted auditing standards (GAAS).

Under both common law and statutory provisions, accountants face potential legal liability in their work. Common law imposes liability for breach of contract, negligence, and fraud. An accountant may also be subject to federal statutory liability under the Securities Act of 1933 and under the Securities Exchange Act of 1934. When violated, these two acts impose civil and criminal liabilities. Considering the many potential sources of legal liability that may be imposed upon accountants, an accountant should be well aware of his or her legal obligations.

POTENTIAL COMMON LAW LIABILITY TO CLIENTS

Under common law, accountants are liable to clients for breach of contract, negligence, or fraud.

Breach of Contract

Under common law, accountants face liability for any breach of contract. An accountant owes a duty to his or her client to honor the terms of the contract and to perform the contract within the stated time period. If the accountant fails to perform as agreed in the contract, then he or she has breached the contract and thus the client has the right to recover damages from the accountant. An accountant may be held liable for expenses incurred by his or her client in securing another accountant, for penalties imposed upon the client in failing to meet time deadlines, and also for any other reasonable and foreseeable monetary losses that arise from the accountant's breach.

When a client brings an action against an accountant for breach of contract, the accountant may not claim, and hope to be successful, that the services rendered conformed to generally accepted accounting and auditing standards. Liability is based upon the accountant's breach of contract—not upon fault. Hence, the accountant may not winningly claim contributory negligence as a defense and assert that his or her client's negligence prohibits the client from recovering. The client may recover notwithstanding any negligence on his or her part.

Liability for Negligence

Accountants occupy a position similar to that of other professionals who render professional services for compensation. When a person holds himself or herself out as an accountant, he or she is held to the care, knowledge, and judgment generally possessed by accountants in the community acting under the same or similar circumstances. An accountant is measured against a hypothetical, reasonably prudent and skillful accountant.

As long as an accountant conforms to generally accepted accounting principles and acts in good faith, he or she will not be held liable to the client for incorrect judgment. As a general rule, an accountant is not required to discover every impropriety, defalcation, or fraud in his or her client's books. If, however, the impropriety, defalcation, or fraud has gone undiscovered because of negligence or failure to perform an express or implied duty, an accountant will be liable for any resulting losses suffered by his or her client. Therefore, an accountant who uncovers suspicious financial transactions and fails to fully investigate the matter or to inform his or her client can be held liable to the client for the resulting loss. Typically, the amount of the loss resulting from an accountant's failure to exercise reasonable care according to the generally accepted standards is substantially higher than the fee the client was to pay the accountant.

A violation of generally accepted accounting principles and generally accepted auditing standards will be considered *prima facie* evidence of negligence by the auditor. Compliance with generally accepted accounting principles and generally accepted auditing standards, however, does not necessarily relieve an accountant from potential legal liability. An accountant will still be held to standards of conduct established by state statutes and by judicial decisions.

If an accountant is deemed guilty of negligence, the client may collect any reasonable and foreseeable damages that arose from the accountant's negligence. An accountant, however, is not without possible defenses to a cause of action for damages based on negligence. Possible defenses include allegations that:

1. The accountant was not negligent.
2. If the accountant was negligent, this negligence was not the proximate cause of the client's losses.
3. The client was contributorily negligent.

Sometimes accountants are hired to perform "write up" work or to prepare unaudited financial statements. While a lesser standard of care is typically required with a "write up," accountants may still be held civilly and criminally liable in this situation. Accountants may be subject to liability for failing, in accordance with standard accounting procedures, to delineate a balance sheet as "unaudited." An accountant will also be held liable for a failure to disclose to a client facts or circumstances that gave rise to a reason to believe that misstatements had been made or that a fraud had been committed.

Liability for Fraud

Actual fraud and constructive fraud present two different circumstances under which an accountant may be found liable. An accountant may be held liable for *actual fraud* when he or she intentionally misstates a "material fact" to mislead his or her client, and the client detrimentally relies on the misstated fact. A material fact is one that a reasonable person would consider important in deciding whether to act. *Constructive fraud*, on the other hand, will be found when an accountant is grossly negligent in the performance of his or her duties. The intentional failure to perform a duty in reckless disregard of the consequences of such a failure would constitute gross negligence on the part of an accountant. Both actual and constructive fraud are potential sources of legal liability under which a client may bring an action against an accountant.

When a client is dissatisfied with the performance of an accounting firm, he or she will often sue on all three common law theories in the alternative. The Federal Rules of Civil Procedure permit a pleader, in a claim or defense, to make two or more statements which are not necessarily consistent with each other. Thus, a plaintiff may sue on several theories. In the following case, the court had to sift through claims for negligence, constructive fraud, and breach of contract. Notice how the court disposes of the latter two counts by its treatment of the negligence claim.

IN THE MATTER OF THE HAWAII CORPORATION

United States District Court, District of Hawaii, 1983. 567 F.Supp. 609.

BACKGROUND AND FACTS *The American Pacific Group (APG), planning a merger with one of its subsidiaries, The Hawaii Corporation (THC), engaged the accounting firm of Peat, Marwick, Mitchell & Co. (PMM) to prepare financial statements for both companies and also to express opinions as to the most advantageous means of combining them. When the merger resulted in an arguably unnecessary loss of $22,000,000, the trustee in reorganization sued PMM on, among others, grounds of accountant malpractice, based on the unusual method PMM used in restructuring the companies. The plaintiff contended that, had PMM used the accounting method generally applied in such transactions, its financial statements would have reflected a more negative picture and the merger would never have occurred.*

PANNER, District Judge.

*   *   *   *

Plaintiff's principal complaint is that the reorganization occurred. Plaintiff argues that, if the proper method of accounting had been applied to the transaction and if the financial facts had been made available, either the THC Board or one or more of the minority shareholders of THC would have prevented the reorganization.

*   *   *   *

Accountants and auditors have the duty to exercise that degree of care, skill and competence exercised by reasonably competent members of their profession under the circumstances. An accountant is not a guarantor. His duty is to act honestly, in good faith, and with reasonable care in the discharge of his professional obligations.

*   *   *   *

An accountant or auditor breaches his professional obligations if, in performing his services, he makes negligent misrepresentations. The standard of liability for negligent misrepresentation is set forth in Section 552 of the Restatement of Torts, Second:

§ 552 Information Negligently Supplied for the Guidance of Others

(1) One who, in the course of his business, profession, or employment, or in any other transaction in which he has a pecuniary interest, supplies false information for the guidance of others in their business transactions, is subject to liability for pecuniary loss caused to them for their justifiable reliance upon the information, if he failed to exercise reasonable care or competence in obtaining or communicating the information.

*   *   *   *

I conclude that the plaintiff has failed to prove by a preponderance of the evidence that the defendant was negligent in the method of accounting for the transaction. It is not necessary to endorse such a procedure for application to all situations. Here it was appropriate. Even if *   *   * purchase accounting should have been used throughout the transaction, the results would have not been significantly different. *   *   *. The income statement on the pro forma statements would not have changed and the figure reported as retained earnings on the balance sheet would have been somewhat higher. Under these circumstances, plaintiff has failed to prove that the merger would not have occurred, either by reason of director action or minority stockholder action.

Analysis of the testimony and the exhibits reflects thoughtful accounting decisions based on judgment in difficult matters.

*   *   *   *

Plaintiff alleges that PMM is liable for fraud because the comfort letter, the financial statements, and pro forma balance sheets that PMM prepared contained material misrepresentations upon which THC relied in embarking on the THC–APG reorganization and related transactions. There is no contention of intentional fraud. Plaintiff asserts the misrepresentations were made with reckless disregard for their truth or falsity.

To prove fraud, plaintiff must show that (1) the defendant made a false representation of material fact, (2) defendant intended to induce the plaintiff to act, (3) the representation was made by the defendant with knowledge that it was false (or without knowledge of its truth or falsity), but plaintiff reasonably believed it was true, and (4) the plaintiff relied to his damage. *   *   * The "knowledge" requirement is satisfied if it is shown that the representations were made with reckless disregard for their truth or falsity. *   *   *

My findings with respect to the negligence claim are dispositive of plaintiff's fraud claim. Plaintiff has failed to prove that the comfort letter, financial statements, or pro forma balance sheets prepared by defendant contained material misrepresentations.

PMM entered into written and oral contracts to perform auditing and accounting services for THC. Plaintiff's breach of contract claim is based upon the allegation that PMM negligently failed to perform its contractual undertakings with due care.

Plaintiff contends that PMM breached its express and implied duties and obligations under the contracts by negligently and recklessly acting as previously set forth, and seeks contract damages including all compensation paid by plaintiff to PMM for the services it rendered.

The requirement that an accountant or auditor exercise that degree of skill and competence reasonably expected of persons in those professions is implied in a contract for professional services. *   *   * Liability follows for breach of contract if there is negligence. *   *   *

In concluding that plaintiff failed to prove by a preponderance of the evidence that defendant was negligent in performing auditing and accounting services for plaintiff, I have also necessarily concluded that plaintiff cannot recover for breach of contract.

*   *   *   *

The court found that the method employed by PMM, while admittedly "creative," did not violate the negligence standard since it produced a result essentially similar to that of the standard method. Furthermore, the court concluded that, even though the accounting was not done according to the usual method, it was arrived at by careful reasoning. Since that standard had been upheld, the court reasoned, there had been no breach of contract, fraud, or negligence. Judgment was for the defendant.

DECISION AND REMEDY

POTENTIAL COMMON LAW LIABILITY TO THIRD PERSONS

Traditionally, an accountant did not owe any duty to a third person with whom he or she had no direct contractual relationship. An accountant's duty was only to his or her client, and violations of the federal securities laws, fraud, and other intentional or reck-

less acts of wrongdoing were the only exceptions to this general rule. Chief Judge Benjamin Cardoza's 1931 decision in *Ultramares Corp.* v. *Touche* was the leading authority for this traditional view.[1] In *Ultramares*, a lender alleged that its reliance on the accountants' negligently prepared statements had

---

1. 255 N.Y. 170, 174 N.E. 441 (1931).

caused it to lose money on loans made to the client. The court, however, refused to impose liability upon the accountants and concluded that the accountants owed a duty of non-negligence only to those persons for whose "primary benefit" the statements were intended. In this case, the client was the only person for whose "primary benefit" the statements were intended.

Over the past few years, however, the *Ultramares* rule has been severely criticized. Accountants perform much of their work for use by persons who are not a party to the contract, and, thus, it is asserted that they should be found liable to these third parties. Consequently, there has been an eroding away of the *Ultramares* rule, and accountants have been exposed to potential liability to third parties.

Understanding an accountant's common law liability to third parties is critical because often, when a business fails, its independent auditor (accountant) may be one of the few potentially solvent defendants. Therefore, in order to hold an accountant liable for negligence, a third party must demonstrate not only that the accountant committed a tort but also that the third party was an "intended beneficiary" of the accountant's work. A person other than the client qualifies as an "intended beneficiary" when the accountant knows or should have known that the work was being done for the benefit of a third party who intended to rely on the accountant's work. Jurisdictions vary as to whether the accountant must be aware that his or her work product is intended for a *particular* third party.

A third party may also hold an accountant liable for actual or constructive fraud. Unlike an action for negligence, a third party need not show any reliance.

In the following case, the accountant was held liable to a third-party creditor for making incorrect financial statements prepared by using nonstandard accounting procedures. The court found the accountant liable, even though the accountant labeled the statements as "unaudited" and included an express disclaimer as to their accuracy.

SEEDKEM, INC. v.
SAFRANEK

United States District Court,
District of Nebraska, 1979.
466 F.Supp. 340.

BACKGROUND AND FACTS   *The defendant, Safranek, prepared regular financial statements for Agri-Products, Inc., a Nebraska company. Based on these documents, Seedkem, Inc., the plaintiff, advanced credit to Agri-Products in excess of $700,000. Later, Seedkem learned that the financial statements were incorrect and had been prepared by nonstandard procedures. The defendant argued that, since he had not certified the statements and had expressly disclaimed any opinion as to their validity, he could not be held liable for their inaccuracy. This action involved a motion to dismiss for failure to state a claim upon which relief could be granted. The federal court attempts to apply Nebraska law, since the present claim is a state common law claim.*

DENNEY, District Judge.

*   *   *   *

The Court notes that the Restatement (Second) of Torts § 552 takes the position that accountants may be liable to a third party, with whom they are not in privity, for negligence in the preparation of a financial statement under certain circumstances. See Restatement (Second) of Torts § 552 (1977). Significantly, both jurisdictions, Indiana and Nebraska, have followed the position taken by the Restatement in the area of strict liability in tort, see Restatement (Second) of Torts § 402A (1965), and have abandoned the requirement of privity in that area. Seemingly, these jurisdictions, when faced with the issue in question, could be expected to follow the position taken by the Restatement in this area as well and abandon the requirement of privity.

However, the defendant argues that this case represents an extreme situation distinguishable from those cases which have rejected the privity requirement and found an accountant liable to a third party. Defendant points out that the cases cited by the plaintiff in support of its position all involved either certified or audited financial statements or express representations by the accountant to the third party as to the accuracy of the statements. Defendant contends that this case, on the other hand, involves unaudited statements containing an express disclaimer of opinion without any contrary representation and is therefore thoroughly distinguishable.

*   *   *   *

The fact that the financial statements were expressly marked "unaudited" and contained an express disclaimer of opinion is not necessarily dispositive at this time. The observations and statements by the Iowa Supreme Court in *Ryan* v. *Kanne*, are particularly persuasive:

> *   *   * Although in this profession a distinction is made between certified audits where greater time and effort are expended to verify book items, and uncertified audits where greater reliance is placed on book items, it is clear to us that accountants, or any other professional persons, must perform those acts that they have agreed to do under the contract and which they claim have been done in order to make the determination set forth and presented in their report. Their liability must be dependent upon their undertaking, not their rejection of dependability. They cannot escape liability for negligence by a general statement that they disclaim its reliability.

> *   *   *   *

> He must perform as agreed whether the work is certified or not. This being so, we have here fact questions as to the substance of the agreement between the parties, as to the care exercised in its performance, and as to the representation made, rather than whether the report was certified or uncertified.

The court denied the motion to dismiss for failure to state a claim upon which relief could be granted. The court held that an accountant can be liable to a third party, who is not in privity, for negligence in preparing financial statements.

DECISION AND REMEDY

POTENTIAL STATUTORY LIABILITY

Potential civil and criminal liabilities against accountants may be imposed by the Securities Act of 1933 and the Securities Exchange Act of 1934.

Liability under Section 11 of the Securities Act of 1933

Accountants frequently prepare and certify the issuer's financial statements that are included in the registration statement. Registration statements are required to be filed with the Securities and Exchange Commission (SEC) prior to an offering of securities. Section 11 of the federal Securities Act of 1933 imposes liability upon accountants for misstatements and omissions of material facts in registration statements. Therefore, an accountant may be found liable if he or she prepared any financial statements included in the registration statement that "contained an untrue statement of a material fact or omitted to state a material fact required to be stated

therein or necessary to make the statements therein not misleading." [2]

Under Section 11 of the 1933 act, an accountant may be held liable by anyone who acquires a security covered by a registration statement. A purchaser of a security need only demonstrate that he or she has suffered a loss on the security. Reliance upon the materially false statement or misleading omission is not an element. Nor is there a requirement of privity between the accountant and the security purchasers.

Section 11 imposes a duty upon accountants to use "due diligence" in the preparation of financial statements included in the registration statement that is filed with the Securities and Exchange Commission prior to an offering of securities. After the purchaser has proved the loss on the security, the accountant bears the burden of showing that he or she exercised "due diligence" in the preparation of the financial statements. Therefore, to disprove liability, the accountant must show that he or she had, after

---

2.   Securities Act of 1933, Section 11(a).

reasonable investigation, reasonable grounds to believe and did believe, at the time such part of the registration statement became effective, that the statements therein were true and that there was no omission of a material fact required to be stated therein or necessary to make the statements therein not misleading.[3] Further, the failure to follow generally accepted accounting principles and generally accepted auditing standards is also proof of a lack of due diligence.

In particular, the due diligence standard places a burden upon accountants to verify information furnished by a corporation's officers and directors. The burden of proving due diligence requires an accountant to demonstrate that he or she is free from negligence or fraud. For example, the accountants in *Escott* v. *BarChris Construction Corp.* were held liable for a failure to detect danger signals in the materials that, under generally accepted accounting standards, required further investigation under the circumstances.[4] Merely asking questions is not always sufficient to satisfy the requirement of due diligence.

Besides proving that he or she has acted with due diligence, an accountant may defend by claiming that:

1. There were no misstatements or omissions; or
2. The misstatements or omissions were not of material facts; or
3. The misstatements or omissions had no causal connection to the plaintiff's loss; or
4. The plaintiff purchaser invested in the securities knowing of the misstatements or omissions.

A purchaser bringing a suit under Section 11 of the Securities Act of 1933 may recover the difference between the amount paid for the security and:

1. The value of the security as of the time the suit was brought; or
2. The price at which the security was disposed of in the market before the suit; or
3. The price at which the security was disposed of after the suit but before judgment if such damages are less than the damages representing the difference between the amount paid for the security at the value as of the time the suit was brought.[5]

Liability under the Securities Exchange Act of 1934

Under Section 18, Section 10b, or Rule 10b–5 of the Securities Exchange Act of 1934, an accountant may be found liable for fraud. A plaintiff has a substantially heavier burden of proof under the 1934 act than under the 1933 act. Unlike the 1933 act, the 1934 act provides that an accountant need not prove due diligence in order to escape liability. Section 18 of the 1934 act imposes civil liability on an accountant who makes or causes to be made in any application, report, or document a statement that at the time and in light of the circumstances was false or misleading with respect to any material fact.[6]

Section 18 liability is narrow in that it applies only to applications, reports, documents, and registration statements filed with the SEC. This remedy is further limited in that it applies only to sellers and purchasers. Under Section 18, a seller or purchaser must prove that:

1. The false or misleading statement affected the price of the security; or
2. The purchaser or seller relied upon the false or misleading statement in making the purchase and was not aware of the inaccuracy of the statement.

Even if a purchaser or seller proves these two elements, an accountant can be exonerated of liability upon proof of "good faith" in the preparation of the financial statement. To demonstrate good faith, an accountant must show that he or she had no knowledge that the financial statement was false and misleading. Acting in good faith requires a total absence of an intention on the part of the accountant to seek an unfair advantage or to defraud another party. Proving a lack of intent to deceive, manipulate, or defraud is frequently referred to as proving a lack of "scienter." Good faith can be further negated by reckless conduct and gross negligence on the part of an accountant. In addition to the good faith defense, accountants have available as a defense the knowledge of the false and misleading financial statement on the part of the buyer or seller.

---

3. Securities Act of 1933, Section 11(b)(3).
4. *Escott* v. *BarChris Construction Corp.*, 283 F.Supp. 643 (S.D.N.Y. 1968).

---

5. Securities Act of 1933, Section 11(3).
6. Securities Exchange Act of 1934, Section 18(a).

A court, under Section 18 of the 1934 act, also has the discretion to assess reasonable costs, including attorneys' fees, against accountants.[7] Sellers and purchasers may further maintain a cause of action "within one year after the discovery of the facts constituting the cause of action and within three years after such cause of action accrued."[8]

The Securities Exchange Act of 1934 further subjects accountants to potential legal liability in its antifraud provisions. Section 10b and SEC Rule 10b–5 contain the antifraud provisions of the 1934 act. As stated in *Herman & MacLean* v. *Huddleston*, "a private right of action under Section 10b of the 1934 act and Rule 10b–5 has been consistently recognized for more than 35 years."[9]

Section 10b makes it unlawful for any person, including accountants, to use, in connection with the purchase or sale of any security registered on a national securities exchange, or any security not so registered, any manipulative or deceptive device or contrivance in contravention of SEC rules and regulations.[10] Rule 10b–5 further makes it unlawful for any person, by use of any means or instrumentality of interstate commerce:

1. To employ any device, scheme, or artifice to defraud;
2. To make any untrue statement of a material fact or to omit to state a material fact necessary in order to make the statements made, in light of the circumstances, not misleading; or
3. To engage in any act, practice, or course of business that operates or would operate as a fraud or deceit upon any person, in connection with the purchase or sale of any security.[11]

Accountants may be held liable only to sellers or purchasers under Section 10b and Rule 10b–5. The scope of these antifraud provisions is extremely wide. Privity is not necessary for a recovery. Under these provisions, an accountant may be found liable not only for fraudulent misstatements of material facts in written material filed with the SEC, but also for any fraudulent oral statements or omissions made in connection with the purchase or sale of any security.

In order for a plaintiff to recover from an accountant under the antifraud provisions of the 1934 act, he or she must, in addition to establishing status as a purchaser or seller, prove *scienter*, some fraudulent action or deception, reliance, materiality, and causation. A plaintiff who fails to establish these elements cannot recover damages from an accountant under Section 10b or Rule 10b–5.

In the following case, the court wrestles with the reliance requirement on finding an accounting firm liable under 10b–5. Ask yourself as you read the case if any evidence exists that actually shows reliance by the plaintiffs.

---

7. Securities Exchange Act of 1934, Section 18(a).
8. Securities Exchange Act of 1934, Section 18(c).
9. 459 U.S. 375, 103 S.Ct. 683 (1983).
10. Securities Exchange Act of 1934, Section 10b.

---

11. Securities Exchange Act of 1934, Rule 10b–5.

BACKGROUND AND FACTS *Westland Minerals Corporation (WMC) was the promoter of a venture in which multiple limited partnerships were formed for the purpose of drilling for oil and gas. WMC requested from the accounting firm of Coopers & Lybrand (C&L), an opinion letter on behalf of one of its investors, a Mr. Muhammed Ali, who desired reassurance concerning the benefits offered by this classic tax "shelter." WMC subsequently showed copies of the letter to other potential investors. Thereafter, C&L concluded that, for the purposes of encouraging potential investors, a more complete letter should be drafted. Hence, WMC was presented with a revised document for use in encouraging potential investors. When the Internal Revenue Service eventually denied deductions taken by the investors, some 210 of them sued C&L, partially on the basis of the revised document of C&L.*

SHARP v. COOPERS & LYBRAND

United States Court of Appeals, Third Circuit, 1981.
649 F.2d 175.

ALDISERT, Circuit Judge.

*   *   *   *

The factual setting of this case combines Caribbean intrigue, creative accounting, and high finance against the backdrop of investors attempting to limit their tax obligations.

*   *   *   *

Here, two opinion letters were issued by C&L. The first went out on July 21, 1971, to WMC and was signed in the firm name by a partner. The letter was in response to a request by WMC in behalf of *one* of its investors. The second letter went out in October, 1971, after a partner, Wright, had learned that WMC was showing copies of the letter to investors generally as part of WMC's sales program. With full knowledge of the letter's intended use—a tool to be used by a securities seller as part of a sales program—the partnership, through a partner, made the calculated decision to send out a more complete letter. Moreover, it was also decided that the letter be signed, not in the name of a partner, but in the partnership name. These facts are central to the important inquiry, whether this activity propelled C&L into a position in which the investing public would place their trust and confidence in it. We determine that it did ascend to that position, and the ultimate issue turns on this determination.

*   *   *   *

Reliance is an element of a plaintiff's action for damages under rule 10b–5. The obvious reason for this requirement is that a plaintiff in a rule 10b–5 action should not be allowed to recover damages when the defendant's wrongful action had no relationship to the plaintiff's loss. Reliance is therefore one aspect of the ubiquitous requirement that losses be causally related to the defendant's wrongful acts. This precept is manifest in the Securities Exchange Act of 1934 in § 28(a), 15 U.S.C. § 78bb(a), which states in part that "no person permitted to maintain a suit for damages under the provisions of this chapter shall recover, through satisfaction of judgment in one or more actions, a total amount in excess of his actual damages on account of the act complained of." Normally, a plaintiff suing under rule 10b–5 bears the burden of proving all the elements of his case. Nevertheless, the necessity of an element to a valid claim does not determine the allocation of the burdens of going forward and persuasion with respect to that element.

The Supreme Court authoritatively addressed the requirement of proving reliance in rule 10b–5 actions in *Affiliated Ute Citizens of Utah* v. *United States*, 406 U.S. 128, 92 S.Ct. 1456, 31 L.Ed.2d 741 (1972), stating:

> Under the circumstances of this case, involving primarily a failure to disclose, positive proof of reliance is not a prerequisite to recovery. All that is necessary is that the facts withheld be material in the sense that a reasonable investor might have considered them important in the making of this decision. This obligation to disclose and this withholding of a material fact establish the requisite element of causation in fact.

The Court has subsequently defined a material omission in the context of proxy statements under rule 14a–9 as "a substantial likelihood that a reasonable [investor] would consider it important. *   *   * [T]here must be a substantial likelihood that the disclosure of the omitted fact would have been viewed by the reasonable investor as having significantly altered the 'total mix' of information made available." We have held this standard of materiality applicable to rule 10b–5 actions as well. *Affiliated Ute* makes clear that in at least some situations a presumption of reliance in favor of the rule 10b–5 plaintiff is proper. Our present task is to determine whether that presumption was properly applied in this case.

Both parties in this case cite decisions indicating that the presumption of reliance is proper in cases of alleged omissions, whereas no presumption arises in cases of alleged misrepresentations. This distinction has led C&L to argue that its wrongful conduct in this case arose from misrepresentations in the opinion letter, whereas the class representatives argue that the violation resulted from the appellant's failure to disclose certain material facts.

We have concluded that both misrepresentations and omissions are present in this case. The jury heard evidence that C&L had misrepresented certain crucial facts in the letter, such as its disclaimer of verification of the facts on which the opinion letter was based and its assertion that cash supplemental to the limited partner's contributions would be borrowed "from suitable banks or other leading agencies. .* * *." The jury also heard evidence that C&L had failed to disclose certain material facts, such as the affiliation between the putative lender, the Bahamian bank, and WMC. A strict application of the omissions-misrepresentation dichotomy would require the trial judge to instruct the jury to presume reliance with regard to the omitted facts, and not to presume reliance with regard to the misrepresented facts. Although this resolution would have great appeal to graduate logicians in a classroom, we are not persuaded to adopt it for use in a courtroom.

* * * *

We agree with the district court that the burden in this case should fall on C&L. The opinion letter issued by C&L was intended to influence the investment decisions of persons interested in WMC partnerships. The appellant undoubtedly foresaw that it would have that effect. As in *Affiliated Ute*, C&L by its action facilitated the transactions at issue but failed to disclose certain facts. Its misrepresentation of other facts should not alleviate its burden of proving nonreliance. Considering the likelihood that investors would rely on the opinion letter, we conclude that the trial judge properly placed the burden of refuting a presumption of reliance on the appellant.

The court held that the accounting firm had violated rule 10b–5 of the Securities and Exchange Act of 1934. Essential to the finding of liability under Rule 10b–5 was the reliance of investors on the letter in their purchase of partnership interests. Note, however, that the court allows reliance to be presumed under these facts; since the defendant had known the letter was going to potential investors, it could assume they would rely on it. At trial, defendant had the burden of refuting that presumption.

**DECISION
AND REMEDY**

If the plaintiff is neither a purchaser nor a seller, the accountant is immune from liability under Section 10b or Rule 10b–5.[12] The plaintiff, in proving *scienter*, must demonstrate an actual intent to deceive, manipulate, or defraud on the part of the accountant. Negligence alone is not sufficient to impose liability.[13] There must also have been some fraudulent action or deception by an accountant in connection with the purchase or sale of securities. The seller or purchaser must have relied upon a

fraudulent statement or omission that was material and caused the loss to the seller or purchaser. Causation may be established by the presence of materiality.

CRIMINAL LIABILITY

An accountant may be found criminally liable under the Securities Act of 1933, the Securities Exchange Act of 1934, the Internal Revenue Code, and under both state and federal criminal codes. Under both the act of 1933 and the act of 1934, accountants may be subject to criminal penalties for *willful conduct*.

---

12. See Blue Chip Stamps v. Manor Drug Stores, 421 U.S. 723, 95 S.Ct. 1917 (1975).
13. See Ernst & Ernst v. Hochfelder, 425 U.S. 185, 96 S.Ct. 1375 (1976).

QUESTIONS AND CASE PROBLEMS

1. Larkin, Inc. retained Howard Perkins to manage its books and to prepare its financial statements. Howard Perkins, a certified public accountant, was authorized to practice in Indiana where he was practicing. After twenty years, Mr. Perkins had become a bit bored with the format of generally accepted accounting principles and decided to be creative. Now Mr. Perkins has a bit of a problem since he is being sued by Molly Tucker, one of Larkin's creditors.

Ms. Tucker alleges that Perkins either knew or should have known that Larkin's financial statements would be distributed to various individuals. Furthermore, she asserts that Perkin's financial statements were negligently prepared and seriously inaccurate. What are the consequences of Larkin's failure to adopt generally accepted accounting standards? Under the traditional *Ultramares* rule, can Ms. Tucker recover damages from Mr. Perkins?

2. The accounting firm of Goldman, Walters, Johnson & Co. prepared financial statements for Lucy's Fashions, Inc. After reviewing the various financial statements, Happydays State Bank agreed to loan Lucy's Fashions, Inc. $35,000 for expansion purposes. When Lucy's Fashions, Inc. declared bankruptcy under Chapter 11 six months later, Happydays State Bank promptly filed an action against Goldman, Walters, Johnson & Co., alleging negligent preparation of financial statements. Assuming that the circuit court has abandoned the *Ultramares* approach, what is the result? What are the policy reasons for holding accountants liable to third parties with whom they are not in privity?

3. In early 1985 Bennett, Inc. offered a substantial number of new common stock shares to the public. Harvey Helms had a long-standing interest in Bennett, Inc., since his grandfather was once president of the company. Upon receiving a prospectus that was both prepared and distributed by Bennett, Inc., Helms was rather dismayed by the pessimism embodied in it. After much debate, Harvey Helms decided to delay purchasing any stock in the company. A few months after deciding not to purchase any shares of Bennett, Inc., Harvey Helms asserts that the prospectus prepared by the accountants was overly pessimistic. Moreover, Helms alleges that the prospectus contains materially misleading statements. How successful will Harvey Helms be in bringing a cause of action, under Rule 10b-5 of the Securities Exchange Act of 1934, against the accountants of Bennett, Inc.?

4. In *White v. Guarente*, a limited partner brought an action in negligence against the general partners as well as against the accountant. The issue in this case was whether accountants who are retained by a *limited partnership* to perform both auditing and tax-return services may be held liable for negligence in the carrying out of those professional services. Should accountants be held responsible in these circumstances? [White v. Guarente, 43 N.Y.2d 356, 372 N.E.2d 315 (1977)]

5. The plaintiffs, Harry and Barry Rosenblum, brought an action against Touch Ross & Co., a prominent accounting firm. The plaintiffs alleged that they had relied upon the correctness of audits in acquiring Giant common stock in conjunction with the sale of their business to Giant. The financial statements of Giant were found to be fraudulent, and the stock that the Rosenblums purchased proved to be worthless. The plaintiffs alleged that Touch's negligence in conducting the audits was the proximate cause of their loss. Is a duty owed to third persons known and intended by the auditor to be recipients of the audit? Furthermore, does an independent auditor owe a duty to anyone when he or she furnishes an opinion with no limitation in the certificate as to whom the company may disseminate the information contained in the financial statements? [Rosenblum v. Adler, 93 N.J. 324, 461 A.2d 138 (1983)]

6. There are several ways in which an auditor may limit or avoid legal liability. An accounting firm was engaged by two car rental companies to determine the net worth of those businesses by preparing an audited statement. At the request of their clients, the accountants did not audit the accounts receivable, made appropriate exceptions to the accounts receivable in the balance sheet, and qualified their accountants' opinion with a similar caveat. After the audit was performed and upon the basis of the figures reflected in the balance sheet, Stephens Industries, Inc. purchased two-thirds of the car rental companies' stock. The car rental businesses thereafter failed, and Stephens Industries, Inc. brought an action against the accounting firm for allegedly having misrepresented the status of the accounts receivable in the audit. What was the result? [Stephen Industries, Inc. v. Haskins and Sells, 438 F.2d 357 (10th Cir., 1971)]

7. Plaintiffs were purchasers of all the stock in companies owned by the defendant sellers. Alleging fraud under the federal securities law and under the New York common law of fraud, the plaintiffs sued the defendant sellers and its accounting firm. What should be the result with respect to the accounting firm, assuming that the treatment according shipping costs and expenses and factoring charges was not in accordance with the generally accepted accounting principles and hence created an inaccurate financial picture in the financial statement? [Berkowitz v. Baron, 428 F.Supp. 1190 (S.D.N.Y., 1977)]

57

The Effect of International Law in a Global Economy

Since World War II, business has become increasingly multinational in character. It is not uncommon, for example, for a U.S. corporation to have investments or manufacturing plants in a foreign country, or for a foreign corporation to have operations within the United States. Because the exchange of goods, services, and ideas on a global level is now a common phenomenon, it is important for the student of business law to have some familiarity with the laws pertaining to international business transactions.

International law consists of a body of laws that are considered to be legally binding among otherwise independent nations. It governs the acts of individuals as well as states. Although no sovereign nation can be compelled, against its will, to obey a law external to itself, nations can and do *voluntarily* agree to be governed in certain respects by international law for the purpose of facilitating international trade and commerce and civilized discourse.

In this chapter we first explore the sources of international law and then examine some selected areas relating to business activities in a global economy: documents facilitating international business transactions (letters of credit and sales contracts); legal principles and doctrines guiding judicial decisions concerning disputes where a foreign element is involved (the *act of state doctrine* and the *principle of comity*); the doctrine of sovereign immunity; and

the application of U.S. antitrust laws in a transnational setting. The chapter concludes with a brief discussion of the proliferation of common markets in the post-war world and the function of common markets in protecting the commercial interests of less powerful nations in a world dominated by superpowers.

SOURCES OF INTERNATIONAL LAW

One important source of international law consists of international customs that have evolved among nations in their relations with one another. Under Article 38(1) of the *Statute* of the International Court of Justice, international custom is referred to as "evidence of a general practice accepted as law." Even though customary law serves as an independent form of law, it is subject to challenges upon various applications. When, for example, does a particular custom evolve into a general practice constituting a law?

Treaties between or among foreign nations provide another source of international law. A *treaty* is an agreement or contract between two or more nations that must be authorized and ratified by the supreme power of each nation. Under Article II, Section 2, of the United States Constitution, the president has the power "by and with the consent of the Senate, to make treaties, provided two-thirds of the Senators present concur."

International organizations and conferences further contribute to what is known as international law. These organizations adopt resolutions, declarations, and other types of standards that often require a particular behavior of nations. The General Assembly of the United Nations, for example, has adopted numerous resolutions and declarations that embody principles of international law. Disputes with respect to these resolutions and declarations may be brought before the United Nations International Court of Justice. In general, however, the Court only has jurisdiction to settle legal disputes when nations voluntarily submit to its jurisdiction.

TRANSACTING BUSINESS ABROAD

Transacting business abroad involves peculiar risks since buyers and sellers are often separated by thousands of miles. Sellers want to avoid delivering goods for which they might not be paid. Buyers desire the assurance that sellers will not be paid until there is evidence that the goods have been shipped. Thus, **letters of credit** have been increasingly used to facilitate international business transactions.

Letters of Credit

In a simple letter-of-credit transaction, the *issuer* (a bank) agrees to issue a letter of credit and to ascertain the occurrence of certain acts by the beneficiary (seller). In return, the *account party* (buyer) promises to reimburse the issuer for the amount paid to the beneficiary. There may also be an *advising bank* that transmits information, and a *paying bank* may be involved to expedite payment under the letter of credit.

Under a letter of credit, the issuer is bound to pay the beneficiary (seller) when the beneficiary has complied with the terms and conditions of the letter of credit. The beneficiary looks to the issuer, not to the account party (buyer), when it presents the documents required by the letter of credit. Typically, the letter of credit will require that the beneficiary deliver a *bill of lading* to prove that shipment has been made. Letters of credit assure beneficiaries

(sellers) of payment while at the same time they assure account parties (buyers) that payment will not be made until the beneficiaries have complied with the terms and conditions of the credit.

The Value of a Letter of Credit The basic principle behind letters of credit is that payment is made *against the documents presented by the beneficiary* and not against the facts that the documents purport to reflect. Thus, in a letter-of-credit transaction, the issuer does not police the underlying contract: A letter of credit is *independent* of the underlying contract between the buyer and the seller. By eliminating the need for banks (issuers) to inquire into whether or not actual conditions have been satisfied, the costs of letters of credit are greatly reduced. Moreover, the use of a letter of credit protects both buyers and sellers.

Compliance with a Letter of Credit In a letter-of-credit transaction, there are generally at least three separate and distinct contracts involved. There is the contract between the account party (buyer) and the beneficiary (seller). Then there is the contract between the issuer (bank) and the account party (buyer). Finally there is the letter of credit itself, which involves the issuer and the beneficiary. Given the fact that these contracts are separate and distinct, the issuer's obligations under the letter of credit do not concern the underlying contract between the buyer and the seller. Rather, it is the issuer's duty to ascertain whether the documents presented by the beneficiary (seller) comply with the terms of the letter of credit.

If the documents presented by the beneficiary comply with the terms of the credit, the issuer (bank) must honor the credit. Sometimes, however, it is difficult to determine exactly what a letter of credit requires. Moreover, the courts are divided as to whether *strict compliance* or *substantial compliance* with the terms of the letter of credit is required. Traditionally, courts required strict compliance with the terms of a letter of credit.

In the following case, the district court discusses the fact that Illinois law has moved away from the traditional standard of "strict compliance" to one of "reasonable compliance."

BACKGROUND AND FACTS *On January 17, 1980, Crocker United Factors, Inc., changed its corporate name to Crocker Commercial Services, Inc. Approximately two weeks later, Countryside Bank issued a letter of credit to Crocker. The credit stated that the drafts must be accompanied by invoices issued to Everyone's Effort, Inc., by Crocker Commercial Services. When Crocker presented the draft for payment, however, the invoices reflected the name of Crocker United Factors, Inc. Both Crocker and Countryside Bank filed cross-motions for summary judgment.*

CROCKER
COMMERCIAL
SERVICES v.
COUNTRYSIDE BANK
United States District Court,
N.D. Illinois, E.D., 1981. 538
F.Supp. 1360.

SHADUR, District Judge.

* * * *

This time of year invariably brings forth a spate of dramas in which the hard-hearted banker is the villain, sometimes regenerate (Scrooge in Dickens' *Christmas Carol*), sometimes unregenerate (as in Frank Capra's *It's a Wonderful Life*). By chance this is the second occasion during the past two weeks in which the Court has had to deal with the unregenerate type—which tries to extricate itself from an unquestioned obligation by the kind of hypertechnical argument that has often tended to give the term "banker" pejorative connotations.

Illinois law however rejects Bank's position. Last year's decision in *First Arlington National Bank* v. *Stathis,* * * * turned away from the "traditional standard" of strict compliance to confirm that *reasonable* compliance with a letter of credit entitles beneficiary to payment.

Under a fair application of the *First Arlington* reasonable compliance doctrine, Crocker is clearly entitled to payment:

(1) Its certification conformed *precisely* to the Letter of Credit by referring to "Crocker Commercial Services." Although it gratuitously enclosed documents that referred to "Crocker United Factors, Inc.," and though that disparity might possibly have relieved Bank of responsibility had it been a real discrepancy, the fact is that *no discrepancy existed.* * * * Because the same corporation was involved, the change in corporate name does not negate "reasonable compliance."

* * * *

There is another and self-sufficient ground that, though not mentioned by either party, also defeats Bank's nit-picking position. Bank's conduct may fairly be viewed as creating either a waiver or an estoppel, for it stood by silently and permitted the Letter of Credit to run out, even though an identification of the claimed deficiencies would have enabled Crocker to cure them.

* * * *

For that reason the failure to make timely objection is a waiver of any curable flaws in the beneficiary's demand. Had Bank voiced its objections to Crocker at any time through January 20, Crocker could have cured the hypertechnical language difficulties now relied upon by Bank. It is only equitable to apply the doctrine of waiver—if the time sequence permits—to bar Bank's purported defenses.

* * * *

Accordingly alternate grounds of waiver or estoppel serve to support summary judgment in Crocker's favor. It should be stressed that this holding is independent of the doctrine of "reasonable compliance," which alone requires the same result.

* * * *

The district court granted Crocker's motion for summary judgment. It concluded that there was no genuine issue of material fact.

DECISION
AND REMEDY

Sales Contracts

As with all commercial contracts, the transnational business contract should be in writing. In addition, this contract should contain a clause which designates the official language to be used in interpreting the terms of the contract. Such a clause promotes a clear and precise understanding of the terms of the contract by each of the parties. The basic contract of sale should include a legal definition of terms, the price and manner of payment, and a provision specifying the acceptable currency for payment. A *force majeure* clause, which protects the parties from forces beyond their control, is also advisable.

It is also important that the parties to a transnational business contract agree in advance as to what law will be applied in the event of a dispute or breach of contract. Such an agreement can be written into the contract in the form of a choice-of-law clause. A choice-of-law clause designates the forum in which adjudication will take place and what substantive law will be applied in the event of any disputes. An arbitration clause may also be included in the contract. When providing for arbitration, it is important that the forum, choice of law, and expertise of the arbitrator are specified in the contract. Many countries recognize the validity of choice-of-law and arbitration clauses and will enforce them in their courts. It is of critical importance, however, that before entering into a transnational business contract both parties be familiar with the laws of the foreign country involved.

CONFLICTS BETWEEN INTERNATIONAL AND MUNICIPAL LAW

Municipal law, or national law, is law that pertains to a particular nation. Because the legal system of each country reflects its cultural, historical, economic, and political background, the laws of each nation differ. Consequently, it is not uncommon for a country's municipal law to come into conflict with international law. Two important principles that have guided the settlement of such conflicts are the *act of state doctrine* and the *principle of comity.*

Act of State Doctrine

The **act of state doctrine** is a judicially created doctrine that provides that the judicial branch of one country will not examine the validity of public acts committed by a recognized foreign government within its own territory. As indicated by the court in *Libra Bank Ltd.* v. *Banco Nacional de Costa Rica,* this doctrine is premised on the theory that the judicial branch should not "pass upon the validity of foreign acts when to do so would vex the harmony of our international relations with that foreign nation."[1]

In the following case, the Supreme Court examines the *act of state doctrine* in the context of an expropriation by the Cuban government. An **expropriation** occurs when a government seizes a privately owned business or privately owned goods for a proper public purpose and awards just compensation. A **confiscation,** on the other hand, occurs when there is a taking without a proper public purpose or an award of just compensation.

---

1. 570 F.Supp. 870, 883 (S.D.N.Y. 1983).

BANCO NACIONAL DE CUBA v. SABBATINO

Supreme Court of the United States, 1964.
376 U.S. 398, 84 S.Ct. 923.

BACKGROUND AND FACTS *The respondent, an American commodity broker, had contracted with a Cuban corporation, largely owned by United States residents, to buy Cuban sugar. When the Cuban government expropriated the corporation's property and rights, the broker entered into a new contract to make payment for the sugar to the petitioner, a Cuban instrumentality. The petitioner delivered the bills of lading and sight draft to the respondent, who accepted the documents, and received payment for the sugar from its customer but refused to deliver the proceeds to the petitioner's agent. The petitioner subsequently filed an action in the Federal District Court for the Southern District of New York alleging conversion of the bills of lading, and it further* *sought to recover the proceeds from the respondent-broker. The Supreme Court discusses the historical background to this expropriation in greater detail.*

Mr. Justice HARLAN delivered the opinion of the Court.

*　*　*　*

The question which brought this case here, and is now found to be the dispositive issue, is whether the so-called act of state doctrine serves to sustain petitioner's claims in this litigation. Such claims are ultimately founded on a decree of the Government of Cuba expropriating certain property, the right to the proceeds of which is here in controversy. The act of state doctrine in its traditional formulation precludes the courts of this country from inquiring into the validity of the public acts a recognized foreign sovereign power committed within its own territory.

*　*　*　*

On July 6, 1960, the Congress of the United States amended the Sugar Act of 1948 to permit a presidentially directed reduction of the sugar quota for Cuba. *　*　* On the same day President Eisenhower exercised the granted power. *　*　* The day of the congressional enactment, the Cuban Council of Ministers adopted "Law No. 851," which characterized this reduction in the Cuban sugar quota as an act of "aggression, for political purposes" on the part of the United States, justifying the taking of countermeasures by Cuba. The law gave the Cuban President and Prime Minister discretionary power to nationalize by forced expropriation property or enterprises in which American nationals had an interest. *　*　* Although a system of compensation was formally provided, the possibility of payment under it may well be deemed illusory.

*　*　*　*

*　*　* The freezing of Cuban assets exemplifies the capacity of the political branches to assure *　*　* that the national interest is protected against a country which is thought to be improperly denying the rights of United States citizens.

*　*　*　*

In these circumstances the question whether the rights acquired by Cuba are enforceable in our courts depends *　*　* upon the act of state doctrine discussed in the succeeding sections of this opinion.

*　*　*　*

We do not believe that this doctrine is compelled either by the inherent nature of sovereign authority, as some of the earlier decisions seem to imply *　*　* or by some principle of international law.

*　*　*　*

If the act of state doctrine is a principle of decision binding on federal and state courts alike but compelled by neither international law nor the Constitution, its continuing vitality depends on its capacity to reflect the proper distribution of functions between the judicial and political branches of the Government on matters bearing upon foreign affairs.

*　*　*　*

When we consider the prospect of the courts characterizing foreign expropriations, however justifiably, as invalid under international law and ineffective to pass title, the wisdom of the precedents is confirmed.

*　*　*　*

*　*　* Following an expropriation of any significance, the Executive engages in diplomacy aimed to assure that United States citizens who are harmed are compensated fairly. *　*　* Judicial determinations of invalidity of title can, on the other hand, have only an occasional impact. *　*　* Such decisions would, if the acts involved were declared invalid, often be likely to give offense to the expropriating country; since the concept of territorial sovereignty is so deep seated, any state may resent the refusal of the courts of another sovereign to accord validity to acts within its territorial borders.

*　*　*　*

However offensive to the public policy of this country and its constituent States an expropriation of this kind may be, we conclude that both the national interest and progress toward the goal of establishing the rule of law among nations are best served by maintaining intact the act of state doctrine in this realm of its application.

*   *   *   *

DECISION AND REMEDY

The Supreme Court reversed the judgment of the Court of Appeals and remanded the case to the district court for proceedings consistent with this opinion. The Court concluded that the act of state doctrine reflects the desirability of presuming the validity of public acts committed by a foreign sovereign power in its own territory, and, thus, New York law regarding foreign expropriations may not be applied. The presumed validity of the expropriation is unaffected by the fact that conversion or breach of contract is a proper cause of action under New York law.

COMMENTS

The judiciary's abstention in such matters reflects the notion of sovereign immunity and the act of state doctrine. Each government is sovereign within its own borders, and the notion of comity *commands that every sovereign nation that voluntarily recognizes the sovereignty of another nation is also bound to respect that nation's sovereign powers.*

The Principle of Comity

The principle of **comity** may also arise when municipal and international law conflict. *Comity* may be defined as a deference by which one nation gives effect to the laws and judicial decrees of another nation. This recognition is based primarily upon respect.

In the recent case of *Allied Bank International v. Banco Credito Agricola de Cartago*, the Second Circuit concluded that the *act of state doctrine* was inapplicable to a dispute between a syndicate of thirty-nine creditor banks and three Costa Rican banks.[2] The court found that the acts of the Costa Rican government had an *extraterritorial effect* and hence fell outside the scope and protection of this doctrine. An extraterritorial effect is one that exists beyond the country's borders. Comity principles were then applied.

In applying the principles of comity, the Second Circuit concluded that acts of foreign governments having an extraterritorial effect should be recognized by courts only when they are consistent with the laws and policy of the United States. Since the Costa Rican government attempted to repudiate private, commercial obligations, the court held that such repudiation was inconsistent with the law and policy of the United States. Even though the Costa Rican government was experiencing international debt

problems, the court recognized the fact that the U.S. government has procedures for resolving these types of difficulties.

THE DOCTRINE OF SOVEREIGN IMMUNITY

When certain conditions are satisfied, the doctrine of **sovereign immunity** immunizes foreign nations from the *jurisdiction* of the United States. In 1976, Congress codified the law of sovereign immunity in the *Foreign Sovereign Immunities Act* (FSIA). The FSIA also modified the law of sovereign immunity in certain respects by expanding the rights that plaintiff creditors have against foreign nations.

The FSIA exclusively governs the circumstances in which an action may be brought against a foreign nation in the United States. Attachment of a foreign nation's property is also covered by this act. One of the primary purposes of the FSIA was to have federal courts, rather than the Department of State, determine claims of foreign sovereign immunity. It was thought that a determination of such an immunity by the courts would increase the degree of certainty in the law of sovereign immunity.

Section 1605 of the FSIA

Section 1605 of the FSIA sets forth the major exceptions to the jurisdictional immunity of a foreign state (country). A foreign state is not immune from the jurisdiction of the courts of the United States

---

2   757 F.2d 516 (2d Cir. 1985).

when the state has "waived its immunity either explicitly or by implication" or when the action is "based upon a commercial activity carried on in the United States by the foreign state."[3]

Issues frequently arise as to the entities that fall within the category of "foreign state." The question of what is a "commercial activity" has also been the

---

3.   U.S.C.A., Section 1605(a)(1), (2).

subject of dispute. Under Section 1603 of the FSIA, a "foreign state" is defined to include both a political subdivision of a foreign state and an instrumentality of a foreign state. A "commercial activity" is defined under Section 1603 to mean a commercial activity that is carried on by the foreign state having substantial contact with the United States.

In the following case, the court had to determine whether the defense of sovereign immunity was available under the FSIA.

BACKGROUND AND FACTS   *The plaintiffs, Texas Trading and three other trading companies, brought an action for breach of contract against the defendants, the Federal Republic of Nigeria and its central bank. The defendants had overbought quantities of cement from the plaintiffs. Unable to accept delivery of the cement, they repudiated the contract, alleging that they were entitled to immunity under the FSIA.*

TEXAS TRADING v. FEDERAL REPUBLIC OF NIGERIA
United States Court of Appeals, Second Circuit, 1981.
647 F.2d 300.

IRVING R. KAUFMAN, Circuit Judge.
*   *   *   *

These four appeals grow out of one of the most enormous commercial disputes in history, and present questions which strike to the very heart of the modern international economic order. An African nation, developing at breakneck speed by virtue of huge exports of high-grade oil, contracted to buy huge quantities of Portland cement, a commodity crucial to the construction of its infrastructure. It overbought, and the country's docks and harbors became clogged with ships waiting to unload. *   *   * Unable to accept delivery of the cement it had bought, the nation repudiated its contracts. *   *   * For the ruling principles here, we must look instead to a new and vaguely-worded statute, the Foreign Sovereign Immunities Act of 1976 *   *   * a law described by its draftsmen as providing only "very modest guidance" on issues of preeminent importance. For answers to those most difficult questions, the authors of the law "decided to put [their] faith in the U.S. courts." Guided by reason, precedent, and equity, we have attempted to give form and substance to the legislative intent.
*   *   *

*   *   *   *

The determination of whether particular behavior is "commercial" is perhaps the most important decision a court faces in an FSIA suit. This problem is significant because the primary purpose of the Act is to "restrict" the immunity of a foreign state to suits involving a foreign state's public acts. *   *   * If the activity is not "commercial," it satisfies none of the three clauses of § 1605(a)(2), and the foreign state is (at least under that subsection) immune from suit. Unfortunately, the definition of "commercial" is the one issue on which the Act provides almost no guidance at all. *   *   * No provision of the Act, however, defines "commercial." Congress deliberately left the meaning open and, as noted above, "put [its] faith in the U.S. courts to work out progressively, on a case-by-case basis . . . the distinction between commercial and governmental." *   *   *
*   *   *   *

Under each of these three standards, Nigeria's cement contracts and letters of credit qualify as "commercial activity." Lord Denning, writing in *Trendtex Trading Corp.* v. *Central Bank of Nigeria,* *   *   * with his usual erudition and clarity, stated: "If a government department goes into the market places of the world and buys boots or cement—as a commercial transaction—that government department should be subject to all the rules of the marketplace." Nigeria's activity here is in the nature of a private contract for the purchase of goods. Its purpose—to build roads, army barracks, whatever—is irrelevant. *   *   *

*   *   *   *

DECISION AND REMEDY *The court of appeals held that under the Foreign Sovereign Immunities Act, the Federal Republic of Nigeria and its central bank were not immune from acts arising out of a breach of contract to purchase cement. This conclusion was based on the court's determination that the contract to purchase the cement was a "commercial activity," and hence the doctrine of sovereign immunity did not apply.*

APPLICATION OF U.S. ANTITRUST LAWS IN A TRANSNATIONAL SETTING

United States antitrust laws have a wide application. They may *subject* persons in foreign nations to their provisions as well as *protect* foreign consumers and competitors from antitrust-violation acts committed by U.S. citizens. Consequently, foreign persons, a term that by definition includes foreign governments, may sue under U.S. antitrust laws in U.S. courts.

Section 1 of the Sherman Act provides for the *extraterritorial effect* of the U.S. antitrust laws.[4] The United States is a major proponent of free competition in the global economy, and thus any conspiracy that has a substantial effect on U.S. commerce is within the reach of the Sherman Act. The act of violation may even occur outside the United States, and foreign governments as well as persons can be sued in violation of U.S. antitrust laws. Yet before U.S. courts will exercise jurisdiction and apply the antitrust laws, it must be shown that the alleged violation had a *substantial effect* on U.S. commerce. U.S. jurisdiction is automatically invoked, however, when a *per se* violation occurs.[5]

A *per se* violation may consist of resale price-fixing and tying or tie-in contracts.[6] If a domestic firm, for example, joins a foreign cartel to control the production, price, or distribution of goods, and this cartel has a *substantial restraining effect* on U.S. commerce, a *per se* violation may exist. Hence, both the domestic firm and the foreign cartel have the potential to be sued in violation of the U.S. antitrust laws.

Amendment of Antitrust Laws

With the enactment of Title IV, the United States has amended the Sherman Act and the Federal Trade Commission Act. Sections 402 and 403 of Title IV limit the application of the Sherman Act and the Federal Trade Commission Act in their application to unfair methods of competition—when such methods or conduct involve U.S. export trade or commerce with foreign nations. The acts are not limited, however, where there is a "direct, substantial, and reasonably foreseeable effect" upon U.S. domestic commerce that results in a claim for damages.

THE PROLIFERATION OF COMMON MARKETS

After World War II, many smaller nations felt that their status in the evolving global economy was

---

4. Extraterritorial effect refers to the effect of U.S. antitrust laws outside the United States.

5. Certain types of restrictive contracts are deemed inherently anticompetitive, and thus in restraint of trade as a matter of law. When such a restrictive contract is entered into, there is said to be a *per se* violation of the antitrust laws. See Chapters 48 and 49 for a more in-depth discussion of *per se* violations.

---

6. A tie-in contract is one in which the seller conditions the sale of a product upon the buyer's agreement to purchase another product produced or distributed by the seller. See also Chapter 49.

threatened by the dominant world powers. To gain economic recognition, they organized and integrated their economies into cohesive groups. An example of one such organization is the European Common Market.

The European Economic Community

Created by the European Economic Community (EEC), the European Common Market presently includes twelve Western European nations. These countries have eliminated public tariffs and private, restrictive agreements among themselves. The EEC promotes free trade and competition within its own

common market in order to protect itself from competition outside the European Common Market.

The EEC came into existence in 1957 with the signing of the Treaty of Rome. Presently, Belgium, France, West Germany, Greece, Denmark, Ireland, Italy, the United Kingdom, Luxembourg, The Netherlands, Spain, and Portugal are members of the EEC. In addition to establishing common tariffs for outside nations and eliminating tariffs among EEC members, the treaty further promotes the free movement of workers, goods, and capital among the member nations.

The following often-cited case illustrates the EEC's regulation of the free movement of workers between the member countries.

BACKGROUND AND FACTS   *In 1968 a government minister in the House of Commons stated that the government considered the practice of Scientology to be socially harmful. Thus, pursuant to government policy, foreign nationals intending to work or study at Scientology establishments were not allowed to enter the United Kingdom. The Home Office announced that the policy would be continued and would apply to members of the European Economic Community. In 1973 the plaintiff, a Dutch national, was offered employment as a secretary within the Church of Scientology at East Grinstead, Sussex. She was subsequently refused entry into the United Kingdom by an immigration officer. The plaintiff then brought an action against the Home Office, declaring that under the EEC Treaty, she should be allowed to enter the United Kingdom. She alleged that refusal had been based solely on the grounds of public policy and that such a refusal was unlawful.*

VAN DUYN v. HOME OFFICE
European Court of Justice, 1974.
Case No. 41/74.

Drafting Judge, J. SORENSEN.
*   *   *   *

The question raises *   *   * the problem of whether a member-State is entitled, on grounds of public policy, to prevent a national of another member-State from taking gainful employment within its territory with a body or organization, it being the case that no similar restriction is placed upon its own nationals.

In this connection, the Treaty, while enshrining the principle of freedom of movement for workers without any discrimination on grounds of nationality, admits, in Article 48(3), limitations justified on grounds of public policy, public security or public health to the rights deriving from this principle. Under the terms of the provisions cited above, the right to accept offers of employment actually made the right to move freely within the territory of member-states for this purpose, and the right to stay in a member-State for the purpose of employment are, among others, all subject to such limitations. Consequently, the effect of such limitations, when they apply, is that leave to enter the territory of a member-State and the right to reside there may be refused to a national of another member-State.

Furthermore, it is a principle of international law, which the EEC treaty cannot be assumed to disregard in the relations between member-States, that a State is precluded from refusing its own nationals the right of entry or residence.

It follows that a member-State, for reasons of public policy, can, where it deems necessary, refuse a national of another member-State the benefit of the principle of freedom of movement for workers in a case where such a national proposes to take up a particular offer of employment even though the member-State does not place a similar restriction upon its own nationals. * * *

Accordingly, Article 48 of the EEC Treaty and Article 3(1) of Directive 64/221 are to be interpreted as meaning that a member-State, in imposing restrictions justified on grounds of public policy, is entitled to take into account, as a matter of personal conduct of the individual concerned, the fact that the individual is associated with some body or organization the activities of which the member-State considers socially harmful but which are not unlawful in that State, despite the fact that no restriction is placed upon nationals of the said member-State who wish to take similar employment with these same bodies or organizations.

* * * *

DECISION AND REMEDY *The Court of Justice determined that a member-State (nation) may exclude persons from entry into its country on the basis of public policy irrespective of the Treaty of Rome, which promotes the free movement of workers among the member nations. Thus the plaintiff was not wrongly denied entry into Great Britain.*

COMMENTS *A European Economic Community provision has limited the freedom-of-movement provision by allowing the exclusion of persons on the basis of public policy, public safety, and public health.*

Other Common Markets

Following World War II, the banding together of countries in close proximities to form economic cooperatives was not uncommon. Although the European Common Market is the most well known of these, there are many others. The Central American states formed the Central American Common Market (CACM); the Caribbean states formed the Caribbean Community (CARICOM); French-speaking African States formed the *Union Douaniére et Econ-omique de l'Afrique Centrale* (UDEAC); and Communist-bloc states formed the Council for Mutual Economic Assistance (COMECON).

Common markets and international economic organizations represent one way to facilitate international business and trade. A basic problem in the international business setting, however, is the fact that both individual nations and groups of nations are at odds over the extent to which free competition on a global level is desirable. The more industrialized and technically advanced nations tend to monopolize certain technological interests by protective measures, such as patents, copyrights, licensing, and registration requirements. It is often the very technology that these countries seek to withhold that the less-developed countries most desire and need for their future development and growth.

QUESTIONS AND CASE PROBLEMS

1. Suppose that Arnold Roth enters into an agreement to purchase widgets from Manufacturers, Inc. Roth further

secures an irrevocable letter of credit from Sunnydays Bank. When Manufacturers, Inc. placed the sixty crates of widgets on board a steamship, it received in return the invoices required under the letter of credit. The purchaser, Arnold Roth, subsequently learns that Manufacturers, Inc. has filled the sixty crates with rubbish—not widgets. Given the fact that an issuer's obligation under a letter of credit is independent of the underlying contract between the buyer and seller, will the issuer be required to pay the draft? See UCC 5-114(2) (a).

2. Verlinden B. V., the plaintiff, entered into a contract for the purchase of 240,000 metric tons of cement by the Federal Republic of Nigeria, the defendant. Verlinden B. V., a Dutch corporation, subsequently sued the Central Bank of Nigeria and alleged that the Central Bank's actions constituted an anticipatory breach. May a federal court exercise subject matter jurisdiction over an action brought by a foreign corporation against a foreign sovereign? Did Congress exceed the scope of Article III by granting federal district courts this jurisdiction? [Verlinden B. V. v. Central Bank of Nigeria, 461 U.S. 480, 103 S.Ct. 1962 (1983)]

3. Issues frequently arise as to whether or not a particular instrument is a "letter of credit" or an ordinary guaranty contract. A letter of credit creates a primary liability, whereas a guaranty contract imposes a secondary liability on the preexisting obligation of another. State statutes prohibit banks from guarantying the debt of another. Consider an instrument that is labeled a "letter of credit." Further assume that the instrument requires the bank (issuer) to do more than simply deal in documents. Is such an instrument a letter of credit or an ordinary guaranty contract? [Wichita Eagle & B. Pub. Co., Inc. v. Pacific Nat. Bk., San Fran., 493 F.2d 1285 (9th Cir. 1974)]

4. A letter of credit was issued by North Carolina National Bank for its customer, Adastra Knittiny Hills, Inc. The credit was to cover Adastra's purchases of acrylic yarn from Courtaulds, the beneficiary. Under the letter of credit, Courtaulds was to present a draft accompanied by a commercial invoice stating that it covers 100 percent acrylic yarn. When Courtaulds presented the draft, the accompanying invoices stated that the goods were "Imported Acrylic Yarn." The packing lists, however, disclosed that the packages contained 100 percent acrylic yarn. The bank refused to honor the draft. Under the traditional view, should the bank be liable to Courtaulds for the amount of the draft? [Courtaulds North America, Inc. v. N. C. Nat. Bank, 528 F.2d 802 (4th Cir. 1975)]

5. Section 1610(d) (1) of the Foreign Sovereign Immunities Act (FSIA) provides that the property of a foreign state that is used for a commercial activity in the U.S. shall not be immune from attachment prior to the entry of a judgment if the foreign state has "explicitly waived its immunity from attachment prior to judgment." Banco Nacional, an instrumentality of the government of Costa Rica, entered into a written agreement with Libra Bank LTD., the plaintiffs. In the agreement, Banco Nacional stated that it did not have "any right of immunity from suit with respect to the Borrower's obligations" under this particular agreement. Did Banco Nacional, the defendant, "explicitly" waive its immunity from prejudgment attachment as required by Section 1610(d)(1) of the FSIA? [Libra Bank LTD v. Banco Nacional de Costa Rica, 676 F.2d 47 (2d Cir. 1982)]

6. Harris Corporation, the plaintiff, entered into a contract with the defendant, National Iranian Radio and Television (NIRT), to manufacture and deliver 144 FM broadcast transmitters to Teheran, Iran. Due to the revolution in Iran, the plaintiff was unable to complete delivery of the transmitters. NIRT attempted to collect on a letter of credit that had been set up to guarantee performance. The plaintiff subsequently brought an action against the defendant seeking to enjoin receipt of payment on the letter of credit. Bank Melli Iran, the issuer, was also made a defendant. Both defendants alleged that the district court lacked jurisdiction over them. From 1969 to 1982, Melli maintained an office in New York City where it carried out significant business transactions. Moreover, NIRT entered into this contract that required performance by Harris in the U.S. and also the training of NIRT personnel in the U.S. Is this action consistent with due process? Has the "minimum contacts" standard established by *International Shoe Co. v. Washington* [326 U.S. 10, 66 S.Ct. 154 (1945)], discussed in Chapter 38, been satisfied? [Harris Corp. v. National Iranian Radio, Etc., 691 F.2d 1344 (11th Cir. 1982)]

FOCUS ON ETHICS

Protection of Property and Other Interests

The legal structures that support our ideas about property are crucial to the continuation of our economic system. Indeed, private property is at the heart of pure capitalist ideology. Nonetheless, alternative views about private property abound; for example, Marxists have often equated private property with theft. Consider some questions relating to property that raise ethical issues.

PATENTS, TRADEMARKS, AND COPYRIGHTS

Personal property includes the rights associated with the ownership of patents, trademarks, and copyrights. In the world of business, it is always possible that one person may intentionally infringe on someone else's patent, trademark, or copyright. The "infringer" reaps the rewards of another's creativity without incurring those expenses associated with the protection of the original item or idea. In turn, the original owner suffers a decrease in profits. Consider a situation where a businessperson took aerial photographs of a competing plant's layout. Then assume that the court ultimately concludes that such conduct is improper and thus orders the defendant not to use any of the information

so obtained. Clearly, in many situations such an order is ineffective. How can you order someone to forget what they have seen?

Furthermore, many businesses will infringe on copyrights and patents when they know that the cost of enforcing these copyrights and patents is prohibitive. In other words, it is not often economically feasible for the owner of a patent, trademark, or copyright to enforce such ownership rights. The expected costs to an owner of a patent desiring to enforce his or her rights include legal fees as well as time spent engaging in such a lawsuit. The expected benefits include any damages awarded in a successful lawsuit, plus any future increase in revenues if the patent, trademark, or copyright is no longer violated. Thus, when an infringement occurs, owners of patents, trademarks, and copyrights will pursue litigation only if the expected benefits exceed the expected costs. Because of this cost-benefit computation and the fact that litigation costs are normally high, the majority of patent, trademark, and copyright infringements in the United States are probably not prosecuted. The ones that are prosecuted usually involve extremely successful products.

THE EXPANDING NATURE OF PERSONAL PROPERTY

Recently a new set of ethical questions has arisen with regard to personal property. Today computer software programs are considered personal property. The incidence of "theft" of computer programs is indeed astounding. Unfortunately, to some individuals, personal property means only *tangible* personal property. These individuals do not consider ethical questions when the theft involves nontangible personal property. How many people think nothing of illegally duplicating copyrighted diskettes? How many people feel compunction about reproducing copyrighted movies?

THE BETAMAX CONTROVERSY

As a result of the recent technological advances in the area of home entertainment, significant ethical issues have arisen. The development of video-cassette recorders (VCRs) certainly makes it possible, and indeed quite tempting, for us to tape TV programs for our viewing convenience. But how far can you go in taping other people's materials? What are the limits? Is it fair to videotape a ball game, play it on your large screen, invite customers to see it—all without paying anything?

This type of recording of copyrighted movies and TV programs has attracted widespread attention. Owners of copyrighted audio-visual works are clearly adversely affected by the home taping of movies and special programs since the copyright owners are not compensated for the copies being made. Remember that the purpose of the copyright laws is to encourage and reward creativity by securing for copyright owners, for a limited time, the exclusive right to reproduce copyrighted works. This limited right clearly provides an economic incentive for people to be creative—and creativity is one of the primary ways by which society progresses.

The Supreme Court case of *Sony Corporation of America v. Universal City Studios* (—— U.S. ——, 104 S.Ct. 774 [1984]), frequently referred to as the "Betamax" case, focused on ethical considerations of the above-mentioned issue of in-home taping of TV movies and programs. The Court specifically addressed the issue of whether the sale of videotape recorders, most certainly to be used for home video recording of free television programs, violates the exclusive right of copyright owners to reproduce copyrighted works. Universal City Studios, owners of copyrights on some TV programs that are broadcast on public airwaves, brought an action against the Sony Corporation, who manufactures and sells home VCRs. The plaintiffs contended that the defendants were liable for copyright infringement as either direct or contributory infringers because the home recording of

their copyrighted programs by Betamax owners constituted a copyright infringement. No relief was sought against any Betamax consumer.

In a five-to-four decision, the majority of the Court held that the sale of the VCRs to the public does not constitute contributory infringement of the plaintiffs' copyrights. The Court concluded that, since many copyright holders who license their works for broadcast on free television would not object to home taping for noncommercial use, the equipment that makes such copying feasible should not be stifled simply because some copyright holders happen to object to this home taping. Furthermore, the Court stated that the plaintiffs had failed to show that noncommercial use of a copyrighted work is harmful or that, if this use should ever become widespread, it would adversely affect the potential market for the plaintiffs' copyrighted works. The fear of copyright owners that they had lost control over their property was disregarded. The district court's theory that it is not implausible that benefits from time-shifting for viewers' convenience could also accrue to the plaintiffs was also restated.

The effect of the Supreme Court's decision is to allow only the VCR manufacturers to benefit from this new market. The Supreme Court accepted the district court's findings of the time-shifting as a noncommercial, nonprofit activity falling within the "fair use" exemption of the copyright laws. But what if the Betamax were used to make copies for a commercial or profit-making purpose? In *Sony,* the Court stated that in such a case the use would presumptively be

unfair and thus not fall within the "fair use" doctrine. In order for a fair-use privilege to be found, the value to the public must override the copyright holder's interest.

The closeness of the *Sony* decision emphasizes the difficulty in dealing with some of the legal ramifications of technological developments. Many people are unhappy with the Supreme Court's decision in this case and are looking to Congress for legislative action. Various proposed items of legislation seek to change the result reached in the Betamax case. Do you believe, for example, that a royalty fee should be paid by VCR manufacturers to copyright owners in return for a license? Solutions such as these are embodied in pending legislation.

COMPUTER PIRACY

Tremendous growth in the microcomputer industry in recent years has also raised numerous ethical considerations. Many people claim that copyright law has failed to keep up with the unethical behavior that is now possible in our legal system. Some types of computer programs are protected under the copyright laws; yet computer software can exist in several forms. In the past, manufacturers of computer software marketed their programs in an unreadable form stored in a silicon chip. But now technology has advanced to the point where programs stored in these silicon chips can be "pirated."

The potential value of pirating computer programs, combined with the uncertainty of the law itself, has encouraged program piracy. Even though some courts will impose liability on this unethical behavior, others refuse to extend protection to a subject matter that has traditionally been found to be outside the copyright laws. Consequently, the computer industry has urged courts to extend copyright protection to computer programs stored in silicon chips. It has also requested the adoption of new legislation to assure adequate protection of computer software. Thus, new situations in which unethical behavior is possible seem to accompany technological advances.

THE QUESTION OF LAND USE CONTROL

Land use control legislation and regulation are prevalent throughout the United States. Often such land use control is undertaken in the name of "the public." But one must realize the consequences of such actions. Consider the effect of legislation altering property owners' rights in coastal sections of the United States. Let's suppose that prior to the legislation, owners of land in coastal areas could use that land in any way they wanted. They could build condominiums, golf courses, or do nothing. After the legislation, a committee is formed that passes judgment on each requested change in the current use of land. Let us suppose that a large amount of unaltered land is desired for coastal areas, even though that land is private property. If the committee routinely does not allow condominiums and housing developments to be built on the land, its market value will fall. Now we are entering into a taking issue, which is part of the Fifth Amendment to the United States Constitution. Government agencies maintain that land use control does not involve a taking because the physical possession of the land remains

in the hands of the private owner. From an economic point of view, however, a taking has occurred because the net worth of the property owner subsequently falls when land use controls restrict the way in which the land can be used.

Who has a greater ethical concern in this issue—the private owner of the land and the potential occupants of condominiums and housing developments on the land or the nonowner who would like to see the land remain undeveloped and use the beaches and surrounding lands? No easy answer is available. Whatever decision is made concerning the use of the land, someone will benefit and someone will lose. Whenever there is a trade-off in terms of who benefits and who loses in the use of an economic resource, we can only make value judgments—we cannot provide a cut-and-dried answer as to what is appropriate.

INSURANCE

In the area of insurance, one of the major ethical concerns involves moral hazard, a topic to which we have referred on several occasions. In the insurance industry moral hazard occurs when individuals or companies have an incentive to act negligently or to engage in activities that will result in payment by an insurance company. For example, the businessperson who takes out a large insurance policy on a building has less incentive to take care that the building is protected from potential fire than an individual without an insurance policy. What is the ethical responsibility of the owner of the building when insurance is in effect? Is he or she exempt from taking precautions against a fire?

The same issue arises for insurance policies that cover losses due to theft. The smaller the deductible in such policies, the less incentive the property owner has to prevent loss due to theft. For example, with insurance in effect, the property owner may have less incentive to install alarm systems, to pay for private patrol service, and so on. Of course, the more claims made on such insurance policies, the higher the average insurance rate per dollar amount insured. Thus, those individuals who are careless about protecting their own property impose costs on all individuals who buy property insurance.

Moral hazard exists with medical insurance also. The smaller the deductible, the greater the incentive for the individual not to practice preventive medicine. What is the ethical responsibility of the individual citizen in terms of providing for his or her own well-being? Because health insurance is available for most individuals in the United States, does that mean that individuals should not be concerned about smoking, being overweight, too much sugar in their diets, and so on? Indeed, it is argued that in the United States, too many resources are devoted to the care of those who are already sick and too few resources to preventive medicine.

Concerning the insurer of property, consider what his or her ethical viewpoint must be. Should the insurer settle when there is a doubt or should he or she require litigation before making payment?

THE WORK OF ACCOUNTANTS DOES NOT GO UNNOTICED

Recently, the situation surrounding ESM Government

Securities, Inc., has brought to light the allegedly unethical behavior of one accountant in particular—Jose Gomez. The Securities and Exchange Commission (SEC) charged Gomez with accepting $125,000 from company officers while issuing false financial statements that were used to lure investors to the Fort Lauderdale firm (March 1985). Quite obviously, auditors are frequently placed in positions in which they can act either ethically or unethically with respect to great sums of money.

When ESM Government Securities, Inc. failed on March 4, 1985, more than two dozen cities and financial institutions may have lost nearly $300 million. The SEC has charged that since 1977 ESM has hidden losses of more than $240 million. In addition, the SEC has further alleged that ESM officers directly transferred money from their personal bank accounts to Gomez's bank account six days after Gomez reviewed the ESM books. When Alexander Grant & Co., the prestigious national accounting firm of which Gomez was a partner, audited ESM's books (through Gomez), it had certified that it was an independent auditor. The SEC, however, has presently charged that because Gomez received money from company directors, the firm was not independent and hence a fraud was committed. In addition, Gomez held himself out as issuing clean financial statements—in other words, not hiding losses.

The fraud *charges* against Jose Gomez have stunned many individuals. The repercussions from the failure of ESM, which are at least *in part* allegedly the result of Gomez's behavior, are tremendous. Thus, even though it is uncertain at

this time whether or not Jose Gomez is guilty of these charges, it is clear that accountants may often come under pressure to act in ways that are less than ethical.

THE "LIVING WILL"

Wills generally deal solely with the distribution of property and take effect *only* upon a client's death. The living will, however, is a different kind of will. This will takes effect during the client's lifetime and concerns the *person,* rather than the *estate,* of the client.

The living will permits the client's physician to withhold or to terminate medical care when such care does not appear to be in the patient's interest and, moreover, is simply prolonging life. To put it mildly, this type of will is very controversial. Many people feel that it is morally wrong to allow a person to consent to the withholding or termination of medical care and treatment. Thus, the question arises: Should we allow members of our society to obtain a living will? Quite often we do protect people from themselves, as is illustrated by the fact that people are required to wear motorcycle helmets and seat belts in many states or by the fact that many drugs are legally prohibited.

Furthermore, even if we are to conclude that the option of procuring a living will is acceptable in our society, the question then arises as to how, and to what extent, we want to recognize the use of living wills. On October 1, 1984, the Wisconsin Natural Death Act became effective. This act sets forth a procedure for obtaining and signing a living will. In addition, the act includes a

specific form that may be used by attorneys, clients, and health care providers. Yet whenever a statute expresses a specific form for dealing with a particular situation, many people are reluctant to seek out variations on the statutory forms.

The question of restrictions upon living wills must also be considered. At what point should we allow patients to terminate life-sustaining procedures? The Wisconsin act, for example, allows life-sustaining procedures to be terminated only if two physicians agree that death will occur within thirty days. The act also permits some kinds of life-support systems to be terminated, but not others. Yet why should we draw the lines here? Some people have suggested that we should ask whether the brain is functioning and whether there is any expectation that the patient will continue to enjoy what is truly life in determining who among us should live or die. Drawing these types of lines is extremely difficult.

It is not unheard of for young, healthy individuals to be injured in a severe automobile accident or to become a victim of a terminal disease. Thus, an individual should be aware of the position of his or her state with respect to these "living wills," as well as the option of leaving a will that concerns the person of the client. If individuals are dissatisfied with the requirements and guidelines of a particular state's "living will" statute or with the fact that a state may not have one, the possibility of amendment or enactment of a statute is always present. As stated throughout these sections on ethics, the law gradually evolves in order to embody society's changing perceptions of what is ethical.

DISCUSSION QUESTIONS

1. Given the expanding nature of personal property today, an appropriate question is "What is the true nature of property?" And indeed, "What is ownership?"

2. What property interests should be protected by law? Does one have a personal property interest in a job? In a spouse? In children?

3. Whose interests should come first in the question of land use control?

4. If an applicant for insurance makes a materially false statement, to what extent is the insurer liable when a subsequent claim is made?

APPENDIX A

HOW TO BRIEF
A CASE

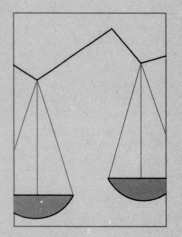

In order to fully understand the law and its implications with respect to business, it is necessary to be able to both read and understand court decisions. A method of case analysis, often referred to as a *briefing*, facilitates such an understanding of the law. There is a fairly standard procedure that may be followed when briefing a case in this book or in any other book. A case must first be read carefully. When you feel that you understand the case, you can prepare a brief of it. Briefing a case while reading the case for the first time does little to enhance your business law education.

Although the format of a brief may vary, it will typically contain the following essentials:

1. Full case citation, including the name of the case and the date it was decided.
2. Facts.
3. Issue(s).
4. Holding.
5. Reasoning (including policy).

In preparing a brief, it is necessary to incorporate all the important facts. A brief, however, by definition should be *brief*. In Chapter 1, the student was exposed to "how to analyze case law." The following illustrates a brief of that same case, *N.L.R.B. v. Bildisco and Bildisco*.

CASE CITATION: **N.L.R.B. v. BILDISCO AND BILDISCO**
United States Supreme Court, 465 U.S. 513, 104 S.Ct. 1188, 1984.

FACTS: The plaintiff, Bildisco, filed a voluntary petition in bankruptcy for reorganization under Chapter 11. The bankruptcy court granted Bildisco permission to reject its collective-bargaining agreement. Subsequently, both the Union and the National Labor Relations Board appealed.

ISSUE(S): The first issue is whether or not the bankruptcy court was correct in permitting Bildisco, as a debtor-in-possession, to reject a collective-bargaining agreement under Section 365(a) of the Bankruptcy Code.

The second issue is whether or not the NRLA can find a debtor-in-possession guilty of an unfair labor practice for unilaterally rejecting or modifying a collective-bargaining agreement before formal rejection by the bankruptcy court.

HOLDING: Rejection of a collective-bargaining agreement under 365(a) of the Bankruptcy Code is permissible if the debtor satisfies certain conditions. If the debtor can show that "the collective-bargaining agreement burdens the estate" and that "the equities balance in favor of rejecting the labor contract," then the bankruptcy court should permit such a rejection. Bildisco satisfied this test.

Bildisco cannot be found guilty of an unfair labor practice by unilaterally breaching a collective-bargaining agreement before formal rejection by the bankruptcy court.

REASONING: In concluding that the bankruptcy court must balance the interests of the affected parties, the Supreme Court is trying to ensure that rejection of such contracts will not be allowed unless Chapter 11's policy of permitting successful rehabilitation of debtors is promoted.

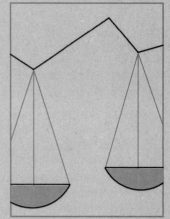

THE CONSTITUTION OF THE UNITED STATES

PREAMBLE

We the People of the United States, in Order to form a more perfect Union, establish Justice, insure domestic Tranquility, provide for the common defence, promote the general Welfare, and secure the Blessings of Liberty to ourselves and our Posterity, do ordain and establish this Constitution for the United States of America.

ARTICLE I

Section 1. All legislative Powers herein granted shall be vested in a Congress of the United States, which shall consist of a Senate and House of Representatives.

Section 2. The House of Representatives shall be composed of Members chosen every second Year by the People of the several States, and the Electors in each State shall have the Qualifications requisite for Electors of the most numerous Branch of the State Legislature.

No Person shall be a Representative who shall not have attained to the Age of twenty five Years, and been seven Years a Citizen of the United States, and who shall not, when elected, be an Inhabitant of that State in which he shall be chosen.

Representatives and direct Taxes shall be apportioned among the several States which may be included within this Union, according to their respective Numbers, which shall be determined by adding to the whole Number of free Persons, including those bound to Service for a Term of Years, and excluding Indians not taxed, three fifths of all other Persons. The actual Enumeration shall be made within three Years after the first Meeting of the Congress of the United States, and within every subsequent Term of ten Years, in such Manner as they shall by Law direct. The Number of Representatives shall not exceed one for every thirty Thousand, but each State shall have at Least one Representative; and until such enumeration shall be made, the State of New Hampshire shall be entitled to chuse three, Massachusetts eight, Rhode Island and Providence Plantations one, Connecticut five, New York six, New Jersey four, Pennsylvania eight, Delaware one, Maryland six, Virginia ten, North Carolina five, South Carolina five, and Georgia three.

When vacancies happen in the Representation from any State, the Executive Authority thereof shall issue Writs of Election to fill such Vacancies.

The House of Representatives shall chuse their Speaker and other Officers; and shall have the sole Power of Impeachment.

Section 3. The Senate of the United States shall be composed of two Senators from each State, chosen by the Legislature thereof, for six Years; and each Senator shall have one Vote.

Immediately after they shall be assembled in Consequence of the first Election, they shall be divided as equally as may be into three Classes. The Seats of the Senators of the first Class shall be vacated at the Expiration of the second Year, of the second Class at the Expiration of the fourth Year, and of the third Class at the Expiration of the sixth Year, so that one third may be chosen every second Year; and if Vacancies happen by Resignation, or otherwise, during the Recess of the Legislature of any State, the Executive thereof may make temporary Appointments until the next Meeting of the Legislature, which shall then fill such Vacancies.

No Person shall be a Senator who shall not have attained to the Age of thirty Years, and been nine Years a Citizen of the United States, and who shall not, when elected, be an Inhabitant of that State for which he shall be chosen.

The Vice President of the United States shall be President of the Senate, but shall have no Vote, unless they be equally divided.

The Senate shall chuse their other Officers, and also a President pro tempore, in the Absence of the Vice President, or when he shall exercise the Office of President of the United States.

The Senate shall have the sole Power to try all Impeachments. When sitting for that Purpose, they shall be on Oath or Affirmation. When the President of the United States is tried, the Chief Justice shall preside: And no Person shall be convicted without the Concurrence of two thirds of the Members present.

Judgment in Cases of Impeachment shall not extend further than to removal from Office, and disqualification to hold and enjoy any Office of honor, Trust, or Profit under the United States: but the Party convicted shall nevertheless be liable and subject to Indictment, Trial, Judgment, and Punishment, according to Law.

Section 4. The Times, Places and Manner of holding Elections for Senators and Representatives, shall be prescribed in each State by the Legislature thereof; but the Congress may at any time by Law make or alter such Regulations, except as to the Places of chusing Senators.

The Congress shall assemble at least once in every Year, and such Meeting shall be on the first Monday in December, unless they shall by Law appoint a different Day.

Section 5. Each House shall be the Judge of the Elections, Returns, and Qualifications of its own Members, and a Majority of each shall constitute a Quorum to do Business; but a smaller Number may adjourn from day to day, and may be authorized to compel the Attendance of absent Members, in such Manner, and under such Penalties as each House may provide.

Each House may determine the Rules of its Proceedings, punish its Members for disorderly Behavior, and, with the Concurrence of two thirds, expel a Member.

Each House shall keep a Journal of its Proceedings, and from time to time publish the same, excepting such Parts as may in their Judgment require Secrecy; and the Yeas and Nays of the Members of either House on any question shall, at the Desire of one fifth of those Present, be entered on the Journal.

Neither House, during the Session of Congress, shall, without the Consent of the other, adjourn for more than three days, nor to any other Place than that in which the two Houses shall be sitting.

Section 6.   The Senators and Representatives shall receive a Compensation for their Services, to be ascertained by Law, and paid out of the Treasury of the United States. They shall in all Cases, except Treason, Felony and Breach of the Peace, be privileged from Arrest during their Attendance at the Session of their respective Houses, and in going to and returning from the same; and for any Speech or Debate in either House, they shall not be questioned in any other Place.

No Senator or Representative shall, during the Time for which he was elected, be appointed to any civil Office under the Authority of the United States, which shall have been created, or the Emoluments whereof shall have been increased during such time; and no Person holding any Office under the United States, shall be a Member of either House during his Continuance in Office.

Section 7.   All Bills for raising Revenue shall originate in the House of Representatives; but the Senate may propose or concur with Amendments as on other Bills.

Every Bill which shall have passed the House of Representatives and the Senate, shall, before it become a Law, be presented to the President of the United States; If he approve he shall sign it, but if not he shall return it, with his Objections to the House in which it shall have originated, who shall enter the Objections at large on their Journal, and proceed to reconsider it. If after such Reconsideration two thirds of that House shall agree to pass the Bill, it shall be sent together with the Objections, to the other House, by which it shall likewise be reconsidered, and if approved by two thirds of that House, it shall become a Law. But in all such Cases the Votes of both Houses shall be determined by Yeas and Nays, and the Names of the Persons voting for and against the Bill shall be entered on the Journal of each House respectively. If any Bill shall not be returned by the President within ten Days (Sundays excepted) after it shall have been presented to him, the Same shall be a Law, in like Manner as if he had signed it, unless the Congress by their Adjournment prevent its Return in which Case it shall not be a Law.

Every Order, Resolution, or Vote, to which the Concurrence of the Senate and House of Representatives may be necessary (except on a question of Adjournment) shall be presented to the President of the United States; and before the Same shall take Effect, shall be approved by him, or being disapproved by him, shall be repassed by two thirds of the Senate and House of Representatives, according to the Rules and Limitations prescribed in the Case of a Bill.

Section 8.   The Congress shall have Power To lay and collect Taxes, Duties, Imposts and Excises, to pay the Debts and provide for the common Defence and general Welfare of the United States; but all Duties, Imposts and Excises shall be uniform throughout the United States;

To borrow Money on the credit of the United States;

To regulate Commerce with foreign Nations, and among the several States, and with the Indian Tribes;

To establish an uniform Rule of Naturalization, and uniform Laws on the subject of Bankruptcies throughout the United States;

To coin Money, regulate the Value thereof, and of foreign Coin, and fix the Standard of Weights and Measures;

To provide for the Punishment of counterfeiting the Securities and current Coin of the United States;

To establish Post Offices and post Roads;

To promote the Progress of Science and useful Arts, by securing for limited Times to Authors and Inventors the exclusive Right to their respective Writings and Discoveries;

To constitute Tribunals inferior to the supreme Court;

To define and punish Piracies and Felonies committed on the high Seas, and Offenses against the Law of Nations;

To declare War, grant Letters of Marque and Reprisal, and make Rules concerning Captures on Land and Water;

To raise and support Armies, but no Appropriation of Money to that Use shall be for a longer Term than two Years;

To provide and maintain a Navy;

To make Rules for the Government and Regulation of the land and naval Forces;

To provide for calling forth the Militia to execute the Laws of the Union, suppress Insurrections and repel Invasions;

To provide for organizing, arming, and disciplining, the Militia, and for governing such Part of them as may be employed in the Service of the United States, reserving to the States respectively, the Appointment of the Officers, and the Authority of training the Militia according to the discipline prescribed by Congress;

To exercise exclusive Legislation in all Cases whatsoever, over such District (not exceeding ten Miles square) as may, by Cession of particular States, and the Acceptance of Congress, become the Seat of the Government of the United States, and to exercise like Authority over all Places purchased by the Consent of the Legislature of the State in which the Same shall be, for the Erection of Forts, Magazines, Arsenals, dock-Yards, and other needful Buildings;—And

To make all Laws which shall be necessary and proper for carrying into Execution the foregoing Powers, and all other Powers vested by this Constitution in the Government of the United States, or in any Department or Officer thereof.

Section 9.   The Migration or Importation of such Persons as any of the States now existing shall think proper to admit, shall not be prohibited by the Congress prior to the Year one thousand eight hundred and eight, but a Tax or duty may be imposed on such Importation, not exceeding ten dollars for each Person.

The privilege of the Writ of Habeas Corpus shall not be suspended, unless when in Cases of Rebellion or Invasion the public Safety may require it.

No Bill of Attainder or ex post facto Law shall be passed.

No Capitation, or other direct, Tax shall be laid, unless in Proportion to the Census or Enumeration herein before directed to be taken.

No Tax or Duty shall be laid on Articles exported from any State.

No Preference shall be given by any Regulation of Commerce or Revenue to the Ports of one State over those of another: nor shall Vessels bound to, or from, one State be obliged to enter, clear, or pay Duties in another.

No Money shall be drawn from the Treasury, but in Consequence of Appropriations made by Law; and a regular Statement and Account of the Receipts and Expenditures of all public Money shall be published from time to time.

No Title of Nobility shall be granted by the United States: And no Person holding any Office of Profit or Trust under them, shall, without the Consent of the Congress, accept of any present, Emolument, Office, or Title, of any kind whatever, from any King, Prince, or foreign State.

Section 10.   No State shall enter into any Treaty, Alliance, or Confederation; grant Letters of Marque and Reprisal; coin Money; emit Bills of Credit; make any Thing but gold and silver Coin a Tender in Payment of Debts; pass any Bill of Attainder, ex post facto Law, or Law impairing the Obligation of Contracts, or grant any Title of Nobility.

No State shall, without the Consent of the Congress, lay any Imposts or Duties on Imports or Exports, except what may be absolutely necessary for executing it's inspection Laws: and the net Produce of all Duties and Imposts, laid by any State on Imports or Exports, shall be for the Use of the Treasury of the United States; and all such Laws shall be subject to the Revision and Controul of the Congress.

No State shall, without the Consent of Congress, lay any Duty of Tonnage, keep Troops, or Ships of War in time of Peace, enter into any Agreement or Compact with another State, or with a foreign Power, or engage in War, unless actually invaded, or in such imminent Danger as will not admit of delay.

ARTICLE II

Section 1.   The executive Power shall be vested in a President of the United States of America. He shall hold his Office during the Term of four Years, and, together with the Vice President, chosen for the same Term, be elected, as follows:

Each State shall appoint, in such Manner as the Legislature thereof may direct, a Number of Electors, equal to the whole Number of Senators and Representatives to which the State may be entitled in the Congress; but no Senator or Representative, or Person holding an Office of Trust or Profit under the United States, shall be appointed an Elector.

The Electors shall meet in their respective States, and vote by Ballot for two Persons, of whom one at least shall not be an Inhabitant of the same State with themselves. And they shall make a List of all the Persons voted for, and of the Number of Votes for each; which List they shall sign and certify, and transmit sealed to the Seat of the Government of the United States, directed to the President of the Senate. The President of the Senate shall, in the Presence of the Senate and House of Representatives, open all the Certificates, and the Votes shall then be counted. The Person having the greatest Number of Votes shall be the President, if such Number be a Majority of the whole Number of Electors appointed; and if there be more than one who have such Majority, and have an equal Number of Votes, then the House of Representatives shall immediately chuse by Ballot one of them for President; and if no Person have a Majority, then from the five highest on the List the said House shall in like

Manner chuse the President. But in chusing the President, the Votes shall be taken by States, the Representation from each State having one Vote; A quorum for this Purpose shall consist of a Member or Members from two thirds of the States, and a Majority of all the States shall be necessary to a Choice. In every Case, after the Choice of the President, the Person having the greater Number of Votes of the Electors shall be the Vice President. But if there should remain two or more who have equal Votes, the Senate shall chuse from them by Ballot the Vice President.

The Congress may determine the Time of chusing the Electors, and the Day on which they shall give their Votes; which Day shall be the same throughout the United States.

No person except a natural born Citizen, or a Citizen of the United States, at the time of the Adoption of this Constitution, shall be eligible to the Office of President; neither shall any Person be eligible to that Office who shall not have attained to the Age of thirty five Years, and been fourteen Years a Resident within the United States.

In Case of the Removal of the President from Office, or of his Death, Resignation or Inability to discharge the Powers and Duties of the said Office, the same shall devolve on the Vice President, and the Congress may by Law provide for the Case of Removal, Death, Resignation or Inability, both of the President and Vice President, declaring what Officer shall then act as President, and such Officer shall act accordingly, until the Disability be removed, or a President shall be elected.

The President shall, at stated Times, receive for his Services, a Compensation, which shall neither be increased nor diminished during the Period for which he shall have been elected, and he shall not receive within that Period any other Emolument from the United States, or any of them.

Before he enter on the Execution of his Office, he shall take the following Oath or Affirmation: "I do solemnly swear (or affirm) that I will faithfully execute the Office of President of the United States, and will to the best of my Ability, preserve, protect and defend the Constitution of the United States."

Section 2. The President shall be Commander in Chief of the Army and Navy of the United States, and of the Militia of the several States, when called into the actual Service of the United States; he may require the Opinion, in writing, of the principal Officer in each of the executive Departments, upon any Subject relating to the Duties of their respective Offices, and he shall have Power to grant Reprieves and Pardons for Offenses against the United States, except in Cases of Impeachment.

He shall have Power, by and with the Advice and Consent of the Senate to make Treaties, provided two thirds of the Senators present concur; and he shall nominate, and by and with the Advice and Consent of the Senate, shall appoint Ambassadors, other public Ministers and Consuls, Judges of the supreme Court, and all other Officers of the United States, whose Appointments are not herein otherwise provided for, and which shall be established by Law; but the Congress may by Law vest the Appointment of such inferior Officers, as they think proper, in the President alone, in the Courts of Law, or in the Heads of Departments.

The President shall have Power to fill up all Vacancies that may happen during the Recess of the Senate, by granting Commissions which shall expire at the End of their next Session.

Section 3. He shall from time to time give to the Congress Information of the State of the Union, and recommend to their Consideration such Measures as he shall judge necessary and expedient; he may, on extraordinary Occasions, convene both Houses, or either of them, and in Case of Disagreement between them, with Respect to the Time of Adjournment, he may adjourn them to such Time as he shall think proper; he shall receive Ambassadors and other public Ministers; he shall take Care that the Laws be faithfully executed, and shall Commission all the Officers of the United States.

Section 4. The President, Vice President and all civil Officers of the United States, shall be removed from Office on Impeachment for, and Conviction of, Treason, Bribery, or other high Crimes and Misdemeanors.

Article III

Section 1. The judicial Power of the United States, shall be vested in one supreme Court, and in such inferior Courts as the Congress may from time to time ordain and establish. The Judges, both of the supreme and inferior Courts, shall hold their Offices during good Behaviour, and shall, at stated Times, receive for their Services a Compensation, which shall not be diminished during their Continuance in Office.

Section 2. The judicial Power shall extend to all Cases, in Law and Equity, arising under this Constitution, the Laws of the United States, and Treaties made, or which shall be made, under their Authority;—to all Cases affecting Ambassadors, other public Ministers and Consuls;—to all Cases of admiralty and maritime Jurisdiction;—to Controversies to which the United States shall be a Party;—to Controversies between two or more States;—between a State and Citizens of another State;—between Citizens of different States;—between Citizens of the same State claiming Lands under Grants of different States, and between a State, or the Citizens thereof, and foreign States, Citizens or Subjects.

In all Cases affecting Ambassadors, other public Ministers and Consuls, and those in which a State shall be a Party, the supreme Court shall have original Jurisdiction. In all the other Cases before mentioned, the supreme Court shall have appellate Jurisdiction, both as to Law and Fact, with such Exceptions, and under such Regulations as the Congress shall make.

The Trial of all Crimes, except in Cases of Impeachment, shall be by Jury; and such Trial shall be held in the State where the said Crimes shall have been committed; but when not committed within any State, the Trial shall be at such Place or Places as the Congress may by Law have directed.

Section 3.   Treason against the United States, shall consist only in levying War against them, or, in adhering to their Enemies, giving them Aid and Comfort. No Person shall be convicted of Treason unless on the Testimony of two Witnesses to the same overt Act, or on Confession in open Court.

The Congress shall have Power to declare the Punishment of Treason, but no Attainder of Treason shall work Corruption of Blood, or Forfeiture except during the Life of the Person attainted.

ARTICLE IV

Section 1.   Full Faith and Credit shall be given in each State to the public Acts, Records, and judicial Proceedings of every other State. And the Congress may by general Laws prescribe the Manner in which such Acts, Records and Proceedings shall be proved, and the Effect thereof.

Section 2.   The Citizens of each State shall be entitled to all Privileges and Immunities of Citizens in the several States.

A Person charged in any State with Treason, Felony, or other Crime, who shall flee from Justice, and be found in another State, shall on Demand of the executive Authority of the State from which he fled, be delivered up, to be removed to the State having Jurisdiction of the Crime.

No Person held to Service or Labour in one State, under the Laws thereof, escaping into another, shall, in Consequence of any Law or Regulation therein, be discharged from such Service or Labour, but shall be delivered up on Claim of the Party to whom such Service or Labour may be due.

Section 3.   New States may be admitted by the Congress into this Union; but no new State shall be formed or erected within the Jurisdiction of any other State; nor any State be formed by the Junction of two or more States,

or Parts of States, without the Consent of the Legislatures of the States concerned as well as of the Congress.

The Congress shall have Power to dispose of and make all needful Rules and Regulations respecting the Territory or other Property belonging to the United States; and nothing in this Constitution shall be so construed as to Prejudice any Claims of the United States, or of any particular State.

Section 4.   The United States shall guarantee to every State in this Union a Republican Form of Government, and shall protect each of them against Invasion; and on Application of the Legislature, or of the Executive (when the Legislature cannot be convened) against domestic Violence.

ARTICLE V

The Congress, whenever two thirds of both Houses shall deem it necessary, shall propose Amendments to this Constitution, or, on the Application of the Legislatures of two thirds of the several States, shall call a Convention for proposing Amendments, which, in either Case, shall be valid to all Intents and Purposes, as part of this Constitution, when ratified by the Legislatures of three fourths of the several States, or by Conventions in three fourths thereof, as the one or the other Mode of Ratification may be proposed by the Congress; Provided that no Amendment which may be made prior to the Year One thousand eight hundred and eight shall in any Manner affect the first and fourth Clauses in the Ninth Section of the first Article; and that no State, without its Consent, shall be deprived of its equal Suffrage in the Senate.

ARTICLE VI

All Debts contracted and Engagements entered into, before the Adoption of this Constitution shall be as valid against the United States under this Constitution, as under the Confederation.

This Constitution, and the Laws of the United States which shall be made in Pursuance thereof; and all Treaties made, or which shall be made, under the Authority of the United States, shall be the supreme Law of the Land; and the Judges in every State shall be bound thereby, any Thing in the Constitution or Laws of any State to the Contrary notwithstanding.

The Senators and Representatives before mentioned, and the Members of the several State Legislatures, and all executive and judicial Officers, both of the United States and of the several States, shall be bound by Oath or Affirmation, to support this Constitution; but no religious Test shall ever be required as a Qualification to any Office or public Trust under the United States.

ARTICLE VII

The Ratification of the Conventions of nine States shall be sufficient for the Establishment of this Constitution between the States so ratifying the Same.

AMENDMENT I [1791]

Congress shall make no law respecting an establishment of religion, or prohibiting the free exercise thereof; or abridging the freedom of speech, or of the press; or the right of the people peaceably to assembly, and to petition the Government for a redress of grievances.

AMENDMENT II [1791]

A well regulated Militia, being necessary to the security of a free State, the right of the people to keep and bear Arms, shall not be infringed.

AMENDMENT III [1791]

No Soldier shall, in time of peace be quartered in any house, without the consent of the Owner, nor in time of war, but in a manner to be prescribed by law.

Amendment IV [1791]

The right of the people to be secure in their persons, houses, papers, and effects, against unreasonable searches and seizures, shall not be violated, and no Warrants shall issue, but upon probable cause, supported by Oath or affirmation, and particularly describing the place to be searched, and the persons or things to be seized.

AMENDMENT V [1791]

No person shall be held to answer for a capital, or otherwise infamous crime, unless on a presentment or indictment of a Grand Jury, except in cases arising in the land or naval forces, or in the Militia, when in actual service in time of War or public danger; nor shall any person be subject for the same offence to be twice put in jeopardy of life or limb; nor shall be compelled in any criminal case to be a witness against himself, nor be deprived of life, liberty, or property, without due process of law; nor shall private property be taken for public use, without just compensation.

AMENDMENT VI [1791]

In all criminal prosecutions, the accused shall enjoy the right to a speedy and public trial, by an impartial jury of the State and district wherein the crime shall have been committed, which district shall have been previously ascertained by law, and to be informed of the nature and cause of the accusation; to be confronted with the witnesses against him; to have compulsory process for obtaining witnesses in his favor, and to have the Assistance of Counsel for his defence.

AMENDMENT VII [1791]

In Suits at common law, where the value in controversy shall exceed twenty dollars, the right of trial by jury shall be preserved, and no fact tried by jury, shall be otherwise re-examined in any Court of the United States, than according to the rules of the common law.

AMENDMENT VIII [1791]

Excessive bail shall not be required, nor excessive fines imposed, nor cruel and unusual punishments inflicted.

AMENDMENT IX [1791]

The enumeration in the Constitution, of certain rights, shall not be construed to deny or disparage others retained by the people.

AMENDMENT X [1791]

The powers not delegated to the United States by the Constitution, nor prohibited by it to the States, are reserved to the States respectively, or to the people.

AMENDMENT XI [1798]

The Judicial power of the United States shall not be construed to extend to any suit in law or equity, commenced or prosecuted against one of the United States by Citizens of another State, or by Citizens or Subjects of any Foreign State.

AMENDMENT XII [1804]

The Electors shall meet in their respective states, and vote by ballot for President and Vice-President, one of whom, at least, shall not be an inhabitant of the same state with themselves; they shall name in their ballots the person voted for as President, and in distinct ballots the person voted for as Vice-President, and they shall make distinct lists of all persons voted for as President, and of all persons voted for as Vice-President, and of the number of votes for each, which lists they shall sign and certify, and transmit sealed to the seat of the government of the United States, directed to the President of the Senate;—The President of the Senate shall, in the presence of the Senate and House of Representatives, open all the certificates and the votes shall then be counted;—The person having the greatest number of votes for President, shall be the President, if such number be a majority of the whole number of Electors appointed; and if no person have such majority, then from the persons having the highest numbers not exceeding three on the list of those voted for as President, the House of Representatives shall choose immediately, by ballot, the President. But in choosing the President, the votes shall be taken by states, the representation from each state having one vote; a quorum for this purpose shall consist of a member or members from two-thirds of the states, and a majority of all states shall be necessary to a choice. And if the House of Representatives shall not choose a President whenever the right of choice shall devolve upon them, before the fourth day of March next following, then the Vice-President shall act as President, as in the case of the death or other constitutional disability of the President.—The person having the greatest number of votes as Vice-President, shall be the Vice-President, if such number be a majority of the whole number of Electors appointed, and if no person have a majority, then from the two highest numbers on the list, the Senate shall choose the Vice-President; a quorum for the purpose shall consist of two-thirds of the whole number of Senators, and a majority of the whole number shall be necessary to a choice. But no person constitutionally ineligible to the office of President shall be eligible to that of Vice-President of the United States.

AMENDMENT XIII [1865]

Section 1. Neither slavery nor involuntary servitude, except as a punishment for crime whereof the party shall have been duly convicted, shall exist within the United States, or any place subject to their jurisdiction.

Section 2. Congress shall have power to enforce this article by appropriate legislation.

AMENDMENT XIV [1868]

Section 1. All persons born or naturalized in the United States, and subject to the jurisdiction thereof, are citizens of the United States and of the State wherein they reside. No State shall make or enforce any law which shall abridge the privileges or immunities of citizens of the United States; nor shall any State deprive any person of life, liberty, or property, without due process of law; nor deny to any person within its jurisdiction the equal protection of the laws.

Section 2. Representatives shall be apportioned among the several States according to their respective numbers, counting the whole number of persons in each State, excluding Indians not taxed. But when the right to vote at any election for the choice of electors for President and Vice President of the United States, Representatives in Congress, the Executive and Judicial officers of a State, or the members of the Legislature thereof, is denied to any of the male inhabitants of such State, being twenty-one years of age, and citizens of the United States, or in any way abridged, except for participation in rebellion, or other crime, the basis of representation therein shall be reduced in the proportion which the number of such male citizens shall bear to the whole number of male citizens twenty-one years of age in such State.

Section 3. No person shall be a Senator or Representative in Congress, or elector of President and Vice President, or hold any office, civil or military, under the United States, or under any State, who having previously taken an oath, as a member of Congress, or as an officer of the United States, or as a member of any State legislature, or as an executive or judicial officer of any State, to support the Constitution of the United States, shall have engaged in insurrection or rebellion against the same, or given aid or comfort to the enemies thereof. But Congress may by a vote of two-thirds of each House, remove such disability.

Section 4. The validity of the public debt of the United States, authorized by law, including debts incurred for payment of pensions and bounties for services in suppressing insurrection or rebellion, shall not be questioned. But neither the United States nor any State shall assume or pay any debt or obligation incurred in aid of insurrection or rebellion against the United States, or any claim for the loss or emancipation of any slave; but all such debts, obligations and claims shall be held illegal and void.

Section 5. The Congress shall have power to enforce, by appropriate legislation, the provisions of this article.

AMENDMENT XV [1870]

Section 1. The right of citizens of the United States to vote shall not be denied or abridged by the United States or by any State on account of race, color, or previous condition of servitude.

Section 2. The Congress shall have power to enforce this article by appropriate legislation.

AMENDMENT XVI [1913]

The Congress shall have power to lay and collect taxes on incomes, from whatever source derived, without apportionment among the several States, and without regard to any census or enumeration.

AMENDMENT XVII [1913]

[1] The Senate of the United States shall be composed of two Senators from each State, elected by the people thereof, for six years; and each Senator shall have one vote. The electors in each State shall have the qualifications requisite for electors of the most numerous branch of the State legislatures.

[2] When vacancies happen in the representation of any State in the Senate, the executive authority of such State shall issue writs of election to fill such vacancies: *Provided*, That the legislature of any State may empower the executive thereof to make temporary appointments until the people fill the vacancies by election as the legislature may direct.

[3] This amendment shall not be so construed as to affect the election or term of any Senator chosen before it becomes valid as part of the Constitution.

AMENDMENT XVIII [1919]

Section 1.   After one year from the ratification of this article the manufacture, sale, or transportation of intoxicating liquors within, the importation thereof into, or the exportation thereof from the United States and all territory subject to the jurisdiction thereof for beverage purposes is hereby prohibited.

Section 2.   The Congress and the several States shall have concurrent power to enforce this article by appropriate legislation.

Section 3.   This article shall be inoperative unless it shall have been ratified as an amendment to the Constitution by the legislatures of the several States, as provided in the Constitution, within seven years from the date of the submission hereof to the States by the Congress.

AMENDMENT XIX [1920]

[1] The right of citizens of the United States to vote shall not be denied or abridged by the United States or by any State on account of sex.

[2] Congress shall have power to enforce this article by appropriate legislation.

AMENDMENT XX [1933]

Section 1.   The terms of the President and Vice President shall end at noon on the 20th day of January, and the terms of Senators and Representatives at noon on the 3d day of January, of the years in which such terms would have ended if this article had not been ratified; and the terms of their successors shall then begin.

Section 2.   The Congress shall assemble at least once in every year, and such meeting shall begin at noon on the 3d day of January, unless they shall by law appoint a different day.

Section 3.   If, at the time fixed for the beginning of the term of the President, the President elect shall have died, the Vice President elect shall become President. If the President shall not have been chosen before the time fixed for the beginning of his term, or if the President elect shall have failed to qualify, then the Vice President elect shall act as President until a President shall have qualified; and the Congress may by law provide for the case wherein neither a President elect nor a Vice President elect shall have qualified, declaring who shall then act as President, or the manner in which one who is to act shall be selected, and such person shall act accordingly until a President or Vice President shall have qualified.

Section 4.   The Congress may by law provide for the case of the death of any of the persons from whom the House of Representatives may choose a President whenever the right of choice shall have devolved upon them, and for the case of the death of any of the persons from whom the Senate may choose a Vice President whenever the right of choice shall have devolved upon them.

Section 5.   Sections 1 and 2 shall take effect on the 15th day of October following the ratification of this article.

Section 6.   This article shall be inoperative unless it shall have been ratified as an amendment to the Constitution by the legislatures of three-fourths of the several States within seven years from the date of its submission.

AMENDMENT XXI [1933]

Section 1.   The eighteenth article of amendment to the Constitution of the United States is hereby repealed.

Section 2.   The transportation or importation into any State, Territory, or possession of the United States for delivery or use therein of intoxicating liquors, in violation of the laws thereof, is hereby prohibited.

Section 3.   This article shall be inoperative unless it shall have been ratified as an amendment to the Constitution by conventions in the several States, as provided in the Constitution, within seven years from the date of the submission hereof to the States by the Congress.

AMENDMENT XXII [1951]

Section 1.   No person shall be elected to the office of the President more than twice, and no person who has held the office of President, or acted as President, for more than two years of a term to which some other person was elected President shall be elected to the office of President more than once. But this Article shall not apply to any person holding the office of President when this Article was proposed by the Congress, and shall not prevent any person who may be holding the office of President, or acting as President, during the term within which this Article becomes operative from holding the office of President or acting as President during the remainder of such term.

Section 2.   This article shall be inoperative unless it shall have been ratified as an amendment to the Constitution by the legislatures of three-fourths of the several States within seven years from the date of its submission to the States by the Congress.

AMENDMENT XXIII [1961]

Section 1.   The District constituting the seat of Government of the United States shall appoint in such manner as the Congress may direct:

A number of electors of President and Vice President equal to the whole number of Senators and Representatives in Congress to which the District would be entitled if it were a State, but in no event more than the least populous state; they shall be in addition to those appointed by the states, but they shall be considered, for the purposes of the election of President and Vice President, to be electors appointed by a state; and they shall meet in the District and perform such duties as provided by the twelfth article of amendment.

Section 2.   The Congress shall have power to enforce this article by appropriate legislation.

Amendment XXIV [1964]

Section 1.   The right of citizens of the United States to vote in any primary or other election for President or Vice President, for electors for President or Vice President, or for Senator or Representative in Congress, shall not be denied or abridged by the United States, or any State by reason of failure to pay any poll tax or other tax.

Section 2.   The Congress shall have power to enforce this article by appropriate legislation.

Amendment XXV [1967]

Section 1.   In case of the removal of the President from office or of his death or resignation, the Vice President shall become President.

Section 2.   Whenever there is a vacancy in the office of the Vice President, the President shall nominate a Vice President who shall take office upon confirmation by a majority vote of both Houses of Congress.

Section 3.   Whenever the President transmits to the President pro tempore of the Senate and the Speaker of the House of Representatives his written declaration that he is unable to discharge the powers and duties of his office, and until he transmits to them a written declaration to the contrary, such powers and duties shall be discharged by the Vice President as Acting President.

Section 4.   Whenever the Vice President and a majority of either the principal officers of the executive departments or of such other body as Congress may by law provide, transmit to the President pro tempore of the Senate and the Speaker of the House of Representatives their written declaration that the President is unable to discharge the powers and duties of his office, the Vice President shall immediately assume the powers and duties of the office as Acting President.

Thereafter, when the President transmits to the President pro tempore of the Senate and the Speaker of the House of Representatives his written declaration that no inability exists, he shall resume the powers and duties of his office unless the Vice President and a majority of either the principal officers of the executive department or of such other body as Congress may by law provide, transmit within four days to the President pro tempore of the Senate and the Speaker of the House of Representatives their written declaration and the President is unable to discharge the powers and duties of his office. Thereupon Congress shall decide the issue, assembling within forty-eight hours for that purpose if not in session. If the Congress, within twenty-one days after receipt of the latter written declaration, or, if Congress is not in session, within twenty-one days after Congress is required to assemble, determines by two-thirds vote of both Houses that the President is unable to discharge the powers and duties of his office, the Vice President shall continue to discharge the same as Acting President; otherwise, the President shall resume the powers and duties of his office.

Amendment XXVI [1971]

Section 1.   The right of citizens of the United States, who are eighteen years of age or older, to vote shall not be denied or abridged by the United States or by any State on account of age.

Section 2.   The Congress shall have power to enforce this article by appropriate legislation.

APPENDIX C

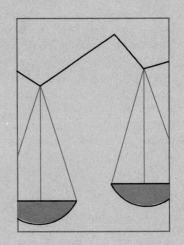

THE UNIFORM
COMMERCIAL
CODE

(Adopted in 52 jurisdictions; all 50 States, although Louisiana has adopted only Articles 1, 3, 4, and 5; the District of Columbia, and the Virgin Islands.)

The Code consists of 10 Articles as follows:

Art.

1. GENERAL PROVISIONS

2. Sales

3. Commercial Paper

4. Bank Deposits and Collections

5. Letters of Credit

6. Bulk Transfers

7. Warehouse Receipts, Bills of Lading and Other Documents of Title

8. Investment Securities

9. Secured Transactions: Sales of Accounts and Chattel Paper

10. Effective Date and Repealer

Article 1
GENERAL PROVISIONS

Part 1 Short Title, Construction, Application and Subject Matter of the Act

§ 1—101. Short Title.

This Act shall be known and may be cited as Uniform Commercial Code.

§ 1—102. Purposes; Rules of Construction; Variation by Agreement.

(1) This Act shall be liberally construed and applied to promote its underlying purposes and policies.

(2) Underlying purposes and policies of this Act are

(a) to simplify, clarify and modernize the law governing commercial transactions;

(b) to permit the continued expansion of commercial practices through custom, usage and agreement of the parties;

(c) to make uniform the law among the various jurisdictions.

(3) The effect of provisions of this Act may be varied by agreement, except as otherwise provided in this Act and except that the obligations of good faith, diligence, reasonableness and care prescribed by this Act may not be disclaimed by agreement but the parties may by agreement determine the standards by which the performance of such

obligations is to be measured if such standards are not manifestly unreasonable.

(4) The presence in certain provisions of this Act of the words "unless otherwise agreed" or words of similar import does not imply that the effect of other provisions may not be varied by agreement under subsection (3).

(5) In this Act unless the context otherwise requires

(a) words in the singular number include the plural, and in the plural include the singular;

(b) words of the masculine gender include the feminine and the neuter, and when the sense so indicates words of the neuter gender may refer to any gender.

§ 1—103. Supplementary General Principles of Law Applicable.

Unless displaced by the particular provisions of this Act, the principles of law and equity, including the law merchant and the law relative to capacity to contract, principal and agent, estoppel, fraud, misrepresentation, duress, coercion, mistake, bankruptcy, or other validating or invalidating cause shall supplement its provisions.

§ 1—104. Construction Against Implicit Repeal.

This Act being a general act intended as a unified coverage of its subject matter, no part of it shall be deemed to be impliedly repealed by subsequent legislation if such construction can reasonably be avoided.

§ 1—105. Territorial Application of the Act; Parties' Power to Choose Applicable Law.

(1) Except as provided hereafter in this section, when a transaction bears a reasonable relation to this state and also to another state or nation the parties may agree that the law either of this state or of such other state or nation shall govern their rights and duties. Failing such agreement this Act applies to transactions bearing an appropriate relation to this state.

(2) Where one of the following provisions of this Act specifies the applicable law, that provision governs and a contrary agreement is effective only to the extent permitted by the law (including the conflict of laws rules) so specified:

Rights of creditors against sold goods. Section 2—402.

Applicability of the Article on Bank Deposits and Collections. Section 4—102.

Bulk transfers subject to the Article on Bulk Transfers. Section 6—102.

Applicability of the Article on Investment Securities. Section 8—106.

Perfection provisions of the Article on Secured Transactions. Section 9—103.

§ 1—106. **Remedies to Be Liberally Administered.**

(1) The remedies provided by this Act shall be liberally administered to the end that the aggrieved party may be put in as good a position as if the other party had fully performed but neither consequential or special nor penal damages may be had except as specifically provided in this Act or by other rule of law.

(2) Any right or obligation declared by this Act is enforceable by action unless the provision declaring it specifies a different and limited effect.

§ 1—107. **Waiver or Renunciation of Claim or Right After Breach.**

Any claim or right arising out of an alleged breach can be discharged in whole or in part without consideration by a written waiver or renunciation signed and delivered by the aggrieved party.

§ 1—108. **Severability.**

If any provision or clause of this Act or application thereof to any person or circumstances is held invalid, such invalidity shall not affect other provisions or applications of the Act which can be given effect without the invalid provision or application, and to this end the provisions of this Act are declared to be severable.

§ 1—109. **Section Captions.**

Section captions are parts of this Act.

Part 2 General Definitions and Principles of Interpretation

§ 1—201. **General Definitions.**

Subject to additional definitions contained in the subsequent Articles of this Act which are applicable to specific Articles or Parts thereof, and unless the context otherwise requires, in this Act:

(1) "Action" in the sense of a judicial proceeding includes recoupment, counterclaim, set-off, suit in equity and any other proceedings in which rights are determined.

(2) "Aggrieved party" means a party entitled to resort to a remedy.

(3) "Agreement" means the bargain of the parties in fact as found in their language or by implication from other circumstances including course of dealing or usage of trade or course of performance as provided in this Act (Sections 1—205 and 2—208). Whether an agreement has legal consequences is determined by the provisions of this Act, if applicable; otherwise by the law of contracts (Section 1—103). (Compare "Contract".)

(4) "Bank" means any person engaged in the business of banking.

(5) "Bearer" means the person in possession of an instrument, document of title, or certified security payable to bearer or indorsed in blank.

(6) "Bill of lading" means a document evidencing the receipt of goods for shipment issued by a person engaged in the business of transporting or forwarding goods, and includes an airbill. "Airbill" means a document serving for air transportation as a bill of lading does for marine or rail transportation, and includes an air consignment note or air waybill.

(7) "Branch" includes a separately incorporated foreign branch of a bank.

(8) "Burden of establishing" a fact means the burden of persuading the triers of fact that the existence of the fact is more probable than its non-existence.

(9) "Buyer in ordinary course of business" means a person who in good faith and without knowledge that the sale to him is in violation of the ownership rights or security interest of a third party in the goods buys in ordinary course from a person in the business of selling goods of that kind but does not include a pawnbroker. All persons who sell minerals or the like (including oil and gas) at wellhead or minehead shall be deemed to be persons in the business of selling goods of that kind. "Buying" may be for cash or by exchange of other property or on secured or unsecured credit and includes receiving goods or documents of title under a pre-existing contract for sale but does not include a transfer in bulk or as security for or in total or partial satisfaction of a money debt.

(10) "Conspicuous": A term or clause is conspicuous when it is so written that a reasonable person against whom it is to operate ought to have noticed it. A printed heading in capitals (as: NON-NEGOTIABLE BILL OF LADING) is conspicuous. Language in the body of a form is "conspicuous" if it is in larger or other contrasting type or color. But in a telegram any stated term is "conspicuous". Whether a term or clause is "conspicuous" or not is for decision by the court.

(11) "Contract" means the total legal obligation which results from the parties' agreement as affected by this Act and any other applicable rules of law. (Compare "Agreement".)

(12) "Creditor" includes a general creditor, a secured creditor, a lien creditor and any representative of creditors, including an assignee for the benefit of creditors, a trustee in bankruptcy, a receiver in equity and an executor or administrator of an insolvent debtor's or assignor's estate.

(13) "Defendant" includes a person in the position of defendant in a cross-action or counterclaim.

(14) "Delivery" with respect to instruments, documents of title, chattel paper, or certificated securities means voluntary transfer of possession.

(15) "Document of title" includes bill of lading, dock warrant, dock receipt, warehouse receipt or order for the delivery of goods, and also any other document which in the regular course of business or financing is treated as adequately evidencing that the person in possession of it is entitled to receive, hold and dispose of the document and the goods it covers. To be a document of title a document must purport to be issued by or addressed to a bailee and purport to cover goods in the bailee's possession which are either identified or afe fungible portions of an identified mass.

(16) "Fault" means wrongful act, omission or breach.

(17) "Fungible" with respect to goods or securities means goods or securities of which any unit is, by nature or usage of trade, the equivalent of any other like unit. Goods which are not fungible shall be deemed fungible for the purposes of this Act to the extent that under a particular agreement or document unlike units are treated as equivalents.

(18) "Genuine" means free of forgery or counterfeiting.

(19) "Good faith" means honesty in fact in the conduct or transaction concerned.

(20) "Holder" means a person who is in possession of a document of title or an instrument or a certificated investment security drawn, issued, or indorsed to him or his order or to bearer or in blank.

(21) To "honor" is to pay or to accept and pay, or where a credit so engages to purchase or discount a draft complying with the terms of the credit.

(22) "Insolvency proceedings" includes any assignment for the benefit of creditors or other proceedings intended to liquidate or rehabilitate the estate of the person involved.

(23) A person is "insolvent" who either has ceased to pay his debts in the ordinary course of business or cannot pay his debts as they become due or is insolvent within the meaning of the federal bankruptcy law.

(24) "Money" means a medium of exchange authorized or adopted by a domestic or foreign government as a part of its currency.

(25) A person has "notice" of a fact when

(a) he has actual knowledge of it; or

(b) he has received a notice or notification of it; or

(c) from all the facts and circumstances known to him at the time in question he has reason to know that it exists.

A person "knows" or has "knowledge" of a fact when he has actual knowledge of it. "Discover" or "learn" or a word or phrase of similar import refers to knowledge rather than to reason to know. The time and circumstances under which a notice or notification may cease to be effective are not determined by this Act.

(26) A person "notifies" or "gives" a notice or notification to another by taking such steps as may be reasonably required to inform the other in ordinary course whether or not such other actually comes to know of it. A person "receives" a notice or notification when

(a) it comes to his attention; or

(b) it is duly delivered at the place of business through which the contract was made or at any other place held out by him as the place for receipt of such communications.

(27) Notice, knowledge or a notice or notification received by an organization is effective for a particular transaction from the time when it is brought to the attention of the individual conducting that transaction, and in any event from the time when it would have been brought to his attention if the organization had exercised due diligence. An organization exercises due diligence if it maintains reasonable routines for communicating significant information to the person conducting the transaction and there is reasonable compliance with the routines. Due diligence does not require an individual acting for the organization to communicate information unless such communication is part of his regular duties or unless he has reason to know of the transaction and that the transaction would be materially affected by the information.

(28) "Organization" includes a corporation, government or governmental subdivision or agency, business trust, estate, trust, partnership or association, two or more persons having a joint or common interest, or any other legal or commercial entity.

(29) "Party", as distinct from "third party", means a person who has engaged in a transaction or made an agreement within this Act.

(30) "Person" includes an individual or an organization (See Section 1—102).

(31) "Presumption" or "presumed" means that the trier of fact must find the existence of the fact presumed unless and until evidence is introduced which would support a finding of its non-existence.

(32) "Purchase" includes taking by sale, discount, negotiation, mortgage, pledge, lien, issue or re-issue, gift or any other voluntary transaction creating an interest in property.

(33) "Purchaser" means a person who takes by purchase.

(34) "Remedy" means any remedial right to which an aggrieved party is entitled with or without resort to a tribunal.

(35) "Representative" includes an agent, an officer of a corporation or association, and a trustee, executor or administrator of an estate, or any other person empowered to act for another.

(36) "Rights" includes remedies.

(37) "Security interest" means an interest in personal property or fixtures which secures payment or performance of an obligation. The retention or reservation of title by a seller of goods notwithstanding shipment or delivery to the buyer (Section 2—401) is limited in effect to a reservation of a "security interest". The term also includes any interest of a buyer of accounts or chattel paper which is subject to Article 9. The special property interest of a buyer of goods on identification of such goods to a contract for sale under Section 2—401 is not a "security interest", but a buyer may also acquire a "security interest" by complying with Article 9. Unless a lease or consignment is intended as security, reservation of title thereunder is not a "security interest" but a consignment is in any event subject to the provisions on consignment sales (Section 2—326). Whether a lease is intended as security is to be determined by the facts of each case; however, (a) the inclusion of an option to purchase does not of itself make the lease one intended for security, and (b) an agreement that upon compliance with the terms of the lease the lessee shall become or has the option to become the owner of the property for no additional consideration or for a nominal consideration does make the lease one intended for security.

(38) "Send" in connection with any writing or notice means to deposit in the mail or deliver for transmission by any other usual means of communication with postage or cost of transmission provided for and properly addressed and in the case of an instrument to an address specified thereon or otherwise agreed, or if there be none to any address reasonable under the circumstances. The receipt of any writing or notice within the time at which it would have arrived if properly sent has the effect of a proper sending.

(39) "Signed" includes any symbol executed or adopted by a party with present intention to authenticate a writing.

(40) "Surety" includes guarantor.

(41) "Telegram" includes a message transmitted by radio, teletype, cable, any mechanical method of transmission, or the like.

(42) "Term" means that portion of an agreement which relates to a particular matter.

(43) "Unauthorized" signature or indorsement means one made without actual, implied or apparent authority and includes a forgery.

(44) "Value". Except as otherwise provided with respect to negotiable instruments and bank collections (Sections 3—303, 4—208 and 4—209) a person gives "value" for rights if he acquires them

(a) in return for a binding commitment to extend credit or for the extension of immediately available credit whether or not drawn upon and whether or not a chargeback is provided for in the event of difficulties in collection; or

(b) as security for or in total or partial satisfaction of a pre-existing claim; or

(c) by accepting delivery pursuant to a preexisting contract for purchase; or

(d) generally, in return for any consideration sufficient to support a simple contract.

(45) "Warehouse receipt" means a receipt issued by a person engaged in the business of storing goods for hire.

(46) "Written" or "writing" includes printing, typewriting or any other intentional reduction to tangible form.

Amended in 1962, 1972 and 1977.

§ 1—202. **Prima Facie Evidence by Third Party Documents.**

A document in due form purporting to be a bill of lading, policy or certificate of insurance, official weigher's or inspector's certificate, consular invoice, or any other document authorized or required by the contract to be issued by a third party shall be prima facie evidence of its own authenticity and genuineness and of the facts stated in the document by the third party.

§ 1—203. **Obligation of Good Faith.**

Every contract or duty within this Act imposes an obligation of good faith in its performance or enforcement.

§ 1—204. **Time; Reasonable Time; "Seasonably".**

(1) Whenever this Act requires any action to be taken within a reasonable time, any time which is not manifestly unreasonable may be fixed by agreement.

(2) What is a reasonable time for taking any action depends on the nature, purpose and circumstances of such action.

(3) An action is taken "seasonably" when it is taken at or within the time agreed or if no time is agreed at or within a reasonable time.

§ 1—205. **Course of Dealing and Usage of Trade.**

(1) A course of dealing is a sequence of previous conduct between the parties to a particular transaction which is fairly to be regarded as establishing a common basis of understanding for interpreting their expressions and other conduct.

(2) A usage of trade is any practice or method of dealing having such regularity of observance in a place, vocation or trade as to justify an expectation that it will be observed with respect to the transaction in question. The existence and scope of such a usage are to be proved as facts. If it is established that such a usage is embodied in a written trade code or similar writing the interpretation of the writing is for the court.

(3) A course of dealing between parties and any usage of trade in the vocation or trade in which they are engaged or of which they are or should be aware give particular meaning to and supplement or qualify terms of an agreement.

(4) The express terms of an agreement and an applicable course of dealing or usage of trade shall be construed wherever reasonable as consistent with each other; but when such construction is unreasonable express terms control both course of dealing and usage of trade and course of dealing controls usage trade.

(5) An applicable usage of trade in the place where any part of performance is to occur shall be used in interpreting the agreement as to that part of the performance.

(6) Evidence of a relevant usage of trade offered by one party is not admissible unless and until he has given the other party such notice as the court finds sufficient to prevent unfair surprise to the latter.

§ 1—206. Statute of Frauds for Kinds of Personal Property Not Otherwise Covered.

(1) Except in the cases described in subsection (2) of this section a contract for the sale of personal property is not enforceable by way of action or defense beyond five thousand dollars in amount or value of remedy unless there is some writing which indicates that a contract for sale has been made between the parties at a defined or stated price, reasonably identifies the subject matter, and is signed by the party against whom enforcement is sought or by his authorized agent.

(2) Subsection (1) of this section does not apply to contracts for the sale of goods (Section 2—201) nor of securities (Section 8—319) nor to security agreements (Section 9—203).

§ 1—207. Performance or Acceptance Under Reservation of Rights.

A party who with explicit reservation of rights performs or promises performance or assents to performance in a manner demanded or offered by the other party does not thereby prejudice the rights reserved. Such words as "without prejudice", "under protest" or the like are sufficient.

§ 1—208. Option to Accelerate at Will.

A term providing that one party or his successor in interest may accelerate payment or performance or require collateral or additional collateral "at will" or "when he deems himself insecure" or in words of similar import shall be construed to mean that he shall have power to do so only if he in good faith believes that the prospect of payment or performance is impaired. The burden of establishing lack of good faith is on the party against whom the power has been exercised.

§ 1—209. Subordinated Obligations

An obligation may be issued as subordinated to payment of another obligation of the person obligated, or a creditor may subordinate his right to payment of an obligation by agreement with either the person obligated or another creditor of the person obligated. Such a subordination does not create a security interest as against either the common debtor or a subordinated creditor. This section shall be construed as declaring the law as it existed prior to the enactment of this section and not as modifying it. Added 1966.

Note: *This new section is proposed as an optional provision to make it clear that a subordination agreement does not create a security interest unless so intended.*

Article 2
SALES

Part 1
Short Title, General Construction and Subject Matter

§ 2—101. Short Title.

This Article shall be known and may be cited as Uniform Commercial Code—Sales.

§ 2—102. Scope; Certain Security and Other Transactions Excluded From This Article.

Unless the context otherwise requires, this Article applies to transactions in goods; it does not apply to any transaction which although in the form of an unconditional contract to sell or present sale is intended to operate only as a security transaction nor does this Article impair or repeal any statute regulating sales to consumers, farmers or other specified classes of buyers.

§ 2—103. Definitions and Index of Definitions.

(1) In this Article unless the context otherwise requires

(a) "Buyer" means a person who buys or contracts to buy goods.

(b) "Good faith" in the case of a merchant means honesty in fact and the observance of reasonable commercial standards of fair dealing in the trade.

(c) "Receipt" of goods means taking physical possession of them.

(d) "Seller" means a person who sells or contracts to sell goods.

(2) Other definitions applying to this Article or to specified Parts thereof, and the sections in which they appear are:

"Acceptance". Section 2—606.
"Banker's credit". Section 2—325.
"Between merchants". Section 2—104.
"Cancellation". Section 2—106(4).
"Commercial unit". Section 2—105.
"Confirmed credit". Section 2—325.
"Conforming to contract". Section 2—106.
"Contract for sale". Section 2—106.
"Cover". Section 2—712.
"Entrusting". Section 2—403.
"Financing agency". Section 2—104.
"Future goods". Section 2—105.
"Goods". Section 2—105.
"Identification". Section 2—501.
"Installment contract". Section 2—612.
"Letter of Credit". Section 2—325.
"Lot". Section 2—105.
"Merchant". Section 2—104.
"Overseas". Section 2—323.
"Person in position of seller". Section 2—707.
"Present sale". Section 2—106.
"Sale". Section 2—106.
"Sale on approval". Section 2—326.
"Sale or return". Section 2—326.
"Termination". Section 2—106.

(3) The following definitions in other Articles apply to this Article:

"Check". Section 3—104.
"Consignee". Section 7—102.
"Consignor". Section 7—102.
"Consumer goods". Section 9—109.
"Dishonor". Section 3—507.
"Draft". Section 3—104.

(4) In addition Article 1 contains general definitions and principles of construction and interpretation applicable throughout this Article.

§ 2—104. Definitions: "Merchant"; "Between Merchants"; "Financing Agency".

(1) "Merchant" means a person who deals in goods of the kind or otherwise by his occupation holds himself out as having knowledge or skill peculiar to the practices or goods involved in the transaction or to whom such knowledge or skill may be attributed by his employment of an agent or broker or other intermediary who by his occupation holds himself out as having such knowledge or skill.

(2) "Financing agency" means a bank, finance company or other person who in the ordinary course of business makes advances against goods or documents of title or who by arrangement with either the seller or the buyer intervenes in ordinary course to make or collect payment due or claimed under the contract for sale, as by purchasing or paying the seller's draft or making advances against it or by merely taking it for collection whether or not documents of title accompany the draft. "Financing agency" includes also a bank or other person who similarly intervenes between persons who are in the position of seller and buyer in respect to the goods (Section 2—707).

(3) "Between merchants" means in any transaction with respect to which both parties are chargeable with the knowledge or skill of merchants.

§ 2—105. Definitions: Transferability; "Goods"; "Future" Goods; "Lot"; "Commercial Unit".

(1) "Goods" means all things (including specially manufactured goods) which are movable at the time of identification to the contract for sale other than the money in which the price is to be paid, investment securities (Article 8) and things in action. "Goods" also includes the unborn young of animals and growing crops and other identified things attached to realty as described in the section on goods to be severed from realty (Section 2—107).

(2) Goods must be both existing and identified before any interest in them can pass. Goods which are not both existing and identified are "future" goods. A purported present sale of future goods or of any interest therein operates as a contract to sell.

(3) There may be a sale of a part interest in existing identified goods.

(4) An undivided share in an identified bulk of fungible goods is sufficiently identified to be sold although the quantity of the bulk is not determined. Any agreed proportion of such a bulk or any quantity thereof agreed upon by number, weight or other measure may to the extent of the seller's interest in the bulk be sold to the buyer who then becomes an owner in common.

(5) "Lot" means a parcel or a single article which is the subject matter of a separate sale or delivery, whether or not it is sufficient to perform the contract.

(6) "Commercial unit" means such a unit of goods as by commercial usage is a single whole for purposes of sale and division of which materially impairs its character or value on the market or in use. A commercial unit may

be a single article (as a machine) or a set of articles (as a suite of furniture or an assortment of sizes) or a quantity (as a bale, gross, or carload) or any other unit treated in use or in the relevant market as a single whole.

§ 2—106. Definitions: "Contract"; "Agreement"; "Contract for Sale"; "Sale"; "Present Sale"; "Conforming" to Contract; "Termination"; "Cancellation".

(1) In this Article unless the context otherwise requires "contract" and "agreement" are limited to those relating to the present or future sale of goods. "Contract for sale" includes both a present sale of goods and a contract to sell goods at a future time. A "sale" consists in the passing of title from the seller to the buyer for a price (Section 2—401). A "present sale" means a sale which is accomplished by the making of the contract.

(2) Goods or conduct including any part of a performance are "conforming" or conform to the contract when they are in accordance with the obligations under the contract.

(3) "Termination" occurs when either party pursuant to a power created by agreement or law puts an end to the contract otherwise than for its breach. On "termination" all obligations which are still executory on both sides are discharged but any right based on prior breach or performance survives.

(4) "Cancellation" occurs when either party puts an end to the contract for breach by the other and its effect is the same as that of "termination" except that the cancelling party also retains any remedy for breach of the whole contract or any unperformed balance.

§ 2—107. Goods to Be Severed From Realty: Recording.

(1) A contract for the sale of minerals or the like (including oil and gas) or a structure or its materials to be removed from realty is a contract for the sale of goods within this Article if they are to be severed by the seller but until severance a purported present sale thereof which is not effective as a transfer of an interest in land is effective only as a contract to sell.

(2) A contract for the sale apart from the land of growing crops or other things attached to realty and capable of severance without material harm thereto but not described in subsection (1) or of timber to be cut is a contract for the sale of goods within this Article whether the subject matter is to be severed by the buyer or by the seller even though it forms part of the realty at the time of contracting, and the parties can by identification effect a present sale before severance.

(3) The provisions of this section are subject to any third party rights provided by the law relating to realty records, and the contract for sale may be executed and recorded as a document transferring an interest in land and shall then constitute notice to third parties of the buyer's rights under the contract for sale.

Part 2 Form, Formation and Readjustment of Contract

§ 2—201. Formal Requirements; Statute of Frauds.

(1) Except as otherwise provided in this section a contract for the sale of goods for the price of $500 or more is not enforceable by way of action or defense unless there is some writing sufficient to indicate that a contract for sale has been made between the parties and signed by the party against whom enforcement is sought or by his authorized agent or broker. A writing is not insufficient because it omits or incorrectly states a term agreed upon but the contract is not enforceable under this paragraph beyond the quantity of goods shown in such writing.

(2) Between merchants if within a reasonable time a writing in confirmation of the contract and sufficient against the sender is received and the party receiving it has reason to know its contents, its satisfies the requirements of subsection (1) against such party unless written notice of objection to its contents is given within ten days after it is received.

(3) A contract which does not satisfy the requirements of subsection (1) but which is valid in other respects is enforceable

(a) if the goods are to be specially manufactured for the buyer and are not suitable for sale to others in the ordinary course of the seller's business and the seller, before notice of repudiation is received and under circumstances which reasonably indicate that the goods are for the buyer, has made either a substantial beginning of their manufacture or commitments for their procurement; or

(b) if the party against whom enforcement is sought admits in his pleading, testimony or otherwise in court that a contract for sale was made, but the contract is not enforceable under this provision beyond the quantity of goods admitted; or

(c) with respect to goods for which payment has been made and accepted or which have been received and accepted (Sec. 2—606).

§ 2—202. Final Written Expression: Parol or Extrinsic Evidence.

Terms with respect to which the confirmatory memoranda of the parties agree or which are otherwise set forth in a writing intended by the parties as a final expression of their agreement with respect to such terms as are included therein may not be contradicted by evidence of any prior agreement or of a contemporaneous oral agreement but may be explained or supplemented

(a) by course of dealing or usage of trade (Section 1—205) or by course of performance (Section 2—208); and

(b) by evidence of consistent additional terms unless the court finds the writing to have been intended also as a complete and exclusive statement of the terms of the agreement.

§ 2—203. Seals Inoperative.

The affixing of a seal to a writing evidencing a contract for sale or an offer to buy or sell goods does not constitute the writing a sealed instrument and the law with respect to sealed instruments does not apply to such a contract or offer.

§ 2—204. Formation in General.

(1) A contract for sale of goods may be made in any manner sufficent to show agreement, including conduct by both parties which recognizes the existence of such a contract.

(2) An agreement sufficient to constitute a contract for sale may be found even though the moment of its making is undetermined.

(3) Even though one or more terms are left open a contract for sale does not fail for indefiniteness if the parties have intended to make a contract and there is a reasonably certain basis for giving an appropriate remedy.

§ 2—205. Firm Offers.

An offer by a merchant to buy or sell goods in a signed writing which by its terms gives assurance that it will be held open is not revocable, for lack of consideration, during the time stated or if no time is stated for a reasonable time, but in no event may such period of irrevocability exceed three months; but any such term of assurance on a form supplied by the offeree must be separately signed by the offeror.

§ 2—206. Offer and Acceptance in Formation of Contract.

(1) Unless other unambiguously indicated by the language or circumstances

(a) an offer to make a contract shall be construed as inviting acceptance in any manner and by any medium reasonable in the circumstances;

(b) an order or other offer to buy goods for prompt or current shipment shall be construed as inviting acceptance either by a prompt promise to ship or by the prompt or current shipment of conforming or non-conforming goods, but such a shipment of non-conforming goods does not constitute an acceptance if the seller seasonably notifies the buyer that the shipment is offered only as an accommodation to the buyer.

(2) Where the beginning of a requested performance is a reasonable mode of acceptance an offeror who is not notified of acceptance within a reasonable time may treat the offer as having lapsed before acceptance.

§ 2—207. Additional Terms in Acceptance or Confirmation.

(1) A definite and seasonable expression of acceptance or a written confirmation which is sent within a reasonable time operates as an acceptance even though it states terms additional to or different from those offered or agreed upon, unless acceptance is expressly made conditional on assent to the additional or different terms.

(2) The additional terms are to be construed as proposals for addition to the contract. Between merchants such terms become part of the contract unless:

(a) the offer expressly limits acceptance to the terms of the offer;

(b) they materially alter it; or

(c) notification of objection to them has already been given or is given within a reasonable time after notice of them is received.

(3) Conduct by both parties which recognizes the existence of a contract is sufficient to establish a contract for sale although the writings of the parties do not otherwise establish a contract. In such case the terms of the particular contract consist of those terms on which the writings of the parties agree, together with any supplementary terms incorporated under any other provisions of this Act.

§ 2—208. Course of Performance or Practical Construction.

(1) Where the contract for sale involves repeated occasions for performance by either party with knowledge of the nature of the performance and opportunity for objection to it by the other, any course of performance accepted or acquiesced in without objection shall be relevant to determine the meaning of the agreement.

(2) The express terms of the agreement and any such course of performance, as well as any course of dealing and usage of trade, shall be construed whenever reasonable as consistent with each other; but when such construction is unreasonable, express terms shall control course of performance and course of performance shall control both course of dealing and usage of trade (Section 1—205).

(3) Subject to the provisions of the next section on modification and waiver, such course of performance shall be relevant to show a waiver or modification of any term inconsistent with such course of performance.

§ 2—209. Modification, Rescission and Waiver.

(1) An agreement modifying a contract within this Article needs no consideration to be binding.

(2) A signed agreement which excludes modification or rescission except by a signed writing cannot be otherwise modified or rescinded, but except as between merchants such a requirement on a form supplied by the merchant must be separately signed by the other party.

(3) The requirements of the statute of frauds section of this Article (Section 2—201) must be satisfied if the contract as modified is within its provisions.

(4) Although an attempt at modification or rescission does not satisfy the requirements of subsection (2) or (3) it can operate as a waiver.

(5) A party who has made a waiver affecting an executory portion of the contract may retract the waiver by reasonable notification received by the other party that strict performance will be required of any term waived, unless the retraction would be unjust in view of a material change of position in reliance on the waiver.

§ 2—210. Delegation of Performance; Assignment of Rights.

(1) A party may perform his duty through a delegate unless otherwise agreed or unless the other party has a substantial interest in having his original promisor perform or control the acts required by the contract. No delegation of performance relieves the party delegating of any duty to perform or any liability for breach.

(2) Unless otherwise agreed all rights of either seller or buyer can be assigned except where the assignment would materially change the duty of the other party, or increase materially the burden or risk imposed on him by his contract, or impair materially his chance of obtaining return performance. A right to damages for breach of the whole contract or a right arising out of the assignor's due performance of his entire obligation can be assigned despite agreement otherwise.

(3) Unless the circumstances indicate the contrary a prohibition of assignment of "the contract" is to be construed as barring only the delegation to the assignee of the assignor's performance.

(4) An assignment of "the contract" or of "all my rights under the contract" or an assignment in similar general terms is an assignment of rights and unless the language or the circumstances (as in an assignment for security) indicate the contrary, it is a delegation of performance of the duties of the assignor and its acceptance by the assignee constitutes a promise by him to perform those duties. This promise is enforceable by either the assignor or the other party to the original contract.

(5) The other party may treat any assignment which delegates performance as creating reasonable grounds for insecurity and may without prejudice to his rights against the assignor demand assurances from the assignee (Section 2—609).

Part 3 General Obligation and Construction of Contract

§ 2—301. General Obligations of Parties.

The obligation of the seller is to transfer and deliver and that of the buyer is to accept and pay in accordance with the contract.

§ 2—302. Unconscionable Contract or Clause.

(1) If the court as a matter of law finds the contract or any clause of the contract to have been unconscionable at the time it was made the court may refuse to enforce the contract, or it may enforce the remainder of the contract without the unconscionable clause, or it may so limit the application of any unconscionable clause as to avoid any unconscionable result.

(2) When it is claimed or appears to the court that the contract or any clause thereof may be unconscionable the parties shall be afforded a reasonable opportunity to present evidence as to its commercial setting, purpose and effect to aid the court in making the determination.

§ 2—303. Allocations or Division of Risks.

Where this Article allocates a risk or a burden as between the parties "unless otherwise agreed", the agreement may not only shift the allocation but may also divide the risk or burden.

§ 2—304. Price Payable in Money, Goods, Realty, or Otherwise.

(1) The price can be made payable in money or otherwise. If it is payable in whole or in part in goods each party is a seller of the goods which he is to transfer.

(2) Even though all or part of the price is payable in an interest in realty the transfer of the goods and the seller's obligations with reference to them are subject to this Article, but not the transfer of the interest in realty or the transferor's obligations in connection therewith.

§ 2—305. Open Price Term.

(1) The parties if they so intend can conclude a contract for sale even though the price is not settled. In such a case the price is a reasonable price at the time for delivery if

(a) nothing is said as to price; or

(b) the price is left to be agreed by the parties and they fail to agree; or

(c) the price is to be fixed in terms of some agreed market or other standard as set or recorded by a third person or agency and it is not so set or recorded.

(2) A price to be fixed by the seller or by the buyer means a price for him to fix in good faith.

(3) When a price left to be fixed otherwise than by agreement of the parties fails to be fixed through fault of one party the other may at his option treat the contract as cancelled or himself fix a reasonable price.

(4) Where, however, the parties intend not to be bound unless the price be fixed or agreed and it is not fixed or agreed there is no contract. In such a case the buyer must return any goods already received or if unable so to do must pay their reasonable value at the time of delivery and the seller must return any portion of the price paid on account.

§ 2—306. Output, Requirements and Exclusive Dealings.

(1) A term which measures the quantity by the output of the seller or the requirements of the buyer means such actual output or requirements as may occur in good faith, except that no quantity unreasonably disproportionate to any stated estimate or in the absence of a stated estimate to any normal or otherwise comparable prior output or requirements may be tendered or demanded.

(2) A lawful agreement by either the seller or the buyer for exclusive dealing in the kind of goods concerned imposes unless otherwise agreed an obligation by the seller to use best efforts to supply the goods and by the buyer to use best efforts to promote their sale.

§ 2—307. Delivery in Single Lot or Several Lots.

Unless otherwise agreed all goods called for by a contract for sale must be tendered in a single delivery and payment is due only on such tender but where the circumstances give either party the right to make or demand delivery in lots the price if it can be apportioned may be demanded for each lot.

§ 2—308. Absence of Specified Place for Delivery.

Unless otherwise agreed

(a) the place for delivery of goods is the seller's place of business or if he has none his residence; but

(b) in a contract for sale of identified goods which to the knowledge of the parties at the time of contracting are in some other place, that place is the place for their delivery; and

(c) documents of title may be delivered through customary banking channels.

§ 2—309. Absence of Specific Time Provisions; Notice of Termination.

(1) The time for shipment or delivery or any other action under a contract if not provided in this Article or agreed upon shall be a reasonable time.

(2) Where the contract provides for successive performances but is indefinite in duration it is valid for a reasonable time but unless otherwise agreed may be terminated at any time by either party.

(3) Termination of a contract by one party except on the happening of an agreed event requires that reasonable notification be received by the other party and an agreement dispensing with notification is invalid if its operation would be unconscionable.

§ 2—310. Open Time for Payment or Running of Credit; Authority to Ship Under Reservation.

Unless otherwise agreed

(a) payment is due at the time and place at which the buyer is to receive the goods even though the place of shipment is the place of delivery; and

(b) if the seller is authorized to send the goods he may ship them under reservation, and may tender the documents of title, but the buyer may inspect the goods after their arrival before payment is due unless such inspection is inconsistent with the terms of the contract (Section 2—513); and

(c) if delivery is authorized and made by way of documents of title otherwise than by subsection (b) then payment is due at the time and place at which the buyer is to receive the documents regardless of where the goods are to be received; and

(d) where the seller is required or authorized to ship the goods on credit the credit period runs from the time of shipment but post-dating the invoice or delaying its dispatch will correspondingly delay the starting of the credit period.

§ 2—311. Options and Cooperation Respecting Performance.

(1) An agreement for sale which is otherwise sufficiently definite (subsection (3) of Section 2—204) to be a contract is not made invalid by the fact that it leaves particulars of performance to be specified by one of the parties. Any such specification must be made in good faith and within limits set by commercial reasonableness.

(2) Unless otherwise agreed specifications relating to assortment of the goods are at the buyer's option and except as otherwise provided in subsections (1)(c) and (3) of Section 2—319 specifications or arrangements relating to shipment are at the seller's option.

(3) Where such specification would materially affect the other party's performance but is not seasonally made or where one party's cooperation is necessary to the agreed performance of the other but is not seasonally forthcoming, the other party in addition to all other remedies

(a) is excused for any resulting delay in his own performance; and

(b) may also either proceed to perform in any reasonable manner or after the time for a material part of his own performance treat the failure to specify or to cooperate as a breach by failure to deliver or accept the goods.

§ 2—312. Warranty of Title and Against Infringement; Buyer's Obligation Against Infringement.

(1) Subject to subsection (2) there is in a contract for sale a warranty by the seller that

(a) the title conveyed shall be good, and its transfer rightful; and

(b) the goods shall be delivered free from any security interest or other lien or encumbrance of which the buyer at the time of contracting has no knowledge.

(2) A warranty under subsection (1) will be excluded or modified only by specific language or by circumstances which give the buyer reason to know that the person selling does not claim title in himself or that he is purporting to sell only such right or title as he or a third person may have.

(3) Unless otherwise agreed a seller who is a merchant regularly dealing in goods of the kind warrants that the goods shall be delivered free of the rightful claim of any third person by way of infringement or the like but a buyer who furnishes specifications to the seller must hold the seller harmless against any such claim which arises out of compliance with the specifications.

§ 2—313. Express Warranties by Affirmation, Promise, Description, Sample.

(1) Express warranties by the seller are created as follows:

(a) Any affirmation of fact or promise made by the seller to the buyer which relates to the goods and becomes part of the basis of the bargain creates an express warranty that the goods shall conform to the affirmation or promise.

(b) Any description of the goods which is made part of the basis of the bargain creates an express warranty that the goods shall conform to the description.

(c) Any sample or model which is made part of the basis of the bargain creates an express warranty that

the whole of the goods shall conform to the sample or model.

(2) It is not necessary to the creation of an express warranty that the seller use formal words such as "warrant" or "guarantee" or that he have a specific intention to make a warranty, but an affirmation merely of the value of the goods or a statement purporting to be merely the seller's opinion or commendation of the goods does not create a warranty.

§ 2—314. Implied Warranty: Merchantability; Usage of Trade.

(1) Unless excluded or modified (Section 2—316), a warranty that the goods shall be merchantable is implied in a contract for their sale if the seller is a merchant with respect to goods of that kind. Under this section the serving for value of food or drink to be consumed either on the premises or elsewhere is a sale.

(2) Goods to be merchantable must be at least such as

(a) pass without objection in the trade under the contract description; and

(b) in the case of fungible goods, are of fair average quality within the description; and

(c) are fit for the ordinary purposes for which such goods are used; and

(d) run, within the variations permitted by the agreement, of even kind, quality and quantity within each unit and among all units involved; and

(e) are adequately contained, packaged, and labeled as the agreement may require; and

(f) conform to the promises or affirmations of fact made on the container or label if any.

(3) Unless excluded or modified (Section 2—316) other implied warranties may arise from course of dealing or usage of trade.

§ 2—315. Implied Warranty: Fitness for Particular Purpose.

Where the seller at the time of contracting has reason to know any particular purpose for which the goods are required and that the buyer is relying on the seller's skill or judgment to select or furnish suitable goods, there is unless excluded or modified under the next section an implied warranty that the goods shall be fit for such purpose.

§ 2—316. Exclusion or Modification of Warranties.

(1) Words or conduct relevant to the creation of an express warranty and words or conduct tending to negate or limit warranty shall be construed wherever reasonable as consistent with each other; but subject to the provisions of this Article on parol or extrinsic evidence (Section

2—202) negation or limitation is inoperative to the extent that such construction is unreasonable.

(2) Subject to subsection (3), to exclude or modify the implied warranty of merchantability or any part of it the language must mention merchantability and in case of a writing must be conspicuous, and to exclude or modify any implied warranty of fitness the exclusion must be by a writing and conspicuous. Language to exclude all implied warranties of fitness is sufficient if it states, for example, that "There are no warranties which extend beyond the description on the face hereof."

(3) Notwithstanding subsection (2)

(a) unless the circumstances indicate otherwise, all implied warranties are excluded by expressions like "as is", "with all faults" or other language which in common understanding calls the buyer's attention to the exclusion of warranties and makes plain that there is no implied warranty; and

(b) when the buyer before entering into the contract has examined the goods or the sample or model as fully as he desired or has refused to examine the goods there is no implied warranty with regard to defects which an examination ought in the circumstances to have revealed to him; and

(c) an implied warranty can also be excluded or modified by course of dealing or course of performance or usage of trade.

(4) Remedies for breach of warranty can be limited in accordance with the provisions of this Article on liquidation or limitation of damages and on contractual modification of remedy (Sections 2—718 and 2—719).

§ 2—317. Cumulation and Conflict of Warranties Express or Implied.

Warranties whether express or implied shall be construed as consistent with each other and as cumulative, but if such construction is unreasonable the intention of the parties shall determine which warranty is dominant. In ascertaining that intention the following rules apply:

(a) Exact or technical specifications displace an inconsistent sample or model or general language of description.

(b) A sample from an existing bulk displaces inconsistent general language of description.

(c) Express warranties displace inconsistent implied warranties other than an implied warranty of fitness for a particular purpose.

§ 2—318. Third Party Beneficiaries of Warranties Express or Implied.

Note: If this Act is introduced in the Congress of the United States this section should be omitted. (States to select one alternative.)

Alternative A

A seller's warranty whether express or implied extends to any natural person who is in the family or household of his buyer or who is a guest in his home if it is reasonable to expect that such person may use, consume or be affected by the goods and who is injured in person by breach of the warranty. A seller may not exclude or limit the operation of this section.

Alternative B

A seller's warranty whether express or implied extends to any natural person who may reasonably be expected to use, consume or be affected by the goods and who is injured in person by breach of the warranty. A seller may not exclude or limit the operation of this section.

Alternative C

A seller's warranty whether express or implied extends to any person who may reasonably be expected to use, consume or be affected by the goods and who is injured by breach of the warranty. A seller may not exclude or limit the operation of this section with respect to injury to the person of an individual to whom the warranty extends. As amended 1966.

§ 2—319. F.O.B. and F.A.S. Terms.

(1) Unless otherwise agreed the term F.O.B. (which means "free on board") at a named place, even though used only in connection with the stated price, is a delivery term under which

(a) when the term is F.O.B. the place of shipment, the seller must at that place ship the goods in the manner provided in this Article (Section 2—504) and bear the expense and risk of putting them into the possession of the carrier; or

(b) when the term is F.O.B. the place of destination, the seller must at his own expense and risk transport the goods to that place and there tender delivery of them in the manner provided in this Article (Section 2—503);

(c) when under either (a) or (b) the term is also F.O.B. vessel, car or other vehicle, the seller must in addition at his own expense and risk load the goods on board. If the term is F.O.B. vessel the buyer must name the vessel and in an appropriate case the seller must comply with the provisions of this Article on the form of bill of lading (Section 2—323).

(2) Unless otherwise agreed the term F.A.S. vessel (which means "free alongside") at a named port, even though used only in connection with the stated price, is a delivery term under which the seller must

(a) at his own expense and risk deliver the goods alongside the vessel in the manner usual in that port or on a dock designated and provided by the buyer; and

(b) obtain and tender a receipt for the goods in exchange for which the carrier is under a duty to issue a bill of lading.

(3) Unless otherwise agreed in any case falling within subsection (1)(a) or (c) or subsection (2) the buyer must seasonably give any needed instructions for making delivery, including when the term is F.A.S. or F.O.B. the loading berth of the vessel and in an appropriate case its name and sailing date. The seller may treat the failure of needed instructions as a failure of cooperation under this Article (Section 2—311). He may also at his option move the goods in any reasonable manner preparatory to delivery or shipment.

(4) Under the term F.O.B. vessel or F.A.S. unless otherwise agreed the buyer must make payment against tender of the required documents and the seller may not tender nor the buyer demand delivery of the goods in substitution for the documents.

§ 2—320. C.I.F. and C. & F. Terms.

(1) The term C.I.F. means that the price includes in a lump sum the cost of the goods and the insurance and freight to the named destination. The term C. & F. or C.F. means that the price so includes cost and freight to the named destination.

(2) Unless otherwise agreed and even though used only in connection with the stated price and destination, the term C.I.F. destination or its equivalent requires the seller at his own expense and risk to

(a) put the goods into the possession of a carrier at the port for shipment and obtain a negotiable bill or bills of lading covering the entire transportation to the named destination; and

(b) load the goods and obtain a receipt from the carrier (which may be contained in the bill of lading) showing that the freight has been paid or provided for; and

(c) obtain a policy or certificate of insurance, including any war risk insurance, of a kind and on terms then current at the port of shipment in the usual amount, in the currency of the contract, shown to cover the same goods covered by the bill of lading and providing for payment of loss to the order of the buyer or for the account of whom it may concern; but the seller may add to the price the amount of the premium for any such war risk insurance; and

(d) prepare an invoice of the goods and procure any other documents required to effect shipment or to comply with the contract; and

(e) forward and tender with commercial promptness all the documents in due form and with any indorsement necessary to perfect the buyer's rights.

(3) Unless otherwise agreed the term C. & F. or its equivalent has the same effect and imposes upon the seller the same obligations and risks as a C.I.F. term except the obligation as to insurance.

(4) Under the term C.I.F. or C. & F. unless otherwise agreed the buyer must make payment against tender of the required documents and the seller may not tender nor the buyer demand delivery of the goods in substitution for the documents.

§ 2—321. C.I.F. or C. & F.: "Net Landed Weights"; "Payment on Arrival"; Warranty of Condition on Arrival.

Under a contract containing a term C.I.F. or C. & F.

(1) Where the price is based on or is to be adjusted according to "net landed weights", "delivered weights", "out turn" quantity or quality or the like, unless otherwise agreed the seller must reasonably estimate the price. The payment due on tender of the documents called for by the contract is the amount so estimated, but after final adjustment of the price a settlement must be made with commercial promptness.

(2) An agreement described in subsection (1) or any warranty of quality or condition of the goods on arrival places upon the seller the risk of ordinary deterioration, shrinkage and the like in transportation but has no effect on the place or time of identification to the contract for sale or delivery or on the passing of the risk of loss.

(3) Unless otherwise agreed where the contract provides for payment on or after arrival of the goods the seller must before payment allow such preliminary inspection as is feasible; but if the goods are lost delivery of the documents and payment are due when the goods should have arrived.

§ 2—322. Delivery "Ex-Ship".

(1) Unless otherwise agreed a term for delivery of goods "ex-ship" (which means from the carrying vessel) or in equivalent language is not restricted to a particular ship and requires delivery from a ship which has reached a place at the named port of destination where goods of the kind are usually discharged.

(2) Under such a term unless otherwise agreed

(a) the seller must discharge all liens arising out of the carriage and furnish the buyer with a direction which puts the carrier under a duty to deliver the goods; and

(b) the risk of loss does not pass to the buyer until the goods leave the ship's tackle or are otherwise properly unloaded.

§ 2—323. Form of Bill of Lading Required in Overseas Shipment; "Overseas".

(1) Where the contract contemplates overseas shipment and contains a term C.I.F. or C. & F. or F.O.B. vessel, the seller unless otherwise agreed must obtain a negotiable bill of lading stating that the goods have been loaded on board or, in the case of a term C.I.F. or C. & F., received for shipment.

(2) Where in a case within subsection (1) a bill of lading has been issued in a set of parts, unless otherwise agreed if the documents are not to be sent from abroad the buyer may demand tender of the full set; otherwise only one part of the bill of lading need be tendered. Even if the agreement expressly requires a full set

(a) due tender of a single part is acceptable within the provisions of this Article on cure of improper delivery (subsection (1) of Section 2—508); and

(b) even though the full set is demanded, if the documents are sent from abroad the person tendering an incomplete set may nevertheless require payment upon furnishing an indemnity which the buyer in good faith deems adequate.

(3) A shipment by water or by air or a contract contemplating such shipment is "overseas" insofar as by usage of trade or agreement it is subject to the commercial, financing or shipping practices characteristic of international deep water commerce.

§ 2—324. "No Arrival, No Sale" Term.

Under a term "no arrival, no sale" or terms of like meaning, unless otherwise agreed,

(a) the seller must properly ship conforming goods and if they arrive by any means he must tender them on arrival but he assumes no obligation that the goods will arrive unless he has caused the non-arrival; and

(b) where without fault of the seller the goods are in part lost or have so deteriorated as no longer to conform to the contract or arrive after the contract time, the buyer may proceed as if there had been casualty to identified goods (Section 2—613).

§ 2—325. "Letter of Credit" Term; "Confirmed Credit".

(1) Failure of the buyer seasonably to furnish an agreed letter of credit is a breach of the contract for sale.

(2) The delivery to seller of a proper letter of credit suspends the buyer's obligation to pay. If the letter of credit is dishonored, the seller may on seasonable notification to the buyer require payment directly from him.

(3) Unless otherwise agreed the term "letter of credit" or "banker's credit" in a contract for sale means an irrevocable credit issued by a financing agency of good repute and, where the shipment is overseas, of good international repute. The term "confirmed credit" means that the credit must also carry the direct obligation of such an agency which does business in the seller's financial market.

§ 2—326. Sale on Approval and Sale or Return; Consignment Sales and Rights of Creditors.

(1) Unless otherwise agreed, if delivered goods may be returned by the buyer even though they conform to the contract, the transaction is

(a) a "sale on approval" if the goods are delivered primarily for use, and

(b) a "sale or return" if the goods are delivered primarily for resale.

(2) Except as provided in subsection (3), goods held on approval are not subject to the claims of the buyer's creditors until acceptance; goods held on sale or return are subject to such claims while in the buyer's possession.

(3) Where goods are delivered to a person for sale and such person maintains a place of business at which he deals in goods of the kind involved, under a name other than the name of the person making delivery, then with respect to claims of creditors of the person conducting the business the goods are deemed to be on sale or return. The provisions of this subsection are applicable even though an agreement purports to reserve title to the person making delivery until payment or resale or uses such words as "on consignment" or "on memorandum". However, this subsection is not applicable if the person making delivery

(a) complies with an applicable law providing for a consignor's interest or the like to be evidenced by a sign, or

(b) establishes that the person conducting the business is generally known by his creditors to be substantially engaged in selling the goods of others, or

(c) complies with the filing provisions of the Article on Secured Transactions (Article 9).

(4) Any "or return" term of a contract for sale is to be treated as a separate contract for sale within the statute of frauds section of this Article (Section 2—201) and as contradicting the sale aspect of the contract within the provisions of this Article on parol or extrinsic evidence (Section 2—202).

§ 2—327. Special Incidents of Sale on Approval and Sale or Return.

(1) Under a sale on approval unless otherwise agreed

(a) although the goods are identified to the contract the risk of loss and the title do not pass to the buyer until acceptance; and

(b) use of the goods consistent with the purpose of trial is not acceptance but failure seasonably to notify the seller of election to return the goods is acceptance, and if the goods conform to the contract acceptance of any part is acceptance of the whole; and

(c) after due notification of election to return, the return is at the seller's risk and expense but a merchant buyer must follow any reasonable instructions.

(2) Under a sale or return unless otherwise agreed

(a) the option to return extends to the whole or any commercial unit of the goods while in substantially their original condition, but must be exercised seasonably; and

(b) the return is at the buyer's risk and expense.

§ 2—328. Sale by Auction.

(1) In a sale by auction if goods are put up in lots each lot is the subject of a separate sale.

(2) A sale by auction is complete when the auctioneer so announces by the fall of the hammer or in other customary manner. Where a bid is made while the hammer is falling in acceptance of a prior bid the auctioneer may in his discretion reopen the bidding or declare the goods sold under the bid on which the hammer was falling.

(3) Such a sale is with reserve unless the goods are in explicit terms put up without reserve. In an auction with reserve the auctioneer may withdraw the goods at any time until he announces completion of the sale. In an auction without reserve, after the auctioneer calls for bids on an article or lot, that article or lot cannot be withdrawn unless no bid is made within a reasonable time. In either case a bidder may retract his bid until the auctioneer's announcement of completion of the sale, but a bidder's retraction does not revive any previous bid.

(4) If the auctioneer knowingly receives a bid on the seller's behalf or the seller makes or procures such as bid, and notice has not been given that liberty for such bidding is reserved, the buyer may at his option avoid the sale or take the goods at the price of the last good faith bid prior to the completion of the sale. This subsection shall not apply to any bid at a forced sale.

Part 4 Title, Creditors and Good Faith Purchasers

§ 2—401. Passing of Title; Reservation for Security; Limited Application of This Section.

Each provision of this Article with regard to the rights, obligations and remedies of the seller, the buyer, purchasers or other third parties applies irrespective of title to the goods except where the provision refers to such title. Insofar as situations are not covered by the other provisions of this Article and matters concerning title became material the following rules apply:

(1) Title to goods cannot pass under a contract for sale prior to their identification to the contract (Section 2—501), and unless otherwise explicitly agreed the buyer acquires by their identification a special property as limited by this Act. Any retention or reservation by the seller of the title (property) in goods shipped or delivered to the buyer is limited in effect to a reservation of a security interest. Subject to these provisions and to the provisions of the Article on Secured Transactions (Article 9), title to goods passes from the seller to the buyer in any manner and on any conditions explicitly agreed on by the parties.

(2) Unless otherwise explicitly agreed title passes to the buyer at the time and place at which the seller completes his performance with reference to the physical delivery of the goods, despite any reservation of a security interest and even though a document of title is to be delivered at a different time or place; and in particular and despite any reservation of a security interest by the bill of lading.

(a) if the contract requires or authorizes the seller to send the goods to the buyer but does not require him to deliver them at destination, title passes to the buyer at the time and place of shipment; but

(b) if the contract requires delivery at destination, title passes on tender there.

(3) Unless otherwise explicitly agreed where delivery is to be made without moving the goods,

(a) if the seller is to deliver a document of title, title passes at the time when and the place where he delivers such documents; or

(b) if the goods are at the time of contracting already identified and no documents are to be delivered, title passes at the time and place of contracting.

(4) A rejection or other refusal by the buyer to receive or retain the goods, whether or not justified, or a justified revocation of acceptance revests title to the goods in the seller. Such revesting occurs by operation of law and is not a "sale".

§ 2—402. Rights of Seller's Creditors Against Sold Goods.

(1) Except as provided in subsections (2) and (3), rights of unsecured creditors of the seller with respect to goods which have been identified to a contract for sale are subject to the buyer's rights to recover the goods under this Article (Sections 2—502 and 2—716).

(2) A creditor of the seller may treat a sale or an identification of goods to a contract for sale as void if as against him a retention of possession by the seller is fraudulent

under any rule of law of the state where the goods are situated, except that retention of possession in good faith and current course of trade by a merchant-seller for a commercially reasonable time after a sale or identification is not fraudulent.

(3) Nothing in this Article shall be deemed to impair the rights of creditors of the seller.

(a) under the provisions of the Article on Secured Transactions (Article 9); or

(b) where identification to the contract or delivery is made not in current course of trade but in satisfaction of or as security for a pre-existing claim for money, security or the like and is made under circumstances which under any rule of law of the state where the goods are situated would apart from this Article constitute the transaction a fraudulent transfer or voidable preference.

§ 2—403. Power to Transfer; Good Faith Purchase of Goods; "Entrusting".

(1) A purchaser of goods acquires all title which his transferor had or had power to transfer except that a purchaser of a limited interest acquires rights only to the extent of the interest purchased. A person with voidable title has power to transfer a good title to a good faith purchaser for value. When goods have been delivered under a transaction of purchase the purchaser has such power even though

(a) the transferor was deceived as to the identity of the purchaser, or

(b) the delivery was in exchange for a check which is later dishonored, or

(c) it was agreed that the transaction was to be a "cash sale", or

(d) the delivery was procured through fraud punishable as larcenous under the criminal law.

(2) Any entrusting of possession of goods to a merchant who deals in goods of that kind gives him power to transfer all rights of the entruster to a buyer in ordinary course of business.

(3) "Entrusting" includes any delivery and any acquiescence in retention of possession regardless of any condition expressed between the parties to the delivery or acquiescence and regardless of whether the procurement of the entrusting or the possessor's disposition of the goods have been such as to be larcenous under the criminal law.

(4) The rights of other purchasers of goods and of lien creditors are governed by the Articles on Secured Transactions (Article 9), Bulk Transfers (Article 6) and Documents of Title (Article 7).

Part 5 Performance

§ 2—501. Insurable Interest in Goods; Manner of Identification of Goods.

(1) The buyer obtains a special property and an insurable interest in goods by identification of existing goods as goods to which the contract refers even though the goods so identified are non-conforming and he has an option to return or reject them. Such identification can be made at any time and in any manner explicitly agreed to by the parties. In the absence of explicit agreement identification occurs

(a) when the contract is made if it is for the sale of goods already existing and identified;

(b) if the contract is for the sale of future goods other than those described in paragraph (c), when goods are shipped, marked or otherwise designated by the seller as goods to which the contract refers;

(c) when the crops are planted or otherwise become growing crops or the young are conceived if the contract is for the sale of unborn young to be born within twelve months after contracting or for the sale of crops to be harvested within twelve months or the next normal harvest season after contracting whichever is longer.

(2) The seller retains an insurable interest in goods so long as title to or any security interest in the goods remains in him and where the identification is by the seller alone he may until default or insolvency or notification to the buyer that the identification is final substitute other goods for those identified.

(3) Nothing in this section impairs any insurable interest recognized under any other statute or rule of law.

§ 2—502. Buyer's Right to Goods on Seller's Insolvency.

(1) Subject to subsection (2) and even though the goods have not been shipped a buyer who has paid a part or all of the price of goods in which he has a special property under the provisions of the immediately preceding section may on making and keeping good a tender of any unpaid portion of their price recover them from the seller if the seller becomes insolvent within ten days after receipt of the first installment on their price.

(2) If the identification creating his special property has been made by the buyer he acquires the right to recover the goods only if they conform to the contract for sale.

§ 2—503. Manner of Seller's Tender of Delivery.

(1) Tender of delivery requires that the seller put and hold conforming goods at the buyer's disposition and give the buyer any notification reasonably necessary to enable him to take delivery. The manner, time and place for tender

are determined by the agreement and this Article, and in particular

(a) tender must be at a reasonable hour, and if it is of goods they must be kept available for the period reasonably necessary to enable the buyer to take possession; but

(b) unless otherwise agreed the buyer must furnish facilities reasonably suited to the receipt of the goods.

(2) Where the case is within the next section respecting shipment tender requires that the seller comply with its provisions.

(3) Where the seller is required to deliver at a particular destination tender requires that he comply with subsection (1) and also in any appropriate case tender documents as described in subsections (4) and (5) of this section.

(4) Where goods are in the possession of a bailee and are to be delivered without being moved

(a) tender requires that the seller either tender a negotiable document of title covering such goods or procure acknowledgment by the bailee of the buyer's right to possession of the goods; but

(b) tender to the buyer of a non-negotiable document of title or of a written direction to the bailee to deliver is sufficient tender unless the buyer seasonably objects, and receipt by the bailee of notification of the buyer's rights fixes those rights as against the bailee and all third persons; but risk of loss of the goods and of any failure by the bailee to honor the non-negotiable document of title or to obey the direction remains on the seller until the buyer has had a reasonable time to present the document or direction, and a refusal by the bailee to honor the document or to obey the direction defeats the tender.

(5) Where the contract requires the seller to deliver documents

(a) he must tender all such documents in correct form, except as provided in this Article with respect to bills of lading in a set (subsection (2) of Section 2—323); and

(b) tender through customary banking channels is sufficient and dishonor of a draft accompanying the documents constitutes non-acceptance or rejection.

§ 2—504. **Shipment by Seller.**

Where the seller is required or authorized to send the goods to the buyer and the contract does not require him to deliver them at a particular destination, then unless otherwise agreed he must

(a) put the goods in the possession of such a carrier and make such a contract for their transportation as may be reasonable having regard to the nature of the goods and other circumstances of the case; and

(b) obtain and promptly deliver or tender in due form any document necessary to enable the buyer to obtain possession of the goods or otherwise required by the agreement or by usage of trade; and

(c) promptly notify the buyer of the shipment.

Failure to notify the buyer under paragraph (c) or to make a proper contract under paragraph (a) is a ground for rejection only if material delay or loss ensues.

§ 2—505. **Seller's Shipment Under Reservation.**

(1) Where the seller has identified goods to the contract by or before shipment:

(a) his procurement of a negotiable bill of lading to his own order or otherwise reserves in him a security interest in the goods. His procurement of the bill to the order of a financing agency or of the buyer indicates in addition only the seller's expectation of transferring that interest to the person named.

(b) a non-negotiable bill of lading to himself or his nominee reserves possession of the goods as security but except in a case of conditional delivery (subsection (2) of Section 2—507) a non-negotiable bill of lading naming the buyer as consignee reserves no security interest even though the seller retains possession of the bill of lading.

(2) When shipment by the seller with reservation of a security interest is in violation of the contract for sale it constitutes an improper contract for transportation within the preceding section but impairs neither the rights given to the buyer by shipment and identification of the goods to the contract nor the seller's powers as a holder of a negotiable document.

§ 2—506. **Rights of Financing Agency.**

(1) A financing agency by paying or purchasing for value a draft which relates to a shipment of goods acquires to the extent of the payment or purchase and in addition to its own rights under the draft and any document of title securing it any rights of the shipper in the goods including the right to stop delivery and the shipper's right to have the draft honored by the buyer.

(2) The right to reimbursement of a financing agency which has in good faith honored or purchased the draft under commitment to or authority from the buyer is not impaired by subsequent discovery of defects with reference to any relevant document which was apparently regular on its face.

§ 2—507. Effect of Seller's Tender; Delivery on Condition.

(1) Tender of delivery is a condition to the buyer's duty to accept the goods and, unless otherwise agreed, to his duty to pay for them. Tender entitles the seller to acceptance of the goods and to payment according to the contract.

(2) Where payment is due and demanded on the delivery to the buyer of goods or documents of title, his right as against the seller to retain or dispose of them is conditional upon his making the payment due.

§ 2—508. Cure by Seller of Improper Tender or Delivery; Replacement.

(1) Where any tender or delivery by the seller is rejected because non-conforming and the time for performance has not yet expired, the seller may seasonally notify the buyer of his intention to cure and may then within the contract time make a conforming delivery.

(2) Where the buyer rejects a non-conforming tender which the seller had reasonable grounds to believe would be acceptable with or without money allowance the seller may if he seasonably notifies the buyer have a further reasonable time to substitute a conforming tender.

§ 2—509. Risk of Loss in the Absence of Breach.

(1) Where the contract requires or authorizes the seller to ship the goods by carrier

    (a) if it does not require him to deliver them at a particular destination, the risk of loss passes to the buyer when the goods are duly delivered to the carrier even though the shipment is under reservation (Section 2—505); but

    (b) if it does require him to deliver them at a particular destination and the goods are there duly tendered while in the possession of the carrier, the risk of loss passes to the buyer when the goods are there duly so tendered as to enable the buyer to take delivery.

(2) Where the goods are held by a bailee to be delivered without being moved, the risk of loss passes to the buyer

    (a) on his receipt of a negotiable document of title covering the goods; or

    (b) on acknowledgment by the bailee of the buyer's right to possession of the goods; or

    (c) after his receipt of a non-negotiable document of title or other written direction to deliver, as provided in subsection (4)(b) of Section 2—503.

(3) In any case not within subsection (1) or (2), the risk of loss passes to the buyer on his receipt of the goods if the seller is a merchant; otherwise the risk passes to the buyer on tender of delivery.

(4) The provisions of this section are subject to contrary agreement of the parties and to the provisions of this Article on sale on approval (Section 2—327) and on effect of breach on risk of loss (Section 2—510).

§ 2—510. Effect of Breach on Risk of Loss.

(1) Where a tender or delivery of goods so fails to conform to the contract as to give a right of rejection the risk of their loss remains on the seller until cure or acceptance.

(2) Where the buyer rightfully revokes acceptance he may to the extent of any deficiency in his effective insurance coverage treat the risk of loss as having rested on the seller from the beginning.

(3) Where the buyer as to conforming goods already identified to the contract for sale repudiates or is otherwise in breach before risk of their loss has passed to him, the seller may to the extent of any deficiency in his effective insurance coverage treat the risk of loss as resting on the buyer for a commercially reasonable time.

§ 2—511. Tender of Payment by Buyer; Payment by Check.

(1) Unless otherwise agreed tender of payment is a condition to the seller's duty to tender and complete any delivery.

(2) Tender of payment is sufficient when made by any means or in any manner current in the ordinary course of business unless the seller demands payment in legal tender and gives any extension of time reasonably necessary to procure it.

(3) Subject to the provisions of this Act on the effect of an instrument on an obligation (Section 3—802), payment by check is conditional and is defeated as between the parties by dishonor of the check on due presentment.

§ 2—512. Payment by Buyer Before Inspection.

(1) Where the contract requires payment before inspection non-conformity of the goods does not excuse the buyer from so making payment unless

    (a) the non-conformity appears without inspection; or

    (b) despite tender of the required documents the circumstances would justify injunction against honor under the provisions of this Act (Section 5—114).

(2) Payment pursuant to subsection (1) does not constitute an acceptance of goods or impair the buyer's right to inspect or any of his remedies.

§ 2—513. Buyer's Right to Inspection of Goods.

(1) Unless otherwise agreed and subject to subsection (3), where goods are tendered or delivered or identified to the contract for sale, the buyer has a right before payment or acceptance to inspect them at any reasonable place and

time and in any reasonable manner. When the seller is required or authorized to send the goods to the buyer, the inspection may be after their arrival.

(2) Expenses of inspection must be borne by the buyer but may be recovered from the seller if the goods do not conform and are rejected.

(3) Unless otherwise agreed and subject to the provisions of this Article on C.I.F. contracts (subsection (3) of Section 2—321), the buyer is not entitled to inspect the goods before payment of the price when the contract provides

(a) for delivery "C.O.D." or on other like terms; or

(b) for payment against documents of title, except where such payment is due only after the goods are to become available for inspection.

(4) A place or method of inspection fixed by the parties is presumed to be exclusive but unless otherwise expressly agreed it does not postpone identification or shift the place for delivery or for passing the risk of loss. If compliance becomes impossible, inspection shall be as provided in this section unless the place or method fixed was clearly intended as an indispensable condition failure of which avoids the contract.

§ 2—514. When Documents Deliverable on Acceptance; When on Payment.

Unless otherwise agreed documents against which a draft is drawn are to be delivered to the drawee on acceptance of the draft if it is payable more than three days after presentment; otherwise, only on payment.

§ 2—515. Preserving Evidence of Goods in Dispute.

In furtherance of the adjustment of any claim or dispute

(a) either party on reasonable notification to the other and for the purpose of ascertaining the facts and preserving evidence has the right to inspect, test and sample the goods including such of them as may be in the possession or control of the other; and

(b) the parties may agree to a third party inspection or survey to determine the conformity or condition of the goods and may agree that the findings shall be binding upon them in any subsequent litigation or adjustment.

Part 6 Breach, Repudiation and Excuse

§ 2—601. Buyer's Rights on Improper Delivery.

Subject to the provisions of this Article on breach in installment contracts (Section 2—612) and unless otherwise agreed under the sections on contractual limitations of remedy (Sections 2—718 and 2—719), if the goods or the tender of delivery fail in any respect to conform to the contract, the buyer may

(a) reject the whole; or

(b) accept the whole; or

(c) accept any commercial unit or units and reject the rest.

§ 2—602. Manner and Effect of Rightful Rejection.

(1) Rejection of goods must be within a reasonable time after their delivery or tender. It is ineffective unless the buyer seasonably notifies the seller.

(2) Subject to the provisions of the two following sections on rejected goods (Sections 2—603 and 2—604),

(a) after rejection any exercise of ownership by the buyer with respect to any commercial unit is wrongful as against the seller; and

(b) if the buyer has before rejection taken physical possession of goods in which he does not have a security interest under the provisions of this Article (subsection (3) of Section 2—711), he is under a duty after rejection to hold them with reasonable care at the seller's disposition for a time sufficient to permit the seller to remove them; but

(c) the buyer has no further obligations with regard to goods rightfully rejected.

(3) The seller's rights with respect to goods wrongfully rejected are governed by the provisions of this Article on Seller's remedies in general (Section 2—703).

§ 2—603. Merchant Buyer's Duties as to Rightfully Rejected Goods.

(1) Subject to any security interest in the buyer (subsection (3) of Section 2—711), when the seller has no agent or place of business at the market of rejection a merchant buyer is under a duty after rejection of goods in his possession or control to follow any reasonable instructions received from the seller with respect to the goods and in the absence of such instructions to make reasonable efforts to sell them for the seller's account if they are perishable or threaten to decline in value speedily. Instructions are not reasonable if on demand indemnity for expenses is not forthcoming.

(2) When the buyer sells goods under subsection (1), he is entitled to reimbursement from the seller or out of the proceeds for reasonable expenses of caring for and selling them, and if the expenses include no selling commission then to such commission as is usual in the trade or if there is none to a reasonable sum not exceeding ten per cent on the gross proceeds.

(3) In complying with this section the buyer is held only to good faith and good faith conduct hereunder is neither acceptance nor conversion nor the basis of an action for damages.

§ 2—604. Buyer's Options as to Salvage of Rightfully Rejected Goods.

Subject to the provisions of the immediately preceding section on perishables if the seller gives no instructions within a reasonable time after notification of rejection the buyer may store the rejected goods for the seller's account or reship them to him or resell them for the seller's account with reimbursement as provided in the preceding section. Such action is not acceptance or conversion.

§ 2—605. Waiver of Buyer's Objections by Failure to Particularize.

(1) The buyer's failure to state in connection with rejection a particular defect which is ascertainable by reasonable inspection precludes him from relying on the unstated defect to justify rejection or to establish breach

(a) where the seller could have cured it if stated seasonably; or

(b) between merchants when the seller has after rejection made a request in writing for a full and final written statement of all defects on which the buyer proposes to rely.

(2) Payment against documents made without reservation of rights precludes recovery of the payment for defects apparent on the face of the documents.

§ 2—606. What Constitutes Acceptance of Goods.

(1) Acceptance of goods occurs when the buyer

(a) after a reasonable opportunity to inspect the goods signifies to the seller that the goods are conforming or that he will take or retain them in spite of their non-conformity; or

(b) fails to make an effective rejection (subsection (1) of Section 2—602), but such acceptance does not occur until the buyer has had a reasonable opportunity to inspect them; or

(c) does any act inconsistent with the seller's ownership; but if such act is wrongful as against the seller it is an acceptance only if ratified by him.

(2) Acceptance of a part of any commercial unit is acceptance of that entire unit.

§ 2—607. Effect of Acceptance; Notice of Breach; Burden of Establishing Breach After Acceptance; Notice of Claim or Litigation to Person Answerable Over.

(1) The buyer must pay at the contract rate for any goods accepted.

(2) Acceptance of goods by the buyer precludes rejection of the goods accepted and if made with knowledge of a non-conformity cannot be revoked because of it unless the acceptance was on the reasonable assumption that the non-conformity would be seasonally cured but acceptance does not of itself impair any other remedy provided by this Article for non-conformity.

(3) Where a tender has been accepted

(a) the buyer must within a reasonable time after he discovers or should have discovered any breach notify the seller of breach or be barred from any remedy; and

(b) if the claim is one for infringement or the like (subsection (3) of Section 2—312) and the buyer is sued as a result of such a breach he must so notify the seller within a reasonable time after he receives notice of the litigation or be barred from any remedy over for liability established by the litigation.

(4) The burden is on the buyer to establish any breach with respect to the goods accepted.

(5) Where the buyer is sued for breach of a warranty or other obligation for which his seller is answerable over

(a) he may give his seller written notice of the litigation. If the notice states that the seller may come in and defend and that if the seller does not do so he will be bound in any action against him by his buyer by any determination of fact common to the two litigations, then unless the seller after seasonable receipt of the notice does come in and defend he is so bound.

(b) if the claim is one for infringement or the like (subsection (3) of Section 2—312) the original seller may demand in writing that his buyer turn over to him control of the litigation including settlement or else be barred from any remedy over and if he also agrees to bear all expense and to satisfy any adverse judgment, then unless the buyer after seasonable receipt of the demand does turn over control the buyer is so barred.

(6) The provisions of subsections (3), (4) and (5) apply to any obligation of a buyer to hold the seller harmless against infringement or the like (subsection (3) of Section 2—312).

§ 2—608. Revocation of Acceptance in Whole or in Part.

(1) The buyer may revoke his acceptance of a lot or commercial unit whose non-conformity substantially impairs its value to him if he has accepted it

(a) on the reasonable assumption that its non-conformity would be cured and it has not been seasonably cured; or

(b) without discovery of such non-conformity if his acceptance was reasonably induced either by the difficulty of discovery before acceptance or by the seller's assurances.

(2) Revocation of acceptance must occur within a reasonable time after the buyer discovers or should have discovered the ground for it and before any substantial change in condition of the goods which is not caused by their own defects. It is not effective until the buyer notifies the seller of it.

(3) A buyer who so revokes has the same rights and duties with regard to the goods involved as if he had rejected them.

§ 2—609. Right to Adequate Assurance of Performance.

(1) A contract for sale imposes an obligation on each party that the other's expectation of receiving due performance will not be impaired. When reasonable grounds for insecurity arise with respect to the performance of either party the other may in writing demand adequate assurance of due performance and until he receives such assurance may if commercially reasonable suspend any performance for which he has not already received the agreed return.

(2) Between merchants the reasonableness of grounds for insecurity and the adequacy of any assurance offered shall be determined according to commercial standards.

(3) Acceptance of any improper delivery or payment does not prejudice the aggrieved party's right to demand adequate assurance of future performance.

(4) After receipt of a justified demand failure to provide within a reasonable time not exceeding thirty days such assurance of due performance as is adequate under the circumstances of the particular case is a repudiation of the contract.

§ 2—610. Anticipatory Repudiation.

When either party repudiates the contract with respect to a performance not yet due the loss of which will substantially impair the value of the contract to the other, the aggrieved party may

(a) for a commercially reasonable time await performance by the repudiating party; or

(b) resort to any remedy for breach (Section 2—703 or Section 2—711), even though he has notified the repudiating party that he would await the latter's performance and has urged retraction; and

(c) in either case suspend his own performance or proceed in accordance with the provisions of this Article on the seller's right to identify goods to the contract notwithstanding breach or to salvage unfinished goods (Section 2—704).

§ 2—611. Retraction of Anticipatory Repudiation.

(1) Until the repudiating party's next performance is due he can retract his repudiation unless the aggrieved party

has since the repudiation cancelled or materially changed his position or otherwise indicated that he considers the repudiation final.

(2) Retraction may be by any method which clearly indicates to the aggrieved party that the repudiating party intends to perform, but must include any assurance justifiably demanded under the provisions of this Article (Section 2—609).

(3) Retraction reinstates the repudiating party's rights under the contract with due excuse and allowance to the aggrieved party for any delay occasioned by the repudiation.

§ 2—612. "Installment Contract"; Breach.

(1) An "installment contract" is one which requires or authorizes the delivery of goods in separate lots to be separately accepted, even though the contract contains a clause "each delivery is a separate contract" or its equivalent.

(2) The buyer may reject any installment which is non-conforming if the non-conformity substantially impairs the value of that installment and cannot be cured or if the non-conformity is a defect in the required documents; but if the non-conformity does not fall within subsection (3) and the seller gives adequate assurance of its cure the buyer must accept that installment.

(3) Whenever non-conformity or default with respect to one or more installments substantially impairs the value of the whole contract there is a breach of the whole. But the aggrieved party reinstates the contract if he accepts a non-conforming installment without seasonably notifying of cancellation or if he brings an action with respect only to past installments or demands performance as to future installments.

§ 2—613. Casualty to Identified Goods.

Where the contract requires for its performance goods identified when the contract is made, and the goods suffer casualty without fault of either party before the risk of loss passes to the buyer, or in a proper case under a "no arrival, no sale" term (Section 2—324) then

(a) if the loss is total the contract is avoided; and

(b) if the loss is partial or the goods have so deteriorated as no longer to conform to the contract the buyer may nevertheless demand inspection and at his option either treat the contract as voided or accept the goods with due allowance from the contract price for the deterioration or the deficiency in quantity but without further right against the seller.

§ 2—614. Substituted Performance.

(1) Where without fault of either party the agreed berthing, loading, or unloading facilities fail or an agreed type

of carrier becomes unavailable or the agreed manner of delivery otherwise becomes commercially impracticable but a commercially reasonable substitute is available, such substitute performance must be tendered and accepted.

(2) If the agreed means or manner of payment fails because of domestic or foreign governmental regulation, the seller may withhold or stop delivery unless the buyer provides a means or manner of payment which is commercially a substantial equivalent. If delivery has already been taken, payment by the means or in the manner provided by the regulation discharges the buyer's obligation unless the regulation is discriminatory, oppressive or predatory.

§ 2—615. Excuse by Failure of Presupposed Conditions.

Except so far as a seller may have assumed a greater obligation and subject to the preceding section on substituted performance:

(a) Delay in delivery or non-delivery in whole or in part by a seller who complies with paragraphs (b) and (c) is not a breach of his duty under a contract for sale if performance as agreed has been made impracticable by the occurrence of a contingency the nonoccurrence of which was a basic assumption on which the contract was made or by compliance in good faith with any applicable foreign or domestic governmental regulation or order whether or not it later proves to be invalid.

(b) Where the causes mentioned in paragraph (a) affect only a part of the seller's capacity to perform, he must allocate production and deliveries among his customers but may at his option include regular customers not then under contract as well as his own requirements for further manufacture. He may so allocate in any manner which is fair and reasonable.

(c) The seller must notify the buyer seasonably that there will be delay or non-delivery and, when allocation is required under paragraph (b), of the estimated quota thus made available for the buyer.

§ 2—616. Procedure on Notice Claiming Excuse.

(1) Where the buyer receives notification of a material or indefinite delay or an allocation justified under the preceding section he may by written notification to the seller as to any delivery concerned, and where the prospective deficiency substantially impairs the value of the whole contract under the provisions of this Article relating to breach of installment contracts (Section 2—612), then also as to the whole,

(a) terminate and thereby discharge any unexecuted portion of the contract; or

(b) modify the contract by agreeing to take his available quota in substitution.

(2) If after receipt of such notification from the seller the buyer fails so to modify the contract within a reasonable time not exceeding thirty days the contract lapses with respect to any deliveries affected.

(3) The provisions of this section may not be negated by agreement except in so far as the seller has assumed a greater obligation under the preceding section.

Part 7 Remedies

§ 2—701. Remedies for Breach of Collateral Contracts Not Impaired.

Remedies for breach of any obligation or promise collateral or ancillary to a contract for sale are not impaired by the provisions of this Article.

§ 2—702. Seller's Remedies on Discovery of Buyer's Insolvency.

(1) Where the seller discovers the buyer to be insolvent he may refuse delivery except for cash including payment for all goods theretofore delivered under the contract, and stop delivery under this Article (Section 2—705).

(2) Where the seller discovers that the buyer has received goods on credit while insolvent he may reclaim the goods upon demand made within ten days after the receipt, but if misrepresentation of solvency has been made to the particular seller in writing within three months before delivery the ten day limitation does not apply. Except as provided in this subsection the seller may not base a right to reclaim goods on the buyer's fraudulent or innocent misrepresentation of solvency or of intent to pay.

(3) The seller's right to reclaim under subsection (2) is subject to the rights of a buyer in ordinary course or other good faith purchaser under this Article (Section 2—403). Successful reclamation of goods excludes all other remedies with respect to them.

§ 2—703. Seller's Remedies in General.

Where the buyer wrongfully rejects or revokes acceptance of goods or fails to make a payment due on or before delivery or repudiates with respect to a part or the whole, then with respect to any goods directly affected and, if the breach is of the whole contract (Section 2—612), then also with respect to the whole undelivered balance, the aggrieved seller may

(a) withhold delivery of such goods;

(b) stop delivery by any bailee as hereafter provided (Section 2—705);

(c) proceed under the next section respecting goods still unidentified to the contract;

(d) resell and recover damages as hereafter provided (Section 2—706);

(e) recover damages for non-acceptance (Section 2—708) or in a proper case the price (Section 2—709);

(f) cancel.

§ 2—704. Seller's Right to Identify Goods to the Contract Notwithstanding Breach or to Salvage Unfinished Goods.

(1) An aggrieved seller under the preceding section may

(a) identify to the contract conforming goods not already identified if at the time he learned of the breach they are in his possession or control;

(b) treat as the subject of resale goods which have demonstrably been intended for the particular contract even though those goods are unfinished.

(2) Where the goods are unfinished an aggrieved seller may in the exercise of reasonable commercial judgment for the purposes of avoiding loss and of effective realization either complete the manufacture and wholly identify the goods to the contract or cease manufacture and resell for scrap or salvage value or proceed in any other reasonable manner.

§ 2—705. Seller's Stoppage of Delivery in Transit or Otherwise.

(1) The seller may stop delivery of goods in the possession of a carrier or other bailee when he discovers the buyer to be insolvent (Section 2—702) and may stop delivery of carload, truckload, planeload or larger shipments of express or freight when the buyer repudiates or fails to make a payment due before delivery or if for any other reason the seller has a right to withhold or reclaim the goods.

(2) As against such buyer the seller may stop delivery until

(a) receipt of the goods by the buyer; or

(b) acknowledgment to the buyer by any bailee of the goods except a carrier that the bailee holds the goods for the buyer; or

(c) such acknowledgment to the buyer by a carrier by reshipment or as warehouseman; or

(d) negotiation to the buyer of any negotiable document of title covering the goods.

(3) (a) To stop delivery the seller must so notify as to enable the bailee by reasonable diligence to prevent delivery of the goods.

(b) After such notification the bailee must hold and deliver the goods according to the directions of the seller but the seller is liable to the bailee for any ensuing charges or damages.

(c) If a negotiable document of title has been issued for goods the bailee is not obliged to obey a notification to stop until surrender of the document.

(d) A carrier who has issued a non-negotiable bill of lading is not obliged to obey a notification to stop received from a person other than the consignor.

§ 2—706. Seller's Resale Including Contract for Resale.

(1) Under the conditions stated in Section 2—703 on seller's remedies, the seller may resell the goods concerned or the undelivered balance thereof. Where the resale is made in good faith and in a commercially reasonable manner the seller may recover the difference between the resale price and the contract price together with any incidental damages allowed under the provisions of this Article (Section 2—710), but less expenses saved in consequence of the buyer's breach.

(2) Except as otherwise provided in subsection (3) or unless otherwise agreed resale may be at public or private sale including sale by way of one or more contracts to sell or of identification to an existing contract of the seller. Sale may be as a unit or in parcels and at any time and place and on any terms but every aspect of the sale including the method, manner, time, place and terms must be commercially reasonable. The resale must be reasonably identified as referring to the broken contract, but it is not necessary that the goods be in existence or that any or all of them have been identified to the contract before the breach.

(3) Where the resale is at private sale the seller must give the buyer reasonable notification of his intention to resell.

(4) Where the resale is at public sale

(a) only identified goods can be sold except where there is a recognized market for a public sale of futures in goods of the kind; and

(b) it must be made at a usual place or market for public sale if one is reasonably available and except in the case of goods which are perishable or threaten to decline in value speedily the seller must give the buyer reasonable notice of the time and place of the resale; and

(c) if the goods are not to be within the view of those attending the sale the notification of sale must state the place where the goods are located and provide for their reasonable inspection by prospective bidders; and

(d) the seller may buy.

(5) A purchaser who buys in good faith at a resale takes the goods free of any rights of the original buyer even though the seller fails to comply with one or more of the requirements of this section.

(6) The seller is not accountable to the buyer for any profit made on any resale. A person in the position of a seller (Section 2—707) or a buyer who has rightfully re-

jected or justifiably revoked acceptance must account for any excess over the amount of his security interest, as hereinafter defined (subsection (3) of Section 2—711).

§ 2—707. "Person in the Position of a Seller".

(1) A "person in the position of a seller" includes as against a principal an agent who has paid or become responsible for the price of goods on behalf of his principal or anyone who otherwise holds a security interest or other right in goods similar to that of a seller.

(2) A person in the position of a seller may as provided in this Article withhold or stop delivery (Section 2—705) and resell (Section 2—706) and recover incidental damages (Section 2—710).

§ 2—708. Seller's Damages for Non-Acceptance or Repudiation.

(1) Subject to subsection (2) and to the provisions of this Article with respect to proof of market price (Section 2—723), the measure of damages for non-acceptance or repudiation by the buyer is the difference between the market price at the time and place for tender and the unpaid contract price together with any incidental damages provided in this Article (Section 2—710), but less expenses saved in consequence of the buyer's breach.

(2) If the measure of damages provided in subsection (1) is inadequate to put the seller in as good a position as performance would have done then the measure of damages is the profit (including reasonable overhead) which the seller would have made from full performance by the buyer, together with any incidental damages provided in this Article (Section 2—710), due allowance for costs reasonably incurred and due credit for payments or proceeds of resale.

§ 2—709. Action for the Price.

(1) When the buyer fails to pay the price as it becomes due the seller may recover, together with any incidental damages under the next section, the price

(a) of goods accepted or of conforming goods lost or damaged within a commercially reasonable time after risk of their loss has passed to the buyer; and

(b) of goods identified to the contract if the seller is unable after reasonable effort to resell them at a reasonable price or the circumstances reasonably indicate that such effort will be unavailing.

(2) Where the seller sues for the price he must hold for the buyer any goods which have been identified to the contract and are still in his control except that if resale becomes possible he may resell them at any time prior to the collection of the judgment. The net proceeds of any such resale must be credited to the buyer and payment of the judgment entitles him to any goods not resold.

(3) After the buyer has wrongfully rejected or revoked acceptance of the goods or has failed to make a payment due or has repudiated (Section 2—610), a seller who is held not entitled to the price under this section shall nevertheless be awarded damages for non-acceptance under the preceding section.

§ 2—710. Seller's Incidental Damages.

Incidental damages to an aggrieved seller include any commercially reasonable charges, expenses or commissions incurred in stopping delivery, in the transportation, care and custody of goods after the buyer's breach, in connection with return or resale of the goods or otherwise resulting from the breach.

§ 2—711. Buyer's Remedies in General; Buyer's Security Interest in Rejected Goods.

(1) Where the seller fails to make delivery or repudiates or the buyer rightfully rejects or justifiably revokes acceptance then with respect to any goods involved, and with respect to the whole if the breach goes to the whole contract (Section 2—612), the buyer may cancel and whether or not he has done so may in addition to recovering so much of the price as has been paid

(a) "cover" and have damages under the next section as to all the goods affected whether or not they have been identified to the contract; or

(b) recover damages for non-delivery as provided in this Article (Section 2—713).

(2) Where the seller fails to deliver or repudiates the buyer may also

(a) if the goods have been identified recover them as provided in this Article (Section 2—502); or

(b) in a proper case obtain specific performance or replevy the goods as provided in this Article (Section 2—716).

(3) On rightful rejection or justifiable revocation of acceptance a buyer has a security interest in goods in his possession or control for any payments made on their price and any expenses reasonably incurred in their inspection, receipt, transportation, care and custody and may hold such goods and resell them in like manner as an aggrieved seller (Section 2—706).

§ 2—712. "Cover"; Buyer's Procurement of Substitute Goods.

(1) After a breach within the preceding section the buyer may "cover" by making in good faith and without unreasonable delay any reasonable purchase of or contract to purchase goods in substitution for those due from the seller.

(2) The buyer may recover from the seller as damages the difference between the cost of cover and the contract price together with any incidental or consequential damages as hereinafter defined (Section 2—715), but less expenses saved in consequence of the seller's breach.

(3) Failure of the buyer to effect cover within this section does not bar him from any other remedy.

§ 2—713. Buyer's Damages for Non-Delivery or Repudiation.

(1) Subject to the provisions of this Article with respect to proof of market price (Section 2—723), the measure of damages for non-delivery or repudiation by the seller is the difference between the market price at the time when the buyer learned of the breach and the contract price together with any incidental and consequential damages provided in this Article (Section 2—715), but less expenses saved in consequence of the seller's breach.

(2) Market price is to be determined as of the place for tender or, in cases of rejection after arrival or revocation of acceptance, as of the place of arrival.

§ 2—714. Buyer's Damages for Breach in Regard to Accepted Goods.

(1) Where the buyer has accepted goods and given notification (subsection (3) of Section 2—607) he may recover as damages for any non-conformity of tender the loss resulting in the ordinary course of events from the seller's breach as determined in any manner which is reasonable.

(2) The measure of damages for breach of warranty is the difference at the time and place of acceptance between the value of the goods accepted and the value they would have had if they had been as warranted, unless special circumstances show proximate damages of a different amount.

(3) In a proper case any incidental and consequential damages under the next section may also be recovered.

§ 2—715. Buyer's Incidental and Consequential Damages.

(1) Incidental damages resulting from the seller's breach include expenses reasonably incurred in inspection, receipt, transportation and care and custody of goods rightfully rejected, any commercially reasonable charges, expenses or commissions in connection with effecting cover and any other reasonable expense incident to the delay or other breach.

(2) Consequential damages resulting from the seller's breach include

(a) any loss resulting from general or particular requirements and needs of which the seller at the time

of contracting had reason to know and which could not reasonably be prevented by cover or otherwise; and

(b) injury to person or property proximately resulting from any breach of warranty.

§ 2—716. Buyer's Right to Specific Performance or Replevin.

(1) Specific performance may be decreed where the goods are unique or in other proper circumstances.

(2) The decree for specific performance may include such terms and conditions as to payment of the price, damages, or other relief as the court may deem just.

(3) The buyer has a right of replevin for goods identified to the contract if after reasonable effort he is unable to effect cover for such goods or the circumstances reasonably indicate that such effort will be unavailing or if the goods have been shipped under reservation and satisfaction of the security interest in them has been made or tendered.

§ 2—717. Deduction of Damages From the Price.

The buyer on notifying the seller of his intention to do so may deduct all or any part of the damages resulting from any breach of the contract from any part of the price still due under the same contract.

§ 2—718. Liquidation or Limitation of Damages; Deposits.

(1) Damages for breach by either party may be liquidated in the agreement but only at an amount which is reasonable in the light of the anticipated or actual harm caused by the breach, the difficulties of proof of loss, and the inconvenience or nonfeasibility of otherwise obtaining an adequate remedy. A term fixing unreasonably large liquidated damages is void as a penalty.

(2) Where the seller justifiably withholds delivery of goods because of the buyer's breach, the buyer is entitled to restitution of any amount by which the sum of his payments exceeds

(a) the amount to which the seller is entitled by virtue of terms liquidating the seller's damages in accordance with subsection (1), or

(b) in the absence of such terms, twenty per cent of the value of the total performance for which the buyer is obligated under the contract or $500, whichever is smaller.

(3) The buyer's right to restitution under subsection (2) is subject to offset to the extent that the seller establishes

(a) a right to recover damages under the provisions of this Article other than subsection (1), and

(b) the amount or value of any benefits received by the buyer directly or indirectly by reason of the contract.

(4) Where a seller has received payment in goods their reasonable value or the proceeds of their resale shall be treated as payments for the purposes of subsection (2); but if the seller has notice of the buyer's breach before reselling goods received in part performance, his resale is subject to the conditions laid down in this Article on resale by an aggrieved seller (Section 2—706).

§ 2—719. Contractual Modification or Limitation of Remedy.

(1) Subject to the provisions of subsections (2) and (3) of this section and of the preceding section on liquidation and limitation of damages,

(a) the agreement may provide for remedies in addition to or in substitution for those provided in this Article and may limit or alter the measure of damages recoverable under this Article, as by limiting the buyer's remedies to return of the goods and repayment of the price or to repair and replacement of non-conforming goods or parts; and

(b) resort to a remedy as provided is optional unless the remedy is expressly agreed to be exclusive, in which case it is the sole remedy.

(2) Where circumstances cause an exclusive or limited remedy to fail of its essential purpose, remedy may be had as provided in this Act.

(3) Consequential damages may be limited or excluded unless the limitation or exclusion is unconscionable. Limitation of consequential damages for injury to the person in the case of consumer goods is prima facie unconscionable but limitation of damages where the loss is commercial is not.

§ 2—720. Effect of "Cancellation" or "Rescission" on Claims for Antecedent Breach.

Unless the contrary intention clearly appears, expressions of "cancellation" or "rescission" of the contract or the like shall not be construed as a renunciation or discharge of any claim in damages for an antecedent breach.

§ 2—721. Remedies for Fraud.

Remedies for material misrepresentation or fraud include all remedies available under this Article for non-fraudulent breach. Neither rescission or a claim for rescission of the contract for sale nor rejection or return of the goods shall bar or be deemed inconsistent with a claim for damages or other remedy.

§ 2—722. Who Can Sue Third Parties for Injury to Goods.

Where a third party so deals with goods which have been identified to a contract for sale as to cause actionable injury to a party to that contract

(a) a right of action against the third party is in either party to the contract for sale who has title to or a security interest or a special property or an insurable interest in the goods; and if the goods have been destroyed or converted a right of action is also in the party who either bore the risk of loss under the contract for sale or has since the injury assumed that risk as against the other;

(b) if at the time of the injury the party plaintiff did not bear the risk of loss as against the other party to the contract for sale and there is no arrangement between them for disposition of the recovery, his suit or settlement is, subject to his own interest, as a fiduciary for the other party to the contract;

(c) either party may with the consent of the other sue for the benefit of whom it may concern.

§ 2—723. Proof of Market Price: Time and Place.

(1) If an action based on anticipatory repudiation comes to trial before the time for performance with respect to some or all of the goods, any damages based on market price (Section 2—708 or Section 2—713) shall be determined according to the price of such goods prevailing at the time when the aggrieved party learned of the repudiation.

(2) If evidence of a price prevailing at the times or places described in this Article is not readily available the price prevailing within any reasonable time before or after the time described or at any other place which in commercial judgment or under usage of trade would serve as a reasonable substitute for the one described may be used, making any proper allowance for the cost of transporting the goods to or from such other place.

(3) Evidence of a relevant price prevailing at a time or place other than the one described in this Article offered by one party is not admissible unless and until he has given the other party such notice as the court finds sufficient to prevent unfair surprise.

§ 2—724. Admissibility of Market Quotations.

Whenever the prevailing price or value of any goods regularly bought and sold in any established commodity market is in issue, reports in official publications or trade journals or in newspapers or periodicals of general circulation published as the reports of such market shall be admissible in evidence. The circumstances of the preparation of such a report may be shown to affect its weight but not its admissibility.

§ 2—725. Statute of Limitations in Contracts for Sale.

(1) An action for breach of any contract for sale must be commenced within four years after the cause of action has accrued. By the original agreement the parties may reduce the period of limitation to not less than one year but may not extend it.

(2) A cause of action accrues when the breach occurs, regardless of the aggrieved party's lack of knowledge of the breach. A breach of warranty occurs when tender of delivery is made, except that where a warranty explicitly extends to future performance of the goods and discovery of the breach must await the time of such performance the cause of action accrues when the breach is or should have been discovered.

(3) Where an action commenced within the time limited by subsection (1) is so terminated as to leave available a remedy by another action for the same breach such other action may be commenced after the expiration of the time limited and within six months after the termination of the first action unless the termination resulted from voluntary discontinuance or from dismissal for failure or neglect to prosecute.

(4) This section does not alter the law on tolling of the statute of limitations nor does it apply to causes of action which have accrued before this Act becomes effective.

Article 3
COMMERCIAL PAPER

Part 1 Short Title, Form and Interpretation

§ 3—101. Short Title.

This Article shall be known and may be cited as Uniform Commercial Code—Commercial Paper.

§ 3—102. Definitions and Index of Definitions.

(1) In this Article unless the context otherwise requires

(a) "Issue" means the first delivery of an instrument to a holder or a remitter.

(b) An "order" is a direction to pay and must be more than an authorization or request. It must identify the person to pay with reasonable certainty. It may be addressed to one or more such persons jointly or in the alternative but not in succession.

(c) A "promise" is an undertaking to pay and must be more than an acknowledgment of an obligation.

(d) "Secondary party" means a drawer or endorser.

(e) "Instrument" means a negotiable instrument.

(2) Other definitions applying to this Article and the sections in which they appear are:
"Acceptance". Section 3—410.
"Accommodation party". Section 3—415.
"Alteration". Section 3—407.
"Certificate of deposit". Section 3—104.
"Certification". Section 3—411.
"Check". Section 3—104.
"Definite time". Section 3—109.
"Dishonor". Section 3—507.
"Draft". Section 3—104.
"Holder in due course". Section 3—302.
"Negotiation". Section 3—202.
"Note". Section 3—104.
"Notice of dishonor". Section 3—508.
"On demand". Section 3—108.
"Presentment". Section 3—504.
"Protest". Section 3—509.
"Restrictive Indorsement". Section 3—205.
"Signature". Section 3—401.

(3) The following definitions in other Articles apply to this Article:
"Account". Section 4—104.
"Banking Day". Section 4—104.
"Clearing House". Section 4—104.
"Collecting Bank". Section 4—105.
"Customer". Section 4—104.
"Depositary Bank". Section 4—105.
"Documentary Draft". Section 4—104.
"Intermediary Bank". Section 4—105.
"Item". Section 4—104.
"Midnight deadline". Section 4—104.
"Payor Bank". Section 4—105.

(4) In addition Article 1 contains general definitions and principles of construction and interpretation applicable throughout this Article.

§ 3—103. Limitations on Scope of Article.

(1) This Article does not apply to money, documents of title or investment securities.

(2) The provisions of this Article are subject to the provisions of the Article on Bank Deposits and Collections (Article 4) and Secured Transactions (Article 9).

§ 3—104. Form of Negotiable Instruments; "Draft"; "Check"; "Certificate of Deposit"; "Note".

(1) Any writing to be a negotiable instrument within this Article must

(a) be signed by the maker or drawer; and

(b) contain an unconditional promise or order to pay a sum certain in money and no other promise, order, obligation or power given by the maker or drawer except as authorized by this Article; and

(c) be payable on demand or at a definite time; and

(d) be payable to order or to bearer.

(2) A writing which complies with the requirements of this section is

(a) a "draft" ("bill of exchange") if it is an order;

(b) a "check" if it is a draft drawn on a bank and payable on demand;

(c) a "certificate of deposit" if it is an acknowledgment by a bank receipt of money with an engagement to repay it;

(d) a "note" if it is a promise other than a certificate of deposit.

(3) As used in other Articles of this Act, and as the context may require, the terms "draft", "check", "certificate of deposit" and "note" may refer to instruments which are not negotiable within this Article as well as to instruments which are so negotiable.

§ 3—105. When Promise or Order Unconditional.

(1) A promise or order otherwise unconditional is not made conditional by the fact that the instrument

(a) is subject to implied or constructive conditions; or

(b) states its consideration, whether performed or promised, or the transaction which gave rise to the instrument, or that the promise or order is made or the instrument matures in accordance with or "as per" such transaction; or

(c) refers to or states that it arises out of a separate agreement or refers to a separate agreement for rights as to prepayment or acceleration; or

(d) states that it is drawn under a letter of credit; or

(e) states that it is secured, whether by mortgage, reservation of title or otherwise; or

(f) indicates a particular account to be debited or any other fund or source from which reimbursement is expected; or

(g) is limited to payment out of a particular fund or the proceeds of a particular source, if the instrument is issued by a government or governmental agency or unit; or

(h) is limited to payment out of the entire assets of a partnership, unincorporated association, trust or estate by or on behalf of which the instrument is issued.

(2) A promise or order is not unconditional if the instrument

(a) states that it is subject to or governed by any other agreement; or

(b) states that it is to be paid only out of a particular fund or source except as provided in this section.

§ 3—106. Sum Certain.

(1) The sum payable is a sum certain even though it is to be paid

(a) with stated interest or by stated installments; or

(b) with stated different rates of interest before and after default or a specified date; or

(c) with a stated discount or addition if paid before or after the date fixed for payment; or

(d) with exchange or less exchange, whether at a fixed rate or at the current rate; or

(e) with costs of collection or an attorney's fee or both upon default.

(2) Nothing in this section shall validate any term which is otherwise illegal.

§ 3—107. Money.

(1) An instrument is payable in money if the medium of exchange in which it is payable is money at the time the instrument is made. An instrument payable in "currency" or "current funds" is payable in money.

(2) A promise or order to pay a sum stated in a foreign currency is for a sum certain in money and, unless a different medium of payment is specified in the instrument, may be satisfied by payment of that number of dollars which the stated foreign currency will purchase at the buying sight rate for that currency on the day on which the instrument is payable or, if payable on demand, on the day of demand. If such an instrument specifies a foreign currency as the medium of payment the instrument is payable in that currency.

§ 3—108. Payable on Demand.

Instruments payable on demand include those payable at sight or on presentation and those in which no time for payment is stated.

§ 3—109. Definite Time.

(1) An instrument is payable at a definite time if by its terms it is payable

(a) on or before a stated date or at a fixed period after a stated date; or

(b) at a fixed period after sight; or

(c) at a definite time subject to any acceleration; or

(d) at a definite time subject to extension at the option of the holder, or to extension to a further definite time at the option of the maker or acceptor or automatically upon or after a specified act or event.

(2) An instrument which by its terms is otherwise payable only upon an act or event uncertain as to time of occurrence is not payable at a definite time even though the act or event has occurred.

§ 3—110. Payable to Order.

(1) An instrument is payable to order when by its terms it is payable to the order or assigns of any person therein specified with reasonable certainty, or to him or his order, or when it is conspicuously designated on its face as "exchange" or the like and names a payee. It may be payable to the order of

(a) the maker or drawer; or

(b) the drawee; or

(c) a payee who is not maker, drawer or drawee; or

(d) two or more payees together or in the alternative; or

(e) an estate, trust or fund, in which case it is payable to the order of the representative of such estate, trust or fund or his successors; or

(f) an office, or an officer by his title as such in which case it is payable to the principal but the incumbent of the office or his successors may act as if he or they were the holder; or

(g) a partnership or unincorporated association, in which case it is payable to the partnership or association and may be indorsed or transferred by any person thereto authorized.

(2) An instrument not payable to order is not made so payable by such words as "payable upon return of this instrument properly indorsed."

(3) An instrument made payable both to order and to bearer is payable to order unless the bearer words are handwritten or typewritten.

§ 3—111. Payable to Bearer.

An instrument is payable to bearer when by its terms it is payable to

(a) bearer or the order of bearer; or

(b) a specified person or bearer; or

(c) "cash" or the order of "cash", or any other indication which does not purport to designate a specific payee.

§ 3—112. Terms and Omissions Not Affecting Negotiability.

(1) The negotiability of an instrument is not affected by

(a) the omission of a statement of any consideration or of the place where the instrument is drawn or payable; or

(b) a statement that collateral has been given to secure obligations either on the instrument or otherwise of an obligor on the instrument or that in case of default on those obligations the holder may realize on or dispose of the collateral; or

(c) a promise or power to maintain or protect collateral or to give additional collateral; or

(d) a term authorizing a confession of judgment on the instrument if it is not paid when due; or

(e) a term purporting to waive the benefit of any law intended for the advantage or protection of any obligor; or

(f) a term in a draft providing that the payee by indorsing or cashing it acknowledges full satisfaction of an obligation of the drawer; or

(g) a statement in a draft drawn in a set of parts (Section 3—801) to the effect that the order is effective only if no other part has been honored.

(2) Nothing in this section shall validate any term which is otherwise illegal.

§ 3—113. Seal.

An instrument otherwise negotiable is within this Article even though it is under a seal.

§ 3—114. Date, Antedating, Postdating.

(1) The negotiability of an instrument is not affected by the fact that it is undated, antedated or postdated.

(2) Where an instrument is antedated or postdated the time when it is payable is determined by the stated date if the instrument is payable on demand or at a fixed period after date.

(3) Where the instrument or any signature thereon is dated, the date is presumed to be correct.

§ 3—115. Incomplete Instruments.

(1) When a paper whose contents at the time of signing show that it is intended to become an instrument is signed while still incomplete in any necessary respect it cannot be enforced until completed, but when it is completed in accordance with authority given it is effective as completed.

(2) If the completion is unauthorized the rules as to material alteration apply (Section 3—407), even though the paper was not delivered by the maker or drawer; but the burden of establishing that any completion is unauthorized is on the party so asserting.

§ 3—116. Instruments Payable to Two or More Persons.

An instrument payable to the order of two or more persons

(a) if in the alternative is payable to any one of them and may be negotiated, discharged or enforced by any of them who has possession of it;

(b) if not in the alternative is payable to all of them and may be negotiated, discharged or enforced only by all of them.

§ 3—117. Instruments Payable With Words of Description.

An instrument made payable to a named person with the addition of words describing him

(a) as agent or officer of a specified person is payable to his principal but the agent or officer may act as if he were the holder;

(b) as any other fiduciary for a specified person or purpose is payable to the payee and may be negotiated, discharged or enforced by him;

(c) in any other manner is payable to the payee unconditionally and the additional words are without effect on subsequent parties.

§ 3—118. Ambiguous Terms and Rules of Construction.

The following rules apply to every instrument:

(a) Where there is doubt whether the instrument is a draft or a note the holder may treat it as either. A draft drawn on the drawer is effective as a note.

(b) Handwritten terms control typewritten and printed terms, and typewritten control printed.

(c) Words control figures except that if the words are ambiguous figures control.

(d) Unless otherwise specified a provision for interest means interest at the judgment rate at the place of payment from the date of the instrument, or if it is undated from the date of issue.

(e) Unless the instrument otherwise specifies two or more persons who sign as maker, acceptor or drawer or indorser and as a part of the same transaction are jointly and severally liable even though the instrument contains such words as "I promise to pay."

(f) Unless otherwise specified consent to extension authorizes a single extension for not longer than the original period. A consent to extension, expressed in the instrument, is binding on secondary parties and accommodation makers. A holder may not exercise his option to extend an instrument over the objection of a maker or acceptor or other party who in accordance with Section 3—604 tenders full payment when the instrument is due.

§ 3—119. Other Writings Affecting Instrument.

(1) As between the obligor and his immediate obligee or any transferee the terms of an instrument may be modified or affected by any other written agreement executed as a part of the same transaction, except that a holder in due course is not affected by any limitation of his rights arising out of the separate written agreement if he had no notice of the limitation when he took the instrument.

(2) A separate agreement does not affect the negotiability of an instrument.

§ 3—120. Instruments "Payable Through" Bank.

An instrument which states that it is "payable through" a bank or the like designates that bank as a collecting bank to make presentment but does not of itself authorize the bank to pay the instrument.

§ 3—121. Instruments Payable at Bank.

Note: If this Act is introduced in the Congress of the United States this section should be omitted.
(States to select either alternative)

Alternative A—

A note or acceptance which states that it is payable at a bank is the equivalent of a draft drawn on the bank payable when it falls due out of any funds of the maker or acceptor in current account or otherwise available for such payment.

Alternative B—

A note or acceptance which states that it is payable at a bank is not of itself an order or authorization to the bank to pay it.

§ 3—122. Accrual of Cause of Action.

(1) A cause of action against a maker or an acceptor accrues

(a) in the case of a time instrument on the day after maturity;

(b) in the case of a demand instrument upon its date or, if no date is stated, on the date of issue.

(2) A cause of action against the obligor of a demand or time certificate of deposit accrues upon demand, but demand on a time certificate may not be made until on or after the date of maturity.

(3) A cause of action against a drawer of a draft or an indorser of any instrument accrues upon demand following dishonor of the instrument. Notice of dishonor is a demand.

(4) Unless an instrument provides otherwise, interest runs at the rate provided by law for a judgment

(a) in the case of a maker, acceptor or other primary obligor of a demand instrument, from the date of demand;

(b) in all other cases from the date of accrual of the cause of action.

Part 2 Transfer and Negotiation

§ 3—201. Transfer: Right to Indorsement.

(1) Transfer of an instrument vests in the transferee such rights as the transferor has therein, except that a transferee who has himself been a party to any fraud or illegality affecting the instrument or who as a prior holder had notice of a defense or claim against it cannot improve his position by taking from a later holder in due course.

(2) A transfer of a security interest in an instrument vests the foregoing rights in the transferee to the extent of the interest transferred.

(3) Unless otherwise agreed any transfer for value of an instrument not then payable to bearer gives the transferee the specifically enforceable right to have the unqualified indorsement of the transferor. Negotiation takes effect only when the indorsement is made and until that time there is no presumption that the transferee is the owner.

§ 3—202. Negotiation.

(1) Negotiation is the transfer of an instrument in such form that the transferee becomes a holder. If the instrument is payable to order it is negotiated by delivery with any necessary indorsement; if payable to bearer it is negotiated by delivery.

(2) An indorsement must be written by or on behalf of the holder and on the instrument or on a paper so firmly affixed thereto as to become a part thereof.

(3) An indorsement is effective for negotiation only when it conveys the entire instrument or any unpaid residue. If it purports to be of less it operates only as a partial assignment.

(4) Words of assignment, condition, waiver, guaranty, limitation or disclaimer of liability and the like accompanying an indorsement do not affect its character as an indorsement.

§ 3—203. Wrong or Misspelled Name.

Where an instrument is made payable to a person under a misspelled name or one other than his own he may indorse in that name or his own or both; but signature in both names may be required by a person paying or giving value for the instrument.

§ 3—204. Special Indorsement; Blank Indorsement.

(1) A special indorsement specifies the person to whom or to whose order it makes the instrument payable. Any instrument specially indorsed becomes payable to the order of the special indorsee and may be further negotiated only by his indorsement.

(2) An indorsement in blank specifies no particular indorsee and may consist of a mere signature. An instrument payable to order and indorsed in blank becomes payable to bearer and may be negotiated by delivery alone until specially indorsed.

(3) The holder may convert a blank indorsement into a special indorsement by writing over the signature of the indorser in blank any contract consistent with the character of the indorsement.

§ 3—205. Restrictive Indorsements.

An indorsement is restrictive which either

(a) is conditional; or

(b) purports to prohibit further transfer of the instrument; or

(c) includes the words "for collection", "for deposit", "pay any bank", or like terms signifying a purpose of deposit or collection; or

(d) otherwise states that it is for the benefit or use of the indorser or of another person.

§ 3—206. Effect of Restrictive Indorsement.

(1) No restrictive indorsement prevents further transfer or negotiation of the instrument.

(2) An intermediary bank, or a payor bank which is not the depositary bank, is neither given notice nor otherwise affected by a restrictive indorsement of any person except the bank's immediate transferor or the person presenting for payment.

(3) Except for an intermediary bank, any transferee under an indorsement which is conditional or includes the words "for collection", "for deposit", "pay any bank", or like terms (subparagraphs (a) and (c) of Section 3—205) must pay or apply any value given by him for or on the security of the instrument consistently with the indorsement and to the extent that he does so he becomes a holder for value. In addition such transferee is a holder in due course if he otherwise complies with the requirements of Section 3—302 on what constitutes a holder in due course.

(4) The first taker under an indorsement for the benefit of the indorser or another person (subparagraph (d) of Section 3—205) must pay or apply any value given by him for or on the security of the instrument consistently with the indorsement and to the extent that he does so he becomes a holder for value. In addition such taker is a holder in due course if he otherwise complies with the requirements of Section 3—302 on what constitutes a holder in due course. A later holder for value is neither given notice nor otherwise affected by such restrictive indorsement unless he has knowledge that a fiduciary or other person has negotiated the instrument in any trans-

action for his own benefit or otherwise in breach of duty (subsection (2) of Section 3—304).

§ 3—207. Negotiation Effective Although It May Be Rescinded.

(1) Negotiation is effective to transfer the instrument although the negotiation is

(a) made by an infant, a corporation exceeding its powers, or any other person without capacity; or

(b) obtained by fraud, duress or mistake of any kind; or

(c) part of an illegal transaction; or

(d) made in breach of duty.

(2) Except as against a subsequent holder in due course such negotiation is in an appropriate case subject to rescission, the declaration of a constructive trust or any other remedy permitted by law.

§ 3—208. Reacquisition.

Where an instrument is returned to or reacquired by a prior party he may cancel any indorsement which is not necessary to his title and reissue or further negotiate the instrument, but any intervening party is discharged as against the reacquiring party and subsequent holders not in due course and if his indorsement has been cancelled is discharged as against subsequent holders in due course as well.

Part 3 Rights of a Holder

§ 3—301. Rights of a Holder.

The holder of an instrument whether or not he is the owner may transfer or negotiate it and, except as otherwise provided in Section 3—603 on payment or satisfaction, discharge it or enforce payment in his own name.

§ 3—302. Holder in Due Course

(1) A holder in due course is a holder who takes the instrument

(a) for value; and

(b) in good faith; and

(c) without notice that it is overdue or has been dishonored or of any defense against or claim to it on the part of any person.

(2) A payee may be a holder in due course.

(3) A holder does not become a holder in due course of an instrument:

(a) by purchase of it at judicial sale or by taking it under legal process; or

(b) by acquiring it in taking over an estate; or

(c) by purchasing it as part of a bulk transaction not in regular course of business of the transferor.

(4) A purchaser of a limited interest can be a holder in due course only to the extent of the interest purchased.

§ 3—303. Taking for Value.

A holder takes the instrument for value

(a) to the extent that the agreed consideration has been performed or that he acquires a security interest in or a lien on the instrument otherwise than by legal process; or

(b) when he takes the instrument in payment of or as security for an antecedent claim against any person whether or not the claim is due; or

(c) when he gives a negotiable instrument for it or makes an irrevocable commitment to a third person.

§ 3—304. Notice to Purchaser.

(1) The purchaser has notice of a claim or defense if

(a) the instrument is so incomplete, bears such visible evidence of forgery or alteration, or is otherwise so irregular as to call into question its validity, terms or ownership or to create an ambiguity as to the party to pay; or

(b) the purchaser has notice that the obligation of any party is voidable in whole or in part, or that all parties have been discharged.

(2) The purchaser has notice of a claim against the instrument when he has knowledge that a fiduciary has negotiated the instrument in payment of or as security for his own debt or in any transaction for his own benefit or otherwise in breach of duty.

(3) The purchaser has notice that an instrument is overdue if he has reason to know

(a) that any part of the principal amount is overdue or that there is an uncured default in payment of another instrument of the same series; or

(b) that acceleration of the instrument has been made; or

(c) that he is taking a demand instrument after demand has been made or more than a reasonable length of time after its issue. A reasonable time for a check drawn and payable within the states and territories of the United States and the District of Columbia is presumed to be thirty days.

(4) Knowledge of the following facts does not of itself give the purchaser notice of a defense or claim

(a) that the instrument is antedated or postdated;

(b) that it was issued or negotiated in return for an executory promise or accompanied by a separate agreement, unless the purchaser has notice that a defense or claim has arisen from the terms thereof;

(c) that any party has signed for accommodation;

(d) that an incomplete instrument has been completed, unless the purchaser has notice of any improper completion;

(e) that any person negotiating the instrument is or was a fiduciary;

(f) that there has been default in payment of interest on the instrument or in payment of any other instrument, except one of the same series.

(5) The filing or recording of a document does not of itself constitute notice within the provisions of this Article to a person who would otherwise be a holder in due course.

(6) To be effective notice must be received at such time and in such manner as to give a reasonable opportunity to act on it.

§ 3—305. Rights of a Holder in Due Course.

To the extent that a holder is a holder in due course he takes the instrument free from

(1) all claims to it on the part of any person; and

(2) all defenses of any party to the instrument with whom the holder has not dealt except

(a) infancy, to the extent that it is a defense to a simple contract; and

(b) such other incapacity, or duress, or illegality of the transaction, as renders the obligation of the party a nullity; and

(c) such misrepresentation as has induced the party to sign the instrument with neither knowledge nor reasonable opportunity to obtain knowledge of its character or its essential terms; and

(d) discharge in insolvency proceedings; and

(e) any other discharge of which the holder has notice when he takes the instrument.

§ 3—306. Rights of One Not Holder in Due Course.

Unless he has the rights of a holder in due course any person takes the instrument subject to

(a) all valid claims to it on the part of any person; and

(b) all defenses of any party which would be available in an action on a simple contract; and

(c) the defenses of want or failure of consideration, non-performance of any condition precedent, non-delivery, or delivery for a special purpose (Section 3—408); and

(d) the defense that he or a person through whom he holds the instrument acquired it by theft, or that payment or satisfaction to such holder would be inconsistent with the terms of a restrictive indorsement. The claim of any third person to the instrument is not otherwise available as a defense to any party liable thereon unless the third person himself defends the action for such party.

§ 3—307. Burden of Establishing Signatures, Defenses and Due Course.

(1) Unless specifically denied in the pleadings each signature on an instrument is admitted. When the effectiveness of a signature is put in issue

(a) the burden of establishing it is on the party claiming under the signature; but

(b) the signature is presumed to be genuine or authorized except where the action is to enforce the obligation of a purported signer who has died or become incompetent before proof is required.

(2) When signatures are admitted or established, production of the instrument entitles a holder to recover on it unless the defendant establishes a defense.

(3) After it is shown that a defense exists a person claiming the rights of a holder in due course has the burden of establishing that he or some person under whom he claims is in all respects a holder in due course.

Part 4 Liability of Parties

§ 3—401. Signature.

(1) No person is liable on an instrument unless his signature appears thereon.

(2) A signature is made by use of any name, including any trade or assumed name, upon an instrument, or by any word or mark used in lieu of a written signature.

§ 3—402. Signature in Ambiguous Capacity.

Unless the instrument clearly indicates that a signature is made in some other capacity it is an indorsement.

§ 3—403. Signature by Authorized Representative.

(1) A signature may be made by an agent or other representative, and his authority to make it may be established as in other cases of representation. No particular form of appointment is necessary to establish such authority.

(2) An authorized representative who signs his own name to an instrument

(a) is personally obligated if the instrument neither names the person represented nor shows that the representative signed in a representative capacity;

(b) except as otherwise established between the immediate parties, is personally obligated if the instrument names the person represented but does not show that the representative signed in a representative capacity, or if the instrument does not name the person represented but does show that the representative signed in a representative capacity.

(3) Except as otherwise established the name of an organization preceded or followed by the name and office of an authorized individual is a signature made in a representative capacity.

§ 3—404. Unauthorized Signatures.

(1) Any unauthorized signature is wholly inoperative as that of the person whose name is signed unless he ratifies it or is precluded from denying it; but it operates as the signature of the unauthorized signer in favor of any person who in good faith pays the instrument or takes it for value.

(2) Any unauthorized signature may be ratified for all purposes of this Article. Such ratification does not of itself affect any rights of the person ratifying against the actual signer.

§ 3—405. Impostors; Signature in Name of Payee.

(1) An indorsement by any person in the name of a named payee is effective if

(a) an impostor by use of the mails or otherwise has induced the maker or drawer to issue the instrument to him or his confederate in the name of the payee; or

(b) a person signing as or on behalf of a maker or drawer intends the payee to have no interest in the instrument; or

(c) an agent or employee of the maker or drawer has supplied him with the name of the payee intending the latter to have no such interest.

(2) Nothing in this section shall affect the criminal or civil liability of the person so indorsing.

§ 3—406. Negligence Contributing to Alteration or Unauthorized Signature.

Any person who by his negligence substantially contributes to a material alteration of the instrument or to the making of an unauthorized signature is precluded from asserting the alteration or lack of authority against a holder in due course or against a drawee or other payor who pays the instrument in good faith and in accordance with the reasonable commercial standards of the drawee's or payor's business.

§ 3—407. Alteration.

(1) Any alteration of an instrument is material which changes the contract of any party thereto in any respect, including any such change in

(a) the number or relations of the parties; or

(b) an incomplete instrument, by completing it otherwise than as authorized; or

(c) the writing as signed, by adding to it or by removing any part of it.

(2) As against any person other than a subsequent holder in due course

(a) alteration by the holder which is both fraudulent and material discharges any party whose contract is thereby changed unless that party assents or is precluded from asserting the defense;

(b) no other alteration discharges any party and the instrument may be enforced according to its original tenor, or as to incomplete instruments according to the authority given.

(3) A subsequent holder in due course may in all cases enforce the instrument according to its original tenor, and when an incomplete instrument has been completed, he may enforce it as completed.

§ 3—408. Consideration.

Want or failure of consideration is a defense as against any person not having the rights of a holder in due course (Section 3—305), except that no consideration is necessary for an instrument or obligation thereon given in payment of or as security for an antecedent obligation of any kind. Nothing in this section shall be taken to displace any statute outside this Act under which a promise is enforceable notwithstanding lack or failure of consideration. Partial failure of consideration is a defense pro tanto whether or not the failure is in an ascertained or liquidated amount.

§ 3—409. Draft Not an Assignment.

(1) A check or other draft does not of itself operate as an assignment of any funds in the hands of the drawee available for its payment, and the drawee is not liable on the instrument until he accepts it.

(2) Nothing in this section shall affect any liability in contract, tort or otherwise arising from any letter of credit or other obligation or representation which is not an acceptance.

§ 3—410. Definition and Operation of Acceptance.

(1) Acceptance is the drawee's signed engagement to honor the draft as presented. It must be written on the draft, and may consist of his signature alone. It becomes operative when completed by delivery or notification.

(2) A draft may be accepted although it has not been signed by the drawer or is otherwise incomplete or is overdue or has been dishonored.

(3) Where the draft is payable at a fixed period after sight and the acceptor fails to date his acceptance the holder may complete it by supplying a date in good faith.

§ 3—411. Certification of a Check.

(1) Certification of a check is acceptance. Where a holder procures certification the drawer and all prior indorsers are discharged.

(2) Unless otherwise agreed a bank has no obligation to certify a check.

(3) A bank may certify a check before returning it for lack of proper indorsement. If it does so the drawer is discharged.

§ 3—412. Acceptance Varying Draft.

(1) Where the drawee's proffered acceptance in any manner varies the draft as presented the holder may refuse the acceptance and treat the draft as dishonored in which case the drawee is entitled to have his acceptance cancelled.

(2) The terms of the draft are not varied by an acceptance to pay at any particular bank or place in the United States, unless the acceptance states that the draft is to be paid only at such bank or place.

(3) Where the holder assents to an acceptance varying the terms of the draft each drawer and indorser who does not affirmatively assent is discharged.

§ 3—413. Contract of Maker, Drawer and Acceptor.

(1) The maker or acceptor engages that he will pay the instrument according to its tenor at the time of his engagement or as completed pursuant to Section 3—115 on incomplete instruments.

(2) The drawer engages that upon dishonor of the draft and any necessary notice of dishonor or protest he will pay the amount of the draft to the holder or to any indorser who takes it up. The drawer may disclaim this liability by drawing without recourse.

(3) By making, drawing or accepting the party admits as against all subsequent parties including the drawee the existence of the payee and his then capacity to indorse.

§ 3—414. Contract of Indorser; Order of Liability.

(1) Unless the indorsement otherwise specifies (as by such words as "without recourse") every indorser engages that upon dishonor and any necessary notice of dishonor and protest he will pay the instrument according to its tenor at the time of his indorsement to the holder or to any subsequent indorser who takes it up, even though the indorser who takes it up was not obligated to do so.

(2) Unless they otherwise agree indorsers are liable to one another in the order in which they indorse, which is presumed to be the order in which their signatures appear on the instrument.

§ 3—415. Contract of Accommodation Party.

(1) An accommodation party is one who signs the instrument in any capacity for the purpose of lending his name to another party to it.

(2) When the instrument has been taken for value before it is due the accommodation party is liable in the capacity in which he has signed even though the taker knows of the accommodation.

(3) As against a holder in due course and without notice of the accommodation oral proof of the accommodation is not admissible to give the accommodation party the benefit of discharges dependent on his character as such. In other cases the accommodation character may be shown by oral proof.

(4) An indorsement which shows that it is not in the chain of title is notice of its accommodation character.

(5) An accommodation party is not liable to the party accommodated, and if he pays the instrument has a right of recourse on the instrument against such party.

§ 3—416. Contract of Guarantor.

(1) "Payment guaranteed" or equivalent words added to a signature mean that the signer engages that if the instrument is not paid when due he will pay it according to its tenor without resort by the holder to any other party.

(2) "Collection guaranteed" or equivalent words added to a signature mean that the signer engages that if the instrument is not paid when due he will pay it according to its tenor, but only after the holder has reduced his claim against the maker or acceptor to judgment and execution has been returned unsatisfied, or after the maker or acceptor has become insolvent or it is otherwise apparent that it is useless to proceed against him.

(3) Words of guaranty which do not otherwise specify guarantee payment.

(4) No words of guaranty added to the signature of a sole maker or acceptor affect his liability on the instrument. Such words added to the signature of one of two or more makers or acceptors create a presumption that the signature is for the accommodation of the others.

(5) When words of guaranty are used presentment, notice of dishonor and protest are not necessary to charge the user.

(6) Any guaranty written on the instrument is enforcible notwithstanding any statute of frauds.

§ 3—417. Warranties on Presentment and Transfer.

(1) Any person who obtains payment or acceptance and any prior transferor warrants to a person who in good faith pays or accepts that

(a) he has a good title to the instrument or is authorized to obtain payment or acceptance on behalf of one who has a good title; and

(b) he has no knowledge that the signature of the maker or drawer is unauthorized, except that this warranty is not given by a holder in due course acting in good faith

(i) to a maker with respect to the maker's own signature; or

(ii) to a drawer with respect to the drawer's own signature, whether or not the drawer is also the drawee; or

(iii) to an acceptor of a draft if the holder in due course took the draft after the acceptance or obtained the acceptance without knowledge that the drawer's signature was unauthorized; and

(c) the instrument has not been materially altered, except that this warranty is not given by a holder in due course acting in good faith

(i) to the maker of a note; or

(ii) to the drawer of a draft whether or not the drawer is also the drawee; or

(iii) to the acceptor of a draft with respect to an alteration made prior to the acceptance if the holder in due course took the draft after the acceptance, even though the acceptance provided "payable as originally drawn" or equivalent terms; or

(iv) to the acceptor of a draft with respect to an alteration made after the acceptance.

(2) Any person who transfers an instrument and receives consideration warrants to his transferee and if the transfer is by indorsement to any subsequent holder who takes the instrument in good faith that

(a) he has a good title to the instrument or is authorized to obtain payment or acceptance on behalf of one who has a good title and the transfer is otherwise rightful; and

(b) all signatures are genuine or authorized; and

(c) the instrument has not been materially altered; and

(d) no defense of any party is good against him; and

(e) he has no knowledge of any insolvency proceeding instituted with respect to the maker or acceptor or the drawer of an unaccepted instrument.

(3) By transferring "without recourse" the transferor limits the obligation stated in subsection (2) (d) to a warranty that he has no knowledge of such a defense.

(4) A selling agent or broker who does not disclose the fact that he is acting only as such gives the warranties

provided in this section, but if he makes such disclosure warrants only his good faith and authority.

§ 3—418. Finality of Payment or Acceptance.

Except for recovery of bank payments as provided in the Article on Bank Deposits and Collections (Article 4) and except for liability for breach of warranty on presentment under the preceding section, payment or acceptance of any instrument is final in favor of a holder in due course, or a person who has in good faith changed his position in reliance on the payment.

§ 3—419. Conversion of Instrument; Innocent Representative.

(1) An instrument is converted when

(a) a drawee to whom it is delivered for acceptance refuses to return it on demand; or

(b) any person to whom it is delivered for payment refuses on demand either to pay or to return it; or

(c) it is paid on a forged indorsement.

(2) In an action against a drawee under subsection (1) the measure of the drawee's liability is the face amount of the instrument. In any other action under subsection (1) the measure of liability is presumed to be the face amount of the instrument.

(3) Subject to the provisions of this Act concerning restrictive indorsements a representative, including a depositary or collecting bank, who has in good faith and in accordance with the reasonable commercial standards applicable to the business of such representative dealt with an instrument or its proceeds on behalf of one who was not the true owner is not liable in conversion or otherwise to the true owner beyond the amount of any proceeds remaining in his hands.

(4) An intermediary bank or payor bank which is not a depositary bank is not liable in conversion solely by reason of the fact that proceeds of an item indorsed restrictively (Sections 3—205 and 3—206) are not paid or applied consistently with the restrictive indorsement of an indorser other than its immediate transferor.

Part 5 Presentment, Notice of Dishonor and Protest

§ 3—501. When Presentment, Notice of Dishonor, and Protest Necessary or Permissible.

(1) Unless excused (Section 3—511) presentment is necessary to charge secondary parties as follows:

(a) presentment for acceptance is necessary to charge the drawer and indorsers of a draft where the draft so provides, or is payable elsewhere than at the residence or place of business of the drawee, or its date of payment depends upon such presentment. The holder may at his option present for acceptance any other draft payable at a stated date;

(b) presentment for payment is necessary to charge any indorser;

(c) in the case of any drawer, the acceptor of a draft payable at a bank or the maker of a note payable at a bank, presentment for payment is necessary, but failure to make presentment discharges such drawer, acceptor or maker only as stated in Section 3—502(1)(b).

(2) Unless excused (Section 3—511)

(a) notice of any dishonor is necessary to charge any indorser;

(b) in the case of any drawer, the acceptor of a draft payable at a bank or the maker of a note payable at a bank, notice of any dishonor is necessary, but failure to give such notice discharges such drawer, acceptor or maker only as stated in Section 3—502(1)(b).

(3) Unless excused (Section 3—511) protest of any dishonor is necessary to charge the drawer and indorsers of any draft which on its face appears to be drawn or payable outside of the states, territories, dependencies, and possessions of the United States, the District of Columbia and the Commonwealth of Puerto Rico. The holder may at his option make protest of any dishonor of any other instrument and in the case of a foreign draft may on insolvency of the acceptor before maturity make protest for better security.

(4) Notwithstanding any provision of this section, neither presentment nor notice of dishonor nor protest is necessary to charge an indorser who has indorsed an instrument after maturity.

§ 3—502. **Unexcused Delay; Discharge.**

(1) Where without excuse any necessary presentment or notice of dishonor is delayed beyond the time when it is due

(a) any indorser is discharged; and

(b) any drawer or the acceptor of a draft payable at a bank or the maker of a note payable at a bank who because the drawee or payor bank becomes insolvent during the delay is deprived of funds maintained with the drawee or payor bank to cover the instrument may discharge his liability by written assignment to the holder of his rights against the drawee or payor bank in respect of such funds, but such drawer, acceptor or maker is not otherwise discharged.

(2) Where without excuse a necessary protest is delayed beyond the time when it is due any drawer or indorser is discharged.

§ 3—503. **Time of Presentment.**

(1) Unless a different time is expressed in the instrument the time for any presentment is determined as follows:

(a) where an instrument is payable at or a fixed period after a stated date any presentment for acceptance must be made on or before the date it is payable;

(b) where an instrument is payable after sight it must either be presented for acceptance or negotiated within a reasonable time after date or issue whichever is later;

(c) where an instrument shows the date on which it is payable presentment for payment is due on that date;

(d) where an instrument is accelerated presentment for payment is due within a reasonable time after the acceleration;

(e) with respect to the liability of any secondary party presentment for acceptance or payment of any other instrument is due within a reasonable time after such party becomes liable thereon.

(2) A reasonable time for presentment is determined by the nature of the instrument, any usage of banking or trade and the facts of the particular case. In the case of an uncertified check which is drawn and payable within the United States and which is not a draft drawn by a bank the following are presumed to be reasonable periods within which to present for payment or to initiate bank collection:

(a) with respect to the liability of the drawer, thirty days after date or issue whichever is later; and

(b) with respect to the liability of an indorser, seven days after his indorsement.

(3) Where any presentment is due on a day which is not a full business day for either the person making presentment or the party to pay or accept, presentment is due on the next following day which is a full business day for both parties.

(4) Presentment to be sufficient must be made at a reasonable hour, and if at a bank during its banking day.

§ 3—504. **How Presentment Made.**

(1) Presentment is a demand for acceptance or payment made upon the maker, acceptor, drawee or other payor by or on behalf of the holder.

(2) Presentment may be made

(a) by mail, in which event the time of presentment is determined by the time of receipt of the mail; or

(b) through a clearing house; or

(c) at the place of acceptance or payment specified in the instrument or if there be none at the place of business or residence of the party to accept or pay. If neither the party to accept or pay nor anyone authorized to act for him is present or accessible at such place presentment is excused.

(3) It may be made

(a) to any one of two or more makers, acceptors, drawees or other payors; or

(b) to any person who has authority to make or refuse the acceptance or payment.

(4) A draft accepted or a note made payable at a bank in the United States must be presented at such bank.

(5) In the cases described in Section 4—210 presentment may be made in the manner and with the result stated in that section.

§ 3—505. Rights of Party to Whom Presentment Is Made.

(1) The party to whom presentment is made may without dishonor require

(a) exhibition of the instrument; and

(b) reasonable identification of the person making presentment and evidence of his authority to make it if made for another; and

(c) that the instrument be produced for acceptance or payment at a place specified in it, or if there be none at any place reasonable in the circumstances; and

(d) a signed receipt on the instrument for any partial or full payment and its surrender upon full payment.

(2) Failure to comply with any such requirement invalidates the presentment but the person presenting has a reasonable time in which to comply and the time for acceptance or payment runs from the time of compliance.

§ 3—506. Time Allowed for Acceptance or Payment.

(1) Acceptance may be deferred without dishonor until the close of the next business day following presentment. The holder may also in a good faith effort to obtain acceptance and without either dishonor of the instrument or discharge of secondary parties allow postponement of acceptance for an additional business day.

(2) Except as a longer time is allowed in the case of documentary drafts drawn under a letter of credit, and unless an earlier time is agreed to by the party to pay, payment of an instrument may be deferred without dishonor pending reasonable examination to determine whether it is properly payable, but payment must be made in any event before the close of business on the day of presentment.

§ 3—507. Dishonor; Holder's Right of Recourse; Term Allowing Re-Presentment.

(1) An instrument is dishonored when

(a) a necessary or optional presentment is duly made and due acceptance or payment is refused or cannot be obtained within the prescribed time or in case of bank collections the instrument is seasonably returned by the midnight deadline (Section 4—301); or

(b) presentment is excused and the instrument is not duly accepted or paid.

(2) Subject to any necessary notice of dishonor and protest, the holder has upon dishonor an immediate right of recourse against the drawers and indorsers.

(3) Return of an instrument for lack of proper indorsement is not dishonor.

(4) A term in a draft or an indorsement thereof allowing a stated time for re-presentment in the event of any dishonor of the draft by nonacceptance if a time draft or by nonpayment if a sight draft gives the holder as against any secondary party bound by the term an option to waive the dishonor without affecting the liability of the secondary party and he may present again up to the end of the stated time.

§ 3—508. Notice of Dishonor.

(1) Notice of dishonor may be given to any person who may be liable on the instrument by or on behalf of the holder or any party who has himself received notice, or any other party who can be compelled to pay the instrument. In addition an agent or bank in whose hands the instrument is dishonored may give notice to his principal or customer or to another agent or bank from which the instrument was received.

(2) Any necessary notice must be given by a bank before its midnight deadline and by any other person before midnight of the third business day after dishonor or receipt of notice of dishonor.

(3) Notice may be given in any reasonable manner. It may be oral or written and in any terms which identify the instrument and state that it has been dishonored. A misdescription which does not mislead the party notified does not vitiate the notice. Sending the instrument bearing a stamp, ticket or writing stating that acceptance or payment has been refused or sending a notice of debit with respect to the instrument is sufficient.

(4) Written notice is given when sent although it is not received.

(5) Notice to one partner is notice to each although the firm has been dissolved.

(6) When any party is in insolvency proceedings instituted after the issue of the instrument notice may be given either to the party or to the representative of his estate.

(7) When any party is dead or incompetent notice may be sent to his last known address or given to his personal representative.

(8) Notice operates for the benefit of all parties who have rights on the instrument against the party notified.

§ 3—509. **Protest; Noting for Protest.**

(1) A protest is a certificate of dishonor made under the hand and seal of a United States consul or vice consul or a notary public or other person authorized to certify dishonor by the law of the place where dishonor occurs. It may be made upon information satisfactory to such person.

(2) The protest must identify the instrument and certify either that due presentment has been made or the reason why it is excused and that the instrument has been dishonored by nonacceptance or nonpayment.

(3) The protest may also certify that notice of dishonor has been given to all parties or to specified parties.

(4) Subject to subsection (5) any necessary protest is due by the time that notice of dishonor is due.

(5) If, before protest is due, an instrument has been noted for protest by the officer to make protest, the protest may be made at any time thereafter as of the date of the noting.

§ 3—510. **Evidence of Dishonor and Notice of Dishonor.**

The following are admissible as evidence and create a presumption of dishonor and of any notice of dishonor therein shown:

(a) a document regular in form as provided in the preceding section which purports to be a protest;

(b) the purported stamp or writing of the drawee, payor bank or presenting bank on the instrument or accompanying it stating that acceptance or payment has been refused for reasons consistent with dishonor;

(c) any book or record of the drawee, payor bank, or any collecting bank kept in the usual course of business which shows dishonor, even though there is no evidence of who made the entry.

§ 3—511. **Waived or Excused Presentment, Protest or Notice of Dishonor or Delay Therein.**

(1) Delay in presentment, protest or notice of dishonor is excused when the party is without notice that it is due or when the delay is caused by circumstances beyond his control and he exercises reasonable diligence after the cause of the delay ceases to operate.

(2) Presentment or notice or protest as the case may be is entirely excused when

(a) the party to be charged has waived it expressly or by implication either before or after it is due; or

(b) such party has himself dishonored the instrument or has countermanded payment or otherwise has no reason to expect or right to require that the instrument be accepted or paid; or

(c) by reasonable diligence the presentment or protest cannot be made or the notice given.

(3) Presentment is also entirely excused when

(a) the maker, acceptor or drawee of any instrument except a documentary draft is dead or in insolvency proceedings instituted after the issue of the instrument; or

(b) acceptance or payment is refused but not for want of proper presentment.

(4) Where a draft has been dishonored by nonacceptance a later presentment for payment and any notice of dishonor and protest for nonpayment are excused unless in the meantime the instrument has been accepted.

(5) A waiver of protest is also a waiver of presentment and of notice of dishonor even though protest is not required.

(6) Where a waiver of presentment or notice or protest is embodied in the instrument itself it is binding upon all parties; but where it is written above the signature of an indorser it binds him only.

Part 6 Discharge

§ 3—601. **Discharge of Parties.**

(1) The extent of the discharge of any party from liability on an instrument is governed by the sections on

(a) payment or satisfaction (Section 3—603); or

(b) tender of payment (Section 3—604); or

(c) cancellation or renunciation (Section 3—605); or

(d) impairment of right of recourse or of collateral (Section 3—606); or

(e) reacquisition of the instrument by a prior party (Section 3—208); or

(f) fraudulent and material alteration (Section 3—407); or

(g) certification of a check (Section 3—411); or

(h) acceptance varying a draft (Section 3—412); or

(i) unexcused delay in presentment or notice of dishonor or protest (Section 3—502).

(2) Any party is also discharged from his liability on an instrument to another party by any other act or agreement with such party which would discharge his simple contract for the payment of money.

(3) The liability of all parties is discharged when any party who has himself no right of action or recourse on the instrument

(a) reacquires the instrument in his own right; or

(b) is discharged under any provision of this Article, except as otherwise provided with respect to discharge for impairment of recourse or of collateral (Section 3—606).

§ 3—602. Effect of Discharge Against Holder in Due Course.

No discharge of any party provided by this Article is effective against a subsequent holder in due course unless he has notice thereof when he takes the instrument.

§ 3—603. Payment or Satisfaction.

(1) The liability of any party is discharged to the extent of his payment or satisfaction to the holder even though it is made with knowledge of a claim of another person to the instrument unless prior to such payment or satisfaction the person making the claim either supplies indemnity deemed adequate by the party seeking the discharge or enjoins payment or satisfaction by order of a court of competent jurisdiction in an action in which the adverse claimant and the holder are parties. This subsection does not, however, result in the discharge of the liability

(a) of a party who in bad faith pays or satisfies a holder who acquired the instrument by theft or who (unless having the rights of a holder in due course) holds through one who so acquired it; or

(b) of a party (other than an intermediary bank or a payor bank which is not a depositary bank) who pays or satisfies the holder of an instrument which has been restrictively indorsed in a manner not consistent with the terms of such restrictive indorsement.

(2) Payment or satisfaction may be made with the consent of the holder by any person including a stranger to the instrument. Surrender of the instrument to such a person gives him the rights of a transferee (Section 3—201).

§ 3—604. Tender of Payment.

(1) Any party making tender of full payment to a holder when or after it is due is discharged to the extent of all subsequent liability for interest, costs and attorney's fees.

(2) The holder's refusal of such tender wholly discharges any party who has a right of recourse against the party making the tender.

(3) Where the maker or acceptor of an instrument payable otherwise than on demand is able and ready to pay at every place of payment specified in the instrument when it is due, it is equivalent to tender.

§ 3—605. Cancellation and Renunciation.

(1) The holder of an instrument may even without consideration discharge any party

(a) in any manner apparent on the face of the instrument or the indorsement, as by intentionally cancelling the instrument or the party's signature by destruction or mutilation, or by striking out the party's signature; or

(b) by renouncing his rights by a writing signed and delivered or by surrender of the instrument to the party to be discharged.

(2) Neither cancellation nor renunciation without surrender of the instrument affects the title thereto.

§ 3—606. Impairment of Recourse or of Collateral.

(1) The holder discharges any party to the instrument to the extent that without such party's consent the holder

(a) without express reservation of rights releases or agrees not to sue any person against whom the party has to the knowledge of the holder a right of recourse or agrees to suspend the right to enforce against such person the instrument or collateral or otherwise discharges such person, except that failure or delay in effecting any required presentment, protest or notice of dishonor with respect to any such person does not discharge any party as to whom presentment, protest or notice of dishonor is effective or unnecessary; or

(b) unjustifiably impairs any collateral for the instrument given by or on behalf of the party or any person against whom he has a right of recourse.

(2) By express reservation of rights against a party with a right of recourse the holder preserves

(a) all his rights against such party as of the time when the instrument was originally due; and

(b) the right of the party to pay the instrument as of that time; and

(c) all rights of such party to recourse against others.

Part 7 Advice of International Sight Draft

§ 3—701. Letter of Advice of International Sight Draft.

(1) A "letter of advice" is a drawer's communication to the drawee that a described draft has been drawn.

(2) Unless otherwise agreed when a bank receives from another bank a letter of advice of an international sight draft the drawee bank may immediately debit the drawer's account and stop the running of interest pro tanto. Such a debit and any resulting credit to any account covering outstanding drafts leaves in the drawer full power to stop payment or otherwise dispose of the amount and creates no trust or interest in favor of the holder.

(3) Unless otherwise agreed and except where a draft is drawn under a credit issued by the drawee, the drawee of

an international sight draft owes the drawer no duty to pay an unadvised draft but if it does so and the draft is genuine, may appropriately debit the drawer's account.

Part 8 Miscellaneous

§ 3—801. **Drafts in a Set.**

(1) Where a draft is drawn in a set of parts, each of which is numbered and expressed to be an order only if no other part has been honored, the whole of the parts constitutes one draft but a taker of any part may become a holder in due course of the draft.

(2) Any person who negotiates, indorses or accepts a single part of a draft drawn in a set thereby becomes liable to any holder in due course of that part as if it were the whole set, but as between different holders in due course to whom different parts have been negotiated the holder whose title first accrues has all rights to the draft and its proceeds.

(3) As against the drawee the first presented part of a draft drawn in a set is the part entitled to payment, or if a time draft to acceptance and payment. Acceptance of any subsequently presented part renders the drawee liable thereon under subsection (2). With respect both to a holder and to the drawer payment of a subsequently presented part of a draft payable at sight has the same effect as payment of a check notwithstanding an effective stop order (Section 4—407).

(4) Except as otherwise provided in this section, where any part of a draft in a set is discharged by payment or otherwise the whole draft is discharged.

§ 3—802. **Effect of Instrument on Obligation for Which It Is Given.**

(1) Unless otherwise agreed where an instrument is taken for an underlying obligation

(a) the obligation is pro tanto discharged if a bank is drawer, maker or acceptor of the instrument and there is no recourse on the instrument against the underlying obligor; and

(b) in any other case the obligation is suspended pro tanto until the instrument is due or if it is payable on demand until its presentment. If the instrument is dishonored action may be maintained on either the instrument or the obligation; discharge of the underlying obligor on the instrument also discharges him on the obligation.

(2) The taking in good faith of a check which is not postdated does not of itself so extend the time on the original obligation as to discharge a surety.

§ 3—803. **Notice to Third Party.**

Where a defendant is sued for breach of an obligation for which a third person is answerable over under this Article he may give the third person written notice of the litigation, and the person notified may then give similar notice to any other person who is answerable over to him under this Article. If the notice states that the person notified may come in and defend and that if the person notified does not do so he will in any action against him by the person giving the notice be bound by any determination of fact common to the two litigations, then unless after seasonable receipt of the notice the person notified does come in and defend he is so bound.

§ 3—804. **Lost, Destroyed or Stolen Instruments.**

The owner of an instrument which is lost, whether by destruction, theft or otherwise, may maintain an action in his own name and recover from any party liable thereon upon due proof of his ownership, the facts which prevent his production of the instrument and its terms. The court may require security indemnifying the defendant against loss by reason of further claims on the instrument.

§ 3—805. **Instruments Not Payable to Order or to Bearer.**

This Article applies to any instrument whose terms do not preclude transfer and which is otherwise negotiable within this Article but which is not payable to order or to bearer, except that there can be no holder in due course of such an instrument.

Article 4
BANK DEPOSITS AND COLLECTIONS

Part 1 General Provisions and Definitions

§ 4—101. **Short Title.**

This Article shall be known and may be cited as Uniform Commercial Code—Bank Deposits and Collections.

§ 4—102. **Applicability.**

(1) To the extent that items within this Article are also within the scope of Articles 3 and 8, they are subject to the provisions of those Articles. In the event of conflict the provisions of this Article govern those of Article 3 but the provisions of Article 8 govern those of this Article.

(2) The liability of a bank for action or non-action with respect to any item handled by it for purposes of presentment, payment or collection is governed by the law of the place where the bank is located. In the case of action or non-action by or at a branch or separate office of a

bank, its liability is governed by the law of the place where the branch or separate office is located.

§ 4—103. **Variation by Agreement; Measure of Damages; Certain Action Constituting Ordinary Care.**

(1) The effect of the provisions of this Article may be varied by agreement except that no agreement can disclaim a bank's responsibility for its own lack of good faith or failure to exercise ordinary care or can limit the measure of damages for such lack or failure; but the parties may by agreement determine the standards by which such responsibility is to be measured if such standards are not manifestly unreasonable.

(2) Federal Reserve regulations and operating letters, clearing house rules, and the like, have the effect of agreements under subsection (1), whether or not specifically assented to by all parties interested in items handled.

(3) Action or non-action approved by this Article or pursuant to Federal Reserve regulations or operating letters constitutes the exercise of ordinary care and, in the absence of special instructions, action or nonaction consistent with clearing house rules and the like or with a general banking usage not disapproved by this Article, prima facie constitutes the exercise of ordinary care.

(4) The specification or approval of certain procedures by this Article does not constitute disapproval of other procedures which may be reasonable under the circumstances.

(5) The measure of damages for failure to exercise ordinary care in handling an item is the amount of the item reduced by an amount which could not have been realized by the use of ordinary care, and where there is bad faith it includes other damages, if any, suffered by the party as a proximate consequence.

§ 4—104. **Definitions and Index of Definitions.**

(1) In this Article unless the context otherwise requires

(a) "Account" means any account with a bank and includes a checking, time, interest or savings account;

(b) "Afternoon" means the period of a day between noon and midnight;

(c) "Banking day" means that part of any day on which a bank is open to the public for carrying on substantially all of its banking functions;

(d) "Clearing house" means any association of banks or other payors regularly clearing items;

(e) "Customer" means any person having an account with a bank or for whom a bank has agreed to collect items and includes a bank carrying an account with another bank;

(f) "Documentary draft" means any negotiable or nonnegotiable draft with accompanying documents, securities or other papers to be delivered against honor of the draft;

(g) "Item" means any instrument for the payment of money even though it is not negotiable but does not include money;

(h) "Midnight deadline" with respect to a bank is midnight on its next banking day following the banking day on which it receives the relevant item or notice or from which the time for taking action commences to run, whichever is later;

(i) "Properly payable" includes the availability of funds for payment at the time of decision to pay or dishonor;

(j) "Settle" means to pay in cash, by clearing house settlement, in a charge or credit or by remittance, or otherwise as instructed. A settlement may be either provisional or final;

(k) "Suspends payments" with respect to a bank means that it has been closed by order of the supervisory authorities, that a public officer has been appointed to take it over or that it ceases or refuses to make payments in the ordinary course of business.

(2) Other definitions applying to this Article and the sections in which they appear are:

"Collecting bank" Section 4—105.
"Depositary bank" Section 4—105.
"Intermediary bank" Section 4—105.
"Payor bank" Section 4—105.
"Presenting bank" Section 4—105.
"Remitting bank" Section 4—105.

(3) The following definitions in other Articles apply to this Article:

"Acceptance" Section 3—410.
"Certificate of deposit" Section 3—104.
"Certification" Section 3—411.
"Check" Section 3—104.
"Draft" Section 3—104.
"Holder in due course" Section 3—302.
"Notice of dishonor" Section 3—508.
"Presentment" Section 3—504.
"Protest" Section 3—509.
"Secondary party" Section 3—102.

(4) In addition Article 1 contains general definitions and principles of construction and interpretation applicable throughout this Article.

§ 4—105. **"Depositary Bank"; "Intermediary Bank"; "Collecting Bank"; "Payor Bank"; "Presenting Bank"; "Remitting Bank".**

In this Article unless the context otherwise requires:

(a) "Depositary bank" means the first bank to which an item is transferred for collection even though it is also the payor bank;

(b) "Payor bank" means a bank by which an item is payable as drawn or accepted;

(c) "Intermediary bank" means any bank to which an item is transferred in course of collection except the depositary or payor bank;

(d) "Collecting bank" means any bank handling the item for collection except the payor bank;

(e) "Presenting bank" means any bank presenting an item except a payor bank;

(f) "Remitting bank" means any payor or intermediary bank remitting for an item.

§ 4—106. Separate Office of a Bank.

A branch or separate office of a bank [maintaining its own deposit ledgers] is a separate bank for the purpose of computing the time within which and determining the place at or to which action may be taken or notices or orders shall be given under this Article and under Article 3.

Note: *The brackets are to make it optional with the several states whether to require a branch to maintain its own deposit ledgers in order to be considered to be a separate bank for certain purposes under Article 4. In some states "maintaining its own deposit ledgers" is a satisfactory test. In others branch banking practices are such that this test would not be suitable.*

§ 4—107. Time of Receipt of Items.

(1) For the purpose of allowing time to process items, prove balances and make the necessary entries on its books to determine its position for the day, a bank may fix an afternoon hour of 2 P.M. or later as a cut-off hour for the handling of money and items and the making of entries on its books.

(2) Any item or deposit of money received on any day after a cut-off hour so fixed or after the close of the banking day may be treated as being received at the opening of the next banking day.

§ 4—108. Delays.

(1) Unless otherwise instructed, a collecting bank in a good faith effort to secure payment may, in the case of specific items and with or without the approval of any person involved, waive, modify or extend time limits imposed or permitted by this Act for a period not in excess of an additional banking day without discharge of secondary parties and without liability to its transferor or any prior party.

(2) Delay by a collecting bank or payor bank beyond time limits prescribed or permitted by this Act or by instructions is excused if caused by interruption of communication facilities, suspension of payments by another bank, war, emergency conditions or other circumstances beyond the control of the bank provided it exercises such diligence as the circumstances require.

§ 4—109. Process of Posting.

The "process of posting" means the usual procedure followed by a payor bank in determining to pay an item and in recording the payment including one or more of the following or other steps as determined by the bank:

(a) verification of any signature;

(b) ascertaining that sufficient funds are available;

(c) affixing a "paid" or other stamp;

(d) entering a charge or entry to a customer's account;

(e) correcting or reversing an entry or erroneous action with respect to the item.

Part 2 Collection of Items: Depositary and Collecting Banks

§ 4—201. Presumption and Duration of Agency Status of Collecting Banks and Provisional Status of Credits; Applicability of Article; Item Indorsed "Pay Any Bank".

(1) Unless a contrary intent clearly appears and prior to the time that a settlement given by a collecting bank for an item is or becomes final (subsection (3) of Section 4—211 and Sections 4—212 and 4—213) the bank is an agent or sub-agent of the owner of the item and any settlement given for the item is provisional. This provision applies regardless of the form of indorsement or lack of indorsement and even though credit given for the item is subject to immediate withdrawal as of right or is in fact withdrawn; but the continuance of ownership of an item by its owner and any rights of the owner to proceeds of the item are subject to rights of a collecting bank such as those resulting from outstanding advances on the item and valid rights of setoff. When an item is handled by banks for purposes of presentment, payment and collection, the relevant provisions of this Article apply even though action of parties clearly establishes that a particular bank has purchased the item and is the owner of it.

(2) After an item has been indorsed with the words "pay any bank" or the like, only a bank may acquire the rights of a holder

(a) until the item has been returned to the customer initiating collection; or

(b) until the item has been specially indorsed by a bank to a person who is not a bank.

§ 4—202. Responsibility for Collection; When Action Seasonable.

(1) A collecting bank must use ordinary care in

(a) presenting an item or sending it for presentment; and

(b) sending notice of dishonor or non-payment or returning an item other than a documentary draft to the bank's transferor [or directly to the depositary bank under subsection (2) of Section 4—212] *(see note to Section 4—212)* after learning that the item has not been paid or accepted as the case may be; and

(c) settling for an item when the bank receives final settlement; and

(d) making or providing for any necessary protest; and

(e) notifying its transferor of any loss or delay in transit within a reasonable time after discovery thereof.

(2) A collecting bank taking proper action before its midnight deadline following receipt of an item, notice or payment acts seasonably; taking proper action within a reasonably longer time may be seasonable but the bank has the burden of so establishing.

(3) Subject to subsection (1)(a), a bank is not liable for the insolvency, neglect, misconduct, mistake or default of another bank or person or for loss or destruction of an item in transit or in the possession of others.

§ 4—203. **Effect of Instructions.**

Subject to the provisions of Article 3 concerning conversion of instruments (Section 3—419) and the provisions of both Article 3 and this Article concerning restrictive indorsements only a collecting bank's transferor can give instructions which affect the bank or constitute notice to it and a collecting bank is not liable to prior parties for any action taken pursuant to such instructions or in accordance with any agreement with its transferor.

§ 4—204. **Methods of Sending and Presenting; Sending Direct to Payor Bank.**

(1) A collecting bank must send items by reasonably prompt method taking into consideration any relevant instructions, the nature of the item, the number of such items on hand, and the cost of collection involved and the method generally used by it or others to present such items.

(2) A collecting bank may send

(a) any item direct to the payor bank;

(b) any item to any non-bank payor if authorized by its transferor; and

(c) any item other than documentary drafts to any non-bank payor, if authorized by Federal Reserve regulation or operating letter, clearing house rule or the like.

(3) Presentment may be made by a presenting bank at a place where the payor bank has requested that presentment be made.

§ 4—205. **Supplying Missing Indorsement; No Notice from Prior Indorsement.**

(1) A depositary bank which has taken an item for collection may supply any indorsement of the customer which is necessary to title unless the item contains the words "payee's indorsement required" or the like. In the absence of such a requirement a statement placed on the item by the depositary bank to the effect that the item was deposited by a customer or credited to his account is effective as the customer's indorsement.

(2) An intermediary bank, or payor bank which is not a depositary bank, is neither given notice nor otherwise affected by a restrictive indorsement of any person except the bank's immediate transferor.

§ 4—206. **Transfer Between Banks.**

Any agreed method which identifies the transferor bank is sufficient for the item's further transfer to another bank.

§ 4—207. **Warranties of Customer and Collecting Bank on Transfer or Presentment of Items; Time for Claims.**

(1) Each customer or collecting bank who obtains payment or acceptance of an item and each prior customer and collecting bank warrants to the payor bank or other payor who in good faith pays or accepts the item that

(a) he has a good title to the item or is authorized to obtain payment or acceptance on behalf of one who has a good title; and

(b) he has no knowledge that the signature of the maker or drawer is unauthorized, except that this warranty is not given by any customer or collecting bank that is a holder in due course and acts in good faith

(i) to a maker with respect to the maker's own signature; or

(ii) to a drawer with respect to the drawer's own signature, whether or not the drawer is also the drawee; or

(iii) to an acceptor of an item if the holder in due course took the item after the acceptance or obtained the acceptance without knowledge that the drawer's signature was unauthorized; and

(c) the item has not been materially altered, except that this warranty is not given by any customer or collecting bank that is a holder in due course and acts in good faith

(i) to the maker of a note; or

(ii) to the drawer of a draft whether or not the drawer is also the drawee; or

(iii) to the acceptor of an item with respect to an alteration made prior to the acceptance if the holder in due course took the item after the acceptance, even though the acceptance provided "payable as originally drawn" or equivalent terms; or

(iv) to the acceptor of an item with respect to an alteration made after the acceptance.

(2) Each customer and collecting bank who transfers an item and receives a settlement or other consideration for it warrants to his transferee and to any subsequent collecting bank who takes the item in good faith that

(a) he has a good title to the item or is authorized to obtain payment or acceptance on behalf of one who has a good title and the transfer is otherwise rightful; and

(b) all signatures are genuine or authorized; and

(c) the item has not been materially altered; and

(d) no defense of any party is good against him; and

(e) he has no knowledge of any insolvency proceeding instituted with respect to the maker or acceptor or the drawer of an unaccepted item.

In addition each customer and collecting bank so transferring an item and receiving a settlement or other consideration engages that upon dishonor and any necessary notice of dishonor and protest he will take up the item.

(3) The warranties and the engagement to honor set forth in the two preceding subsections arise notwithstanding the absence of indorsement or words of guaranty or warranty in the transfer or presentment and a collecting bank remains liable for their breach despite remittance to its transferor. Damages for breach of such warranties or engagement to honor shall not exceed the consideration received by the customer or collecting bank responsible plus finance charges and expenses related to the item, if any.

(4) Unless a claim for breach of warranty under this section is made within a reasonable time after the person claiming learns of the breach, the person liable is discharged to the extent of any loss caused by the delay in making claim.

§ 4—208. **Security Interest of Collecting Bank in Items, Accompanying Documents and Proceeds.**

(1) A bank has a security interest in an item and any accompanying documents or the proceeds of either

(a) in case of an item deposited in an account to the extent to which credit given for the item has been withdrawn or applied;

(b) in case of an item for which it has given credit available for withdrawal as of right, to the extent of the credit given whether or not the credit is drawn

upon and whether or not there is a right of charge-back; or

(c) if it makes an advance on or against the item.

(2) When credit which has been given for several items received at one time or pursuant to a single agreement is withdrawn or applied in part the security interest remains upon all the items, any accompanying documents or the proceeds of either. For the purpose of this section, credits first given are first withdrawn.

(3) Receipt by a collecting bank of a final settlement for an item is a realization on its security interest in the item, accompanying documents and proceeds. To the extent and so long as the bank does not receive final settlement for the item or give up possession of the item or accompanying documents for purposes other than collection, the security interest continues and is subject to the provisions of Article 9 except that

(a) no security agreement is necessary to make the security interest enforceable (subsection (1)(a) of Section 9—203); and

(b) no filing is required to perfect the security interest; and

(c) the security interest has priority over conflicting perfected security interests in the item, accompanying documents or proceeds.

§ 4—209. **When Bank Gives Value for Purposes of Holder in Due Course.**

For purposes of determining its status as a holder in due course, the bank has given value to the extent that it has a security interest in an item provided that the bank otherwise complies with the requirements of Section 3—302 on what constitutes a holder in due course.

§ 4—210. **Presentment by Notice of Item Not Payable by, Through or at a Bank; Liability of Secondary Parties.**

(1) Unless otherwise instructed, a collecting bank may present an item not payable by, through or at a bank by sending to the party to accept or pay a written notice that the bank holds the item for acceptance or payment. The notice must be sent in time to be received on or before the day when presentment is due and the bank must meet any requirement of the party to accept or pay under Section 3—505 by the close of the bank's next banking day after it knows of the requirement.

(2) Where presentment is made by notice and neither honor nor request for compliance with a requirement under Section 3—505 is received by the close of business on the day after maturity or in the case of demand items by the close of business on the third banking day after notice was sent, the presenting bank may treat the item

as dishonored and charge any secondary party by sending him notice of the facts.

§ 4—211. Media of Remittance; Provisional and Final Settlement in Remittance Cases.

(1) A collecting bank may take in settlement of an item

(a) a check of the remitting bank or of another bank on any bank except the remitting bank; or

(b) a cashier's check or similar primary obligation of a remitting bank which is a member of or clears through a member of the same clearing house or group as the collecting bank; or

(c) appropriate authority to charge an account of the remitting bank or of another bank with the collecting bank; or

(d) if the item is drawn upon or payable by a person other than a bank, a cashier's check, certified check or other bank check or obligation.

(2) If before its midnight deadline the collecting bank properly dishonors a remittance check or authorization to charge on itself or presents or forwards for collection a remittance instrument of or on another bank which is of a kind approved by subsection (1) or has not been authorized by it, the collecting bank is not liable to prior parties in the event of the dishonor of such check, instrument or authorization.

(3) A settlement for an item by means of a remittance instrument or authorization to charge is or becomes a final settlement as to both the person making and the person receiving the settlement

(a) if the remittance instrument or authorization to charge is of a kind approved by subsection (1) or has not been authorized by the person receiving the settlement and in either case the person receiving the settlement acts seasonably before its midnight deadline in presenting, forwarding for collection or paying the instrument or authorization,—at the time the remittance instrument or authorization is finally paid by the payor by which it is payable;

(b) if the person receiving the settlement has authorized remittance by a non-bank check or obligation or by a cashier's check or similar primary obligation of or a check upon the payor or other remitting bank which is not of a kind approved by subsection (1)(b),—at the time of the receipt of such remittance check or obligation; or

(c) if in a case not covered by sub-paragraphs (a) or (b) the person receiving the settlement fails to seasonably present, forward for collection, pay or return a remittance instrument or authorization to it to charge

before its midnight deadline,—at such midnight deadline.

§ 4—212. Right of Charge-Back or Refund.

(1) If a collecting bank has made provisional settlement with its customer for an item and itself fails by reason of dishonor, suspension of payments by a bank or otherwise to receive a settlement for the item which is or becomes final, the bank may revoke the settlement given by it, charge back the amount of any credit given for the item to its customer's account or obtain refund from its customer whether or not it is able to return the items if by its midnight deadline or within a longer reasonable time after it learns the facts it returns the item or sends notification of the facts. These rights to revoke, charge-back and obtain refund terminate if and when a settlement for the item received by the bank is or becomes final (subsection (3) of Section 4—211 and subsections (2) and (3) of Section 4—213).

[(2) Within the time and manner prescribed by this section and Section 4—301, an intermediary or payor bank, as the case may be, may return an unpaid item directly to the depositary bank and may send for collection a draft on the depositary bank and obtain reimbursement. In such case, if the depositary bank has received provisional settlement for the item, it must reimburse the bank drawing the draft and any provisional credits for the item between banks shall become and remain final.]

Note: *Direct returns is recognized as an innovation that is not yet established bank practice, and therefore, Paragraph 2 has been bracketed. Some lawyers have doubts whether it should be included in legislation or left to development by agreement.*

(3) A depositary bank which is also the payor may charge-back the amount of an item to its customer's account or obtain refund in accordance with the section governing return of an item received by a payor bank for credit on its books (Section 4—301).

(4) The right to charge-back is not affected by

(a) prior use of the credit given for the item; or

(b) failure by any bank to exercise ordinary care with respect to the item but any bank so failing remains liable.

(5) A failure to charge-back or claim refund does not affect other rights of the bank against the customer or any other party.

(6) If credit is given in dollars as the equivalent of the value of an item payable in a foreign currency the dollar amount of any charge-back or refund shall be calculated on the basis of the buying sight rate for the foreign currency prevailing on the day when the person entitled to the charge-back or refund learns that it will not receive payment in ordinary course.

§ 4—213. Final Payment of Item by Payor Bank; When Provisional Debits and Credits Become Final; When Certain Credits Become Available for Withdrawal.

(1) An item is finally paid by a payor bank when the bank has done any of the following, whichever happens first:

(a) paid the item in cash; or

(b) settled for the item without reserving a right to revoke the settlement and without having such right under statute, clearing house rule or agreement; or

(c) completed the process of posting the item to the indicated account of the drawer, maker or other person to be charged therewith; or

(d) made a provisional settlement for the item and failed to revoke the settlement in the time and manner permitted by statute, clearing house rule or agreement.

Upon a final payment under subparagraphs (b), (c) or (d) the payor bank shall be accountable for the amount of the item.

(2) If provisional settlement for an item between the presenting and payor banks is made through a clearing house or by debits or credits in an account between them, then to the extent that provisional debits or credits for the item are entered in accounts between the presenting and payor banks or between the presenting and successive prior collecting banks seriatim, they become final upon final payment of the item by the payor bank.

(3) If a collecting bank receives a settlement for an item which is or becomes final (subsection (3) of Section 4—211, subsection (2) of Section 4—213) the bank is accountable to its customer for the amount of the item and any provisional credit given for the item in an account with its customer becomes final.

(4) Subject to any right of the bank to apply the credit to an obligation of the customer, credit given by a bank for an item in an account with its customer becomes available for withdrawal as of right

(a) in any case where the bank has received a provisional settlement for the item,—when such settlement becomes final and the bank has had a reasonable time to learn that the settlement is final;

(b) in any case where the bank is both a depositary bank and a payor bank and the item is finally paid,—at the opening of the bank's second banking day following receipt of the item.

(5) A deposit of money in a bank is final when made but, subject to any right of the bank to apply the deposit to an obligation of the customer, the deposit becomes available for withdrawal as of right at the opening of the bank's next banking day following receipt of the deposit.

§ 4—214. Insolvency and Preference.

(1) Any item in or coming into the possession of a payor or collecting bank which suspends payment and which item is not finally paid shall be returned by the receiver, trustee or agent in charge of the closed bank to the presenting bank or the closed bank's customer.

(2) If a payor bank finally pays an item and suspends payments without making a settlement for the item with its customer or the presenting bank which settlement is or becomes final, the owner of the item has a preferred claim against the payor bank.

(3) If a payor bank gives or a collecting bank gives or receives a provisional settlement for an item and thereafter suspends payments, the suspension does not prevent or interfere with the settlement becoming final if such finality occurs automatically upon the lapse of certain time or the happening of certain events (subsection (3) of Section 4—211, subsections (1)(d), (2) and (3) of Section 4—213).

(4) If a collecting bank receives from subsequent parties settlement for an item which settlement is or becomes final and suspends payments without making a settlement for the item with its customer which is or becomes final, the owner of the item has a preferred claim against such collecting bank.

Part 3 Collection of Items: Payor Banks

§ 4—301. Deferred Posting; Recovery of Payment by Return of Items; Time of Dishonor.

(1) Where an authorized settlement for a demand item (other than a documentary draft) received by a payor bank otherwise than for immediate payment over the counter has been made before midnight of the banking day of receipt the payor bank may revoke the settlement and recover any payment if before it has made final payment (subsection (1) of Section 4—213) and before its midnight deadline it

(a) returns the item; or

(b) sends written notice of dishonor or nonpayment if the item is held for protest or is otherwise unavailable for return.

(2) If a demand item is received by a payor bank for credit on its books it may return such item or send notice of dishonor and may revoke any credit given or recover the amount thereof withdrawn by its customer, if it acts within the time limit and in the manner specified in the preceding subsection.

(3) Unless previous notice of dishonor has been sent an item is dishonored at the time when for purposes of dishonor it is returned or notice sent in accordance with this section.

(4) An item is returned:

(a) as to an item received through a clearing house, when it is delivered to the presenting or last collecting bank or to the clearing house or is sent or delivered in accordance with its rules; or

(b) in all other cases, when it is sent or delivered to the bank's customer or transferor or pursuant to his instructions.

§ 4—302. Payor Bank's Responsibility for Late Return of Item.

In the absence of a valid defense such as breach of a presentment warranty (subsection (1) of Section 4—207), settlement effected or the like, if an item is presented on and received by a payor bank the bank is accountable for the amount of

(a) a demand item other than a documentary draft whether properly payable or not if the bank, in any case where it is not also the depositary bank, retains the item beyond midnight of the banking day of receipt without settling for it or, regardless of whether it is also the depositary bank, does not pay or return the item or send notice of dishonor until after its midnight deadline; or

(b) any other properly payable item unless within the time allowed for acceptance or payment of that item the bank either accepts or pays the item or returns it and accompanying documents.

§ 4—303. When Items Subject to Notice, Stop-Order, Legal Process or Setoff; Order in Which Items May Be Charged or Certified.

(1) Any knowledge, notice or stop-order received by, legal process served upon or setoff exercised by a payor bank, whether or not effective under other rules of law to terminate, suspend or modify the bank's right or duty to pay an item or to charge its customer's account for the item, comes too late to so terminate, suspend or modify such right or duty if the knowledge, notice, stop-order or legal process is received or served and a reasonable time for the bank to act thereon expires or the setoff is exercised after the bank has done any of the following:

(a) accepted or certified the item;

(b) paid the item in cash;

(c) settled for the item without reserving a right to revoke the settlement and without having such right under statute, clearing house rule or agreement;

(d) completed the process of posting the item to the indicated account of the drawer, maker or other person to be charged therewith or otherwise has evidenced by examination of such indicated account and by action its decision to pay the item; or

(e) become accountable for the amount of the item under subsection (1)(d) of Section 4—213 and Section 4—302 dealing with the payor bank's responsibility for late return of items.

(2) Subject to the provisions of subsection (1) items may be accepted, paid, certified or charged to the indicated account of its customer in any order convenient to the bank.

Part 4 Relationship Between Payor Bank and Its Customer

§ 4—401. When Bank May Charge Customer's Account.

(1) As against its customer, a bank may charge against his account any item which is otherwise properly payable from that account even though the charge creates an overdraft.

(2) A bank which in good faith makes payment to a holder may charge the indicated account of its customer according to

(a) the original tenor of his altered item; or

(b) the tenor of his completed item, even though the bank knows the item has been completed unless the bank has notice that the completion was improper.

§ 4—402. Bank's Liability to Customer for Wrongful Dishonor.

A payor bank is liable to its customer for damages proximately caused by the wrongful dishonor of an item. When the dishonor occurs through mistake liability is limited to actual damages proved. If so proximately caused and proved damages may include damages for an arrest or prosecution of the customer or other consequential damages. Whether any consequential damages are proximately caused by the wrongful dishonor is a question of fact to be determined in each case.

§ 4—403. Customer's Right to Stop Payment; Burden of Proof of Loss.

(1) A customer may by order to his bank stop payment of any item payable for his account but the order must be received at such time and in such manner as to afford the bank a reasonable opportunity to act on it prior to any action by the bank with respect to the item described in Section 4—303.

(2) An oral order is binding upon the bank only for fourteen calendar days unless confirmed in writing within that period. A written order is effective for only six months unless renewed in writing.

(3) The burden of establishing the fact and amount of loss resulting from the payment of an item contrary to a binding stop payment order is on the customer.

§ 4—404. Bank Not Obligated to Pay Check More Than Six Months Old.

A bank is under no obligation to a customer having a checking account to pay a check, other than a certified check, which is presented more than six months after its date, but it may charge its customer's account for a payment made thereafter in good faith.

§ 4—405. Death or Incompetence of Customer.

(1) A payor or collecting bank's authority to accept, pay or collect an item or to account for proceeds of its collection if otherwise effective is not rendered ineffective by incompetence of a customer of either bank existing at the time the item is issued or its collection is undertaken if the bank does not know of an adjudication of incompetence. Neither death nor incompetence of a customer revokes such authority to accept, pay, collect or account until the bank knows of the fact of death or of an adjudication of incompetence and has reasonable opportunity to act on it.

(2) Even with knowledge a bank may for 10 days after the date of death pay or certify checks drawn on or prior to that date unless ordered to stop payment by a person claiming an interest in the account.

§ 4—406. Customer's Duty to Discover and Report Unauthorized Signature or Alteration.

(1) When a bank sends to its customer a statement of account accompanied by items paid in good faith in support of the debit entries or holds the statement and items pursuant to a request or instructions of its customer or otherwise in a reasonable manner makes the statement and items available to the customer, the customer must exercise reasonable care and promptness to examine the statement and items to discover his unauthorized signature or any alteration on an item and must notify the bank promptly after discovery thereof.

(2) If the bank establishes that the customer failed with respect to an item to comply with the duties imposed on the customer by subsection (1) the customer is precluded from asserting against the bank

   (a) his unauthorized signature or any alteration on the item if the bank also establishes that it suffered a loss by reason of such failure; and

   (b) an unauthorized signature or alteration by the same wrongdoer on any other item paid in good faith by the bank after the first item and statement was available to the customer for a reasonable period not exceeding fourteen calendar days and before the bank receives notification from the customer of any such unauthorized signature or alteration.

(3) The preclusion under subsection (2) does not apply if the customer establishes lack of ordinary care on the part of the bank in paying the item(s).

(4) Without regard to care or lack of care of either the customer or the bank a customer who does not within one year from the time the statement and items are made available to the customer (subsection (1)) discover and report his unauthorized signature or any alteration on the face or back of the item or does not within three years from that time discover and report any unauthorized indorsement is precluded from asserting against the bank such unauthorized signature or indorsement or such alteration.

(5) If under this section a payor bank has a valid defense against a claim of a customer upon or resulting from payment of an item and waives or fails upon request to assert the defense the bank may not assert against any collecting bank or other prior party presenting or transferring the item a claim based upon the unauthorized signature or alteration giving rise to the customer's claim.

§ 4—407. Payor Bank's Right to Subrogation on Improper Payment.

If a payor bank has paid an item over the stop payment order of the drawer or maker or otherwise under circumstances giving a basis for objection by the drawer or maker, to prevent unjust enrichment and only to the extent necessary to prevent loss to the bank by reason of its payment of the item, the payor bank shall be subrogated to the rights

   (a) of any holder in due course on the item against the drawer or maker; and

   (b) of the payee or any other holder of the item against the drawer or maker either on the item or under the transaction out of which the item arose; and

   (c) of the drawer or maker against the payee or any other holder of the item with respect to the transaction out of which the item arose.

Part 5 Collection of Documentary Drafts

§ 4—501. Handling of Documentary Drafts; Duty to Send for Presentment and to Notify Customer of Dishonor.

A bank which takes a documentary draft for collection must present or send the draft and accompanying documents for presentment and upon learning that the draft has not been paid or accepted in due course must seasonably notify its customer of such fact even though it may have discounted or bought the draft or extended credit available for withdrawal as of right.

§ 4—502. Presentment of "On Arrival" Drafts.

When a draft or the relevant instructions require presentment "on arrival", "when goods arrive" or the like, the collecting bank need not present until in its judgment a reasonable time for arrival of the goods has expired. Refusal to pay or accept because the goods have not arrived is not dishonor; the bank must notify its transferor of such refusal but need not present the draft again until it is instructed to do so or learns of the arrival of the goods.

§ 4—503. Responsibility of Presenting Bank for Documents and Goods; Report of Reasons for Dishonor; Referee in Case of Need.

Unless otherwise instructed and except as provided in Article 5 a bank presenting a documentary draft

(a) must deliver the documents to the drawee on acceptance of the draft if it is payable more than three days after presentment; otherwise, only on payment; and

(b) upon dishonor, either in the case of presentment for acceptance or presentment for payment, may seek and follow instructions from any referee in case of need designated in the draft or if the presenting bank does not choose to utilize his services it must use diligence and good faith to ascertain the reason for dishonor, must notify its transferor of the dishonor and of the results of its effort to ascertain the reasons therefor and must request instructions.

But the presenting bank is under no obligation with respect to goods represented by the documents except to follow any reasonable instructions seasonably received; it has a right to reimbursement for any expense incurred in following instructions and to prepayment of or indemnity for such expenses.

§ 4—504. Privilege of Presenting Bank to Deal With Goods; Security Interest for Expenses.

(1) A presenting bank which, following the dishonor of a documentary draft, has seasonably requested instructions but does not receive them within a reasonable time may store, sell, or otherwise deal with the goods in any reasonable manner.

(2) For its reasonable expenses incurred by action under subsection (1) the presenting bank has a lien upon the goods or their proceeds, which may be foreclosed in the same manner as an unpaid seller's lien.

Article 5
LETTERS OF CREDIT

§ 5—101. Short Title.

This Article shall be known and may be cited as Uniform Commercial Code—Letters of Credit.

§ 5—102. Scope.

(1) This Article applies

(a) to a credit issued by a bank if the credit requires a documentary draft or a documentary demand for payment; and

(b) to a credit issued by a person other than a bank if the credit requires that the draft or demand for payment be accompanied by a document of title; and

(c) to a credit issued by a bank or other person if the credit is not within subparagraphs (a) or (b) but conspicuously states that it is a letter of credit or is conspicuously so entitled.

(2) Unless the engagement meets the requirements of subsection (1), this Article does not apply to engagements to make advances or to honor drafts or demands for payment, to authorities to pay or purchase, to guarantees or to general agreements.

(3) This Article deals with some but not all of the rules and concepts of letters of credit as such rules or concepts have developed prior to this act or may hereafter develop. The fact that this Article states a rule does not by itself require, imply or negate application of the same or a converse rule to a situation not provided for or to a person not specified by this Article.

§ 5—103. Definitions.

(1) In this Article unless the context otherwise requires

(a) "Credit" or "letter of credit" means an engagement by a bank or other person made at the request of a customer and of a kind within the scope of this Article (Section 5—102) that the issuer will honor drafts or other demands for payment upon compliance with the conditions specified in the credit. A credit may be either revocable or irrevocable. The engagement may be either an agreement to honor or a statement that the bank or other person is authorized to honor.

(b) A "documentary draft" or a "documentary demand for payment" is one honor of which is conditioned upon the presentation of a document or documents. "Document" means any paper including document of title, security, invoice, certificate, notice of default and the like.

(c) An "issuer" is a bank or other person issuing a credit.

(d) A "beneficiary" of a credit is a person who is entitled under its terms to draw or demand payment.

(e) An "advising bank" is a bank which gives notification of the issuance of a credit by another bank.

(f) A "confirming bank" is a bank which engages either that it will itself honor a credit already issued by another bank or that such a credit will be honored by the issuer or a third bank.

(g) A "customer" is a buyer or other person who causes an issuer to issue a credit. The term also includes a bank which procures issuance or confirmation on behalf of that bank's customer.

(2) Other definitions applying to this Article and the sections in which they appear are:
"Notation of Credit". Section 5—108.
"Presenter". Section 5—112(3).

(3) Definitions in other Articles applying to this Article and the sections in which they appear are:
"Accept" or "Acceptance". Section 3—410.
"Contract for sale". Section 2—106.
"Draft". Section 3—104.
"Holder in due course". Section 3—302.
"Midnight deadline". Section 4—104.
"Security". Section 8—102.

(4) In addition, Article 1 contains general definitions and principles of construction and interpretation applicable throughout this Article.

§ 5—104. Formal Requirements; Signing.

(1) Except as otherwise required in subsection (1)(c) of Section 5—102 on scope, no particular form of phrasing is required for a credit. A credit must be in writing and signed by the issuer and a confirmation must be in writing and signed by the confirming bank. A modification of the terms of a credit or confirmation must be signed by the issuer or confirming bank.

(2) A telegram may be a sufficient signed writing if it identifies its sender by an authorized authentication. The authentication may be in code and the authorized naming of the issuer in an advice of credit is a sufficient signing.

§ 5—105. Consideration.

No consideration is necessary to establish a credit or to enlarge or otherwise modify its terms.

§ 5—106. Time and Effect of Establishment of Credit.

(1) Unless otherwise agreed a credit is established

(a) as regards the customer as soon as a letter of credit is sent to him or the letter of credit or an authorized written advice of its issuance is sent to the beneficiary; and

(b) as regards the beneficiary when he receives a letter of credit or an authorized written advice of its issuance.

(2) Unless otherwise agreed once an irrevocable credit is established as regards the customer it can be modified or revoked only with the consent of the customer and once

it is established as regards the beneficiary it can be modified or revoked only with his consent.

(3) Unless otherwise agreed after a revocable credit is established it may be modified or revoked by the issuer without notice to or consent from the customer or beneficiary.

(4) Notwithstanding any modification or revocation of a revocable credit any person authorized to honor or negotiate under the terms of the original credit is entitled to reimbursement for or honor of any draft or demand for payment duly honored or negotiated before receipt of notice of the modification or revocation and the issuer in turn is entitled to reimbursement from its customer.

§ 5—107. Advice of Credit; Confirmation; Error in Statement of Terms.

(1) Unless otherwise specified an advising bank by advising a credit issued by another bank does not assume any obligation to honor drafts drawn or demands for payment made under the credit but it does assume obligation for the accuracy of its own statement.

(2) A confirming bank by confirming a credit becomes directly obligated on the credit to the extent of its confirmation as though it were its issuer and acquires the rights of an issuer.

(3) Even though an advising bank incorrectly advises the terms of a credit it has been authorized to advise the credit is established as against the issuer to the extent of its original terms.

(4) Unless otherwise specified the customer bears as against the issuer all risks of transmission and reasonable translation or interpretation of any message relating to a credit.

§ 5—108. "Notation Credit"; Exhaustion of Credit.

(1) A credit which specifies that any person purchasing or paying drafts drawn or demands for payment made under it must note the amount of the draft or demand on the letter or advice of credit is a "notation credit".

(2) Under a notation credit

(a) a person paying the beneficiary or purchasing a draft or demand for payment from him acquires a right to honor only if the appropriate notation is made and by transferring or forwarding for honor the documents under the credit such a person warrants to the issuer that the notation has been made; and

(b) unless the credit or a signed statement that an appropriate notation has been made accompanies the draft or demand for payment the issuer may delay honor until evidence of notation has been procured which is satisfactory to it but its obligation and that of its customer continue for a reasonable time not exceeding thirty days to obtain such evidence.

(3) If the credit is not a notation credit

(a) the issuer may honor complying drafts or demands for payment presented to it in the order in which they are presented and is discharged pro tanto by honor of any such draft or demand;

(b) as between competing good faith purchasers of complying drafts or demands the person first purchasing his priority over a subsequent purchaser even though the later purchased draft or demand has been first honored.

§ 5—109. Issuer's Obligation to Its Customer.

(1) An issuer's obligation to its customer includes good faith and observance of any general banking usage but unless otherwise agreed does not include liability or responsibility

(a) for performance of the underlying contract for sale or other transaction between the customer and the beneficiary; or

(b) for any act or omission of any person other than itself or its own branch or for loss or destruction of a draft, demand or document in transit or in the possession of others; or

(c) based on knowledge or lack of knowledge of any usage of any particular trade.

(2) An issuer must examine documents with care so as to ascertain that on their face they appear to comply with the terms of the credit but unless otherwise agreed assumes no liability or responsibility for the genuineness, falsification or effect of any document which appears on such examination to be regular on its face.

(3) A non-bank issuer is not bound by any banking usage of which it has no knowledge.

§ 5—110. Availability of Credit in Portions; Presenter's Reservation of Lien or Claim.

(1) Unless otherwise specified a credit may be used in portions in the discretion of the beneficiary.

(2) Unless otherwise specified a person by presenting a documentary draft or demand for payment under a credit relinquishes upon its honor all claims to the documents and a person by transferring such draft or demand or causing such presentment authorizes such relinquishment. An explicit reservation of claim makes the draft or demand non-complying.

§ 5—111. Warranties on Transfer and Presentment.

(1) Unless otherwise agreed the beneficiary by transferring or presenting a documentary draft or demand for payment warrants to all interested parties that the necessary conditions of the credit have been complied with. This is in addition to any warranties arising under Articles 3, 4, 7 and 8.

(2) Unless otherwise agreed a negotiating, advising, confirming, collecting or issuing bank presenting or transferring a draft or demand for payment under a credit warrants only the matters warranted by a collecting bank under Article 4 and any such bank transferring a document warrants only the matters warranted by an intermediary under Articles 7 and 8.

§ 5—112. Time Allowed for Honor or Rejection; Withholding Honor or Rejection by Consent; "Presenter".

(1) A bank to which a documentary draft or demand for payment is presented under a credit may without dishonor of the draft, demand or credit

(a) defer honor until the close of the third banking day following receipt of the documents; and

(b) further defer honor if the presenter has expressly or impliedly consented thereto.

Failure to honor within the time here specified constitutes dishonor of the draft or demand and of the credit [except as otherwise provided in subsection (4) of Section 5—114 on conditional payment].

Note: *The bracketed language in the last sentence of subsection (1) should be included only if the optional provisions of Section 5—114(4) and (5) are included.*

(2) Upon dishonor the bank may unless otherwise instructed fulfill its duty to return the draft or demand and the documents by holding them at the disposal of the presenter and sending him an advice to that effect.

(3) "Presenter" means any person presenting a draft or demand for payment for honor under a credit even though that person is a confirming bank or other correspondent which is acting under an issuer's authorization.

§ 5—113. Indemnities.

(1) A bank seeking to obtain (whether for itself or another) honor, negotiation or reimbursement under a credit may give an indemnity to induce such honor, negotiation or reimbursement.

(2) An indemnity agreement inducing honor, negotiation or reimbursement

(a) unless otherwise explicitly agreed applies to defects in the documents but not in the goods; and

(b) unless a longer time is explicitly agreed expires at the end of ten business days following receipt of the documents by the ultimate customer unless notice of objection is sent before such expiration date. The ultimate customer may send notice of objection to the person from whom he received the documents and any bank receiving such notice is under a duty to send notice to its transferor before its midnight deadline.

§ 5—114. Issuer's Duty and Privilege to Honor; Right to Reimbursement.

(1) An issuer must honor a draft or demand for payment which complies with the terms of the relevant credit regardless of whether the goods or documents conform to the underlying contract for sale or other contract between the customer and the beneficiary. The issuer is not excused from honor of such a draft or demand by reason of an additional general term that all documents must be satisfactory to the issuer, but an issuer may require that specified documents must be satisfactory to it.

(2) Unless otherwise agreed when documents appear on their face to comply with the terms of a credit but a required document does not in fact conform to the warranties made on negotiation or transfer of a document of title (Section 7—507) or of a certificated security (Section 8—306) or is forged or fraudulent or there is fraud in the transaction:

(a) the issuer must honor the draft or demand for payment if honor is demanded by a negotiating bank or other holder of the draft or demand which has taken the draft or demand under the credit and under circumstances which would make it a holder in due course (Section 3—302) and in an appropriate case would make it a person to whom a document of title has been duly negotiated (Section 7—502) or a bona fide purchaser of a certificated security (Section 8—302); and

(b) in all other cases as against its customer, an issuer acting in good faith may honor the draft or demand for payment despite notification from the customer of fraud, forgery or other defect not apparent on the face of the documents but a court of appropriate jurisdiction may enjoin such honor.

(3) Unless otherwise agreed an issuer which has duly honored a draft or demand for payment is entitled to immediate reimbursement of any payment made under the credit and to be put in effectively available funds not later than the day before maturity of any acceptance made under the credit.

[(4) When a credit provides for payment by the issuer on receipt of notice that the required documents are in the possession of a correspondent or other agent of the issuer

(a) any payment made on receipt of such notice is conditional; and

(b) the issuer may reject documents which do not comply with the credit if it does so within three banking days following its receipt of the documents; and

(c) in the event of such rejection, the issuer is entitled by charge back or otherwise to return of the payment made.]

[(5) In the case covered by subsection (4) failure to reject documents within the time specified in sub-paragraph (b) constitutes acceptance of the documents and makes the payment final in favor of the beneficiary.]

Note: *Subsections (4) and (5) are bracketed as optional. If they are included the bracketed language in the last sentence of Section 5—112(1) should also be included.*

§ 5—115. Remedy for Improper Dishonor or Anticipatory Repudiation.

(1) When an issuer wrongfully dishonors a draft or demand for payment presented under a credit the person entitled to honor has with respect to any documents the rights of a person in the position of a seller (Section 2—707) and may recover from the issuer the face amount of the draft or demand together with incidental damages under Section 2—710 on seller's incidental damages and interest but less any amount realized by resale or other use or disposition of the subject matter of the transaction. In the event no resale or other utilization is made the documents, goods or other subject matter involved in the transaction must be turned over to the issuer on payment of judgment.

(2) When an issuer wrongfully cancels or otherwise repudiates a credit before presentment of a draft or demand for payment drawn under it the beneficiary has the rights of a seller after anticipatory repudiation by the buyer under Section 2—610 if he learns of the repudiation in time reasonably to avoid procurement of the required documents. Otherwise the beneficiary has an immediate right of action for wrongful dishonor.

§ 5—116. Transfer and Assignment.

(1) The right to draw under a credit can be transferred or assigned only when the credit is expressly designated as transferable or assignable.

(2) Even through the credit specifically states that it is nontransferable or nonassignable the beneficiary may before performance of the conditions of the credit assign his right to proceeds. Such an assignment is an assignment of an account under Article 9 on Secured Transactions and is governed by that Article except that

(a) the assignment is ineffective until the letter of credit or advice of credit is delivered to the assignee which delivery constitutes perfection of the security interest under Article 9; and

(b) the issuer may honor drafts or demands for payment drawn under the credit until it receives a notification of the assignment signed by the beneficiary which reasonably identifies the credit involved in the assignment and contains a request to pay the assignee; and

(c) after what reasonably appears to be such a notification has been received the issuer may without dishonor refuse to accept or pay even to a person otherwise entitled to honor until the letter of credit or advice of credit is exhibited to the issuer.

(3) Except where the beneficiary has effectively assigned his right to draw or his right to proceeds, nothing in this section limits his right to transfer or negotiate drafts or demands drawn under the credit.

§ 5—117. Insolvency of Bank Holding Funds for Documentary Credit.

(1) Where an issuer or an advising or confirming bank or a bank which has for a customer procured issuance of a credit by another bank becomes insolvent before final payment under the credit and the credit is one to which this Article is made applicable by paragraphs (a) or (b) of Section 5—102(1) on scope, the receipt or allocation of funds or collateral to secure or meet obligations under the credit shall have the following results:

(a) to the extent of any funds or collateral turned over after or before the insolvency as indemnity against or specifically for the purpose of payment of drafts or demands for payment drawn under the designated credit, the drafts or demands are entitled to payment in preference over depositors or other general creditors of the issuer or bank; and

(b) on expiration of the credit or surrender of the beneficiary's rights under it unused any person who has given such funds or collateral is similarly entitled to return thereof; and

(c) a charge to a general or current account with a bank if specifically consented to for the purpose of indemnity against or payment of drafts or demands for payment drawn under the designated credit falls under the same rules as if the funds had been drawn out in cash and then turned over with specific instructions.

(2) After honor or reimbursement under this section the customer or other person for whose account the insolvent bank has acted is entitled to receive the documents involved.

Article 6
BULK TRANSFERS

§ 6—101. Short Title.

This Article shall be known and may be cited as Uniform Commercial Code—Bulk Transfers.

§ 6—102. "Bulk Transfers"; Transfers of Equipment; Enterprises Subject to This Article; Bulk Transfers Subject to This Article.

(1) A "bulk transfer" is any transfer in bulk and not in the ordinary course of the transferor's business of a major part of the materials, supplies, merchandise or other inventory (Section 9—109) of an enterprise subject to this Article.

(2) A transfer of a substantial part of the equipment (Section 9—109) of such an enterprise is a bulk transfer if it is made in connection with a bulk transfer of inventory, but not otherwise.

(3) The enterprises subject to this Article are all those whose principal business is the sale of merchandise from stock, including those who manufacture what they sell.

(4) Except as limited by the following section all bulk transfers of goods located within this state are subject to this Article.

§ 6—103. Transfers Excepted From This Article.

The following transfers are not subject to this Article:

(1) Those made to give security for the performance of an obligation;

(2) General assignments for the benefit of all the creditors of the transferor, and subsequent transfers by the assignee thereunder;

(3) Transfers in settlement or realization of a lien or other security interests;

(4) Sales by executors, administrators, receivers, trustees in bankruptcy, or any public officer under judicial process;

(5) Sales made in the course of judicial or administrative proceedings for the dissolution or reorganization of a corporation and of which notice is sent to the creditors of the corporation pursuant to order of the court or administrative agency;

(6) Transfers to a person maintaining a known place of business in this State who becomes bound to pay the debts of the transferor in full and gives public notice of that fact, and who is solvent after becoming so bound;

(7) A transfer to a new business enterprise organized to take over and continue the business, if public notice of the transaction is given and the new enterprise assumes the debts of the transferor and he receives nothing from the transaction except an interest in the new enterprise junior to the claims of creditors;

(8) Transfers of property which is exempt from execution.

Public notice under subsection (6) or subsection (7) may be given by publishing once a week for two consecutive weeks in a newspaper of general circulation where the transferor had its principal place of business in this state an advertisement including the names and addresses of the transferor and transferee and the effective date of the transfer.

§ 6—104. Schedule of Property, List of Creditors.

(1) Except as provided with respect to auction sales (Section 6—108), a bulk transfer subject to this Article is ineffective against any creditor of the transferor unless:

> (a) The transferee requires the transferor to furnish a list of his existing creditors prepared as stated in this section; and

> (b) The parties prepare a schedule of the property transferred sufficient to identify it; and

> (c) The transferee preserves the list and schedule for six months next following the transfer and permits inspection of either or both and copying therefrom at all reasonable hours by any creditor of the transferor, or files the list and schedule in (a public office to be here identified).

(2) The list of creditors must be signed and sworn to or affirmed by the transferor or his agent. It must contain the names and business addresses of all creditors of the transferor, with the amounts when known, and also the names of all persons who are known to the transferor to assert claims against him even though such claims are disputed. If the transferor is the obligor of an outstanding issue of bonds, debentures or the like as to which there is an indenture trustee, the list of creditors need include only the name and address of the indenture trustee and the aggregate outstanding principal amount of the issue.

(3) Responsibility for the completeness and accuracy of the list of creditors rests on the transferor, and the transfer is not rendered ineffective by errors or omissions therein unless the transferee is shown to have had knowledge.

§ 6—105. Notice to Creditors.

In addition to the requirements of the preceding section, any bulk transfer subject to this Article except one made by auction sale (Section 6—108) is ineffective against any creditor of the transferor unless at least ten days before he takes possession of the goods or pays for them, whichever happens first, the transferee gives notice of the transfer in the manner and to the persons hereafter provided (Section 6—107).

[§ 6—106. Application of the Proceeds.

In addition to the requirements of the two preceding sections:

(1) Upon every bulk transfer subject to this Article for which new consideration becomes payable except those made by sale at auction it is the duty of the transferee to assure that such consideration is applied so far as necessary

to pay those debts of the transferor which are either shown on the list furnished by the transferor (Section 6—104) or filed in writing in the place stated in the notice (Section 6—107) within thirty days after the mailing of such notice. This duty of the transferee runs to all the holders of such debts, and may be enforced by any of them for the benefit of all.

(2) If any of said debts are in dispute the necessary sum may be withheld from distribution until the dispute is settled or adjudicated.

(3) If the consideration payable is not enough to pay all of the said debts in full distribution shall be made pro rata.]

Note: *This section is bracketed to indicate division of opinion as to whether or not it is a wise provision, and to suggest that this is a point on which State enactments may differ without serious damage to the principle of uniformity. In any State where this section is omitted, the following parts of sections, also bracketed in the text, should also be omitted, namely:*

Section 6—107(2)(e).
> *6—108(3)(c).*
> *6—109(2).*

In any State where this section is enacted, these other provisions should be also.

Optional Subsection (4)

[(4) The transferee may within ten days after he takes possession of the goods pay the consideration into the (specify court) in the county where the transferor had its principal place of business in this state and thereafter may discharge his duty under this section by giving notice by registered or certified mail to all the persons to whom the duty runs that the consideration has been paid into that court and that they should file their claims there. On motion of any interested party, the court may order the distribution of the consideration to the persons entitled to it.]

Note: *Optional subsection (4) is recommended for those states which do not have a general statute providing for payment of money into court.*

§ 6—107. The Notice.

(1) The notice to creditors (Section 6—105) shall state:

> (a) that a bulk transfer is about to be made; and

> (b) the names and business addresses of the transferor and transferee, and all other business names and addresses used by the transferor within three years last past so far as known to the transferee; and

> (c) whether or not all the debts of the transferor are to be paid in full as they fall due as a result of the transaction, and if so, the address to which creditors should send their bills.

(2) If the debts of the transferor are not to be paid in full as they fall due or if the transferee is in doubt on that point then the notice shall state further:

    (a) the location and general description of the property to be transferred and the estimated total of the transferor's debts;

    (b) the address where the schedule of property and list of creditors (Section 6—104) may be inspected;

    (c) whether the transfer is to pay existing debts and if so the amount of such debts and to whom owing;

    (d) whether the transfer is for new consideration and if so the amount of such consideration and the time and place of payment; [and]

    [(e) if for new consideration the time and place where creditors of the transferor are to file their claims.]

(3) The notice in any case shall be delivered personally or sent by registered or certified mail to all the persons shown on the list of creditors furnished by the transferor (Section 6—104) and to all other persons who are known to the transferee to hold or assert claims against the transferor.

§ 6—108. **Auction Sales; "Auctioneer".**

(1) A bulk transfer is subject to this Article even though it is by sale at auction, but only in the manner and with the results stated in this section.

(2) The transferor shall furnish a list of his creditors and assist in the preparation of a schedule of the property to be sold, both prepared as before stated (Section 6—104).

(3) The person or persons other than the transferor who direct, control or are responsible for the auction are collectively called the "auctioneer". The auctioneer shall:

    (a) receive and retain the list of creditors and prepare and retain the schedule of property for the period stated in this Article (Section 6—104);

    (b) give notice of the auction personally or by registered or certified mail at least ten days before it occurs to all persons shown on the list of creditors and to all other persons who are known to him to hold or assert claims against the transferor; [and]

    [(c) assure that the net proceeds of the auction are applied as provided in this Article (Section 6—106).]

(4) Failure of the auctioneer to perform any of these duties does not affect the validity of the sale or the title of the purchasers, but if the auctioneer knows that the auction constitutes a bulk transfer such failure renders the auctioneer liable to the creditors of the transferor as a class for the sums owing to them from the transferor up to but not exceeding the net proceeds of the auction. If the auctioneer consists of several persons their liability is joint and several.

§ 6—109. **What Creditors Protected; [Credit for Payment to Particular Creditors].**

(1) The creditors of the transferor mentioned in this Article are those holding claims based on transactions or events occurring before the bulk transfer, but creditors who become such after notice to creditors is given (Sections 6—105 and 6—107) are not entitled to notice.

[(2) Against the aggregate obligation imposed by the provisions of this Article concerning the application of the proceeds (Section 6—106 and subsection (3)(c) of 6—108) the transferee or auctioneer is entitled to credit for sums paid to particular creditors of the transferor, not exceeding the sums believed in good faith at the time of the payment to be properly payable to such creditors.]

§ 6—110. **Subsequent Transfers.**

When the title of a transferee to property is subject to a defect by reason of his non-compliance with the requirements of this Article, then:

(1) a purchaser of any of such property from such transferee who pays no value or who takes with notice of such non-compliance takes subject to such defect, but

(2) a purchaser for value in good faith and without such notice takes free of such defect.

§ 6—111. **Limitation of Actions and Levies.**

No action under this Article shall be brought nor levy made more than six months after the date on which the transferee took possession of the goods unless the transfer has been concealed. If the transfer has been concealed, actions may be brought or levies made within six months after its discovery.

Note to Article 6: *Section 6—106 is bracketed to indicate division of opinion as to whether or not it is a wise provision, and to suggest that this is a point on which State enactments may differ without serious damage to the principle of uniformity.*

In any State where Section 6—106 is not enacted, the following parts of sections, also bracketed in the text, should also be omitted, namely:
Sec. 6—107(2)(e).
    6—108(3)(c).
    6—109(2).
In any State where Section 6—106 is enacted, these other provisions should be also.

Article 7
Warehouse Receipts, Bills of Lading and Other Documents of Title

Part 1 General

§ 7—101. **Short Title.**

This Article shall be known and may be cited as Uniform Commercial Code—Documents of Title.

§ 7—102. **Definitions and Index of Definitions.**

(1) In this Article, unless the context otherwise requires:

(a) "Bailee" means the person who by a warehouse receipt, bill of lading or other document of title acknowledges possession of goods and contracts to deliver them.

(b) "Consignee" means the person named in a bill to whom or to whose order the bill promises delivery.

(c) "Consignor" means the person named in a bill as the person from whom the goods have been received for shipment.

(d) "Delivery order" means a written order to deliver goods directed to a warehouseman, carrier or other person who in the ordinary course of business issues warehouse receipts or bills of lading.

(e) "Document" means document of title as defined in the general definitions in Article 1 (Section 1—201).

(f) "Goods" means all things which are treated as movable for the purposes of a contract of storage or transportation.

(g) "Issuer" means a bailee who issues a document except that in relation to an unaccepted delivery order it means the person who orders the possessor of goods to deliver. Issuer includes any person for whom an agent or employee purports to act in issuing a document if the agent or employee has real or apparent authority to issue documents, notwithstanding that the issuer received no goods or that the goods were misdescribed or that in any other respect the agent or employee violated his instructions.

(h) "Warehouseman" is a person engaged in the business of storing goods for hire.

(2) Other definitions applying to this Article or to specified Parts thereof, and the sections in which they appear are:
"Duly negotiate". Section 7—501.
"Person entitled under the document". Section 7—403(4).

(3) Definitions in other Articles applying to this Article and the sections in which they appear are:
"Contract for sale". Section 2—106.
"Overseas". Section 2—323.
"Receipt" of goods. Section 2—103.

(4) In addition Article 1 contains general definitions and principles of construction and interpretation applicable throughout this Article.

§ 7—103. **Relation of Article to Treaty, Statute, Tariff, Classification or Regulation.**

To the extent that any treaty or statute of the United States, regulatory statute of this State or tariff, classification or regulation filed or issued pursuant thereto is applicable, the provisions of this Article are subject thereto.

§ 7—104. **Negotiable and Non-Negotiable Warehouse Receipt, Bill of Lading or Other Document of Title.**

(1) A warehouse receipt, bill of lading or other document of title is negotiable

(a) if by its terms the goods are to be delivered to bearer or to the order of a named person; or

(b) where recognized in overseas trade, if it runs to a named person or assigns.

(2) Any other document is non-negotiable. A bill of lading in which it is stated that the goods are consigned to a named person is not made negotiable by a provision that the goods are to be delivered only against a written order signed by the same or another named person.

§ 7—105. **Construction Against Negative Implication.**

The omission from either Part 2 or Part 3 of this Article of a provision corresponding to a provision made in the other Part does not imply that a corresponding rule of law is not applicable.

Part 2 Warehouse Receipts: Special Provisions

§ 7—201. **Who May Issue a Warehouse Receipt; Storage Under Government Bond.**

(1) A warehouse receipt may be issued by any warehouseman.

(2) Where goods including distilled spirits and agricultural commodities are stored under a statute requiring a bond against withdrawal or a license for the issuance of receipts in the nature of warehouse receipts, a receipt issued for the goods has like effect as a warehouse receipt even though issued by a person who is the owner of the goods and is not a warehouseman.

§ 7—202. **Form of Warehouse Receipt; Essential Terms; Optional Terms.**

(1) A warehouse receipt need not be in any particular form.

(2) Unless a warehouse receipt embodies within its written or printed terms each of the following, the warehouseman is liable for damages caused by the omission to a person injured thereby:

(a) the location of the warehouse where the goods are stored;

(b) the date of issue of the receipt;

(c) the consecutive number of the receipt;

(d) a statement whether the goods received will be delivered to the bearer, to a specified person, or to a specified person or his order;

(e) the rate of storage and handling charges, except that where goods are stored under a field warehousing arrangement a statement of that fact is sufficient on a non-negotiable receipt;

(f) a description of the goods or of the packages containing them;

(g) the signature of the warehouseman, which may be made by his authorized agent;

(h) if the receipt is issued for goods of which the warehouseman is owner, either solely or jointly or in common with others, the fact of such ownership; and

(i) a statement of the amount of advances made and of liabilities incurred for which the warehouseman claims a lien or security interest (Section 7—209). If the precise amount of such advances made or of such liabilities incurred is, at the time of the issue of the receipt, unknown to the warehouseman or to his agent who issues it, a statement of the fact that advances have been made or liabilities incurred and the purpose thereof is sufficient.

(3) A warehouseman may insert in his receipt any other terms which are not contrary to the provisions of this Act and do not impair his obligation of delivery (Section 7—403) or his duty of care (Section 7—204). Any contrary provisions shall be ineffective.

§ 7—203. Liability for Non-Receipt or Misdescription.

A party to or purchaser for value in good faith of a document of title other than a bill of lading relying in either case upon the description therein of the goods may recover from the issuer damages caused by the non-receipt or misdescription of the goods, except to the extent that the document conspicuously indicates that the issuer does not know whether any part or all of the goods in fact were received or conform to the description, as where the description is in terms of marks or labels or kind, quantity or condition, or the receipt or description is qualified by "contents, condition and quality unknown", "said to contain" or the like, if such indication be true, or the party or purchaser otherwise has notice.

§ 7—204. Duty of Care; Contractual Limitation of Warehouseman's Liability.

(1) A warehouseman is liable for damages for loss of or injury to the goods caused by his failure to exercise such care in regard to them as a reasonably careful man would exercise under like circumstances but unless otherwise agreed he is not liable for damages which could not have been avoided by the exercise of such care.

(2) Damages may be limited by a term in the warehouse receipt or storage agreement limiting the amount of lia-bility in case of loss or damage, and setting forth a specific liability per article or item, or value per unit of weight, beyond which the warehouseman shall not be liable; provided, however, that such liability may on written request of the bailor at the time of signing such storage agreement or within a reasonable time after receipt of the warehouse receipt be increased on part or all of the goods thereunder, in which event increased rates may be charged based on such increased valuation, but that no such increase shall be permitted contrary to a lawful limitation of liability contained in the warehouseman's tariff, if any. No such limitation is effective with respect to the warehouseman's liability for conversion to his own use.

(3) Reasonable provisions as to the time and manner of presenting claims and instituting actions based on the bailment may be included in the warehouse receipt or tariff.

(4) This section does not impair or repeal . . .

Note: *Insert in subsection (4) a reference to any statute which imposes a higher responsibility upon the warehouseman or invalidates contractual limitations which would be permissible under this Article.*

§ 7—205. Title Under Warehouse Receipt Defeated in Certain Cases.

A buyer in the ordinary course of business of fungible goods sold and delivered by a warehouseman who is also in the business of buying and selling such goods takes free of any claim under a warehouse receipt even though it has been duly negotiated.

§ 7—206. Termination of Storage at Warehouseman's Option.

(1) A warehouseman may on notifying the person on whose account the goods are held and any other person known to claim an interest in the goods require payment of any charges and removal of the goods from the warehouse at the termination of the period of storage fixed by the document, or, if no period is fixed, within a stated period not less than thirty days after the notification. If the goods are not removed before the date specified in the notification, the warehouseman may sell them in accordance with the provisions of the section on enforcement of a warehouseman's lien (Section 7—210).

(2) If a warehouseman in good faith believes that the goods are about to deteriorate or decline in value to less than the amount of his lien within the time prescribed in subsection (1) for notification, advertisement and sale, the warehouseman may specify in the notification any reasonable shorter time for removal of the goods and in case the goods are not removed, may sell them at public sale held not less than one week after a single advertisement or posting.

(3) If as a result of a quality or condition of the goods of which the warehouseman had no notice at the time of deposit the goods are a hazard to other property or to the warehouse or to persons, the warehouseman may sell the goods at public or private sale without advertisement on reasonable notification to all persons known to claim an interest in the goods. If the warehouseman after a reasonable effort is unable to sell the goods he may dispose of them in any lawful manner and shall incur no liability by reason of such disposition.

(4) The warehouseman must deliver the goods to any person entitled to them under this Article upon due demand made at any time prior to sale or other disposition under this section.

(5) The warehouseman may satisfy his lien from the proceeds of any sale or disposition under this section but must hold the balance for delivery on the demand of any person to whom he would have been bound to deliver the goods.

§ 7—207. Goods Must Be Kept Separate; Fungible Goods.

(1) Unless the warehouse receipt otherwise provides, a warehouseman must keep separate the goods covered by each receipt so as to permit at all times identification and delivery of those goods except that different lots of fungible goods may be commingled.

(2) Fungible goods so commingled are owned in common by the persons entitled thereto and the warehouseman is severally liable to each owner for that owner's share. Where because of overissue a mass of fungible goods is insufficient to meet all the receipts which the warehouseman has issued against it, the persons entitled include all holders to whom overissued receipts have been duly negotiated.

§ 7—208. Altered Warehouse Receipts.

Where a blank in a negotiable warehouse receipt has been filled in without authority, a purchaser for value and without notice of the want of authority may treat the insertion as authorized. Any other unauthorized alteration leaves any receipt enforceable against the issuer according to its original tenor.

§ 7—209. Lien of Warehouseman.

(1) A warehouseman has a lien against the bailor on the goods covered by a warehouse receipt or on the proceeds thereof in his possession for charges for storage or transportation (including demurrage and terminal charges), insurance, labor, or charges present or future in relation to the goods, and for expenses necessary for preservation of the goods or reasonably incurred in their sale pursuant to law. If the person on whose account the goods are held

is liable for like charges or expenses in relation to other goods whenever deposited and it is stated in the receipt that a lien is claimed for charges and expenses in relation to other goods, the warehouseman also has a lien against him for such charges and expenses whether or not the other goods have been delivered by the warehouseman. But against a person to whom a negotiable warehouse receipt is duly negotiated a warehouseman's lien is limited to charges in an amount or at a rate specified on the receipt or if no charges are so specified then to a reasonable charge for storage of the goods covered by the receipt subsequent to the date of the receipt.

(2) The warehouseman may also reserve a security interest against the bailor for a maximum amount specified on the receipt for charges other than those specified in subsection (1), such as for money advanced and interest. Such a security interest is governed by the Article on Secured Transactions (Article 9).

(3) (a) A warehouseman's lien for charges and expenses under subsection (1) or a security interest under subsection (2) is also effective against any person who so entrusted the bailor with possession of the goods that a pledge of them by him to a good faith purchaser for value would have been valid but is not effective against a person as to whom the document confers no right in the goods covered by it under Section 7—503.

  (b) A warehouseman's lien on household goods for charges and expenses in relation to the goods under subsection (1) is also effective against all persons if the depositor was the legal possessor of the goods at the time of deposit. "Household goods" means furniture, furnishings and personal effects used by the depositor in a dwelling.

(4) A warehouseman loses his lien on any goods which he voluntarily delivers or which he unjustifiably refuses to deliver.

§ 7—210. Enforcement of Warehouseman's Lien.

(1) Except as provided in subsection (2), a warehouseman's lien may be enforced by public or private sale of the goods in bloc or in parcels, at any time or place and on any terms which are commercially reasonable, after notifying all persons known to claim an interest in the goods. Such notification must include a statement of the amount due, the nature of the proposed sale and the time and place of any public sale. The fact that a better price could have been obtained by a sale at a different time or in a different method from that selected by the warehouseman is not of itself sufficient to establish that the sale was not made in a commercially reasonable manner. If the warehouseman either sells the goods in the usual manner in any recognized market therefor, or if he sells

at the price current in such market at the time of his sale, or if he has otherwise sold in conformity with commercially reasonable practices among dealers in the type of goods sold, he has sold in a commercially reasonable manner. A sale of more goods than apparently necessary to be offered to insure satisfaction of the obligation is not commercially reasonable except in cases covered by the preceding sentence.

(2) A warehouseman's lien on goods other than goods stored by a merchant in the course of his business may be enforced only as follows:

(a) All persons known to claim an interest in the goods must be notified.

(b) The notification must be delivered in person or sent by registered or certified letter to the last known address of any person to be notified.

(c) The notification must include an itemized statement of the claim, a description of the goods subject to the lien, a demand for payment within a specified time not less than ten days after receipt of the notification, and a conspicuous statement that unless the claim is paid within the time the goods will be advertised for sale and sold by auction at a specified time and place.

(d) The sale must conform to the terms of the notification.

(e) The sale must be held at the nearest suitable place to that where the goods are held or stored.

(f) After the expiration of the time given in the notification, an advertisement of the sale must be published once a week for two weeks consecutively in a newspaper of general circulation where the sale is to be held. The advertisement must include a description of the goods, the name of the person on whose account they are being held, and the time and place of the sale. The sale must take place at least fifteen days after the first publication. If there is no newspaper of general circulation where the sale is to be held, the advertisement must be posted at least ten days before the sale in not less than six conspicuous places in the neighborhood of the proposed sale.

(3) Before any sale pursuant to this section any person claiming a right in the goods may pay the amount necessary to satisfy the lien and the reasonable expenses incurred under this section. In that event the goods must not be sold, but must be retained by the warehouseman subject to the terms of the receipt and this Article.

(4) The warehouseman may buy at any public sale pursuant to this section.

(5) A purchaser in good faith of goods sold to enforce a warehouseman's lien takes the goods free of any rights of persons against whom the lien was valid, despite non-compliance by the warehouseman with the requirements of this section.

(6) The warehouseman may satisfy his lien from the proceeds of any sale pursuant to this section but must hold the balance, if any, for delivery on demand to any person to whom he would have been bound to deliver the goods.

(7) The rights provided by this section shall be in addition to all other rights allowed by law to a creditor against his debtor.

(8) Where a lien is on goods stored by a merchant in the course of his business the lien may be enforced in accordance with either subsection (1) or (2).

(9) The warehouseman is liable for damages caused by failure to comply with the requirements for sale under this section and in case of willful violation is liable for conversion.

Part 3 Bills of Lading: Special Provisions

§ 7—301. Liability for Non-Receipt or Misdescription; "Said to Contain"; "Shipper's Load and Count"; Improper Handling.

(1) A consignee of a non-negotiable bill who has given value in good faith or a holder to whom a negotiable bill has been duly negotiated relying in either case upon the description therein of the goods, or upon the date therein shown, may recover from the issuer damages caused by the misdating of the bill or the non-receipt or misdescription of the goods, except to the extent that the document indicates that the issuer does not know whether any part of all of the goods in fact were received or conform to the description, as where the description is in terms of marks or labels or kind, quantity, or condition or the receipt or description is qualified by "contents or condition of contents of packages unknown", "said to contain", "shipper's weight, load and count" or the like, if such indication be true.

(2) When goods are loaded by an issuer who is a common carrier, the issuer must count the packages of goods if package freight and ascertain the kind and quantity if bulk freight. In such cases "shipper's weight, load and count" or other words indicating that the description was made by the shipper are ineffective except as to freight concealed by packages.

(3) When bulk freight is loaded by a shipper who makes available to the issuer adequate facilities for weighing such freight, an issuer who is a common carrier must ascertain the kind and quantity within a reasonable time after receiving the written request of the shipper to do so. In such cases "shipper's weight" or other words of like purport are ineffective.

(4) The issuer may by inserting in the bill the words "shipper's weight, load and count" or other words of like purport indicate that the goods were loaded by the shipper; and if such statement be true the issuer shall not be liable for damages caused by the improper loading. But their omission does not imply liability for such damages.

(5) The shipper shall be deemed to have guaranteed to the issuer the accuracy at the time of shipment of the description, marks, labels, number, kind, quantity, condition and weight, as furnished by him; and the shipper shall indemnify the issuer against damage caused by inaccuracies in such particulars. The right of the issuer to such indemnity shall in no way limit his responsibility and liability under the contract of carriage to any person other than the shipper.

§ 7—302. Through Bills of Lading and Similar Documents.

(1) The issuer of a through bill of lading or other document embodying an undertaking to be performed in part by persons acting as its agents or by connecting carriers is liable to anyone entitled to recover on the document for any breach by such other persons or by a connecting carrier of its obligation under the document but to the extent that the bill covers an undertaking to be performed overseas or in territory not contiguous to the continental United States or an undertaking including matters other than transportation this liability may be varied by agreement of the parties.

(2) Where goods covered by a through bill of lading or other document embodying an undertaking to be performed in part by persons other than the issuer are received by any such person, he is subject with respect to his own performance while the goods are in his possession to the obligation of the issuer. His obligation is discharged by delivery of the goods to another such person pursuant to the document, and does not include liability for breach by any other such persons or by the issuer.

(3) The issuer of such through bill of lading or other document shall be entitled to recover from the connecting carrier or such other person in possession of the goods when the breach of the obligation under the document occurred, the amount it may be required to pay to anyone entitled to recover on the document therefor, as may be evidenced by any receipt, judgment, or transcript thereof, and the amount of any expense reasonably incurred by it in defending any action brought by anyone entitled to recover on the document therefor.

§ 7—303. Diversion; Reconsignment; Change of Instructions.

(1) Unless the bill of lading otherwise provides, the carrier may deliver the goods to a person or destination other than that stated in the bill or may otherwise dispose of the goods on instructions from

(a) the holder of a negotiable bill; or

(b) the consignor on a non-negotiable bill notwithstanding contrary instructions from the consignee; or

(c) the consignee on a non-negotiable bill in the absence of contrary instructions from the consignor, if the goods have arrived at the billed destination or if the consignee is in possession of the bill; or

(d) the consignee on a non-negotiable bill if he is entitled as against the consignor to dispose of them.

(2) Unless such instructions are noted on a negotiable bill of lading, a person to whom the bill is duly negotiated can hold the bailee according to the original terms.

§ 7—304. Bills of Lading in a Set.

(1) Except where customary in overseas transportation, a bill of lading must not be issued in a set of parts. The issuer is liable for damages caused by violation of this subsection.

(2) Where a bill of lading is lawfully drawn in a set of parts, each of which is numbered and expressed to be valid only if the goods have not been delivered against any other part, the whole of the parts constitute one bill.

(3) Where a bill of lading is lawfully issued in a set of parts and different parts are negotiated to different persons, the title of the holder to whom the first due negotiation is made prevails as to both the document and the goods even though any later holder may have received the goods from the carrier in good faith and discharged the carrier's obligation by surrender of his part.

(4) Any person who negotiates or transfers a single part of a bill of lading drawn in a set is liable to holders of that part as if it were the whole set.

(5) The bailee is obliged to deliver in accordance with Part 4 of this Article against the first presented part of a bill of lading lawfully drawn in a set. Such delivery discharges the bailee's obligation on the whole bill.

§ 7—305. Destination Bills.

(1) Instead of issuing a bill of lading to the consignor at the place of shipment a carrier may at the request of the consignor procure the bill to be issued at destination or at any other place designated in the request.

(2) Upon request of anyone entitled as against the carrier to control the goods while in transit and on surrender of any outstanding bill of lading or other receipt covering such goods, the issuer may procure a substitute bill to be issued at any place designated in the request.

§ 7—306. **Altered Bills of Lading.**

An unauthorized alteration or filling in of a blank in a bill of lading leaves the bill enforceable according to its original tenor.

§ 7—307. **Lien of Carrier.**

(1) A carrier has a lien on the goods covered by a bill of lading for charges subsequent to the date of its receipt of the goods for storage or transportation (including demurrage and terminal charges) and for expenses necessary for preservation of the goods incident to their transportation or reasonably incurred in their sale pursuant to law. But against a purchaser for value of a negotiable bill of lading a carrier's lien is limited to charges stated in the bill or the applicable tariffs, or if no charges are stated then to a reasonable charge.

(2) A lien for charges and expenses under subsection (1) on goods which the carrier was required by law to receive for transportation is effective against the consignor or any person entitled to the goods unless the carrier had notice that the consignor lacked authority to subject the goods to such charges and expenses. Any other lien under subsection (1) is effective against the consignor and any person who permitted the bailor to have control or possession of the goods unless the carrier had notice that the bailor lacked such authority.

(3) A carrier loses his lien on any goods which he voluntarily delivers or which he unjustifiably refuses to deliver.

§ 7—308. **Enforcement of Carrier's Lien.**

(1) A carrier's lien may be enforced by public or private sale of the goods, in bloc or in parcels, at any time or place and on any terms which are commercially reasonable, after notifying all persons known to claim an interest in the goods. Such notification must include a statement of the amount due, the nature of the proposed sale and the time and place of any public sale. The fact that a better price could have been obtained by a sale at a different time or in a different method from that selected by the carrier is not of itself sufficient to establish that the sale was not made in a commercially reasonable manner. If the carrier either sells the goods in the usual manner in any recognized market therefor or if he sells at the price current in such market at the time of his sale or if he has otherwise sold in conformity with commercially reasonable practices among dealers in the type of goods sold he has sold in a commercially reasonable manner. A sale of more goods than apparently necessary to be offered to ensure satisfaction of the obligation is not commercially reasonable except in cases covered by the preceding sentence.

(2) Before any sale pursuant to this section any person claiming a right in the goods may pay the amount nec-

essary to satisfy the lien and the reasonable expenses incurred under this section. In that event the goods must not be sold, but must be retained by the carrier subject to the terms of the bill and this Article.

(3) The carrier may buy at any public sale pursuant to this section.

(4) A purchaser in good faith of goods sold to enforce a carrier's lien takes the goods free of any rights of persons against whom the lien was valid, despite noncompliance by the carrier with the requirements of this section.

(5) The carrier may satisfy his lien from the proceeds of any sale pursuant to this section but must hold the balance, if any, for delivery on demand to any person to whom he would have been bound to deliver the goods.

(6) The rights provided by this section shall be in addition to all other rights allowed by law to a creditor against his debtor.

(7) A carrier's lien may be enforced in accordance with either subsection (1) or the procedure set forth in subsection (2) of Section 7—210.

(8) The carrier is liable for damages caused by failure to comply with the requirements for sale under this section and in case of willful violation is liable for conversion.

§ 7—309. **Duty of Care; Contractual Limitation of Carrier's Liability.**

(1) A carrier who issues a bill of lading whether negotiable or non-negotiable must exercise the degree of care in relation to the goods which a reasonably careful man would exercise under like circumstances. This subsection does not repeal or change any law or rule of law which imposes liability upon a common carrier for damages not caused by its negligence.

(2) Damages may be limited by a provision that the carrier's liability shall not exceed a value stated in the document if the carrier's rates are dependent upon value and the consignor by the carrier's tariff is afforded an opportunity to declare a higher value or a value as lawfully provided in the tariff, or where no tariff is filed he is otherwise advised of such opportunity; but no such limitation is effective with respect to the carrier's liability for conversion to its own use.

(3) Reasonable provisions as to the time and manner of presenting claims and instituting actions based on the shipment may be included in a bill of lading or tariff.

Part 4 Warehouse Receipts and Bills of Lading: General Obligations

§ 7—401. **Irregularities in Issue of Receipt or Bill or Conduct of Issuer.**

The obligations imposed by this Article on an issuer apply to a document of title regardless of the fact that

(a) the document may not comply with the requirements of this Article or of any other law or regulation regarding its issue, form or content; or

(b) the issuer may have violated laws regulating the conduct of his business; or

(c) the goods covered by the document were owned by the bailee at the time the document was issued; or

(d) the person issuing the document does not come within the definition of warehouseman if it purports to be a warehouse receipt.

§ 7—402. Duplicate Receipt or Bill; Overissue.

Neither a duplicate nor any other document of title purporting to cover goods already represented by an outstanding document of the same issuer confers any right in the goods, except as provided in the case of bills in a set, overissue of documents for fungible goods and substitutes for lost, stolen or destroyed documents. But the issuer is liable for damages caused by his overissue or failure to identify a duplicate document as such by conspicuous notation on its face.

§ 7—403. Obligation of Warehouseman or Carrier to Deliver; Excuse.

(1) The bailee must deliver the goods to a person entitled under the document who complies with subsections (2) and (3), unless and to the extent that the bailee establishes any of the following:

(a) delivery of the goods to a person whose receipt was rightful as against the claimant;

(b) damage to or delay, loss or destruction of the goods for which the bailee is not liable [, but the burden of establishing negligence in such cases is on the person entitled under the document];

Note: *The brackets in (1)(b) indicate that State enactments may differ on this point without serious damage to the principle of uniformity.*

(c) previous sale or other disposition of the goods in lawful enforcement of a lien or on warehouseman's lawful termination of storage;

(d) the exercise by a seller of his right to stop delivery pursuant to the provisions of the Article on Sales (Section 2—705);

(e) a diversion, reconsignment or other disposition pursuant to the provisions of this Article (Section 7—303) or tariff regulating such right;

(f) release, satisfaction or any other fact affording a personal defense against the claimant;

(g) any other lawful excuse.

(2) A person claiming goods covered by a document of title must satisfy the bailee's lien where the bailee so requests or where the bailee is prohibited by law from delivering the goods until the charges are paid.

(3) Unless the person claiming is one against whom the document confers no right under Sec. 7—503(1), he must surrender for cancellation or notation of partial deliveries any outstanding negotiable document covering the goods, and the bailee must cancel the document or conspicuously note the partial delivery thereon or be liable to any person to whom the document is duly negotiated.

(4) "Person entitled under the document" means holder in the case of a negotiable document, or the person to whom delivery is to be made by the terms of or pursuant to written instructions under a non-negotiable document.

§ 7—404. No Liability for Good Faith Delivery Pursuant to Receipt or Bill.

A bailee who in good faith including observance of reasonable commercial standards has received goods and delivered or otherwise disposed of them according to the terms of the document of title or pursuant to this Article is not liable therefor. This rule applies even though the person from whom he received the goods had no authority to procure the document or to dispose of the goods and even though the person to whom he delivered the goods had no authority to receive them.

Part 5 Warehouse Receipts and Bills of Lading: Negotiation and Transfer

§ 7—501. Form of Negotiation and Requirements of "Due Negotiation".

(1) A negotiable document of title running to the order of a named person is negotiated by his indorsement and delivery. After his indorsement in blank or to bearer any person can negotiate it by delivery alone.

(2) (a) A negotiable document of title is also negotiated by delivery alone when by its original terms it runs to bearer.

(b) When a document running to the order of a named person is delivered to him the effect is the same as if the document had been negotiated.

(3) Negotiation of a negotiable document of title after it has been indorsed to a specified person requires indorsement by the special indorsee as well as delivery.

(4) A negotiable document of title is "duly negotiated" when it is negotiated in the manner stated in this section to a holder who purchases it in good faith without notice of any defense against or claim to it on the part of any person and for value, unless it is established that the negotiation is not in the regular course of business or financing or involves receiving the document in settlement or payment of a money obligation.

(5) Indorsement of a non-negotiable document neither makes it negotiable nor adds to the transferee's rights.

(6) The naming in a negotiable bill of a person to be notified of the arrival of the goods does not limit the negotiability of the bill nor constitute notice to a purchaser thereof of any interest of such person in the goods.

§ 7—502. Rights Acquired by Due Negotiation.

(1) Subject to the following section and to the provisions of Section 7—205 on fungible goods, a holder to whom a negotiable document of title has been duly negotiated acquires thereby:

   (a) title to the document;

   (b) title to the goods;

   (c) all rights accruing under the law of agency or estoppel, including rights to goods delivered to the bailee after the document was issued; and

   (d) the direct obligation of the issuer to hold or deliver the goods according to the terms of the document free of any defense or claim by him except those arising under the terms of the document or under this Article. In the case of a delivery order the bailee's obligation accrues only upon acceptance and the obligation acquired by the holder is that the issuer and any indorser will procure the acceptance of the bailee.

(2) Subject to the following section, title and rights so acquired are not defeated by any stoppage of the goods represented by the document or by surrender of such goods by the bailee, and are not impaired even though the negotiation or any prior negotiation constituted a breach of duty or even though any person has been deprived of possession of the document by misrepresentation, fraud, accident, mistake, duress, loss, theft or conversion, or even though a previous sale or other transfer of the goods or document has been made to a third person.

§ 7—503. Document of Title to Goods Defeated in Certain Cases.

(1) A document of title confers no right in goods against a person who before issuance of the document had a legal interest or a perfected security interest in them and who neither

   (a) delivered or entrusted them or any document of title covering them to the bailor or his nominee with actual or apparent authority to ship, store or sell or with power to obtain delivery under this Article (Section 7—403) or with power of disposition under this Act (Sections 2—403 and 9—307) or other statute or rule of law; nor

   (b) acquiesced in the procurement by the bailor or his nominee of any document of title.

(2) Title to goods based upon an unaccepted delivery order is subject to the rights of anyone to whom a negotiable warehouse receipt or bill of lading covering the goods has been duly negotiated. Such a title may be defeated under the next section to the same extent as the rights of the issuer or a transferee from the issuer.

(3) Title to goods based upon a bill of lading issued to a freight forwarder is subject to the rights of anyone to whom a bill issued by the freight forwarder is duly negotiated; but delivery by the carrier in accordance with Part 4 of this Article pursuant to its own bill of lading discharges the carrier's obligation to deliver.

§ 7—504. Rights Acquired in the Absence of Due Negotiation; Effect of Diversion; Seller's Stoppage of Delivery.

(1) A transferee of a document, whether negotiable or non-negotiable, to whom the document has been delivered but not duly negotiated, acquires the title and rights which his transferor had or had actual authority to convey.

(2) In the case of a non-negotiable document, until but not after the bailee receives notification of the transfer, the rights of the transferee may be defeated

   (a) by those creditors of the transferor who could treat the sale as void under Section 2—402; or

   (b) by a buyer from the transferor in ordinary course of business if the bailee has delivered the goods to the buyer or received notification of his rights; or

   (c) as against the bailee by good faith dealings of the bailee with the transferor.

(3) A diversion or other change of shipping instructions by the consignor in a non-negotiable bill of lading which causes the bailee not to deliver to the consignee defeats the consignee's title to the goods if they have been delivered to a buyer in ordinary course of business and in any event defeats the consignee's rights against the bailee.

(4) Delivery pursuant to a non-negotiable document may be stopped by a seller under Section 2—705, and subject to the requirement of due notification there provided. A bailee honoring the seller's instructions is entitled to be indemnified by the seller against any resulting loss or expense.

§ 7—505. Indorser Not a Guarantor for Other Parties.

The indorsement of a document of title issued by a bailee does not make the indorser liable for any default by the bailee or by previous indorsers.

§ 7—506. Delivery Without Indorsement: Right to Compel Indorsement.

The transferee of a negotiable document of title has a specifically enforceable right to have his transferor supply any necessary indorsement but the transfer becomes a negotiation only as of the time the indorsement is supplied.

§ 7—507. Warranties on Negotiation or Transfer of Receipt or Bill.

Where a person negotiates or transfers a document of title for value otherwise than as a mere intermediary under the next following section, then unless otherwise agreed he warrants to his immediate purchaser only in addition to any warranty made in selling the goods

(a) that the document is genuine; and

(b) that he has no knowledge of any fact which would impair its validity or worth; and

(c) that his negotiation or transfer is rightful and fully effective with respect to the title to the document and the goods it represents.

§ 7—508. Warranties of Collecting Bank as to Documents.

A collecting bank or other intermediary known to be entrusted with documents on behalf of another or with collection of a draft or other claim against delivery of documents warrants by such delivery of the documents only its own good faith and authority. This rule applies even though the intermediary has purchased or made advances against the claim or draft to be collected.

§ 7—509. Receipt or Bill: When Adequate Compliance With Commercial Contract.

The question whether a document is adequate to fulfill the obligations of a contract for sale or the conditions of a credit is governed by the Articles on Sales (Article 2) and on Letters of Credit (Article 5).

Part 6 Warehouse Receipts and Bills of Lading: Miscellaneous Provisions

§ 7—601. Lost and Missing Documents.

(1) If a document has been lost, stolen or destroyed, a court may order delivery of the goods or issuance of a substitute document and the bailee may without liability to any person comply with such order. If the document was negotiable the claimant must post security approved by the court to indemnify any person who may suffer loss as a result of non-surrender of the document. If the document was not negotiable, such security may be required at the discretion of the court. The court may also in its discretion order payment of the bailee's reasonable costs and counsel fees.

(2) A bailee who without court order delivers goods to a person claiming under a missing negotiable document is liable to any person injured thereby, and if the delivery is not in good faith becomes liable for conversion. Delivery in good faith is not conversion if made in accordance with a filed classification or tariff or, where no classification or tariff is filed, if the claimant posts security with the bailee in an amount at least double the value of the goods at the time of posting to indemnify any person injured by the delivery who files a notice of claim within one year after the delivery.

§ 7—602. Attachment of Goods Covered by a Negotiable Document.

Except where the document was originally issued upon delivery of the goods by a person who had no power to dispose of them, no lien attaches by virtue of any judicial process to goods in the possession of a bailee for which a negotiable document of title is outstanding unless the document be first surrendered to the bailee or its negotiation enjoined, and the bailee shall not be compelled to deliver the goods pursuant to process until the document is surrendered to him or impounded by the court. One who purchases the document for value without notice of the process or injunction takes free of the lien imposed by judicial process.

§ 7—603. Conflicting Claims; Interpleader.

If more than one person claims title or possession of the goods, the bailee is excused from delivery until he has had a reasonable time to ascertain the validity of the adverse claims or to bring an action to compel all claimants to interplead and may compel such interpleader, either in defending an action for non-delivery of the goods, or by original action, whichever is appropriate.

Article 8
INVESTMENT SECURITIES

Part 1 Short Title and General Matters

§ 8—101. Short Title.

This Article shall be known and may be cited as Uniform Commercial Code—Investment Securities.

§ 8—102. Definitions and Index of Definitions.

(1) In this Article, unless the context otherwise requires:

(a) A "certificated security" is a share, participation, or other interest in property of or an enterprise of the issuer or an obligation of the issuer which is

(i) represented by an instrument issued in bearer or registered form;

(ii) of a type commonly dealt in on securities exchanges or markets or commonly recognized in any area in which it is issued or dealt in as a medium for investment; and

(iii) either one of a class or series or by its terms divisible into a class or series of shares, participations, interests, or obligations.

(b) An "uncertificated security" is a share, participation, or other interest in property or an enterprise of the issuer or an obligation of the issuer which is

(i) not represented by an instrument and the transfer of which is registered upon books maintained for that purpose by or on behalf of the issuer;

(ii) of a type commonly dealt in on securities exchanges or markets; and

(iii) either one of a class or series or by its terms divisible into a class or series of shares, participations, interests, or obligations.

(c) A "security" is either a certificated or an uncertificated security. If a security is certificated, the terms "security" and "certificated security" may mean either the intangible interest, the instrument representing that interest, or both, as the context requires. A writing that is a certificated security is governed by this Article and not by Article 3, even though it also meets the requirements of that Article. This Article does not apply to money. If a certificated security has been retained by or surrendered to the issuer or its transfer agent for reasons other than registration of transfer, other temporary purpose, payment, exchange, or acquisition by the issuer, that security shall be treated as an uncertificated security for purposes of this Article.

(d) A certificated security is in "registered form" if

(i) it specifies a person entitled to the security or the rights it represents; and

(ii) its transfer may be registered upon books maintained for that purpose by or on behalf of the issuer, or the security so states.

(e) A certificated security is in "bearer form" if it runs to bearer according to its terms and not by reason of any indorsement.

(2) A "subsequent purchaser" is a person who takes other than by original issue.

(3) A "clearing corporation" is a corporation registered as a "clearing agency" under the federal securities laws or a corporation:

(a) at least 90 percent of whose capital stock is held by or for one or more organizations, none of which, other than a national securities exchange or association, holds in excess of 20 percent of the capital stock of the corporation, and each of which is

(i) subject to supervision or regulation pursuant to the provisions of federal or state banking laws or state insurance laws,

(ii) a broker or dealer or investment company registered under the federal securities laws, or

(iii) a national securities exchange or association registered under the federal securities laws; and

(b) any remaining capital stock of which is held by individuals who have purchased it at or prior to the time of their taking office as directors of the corporation and who have purchased only so much of the capital stock as is necessary to permit them to qualify as directors.

(4) A "custodian bank" is a bank or trust company that is supervised and examined by state or federal authority having supervision over banks and is acting as custodian for a clearing corporation.

(5) Other definitions applying to this Article or to specified Parts thereof and the sections in which they appear are:

"Adverse claim". Section 8—302.
"Bona fide purchaser". Section 8—302.
"Broker". Section 8—303.
"Debtor". Section 9—105.
"Financial intermediary". Section 8—313.
"Guarantee of the signature". Section 8—402.
"Initial transaction statement". Section 8—408.
"Instruction". Section 8—308.
"Intermediary bank". Section 4—105.
"Issuer". Section 8—201.
"Overissue". Section 8—104.
"Secured Party". Section 9—105.
"Security Agreement". Section 9—105.

(6) In addition, Article 1 contains general definitions and principles of construction and interpretation applicable throughout this Article.

Amended in 1962, 1973 and 1977.

§ 8—103. Issuer's Lien.

A lien upon a security in favor of an issuer thereof is valid against a purchaser only if:

(a) the security is certificated and the right of the issuer to the lien is noted conspicuously thereon; or

(b) the security is uncertificated and a notation of the right of the issuer to the lien is contained in the initial transaction statement sent to the purchaser or, if his interest is transferred to him other than by registration of transfer, pledge, or release, the initial transaction statement sent to the registered owner or the registered pledgee.

Amended in 1977.

§ 8—104. **Effect of Overissue; "Overissue".**

(1) The provisions of this Article which validate a security or compel its issue or reissue do not apply to the extent that validation, issue, or reissue would result in overissue; but if:

(a) an identical security which does not constitute an overissue is reasonably available for purchase, the person entitled to issue or validation may compel the issuer to purchase the security for him and either to deliver a certificated security or to register the transfer of an uncertificated security to him, against surrender of any certificated security he holds; or

(b) a security is not so available for purchase, the person entitled to issue or validation may recover from the issuer the price he or the last purchaser for value paid for it with interest from the date of his demand.

(2) "Overissue" means the issue of securities in excess of the amount the issuer has corporate power to issue.

Amended in 1977.

§ 8—105. **Certificated Securities Negotiable; Statements and Instructions Not Negotiable; Presumptions.**

(1) Certificated securities governed by this Article are negotiable instruments.

(2) Statements (Section 8—408), notices, or the like, sent by the issuer of uncertificated securities and instructions (Section 8—308) are neither negotiable instruments nor certificated securities.

(3) In any action on a security:

(a) unless specifically denied in the pleadings, each signature on a certificated security, in a necessary indorsement, on an initial transaction statement, or on an instruction, is admitted;

(b) if the effectiveness of a signature is put in issue, the burden of establishing it is on the party claiming under the signature, but the signature is presumed to be genuine or authorized;

(c) if signatures on a certificated security are admitted or established, production of the security entitles a holder to recover on it unless the defendant establishes a defense or a defect going to the validity of the security;

(d) if signatures on an initial transaction statement are admitted or established, the facts stated in the statement are presumed to be true as of the time of its issuance; and

(e) after it is shown that a defense or defect exists, the plaintiff has the burden of establishing that he or some person under whom he claims is a person against whom the defense or defect is ineffective (Section 8—202).

Amended in 1977.

§ 8—106. **Applicability.**

The law (including the conflict of laws rules) of the jurisdiction of organization of the issuer governs the validity of a security, the effectiveness of registration by the issuer, and the rights and duties of the issuer with respect to:

(a) registration of transfer of a certificated security;

(b) registration of transfer, pledge, or release of an uncertificated security; and

(c) sending of statements of uncertificated securities.

Amended in 1977.

§ 8—107. **Securities Transferable; Action for Price.**

(1) Unless otherwise agreed and subject to any applicable law or regulation respecting short sales, a person obligated to transfer securities may transfer any certificated security of the specified issue in bearer form or registered in the name of the transferee, or indorsed to him or in blank, or he may transfer an equivalent uncertificated security to the transferee or a person designated by the transferee.

(2) If the buyer fails to pay the price as it comes due under a contract of sale, the seller may recover the price of:

(a) certificated securities accepted by the buyer;

(b) uncertificated securities that have been transferred to the buyer or a person designated by the buyer; and

(c) other securities if efforts at their resale would be unduly burdensome or if there is no readily available market for their resale.

Amended in 1977.

§ 8—108. **Registration of Pledge and Release of Uncertificated Securities.**

A security interest in an uncertificated security may be evidenced by the registration of pledge to the secured party or a person designated by him. There can be no more than one registered pledge of an uncertificated security at any time. The registered owner of an uncertificated security is the person in whose name the security is registered, even if the security is subject to a registered pledge. The rights of a registered pledgee of an uncertificated security under this Article are terminated by the registration of release.

Added in 1977.

Part 2 Issue—Issuer

§ 8—201. **"Issuer"**

(1) With respect to obligations on or defenses to a security, "issuer" includes a person who:

(a) places or authorizes the placing of his name on a certificated security (otherwise than as authenticating trustee, registrar, transfer agent, or the like) to evidence that it represents a share, participation, or other interest in his property or in an enterprise, or to evidence his duty to perform an obligation represented by the certificated security;

(b) creates shares, participations, or other interests in his property or in an enterprise or undertakes obligations, which shares, participations, interests, or obligations are uncertificated securities;

(c) directly or indirectly creates fractional interests in his rights or property, which fractional interests are represented by certificated securities; or

(d) becomes responsible for or in place of any other person described as an issuer in this section.

(2) With respect to obligations on or defenses to a security, a guarantor is an issuer to the extent of his guaranty, whether or not his obligation is noted on a certificated security or on statements of uncertificated securities sent pursuant to Section 8—408.

(3) With respect to registration of transfer, pledge, or release (Part 4 of this Article), "issuer" means a person on whose behalf transfer books are maintained.

Amended in 1977.

§ 8—202. Issuer's Responsibility and Defenses; Notice of Defect or Defense.

(1) Even against a purchaser for value and without notice, the terms of a security include:

(a) if the security is certificated, those stated on the security;

(b) if the security is uncertificated, those contained in the initial transaction statement sent to such purchaser or, if his interest is transferred to him other than by registration of transfer, pledge, or release, the initial transaction statement sent to the registered owner or registered pledgee; and

(c) those made part of the security by reference, on the certificated security or in the initial transaction statement, to another instrument, indenture, or document or to a constitution, statute, ordinance, rule, regulation, order or the like, to the extent that the terms referred to do not conflict with the terms stated on the certificated security or contained in the statement. A reference under this paragraph does not of itself charge a purchaser for value with notice of a defect going to the validity of the security, even though the certificated security or statement expressly states that a person accepting it admits notice.

(2) A certificated security in the hands of a purchaser for value or an uncertificated security as to which an initial transaction statement has been sent to a purchaser for value, other than a security issued by a government or governmental agency or unit, even though issued with a defect going to its validity, is valid with respect to the purchaser if he is without notice of the particular defect unless the defect involves a violation of constitutional provisions, in which case the security is valid with respect to a subsequent purchaser for value and without notice of the defect. This subsection applies to an issuer that is a government or governmental agency or unit only if either there has been substantial compliance with the legal requirements governing the issue or the issuer has received a substantial consideration for the issue as a whole or for the particular security and a stated purpose of the issue is one for which the issuer has power to borrow money or issue the security.

(3) Except as provided in the case of certain unauthorized signatures (Section 8—205), lack of genuineness of a certificated security or an initial transaction statement is a complete defense, even against a purchaser for value and without notice.

(4) All other defenses of the issuer of a certificated or uncertificated security, including nondelivery and conditional delivery of a certificated security, are ineffective against a purchaser for value who has taken without notice of the particular defense.

(5) Nothing in this section shall be construed to affect the right of a party to a "when, as and if issued" or a "when distributed" contract to cancel the contract in the event of a material change in the character of the security that is the subject of the contract or in the plan or arrangement pursuant to which the security is to be issued or distributed.

Amended in 1977.

§ 8—203. Staleness as Notice of Defects or Defenses.

(1) After an act or event creating a right to immediate performance of the principal obligation represented by a certificated security or that sets a date on or after which the security is to be presented or surrendered for redemption or exchange, a purchaser is charged with notice of any defect in its issue or defense of the issuer if:

(a) the act or event is one requiring the payment of money, the delivery of certificated securities, the registration of transfer of uncertificated securities, or any of these on presentation or surrender of the certificated security, the funds or securities are available on the date set for payment or exchange, and he takes the security more than one year after that date; and

(b) the act or event is not covered by paragraph (a) and he takes the security more than 2 years after the date set for surrender or presentation or the date on which performance became due.

(2) A call that has been revoked is not within subsection (1).

Amended in 1977.

§ 8—204. **Effect of Issuer's Restrictions on Transfer.**

A restriction on transfer of a security imposed by the issuer, even if otherwise lawful, is ineffective against any person without actual knowledge of it unless:

(a) the security is certificated and the restriction is noted conspicuously thereon; or

(b) the security is uncertificated and a notation of the restriction is contained in the initial transaction statement sent to the person or, if his interest is transferred to him other than by registration of transfer, pledge, or release, the initial transaction statement sent to the registered owner or the registered pledgee.

Amended in 1977.

§ 8—205. **Effect of Unauthorized Signature on Certificated Security or Initial Transaction Statement.**

An unauthorized signature placed on a certificated security prior to or in the course of issue or placed on an initial transaction statement is ineffective, but the signature is effective in favor of a purchaser for value of the certificated security or a purchaser for value of an uncertificated security to whom the initial transaction statement has been sent, if the purchaser is without notice of the lack of authority and the signing has been done by:

(a) an authenticating trustee, registrar, transfer agent, or other person entrusted by the issuer with the signing of the security, of similar securities, or of initial transaction statements or the immediate preparation for signing of any of them; or

(b) an employee of the issuer, or of any of the foregoing, entrusted with responsible handling of the security or initial transaction statement.

Amended in 1977.

§ 8—206. **Completion or Alteration of Certificated Security or Initial Transaction Statement.**

(1) If a certificated security contains the signatures necessary to its issue or transfer but is incomplete in any other respect:

(a) any person may complete it by filling in the blanks as authorized; and

(b) even though the blanks are incorrectly filled in, the security as completed is enforceable by a purchaser

who took it for value and without notice of the incorrectness.

(2) A complete certificated security that has been improperly altered, even though fraudulently, remains enforceable, but only according to its original terms.

(3) If an initial transaction statement contains the signatures necessary to its validity, but is incomplete in any other respect:

(a) any person may complete it by filling in the blanks as authorized; and

(b) even though the blanks are incorrectly filled in, the statement as completed is effective in favor of the person to whom it is sent if he purchased the security referred to therein for value and without notice of the incorrectness.

(4) A complete initial transaction statement that has been improperly altered, even though fraudulently, is effective in favor of a purchaser to whom it has been sent, but only according to its original terms.

Amended in 1977.

§ 8—207. **Rights and Duties of Issuer With Respect to Registered Owners and Registered Pledgees.**

(1) Prior to due presentment for registration of transfer of a certificated security in registered form, the issuer or indenture trustee may treat the registered owner as the person exclusively entitled to vote, to receive notifications, and otherwise to exercise all the rights and powers of an owner.

(2) Subject to the provisions of subsections (3), (4), and (6), the issuer or indenture trustee may treat the registered owner of an uncertificated security as the person exclusively entitled to vote, to receive notifications, and otherwise to exercise all the rights and powers of an owner.

(3) The registered owner of an uncertificated security that is subject to a registered pledge is not entitled to registration of transfer prior to the due presentment to the issuer of a release instruction. The exercise of conversion rights with respect to a convertible uncertificated security is a transfer within the meaning of this section.

(4) Upon due presentment of a transfer instruction from the registered pledgee of an uncertificated security, the issuer shall:

(a) register the transfer of the security to the new owner free of pledge, if the instruction specifies a new owner (who may be the registered pledgee) and does not specify a pledgee;

(b) register the transfer of the security to the new owner subject to the interest of the existing pledgee, if the instruction specifies a new owner and the existing pledgee; or

(c) register the release of the security from the existing pledge and register the pledge of the security to the other pledgee, if the instruction specifies the existing owner and another pledgee.

(5) Continuity of perfection of a security interest is not broken by registration of transfer under subsection (4)(b) or by registration of release and pledge under subsection (4)(c), if the security interest is assigned.

(6) If an uncertificated security is subject to a registered pledge:

(a) any uncertificated securities issued in exchange for or distributed with respect to the pledged security shall be registered subject to the pledge;

(b) any certificated securities issued in exchange for or distributed with respect to the pledged security shall be delivered to the registered pledgee; and

(c) any money paid in exchange for or in redemption of part or all of the security shall be paid to the registered pledgee.

(7) Nothing in this Article shall be construed to affect the liability of the registered owner of a security for calls, assessments, or the like.

Amended in 1977.

§ 8—208. Effect of Signature of Authenticating Trustee, Registrar, or Transfer Agent.

(1) A person placing his signature upon a certificated security or an initial transaction statement as authenticating trustee, registrar, transfer agent, or the like, warrants to a purchaser for value of the certificated security or a purchaser for value of an uncertificated security to whom the initial transaction statement has been sent, if the purchaser is without notice of the particular defect, that:

(a) the certificated security or initial transaction statement is genuine;

(b) his own participation in the issue or registration of the transfer, pledge, or release of the security is within his capacity and within the scope of the authority received by him from the issuer; and

(c) he has reasonable grounds to believe the security is in the form and within the amount the issuer is authorized to issue.

(2) Unless otherwise agreed, a person by so placing his signature does not assume responsibility for the validity of the security in other respects.

Amended in 1962 and 1977.

Part 3 Transfer

§ 8—301. Rights Acquired by Purchaser.

(1) Upon transfer of a security to a purchaser (Section 8—313), the purchaser acquires the rights in the security which his transferor had or had actual authority to convey unless the purchaser's rights are limited by Section 8—302(4).

(2) A transferee of a limited interest acquires rights only to the extent of the interest transferred. The creation or release of a security interest in a security is the transfer of a limited interest in that security.

Amended in 1977.

§ 8—302. "Bona Fide Purchaser"; "Adverse Claim"; Title Acquired by Bona Fide Purchaser.

(1) A "bona fide purchaser" is a purchaser for value in good faith and without notice of any adverse claim:

(a) who takes delivery of a certificated security in bearer form or in registered form, issued or indorsed to him or in blank;

(b) to whom the transfer, pledge, or release of an uncertificated security is registered on the books of the issuer; or

(c) to whom a security is transferred under the provisions of paragraph (c), (d)(i), or (g) of Section 8—313(1).

(2) "Adverse claim" includes a claim that a transfer was or would be wrongful or that a particular adverse person is the owner of or has an interest in the security.

(3) A bona fide purchaser in addition to acquiring the rights of a purchaser (Section 8—301) also acquires his interest in the security free of any adverse claim.

(4) Notwithstanding Section 8—301(1), the transferee of a particular certificated security who has been a party to any fraud or illegality affecting the security, or who as a prior holder of that certificated security had notice of an adverse claim, cannot improve his position by taking from a bona fide purchaser.

Amended in 1977.

§ 8—303. "Broker".

"Broker" means a person engaged for all or part of his time in the business of buying and selling securities, who in the transaction concerned acts for, buys a security from, or sells a security to, a customer. Nothing in this Article determines the capacity in which a person acts for purposes of any other statute or rule to which the person is subject.

§ 8—304. Notice to Purchaser of Adverse Claims.

(1) A purchaser (including a broker for the seller or buyer, but excluding an intermediary bank) of a certificated security is charged with notice of adverse claims if:

(a) the security, whether in bearer or registered form, has been indorsed "for collection" or "for surrender" or for some other purpose not involving transfer; or

(b) the security is in bearer form and has on it an unambiguous statement that it is the property of a person other than the transferor. The mere writing of a name on a security is not such a statement.

(2) A purchaser (including a broker for the seller or buyer, but excluding an intermediary bank) to whom the transfer, pledge, or release of an uncertificated security is registered is charged with notice of adverse claims as to which the issuer has a duty under Section 8—403(4) at the time of registration and which are noted in the initial transaction statement sent to the purchaser or, if his interest is transferred to him other than by registration of transfer, pledge, or release, the initial transaction statement sent to the registered owner or the registered pledgee.

(3) The fact that the purchaser (including a broker for the seller or buyer) of a certificated or uncertificated security has notice that the security is held for a third person or is registered in the name of or indorsed by a fiduciary does not create a duty of inquiry into the rightfulness of the transfer or constitute constructive notice of adverse claims. However, if the purchaser (excluding an intermediary bank) has knowledge that the proceeds are being used or that the transaction is for the individual benefit of the fiduciary or otherwise in breach of duty, the purchaser is charged with notice of adverse claims.

Amended in 1977.

§ 8—305. Staleness as Notice of Adverse Claims.

An act or event that creates a right to immediate performance of the principal obligation represented by a certificated security or sets a date on or after which a certificated security is to be presented or surrendered for redemption or exchange does not itself constitute any notice of adverse claims except in the case of a transfer:

(a) after one year from any date set for presentment or surrender for redemption or exchange; or

(b) after 6 months from any date set for payment of money against presentation or surrender of the security if funds are available for payment on that date.

Amended in 1977.

§ 8—306. Warranties on Presentment and Transfer of Certificated Securities; Warranties of Originators of Instructions.

(1) A person who presents a certificated security for registration of transfer or for payment or exchange warrants to the issuer that he is entitled to the registration, payment, or exchange. But, a purchaser for value and without notice of adverse claims who receives a new, reissued, or re-registered certificated security on registration of transfer or receives an initial transaction statement confirming the registration of transfer of an equivalent uncertificated security to him warrants only that he has no knowledge of any unauthorized signature (Section 8—311) in a necessary indorsement.

(2) A person by transferring a certificated security to a purchaser for value warrants only that:

(a) his transfer is effective and rightful;

(b) the security is genuine and has not been materially altered; and

(c) he knows of no fact which might impair the validity of the security.

(3) If a certificated security is delivered by an intermediary known to be entrusted with delivery of the security on behalf of another or with collection of a draft or other claim against delivery, the intermediary by delivery warrants only his own good faith and authority, even though he has purchased or made advances against the claim to be collected against the delivery.

(4) A pledgee or other holder for security who redelivers a certificated security received, or after payment and on order of the debtor delivers that security to a third person, makes only the warranties of an intermediary under subsection (3).

(5) A person who originates an instruction warrants to the issuer that:

(a) he is an appropriate person to originate the instruction; and

(b) at the time the instruction is presented to the issuer he will be entitled to the registration of transfer, pledge, or release.

(6) A person who originates an instruction warrants to any person specially guaranteeing his signature (subsection 8—312(3)) that:

(a) he is an appropriate person to originate the instruction; and

(b) at the time the instruction is presented to the issuer

(i) he will be entitled to the registration of transfer, pledge, or release; and

(ii) the transfer, pledge, or release requested in the instruction will be registered by the issuer free from all liens, security interests, restrictions, and claims other than those specified in the instruction.

(7) A person who originates an instruction warrants to a purchaser for value and to any person guaranteeing the instruction (Section 8—312(6)) that:

(a) he is an appropriate person to originate the instruction;

(b) the uncertificated security referred to therein is valid; and

(c) at the time the instruction is presented to the issuer

(i) the transferor will be entitled to the registration of transfer, pledge, or release;

(ii) the transfer, pledge, or release requested in the instruction will be registered by the issuer free from all liens, security interests, restrictions, and claims other than those specified in the instruction; and

(iii) the requested transfer, pledge, or release will be rightful.

(8) If a secured party is the registered pledgee or the registered owner of an uncertificated security, a person who originates an instruction of release or transfer to the debtor or, after payment and on order of the debtor, a transfer instruction to a third person, warrants to the debtor or the third person only that he is an appropriate person to originate the instruction and, at the time the instruction is presented to the issuer, the transferor will be entitled to the registration of release or transfer. If a transfer instruction to a third person who is a purchaser for value is originated on order of the debtor, the debtor makes to the purchaser the warranties of paragraphs (b), (c)(ii) and (c)(iii) of subsection (7).

(9) A person who transfers an uncertificated security to a purchaser for value and does not originate an instruction in connection with the transfer warrants only that:

(a) his transfer is effective and rightful; and

(b) the uncertificated security is valid.

(10) A broker gives to his customer and to the issuer and a purchaser the applicable warranties provided in this section and has the rights and privileges of a purchaser under this section. The warranties of and in favor of the broker, acting as an agent are in addition to applicable warranties given by and in favor of his customer.

Amended in 1962 and 1977.

§ 8—307. Effect of Delivery Without Indorsement; Right to Compel Indorsement.

If a certificated security in registered form has been delivered to a purchaser without a necessary indorsement

he may become a bona fide purchaser only as of the time the indorsement is supplied; but against the transferor, the transfer is complete upon delivery and the purchaser has a specifically enforceable right to have any necessary indorsement supplied.

Amended in 1977.

§ 8—308. Indorsements; Instructions.

(1) An indorsement of a certificated security in registered form is made when an appropriate person signs on it or on a separate document an assignment or transfer of the security or a power to assign or transfer it or his signature is written without more upon the back of the security.

(2) An indorsement may be in blank or special. An indorsement in blank includes an indorsement to bearer. A special indorsement specifies to whom the security is to be transferred, or who has power to transfer it. A holder may convert a blank indorsement into a special indorsement.

(3) An indorsement purporting to be only of part of a certificated security representing units intended by the issuer to be separately transferable is effective to the extent of the indorsement.

(4) An "instruction" is an order to the issuer of an uncertificated security requesting that the transfer, pledge, or release from pledge of the uncertificated security specified therein be registered.

(5) An instruction originated by an appropriate person is:

(a) a writing signed by an appropriate person; or

(b) a communication to the issuer in any form agreed upon in a writing signed by the issuer and an appropriate person.

If an instruction has been originated by an appropriate person but is incomplete in any other respect, any person may complete it as authorized and the issuer may rely on it as completed even though it has been completed incorrectly.

(6) "An appropriate person" in subsection (1) means the person specified by the certificated security or by special indorsement to be entitled to the security.

(7) "An appropriate person" in subsection (5) means:

(a) for an instruction to transfer or pledge an uncertificated security which is then not subject to a registered pledge, the registered owner; or

(b) for an instruction to transfer or release an uncertificated security which is then subject to a registered pledge, the registered pledgee.

(8) In addition to the persons designated in subsections (6) and (7), "an appropriate person" in subsections (1) and (5) includes:

(a) if the person designated is described as a fiduciary but is no longer serving in the described capacity, either that person or his successor;

(b) if the persons designated are described as more than one person as fiduciaries and one or more are no longer serving in the described capacity, the remaining fiduciary or fiduciaries, whether or not a successor has been appointed or qualified;

(c) if the person designated is an individual and is without capacity to act by virtue of death, incompetence, infancy, or otherwise, his executor, administrator, guardian, or like fiduciary;

(d) if the persons designated are described as more than one person as tenants by the entirety or with right of survivorship and by reason of death all cannot sign, the survivor or survivors;

(e) a person having power to sign under applicable law or controlling instrument; and

(f) to the extent that the person designated or any of the foregoing persons may act through an agent, his authorized agent.

(9) Unless otherwise agreed, the indorser of a certificated security by his indorsement or the originator of an instruction by his origination assumes no obligation that the security will be honored by the issuer but only the obligations provided in Section 8—306.

(10) Whether the person signing is appropriate is determined as of the date of signing and an indorsement made by or an instruction originated by him does not become unauthorized for the purposes of this Article by virtue of any subsequent change of circumstances.

(11) Failure of a fiduciary to comply with a controlling instrument or with the law of the state having jurisdiction of the fiduciary relationship, including any law requiring the fiduciary to obtain court approval of the transfer, pledge, or release, does not render his indorsement or an instruction originated by him unauthorized for the purposes of this Article.

Amended in 1962 and 1977.

§ 8—309. Effect of Indorsement Without Delivery.

An indorsement of a certificated security, whether special or in blank, does not constitute a transfer until delivery of the certificated security on which it appears or, if the indorsement is on a separate document, until delivery of both the document and the certificated security.

Amended in 1977.

§ 8—310. Indorsement of Certificated Security in Bearer Form.

An indorsement of a certificated security in bearer form may give notice of adverse claims (Section 8—304) but

does not otherwise affect any right to registration the holder possesses.

Amended in 1977.

§ 8—311. Effect of Unauthorized Indorsement or Instruction.

Unless the owner or pledgee has ratified an unauthorized indorsement or instruction or is otherwise precluded from asserting its ineffectiveness:

(a) he may assert its ineffectiveness against the issuer or any purchaser, other than a purchaser for value and without notice of adverse claims, who has in good faith received a new, reissued, or re-registered certificated security on registration of transfer or received an initial transaction statement confirming the registration of transfer, pledge, or release of an equivalent uncertificated security to him; and

(b) an issuer who registers the transfer of a certificated security upon the unauthorized indorsement or who registers the transfer, pledge, or release of an uncertificated security upon the unauthorized instruction is subject to liability for improper registration (Section 8—404).

Amended in 1977.

§ 8—312. Effect of Guaranteeing Signature, Indorsement or Instruction.

(1) Any person guaranteeing a signature of an indorser of a certificated security warrants that at the time of signing:

(a) the signature was genuine;

(b) the signer was an appropriate person to indorse (Section 8—308); and

(c) the signer had legal capacity to sign.

(2) Any person guaranteeing a signature of the originator of an instruction warrants that at the time of signing:

(a) the signature was genuine;

(b) the signer was an appropriate person to originate the instruction (Section 8—308) if the person specified in the instruction as the registered owner or registered pledgee of the uncertificated security was, in fact, the registered owner or registered pledgee of the security, as to which fact the signature guarantor makes no warranty;

(c) the signer had legal capacity to sign; and

(d) the taxpayer identification number, if any, appearing on the instruction as that of the registered owner or registered pledgee was the taxpayer identification number of the signer or of the owner or pledgee for whom the signer was acting.

(3) Any person specially guaranteeing the signature of the originator of an instruction makes not only the warranties

of a signature guarantor (subsection (2)) but also warrants that at the time the instruction is presented to the issuer:

(a) the person specified in the instruction as the registered owner or registered pledgee of the uncertificated security will be the registered owner or registered pledgee; and

(b) the transfer, pledge, or release of the uncertificated security requested in the instruction will be registered by the issuer free from all liens, security interests, restrictions, and claims other than those specified in the instruction.

(4) The guarantor under subsections (1) and (2) or the special guarantor under subsection (3) does not otherwise warrant the rightfulness of the particular transfer, pledge, or release.

(5) Any person guaranteeing an indorsement of a certificated security makes not only the warranties of a signature guarantor under subsection (1) but also warrants the rightfulness of the particular transfer in all respects.

(6) Any person guaranteeing an instruction requesting the transfer, pledge, or release of an uncertificated security makes not only the warranties of a special signature guarantor under subsection (3) but also warrants the rightfulness of the particular transfer, pledge, or release in all respects.

(7) No issuer may require a special guarantee of signature (subsection (3)), a guarantee of indorsement (subsection (5)), or a guarantee of instruction (subsection (6)) as a condition to registration of transfer, pledge, or release.

(8) The foregoing warranties are made to any person taking or dealing with the security in reliance on the guarantee, and the guarantor is liable to the person for any loss resulting from breach of the warranties.

Amended in 1977.

§ 8—313. When Transfer to Purchaser Occurs; Financial Intermediary as Bona Fide Purchaser; "Financial Intermediary".

(1) Transfer of a security or a limited interest (including a security interest) therein to a purchaser occurs only:

(a) at the time he or a person designated by him acquires possession of a certificated security;

(b) at the time the transfer, pledge, or release of an uncertificated security is registered to him or a person designated by him;

(c) at the time his financial intermediary acquires possession of a certificated security specially indorsed to or issued in the name of the purchaser;

(d) at the time a financial intermediary, not a clearing corporation, sends him confirmation of the purchase

and also by book entry or otherwise identifies as belonging to the purchaser

(i) a specific certificated security in the financial intermediary's possession;

(ii) a quantity of securities that constitute or are part of a fungible bulk of certificated securities in the financial intermediary's possession or of uncertificated securities registered in the name of the financial intermediary; or

(iii) a quantity of securities that constitute or are part of a fungible bulk of securities shown on the account of the financial intermediary on the books of another financial intermediary;

(e) with respect to an identified certificated security to be delivered while still in the possession of a third person, not a financial intermediary, at the time that person acknowledges that he holds for the purchaser;

(f) with respect to a specific uncertificated security the pledge or transfer of which has been registered to a third person, not a financial intermediary, at the time that person acknowledges that he holds for the purchaser;

(g) at the time appropriate entries to the account of the purchaser or a person designated by him on the books of a clearing corporation are made under Section 8—320;

(h) with respect to the transfer of a security interest where the debtor has signed a security agreement containing a description of the security, at the time a written notification, which, in the case of the creation of the security interest, is signed by the debtor (which may be a copy of the security agreement) or which, in the case of the release or assignment of the security interest created pursuant to this paragraph, is signed by the secured party, is received by

(i) a financial intermediary on whose books the interest of the transferor in the security appears;

(ii) a third person, not a financial intermediary, in possession of the security, if it is certificated;

(iii) a third person, not a financial intermediary, who is the registered owner of the security, if it is uncertificated and not subject to a registered pledge; or

(iv) a third person, not a financial intermediary, who is the registered pledgee of the security, if it is uncertificated and subject to a registered pledge;

(i) with respect to the transfer of a security interest where the transferor has signed a security agreement containing a description of the security, at the time new value is given by the secured party; or

(j) with respect to the transfer of a security interest where the secured party is a financial intermediary and the security has already been transferred to the financial intermediary under paragraphs (a), (b), (c), (d), or (g), at the time the transferor has signed a security agreement containing a description of the security and value is given by the secured party.

(2) The purchaser is the owner of a security held for him by a financial intermediary, but cannot be a bona fide purchaser of a security so held except in the circumstances specified in paragraphs (c), (d)(i), and (g) of subsection (1). If a security so held is part of a fungible bulk, as in the circumstances specified in paragraphs (d)(ii) and (d)(iii) of subsection (1), the purchaser is the owner of a proportionate property interest in the fungible bulk.

(3) Notice of an adverse claim received by the financial intermediary or by the purchaser after the financial intermediary takes delivery of a certificated security as a holder for value or after the transfer, pledge, or release of an uncertificated security has been registered free of the claim to a financial intermediary who has given value is not effective either as to the financial intermediary or as to the purchaser. However, as between the financial intermediary and the purchaser the purchaser may demand transfer of an equivalent security as to which no notice of adverse claim has been received.

(4) A "financial intermediary" is a bank, broker, clearing corporation, or other person (or the nominee of any of them) which in the ordinary course of its business maintains security accounts for its customers and is acting in that capacity. A financial intermediary may have a security interest in securities held in account for its customer.

Amended in 1962 and 1977.

§ 8—314. Duty to Transfer, When Completed

(1) Unless otherwise agreed, if a sale of a security is made on an exchange or otherwise through brokers:

(a) the selling customer fulfills his duty to transfer at the time he:

(i) places a certificated security in the possession of the selling broker or a person designated by the broker;

(ii) causes an uncertificated security to be registered in the name of the selling broker or a person designated by the broker;

(iii) if requested, causes an acknowledgment to be made to the selling broker that a certificated or uncertificated security is held for the broker; or

(iv) places in the possession of the selling broker or of a person designated by the broker a transfer instruction for an uncertificated security, provid-

ing the issuer does not refuse to register the requested transfer if the instruction is presented to the issuer for registration within 30 days thereafter; and

(b) the selling broker, including a correspondent broker acting for a selling customer, fulfills his duty to transfer at the time he:

(i) places a certificated security in the possession of the buying broker or a person designated by the buying broker;

(ii) causes an uncertificated security to be registered in the name of the buying broker or a person designated by the buying broker;

(iii) places in the possession of the buying broker or of a person designated by the buying broker a transfer instruction for an uncertificated security, providing the issuer does not refuse to register the requested transfer if the instruction is presented to the issuer for registration within 30 days thereafter; or

(iv) effects clearance of the sale in accordance with the rules of the exchange on which the transaction took place.

(2) Except as provided in this section or unless otherwise agreed, a transferor's duty to transfer a security under a contract of purchase is not fulfilled until he:

(a) places a certificated security in form to be negotiated by the purchaser in the possession of the purchaser or of a person designated by the purchaser;

(b) causes an uncertificated security to be registered in the name of the purchaser or a person designated by the purchaser; or

(c) if the purchaser requests, causes an acknowledgment to be made to the purchaser that a certificated or uncertificated security is held for the purchaser.

(3) Unless made on an exchange, a sale to a broker purchasing for his own account is within subsection (2) and not within subsection (1).

Amended in 1977.

§ 8—315. Action Against Transferee Based Upon Wrongful Transfer

(1) Any person against whom the transfer of a security is wrongful for any reason, including his incapacity, as against anyone except a bona fide purchaser, may:

(a) reclaim possession of the certificated security wrongfully transferred;

(b) obtain possession of any new certificated security representing all or part of the same rights;

(c) compel the origination of an instruction to transfer to him or a person designated by him an uncertificated security constituting all or part of the same rights; or

(d) have damages.

(2) If the transfer is wrongful because of an unauthorized indorsement of a certificated security, the owner may also reclaim or obtain possession of the security or a new certificated security, even from a bona fide purchaser, if the ineffectiveness of the purported indorsement can be asserted against him under the provisions of this Article on unauthorized indorsements (Section 8—311).

(3) The right to obtain or reclaim possession of a certificated security or to compel the origination of a transfer instruction may be specifically enforced and the transfer of a certificated or uncertificated security enjoined and a certificated security impounded pending the litigation.

Amended in 1977.

§ 8—316. Purchaser's Right to Requisites for Registration of Transfer, Pledge, or Release on Books

Unless otherwise agreed, the transferor of a certificated security or the transferor, pledgor, or pledgee of an uncertificated security on due demand must supply his purchaser with any proof of his authority to transfer, pledge, or release or with any other requisite necessary to obtain registration of the transfer, pledge, or release of the security; but if the transfer, pledge, or release is not for value, a transferor, pledgor, or pledgee need not do so unless the purchaser furnishes the necessary expenses. Failure within a reasonable time to comply with a demand made gives the purchaser the right to reject or rescind the transfer, pledge, or release.

Amended in 1977.

§ 8—317. Creditors' Rights

(1) Subject to the exceptions in subsections (3) and (4), no attachment or levy upon a certificated security or any share or other interest represented thereby which is outstanding is valid until the security is actually seized by the officer making the attachment or levy, but a certificated security which has been surrendered to the issuer may be reached by a creditor by legal process at the issuer's chief executive office in the United States.

(2) An uncertificated security registered in the name of the debtor may not be reached by a creditor except by legal process at the issuer's chief executive office in the United States.

(3) The interest of a debtor in a certificated security that is in the possession of a secured party not a financial intermediary or in an uncertificated security registered in the name of a secured party not a financial intermediary (or in the name of a nominee of the secured party) may

be reached by a creditor by legal process upon the secured party.

(4) The interest of a debtor in a certificated security that is in the possession of or registered in the name of a financial intermediary or in an uncertificated security registered in the name of a financial intermediary may be reached by a creditor by legal process upon the financial intermediary on whose books the interest of the debtor appears.

(5) Unless otherwise provided by law, a creditor's lien upon the interest of a debtor in a security obtained pursuant to subsection (3) or (4) is not a restraint on the transfer of the security, free of the lien, to a third party for new value; but in the event of a transfer, the lien applies to the proceeds of the transfer in the hands of the secured party or financial intermediary, subject to any claims having priority.

(6) A creditor whose debtor is the owner of a security is entitled to aid from courts of appropriate jurisdiction, by injunction or otherwise, in reaching the security or in satisfying the claim by means allowed at law or in equity in regard to property that cannot readily be reached by ordinary legal process.

Amended in 1977.

§ 8—318. No Conversion by Good Faith Conduct

An agent or bailee who in good faith (including observance of reasonable commercial standards if he is in the business of buying, selling, or otherwise dealing with securities) has received certificated securities and sold, pledged, or delivered them or has sold or caused the transfer or pledge of uncertificated securities over which he had control according to the instructions of his principal, is not liable for conversion or for participation in breach of fiduciary duty although the principal had no right so to deal with the securities.

Amended in 1977.

§ 8—319. Statute of Frauds

A contract for the sale of securities is not enforceable by way of action or defense unless:

(a) there is some writing signed by the party against whom enforcement is sought or by his authorized agent or broker, sufficient to indicate that a contract has been made for sale of a stated quantity of described securities at a defined or stated price;

(b) delivery of a certificated security or transfer instruction has been accepted, or transfer of an uncertificated security has been registered and the transferee has failed to send written objection to the issuer within 10 days after receipt of the initial transaction statement confirming the registration, or payment has been made, but the contract is enforceable under this provision only to the extent of the delivery, registration, or payment;

(c) within a reasonable time a writing in confirmation of the sale or purchase and sufficient against the sender under paragraph (a) has been received by the party against whom enforcement is sought and he has failed to send written objection to its contents within 10 days after its receipt; or

(d) the party against whom enforcement is sought admits in his pleading, testimony, or otherwise in court that a contract was made for the sale of a stated quantity of described securities at a defined or stated price.

Amended in 1977.

§ 8—320. Transfer or Pledge Within Central Depository System

(1) In addition to other methods, a transfer, pledge, or release of a security or any interest therein may be effected by the making of appropriate entries on the books of a clearing corporation reducing the account of the transferor, pledgor, or pledgee and increasing the account of the transferee, pledgee, or pledgor by the amount of the obligation or the number of shares or rights transferred, pledged, or released, if the security is shown on the account of a transferor, pledgor, or pledgee on the books of the clearing corporation; is subject to the control of the clearing corporation; and

(a) if certificated,

(i) is in the custody of the clearing corporation, another clearing corporation, a custodian bank, or a nominee of any of them; and

(ii) is in bearer form or indorsed in blank by an appropriate person or registered in the name of the clearing corporation, a custodian bank, or a nominee of any of them; or

(b) if uncertificated, is registered in the name of the clearing corporation, another clearing corporation, a custodian bank, or a nominee of any of them.

(2) Under this section entries may be made with respect to like securities or interests therein as a part of a fungible bulk and may refer merely to a quantity of a particular security without reference to the name of the registered owner, certificate or bond number, or the like, and, in appropriate cases, may be on a net basis taking into account other transfers, pledges, or releases of the same security.

(3) A transfer under this section is effective (Section 8—313) and the purchaser acquires the rights of the transferor (Section 8—301). A pledge or release under this section is the transfer of a limited interest. If a pledge or the creation of a security interest is intended, the security interest is perfected at the time when both value is given

by the pledgee and the appropriate entries are made (Section 8—321). A transferee or pledgee under this section may be a bona fide purchaser (Section 8—302).

(4) A transfer or pledge under this section is not a registration of transfer under Part 4.

(5) That entries made on the books of the clearing corporation as provided in subsection (1) are not appropriate does not affect the validity or effect of the entries or the liabilities or obligations of the clearing corporation to any person adversely affected thereby.

Added in 1962; amended in 1977.

§ 8—321. Enforceability, Attachment, Perfection and Termination of Security Interests

(1) A security interest in a security is enforceable and can attach only if it is transferred to the secured party or a person designated by him pursuant to a provision of Section 8—313(1).

(2) A security interest so transferred pursuant to agreement by a transferor who has rights in the security to a transferee who has given value is a perfected security interest, but a security interest that has been transferred solely under paragraph (i) of Section 8—313(1) becomes unperfected after 21 days unless, within that time, the requirements for transfer under any other provision of Section 8—313(1) are satisfied.

(3) A security interest in a security is subject to the provisions of Article 9, but:

(a) no filing is required to perfect the security interest; and

(b) no written security agreement signed by the debtor is necessary to make the security interest enforceable, except as provided in paragraph (h), (i), or (j) of Section 8—313(1). The secured party has the rights and duties provided under Section 9—207, to the extent they are applicable, whether or not the security is certificated, and, if certificated, whether or not it is in his possession.

(4) Unless otherwise agreed, a security interest in a security is terminated by transfer to the debtor or a person designated by him pursuant to a provision of Section 8—313(1). If a security is thus transferred, the security interest, if not terminated, becomes unperfected unless the security is certificated and is delivered to the debtor for the purpose of ultimate sale or exchange or presentation, collection, renewal, or registration of transfer. In that case, the security interest becomes unperfected after 21 days unless, within that time, the security (or securities for which it has been exchanged) is transferred to the secured party or a person designated by him pursuant to a provision of Section 8—313(1).

Added in 1977.

Part 4 Registration

§ 8—401. **Duty of Issuer to Register Transfer, Pledge, or Release**

(1) If a certificated security in registered form is presented to the issuer with a request to register transfer or an instruction is presented to the issuer with a request to register transfer, pledge, or release, the issuer shall register the transfer, pledge, or release as requested if:

> (a) the security is indorsed or the instruction was originated by the appropriate person or persons (Section 8—308);

> (b) reasonable assurance is given that those indorsements or instructions are genuine and effective (Section 8—402);

> (c) the issuer has no duty as to adverse claims or has discharged the duty (Section 8—403);

> (d) any applicable law relating to the collection of taxes has been complied with; and

> (e) the transfer, pledge, or release is in fact rightful or is to a bona fide purchaser.

(2) If an issuer is under a duty to register a transfer, pledge, or release of a security, the issuer is also liable to the person presenting a certificated security or an instruction for registration or his principal for loss resulting from any unreasonable delay in registration or from failure or refusal to register the transfer, pledge, or release.

Amended in 1977.

§ 8—402. **Assurance that Indorsements and Instructions Are Effective**

(1) The issuer may require the following assurance that each necessary indorsement of a certificated security or each instruction (Section 8—308) is genuine and effective:

> (a) in all cases, a guarantee of the signature (Section 8—312(1) or (2)) of the person indorsing a certificated security or originating an instruction including, in the case of an instruction, a warranty of the taxpayer identification number or, in the absence thereof, other reasonable assurance of identity;

> (b) if the indorsement is made or the instruction is originated by an agent, appropriate assurance of authority to sign;

> (c) if the indorsement is made or the instruction is originated by a fiduciary, appropriate evidence of appointment or incumbency;

> (d) if there is more than one fiduciary, reasonable assurance that all who are required to sign have done so; and

> (e) if the indorsement is made or the instruction is originated by a person not covered by any of the foregoing, assurance appropriate to the case corresponding as nearly as may be to the foregoing.

(2) A "guarantee of the signature" in subsection (1) means a guarantee signed by or on behalf of a person reasonably believed by the issuer to be responsible. The issuer may adopt standards with respect to responsibility if they are not manifestly unreasonable.

(3) "Appropriate evidence of appointment or incumbency" in subsection (1) means:

> (a) in the case of a fiduciary appointed or qualified by a court, a certificate issued by or under the direction or supervision of that court or an officer thereof and dated within 60 days before the date of presentation for transfer, pledge, or release; or

> (b) in any other case, a copy of a document showing the appointment or a certificate issued by or on behalf of a person reasonably believed by the issuer to be responsible or, in the absence of that document or certificate, other evidence reasonably deemed by the issuer to be appropriate. The issuer may adopt standards with respect to the evidence if they are not manifestly unreasonable. The issuer is not charged with notice of the contents of any document obtained pursuant to this paragraph (b) except to the extent that the contents relate directly to the appointment or incumbency.

(4) The issuer may elect to require reasonable assurance beyond that specified in this section, but if it does so and, for a purpose other than that specified in subsection (3)(b), both requires and obtains a copy of a will, trust, indenture, articles of co-partnership, by-laws, or other controlling instrument, it is charged with notice of all matters contained therein affecting the transfer, pledge, or release.

Amended in 1977.

§ 8—403. **Issuer's Duty as to Adverse Claims**

(1) An issuer to whom a certificated security is presented for registration shall inquire into adverse claims if:

> (a) a written notification of an adverse claim is received at a time and in a manner affording the issuer a reasonable opportunity to act on it prior to the issuance of a new, reissued, or re-registered certificated security, and the notification identifies the claimant, the registered owner, and the issue of which the security is a part, and provides an address for communications directed to the claimant; or

> (b) the issuer is charged with notice of an adverse claim from a controlling instrument it has elected to require under Section 8—402(4).

(2) The issuer may discharge any duty of inquiry by any reasonable means, including notifying an adverse claimant by registered or certified mail at the address furnished by him or, if there be no such address, at his residence or regular place of business that the certificated security has been presented for registration of transfer by a named person, and that the transfer will be registered unless within 30 days from the date of mailing the notification, either:

(a) an appropriate restraining order, injunction, or other process issues from a court of competent jurisdiction; or

(b) there is filed with the issuer an indemnity bond, sufficient in the issuer's judgment to protect the issuer and any transfer agent, registrar, or other agent of the issuer involved from any loss it or they may suffer by complying with the adverse claim.

(3) Unless an issuer is charged with notice of an adverse claim from a controlling instrument which it has elected to require under Section 8—402(4) or receives notification of an adverse claim under subsection (1), if a certificated security presented for registration is indorsed by the appropriate person or persons the issuer is under no duty to inquire into adverse claims. In particular:

(a) an issuer registering a certificated security in the name of a person who is a fiduciary or who is described as a fiduciary is not bound to inquire into the existence, extent, or correct description of the fiduciary relationship; and thereafter the issuer may assume without inquiry that the newly registered owner continues to be the fiduciary until the issuer receives written notice that the fiduciary is no longer acting as such with respect to the particular security;

(b) an issuer registering transfer on an indorsement by a fiduciary is not bound to inquire whether the transfer is made in compliance with a controlling instrument or with the law of the state having jurisdiction of the fiduciary relationship, including any law requiring the fiduciary to obtain court approval of the transfer; and

(c) the issuer is not charged with notice of the contents of any court record or file or other recorded or unrecorded document even though the document is in its possession and even though the transfer is made on the indorsement of a fiduciary to the fiduciary himself or to his nominee.

(4) An issuer is under no duty as to adverse claims with respect to an uncertificated security except:

(a) claims embodied in a restraining order, injunction, or other legal process served upon the issuer if the process was served at a time and in a manner affording the issuer a reasonable opportunity to act on

it in accordance with the requirements of subsection (5);

(b) claims of which the issuer has received a written notification from the registered owner or the registered pledgee if the notification was received at a time and in a manner affording the issuer a reasonable opportunity to act on it in accordance with the requirements of subsection (5);

(c) claims (including restrictions on transfer not imposed by the issuer) to which the registration of transfer to the present registered owner was subject and were so noted in the initial transaction statement sent to him; and

(d) claims as to which an issuer is charged with notice from a controlling instrument it has elected to require under Section 8—402(4).

(5) If the issuer of an uncertificated security is under a duty as to an adverse claim, he discharges that duty by:

(a) including a notation of the claim in any statements sent with respect to the security under Sections 8—408(3), (6), and (7); and

(b) refusing to register the transfer or pledge of the security unless the nature of the claim does not preclude transfer or pledge subject thereto.

(6) If the transfer or pledge of the security is registered subject to an adverse claim, a notation of the claim must be included in the initial transaction statement and all subsequent statements sent to the transferee and pledgee under Section 8—408.

(7) Notwithstanding subsections (4) and (5), if an uncertificated security was subject to a registered pledge at the time the issuer first came under a duty as to a particular adverse claim, the issuer has no duty as to that claim if transfer of the security is requested by the registered pledgee or an appropriate person acting for the registered pledgee unless:

(a) the claim was embodied in legal process which expressly provides otherwise;

(b) the claim was asserted in a written notification from the registered pledgee;

(c) the claim was one as to which the issuer was charged with notice from a controlling instrument it required under Section 8—402(4) in connection with the pledgee's request for transfer; or

(d) the transfer requested is to the registered owner.

Amended in 1977.

§ 8—404. Liability and Non-Liability for Registration

(1) Except as provided in any law relating to the collection of taxes, the issuer is not liable to the owner, pledgee, or

any other person suffering loss as a result of the registration of a transfer, pledge, or release of a security if:

(a) there were on or with a certificated security the necessary indorsements or the issuer had received an instruction originated by an appropriate person (Section 8—308); and

(b) the issuer had no duty as to adverse claims or has discharged the duty (Section 8—403).

(2) If an issuer has registered a transfer of a certificated security to a person not entitled to it, the issuer on demand shall deliver a like security to the true owner unless:

(a) the registration was pursuant to subsection (1);

(b) the owner is precluded from asserting any claim for registering the transfer under Section 8—405(1); or

(c) the delivery would result in overissue, in which case the issuer's liability is governed by Section 8—104.

(3) If an issuer has improperly registered a transfer, pledge, or release of an uncertificated security, the issuer on demand from the injured party shall restore the records as to the injured party to the condition that would have obtained if the improper registration had not been made unless:

(a) the registration was pursuant to subsection (1); or

(b) the registration would result in overissue, in which case the issuer's liability is governed by Section 8—104.

Amended in 1977.

§ 8—405. Lost, Destroyed, and Stolen Certificated Securities

(1) If a certificated security has been lost, apparently destroyed, or wrongfully taken, and the owner fails to notify the issuer of that fact within a reasonable time after he has notice of it and the issuer registers a transfer of the security before receiving notification, the owner is precluded from asserting against the issuer any claim for registering the transfer under Section 8—404 or any claim to a new security under this section.

(2) If the owner of a certificated security claims that the security has been lost, destroyed, or wrongfully taken, the issuer shall issue a new certificated security or, at the option of the issuer, an equivalent uncertificated security in place of the original security if the owner:

(a) so requests before the issuer has notice that the security has been acquired by a bona fide purchaser;

(b) files with the issuer a sufficient indemnity bond; and

(c) satisfies any other reasonable requirements imposed by the issuer.

(3) If, after the issue of a new certificated or uncertificated security, a bona fide purchaser of the original certificated security presents it for registration of transfer, the issuer shall register the transfer unless registration would result in overissue, in which event the issuer's liability is governed by Section 8—104. In addition to any rights on the indemnity bond, the issuer may recover the new certificated security from the person to whom it was issued or any person taking under him except a bona fide purchaser or may cancel the uncertificated security unless a bona fide purchaser or any person taking under a bona fide purchaser is then the registered owner or registered pledgee thereof.

Amended in 1977.

§ 8—406. Duty of Authenticating Trustee, Transfer Agent, or Registrar

(1) If a person acts as authenticating trustee, transfer agent, registrar, or other agent for an issuer in the registration of transfers of its certificated securities or in the registration of transfers, pledges, and releases of its uncertificated securities, in the issue of new securities, or in the cancellation of surrendered securities:

(a) he is under a duty to the issuer to exercise good faith and due diligence in performing his functions; and

(b) with regard to the particular functions he performs, he has the same obligation to the holder or owner of a certificated security or to the owner or pledgee of an uncertificated security and has the same rights and privileges as the issuer has in regard to those functions.

(2) Notice to an authenticating trustee, transfer agent, registrar or other agent is notice to the issuer with respect to the functions performed by the agent.

Amended in 1977.

§ 8—407. Exchangeability of Securities

(1) No issuer is subject to the requirements of this section unless it regularly maintains a system for issuing the class of securities involved under which both certificated and uncertificated securities are regularly issued to the category of owners, which includes the person in whose name the new security is to be registered.

(2) Upon surrender of a certificated security with all necessary indorsements and presentation of a written request by the person surrendering the security, the issuer, if he has no duty as to adverse claims or has discharged the duty (Section 8—403), shall issue to the person or a person designated by him an equivalent uncertificated security

subject to all liens, restrictions, and claims that were noted on the certificated security.

(3) Upon receipt of a transfer instruction originated by an appropriate person who so requests, the issuer of an uncertificated security shall cancel the uncertificated security and issue an equivalent certificated security on which must be noted conspicuously any liens and restrictions of the issuer and any adverse claims (as to which the issuer has a duty under Section 8—403(4)) to which the uncertificated security was subject. The certificated security shall be registered in the name of and delivered to:

(a) the registered owner, if the uncertificated security was not subject to a registered pledge; or

(b) the registered pledgee, if the uncertificated security was subject to a registered pledge.

Added in 1977.

§ 8—408. Statements of Uncertificated Securities

(1) Within 2 business days after the transfer of an uncertificated security has been registered, the issuer shall send to the new registered owner and, if the security has been transferred subject to a registered pledge, to the registered pledgee a written statement containing:

(a) a description of the issue of which the uncertificated security is a part;

(b) the number of shares or units transferred;

(c) the name and address and any taxpayer identification number of the new registered owner and, if the security has been transferred subject to a registered pledge, the name and address and any taxpayer identification number of the registered pledgee;

(d) a notation of any liens and restrictions of the issuer and any adverse claims (as to which the issuer has a duty under Section 8—403(4)) to which the uncertificated security is or may be subject at the time of registration or a statement that there are none of those liens, restrictions, or adverse claims; and

(e) the date the transfer was registered.

(2) Within 2 business days after the pledge of an uncertificated security has been registered, the issuer shall send to the registered owner and the registered pledgee a written statement containing:

(a) a description of the issue of which the uncertificated security is a part;

(b) the number of shares or units pledged;

(c) the name and address and any taxpayer identification number of the registered owner and the registered pledgee;

(d) a notation of any liens and restrictions of the issuer and any adverse claims (as to which the issuer has a duty under Section 8—403(4)) to which the uncertificated security is or may be subject at the time of registration or a statement that there are none of those liens, restrictions, or adverse claims; and

(e) the date the pledge was registered.

(3) Within 2 business days after the release from pledge of an uncertificated security has been registered, the issuer shall send to the registered owner and the pledgee whose interest was released a written statement containing:

(a) a description of the issue of which the uncertificated security is a part;

(b) the number of shares or units released from pledge;

(c) the name and address and any taxpayer identification number of the registered owner and the pledgee whose interest was released;

(d) a notation of any liens and restrictions of the issuer and any adverse claims (as to which the issuer has a duty under Section 8—403(4)) to which the uncertificated security is or may be subject at the time of registration or a statement that there are none of those liens, restrictions, or adverse claims; and

(e) the date the release was registered.

(4) An "initial transaction statement" is the statement sent to:

(a) the new registered owner and, if applicable, to the registered pledgee pursuant to subsection (1);

(b) the registered pledgee pursuant to subsection (2); or

(c) the registered owner pursuant to subsection (3).

Each initial transaction statement shall be signed by or on behalf of the issuer and must be identified as "Initial Transaction Statement".

(5) Within 2 business days after the transfer of an uncertificated security has been registered, the issuer shall send to the former registered owner and the former registered pledgee, if any, a written statement containing:

(a) a description of the issue of which the uncertificated security is a part;

(b) the number of shares or units transferred;

(c) the name and address and any taxpayer identification number of the former registered owner and of any former registered pledgee; and

(d) the date the transfer was registered.

(6) At periodic intervals no less frequent than annually and at any time upon the reasonable written request of

the registered owner, the issuer shall send to the registered owner of each uncertificated security a dated written statement containing:

(a) a description of the issue of which the uncertificated security is a part;

(b) the name and address and any taxpayer identification number of the registered owner;

(c) the number of shares or units of the uncertificated security registered in the name of the registered owner on the date of the statement;

(d) the name and address and any taxpayer identification number of any registered pledgee and the number of shares or units subject to the pledge; and

(e) a notation of any liens and restrictions of the issuer and any adverse claims (as to which the issuer has a duty under Section 8—403(4)) to which the uncertificated security is or may be subject or a statement that there are none of those liens, restrictions, or adverse claims.

(7) At periodic intervals no less frequent than annually and at any time upon the reasonable written request of the registered pledgee, the issuer shall send to the registered pledgee of each uncertificated security a dated written statement containing:

(a) a description of the issue of which the uncertificated security is a part;

(b) the name and address and any taxpayer identification number of the registered owner;

(c) the name and address and any taxpayer identification number of the registered pledgee;

(d) the number of shares or units subject to the pledge; and

(e) a notation of any liens and restrictions of the issuer and any adverse claims (as to which the issuer has a duty under Section 8—403(4)) to which the uncertificated security is or may be subject or a statement that there are none of those liens, restrictions, or adverse claims.

(8) If the issuer sends the statements described in subsections (6) and (7) at periodic intervals no less frequent than quarterly, the issuer is not obliged to send additional statements upon request unless the owner or pledgee requesting them pays to the issuer the reasonable cost of furnishing them.

(9) Each statement sent pursuant to this section must bear a conspicuous legend reading substantially as follows: "This statement is merely a record of the rights of the addressee as of the time of its issuance. Delivery of this statement, of itself, confers no rights on the recipient. This statement is neither a negotiable instrument nor a security."

Added in 1977.

Article 9
Secured Transactions; Sales of Accounts and Chattel Paper

Note: *The adoption of this Article should be accompanied by the repeal of existing statutes dealing with conditional sales, trust receipts, factor's liens where the factor is given a non-possessory lien, chattel mortgages, crop mortgages, mortgages on railroad equipment, assignment of accounts and generally statutes regulating security interests in personal property.*

Where the state has a retail installment selling act or small loan act, that legislation should be carefully examined to determine what changes in those acts are needed to conform them to this Article. This Article primarily sets out rules defining rights of a secured party against persons dealing with the debtor; it does not prescribe regulations and controls which may be necessary to curb abuses arising in the small loan business or in the financing of consumer purchases on credit. Accordingly there is no intention to repeal existing regulatory acts in those fields by enactment or re-enactment of Article 9. See Section 9—203(4) and the Note thereto.

Part 1 Short Title, Applicability and Definitions

§ 9—101. **Short Title.**

This Article shall be known and may be cited as Uniform Commercial Code—Secured Transactions.

§ 9—102. **Policy and Subject Matter of Article.**

(1) Except as otherwise provided in Section 9—104 on excluded transactions, this Article applies

(a) to any transaction (regardless of its form) which is intended to create a security interest in personal property or fixtures including goods, documents, instruments, general intangibles, chattel paper or accounts; and also

(b) to any sale of accounts or chattel paper.

(2) This Article applies to security interests created by contract including pledge, assignment, chattel mortgage, chattel trust, trust deed, factor's lien, equipment trust, conditional sale, trust receipt, other lien or title retention contract and lease or consignment intended as security. This Article does not apply to statutory liens except as provided in Section 9—310.

(3) The application of this Article to a security interest in a secured obligation is not affected by the fact that the obligation is itself secured by a transaction or interest to which this Article does not apply. Amended in 1972.

§ 9—103. Perfection of Security Interest in Multiple State Transactions

(1) Documents, instruments and ordinary goods.

(a) This subsection applies to documents and instruments and to goods other than those covered by a certificate of title described in subsection (2), mobile goods described in subsection (3), and minerals described in subsection (5).

(b) Except as otherwise provided in this subsection, perfection and the effect of perfection or non-perfection of a security interest in collateral are governed by the law of the jurisdiction where the collateral is when the last event occurs on which is based the assertion that the security interest is perfected or unperfected.

(c) If the parties to a transaction creating a purchase money security interest in goods in one jurisdiction understand at the time that the security interest attaches that the goods will be kept in another jurisdiction, then the law of the other jurisdiction governs the perfection and the effect of perfection or non-perfection of the security interest from the time it attaches until thirty days after the debtor receives possession of the goods and thereafter if the goods are taken to the other jurisdiction before the end of the thirty-day period.

(d) When collateral is brought into and kept in this state while subject to a security interest perfected under the law of the jurisdiction from which the collateral was removed, the security interest remains perfected, but if action is required by Part 3 of this Article to perfect the security interest,

(i) if the action is not taken before the expiration of the period of perfection in the other jurisdiction or the end of four months after the collateral is brought into this state, whichever period first expires, the security interest becomes unperfected at the end of that period and is thereafter deemed to have been unperfected as against a person who became a purchaser after removal;

(ii) if the action is taken before the expiration of the period specified in subparagraph (i), the security interest continues perfected thereafter;

(iii) for the purpose of priority over a buyer of consumer goods (subsection (2) of Section 9—307), the period of the effectiveness of a filing in the jurisdiction from which the collateral is removed is governed by the rules with respect to perfection in subparagraphs (i) and (ii).

(2) Certificate of title.

(a) This subsection applies to goods covered by a certificate of title issued under a statute of this state or of another jurisdiction under the law of which indication of a security interest on the certificate is required as a condition of perfection.

(b) Except as otherwise provided in this subsection, perfection and the effect of perfection or non-perfection of the security interest are governed by the law (including the conflict of laws rules) of the jurisdiction issuing the certificate until four months after the goods are removed from that jurisdiction and thereafter until the goods are registered in another jurisdiction, but in any event not beyond surrender of the certificate. After the expiration of that period, the goods are not covered by the certificate of title within the meaning of this section.

(c) Except with respect to the rights of a buyer described in the next paragraph, a security interest, perfected in another jurisdiction otherwise than by notation on a certificate of title, in goods brought into this state and thereafter covered by a certificate of title issued by this state is subject to the rules stated in paragraph (d) of subsection (1).

(d) If goods are brought into this state while a security interest therein is perfected in any manner under the law of the jurisdiction from which the goods are removed and a certificate of title is issued by this state and the certificate does not show that the goods are subject to the security interest or that they may be subject to security interests not shown on the certificate, the security interest is subordinate to the rights of a buyer of the goods who is not in the business of selling goods of that kind to the extent that he gives value and receives delivery of the goods after issuance of the certificate and without knowledge of the security interest.

(3) Accounts, general intangibles and mobile goods.

(a) This subsection applies to accounts (other than an account described in subsection (5) on minerals) and general intangibles (other than uncertificated securities) and to goods which are mobile and which are of a type normally used in more than one jurisdiction, such as motor vehicles, trailers, rolling stock, airplanes, shipping containers, road building and construction machinery and commercial harvesting machinery and the like, if the goods are equipment or are inventory leased or held for lease by the debtor to others, and are not covered by a certificate of title described in subsection (2).

(b) The law (including the conflict of laws rules) of the jurisdiction in which the debtor is located governs the perfection and the effect of perfection or non-perfection of the security interest.

(c) If, however, the debtor is located in a jurisdiction which is not a part of the United States, and which does not provide for perfection of the security interest by filing or recording in that jurisdiction, the law of the jurisdiction in the United States in which the debtor has its major executive office in the United States governs the perfection and the effect of perfection or non-perfection of the security interest through filing. In the alternative, if the debtor is located in a jurisdiction which is not a part of the United States or Canada and the collateral is accounts or general intangibles for money due or to become due, the security interest may be perfected by notification to the account debtor. As used in this paragraph, "United States" includes its territories and possessions and the Commonwealth of Puerto Rico.

(d) A debtor shall be deemed located at his place of business if he has one, at his chief executive office if he has more than one place of business, otherwise at his residence. If, however, the debtor is a foreign air carrier under the Federal Aviation Act of 1958, as amended, it shall be deemed located at the designated office of the agent upon whom service of process may be made on behalf of the foreign air carrier.

(e) A security interest perfected under the law of the jurisdiction of the location of the debtor is perfected until the expiration of four months after a change of the debtor's location to another jurisdiction, or until perfection would have ceased by the law of the first jurisdiction, whichever period first expires. Unless perfected in the new jurisdiction before the end of that period, it becomes unperfected thereafter and is deemed to have been unperfected as against a person who became a purchaser after the change.

(4) Chattel paper.

The rules stated for goods in subsection (1) apply to a possessory security interest in chattel paper. The rules stated for accounts in subsection (3) apply to a non-possessory security interest in chattel paper, but the security interest may not be perfected by notification to the account debtor.

(5) Minerals.

Perfection and the effect of perfection or non-perfection of a security interest which is created by a debtor who has an interest in minerals or the like (including oil and gas) before extraction and which attaches thereto as extracted, or which attaches to an account resulting from the sale thereof at the wellhead or minehead are governed by the law (including the conflict of laws rules) of the jurisdiction wherein the wellhead or minehead is located.

(6) Uncertificated securities.

The law (including the conflict of laws rules) of the jurisdiction of organization of the issuer governs the per-

fection and the effect of perfection or non-perfection of a security interest in uncertificated securities.

Amended in 1972 and 1977.

§ 9—104. **Transactions Excluded From Article.**

This Article does not apply

(a) to a security interest subject to any statute of the United States, to the extent that such statute governs the rights of parties to and third parties affected by transactions in particular types of property; or

(b) to a landlord's lien; or

(c) to a lien given by statute or other rule of law for services or materials except as provided in Section 9—310 on priority of such liens; or

(d) to a transfer of a claim for wages, salary or other compensation of an employee; or

(e) to a transfer by a government or governmental subdivision or agency; or

(f) to a sale of accounts or chattel paper as part of a sale of the business out of which they arose, or an assignment of accounts or chattel paper which is for the purpose of collection only, or a transfer of a right to payment under a contract to an assignee who is also to do the performance under the contract or a transfer of a single account to an assignee in whole or partial satisfaction of a preexisting indebtedness; or

(g) to a transfer of an interest in or claim in or under any policy of insurance, except as provided with respect to proceeds (Section 9—306) and priorities in proceeds (Section 9—312); or

(h) to a right represented by a judgment (other than a judgment taken on a right to payment which was collateral); or

(i) to any right of set-off; or

(j) except to the extent that provision is made for fixtures in Section 9—313, to the creation or transfer of an interest in or lien on real estate, including a lease or rents thereunder; or

(k) to a transfer in whole or in part of any claim arising out of tort; or

(l) to a transfer of an interest in any deposit account (subsection (1) of Section 9—105), except as provided with respect to proceeds (Section 9—306) and priorities in proceeds (Section 9—312).

Amended in 1972.

§ 9—105. **Definitions and Index of Definitions**

(1) In this Article unless the context otherwise requires:

(a) "Account debtor" means the person who is obligated on an account, chattel paper or general intangible;

(b) "Chattel paper" means a writing or writings which evidence both a monetary obligation and a security interest in or a lease of specific goods, but a charter or other contract involving the use or hire of a vessel is not chattel paper. When a transaction is evidenced both by such a security agreement or a lease and by an instrument or a series of instruments, the group of writings taken together constitutes chattel paper;

(c) "Collateral" means the property subject to a security interest, and includes accounts and chattel paper which have been sold;

(d) "Debtor" means the person who owes payment or other performance of the obligation secured, whether or not he owns or has rights in the collateral, and includes the seller of accounts or chattel paper. Where the debtor and the owner of the collateral are not the same person, the term "debtor" means the owner of the collateral in any provision of the Article dealing with the collateral, the obligor in any provision dealing with the obligation, and may include both where the context so requires;

(e) "Deposit account" means a demand, time, savings, passbook or like account maintained with a bank, savings and loan association, credit union or like organization, other than an account evidenced by a certificate of deposit;

(f) "Document" means document of title as defined in the general definitions of Article 1 (Section 1—201), and a receipt of the kind described in subsection (2) of Section 7—201;

(g) "Encumbrance" includes real estate mortgages and other liens on real estate and all other rights in real estate that are not ownership interests;

(h) "Goods" includes all things which are movable at the time the security interest attaches or which are fixtures (Section 9—313), but does not include money, documents, instruments, accounts, chattel paper, general intangibles, or minerals or the like (including oil and gas) before extraction. "Goods" also includes standing timber which is to be cut and removed under a conveyance or contract for sale, the unborn young of animals, and growing crops;

(i) "Instrument" means a negotiable instrument (defined in Section 3—104), or a certificated security (defined in Section 8—102) or any other writing which evidences a right to the payment of money and is not itself a security agreement or lease and is of a type which is in ordinary course of business transferred by delivery with any necessary indorsement or assignment;

(j) "Mortgage" means a consensual interest created by a real estate mortgage, a trust deed on real estate, or the like;

(k) An advance is made "pursuant to commitment" if the secured party has bound himself to make it, whether or not a subsequent event of default or other event not within his control has relieved or may relieve him from his obligation;

(l) "Security agreement" means an agreement which creates or provides for a security interest;

(m) "Secured party" means a lender, seller or other person in whose favor there is a security interest, including a person to whom accounts or chattel paper have been sold. When the holders of obligations issued under an indenture of trust, equipment trust agreement or the like are represented by a trustee or other person, the representative is the secured party;

(n) "Transmitting utility" means any person primarily engaged in the railroad, street railway or trolley bus business, the electric or electronics communications transmission business, the transmission of goods by pipeline, or the transmission or the production and transmission of electricity, steam, gas or water, or the provision of sewer service.

(2) Other definitions applying to this Article and the sections in which they appear are:
"Account". Section 9—106.
"Attach". Section 9—203.
"Construction mortgage". Section 9—313(1).
"Consumer goods". Section 9—109(1).
"Equipment". Section 9—109(2).
"Farm products". Section 9—109(3).
"Fixture". Section 9—313(1).
"Fixture filing". Section 9—313(1).
"General intangibles". Section 9—106.
"Inventory". Section 9—109(4).
"Lien creditor". Section 9—301(3).
"Proceeds". Section 9—306(1).
"Purchase money security interest". Section 9—107.
"United States". Section 9—103.

(3) The following definitions in other Articles apply to this Article:
"Check". Section 3—104.
"Contract for sale". Section 2—106.
"Holder in due course". Section 3—302.
"Note". Section 3—104.
"Sale". Section 2—106.

(4) In addition Article 1 contains general definitions and principles of construction and interpretation applicable throughout this Article.

Amended in 1966, 1972 and 1977.

§ 9—106. Definitions: "Account"; "General Intangibles".

"Account" means any right to payment for goods sold or leased or for services rendered which is not evidenced by an instrument or chattel paper, whether or not it has been earned by performance. "General intangibles" means any personal property (including things in action) other than goods, accounts, chattel paper, documents, instruments, and money. All rights to payment earned or unearned under a charter or other contract involving the use or hire of a vessel and all rights incident to the charter or contract are accounts.

§ 9—107. Definitions: "Purchase Money Security Interest".

A security interest is a "purchase money security interest" to the extent that it is

(a) taken or retained by the seller of the collateral to secure all or part of its price; or

(b) taken by a person who by making advances or incurring an obligation gives value to enable the debtor to acquire rights in or the use of collateral if such value is in fact so used.

§ 9—108. When After-Acquired Collateral Not Security for Antecedent Debt.

Where a secured party makes an advance, incurs an obligation, releases a perfected security interest, or otherwise gives new value which is to be secured in whole or in part by after-acquired property his security interest in the after-acquired collateral shall be deemed to be taken for new value and not as security for an antecedent debt if the debtor acquires his rights in such collateral either in the ordinary course of his business or under a contract of purchase made pursuant to the security agreement within a reasonable time after new value is given.

§ 9—109. Classification of Goods; "Consumer Goods"; "Equipment"; "Farm Products"; "Inventory".

Goods are

(1) "consumer goods" if they are used or bought for use primarily for personal, family or household purposes;

(2) "equipment" if they are used or bought for use primarily in business (including farming or a profession) or by a debtor who is a non-profit organization or a governmental subdivision or agency or if the goods are not included in the definitions of inventory, farm products or consumer goods;

(3) "farm products" if they are crops or livestock or supplies used or produced in farming operations or if they are products of crops or livestock in their unmanufactured states (such as ginned cotton, wool-clip, maple syrup, milk and eggs), and if they are in the possession of a debtor engaged in raising, fattening, grazing or other farming operations. If goods are farm products they are neither equipment nor inventory;

(4) "inventory" if they are held by a person who holds them for sale or lease or to be furnished under contracts of service or if he has so furnished them, or if they are raw materials, work in process or materials used or consumed in a business. Inventory of a person is not to be classified as his equipment.

§ 9—110. Sufficiency of Description.

For purposes of this Article any description of personal property or real estate is sufficient whether or not it is specific if it reasonably identifies what is described.

§ 9—111. Applicability of Bulk Transfer Laws.

The creation of a security interest is not a bulk transfer under Article 6 (see Section 6—103).

§ 9—112. Where Collateral Is Not Owned by Debtor.

Unless otherwise agreed, when a secured party knows that collateral is owned by a person who is not the debtor, the owner of the collateral is entitled to receive from the secured party any surplus under Section 9—502(2) or under Section 9—504(1), and is not liable for the debt or for any deficiency after resale, and he has the same right as the debtor

(a) to receive statements under Section 9—208;

(b) to receive notice of and to object to a secured party's proposal to retain the collateral in satisfaction of the indebtedness under Section 9—505;

(c) to redeem the collateral under Section 9—506;

(d) to obtain injunctive or other relief under Section 9—507(1); and

(e) to recover losses caused to him under Section 9—208(2).

§ 9—113. Security Interests Arising Under Article on Sales.

A security interest arising solely under the Article on Sales (Article 2) is subject to the provisions of this Article except that to the extent that and so long as the debtor does not have or does not lawfully obtain possession of the goods

(a) no security agreement is necessary to make the security interest enforceable; and

(b) no filing is required to perfect the security interest; and

(c) the rights of the secured party on default by the debtor are governed by the Article on Sales (Article 2).

§ 9—114. Consignment.

(1) A person who delivers goods under a consignment which is not a security interest and who would be required to file under this Article by paragraph (3)(c) of Section 2—326 has priority over a secured party who is or becomes a creditor of the consignee and who would have a perfected security interest in the goods if they were the property of the consignee, and also has priority with respect to identifiable cash proceeds received on or before delivery of the goods to a buyer, if

(a) the consignor complies with the filing provision of the Article on Sales with respect to consignments (paragraph (3)(c) of Section 2—326) before the consignee receives possession of the goods; and

(b) the consignor gives notification in writing to the holder of the security interest if the holder has filed a financing statement covering the same types of goods before the date of the filing made by the consignor; and

(c) the holder of the security interest receives the notification within five years before the consignee receives possession of the goods; and

(d) the notification states that the consignor expects to deliver goods on consignment to the consignee, describing the goods by item or type.

(2) In the case of a consignment which is not a security interest and in which the requirements of the preceding subsection have not been met, a person who delivers goods to another is subordinate to a person who would have a perfected security interest in the goods if they were the property of the debtor.

Part 2 Validity of Security Agreement and Rights of Parties Thereto

§ 9—201. General Validity of Security Agreement.

Except as otherwise provided by this Act a security agreement is effective according to its terms between the parties, against purchasers of the collateral and against creditors. Nothing in this Article validates any charge or practice illegal under any statute or regulation thereunder governing usury, small loans, retail installment sales, or the like, or extends the application of any such statute or regulation to any transaction not otherwise subject thereto.

§ 9—202. Title to Collateral Immaterial.

Each provision of this Article with regard to rights, obligations and remedies applies whether title to collateral is in the secured party or in the debtor.

§ 9—203. Attachment and Enforceability of Security Interest; Proceeds; Formal Requisites

(1) Subject to the provisions of Section 4—208 on the security interest of a collecting bank, Section 8—321 on security interests in securities and Section 9—113 on a security interest arising under the Article on Sales, a security interest is not enforceable against the debtor or third parties with respect to the collateral and does not attach unless:

(a) the collateral is in the possession of the secured party pursuant to agreement, or the debtor has signed a security agreement which contains a description of the collateral and in addition, when the security interest covers crops growing or to be grown or timber to be cut, a description of the land concerned;

(b) value has been given; and

(c) the debtor has rights in the collateral.

(2) A security interest attaches when it becomes enforceable against the debtor with respect to the collateral. Attachment occurs as soon as all of the events specified in subsection (1) have taken place unless explicit agreement postpones the time of attaching.

(3) Unless otherwise agreed a security agreement gives the secured party the rights to proceeds provided by Section 9—306.

(4) A transaction, although subject to this Article, is also subject to . . . .*, and in the case of conflict between the provisions of this Article and any such statute, the provisions of such statute control. Failure to comply with any applicable statute has only the effect which is specified therein.

Amended in 1972 and 1977.

Note: At * in subsection (4) insert reference to any local statute regulating small loans, retail installment sales and the like.

The foregoing subsection (4) is designed to make it clear that certain transactions, although subject to this Article, must also comply with other applicable legislation.

This Article is designed to regulate all the "security" aspects of transactions within its scope. There is, however, much regulatory legislation, particularly in the consumer field, which supplements this Article and should not be repealed by its enactment. Examples are small loan acts, retail installment selling acts and the like. Such acts may provide for licensing and rate regulation and may prescribe particular forms of contract. Such provisions should remain in force despite the enactment of this Article. On the other hand if a retail installment selling act contains provisions on filing, rights on default, etc., such provisions should be repealed as in-

consistent with this Article except that inconsistent provisions as to deficiencies, penalties, etc., in the Uniform Consumer Credit Code and other recent related legislation should remain because those statutes were drafted after the substantial enactment of the Article and with the intention of modifying certain provisions of this Article as to consumer credit.

§ 9—204. After-Acquired Property; Future Advances.

(1) Except as provided in subsection (2), a security agreement may provide that any or all obligations covered by the security agreement are to be secured by after-acquired collateral.

(2) No security interest attaches under an after-acquired property clause to consumer goods other than accessions (Section 9—314) when given as additional security unless the debtor acquires rights in them within ten days after the secured party gives value.

(3) Obligations covered by a security agreement may include future advances or other value whether or not the advances or value are given pursuant to commitment (subsection (1) of Section 9—105).

§ 9—205. Use or Disposition of Collateral Without Accounting Permissible.

A security interest is not invalid or fraudulent against creditors by reason of liberty in the debtor to use, commingle or dispose of all or part of the collateral (including returned or repossessed goods) or to collect or compromise accounts or chattel paper, or to accept the return of goods or make repossessions, or to use, commingle or dispose of proceeds, or by reason of the failure of the secured party to require the debtor to account for proceeds or replace collateral. This section does not relax the requirements of possession where perfection of a security interest depends upon possession of the collateral by the secured party or by a bailee.

§ 9—206. Agreement Not to Assert Defenses Against Assignee; Modification of Sales Warranties Where Security Agreement Exists.

(1) Subject to any statute or decision which establishes a different rule for buyers or lessees of consumer goods, an agreement by a buyer or lessee that he will not assert against an assignee any claim or defense which he may have against the seller or lessor is enforceable by an assignee who takes his assignment for value, in good faith and without notice of a claim or defense, except as to defenses of a type which may be asserted against a holder in due course of a negotiable instrument under the Article on Commercial Paper (Article 3). A buyer who as part of one transaction signs both a negotiable instrument and a security agreement makes such an agreement.

(2) When a seller retains a purchase money security interest in goods the Article on Sales (Article 2) governs the sale and any disclaimer, limitation or modification of the seller's warranties.

§ 9—207. Rights and Duties When Collateral is in Secured Party's Possession.

(1) A secured party must use reasonable care in the custody and preservation of collateral in his possession. In the case of an instrument or chattel paper reasonable care includes taking necessary steps to preserve rights against prior parties unless otherwise agreed.

(2) Unless otherwise agreed, when collateral is in the secured party's possession

(a) reasonable expenses (including the cost of any insurance and payment of taxes or other charges) incurred in the custody, preservation, use or operation of the collateral are chargeable to the debtor and are secured by the collateral;

(b) the risk of accidental loss or damage is on the debtor to the extent of any deficiency in any effective insurance coverage;

(c) the secured party may hold as additional security any increase or profits (except money) received from the collateral, but money so received, unless remitted to the debtor, shall be applied in reduction of the secured obligation;

(d) the secured party must keep the collateral identifiable but fungible collateral may be commingled;

(e) the secured party may repledge the collateral upon terms which do not impair the debtor's right to redeem it.

(3) A secured party is liable for any loss caused by his failure to meet any obligation imposed by the preceding subsections but does not lose his security interest.

(4) A secured party may use or operate the collateral for the purpose of preserving the collateral or its value or pursuant to the order of a court of appropriate jurisdiction or, except in the case of consumer goods, in the manner and to the extent provided in the security agreement.

§ 9—208. Request for Statement of Account or List of Collateral.

(1) A debtor may sign a statement indicating what he believes to be the aggregate amount of unpaid indebtedness as of a specified date and may send it to the secured party with a request that the statement be approved or corrected and returned to the debtor. When the security agreement or any other record kept by the secured party

identifies the collateral a debtor may similarly request the secured party to approve or correct a list of the collateral.

(2) The secured party must comply with such a request within two weeks after receipt by sending a written correction or approval. If the secured party claims a security interest in all of a particular type of collateral owned by the debtor he may indicate that fact in his reply and need not approve or correct an itemized list of such collateral. If the secured party without reasonable excuse fails to comply he is liable for any loss caused to the debtor thereby; and if the debtor has properly included in his request a good faith statement of the obligation or a list of the collateral or both the secured party may claim a security interest only as shown in the statement against persons misled by his failure to comply. If he no longer has an interest in the obligation or collateral at the time the request is received he must disclose the name and address of any successor in interest known to him and he is liable for any loss caused to the debtor as a result of failure to disclose. A successor in interest is not subject to this section until a request is received by him.

(3) A debtor is entitled to such a statement once every six months without charge. The secured party may require payment of a charge not exceeding $10 for each additional statement furnished.

Part 3 Rights of Third Parties; Perfected and Unperfected Security Interests; Rules of Priority

§ 9—301. Persons Who Take Priority Over Unperfected Security Interests; Rights of "Lien Creditor".

(1) Except as otherwise provided in subsection (2), an unperfected security interest is subordinate to the rights of

(a) persons entitled to priority under Section 9—312;

(b) a person who becomes a lien creditor before the security interest is perfected;

(c) in the case of goods, instruments, documents, and chattel paper, a person who is not a secured party and who is a transferee in bulk or other buyer not in ordinary course of business or is a buyer of farm products in ordinary course of business, to the extent that he gives value and receives delivery of the collateral without knowledge of the security interest and before it is perfected;

(d) in the case of accounts and general intangibles, a person who is not a secured party and who is a transferee to the extent that he gives value without knowledge of the security interest and before it is perfected.

(2) If the secured party files with respect to a purchase money security interest before or within ten days after the debtor receives possession of the collateral, he takes priority over the rights of a transferee in bulk or of a lien creditor which arise between the time the security interest attaches and the time of filing.

(3) A "lien creditor" means a creditor who has acquired a lien on the property involved by attachment, levy or the like and includes an assignee for benefit of creditors from the time of assignment, and a trustee in bankruptcy from the date of the filing of the petition or a receiver in equity from the time of appointment.

(4) A person who becomes a lien creditor while a security interest is perfected takes subject to the security interest only to the extent that it secures advances made before he becomes a lien creditor or within 45 days thereafter or made without knowledge of the lien or pursuant to a commitment entered into without knowledge of the lien.

§ 9—302. When Filing Is Required to Perfect Security Interest; Security Interests to Which Filing Provisions of This Article Do Not Apply

(1) A financing statement must be filed to perfect all security interests except the following:

(a) a security interest in collateral in possession of the secured party under Section 9—305;

(b) a security interest temporarily perfected in instruments or documents without delivery under Section 9—304 or in proceeds for a 10 day period under Section 9—306;

(c) a security interest created by an assignment of a beneficial interest in a trust or a decedent's estate;

(d) a purchase money security interest in consumer goods; but filing is required for a motor vehicle required to be registered; and fixture filing is required for priority over conflicting interests in fixtures to the extent provided in Section 9—313;

(e) an assignment of accounts which does not alone or in conjunction with other assignments to the same assignee transfer a significant part of the outstanding accounts of the assignor;

(f) a security interest of a collecting bank (Section 4—208) or in securities (Section 8—321) or arising under the Article on Sales (see Section 9—113) or covered in subsection (3) of this section;

(g) an assignment for the benefit of all the creditors of the transferor, and subsequent transfers by the assignee thereunder.

(2) If a secured party assigns a perfected security interest, no filing under this Article is required in order to continue

the perfected status of the security interest against creditors of and transferees from the original debtor.

(3) The filing of a financing statement otherwise required by this Article is not necessary or effective to perfect a security interest in property subject to

(a) a statute or treaty of the United States which provides for a national or international registration or a national or international certificate of title or which specifies a place of filing different from that specified in this Article for filing of the security interest; or

(b) the following statutes of this state; [list any certificate of title statute covering automobiles, trailers, mobile homes, boats, farm tractors, or the like, and any central filing statute.]; but during any period in which collateral is inventory held for sale by a person who is in the business of selling goods of that kind, the filing provisions of this Article (Part 4) apply to a security interest in that collateral created by him as debtor; or

(c) a certificate of title statute of another jurisdiction under the law of which indication of a security interest on the certificate is required as a condition of perfection (subsection (2) of Section 9—103).

(4) Compliance with a statute or treaty described in subsection (3) is equivalent to the filing of a financing statement under this Article, and a security interest in property subject to the statute or treaty can be perfected only by compliance therewith except as provided in Section 9—103 on multiple state transactions. Duration and renewal of perfection of a security interest perfected by compliance with the statute or treaty are governed by the provisions of the statute or treaty; in other respects the security interest is subject to this Article.

Amended in 1972 and 1977.

§ 9—303. When Security Interest Is Perfected; Continuity of Perfection.

(1) A security interest is perfected when it has attached and when all of the applicable steps required for perfection have been taken. Such steps are specified in Sections 9—302, 9—304, 9—305 and 9—306. If such steps are taken before the security interest attaches, it is perfected at the time when it attaches.

(2) If a security interest is originally perfected in any way permitted under this Article and is subsequently perfected in some other way under this Article, without an intermediate period when it was unperfected, the security interest shall be deemed to be perfected continuously for the purposes of this Article.

§ 9—304. Perfection of Security Interest in Instruments, Documents, and Goods Covered by Documents; Perfection by Permissive Filing; Temporary Perfection Without Filing or Transfer of Possession

(1) A security interest in chattel paper or negotiable documents may be perfected by filing. A security interest in money or instruments (other than certificated securities or instruments which constitute part of chattel paper) can be perfected only by the secured party's taking possession, except as provided in subsections (4) and (5) of this section and subsections (2) and (3) of Section 9—306 on proceeds.

(2) During the period that goods are in the possession of the issuer of a negotiable document therefor, a security interest in the goods is perfected by perfecting a security interest in the document, and any security interest in the goods otherwise perfected during such period is subject thereto.

(3) A security interest in goods in the possession of a bailee other than one who has issued a negotiable document therefor is perfected by issuance of a document in the name of the secured party or by the bailee's receipt of notification of the secured party's interest or by filing as to the goods.

(4) A security interest in instruments (other than certificated securities) or negotiable documents is perfected without filing or the taking of possession for a period of 21 days from the time it attaches to the extent that it arises for new value given under a written security agreement.

(5) A security interest remains perfected for a period of 21 days without filing where a secured party having a perfected security interest in an instrument (other than a certificated security), a negotiable document or goods in possession of a bailee other than one who has issued a negotiable document therefor

(a) makes available to the debtor the goods or documents representing the goods for the purpose of ultimate sale or exchange or for the purpose of loading, unloading, storing, shipping, transshipping, manufacturing, processing or otherwise dealing with them in a manner preliminary to their sale or exchange, but priority between conflicting security interests in the goods is subject to subsection (3) of Section 9—312; or

(b) delivers the instrument to the debtor for the purpose of ultimate sale or exchange or of presentation, collection, renewal or registration of transfer.

(6) After the 21 day period in subsections (4) and (5) perfection depends upon compliance with applicable provisions of this Article.

Amended in 1972 and 1977.

§ 9—305. **When Possession by Secured Party Perfects Security Interest Without Filing**

A security interest in letters of credit and advices of credit (subsection (2)(a) of Section 5—116), goods, instruments (other than certificated securities), money, negotiable documents, or chattel paper may be perfected by the secured party's taking possession of the collateral. If such collateral other than goods covered by a negotiable document is held by a bailee, the secured party is deemed to have possession from the time the bailee receives notification of the secured party's interest. A security interest is perfected by possession from the time possession is taken without a relation back and continues only so long as possession is retained, unless otherwise specified in this Article. The security interest may be otherwise perfected as provided in this Article before or after the period of possession by the secured party.

Amended in 1972 and 1977.

§ 9—306. **"Proceeds"; Secured Party's Rights on Disposition of Collateral.**

(1) "Proceeds" includes whatever is received upon the sale, exchange, collection or other disposition of collateral or proceeds. Insurance payable by reason of loss or damage to the collateral is proceeds, except to the extent that it is payable to a person other than a party to the security agreement. Money, checks, deposit accounts, and the like are "cash proceeds". All other proceeds are "non-cash proceeds".

(2) Except where this Article otherwise provides, a security interest continues in collateral notwithstanding sale, exchange or other disposition thereof unless the disposition was authorized by the secured party in the security agreement or otherwise, and also continues in any identifiable proceeds including collections received by the debtor.

(3) The security interest in proceeds is a continuously perfected security interest if the interest in the original collateral was perfected but it ceases to be a perfected security interest and becomes unperfected ten days after receipt of the proceeds by the debtor unless

    (a) a filed financing statement covers the original collateral and the proceeds are collateral in which a security interest may be perfected by filing in the office or offices where the financing statement has been filed and, if the proceeds are acquired with cash proceeds, the description of collateral in the financing statement indicates the types of property constituting the proceeds; or

    (b) a filed financing statement covers the original collateral and the proceeds are identifiable cash proceeds; or

    (c) the security interest in the proceeds is perfected before the expiration of the ten day period.

Except as provided in this section, a security interest in proceeds can be perfected only by the methods or under the circumstances permitted in this Article for original collateral of the same type.

(4) In the event of insolvency proceedings instituted by or against a debtor, a secured party with a perfected security interest in proceeds has a perfected security interest only in the following proceeds:

    (a) in identifiable non-cash proceeds and in separate deposit accounts containing only proceeds;

    (b) in identifiable cash proceeds in the form of money which is neither commingled with other money nor deposited in a deposit account prior to the insolvency proceedings;

    (c) in identifiable cash proceeds in the form of checks and the like which are not deposited in a deposit account prior to the insolvency proceedings; and

    (d) in all cash and deposit accounts of the debtor in which proceeds have been commingled with other funds, but the perfected security interest under this paragraph (d) is

        (i) subject to any right to set-off; and

        (ii) limited to an amount not greater than the amount of any cash proceeds received by the debtor within ten days before the institution of the insolvency proceedings less the sum of (I) the payments to the secured party on account of cash proceeds received by the debtor during such period and (II) the cash proceeds received by the debtor during such period to which the secured party is entitled under paragraphs (a) through (c) of this subsection (4).

(5) If a sale of goods results in an account or chattel paper which is transferred by the seller to a secured party, and if the goods are returned to or are repossessed by the seller or the secured party, the following rules determine priorities:

    (a) If the goods were collateral at the time of sale, for an indebtedness of the seller which is still unpaid, the original security interest attaches again to the goods and continues as a perfected security interest if it was perfected at the time when the goods were sold. If the security interest was originally perfected by a filing which is still effective, nothing further is required to continue the perfected status; in any other case, the secured party must take possession of the returned or repossessed goods or must file.

    (b) An unpaid transferee of the chattel paper has a security interest in the goods against the transferor.

Such security interest is prior to a security interest asserted under paragraph (a) to the extent that the transferee of the chattel paper was entitled to priority under Section 9—308.

(c) An unpaid transferee of the account has a security interest in the goods against the transferor. Such security interest is subordinate to a security interest asserted under paragraph (a).

(d) A security interest of an unpaid transferee asserted under paragraph (b) or (c) must be perfected for protection against creditors of the transferor and purchasers of the returned or repossessed goods.

§ 9—307. Protection of Buyers of Goods.

(1) A buyer in ordinary course of business (subsection (9) of Section 1—201) other than a person buying farm products from a person engaged in farming operations takes free of a security interest created by his seller even though the security interest is perfected and even though the buyer knows of its existence.

(2) In the case of consumer goods, a buyer takes free of a security interest even though perfected if he buys without knowledge of the security interest, for value and for his own personal, family or household purposes unless prior to the purchase the secured party has filed a financing statement covering such goods.

(3) A buyer other than a buyer in ordinary course of business (subsection (1) of this section) takes free of a security interest to the extent that it secures future advances made after the secured party acquires knowledge of the purchase, or more than 45 days after the purchase, whichever first occurs, unless made pursuant to a commitment entered into without knowledge of the purchase and before the expiration of the 45 day period.

§ 9—308. Purchase of Chattel Paper and Instruments.

A purchaser of chattel paper or an instrument who gives new value and takes possession of it in the ordinary course of his business has priority over a security interest in the chattel paper or instrument

    (a) which is perfected under Section 9—304 (permissive filing and temporary perfection) or under Section 9—306 (perfection as to proceeds) if he acts without knowledge that the specific paper or instrument is subject to a security interest; or

    (b) which is claimed merely as proceeds of inventory subject to a security interest (Section 9—306) even though he knows that the specific paper or instrument is subject to the security interest.

§ 9—309. Protection of Purchasers of Instruments, Documents and Securities

Nothing in this Article limits the rights of a holder in due course of a negotiable instrument (Section 3—302) or a holder to whom a negotiable document of title has been duly negotiated (Section 7—501) or a bona fide purchaser of a security (Section 8—302) and the holders or purchasers take priority over an earlier security interest even though perfected. Filing under this Article does not constitute notice of the security interest to such holders or purchasers.

Amended in 1977.

§ 9—310. Priority of Certain Liens Arising by Operation of Law.

When a person in the ordinary course of his business furnishes services or materials with respect to goods subject to a security interest, a lien upon goods in the possession of such person given by statute or rule of law for such materials or services takes priority over a perfected security interest unless the lien is statutory and the statute expressly provides otherwise.

§ 9—311. Alienability of Debtor's Rights: Judicial Process.

The debtor's rights in collateral may be voluntarily or involuntarily transferred (by way of sale, creation of a security interest, attachment, levy, garnishment or other judicial process) notwithstanding a provision in the security agreement prohibiting any transfer or making the transfer constitute a default.

§ 9—312. Priorities Among Conflicting Security Interests in the Same Collateral

(1) The rules of priority stated in other sections of this Part and in the following sections shall govern when applicable: Section 4—208 with respect to the security interests of collecting banks in items being collected, accompanying documents and proceeds; Section 9—103 on security interests related to other jurisdictions; Section 9—114 on consignments.

(2) A perfected security interest in crops for new value given to enable the debtor to produce the crops during the production season and given not more than three months before the crops become growing crops by planting or otherwise takes priority over an earlier perfected security interest to the extent that such earlier interest secures obligations due more than six months before the crops become growing crops by planting or otherwise, even though the person giving new value had knowledge of the earlier security interest.

(3) A perfected purchase money security interest in inventory has priority over a conflicting security interest in the same inventory and also has priority in identifiable

cash proceeds received on or before the delivery of the inventory to a buyer if

(a) the purchase money security interest is perfected at the time the debtor receives possession of the inventory; and

(b) the purchase money secured party gives notification in writing to the holder of the conflicting security interest if the holder had filed a financing statement covering the same types of inventory (i) before the date of the filing made by the purchase money secured party, or (ii) before the beginning of the 21 day period where the purchase money security interest is temporarily perfected without filing or possession (subsection (5) of Section 9—304); and

(c) the holder of the conflicting security interest receives the notification within five years before the debtor receives possession of the inventory; and

(d) the notification states that the person giving the notice has or expects to acquire a purchase money security interest in inventory of the debtor, describing such inventory by item or type.

(4) A purchase money security interest in collateral other than inventory has priority over a conflicting security interest in the same collateral or its proceeds if the purchase money security interest is perfected at the time the debtor receives possession of the collateral or within ten days thereafter.

(5) In all cases not governed by other rules stated in this section (including cases of purchase money security interests which do not qualify for the special priorities set forth in subsections (3) and (4) of this section), priority between conflicting security interests in the same collateral shall be determined according to the following rules:

(a) Conflicting security interests rank according to priority in time of filing or perfection. Priority dates from the time a filing is first made covering the collateral or the time the security interest is first perfected, whichever is earlier, provided that there is no period thereafter when there is neither filing nor perfection.

(b) So long as conflicting security interests are unperfected, the first to attach has priority.

(6) For the purposes of subsection (5) a date of filing or perfection as to collateral is also a date of filing or perfection as to proceeds.

(7) If future advances are made while a security interest is perfected by filing, the taking of possession, or under Section 8—321 on securities, the security interest has the same priority for the purposes of subsection (5) with respect to the future advances as it does with respect to the first advance. If a commitment is made before or while the security interest is so perfected, the security interest has the same priority with respect to advances made pursuant thereto. In other cases a perfected security interest has priority from the date the advance is made.

Amended in 1972 and 1977.

§ 9—313. Priority of Security Interests in Fixtures.

(1) In this section and in the provisions of Part 4 of this Article referring to fixture filing, unless the context otherwise requires

(a) goods are "fixtures" when they become so related to particular real estate that an interest in them arises under real estate law

(b) a "fixture filing" is the filing in the office where a mortgage on the real estate would be filed or recorded of a financing statement covering goods which are or are to become fixtures and conforming to the requirements of subsection (5) of Section 9—402

(c) a mortgage is a "construction mortgage" to the extent that it secures an obligation incurred for the construction of an improvement on land including the acquisition cost of the land, if the recorded writing so indicates.

(2) A security interest under this Article may be created in goods which are fixtures or may continue in goods which become fixtures, but no security interest exists under this Article in ordinary building materials incorporated into an improvement on land.

(3) This Article does not prevent creation of an encumbrance upon fixtures pursuant to real estate law.

(4) A perfected security interest in fixtures has priority over the conflicting interest of an encumbrancer or owner of the real estate where

(a) the security interest is a purchase money security interest, the interest of the encumbrancer or owner arises before the goods become fixtures, the security interest is perfected by a fixture filing before the goods become fixtures or within ten days thereafter, and the debtor has an interest of record in the real estate or is in possession of the real estate; or

(b) the security interest is perfected by a fixture filing before the interest of the encumbrancer or owner is of record, the security interest has priority over any conflicting interest of a predecessor in title of the encumbrancer or owner, and the debtor has an interest of record in the real estate or is in possession of the real estate; or

(c) the fixtures are readily removable factory or office machines or readily removable replacements of domestic appliances which are consumer goods, and before the goods become fixtures the security interest is perfected by any method permitted by this Article; or

(d) the conflicting interest is a lien on the real estate obtained by legal or equitable proceedings after the security interest was perfected by any method permitted by this Article.

(5) A security interest in fixtures, whether or not perfected, has priority over the conflicting interest of an encumbrancer or owner of the real estate where

(a) the encumbrancer or owner has consented in writing to the security interest or has disclaimed an interest in the goods as fixtures; or

(b) the debtor has a right to remove the goods as against the encumbrancer or owner. If the debtor's right terminates, the priority of the security interest continues for a reasonable time.

(6) Notwithstanding paragraph (a) of subsection (4) but otherwise subject to subsections (4) and (5), a security interest in fixtures is subordinate to a construction mortgage recorded before the goods become fixtures if the goods become fixtures before the completion of the construction. To the extent that it is given to refinance a construction mortgage, a mortgage has this priority to the same extent as the construction mortgage.

(7) In cases not within the preceding subsections, a security interest in fixtures is subordinate to the conflicting interest of an encumbrancer or owner of the related real estate who is not the debtor.

(8) When the secured party has priority over all owners and encumbrancers of the real estate, he may, on default, subject to the provisions of Part 5, remove his collateral from the real estate but he must reimburse any encumbrancer or owner of the real estate who is not the debtor and who has not otherwise agreed for the cost of repair of any physical injury, but not for any diminution in value of the real estate caused by the absence of the goods removed or by any necessity of replacing them. A person entitled to reimbursement may refuse permission to remove until the secured party gives adequate security for the performance of this obligation.

§ 9—314. Accessions.

(1) A security interest in goods which attaches before they are installed in or affixed to other goods takes priority as to the goods installed or affixed (called in this section "accessions") over the claims of all persons to the whole except as stated in subsection (3) and subject to Section 9—315(1).

(2) A security interest which attaches to goods after they become part of a whole is valid against all persons subsequently acquiring interests in the whole except as stated in subsection (3) but is invalid against any person with an interest in the whole at the time the security interest attaches to the goods who has not in writing consented to the security interest or disclaimed an interest in the goods as part of the whole.

(3) The security interests described in subsections (1) and (2) do not take priority over

(a) a subsequent purchaser for value of any interest in the whole; or

(b) a creditor with a lien on the whole subsequently obtained by judicial proceedings; or

(c) a creditor with a prior perfected security interest in the whole to the extent that he makes subsequent advances

if the subsequent purchase is made, the lien by judicial proceedings obtained or the subsequent advance under the prior perfected security interest is made or contracted for without knowledge of the security interest and before it is perfected. A purchaser of the whole at a foreclosure sale other than the holder of a perfected security interest purchasing at his own foreclosure sale is a subsequent purchaser within this section.

(4) When under subsections (1) or (2) and (3) a secured party has an interest in accessions which has priority over the claims of all persons who have interests in the whole, he may on default subject to the provisions of Part 5 remove his collateral from the whole but he must reimburse any encumbrancer or owner of the whole who is not the debtor and who has not otherwise agreed for the cost of repair of any physical injury but not for any diminution in value of the whole caused by the absence of the goods removed or by any necessity for replacing them. A person entitled to reimbursement may refuse permission to remove until the secured party gives adequate security for the performance of this obligation.

§ 9—315. Priority When Goods Are Commingled or Processed.

(1) If a security interest in goods was perfected and subsequently the goods or a part thereof have become part of a product or mass, the security interest continues in the product or mass if

(a) the goods are so manufactured, processed, assembled or commingled that their identity is lost in the product or mass; or

(b) a financing statement covering the original goods also covers the product into which the goods have been manufactured, processed or assembled.

In a case to which paragraph (b) applies, no separate security interest in that part of the original goods which has been manufactured, processed or assembled into the product may be claimed under Section 9—314.

(2) When under subsection (1) more than one security interest attaches to the product or mass, they rank equally according to the ratio that the cost of the goods to which each interest originally attached bears to the cost of the total product or mass.

§ 9—316. **Priority Subject to Subordination.**

Nothing in this Article prevents subordination by agreement by any person entitled to priority.

§ 9—317. **Secured Party Not Obligated on Contract of Debtor.**

The mere existence of a security interest or authority given to the debtor to dispose of or use collateral does not impose contract or tort liability upon the secured party for the debtor's acts or omissions.

§ 9—318. **Defenses Against Assignee; Modification of Contract After Notification of Assignment; Term Prohibiting Assignment Ineffective; Identification and Proof of Assignment.**

(1) Unless an account debtor has made an enforceable agreement not to assert defenses or claims arising out of a sale as provided in Section 9—206 the rights of an assignee are subject to

(a) all the terms of the contract between the account debtor and assignor and any defense or claim arising therefrom; and

(b) any other defense or claim of the account debtor against the assignor which accrues before the account debtor receives notification of the assignment.

(2) So far as the right to payment or a part thereof under an assigned contract has not been fully earned by performance, and notwithstanding notification of the assignment, any modification of or substitution for the contract made in good faith and in accordance with reasonable commercial standards is effective against an assignee unless the account debtor has otherwise agreed but the assignee acquires corresponding rights under the modified or substituted contract. The assignment may provide that such modification or substitution is a breach by the assignor.

(3) The account debtor is authorized to pay the assignor until the account debtor receives notification that the amount due or to become due has been assigned and that payment is to be made to the assignee. A notification which does not reasonably identify the rights assigned is ineffective. If requested by the account debtor, the assignee must seasonably furnish reasonable proof that the assignment has been made and unless he does so the account debtor may pay the assignor.

(4) A term in any contract between an account debtor and an assignor is ineffective if it prohibits assignment of

an account or prohibits creation of a security interest in a general intangible for money due or to become due or requires the account debtor's consent to such assignment or security interest.

Part 4 Filing

§ 9—401. **Place of Filing; Erroneous Filing; Removal of Collateral.**

First Alternative Subsection (1)

(1) The proper place to file in order to perfect a security interest is as follows:

(a) when the collateral is timber to be cut or is minerals or the like (including oil and gas) or accounts subject to subsection (5) of Section 9—103, or when the financing statement is filed as a fixture filing (Section 9—313) and the collateral is goods which are or are to become fixtures, then in the office where a mortgage on the real estate would be filed or recorded;

(b) in all other cases, in the office of the [Secretary of State].

Second Alternative Subsection (1)

(1) The proper place to file in order to perfect a security interest is as follows:

(a) when the collateral is equipment used in farming operations, or farm products, or accounts or general intangibles arising from or relating to the sale of farm products by a farmer, or consumer goods, then in the office of the . . . . in the county of the debtor's residence or if the debtor is not a resident of this state then in the office of the . . . . in the county where the goods are kept, and in addition when the collateral is crops growing or to be grown in the office of the . . . . in the county where the land is located;

(b) when the collateral is timber to be cut or is minerals or the like (including oil and gas) or accounts subject to subsection (5) of Section 9—103, or when the financing statement is filed as a fixture filing (Section 9—313) and the collateral is goods which are or are to become fixtures, then in the office where a mortgage on the real estate would be filed or recorded;

(c) in all other cases, in the office of the [Secretary of State].

Third Alternative Subsection (1)

(1) The proper place to file in order to perfect a security interest is as follows:

(a) when the collateral is equipment used in farming operations, or farm products, or accounts or general intangibles arising from or relating to the sale of farm products by a farmer, or consumer goods, then in the office of the . . . . in the county of the debtor's residence or if the debtor is not a resident of this state then in the office of the . . . . in the county where the goods are kept, and in addition when the collateral is crops growing or to be grown in the office of the . . . . in the county where the land is located;

(b) when the collateral is timber to be cut or is minerals or the like (including oil and gas) or accounts subject to subsection (5) of Section 9—103, or when the financing statement is filed as a fixture filing (Section 9—313) and the collateral is goods which are or are to become fixtures, then in the office where a mortgage on the real estate would be filed or recorded;

(c) in all other cases, in the office of the [Secretary of State] and in addition, if the debtor has a place of business in only one county of this state, also in the office of . . . . of such county, or, if the debtor has no place of business in this state, but resides in the state, also in the office of . . . . of the county in which he resides.

Note: *One of the three alternatives should be selected as subsection (1).*

(2) A filing which is made in good faith in an improper place or not in all of the places required by this section is nevertheless effective with regard to any collateral as to which the filing complied with the requirements of this Article and is also effective with regard to collateral covered by the financing statement against any person who has knowledge of the contents of such financing statement.

(3) A filing which is made in the proper place in this state continues effective even though the debtor's residence or place of business or the location of the collateral or its use, whichever controlled the original filing, is thereafter changed.

Alternative Subsection (3)

[(3) A filing which is made in the proper county continues effective for four months after a change to another county of the debtor's residence or place of business or the location of the collateral, whichever controlled the original filing. It becomes ineffective thereafter unless a copy of the financing statement signed by the secured party is filed in the new county within said period. The security interest may also be perfected in the new county after the expiration of the four-month period; in such case perfection dates from the time of perfection in the new county. A change in the use of the collateral does not impair the effectiveness of the original filing.]

(4) The rules stated in Section 9—103 determine whether filing is necessary in this state.

(5) Notwithstanding the preceding subsections, and subject to subsection (3) of Section 9—302, the proper place to file in order to perfect a security interest in collateral, including fixtures, of a transmitting utility is the office of the [Secretary of State]. This filing constitutes a fixture filing (Section 9—313) as to the collateral described therein which is or is to become fixtures.

(6) For the purposes of this section, the residence of an organization is its place of business if it has one or its chief executive office if it has more than one place of business.

Note: *Subsection (6) should be used only if the state chooses the Second or Third Alternative Subsection (1).*

§ 9—402. **Formal Requisites of Financing Statement; Amendments; Mortgage as Financing Statement.**

(1) A financing statement is sufficient if it gives the names of the debtor and the secured party, is signed by the debtor, gives an address of the secured party from which information concerning the security interest may be obtained, gives a mailing address of the debtor and contains a statement indicating the types, or describing the items, of collateral. A financing statement may be filed before a security agreement is made or a security interest otherwise attaches. When the financing statement covers crops growing or to be grown, the statement must also contain a description of the real estate concerned. When the financing statement covers timber to be cut or covers minerals or the like (including oil and gas) or accounts subject to subsection (5) of Section 9—103, or when the financing statement is filed as a fixture filing (Section 9—313) and the collateral is goods which are or are to become fixtures, the statement must also comply with subsection (5). A copy of the security agreement is sufficient as a financing statement if it contains the above information and is signed by the debtor. A carbon, photographic or other reproduction of a security agreement or a financing statement is sufficient as a financing statement if the security agreement so provides or if the original has been filed in this state.

(2) A financing statement which otherwise complies with subsection (1) is sufficient when it is signed by the secured party instead of the debtor if it is filed to perfect a security interest in

(a) collateral already subject to a security interest in another jurisdiction when it is brought into this state, or when the debtor's location is changed to this state. Such a financing statement must state that the collateral was brought into this state or that the debtor's location was changed to this state under such circumstances; or

(b) proceeds under Section 9—306 if the security interest in the original collateral was perfected. Such a financing statement must describe the original collateral; or

(c) collateral as to which the filing has lapsed; or

(d) collateral acquired after a change of name, identity or corporate structure of the debtor (subsection (7)).

(3) A form substantially as follows is sufficient to comply with subsection (1):

Name of debtor (or assignor) . . . .
Address . . . .
Name of secured party (or assignee) . . . .
Address . . . .
1. This financing statement covers the following types (or items) of property:
  (Describe) . . . .
2. (If collateral is crops) The above described crops are growing or are to be grown on:
  (Describe Real Estate) . . . .
3. (If applicable) The above goods are to become fixtures on *
*Where appropriate substitute either "The above timber is standing on . . . ." or "The above minerals or the like (including oil and gas) or accounts will be financed at the wellhead or minehead of the well or mine located on . . . ."
  (Describe Real Estate) . . . .
and this financing statement is to be filed [for record] in the real estate records. (If the debtor does not have an interest of record) The name of a record owner is

. . . .

4. (If products of collateral are claimed) Products of the collateral are also covered.
(use . . . .
whichever   Signature of Debtor (or Assignor)

is   . . . .
applicable)   Signature of Secured Party
    (or Assignee)

(4) A financing statement may be amended by filing a writing signed by both the debtor and the secured party. An amendment does not extend the period of effectiveness of a financing statement. If any amendment adds collateral, it is effective as to the added collateral only from the filing date of the amendment. In this Article, unless the context otherwise requires, the term "financing statement" means the original financing statement and any amendments.

(5) A financing statement covering timber to be cut or covering minerals or the like (including oil and gas) or accounts subject to subsection (5) of Section 9—103, or a financing statement filed as a future filing (Section 9—313) where the debtor is not a transmitting utility, must show that it covers this type of collateral, must recite that it is to be filed [for record] in the real estate records, and the financing statement must contain a description of the real estate [sufficient if it were contained in a mortgage of the real estate to give constructive notice of the mortgage under the law of this state]. If the debtor does not have an interest of record in the real estate, the financing statement must show the name of a record owner.

(6) A mortgage is effective as a financing statement filed as a fixture filing from the date of its recording if

(a) the goods are described in the mortgage by item or type; and

(b) the goods are or are to become fixtures related to the real estate described in the mortgage; and

(c) the mortgage complies with the requirements for a financing statement in this section other than a recital that it is to be filed in the real estate records; and

(d) the mortgage is duly recorded.

No fee with reference to the financing statement is required other than the regular recording and satisfaction fees with respect to the mortgage.

(7) A financing statement sufficiently shows the name of the debtor if it gives the individual, partnership or corporate name of the debtor, whether or not it adds other trade names or names of partners. Where the debtor so changes his name or in the case of an organization its name, identity or corporate structure that a filed financing statement becomes seriously misleading, the filing is not effective to perfect a security interest in collateral acquired by the debtor more than four months after the change, unless a new appropriate financing statement is filed before the expiration of that time. A filed financing statement remains effective with respect to collateral transferred by the debtor even though the secured party knows of or consents to the transfer.

(8) A financing statement substantially complying with the requirements of this section is effective even though it contains minor errors which are not seriously misleading.

Note: *Language in brackets is optional.*

Note: *Where the state has any special recording system for real estate other than the usual grantor-grantee index (as, for instance, a tract system or a title registration or Torrens system) local adaptations of subsection (5) and Section 9—403(7) may be necessary. See Mass.Gen.Laws Chapter 106, Section 9—409.*

§ 9—403. What Constitutes Filing; Duration of Filing; Effect of Lapsed Filing; Duties of Filing Officer.

(1) Presentation for filing of a financing statement and tender of the filing fee or acceptance of the statement by the filing officer constitutes filing under this Article.

(2) Except as provided in subsection (6) a filed financing statement is effective for a period of five years from the date of filing. The effectiveness of a filed financing statement lapses on the expiration of the five year period unless a continuation statement is filed prior to the lapse. If a security interest perfected by filing exists at the time insolvency proceedings are commenced by or against the debtor, the security interest remains perfected until termination of the insolvency proceedings and thereafter for a period of sixty days or until expiration of the five year period, whichever occurs later. Upon lapse the security interest becomes unperfected, unless it is perfected without filing. If the security interest becomes unperfected upon lapse, it is deemed to have been unperfected as against a person who became a purchaser or lien creditor before lapse.

(3) A continuation statement may be filed by the secured party within six months prior to the expiration of the five year period specified in subsection (2). Any such continuation statement must be signed by the secured party, identify the original statement by file number and state that the original statement is still effective. A continuation statement signed by a person other than the secured party of record must be accompanied by a separate written statement of assignment signed by the secured party of record and complying with subsection (2) of Section 9—405, including payment of the required fee. Upon timely filing of the continuation statement, the effectiveness of the original statement is continued for five years after the last date to which the filing was effective whereupon it lapses in the same manner as provided in subsection (2) unless another continuation statement is filed prior to such lapse. Succeeding continuation statements may be filed in the same manner to continue the effectiveness of the original statement. Unless a statute on disposition of public records provides otherwise, the filing officer may remove a lapsed statement from the files and destroy it immediately if he has retained a microfilm or other photographic record, or in other cases after one year after the lapse. The filing officer shall so arrange matters by physical annexation of financing statements to continuation statements or other related filings, or by other means, that if he physically destroys the financing statements of a period more than five years past, those which have been continued by a continuation statement or which are still effective under subsection (6) shall be retained.

(4) Except as provided in subsection (7) a filing officer shall mark each statement with a file number and with the date and hour of filing and shall hold the statement or a microfilm or other photographic copy thereof for public inspection. In addition the filing officer shall index the statement according to the name of the debtor and shall note in the index the file number and the address of the debtor given in the statement.

(5) The uniform fee for filing and indexing and for stamping a copy furnished by the secured party to show the date and place of filing for an original financing statement or for a continuation statement shall be $. . . . . if the statement is in the standard form prescribed by the [Secretary of State] and otherwise shall be $. . . . ., plus in each case, if the financing statement is subject to subsection (5) of Section 9—402, $. . . . . . . The uniform fee for each name more than one required to be indexed shall be $. . . . . The secured party may at his option show a trade name for any person and an extra uniform indexing fee of $. . . . . . . shall be paid with respect thereto.

(6) If the debtor is a transmitting utility (subsection (5) of Section 9—401) and a filed financing statement so states, it is effective until a termination statement is filed. A real estate mortgage which is effective as a fixture filing under subsection (6) of Section 9—402 remains effective as a fixture filing until the mortgage is released or satisfied of record or its effectiveness otherwise terminates as to the real estate.

(7) When a financing statement covers timber to be cut or covers minerals or the like (including oil and gas) or accounts subject to subsection (5) of Section 9—103, or is filed as a fixture filing, [it shall be filed for record and] the filing officer shall index it under the names of the debtor and any owner of record shown on the financing statement in the same fashion as if they were the mortgagors in a mortgage of the real estate described, and, to the extent that the law of this state provides for indexing of mortgages under the name of the mortgagee, under the name of the secured party as if he were the mortgagee thereunder, or where indexing is by description in the same fashion as if the financing statement were a mortgage of the real estate described.

Note: *In states in which writings will not appear in the real estate records and indices unless actually recorded the bracketed language in subsection (7) should be used.*

§ 9—404. Termination Statement.

(1) If a financing statement covering consumer goods is filed on or after . . . ., then within one month or within ten days following written demand by the debtor after there is no outstanding secured obligation and no

commitment to make advances, incur obligations or otherwise give value, the secured party must file with each filing officer with whom the financing statement was filed, a termination statement to the effect that he no longer claims a security interest under the financing statement, which shall be identified by file number. In other cases whenever there is no outstanding secured obligation and no commitment to make advances, incur obligations or otherwise give value, the secured party must on written demand by the debtor send the debtor, for each filing officer with whom the financing statement was filed, a termination statement to the effect that he no longer claims a security interest under the financing statement, which shall be identified by file number. A termination statement signed by a person other than the secured party of record must be accompanied by a separate written statement of assignment signed by the secured party of record complying with subsection (2) of Section 9—405, including payment of the required fee. If the affected secured party fails to file such a termination statement as required by this subsection, or to send such a termination statement within ten days after proper demand therefor, he shall be liable to the debtor for one hundred dollars, and in addition for any loss caused to the debtor by such failure.

(2) On presentation to the filing officer of such a termination statement he must note it in the index. If he has received the termination statement in duplicate, he shall return one copy of the termination statement to the secured party stamped to show the time of receipt thereof. If the filing officer has a microfilm or other photographic record of the financing statement, and of any related continuation statement, statement of assignment and statement of release, he may remove the originals from the files at any time after receipt of the termination statement, or if he has no such record, he may remove them from the files at any time after one year after receipt of the termination statement.

(3) If the termination statement is in the standard form prescribed by the [Secretary of State], the uniform fee for filing and indexing the termination statement shall be $. . . . ., and otherwise shall be $. . . . ., plus in each case an additional fee of $. . . . . . . for each name more than one against which the termination statement is required to be indexed.

Note: *The date to be inserted should be the effective date of the revised Article 9.*

§ 9—405. Assignment of Security Interest; Duties of Filing Officer; Fees.

(1) A financing statement may disclose an assignment of a security interest in the collateral described in the financing statement by indication in the financing statement of the name and address of the assignee or by an assignment itself or a copy thereof on the face or back of the statement. On presentation to the filing officer of such a financing statement the filing officer shall mark the same as provided in Section 9—403(4). The uniform fee for filing, indexing and furnishing filing data for a financing statement so indicating an assignment shall be $. . . . . . . if the statement is in the standard form prescribed by the [Secretary of State] and otherwise shall be $. . . . ., plus in each case an additional fee of $. . . . . . . for each name more than one against which the financing statement is required to be indexed.

(2) A secured party may assign of record all or part of his rights under a financing statement by the filing in the place where the original financing statement was filed of a separate written statement of assignment signed by the secured party of record and setting forth the name of the secured party of record and the debtor, the file number and the date of filing of the financing statement and the name and address of the assignee and containing a description of the collateral assigned. A copy of the assignment is sufficient as a separate statement if it complies with the preceding sentence. On presentation to the filing officer of such a separate statement, the filing officer shall mark such separate statement with the date and hour of the filing. He shall note the assignment on the index of the financing statement, or in the case of a fixture filing, or a filing covering timber to be cut, or covering minerals or the like (including oil and gas) or accounts subject to subsection (5) of Section 9—103, he shall index the assignment under the name of the assignor as grantor and, to the extent that the law of this state provides for indexing the assignment of a mortgage under the name of the assignee, he shall index the assignment of the financing statement under the name of the assignee. The uniform fee for filing, indexing and furnishing filing data about such a separate statement of assignment shall be $. . . . . . if the statement is in the standard form prescribed by the [Secretary of State] and otherwise shall be $. . . . . ., plus in each case an additional fee of $. . . . . . for each name more than one against which the statement of assignment is required to be indexed. Notwithstanding the provisions of this subsection, an assignment of record of a security interest in a fixture contained in a mortgage effective as a fixture filing (subsection (6) of Section 9—402) may be made only by an assignment of the mortgage in the manner provided by the law of this state other than this Act.

(3) After the disclosure or filing of an assignment under this section, the assignee is the secured party of record.

§ 9—406. Release of Collateral; Duties of Filing Officer; Fees.

A secured party of record may by his signed statement release all or a part of any collateral described in a filed financing statement. The statement of release is sufficient if it contains a description of the collateral being released, the name and address of the debtor, the name and address of the secured party, and the file number of the financing statement. A statement of release signed by a person other than the secured party of record must be accompanied by a separate written statement of assignment signed by the secured party of record and complying with subsection (2) of Section 9—405, including payment of the required fee. Upon presentation of such a statement of release to the filing officer he shall mark the statement with the hour and date of filing and shall note the same upon the margin of the index of the filing of the financing statement. The uniform fee for filing and noting such a statement of release shall be $...... if the statement is in the standard form prescribed by the [Secretary of State] and otherwise shall be $......, plus in each case an additional fee of $...... for each name more than one against which the statement of release is required to be indexed. Amended in 1972.

§ 9—407. Information From Filing Officer.

[(1) If the person filing any financing statement, termination statement, statement of assignment, or statement of release, furnishes the filing officer a copy thereof, the filing officer shall upon request note upon the copy the file number and date and hour of the filing of the original and deliver or send the copy to such person.]

[(2) Upon request of any person, the filing officer shall issue his certificate showing whether there is on file on the date and hour stated therein, any presently effective financing statement naming a particular debtor and any statement of assignment thereof and if there is, giving the date and hour of filing of each such statement and the names and addresses of each secured party therein. The uniform fee for such a certificate shall be $...... if the request for the certificate is in the standard form prescribed by the [Secretary of State] and otherwise shall be $....... Upon request the filing officer shall furnish a copy of any filed financing statement or statement of assignment for a uniform fee of $...... per page.]

Note: *This section is proposed as an optional provision to require filing officers to furnish certificates. Local law and practices should be consulted with regard to the advisability of adoption.*

§ 9—408. Financing Statements Covering Consigned or Leased Goods.

A consignor or lessor of goods may file a financing statement using the terms "consignor," "consignee," "lessor," "lessee" or the like instead of the terms specified in Section 9—402. The provisions of this Part shall apply as appropriate to such a financing statement but its filing shall not of itself be a factor in determining whether or not the consignment or lease is intended as security (Section 1—

201(37)). However, if it is determined for other reasons that the consignment or lease is so intended, a security interest of the consignor or lessor which attaches to the consigned or leased goods is perfected by such filing.

Part 5 Default

§ 9—501. Default; Procedure When Security Agreement Covers Both Real and Personal Property.

(1) When a debtor is in default under a security agreement, a secured party has the rights and remedies provided in this Part and except as limited by subsection (3) those provided in the security agreement. He may reduce his claim to judgment, foreclose or otherwise enforce the security interest by any available judicial procedure. If the collateral is documents the secured party may proceed either as to the documents or as to the goods covered thereby. A secured party in possession has the rights, remedies and duties provided in Section 9—207. The rights and remedies referred to in this subsection are cumulative.

(2) After default, the debtor has the rights and remedies provided in this Part, those provided in the security agreement and those provided in Section 9—207.

(3) To the extent that they give rights to the debtor and impose duties on the secured party, the rules stated in the subsections referred to below may not be waived or varied except as provided with respect to compulsory disposition of collateral (subsection (3) of Section 9—504 and Section 9—505) and with respect to redemption of collateral (Section 9—506) but the parties may by agreement determine the standards by which the fulfillment of these rights and duties is to be measured if such standards are not manifestly unreasonable:

(a) subsection (2) of Section 9—502 and subsection (2) of Section 9—504 insofar as they require accounting for surplus proceeds of collateral;

(b) subsection (3) of Section 9—504 and subsection (1) of Section 9—505 which deal with disposition of collateral;

(c) subsection (2) of Section 9—505 which deals with acceptance of collateral as discharge of obligation;

(d) Section 9—506 which deals with redemption of collateral; and

(e) subsection (1) of Section 9—507 which deals with the secured party's liability for failure to comply with this Part.

(4) If the security agreement covers both real and personal property, the secured party may proceed under this Part as to the personal property or he may proceed as to both the real and the personal property in accordance with his

rights and remedies in respect of the real property in which case the provisions of this Part do not apply.

(5) When a secured party has reduced his claim to judgment the lien of any levy which may be made upon his collateral by virture of any execution based upon the judgment shall relate back to the date of the perfection of the security interest in such collateral. A judicial sale, pursuant to such execution, is a foreclosure of the security interest by judicial procedure within the meaning of this section, and the secured party may purchase at the sale and thereafter hold the collateral free of any other requirements of this Article.

§ 9—502. Collection Rights of Secured Party.

(1) When so agreed and in any event on default the secured party is entitled to notify an account debtor or the obligor on an instrument to make payment to him whether or not the assignor was theretofore making collections on the collateral, and also to take control of any proceeds to which he is entitled under Section 9—306.

(2) A secured party who by agreement is entitled to charge back uncollected collateral or otherwise to full or limited recourse against the debtor and who undertakes to collect from the account debtors or obligors must proceed in a commercially reasonable manner and may deduct his reasonable expenses of realization from the collections. If the security agreement secures an indebtedness, the secured party must account to the debtor for any surplus, and unless otherwise agreed, the debtor is liable for any deficiency. But, if the underlying transaction was a sale of accounts or chattel paper, the debtor is entitled to any surplus or is liable for any deficiency only if the security agreement so provides.

§ 9—503. Secured Party's Right to Take Possession After Default.

Unless otherwise agreed a secured party has on default the right to take possession of the collateral. In taking possession a secured party may proceed without judicial process if this can be done without breach of the peace or may proceed by action. If the security agreement so provides the secured party may require the debtor to assemble the collateral and make it available to the secured party at a place to be designated by the secured party which is reasonably convenient to both parties. Without removal a secured party may render equipment unusable, and may dispose of collateral on the debtor's premises under Section 9—504.

§ 9—504. Secured Party's Right to Dispose of Collateral After Default; Effect of Disposition.

(1) A secured party after default may sell, lease or otherwise dispose of any or all of the collateral in its then condition or following any commercially reasonable preparation or processing. Any sale of goods is subject to the Article on Sales (Article 2). The proceeds of disposition shall be applied in the order following to

(a) the reasonable expenses of retaking, holding, preparing for sale or lease, selling, leasing and the like and, to the extent provided for in the agreement and not prohibited by law, the reasonable attorneys' fees and legal expenses incurred by the secured party;

(b) the satisfaction of indebtedness secured by the security interest under which the disposition is made;

(c) the satisfaction of indebtedness secured by any subordinate security interest in the collateral if written notification of demand therefor is received before distribution of the proceeds is completed. If requested by the secured party, the holder of a subordinate security interest must seasonably furnish reasonable proof of his interest, and unless he does so, the secured party need not comply with his demand.

(2) If the security interest secures an indebtedness, the secured party must account to the debtor for any surplus, and, unless otherwise agreed, the debtor is liable for any deficiency. But if the underlying transaction was a sale of accounts or chattel paper, the debtor is entitled to any surplus or is liable for any deficiency only if the security agreement so provides.

(3) Disposition of the collateral may be by public or private proceedings and may be made by way of one or more contracts. Sale or other disposition may be as a unit or in parcels and at any time and place and on any terms but every aspect of the disposition including the method, manner, time, place and terms must be commercially reasonable. Unless collateral is perishable or threatens to decline speedily in value or is of a type customarily sold on a recognized market, reasonable notification of the time and place of any public sale or reasonable notification of the time after which any private sale or other intended disposition is to be made shall be sent by the secured party to the debtor, if he has not signed after default a statement renouncing or modifying his right to notification of sale. In the case of consumer goods no other notification need be sent. In other cases notification shall be sent to any other secured party from whom the secured party has received (before sending his notification to the debtor or before the debtor's renunciation of his rights) written notice of a claim of an interest in the collateral. The secured party may buy at any public sale and if the collateral is of a type customarily sold in a recognized market or is of a type which is the subject of widely distributed standard price quotations he may buy at private sale.

(4) When collateral is disposed of by a secured party after default, the disposition transfers to a purchaser for value

all of the debtor's rights therein, discharges the security interest under which it is made and any security interest or lien subordinate thereto. The purchaser takes free of all such rights and interests even though the secured party fails to comply with the requirements of this Part or of any judicial proceedings

(a) in the case of a public sale, if the purchaser has no knowledge of any defects in the sale and if he does not buy in collusion with the secured party, other bidders or the person conducting the sale; or

(b) in any other case, if the purchaser acts in good faith.

(5) A person who is liable to a secured party under a guaranty, indorsement, repurchase agreement or the like and who receives a transfer of collateral from the secured party or is subrogated to his rights has thereafter the rights and duties of the secured party. Such a transfer of collateral is not a sale or disposition of the collateral under this Article.

§ 9—505. Compulsory Disposition of Collateral; Acceptance of the Collateral as Discharge of Obligation.

(1) If the debtor has paid sixty per cent of the cash price in the case of a purchase money security interest in consumer goods or sixty per cent of the loan in the case of another security interest in consumer goods, and has not signed after default a statement renouncing or modifying his rights under this Part a secured party who has taken possession of collateral must dispose of it under Section 9—504 and if he fails to do so within ninety days after he takes possession the debtor at his option may recover in conversion or under Section 9—507(1) on secured party's liability.

(2) In any other case involving consumer goods or any other collateral a secured party in possession may, after default, propose to retain the collateral in satisfaction of the obligation. Written notice of such proposal shall be sent to the debtor if he has not signed after default a statement renouncing or modifying his rights under this subsection. In the case of consumer goods no other notice need be given. In other cases notice shall be sent to any other secured party from whom the secured party has received (before sending his notice to the debtor or before the debtor's renunciation of his rights) written notice of a claim of an interest in the collateral. If the secured party receives objection in writing from a person entitled to receive notification within twenty-one days after the notice was sent, the secured party must dispose of the collateral under Section 9—504. In the absence of such written objection the secured party may retain the collateral in satisfaction of the debtor's obligation. Amended in 1972.

§ 9—506. Debtor's Right to Redeem Collateral.

At any time before the secured party has disposed of collateral or entered into a contract for its disposition under Section 9—504 or before the obligation has been discharged under Section 9—505(2) the debtor or any other secured party may unless otherwise agreed in writing after default redeem the collateral by tendering fulfillment of all obligations secured by the collateral as well as the expenses reasonably incurred by the secured party in retaking, holding and preparing the collateral for disposition, in arranging for the sale, and to the extent provided in the agreement and not prohibited by law, his reasonable attorneys' fees and legal expenses.

§ 9—507. Secured Party's Liability for Failure to Comply With This Part.

(1) If it is established that the secured party is not proceeding in accordance with the provisions of this Part disposition may be ordered or restrained on appropriate terms and conditions. If the disposition has occurred the debtor or any person entitled to notification or whose security interest has been made known to the secured party prior to the disposition has a right to recover from the secured party any loss caused by a failure to comply with the provisions of this Part. If the collateral is consumer goods, the debtor has a right to recover in any event an amount not less than the credit service charge plus ten per cent of the principal amount of the debt or the time price differential plus 10 per cent of the cash price.

(2) The fact that a better price could have been obtained by a sale at a different time or in a different method from that selected by the secured party is not of itself sufficient to establish that the sale was not made in a commercially reasonable manner. If the secured party either sells the collateral in the usual manner in any recognized market therefor or if he sells at the price current in such market at the time of his sale or if he has otherwise sold in conformity with reasonable commercial practices among dealers in the type of property sold he has sold in a commercially reasonable manner. The principles stated in the two preceding sentences with respect to sales also apply as may be appropriate to other types of disposition. A disposition which has been approved in any judicial proceeding or by any bona fide creditors' committee or representative of creditors shall conclusively be deemed to be commercially reasonable, but this sentence does not indicate that any such approval must be obtained in any case nor does it indicate that any disposition not so approved is not commercially reasonable.

Article 10
EFFECTIVE DATE AND REPEALER

10—101. **Effective Date.**

This Act shall become effective at midnight on December 31st following its enactment. It applies to transactions entered into and events occurring after that date.

§ 10—102. **Specific Repealer; Provision for Transition.**

(1) The following acts and all other acts and parts of acts inconsistent herewith are hereby repealed:

(Here should follow the acts to be specifically repealed including the following:

    Uniform Negotiable Instruments Act
    Uniform Warehouse Receipts Act
    Uniform Sales Act
    Uniform Bills of Lading Act
    Uniform Stock Transfer Act
    Uniform Conditional Sales Act
    Uniform Trust Receipts Act
        Also any acts regulating:
    Bank collections
    Bulk sales
    Chattel mortgages
    Conditional sales
    Factor's lien acts
    Farm storage of grain and similar acts
    Assignment of accounts receivable)

(2) Transactions validly entered into before the effective date specified in Section 10—101 and the rights, duties and interests flowing from them remain valid thereafter and may be terminated, completed, consummated or enforced as required or permitted by any statute or other law amended or repealed by this Act as though such repeal or amendment had not occurred.

Note: *Subsection (1) should be separately prepared for each state. The foregoing is a list of statutes to be checked.*

§ 10—103. **General Repealer.**

Except as provided in the following section, all acts and parts of acts inconsistent with this Act are hereby repealed.

§ 10—104. **Laws Not Repealed.**

(1) The Article on Documents of Title (Article 7) does not repeal or modify any laws prescribing the form or contents of documents of title or the services or facilities to be afforded by bailees, or otherwise regulating bailees' businesses in respects not specifically dealt with herein; but the fact that such laws are violated does not affect the status of a document of title which otherwise complies with the definition of a document of title (Section 1—201).

[(2) This Act does not repeal . . . .*, cited as the Uniform Act for the Simplification of Fiduciary Security Transfers, and if in any respect there is any inconsistency between that Act and the Article of this Act on investment securities (Article 8) the provisions of the former Act shall control.]

Note: *At * in subsection (2) insert the statutory reference to the Uniform Act for the Simplification of Fiduciary Security Transfers if such Act has previously been enacted. If it has not been enacted, omit subsection (2).*

Article 11
(REPORTERS' DRAFT) EFFECTIVE DATE AND TRANSITION PROVISIONS

This material has been numbered Article 11 to distinguish it from Article 10, the transition provision of the 1962 Code, which may still remain in effect in some states to cover transition problems from pre-Code law to the original Uniform Commercial Code. Adaptation may be necessary in particular states. The terms "[old Code]" and "[new Code]" and "[old U.C.C.]" and "[new U.C.C.]" are used herein, and should be suitably changed in each state.

Note: *This draft was prepared by the Reporters and has not been passed upon by the Review Committee, the Permanent Editorial Board, the American Law Institute, or the National Conference of Commissioners on Uniform State Laws. It is submitted as a working draft which may be adapted as appropriate in each state.*

§ 11—101. **Effective Date.**

This Act shall become effective at 12:01 A.M. on _____ , 19___.

§ 11—102. **Preservation of Old Transition Provision.**

The provisions of [here insert reference to the original transition provision in the particular state] shall continue to apply to [the new U.C.C.] and for this purpose the [old U.C.C. and new U.C.C.] shall be considered one continuous statute.

§ 11—103. **Transition to [New Code]—General Rule.**

Transactions validly entered into after [effective date of old U.C.C.] and before [effective date of new U.C.C.], and which were subject to the provisions of [old U.C.C.] and which would be subject to this Act as amended if they had been entered into after the effective date of [new U.C.C.] and the rights, duties and interests flowing from such transactions remain valid after the latter date and may be terminated, completed, consummated or enforced as required or permitted by the [new U.C.C.]. Security interests arising out of such transactions which are perfected when [new U.C.C.] becomes effective shall remain perfected until they lapse as provided in [new U.C.C.], and may be continued as permitted by [new U.C.C.], except as stated in Section 11—105.

§ 11—104. Transition Provision on Change of Requirement of Filing.

A security interest for the perfection of which filing or the taking of possession was required under [old U.C.C.] and which attached prior to the effective date of [new U.C.C.] but was not perfected shall be deemed perfected on the effective date of [new U.C.C.] if [new U.C.C.] permits perfection without filing or authorizes filing in the office or offices where a prior ineffective filing was made.

§ 11—105. Transition Provision on Change of Place of Filing.

(1) A financing statement or continuation statement filed prior to [effective date of new U.C.C.] which shall not have lapsed prior to [the effective date of new U.C.C.] shall remain effective for the period provided in the [old Code], but not less than five years after the filing.

(2) With respect to any collateral acquired by the debtor subsequent to the effective date of [new U.C.C.], any effective financing statement or continuation statement described in this section shall apply only if the filing or filings are in the office or offices that would be appropriate to perfect the security interests in the new collateral under [new U.C.C.].

(3) The effectiveness of any financing statement or continuation statement filed prior to [effective date of new U.C.C.] may be continued by a continuation statement as permitted by [new U.C.C.], except that if [new U.C.C.] requires a filing in an office where there was no previous financing statement, a new financing statement conforming to Section 11—106 shall be filed in that office.

(4) If the record of a mortgage of real estate would have been effective as a fixture filing of goods described therein if [new U.C.C.] had been in effect on the date of recording the mortgage, the mortgage shall be deemed effective as a fixture filing as to such goods under subsection (6) of Section 9—402 of the [new U.C.C.] on the effective date of [new U.C.C.].

§ 11—106. Required Refilings.

(1) If a security interest is perfected or has priority when this Act takes effect as to all persons or as to certain persons without any filing or recording, and if the filing of a financing statement would be required for the perfection or priority of the security interest against those persons under [new U.C.C.], the perfection and priority rights of the security interest continue until 3 years after the ef-

fective date of [new U.C.C.]. The perfection will then lapse unless a financing statement is filed as provided in subsection (4) or unless the security interest is perfected otherwise than by filing.

(2) If a security interest is perfected when [new U.C.C.] takes effect under a law other than [U.C.C.] which requires no further filing, refiling or recording to continue its perfection, perfection continues until and will lapse 3 years after [new U.C.C.] takes effect, unless a financing statement is filed as provided in subsection (4) or unless the security interest is perfected otherwise than by filing, or unless under subsection (3) of Section 9—302 the other law continues to govern filing.

(3) If a security interest is perfected by a filing, refiling or recording under a law repealed by this Act which required further filing, refiling or recording to continue its perfection, perfection continues and will lapse on the date provided by the law so repealed for such further filing, refiling or recording unless a financing statement is filed as provided in subsection (4) or unless the security interest is perfected otherwise than by filing.

(4) A financing statement may be filed within six months before the perfection of a security interest would otherwise lapse. Any such financing statement may be signed by either the debtor or the secured party. It must identify the security agreement, statement or notice (however denominated in any statute or other law repealed or modified by this Act), state the office where and the date when the last filing, refiling or recording, if any, was made with respect thereto, and the filing number, if any, or book and page, if any, of recording and further state that the security agreement, statement or notice, however denominated, in another filing office under the [U.C.C.] or under any statute or other law repealed or modified by this Act is still effective. Section 9—401 and Section 9—103 determine the proper place to file such a financing statement. Except as specified in this subsection, the provisions of Section 9—403(3) for continuation statements apply to such a financing statement.

§ 11—107. Transition Provisions as to Priorities.

Except as otherwise provided in [Article 11], [old U.C.C.] shall apply to any questions of priority if the positions of the parties were fixed prior to the effective date of [new U.C.C.]. In other cases questions of priority shall be determined by [new U.C.C.].

§ 11—108. Presumption that Rule of Law Continues Unchanged.

Unless a change in law has clearly been made, the provisions of [new U.C.C.] shall be deemed declaratory of the meaning of the [old U.C.C.].

1978 OFFICIAL TEXT—UCC

The preceding articles and sections constitute the 1978 official text of the Uniform Commercial Code. As of May 31, 1985, the following states had adopted most of the proposed amendments of 1972, which was the year of the most recent major changes. The other states basically follow the original text plus amendments proposed in the 1960s.

1972 Amendments

States	Effective Date	States	Effective Date
Alabama	2/01/82	Nebraska	7/19/80
Alaska	7/01/83	Nevada	7/01/75
Arizona	1/01/76	New Hampshire	8/21/79
Arkansas	1/01/74	New Jersey	12/01/81
California	1/01/76	New Mexico	6/14/85
Colorado	1/01/78	New York	7/02/78
Connecticut	10/01/76	North Carolina	7/01/76
Delaware	1/01/84	North Dakota	1/01/74
Florida	1/01/80	Ohio	1/01/79
Georgia	7/01/78	Oklahoma	10/19/81
Hawaii	7/01/79	Oregon	1/01/74
Idaho	7/01/79	Pennsylvania	5/25/83
Illinois	7/01/73	Rhode Island	1/01/80
Iowa	1/01/75	South Dakota	7/01/83
Kansas	1/01/76	Texas	1/01/74
Maine	1/01/78	Utah	7/01/77
Maryland	1/01/81	Virginia	7/01/74
Massachusetts	1/01/80	Washington	7/01/82
Michigan	1/01/79	West Virginia	7/01/75
Minnesota	1/01/77	Wisconsin	7/01/74
Mississippi	4/01/78	Wyoming	9/01/83
Montana	10/01/83		

APPENDIX D

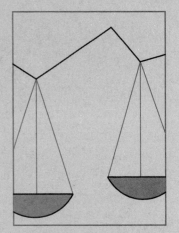

THE UNIFORM
PARTNERSHIP
ACT

(Adopted in 48 States [except Georgia and Louisiana], the District of Columbia, the Virgin Islands, and Guam. The adoptions by Alabama and Nebraska do not follow the official text in every respect, but are substantially similar, with local variations.)

The Act consists of 7 Parts as follows:

I. Preliminary Provisions

II. Nature of Partnership

III. Relations of Partners to Persons Dealing with the Partnership

IV. Relations of Partners to One Another

V. Property Rights of a Partner

VI. Dissolution and Winding Up

VII. Miscellaneous Provisions

An Act to make uniform the Law of Partnerships

Be it enacted, etc.:

Part I Preliminary Provisions

Sec. 1. Name of Act

This act may be cited as Uniform Partnership Act.

Sec. 2. Definition of Terms

In this act, "Court" includes every court and judge having jurisdiction in the case.

"Business" includes every trade, occupation, or profession.

"Person" includes individuals, partnerships, corporations, and other associations.

"Bankrupt" includes bankrupt under the Federal Bankruptcy Act or insolvent under any state insolvent act.

"Conveyance" includes every assignment, lease, mortgage, or encumbrance.

"Real property" includes land and any interest or estate in land.

Sec. 3. Interpretation of Knowledge and Notice

(1) A person has "knowledge" of a fact within the meaning of this act not only when he has actual knowledge thereof, but also when he has knowledge of such other facts as in the circumstances shows bad faith.

(2) A person has "notice" of a fact within the meaning of this act when the person who claims the benefit of the notice:

(a) States the fact to such person, or

(b) Delivers through the mail, or by other means of communication, a written statement of the fact to such person or to a proper person at his place of business or residence.

Sec. 4. Rules of Construction

(1) The rule that statutes in derogation of the common law are to be strictly construed shall have no application to this act.

(2) The law of estoppel shall apply under this act.

(3) The law of agency shall apply under this act.

(4) This act shall be so interpreted and construed as to effect its general purpose to make uniform the law of those states which enact it.

(5) This act shall not be construed so as to impair the obligations of any contract existing when the act goes into effect, nor to affect any action or proceedings begun or right accrued before this act takes effect.

Sec. 5. Rules for Cases Not Provided for in this Act.

In any case not provided for in this act the rules of law and equity, including the law merchant, shall govern.

Part II Nature of Partnership

Sec. 6. Partnership Defined

(1) A partnership is an association of two or more persons to carry on as co-owners a business for profit.

(2) But any association formed under any other statute of this state, or any statute adopted by authority, other than the authority of this state, is not a partnership under this act, unless such association would have been a partnership in this state prior to the adoption of this act; but this act shall apply to limited partnerships except in so far as the statutes relating to such partnerships are inconsistent herewith.

Sec. 7. Rules for Determining the Existence of a Partnership

In determining whether a partnership exists, these rules shall apply:

(1) Except as provided by Section 16 persons who are not partners as to each other are not partners as to third persons.

(2) Joint tenancy, tenancy in common, tenancy by the entireties, joint property, common property, or part ownership does not of itself establish a partnership, whether such co-owners do or do not share any profits made by the use of the property.

(3) The sharing of gross returns does not of itself establish a partnership, whether or not the persons sharing them have a joint or common right or interest in any property from which the returns are derived.

(4) The receipt by a person of a share of the profits of a business is prima facie evidence that he is a partner in the business, but no such inference shall be drawn if such profits were received in payment:

(a) As a debt by installments or otherwise,

(b) As wages of an employee or rent to a landlord,

(c) As an annuity to a widow or representative of a deceased partner,

(d) As interest on a loan, though the amount of payment vary with the profits of the business.

(e) As the consideration for the sale of a good-will of a business or other property by installments or otherwise.

Sec. 8. **Partnership Property**

(1) All property originally brought into the partnership stock or subsequently acquired by purchase or otherwise, on account of the partnership, is partnership property.

(2) Unless the contrary intention appears, property acquired with partnership funds is partnership property.

(3) Any estate in real property may be acquired in the partnership name. Title so acquired can be conveyed only in the partnership name.

(4) A conveyance to a partnership in the partnership name, though without words of inheritance, passes the entire estate of the grantor unless a contrary intent appears.

Part III Relations of Partners to Persons Dealing with the Partnership

Sec. 9. **Partner Agent of Partnership as to Partnership Business**

(1) Every partner is an agent of the partnership for the purpose of its business, and the act of every partner, including the execution in the partnership name of any instrument, for apparently carrying on in the usual way the business of the partnership of which he is a member binds the partnership, unless the partner so acting has in fact no authority to act for the partnership in the particular matter, and the person with whom he is dealing has knowledge of the fact that he has no such authority.

(2) An act of a partner which is not apparently for the carrying on of the business of the partnership in the usual way does not bind the partnership unless authorized by the other partners.

(3) Unless authorized by the other partners or unless they have abandoned the business, one or more but less than all the partners have no authority to:

(a) Assign the partnership property in trust for creditors or on the assignee's promise to pay the debts of the partnership,

(b) Dispose of the good-will of the business,

(c) Do any other act which would make it impossible to carry on the ordinary business of a partnership,

(d) Confess a judgment,

(e) Submit a partnership claim or liability to arbitration or reference.

(4) No act of a partner in contravention of a restriction on authority shall bind the partnership to persons having knowledge of the restriction.

Sec. 10. **Conveyance of Real Property of the Partnership**

(1) Where title to real property is in the partnership name, any partner may convey title to such property by a conveyance executed in the partnership name; but the partnership may recover such property unless the partner's act binds the partnership under the provisions of paragraph (1) of section 9, or unless such property has been conveyed by the grantee or a person claiming through such grantee to a holder for value without knowledge that the partner, in making the conveyance, has exceeded his authority.

(2) Where title to real property is in the name of the partnership, a conveyance executed by a partner, in his own name, passes the equitable interest of the partnership, provided the act is one within the authority of the partner under the provisions of paragraph (1) of section 9.

(3) Where title to real property is in the name of one or more but not all the partners, and the record does not disclose the right of the partnership, the partners in whose name the title stands may convey title to such property, but the partnership may recover such property if the partners' act does not bind the partnership under the provisions of paragraph (1) of section 9, unless the purchaser or his assignee, is a holder for value, without knowledge.

(4) Where the title to real property is in the name of one or more or all the partners, or in a third person in trust for the partnership, a conveyance executed by a partner in the partnership name, or in his own name, passes the equitable interest of the partnership, provided the act is one within the authority of the partner under the provisions of paragraph (1) of section 9.

(5) Where the title to real property is in the names of all the partners a conveyance executed by all the partners passes all their rights in such property.

Sec. 11. **Partnership Bound by Admission of Partner**

An admission or representation made by any partner concerning partnership affairs within the scope of his authority as conferred by this act is evidence against the partnership.

Sec. 12. Partnership Charged with Knowledge of or Notice to Partner

Notice to any partner of any matter relating to partnership affairs, and the knowledge of the partner acting in the particular matter, acquired while a partner or then present to his mind, and the knowledge of any other partner who reasonably could and should have communicated it to the acting partner, operate as notice to or knowledge of the partnership, except in the case of a fraud on the partnership committed by or with the consent of that partner.

Sec. 13. Partnership Bound by Partner's Wrongful Act

Where, by any wrongful act or omission of any partner acting in the ordinary course of the business of the partnership or with the authority of his co-partners, loss or injury is caused to any person, not being a partner in the partnership, or any penalty is incurred, the partnership is liable therefor to the same extent as the partner so acting or omitting to act.

Sec. 14. Partnership Bound by Partner's Breach of Trust

The partnership is bound to make good the loss:

(a) Where one partner acting within the scope of his apparent authority receives money or property of a third person and misapplies it; and

(b) Where the partnership in the course of its business receives money or property of a third person and the money or property so received is misapplied by any partner while it is in the custody of the partnership.

Sec. 15. Nature of Partner's Liability

All partners are liable

(a) Jointly and severally for everything chargeable to the partnership under sections 13 and 14.

(b) Jointly for all other debts and obligations of the partnership; but any partner may enter into a separate obligation to perform a partnership contract.

Sec. 16. Partner by Estoppel

(1) When a person, by words spoken or written or by conduct, represents himself, or consents to another representing him to any one, as a partner in an existing partnership or with one or more persons not actual partners, he is liable to any such person to whom such representation has been made, who has, on the faith of such representation, given credit to the actual or apparent partnership, and if he has made such representation or consented to its being made in a public manner he is liable to such person, whether the representation has or has not

been made or communicated to such person so giving credit by or with the knowledge of the apparent partner making the representation or consenting to its being made.

(a) When a partnership liability results, he is liable as though he were an actual member of the partnership.

(b) When no partnership liability results, he is liable jointly with the other persons, if any, so consenting to the contract or representation as to incur liability, otherwise separately.

(2) When a person has been thus represented to be a partner in an existing partnership, or with one or more persons not actual partners, he is an agent of the persons consenting to such representation to bind them to the same extent and in the same manner as though he were a partner in fact, with respect to persons who rely upon the representation. Where all the members of the existing partnership consent to the representation, a partnership act or obligation results; but in all other cases it is the joint act or obligation of the person acting and the persons consenting to the representation.

Sec. 17. Liability of Incoming Partner

A person admitted as a partner into an existing partnership is liable for all the obligations of the partnership arising before his admission as though he had been a partner when such obligations were incurred, except that this liability shall be satisfied only out of partnership property.

Part IV Relations of Partners to One Another

Sec. 18. Rules Determining Rights and Duties of Partners

The rights and duties of the partners in relation to the partnership shall be determined, subject to any agreement between them, by the following rules:

(a) Each partner shall be repaid his contributions, whether by way of capital or advances to the partnership property and share equally in the profits and surplus remaining after all liabilities, including those to partners, are satisfied; and must contribute towards the losses, whether of capital or otherwise, sustained by the partnership according to his share in the profits.

(b) The partnership must indemnify every partner in respect of payments made and personal liabilities reasonably incurred by him in the ordinary and proper conduct of its business, or for the preservation of its business or property.

(c) A partner, who in aid of the partnership makes any payment or advance beyond the amount of capital which he agreed to contribute, shall be paid interest from the date of the payment or advance.

(d) A partner shall receive interest on the capital contributed by him only from the date when repayment should be made.

(e) All partners have equal rights in the management and conduct of the partnership business.

(f) No partner is entitled to remuneration for acting in the partnership business, except that a surviving partner is entitled to reasonable compensation for his services in winding up the partnership affairs.

(g) No person can become a member of a partnership without the consent of all the partners.

(h) Any difference arising as to ordinary matters connected with the partnership business may be decided by a majority of the partners; but no act in contravention of any agreement between the partners may be done rightfully without the consent of all the partners.

Sec. 19. Partnership Books

The partnership books shall be kept, subject to any agreement between the partners, at the principal place of business of the partnership, and every partner shall at all times have access to and may inspect and copy any of them.

Sec. 20. Duty of Partners to Render Information

Partners shall render on demand true and full information of all things affecting the partnership to any partner or the legal representative of any deceased partner or partner under legal disability.

Sec. 21. Partner Accountable as a Fiduciary

(1) Every partner must account to the partnership for any benefit, and hold as trustee for it any profits derived by him without the consent of the other partners from any transaction connected with the formation, conduct, or liquidation of the partnership or from any use by him of its property.

(2) This section applies also to the representatives of a deceased partner engaged in the liquidation of the affairs of the partnership as the personal representatives of the last surviving partner.

Sec. 22. Right to an Account

Any partner shall have the right to a formal account as to partnership affairs:

(a) If he is wrongfully excluded from the partnership business or possession of its property by his co-partners,

(b) If the right exists under the terms of any agreement,

(c) As provided by section 21,

(d) Whenever other circumstances render it just and reasonable.

Sec. 23. Continuation of Partnership Beyond Fixed Term

(1) When a partnership for a fixed term or particular undertaking is continued after the termination of such term or particular undertaking without any express agreement, the rights and duties of the partners remain the same as they were at such termination, so far as is consistent with a partnership at will.

(2) A continuation of the business by the partners or such of them as habitually acted therein during the term, without any settlement or liquidation of the partnership affairs, is prima facie evidence of a continuation of the partnership.

Part V Property Rights of a Partner

Sec. 24. Extent of Property Rights of a Partner

The property rights of a partner are (1) his rights in specific partnership property, (2) his interest in the partnership, and (3) his right to participate in the management.

Sec. 25. Nature of a Partner's Right in Specific Partnership Property

(1) A partner is co-owner with his partners of specific partnership property holding as a tenant in partnership.

(2) The incidents of this tenancy are such that:

(a) A partner, subject to the provisions of this act and to any agreement between the partners, has an equal right with his partners to possess specific partnership property for partnership purposes; but he has no right to possess such property for any other purpose without the consent of his partners.

(b) A partner's right in specific partnership property is not assignable except in connection with the assignment of rights of all the partners in the same property.

(c) A partner's right in specific partnership property is not subject to attachment or execution, except on a claim against the partnership. When partnership property is attached for a partnership debt the partners, or any of them, or the representatives of a deceased partner, cannot claim any right under the homestead or exemption laws.

(d) On the death of a partner his right in specific partnership property vests in the surviving partner or partners, except where the deceased was the last surviving partner, when his right in such property vests in his legal representative. Such surviving partner or partners, or the legal representative of the last surviving partner, has no right to possess the partnership property for any but a partnership purpose.

(e) A partner's right in specific partnership property is not subject to dower, curtesy, or allowances to widows, heirs, or next of kin.

Sec. 26. Nature of Partner's Interest in the Partnership

A partner's interest in the partnership is his share of the profits and surplus, and the same is personal property.

Sec. 27. Assignment of Partner's Interest

(1) A conveyance by a partner of his interest in the partnership does not of itself dissolve the partnership, nor, as against the other partners in the absence of agreement, entitle the assignee, during the continuance of the partnership, to interfere in the management or administration of the partnership business or affairs, or to require any information or account of partnership transactions, or to inspect the partnership books; but it merely entitles the assignee to receive in accordance with his contract the profits to which the assigning partner would otherwise be entitled.

(2) In case of a dissolution of the partnership, the assignee is entitled to receive his assignor's interest and may require an account from the date only of the last account agreed to by all the partners.

Sec. 28. Partner's Interest Subject to Charging Order

(1) On due application to a competent court by any judgment creditor of a partner, the court which entered the judgment, order, or decree, or any other court, may charge the interest of the debtor partner with payment of the unsatisfied amount of such judgment debt with interest thereon; and may then or later appoint a receiver of his share of the profits, and of any other money due or to fall due to him in respect of the partnership, and make all other orders, directions, accounts and inquiries which the debtor partner might have made, or which the circumstances of the case may require.

(2) The interest charged may be redeemed at any time before foreclosure, or in case of a sale being directed by the court may be purchased without thereby causing a dissolution:

(a) With separate property, by any one or more of the partners, or

(b) With partnership property, by any one or more of the partners with the consent of all the partners whose interests are not so charged or sold.

(3) Nothing in this act shall be held to deprive a partner of his right, if any, under the exemption laws, as regards his interest in the partnership.

Part VI Dissolution and Winding up

Sec. 29. Dissolution Defined

The dissolution of a partnership is the change in the relation of the partners caused by any partner ceasing to be associated in the carrying on as distinguished from the winding up of the business.

Sec. 30. Partnership not Terminated by Dissolution

On dissolution the partnership is not terminated, but continues until the winding up of partnership affairs is completed.

Sec. 31. Causes of Dissolution

Dissolution is caused:

(1) Without violation of the agreement between the partners,

(a) By the termination of the definite term or particular undertaking specified in the agreement,

(b) By the express will of any partner when no definite term or particular undertaking is specified,

(c) By the express will of all the partners who have not assigned their interests or suffered them to be charged for their separate debts, either before or after the termination of any specified term or particular undertaking,

(d) By the expulsion of any partner from the business bona fide in accordance with such a power conferred by the agreement between the partners;

(2) In contravention of the agreement between the partners, where the circumstances do not permit a dissolution under any other provision of this section, by the express will of any partner at any time;

(3) By any event which makes it unlawful for the business of the partnership to be carried on or for the members to carry it on in partnership;

(4) By the death of any partner;

(5) By the bankruptcy of any partner or the partnership;

(6) By decree of court under section 32.

Sec. 32. Dissolution by Decree of Court

(1) On application by or for a partner the court shall decree a dissolution whenever:

(a) A partner has been declared a lunatic in any judicial proceeding or is shown to be of unsound mind,

(b) A partner becomes in any other way incapable of performing his part of the partnership contract,

(c) A partner has been guilty of such conduct as tends to affect prejudicially the carrying on of the business,

(d) A partner wilfully or persistently commits a breach of the partnership agreement, or otherwise so conducts himself in matters relating to the partnership business that it is not reasonably practicable to carry on the business in partnership with him,

(e) The business of the partnership can only be carried on at a loss,

(f) Other circumstances render a dissolution equitable.

(2) On the application of the purchaser of a partner's interest under sections 28 or 29 [should read 27 or 28];

(a) After the termination of the specified term or particular undertaking,

(b) At any time if the partnership was a partnership at will when the interest was assigned or when the charging order was issued.

Sec. 33. General Effect of Dissolution on Authority of Partner

Except so far as may be necessary to wind up partnership affairs or to complete transactions begun but not then finished, dissolution terminates all authority of any partner to act for the partnership,

(1) With respect to the partners,

(a) When the dissolution is not by the act, bankruptcy or death of a partner; or

(b) When the dissolution is by such act, bankruptcy or death of a partner, in cases where section 34 so requires.

(2) With respect to persons not partners, as declared in section 35.

Sec. 34. Rights of Partner to Contribution from Co-partners After Dissolution

Where the dissolution is caused by the act, death or bankruptcy of a partner, each partner is liable to his copartners for his share of any liability created by any partner acting for the partnership as if the partnership had not been dissolved unless

(a) The dissolution being by act of any partner, the partner acting for the partnership had knowledge of the dissolution, or

(b) The dissolution being by the death or bankruptcy of a partner, the partner acting for the partnership had knowledge or notice of the death or bankruptcy.

Sec. 35. Power of Partner to Bind Partnership to Third Persons After Dissolution

(1) After dissolution a partner can bind the partnership except as provided in Paragraph (3).

(a) By any act appropriate for winding up partnership affairs or completing transactions unfinished at dissolution;

(b) By any transaction which would bind the partnership if dissolution had not taken place, provided the other party to the transaction

(I) Had extended credit to the partnership prior to dissolution and had no knowledge or notice of the dissolution; or

(II) Though he had not so extended credit, had nevertheless known of the partnership prior to dissolution, and, having no knowledge or notice of dissolution, the fact of dissolution had not been advertised in a newspaper of general circulation in the place (or in each place if more than one) at which the partnership business was regularly carried on.

(2) The liability of a partner under paragraph (1b) shall be satisfied out of partnership assets alone when such partner had been prior to dissolution

(a) Unknown as a partner to the person with whom the contract is made; and

(b) So far unknown and inactive in partnership affairs that the business reputation of the partnership could not be said to have been in any degree due to his connection with it.

(3) The partnership is in no case bound by any act of a partner after dissolution

(a) Where the partnership is dissolved because it is unlawful to carry on the business, unless the act is appropriate for winding up partnership affairs; or

(b) Where the partner has become bankrupt; or

(c) Where the partner has no authority to wind up partnership affairs; except by a transaction with one who

(I) Had extended credit to the partnership prior to dissolution and had no knowledge or notice of his want of authority; or

(II) Had not extended credit to the partnership prior to dissolution, and, having no knowledge or notice of his want of authority, the fact of his want of authority has not been advertised in the manner provided for advertising the fact of dissolution in paragraph (1bII).

(4) Nothing in this section shall affect the liability under Section 16 of any person who after dissolution represents himself or consents to another representing him as a partner in a partnership engaged in carrying on business.

Sec. 36. Effect of Dissolution on Partner's Existing Liability

(1) The dissolution of the partnership does not of itself discharge the existing liability of any partner.

(2) A partner is discharged from any existing liability upon dissolution of the partnership by an agreement to that effect between himself, the partnership creditor and the person or partnership continuing the business; and such agreement may be inferred from the course of dealing between the creditor having knowledge of the dissolution and the person or partnership continuing the business.

(3) Where a person agrees to assume the existing obligations of a dissolved partnership, the partners whose obligations have been assumed shall be discharged from any liability to any creditor of the partnership who, knowing of the agreement, consents to a material alteration in the nature or time of payment of such obligations.

(4) The individual property of a deceased partner shall be liable for all obligations of the partnership incurred while he was a partner but subject to the prior payment of his separate debts.

Sec. 37. Right to Wind Up

Unless otherwise agreed the partners who have not wrongfully dissolved the partnership or the legal representative of the last surviving partner, not bankrupt, has the right to wind up the partnership affairs; provided, however, that any partner, his legal representative or his assignee, upon cause shown, may obtain winding up by the court.

Sec. 38. Rights of Partners to Application of Partnership Property

(1) When dissolution is caused in any way, except in contravention of the partnership agreement, each partner, as against his co-partners and all persons claiming through them in respect of their interests in the partnership, unless otherwise agreed, may have the partnership property applied to discharge its liabilities, and the surplus applied to pay in cash the net amount owing to the respective partners. But if dissolution is caused by expulsion of a partner, bona fide under the partnership agreement and if the expelled partner is discharged from all partnership liabilities, either by payment or agreement under section 36(2), he shall receive in cash only the net amount due him from the partnership.

(2) When dissolution is caused in contravention of the partnership agreement the rights of the partners shall be as follows:

(a) Each partner who has not caused dissolution wrongfully shall have,

(I) All the rights specified in paragraph (1) of this section, and

(II) The right, as against each partner who has caused the dissolution wrongfully, to damages for breach of the agreement.

(b) The partners who have not caused the dissolution wrongfully, if they all desire to continue the business in the same name, either by themselves or jointly with others, may do so, during the agreed term for the partnership and for that purpose may possess the partnership property, provided they secure the payment by bond approved by the court, or pay to any partner who has caused the dissolution wrongfully, the value of his interest in the partnership at the dissolution, less any damages recoverable under clause (2a II) of the section, and in like manner indemnify him against all present or future partnership liabilities.

(c) A partner who has caused the dissolution wrongfully shall have:

(I) If the business is not continued under the provisions of paragraph (2b) all the rights of a partner under paragraph (1), subject to clause (2a II), of this section,

(II) If the business is continued under paragraph (2b) of this section the right as against his co-partners and all claiming through them in respect of their interests in the partnership, to have the value of his interest in the partnership, less any damages caused to his co-partners by the dissolution, ascertained and paid to him in cash, or the payment secured by bond approved by the court, and to be released from all existing liabilities of the partnership; but in ascertaining the value of the partner's interest the value of the good-will of the business shall not be considered.

Sec. 39. Rights Where Partnership is Dissolved for Fraud or Misrepresentation

Where a partnership contract is rescinded on the ground of the fraud or misrepresentation of one of the parties thereto, the party entitled to rescind is, without prejudice to any other right, entitled,

(a) To a lien on, or right of retention of, the surplus of the partnership property after satisfying the partnership liabilities to third persons for any sum of money paid by him for the purchase of an interest in the partnership and for any capital or advances contributed by him; and

(b) To stand, after all liabilities to third persons have been satisfied, in the place of the creditors of the partnership for any payments made by him in respect of the partnership liabilities; and

(c) To be indemnified by the person guilty of the fraud or making the representation against all debts and liabilities of the partnership.

Sec. 40. **Rules for Distribution**

In settling accounts between the partners after dissolution, the following rules shall be observed, subject to any agreement to the contrary:

(a) The assets of the partnership are:

(I) The partnership property,

(II) The contributions of the partners necessary for the payment of all the liabilities specified in clause (b) of this paragraph.

(b) The liabilities of the partnership shall rank in order of payment, as follows:

(I) Those owing to creditors other than partners,

(II) Those owing to partners other than for capital and profits,

(III) Those owing to partners in respect of capital,

(IV) Those owing to partners in respect of profits.

(c) The assets shall be applied in the order of their declaration in clause (a) of this paragraph to the satisfaction of the liabilities.

(d) The partners shall contribute, as provided by section 18(a) the amount necessary to satisfy the liabilities; but if any, but not all, of the partners are insolvent, or, not being subject to process, refuse to contribute, the other partners shall contribute their share of the liabilities, and, in the relative proportions in which they share the profits, the additional amount necessary to pay the liabilities.

(e) An assignee for the benefit of creditors or any person appointed by the court shall have the right to enforce the contributions specified in clause (d) of this paragraph.

(f) Any partner or his legal representative shall have the right to enforce the contributions specified in clause (d) of this paragraph, to the extent of the amount which he has paid in excess of his share of the liability.

(g) The individual property of a deceased partner shall be liable for the contributions specified in clause (d) of this paragraph.

(h) When partnership property and the individual properties of the partners are in possession of a court for distribution, partnership creditors shall have priority on partnership property and separate creditors on individual property, saving the rights of lien or secured creditors as heretofore.

(i) Where a partner has become bankrupt or his estate is insolvent the claims against his separate property shall rank in the following order:

(I) Those owing to separate creditors,

(II) Those owing to partnership creditors,

(III) Those owing to partners by way of contribution.

Sec. 41. **Liability of Persons Continuing the Business in Certain Cases**

(1) When any new partner is admitted into an existing partnership, or when any partner retires and assigns (or the representative of the deceased partner assigns) his rights in partnership property to two or more of the partners, or to one or more of the partners and one or more third persons, if the business is continued without liquidation of the partnership affairs, creditors of the first or dissolved partnership are also creditors of the partnership so continuing the business.

(2) When all but one partner retire and assign (or the representative of a deceased partner assigns) their rights in partnership property to the remaining partner, who continues the business without liquidation of partnership affairs, either alone or with others, creditors of the dissolved partnership are also creditors of the person or partnership so continuing the business.

(3) When any partner retires or dies and the business of the dissolved partnership is continued as set forth in paragraphs (1) and (2) of this section, with the consent of the retired partners or the representative of the deceased partner, but without any assignment of his right in partnership property, rights of creditors of the dissolved partnership and of the creditors of the person or partnership continuing the business shall be as if such assignment had been made.

(4) When all the partners or their representatives assign their rights in partnership property to one or more third persons who promise to pay the debts and who continue the business of the dissolved partnership, creditors of the dissolved partnership are also creditors of the person or partnership continuing the business.

(5) When any partner wrongfully causes a dissolution and the remaining partners continue the business under the provisions of section 38(2b), either alone or with others, and without liquidation of the partnership affairs, creditors of the dissolved partnership are also creditors of the person or partnership continuing the business.

(6) When a partner is expelled and the remaining partners continue the business either alone or with others, without liquidation of the partnership affairs, creditors of the dissolved partnership are also creditors of the person or partnership continuing the business.

(7) The liability of a third person becoming a partner in the partnership continuing the business, under this section, to the creditors of the dissolved partnership shall be satisfied out of partnership property only.

(8) When the business of a partnership after dissolution is continued under any conditions set forth in this section the creditors of the dissolved partnership, as against the

separate creditors of the retiring or deceased partner or the representative of the deceased partner, have a prior right to any claim of the retired partner or the representative of the deceased partner against the person or partnership continuing the business, on account of the retired or deceased partner's interest in the dissolved partnership or on account of any consideration promised for such interest or for his right in partnership property.

(9) Nothing in this section shall be held to modify any right of creditors to set aside any assignment on the ground of fraud.

(10) The use by the person or partnership continuing the business of the partnership name, or the name of a deceased partner as part thereof, shall not of itself make the individual property of the deceased partner liable for any debts contracted by such person or partnership.

Sec. 42. Rights of Retiring or Estate of Deceased Partner When the Business is Continued

When any partner retires or dies, and the business is continued under any of the conditions set forth in section 41 (1, 2, 3, 5, 6), or section 38(2b) without any settlement of accounts as between him or his estate and the person or partnership continuing the business, unless otherwise agreed, he or his legal representative as against such persons or partnership may have the value of his interest at the date of dissolution ascertained, and shall receive as an ordinary creditor an amount equal to the value of his interest in the dissolved partnership with interest, or, at his option or at the option of his legal representative, in lieu of interest, the profits attributable to the use of his right in the property of the dissolved partnership; provided that the creditors of the dissolved partnership as against the separate creditors, or the representative of the retired or deceased partner, shall have priority on any claim arising under this section, as provided by section 41(8) of this act.

Sec. 43. Accrual of Actions

The right to an account of his interest shall accrue to any partner, or his legal representative, as against the winding up partners or the surviving partners or the person or partnership continuing the business, at the date of dissolution, in the absence of any agreement to the contrary.

Part VII Miscellaneous Provisions

Sec. 44. When Act Takes Effect

This act shall take effect on the ___ day of ___ one thousand nine hundred and ___.

Sec. 45. Legislation Repealed

All acts or parts of acts inconsistent with this act are hereby repealed.

APPENDIX E

UNIFORM
LIMITED
PARTNERSHIP
ACT

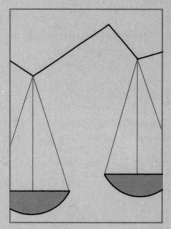

(Adopted in 27 States: Alaska, Florida, Georgia, Hawaii, Illinois, Indiana, Kentucky, Maine, Mississippi, Missouri, Nevada, New Hampshire, New Mexico, New York, North Carolina, North Dakota, Ohio, Oregon, Pennsylvania, Rhode Island, South Carolina, South Dakota, Tennessee, Texas, Utah, Vermont, and Virginia. Also adopted in the District of Columbia, and the Virgin Islands.)

Sec. 1. Limited Partnership Defined

A limited partnership is a partnership formed by two or more persons under the provisions of Section 2, having as members one or more general partners and one or more limited partners. The limited partners as such shall not be bound by the obligations of the partnership.

Sec. 2. Formation

(1) Two or more persons desiring to form a limited partnership shall

(a) Sign and swear to a certificate, which shall state

I. The name of the partnership,

II. The character of the business,

III. The location of the principal place of business,

IV. The name and place of residence of each member; general and limited partners being respectively designated,

V. The term for which the partnership is to exist,

VI. The amount of cash and a description of and the agreed value of the other property contributed by each limited partner,

VII. The additional contributions, if any, agreed to be made by each limited partner and the times at which or events on the happening of which they shall be made,

VIII. The time, if agreed upon, when the contribution of each limited partner is to be returned,

IX. The share of the profits or the other compensation by way of income which each limited partner shall receive by reason of his contribution,

X. The right, if given, of a limited partner to substitute an assignee as contributor in his place, and the terms and conditions of the substitution,

XI. The right, if given, of the partners to admit additional limited partners,

XII. The right, if given, of one or more of the limited partners to priority over other limited partners, as to contributions or as to compensation by way of income, and the nature of such priority,

XIII. The right, if given, of the remaining general partner or partners to continue the business on the death, retirement or insanity of a general partner, and

XIV. The right, if given, of a limited partner to demand and receive property other than cash in return for his contribution.

(b) File for record the certificate in the office of [here designate the proper office].

(2) A limited partnership is formed if there has been substantial compliance in good faith with the requirements of paragraph (1).

Sec. 3. Business Which May Be Carried On

A limited partnership may carry on any business which a partnership without limited partners may carry on, except [here designate the business to be prohibited].

Sec. 4. Character of Limited Partner's Contribution

The contributions of a limited partner may be cash or other property, but not services.

Sec. 5. A Name Not to Contain Surname of Limited Partner; Exceptions

(1) The surname of a limited partner shall not appear in the partnership name, unless

(a) It is also the surname of a general partner, or

(b) Prior to the time when the limited partner became such the business had been carried on under a name in which his surname appeared.

(2) A limited partner whose name appears in a partnership name contrary to the provisions of paragraph (1) is liable as a general partner to partnership creditors who extend credit to the partnership without actual knowledge that he is not a general partner.

Sec. 6. Liability for False Statements in Certificate

If the certificate contains a false statement, one who suffers loss by reliance on such statement may hold liable any party to the certificate who knew the statement to be false.

(a) At the time he signed the certificate, or

(b) Subsequently, but within a sufficient time before the statement was relied upon to enable him to cancel or amend the certificate, or to file a petition for its cancellation or amendment as provided in Section 25(3).

Sec. 7. Limited Partner Not Liable to Creditors

A limited partner shall not become liable as a general partner unless, in addition to the exercise of his rights and powers as a limited partner, he takes part in the control of the business.

Sec. 8. **Admission of Additional Limited Partners**

After the formation of a limited partnership, additional limited partners may be admitted upon filing an amendment to the original certificate in accordance with the requirements of Section 25.

Sec. 9. **Rights, Powers and Liabilities of a General Partner**

(1) A general partner shall have all the rights and powers and be subject to all the restrictions and liabilities of a partner in a partnership without limited partners, except that without the written consent or ratification of the specific act by all the limited partners, a general partner or all of the general partners have no authority to

(a) Do any act in contravention of the certificate,

(b) Do any act which would make it impossible to carry on the ordinary business of the partnership,

(c) Confess a judgment against the partnership,

(d) Possess partnership property, or assign their rights in specific partnership property, for other than a partnership purpose,

(e) Admit a person as a general partner,

(f) Admit a person as a limited partner, unless the right so to do is given in the certificate,

(g) Continue the business with partnership property on the death, retirement or insanity of a general partner, unless the right so to do is given in the certificate.

Sec. 10. **Rights of a Limited Partner**

(1) A limited partner shall have the same rights as a general partner to

(a) Have the partnership books kept at the principal place of business of the partnership, and at all times to inspect and copy any of them.

(b) Have on demand true and full information of all things affecting the partnership, and a formal account of partnership affairs whenever circumstances render it just and reasonable, and

(c) Have dissolution and winding up by decree of court.

(2) A limited partner shall have the right to receive a share of the profits or other compensation by way of income, and to the return of his contribution as provided in Sections 15 and 16.

Sec. 11. **Status of Person Erroneously Believing Himself a Limited Partner**

A person who has contributed to the capital of a business conducted by a person or partnership erroneously believing that he has become a limited partner in a limited partnership, is not, by reason of his exercise of the rights of a limited partner, a general partner with the person or in the partnership carrying on the business, or bound by the obligations of such person or partnership; provided that on ascertaining the mistake he promptly renounces his interest in the profits of the business, or other compensation by way of income.

Sec. 12. **One Person Both General and Limited Partner**

(1) A person may be a general partner and a limited partner in the same partnership at the same time.

(2) A person who is a general, and also at the same time a limited partner, shall have all the rights and powers and be subject to all the restrictions of a general partner; except that, in respect to his contribution, he shall have the rights against the other members which he would have had if he were not also a general partner.

Sec. 13. **Loans and Other Business Transactions with Limited Partner**

(1) A limited partner also may loan money to and transact other business with the partnership, and, unless he is also a general partner, receive on account of resulting claims against the partnership, with general creditors, a pro rata share of the assets. No limited partner shall in respect to any such claim

(a) Receive or hold as collateral security any partnership property, or

(b) Receive from a general partner or the partnership any payment, conveyance, or release from liability, if at the time the assets of the partnership are not sufficient to discharge partnership liabilities to persons not claiming as general or limited partners,

(2) The receiving of collateral security, or a payment, conveyance, or release in violation of the provisions of paragraph (1) is a fraud on the creditors of the partnership.

Sec. 14. **Relation of Limited Partners Inter Se**

Where there are several limited partners the members may agree that one or more of the limited partners shall have a priority over other limited partners as to the return of their contributions, as to their compensation by way of income, or as to any other matter. If such an agreement is made it shall be stated in the certificate, and in the absence of such a statement all the limited partners shall stand upon equal footing.

Sec. 15. **Compensation of Limited Partner**

A limited partner may receive from the partnership the share of the profits or the compensation by way of income stipulated for in the certificate; provided, that after such payment is made, whether from the property of the partnership or that of a general partner, the partnership assets are in excess of all liabilities of the partnership except liabilities to limited partners on account of their contributions and to general partners.

Sec. 16. Withdrawal or Reduction of Limited Partner's Contribution

(1) A limited partner shall not receive from a general partner or out of partnership property any part of his contribution until

(a) All liabilities of the partnership, except liabilities to general partners and to limited partners on account of their contributions, have been paid or there remains property of the partnership sufficient to pay them,

(b) The consent of all members is had, unless the return of the contribution may be rightfully demanded under the provisions of paragraph (2), and

(c) The certificate is cancelled or so amended as to set forth the withdrawal or reduction.

(2) Subject to the provisions of paragraph (1) a limited partner may rightfully demand the return of his contribution

(a) On the dissolution of a partnership, or

(b) When the date specified in the certificate for its return has arrived, or

(c) After he has given six months' notice in writing to all other members, if no time is specified in the certificate either for the return of the contribution or for the dissolution of the partnership,

(3) In the absence of any statement in the certificate to the contrary or the consent of all members, a limited partner, irrespective of the nature of his contribution, has only the right to demand and receive cash in return for his contribution.

(4) A limited partner may have the partnership dissolved and its affairs wound up when

(a) He rightfully but unsuccessfully demands the return of his contribution, or

(b) The other liabilities of the partnership have not been paid, or the partnership property is insufficient for their payment as required by paragraph (1a) and the limited partner would otherwise be entitled to the return of his contribution.

Sec. 17. Liability of Limited Partner to Partnership

(1) A limited partner is liable to the partnership

(a) For the difference between his contribution as actually made and that stated in the certificate as having been made, and

(b) For any unpaid contribution which he agreed in the certificate to make in the future at the time and on the conditions stated in the certificate.

(2) A limited partner holds as trustee for the partnership

(a) Specific property stated in the certificate as contributed by him, but which was not contributed or which has been wrongfully returned, and

(b) Money or other property wrongfully paid or conveyed to him on account of his contribution.

(3) The liabilities of a limited partner as set forth in this section can be waived or compromised only by the consent of all members; but a waiver or compromise shall not affect the right of a creditor of a partnership who extended credit or whose claim arose after the filing and before a cancellation or amendment of the certificate, to enforce such liabilities.

(4) When a contributor has rightfully received the return in whole or in part of the capital of his contribution, he is nevertheless liable to the partnership for any sum, not in excess of such return with interest, necessary to discharge its liabilities to all creditors who extended credit or whose claims arose before such return.

Sec. 18. Nature of Limited Partner's Interest in Partnership

A limited partner's interest in the partnership is personal property.

Sec. 19. Assignment of Limited Partner's Interest

(1) A limited partner's interest is assignable.

(2) A substituted limited partner is a person admitted to all the rights of a limited partner who has died or has assigned his interest in a partnership.

(3) An assignee, who does not become a substituted limited partner, has no right to require any information or account of the partnership transactions or to inspect the partnership books; he is only entitled to receive the share of the profits or other compensation by way of income, or the return of his contribution, to which his assignor would otherwise be entitled.

(4) An assignee shall have the right to become a substituted limited partner if all the members (except the assignor) consent thereto or if the assignor, being thereunto empowered by the certificate, gives the assignee that right.

(5) An assignee becomes a substituted limited partner when the certificate is appropriately amended in accordance with Section 25.

(6) The substituted limited partner has all the rights and powers, and is subject to all the restrictions and liabilities of his assignor, except those liabilities of which he was

ignorant at the time he became a limited partner and which could not be ascertained from the certificate.

(7) The substitution of the assignee as a limited partner does not release the assignor from liability to the partnership under Sections 6 and 17.

Sec. 20. Effect of Retirement, Death or Insanity of a General Partner

The retirement, death or insanity of a general partner dissolves the partnership, unless the business is continued by the remaining general partners

(a) Under a right so to do stated in the certificate, or

(b) With the consent of all members.

Sec. 21. Death of Limited Partner

(1) On the death of a limited partner his executor or administrator shall have all the rights of a limited partner for the purpose of settling his estate, and such power as the deceased had to constitute his assignee a substituted limited partner.

(2) The estate of a deceased limited partner shall be liable for all his liabilities as a limited partner.

Sec. 22. Rights of Creditors of Limited Partner

(1) On due application to a court of competent jurisdiction by any judgment creditor of a limited partner, the court may charge the interest of the indebted limited partner with payment of the unsatisfied amount of the judgment debt; and may appoint a receiver, and make all other orders, directions, and inquiries which the circumstances of the case may require.

(2) The interest may be redeemed with the separate property of any general partner, but may not be redeemed with partnership property.

(3) The remedies conferred by paragraph (1) shall not be deemed exclusive of others which may exist.

(4) Nothing in this act shall be held to deprive a limited partner of his statutory exemption.

Sec. 23. Distribution of Assets

(1) In settling accounts after dissolution the liabilities of the partnership shall be entitled to payment in the following order:

(a) Those to creditors, in the order of priority as provided by law, except those to limited partners on account of their contributions, and to general partners,

(b) Those to limited partners in respect to their share of the profits and other compensation by way of income on their contributions,

(c) Those to limited partners in respect to the capital of their contributions,

(d) Those to general partners other than for capital and profits,

(e) Those to general partners in respect to profits,

(f) Those to general partners in respect to capital.

(2) Subject to any statement in the certificate or to subsequent agreement, limited partners share in the partnership assets in respect to their claims for capital, and in respect to their claims for profits or for compensation by way of income on their contributions respectively, in proportion to the respective amounts of such claims.

Sec. 24. When Certificate Shall Be Cancelled or Amended

(1) The certificate shall be cancelled when the partnership is dissolved or all limited partners cease to be such.

(2) A certificate shall be amended when

(a) There is a change in the name of the partnership or in the amount or character of the contribution of any limited partner,

(b) A person is substituted as a limited partner,

(c) An additional limited partner is admitted,

(d) A person is admitted as a general partner,

(e) A general partner retires, dies or becomes insane, and the business is continued under Section 20,

(f) There is a change in the character of the business of the partnership,

(g) There is a false or erroneous statement in the certificate,

(h) There is a change in the time as stated in the certificate for the dissolution of the partnership or for the return of a contribution,

(i) A time is fixed for the dissolution of the partnership, or the return of a contribution, no time having been specified in the certificate, or

(j) The members desire to make a change in any other statement in the certificate in order that it shall accurately represent the agreement between them.

Sec. 25. Requirements for Amendment and for Cancellation of Certificate

(1) The writing to amend a certificate shall

(a) Conform to the requirements of Section 2(1a) as far as necessary to set forth clearly the change in the certificate which it is desired to make, and

(b) Be signed and sworn to by all members, and an amendment substituting a limited partner or adding a limited or general partner shall be signed also by the member to be substituted or added, and when a limited partner is to be substituted, the amendment shall also be signed by the assigning limited partner.

(2) The writing to cancel a certificate shall be signed by all members.

(3) A person desiring the cancellation or amendment of a certificate, if any person designated in paragraphs (1) and (2) as a person who must execute the writing refuses to do so, may petition the [here designate the proper court] to direct a cancellation or amendment thereof.

(4) If the court finds that the petitioner has a right to have the writing executed by a person who refuses to do so, it shall order the [here designate the responsible official in the office designated in Section 2] in the office where the certificate is recorded to record the cancellation or amendment of the certificate; and where the certificate is to be amended, the court shall also cause to be filed for record in said office a certified copy of its decree setting forth the amendment.

(5) A certificate is amended or cancelled when there is filed for record in the office [here designate the office designated in Section 2] where the certificate is recorded

(a) A writing in accordance with the provisions of paragraph (1), or (2) or

(b) A certified copy of the order of court in accordance with the provisions of paragraph (4).

(6) After the certificate is duly amended in accordance with this section, the amended certificate shall thereafter be for all purposes the certificate provided for by this act.

Sec. 26. Parties to Actions

A contributor, unless he is a general partner, is not a proper party to proceedings by or against a partnership, except where the object is to enforce a limited partner's right against or liability to the partnership.

Sec. 27. Name of Act

This act may be cited as The Uniform Limited Partnership Act.

Sec. 28. Rules of Construction

(1) The rule that statutes in derogation of the common law are to be strictly construed shall have no application to this act.

(2) This act shall be so interpreted and construed as to effect its general purpose to make uniform the law of those states which enact it.

(3) This act shall not be so construed as to impair the obligations of any contract existing when the act goes into effect, nor to affect any action or proceedings begun or right accrued before this act takes effect.

Sec. 29. Rules for Cases Not Provided for in This Act

In any case not provided for in this act the rules of law and equity, including the law merchant, shall govern.

Sec. 30. Provisions for Existing Limited Partnerships

(1) A limited partnership formed under any statute of this state prior to the adoption of this act, may become a limited partnership under this act by complying with the provisions of Section 2; provided the certificate sets forth

(a) The amount of the original contribution of each limited partner, and the time when the contribution was made, and

(b) That the property of the partnership exceeds the amount sufficient to discharge its liabilities to persons not claiming as general or limited partners by an amount greater than the sum of the contributions of its limited partners.

(2) A limited partnership formed under any statute of this state prior to the adoption of this act, until or unless it becomes a limited partnership under this act, shall continue to be governed by the provisions of [here insert proper reference to the existing limited partnership act or acts], except that such partnership shall not be renewed unless so provided in the original agreement.

Sec. 31. Act [Acts] Repealed

Except as affecting existing limited partnerships to the extent set forth in Section 30, the act (acts) of [here designate the existing limited partnership act or acts] is (are) hereby repealed.

APPENDIX F

REVISED
UNIFORM
LIMITED
PARTNERSHIP
ACT

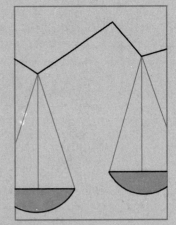

*(Adopted August 5, 1976, by the National Conference of Commissioners on Uniform State Laws, it is intended to replace the existing Uniform Limited Partnership Act (Appendix E). It has been adopted in 22 States: Alabama, Arizona, Arkansas, California, Colorado, Connecticut, Delaware, Idaho, Iowa, Kansas, Maryland, Massachusetts, Michigan, Minnesota, Montana, Nebraska, New Jersey, Oklahoma, Washington, West Virginia, Wisconsin, and Wyoming.

The Act consists of 11 Articles as follows:

1. General Provisions
2. Formation; Certificate of Limited Partnership
3. Limited Partners
4. General Partners
5. Finance
6. Distributions and Withdrawal
7. Assignment of Partnership Interests
8. Dissolution
9. Foreign Limited Partnerships
10. Derivative Actions
11. Miscellaneous

Article 1
GENERAL PROVISIONS

Sec. 101. **Definitions**

As used in this Act, unless the context otherwise requires:

(1) "Certificate of limited partnership" means the certificate referred to in Section 201, and the certificate as amended.

(2) "Contribution" means any cash, property, services rendered, or a promissory note or other binding obligation to contribute cash or property or to perform services, which a partner contributes to a limited partnership in his capacity as a partner.

(3) "Event of withdrawal of a general partner" means an event that causes a person to cease to be a general partner as provided in Section 402.

(4) "Foreign limited partnership" means a partnership formed under the laws of any State other than this State and having as partners one or more general partners and one or more limited partners.

---

*At its annual conference in August 1985, the National Conference of Commissioners on Uniform State Laws approved amendments to the "Revised Uniform Partnership Act." Since at the time of the printing of this text no states have adopted these amendments, they are *not* included.

(5) "General partner" means a person who has been admitted to a limited partnership as a general partner in accordance with the partnership agreement and named in the certificate of limited partnership as a general partner.

(6) "Limited partner" means a person who has been admitted to a limited partnership as a limited partner in accordance with the partnership agreement and named in the certificate of limited partnership as a limited partner.

(7) "Limited partnership" and "domestic limited partnership" mean a partnership formed by 2 or more persons under the laws of this State and having one or more general partners and one or more limited partners.

(8) "Partner" means any limited partner or general partner.

(9) "Partnership agreement" means any valid agreement, written or oral, of the partners as to the affairs of a limited partnership and the conduct of its business.

(10) "Partnership interest" means a partner's share of the profits and losses of a limited partnership and the right to receive distributions of partnership assets.

(11) "Person" means a natural person, partnership, limited partnership (domestic or foreign), trust, estate, association, or corporation.

(12) "State" means a state, territory, or possession of the United States, the District of Columbia, or the Commonwealth of Puerto Rico.

Sec. 102. **Name**

The name of each limited partnership as set forth in its certificate of limited partnership:

(1) shall contain without abbreviation the words "limited partnership";

(2) may not contain the name of a limited partner unless (i) it is also the name of a general partner or the corporate name of a corporate general partner, or (ii) the business of the limited partnership had been carried on under that name before the admission of that limited partner;

(3) may not contain any word or phrase indicating or implying that it is organized other than for a purpose stated in its certificate of limited partnership;

(4) may not be the same as, or deceptively similar to, the name of any corporation or limited partnership organized under the laws of this State or licensed or registered as a foreign corporation or limited partnership in this State; and

(5) may not contain the following words [here insert prohibited words].

Sec. 103. **Reservation of Name**

(a) The exclusive right to the use of a name may be reserved by:

(1) any person intending to organize a limited partnership under this Act and to adopt that name;

(2) any domestic limited partnership or any foreign limited partnership registered in this State which, in either case, intends to adopt that name;

(3) any foreign limited partnership intending to register in this State and to adopt that name; and

(4) any person intending to organize a foreign limited partnership and intending to have it register in this State and adopt that name.

(b) The reservation shall be made by filing with the Secretary of State an application, executed by the applicant, to reserve a specified name. If the Secretary of State finds that the name is available for use by a domestic or foreign limited partnership, he shall reserve the name for the exclusive use of the applicant for a period of 120 days. Once having reserved a name, the same applicant may not again reserve the same name until more than 60 days after the expiration of the last 120-day period for which that applicant reserved that name. The right to the exclusive use of a reserved name may be transferred to any other person by filing in the office of the Secretary of State a notice of the transfer, executed by the applicant for whom the name was reserved and specifying the name and address of the transferee.

Sec. 104. Specified Office and Agent

Each limited partnership shall continuously maintain in this State:

(1) an office, which may but need not be a place of its business in this State, at which shall be kept the records required by Section 105 to be maintained; and

(2) an agent for service of process on the limited partnership, which agent must be an individual resident of this State, a domestic corporation, or a foreign corporation authorized to do business in this State.

Sec. 105. Records to be Kept

Each limited partnership shall keep at the office referred to in Section 104(1) the following: (1) a current list of the full name and last known business address of each partner set forth in alphabetical order, (2) a copy of the certificate of limited partnership and all certificates of amendment thereto, together with executed copies of any powers of attorney pursuant to which any certificate has been executed, (3) copies of the limited partnership's federal, state, and local income tax returns and reports, if any, for the 3 most recent years, and (4) copies of any then effective written partnership agreements and of any financial statements of the limited partnership for the 3 most recent years. These records are subject to inspection and copying at the reasonable request, and at the expense, of any partner during ordinary business hours.

Sec. 106. Nature of Business

A limited partnership may carry on any business that a partnership without limited partners may carry on except [here designate prohibited activities].

Sec. 107. Business Transactions of Partner With the Partnership

Except as provided in the partnership agreement, a partner may lend money to and transact other business with the limited partnership and, subject to other applicable law, has the same rights and obligations with respect thereto as a person who is not a partner.

Article 2
FORMATION; CERTIFICATE OF LIMITED PARTNERSHIP

Sec. 201. Certificate of Limited Partnership

(a) In order to form a limited partnership two or more persons must execute a certificate of limited partnership. The certificate shall be filed in the office of the Secretary of State and set forth:

(1) the name of the limited partnership;

(2) the general character of its business;

(3) the address of the office and the name and address of the agent for service of process required to be maintained by Section 104;

(4) the name and the business address of each partner (specifying separately the general partners and limited partners);

(5) the amount of cash and a description and statement of the agreed value of the other property or services contributed by each partner and which each partner has agreed to contribute in the future;

(6) the times at which or events on the happening of which any additional contributions agreed to be made by each partner are to be made;

(7) any power of a limited partner to grant the right to become a limited partner to an assignee of any part of his partnership interest and the terms and conditions of the power;

(8) if agreed upon, the time at which or the events on the happening of which a partner may terminate his membership in the limited partnership and the amount of, or the method of determining, the distribution to which he may be entitled respecting his partnership interest, and the terms and conditions of the termination and distribution;

(9) any right of a partner to receive distributions of property, including cash from the limited partnership;

(10) any right of a partner to receive, or of a general partner to make, distributions to a partner which include a return of all or any part of the partner's contribution;

(11) any time at which or events upon the happening of which the limited partnership is to be dissolved and its affairs wound up;

(12) any right of the remaining general partners to continue the business on the happening of an event of withdrawal of a general partner; and

(13) any other matters the partners determine to include therein.

(b) A limited partnership is formed at the time of the filing of the certificate of limited partnership in the office of the Secretary of State or at any later time specified in the certificate of limited partnership if, in each case, there has been substantial compliance with the requirements of this section.

Sec. 202. Amendment to Certificate

(a) A certificate of limited partnership is amended by filing a certificate of amendment thereto in the office of the Secretary of State. The certificate shall set forth:

(1) the name of the limited partnership;

(2) the date of filing of the certificate; and

(3) the amendments to the certificate.

(b) Within 30 days after the happening of any of the following events an amendment to a certificate of limited partnership reflecting the occurrence of the event or events shall be filed:

(1) a change in the amount or character of the contribution of any partner, or in any partner's obligation to make a contribution;

(2) the admission of a new partner;

(3) the withdrawal of a partner; or

(4) the continuation of the business under Section 801 after an event of withdrawal of a general partner.

(c) A general partner who becomes aware that any statement in a certificate of limited partnership was false when made or that any arrangements or other facts described have changed, making the certificate inaccurate in any respect, shall promptly amend the certificate, but an amendment to show a change of address of a limited partner need be filed only once every 12 months.

(d) A certificate of limited partnership may be amended at any time for any other proper purpose the general partners may determine.

(e) No person has any liability because an amendment to a certificate of limited partnership has not been filed to reflect the occurrence of any event referred to in subsection (b) of this Section if the amendment is filed within the 30-day period specified in subsection (b).

Sec. 203. Cancellation of Certificate

A certificate of limited partnership shall be cancelled upon the dissolution and the commencement of winding up of the partnership and at any other time there are no limited partners. A certificate of cancellation shall be filed in the office of the Secretary of State and shall set forth:

(1) the name of the limited partnership;

(2) the date of filing of its certificate of limited partnership;

(3) the reason for filing the certificate of cancellation;

(4) the effective date (which shall be a date certain) of cancellation if it is not to be effective upon the filing of the certificate; and

(5) any other information the general partners filing the certificate may determine.

Sec. 204. Execution of Certificates

(a) Each certificate required by this Article to be filed in the office of the Secretary of State shall be executed in the following manner:

(1) each original certificate of limited partnership must be signed by each partner named therein;

(2) each certificate of amendment must be signed by at least one general partner and by each other partner designated in the certificate as a new partner or whose contribution is described as having been increased; and

(3) each certificate of cancellation must be signed by all general partners.

(b) Any person may sign a certificate by an attorney-in-fact, but a power of attorney to sign a certificate relating to the admission, or increased contribution, of a partner must specifically describe the admission or increase.

(c) The execution of a certificate by a general partner constitutes an affirmation under the penalties of perjury that the facts stated therein are true.

Sec. 205. Amendment or Cancellation by Judicial Act

If a person required by Section 204 to execute a certificate of amendment or cancellation fail or refuse to do so, any other partner, and any assignee of a partnership interest, who is adversely affected by the failure or refusal, may petition the [here designate the proper court] to direct the amendment or cancellation. If the court finds that the amendment or cancellation is proper and that the person so designated has failed or refused to execute the certificate, it shall order the Secretary of State to record an appropriate certificate of amendment or cancellation.

Sec. 206. **Filing in the Office of the Secretary of State**

(a) Two signed copies of the certificate of limited partnership and of any certificates of amendment or cancellation (or of any judicial decree of amendment or cancellation) shall be delivered to the Secretary of State. A person who executes a certificate as an agent or fiduciary need not exhibit evidence of his authority as a prerequisite to filing. Unless the Secretary of State finds that any certificate does not conform to law, upon receipt of all filing fees required by law he shall:

(1) endorse on each duplicate original the word "Filed" and the day, month, and year of the filing thereof;

(2) file one duplicate original in his office; and

(3) return the other duplicate original to the person who filed it or his representative.

(b) Upon the filing of a certificate of amendment (or judicial decree of amendment) in the office of the Secretary of State, the certificate of limited partnership shall be amended as set forth therein, and upon the effective date of a certificate of cancellation (or a judicial decree thereof), the certificate of limited partnership is cancelled.

Sec. 207. **Liability for False Statement in Certificate**

If any certificate of limited partnership or certificate of amendment or cancellation contains a false statement, one who suffers loss by reliance on the statement may recover damages for the loss from:

(1) any person who executes the certificate, or causes another to execute it on his behalf, and knew, and any general partner who knew or should have known, the statement to be false at the time the certificate was executed; and

(2) any general partner who thereafter knows or should have known that any arrangement or other fact described in the certificate have changed, making the statement inaccurate in any respect within a sufficient time before the statement was relied upon reasonably to have enabled that general partner to cancel or amend the certificate, or to file a petition for its cancellation or amendment under Section 205.

Sec. 208. **Notice**

The fact that a certificate of limited partnership is on file in the office of the Secretary of State is notice that the partnership is a limited partnership and the persons designated therein as limited partners are limited partners, but is not notice of any other fact.

Sec. 209. **Delivery of Certificates to Limited Partners**

Upon the return by the Secretary of State pursuant to Section 206 of a certificate marked "Filed," the general partners shall promptly deliver or mail a copy of the certificate of limited partnership and each certificate to each limited partner unless the partnership agreement provides otherwise.

Article 3
LIMITED PARTNERS

Sec. 301. **Admission of Additional Limited Partners**

(a) After the filing of a limited partnership's original certificate of limited partnership, a person may be admitted as an additional limited partner:

(1) in the case of a person acquiring a partnership interest directly from the limited partnership, upon the compliance with the partnership agreement or, if the partnership agreement does not so provide, upon the written consent of all partners; and

(2) in the case of an assignee of a partnership interest of a partner who has the power, as provided in Section 704, to grant the assignee the right to become a limited partner, upon the exercise of that power and compliance with any conditions limiting the grant or exercise of the power.

(b) In each case under subsection (a), the person acquiring the partnership interest becomes a limited partner only upon amendment of the certificate of limited partnership reflecting that fact.

Sec. 302. **Voting**

Subject to Section 303, the partnership agreement may grant to all or a specified group of the limited partners the right to vote (on a per capita or any other basis) upon any matter.

Sec. 303. **Liability to Third Parties**

(a) Except as provided in subsection (d), a limited partner is not liable for the obligations of a limited partnership unless he is also a general partner or, in addition to the exercise of his rights and powers as a limited partner, he takes part in the control of the business. However, if the limited partner's participation in the control of the business is not substantially the same as the exercise of the powers of a general partner, he is liable only to persons who transact business with the limited partnership with actual knowledge of his participation in control.

(b) A limited partner does not participate in the control of the business within the meaning of subsection (a) solely by doing one or more of the following:

(1) being a contractor for or an agent or employee of the limited partnership or of a general partner;

(2) consulting with and advising a general partner with respect to the business of the limited partnership;

(3) acting as surety for the limited partnership;

(4) approving or disapproving an amendment to the partnership agreement; or

(5) voting on one or more of the following matters:

(i) the dissolution and winding up of the limited partnership;

(ii) the sale, exchange, lease, mortgage, pledge, or other transfer of all or substantially all of the assets of the limited partnership other than in the ordinary course of its business;

(iii) the incurrence of indebtedness by the limited partnership other than in the ordinary course of its business;

(iv) a change in the nature of the business; or

(v) the removal of a general partner.

(c) The enumeration in subsection (b) does not mean that the possession or exercise of any other powers by a limited partner constitutes participation by him in the business of the limited partnership.

(d) A limited partner who knowingly permits his name to be used in the name of the limited partnership, except under circumstances permitted by Section 102(2)(i), is liable to creditors who extend credit to the limited partnership without actual knowledge that the limited partner is not a general partner.

Sec. 304. **Person Erroneously Believing Himself Limited Partner**

(a) Except as provided in subsection (b), a person who makes a contribution to a business enterprise and erroneously but in good faith believes that he has become a limited partner in the enterprise is not a general partner in the enterprise and is not bound by its obligations by reason of making the contribution, receiving distributions from the enterprise, or exercising any rights of a limited partner, if, on ascertaining the mistake, he:

(1) causes an appropriate certificate of limited partnership or a certificate of amendment to be executed and filed; or

(2) withdraws from future equity participation in the enterprise.

(b) Any person who makes a contribution of the kind described in subsection (a) is liable as a general partner to any third party who transacts business with the enterprise (i) before the person withdraws and an appropriate certificate is filed to show withdrawal, or (ii) before an appropriate certificate is filed to show his status as a limited partner and, in the case of an amendment, after expiration of the 30-day period for filing an amendment relating to the person as a limited partner under Section 202, but in

either case only if the third party actually believed in good faith that the person was a general partner at the time of the transaction.

Sec. 305. **Information**

Each limited partner has the right to:

(1) inspect and copy any of the partnership records required to be maintained by Section 105; and

(2) obtain from the general partners from time to time upon reasonable demand (i) true and full information regarding the state of the business and financial condition of the limited partnership, (ii) promptly after becoming available, a copy of the limited partnership's federal, state, and local income tax returns for each year, and (iii) other information regarding the affairs of the limited partnership as is just and reasonable.

Article 4
GENERAL PARTNERS

Sec. 401. **Admission of Additional General Partners**

After the filing of a limited partnership's original certificate of limited partnership, additional general partners may be admitted only with the specific written consent of each partner.

Sec. 402. **Events of Withdrawal**

Except as approved by the specific written consent of all partners at the time, a person ceases to be a general partner of a limited partnership upon the happening of any of the following events:

(1) the general partner withdraws from the limited partnership as provided in Section 602;

(2) the general partner ceases to be a member of the limited partnership as provided in Section 702;

(3) the general partner is removed as a general partner in accordance with the partnership agreement;

(4) unless otherwise provided in the certificate of limited partnership, the general partner: (i) makes an assignment for the benefit of creditors; (ii) files a voluntary petition in bankruptcy; (iii) is adjudicated a bankrupt or insolvent; (iv) files a petition or answer seeking for himself any reorganization, arrangement, composition, readjustment, liquidation, dissolution, or similar relief under any statute, law, or regulation; (v) files an answer or other pleading admitting or failing to contest the material allegations of a petition filed against him in any proceeding of this nature; or (vi) seeks, consents to, or acquiesces in the appointment of a trustee, receiver, or liquidator of the general partner or of all or any substantial part of his properties;

(5) unless otherwise provided in the certificate of limited partnership, [120] days after the commencement of any proceeding against the general partner seeking any reorganization, arrangement, composition, readjustment, liquidation, dissolution, or similar relief under any statute, law, or regulation, the proceeding has not been dismissed, or if within [90] days after the appointment without his consent or acquiescence of any trustee, receiver, or liquidator of the general partner or of all or any substantial part of his properties, the appointment is not vacated or stayed, or within [90] days after the expiration of any such stay, the appointment is not vacated;

(6) in the case of a general partner who is a natural person

　(i) his death; or

　(ii) the entry by a court of competent jurisdiction adjudicating him incompetent to manage his person or his estate;

(7) in the case of a general partner who is acting as a general partner by virture of being a trustee of a trust, the termination of the trust (but not merely the substitution of a new trustee);

(8) in the case of a general partner that is a separate partnership, the dissolution and commencement of winding up of the partnership;

(9) in the case of a general partner that is a corporation, the filing of a certificate of dissolution, or its equivalent, for the corporation or the revocation of its charter; and

(10) in the case of an estate, the distribution by the fiduciary of the estate's entire interest in the partnership.

Sec. 403. General Powers and Liabilities

(a) Except as provided in this Act or in the partnership agreement, a general partner of a limited partnership has the rights and powers and is subject to the restrictions of a partner in a partnership without limited partners.

(b) Except as provided in this Act, a general partner of a limited partnership has the liabilities of a partner in a partnership without limited partners to persons other than the partnership and the other partners. Except as provided in this Act or in the partnership agreement, a general partner of a limited partnership has the liabilities of a partner in a partnership without limited partners to the partnership and to the other partners.

Sec. 404. Contributions by a General Partner

A general partner of a limited partnership may make contribution to the partnership and share in the profits and losses of, and in distributions from, the limited partnership as a general partner. A general partner also may make contributions to and share in profits, losses, and distributions as a limited partner. A person who is both a general partner and a limited partner has the rights and powers, and is subject to the restrictions and liabilities, of a general partner and, except as provided in the partnership agreement, also has the powers, and is subject to the restrictions, of a limited partner to the extent of his participation in the partnership as a limited partner.

Sec. 405. Voting

The partnership agreement may grant to all or certain identified general partners the right to vote (on a per capita or any other basis), separately or with all or any class of the limited partners, on any matter.

Article 5
FINANCE

Sec. 501. Form of Contributions

The contribution of a partner may be in cash, property, or services rendered, or a promissory note or other obligation to contribute cash or property or to perform services.

Sec. 502. Liability for Contributions

(a) Except as otherwise provided in the certificate of limited partnership, a partner is obligated to the limited partnership to perform any promise to contribute cash or property or to perform services even if he is unable to perform because of death, disability or any other reason. If a partner does not make the required contribution of property or services, he is obligated at the option of the limited partnership to contribute cash equal to that portion of the value (as stated in the certificate of limited partnership) of the stated contribution that has not been made.

(b) Unless otherwise provided in the partnership agreement, the obligation of a partner to make a contribution or return money or other property paid or distributed in violation of this Act may be compromised only by consent of all of the partners. Notwithstanding the compromise, a creditor of a limited partnership who extends credit, or whose claim arises, after the filing of the certificate of limited partnership or an amendment thereto which, in either case, reflects the obligation and before the amendment or cancellation thereof to reflect the compromise, may enforce the original obligation.

Sec. 503. Sharing of Profits and Losses

The profits and losses of a limited partnership shall be allocated among the partners, and among classes of partners, in the manner provided in the partnership agreement. If the partnership agreement does not so provide, profits and losses shall be allocated on the basis of the value (as stated in the certificate of limited partnership) of the contributions made by each partner to the extent they have been received by the partnership and have not been returned.

Sec. 504. Sharing of Distributions

Distributions of cash or other assets of a limited partnership shall be allocated among the partners, and among classes of partners, in the manner provided in the partnership agreement. If the partnership agreement does not so provide, distributions shall be made on the basis of the value (as stated in the certificate of limited partnership) of the contributions made by each partner to the extent they have not been received by the partnership and have not been returned.

Article 6
DISTRIBUTIONS AND WITHDRAWAL

Sec. 601. Interim Distributions

Except as provided in this Article, a partner is entitled to receive distributions from a limited partnership before his withdrawal from the limited partnership and before the dissolution and winding up thereof:

(1) to the extent and at the times or upon the happening of the events specified in the partnership agreement; and

(2) if any distribution constitutes a return of any part of his contribution under Section 608(c), to the extent and at the times or upon the happening of the events specified in the certificate of limited partnership.

Sec. 602. Withdrawal of General Partner

A general partner may withdraw from a limited partnership at any time by giving written notice to the other partners, but if the withdrawal violates the partnership agreement, the limited partnership may recover from the withdrawing general partner damages for breach of the partnership agreement and offset the damages against the amount otherwise distributable to him.

Sec. 603. Withdrawal of Limited Partner

A limited partner may withdraw from a limited partnership at the time or upon the happening of the events specified in the certificate of limited partnership and in accordance with the partnership agreement. If the certificate does not specify the time or the events upon the happening of which a limited partner may withdraw or a definite time for the dissolution and winding up of the limited partnership, a limited partner may withdraw upon not less than 6 months' prior written notice to each general partner at his address on the books of the limited partnership at its office in this State.

Sec. 604. Distribution Upon Withdrawal

Except as provided in this Article, upon withdrawal any withdrawing partner is entitled to receive any distribution to which he is entitled under the partnership agreement and, if not otherwise provided in the agreement, he is entitled to receive, within a reasonable time after withdrawal, the fair value of his interest in the limited partnership as of the date of withdrawal based upon his right to share in distributions from the limited partnership.

Sec. 605. Distribution in Kind

Except as provided in the certificate of limited partnership, a partner, regardless of the nature of his contribution, has no right to demand and receive any distribution from a limited partnership in any form other than cash. Except as provided in the partnership agreement, a partner may not be compelled to accept a distribution of any asset in kind from a limited partnership to the extent that the percentage of the asset distributed to him exceeds a percentage of that asset which is equal to the percentage in which he shares in distributions from the limited partnership.

Sec. 606. Right to Distribution

At the time a partner becomes entitled to receive a distribution, he has the status of, and is entitled to all remedies available to, a creditor of the limited partnership with respect to the distribution.

Sec. 607. Limitations on Distribution

A partner may not receive a distribution from a limited partnership to the extent that, after giving effect to the distribution, all liabilities of the limited partnership, other than liabilities to partners on account of their partnership interests, exceed the fair value of the partnership assets.

Sec. 608. Liability Upon Return of Contributions

(a) If a partner has received the return of any part of his contribution without violation of the partnership agreement or this Act, he is liable to the limited partnership for a period of one year thereafter for the amount of the returned contribution, but only to the extent necessary to discharge the limited partnership's liabilities to creditors who extended credit to the limited partnership during the period the contribution was held by the partnership.

(b) If a partner has received the return of any part of his contribution in violation of the partnership agreement or this Act, he is liable to the limited partnership for a period of 6 years thereafter for the amount of the contribution wrongfully returned.

(c) A partner receives a return of his contribution to the extent that a distribution to him reduces his share of the fair value of the net assets of the limited partnership below the value (as set forth in the certificate of limited partnership) of his contributions which has not been distributed to him.

Article 7
ASSIGNMENT OF PARTNERSHIP INTERESTS

Sec. 701. **Nature of Partnership Interest**

A partnership interest is personal property.

Sec. 702. **Assignment of Partnership Interest**

Except as provided in the partnership agreement, a partnership interest is assignable in whole or in part. An assignment of a partnership interest does not dissolve a limited partnership or entitle the assignee to become or to exercise any rights of a partner. An assignment entitles the assignee to receive, to the extent assigned, only the distribution to which the assignor would be entitled. Except as provided in the partnership agreement, a partner ceases to be a partner upon assignment of all his partnership interest.

Sec. 703. **Rights of Creditor**

On application to a court of competent jurisdiction by any judgment creditor of a partner, the court may charge the partnership interest of the partner with payment of the unsatisfied amount of the judgment with interest. To the extent so charged, the judgment creditor has only the rights of an assignee of the partnership interest. This Act does not deprive any partner of the benefit of any exemption laws applicable to his partnership interest.

Sec. 704. **Right of Assignee to Become Limited Partner**

(a) An assignee of a partnership interest, including an assignee of a general partner, may become a limited partner if and to the extent that (1) the assignor gives the assignee that right in accordance with authority described in the certificate of limited partnership, or (2) all other partners consent.

(b) An assignee who has become a limited partner has, to the extent assigned, the rights and powers, and is subject to the restrictions and liabilities, of a limited partner under the partnership agreement and this Act. An assignee who becomes a limited partner also is liable for the obligations of his assignor to make and return contributions as provided in Article 6. However, the assignee is not obligated for liabilities unknown to the assignee at the time he became a limited partner and which could not be ascertained from the certificate of limited partnership.

(c) If an assignee of a partnership interest becomes a limited partner, the assignor is not released from his liability to the limited partnership under Sections 207 and 502.

Sec. 705. **Power of Estate of Deceased or Incompetent Partner**

If a partner who is an individual dies or a court of competent jurisdiction adjudges him to be incompetent to manage his person or his property, the partner's executor, administrator, guardian, conservator, or other legal representative may exercise all of the partner's rights for the purpose of settling his estate or administering his property, including any power the partner had to give an assignee the right to become a limited partner. If a partner is a corporation, trust, or other entity and is dissolved or terminated, the powers of that partner may be exercised by its legal representative or successor.

Article 8
DISSOLUTION

Sec. 801. **Nonjudicial Dissolution**

A limited partnership is dissolved and its affairs shall be wound up upon the happening of the first to occur of the following:

(1) at the time or upon the happening of events specified in the certificate of limited partnership;

(2) written consent of all partners;

(3) an event of withdrawal of a general partner unless at the time there is at least one other general partner and the certificate of limited partnership permits the business of the limited partnership to be carried on by the remaining general partner and that partner does so, but the limited partnership is not dissolved and is not required to be wound up by reason of any event of withdrawal if, within 90 days after the withdrawal, all partners agree in writing to continue the business of the limited partnership and to the appointment of one or more additional general partners if necessary or desired; or

(4) entry of a decree of judicial dissolution under Section 802.

Sec. 802. **Judicial Dissolution**

On application by or for a partner the [here designate the proper court] court may decree a dissolution of a limited partnership whenever it is not reasonably practicable to carry on the business in conformity with the partnership agreement.

Sec. 803. **Winding Up**

Except as provided in the partnership agreement, the general partners who have not wrongfully dissolved a limited partnership or, if none, the limited partners, may wind up the limited partnership's affairs; but the [here designate the proper court] court may wind up the limited partnership's affairs upon application of any partner, his legal representative, or assignee.

Sec. 804. **Distribution of Assets**

Upon the winding up of a limited partnership, the assets shall be distributed as follows:

(1) to creditors, including partners who are creditors, to the extent otherwise permitted by law, in satisfaction of liabilities of the limited partnership other than liabilities for distributions to partners under Section 601 or 604;

(2) except as provided in the partnership agreement, to partners and former partners in satisfaction of liabilities for distributions under Section 601 or 604; and

(3) except as provided in the partnership agreement, to partners *first* for the return of their contributions and *secondly* respecting their partnership interests, in the proportions in which the partners share in distributions.

Article 9
FOREIGN LIMITED PARTNERSHIPS

Sec. 901. **Law Governing**

Subject to the Constitution of this State, (1) the laws of the state under which a foreign limited partnership is organized govern its organization and internal affairs and the liability of its limited partners, and (2) a foreign limited partnership may not be denied registration by reason of any difference between those laws and the laws of this State.

Sec. 902. **Registration**

Before transacting business in this State, a foreign limited partnership shall register with the Secretary of State. In order to register, a foreign limited partnership shall submit to the Secretary of State, in duplicate, an application for registration as a foreign limited partnership, signed and sworn to by a general partner and setting forth:

(1) the name of the foreign limited partnership and, if different, the name under which it proposes to register and transact business in this State;

(2) the state and date of its formation;

(3) the general character of the business it proposes to transact in this State;

(4) the name and address of any agent for service of process on the foreign limited partnership whom the foreign limited partnership elects to appoint, the agent must be an individual resident of this State, a domestic corpora-

tion, or a foreign corporation having a place of business in, and authorized to do business in this State;

(5) a statement that the Secretary of State is appointed the agent of the foreign limited partnership for service of process if no agent has been appointed under paragraph (4) or, if appointed, the agent's authority has been revoked or if the agent cannot be found or served with the exercise of reasonable diligence;

(6) the address of the office required to be maintained in the State of its organization by the laws of that State or, if not so required, of the principal office of the foreign limited partnership; and

(7) If the certificate of limited partnership filed in the foreign limited partnership's state of organization is not required to include the names and business addresses of the partners, a list of the names and addresses.

Sec. 903. **Issuance of Registration**

(a) If the Secretary of State finds that an application for registration conforms to law and all requisite fees have been paid, he shall:

(1) endorse on the application the word "Filed", and the month, day, and year of the filing thereof;

(2) file in his office a duplicate original of the application; and

(3) issue a certificate of registration to transact business in this State.

(b) The certificate of registration, together with a duplicate original of the application, shall be returned to the person who filed the application or his representative.

Sec. 904. **Name**

A foreign limited partnership may register with the Secretary of State under any name (whether or not it is the name under which it is registered in its state of organization) that includes without abbreviation the words "limited partnership" and that could be registered by a domestic limited partnership.

Sec. 905. **Changes and Amendments**

If any statement in the application for registration of a foreign limited partnership was false when made or any arrangements or other facts described have changed, making the application inaccurate in any respect, the foreign limited partnership shall promptly file in the office of the Secretary of State a certificate, signed and sworn to by a general partner, correcting the statement.

Sec. 906. **Cancellation of Registration**

A foreign limited partnership may cancel its registration by filing with the Secretary of State a certificate of cancellation signed and sworn to by a general partner. A cancellation does not terminate the authority of the Secretary of State to accept service of process on the foreign limited partnership with respect to [claims for relief] [causes of action] arising out of the transaction of business in this State.

Sec. 907. **Transaction of Business Without Registration**

(a) A foreign limited partnership transacting business in this State may not maintain any action, suit, or proceeding in any court of this State until it has registered in this State.

(b) The failure of a foreign limited partnership to register in this State does not impair the validity of any contract or act of the foreign limited partnership or prevent the foreign limited partnership from defending any action, suit, or proceeding in any court of this State.

(c) A limited partner of a foreign limited partnership is not liable as a general partner of the foreign limited partnership solely by reason of having transacted business in this State without registration.

(d) A foreign limited partnership, by transacting business in this State without registration, appoints the Secretary of State as its agent for service of process with respect to [claims for relief] [causes of action] arising out of the transaction of business in this State.

Sec. 908. **Action by [Appropriate Official]**

The [appropriate official may bring an action to restrain a foreign limited partnership from transacting business in this State in violation of this Article.

Article 10
DERIVATIVE ACTIONS

Sec. 1001. **Right of Action**

A limited partner may bring an action in the right of a limited partnership to recover a judgment in its favor if general partners with authority to do so have refused to bring the action or if an effort to cause those general partners to bring the action is not likely to succeed.

Sec. 1002. **Proper Plaintiff**

In a derivative action, the plaintiff must be a partner at the time of bringing the action and (1) at the time of the transaction of which he complains or (2) his status as a partner had devolved upon him by operation of law or pursuant to the terms of the partnership agreement from a person who was a partner at the time of the transaction.

Sec. 1003. **Pleading**

In any derivative action, the complaint shall set forth with particularity the effort of the plaintiff to secure initiation of the action by a general partner or the reasons for not making the effort.

Sec. 1004. **Expenses**

If a derivative action is successful, in whole or in part, or if anything is received by the plaintiff as a result of a judgment, compromise, or settlement of an action or claim, the court may award the plaintiff reasonable expenses, including reasonable attorney's fees, and shall direct him to remit to the limited partnership the remainder of those proceeds received by him.

Article 11
MISCELLANEOUS

Sec. 1101. **Construction and Application**

This Act shall be so applied and construed to effectuate its general purpose to make uniform the law with respect to the subject of this Act among states enacting it.

Sec. 1102. **Short Title**

This Act may be cited as the Uniform Limited Partnership Act.

Sec. 1103. **Severability**

If any provision of this Act or its application to any person or circumstance is held invalid, the invalidity does not affect other provisions or applications of the Act which can be given effect without the invalid provision or application, and to this end the provisions of this Act are severable.

Sec. 1104. **Effective Date, Extended Effective Date and Repeal**

Except as set forth below, the effective date of this Act is _____ and the following Acts [list prior limited partnership acts] are hereby repealed:

(1) The existing provisions for execution and filing of certificates of limited partnerships and amendments thereunder and cancellations thereof continue in effect until [specify time required to create central filing system], the extended effective date, and Sections 102, 103, 104, 105, 201, 202, 203, 204 and 206 are not effective until the extended effective date.

(2) Section 402, specifying the conditions under which a general partner ceases to be a member of a limited part-

nership, is not effective until the extended effective date, and the applicable provisions of existing law continue to govern until the extended effective date.

(3) Sections 501, 502 and 608 apply only to contributions and distributions made after the effective date of this Act.

(4) Section 704 applies only to assignments made after the effective date of this Act.

(5) Article 9, dealing with registration of foreign limited partnerships, is not effective until the extended effective date.

Sec. 1105. **Rules for Cases Not Provided for in This Act**

In any case not provided for in this Act the provisions of the Uniform Partnership Act govern.

APPENDIX G

THE MODEL BUSINESS CORPORATION ACT

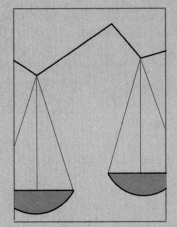

§ 1. Short Title*

This Act shall be known and may be cited as the ". . . . .† Business Corporation Act."

§ 2. Definitions

As used in this Act, unless the context otherwise requires, the term:

(a) "Corporation" or "domestic corporation" means a corporation for profit subject to the provisions of this Act, except a foreign corporation.

(b) "Foreign corporation" means a corporation for profit organized under laws other than the laws of this State for a purpose or purposes for which a corporation may be organized under this Act.

(c) "Articles of incorporation" means the original or restated articles of incorporation or articles of consolidation and all amendments thereto including articles of merger.

(d) "Shares" means the units into which the proprietary interests in a corporation are divided.

(e) "Subscriber" means one who subscribes for shares in a corporation, whether before or after incorporation.

(f) "Shareholder" means one who is a holder of record of shares in a corporation. If the articles of incorporation or the by-laws so provide, the board of directors may adopt by resolution a procedure whereby a shareholder of the corporation may certify in writing to the corporation that all or a portion of the shares registered in the name of such shareholder are held for the account of a specified person or persons. The resolution shall set forth (1) the classification of shareholder who may certify, (2) the purpose or purposes for which the certification may be made, (3) the form of certification and information to be con-

---

*[By the Editor] The Model Business Corporation Act prepared by the Committee on Corporate Laws (Section of Corporation, Banking and Business Law) of the American Bar Association was originally patterned after the Illinois Business Corporation Act of 1933. It was first published as a complete act in 1950. In subsequent years several revisions, addenda and optional or alternative provisions were added. The Act was substantially revised and renumbered in 1969.

This Act should be distinguished from the Model Business Corporation Act promulgated in 1928 by the Commissioners on Uniform State Laws under the name "Uniform Business Corporation Act" and renamed Model Business Corporation Act in 1943. This Uniform Act was withdrawn in 1957.

The Model Business Corporation Act has been influential in the codification of corporation statutes in more than 35 states. However, there is no state that has totally adopted it in its current form. Moreover, since the Model Act itself has been substantially modified from time to time, there is considerable variation among the statutes of the states that used this Act as a model.

†Insert name of State.

tained therein, (4) if the certification is with respect to a record date or closing of the stock transfer books within which the certification must be received by the corporation and (5) such other provisions with respect to the procedure as are deemed necessary or desirable. Upon receipt by the corporation of a certification complying with the procedure, the persons specified in the certification shall be deemed, for the purpose or purposes set forth in the certification, to be the holders of record of the number of shares specified in place of the shareholder making the certification.

(g) "Authorized shares" means the shares of all classes which the corporation is authorized to issue.

(h) "Employee" includes officers but not directors. A director may accept duties which make him also an employee.

(i) "Distribution" means a direct or indirect transfer of money or other property (except its own shares) or incurrence of indebtedness, by a corporation to or for the benefit of any of its shareholders in respect of any of its shares, whether by dividend or by purchase, redemption or other acquisition of its shares, or otherwise.

§ 3. Purposes

Corporations may be organized under this Act for any lawful purpose or purposes, except for the purpose of banking or insurance.

§ 4. General Powers

Each corporation shall have power:

(a) To have perpetual succession by its corporate name unless a limited period of duration is stated in its articles of incorporation.

(b) To sue and be sued, complain and defend, in its corporate name.

(c) To have a corporate seal which may be altered at pleasure, and to use the same by causing it, or a facsimile thereof, to be impressed or affixed or in any other manner reproduced.

(d) To purchase, take, receive, lease, or otherwise acquire, own, hold, improve, use and otherwise deal in and with, real or personal property, or any interest therein, wherever situated.

(e) To sell, convey, mortgage, pledge, lease, exchange, transfer and otherwise dispose of all or any part of its property and assets.

(f) To lend money and use its credit to assist its employees.

(g) To purchase, take, receive, subscribe for, or otherwise acquire, own, hold, vote, use, employ, sell, mortgage, lend, pledge, or otherwise dispose of, and otherwise use and deal in and with, shares or other interests in, or obligations of, other domestic or foreign corporations, associations, partnerships or individuals, or direct or indirect obligations of the United States or of any other government, state, territory, governmental district or municipality or of any instrumentality thereof.

(h) To make contracts and guarantees and incur liabilities, borrow money at such rates of interest as the corporation may determine, issue its notes, bonds, and other obligations, and secure any of its obligations by mortgage or pledge of all or any of its property, franchises and income.

(i) To lend money for its corporate purposes, invest and reinvest its funds, and take and hold real and personal property as security for the payment of funds so loaned or invested.

(j) To conduct its business, carry on its operations and have offices and exercise the powers granted by this Act, within or without this State.

(k) To elect or appoint officers and agents of the corporation, and define their duties and fix their compensation.

(l) To make and alter by-laws, not inconsistent with its articles of incorporation or with the laws of this State, for the administration and regulation of the affairs of the corporation.

(m) To make donations for the public welfare or for charitable, scientific or educational purposes.

(n) To transact any lawful business which the board of directors shall find will be in aid of governmental policy.

(o) To pay pensions and establish pension plans, pension trusts, profit sharing plans, stock bonus plans, stock option plans and other incentive plans for any or all of its directors, officers and employees.

(p) To be a promoter, partner, member, associate, or manager of any partnership, joint venture, trust or other enterprise.

(q) To have and exercise all powers necessary or convenient to effect its purposes.

§ 5. Indemnification of Directors and Officers

(a) As used in this section:

(1) "Director" means any person who is or was a director of the corporation and any person who, while a director of the corporation, is or was serving at the request of the corporation as a director, officer, partner, trustee, employee or agent of another foreign or domestic corporation, partnership, joint venture, trust, other enterprise or employee benefit plan.

(2) "Corporation" includes any domestic or foreign predecessor entity of the corporation in a merger, consolida-

tion or other transaction in which the predecessor's existence ceased upon consummation of such transaction.

(3) "Expenses" include attorneys' fees.

(4) "Official capacity" means

(A) when used with respect to a director, the office of director in the corporation, and

(B) when used with respect to a person other than a director, as contemplated in subsection (i), the elective or appointive office in the corporation held by the officer or the employment or agency relationship undertaken by the employee or agent in behalf of the corporation,

but in each case does not include service for any other foreign or domestic corporation or any partnership, joint venture, trust, other enterprise, or employee benefit plan.

(5) "Party" includes a person who was, is, or is threatened to be made, a named defendant or respondent in a proceeding.

(6) "Proceeding" means any threatened, pending or completed action, suit or proceeding, whether civil, criminal, administrative or investigative.

(b) A corporation shall have power to indemnify any person made a party to any proceeding by reason of the fact that he is or was a director if

(1) he conducted himself in good faith; and

(2) he reasonably believed

(A) in the case of conduct in his official capacity with the corporation, that his conduct was in its best interests, and

(B) in all other cases, that his conduct was at least not opposed to its best interests; and

(3) in the case of any criminal proceeding, he had no reasonable cause to believe his conduct was unlawful.

Indemnification may be made against judgments, penalties, fines, settlements and reasonable expenses, actually incurred by the person in connection with the proceeding; except that if the proceeding was by or in the right of the corporation, indemnification may be made only against such reasonable expenses and shall not be made in respect of any proceeding in which the person shall have been adjudged to be liable to the corporation. The termination of any proceeding by judgment, order, settlement, conviction, or upon a plea of nolo contendere or its equivalent, shall not, of itself, be determinative that the person did not meet the requisite standard of conduct set forth in this subsection (b).

(c) A director shall not be indemnified under subsection (b) in respect of any proceeding charging improper personal benefit to him, whether or not involving action in his official capacity, in which he shall have been adjudged to be liable on the basis that personal benefit was improperly received by him.

(d) Unless limited by the articles of incorporation,

(1) a director who has been wholly successful, on the merits or otherwise, in the defense of any proceeding referred to in subsection (b) shall be indemnified against reasonable expenses incurred by him in connection with the proceeding; and

(2) a court of appropriate jurisdiction, upon application of a director and such notice as the court shall require, shall have authority to order indemnification in the following circumstances:

 (A) if it determines a director is entitled to reimbursement under clause (1), the court shall order indemnification, in which case the director shall also be entitled to recover the expenses of securing such reimbursement; or

 (B) if it determines that the director is fairly and reasonably entitled to indemnification in view of all the relevant circumstances, whether or not he has met the standard of conduct set forth in subsection (b) or has been adjudged liable in the circumstances described in subsection (c), the court may order such indemnification as the court shall deem proper, except that indemnification with respect to any proceeding by or in the right of the corporation or in which liability shall have been adjudged in the circumstances described in subsection (c) shall be limited to expenses.

A court of appropriate jurisdiction may be the same court in which the proceeding involving the director's liability took place.

(e) No indemnification under subsection (b) shall be made by the corporation unless authorized in the specific case after a determination has been made that indemnification of the director is permissible in the circumstances because he has met the standard of conduct set forth in subsection (b). Such determination shall be made:

(1) by the board of directors by a majority vote of a quorum consisting of directors not at the time parties to the proceeding; or

(2) if such a quorum cannot be obtained, then by a majority vote of a committee of the board, duly designated to act in the matter by a majority vote of the full board (in which designation directors who are parties may participate), consisting solely of two or more directors not at the time parties to the proceeding; or

(3) by special legal counsel, selected by the board of directors or a committee thereof by vote as set forth in clauses (1) or (2) of this subsection (e), or, if the requisite quorum of the full board cannot be obtained therefor and

such committee cannot be established, by a majority vote of the full board (in which selection directors who are parties may participate); or

(4) by the shareholders.

Authorization of indemnification and determination as to reasonableness of expenses shall be made in the same manner as the determination that indemnification is permissible, except that if the determination that indemnification is permissible is made by special legal counsel, authorization of indemnification and determination as to reasonableness of expenses shall be made in a manner specified in clause (3) in the preceding sentence for the selection of such counsel. Shares held by directors who are parties to the proceeding shall not be voted on the subject matter under this subsection (e).

(f) Reasonable expenses incurred by a director who is a party to a proceeding may be paid or reimbursed by the corporation in advance of the final disposition of such proceeding upon receipt by the corporation of

(1) a written affirmation by the director of his good faith belief that he has met the standard of conduct necessary for indemnification by the corporation as authorized in this section, and

(2) a written undertaking by or on behalf of the director to repay such amount if it shall ultimately be determined that he has not met such standard of conduct, and after a determination that the facts then known to those making the determination would not preclude indemnification under this section. The undertaking required by clause (2) shall be an unlimited general obligation of the director but need not be secured and may be accepted without reference to financial ability to make repayment. Determinations and authorizations of payments under this subsection (f) shall be made in the manner specified in subsection (e).

(g) No provision for the corporation to indemnify or to advance expenses to a director who is made a party to a proceeding, whether contained in the articles of incorporation, the by-laws, a resolution of shareholders or directors, an agreement or otherwise (except as contemplated by subsection (j)), shall be valid unless consistent with this section or, to the extent that indemnity hereunder is limited by the articles of incorporation, consistent therewith. Nothing contained in this section shall limit the corporation's power to pay or reimburse expenses incurred by a director in connection with his appearance as a witness in a proceeding at a time when he has not been made a named defendant or respondent in the proceeding.

(h) For purposes of this section, the corporation shall be deemed to have requested a director to serve an employee benefit plan whenever the performance by him of his duties to the corporation also imposes duties on, or otherwise involves services by, him to the plan or participants or beneficiaries of the plan; excise taxes assessed on a director with respect to an employee benefit plan pursuant to applicable law shall be deemed "fines"; and action taken or omitted by him with respect to an employee benefit plan in the performance of his duties for a purpose reasonably believed by him to be in the interest of the participants and beneficiaries of the plan shall be deemed to be for a purpose which is not opposed to the best interests of the corporation.

(i) Unless limited by the articles of incorporation,

(1) an officer of the corporation shall be indemnified as and to the same extent provided in subsection (d) for a director and shall be entitled to the same extent as a director to seek indemnification pursuant to the provisions of subsection (d);

(2) a corporation shall have the power to indemnify and to advance expenses to an officer, employee or agent of the corporation to the same extent that it may indemnify and advance expenses to directors pursuant to this section; and

(3) a corporation, in addition, shall have the power to indemnify and to advance expenses to an officer, employee or agent who is not a director to such further extent, consistent with law, as may be provided by its articles of incorporation, by-laws, general or specific action of its board of directors, or contract.

(j) A corporation shall have power to purchase and maintain insurance on behalf of any person who is or was a director, officer, employee or agent of the corporation, or who, while a director, officer, employee or agent of the corporation, is or was serving at the request of the corporation as a director, officer, partner, trustee, employee or agent of another foreign or domestic corporation, partnership, joint venture, trust, other enterprise or employee benefit plan, against any liability asserted against him and incurred by him in any such capacity or arising out of his status as such, whether or not the corporation would have the power to indemnify him against such liability under the provisions of this section.

(k) Any indemnification of, or advance of expenses to, a director in accordance with this section, if arising out of a proceeding by or in the right of the corporation, shall be reported in writing to the shareholders with or before the notice of the next shareholders' meeting.

§ 6. Power of Corporation to Acquire Its Own Shares

A corporation shall have the power to acquire its own shares. All of its own shares acquired by a corporation shall, upon acquisition, constitute authorized but unissued shares, unless the articles of incorporation provide that they shall not be reissued, in which case the au-

thorized shares shall be reduced by the number of shares acquired.

If the number of authorized shares is reduced by an acquisition, the corporation shall, not later than the time it files its next annual report under this Act with the Secretary of State, file a statement of cancellation showing the reduction in the authorized shares. The statement of cancellation shall be executed in duplicate by the corporation by its president or a vice president and by its secretary or an assistant secretary, and verified by one of the officers signing such statement, and shall set forth:

(a) The name of the corporation.

(b) The number of acquired shares cancelled, itemized by classes and series.

(c) The aggregate number of authorized shares, itemized by classes and series, after giving effect to such cancellation.

Duplicate originals of such statement shall be delivered to the Secretary of State. If the Secretary of State finds that such statement conforms to law, he shall, when all fees and franchise taxes have been paid as in this Act prescribed:

(1) Endorse on each of such duplicate originals the word "Filed", and the month, day and year of the filing thereof.

(2) File one of such duplicate originals in his office.

(3) Return the other duplicate original to the corporation or its representative.

§ 7. Defense of Ultra Vires

No act of a corporation and no conveyance or transfer of real or personal property to or by a corporation shall be invalid by reason of the fact that the corporation was without capacity or power to do such act or to make or receive such conveyance or transfer, but such lack of capacity or power may be asserted:

(a) In a proceeding by a shareholder against the corporation to enjoin the doing of any act or the transfer of real or personal property by or to the corporation. If the unauthorized act or transfer sought to be enjoined is being, or is to be, performed or made pursuant to a contract to which the corporation is a party, the court may, if all of the parties to the contract are parties to the proceeding and if it deems the same to be equitable, set aside and enjoin the performance of such contract, and in so doing may allow to the corporation or to the other parties to the contract, as the case may be, compensation for the loss or damage sustained by either of them which may result from the action of the court in setting aside and enjoining the performance of such contract, but anticipated profits to be derived from the performance of the contract shall not be awarded by the court as a loss or damage sustained.

(b) In a proceeding by the corporation, whether acting directly or through a receiver, trustee, or other legal representative, or through shareholders in a representative suit, against the incumbent or former officers or directors of the corporation.

(c) In a proceeding by the Attorney General, as provided in this Act, to dissolve the corporation, or in a proceeding by the Attorney General to enjoin the corporation from the transaction of unauthorized business.

§ 8. Corporate Name

The corporate name:

(a) Shall contain the word "corporation," "company," "incorporated" or "limited," or shall contain an abbreviation of one of such words.

(b) Shall not contain any word or phrase which indicates or implies that it is organized for any purpose other than one or more of the purposes contained in its articles of incorporation.

(c) Shall not be the same as, or deceptively similar to, the name of any domestic corporation existing under the laws of this State or any foreign corporation authorized to transact business in this State, or a name the exclusive right to which is, at the time, reserved in the manner provided in this Act, or the name of a corporation which has in effect a registration of its corporate name as provided in this Act, except that this provision shall not apply if the applicant files with the Secretary of State either of the following: (1) the written consent of such other corporation or holder of a reserved or registered name to use the same or deceptively similar name and one or more words are added to make such name distinguishable from such other name, or (2) a certified copy of a final decree of a court of competent jurisdiction establishing the prior right of the applicant to the use of such name in this State.

A corporation with which another corporation, domestic or foreign, is merged, or which is formed by the reorganization or consolidation of one or more domestic or foreign corporations or upon a sale, lease or other disposition to or exchange with, a domestic corporation of all or substantially all the assets of another corporation, domestic or foreign, including its name, may have the same name as that used in this State by any of such corporations if such other corporation was organized under the laws of, or is authorized to transact business in, this State.

§ 9. Reserved Name

The exclusive right to the use of a corporate name may be reserved by:

(a) Any person intending to organize a corporation under this Act.

(b) Any domestic corporation intending to change its name.

(c) Any foreign corporation intending to make application for a certificate of authority to transact business in this State.

(d) Any foreign corporation authorized to transact business in this State and intending to change its name.

(e) Any person intending to organize a foreign corporation and intending to have such corporation make application for a certificate of authority to transact business in this State.

The reservation shall be made by filing with the Secretary of State an application to reserve a specified corporate name, executed by the applicant. If the Secretary of State finds that the name is available for corporate use, he shall reserve the same for the exclusive use of the applicant for a period of one hundred and twenty days.

The right to the exclusive use of a specified corporate name so reserved may be transferred to any other person or corporation by filing in the office of the Secretary of State a notice of such transfer, executed by the applicant for whom the name was reserved, and specifying the name and address of the transferee.

§ 10. Registered Name

Any corporation organized and existing under the laws of any state or territory of the United States may register its corporate name under this Act, provided its corporate name is not the same as, or deceptively similar to, the name of any domestic corporation existing under the laws of this State, or the name of any foreign corporation authorized to transact business in this State, or any corporate name reserved or registered under this Act.

Such registration shall be made by:

(a) Filing with the Secretary of State (1) an application for registration executed by the corporation by an officer thereof, setting forth the name of the corporation, the state or territory under the laws of which it is incorporated, the date of its incorporation, a statement that it is carrying on or doing business, and a brief statement of the business in which it is engaged, and (2) a certificate setting forth that such corporation is in good standing under the laws of the state or territory wherein it is organized, executed by the Secretary of State of such state or territory or by such other official as may have custody of the records pertaining to corporations, and

(b) Paying to the Secretary of State a registration fee in the amount of . . . . for each month, or fraction thereof, between the date of filing such application and December 31st of the calendar year in which such application is filed.

Such registration shall be effective until the close of the calendar year in which the application for registration is filed.

§ 11. Renewal of Registered Name

A corporation which has in effect a registration of its corporate name, may renew such registration from year to year by annually filing an application for renewal setting forth the facts required to be set forth in an original application for registration and a certificate of good standing as required for the original registration and by paying a fee of . . . . A renewal application may be filed between the first day of October and the thirty-first day of December in each year, and shall extend the registration for the following calendar year.

§ 12. Registered Office and Registered Agent

Each corporation shall have and continuously maintain in this State:

(a) A registered office which may be, but need not be, the same as its place of business.

(b) A registered agent, which agent may be either an individual resident in this State whose business office is identical with such registered office, or a domestic corporation, or a foreign corporation authorized to transact business in this State, having a business office identical with such registered office.

§ 13. Change of Registered Office or Registered Agent

A corporation may change its registered office or change its registered agent, or both, upon filing in the office of the Secretary of State a statement setting forth:

(a) The name of the corporation.

(b) The address of its then registered office.

(c) If the address of its registered office is to be changed, the address to which the registered office is to be changed.

(d) The name of its then registered agent.

(e) If its registered agent is to be changed, the name of its successor registered agent.

(f) That the address of its registered office and the address of the business office of its registered agent, as changed, will be identical.

(g) That such change was authorized by resolution duly adopted by its board of directors.

Such statement shall be executed by the corporation by its president, or a vice president, and verified by him, and delivered to the Secretary of State. If the Secretary of State finds that such statement conforms to the provisions of this Act, he shall file such statement in his office, and upon such filing the change of address of the registered office, or the appointment of a new registered agent, or both, as the case may be, shall become effective.

Any registered agent of a corporation may resign as such agent upon filing a written notice thereof, executed in duplicate, with the Secretary of State, who shall forth-with mail a copy thereof to the corporation at its registered office. The appointment of such agent shall terminate upon the expiration of thirty days after receipt of such notice by the Secretary of State.

If a registered agent changes his or its business address to another place within the same . . . . ,* he or it may change such address and the address of the registered office of any corporation of which he or it is registered agent by filing a statement as required above except that it need be signed only by the registered agent and need not be responsive to (e) or (g) and must recite that a copy of the statement has been mailed to the corporation.

§ 14. Service of Process on Corporation

The registered agent so appointed by a corporation shall be an agent of such corporation upon whom any process, notice or demand required or permitted by law to be served upon the corporation may be served.

Whenever a corporation shall fail to appoint or maintain a registered agent in this State, or whenever its registered agent cannot with reasonable diligence be found at the registered office, then the Secretary of State shall be an agent of such corporation upon whom any such process, notice, or demand may be served. Service on the Secretary of State of any such process, notice, or demand shall be made by delivering to and leaving with him, or with any clerk having charge of the corporation department of his office, duplicate copies of such process, notice or demand. In the event any such process, notice or demand is served on the Secretary of State, he shall immediately cause one of the copies thereof to be forwarded by registered mail, addressed to the corporation at its registered office. Any service so had on the Secretary of State shall be returnable in not less than thirty days.

The Secretary of State shall keep a record of all processes, notices and demands served upon him under this section, and shall record therein the time of such service and his action with reference thereto.

Nothing herein contained shall limit or affect the right to serve any process, notice or demand required or permitted by law to be served upon a corporation in any other manner now or hereafter permitted by law.

§ 15. Authorized Shares

Each corporation shall have power to create and issue the number of shares stated in its articles of incorporation. Such shares may be divided into one or more classes with such designations, preferences, limitations, and relative rights as shall be stated in the articles of incorporation. The articles of incorporation may limit or deny the voting rights of or provide special voting rights for the shares of

---

*Supply designation of jurisdiction, such as county, etc., in accordance with local practice.

any class to the extent not inconsistent with the provisions of this Act.

Without limiting the authority herein contained, a corporation, when so provided in its articles of incorporation, may issue shares of preferred or special classes:

(a) Subject to the right of the corporation to redeem any of such shares at the price fixed by the articles of incorporation for the redemption thereof.

(b) Entitling the holders thereof to cumulative, noncumulative or partially cumulative dividends.

(c) Having preference over any other class or classes of shares as to the payment of dividends.

(d) Having preference in the assets of the corporation over any other class or classes of shares upon the voluntary or involuntary liquidation of the corporation.

(e) Convertible into shares of any other class or into shares of any series of the same or any other class, except a class having prior or superior rights and preferences as to dividends or distribution of assets upon liquidation.

§ 16. Issuance of Shares of Preferred or Special Classes in Series

If the articles of incorporation so provide, the shares of any preferred or special class may be divided into and issued in series. If the shares of any such class are to be issued in series, then each series shall be so designated as to distinguish the shares thereof from the shares of all other series and classes. Any or all of the series of any such class and the variations in the relative rights and preferences as between different series may be fixed and determined by the articles of incorporation, but all shares of the same class shall be identical except as to the following relative rights and preferences, as to which there may be variations between different series:

(A) The rate of dividend.

(B) Whether shares may be redeemed and, if so, the redemption price and the terms and conditions of redemption.

(C) The amount payable upon shares in the event of voluntary and involuntary liquidation.

(D) Sinking fund provisions, if any, for the redemption or purchase of shares.

(E) The terms and conditions, if any, on which shares may be converted.

(F) Voting rights, if any.

If the articles of incorporation shall expressly vest authority in the board of directors, then, to the extent that the articles of incorporation shall not have established series and fixed and determined the variations in the relative rights and preferences as between series, the board of directors shall have authority to divide any or all of such classes into series and, within the limitations set forth in this section and in the articles of incorporation, fix and determine the relative rights and preferences of the shares of any series so established.

In order for the board of directors to establish a series, where authority so to do is contained in the articles of incorporation, the board of directors shall adopt a resolution setting forth the designation of the series and fixing and determining the relative rights and preferences thereof, or so much thereof as shall not be fixed and determined by the articles of incorporation.

Prior to the issue of any shares of a series established by resolution adopted by the board of directors, the corporation shall file in the office of the Secretary of State a statement setting forth:

(a) The name of the corporation.

(b) A copy of the resolution establishing and designating the series, and fixing and determining the relative rights and preferences thereof.

(c) The date of adoption of such resolution.

(d) That such resolution was duly adopted by the board of directors.

Such statement shall be executed in duplicate by the corporation by its president or a vice president and by its secretary or an assistant secretary, and verified by one of the officers signing such statement, and shall be delivered to the Secretary of State. If the Secretary of State finds that such statement conforms to law, he shall, when all franchise taxes and fees have been paid as in this Act prescribed:

(1) Endorse on each of such duplicate originals the word "Filed," and the month, day, and year of the filing thereof.

(2) File one of such duplicate originals in his office.

(3) Return the other duplicate original to the corporation or its representative.

Upon the filing of such statement by the Secretary of State, the resolution establishing and designating the series and fixing and determining the relative rights and preferences thereof shall become effective and shall constitute an amendment of the articles of incorporation.

§ 17. Subscriptions for Shares

A subscription for shares of a corporation to be organized shall be irrevocable for a period of six months, unless otherwise provided by the terms of the subscription agreement or unless all of the subscribers consent to the revocation of such subscription.

Unless otherwise provided in the subscription agreement, subscriptions for shares, whether made before or after the organization of a corporation, shall be paid in full at such time, or in such installments and at such times, as shall be determined by the board of directors. Any call made by the board of directors for payment on subscriptions shall be uniform as to all shares of the same class or as to all shares of the same series, as the case may be. In case of default in the payment of any installment or call when such payment is due, the corporation may proceed to collect the amount due in the same manner as any debt due the corporation. The by-laws may prescribe other penalties for failure to pay installments or calls that may become due, but no penalty working a forfeiture of a subscription, or of the amounts paid thereon, shall be declared as against any subscriber unless the amount due thereon shall remain unpaid for a period of twenty days after written demand has been made therefor. If mailed, such written demand shall be deemed to be made when deposited in the United States mail in a sealed envelope addressed to the subscriber at his last post-office address known to the corporation, with postage thereon prepaid. In the event of the sale of any shares by reason of any forfeiture, the excess of proceeds realized over the amount due and unpaid on such shares shall be paid to the delinquent subscriber or to his legal representative.

§ 18. Issuance of Shares

Subject to any restrictions in the articles of incorporation:

(a) Shares may be issued for such consideration as shall be authorized by the board of directors establishing a price (in money or other consideration) or a minimum price or general formula or method by which the price will be determined; and

(b) Upon authorization by the board of directors, the corporation may issue its own shares in exchange for or in conversion of its outstanding shares, or distribute its own shares, pro rata to its shareholders or the shareholders of one or more classes or series, to effectuate stock dividends or splits, and any such transaction shall not require consideration; provided, that no such issuance of shares of any class or series shall be made to the holders of shares of any other class or series unless it is either expressly provided for in the articles of incorporation, or is authorized by an affirmative vote or the written consent of the holders of at least a majority of the outstanding shares of the class or series in which the distribution is to be made.

§ 19. Payment for Shares

The consideration for the issuance of shares may be paid, in whole or in part, in money, in other property, tangible or intangible, or in labor or services actually performed for the corporation. When payment of the consideration for which shares are to be issued shall have been received by the corporation, such shares shall be nonassessable.

Neither promissory notes nor future services shall constitute payment or part payment for the issuance of shares of a corporation.

In the absence of fraud in the transaction, the judgment of the board of directors or the shareholders, as the case may be, as to the value of the consideration received for shares shall be conclusive.

§ 20. Stock Rights and Options

Subject to any provisions in respect thereof set forth in its articles of incorporation, a corporation may create and issue, whether or not in connection with the issuance and sale of any of its shares or other securities, rights or options entitling the holders thereof to purchase from the corporation shares of any class or classes. Such rights or options shall be evidenced in such manner as the board of directors shall approve and, subject to the provisions of the articles of incorporation, shall set forth the terms upon which, the time or times within which and the price or prices at which such shares may be purchased from the corporation upon the exercise of any such right or option. If such rights or options are to be issued to directors, officers or employees as such of the corporation or of any subsidiary thereof, and not to the shareholders generally, their issuance shall be approved by the affirmative vote of the holders of a majority of the shares entitled to vote thereon or shall be authorized by and consistent with a plan approved or ratified by such a vote of shareholders. In the absence of fraud in the transaction, the judgment of the board of directors as to the adequacy of the consideration received for such rights or options shall be conclusive.

§ 21. Determination of Amount of Stated Capital

[Repealed in 1979].

§ 22. Expenses of Organization, Reorganization and Financing

The reasonable charges and expenses of organization or reorganization of a corporation, and the reasonable expenses of and compensation for the sale or underwriting of its shares, may be paid or allowed by such corporation out of the consideration received by it in payment for its shares without thereby rendering such shares assessable.

§ 23. Shares Represented by Certificates and Uncertified Shares

The shares of a corporation shall be represented by certificates or shall be uncertificated shares. Certificates shall be signed by the chairman or vice-chairman of the board of directors or the president or a vice president and by the treasurer or an assistant treasurer or the secretary or an assistant secretary of the corporation, and may be sealed with the seal of the corporation or a facsimile thereof. Any of or all the signatures upon a certificate may be a facsimile. In case any officer, transfer agent or registrar who has signed or whose facsimile signature has been placed upon such certificate shall have ceased to be such officer, transfer agent or registrar before such certificate is issued, it may be issued by the corporation with the same effect as if he were such officer, transfer agent or registrar at the date of its issue.

Every certificate representing shares issued by a corporation which is authorized to issue shares of more than one class shall set forth upon the face or back of the certificate, or shall state that the corporation will furnish to any shareholder upon request and without charge, a full statement of the designations, preferences, limitations, and relative rights of the shares of each class authorized to be issued, and if the corporation is authorized to issue any preferred or special class in series, the variations in the relative rights and preferences between the shares of each such series so far as the same have been fixed and determined and the authority of the board of directors to fix and determine the relative rights and preferences of subsequent series.

Each certificate representing shares shall state upon the face thereof:

(a) That the corporation is organized under the laws of this State.

(b) The name of the person to whom issued.

(c) The number and class of shares, and the designation of the series, if any, which such certificate represents.

(d) The par value of each share represented by such certificate, or a statement that the shares are without par value.

No certificate shall be issued for any share until such share is fully paid.

Unless otherwise provided by the articles of incorporation or by-laws, the board of directors of a corporation may provide by resolution that some or all of any or all classes and series of its shares shall be uncertificated shares, provided that such resolution shall not apply to shares represented by a certificate until such certificate is surrendered to the corporation. Within a reasonable time after the issuance or transfer of uncertificated shares, the corporation shall send to the registered owner thereof a written notice containing the information required to be set forth or stated on certificates pursuant to the second and third paragraphs of this section. Except as otherwise expressly provided by law, the rights and obligations of the holders of uncertificated shares and the rights and obligations of the holders of certificates representing shares of the same class and series shall be identical.

§ 24. Fractional Shares

A corporation may (1) issue fractions of a share, either represented by a certificate or uncertificated, (2) arrange

for the disposition of fractional interests by those entitled thereto, (3) pay in money the fair value of fractions of a share as of a time when those entitled to receive such fractions are determined, or (4) issue scrip in registered or bearer form which shall entitle the holder to receive a certificate for a full share or an uncertificated full share upon the surrender of such scrip aggregating a full share. A certificate for a fractional share or an uncertificated fractional share shall, but scrip shall not unless otherwise provided therein, entitle the holder to exercise voting rights, to receive dividends thereon, and to participate in any of the assets of the corporation in the event of liquidation. The board of directors may cause scrip to be issued subject to the condition that it shall become void if not exchanged for certificates representing full shares or uncertificated full shares before a specified date, or subject to the condition that the shares for which scrip is exchangeable may be sold by the corporation and the proceeds thereof distributed to the holders of scrip, or subject to any other conditions which the board of directors may deem advisable.

§ 25. Liability of Subscribers and Shareholders

A holder of or subscriber to shares of a corporation shall be under no obligation to the corporation or its creditors with respect to such shares other than the obligation to pay to the corporation the full consideration for which such shares were issued or to be issued.

Any person becoming an assignee or transferee of shares or of a subscription for shares in good faith and without knowledge or notice that the full consideration therefor has not been paid shall not be personally liable to the corporation or its creditors for any unpaid portion of such consideration.

An executor, administrator, conservator, guardian, trustee, assignee for the benefit of creditors, or receiver shall not be personally liable to the corporation as a holder of or subscriber to shares of a corporation but the estate and funds in his hands shall be so liable.

No pledgee or other holder of shares as collateral security shall be personally liable as a shareholder.

§ 26. Shareholders' Preemptive Rights

The shareholders of a corporation shall have no preemptive right to acquire unissued shares of the corporation, or securities of the corporation convertible into or carrying a right to subscribe to or acquire shares, except to the extent, if any, that such right is provided in the articles of incorporation.

§ 26A. Shareholders' Preemptive Rights [Alternative]

Except to the extent limited or denied by this section or by the articles of incorporation, shareholders shall have a preemptive right to acquire unissued shares or securities convertible into such shares or carrying a right to subscribe to or acquire shares.

Unless otherwise provided in the articles of incorporation,

(a) No preemptive right shall exist

(1) to acquire any shares issued to directors, officers or employees pursuant to approval by the affirmative vote of the holders of a majority of the shares entitled to vote thereon or when authorized by and consistent with a plan theretofore approved by such a vote of shareholders; or

(2) to acquire any shares sold otherwise than for money.

(b) Holders of shares of any class that is preferred or limited as to dividends or assets shall not be entitled to any preemptive right.

(c) Holders of shares of common stock shall not be entitled to any preemptive right to shares of any class that is preferred or limited as to dividends or assets or to any obligations, unless convertible into shares of common stock or carrying a right to subscribe to or acquire shares of common stock.

(d) Holders of common stock without voting power shall have no preemptive right to shares of common stock with voting power.

(e) The preemptive right shall be only an opportunity to acquire shares or other securities under such terms and conditions as the board of directors may fix for the purpose of providing a fair and reasonable opportunity for the exercise of such right.

§ 27. By-Laws

The initial by-laws of a corporation shall be adopted by its board of directors. The power to alter, amend or repeal the by-laws or adopt new by-laws, subject to repeal or change by action of the shareholders, shall be vested in the board of directors unless reserved to the shareholders by the articles of incorporation. The by-laws may contain any provisions for the regulation and management of the affairs of the corporation not inconsistent with law or the articles of incorporation.

§ 27A. By-Laws and Other Powers in Emergency [Optional]

The board of directors of any corporation may adopt emergency by-laws, subject to repeal or change by action of the shareholders, which shall, notwithstanding any different provision elsewhere in this Act or in the articles of incorporation or by-laws, be operative during any emergency in the conduct of the business of the corporation resulting from an attack on the United States or any nuclear or atomic disaster. The emergency by-laws may make any provision that may be practical and necessary for the circumstances of the emergency, including provisions that:

(a) A meeting of the board of directors may be called by any officer or director in such manner and under such conditions as shall be prescribed in the emergency by-laws;

(b) The director or directors in attendance at the meeting, or any greater number fixed by the emergency by-laws, shall constitute a quorum; and

(c) The officers or other persons designated on a list approved by the board of directors before the emergency, all in such order of priority and subject to such conditions, and for such period of time (not longer than reasonably necessary after the termination of the emergency) as may be provided in the emergency by-laws or in the resolution approving the list shall, to the extent required to provide a quorum at any meeting of the board of directors, be deemed directors for such meeting.

The board of directors, either before or during any such emergency, may provide, and from time to time modify, lines of succession in the event that during such an emergency any or all officers or agents of the corporation shall for any reason be rendered incapable of discharging their duties.

The board of directors, either before or during any such emergency, may, effective in the emergency, change the head office or designate several alternative head offices or regional offices, or authorize the officers so to do.

To the extent not inconsistent with any emergency by-laws so adopted, the by-laws of the corporation shall remain in effect during any such emergency and upon its termination the emergency by-laws shall cease to be operative.

Unless otherwise provided in emergency by-laws, notice of any meeting of the board of directors during any such emergency may be given only to such of the directors as it may be feasible to reach at the time and by such means as may be feasible at the time, including publication or radio.

To the extent required to constitute a quorum at any meeting of the board of directors during any such emergency, the officers of the corporation who are present shall, unless otherwise provided in emergency by-laws, be deemed, in order of rank and within the same rank in order of seniority, directors for such meeting.

No officer, director or employee acting in accordance with any emergency by-laws shall be liable except for willful misconduct. No officer, director or employee shall be liable for any action taken by him in good faith in such an emergency in furtherance of the ordinary business affairs of the corporation even though not authorized by the by-laws then in effect.

§ 28. Meetings of Shareholders

Meetings of shareholders may be held at such place within or without this State as may be stated in or fixed in accordance with the by-laws. If no other place is stated or so fixed, meetings shall be held at the registered office of the corporation.

An annual meeting of the shareholders shall be held at such time as may be stated in or fixed in accordance with the by-laws. If the annual meeting is not held within any thirteen-month period the Court of . . . . may, on the application of any shareholder, summarily order a meeting to be held.

Special meetings of the shareholders may be called by the board of directors, the holders of not less than one-tenth of all the shares entitled to vote at the meeting, or such other persons as may be authorized in the articles of incorporation or the by-laws.

§ 29. Notice of Shareholders' Meetings

Written notice stating the place, day and hour of the meeting and, in case of a special meeting, the purpose or purposes for which the meeting is called, shall be delivered not less than ten nor more than fifty days before the date of the meeting, either personally or by mail, by or at the direction of the president, the secretary, or the officer or persons calling the meeting, to each shareholder of record entitled to vote at such meeting. If mailed, such notice shall be deemed to be delivered when deposited in the United States mail addressed to the shareholder at his address as it appears on the stock transfer books of the corporation, with postage thereon prepaid.

§ 30. Closing of Transfer Books and Fixing Record Date

For the purpose of determining shareholders entitled to notice of or to vote at any meeting of shareholders or any adjournment thereof, or entitled to receive payment of any dividend, or in order to make a determination of shareholders for any other proper purpose, the board of directors of a corporation may provide that the stock transfer books shall be closed for a stated period but not to exceed, in any case, fifty days. If the stock transfer books shall be closed for the purpose of determining shareholders entitled to notice of or to vote at a meeting of shareholders, such books shall be closed for at least ten days immediately preceding such meeting. In lieu of closing the stock transfer books, the by-laws, or in the absence of an applicable by-law the board of directors, may fix in advance a date as the record date for any such determination of shareholders, such date in any case to be not more than fifty days and, in case of a meeting of shareholders, not less than ten days prior to the date on which the particular action, requiring such determination of shareholders, is to be taken. If the stock transfer books are not closed and no record date is fixed for the determination of shareholders entitled to notice of or to vote at a meeting of shareholders, or shareholders entitled to receive payment

of a dividend, the date on which notice of the meeting is mailed or the date on which the resolution of the board of directors declaring such dividend is adopted, as the case may be, shall be the record date for such determination of shareholders. When a determination of shareholders entitled to vote at any meeting of shareholders has been made as provided in this section, such determination shall apply to any adjournment thereof.

§ 31. Voting Record

The officer or agent having charge of the stock transfer books for shares of a corporation shall make a complete record of the shareholders entitled to vote at such meeting or any adjournment thereof, arranged in alphabetical order, with the address of and the number of shares held by each. Such record shall be produced and kept open at the time and place of the meeting and shall be subject to the inspection of any shareholder during the whole time of the meeting for the purposes thereof.

Failure to comply with the requirements of this section shall not affect the validity of any action taken at such meeting.

An officer or agent having charge of the stock transfer books who shall fail to prepare the record of shareholders, or produce and keep it open for inspection at the meeting, as provided in this section, shall be liable to any shareholder suffering damage on account of such failure, to the extent of such damage.

§ 32. Quorum of Shareholders

Unless otherwise provided in the articles of incorporation, a majority of the shares entitled to vote, represented in person or by proxy, shall constitute a quorum at a meeting of shareholders, but in no event shall a quorum consist of less than one-third of the shares entitled to vote at the meeting. If a quorum is present, the affirmative vote of the majority of the shares represented at the meeting and entitled to vote on the subject matter shall be the act of the shareholders, unless the vote of a greater number or voting by classes is required by this Act or the articles of incorporation or by-laws.

§ 33. Voting of Shares

Each outstanding share, regardless of class, shall be entitled to one vote on each matter submitted to a vote at a meeting of shareholders, except as may be otherwise provided in the articles of incorporation. If the articles of incorporation provide for more or less than one vote for any share, on any matter, every reference in this Act to a majority or other proportion of shares shall refer to such a majority or other proportion of votes entitled to be cast.

Shares held by another corporation if a majority of the shares entitled to vote for the election of directors of such other corporation is held by the corporation, shall not be voted at any meeting or counted in determining the total number of outstanding shares at any given time.

A shareholder may vote either in person or by proxy executed in writing by the shareholder or by his duly authorized attorney-in-fact. No proxy shall be valid after eleven months from the date of its execution, unless otherwise provided in the proxy.

[Either of the following prefatory phrases may be inserted here: "The articles of incorporation may provide that" or "Unless the articles of incorporation otherwise provide"] . . . at each election for directors every shareholder entitled to vote at such election shall have the right to vote, in person or by proxy, the number of shares owned by him for as many persons as there are directors to be elected and for whose election he has a right to vote, or to cumulate his votes by giving one candidate as many votes as the number of such directors multiplied by the number of his shares shall equal, or by distributing such votes on the same principle among any number of such candidates.

Shares standing in the name of another corporation, domestic or foreign, may be voted by such officer, agent or proxy as the by-laws of such other corporation may prescribe, or, in the absence of such provision, as the board of directors of such other corporation may determine.

Shares held by an administrator, executor, guardian or conservator may be voted by him, either in person or by proxy, without a transfer of such shares into his name. Shares standing in the name of a trustee may be voted by him, either in person or by proxy, but no trustee shall be entitled to vote shares held by him without a transfer of such shares into his name.

Shares standing in the name of a receiver may be voted by such receiver, and shares held by or under the control of a receiver may be voted by such receiver without the transfer thereof into his name if authority so to do be contained in an appropriate order of the court by which such receiver was appointed.

A shareholder whose shares are pledged shall be entitled to vote such shares until the shares have been transferred into the name of the pledgee, and thereafter the pledgee shall be entitled to vote the shares so transferred.

On and after the date on which written notice of redemption of redeemable shares has been mailed to the holders thereof and a sum sufficient to redeem such shares has been deposited with a bank or trust company with irrevocable instruction and authority to pay the redemption price to the holders thereof upon surrender of certificates therefor, such shares shall not be entitled to vote on any matter and shall not be deemed to be outstanding shares.

§ 34. Voting Trusts and Agreements Among Shareholders

Any number of shareholders of a corporation may create a voting trust for the purpose of conferring upon a trustee or trustees the right to vote or otherwise represent their shares, for a period of not to exceed ten years, by entering into a written voting trust agreement specifying the terms and conditions of the voting trust, by depositing a counterpart of the agreement with the corporation at its registered office, and by transferring their shares to such trustee or trustees for the purposes of the agreement. Such trustee or trustees shall keep a record of the holders of voting trust certificates evidencing a beneficial interest in the voting trust, giving the names and addresses of all such holders and the number and class of the shares in respect of which the voting trust certificates held by each are issued, and shall deposit a copy of such record with the corporation at its registered office. The counterpart of the voting trust agreement and the copy of such record so deposited with the corporation shall be subject to the same right of examination by a shareholder of the corporation, in person or by agent or attorney, as are the books and records of the corporation, and such counterpart and such copy of such record shall be subject to examination by any holder of record of voting trust certificates, either in person or by agent or attorney, at any reasonable time for any proper purpose.

Agreements among shareholders regarding the voting of their shares shall be valid and enforceable in accordance with their terms. Such agreements shall not be subject to the provisions of this section regarding voting trusts.

§ 35. Board of Directors

All corporate powers shall be exercised by or under authority of, and the business and affairs of a corporation shall be managed under the direction of, a board of directors except as may be otherwise provided in this Act or the articles of incorporation. If any such provision is made in the articles of incorporation, the powers and duties conferred or imposed upon the board of directors by this Act shall be exercised or performed to such extent and by such person or persons as shall be provided in the articles of incorporation. Directors need not be residents of this State or shareholders of the corporation unless the articles of incorporation or by-laws so require. The articles of incorporation or by-laws may prescribe other qualifications for directors. The board of directors shall have authority to fix the compensation of directors unless otherwise provided in the articles of incorporation.

A director shall perform his duties as a director, including his duties as a member of any committee of the board upon which he may serve, in good faith, in a manner he reasonably believes to be in the best interests of the corporation, and with such care as an ordinarily prudent person in a like position would use under similar circumstances. In performing his duties, a director shall be entitled to rely on information, opinions, reports or statements, including financial statements and other financial data, in each case prepared or presented by:

(a) one or more officers or employees of the corporation whom the director reasonably believes to be reliable and competent in the matters presented,

(b) counsel, public accountants or other persons as to matters which the director reasonably believes to be within such person's professional or expert competence, or

(c) a committee of the board upon which he does not serve, duly designated in accordance with a provision of the articles of incorporation or the by-laws, as to matters within its designated authority, which committee the director reasonably believes to merit confidence,

but he shall not be considered to be acting in good faith if he has knowledge concerning the matter in question that would cause such reliance to be unwarranted. A person who so performs his duties shall have no liability by reason of being or having been a director of the corporation.

A director of a corporation who is present at a meeting of its board of directors at which action on any corporate matter is taken shall be presumed to have assented to the action taken unless his dissent shall be entered in the minutes of the meeting or unless he shall file his written dissent to such action with the secretary of the meeting before the adjournment thereof or shall forward such dissent by registered mail to the secretary of the corporation immediately after the adjournment of the meeting. Such right to dissent shall not apply to a director who voted in favor of such action.

§ 36. Number and Election of Directors

The board of directors of a corporation shall consist of one or more members. The number of directors shall be fixed by, or in the manner provided in, the articles of incorporation or the by-laws, except as to the number constituting the initial board of directors, which number shall be fixed by the articles of incorporation. The number of directors may be increased or decreased from time to time by amendment to, or in the manner provided in, the articles of incorporation or the by-laws, but no decrease shall have the effect of shortening the term of any incumbent director. In the absence of a by-law providing for the number of directors, the number shall be the same as that provided for in the articles of incorporation. The names and addresses of the members of the first board of directors shall be stated in the articles of incorporation. Such persons shall hold office until the first annual meeting of shareholders, and until their successors shall have

been elected and qualified. At the first annual meeting of shareholders and at each annual meeting thereafter the shareholders shall elect directors to hold office until the next succeeding annual meeting, except in case of the classification of directors as permitted by this Act. Each director shall hold office for the term for which he is elected and until his successor shall have been elected and qualified.

§ 37. Classification of Directors

When the board of directors shall consist of nine or more members, in lieu of electing the whole number of directors annually, the articles of incorporation may provide that the directors be divided into either two or three classes, each class to be as nearly equal in number as possible, the term of office of directors of the first class to expire at the first annual meeting of shareholders after their election, that of the second class to expire at the second annual meeting after their election, and that of the third class, if any, to expire at the third annual meeting after their election. At each annual meeting after such classification the number of directors equal to the number of the class whose term expires at the time of such meeting shall be elected to hold office until the second succeeding annual meeting, if there be two classes, or until the third succeeding annual meeting, if there be three classes. No classification of directors shall be effective prior to the first annual meeting of shareholders.

§ 38. Vacancies

Any vacancy occurring in the board of directors may be filled by the affirmative vote of a majority of the remaining directors though less than a quorum of the board of directors. A director elected to fill a vacancy shall be elected for the unexpired term of his predecessor in office. Any directorship to be filled by reason of an increase in the number of directors may be filled by the board of directors for a term of office continuing only until the next election of directors by the shareholders.

§ 39. Removal of Directors

At a meeting of shareholders called expressly for that purpose, directors may be removed in the manner provided in this section. Any director or the entire board of directors may be removed, with or without cause, by a vote of the holders of a majority of the shares then entitled to vote at an election of directors.

In the case of a corporation having cumulative voting, if less than the entire board is to be removed, no one of the directors may be removed if the votes cast against his removal would be sufficient to elect him if then cumulatively voted at an election of the entire board of directors, or, if there be classes of directors, at an election of the class of directors of which he is a part.

Whenever the holders of the shares of any class are entitled to elect one or more directors by the provisions of the articles of incorporation, the provisions of this section shall apply, in respect to the removal of a director or directors so elected, to the vote of the holders of the outstanding shares of that class and not to the vote of the outstanding shares as a whole.

§ 40. Quorum of Directors

A majority of the number of directors fixed by or in the manner provided in the by-laws or in the absence of a by-law fixing or providing for the number of directors, then of the number stated in the articles of incorporation, shall constitute a quorum for the transaction of business unless a greater number is required by the articles of incorporation or the by-laws. The act of the majority of the directors present at a meeting at which a quorum is present shall be the act of the board of directors, unless the act of a greater number is required by the articles of incorporation or the by-laws.

§ 41. Director Conflicts of Interest

No contract or other transaction between a corporation and one or more of its directors or any other corporation, firm, association or entity in which one or more of its directors are directors or officers or are financially interested, shall be either void or voidable because of such relationship or interest or because such director or directors are present at the meeting of the board of directors or a committee thereof which authorizes, approves or ratifies such contract or transaction or because his or their votes are counted for such purpose, if:

(a) the fact of such relationship or interest is disclosed or known to the board of directors or committee which authorizes, approves or ratifies the contract or transaction by a vote or consent sufficient for the purpose without counting the votes or consents of such interested directors; or

(b) the fact of such relationship or interest is disclosed or known to the shareholders entitled to vote and they authorize, approve or ratify such contract or transaction by vote or written consent; or

(c) the contract or transaction is fair and reasonable to the corporation.

Common or interested directors may be counted in determining the presence of a quorum at a meeting of the board of directors or a committee thereof which authorizes, approves or ratifies such contract or transaction.

§ 42. Executive and Other Committees

If the articles of incorporation or the by-laws so provide, the board of directors, by resolution adopted by a majority of the full board of directors, may designate from among

its members an executive committee and one or more other committees each of which, to the extent provided in such resolution or in the articles of incorporation or the by-laws of the corporation, shall have and may exercise all the authority of the board of directors, except that no such committee shall have authority to (i) authorize distributions, (ii) approve or recommend to shareholders actions or proposals required by this Act to be approved by shareholders, (iii) designate candidates for the office of director, for purposes of proxy solicitation or otherwise, or fill vancancies on the board of directors or any committee thereof, (iv) amend the by-laws, (v) approve a plan of merger not requiring shareholder approval, (vi) authorize or approve the reacquisition of shares unless pursuant to a general formula or method specified by the board of directors, or (vii) authorize or approve the issuance or sale of, or any contract to issue or sell, shares or designate the terms of a series of a class of shares, provided that the board of directors, having acted regarding general authorization for the issuance or sale of shares, or any contract therefor, and, in the case of a series, the designation thereof, may, pursuant to a general formula or method specified by the board by resolution or by adoption of a stock option or other plan, authorize a committee to fix the terms of any contract for the sale of the shares and to fix the terms upon which such shares may be issued or sold, including, without limitation, the price, the dividend rate, provisions for redemption, sinking fund, conversion, voting or preferential rights, and provisions for other features of a class of shares, or a series of a class of shares, with full power in such committee to adopt any final resolution setting forth all the terms thereof and to authorize the statement of the terms of a series for filing with the Secretary of State under this Act.

Neither the designation of any such committee, the delegation thereto of authority, nor action by such committee pursuant to such authority shall alone constitute compliance by any member of the board of directors, not a member of the committee in question, with his responsibility to act in good faith, in a manner he reasonably believes to be in the best interests of the corporation, and with such care as an ordinarily prudent person in a like position would use under similar circumstances.

§ 43. Place and Notice of Directors' Meetings; Committee Meetings

Meetings of the board of directors, regular or special, may be held either within or without this State.

Regular meetings of the board of directors or any committee designated thereby may be held with or without notice as prescribed in the by-laws. Special meetings of the board of directors or any committee designated thereby shall be held upon such notice as is prescribed in the by-laws. Attendance of a director at a meeting shall constitute a waiver of notice of such meeting, except where a director attends a meeting for the express purpose of objecting to the transaction of any business because the meeting is not lawfully called or convened. Neither the business to be transacted at, nor the purpose of, any regular or special meeting of the board of directors or any committee designated thereby need be specified in the notice or waiver of notice of such meeting unless required by the by-laws.

Except as may be otherwise restricted by the articles of incorporation or by-laws, members of the board of directors or any committee designated thereby may participate in a meeting of such board or committee by means of a conference telephone or similar communications equipment by means of which all persons participating in the meeting can hear each other at the same time and participation by such means shall constitute presence in person at a meeting.

§ 44. Action by Directors Without a Meeting

Unless otherwise provided by the articles of incorporation or by-laws, any action required by this Act to be taken at a meeting of the directors of a corporation, or any action which may be taken at a meeting of the directors or of a committee, may be taken without a meeting if a consent in writing, setting forth the action so taken, shall be signed by all of the directors, or all of the members of the committee, as the case may be. Such consent shall have the same effect as a unanimous vote.

§ 45. Distributions to Shareholders

Subject to any restrictions in the articles of incorporation, the board of directors may authorize and the corporation may make distributions, except that no distribution may be made if, after giving effect thereto, either:

(a) the corporation would be unable to pay its debts as they become due in the usual course of its business; or

(b) the corporation's total assets would be less than the sum of its total liabilities and (unless the articles of incorporation otherwise permit) the maximum amount that then would be payable, in any liquidation, in respect of all outstanding shares having preferential rights in liquidation.

Determinations under subparagraph (b) may be based upon (i) financial statements prepared on the basis of accounting practices and principles that are reasonable in the circumstances, or (ii) a fair valuation or other method that is reasonable in the circumstances.

In the case of a purchase, redemption or other acquisition of a corporation's shares, the effect of a distribution shall be measured as of the date money or other property is transferred or debt is incurred by the corporation, or as of the date the shareholder ceases to be a shareholder of the corporation with respect to such shares,

whichever is earlier. In all other cases, the effect of a distribution shall be measured as of the date of its authorization if payment occurs 120 days or less following the date of authorization, or as of the date of payment if payment occurs more than 120 days following the date of authorization.

Indebtedness of a corporation incurred or issued to a shareholder in a distribution in accordance with this Section shall be on a parity with the indebtedness of the corporation to its general unsecured creditors except to the extent subordinated by agreement.

§ 46. Distributions from Capital Surplus

[Repealed in 1979].

§ 47. Loans to Employees and Directors

A corporation shall not lend money to or use its credit to assist its directors without authorization in the particular case by its shareholders, but may lend money to and use its credit to assist any employee of the corporation or of a subsidiary, including any such employee who is a director of the corporation, if the board of directors decides that such loan or assistance may benefit the corporation.

§ 48. Liability of Directors in Certain Cases

In addition to any other liabilities, a director who votes for or assents to any distribution contrary to the provisions of this Act or contrary to any restrictions contained in the articles of incorporation, shall, unless he complies with the standard provided in this Act for the performance of the duties of directors, be liable to the corporation, jointly and severally with all other directors so voting or assenting, for the amount of such dividend which is paid or the value of such distribution in excess of the amount of such distribution which could have been made without a violation of the provisions of this Act or the restrictions in the articles of incorporation.

Any director against whom a claim shall be asserted under or pursuant to this section for the making of a distribution and who shall be held liable thereon, shall be entitled to contribution from the shareholders who accepted or received any such distribution, knowing such distribution to have been made in violation of this Act, in proportion to the amounts received by them.

Any director against whom a claim shall be asserted under or pursuant to this section shall be entitled to contribution from any other director who voted for or assented to the action upon which the claim is asserted and who did not comply with the standard provided in this Act for the performance of the duties of directors.

§ 49. Provisions Relating to Actions by Shareholders

No action shall be brought in this State by a shareholder in the right of a domestic or foreign corporation unless the plaintiff was a holder of record of shares or of voting trust certificates therefor at the time of the transaction of which he complains, or his shares or voting trust certificates thereafter devolved upon him by operation of law from a person who was a holder of record at such time.

In any action hereafter instituted in the right of any domestic or foreign corporation by the holder or holders of record of shares of such corporation or of voting trust certificates therefor, the court having jurisdiction, upon final judgment and a finding that the action was brought without reasonable cause, may require the plaintiff or plaintiffs to pay to the parties named as defendant the reasonable expenses, including fees of attorneys, incurred by them in the defense of such action.

In any action now pending or hereafter instituted or maintained in the right of any domestic or foreign corporation by the holder or holders of record of less than five per cent of the outstanding shares of any class of such corporation or of voting trust certificates therefor, unless the shares or voting trust certificates so held have a market value in excess of twenty-five thousand dollars, the corporation in whose right such action is brought shall be entitled at any time before final judgment to require the plaintiff or plaintiffs to give security for the reasonable expenses, including fees of attorneys, that may be incurred by it in connection with such action or may be incurred by other parties named as defendant for which it may become legally liable. Market value shall be determined as of the date that the plaintiff institutes the action or, in the case of an intervenor, as of the date that he becomes a party to the action. The amount of such security may from time to time be increased or decreased, in the discretion of the court, upon showing that the security provided has or may become inadequate or is excessive. The corporation shall have recourse to such security in such amount as the court having jurisdiction shall determine upon the termination of such action, whether or not the court finds the action was brought without reasonable cause.

§ 50. Officers

The officers of a corporation shall consist of a president, one or more vice presidents as may be prescribed by the by-laws, a secretary, and a treasurer, each of whom shall be elected by the board of directors at such time and in such manner as may be prescribed by the by-laws. Such other officers and assistant officers and agents as may be deemed necessary may be elected or appointed by the board of directors or chosen in such other manner as may be prescribed by the by-laws. Any two or more offices may be held by the same person, except the offices of president and secretary.

All officers and agents of the corporation, as between themselves and the corporation, shall have such authority and perform such duties in the management of the cor-

poration as may be provided in the by-laws, or as may be determined by resolution of the board of directors nc' inconsistent with the by-laws.

§ 51. Removal of Officers

Any officer or agent may be removed by the board of directors whenever in its judgment the best interests of the corporation will be served thereby, but such removal shall be without prejudice to the contract rights, if any, of the person so removed. Election or appointment of ar officer or agent shall not of itself create contract rights.

§ 52. Books and Records: Financial Reports to Shareholders; Examination of Records

Each corporation shall keep correct and complete books and records of account and shall keep minutes of the proceedings of its shareholders and board of directors and shall keep at its registered office or principal place of business, or at the office of its transfer agent or registrar, a record of its shareholders, giving the names and addresses of all shareholders and the number and class of the shares held by each. Any books, records and minutes may be in written form or in any other form capable of being converted into written form within a reasonable time.

Any person who shall have been a holder of record of shares or of voting trust certificates therefor at least six months immediately preceding his demand or shall be the holder of record of, or the holder of record of voting trust certificates for, at least five percent of all the outstanding shares of the corporation, upon written demand stating the purpose thereof, shall have the right to examine, in person, or by agent or attorney, at any reasonable time or times, for any proper purpose its relevant books and records of account, minutes, and record of shareholders and to make extracts therefrom.

Any officer or agent who, or a corporation which, shall refuse to allow any such shareholder or holder of voting trust certificates, or his agent or attorney, so to examine and make extracts from its books and records of account, minutes, and record of shareholders, for any proper purpose, shall be liable to such shareholder or holder of voting trust certificates in a penalty of ten per cent of the value of the shares owned by such shareholder, or in respect of which such voting trust certificates are issued, in addition to any other damages or remedy afforded him by law. It shall be a defense to any action for penalties under this section that the person suing therefor has within two years sold or offered for sale any list of shareholders or of holders of voting trust certificates for shares of such corporation or any other corporation or has aided or abetted any person in procuring any list of shareholders or of holders of voting trust certificates for any such purpose, or has improperly used any information secured through any prior examination of the books and records of account, or minutes, or record of shareholders or of holders of voting trust certificates for shares of such corporation or any other corporation, or was not acting in good faith or for a proper purpose in making his demand.

Nothing herein contained shall impair the power of any court of competent jurisdiction, upon proof by a shareholder or holder of voting trust certificates of proper purpose, irrespective of the period of time during which such shareholder or holder of voting trust certificates shall have been a shareholder of record or a holder of record of voting trust certificates, and irrespective of the number of shares held by him or represented by voting trust certificates held by him, to compel the production for examination by such shareholder or holder of voting trust certificates of the books and records of account, minutes and record of shareholders of a corporation.

Each corporation shall furnish to its shareholders annual financial statements, including at least a balance sheet as of the end of each fiscal year and a statement of income for such fiscal year, which shall be prepared on the basis of generally accepted accounting principles, if the corporation prepares financial statements for such fiscal year on that basis for any purpose, and may be consolidated statements of the corporation and one or more of its subsidiaries. The financial statements shall be mailed by the corporation to each of its shareholders within 120 days after the close of each fiscal year and, after such mailing and upon written request, shall be mailed by the corporation to any shareholder (or holder of a voting trust certificate for its shares) to whom a copy of the most recent annual financial statements has not previously been mailed. In the case of statements audited by a public accountant, each copy shall be accompanied by a report setting forth his opinion thereon; in other cases, each copy shall be accompanied by a statement of the president or the person in charge of the corporation's financial accounting records (1) stating his reasonable belief as to whether or not the financial statements were prepared in accordance with generally accepted accounting principles and, if not, describing the basis of presentation, and (2) describing any respects in which the financial statements were not prepared on a basis consistent with those prepared for the previous year.

§ 53. Incorporators

One or more persons, or a domestic or foreign corporation, may act as incorporator or incorporators of a corporation by signing and delivering in duplicate to the Secretary of State articles of incorporation for such corporation.

§ 54. Articles of Incorporation

The articles of incorporation shall set forth:

(a) The name of the corporation.

(b) The period of duration, which may be perpetual.

(c) The purpose or purposes for which the corporation is organized which may be stated to be, or to include, the transaction of any or all lawful business for which corporations may be incorporated under this Act.

(d) The aggregate number of shares which the corporation shall have authority to issue and, if such shares are to be divided into classes, the number of shares of each class.

(e) If the shares are to be divided into classes, the designation of each class and a statement of the preferences, limitations and relative rights in respect of the shares of each class.

(f) If the corporation is to issue the shares of any preferred or special class in series, then the designation of each series and a statement of the variations in the relative rights and preferences as between series insofar as the same are to be fixed in the articles of incorporation, and a statement of any authority to be vested in the board of directors to establish series and fix and determine the variations in the relative rights and preferences as between series.

(g) If any preemptive right is to be granted to shareholders, the provisions therefor.

(h) The address of its initial registered office, and the name of its initial registered agent at such address.

(i) The number of directors constituting the initial board of directors and the names and addresses of the persons who are to serve as directors until the first annual meeting of shareholders or until their successors be elected and qualify.

(j) The name and address of each incorporator.

In addition to provisions required therein, the articles of incorporation may also contain provisions not inconsistent with law regarding:

(1) the direction of the management of the business and the regulation of the affairs of the corporation;

(2) the definition, limitation and regulation of the powers of the corporation, the directors, and the shareholders, or any class of the shareholders, including restrictions on the transfer of shares;

(3) the par value of any authorized shares or class of shares;

(4) any provision which under this Act is required or permitted to be set forth in the by-laws.

It shall not be necessary to set forth in the articles of incorporation any of the corporate powers enumerated in this Act.

§ 55. Filing of Articles of Incorporation

Duplicate originals of the articles of incorporation shall be delivered to the Secretary of State. If the Secretary of State finds that the articles of incorporation conform to law, he shall, when all fees have been paid as in this Act prescribed:

(a) Endorse on each of such duplicate originals the word "Filed," and the month, day and year of the filing thereof.

(b) File one of such duplicate originals in his office.

(c) Issue a certificate of incorporation to which he shall affix the other duplicate original.

The certificate of incorporation, together with the duplicate original of the articles of incorporation affixed thereto by the Secretary of State, shall be returned to the incorporators or their representative.

§ 56. Effect of Issuance of Certificate of Incorporation

Upon the issuance of the certificate of incorporation, the corporate existence shall begin, and such certificate of incorporation shall be conclusive evidence that all conditions precedent required to be performed by the incorporators have been complied with and that the corporation has been incorporated under this Act, except as against this State in a proceeding to cancel or revoke the certificate of incorporation or for involuntary dissolution of the corporation.

§ 57. Organization Meeting of Directors

After the issuance of the certificate of incorporation an organization meeting of the board of directors named in the articles of incorporation shall be held, either within or without this State, at the call of a majority of the directors named in the articles of incorporation, for the purpose of adopting by-laws, electing officers and transacting such other business as may come before the meeting. The directors calling the meeting shall give at least three days' notice thereof by mail to each director so named, stating the time and place of the meeting.

§ 58. Right to Amend Articles of Incorporation

A corporation may amend its articles of incorporation, from time to time, in any and as many respects as may be desired, so long as its articles of incorporation as amended contain only such provisions as might be lawfully contained in original articles of incorporation at the time of making such amendment, and, if a change in shares or the rights of shareholders, or an exchange, reclassification or cancellation of shares or rights of shareholders is to be made, such provisions as may be necessary to effect such change, exchange, reclassification or cancellation.

In particular, and without limitation upon such general power of amendment, a corporation may amend its articles of incorporation, from time to time, so as:

(a) To change its corporate name.

(b) To change its period of duration.

(c) To change, enlarge or diminish its corporate purposes.

(d) To increase or decrease the aggregate number of shares, or shares of any class, which the corporation has authority to issue.

(e) To provide, change or eliminate any provision with respect to the par value of any shares or class of shares.

(f) To exchange, classify, reclassify or cancel all or any part of its shares, whether issued or unissued.

(g) To change the designation of all or any part of its shares, whether issued or unissued, and to change the preferences, limitations, and the relative rights in respect of all or any part of its shares, whether issued or unissued.

(h) To change the shares of any class, whether issued or unissued [sic] into a different number of shares of the same class or into the same or a different number of shares of other classes.

(i) To create new classes of shares having rights and preferences either prior and superior or subordinate and inferior to the shares of any class then authorized, whether issued or unissued.

(j) To cancel or otherwise affect the right of the holders of the shares of any class to receive dividends which have accrued but have not been declared.

(k) To divide any preferred or special class of shares, whether issued or unissued, into series and fix and determine the designations of such series and the variations in the relative rights and preferences as between the shares of such series.

(l) To authorize the board of directors to establish, out of authorized but unissued shares, series of any preferred or special class of shares and fix and determine the relative rights and preferences of the shares of any series so established.

(m) To authorize the board of directors to fix and determine the relative rights and preferences of the authorized but unissued shares of series theretofore established in respect of which either the relative rights and preferences have not been fixed and determined or the relative rights and preferences theretofore fixed and determined are to be changed.

(n) To revoke, diminish, or enlarge the authority of the board of directors to establish series out of authorized but unissued shares of any preferred or special class and fix and determine the relative rights and preferences of the shares of any series so established.

(o) To limit, deny or grant to shareholders of any class the preemptive right to acquire additional shares of the corporation, whether then or thereafter authorized.

§ 59. Procedure to Amend Articles of Incorporation

Amendments to the articles of incorporation shall be made in the following manner:

(a) The board of directors shall adopt a resolution setting forth the proposed amendment and, if shares have been issued, directing that it be submitted to a vote at a meeting of shareholders, which may be either the annual or a special meeting. If no shares have been issued, the amendment shall be adopted by resolution of the board of directors and the provisions for adoption by shareholders shall not apply. If the corporation has only one class of shares outstanding, an amendment solely to change the number of authorized shares to effectuate a split of, or stock dividend in, the corporation's own shares, or solely to do so and to change the number of authorized shares in proportion thereto, may be adopted by the board of directors; and the provisions for adoption by shareholders shall not apply, unless otherwise provided by the articles of incorporation. The resolution may incorporate the proposed amendment in restated articles of incorporation which contain a statement that except for the designated amendment the restated articles of incorporation correctly set forth without change the corresponding provisions of the articles of incorporation as theretofore amended, and that the restated articles of incorporation together with the designated amendment supersede the original articles of incorporation and all amendments thereto.

(b) Written notice setting forth the proposed amendment or a summary of the changes to be effected thereby shall be given to each shareholder of record entitled to vote thereon within the time and in the manner provided in this Act for the giving of notice of meetings of shareholders. If the meeting be an annual meeting, the proposed amendment of such summary may be included in the notice of such annual meeting.

(c) At such meeting a vote of the shareholders entitled to vote thereon shall be taken on the proposed amendment. The proposed amendment shall be adopted upon receiving the affirmative vote of the holders of a majority of the shares entitled to vote thereon, unless any class of shares is entitled to vote thereon as a class, in which event the proposed amendment shall be adopted upon receiving the affirmative vote of the holders of a majority of the shares of each class of shares entitled to vote thereon as a class and of the total shares entitled to vote thereon.

Any number of amendments may be submitted to the shareholders, and voted upon by them, at one meeting.

§ 60. Class Voting on Amendments

The holders of the outstanding shares of a class shall be entitled to vote as a class upon a proposed amendment, whether or not entitled to vote thereon by the provisions of the articles of incorporation, if the amendment would:

(a) Increase or decrease the aggregate number of authorized shares of such class.

(b) Effect an exchange, reclassification or cancellation of all or part of the shares of such class.

(c) Effect an exchange, or create a right of exchange, of all or any part of the shares of another class into the shares of such class.

(d) Change the designations, preferences, limitations or relative rights of the shares of such class.

(e) Change the shares of such class into the same or a different number of shares of the same class or another class or classes.

(f) Create a new class of shares having rights and preferences prior and superior to the shares of such class, or increase the rights and preferences or the number of authorized shares, of any class having rights and preferences prior or superior to the shares of such class.

(g) In the case of a preferred or special class of shares, divide the shares of such class into series and fix and determine the designation of such series and the variations in the relative rights and preferences between the shares of such series, or authorize the board of directors to do so.

(h) Limit or deny any existing preemptive rights of the shares of such class.

(i) Cancel or otherwise affect dividends on the shares of such class which have accrued but have not been declared.

§ 61. Articles of Amendment

The articles of amendment shall be executed in duplicate by the corporation by its president or a vice president and by its secretary or an assistant secretary, and verified by one of the officers signing such articles, and shall set forth:

(a) The name of the corporation.

(b) The amendments so adopted.

(c) The date of the adoption of the amendment by the shareholders, or by the board of directors where no shares have been issued.

(d) The number of shares outstanding, and the number of shares entitled to vote thereon, and if the shares of any class are entitled to vote thereon as a class, the designation and number of outstanding shares entitled to vote thereon of each such class.

(e) The number of shares voted for and against such amendment, respectively, and, if the shares of any class are entitled to vote thereon as a class, the number of shares of each such class voted for and against such amendment, respectively, or if no shares have been issued, a statement to that effect.

(f) If such amendment provides for an exchange, reclassification or cancellation of issued shares, and if the manner in which the same shall be effected is not set forth in the amendment, then a statement of the manner in which the same shall be effected.

§ 62. Filing of Articles of Amendment

Duplicate originals of the articles of amendment shall be delivered to the Secretary of State. If the Secretary of State finds that the articles of amendment conform to law, he shall, when all fees and franchise taxes have been paid as in this Act prescribed:

(a) Endorse on each of such duplicate originals the word "Filed," and the month, day and year of the filing thereof.

(b) File one of such duplicate originals in his office.

(c) Issue a certificate of amendment to which he shall affix the other duplicate original.

The certificate of amendment, together with the duplicate original of the articles of amendment affixed thereto by the Secretary of State, shall be returned to the corporation or its representative.

§ 63. Effect of Certificate of Amendment

Upon the issuance of the certificate of amendment by the Secretary of State, the amendment shall become effective and the articles of incorporation shall be deemed to be amended accordingly.

No amendment shall affect any existing cause of action in favor of or against such corporation, or any pending suit to which such corporation shall be a party, or the existing rights of persons other than shareholders; and, in the event the corporate name shall be changed by amendment, no suit brought by or against such corporation under its former name shall abate for that reason.

§ 64. Restated Articles of Incorporation

A domestic corporation may at any time restate its articles of incorporation as theretofore amended, by a resolution adopted by the board of directors.

Upon the adoption of such resolution, restated articles of incorporation shall be executed in duplicate by the corporation by its president or a vice president and by its secretary or assistant secretary and verified by one of the officers signing such articles and shall set forth all of the operative provisions of the articles of incorporation as theretofore amended together with a statement that the restated articles of incorporation correctly set forth without change the corresponding provisions of the articles of incorporation as theretofore amended and that the restated articles of incorporation supersede the original articles of incorporation and all amendments thereto.

Duplicate originals of the restated articles of incorporation shall be delivered to the Secretary of State. If the Secretary of State finds that such restated articles of incorporation conform to law, he shall, when all fees and franchise taxes have been paid as in this Act prescribed:

(1) Endorse on each of such duplicate originals the word "Filed," and the month, day and year of the filing thereof.

(2) File one of such duplicate originals in his office.

(3) Issue a restated certificate of incorporation, to which he shall affix the other duplicate original.

The restated certificate of incorporation, together with the duplicate original of the restated articles of incorporation affixed thereto by the Secretary of State, shall be returned to the corporation or its representative.

Upon the issuance of the restated certificate of incorporation by the Secretary of State, the restated articles of incorporation shall become effective and shall supersede the original articles of incorporation and all amendments thereto.

§ 65. Amendment of Articles of Incorporation in Reorganization Proceedings

Whenever a plan of reorganization of a corporation has been confirmed by decree or order of a court of competent jurisdiction in proceedings for the reorganization of such corporation, pursuant to the provisions of any applicable statute of the United States relating to reorganizations of corporations, the articles of incorporation of the corporation may be amended, in the manner provided in this section, in as many respects as may be necessary to carry out the plan and put it into effect, so long as the articles of incorporation as amended contain only such provisions as might be lawfully contained in original articles of incorporation at the time of making such amendment.

In particular and without limitation upon such general power of amendment, the articles of incorporation may be amended for such purpose so as to:

(A) Change the corporate name, period of duration or corporate purposes of the corporation;

(B) Repeal, alter or amend the by-laws of the corporation;

(C) Change the aggregate number of shares or shares of any class, which the corporation has authority to issue;

(D) Change the preferences, limitations and relative rights in respect of all or any part of the shares of the corporation, and classify, reclassify or cancel all or any part thereof, whether issued or unissued;

(E) Authorize the issuance of bonds, debentures or other obligations of the corporation, whether or not convertible into shares of any class or bearing warrants or other evidences of optional rights to purchase or subscribe for shares of any class, and fix the terms and conditions thereof; and

(F) Constitute or reconstitute and classify or reclassify the board of directors of the corporation, and appoint directors and officers in place of or in addition to all or any of the directors or officers then in office.

Amendments to the articles of incorporation pursuant to this section shall be made in the following manner:

(a) Articles of amendment approved by decree or order of such court shall be executed and verified in duplicate by such person or persons as the court shall designate or appoint for the purpose, and shall set forth the name of the corporation, the amendments of the articles of incorporation approved by the court, the date of the decree or order approving the articles of amendment, the title of the proceedings in which the decree or order was entered, and a statement that such decree or order was entered by a court having jurisdiction of the proceedings for the reorganization of the corporation pursuant to the provisions of an applicable statute of the United States.

(b) Duplicate originals of the articles of amendment shall be delivered to the Secretary of State. If the Secretary of State finds that the articles of amendment conform to law, he shall, when all fees and franchise taxes have been paid as in this Act prescribed:

(1) Endorse on each of such duplicate originals the word "Filed," and the month, day and year of the filing thereof.

(2) File one of such duplicate originals in his office.

(3) Issue a certificate of amendment to which he shall affix the other duplicate original.

The certificate of amendment, together with the duplicate original of the articles of amendment affixed thereto by the Secretary of State, shall be returned to the corporation or its representative.

Upon the issuance of the certificate of amendment by the Secretary of State, the amendment shall become effective and the articles of incorporation shall be deemed to be amended accordingly, without any action thereon by the directors or shareholders of the corporation and with the same effect as if the amendments had been adopted by unanimous action of the directors and shareholders of the corporation.

§ 66. Restriction on Redemption or Purchase of Redeemable Shares

[Repealed in 1979].

§ 67. Cancellation of Redeemable Shares by Redemption or Purchase

[Repealed in 1979].

§ 68. Cancellation of Other Reacquired Shares

[Repealed in 1979].

§ 69. Reduction of Stated Capital in Certain Cases

[Repealed in 1979].

§ 70. Special Provisions Relating to Surplus and Reserves

[Repealed in 1979].

§ 71. Procedure for Merger

Any two or more domestic corporations may merge into one of such corporations pursuant to a plan of merger approved in the manner provided in this Act.

The board of directors of each corporation shall, by resolution adopted by each such board, approve a plan of merger setting forth:

(a) The names of the corporations proposing to merge, and the name of the corporation into which they propose to merge, which is hereinafter designated as the surviving corporation.

(b) The terms and conditions of the proposed merger.

(c) The manner and basis of converting the shares of each corporation into shares, obligations or other securities of the surviving corporation or of any other corporation or, in whole or in part, into cash or other property.

(d) A statement of any changes in the articles of incorporation of the surviving corporation to be effected by such merger.

(e) Such other provisions with respect to the proposed merger as are deemed necessary or desirable.

§ 72. Procedure for Consolidation

Any two or more domestic corporations may consolidate into a new corporation pursuant to a plan of consolidation approved in the manner provided in this Act.

The board of directors of each corporation shall, by a resolution adopted by each such board, approve a plan of consolidation setting forth:

(a) The names of the corporations proposing to consolidate, and the name of the new corporation into which they propose to consolidate, which is hereinafter designated as the new corporation.

(b) The terms and conditions of the proposed consolidation.

(c) The manner and basis of converting the shares of each corporation into shares, obligations or other securities of the new corporation or of any other corporation or, in whole or in part, into cash or other property.

(d) With respect to the new corporation, all of the statements required to be set forth in articles of incorporation for corporations organized under this Act.

(e) Such other provisions with respect to the proposed consolidation as are deemed necessary or desirable.

§ 72A. Procedure for Share Exchange

All the issued or all the outstanding shares of one or more classes of any domestic corporation may be acquired through the exchange of all such shares of such class or classes by another domestic or foreign corporation pursuant to a plan of exchange approved in the manner provided in this Act.

The board of directors of each corporation shall, by resolution adopted by each such board, approve a plan of exchange setting forth:

(a) The name of the corporation the shares of which are proposed to be acquired by exchange and the name of the corporation to acquire the shares of such corporation in the exchange, which is hereinafter designated as the acquiring corporation.

(b) The terms and conditions of the proposed exchange.

(c) The manner and basis of exchanging the shares to be acquired for shares, obligations or other securities of the acquiring corporation or any other corporation, or, in whole or in part, for cash or other property.

(d) Such other provisions with respect to the proposed exchange as are deemed necessary or desirable.

The procedure authorized by this section shall not be deemed to limit the power of a corporation to acquire all or part of the shares of any class or classes of a corporation through a voluntary exchange or otherwise by agreement with the shareholders.

§ 73. Approval by Shareholders

(a) The board of directors of each corporation in the case of a merger or consolidation, and the board of directors of the corporation the shares of which are to be acquired in the case of an exchange, upon approving such plan of merger, consolidation or exchange, shall, by resolution, direct that the plan be submitted to a vote at a meeting of its shareholders, which may be either an annual or a special meeting. Written notice shall be given to each shareholder of record, whether or not entitled to vote at such meeting, not less than twenty days before such meeting, in the manner provided in this Act for the giving of notice of meetings of shareholders, and, whether the meeting be an annual or a special meeting, shall state that the purpose or one of the purposes is to consider the proposed plan of merger, consolidation or exchange. A copy or a summary of the plan of merger, consolidation or exchange, as the case may be, shall be included in or enclosed with such notice.

(b) At each such meeting, a vote of the shareholders shall be taken on the proposed plan. The plan shall be approved upon receiving the affirmative vote of the holders of a majority of the shares entitled to vote thereon of each such corporation, unless any class of shares of any such corporation is entitled to vote thereon as a class, in which event, as to such corporation, the plan shall be approved upon receiving the affirmative vote of the holders of a majority of the shares of each class of shares entitled to vote thereon as a class and of the total shares entitled to vote thereon. Any class of shares of any such corporation shall be entitled to vote as a class if any such plan contains any provision which, if contained in a proposed amendment to articles of incorporation, would entitle such class of shares to vote as a class and, in the case of an exchange, if the class is included in the exchange.

(c) After such approval by a vote of the shareholders of each such corporation, and at any time prior to the filing of the articles of merger, consolidation or exchange, the merger, consolidation or exchange may be abandoned pursuant to provisions therefor, if any, set forth in the plan.

(d) (1) Notwithstanding the provisions of subsections (a) and (b), submission of a plan of merger to a vote at a meeting of shareholders of a surviving corporation shall not be required if:

(i) the articles of incorporation of the surviving corporation do not differ except in name from those of the corporation before the merger,

(ii) each holder of shares of the surviving corporation which were outstanding immediately before the effective date of the merger is to hold the same number of shares with identical rights immediately after,

(iii) the number of voting shares outstanding immediately after the merger, plus the number of voting shares issuable on conversion of other securities issued by virtue of the terms of the merger and on exercise of rights and warrants so issued, will not exceed by more than 20 percent the number of voting shares outstanding immediately before the merger, and

(iv) the number of participating shares outstanding immediately after the merger, plus the number of participating shares issuable on conversion of other securities issued by virtue of the terms of the merger and on exercise of rights and warrants so issued, will not exceed by more than 20 percent the number of participating shares outstanding immediately before the merger.

(2) As used in this subsection:

(i) "voting shares" means shares which entitle their holders to vote unconditionally in elections of directors;

(ii) "participating shares" means shares which entitle their holders to participate without limitation in distribution of earnings or surplus.

§ 74. Articles of Merger, Consolidation or Exchange

(a) Upon receiving the approvals required by Sections 71, 72 and 73, articles of merger or articles of consolidation shall be executed in duplicate by each corporation by its president or a vice president and by its secretary or an assistant secretary, and verified by one of the officers of each corporation signing such articles, and shall set forth:

(1) The plan of merger or the plan of consolidation;

(2) As to each corporation, either (i) the number of shares outstanding, and, if the shares of any class are entitled to vote as a class, the designation and number of outstanding shares of each such class, or (ii) a statement that the vote of shareholders is not required by virtue of subsection 73(d);

(3) As to each corporation the approval of whose shareholders is required, the number of shares voted for and against such plan, respectively, and, if the shares of any class are entitled to vote as a class, the number of shares of each such class voted for and against such plan, respectively.

(b) Duplicate originals of the articles of merger, consolidation or exchange shall be delivered to the Secretary of State. If the Secretary of State finds that such articles conform to law, he shall, when all fees and franchise taxes have been paid as in this Act prescribed:

(1) Endorse on each of such duplicate originals the word "Filed," and the month, day and year of the filing thereof.

(2) File one of such duplicate originals in his office.

(3) Issue a certificate of merger, consolidation or exchange to which he shall affix the other duplicate original.

(c) The certificate of merger, consolidation or exchange together with the duplicate original of the articles affixed thereto by the Secretary of State, shall be returned to the surviving, new or acquiring corporation, as the case may be, or its representative.

§ 75. Merger of Subsidiary Corporation

Any corporation owning at least ninety per cent of the outstanding shares of each class of another corporation may merge such other corporation into itself without approval by a vote of the shareholders of either corporation. Its board of directors shall, by resolution, approve a plan of merger setting forth:

(A) The name of the subsidiary corporation and the name of the corporation owning at least ninety per cent of its

shares, which is hereinafter designated as the surviving corporation.

(B) The manner and basis of converting the shares of the subsidiary corporation into shares, obligations or other securities of the surviving corporation or of any other corporation or, in whole or in part, into cash or other property.

A copy of such plan of merger shall be mailed to each shareholder of record of the subsidiary corporation.

Articles of merger shall be executed in duplicate by the surviving corporation by its president or a vice president and by its secretary or an assistant secretary, and verified by one of its officers signing such articles, and shall set forth:

(a) The plan of merger;

(b) The number of outstanding shares of each class of the subsidiary corporation and the number of such shares of each class owned by the surviving corporation; and

(c) The date of the mailing to shareholders of the subsidiary corporation of a copy of the plan of merger.

On and after the thirtieth day after the mailing of a copy of the plan of merger to shareholders of the subsidiary corporation or upon the waiver thereof by the holders of all outstanding shares duplicate originals of the articles of merger shall be delivered to the Secretary of State. If the Secretary of State finds that such articles conform to law, he shall, when all fees and franchise taxes have been paid as in this Act prescribed:

(1) Endorse on each of such duplicate originals the word "Filed," and the month, day and year of the filing thereof,

(2) File one of such duplicate originals in his office, and

(3) Issue a certificate of merger to which he shall affix the other duplicate original.

The certificate of merger, together with the duplicate original of the articles of merger affixed thereto by the Secretary of State, shall be returned to the surviving corporation or its representative.

§ 76. Effect of Merger, Consolidation or Exchange

Upon the issuance of the certificate of merger or the certificate of consolidation by the Secretary of State, the merger or consolidation shall be effected.

When such merger or consolidation has been effective:

(a) The several corporations parties to the plan of merger or consolidation shall be a single corporation, which, in the case of a merger, shall be that corporation designated in the plan of merger as the surviving corporation, and, in the case of a consolidation, shall be the new corporation provided for in the plan of consolidation.

(b) The separate existence of all corporations parties to the plan of merger or consolidation, except the surviving or new corporation, shall cease.

(c) Such surviving or new corporation shall have all the rights, privileges, immunities and powers and shall be subject to all the duties and liabilities of a corporation organized under this Act.

(d) Such surviving or new corporation shall thereupon and thereafter possess all the rights, privileges, immunities, and franchises, of a public as well as of a private nature, of each of the merging or consolidating corporations; and all property, real, personal and mixed, and all debts due on whatever account, including subscriptions to shares, and all other choses in action, and all and every other interest of or belonging to or due to each of the corporations so merged or consolidated, shall be taken and deemed to be transferred to and vested in such single corporation without further act or deed; and the title to any real estate, or any interest therein, vested in any of such corporations shall not revert or be in any way impaired by reason of such merger or consolidation.

(e) Such surviving or new corporation shall thenceforth be responsible and liable for all the liabilities and obligations of each of the corporations so merged or consolidated; and any claim existing or action or proceeding pending by or against any of such corporations may be prosecuted as if such merger or consolidation had not taken place, or such surviving or new corporation may be substituted in its place. Neither the rights of creditors nor any liens upon the property of any such corporation shall be impaired by such merger or consolidation.

(f) In the case of a merger, the articles of incorporation of the surviving corporation shall be deemed to be amended to the extent, if any, that changes in its articles of incorporation are stated in the plan of merger; and, in the case of a consolidation, the statements set forth in the articles of consolidation and which are required or permitted to be set forth in the articles of incorporation of corporations organized under this Act shall be deemed to be the original articles of incorporation of the new corporation.

§ 77. Merger, Consolidation or Exchange of Shares Between Domestic and Foreign Corporations

One or more foreign corporations and one or more domestic corporations may be merged or consolidated in the following manner, if such merger or consolidation is permitted by the laws of the state under which each such foreign corporation is organized:

(a) Each domestic corporation shall comply with the provisions of this Act with respect to the merger or consolidation, as the case may be, of domestic corporations and each foreign corporation shall comply with the applicable provisions of the laws of the state under which it is organized.

(b) If the surviving or new corporation, as the case may be, is to be governed by the laws of any state other than this State, it shall comply with the provisions of this Act with respect to foreign corporations if it is to transact business in this State, and in every case it shall file with the Secretary of State of this State:

(1) An agreement that it may be served with process in this State in any proceeding for the enforcement of any obligation of any domestic corporation which is a party to such merger or consolidation and in any proceeding for the enforcement of the rights of a dissenting shareholder of any such domestic corporation against the surviving or new corporation;

(2) An irrevocable appointment of the Secretary of State of this State as its agent to accept service of process in any such proceeding; and

(3) An agreement that it will promptly pay to the dissenting shareholders of any such domestic corporation the amount, if any, to which they shall be entitled under the provisions of this Act with respect to the rights of dissenting shareholders.

The effect of such merger or consolidation shall be the same as in the case of the merger or consolidation of domestic corporations, if the surviving or new corporation is to be governed by the laws of this State. If the surviving or new corporation is to be governed by the laws of any state other than this State, the effect of such merger or consolidation shall be the same as in the case of the merger or consolidation of domestic corporations except insofar as the laws of such other state provide otherwise.

At any time prior to the filing of the articles of merger or consolidation, the merger or consolidation may be abandoned pursuant to provisions therefor, if any, set forth in the plan of merger or consolidation.

§ 78. Sale of Assets in Regular Course of Business and Mortgage or Pledge of Assets

The sale, lease, exchange, or other disposition of all, or substantially all, the property and assets of a corporation in the usual and regular course of its business and the mortgage or pledge of any or all property and assets of a corporation whether or not in the usual and regular course of business may be made upon such terms and conditions and for such consideration, which may consist in whole or in part of cash or other property, including shares, obligations or other securities of any other corporation, domestic or foreign, as shall be authorized by its board of directors; and in any such case no authorization or consent of the shareholders shall be required.

§ 79. Sale of Assets Other Than in Regular Course of Business

A sale, lease, exchange, or other disposition of all, or substantially all, the property and assets, with or without the good will, of a corporation, if not in the usual and regular course of its business, may be made upon such terms and conditions and for such consideration, which may consist in whole or in part of cash or other property, including shares, obligations or other securities of any other corporation, domestic or foreign, as may be authorized in the following manner:

(a) The board of directors shall adopt a resolution recommending such sale, lease, exchange, or other disposition and directing the submission thereof to a vote at a meeting of shareholders, which may be either an annual or a special meeting.

(b) Written notice shall be given to each shareholder of record, whether or not entitled to vote at such meeting, not less than twenty days before such meeting, in the manner provided in this Act for the giving of notice of meetings of shareholders, and, whether the meeting be an annual or a special meeting, shall state that the purpose, or one of the purposes is to consider the proposed sale, lease, exchange, or other disposition.

(c) At such meeting the shareholders may authorize such sale, lease, exchange, or other disposition and may fix, or may authorize the board of directors to fix, any or all of the terms and conditions thereof and the consideration to be received by the corporation therefor. Such authorization shall require the affirmative vote of the holders of a majority of the shares of the corporation entitled to vote thereon, unless any class of shares is entitled to vote thereon as a class, in which event such authorization shall require the affirmative vote of the holders of a majority of the shares of each class of shares entitled to vote as a class thereon and of the total shares entitled to vote thereon.

(d) After such authorization by a vote of shareholders, the board of directors nevertheless, in its discretion, may abandon such sale, lease, exchange, or other disposition of assets, subject to the rights of third parties under any contracts relating thereto, without further action or approval by shareholders.

§ 80. Right of Shareholders to Dissent and Obtain Payment for Shares

(a) Any shareholder of a corporation shall have the right to dissent from, and to obtain payment for his shares in the event of, any of the following corporate actions:

(1) Any plan of merger or consolidation to which the corporation is a party, except as provided in subsection (c);

(2) Any sale or exchange of all or substantially all of the property and assets of the corporation not made in the usual or regular course of its business, including a sale in dissolution, but not including a sale pursuant to an order of a court having jurisdiction in the premises or a sale for cash on terms requiring that all or substantially all of the net proceeds of sale be distributed to the shareholders in accordance with their respective interests within one year after the date of sale;

(3) Any plan of exchange to which the corporation is a party as the corporation the shares of which are to be acquired;

(4) Any amendment of the articles of incorporation which materially and adversely affects the rights appurtenant to the shares of the dissenting shareholder in that it:

(i) alters or abolishes a preferential right of such shares;

(ii) creates, alters or abolishes a right in respect of the redemption of such shares, including a provision respecting a sinking fund for the redemption or repurchase of such shares;

(iii) alters or abolishes a preemptive right of the holder of such shares to acquire shares or other securities;

(iv) excludes or limits the right of the holder of such shares to vote on any matter, or to cumulate his votes, except as such right may be limited by dilution through the issuance of shares or other securities with similar voting rights; or

(5) Any other corporate action taken pursuant to a shareholder vote with respect to which the articles of incorporation, the bylaws, or a resolution of the board of directors directs that dissenting shareholders shall have a right to obtain payment for their shares.

(b) (1) A record holder of shares may assert dissenters' rights as to less than all of the shares registered in his name only if he dissents with respect to all the shares beneficially owned by any one person, and discloses the name and address of the person or persons on whose behalf he dissents. In that event, his rights shall be determined as if the shares as to which he has dissented and his other shares were registered in the names of different shareholders.

(2) A beneficial owner of shares who is not the record holder may assert dissenters' rights with respect to shares held on his behalf, and shall be treated as a dissenting shareholder under the terms of this section and section 81 if he submits to the corporation at the time of or before the assertion of these rights a written consent of the record holder.

(c) The right to obtain payment under this section shall not apply to the shareholders of the surviving corporation in a merger if a vote of the shareholders of such corporation is not necessary to authorize such merger.

(d) A shareholder of a corporation who has a right under this section to obtain payment for his shares shall have no right at law or in equity to attack the validity of the corporate action that gives rise to his right to obtain payment, nor to have the action set aside or rescinded, except when the corporate action is unlawful or fraudulent with regard to the complaining shareholder or to the corporation.

§ 81. Procedures for Protection of Dissenters' Rights

(a) As used in this section:

(1) "Dissenter" means a shareholder or beneficial owner who is entitled to and does assert dissenters' rights under section 80, and who has performed every act required up to the time involved for the assertion of such rights.

(2) "Corporation" means the issuer of the shares held by the dissenter before the corporate action, or the successor by merger or consolidation of that issuer.

(3) "Fair value" of shares means their value immediately before the effectuation of the corporate action to which the dissenter objects, excluding any appreciation or depreciation in anticipation of such corporate action unless such exclusion would be inequitable.

(4) "Interest" means interest from the effective date of the corporate action until the date of payment, at the average rate currently paid by the corporation on its principal bank loans, or, if none, at such rate as is fair and equitable under all the circumstances.

(b) If a proposed corporate action which would give rise to dissenters' rights under section 80(a) is submitted to a vote at a meeting of shareholders, the notice of meeting shall notify all shareholders that they have or may have a right to dissent and obtain payment for their shares by complying with the terms of this section, and shall be accompanied by a copy of sections 80 and 81 of this Act.

(c) If the proposed corporate action is submitted to a vote at a meeting of shareholders, any shareholder who wishes to dissent and obtain payment for his shares must file with the corporation, prior to the vote, a written notice of intention to demand that he be paid fair compensation for his shares if the proposed action is effectuated, and shall refrain from voting his shares in approval of such action. A shareholder who fails in either respect shall acquire no right to payment for his shares under this section or section 80.

(d) If the proposed corporate action is approved by the required vote at a meeting of shareholders, the corporation shall mail a further notice to all shareholders who gave due notice of intention to demand payment and who refrained from voting in favor of the proposed action. If the proposed corporate action is to be taken without a vote of shareholders, the corporation shall send to all shareholders who are entitled to dissent and demand payment for their shares a notice of the adoption of the plan of corporate action. The notice shall (1) state where and when a demand for payment must be sent and certificates of certificated shares must be deposited in order to obtain payment, (2) inform holders of uncertificated shares to what extent transfer of shares will be restricted from the time that demand for payment is received, (3) supply a form for demanding payment which includes a request for certification of the date on which the shareholder, or the person on whose behalf the shareholder dissents, acquired beneficial ownership of the shares, and (4) be accompanied by a copy of sections 80 and 81 of this Act. The time set for the demand and deposit shall be not less than 30 days from the mailing of the notice.

(e) A shareholder who fails to demand payment, or fails (in the case of certificated shares) to deposit certificates, as required by a notice pursuant to subsection (d) shall have no right under this section or section 80 to receive payment for his shares. If the shares are not represented by certificates, the corporation may restrict their transfer from the time of receipt of demand for payment until effectuation of the proposed corporate action, or the release of restrictions under the terms of subsection (f). The dissenter shall retain all other rights of a shareholder until these rights are modified by effectuation of the proposed corporate action.

(f) (1) Within 60 days after the date set for demanding payment and depositing certificates, if the corporation has not effectuated the proposed corporate action and remitted payment for shares pursuant to paragraph (3), it shall return any certificates that have been deposited, and release uncertificated shares from any transfer restrictions imposed by reason of the demand for payment.

(2) When uncertificated shares have been released from transfer restrictions, and deposited certificates have been returned, the corporation may at any later time send a new notice conforming to the requirements of subsection (d), with like effect.

(3) Immediately upon effectuation of the proposed corporate action, or upon receipt of demand for payment if the corporate action has already been effectuated, the corporation shall remit to dissenters who have made demand and (if their shares are certificated) have deposited their certificates the amount which the corporation estimates to be the fair value of the shares, with interest if

any has accrued. The remittance shall be accompanied by:

(i) the corporation's closing balance sheet and statement of income for a fiscal year ending not more than 16 months before the date of remittance, together with the latest available interim financial statements;

(ii) a statement of the corporation's estimate of fair value of the shares; and

(iii) a notice of the dissenter's right to demand supplemental payment, accompanied by a copy of sections 80 and 81 of this Act.

(g) (1) If the corporation fails to remit as required by subsection (f), or if the dissenter believes that the amount remitted is less than the fair value of his shares, or that the interest is not correctly determined, he may send the corporation his own estimate of the value of the shares or of the interest, and demand payment of the deficiency.

(2) If the dissenter does not file such an estimate within 30 days after the corporation's mailing of its remittance, he shall be entitled to no more than the amount remitted.

(h) (1) Within 60 days after receiving a demand for payment pursuant to subsection (g), if any such demands for payment remain unsettled, the corporation shall file in an appropriate court a petition requesting that the fair value of the shares and interest thereon be determined by the court.

(2) An appropriate court shall be a court of competent jurisdiction in the county of this state where the registered office of the corporation is located. If, in the case of a merger or consolidation or exchange of shares, the corporation is a foreign corporation without a registered office in this state, the petition shall be filed in the county where the registered office of the domestic corporation was last located.

(3) All dissenters, wherever residing, whose demands have not been settled shall be made parties to the proceeding as in an action against their shares. A copy of the petition shall be served on each such dissenter; if a dissenter is a nonresident, the copy may be served on him by registered or certified mail or by publication as provided by law.

(4) The jurisdiction of the court shall be plenary and exclusive. The court may appoint one or more persons as appraisers to receive evidence and recommend a decision on the question of fair value. The appraisers shall have such power and authority as shall be specified in the order of their appointment or in any amendment thereof. The dissenters shall be entitled to discovery in the same manner as parties in other civil suits.

(5) All dissenters who are made parties shall be entitled to judgment for the amount by which the fair value of their shares is found to exceed the amount previously remitted, with interest.

(6) If the corporation fails to file a petition as provided in paragraph (1) of this subsection, each dissenter who made a demand and who has not already settled his claim against the corporation shall be paid by the corporation the amount demanded by him, with interest, and may sue therefor in an appropriate court.

(i) (1) The costs and expenses of any proceeding under subsection (h), including the reasonable compensation and expenses of appraisers appointed by the court, shall be determined by the court and assessed against the corporation, except that any part of the costs and expenses may be apportioned and assessed as the court may deem equitable against all or some of the dissenters who are parties and whose action in demanding supplemental payment the court finds to be arbitrary, vexatious, or not in good faith.

(2) Fees and expenses of counsel and of experts for the respective parties may be assessed as the court may deem equitable against the corporation and in favor of any or all dissenters if the corporation failed to comply substantially with the requirements of this section, and may be assessed against either the corporation or a dissenter, in favor of any other party, if the court finds that the party against whom the fees and expenses are assessed acted arbitrarily, vexatiously, or not in good faith in respect to the rights provided by this Section and Section 80.

(3) If the court finds that the services of counsel for any dissenter were of substantial benefit to other dissenters similarly situated, and should not be assessed against the corporation, it may award to these counsel reasonable fees to be paid out of the amounts awarded to the dissenters who were benefitted.

(j) (1) Notwithstanding the foregoing provisions of this section, the corporation may elect to withhold the remittance required by subsection (f) from any dissenter with respect to shares of which the dissenter (or the person on whose behalf the dissenter acts) was not the beneficial owner on the date of the first announcement to news media or to shareholders of the terms of the proposed corporate action. With respect to such shares, the corporation shall, upon effectuating the corporate action, state to each dissenter its estimate of the fair value of the shares, state the rate of interest to be used (explaining the basis thereof), and offer to pay the resulting amounts on receiving the dissenter's agreement to accept them in full satisfaction.

(2) If the dissenter believes that the amount offered is less than the fair value of the shares and interest determined according to this section, he may within 30 days after the date of mailing of the corporation's offer, mail the cor-

poration his own estimate of fair value and interest, and demand their payment. If the dissenter fails to do so, he shall be entitled to no more than the corporation's offer.

(3) If the dissenter makes a demand as provided in paragraph (2), the provisions of subsections (h) and (i) shall apply to further proceedings on the dissenter's demand.

§ 82. Voluntary Dissolution by Incorporators

A corporation which has not commenced business and which has not issued any shares, may be voluntarily dissolved by its incorporators at any time in the following manner:

(a) Articles of dissolution shall be executed in duplicate by a majority of the incorporators, and verified by them, and shall set forth:

   (1) The name of the corporation.

   (2) The date of issuance of its certificate of incorporation.

   (3) That none of its shares has been issued.

   (4) That the corporation has not commenced business.

   (5) That the amount, if any, actually paid in on subscriptions for its shares, less any part thereof disbursed for necessary expenses, has been returned to those entitled thereto.

   (6) That no debts of the corporation remain unpaid.

   (7) That a majority of the incorporators elect that the corporation be dissolved.

(b) Duplicate originals of the articles of dissolution shall be delivered to the Secretary of State. If the Secretary of State finds that the articles of dissolution conform to law, he shall, when all fees and franchise taxes have been paid as in this Act prescribed:

   (1) Endorse on each of such duplicate originals the word "Filed," and the month, day and year of the filing thereof.

   (2) File one of such duplicate originals in his office.

   (3) Issue a certificate of dissolution to which he shall affix the other duplicate original.

The certificate of dissolution, together with the duplicate original of the articles of dissolution affixed thereto by the Secretary of State, shall be returned to the incorporators or their representative. Upon the issuance of such certificate of dissolution by the Secretary of State, the existence of the corporation shall cease.

§ 83. Voluntary Dissolution by Consent of Shareholders

A corporation may be voluntarily dissolved by the written consent of all of its shareholders.

Upon the execution of such written consent, a statement of intent to dissolve shall be executed in duplicate by the corporation by its president or a vice president and by its secretary or an assistant secretary, and verified by one of the officers signing such statement, which statement shall set forth:

(a) The name of the corporation.

(b) The names and respective addresses of its officers.

(c) The names and respective addresses of its directors.

(d) A copy of the written consent signed by all shareholders of the corporation.

(e) A statement that such written consent has been signed by all shareholders of the corporation or signed in their names by their attorneys thereunto duly authorized.

§ 84. Voluntary Dissolution by Act of Corporation

A corporation may be dissolved by the act of the corporation, when authorized in the following manner:

(a) The board of directors shall adopt a resolution recommending that the corporation be dissolved, and directing that the question of such dissolution be submitted to a vote at a meeting of shareholders, which may be either an annual or a special meeting.

(b) Written notice shall be given to each shareholder of record entitled to vote at such meeting within the time and in the manner provided in this Act for the giving of notice of meetings of shareholders, and, whether the meeting be an annual or special meeting, shall state that the purpose, or one of the purposes, of such meeting is to consider the advisability of dissolving the corporation.

(c) At such meeting a vote of shareholders entitled to vote thereat shall be taken on a resolution to dissolve the corporation. Such resolution shall be adopted upon receiving the affirmative vote of the holders of a majority of the shares of the corporation entitled to vote thereon, unless any class of shares is entitled to vote thereon as a class, in which event the resolution shall be adopted upon receiving the affirmative vote of the holders of a majority of the shares of each class of shares entitled to vote thereon as a class and of the total shares entitled to vote thereon.

(d) Upon the adoption of such resolution, a statement of intent to dissolve shall be executed in duplicate by the corporation by its president or a vice president and by its secretary or an assistant secretary, and verified by one of the officers signing such statement, which statement shall set forth:

   (1) The name of the corporation.

   (2) The names and respective addresses of its officers.

   (3) The names and respective addresses of its directors.

(4) A copy of the resolution adopted by the shareholders authorizing the dissolution of the corporation.

(5) The number of shares outstanding, and, if the shares of any class are entitled to vote as a class, the designation and number of outstanding shares of each such class.

(6) The number of shares voted for and against the resolution, respectively, and, if the shares of any class are entitled to vote as a class, the number of shares of each such class voted for and against the resolution, respectively.

§ 85. Filing of Statement of Intent to Dissolve

Duplicate originals of the statement of intent to dissolve, whether by consent of shareholders or by act of the corporation, shall be delivered to the Secretary of State. If the Secretary of State finds that such statement conforms to law, he shall, when all fees and franchise taxes have been paid as in this Act prescribed:

(a) Endorse on each of such duplicate originals the word "Filed," and the month, day and year of the filing thereof.

(b) File one of such duplicate originals in his office.

(c) Return the other duplicate original to the corporation or its representative.

§ 86. Effect of Statement of Intent to Dissolve

Upon the filing by the Secretary of State of a statement of intent to dissolve, whether by consent of shareholders or by act of the corporation, the corporation shall cease to carry on its business, except insofar as may be necessary for the winding up thereof, but its corporate existence shall continue until a certificate of dissolution has been issued by the Secretary of State or until a decree dissolving the corporation has been entered by a court of competent jurisdiction as in this Act provided.

§ 87. Procedure after Filing of Statement of Intent to Dissolve

After the filing by the Secretary of State of a statement of intent to dissolve:

(a) The corporation shall immediately cause notice thereof to be mailed to each known creditor of the corporation.

(b) The corporation shall proceed to collect its assets, convey and dispose of such of its properties as are not to be distributed in kind to its shareholders, pay, satisfy and discharge its liabilities and obligations and do all other acts required to liquidate its business and affairs, and, after paying or adequately providing for the payment of all its obligations, distribute the remainder of its assets, either in cash or in kind, among its shareholders according to their respective rights and interests.

(c) The corporation, at any time during the liquidation of its business and affairs, may make application to a court of competent jurisdiction within the state and judicial subdivision in which the registered office or principal place of business of the corporation is situated, to have the liquidation continued under the supervision of the court as provided in this Act.

§ 88. Revocation of Voluntary Dissolution Proceedings by Consent of Shareholders

By the written consent of all of its shareholders, a corporation may, at any time prior to the issuance of a certificate of dissolution by the Secretary of State, revoke voluntary dissolution proceedings theretofore taken, in the following manner:

Upon the execution of such written consent, a statement of revocation of voluntary dissolution proceedings shall be executed in duplicate by the corporation by its president or a vice president and by its secretary or an assistant secretary, and verified by one of the officers signing such statement, which statement shall set forth:

(a) The name of the corporation.

(b) The names and respective addresses of its officers.

(c) The names and respective addresses of its directors.

(d) A copy of the written consent signed by all shareholders of the corporation revoking such voluntary dissolution proceedings.

(e) That such written consent has been signed by all shareholders of the corporation or signed in their names by their attorneys thereunto duly authorized.

§ 89. Revocation of Voluntary Dissolution Proceedings by Act of Corporation

By the act of the corporation, a corporation may, at any time prior to the issuance of a certificate of dissolution by the Secretary of State, revoke voluntary dissolution proceedings theretofore taken, in the following manner:

(a) The board of directors shall adopt a resolution recommending that the voluntary dissolution proceedings be revoked, and directing that the question of such revocation be submitted to a vote at a special meeting of shareholders.

(b) Written notice, stating that the purpose or one of the purposes of such meeting is to consider the advisability of revoking the voluntary dissolution proceedings, shall be given to each shareholder of record entitled to vote at such meeting within the time and in the manner provided in this Act for the giving of notice of special meetings of shareholders.

(c) At such meeting a vote of the shareholders entitled to vote thereat shall be taken on a resolution to revoke the voluntary dissolution proceedings, which shall require for its adoption the affirmative vote of the holders of a majority of the shares entitled to vote thereon.

(d) Upon the adoption of such resolution, a statement of revocation of voluntary dissolution proceedings shall be executed in duplicate by the corporation by its president or a vice president and by its secretary or an assistant secretary, and verified by one of the officers signing such statement, which statement shall set forth:

(1) The name of the corporation.

(2) The names and respective addresses of its officers.

(3) The names and respective addresses of its directors.

(4) A copy of the resolution adopted by the shareholders revoking the voluntary dissolution proceedings.

(5) The number of shares outstanding.

(6) The number of shares voted for and against the resolution, respectively.

§ 90. Filing of Statement of Revocation of Voluntary Dissolution Proceedings

Duplicate originals of the statement of revocation of voluntary dissolution proceedings, whether by consent of shareholders or by act of the corporation, shall be delivered to the Secretary of State. If the Secretary of State finds that such statement conforms to law, he shall, when all fees and franchise taxes have been paid as in this Act prescribed:

(a) Endorse on each of such duplicate originals the word "Filed," and the month, day and year of the filing thereof.

(b) File one of such duplicate originals in his office.

(c) Return the other duplicate original to the corporation or its representative.

§ 91. Effect of Statement of Revocation of Voluntary Dissolution Proceedings

Upon the filing by the Secretary of State of a statement of revocation of voluntary dissolution proceedings, whether by consent of shareholders or by act of the corporation, the revocation of the voluntary dissolution proceedings shall become effective and the corporation may again carry on its business.

§ 92. Articles of Dissolution

If voluntary dissolution proceedings have not been revoked, then when all debts, liabilities and obligations of the corporation have been paid and discharged, or adequate provision has been made therefor, and all of the remaining property and assets of the corporation have been distributed to its shareholders, articles of dissolution shall be executed in duplicate by the corporation by its president or a vice president and by its secretary or an assistant

secretary, and verified by one of the officers signing such statement, which statement shall set forth:

(a) The name of the corporation.

(b) That the Secretary of State has theretofore filed a statement of intent to dissolve the corporation, and the date on which such statement was filed.

(c) That all debts, obligations and liabilities of the corporation have been paid and discharged or that adequate provision has been made therefor.

(d) That all the remaining property and assets of the corporation have been distributed among its shareholders in accordance with their respective rights and interests.

(e) That there are no suits pending against the corporation in any court, or that adequate provision has been made for the satisfaction of any judgment, order or decree which may be entered against it in any pending suit.

§ 93. Filing of Articles of Dissolution

Duplicate originals of such articles of dissolution shall be delivered to the Secretary of State. If the Secretary of State finds that such articles of dissolution conform to law, he shall, when all fees and franchise taxes have been paid as in this Act prescribed:

(a) Endorse on each of such duplicate originals the word "Filed," and the month, day and year of the filing thereof.

(b) File one of such duplicate originals in his office.

(c) Issue a certificate of dissolution to which he shall affix the other duplicate original.

The certificate of dissolution, together with the duplicate original of the articles of dissolution affixed thereto by the Secretary of State, shall be returned to the representative of the dissolved corporation. Upon the issuance of such certificate of dissolution the existence of the corporation shall cease, except for the purpose of suits, other proceedings and appropriate corporate action by shareholders, directors and officers as provided in this Act.

§ 94. Involuntary Dissolution

A corporation may be dissolved involuntarily by a decree of the . . . . court in an action filed by the Attorney General when it is established that:

(a) The corporation has failed to file its annual report within the time required by this Act, or has failed to pay its franchise tax on or before the first day of August of the year in which such franchise tax becomes due and payable; or

(b) The corporation procured its articles of incorporation through fraud; or

(c) The corporation has continued to exceed or abuse the authority conferred upon it by law; or

(d) The corporation has failed for thirty days to appoint and maintain a registered agent in this State; or

(e) The corporation has failed for thirty days after change of its registered office or registered agent to file in the office of the Secretary of State a statement of such change.

§ 95. Notification to Attorney General

The Secretary of State, on or before the last day of December of each year, shall certify to the Attorney General the names of all corporations which have failed to file their annual reports or to pay franchise taxes in accordance with the provisions of this Act, together with the facts pertinent thereto. He shall also certify, from time to time, the names of all corporations which have given other cause for dissolution as provided in this Act, together with the facts pertinent thereto. Whenever the Secretary of State shall certify the name of a corporation to the Attorney General as having given any cause for dissolution, the Secretary of State shall concurrently mail to the corporation at its registered office a notice that such certification has been made. Upon the receipt of such certification, the Attorney General shall file an action in the name of the State against such corporation for its dissolution. Every such certificate from the Secretary of State to the Attorney General pertaining to the failure of a corporation to file an annual report or pay a franchise tax shall be taken and received in all courts as prima facie evidence of the facts therein stated. If, before action is filed, the corporation shall file its annual report or pay its franchise tax, together with all penalties thereon, or shall appoint or maintain a registered agent as provided in this Act, or shall file with the Secretary of State the required statement of change of registered office or registered agent, such fact shall be forthwith certified by the Secretary of State to the Attorney General and he shall not file an action against such corporation for such cause. If, after action is filed, the corporation shall file its annual report or pay its franchise tax, together with all penalties thereon, or shall appoint or maintain a registered agent as provided in this Act, or shall file with the Secretary of State the required statement of change of registered office or registered agent, and shall pay the costs of such action, the action for such cause shall abate.

§ 96. Venue and Process

Every action for the involuntary dissolution of a corporation shall be commenced by the Attorney General either in the . . . . court of the county in which the registered office of the corporation is situated, or in the . . . . court of . . . . county. Summons shall issue and be served as in other civil actions. If process is returned not found, the Attorney General shall cause publication to be made as in other civil cases in some newspaper published in the county where the registered office

of the corporation is situated, containing a notice of the pendency of such action, the title of the court, the title of the action, and the date on or after which default may be entered. The Attorney General may include in one notice the names of any number of corporations against which actions are then pending in the same court. The Attorney General shall cause a copy of such notice to be mailed to the corporation at its registered office within ten days after the first publication thereof. The certificate of the Attorney General of the mailing of such notice shall be prima facie evidence thereof. Such notice shall be published at least once each week for two successive weeks, and the first publication thereof may begin at any time after the summons has been returned. Unless a corporation shall have been served with summons, no default shall be taken against it earlier than thirty days after the first publication of such notice.

§ 97. Jurisdiction of Court to Liquidate Assets and Business of Corporation

The . . . . courts shall have full power to liquidate the assets and business of a corporation:

(a) In an action by a shareholder when it is established:

(1) That the directors are deadlocked in the management of the corporate affairs and the shareholders are unable to break the deadlock, and that irreparable injury to the corporation is being suffered or is threatened by reason thereof; or

(2) That the acts of the directors or those in control of the corporation are illegal, oppressive or fraudulent; or

(3) That the shareholders are deadlocked in voting power, and have failed, for a period which includes at least two consecutive annual meeting dates, to elect successors to directors whose terms have expired or would have expired upon the election of their successors; or

(4) That the corporate assets are being misapplied or wasted.

(b) In an action by a creditor:

(1) When the claim of the creditor has been reduced to judgment and an execution thereon returned unsatisfied and it is established that the corporation is insolvent; or

(2) When the corporation has admitted in writing that the claim of the creditor is due and owing and it is established that the corporation is insolvent.

(c) Upon application by a corporation which has filed a statement of intent to dissolve, as provided in this Act, to have its liquidation continued under the supervision of the court.

(d) When an action has been filed by the Attorney General to dissolve a corporation and it is established that liquidation of its business and affairs should precede the entry of a decree of dissolution.

Proceedings under clause (a), (b) or (c) of this section shall be brought in the county in which the registered office or the principal office of the corporation is situated.

It shall not be necessary to make shareholders parties to any such action or proceeding unless relief is sought against them personally.

§ 98. Procedure in Liquidation of Corporation by Court

In proceedings to liquidate the assets and business of a corporation the court shall have power to issue injunctions, to appoint a receiver or receivers pendente lite, with such powers and duties as the court, from time to time, may direct, and to take such other proceedings as may be requisite to preserve the corporate assets wherever situated, and carry on the business of the corporation until a full hearing can be had.

After a hearing had upon such notice as the court may direct to be given to all parties to the proceedings and to any other parties in interest designated by the court, the court may appoint a liquidating receiver or receivers with authority to collect the assets of the corporation, including all amounts owing to the corporation by subscribers on account of any unpaid portion of the consideration for the issuance of shares. Such liquidating receiver or receivers shall have authority, subject to the order of the court, to sell, convey and dispose of all or any part of the assets of the corporation wherever situated, either at public or private sale. The assets of the corporation or the proceeds resulting from a sale, conveyance or other disposition thereof shall be applied to the expenses of such liquidation and to the payment of the liabilities and obligations of the corporation, and any remaining assets or proceeds shall be distributed among its shareholders according to their respective rights and interests. The order appointing such liquidating receiver or receivers shall state their powers and duties. Such powers and duties may be increased or diminished at any time during the proceedings.

The court shall have power to allow from time to time as expenses of the liquidation compensation to the receiver or receivers and to attorneys in the proceeding, and to direct the payment thereof out of the assets of the corporation or the proceeds of any sale or disposition of such assets.

A receiver of a corporation appointed under the provisions of this section shall have authority to sue and defend in all courts in his own name as receiver of such corporation. The court appointing such receiver shall have

exclusive jurisdiction of the corporation and its property, wherever situated.

§ 99. Qualifications of Receivers

A receiver shall in all cases be a natural person or a corporation authorized to act as receiver, which corporation may be a domestic corporation or a foreign corporation authorized to transact business in this State, and shall in all cases give such bond as the court may direct with such sureties as the court may require.

§ 100. Filing of Claims in Liquidation Proceedings

In proceedings to liquidate the assets and business of a corporation the court may require all creditors of the corporation to file with the clerk of the court or with the receiver, in such form as the court may prescribe, proofs under oath of their respective claims. If the court requires the filing of claims it shall fix a date, which shall be not less than four months from the date of the order, as the last day for the filing of claims, and shall prescribe the notice that shall be given to creditors and claimants of the date so fixed. Prior to the date so fixed, the court may extend the time for the filing of claims. Creditors and claimants failing to file proofs of claim on or before the date so fixed may be barred, by order of court, from participating in the distribution of the assets of the corporation.

§ 101. Discontinuance of Liquidation Proceedings

The liquidation of the assets and business of a corporation may be discontinued at any time during the liquidation proceedings when it is established that cause for liquidation no longer exists. In such event the court shall dismiss the proceedings and direct the receiver to redeliver to the corporation all its remaining property and assets.

§ 102. Decree of Involuntary Dissolution

In proceedings to liquidate the assets and business of a corporation, when the costs and expenses of such proceedings and all debts, obligations and liabilities of the corporation shall have been paid and discharged and all of its remaining property and assets distributed to its shareholders, or in case its property and assets are not sufficient to satisfy and discharge such costs, expenses, debts and obligations, all the property and assets have been applied so far as they will go to their payment, the court shall enter a decree dissolving the corporation, whereupon the existence of the corporation shall cease.

§ 103. Filing of Decree of Dissolution

In case the court shall enter a decree dissolving a corporation, it shall be the duty of the clerk of such court to cause a certified copy of the decree to be filed with the

Secretary of State. No fee shall be charged by the Secretary of State for the filing thereof.

§ 104. Deposit with State Treasurer of Amount Due Certain Shareholders

Upon the voluntary or involuntary dissolution of a corporation, the portion of the assets distributable to a creditor or shareholder who is unknown or cannot be found, or who is under disability and there is no person legally competent to receive such distributive portion, shall be reduced to cash and deposited with the State Treasurer and shall be paid over to such creditor or shareholder or to his legal representative upon proof satisfactory to the State Treasurer of his right thereto.

§ 105. Survival of Remedy after Dissolution

The dissolution of a corporation either (1) by the issuance of a certificate of dissolution by the Secretary of State, or (2) by a decree of court when the court has not liquidated the assets and business of the corporation as provided in this Act, or (3) by expiration of its period of duration, shall not take away or impair any remedy available to or against such corporation, its directors, officers, or shareholders, for any right or claim existing, or any liability incurred, prior to such dissolution if action or other proceeding thereon is commenced within two years after the date of such dissolution. Any such action or proceeding by or against the corporation may be prosecuted or defended by the corporation in its corporate name. The shareholders, directors and officers shall have power to take such corporate or other action as shall be appropriate to protect such remedy, right or claim. If such corporation was dissolved by the expiration of its period of duration, such corporation may amend its articles of incorporation at any time during such period of two years so as to extend its period of duration.

§ 106. Admission of Foreign Corporation

No foreign corporation shall have the right to transact business in this State until it shall have procured a certificate of authority so to do from the Secretary of State. No foreign corporation shall be entitled to procure a certificate of authority under this Act to transact in this State any business which a corporation organized under this Act is not permitted to transact. A foreign corporation shall not be denied a certificate of authority by reason of the fact that the laws of the state or country under which such corporation is organized governing its organization and internal affairs differ from the laws of this State, and nothing in this Act contained shall be construed to authorize this State to regulate the organization or the internal affairs of such corporation.

Without excluding other activities which may not constitute transacting business in this State, a foreign corporation shall not be considered to be transacting business in this State, for the purposes of this Act, by reason of carrying on in this State any one or more of the following activities:

(a) Maintaining or defending any action or suit or any administrative or arbitration proceeding, or effecting the settlement thereof or the settlement of claims or disputes.

(b) Holding meetings of its directors or shareholders or carrying on other activities concerning its internal affairs.

(c) Maintaining bank accounts.

(d) Maintaining offices or agencies for the transfer, exchange and registration of its securities, or appointing and maintaining trustees or depositaries with relation to its securities.

(e) Effecting sales through independent contractors.

(f) Soliciting or procuring orders, whether by mail or through employees or agents or otherwise, where such orders require acceptance without this State before becoming binding contracts.

(g) Creating as borrower or lender, or acquiring, indebtedness or mortgages or other security interests in real or personal property.

(h) Securing or collecting debts or enforcing any rights in property securing the same.

(i) Transacting any business in interstate commerce.

(j) Conducting an isolated transaction completed within a period of thirty days and not in the course of a number of repeated transactions of like nature.

§ 107. Powers of Foreign Corporation

A foreign corporation which shall have received a certificate of authority under this Act shall, until a certificate of revocation or of withdrawal shall have been issued as provided in this Act, enjoy the same, but no greater, rights and privileges as a domestic corporation organized for the purposes set forth in the application pursuant to which such certificate of authority is issued; and, except as in this Act otherwise provided, shall be subject to the same duties, restrictions, penalties and liabilities now or hereafter imposed upon a domestic corporation of like character.

§ 108. Corporate Name of Foreign Corporation

No certificate of authority shall be issued to a foreign corporation unless the corporate name of such corporation:

(a) Shall contain the word "corporation," "company," "incorporated," or "limited," or shall contain an abbreviation of one of such words, or such corporation shall, for use in this State, add at the end of its name one of such words or an abbreviation thereof.

(b) Shall not contain any word or phrase which indicates or implies that it is organized for any purpose other than one or more of the purposes contained in its articles of incorporation or that it is authorized or empowered to conduct the business of banking or insurance.

(c) Shall not be the same as, or deceptively similar to, the name of any domestic corporation existing under the laws of this State or any foreign corporation authorized to transact business in this State, or a name the exclusive right to which is, at the time, reserved in the manner provided in this Act, or the name of a corporation which has in effect a registration of its name as provided in this Act except that this provision shall not apply if the foreign corporation applying for a certificate of authority files with the Secretary of State any one of the following:

(1) a resolution of its board of directors adopting a fictitious name for use in transacting business in this State which fictitious name is not deceptively similar to the name of any domestic corporation or of any foreign corporation authorized to transact business in this State or to any name reserved or registered as provided in this Act, or

(2) the written consent of such other corporation or holder of a reserved or registered name to use the same or deceptively similar name and one or more words are added to make such name distinguishable from such other name, or

(3) a certified copy of a final decree of a court of competent jurisdiction establishing the prior right of such foreign corporation to the use of such name in this State.

§ 109. Change of Name by Foreign Corporation

Whenever a foreign corporation which is authorized to transact business in this State shall change its name to one under which a certificate of authority would not be granted to it on application therefor, the certificate of authority of such corporation shall be suspended and it shall not thereafter transact any business in this State until it has changed its name to a name which is available to it under the laws of this State or has otherwise complied with the provisions of this Act.

§ 110. Application for Certificate of Authority

A foreign corporation, in order to procure a certificate of authority to transact business in this State, shall make application therefor to the Secretary of State, which application shall set forth:

(a) The name of the corporation and the state or county under the laws of which it is incorporated.

(b) If the name of the corporation does not contain the word "corporation," "company," "incorporated," or "lim-

ited," or does not contain an abbreviation of one of such words, then the name of the corporation with the word or abbreviation which it elects to add thereto for use in this State.

(c) The date of incorporation and the period of duration of the corporation.

(d) The address of the principal office of the corporation in the state or country under the laws of which it is incorporated.

(e) The address of the proposed registered office of the corporation in this State, and the name of its proposed registered agent in this State at such address.

(f) The purpose or purposes of the corporation which it proposes to pursue in the transaction of business in this State.

(g) The names and respective addresses of the directors and officers of the corporation.

(h) A statement of the aggregate number of shares which the corporation has authority to issue, itemized by classes and series, if any, within a class.

(i) A statement of the aggregate number of issued shares, itemized by class and by series, if any, within each class.

(j) An estimate, expressed in dollars, of the value of all property to be owned by the corporation for the following year, wherever located, and an estimate of the value of the property of the corporation to be located within this State during such year, and an estimate, expressed in dollars of the gross amount of business which will be transacted by the corporation during such year, and an estimate of the gross amount thereof which will be transacted by the corporation at or from places of business in this State during such year.

(k) Such additional information as may be necessary or appropriate in order to enable the Secretary of State to determine whether such corporation is entitled to a certificate of authority to transact business in this State and to determine and assess the fees and franchise taxes payable as in this Act prescribed.

Such application shall be made on forms prescribed and furnished by the Secretary of State and shall be executed in duplicate by the corporation by its president or a vice president and by its secretary or an assistant secretary, and verified by one of the officers signing such application.

§ 111. Filing of Application for Certificate of Authority

Duplicate originals of the application of the corporation for a certificate of authority shall be delivered to the Secretary of State, together with a copy of its articles of incorporation and all amendments thereto, duly authenticated by the proper officer of the state or country under the laws of which it is incorporated.

If the Secretary of State finds that such application conforms to law, he shall, when all fees and franchise taxes have been paid as in this Act prescribed:

(a) Endorse on each of such documents the word "Filed," and the month, day and year of the filing thereof.

(b) File in his office one of such duplicate originals of the application and the copy of the articles of incorporation and amendments thereto.

(c) Issue a certificate of authority to transact business in this State to which he shall affix the other duplicate original application.

The certificate of authority, together with the duplicate original of the application affixed thereto by the Secretary of State, shall be returned to the corporation or its representative.

§ 112. Effect of Certificate of Authority

Upon the issuance of a certificate of authority by the Secretary of State, the corporation shall be authorized to transact business in this State for those purposes set forth in its application, subject, however, to the right of this State to suspend or to revoke such authority as provided in this Act.

§ 113. Registered Office and Registered Agent of Foreign Corporation

Each foreign corporation authorized to transact business in this State shall have and continuously maintain in this State:

(a) A registered office which may be, but need not be, the same as its place of business in this State.

(b) A registered agent, which agent may be either an individual resident in this State whose business office is identical with such registered office, or a domestic corporation, or a foreign corporation authorized to transact business in this State, having a business office identical with such registered office.

§ 114. Change of Registered Office or Registered Agent of Foreign Corporation

A foreign corporation authorized to transact business in this State may change its registered office or change its registered agent, or both, upon filing in the office of the Secretary of State a statement setting forth:

(a) The name of the corporation.

(b) The address of its then registered office.

(c) If the address of its registered office be changed, the address to which the registered office is to be changed.

(d) The name of its then registered agent.

(e) If its registered agent be changed, the name of its successor registered agent.

(f) That the address of its registered office and the address of the business office of its registered agent, as changed, will be identical.

(g) That such change was authorized by resolution duly adopted by its board of directors.

Such statement shall be executed by the corporation by its president or a vice president, and verified by him, and delivered to the Secretary of State. If the Secretary of State finds that such statement conforms to the provisions of this Act, he shall file such statement in his office, and upon such filing the change of address of the registered office, or the appointment of a new registered agent, or both, as the case may be, shall become effective.

Any registered agent of a foreign corporation may resign as such agent upon filing a written notice thereof, executed in duplicate, with the Secretary of State, who shall forthwith mail a copy thereof to the corporation at its principal office in the state or country under the laws of which it is incorporated. The appointment of such agent shall terminate upon the expiration of thirty days after receipt of such notice by the Secretary of State.

If a registered agent changes his or its business address to another place within the same . . . .*, he or it may change such address and the address of the registered office of any corporation of which he or it is registered agent by filing a statement as required above except that it need be signed only by the registered agent and need not be responsive to (e) or (g) and must recite that a copy of the statement has been mailed to the corporation.

§ 115. Service of Process on Foreign Corporation

The registered agent so appointed by a foreign corporation authorized to transact business in this State shall be an agent of such corporation upon whom any process, notice or demand required or permitted by law to be served upon the corporation may be served.

Whenever a foreign corporation authorized to transact business in this State shall fail to appoint or maintain a registered agent in this State, or whenever any such registered agent cannot with reasonable diligence be found at the registered office, or whenever the certificate of authority of a foreign corporation shall be suspended or revoked, then the Secretary of State shall be an agent of such corporation upon whom any such process, notice, or demand may be served. Service on the Secretary of State of any such process, notice or demand shall be made by delivering to and leaving with him, or with any clerk having charge of the corporation department of his office,

*Supply designation of jurisdiction, such as county, etc. in accordance with local practice.

duplicate copies of such process, notice or demand. In the event any such process, notice or demand is served on the Secretary of State, he shall immediately cause one of such copies thereof to be forwarded by registered mail, addressed to the corporation at its principal office in the state or country under the laws of which it is incorporated. Any service so had on the Secretary of State shall be returnable in not less than thirty days.

The Secretary of State shall keep a record of all processes, notices and demands served upon him under this section, and shall record therein the time of such service and his action with reference thereto.

Nothing herein contained shall limit or affect the right to serve any process, notice or demand, required or permitted by law to be served upon a foreign corporation in any other manner now or hereafter permitted by law.

§ 116. Amendment to Articles of Incorporation of Foreign Corporation

Whenever the articles of incorporation of a foreign corporation authorized to transact business in this State are amended, such foreign corporation shall, within thirty days after such amendment becomes effective, file in the office of the Secretary of State a copy of such amendment duly authenticated by the proper officer of the state or country under the laws of which it is incorporated; but the filing thereof shall not of itself enlarge or alter the purpose or purposes which such corporation is authorized to pursue in the transaction of business in this State, nor authorize such corporation to transact business in this State under any other name than the name set forth in its certificate of authority.

§ 117. Merger of Foreign Corporation Authorized to Transact Business in This State

Whenever a foreign corporation authorized to transact business in this State shall be a party to a statutory merger permitted by the laws of the state or country under the laws of which it is incorporated, and such corporation shall be the surviving corporation, it shall, within thirty days after such merger becomes effective, file with the Secretary of State a copy of the articles of merger duly authenticated by the proper officer of the state or country under the laws of which such statutory merger was effected; and it shall not be necessary for such corporation to procure either a new or amended certificate of authority to transact business in this State unless the name of such corporation be changed thereby or unless the corporation desires to pursue in this State other or additional purposes than those which it is then authorized to transact in this State.

§ 118. Amended Certificate of Authority

A foreign corporation authorized to transact business in this State shall procure an amended certificate of authority in the event it changes its corporate name, or desires to pursue in this State other or additional purposes than those set forth in its prior application for a certificate of authority, by making application therefor to the Secretary of State.

The requirements in respect to the form and contents of such application, the manner of its execution, the filing of duplicate originals thereof with the Secretary of State, the issuance of an amended certificate of authority and the effect thereof, shall be the same as in the case of an original application for a certificate of authority.

§ 119. Withdrawal of Foreign Corporation

A foreign corporation authorized to transact business in this State may withdraw from this State upon procuring from the Secretary of State a certificate of withdrawal. In order to procure such certificate of withdrawal, such foreign corporation shall deliver to the Secretary of State an application for withdrawal, which shall set forth:

(a) The name of the corporation and the state or country under the laws of which it is incorporated.

(b) That the corporation is not transacting business in this State.

(c) That the corporation surrenders its authority to transact business in this State.

(d) That the corporation revokes the authority of its registered agent in this State to accept service of process and consents that service of process in any action, suit or proceeding based upon any cause of action arising in this State during the time the corporation was authorized to transact business in this State may thereafter be made on such corporation by service thereof on the Secretary of State.

(e) A post-office address to which the Secretary of State may mail a copy of any process against the corporation that may be served on him.

(f) A statement of the aggregate number of shares which the corporation has authority to issue, itemized by class and series, if any, within each class, as of the date of such application.

(g) A statement of the aggregate number of issued shares, itemized by class and series, if any, within each class, as of the date of such application.

(h) Such additional information as may be necessary or appropriate in order to enable the Secretary of State to determine and assess any unpaid fees or franchise taxes payable by such foreign corporation as in this Act prescribed.

The application for withdrawal shall be made on forms prescribed and furnished by the Secretary of State and shall be executed by the corporation by its president or a vice president and by its secretary or an assistant secretary, and verified by one of the officers signing the application, or, if the corporation is in the hands of a receiver or trustee, shall be executed on behalf of the corporation by such receiver or trustee and verified by him.

§ 120. Filing of Application for Withdrawal

Duplicate originals of such application for withdrawal shall be delivered to the Secretary of State. If the Secretary of State finds that such application conforms to the provisions of this Act, he shall, when all fees and franchise taxes have been paid as in this Act prescribed:

(a) Endorse on each of such duplicate originals the word "Filed," and the month, day and year of the filing thereof.

(b) File one of such duplicate originals in his office.

(c) Issue a certificate of withdrawal to which he shall affix the other duplicate original.

The certificate of withdrawal, together with the duplicate original of the application for withdrawal affixed thereto by the Secretary of State, shall be returned to the corporation or its representative. Upon the issuance of such certificate of withdrawal, the authority of the corporation to transact business in this State shall cease.

§ 121. Revocation of Certificate of Authority

The certificate of authority of a foreign corporation to transact business in this State may be revoked by the Secretary of State upon the conditions prescribed in this section when:

(a) The corporation has failed to file its annual report within the time required by this Act, or has failed to pay any fees, franchise taxes or penalties prescribed by this Act when they have become due and payable; or

(b) The corporation has failed to appoint and maintain a registered agent in this State as required by this Act; or

(c) The corporation has failed, after change of its registered office or registered agent, to file in the office of the Secretary of State a statement of such change as required by this Act; or

(d) The corporation has failed to file in the office of the Secretary of State any amendment to its articles of incorporation or any articles of merger within the time prescribed by this Act; or

(e) A misrepresentation has been made of any material matter in any application, report, affidavit, or other document submitted by such corporation pursuant to this Act.

No certificate of authority of a foreign corporation shall be revoked by the Secretary of State unless (1) he shall have given the corporation not less than sixty days' notice thereof by mail addressed to its registered office in this State, and (2) the corporation shall fail prior to revocation to file such annual report, or pay such fees, franchise taxes or penalties, or file the required statement of change of registered agent or registered office, or file such articles of amendment or articles of merger, or correct such misrepresentation.

§ 122. Issuance of Certificate of Revocation

Upon revoking any such certificate of authority, the Secretary of State shall:

(a) Issue a certificate of revocation in duplicate.

(b) File one of such certificates in his office.

(c) Mail to such corporation at its registered office in this State a notice of such revocation accompanied by one of such certificates.

Upon the issuance of such certificate of revocation, the authority of the corporation to transact business in this State shall cease.

§ 123. Application to Corporations Heretofore Authorized to Transact Business in This State

Foreign corporations which are duly authorized to transact business in this State at the time this Act takes effect, for a purpose or purposes for which a corporation might secure such authority under this Act, shall, subject to the limitations set forth in their respective certificates of authority, be entitled to all the rights and privileges applicable to foreign corporations procuring certificates of authority to transact business in this State under this Act, and from the time this Act takes effect such corporations shall be subject to all the limitations, restrictions, liabilities, and duties prescribed herein for foreign corporations procuring certificates of authority to transact business in this State under this Act.

§ 124. Transacting Business Without Certificate of Authority

No foreign corporation transacting business in this State without a certificate of authority shall be permitted to maintain any action, suit or proceeding in any court of this State, until such corporation shall have obtained a certificate of authority. Nor shall any action, suit or proceeding be maintained in any court of this State by any successor or assignee of such corporation on any right, claim or demand arising out of the transaction of business by such corporation in this State, until a certificate of authority shall have been obtained by such corporation or by a corporation which has acquired all or substantially all of its assets.

The failure of a foreign corporation to obtain a certificate of authority to transact business in this State shall not impair the validity of any contract or act of such corporation, and shall not prevent such corporation from defending any action, suit or proceeding in any court of this State.

A foreign corporation which transacts business in this State without a certificate of authority shall be liable to this State, for the years or parts thereof during which it transacted business in this State without a certificate of authority, in an amount equal to all fees and franchise taxes which would have been imposed by this Act upon such corporation had it duly applied for and received a certificate of authority to transact business in this State as required by this Act and thereafter filed all reports required by this Act, plus all penalties imposed by this Act for failure to pay such fees and franchise taxes. The Attorney General shall bring proceedings to recover all amounts due this State under the provisions of this Section.

§ 125. Annual Report of Domestic and Foreign Corporations

Each domestic corporation, and each foreign corporation authorized to transact business in this State, shall file, within the time prescribed by this Act, an annual report setting forth:

(a) The name of the corporation and the state or country under the laws of which it is incorporated.

(b) The address of the registered office of the corporation in this State, and the name of its registered agent in this State at such address, and, in case of a foreign corporation, the address of its principal office in the state or country under the laws of which it is incorporated.

(c) A brief statement of the character of the business in which the corporation is actually engaged in this State.

(d) The names and respective addresses of the directors and officers of the corporation.

(e) A statement of the aggregate number of shares which the corporation has authority to issue, itemized by class and series, if any, within each class.

(f) A statement of the aggregate number of issued shares, itemized by class and series, if any, within each class.

(g) A statement, expressed in dollars, of the value of all the property owned by the corporation, wherever located, and the value of the property of the corporation located within this State, and a statement, expressed in dollars, of the gross amount of business transacted by the corporation for the twelve months ended on the thirty-first day of December preceding the date herein provided for the filing of such report and the gross amount thereof transacted by the corporation at or from places of business in this State. If, on the thirty-first day of December preceding the time herein provided for the filing of such report, the corporation had not been in existence for a period of twelve months, or in the case of a foreign corporation had not been authorized to transact business in this State for a period of twelve months, the statement with respect to business transacted shall be furnished for the period between the date of incorporation or the date of its authorization to transact business in this State, as the case may be, and such thirty-first day of December. If all the property of the corporation is located in this State and all of its business is transacted at or from places of business in this State, then the information required by this subparagraph need not be set forth in such report.

(h) Such additional information as may be necessary or appropriate in order to enable the Secretary of State to determine and assess the proper amount of franchise taxes payable by such corporation.

Such annual report shall be made on forms prescribed and furnished by the Secretary of State, and the information therein contained shall be given as of the date of the execution of the report, except as to the information required by subparagraphs (g) and (h) which shall be given as of the close of business on the thirty-first day of December next preceding the date herein provided for the filing of such report. It shall be executed by the corporation by its president, a vice president, secretary, an assistant secretary, or treasurer, and verified by the officer executing the report, or, if the corporation is in the hands of a receiver or trustee, it shall be executed on behalf of the corporation and verified by such receiver or trustee.

§ 126. Filing of Annual Report of Domestic and Foreign Corporations

Such annual report of a domestic or foreign corporation shall be delivered to the Secretary of State between the first day of January and the first day of March of each year, except that the first annual report of a domestic or foreign corporation shall be filed between the first day of January and the first day of March of the year next succeeding the calendar year in which its certificate of incorporation or its certificate of authority, as the case may be, was issued by the Secretary of State. Proof to the satisfaction of the Secretary of State that prior to the first day of March such report was deposited in the United States mail in a sealed envelope, properly addressed, with postage prepaid, shall be deemed a compliance with this requirement. If the Secretary of State finds that such report conforms to the requirements of this Act, he shall file the same. If he finds that it does not so conform, he shall promptly return the same to the corporation for any necessary corrections, in which event the penalties hereinafter prescribed for failure to file such report within the time hereinabove provided shall not apply, if such report is corrected to conform to the requirements of this Act and returned to the Secretary of State within thirty days from the date on which it was mailed to the corporation by the Secretary of State.

§ 127. Fees, Franchise Taxes and Charges to be Collected by Secretary of State

The Secretary of State shall charge and collect in accordance with the provisions of this Act:

(a) Fees for filing documents and issuing certificates.

(b) Miscellaneous charges.

(c) License fees.

(d) Franchise taxes.

§ 128. Fees for Filing Documents and Issuing Certificates

The Secretary of State shall charge and collect for:

(a) Filing articles of incorporation and issuing a certificate of incorporation, ... dollars.

(b) Filing articles of amendment and issuing a certificate of amendment, ... dollars.

(c) Filing restated articles of incorporation, ... dollars.

(d) Filing articles of merger or consolidation and issuing a certificate of merger or consolidation, ... dollars.

(e) Filing an application to reserve a corporate name, ... dollars.

(f) Filing a notice of transfer of a reserved corporate name, ... dollars.

(g) Filing a statement of change of address of registered office or change of registered agent or both, ... dollars.

(h) Filing a statement of the establishment of a series of shares, ... dollars.

(i) Filing a statement of intent to dissolve, ... dollars.

(j) Filing a statement of revocation of voluntary dissolution proceedings, ... dollars.

(k) Filing articles of dissolution, ... dollars.

(l) Filing an application of a foreign corporation for a certificate of authority to transact business in this State and issuing a certificate of authority, ... dollars.

(m) Filing an application of a foreign corporation for an amended certificate of authority to transact business in this State and issuing an amended certificate of authority, ... dollars.

(n) Filing a copy of an amendment to the articles of incorporation of a foreign corporation holding a certificate of authority to transact business in this State, ... dollars.

(o) Filing a copy of articles of merger of a foreign corporation holding a certificate of authority to transact business in this State, ... dollars.

(p) Filing an application for withdrawal of a foreign corporation and issuing a certificate of withdrawal, ... dollars.

(q) Filing any other statement or report, except an annual report, of a domestic or foreign corporation, ... dollars.

§ 129. Miscellaneous Charges

The Secretary of State shall charge and collect:

(a) For furnishing a certified copy of any document, instrument, or paper relating to a corporation, ... cents per page and .... dollars for the certificate and affixing the seal thereto.

(b) At the time of any service of process on him as resident agent of a corporation, ... dollars, which amount may be recovered as taxable costs by the party to the suit or action causing such service to be made if such party prevails in the suit or action.

§ 130. License Fees Payable by Domestic Corporations

The Secretary of State shall charge and collect from each domestic corporation license fees, based upon the number of shares which it will have authority to issue or the increase in the number of shares which it will have authority to issue, at the time of:

(a) Filing articles of incorporation;

(b) Filing articles of amendment increasing the number of authorized shares; and

(c) Filing articles of merger or consolidation increasing the number of authorized shares which the surviving or new corporation, if a domestic corporation, will have the authority to issue above the aggregate number of shares which the constituent domestic corporations and constituent foreign corporations authorized to transact business in this State had authority to issue.

The license fees shall be at the rate of .... cents per share up to and including the first 10,000 authorized shares, ... cents per share for each authorized share in excess of 10,000 shares up to and including 100,000 shares, and .... cents per share for each authorized share in excess of 100,000 shares.

The license fees payable on an increase in the number of authorized shares shall be imposed only on the increased number of shares, and the number of previously authorized shares shall be taken into account in determining the rate applicable to the increased number of authorized shares.

§ 131. License Fees Payable by Foreign Corporations

The Secretary of State shall charge and collect from each foreign corporation license fees, based upon the proportion represented in this State of the number of shares which it has authority to issue or the increase in the number of shares which it has authority to issue, at the time of:

(a) Filing an application for a certificate of authority to transact business in this State;

(b) Filing articles of amendment which increased the number of authorized shares; and

(c) Filing articles of merger or consolidation which increased the number of authorized shares which the surviving or new corporation, if a foreign corporation, has authority to issue above the aggregate number of shares which the constituent domestic corporations and constituent foreign corporations authorized to transact business in this State had authority to issue.

The license fees shall be at the rate of …….. cents per share up to and including the first 10,000 authorized shares represented in this State, …….. cents per share for each authorized share in excess of 10,000 shares up to and including 100,000 shares represented in this State, and …….. cents per share for each authorized share in excess of 100,000 shares represented in this State.

The license fees payable on an increase in the number of authorized shares shall be imposed only on the increased number of such shares represented in this State, and the number of previously authorized shares represented in this State shall be taken into account in determining the rate applicable to the increased number of authorized shares.

The number of authorized shares represented in this State shall be that proportion of its total authorized shares which the sum of the value of its property located in this State and the gross amount of business transacted by it at or from places of business in this State bears to the sum of the value of all of its property, wherever located, and the gross amount of its business, wherever transacted. Such proportion shall be determined from information contained in the application for a certificate of authority to transact business in this State until the filing of an annual report and thereafter from information contained in the latest annual report filed by the corporation.

§ 132. Franchise Taxes Payable by Domestic Corporations

The Secretary of State shall charge and collect from each domestic corporation an initial franchise tax at the time of filing its articles of incorporation at the rate of one-twelfth of one-half of the license fee payable by such corporation under the provisions of this Act at the time of filing its articles of incorporation, for each calendar month, or fraction thereof, between the date of the issuance of the certificate of incorporation by the Secretary

of State and the first day of July of the next succeeding calendar year.

The Secretary of State shall charge and collect from each domestic corporation an annual franchise tax, payable in advance for the period from July 1 in each year to July 1 in the succeeding year, beginning July 1 in the calendar year in which such corporation is required to file its first annual report under this Act, (Alternative 1: at the rate of …………. of …….. per cent of the amount represented in this State of the stated capital of the corporation, as determined in accordance with accounting practices and principles that are reasonable in the circumstances, as disclosed by the latest report filed by the corporation with the Secretary of State) (Alternative 2: at the rate of …….. cents per share up to and including the first 10,000 issued and outstanding shares, and …….. cents per share for each issued and outstanding share in excess of 10,000 shares up to and including 100,000 shares, and …….. cents per share for each issued and outstanding share in excess of 100,000 shares).

[If Alternative 2 is enacted, the following paragraph should be deleted.]

The amount represented in this State of the stated capital of the corporation shall be that proportion of its stated capital which the sum of the value of its property located in this State and the gross amount of business transacted by it at or from places of business in this State bears to the sum of the value of all of its property, wherever located, and the gross amount of its business, wherever transacted.

§ 133. Franchise Taxes Payable by Foreign Corporations

The Secretary of State shall charge and collect from each foreign corporation authorized to transact business in this State an initial franchise tax at the time of filing its application for a certificate of authority at the rate of one-twelfth of one-half of the license fee payable by such corporation under the provisions of this Act at the time of filing such application, for each month, or fraction thereof, between the date of the issuance of the certificate of authority by the Secretary of State and the first day of July of the next succeeding calendar year.

The Secretary of State shall charge and collect from each foreign corporation authorized to transact business in this State an annual franchise tax, payable in advance for the period from July 1 in each year to July 1 in the succeeding year, beginning July 1 in the calendar year in which such corporation is required to file its first annual report under this Act, (Alternative 1: at the rate of …….. per cent of the amount represented in this State of the stated capital of the corporation, as determined in accordance with accounting practices and principles that are reasonable in the circumstances, as disclosed by the latest annual report filed by the corporation with the Secretary of State) (Alternative 2: at a rate of .... cents per share up to and including the first 10,000 issued and outstanding shares represented in this State, and .... cents per share for each issued and outstanding share in excess of 10,000 shares up to and including 100,000 shares represented in this State, and .... cents per share for each issued and outstanding share in excess of 100,000 shares represented in this State).

[If Alternative 2 is enacted, the following paragraph should be deleted.]

The amount represented in this State of the stated capital of the corporation shall be that proportion of its stated capital which the sum of the value of its property located in this State and the gross amount of business transacted by it at or from places of business in this State bears to the sum of the value of all of its property, wherever located, and the gross amount of its business, wherever transacted.

§ 134. Assessment and Collection of Annual Franchise Taxes

It shall be the duty of the Secretary of State to collect all annual franchise taxes and penalties imposed by, or assessed in accordance with, this Act.

Between the first day of March and the first day of June of each year, the Secretary of State shall assess against each corporation, domestic and foreign, required to file an annual report in such year, the franchise tax payable by it for the period from July 1 of such year to July 1 of the succeeding year in accordance with the provisions of this Act, and, if it has failed to file its annual report within the time prescribed by this Act, the penalty imposed by this Act upon such corporation for its failure so to do; and shall mail a written notice to each corporation against which such tax is assessed, addressed to such corporation at its registered office in this State, notifying the corporation (1) of the amount of franchise tax assessed against it for the ensuing year and the amount of penalty, if any, assessed against it for failure to file its annual report; (2) that objections, if any, to such assessment will be heard by the officer making the assessment on or before the fifteenth day of June of such year, upon receipt of a request from the corporation; and (3) that such tax and penalty shall be payable to the Secretary of State on the first day of July next succeeding the date of the notice. Failure to receive such notice shall not relieve the corporation of its obligation to pay the tax and any penalty assessed, or invalidate the assessment thereof.

The Secretary of State shall have power to hear and determine objections to any assessment of franchise tax at any time after such assessment and, after hearing, to change or modify any such assessment. In the event of

any adjustment of franchise tax with respect to which a penalty has been assessed for failure to file an annual report, the penalty shall be adjusted in accordance with the provisions of this Act imposing such penalty.

All annual franchise taxes and all penalties for failure to file annual reports shall be due and payable on the first day of July of each year. If the annual franchise tax assessed against any corporation subject to the provisions of this Act, together with all penalties assessed thereon, shall not be paid to the Secretary of State on or before the thirty-first day of July of the year in which such tax is due and payable, the Secretary of State shall certify such fact to the Attorney General on or before the fifteenth day of November of such year, whereupon the Attorney General may institute an action against such corporation in the name of this State, in any court of competent jurisdiction, for the recovery of the amount of such franchise tax and penalties, together with the cost of suit, and prosecute the same to final judgment.

For the purpose of enforcing collection, all annual franchise taxes assessed in accordance with this Act, and all penalties assessed thereon and all interest and costs that shall accrue in connection with the collection thereof, shall be a prior and first lien on the real and personal property of the corporation from and including the first day of July of the year when such franchise taxes become due and payable until such taxes, penalties, interest, and costs shall have been paid.

§ 135. Penalties Imposed Upon Corporations

Each corporation, domestic or foreign, that fails or refuses to file its annual report for any year within the time prescribed by this Act shall be subject to a penalty of ten per cent of the amount of the franchise tax assessed against it for the period beginning July 1 of the year in which such report should have been filed. Such penalty shall be assessed by the Secretary of State at the time of the assessment of the franchise tax. If the amount of the franchise tax as originally assessed against such corporation be thereafter adjusted in accordance with the provisions of this Act, the amount of the penalty shall be likewise adjusted to ten per cent of the amount of the adjusted franchise tax. The amount of the franchise tax and the amount of the penalty shall be separately stated in any notice to the corporation with respect thereto.

If the franchise tax assessed in accordance with the provisions of this Act shall not be paid on or before the thirty-first day of July, it shall be deemed to be delinquent, and there shall be added a penalty of one per cent for each month or part of month that the same is delinquent, commencing with the month of August.

Each corporation, domestic or foreign, that fails or refuses to answer truthfully and fully within the time prescribed by this Act interrogatories propounded by the Secretary of State in accordance with the provisions of this Act, shall be deemed to be guilty of a misdemeanor and upon conviction thereof may be fined in any amount not exceeding five hundred dollars.

§ 136. Penalties Imposed Upon Officers and Directors

Each officer and director of a corporation, domestic or foreign, who fails or refuses within the time prescribed by this Act to answer truthfully and fully interrogatories propounded to him by the Secretary of State in accordance with the provisions of this Act, or who signs any articles, statement, report, application or other document filed with the Secretary of State which is known to such officer or director to be false in any material respect, shall be deemed to be guilty of a misdemeanor, and upon conviction thereof may be fined in any amount not exceeding .... dollars.

§ 137. Interrogatories by Secretary of State

The Secretary of State may propound to any corporation, domestic or foreign, subject to the provisions of this Act, and to any officer or director thereof, such interrogatories as may be reasonably necessary and proper to enable him to ascertain whether such corporation has complied with all the provisions of this Act applicable to such corporation. Such interrogatories shall be answered within thirty days after the mailing thereof, or within such additional time as shall be fixed by the Secretary of State, and the answers thereto shall be full and complete and shall be made in writing and under oath. If such interrogatories be directed to an individual they shall be answered by him, and if directed to a corporation they shall be answered by the president, vice president, secretary or assistant secretary thereof. The Secretary of State need not file any document to which such interrogatories relate until such interrogatories be answered as herein provided, and not then if the answers thereto disclose that such document is not in conformity with the provisions of this Act. The Secretary of State shall certify to the Attorney General, for such action as the Attorney General may deem appropriate, all interrogatories and answers thereto which disclose a violation of any of the provisions of this Act.

§ 138. Information Disclosed by Interrogatories

Interrogatories propounded by the Secretary of State and the answers thereto shall not be open to public inspection nor shall the Secretary of State disclose any facts or information obtained therefrom except insofar as his official duty may require the same to be made public or in the event such interrogatories or the answers thereto are required for evidence in any criminal proceedings or in any other action by this State.

§ 139. Powers of Secretary of State

The Secretary of State shall have the power and authority reasonably necessary to enable him to administer this Act efficiently and to perform the duties therein imposed upon him.

§ 140. Appeal from Secretary of State

If the Secretary of State shall fail to approve any articles of incorporation, amendment, merger, consolidation or dissolution, or any other document required by this Act to be approved by the Secretary of State before the same shall be filed in his office, he shall, within ten days after the delivery thereof to him, give written notice of his disapproval to the person or corporation, domestic or foreign, delivering the same, specifying the reasons therefor. From such disapproval such person or corporation may appeal to the .... court of the county in which the registered office of such corporation is, or is proposed to be, situated by filing with the clerk of such court a petition setting forth a copy of the articles or other document sought to be filed and a copy of the written disapproval thereof by the Secretary of State; whereupon the matter shall be tried de novo by the court, and the court shall either sustain the action of the Secretary of State or direct him to take such action as the court may deem proper.

If the Secretary of State shall revoke the certificate of authority to transact business in this State of any foreign corporation, pursuant to the provisions of this Act, such foreign corporation may likewise appeal to the .... court of the county where the registered office of such corporation in this State is situated, by filing with the clerk of such court a petition setting forth a copy of its certificate of authority to transact business in this State and a copy of the notice of revocation given by the Secretary of State; whereupon the matter shall be tried de novo by the court, and the court shall either sustain the action of the Secretary of State or direct him to take such action as the court may deem proper.

Appeals from all final orders and judgments entered by the .... court under this section in review of any ruling or decision of the Secretary of State may be taken as in other civil actions.

§ 141. Certificates and Certified Copies to be Received in Evidence

All certificates issued by the Secretary of State in accordance with the provisions of this Act, and all copies of documents filed in his office in accordance with the provisions of this Act when certified by him, shall be taken and received in all courts, public offices, and official bodies as prima facie evidence of the facts therein stated. A certificate by the Secretary of State under the great seal of this State, as to the existence or non-existence of the facts relating to corporations shall be taken and received in all courts, public offices, and official bodies as prima facie evidence of the existence or non-existence of the facts therein stated.

§ 142. Forms to be Furnished by Secretary of State

All reports required by this Act to be filed in the office of the Secretary of State shall be made on forms which shall be prescribed and furnished by the Secretary of State. Forms for all other documents to be filed in the office of the Secretary of State shall be furnished by the Secretary of State on request therefor, but the use thereof, unless otherwise specifically prescribed in this Act, shall not be mandatory.

§ 143. Greater Voting Requirements

Whenever, with respect to any action to be taken by the shareholders of a corporation, the articles of incorporation require the vote or concurrence of the holders of a greater proportion of the shares, or of any class or series thereof, than required by this Act with respect to such action, the provisions of the articles of incorporation shall control.

§ 144. Waiver of Notice

Whenever any notice is required to be given to any shareholder or director of a corporation under the provisions of this Act or under the provisions of the articles of incorporation or by-laws of the corporation, a waiver thereof in writing signed by the person or persons entitled to such notice, whether before or after the time stated therein, shall be equivalent to the giving of such notice.

§ 145. Action by Shareholders Without a Meeting

Any action required by this Act to be taken at a meeting of the shareholders of a corporation, or any action which may be taken at a meeting of the shareholders, may be taken without a meeting if a consent in writing, setting forth the action so taken, shall be signed by all of the shareholders entitled to vote with respect to the subject matter thereof.

Such consent shall have the same effect as a unanimous vote of shareholders, and may be stated as such in any articles or document filed with the Secretary of State under this Act.

§ 146. Unauthorized Assumption of Corporate Powers

All persons who assume to act as a corporation without authority so to do shall be jointly and severally liable for all debts and liabilities incurred or arising as a result thereof.

§ 147. Application to Existing Corporations

The provisions of this Act shall apply to all existing corporations organized under any general act of this State providing for the organization of corporations for a purpose or purposes for which a corporation might be or-

ganized under this Act, where the power has been reserved to amend, repeal or modify the act under which such corporation was organized and where such act is repealed by this Act.

§ 148. Application to Foreign and Interstate Commerce

The provisions of this Act shall apply to commerce with foreign nations and among the several states only insofar as the same may be permitted under the provisions of the Constitution of the United States.

§ 149. Reservation of Power

The ....* shall at all times have power to prescribe such regulations, provisions and limitations as it may deem advisable, which regulations, provisions and limitations shall be binding upon any and all corporations subject to the provisions of this Act, and the ....* shall have power to amend, repeal or modify this Act at pleasure.

*Insert name of legislative body.

§ 150. Effect of Repeal of Prior Acts

The repeal of a prior act by this Act shall not affect any right accrued or established, or any liability or penalty incurred, under the provisions of such act, prior to the repeal thereof.

§ 151. Effect of Invalidity of Part of this Act

If a court of competent jurisdiction shall adjudge to be invalid or unconstitutional any clause, sentence, paragraph, section or part of this Act, such judgment or decree shall not affect, impair, invalidate or nullify the remainder of this Act, but the effect thereof shall be confined to the clause, sentence, paragraph, section or part of this Act so adjudged to be invalid or unconstitutional.

§ 152. Exclusivity of Certain Provisions [Optional]

In circumstances to which section 45 and related sections of this Act are applicable, such provisions supersede the applicability of any other statutes of this state with respect to the legality of distributions.

§ 153. Repeal of Prior Acts
(Insert appropriate provisions) ....

SPECIAL COMMENTS—CLOSE CORPORATIONS

In view of the increasing importance of close corporations, both for the small family business and for the larger undertakings conducted by some small number of other corporations, this liberalizing trend has now been followed by the 1969 Amendments to the Model Act. The first sentence of section 35, providing that the business of the corporation shall be managed by a board of directors, was supplemented by a new clause "except as may be otherwise provided in the articles of incorporation." This permits the shareholders to take over and exercise the functions of the directors by appropriate provision to that effect in the articles, or to allocate functions between the directors and shareholders in such manner as may be desired. Taken with other provisions of the Model Act, which are here enumerated for convenience, this rounds out the adaptability of the Model Act for all the needs of a close corporation:

(1) By section 4(*l*) the by-laws may make any provision for the regulation of the affairs of the corporation that is not inconsistent with the articles or the laws of the incorporating state.

(2) By section 15 shares may be divided into several classes and the articles may limit or deny the voting rights of or provide special voting rights for the shares of any class to the extent not inconsistent with the Model Act. The narrow limits of this exception are revealed by section 33 which provides that each outstanding share, regardless of class, shall be entitled to one vote on each matter submitted to a vote at a meeting of the shareholders "except as may be otherwise provided in the articles of incorporation," thus expressly authorizing more than one vote per share or less than one vote per share, either generally or in respect to particular matters.

(3) By section 16 item (F) the shares of any preferred or special class may be issued in series and there may be variations between different series in numerous respects, including specifically the matter of voting rights, if any.

(4) By section 32 the articles may reduce a quorum of shareholders to not less than one-third of the shares entitled to vote, or leave the quorum at the standard of a majority or, as confirmed by section 143, increase the number to any desired point.

(5) By section 34 agreements among shareholders regarding the voting of their shares are made valid and enforceable in accordance with their terms without limitation in time. These could relate to the election or compensation of directors or officers or the creation of various types of securities for new financing or the conduct of business of various kinds or dividend policy or mergers and consolidations or other transactions without limit.

(6) The flexibility permitted by the revision of section 35 in the distribution or reallocation of authority among directors and stockholders has already been mentioned.

(7) Under section 36 the number of directors may be fixed by the by-laws at one or such greater number as may best serve the interests of the shareholders and that number may be increased or decreased from time to time by amendment to, or in the manner provided in, the articles or the by-laws, subject to any limiting provision adopted pursuant to law, such as an agreed requirement for a unanimous vote by directors for any such change or a requirement that amendments to the by-laws be made by shareholder vote. Similarly, under section 53, the incorporation may be effected by a single incorporator or by more as may be desired.

(8) By section 37 directors may be classified. While this relates to directors classified in such manner that the term of office of a specified proportion terminates in each year, the Model Act does not forbid the election of separate directors by separate classes of stock.

(9) Section 40 permits the articles or the by-laws to require more than a majority of the directors to constitute a quorum for the transaction of business and also permits the articles or by-laws to require the act of a greater number than a majority of those present at a meeting where a quorum is present before any specified business may be transacted. Or a unanimous vote of all directors may be required. This may be utilized to confer a right of veto on any designated class in order to protect its special interests.

(10) By section 50 the authority and duties of the respective officers and agents of the corporation may be tailored and prescribed in the by-laws, or consistently with the by-laws, in such manner as the needs of the shareholders may indicate.

(11) By section 54 the articles may include any desired provision for the regulation of the internal affairs of the corporation, including, in particular, "any provision restricting the transfer of shares." This expressly validates agreements for prior offering of shares to the corporation or other shareholders. All such restrictions must, of course, be clearly shown on the stock certificate as required by the Uniform Commercial Code. A similarly broad provision for the contents of the by-laws is contained in section 27.

(12) By sections 60, 73 and 79, respectively, a class vote may be required for an amendment to the articles, for any merger or consolidation or for a sale of assets other than in the regular course of business.

(13) Section 143 permits the articles to require, for any particular action by the shareholders, the vote or concurrence of the holders of a greater proportion of the shares, or of any class or series thereof, than the Model Act itself requires.

(14) Section 44 permits action by directors without a meeting and section 145 permits the same for shareholders, while section 144 contains a broad provision on waiver of notice. Thus the formality of meetings may, where desired, be eliminated in whole or in part, except for the annual meeting required by section 28.

Under these provisions protection may be afforded for a great diversity of interests. By way of illustration, the shares may be divided into different classes with different voting rights and each class may be permitted to elect a different director. Or some classes may be permitted to vote on certain transactions, but not all. Even more drastically, some classes may be denied all voting rights whatever. Thus a family could provide for equal participation in the profits of the venture, but restrict the power of management to selected members. The advantages of having a known group of business associates may be safeguarded by restrictions on the transfer of shares. Most commonly this takes the form of a requirement for *pro rata* offering to the other shareholders before selling to an outsider. Or the other shareholders may be given an option, in the event of death or a proposed transfer, to buy the stock *pro rata*. The same option may be given to the corporation. The purchase price may be fixed by any agreed formula, such as adjusted book value or some multiple of recent earnings. Or stockholder agreements may be used to assure that, at least for a limited number of years, all shares will be voted for certain directors and officers, or in a certain way on other corporate matters. Cumulative voting may be provided for, by which each shareholder has a number of votes equal to the number of his shares multiplied by the number of directors to be elected, with the privilege of casting all of his votes for a single candidate, or dividing them as he may wish. This helps minorities obtain representation on the board of directors. Thus the holder of one-fourth of the shares voting, plus one share, is sure of electing one of three directors. The preemptive right is another important protection in the case of close corporations, since it assures each stockholder a right to maintain his proportionate interest. Still more definite protection is afforded by provisions in the articles that prohibit particular transactions except with the assent of a specified percentage of all outstanding shares or of each class of shares. Much the same protection can sometimes be obtained by requiring a specially large quorum for the election of directors, or a specially large vote, or even unanimous vote, by directors for the authorization of particular transactions. Quite the opposite situation exists if one of the participants is to be an inactive investor, for whom non-voting preferred stock, with its prior right to a return from earnings, may be sufficient. But even here he may require a veto power over major transactions, such as the issuance of debt, the issuance of additional preferred shares or mergers or consolidations. Or the preferred shareholders may be given as a class the right to elect one or more of the directors, particularly in the event that dividends should be in arrears.

These possibilities are listed merely as illustrations and not in any sense as exhausting the variations permissible under the Model Act.

APPENDIX H

SELECTED PROVISIONS OF THE REVISED MODEL BUSINESS CORPORATION ACT*

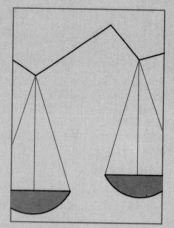

✳ ✳ ✳   ✳ ✳ ✳

§ 2.04. Liability for Preincorporation Transactions

All persons purporting to act as or on behalf of a corporation, knowing there was no incorporation under this
Act, are jointly and severally liable for all liabilities created
while so acting.

✳ ✳ ✳

§ 2.06. Bylaws

(a) The incorporators or board of directors of a corporation shall adopt initial bylaws for the corporation.

(b) The bylaws of a corporation may contain any provision
for managing the business and regulating the affairs of the
corporation that is not inconsistent with law or the articles
of incorporation.

✳ ✳ ✳

§ 6.21. Issuance of Shares

(a) The powers granted in this section to the board of
directors may be reserved to the shareholders by the articles of incorporation.

(b) The board of directors may authorize shares to be
issued for consideration consisting of any tangible or intangible property or benefit to the corporation, including
cash, promissory notes, services performed, contracts for
services to be performed, or other securities of the corporation.

(c) Before the corporation issues shares, the board of directors must determine that the consideration received or
to be received for shares to be issued is adequate. That
determination by the board of directors is conclusive insofar as the adequacy of consideration for the issuance of
shares relates to whether the shares are validly issued, fully
paid, and nonassessable.

(d) When the corporation receives the consideration for
which the board of directors authorized the issuance of
shares, the shares issued therefor are fully paid and nonassessable.

(e) The corporation may place in escrow shares issued for
a contract for future services or benefits or a promissory
note, or make other arrangements to restrict the transfer
of the shares, and may credit distributions in respect of
the shares against their purchase price, until the services
are performed, the note is paid, or the benefits received.
If the services are not performed, the note is not paid, or
the benefits are not received, the shares escrowed or restricted and the distributions credited may be cancelled
in whole or part.

*Reprinted with permission of the American Bar Foundation,
Chicago, Illinois.

§ 7.01. Annual Meeting

(a) A corporation shall hold a meeting of shareholders
annually at a time stated in or fixed in accordance with
the bylaws.

(b) Annual shareholders' meetings may be held in or out
of this state at the place stated in or fixed in accordance
with the bylaws. If no place is stated in or fixed in accordance with the bylaws, annual meetings shall be held
at the corporation's principal office.

(c) The failure to hold an annual meeting at the time
stated in or fixed in accordance with a corporation's bylaws
does not affect the validity of any corporate action.

✳ ✳ ✳

§ 7.03. Court-Ordered Meeting

(a) The [name or describe] court of the county where a
corporation's principal office (or, if none in this state, its
registered office) is located may summarily order a meeting to be held:

(1) On application of any shareholder of the corporation entitled to participate in an annual meeting if
an annual meeting was not held within the earlier of
6 months after the end of the corporation's fiscal year
or 15 months after its last annual meeting; or

(2) on application of a shareholder who signed a demand for a special meeting valid under section 7.02
if:

(i) notice of the special meeting was given within
30 days after the date the demand was delivered
to the corporation's secretary; or

(ii) the special meeting was not held in accordance
with the notice.

(b) The court may fix the time and place of the meeting,
determine the shares entitled to participate in the meeting,
specify a record date for determining shareholders entitled
to notice of and to vote at the meeting, prescribe the form
and content of the meeting notice, fix the quorum required for specific matters to be considered at the meeting
(or direct that the votes represented at the meeting constitute a quorum for action on those matters), and enter
other orders necessary to accomplish the purpose or purposes of the meeting.

✳ ✳ ✳

§ 7.27. Greater Quorum or Voting Requirements

(a) The articles of incorporation may provide for a greater
quorum or voting requirement for shareholders (or voting
groups of shareholders) than is provided by this Act.

(b) An amendment to the articles of incorporation that
adds, changes, or deletes a greater quorum or voting re-

quirement must meet the same quorum requirement and be adopted by the same vote and voting groups required to take action under the quorum and voting requirements then in effect or proposed to be adopted, whichever is greater.

* * *

§ 7.40. Procedure in Derivative Proceedings

(a) A person may not commence a proceeding in the right of a domestic or foreign corporation unless he was a shareholder of the corporation when the transaction complained of occurred or unless he became a shareholder through transfer by operation of law from one who was a shareholder at that time.

(b) A complaint in a proceeding brought in the right of a corporation must be verified and allege with particularity the demand made, if any, to obtain action by the board of directors and either that the demand was refused or ignored or why he did not make the demand. Whether or not a demand for action was made, if the corporation commences an investigation of the changes made in the demand or complaint, the court may stay any proceeding until the investigation is completed.

(c) A proceeding commenced under this section may not be discontinued or settled without the court's approval. If the court determines that a proposed discontinuance or settlement will substantially affect the interest of the corporation's shareholders or a class of shareholders, the court shall direct that notice be given the shareholders affected.

(d) On termination of the proceeding the court may require the plaintiff to pay any defendant's reasonable expenses (including counsel fees) incurred in defending the proceeding if it finds that the proceeding was commenced without reasonable cause.

(e) For purposes of this section, "shareholder" includes a beneficial owner whose shares are held in a voting trust or held by a nominee on his behalf.

§ 8.01. Requirement for and Duties of Board of Directors

(a) Except as provided in subsection (c), each corporation must have a board of directors.

(b) All corporate powers shall be exercised by or under the authority of, and the business and affairs of the corporation managed under the direction of, its board of directors, subject to any limitation set forth in the articles of incorporation.

(c) A corporation having 50 or fewer shareholders may dispense with or limit the authority of a board of directors by describing in its articles of incorporation who will perform some or all of the duties of a board of directors.

* * *

§ 8.03. Number and Election Of Directors

(a) A board of directors must consist of one or more individuals, with the number specified in or fixed in accordance with the articles of incorporation or bylaws.

(b) If a board of directors has power to fix or change the number of directors, the board may increase or decrease by 30 percent or less the number of directors last approved by the shareholders, but only the shareholders may increase or decrease by more than 30 percent the number of directors last approved by the shareholders.

(c) The articles of incorporation or bylaws may establish a variable range for the size of the board of directors by fixing a minimum and maximum number of directors. If a variable range is established, the number of directors may be fixed or changed from time to time, within the minimum and maximum, by the shareholders or the board of directors. After shares are issued, only the shareholders may change the range for the size of the board or change from a fixed to a variable-range size board or vice versa.

(d) Directors are elected at the first annual shareholders' meeting and at each annual meeting thereafter unless their terms are staggered under section 8.06.

§ 8.04. Election of Directors by Certain Classes of Shareholders

If the articles of incorporation authorize dividing the shares into classes, the articles may also authorize the election of all or a specified number of directors by the holders of one or more authorized classes of shares. Each class (or classes) of shares entitled to elect one or more directors is a separate voting group for purposes of the election of directors.

* * *

§ 8.08. Removal of Directors by Shareholders

(a) The shareholders may remove one or more directors with or without cause unless the articles of incorporation provide that directors may be removed only for cause.

(b) If a director is elected by a voting group of shareholders, only the shareholders of that voting group may participate in the vote to remove him.

(c) If cumulative voting is authorized, a director may not be removed if the number of votes sufficient to elect him under cumulative voting is voted against his removal. If cumulative voting is not authorized, a director may be removed only if the number of votes cast to remove him exceeds the number of votes cast not to remove him.

(d) A director may be removed by the shareholders only at a meeting called for the purpose of removing him and the meeting notice must state that the purpose, or one of the purposes, of the meeting is removal of the director.

* * *

§ 8.24. Quorum and Voting

(a) Unless the articles of incorporation or bylaws require a greater number, a quorum of a board of directors consists of:

(1) a majority of the fixed number of directors if the corporation has a fixed board size; or

(2) a majority of the number of directors prescribed, or if no number is prescribed the number in office immediately before the meeting begins, if the corporation has a variable range size board.

(b) The articles of incorporation or bylaws may authorize a quorum of a board of directors to consist of no fewer than one-third of the fixed or prescribed number of directors determined under subsection (a).

(c) If a quorum is present when a vote is taken, the affirmative vote of a majority of directors present is the act of the board of directors unless the articles of incorporation or bylaws require the vote of a greater number of directors.

(d) A director who is present at a meeting of the board of directors or a committee of the board of directors when corporate action is taken is deemed to have assented to the action taken unless: (1) he objects at the beginning of the meeting (or promptly upon his arrival) to holding it or transacting business at the meeting; (2) his dissent or abstention from the action taken is entered in the minutes of the meeting; or (3) he delivers written notice of his dissent or abstention to the presiding officer of the meeting before its adjournment or to the corporation immediately after adjournment of the meeting. The right of dissent or abstention is not available to a director who votes in favor of the action taken.

§ 8.25. Committees

(a) Unless the articles of incorporation or bylaws provide otherwise, a board of directors may create one or more committees and appoint members of the board of directors to serve on them. Each committee may have two or more members, who serve at the pleasure of the board of directors.

(b) The creation of a committee and appointment of members to it must be approved by the greater of (1) a majority of all the directors in office when the action is taken or (2) the number of directors required by the articles of incorporation or bylaws to take action under section 8.24.

(c) Sections 8.20 through 8.24, which govern meetings, action without meetings, notice and waiver of notice, and

quorum and voting requirements of the board of directors, apply to committees and their members as well.

(d) To the extent specified by the board of directors or in the articles of incorporation or bylaws, each committee may exercise the authority of the board of directors under section 8.01.

(e) A committee may not, however:

(1) authorize distributions;

(2) approve or propose to shareholders action that this Act requires to be approved by shareholders;

(3) fill vacancies on the board of directors or on any of its committees;

(4) amend articles of incorporation pursuant to section 10.02;

(5) adopt, amend, or repeal bylaws;

(6) approve a plan of merger not requiring shareholder approval;

(7) authorize or approve reacquisition of shares, except according to a formula or method prescribed by the board of directors; or

(8) authorize or approve the issuance or sale or contract for sale of shares, or determine the designation and relative rights, preferences, and limitations of a class or series of shares, except that the board of directors may authorize a committee (or a senior executive officer of the corporation) to do so within limits specifically prescribed by the board of directors.

(f) The creation of, delegation of authority to, or action by a committee does not alone constitute compliance by a director with the standards of conduct described in section 8.30.

* * *

§ 8.30. General Standards for Directors

(a) A director shall discharge his duties as a director, including his duties as a member of a committee:

(1) in good faith;

(2) with the care an ordinarily prudent person in a like position would exercise under similar circumstances; and

(3) in a manner he reasonably believes to be in the best interests of the corporation.

(b) In discharging his duties a director is entitled to rely on information, opinions, reports, or statements, including financial statements and other financial data, if prepared or presented by:

(1) one or more officers or employees of the corporation whom the director reasonably believes to be reliable and competent in the matters presented;

(2) legal counsel, public accountants, or other persons as to matters the director reasonably believes are within the person's professional or expert competence; or

(3) a committee of the board of directors of which he is not a member if the director reasonably believes the committee merits confidence.

(c) A director is not acting in good faith if he has knowledge concerning the matter in question that makes reliance otherwise permitted by subsection (b) unwarranted.

(d) A director is not liable for any action taken as a director, or any failure to take any action, if he performed the duties of his office in compliance with this section.

§ 8.31. Director Conflict of Interest

(a) A conflict of interest transaction is a transaction with the corporation in which a director of the corporation has a direct or indirect interest. A conflict of interest transaction is not voidable by the corporation solely because of the director's interest in the transaction if any one of the following is true:

(1) the material facts of the transaction and the director's interest were disclosed or known to the board of directors or a committee of the board of directors and the board of directors or committee authorized, approved, or ratified the transaction;

(2) the material facts of the transaction and the director's interest were disclosed or known to the shareholders entitled to vote and they authorized, approved, or ratified the transaction; or

(3) the transaction was fair to the corporation.

(b) For purposes of this section, a director of the corporation has an indirect interest in a transaction if (1) another entity in which he has a material financial interest or in which he is a general partner is a party to the transaction or (2) another entity of which he is a director, officer, or trustee is a party to the transaction and the transaction is or should be considered by the board of directors of the corporation.

(c) For purposes of subsection (a)(1), a conflict of interest transaction is authorized, approved, or ratified if it receives the affirmative vote of a majority of the directors on the board of directors (or on the committee) who have no direct or indirect interest in the transaction, but a transaction may not be authorized, approved, or ratified under this section by a single director. If a majority of the directors who have no direct or indirect interest in the transaction vote to authorize, approve, or ratify the transaction, a quorum is present for the purpose of taking action under this section. The presence of, or vote cast by, a director with a direct or indirect interest in the transaction does not affect the validity of any action taken under subsection

(a)(1) if the transaction is otherwise authorized, approved, or ratified as provided in that subsection.

(d) For purposes of subsection (a)(2), a conflict of interest transaction is authorized, approved, or ratified if it receives the vote of a majority of the shares entitled to be counted under this subsection. Shares owned by or voted under the control of a director who has a direct or indirect interest in the transaction, and shares owned by or voted under the control of an entity described in subsection (b)(1), may not be counted in a vote of shareholders to determine whether to authorize, approve, or ratify a conflict of interest transaction under subsection (a)(2). The vote of those shares, however, shall be counted in determining whether the transaction is approved under other sections of this Act. A majority of the shares, whether or not present, that are entitled to be counted in a vote on the transaction under this subsection constitutes a quorum for the purpose of taking action under this section.

§ 8.32. Loans to Directors

(a) Except as provided by subsection (c), a corporation may not lend money to or guarantee the obligation of a director of the corporation unless:

(1) the particular loan or guarantee is approved by a majority of the votes represented by the outstanding voting shares of all classes, voting as a single voting group, except the votes of shares owned by or voted under the control of the benefited director; or

(2) the corporation's board of directors determines that the loan or guarantee benefits the corporation and either approves the specific loan or guarantee or a general plan authorizing loans and guarantees.

(b) The fact that a loan or guarantee is made in violation of this section does not affect the borrower's liability on the loan.

(c) This section does not apply to loans and guarantees authorized by statute regulating any special class of corporations.

* * *

§ 8.40. Required Officers

(a) A corporation has the officers described in its bylaws or appointed by the board of directors in accordance with the bylaws.

(b) A duly appointed officer may appoint one or more officers or assistant officers if authorized by the bylaws or the board of directors.

(c) The bylaws or the board of directors shall delegate to one of the officers responsibility for preparing minutes of the directors' and shareholders' meetings and for authenticating records of the corporation.

(d) The same individual may simultaneously hold more than one office in a corporation.

* * *

§ 8.42. Standards of Conduct for Officers

(a) An officer with discretionary authority shall discharge his duties under that authority:

(1) in good faith;

(2) with the care an ordinarily prudent person in a like position would exercise under similar circumstances; and

(3) in a manner he reasonably believes to be in the best interests of the corporation.

(b) In discharging his duties an officer is entitled to rely on information, opinions, reports, or statements, including financial statements and other financial data, if prepared or presented by:

(1) one or more officers or employees of the corporation whom the officer reasonably believes to be reliable and competent in the matters presented; or

(2) legal counsel, public accountants, or other persons as to matters the officer reasonably believes are within the person's professional or expert competence.

(c) An officer is not acting in good faith if he has knowledge concerning the matter in question that makes reliance otherwise permitted by subsection (b) unwarranted.

(d) An officer is not liable for any action taken as an officer, or any failure to take any action, if he performed the duties of his office in compliance with this section.

* * *

§ 10.02. Amendment by Board of Directors

Unless the articles of incorporation provide otherwise, a corporation's board of directors may adopt one or more amendments to the corporation's articles of incorporation without shareholder action:

(1) to extend the duration of the corporation if it was incorporated at a time when limited duration was required by law;

(2) to delete the names and addresses of the initial directors;

(3) to delete the name and address of the initial registered agent or registered office, if a statement of change is on file with the secretary of state;

(4) to change each issued and unissued authorized share of an outstanding class into a greater number of whole shares if the corporation has only shares of that class outstanding;

(5) to change the corporate name by substituting the word "corporation," "incorporated," "company," "limited," or the abbreviation "corp.," "inc.," "co.," or "ltd.," for a similar word or abbreviation in the name, or by adding, deleting, or changing a geographical attribution for the name; or

(6) to make any other change expressly permitted by this Act to be made without shareholder action.

§ 10.03. Amendment by Board of Directors and Shareholders

(a) A corporation's board of directors may propose one or more amendments to the articles of incorporation for submission to the shareholders.

(b) For the amendment to be adopted:

(1) the board of directors must recommend the amendment to the shareholders unless the board of directors determines that because of conflict of interest or other special circumstances it should make no recommendation and communicates the basis for its determination to the shareholders with the amendment; and

(2) the shareholders entitled to vote on the amendment must approve the amendment as provided in subsection (e).

(c) The board of directors may condition its submission of the proposed amendment on any basis.

(d) The corporation shall notify each shareholder, whether or not entitled to vote, of the proposed shareholders' meeting in accordance with section 7.05. The notice of meeting must also state that the purpose, or one of the purposes, of the meeting is to consider the proposed amendment and contain or be accompanied by a copy or summary of the amendment.

(e) Unless this Act, the articles of incorporation, or the board of directors (acting pursuant to subsection (c)) require a greater vote or a vote by voting groups, the amendment to be adopted must be approved by:

(1) a majority of the votes entitled to be cast on the amendment by any voting group with respect to which the amendment would create dissenters' rights; and

(2) the votes required by sections 7.25 and 7.26 by every other voting group entitled to vote on the amendment.

§ 10.04. Voting on Amendments by Voting Groups

(a) The holders of the outstanding shares of a class are entitled to vote as a separate voting group (if shareholder voting is otherwise required by this Act) on a proposed amendment if the amendment would:

(1) increase or decrease the aggregate number of authorized shares of the class;

(2) effect an exchange or reclassification of all or part of the shares of the class into shares of another class;

(3) effect an exchange or reclassification, or create the right of exchange, of all or part of the shares of another class into shares of the class;

(4) change the designation, rights, preferences, or limitations of all or part of the shares of the class;

(5) change the shares of all or part of the class into a different number of shares of the same class;

(6) create a new class of shares having rights or preferences with respect to distributions or to dissolution that are prior, superior, or substantially equal to the shares of the class;

(7) increase the rights, preferences, or number of authorized shares of any class that, after giving effect to the amendment, have rights or preferences with respect to distributions or to dissolution that are prior, superior, or substantially equal to the shares of the class;

(8) limit or deny an existing preemptive right of all or part of the shares of the class; or

(9) cancel or otherwise affect rights to distributions or dividends that have accumulated but not yet been declared on all or part of the shares of the class.

(b) If a proposed amendment would affect a series of a class of shares in one or more of the ways described in subsection (a), the shares of that series are entitled to vote as a separate voting group on the proposed amendment.

(c) If a proposed amendment that entitles two or more series of shares to vote as separate voting groups under this section would affect those two or more series in the same or a substantially similar way, the shares of all the series so affected must vote together as a single voting group on the proposed amendment.

(d) A class or series of shares is entitled to the voting rights granted by this section although the articles of incorporation provide that the shares are nonvoting shares.

* * *

§ 11.01. Merger

(a) One or more corporations may merge into another corporation if the board of directors of each corporation adopts and its shareholders (if required by section 11.03) approve a plan of merger.

(b) The plan of merger must set forth:

(1) the name of each corporation planning to merge and the name of the surviving corporation into which each other corporation plans to merge;

(2) the terms and conditions of the merger; and

(3) the manner and basis of converting the shares of each corporation into shares, obligations, or other securities of the surviving or any other corporation or into cash or other property in whole or part.

(c) The plan of merger may set forth:

(1) amendments to the articles of incorporation of the surviving corporation; and

(2) other provisions relating to the merger.

* * *

§ 14.07. Unknown Claims Against Dissolved Corporation

(a) A dissolved corporation may also publish notice of its dissolution and request that persons with claims against the corporation present them in accordance with the notice.

(b) The notice must:

(1) be published one time in a newspaper of general circulation in the county where the dissolved corporation's principal office (or, if none in this state, its registered office) is or was last located;

(2) describe the information that must be included in a claim and provide a mailing address where the claim may be sent; and

(3) state that a claim against the corporation will be barred unless a proceeding to enforce the claim is commenced within five years after the publication of the notice.

(c) If the dissolved corporation publishes a newspaper notice in accordance with subsection (b), the claim of each of the following claimants is barred unless the claimant commences a proceeding to enforce the claim against the dissolved corporation within five years after the publication date of the newspaper notice:

(1) a claimant who did not receive written notice under section 14.06;

(2) a claimant whose claim was timely sent to the dissolved corporation but not acted on;

(3) a claimant whose claim is contingent or based on an event occurring after the effective date of dissolution.

(d) A claim may be enforced under this section:

(1) against the dissolved corporation, to the extent of its undistributed assets; or

(2) if the assets have been distributed in liquidation, against a shareholder of the dissolved corporation to the extent of his pro rata share of the claim or the corporate assets distributed to him in liquidation, whichever is less, but a shareholder's total liability for

all claims under this section may not exeed the total amount of assets distributed to him.

§ 14.20. Grounds for Administrative Dissolution

The secretary of state may commence a proceeding under section 14.21 to administratively dissolve a corporation if:

(1) the corporation does not pay within 60 days after they are due any franchise taxes or penalties imposed by this Act or other law;

(2) the corporation does not deliver its annual report to the secretary of state within 60 days after it is due;

(3) the corporation is without a registered agent or registered office in this state for 60 days or more;

(4) the corporation does not notify the secretary of state within 60 days that its registered agent or registered office has been changed, that its registered agent has resigned, or that its registered office has been discontinued; or

(5) the corporation's period of duration stated in its articles of incorporation expires.

*   *   *

§ 14.30. Grounds For Judicial Dissolution

The [name or describe court or courts] may dissolve a corporation:

(1) in a proceeding by the attorney general if it is established that:

   (i) the corporation obtained its articles of incorporation through fraud; or

   (ii) the corporation has continued to exceed or abuse the authority conferred upon it by law;

(2) in a proceeding by a shareholder if it is established that:

   (i) the directors are deadlocked in the management of the corporate affairs, the shareholders are unable to break the deadlock, and irreparable injury to the corporation is threatened or being suffered, or the business and affairs of the corporation can no longer be conducted to the advantage of the shareholders generally, because of the deadlock;

   (ii) the directors or those in control of the corporation have acted, are acting, or will act in a manner that is illegal, oppressive, or fraudulent;

   (iii) the shareholders are deadlocked in voting power and have failed, for a period that includes at least two consecutive annual meeting dates, to elect successors to directors whose terms have expired; or

   (iv) the corporate assets are being misapplied or wasted;

(3) in a proceeding by a creditor if it is established that:

   (i) the creditor's claim has been reduced to judgment, the execution on the judgment returned unsatisfied, and the corporation is insolvent; or

   (ii) the corporation has admitted in writing that the creditor's claim is due and owing and the corporation is insolvent; or

(4) in a proceeding by the corporation to have its voluntary dissolution continued under court supervision.

*   *   *

§ 15.01 Authority to Transact Business Required

(a) A foreign corporation may not transact business in this state until it obtains a certificate of authority from the secretary of state.

(b) The following activities, among others, do not constitute transacting business within the meaning of subsection (a):

   (1) maintaining, defending, or settling any proceeding;

   (2) holding meetings of the board of directors or shareholders or carrying on other activities concerning internal corporate affairs;

   (3) maintaining bank accounts;

   (4) maintaining offices or agencies for the transfer, exchange, and registration of the corporation's own securities or maintaining trustees or depositaries with respect to those securities;

   (5) selling through independent contractors;

   (6) soliciting or obtaining orders, whether by mail or through employees or agents or otherwise, if the orders require acceptance outside this state before they become contracts;

   (7) creating or acquiring indebtedness, mortgages, and security interests in real or personal property;

   (8) securing or collecting debts or enforcing mortgages and security interests in property securing the debts;

   (9) owning, without more, real or personal property;

   (10) conducting an isolated transaction that is completed within 30 days and that is not one in the course of repeated transactions of a like nature;

   (11) transacting business in interstate commerce.

(c) The list of activities in subsection (b) is not exhaustive.

*   *   *

§ 16.02. Inspection of Records by Shareholders

(a) A shareholder of a corporation is entitled to inspect and copy, during regular business hours at the corporation's principal office, any of the records of the corporation described in section 16.01(e) if he gives the corporation written notice of his demand at least five business days before the date on which he wishes to inspect and copy.

(b) A shareholder of a corporation is entitled to inspect and copy, during regular business hours at a reasonable location specified by the corporation, any of the following records of the corporation if the shareholder meets the requirements of subsection (c) and gives the corporation written notice of his demand at least five business days before the date on which he wishes to inspect and copy:

    (1) excerpts from minutes of any meeting of the board of directors, records of any action of a committee of the board of directors while acting in place of the board of directors on behalf of the corporation, minutes of any meeting of the shareholders, and records of action taken by the shareholders or board of directors without a meeting, to the extent not subject to inspection under section 16.02(a);

    (2) accounting records of the corporation; and

    (3) the record of shareholders.

(c) A shareholder may inspect and copy the records identified in subsection (b) only if:

    (1) his demand is made in good faith and for a proper purpose;

    (2) he describes with reasonable particularity his purpose and the records he desires to inspect; and

    (3) the records are directly connected with his purpose.

(d) The right of inspection granted by this section may not be abolished or limited by a corporation's articles of incorporation or bylaws.

(e) This section does not affect:

    (1) the right of a shareholder to inspect records under section 7.20 or, if the shareholder is in litigation with the corporation, to the same extent as any other litigant;

    (2) the power of a court, independently of this Act, to compel the production of corporate records for examination.

§ 16.03. Scope of Inspection Right

(a) A shareholder's agent or attorney has the same inspection and copying rights as the shareholder he represents.

(b) The right to copy records under section 16.02 includes, if reasonable, the right to receive copies made by photographic, xerographic, or other means.

(c) The corporation may impose a reasonable charge, covering the costs of labor and material, for copies of any documents provided to the shareholder. The charge may not exceed the estimated cost of production or reproduction of the records.

(d) The corporation may comply with a shareholder's demand to inspect the record of shareholders under section 16.02(b)(3) by providing him with a list of its shareholders that was compiled no earlier than the date of the shareholder's demand.

*   *   *

§ 16.21. Other Reports to Shareholders

(a) If a corporation indemnifies or advances expenses to a director under section 8.51, 8.52, 8.53, or 8.54 in connection with a proceeding by or in the right of the corporation, the corporation shall report the indemnification or advance in writing to the shareholders with or before the notice of the next shareholders' meeting.

(b) If a corporation issues or authorizes the issuance of shares for promissory notes or for promises to render services in the future, the corporation shall report in writing to the shareholders the number of shares authorized or issued, and the consideration received by the corporation, with or before the notice of the next shareholders' meeting.

*   *   *

GLOSSARY

A

abandoned property Property over which the owner has given up dominion and control with no intention of recovering it.

abuse of discretion Clearly erroneous judgment; usually used in reference to action taken by an administrative agency or judge which has no foundation in fact or in law.

acceleration clause A clause in a contract for rent, or for installment payments, which provides that all future payments will become due immediately upon the failure to tender timely payments or upon the occurrence of an event. (see *installment contracts, tender, severable contracts*)

acceptance (1) In contract law the offeree's notification to the offeror that the offeree agrees to be bound by the terms of the offeror's proposal. Although historically acceptance had to be in the exact manner specified by the offeror, the trend is to allow acceptance by any means which will reasonably notify the offeror of the acceptance. (2) In commercial paper law, the drawee's signed agreement to pay a draft when presented.

acceptor The person (the drawee) who accepts a draft and who engages to be primarily responsible for its payment.

accession (1) The changing (through manufacturing) of one good into a new good (*i.e.*, flour into bread). (2) The right to all that which one's property produces (*i.e.*, fruit from trees) or to that which becomes added to or incorporated to that property (*i.e.*, buildings on one's land). (3) The right, upon payment for the original materials, to keep an article manufactured out of goods which were innocently converted. (see *conversion*)

accommodation party A person who signs an instrument for the purpose of lending that person's credit to another party on that instrument.

accord An agreement between two persons, one of whom has a right of action against the other, to settle the dispute.

accord and satisfaction An agreement and payment (or other performance) between two parties, one of whom has a right of action against the other. After the agreement has been made and payment or other performance has been tendered, the "accord and satisfaction" is complete.

account (1) An intangible concept of individualized funds maintained by banks for each depositor. (2) A right to payment for goods sold or leased, or services rendered, which is not evidenced by an instrument or chattel paper (such as an account receivable).

act of state doctrine A judicially created doctrine. The act of state doctrine provides that the judicial branch will not examine the validity of acts by a foreign nation within its own territory.

actual authority The power of an agent to bind its principal where such power derives either from express or implied agreement between the principal and the agent.

actus reus The "guilty act." The *actus reus* is the physical aspect of a crime, whereas the *mens rea* (guilty mind) involves the psychological or intent factor.

adhesion contracts Standard "form" contracts, such as those between a large retailer and a consumer, whereby the stronger party dictates the terms.

administrative law A body of law created by administrative agencies such as the SEC and FTC in the form of rules, regulations, orders, and decisions to carry out their duties and responsibilities. This law can initially be enforced by these agencies, outside the judicial process.

administrative process Procedures used which govern an agency's powers in the enforcement of administrative law.

administrator (-trix) One who is appointed by a court to handle the probate (disposition) of a person's estate if that person dies intestate. (see *estate, will, intestacy laws*)

adverse possession The acquisition of title to real property by occupying it, with the knowledge of the owner, for a period of time specified by state statutes.

affirmative defense A response to a plaintiff's claim which attacks the plaintiff's *legal* right to bring an action, as opposed to attacking the truth of the claim. Running of the statute of limitations is an example of an affirmative defense.

after-acquired property Property of the debtor which is acquired after a security transaction with a secured party is created. This may also refer to property acquired by a testator after execution of his or her will. Property acquired after the date of the agreement usually becomes additional security for payment of the indebtedness if an after-acquired property is included in the agreement. (see UCC 9–204)

agency A relationship between two persons where, by agreement or otherwise, one is bound by the words and acts of the other. The former is a *principal;* the latter is an *agent.*

agency by estoppel Agency created by operation of law and established by proof of acts of the principal which would lead a third person to reasonably believe an agency exists.

agent A person authorized by another to act for or in place of him or her.

agreement A meeting of two or more minds. Often used as a synonym for contract.

alien corporation A corporation formed in another country but doing business in the United States is referred to within the United States as an alien corporation.

allonge A piece of paper firmly attached to a negotiable instrument, upon which transferees can make indorsements if there is no room left on the instrument itself.

American Arbitration Association (AAA) The major organization offering arbitration services in the United States. Arbitration is becoming an increasingly popular alternative to the court system and its formalities.

answer The defendant's response to the complaint. Filing of the complaint and answer are governed by rules of procedure.

antecedent claim A preexisting claim. In the law of negotiable instruments, a holder takes for value if he or she takes the instrument for an antecedent claim against any person whether or not the claim is due. UCC 3–303(b)

anticipatory breach or **anticipatory repudiation** The assertion by a party that he or she will not perform an obligation which the party is contractually obligated to perform at a future time.

apparent authority Such authority as a reasonable person would assume an agent has in light of the conduct of the principal. Apparent authority cannot be established solely by the conduct of the agent and must be based upon the conduct of the principal.

appeal An appeal to a request for a legal proceeding in which a higher court rehears the decision of a lower court.

appellant The party who invokes the appellate jurisdiction of a superior court. The appellant may be either the plaintiff or the defendant.

appellee The party against whom an appeal is taken.

appraisal right A dissenting shareholder's right to object to an extraordinary transaction of the corporation, such as a merger or consolidation, have his or her shares appraised, and be paid the fair market value by the corporation. (see Model Business Corporation Act, §§ 80–81)

appropriation In tort law, the act of making a thing one's own or exercising or making use of an object to subserve one's own interest. When the act is wrongful, a tort is committed.

arbitrary and capricious Without basis in fact or law. Without a rational basis.

arbitration The settling of a dispute by submitting it to a disinterested third party other than a court.

arbitration clause A clause in a contract which provides that in case of dispute the parties will determine their rights by arbitration rather than through the judicial system.

arson The malicious burning of another's dwelling. Some statutes have expanded this to include any real property regardless of ownership, and the destruction of property by other means, *e.g.,* explosion.

articles of incorporation The instrument under which a corporation is formed which serves as a request to a state to be treated as a corporation under that state's laws.

articles of partnership The written contract by which parties enter into a partnership to be governed by the terms set forth in the contract.

artisan's lien A possessory lien given to a person who has made improvements and added value to another person's personal property as security for payment for services performed.

assault Any word or action intended to cause the person to whom it is directed to be in fear of immediate physical harm; a reasonably believable threat. (see *battery*)

assault and battery An intentional, unlawful threat of bodily harm and the carrying out of the threat.

assignment The act of transferring to another all or part of one's property, interest, or rights.

assumption of risk A doctrine whereby a plaintiff may not recover for injuries or damages suffered to which he or she assents. A defense if the plaintiff has knowledge of and appreciates a danger and voluntarily exposes himself or herself to the danger.

attachment (1) In a secured transaction, the process by which a security interest in the property of another becomes enforceable. Attachment may occur upon the taking possession of the property or upon the signing of a security agreement by the person pledging the property as collateral. (2) The legal process of seizing another's property in accordance with a writ or judicial order for the purpose of securing satisfaction of a judgment yet to be rendered.

authorized shares That capital stock which the charter or articles of incorporation permits the corporation to sell.

B

bailee One to whom goods are entrusted by a bailor.

bailment An agreement to entrust goods or personal property of one person (bailor) to another (bailee) with the obligation of the bailee to return the bailed property to the bailor or dispose of the property as directed.

bailor One who entrusts goods to a bailee.

bankruptcy Proceedings under law, initiated either by a person or business entity or by its creditors seeking to have the bankrupt's assets distributed among its creditors, thus discharging the debtor's debts.

battery The unprivileged, intentional touching of another. (see *assault*)

bearer A person in possession of an instrument payable to bearer or indorsed in blank.

bearer instrument In the law of commercial paper, any instrument which runs to the bearer. It includes instruments payable to the bearer or to "cash."

beneficiary One who holds equitable title to property being held in trust, such property being cared for by the trustee. (see *fiduciary duty*)

bequest A gift by will of personal property (from the verb—to bequeath).

bilateral contract A contract which includes the exchange of a promise for a promise (as compared to a unilateral contract).

bill of lading A document which serves both as evidence of the receipt of goods for shipment and as documentary evidence of title to the goods.

Bill of Rights The Bill of Rights consists of the first ten amendments to the Constitution.

binder A written, temporary insurance policy. (see *policy*)

blank indorsement One made by the mere writing of the indorser's name on the back of an instrument. Such indorsement causes an instrument, otherwise payable to order, to become payable to bearer and negotiated only by delivery.

blanket policy A policy covering more than one type of property in one location, or one or more types of property at more than one location.

"Blue Sky" laws Another name for state laws which regulate the offer and sale of securities.

bond A certificate which evidences a corporate debt. It is a security which involves no ownership interest in the issuing corporation.

bond indenture An instrument of secured indebtedness issued by a corporation.

breach of contract Failure, without legal excuse, of a promisor to perform the obligations of a contract.

burglary The unlawful entry, usually at night, into a building with the intent to commit theft. (Some state statutes expand this to include the intent to commit any crime.)

business tort A noncontractual breach of a legal duty by one party that directly results in damage or injury to another.

bylaws The rules which a business firm adopts in order to control the conduct of its internal affairs.

C

capital stock The amount of money or property contributed by shareholders to be used as a corporation's financial foundation. The total amount of stock representing ownership of a business (including preferred and common stock).

case law Case law consists of the rules of law announced in court decisions. It includes the aggregate of reported cases that interpret statutes, regulations, and constitutional provisions.

cashier's check A draft drawn by a bank on itself.

causa mortis gift A gift made by a donor in contemplation of his or her imminent death. If the donor does not die of that ailment, the gift is revoked.

causation in fact An act or omission without which an event would not have occurred. (Prosser and Keaton on Torts, 5th Ed., pp. 264–265)

cause of action A legal right of redress against another; it includes both the right to sue and the right to recover in a court of law or equity.

caveat emptor (Latin) Literally, "let the buyer beware."

cease and desist order An administrative or judicial order prohibiting a business firm from conducting the activities which an agency or a court has deemed illegal.

certificate of deposit An instrument evidencing a promissory acknowledgement by a bank of a receipt of money with an engagement to repay it. (see UCC 3–104(2)(c))

certified check A check drawn by an individual on his or her own account but bearing a guarantee (acceptance) by a bank that the bank will pay the check regardless of whether the drawer's account contains adequate funds at the time the check is presented.

chancellor In the early King's Court, individuals petitioned the king for relief when they could not obtain an adequate remedy in a court of law. These petitions were decided by the chancellor, who was an advisor to the king.

charitable trust One in which property held by a trustee must be used for charitable purposes (advancement of health, religion, etc.).

charter The basic document issued by a sovereign power under which a corporation is organized, setting forth the corporation's and shareholders' rights and duties (certificate or articles of incorporation).

chattel Tangible personal property.

chattel paper Any writing or writings which evidences both a security interest in collateral and a money obligation with respect to the collateral.

check A draft drawn on a bank, signed by the drawer, and payable on demand.

checks and balances An arrangement of governmental powers whereby powers of one governmental branch check or balance those of other branches.

citation A citation indicates where a particular constitutional provision, statute, reported case, or article may be found; also an order for a defendant to appear in court or indicating that a person has violated a legal rule.

civil law (1) That branch of law which deals with the definition and enforcement of all private or public rights, as opposed to criminal matters. (2) Codified law compiled by the early Roman jurists, which is still in force in many Western European states and which is the foundation for the law in Louisiana, as distinguished from common law.

class action suit A legal action in which a group of persons are represented by one or a few persons in a lawsuit. The class can be either a plaintiff or a defendant.

close corporation A corporation whose shareholders are limited to a small group of persons, often including only family members. The rights of shareholders of a close corporation usually are restricted regarding transfer of shares to others.

closed shop A place of employment that requires union membership as a condition of employment. Unlawful under Taft-Hartley Act.

closing argument Closing arguments are made after the plaintiff(s) and defendant(s) have rested their cases. Closing arguments are made prior to the jury charges.

codicil A written supplement to, or modification of, a will. Codicils must be executed with the same formalities as a will.

collateral Property in which the secured party has an interest, as security in case of nonpayment by the debtor.

collecting bank Any bank handling an item for collection, except the payor bank.

comity Comity may be defined as a deference by which one nation gives effect to the laws and judicial decrees of another nation. This recognition is based primarily upon respect.

commercial paper Under UCC Article 3, negotiable instruments, which are signed writings by which the maker or drawer promises or orders a drawee (unconditionally) to pay a certain amount of money to the order of the bearer of the paper.

common law That body of law developed from custom or judicial decisions in English and American courts, not attributable to a legislature.

common stock Shares of ownership in a corporation which are lowest in priority with respect to payment of dividends and distribution of the corporation's assets upon dissolution. (see *preferred stock*)

comparative negligence A concept in tort law whereby liability for injuries resulting from negligent acts is shared by all persons who were guilty of negligence, including the injured party, on the basis of each person's proportionate carelessness.

compensatory damages A money award equivalent to the actual value of injuries or damages sustained by the aggrieved party.

complaint The pleading made by a plaintiff or a charge by the state to a judicial officer alleging wrongdoing on the part of the defendant. Thus, the plaintiff is also referred to as the complainant.

concurrent conditions Conditions which must occur or be performed at the same time; they are mutually dependent. No obligations arise until these conditions are simultaneously performed.

concurrent estates Estates in land held by two or more persons simultaneously. (see *joint tenancy* and *tenancy in common*)

concurrent jurisdiction Concurrent jurisdiction exists when two different courts have the power to hear a case. For example, some cases can be heard in a federal or a state court. When a case can only be tried in federal court, or only in state court, jurisdiction is "exclusive."

condition A qualification, provision, or clause in a contractual agreement, the occurrence of which creates, suspends, or terminates the obligations of the contracting parties.

condition precedent A condition in a contractual agreement which must be met before the other party's obligations arise.

condition subsequent A condition in a contract which, if not met, discharges the obligation of the other party.

conditional indorsement One by which the indorser attaches a present or subsequent condition to his liability.

confiscation Confiscation occurs when there is a taking without a proper public purpose or an award of just compensation.

confusion The mixing together of goods of two or more owners so that the independent goods cannot be identified.

conglomerate mergers Mergers between firms which do not compete with each other because they are in different industries, as opposed to horizontal and vertical mergers.

consent Voluntary agreement to submit to a proposition or an act of another. A concurrence of wills.

consent decree A judgment entered, by a court, by the agreement of the parties. In a consent decree neither party admits guilt or wrongdoing.

consequential damages Special damages, which compensate for loss that is indirect or immediate (*i.e.*, lost profits). The special damages must have been reasonably foreseeable at the time the breach or injury oc-

curred, in order for the plaintiff to collect them. (see UCC 2–715(2))

consideration That which motivates the exchange of promises or performance in a contractual agreement. The consideration, which must be present to make the contract legally binding, must be a detriment to the promisee (something of legal value, legally sufficient, and bargained for) or a benefit to the promisor. (see *contract*)

consolidation A contractual and statutory process whereby two or more corporations join to become a completely new corporation. The original corporations cease to exist, and the new corporation acquires all their assets and liabilities (*i.e.*, A + B = C).

constructive delivery The recognition of the act of intending that title to property be transferred to someone, even though the actual, physical delivery of the property is not made (because of difficulty, impossibility) (*e.g.*, the transfer of a key to a safe constructively delivers the contents of the safe).

constructive/implied conditions Conditions or qualifications to a promise which arise from the very nature of the promise and which the law recognizes as conditioning the promise even though not expressly stated.

constructive trust A trust created by operation of law against one who wrongfully has obtained or holds legal right to property which he should not, in equity and good conscience, hold and enjoy.

consumer goods Goods which are purchased primarily for personal, family, or household use.

contract A set of promises constituting an agreement between parties, giving each a legal duty to the other and also the right to seek a remedy for the breach of the promises/duties owed to each. The elements of an enforceable contract are competent parties, a proper or legal purpose, consideration (an exchange of promises/duties), and mutuality of agreement and of obligation.

contracts implied-in-law Contracts imposed upon parties by law, in the interest of justice, to prevent unjust enrichment even though the parties never intended to voluntarily enter into a contract (sometimes referred to as a quasi-contract).

contracts under seal Formal agreements in which the seal is a substitute for *consideration*. A court will not invalidate a contract under seal for lack of consideration.

contractual capacity The threshold mental capacity required by the law for a party who enters into a contract to be bound by that contract.

contributory negligence Any negligent act by a complaining party which contributed to or caused the complaining party's injuries. Contributory negligence is an absolute bar to recovery in some jurisdictions. (see *comparative negligence, affirmative defense*)

conversion The wrongful taking or retaining possession of property which belongs to another.

copyright The exclusive right of "authors" to publish, print, or sell an intellectual production for a statutory period of time (presently, for an identified author, his or her lifetime plus fifty years, and for anonymous or pseudonymous authors, seventy-five years from publication or one hundred years from creation). It has the same monopolistic nature as a patent or trademark, but a copyright differs from them in that it applies exclusively to works of art and literature. (See 18 C.J.S. Copyrights and Library Property § 1)

corporation An association of persons created by statute as a legal entity. The law treats the corporation itself as a person which can sue and be sued. The corporation is distinct from the individuals who comprise it (shareholders). The corporation survives the death of its investors, as the shares can usually be transferred. (see *domestic, foreign,* and *close corporations*)

counterclaim A pleading by a defendant against the plaintiff in which the defendant states a claim for damages (or to defeat plaintiff's action) resulting from allegedly wrongful acts of the plaintiff.

counter-offer An offeree's response to an offeror in which the offeree rejects the original offer and at the same time makes a new offer.

course of dealing The understandings which arise between two parties with respect to performance expected, developed over a period of time by a number of transactions establishing a particular conduct between the two parties.

course of performance The understandings of performance which develop by conduct without objection between two parties during the performance of an executory contract.

courts at law Under the Federal Rules of Civil Procedure, law and equity actions have been merged procedurally. In the early King's Court, however, courts of law were separate from the courts of equity, and the remedies in the two courts were also separate and distinct.

covenant for quiet enjoyment A promise by the landlord or grantor that the tenant or grantee will not be evicted or disturbed by the grantor or a person having a lien or superior title.

covenant running with the land An executory promise made between a grantor and a grantee which binds them and subsequent owners of the land by the covenant.

creditor beneficiary A creditor who has rights in a contract made by the debtor and a third person, where the terms of the·contract obligate the third person to pay the debt owed to the creditor. The creditor beneficiary can enforce the debt against either party.

crime A broad term for violations of law which are punishable by the state or nation. Crimes are codified by legislatures, and their objective is the protection of the public. (see *civil law, criminal law*)

crimes *mala in se* Acts which are morally wrong/wrong in themselves, such as murder, rape, arson, larceny, etc. (see *crimes mala prohibita*)

crimes *mala prohibita* Acts which are prohibited by statute as infringing on others' rights, but which are not necessarily wrong in themselves. (see *crimes mala in se*)

criminal law Governs and defines those actions which are crimes and which subject the convicted offender to punishment imposed by the state.

cross-complaint See counterclaim.

cure The right of a party who tenders non-conforming performance to correct his or her performance within the contract period. (see UCC 3–508)

cy pres A doctrine in the law of trusts and wills under which a grantor's (or testator's) wishes will be carried out "as nearly as possible" even though the grant (bequest or devise) is illegal or impossible in its original form.

D

damages Money sought as a remedy for a breach of contract action or for tortious acts.

debt A sum of money due by certain and express agreement.

debt securities Securities which are of such duration that they evidence an obligation of the corporation to repay the holder, rather than evidencing an investment by the holder in exchange for stock.

debtor A person who owes a sum of money or other obligations to another.

deceit A false representation of facts made recklessly, maliciously, or with knowledge of its falsity, which causes the injured person to rely on the misrepresentation. (see *fraud*)

deed A document by which title to property (usually real property) is passed.

deed of trust An instrument or document used in some states as a security device as a type of mortgage whereby legal title to real property is transferred to a trustee to secure the repayment of a sum of money or the performance of other conditions. (see *mortgage*)

de facto corporation A business which holds itself out as a corporation but which has not been organized in substantial compliance with state corporation law.

defamation Anything published or publicly spoken which causes injury to another's good name, reputation, or character. (see *slander, libel*)

defendant The party against whom an action or suit is brought.

defense of others The legally recognized privilege in which a defender may do whatever the person attacked would do to protect himself. Whether one was justified and used reasonable force in the protection of another is judged on the same criteria as the privilege of self-defense. (Prosser and Keaton on Torts, 5th Ed. pp. 129–131)

defense of property The legally recognized privilege of a person to defend his or her property. One may only use the amount of force necessary to protect his or her property, as the use of even slightly greater force will be deemed wrongful. (Prosser and Keaton on Torts, 5th Ed., pp. 131–137)

de jure corporation A corporation which has been organized substantially in compliance with state corporation laws.

delegation of duties The act of transferring to another all or part of one's duties arising under a contract.

demand deposit Funds accepted by a bank subject to immediate withdrawal, in contrast to a time deposit which requires depositor to wait a specific time before withdrawing or pay a penalty for early withdrawal.

demurrer A pleading in which a defendant admits to the facts as alleged by the plaintiff but asserts that the plaintiff's claim fails to state a cause of action (*i.e.*, has no basis in law).

depositary bank The first bank to which an item is transferred for collection even though it may also be the payor bank. (see UCC 4–105(a))

deposition A generic term which refers to any written evidence verified by oath. As a legal term, it is usually limited to the testimony of a witness taken under oath, with the opportunity of cross examination, in answer to interrogatories. (See 26A C.J.S. Depositions § 1)

derivative suit A suit by a shareholder to enforce a corporate cause of action against a third person.

devise To make a gift of real property by a will.

disaffirmance The repudiation of an obligation.

discharge The termination of one's obligation. In contract law, discharge occurs when the parties have fully performed their contractual obligations or when events, conduct of the parties, or operation of the law release the parties from further performance.

discharge in bankruptcy The release of a bankrupt from all debts which are provable, except those specifically excepted from discharge by statute.

disclosed principal A principal whose identity and existence as a principal is known by a third person at the time a transaction is conducted by an agent.

discovery A method by which opposing parties may obtain information from each other to prepare for trial. Generally governed by rules of procedure, but may be controlled by the court.

dishonor The refusal to pay or to accept an instrument which has been properly presented. (see UCC 3–507)

dissolution The formal disbanding of a partnership. Can take place by agreement of the parties, death of a partner, or court order. (see *partnership at will*)

diversity of citizenship Under Article III, Section 2, of the Constitution, diversity of citizenship provides a basis for federal court jurisdiction over a lawsuit between citizens of different states.

dividend A distribution to corporate shareholders, disbursed in proportion to the number of shares held.

documents of title Paper exchanged in the regular course of business which evidence the right to possession of goods (*e.g.*, bills of lading, warehouse receipts, etc.).

domestic corporation In a given state, a corporation which is doing business and is organized under the laws of that state.

donee beneficiary A person not a party to a contract but to whom the benefits of a contract flow as a direct result of an intention to make a gift to that person.

draft Any instrument drawn on any person (including a bank) which orders that person to pay a certain sum of money. (see UCC 3–104)

drawee The person who is ordered to pay on an instrument. With a check, the bank is always the drawee.

drawer A person who initiates a draft (including a check), thereby ordering the drawee to pay.

due process An individual's right not to be deprived of life, liberty, or property without a fair hearing.

duress Any unlawful threat or coercion used by a person to induce another to act (or to refrain from acting) in a manner he or she otherwise would not (or would).

E

easement A nonpossessory right to use another's property in a manner established by either express or implied agreement.

easement appurtenant An easement on a "servient estate," which serves a "dominant estate." An easement created for the benefit of another tract of land.

easement in gross The personal right to use another's land which is not dependent upon ownership of land by the holder of the easement.

embezzlement The fraudulent appropriation of money or other property by a person to whom the money or property has been entrusted.

eminent domain The power of a government to take land for public use from private citizens for a fair compensation.

employee A person who works for an employer for salary or wages.

endowment policy In life insurance, a policy which is payable when the insured reaches a given age, or upon his or her death, if that occurs earlier.

equal dignity statute In most states, express authority given an agent must be in writing if the contract to be made on behalf of the principal is required to be in writing.

equitable principles and maxims Equitable principles and maxims are frequently involved in equity jurisdiction. They are propositions or general statements of rules of law.

equitable servitude A restriction on the use of land enforceable in a court of equity.

equity The system of remedial justice, separate from the common law, based upon settled rules of fairness, justice, and honesty.

equity of redemption The right of a mortgagor to redeem or purchase the property, after the mortgagor has breached the mortgage agreement, prior to foreclosure proceedings.

equity securities Securities or shares of capital stock representing an ownership interest in a corporation rather than debt.

estate The extent of ownership or interest that one has in property.

estop To stop, bar, or impede.

estray statutes Laws dealing with a person's rights in property whose ownership is unknown.

exclusive dealing contract An agreement under which a producer of goods agrees to sell its goods exclusively through one distributor.

exclusive jurisdiction Jurisdiction is exclusive when a case can only be heard in a particular court.

exculpatory contract or clause A contract or contract clause which releases one of the parties from liability for his or her wrongful acts.

executed contract A contract which has been completely performed by both parties.

executor (-trix) A person either expressly or by implication appointed by a testator to see that his or her will is administered appropriately. (see *will, testator*)

executory contract A contract that has not as yet been fully completed or performed.

executory interest A future interest held by a third person (not the grantor) which either cuts short (shifting) or begins some time after (springing) the natural termination of the preceding estate.

exemplary damages Damages above those which will compensate a victim for his or her loss, intended to solace plaintiff for aggravations of the original wrong, or to punish the defendant for evil behavior or to make an example of the defendant. Also called punitive damages.

express condition A qualification or condition upon which a promise is based and which is stated in the body of the contract. (see *condition*)

express contract A contract which is either oral and/or written (as opposed to an *implied contract*).

express warranty A promise, ancillary to an underlying sales agreement, which is included in the written or oral terms of the sales agreement under which the promisor assures the quality, description, or performance of the goods.

expropriation Expropriation occurs when a government seizes a privately owned business or privately owned goods for a proper public purpose and awards just compensation.

ex-ship Words in a contract for the sale of goods denoting that risk of loss shall pass to the buyer upon the goods leaving the ship. Buyer is responsible for any subsequent landing charges. (see UCC 2–322)

F

fair trade laws State statutes which permit manufacturers or distributors of namebrand goods to fix minimum retail resale prices. These statutes are no longer valid.

F.A.S. "Free alongside ship"; delivery term under which the seller is obligated to deliver goods to a specified loading dock and bears expense and risk of loss up to that point. (see UCC 2–319(2))

featherbedding Employee practices, primarily stemming from a desire on the part of employees to insure job security in the face of technological improvements, in which the number of employees used, or amount of time consumed, to work on a job is unnecessarily high.

federal question A federal question provides jurisdiction for federal courts. This jurisdiction arises from Article III, Section 2, of the Constitution. Federal questions may pertain to the U.S. Constitution, acts of Congress, or treaties.

federalism A form of government in which sovereign power is divided between a central governing authority and the member states of a political union. The United States has a federal form of government.

fee simple absolute An estate or interest in land with no time, disposition, or descendibility limitations.

fee simple defeasible An estate which can be taken away (by the prior grantor) upon the occurrence or nonoccurrence of a specified event.

felony A crime which carries the most severe sanctions, usually ranging from one year in a state or federal prison to the forfeiture of one's life (*i.e.*, arson, murder, rape, robbery).

felony murder At common law, the intent to commit a felony unrelated to a homicide was sufficient to meet the *mens rea* requirement for murder. Because of the many new statutory felonies that pose little threat of death or bodily harm to anyone, this doctrine has been limited by courts and legislatures.

ficticious payee A payee on a negotiable instrument, whom the maker or drawer does not intend to have an interest in the instrument. A payee imposter comes under the definition of a fictitious payee. Frequently an unscrupulous employee or agent supplies the maker or drawer, or drafts the instrument, with the name of the fictitious payee. Indorsements by fictitious payees are not forgeries under negotiable instruments law. (see UCC 3–405)

fiduciary duty A duty to act for someone else's benefit, while subordinating one's personal interests to that of the other person. It is the highest standard of duty implied by law (*e.g.*, trustee, guardian).

financing statement A document setting out a secured party's security interest in goods. When the document is filed with the appropriate government agency, all potential lenders and third parties are put on constructive notice of the security interest.

firm offer A signed writing by a merchant who promises to keep an offer open. Unlike an option, no consideration need be given to make the offer irrevocable. (see UCC 2–205)

fixture A thing which was once personal property, but has become attached to real property in such a way that it takes on the characteristics of real property and becomes part of that real property. (see *chattel, personal property, real property*)

floater policy A policy of insurance which is issued to cover items which have no fixed location.

floating lien A security interest retained in collateral even when the collateral changes in character, classification, or location.

floating zone A concept in zoning whereby land use is predetermined by reserving specified portions of an entire area for particular uses while not immediately assigning particular parcels to a certain use.

F.O.B. "Free on board"; a delivery term which requires a seller to ship goods and bear the expense and risk of loss to the F.O.B. point designated. (see UCC 2–319(1))

forebearance Refraining from doing something that one has a legal right to do.

foreclosure A proceeding in equity whereby a mortgagee either takes title to or forces the sale of the mortgagor's property in satisfaction of a debt.

foreign corporation In any given state, a corporation which does business in the state without being incorporated therein.

forgery The false or unauthorized signature of a document, or the false making of a document, with the intent to defraud. (see *fraud*)

form Generally the legal or technical requirements for negotiable instruments, juridical proceedings, or the construction of legal documents or processes.

formal contract An agreement or contract which by law requires for its validity a specific form, such as executed under seal or in the presence of witnesses or both.

forum selection clause A clause in a contract preselecting a particular forum, such as a given state, country, court or administrative proceeding, for the resolution of a dispute. Usually upheld unless the clause is designed to discourage litigation.

franchise The Federal Trade Commission has defined a franchise as "an arrangement in which the owner of a trademark, a trade name, or a copyright licenses others, under specified conditions or limitations, to use the trademark, trade name, or copyright in purveying goods or services."

fraud Any misrepresentation, either by misstatement or omission of a material fact, knowingly made with the intention of misrepresentation to another and on which a reasonable person would and does rely to his or her detriment.

freehold estate An estate for life or in fee; an estate of uncertain duration.

frustration of purpose doctrine A court-created doctrine under which a party to a contract will be relieved of his or her duty to perform when the objective purpose for performance no longer exists (due to reasons beyond that party's control).

fungible Goods or securities which cannot be distinguished from other goods or securities of the same type (*e.g.*, bushels of wheat, apples of the same brand).

future estates A future estate is one which is not at present possessory but which will or may commence in possession in the future. Remainders and reversions are future estates.

future interest A present interest in land in which the right of enjoyment or possession is in the future.

G

garnishment A legal process whereby a creditor appropriates the debtor's property or wages which are in the hands of a third party.

general intangibles Any personal property other than goods, accounts, contract rights, chattel paper, documents, or instruments. (see UCC 9–106)

gift Any voluntary transfer of property to another which is without consideration, past or present.

gift causa mortis See causa mortis gift.

gift inter vivos See inter vivos gift.

good faith Honesty in fact as well as honesty in the conduct or transaction concerned. (see UCC 1–201(19))

good faith purchaser A purchaser who buys without notice of circumstance which would put a person of ordinary prudence on inquiry as to the title, or as to an impediment on the title, of a seller. Sometimes used interchangeably with a "buyer in ordinary course of business" when the seller is a merchant. (see UCC 1–201(9), 2–403)

goods Any tangible and moveable personal property. (see UCC 2–105(1))

grace period A span of time (usually one month) after an insurance policy premium (payment) was due, during which the policy remains in effect. (see *policy*)

grand jury A body of people (not less than twelve nor more than twenty-three) selected to conduct fact finding hearings for the purpose of issuing true bills for criminal offenses. The grand jury does not adjudicate, it only accuses. The grand jurors need only to find probable cause in order to indict someone, as opposed to the exclusion of reasonable doubt standard which is necessary to convict someone of a crime. In certain situations, the state or U.S. prosecutor can issue an information, rather than seek a grand-jury indictment. (see *information, true bill*)

grantor One who transfers property or creates a trust.

guaranty An agreement in which the guarantor agrees to satisfy the debt of another (the debtor), only if and when the debtor fails to repay (secondarily liable).

H

holder A person "who is in possession of a document of title or negotiable instrument or a certificated investment security drawn, issued, or indorsed to him or his order or to bearer or blank." (see UCC 1–201(20))

holder in due course A person who is a holder of an instrument who took it in good faith, for value, and without notice that the instrument is overdue or has been dishonored or that any defense or claim exists against it. (see UCC 3–302(1))

holder through a holder in due course One who acquires the rights of a holder in due course by taking the instrument in good faith through a holder in due course. (see UCC 3–201(1); referred to as the "shelter" rule)

holographic will A will written entirely in the signer's handwriting, usually not witnessed.

homestead exemption A law allowing a householder/head of a family to designate his or her house and adjoining land a homestead, and exempting it from liability for his or her general debts.

horizontal merger A merger between two companies which compete in the marketplace.

hotelkeeper's lien A possessory or statutory lien allowing the hotelkeeper or innkeeper to take the personal property of a guest, brought into the hotel, as security for nonpayment of the guest's bill (debt).

I

identification Proof that a thing is what it is purported or represented to be.

implied authority The power of an agent to act on behalf of his principal which is inferred from the responsibilities imposed on the agent or necessary to carry out an agent's express authority.

implied-in-fact contract A contract formed in whole or in part from the conduct of the parties. (as opposed to an express contract)

implied warranty A guarantee which the law implies either through the situation of the parties or the nature of the transaction. (see *usage of trade, course of dealing*)

implied warranty of merchantability See *warranty of merchantability* and UCC 2–314.

impossibility of performance A doctrine under which a party to a contract is relieved of his or her duty to perform when performance has become impossible or totally impracticable (through no fault of the party).

imposter One who, with the intent to deceive, pretends to be somebody else.

impracticability (commercial impracticability) A broadened interpretation of the doctrine of impossibility which holds that a party to a contract for the sale of goods will be relieved of his or her duty to perform when the premise (*e.g.*, existence of certain goods) on which the contract was based no longer exists due to unforeseeable events. (see UCC 2–615)

incidental beneficiary A person who indirectly receives, or will receive, a benefit as the result of a contract entered into by other parties. The incidental beneficiary is neither a donee beneficiary nor a creditor

beneficiary and thus has no right to enforce the contract.

incidental damages Damages resulting from a breach of a contract, including all reasonable expenses incurred because of the breach. (see UCC 2–710 and 2–715(1))

indemnification To compensate one for a loss or to reimburse one for expenses incurred.

indenture A bond document which specifies the details of the bond agreement between the borrower and the lender. This document usually includes a detailed description of the pledged assets, identification and duties of the trustee, and provisions for retirement of the bond. (see *bond*)

indictment A charge or written accusation issued by a grand jury that a named person has committed a crime. Referred to as a "true bill."

indorsee The one to whom a negotiable instrument is transferred by indorsement.

indorsement A signature placed on an instrument or a document of title for the purpose of transferring one's ownership in the instrument or document of title. (see UCC 3–202)

indorser One who, being the payee or holder of a negotiable instrument, signs by indorsement on the back of it.

informal contract A contract that does not require a specified form or formality for its validity.

information A formal accusation or complaint issued in certain types of actions by a prosecuting attorney or other law officer without an indictment. The types of actions are set forth in the rules of states or the Federal Rules of Criminal Procedure. (see *grand jury, true bill*)

injunction An order by a court requiring a person to act or refrain from acting in a certain manner.

innocent misrepresentation A false statement of fact or an act made in good faith which deceives and causes harm or injury to another.

in pari delicto At equal fault.

in personam jurisdiction *In personam* jurisdiction refers to the power that a court has over the "person" involved in the action.

in rem jurisdiction *In rem* jurisdiction refers to an action that is taken directly against the defendant's property. The term may be contrasted with *in personam* jurisdiction.

insolvency The financial state of a person when liabilities exceed the value of his or her assets *or* when that person "either has ceased to pay his debts in the ordinary course of business or cannot pay his debts as they come due." (see UCC 1–201(23))

installment contract A contract whereby either property purchased or payments due, or both, are made periodically. (see UCC 2–612)

instrument A formal or legal document in writing. Under the UCC, a negotiable instrument. (see UCC 3–102(e))

insurable interest An interest either in a person's life or well-being or in property which is sufficiently substantial that insuring against injury to the person or damage to the property will not amount to a mere wagering contract.

intangible property A property right, usually represented by a document or certificate which has no intrinsic value, which evidences a valuable ownership interest.

intent Action(s) by a person in a state of mind by design, resolve, or determination.

intentional tort A tort in which the actor is expressly or impliedly judged to have possessed intent or purpose to injure.

intermediary bank Any bank to which an item is transferred in the course of collection, except the depositary or payor bank. (see UCC 4–105(c))

international law International law consists of those laws that govern relations between nations. International customs and treaties are generally considered to be the two most important sources of international law.

interrogatories Interrogatories are a series of written questions for which written answers are prepared and then signed under oath.

inter vivos gift A gift made by a living person which is not in contemplation of death.

inter vivos trust A trust created and effective by the grantor (settlor) during the grantor's lifetime (*i.e.*, a trust not established by a will).

intestacy laws State laws determining the division and descent of an intestate's (one who dies with no will) estate.

intestate (Dying) without a valid will.

inventory Goods held for sale or lease or to be furnished under contracts of service, including work in process and materials used or consumed in a business.

Inventory of a person is not to be classified as equipment. (see UCC 9–109(4))

invitee A person who, either expressly or impliedly, is privileged to enter upon another's land. The inviter owes the invitee the duty to exercise reasonable care to protect an individual from harm (*e.g.*, a customer in a store, the postman).

involuntary bankruptcy A proceeding against an insolvent debtor which is initiated by the debtor's creditors.

irrevocable offer An offer which cannot be revoked or recalled by the offeror without liability. (see UCC 2–205, firm offers)

issue The first delivery of an instrument to a holder or a remitter. (see UCC 3–102(1))

issued shares Stock which has been authorized and sold to subscribers. Such may include treasury shares. (see *authorized* and *treasury shares*)

J

joint and several liability Liability of a group of persons for the same act (or failure to act) whereby a claimant may sue one or more of the parties separately or all of them together.

joint liability Liability of a group of persons for the same wrongful act (or failure to act) whereby when one is sued, that party can insist that the others be sued as co-defendants.

joint tenancy The ownership interest of two or more co-owners of property whereby each owns an undivided portion of the property. The key feature of joint tenancy is the "right of survivorship" whereby, upon the death of one of the joint tenants, his or her interest automatically passes to the others and cannot be transferred by the will of the deceased.

judgment creditor A person in whose favor a money judgment has been entered by a court of law and who has not yet been paid.

judgment debt A monetary obligation which is either evidenced by a written record, or brought about by successful legal action against the debtor.

judgment n.o.v. A judgment n.o.v. is a judgment that may be entered by the court for the plaintiff (or the defendant) after there has been a jury verdict for the defendant (or plaintiff).

judgment rate of interest A rate of interest fixed by statute which is applied to a monetary judgment from the moment the judgment is awarded by a court until the judgment is paid or terminated. (see *judgment debt*)

judicial review The authority of a court to re-examine a previously considered dispute, especially the appeal of a lower court or the decision of an administrative agency.

jurisdiction The authority of a court to hear and decide a specific action.

jurisprudence The science or philosophy of law.

justice Justice is generally perceived as one of the primary goals of our legal system. The term refers to the ideal of being just, impartial, and fair.

L

laches The equitable doctrine which bars a party's right due to neglect for an unreasonable length of time to do what should have been done.

laissez-faire A doctrine advocating government restraint in regulation of business.

larceny The act of taking another's personal property unlawfully. Some states classify larceny as either grand or petit, depending on the property's value.

law Enforceable rules of conduct to be followed by citizens of a society, as pronounced by that society's government.

law merchant Relates chiefly to rules resulting from resolution of disputes and transactions of merchants, mariners, and other commercial traders. Consists chiefly of the general customs of the trades, which remain law unless displaced by specific statutes. (see UCC 1–103)

lease A transfer by the landlord/lessor of real or personal property to the tenant/lessee for a period of time, for a consideration (usually the payment of rent). Upon termination of the lease, the property reverts to the lessor.

leasehold estate An estate in realty held by a tenant under a lease. In every leasehold estate, the tenant has a qualified right to possess and/or use the land.

legal rate of interest A rate of interest fixed by statute as either the maximum rate of interest permitted to be charged by law, or a rate of interest to be applied when the parties to a contract intend an interest rate to be paid but do not fix the rate in the contract. Even in the latter case, frequently this rate is the same as the statutory maximum rate permitted.

legality Lawfulness.

legally sufficient consideration Consideration which the law recognizes as legally adequate to support a valid contract. (see *consideration*)

lessee A person who pays for the use or possession of another's property.

lessor A property owner who allows others to use his or her property in exchange for payment of rent.

letter of credit A written instrument, usually issued by a bank on behalf of a customer or other person, in which the issuer promises to honor drafts or other demands for payment by third persons in accordance with the terms of the instrument. (see UCC 5–103(1)(a))

levy A legal seizure of property in order to obtain money.

libel A written defamation of one's character or reputation. The press is, to a limited degree, protected from libel actions by the First Amendment.

license A revocable privilege to enter on the land of another.

lien An encumbrance upon a property, to satisfy or protect a claim for payment of a debt.

lien creditor One whose debt or claim is secured by a lien on particular property, as distinguished from a general creditor, who has no such security.

life estate An interest in land which exists only for the duration of the life of some person, usually the holder of the estate.

limited liability A concept in corporation or limited partnership law whereby the shareholders' or limited partners' liability for debts incurred by the corporation or limited partnership are limited to the money which the shareholders or limited partners invested in the corporation or limited partnership.

limited partnership A partnership consisting of one or more general partners who carry on the business as well as contribute assets and who are liable to the full extent of their personal assets for debts of the partnership, and of one or more limited partners, who contribute only assets and who are liable only up to the amount contributed by them.

limited payment life A type of life insurance for which premiums are payable for a definite period, after which the policy is fully paid.

liquidated damages An amount, stipulated in the contract, which the parties believe to be a reasonable estimation of the damages which will occur in the event of a breach.

liquidated debt A debt which is for a known or ascertainable sum of money, the amount of which cannot be disputed by either the debtor or creditor.

liquidation The sale of the assets of a business or an individual for cash and the distribution of the cash received to creditors with the balance going to the owner(s).

long arm statute Through long arm statutes, states permit personal jurisdiction to be obtained over nonresident individuals and corporations. Individuals or corporations, however, must have certain "minimum contacts" with that state.

lost property Property which the owner has involuntarily parted with and does not know where to find or recover it.

M

maker One who issues a promissory note or certificate of deposit (*i.e.*, one who promises to pay a certain sum to the holder of the note or CD). (see *drawer*)

marshalling assets The arrangement or ranking of assets in a certain order towards the payment of debts. In equity, when two creditors have recourse to the same property of the debtor, but one has recourse to other property of the debtor, that creditor must resort first to those assets of the debtor not available to the other creditor.

mechanic's lien A statutory lien filed against the entire realty for labor, services, or materials performed in improving or repairing the realty.

merchant A person "who deals in goods of the kind" or who "holds himself out as having knowledge or skills peculiar" to the trade or goods involved, or to whom such skills can be attributed because of the nature of his or her employment. (see UCC 2–104(1))

merchant's firm offer A signed, written offer to buy or sell goods, which by its terms will be held open for a certain time, without requiring consideration. The UCC limits merchants' firm offers to a maximum of three months. (see *firm offer*, UCC 2–205)

merger A contractual process by which one corporation (the surviving corporation) acquires all the assets and liabilities of another corporation (the merged corporation). The shareholders of the merged corporation receive either payment for their shares or shares in the surviving corporation (*i.e.*, A + B = A).

mirror image rule A common law rule which requires, for a valid contractual agreement, that the terms of an offeree's acceptance must adhere exactly to the terms of the offeror's offer.

misdemeanors Lesser crimes, punishable by fine or imprisonment in other than a state or federal penitentiary, as opposed to felonies. (see *felony*)

mislaid property Property which the owner has voluntarily parted with, with the intention of retrieving it later, but which cannot now be found. Does not include intentionally hidden property. (see *lost property*)

mitigation of damages A doctrine which imposes on an injured party the duty to exercise reasonable diligence in attempting to minimize his or her damages after an injury has been inflicted. This is sometimes called the doctrine of "avoidable consequences." (see *damages*)

mortgage A written instrument giving a creditor (the mortgagee) an interest (lien) in the debtor's (mortgagor's) property as security for a debt.

mortgagee The creditor who takes the security interest under the mortgage agreement.

mortgagor The debtor who pledges collateral in a mortgage agreement.

motion to dismiss See demurrer.

municipal law Municipal or national law (as opposed to international law) is that law which pertains to a particular nation. It is not uncommon for a country's municipal law to come into conflict with international law.

mutual assent A meeting of the minds and a manifestation of intent of the parties to a contract, whereby each party agrees to the terms and conditions in both the same sense and meaning.

mutual rescission An agreement between the parties to cancel their contract, releasing the parties from further obligations under the contract. The object of the agreement is to restore the parties to positions they would have occupied had no contract ever been made. (see *rescission*)

N

natural law Certain individuals believe that natural law exists. They assert that there are certain rules and principles for the guidance of human conduct that may be discovered through the use of reason.

necessaries Goods and services, such as food, shelter, clothing and employment, which are legally deemed essential for a person's well-being.

negative easement A burden on land whereby the landowner is restricted under an easement agreement not to use his property in a certain way (*e.g.*, not to build a building higher than four stories so as to preserve an adjacent landholder's view).

negligence Conduct which falls below that standard of care which would be exercised by a "reasonable person" in relation to the protection of others. A legal duty is inherent in negligence. (see *tort*)

negotiable instruments A written and signed unconditional promise or order to pay a specified sum of money on demand or at a definite time payable to order or bearer. (see UCC 3–104(1))

negotiation The transferring of a negotiable instrument to another in such form that the transferee becomes a holder. (see UCC 3–202)

nominal damages An award of damages whereby a court recognizes that there has been a technical breach of duty but has found that no financial loss or injury has resulted from the breach of duty.

nonconforming use A use which does not comply to present zoning provisions but which previously existed lawfully and was created in good faith prior to the revision, amendment, or enactment of the zoning provision.

novation A mutual agreement for the release of an old debt or debtor with the substitution of a new one, whereby the old debt is extinguished.

nuisance An act which interferes unlawfully with a person's possession or ability to use his or her property.

O

objective theory of contracts The view taken by American law that contracting parties shall only be bound by terms which can be actually inferred from promises made. Contract law does not examine a contracting party's subjective intent or underlying motive.

offer A proposal to do something by an offeror which creates in the offeree a legal power to bind the offeror to the terms of the proposal by accepting the offer.

offeree One to whom an offer is made.

offeror A person who makes an offer.

open policy An insurance policy in which the value of the object insured is left by parties to be estimated in case of loss. (see *valued policy*)

option contract A contract whereby the offeror cannot revoke his or her offer for a stipulated time period, and the offeree can accept or reject during this period without fear of the offer being made to another person. The offeree must give consideration for the option (the irrevocable offer) to be enforceable.

order paper A negotiable instrument which is payable to a specific payee or to any person the payee, by his or her indorsement, designates. (see UCC 3–110 and 3–204)

ordinary bailment A transfer of goods or personal property to the bailee in trust for the bailor, with the bailee to hold the goods according to the bailment agreement for the benefit of the bailor, bailee, or both. Upon termination, the bailee is required to return the bailed property to the bailor or dispose of it according to the bailor's directions. The bailee is responsible for exercising due care toward the goods.

output contract A binding agreement where a seller agrees to deliver/sell the seller's entire output of a good (an unspecified amount at the time of agreement) to a buyer, and the buyer agrees to buy all of the goods supplied.

outstanding shares Issued shares of stock less treasury shares. (see *issued shares, treasury shares*)

P

parol evidence rule A substantive rule of contracts under which a court will not receive into evidence oral or written statements made prior to or contemporaneous with a written agreement where the court finds that the written agreement was intended by the parties to be a final, complete, and unambiguous expression of their agreement.

partially disclosed principal A principal whose identity is unknown by the third party, but the third party knows that the agent is or may be acting for a principal at the time the contract is made.

partnership An association of two or more persons to carry on, as co-owners, a business for profit. (see UPA Section 6(1))

partnership at will A partnership which, by the terms of the articles of partnership, may be dissolved at any time by any of the partners.

partnership by estoppel Two or more persons who hold themselves out as partners to a third person, when in fact they are not partners, are barred from claiming they are not partners.

past consideration An act done before the contract is made, which is ordinarily by itself no consideration for a later promise to pay for the act.

patent A government grant to an inventor giving the inventor the exclusive right or privilege to make, use, or sell his or her invention for a limited time period (presently seventeen years). The word "patent" ordinarily refers to some invention and designates either the instrument by which patent rights are evidenced or the patent itself. (See 69 C.J.S. Patents § 1)

payee A person to whom an instrument is made payable.

payor bank A bank by which an item is payable as drawn (or is payable as accepted). (see UCC 4–105(b))

penalty A sum inserted in a contract, not as a measure of compensation for its breach, but rather as punishment for a default. The agreement as to the amount will not be enforced, and recovery will be limited to actual damages.

per capita The method of distribution of property whereby the heirs to an intestate's estate share and share alike. (antithesis of *per stirpes*)

perfect tender rule A strict doctrine, whereby tender of performance/goods which does not exactly conform to the contract can properly be rejected. (see *tender, substantial performance*)

perfection The method by which a secured party obtains a priority by notice that the security interest in the debtor's collateral cannot be challenged by a subsequent party. Usually accomplished by filing a financing statement at a location set out in the state statute. (see *secured party, security interest, financing statement*)

periodic tendency A lease interest in land for an indefinite period where payment of rent is at fixed intervals, such as week to week, month to month, year to year.

per se By itself, without reference to other matters.

personal property Property which is movable; any property which is not real property. (see *real property*)

per stirpes A manner of distribution of property whereby a class or group of distributees take the share which their deceased ancestor would have been entitled to (*e.g.*, A dies leaving one son, B, and two grandchildren of deceased daughter C. B takes one-half and the two grandchildren each take one-quarter—see *per capita*).

piercing the corporate veil A court's act of ignoring the separate legal existence of the corporation and thereby holding the corporation's shareholders personally liable for the corporation's wrongdoings.

plaintiff The party bringing an action.

plat A chart or map, usually filed with a municipal or county clerk, which delineates the parcels into which a large tract of land has been subdivided.

plat map A plat which gives legal descriptions of pieces of property by lot, street, and block numbers.

pleadings Statements by the plaintiff and the defendant which detail the facts, charges, and defenses. Modern rules simplify common law pleading, often requiring only the complaint, answer, and sometimes a reply to the answer.

pledge The bailment of personal property to a creditor as security for the payment of a debt.

police powers States possess police powers as part of their inherent sovereignty. These powers may be exercised to protect or promote the public health, safety, morals, or general welfare.

policy In insurance, the contract of indemnity against a contingent loss between the insurer and insured.

possibility of reverter A future interest in land which a grantor retains after conveying property subject to a condition subsequent. (see *future interest*)

power of attorney A document or instrument authorizing another to act as one's agent or attorney.

power of termination A future interest in land which results when a grantor conveys land subject to a condition subsequent but also conditions the reversion of the land on the affirmative retaking of possession either by the grantor or his/her heirs.

precedent A court decision which furnishes an example or authority for deciding subsequent cases in which identical or similar facts are presented. (see *stare decisis*)

pre-emptive right A shareholder's right to purchase newly issued stock of a corporation, before it is offered to any outside buyers, equal in percentage to shares presently held, enabling the shareholder to maintain proportionate ownership and voice in the corporation.

preferential transfer A transfer by an insolvent debtor to one or more of his or her creditors whereby the creditor to whom the property was transferred is put in a better position than other creditors with respect to their priority claims to the assets of the insolvent. (see Bankruptcy Reform Act–Section 547)

preferred stock Classes of stock which have priority over common stock both as to payment of dividends and distribution of assets upon the corporation's dissolution.

premium In insurance, the price for insurance protection for a specified period of exposure.

prenuptial agreement An agreement made by the parties to a marriage prior to the marriage. If the consideration for the agreement is the forthcoming marriage, there must be a signed writing to make the agreement enforceable. (see *Statute of Frauds*)

prescription The acquiring of an easement (or profit) by continuous and open use of land owned by another for a prescribed statutory period. (see *adverse possession*)

presentment Demand by a holder of a commercial paper for payment (or acceptance). (see UCC 3–504(1))

presentment warranty A warranty impliedly made, by any person who seeks payment or acceptance of a negotiable instrument to any person who in good faith pays or accepts the instrument, that the party presenting has good title to the instrument or is authorized to obtain payment or acceptance on behalf of a person who has good title; has no knowledge that the signature of a maker or the drawer is unauthorized; and that the instrument has not been materially altered. (see UCC 3–417(1), 3–418)

price discrimination Exists when two competing buyers pay two different prices for an identical product or service.

prima facie (Latin) "at first sight." Something that is considered true because, on the face of it, it appears to be true. A presumption until disproved by contrary evidence.

principal In agency, a person who, by agreement or otherwise, authorizes an agent to act on his or her behalf such that the acts of the agent become binding on the principal.

private law That portion of the law which defines, regulates, enforces, and administers relationships among individuals, associations, and corporations, in contradistinction to public law. (see *public law*)

privilege In tort law, the ability to act contrary to another person's right without that person having legal redress for such acts. Privilege is usually raised as a defense, such as where A attacks B, B has a privilege to fight back to reasonably protect himself or herself without B being liable for the tort of assault and battery. (see *assault and battery*)

privity of contract The relationship which exists between the promisor and promisee of a contract.

probable cause Reasonable grounds to believe the existence of facts warranting certain actions such as the search or arrest of a person.

probate The process of proving and validating a will, and the settling of all matters pertaining to administration, guardianship, and like matters.

probate court A special court, in some jurisdictions, having jurisdiction of proceedings concerning the settlement of a person's estate. (see *jurisdiction, estate, probate*)

procedural law Rules which deal with the manner of bringing an action. Sometimes referred to as adjective law as opposed to substantive law. (see *substantive law*)

procedure The manner by which parties and courts must act when bringing an action, whether civil, criminal, or administrative. Includes pleading, process of service, evidence, and practice.

proceeds In secured transactions law, whatever is received when the collateral is sold, exchanged, collected, or otherwise disposed of, such as insurance payments from destroyed or lost collateral. Money, checks, and the like are "cash proceeds," while all other proceeds received are "noncash proceeds." (see UCC 9–306)

profit In real property law, the right to enter upon and remove things from the property of another (*e.g.*, the right to enter onto a person's land and remove sand and gravel therefrom). Sometimes referred to as profits *a prendre*.

promise A declaration which binds the person who makes it (promisor) to do or forbear from a certain act. The person to whom the promise is made (promisee) has a right to expect or demand the performance of some particular thing.

promisee The person to whom a promise is made.

promisor The person who makes a promise.

promissory estoppel A doctrine which arises when there is a promise which the promisor should reasonably expect to induce action or forbearance of a definite and substantial character on the part of the promisee, and which does induce such action or forbearance in reliance thereon; such a promise is binding if injustice can be avoided only through enforcement of the promise.

promissory note A written instrument signed by a maker unconditionally promising to pay a sum certain in money to a payee or a holder on demand or on a specified date. (see UCC 3–104)

promoter An entrepreneur who participates in the organization of a newly formed corporation, usually by issuing a prospectus, procuring subscriptions to the stock, making contract purchases, securing a charter, and the like. Promoters generally assume substantial risks in organizing new corporations, but also stand to realize significant profits from their efforts.

property Anything subject to being used, possessed, and disposed of; need not be tangible ("rights" are property).

proximate cause The "next" or "substantial" cause; in tort law, a concept used to determine whether a plaintiff's injury was the natural and continuous result of a defendant's negligent act. If the negligent act of a defendant was the sole cause or was a substantial cause of injuries to a plaintiff, the defendant will be liable to the plaintiff.

proxy In corporation law, a written agreement between a stockholder and another under which the stockholder authorizes the other to vote the stockholder's shares in a certain manner.

public law That portion of law that defines rights and duties with either the operation of government, or the relationships between the government and individuals, associations, and corporations. (see *private law*)

punitive damages Compensation in excess of actual or consequential damages. They are awarded in order to punish the wrongdoer, and will be awarded only in cases involving willful or malicious misconduct. (see *exemplary damages*)

purchase money security interest A security interest to the extent that it is: (1) taken or retained by a seller of the collateral to secure all or part of its price; or (2) taken by a creditor who, by making advances or incurring an obligation, gives value to enable the debtor to acquire rights in or use of collateral, if such value is in fact so used. (see UCC 9–107)

Q

qualified indorsement An indorsement on a negotiable instrument under which the indorser disclaims to subsequent holders secondary liability on the instrument; under a qualified indorsement, however, an indorser still gives the normal transfer warranties except the qualified indorser warrants only that "he has no knowledge" that a defense of "any party is good against him . . . ." The most common qualified indorsement is "without recourse." (see UCC 3–417(2)(3))

quasi-contract An obligation or contract imposed by law, in the absence of agreement, to prevent unjust enrichment. Sometimes referred to as implied-in-law contracts (as a legal fiction) to distinguish them from

implied-in-fact contracts (voluntary agreements inferred from the parties' conduct). (see *contract, implied-in-fact contract*)

quasi in rem jurisdiction This refers to proceedings that are brought against the defendant personally. Yet it is the defendant's interest in the property that serves as the basis of the jurisdiction.

quasi-judicial power The power of an administrative agency to adjudicate the rights of persons before it.

quasi-legislative The power of an administrative agency to engage in rule-making.

quitclaim deed A deed conveying whatever title or interest the grantor has in the real property, but warranting nothing, not even the transferor's title, to the grantee.

quorum The number of persons who must be present (or shares represented) at a meeting in order for valid actions taken at the meeting. (see Model Business Corporation Act, §§ 32 and 40)

R

rate-making power Government power to determine and set rates for business (*e.g.*, wage rate, prices).

ratification In contract law, the act of adopting or confirming a previous act which without ratification would not be an enforceable contractual obligation, or confirming an obligation by one without the authority to make or do (or who was incompetent at the time the contract was made). The act of ratification causes the obligation to be binding as if such was valid and enforceable in the first instance.

reality of assent Despite the apparent mutual assent of the parties, a defect exists in the intention or minds of the parties (such as fraud, duress, undue influence, or mistake) which can render the contract void or voidable. (see *mutual assent, duress, fraud,* and *undue influence*)

real property Property consisting of land and buildings thereupon, which are stationary, as opposed to personal property, which can be moved. In the absence of a contract, real property includes things growing on the land before they are severed (such as timber) as well as fixtures. (see UCC 2–107)

reasonable doubt The standard used to determine the guilt or innocence of a person criminally charged. To be guilty of a crime, one must be proved guilty "beyond and to the exclusion of every reasonable doubt." A doubt that would cause prudent persons to hesitate before acting in matters important to themselves.

rebuttal A rebuttal refers to evidence that is given by one party to refute evidence that has been introduced by an adverse party.

recognizance A formal obligation to do a certain act as recorded and required by a court, such as an obligation to return or reappear before a court without putting up a bail bond.

recording statutes Recording statutes for deeds, mortgages, etc. are enacted to provide notice to future purchasers, creditors, and encumbrancers of an existing claim.

reformation A court-ordered correction of a written instrument to cause it to reflect the true intentions of the parties.

rejection An offeree's communication to an offeror that the offeree refuses to accept the terms of the proposal made by the offeror. (see *counter-offer*)

rejoinder In a rejoinder, the defendant's attorney answers the plaintiff's rebuttal.

release The relinquishment, concession, or giving up of a right, claim, or privilege, by the person in whom it exists or to whom it accrues, to the person against whom it might have been enforced or demanded.

remainder A future interest in property held by a person other than a grantor which occurs at the natural termination of the preceding estate. For example, G transfers real property in trust with income therefrom to A for life with the remainder to B upon A's death. B has a remainder interest. A remainder is a present right to a future interest in property and can either be vested or contingent.

remand The act of an appellate court when it sends a case back to the trial court and orders the trial court to conduct limited new hearings or an entirely new trial, or to take some other further action.

remedy The term remedy refers to the rights that are given to individuals, by law or by contract, upon the happening of a particular event.

remedy at law A remedy at law is a legal remedy that is available in a court of law. Money damages are awarded as a remedy at law. This remedy is to be distinguished from a remedy in equity.

remedy in equity A remedy allowed by courts in situations where remedies at law are not appropriate. Remedies in equity are based on settled rules of fairness, justice, and honesty.

replevin An action in equity brought to recover possession of personal property unlawfully held by another. (see *conversion*, UCC 2–716(3))

reply Procedurally, a plaintiff's response to a defendant's answer.

repudiation The rejection of a contract due to the unconditional refusal by one of the parties to perform. (see UCC 2–610, 2–703, 2–711)

requirements contract An agreement under which a promisor promises to supply the promisee with all the goods and/or services the promisee might require from period to period. While such contracts were at one time void for indefiniteness of amount, they are now universally valid. (see UCC 2–306(1))

rescission A remedy whereby the contract is cancelled and the parties are returned to the positions they occupied before the contract was made. May be done through mutual consent of the parties, by their conduct, or by the decree of a court of equity.

res judicata A rule that prohibits the same factual dispute between two parties to be retried by a court after final judgment has been entered by a trial court and all appeals have been exhausted (or the time for appeal has passed).

respondeat superior A principle of law whereby an employer is held liable for the wrongful acts committed by employees while within the scope of their employment. (see *vicarious liability*)

restitution An equitable remedy under which a person is restored to his or her original position prior to loss or injury, or placed in the same position as if a breach had not occurred. (see UCC 2–718)

restrictive indorsement Any indorsement of a negotiable instrument which purports to condition or prohibit further transfer of the instrument. As against payor and intermediary banks, such indorsements are usually ineffective. (see UCC 3–205)

resulting trust A trust implied in law from the intentions of the parties to a given transaction. A trust in which a party holds legal title for the benefit of another, although without expressed intent to do so, because the presumption of such intent arises by operation of law.

reversion A future interest under which a grantor retains a present right to a future interest in property which the grantor conveys to another; usually the residue of a life estate. The reversion is always a vested property right.

revocation The recall of some power, authority, or thing granted, or a destroying or making void of some will, deed, or offer that had been valid until revoked.

right of contribution In tort law, the right of a tortfeasor against whom judgment has been rendered to recover proportional shares of judgment from other joint tortfeasors whose negligence contributed to the injury and who are also liable to the plaintiff.

right of redemption The right to free property from the encumbrance of a foreclosure or judicial sale, or to recover the title passing thereby, by paying what is due, with all costs and interest. Includes both equity and statutory periods of redemption.

right of reimbursement The legal right of a person to be restored, repaid, or indemnified for costs, expenses, or losses incurred or expended on behalf of another.

right-to-work laws State laws generally providing that employees are not to be required to join a union as a condition of receiving or retaining employment.

risk A specified contingency or peril.

robbery Theft from a person, accompanied by force or fear of force. (see *assault, battery*)

rule against perpetuities A rule against remoteness in vesting which states: "no interest in property is good unless it must vest, if at all, not later than 21 years, plus a period of gestation, after some life or lives in being at the time of creation of the interest."

Rule 10b-5 A rule by the Securities and Exchange Commission which makes it unlawful, in connection with the purchase or sale of any security, to make any untrue statement of a material fact or to omit to state a material fact necessary in order to make the statements made, in light of circumstances under which they were made, not misleading. (see 10-b of Securities Exchange Act, 15 U.S.C.A. 78(j)(b))

S

sale The passing of title to property from the seller to the buyer for a price. (see UCC 2–106(1))

sale on approval A type of conditional sale which becomes absolute only when the buyer, on trial, approves or is satisfied with the good(s) sold. Besides expressly approving the goods, approval may be inferred if the buyer keeps the goods beyond a reasonable time, or does any act with the goods which is inconsistent with the seller's ownership. (see *sale or return*, UCC 2–326 and 2–327)

sale or return A type of conditional sale wherein title and possession pass from the seller to the buyer; however, the buyer retains the option to rescind or return the goods during a specified period even though the goods conform to the contract. (see *sale on approval*, UCC 3–236 and UCC 2–327)

satisfaction The tender of substitute performance in return for the relinquishment of the right of action on a prior obligation. (see *accord and satisfaction*)

scienter Guilty knowledge of the defendant as to the act or omission which led to the injury or conduct complained of.

scope of employment The activities in which an employee engages in the carrying out of the employer's business which are reasonably foreseeable by the employer. (see *respondeat superior, vicarious liability*)

S corporation A close business corporation which has met certain requirements as set out by the Internal Revenue Code qualifies for special income tax treatment. Essentially, an S corporation is taxed the same as a partnership while at the same time allowing the corporation's owners to enjoy the privilege of limited liability.

secondary boycott Refusal to work for, purchase from, or handle products of secondary employer with whom the union has no dispute, with the object of forcing such employer to stop doing business with the primary employer with whom the union has a labor dispute.

secured Supported or backed by security or collateral, such as a mortgage, lien, pledge, or other security interest.

secured party The lender, seller, or other person in whose favor there is a security interest. (see *security interest*, UCC 9–105(1)(m))

secured transaction Any transaction, regardless of its form, which is intended to create a security interest in personal property or fixtures, including goods, documents, and other intangibles. (see UCC 9–105)

securities Stock certificates, bonds, notes, debentures, warrants, or other documents given as evidence of an ownership interest in the corporation or as a promise of repayment by the corporation.

security agreement An agreement which creates or provides for a security interest. (see *security interest*, UCC 9–105(1)(l))

security interest An interest in personal property or fixtures which secures payment or performance of an obligation. (see UCC 1–201(37))

self-defense The legally recognized privilege to protect one's self or one's property against injury by another. The privilege of self-defense only protects acts which are reasonably necessary to protect one's self or one's property.

service mark A mark used in the sale or advertising of services, such as to distinguish the services of one person from the services of others. Titles, character names, and other distinctive features of radio and television programs may be registered as service marks.

severable contract A contract which includes two or more promises which can be acted on separately such that the failure to perform one promise does not necessarily put the promisor in breach of the entire agreement.

shareholder The holder of an ownership interest by shares of stock in a corporation or joint-stock company.

shelter principle A holder of a negotiable instrument who cannot qualify as a holder in due course, but who derives his or her title through a holder in due course, acquires the rights of a holder in due course. (see UCC 3-201 and *assignment*)

shipment contract Any agreement for the sale of goods under which the seller is authorized or required only to bear the expense of putting the goods in the hands of a common carrier and bears the risk of loss only up to that point. A contract for the sale of goods which is silent on a delivery term is presumed to be a shipment contract. (see UCC 2–319, 2–504, 2–509(1))

shop right doctrine An employer's privilege to use an invention developed during work hours by an employee using employer's equipment and/or materials, without compensating that employee.

short-form merger A merger between a parent corporation and a subsidiary corporation where the parent corporation owns at least ninety percent of the outstanding shares of each class of stock issued by the subsidiary corporation. These mergers can be accomplished without shareholder approval of either corporation. (see Model Business Corporation Act § 75)

short-swing profits Profits made on the purchase and sale of stock of a corporation within a six-month period by an insider.

sight draft A draft which is payable upon proper presentment. (see UCC 3–108, 3–109(1)(b))

signature The name or mark of a person, written by that person at his or her direction. In commercial law, any name, word, or mark used with the intention to authenticate a writing constitutes a signature. (see UCC 1–201(39), 3–401(2))

slander An oral defamation of one's character, reputation, business, or property rights. (see *libel*)

sole proprietorship A business which is owned and operated by a single person (or his or her immediate family) which is not a partnership or a corporation incorporated under the laws of the domiciliary state. (see *partnership, corporation*)

sovereign immunity Sovereign immunity is a doctrine under which a nonsovereign party is precluded from asserting a cause of action against a sovereign party unless the sovereign party consents.

special bailment Generally a bailment in which by law a bailee is given greater duties and liabilities than those imposed on an ordinary bailee. Innkeepers and common carrier bailees are examples. (see *bailment, ordinary bailment, strict liability*)

special indorsement An indorsement of an instrument specifying to whom or to whose order the instrument is payable. (see UCC 3–204(1))

specific performance An equitable remedy, whereby the court orders one of the parties to a contract to perform duties under the contract. Usually granted when money damages would be an inadequate remedy and the object of the contract is unique (*e.g.*, purchase and sale of real property). (see UCC 2–716(1)(2))

spendthrift trust A trust created to protect the beneficiary from spending all the money he or she is entitled to. Only a certain portion of the total amount is given to the beneficiary at any one time, and most states prohibit creditors from attaching assets of the trust.

stale check A check, other than a certified check, which is presented more than six months after its date. (see UCC 4–404)

standing to sue The requirement of standing to sue means that an individual must have a sufficient stake in a controversy in order to sue. The plaintiff must demonstrate that he or she either is injured or has been threatened with injury.

stare decisis A flexible doctrine of the courts, recognizing the value of following prior decisions (precedents) in cases similar to the one before the court— the practice by the courts of being consistent with prior decisions based on similar facts. (see *precedent*)

Statute of Frauds The statutory requirement (based on English common law) that certain types of contracts be written to be enforceable (*e.g.*, contracts for the sale of goods priced at $500 or more; contracts for the sale of land; contracts which cannot, by their terms, be performed within a year; and contracts to guaranty the debt of another). (see UCC 2–201)

statute of limitations Statutes of the federal government and the various states setting maximum time periods during which certain actions can be brought or rights enforced. After the time period set out in the applicable statute of limitations has run, no legal action can be brought regardless of whether any cause of action ever existed. (see *laches* for equitable doctrine)

statutory law Laws which are enacted by a legislative body (as opposed to constitutional law, administrative law or case law).

statutory period of redemption A time period (usually set by state statute) during which a defaulted mortgage, land contract, etc. can be redeemed after foreclosure or judicial sale. (see *right of redemption*)

stock warrant A certificate commonly attached to preferred stock and bonds granting one the right to buy shares of stock, usually within a set time period.

stop payment order An order by a drawer of a draft or check directing the drawer's bank not to pay a check. (see UCC 4–403)

strict liability Liability regardless of fault. Under tort law, strict liability is imposed on any merchant seller who introduces into commerce any good which is unreasonably dangerous when in a defective condition.

sublease A lease executed by the lessee of land to a third person, conveying the same interest which the lessee enjoys, but for a shorter term than that for which the lessee holds (as compared to assignment, where the lessee transfers the entire unexpired term of the leasehold to a third party).

subrogation The substitution of one person in the place of another giving the former the same legal rights which the latter had. Subrogation appears most frequently in construction contracts, insurance contracts, suretyship, and negotiable instrument law.

substantial performance A doctrine of commercial reasonableness which recognizes that the rendering of a performance which does not exactly meet the terms of the agreement (slight deviation) will be looked upon as fulfillment of the obligation, less the damages which result from any deviation from the promised performance. (see *condition*, which does not permit deviation)

substantive law Laws which define the rights and duties of individuals with respect to each other, as opposed to procedural law which defines the manner in which these rights and duties may be enforced.

summary judgment A judgment entered by a trial court prior to trial which is based upon the valid assertion by one of the parties that there are no disputed issues of fact which would necessitate a trial.

surety One who agrees to pay the debt of another. A strict surety is liable to the creditor, even if the creditor does not seek to collect from the principal debtor first at due date. (see *suretyship, guaranty*)

suretyship The relationship among three parties whereby one person (the surety) guarantees payment of a debtor's debt owed to a creditor or acts as a co-debtor. (see *guaranty*)

surviving corporation The corporation which, through a merger, acquires the assets and liabilities of another corporation.

sympathy strike A strike in which a union strikes not to gain concessions for itself, but to aid another union's objectives.

T

tangible personal property Property, which can be moved, which has physical substance, and which can be distinguished by the five senses; corporeal property. (see *intangible property*)

tenancy at sufferance The situation whereby one who, after rightfully being in possession of leased premises, continues to occupy the property after the lease has been terminated. The tenant has no estate in the land. He or she occupies only because the person entitled to evict has not done so.

tenancy at will The right of a tenant to remain in possession of land with permission of the landlord until either the tenant or the landlord chooses to terminate the tenancy.

tenancy by the entirety The joint ownership of property by husband and wife. Neither party can alienate or encumber the property without the consent of the other. It is inherited by the survivor of the two, and dissolution of marriage transforms it to tenancy in common.

tenancy for years A non-freehold estate/lease for a specified number of years, at which time the interest reverts to the grantor.

tenancy from period to period (periodic tenancy) A non-freehold estate/lease which exists for a specified period of one year or less, automatically renewed for a like period until terminated (*e.g.*, month-to-month).

tenancy in common Co-ownership of property whereby each party owns an undivided interest that passes to his or her heirs at death. (see *joint tenancy*)

tender A timely offer, or expression of willingness, to pay a debt or perform an obligation.

term A word or phrase in a contract, instrument, or agreement which relates to a particular matter; also a fixed period of time. (see UCC 1–201(42))

testamentary trust A trust which is created by will and therefore does not take effect until the death of the testator.

testate Leaving a valid will; when a person dies leaving a valid will, he or she dies testate. (see *intestate*)

testator (-trix) One who makes and executes a will. (see *will*)

third party beneficiary contract A contract between two or more parties, the performance of which is intended to directly benefit a third party, thus giving the third party a right to file suit for breach of contract by either of the original contracting parties. (see *donee beneficiary* and *creditor beneficiary*)

title The formal right of ownership of property.

title insurance An insurance policy which insures against defects in the title to real property.

tort Civil (as opposed to criminal) wrongs not arising from a breach of contract; a breach of a legal duty owed by the defendant to the plaintiff. That breach must be the proximate cause of the harm done to plaintiff. (see *proximate cause, negligence*)

tortfeasor One who commits a personal wrong (or a tort).

totten trust A trust created by the deposit of a person's own money in his or her own name as a trustee for another. It is a tentative trust, revocable at will until the depositor dies or completes the gift in his or her lifetime by some unequivocal act or declaration.

trade acceptance A bill of exchange/draft drawn by the seller of goods on the purchaser and accepted by such purchaser. Once accepted, the purchaser becomes primarily liable to pay the draft. (see UCC 3–413(1))

trade fixture Articles placed in or attached to buildings by the tenant, to carry on the tenant's business. Such fixtures usually retain the character of personal property.

trademark A word or symbol which has become sufficiently associated with a good (common law) or has been registered with a government agency. Once established, the owner has exclusive use and has the right to bring a legal action against those who infringe upon the protection given the trademark. The remedy may be criminal, money damages, or an injunction against the defendant. (see *injunction*)

trade name A name used in commercial activity to designate a particular business, or place at which a business is located, or a class of goods. Trade names can be exclusive or non-exclusive. They differ from trademarks, because trade names are not usually affixed to goods sent into the market. Examples of trade names are Sears, Safeway, Firestone, and Austin Vacuum Cleaner Co. (see 87 C.J.S. Trademarks, Trade Names, and Competition § 8)

traveler's check An instrument purchased from a bank, express company, or the like, in various denominations, which can be used as cash upon a second signature by the purchaser. It has the characteristics of a cashier's check. (see *cashier's check*)

treasury shares Shares of corporate stock which have been issued as fully paid that are subsequently reacquired by the corporation.

trespass Any wrongful transgression or offense against the property of another.

trespass to land At common law, the mere intentional or unintentional passing over another person's land uninvited, regardless whether any physical damage was done to the land. Today a majority of courts find trespass only in cases of intentional intrusion, negligence, or some "abnormally dangerous activity" on the part of the defendant. (see Restatement, Second, Torts, Section 166)

trespass to personalty Same as trespass.

true bill Often called an indictment, the true bill is issued by the grand jury after a finding of probable cause to accuse a person of a criminal offense. (see *information, grand jury*)

trustee One who holds legal title to property "in trust" for the benefit of another person (beneficiary) and who must carry out specific duties with regard to the property. The trustee owes a fiduciary duty to the beneficiary. (see *fiduciary duty*)

trustee in bankruptcy The person appointed to administer the estate of a bankrupt (debtor).

tying agreement A requirement in a contract between a buyer and seller whereby the buyer of a specific good is obligated to purchase additional products or services.

U

ultra vires Activities of a corporation's managers which are outside the scope of the power granted them by its charter or the laws of the state of incorporation.

unconscionable contract or clause A contract or clause which is void as against public policy because one party, as a result of his or her disproportionate bargaining power, is forced to accept terms which are unfairly burdensome and which unfairly benefit the dominating party. (see UCC 2–302)

underwriter In insurance law, the one assuming a risk in return for the payment of a premium; the insurer. In securities law, any person, banker, or syndicate that guarantees a definite sum of money to a business or government in return for the issue of stock or bonds, usually for resale purposes.

undisclosed principal A principal whose identity is unknown by a third person, and the third person has no knowledge that the agent is acting in an agency capacity at the time the contract is made. (see and compare to *disclosed* and *partially disclosed principal*)

undue influence Abuse of one's position of influence or relationship with another person by overcoming that person's free will, persuading that person to act or refrain from acting in a certain manner. (see *duress*)

unenforceable contract A contract having no legal effect or force in a court action.

unilateral contract A contract under which promise of payment or performance is given in exchange for the full performance by the other party (as opposed to a promise to perform by the other party). (see *bilateral contract*)

union shop All workers, once employed, must become union members within a specified period of time as a condition of their continued employment.

unliquidated debt An obligation which has not been reduced to a specific money amount; also, there may be a bona fide dispute between the parties as to this undetermined amount. (see *liquidated debt*)

usage of trade The prevailing and accepted customs within a particular trade or industry. It is implied that merchants are cognizant of the usage of their trade. A usage of trade is any practice or method of dealing having such regularity of observance in a place, vocation, or trade as to justify an expectation that it will be observed with respect to the transaction in question. (see UCC 1–205, *course of dealing*)

usury Charging interest on a debt above the statutory maximum, as defined by various state statutes. A contract which includes a usurious interest rate is illegal.

V

valid contract A properly constituted contract having legal strength or force. (see *unenforceable contract*)

valued policy A policy in which there is a definite valuation amount placed on the property insured by agreement between the insurer and insured, and that value is paid upon loss (as opposed to an *open policy*).

venue The geographical district in which the action is tried and from which the jury is selected. (see *jurisdiction*)

vertical merger A combining of two firms, one of which purchases goods for resale from the other. If a producer or wholesaler acquires a retailer, it is a *forward* merger. If a retailer or distributor acquires its producer, it is a *backward* merger. (see *merger*)

vertical price-fixing contract An illegal agreement to maintain prices between producers and wholesalers or distributors, between producers and retailers, or between wholesalers or distributors and retailers.

vicarious liability Responsibility for someone else's actions, arising out of some legal relationship. (see *respondeat superior*)

void Having no legal force or binding effect. (see *valid contract*, *unenforceable contract*)

voidable That which may be legally annulled at the option of one of the parties.

voluntary bankruptcy A bankruptcy proceeding which is initiated by the debtor. (see *involuntary bankruptcy*)

voting trust The transfer of title by stockholders of shares of a corporation to a trustee who is authorized to vote the shares on their behalf.

W

wait and see doctrine When determining whether or not a contingent interest violates the Rule Against Perpetuities, many states have enacted laws which permit the court to look at the condition when the contingency occurs and not as the Rule mandates, at the creation of the interest. If an interest *does* vest before the perpetuities rule expires it is valid, even though the interest at creation was in violation. In some states this is called the second look doctrine.

waiver An intentional, knowing relinquishment of a legal right. (see *release*)

warehouseman A person engaged in the business of receiving and storing goods for hire. (see UCC 7–102(1)(h))

warehouse receipt A receipt issued by a person engaged in the business of storing goods for hire; it is a document of title. (see UCC 1–201(46), 7–201, 7–202)

warranty In sales law, a statement or representation made by a seller of goods, or implied by law, as a part of a contract of sale, having reference to and ensuring the character, quality, fitness of purpose, or title of the goods. (see UCC 2–312, 2–313, 2–314, 2–315)

warranty deed A deed under which the grantor guarantees to the grantee that the grantor has title to the property conveyed in the deed, that there are no encumbrances on the property other than what the grantor has represented, and that the grantee will enjoy quiet possession.

warranty of merchantability A promise by a merchant seller of goods that they are reasonably fit for the general purpose for which they are sold, are properly packaged and labeled, and are of proper quality. (see UCC 2–314)

warranty of possession In a lease contract, a warranty by the landlord that the premises have been leased to only one tenant and that the premises will be available as the agreed time.

watered stock Stock issued by a corporation as if fully paid for, when in fact less than par value has been paid.

white collar crime White collar crime refers to nonviolent crimes committed by corporations and individuals. Embezzlement and theft are two examples of white collar crime.

whole life A life insurance policy in which the insured pays a level premium for his or her entire life and in which there is a constantly accumulating cash value against which the insured can withdraw or borrow. Sometimes referred to as straight life insurance.

will An instrument directing what is to be done with a person's property upon his or her death, made by that person and revocable during his or her lifetime. No interests pass until the testator dies. (see *testator*)

winding up The settling of accounts and liquidation of assets of a partnership or corporation just prior to dissolution.

workers' compensation statutes State statutes which provide for fixed awards to employees or their dependents in case of employment-related accidents or diseases, dispensing with proof of negligence and legal actions.

workouts A common law or bankruptcy composition with creditors whereby a debtor enters into an agreement with a creditor or creditors for a payment or plan to discharge the debtor's debt(s).

writ A written court order or a judicial process, directing that a sheriff, judge, or other judicial officer do what is commanded by the writ. A granted "writ of certiorari" commands the inferior court to send the record of the case to the issuing court, which will take appellate jurisdiction.

writ of attachment A writ employed to enforce obedience to an order or judgment of the court. The writ may take the form of taking or seizing property or persons to bring them under the control of the court.

writ of certiorari An order by the appellate court which is used when the court has discretion on whether to hear an appeal. If the writ is denied, the court refuses to hear the appeal and, in effect, the judgment of the lower court stands unchanged. If the writ is granted, then it has the effect of ordering the lower court to certify the record and send it up to the higher court which has used its discretion to hear the appeal. (see *writ*)

writ of execution A writ which puts in force a court's decree or judgment.

Z

zoning The division of land of an entire city or county by legislative regulation whereby the legislature prescribes certain general or particular uses for various segments of the land, including structural and architectural design.

INDEX

A

Abatement, 895
AAA. *See* American Arbitration Association
Ability, legal. *See* Contracts, capacity in
Abstract, 49
Acceptance: of a gift, 840
  partial, of sales contracts, 342
  revocation of, 321
  of a sales contract, 296–301, 339–42
Acceptor: *defined*, 401
  liability of, 446
Accession, personal property and, 840–41
Accommodation: notice of, 297
  party, 403
  and negotiable instruments, 448
Accord: *defined*, 255
  and satisfaction, 157–60
  case illustrating, 158–60
Account party to a letter of credit, 944
Accountants' ethics and, 957
  liability of, 932–42
    to clients, 932–35
    criminal, 941
    statutory, 937–41
    to third persons, 935–36
Accounting: agent's duty of, 561
  of partnership assets, partners' right to, 624–25, 627 n.17
Accounts, security interest in, 486 n.3, 489, 491, 492
Acid pollution, and government regulation, 780
Act: guilty, 93
  of state doctrine, in international law, 946
  case illustrating, 946–48
Act for the Prevention of Frauds and Perjuries, An (1677), 217
Act to Regulate Commerce (1887), 750
Activity, commercial, *defined*, 949
Acts of God, 860
Actus reus, 93 n.1
Ademption, 895
Adequate protection, concept of, 530
Adjudication, administrative, 756
Administrator (administratrix), 849, 909
Administrative Procedure Act (APA), 754
Admission: of an oral contract, and its enforceability, 225, 303
  request for, 47
Advances, future, security interest in, 492–93
Adverse possession, transfer of real estate by, 877
Advertisements, and contractual offers, 128–31

case illustrating, 129–31
Advertising: bait-and-switch, 765
  case illustrating, 765–66
  and consumer protection, 762–66
  deceptive, *defined*, 763
    case illustrating, 763–65
  and the First Amendment, 28
  sale of securities and, 716
Affidavit, 46
Age, misstatement of, on insurance policies, 925. *See also* Minors
Agency, 553–94
  administrative: for consumer protection, 761–62
    and environmental protection, 777
    listed, 755
    powers of, 749–50, 753–57
  coupled with an interest, termination of, 580, 581 n.
  defined, 553
  ethics and, 591–92
  exclusive, 882
  minors and, 557
  nature of, 553
  relationship, 553–59
    case illustrating, 555–56
    concept summary, 555
  formation of, 556–59
    concept summary, 558
  termination of, 579–83
    concept summary, 583
    by act of the parties, 579–81
    notice required in, 583
    by operation of law, 581–82
Agent (*see also* Subagent): acceptance of contract by, 142
  authority of, 567–75
  consignment of goods through, and antitrust law, 808
  corporate, 662
  and delivery of gifts, 838
  duty of, to principal, 559–62
  escrow, 885
  franchisee as, 739
  indorsement by, 426
  insurance, 914
  legal capacity of, 557
  liability of—for contracts, 575–77
    personal, 406
    for torts, 577–79
  partner as, 628
  remedies of, against principal, 563
  rights of, 563
  signature of, 406
    on negotiable instruments, 443–45
  warranties of, 577
Agreement: agency, 557
  implied, 557
  oral, 556–57

to agree, and contractual offers, 131
bailment, 848, 850–51
buy-out, 711
in contracts, 115, 125–47
creditors' composition, 162, 518
family settlement, and a will, 910
franchise. *See* Franchise contract
mutual, for terminating an agency, 580
to obstruct legal process, 196
oral, 557
  of a partnership, 607
  of rescission, 253
partnership—to dissolve, 615
  written, 607
and passage of title, 313
and perfect tender, 333
prenuptial, 224
reaffirmation, 163, 538
repurchase, and bankruptcy, 543
resale price maintenance, 190
retail charge (revolving charge account), 183
and risk of loss, 314
security, 482–85
  creditors' rights and, 497–99
  debtors' rights in, 499
  defined, 482
  illustrated, 483–84
  termination of, 503–04
  written, 482
shareholder—in close corporations, 649–51
  case illustrating, 650–51
  voting, 685
subscription, for a corporation, 659
substituted, for discharge of contract, 254–55
voting trust, 685
written, for covenant running with the land, 888
Agriculture, exemption of, from antitrust laws, 797
Air: pollution of, and government regulation, 778–80
  property rights to, 865–66
Alcoholic, contractual capacity of an, 179
Alienation, restraint against, 235 n.4
  case illustrating, 237–39
Aliens, contracts and, 180
Allonge, indorsement on, 419
  case illustrating, 422
Alteration: of check, and payment of, 474
  certified, 464
  case illustrating, 464–65
  material—of a contract, 298
    as defense against liability on

negotiable instruments, 453
American Arbitration Association (AAA),
     50
American Bar Association, 897
     Committee on Corporate Laws, 644
American Law Institute, 113, 115 n.,
     136
     Model Penal Code, 91, 93, 94
Annuity, 924
Annulment, and the revocation of a will,
     903
Answer, defendant's, in a court case, 44
Antitrust laws: enforcement of 803–18
     ethics of 830–31
     exemption from, 797–800
     franchises and 733, 739
     and foreign nations, 950
     and government regulation, 798–818
     history of 798–90
APA. *See* Administrative Procedure Act
Appeal: procedures for, 48–50
     right of, and the Supreme Court, 41
Appraisal, shareholders' rights of, 706–10
     cases illustrating, 707–08, 709–10
Appropriation, 87–88
Appurtenant, easement, 886
Arbitration, 50, 196
     clause on, and effect of, *case
          illustrating*, 298, 301
     transnational, 944
Arrangement: reciprocal buying, and
          antitrust laws, 812
     tying, 810, 811
Arrest: false. *See* Imprisonment, false
     procedure for, 98
Arson, 100
Articles: of incorporation, 660–62
     of merger, 704
     of partnership, 607
Assault, 53, 54
Assent: to limitation of liability, 277
     mutuality of, in contracts, 125–26
     reality of (genuineness), in contracts,
          115, 201–14
Assets: assignment of, creditor's rights in,
          518
     distribution of—from a partnership,
          621
          from a limited partnership, 640–41
     purchase of corporate, 710–11
     residual, of an estate, *case illustrating*,
          895–97
Assignment: of insurance policies—fire,
          927
     life, 925
     of a lease, 875
     rights of—and anti assignment clauses,
          235 n.4, 236–39
     consideration for, 234
     creditor's, of assets, 518
     and delegation of duties, 233–39,
          241
     notice of, 239
     and priority in performance, 239
     prohibited, 235–36
          case illustrating, 235–36

revocation of, 234
     and Statute of Frauds, 234
     of secured interest collateral, 497–98
     transfer of negotiable instruments by,
          405, 409, 418
Association: joint stock company, 599,
          643
     limited partnership, 641
     professional (P.A.), 652
Assurance, right of, in sales contracts,
          338
Attachment, concept of, with a security
          interest, 485, 486
Attorney-in-fact, agent as, 567 n.1
Auction, and contractual offers, 131
Authority: agent's—apparent. *See*
          Estoppel, agency by
     express, 567–69
     implied, 570
     apparent, and antitrust regulation, 804
Authorization, and acceptance of
          contracts, 145–46
Automobile: financing, chattel paper in,
          497
     insurance of, 929–30
     pollution from, and government
          regulation 778–79
     secured interest in, 493–94
Automobile Dealers' Day in Court Act,
          730, 732, 735, 737
Avoidance, of contract, principal's right
          to, 563
     case illustrating, 563–65. *See also*
          Contract, void

B

Bailee: acknowledgment of buyer's rights
          by, 332
     defined, 848
     involuntary, 842 n.5, n.7
     liabilities of, 853, 854, 855
     right of, 852–53
          concept summary, 858
          possession, 842
     and risk of loss, 316, 318
Bailor: *defined*, 848
     duties of, 859
     rights of, 859
Bailment, 848–64
     common carriers and, 859–62
     constructive. *See* Bailment,
          involuntary
     contractual. *See* Bailment, material
          benefit
     defined, 848
     delivery and, 850
     distinguished from a lease, *case
          illustrating*, 849–50
     elements of, 848–51
     of fungible goods, 851
     gratuitous, 851
          compensation and, 853
     innkeeper's, 863
     involuntary (constructive), 850
     limitation of, to personal property,
          848–48

mutual benefit (contractual), 851
     compensation in, 852
     duties of bailor in, 859, 860
     ordinary, 851–52
     for the sole benefit of the bailee,
          851–52, 859
     special, 851, 859–63
     termination of, 859
     voluntary, 849 n.
     and warehouse companies, 862–63
Bank: charges, appropriate, 509
     collecting, *defined*, 475
     collection process of, 471–77
     depositary, *defined*, 475
     duties of, toward customers, 465–77
     intermediary, *defined*, 475
     paying, on a letter of credit, 944
     payor, *defined*, 475
     relationship with customers, 465
          concept summary, 476
Banking system: and checks, 461–80
     ethics and, 509
Bankruptcy (*see also* Insolvency), 472–45
     Chapter: 7 liquidations in, 528–38
          in, 538–41, 548
     13 plans for, 541–43
     as defense against liability on
          negotiable instruments, 453
     and discharge of contract, 256
     and ethics, 546–49
     fraudulent, 103–04
     involuntary, petition for, 529
     partnership and, 604–605, 616, 638
     promises to pay debts discharged by,
          163
     scam, 103–04
     of special business functions, 543–44
     and termination of an agency, 582
     voluntary, petition for, 528–29
Bankruptcy Act (1898), 527
Bankruptcy Amendments and Federal
          Judgeship Act (1984), 37, 103, 163,
          527–28
Bankruptcy Reform Act (1978), 103,
          163, 346, 527, 528
Baseball, exemption of, from antitrust
          laws, 797–98
Basis of the bargain, concept of, 366
     case illustrating, 366–67
Battery, 53–54
BBB. *See* Better Business Bureau
Bearer, *defined*, 402
Bearer paper (instrument), 414
     case illustrating, 414–15
     conversion of, to order paper, 419
     indorsement of, 419, 420
     negotiation of, 419
Beneficiary: creditor, 241
     donee, 241 n.11, 243
     incidental, 241, 243
     rights of, under a will, 903
     third party. *See* Third party,
          beneficiary
Benefits, insurance, 924
Behavior, changes in ethical, 109
Bequest, 894–95

Better Business Bureau (BBB), and
  consumer protection, 762
Bid, take-over, 711
Bill of lading, 316, 944
  illustrated, 319
Bill of Rights, The, 18
  and business, 25
Billing, government regulation of
  disputes about, 773
Bills of exchange. *See* Drafts
Bills of Exchange Act (1882), 397
Binder, insurance, 917
Blue sky laws, 727, 738
Bond: callable, 670
  chattel mortgage, 670
  collateral trust, 670
  convertible, 670
  corporate, 669
  criminal recognizance, 122
  equipment trust (chattel mortgage),
    670
  as fixed income securities, 669–70
  indenture, 669
  mortgage, 669–70
  surety, 122
  compared with stocks, 671
Books, right to inspect. *See* Records,
  business
Boycott: group, and antitrust regulations,
  805
  secondary, 820–21
Broadcasting, government regulation of,
  751
Bribery of foreign officials, 101–03
  commercial, *case illustrating*, 102–03
  ethics and, 109
Broker, insurance, 914
Bubble Act (1720), 643
Bulk sale. *See* Transfer, bulk
Business: crimes affecting, 99–105
  entering wrongfully, tort of, 79–81
  ethics of. *See* Ethics, business
  relationship, wrongful interference
    with, 77–79
  responsibility of, for the environment,
    830
  transacting abroad, 944–48
  trust, 599
Business organizations, 597–741
  corporations, 643–745
    and ethics, 742–45
  franchises, 730–41
  partnerships, 597–98, 600, 602–42
    limited, 632–42
  sole proprietorships, 597, 599–600
Burglary, 99
Buyer: in the ordinary course of business,
  defined, 346 n., 495
  and security interest in merchandise,
    495
    case illustrating, 495–96
  for real estate, 882
  remedies of, in breach of contract,
    350–56
    concept summary, 356
Buying, reciprocal, 812

Bylaws, corporate, 661–62
Bystanders, strict liability to, 393
  case illustrating, 393–94

C

Cancellation: of a contract—buyer's right
  to, 352
  seller's right to, 349
  of an insurance policy, 921, 927
  of a negotiable instrument—as a
    defense, 457
  and discharge of, 458
Capacity: contractual, 115, 168–80
  legal, and partnership, 610
  testamentary, 897–98
    case illustrating, 898–99
Capital: need for, and choice of business
  organization, 602
  stated, of a corporation, 672
Capitalization, inadequate, of a
  corporation, 665
    case illustrating, 665
Cardozo, Justice, on loyalty, 690
Care: corporate directors' duty of,
  689–80
  standard of, and bailments, 851–52
Carrier: common, and bailments, 859–
  62
  securities of, exempt from registration,
    717
  substitution of, and perfect tender, 334
Carrier cases: delivery of, 332–33
  and risk of loss, 314–15
Case law. *See* Law, case
Cases, non-carrier, delivery of, 332
Cash: surrender fund, 924
  value, of an insurance policy, 924
Catalogues, and contractual offers, 128
Causa mortis, donation of gift in, 840
Causation, 65–68
  as defense against negligence, 386
Cause: legal. *See* Cause, proximate
  probable, *defined*, 98
  proximate (legal), 66–68, 387
    case illustrating, 66–67
Caveat emptor, in real estate
  transactions, 880, 882
CCPA. *See* Consumer Credit Protection
  Act
CDs. *See* Certificates of deposit
Celler-Kefauver Anti-Merger Act, 796,
  812, 813
Certificate: of authority, for foreign
  corporations, 646
  of co-partnership, 605
  of deposit (CDs), 398
    described, 400, 401, 402
    promise to pay, 407
    presentment of, 447
  of incorporation, 662
  of limited partnership, 633, 635, 636
    (illustrated)
  stock, 693
    preferred, *illustrated*, 673
  voting trust, 685

Certification: of checks, 462–65
  mark, 83
C&F (cost and freight), 315
  and delivery, 333
  and payment, 339
Chain-style business, as a franchise, 731
Chandler Act (1938), 527
Change of circumstances, and
  termination of an agency, 582
Chapter 7; 11; 13. *See* Bankruptcy
Charity: corporation formed for, 649
  enforceability of promises to subscribe
    to, 165
  securities of, exempt from registration,
    717
Chattel, personal property as, 836
  paper, security interest in, 489, 491,
    497
Checks: and the banking system, 461–80
  cashier's, 461–62
  certification of, 446–47
  certified, 461–65
  clearance of, 477, 478
  described, 399, 401, 402
  honoring, bank's duties in, 465–74
  presentment of, 447
  stale, 467
    case illustrating, 467–68
  traveler's, 461, 463
  as unconditional order, 407
    payable on demand, 412
Child labor, 827
Children, inheritance by. *See* Heirs
Chose in action, 704
  case illustrating, 704–06
CIF (cost, insurance, and freight), 315
  and delivery, 333
  and payment, 339
Citations of court cases, how to read,
  11–12
Citizenship, diversity of, 40–41
Civil rights, and employment laws,
  821–24
Civil Rights Act (1964), 195 n.
  and the Commerce Clause, 19
  provisions of, 821–22
Claim, antecedent, and the
  holder-in-due-course of a
    negotiable instrument, 433
Claims: disputed (unliquidated), in
  Chapter 7 liquidation, 534
  settlement of, 157–60
Clarkson, K. W., R. L. Miller, and J. J.
  Muris ("Liquidated Damages v.
    Penalty: Sense or Nonsense"), 296
Clause: acceleration, on negotiable
  instruments, 412–13
  add-on, ethics of, 546–47
  arbitration, 196, 944
  choice-of-law, 944
  exculpatory, 191–93, 276
    and assignability of rights, 236
    and bailments, 853
    and remedies, 276–77
  extension, on negotiable instruments,
    413

force majeure, 946
forum selection, 196
incontestable, in life insurance policy, 925
limitation of liability. *See* Clause, exculpatory
occupancy, in fire insurance, 927
pro rata, in fire insurance, 926–27
residuary, in a will, 895
unconscionable, 191
and remedies, 277–78
Clayton Act, 188n., 710, 753, 795, 796, 797, 805, 811
on anticompetitive mergers, 812, 814, 816
Clean Air Act, 778, 780
Clean Water Act (1972), 781
Clearinghouse, automated, in banking, 478
Closed shop, illegality of, 820
Closing: argument, 48
of a real estate sale, 885
costs of, and government regulation, 770
C.O.D. shipments, 339
Code, the. *See* Uniform Commercial Code
Codicil, 901
Coinsurance, 926
Collateral: assembly of, in default, 500–01
classification of, and place for filing financial statement, 489–95
illustration of, 491
creditor's right to take possession of, in default, 500–01
debtor's rights in, 485
defined, 482, 491–92
description of, and security interest, 486, 488–93
case illustrating, 488–89
disposition of, by creditor, in default, 501–03
case illustrating, 502–03
duty of care of, 499, 500
fungible, 499
movement of, and security interest, 493–94
note, 500
priority of secured interest in, 494
concept summary, 498
sale of, and security interest in the proceeds, 490, 492
security interest in, assignment of, 497–98
surrender of, and discharge of a negotiable instrument, 459
transfer of, and perfection, 486
Collective bargaining: and bankruptcy, 544
legislation on, 819–20
Collective mark, 83
Collection direct (indirect). *See* Notification (nonnotification), chattel paper and
Comity, principle of, in international law, 948
Commenda, 632

Commerce Clause, of the U.S. Constitution, 18–19
Commerce Clearing House *(Blue Sky Law Reporter),* 727 n.
Commercial paper, 397–403
collectibility of, 398
defined, 397
exemption of, from offerings registration, 717
functions of 397–98
holder-in-due-course, rights of, 429–40
legal conditions on payment of, 407–09
liability and, 442–452
negotiability of, 405–17
parties to, 401–03
signatures on, 442–49
transferability of, 418–26
types of instruments as, 398–400, 401
warranty liability and, 442, 450–52
Commercial reasonableness, 296
ethics and, 507
Commission, act of *(actus reus;* guilty act), and criminal liability, 93
Committee, executive, of a corporation, 687
Common markets, 950–52
Communication, privileged, 57
Communications, government regulation of, 751
Compensation, 65
bailee's right to, 852–53
directors', 686, 693
in an employment contract, 584
legal, for injury in the workplace, 824
partners', from the partnership, 624
principal's duty of, 562
unemployment, government regulation of, 826
Competence (legal ability). *See* Contracts, capacity in
Competition: and Chapter 11 reorganization, 549
ethics and, 506–07
fair, 77
case illustrating, 77–78
potential, and government regulation, 796
predatory, 79–81
case illustrating, 79–81
Complaint (declaration; petition), 42–44
amended, 44
Compliance, with a letter of credit, 944
case illustrating, 945
Compositions. *See* Agreements, creditors' composition
Compromise, legal, 255
Computers: crime and, 101
programs for, as personal property, 836, 845
piracy of, 954, 955–56
Concepts, summaries of *(See also* Doctrine; Rule; Test):
agency, termination of, 583
agent-principal relationship, formation of, 558
bailee, rights and duties of, 858

bank-customer relationships, 476
collateral, priority of debtors' claims to, 498
contracts: discharge of, 260
valid, under the Statute of Frauds, 228
negotiable instruments: indorsers of, transfer warranty liability for, 452
requirements for, 415–16
valid defenses for holder of, 457
offer, methods of terminating, 143
passage of title and risk of loss, 318
real property, forms of ownership of, 877
remedies: of the buyer, for breach of contract by seller, 356
available to creditors, 523
stocks, 674
warrants under the UCC, 380
wills, 904
Concerted action, and antitrust regulation, 803–04
Condition, contractual, 246–49
concurrent, 248, 249
constructive, 249
defined, 247
express, 248
implied— -in-fact, 248–49
-in-law (constructive), 249
and performance, 250–52
case illustrating, 250–51
precedent, 247, 252
case illustrating, 247–48
subsequent, 247, 248
time as, 253
Conduct, improper, and the dissolution of a partnership, 617
Confirmation: of a sales contract, 302
written, of an oral contract, 225
Confiscation, 946
of land, 888–89
Confusion, *defined,* 841
Conscience. *See* Contract, unconscionable
Consent, as defense against criminal liability, 54, 95
Consideration, in contracts, 149–65
adequacy of, 151–55, 203
case illustrating, 152–53
and assignability of contracts, 234
defined, 149, 150–51
good, 151
insurance premium as, 913–14
legal sufficiency of, 234
in oral contracts, 221
past, 151, 160–62
case illustrating, 160–62
and the preexisting duty rule, 154–55
problems with, 156–65
and promise of marriage, 224
requirements of, 149–51
in a sales contract, 301–02
statements of, and negotiable instruments, 427–28
and value of negotiable instruments, 432
want of, *case illustrating,* 194–95
Consolidation, corporate, 703, 704, 706

Constitution, the U.S., 6, 17–31, 98
Consumer: and corporate responsibility, 744
  debtor, protection for, 524–25
  products, government regulation of, 751
  protection of: and credit, 770–74
    in franchising, 737
    by government regulation, 760–76
    legislation for, 760–62, 768–69
    and real estate, 769–70
Consumer Credit Protection Act (CCPA) (Truth-in-Lending Act), 183 n.2, 516 n.3, 524, 760, 769, 770–74
Consumer Product Safety Act (1972), 768, 769
Consumer Product Safety Commission (CPSC), 508, 509, 749, 751, 768, 769
Contacts, corporate, 646
  case illustrating, 647–48
Contracts, 113–283
  abeyance of, 180
  acceptance—authorization and, 145–46
    communication of, 145
    of offer in, 142–47
    silence as, 144
    by third parties, 142–43
    unequivocal, 143–44
  adhesion, 193
    and unconscionability, 214
  agreement in, 115, 125–47
  aliens and, 180
  alteration of, and discharge, 255
  assent—genuine, to, 201–14
    mutual in, 125–26
  bailee's, to return bailed property, 854
  bilateral, 115–17
    acceptance of, 145–47
    assignment relationships in, 233–34
    case illustrating, 116–17
  breach of, 263–78. See also Contract, remedy for breach of
    accountant's liability for, 932–33
    anticipatory, 256–57
    as defense against liability on negotiable instruments, 454
    deliberate, 264 n.4
    material, 249, 250, 252–53, 256–57
    minor, 252
    nondeliberate, 264 n.4
    waiver of, 276
  capacity in, 168–80
    and ethics, 281–82
  classification of, 115–22
    concept summary, 123
  to commit—a crime, 186
    a tort, 195–96
  communication of offer in, 134–36
  condition precedent in, 339
  conditions in, 246–49
  consideration in, 149–65
  construction—and damages, 264–66
    and specific performance, 273 n.16
  defined, 115
  delegation of duties under, 239–41

for delivery without shipment, and passage of title, 314
destination—delivery of, 332–33
  and passage of title, 314
  and risk of loss, 314–15
between directors and a corporation, 692
discharge of, 246–60
  by accord, 255
  by agreement, 253–55
  by anticipatory breach (repudiation), 256–57
  in bankruptcy, 256
  concept summary, 260
  impliedly, 254
  by impossibility of performance, 257–60
  by law, 186, 255–56
  by novation, 254–55
  by performance, 249–53
  by rescission, 253–54
  by satisfaction, 255
  under statutes of limitations, 254–56
discriminatory, legality of, 195
divisible. See Contract, severable
duress, made under, 122
employment, 583, 584–89
  termination of, 586
exclusive dealing, 156
executed, 122
  and disaffirmance, 169
  illegality and, 197
  rescission of, 254
  and Sunday laws, 185
executory, 122
  and disaffirmance, 169
  and illegality, 196–97
  rescission of, 254
express, 117, 120
  case illustrating, 118–19, 120–21
  written, agency agreement as, 557
ex-ship, and delivery, 333
form of, 217–32
formal, 121–22
franchise, 731–37, 738–39
  good faith in, case illustrating, 330–31
fraudulent, 122, 205–12
freedom—from, 114
  of, 114, 152
function of, 114
futures, 184
good faith in, 735
hot cargo, 820–21
ignorance in, 197
illegal, 182–86
  withdrawal from, 197–98
implied— -in-fact, 117, 114
  case illustrating, 118–19
  -in-law. See Contract, quasi-in
  partnerships, 687
incomplete, and parol evidence, 227
informal (simple), 122
and insanity, 179–80
installment–defined, 334
  and perfect tender, 334–35
insurance as, 913, 916–23

exception of, from registration, 717
integration of, and admissibility of parol evidence, case illustrating, 229–30
intention in—of offer, 126–31
  and third party beneficiaries, 241, 243
and intoxication, 176–79
  case illustrating, 177–79
investment, defined, 738
law of, and ethics, 280–83
legality of, 115, 182–98
married women and, 180
between merchants, 140
mistaken, 122
modifications to, 227, 302, 303
  oral, and parol evidence, 228
for necessaries, 173–75
  minors and, 168–76
non-offer in, 126–31
non-voidable, minors and, 176
objective theory of, 117–18, 125–26
  case illustrating, 118–19
  requirements of, 126–36
offer in, termination of, 136–42
  by action of the parties, 136–40
  concept summary, 143
  by operation of the law, 140–42
open listing, 882
option, 137, 296 n.4
  to cancel, 156–57
oral, 122
  assignability of, 234
  enforceability of, 186, 217, 219, 220, 221–22
  for land, 219
  memorandum of, 225–27, 228
  reformation and, 274–75
  for sale of goods, 302–303
  and statutes of limitations, 255
output, 134, 156
performance of, 246–53
  and the Statute of Frauds, 219–20
personal—and assignability, 235
  case illustrating, 235–36
  and specific performance, 272–73
preliminary negotiations in, 127–28
  case illustrating, 127–28
privity of, 233, 242
of protected persons, 197
and public policy, 186–96
quasi- (implied-in-law), 79, 119–21
  case illustrating, 120–21
  and bulk transfers, 323
  ethics of, 281
  insanity and, 179
  and intoxication, 179
  minors' liability for necessaries in, 173
  recovery under, 275
ratification of, 122
  by minors, 175–76
rescission of, 272
  and consideration, 154
  in franchising, 210
remedy for breach of, 263, 272–78
  damages as, 263–71
  defined, 246

election of, 275–76
limitations on, 270–76
quasi-, 275
reformation as, 274–75
specific performance as, 272–74
requirements, 134
  and antitrust laws, 811
  and ethics, 508
  and uncertainty of performance,
    155, 156
requirements of, 114–15
in restraint of trade, 188–90
sales—of goods. *See* Sales of goods,
  contract for
  of real estate, 882–85
seal on, 122 n.4
service, as an express warranty, 381
severable (divisible), 198
shipment—delivery of, 332
  and passage of title, 314
  and risk of loss, 314
simple. *See* Contract, informal
standard form, as unconscionable,
  214, 307
suspension of, 260
third party beneficiary, 233, 241–44
  rights in, 233, 241–44
  theory of, *case illustrating*, 242
terms of—agreement in, 125
  definite, 131–34
  indefinite, cure of, 134
tie-in, 950
with unlicensed parties, 185–86
ultra vires, 680
unconscionable, 274
  and legality, 191–95
  in sale of goods, 306–307
undue influence and, 212
unenforceable, 122, 142, 201
unilateral, 115–16
  revocability of, 138
"under seal," 121–22
  valid, 122, 142, 176–79
    insanity and, 179–80
  void, 122
    and insanity, 179
    married women and, 180
    parol evidence and, 227
    public policy and, 186
    by reason of illegality, 196–97
    ultra vires, 680
    usury and, 183
  voidable—for alteration, 255 n.16
    between directors and a corporation,
      692
    for duress, 212–14
    for fraud, 205–12
    insanity and, 179
    for intoxication, 176–77
    when made by minors, 122, 168,
      178, 610
    for mistakes in, 201–204
    and parol evidence, 227
    of partnership with a minor, 610
    for undue influence, 212
  written, 217–30

and assignability, 234
and statutes of limitations, 255
Contractor, independent: *defined*, 554
  franchisee as, 739
  liability of principal toward, 579
  relationship of, with principal, 553,
    554–55
Contractual relationship, wrongful
  interference with, 75–77
  case illustrating, 76–77
Contribution, right of, 521
Conversion: *defined*, 171
  distinguished from theft, 62–63
    case illustrating, 62–63
  liabilty for in mis-delivery of bailed
    goods, 854
    cases illustrating, 854–55, 856–57
  and mistake of fact, 95
Conveyance, fraudulent, 522
Cooperation, duty of, 329, 338, 526
Cooperative, business organization as,
  599
Copyright: government regulation of, 752
  infringement of, 85–87
    and ethics, 954–55
    warranty against, 365
  as personal property, 845–46
Copyright Act, 85
Coronation cases, 259–60
Corporate veil, 645
  piercing, 663–67
    cases illustrating, 663–64, 665
Corporations, 643–747
  acquiring, 710–11
  adoption of promoter's contract by,
    657
  agent of, 662
  alien, 646
  board of directors of, 645
  bonds, 669–70
  borrowing by, authority for, 677
    case illustrating, 678–79
  business, 598
  bylaws of, 661–62
  C, 651
  capital structure of, 660–61
  and Chapter 11 reorganization, 538
  close (closed; closely held; family;
    privately held), 648, 649–51
    defined, 650
    dissolution of, *case illustrating*,
      712–13
    incorporation of, 660
    preemptive rights in, 694
    share transfers in, 699
  consolidation, 703, 704–06
  control of, 742
  crimes of, 30, 104–05, 644
  de facto, 663
  de jure, 662–63
  directors of, 689–93
    and management, 685–87
  dissolution of, and shareholders' rights,
    699–700. *See also* Corporation,
    termination of
  dividends in, 694–97

domestic, 646, 706
duration of, 660
duty of—to the consumer, 744
  directors to, 689–92
  to employees, 744–45
  to shareholders, 745
eleemosynary. *See* Corporation,
  nonprofit
by estoppel, 663
family. *See* Corporation, close
financing, 669–74
foreign, 646–48, 706
formation of. *See* Incorporation
franchising and, 730–41
history of, 643
internal organization of, 661–62
as a "legal person," 644, 677
liability of, 681. *See also* Directors,
  liability of; Shareholders, liabilities
  of
management of, 684–87
merger of, 703–11
name of, 660
nature of, 644–46, 660
nonprofit (eleemosynary; not-for-
  profit), 648–49
officers of, 646, 693
as partner, 610
partnership, compared with, 600
  concept summary, 601
philanthropy of, 743–44
powers of, 677–81
privately-held. *See* Corporation, close
professional (P.C.), 652–54
  case illustrating, 653
public, 648
purpose of, 660
registered office of, 662
regulation of securities of, 715–26,
  727
rights in, 693–700
service (S.C.), 652
shareholders in, 645
  and management of, 681–85
  rights of, in, 693–700
social responsibility of, 742–44
statute and, 643–44
stocks of, 670–74
  concept summary, 674
subchapter S, 651–52
surviving, 703, 704
target, 711
taxation of, 601, 646
  and benefits to, 668–69
termination of, 711–13. *See also*
  Corporation, dissolution of
veil of. *See* Corporate veil
voting rights in, 670
Cost—and freight. *See* C&F
  insurance, and freight. *See* C.I.F.
Council of Better Business Bureaus, Inc.,
  762
Council of Environmental Quality, 778
Counterclaim (cross-complaint), 44
Counteroffer, and termination of a
  contract, 145

Course: of dealing (usage of trade)—and
   implied warranty, 374, 380
   and parol evidence, 227, 303–304
     case illustrating, 304–305
   of performance, and implied warranty,
     374, 380
Court: probate, 894, 908
   Supreme, 37–38, 40
     jurisdiction of, 41–42
Courts, in the U.S., 34–48
   of Appeal (appellate), 36, 37, 39
   discussed, 33
   district (federal trial), 37, 39
   federal trial. *See* Courts, district
   judicial procedure through, 42–50
   of record, 35
Covenant: against encumbrances, 878
   against grantor's acts, deed with, 880
   not to compete (restrictive), 198
     in employment contracts, 584
     legality of, 188–90
     reformation of, 275
   not to sue (release), 160
   of quiet enjoyment, 866, 873, 878
     case illustrating, 878–80
   reformation of, by the courts, 188–89
   restrictive. *See* Covenant not to
     compete
   of the right to convey, 878
   running with the land, 887–88
   of seisin, 878
     case illustrating, 878–80
Cover, buyer's right of, 352–53
CPSC. *See* Consumer Product Safety
   Commission
Cram-down provision, for acceptance of
   Chapter 11 plan for reorganization,
   541
Crashworthiness, and liability, 394–95
Credit: commercial paper as, 398
   and consumer protection, 770–74
   line of, security interest in, 492–93
Credit cards, government regulation of,
   99, 773
Credit report: access to, 774
   government regulation of, 773–74
Creditors: claims of, in Chapter 7
     liquidation, 534
   committees of, in Chapter 11
     reorganization, 540
   liability to, of limited partners, 638
   meeting, of, 530
   rights of, 513–22
     in life insurance policies, 924
     in security agreements, 497–99
   secured, 481
     and automatic stay, 529
     and distribution of property in
       Chapter 7 liquidation, 534
   unsecured—and Chapter 13 plans,
     542
     priority among, in Chapter 7
       liquidation, 534–35
Crime: against business, 99–105
   classification of, 91–93
   computer. *See* Computers

corporate, 104–105
   liability for, 681
   defined, 90–91
   federal, 93
   state, 93
   white-collar, 101–105
     and ethics, 108–109
Crops: as personal property, 866
   sale of growing, 289
Cross-examination, 48
Cross-complaint. *See* Counterclaim
Cure, for nonconforming goods, and
   tender, 333–34
Curia Regis, 5
Customer: buyer's, and suit brought by,
   355
   restrictions on, and antitrade laws, 809
     case illustrating, 809–10
Customer bank communication system.
   See Teller machines
Customs, international, and law, 943

D

Damages for breach of contract, 263–71
   assignability of, 235 n.4
   buyer's rights to sue for, 353
     and accepted goods, 353–56
   compensatory, 263–66
     case illustrating, 265–66
   consequential (special), 266–68,
     277–78
     buyer's right to, 353
     limited, 361
   defined, 263
   exemplary. *See* Damages, punitive
     fraud and, 210
   incidental, *defined*, 347, 348
   limitation of, 358–59
     case illustrating, 359–61
   liquidated, 269, 271, 358
     case illustrating, 269–71
   measure of, 353–56
     in the termination of a franchise,
       735
   mitigation of, 269, 348
   nominal, 268–69
   punitive (exemplary), 268
     for fraud, 210
   special. *See* Damages, consequential
   treble, under the Sherman Act, 791
   for wrongful repudiation, 348
     case illustrating, 348–50
Danger, abnormal, and liability, 71–72
   case illustrating, 71–72
   defined, 72
   in the workplace, employer's liability
     for, 588–89
Date, on negotiable instruments, 415
Davis-Bacon Act (1931), 827
Deal, refusals to, and antitrust violations,
   810, 811
Dealing, exclusive, and antitrust
   arrangements, 811

Death: benefits, 924, 930
   of contracting party and termination of
     a contract, 142
   of a customer, banks' duties upon,
     468–69
   legal, of a corporate "person," 711
   of a partner, and the dissolution of the
     partnership, 615–16, 619
   and termination of an agency, 581–82
Debenture, 669
Debt: government regulation of
     collection of, 774
   homestead exemption from 521 n.,
     522–24
   liquidated, *defined*, 157
   priority, under Chapter 13 plans,
     542–43
   and promises to pay, 162–63
     collateral, 220–23
   reaffirmation of, 163
   secured. *See* Security interest
     status of, for debtor's information, 499
Debtor: consumer as, *defined*, 528 n.7
   defined, 482
   -in-possession, in Chapter 11
     reorganization, 540
   rights of, 522–25
     in collateral, 485
     in security agreement, 499
Deceit. *See* Misrepresentation
Deception, intentional, as fraud, 209–10
   case illustrating, 210–11. *See also*
     Misrepresentation
Declaration. *See* Complaint
Decree, judicial, and dissolution of a
   partnership, 617
Deed: bargain and sale (grant deed), 880
   conveyance of real property by,
     877–80
   easement created by, 887
   grant. *See* Deed, bargain and sale
     profit created by, 887
   quitclaim, 880, 881
   special warranty, 880
   of trust, *defined*, 521
   valid, requirements of, 878
Defamation, 26–28, 56–59
   case illustrating, 57–59
   business torts on, 59
Default, on security interest, 499–503
Defects, disclosure of, as a bailor's duty,
   859
Defense: affirmative, 44, 46
   against accountant's liability for
     negligence, 933
   against actions of strict liability,
     391–93
   against assault, 54
   against battery, 54
   against a contract, 115, 218, 226. *See
     also* Contract, assent to; Contract,
     form of
   against conversion, 63
   against criminal liability, 94–98
   against defamation, 57
   insurers', against payment, 921–23

against liability—under duty of due diligence, 938
  on negotiable instruments, 452–58
against negligence, 68–71
of others, 54
of property, 54
self-. *See* Self-defense
of the surety, 520–21
against tort for wrongful interference, 78–79
against trespass, 61, 62
waiver of, against breach of contract, 361
Delivery: constructive, 837–38
and a bailment, 850
ex-ship, and risk of loss, 315
of a gift, 837–38
open terms of, in sales contract, 294
physical, and bailment, 850
place of, 332–33
of possession, in a bailment, 849–50
  case illustrating, 849–50
seller's rights over, as remedy, 345–46
tender of, 331–32
and risk of loss, 316
without movement of goods, and risk of loss, 316
Demand payment, of negotiable instruments, 412
Demurrer. *See* Motion to dismiss
Department of Health and Human Services, 766
Department of Housing and Urban Development (HUD), 762, 770
Deposits: bank's duties in accepting, 471–77
demand, 401
Descent, rules of, 903. *See also* Heirs
Design, patents for, 845
Detriment, legal, 149
  case illustrating, 150–51
Devise, 894–95
Difficulties, unforeseen, and contract law, 155
Directors, corporate, 654, 685–87
as agents, 689
compensation of, 686
dismissal of, 682, 685–86
  case illustrating, 682–83
duties, fiduciary, of, 689–92
election of, 685
liability of, in corporate business, 639, 686, 697
management by, 685–87
qualifications of, 686
responsibilities of, 686
rights of, 692–93
term of office, 685–86
as trustees, 689
Disaffirmance:
of contract, and insanity, 179
defined, 169
minors' rights to, 168–75
  case illustrating, 70–71
of a negotiable instrument, 453–54
Discharge: contractual, 246–60

of debt—under Chapter 7 liquidation, 535–38
  under Chapter 13 plan, 542
  hardship, 543
of a negotiable instrument, 458–59
Disclosure, requirements for: in credit transactions, 770–72
  case illustrating, 771–72
and franchising contracts, 738–39
in real estate, 769–70
and security trading (Rule 10b–5), 719–26
timing of, 719
Discounting, 398
of negotiable instruments, 432
Discovery, rules of pre-trial, 46–47
Discrimination: ethics of reverse, 829–30
illegality of, in employment, 821
Dishonor: of checks, *case illustrating* bank's wrongful, 466–67
of foreign drafts, 448
of a negotiable instrument—notice of, 447–48
secondary liability and, 447
Dismissal: of actions, 46
of petition for bankruptcy, 538–39
  case illustrating, 539–41
Disposition of collateral, in default, 501–03
  case illustrating, 502–03
Dissent, notice of, in corporate mergers, 707
Dissolution (*see also* Termination): of a corporation, 711–13
involuntary, 713
of a limited partnership, 640–41
of a partnership, 614–18
Distress, mental, and tort law, 56
Distribution: of an estate, laws of, 903–07
of goods, and antitrust regulations, 808–10
Distributorship, as a franchise, 731
Dividends: illegal, 697
on preferred stock, 672
shareholders' rights to, 694–97
  case illustrating, 695–96
sources of, 694–95
stock, 694
exemption of, from registration, 717
Divorce: and the revocation of a will, 903
and tenancy, 875
Doctrine (*see also* Rule): act of state, 946
  case illustrating, 946–48
affectation, and interstate commerce, 19, 20, 750
  case illustrating, 19–20
of commercial impracticality, 257–58
of crashworthiness, 394–95
of "danger inviting rescue," 68
  case illustrating, 68–69
of detriment-benefit, 150–51
of detrimental reliance (promissory estoppel), 63–65
of election of remedies, 275–76

of "fair use," 85
of freedom of contract, 152
of frustration of purpose, 259–60
  and ethics, 281
of the holder-in-due-course, 405
of impossibility of performance, 280–81
of laches, 9–10
of "last clear chance," 70
of marshalling assets, 604
of mitigation of damages, 269
of perfect tender, 333
of *respondeat superior*—and agent's negligence, 578, 579
  and corporate liability, 681
  and employer's liability, 587, 589
  ethics and, 593–94
of selective incorporation, 25
shop right, 584
of sovereign immunity, 948–50
of standing to sue, 25
of *stare decisis,* 5–6
of state action, and immunity from antitrust laws, 799–800
of strict liability, 387–90
ultra vires (beyond powers), 697–81
of unjust enrichment, 282
DOS. *See* Mortgage, due-on-sale provisions in
Drafts (bills of exchange), 397
demand. *See* Draft, sight
described, 398–99
foreign, dishonor of, 448
presentment of, 447
sight (demand), 399, 401
  payment due on, 412
time, 399
as unconditional order, 407
Drawee: *defined,* 402
identification of, and negotiability, 407
Drawer: *defined,* 402
request for certification of check by, 462–63
Due diligence, accountant's duty of, 937–38
Due process, 31
Duress: contracts entered under, 198, 212–14
  case illustrating, 213–14
as defense against liability—criminal, 95–96
  on negotiable instruments, 454
extreme, 454
ordinary, 457
Durham role, and insanity as a defense, 95
Duty: accountant's, of due diligence, 937–38
agent's, to principal, ethics of, 592
bailee's, 853–59
  concept summary, 858
bailor's, 859
breach of, 65
of care, 64–65
  bailee's 858–59
  and products liability, 383–84, 386

delegation of contractual, 239–41
term of, 240
liability in, 240–41
prohibited, 240
of directors, 689–92
fiduciary, 627
of officers, 693
of restitution, 169–70
of restoration, 169
to speak, 144–45
Dyer's Case, 789

E

Earnings, retained, and dividends, 694
Easement, 218, 886–87
Education, requirements of and
employment discrimination, 822
case illustrating, 822–24
ECC. See European Economic
Community
Efficiency, ethics of economic, 831
EFTS. See Electronic funds transfer
systems
Electronic funds transfer system (EFTS),
477–79
Embezzlement, 100
Emergency, and agent's powers, 572
Eminent domain, transfer of real
property by, 876–77, 888
Employee: corporate responsibility for,
744–45
key, and contractual rights, 76
relationship of, with employer,
554–55, 583–84
rights of, laws establishing, 820
wrongful discharge of, case
illustrating, 107–08
Employee Retirement Income Security
Act (ERISA) (1974), 826
Employer: protection of, against
employees, 820
relationship of, as master or principal,
with employees, 554–55, 583–84
Employment: contract—enforceability of,
case illustrating, 132–33
and restrictive covenants, 188, 190
termination of, 157
discrimination in, and ethics, 829–30
government regulation of, 819–28
torts, 586–89
Endangered Species Act (1973), 786
Entrapment, as defense against criminal
liability, 96–97
case illustrating, 96–97
Entrustment, and sale of goods, 326
Entry, in foreclosure, 521
Environment, protection of, by
government regulation, 777–88
history of, 777
and judicial limits of business
activities, 785–86
case illustrating, 786–87
Environmental impact statement, 778
Environmental Protection Agency (EPA),
747, 778, 780, 782–83, 785

EPA. See Environmental Protection
Agency
Equal Credit Opportunity Act (1974),
773
Equal Employment Opportunity Act
(1972), 822
Equal Opportunity, legislation on,
821–24
Equipment, security interest in, 489–90,
491
Equity: action in—adequacy of
consideration, 152
for dividends, 695
case illustrating, 695–96
distinguished from law, 9–10
ERISA. See Employee Retirement
Income Security Act
Espionage, industrial, 102
Estate (see also Ownership):
administration of, 908–10
concurrent, 875–76
distribution of, 903–07
in fee, 869–70
freehold, 869–71
future, 885
in land, 869–72
leasehold, 871
life, 218, 870–71
nonfreehold, 871–73
nonpossessory, 885
privity of, 888
in property, and Chapter 7 liquidation,
530–31
Estoppel: agency by (apparent authority),
558, 570
case illustrating, 571–72
and ethics, 592
corporation by, 663
of insurer's defense against payment,
923
partnership by, 605, 613
promissory (doctrine of detrimental
reliance), 138, 163–65
case illustrating, 163–65
Ethics: in agency relationships, 592–94
business, 742–45
defined, 107–09
of commercial transactions, 506–09
and contract law, 280–83
of creditor's rights, and bankruptcy,
546–49
and economics, 546–47
and efficiency, 282–83
and government regulations, 829–31
and the protection of property, 954–58
of quasi-contractual remedy, 282
European Common Market, 951
European Economic Community (ECC),
951
Eviction, constructive, 873
Evidence: oral. See Evidence, parol
parol (oral)—admissibility of, in a sales
contract, 303–06
and signature, 406, 442
and written contracts, 227–30
Examination, during trial, 48

Exchange securities, exemption of, from
registration, 717
Exclusionary practices, and antitrust
laws, 810–11
Executor (executrix), 894, 909
Exemptions: from antitrust laws,
797–800
from estate in property in Chapter 7
liquidation, 531
Homestead, 521 n., 522–24
from securities registration, 716–17
Expertise and warranty, 368
Expropriation, 946

F

Fact: mistake of. See Mistake
seller's affirmation of, as warranty, 368
Factor, assignment of accounts receivable
to, 486
Fair Credit Billing Act (1974), 773
Fair Credit Reporting Act (1974), 773
Fair Debt Collection Practices Act
(FDCPA) (1977), 774
Fair Labor Standards Act (Wage-Hour
Law), 827
Fair Packaging and Labeling Law (1976),
568
Fair trade, 808
Fair use of copyright material, 846
ethics and, 955
Fairness in contracts, 151–55, 280–83
and inequity of the contractors'
bargaining power, 193.
False pretenses, obtaining goods by, 100.
See also Misrepresentation
Family, protection of, and inheritance,
894
Farm products, security interest in, 489,
491
Farmer, defined, 529 n.10
F.A.S. (free alongside), 315, 333
FCC. See Federal Communications
Commission
FDA. See Food and Drug Administration
FDCPA. See Fair Debt Collection
Practices Act
Federal Communications Commission
(FCC), 751
Federal Elections Campaign Act, 677 n.
Federal Insurance Contributions Act
(FICA), 826
Federal Judgeship Act. See Bankruptcy
Amendments
Federal Reserve Board of Governors,
766, 770
Federal Reserve System, 477, 478
Federal Rules of Civil Procedure,
933–34
Federal Trade Commission (FTC), 129,
361, 379, 524, 730, 737, 739,
761–67 passim
and antitrust enforcement, 795–96,
803, 808, 811, 812
Federal Trust Commission Act (1914),
188, 761, 762, 795–96, 950

Federal Unemployment Tax Act
 (FUTA), 826
Federal Water Pollution Control Act
 (1965), 780, 782
Federalism, 12–18
Fee simple absolute (fee simple), 218
 n.4, 836
 defeasible, 869–70
 determinable, 870, 886
 ownership rights in, 869
Felony, 91–92
 grand larceny as, 100
 statutes of limitations and, 97
FICA. *See* Federal Insurance
 Contributions Act
Fiction, legal, 119
Fifth Amendment, suspension of, 98
Filing: to perfect a security interest,
 486–90
 information on, 497
 locality of, 489–90
 illustrated, 491
 of plan for Chapter 11 reorganization,
 538, 540
Financing: corporate, 669–74
 statement—filing, to perfect a security
 interest, 486–90
 illustrated, 487
 amendment of, 499
Fire, insurance against, 100, 925–27
First refusal, on transfer of shares, 699
Fitness, warranty of, 375–76, 380
Fixtures (*see also* Things attached):
 defined, 835–36
 as property, 866–69
 case illustrating, 867–69
 security interest in, 486 n.3, 491
Flammable Fabrics Act (1953), 768
F.O.B. (free on board): and delivery, 333
 and risk of loss, 314, 315
 case illustrating, 315–16
Food and Drug Administration (FDA),
 752, 768
Food, Drug, and Cosmetic Act (1938),
 752, 768
Forbearance, 149
 case illustrating, 150–51
Force: superseding intervening, and
 negligence, 68–69
 use of, in self-defense, 96
Foreclosure, methods of, 521–22
Foreign: currency, for payment of
 negotiable instruments, 411
 officials, bribery of, 101–102
 trade, and international law, 943–53
Foreign Corrupt Practices Act (1977),
 101
Foreign Sovereign Immunities Act
 (FSIA) (1976), 948–49, 950
Forgery, 99
 of negotiable instruments, 437, 453
Form, of contracts, 115, 217–30
France, Commercial Code (1707) of,
 632
Franchise: acquiring, 731
 business organization of, 731–32
 contract, 731–37, 738–39

damages for termination of, 735–37
 defined, 730, 731
 FTC rule on, 739
 location of, 731–32
 payment for, 731
 prices and, 733
 termination of, 733–35
 territorial exclusivity of, 732
 case illustrating, 732–33
 types of, 731
Franchising, 730–41
 antitrust laws and, 739
 and consumer protection, 737
 law of, 730–31
 regulation of, 737–39
 relationship in, between franchisor and
 franchisee, 739
Fraud (*see also* Misrepresentation), 100
 accountant's liability for, 933–34,
 938–41
 bankruptcy as, 103–04
 bulk transfer as, 522
 constructive, accountant's, 933
 case illustrating, 934–35
 in execution (*in factum*), 453
 in fact, 522
 and holder's defense, in liability on
 negotiable instruments, 453
 and illegal contracts, 198
 implied in law, 522
 in inception, 453
 in the inducement, as defense against
 liability on negotiable instruments,
 454
 case illustrating, 454–56
 and intoxication, 177
 mail, and franchising, 739
 misrepresentation and, 205–12, 387,
 578
 and sham transactions, 326
Free alongside. *See* F.A.S.
Free on board. See F.O.B.
Fringe benefits, corporate, 668
FSIA. *See* Foreign Sovereign
 Immunities Act
FTC. *See* Federal Trade Commission
FUTA. *See* Federal Unemployment
 Tax Act

G

Gambling, 184
 case illustrating, 184–85
Garn-St. Germain Act (1982), 237
Garnishment, 516–18
 case illustrating, 517–18
 ethics and, 547
Gas service, as personal property, 836
Gasoline, lead content, *case illustrating*,
 779–80
Gift: acquisition of personal property by,
 837–40
 causa mortis, 840
 effective, 837–40
 inter vivos, 840
 transfer of property by will as, 895–96
Good faith: accountants', 938–39

defined, 507
 and ethics, 507–08
 and holders-in-due-course, 433–34
 case illustrating, 434
 in sales contracts, 329
 case illustrating, 330–31
Goods (*see also* Property, personal):
 buyer's right to reject, 351
 consumer—as collateral, and
 disposition of in default, 501
 defined, 486
 security interest in, 468, 491
 defined, 289
 fungible—as collateral, 499
 defined, 841
 and passage of title, 313
 future, 312
 identified—delivery of, 332
 destruction of, and perfect tender,
 337–38
 recovery of, 351–52
 in transit, and breach of sales contract,
 346
 merchantable, *defined*, 370
 nonconforming, 297
 damages for, 355
 rejection of, 351
 retention of, and fraud, 326
 sale of. *See* Sale of goods
 second-hand, and security interest,
 496–97
 seller's rights in, as remedy, 346–48
 tangible, security interest in, 489–90,
 491
Government regulation, 749–831
 and antitrust laws, 798–818
 consumer protection by, 760–76
 and employment laws, 819–28
 and environmental protection, 777–88
 ethics of, 829–31
 history of, 749–50
 and labor relations, 819–21
 scope of, 750–58
 types of, *illustrated*, 753
Grain storage facilities, bankruptcy of,
 543
Grandchildren, and inheritance,
 906–07
Gross, profit in, 886–87
Guaranty, 518, 519–21
 case illustrating, 519–20
 promise of, 221

H

Habitability, warranty of, 873, 880, 882
Hand, Judge Learned, on the meaning of
 words, 126 n.6
Handwriting: on negotiable instruments,
 415
 a will in, 899
Hawkland, (*Commercial Paper and Bank
 Deposits and Collections*), 454 n.
Hazard: abnormal, and principal's strict
 liability, 579
 moral, 508–09, 548, 956
HDC. *See* Holder-in-due-course

Health, protection of: for consumers, 767–68
  and employment, 824
  government regulation of, 751–52
Hearing, pretrial, 47
Heirs, precedence among, in distribution of intestate estate's, 903–07
Hold harmless, agreement to, 365
Holder: *defined*, 402
  request for certification of check by, 463–64
  through a holder-in-due-course, 438
    case illustrating, 438–39
Holder-in-due-course (HDC): *defined*, 402–03, 430
  federal limits on rights of, 439–40
  indorsement and, 419, 423 n.5, 426
  lack of status as, 433
  and presentment warranty, 450
  requirements for status of, 430–38
  rights of, 429–40
  rule on, 524–25
  and stop payment orders, 469–70
Holdsworth, W. (*History of English Law*), 632 n.
Homeowners', insurance policies for, 925, 927–29
  forms of, 927
    illustrated, 928–29
Homestead, statutory exemption of, for debtors, 521 n., 522–24
Hours of employment, maximum, 827
HUD. *See* Department of Housing and Urban Development

I

ICC. *See* Interstate Commerce Commission
Identification of goods—used as collateral, 499
  for sale, *defined*, 312–13
Illegality: as a defense against liability on a negotiable instrument, 454, 457
  and dissolution of a partnership, 616
    case illustrating, 616
  effect of, on contracts, 142, 196–98
  supervening, 142
Illegitimacy, and the laws of inheritance, 904
  case illustrating, 905–06
Illinois Business Corporation Act (1933), 644
Immunity, as a defense against criminal liability, 98
  sovereign. *See* Foreign trade
Impairment, substantial, 334
Implication, easement (profit) created by, 887
Impossibility, of performance: doctrine of, in contract law, 280–81
  impossibility, objective, 257
    case illustrating, 258–59
  temporary, and suspension of contracts, 260
  and termination of an agency, 582

Imposter, and negotiable instruments, 423–24
Impracticality: business, and the dissolution of a partnership, 617
  and contract performance, *case illustrating*, 335–37
Imprisonment, false (false arrest), 54–56
  case illustrating, 55–56
Incapacity, mental: as defense against liability on a negotiable instrument, 454, 457
  and the dissolution of a partnership, 617
Incompetence: of contracting party, and termination of the contract, 142
  of a customer, bank's duties in, 468
Incorporation: articles of, 660–62
  illustrated, 661
  benefits of, 668–69
  costs of, 667–68
  improper, 662
  procedures for, 656, 659–63
Indemnification: directors' rights to, 693
  principal's—duty of, 562
    rights of, from agents, 566
Indemnity, 916
Independent contractor. *See* Contractor, independent
Indictment (an information), 98–99
Individuals, eligibility of, for Chapter 13 plans, 541
Indorsee, *defined*, 402
Indorsement: agency, 422–23
  by bank, 426
  blank, 419–20
  conditional, 421, 423 n.1
  deposit or collection, 421
  forged, 423–25
    bank's duties and, 472
  missing, on a check, 468
  of negotiable instruments, 419–26
    and transfer warranties, 450, 452
  nonstandard, 425–26
  prohibiting further indorsement, 421
  qualified, 420–21
    and liability, 445 n.
  restrictive, 421–23, 458
    case illustrating, 422
    bank's liability for, 475
  special, 418, 419
  trust, 422–23
  unqualified, 447
  wrongful, *case illustrating*, 424–25
Indorser: accommodation, 448
  case illustrating, 451–52
  defined, 402
Infancy, as a defense against criminal liability, 94
Infant. *See* Minor
Influence, undue: as defense against liability on a negotiable instrument, 457
  and illegal contracts, 198
  and the validity of a will, 900
Information, an. *See* Indictment
Infringement: of copyright. *See* Copyright
  of patent. *See* Patent

of title, warranty against, 365
of trademark. *See* Trademark
Inheritance: rules of descent for, 903–07
  transfer of property by—personal, 840
    real, 876
Injunction, 10, 64
  eighty-day, in labor disputes, 820
Injury: and employment, laws on, 824
  to innocent party, and rescission of contract, 210
  legal, 65
Innkeeper, bailments and, 862–63
  lien of, 514
Innovation, government regulation of, 752
In pari delicto, 196, 616
Insanity: and contractual capacity, 179–80
  as a defense against criminal liability, 94–95
  and the dissolution of a partnership, 610, 617
Insider trading in securities, regulation on, 719–26
Insolvency (*see also* Bankruptcy): balance sheet, 529 n.11
  buyer's rights in, 351–52
  equitable, 529 n.11
  and illegal dividends, 697
  and a partnership, 616
  seller's rights in, 346–47, 351
  and termination of an agency, 582 n.13
Inspection: buyer's right of, 339
  and warranties, 376
  of food, and government regulation, 767
  by OSHA, *case illustrating*, 824–26
  rights of. *See* Records, business
Installment: contract. *See* Contract, installment
  note: *see* Note, installment
Instrument: *defined*, 497
  demand, 401
  negotiable. *See* Negotiable instruments
  nonnegotiable, 401
  order. *See* Order paper
  security interest in, 491, 497
  time, 401
Insurance, 913–31
  arson and, 100
  automobile, 929–30
  comprehensive, 929, 930
  collision, 929–30
  contracts for—enforceable, 197
    vesting of rights in, 244
  coverage of, and timing, 917
    case illustrating, 917–19
  disability, 668, 826
  endowment, 923
  exemption of industry from antitrust laws, 799
  fire, 100, 925–27
  as a fringe benefit, 668
  home protection, 924
  key person, 916
  liability—automobile, 929

for corporate directors, 639
  personal, 927
life, 923–25
  limited payment, 923
  mutual, 924
  termination of, 925
  whole, 923, 924–25
for medical payments, 930
as a minor's necessary, 175
moral hazard and, 956
mortgage term, 924
old age, legislation on, 826
policy, 913
  anti-assignment clauses in, 237
  blanket, 925
  complete performance and, 250
  floater, 926, 929
  interpreting, 920
  open, 926
  specific, 925
  umbrella, 929
  valued, 926
retirement, 826
and risk of loss, 326–27
survivors', legislation on, 826
term, 668, 923–24
  extended, 924
  mortgage, 924
title, 882
types, 923–30
Insured, 914
Insurer, 914
Intangibles, general, security interest in,
  489, 492
Intent: donative, and a gift, 838
  case illustrating, 838–39
  (state of mind: *mens rea* or evil intent)
    and criminal liability, 93, 95
Intention, and contract law, 178
  offer and, 126–31
  statement of, 126–27
Interest: conflict of, 196, 692
  executory, 885, 886
    shifting, 886
  future, 885
    in land, 870
  insurable, 184, 326–27, 914
    case illustrating, 915–96
  nonpossessory, 886–87
  partner's, in the partnership, 624, 625
  present possessory, 885
  promissory, a lease of personal
    property as, 835
  property, as real estate lease as, 835
  security. *See* Security interest
Interest rate (*see also* Usury): judgment,
  182, 415
  legal, 182
  and negotiable instruments, 415
Interference: permissive, 79
  wrongful, 75–79
Internal Revenue Code, 941
  Subchapter S of, 651
International Court of Justice, 943, 944
Interrogatories, 47

Interstate commerce, and government
  regulation, 750, 754
  and the Commerce Clause, 18–22
  cases illustrating, 19–20, 21–22
Interstate Commerce Commission (ICC),
  750, 754
Interstate Land Sale Full Disclosure Act,
  762, 770
Inter vivos donation of gift, 840
Intestacy: laws of, 903
  and title to property, 893, 894
Intoxication: contracts made under,
  176–79
  case illustrating, 177–79
  as defense against criminal liability, 94
Inventory: floating lien on, 493
  and purchase money priority rules,
    494–95
  security interest in, 489, 490, 491
Investing, social, 744
Investment (*see also* Securities):
  companies, government regulation
    of, 726–27, 752
  group. *See* Syndicate
Investment Company Act (1940), 726
  Amendments (1970), 726
Investors, protection of. *See* Securities
  regulation
"Irresistible impulse" test, of insanity, 95
Issue, *defined,* 402
Issuer, of a letter of credit, 944

J

Jentz, Gaylord A. ("Federal Regulation
  of Advertising: False
  Representation"), 763
Joint: stock company (association), 599,
  643
  tenancy with right of survivorship,
    836, 875–76
    and distribution of an estate, 910
  venture, 598–99, 610
Judgment: deficiency—in default, 503
  in foreclosure, 522
  n.o.v., 48
  recovery of, and statutes of limitations,
    255
Jurisdiction, 33–34
  appellate, 34, 41
  concurrent, 41
  congressional limitations of, 40
  defined, 33
  exclusive, 41
  of federal courts, 40–41, 646
  over foreign corporations, 646
  over foreign nations, in the U.S.,
    948–59, 950
  general, 36
  limited, 35, 37, 40
  original, 34, 35
  and perfected security interest, 493–94
  in personam, 33, 41
  quasi in rem, 33

  in rem, 33
  under the Sherman Act, 791
  subject matter, 34
Jurisprudence, philosophies of, 4–5
Jury, 47, 48

K

Kickback. *See* Bribery
Keeton, *et al. (Prosser and Keeton on
  Torts)* 393 n.4

L

Labor (*see also* Employees; Employment):
  exemption of, from antitrust laws,
    797
  government regulation of relationships,
    819–20
Labor-Management Relations Act (Taft-
  Hartley Act) (1947), 820
Labor-Management Reporting and
  Disclosure Act (Landrum-Griffin
  Act) (1959), 820–21
Laches, equitable doctrine of, 9–10
Land (*see also* Real estate): as real
  property, 865
  sale of—contracts for, 218–19,
    and damages, 264
    and specific performance, 272
  trespass to, 60–61
  use of, limitations on, 887–91
    ethics of, 956
Landlord, warranties given by, 873
Landrum Griffin Act. *See* Labor-
  Management Reporting and
  Disclosure Act
Lanham Act (1946), 752
Larcency, 99–100, 101
Law, Laws: adjective. *See* Law,
  procedural
  administrative, 7, 756–57
  American, sources of, 5–8
  antitrust, 733, 790–800
    and foreign nations, 950
  business (commercial), sources of, 7–8
  case, 5
    procedure for analyzing, 11, 13–15
    records of, 10–11
  civil, 8–9
    distinguished from criminal law,
    concept summary, 104
  commercial. *See* Law, business
  common—and accountants' liability,
    932–37
    conveyance of fee simple absolute
    by, 869
    development of, 5–6
    and environmental protection, 777
    and inheritance, 893
    and the origins of antitrust laws,
    789–90
  constitutional, 8, 760–61
  contract, 113–283, 429–30

criminal, 8, 9, 90–105
  distinguished—from civil law, 90
    from tort law, 52–53
disclosure, 524
equity, 9–10
fair trade, 190
international, 943–53
mercantile (sale of goods), 287–396
Merchant (*Lex Mercantoria*), 287,
  397, 442
misrepresentations of, as fraud,
  208–09
  case illustrating, 208–09
mistake of, 95
municipal (national), and international
  law, 946–48
national. *See* Law, municipal
natural, 4
operation of—and agency, 558,
  581–82
  and contract discharge, 140–42,
    255–56
  and the dissolution of a partnership,
    615–16
  and the revocation of a will,
    902–903
perceptions of, 3–4
private, 8, 9
procedural (adjective), 8
public, 8, 9
of sale of goods. *See* Law, mercantile
statutory, 7
substantive, 8
tort—distinguished from criminal law,
  52–53
  scope of, 52
Lease, 219
  assignment of, 875
    prohibited, 236
  defined, 873
  distinguished from a bailment, *case
    illustrating*, 849–50
  exculpatory clauses in, 191
    case illustrating, 191–93
  as an implied warranty, 395
  management of, in bankruptcy, 543
  standard forms for, 214
Legacy, 894–95
Lessors, strict liability of, 395
Letter of credit, 400–01, 944–45
  as recognizance, 122
  security interest in, 492–93
Lex Mercantoria (Law Merchant), 287,
  397, 442
Liability (*see also* Duties):
  of an acceptor, 401
  accountant's, 932–42
  agent's, 406, 575–79
  bailee's, 853–55
  bailor's, 859
  bank's, 475, 478–79
  basis of, 387
  commercial paper and, 442–60
  consumers', 479. *See also* Consumer,
    protection of

corporate, 681. *See also* Directors,
  liabilities of; Shareholders, liabilities
  of
in credit card transactions, 773
criminal, 93–98
  accountant's, 941
  corporate, 681
  defenses against, 94–94
  elements of, 93
for danger, 71–72, 579, 588–89
defense against—due diligence as, 938
  for negotiable instruments, 452–58
  personal, 454–58
  real, 452–54
in delegation of contractual duties,
  240–41
employers', 587–89, 593–94, 824
of franchisor, for franchisee, 739
of indorsers, 419, 420
in insurance contracts, 924–25
joint, 628–29
  and several, 629
limitation of, 276–77, 635, 637–39,
  853. *See also* Clause, exculpatory
maker's, 446
minor's, 173, 176
for misrepresentation, 387, 578, 613
for negligence, 383–95, 578–79,
  587–88, 933
  defense against, 68–71
on negotiable instruments, 442–49,
  452–58, 459
of owners, in businesses, 601
parents', for children, 176
of partners, 128–29, 579, 629,
  634–35, 638–39
in a partnership, 604, 613, 628–29,
  634–35
  limited, 635, 637–39
personal, 406, 443–45, 634–35,
  637–39, 656–69
primary, and negotiable instruments,
  445–46, 448
principal's, 575–79
product, 73, 383–95, 508–09, 769
of a promoter, 657
for safety in the workplace, 587
secondary—for a certified check, 463
  guaranty and, 519
  on negotiable instruments, 446,
    447, 448
  and the Statute of Frauds, 221–24
self-defense and, 54, 96
for servants, 588
of shareholders, 653, 662–67, 697,
  700
strict (liability without fault), 71–73,
  387–95
  defenses against, 391–93
  principal's, 579
  requirements of, 390–91
  in special bailments, 860
  suppliers', 395
tenants', for rent, 875
and third-party beneficiaries of

warranties, 375
  of a tipee, 724
  vicarious, 86
  warranty, 450–52
  without fault. *See* Liability, strict
Libel (*see also* Defamation), 56
  trade, 88
Library, reproduction of copyright
  material by, 846
License, as a revocable right, 887
Licensing, statutes on, 185–86
Lien: artisan's, 514, 853
  bailee's, 853
  creditor's, 494
  on a debtor's property, 534
  floating, concept of, 493–94
  hotelkeeper's, 514
  mechanic's, 513
  mortgage as, 885
  on a negotiable instrument, as value,
    432
  possessory, 514
  seller's, 350
  state, 218 n.5
  warranty of absence of, 365
Limitations: good faith, on output
    contracts, 156
  on liability. *See* Liability, limitations
    on
  on recovery, and strict liability, 391
  statute. *See* Statute of limitations
Liquidation (*see also* Bankruptcy,
    Chapter 7): corporate termination
    as, 711, 713
  of damages. *See* Damages, liquidated
  of debt. *See* Debt, liquidation of
Litigation, private, and environmental
    protection, 778
Loans: add-on interest, 183
  installment, and usury, 183
  as a minor's necessary, 175
  nonpayment of, and ethics, 546
  shareholders', to a corporation, 666
    case illustrating, 666–67
Lobbying, legality of, 196
Locus sigilli (L.S.), 122 n.4
Loss: material, and rejection of
    shipment, 332
  mitigation of, by seller, 347
  proof of, in fire insurance, 927
  risk of. *See* Risk of loss
  shipper's, 860
    case illustrating, 860–62
  of use, and breach of contract, 265
Loyalty: agent's duty of, 559
    case illustrating, 560–61
  corporate directors' duty of, 690–92
    case illustrating, 691–92
  defined, 690
L.S. *See Locus sigilli*

M

McCarran-Ferguson Act (1945), 799

McCoy, C., *et al.* (*Ethics in the Corporate Policy Process: An Introduction*), 107
McGee, John S. ("Predatory Price Cutting: The Standard Oil [New Jersey] Case"), 790 n.3
M'Naghton test, of insanity, 94–95
Magnuson-Moss Warranty Act, 379–81
Maker: accommodation, 403
  and negotiable instruments, 448
  defined, 402
  liability of, 446
Malpractice, in a professional corporation, 653–54
Management: of close corporations, 649
  partner's rights in, 623
Manufacturing plant, as a franchise, 731
Mail-order transactions, 767
Mails, use of, to defraud, 100
Majority, age of, 168
Market: division of, and antitrust laws, 805
  relevant, and monopolization, 807–08, 811
Marriage: promise of, 224
  and revocation of a will, 902–03
  and women's freedom to contract, 180
Married Women's Property Acts, 180 n.8
Master (*see also* Employer) and servant, relationship between, 553, 554
MBCA. *See* Model Business Corporation Act
Medical plan, as a fringe benefit, 668–69
Medicare, 826
Meeting: corporate organizational, 662
  directors', 686–87
  shareholders', 684–85
Memorandum of a contract: oral, 228
  written, 225–27
  case illustrating, 226–27
Mens rea (evil intent), 93, 95
Merchandise, unsolicited, 144, 766–67
Merchants: contracts between, 140
  additional terms in, 298–99, 301
    case illustrating, 298, 301
  oral, 225
  the Statute of Frauds, 302
  defined, 290
    case illustrating, 290–92
  ethical standards for, 507, 508
  firm offer by, 296
  and implied warranties, 370
  right of, to reject nonconforming goods, 351
  seller as, and risk of loss, 316
  and warranty of title infringement, 365
Merchantability, warranty of, 375–76, 380
Merger, corporate, 703–11
  anticompetitive, 812–16
  conglomerate, legality of, 814
  production extension, *case illustrating*, 815–16
  defined, 703
  horizontal, legality of, 812
    case illustrating, 812–14

parent-subsidy, 706
procedure for, 706
short-form (parent-subsidy), 706
vertical, legality of, 814
Mind: sound, concept of: 897–98. *See also* Incapacity, mental; Insanity
  state of. *See* Intent
Minerals: sale of, 289
  security interest in, 486 n.3
Minors (infants): agency and, 557
  contractual capacity of, 168–76
  and ethics, 281–82
  defined, 168
  liability of, for torts, 176
  and non-voidable contracts, 176
  partnership with, 610
Misrepresentation (deceit; fraud), 59–60, 205–12
  of age, by a minor, 171–73
    case illustrating, 172–73
  agent's, and liability of principal, 578
  innocent, 212, 578
  and liability, 387, 578, 613
  material, 211
  negligent, 212
  of a partnership, 613
Minority, status of, as defense against liability, 453
Mis-delivery of bailed goods, 854
  case illustrating, 854–55
Misdemeanor: *defined*, 92
  petit larceny as, 100
Mistake: in contracts, 201–04
  and ethics, 281
  and parol evidence, 228–29
  bilateral. *See* Mistake, mutual
  as defense against criminal liability, 95
  of fact (identity), 95, 201, 202–03
    cases illustrating, 202–03, 203–04
    defined, 204
  in identity. *See* Mistake, of fact
  mathematical, and enforceability of contracts, 202
  mutual (bilateral), 201, 202–04
    case illustrating, 203–04
  unilateral, 201–02
  in value, 203
Model Act. *See* Model Business Corporation Act
Model Business Corporation Act (MBCA) (1933), 610, 643–44, 659, 661, 663, 680, 686 n.10, 690, 692, 693, 697, 700, 701
Model Nonprofit Corporation Act, 648–49
Model Penal Code, 91, 93, 94
Money: assignment of right to receive, 235 n.4
  commercial paper as substitute for, 397–98
  payment in, and negotiability of instruments, 411–12
  purchase. *See* Purchase money
Monopolization, and antitrust regulation, 807–08
Monopoly. *See* Antitrust laws; Trade,

restraint of
Mortgage, 218
  anti-assignment clauses in, 236–37
  assumption of, as a third party beneficiary contract, 242–43
  due-on-sale (DOS) provisions in, 237
  foreclosure, 521–22
  note, 400
  obtaining, 885
  purchase money (first), 885
  security by, and negotiability, 409
  term insurance (home protection), 924
Motion: for a directed verdict, 48
  to dismiss (demurrer), 44
  for judgment on the pleadings, 46
  for a new trial, 48
  for summary judgment, 46
Motorist, uninsured, coverage for, 930
Murder: felonious, 91–92, 96
  case illustrating, 91–92
  statute of limitation on, 97
Music, recorded, as personal property, 836
Mutual funds, regulation of, 726–27

N

Name: corporate, 660
  correction of, in indorsement, 426
  generic, trademark as, 83–84, 752–53, 845
National Association of Realtors (*Real Estate Sales Handbook*), 182 n.
National Commission on Product Safety, 768
National Conference of Commissioners on Uniform Laws, 397, 524, 633, 897
National Energy Act (1978), 780
National Environmental Policy Act (NEPA) (1970), 778
National Hispanic Business Agenda, 743
National Labor Relations Act (Wagner Act) (1935), 750, 797, 819
National Organization for Women, 743–44
National Reporter System (*West*), 11
Necessaries, contract for: and insanity, 179
  minors' disaffirmance of, 173–75
Necessity, easement created by, 887
Need, economic, as duress, 213
Negligence, 64–71
  case illustrating, 70–71
  accountant's liability for, 933
    cases illustrating, 934–35, 936–37
  agent's, and liability of principal, 578–79
  comparative, 69–70, 387, 393
  confusion by, 841
  contributory, 69, 386, 387, 393
  customer's, with checks, 471–74
    case illustrating, 472–74
  defenses to, 386–87
  defined, 383
  employee's, and liability of employer, 587–88

liability for, 383–95, 578–79, 587–88, 933
per se, 387
presumption of bailee's, 856
case illustrating, 856–58
Negotiable instruments, 401
and accommodation parties, 448–49
claims against. *See* Negotiable instruments, defenses against
completion of unauthorized, as a defense, 457–58
defenses against liability on, 436, 452–58
defined, 401
demand, overdue, 435
discharge of, 458–49
dishonor of, 436, 447–48
incomplete, 436
irregular, 436–37
and recognizance, 122
negotiability of—factors not affecting, 415
and reference to another agreement, 408
requirements for, 405–15
negotiation of, 418–19
defined, 418
overdue, 435
and rights to assign, 235 n.4
security interest in, 491
signature on, and liability, 442–49
time, overdue, 435
as value, 433
warranty liability and, 450–52
case illustrating, 451–52
Noise Control Acts (1970, 1972), 782
Noise pollution and government regulation, 782–83
Nondelivery, of a negotiable instrument, as a defense, 458
Nonmerchants: contracts between, 140
and additional terms in, 298
sellers as, and risk of loss, 316
Nonnotification (indirect collection), chattel paper and, 497
Nonowners, sales by, 323–26
Norris-La Guardia Act (1932), 819
Note: installment, 400
overdue, 435
promissory, 397
described, 399–400, 401, 402
negotiability of, *case illustrating*, 408–09
presentment of, 447
Notice: constructive, 633, 635
defined, 582 n.15
of defect, and holder-in-due-course of a negotiable instrument, 435–38
of a partnership dissolution, 617–18
Notification: agent's duty of, 559
of contractual acceptance, 145
(direct collection), and chattel paper, 497
required, in the termination of an agency, 582
Novation: *defined*, 283
and discharge of contract, 254–55

and liability of a corporate promoter, 657
Nuisance, 63–64

O

OASDI. *See* Old Age, Survivors, and Disability Insurance
Obedience, agent's duty of, 561
Obligation: contractual, and the statutes of limitations, 255–56
moral, as consideration, 151
case illustrating, 160–62
voidable, on negotiable instruments, 437
Occupational Safety and Health Act (OSHA) (1970), 587 n., 749, 824–26
Offense, petty, *defined*, 92
Offer, contractual: acceptance of, 142–47
firm, 137, 296
irrevocable, 137–39, 142
rejection of, 139–40
reliance on, and revocability, 137–39
case illustrating, 138–39
requirements for, 126–36
for a sale of goods, 292–96
termination of, 136–42
Offerings, securities: private, 716
regulations affecting, 716–18
Officers, of a corporation, 646, 693
delegation of powers to, 687
indorsement by, 426
Old Age, Survivors, and Disability Insurance (OASDI), 826
Omission, act of, and criminal liability, 93
"On-us item," 476
Opinion: expression of, and contract law, 126
statement of—as fraud, 205–208
and warranty, 368
Option: contract, 137, 142
to purchase, bailment with, 851
stock warrant, 694
Order: cease and desist, 766
changing, 625
to pay, unconditional, and negotiability, 406–09
stop payment, 469–70
case illustrating, 470
ethics and, 509
for relief, in bankruptcy, 529
Order paper (order instruments), 413–14
conversion of, to bearer paper, 419, 420
indorsement of, 419, 420
negotiation of, 418–19
unindorsed, 426
OSHA. *See* Occupational Safety and Health Act
Overdrafts, and the dishonoring of checks, 466–67, 471
Overtime, laws on, 827
Ownership (*see also* Estate): concurrent, 875–76

of property, 836–37
real, *concept summary*, 872
rights of—and gifts, 838
in real property, 869–72
transfer of, 876–85

P

P.A. *See* Association, professional
"Palimony," *case illustrating*, 186–88
Paper label case, the, 108
Par value, 671–72
Parents, liability of, for children, 176
Partition, transfer of tenancy by, 876
Partner: admission of new, and dissolution of the partnership, 615
authority of, 629–30
a corporation as, 610
death of, 615–16
duties of, 627–28
case illustrating, 627–28
general, liability of, 635, 638
case illustrating, 638–39
incoming, liability of, 629
joint liability of, 628–29, 634
limited—liability of, 597
personnel, 634, 635, 638
management of partnership by, 635
number of, permissible, 635
restrictions on authority of, 639
rights of, 639
notice to, of a dissolution of the partnership, 617
case illustrating, 617–18
power of—general agency, 628–30
to withdraw, 615
rights of, 623–27
in partnership property, 625–27
transfer of interest of, 615
Partnership, 597–98, 623–31
accounting of assets of, 624–25, 627 n.17
agreement of, formalities, 607
aggregate theory of, 604
articles of, 607
bankruptcy of, 604–05
capacity, legal, of, 604
certificate of, 598
compared with a corporation, 600
concept summary, 601
and conveyance of property, 605
defined, 603
dissolution of, 614–18
duration of, 607, 610
by estoppel, 605, 613
formation of, 605–13
general, characteristics of, 634–35
indication of, 610–12
case illustrating, 611–12
judgments against, 604
law of, 603–05
as a legal entity, 604–05
liability in, 604, 613, 634–35. *See also* Partner, general; Partner, limited
joint, 628–29

limited, 598, 632–42
  defined, 632
  dissolution of, 640–41
  formation of, 633, 635
  history of, 632–33
  liability in, 635, 637–39
  revised, characteristics of, 634–35
  use of, 640
mutual consent in, 610
property and, 611, 613
rights in, of partners, 623–26
taxation of, 605, 611
for a term, 607
termination of, 613–21
  case illustrating, 614–15
trading and non-trading, 629
true, 605
  case illustrating, 605–07
types of, *concept summary*, 634–35
at will, 607, 610, 615
winding up, 614, 618–21, 624
  case illustrating, 619–21
Patents: government regulation of, 752
infringement of, 85
  and ethics, 954
  warranty against, 365
as personal property, 845
Payee: *defined*, 402
fictitious, 424
as holder-in-due-course, 437
multiple, and indorsement, 426
Payment: of debt under Chapter 13 plan,
  541
discharge by, on a negotiable
  instrument, 457, 458
for a franchise, 731
open term, in a sales contract, 293
as order or promise, 401
for sales contracts, 293, 339
source of, and negotiable instruments,
  409
tenants obligation of, 875
Payoff. *See* Bribery
P.C. *See* Corporation, professional
Penalty, *defined*, 269
Pension plans: corporate, 668
government regulation of private, 826
Perfection, of a security interest, 485–90
improper, *case illustrating*, 532–33
priority rules on, 494–97
  concept summary, 498
in second-hand goods, 496–97
voiding, 490
Per capita, distribution of an estate by,
  907
Performance, contractual: agent's duty of,
  559
and breach of contract, 264–66,
  272–74
complete, 249–50
defined, 115
and discharge of contract, 249–53,
  257–60
duty of, and assignability of rights, 235
impossibility of, and discharge of
  contract, 257–60
  case illustrating, 258–59

inferior, 249, 250
partial, 134, 303
  and illegal contracts, 197–98
  recovery and, 275
  revocability and, 138
  and the Statute of Frauds, 219, 224
for a sale of goods, 329–38
  concurrent conditions of, 331
  course of, 306
  partial, 303
to the satisfaction of another, 252
specific, 10, 219
  buyer's right to, 352
  as remedy for breach of contract,
    272–74
  and unconscionable contracts, 307
substantial, 249, 250–51, 252
  case illustrating, 250–51
  and breach of contract, 264
suspended, 342
time taken, 253
uncertain, 155–57
Personalty. *See* Property, personal
Per stirpes, 906–07
Petition (*see also* Complaint),
  bankruptcy, filing: for Chapter 7
    liquidation, 528–29
  for Chapter 13 plan, 541
Plan: for Chapter 11 reorganization,
  540–41
for Chapter 13 adjustment of debts,
  541–42
zero, 542
Plants: patents for, 845
as real property, 866
Plea bargaining, 98, 101
Pleadings, 42–46
responsive, 44
Point of sale systems, banking and, 477
Points, *defined*, 182 n.
Policy: insurance. *See* Insurance policy
public, law and, 186–96
social, and inheritance, 894
Political contributions, by corporations,
  677 n.
Pollock, *(Torts)*, 80
Pollution: control of and cost, 830
and government regulation, 778–83
Possession: acquiring personal property
  by, 837
bailee's right of, 852
creditors' right to take, on default,
  500–01
delivery of, without title, 849–50
Postal Reorganization Act (1970), 144,
  766–67
Posting, deferred (delayed return), 477
Power: of attorney, 557 n.
agent's, 567
  illustrated, 568
  case illustrating, 569
government's, of condemnation
  (eminent domain), 876–77
of sale, in foreclosure, 521
Powers: of administrative agencies
  (judicial, executive, and legislative),
  749–50, 753–57

of the Consumer Product Safety
  Commission, 769
corporate, 677–81
directors' delegation of, 687
of the federal government, 18. *See also*
  Government regulation
general agency, of partners, 628–39
police, of a state, 20–22, 888
rulemaking, 754–56
shareholders' in corporate
  management, 681–85
Precedent, 5–6, 41
Prediction, as fraud, 205
Preemption, 23–24
Preference, in debt payment, 533–34
Premium, insurance, 913
Prescription, easement (profit) created by,
  887
Presentment of a negotiable instrument:
  proper, 447, 448
and warranty, 450–51
Price: discrimination—and
  monopolization, 811
statutes on, 796, 797
in franchises, and antitrust regulations,
  733
open term of, in a sales contract,
  292–93
  case illustrating, 293–94
resale, 808
seller's right to recover, 348
Price list, and contractual offers, 129
Principal (*see also* Employer): and agent,
  relationship between, 553, 554
disclosed, 575
duty of—to agent, 562, 592–93
  and ethics, 592–93
and employee, relationship between,
  553
and independent contractor,
  relationship between, 553, 554–55
liability—for contracts, 575–77
  for subagents, 579
  for torts, 577–79
partially disclosed, 575
remedies of, against agents, 563–66
rights of, 563
undisclosed, 575–76
  case illustrating, 576–77
Privacy, invasion of right to, 59
Privity: of contract, 374, 384, 386
of estate, 888
Probate, of a will, 894, 908, 910
Procedure, 42, 98–99, 910
Proceedings, core, 528 n.5
Proceeds from disposition of collateral, in
  default, 503
Processing plant, as a franchise, 731
Product (property), disparagement of, 88
Product liability. *See* Liability, product
Production, acquisition of personal
  property by, 837
Professionals, and antitrust laws, 798
  case illustrating, 798–99
Profit, nonpossessory interest as, 886–87
Profits: net, and dividends, 695
"short-swing," 726

Profit sharing plans, corporate, 668
Promise: absolute, 246, 252
  collateral (secondary), and the Statute
    of Frauds, 220–24
  in a contract, 115–16
  enforceable without consideration,
    162–65
  express, 162
  illusory, 155, 156
  of marriage, for consideration, 224
  oral, 220–22
  to pay—debts for another, 221–24
    debts of an estate, personally, 221
    unconditional, and negotiability,
      406–09
  secondary. *See* Promises, collateral
  waiver as, 276 n.19
  written, as an express warranty, 381
Promissory note. *See* Note, promissory
Promoter, corporate, 656–59
Property: abandoned, 844–45
  after-acquired, security interest in, 492
  bailed, right to use, 852
  community, 836, 837, 876
  defense of, 54
  definition of, and crime, 99, 101
  disparagement of, 88
  distribution of—in Chapter 7
    liquidation, 534–35
    in intestacy, 903–04, 906–07
  ethics of the protection of, 954–58
  insurance for, 927
  legal protection of, 835
  lost, 842
    estray statute and, *case illustrating*,
      842–44
    treasure trove as, 845
  mislaid, 841–42
  and a nonmarital relationship, 186–88
  ownership of, rights in, 836–37
  partnership and, 611, 613
    conveyance of, 605
    joint ownership of, 611
    and partners' rights in, 625–27
  personal (personalty), 218, 835–47
    acquisition of, 837–41
    bailment and, 848–49
    distinguished from real, 835–36
    intangible, 836
    delivery of, 838
    nature of, 835–36
    ownership of, and accession,
      840–41
    scope of, expanding, 836
    special types of, 845–46
    tangible, 836
    transfer of, by inheritance, 840
    trespass to, 61–62
  private, and inheritance, 894
  real. *See* Real estate
  tangible, bailment of, 848–49
  transfer of, 103
  wrongs against, 60–64
Prospectus of corporate securities
  offerings, 656, 716
Prosser, W. (*Law of Torts*), 78
Protection, equal, 31

Protest, notice of dishonor as, 448
Proxy, 684, 685, 687 n., 726
Public: officials, bribery of, 102
  policy. *See* Policy, public
Publication, of a will, 900
Puffing, 60, 368
  case illustrating, 368–70
Punishment, purpose of, in the legal
  system, 90–91
Purchase: money, 485, 486, 494–95,
  501
  order, *illustrated*, 299–301
  of personal property, 837. *See also*
    Goods
Purchaser, bona fide, *defined*, 169 n.
Purpose, achievement of, and
  termination of an agency, 579–80

Q

Qualifications: of corporate officers, 687
  and employment discrimination, 821,
    822
  case illustrating, 822–24
Quality control, franchising and, 731
Quantum meruit (recovery of fair value),
  265, 275
Quorum: of directors, 687
  of shareholders, 684
Quotas, illegality of, in affirmative action
  programs, 829

R

Ratification: agency by, 557–58
  an agent's, 572–74
    case illustrating, 574–75
  of contract—
    and insanity, 179
    and intoxication, 179
    by a minor, 169, 175–76
    express, 175, 179, 573
    implied, 176–77, 179, 573
Reacquisition, of a negotiable
  instrument, and discharge, 458–59
Reaffirmation, of debt, and Chapter 7
  liquidation, 538
Real Estate (real property; reality; *see also*
  Land), 218, 835, 865–92
  assignment of rights in, 235 n.4,
    236–37
  consumer protection and, 769–70
  goods associated with, 289
  nature of, 865–69
  ownership of, 869–72
    concept summary, 874
  rescission of, 253
  rights in, 836–37
  sale of, 882–85
    foreclosure, 521–22
Real Estate Settlement Procedures Act,
  770
Realism, legal, 5
Realty. *See* Real estate
Reason, development of rule of, 790,
  792

case illustrating, 792–94
"Reasonable person" standard, 65
Rebuttal, 48
Receivership, shareholders' petition for,
  700
Recognizance, 122
Records: business (books), inspection of,
  29
  case illustrating, 29–30
  rights of—by directors, 692–93
  by partners, 624
  by shareholders, 697
  of court decisions, publication of,
    10–11
Recourse, impairment of, and discharge
  of a negotiable instrument, 459
Recycling, government regulation of, 783
  case illustrating, 784–85
Red herring prospectus, 716
Redemption: equity of, and foreclosure
  sale, 552
  rights, of debtors, in security
    agreements, 501
Reformation, of a contract, 274–75
Refusals to deal, joint, and antitrust
  regulations, 805
  case illustrating, 806–07
Registration, of securities, 716–18
  exemption from, 716–17
  violations of, *case illustrating*, 717–18
Registration statement, 716
  and accountant's liability, 937–38
Regulation: of franchising, 737–39
  government. *See* Government
    regulation
  of securities. *See* Securities regulation
Regulation Z, on credit provisions, 766
Reimbursement: principal's duty of, 562
  right of, 521
Rejoinder, 48
Relationship, fiduciary: agency as, 559
  and fraudulent silence, 209
  ethics and, 592
  undue influence and, 212
Release (covenant not to sue), 160
Religion, freedom of, under the
  Constitution, 28
  tenets of, and employment
    discrimination, 821
Remainder, 885, 886
Remedies: agent's, against principal, 563
  for breach of contract, 272–78
  contractual provisions about, 358–61
  creditors', *concept summary*, 523
  for default in debt, 499–503
  election of, 275–76
  limitations on, 276–78
  principal's, against agent, 563–65
  recovery and quasi-contract as, 275
  ethics of, 282
  reformation as, 274–75
  rescission, 272
  restitution, 272
  in a sales contract, 339–40, 345–61
  limitations on, 327–78
  sellers', 345–50
  concept summary, 351

under the Sherman Act, 792
sole, 359
specific performance as, 272–74
waiver as, 276
Remote service units. *See* Teller
machines
Renfrew, Charles B. ("The Paper Label
Sentences: An Evaluation"), 108
Rent, tenant's liability for, 875
Renters, insurance for, 927
Renunciation: of authority by an agent,
580
by the limited partner, and liability,
638
Replevin, buyer's right to, 352
ethics and, 547
Reports, 10
Reporting, required of corporate insiders
on securities trading (Securities
Exchange Act, Section 16b), 726
Representative, personal, in
administration of an estate, 908
duties of, *illustrated*, 909
Repudiation, of a contract: anticipatory,
256–57, 342
seller's right to stop delivery, 346
wrongful, 348
Repurchase agreements (REPOs), and
bankruptcy, 543
Reputation, disparagement of, 88. *See
also* Defamation
Resale: of goods, 347–48
price-maintenance (fair trade), and
antitrust regulations, 808
Rescission, 10, 272, 364 n.
of contract—and consideration, 154
discharge by, 253–54
right of, 770
of reaffirmation agreement, 538
as revocation of acceptance, 340–41
Res judicata, partner's liability and, 629
Restatement of the Law of Contracts,
113, 115
Restatement, Second, Torts, on the
application of the doctrine
of strict liability, 388
Restitution, 272
and disaffirmance, 179
duty of, 169–70
case illustrating, 170–71
Restoration, duty of, 169
case illustrating, 170–71
Restraint of trade, 789–90
antitrust enforcement and: horizontal,
803–08
the Sherman Act, 790–95
vertical, 808–12
Retirement. *See* Insurance, retirement
Return, delayed. *See* Posting, deferred
Revenue Act (1978), 669
Reversion, 885–86
Reverter, possibility of, 885, 886
Review, judicial. *See* judicial review
de novo, 757
Revised Model Business Corporation Act
(RMBCA) (1984), 644

Revised Uniform Limited Partnership Act
(RULPA), 633
Revocation: of acceptance, in a sales
contract, 339–42
case illustrating, 340–42
of assignment, contractual, 234
of authority, by principal, 580
of check certification, 464
declaration of, 901
of discharge, in Chapter 7 liquidation,
538
of a gift, *causa mortis*, 840
notice of, 342
of offer, contractual, 136–37
of a subscription agreement, 659
of a will, 900–903
Revolving charge account, 183
Reward, 134–36
case illustrating, 135–36
void, 196
Right (*see also* Duty): appraisal,
706–11
of compensation, for directors, 693
of inspection, 692–93, 697–99
of indemnification, 693
of participation, 692
preemptive, shareholders', 694
of possession, bailee's, 852
to sell, exclusive, 882
of subrogation, 916
of survivorship, 875–76
to transfer shares, 699
to use bailed property, 852
to vote, shareholders', 697
to work, 820
Rights: agents', 563
air, 865–66
of assignment. *See* Assignment, rights
of
bailee's, 852–53
bailor's, 859
civil. *See* Civil rights
contract, 75–77
creditors', 518, 925
of debtor, in collateral, 485
of directors, 692–93
dividend, 694–97
of a franchisee, 735
of holder-in-due-course, 429–41
of a limited partner, 639
of officers, corporate, 693
of ownership, 838, 869–72
of principals, 563
of property, 836–37, 869–72
of the surety, 521
shareholders', 693–700, 706–10
in stock warrants, 694
subsurface, 865, 866
surface, 866
trustee's voidable, 533
vesting of, 243–44
under a will, 903
Risk: assumption of—as defense against
negligence, 69–71, 386
case illustrating, 70–71
and strict liability, 391

insurance, 913
of loss, 314–28
concept summary, 318
and insurance against, 326–27
sale—on approval, and, 318, 321
and security interest, 327
pooling, 913
Robbery, 99
Robinson-Patman Act, 796, 797, 811,
831
RMBCA. *See* Revised Model Business
Corporation Act
Rule (*see also* Doctrine): acceptance upon
dispatch (mailbox rule), 145
administrative agency, 754–56
of automatic perfection, 486
best efforts, 156
of construction, and sales contracts,
306
depositary, 146
diminished-value, and contract
performance, 251
English, on priority of assignment
rights, 239 n.
equal dignity, 557 n., 567
fictitious payee, 423, 424
franchise (FTC), 739
holder-in-due-course (FTC), 456
imposter, 423
leading object. *See* Rule, main
purpose
mailbox, 145
main purpose (leading object), 222
case illustrating, 222–24
Massachusetts, on priority of
assignment rights, 239 n.
mirror image, 140, 143, 297
New York, on priority of assignment
rights, 239 n.
perfect tender, 333–38
of preexisting duty, 154–55
for priority of security interests, 494
of reason, 810, 811
reasonable person, 252
10b–5. *See* Securities and Exchange
Commission
Rulemaking, 754–56
notice-and-comment, 754–55
RULPA. *See* Revised Uniform Limited
Partnership Act

S

Sabbath. *See* Sunday laws
Safe deposit box, as bailment, 850
"Safe-harbor" provisions, 785
Safety, workplace, 824
and ethics, 593
government regulation, 751–52
and liability, 587
principal's duty to provide, 562
Sale: of goods (*see also* Goods), 287–396
on approval—as a bailment, 851
risk of loss, 318, 321
contract for—acceptance in, 296–301,
339–42

additional terms in, 297–98, 301
case illustrating, 298, 301
breach of, 297, 345–61
and risk of loss, 321–22
buyer's obligations in, 338–42
consideration in, 154–55, 301–302
formation of, 292–310
material alteration of, 298
modification of, 154–55
offer in, 292–96
ongoing, 295–96
oral, 302–303
and parol evidence, 303–306
payment of, 339
performance of, 329–38
and products liability, 383–95
remedies for breach of, 345–61
limitation of, 277–78
repudiation, anticipatory, of, 342
revocation of acceptance of, 339–42
rules of, *concept summary*, 309–10
and the Statute of Frauds, 224–25, 302–303
terms of, delivery, 333
transnational, 946
unconscionability in, 306–309
warranties in, 364–82
damages, 264
defined, 287, 288–89
door-to-door, 767
ethics and, 506–509
government regulation, 766–67
and passage of title, 312–14
proceeds from and security interest, 490, 492
rescission of, 253
or return, 318, 321
and risk of loss, 314–18
and the statutes of limitations, 255
and the UCC, 288
rules for, *summarized*, 309–10
Sale, of real estate. *See* Real estate
Sanctions, under the Sherman Act, 792
Satisfaction, *defined*, 255
S.C. *See* Corporation, service
Scienter (guilty knowledge), 209–10, 212
accountant's lack of, 938, 941
Seal, on a contract, 122 n.4, 125 n.1
Search warrants. *See* Warrants
SEC. *See* Securities Exchange Commission
Secrecy, and computer crime, 101
Secured party, *defined*, 482
Securities, investment (*see also* Bonds, shares, stock):
corporate, 669–74
debt (bonds), 669–70
equity (stocks), 668
fixed income, 669–70
registration of, 716–18
regulation of, 715–27
transactions in, 288 n.
Securities Act (1933), 715–16, 727, 738, 757, 770, 932, 937–38, 941
Securities Act Amendments (1975), 726
Securities Exchange Act (1934), 715,

719–26, 727, 757, 932, 938–41
Securities Exchange Commission (SEC):
responsibilities of, 715
Rule 10b–5 of, on disclosure in securities trading, 719–27
application of, 723–26
Security interest (secured debt): buyer's right to retain, 352
creating, 482–85
default on, 499–503
defined, 482
perfection of, 485–90
duration of, 494
purchase money, 485, 486, 494–95, 501
and priority of claim to, 494–97
concept summary, 498
and risk of loss, 327
in unsecured stock, 489
Seisin. *See* Covenant of seisin
Self-defense, liability and, 54, 96
Self-incrimination, a corporation and, 29
Sentencing, in white-collar crime, 108
Servant (*see also* Employee): *defined*, 554
borrowed, and tort liability, 588
Service, of summons, 44
Service mark, 81
Services, sales of, with goods, 289
Servitude: equitable, 888
involuntary, 273
Sham transaction, and contractual offers, 131
Shareholder, corporate, 645
agreement by, in a close corporation, 649–51
appraisal rights of, 706–10
approval by, 708–11
case illustrating, 709–10
as creditor, 683–84
duty of corporation to, 745
liability—for illegal dividends, 697, 700
personal, 662–67
cases illustrating, 662–64, 665
in a professional corporation, 653
majority, 700
powers of, in corporate management, 681–85
rights of, 693–700, 706–10
voting by, 684–85
Shares (*see also* Bonds; Stocks):
authorized, 671
compared with bonds, 671
fair value of, 707–708
issued, 671
outstanding, 671
ownership of, 699
par value of, 671–72
transfer of—in close corporations, 649–50
in limited partnership association, 641
as a shareholder right, 699
treasury, 671
valuation of, in a corporate merger, 707

case illustrating, 707–708
watered, and shareholders' liability, 700
Shelter principle, and rights of holders-in-due-course, 438
Sherman Antitrust Act (1890), 20, 188n., 739, 753, 790, 797, 799, 800, 805, 807, 950
discussed, 790–92
interpretation of, by the courts, 792
Shoplifting, 54–56
Signature: *defined*, 442
forged, on checks, 471–72
on negotiable instruments, 406
and liability, 442–49
of organizations on, 445
unauthorized, 423–24, 442–43
on a sales contract, 296 n.5
on a will, 900
Silence, fraudulent, 209
Sinking fund, 669
Slander, 56
of quality (trade libel), 88
of title, 88
Small businesses: eligibility of, for Chapter 13 plans, 54
exemption of securities of, from registration, 716
Smoking, and consumer protection, 768
Snail darter, *case about*, 786–87
Social Security, legislation on, 826
Social Security Act (1934), 826
Sole proprietorship, 597, 599–600
South Sea Bubble, 643
Sovereign immunity, and international law, 948–50
case illustrating, 948–50
Soviet Union, contract law in, 113 n.
Speech, freedom of, under the Constitution, 26–28
case illustrating, 26–27
Spending power, of Congress, as defined by the Constitution, 25
Sport, professional: and employers' liability for injuries, 593–94
exemptions of, from antitrust laws, 797–98
Spouse, surviving, share of estate for, 903, 906
Stabilization, in the securities market, *defined*, 719
Standard, *prima facie* case, 99
Standing to sue. *See* Sue
Stare decisis, doctrine of, 5–6
State: chartering of a corporation by, 659–60
foreign, *defined*, 949
police powers of, 20–21, 888
case illustrating, 21–22
Statute; Statutes: antitrust, 790–92, 794–96
summary of, 797
estray, 842
case illustrating, 842–44
of Frauds—applicability of, to merchants, *case illustrating*, 290–92

and agency agreements, 556 n.
and assignability of contracts, 234
  discussed, 217–30
  concept summary of, 228
  and a sales contract, 302–303
  and partnership agreements, 607
  and real estate contracts, 882
of limitations, 10
  as defense against criminal liability,
    97–98
  and discharge of contracts, 255–56
  and promises to pay debts, 162–63
  and UCC actions, 356–58
  and unenforceable contracts, 122
long arm, 34, 41
notice-race, 880
pure notice, 880
race, 880
recording, for real estate deeds, 880
Stay, automatic, in bankruptcy
  proceedings, 529–30, 541
Stepchildren, and inheritance, 904
Stock (*see also* Bonds, Shares): callable
    preferred, 672
  common, 670–72
  convertible preferred, 672
  corporate, 670–74
    concept summary, 674
  cumulative preferred, 672
  loss of certificate of, 693
  participating preferred, 672
  preferred, 672–74
  purchase of, and corporate mergers,
    711
  redeemable (callable) preferred, 672
  splits, exemption of, from registration,
    717
  subscriptions, and shareholders'
    liabilities, 700
  unissued, security interest in, 489
  warrant, 694
Stockholder (*see also* Shareholder):
    personal liability of, 662–67
  cases illustrating, 662–64, 665
  preferred, in a corporation, 672, 674
Stolen goods, 100
  conversion and, 63
Stop-payment order. *See* Order, stop
    payment
Subagent: duties of, to principal, 561–62
  indemnification for, 562
  principal's liability for, 579
  unauthorized, 562
Subchapter S Revision Act (1982), 651
Subleasing, 875
Subrogation, right of, 521
Subscriber, pre-incorporation, 659
Substantial factor test, 65
Subsurface, property rights in, 865, 866
Sue: right to—of a limited partner, 639
  of a shareholder, 682
  standing to, 25, 233, 645, 791
Sufficiency, legal: of consideration,
    149–50
  of the writing, in a contract, 224,
    225–27, 302–03

Suit, derivative, 645, 680
Sum certain in money, and negotiability
    of an instrument, 409–12
  case illustrating, 410–11
Summary: of concepts. *See* Concepts
  procedures, in estate administration,
    910
Summons, 44, 45
Sunday (Sabbath) laws, 185
Suppliers, strict liability of, 395
Supremacy Clause, of the Constitution,
    23
  case illustrating, 23–24
Supreme Court. *See* Court, Supreme
Surety, 518, 519, 520–21
Suretyship, promise of, 221
Surplus, earned, and dividends, 695
Symbol, of copyright, 85
Syndicate (investment group), 599

T

Taft-Hartley Act. *See* Labor-Management
    relations Act
Taxation: constitutional power of, 25
  corporate, 646
  of a partnership, 605
  of professional corporations, 654
  of subchapter S corporations, 652
Taxes: federal estate, 910
  state inheritance, 910
Telephone service, as personal property,
    836
Television: ethics of recording from,
    954–55
  government regulation of, 751
Teller machines (customer bank
    communication systems; remote
    service units), 477
Tenancy: in common, 836, 841, 875
  by the entirety, 836, 837, 876
  from period to period, 871
  by sufferance, 871–72
  termination of, 872
    case illustrating, 872
  at will, 871
  for years, 871
Tenant, duties of, 875
  life, 870–71
  in partnership, 605, 625
Tender: *defined,* 331 n.
  of delivery, 331–38
    rule of perfect, 333–38
    and statute of limitations, 356
  offer, 711
Termination (*see also* Dissolution): of a
    bailment, 859
  of a corporation, 711–13
  of an easement, 887
  of a franchise agreement, 733–37
    case illustrating, 733–35
  of life insurance policies, 925
  of a partnership, 613–21
    case illustrating, 614–15
  power of, 885
  of a profit, 887

of a security agreement, 503–04
of tenancy, 872
  case illustrating, 872
Terms, of a contract: additional, and
    parol evidence, 303
  open, 292–95
    case illustrating, 293–94
  and risk of loss, 315
Territory, marketing restrictions on, and
    antitrust laws, 809
  case illustrating, 809–10
Test: "arbitrary and capricious," 757
  of insanity, 94–95
  of reasonable doubt, 99
  substantial evidence, 757
  "unwarranted by the facts," 757
Testament, will as, and private property,
    894
Testator (testatrix), 894
Testing, and employment, 822
Theft, of a negotiable instrument, 458
Things attached (*see also* Fixtures), 289
Third party: beneficiaries—rights of, in
    contracts, 233, 241–44
  and warranties, 374–75
  notice to—of the dissolution of a
    partnership, 618
  of the termination of an agency, 583
Timber: sale of 289
  security interest in, 486 n.3
Time: lapse of, and termination—of an
    agency, 579
  of a contract, 140–42
    case illustrating, 141–42
  limit of, on warranty, 381
  specified, for payment of negotiable
    instruments, 412
Timeliness, in contract acceptance,
    145–46
Timesharing, bankruptcy, 543–44
Tippee, liability of, 719, 724
  case illustrating, 724–26
Title: chain of, 885
  disclaimers of warranty of, 366
  document of, 314, 316
    and delivery, 332
    and payment, 339
    security interest in, 489, 491
  examination, 885
  good, 364–65
  imperfect, and sale of goods, 323–26
  insurance, 882
  marketable, 880
  passage of, 312–14, 318, 321
    concept summary, 318
  state, 218 n.5
  void, and sale of goods, 323–24
  voidable, and sale of goods, 324
    case illustrating, 324–26
  warrant of, 364–66, 380
Tombstone advertisements, 716
Torts, 52–74
  business, 75–89
  categories of, 53–73
  contract for, 195–96
  corporate liability for, 681

intentional, 53–64
  minor's liability for, 176
  unintentional (negligence), 64–71
Toxic substances, government regulation of, 783
Trade: acceptances, 399
  as unconditional order, 407
  associations, and antitrust regulation, 804
    case illustrating, 804
  mark: franchise licensing arrangements of, and antitrust laws, 739
    government regulation of, 752–53
    infringement of, 81–83
    as personal property, 845
  name, infringement upon, 83–84
    case illustrating, 83–84
  restraint of. *See* Restraint of trade
  secrets, theft of, 87
Transaction, secured, 481–505
  creditors' rights in, 518
Transfer: bulk (bulk sale)—creditors' rights in, 522
  defined, 288 n., 322–23
  and priority of secured interest claims, 494
  requirements in, 323
  fraudulent, 534
Transportation, government regulation of, 750
Treasure trove, 845
Treaty, 943–44
Treaty of Rome, 952
Trespass: to land, 60–61
  case illustrating, 61
  and ownership of abandoned property, 844–45
  to personal property, 61–62
Trial: criminal, 99
  jury, 47–48
Truth-in-Lending Act. *See* Consumer Credit Protection Act
Trusts, 907–908
  charitable, 908
  constructive, 563, 692, 908
  express, 907
  funds, misapplication of, 100
  inter-vivos, 894, 907, 908
  and monopoly, 790
  property, *defined*, 907
  resulting, 908
  spendthrift, 908
  testamentary, 907
  totten, 908
  voting, 685
Trustee: in Chapter 7 liquidation, 530
  powers of, 531–34
    case illustrating, 532–33
Tying arrangement, and antitrust laws, 810, 811

U

UCC. *See* Uniform Commercial Code

UCCC. *See* Uniform Consumer Credit Code
ULPA. *See* Uniform Limited Partnership Act
Ultra vires. See Doctrine, *ultra vires*
Unconditionality, *defined*, for negotiable instruments, 407
Unconscionability: and adhesion contracts, 214
  and consumer protection, 760
  defined, 195
  ethics and, 281
  in sales contracts, 306–309
  and the termination of franchises, 735
  and warranty disclaimers, 376
    case illustrating, 376–79
Underwriter, 914
Unemployment, government compensation for, 826
Unemployment Insurance Fund, 826
Unfair Trade Practices Act, 733
Uniform Commercial Code (UCC) (the Code): on definiteness of contract terms, 133–34
  development of, 7–8
  discussed, 288
  and franchises, 735
  law of secured transactions, article 9 on, 481–82
  unconscionability concept in, 193–94
Uniform Consumer Credit Code (UCCC): provisions of, 524
  scope of, 774
  unconscionability in, 193
Uniform Limited Partnership Act (ULPA), 598, 633
Uniform Negotiable Instruments Law (1896), 397
Uniform Partnership Act (UPA), 597, 603, 610, 615, 624
Uniform Probate code (UPC), 897
Uniform Securities Act, 727
Unions: exemption of, from antitrust laws, 797
  legislation about, 819–21
Union shop, 820
Unit, commercial, *defined*, 342
United Nations, General Assembly of, and international law, 944
UPA. *See* Uniform Partnership Act
UPC. *See* Uniform Probate Code
Usage of trade. *See* Course of dealing
Usury, 182–83
Utilities, government regulation of, 751

V

Value: giving, and secured interest, 482, 485, 494
  in negotiable instruments, and holders-in-due-course, 430–33
    case illustrating, 431–32
Variance, zoning, 889
  case illustrating, 889–91
Vegetation, as property, 866

Venue, and jurisdiction, 34, 42
Violation: *per se*, of the Sherman Act, 794–95, 805, 950
  petty offense as, *defined*, 92–93
Vote, shareholders', 682, 684–85
  right to, 697
Voting: cumulative, 684–85
  list, 684
  rights, in a corporation, 670, 697

W

Wage-Hour Law. *See* Fair Labor Standards Act
Wages, minimum, 827
Wagner Act. *See* National Labor Relations Act
Waiver, of breach of contract, 276
Walsh-Healey Public Contract Act (1936), 825, 827
War, and termination of an agency, 582
Warehouse: company, bailments and, 862
  receipt, *illustrated*, 320
  negotiability of, 862
Warrants: search, constitutional regulation of, 28–29
  for inspection of workplaces, *case illustrating*, 824–26
  stock, 694
Warranty: agent's, 577
  breach of, and damages, 353–55
    case illustrating, 354–55
  on commercial paper, 442, 450–52
  concept of, 364
    summarized, 380
  deed—general, 878
    special, 880
  disclaimers of, 375–79
  ethics and, 508
  express, 366–70, 380
    disclaimer of, 375
    and third-party beneficiaries, 374–75
  of fitness, in bailments, 859
  full, 376
  future performance and statutes of limitations, 356
    case illustrating, 357
  of habitability, 873, 880, 882
  implied, 370–74, 381
    and course of dealing, 374
    and course of performance, 374
    disclaimer of, 375–76
    of fitness, 372–73
    of habitability, 873
    lease as, 395
    of merchantability, 370
    on negotiable instruments, 450
    and third party beneficiaries, 374–75
    and usage of trade, 374
  legal theory of, 383–88
  limited, 376–77
  overlapping, 374

of possession, 873
presentment, on negotiable
    instruments, 450–51
of title, 364–66, 380
transfer, on negotiable instruments,
    450
    concept summary, 452
Waste: disposal, government regulation
    of, 783–85
economic, 265
hazardous, 785
of real property, 869, 870
Water: pollution, and government
    regulation, 780–82
case illustrating, 781–82
service, as personal property, 836
Whistle-blowing, ethics of, 109
Williams-Steger Occupational Safety and
    Health Act (OSHA), 751–52
Wills, 894–907
concept summary, 904
death-bed. *See* Will, nuncupative
formal requirements of, 899–900
holographic (olographic), 899, 900

living, ethics and, 957
nuncupative (death-bed), 900
oral, 899, 900
revocation of, 900–903
terms used in, 894
transfer of—personal property by, 840
    real property by, 876
Winding up, of a partnership, 614,
    618–21
case illustrating, 619–21
limited, 640
and partners' compensation, 624
Witness, to a will, 900
Women: discrimination against, in
    employment, 821–22
married, contractual capacity of, 180
Words, and figures on negotiable
    instruments, 415
Workers' free movement of, in the EEC,
    case illustrating, 951–52
Workers' compensation, 73–824
Workout, as an alternative to bankruptcy,
    538
Workplaces. *See* Safety, in the workplace

Writ: of attachment, 515
case illustrating, 515–16
of certiorari, 41–42, 50
of entry, 521
of execution, 514
Writing: in agents' contracts, 567, 569
for bailment agreements, 851
as a contractual requirement, 125 n.1
and negotiable instruments, 405–406
sufficiency of the, 224, 225–27
    in sales contracts, 302–303
of a will, 899–900
    and revocation by another, *case
    illustrating*, 901–902

Z

Zone, floating, 899
Zoning, of land, 888–91